THE EVERETT D. GRAFF COLLECTION

EVERETT D. GRAFF
1885-1964

THE NEWBERRY LIBRARY, *Chicago*

A Catalogue of

THE EVERETT D. GRAFF

COLLECTION

of

WESTERN AMERICANA

Compiled by

COLTON STORM

CHICAGO

Published for THE NEWBERRY LIBRARY

by THE UNIVERSITY OF CHICAGO PRESS

1968

Library of Congress Catalog Card Number: 66-20577
The Newberry Library, Chicago 60610

THE UNIVERSITY OF CHICAGO PRESS, CHICAGO 60637
The University of Chicago Press, Ltd., London W.C. 1

Foreword

Everett D. Graff was one of the finest book collectors I have ever known. He understood the importance of the contents of his books and appreciated them as physical objects. His enthusiasm was unflagging over a long period of time; he never begrudged the time, energy, and money he spent collecting books. He often said that his only regrets were for the books he failed to buy. Always, his principal object was the acquisition of the records of knowledge about the West.

Mr. Graff believed that the best way to appreciate knowledge is to share it. He was firmly convinced that great libraries are sources of strength for a democracy, and he was always willing to support scholarly collections and libraries. He joined the Board of Trustees of The Newberry Library in 1948, and was elected President of the Board in 1952. Probably at that time he recognized that his interest in the Library would lead eventually, as it did in 1964, to the incorporation of his collection into the already strong holdings of the Newberry.

Books were not Mr. Graff's only enthusiasm. He was a member of the Art Institute of Chicago, serving for many years on its Board of Trustees and as President of the Board for five years. There was nothing half-hearted about his love of great paintings, sculpture, and architecture. He not only appreciated them visually and tactually, but studied many written works about art. His collection of fine art books (kept wholly separate from his Americana) is a kind of evidence of the care with which he approached the subjects in which he was interested. He knew the writings of Berenson and Cooke and other critics and historians of art almost as well as he knew his Western books. His many excursions with Mrs. Graff to the art galleries of the world and the great monuments of the ancient world fortified his reading and deepened his appreciation of beauty. He believed firmly that fine paintings and sculptures and *objets d'art* must be lived with to be appreciated fully. In his personal collection, paintings by Goya, Cranach, Quentin Matsys, drawings by Tiepolo and Hokusai, among many others, were the background in which he lived. He believed in sharing this background with his friends and in displaying for them his own appreciation of the beauties of his unusual Tanagra figure of the standing woman, his jadeite Mayan carving, and his exquisite collection of Chinese porcelains.

Books and paintings by themselves did not satisfy the instincts of the connoisseur in Mr. Graff. He enriched his life and that of his friends by his deep devotion to music. For many years he regularly attended the concerts of the Chicago Symphony Orchestra. When he was abroad he made certain that he heard the great orchestras of Europe and the British Isles. Again, through his reading, he found knowledge and understanding of music beyond that of the common music lover. His conversations with musicians and critics added appreciably to his knowledge of the performance of music. He was also devoted to opera and supported local performances assiduously and attended many performances abroad. With music and paintings and books he lived a full life rich with beauty.

Mr. Graff was that rare kind of person who enhances the lives of those who knew him. The many hours I spent with him are among the most treasured memories I have. One of the great joys of knowing him was the realization that his special knowledge was always at the command of his friends. The days I spent discussing his books, bibliographically and textually, listening to great performances of Berlioz, of Beethoven, of Verdi, of Ravel, of Fauré, to performances of Horowitz and Piatigorsky, and of orchestras under Münch, Reiner, and Walter, while seeing on the walls an Italian primitive painting, a Flemish skating scene, or a pair of exquisite illuminated initials from a Renaissance antiphonal, I could never forget. I shall always treasure those hours spent in peaceful appreciation of the enthusiasms of a great collector. We always came back to books—books which meant so much to him, which had entwined themselves in almost every part of his living. Books quoted for his consideration were discussed in elaborate detail. They were sent on approval. The packages were unwrapped with a sense of excitement carried over from the initial discovery. The careful examination of each leaf, the reading of a snatch from this page or that, eventually the decision either to reject it or purchase it—these are all part of the excitement of living with books that was of such great importance in the life of Everett Graff. The way in which he shared his enthusiasm for books and music and art and the ideas of human beings from the past and in the present enriched my life more than I can well express.

Acknowledgments

Were I to list those friends and acquaintances who have helped me compile this catalogue, the pages and pages of names would run from Adams to Zeitlin and back. Every person I have known in thirty-five years among rare books has helped in one way or another. To all of my friends and acquaintances and to an infinitude of institutions, whether I have known them face to face or only through correspondence, I acknowledge a great debt of gratitude which I can never discharge. I repeat for them, in sincerity, the words of a gallant eighteenth-century gentleman: "With all the warmth of my heart, I give you thanks for your Excellency's profuse kindness to me."

COLTON STORM

Table of Contents

Introduction

I

The Everett D. Graff Collection of Western Americana is a remarkable gathering of source materials about the country west of the Mississippi River, recording its history both in broad general terms and in fascinating detail. The collection of about ten thousand books, pamphlets, maps, broadsides, and manuscripts of high quality relating to exploration, settlement, and development was formed over a period of more than forty years by a collector who was truly a connoisseur. Included are important materials describing personal experiences of the French and English in areas east of the Mississippi and great rarities reporting explorations of the Spanish in the far Southwest. There are also numerous works describing German, Russian, and Spanish experiences along the far Northwest coast. However, the bulk of the collection deals with the exploration and settlement of the trans-Mississippi West by men and women from "the States." Since the earliest successful expedition west of the Mississippi River was conducted by Captains Lewis and Clark under the auspices of Thomas Jefferson from 1804 to 1806, the most substantial part of the collection falls within the nineteenth century.

Mr. Graff was one of that remarkable breed of men, rare book collectors willing to gamble their judgment against the verdict of time. The high quality of his collection ensures that he won his wager. His success came from a highly developed ability to coördinate his treasures so that the many parts are closely related and support one another. Quite simply, the collection as a whole is of far greater value than the individual parts. His desire to collect source materials relating to exploration and early settlement was interpreted broadly enough to include not only the Lewis and Clark expedition, but the fur trade as exemplified by Jedediah Smith, who discovered South Pass, the most-used route to California; the Mormon treks of 1846 and 1849; the California gold rush of 1849; the later famous gold rushes to Colorado in 1859, to Montana and Idaho in 1864, to the Black Hills of the Dakotas in 1874, and to Alaska in 1898; narratives of overland travel throughout the nineteenth century; the surveys for transcontinental railroads in the 1850's; the earlier methods of transportation and freighting by such firms as Russell, Majors, and Waddell; the pony express; the cattle industry, including the dramatic drives north from Texas and west to California; great western ranches of the 1870's and 1880's; early town, county, and state histories; early maps; military protection to travelers and settlers; army camps and forts; the difficulties which traders, civilian settlers, and the Army had with local

Indians; the "bad men" of the West, particularly after the Civil War; law enforcement in general, including the various vigilante organizations; records of early settlers, including social conditions and customs. In short, there is scarcely an activity of the Western pioneer which is not treated extensively. In the development of his collection, Mr. Graff knew that eventually provisions should be made to ensure that the collection was not dispersed. For nearly half of his collecting years, he concentrated on securing the finest copies available of rarer Western books, believing that any institution which received his collection should be able to provide the background books and scholarly apparatus for the proper use of the rarities in which he was interested.

Mr. Graff was an unusual collector in that he not only gathered the books which interested him but read them and read them carefully. Of his entire collection, there were very few books which he did not know in detail. He could read French and German easily enough to know something at firsthand about the books in those languages which he had purchased. On the Spanish materials he followed the advice of the late Henry R. Wagner. The works in English were his particular delight and pleasure. One of the reasons that his collection, viewed as a whole, seems so extraordinary is that he was able to understand the books he owned and to relate one book or manuscript to dozens of others in his collection. In the later years of his collecting, a single reason was not enough to add a book to the collection. There had to be several reasons and a close relation between the new addition and other books already on his shelves. Rarity by itself had relatively little attraction for him. The correlation of his books, as far as subject is concerned, makes the whole body an exceptionally useful mass of material. In its field the Graff Collection must be considered an extraordinary achievement.

II

In 1946 the William L. Clements Library at the University of Michigan invited Mr. Graff to select fifty books from his collection relating to Texas for an exhibition to commemorate the 100th anniversary of the annexation of Texas by the United States. When the exhibition was opened, Wright Howes addressed the guests, and a catalogue entitled *Fifty Texas Rarities* was issued. (Incidentally, there were two editions of the catalogue, one limited to fifty copies and the other without limitation notice.) In cooperation with Mr. Graff, I prepared the catalogue for the exhibition. After that time Mr. Graff and I carried on a desultory correspondence relating principally to books. Ten years later Mr. Graff and Stanley Pargellis, then Librarian of The Newberry Library, invited me to come to Chicago and catalogue the entire Graff Collection.

I accepted the invitation and expected to have the work finished in three or four years. A survey of the entire collection convinced me that it was of such importance that a full and detailed catalogue would be of value to librarians, scholars, and book collectors. A plan of procedure was drawn up and approved. The work then commenced and was carried to completion on the principles approved. We planned to describe each book, map, broadside, pamphlet, newspaper, and manuscript in ful detail. This meant a complete examination of every item in the collection and full collations of about ten thousand pieces. From the original worksheets incorporating all of the information derived from the materials themselves, catalogue descriptions were drawn for a printed catalogue. When the final manuscript was being readied for the printer, it was decided that certain drastic changes should be made to shorten the manuscript. The decision was not an easy one for either Mr. Graff or the compiler. First of all, it was decided to limit the catalogue essentially to source materials and to include only those secondary works of exceptional interest or value. Lined-off title pages were reduced to short titles and the imprints formalized for easy use. The physical descriptions were retained almost in full, although descriptions of bindings were reduced to materials only. Provenance was retained only for owners of outstanding significance. The number of references to bibliographical listings was scaled down materially to record only important appearances. Finally, the comments appended to the descriptions were in large part eliminated. The resulting catalogue is not on the scale first designed, but it is, we hope, a useful addition to bibliographical knowledge.

The catalogue of the Graff Collection is not a bibliography. It was not designed as such and should not be used as a bibliography. It comprises descriptions of specific copies owned by Mr. Graff. We are very much aware that in the future the Graff catalogue will be referred to, and that the Graff copies may be considered bibliographically more desirable than other copies. This is not necessarily true, and yet there seems to be no way of preventing it except by stating categorically that these are descriptions of the Graff copies and are not necessarily to be considered standard. Variations from normal, when those variations are known for certain, are usually indicated. If we have been unable to determine priority or preference of one state or issue over the Graff copy, the Graff copy has been described without comment.

The arrangement of the catalogue is alphabetical, and each entry carries its own number; references in the index are to numbers in the catalogue. For the most part, either the Library of Congress headings or The Newberry Library headings have been used for the entries. In a few cases Mr. Graff and I disagreed with both the Library of Congress and The Newberry Library, and chose our own entries; however, it is easy enough to use the index and locate the item no matter what the heading may be. Punctuation of the short titles has been formalized. Regardless of the order in which they appear on the title-page, place of publication, publisher, and date have been recorded in that order. Single maps are described in full—the whole title lined off as in the original and important subsidiary information given.

Collations are given by signature for all books printed before 1821 and for a few later books, when the format is bibliographically important, peculiar, difficult, or exceptionally interesting. The collation by signature is followed by collation by pagination. Blank pages are indicated and blank leaves noted wherever those blanks complete a section. Square brackets have been used to indicate unsigned or unpaginated sections or pages. If a signature or a page number is given within square brackets followed by a hyphen and the latter followed by a signature or a page number within square brackets, the sections or the pages between the first and the last are signed or numbered. Where noted, mispagination or erratic pagination has been given within parentheses immediately after the collation by pagination. The size of the title leaf is given in centimeters with the vertical measurement first and the horizontal measurement second; in each instance the number of illustrations and maps is given and, in most instances, whether or not the illustrations are listed. Illustrations have not been described in detail. The maps, in books, are given in complete detail with all printed or engraved information lined off; flourishes, however, usually have been omitted. Significant marginal and side notes have been given as well as insets. Map measurements have been taken in centimeters with vertical measurements first, and, as with title leaves, measurements have been taken across the center of the map. Unless otherwise stated (i.e., "page size" or "platemark") the limits used for the measurements are the neat line. The binding, of course, is for the Graff copy only, and unless otherwise stated it may be assumed that the text edges are as issued. A notation about books and pamphlets enclosed in folding cases or slipcases is given for the convenience of The Newberry Library staff. At the end of the physical description major defects are noted briefly; otherwise it may be assumed that the books are in better than good condition.

Records have been made of the former ownership of all copies of books and manuscripts in the Graff Collection, but for the catalogue only the significant former owners are given under the heading *Prov.* (for "provenance"). The section of references (*Ref.*) contains citations to descriptions in lists and bibliographies. The citations are given generally for comparison or because those descriptions contain additional information. The user may assume that the Graff copies are identical with those references cited, except where the citation is followed by "see." In the latter cases the Graff copy is similar to or related to the copy described; for instance, "Sabin 97836 see" means that the copy described by Sabin is not identical with the Graff copy, but is closely related to it. "*Ref.:*" followed by a blank indicates that a description was not found in a bibliography or check list.

The paragraph of comments following the references is designed to indicate the character of the contents if the title-page does not make the principal subject of the book immediately apparent. In addition, a number of attempts at evaluation of the book from the textual point of view have been made by Mr. Graff as the result of reading and studying the book in question; such annotations are initialed EDG. In a few instances quotations from bibliographies and historians have been used to guide the user. A very large majority of the books are well enough known that they do not need comment.

All of the books in the collection are assumed to be first editions unless otherwise indicated. Under the heading *Editions*, only known earlier editions are listed. If the Graff copy is not a first edition, earlier editions listed under this heading will give an idea of the position of the Graff copy. In general, if a later edition was chosen by Mr. Graff for inclusion in his collection, it is to be preferred textually.

Books and pamphlets bound together have been entered under the initial piece in the volume. The complete list of contents is given at this point and the individual items are described under the headings used in the list.

Maps either separate or in books are described in full through 1874 with one or two exceptions. Abbreviations have been avoided and those which are used should be immediately understood.

A list of the bibliographies and checklists referred to under the heading "References" will be found preceding the text of the catalogue.

Finally, it may be said again, the present work is not a bibliography, but a catalogue of specific copies owned by Everett D. Graff. It contains descriptions of the primary works collected by him and bequeathed to The Newberry Library at his death in 1964. It does not, however, record the whole of the Graff Collection now at the Library, because books have been added to the collection since 1964 with funds left by him for that purpose. Moreover, a small number of rarities (marked with an asterisk after the title) were sold at auction in May, 1966. Mr. Graff was a collector whose standards were extremely high, as readers of the present catalogue will readily note; he was also firmly committed to the principle of selling duplicates, so that other collectors might have the opportunity of owning works important to them. In accordance with his wishes, whenever the Library already owned a finer copy of a work than that in the Graff Collection, the Graff copy was sold and the money realized by that sale held for purchasing appropriate other works. If finer copies than those owned by Mr. Graff should turn up in the future—an eventuality which, considering his standards of quality, cannot happen often—the Library may again decide to improve its present copy. The reader is warned, therefore, that while in the vast majority of instances he can expect to find at the Newberry the copy described in this catalogue, occasionally he will find, instead, a superior copy in another of the Newberry's collections or in the Graff Collection itself. A larger number of works, chiefly twentieth-century publications, were also sold at auction. They are also indicated by asterisks in the catalogue. These works were duplicated in the Library's holdings and were sold in accordance with Mr. Graff's wishes to provide further funds for acquisitions.

Library Location Symbols

AzTP	Arizona Pioneers' Historical Society, Tucson
AzU	University of Arizona, Tucson
CSfU	University of San Francisco
CSmH	Huntington Library, San Marino
CU-B	Bancroft Library, University of California, Berkeley
CoHi	Colorado State Historical Society, Denver
CtY	Yale University, New Haven
DLC	Library of Congress, Washington
ICHi	Chicago Historical Society
ICN	Newberry Library, Chicago
ICN (Ayer)	Newberry Library, Chicago (Edward E. Ayer Collection)
IaHi	State Historical Society of Iowa, Iowa City
MH	Harvard University, Cambridge
MHi	Massachusetts Historical Society, Boston
MWA	American Antiquarian Society, Worcester
MnHi	Minnesota Historical Society, St. Paul
MoHi	Missouri State Historical Society, Columbia
NN	New York Public Library
OC	Cincinnati Public Library
OCHP	Historical and Philosophical Society of Ohio, Cincinnati
OClM	Cleveland Medical Library
PHC	Haverford College, Haverford
PHi	Historical Society of Pennsylvania, Philadelphia
PPL-R	Library Company of Philadelphia (Ridgeway Branch)
PPiU	University of Pittsburgh
RPJCB	John Carter Brown Library, Brown University, Providence
TxU	University of Texas, Austin
WHi	State Historical Society of Wisconsin, Madison

References

Adair: Adair, James, *History of the American Indians*. Edited by Samuel Cole Williams. Johnson City, Tennessee, 1930.

Adams: Adams, Ramon F., *Six-Guns & Saddle Leather*. Norman, 1954.

Adams (*Ramp. Herd*): Adams, Ramon F., *The Rampaging Herd*. Norman, 1959.

Adams, F. B.: Adams, Frederick B., Jr., *Radical Literature in America*. Stamford, Connecticut, 1939.

AII: For a complete list of the American Imprints Inventories, see either Constance Winchell, *A Guide to Reference Books* (Chicago, 1951), item A163; or Douglas McMurtrie, "The Bibliography of American Imprints," *Publishers' Weekly*, CXLIV (1943), 1939–44. Note that the volumes of the Wisconsin Inventory are separately paged.

Allen (*Arkansas*): Allen, Albert H., *Arkansas Imprints, 1821–1876*. New York, 1947.

Allen (*Dakota*): Allen, Albert H., *Dakota Imprints, 1858–1889*. New York, 1947.

Auerbach: Parke-Bernet Galleries, Inc., *The Distinguished Collection of Western Americana . . . Formed by . . . Herbert S. Auerbach*. Sales 893 and 997. New York, 1947–48. 2 parts.

Ayer: Newberry Library, *Narratives of Captivity among the Indians of North America . . . in the Edward E. Ayer Collection*. Chicago, 1912. Supplement, compiled by Clara A. Smith (Chicago, 1928).

Bancroft (*Arizona*): Bancroft, Hubert Howe, *History of Arizona and New Mexico, 1530–1888*. San Francisco, 1889.

Bancroft (*California*): Bancroft, Hubert Howe, *History of California*. San Francisco, 1884–90. 7 volumes.

Bancroft (*NW Coast*): Bancroft, Hubert Howe, *History of the Northwest Coast*. San Francisco, 1884–86. 2 volumes.

Bancroft (*Popular Tribunals*): Bancroft, Hubert Howe, *Popular Tribunals*. San Francisco, 1887. 2 volumes.

Barba: Barba, Preston Albert, *The Life and Works of Friedrich Armand Strubberg*. Philadelphia, 1913.

Barrett: Barrett, Ellen C., *Baja California, 1535–1956*. Los Angeles, 1957.

Bay: Bay, Jens Christian, *Three Handfuls of Western Books*. Second edition. Cedar Rapids, 1941. Reprinted from his *The Fortune of Books* (Chicago, 1941), pp. 315–442.

Belknap: Belknap, George N., *McMurtrie's Oregon Imprints: A Supplement*. Portland, 1950–63. 4 volumes. Reprinted from the *Oregon Historical Quarterly*, LI (1950), 239–72; LV (1954), 99–144; LIX (1958), 208–45; LXIV (1963), 137–82.

Beristain: Beristain de Souza, José Mariano, *Biblioteca hispanoamericana setentrional*. Amecameca, 1883–97. 4 volumes. Adiciones y correciones (México, 1898).

Bib. Nat.: Bibliothèque Nationale (Paris), *Catalogue général des livres imprimés de la Bibliothèque Nationale*. Paris, 1897– .

Biesele: Biesele, Rudolph Leopold, *The History of the German Settlements in Texas, 1831–1861*. Austin, 1930.

Blanck: Blanck, Jacob, *Bibliography of American Literature*. New Haven, 1955– .

Blumann & Thomas: California Library Association, *California Local History*. Edited by Ethel Blumann and Mabel W. Thomas. Stanford, 1950.

Boggess: Boggess, Arthur Clinton, *The Settlement of Illinois, 1778–1830*. Chicago, 1908.

Bradford: Bradford, Thomas Lindsley, *The Bibliographer's Manual of American History*. Edited and revised by Stan. V. Henkels. Philadelphia, 1907–10. 5 volumes.

Bradsher: Bradsher, Earl L., *Mathew Carey*. New York, 1912.

Braislin: Anderson Galleries, *The Important American Library Formed by Dr. William C. Braislin*. Sales 2149 and 2156. New York, 1927. 2 parts.

Brinley: *Catalogue of the American Library of the Late Mr. George Brinley*. Hartford, Connecticut, 1878–93. 5 volumes.

Brit. Mus.: British Museum, *Catalogue of the Printed Books*. London, 1881–1905.

Buck: Buck, Solon Justus, *Travel and Description, 1765–1865*. Springfield, 1914.

Buley: Buley, Roscoe Carlyle, *The Old Northwest Pioneer Period, 1815–1840*. Indianapolis, 1950. 2 volumes.

Butler: Butler, Ruth Lapham, *A Bibliographical Check List of North and Middle American Indian Linguistics in the Edward E. Ayer Collection*. Chicago, 1941. 2 volumes. (In the references, the names of the linguistic sections are given in parentheses.)

Byrd: Byrd, Cecil K., *A Bibliography of Illinois Imprints, 1814–58*. Chicago, 1966.

Byrd & Peckham: Byrd, Cecil K., and Howard H. Peckham, *A Bibliography of Indiana Imprints, 1804–1853*. Indianapolis, 1955.

Carayon: Carayon, Auguste, *Bibliographie historique de la Compagnie de Jésus*. Paris, 1864.

Carroll: Carroll, Horace Bailey, *Texas County Histories*. Austin, 1943.

Caxton Club (Lowe): Lowe, John Williamson, *Catalogue of a Collection of Books and Manuscripts on the War of 1812, and Other Americana*. Chicago, 1917.

Church: Cole, George Watson, *A Catalogue of Books Relating to . . . America Forming a Part of the Library of E. D. Church*. New York, 1907. 5 volumes.

Clagett: Clagett, Helen L., *A Guide to the Law and Legal Literature of the Mexican States*. Washington, 1947.

Clark: Clark, Thomas D., *Travels in the Old South*. Norman, 1956–59. 3 volumes.

Clark (*New South*): Clark, Thomas D., *Travels in the New South*. Norman, 1962. 2 volumes.

Clements Library (*Michigan*): William L. Clements Library, *One Hundred Michigan Rarities*. Ann Arbor, 1950.

Clements Library (*Ohio*): William L. Clements Library, *Fifty Ohio Rarities, 1653–1802*. Ann Arbor, 1953.

Clements Library (*Texas*): William L. Clements Library, *Fifty Texas Rarities. Selected from the Library of Mr. Everett D. Graff*. [Compiled by Colton Storm.] Ann Arbor, 1946.

Cook: Cook, Luella E., "Histories of Iowa Counties," *The Iowa Journal of History and Politics*, XXXVI (1938), 115–51.

Coulter: Coulter, E. Merton, *Travels in the Confederate States*. Norman, 1948.

Cowan: Cowan, Robert Ernest, and Robert Granniss Cowan, *A Bibliography of the History of California, 1510–1930*. San Francisco, 1933. 3 volumes.

Cowan (1914): Cowan, Robert Ernest, *A Bibliography of the History of California and the Pacific West, 1510–1906*. San Francisco, 1914.

Cox: Cox, Edward Godfrey, *A Reference Guide to the Literature of Travel*. Seattle, 1935–38. 2 volumes.

Crane: Crane, Verner W., *The Southern Frontier, 1670–1732*. Durham, 1928.

Cuthbertson & Ewers: Cuthbertson, Stuart, and John C. Ewers, *A Preliminary Bibliography on the American Fur Trade*. St. Louis, 1939.

DAB: *Dictionary of American Biography*. New York, 1943–58. 23 volumes.

Daniel: Daniel, Price, Jr., *Texas and the West, Featuring the Writings of J. Frank Dobie*. Catalogue 24. Waco, Texas, [1963].

Darlow & Moule: Darlow, T. H., and H. F. Moule, *Historical Catalogue of the Printed Editions of Holy Scripture*. London, 1903–11. 2 volumes.

Dellenbaugh: Dellenbaugh, Frederick S., *Books by American Travellers and Explorers from 1846 to 1900*. New York, 1920. Reprinted from the *Cambridge History of American Literature* (Cambridge and New York, 1921), III, 131–70; IV, 681–728.

De Renne: *Catalogue of the Wymberley Jones De Renne Georgia Library at Wormsloe*. Wormsloe, Georgia, 1931. 3 volumes.

Dobie: Dobie, J. Frank, *Guide to Life and Literature of the Southwest*. Revised edition. Dallas, 1952.

Dunbar: Dunbar, Seymour, *A History of Travel in America*. Indianapolis, 1915. 4 volumes.

Dustin: Dustin, Fred, "Bibliography of the Battle of the Little Big Horn," in W. A. Graham, *The Custer Myth* (Harrisburg, Pennsylvania, 1953), pp. 380–405.

Dykes: Dykes, J. C., *Billy the Kid*. Albuquerque, 1952.

Eberstadt: Eberstadt, Edward, & Sons, Catalogues 103–138. New York, 1935–56. Reprinted as *The Annotated Eberstadt Catalogs of Americana, Numbers 103 to 138, 1935–1956* (New York, 1965), 4 volumes.

Edwards: Edwards, E. I., *Desert Voices*. Los Angeles, 1958.

Evans: Evans, Charles, *American Bibliography . . . 1639 Down to . . . 1800*. Chicago, 1903–59. 14 volumes.

Farquhar: Farquhar, Francis P., *The Books of the Colorado River & the Grand Canyon*. Los Angeles, 1953.

Farquhar (*Yosemite*): Farquhar, Francis P., *Yosemite, the Big Trees, and the High Sierra.* Berkeley and Los Angeles, 1948.

Faust: Faust, Albert B., *Charles Sealsfield (Carl Postl)*. Baltimore, 1891.

Fenton: Fenton, William Nelson, *American Indian and White Relations to 1830.* Chapel Hill, 1957.

Field: Field, Thomas W., *An Essay towards an Indian Bibliography.* New York, 1873.

Fitzpatrick: Fitzpatrick, T. J., *Bibliography of the Iowa Territorial Documents.* Iowa City, 1907. Reprinted from the *Iowa Journal of History and Politics*, V (1907), 234–69.

Ford: Ford, Worthington Chauncey, *List of the Benjamin Franklin Papers in the Library of Congress.* Washington, 1905.

Foreman: Foreman, Carolyn Thomas, *Oklahoma Imprints, 1835–1907.* Norman, 1936.

Freeman: Freeman, Douglas Southall, *The South to Posterity.* New York, 1939.

Gaer: Gaer, Joseph, *Bibliography of California Literature: Pre-Gold Rush Period.* No place, [1935].

Gilman: Gilman, Marcus D., *The Bibliography of Vermont.* Burlington, 1897.

Golder (*March of the Mormon Battalion*): Golder, Frank Alfred, *The March of the Mormon Battalion.* New York, 1928.

Gómez & González: Gómez, Néstor Herrera, and Silvino M. González, *Apuntes para una bibliografía militar de México, 1536–1936.* México, 1937.

Graham: Graham, W. A., *The Custer Myth.* Harrisburg, Pennsylvania, 1953.

Greely: Greely, A. W., *Public Documents of the First Fourteen Congresses, 1789–1817.* Washington, 1900.

Greenly (*Camels*): Greenly, Albert H., *Camels in America.* New York, 1952.

Greenly (*Lahontan*): Greenly, A. H., *Lahontan: An Essay and Bibliography.* [New York, 1954]. Reprinted from the Bibliographical Society of America *Papers*, XLVIII (1954), 334–89.

Greenly (*Michigan*): Greenly, Albert Harry, *A Selective Bibliography . . . Relating to Michigan History.* Lunenberg, Vermont, 1958.

Greenwood: Greenwood, Robert, *California Imprints, 1833–1862.* Los Gatos, 1961.

Gregory: Gregory, Winifred, *American Newspapers, 1821–1936.* New York, 1937.

Grolier: Grolier Club, *One Hundred Influential American Books.* New York, 1947.

Hafen: Hafen, LeRoy R., *Pike's Peak Gold Rush Guidebooks of 1859.* Glendale, California, 1941.

Hanna-Powell: Hanna, Phil Townsend, *Libros Californianos.* Revised by Lawrence Clark Powell. Los Angeles, 1958.

Hargrett (*Bibliography*): Hargrett, Lester, *A Bibliography of the Constitutions and Laws of the American Indians.* Cambridge, 1947.

Hargrett (*Oklahoma*): Hargrett, Lester, *Oklahoma Imprints, 1835–1890.* New York, 1951.

Harrisse: Harrisse, Henry, *Notes pour servir à l'histoire, à la bibliographie et à la cartographie de la Nouvelle-France . . . 1545–1700.* Paris, 1872.

Harwell: Harwell, Richard, *More Confederate Imprints.* Richmond, 1957. 2 volumes.

Hawley & Farley: Hawley, Lorene Anderson, and Alan W. Farley, *Kansas Imprints, 1854–1876: A Supplement.* Topeka, 1958.

Heartman (*Brackenridge*): Heartman, Charles F., *A Bibliography of the Writings of Hugh Henry Brackenridge.* New York, 1917.

Heller & Magee: Heller, Eleanor Raas, and David Magee, *Bibliography of the Grabhorn Press, 1915–1940.* San Francisco, 1940.

Hildeburn: Hildeburn, Charles R., *A Century of Printing: The Issues of the Press in Pennsylvania, 1685–1784.* Philadelphia, 1885–86. 2 volumes. Supplement by Edith S. Taylor, *Supplement to Hildeburn's Century of Printing, 1776–1784* (Master's thesis, Columbia University, 1935).

Hodge: Hodge, Frederick Webb, *Handbook of American Indians North of Mexico.* Washington, 1912. 2 volumes.

Holliday: Parke-Bernet Galleries, Inc., *Western Americana . . . Collection Formed by W. J. Holliday.* Sale 1513. New York, 1954.

Holmes: Holmes, Sir Maurice, *Captain James Cook, R.N., F.R.S., a Bibliographical Excursion.* London, 1952.

Howell: Howell, John, *The Oregon Country.* Catalogue 32. San Francisco, 1958.

Howes: Howes, Wright, *U.S.iana (1650–1950).* Revised edition. New York, 1962.

Howes (1954): Howes, Wright, *U.S.-iana (1700–1950).* New York, 1954.

Hubach: Hubach, Robert R., *Early Midwestern Travel Narratives . . . 1634–1850.* Detroit, 1961.

Hunt: Quinby, Jane, and Allan Stevenson, *Catalogue of Botanical Books in the Collection of Rachel McMasters Miller Hunt.* Pittsburgh, 1958–61. 4 volumes.

Icazbalceta: Icazbalceta, Joaquín García, *Bibliografía mexicana del siglo XVI*. México, 1954.

JCB: John Carter Brown Library, *Bibliotheca Americana*. Providence, 1919–32. 3 volumes.

JCB (*In Retrospect*): John Carter Brown Library, *In Retrospect, 1923–1949*. Providence, 1949.

Jefferson (Sowerby): Sowerby, E. Millicent, *Catalogue of the Library of Thomas Jefferson*. Washington, 1952–59. 5 volumes.

Jennewein: Jennewein, J. Leonard, *Black Hills Booktrails*. Mitchell, South Dakota, 1962.

Jillson: Jillson, Willard Rouse, *A Bibliography of Early Western Travel in Kentucky, 1674–1824*. Louisville, 1944.

Jillson (*RKB*): Jillson, Willard Rouse, *Rare Kentucky Books, 1776–1926*. Louisville, 1939.

Jillson (*Smith*): Jillson, Willard Rouse, *A Bibliography of . . . Col. James Smith*. Frankfort, Kentucky, 1947.

Johannsen: Johannsen, Albert, *The House of Beadle and Adams*. Norman, 1950–62. 3 volumes.

Johnson (Blanck): Johnson, Merle, *American First Editions*. Fourth edition, revised by Jacob Blanck. New York, 1942.

Jones: Eames, Wilberforce, *Americana Collection of Herschel V. Jones*. New York, 1938.

Karpinski: Karpinski, Louis C., *Bibliography of the Printed Maps of Michigan, 1804–1880*. Lansing, 1931.

Kimball: Kimball, J. P., *Laws and Decrees of the State of Coahuila and Texas*. Houston, 1839.

Kingsborough: Kingsborough, Edward King, Viscount, *Antiquities of Mexico*. London, 1830–48. 9 volumes.

Kluckhohn & Spencer: Kluckhohn, Clyde, and Katherine Spencer, *A Bibliography of the Navaho Indians*. New York, 1940.

Langfeld & Blackburn: Langfeld, William R., and Philip C. Blackburn, *Washington Irving, a Bibliography*. New York, 1933.

Leclerc: Leclerc, Charles. *Bibliotheca americana*. Paris, 1867–78. 2 parts. Two supplements (Paris, 1881–87).

Legler: Legler, Henry Eduard, *Early Wisconsin Imprints*. Madison, 1904. Reprinted from the State Historical Society of Wisconsin *Proceedings* (1903), pp. 118–38.

LHOTUS: Spiller, Robert E., and others, *Literary History of the United States*. New York, 1948. 3 volumes.

Littell: Parke-Bernet Galleries, Inc., *The Distinguished Collection of Americana Formed by C. G. Littell*. Sale 631. New York, 1945.

Lutrell: Lutrell, Estelle, *Newspapers and Periodicals of Arizona, 1859–1911*. Tucson, 1950.

McDade: McDade, Thomas M., *The Annals of Murder*. Norman, 1961.

McMurtrie (*Chicago*): McMurtrie, Douglas C., *A Bibliography of Chicago Imprints, 1835–1850*. Chicago, 1944.

McMurtrie (*Florida*): McMurtrie, Douglas C., *A Preliminary Short-Title Check List of Books, Pamphlets and Broadsides Printed in Florida, 1784–1860*. Jacksonville, 1937.

McMurtrie (*The General Epistle of the Latter Day Saints*): McMurtrie, Douglas C., *The General Epistle of the Latter Day Saints*. Chicago, 1935.

McMurtrie (*Louisiana*): McMurtrie, Douglas C., *Louisiana Imprints, 1768–1810*. Hattiesburg, Mississippi, 1942.

McMurtrie (*Mississippi*): McMurtrie, Douglas C., *A Bibliography of Mississippi Imprints, 1798–1830*. Beauvoir Community, Mississippi, 1945.

McMurtrie (*Montana*): McMurtrie, Douglas C., *Montana Imprints, 1864–1880*. Chicago, 1937.

McMurtrie (*New Mexico*): McMurtrie, Douglas C., "The History of Early Printing in New Mexico, with a Bibliography of the Known Issues of the New Mexican Press, 1834–1860," *New Mexico Historical Review*, IV (1929), 372–410. Supplement in VII (1932), 165–75.

McMurtrie (*New Orleans*): McMurtrie, Douglas C., *Early Printing in New Orleans, 1764–1810, with a Bibliography of the Issues of the Louisiana Press*. New Orleans, 1929.

McMurtrie (*Oregon*): McMurtrie, Douglas C., *Oregon Imprints, 1847–1870*. Eugene, 1950.

McMurtrie (*Peoria*): McMurtrie, Douglas C., *A Bibliography of Peoria Imprints, 1835–1860*. Springfield, 1934. Reprinted from the Illinois State Historical Society *Journal*, XXVII (1934), 202–27.

McMurtrie (*Pioneer Press*): McMurtrie, Douglas C., and Albert H. Allen, *A Forgotten Pioneer Press of Kansas*. Chicago, 1930.

McMurtrie (*Tennessee*): McMurtrie, Douglas C., *Early Printing in Tennessee, with a Bibliography of the Issues of the Tennessee Press, 1793–1830*. Chicago, 1933.

McMurtrie (*Utah*): McMurtrie, Douglas C., *The Beginnings of Printing in Utah, with a Bibliography of the Issues of the Utah Press, *1849–1860*. Chicago, 1931.

McMurtrie (*Wisconsin*): McMurtrie, Douglas C., *Early Printing in Wisconsin, with a Bibliography of the Issues of the Press, 1833–1850*. Seattle, 1931.

McMurtrie (*Wyoming*): McMurtrie, Douglas C., *Early Printing in Wyoming and the Black Hills*. Hattiesburg, Mississippi, 1943. Reprinted from the Bibliographical Society of America *Papers*, XXXVI (1942), 267–304; XXXVII (1943), 37–60.

McMurtrie & Allen (*Colorado*): McMurtrie, Douglas C., and Albert H. Allen, *Early Printing in Colorado . . . 1859 to 1876*. Denver, 1935. Supplement (Evanston, 1943).

McMurtrie & Allen (*Meeker*): McMurtrie, Douglas C., and Albert H. Allen, *Jotham Meeker, Pioneer Printer of Kansas, with a Bibliography of the Known Issues of the Baptist Mission Press at Shawanoe, Stockbridge, and Ottawa, 1834–1854*. Chicago, 1930.

Magee: Magee, David, *The Hundredth Book: A Bibliography of the Publications of the Book Club of California*. San Francisco, 1958.

Magee & Magee: Magee, Dorothy, and David Magee, *Bibliography of the Grabhorn Press, 1940–1956*. San Francisco, 1957.

Malone: Malone, Rose Mary, *Wyomingana*. Denver, 1950.

Matthews: Matthews, William, *American Diaries . . . Prior to . . . 1861*. Berkeley, 1945.

Meany: Meany, Edmond S., "Newspapers of Washington Territory." *Washington Historical Quarterly*, XIII (1922), 181–95, 251–68; XIV (1923), 21–29, 100–107, 186–200, 269–90.

Medina (*BHA*): Medina, José Toribio, *Biblioteca hispano-americana (1493–1810)*. Santiago de Chile, 1898–1907. 7 volumes.

Medina (*Mexico*): Medina, José Toribio, *La imprenta en México (1539–1821)*. Santiago de Chile, 1907–12. 8 volumes.

Meine: Meine, Franklin J., *American Humor, an Exhibition [at] The Newberry Library*. Chicago, 1939.

Meisel: Meisel, Max, *A Bibliography of American Natural History*. Brooklyn, 1924–29. 3 volumes.

Mitchell Library: Mitchell Library, Sydney, New South Wales, *Bibliography of Captain James Cook*. Sydney, 1928.

Moffit: Moffit, Alexander, "A Checklist of Iowa Imprints, 1837–1860," *Iowa Journal of History and Politics*, XXXVI (1938), 3–95.

Monaghan: Monaghan, Frank, *French Travellers in the United States, 1765–1932*. With a Supplement by Samuel J. Morino. New York, 1961.

Monaghan (*Lincoln*): Monaghan, James, *Lincoln Bibliography, 1839–1939*. Springfield, 1943–45. 2 volumes.

Morgan I: Morgan, Dale L., "A Bibliography of the Church of Jesus Christ of Latter Day Saints (Bickertonite)," *Western Humanities Review*, IV (1950), 45–70.

Morgan II: Morgan, Dale L., "A Bibliography of the Church of Jesus Christ of Latter Day Saints (Strangite)," *Western Humanities Review*, V (1951), 43–114.

Morgan III: Morgan, Dale L., *A Bibliography of the Churches of the Dispersion*. No place, [1953].

Morgan (*Pritchard*): Morgan, Dale L., editor, *The Overland Diary of James A. Pritchard with a . . . Bibliography . . . of Travel by All Known Diarists West across South Pass in 1849*. Denver, 1959.

Mott: Mott, Howard S., Jr., *Three Hundred Years of American Humor (1637–1936)*. Catalogue 5. New York, [1937].

Mott (*Amer. Mag.*): Mott, Frank Luther, *A History of American Magazines*. Cambridge, 1930–37. 4 volumes.

Mott (*Iowa*): Mott, Frank Luther, *Literature of Pioneer Life in Iowa*. Iowa City, 1923.

Munk (*Alliot*): Alliot, Hector, *Bibliography of Arizona . . . Literature Collected by Joseph Amasa Munk*. Los Angeles, 1914.

National Parks (*Yellowstone*): United States. National Park Service, *A Bibliography of National Parks and Monuments West of the Mississippi River*. No place, 1941. 2 volumes.

Nicholson: Nicholson, John Page, *Catalogue of Library of . . . John Page Nicholson . . . Relating to the War of the Rebellion, 1861–1866*. Philadelphia, 1914.

NYPL: New York Public Library, *List of Works . . . Relating to the Mormons*. New York, 1909. Reprinted from the New York Public Library *Bulletin*, XIII (1909), 183–239.

Palau: Palau y Dulcet, Antonio, *Manual del librero hispano-americano*. Segunda edición. Barcelona, 1948– .

Paltsits: Paltsits, Victor Hugo, "Bibliographical Data," in *Original Journals of the Lewis and Clark Expedition*, edited by Reuben Gold Thwaites (New York, 1904), I, lxi–xciii.

Paullin: American Art Association, Inc., *The Important American Library Collected by*

George W. Paullin. Sold April 1–3; April 29–30 and May 1, 1929. New York, 1929. 2 parts.

Peckham (*Captured by Indians*): Peckham, Howard, *Captured by Indians.* New Brunswick, New Jersey, 1954.

Peel: Peel, Bruce Braden, *A Bibliography of the Prairie Provinces to 1953.* Toronto, 1956. Supplement (Toronto, 1963).

Petersen: Petersen, William J., *Iowa History Reference Guide.* Iowa City, 1952.

Phillips: Phillips, John C., *American Game Mammals and Birds.* Boston, 1930.

Phillips (*Atlases*): Phillips, Philip Lee, *A List of Geographical Atlases in the Library of Congress.* Washington, 1909–20. 4 volumes. Continued by Clara Egli LeGear (Washington, 1958–   ).

Phillips (*Maps*): Phillips, P. Lee, *A List of Maps of America in the Library of Congress.* Washington, 1901.

Pilling: Pilling, James Constantine, *Proof-Sheets of a Bibliography of the Languages of the North American Indians.* Washington, 1885.

Pilling (*Alg.*): Pilling, James Constantine, *Bibliography of the Algonquian Languages.* Washington, 1891.

Pilling (*Muskhogean*): Pilling, James Constantine, *Bibliography of the Muskhogean Languages.* Washington, 1889.

Pilling (*Sal.*): Pilling, James Constantine, *Bibliography of the Salishan Languages.* Washington, 1893.

Poore: Poore, Ben. Perley, *A Descriptive Catalogue of the Government Publications of the United States . . . 1774– . . . 1881.* Washington, 1885.

Rader: Rader, Jesse L., *South of Forty.* Norman, 1947.

Railway Economics: Bureau of Railway Economics, *Railway Economics.* Chicago, 1912.

Raines: Raines, C. W., *A Bibliography of Texas.* Austin, 1896.

Rascoe: Rascoe, Burton, *Belle Starr, "The Bandit Queen."* New York, 1941.

Robertson (*Relaçam Verdadeira*): Robertson, James Alexander, translator, *True Relation.* Deland, Florida, 1932–33. 2 volumes.

Robles (*Coahuila y Texas*): Alessio Robles, Vito, *Coahuila y Texas desde la consumación de la independencia.* México, 1945–46. 2 volumes.

Robles (*La Primera Imprenta*): Alessio Robles, Vito, *La Primera Imprenta en Coahuila.* México, 1932.

Rusk: Rusk, Ralph Leslie, *The Literature of the Middle Western Frontier.* New York, 1925. 2 volumes.

Russell: Russell, Carl P., *A Concise History of Scientists and Scientific Investigations in Yellowstone National Park.* No place, [1934].

Sabin: Sabin, Joseph, *Bibliotheca Americana: A Dictionary of Books Relating to America.* New York, 1868–1936. 29 volumes.

Saunders: Saunders, Lyle, *A Guide to Materials Bearing on Cultural Relations in New Mexico.* Albuquerque, 1944.

Seitz: Seitz, Don C., *Paul Jones.* New York, 1917.

Shaw & Shoemaker: Shaw, Ralph Robert, and Richard H. Shoemaker, *American Bibliography; a Preliminary Checklist for 1801–19.* New York, 1958–66. 22 volumes.

Smith: Smith, Charles W., *Pacific Northwest Americana.* Third edition, revised by Isabel Mayhew. Portland, 1950.

Smith (1921): Smith, Charles Wesley, *Pacific Northwest Americana.* Second edition. New York, 1921.

Smith, W. W.: Smith, Walter W., "The Periodical Literature of the Latter Day Saints." *Journal of History*, XIV (1921), 257–99.

Smyth: Smyth, Albert Henry, *The Philadelphia Magazines and Their Contributors, 1741–1850.* Philadelphia, 1892.

Soliday: Decker, Peter, *Americana . . . Relating to . . . the Pacific Northwest.* Catalogues 17–21; collection of George W. Soliday. New York, 1941. 5 parts.

Staton & Tremaine: Staton, Frances M., and Marie Tremaine, *A Bibliography of Canadiana.* Toronto, 1934. Supplement, edited by Gertrude M. Boyle (Toronto, 1959).

STC: Pollard, A. W., and G. R. Redgrave, *A Short-Title Catalogue of Books . . . 1475–1640.* London, 1926.

Steele: Steele, Lavinia, *Check List of the Publications of the State of Iowa.* Des Moines, 1904.

Stevens (*Nuggets*): Stevens, Henry, *Historical Nuggets.* London, 1862. 2 volumes.

Stevens & Tree: Stevens, Henry, and Roland Tree, "Comparative Cartography," in *Essays Honoring Lawrence C. Wroth* (Portland, Maine, 1951), pp. 305–63.

Streeter: Streeter, Thomas W., *Bibliography of Texas, 1795–1845.* Cambridge, 1955–60. 5 volumes.

Streeter (*Americana—Beginnings*): Streeter, Thomas W., *Americana—Beginnings*. Morristown, New Jersey, 1952.

Streit: Streit, Robert, and others, *Bibliotheca Missionum*. Münster, 1916– .

Swanton: Swanton, John R., *The Indians of the Southeastern United States*. Washington, 1946.

Thomson: Thomson, Peter G., *A Bibliography of the State of Ohio*. Cincinnati, 1880.

Tinker: Tinker, Edward Larocque, *Les écrits de langue française en Louisiane au XIXe siècle*. Paris, 1932.

Trumbull (*Books Printed in Conn.*): Trumbull, James Hammond, *List of Books Printed in Connecticut, 1709–1800*. Hartford, 1904. Supplements I–II, by Albert Carlos Gates (Hartford, 1938–47), 2 volumes.

Uriarte: Uriarte, J. Eug. de, and Mariano Lecina, *Cátalogo razonado . . . de la Compañía de Jesús . . . (1540–1773)*. Madrid, 1904–16. 5 volumes.

Vail: Vail, R. W. G., *The Voice of the Old Frontier*. Philadelphia, 1949.

Vail (*Gold Fever*): Vail, R. W. G., "Gold Fever." New-York Historical Society *Quarterly*, XXXIII (1949), 237–71.

Vandale: Winkler, E. W., "The Vandale Collection of Texana." *Southwestern Historical Quarterly*, LIV (1950–51), 27–61.

Wagner (*California Imprints*): Wagner, Henry R., *California Imprints, August 1846—June 1851*. Berkeley, 1922.

Wagner (*Cart. of NW Coast*): Wagner, Henry R., *The Cartography of the Northwest Coast of America to . . . 1800*. Berkeley, 1937. 2 volumes.

Wagner (*New Mexico*): Wagner, Henry R., *New Mexico Spanish Press, 1834–1845*. No place, 1937. Reprinted from the *New Mexico Historical Review*, XII (1937), 1–40.

Wagner (*SS*): Wagner, Henry R., *The Spanish Southwest, 1542–1794*. Albuquerque, 1937. 2 volumes.

Wagner-Camp: Wagner, Henry R., *The Plains and the Rockies*. Third edition, revised by Charles L. Camp. Columbus, 1953.

Walker: Walker, Mary Alden, *The Beginnings of Printing in . . . Indiana . . . to 1850*. Crawfordsville, 1934.

Wheat (*Gold Region*): Wheat, Carl I., *The Maps of the California Gold Region, 1848–1857*. San Francisco, 1942.

Wheat (*Gold Rush*): Wheat, Carl I., *Books of the California Gold Rush*. San Francisco, 1949.

Wheat (*Transmississippi*): Wheat, Carl I., *Mapping the Transmississippi West, 1540–1861*. San Francisco, 1957–63. 5 volumes.

Wickersham: Wickersham, James, *A Bibliography of Alaskan Literature, 1724–1924*. Cordova, Alaska, 1927.

Wilcox: Wilcox, Virginia Lee, *Colorado: A Selected Bibliography of Its Literature, 1858–1952*. Denver, 1954.

Wilkie: Wilkie, Florence, *Early Printing in Ohio, 1793–1820, with a Checklist of Ohio Imprints for That Period*. Master's thesis, Columbia University, 1933.

Wing: Wing, Donald, *Short-Title Catalogue of Books . . . 1641–1700*. New York, 1945–51. 3 volumes.

Winkler: Winkler, Ernest W., *Check List of Texas Imprints, 1846–1860*. Austin, 1949.

Winkler & Friend: Winkler, Ernest W., and Llerena Friend, *Check List of Texas Imprints, 1861–1876*. Austin, 1963.

Winsor: Winsor, Justin. *Narrative and Critical History of America*. Boston, 1884–89. 8 volumes.

Wirick: Wirick, Harriet P., *A Checklist and Study of Illinois Imprints through 1850*. Master's thesis, University of Illinois, 1932.

Woodward: Banks & Co., *Bibliothica Scallawagiana. Catalogue . . . Relating to Mormonism and the Mormons . . . Gatherings of Charles L. Woodward*. Sold January 19, 1880. [New York, 1880.]

Wright I: Wright, Lyle, *American Fiction, 1774–1850*. San Marino, California, 1948.

Wright II: Wright, Lyle, *American Fiction, 1851–1875*. San Marino, California, 1957.

Wroth (*Acts*): Wroth, Lawrence C., and Gertrude L. Annan, *Acts of French Royal Administration*. New York, 1930. Reprinted from the New York Public Library *Bulletin*, XXXIII (1929), 789–800, 868–93; XXXIV (1930), 21–55, 87–126, 155–93.

Wroth (*American Bookshelf*): Wroth, Lawrence C., *An American Bookshelf, 1755*. Philadelphia, 1934.

Zamorano Eighty: Zamorano Club, *The Zamorano 80*. Los Angeles, 1945.

The Catalogue

A

1 ABBEY, JAMES

CALIFORNIA. A TRIP ACROSS THE PLAINS, IN THE SPRING OF 1850, BEING A DAILY RECORD OF INCIDENTS . . . SKETCHES OF THE COUNTRY, DISTANCES FROM CAMP TO CAMP. ETC. . . . NEW ALBANY, IND.: KENT & NORMAN, AND J. R. NUNEMACHER, 1850.

[1]–64. 17.4 x 11.2 cm. Light brown printed wrappers with title on front wrapper, advertisements on verso of front and recto and verso of back wrapper. Backstrip supplied, wrapper repairs. In a red cloth folder.

Ref.: Byrd & Peckham 1615; Cowan p. 1; Howes A5; Wagner-Camp 178

The first parts of the work appeared during May, June, and July, 1850, as a series of letters in the *New Albany Ledger*. It is a day by day account written in a rather exuberant style by a young man who enjoyed his experiences.

2 ABBOTT, CARLISLE S.

RECOLLECTIONS OF A CALIFORNIA PIONEER . . . NEW YORK: NEALE PUBLISHING COMPANY, MCMXVII.

[1]–235, [236 blank]. 18.7 x 12.7 cm. Frontispiece. Orange cloth.

Ref.: Cowan p. 1

Personal narrative of a trip overland in 1850, and experiences in the California mines.

3 [ABBOTT, JAMES B.]

[Wrapper title] MEMORIAL IN BEHALF OF THE "BLACK BOB" BAND OF SHAWNEE INDIANS, IN FAVOR OF THE ISSUANCE OF PATENTS TO THEIR LAND IN SEVERALTY . . . WASHINGTON, D.C.: POWELL, GINCK & CO., 1870.

[1]–22, [23–4 blank]. 22.1 x 14.7 cm. Tan printed wrappers with title on front wrapper.

Ref.:

Black Bob was a Shawnee chief who led part of his tribe from their lands in Eastern Missouri to Kansas about 1826.

4 [ABEL, HENRY I.]

[Broadside] GEOGRAPHICAL, GEOLOGICAL AND STATISTICAL CHART OF WISCONSIN & IOWA. DESIGNED ESPECIALLY FOR THE USE OF EMIGRANTS AND TRAVELLERS . . . PHILADELPHIA: HENRY I. ABEL, 1838.

Broadside, 51.8 x 66.1 cm. Accompanied by a map: Map / of the settled part / of / Wisconsin Territory / compiled from / the latest Authorities / Philadelphia: Published by / Hinman & Dutton N.º 6 North Fifth Street. / Compiled and engraved 1838 by J. H. Young Philad.ª / [at foot:]

Entered according to Act of Congress, in the year 1837, by Hinman & Dutton, in the Clerk's office of the District Court of the eastern district of Pennsylvania. / 54.6 x 44.3 cm. Scale: 18 miles to one inch. *Inset:* The / Entire Territory of / Wisconsin. / As / Established by Act of Congress, / April 10, 1836. / 18.2 x 25.5 cm. No scale given. Map and broadside folded into green cloth covers, 15.5 x 9 cm., printed paper label, 3.9 x 6.3 cm.: Travellers & Emigrants Guide / to / Wisconsin & Iowa. / By Henry I. Abel. / Accompanied with a new and / Improved Map of those Territories, / With the addition of parts of / Illinois, Indiana & Michigan. / [within typographical border].

Ref.: AII (*Wisconsin*) 527; Sabin 49

An early work relating to Iowa, Abel's map and broadside comprise one of the first few works containing reliable information about the northern part of the Old Northwest Territory. The T. W. Streeter copy of the map shows Aug. Mitchell as the compiler in the cartouche.

5 ABERT, JAMES W.

[Wrapper title] . . . A REPORT AND MAP OF THE EXAMINATION OF NEW MEXICO . . . WASHINGTON: 1848.

[i–ii blank], [1]–132, [133–34 blank]. (Pages [i–ii] and [133–34] used as fly-leaves.) 25 x 16 cm. 21 lithographic views, three plates of fossils, and a folding map. (Plate 3 is present in duplicate.) Map: Map / of the / Territory of New Mexico, / made by order of / Brig. Gen. S. W. Kearny, / under instructions from / Lieut. W. H. Emory, U. S. T. E. / by / Lieut's [!] J. W. Abert and W. G. Peck, U. S. T. E. / 1846–7. / C. B. Graham's Lith.ʸ Washington. / 64.7 x 49.8 cm. Scale: 10 miles to one inch. Tan printed wrappers with title on front wrapper, uncut. New blank back wrapper. In a green buckram case.

Ref.: Howes A11; Matthews p. 297; Rader 3344; Raines p. 1; Sabin 57; Saunders 2691; Wagner-Camp 143

The caption title on page [1] reads: 30th Congress, [Senate.] Executive, / 1st Session. No. 23. / [rule] [rule] / Report / of / The Secretary of War, / Communicating, in / Answer to a resolution of the Senate, a report and map of the ex-/ amination of New Mexico, made by Lieutenant J. W. Abert, of / the topographical corps. / . . . [Serial 506.]

Editions: Included in Emory, W. H.: *Notes of a Military Reconnoissance . . . Made in 1846-7 . . .* Washington, 1848, pages [418]–548. 30th Congress, 1st Session, House, Executive Document 41, Serial 517. Also published in New York, 1848.

6 ABERT, JAMES W.

[Caption title] . . . A REPORT OF AN EXPEDITION LED BY LIEUTENANT ABERT, ON THE UPPER ARKANSAS AND THROUGH THE COUNTRY OF THE CAMANCHE INDIANS, IN THE FALL OF THE YEAR 1845 . . .

[1]–75, [76 blank]. 22.7 x 14.3 cm. Two maps and 11 views. Map: Map / Shewing the Route pursued by the Exploring Expedition to / New Mexico / and the / Southern Rocky Mountains / made under the orders of / Captain J. C. Fremont U. S. Topographical Engineers / and conducted by / Lieut. J. W. Abert, assisted by Lieut. W. G. Peck, U. S. T. E. / during the year 1845. / 48.7 x 72.3 cm. Scale: About 31 1/2 miles to one inch. Map: Sketch / of a Day's Travel. / 20.5 x 12.9 cm. Scale: 4 miles to one inch. Rebound in new red cloth.

Ref.: Howes A10; Matthews p. 297; Munk (Alliot) p. 17; Sabin 59; Wagner-Camp 120

29th Congress, 1st Session, Senate, Document 438, Serial 477. [Washington, 1846.]

A famous and important report. The views include the noted plate of Bent's Fort.

7 ABINGDON ASSOCIATION OF SETTLERS

[Caption title] CONSTITUTION & BY-LAWS OF ABINGTON[!] ASSOCIATION OF SETTLERS. AT A NUMEROUS MEETING OF THE INHABITANTS ON THE UPPER DES PLAINES RIVER HELD PURSUANT TO NOTICE, AT INDEPENDENCE GROVE, ON FRIDAY THE 2D DEC. 1836, . . .

[1]–8. 16.7 x 14 cm. Stabbed, unbound, uncut. In a blue cloth case.

Prov.: Inscribed on page [1] by Elijah Middlebrook Haines: Printed by Rev. Jason Lathrop [i.e. Lothrop] / in South port Wis 1839 /.

Ref.: AII (*Wisconsin*) 529

The Abingdon Association was the first attempt to establish a form of local government in the area of present day Waukegan, Illinois. Abingdon was located about five miles west and slightly south of Waukegan and about three miles north of Libertyville on the Des Plaines River.

Elijah M. Haines, in his *Historical and Statistical Sketches of Lake County* . . . 1852, pages 8–15, described the events leading to the establishment of the Abingdon Association and printed this Constitution.

The Reverend Jason Lothrop described the handmade press on which he had printed this pamphlet in *Second Annual Report and Collections of the State Historical Society of Wisconsin* . . . Madison, 1856, pages 461–62. His earliest pieces were printed in 1835. Lothrop's seems to have been the second press in Wisconsin and the first in Pike River (later Southport, finally Kenosha).

8 ABNEY, A. H.

LIFE AND ADVENTURES OF L. D. LAFFERTY; BEING A TRUE BIOGRAPHY OF ONE OF THE MOST REMARKABLE MEN OF THE GREAT SOUTHWEST . . . NEW YORK: H. S. GOODSPEED & CO.

[1]–219, [220 blank]. 18.6 x 12.5 cm. Two portraits and two illustrations included in pagination. Green cloth, front cover gilt stamped, backstrip in black.

Ref.: Adams (*Ramp. Herd*) 6; Howes A15; Raines p. 1

Copyrighted 1875. The author used his imagination freely in describing his cowboy adventures in Arkansas and Texas.

9 ACUNA, JUAN DE, MARQUES DE CASA-FUERTE

RECOPILACION DE LAS ORDENES DE S. M. Y REGLAMENTO, QUE HA DE OBSERVAR EL BATALLON DE MARINA DE LA ARMADA DE BARLOVENTO . . . MEXICO: DONA MARIA DE RIVERA, 1744.

A², B⁴. [i–ii], 1–10. 28 x 19.4 cm. Twenty printed documents bound together, early nineteenth century mottled calf, gilt back, yellow edges.

Ref.: Palau 252548

Bound with the following printed documents:

BUCARELLI Y URSUA, ANTONIO MARIA: . . . Instruccion para el Govierno interior y buen Régimen de la Guarnacion del Presidio del Carmen . . . [1774]. Number 461.

BUCARELLI Y URSUA, ANTONIO MARIA: . . . Instruccion y Metodo con que se ha de Establecer el Hospital para la Tropa de la Guarnacion del Presidio de Nuestra Señora del Carmen . . . [1774]. Number 462.

BUCARELLI Y URSUA, ANTONIO MARIA: Reglamento Provisional para el Prest, Vestuario, Gratificaciones, Hospitalidad, Recluta, Disciplina y total Govierno . . . Presidio . . . del Carmen . . . 1774. Number 463.

BUCARELLI Y URSUA, ANTONIO MARIA: Reglamento Provisional que han de Observar el Tesorero Pagador y el Guarda Almacen del Real Fuerte de S. Carlos de Perote . . . 1778. Number 464.

CALIFORNIA (PROVINCE): Reglamento para el Gobierno de la Provincia de Californias . . . 1784. Number 546.

CROIX, CARLOS FRANCISCO: Instruccion para formar una Linea ó Cordon de quince Presidios . . . [1771]. Number 925.

CROIX, CARLOS FRANCISCO: Ordenanzas de la

Real Renta de la Polvora . . . 1787. Number 926.

GALVEZ, BERNARDO DE: . . . Instruccion Formada en Virtud de Real Orden de S. M. . . . [1786]. Number 1498.

GALVEZ, JOSE DE: Ordenanzas de la Real Renta de los Naypes . . . 1777. Number 1499.

GUEMES PACHECO, JUAN VICENTE DE: Ordenanza para la Formacion de los Autos de Visitas y Padrones . . . 1793. Number 1683.

GUEMES PACHECO, JUAN VICENTE DE: Reglamento para los Mercados de México . . . 1791. Number 1684.

LINCE GONZALEZ, JOSE ANTONIO: Reglamento, u Ordenanzas de Ensayadores . . . 1789. Number 2492.

MEXICO. REAL AUDIENCIA: Nueves Instrucciones para el Juzgado de Bienes de Difuntos de la Real Audiencia . . . 1805. Number 2773.

SPAIN. Laws, Statutes, etc., Charles III: Pragmatica Sancion . . . por la qual se Prohibe la Introducion y Uso en estos Reynos de los Tegidos de Algodon . . . 1771. Number 3910.

SPAIN. Laws, Statutes, etc., Charles III: Superintendencia y Juzgado Privativo del Ramo del Papel Sellado . . . 1785. Number 3914.

SPAIN. Laws, Statutes, etc., Charles III: Real Decreto . . . Ampliar la Concesion del Comercio libre . . . 1778. Number 3911.

SPAIN. Charles IV: El Señor Príncipe de la Paz me dice lo que sigue en Oficio de 29 de Diciembre último . . . [1796]. Number 3916.

SPAIN. Laws, Statutes, etc., Charles IV: Con Real Órden de primero de Diciembre próximo . . . [1805]. Number 3915.

VALCAREL Y BAQUERIZO, DOMINGO: Instruccion del Papel Sellado . . . [1774]. Number 4452.

10 ADAIR, JAMES

THE HISTORY OF THE AMERICAN INDIANS, PARTICULARLY THOSE NATIONS ADJOINING TO THE MISSISIPPI[!], EAST AND WEST FLORIDA, GEORGIA, SOUTH AND NORTH CAROLINA, AND VIRGINIA . . . LONDON: PRINTED FOR EDWARD AND CHARLES DILLY, MDCCLXXV.

[*]², A-Nnn⁴. [i–xii], [1]–464. (Page 101 mispaginated 102.) 26.7 x 21 cm. Map: A Map / of the / American Indian Nations, / adjoining to the / Mississippi, West & East Florida, / Georgia, / S. & N. Carolina, / Virginia. &c. / [lower right:] Jno. Lodge Sculp. / 32.6 x 24.1 cm. Scale: about 100 miles to one inch. Contemporary sprinkled calf, gilt backstrip, blind double fillets on sides. Rebacked, preserving most of original.

Ref.: Field 11; Howes A38; Pilling 18; Sabin 155; Swanton p. 828; Vail 643

Adair's work is difficult to appraise because of his theories regarding the Jewish origin of the American Indians. Nevertheless, he was an intelligent observer. Vail calls it a "standard work," and Swanton considers it "basal" to everything in the Southeast.

11 ADAM, GEORGE

THE DREADFUL SUFFERINGS AND THRILLING ADVENTURES OF AN OVERLAND PARTY OF EMIGRANTS TO CALIFORNIA . . . COMPILED FROM THE JOURNAL OF MR. GEORGE ADAM . . . BY PROF. WM. BESCHKE. ST. LOUIS, MO.: PUBLISHED BY BARCLAY & CO., 1850.

[iii]–[x], [11]–60. 23 x 14.5 cm. Five illustrations, two of which are included in the pagination. Gray printed wrappers with title on front wrapper, Lacks back wrapper. In a red cloth case.

Ref.: AII (*Missouri*) 535; Cowan p. 51; Howes B396; Wagner-Camp 179

This company, known as the "California phalanx," was formed in New Orleans, October, 1849, and journeyed by the southern Platte route. The contents of this work and the illustrations are of a highly lurid character.—Cowan

There were also 70- and 72-page editions with the same imprint. While priority has not been determined, the 60-page edition seems to be earlier and is certainly less frequently found.

12 ADAM, WILLIAM

ONE GOD, THE FATHER. A SERMON, PREACHED AT . . . ELGIN, KANE COUNTY, ILL. . . . CHICAGO: PRINTED BY ROBERT FERGUS, 1848.

[1]–20. 21.8 x 12.8 cm. Pale blue printed wrappers with title on front wrapper.

Ref.: Byrd 1262; McMurtrie (*Chicago*) 133

13 ADAMS, ANDY

THE LOG OF A COWBOY. A NARRATIVE OF THE OLD TRAIL DAYS . . . BOSTON: HOUGHTON, MIFFLIN AND COMPANY, 1903.* ¹

[i–x], [1]–[388]. 18.8 x 12.5 cm. Six illustrations listed. Olive-green pictorial cloth.

Ref.: Dobie pp. 94–5; Howes A45

If all other books on trail driving were destroyed, a reader could still get a just and authentic conception of trail men, trail work, range cattle, cow horses, and the cow country in general from *The Log of a Cowboy*.—Dobie

¹ The asterisk in this, as in following entries, indicates that the present copy is no longer in the Graff Collection; however, another copy can be found in The Newberry Library collections. For a fuller explanation, see the Introduction, p. xv.

14 [ADAMS, EPHRAIM]

THE IOWA BAND. BOSTON: CONGREGATIONAL PUB-
LISHING SOCIETY, 1870.

[1]–184. 18.7 x 11.8 cm. Illustrated. Green cloth,
title in gilt on backstrip.

> *Ref.:* Mott (*Iowa*) p. 62
> Pioneers in Iowa.

15 ADAMS, JAMES CAPEN [?] [JOHN? WILLIAM?]

[Wrapper title, supplied from another copy]
LIFE OF J. C. ADAMS, KNOWN AS OLD ADAMS, OLD
GRIZZLY ADAMS . . . NEW YORK, 1860.

[1]–53, [54 blank]. 15.5 x 14 cm. Rebound in red
morocco. Lacks pictorial wrappers.

> *Ref.:* Cowan p. 3; Howes A57; Wagner-
> Camp 347

The *Life of J. C. Adams* was prepared as publicity at the time Barnum exhibited Adams' collection of wild animals in New York. Adams
probably supplied some of the information, but
the results do not compare favorably with
Hittell's work.

There are two editions of the work, the earlier
containing only 29 pages of text.

Laid in is an original photograph of Adams
and a grizzly bear.

16 ADAMS, JAMES CAPEN

[Photograph] ORIGINAL PHOTOGRAPH OF JOHN
CAPEN ADAMS AND A GRIZZLY BEAR. Full length,
standing. 9.6 x 5.5 cm. mounted on card 10 x 6.4
cm.

The photographer's name is not given. The
photograph was probably made for publicity
purposes during Adams' association with P. T.
Barnum. It is unclear whether or not the bear is
alive. Adams is. Laid in *Life of J. C. Adams* . . .
1860.

17 ADAMS, SAMUEL

[Caption title] . . . COMMUNICATION FROM CAP-
TAIN SAMUEL ADAMS RELATIVE TO THE EXPLORA-
TION OF THE COLORADO RIVER TO ITS TRIBU-
TARIES . . .

[1]–20. 22.7 x 14.5 cm. Rebound in red cloth.

> *Ref.:*
> 41st Congress, 3rd Session, House, Miscella-
> neous Document No. 12, Serial 1462. [Washing-
> ton: Government Printing Office, 1870.]

Included in the material relative to Adams'
petition for expenses in connection with his exploration is a diary of an expedition in 1869
down the Blue and Grand Rivers into the Colorado.

18 ADAMS, WILLIAM L.

OREGON AS IT IS; ITS PRESENT AND FUTURE . . .
PORTLAND: "BULLETIN" STEAM BOOK AND JOB
PRINTING ROOMS, 1873.

[1]–[63], [64 blank]. 21.1 x 14.4 cm. Green printed wrappers with title on front wrapper, advertisements on versos of front and back wrappers.

> *Ref.:* Howes A74; Smith 52

The first guide to the Northwest printed in
Oregon.

19 ADAMSON, ARCHIBALD R.

NORTH PLATTE AND ITS ASSOCIATIONS . . . THE
EVENING TELEGRAPH. NORTH PLATTE, NEBRASKA.

[i–iv], 1–241, [242–44 Index]. 18.3 x 13.3 cm.
Frontispiece, two plates and 14 text illustrations,
unlisted. Blue ribbed cloth, red edges.

> *Prov.:* Inscribed on page [i]: Presented to /
> Mr James R. Williams, / with kind regard of /
> The Author. / —North Platte, Neb. / April 6.
> 1914. /
> *Ref.:*
> Copyrighted 1910. Contains local informa-
> tion on the building of the Union Pacific Rail-
> road and on Indian troubles in eastern Ne-
> braska.

20 ADDRESS. TO THE HUNTERS . . .

[Caption title] ADDRESS. TO THE HUNTERS AFTER
THE NINETY DAYS' SCOUT. BY VOX BUFFALO-
REM . . . /

[1–4]. 21.7 x 14 cm. Unbound leaflet.

> *Ref.:*
> Dated at the end: Reynolds City, Texas,
> Sept. 16, 1877. / [From Dodge City *Times*, Sept.
> 29, 1877.] /

The twenty-seven-line "poem" is laid in
Cook, John R.: *The Border and the Buffalo* . . .
1907. It may have been written by Cook.

21 ADELAIDE GALLERY, London

[Broadside] MAMMOTH TREE FROM CALIFORNIA.
363 FEET IN HEIGHT. 31 FEET IN DIAMETER AT
THE BASE . . . KNOWN AS THE WELLINGTONEA
GIGANTEA, OF LINLEY; AND WASHINGTONEA GI-
GANTEA, OF AMERICANS . . . NOW OPEN, DAILY,
FROM TEN A. M. UNTIL EIGHT P. M. ADMISSION.
– – – ONE SHILLING.

Broadside, 25.4 x 12.6 cm. Text, 13.7 x 10.7 cm.

> *Ref.:* Farquhar (*Yosemite*) 3 note see
> Dated in manuscript in lower margin: July,
> 1858. /

22 ADNEY, TAPPAN

THE KLONDIKE STAMPEDE . . . NEW YORK: HAR-
PER & BROTHERS . . . 1900.*

[i]–[xiv, xiv blank], 1–[471], [472 blank]. 20.2 x
13.4 cm. 146 illustrations listed. Red cloth.

Ref.: Howes (1954) 92; Smith 59; Wickersham 4272

One of the better contemporary accounts of the Klondike "rush."

23 AINSA, JOSEPH Y.

HISTORY OF THE CRABB EXPEDITION INTO N. SONORA . . . PHOENIX, 1951.

[i–xii], 1–[52]. 20.2 x 13.9 cm. White printed wrappers with title on front wrapper, cut on verso of back wrapper, stapled.

Ref.:

Typographical errors are not listed as these mistakes will not alter the meaning of the words. —page [52]

24 AINSWORTH, DANFORTH H.

RECOLLECTIONS OF A CIVIL ENGINEER. EXPERIENCE IN NEW YORK, IOWA, NEBRASKA, DAKOTA, ILLINOIS, MISSOURI, MINNESOTA AND COLORADO . . . NEWTON, IOWA, 1901.

[i–ii], [1]–192. 20.6 x 13.9 cm. Orange boards, black cloth backstrip.

Prov.: Presentation copy, inscribed on the front endleaf: J. D. Edmundson. / Nov. 7th 1901. / Presented by the Author. / With bookplate and signature of J. D. Edmundson.

Ref.: Howes A90; Mott (*Iowa*) pp. 83–4

Ainsworth's vivid account of railroad building, civil engineering, farm and pioneer life was apparently compiled from day-by-day diaries which are occasionally quoted or mentioned.

25 AITKEN, W.

A JOURNEY UP THE MISSISSIPPI RIVER, FROM ITS MOUTH TO NAUVOO, THE CITY OF THE LATTER DAY SAINTS . . . ASHTON-UNDER-LYNE: PRINTED BY W. B. MICKLETHWAITE.

[1]–58, [59–60 blank]. 21.5 x 13.9 cm. Yellow printed wrappers with title on front wrapper, advertisement on verso of back wrapper. In a green cloth case.

Ref.: Howes A92

Aitken was not favorably impressed by the Mormons. His pamphlet was first published by Williamson in 1845; the present second edition appeared the following year.

Editions: Ashton-under-Lyne [1845].

26 AKEN, DAVID

[Wrapper title] PIONEERS OF THE BLACK HILLS; OR, GORDON'S STOCKADE PARTY OF 1874 . . . *

[1]–151, [152 blank]. 16.7 x 12.3 cm. Nine illustrations. Cream printed wrappers with title on front wrapper. In a red cloth jacket, blue leather label.

Prov.: Herschel V. Jones copy.

Ref.: Howes A93; Jones 1737

Although the Federal government had denied civilians access to the gold fields discovered in the Black Hills by Custer's command in 1874, Charles Collins, editor of the *Sioux City Times*, organized a party of twenty-eight adventurers to prospect. They established Gordon's Stockade on French Creek. It was disbanded by Federal troops in 1875.

The text of the work was printed in the *Custer Chronicle*, January 7 to May 20, 1911. If it appeared in book form at that time, such an edition has not been identified. The present edition was printed at Milwaukee about 1920.

27 AKIN, JAMES

[Wrapper title] . . . THE JOURNAL OF JAMES AKIN, JR. EDITED BY EDWARD EVERETT DALE. NORMAN: UNIVERSITY OF OKLAHOMA, 1919.*

[1]–32. 21.7 x 15 cm. Gray printed wrappers.

Ref.: Howes A95

The diarist, an eighteen-year-old boy, kept a day-by-day record of his 1852 overland journey from Southampton, Iowa, to Oregon.

28 ALASKAN & YUKON RIVER GOLD-FIELDS BUREAU OF INFORMATION

[Map] MINER'S / GUIDE MAP / TO / ALASKAN & YUKON RIVER / GOLDFIELDS. / COMPILED BY THE / ALASKAN & YUKON RIVER GOLDFIELDS / BUREAU OF INFORMATION. / CARL UHLIG, / PRESIDENT. / JAS. M. STREETER, MANAGER. / SAN FRANCISCO CALIFORNIA / JANUARY 1898. / COPYRIGHTED. 1898. / [lower right:] LITH. DAKIN PUB. CO. 320 SANSOME ST. S. F. /

Map, 65 x 97.3 cm. No scale given.

Ref.:

Thomas W. Streeter had this as part of a sixteen-page pamphlet. The map was probably issued separately also.

29 ALDRICH, LORENZO D.

A JOURNAL OF THE OVERLAND ROUTE TO CALIFORNIA! AND THE GOLD MINES . . . LANSINGBURGH, N. Y.: ALEXR. KIRKPATRICK, 1851.

[1]–48. 21.5 x 12.7 cm. Tan printed wrappers, with title on front wrapper. Corner of front wrapper torn off affecting upper right border and one letter. In a large red cloth case.

Ref.: Cowan p. 6; Howes A109; Jones 1255; Wagner-Camp 194

Aldrich's *Journal*, published posthumously, is the scarce and interesting overland narrative which contains the earliest printed account of a civilian crossing of Arizona. Aldrich and his party took the southern route via Fort Smith, Santa Fé, Tucson, the Gila River, and San Diego. The author died in 1851, two weeks after he had returned home.

Accompanying the pamphlet are two Autograph Letters, signed by Alexander McDonnell, a member of Aldrich's party, relating adventures of the party mining in California. See Number 2601.

30 ALDRIDGE, REGINALD

RANCH NOTES IN KANSAS, COLORADO, THE INDIAN TERRITORY AND NORTHERN TEXAS . . . LONDON: LONGMANS, GREEN, AND CO., 1884.

[i–viii], [1]–227, [228 blank], [229–32 advertisements], [1]–12 advertisements (not on text paper). 18.1 x 12 cm. Four illustrations. Blue cloth.

Prov.: Publisher's embossed presentation stamp on title-leaf.

Ref.: Adams (*Ramv. Herd*) 23; Howes A110; Rader 83

This is one of the standard books on cattle. The author was a partner of Benjamin S. Miller in the ranching business in the states and territories mentioned.—Adams

31 ALEXANDER, TONY

AUTOGRAPH LETTER, SIGNED. 1926 April 23, Seattle, Washington. One page, quarto. To Fred Lockley.

Regarding plans for a cougar hunt on Olympic Peninsula. Laid in the writer's *Experiences of a Trapper and Hunter* . . . 1924.

32 ALEXANDER, TONY

EXPERIENCES OF A TRAPPER AND HUNTER FROM YOUTH TO OLD AGE . . . COPYRIGHTED SEPTEMBER, 1924 BY TONY ALEXANDER, LINNTON, OREGON.

[i–iv], [1]–119, [120 blank]. 21.5 x 15 cm. 34 illustrations unlisted. White printed wrappers.

Prov.: Inscribed by the author on the title-page in pencil: With regards / of the Author / T. Alexander / .

Ref.: Howes A121

With an Autograph Letter, signed by the author laid in. Alexander's work relates mostly to experiences in the Far Northwest.

33 ALEXANDER COLLEGE, Dubuque, Iowa

SECOND ANNUAL CATALOGUE AND CIRCULAR . . . DUBUQUE: PUBLISHED BY ORDER OF THE TRUSTEES, 1855.

[1]–16. 20.8 x 14.4 cm. White printed glazed wrappers, with title on front wrapper.

Ref.: AII (*Iowa*) 79

This is the copy located in AII (*Iowa*).

34 ALEXANDRE, PHILIP L.

ALEXANDRE'S . . . COMPENDIUM. FACTS ABOUT OKLAHOMA CITY IN DETAIL, OKLAHOMA TERRITORY IN GENERAL, KIOWA & COMANCHE COUNTRY IN PARTICULAR . . . OKLAHOMA CITY: PHILIP L. ALEXANDRE.

[i]–[vi], [1]–[209], [210 blank]. 14.8 x 8.7 cm. Ten illustrations unlisted. Printed maroon boards.

Ref.: Howes A125

Copyrighted 1901. The Library of Congress describes a copy of 183 pages only.

35 ALEXIS OF RUSSIA, GRAND DUKE

HIS IMPERIAL HIGHNESS THE GRAND DUKE ALEXIS IN THE UNITED STATES OF AMERICA DURING THE WINTER OF 1871–72 . . . CAMBRIDGE: PRINTED AT THE RIVERSIDE PRESS, 1872.

[i–iv], [1]–[223], [224 blank]. 25.4 x 16.8 cm. Frontispiece. Original brown morocco, gilt, gilt edges, by the Riverside Press.

Prov.: Rubber stamp on title-page: Bibliothèque de Tsarskoe Selo. American Antiquarian Society copy, without identifying marks.

Ref.: Howes A126

Includes a description of a great buffalo hunt staged by General Sheridan in honor of the Grand Duke Alexis near Fort McPherson, Nebraska.

36 ALLEN, MISS A. J.

TEN YEARS IN OREGON. TRAVELS AND ADVENTURES OF DOCTOR E. WHITE AND LADY WEST OF THE ROCKY MOUNTAINS . . . ITHACA, N.Y.: MACK, ANDRUS, & CO., 1848.

[i blank, ii frontispiece], [iii]–xvi, [17]–399, [400 blank]. 19.3 x 12.1 cm. Frontispiece portraits of Dr. and Mrs. White. Original sheepskin, black leather label on backstrip.

Ref.: Howes A131; Smith 114; Wagner-Camp 144

First Edition. First Issue. An Appendix, consisting of passages from Frémont's *Narrative* . . . 1845, continues pages 401–430 in the Second Issue. Wagner-Camp 144 contains the curious suggestion that the 430-page issue might be earlier.

Dr. White and Lady went overland to Oregon in 1842 and returned in 1845.

37 ALLEN, MISS A. J.

THE SAME.

[i–ii blank], [iii]–xvi, 17–430. 19.6 x 12.4 cm. Black ribbed cloth, blind embossed panels on covers, backstrip gilt.

First Edition. Second Issue. The added Appendix, pages 401–30, is present. No frontispiece portraits were included with this issue.

38 ALLEN, BEVERLEY, & OTHERS

[Caption title] CITY OF JEFFERSON, MISSOURI, OFFICE OF SECRETARY OF STATE, 1841. SIR,—PURSUANT TO A RESOLUTION OF THE GENERAL ASSEMBLY OF THE STATE OF MISSOURI, I HAVE THE HONOR TO FORWARD TO YOU A COPY OF THE CORRESPONDENCE, ON FILE IN THIS DEPARTMENT, BETWEEN BEVERLEY ALLEN, ESQ., A MEMBER OF THE GENERAL ASSEMBLY, AND OTHER MEMBERS OF THE CONVENTION WHICH FORMED THE CONSTITUTION OF THIS STATE . . . JAMES L. MINOR, (COPY) SEC. OF STATE.

[1]–15, [16 blank]. 21.5 x 13.5 cm. Stabbed, unbound.

Ref.: AII (*Missouri*) 289

The correspondence relates to the northern boundary of Missouri.

39 [ALLEN, LIEUTENANT G. N.]

[Wrapper title] MEXICAN TREACHERIES AND CRUELTIES. INCIDENTS AND SUFFERINGS IN THE MEXICAN WAR . . . BOSTON: 1848.

[1–32]. 21.9 x 14.9 cm. Two full-page and 16 text woodcuts. Tan printed wrappers, advertisement on verso of back wrapper. In green cloth case.

Ref.: Howes A140

Editions: Boston, 1847.

40 ALLEN, JAMES

[Broadside] THE ACCOMPANYING MAP, WAS REDUCED FROM THE ORIGINAL . . . CHICAGO, ILL. JAN. 2, 1835. J. ALLEN.

Broadside, 21.9 x 26.6 cm. Text, 14 x 10.7 cm.

Ref.: Byrd 216

The second Chicago imprint, aside from newspapers. The broadside accompanies the map and report of Lieutenant Allen's and H. R. Schoolcraft's visit to the Northwest Indians in 1832 in 23rd Congress, 1st Session, Document Number 323, House of Representatives, War Department. The broadside was intended "to correct some of its [i.e. the map's] principal omissions and defects."

The appointment of Lieutenant Allen as Superintendent of the Harbor at Chicago was announced in the Chicago *Democrat* for February 4, 1834. The account books of John Calhoun, Chicago's first printer and publisher of the *Democrat*, now in the collections of the Chicago Historical Society, contain a record of a charge of $1.50 against Lieutenant Allen for 100 copies of an errata sheet for a report. The charge is dated January, 1835.

No other copy of this broadside has been found.

41 ALLEN, JAMES

[Caption title] . . . CAPTAIN J. ALLEN'S EXPEDITION . . . THE REPORT, JOURNAL, AND MAP OF CAPTAIN J. ALLEN . . . OF HIS EXPEDITION TO THE HEADS OF THE RIVERS DES MOINES, BLUE EARTH, &C., IN THE NORTHWEST . . .

[i]–18. 23.8 x 15.1 cm. Rebound in new red cloth.

Ref.:

29th Congress, 1st Session, House, Document No. 168, Serial 485. [Washington, 1846.]

Printer's imprint at left foot of page [1]: [short rule] / Ritchie & Heiss, printers. /

The map mentioned on page [1] was not issued.

42 ALLEN, JOEL A.

. . . THE AMERICAN BISONS, LIVING AND EXTINCT . . . CAMBRIDGE: UNIVERSITY PRESS, 1876.

[i–x, x blank], [1]–246. 29.7 x 23 cm. 12 plates, each with leaf of text, and a map: Map of / North America / Kentucky Geological Survey / 1876 / N. S. Shaler, Director. / L. Trouvelot, Artist / . . . / Compiled from / the Maps of Stieler's Atlas, the Isothermal Maps of Schott, records of the U. S. Coast Survey and other Authorities. / A. Meisel, Lith. 64 Federal St. / 63.5 x 74.5 cm. No scale given. Gray printed wrappers with title on front wrapper, advertisements on recto and verso of back wrapper. In a brown buckram case.

Prov.: Printed presentation slip from Alexander Agassiz tipped in.

Ref.: Howes A149; Meisel III p. 304

The first important work on the American bison. Comprises Volume IV, Number 10, of *Memoirs of the Museum of Comparative Zoölogy, at Harvard College.*

43 [ALLEN, THOMAS]

THE COMMERCE AND NAVIGATION OF THE VALLEY OF THE MISSISSIPPI; AND ALSO THAT APPERTAINING TO THE CITY OF ST. LOUIS: CONSIDERED, WITH REFERENCE TO THE IMPROVEMENT, BY THE GENERAL GOVERNMENT, OF THE MISSISSIPPI RIVER AND ITS PRINCIPAL TRIBUTARIES . . . ST. LOUIS, MO.: PRINTED BY CHAMBERS & KNAPP.

[1]–32. 22.1 x 14.7 cm. Pink printed wrappers, with title on front wrapper.

Ref.: AII (*Missouri*) 507; Buck 414; Howes A158

Published in 1847. The report is signed on page 28 by Thomas Allen as chairman. The Appendix, pages 29–32, includes a letter from Thomas Hart Benton which was ordered to be printed with the report of the convention.

44 ALLEN, WILLIAM A.

ADVENTURES WITH INDIANS AND GAME, OR TWEN-
TY YEARS IN THE ROCKY MOUNTAINS . . . CHICA-
GO: A. W. BOWEN & CO., 1903.

[1]–112, blank page, [113–14], blank page, 115–
250, 253–64, 267–302. 22.1 x 14.7 cm. 28 illustrations. (Plates listed incorrectly.) Half maroon
leather, gilt top.

   Ref.: Howes A165

The author, known to his friends as "Montana Allen," tells some wild and possible tales
of pioneer life in the West.

45 ALLEN, WILLIAM A.

THE SHEEP EATERS . . . NEW YORK: THE SHAKES-
PEARE PRESS, 1913.*

[1]–78. 18.7 x 12.5 cm. Six illustrations. Brown
cloth.

   Ref.: Howes A166; Smith 138

The Sheep Eaters or Tukuarika were a subdivision of the Western Shoshoni. After about
1907, they were not separately enumerated.

46 ALLISON, EDWIN H.

THE SURRENDER OF SITTING BULL, BEING A FULL
AND COMPLETE HISTORY OF THE NEGOTIATIONS
. . . WHICH RESULTED IN THE SURRENDER OF SIT-
TING BULL AND HIS ENTIRE BAND OF HOSTILE
SIOUX IN 1881 . . . DAYTON, OHIO: THE WALKER
LITHO. AND PRINTING CO., 1891.

[1]–85, [86 blank]. 19.4 x 13.1 cm. Plan of Sitting Bull's Lodge. Gray printed wrappers with
title on front wrapper. In a brown cloth case.

   Ref.: Burdick (*Tales from Buffalo Land . . .*
1940) p. 26; Howes A173; *South Dakota Historical Collections*, VI, pp. [229]–272

Copyrighted in 1891 by E. H. Allison. Doane
Robinson in *South Dakota Historical Collections*
gives the copyright date 1892.

Burdick states the text was published in a
newspaper in 1881 and states further that Gus
Hedderich (on authority of his widow) wrote
the story for Allison. Hedderich was one of the
sutlers at Fort Buford when Sitting Bull surrendered. There is a holographic version of the
Allison story, presumably in Allison's handwriting, among the Miscellaneous Manuscripts at
the Clements Library.

Allison was born in Macomb County, Michigan, in 1847. After service in the Army during
the Civil War, he went to the Dakotas in 1867
where he married into the Brulé tribe and became proficient as an Indian interpreter. He
lived in Dayton, Ohio, from 1891 to 1898, according to Ernest Wessen, returned then to
Pierre, South Dakota, and died some time after
1912. Allison's activities are described in General Terry's report of the Department of Dakota
for 1880.

47 ALVAREZ, JOSE MARIA

[Caption title] DEL LIB. 2 DE ALVAREZ . . .

[i–ii], [1]–49, [50 blank], [1–32, 1–16]. (Page 49
mispaginated 43.) 15 x 10 cm. Contemporary local binding with covers made from discarded
leaves covered with flowered cotton print cloth;
front endpaper is a discarded leaf bearing pages
33–34 of the present pamphlet pasted in inverted,
back endpaper is a discarded leaf bearing pages
39–40; inserted at end of third section is a mutilated leaf bearing pages 33–34. In a brown cloth
case.

   Prov.: On first leaf and pages 7, 41, [50],
and on the final leaf, signatures of Rafael and
Liandro Alarick.

   Ref.: Sabin 979 see

The imprint on page 49 reads: Taos 1843 /
Imprenta del P. A. J. M. á cargo de J. M. B. /
The second and third sections are without im-
print but are obviously from Baca's press.

The caption title above is followed by a table
of contents, with verso blank. The table lists
Titulos I–XX and XXII and also a "Forma de
hacer testamentos." The Titulos are extracts and
condensations from Alvarez: *Instituciones de
Derecho Real de Castilla y de Indias . . .* Guatemala, 1818–1820 (Sabin 979) parts of which had
been published by Baca in 1842 (Wagner: *New
Mex.* 20). The source of the chapter on making
wills has not been identified.

The second section of the volume, also with
caption title only, is: Leyes y axiomas del derecho traducidos / de latin al Castellano, de la
coleccion que / al fin del libro quinto titulo 41 de
verbo-/rum significatione pone el canonista
Mu-/rillo en su obra de las decretales. / These are
extracts and condensations from the final chapter of Murillo Velarde: *Cursus Juris Canonici,
Hispani, et Indici . . .* Madrid, 1743 (Palau y
Dulcet 186206).

The third section is incomplete. Page 1 is
headed: Del Tomo Tercero de Alvarez / Titulo
XXIV. / De la compra y venta. / It is a single
chapter from the Alvarez work noted above.

The purpose of printing this material is ob-
scure; perhaps the publisher had in mind a kind
of do-it-yourself compendium of laws.

The binding is closely similar to one described
by Wagner in his list of New Mexico imprints,
no. 20.

No other copy of this pamphlet or any of its
parts has been located.

48 ALVORD, HENRY E.

REPORT OF SPECIAL COMMISSIONERS TO VISIT THE KIOWAS AND COMANCHES, ARRAPAHOES AND CHEYENNES, CADDOES, WICHITAS, AND AFFILIATED BANDS, IN THE INDIAN TERRITORY . . . WASHINGTON: GOVERNMENT PRINTING OFFICE, 1872.

[i–ii], [1]–22. 23 x 14.9 cm. Buff printed wrappers, with title on front wrapper.

Prov.: Inscribed on front wrapper, above and beside author's name: Compliments / of / .

Ref.:

The *Report* appeared also in *Annual Report of the Commissioner of Indian Affairs to the Secretary of the Interior for the Year 1872* (Washington, 1872) and in House Executive Documents, 42nd Congress, 3rd Session, Vol. 3, Pt. 1, Doc. 1, Pt. 5, Appendix E, Serial 1561. The present pamphlet is from the same type setting as the others, but the arrangement of pages 19–21 differs slightly; there is also (page 22) a list headed: Indian Delegation to Washington. / which is not present in the other two printings.

49 AMERICAN ANTIQUARIAN SOCIETY, Worcester, Massachusetts

ARCHAEOLOGIA AMERICANA. TRANSACTIONS AND COLLECTIONS OF THE AMERICAN ANTIQUARIAN SOCIETY. VOLUME II. CAMBRIDGE: PRINTED FOR THE SOCIETY, AT THE UNIVERSITY PRESS, 1836.*

[i]–xxx, [xxxi–xxxii fly-title], [1]–573, [574 blank, 575 errata, 576 blank]. 24.2 x 14.4 cm. Map: Map / of the / Indian Tribes / of / North America / about 1600 A. D. / along the Atlantic; / & about 1800 A. D. / westwardly. / [rule] / Published by the Amer: Antiq: Soc: / From a drawing by Hon. A. Gallatin. / Pendleton's Lithography. / 38 x 41.1 cm. No scale given. Gray boards, green cloth back, printed white paper label, uncut.

Prov.: Signature inside front cover: Maria Edgeworth /. Also pencilled shelf-mark: Library B-7 /.

Ref.: Field 46; Howes G30; Sabin 1049; Wagner-Camp 35 note

Contains "A Synopsis of the Indian Tribes within the United States East of the Rocky Mountains, and in the British and Russian Possessions of North America. By the Hon. Albert Gallatin." Pages [xxxi]–422.

Also contains Daniel Gookin's "An Historical Account of the Doings and Sufferings of the Christian Indians in New England, in the Years 1675, 1676, 1677 . . ." Pages [423]–534.

Maria Edgeworth was a successful Irish novelist of the first half of the nineteenth century.

50 AMERICAN HOME MISSIONARY SOCIETY

[Broadside] THE FRUIT OF HOME MISSIONS. [short rule] [35 lines] JOSEPH E. ROY, AGENT A.H.M.S. CHICAGO.

Broadside, 20.2 x 12.4 cm. Text, 17.2 x 9.2 cm. Printed on light yellow paper.

Neither place nor date of printing is given. Possibly Chicago, 1865.

Laid in Turner, E. B.: *Reminiscences of Morris . . . 1865.*

51 AMERICAN MUSEUM, THE

THE AMERICAN MUSEUM; OR, UNIVERSAL MAGAZINE . . . FOR THE YEAR 1792. JANUARY TO JUNE. PHILADELPHIA: M. CAREY, M.DCC.XCII.

2A–2I⁴. [i–ii], [181]–248. 21.3 x 13.1 cm. Rebound in blue half morocco, gilt top, uncut.

Ref.: Bradsher pp. 4–9; Mott (*Amer. Mag.*) I pp. 100–03; Sabin 1162; Smyth pp. 67–73

The last volume of the magazine, which had been started in 1787, contains a paragraph on page 216 headed: "Western Discoveries." There it is stated that a British agent named Stuart spent four years traveling in the West, and that he reached the head of the Missouri within 500 miles of the Pacific, but was prevented from going further by Indian wars. The paragraph has been reprinted in the prefatory note to Poe: *The Journal of Julius Rodman*, San Francisco: Colt Press, 1947, page [iv].

52 AMERICAN SKETCH BOOK, THE

[Wrapper title] VOL. V. TEXAS PIONEER MAGAZINE. NO 11. THE AMERICAN SKETCH BOOK. AN HISTORICAL AND HOME MONTHLY. AUSTIN, TEXAS: SKETCH BOOK PUBLISHING HOUSE, 1879.

[67]–130. 23.4 x 14.7 cm. Pale green printed wrappers with title on front wrapper, advertisements on verso of back wrapper.

Ref.: Gregory p. 213

Mrs. Bella French Swisher was editor and publisher.

This issue contains, among other materials, "Historical Sketch of Anderson County, Texas" and "Sketches of Texas Pioneers" by Kate Efnor, pages 67–86 and 86–90; "Remembrances of Texas and Texas People" by John M. Swisher, pages [93]–102; and "Fifty-One Year's Reminiscences of Texas" by Frank W. Johnson, pages [115]–122. The magazine was established in LaCrosse, Wisconsin, in 1874 and the last number, Volume VII, No. 4 appeared in 1883. Miss Gregory locates only one complete file in the American Geographical Society Library.

53 AMERICAN SOCIETY FOR ENCOURAGING THE SETTLEMENT OF THE OREGON TERRITORY

[Broadside] NO. [in manuscript: 79] THIS CERTIFIES THAT [space] HAS PAID TWENTY DOLLARS TO THE AMERICAN SOCIETY FOR ENCOURAGING THE SETTLEMENT OF THE OREGON TERRITORY, AS A PLEDGE . . .

Broadside, 16.9 x 21 cm. Text, 14.2 x 15.7 cm.

The wax and paper seal of the Society appears in the upper left corner. The signatures of the president, J M Nisb[et] and R. P. Williams are vigorously crossed out.

Laid in Kelley: *A General Circular . . .* 1831.

54 AMERICAN TURF REGISTER

[Caption title] AMERICAN TURF REGISTER AND SPORTING MAGAZINE. VOL. VIII. MAY, JULY, NOVEMBER, 1837. NOS. 9, 10, 12.

[385]–432, [433]–480, 529–576. 22.2 x 13.3 cm. Rebound together in brown half calf.

Ref.: Wagner-Camp 64a

Each number contains a letter by William Marshall Anderson, a companion of Sublette, as follows:

"Adventures in the Rocky Mountains." Signed: Marshall. Undated. Pages 409–12.

"Scenes in the West—The Platte, &c." Signed: W. Marshall. Dated May 27th, 1837. Pages 454–57.

"Scenes and Things in the West." Signed: W. M. A. Dated September 29, 1837. Pages 549–52.

The letters were discovered and recorded by Bernard DeVoto for his *Across the Wide Missouri . . .* 1947. They were printed separately under the title *Adventures in the Rocky Mountains in 1834 . . .* (New York, 1951). The manuscript of Anderson's 1834 journal, which is the basis for dating the letters, was sold in the W. J. Holliday Sale, 1954.

55 AMES, JOHN H.

LINCOLN, THE CAPITAL OF NEBRASKA . . . LINCOLN: STATE JOURNAL POWER PRESS PRINT, 1870.

[1]–30, [1–6 advertisements]. 24.7 x 15.6 cm. Buff printed wrappers, with title on front wrapper, advertisements on recto and verso of back wrapper, uncut, unopened.

Ref.: AII (*Nebraska*) 153; Howes A219

56 AMITY COLLEGE, College Springs, Iowa

[Broadside] FOR VALUE RECEIVED WE, THE TRUSTEES OF AMITY COLLEGE ASSOCIATION, OF PAGE COUNTY, IOWA, HEREBY GRANT TO . . .

Broadside, 12.5 x 20 cm. Text, 10 x 18.8 cm.

Ref.:

Each share in the Amity College Association was good for a scholarship of five years gratuitous instruction which could be used, rented, or sold.

College Springs was about twelve miles south of Clarinda, Iowa. The first class in the Academic Department of Amity College was organized in 1857 with thirty students; by 1876–77 the enrollment had reached 106. When I was a boy in Clarinda in the 1890's the College was still going strong.—EDG

57 AMPHLETT, WILLIAM

THE EMIGRANT'S DIRECTORY TO THE WESTERN STATES OF NORTH AMERICA . . . LONDON: LONGMAN, HURST, REES, ORME, AND BROWNE . . . 1819.

[A]⁴, B-O⁸. [i]–viii, [1]–208. (Page vi mispaginated v.) 19.5 x 11.9 cm. Contemporary marbled boards, calf back and corners.

Prov.: Toft Hall bookplate.

Ref.: Buck 133; Buley II p. 642; Howes A223; Rusk I p. 129; Sabin 1349; Thomson 16

The first quarter of this well-written little book is in the form of a diary or journal. The balance comprises itineraries, descriptions, statistics, etc., relating to the country between Pittsburgh and Texas. Not all the material is original; Amphlett lists several of his sources in the preface. He is considerably less partial than many other writers of the time.

58 ANALECTIC MAGAZINE, THE

THE ANALECTIC MAGAZINE. (NEW SERIES.) . . . VOL. I. NOS. I–V. JANUARY–MAY, 1820. PHILADELPHIA: PRINTED AND PUBLISHED BY JAMES MAXWELL, 1820.

[i–ii], [i–ii], [1]–440. 21.3 x 13.3 cm. Three colored engravings and nine in black and white, unlisted. Marbled boards, calf back and corners, leather label on backstrip.

Ref.: Sabin 1358; Wagner-Camp 18

The title-page for the first part is not present. Contains "Notes on the Missouri River, and some of the Native Tribes in its Neighbourhood.—By a Military Gentleman attached to the Yellow Stone Expedition in 1819." Pages 293–313, 347–75. But the "Notes" cover only the author's trip from Fort Osage to Council Bluffs.

59 ANDERSON, ALEXANDER C.

[Cover title] . . . HAND-BOOK AND MAP TO THE GOLD REGION OF FRAZER'S AND THOMPSON'S RIVERS, WITH TABLE OF DISTANCES . . . SAN FRANCISCO: PUBLISHED BY J. J. LE COUNT, 1858.

[1]–31, [32 blank]. 14.6 x 9.2 cm. Map: Published / by / J. J. LeCount / San Francisco Cᵃ /

Map / showing the different / Routes of Communication / with the / Gold Region on Frasers River / Compiled from Original Notes / By / / Alexander C: Anderson. / Scale of English Miles / [diagrammatic scale: about 16 miles to one inch] / Lith.ʸ of Britton & Rey. S. Francisco. / [below border:] Entered according to act of Congress in the year 1858 by Alexander Anderson in the clerks office of the district Court of the Northern D.ᵗ of California. / 38.7 x 50.1 cm. Scale as above. *Inset:* An approximate / Sketch / showing the / Extension of the Route / Downwards. / 12.4 x 16.4 cm. Scale not given. Tan printed boards with title on front cover, advertisements on inner covers and on outer back cover, black leather backstrip. In a red cloth folder.

Ref.: Smith 223; Soliday I 132

The author was an official of the Hudson's Bay Company. He was intimately acquainted with the routes to the new gold fields and set out his knowledge carefully and succinctly. The Chinook jargon is described on pages [25]–31.

60 ANDERSON, MABEL W.

LIFE OF GENERAL STAND WATIE. THE ONLY INDIAN BRIGADIER GENERAL OF THE CONFEDERATE ARMY AND THE LAST GENERAL TO SURRENDER.*

[1]–58, [59–60 blank]. 22.1 x 14.7 cm. Gray printed wrappers.

Ref.: Howes A232

Prov.: Signed twice by the author.

Copyrighted 1915. Published at Pryor, Oklahoma.

A good story about an interesting man.— EDG

61 ANDERSON, W. F.

MAP OF SOUTHERN IDAHO AND THE ADJACENT REGIONS, BY JUDGE W. E. ANDERSON, . . . WITH AN ACCOMPANIMENT, COMPILED BY CHAS. DRAYTON GIBBES, C. E. . . . SAN FRANCISCO, CAL.: PUBLISHED BY WARREN HOLT.

[1–3]⁸, [4]⁴. [1]–55, [56 blank]. 19.3 x 11.7 cm. Map: Territory of Idaho / South / of / Salmon River and Rocky Mountains / Designed as a Guide to all the / Mining Districts / of the included Country / Made from personal observation and information furnished by resident miners, prospectors, scouts and army guides / By W. F. Anderson of Bonanza, Idaho April 1880. / Drawn and Compilation [!] from U. S. Land Surveys; from Scout map of Headwaters of Salmon River, Lt. Geo. S. Wilson, / 12th U. S. Infantry: from Government map of Yellowstone National Park, and other official data. / By C. D. Gibbes, C. E. San Francisco, April 1880. / Scale 10 Miles to one inch. / Published by Warren Holt, 717 Montg'ry S.ᵗ / San Francisco, Cal. / 1880. / E. Bosqui & Co. Lith. S.F. / [at lower left:] Entered according to Act of Congress, in the year 1880 by Warren Holt in the Office of the Librarian of Congress, at Washington, D.C. / 90 x 118 cm. Scale: 10 miles to one inch. Stabbed, first leaf partly pasted to front inner cover of red cloth folder (20.8 x 11.7 cm.), map folded and pasted to inner back cover, title in gilt on front cover.

Ref.: Howes A236

Pages 33–[56] are printed on slightly thinner and shinier paper. The imprint on page [7] reads: San Francisco. / Crowe & Cooke, Engravers and Printers, 22 Montg'ry St. / 1880. /

This very uncommon map contains details of the area previously unpublished. The map was apparently quite popular and seems to have been used roughly, for few copies have survived.

62 ANDREW, JAMES O.

MISCELLANIES: COMPRISING LETTERS, ESSAYS, AND ADDRESSES . . . LOUISVILLE: PUBLISHED BY MORTON & GRISWOLD, 1854.

[i]–viii, [9]–395, [396 blank]. 18.9 x 11.6 cm. Gray cloth, blind embossed panels on sides, title in gilt on backstrip.

Ref.: Howes A250

The letters relating to the author's travels in Illinois, Arkansas, Iowa, and Texas during the Forties are much above the usual ranting of such preachers during those days. Andrew was a cultured man even though a controversialist.— EDG

63 ANGEL, MYRON

EXPOSITION UNIVERSELLE DU 1867. ETATS-UNIS D'AMERIQUE. LA NEVADA ORIENTALE GEOGRAPHIE, RESSOURCES, CLIMAT ET ETAT SOCIAL . . . PARIS: IMPRIMERIE GENERALE DE CH. LAHURE, 1867.

[i]–viii, [1]–164. 17.5 x 11.5 cm. Orange printed wrappers laid in black cloth covers.

Ref.: Howes A276

English and French texts appear on opposite pages.

64 ANGEL, MYRON

HISTORY OF NEVADA WITH ILLUSTRATIONS AND BIOGRAPHICAL SKETCHES OF ITS PROMINENT MEN AND PIONEERS. OAKLAND, CAL.: THOMPSON & WEST, / 1881.

[i]–[xvi], [17]–680. 29.5 x 21.5 cm. Illustrations and portraits listed. Original green cloth, new morocco back strip.

Prov.: Printed label inside front cover: Compliments of / Capt. J. F. Seymour. /

Ref.: AII (*Nevada*) 514; Howes A273
Myron Angel, who acted as general editor, was assisted by J. D. Mason, M. D. Fairchild, C. K. Robinson, and others. Special articles were prepared by William Wright (Dan De Quille), H. G. Shaw, D. R. Sessions, and C. N. Harris.

65 ANNALS OF A WESTERN MISSIONARY

ANNALS OF A WESTERN MISSIONARY. A MONTHLY PAMPHLET . . . NO. 1[–2] FEBRUARY, 1853 [–MARCH, 1853.] PUBLISHED BY FINCH & McCABE, CEDAR RAPIDS, IOWA.* (No. 2)

[1]–32. [1]–32. 20.7 x 13.4 cm. Sewn, removed from bound volume.

Ref.: Sabin 1588
The editor and publisher was the Rev. C. C. Townsend. He explains in the first number that the issues were printed on a "little press and font in our narrow 8 by 10 study." The earliest Cedar Rapids imprints located by Moffit and in AII (*Iowa*) are 1857, although the *Progressive Times* had been established in 1851.

No complete run of the periodical has been located. There were two volumes (1853–54) in the first series and four volumes in a new series (1864–67). AII (*Iowa*) 98 describes a sixteen-page number dated from Iowa City, January, 1855. Scattered numbers of the six volumes have been found in ICN, MH, NN, OCHP, PHi, and WHi.

The ICN copy of Part 2 shows the reading Qurato in line 6.

66 ANNEWALT, E. H., *Compiler*

MOUNT PLEASANT CITY DIRECTORY; CONTAINING A CATALOGUE OF INHABITANTS . . . TO WHICH IS PREFIXED A HISTORICAL SKETCH OF THE CITY. BURLINGTON: DAILY GAZETTE BOOK AND JOB PRINTING HOUSE, 1870.

[1]–67, [68 blank]. 21 x 13.7 cm. Two illustrations and five vignettes, unlisted. Blue printed boards, roan backstrip, advertisements on covers, advertisements mounted inside covers.

Ref.: Howes A284
There are seven unpaginated advertisement leaves interspersed through the text.

67 ANSALDO, MATHEO

. . . EMPLEOS APOSTOLICOS, Y RELIGIOSAS VIRTUDES DEL FERVEROSO P. JOSEPH XAVIER DE MOLINA . . .

A–H⁴. [1]–64. (Page 38 mispaginated 37.) 19.4 x 14 cm. Rebound in light brown morocco. Remnant of marginal tab on first leaf.

Ref.: Carayon 2307; Jones 450; Medina (*Mexico*) 3639; Streit III 470; Wagner (*SS*) 114

Printed at Mexico City by Doña Maria de Rivera in 1743.

Father Molina, whose travels in Pimería Alta are described by Ansaldo, died on April 21, 1741. Ansaldo's biography is dated at the end: Mexico, y Mayo 25. de 1742. Wagner states that he once owned "a number of lives written" by Ansaldo. Medina and Streit list five other similar titles including a life of Father Estrada which carries a colophon reading in part: Esta, y las antecedentes Cartas, impressas con las licencias necesarias en Mexico, en la Imprenta Real del Superior Gobierno, y del Nuevo Rezado, de Doña Maria de Rivera, en el Empedradillo, Año de 1743.

The present work is probably one of the "antecedentes Cartas" referred to in the colophon above. Dr. Wilberforce Eames apparently reached the same conclusion, for he dated the Jones copy 1743 instead of using the 1742 date suggested by Wagner.

Wagner gives a reproduction of the title-page of this work on page 388, but it does not show a rule border, as in the Graff copy. Medina mentions filet borders; Streit does not.

68 ANTI–HORSE THIEF SOCIETY OF MISSOURI

[Wrapper title] CONSTITUTION AND BY-LAWS OF THE GRAND ORDER OF THE ANTI–HORSE THIEF SOCIETY OF MISSOURI. KEOKUK: R. B. OGDEN, STEAM PRINTING HOUSE, 1875.

[1]–12. 14.5 x 9 cm. Yellow printed wrappers, with title on front wrapper.

Ref.:
Apparently the earliest printing of the Constitution and By-Laws of one of the most active organizations of its kind.

69 ANTI–HORSE THIEF SOCIETY OF MISSOURI

[Wrapper title] CONSTITUTION OF THE GRAND AND SUBORDINATE ORDERS OF THE A. H. T. A. OF MISSOURI. REVISED 1887. PALMYRA, MO.: HERALD PRINT.

[1]–[16]. 14.4 x 9.7 cm. Green printed wrappers, with title on front wrapper.

Ref.:

70 APPEL APOSTOLIQUE . . .

APPEL APOSTOLIQUE ADDRESSE AUX REVERENDS PASTEURS DE TOUS LES CULTES AU SUJET DE LA REVELATION DES MYSTERES DU CHRISTIANISME . . . EN VENTE: AU BUREAU DE L'ETOILE DU KANSAS ET DE L'IOWA. A CORNING, POST-OFFICE, ADAMS COUNTY. IOWA. MDCCCLXXVIII.

[1]–23, [24 advertisement]. 21.2 x 12.5 cm. Folded, unbound, mostly unopened, uncut.
Ref.:
Note at foot of page 23: (A continuer.)

71 APPLE, CHARLES, *Compiler*

CHEYENNE DIRECTORY . . . CHEYENNE, WYOMING: THE LEADER STEAM PRINT, 1895.

[1–86]. 24.5 x 15.2 cm. 24 illustrations and portraits inserted as each third leaf, except the last three plates which are separated by only one leaf of text each. Brown cloth, printed advertisements on covers, advertisements pasted to inner covers.
Prov.: Signature in pencil on front fly-leaf: T. J. Carr/.
Ref.:
Thomas Jefferson Carr was one of the famous law enforcement officers of the last quarter of the nineteenth century. His career is described in Cook, D. J.: *Hands Up! . . .* 1882.

Laid in are twenty newspaper and magazine clippings relating to Carr and to law enforcement in the West. There is also a photograph of J. F. Moretton, signed and presented to Carr. There is also laid in an original pencil drawing, signed John Smith, of a barroom murder, with note at top: Fort D. A. Russell. Wyoming Territory. / December 11ᵗʰ A.D. 1877. / Size: 24.7 x 19.6 cm.

72 APPLEGATE, E. L.

DOCUMENT, SIGNED. 1871 January 9, Eugene City, Oregon. One page, 31.8 x 19.5 cm.

Appointment of Loren L. Williams as Surveyor of Mining Claims, Mining District No. 2. Inserted in Manuscript Journals of Loren L. Williams, Volume IV.

73 APPLEGATE, JESSE

AUTOGRAPH LETTER, SIGNED. 1865 January 12, Yoncalla, Oregon. One page, 31.5 x 19.8 cm. To Loren L. Williams.

Inserted in Manuscript Journals of Loren L. Williams, Volume III.

74 APPLEGATE, JESSE A.

A DAY WITH THE COW COLUMN IN 1843 . . . RECOLLECTIONS OF MY BOYHOOD . . . EDITED . . . BY JOSEPH SCHAFER . . . CHICAGO: CAXTON CLUB, 1934.*

[i]–[xviii, xviii blank], [1]–207, [208 colophon]. 19 x 14 cm. Cloth, red top, uncut.
Ref.: Howes A294
Limited to 300 copies. Part of the work had been published at Roseburg, Oregon, in 1914 as *Recollections of My Boyhood . . .*

75 APPLEGATE, JESSE A.

RECOLLECTIONS OF MY BOYHOOD . . . ROSEBURG, OREGON: REVIEW PUBLISHING CO., 1914.

[1]–99, [100 blank]. 20.9 x 14.2 cm. Pictorial wrappers. In a brown cloth case.
Ref.: Howes A294; Wagner-Camp 174 (note)
Applegate, an Oregon pioneer of 1843, laid out the southern route or "Applegate Trail" to Oregon in 1845.

76 APPLER, AUGUSTUS C.

THE GUERRILLAS OF THE WEST; OR, THE LIFE, CHARACTER AND DARING EXPLOITS OF THE YOUNGER BROTHERS WITH A SKETCH OF THE LIFE OF HENRY W. YOUNGER, FATHER OF THE YOUNGER BROTHERS, WHO WAS ASSASSINATED AND ROBBED BY A BAND OF JAYHAWKERS. ALSO THE WAR RECORD OF QUANTRELL DURING THE THREE YEARS THAT COLE AND JAMES YOUNGER WERE WITH HIM ALSO A SKETCH OF THE LIFE OF THE JAMES BOYS . . . ST. LOUIS: EUREKA PUBLISHING COMPANY, 1876.

[i]–iv, [1]–208. 21.5 x 14.5 cm. Four plates, one used twice. Green cloth, gilt stamped on front cover.
Ref.: Adams 31; Howes A295; Rader 160
Adams describes an 1875 edition with the imprint: "St. Louis, John T. Appler, publisher and proprietor, 1875." which collates "iv, 208," and carries the cover title "Younger Brothers." His 1876 edition with the Eureka imprint collates "iv, 5–224." Howes does not mention the 1875 edition and collates the 1876 as "208."

This book served as the fountainhead for many later and less accurate volumes.—Adams.

77 ARCHBOLD, ANN

A BOOK FOR THE MARRIED AND SINGLE, THE GRAVE AND THE GAY: AND ESPECIALLY DESIGNED FOR STEAMBOAT PASSENGERS. EAST PLAINFIELD, OHIO: PRINTED AT THE OFFICE OF THE "PRACTICAL PREACHER," 1850.*

[i]–xiv, [15]–192. 14.1 x 10 cm. Black cloth, white printed paper label on back.
Ref.: Howes A299
Miss Archbold traveled alone in the 1840's on Ohio and Mississippi steamboats, by buggy across Indiana, Illinois and Missouri, and into Kansas, and by stage in several states. While she condemns the actions and morals of some of her fellow passengers (for dancing, swearing, tippling, and incivility), she presents a good description of public behaviour, attitudes, manners and customs of her time.

Her travels eventually brought the author to the Old Shawnee [Methodist] Mission School, near the present town of Turner, in Wyandotte County, Kansas. There she taught in 1848 and 1850, and there she gathered materials for her sketches of Indian customs, scenes, and activities.

A strip of paper bearing the copyright notice is mounted on the verso of the title-leaf. The Ayer copy shows page vii mispaginated vi.

78 ARGYLE, ANNIE

CUPID'S ALBUM. BY ARCHIE ARGYLE. NEW YORK: M. DOOLADY . . . 1866.

[1–4], [i]–vi, [7]–332. 18.6 x 12.3 cm. Green cloth.
Ref.: Howes A306

Included is an interesting account of an overland trip from St. Joseph to California in 1864, via the Platte, Fort Bridger, Salt Lake City, and Virginia City.

79 ARIZONA CITIZEN, Tucson

[Newspaper] ARIZONA CITIZEN. VOL. IV. TUCSON, PIMA COUNTY, A. T., SATURDAY, APRIL 11, 1874. [NO. 27. . . .

[1–4]. 46.4 x 35 cm. Unbound.
Ref.: Lutrell pp. 56–7.

Miss Lutrell locates only three copies of this number, at AzTP, AzU, CU-B.

80 ARIZONA TERRITORY

[Map] OFFICIAL MAP / OF THE / TERRITORY OF ARIZONA. / WITH ALL THE RECENT EXPLORATIONS / COMPILED BY RICHARD GIRD C. E. COMMISSIONER. / APPROVED BY JOHN N. GOODWIN, GOVERNOR. / IN ACCORDANCE WITH AN ACT OF THE LEGISLATURE, APPROVED OCT. 23^D 1864. / WE HEREBY CERTIFY, THAT THIS IS THE OFFICIAL MAP / OF THE TERRITORY OF ARIZONA, AND APPROVE THE SAME. / JOHN N. GOODWIN / GOVERNOR. / R. C. McCORMICK / SECRETARY. / [at left of preceding two names is Seal of the Territory and at left of Seal the following three lines:] PRESCOTT / OCTOBER 12TH. / 1856. / PUBLISHED BY A. GENSOUL. / PACIFIC MAP DEPOT. / N^Q 511. MONTGOMERY ST. SAN FRANCISCO. / [lower right:] LITH. BRITTON & CO. SAN FRANCISCO. /

Map, 89.5 x 90.7 cm. Scale: 15 miles to one inch. Folded into light red cloth covers, 15.7 x 10 cm., with gilt title on front cover within blind borders: Gird's / Official Map / of the Territory of / Arizona. / [decorative rule] / A. Gensoul, Publisher. /
Ref.:

Advertisements of G. W. & C. B. Colton appear inside front cover.

81 ARIZONA TERRITORY. Laws, Statutes, etc.

MINING LAW OF THE TERRITORY OF ARINONA[!]. PRESCOTT: OFFICE OF THE ARIZONA MINER, 1864.

[A–C]⁴, [D]². [i–ii], [1]–12, [blank leaf], 13–18, [blank leaf], 19–21, [22 colophon]. 22 x 14.7 cm. Stabbed, unbound, uncut.
Prov.: Inscribed on title-page: Recorders Office / Jany. '66 /.
Ref.: AII (*Arizona*) 4; Munk (Alliot) p. 154

The colophon reads as follows: Issued as a supplement to the Arizona Miner, and for / sale at the office of that paper in Prescott. / Price fifty cents per copy. /

82 ARIZONA TERRITORY. Legislative Assembly

MEMORIAL AND AFFIDAVITS SHOWING OUTRAGES PERPETRATED BY THE APACHE INDIANS, IN THE TERRITORY OF ARIZONA, FOR THE YEARS 1869 AND 1870 . . . SAN FRANCISCO: FRANCIS & VALENTINE, 1871.

[1]–32. 23 x 14.5 cm. Stabbed, laid in gray printed wrappers, with title on front wrapper, contents listed on verso of front wrapper. In a red cloth folder.
Prov.: Signature partially erased from front wrapper: W H Brown /. Marginal notes throughout in pencil.
Ref.: Howes D372

The annotator was keenly aware of the "outrages" and adds some interesting notes in the margins.

83 ARIZONA TERRITORY. Legislative Assembly

MEMORIAL FROM THE LEGISLATURE OF ARIZONA IN THE MATTER OF THE BOUNDARY BETWEEN ARIZONA AND CALIFORNIA.

[1]–4. 22.2 x 14.4 cm. Unbound, removed from bound volume.
Ref.:

Dated at end: November 3, 1864. Printed by O. M. Clayes, state printer, but Mr. Clayes's state has not yet been determined.

84 ARKANSAS GRANT, THE

THE ARKANSAS GRANT. A BRIEF HISTORY FROM THE TIME THE GRANT WAS MADE BY THE MEXICAN GOVERNMENT IN 1832 . . . COMPILED FROM THE OFFICIAL RECORDS, 1901.

[1]–62. 22.6 x 15.1 cm. Brown cloth.
Ref.:

Printed at Washington, D.C. Concerns the Beales Grant.

85 ARLEGUI, JOSEPH

CHRONICA DE LA PROVINCIA DE N. S. P. S. FRAN-CISCO DE ZACATECAS . . . EN MEXICO POR JOSEPH BERNARDO DE HOGAL . . . 1737.

[*]¹, ¶–¶¶¶⁴, ¶¶¶² A-Ggg⁴, Hhh², [**]¹. (Stubs of [*]² and [**]² are present.) [i]–xxx, [1]–412, [413–29 index, 430 blank]. (Page 234 mispaginated 342.) 20.4 x 14.7 cm. Woodcut on page [4]. Contemporary vellum, painted manuscript shelf mark (partially erased) and manuscript title reading down backstrip: Arlegui Chron. de Zacateˢ / . Remnants of leather ties.

Prov.: Below third line on title-page: Pertenece â la Libreria del Colegio de la Snŝa Cruz de Queretaro /. Branded on top edge: Ⓒ

Ref.: Jones 443; Medina (*Mexico*) 3451; Sabin 1998, 52106; Streit III 399; Wagner (*SS*) 99

A valuable chronicle containing much information about mines in Zacatecas as well as about the establishment of missions. A short account of Antonio de Espejo's discoveries in New Mexico is included.

86 ARMES, GEORGE A.

UPS AND DOWNS OF AN ARMY OFFICER . . . WASHINGTON, 1900.

[i]–[xx], 1–784. 21.8 x 14.8 cm. 107 illustrations listed. Calf, gilt back.

Prov.: Inscribed on blank leaf at front: Compliments of the / Author to his friend / Hon. Park W. Pitman / El Paso Texas / G. A. Armes / U.S.A. / Aug. 27ᵗʰ 1915— /.

Ref.: Howes A316

The author served at several posts in the West after the Civil War—Kansas, Colorado, the Dakotas. In 1870, Armes was dismissed from the Army by court martial and lived in Washington for the next thirty years trying for re-instatement, but without success. According to his story, he was a meritorious officer unjustly treated. Congress passed legislation for his reinstatement but Grant refused to sign the bill.—EDG

87 ARMSTRONG, A. N.

OREGON: COMPRISING A BRIEF HISTORY AND FULL DESCRIPTION OF THE TERRITORIES OF OREGON AND WASHINGTON . . . CHICAGO: PUBLISHED BY CHAS. SCOTT & CO., 1857.

[i]–vi, [7]–147, [148 blank]. 18.9 x 11.5 cm. Gray cloth.

Ref.: AII (*Chicago*) 229; Byrd 2566; Howes A318

The author was a government surveyor for three years in Oregon.

88 ARMSTRONG, BENJAMIN G.

EARLY LIFE AMONG THE INDIANS. REMINISCENCES FROM THE LIFE OF BENJ. G. ARMSTRONG . . . DICTATED TO AND WRITTEN BY THOS. P. WENTWORTH . . . ASHLAND, WIS. PRESS OF A. W. BOWRON, 1892.

[1]–266. 19.3 x 13.2 cm. Two frontispieces and sixteen plates. Red pictorial cloth.

Ref.: Howes A319

Armstrong's reminiscences contain valuable information about the early fur trade in Wisconsin and Minnesota and about treaties with the Indians of the area in 1835, 1837, 1842, and 1854.

89 ARMSTRONG, MOSES K.

THE EARLY EMPIRE BUILDERS OF THE GREAT WEST . . . ST. PAUL, MINN.: PUBLISHED BY E. W. PORTER, 1901.

[i]–[x], [1]–456. 22.9 x 14.9 cm. 23 plates listed. Red cloth.

Ref.:

90 ARMSTRONG, MOSES K.

HISTORY AND RESOURCES OF DAKOTA, MONTANA, AND IDAHO. TO WHICH IS APPENDED A MAP OF THE NORTHWEST. YANKTON, DAKOTA TERRITORY: GEO. W. KINGSBURY, 1866.*

[1]–72. 18.2 x 11.6 cm. Map attached to front wrapper: Nebraska, / Kansas, Dakota / Colorado / -and- / Montana. / [below neat line at right:] Eng. by Oliver J. Stuart, N.Y. / [along right margin, reading down:] McNally's System of Geography, Map N⁰ 18.) / 21.2 x 26.7 cm. Scale: about 120 miles to one inch. Silked. Green printed wrappers, with title on front wrapper, contents on verso of front wrapper, advertisements on recto and verso of back wrapper. In a green half morocco case.

Ref.: Allen (*Dakota*) 35; Howes A322

The first history of the Dakotas.

91 ARMSTRONG, NEVILL A. D.

YUKON YESTERDAYS. THIRTY YEARS OF ADVENTURE IN THE KLONDIKE . . . LONDON: JOHN LONG, LTD. . . . MCMXXXVI.

[1]–287, [288 blank], [1]–8 advertisements. 22.9 x 15.3 cm. Two maps on endpapers and 54 illustrations listed. Black cloth.

Ref.: Smith 294

92 ARMY AND NAVY CHRONICLE, THE

[THE ARMY AND NAVY CHRONICLE. VOLS. II–IX. WASHINGTON, 1836–39.]*

Eight volumes, various bindings. Lacks five numbers of Vol. V.

Ref.: Sabin 4230

"Summer on the Prairie," signed F., appears in Vol. II, pages 277–78, 292–93, 311–12, 321–22, 337–38, 353–54, 369–70, 385–86, and Vol. III, pages 1–2, 17–18, 33–34.

"Dragoon Expedition. Fort Leavenworth, Oct. 3, 1839.", signed ø, appears in Vol. IX, pages 285–86.

93 [ARNOLD, HENRY V.]

THE EARLY HISTORY OF THE DEVILS LAKE COUNTRY, INCLUDING THE PERIOD OF THE EARLY SETTLEMENTS. LARIMORE, N. D.: PRINTED BY H. V. ARNOLD, 1920.*

[1]–105, [106 advertisement]. 17.9 x 12.9 cm. Gray-green printed wrappers. In yellow cloth case.

Ref.: Howes A328

Note in pencil on endpaper: Only 46 printed /.

"Our pamphlets are not printed in any newspaper office, but at our home instead and on a press that was devised out of a common copy press which prints only one page at a time on four paged sheets."—Note on verso of title-leaf. "About 1917 the first two chapters were worked off the press . . . Last year this work was pushed forward again to page 48, when winter stopped further work on it until spring . . ."—Preface.

94 ARNY, WILLIAM F. M.

[Wrapper title] . . . CENTENNIAL HISTORICAL ORATION . . . "SANTA FE, NEW MEXICO—THE OLDEST CITY IN NORTH AMERICA." . . . SANTA FE: WILLIAMS & SHAW, PRINTERS, 1876.

[1]–64. 21.4 x 14.5 cm. Lavender printed wrappers, with title on front wrapper, note on verso of back wrapper.

Ref.: AII (*New Mexico*) 278; Howes A333

A summary of the history of Santa Fé.

95 [ARRINGTON, ALFRED W.]

THE DESPERADOES OF THE SOUTH-WEST: CONTAINING AN ACCOUNT OF THE CANE-HILL MURDERS, TOGETHER WITH THE LIVES OF SEVERAL OF THE MOST NOTORIOUS REGULATORS AND MODERATORS OF THAT REGION. BY CHARLES SUMMERFIELD. NEW-YORK: WILLIAM H. GRAHAM, 1847.

[i]–iv, [5]–48. 24.1 x 15.3 cm. Woodcut frontispiece and woodcuts on title-page and page 11. Blue printed wrappers, with title on front wrapper. In a red cloth case.

Ref.: Adams 35; Howes A338

The present copy carries 44 lines on page 48 and the printer's imprint appears on the verso of the title-leaf. There may have been a line of text under the author's name on the title-page, as

there is on the front wrapper; either the line failed to print or was deliberately blocked out.

Charles Summerfield was the pseudonym of Alfred W. Arrington.

96 ASBURY, HENRY

REMINISCENCES OF QUINCY, ILLINOIS . . . QUINCY: D. WILCOX & SONS, PRINTERS, 1882.

[1]–224. 22.8 x 15 cm. Frontispiece. Black cloth, title in gilt on backstrip.

Prov.: Name erased from inner front cover: ——— Henry Asbury /.

Ref.: Howes (1954) 345

The Mormon troubles in Illinois are described on pages 153–69.

97 [ASHE, THOMAS]

TRAVELS IN AMERICA, PERFORMED IN 1806, FOR THE PURPOSE OF EXPLORING THE RIVERS ALLEGHANY, MONONGAHELA, OHIO, AND MISSISSIPPI, AND ASCERTAINING THE PRODUCE AND CONDITION OF THEIR BANKS AND VICINITY. LONDON: PRINTED FOR RICHARD PHILLIPS, 1808.

[*]², [A]², B–O¹², P⁸. [i]–iv, [i]–iv, [1]–328. [A]¹, B⁴, C–O¹². [i–ii], [1]–152, 151–292, [283–94 Contents]. [A]¹, B–O¹². [i–ii], [1]–310, [311–12 Contents]. 17.7 x 10.3 to 18.9 x 9.8 cm. Three volumes, gray-blue boards, tan paper backstrips, uncut. Manuscript labels on backstrips, backs worn, part of first backstrip torn off.

Ref.: Bradford 134; Buck 68; Clark I 134; Howes A352; Jones 724; Sabin 2180; Thomson 45

Enlivened by misrepresentation and exaggeration, Ashe's account is interesting and highly readable.—Clark

98 [ASHLEY, WILLIAM H.]

[Caption title] 20TH CONGRESS, [CONFIDENTIAL.] 1ST SESSION. IN SENATE OF THE UNITED STATES. JANUARY 9, 1828. THE FOLLOWING LETTER WAS ORDERED TO BE PRINTED, IN CONFIDENCE, FOR THE USE OF THE SENATE. ST. LOUIS, NOVEMBER 12TH, 1827. . . [at foot of page 2:] YOUR VERY OBEDIENT SERVANT, W. H. ASHLEY. HON. THOMAS H. BENTON.

[1]–2. 21.8 x 13.7 cm.

BOUND WITH:

20TH CONGRESS, [CONFIDENTIAL.] 1ST SESSION. DOCUMENTS IN RELATION TO THE BOUNDARY OF THE UNITED STATES, WEST OF THE ROCKY MOUNTAINS, ACCOMPANYING THE PRESIDENT'S MESSAGE OF DECEMBER 12, 1827 . . . WASHINGTON: PRINTED BY DUFF GREEN. 1828.

[1]–83, [84 blank]. Two pieces bound together, new black cloth.

Ref.: Howes D381; Wagner-Camp 36

The first of the two pieces seems to have been unnoticed by other bibliographers. Wagner-Camp and Dale Morgan report later printings, but not this one dated January 9, 1828. The same letter by Ashley is repeated on pages 82–83 of the second document, and in 20th Congress, 2nd Session, Executive Document 67, Serial 181.

99 [ASHLEY, WILLIAM H.]

[Caption title] . . . RESOLVED, THAT THE COMMITTEE ON INDIAN AFFAIRS BE INSTRUCTED TO INQUIRE INTO THE PRESENT CONDITION OF THE FUR TRADE WITHIN THE LIMITS OF THE UNITED STATES, AND TO REPORT WHAT MEASURES, IF ANY, ARE NECESSARY TO THE SAFE AND SUCCESSFUL PROSECUTION OF THAT TRADE BY CITIZENS OF THE UNITED STATES . . . MR. BENTON MADE THE FOLLOWING REPORT . . .

[1]–19, [20 blank]. 22.3 x 14.3 cm. Rebound in new red cloth.

Ref.: Wagner-Camp 37

20th Congress, 2nd Session, Senate, Document No. 67, Serial 181. [Washington, 1829.]

Contains W. H. Ashley's letter of November 12, 1827, to Thomas Hart Benton on pages 11–12 and a second letter dated January 20, 1829, pages 12–15, both relating to the fur trade.

100 ASHLEY, WILLIAM H., JOSHUA PILCHER, & OTHERS

[Caption title] . . . MESSAGE FROM THE PRESIDENT OF THE UNITED STATES . . . RELATIVE TO THE BRITISH ESTABLISHMENTS ON THE COLUMBIA, AND THE STATE OF THE FUR TRADE, &C. . . . THE ENCLOSED COMMUNICATION FROM GEN. W. H. ASHLEY, JOSHUA PILCHER, AND FROM J. D. SMITH, DAVID E. JACKSON, AND W. L. SUBLETTE, CONTAINS ALL THE INFORMATION TO BE FOUND IN THIS DEPARTMENT ON THE SUBJECT OF THE RESOLUTION OF THE SENATE OF THE 21ST INSTANT. VERY RESPECTFULLY, J. H. EATON. . . .

[1]–36. 22.4 x 14.2 cm. Removed from bound volume, unbound. In a brown cloth case.

Ref.: Wagner-Camp 44

21st Congress, 2nd Session, Senate, Document No. 39, Serial 203. [Washington, 1831.]

101 ASHTABULA [Ohio] SENTINEL

[Newspaper] ASHTABULA S[ENTINEL]. VOLUME XXVIII. JEFFERSON, OHIO, THURSDAY, [APRIL 7, 1859. NUMBER 14.]

Newspaper, [109]–116. 49.3 x 33.4 cm. Unbound. Part of first leaf cut away.

John Udell's letter of March 5, 1859, dated from Alberquerque[!], New Mexico, occupies the first two columns on page 113. The letter contains a long description of his troubles with the Indians.

102 ATHERTON, GERTRUDE

THE SPLENDID IDLE FORTIES . . . NEW YORK: THE MACMILLAN COMPANY, 1902.

[i]–[x], [1]–389, [390 blank]. 19.2 x 13 cm. Eight illustrations listed. Red pictorial ribbed cloth.

Prov.: Inscribed on front endleaf: [?] a few per-/sonal adventures / in all [?] old / California times Some / of the stories founded / on fact. Others, like / Pearls of the Lareto, en-/tirely original / Gertrude Atherton / For Mrs. B. F. Hart /. Mounted above the inscription is a return label addressed by the author.

Ref.: Johnson (Blanck), p. 28; Zamorano Eighty 1

103 ATHERTON, WILLIAM

NARRATIVE OF THE SUFFERING & DEFEAT OF THE NORTH-WESTERN ARMY, UNDER GENERAL WINCHESTER: MASSACRE OF THE PRISONERS: SIXTEEN MONTHS IMPRISONMENT OF THE WRITER AND OTHERS WITH THE INDIANS AND BRITISH. FRANKFORT, KY.: PRINTED FOR THE AUTHOR BY A. G. HODGES, 1842.

[1]–152, [153–56 blank]. 16.3 x 10.3 cm. Tan boards, sheep back, printed white paper label on front cover.

Ref.: Caxton Club (Lowe) 52; Field 52; Howes A366; Jones 1058; Sabin 2273; Thomson 47

Atherton gives a good personal narrative of the Raisin River Massacre and the events leading up to it. A generous share of the work is devoted to his subsequent adventures as a prisoner of war.

In the ICN copy, the "3" in the pagination on page 53 is much raised above the line. Neither the Graff nor the ICN (Ayer) copy shows this error.

104 [ATKINSON, H., & OTHERS]

. . . EXPEDITION UP THE MISSOURI. LETTER FROM THE SECRETARY OF WAR . . . RESPECTING THE MOVEMENTS OF THE EXPEDITION WHICH LATELY ASCENDED THE MISSOURI RIVER, &C. . . . WASHINGTON: PRINTED BY GALES & SEATON, 1826.

[1]–16. 24.2 x 15.2 cm. Original folded gathering, uncut, unopened.

Ref.: Wagner-Camp 32

19th Congress, 1st Session, House, Document No. 117, Serial 136.

105 ATLANTIC AND PACIFIC JUNCTION AND COSTA RICA COLONISATION COMPANY, THE

[Caption title] (PRIVATE.) NEW ROUTE TO CALIFORNIA, AND UNION OF THE ATLANTIC AND PA-

CIFIC, BY ROAD, RAILWAY, OR CANAL. WITH NEW HOMES FOR EMIGRANTS IN THE FREE COLONY OF COSTA RICA . . .

[1]–16. 20.3 x 13.3 cm. Unbound, removed from bound volume.

Ref.:

An early proposal for a railroad between the two oceans.

106 ATSON, WILLIAM

HEART WHISPERS; OR, A PEEP BEHIND THE FAMILY CURTAIN, INTERSPERSED WITH SKETCHES OF A TOUR THROUGH NINE SOUTHERN STATES. MEMPHIS: CLEAVES & VADEN, 1859.*

[i]–xvi, [25]–368. 18 x 11.5 cm. Black cloth, blind embossed sides, title in gilt on backstrip.

Ref.: Howes A374; Sabin 2321

Copies are also found with the imprint: Philadelphia: H. Cowperthwait & Co., 1859.

107 ATTENTION, VOLUNTEERS!

[Broadside] ATTENTION, VOLUNTEERS! CAPT. STAPP'S COMPANY OF MOUNTED VOLUNTEERS, HAVE BEEN ACCEPTED BY THE WAR DEPARTMENT, . . . G. C. LANPHERE, 1ST LIEUT. G. W. PALMER, 1ST 2D LIEUT. D. S. COWEN, 2D 2D LIEUT. MONMOUTH, JULY 10, 1847.

Broadside, 21.5 x 17.6 cm. Text, 21.1 x 16.7 cm.

Ref.: Byrd 1251

108 AUBRY, FRANCOIS XAVIER

[Caption title] DIARY OF A JOURNEY THROUGH ARIZONA. FROM THE RAILROAD RECORD. . . .

[1]–12, [13–16 blank]. 22.4 x 14.5 cm. Sewn, unbound. In a brown morocco case.

Ref.:

Apparently the first separate printing of Aubry's Journal from Tejon Pass, July 10, to Albuquerque, September 10, 1853. Reprinted from the *Railroad Record*, 1866.

The Journal appeared first in the *Santa Fé Weekly Gazette* for September 24, 1853. It was reprinted in the *San Francisco Daily Herald* for December 5–6, 1853; the *Daily Alta California* for January 25, 1854; the *Daily Missouri Republican* for March 19 and April 18, 1854; and the *Western Journal & Civilian*, 1854, Vol. 11, pages 84–96. It was quoted in full in Gwin: *Speeches of Mr. Gwin, of California, on the National Railroad Bill* . . . Washington, 1853. (See number 1697.)

109 AUDUBON, JOHN J.

AUTOGRAPH MANUSCRIPT JOURNAL: Copy of my Journal from Fort Union [undeciphered word ending: eway] / Commencing Aug^T 16TH at 12

o'clock, the moment of our / departure. [flourish] /.

Seventeen pages, 31.5 x 18.9 cm., removed from bound notebook, stabbed with old string.

The manuscript journal covers the period August 16 to November 6, 1843.

Maria R. Audubon, the author's granddaughter, published a journal which she claimed was found "in the back of an old secretary" in August, 1896. The version she published differs from the present manuscript, and is somewhat condensed. All of the information in the printed version is present in this manuscript copy, but not all of the material in the latter is found in the printed version, even in condensed form. The present manuscript is about fifteen hundred words longer than the printed version. Certain portions, including for example, the measurements of a grizzly bear shot on August 22, are omitted entirely. Parts of the manuscript are crossed out in pencil; these sections are not included in the printed version.

110 AUDUBON, JOHN J.

AUTOGRAPH LETTER, SIGNED WITH INITIALS (retained copy). 1845 January 8, no place. Four pages, 31.5 x 18.9 cm. To John Bachman.

This is a letter in which Audubon denies the charge of a third party that he intended to claim the *Quadrupeds*, on which Bachman and Audubon were working together, as his work alone. It contains information about the state of the work and concludes with a warm expression of friendship and affection for the recipient.

The letter accompanies and is attached to Audubon's manuscript Journal for August to November, 1843.

111 AUDUBON, JOHN W.

ILLUSTRATED NOTES OF AN EXPEDITION THROUGH MEXICO AND CALIFORNIA . . . NEW-YORK: PUBLISHED BY J. W. AUDUBON, 1852.

[i–iv], [1]–48. 44.1 x 33 cm. Four colored lithographs: [1] [upper left corner:] N° I. [upper right corner:] Pl. 1. / [lower left:] On Stone by E. Gildemeister. [centre:] Entered according to act of Congress in the year 1851 by J. W. Audubon, in the Clerk's Office of the District Court of the Southern District of N.Y. [right:] Print. by Nagel & Weingærtner. / [centre:] From Nature by J. W. Audubon A. N. A. / Fourth of July Camp / Published by Audubon 34 Liberty Str. and Nagel & Weingærtner 74 Fulton Str. N.Y. / 25 x 32.7 cm. [2] [lower left:] On Stone by Gildemeister. [centre:] From Nature by J. W. Audubon A. N. A. [lower left:] Lith. & Print. by

Nagel & Weingærtner / The Night Watch / 25.1 x 32.5 cm. [3] [upper left:] N° I. [upper right:] Pl. 3. / [lower left:] On Stone by E Gildemeister / [centre:] Entered according to act of Congress in the year 1851 by J. W. Audubon, in the Clerk's Office of the District Court of the Southern District of N.Y. [lower right:] Print by Nagel & Weingærtner / [centre:] From Nature by J. W. Audubon A. N. A. / Cañon, Jesus Maria / [centre:] Published by Audubon 34 Liberty Str. and Nagel & Weingærtner 74 Fulton Str. N.Y. / 25.4 x 33 cm. [4] [upper left:] N° I. [upper right:] Pl. 4. / [lower left:] On Stone by E. Gildemeister. [centre:] Entered according to act of Congress in the year 1851 by J. W. Audubon, in the Clerk's Office of the District Court of the Southern District of N.Y. [right:] Print. by Nagel & Weingærtner. / [centre:] From Nature by J. W. Audubon A. N. A. / Jesus Maria / Published by Audubon 34 Liberty Str. and Nagel & Weingærtner 74 Fulton Str. N.Y. / 25.1 x 32.8 cm. Brown printed wrappers bound into half red levant morocco, gilt top. Title on front wrapper.

Prov.: Ruthven Deane bookplate, and with a long note by him on first blank leaf.

Ref.: Bay p. 349; Cowan p. 23; Howes A390; Sabin 2372; Wagner-Camp 208

Only the first part of the projected work was published. It was issued with plates either plain or colored.

112 AUDUBON, MARIA R.

AUDUBON AND HIS JOURNALS. . . . NEW YORK: CHARLES SCRIBNER'S SONS, 1897.

[i]–xiv, [1] 532. [i]–viii, [1]–554, [555 list of facsimiles, 556 blank]. 22.2 x 15 cm. 46 illustrations listed. Two volumes, dark gray cloth, gilt tops, uncut.

Prov.: Bookplates of Ruthven Deane, Maria R. Audubon, and Florence Audubon.

Ref.: Howes A391; Hubach p. 120

Extensively extra-illustrated with original photographs, manuscripts, letters, etc. by Maria R. Audubon and Ruthven Deane, including an autograph letter from Miss Audubon presenting the two volumes to Mr. Deane.

113 AULNEAU COLLECTION

RARE OR UNPUBLISHED DOCUMENTS. II. THE AULNEAU COLLECTION, 1734–1745. EDITED BY THE REV. ARTHUR E. JONES . . . MONTREAL: ARCHIVES OF ST. MARY'S COLLEGE, 1893.

[1]–160. 21 x 14.7 cm. Pink printed wrappers bound into board covers with morocco back.

Prov.: Bookplate of G. Ducharme.

Ref.:

Father Jean Aulneau was killed by Indians in 1734, when he was on an expedition with the younger Verendrye near Mackinac.

114 AUSTIN, MARY

THE LAND OF LITTLE RAIN . . . BOSTON: HOUGHTON, MIFFLIN AND COMPANY, 1903.*

[i]–[xvi], [1]–[281], [282 colophon]. 21.5 x 16 cm. Illustrations and marginal sketches unlisted. Olive-green pictorial ribbed cloth.

Ref.: Cowan p. 24; Howes A400; Zamorano Eighty 2

115 AUSTIN, STEPHEN F.

AN ADDRESS DELIVERED . . . ON THE 7TH OF MARCH, 1836. LEXINGTON: J. CLARKE & CO. PRINTERS. 1836.

[1]–30. 17.4 x 11.1 cm. Pink printed wrappers, with title on front wrapper. In a red cloth case.

Prov.: Signature on front wrapper: John M Holley /, and on title-page: John M Holleys — /.

Ref.: Clements Library (*Texas*) 13; Howes A402; NYPL (*Bulletin*) XLI p. 83; Rader 212; Sabin 2426; Streeter 1181

Austin *always* had Texas on his mind.

116 AUSTIN, STEPHEN F.

ESPOSICION AL PUBLICO SOBRE LOS ASUNTOS DE TEJAS . . . MEGICO: EN CASA DE CORNELIO C. SEBRING, 1835.

[1]–32. (Page 29 mispaginated 21.) 20.5 x 14 cm. Stabbed, unbound. In a brown cloth case.

Ref.: Clements Library (*Texas*) 11; Howes A403; NYPL (*Bulletin*) XLI p. 82; Rader 213; Raines p. 15; Streeter 817

Austin went to Mexico City reluctantly to argue for a measure of autonomy for Texas. He argued himself into jail (charged with disloyalty), where he spent his time composing this explanation of the attitude of Texans toward Mexico.

117 AUSTIN, STEPHEN F.

[Map] [vignette] / MAP / OF / TEXAS / WITH PARTS OF THE ADJOINING STATES / COMPILED BY STEPHEN F. AUSTIN / PUBLISHED BY H. S. TANNER PHILADELPHIA / NOTE. THE LATITUDE AND LONGITUDE OF SALTILLO MONTEREY / LAREDO BEXAR NACOGDOCHES AND THE POINT WHERE THE BOUND-/-ARY LINE LEAVES THE SABINE ARE FROM THE OBSERVATIONS OF / GENERAL TERAN OF THE MEXICAN ARMY. / SCALE OF MILES. / [diagrammatic scale: about 24 miles to one inch] / ENGRAVED BY JOHN & WM. W. WARR PHILAD.ᴬ / [lower left:] ENTERED ACCORDING TO ACT OF CONGRESS THE 17ᵀᴴ DAY OF MARCH 1830 BY H. S. TANNER OF THE STATE OF PENNSYLVANIA. /

Map, 74.2 x 61.5 cm. Folded into a red straight-grain leather folder, 15.1 x 8.5 cm.

Ref.: Howes A404; NYPL (*Bulletin*) XLI p. 80; Phillips (*Maps*) p. 841; Streeter 1115

118 [AUSTIN, STEPHEN F.]

TRANSLATION OF THE LAWS, ORDERS, AND CON-TRACTS, ON COLONIZATION, FROM JANUARY, 1821, UP TO THIS TIME, IN VIRTUE OF WHICH COL. STEPHEN F. AUSTIN, HAS INTRODUCED AND SETTLED FOREIGN EMIGRANTS IN TEXAS, WITH AN EXPLANA-TORY INTRODUCTION. SAN FILIPE[!] DE AUSTIN, TEXAS: PRINTED BY GODWIN B. COTTEN, 1829.

[i]–[70], [71 errata, 72 blank]. 18.3 x 12.2 cm. Rebound in brown half morocco.

Prov.: Signature on title-page: P. W. Gray. / and on preliminary blank leaf: W. F. Gray /. Bookplate of C. R. Wharton and a long manu-script note by him on a fly leaf identifying W. F. Gray and his son P. W. Gray and commenting on W. F. Gray's diary. Part of rubber stamp: Austin / three times in outer margin of title. A few manuscript notes in text.

Ref.: Howes 144; Raines p. 15; Sabin 94945; Streeter 12

The Gray diary has been published. The au-thor mentions the purchase of this volume in the diary.

119 AUSTIN, STEPHEN F.

TRANSLATION OF THE LAWS, ORDERS AND CON-TRACTS, ON COLONIZATION, FROM JANUARY 1821, UP TO 1829 . . . COLUMBIA: RE-PRINTED BY BOR-DEN & MOORE, PUBLIC PRINTERS, 1837.

[1]–81, [82 blank]. 20.2 x 13.1 cm. Rebound in gray buckram, red leather label.

Prov.: Inscribed at top of title-page: From Algernon Thompson / To Rob.ᵗ A. Campbell / 1840. / Along inner margin of title-page, reading up: Thomas Benjamin Jefferson Hadley /.

Ref.: Howes T144; Raines p. 15; Sabin 94945; Streeter 186

Editions: San Filipe[!] de Austin, 1829.

120 AUZIAS-TURENNE, RAYMOND

. . . VOYAGE AU PAYS DES MINES D'OR, LE KLON-DIKE . . . PARIS: CALMANN LEVY, EDITEUR . . . 1899.

[i–vi], [1]–318, [319–20 Table]. 18.6 x 12 cm. 40 illustrations and two maps. White printed wrap-pers, uncut, unopened. In a green buckram case.

Ref.: Howes A415; Smith 381; Wickersham 4275

Editions: Paris, 1898.

121 AVERELL, WILLIAM WOODS

AUTOGRAPH MANUSCRIPT [Reminiscences]. 91 pages, 31.3 x 19.7 to 25.1 x 19.9 cm. Written partly in pencil. Fragile.

Averell was born in 1832, entered the United States Military Academy at West Point in 1851, was graduated four years later, and served at Jackson Barracks, Mo., for his first Army as-signment. After training at the Cavalry School for Practice in Carlisle, Penna., he went to New Mexico in 1857 for field duty, and for the next two years was actively engaged in skirmishes with the Indians. He secured a leave of absence because of wounds received and remained inac-tive until the Civil War. During that conflict he distinguished himself as a cavalry officer under McClellan, Sheridan, and Hooker, eventually achieving the rank of Brevet Brigadier General. In May, 1865, he resigned from the Army and entered private life. His career as a manufacturer and engineer was successful. Toward the end of his life (he died in 1900) he started the present uncompleted reminiscences. The completed sec-tions deal principally with his Army life in the Southwest.

122 AVERILL, CHARLES E.

LIFE IN CALIFORNIA; OR, THE TREASURE-SEEKERS' EXPEDITION. A SEQUEL TO KIT CARSON, THE PRINCE OF THE GOLD-HUNTERS. BOSTON: PRINTED AND PUBLISHED BY GEORGE H. WILLIAMS.

[i–iv], 9–100. 25.5 x 17 cm. Woodcut. Yellow printed wrappers with title on front wrapper, advertisement on verso of front wrapper. Lacks back wrapper, front wrapper partly defective.

Ref.: Cowan p. 24; Howes A418

Howes dates this edition [1865], although it was copyrighted in 1849. In 1857 it appeared as *Rob Roy of the Rocky Mountains* . . .

Editions: Boston, 1849; New York, 1849; Boston, 1850.

123 AVERY, A.

HAND-BOOK AND TRAVELERS' GUIDE OF NEW MEXI-CO . . . DENVER, COLO.: E. PRICE & CO., 1881.

[1]–33, unpaginated illustration, 33–106, [1–14 advertisements]. 14.8 x 11.3 cm. Two woodcuts, five text illustrations and a map, unlisted. Map: [Routes from El Paso to Pueblo.] 13.3 x 10.2 cm. No scale given. Light green printed wrap-pers, with title on front wrapper, advertisements on verso of front wrapper and on recto and verso of back wrapper. In a green half morocco case.

Prov.: Bookplate of C. G. Littell.

Ref.: Howes A420

An account of an overland trip from Fort

Ellsworth begins on page 47. Laid in is an eight-page foldout advertising the author's leather business.

124 AVERY, A.

[Cover title] A. AVERY, MANUFACTURER OF GLOVES, BUCKSKIN CLOTHING, AND LEATHER NOVELTIES. 301 FIFTEENTH STREET, DENVER, = COLORADO. P.O. BOX 2628. E. PRICE & CO., PRINTERS.

[1–8] foldout. 13.3 x 30.7 cm. folded to 13.3 x 7.8 cm. Unbound.

Laid in Avery: *Hand-Book and Travelers' Guide* . . . 1881.

125 AVERY, J. H.

THE LAND OF OPHIR, IDEAL AND REAL. A DISCOURSE DELIVERED AT AUSTINBURG, OHIO, BEFORE A COMPANY ABOUT PROCEEDING TO CALIFORNIA . . . NEW YORK: PRINTED BY EDWARD O. JENKINS, 1853.

[1]–15, [16 blank]. 22.9 x 15 cm. Tan printed wrappers with title on front wrapper. In a blue cloth folder.

Ref.:

Bon voyage!

126 AYER, I. WINSLOW

LIFE IN THE WILDS OF AMERICA, AND WONDERS OF THE WEST IN AND BEYOND THE BOUNDS OF CIVILIZATION . . . GRAND RAPIDS: THE CENTRAL PUBLISHING COMPANY, 1880.

[1]–528. 21.5 x 14.6 cm. Illustrations unlisted. Green cloth, stamped in black and gilt.

Ref.: Howes A427

The author's accounts of his own adventures are almost wholly imaginary.

127 AYERS, JAMES J.

GOLD AND SUNSHINE. REMINISCENCES OF EARLY CALIFORNIA . . . BOSTON: THE GORHAM PRESS [1922].

[i]–[xvi, xvi blank], 11–359, [360 blank]. 20.6 x 14 cm. 16 plates and pictorial endpapers listed. Red cloth, fore and lower edges uncut.

Ref.: Cowan p. 26

B

128 [BABCOCK, O. E.]

[Caption title] . . . MILITARY POSTS. LETTER FROM THE SECRETARY OF WAR . . . TRANSMITTING A REPORT OF INSPECTION OF MILITARY POSTS . . .

[1]–15, [16 blank]. 24.6 x 14.9 cm. Unbound, uncut.

Ref.:

39th Congress, 2nd Session, House, Executive Document No. 20, Serial 1288. [Washington: Government Printing Office, 1867.]

The report, dated October 5, 1866, was made by Brevet Brigadier General O. E. Babcock.

129 BABCOCK, RUFUS

FORTY YEARS OF PIONEER LIFE. MEMOIR OF JOHN MASON PECK, D.D. EDITED FROM HIS JOURNALS AND CORRESPONDENCE . . . PHILADELPHIA: AMERICAN BAPTIST PUBLICATION SOCIETY.

[1]–360. 19.4 x 12.2 cm. Portrait. Blue-purple cloth, blind embossed sides, title in gilt on backstrip.

Ref.: Buck 110; Howes B6; Sabin 2574

Published in 1864. Peck was an Illinois Pioneer.

130 BACK, SIR GEORGE

NARRATIVE OF THE ARCTIC LAND EXPEDITION TO THE MOUTH OF THE GREAT FISH RIVER, AND ALONG THE SHORES OF THE ARCTIC OCEAN, IN THE YEARS 1833, 1834, AND 1835 . . . LONDON: JOHN MURRAY, MDCCCXXXVI.

[i]–[xii, xii blank], [1]–663, [664 colophon]. 28.4 x 22.2 cm. 16 plates and a map: Map of the / Discoveries and Route / of the / Arctic Land Expedition, / in the Years 1833 & 1834. / Surveyed and Drawn / by / Captain Back, R. N. / [diagrammatic scale: about 38 English miles to one inch] / Reference / [three lines] / [lower centre:] London: John Murray, Albemarle Street, 1836. [lower right:] John Arrowsmith. / 37.6 x 48.1 cm. Scale as above. *Inset:* [Arctic Canada]. 15.7 x 23.9 cm. No scale given. Plum cloth, blind stamped sides, gilt back, uncut, unopened.

Ref.: Field 63; Sabin 2613; Smith 393; Staton & Tremaine 1873; Winsor VIII p. 119

Large and Superior Paper copy, with the plates printed on India paper. Fourteen illustrations are listed, but there are two additional plates following the last plate listed.

131 BACON, EDWARD

AMONG THE COTTON THIEVES. . . DETROIT: THE FREE PRESS STEAM BOOK AND JOB PRINTING HOUSE, 1867.

[1]–299, [300 blank]. 23 x 14.6 cm. Dark yellow printed wrappers with title on front wrapper, and with title on backstrip reading down.

Ref.: Coulter 14; Howes B20; Nicholson p. 50

Bacon's account of cotton thievery and other skullduggery among Union soldiers and officers covers activities in Louisiana near Baton Rouge, Port Hudson, Lake Maurepas, and New Orleans.

132 BACON, EPHRAIM

AUTOBIOGRAPHY. A NARRATIVE OF THE PRINCIPAL INCIDENTS IN THE LIFE OF EPHRAIM BACON: FOR TWENTY YEARS A PROFESSED BELIEVER, AND ZEALOUS PROPAGATOR OF INFIDEL SENTIMENTS: SUBSEQUENTLY, AN HUMBLE DISCIPLE OF THE MEEK AND LOWLY JESUS, AND MEMBER OF THE PROTESTANT EPISCOPAL CHURCH . . . DES MOINES, IOWA.: N. W. MILLS & CO. PRINTERS, 1857.

[i–ii], [1]–14. 20.5 x 13 cm. Stabbed, uncut.
Ref.:

133 BACQUEVILLE DE LA POTHERIE, CLAUDE CHARLES LE ROY

HISTOIRE DE L'AMERIQUE SEPTENTRIONALE . . . A PARIS: JEAN-LUC NION, M.DCC.XXII.

[*]², ã⁴, A⁴, B⁵, C–Gg⁶, Hh². [*]², A–Gg⁶. [*]², A–Dd⁶, Ee². [*]², A⁵, B–Z⁶, Aa². [i–xiv], 1–10, 15–216, 227–370, [371–74 Table]. (Pages [i–ii] blank, pagination 11–14 omitted, pages 214–16 mispaginated 124–26.) [i–iv], 1–168, 173–356, [357–63 Table, 364 blank]. (Pages [i–ii] blank, pagination 169–72 omitted.) [i–xiv], [1]–158, 157–310, [311–16 Table]. (Pages [i–ii] blank, pagination 157–58 repeated.) [i–iv], 1–271, [272–76 Table and Licence]. (Pages [i–ii] blank.) 15.4 x 8.8 cm. 20 engraved plates, engraved title-pages, three engraved maps. Map: Carte / de la Baye et Detroit / d'Hudson / [upper right:] Tom. 1 pag. 56. / 11.7 x 16.2 cm. No scale given. Map: Carte / du Gouvernement du / Montreal. / [upper right:] Tom. 1 pag. 311. / 12.8 x 7.5 cm. No scale given. Map: Carte / Generalle / de la / Nouvelle / France. / [upper right:] Tom. 2. pag. 1. / 13 x 16.3 cm. No scale given. Four volumes, contemporary full calf, gilt backstrips, red labels, red edges. The binding of the second volume differs slightly from the others.

Ref.: Field 66; Howes B23; Jones 413; Leclerc 98; Sabin 2692

Jacques Le Long: *Bibliothèque Historique de la France* . . . Paris, 1719, under entry 15876, gives the following description: "Nouveau Voïage de Canada, ou de la Nouvelle France, avec les Guerres des François avec les Anglois & les Originaires du Païs: par Le Roy de la Poterie; quatre volumes en douze, Paris, 1716." No such 1716 edition has as yet been reported. However, Le Long described both printed books and manuscripts and it is possible that in 1719 he was referring either to a manuscript by Bacqueville or to a projected work which was not published.

The present work bears on the last page of the final volume a permission to publish dated June 9, 1702, although the Privilege in the first volume is dated May 2, 1721. This was issued to François Didot of Paris and was shared also by Jean-Luc Nion of Paris and Jean Baptiste Machuël Père of Rouen. Thus, the Rouen edition of the same year probably followed the Paris edition of 1722. The sheets of the 1722 editions are identical except for the title-pages; the Amsterdam, 1723 edition and the 1750 editions are from the same printing, but omit the prefatory matter in the first volume.

134 BAD LANDS COW BOY, THE

[Newspaper] THE BAD LANDS COW BOY. VOLUME 2, NUMBER 31. MEDORA, DAKOTA, SEPTEMBER 3, 1885...

[1–4]. 60.7 x 44.6 cm. Unbound.
Ref.:
The editor was A. T. Packard. There is a notice of a meeting, signed by Theodore Roosevelt, and there is also a note about Granville Stuart.

135 BADGER, JOSEPH

A MEMOIR OF REV. JOSEPH BADGER; CONTAINING AN AUTOBIOGRAPHY AND SELECTIONS FROM HIS PRIVATE JOURNAL AND CORRESPONDENCE. HUDSON, OHIO: SAWYER, INGERSOLL AND COMPANY, 1851.

[1]–185, [186 blank, 187–88 advertisement]. 17.9 x 11.2 cm. Portrait. Black cloth.

Ref.: Howes B25; Sabin 47496

The *Memoir* covers experiences in the Revolutionary War; in the War of 1812; travels of the author in New England, Pennsylvania, Ohio, and Michigan; and missionary work among the Wyandottes (1806–12) as well as pastorates in the Connecticut Western Reserve. Substantially the same material had been printed earlier in the *American Quarterly Register*, Vol. XIII, pages 317–28. The preface, editorial work, and additions were by Henry N. Day whose *Elements of the Art of Rhetoric* . . . is advertised on pages [187–88].

136 [BAEDEKER, JULIUS]

[Map] KARTE DES STAATES / TEXAS / (AUFGENOMMEN IN DIE UNION 1846.) / NACH DER NEUESTEN EINTHEILUNG. / 1849. / [lower left:] VERLAG V. J. BADEKER IN ELBERFELD. / [lower right:] LITH. BEI FR. KOENEN, ELBERFELD. / *Inset:* Plan von Castroville. / 6.6 x 8.2 cm. No scale given. *Inset:* Plan / von / Neu-Braunfels / und / Comalstadt. / 5.4 x 8.1 cm. No scale given.

Map, 28.7 x 36.3 cm. No scale given. Folded into gray board folder, 17 x 10.4 cm., brown cloth backstrip, advertisement on verso of back cover and on verso of front cover.
Ref.:
The Texas flag is printed in color.

137 [BAEGERT, JACOB]

NACHRICHTEN / VON DER / AMERIKANISCHEN HALBINSEL / CALIFORNIEN: MIT EINEM / ZWEY-FACHEN / ANHANG FALSCHER NACHRICHTEN. . . MANNHEIM: / GEDRUCKT IN DER CHURSURSTL. HOF- UND ACAADEMIE- / BUCKDRUCKERY, 1772. /

[*]⁸, A-Y⁸, Z⁴. [1–16], [1]–358, [359 errata, 360 blank]. 16.6 x 10.2 cm. Two plates and a map: California / per / P. Ferdinandum Con-/sak S. I. / et alios / [lower left:] E. V. sc. / [three lines of text below neat line] 22 x 17.4 cm. Scale: about 55 *horae itineris* to one inch. Contemporary half vellum, marbled board sides, printed paper label, red sprinkled edges.

Prov.: Manuscript note on title-page: ex libris Univ. Kn. v. Cloth (?) Ao 1774 /. Shelfmark on front endleaf: XXXI K 19 /.

Ref.: Bradford 332; Cowan p. 27; Howes B29; Sabin 4363; Streit III 937; Wagner (*Cart. of NW Coast*) 631; Wagner (*SS*) 157

Streit describes a 1771 edition which he locates in the British Museum. However, the new edition of the British Museum Catalogue lists the 1772 edition as its earliest. The other bibliographies mentioned above list 1772 as the first edition. The English translation by Brandenburg and Baumann published by the University of California mentions, but does not describe, a 1771 edition. It is doubtful that a 1771 edition exists.

138 BAILEY, GILBERT S.

HISTORY OF THE ILLINOIS RIVER BAPTIST ASSOCIATION, AND OF ITS CHURCHES . . . NEW YORK: SHELDON, BLAKEMAN & CO., 1857.

[i]–vi, [7]–146. 14.9 x 9.6 cm. Plum cloth, blind embossed borders on sides, title in gilt on front cover.

Ref.:

139 BAILEY, WASHINGTON

A TRIP TO CALIFORNIA IN 1853 . . . RECOLLECTIONS OF A GOLD SEEKING TRIP BY OX TRAIN ACROSS THE PLAINS AND MOUNTAINS . . . LEROY JOURNAL PRINTING COMPANY, 1915.*

[i–ii], [1]-50, [51–2 blank]. 22.2 x 15.2 cm. Portrait. Brown printed wrappers with title on front wrapper.

Prov.: Inscribed in pencil on initial blank leaf: Dec. 30, 1915—This thrilling / sketch presented by the venerable / Washington Bailey to W. H. Porter /.

Ref.: Cowan p. 28; Howes B35

Printed at LeRoy, Illinois. There is an errata slip following page 46, 11.4 x 15.2 cm.

140 BAILY, FRANCIS

JOURNAL OF A TOUR IN UNSETTLED PARTS OF NORTH AMERICA IN 1796 & 1797 . . . LONDON: BAILY BROTHERS, MDCCCLVI.

[i]–xii, [1]–439, [440 blank]. 22.4 x 14.3 cm. Brown cloth, blind embossed sides, gilt title on backstrip, uncut.

Prov.: Inscribed on the title-page: W: H: Ogden: Esqᵉ / Southampton, / Harts / with Mr Baily's kind / regards, /.

Ref.: Buck 52; Clark II 74; Howes B40; Jones 1345; Rader 230; Sabin 2770; Thomson 55

A travel journal of the late eighteenth century which remained unpublished for more than fifty years. The prefatory memoir was written by Sir John Herschel.

141 [BAIRD, ROBERT]

VIEW OF THE VALLEY OF THE MISSISSIPPI: OR THE EMIGRANT'S AND TRAVELLER'S GUIDE TO THE WEST. PHILADELPHIA: PUBLISHED BY H. S. TANNER, 1832.

[i]–xii, [1]–341, [342 blank], [1]–10 advertisements. 18.5 x 10.9 cm. 15 engraved maps, unlisted. Map: / United States / [above neat line:] Frontispiece / [lower right:] J. Knight Sc. / 13.4 x 6.1 cm. Scale: about 260 miles to one inch. Map: New York / [upper right:] Page 8. / 12.4 x 15.7 cm. Scale: 70 miles to one inch. Map: Pennsylvania / and / New Jersey / [upper right:] Page 95. / 12.2 x 15.4 cm. Scale: 70 miles to one inch. Plan: Pittsburgh / [upper right:] Page 101. / 8.6 x 15.2 cm. Scale: about 65 miles to one inch. Map: Ohio / and / Indiana / [upper right:] Page 127. / 12.4 x 15.7 cm. Scale: 70 miles to one inch. Plan: Cincinnati / [upper right:] Page 137. / 8.6 x 15.7 cm. Scale: 1200 feet to one inch. Map: Michigan / [upper right:] Page 164. / [lower right:] E. B. Dawson Sc. / 13.6 x 16.9 cm. Scale: about 120 miles to one inch. *Inset:* Environs of Detroit / 5 x 4.4 cm. Scale: about 32 miles to one inch. Map: Kentucky / and Tennessee / [upper right:] Page 176. / [lower right:] J. Knight Sc. / 12.7 x 16.3 cm. Scale: about 65 miles to one inch. Plan: Louisville / [upper right:] Page 180. / 7.9 x 15.5 cm. Scale: 3200 feet to one inch. Map: Illinois / and / Missouri / [upper right:] Page 200. / [lower right:] J. Knight Sc. / 15.7 x 12.7 cm. Scale: about 65 miles to one inch. *Inset:* Missouri River / West Part / 2.2 x 2.9 cm. Scale: about 65 miles to one inch. Plans: [Four plans] Environs of Sᵗ Louis /, Lead Region /, Environs of Lexington /, and Environs of Nashville / [upper right:] Page 228. / [lower right:] J. Knight Sc. / Each plan: 7.6 x 6.7 cm. Scale: about 18

miles to one inch. Map: Louisiana / and / Mississippi / [upper right:] Page 247. / [lower right:] J. Knight Sc. / 15.7 x 12.7 cm. Scale: about 65 miles to one inch. Plans: [Three plans] Environs of Mobile / 7.8 x 6.8 cm. Scale: about 18 miles to one inch. Environs of Pensacola / 7.8 x 6.8 cm. Scale: about 18 miles to one inch. New Orleans / 7.8 x 13.6 cm. Scale: 2000 feet to one inch. [upper right:] / Page 264. / Map: Georgia / and / Alabama / [upper right:] Page 276. / [lower right:] J. Knight Sc. / 12.9 x 16.4 cm. Scale: 70 miles to one inch. Plum cloth with original printed white label on backstrip, 4.6 x 2.8 cm.

Ref.: Buck 249; Clark III 10; Howes B45; Hubach p. 67; Sabin 2594 see

The work is based in large measure on Peck's *Guide for Emigrants* . . . Boston, 1831, although there are some passages developed from personal observation. Buck and Sabin ascribe the work to Robert Bache; DLC to Robert Baird. The maps, redrawn in lithograph, were used later for Traugott Bromme's *Rathgeber für Auswanderungslustige* . . . Stuttgart, 1846.

142 BAKER, HOZIAL H.

OVERLAND JOURNEY TO CARSON VALLEY, UTAH; THROUGH KANSAS, NEBRASKA AND UTAH; ALSO, RETURN TRIP, FROM SAN FRANCISCO TO SENECA FALLS, VIA. THE ISTHMUS . . . SENECA FALLS, N.Y.: PUBLISHED BY F. M. BAKER 1861.

[1]–38. 20.2 x 14.5 cm. Portrait and seven illustrations in the text. Yellow printed wrappers, with title on front wrapper. Lacks back wrapper. In a maroon morocco pull off case.

Ref.: Howes 1349; Wagner-Camp 367a

The frontispiece portrait is captioned in manuscript: Mr Baker /.

143 BALDRIDGE, SAMUEL C.

SKETCHES OF THE LIFE AND TIMES OF THE REV. STEPHEN BLISS, A.M. WITH NOTICES OF HIS CO-LABORERS: REV. ISAAC BENNET, REV. B. F. SPILMAN, REV. JOHN SILLIMAN, REV. JOSEPH BUTLER, REV. SAMUEL T. SCOTT, ETC. . . . CINCINNATI: ELM STREET PRINTING COMPANY, 1870.

[1–2], [i]–[viii, viii blank], 7–280. 16.1 x 11 cm. Black cloth, title in gilt on backstrip.

Prov.: Inscribed in pencil on front endleaf: in pleasant memory / of many kindnesses in former / days by the author— / Hanover, Ind. / June 5, 1897. / [In another hand:] Rev. S. C. Baldridge / Died as pastor in Hanover / a few months after the / above date. /

Ref.:

Bliss was a Presbyterian minister in Illinois.

Preceding the title-page is a short title printed in red. Pages [1–2] are a half-title.

144 BALDWIN, ALICE BLACKWOOD

MEMOIRS OF THE LATE FRANK D. BALDWIN . . . EDITED BY BRIGADIER GENERAL W. C. BROWN, COLONEL C. C. SMITH, AND E. A. BRININSTOOL. LOS ANGELES: WETZEL PUBLISHING CO., INC. 1929.

[i]–[xvi, xvi blank], [1]–204. (Pages [i–ii] blank.) 22.8 x 15.9 cm. 12 illustrations listed. Blue cloth.

Ref.: Howes B58

General Baldwin campaigned against Indians all over the West and was the only officer to receive twice the Medal of Honor.—Howes

145 BALDWIN, H. P.

AUTOGRAPH LETTER, SIGNED. 1872 January 10, Detroit, Michigan. One page, 24.7 x 18.3 cm. To Loren L. Williams.

Thanks for his donation to sufferers from the Michigan Fire. Inserted in Manuscript Journals of Loren L. Williams, Volume IV.

146 BALDWIN, JOSEPH G.

THE FLUSH TIMES OF ALABAMA AND MISSISSIPPI . . . NEW YORK: D. APPLETON AND COMPANY, M.DCCC.LIII.

[i–ii], [i]–x, [1]–330, [331–36 advertisements, 1–12 advertisements]. 18.1 x 11.9 cm. Black-green cloth. Pages [iii]–vi supplied from another edition, pages [ix]–x missing, apparently recased.

Ref.: Blanck 580; Clark III 124; Howes B62; LHOTUS III 204; Meine 51; Mott 36; Sabin 2898

The most famous of the lawless-frontier collections and a landmark in the development of humor in the Old Southwest . . . LHOTUS.

147 [BALDWIN, THERON]

HISTORICAL SKETCH OF THE ORIGIN, PROGRESS, AND WANTS, OF ILLINOIS COLLEGE. MAY, 1832. NEW-YORK: JOHN T. WEST, MDCCCXXXII.

[1]–16. 22.5 x 14.1 cm. Pink printed wrappers, with title on front wrapper.

Ref.:

The pamphlet is signed on page 16: Theron Baldwin, / Trustee and Agent of Illinois College. /

148 BALDWIN & CO.

[Map] BALDWIN'S MAP / OF / MINING CLAIMS, / NEAR / LEADVILLE / CALIFORNIA MINING DISTRICT, / LAKE CO. COLORADO. / JAN.Y 1879. / SCALE / [diagrammatic scale: about 800 feet to one inch] / 800 FT TO THE INCH 66 INCHES— 1 MILE. / LITH. W. J. MORGAN & CO. CLEVELAND,

O. / F. L. SIZER; / DRAUGHTSMAN / [on mounted strip of paper 1.6 x 21.6 cm.:] ENTERED ACCORDING TO ACT OF CONGRESS A. D. 1879, BY BALDWIN & CO., WITH THE LIBRARIAN OF CONGRESS, AT WASHINGTON, D.C. /

Map, 65.7 x 93.8 cm. Scale as above. Mounted on cloth, folded into brown cloth covers, 18.4 x 10.2 cm.

> *Ref.:* Phillips (*Maps*) p. 357

149 BALDWIN & DODGE, Council Bluffs, Iowa

[Broadside] [Eight one dollar notes printed on on sheet, each as follows:] COUNCIL BLUFFS . . . BANKING HOUSE OF BALDWIN & DODGE, / PAY TO OR BEARER ONE DOLLAR IN CURRENT BANK NOTES . . .

Broadside, 35 x 42.8 cm. Text, 31.5 x 17.3 cm. Each note: 7.4 x 17.3 cm.

> *Ref.:*
> Unused, unsigned sheet. No place of printing indicated; dated: 185 /.

150 BALDWIN & DODGE, Council Bluffs, Iowa

[Broadside] [Eight two dollar notes printed on one sheet, each as follows: COUNCIL BLUFFS . . . STATE OF IOWA. BANKING HOUSE OF BALDWIN & DODGE, PAY TO OR BEARER TWO DOLLARS IN CURRENT BANK NOTES 185 . LITH OF ED. MENDEL, CHICAGO, ILL.

Broadside, 34.9 x 43.4 cm. Text, 29 x 35.8 cm. Each note: 6.9 x 17.7 cm.

> *Ref.:*
> Unused, unsigned sheet. Dated: 185 /.

151 BALESTIER, JOSEPH N.

THE ANNALS OF CHICAGO; A LECTURE DELIVERED BEFORE THE CHICAGO LYCEUM, JANUARY 21, 1840. CHICAGO: EDWARD H. RUDD, MDCCCXL.

[1]–24. 20.1 x 13.1 cm. Printed buff wrappers with title on front wrapper.

> *Prov.:* Inscribed on the front wrapper: Boston Courier /, and on the title-page: An old correspondent of the / N. Eng. Magazine to the former / Editor of the same— /.
> *Ref.:* Byrd 491; Howes B64; McMurtrie (*Chicago*) 27; Sabin 2928
> The pamphlet is described and discussed in *Chicago History*, Vol. II, No. 1, Fall, 1948. It was reprinted later in the Fergus Reprints with an introduction by the author.

152 BALL, JOHN

AUTOBIOGRAPHY . . . COMPILED BY HIS DAUGHTERS KATE BALL POWERS, FLORA BALL HOPKINS, LUCY BALL. GRAND RAPIDS: THE DEAN-HICKS COMPANY, 1925.

[i]–[xii, xii blank], [1]–[230], [231–2 blank]. 21.7 x 15.2 cm. Eight illustrations listed. Green cloth.

> *Ref.:* Smith 474
> Ball accompanied Wyeth to Oregon in 1832.
> *Editions:* Grand Rapids, 1924.

153 BALLANTYNE, ROBERT M.

THE GOLDEN DREAM; OR, ADVENTURES IN THE FAR WEST . . . LONDON: JOHN F. SHAW AND CO., M.DCCC.LXI.

[i]–viii, [1]–358, [1]–2, [1]–24 advertisements. 16.4 x 11.1 cm. Four illustrations. Light plum embossed cloth.

> *Ref.:* Sabin 2952; Smith 478
> Sabin's date of 1854 is apparently an error. The earliest edition located is London: J. Nisbet & Co., 1860.

154 BALLANTYNE, ROBERT M.

HUDSON'S BAY; OR, EVERY-DAY LIFE IN THE WILDS OF NORTH AMERICA . . . EDINBURGH: FOR PRIVATE CIRCULATION, M.DCCC.XLVIII.

[i]–x, [xi–xii fly-title], [1]–328. 19.1 x 12.3 cm. Frontispiece, three plates, and text illustrations. Black cloth. In a green cloth case.

> *Ref.:* Sabin 2952; Smith 480; Wagner-Camp 144a
> Ballantyne's adventures began in 1841 from York Factory. While he recapitulates much history of the Hudson's Bay Company, he also quotes extensively from the journal he kept during his travels.

155 BANCROFT, HUBERT H.

THE WORKS OF HUBERT HOWE BANCROFT. VOLUME I [–XXXIX] . . . SAN FRANCISCO: THE HISTORY COMPANY, 1886 [–1890]. 39 volumes, 8vo, light brown straight-grained calf, gilt, marbled edges, beveled covers. Howes B91

156 BANGS, JOHN K.

TYPEWRITTEN LETTER, SIGNED. 1900 January 2, New York. One page, octavo. To Robert G. Carter.

> Refusing to publish an account of Henry W. Lawton's Capture of Geronimo. In Lawton Scrapbook.

157 BANGS, STEPHEN D.

[Cover title] PAPILLION, NEBRASKA, JULY 4TH, 1876. S. D. BANGS' CENTENNIAL HISTORY OF SARPY COUNTY. PAPILLION TIMES PRINT.

[1–9], [10 blank]. 24 x 15.7 cm. Violet printed wrappers with title on front wrapper.

Ref.: AII (*Nebraska*) 391

158 BANNACK, MONTANA. Theatre

[Broadside] THEATRE. BANNACK, MON. TER. A GRAND BILL TO-NIGHT. ON SATURDAY OCT 16 1862 THE TRAGEDY IN 5 ACTS OF KING EDWARD IV. EDWARD IV, KING OF ENGLAND. J. A. HOSMER . . .

Broadside, 19 x 12.3 cm. Text, 9 x 7.2 cm.

The Hosmer family engaged in lively dramatic activities, as is shown by this broadside and other Hosmer material in the Graff Collection. For a while, they owned a printing press.

159 BAPTISTS. ARKANSAS. Concord General Association, 1868

PROCEEDINGS OF THE SECOND ANNIVERSARY OF THE CONCORD GENERAL ASSOCIATION OF BAPTISTS . . . BEGINNING AUGUST 7, 1868 . . . FORT SMITH: PRINTED AT THE FORT SMITH HERALD OFFICE, 1868.

[1]–8. 20.8 x 14.9 cm. Blue printed wrappers with title on front wrapper.

Ref.: Allen (*Arkansas*) 544

160 BAPTISTS. ARKANSAS. Dardanelle Baptist Association, 1868

PROCEEDINGS OF THE FOURTEENTH ANNIVERSARY . . . OF THE DARDANELLE BAPTIST ASSOCIATION, HELD . . . SEPTEMBER 26TH, 27TH AND 28TH 1868 . . . FORT SMITH, ARK: PRINTED BY JOHN F. WHEELER, AT THE HERALD OFFICE, 1869.

[1]–12, folding table. 21.7 x 14 cm. Pink printed wrappers with title on front wrapper, advertisement on verso of back wrapper.

Ref.:

161 BAPTISTS. ILLINOIS. United Baptist Illinois Association, 1821

[Broadside] MINUTES OF THE UNITED BAPTIST ILLINOIS ASSOCIATION, HELD AT THE MEETING-HOUSE AT RICHLAND CREEK CHURCH, ON THE FOURTH SATURDAY OF AUGUST, THE 25TH, 1821, AND FOLLOWING DAYS . . . (SIGNED) WILLIAM JONES, MODERATOR. JAMES TUNNELL, CLERK.

Broadside, 28 x 22.5 cm. Text, 19.7 x 19.9 cm.

Ref.: Byrd 23

The minutes includes a list of the Churches and names of the delegates. Paragraph 19 reads: Agree to print 300 copies of our Minutes, and Brother William / Kinney superintend same. / Kinney was a delegate from Richland Creek Church, St. Clair County. McMurtrie thought this was printed in Illinois, although it may well have been done at St. Louis.—EDG

162 BAPTISTS. INDIAN TERRITORY. Choctaw and Chickasaw Baptist Association, 1874

MINUTES OF THE THIRD ANNUAL MEETING OF THE CHOCTAW AND CHICKASAW BAPTIST ASSOCIATION, HELD AT ATOKA, CHOCTAW NATION, INDIAN TERRITORY, JULY 17TH, 18TH AND 19TH, 1874. SAINT LOUIS: BARNES & BEYNON.

[1]–22, [23–4 blank]. 23.1 x 14.9 cm. Yellow printed wrappers with title on front wrapper and with date 1874 in imprint.

Ref.:

163 BAPTISTS. INDIAN TERRITORY. Choctaw and Chickasaw Baptist Association, 1877

. . . MINUTES OF THE SIXTH ANNUAL MEETING OF THE CHOCTAW AND CHICKASAW BAPTIST ASSOCIATION, . . . COMMENCING ON FRIDAY, AUGUST 10, 1877. ST. LOUIS: WRIGHT & FLEMING, 1877.

[1]–[14], [15–6 blank]. 21.8 x 15.3 cm. Pink printed wrappers with title on front wrapper.

Ref.:

164 BAPTISTS. INDIAN TERRITORY. Choctaw and Chickasaw Baptist Association, 1878

. . . MINUTES OF THE SEVENTH ANNUAL MEETING OF THE CHOCTAW AND CHICKASAW BAPTIST ASSOCIATION . . . COMMENCING ON FRIDAY, AUGUST 9TH, 1878. ST. LOUIS: LEWIS E. KLINE, PUBLISHER.

[1]–[14], [15–6 blank]. 22.1 x 15 cm. Tan printed wrappers with title on front wrapper.

Ref.:

Published in 1878.

165 BAPTISTS. INDIAN TERRITORY. Choctaw and Chickasaw Baptist Association, 1879

MINUTES OF THE EIGHTH ANNUAL MEETING OF THE CHOCTAW AND CHICKASAW BAPTIST ASSOCIATION . . . COMMENCING ON FRIDAY, SEPTEMBER 19TH, 1879. DENISON, TEXAS: PRINTED BY M. F. DEARING, 1879.

[1]–[12]. 21.4 x 14.8 cm. Blue printed wrappers with title on front wrapper.

Ref.:

166 BAPTISTS. INDIAN TERRITORY. Choctaw and Chickasaw Baptist Association, 1880

MINUTES OF THE NINTH ANNUAL MEETING OF THE CHOCTAW AND CHICKASAW BAPTIST ASSOCIATION . . . COMMENCING ON FRIDAY, SEPT. 20TH, 1880. MUSKOGEE, INDIAN TERRITORY: INDIAN JOURNAL OFFICE, 1880.

[i–ii blank], [1]–13, [14 blank]. 22.3 x 14.9 cm. Cream printed wrappers with title on front wrapper.
Ref.:

167 BAPTISTS. INDIAN TERRITORY. Choctaw and Chickasaw Baptist Association, 1881

MINUTES OF THE TENTH ANNUAL MEETING OF THE CHOCTAW AND CHICKASAW BAPTIST ASSOCIATION . . . COMMENCING ON FRIDAY, AUGUST 26TH, 1881 . . . ST. LOUIS: AMERICAN BAPTIST FLAG OFFICE, 1881.

[1]–[15], [16 blank]. 22.4 x 14.3 cm. Gray printed wrappers with title on front wrapper, advertisement on verso of back wrapper.
Ref.:

168 BAPTISTS. INDIAN TERRITORY. Choctaw and Chickasaw Baptist Association, 1889

MINUTES OF THE NINETEENTH ANNUAL MEETING OF THE CHOCTAW AND CHICKASAW BAPTIST ASSOCIATION . . . COMMENCING AUGUST 23, 1889 . . . ATOKA, INDIAN TERRITORY: INDIAN CITIZEN PRINT, 1889.

[1]–[19], [20 blank]. 22.6 x 15.1 cm. Gray printed wrappers with title on front wrapper, advertisement on verso of back wrapper.
Ref.: Hargrett (*Oklahoma*) 638

169 BAPTISTS. INDIAN TERRITORY. Choctaw and Chickasaw Baptist Association, 1890

MINUTES OF THE TWENTIETH ANNUAL MEETING OF THE CHOCTAW AND CHICKASAW BAPTIST ASSOCIATION . . . COMMENCING AUGUST 22, 1890 . . . ATOKA, INDIAN TERRITORY: INDIAN CITIZEN PRINT, 1890.

[1]–[20]. 22.3 x 15.1 cm. Blue printed wrappers with title on front wrapper, advertisement on verso of back wrapper.
Ref.: Hargrett (*Oklahoma*) 680

170 BAPTISTS. INDIAN TERRITORY. Baptist Missionary and Educational Convention of the Indian Territory, 1885–86

PROCEEDINGS OF THE BAPTIST MISSIONARY AND EDUCATIONAL CONVENTION OF THE INDIAN TERRITORY. HELD . . . JUNE 5TH AND 6TH, 1885, AND . . . JULY 15TH, 16TH AND 17TH, 1886 . . . OTTAWA, KANSAS: KESSLER & SUMNER, PRINTERS.

[1]–15, [16 blank]. 22.4 x 15 cm. Mustard printed wrappers, with title on front wrapper.
Ref.:
Published in 1886.

171 BAPTISTS. INDIAN TERRITORY. Baptist Missionary and Educational Convention of the Indian Territory, 1887–89

PROCEEDINGS OF THE BAPTIST MISSIONARY AND EDUCATIONAL CONVENTION OF THE INDIAN TERRITORY. HELD . . . SEPTEMBER 9TH AND 10TH, 1887, SEPTEMBER 11TH, 1888, AND . . . SEPTEMBER 13TH AND 14TH, 1889 . . . OTTAWA, KANSAS: J. P. KESSLER, PROPRIETOR HERALD AND BOOK AND JOB PRINTER, 1889.

[1]–20. 23.2 x 15.2 cm. Pale gray printed wrappers with title on front wrapper, advertisement on verso of back wrapper.
Ref.:

172 BAPTISTS. IOWA. State Convention, 1850

MINUTES OF THE NINTH ANNIVERSARY OF THE IOWA BAPTISTS CONVENTION, HELD . . . AT MT. PLEASANT, MAY 31ST, AND JUNE 1ST AND 2D, 1850 . . . MUSCATINE, IOWA: H. D. LA. COSSITT, 1850.

[1]–[16]. 21.4 x 13.8 cm. Removed from bound volume, unbound.
Ref.: AII (*Iowa, Supp.*) 66; Moffit 66

173 BAPTISTS. MISSISSIPPI. Yazoo Association

MINUTES OF THE YAZOO BAPTIST ASSOCIATION, CONVENED AT TILDEBOGUE CHURCH, ON THE 7TH MARCH A. D. 1835. LEXINGTON, MI. PRINTED AT THE OFFICE OF THE LEXINGTON GAZETTE, 1836.

[1]–[8]. 17.6 x 12.4 cm. Stabbed, roughly trimmed.
Prov.: Inscribed in lower margin of title-page: Rev J Mercer Washington Ga— /
Ref.:
Three hundred copies were printed (at a cost of $35, printed and stitched). The congregations numbered 178 members at the time; the additional copies were for distribution among sister Associations.

No other copy of this pamphlet has been located nor have copies of the *Lexington Gazette* been found. The quality of the printing indicates that the printer was little more than an amateur.

The historians of the Baptists in Mississippi (Z. T. Leavell and T. J. Bailey) apparently did not have access to this pamphlet in 1904, since they were unable to list the ten churches forming the Yazoo Association which was, at that time, the oldest Association in Northern Mississippi.

174 BAPTISTS. MISSISSIPPI. Zion Association

MINUTES OF THE THIRD ANNUAL SESSION OF THE ZION ASSOCIATION, HELD AT FELLOWSHIP MEETING-

HOUSE, IN CHOCTAW COUNTY, ON THE 19TH AND 21ST DAYS OF OCTOBER, 1839. GRENADA: PRINTED AT THE "SOUTHERN REPORTER" OFFICE, 1839.

[1]–[8]. 24 x 14 cm. Unbound, uncut, unopened. Remnants of wafer and sealing wax on title-page.

Prov.: Inscribed on title-page: J. Mercer & W. H. Stokes Washington Ga By Jo Mor[ris] Middlet[on] Miss /.

Ref.:

Six hundred copies were ordered printed. No other copy of the work has been located and no other mention of the *Southern Reporter* has been found. Note that both this pamphlet and the *Minutes of the Yazoo Association* came from the Rev. J. Mercer.

175 BAPTISTS. TENNESSEE. Concord Association.

[Caption title] MINUTES OF THE CONCORD BAPTIST ASSOCIATION, HELD AT ANTIOCH, DAVIDSON COUNTY, SEPTEMBER 1, 2 & 3, 1832 . . .

[1]–8. 25.4 x 15.6 cm. Unbound, removed from a bound volume.

Ref.:

One thousand copies were printed at Nashville by Hunt, Tardiff & Co., according to a note at the foot of page 8, at a cost of $20. AII (*Tennessee*) cites editions for several other years, but the minutes for 1832 seem to have survived in this copy only.

The Concord Association was a flourishing organization in 1832. There were seventeen member churches with 1156 communicants in the congregations. The *Minutes* occupy little more than two pages; the rest of the text carries one of the famous *Circulars* on church doctrine.

176 BAPTISTS. TEXAS. Baptist General Association of Texas, 1868

[Wrapper title] PROCEEDINGS OF THE FIRST ANNUAL SESSION OF THE BAPTIST GENERAL ASSOCIATION OF TEXAS HELD . . . ON THE 17TH, 18TH AND 20TH JULY, 1868 . . . HOUSTON, TEXAS: TEXAS BAPTIST HERALD, 1868.

[1]–28. 20.8 x 13.5 cm. Green printed wrappers with title on front wrapper.

Ref.:

177 BAPTISTS. TEXAS. Baptist State Convention of Texas, 1867

[Wrapper title] MINUTES OF THE TWENTIETH ANNUAL SESSION OF THE BAPTIST STATE CONVENTION OF TEXAS, HELD . . . ON SATURDAY, NOVEMBER 30, 1867 . . . HOUSTON, TEXAS: TEXAS BAPTIST HERALD, 1868.

[1]–39, [40 blank]. 20.8 x 13.8 cm. Tan printed wrappers with title on front wrapper and advertisements on verso of front and recto and verso of back wrapper.

Ref.:

178 BAPTISTS. TEXAS. Baptist State Convention of Texas, 1868

[Wrapper title] MINUTES OF THE TWENTY-FIRST ANNUAL SESSION OF THE BAPTIST STATE CONVENTION, OF TEXAS. HELD . . . OCTOBER 3D., 5TH AND 6TH, 1868 . . . HOUSTON, TEXAS: TEXAS BAPTIST HERALD, 1868.

[1]–27, [28 blank]. 21.5 x 14.3 cm. Blue printed wrappers with title on front wrapper and with advertisements on verso of front and recto and verso of back wrapper.

Ref.:

179 BAPTISTS. TEXAS. Sister Grove Baptist Association, 1867

MINUTES OF THE FIFTEENTH ANNUAL SESSION OF THE SISTER GROVE BAPTIST ASSOCIATION, HELD . . . SEPTEMBER 13TH–16TH, A.D., 1867. HOUSTON, TEXAS: TEXAS BAPTIST HERALD, 1867.

[1]–16. 20.6 x 13.4 cm. Blue printed wrappers with title on front wrapper.

Ref.:

180 BARBOUR, JAMES

MANUSCRIPT LETTER (copy). 1825 March 16, Department of War. Three pages, 24.7 x 19.8 cm. To Benjamin H. Reeves, George C. Sibley, and Pierre Menard. In Mather Papers.

Instructions to Commissioners of the Santa Fé Road Commission regarding keeping of accounts.

ANOTHER COPY. With three-line postscript relating to Thomas Mather as successor to Pierre Menard. With original cover. In Mather papers.

181 [BARCIA CARBALLIDO Y ZUNIGA, ANDRES GONZALEZ DE]

ENSAYO CRONOLOGICO, PARA LA HISTORIA GENERAL DE LA FLORIDA . . . MADRID: EN LA OFICINA REAL, ANO DE CIƆ IƆCCXIIJ.

[¶]–¶¶², ¶¶¶¹, ❡ –❡7², ❡ 8¹, large folding table, A-Zzzz², ❡ –❡13², ❡14¹. [i–xl], 1–367, [368 blank], [369–422]. 29.9 x 19.8 cm. Genealogical table between pages 150–51. Limp vellum.

Prov.: Shelfmark in pencil inside front cover: *3–10.* /

Ref.: Howes B130; Medina (*BHA*) 7885; Raines p. 22; Streit II 157; Sabin 3349; Wagner (*SS*) 84

The *Ensayo Cronologico* was designed as the second part of Barcia's edition of Garcilaso de la Vega's *La Florida*. . . . It contains accounts of Cabeza de Vaca, De Soto, La Salle, and Coronado among others. The introduction is especially valuable. The text also contains much of value relating to the French and the English in North America.

182 BARDE, ALEXANDRE

HISTOIRE DES COMITES DE VIGILANCE AUX ATTAKAPAS . . . SAINT-JEAN-BAPTISTE (LOUISIANE): IMPRIMERIE DU MESCHACEBE DE L'AVANT-COUREUR, 1861.

[1–4], [i]–vi, [7]–428. 17.1 x 12.1 cm. Rebound in green half morocco, marbled board sides, gilt top.

Ref.: Howes B134; Tinker pp. 22–9

L'Attakapas means literally "the cannibal" and is the name of a plain about 150 miles north of New Orleans. The author lived for some time at the plantation of Major Aurélian St.-Julian, the head of the Comités de Vigilance.

Two maps have been inserted in the present copy: Map of the / French, English & Spanish / Possessions / in North America in / 1745. / W. Kemble Sc. / [below neat line:] Harper & Brothers, New York. / 19.8 x 21.1 cm. No scale given. Map: Early French Missions / in the remote Western regions of / Canada or New France. / [at top, in border:] Copy of the Map attached to the Relations of the Jesuits of New France in 1670 & 1671. / 10.4 x 18.5 cm. (page size). Scale: 37 leagues to one inch.

183 BARDE, FREDERICK S.

LIFE AND ADVENTURES OF "BILLY" DIXON OF ADOBE WALLS, TEXAS PANHANDLE. A NARRATIVE IN WHICH IS DESCRIBED MANY THINGS RELATING TO THE EARLY SOUTHWEST, WITH AN ACCOUNT OF THE FIGHT BETWEEN INDIANS AND BUFFALO HUNTERS AT ADOBE WALLS, AND THE DESPERATE ENGAGEMENT AT BUFFALO WALLOW, FOR WHICH CONGRESS VOTED THE MEDAL OF HONOR TO THE SURVIVORS . . . GUTHRIE, OKLAHOMA.*

[1]–320. (Pages [1–2] blank.) 19.6 x 13.5 cm. 16 illustrations listed. Dark blue cloth.

Ref.: Howes B135

Copyrighted 1914. Tipped in following the title-leaf is a typed note referring the reader to the end of the volume for index and list of illustrations. Inserted at the end is the following: Addendum / To / "The Life of Billie Dixon" / [within decorative border]. [1–8]. 19.3 x 12 cm. Signed on the title-page: O.S. Clark. / Attica. / Ind. / See Number 741. Clark was also the author of a biography of Clay Allison.

184 BARKER, BENJAMIN

THE INDIAN BUCANIER; OR, THE TRAPPER'S DAUGHTER. A ROMANCE OF OREGON . . . BOSTON: PUBLISHED BY F. GLEASON, 1847.

[i–ii], [5]–50. 21.4 x 14.6 cm. Yellow printed pictorial wrappers with title on front wrapper, advertisements on verso of front and recto and verso of back wrapper, uncut.

Ref.: Wright I 271

Said to be the first Oregon novel.

185 BARKER, STEPHEN

[Broadside] SHALL KANSAS BE FREE? DEAR SIR: IF THE ABOVE QUESTION IS OF INTEREST TO YOU, I BEG OF YOU TO READ THIS CIRCULAR. AT LAWRENCE, IN KANSAS TERRITORY, A LARGE AND WELL EDITED PAPER CALLED THE KANSAS HERALD OF FREEDOM! IS PUBLISHED WEEKLY . . . LAWRENCE ALREADY CONTAINS ABOUT A HUNDRED HOUSES AND OVER ONE THOUSAND PEOPLE. STEPHEN BARKER. BOSTON, FEBRUARY 7TH, 1855.

Broadside, 15.3 x 12.5 cm. Text, 13 x 9.5 cm.

Ref.:

Probably printed at Boston.

186 [BARNARD, HELEN M.]

[COVER title] THE CHORPENNING CLAIM. M'INTOSH, PRINTER, WASINGTON[!] D.C.

[1]–22. 21.5 x 14.5 cm. Blue printed wrappers, with title on front wrapper.

This review of a famous case relating to Transmississippi mail contracts is signed on page 22 by Helen M. Barnard. Small hope is expressed that the case would ever be solved equitably. Probably printed in 1871.

187 BARNEBY, WILLIAM H.

LIFE AND LABOUR IN THE FAR, FAR WEST: BEING NOTES OF A TOUR IN THE WESTERN STATES, BRITISH COLUMBIA, MANITOBA, AND THE NORTH-WEST TERRITORY . . . LONDON: CASSELL & COMPANY, LIMITED . . . 1884.

[i]–xvi, [1]–432, 1–8 advertisements. 22 x 14 cm. Map: Part of the / United States / and / Canada. / To accompany / "Life & Labour in the Far, Far West" / By W. Henry Barneby. / [lower right:] Edwd Weller, lith., Red Lion Square. / [lower centre:] Cassell & Company, Limited. / 54.1 x 68.3 cm. Scale: 70 English miles to one inch. Red cloth, uncut.

Prov.: Inscribed on half-title: To / ——— Egan Esq. / Canadian Pacific Railway. / With The Author's compliments / & those of A. C. Mitchell. / June 2—1884. / Signature on title-page: J M Egan /.

Ref.: Smith 559

The recipient was John M. Egan, president of the Canadian Pacific Railroad.

188 BARNES, DEMAS

FROM THE ATLANTIC TO THE PACIFIC, OVERLAND. A SERIES OF LETTERS, BY DEMAS BARNES, DESCRIBING A TRIP FROM NEW YORK, VIA CHICAGO, ATCHISON, THE GREAT PLAINS, DENVER, THE ROCKY MOUNTAINS, CENTRAL CITY, COLORADO, DAKOTA, PIKE'S PEAK, LARAMIE PARK, BRIDGER'S PASS, SALT LAKE CITY, UTAH, NEVADA, AUSTIN, WASHOE, VIRGINIA CITY, THE SIERRAS AND CALIFORNIA, TO SAN FRANCISCO, THENCE HOME, BY ACAPULCO, AND THE ISTHMUS OF PANAMA. NEW YORK: D. VAN NOSTRAND, 1866.

[1]–136. 18.8 x 12.7 cm. Portrait. Dark brown cloth, with title on front cover in gilt and on back cover in blind.
    Ref.: Howes B153
    The author's itinerary is well described on the title-page. The text appeared first as letters in the *Brooklyn Eagle*, in 1866.

189 BARNES, WILL C.

APACHES & LONGHORNS . . . LOS ANGELES: THE WARD RITCHIE PRESS, MCMXLI.*

[i]–xxiii, [xxiv blank], [1]–210. 21 x 14.3 cm. 18 illustrations listed. Buff cloth. In dust jacket.
    Ref.: Adams (*Ramp. Herd*) 208
    A grand book of Arizona experiences.—EDG

190 BARNES, WILL C.

WESTERN GRAZING GROUNDS AND FOREST RANGES . . . CHICAGO: THE BREEDERS' GAZETTE, 1913.

[1]–390. 19.1 x 13.1 cm. Illustrations listed, some in color. Green cloth.
    Ref.: Adams (*Ramp. Herd*) 212; Howes B157
    Barnes was Inspector of Grazing, United States Forest Service, when he published his first book.

191 BARNETT, JOEL

A LONG TRIP IN A PRAIRIE SCHOONER . . . WHITTIER, CALIF. [WESTERN STATIONERY COMPANY, 1928].

[1]–134 [1–2 blank]. 19.7 x 13.4 cm. Two portraits unlisted. Red cloth.
    Prov.: Bookplate of Robert E. Cowan.
    Ref.: Smith 579
    Keokuk County, Iowa, to Oregon in 1859.

192 BARNEY, LIBEUS

EARLY-DAY LETTERS FROM AURARIA (NOW DENVER) . . . BENNINGTON, VERMONT, 1859–1860.

[1]–88. 23.5 x 15.6 cm. Portrait. Green printed wrappers with title on front wrapper. Rebacked.
    Ref.: Howes B159; Wagner-Camp 349; Wilcox p. 11
    Reprinted from issues of the *Bennington Banner*, Bennington, Vermont, for 1859–60, in 1907. The imprint on the verso of the title-leaf reads as follows: [rule] / A. J. Ludditt Press, 1409–1411 Lawrence St. / Denver, Colorado. / [rule] /.

193 BARRA, EZEKIEL I.

A TALE OF TWO OCEANS; A NEW STORY BY AN OLD CALIFORNIAN . . . AN ACCOUNT OF A VOYAGE FROM PHILADELPHIA TO SAN FRANCISCO, AROUND CAPE HORN, YEARS 1849–50 . . . SAN FRANCISCO, 1893.

[1]–198. 22.9 x 14.7 cm. Two full-page and five text illustrations, unlisted. Gray printed wrappers, with title printed in blue on front wrapper.
    Ref.: Cowan p. 35; Howes (1954) 590

194 BARREIRO, ANTONIO

OJEADA SOBRE NUEVO-MEXICO, QUE DA UNA IDEA DE SUS PRODUCIONES NATURALES, Y DE ALGUNAS OTRAS COSAS QUE SE CONSIDERAN OPORTUNAS PARA MAJORAR SU ESTADO, E IR PROPORCIONANDO SU FUTURA FELICIDAD . . . PUEBLA: IMPRENTA DEL CIUDADANO JOSE MARIA CAMPOS, 1832.

[1]–42, [1–3], [4 blank], [1]–10. 20.2 x 14.2 cm. Old glazed marbled wrappers.
    Ref.: Bloom (*New Mexico Historical Review*, Vol. III, 1928, pp. 73–96, 145–78); Bloom 2 (Historical Society of New Mexico *Publications in History*, Vol. 5, 1929); Carroll & Haggard: *Three New Mexico Chronicles*, Quivira Society Vol. XI; Howes B169; Saunders 2443
    The chief value of the work . . . lies in the discriminating yet sympathetic picture which it gives of New Mexico as it then was, presented not by one who had grown up within the territory but by one of cultured mind and legal training who had come to New Mexico from *la tierra afuera*, the outer world, and who wrote therefore with a cosmopolitan point of view.—Bloom 2

195 [BARROWS, WILLIAM]

[Wrapper title] EIGHT WEEKS ON THE FRONTIER.
[1]–24. 15.3 x 9.4 cm. Tan printed wrappers with title on front wrapper. In a brown cloth folder.
    Ref.: Howes B187
    The caption title on page [1] differs slightly: Eight weeks / Among our Missionaries / At the Front. / The pamphlet is signed at the end: W. Barrows, Sec'y. / Mass. H. M. Society, / Congregational House, / Boston, March, 1876. /

196 [BARROWS, WILLIAM]

THE GENERAL; OR, TWELVE NIGHTS IN THE HUNTER'S CAMP. A NARRATIVE OF REAL LIFE . . . BOSTON: LEE AND SHEPARD, 1869.

[i]–iv, 1–268. 16.9 x 11 cm. Four illustrations. Green cloth.

Ref.: Howes B188; Mott (*Iowa*) p. 35

The title is misleading. This is a biography of the author's brother, General Willard Barrows, an Iowa pioneer. General Barrows issued the first map of Iowa in 1845, wrote a history of Scott County, crossed the Plains in 1850, and was in Idaho and Montana in the sixties.— EDG

197 BARRY, THEODORE A., & BENJAMIN A. PATTEN

MEN AND MEMORIES OF SAN FRANCISCO, IN THE "SPRING OF '50." . . . SAN FRANCISCO: A. L. BANCROFT & COMPANY, 1873.

[1]–296. 18.8 x 12.1 cm. Green cloth, blind embossed sides, title stamped in gilt on backstrip and front cover.

Prov.: Signed on front endleaf: John Bidwell / and on preliminary blank leaf: John Bidwell / July 30, 1873. /

Ref.: Blumann & Thomas 2856; Cowan p. 36; Howes B192

One of the most interesting works upon "Old San Francisco."—Cowan. John Bidwell was a member of the first overland party to California from Missouri.

198 BARTLETT, JOHN R.

PERSONAL NARRATIVE OF EXPLORATIONS AND INCIDENTS IN TEXAS, NEW MEXICO, CALIFORNIA, SONORA, AND CHIHUAHUA, CONNECTED WITH THE UNITED STATES AND MEXICAN BOUNDARY COMMISSION, DURING THE YEARS 1850, '51, '52 AND '53 . . . NEW YORK: D. APPLETON & COMPANY, M.DCCC.LIV.

[1–2], [i]–xxii, [1]–506, [1–6 advertisements]. [1–2], [i]–[xviii, xviii blank], [1]–624. 23.2 x 14.2 cm. 110 illustrations listed and a map: General Map / Showing the Countries Explored & Surveyed / by the / United States & Mexican / Boundary Commission, / in the Years 1850, 51, 52, & 53, / Under the direction of / John R. Bartlett, / U.S. Commissioner. / [lower left corner:] J. H. Colton & Cº Nº 172 William St. New York. / D. McLellan. Print 26 Spruce St. / 28.8 x 49.2 cm. Scale: 100 miles to one inch. Two volumes, dark gray cloth, blind embossed sides, title in gilt on backstrips.

Ref.: Cowan p. 36; Howes B201; Rader 287; Raines p. 22; Sabin 3746; Saunders 2721; Wagner-Camp 234

Bartlett's *Personal Narrative* is an essential book for the Southwest and an interesting one, too. The author was a contentious individual who caused a good deal of trouble for himself. A number of incidents described by Bartlett have been differently interpreted by his associates.

199 BARTON, H. M.

A TRIP TO THE YOSEMITE VALLEY, AND THE MARIPOSA GROVE OF BIG TREES, CALIFORNIA . . . DUBLIN: PRINTED AT THE UNIVERSITY PRESS, 1885.

[i–ii], [1]–49, [50 blank]. 15.1 x 11.3 cm. Three photographs, mounted. Purple cloth, title in gilt on front cover within decorative border.

Prov.: Inscription clipped from top of title-page, but leaving two lines: from / HMB /. Probably the author.

Ref.:

200 BARTON & HOBBS, Storm Lake, Iowa

THE SETTLER'S GUIDE, CONTAINING A DESCRIPTION OF BUENA VISTA COUNTY, IN WHICH IS THE CITY OF STORM LAKE. BY BARTON & HOBBS, REAL ESTATE, TAX-PAYING AGENTS & BANKERS. STORM LAKE, BUENA VISTA CO., IOWA.

[1]–48, 30–1, [51–2 blank], [53–64 advertisements]. (Pages 49–50 mispaginated 30–1.) 19.4 x 12.6 cm. Map: Miniature / Map of the State of Iowa / Des Moines, Iowa / Mills & Cº / [below map:] Entered according to Act of Congress in the Year 1870 by Mills & Co in the Clerks Office of the District Court of the United States for the District of Iowa. / Barton & Hobbs, / Real Estate and Tax Paying Agents, / Storm Lake, Iowa. / 14.2 x 18.8 cm. Scale: 50 miles to one inch. Cream printed wrappers with title on front wrapper, advertisements on verso of front and recto and verso of back wrapper.

Ref.:

The only copy located. Printed by Vestal & Young in 1872, according to the front wrapper.

Climate, history, soil, productions, railroads, institutions, etc. are covered in this pamphlet describing Buena Vista County. The area immediately near Storm Lake is described in detail.

201 BARTON & HOBBS, Storm Lake, Iowa

[Broadside] TO TAX PAYERS. BARTON & HOBBS, REAL ESTATE AGENTS, STORM LAKE, IOWA.

Broadside, 11.5 x 15.3 cm. Text, 8.6 x 11.4 cm.

Laid in Barton & Hobbs: *The Settler's Guide* . . . [1872].

202 BASCOM, MAJOR DICK

THE CARPET-BAGGER IN TENNESSEE. BY MAJOR DICK BASCOM.

[1]–202, 203–08 advertisements. 21.2 x 14 cm. Rebound in marbled boards with black cloth backstrip.

Ref.: Howes B224; Wright II 233

Copyrighted 1869 by J. Jay Buck of Clarksville, Tennessee. A tale of Reconstruction in Tennessee.

203 BASKIN, ROBERT N.

REMINISCENCES OF EARLY UTAH . . . COPYRIGHT 1914 . . .*

[i–ii], [1]–252. 22.9 x 15 cm. Six illustrations listed. Light gray-green cloth.

Ref.: Howes B226

Published at Salt Lake City. The author was Chief Justice of the Supreme Court of Utah. Baskin believed Whiting's history of Utah contained serious errors and tried to correct them in this work.

204 BASS, WILLIAM W., Editor

ADVENTURES IN THE CANYONS OF THE COLORADO BY TWO OF ITS EARLIEST EXPLORERS, JAMES WHITE AND W. W. HAWKINS . . . GRAND CANYON, ARIZONA: PUBLISHED BY THE AUTHOR, 1920.

[1]–38. (Page [1] blank, page [2] frontispiece.) 19.9 x 13.5 cm. Eight illustrations, unlisted. Green printed wrappers bound into gray boards, yellow cloth backstrip.

Ref.: Farquhar (*Colorado River*) 49; Howes B229

205 BATCHELDER, GEORGE A.

A SKETCH OF THE HISTORY AND RESOURCES OF DAKOTA TERRITORY . . . YANKTON: PRESS STEAM POWER PRINTING COMPANY, 1870.*

[1]–56. 22.7 x 15.2 cm. Map: Map of / Dakota in Miniature, / [below map:] designed to accompany the work on / Dakota / by the / Hon. George A. Batchelder. / Secretary of Dakota Territory. / 12 x 12.4 cm. No scale given. Blue printed wrappers with title on front wrapper, seal of Territory on verso of back wrapper. In a red half morocco case.

Prov.: Inscribed in pencil at the top of the front wrapper: Author's Compliments. /

Ref.: Allen (*Dakota*) 73; Bradford 286; Howes B231; Jones 1522

Batchelder produced a somewhat better than average promotion piece for Dakota.

206 BATE, WALTER N.

FRONTIER LEGEND. TEXAS FINALE OF CAPT. WILLIAM F. DRANNAN PSEUDO FRONTIER COMRADE OF KIT CARSON . . . NEW BERN, NORTH CAROLINA: OWEN G. DUNN COMPANY, 1954.*

[1]–[69], [70 blank]. 22.8 x 15.2 cm. Illustrated. Printed wrappers.

Prov.: Inscribed and signed by the author on verso of title-page.

Ref.:

Bate suggests that Mrs. Drannan wrote the books in which Drannan posed as a companion of Kit Carson.

207 BATES, EDWARD

EDWARD BATES AGAINST THOMAS BENTON. ST. LOUIS: CHARLESS AND PASCHALL, 1828.

[1]–12. 19.1 x 12 cm. Rebound in blue half morocco.

Prov.: Signature on title-page: Benjamin Morrell, Esq /.

Ref.: AII (*Missouri*) 93; Sabin 3929

Bates attacked Benton on several grounds relating to the Spanish Land Claims in Missouri and Arkansas. The former owner was probably the noted South Seas sealing captain.

208 BATTEY, THOMAS C.

THE LIFE AND ADVENTURES OF A QUAKER AMONG THE INDIANS . . . BOSTON: LEE AND SHEPARD, 1875.

[i]–xii, 9–339, [340 blank]. 19.5 x 13.6 cm. Eight illustrations listed. Green cloth, decorative bands in black on covers and backstrip, title in gilt on backstrip.

Ref.: Howes (1954) 660; Rader 298

Battey's experiences were among the Kiowas, principally, but he was also associated with Comanches, Apaches, Caddoes, and Kickapoos.

209 BATTY, JOSEPH

OVER THE WILDS TO CALIFORNIA; OR, EIGHT YEARS FROM HOME . . . LEEDS: J. PARROTT, M DCCC LXVII.

[i–iv, iv blank], [1]–64. 15.8 x 10.1 cm. Black cloth, blind embossed borders on sides, title in gilt on front cover. In a red half morocco case.

Ref.: Cowan p. 39; Howes B240

Batty's narrative, although written in general terms with little reference to specific places, is charming and interesting. Dates are not given, but he seems to have left England in 1858 or 1859 to live with his brother's family about twenty-five miles northwest of Madison, Wisconsin. Shortly afterwards, he went overland to California where he tried mining and farming without success and eventually returned by sea to New York and from there home to Leeds.

210 BAUGHMAN, THEODORE

BAUGHMAN, THE OKLAHOMA SCOUT. PERSONAL REMINISCENCES . . . CHICAGO: BELFORD, CLARKE & CO., 1886.

[1–2], [5]–215, [216 blank]. 17.6 x 12 cm. Frontispiece portrait and 11 plates listed. Yellow cloth.

Ref.: Adams (*Ramp. Herd*) 224; Howes B244; Rader 302

Among Baughman's reminiscences of the cattle trade there is interesting and valuable information about Kansas and Oklahoma in the early days. Andy Adams, in *Cattle Brands*, refers to Baughman or "Baugh" as foreman in charge of a drive from Texas to Dodge City. Adams was a hand in the drive and tells several stories about Baughman.

211 BEADLE, ERASTUS F.

TO NEBRASKA IN '57. A DIARY . . . [NEW YORK:] NEW YORK PUBLIC LIBRARY, 1923.*

[1]–89, [90 blank]. 25.2 x 17.7 cm. Three illustrations. Tan printed wrappers with titles on front wrapper.

Ref.:

212 BEADLE, JOHN H.

THE UNDEVELOPED WEST; OR, FIVE YEARS IN THE TERRITORIES: BEING A COMPLETE HISTORY OF THAT VAST REGION BETWEEN THE MISSISSIPPI AND THE PACIFIC . . . PHILADELPHIA: NATIONAL PUBLISHING COMPANY.

[1–2], 15–823, [824 blank], [825–32 advertisements]. 21 x 13.8 cm. 244 illustrations listed. Plum cloth.

Ref.: Howes B269; Rader 307; Wagner-Camp 103 note

Copyrighted 1873.

213 BEADLE COUNTY, SOUTH DAKO-
TA. County Commissioners, *publishers.*

DEVELOPMENT AND RESOURCES OF BEADLE COUNTY IN THE NEW STATE OF SOUTH DAKOTA . . . PUBLISHED AND ENDORSED BY THE COUNTY COMMISSIONERS. 1889.

[1]–[48]. 22 x 15 cm. Illustrations and maps. Pink printed wrappers with title on front wrapper; map on verso of front wrapper and map on recto of back wrapper.

Ref.: Allen (*Dakota*) 671

On page [48], below map: Published by the Daily Times. Huron, Dak. /

214 BEALE, EDWIN F.

[Caption title] . . . WAGON ROAD—FORT SMITH TO COLORADO RIVER. LETTER OF THE SECRETARY

OF WAR, TRANSMITTING THE REPORT OF MR. BEALE, RELATING TO THE CONSTRUCTION OF A WAGON ROAD FROM FORT SMITH TO THE COLORADO RIVER . . .

[1]–91, [92 blank]. 22.5 x 14.5 cm. Map: Map / Showing the Route of / E. F. Beale / from / Fort Smith, Ark. / to / Alburquerque [!] N.M. / 1858–9. / [upper right:] H. R. Ex: Doc: N⁰ 42. 36ᵗʰ Cong: 1ˢᵗ Session. / [lower left:] Lith. of J. Bien, 180 Broadway N.Y. / 17.2 x 124 cm. Scale: 15 1/2 miles to one inch. Rebound in new red cloth.

Ref.: Howes B272; Munk (Alliot) p. 26; Saunders 2727; Wagner-Camp 350

36th Congress, 1st Session, House, Executive Document No. 42, Serial 1048. [Washington, 1860.]

215 BEALE, EDWIN F., & AMIEL W. WHIPPLE

[Caption title] . . . REPORT OF THE SECRETARY OF WAR, COMMUNICATING . . . A REPORT OF E. F. BEALE OF HIS EXPLORATION FOR A WAGON ROAD FROM FORT DEFIANCE, IN NEW MEXICO, TO THE WESTERN BORDERS OF CALIFORNIA . . .

[1]–5, [6 blank]. 22.8 x 14.3 cm.

BOUND WITH:

. . . WAGON ROAD FROM FORT DEFIANCE TO THE COLORADO RIVER . . .

[1]–87, [88 blank]. Two pamphlets bound together, full contemporary sprinkled calf, black leather labels on front cover and backstrip, sprinkled edges.

Prov.: Inscribed on blank leaf at front: To my wife with / affectionate love / E F. Beale. / Chester / Sept 3ʳᵈ 1858 / [underline] / To Mʳ Kingsley [!] / with kind regards of / E F. Beale / Lafayette Square / May 21ˢᵗ 1884 / [underline] /. Signature on front cover: E. W. Kinsley /.

Ref.: Howes B271; Munk (Alliot) p. 28; Wagner-Camp 297 note

35th Congress, 1st Session, Senate, Executive Document No. 43, Serial 922. [Washington, 1858.]

35th Congress, 1st Session, House, Executive Document No. 124, Serial 959. [Washington, 1858.]

Some marginal annotations, corrections, etc., probably by both Beale and Kinsley.

The first title is the preliminary report of the reconnaissance and the second title is the final report, but the latter lacks the map. See Number 216 for a copy with map.

216 [BEALE, EDWIN F., & AMIEL W. WHIPPLE]

[Caption title] . . . WAGON ROAD FROM FORT DEFIANCE TO THE COLORADO RIVER. LETTER FROM THE SECRETARY OF WAR, TRANSMITTING THE REPORT OF THE SUPERINTENDENT OF THE WAGON ROAD FROM FORT DEFIANCE TO THE COLORADO RIVER . . .

[1]–87, [88 blank]. 22.9 x 14.5 cm. Map: Preliminary Map / of the Western Portion of the Reconnaissance and Survey / for a Pacific Rail Road Route near the 35.th Par. / made by Capt A. W. Whipple, T. E. in 1853–4. / With Additions showing the Route of the Proposed / Wagon Road from Fort Defiance to the Colorado / together with several lateral Explorations. / by E. F. Beale Supt. / 1857–8. / Scale: 1: 900,000. / Lith. of J. Bien, 60 Fulton Street N.Y. / [upper right:] (House Ex. Doc. N⁰ 124.—1.st Session 35.th Con / 66.5 x 124.3 cm. Scale: as above. Rebound in red cloth.

Prov.: Frederick S. Dellenbaugh's copy.

Ref.: Howes B271; Munk (Alliot) p. 28; Wagner-Camp 297

35th Congress, 1st Session, House, Executive Document No. 124, Serial 959. [Washington, 1858.]

Beale's final report carries his journal. Aubry's trail of 1854 is indicaled on the map. A manuscript note, in pencil, initialed by Dellenbaugh appears on page 77.

217 BEALE, GEORGE P., & GEORGE BAKER

CONFESSIONS OF GEO. P. BEALE AND GEO. BAKER HUNG AT SALEM, OREGON, MAY 17, 1865, FOR THE MURDER OF DANIEL DELANEY, SEN. . . . SALEM, OREGON: OREGON STATESMAN POWER PRESS. 1865.

[1]–32. 19.9 x 14 cm. Green printed wrappers with title on front wrapper.

Ref.: McDade 78; McMurtrie (*Oregon*) 297

218 BEALL, JOHN B.

IN BARRACK AND FIELD. POEMS AND SKETCHES OF ARMY LIFE. NASHVILLE, TENN.: SMITH & LAMAR, 1906.

[1]–420. 18.1 x 12.2 cm. Portrait. Green pictorial cloth, advertisement on recto of back endleaf.

Ref.:

Enlisting as a common soldier in 1855, Beall took part in the "Kansas troubles" of the period, while stationed at Forts Leavenworth and Scott. In 1857, he accompanied the expedition to mark the southern boundary of Kansas, and in his book includes his day-by-day diary of the overland trip covering the period May to September. He was stationed at Fort Washita during the year 1858.—EDG

219 BEAN, EDWIN F.

BEAN'S HISTORY AND DIRECTORY OF NEVADA COUNTY, CALIFORNIA. CONTAINING A COMPLETE HISTORY OF THE COUNTY, WITH SKETCHES OF THE VARIOUS TOWNS AND MINING CAMPS, THE NAMES AND OCCUPATION OF RESIDENTS; ALSO, FULL STATISTICS OF MINING AND ALL OTHER INDUSTRIAL RESOURCES. NEVADA: PRINTED AT THE DAILY GAZETTE BOOK AND JOB OFFICE, 1867.

[I]–VI, [i–vi], [1]–424. (Some inserted advertisements on colored paper.) 21.8 x 13.7 cm. Light blue printed boards, black roan backstrip, outer and inner covers carry advertisements.

Ref.: Howes B278

All the known advertisements are present. Between pages IV and V there is a small slip advertising Hermann Ernst, Book-Binder, Nevada City, California.

220 BEAUCHAMP, JEREBOAM O.

THE CONFESSION OF JEREBOAM O. BEAUCHAMP. WHO WAS EXECUTED AT FRANKFORT, KY ON THE 7TH OF JULY, 1826. FOR THE MURDER OF COL. SOLOMON P. SHARP . . . BLOOMFIELD, KY.: PRINTED FOR THE PUBLISHER, 1826.

[1]–107, [108 blank], [113]–134. (Pages 109–12 omitted in pagination; pages 113, 116, 123, 131 unpaginated.) 19.1 x 12.3 cm. Rebound in green half morocco. Lacks a final blank leaf.

Ref.: Howes B284; Jillson (*RKB*) p. 74; Jillson: "The Beauchamp-Sharp Tragedy in American Literature" in *The Register* of the Kentucky State Historical Society, Vol. 36 (1938); Rusk I, p. 73; Sabin 4159

The irregular pagination noted above is common to other copies located.

The Beauchamp-Sharp tragedy has long been a popular source in American literature. "Hoffman's *Greyslaer*, for example, was partly based on the famous Beauchamp murder case in Kentucky, which was itself the subject of two novels by William Gilmore Simms [*Beauchampe* (1842) and *Charlmonte* (1856)] and even furnished some of the groundwork for Poe's 'Politian' . . ."—Rusk. As early as 1938, Jillson found forty-eight editions, accounts, plays, novels, poems, etc. based on the tragedy. He did not, of course, list the famous modern novel by Robert Penn Warren: *World Enough and Time*, published in 1950.

221 BEAUGRAND, HONORE

SIX MOIS DANS LES MONTAGNES-ROCHEUSES, COLO-RADO—UTAH—NOUVEAU MEXIQUE . . . MON-TREAL: GRANGER FRERES, 1890.

[i blank], [1]–[324], [325 blank]. 23.2 x 15.3 cm. Map, 45 plates, unlisted, mostly included in pagination, and cuts in text. Cream printed wrappers with title on front wrapper, cut on verso of back wrapper, uncut, unopened.

Ref.: Howes (1954) 709; Monaghan 155

222 BEAUMONT, WILLIAM

EXPERIMENTS AND OBSERVATIONS ON THE GASTRIC JUICE, AND THE PHYSIOLOGY OF DIGESTION . . . PLATTSBURGH: PRINTED BY F. P. ALLEN, 1833.

[1]–280. 22.6 x 13.7 cm. Brown sheep. Binding repaired at corners, rebacked, new leather label. In a brown half morocco case.

Prov.: Inscribed by the author in pencil on the title-page: For Mrs Genl Hamilton / with the best respects of the / *Author* /. Signature on title-page: Elizth Hamilton /. Inscribed on the front endleaf: Given by / Philip Schuyler / to W. M. / With the bookplate of Dr. S. Weir Mitchell. Mrs. Hamilton was the widow of Alexander Hamilton and Philip Schuyler was one of her nephews.

Ref.: Grolier 38; Howes B291

Beaumont's work is one of the half-dozen great contributions to medical knowledge.

In the preface to the second edition (see next item), the writer states there were three thousand copies of the first edition printed. Myer, in his *Life and Letters of William Beaumont* (page 204) states that Beaumont had fifty copies of the first edition bound in full sheep for presentation.

223 BEAUMONT, WILLIAM

THE PHYSIOLOGY OF DIGESTION . . . CORRECTED BY SAMUEL BEAUMONT, M.D. BURLINGTON: CHAUNCEY GOODRICH, 1847.

[1]–[304]. 19.1 x 12 cm. Black cloth, blind embossed sides, title in gilt on backstrip.

Ref.: Howes B291
Editions: Plattsburgh, 1833.

224 BECK, LEWIS C.

A GAZETTEER OF THE STATES OF ILLINOIS AND MIS-SOURI; CONTAINING A GENERAL VIEW OF EACH STATE . . . 1823.

[i]–[viii], [9]–352. 23.4 x 14.8 cm. One illustration, five maps and plans. Map: Map / of the / States / of / Illinois & Missouri / by / Lewis C. Beck A.M. / Scale 24 miles to the inch / [diagrammatic scale as above] / Balch, Rawdon & Cº fc. / 48.3 x 44.4 cm. Scale as above. Plan: Plan / of / Fort Chartres / on the / Mississip-pi / Scale of Feet / [diagrammatic scale: 125 feet to one inch] /. 12.3 x 19.4 cm. (plate mark). Scale as above. Plan: P. II./ Plan of Vandalia / the / Capital / of The / State of Illinois /. 19.5 x 11.7 cm. (plate mark). No scale given. Plan: P. IV. / Plan / of / St Louis, / Including the late / Additions / [decorative rule] / Engraved for / Beck's Gazetteer 1822 /. 17.6 x 43 cm. No scale given. Plan: [Sand bar before St. Louis.] [upper left:] P. V. / 20.6 x 22.7 cm. (plate mark). No scale given. Blue-gray boards, tan paper backstrip, with salmon printed label, 3.3 x 2.5 cm., uncut, mostly unopened. In a green full morocco pull off case.

Ref.: Bradford 324; Buck 180; Howes B297; Jones 848; Sabin 4231

Beck's popular *Gazetteer* was widely used at the time of publication and is still important for the detailed information about local communities as they were then.

225 BECKNELL, WILLIAM

[Cover title] THE JOURNALS OF CAPT. THOMAS BECKNELL FROM BOONE'S LICK TO SANTA FE AND FROM SANTA CRUZ TO GREEN RIVER . . . COLUM-BIA, MISSOURI: STATE HISTORICAL SOCIETY OF MIS-SOURI, 1910.

[75]–84. 22.9 x 15 cm. Printed gray wrappers.
Ref.:

Off-print from the *Missouri Historical Review*, Vol. 4, No. 2, January, 1910. Thomas has been changed in manuscript to William on the front wrapper and on page [75]. One other manuscript correction in a footnote.

226 BECKWITH, C., & ORVILLE H. BROWNING

ARGUMENTS IN THE CASE OF ISAAC H. BURCH VS. MARY W. BURCH . . . CHICAGO: SCOTT & COM-PANY, 1861.

[i–iv], [1]–162, [163–64 blank], [1]–91, [92–4 blank]. 22.3 x 14 cm. Brown cloth, title in gilt on backstrip.

Ref.: AII (*Chicago*) 520; Sabin 4256

The case argued here was a notorious divorce case with trimmings. Errata on page [i].

227 BEDFORD, HILORY G.

TEXAS INDIAN TROUBLES. THE MOST THRILLING EVENTS IN THE HISTORY OF TEXAS . . . DALLAS: HARGREAVES PRINTING CO., INC., 1905.

[1]–249, [250 blank]. 20.8 x 14.4 cm. Five illustrations listed. Pale blue pictorial cloth.

Ref.: Howes B303

228 BEDFORD & GEORGE [T. W. BED-
FORD and HUDSON GEORGE],
Brownville, Nebraska

[Map] MAP OF THE NEMAHA LAND DISTRICT NE-
BRASKA TERRITORY / COMPILED AND DRAWN FROM
NOTES PROCURED FROM THE U.S. LAND OFFICE AT
BROWNVILLE, N.T. / BY BEDFORD & GEORGE CIV.
ENG⁹ / [upper right:] LITHOGRAPHED BY TH.
SCHRADER / Nº 42 SECOND-STREET ST. LOUIS / FOR /
BEDFORD AND GEORGE / SURVEYORS, CIVIL ENGI-
NEERS AND GENERAL LAND AGENTS / BROWNVILLE,
N.T. / [lower left:] ENTERED ACCORDING TO THE
ACT OF CONGRESS IN THE YEAR 1858 BY BEDFORD
AND GEORGE IN THE CLERKS OFFICE OF THE U.S.
DISTRICT COURT OF THE SECOND / JUDICIAL DIS-
TRICT OF THE TERRITORY OF NEBRASKA. /

Map, 53.1 x 139.3 cm. No scale given. Folded
into black cloth covers, 14.7 x 9.8 cm., with
printed label on front cover.
Ref.:

229 BEEBE, HENRY S.

THE HISTORY OF PERU. PERU, ILLS.: J. F. LINTON,
1858.

[i–iv], [1]–162, [163–64 blank]. 14.5 x 10.6 cm.
Gray printed wrappers with title on front
wrapper. In a pink board case.
Ref.: Byrd 2856; Howes B306

230 BEECHER ISLAND ANNUAL, THE

[Wrapper title] THE BEECHER ISLAND ANNUAL.
ROBERT LYNAM, EDITOR. VOLUME IV . . . WRAY,
COLO.: PUBLISHED BY THE BEECHER ISLAND
BATTLE MEMORIAL ASSOCIATION, 1908.

[i–viii], [1]–36, [37–40 advertisements]. 22.5 x
15.6 cm. Numerous illustrations and maps.
Green printed wrappers with title on front wrapper, programme on verso of front wrapper, advertisement on recto of back wrapper, cut on
verso of back wrapper.
Ref.:

In addition to the programme noted above,
the *Annual* contains an account of the Fortieth
Reunion of the Battle, a history of the Beecher
Island Battle Memorial Association, and a history of the battle itself, the last two articles from
the pen of Judge E. S. Ricker of Grand Junction,
Colo. The pamphlet contains many illustrations
and portraits of participants.

231 BEECHER ISLAND ANNUAL, THE

THE SAME . . . VOLUME V . . . 1917.

[i–xx], 1–[56], [57–68 advertisements]. 22.5 x
15.6 cm. Illustrations, unlisted. Gray wrappers
with title on front wrapper, advertisements on
verso of front and recto and verso of back wrapper.

This volume of the *Annual* contains an article
by Thomas Ranahan about the events leading up
to the battle, General Forsyth's account of the
battle from his *Thrilling Days in Army Life*, a
sketch of Forsyth's career, and stories of the
battle by H. Tucker, Eli Zigler, Thomas B.
Murphy, John Hurst, A. J. Pliley, Scout Schle-
singer, and others.

232 BEESON, JOHN

[Caption title] ARE WE NOT MEN AND BRETHREN?
AN ADDRESS TO THE PEOPLE OF THE UNITED STATES
. . .

[1]–[8]. 23 x 14.5 cm. Unbound.
Ref.:

Page [8] is a prospectus for Beeson's projected periodical *The Calumet* dated Boston, November 30. *The Calumet* was intended for publication in January, 1860, but did not appear until
the following month. The present pamphlet was
printed in Boston, probably in December, 1859.

233 BEESON, JOHN

A PLEA FOR THE INDIANS; WITH FACTS AND FEA-
TURES OF THE LATE WAR IN OREGON . . . NEW
YORK: PUBLISHED BY JOHN BEESON, 1857.

[i]–viii, [9]–143, [144 advertisements]. 18.6 x
12.3 cm. Green printed wrappers with title on
front wrapper within decorative border. In a
blue half morocco case.
Prov.: Bookplate of Henry W. Poor. Duplicate note of Henry E. Huntington Library.
Ref.: Howell 19; Howes B314; Sabin 4360;
Smith 709; Wagner-Camp 284

The work refers to the Rogue River affair.

234 BEESON, JOHN

[Broadside] TO THE AMERICAN PUBLIC. I AD-
DRESS YOU BECAUSE THERE IS A CONDITION OF
THINGS WHICH EITHER IS NOT KNOWN, OR IS NOT
DULY CONSIDERED; AND AS A CONSEQUENCE THERE
IS DANGER OF WRONG LEGISLATION. THE CHIEF
MISTAKE CONSISTS IN THE PREVALENT IDEA THAT
THE INDIANS OF THIS TERRITORY ARE BUT SAVAGES,
AND THAT THEIR COUNTRY CAN BE MONOPOLIZED
BY RAILWAY SPECULATORS AND GOVERNED BY THE
APPOINTEES OF THE PRESIDENT OF THE UNITED
STATES, INSTEAD OF THOSE OF THEIR OWN SELEC-
TION. NOW THE FACT IS, SO FAR FROM BEING
"IGNORANT SAVAGES," MANY OF THEM ARE HIGHLY
EDUCATED AND INTELLIGENT PEOPLE. . . . RE-
SPECTFULLY, JOHN BEESON. FORT GIBSON, INDIAN
TER., JAN. 12, 1874.

Broadside, 34 x 15.1 cm. Text, 29.5 x 11.1 cm.
Ref.:

There is one manuscript correction in the text
and there are two annotations in the margin.

235 BELDEN, GEORGE P.

BELDEN, THE WHITE CHIEF; OR, TWELVE YEARS
AMONG THE WILD INDIANS OF THE PLAINS . . .
CINCINNATI: C. F. VENT, 1870.

[i]–iv, [5]–13, [14 blank], xv–xvi, [17]–513, [514
blank]. 21.5 x 14.6 cm. 55 illustrations listed.
Blue cloth, gilt vignettes on covers, gilt title on
backstrip: Belden / the / White Chief / Illustrated /.

Ref.: Howes B781; Rader 326

Belden's veracity has often been questioned.
Edited by General James S. Brisbin.

236 BELDEN, GEORGE P.

THE SAME, except for additional line in imprint.
[i]–iv, [5]–13, [14 blank], xv–xvi, [17]–22, 33,
54–56, 96, 99, 103, 117, 119–21, 124, 129–30, 240,
256, [1–24]. 19.5 x 13.2 cm. Seven plates, text
illustrations, unlisted. Plum cloth, blind vignettes on sides, gilt backstrip mounted inside
front cover.

Salesman's dummy. The colon after Chicago
in the imprint is defective (as in the preceding
number), and there is an added line. The last
twenty-four pages are for subscribers' names,
addresses, etc.

Preceding the last section is an inserted prospectus: [Folded broadside, 34.1 x 19.2 cm.:]
Prospectus of / Belden: The White Chief; / [73
lines] We, the subscribers will take and pay for
the number of copies of the above work, when /
delivered in accordance with the above conditions. / The broadside is printed on pale blue
paper. Text size: 32.9 x 18.2 cm.

237 BELDEN, GEORGE P.

BRISBIN'S STORIES OF THE PLAINS; OR, TWELVE
YEARS AMONG THE WILD INDIANS . . . ST. LOUIS:
ANCHOR PUBLISHING COMPANY . . . 1881.

[i]–iv, [5]–13, [14 blank], xv–xvi, [17]–541, [542
advertisement]. 18.5 x 12.3 cm. 56 illustrations
listed. Light brown cloth, gilt vignette on front
cover, blind vignette on back cover, title in gilt
on backstrip.

Ref.: Howes B781

This is a reprint of *Belden, the White Chief*
with additional material at the end and one
added plate.

238 BELISLE, DAVID W.

THE AMERICAN FAMILY ROBINSON; OR, THE ADVEN-
TURES OF A FAMILY LOST IN THE GREAT DESERT OF
THE WEST . . . PHILADELPHIA: WILLIS P. HAZARD,
1854.

[i]–viii, [9]–360. 18.6 x 12.5 cm. Four plates,
unlisted. Black cloth, gilt, gilt edges.

Ref.: Howes 745; Sabin 4426; Wagner-Camp
236; Wright II 250

Juvenile, with plates after Carl Bodmer.

239 BELKNAP, JEREMY

A DISCOURSE, INTENDED TO COMMEMORATE THE
DISCOVERY OF AMERICA BY CHRISTOPHER COLUM-
BUS . . . BOSTON: BELKNAP AND HALL, MDCCXCII.

A-R⁴. [1]–132, [133–34 advertisements, 135–36
blank]. Bound with Number 3867.

Ref.: Evans 24085; Sabin 4431

240 BELL, HORACE

REMINISCENCES OF A RANGER; OR EARLY TIMES IN
SOUTHERN CALIFORNIA. LOS ANGELES: YARNELL,
CAYSTILE & MATHES, 1881.

[1]–457, [458 blank]. (Pages [1–2] blank.)
22.5 x 14.2 cm. Red pictorial cloth, title and
vignettes on front cover and title on backstrip in
gilt.

Prov.: Inscribed on front endleaf: With the
Authors Compliments / Horace Bell / [flour-
ish] /. Above the inscription, in a different hand:
E. H. Coffin Esq / St Louis Mo /.

Ref.: Adams 92; Cowan p. 44; Howes B325;
Zamorano Eighty 5

Bell has written more minutely upon the
"seamy side" of society than any other California author, and there is a fascination about
his book. From the long lists given of murderous
villains, thieving scoundrels, and other unholy
characters, it would appear that the polite society of the south in those days was neither large
nor extensive.—Cowan.

Bell was a member of Walker's filibustering
expedition.

241 BELL, J. F.

[Caption title] A REPLY TO THE BARE-FACED
FALSEHOODS AND MISREPRESENTATIONS OF MR.
JOHN THEOBALD . . .

[1]–8. Bound with Number 3346.

Ref.:

Printed in Washington in 1844.

242 BELL, JAMES G.

A LOG OF THE TEXAS-CALIFORNIA CATTLE TRAIL,
1854 . . . EDITED BY J. EVETTS HALEY. REPRINTED
FROM THE SOUTHWESTERN HISTORICAL QUAR-
TERLY, 1932.

[1]–[79], [80 blank]. 23.2 x 15.2 cm. Blue printed
wrappers, with title on front wrapper.

Ref.: Adams (*Ramp. Herd*) 235; Dobie pp.
103–04; Howes B326; Saunders 328

Published at Austin, Texas. With an Autograph Letter, signed, by the editor laid in.

243 BELL, JOHN T.

HISTORY OF WASHINGTON COUNTY, NEBRASKA. ITS EARLY SETTLEMENT AND PRESENT STATUS . . . OMAHA, NEB.: PRINTED AT THE HERALD STEAM BOOK AND JOB PRINTING HOUSE, JULY, 1876.

[1]–64, [65–70 advertisements, 71–2 blank]. 21.6 x 14.6 cm. Tan printed wrappers with title on front wrapper, cut of "Blair High School" on verso of back wrapper.

Ref.: AII (*Nebraska*) 392; Howes B327

244 BELL, JOHN T.

TRAMPS AND TRIUMPHS OF THE SECOND IOWA INFANTRY, BRIEFLY SKETCHED . . . OMAHA: GIBSON, MILLER & RICHARDSON, 1886.

[1]–32. 21.5 x 13.6 cm. Orange printed front wrapper, with title as above within rule border, bound in contemporary black cloth, title in gilt on backstrip, and with 54 leaves of filler.

Ref.: Coulter 25; Nicholson p. 74

While Coulter finds it of little value as a travel record, Bell's account is an interesting personal narrative of wartime adventure.

245 BELL, JOSIAS F.

[Manuscript] SKETCHES OF A JOURNEY BY JOSIAS FENDALL BELL. 1841–44. 156 pages, 18.2 x 14.4 cm. Bound in marbled boards, green leather backstrip. Worn. In a green half morocco case.

The diary covers the author's travels across country from Smithsboro, Pennsylvania, which place he left on April 19, 1841. He went by way of St. Louis, Missouri, and Peoria, Illinois, to Boonville, Missouri, where he joined James and Samuel Magoffin. They set out for Santa Fé on July 20, going by way of Las Vegas, New Mexico, and arrived in Santa Fé on October 12. Bell's description of the journey over the Santa Fé Trail is succinct and well told. He continued toward the West Coast via Chihuahua (where he heard about Robert McKnight, the famous earlier Santa Fé trader who was then mining silver at Barrance Colorado), Guaymas, Mazatlan, and Monterrey which he reached on April 15, 1843. He left Monterrey on September 14, 1843, returning by ship via Cape Horn to New Bedford.

Bell's purpose in taking the journey was to regain his health; he chose an arduous method. When he set out he was twenty-six years old, a journeyman shoemaker, slightly deaf, and troubled by a club foot. His diary is a good personal account of a long journey.

The original manuscript is accompanied by a bound, edited typed transcript.

246 BELL, WILLIAM A.

NEW TRACKS IN NORTH AMERICA. A JOURNAL OF TRAVEL AND ADVENTURE WHILST ENGAGED IN THE SURVEY FOR A SOUTHERN RAILROAD TO THE PACIFIC OCEAN DURING 1867–8 . . . LONDON: CHAPMAN AND HALL, 1869.

[i]–[lxviii, lxviii blank], [1]–236. [i]–x, x blank], [1]–322. 22 x 15 cm. 45 illustrations and one map listed. Map: Map / of the / South-Western Portion / of the / United States, / and of / Sonora and Chihuahua. / Illustrating Travels by Dr. W. A. Bell. / Compiled by E. G. Ravenstein, F. R. G. S. &c. / Scale 1:6,000,000 (95 miles to 1 inch) / [diagrammatic scale] / . . . [lower centre:] London: Chapman & Hall, 1869. / 32.1 x 36.3 cm. Scale as above. *Inset:* Lower / California / continued. / 5.5 x 5.8 cm. Scale as above. Two volumes, brown cloth, blind embossed sides, title in gilt on backstrips, uncut, unopened.

Ref.: Cowan p. 45; Howes B330; Rader 330

Contains firsthand accounts of Indians in Arizona and New Mexico.

247 BELL COUNTY, TEXAS . . .

[Broadside] 1876. BELL COUNTY, TEXAS. 1877. A GENERAL INVITATION TO WORTHY PEOPLE. BELL COUNTY IS SITUATED . . . THE FOLLOWING GENTLEMEN CITIZENS OF BELL COUNTY WILL CHEERFULLY REPLY TO ANY LETTERS OF ENQUIRY, AND INVITE CORRESPONDENCE FROM ALL PARTIES WHO HAVE A DESIRE OF SETTLING IN TEXAS. L. A. GRIFFITH, SALADO, [21 names].

Broadside, 42.8 x 27.7 cm. Text, 33 x 22.6 cm.

The place of printing is not mentioned. The broadside is remarkably close in character to a similar advertising broadside for Rusk County, Texas.

248 BELLEVILLE, ILLINOIS

REVISED ORDINANCES OF THE CITY OF BELLEVILLE, WITH THE CITY CHARTER AND AMENDMENTS . . . TOGETHER WITH A BRIEF HISTORY OF BELLEVILLE, BY EX-GOVERNOR JOHN REYNOLDS . . . BELLEVILLE, ILL: PRINTED BY G. A. HARVEY, 1862.

[1]–191, [192 blank], [i]–xii. 22.7 x 14.6 cm. Rebound in dark blue cloth, blind borders on sides, blind bands on backstrip.

Ref.: Howes B336

249 BENAVIDES, ALONSO DE

MEMORIAL QVE FRAY IVAN DE SANTANDER . . . PRESENTA A LA MAGESTAD CATOLICA DEL REY DON FELIPE QVARTO NVESTRO SENOR . . . EN MADRID EN LA IMPRENTA REAL. ANO M. DC. XXX.

[B4], A⁴, B³, C–G⁴, H², I–O⁴. [i–ii], [1]–109, [110–12 blank]. (Pages 51, 52, 53, 54, 66, 99, 87, and 10 are mispaginations for pages 15, 16, 17,

18, 64, 69, 85, and 109; pages 19, 20, 60–3 omitted in pagination.) 20.1 x 14 cm. Full limp vellum, leather ties (one missing). Outer half of last blank leaf torn off. In a red half morocco case.

Prov.: Inscribed on front endleaf: [paraph] / Relaz^on Nueba de la / Nuebo mejico y nueba[s] / Copannia^s / Vitoria / Santander /. On the verso of the same leaf, in a later hand: Joy De Juan José Arenos /. On the front cover, reading up: DesCubrimiento del / Nuevo Mejico / Año de 1626 / en 20 de Junio /. Henry R. Wagner-Herschel V. Jones copy.

Ref.: Beristain I pp. 154–55; Jones 233; Medina (*BHA*) 868; Rader 331; Sabin 4636, 76810; Streit II 1583; Wagner (*SS*) 33

Wagner deals with the states of the *Memorial* in some detail, using the Ayer copy as one variety. The present copy differs from the Ayer copy and agrees with both the Library of Congress and Wagner copies. The present copy, however, is not the copy illustrated in Wagner (*SS*). Both Ayer and Graff copies show two manuscript corrections on page 21 unmentioned by Wagner.

250 BENAVIDES, ALONSO DE

THE MEMORIAL . . . TRANSLATED BY MRS. EDWARD E. AYER . . . CHICAGO; PRIVATELY PRINTED, 1916.*

[i]–[xiv, xiv blank], [1]–309, [310 blank, 311 colophon, 312 blank]. 22.6 x 16 cm. 44 illustrations listed. Half brown buckram, yellow cloth sides, gilt top, uncut.

Ref.:
Limited to 300 copies.

251 BENAVIDES, ALONSO DE

TANTO QVE SE SACO DE UNA CARTA . . .

[*Colophon:*] Con Licencia de los Superiores. / Impresso en Mexico: por Joseph Bernardo de / Hogal, Ministro, ê Impressor del Real, y / Apostolico Tribunal de la Santa Cruzada en / toda esta Nueva-España, Año de 1730. /

¶^8. [i–vi], 1–10. 14.1 x 10 cm. Engraved frontispiece: La Ve Me Maria de Iesus de Agreda, Predicando / â los Chichimecos del Nuebomexico. Antt^o Castro f^t / Sewn into later brown paper wrappers. In a red half morocco case.

Prov.: Henry R. Wagner-Herschel V. Jones copy.

Ref.: Jones 436; Medina (*Mexico*) 3106; Palau 2751; Streit III 295; Wagner (*SS*) 92

Wagner lists the present edition first and describes two other editions which he considers later. Streit calls this the third edition, describing as the first an undated edition which Wagner designates the third (92b). Streit does not list a second edition.

The present copy belonged formerly to Henry R. Wagner, but the reproduction of the title-page in Wagner (*SS*) is faulty, apparently touched up by the engraver.

252 BENJAMIN, ISRAEL JOSEPH, II

[General title:] DREI JAHRE IN AMERIKA 1859– 1862 . . . HANNOVER, 1862.

[I]–XVI, [1]–384. [II]–[VIII, VIII blank], 1–168. [II]–[XII, XII blank], 1–132. 20.8 x 13.7 cm. Portrait. Three parts bound in two volumes, red cloth, gilt, gilt edges. Some stains.

Ref.: Cowan p. 46; Howes B351; Sabin 4698

These are the observations of a careful traveler who was able to record his personal narrative vividly. Each of the three parts carries a separate title-page in addition to the general title-page.

253 BENJAMIN, MARCUS

JOHN BIDWELL, PIONEER. A SKETCH OF HIS CAREER. WASHINGTON, 1907.*

[i–iv], 1–52. 25.6 x 19 cm. Five illustrations, unlisted. White printed wrappers bound into original half brown leather, white board sides with title in gilt on front cover and backstrip, gilt top, uncut.

Ref.: Cowan p. 47; Howes B353; Wagner-Camp 88 note.

Contains a good account of Bidwell's overland trip, his life with Sutter, and his later successes.

254 BENNETT, EMERSON

THE BORDER ROVER . . . PHILADELPHIA: T. B. PETERSON . . .

33–524, 1–[20] advertisements. 18.4 x 12.2 cm. Brown cloth.

Ref.: Blanck 1080; Wagner-Camp 285; Wright II 269

Copyrighted 1857. The scene is Bent's Fort.

255 BENNETT, EMERSON

LENI-LEOTI: OR, ADVENTURES IN THE FAR WEST . . . CINCINNATI & ST. LOUIS: STRATTON & BARNARD . . . 1849.

[i–ii], [11]–117, [118 blank]. 23 x 14 cm. Terra cotta printed wrappers. In red buckram case.

Ref.: Blanck 1055; Howes B354; Sabin 4723; Smith 757; Wagner-Camp 163; Wright I 300.

256 BENNETT, EMERSON

THE PRAIRIE FLOWER . . . CINCINNATI: STRATTON & BARNARD, 1849.

[i–iv], [9]–128. 22.2 x 13 cm. Rebound in red cloth. Some outer edges bled.

Ref.: Blanck 1054; Howes B355; Sabin 4723; Wagner-Camp 162; Wright I 304

257 BENNETT, EMERSON

ANOTHER COPY. 22.7 x 13.8 cm. Rebound in brown boards, leather label.

258 BENNETT, EMERSON

WILD SCENES ON THE FRONTIERS; OR, HEROES OF THE WEST . . . PHILADELPHIA: HAMELIN & CO. . . . 1859.

[3]–8, 15–408, 419–421, [422 blank]. 19.5 x 12.8 cm. Double frontispiece and six plates. Black cloth, gilt title on backstrip.
  Ref.: Blanck 1083; Sabin 4723; Wagner-Camp 317a; Wright II 287

259 BENNETT, ESTELLINE

OLD DEADWOOD DAYS . . . NEW YORK: J. H. SEARS & COMPANY, INC., [1928].*

[1–2, 2 blank], [i]–[xii, xii blank], [1]–300. 20.3 x 3.7 cm. 12 illustrations listed. Orange cloth.
  Ref.: Adams 98; Howes B356

260 BENNETT, FRED E.

FRED BENNETT, THE MORMON DETECTIVE; OR, ADVENTURES IN THE WILD WEST . . . CHICAGO: LAIRD & LEE, 1887.

[11]–283, [284–92 advertisements]. 18.8 x 13 cm. Seven illustrations and a portrait, unlisted. Light brown cloth with maroon cloth backstrip.
  Ref.:
Another edition contains an appendix.

261 BENNETT, JAMES

[Wrapper title] OVERLAND JOURNEY TO CALIFORNIA. JOURNAL OF JAMES BENNETT WHOSE PARTY LEFT NEW HARMONY IN 1850 AND CROSSED THE PLAINS AND MOUNTAINS UNTIL THE GOLDEN WEST WAS REACHED. NEW HARMONY, INDIANA: TIMES PRINT, 1906.

1–45, [46–8 blank]. 21.6 x 13.9 cm. Buff printed wrappers with title on front wrapper.
  Prov.: Inscribed in pencil on inside front wrapper: To Everett D Graff Esq from his friend, / the publisher. This little brochure was produced / by the Shears and Camera and was prepared for / publication during several bleary nights in which / its producer was on a jag across the continence. / Once again Sober I perceive that it looks more / like a crazy-quilt than a specimen of printing / but then, for the sake of the record, consider: The / border-title is clipped from a Riley Root wrapper; the imprint from a German-English dictionary; the notice of edition from some of my old catalogs; the column-lines

from the Evening Post and / lastly, the pagination numbers from an im-/maculate and "as new" copy of Mrs Post's book / on table manners and etiquette, a gift from / my wife the day after we were married. / E E /.
  Ref.: Howes B357a
The "notice of edition" on the inner front wrapper reads: Printed in an edition of / 200 copies / from the files of the / New Harmony Times / wherein the journal appeared / serially March 16–August 3, 1906 / Edward Eberstadt / 55 West 42nd Street, New York /.
  The text, in two columns, is a facsimile from the *New Harmony Times.* The pamphlet was published in 1932.

262 BENNETT, JOHN C.

THE HISTORY OF THE SAINTS; OR, AN EXPOSE OF JOE SMITH AND MORMONISM . . . BOSTON: LELAND & WHITING, 1842.

[i]–ii, [1]–344. 18.7 x 11.7 cm. Four illustrations, unlisted. Black cloth, blind embossed borders on sides, title in gilt on front cover.
  Ref.: Howes B358; Sabin 4733; Woodward 13

263 BENNETT, WILLIAM P.

THE FIRST BABY IN CAMP. A FULL ACCOUNT OF THE SCENES AND ADVENTURES DURING THE PIONEER DAYS OF '49 . . . SALT LAKE CITY: THE RANCHER PUBLISHING CO., 1893.

[1]–68, [69 blank, 70 advertisement]. 17.5 x 11.8 cm. Pale yellow printed wrappers with title on front wrapper.
  Ref.:
The large print described on the title-page is not present.

264 BENSCHOTER, GEORGE E.

1873. 1897. BOOK OF FACTS CONCERNING THE EARLY SETTLEMENT OF SHERMAN COUNTY . . . LOUP CITY, NEBRASKA: LOUP CITY NORTHWESTERN PRINT.*

[i–vi, vi blank], [1]–76, [77–8 blank]. (Pages [1–2] blank.) 18.2 x 13.8 cm. Printed yellow wrappers with title on front wrapper. Backstrip supported by strip of tan cloth, upper right corner of wrapper and first nine leaves moused.
  Ref.: Adams (*Ramp. Herd*) 244; Howes B359a
Published in 1897.
  The author arrived in Sherman County on July 4, 1873, and camped four miles from the future location of Loup City. He gives interesting stories of pioneer life including the perilous adventures of Judge Wall with the notorious Olive gang of cowboy thugs.

265 BENSON, HENRY C.

LIFE AMONG THE CHOCTAW INDIANS, AND SKETCHES OF THE SOUTH-WEST . . . CINCINNATI: PUBLISHED BY L. SWORMSTEDT & A. POE, 1860.

[1]–314. 18.4 x 11.7 cm. Black cloth, blind embossed sides, title in gilt on backstrip.

Ref.: Field 113; Howes B360a; Rader 342; Sabin 4750

266 BENSON, HENRY E., *Defendant*

[Caption title] CHARLES A. LOREN, VS. HENRY E. BENSON. IN THE CIRCUIT COURT FOR THE COUNTY OF WAYNE. TO THE HON. THE JUSTICES OF THE SUPREME COURT OF THE STATE OF MICHIGAN: CASE RESERVED. . . .

[1]–18, [19–20 blank]. Bound with related materials in contemporary black half calf, Number 2082.

Ref.:

See under ILLINOIS CENTRAL RAILROAD COMPANY.

267 BENT, JOSEPH A.

HAND-BOOK OF KANSAS . . . CHICAGO: PUBLISHED BY RUFUS BLANCHARD, 1869.

[1]–77, [78 blank]. 14.5 x 9 cm. Map attached to inner back cover: Map of / Kansas / Engraved & Publishld[!] by / Rufus Blanchard, 146 Lake St. / Chicago / 1869. / [at foot:] Lith. Cha⁵ Shober & Co. Chicago. / 42.5 x 54.7 cm. Scale: 18 miles to one inch. Black cloth, blind embossed borders on sides, title in gilt on front cover.

Ref.: AII (*Chicago*) 1443; Howes B361

268 BENTON, JESSE

AN ADDRESS TO THE PEOPLE OF THE UNITED STATES, ON THE PRESIDENTIAL ELECTION . . . NASHVILLE: PRINTED BY JOSEPH NORVELL, 1824.

[1]–34. 18 x 11 cm. Rebound in old marbled boards, new leather back. Title-leaf supplied in facsimile on old paper.

Ref.: AII (*Tennessee*) 273; Howes B364; McMurtrie (*Tennessee*) 221; Sabin 4781

A vicious attack on Andrew Jackson. A dozen years earlier, Jesse Benton or his brother Thomas Hart Benton had shot Jackson during a quarrel. Jesse had no hesitancy about trying to damage Jackson again.

269 BENTON, JOSEPH A.

CALIFORNIA AS SHE WAS: AS SHE IS: AS SHE IS TO BE: A DISCOURSE DELIVERED AT THE FIRST CHURCH OF CHRIST, IN SIXTH STREET, SACRAMENTO CITY; ON THE OCCASION OF THE ANNUAL THANKSGIVING, NOVEMBER 30, 1850 . . . SACRAMENTO CITY: PLACER TIMES PRESS, 1850.

[1]–16. 21.7 x 13.5 cm. Rebound in full calf, green leather label on backstrip.

Ref.: AII (*California*) 118; Bradford 357; Cowan p. 48; Greenwood 161; Wagner (*California Imprints*) 96

The second pamphlet printed in Sacramento.

270 BENTON, THOMAS H.

[Caption title] LETTER FROM COL. BENTON TO THE PEOPLE OF MISSOURI. CENTRAL NATIONAL HIGHWAY FROM THE MISSISSIPPI RIVER TO THE PACIFIC. . . .

[1]–24. 24 x 16 cm. Stabbed, uncut. In a dark blue cloth case.

Ref.: Howes B368; Sabin 4786; Wagner-Camp 221

Signed Thomas H. Benton and dated Washington, March 4, 1853 on page 16. Pages [17]–24 comprise the Appendix. Contains the probable first printing of Leroux's statement to Benton of his activities with Ashley and Henry and his residence in Taos, dated March 1, 1853. Also contains Frémont's letter to the Philadelphia Railroad Convention, April, 1850.

Probably printed at Washington in 1853. The date given in Wagner-Camp 221 is a typographical error.

Editions: [Washington, 1849] (In part only.) [St. Louis, 1853].

271 BENTON, THOMAS H.

SELECTIONS OF EDITORIAL ARTICLES FROM THE ST. LOUIS ENQUIRER, ON THE SUBJECT OF OREGON AND TEXAS . . . 1818–19 . . . ST. LOUIS: MISSOURIAN OFFICE, 1844.

[i]–iv, [5]–45, [46 blank]. 22.6 x 14.2 cm. Removed from bound volume, unbound. Pages [1]–8 present in duplicate.

Ref.: AII (*Missouri*) 394; Howes B369; Smith 772

In 1844, Benton had been accused of inconsistencies in his statements in relation to Texas and Oregon. The present pamphlet was prepared to clarify his positions.

272 BENTON, THOMAS H.

SPEECH OF MR. BENTON, OF MISSOURI, ON THE PACIFIC RAILROAD BILL, AND THE PHYSICAL GEOGRAPHY OF THE COUNTRY BETWEEN THE STATES OF MISSOURI AND CALIFORNIA . . . WASHINGTON: PRINTED AT THE CONGRESSIONAL GLOBE OFFICE, 1855.

[1]–21, [22–4 blank]. 21.5 x 14.3 cm. Rebound in brown wrappers.

Ref.: Howes (1954) 793; Wagner-Camp 237

273 BENTON, THOMAS H.

MERCANTILE LIBRARY ASSOCIATION OF BOSTON—
WESTERN GEOGRAPHY, AND PACIFIC OCEAN RAIL-
ROAD . . . WASHINGTON: PRINTED BY J. T. AND
LEM. TOWERS, 1854.

[1]–24. 22.8 x 14.6 cm. Light blue printed wrap-
pers with title on front wrapper. In a green cloth
case.
   Prov.: J. W. Holliday copy.
   Ref.: Howes B366; Wagner-Camp 237
   Editions: [Baltimore, 1854].

274 BENTON, THOMAS H.

[Caption title] SUPPLEMENT TO THE MISSOURI
DEMOCRAT. LETTER FROM COL. BENTON TO THE
PEOPLE OF MISSOURI. CENTRAL NATIONAL HIGH-
WAY FROM THE MISSISSIPPI RIVER TO THE PACIFIC.
. . .

[1]–14, [15–16 blank]. 23.4 x 14.3 cm. Rebound
in blue boards, black cloth back.
   Ref.: Wagner-Camp 221
   Published in St. Louis in 1853. On page 14 is
the following passage: . . . / Read and Circulate. / [rule] / Copies of this Letter may be had
by addressing the office of the / Missouri Democrat, St. Louis, Mo.

**275 BENTON COUNTY (Minnesota) AGRI-
CULTURAL SOCIETY**

PROCEEDINGS OF THE BENTON COUNTY AGRICUL-
TURAL SOCIETY, HELD AT SAUK RAPIDS, DEC. 12TH
& 13TH, 1853. ST. ANTHONY, MINNESOTA: PRINTED
BY PRESCOTT & JONES, 1854.

[1]–23, [24 blank]. (Pages [1–2] blank.) 21 x 12.5
cm. Stabbed.
   Ref.: AII (*Minnesota*) 67
   The "Address of Governor William A. Gorman" appears on pages 6–19.

276 BERGHOLD, ALEXANDER

THE INDIANS' REVENGE; OR, DAYS OF HORROR.
SOME APPALLING EVENTS IN THE HISTORY OF THE
SIOUX . . . SAN FRANCISCO: P. J. THOMAS, PRINTER,
1891.*

[1]–240. 17 x 11.2 cm. Seven illustrations, un-
listed. Brown pictorial cloth.
   Ref.: Howes B373
   An "Appalling" tale.
   Editions: New Ulm, Minn., 1876. (In German
as *Indianer-rache* . . .)

277 BERKELEY, GRANTLEY F.

THE ENGLISH SPORTSMAN IN THE WESTERN PRAI-
RIES . . . LONDON: HURST AND BLACKETT, PUB-
LISHERS, 1861.

[i]–[xiv, xiv blank], [1]–431, [432 blank], [1]–
[16] advertisements. 25.1 x 16 cm. Nine illustrations and one vignette listed. Purple cloth, uncut.
   Ref.: Howes B374; Sabin 4883; Wagner-
Camp 368
   Contains good descriptions of buffalo hunts
in western Kansas.

**278 BERLANDIER, LUIS, & RAFAEL
CHOVEL**

DIARIO DE VIAGE LA COMISION DE LIMITES . . .
MEXICO: TIPOGRAPHIA DE JUAN NAVARRO, 1850.

[1]–298, [299 index, 300 blank]. 23 x 15.5 cm.
Portrait. Blue boards, blue leather backstrip.
   Ref.: Gómez & González 467; Howes B379;
Raines p. 24
   Berlandier spent the years 1827 to 1831 ex-
ploring the north and western boundaries of
Mexico at the request of the Mexican Boundary
Commission. The day-by-day records of the ex-
pedition were published in this volume, possibly
as an aftermath of the Mexican War.
   Both Howes and Raines call for two maps
which are not in the present copy. Copies with
two maps have not been found and it is doubtful
that they were issued.

**279 BERNHARD KARL, HERZOG ZU
SACHSEN-WEIMAR-EISENACH**

REISE . . . DURCH NORD-AMERIKA IN DEN JAHREN
1825 UND 1826 . . . WEIMAR: BEI WILHELM HOFF-
MANN, 1828.

[1–2], [I]–[XXXII], [1]–317, [318–20 blank]. [I]–
[VI], [1]–324, [325–28 advertisements]. 24.3 x
14.5 cm. Three engraved views, eight plans and
charts, and 27 vignettes in the text. Map: Plan /
von der Stadt / New-York /. 28.3 x 33 cm.
Scale: 1/4 mile to one inch. Map: New York /
und / Umgebungen. / 13.8 x 7.9 cm. No scale
given. Map: Plan / von / Philadelphia / [lower
left:] Carl Metzeroth sc. / 35.6 x 43 cm. Scale:
1250 feet to one inch. Map: Plan / von / Pittsburgh / und / Umgebungen /. 30.2 x 25.5 cm.
Scale: 550 yards to one inch. Map: Plymouth
und Umgebungen. / 15.1 x 18.1 cm. Scale:
about 5/8 mile to one inch. Map: New York /
und / Umgebungen /. 13.9 x 7.9 cm. No scale
given. Map: Ohio /. 24.7 x 20.2 cm. Scale: 31
miles to one inch. Map: Vereinigten Staaten /
von / Nord-America / Weimar / Im Verlage bei
Wilh. Hoffmann / 1828. / 41 x 51.6 cm. Scale:
120 miles to one inch. Plan: Universitaet von
Virginia /. 24.3 x 17.8 cm. (page size). No scale
given. Two volumes bound together, light green
cloth, white printed label on backstrip, 6 x 8.7
cm., uncut.

Ref.: Buck 198; Clark III 14; Howes B385; Sabin 4953

Bernhard Karl tells much of interest about his trip, despite the fact that most of his descriptions of towns visited are taken from the works of others.

280 BERTHOUD, EDWARD L.

JEFFERSON COUNTY, COLORADO: A STATISTICAL REVIEW OF ITS AGRICULTURAL, MINING, MANUFACTURING AND PASTORAL RESOURCES . . . GOLDEN CITY: PRINTED AT THE COLORADO TRANSCRIPT OFFICE, 1868.

[1]–7, [8 advertisement]. 19.9 x 13.4 cm. Removed from bound volume, unbound.

Prov.: Inscribed in pencil on title-page: Comp. of G. W. /

Ref.: Howes B392; McMurtrie & Allen (*Colorado*) 98

This is probably McMurtrie & Allen 98. The inscription on the title-page was by George West, proprietor of the *Colorado Transcript*, who had apparently sent another copy to the *Denver Post*. An enlarged edition was published at Golden City in 1882.

281 BERTRAND, L. A.

MEMOIRES D'UN MORMON . . . PARIS: COLLECTION HETZEL.

[i–iv], [1]–323, [324 blank]. 18.2 x 11.4 cm. Rebound in blue half morocco, gilt top, uncut, original green printed wrappers bound in.

Ref.: Howes (1954) 824; Monaghan 212; Woodward 14

This is the first book by a French Mormon.— Monaghan. The work was published in 1862.

Editions: Paris: P. Jung [1862].

282 BESOM, A.

PAWNEE COUNTY, NEBRASKA. AS IT WAS, IS, AND IS TO BE, WITH A NEW COUNTY MAP AND DIRECTORY . . . ATCHISON, KANSAS: THE IMMIGRANT UNION, 1878.

[1]–[83], [84 blank]. 17 x 12.3 cm. Illustrated with vignettes, portraits, plate, and map, unlisted: Map: [Pawnee County] [lower centre:] Lands of Ford Lewis marked (X). See Advertisement. / 10.1 x 13.3 cm. No scale given. Black cloth, blind rule borders on sides, title in gilt on front cover.

Ref.: Howes B399

283 BESTE, JOHN R.

THE WABASH: OR, ADVENTURES OF AN ENGLISH GENTLEMAN'S FAMILY IN THE INTERIOR OF AMERICA . . . LONDON: HURST AND BLACKETT, 1855.

[1–4], [i]–viii, [1]–329, [330 blank]. [i]–viii, [1]–352. 19.7 x 12.1 cm. Two plates, tinted, unlisted. Two volumes, blue cloth, blind embossed borders on sides, title in gilt on backstrips, uncut. In contemporary protective blue cloth covers, with printed paper labels.

Prov.: The first protective cover carries remnants of the label of the Yeovil Ladies' Book Society.

Ref.: Buck 489; Clark III 274; Howes B401; Jones 1327; Sabin 5056

A sober, perceptive account of considerable value.

284 BIBLE. NEW TESTAMENT

THE NEW TESTAMENT . . . TRANSLATED INTO THE OTTAWA LANGUAGE BY JOTHAM MEEKER . . . REVISED . . . BY REV. FRANCIS BARKER. SHAWANOE BAPTIST MISSION PRESS, J. G. PRATT, PRINTER. 1841.

[1]–125, [126 blank]. 15.7 x 10.3 cm. Contemporary sprinkled sheep.

Prov.: Inscribed on front endleaf: Rev. B. F. Brabrook / From his friend / & brother / Jotham Meeker. / Ottawa Mission / April 7, 1844. /

Ref.: McMurtrie & Allen (*Meeker*) 67; Pilling 2540

One of 500 copies printed. The Ottawa title appears on the verso of the title-page.

285 BIBLE. NEW TESTAMENT. Gospel according to St. John

TRANSLATION OF JOHN'S GOSPEL . . . BY FRANCIS BARKER. STOCKBRIDGE, IND. TER.: PRESS OF AM. BAPTIST BD. OF FOR. MISSIONS, 1846.

[1]–90. 16.5 x 10.7 cm. Contemporary sprinkled sheep. Front hinge and backstrip defective, lacks front endleaf.

Ref.: Foreman p. 34; McMurtrie & Allen (*Meeker*) 76

On the verso of the title-page above, there is a Shawnee title-page.

This may be the earliest Stockbridge, Kansas, imprint.

286 BIBLE. NEW TESTAMENT. Gospels

THE HISTORY OF OUR LORD AND SAVIOUR JESUS CHRIST; COMPREHENDING ALL THAT THE FOUR EVANGELISTS HAVE RECORDED CONCERNING HIM . . . BY THE REV. SAMUEL LEIBERKUHN, M. A. TRANSLATED INTO THE DELAWARE LANGUAGE, IN 1806, BY REV. DAVID ZEISBERGER . . . RE-TRANSLATED . . . BY I. D. BLANCHARD. SHAWANOE BAPTIST MISSION: J. MEEKER, 1837.

[1]–221, [222 blank]. 16 x 10.1 cm. Contemporary sprinkled sheep, with old dark blue leather backstrip applied.

Ref.: McMurtrie & Allen (*Meeker*) 57; Pilling (*Alg.*) p. 547

The Delaware language title-page appears on page [3].

A newspaper clipping dated 1861 mounted on the inside front cover comprises a message from the Delaware Nation offering their services to the Union during the Civil War.

287 BIBLE. OLD AND NEW TESTAMENTS

THE HOLY BIBLE, CONTAINING THE OLD AND NEW TESTAMENTS . . . NEW YORK: AMERICAN BIBLE SOCIETY, 1857.

[i–ii], [1]–1278. 14.5 x 9.1 cm. Sheepskin, black leather label on backstrip, lettered in gilt on front cover: Presented by / Russell, Majors & Waddell / 1858. /

Prov.: Presented by Russell, Majors & Waddell to George F. Smith, with the latter's signature in pencil on front endleaf.

Ref.: Darlow & Moule 1198

This is one of the famous Bibles presented by the firm of Russell, Majors & Waddell to each of their stage coach and wagon drivers. George F. Smith operated a clothing store in Council Bluffs which was, according to his daughter, a stage coach stop. Laid in is a card inscribed and signed by Vinnie Smith Jefferis: I am the Daughter of Geo. T.[!] Smith / this bible was left by the Russell / Majors & Waddell at my Father's / Store / Vinnie Smith Jefferis /.

288 BIDDLE, ELLEN McGOWAN

REMINISCENCES OF A SOLDIER'S WIFE . . . PHILADELPHIA: J. B. LIPPINCOTT COMPANY, 1907.*

[1]–259, [260 blank]. 19.3 x 13.2 cm. 14 illustrations listed. Gray-blue pictorial cloth, gilt top, uncut.

Ref.: Howes B426

A very good account of Army life at western posts after the Civil War.—EDG

289 BIDDLE, ELLEN McGOWAN

ANOTHER COPY. With signature of Lydia Spencer Lane, author of *I Married a Soldier* . . . 1893.*

290 [BIDDLE, THOMAS, & H. ATKINSON]

[LETTERS OF THOMAS BIDDLE AND H. ATKINSON ON TRADE AND INTERCOURSE WITH THE INDIANS.] Extract from *American State Papers. Documents, Legislative and Executive, of the Congress of the United States . . . December 4, 1815 . . . March 3, 1827 . . . [Indian Affairs, Vol. II] . . .* Washington: Gales and Seaton, 1834.

201–04. 33 x 20.3 cm. Bound in marbled boards with green morocco backstrip.

Ref.:

The two letters are included in a Report of the Committee on Indian Affairs communicated to the Senate February 16, 1820, 16th Congress, 1st Session. The report is No. 163 in the *American State Papers*. The letters contain much of interest about the fur trade and the Indian trade in the early years, i.e. 1809–20. The Biddle letter to Colonel H. Atkinson is dated from Camp Missouri, Missouri River, October 19, 1819, and the extract from a letter by Colonel Atkinson to the Secretary of War (Calhoun) is dated from St. Louis, November 23, 1819. Among the traders mentioned are Manuel Lisa, the Missouri Fur Co., McClinnon and Crooks, John Jacob Astor, Francis Chouteau, and others.

291 BIDWELL, JOHN

AUTOGRAPH LETTER, SIGNED, in blue pencil. 1895 September 30, Chico, California. To Mr. Davis. One page, 22.1 x 14.3 cm.

In reply to a request for a photograph. He sent it. Laid in Royce, C. C.: *John Bidwell, Pioneer . . .* 1906.

292 BIDWELL, JOHN

ECHOES OF THE PAST . . .*

[i–iv], [1]–91, [92 blank]. 17.7 x 13 cm. Vignette and three illustrations, unlisted. Dark green printed wrappers bound into gray boards, yellow cloth backstrip.

Ref.: Cowan p. 52; Howes B432

Published at Chico, California, in 1914.

293 [BIDWELL, JOHN]

[Wrapper title] MEMORIAL EXERCISES FOR GENERAL JOHN BIDWELL (DIED APRIL 4, 1900). HELD UNDER THE DIRECTION OF THE COUNTY OFFICERS OF BUTTE COUNTY, IN THE COURT-HOUSE AT OROVILLE, CALIFORNIA MAY 7, 1900.

[1–31, 32 blank]. 25 x 13 cm. Portrait. Purple printed wrappers with title on front wrapper, wallet fold on front wrapper, uncut.

Ref.: Cowan p. 52

294 BIEBER, RALPH P., Editor

[Wrapper title] THE PAPERS OF JAMES J. WEBB, SANTA FE MERCHANT, 1844–1861 . . . [ST. LOUIS: WASHINGTON UNIVERSITY] 1924.*

255–305, [306 blank]. 26.8 x 18 cm. Portrait. Printed green wrappers with title on front wrapper, bound into gray boards, yellow cloth backstrip.

Ref.:

295 BIG CREEK MINING DISTRICT, NE-VADA

[Broadside] LAWS OF BIG CREEK MINING DISTRICT, ADOPTED FEB. 13TH, 1864 . . . C. F. NEWCOMB, CH'N.

Broadside, 30.7 x 13.5 cm. Text, 25.8 x 10.6 cm.
Ref.:
Mining districts throughout the West often were permitted to draw up their own laws. These were occasionally printed in newspapers, but other printings of such laws separately have seldom been found.

296 BIGELOW, JOHN

MEMOIR OF THE LIFE AND PUBLIC SERVICES OF JOHN CHARLES FREMONT . . . NEW YORK: DERBY & JACKSON, 1856.

[i]–x, [11]–480. 18.5 x 12.3 cm. Brown cloth.
Prov.: Bookplate of Frederick W. Dau.
Ref.: Sabin 5306; Wagner-Camp 271a
A campaign biography published when Frémont was the first presidential candidate of the new Republican Party.

297 BIGGERS, DONALD H.

FROM CATTLE RANGE TO COTTON PATCH. A SERIES OF HISTORICAL SKETCHES DEALING WITH THE INDUSTRIAL, SOCIAL AND COMMERCIAL EVOLUTIONS THAT HAVE TAKEN PLACE IN WESTERN TEXAS . . . ABILENE, TEXAS: PRESS OF THE ABILENE PRINTING CO.

[i–vi], [1]–30, 47–[142], [142]–156, [157 blank]. (From second [142] to end, even pagination on rectos.) 21.9 x 14.7 cm. Illustrations unlisted, but included in pagination. Light brown printed wrappers with title on front wrapper.
Ref.: Howes B439; Vandale 15
The latest date mentioned in the text is 1902; the work was probably published in that year or the next.

298 [BILSON, BENJAMIN(?)]

THE HUNTERS OF KENTUCKY; OR THE TRIALS AND TOILS OF TRAPPERS AND TRADERS, DURING AN EXPEDITION TO THE ROCKY MOUNTAINS, NEW MEXICO, AND CALIFORNIA . . . NEW YORK: WM. H. GRAHAM, 1847.

[1]–100, [101–04 advertisements]. 23.9 x 15 cm. Brown printed wrappers with title on front wrapper, advertisements on verso of back wrapper. In a blue half morocco case.
Ref.: Cowan p. 54; Field 135; Howes B452; Jones 1152; Sabin 33941; Wagner-Camp 45
This work is a reproduction of Pattie's narrative, which the penury of the thieving writer's imagination has not empowered him to clothe with new language, or interleave with new incidents . . . —Field

299 BIRGE, JULIUS C.

THE AWAKENING OF THE DESERT . . . BOSTON: RICHARD G. BADGER.

[1]–429, [430 blank]. 19 x 13 cm. 25 illustrations listed, endpaper maps. Red cloth, fore and lower edges uncut.
Prov.: Inscribed on recto of frontispiece: To Rev Elmer I Goshen / With sincere regards / and best wishes of / Julius C Birge / St Louis Nov 1915 /.
Ref.: Howes B463, Rader 363
Copyrighted 1912. Although a latecomer, Birge's account of his trip overland in 1866 from Whitewater, Wisconsin, to Salt Lake City, is a fine first hand narrative. He returned by stage coach via Denver.

300 BIRKBECK, MORRIS

AN ADDRESS TO THE FARMERS OF GREAT BRITAIN . . . LONDON: PRINTED FOR JAMES RIDGWAY, 1822.

[1]–iv, [5]–52. 20.5 x 12.8 cm. Rebound in mottled half calf, gilt edges.
Ref.: Buck 173; Howes B464; Sabin 5563
An Address is a continuation of Birkbeck's arguments in favor of an English colony in Illinois and a statement of current conditions.

301 BIRKBECK, MORRIS

AN APPEAL TO THE PEOPLE OF ILLINOIS, ON THE QUESTION OF A CONVENTION . . . SHAWNEETOWN: PRINTED BY E. JONES, JULY, 1823.

[A]^1, [B–D]^4. [1]–21, [unpaginated blank page], [22]–25. (Even pagination on rectos, 22–25.) 20.3 x 13.8 cm. Removed from bound volume, unbound, uncut. Strip torn from top of title-leaf.
Prov.: Herschel V. Jones copy.
Ref.: Byrd 35; Howes B465; Jones 849; Sabin 5564
The *Appeal* ends on page 21, the verso of which is blank and not included in pagination. Page [22] is headed "Postscript" and is signed at the end M. Birkbeck.
This is not another edition of *An Impartial Appeal . . . on the Injurious Effects of Slave Labour . . .* 1824.

302 BIRKBECK, MORRIS

EXTRACTS FROM A SUPPLEMENTARY LETTER FROM THE ILLINOIS, DATED JANUARY 31ST, 1819 . . . NEW-YORK: PUBLISHED BY C. WILEY AND CO., 1819.

[1]–4^4. [1]–29, [30–2 blank]. 22.3 x 14.9 cm. Tan printed wrappers with title on front wrapper. In a blue half morocco case.

Ref.: Buck 134; Howes B466; Sabin 5565

The interesting part of this pamphlet is Birkbeck's temperate reply to Cobbett's intemperate attack.

303 BIRKBECK, MORRIS

LETTERS FROM ILLINOIS . . . PHILADELPHIA: PUBLISHED BY M. CAREY AND SON, 1818.

1^2, 2–13^6, 14^4. [i]–[xvi, xvi blank], [17]–154, [155–56 blank]. 19 x 11.7 cm. Map: United States. / [upper right:] N° VIII. / [lower centre:] Published 1st June 1816 by J. Melish. Philadelphia. Improved to 1818. / 24.6 x 34.7 cm. Scale: 120 miles to one inch. Map: English Prairie / and / Adjacent Country. / [lower left:] T. V. K. &. Co. Sc / [lower right:] J. Melish Del. / 17.1 x 11.7 cm. Scale: about 16 miles to one inch. Tan printed boards, with title on front cover, advertisement on back cover, title on backstrip, uncut.

Ref.: Buck 105; Howes B467; Jones 795; Sabin 5567

Pages [i–ii] carry advertisements. The letters contain a great deal of important information about social and economic conditions in Illinois.

304 BIRKBECK, MORRIS

NOTES ON A JOURNEY IN AMERICA, FROM THE COAST OF VIRGINIA TO THE TERRITORY OF ILLINOIS. WITH PROPOSALS FOR THE ESTABLISHMENT OF A COLONY OF ENGLISH . . . PHILADELPHIA: PUBLISHED BY CALEB RICHARDSON, 1817.

A^2, B–Q^6, R^4. [i–iv (iii–iv blank)], [3]–189, [190 blank]. 19.7 x 11.4 cm. Pale gray-green printed boards with title on front cover, advertisement on back cover, title on backstrip, uncut. In a maroon cloth case.

Ref.: Buck 95; Howes B468; Sabin 5569

305 BISBEE, WILLIAM H.

THROUGH FOUR AMERICAN WARS . . . BOSTON: MEADOR PUBLISHING COMPANY, MCMXXXI.

[1]–281, [282 blank]. (Errata slip, 1.9 x 10.2 cm., mounted on page 161.) 20.7 x 14 cm. 16 illustrations listed. Dark blue cloth, fore and lower edges uncut.

Prov.: Signature on front endleaf: William H. Bisbee / Brig. Genl. / U.S. Army. /

Ref.:

"Bisbee, who served at Fort Kearney for several months in the fall of 1866, is quite critical of Carrington and ridicules his Civil War record. He states his belief that Fetterman (with whom he had served during the Civil War) did not dis-obey Carrington's orders. He also claims that evidence by several living eyewitnesses to this effect exists in the files of the 'Order of Indian Wars' in Washington, D.C. Bisbee's reminiscences were written when he was 79 or 80, about 55 years after the events of 1866."—EDG. The archives of the Order of Indian Wars which were deposited in the library of the War College at Washington have not yet yielded the evidence described by General Bisbee regarding Carrington and Fetterman.

306 BISHOP, ALBERT W.

LOYALTY ON THE FRONTIER; OR, SKETCHES OF UNION MEN OF THE SOUTH-WEST; WITH INCIDENTS AND ADVENTURES IN REBELLION ON THE BORDER . . . ST. LOUIS: R. P. STUDLEY AND CO., 1863.

[1]–228. 19.2 x 12.7 cm. Dark green cloth, blind embossed sides, title in gilt on backstrip.

Prov.: Inscribed in pencil on front blank leaf: To Mrs. Mollie Merrill / Compliments of / M. La Rue Harrison / Feb 21. 1871 / See Page 51 /.

Ref.: Howes B474; Nicholson p. 85; Sabin 5599

Colonel Harrison is mentioned on page 51 and on page 225.

307 BISHOP, ALBERT W.

ANOTHER COPY

Red cloth stamping on back differs.

308 BISHOP, W. W.

A JOURNAL OF THE TWELVE MONTHS CAMPAIGN OF GEN. SHIELDS' BRIGADE, IN MEXICO. IN THE YEARS 1846-7. COMPILED FROM NOTES OF LIEUTENANTS J. J. ADAMS & H. C. DUNBAR . . . ST. LOUIS: CATHCART, PRESCOTT & CO., 1847.

[1]–48. 22 x 14.4 cm. Buff printed wrappers with title on front wrapper.

Ref.: AII (*Missouri*) 512; Howes B479; Sabin 5625

A good first hand account of an Illinois regiment in the Mexican War.

309 BISMARCK TRIBUNE

[Newspaper] BISMARCK TRIBUNE. VOL. 3. BISMARCK, D. T., THURSDAY, JULY 6, 1876, NO. 52. EXTRA.

Newspaper, [1–4]. 47.5 x 31.7 cm. Unbound.

Ref.: Dustin 17 see; Graham pp. 349–51

The account of the Custer battle occupies four and one-half columns on the first page. The account was also printed as a broadside, probably on the same day.

General Terry wrote a dispatch to his superior officer on June 27th which was sent with

Scout Taylor via the riverboat "Far West." Taylor stayed on the "Far West" until it tied up at the mouth of the Big Horn River on the night of June 30th. He left the next morning for his long ride of 175 miles to Fort Ellis and Bozeman, the latter place being the nearest telegraph station. Taylor's story was first published in eastern papers on July 5th. The Terry account did not reach the public until July 7th. The "Far West" carrying the wounded and Captain Smith with confidential dispatches for General Sheridan tied up at Bismarck on July 5th at 11 p.m. The first complete account of the Battle of the Little Big Horn was published in the *Bismarck Tribune* on the morning of July 6th. The Taylor story, consisting of a dozen or so lines, was published in the Helena *Independent* and several other western papers. Colonel Lounsberry, in his *Early History of North Dakota . . .* 1919, states that the first publication giving substantial information came from Bismarck and that, aside from a bulletin (five lines) sent by the *Tribune* to the *New York Herald* and which was printed on July 6th, the first account was published in the *Bismarck Tribune.*—EDG

310 BLACK, HAMILTON M., *Plaintiff*

[Caption title] HAMILTON M. BLACK, ET. AL. VS. WILLIAM PHELPS ET. AL. TO ANNUL DECREE OF PARTITION OF DISTRICT COURT OF HALF-BREED SAC AND FOX RESERVATION, OF LEE COUNTY, IOWA. . . .

[1]–54. 22.8 x 14 cm. Rebound in red cloth.

Ref.: AII (*Iowa*) 101

The following imprint appears on page 54: J. B. Howell & Co., Prs., Keokuk. / The brief was printed in 1856. The seal of Lee County is embossed in the last leaf.

A former owner, apparently knowledgeable about the case, has annotated the pamphlet in pencil with comments about the statements recorded.

311 [BLACK, JEREMIAH S.]

[Caption title] IN RE CHORPENNING. TO THE COMMITTEE ON THE JUDICIARY, FORTY-THIRD CONGRESS: . . .

[1–4] 21.6 x 14.3 cm. Removed from bound volume, unbound. In a red cloth box with other Chorpenning materials.

Ref.:

Published in Washington, 1874. Signed on page 4: J. S. Black. Black was arguing here against the validity of the Joint Resolution of Congress passed on February 9, 1871, to repeal the Joint Resolution of July 15, 1870, under which the Postmaster General had made an award to Chorpenning.

312 BLACK, WILLIAM P., & OTHERS

WAR SKETCHES . . . OF ARKANSAW . . . MULDROW, I.T., 1895.

[1]–232. (Pages [1–2] blank.) 17.1 x 12.4 cm. Three portraits, unlisted. Blue printed wrappers with title on front wrapper. In a red cloth folder.

Ref.: Howes B488

The text breaks off in the middle of a sentence on page 12. A new sentence begins on page 13. Pagination of pages 166–67 reversed.

313 BLACK HAWK, SAUK CHIEF

LIFE OF MA-KA-TAI-ME-SHE-KIA-KIAK OR BLACK HAWK . . . DICTATED BY HIMSELF. J. B. PATTERSON, OF ROCK ISLAND, ILLINOIS, EDITOR AND PROPRIETOR. CINCINNATI, 1833.

[i]–[xii, xii blank], [13]–155, [156 blank]. 17.5 x 10.7 cm. Tan boards, tan cloth backstrip.

Ref.: Howes P120; Pilling (*Alg.*) 49; Sabin 5675

Black Hawk's narrative is one of the very few important American Indian autobiographies. The work was copyrighted by J. B. Patterson on November 13, 1833, in Illinois. The more common edition was published in Boston the following year.

314 BLACK HAWK, SAUK CHIEF

THE SAME . . . BOSTON: RUSSELL, ODIORNE & METCALF, 1834.

[1]–155, [156 blank]. 19 x 12 cm. Portrait by Pendleton, Boston. Pale green boards, printed paper label on front cover.

Ref.: Howes P120; Jones 948; Pilling (*Alg.*) 49; Sabin 5675

The imprint on the verso of the title-leaf, below a rule, reads as follows: Charles Gordon Greene, Printer, / 19 Water Street. /

Editions: Cincinnati, 1833.

315 BLACK HILLS EXPLORING AND MINING ASSOCIATION

[Broadside] NEW AND SHORT ROUTE TO THE GOLD MINES OF THE BLACK HILLS, MONTANA AND IDAHO. 400 MILES OF TRAVEL SAVED. THE "BLACK HILLS EXPLORING AND MINING ASSOCIATION" DESIRES TO CALL THE ATTENTION OF MINERS AND EMIGRANTS TO THE NEW AND SHORT ROUTE TO THE GOLD MINES WHICH PASSES THROUGH SIOUX CITY, IOWA, AND YANKTON, D.T. . . . YANKTON, D.T. APRIL 18TH, 1865. HON. WALTER A. BURLEIGH HAS JUST RETURNED FROM GEN. POPE'S HEADQUARTERS, AND BRINGS THE INFORMATION THAT ORDERS HAVE BEEN ISSUED PROVIDING FOR AN AMPLE MILITARY FORCE TO ACCOMPANY SUPT'T BROOKINGS' ROAD PARTY. AN

INFANTRY FORCE OF 200 MEN WILL ALSO ESCORT COL. SAWYER THROUGH FROM THE MOUTH OF THE NIOBRARA.

Broadside, 45 x 31.6 cm. Text, 40.5 x 28 cm.

Ref.: Allen (*Dakota*) 25
Printed at Yankton.

George N. Propper's report as surveyor and engineer, dated October 31, 1865, will be found in 39th Congress, 1st Session, Executive Document No. 58. The survey for the road started on the Missouri River opposite the mouth of the Cheyenne River and ran east to the Minnesota border. Propper claims the lack of military protection, promised so glibly in the broadside, prevented surveying west of the Missouri. The report of W. W. Brookings dated November 1, 1865, was printed with the report of Lieut. Col. James H. Simpson, page 124.—EDG

316 BLACK HILLS GOLD FIELDS, THE

[Caption title] THE BLACK HILLS GOLD FIELDS AND HOW TO REACH THEM! WITH MAP OF DISTANCES, AND FARES FROM THE VARIOUS POINTS; ALSO COST OF OUTFIT, AND FULL INFORMATION OF THE COUNTRY BY ONE WHO HAS BEEN THERE. . . .

[1]–8. 24 x 16 cm. Map: Routes to the Black Hills Gold Fields. / 19 x 27.2 cm. No scale given. Double-page spread on pages [4–5], white on dark green. Unbound, laid in new orange cloth folder. In a green cloth case.

Ref.:
Imprint at foot of page 8: Published by / W. Norris & Co., 242 East Madison Street, / Chicago, Ills. / For Sale by all News Dealers. / [line inked out:] (Price 25 Cents.) / Price 10 cts. / Issued in 1875.

Much of the information here given was supplied by John Gordon of "Gordon's Stockade Party of 1874" and Eph Witcher, "lately returned" from the Sioux City expedition of the previous October. Witcher is named as guide of the proposed expedition from Chicago scheduled to leave about the fifteenth of April.—EDG

317 BLACK HILLS NEWS-LETTER AND MINING REPORTER, THE

[Newspaper] THE BLACK HILLS NEWS-LETTER AND MINING REPORTER. BY HARRY J. NORTON, AUTHOR OF "WONDERLAND." . . .

Newspaper, [1–8]. 26.6 x 20.6 cm. Unbound.

Ref.: McMurtrie (*Wyoming*) p. 69

Page [7] is set up as a letterhead and is blank otherwise. The newspaper, although without volume or issue number, appeared more than once, if the text is to be believed. McMurtrie found three references to the paper in other Wyoming newspapers. The second page is a di-

rectory of the leading firms in Deadwood. No place of publication is given, but it is fairly certain that Deadwood was Norton's base of operations in 1878. From the text and advertisements, the date of publication is clearly 1878.

318 BLACKMORE, WILLIAM

COLORADO: ITS RESOURCES, PARKS, AND PROSPECTS AS A NEW FIELD FOR EMIGRATION . . . LONDON: SAMPSON LOW, SON, AND MARSTON, 1869.

[i–ii], [1]–217, [218 blank]. 27.4 x 21.5 cm. Five mounted photographs and three maps, unlisted. Map: Map of the / United States / Shewing the / New and Projected Lines of Railway / to the / Pacific Ocean. / [decorative rule] / C. W. Bacon, 127, Strand, London. / 1869. / 40 x 67.2 cm. Scale: 100 miles to one inch. Map: Map of / Colorado / Embracing the / Central Gold Region. / Drawn by Frederick J. Ebert / under direction of the / Governor Wᵐ Gilpin. / [rule] / 1869. / [lower right:] Drawn by C. W. Bacon & Cᵒ 127 Strand. / 46.8 x 65.3 cm. Scale: 12 miles to one inch. Map: Map of the / Trenchara and Costilla Estates / Forming the / Sangre de Christo Grant / Situate in / San Luis Valley / Colorado Territory. / [lower right:] Witherby & Co. Litho. Birchin Lane /. 57.9 x 45.5 cm. Scale: 106 2/3 chains to one inch. Green cloth, title in gilt on front cover and backstrip.

Ref.: Howes C607; Wilcox p. 15

An elaborate land-selling advertisement.

Editions: London: Privately printed, 1869.

319 [BLAKE, J. A., & F. C. WILLETT, *Compilers*]

SKETCH OF BOULDER, COLORADO . . . DENVER, COL.: BLAKE & WILLETT, PUBLISHERS, 1873.

[1]–11, 12–15 advertisements, [16 ornament]. 15.1 x 10.3 cm. Map on page [3]: Map of Boulder and Vicinity. / [lower left:] C. Bohm D. & Eng. Denver Col / 12.6 x 6.1 cm. No scale given. Stitched.

Ref.: McMurtrie & Allen (*Colorado*) 166; Wilcox p. 15

McMurtrie & Allen omit the colon after Col. in the imprint. The second section, pages 12–15, comprises a business directory of Boulder.

320 BLAKISTON, THOMAS W.

[Wrapper title] REPORT OF THE EXPLORATION OF TWO PASSES THROUGH THE ROCKY MOUNTAINS, IN 1858 . . . WOOLWICH: PRINTED AT THE ROYAL ARTILLERY INSTITUTION, M.DCCC.LIX.

[1]–18. 22.1 x 14.3 cm. Map: The / Kootanie and Boundary / Passes / of the / Rocky Mountains. / Explored in 1858 by / Lieutenant (now Captain) Blakiston, / Royal Artillery. / [lower

right:] Lithographed at the Royal Artillery Institution. / [lower centre:] Scale of Geog¹ Miles 8 1/3 to an Inch. / [diagrammatic scale as above] /. On same sheet at right: two sections of map. Maps: 19.8 x 19.8 cm. Sheet: 22.3 x 57.3 cm. Resewn into strawboard covers, blue paper backstrip, original printed front wrapper mounted on front cover.

Ref.: Wagner-Camp 318

This report appears as pages 237–54 of *Occasional Papers of the Royal Artillery Institution*, No. 12, May, 1859. Wagner-Camp 318 notes only this copy as a separate.

321 BLAKISTON, THOMAS W.

[Caption title] ART. XXXV.—REPORT ON THE EXPLORATION OF TWO PASSES, (THE KOOTANIE AND BOUNDARY PASSES) OF THE ROCKY MOUNTAINS IN 1858; BY CAPTAIN BLAKISTON, ROYAL ARTILLERY. (WITH A MAP.)*[!] . . .

319–346. (Blakiston's article; 320–345.) 21.3 x 12.7 cm. Map: The / Kootanie and Boundary / Passes / of the / Rocky Mountains / Explored in 1858 by / Lieutenant (now Captain) Blakiston / Royal Artillery. / [lower centre:] Lith by Punderson & Crisand, New Haven Conn. / With diagram headed: Sections /, on right half of sheet. Map: 19.7 x 19.3 cm. Scale: about eight miles to one inch. Sheet: 21.2 x 43 cm. Stapled into gray boards, black cloth backstrip, typed label on front cover.

Ref.: Wagner-Camp 318

Extract from *American Journal of Science and Arts*, Second Series, Vol. XXVIII, No. 84, [New Haven], November, 1859. Also includes, as an appendix, an extract from an address by Sir R. I. Murchison on the Palliser Expedition of which Blakiston was also a member.

Editions: Woolwich, 1859.

322 BLANCHARD, JONATHAN

MEMOIR OF REV. LEVI SPENCER: SUCCESSIVELY PASTOR OF THE CONGREGATIONAL CHURCH AT CANTON, BLOOMINGTON, AND PEORIA, ILLINOIS . . . CINCINNATI: AMERICAN REFORM TRACT AND BOOK SOCIETY, 1856.

[i]–vi, [7]–192. (Page [i] blank, page [ii] frontispiece.) 14.8 x 9.6 cm. Portrait. Brown cloth, blind embossed sides, title in gilt on backstrip.

Ref.: Howes B504

323 BLANCHARD, P., & ADRIEN DAUZATS

SAN JUAN DE ULUA OU RELATION DE L'EXPEDITION FRANCAISE AU MEXIQUE, SOUS LES ORDRES DE M. LE CONTRE-AMIRAL BAUDIN . . . SUIVI DE NOTES ET DOCUMENTS, ET D'UN APERCU GENERAL SUR L'ETAT ACTUEL DE TEXAS, PAR M. E. MAISSIN . . . PARIS: CHEZ GIDE, EDITEUR, 1859.

[I]–XII, [1]–591, [592 blank]. 28.3 x 18.4 cm. 18 plates (wood engravings printed on India paper) and 34 vignettes. Contemporary dark blue half morocco, blue marbled sides, backstrip gilt, gilt top, uncut.

Prov.: Louis Phillippe's copy, with his crowned cypher in gilt on the backstrip and with the rubber stamp of the Bibliothèque du Château d'Eu, including the king's initials, on the title-pages.

Ref.: Howes B507; Sabin 5832

Large Paper copy, with all the plates and vignettes.

324 BLANCHARD, RUFUS

HAND-BOOK OF IOWA; DESCRIBING ITS AGRICULTURAL, COMMERCIAL AND MANUFACTURING RESOURCES AND OTHER CAPABILITIES OF PRODUCING WEALTH, ALSO, ITS PHYSICAL GEOGRAPHY AND GEOLOGY . . . CHICAGO: PUBLISHED BY RUFUS BLANCHARD, 1869.

[i–ii], [5]–92, [93–94 Contents]. 14.5 x 9.8 cm. Map: Map of / Iowa / Compiled and Published / by / Rufus Blanchard, / 146 Lake St. / Chicago, / 1869. / [at lower left:] Lith. Chas. Shober & Co. Chicago. / 40.8 x 51.6 cm. Scale: 20 miles to one inch. Black cloth.

Ref.: Howes B509

Editions: Chicago, 1867.

325 BLANCHARD, RUFUS

[Map] MAP OF / CHICAGO / [decorative rule] / RUFUS BLANCHARD, / 52 LA SALLE STREET. / 1857. /

Map, 75.6 x 58.7 cm. No scale given. Folded into maroon cloth covers, 15 x 9.6 cm., title in gilt on front cover: Blanchard's / Map of / Chicago. /-1857-/.

Prov.: Signature in pencil inside front cover: John Ritchie /.

Ref.: Byrd 2599

Below the title, in the right margin, is given information about Chicago under the following headings: Omnibus Lines, Legal Hack or Cab Fare, Chicago in 1812 [outlined along the lakeshore], Schools, Churches, Population . . .

326 BLAND, THOMAS A.

LIFE OF ALFRED B. MEACHAM . . . THE TRAGEDY OF THE LAVA BEDS . . . WASHINGTON: T. A. & M. C. BLAND, 1883.

[1]–30, [1]–48. 20.1 x 12.6 cm. Illustrations unlisted. Black cloth.

Prov.: Signature on title-page in indelible pencil: Bishop Whipple /.

Ref.:
Laid in is a copy of General Orders No. 3, Washington, April 14, 1872, 2 pages, announcing the death of General Canby.

327 [BLANE, WILLIAM N.]

AN EXCURSION THROUGH THE UNITED STATES AND CANADA DURING THE YEARS 1822–23 . . . LONDON: BALDWIN, CRADOCK, AND JOY, 1824.

[i–iv], [1]–511, [512 blank], [1–8 advertisements], [1–14 advertisements (pages 15–16 apparently torn out)]. 22.3 x 14.2 cm. Map: United States / of / America, / Compiled from the latest & best Authorities / by / John Melish. / 1820 / [upper right:] To face yᵉ Title. / [lower right:] Engraved by Sidʸ Hall, Bury Strᵗ Bloomsbʸ / [lower centre:] London, Published by Baldwin, Cradock & Joy, Paternoster Row, June 1824. / 39 x 47.8 cm. Scale: 120 miles to one inch. Map: The / Straits of Niagara / From a Map by Mʳ Darby. / [upper right:] Page 406. / [lower right: as in preceding map] / [lower centre: as in preceding map] 16.1 x 36.3 cm. Scale: about two miles to one inch. *Inset:* . . . Vertical Section of the Great Slope which occasions the Falls . . . 5 x 16.3 cm. Scale: about one mile to one inch. Statistical Table: Statistical View of the Commerce of the United States . . . Blue boards, tan paper backstrip, white printed label on backstrip, 7.6 x 3.7 cm., uncut.

Prov.: Name scratched from front cover: Leicester [?] / 1824 /. On verso of front endleaf: Litʸ Gazette / [underline] / [printed notice of the work, mounted] / In this Opinion I entirely / concur—& strongly / recommend the Perusal of this / Publication to correct yᵉ erronious[!] / opinions very generally adopted / wᵗʰ regard to the Americans— / L. 1824 /.

Ref.: Buck 174; Clark III 184; Howes B521; Sabin 5872

Sabin gives Captain Blaney as the author. An errata slip mentioned by Howes is not present in this copy.

Blane's journal covers his travels in Indiana, Illinois, and Missouri.

328 BLEDSOE, ANTHONY J.

INDIAN WARS OF THE NORTHWEST. A CALIFORNIA SKETCH. . . SAN FRANCISCO: BACON & COMPANY, 1885.

[5]–505, [506 blank]. 22.5 x 14.5 cm. Dark slate cloth, decorative bands in black and title in gilt on front cover, bands in blind on back cover, title in gilt on backstrip. Lacks two blank leaves before title-leaf.

Ref.: Blumann & Thomas 771; Cowan p. 57; Howell 22; Howes B529

An errata slip, 2.9 x 13.2 cm., is tipped to page [9]. Cowan's collation is same as above without mention of excised initial leaf.

Includes an account of the overland expedition of the Gregg party in 1849 as well as Del Norte County history.

329 BLISS, CHARLES R.

THE NEW WEST, NEW MEXICO . . . BOSTON: FRANK WOOD, 1879.

[1]–90. 23 x 15 cm. Map included in pagination, vignettes. Blue printed wrappers with title on front wrapper.

Ref.: Saunders 2752

330 BLISS, EDWARD

A BRIEF HISTORY OF THE NEW GOLD REGIONS OF COLORADO TERRITORY . . . NEW-YORK: JOHN W. AMERMAN, 1864.

[1]–30, [31 map, 32 blank]. 22.7 x 14.3 cm. Map: A Map of the Route / from the Missouri River to Denver, Colorado. / Distance, 650 Miles. / [lower right corner:] Cox & Holloway Sc. N.Y. / 7.4 x 16.6 cm. No scale given. Stabbed. In brown half morocco case.

Prov.: Herschel V. Jones copy.

Ref.: Howes B534; Jones 1466; Sabin 5917; Wagner-Camp 397

331 BLODGETT, HENRY W.

AUTOBIOGRAPHY . . . WAUKEGAN, 1906.*

[i–ii], [1]–102. 23 x 15.2 cm. Gray buckram.

Ref.: Howes B540

Privately printed, uncopyrighted.

An excellent narrative of early Illinois. Smitten with "Western Fever," Blodgett's father brought his family out from Amherst, Massachusetts in 1830. In the spring of 1831, he settled about five miles south of the present town of Naperville. On the way from Detroit by wagon team, considerable time was spent in the village of Chicago. The narrative deals principally with Indian affairs and the Black Hawk War.—EDG

332 BLOOM, S., *Plattsmouth, Nebraska*

[Trade card] S. BLOOM, DEALER IN CLOTHING, AND GENT'S FURNISHING GOODS. GENERAL ASSORTMENT OF MINERS OUTFITTING ARTICLES. PLATTSMOUTH, - NEBRASKA . . .

Broadside on stiff card, 5.6 x 8.6 cm.

333 [BLUE, DANIEL]

THRILLING NARRATIVE OF THE ADVENTURES, SUFFERINGS AND STARVATION OF PIKE'S PEAK GOLD SEEKERS ON THE PLAINS OF THE WEST IN THE WINTER AND SPRING OF 1859. BY ONE OF THE SURVIVORS. WHITESIDE COUNTY, ILLINOIS, 1860.

[i–ii], [1]–21, [22 blank]. 21 x 13.5 cm. Brown printed wrappers with title on front wrapper.

Ref.: Howes B552; Wagner-Camp 350b

The Morrison, Illinois, reprint issued about 1890.

Editions: Whiteside County, Ill. [Chicago], 1860.

334 BLUFF CITY ENGINE COMPANY NO. 1, *Council Bluffs, Iowa*

EIGHTH ANNUAL BALL OF THE BLUFF CITY ENGINE COMPANY NO. 1 AT DOHANY'S HALL, WEDNESDAY EVENING, FEBRUARY 22, 1875. THE HONOR OF YOUR COMPANY WITH LADIES IS MOST RESPECTFULLY SOLICITED.

[1–4]. (Pages [2–3] blank.) 17.9 x 11.4 cm. Unbound leaflet, fold at right margin.

Ref.:

Imprint at foot of page [4]: [rule] / Evening Globe Print. /

335 [BLUNT, EDMUND M.]

TRAVELLERS GUIDE TO AND THROUGH THE STATE OF OHIO. NEW YORK: SOLD BY D. H. BURR, 1832.

[1]–16. 11.7 x 7.3 cm. Folding map: The / Travellers Pocket Map / of / Ohio / with its / Canals, Roads and Distances, / by Stage & Steam Boat Routes. / Published by / Edmund Blunt, / New York. / 1832. / [short decorative rule] / Drawn and Engraved by William Hooker, New York. / 35.3 x 40.5 cm. Scale: 25 miles to one inch. Buff roan folder, title in gilt on front cover.

Ref.: Howes B558; Thomson 98 see

Thomson describes only an 1833 edition which seems (with 28 pages) to be a different work.

336 BODMAN, ALBERT H., *Publisher*

[Wrapper title] 1859 THE HAND BOOK OF CHICAGO, OR STRANGERS GUIDE TO POINTS OF INTEREST IN AND ABOUT THE CITY. CHICAGO, ILL.: PUBLISHED BY ALBERT HOLMES BODMAN, 1859.

[1–8], 5–129, [130–131 advertisements], [132 blank]. 16.1 x 10.4 cm. White printed wrappers, with title on front wrapper, advertisements on verso of front and on recto and verso of back wrapper.

Ref.: AII (*Chicago*) 457; Howes B565; Sabin 30202

According to AII (*Chicago*), the Illinois Historical Society copy was copyrighted in 1860 instead of 1859. The date is 1859, although faint and easily confused.

337 BOGY, JOSEPH

[Caption title] . . . PETITION OF JOSEPH BOGY, PRAYING COMPENSATION FOR SPOLIATIONS ON HIS PROPERTY BY A NUMEROUS PARTY OF CHOCTAW INDIANS, THEN AT PEACE WITH THE UNITED STATES, WHILST ON A TRADING EXPEDITION ON THE ARKANSAS RIVER, UNDER AUTHORITY OF A LICENSE DERIVED FROM THE UNITED STATES . . .

[1]–14, [15–16 blank]. 22.3 x 14.1 cm. Rebound in new red cloth.

Ref.:

24th Congress, 1st Session, Senate, Document No. 23, Serial 280. [Washington, 1835.]

Page [1], lower left corner: [short rule] / [Gales & Seaton, print.] /

Mentions meeting Zebulon Montgomery Pike on the Arkansas River in 1807, page 11.—EDG

338 BOISE, IDAHO. Board of Trade

[Broadsheet] BOISE CITY AND SOUTHWESTERN IDAHO. RESOURCES, PROGRESS AND PROSPECTS. INFORMATION FOR INTENDING SETTLERS, COMPILED UNDER DIRECTION OF THE BOISE CITY BOARD OF TRADE . . .

Broadsheet, 63.3 x 91.2 cm. Unbound, folded to about 20.4 x 10.9 cm., 24 printed sections, including title as above.

Ref.:

On the verso of the broadsheet is a map: The Inter-Mountain District / comprising / Idaho, Montana, Wyoming and Washington / Territories, the State of Oregon, / and Portions of California, Nevada, / Utah and Colorado. / [rule] / Showing the present and prospective railway connections of / Boise City. / [rule] / Published by the Boise City Board of Trade. / 1887–1888. / [rule] / [at left: 4 lines of references] [at right:] Address, / Chas. A. Clark, / Corresponding Secretary. / 59.4 x 87.3 cm. No scale given.

339 BOISE NEWS

[Newspaper] BOISE NEWS. / VOL. I. BANNOCK CITY, I.T., OCT. 13, 1863. NO. 3 . . .

[1–4]. 48.2 x 33.1 cm. Unbound.

Ref.: AII (*Idaho*) 13 note

Contains Governor W. H. Wallace's proclamation of September 22, 1863, outlining conditions for the first Idaho elections. The issue also contains various mining laws. The governor's proclamation was also printed separately.

340 BOLDUC, JEAN-BAPTISTE Z.

MISSION DE LA COLOMBIE . . . QUEBEC: DE L'IMPRIMERIE DE J.-B. FRECHETTE, PERE.*

[1]–95, [96 blank]. 19 x 12.5 cm. Rebound in green half morocco, gilt top.

Ref.: Cowan (1914) p. 21; Howes B573;

Sabin 6181; Smith 927; Staton & Tremaine 5254; Streit III 2292; Wagner-Camp 93

The work was published in 1843 or 1844; continuations appeared in 1844 and 1845.

Father Bolduc was one of the early Catholic missionaries in Oregon. The larger part of the edition of this work was burned in the printing office, and it is, in consequence, extremely scarce.—Cowan

341 BOLLER, HENRY A.

AMONG THE INDIANS. EIGHT YEARS IN THE FAR WEST: 1858–1866. EMBRACING SKETCHES OF MONTANA AND SALT LAKE . . . PHILADELPHIA: T. ELLWOOD ZELL, 1868.

[i]–xvi, 17–428. 19 x 12.6 cm. Folding map: Map / of Localities / to accompany / "Among the Indians" / T. Ellwood Zell, Publisher. / Philadelphia. / 1868. / 30.5 x 48.5 cm. Scale: about 58 miles to one inch. Blue cloth, gilt title on backstrip: Among / the / Indians / Boller / [publisher's monogram] /.

Prov.: Inscribed by the author: To / Cousin Jane / With affectionate Regards of / The Author / Philadᵃ Oct. 31ˢᵗ 1867 /.

Ref.: Field 147; Howes B579; Sabin 6221; Smith 928

The date of the inscription indicates the book was in print before the year on the title-page.

342 BOLLER, HENRY A.

THE SAME.

19.7 x 13 cm. Black cloth, printed paper label: Among / the / Indians; / Eight Years / in the / Far West. / 1858–66. / [rule] / Henry A. Boller. /; uncut.

343 BOND, FRED G.

FLATBOATING ON THE YELLOWSTONE, 1877 . . . NEW YORK: NEW YORK PUBLIC LIBRARY, 1925.*

[1]–22. 25.3 x 17.8 cm. Portrait. Gray printed wrappers, with title on front wrapper.

Ref.: Howes (1954) 1013

The trip described was from Fort Keogh to Fort Buford. Bond had for passengers twenty-two Nez Perces Indians and General Miles was on board for the first two days. Bond doesn't appear to have been one of Miles's admirers.—EDG

344 BONDI, AUGUST

AUTOBIOGRAPHY . . . 1833–1907. GALESBURG, ILLINOIS: WAGONER PRINTING COMPANY, 1910.*

[1]–[178]. 23.2 x 15.3 cm. 13 illustrations, unlisted. Dark blue buckram, gilt top.

Ref.: Howes B595

Includes experiences in Kansas, Missouri, Texas, Illinois, Arkansas, the Civil War, etc.—EDG

345 BONNELL, GEORGE W.

TOPOGRAPHICAL DESCRIPTION OF TEXAS. TO WHICH IS ADDED AN ACCOUNT OF THE INDIAN TRIBES . . . AUSTIN: PUBLISHED BY CLARK, WING, & BROWN, 1840.

[i]–viii, [7]–127, [128 blank], 130–150, [151 blank]. (Pages 130–150 show even numbers on rectos.] 14.6 x 9.2 cm. Rough brown cloth, beveled edges.

Prov.: Inscribed on front fly-leaf: From / Memucan Hunt / to his Sister / Mrs Mary A. Nelson / Iron Banks / Kentucky / Conveyed through / the politeness of / Gen. A. Sidney Johnston /.

Ref.: Bradford 446; Clements Library (*Texas*) 21; Field 148; Howes B600; Rader 402; Raines p. 27; Sabin 6317; Streeter 380

The earlier of two issues described by Streeter. The running head and pagination are both present on page 130. "This is the first book or pamphlet published in Texas giving an account of the country."—Streeter

Memucan Hunt, at one time Secretary of the Texas Navy, was Minister Plenipotentiary and Envoy Extraordinary from the Republic of Texas to the United States. Albert Sidney Johnston was Secretary of War, of Texas, that is.

346 BONNELL, GEORGE W.

ANOTHER COPY. 14.5 x 9.3 cm. Buff printed boards with title on front cover within decorative border, advertisements on back cover.

Ref.: Clements Library (*Texas*) 21; Streeter 380A

The second of two issues described by Streeter.

347 BONNER, T. D., *Editor*

THE LIFE AND ADVENTURES OF JAMES P. BECKWOURTH, MOUNTAINEER, SCOUT, AND PIONEER, AND CHIEF OF THE CROW NATION OF INDIANS . . . NEW YORK: HARPER & BROTHERS, 1856.

[i]–xii, [13]–537, [538 blank]. 19.4 x 12.5 cm. Illustrations unlisted. Brown cloth.

Ref.: Blumann & Thomas 2330; Buck 156; Cowan p. 41; Dobie p. 71; Field 149; Howes B601; Rader 322; Sabin 4265; Smith 695; Wagner-Camp 272

Beckwourth's life is a classic of pioneer days in the West. Compare Dobie's comment with De Voto's estimate of his character in the 1931 reprint which he edited.

348 BONNER, T. D., *Editor*

THE SAME. LONDON: SAMPSON LOW, SON, & CO. . . . 1856.

18.7 x 12.2 cm. Contemporary green calf, gilt, with gilt wreath on front cover enclosing: Chatham House / Academy / Ramsgate. / Red leather label, gilt edges.

A school prize binding.

349 BONNEVILLE, BENJAMIN L. E.

AUTOGRAPH LETTER, SIGNED. 1835 October 30, Washington, D.C., n.d. Two pages, 24.9 x 19.4 cm. To General John Mason.

Thanks for a favor.

350 [BONNEVILLE, R. C., & SYLVESTER MOWRY]

[Extract] [caption title] . . . REPORT . . . No. 126. SANTA FE, NEW MEIXICO[!], SEPTEMBER 22, 1857 . . .

581 (end of preceding report), 582–594. 22.5 x 14.3 cm. Rebound in new red cloth.

Ref.: Wagner-Camp 293 note

Extracts from Report of the Secretary of the Interior, 35th Congress, 1st Session, Executive Document No. 11, Serial 919.

The first of the two reports, (No. 126) by Colonel R. C. Bonneville, contains a description of the upper Gila River area in Arizona, pages 582–84. The second report (No. 127) is by Lieutenant Sylvester Mowry and comprises a memoir on the Indian tribes of Arizona, pages 584–93.

Pages 593–94 contain No. 128 (By Garland Hunt from Salt Lake City) and part of No. 129.

351 BONNEY, EDWARD

[Pictorial title-page] BANDITTI OF THE PRAIRIES; OR, THE MURDERER'S DOOM!! A TALE OF THE MISSISSIPPI VALLEY, CHICAGO: EDWARD BONNEY, 1850.

[i–iv], [9]–196, [197–202 blank]. 21.2 x 13.7 cm. Illustrations on text paper not included in pagination facing pages [9], 26, 27, 43, 48, 50, 56, 92, 104, 126, 151, 153, 176, 178. Blue printed wrappers with title on front wrapper. Strip across top of front cover supplied. In a blue cloth case.

Ref.: Adams 112; Byrd 1545; Howes B606; McMurtrie (*Chicago*) 200 Monaghan, J. (*Journal*, Ill. State Hist. Soc., Vol. XXXIX, 1946) pp. 361–65; Mott (*Iowa*) pp. 35–36; Rader 404

Edward Bonney, the presumed author and private detective who tracked down the murderers of Colonel George Davenport, published this sensational account in 1850. At least eight editions have been identified. Some members of the loosely organized band described by Bonney were Mormons or claimed sanctuary in Nauvoo;

contemporary Mormon comments about Bonney are uncomplimentary. The band terrorized the upper Mississippi Valley from 1843 to 1848.

A. T. Andreass, the historian of Chicago, attributed the authorship of this work to Henry A. Clark, author of *The War Scout of 1812* . . . Chicago, 1850. Several years ago, a manuscript copy of the *Banditti* purportedly in the handwriting of Bonney was offered for sale. It resembles the printed version, but it seems probable that a more experienced writer than Bonney "edited" the work for publication.

352 BONNEY, EDWARD

ANOTHER EDITION. . . . FIFTIETH THOUSAND. CHICAGO: D. B. COOKE & CO., 1858.

[i–iv, iv blank], [9]–196. 21.9 x 23.7 cm. Illustrations on text paper not included in pagination facing pages 26, 26, 43, 49, 63, 73, 75, 89, 103, 117, 131, 145, 159, 173. Pale gray-green pictorial wrappers: Banditti / of the / Prairies, / or the / Murderer's Doom!! / A Tale / of the / Mississippi Valley, / by / Edward Bonney. / Chicago: / D. B. Cooke & Co., / Portland Block. / 1858. / [above pictorial title:] Price Fifty Cents. / Backstrip and back wrapper supplied. In a blue-green cloth case.

Ref.: Byrd 2859

Copyrighted in 1855 by D. B. Cooke.

353 BOOK OF PRICES, THE, *Muscatine, Iowa*

THE BOOK OF PRICES OF THE HOUSE-CARPENTERS AND JOINERS OF THE CITY OF MUSCATINE, IOWA. ADOPTED OCTOBER 31, A.D. 1851. MUSCATINE: PRINTED BY H. D. LA COSSITT, 1851.

[1] 92, [93–4 Index]. 14.2 x 10.2 cm. Original sheep.

Prov.: Signature of J. P. Walton on title-page, on front cover: J P Walton / Muscatine Iowa / Feb 11th 1852 /.

Ref.:

No other copy has been located.

J. P. Walton went to Muscatine in 1838 and lived to write his pioneer recollections which are the best to be found on the vicinity.—EDG

The name of W. Davidson has been added in pencil at the foot of the list on page [2].

354 BOOK OF PRICES, THE, *Peoria, Illinois*

THE BOOK OF PRICES, OF THE JOURNEYMAN HOUSE CARPENTERS & JOINERS, OF PEORIA. ADOPTED, MARCH 2, 1836. PEORIA: PRINTED BY J. L. MARSH, 1836.

[1]–22, [23–4 blank]. 16.7 x 10.1 cm. Stabbed.

Ref.: Byrd 265

No other copy located.

355 BOOK OF PRICES, THE, *Zanesville and Putnam, Ohio*

THE BOOK OF PRICES ADOPTED BY THE HOUSE CAR-
PENTERS OF THE TOWNS OF ZANESVILLE & PUTNAM,
MARCH 22, 1828. ZANESVILLE: PRINTED BY PETERS
& PELHAM, 1828.

[1]–15, [16], [i–iv (ii–vi blank)]. 19.5 x 13 cm.
Unbound, removed from bound volume. Pages
[i–iv] were added to carry a full page of errata
(page [i]); the paper differs from the text paper.
Lacks most of last blank leaf.
Ref.:
No other copy of this pamphlet has been lo-
cated.

The earliest schedule of uniform prices located was published in Philadelphia in 1786;
others for 1801, 1808, 1819, and 1827 had also
appeared. Two of those for 1819 were issued in
Canton and Cincinnati.

356 [BORDLEY, JOHN B.]

[SKETCHES ON ROTATIONS OF CROPS . . . PHILA-
DELPHIA: CHARLES CIST, 1796.]

A–H⁴, I⁶. (I6 blank). [1]–76, [77–8 blank]. Lacks
title-leaf. Bound with Number 3867.
Ref.: Evans 30103(?); Sabin 6415

357 BORRETT, GEORGE T.

LETTERS FROM CANADA AND THE UNITED STATES
. . . LONDON: PRINTED FOR PRIVATE CIRCULATION,
1865.

[i–iv], [1]–294. 18.8 x 12.8 cm. Red cloth, blind
embossed borders and panels on sides, title in
gilt on backstrip, uncut.
Ref.: Buck 644 see; Howes B621; Sabin 6433
see

The work was circulated privately in 1865 and
published the following year with a slightly different title. Borrett visited Chicago in 1864. Buck
and Sabin cite an edition dated 1866.

358 BORTHWICK, J. D.

THREE YEARS IN CALIFORNIA . . . EDINBURGH:
WILLIAM BLACKWOOD AND SONS, MDCCCLVII.

[i]–[viii, viii blank], [1]–384, [1]–16 advertisements. 22 x 14.2 cm. Eight illustrations listed.
Red cloth, blind embossed sides, title stamped in
gilt on backstrip, uncut.
Ref.: Blumann & Thomas 5166; Bradford
455; Cowan p. 64; Howes B622; Sabin 6436

Borthwick spent some time in 1851 as a miner
at Weaver Creek. His book presents a faithful
and graphic picture of his mining experiences
and of conditions at this time.—Cowan

359 [BOSQUI, EDWARD]

MEMOIRS.

[1]–281, [282]. 24 x 15 cm. Brown half morocco,
gilt top, uncut.
Prov.: Inscribed on title-page: To / Hiram R
Bloomer / from his friend / Edward Bosqui /.
Ref.: Barrett 2726; Blumann & Thomas
2883; Cowan p. 64; Howes B623

Bosqui was a printer who reached San Francisco in July, 1850. His reminiscences are especially interesting for the knowledge they give of
printing and publishing in San Francisco.

Cowan states that fifty copies only were
printed. However, Mr. P. K. Bekeart has written
that he has found two records that only thirty
copies were printed. The University of San Francisco copy, which is accompanied by eleven letters to Bosqui about the book, carries a note in
an unidentified hand stating there were only
twenty copies printed.
Copies: CSfU, CSmH, P. K. Bekeart, E. L.
Bosqui, Mrs. Archie Treat.

360 BOSS, HENRY R.

SKETCHES OF THE HISTORY OF OGLE COUNTY, ILL.,
AND THE EARLY SETTLEMENTS OF THE NORTHWEST
. . . POLO, ILLINOIS: PUBLISHED BY HENRY R.
BOSS, 1859.*

[i–iv], [1]–75, 76–80 advertisements. 21 x 14.5
cm. Brown cloth.
Ref.: Bradford 456; Buck 1009; Howes
B624

The first history of Ogle County. Buck calls
for only 76 pages; Howes calls for two preliminary pages and 88 pages; the ICN copy shows
four preliminary pages, 75 pages of text, and advertisements on pages 76–88.

361 BOSSU, JEAN BERNARD

NOUVEAUX VOYAGES AUX INDES OCCIDENTALES . . .
A PARIS, CHEZ LE JAY, M. DCC. LXVIII.

a¹⁰, A–K¹², L². [i]–xx, [1]–244. [a]², A–L¹². [i–iv],
[1]–[255], 256–64 advertisements. 17.7 x 10.9
cm. Four engraved illustrations, unlisted. Two
volumes, gray wrappers, manuscript titles on
backstrips, uncut. Backstrips partially chipped
away. In a gray cloth case.
Ref.: Clark II 5; Field 156; Howes B626;
Hubach p. 13; Monaghan 261; Sabin 6465

Bossu's first and second voyages.

Sabin's 1768 edition carried *Seconde édition*
on the title-page.

362 BOSSU, JEAN BERNARD

NOUVEAUX VOYAGES DANS L'AMERIQUE SEPTEN-
TRIONALE, CONTENANT UNE COLLECTION DE LET-

TRES . . . A AMSTERDAM, CHEZ CHANGUION, A LA BOURSE, M. DCC. LXXVII.

a⁸, A–Aa⁸, Bb⁴. [i]–xvi, [1]–392. 19.4 x 10.9 cm. Four illustrations, unlisted. Contemporary full mottled calf, gilt fillet borders on sides, gilt back, red morocco label, red edges.

Prov.: Bookplate of Philoe Pontov.

Ref.: Field 158; Howes B627; Hubach p. 13 note; Monaghan 267; Sabin 6470

Printed in Paris, with a false place of publication.

Bossu's account of his third voyage to the New World.

363 BOSSU, JEAN BERNARD

TRAVELS THROUGH THAT PART OF NORTH AMERICA FORMERLY CALLED LOUISIANA . . . LONDON: PRINTED FOR T. DAVIES, M DCC LXXI.

A⁴, B–Cc⁸, Dd⁴. [i]–viii, [1]–407. A²,B–Ee⁸. [i]–iv], [1]–432. 20.2 x 12.6 cm. Two volumes, contemporary full sprinkled calf, gilt fillets on backstrips, dark green and red labels, yellow sprinkled edges.

Prov.: Bookplates of S. S. Dashwood.

Ref.: Clark II 5; Field 157; Howes B626; Hunt 619 note; Monaghan 264; Sabin 6466

Bossu's first and second voyages to America. His third voyage did not appear in English.

364 BOUCARD, ADOLPHE

TRAVELS OF A NATURALIST. A RECORD OF ADVENTURES, DISCOVERIES, HISTORY AND CUSTOMS OF AMERICAN AND INDIAN HABITS AND DESCRIPTIONS OF ANIMALS, CHIEFLY MADE IN NORTH AMERICA, CALIFORNIA, MEXICO, CENTRAL AMERICA, COLOMBIA, CHILI, ETC. . . . LONDON, 1894.

[i]–viii, [i]–ii, [1]–204. 21.2 x 14 cm. Portrait. Brown cloth.

Ref.: Cowan p. 65; Howes (1954) 1058; Rader 412

A preliminary half-title on the first page [i] reads: Travels / of a / Naturalist. / By / A. Boucard. / [short rule] / London, 1894. /

Among Boucard's travels was a journey to California overland in 1851.

365 BOURKE, JOHN G.

AN APACHE CAMPAIGN IN THE SIERRA MADRE. AN ACCOUNT OF THE EXPEDITION IN PURSUIT OF THE HOSTILE CHIRICAHUA APACHES IN THE SPRING OF 1883 . . . NEW YORK: CHARLES SCRIBNER'S SONS, 1886.

[i]–[vi, vi blank], [1]–112, [113–14 blank, 115–30 advertisements]. 18.6 x 12.7 cm. 12 illustrations listed. Yellow pictorial cloth, title stamped in black on front cover and in gilt on backstrip.

Ref.: Howes B652; Munk (Alliot) p. 35; Rader 424

366 BOURKE, JOHN G.

[Cover title] REPRINTED FROM JOURNAL MILITARY SERVICE INSTITUTION. MACKENZIE'S LAST FIGHT WITH THE CHEYENNES: A WINTER CAMPAIGN IN WYOMING AND MONTANA . . . GOVERNOR'S ISLAND, N. Y. H.: 1890.

[1]–44. 23.2 x 15.5 cm. Portrait. Removed from bound volume, pale blue front wrapper only. In a red cloth case.

Prov.: Small manuscript slip inserted before frontispiece: Compliments of / The Author. /

Ref.: Howes B653; Jones 1657

367 BOURKE, JOHN G.

ON THE BORDER WITH CROOK . . . NEW YORK: CHARLES SCRIBNER'S SONS, 1891.

[i]–[xvi], 1–491, [492 blank], [1]–4 advertisements. 22 x 14.6 cm. Seven illustrations listed. Dark red pictorial cloth, stamped in silver.

Ref.: Dobie pp. 32, 85; Howes B654; Jennewein 61; Munk (Alliot) p. 36; Rader 426

A truly great book, on both Apaches and Arizona frontier.—Dobie

368 BOURKE, JOHN G.

THE SNAKE-DANCE OF THE MOQUIS OF ARIZONA BEING A NARRATIVE OF A JOURNEY FROM SANTA FE, NEW MEXICO, TO THE VILLAGES OF THE MOQUI INDIANS OF ARIZONA, WITH A DESCRIPTION OF THE MANNERS AND CUSTOMS OF THIS PECULIAR PEOPLE, AND ESPECIALLY OF THE REVOLTING RELIGIOUS RITE, THE SNAKE-DANCE . . . NEW YORK: CHARLES SCRIBNER'S SONS, 1884.

[iii]–[xviii, xviii blank], [1]–371, [372 blank]. 21.9 x 14.3 cm. 31 plates listed. Dark green pictorial cloth, uncut.

Ref.: Howes B655; Munk (Alliot) p. 36; Saunders 1471

The Moqui Indians of Arizona are, of course, the Hopi. The snake-dance is still performed, but is too fascinating to be called "revolting" today.

369 BOWLBY, RICHARD

KANSAS, THE SEAT OF WAR IN AMERICA . . . LONDON: EFFINGHAM WILSON, 1856.

[1]–36. 21.1 x 13.4 cm. Removed from bound volume, sewn, unbound.

Ref.: Howes B666

The author apparently never got closer to Kansas than Washington, D.C., and is indebted to other publications for all his data.—EDG

370 BOWLES, SAMUEL

ACROSS THE CONTINENT: A SUMMER'S JOURNEY TO THE ROCKY MOUNTAINS, THE MORMONS, AND THE PACIFIC STATES, WITH SPEAKER COLFAX ... SPRINGFIELD, MASS.: SAMUEL BOWLES & COMPANY, 1865.

[1–2 advertisement], [i]–[xx, xx blank], 1–[438], 1–6 advertisements. 19.1 x 12.2 cm. Map: Map of the / Territories & Pacific States / to Accompany / "Across the Continent" / By Samuel Bowles, / [3 lines] / Engraved by J. H. Goldthwait Printed by G. W. & C. B. Colton N. Y. / [lower left:] Entered according to Act of Congress in the Year 1865, by J. H. Goldthwait in the Clerks Office of the district Court of the U.S. for the South^n Dist^t of New York. / 34.4 x 45.5 cm. Scale: 110 miles to one inch. *Inset:* Plan of / Central California / on an / Enlarged Scale. / 13.1 x 14.8 cm. No scale given. Brown cloth, title in gilt on backstrip.

Ref.: Cowan p. 67; Howell 25; Howes (1954) 1089; Rader 431; Sabin 7077; Smith 982; Wagner-Camp 410

Among the states and territories visited by Bowles were Utah, Oregon, Washington, California, and Nevada.

371 BOWRON, WATSON, *Compiler*

HENRY COUNTY DIRECTORY, 1859–'60. CONTAINING A HISTORY OF THE COUNTY ... BURLINGTON, IOWA: WATSON BOWRON.

[1]–4 advertisements [5]–127, 128–32 advertisements. 17.6 x 11 cm. Yellow printed boards, black cloth backstrip, with title on front cover, advertisements on back cover and on both inner covers.

Ref.: Howes B670; Moffit 435

Advertisements also interspersed throughout the volume.

Probably printed in Burlington by the Hawkeye book and job establishment.—Moffit

372 BOX, MICHAEL JAMES

... ADVENTURES AND EXPLORATIONS IN NEW AND OLD MEXICO ... NEW-YORK: DERBY & JACKSON, 1861.

[1]–344. 18.2 x 12.3 cm. Brown cloth, blind embossed sides, title in gilt on backstrip.

Prov.: Inscribed on inner front covers: Chas. E. Nougues / La Paz S. Cal. / June 19th 1865 / Al estimade Señor / Francis W. Davis Md / H. M. S. Alert / with regards / of Chas. E. Nougues / [flourish] /.

Ref.: Howes B671

This excellent narrative is based on the author's personal experiences, especially as a member of the Texas Rangers.

373 BOYCE, JAMES R.

FACTS ABOUT MONTANA TERRITORY AND THE WAY TO GET THERE. HELENA, MONTANA, MARCH 5, 1872 ... CONTRIBUTED TO THE ROCKY MOUNTAIN GAZETTE, BY J. R. BOYCE, SR.

[1]–24. 23 x 14.7 cm. Rebound in brown half calf.

Ref.: Adams (*Ramp. Herd*) 294; Howes B672; McMurtrie (*Montana*) 64; Smith (1921) 395

Published at Helena, Montana, in 1872. In addition to the letter by Major Boyce there is a letter from Governor Potts which had been published in the *Philadelphia Enquirer* for April 22, 1872.

374 BOYD, F. A. (MRS ORSEMUS BRONSON)

CAVALRY LIFE IN TENT AND FIELD ... NEW YORK: J. SELWYN TAIT & SONS, 1894.

[1]–376. 18.3 x 12.3 cm. Portrait. Blue pictorial cloth.

Prov.: Inscribed on blank leaf at front: Senator Palmer / with best / regards and / gratitude / from the author / F A Boyd /.

Ref.: Howes B674

375 BOYD, ROBERT K.

THE BATTLE OF BIRCH COULEE. A WOUNDED MAN'S DESCRIPTION ... AN ADDRESS ... SONS OF VETERANS AT EAU CLAIRE, WISCONSIN IN JANUARY 1925 ... COPYRIGHT 1925 BY ROBERT K. BOYD.*

[1]–23, [24 colophon]. 20.4 x 13.2 cm. Two manuscript maps: [Southern parts of Minnesota and South Dakota]. 19 x 51.1 cm. (paper size). No scale given. [Birch Coulée and vicinity]. 19 x 25.1 cm. (paper size). No scale given. Brown printed wrappers. In a red cloth case.

Prov.: Signed by the author on the title-page: Robert K. Boyd / Eau Claire Wis / September 1925 /. Numerals 93 at foot of front cover, possibly by the author.

Ref.:

Printed at Eau Claire by the Herges Printing Company.

376 BOYNTON, CHARLES B., and T. B. MASON

A JOURNEY THROUGH KANSAS; WITH SKETCHES OF NEBRASKA: DESCRIBING THE COUNTRY, CLIMATE, SOIL, MINERAL, MANUFACTURING, AND OTHER RESOURCES. THE RESULTS OF A TOUR MADE IN THE AUTUMN OF 1854 ... CINCINNATI: MOORE, WILSTACH, KEYS & CO., 1855.

[i]–x, [1]–216. 19.9 x 11.7 cm. Map: Map of Kansas / with portions of / Nebraska etc. / Redrawn from official sources with emendations /

by H. V. Boynton. / Moore, Wilstach, Keys & Co. Publishers, Cin. / [lower left:] Middleton, Wallace & Co. Cin. / 13.3 x 17.1 cm. No scale given. Green printed wrappers with title on front wrapper within thick and thin rule borders, advertisements on verso of front and recto and verso of back wrapper. In a blue cloth case.

Ref.: Dolbee ("The Second Book on Kansas" in *Kansas Historical Quarterly*, Vol. IV, No. 2, May, 1935); Howes B677; Wagner-Camp 250

Miss Dolbee reports no copies in wrappers and describes only three Kansas copies in board covers with leather backs and corners.

377 BRACKENRIDGE, HENRY M.

JOURNAL OF A VOYAGE UP THE RIVER MISSOURI; PERFORMED IN EIGHTEEN HUNDRED AND ELEVEN . . . SECOND EDITION, REVISED AND ENLARGED BY THE AUTHOR . . . BALTIMORE: PUBLISHED BY COALE AND MAXWELL, 1815.

[*]⁴, A–U⁶, X⁴. [i]–viii, [1]–244, 246–47. (Page 245 omitted from pagination.) 19.2 x 10.6 cm. Gray-green printed boards with title as above on front cover within decorative border, except for date 1816; advertisements on back cover, uncut. Rebacked with matching plain paper. In a green cloth case.

Prov.: William C. Braislin copy.

Ref.: Bradford 498; Braislin 217; Clark II 136; Howes B658; Jones 773; Matthews p. 217; Rader 443 note; Sabin 7168; Shaw & Shoemaker 34189; Wagner-Camp 12

The first separate edition of the *Journal* which had appeared as part of *Views of Louisiana* . . . Pittsburgh, 1814. The volume also contains as an appendix a forty-two-page account by John Sibley of his journey from Fort Clark, Missouri, to the Arkansas River.

The voyage described by Brackenridge was made in the company of Manuel Lisa in 1811.

378 BRACKENRIDGE, HENRY M.

RECOLLECTIONS OF PERSONS AND PLACES IN THE WEST . . . SECOND EDITION, ENLARGED. PHILADELPHIA: J. B. LIPPINCOTT & CO., 1868.

[i]–viii, 9–331, [332 blank], [i–iv advertisements]. 18.8 x 12.2 cm. Blue cloth.

Ref.: Howes B687

The second edition contains ten added chapters and an appendix.

379 BRACKENRIDGE, HENRY M.

VIEWS OF LOUISIANA; TOGETHER WITH A JOURNAL OF A VOYAGE UP THE MISSOURI RIVER IN 1811 . . . PITTSBURGH: PRINTED AND PUBLISHED BY CRAMER, APEAR AND EICHBAUM, 1814.

[A]–Oo⁴. [1]–304. 21.1 x 12.8 cm. Original tree calf, red leather label on backstrip.

Prov.: Inscribed on the title-page: From the Author /, and with the signature of Jacob Price on the same page, and with his book label on the inner front cover.

Ref.: Bradford 496; Clark II 136; Howes B688; Hubach p. 43; Jones 767; Matthews p. 217; Rader 443; Raines p. 30; Shaw & Shoemaker 30979; Wagner-Camp 12

Howes has found copies in both full calf and in boards; the latter have all been trimmed and are slightly less tall than copies in original calf.

380 [BRACKENRIDGE, HUGH H., *Editor*]

NARRATIVES OF A LATE EXPEDITION AGAINST THE INDIANS; WITH AN ACCOUNT OF THE BARBAROUS EXECUTION OF COL. CRAWFORD; AND THE WONDERFUL ESCAPE OF DR. KNIGHT AND JOHN SLOVER FROM CAPTIVITY, IN 1782. PHILADELPHIA: PRINTED BY FRANCIS BAILEY, M,DCC,LXXXIII.

[A]–E³ [1]–38. 14.8 x 9.3 cm. Rebound in old marbled boards, new calf back. Lacks E4, blank.

Prov.: Most of name trimmed from upper margin of page [3].

Ref.: Evans 17993; Heartman (*Brackenridge*) 12; Hildeburn 4262 (Taylor Supplement 358, 359); Howes K214; Peckham (*Captured by Indians*) pp. 133–46; Sabin 38109; Thomson 582; Vail 684, 1201–04

First Edition. The Darlington Library copy is misdated 1773.

Dr. John Knight wrote his own account which was edited by Brackenridge. The editor took Slover's account (he could not write) by dictation and perfected it for publication. The two narratives, with a covering letter, were offered by Brackenridge to Francis Bailey who printed the work in the *Freeman's Journal*, April 30 to May 21, 1783. The work was fantastically successful and became one of the most popular examples in Captivity literature. For an extensive list of other editions, see the Ayer catalogues.

381 BRACKETT, ALBERT G.

HISTORY OF THE UNITED STATES CAVALRY, FROM THE FORMATION OF THE FEDERAL GOVERNMENT TO THE 1ST OF JUNE, 1863. TO WHICH IS ADDED A LIST OF ALL THE CAVALRY REGIMENTS, WITH THE NAMES OF THEIR COMMANDERS WHICH HAVE BEEN IN THE UNITED STATES SERVICE SINCE THE BREAKING OUT OF THE REBELLION . . . NEW YORK: HARPER & BROTHERS, 1865.

[i–ii blank], [iii]–xii, [13]–337, [338 blank], [339–40 advertisements]. 18.7 x 12.4 cm. Two maps and five illustrations listed. Green cloth, blind fillet borders on sides, gilt vignette on front cover, same in blind on back cover, title in gilt on backstrip.

Ref.: Howes B692; Wagner-Camp 411

The campaigns of Cooke, Doniphan, Frémont, and Johnston are among those described.

382 [BRACKETT, GEORGE A.]

A WINTER EVENING'S TALE. NEW YORK: PRINTED FOR THE AUTHOR, 1880.

[1]–31, [32 blank]. 24.7 x 17.1 cm. Four inserted photographs, five full-page illustrations, two illustrations in text. Green cloth, title in gilt on front cover.

Prov.: Inscribed on blank leaf at front: Wishing you happiness this / Christmas and New Year from / Thomas S. Brackett (grandson) / December 24, 1931 / Minneapolis /.

Ref.: Howes B693

Probably only a small edition of this privately printed work was published. The author was a beef contractor with General Sibley. The present volume contains an account of his experiences during the Sioux War of 1862. A copy in the Minnesota Historical Society was purchased from the author in 1880; their records indicate his name as above and add that his portrait appears facing page 6.

383 BRADBURY, JOHN

TRAVELS IN THE INTERIOR OF AMERICA, IN THE YEARS 1809, 1810, AND 1811; INCLUDING A DESCRIPTION OF UPPER LOUISIANA, TOGETHER WITH THE STATES OF OHIO, KENTUCKY, INDIANA, AND TENNESSEE, WITH THE ILLINOIS AND WESTERN TERRITORIES, AND CONTAINING REMARKS AND OBSERVATIONS USEFUL TO PERSONS EMIGRATING TO THOSE COUNTRIES . . . LIVERPOOL: PRINTED FOR THE AUTHOR, 1817.

[A]⁴, b², B–Z⁸, Aa². [i]–xii, [9]–364. 22.6 x 14 cm. Gray boards with tan paper backstrip, white printed label on backstrip, 4.5 x 3 cm. Front endpapers supplied, but not laid down. In a brown cloth case.

Ref.: Bradford 502; Buck 89; Butler (*Osage*) 1; Howes B695; Jones 784; Pilling 433; Rader 449; Sabin 7207; Thomson 111; Wagner-Camp 14

This is a fair and informing general description of western life and conditions . . . —Buck

384 BRADBURY, JOHN

THE SAME . . . SECOND EDITION . . . LONDON: PUBLISHED BY SHERWOOD, NEELY, AND JONES, 1819.

[*]¹, [A]–X⁸, Y⁴, Z¹. [1]–xiv, [17]–346. 22 x 13.7 cm. Map: Map / of the / United States / of /

America; / [thin and thick rules] / Comprehending the / Western Territory / with the Course of the / Missouri. / Engraved for / Bradbury's Travels. / 30.5 x 40.5 cm. No scale given. Contemporary or original gray boards, new gray paper backstrip, with original white printed label, 4.7 x 3.6 cm., uncut. Label slightly defective. In a light red cloth case.

The second and better edition, with a map.

385 BRADFORD, WARD

BIOGRAPHICAL SKETCHES OF THE LIFE OF MAJOR WARD BRADFORD, (OLD PIONEER) AS RELATED BY THE AUTHOR, WHO IS EIGHTY-FOUR YEARS OF AGE AND NEARLY BLIND . . . PUBLISHED FOR THE AUTHOR.

[1]–95, [96 blank]. (Page [1] blank, page [2] portrait.) 17 x 11.5 cm. Portrait and two illustrations. Salmon printed wrappers with title on front wrapper. In a blue half morocco case.

Ref.: Howes B702

The author was living at Fresno, California, when the book was written. Much of the narrative relates to Nevada. One episode, late in the book, is dated 1882. Probably printed at Fresno in 1892.

386 BRADSTREET, NATHAN

A DISCOURSE, DELIVERED AT HOPKINTON, BEFORE THE HONORABLE LEGISLATURE OF THE STATE OF NEW-HAMPSHIRE, AT THE ANNUAL ELECTION, JUNE 4, 1807 . . . AMHERST: PRINTED BY JOSEPH CUSHING . . . JUNE—1807.

[A]–C⁴. [1]–24. Bound with Number 3289.

Ref.: Sabin 7308; Shaw & Shoemaker 12199

387 BRADY, WILLIAM

GLIMPSES OF TEXAS: ITS DIVISIONS, RESOURCES, DEVELOPMENT AND PROSPECTS . . . HOUSTON, 1871.

[1]–83, 84–104 advertisements, [105 index, 106 pasted down on back cover]. 17.7 x 11 cm. Map: Map of / Texas / To Accompany / "Brady's Glimpses of Texas." / E. H. Cushing. Houston, Texas, 1871. / Scale of Miles. / [diagrammatic scale: 60 miles to one inch] / Entered according to Act of Congress in the year 1871 by G. W. & C. B. Colton & Co. / in the Office of the Librarian of Congress, at Washington. / 30.2 x 37.7 cm. Scale: 60 miles to one inch. *Inset:* General Map / of the / United States / and / Mexico / 12.1 x 17.2 cm. No scale indicated. *Inset:* Plan of / the Environs of / Houston / Showing its / Railroad & Water Connections. / Statute Miles / [diagrammatic scale; 19 miles to one inch] / 10.5 x 15.1 cm. Scale as above. Black cloth, title in gilt on front cover.

Ref.: Adams (*Ramp. Herd*) 303; Howes B714; Rader 460; Raines p. 30

Devoted to the enticement of immigrants.

388 BRAINERD, A.

ATCHISON CITY AND BUSINESS DIRECTORY FOR 1870–1. CONTAINING . . . A . . . SKETCH OF THE CITY . . . ATCHISON, KAN.: CHAMPION AND PRESS BOOK AND JOB PRINTING ESTABLISHMENT, 1870.

[1]–[124]. 20.3 x 13.4 cm. Removed from bound volume, sewn, unbound. Lacks wrappers.

Ref.: AII (*Kansas*) 741

Pages 113–[124] are printed on colored paper. AII (*Kansas*) calls for only 120 pages; in the present copy, the final four are unnumbered, but clearly part of the original work. Pages 117–[124] are advertisements.

389 BRAKE, HEZEKIAH

ON TWO CONTINENTS. A LONG LIFE'S EXPERIENCE . . . TOPEKA, KANSAS: PUBLISHED BY THE AUTHOR, 1896.*

[1]–240. 19.1 x 13.3 cm. Two portraits. Red cloth.

Ref.: Adams (*Ramp. Herd*) 304; Howes B718; Rader 462

In the 1850's and 1860's, Brake drifted from Minnesota to New Mexico and back to Kansas, where he settled.

390 BRALY, JOHN HYDE

MEMORY PICTURES: AN AUTOBIOGRAPHY . . .

[i–iv], [1]–263, [264 blank], [265–68]. 23.8 x 16 cm. 22 illustrations listed. Brown pictorial boards, brown cloth backstrip, fore and lower edges uncut.

Prov.: Mounted on the recto of the dedication leaf there is a small printed slip of presentation with the recipient's name filled in in manuscript: Mr and Mrs Lewis McLeure / Oct 15 1912 /.

Ref.: Cowan p. 69

Limited edition of which this is copy No. 63. Copyrighted in 1912. The verso of the title-leaf bears the following imprint: From the Press of / The Neuner Company / Los Angeles /. The final four leaves were added after the volume had been prepared for publication; they contain additional complimentary letters.

The author describes his boyhood in Missouri and his overland trip to California in the spring of 1847. On his way, he met General Kearny returning from California. Kearny told him he and his party were too late to cross the mountains to California, so they took the Oregon Road down the Snake River. Braly stayed for awhile with Dr. Whitman, but due to a premonition on his mother's part, he left the mission just two weeks before the massacre. By the spring of 1849, he was in California where he remained.—EDG

391 BRANSTETTER, PETER L.

LIFE AND TRAVELS . . . ST. JOSEPH, MO.: PUBLISHED BY MESSENGER OF PEACE.

[i–viii], [9]–203, [204 blank]. 16.6 x 11.4 cm. Portrait. Black leather, title in gilt on front cover.

Ref.: Howes B723

Printed twenty-three years after the death of the author, the uncopyrighted work was published to preserve for his descendants and friends Branstetter's writings. The first portion of the volume, some seventy pages, contains the author's diary of his overland trip to California in 1850, experiences gold mining in California, and an account of his return overland in the summer of 1851.

The introduction is dated from Curryville, Missouri, March 15, 1913. Careful searches over a number of years in the vicinity of St. Joseph have failed to turn up another copy.

392 BRAY, ELIZABETH McCULLOUGH, *Compiler and Editor*

JUDGE G. C. R. MITCHELL. MEMOIRS AND MEMORIALS . . . DAVENPORT, IOWA: FIDLAR & CHAMBERS, 1915.

[i–ii], [1]–96. 23.4 x 16.1 cm. Portrait and nine illustrations. Blue cloth, uncut.

Prov.: Printed presentation slip to Hiram Bruce Dillon tipped in at front.

Ref.: Howes B735

At the home of Colonel George Davenport, Government Island, a meeting was held on February 23, 1836, to found the town of Davenport. At this meeting, six of the eight original owners were present, including Antoine Le Claire and Colonel Davenport. Gilbert Chris Russell Mitchell was also present, although his signature does not appear on the document. The text of the entire document is in his fine, clear handwriting; it was probably one of the first acts of his professional career at Davenport. For years he acted as consulting attorney for Le Claire and Davenport, both of whom were fond of the young man.—EDG

The original manuscript of the document drawn up by Mitchell for Le Claire and Davenport on February 23, 1836, is in the Graff Collection.

393 BRAYTON, MATTHEW

THE INDIAN CAPTIVE . . . CLEVELAND, O.: FAIRBANKS, BENEDICT & CO., 1860.

[1]–68. 16 x 10.3 cm. Green printed wrappers, with title on front wrapper. In a red cloth case.

Ref.: Greenly (*Michigan*) 32; Howes B736; Peckham (*Captured by Indians*) pp. 168–183; Thomson 115; Wagner-Camp 351

Although Brayton was captured as a child in northwestern Ohio, much of his narrative concerns his wanderings in the far west—as far west as California and Oregon. Essentially this is an authentic account. Ernest J. Wessen is of the opinion that the narrative was written for Brayton by John H. A. Bone.

A note in the second edition (1896) states that after Brayton's return, he lived for a while in Carey and Fostoria, Ohio, enlisted in an Indiana regiment during the Civil War, and died at Pittsburgh Landing in 1862.

The first edition also appears in printed boards. Other than the bindings, there seem to be no differences between the two varieties.

394 BRAYTON, MATTHEW

THE SAME . . . FOSTORIA, OHIO: THE GRAY PRINTING COMPANY, 1896.

[1]–70, [71–2 blank]. 14.5 x 11.5 cm. White boards with title on front cover, white cloth backstrip.

Ref.: Howes B736
Second edition.
Editions: Cleveland, 1860.

395 BREAKENRIDGE, WILLIAM M.

HELLDORADO. BRINGING THE LAW TO THE MESQUITE . . . BOSTON: HOUGHTON, MIFFLIN COMPANY.

[i]–[xx, xx blank], 1–256. 22.5 x 15 cm. 21 illustrations listed. Tan cloth.

Prov.: Inscribed on the front endleaf: Cordially Yours / William M. Breakenridge / Tucson, Ariz. 3/24/30 /. And: Old Pueblo Club / [rule] / Charles A. Ewing / [preceding three lines in pencil].

Ref.: Adams 125; Adams (*Ramp. Herd*) 315; Howes B739; Rader 469; Saunders 2768
Copyrighted 1928.
Editions: Boston, 1928.

396 BREEN, PATRICK

THE DIARY OF PATRICK BREEN RECOUNTING THE ORDEAL OF THE DONNER PARTY SNOWBOUND IN THE SIERRA 1846–47. INTRODUCTION & NOTES BY GEORGE R. STEWART. SAN FRANCISCO: THE BOOK CLUB OF CALIFORNIA, 1946.

[1]–[68], [69 colophon, 70 blank]. 21.2 x 13.3 cm. 30 pages of facsimile. Decorated green boards, white cloth backstrip.

Ref.:
Limited to 300 copies.

397 BREESE, SIDNEY

THE EARLY HISTORY OF ILLINOIS, FROM ITS DISCOVERY BY THE FRENCH, IN 1673, UNTIL ITS CESSION TO GREAT BRITAIN IN 1763, INCLUDING THE NARRATIVE OF MARQUETTE'S DISCOVERY OF THE MISSISSIPPI . . . CHICAGO: E. B. MYERS & COMPANY, 1884.

[i]–[xiv, xiv blank], [1]–422. 22.9 x 14.9 cm. Portrait and three maps. Gray-green cloth.

Ref.: Howes B743

398 [BRENNAN, JOHN]

CONDITION AND RESOURCES OF SOUTHERN DAKOTA. PROSPECTIVE TRADE AND TRAVEL OF THE DAKOTA SOUTHERN RAILROAD . . . SIOUX CITY, IOWA: DAILY JOURNAL PRINTING HOUSE AND BINDERY, 1872.

[1]–54, [55–56 blank]. 18.7 x 12.4 cm. Map: Map of / Dakota / W. D. Baker, Chicago, Western Agent for Fisk & Russell, N.Y. / 28.1 x 34 cm. No scale given. Tan printed wrappers with title on front wrapper.

Ref.:

399 [BRIGGS, CHARLES W.]

THE REIGN OF TERROR IN KANZAS: AS ENCOURAGED BY PRESIDENT PIERCE, AND CARRIED OUT BY THE SOUTHERN SLAVE POWER . . . BOSTON: PUBLISHED BY CHARLES W. BRIGGS, 1856.*

[3]–34. 21.2 x 13.8 cm. Seven illustrations in the text. Pink printed wrappers with title on front wrapper. Lacks back wrapper.

Ref.: Howes B771; Sabin 37080
An extraordinary, inflammatory pamphlet.

400 BRIGHAM, ALASCO D.

AURORA CITY DIRECTORY AND BUSINESS ADVERTISER, FOR 1858 & 1859 . . . AURORA, ILLINOIS: PRINTED AT THE "BEACON" GENERAL PRINTING AND BOOKBINDING HOUSE, 1858.

[1]–[120]. [Advertisement on brown endpapers, two leaves of advertisements on brown paper inserted at front.] 19.9 x 12.9 cm. Printed green boards, advertisements on front and back covers, calf backstrip.

Ref.: Byrd 2861; Howes B775
Pages [5]–32 comprise a history of Aurora by Augustus Harman.

401 BRINGAS DE MANZANEDA Y ENCINAS, DIEGO MIGUEL

SERMON QUE EN LAS SOLEMNES HONRAS CELEBRADAS EN OBSEQUIO DE LOS VV. PP. PREDICADORES APOSTOLICOS FR. FRANCISCO TOMAS HERMENEGILDO GARCES: FR. JUAN MARCELO DIAZ: FR. JOSE MATIAS MORENO: FR. JUAN ANTONIO BARRENECHE: MISSIONEROS . . . ENTRE LOS GENTILES YUMAS, Y MUERTOS EN ELLAS GLORIOSAMENTE A MANOS DE LOS MISMOS BARBAROS EN LOS DIAS 17 Y 19 DE JULIO DE 1781 . . . MADRID, ANO 1819. EN LA IMPRENTA DE D. FERMIN VILLALPANDO, IMPRESOR DE CAMARA DE S. M.

[1]–12⁴. [1]–94, [95–96 blank]. 18.6 x 13.5 cm. Rebound in full brown morocco, blind fillet borders, red edges, by The Lakeside Press.

Ref.: Howes M269; Jones 805; Leclerc 1192, 2570; Sabin 44440; Streeter 1067; Streit III 1500; Wagner (*SS*) 174a

In eulogizing the martyred priests, the author gives a good deal about the history of New Mexico and Arizona Franciscan missions.

402 BRINKERHOFF, HENRY R.

NAH-NEE-TA, A TALE OF THE NAVAJOS . . . WASHINGTON: J. H. SOULE & CO., 1886.

[1–2], [i]–[vi, vi blank], [1]–236. 18.1 x 13.4 cm. Green cloth, title in gilt on backstrip.

Prov.: Inscribed on blank leaf at front: Mary S. Thayer. / Feb. 1. 1888. /

Ref.: Kluckhohn & Spencer p. 82; Saunders 3707

The author was stationed in western New Mexico for several years following the Civil War.

403 BRINKERHUFF, DICK

[Wrapper title] LIFE AND ADVENTURES OF DICK BRINKERHUFF ONE OF CUSTAR'S OLDEST PIONEERS AND WELL KNOWN THROUGHOUT WOOD COUNTY . . . PUBLISHED IN THE CUSTAR NEWS IN 1915.

[1]–31, [32 blank]. 23.6 x 14.7 cm. Semi-stiff printed wrappers with title on front wrapper. Rebacked with red cloth.

Ref.: Howes B777

Published at Custar, Ohio, in 1915.

Brinkerhuff says he went to California overland in 1850 and returned to Ohio in 1855. He went west again in 1857, including a stay in Iowa, and spent much of the rest of his life on the Plains and in California.

404 BRISTOL, SHERLOCK

THE PIONEER PREACHER: AN AUTOBIOGRAPHY . . . NEW YORK: FLEMING H. REVELL.

[i]–viii, 9–330, [1–6 advertisements]. 19 x 13.2 cm. Six plates. Brown cloth, blind embossed bands on sides, title stamped in gilt on backstrip

Ref.: Cowan p. 72; Howes (1954) 1210

Copyrighted 1887. There was an edition with a slightly different title and with a Chicago imprint only bearing the same copyright date. The present edition probably was not published until 1888.

Includes his 1852 trip to Oregon and experiences in California and Idaho mining camps.—Howes

405 BRISTOW, G. O.

LOST ON GRAND RIVER, NOWATA, I. T,[!]: CHEROKEE AIR PUBLISHING COMPANY, 1900.

[i–ii], [1]–131, [132 blank]. 16.7 x 11.8 cm. Tan printed wrappers with title on front wrapper. In a blue cloth case.

Ref.: Howes B788

The author describes his personal experiences as an unwilling member of one of the gangs of desperadoes operating in Indian Territory during the 1890's.—EDG

406 BRITISH COLUMBIA DEVELOPMENT ASSOCIATION, LIMITED, THE

. . . KLONDYKE. THE YUKON (KLONDYKE) MINES, AND HOW TO REACH THEM. LONDON: PRINTED AND PUBLISHED BY CROWTHER & GOODMAN.

[1]–32. 16.1 x 10.2 cm. Folding map: British Columbia Development Assⁿ / [rule] / Limited. / [rule] / Map Shewing the / "White Pass" Route to / [rule] / Yukon Goldfields viâ / Skagway Bay. / [double rule] / [lower centre:] Crowther & Goodman, Designers & Printers, 133, Fenchurch Sᵗ E.C. / 18.2 x 30.4 cm. No scale given. Red cloth with title in gilt on front cover.

Ref.:

Published in 1898 or 1899.

407 BROKE, HORATIO G.

WITH SACK AND STOCK IN ALASKA . . . LONDON: LONGMANS, GREEN, AND CO., 1891.

[i]–[xii, xii blank]. [1]–258, [259–60 blank], [1]–16 advertisements. 19.1 x 12.1 cm. Folding map. Blue cloth, uncut.

Ref.: Wickersham 4935

408 BROMLEY, GEORGE T.

THE LONG AGO AND THE LATER ON; OR, RECOLLECTIONS OF EIGHTY YEARS . . . SAN FRANCISCO: A. M. ROBERTSON, MCMIV.*

[i]–[xvi, xvi blank], 1–289, [290 blank]. 19.5 x 13 cm. Portrait. Red cloth, red top, uncut.

Ref.: Cowan p. 73

RATHGEBER FUR AUSWANDERUNGSLUSTIGE. BIE
UND WOHIN FOLLEN WIR AUSWANDERN: NACH
DEN VEREINIGTEN STAATEN ODER BRITISCH NORD-
AMERIKA . . . TEXAS . . . DIE MUSQUITOKUSTE—
SUD-AMERIKA ODER WESTINDIEN—AFRIKA ODER
ASIEN—SUD-AUSTRALIEN ODER NEU-SEELAND,—
SOLLEN WIR NACH RUSSLAND ODER POLEN . . .
STUTTGART: HOFFMANN'SCHE VERLAGS-BUCH-
HANDLUNG, 1846.

[I]–IV, [1]–[347], [348 blank]. 20.3 x 13.5 cm.
Map: Nord-America / 20.7 x 27.7 cm. Scale:
about 140 miles to one inch. Map: Karte / der /
Vereinigten Staaten / von / Nord-America. /
Neu Braunschweigs, der Beiden Canadas / und
Texas. / [upper right:] zu Bromme's Atlas Nº /
[lower left:] Lith. von H. P. Jahn. 24.8 x 39.2
cm. Scale: about 200 miles to one inch. *Inset:*
Das / Oregon Gebeit. / 9.5 x 9.9 cm. No scale
given. Map: [Plans of Boston, New York, Baltimore and Washington, and Philadelphia]. Each
8 x 6.5 cm. Scales: various. Map: New York /.
[upper right:] Bromme's kl. Atlas Nº 2. / 12.3 x
15.2 cm. Scale: 70 miles to one inch. Map:
Pennsylvania / und / New Jersey /. [upper
right:] Bromme's kl. Atlas Nº 3. / 12 x 14.8 cm.
Scale: 70 miles to one inch. Map: Ohio / und /
Indiana /. [upper right:] Bromme's kl. Atlas
Nº 5. / 12.2 x 15.1 cm. Scale: 70 miles to one
inch. Map: Illinois / und / Missouri /. [upper
right:] zu Bromme's kl. Atlas Nº 9. / 15.3 x 12.8
cm. Scale: about 70 miles to one inch. Map:
Michigan / und / Wisconsing [!]. / [upper right:]
Bromme's kl. Atlas Nº 10. / 13.2 x 16.3 cm.
Scale: 125 miles to one inch. *Inset:* Umgebung
von Detroit /. 5.1 x 4.1 cm. Scale: about 35 miles
to one inch. Map: [Plans of St. Louis, Blei District, Lexington, and Nashville.] Each 7.9 x 6.6
cm. Scales: about 20 miles to one inch. Map:
Virginia / Maryland / und / Delaware /. [upper
right:] Bromme's kl. Atlas Nº 4 / 12.4 x 15.4 cm.
Scale: 70 miles to one inch. Map: Kentucky /
und / Tennessee /. [upper right:] Bromme's kl.
Atlas Nº 6. / 12.5 x 15.9 cm. Scale: 70 miles to
one inch. Map: Georgia / und / Alabama /.
[upper right:] zu Bromme's kl. Atlas Nº 7. /
12.7 x 15.9 cm. Scale: 70 miles to one inch.
Map: Louisiana / und / Mississippi /. [upper
right:] zu Bromme's kl. Atlas N.º 8. / 15.3 x 12.5
cm. Scale: 70 miles to one inch. Map: [Three
plans:] [1] Umgebung / von / Quebec. / 6.5 x 7.9
cm. Scale: about 11 miles to one inch. [2] Umgebung / von / Montreal /. 6.5 x 8 cm. Scale:
about 11 miles to one inch. [3] Hudson / River /.
6.8 x 16.1 cm. Scale: about 21 miles to one inch.
Whole map: 13.5 x 16.1 cm. Map: Süd-Ameri-

ca. / 27.7 x 20.6 cm. Scale: about 130 miles to
one inch. Map: Australien. / 20.7 x 17.6 cm.
Scale: about 240 miles to one inch. Map: [Die
untern Donauländer.] 13.3 x 16.3 cm. No scale
given. Original white printed boards, with title
on front cover within decorative border, adver-
tisements on back cover, title on backstrip:
[double rule] / Bromme / Rathgeber / für /
Auswander. / [double rule] /.
  Prov.: Rubber stamp of Grosseherzogliche
Luxemburgische on title-page:
  Ref.: Buck 357; Howes B800; Sabin 8216
  The earliest edition of this work, under the
title *Reisen durch die Vereinigten Staaten und
Ober-Canada . . . ,* was published in 1834–35.
Clark III 16 details Bromme's travels in the
South, but does not mention this edition. The
small maps were derived from Baird: *View of the
Valley of the Mississippi . . . 1832.*

410 BRONSON, EDGAR B.

REMINISCENCES OF A RANCHMAN . . . NEW YORK:
THE McCLURE COMPANY, MCMVIII.

[i]–[vi, vi blank], [1]–314. 19.4 x 13 cm. Green
cloth, lower edges uncut.
  Ref.: Adams: (*Ramp. Herd*) 330; Howes
B802; Rader 498

411 BRONSON, EDGAR B.

THE VANGUARD . . . NEW YORK: GEORGE H.
DORAN COMPANY.

[i–ii], [1]–316. 19.1 x 13 cm. Brown pictorial
cloth, pictorial endpapers.
  Prov.: E. A. Brininstool's copy, with bookplate and notes as described below.
  Ref.: Adams (*Ramp. Herd*) 331
  Copyrighted 1914.
  Signed by E. A. Brininstool on half-title.
Photograph of Mr. and Mrs. Clark B. Stocking
mounted on title-page and with initialed annotations by Brininstool. Photograph of Stocking
mounted on dedication leaf, annotated by
Brininstool and inscribed below the dedication
by Clark B. Stocking. Laid in is an autograph
note by Brininstool, in pencil, signed with initials stating that *The Vanguard* is the life story of
Clark B. Stocking. According to Brininstool,
Bronson gave Stocking $1000 for the story and
agreed to make him famous. Also laid in is a
card, 7.7 x 13.2 cm., advertising the *West Coast
Magazine* which was carrying Stocking's reminiscences. On the verso is a manuscript menu
headed: For Dinner At the old / Guard's
Tepee / . . . / Dated at the end in another hand,
April 11, 1919.

412 BROOKS, ELISHA

A PIONEER MOTHER OF CALIFORNIA . . . SAN
FRANCISCO: HARR WAGNER PUBLISHING CO., 1922.

[1]–61, [62 blank]. 19.6 x 13.5 cm. Two portraits.
Green buckram.

Ref.: Cowan p. 74; Howes B815

The first edition of this work, also published
in 1922, was limited to 100 copies. The second
edition includes corrections by the author. The
narrative describes a trip across the plains in
1852, when the author, then aged eleven years,
went with his mother to join his father who had
gone overland in 1850.—EDG

Editions: San Francisco, 1922.

413 BROSS, WILLIAM

[Caption title] IMMORTALITY. ALL LIFE CONDI-
TIONALLY IMMORTAL. A PAPER READ BEFORE
THE AMERICAN ASSOCIATION FOR THE ADVANCE-
MENT OF SCIENCE . . . AUGUST 19, 1877 . . . JAN-
SEN, MC CLURG & CO. . . .

[1–8]. 22.5 x 15 cm. Stapled, unbound.

Ref.:

Printed at Chicago in 1877.

414 [BROSS, WILLIAM]

ROCK ISLAND AND ITS SURROUNDINGS, IN 1853.
DAVENPORT: PUBLISHED BY SANDERS & DAVIS,
1854.

[1]–36. 20.6 x 13.3 cm. Map on verso of front
wrapper: [schematic birds' eye view of Rock
Island and Vicinity]. [lower centre:] Sold by
Richards & Allen, Moline. / 7.9 x 16 cm., oval.
Scale: about 3 miles to one inch. Rebound in
three quarter blue morocco, original front
wrapper bound in.

Ref.: AII (*Chicago*) 78; Byrd 2068; Howes
B810; Moffit 145; Sabin 72396

On the verso of the title-page, there is a note
headed: Explanatory / which is dated: Office of
the Chicago Democratic Press, / Chicago, Ill.
January, 1854. On the verso of the front wrapper, under the map, there is a line reading: Sold
by Richards & Allen, Moline. / The pamphlet
was undoubtedly printed in Chicago, since these
letters, written by one of the editors, were originally printed in the Chicago *Democratic Press.*
According to Howes, some copies carry a Chicago imprint and some a Rock Island imprint.

415 BROSS, WILLIAM

HISTORY OF CHICAGO . . . WHAT I REMEMBER OF
EARLY CHICAGO . . . CHICAGO: JANSEN, MC CLURG
& CO., 1876.

[1]–126, [127–28 advertisements]. 23.2 x 14.6 cm.
Gray printed wrappers, with title on front wrapper, advertisements on recto and verso of back
wrapper.

Ref.: Howes (1954) 1247

Contains an account of the first Chicago
charter.

416 BROUGHTON, WILLIAM ROBERT

A VOYAGE OF DISCOVERY TO THE NORTH PACIFIC
OCEAN . . . IN THE YEARS 1795, 1796, 1797, 1798
. . . LONDON: PRINTED FOR T. CADELL AND W.
DAVIES, 1804.*

A⁴, a⁴, b², B–3D⁴, 3E². [i]–xx, [1]–393, [394],
[1–2 advertisement]. 26.2 x 20.5 cm. Six plates,
a map and two charts: Map: A Chart / of the /
of the / N.E. Coast of Asia, / [swelled rule] and
[swelled rule] / Japanese Isles / With the Track
of His Majesty's Sloop Providence / and her
Tender in 1796 and 1797 / under the Command
of / Wᵐ Robᵗ Broughton Esqʳ / [decorative
rule] / T. G. Vashon Delin. / [upper right:] To
face the Title. / [lower centre:] London Published May 1ˢᵗ 1804 by Cadell & Davies Strand. /
[lower right:] S. I. Neele, sculp. 352 Strand. /
55 x 70 cm. No scale given. Map: [1] Sketch /
of / Thosan Harbor, / on the S.E. Coast of
Corea / By / Capt. W. R. Broughton, / 1797. /
24.1 x 23.4 cm. Scale: about 4/5 nautical mile to
one inch. [2] The Sketch / of / Mapachan
Roads, / in the / Island of Lieuchieux / By /
Captⁿ W. R. Broughton, / 1797. / 12 x 16.3 cm.
No scale given. [3] Plan / of / Endermo Harbor
in the Island of Matamay / by Captⁿ W. R.
Broughton, / 1797. / 12 x 16.3 cm. Scale: about
1/2 league to one inch. Three maps on one sheet;
[upper right:] Page 96 / [lower centre:] [approxi-
mately same as preceding map] [lower right:]
Neele sculp. 352 Strand. / Map: A Chart / From
the South Point / of Formoso to / Great
Lieuchieux, / including the Islands of / Madjicosemah / By / Capt. W. R. Broughton. /
1797. / [upper right:] Page 147. / [lower centre
and lower right:] [same as preceding]. 44.5 x 61.3
cm. No scale given. Contemporary mottled calf,
red leather label, green edges. In a brown cloth
case.

Ref.: Cox II 32; Eberstadt (Catalogue 119)
98; Howes B821; Sabin 8423; Smith 485; Wagner (*Cart. of NW Coast*) p. 232 *et seq.*

Visited Nootka and sailed down the coast to
California; in further explorations he solved
what La Perouse had first attempted, the puzzle
of the Aleutians, Japan and Korea. Great
Britain's claim to the Oregon country was based
largely on Broughton's exploration of the mouth
of the Columbia.—Howes

417 BROUILLET, JEAN BAPTISTE ABRA-HAM

AUTHENTIC ACCOUNT OF THE MURDER OF DR. WHITMAN AND OTHER MISSIONARIES, BY THE CAYUSE INDIANS OF OREGON, IN 1847 . . . PORTLAND, OREGON: S. J. MC CORMICK, PUBLISHER, 1869.

[1]–108. 18.8 x 11.5 cm. Tan printed wrappers with title on front wrapper. In a red cloth folder.

Ref.: Cowan (1914) p. 25 note; Howell 32; Howes B822; Jones 1515; McMurtrie (*Oregon*) 513; Smith 487; Streit III 2567; Wagner-Camp see 164

The Introduction, signed and dated: J. B. A. Brouillet, V. G. Walla Walla, August, 1869, contains the statement that "The first edition of this pamphlet, written in 1848 and issued in 1853, has become exhausted . . . " The Appendix comprises extracts from Hines' *History of Oregon* and a letter of Sir James Douglas.

Editions: New York, 1853 (*Protestantism in Oregon*).

418 BROUILLET, JEAN BAPTISTE ABRA-HAM

PROTESTANTISM IN OREGON. ACCOUNT OF THE MURDER OF DR. WHITMAN, AND THE UNGRATEFUL CALUMNIES OF H. H. SPALDING, PROTESTANT MISSIONARY . . . NEW-YORK: M. T. COZANS, MDCCCLIII.

[i]–[iv, iv blank], [1]–107, [108 blank]. (Page 87 mispaginated 78.) 18.9 x 11.1 cm. Yellow printed wrappers with title on front wrapper, bound into three quarter red morocco covers.

Ref.: Cowan (1914) p. 25; Howes B822; Jones 1297; Smith 486; Streit III 2395; Wagner-Camp 164 see

The Preface, which is signed J. A. McM. New York, June, 1853, explains that "these pages, which appeared recently in the columns of the New York Freeman's Journal, will form an interesting and authentic chapter in the history of Protestant Missions."

In manuscript above the title on the front wrapper: Catholicism / and /.

419 BROWN, BENJAMIN

TESTIMONIES FOR THE TRUTH: A RECORD OF MANIFESTATIONS OF THE POWER OF GOD, MIRACULOUS AND PROVIDENTIAL, WITNESSED IN THE TRAVELS AND EXPERIENCE OF BENJAMIN BROWN, HIGH PRIEST IN THE CHURCH OF JESUS CHRIST OF LATTER-DAY SAINTS . . . LIVERPOOL: PUBLISHED BY S. W. RICHARDS, 1853.

[1]–32. Bound with Number 3346.
Ref.: Howes B828
Contains an overland narrative.

420 BROWN, CHARLES E.

PERSONAL RECOLLECTIONS, / 1813–1893 . . .

[i–viii], [1]–222, [223–24 blank], [1]–21, [22 colophon]. 20.5 x 14.4 cm. 55 illustrations listed. Limp black leather, title in gilt on backstrip, gilt edges, rounded corners.
Ref.: Mott (*Iowa*) p. 84
Printed at Ottumwa, Iowa, 1907.

421 BROWN, HENRY

THE HISTORY OF ILLINOIS . . . NEW-YORK: J. WINCHESTER, NEW WORLD PRESS, MDCCCXLIV.

[i]–x, [1]–492, [1–10 advertisements]. 21.8 x 13.8 cm. Map: Guide / through / Ohio, Michigan, Indiana, Illinois, / Missouri, Wisconsin & Iowa. / Showing the Township Lines of the / United States Surveys, / Location of Cities, Towns, Villages, Post Hamlets, Canals, Rail and Stage Roads. / By J. Calvin Smith. / New York. / Published by J. M. Colton, 86 Cedar St. / —1844.— / [lower right:] Engraved by S. Stiles, Sherman & Smith / [centre, below neat line:] Entered according to Act of Congress in the year 1840 by J. C. Smith, in the Clerks office of the District Court of the Southern district of New York /. 48.4 x 62.2 cm. Scale: 35 miles to one inch. Dark blue cloth, blind embossed panels on sides.
Ref.: Howes B839
⌐Chronologically the first, intrinsically the worst, history of this state.—Howes

422 BROWN, HENRY

AN ORATION, DELIVERED . . . ON THE FOURTH OF JULY, 1846. CHICAGO: PRINTED BY R. CRAWFORD WILSON, 1846.

[1]–24. 21.9 x 14.3 cm. Stabbed, unbound.
Ref.: Byrd 1042a
A hitherto unrecorded Chicago imprint and the only known imprint of R. Crawford Wilson.

423 BROWN, JAMES

AN ADDRESS TO THE PUBLIC, ACCOMPANIED BY DOCUMENTS, EXPOSING THE MISREPRESENTATIONS, CALUMNIES AND FALSEHOODS, CONTAINED IN THE PAMPHLET OF ELISHA I. HALL, OF FREDERICK COUNTY, VIRGINIA . . . LEXINGTON: PRINTED BY DANIEL BRADFORD.

[A]–L[4,2] (lacks L4, blank). [1]–65, [66]. 17.5 x 11 cm. Half brown calf, red leather label on front cover. Part of last leaf defective affecting text slightly.
Ref.: AII (*Kentucky*) 172; Howes B844
How violent public quarrels could be in the

early years of the nineteenth century is well illustrated by this pamphlet and the related *Observations and Documents, &c.* by Elisha I. Hall. The latter was published in 1802 and the former in 1803.

It is probably impossible to decide today which writer was justified, but it should be pointed out that Mr. Hall disappeared, while Mr. Brown became a senator from Louisiana after he left Kentucky. The present work contains references to both Philip Nolan and Lieut. William Clark.

424 BROWN, JAMES H.

THE SALEM DIRECTORY FOR 1871: EMBRACING A GENERAL DIRECTORY OF RESIDENTS, AND A BUSINESS DIRECTORY . . . AND THE HISTORY OF SALEM . . . SALEM, OREGON: PUBLISHED BY SNYDER & COOK, 1871.

[i]–vi, [1]–128, [3]–86, i–[vi, vi blank]. (First page [i] raised from inner front cover, second page [vi] pasted to inner back cover; colored advertising leaves interspersed.) 20.9 x 14.4 cm. Diagram of the City of Salem. / inserted before title-page, apparently from another copy. Tan printed boards, black roan backstrip, remounted on cloth, with short title and advertisements on front cover.

Ref.: Howes B847; Smith 490

Compiled by the Oregon historian James Henry Brown, this *Directory* contains an excellent history of Salem by the Rev. L. H. Judson. It is a fine record of the early settlement of Oregon and includes an account of the successive parties of overland emigrants. According to McMurtrie, there was a Salem directory for 1867, although no copy has been found. The compiler called this the "first *real* Directory."—EDG

The Appendix contains the City Charter and the Amended Charter (1868), the City Laws (1870), an Index to the City Laws, etc.

425 BROWN, JAMES S.

CALIFORNIA GOLD. AN AUTHENTIC HISTORY OF THE FIRST FIND WITH THE NAMES OF THOSE INTERESTED IN THE DISCOVERY . . . OAKLAND: PACIFIC PRESS PUBLISHING COMPANY, 1894.

[1]–20. 18.1 x 12.5 cm. Portrait. Gray printed wrappers, with title on front wrapper.

Ref.: Blumann & Thomas 803; Cowan p. 77; Howes B848, Wheat (*Gold Rush*) 22 see

Brown was working for Marshall at Coloma and was present when gold was discovered.—Wheat

426 BROWN, JAMES S.

LIFE OF A PIONEER, BEING THE AUTOBIOGRAPHY OF JAMES S. BROWN. SALT LAKE CITY, UTAH: GEO. Q. CANNON & SONS CO., 1900.*

[i]–[xx, xx blank], [9]–520. 21.5 x 14.3 cm. Seven illustrations listed. Brown cloth.

Ref.: Cowan p. 77; Howes B849; Wheat (*Gold Rush*) 22 see

The writer went overland with the Mormon Battalion to California in 1846 and was present when the first gold was discovered at Sutter's Mill.—EDG

427 BROWN, JESSE, & A. M. WILLARD

THE BLACK HILLS TRAILS: A HISTORY OF THE STRUGGLES OF THE PIONEERS IN THE WINNING OF THE BLACK HILLS . . . RAPID CITY, SOUTH DAKOTA: RAPID CITY JOURNAL COMPANY, 1924.

[1]–572. 22.8 x 14.6 cm. 54 illustrations listed. Green cloth.

Prov.: Inscribed on inside front cover: Kind Regards / To / Luke Voorhees / The grand old Scout / By Jesse Brown. & / A.. M.. Willard.. /

Ref.: Adams 137; Adams (*Ramp. Herd*) 342; Howes B850; Jennewein 126

Luke Voorhees was one of the most famous scouts and pioneers of the Black Hills country.

428 BROWN, JOHN

TWENTY-FIVE YEARS A PARSON IN THE WILD WEST, BEING THE EXPERIENCE OF PARSON RALPH RILEY . . . FALL RIVER, MASS.: PRINTED FOR THE AUTHOR, 1896.

[1]–215, [216 blank]. 18 x 12.4 cm. Portrait. Blue cloth.

Ref.: Adams 138; Adams (*Ramp. Herd*) 343; Rader 511

Cowboy and ranch life in Texas and Nevada.

429 BROWN, JOHN HENRY

REMINISCENCES AND INCIDENTS, OF "THE EARLY DAYS" OF SAN FRANCISCO . . . SAN FRANCISCO: MISSION JOURNAL PUBLISHING CO.

[1–106]. 22.3 x 14 cm. Folding map: [San Francisco, Pine to Broadway, Mason to Montgomery Streets], 19.1 x 26.9 cm. No scale given. Yellow cloth, title in gilt on front cover, blind ornaments at top and bottom.

Ref.: Blumann & Thomas 2901; Cowan p. 77; Howes B853

Published in 1886.

A little work of much historical value but it contains a great number of misspelled proper names.—Cowan

The final eight pages contain descriptions of forty-eight parcels of land located on the folding plan mentioned above.

430 BROWN, JOSEPH C.

AUTOGRAPH LETTER, SIGNED. 1826 October 30, St. Louis. Two pages, 31 x 20 cm. To Thomas Mather. In Mather papers.

Regarding the return of Sibley from Santa Fé and other business of the Road Commission. Brown was official surveyor of the Commission.

431 BROWN, NAT. P., and JOHN K. DALLISON

BROWN & DALLISON'S NEVADA, GRASS VALLEY AND ROUGH AND READY DIRECTORY, FOR THE YEAR COMMENCING JANUARY 1ST, 1856 . . . SAN FRANCISCO: PRINTED AT THE TOWN TALK OFFICE, 1856.

[i–vi advertisements], [1]–[86], 89–101, [102 blank], [103–10 advertisements], [111–12 blank], [113–16], [i–iv advertisements on pink paper], [117–18 advertisements], [119]–33, [134 blank], [135–52 advertisements]. 20.4 x 17.6 cm. Green printed boards with brown leather backstrip, gilt label, advertisements on pink paper mounted on inner covers. Rebacked preserving part of backstrip and all of the label.

Ref.: Blumann & Thomas 2225; Cowan p. 171; Greenwood 718; Howes B861

The historical sketch was written by Aaron Augustus Sargent. Believed to be the first Nevada City Directory.

Pages 87–8 were skipped in the pagination; the gathering is complete.

432 BROWN, SAMUEL

A THRILLING NARRATIVE OF THE HORRIBLE SUFFERINGS & MIRACULOUS ESCAPE OF SAMUEL BROWN, RESIDENT OF HARRISON CO., O., WHO WAS THROWN FROM HIS HORSE ON THE PRAIRIE, IN THE STATE OF IOWA, DECEMBER 17TH, A.D. 1850, BEING FOUR DAYS & FOUR NIGHTS EXPOSED TO THE INCLEMENCY OF THE SEVEREST FREEZING WEATHER THAT HAD BEEN FELT IN THAT COUNTRY FOR MANY YEARS; HAVING ONE OF HIS LEGS BROKEN, AND BOTH FROZEN, AND BEING WITHOUT FOOD OR SHELTER, SURROUNDED BY WOLVES BOTH NIGHT AND DAY. CONTAINING, ALSO, AN ACCOUNT OF THE HORRIBLE MANNER IN WHICH ONE OF HIS LEGS WAS AMPUTATED BY TWO IOWA SURGEONS . . . UHRICHSVILLE, OHIO. JAMES ILER, 1852.

[1]–63, [64 blank]. 18.3 x 12.4 cm. Restabbed, unbound. In a red cloth case.

Ref.: Howes B865

A grim experience.

433 BROWN, SAMUEL R.

THE WESTERN GAZETTEER; OR EMIGRANT'S DIRECTORY, CONTAINING A GEOGRAPHICAL DESCRIPTION OF THE WESTERN STATES AND TERRITORIES . . . AUBURN, N.Y.: PRINTED BY H. C. SOUTHWICK, 1817.

A–Xx⁴. [i]–vi, [7]–352. 22 x 14 cm. Gray boards, printed white label, 3.4 x 2.4 cm., on backstrip, uncut.

Ref.: Buck 96; Clark II 186; Howes B867; Sabin 8558; Thomson 129

With a three-line errata slip, 2.2 x 10.2 cm., mounted on blank leaf facing page 352. I have seen one other copy of the first edition with 352 pages (later printings have 360 pages), but in that copy the errata slip contained five lines of text.—EDG

434 BROWN, W. C.

BROWN'S MARYSVILLE DIRECTORY FOR THE YEAR COMMENCING MARCH, 1861: EMBRACING A GENERAL AND BUSINESS REGISTER OF CITIZENS . . . HISTORICAL SKETCHES OF INDUSTRIAL ENTERPRISES, BENEVOLENT AND CHARITABLE ASSOCIATIONS, ETC. . . . MARYSVILLE: PRINTED AT THE OFFICE OF THE DAILY CALIFORNIA EXPRESS, 1861.

[1]–[120], interspersed advertisements on pink, white, and green paper. 20.1 x 13.5 cm. Gray printed boards with black leather backstrip, advertisements on back and front covers, with short title forming border on front cover, four pages (on three leaves) of advertisements on blue paper at front and same on green paper at back (half of one leaf cut away).

Ref.: Blumann & Thomas 4829; Greenwood 1493

435 BROWN, WILLIAM H.

THE EARLY HISTORY OF THE STATE OF ILLINOIS. A LECTURE, . . . DELIVERED BEFORE THE CHICAGO LYCEUM, ON THE EIGHTH DAY OF DECEMBER, 1840 . . . CHICAGO: HOLCOMB & CO., 1840.

[1]–16. 21.6 x 12.9 cm. Rebound in full blue crushed levant morocco, gilt fillet borders on sides, gilt backstrip, title in gilt on front cover, gilt inner dentelles, by Scroll Bindery. In a blue cloth folder and half calf case.

Ref.: Byrd 513; McMurtrie (*Chicago*) 29

The work was reprinted in Volume 14 of the Fergus Reprints.

436 BROWN, WILLIAM H.

MEMOIR OF THE LATE HON. DANIEL P. COOK: READ BEFORE THE CHICAGO HISTORICAL SOCIETY, JUNE 9, 1857 . . . CHICAGO: SCRIPPS, BROSS & SPEARS, 1857.

[1]–30, [31–32 blank]. 21.5 x 13.7 cm. Removed from bound volume, unbound.

Ref.: AII (*Chicago*) 234; Byrd 2603; Sabin 8581

The Chicago Historical Society was organized April 24, 1856. Other than promotional materials, this is the first publication of the Society.

437 BROWNE, JOHN ROSS

ADVENTURES IN THE APACHE COUNTRY; A TOUR THROUGH ARIZONA AND SONORA, WITH NOTES ON THE SILVER REGIONS OF NEVADA . . . NEW YORK: HARPER & BROTHERS, PUBLISHERS, 1869.

[1]–535, [536 blank], [1]–4 advertisements. (Page [1] advertisement, page [2] blank.) 18.6 x 11.8 cm. 155 illustrations listed. Blue cloth.

Ref.: Bradford 610; Edwards pp. 24–5; Farquhar 26; Field 197; Howes B875; Munk (Alliot) p. 40; Rader 519; Sabin 8656

438 BROWNE, JOHN ROSS

[Caption title] . . . REPORT . . . ON THE LATE INDIAN WAR IN OREGON AND WASHINGTON TERRITORIES . . .

[1]–66. 22 x 14.5 cm. Removed from bound volume, unbound. In a green cloth case.

Prov.: Signed on page [1]: B. F. Dowell /.
Ref.: Howes B878; Smith (1921) 4110

35th Congress, 1st Session, Senate, Executive Document No. 40, Serial 929. [Washington, 1858.]

Browne's report is in the form of a letter dated from San Francisco, December 4, 1857, and occupies only pages 2–13. The rest of the volume contains J. B. A. Brouillet: "Account of the Murder of Dr. Whitman, and the Ungrateful Calumnies of H. H. Spalding . . . ," pages 13–66. The *Account* had appeared first in New York in 1853 and was reprinted shortly before the present printing in the *New York Freeman's Journal.*

The letter by Browne is a general review of Indian-white relations from the time of Lewis and Clark.

Mounted at the foot of page 66 is a slip, 6.5 x 14.5 cm., headed [S. R. 22.] / Joint Resolution declaring the meaning of the second section of the act of the second / of March, eighteen hundred and sixty-one, relative to property lost in the military service. / [12 lines] / Approved March 28, 1867. /

The slip relates to compensation claims for property lost during the Indian hostilities in Washington and Oregon in 1855–56.

439 BROWNLOW, WILLIAM G.

HELPS TO THE STUDY OF PRESBYTERIANISM OR, AN UNSOPHISTICATED EXPOSITION OF CALVINISM . . . TO WHICH IS ADDED A BRIEF ACCOUNT OF THE LIFE AND TRAVELS OF THE AUTHOR . . . KNOXVILLE, T.: F. S. HEISKELL, PRINTER, 1834.

[i]–[xiv, xiv blank], [15]–299, [300 blank]. 19.3 x 11.1 cm. Tan boards, mottled calf back, with brown leather label.

Ref.: AII (*Tennessee*) 527; Howes B882

Brownlow was governor of Tennessee from 1865 to 1869. His *Helps* is particularly interesting because of the narrative of his life on pages 241–94, the balance of the volume being an attack on the Presbyterian Church.

440 BROWNSON, ORESTES A.

A REVIEW OF THE SERMON BY DR. POTTS, ON THE DANGERS OF JESUIT INSTRUCTION, PREACHED AT THE SECOND PRESBYTERIAN CHURCH, ST. LOUIS, ON THE 25TH SEPTEMBER, 1845 . . . ST. LOUIS: "NEWSLETTER" PUBLICATION OFFICE, 1846.

[1]–23, [24 blank]. 22.4 x 13.5 cm. Buff printed wrappers with title on front wrapper.

Ref.: AII (*Missouri*) 472

441 BROWNSON, ORESTES A., JR.

ANNIE: A TRAGIC DRAMINA, IN FOUR ACTS . . . DUBUQUE, IOWA: PUBLISHED BY PALMER & BRO., 1869.

[1]–23, [24 blank]. 18 x 10.5 cm. Bound with eight other works, contemporary marbled boards, light red scored calf backstrip.

Ref.:

442 BROWNSON, ORESTES A., JR.

CARL EHRLICHKEIT: A DRAMINA, IN THREE ACTS . . . DUBUQUE, IOWA.

[1]–36. 18 x 10.5 cm. Bound with eight other works, contemporary marbled boards, light red scored calf backstrip.

Ref.:
Published in 1869 or 1870.
Pages 13–16 printed on yellow paper.

443 BROWNSON, ORESTES A., JR.

CAROLINE: A COMIC DRAMINA, IN TWO ACTS . . . DUBUQUE: PALMER & BROS., 1870.

[1]–20, [21]–24. One illustration. 18 x 10.5 cm. Bound with eight other works, contemporary marbled boards, light red scored calf backstrip.

Ref.:
Pages [21]–24: [caption title] Coriolanus: / An Historical Dramina, / By O. A. Brownson, Jr. / [decorative rule] / . . .

444 BROWNSON, ORESTES A., JR.

EXAMINATION QUESTIONS FOR REVIEW PURPOSES . . . DUBUQUE, IOWA.

[1]–20. 18 x 10.5 cm. Two illustrations and numerous vignettes. Bound with eight other works, contemporary marbled boards, light red scored calf backstrip.

Ref.:
Published in 1869 or 1870.

445 BROWNSON, ORESTES A., JR.

THE FOREIGNER IN AMERICA: A COMIC DRAMINA, IN FOUR ACTS . . . DUBUQUE, IOWA.

[1]–39, [40 advertisement]. 18 x 10.5 cm. Bound with eight other works, contemporary marbled boards, light red scored calf backstrip.
Ref.:
Published in 1869 or 1870.

446 BROWNSON, ORESTES A., JR.

PLURIMA: AD USUM CEUX QUI EN VEULENT. DUBUQUE, IOWA.

[1–4]. 18 x 10.5 cm. Bound with eight other works, contemporary marbled boards, light red scored calf backstrip.
Ref.:
Published in 1869 or 1870.

447 BROWNSON, ORESTES A., JR.

SIMPSON: A COMIC DRAMINA . . . DUBUQUE.

[1]–32. 18 x 10.5 cm. Vignettes. Bound with eight other works, contemporary marbled boards, light red scored calf backstrip.
Ref.:
Pages [1]–4 printed in green, vignettes on pages 29 and 32 printed in green.
Published in 1869 or 1870.

448 BROWNSON, ORESTES A., JR.

THE TEN SQUAWS: A SERIO-COMIC DRAMINA, IN FOUR ACTS . . . DUBUQUE, IOWA, 1870.

[1]–36. 18 x 10.5 cm. Two illustrations and numerous vignettes. Bound with eight other works, contemporary marbled boards, light red scored calf backstrip.
Ref.:

449 BRUCE, MINER W.

ALASKA: ITS HISTORY AND RESOURCES, GOLD FIELDS, ROUTES, AND SCENERY . . . SEATTLE, WASHINGTON: LOWMAN & HANFORD STATIONERY AND PRINTING CO., 1895.

[1]–128, [129 Table, 130 blank, 131 advertisements, 132 blank]. 23.2 x 15.5 cm. 45 illustrations and large folding map listed. Gray pictorial cloth.
Ref.: Smith 1204; Wickersham 4058
The map was also published separately. See following number.

450 BRUCE, MINER W.

[Map] M. W. BRUCE'S / MAP OF / ALASKA. / PUBLISHED BY / LOWMAN & HANFORD STATIONERY AND PRINTING CO., / SEATTLE, WASHINGTON. / (COPYRIGHTED) / 1895. / SCALE OF MILES / [diagrammatic scale: 23 miles to one inch] / [lower centre:] TRANSFERRED TO STONE AND PRINTED BY LOWMAN & HANFORD, SEATTLE, WASHINGTON. / *Inset:* Tourist Route / —from— / Puget Sound to Alaska. / Scale of Miles / [diagrammatic scale: 25 miles to one inch] / 19.2 x 26.7 cm. *Inset:* [Alaska Peninsula and Aleutian Islands.] 10.2 x 25.3 cm. Scale: 75 miles to one inch.

Map, 55.9 x 86 cm. Scale: 23 miles to one inch. Folded and laid in blue cloth covers, 17.5 x 11 cm., with title in blue on front cover: Bruce's / Map of / Alaska / Published by / Lowman & Hanford / Stationery and Printing Company / Seattle, Wash. / 1895 /.
Ref.: Phillips (*Maps*) p. 95

451 BRUFFEY, GEORGE A.

EIGHTY-ONE YEARS IN THE WEST . . . BUTTE, MONTANA: THE BUTTE MINER COMPANY PRINTERS, 1925.

[1]–152. 19.5 x 13.7 cm. Portrait. Gray printed wrappers.
Ref.: Adams 139; Howes B891; Smith 1211
Montana vigilantes, etc.

452 BRUNSON, ALFRED

AUTOGRAPH LETTER, SIGNED. 1841 September 17, Prairie du Chien, Wisconsin Territory. Eight pages, 32.2 x 19.7 cm. To Secretary of War John Bell.

A fine letter in which the writer proposes a future series of states west of the Mississippi for Indian tribes. Brunson's experiences as a missionary among the Indians led him to think well of them. His proposal, which included a return of Upper Michigan to Wisconsin, was humane and sensible—probably too sensible for acceptance by the War Department.

453 BRUNSON, ALFRED

[Caption title] NORTHERN WISKONSAN. A DESCRIPTION OF THE NORTHERN PART OF THIS TERRITORY . . . MADISON, DECEMBER 15, 1843.

[1]–16. 21.5 x 13.6 cm. Stabbed, unbound. In a dark red half morocco case.
Prov.: Herschel V. Jones copy.
Ref.: AII (*Wisconsin*) 169; Jones 1067; Sabin 8760
This is the earliest printed report on the northern part of Wisconsin by a careful observer. There was another edition, without date, of twelve pages.

454 BRUNSON, ALFRED

PRAIRIE DU CHIEN. ITS PRESENT POSITION AND FUTURE PROSPECTS . . . MILWAUKEE: DAILY SENTINEL STEAM POWER PRESS, 1857.

[1]–12. 19.6 x 12 cm. Green printed wrappers with title on front wrapper.

Prov.: Signature at top of front wrapper: H R Searles Esq / Signature at lower right corner: C King /. Addressed to Searles in New York on back wrapper with paid stamp and postmark of Prairie du Chien dated Feb 25.

Ref.: AII (*Wisconsin*) 275; Jones 1366; Sabin 8761

Brunson also believed in the great future of Prairie du Chien.

455 BRUNSON, ALFRED

A WESTERN PIONEER: OR, INCIDENTS OF THE LIFE AND TIMES . . . EMBRACING A PERIOD OF OVER SEVENTY YEARS . . . CINCINNATI: HITCHCOCK AND WALDEN, 1872 [–1879].

[1]–418. [1]–413, [414 blank]. 19.2 x 12.2 cm. Two volumes, black cloth, decorative blind borders and panels on first volume, fillet borders in blind on second, gilt titles on backstrips.

Ref.: Howes B897

Although essentially a religious autobiography, there is much of interest to the historian of early times in Western Pennsylvania, Ohio, Indiana, and particularly Illinois and Wisconsin.

456 BRYAN, ROGER B.

AN AVERAGE AMERICAN ARMY OFFICER. AN AUTOBIOGRAPHY . . . SAN DIEGO, CALIFORNIA: BUCK-MOLINA CO., PRINTERS, 1914.

[1]–[167], [168 blank]. (Pages [1–2] blank.) 17.9 x 12 6 cm. Five illustrations listed. Tan printed wrappers.

Prov.: Printed presentation slip from the author laid in.

Ref.: Howes B899

Bryan had tours of duty at Fort Custer, Fort Walla Walla, Fort Leavenworth, Fort Huachuca, Fort Wingate, and elsewhere.

457 BRYANT, EDWIN

WHAT I SAW IN CALIFORNIA: BEING THE JOURNAL OF A TOUR, BY THE EMIGRANT ROUTE AND SOUTH PASS OF THE ROCKY MOUNTAINS, ACROSS THE CONTINENT OF NORTH AMERICA, THE GREAT DESERT BASIN, AND THROUGH CALIFORNIA, IN THE YEARS 1846, 1847 . . . NEW YORK: D. APPLETON & COMPANY, M DCCC XLVIII.

[1]–455, [456 blank]. 18.3 x 12.1 cm. Blue cloth, blind embossed sides, title stamped in gilt on backstrip.

Ref.: Barrett 375; Blumann & Thomas 4872; Bradford 632; Cowan p. 81; Howes B903; Wagner-Camp 146; Wheat (*Gold Rush*) 26

Although this is a faithful account of an overland journey, its usefulness was marred because there was no map. The lack was supplied starting with the fifth edition.

Laid in is an Autograph Letter, signed by W. D. Gallagher.

458 BRYANT, EDWIN

THE SAME . . . SIXTH EDITION, WITH AN APPENDIX, CONTAINING ACCOUNTS OF THE GOLD MINES, VARIOUS ROUTES, OUTFIT, ETC., ETC. NEW-YORK: D. APPLETON & COMPANY, MDCCCXLIX.

[1]–480. 18.2 x 12.1 cm. Frontispiece map of California around San Francisco. Map: Map of / California, / Oregon, Texas, / and the Territories adjoining / with Routes &c. / Published by J. H. Colton, / Nº 86, Cedar S.ᵗ, New York, / 1849. / Scale of Statute Miles. / [diagrammatic scale: 100 miles to one inch] / Ackermans lith 120 Fulton Sᵗ N.Y. / [lower left:] Entered according to Act of Congress in the year 1849 by J. H. Colton in the Clerk's Office of the District Court for the Southern District of New York. / [lower centre:] D. Appleton & Co. New York. / 52.8 x 46 cm. Scale: as above. Blue cloth, blind embossed sides, title stamped in gilt on backstrip.

Ref.: Wheat (*Gold Region*) 67, 73(?); Wheat (*Transmississippi*) 593(?)

459 BRYANT, THOMAS J.

HISTORY OF THE FIRST REGIMENT ILLINOIS VOLUNTEER INFANTRY, AND COMPANY D, FOURTEENTH REGIMENT . . .

[i–iv], [1–174]. [1–154]. 13.8 x 9.5 cm. Two volumes, black cloth, titles in gilt on backstrip.

Prov.: Each volume inscribed in pencil: Thomas Bryant from Pa /.

Ref.:

The two volumes comprising this *History* are made up from newspaper clippings from the *Carrollton* (Illinois) *Press* in which Bryant published his reminiscences. A printed title-page (as above) was prepared for each volume. The first volume contains seven chapters about the Mexican War and six chapters about the Civil War. The second volume is devoted wholly to the latter war. The author intended to "give the student of history an idea of the state of things and feeling that existed north and south, immediately proceeding[!] the out brake[!] of the Rebellion."

Bryant was elected captain of the first full company formed at Greenfield, Illinois, shortly after the firing on Fort Sumter. The company went into training at Jacksonville, Illinois on May 9, 1861.

Throughout the two volumes, there are numerous changes and corrections, mostly single words, made with printed slips pasted over the original versions. The type used for the corrections is not identical with the type used for the original text.

460 BUACHE, PHILIPPE

CONSIDERATIONS GEOGRAPHIQUES ET PHYSIQUES SUR LES NOUVELLES DECOUVERTES AU NORD DE LA GRANDE MER, APPELLE'E VULGAIREMENT LA MER DU SUD . . . A PARIS, M.DCC.LIII.

A^{4+1}, B–F^4, G^{6+1}, H^6, I–R^4, S–V^2. (G1 is unsigned; the gathering may have been an eight with G8 either excised or used for the fifth leaf of A. Other gatherings of four are signed through the second leaf while H is signed through Hiii and G through Giv.) [1]–7, 6–49, [50 blank], 51–158. (Pages 151–54 are present in duplicate.) 24.6 x 20 cm. Fourteen maps on eleven plates / and five plates of views: [1] Carte des Nouvelles Découverts / entre la partie Orient^{le} de l'Asie et l'Occid^{le} de l'Amerique / Avec des Vuës sur la Gr^{de} Terre reconnuë par les Russes en 1741. / et sur la Mer de l'Ouest et autres communications de Mers. / Dressée par Phil. Buache P^{er} Geographe du Roi, / Presentée à l'Acad. des Sciences le 9. Août 1752 / et approuvée dans son Assemblée / du 6. Septembre suivant. / [upper right corner:] Iere Carte du Mem. lû à l'Acad. le 9. Août 1752. / Avant / l'Exposé / [lower left:] Publiée sous le Privilege de l'Acad. des Sciences / [lower right:] A Paris sur le Quay de l'Horloge du Palais /. 21.9 x 32 cm. Scale: 160 French marine leagues to one inch. [2–3 on one plate] Réduction d'une Carte publiée à Nuremberg / représentant l'une des Premieres Idées qu'on s'est formé / du Kamchatka et de ses Environs / pour les pag. 10. et 11. des Considérations Géog? &c. / 20.4 x 10.6 cm. No scale indicated. [and] Vues des Glaces / au milieu desquelles / l'on voit la Pêche qui se fait / au Nord-Est de l'Asie. / Extraite d'apres la Carte de l'Empire / Russien en langue Russe / Par Philippe Buache. / 1753. / 20.4 x 20.6 cm. No scale indicated. [upper right corner:] IVe Carte relative au Mém. lû à l'Académie le 9. Août 1752. Page / 9 [lower left corner:] Publiée sous le Privilége de l'Acad. des Sciences du 7. Juillet 1753 /. 22 x 32.6 cm. (plate mark). [4] Carte / des Découv^{tes} de l'Am^{al} de Fonte selon la Carte Angloise / donnée par l'Ecrivain du Vaisseau la Californie / dans son Voyage à la Baye d'Hudson / Avec les Terres vuës et reconnues par les Russes / Et une Comparaison du Résultat des Cartes / du 16e et 17e Siecle au sujet du / Détroit d'Anian. / [short rule] / Dressée / Par Philippe Buache P^{er} Géog. du Roy / et de l'Académie des Sciences. / [upper right:] IIe Carte du Mém. lû à l'Acad. le 9. Août 1752. Page 13 / [lower centre:] Publiée sous le Privilége de l'Académie R^{le} des Sciences. / 21.8 x 32.3 cm. Scale: about 465 English miles to one inch. [5] Carte du Géometrique / des Découvertes de l'Amiral de Fonte / Et de son Capitaine Bernarda / Comparée avec le Systeme de la Carte Angloise / publiée par l'Ecrivain du Vaisseau la Californie. / Dressée et Présentée à l'Acad? des Sciences / Par Philippe Buache. / [upper right:] IIIe Carte du Mem. lû à l'Acad. le 9. Août 1752. Pag. 16. / [lower centre:] Publiée sous le Privilége de l'Acad. R^{le} des Sc. du 6. Sept^{bre} 1752. A Paris, sur le Quay de l'Horloge /. 22.4 x 32.4 cm. Scale: about 90 French marine leagues to one inch. [6] Essai d'une Carte que Mr Guillaume Delisle P^{er} Géographe du Roy / et de l'Académie des Sciences avoit joint à son Mémoire présenté à la Cour en 1717. Sur la / Mer de l'Ouest. / [upper right:] Veme Carte du Mém. lû à l'Acad. le 9. Août 1752. Page / 25 /. [lower centre:] Cette Carte a rapport à la Seconde partie des Eclaircissemens du Mémoire / Présenté et lû à l'Académie des Sciences le 9. Août 1752. par Phil. Buache. / 23. x 16.6 cm. No scale indicated. [7–8 on one plate] Cartes des Terres aux environs du Japon / ou du Nord-Est de l'Asie et du Nord-Ouest de l'Amerique Extraite d'une Carte Japonnoise de l'Univers / apportée en Europe par Kæmpfer et déposé dans le Cabinet de feu Mr Hans-Sloane / Président de la Société R^{le} de Londres. 16.4 x 26.5 cm. No scale indicated. Cartes des Terres nouvellement connues au Nord de la Mer du Sud / tant du Côté de l'Asie que du Côte de l'Amerique. / Réduite d'après les Cartes présentées à l'Acad. des Sc. au mois d'Août 1752. Avec la Route des Chinois en Amérique vers l'an 458. de J. C. / tracée sur les connoiss^{ces} Géographiques / que Mr de Guignes a tirées des / Annales Chinoises / Par Philippe Buache. / 16.2 x 22.5 cm. No scale indicated. [upper left corner:] Publiée sous le Privilége de l'Académie des Sc. / [upper right corner:] VIe Carte rélative au Mém. lû à l'Acad. le 9. Août 1752. / Page 47 / [lower centre:] A Paris, sur le Quay de l'Horloge du Palais. / [Between the two maps are eleven lines of text.] 38.9 x 28.2 cm. [9–10 on one plate] La Californie d'après une très grande Carte Espagnole / M. S^{te} de l'Amerique Dressée à Florence en 1604 par Mathieu Neron Pecciolen. Cosmog? / [Inset:] Partie de la Californie tirée de l'Amerique / Sept^{le} publiée en 1700 par Guillaume Delisle; / 7.8 x 7.3 cm. (neat line). No scale indicated. 21 x 14.7 cm. Scale: 300 Italian miles to one inch. Carte du Passage par Terre à la / California / découvert en 1701. par le R. P. Kino Jesuite / Avec les N^lles Miss^ons des P. P. de la Compagnie / donnée en 1705 dans le Tome 5. / des Lettres Edifiantes. / 21.1 x 16.2 cm. Scale: about 27 leagues to one inch. [upper right corner:] IXe Carte pour le 3e Partie des Considérations &c. Page 71. / [lower right:] A Paris sur le Quay de l'Horloge. Sous le Privilege de l'Acad^e des Sc. du 24 Juill. 1754. / Delahaye l'Ainé Sculp. / 22 x 32.3 cm. [11] Carte / de l'Isle de Ieso / et de ses Environs / pour servir à concilier les / differentes idées que l'on en a eues / jusqu'à présent. / Dressée par Philippe Buache / de l'Académie des Sciences / et P^er Géographe du Roi. / 1754. / [Inset:] Province / d'Osju / du Nord de l'Isle Nipon / Japon / Extrait de la Carte de l'Hist^re de Kæmpfer / 7.6 x 6.5 cm. No scale indicated. [Inset:] Province d'Osju / Japon / Extrait donné par Scheuchzer /. 7 x 6.5 cm. No scale indicated. [Inset:] Extrait de la Carte / Originale Manuscrite de Texeira / où l'on voit de Détroit d'Anian / qui ne se trouve point sur celle q^e Thevenot / a publiée en 1664. / 7.6 x 25 cm. No scale indicated. [upper right:] Xe Carte pour le 3e Partie des Considérations &c. / [lower left:] Delahaye l'Ainé sculpsit /. 39.1 x 28 cm. (plate mark). Scale: 35 Dutch miles to one inch. [12] Carte du Royaume et des Isles de Lieou-Kieou / Réduite d'après les Cartes Manuscrites que le R. P. Gaubil a dressées en Chine / le 6 Novembre 1752. / [upper right:] XIe pour la 3e Partie des Considérations &c. Pag. / 132 / [lower centre:] Dressée par Phil. Buache et publiée sous le Privilege de l'Acad^e des Sc. / du 4. Septembre 1754. / 34.3 x 24.4 cm. (plate mark). Scale: 26 French marine leagues to one inch. [13] Carte Marine des Parties Septentrionales de la Grande Mer, et de l'Ocean, / Où l'on réuni diverses Vues Phisiques, Et où l'on voit particulierement les Terreins inclinés vers chaque Mer, / et dont es Eaux s'y déchargent depuis les Chaînes de Montagnes. / Dressée et Présentée à l'Acad. des Sc. le 9. Aoust 1752. par Phil. Buache. [Inset:] [Arctic Polar map.] 7.5 cm. diameter. No scale indicated. [upper right:] VIIe Carte pour la 3e Partie des Considérations &c. / [upper right corner:] Page / 142 /. 21.6 x 50.8 cm. (plate mark). No scale indicated. [14] Carte Physique / des Terreins / les plus élevés de la / Partie Occidentale / du Canada; / Où l'on voit les Nouvelles / Découvertes des Officiers / François à l'Ouest du Lac / Supérieur; Avec les Rivieres et les / Lacs dont M. Jeremie a parlé dans la / Relation de la Baye de Hudson. / Dressée par Philippe Buache. [Inset:] Réduction de la Carte Tracée par le Sauvage Ochagach et

autres, / laquelle a donnée lieu aux Découvertes des Officiers François representée dans la Carte cy jointe. / 8.7 x 25.5 cm. Scale: 20 leagues to one inch. [upper left:] Publiée sous le Privilege de l'Académie des Sciences, du 4 Septembre 1754 / [upper right:] VIIIe Carte pour la 3e et derniere Partie / des Considérations, &c. / [upper right corner:] Page 146 / [lower left corner:] Delahaye l'Ainé Sculpsit / 24.1 x 34.7 cm. (plate mark). Scale: 75 leagues to one inch. [15] Vues / des Cotes / de la / Terre ou Isle d'Eso / de celle de la Compagnie / et des Etats / Dessinnées sur les Lieux en 1643. / par les Hollandois / du Vaisseau le Kastrikum / lors de leur expedition pour la décou-/verte des Païs au Nord du Japon. / [Plan and five views of coasts.] [upper right:] XIIe Carte ou Vûes / pour les Considérations &c. / Planche I. / [upper right corner:] A la fin du Volume / [below centre, but above bottom inset view:] A Paris Sur le Quay de l'Horloge / du Palais / ou se trouvent les Cartes de l'Atlas Géographique de Guill. Delisle P^er Géographe du Roy, / et de Phil. Buache, de l'acad^e des Sciences / 21.7 x 51 cm. (plate mark). Scale: about 7/8 Dutch mile to one inch. [16] [Seven views of coasts.] [upper right:] Planche 2e / 22 x 51.4 cm. (plate mark). [17] [Seven views of coasts.] [upper right:] Planche 3e / 22.5 x 52 cm. (plate mark). [18] Plan de la Côte entre le Pic Antoine et l'Isle des Etats / [Five views of coasts and one plan.] [upper right:] Planche 4^e / 22.4 x 51.9 cm. (plate mark). [19] [Six views of coasts.] [upper right:] Planche 5e / et derniere /. 21.6 x 50.4 cm. (plate mark). Contemporary green vellum, maroon leather label on backstrip, red edges.

Ref.: Howes B908; Sabin 8832; Wagner (*Cart. of NW Coast*) pp. 158–62; Wickersham 5916

Some copies of Buache's *Considérations* contain a three-page "Exposé" and a four-page "Liste des Cartes," neither of which is present in this copy. The maps are bound in their proper places.

In many respects, Buache's *Considérations* is a curious and frustrating work. The author, being one of the principal French geographers of his time, was in the unfortunate position of trying to defend the French view of the cartography of the north Pacific after the earlier conjectures had been pretty thoroughly proven erroneous. His arguments are ingenious in many instances, and his method of ignoring or perverting evidence which does not fit the French theories is fascinating. As soon as the work was issued it was attacked bitterly from all sides.

461 BUCARELI Y URSUA, ANTONIO MARIA

[Caption title]. . . INSTRUCCION PARA EL GO-VIERNO INTERIOR Y BUEN REGIMEN DE LA GUAR-NICION DEL PRESIDIO DEL CARMEN, . . .

I–O². 1–23, [24 blank]. 28 x 19.8 cm. Bound with Number 9.

Ref.: Medina (*Mexico*) 5674

Signed at the end: México trece de Octubre de mil se-/tecientos setenta y quatro. / El B. Fr. D. Antonio Bucareli, / y Ursúa. /

462 BUCARELI Y URSUA, ANTONIO MARIA

[Caption title] . . . INSTRUCCION Y METODO CON QUE SE HA DE ESTABLECER EL HOSPITAL PARA LA TROPA DE LA GUARNICION DEL PRESIDIO DE NUESTRA SENORA DEL CARMEN, . . .

P–S². 1–15, [16 blank]. 28 x 19.8 cm. Bound with Number 9.

Ref.: Medina (*Mexico*) 5674

At foot of page 15: El B. Fr. D. Antonio Bucareli, / y Ursúa. / Es conforme en todo á el Reglamento é Ins-/trucciones originales, de que certifico. Méxi-/co trece de Octubre de mil setecientos setenta / y quatro. /

463 BUCARELI Y URSUA, ANTONIO MARIA

REGLAMENTO PROVISIONAL PARA EL PREST, VES-TUARIO, GRATIFICACIONES, HOSPITALIDAD, RECLU-TA, DISCIPLINA Y TOTAL GOVIERNO DE LA TROPA QUE DEBE GUARNECER EL PRESIDIO DE NUESTRA SENORA DEL CARMEN DE LA ISLA DE TRIS EN LA LAGUNA DE TERMINO . . . EN MEXICO: EN LA IMPRENTA DE D. FELIPE DE ZUNIGA Y ONTIVEROS, 1774.

[*]¹, [A]–H², [i–ii], 1–32. 28 x 19.8 cm. Bound with Number 9.

Ref.: Medina (*Mexico*) 5674

464 BUCARELI Y URSUA, ANTONIO MARIA

REGLAMENTO PROVISIONAL QUE HAN DE OBSERVAR EL TESORERO PAGADOR Y EL GUARDA ALMACEN DEL REAL FUERTE DE S. CARLOS DE PEROTE . . . MEXICO, POR D. FELIPE DE ZUNIGA Y ONTIVEROS, 1778.

[*]¹, A–O². [i–ii], 1–56. 28 x 19.8 cm. Bound with Number 9.

Ref.: Medina (*Mexico*) 6088

465 BUDLONG, CAROLINE DALE

MEMORIES. PIONEER DAYS IN OREGON AND WASH-INGTON TERRITORY . . . EUGENE, OREGON: PIC-TURE PRESS PRINTERS.

[i]–[viii]. 1–45, [46 blank]. 19 x 13.8 cm. 12 illus-trations. Green flocked printed wrappers.

Ref.:

Printed in 1919. Limited to 125 copies, ac-cording to a pencil note on a front blank leaf, by Fred Lockley.

466 BUEL, JAMES W.

THE BORDER OUTLAWS. AN AUTHENTIC AND THRILLING HISTORY OF THE MOST NOTED BANDITS OF ANCIENT OR MODERN TIMES, THE YOUNGER BROTHERS, JESSE AND FRANK JAMES, AND THEIR COMRADES IN CRIME . . . ST. LOUIS, MO.: HISTORI-CAL PUBLISHING COMPANY, 1881.

BOUND WITH:

THE BORDER BANDITS. AN AUTHENTIC AND THRILL-ING HISTORY OF THE NOTED OUTLAWS, JESSE AND FRANK JAMES, AND THEIR BANDS OF HIGHWAY-MEN . . . ST. LOUIS, MO.: HISTORICAL PUBLISHING COMPANY, 1881.

[1]–252, [253–54 blank]. [1]–148. (Pages [1–2] in each volume are the frontispiece.) 18.2 x 12.5 cm. 23 and 13 illustrations respectively, listed. Two volumes bound together in brown cloth, pictorial borders in blind on covers, title in gilt on backstrip and front cover, in blind on back cover.

Ref.: Adams 142; Howes B933; Jones 1616; Rader 531 note

The two works were issued several times both separately and together.

467 BUEL, JAMES W.

HEROES OF THE PLAINS; OR, LIVES AND WONDERFUL ADVENTURES OF WILD BILL, BUFFALO BILL, KIT CARSON, CAPT. PAYNE, CAPT. JACK, TEXAS JACK, CALIFORNIA JOE, AND OTHER CELEBRATED INDIAN FIGHTERS, SCOUTS, HUNTERS AND GUIDES INCLUD-ING A TRUE AND THRILLING HISTORY OF GEN. CUSTER'S FAMOUS "LAST FIGHT" ON THE LITTLE BIG HORN, WITH SITTING BULL . . . ST. LOUIS, MO.: N. D. THOMPSON & CO., 1881.

[9]–548. 20.2 x 13.5 cm. 16 colored plates and 72 black and white illustrations. Brick pictorial cloth.

Ref.: Adams 143; Howes B943; Jennewein 110

The work was issued with several imprints.

468 BUEL, JAMES W.

LIFE AND MARVELOUS ADVENTURES OF WILD BILL, THE SCOUT . . . CHICAGO: BELFORD, CLARKE & CO. 1880.*

[1]–[93], [94 blank]. 17.4 x 12 cm. Eight illustra-tions, unlisted. Gray printed wrappers, title

within pictorial border. In a dark blue cloth folder.

Ref.: Adams 145; Howes B935

The date on the wrapper is 1881.

It is difficult to suppose that either the original "Wild Bill" Hickok or his television reincarnation would recognize Buel's fancies.

469 BUEL, JAMES W.

THE SAME. 1888. Tan pictorial wrappers, similar to preceding, dated 1886.

470 BUFFALO CHILD LONG LANCE, Blood Indian Chief

TYPEWRITTEN LETTER, SIGNED "Long Lance." 1931 January 9, Roosevelt Field Hotel, Mineola, L.I. One page, 21.4 x 13.9 cm. To Mrs. S. A. Tucker.

Laid in the writer's *Long Lance* . . . 1929.

471 BUFFALO CHILD LONG LANCE, Blood Indian Chief

LONG LANCE . . . NEW YORK: COSMOPOLITAN BOOK CORPORATION, 1929.

[i]–[xviii, xviii blank], 1–278. 19.6 x 12.9 cm. Illustrations listed. Rust cloth.

Prov.: Inscribed on front fly-leaf: With kindest wishes / to my friend— / Mrs. S. A. Tucker / Long Lance / Dec. 26, '30. /

Ref.: Dobie p. 34

Tipped in at the front is a Typewritten Letter signed by the author to Mrs. Tucker. Also laid in is a typed manuscript poem, possibly by the author and the carbon copy of an interesting letter by J. Frank Dobie about the author.

472 BUFFUM, E. GOULD

SIX MONTHS IN THE GOLD MINES; FROM A JOURNAL OF THREE YEARS' RESIDENCE IN UPPER AND LOWER CALIFORNIA, 1847–8–9 . . . PHILADELPHIA: LEA AND BLANCHARD, 1850.

[v]–xxiv, [25]–172, [1–44 advertisements]. 19.3 x 12.3 cm. Black cloth, blind embossed sides, title in gilt on backstrip.

Ref.: Barrett 389; Blumann & Thomas 4876; Cowan p. 83; Howes B943; Jones 1229; Sabin 9067; Wheat (*Gold Rush*) 28

One of the chiefest sources of authority for the history of that period.—Cowan

473 BULLOCH, JAMES D.

THE SECRET SERVICE OF THE CONFEDERATE STATES IN EUROPE OR, HOW THE CONFEDERATE CRUISERS WERE EQUIPPED . . . NEW YORK: G. P. PUTNAM'S SONS, 1884.

[i]–x, [1]–460 (errata slip, 10.9 x 14 cm., between pages [ii–iii]). [i]–[vi, vi blank], [1]–438. 22 x 14.1

cm. Two volumes, purple cloth, printed white paper labels on backstrips, uncut, unopened.

Ref.: Howes B949

This American edition was printed in England.

Editions: London, 1883.

474 BULLOCK, WILLIAM

SKETCH OF A JOURNEY THROUGH THE WESTERN STATES OF NORTH AMERICA, FROM NEW ORLEANS, BY THE MISSISSIPPI, OHIO, CITY OF CINCINNATI AND FALLS OF NIAGARA, TO NEW YORK, IN 1827 . . . LONDON: JOHN MILLER, 1827.*

[1–2], [i]–[xxxii, xxxii blank], [i]–viii, [1]–135, [136 blank]. (Pages [95–6] blank.) 18.8 x 11 cm. Plan: Plan of a proposed Rural Town, to be called Hygeia, / The Property of W. Bullock / on the River Ohio, Kentucky, in the United States of America, / Designed by I. B. Papworth, / Architect to the King of Wirtemburg, &c. &c. / 35.3 x 59.5 cm. Scale: 430 yards to one inch. Map: United States / of / America. / 18.6 x 20.4 cm. No scale given. Contemporary half blue straight-grain calf, gilt backstrip, gilt top, uncut.

Ref.: Clark III 18; Howes B950; Thomson 135

The journey described is Bullock's return from Mexico to England. On the way, he bought property in Kentucky and later returned with his family to settle there. The plan of Hygeia is fascinating.

The second part of the volume is a London reprint of the Drake and Mansfield description of Cincinnati with a separate title-page on page [iii]: Cincinnati / in / 1826. / [rule] / By B. Drake and E. D. Mansfield. / [rule] / Cincinnati: / Printed by Morgan, Lodge, and Fisher. / [short rule] / February, 1827. /

475 BUNN, MATTHEW

A JOURNAL OF THE ADVENTURES OF MATTHEW BUNN . . . WHO ENLISTED WITH ENSIGN JOHN TILLINGHAST . . . IN THE YEAR 1791, ON AN EXPEDITION INTO THE WESTERN COUNTRY; — WAS TAKEN BY THE SAVAGES, AND MADE HIS ESCAPE INTO DETROIT THE 30TH OF APRIL, 1792 . . . PROVIDENCE: PRINTED FOR THE AUTHOR.

[A]–C⁴. [1]–24. 24 x 14 cm. Rebound in calf, blind tooled, leather label on backstrip, uncut. Title-leaf partly defective affecting two words.

Ref.: Evans 30135; Howes B952; Sabin 9185 see; Vail 1052–54

An address "To the Public" on the verso of the title-page is dated December 10, 1795.

This is the only known copy of the First Edition. It was imperfectly described by Evans who apparently saw an advertisement only. It is the copy sold at the American-Anderson Galleries on March 3, 1936, lot 53.

Matthew Bunn's *Journal* is an invaluable record of the Niagara frontier during the latter years of the eighteenth century. Much of the material is not found elsewhere in contemporary printings. Four editions were published in two years. The first edition differs in some details from later editions and carries the author's adventures only as far as his arrival in Detroit. All of the early editions seem to have been issued for the support of the author.

A facsimile edition of this copy was issued by The Newberry Library in 1962.

476 BUNN, MATTHEW

A JOURNAL OF THE ADVENTURES OF MATTHEW BUNN . . . A FACSIMILE OF THE COPY IN THE EVERETT D. GRAFF COLLECTION AT THE NEWBERRY LIBRARY. CHICAGO, 1962.

[i–vi, vi blank], [1]–24. 26 x 15.2 cm. 24 pages of facsimile. Gray printed wrappers.
Ref.:
Limited to 2000 copies.

477 BURCH, JOHN P.

CHARLES W. QUANTRELL. A TRUE HISTORY OF HIS GUERILLA WARFARE AND THE MISSOURI AND KANSAS BORDER DURING THE CIVIL WAR OF 1861 TO 1865 . . .*

1–266. 19.5 x 13.2 cm. Illustrations unlisted. Red cloth. In dust jacket.
Ref.: Adams 151; Rader 536
Copyrighted 1923 in Vega, Texas. The author claimed his information came from Captain Harrison Trow.

478 BURDICK, USHER L.

LIFE AND EXPLOITS OF JOHN GOODALL . . . WATFORD CITY, NORTH DAKOTA: THE MC KENZIE COUNTY FARMER, 1931.*

[1]–29, [30–2 blank]. 23 x 15.5 cm. Two illustrations. Salmon printed wrappers.
Ref.: Adams (*Ramp. Herd*) 160
Goodall was associated with the Marquis de Mores for a number of years in charge of his cattle and cattle ranches in which capacity he became well acquainted with Theodore Roosevelt.—EDG

479 BURDICK, USHER L.

TALES FROM BUFFALO LAND. THE STORY OF FORT BUFORD . . . BALTIMORE: WIRTH BROTHERS, 1940.

[1]–215, [216 colophon]. 19.8 x 12.7 cm. 13 illustrations listed. Red cloth, fore and lower edges uncut.

Ref.: Adams 155; Adams (*Ramp. Herd*) 365
Contains information about Scout Allison and Sitting Bull.

480 BURGESS, JOHN

PLEASANT RECOLLECTIONS OF CHARACTERS AND WORKS OF NOBLE MEN, WITH OLD SCENES AND MERRY TIMES OF LONG, LONG AGO . . . CINCINNATI: PRINTED BY CRANSTON & STOWE, FOR THE AUTHOR, 1887.*

[1]–460. 18.8 x 12.2 cm. Yellow cloth, decorative bands stamped in black on front cover and in blind on back cover, title in gilt on backstrip and front cover.
Ref.:

481 BURGESS, JOHN

SEMI-CENTENNIAL REMINISCENCE SERMON . . . BY THE REQUEST OF THE IOWA ANNUAL CONFERENCE . . . CINCINNATI: PRINTED BY CRANSTON & CURTS, 1894.

[1]–32. 22.5 x 15 cm. Gray printed wrappers with title on front wrapper.
Ref.:

482 BURGUM, JESSAMINE S.

ZEZULA; OR, PIONEER DAYS IN THE SMOKY WATER COUNTRY. A COLLECTION OF HISTORICAL SKETCHES . . . OF THE EARLY AND ROMANTIC HISTORY OF DAKOTA TERRITORY ALONG THE MISSOURI RIVER . . . VALLEY CITY, N.D.: PUBLISHED BY GETCHELL & NEILSEN.*

[i–x, x blank], 1–195, [196 blank]. 21.6 x 14.6 cm. 25 illustrations listed. Orange pictorial cloth.
Ref.:
Copyrighted 1937. Frontispiece portrait signed by the author.

483 BURK, MARTHA CANNARY

[Photograph] [An alleged photograph of Calamity Jane, on horseback, accoutred.]

18.5 x 11.1 cm. mounted on card 20.2 x 12.7 cm.

Inscribed under the photograph in pencil: Calamity Jane /. Further inscribed on verso: To my sweet Everett / from his / Sweetie Pie / "Calamity" Jane / — / 1888 / = /. The handwriting bears a startling similarity to that of the late Edward Eberstadt.

484 BURK, MARTHA CANNARY

[Wrapper title] LIFE AND ADVENTURES OF CALAMITY JANE. BY HERSELF.*

[1]–7, [8, ornament in centre]. 16.5 x 10.5 cm. Light tan printed wrappers with title on front wrapper. Lower outer corners of last leaf and wrapper chewed off, not affecting text.
Ref.: Adams 156; Jennewein 115

The pamphlet was designed for sale at public performances of Calamity Jane's skill as a marksman.

Many years ago, Eberstadt had a copy which measured 15.9 x 10 cm. with eight pages of text as in this copy. The portrait on the front wrappers was identical, but the border and type ornaments differed. The Eberstadt copy carried an imprint on the front wrapper: Post Print, Livingston, Mont. / —EDG

Neither place nor date is given in the present copy. Adams suggests the Livingston, Montana, edition is a reprint.

485   BURKE, EMILY P.

REMINISCENCES OF GEORGIA . . . JAMES M. FITCH, MDCCCL.

[i]–viii, [1]–252. 16.9 x 10.5 cm. Portrait. Brown cloth, blind embossed sides, title in gilt on backstrip.

Ref.: Clark III 281; De Renne p. 530; Howes B981

Published at Oberlin, Ohio, where Fitch printed the *Oberlin Evangelist*.

Her sharply etched pictures in miniature . . . give some of the detailed information that comes from intimate association and observation not noted in most of the travel accounts.—Clark

486   BURKE, JOHN M.

"BUFFALO BILL" FROM PRAIRIE TO PALACE. AN AUTHENTIC HISTORY OF THE WILD WEST WITH SKETCHES, STORIES OF ADVENTURE, AND ANECDOTES OF "BUFFALO BILL," THE HERO OF THE PLAINS . . . CHICAGO: RAND, McNALLY & COMPANY, 1893.

[1]–275, [276 advertisement]. 18.9 x 13.3 cm. Illustrations unlisted. Dark red cloth, with portrait on cover.

Prov.: Inscribed on the front fly-leaf: Chicago Ill / Buffalo Bills Wild West, / Sept 16—1893 / Presented to M. A. Blumenfeld / by / Major J. M. Burke. /

Ref.: Adams 157; Howes B982; Rader 544

The author was closely associated with Cody for many years.

Burke, according to Don Russell, "was one of the founders of the art of press-agentry, and to him goes much of the credit for making the name of Buffalo Bill a household word."

487   BURKE, WILLIAM S.

DIRECTORY OF THE CITY OF COUNCIL BLUFFS AND EMIGRANTS' GUIDE TO THE GOLD REGIONS OF THE WEST. COUNCIL BLUFFS, IOWA: NONPAREIL PRINTING COMPANY, 1866.

[1–8 advertisements], [i]–xxiv, [1]–32, [1–8 advertisements]. 21 x 13.3 cm. Map: North Platte Route / to the / Gold Mines /. 11.1 x 56.2 cm. No scale given. Six boxed advertisements in margin above map. Yellow printed wrappers with title on front wrapper. Back wrapper, backstrip, and inner margin of front wrapper supplied. In a green cloth case.

Prov.: IaHi copy with numerals stamped on page [iii] and with letter of release.

Ref.: Howes B984; Sabin 9320

In addition to the directory, there is a section devoted to Council Bluffs, the routes across the plains, and a seven-page Emigrants' Guide.

488   BURKE, WILLIAM S., and J. L. ROCK

THE HISTORY OF LEAVENWORTH, THE METROPOLIS OF KANSAS, AND THE CHIEF COMMERCIAL CENTER WEST OF THE MISSOURI RIVER . . . LEAVENWORTH, KANSAS: THE LEAVENWORTH TIMES BOOK AND JOB PRINTING ESTABLISHMENT, 1880.

[1]–[88], with inserted leaves of advertisements before pages 73, 81, and after [88]. 22.1 x 14.4 cm. Woodcuts in text and on verso of back wrapper. Buff printed wrappers with title on front wrapper, advertisements on verso of front and recto of back wrapper, large cut on verso of back wrapper.

Ref.: Howes B985

489   BURKLEY, FRANK J.

THE FADED FRONTIER . . . OMAHA, NEBRASKA: BURKLEY ENVELOPE AND PRINTING CO., 1935.*

[1]–[442]. 22.9 x 15.2 cm. 27 illustrations. Red cloth.

Prov.: Inscribed on front fly-leaf: To my friend / George B. Thummel / with the compliments of the / author / Frank J Burkley /.

Ref.: Howes B989

Burkley was one of the pioneers of Omaha and his volume contains many fascinating details.

490   BURLEND, REBECCA

A TRUE PICTURE OF EMIGRATION: OR FOURTEEN YEARS IN THE INTERIOR OF NORTH AMERICA; BEING A FULL AND IMPARTIAL ACCOUNT OF THE VARIOUS DIFFICULTIES AND ULTIMATE SUCCESS OF AN ENGLISH FAMILY WHO EMIGRATED FROM BARWICK-IN-ELMET, NEAR LEEDS, IN THE YEAR 1831. LONDON: PUBLISHED BY G. BERGER.

[3]–62. 17.7 x 10.9 cm. Buff printed wrappers with title on front wrapper and advertisements on verso of back wrapper.

Ref.: Buck 235; Clark III 19; Howes B992; Hubach p. 70.

The greater part of the pamphlet is devoted to

the trials and experiences of the first few years [in Pike County, Illinois] and it is an excellent picture of frontier life.—Buck

The work was published in 1848. While Mrs. Burlend is the presumed author, and undoubtedly supplied most of the information, the work was probably composed by her son.

491 BURLINGTON, IOWA. Citizens

THE SEMI-CENTENNIAL OF IOWA. A RECORD OF THE COMMEMORATION OF THE FIFTIETH ANNIVERSARY OF THE SETTLEMENT OF IOWA, HELD AT BURLINGTON, JUNE 1, 1883. BURLINGTON: HAWKEYE BOOK AND JOB PRINTING HOUSE, 1883.

[1]–104. 21 x 14 cm. Blue printed wrappers, with title as above within decorative border on front wrapper.

Ref.: Mott (*Iowa*) p. 65

Included is an historical address by A. C. Dodge.

492 BURLINGTON & MISSOURI RIVER RAILROAD COMPANY

[Broadside] LAND DEPARTMENT, BURLINGTON & MISSOURI R. R. CO. IN NEBRASKA . . . PREMIUMS FOR LAND IMPROVEMENTS. SPLENDID INDUCEMENTS OFFERED BY THE BURLINGTON & MISSOURI RIVER RAILROAD COMPANY IN NEBRASKA, TO ACTUAL SETTLERS WHO BUY LAND ON TEN YEARS' CREDIT AT ANY TIME BETWEEN JANUARY 1ST AND DECEMBER 31ST, 1873 . . . APPLY TO GEO. S. HARRIS, LAND COMMISSIONER, FOR IOWA LANDS, AT BURLINGTON, IOWA; FOR NEBRASKA LANDS, AT LINCOLN, NEBRASKA . . . W. H. WISNER, GENERAL AGENT, 59 SOUTH CLARK STREET, CHICAGO, ILL.

Broadside, 28.4 x 20 cm. Text, 24.8 x 17.2 cm.

Ref.:

Probably printed at Burlington in 1872.

493 BURLINGTON & MISSOURI RIVER RAILROAD COMPANY

[Wrapper title] VIEWS AND DESCRIPTIONS OF BURLINGTON & MISSOURI RIVER RAILROAD LANDS, WITH IMPORTANT INFORMATION CONCERNING WHERE AND HOW TO SELECT AND PURCHASE FARMS IN IOWA AND NEBRASKA, ON TEN YEARS' CREDIT. ISSUED BY THE LAND DEPARTMENT OF THE BURLINGTON & MO. RIVER RAILROAD CO., BURLINGTON, IOWA, AND LINCOLN, NEB. ACRES, BLACKMAR & CO., STEAM PRINTERS, BURLINGTON, IOWA.

[1–40]. 24.3 x 18 cm. 20 plates. Dark green cloth, with original blue wrappers bound in, title in gilt on front cover.

Ref.: Howes B994; *Railway Economics* p. 187

Published in 1872. The copy described in *Railway Economics* comprises 42 pages.

494 BURLINGTON & MISSOURI RIVER RAILROAD COMPANY

HOW TO GO WEST. A GUIDE TO SOUTHERN IOWA, NEBRASKA, KANSAS, CALIFORNIA, AND THE WHOLE GREAT WEST . . . CHICAGO: HORTON & LEONARD, 1872.

[1]–73, [74 blank]. 21.5 x 11.9 cm. Three folding maps, seven page maps, and plates. Glazed pink printed wrappers with title on front wrapper. In a red cloth case.

Ref.: Howes H699

495 BURNET, DAVID G.

REVIEW OF THE LIFE OF GEN. SAM HOUSTON, AS RECENTLY PUBLISHED IN WASHINGTON CITY, BY J. T. TOWERS . . . GALVESTON: NEWS POWER PRESS PRINT, 1852.

[1]–15, [16 blank]. 21 x 13.5 cm. Removed from bound volume, unbound. In a green cloth case.

Ref.: Raines p. 37; Winkler 295

Comprises a bitter attack on Houston and his pretensions. "Harsh, but not without provocation."—Raines

496 BURNETT, PETER H.

RECOLLECTIONS AND OPINIONS OF AN OLD PIONEER. NEW YORK: D. APPLETON AND COMPANY, 1880.

[i]–[xiv, xiv blank], [1]–448, [449–54 advertisements]. 19.5 x 12.5 cm. Brown cloth, gilt and black border and centre panel on front cover, blind borders on back cover, title in gilt and black on backstrip.

Ref.: Cowan p. 86; Howes B1000; Smith 1282

Burnett's autobiography includes an account of his trip across the country in 1843.

497 BURNEY, DAVID

AUTOGRAPH DOCUMENT, SIGNED. 1801 March 2, no place. One page, 13.3 x 18.8 cm.

Bill and receipt for payment of account of Philip Nolan with David Burney for care of horses. The payment was made by William Dunbar for Nolan. Docketed on the verso by Nolan.

498 BURNHAM, FREDERICK R.

SCOUTING ON TWO CONTINENTS . . . GARDEN CITY: DOUBLEDAY, PAGE & COMPANY, 1926.

[i]–[xxiv, xxiv blank], 1–370. 22.7 x 15.2 cm. 31 illustrations listed. Maroon cloth, yellow top.

Prov.: Inscribed in pencil on front endleaf: From Walter Grey / Dec. 25—1926 / Frederick S. Dellenbaugh /.

Ref.: Adams 159; Adams (*Ramp. Herd*) 373; Dobie p. 85

The first seven chapters relate adventures in the United States, particularly the Southwest. Tipped in at the front is a Typewritten Letter, signed, by John Hays Hammond. 1926 September 17, Lookout Hill, Gloucester, Mass. One page, 19.9 x 14.7 cm. To Frederick S. Dellenbaugh. The letter relates to the book. Hammond wrote a three-page foreword.

499 BURNHAM, JOHN H.

HISTORY OF BLOOMINGTON AND NORMAL, IN MC LEAN COUNTY, ILLINOIS. BLOOMINGTON: J. H. BURNHAM, 1879.

[1]–[145], [146 blank]. 23.9 x 15.7 cm. Portrait, plate, and text illustrations. Brown cloth, blind embossed sides, title in gilt on backstrip.

Prov.: Inscribed on blank leaf at front: Bloomington—Ill— / Dec. 20 / 1888. / With the kind regards of / J. H. Burnham /.

Ref.: Bradford 666

The history of Bloomington and Normal, herewith given, was written for the history of McLean County, Illinois, published by Le Baron & Co., of Chicago and appears in the body of that work . . . —Preface

500 BURNS, B. J., and Others

DOCUMENT, SIGNED by B. J. Burns, S. F. Chadwick, and others. 1851, December 23, Scottsburg, Oregon. Three pages, 25 x 19.6 cm.

Subscription for the benefit of Loren L. Williams, with the names of forty-two subscribers and the amounts of their contributions. Inserted in Manuscript Journals of Loren L. Williams, Volume I.

501 BURNS, WALTER N.

THE SAGA OF BILLY THE KID . . . GARDEN CITY: DOUBLEDAY, PAGE AND COMPANY, 1926.

[i–x, x blank], 1–322. 20.5 x 13.8 cm. Pictorial endpapers. Green cloth, orange top, uncut.

Ref.: Adams 161; Dobie p. 140; Dykes 107; Rader 547; Rascoe 308; Saunders 2786

502 BURR, AARON

AUTOGRAPH LETTER IN CYPHER. [1806] July 22, no place. Two pages, 34.5 x 22.6 cm. Silked. To James Wilkinson.

An important letter relating to plans for "Some grand Project" between Burr and Wilkinson. At the foot of the second page and extending onto the third page there is the following unsigned statement by Wilkinson: I do Solemnly swear that this is the Original letter, delivered to me by Samuel Swartwout from Aaron Burr, at Natchitoches about the 5th or 8th of October last, and that the annexed letter from the Said Burr, in his proper Manuscript, bearing date

"Philadelphia 25th of July 1806"—was delivered to me at the Same time by the Said Swartwout, that the Cypher from which this letter has been executed was employed between myself and the Said Burr since the Year 1799, or 1800—And I do further more Swear, that I do not recollect the purport of the letter refferred to by the said Burr, as bearing the date the 13th May last, as I have kept no Copy of it, but Suppose it was one of Several Short notes written to him with the design to extract from him the particulars of Some grand Project, which he mentioned to me in general terms for the first and only time, during his visit to St Louis in the Autumn 1805—And I do further Swear that this letter contains the first and only intimation I have ever received from the Said Burr, except by his Agents, Swartwout and Bollman, of any intention hostile to the Laws or Government of the United States— And I further Swear that the letter which I received by Doctor Erick Bollman from the Said Burr is a Duplicate of this letter, with the following exceptions, that it is dated the 29th instead of the 22nd of July, and bears the following Postscript—"\—o / c —o ⌒ | –o ooo — o — equally confidential and better informed on the Subject will hand this Duplicate"—And I further Swear that the preceeding Hieroglyphics represent "Doctor Bollman" in the Cypher herein referred to—

The fourth page bears the following note by Burr: 13. [space] a [space] 45. /, and a docket by Wilkinson: 27 / Burrs Letter / 22nd. July, / by Swarwout /.

For related Burr-Wilkinson manuscript materials, see also the following three numbers and under David Burney (Number 497), Beverly Chew (Number 673), Julian Depestre (Number 1056), Jacob Dunbaugh (Number 1166), Gideon Granger (Number 1613), John W. Hunt (Number 2014), F. Lintot (Number 2505), John McKee (Numbers 2622 to 2625), John Marshall (Number 2690), John Minor (Number 2825), Philip Nolan (Number 3025), United States, Congress, House (Number 4372), and James Wilkinson (Numbers 4663 to 4670).

503 BURR, AARON

AUTOGRAPH LETTER IN CYPHER. [1806] July 29, no place. Two pages, 34.5 x 22.6 cm. To James Wilkinson.

The duplicate referred to by Wilkinson, with the added sentence about Dr. Bollman. The fourth page bears the following by Burr: 13. [space] 45. /, and the following docket by Wilkinson: Burrs Letter / July 29th. 07 / By Bollman /.

504 BURR, AARON

DOCUMENT, SIGNED. 1807 January 16, Cole's Creek, Louisiana Territory. Three pages, 25.8 x 20.8 cm. Silked.

Agreement for a meeting between Aaron Burr and Acting Governor Cowles Meade and for the safety of the two principals and their parties. Signed for Governor Meade by W. B. Shields and G. Poindexter, by Aaron Burr for himself, and by Thomas Fitzgerald as witness.

Burr was in flight after the fall of Blennerhasset's Island. The result of the meeting arranged above was Burr's appearance before Judge Rodney who bound him over for action by a Grand Jury.

505 BURR, AARON

THE PRIVATE JOURNAL OF AARON BURR . . . ROCHESTER, N.Y., 1903.*

[1–6, 6 blank], i–xiv, [xv–xvi blank], 1–501, [502 blank]. [i–iv], 1–503, [504 blank]. 24 x 16 cm. Frontispiece portraits. Two volumes, blue boards, blue cloth backstrips, printed white paper labels, uncut.
Prov.: Presentation copy from the owner, W. K. Bixby, to the Hon. Willis Vickery.
Ref.: Howes B1011
Limited to 250 copies.

506 BURR, AARON, *Defendant*

THE TRIAL OF COL. AARON BURR, ON AN INDICTMENT FOR TREASON, BEFORE THE CIRCUIT COURT OF THE UNITED STATES, HELD IN RICHMOND, (VIRGINIA), MAY TERM, 1807: INCLUDING THE ARGUMENTS AND DECISIONS ON ALL THE MOTIONS MADE DURING THE EXAMINATION AND TRIAL, AND ON THE MOTION FOR AN ATTACHMENT AGAINST GEN. WILKINSON. TAKEN IN SHORT-HAND BY T. CARPENTER. WASHINGTON CITY: PRINTED BY WESTCOTT & CO., 1807–1808.

[*]², [A]–S⁴, [T]², [A2]–R2⁴. ([T2] blank.) [A]–S⁴, T³, U–Ll⁴, Mmm². [A]–Eee⁴, Fff⁴⁺¹, [A]–G⁴. (G4 blank.) [1]–[148], [1–2 blank], [3]–135, [136 blank], [137 publishers' note], [138 blank]. [1]–465, [466 blank]. [1]–418, [i]–l, [1–4], [5–6 blank]. 22.7 x 13.6 cm. Three volumes, gray boards, new tan paper backs, new printed white paper labels, uncut. Resewn, lacks front endleaf in Vol. III, some pencil notes.
Ref.: Howes B1013; Sabin 9433; Shaw & Shoemaker 13732
The earlier of two contemporary accounts, the work details the most exciting trial held in this country during the first half of the nineteenth century. Chief Justice Marshall's rulings on aspects of treason had far-reaching effects;

their influence was observable in trials held during and after World War II.

507 BURROUGHS & MEERS, *Publishers*

POCKET ALMANAC AND RECEIPT BOOK FOR 1867. CHICAGO: PRINTED BY BURROUGHS & MEERS, 1866.

[1]–112. 10.5 x 7.1 cm. Yellow printed wrappers with title on front wrapper, advertisements on verso of front and recto and verso of back wrapper.
Ref.:
The text is interspersed with numerous advertisements.

508 BURROWS, JOHN M. D.

FIFTY YEARS IN IOWA: BEING . . . PERSONAL REMINISCENCES OF . . . MEN AND EVENTS, SOCIAL LIFE, INDUSTRIAL INTERESTS, PHYSICAL DEVELOPMENT, AND COMMERCIAL PROGRESS OF DAVENPORT AND SCOTT COUNTY, DURING THE PERIOD FROM 1838 TO 1888. DAVENPORT, IOWA: GLASS & COMPANY, 1888.

[i]–[xii, xii blank], [1]–182. 18.5 x 12.5 cm. Two portraits, unlisted. Brown cloth, blind embossed bands on covers, title in gilt on front cover.
Ref.: Howes B1023; Mott (*Iowa*) p. 84
One of the best books of pioneer reminiscences.—Mott

509 BURT, MARTIN

NEW TRAVELS TO THE WEST. BEING AN EXTRACT OF A LETTER FROM MARTIN BURT TO AARON BURT. DATED JANUARY 6, 1817. PRINTED FOR THE PUBLISHER. 1818.

[1]⁸. [1]–16. 15.7 x 11.5 cm. Stabbed, unbound, uncut. In a blue half morocco case.
Ref.:
Aaron Burt was a distant cousin of Martin. He had settled in Manlius, New York. The pamphlet may have been printed at Batavia. Martin Burt reports here on his experiences in the Illinois-Missouri country with great enthusiasm. However, when it came to settling down, he chose Portage County, Ohio.

No other copy of this pamphlet has been located.

510 BURT, SILAS W., & EDWARD L. BERTHOUD

THE ROCKY MOUNTAIN GOLD REGIONS CONTAINING SKETCHES OF ITS HISTORY, GEOGRAPHY, BOTANY, GEOLOGY, MINERALOGY AND GOLD MINES, AND THEIR PRESENT OPERATIONS . . . DENVER CITY, J. T.: PUBLISHED BY THE ROCKY MOUNTAIN NEWS PRINTING CO., 1861.

[1]–132, [133–40 advertisements]. 19.9 x 12.8 cm. Rebound in dark brown calf, black leather label on backstrip, by The Lakeside Press.

Ref.: Howes B1026; McMurtrie & Allen (*Colorado*) 15; Wagner-Camp 369; Wilcox pp. 19–20

Although two maps are mentioned on the title-page, there are no known copies with the maps present originally. According to a news article in the *Daily Rocky Mountain News* for November 13, 1860, the map of the Quartz Mining Region of the Rocky Mountains by Burt and Berthoud was offered separately for twenty-five cents.

Mr. James G. Hodgson, formerly of the Colorado State University Library, has studied this work carefully and has concluded that this is a unique copy, each of the known copies differing in the number and arrangement of advertisements at the end. Mr. Hodgson's conclusions have been published with a facsimile edition of the work. See next item.

511 BURT, SILAS W., and EDWARD L. BERTHOUD

[Map] SKETCH / OF THE / QUARTZ MINING RE-GION / OF THE / ROCKY MOUNTAIN, / INCLUDING THE ADJACENT COUNTRY WITH THE PRINCIPAL ROADS, STREAMS, & TOWNS / BY / S. W. BURT & E. L. BERTHOUD, / CIVIL AND MINING ENG^{RS}. / CENTRAL CITY & GOLDEN CITY / 1860. / [ornamental rule] / ROCKY MOUNTAIN NEWS PRINTING C.^{O} DENVER CITY. / [lower left, below neat line:] LITH OF ED.^{W} MENDEL, CHICAGO. / *Inset:* Sketch of Routes to the Rocky Mountain Gold Regions / Burt & Berthoud Civil Engineers. / 9.9 x 20.2 cm. No scale given.

Map, 48.6 x 66.8 cm. Scale not given.
Ref.:

512 BURTON, SIR RICHARD F.

THE CITY OF THE SAINTS AND ACROSS THE ROCKY MOUNTAINS TO CALIFORNIA . . . LONDON: LONG-MAN, GREEN, LONGMAN, AND ROBERTS, 1861.

[i]–[xii], [1]–707, [708 colophon]. 22.2 x 14.5 cm. 21 illustrations and maps listed. Green cloth, uncut, advertisements on inner covers.
Prov.: Bookplate of J. A. Froude. Embossed stamp through title-leaf and following leaf: Presented / by / the / Publishers /.
Ref.: Adams 167; Bradford 680; Cowan p. 87; Howes B1033; Sabin 9497; Wagner-Camp 370

513 BURTON'S GENTLEMAN'S MAGAZINE

BURTON'S GENTLEMAN'S MAGAZINE. VOLUME VI [–VII]. FROM JANUARY TO JUNE [–FROM JULY TO DECEMBER] . . . PHILADELPHIA: PUBLISHED BY WILLIAM E. BURTON[–GEORGE R. GRAHAM], 1840.

[i]–iv, [11]–194. [i]–iv, [11]–198. 24.7 x 15.4 cm. Engraved frontispiece and title-page, thirteen engraved plates and several cuts in text, unlisted. Two volumes (twelve parts) bound together, contemporary marbled boards with green calf backstrip and corners, gilt, sprinkled edges.
Ref.: Wagner-Camp 82

Contains Edgar Allan Poe's "The Journal of Julius Rodman." Pages [44]–47, [80]–85, [109]–113, [179]–183, [206]–210, [255]–259.

514 BUSBY, ALLIE B.

TWO SUMMERS AMONG THE MUSQUAKIES, RELATING TO THE EARLY HISTORY OF THE SAC AND FOX TRIBE . . . VINTON, IOWA: HERALD BOOK AND JOB ROOMS, 1886.

[i]–viii, [9]–238. 19.1 x 13.1 cm. Dark brown cloth, blind fillet borders and corner ornaments with quotation in gilt on front cover, title in gilt on backstrip.
Ref.: Howes B1037; Mott (*Iowa*) p. 64

Errata slip, 6.5 x 13 cm., inserted following title-leaf.

515 BUSHNELL, JOSEPH P.

BUSHNELL'S BUSINESS & RESIDENCE DIRECTORY OF COUNCIL BLUFFS, CONTAINING A HISTORY AND GENERAL REVIEW OF THE CITY AND WHAT IT CONTAINS. ALSO A MAP OF CITY AND RAILROADS. JULY 1ST, 1868! . . . COUNCIL BLUFFS, IOWA: NONPAREIL PRINTING COMPANY, 1898[!].

[1]–120. 22.2 x 14 cm. Map: [Map of Council Bluffs] on page 27, 7.3 x 9.6 cm. No scale given. Tan printed boards with brown cloth backstrip, title at top of front cover, advertisements below, advertisements on back cover.
Refs.: Howes B1044

The title-page is misdated 1898 instead of 1868. The map mentioned on the title-page does not accompany the book.

516 BUSHNELL, WILLIAM H.

PRAIRIE FIRE! A TALE OF EARLY ILLINOIS . . . CHICAGO: WALTER B. SLOAN, 1854.

[1]–96. 22 x 14.6 cm. Contemporary brown marbled boards, black roan backstrip.
Prov.: Inscribed in pencil on front endleaf: Josephine L. Palmer / From / R. G. S. / Signature in pencil on page [3]: Josephine L. Palmer / Fayette / Maine /. Manuscript note in pencil in unidentified hand at foot of page 96: I could not send this No / sooner on acct. of delay / in printing. /
Ref.: AII (*Chicago*) 116 see; Wright II 438 see

An apparently hitherto unnoted 1854 edition. Both AII (*Chicago*) and Wright list only an 1855 edition, with the same collation.

517 BUTLER, JAMES D.

NEBRASKA. ITS CHARACTERISTICS AND PROSPECTS
. . .

[1]–36, [i]–ii, [37–8]. 19.7 x 13.4 cm. Illustrations in text. Sewn, unbound.

Ref.: AII (*Nebraska*) 454; Howes B1054

The copyright notice in favor of G. S. Harris dated 1873 appears at the foot of page [3]. No place of printing is indicated, but the advertisement of George S. Harris, Land Commissioner, at Burlington, Iowa, appears on page [37]. The work may have been printed in Iowa.

Editions: [Nebraska City, 1871].

518 BUTLER, SIR WILLIAM F.

FAR OUT: ROVINGS RETOLD . . . LONDON: WM. ISBISTER, LIMITED, 1881.

[i]–xx, [1]–329, [330 advertisements], ii–iii advertisements. 17.5 x 11.9 cm. Olive pictorial cloth, top edges uncut, partly unopened.

Ref.: Smith 1323

519 BUTLER, SIR WILLIAM F.

THE GREAT LONE LAND: A NARRATIVE OF TRAVEL AND ADVENTURE IN THE NORTHWEST OF AMERICA . . . LONDON: SAMPSON, LOW, MARSTON, LOW, & SEARLE, 1872.

[i]–[xii, xii blank], [1]–388. 21.7 x 14.1 cm. Six illustrations and one map listed. Pictorial brown cloth, uncut.

Ref.: Smith 1326

The Appendix contains Butler's report of his journey from Fort Garry to Rocky Mountain House and back during the winter of 1870–71. It had been printed previously, in 1871, as an official document of the Canadian Government.

Editions: Ottawa, 1871.

520 BUTLER, SIR WILLIAM F.

REPORT BY LIEUTENANT BUTLER, (69TH REGT.) OF HIS JOURNEY FROM FORT GARRY TO ROCKY MOUNTAIN HOUSE AND BACK, UNDER INSTRUCTIONS FROM THE LIEUT.-GOVERNOR OF MANITOBA, DURING THE WINTER OF 1870–71. OTTAWA: PRINTED BY THE TIMES PRINTING & PUBLISHING CO., 1871.

[i–ii], [1]–29, [30 blank]. 23.9 x 15 cm. Rebound in red half morocco. Manuscript pagination, 209–39.

Ref.: Howes B1061

The *Report* appears also as an appendix to Butler's *The Great Lone Land* . . . London, 1872.

There is another separate printing, without title-page, in twenty-four pages.

521 BUTLER, SIR WILLIAM F.

SIR WILLIAM BUTLER AN AUTOBIOGRAPHY . . . LONDON: CONSTABLE AND COMPANY, LTD., 1911.*

[i]–[xii, xii blank], [1]–476. 22.9 x 14.6 cm. Four plates, two maps. Blue cloth, uncut.

Ref.:

522 BUTLER, SIR WILLIAM F.

THE WILD NORTH LAND: BEING THE STORY OF A WINTER JOURNEY, WITH DOGS, ACROSS NORTHERN NORTH AMERICA . . . LONDON: SAMPSON LOW, MARSTON, LOW, & SEARLE, 1873.

[i]–[xii, xii blank], [1]–358, [359–60 blank], [1]–48 advertisements. 21.7 x 14.1 cm. 16 illustrations and one map listed. Green cloth, uncut.

Ref.: Smith 1339

523 BUTTERFIELD, CONSUL W.

HISTORY OF THE GIRTYS BEING A CONCISE ACCOUNT OF THE GIRTY BROTHERS—THOMAS, SIMON, JAMES AND GEORGE, AND OF THEIR HALF-BROTHER, JOHN TURNER—ALSO OF THE PART TAKEN BY THEM IN LORD DUNMORE'S WAR, IN THE WESTERN BORDER WAR OF THE REVOLUTION, AND IN THE INDIAN WAR OF 1790–95 . . . CINCINNATI: ROBERT CLARKE & CO., 1890.

[i]–[xiv, xiv blank], [1]–[426]. 23.1 x 15.3 cm. Green cloth.

Ref.: Bradford 704; Howes B1066

Butterfield's liveliest work contains considerable material about Indian captivities, including the notorious affairs of Knight and Slover.

524 BUTTERFIELD, CONSUL W.

HISTORY OF THE DISCOVERY OF THE NORTHWEST BY JOHN NICOLET IN 1634. WITH A SKETCH OF HIS LIFE . . . CINCINNATI: ROBERT CLARKE & CO., 1881.

[i]–[x, x blank], 11–113, [114 blank], [1]–8 advertisements. 19.6 x 13.7 cm. Green cloth.

Ref.: Bradford 701; Howes B1065

525 BUTTERFIELD, F. E., & C. M. RUNDLETT, *Compilers*

DIRECTORY OF THE CITY OF DALLAS, CAREFULLY ARRANGED AND PREPARED . . . FOR THE YEAR 1875.

[1]–140. 22.6 x 14.8 cm. Portrait of J. C. McCoy. Printed white boards, black cloth back, advertisements on outer and inner covers and recto of front endleaf.

Ref.: Howes B1069; Winkler & Friend 3373
Published at Dallas in 1874.

526 BUTTERFIELD, JOHN

[Broadside] [Map:] SKELETON MAP OF THE OVERLAND MAIL ROUTE TO CALIFORNIA. ROUTE ADOPTED BY THE DEPARTMENT TRACED IN GREEN. ROUTE PROPOSED BY JOHN BUTTERFIELD AND OTHERS (WHO WERE THE LOWEST BIDDERS) IN RED. [20.8 x 33.4 cm. No scale given.] [26 lines]

Broadside, 43.5 x 33.4 cm. Text, 40.5 x 33.4 cm.

Ref.: Conkling & Conkling: *The Butterfield Overland Mail* . . . Glendale, California, 1947, Vol. I pp. 103–20.

The upper half consists of the map described above while the lower half comprises the text. In the text, Butterfield presses the advantages of his route over that chosen. The broadside was circulated by parties dissatisfied with the decision of Postmaster General Brown of Tennessee to take the road through Tennessee and bypass northern cities.

No place of printing is indicated. The date is 1857.

527 BUTTERWICK, THOMAS

THE CHRISTIAN CITIZEN . . . KEWANEE: ADVERTISER BOOK AND JOB OFFICE, 1862.

[1]–110. 12.9 x 8.3 cm. Contemporary marbled boards, rebacked with black cloth.

Prov.: Inscription inside back cover: This book written by grand-/pa Butterwick—first book published in Kewanee. / A B / [underline] /

Ref.:

528 BUTTRICK, DANIEL S.

ANTIQUITIES OF THE CHEROKEE INDIANS . . . VINITA: INDIAN CHIEFTAIN, 1884.

[i]–vi, [1]–20. 23.3 x 16 cm. Buff printed wrappers with title on front wrapper.

Ref.: Hargrett (*Oklahoma*) 522; Howes B1072

The editor was William Potter Ross.

529 BUTTRICK, TILLY, JR.

VOYAGES, TRAVELS AND DISCOVERIES OF TILLY BUTTRICK, JR. BOSTON: PRINTED FOR THE AUTHOR. JOHN PUTNAM, PRINTER. 1831.

[1]–58, [59–60 blank]. 17.6 x 11.2 cm. Original or contemporary blue wrappers, title on front cover in manuscript. In a blue half morocco case.

Ref.: Bay 345; Howes B1073; Jones 912; Rusk I, p. 121; Sabin 9679; Thomson 148

Rusk condemns the work as being "perhaps as dull as could well have been written" yet a careful reading reveals it as a good account by a casual traveller which tells much of interest about the hardships of pioneer life. Buttrick made several journeys through the Ohio and Mississippi valleys as far as New Orleans and covered a large part of the old West.

530 BUTTRICKE, GEORGE

AFFAIRS AT FORT CHARTRES, 1768–1781. ALBANY: J. MUNSELL, 1864.

[1]–12 23.1 x 18.3 cm. Rebound in half maroon morocco, gilt top, original tan printed wrappers bound in.

Prov.: John G. Shea's copy with two notes by him in pencil on the verso of front endleaf and verso of original front wrapper.

Ref.: Buck 18

The original work comprises a series of letters by Ensign Buttricke to Captain Charles Barnsley. It is extra-illustrated with the following materials:

Lithographic portrait of Governor John Reynolds of Illinois.

Photograph of John G. Shea, inscribed and signed.

Facsimile of Hutchins' *Plan of the Several Villages in the Illinois Country.*

An unidentified eight-page article about Fort Chartres excerpted from a magazine.

Autograph Letter, signed, by John Wilkins. 1770 July 28, Fort Chartres. One page, 24.1 x 18.6 cm. To James Rumsey. Regarding the quality of whiskey left by a Mr. Bradley. Wilkins was the British commandant at Fort Chartres when the letter was written.

531 BYRNE, WILLIAM S.

DIRECTORY OF GRASS VALLEY TOWNSHIP FOR 1865 CONTAINING A HISTORICAL SKETCH OF GRASS VALLEY, OF ALLISON RANCH, AND FOREST SPRINGS . . . SAN FRANCISCO: PRINTED BY CHARLES F. ROBBINS AND COMPANY, 1865.

[iii]–xxix, xxx blank], [1]–144. 22.3 x 14.3 cm. Green printed boards, with advertisements on inner and outer covers, black roan backstrip.

Ref.: Blumann & Thomas 2228; Bradford 713; Cowan p. 90; Howes B1080

Pages [i–ii] may be missing, although page [iii] bears a signature 1; possibly the publisher counted the front cover as pages [i–ii].

C

532 CABET, ETIENNE

COLONY OR REPUBLIC OF ICARIA IN THE UNITED STATES OF AMERICA, ITS HISTORY. ICARIAN SYSTEM OR DOCTRINE.—SOCIAL AND POLITICAL ORGANIZATION.—ICARIAN COMMUNE.—ADVANTAGES OF COMMUNITY.—ICARIAN CONSTITUTION—PRINCIPAL LAWS OF THE COLONY.—MODE AND CONDITIONS OF ADMISSION . . . NAUVOO (ILLINOIS): ICARIAN PRINTING OFFICE, 1852.

[i–ii, ii blank], [1]–[20], [21–2 blank]. 26 x 16.2 cm. Gray-green wrappers bound into brown cloth.

Prov.: U.S. Geological Survey Library stamps, C. G. Littell bookplate.

Ref.: Byrd 1823; Howes C6; Littell 520; Sabin 9783

One of the most important pamphlets relating to the Icarian Illinois experiment.

533 CACKLER, CHRISTIAN

[Caption title] RECOLLECTIONS OF AN OLD SETTLER . . .

[1]–38. 22 x 14 cm. Peach wrappers.

Prov.: Pencil note on front wrapper by Wallace H. Cathcart. Numerals in ink in upper left corner: 466 /.

Ref.: Howes C13

According to the text, the *Recollections* of early pioneer life in Ohio, where the author settled in 1804, was written in 1870. There is no date of publication given in this edition, but the front wrapper of the second edition notes the original edition was published in 1874. Howes states the place of printing was Kent, Ohio.

534 CADWALADER, ALLEN

MAP AND GUIDE TO THE WHITE PINE MINES AND THE REGION OF COUNTRY ADJACENT, IN EASTERN NEVADA, WITH COMPLETE DATA TO APRIL, 1869, REGARDING THE TOPOGRAPHY, CLIMATE, GEOLOGICAL FORMATION, CHARACTER OF ORES, VEIN SYSTEM OF THE DISTRICT, TABLES OF ALTITUDES, DISTANCES, ETC. DESCRIPTIONS OF TOWNS, MINES, MILL SITES, AND OTHER IMPROVEMENTS . . . SAN FRANCISCO: H. H. BANCROFT & COMPANY, APRIL, 1869.

[1]–31, [32 blank and pasted to inner back cover]. 16.4 x 10.1 cm. Two maps on one sheet. [At left:] Map / of the / White Pine Range, / Compiled by A. Cadwalader / Published by / H. H. Bancroft & Company, / San Francisco April, 1869. / Lith. Geo. H. Baker, / 408 California St. / Scale, —11 6/10 Miles to the inch. 61.2 x 14.4 cm. [At right:] Map / of the / White Pine / Mining District, / Compiled by A. Cadwalader / Published by / H. H. Bancroft & Company, / San Francisco April, 1869. / Lith. Geo. H. Baker, /408 California St. / Scale,—4 inches to the Mile. 61.2 x 37.8 cm. Whole map including border: 62 x 55 cm. Black cloth, title stamped (possibly in silver) on front cover: Cadwalader's / Map and Guide to the / White Pine Mines /. Waterstained. In a brown cloth case.

Ref.:

Advertisement of publisher inside front cover.

535 CADY, JOHN H.

ARIZONA'S YESTERDAY. BEING THE NARRATIVE OF JOHN H. CADY, PIONEER. REWRITTEN AND REVISED BY BASIL DILLON WOON. 1915.*

[1]–127, [128 blank]. 17.4 x 12.3 cm. Illustrations unlisted. Gray-green pictorial wrappers, uncut.

Ref.: Adams (*Ramp. Herd*) 391; Howes C16; Jones 1731

The copyright notice on the verso of the title-page in behalf of John H. Cady is dated 1916. The dedication is dated from Patagonia, Arizona, 1915. Printed at Los Angeles.

536 CAIN, JOSEPH & ARIEH C. BROWER

[COPY RIGHT SECURED] MORMON WAY-BILL, TO THE GOLD MINES, FROM THE PACIFIC SPRINGS, BY THE NORTHERN & SOUTHERN ROUTES, VIZ. FORT HALL, SALT LAKE, AND LOS ANGELOS, INCLUDING SUBLET'S HUDSPETH'S, AND THE VARIOUS CUT-OFF'S; ALSO—FROM LOS ANGELOS TO ST. FRANCISCO, BY COAST ROUTE, WITH THE DISTANCES TO THE DIFFERENT RIVERS IN CALIFORNIA;—TOGETHER WITH IMPORTANT INFORMATION TO EMIGRANTS . . . G. S. L. CITY, DESERET; W. RICHARDS, 1851.

[1]–[40]. 13.5 x 10.7 cm. Stabbed, uncut. In a red cloth case.

Ref.: Auerbach I, 144; Cowan pp. 91–2; Howes C18; Wagner-Camp 196

Howes calls this the "First overland guide printed west of Missouri." Printed on tan paper.

537 CAIRD, SIR JAMES

PRAIRIE FARMING IN AMERICA. WITH NOTES BY THE WAY ON CANADA AND THE UNITED STATES . . . LONDON: LONGMAN, BROWN, GREEN, LONGMANS, & ROBERTS, 1859.

[i]–viii, [1]–128. 18.2 x 12 cm. Map: Emigrant's Railway Guide / Map of North America / [lower centre:] J. Wyld Charing Cross East London. / 14.8 x 21.4 cm. No scale given. *Inset:* British Isles. / on the Same Scale./ 7.9 x 6.3 cm. No scale given. Green cloth, blind embossed borders on sides, title in gilt on backstrip, advertisements on endpapers, uncut.

Ref.: Buck 587; Howes C19

538 CALDWELL, GEORGE R.

"STRINGS" FROM A WYOMING LYRE. WINCHESTER WILLIAM AND OTHER TALES . . . RAWLINS, WYO.: THE JOURNAL PRESS, 1897.

[i–x], [1]–177, [178–80 blank]. ([i] blank, [ii–iii] Contents, [iv] blank, [v–vi] blank, inserted portrait, verso blank, [vii] blank, [viii–ix] The Dutchman's Soliloquy, [x] blank, inserted colored portrait, verso blank, [1] title, 2–177 text, [17?80] blank). 18.2 x 12.4 cm. Illustrations unlisted. Gray printed wrappers with title on front wrapper. In a gray cloth case.

Prov.: Inscribed in pencil on front wrapper: Compliments / of / Author / [flourish] /.

Ref.:

The contents had appeared previously in the *Platte Valley Lyre* of Saratoga, Wyoming, during the 1880's. There is no mention in McMurtrie (*Wyoming*) of a printing plant in Saratoga at that time.

539 CALIFORNIA. Constitution

CONSTITUTION OF THE STATE OF CALIFORNIA. SAN FRANCISCO: PRINTED AT THE OFFICE OF THE ALTA CALIFORNIA, 1849.

[1]–19, [20 blank]. 22.3 x 14.5 cm. Removed from bound volume, unbound.

Ref.: AII (*California*) 89; Cowan p. 140; Greenwood 124; Sabin 9998; Wagner (*California Imprints*) 37

The first appearance of the constitution in book form, and one of the earliest works printed in San Francisco.—Cowan

Governor Riley's proclamation of October 12, 1849, calling for a statewide vote on the Constitution appears on the verso of the title-page. According to Cowan, 8000 copies were printed, in English, and 2000 copies in Spanish.

540 CALIFORNIA. Constitutional Convention

REPORT OF THE DEBATES IN THE CONVENTION IN CALIFORNIA, ON THE FORMATION OF THE STATE CONSTITUTION, IN SEPTEMBER AND OCTOBER, 1849. BY J. ROSS BROWNE. WASHINGTON: PRINTED BY JOHN T. TOWERS, 1850.

[1]–479, [480 blank], [I]–[XLVII], [XLVIII blank]. 22.4 x 14.5 cm. Dark brown cloth, blind embossed sides, title in gilt on backstrip.

Ref.: Bradford 611; Cowan p. 79; Jones 1228

An exhaustive account of the acts and proceedings of this most remarkable assembly. Browne was the only shorthand reporter in California at that time, and for this work he received $10,000.—Cowan

541 CALIFORNIA. GOVERNOR (John Bigler)

GOVERNOR'S ANNUAL MESSAGE TO THE LEGISLATURE OF THE STATE OF CALIFORNIA, ASSEMBLED AT SACRAMENTO, JAN. 1, 1855. B. B. REDDING, STATE PRINTER.

[1]–40. 24.1 x 15.5 cm. Blue printed wrappers with title on front wrapper.

Prov.: Inscribed on front wrapper: Respects of John Bigler /.

Ref.: Cowan p. 53; Howes B445(?)

Printed at Sacramento. Cowan lists also an edition of 110 pages.

542 CALIFORNIA. GOVERNOR (John Bigler)

IN THE SENATE.[ ]SESSION OF 1852. OFFICIAL CORRESPONDENCE BETWEEN THE GOVERNOR OF CALIFORNIA, THE U.S. INDIAN AGENTS FOR CALIFORNIA, AND THE COMMANDER OF THE U. STATES TROOPS NOW IN CALIFORNIA, IN RELATION TO RECENT INDIAN DIFFICULTIES IN THE NORTHERN PART OF THE STATE. [SACRAMENTO(?)] EUGENE CASSERLY, STATE PRINTER.

[1]–37, [38–40 blank]. 18.8 x 13.7 cm. Removed from bound volume, unbound, uncut.

Ref.:

Signed at the end by Governor John Bigler.

Casserly, Callendar y Cia. are listed by Greenwood as printers in San Francisco in 1851, but Casserly alone is not listed. However, Greenwood 318 carries the imprint: [Sacramento]: Eugene Casserly, state printer, 1852.

543 CALIFORNIA. LEGISLATURE. (Committee on Public Buildings and Grounds)

REPORT OF THE COMMITTEE ON PUBLIC BUILDINGS AND GROUNDS, IN RELATION TO THE PERMANENT LOCATION OF THE SEAT OF GOVERNMENT. BY MR. BRODERICK. APRIL 3, 1850.

[1]–16. 22 x 16 cm. Stabbed, unbound.

Prov.: Signature on title-page: Capt. Day 2.ᵈ Inf: /.

Ref.: Greenwood 183; Wagner (*California Imprints*) 176

The place of printing is not given.

The signature on the title-page may be that of Hannibal Day, of Vermont, Brevet Brigadier General in 1865.

544 CALIFORNIA. LEGISLATURE. Senate. (Committee on Internal Improvements)

DOCUMENT NO, 22. IN SENATE.] [SESSION 1855 REPORT OF THE COMMITTEE ON INTERNAL IMPROVEMENTS WITH REFERENCE TO A ROAD ACROSS THE SIERRA NEVADA SUBMITTED APRIL 10, 1855. B. B. REDDING, STATE PRINTER.

[1]–13, [14–6 blank]. 21.8 x 14.3 cm. Removed from bound volume, unbound.

Prov.: Bookplate of Robert E. Cowan.

Ref.: Cowan p. 194; Wagner-Camp 253a see Printed at Sacramento.

The famous "lost" guide book of O. B. Huntington is mentioned in the *Report* as having been published in Salt Lake City in 1854 or 1855 and that "it" was on the way to New York to be reprinted under copyright.—EDG

545 CALIFORNIA. LEGISLATURE. Senate
(Committee on Public Lands)

IN SENATE, SESSION OF 1853. REPORT OF COMMIT-
TEE AND STATEMENT OF CAPTAIN JOSEPH WALKER
BEFORE THEM ON THE PRACTICABILITY OF A RAIL-
ROAD FROM SAN FRANCISCO TO THE UNITED STATES.
GEORGE KERR, STATE PRINTER.

[1]–7, [8 blank]. 24.2 x 15.2 cm. Unbound leaflet, uncut, unopened.
    Ref.:
The *Statement* by the famous Captain
Walker, who commanded one of the very early
expeditions which crossed the plains to California, was unknown until John Howell found a
small cache, less than ten copies.—EDG

546 CALIFORNIA PROVINCE.

REGLAMENTO PARA EL GOBIERNO DE LA PROVINCIA
DE CALIFORNIAS. APROBADO POR S. M. EN REAL
ORDEN DE 24. DE OCTUBRE DE 1781. EN MEXICO:
D. FELIPE DE ZUNIGA Y ONTIVEROS, ANO DE 1784.

[*]¹, [A]–I², [K]¹. [i–ii], 1–[38]. 28 x 19.8 cm.
Bound with Number 9.
    Ref.: Hanna-Powell pp. 16, 20, 24; Howes
C60; Medina (*Mexico*) 7503; Wagner (*SS*) 166;
Zamorano Eighty 62
California was governed by these regulations
until the independence of Mexico. The *Regla-
mento* was issued at San Carlos de Monterrey on
June 1, 1779, by Félipe de Neve. Cowan, Bliss,
and Wagner all chose this as one of the twenty
most important California books.
Leaves [*]1 and K1 may have been printed as
a wraparound. Gathering E is unsigned.

547 CALIFORNIA TERRITORY. Governor
(R. B. Mason)

[Broadside] POLICE REGULATIONS, FOR THE HAR-
BORS OF CALIFORNIA. 1ST. THE HARBOR MASTER
SHALL VISIT ALL MERCHANT VESSELS IMMEDIATELY
ON THEIR ARRIVAL . . . DONE AT MONTEREY, THIS
15TH DAY OF SEPTEMBER, 1847. W. BRANFORD
SHUBRICK, COMD'G U.S. NAVAL FORCES, IN THE
PACIFIC OCEAN. R. B. MASON, COL. 1ST DRAG., AND
GOV. OF CALIFORNIA.

Broadside: 31.2 x 21.5 cm. Text: 27.2 x 15.1 cm.
    Prov.: Templeton Crocker copy.
    Ref.: AII (*California*) 70; Greenwood 92;
Wagner (*California Imprints*) 12

548 CALIFORNIA TERRITORY. Governor
(Bennett Riley)

[Broadside] PROCLAMATION TO THE PEOPLE OF
CALIFORNIA . . . GIVEN AT MONTEREY, CALIFORNIA,
THIS THIRD DAY OF JUNE, A.D. 1849. (SIGNED)
B. RILEY, BREVET BRIG. GENL. U.S.A., AND GOV-
ERNOR OF CALIFORNIA. OFFICIAL—H. W. HALLECK,
BVT. CAPT. AND SECRETARY OF STATE.

Broadside, 41.3 x 33.4 cm. Text: 33.3 x 26.2 cm.
    Ref.: AII (*California*) 92; Greenwood 119;
Wagner (*California Imprints*) 31
Governor Riley's Proclamation called for an
election of delegates to meet at Monterey on
September first to form a state constitution or a
plan for a territorial government, and also assigned the election districts.—EDG

549 CALIFORNIA TERRITORY. State Department

[Broadside] [two columns, left:] CIRCULAR TO
INDIAN AGENTS AND OTHERS. STATE DEPARTMENT
OF THE TERRITORY OF CAL. MONTEREY, SEPTEMBER,
6TH 1847. IN ORDER TO HAVE SOME MEANS OF
DISTINGUISHING BETWEEN THE FRIENDLY INDIANS
OF THE SETTLEMENTS AND THE HORSE THIEVES
AND MARAUDERS . . . H. W. HALLECK, LIEUT. OF
ENG'RS AND SEC'Y OF STATE FOR CALIFORNIA.
[vertical rule separating column at right:] CIR-
CULAR A LOS AGENTES DE INDIOS Y OTROS' DE-
PARTAMTO[!] DE ESTAD[!] DEL TERITORIO[!] DE
CAL. MONTEREY, SETIEMBRE 6 DE 1847. CON EL
EBJETO DE EN CONTRAR ALGUN MODO PARA
DISTINGUIR ENTRE LOS INDIOS AMIGOS . . . H. W.
HALLECK, LENIENTE DE INGEN. Y SCRIO. DE ESTADO
PAR EL TERRITORIO DE CALIFARNIA[!].

Broadside, 16.7 x 20.9 cm. Text, 9.9 x 13.6 cm.
    Ref.:
A hitherto undescribed broadside. Inscribed
on the verso: Monterey Califa / Sept 6ᵗʰ 1847. /
[underline] / Circular to Indian / Agents / [un-
derline] /. The inscription has been written over
an undeciphered pencil note of two lines.

550 CALIFORNIAN

[Newspaper] CALIFORNIAN. VOL. I. MONTEREY,
SATURDAY, FEBRUARY 27[—MARCH, 6], 1847. NO.
28[–29].

[1–4]. [1–4]. 30.8 x 20.8 cm. Two issues, unbound.
    Prov.: Signature at head of March 6 issue:
Capt Wᵐ Merwin /.
    Ref.:
These two issues contain the "Journal of
Thomas O. Larkin, Esq., late U.S. Consul, while
prisoner to the Californians, from the 15th Nov.
1847[!], till his release at the taking of the Pueblo
of Los Angeles." The issue of March 6 contains
Kearny's proclamation on his assumption of the
duties of governor. Although dated March first
in this printing, according to Wagner, the
proclamation was not issued until March 4.
There is also an article about a destructive
storm on the coast of Florida—perhaps the

opening gun in the war between California and Florida over their respective climates.

Published by Colton & Semple.

551 CALKINS, FRANKLIN W.

INDIAN TALES . . . CHICAGO: DONOHUE, HENNE-BERRY & CO.*

[1]–150. 19.4 x 13.1 cm. Seven illustrations, unlisted. Green pictorial cloth, red top.

Ref.:

Copyrighted 1893. Contains a diary of an expedition from Fort Laramie to the Black Hills of Dakota.

552 CALLAWAY, D.

AUTOGRAPH DOCUMENT, SIGNED. 1812 April 21, St. Charles. One page, 12.5 x 19.1 cm. Addressed to Daniel Cogan.

A demand by Callaway that Cogan start legal action to secure money due from Robert Mc-Knight. From the William Clark Papers.

553 CALLISON, JOHN J.

BILL JONES OF PARADISE VALLEY, OKLAHOMA. HIS LIFE AND ADVENTURES FOR OVER FORTY YEARS IN THE GREAT SOUTHWEST . . . KINGFISHER, OKLA-HOMA.

[1]–328. 18.7 x 12.5 cm. 24 illustrations listed. Red cloth.

Ref.: Adams 174; Adams (*Ramp. Herd*) 398; Howes C74a; Rader 573

Printed in Chicago, copyrighted 1914.

554 CALLISON, MINEEBA

AUTOGRAPH LETTER, SIGNED. 1865 August 2, Camp Watson, Oregon. Two pages, 19.6 x 12.1 cm. To Loren L. Williams.

With Autograph Note, signed, by Callison appended. Inserted in Manuscript Journals of Loren L. Williams, Volume III.

555 CALUMET, THE

[Wrapper title] VOL. 1. OFFICE 55 BROADWAY, N.Y. NO. 1. THE CALUMET. CONTENTS . . . JOHN BEESON, EDITOR AND PUBLISHER.

[1]–32. 23.5 x 14.5 cm. Two portraits. Yellow printed wrappers with title on front wrapper, text on verso of front wrapper, map on recto of back wrapper, prospectus on verso of back wrapper.

Ref.:

The Calumet No. 1, published in 1860, contains the first installment of the autobiography of John Beeson. Only this first number was published.

556 CAMP, C. ROLLIN

FIRST ANNUAL DIRECTORY OF FORT SCOTT. FOR 1875. COMPRISING A COMPLETE DIRECTORY OF THE CITY . . . ALSO A HISTORY OF FORT SCOTT . . . FORT SCOTT: PRINTED AT THE MONITOR STEAM PUBLISHING HOUSE, 1875.

[1]–[130], single advertisement leaves inserted before pages 9 and 73, two leaves of advertisement inserted before title-leaf and two at end. 22 x 13.7 cm. Yellow wrappers, bound into half dark blue crinkled calf, marbled sides, printed yellow paper label on front cover.

Ref.:

The first Fort Scott, Kansas, directory appeared in 1865.

557 CAMPBELL, ALBERT H.

LETTER FROM ALBERT H. CAMPBELL TO HON. GUY M. BRYAN, OF TEXAS, IN RELATION TO THE PACIFIC RAILROAD. WASHINGTON: 1858.

[1]–18. 23.6 x 15 cm. Stabbed, unbound, uncut, unopened.

Ref.: Railway Economics p. 281

558 [CAMPBELL, ALBERT H.]

[Caption title] . . . REPORTS UPON THE PACIFIC WAGON ROADS CONSTRUCTED UNDER THE DIRECTION OF THAT DEPARTMENT [INTERIOR] . . .

[1]–125, [126 blank]. 23 x 14.8 cm. Six maps. Map: Department of the Interior / Pacific Wagon Roads, / [decorative rule] / Map / of the / Fort Ridgely & South Pass Road / To accompany the report of / William. H. Nobles, Superintendent, / by Samuel. A. Medary, Eng^r / 1858. / T. S. Wagner's Lith, Philad^a / [upper right:] (Sen. Ex Doc. N° 36–Ho. Ex: Doc. N° 108—2^d Sess: 35 Cong.) / [lower left:] Drawn by John R. Key / 46.7 x 82 cm. Scale: 8 miles to one inch. Map: Department of the Interior / Pacific Wagon Roads. / [rule] / Preliminary Map / of the / Central Division / Ft. Kearney South Pass & Honey Lake / Wagon-Road / Surveyed and worked under the Direction of / F. W. Lander, Sup^t / by / W. H. Wagner, Eng^r / 1857–58. / Scale / [diagrammatic scale: about 9 1/2 miles to one inch.] / T. S. Wagner's Lith. Philad^a / [upper right:] (Sen. Ex: Doc. N° 36–Ho. Ex: Doc. N° 108–2^d Sess: 35' Cong.) / 52.1 x 86.3 cm. Scale as above. Map: Dep^t of the Interior / Pacific Wagon Roads. / [rule] / Map / of the / Fort Kearney South Pass / and / Honey Lake Road / Surveyed under the direction of John Kirk, Sup^{dt} / by F. A. Bishop Engineer / 1857 / Scale 1/720,000 / Scale of Statute Miles / [diagrammatic scale: 11 1/2 miles to one inch] / Thos S. Wagner's Lith Philad^a / 54.2 x 88.3 cm. Scale as above. Map: Dep^t of the Interior / Pa-

cific Wagon Roads. / [decorative rule] / Map Nº 1 / El Paso & Fort Yuma Wagon Road / J. B. Leach, Superintendent. / [rule] / Made under the direction of N. H. Hutton, Chief Engr / Assisted by G. C. Wharton, Prinl Asst Engr / W. D. Cress and P. G. Hume, Assts / 1857–8 / Scale 1/600,000. / [diagrammatic scale: 9 1/2 miles to one inch] / Thos S. Wagner Lith. 38 Hudson St Philada / [upper right:] (Sen. Ex: Doc. Nº 36–Ho. Ex: Doc. Nº 108—2d Sess: 35' Cong.) / 56.3 x 92.1 cm. Scale as above. Map: Dept of the Interior / Pacific Wagon Roads / [decorative rule] / Map Nº 2 / of the / El Paso & Fort Yuma Wagon Road / J. B. Leach Superintendent / [double rule] / Made under the direction of N. H. Hutton, Chief Engr / Assisted by G. C. Wharton Prin: Asst Engr / W. D. Cress and P. G. Hume, Assts / 1857–8 / Scale 1/600,000 / [8 lines of notes] / [diagrammatic scale: ten miles to one inch] / T. S. Wagner's Lith. Philada / [upper right:] (Sen. Ex: Doc. Nº 36–Ho. Ex. Doc: Nº 108—2d Sess. 35 Cong) / 55.6 x 89.2 cm. Scale as indicated. Map: Department of the Interior / Pacific Wagon Roads / [thin and thick rules] / Map / of the / Wagon-Road / from / Platte River / via / Omaha Reserve and Dakota City / to / Running Water River / [decorative rule] / Geo. L. Sites, Supt / [decorative rule] / 1858 / Scale / 10 Miles—1 Inch / T. S. Wagner's Lith Philada / [upper right:] (Sen. Ex. Doc. Nº 36–Ho. Ex. Doc. Nº 108—2d Sess. 35th Cong.) / 67 x 60.6 cm. Scale as indicated. Rebound in red cloth.

Ref.: Howes C86; Wagner-Camp 321

35th Congress, 2nd Session, Senate, Executive Document No. 36, Serial 981. [Washington, 1859.]

The Senate version probably preceded the House printing, for the latter body ordered the report to be printed on March 1 while the Senate had ordered it on February 26. The two printings may be identified by the first page of each and by the differing notes on signature pages, i.e. the Senate version reads: Ex. Doc. 36—, and the House printing reads: H. Ex. Doc. 108— /.

559 [CAMPBELL, ALBERT H.]

[Caption title] . . . PACIFIC WAGON ROADS . . . A REPORT UPON THE SEVERAL WAGON ROADS CONSTRUCTED UNDER THE DIRECTION OF THE INTERIOR DEPARTMENT . . .

[1]–125, [126 blank]. 22.6 x 14 cm. Six maps, as in preceding work. Rebound in green cloth, sprinkled edges.

Prov.: W. J. Holliday copy.

Ref.: Howes C86; Wagner-Camp 321

35th Congress, 2nd Session, House, Execu-

tive Document No. 108, Serial 1008. [Washington, 1859.]

In this printing, on pages 16 and 125 slugs have slipped out of place and have left impressions at ends of lines.

560 CAMPBELL, JOHN L.

IDAHO: SIX MONTHS IN THE NEW GOLD DIGGINGS. THE EMIGRANT'S GUIDE OVERLAND. ITINERARY OF THE ROUTES, FEATURES OF THE COUNTRY, JOURNAL OF RESIDENCE, ETC. ETC. . . . NEW YORK: PUBLISHED BY J. L. CAMPBELL, 1864.

[1]–48, [9]2. [1]–52, 53–62 advertisements, [1–4 advertisements on mauve paper]. 21.7 x 13.3 cm. Vignette and four full page illustrations, included in pagination, and a map: [Map of the Northwest, Canada to the southern line of Kansas, Des Moines to the Pacific.] 9 x 16.8 cm. No scale given. Yellow pictorial wrappers printed in red and black, with title on front wrapper: [except for imprints, all within pictorial design:] Idaho. / Six Months / in the / New Gold Regions. / The Emigrant's Guide / New-York: / Sinclair Tousey / 1864. / [below pictorial title:] Tribune Print, 51 Clark Street, Chicago. /; Tousey advertisements on verso of back wrapper, verso of front and recto of back wrappers blank. Wrappers are of printed yellow (not yellow paper) and are semi-glazed. In a dark red half morocco case.

Ref.: Howes C97; Sabin 10253; Smith 580; Wagner-Camp 398

The 1864 copyright on the verso of the title-leaf is in favor of the author. The printer's imprint at lower left of the same page reads: [rule] / Tribune Book and Job Office, / 51 Clark Street. / The sketch map, an integral part of the first gathering, is used as a frontispiece; the recto is blank.

The text, with caption: Idaho. / [diamond rule] / . . . , begins on page [5]. The second section starts on page 40, with caption: How to Go to Idaho. / [rule] / Description of Outfitting Points. / [short rule] / . . . Section three comprises only page 46 with the caption under the running head: The South Route from Fort Kearney. / Section four starts on page 47, with the caption under the running head: The Emigrant's Guide / from the Missouri River to Idaho. / [short rule] / . . . Pages 53–62 carry advertisements (business cards) on text paper. Page 62 is followed by four unnumbered pages of transportation advertisements printed on mauve paper. In the centre of the fourth page, printed at right angles to the other two advertisements is a notice: Just Issued. / [decorative rule] / Campbell's Map / of / Idaho. / [13 lines] / [pointing hand] It will shortly follow this Book. / Price 25 Cents. / [two lines] / J. L. Campbell, / Box 3179, Chicago, Ill. /

The present copy carries no advertisement on the recto of the frontispiece map. The map shows the country only as far east as Des Moines and does not mention Montana. There is no reference to Campbell by name on page 9. The recto of the back wrapper is blank.

The order of printings of this popular little pamphlet remains an unsolved problem. It is unlikely that the version described by Wagner-Camp is the earliest, or that it preceded the present copy. Sinclair Tousey was succeeded in February of 1864 by the American News Company, formed by Sinclair Tousey and Dexter, Hamilton & Co. [See Johannsen I p. 47 and New York *Tribune*, February 6 & 9, 1864.] Thus, the Campbell book was probably published before the end of February, 1864.

John R. Walsh, whose imprint appears on the copy described by Wagner-Camp, according to Andreass' history of Chicago, various Chicago directories, and the researches of Miss Margaret Scriven of the Chicago Historical Society, was a clerk with John McNally in 1861, started his own business as a newspaper depot in the same year, and is listed at several addresses in that capacity through 1863. (The Chicago Historical Society owns at least one book dated 1861 with a John R. Walsh imprint.) In the 1864–65 directory, Walsh described himself as wholesale news agent and bookseller, not as a publisher. In 1866, Walsh became manager of the Western News Company.

It is possible that Walsh's imprint appeared on early copies of the Campbell work, especially since the author is believed to have been a Chicago journalist, and certainly, in this case, acted as his own publisher. However, Sinclair Tousey and other distributors normally bought whole printings for distribution, and Tousey was at that time an important national outlet. It would have been much to Campbell's advantage to sell to Tousey, so it seems likely that the New York imprint on the front wrapper should be preferred over the Walsh imprint.

561 [CAMPBELL, JOHN P.]

THE PASSENGER; OR A RELIGIOUS RAMBLE THROUGH KENTUCKY AND OHIO . . . LEXINGTON: PRINTED BY D. BRADFORD, 1804.

[A]⁴, B², C⁴. A⁴, B², C⁴, D². [1]–19, [20 blank]. [1]–22, [23–24 blank]. 19 x 12.5 cm. Two parts, unbound, stabbed, uncut. Each part stabbed separately and then stabbed together.

Ref.: AII (*Kentucky*) 201; Howes C98

Campbell was a minister at Chillicothe, Ohio. The contents of his pamphlet are purely theological maunderings.

562 CAMPBELL, ROBERT

THE DISCOVERY AND EXPLORATION OF THE YOUCON (PELLY) RIVER BY THE DISCOVERER . . . WINNIPEG: MANITOBA FREE PRESS PRINT, 1885.

[1]–18. 14.4 x 9.4 cm. Rebound in black half morocco, printed wrappers bound in.
Ref.: Smith 1450

Robert Campbell, F. R. G. S., is not to be confused with Robert Campbell, R. M. F. C. (Rocky Mountain Fur Company).

563 CAMPBELL, THOMPSON

SPEECH OF HON. THOMPSON CAMPBELL, OF ILL., AGAINST THE KEOKUK AND DUBUQUE RAILROAD. DELIVERED IN THE HOUSE OF REPRESENTATIVES, MAY 28, 1852. WASHINGTON: PRINTED AT THE CONGRESSIONAL GLOBE OFFICE, 1852.

[1]–15, [16 blank]. 21.9 x 14 cm. Removed from bound volume, unbound.
Ref.:

564 CAMPBELL, WILLIAM C.

A COLORADO COLONEL AND OTHER SKETCHES . . . TOPEKA, KANSAS: CRANE & COMPANY, 1901.*

[1]–402. 19.5 x 13.3 cm. Illustrations unlisted. Blue-green pictorial cloth, gilt top.
Prov.: Inscribed on front fly-leaf: To my old friends, / Mr. & Mrs. C. N. Sterry, / With Compliments / of / W. C. Campbell. / Prescott, Ariz. / Jan. 30, 1902. /
Ref.: Adams (*Ramp. Herd*) 406

Portrait of the author mounted on the inner front cover.

565 CAMPBELL & HOOGS, San Francisco

[Caption title] CAMPBELL & HOOGS' DIRECTORY, FOR FEBRUARY; 1850. PUBLISHED MONTHLY AT THE OFFICE OF THE PROPRIETORS, IN CLAY STREET, NEAR MONTGOMERY, SOUTH SIDE, UP STAIRS. . . .

[1–4, 4 blank]. 32.3 x 22 cm. Unbound leaflet.
Ref.: AII (*California*) 124 see; Cowan p. 174 see; Greenwood 194; Wagner (*California Imprints*) 53 see

This is the first directory of any kind issued for San Francisco. Wagner only surmised the existence of a February issue while Cowan guessed none was issued. AII (*California*) lists the March issue.

566 CAMPION, J. S.

ON THE FRONTIER. REMINISCENCES OF WILD SPORTS, PERSONAL ADVENTURES AND STRANGE SCENES . . . LONDON: CHAPMAN & HALL, 1878.

[i]–[xvi, xvi blank], [1]–372. 22 x 14 cm. Eight illustrations listed. Gray cloth.

Ref.: Howes C105; Rader 583

567 CANADA. PARLIAMENT. Commons (Select Committee)

REPORT OF THE SELECT COMMITTEE IN RE CHARLES BREMNER'S FURS . . . OTTAWA: PRINTED BY BROWN CHAMBERLAIN, 1890.

[i]–iv, 1–45, [46 blank]. 24.9 x 18.4 cm. Blue printed wrappers with title as above on front wrapper.

Ref.:

568 CANADIAN PACIFIC RAILWAY

CANADIAN PACIFIC RAILWAY. SANFORD FLEMING, C.M.G., ENGINEER-IN-CHIEF. REPORTS AND DOCUMENTS IN REFERENCE TO THE LOCATION OF THE LINE AND A WESTERN TERMINAL HARBOUR. 1878. OTTAWA: PRINTED BY MACLEAN, ROGER & CO., 1878.

[1]–104. 25.1 x 16.2 cm. Three folding maps. Gray-green printed wrappers with title on front wrapper as above within thick and thin rules.

Prov.: Signature on front wrapper: Jewell [?] Egan /.

Ref.: Railway Economics p. 336; Smith 1461

569 CANADIAN PACIFIC RAILWAY

THE CANADIAN PACIFIC RAILWAY. AN APPEAL TO PUBLIC OPINION AGAINST THE RAILWAY BEING CARRIED ACROSS THE SELKIRK RANGE, THAT ROUTE BEING OBJECTIONABLE FROM THE DANGER OF FALLS FROM GLACIERS AND FROM AVALANCHES, ALSO, GENERALLY ON OTHER MATTERS. BY PHILO. VERITAS. MONTREAL: WM. DRYSDALE & CO., 1885.

[1]–100. 21.7 x 15 cm. Map: A Section of the Map / of the / North West / Showing Present Location / of C. P. R. R. over the / Selkirk Range /. 44.5 x 33.4 cm. No scale given. Blue printed wrappers with title on front wrapper, copyright notice on verso of front wrapper.

Ref.: Railway Economics p. 337

570 CANADIAN PACIFIC RAILWAY

[Wrapper title] TO THE KLONDIKE AND GOLD FIELDS OF THE YUKON BY THE CANADIAN PACIFIC RAILWAY.

[1]–28. 22.7 x 10.4 cm. Illustrations unlisted. Red and gold printed wrappers with title on front wrapper, map on verso of front wrapper, cut on recto of back wrapper,

Ref.:
Published before April, 1898, probably during the winter of 1897–98.

571 CANFIELD, CHAUNCEY L., *Editor*

THE DIARY OF A FORTY-NINER. EDITED BY CHAUNCEY L. CANFIELD. NEW YORK: MORGAN SHEPARD COMPANY, MCMVI.*

[i]–[xxii], 1–231, [232 blank]. 20.8 x 15.6 cm. Map. Brown pictorial boards, red buckram backstrip, green top.

Ref.: Blumann & Thomas 2195; Cowan p. 104; Howes C111; Matthews p. 326

The diary was kept by Alfred T. Jackson, a pioneer California miner, from May 18, 1850 to June 17, 1852. Blumann & Thomas attribute the original material to Lewis Hanchett.

In a letter dated August 9, 1933, Cowan wrote to C. G. Littell that the authenticity of the diary had been questioned frequently. Cowan had asked Canfield about it in 1910, but received no conclusive answer.—EDG

572 CANFIELD, THOMAS H.

LIFE OF THOMAS HAWLEY CANFIELD HIS EARLY EFFORTS TO OPEN A ROUTE FOR THE TRANSPORTATION OF THE PRODUCTS OF THE WEST TO NEW ENGLAND, BY WAY OF THE GREAT LAKES ST. LAWRENCE RIVER AND VERMONT RAILROADS, AND HIS CONNECTIONS WITH THE EARLY HISTORY OF THE NORTHERN PACIFIC RAILROAD, FROM THE HISTORY OF THE RED RIVER VALLEY, NORTH DAKOTA, AND PARK REGION OF NORTHWESTERN MINNESOTA . . . BURLINGTON, VERMONT, 1889.

[1]–48. 26.7 x 19.7 cm. Portrait. Blue cloth, gilt edges.

Prov.: Printed presentation slip pasted inside front cover, inscribed: Presented to / Mr. Charles W. Braislin / by Emily Canfield / . . . April 13 1921 / Chicago, Illinois /.

Ref.: Braislin 327; Howes C113; *Railway Economics* p. 11; Smith 1472

According to the printed presentation slip, this is an offprint of the sketch from *History of Red River Valley, North Dakota and Park Region of Northwestern Minnesota* . . .

573 CANFIELD, THOMAS H.

NORTHERN PACIFIC RAILROAD. PARTIAL REPORT TO THE BOARD OF DIRECTORS, OF A PORTION OF A RECONNOISSANCE MADE IN THE SUMMER OF 1869, BETWEEN LAKE SUPERIOR AND THE PACIFIC OCEAN . . . ACCOMPANIED WITH NOTES ON PUGET SOUND . . . FOR PRIVATE CIRCULATION ONLY. MAY, 1870.

[1]–96, [97–100 blank], [1]–44. 22.5 x 14.2 cm. Two maps: Map of the / Harbors of / Puget Sound / and / Cowlitz Valley / Washington Ter-

ritory / From the United States Land Surveys. / Explanation. / [6 lines] / Scale of Miles. / [diagrammatic scale: 4 miles to one inch] / [upper right corner:] Engraved, Printed and Manufactured by / G. W. & C. B. Colton & Co. / N⁰ 172 William Sᵗ New York. / [lower right:] Entered according to Act of Congress in the year 1870 by G. W. & C. B. Colton & Co in the Clerks Office of the District Court of the United States for the Eastern District of New York. / 150.2 x 39.2 cm. Scale: four miles to one inch. Map: Map of the Country / West of / Dakota to the Pacific Ocean / From the latest Explorations and Surveys / To Accompany the Report of / Thoˢ H. Canfield Director. / Northern Pacific R. R. / May, 1870. / [at right, above centre:] Compiled Printed and / Published by G. W. & C. B. Colton & Cᵒ / No. 172 William Sᵗ / New York /. 50.5 x 61.5 cm. Scale: 50 miles to one inch. *Inset:* Map of / San Juan / or / Haro Archipelago / Showing the / Boundaries claimed by / the United States and / Great Britain /. 12.8 x 9 cm. Scale: about 18 miles to one inch. *Inset:* Our Northwest Territories" / Scale of Statute Miles / [diagrammatic scale: about 240 miles to one inch] / [lower right:] Drawn Engraved & Printed by G. W. & C. B. Colton & Cᵒ New York. / 8.5 x 22 cm. Scale: about 240 miles to one inch. *Insets:* Two printed tables. White printed wrappers with title within thick and thin rule borders. In a red cloth case.

Ref.: Howes C114; *Railway Economics* p. 243; Smith 1473

Printed in New York.

There is a separate title-page for the section on Puget Sound by Samuel Wilkeson.

574 CANN, L. H.

AUTOGRAPH LETTER, SIGNED. 1873 December 9, Salem, Oregon. One page, 24.7 x 19 cm. To Loren L. Williams.

Inserted in Manuscript Journals of Loren L. Williams, Volume IV.

575 CANNON, MILES

WAIILAPTU: ITS RISE AND FALL, 1836–1847. A STORY OF PIONEER DAYS IN THE PACIFIC NORTHWEST . . . FEATURING THE JOURNEY OF NARCISSA PRENTISS WHITMAN . . . HER DREADFUL MASSACRE . . . THE TAKING INTO CAPTIVITY OF TWO SCORE WOMEN AND GIRLS . . . THE FINAL RESCUE, ETC. . . . BOISE, IDAHO: CAPITAL NEWS JOB ROOMS, 1915.*

[i]–[x, x blank], [1]–171, [172–74 blank]. 22.8 x 15.1 cm. Fifteen illustrations unlisted. Green printed pictorial wrappers.

Ref.: Smith 1474

576 CANTON, FRANK M.

FRONTIER TRAILS. THE AUTOBIOGRAPHY OF FRANK M. CANTON . . . BOSTON, 1930.*

[i]–[xviii, xviii blank], [1]–237, [238 blank]. 20.6 x 14 cm. 12 illustrations listed. Red cloth, yellow top, uncut.

Prov.: Inscribed on fly-leaf: That you may enjoy this / book, is the wish of, / Mrs Frank M. Canton. /

Ref.: Adams 176; Adams (*Ramp. Herd*) 409; Dobie p. 98; Howes C118; Rader 588; Saunders 2792

He only thought of guns and killings . . . they seemed to be on his mind all the time . . . —A contemporary, quoted by Horan and Sann: *Pictorial History of the West.*

577 CANTON TOWN COMPANY, Canton, Nebraska

[Broadside] ONE SHARE. N⁰ 23 [numeral in manuscript on gray ground] THIS ENTITLES [gray multiple bar rule] TO ONE SHARE IN CANTON, EACH SHARE BEING AN UNDIVIDED TWO-HUNDREDTH PART OF THE LAND, TOWN SITE, AND LOTS CLAIMED BY THE CANTON TOWN COMPANY. CANTON, N. T., 1857. EXPLANATION.—CANTON IS LOCATED ON THE WAHOO CREEK, ON THE DIRECT LINE OF THE PLATTE VALLEY AND PACIFIC RAILROAD.

Broadside, 11 x 20.1 cm. Text, 8.5 x 18.2 cm.

Ref.:

Signed in manuscript by D. H. Wheeler and W. H. Bassett. Dated January 1, 1857. Made out to D. H. Wheeler, with his signature on the verso.

578 CAPITOL HYDRAULIC COMPANY, Denver, Colorado

[Broadside] [in border, left corner:] 500,000 [in border, right corner:] 500,000 [in box, centre:] NO. CAPITOL HYDRAULIC COMPANY INCORPORATED BY THE LEGISLATURE OF KANSAS TERRITORY FEB. 11ᵗʰ 1860. [map: map showing the Lines and Lands of the Capitol Hydraulic Company. Denver, Oct. 1860. 8.1 x 18.1 cm. No scale given.] [at left of map:] CAPITAL STOCK [in box, 2 lines:] 500,000 DOLLARS. [vignette] [at right of map:] SHARES [in box, 2 lines:] 100 DOLLARS. [vignette] [below map:] THIS CERTIFIES THAT . . . A. McLEAN LITH., COR. 3ᵈ & PINE. ST. LOUIS.

Broadside on bank note paper, 23.8 x 32 cm. Text, including border, 21.2 x 32.1 cm.

Ref.:

579 CAPRON, EDWIN R.

TWELVE AUTOGRAPH LETTERS, SIGNED. 1865 January 30 to October 13, Fort Kearney, Cottonwood Springs, and Nebraska City. Forty-one pages, octavo and quarto. To members of his family.

The series of letters contains good descriptions of military life at western posts during 1865. At the time of the first letter, Capron's parents had not heard from him for six years.

Accompanying the correspondence are a letter from Capron's parents, a letter from his sister, a letter by Henry C. Barrett to Miss Nannie Fairley, and another letter by Capron's sister (returned to sender) in which she complains she has not heard from him for nine years. Evidently, Capron was not a steady letter-writer. With the letters is a daguerreotype portrait of Capron.

580 CAPRON, ELISHA S.

HISTORY OF CALIFORNIA, FROM ITS DISCOVERY TO THE PRESENT TIME . . . A JOURNAL OF THE VOYAGE FROM NEW YORK, VIA NICARAGUA, TO SAN FRANCISCO, AND BACK, VIA PANAMA . . . BOSTON: PUBLISHED BY JOHN P. JEWETT & COMPANY, 1854.*

[I]–[XII, XII blank], 1–356. 18.3 x 11.5 cm. Map: California / 1854. / Published by J. H. Colton, Nº 86 Cedar St New York. / Scale of Miles. / [diagrammatic scale: about 50 miles to one inch] / Entered according to Act of Congress, in the year 1853, by J. H. Colton, in the Clerks Office of the District Court for the Southern District of New York. / 40 x 32 cm. Scale: about 50 miles to one inch. *Inset:* City of / San Francisco /. 14.9 x 14 cm. Scale: 1/2 mile to one inch. Brown cloth, blind embossed sides, title in gilt on backstrip.
Ref.: Blumann & Thomas 4909; Bradford 769; Cowan p. 104; Howes C127; Jones 1309

581 CAPRON, V [or N]. and J. P.

AUTOGRAPH LETTER, SIGNED. 1845 July 20, Keosauqua, Iowa.

Three pages, 31.3 x 20.2 cm. To John P. Capron.

The letter consists of family news and the following passage at the foot of the second page: There has been quite a number of people emegranted from this territory this Spring to oregon about three hundred wagons and three thousand Cattle I dont know the exact number of people their ware to baptist preachers went out as missionarys one the Rev H Johnson from here it creatid quite an excitement for awhile . . .

582 CARDINELL, CHARLES

[Wrapper title] . . . ADVENTURES ON THE PLAINS . . . SAN FRANCISCO: CALIFORNIA HISTORICAL SOCIETY, 1922.

[1]–15, [16 blank]. 25.4 x 17.1 cm. Buff printed wrappers.
Ref.: Edwards p. 28
Limited to 100 copies.

583 [CAREY, T. J.]

. . . KLONDIKE AND ALL ABOUT IT. BY A PRACTICAL MINING ENGINEER. NEW YORK: EXCELSIOR PUBLISHING HOUSE, 1896 [1897].

[1]–143, [144 advertisements]. 18 x 12.3 cm. Illustration and folding map. Printed white wrappers. Wrappers slightly chipped. In a tan cloth case.
Ref.: Howes C143; Wickersham 3900

584 CAREY & HART, Philadelphia

LETTER, SIGNED Carey & Hart. 1846 May 14, Philadelphia. One page, 26.5 x 20.9 cm. To Rufus B. Sage.

Specifications for printing a specimen page of Sage's *Scenes in the Rocky Mountains* . . . which was published by Carey & Hart in 1846. The letterpaper used is bordered with black and carries an announcement at the head of the dissolution of the firm of Carey & Hart.

Laid in the wrappered copy of Sage's book.

585 CARLETON, GUY H.

[Map] SECTIONAL / MAP / OF / THE STATE OF / IOWA / COMPILED FROM THE / UNITED STATES SURVEYS / ALSO EXHIBITING THE / INTERNAL IMPROVEMENTS, DISTANCES BETWEEN TOWNS / & VILLAGES, LINES OF PROJECTED RAIL ROADS, &C. &C. / DRAWN AND PUBLISHED BY / GUY H. CARLETON, DEP. SUR. U.S. / DUBUQUE, Iowa. / 1854 / [lower right:] ENTERED ACCORDING TO ACT OF CONGRESS JULY 11, 1850, BY GUY H. CARLETON, IN THE CLERK'S OFFICE OF THE DISTRICT COURT OF THE DISTRICT OF MICHIGAN. *Inset:* Vicinity of / Dubuque the Lead Region / and part of / Illinois & Wisconsin. / 15.8 x 16.2 cm. Scale: No scale given. *Inset:* Des Moines River / Improvement. / 4.6 x 50.7 cm. Scale: No scale given.

Map, 67.2 x 100.5 cm. Scale: 9 miles to one inch. Folded into brown leather covers, 14.1 x 8.8 cm., lettered in gilt on front cover: Carlton's [!] / Sectional / Map of / Iowa /.
Ref.:
Extensive text about the state appears in a box at left of map headed: Public Lands. /

586 CARLETON, JAMES H.

REPORT ON THE SUBJECT OF THE MASSACRE AT THE MOUNTAIN MEADOWS, IN UTAH TERRITORY, IN SEPTEMBER, 1857, OF ONE HUNDRED AND TWENTY MEN, WOMEN AND CHILDREN, WHO WERE FROM ARKANSAS . . . AND REPORT OF THE HON. WILLIAM C. MITCHELL, RELATIVE TO THE SEVENTEEN SURVIVING CHILDREN WHO WERE BROUGHT BACK BY THE AUTHORITIES OF THE U.S. AFTER THEIR PARENTS AND OTHERS, WITH WHOM THEY WERE EMIGRATING, HAD BEEN MURDERED. LITTLE ROCK: TRUE DEMOCRAT STEAM PRESS PRINT, 1860.

[1]–32. 22.7 x 14.1 cm. Removed from bound volume, unbound. In a green cloth case.

Ref.: Allen (*Arkansas*) 396; Brooks, J.: *The Mountain Meadows Massacre . . .* Stanford: Stanford University Press [1950] p. 231; Howes C147; Wagner-Camp 354

587 CARLILE, PRICE & McGAVOCK, Pueblo, Colorado

MANUSCRIPT DOCUMENT. 1889 January 19, Pueblo, Colorado. Two pages, 35.3 x 21 cm.

Invoice for the Pike's Peak Toll Road, including cost of right of way, surveying, labor, printing tickets, building tollgate, entertaining the press, etc. Comprises fifty-seven entries.

588 CARNEGIE, JAMES, NINTH EARL OF SOUTHESK

SASKATCHEWAN AND THE ROCKY MOUNTAINS, A DIARY AND NARRATIVE OF TRAVEL, SPORT, AND ADVENTURE, DURING A JOURNEY THROUGH THE HUDSON'S BAY COMPANY'S TERRITORIES, IN 1859 AND 1860 . . . EDINBURGH: EDMONSTON AND DOUGLAS, 1875.

[i]–xxx, [1]–448. (Pages [1–2] blank.) 21.8 x 14.5 cm. 31 illustrations and two maps listed. Folding map on cloth: Sketch Map of / Part of the Rocky Mountains / Showing / Lord Southesk's route / Aug.t and Sep.t 1859. / [lower right:] W. & A. K. Johnston. Edinburgh. / 18.1 x 27 cm. No scale given. Folding map on cloth: Map of / Lord Southesk's Route / from Crow-wing to Rocky Mountains. / [rule] / [lower right:] W. & A. K. Johnston. Edinburgh. / 18.1 x 31.4 cm. No scale given. Dark blue cloth, gilt title on front cover, uncut.

Ref.: Peel 333; Sabin 88549

589 CARR, JOHN

EARLY TIMES IN MIDDLE TENNESSEE . . . NASHVILLE, TENN.: PUBLISHED FOR THE AUTHOR, 1857.

[i]–[vi, vi blank], 7–248. 14.9 x 9.5 cm. Black or very dark brown cloth. In a full brown morocco case.

Ref.: Bradford 783; Howes C166; Jones 1368; Sabin 11024

Copies are found with another imprint: Nashville, Tenn.: / Published for Elisha Carr, / (Nephew of the Author,) / By E. Stevenson & F. A. Owen. / 1857. / In the ICN (Ayer) and ICN copies, the Introduction occupies pages iii–vi while in the present copy page [vi] is blank. The text is identical except for one comma.

The first part of the work is a history of religious activities in Tennessee, but the section includes also a goodly number of biographical sketches of early settlers and anecdotes from pioneer life. Pages 186–241 carry an excellent narrative of the adventures of John Carr, comprising a number of Indian tales. This section was reprinted from the Wales and Roberts edition of *Indian Battles . . .* [1853].

590 CARR, JOHN

PIONEER DAYS IN CALIFORNIA . . . EUREKA, CALIFORNIA: TIMES PUBLISHING COMPANY, 1891.

[5]–452. (Pages [5–6] blank,) 21.5 x 14.3 cm. Portrait. Dark green cloth, front cover stamped in black, back cover embossed in blind, title in gilt on backstrip.

Ref.: Blumann & Thomas 900; Cowan p. 106; Howes C167

Includes adventures overland from Peoria, Illinois, to Hangtown, California, via Forts Leavenworth, Laramie, Bridger (where he met Jim Bridger), and Salt Lake City. Also includes mining adventures in California.—EDG

591 CARRIGAN, WILHELMINA B.

CAPTURED BY THE INDIANS: REMINISCENCES OF PIONEER LIFE IN MINNESOTA . . . FOREST CITY, S.D.: FOREST CITY PRESS, 1907.

[i–ii], [1]–40, [41 vignette, 42 blank]. 21.8 x 14 cm. Portrait on verso of title-leaf. Gray printed wrappers with title on front wrapper. In a red cloth case.

Ref.: Ayer (*Supp.*) 28; Howes C171; Jones 1715

The work was originally published in serial form in the Buffalo Lake, Minn. *News* during January, 1903. The Ayer and Jones references listed above are to the Buffalo Lake, 1912 edition.

592 CARRINGTON, FRANCES C.

MY ARMY LIFE AND THE FORT PHIL. KEARNEY MASSACRE WITH AN ACCOUNT OF THE CELEBRATION OF "WYOMING OPENED" . . . PHILADELPHIA: J. B. LIPPINCOTT COMPANY, 1910.

[1]–[318]. 19.8 x 13.6 cm. 41 illustrations and maps listed. Dark green cloth, title in gilt on front cover and backstrip.

Ref.: Howes C172; Malone p. 2; Rader 600

Laid in is an Autograph Note, signed, by Henry B. Carrington to Miss Frances Ten Eyck, thanking her for a letter about Mrs. Carrington's book. Also laid in is a printed letter by William A. Mowry headed: In-Re My Army Life . . .

Mrs. Frances C. Carrington, the General's second wife, was the widow of Colonel G. W. Grummond who was killed in the Fetterman Massacre. Her maiden name was Courtney.

593 CARRINGTON, HENRY B.

[Caption title] COLONEL CARRINGTON'S OFFICIAL REPORT OF THE PHIL KEARNEY MASSACRE. (PUBLISHED BY PERMISSION OF THE WAR DEPARTMENT.) . . .

[1]–8. 19.5 x 13 cm. Unbound.

Ref.:

This report, dated Headquarters Post, Fort Philip Kearney, Dacotah Territory, January 2ᵈ, 1867, and signed by Henry B. Carrington, Colonel 18ᵗʰ U.S. Infantry was withheld from publication by General Grant at the time of its receipt. It was printed by permission of General Sherman at the time of the publication of Mrs. Carrington's *Absaraka . . .* 1869 (second edition). The first official publication did not appear until 1887. In Hebard and Brininstool: *The Bozeman Trail . . .* Cleveland, 1922, pages 339–40, Carrington is quoted as having said the report was first published in 1869 in the second edition of *Absaraka.* An examination of copies of the 1868, 1869, and 1878 editions discloses nothing of this nature. The report was, however, printed and reprinted in Carrington's *The Indian Question . . .* 1884 and 1909.—EDG

The present copy was probably printed in 1869 and may have been intended for insertion in *Absaraka . . .* 1869. There are no indications of printer or date of printing.

594 CARRINGTON, HENRY B.

THE INDIAN QUESTION. AN ADDRESS . . . BOSTON: CHARLES H. WHITING, 1884.

[1]–32. 22.5 x 14.8 cm. Map: (Map Nº 1.) Carringtons Outline of Indian Operations on the Plains. / 28.8 x 46.3 cm. No scale given. Light brown cloth, blind bands on covers, title in gilt on front cover.

Prov.: Inscribed on front endleaf: Dr. W. Thornton Parker— / [underline] / form Adjt Soc Vet. Indian Wars / from / Gen—[following name stamped in blue:] Henry B. Carrington / [name underlined] / U S Army— / Historian /

[underline] / Society of Veterans / [underline] / Indian Wars U. S A / [underline] /. Bookplate of Dr. William Thornton Parker.

Ref.: Howes C174

A valuable gathering of records relating to Carrington's experiences with the Indians of the Western Plains, including the first open publication of the official report on the Fort Phil Kearney Massacre.

595 CARRINGTON, HENRY B.

AUTOGRAPH NOTE, SIGNED. 1910 July 17, Hyde Park, Massachusetts. One page, 16.3 x 13 cm. To Miss Frances Ten Eyck.

Written for Mrs. Carrington, the writer thanks the recipient for her kind remarks about Mrs. Carrington's book.

Laid in Carrington: *My Army Life . . .* 1910.

596 CARRINGTON, MARGARET I.

AB-SA-RA-KA HOME OF THE CROWS: BEING THE EXPERIENCE OF AN OFFICER'S WIFE ON THE PLAINS . . . PHILADELPHIA: J. B. LIPPINCOTT & CO., 1868.

[i]–xii, 13–284. 18.6 x 11.8 cm. Text illustrations and map unlisted. Map: [Map of Ab-sa-ra-ka, Nebraska City to Salt Lake City, Fort Kearney to Silver City]. 20.5 x 40.3 cm. No scale given. Green cloth, blind fillet borders on sides, title in gilt on backstrip.

Ref.: Field 244; Howes C175; Jones 1504; Malone p. 2; Sabin 11061; Smith 1536

An excellent personal account fortified by invaluable additional material from the author's husband, Colonel Henry B. Carrington.

597 CARRINGTON, MARGARET I.

THE SAME. PHILADELPHIA, 1879.

[i]–xx, 13–378, 379–83 advertisements, [384 blank]. 18.6 x 12.4 cm. 15 illustrations and two maps listed. Map: (Map Nº 1) Carrington's Outline of Indian Operations on the Plains. / 28.1 x 45.9 cm. No scale given. Map: (Map Nº 11.) Carrington's Outline of Indian Operations on the Plains. / 14.1 x 18.3 cm. No scale given. Dark orange cloth, black and gilt bands and gilt vignette on front cover, title in gilt on backstrip.

Prov.: Inscribed on front blank leaf: Mr Lake / with regards of the author / Henry B. Carrington / Col U.S.A. / Dec. 5 1878. /

Ref.: Howes C175; Malone p. 2; Rader 601; Sabin 11061; Smith 1538

The inscription in the front of the volume is curious; one wonders how literally to read it.

598 [CARRINGTON, MARGARET I.]

OCEAN TO OCEAN. PACIFIC RAILROAD AND ADJOINING TERRITORIES WITH DISTANCES AND FARES OF

TRAVEL FROM AMERICAN CITIES. PHILADELPHIA: J. B. LIPPINCOTT & CO., 1869.

[1]–31, 32 advertisement. 16.4 x 10.6 cm. Map: [Area from Omaha to Salt Lake City, Fort Kearney to Montana City.] 20.4 x 40.4 cm. No scale given. Green cloth, title in gilt on front cover.

Prov.: Inscribed on inside front cover: [monogram:] FHR(?) / Apr. 15. 85 / Comps of Genl Carrington / [underline] /.

Ref.: Howes C176

Although authorship is attributed to Mrs. Carrington, the General probably wrote this little guide.

599 CARROLL, GEORGE R.

PIONEER LIFE IN AND AROUND CEDAR RAPIDS, IOWA. FROM 1839 TO 1849 . . . CEDAR RAPIDS, IOWA: TIME PRINTING AND BINDING HOUSE, 1895.

[III]–XII, [1]–251, [252 blank]. 19.5 x 13.5 cm. Ten illustrations listed. Dark green cloth, blind embossed bands on sides, gilt vignette on front cover, title in gilt on backstrip.

Prov.: Signature on front endleaf: W R Hinman /.

Ref.: Howes C180; Mott (*Iowa*) p. 85; Petersen p. 86

Anecdotal and entertaining work.—Mott

600 CARSON, CHRISTOPHER

ORIGINAL PHOTOGRAPHIC PORTRAIT, bust length, vignette, subject turned slightly toward his left. 8.9 x 5.5 cm., mounted on thin cardboard, 10.1 x 6.2 cm.

Manuscript signature at foot: C Carson /. On verso: Published by / E. & H. T. Anthony, / 501 Broadway, / New York. / [device] / from / Photographic Negative / in / Brady's / National Portrait Gallery. /

601 CARSON, CHRISTOPHER

ORIGINAL DAGUERREOTYPE PORTRAIT, waist length, nearly full face. 8 x 5.7 cm., in mat with rounded corners, in ornate gold colored frame, 11 x 8.4 cm.

The mount is inscribed: Taken by T. M. ͨEwen in / Santa Fe New Mexico / in 1859 / Kit Carson / [underline] / [vertical bracket] Of New Mexico /. From the Connelly Collection.—EDG

602 CARSON, CHRISTOPHER

[Forgery] AUTOGRAPH LETTER, SIGNED. 1848 August, Taos. One page, 20.1 x 13.1 cm. To Mrs. John C. Frémont.

An amusing forgery. Accompanied by a letter from Edward Eberstadt presenting the above to EDG.

603 CARSON, CHRISTOPHER

KIT CARSON'S OWN STORY OF HIS LIFE AS DICTATED TO COL. AND MRS. C. D. PETERS . . . EDITED BY BLANCHE C. GRANT. TAOS, NEW MEXICO, 1926.*

Ref.: Howes C182; Rader 606; Saunders 2802; Wagner-Camp 306 note

Signed by the editor.

Editions: New York, 1858.

604 CARSON, JAMES H.

EARLY RECOLLECTIONS OF THE MINES, AND A DESCRIPTION OF THE GREAT TULARE VALLEY . . . STOCKTON: PUBLISHED TO ACCOMPANY THE STEAMER EDITION OF THE "SAN JOAQUIN REPUBLICAN," 1852.

[1]–64. 20.3 x 14.1 cm. Map: Map / of the / Southern Mines / By / C. D. Gibbes. / 1852 / [2 lines] / Lith. of Quirot & Co. corner Calif.ᵃ & Mong.ʸ Sᵗˢ S. F. 18.7 x 24.4 cm. Scale: 20 miles to one inch. Tan printed wrappers with title on front wrapper. In a red half morocco case.

Prov.: Inscribed on front wrapper: Mercantile Library Association / Cincinnati / Ohio /. Henry E. Huntington copy, inscribed on last page in pencil: HEH dup /. Herschel V. Jones copy.

Ref.: AII (*California*) 191; Blumann & Thomas 5174; Bradford 787; Cowan p. 107; Howes C183; Jones 1273; Sabin 11084

The first book printed in Stockton . . . The first edition did not appear in book form, having been issued as a supplement to the "San Joaquin Republican" . . . —Cowan

605 CARSON, THOMAS

RANCHING, SPORT AND TRAVEL . . . LONDON: T. FISHER UNWIN, 1911.

[1]–316. 21.8 x 14.4 cm. 18 illustrations listed. Dark blue cloth, gilt top, uncut.

Ref.: Adams (*Ramp. Herd*) 422; Howes C184; Rader 607

A good tale of cattle ranching, Indians, cowboys, and mustang hunting in Arizona and New Mexico during the 1880's.

606 CARSTARPHEN, JAMES E.

[Wrapper title] MY TRIP TO CALIFORNIA IN '49. [1–8]. 21.6 x 14.9 cm. Portrait in text. Pale green printed wrappers with title as above on front wrapper.

Prov.: Bookplate of Henry R. Wagner.

Ref.: Cowan p. 107

Published at Louisiana, Missouri, 1914.

The sketchy account of Carstarphen's overland trip occupies only a small portion of these reminiscences.—EDG

607 CARTER, CHARLES M.

SHOOTING IN THE EARLY DAYS FROM 1863 TO 1919 . . . ST. JOSEPH, MISSOURI: PRINTED FOR PRIVATE DISTRIBUTION, DECEMBER, 1919 . . .

[1]–38, [39–40 blank]. 20.4 x 13.5 cm. Portrait. Green printed wrappers.

Ref.:

Printed and manuscript presentation form on title-page, including author's signature.

608 CARTER, CHARLES W.

THE EXODUS OF 1847 BEING A FULL AND INTERESTING ACCOUNT OF THE THRILLING EXPERIENCES OF THE LATTER DAY SAINTS JOURNEY, FROM THEIR HOMES IN THE UNITED STATES TO THE UNKNOWN REGION OF MEXICO, WHERE THEY BUILT UP WHAT IS KNOWN AS THE SALT LAKE VALLEY, AND UNFURLED THE STARS AND STRIPES UPON ENSIGN PEAK . . . SALT LAKE CITY: THE UTAH LITHOGRAPHING CO., 1897.

[1]–14, [15 blank, 16 advertisements]. 16.8 x 13.5 cm. Green pictorial wrappers, with title on front wrapper and advertisements on verso of front and recto and verso of back wrappers.

Ref.:

609 CARTER, E. S.

THE LIFE AND ADVENTURES OF E. S. CARTER INCLUDING A TRIP ACROSS THE PLAINS AND MOUNTAINS IN 1852, INDIAN WARS IN THE EARLY DAYS OF OREGON IN THE YEARS 1854–5–6. LIFE AND EXPERIENCE IN THE GOLD FIELDS OF CALIFORNIA, AND FIVE YEARS' TRAVEL IN NEW MEXICO . . . ST. JOSEPH, MO.: COMBE PRINTING COMPANY, 1896.

[1]–145, [146–48 blank]. 19.2 x 13.2 cm. Maroon wrappers with title in gilt on front wrapper. In a red cloth case.

Ref.: Braislin 340; Howes C186; Rader 609

Mounted on the verso of the title-leaf there is a small label on which is printed: Copyrighted /; this is followed by the date 1896 in manuscript and below the label, also in manuscript, appear the words: by E. S. Carter /.

The Braislin Catalogue reports "it is believed that nearly every copy was destroyed by fire in the printing office before distribution."

610 CARTER, O. L.

AUTOGRAPH LETTER, SIGNED, by O. L. Carter. 1888 February 16, Roseburg, Oregon. One page, 21.5 x 13.5 cm. To James H. Twogood. Regarding Twogood's claims.

611 CARTER, O. L.

AUTOGRAPH LETTER, SIGNED, by O. L. Carter. 1888 March 2, Roseburg, Ore. Two pages, 25.3 x 21 cm. To Twogood. Re his claims. Accompanied by a one-page Memorandum giving instructions.

612 CARTER, W. A.

HISTORY OF FANNIN COUNTY, TEXAS. HISTORY, STATISTICS AND BIOGRAPHIES. BUSINESS CARDS, ETC. . . . BONHAM, TEXAS, 1885.

[1]–128, [1–15 "Business cards," 16 blank]. (Pages [1–2] blank.) Plum cloth, blind embossed borders on sides, title in gilt on front cover.

Ref.: Carroll p. 53; Howes C199

Among the more interesting passages in this volume are the reminiscences of Judge J. P. Simpson, one of the pioneers of the county.

613 CARTER, W. A.

[Broadside] TO CATTLE SHIPPERS! . . . W. A. CARTER, FORT BRIDGER, WY, TY. JULY 2D, 1877.

Broadside, 30.6 x 22.8 cm. Text, 25.4 x 16.5 cm.

Ref.:

The broadside is an invitation to cattle owners to sell their cattle to Carter or ship them via the Union Pacific Railroad from "ten miles east of Carter Station."

Carter issued another broadside, in the same year, which is headed: Cattle Men Read This! / and is dated at the end from Fort Bridger, July 2, 1877. A copy of this is in the Union Pacific Museum at Omaha, Nebraska.

614 CARTER, WILLIAM H.

FROM YORKTOWN TO SANTIAGO WITH THE SIXTH U.S. CAVALRY . . . BALTIMORE: THE LORD BALTIMORE PRESS, 1900.*

[i]–[viii, viii blank], [1]–317, [318 blank]. 22.5 x 15.2 cm. 13 illustrations listed. Yellow pictorial cloth, gilt top, uncut.

Ref.: Munk (Alliot) p. 39; Nicholson p. 139

615 CARTER, WILLIAM H.

OLD ARMY SKETCHES . . . BALTIMORE: THE LORD BALTIMORE PRESS, 1906.*

[1]–203, [204 blank]. 19 x 13 cm. Five illustrations listed, illustrations in text unlisted. Blue cloth, gilt top, uncut.

Ref.: Howes C202; Munk (Alliot) p. 39; Nicholson p. 139

616 CARTWRIGHT, DAVID W.

NATURAL HISTORY OF WESTERN WILD ANIMALS AND GUIDE FOR HUNTERS, TRAPPERS, AND SPORTSMEN; EMBRACING OBSERVATIONS ON THE ART OF HUNTING AND TRAPPING . . . TOLEDO, OHIO.: BLADE PRINTING & PAPER COMPANY, 1875.

[i]–[xii, xii blank], [1]–280. 19.5 x 12.6 cm. 19 illustrations listed. Dark brown cloth, blind embossed borders, vignettes on sides, title stamped
in gilt on backstrip.

Ref.: Cowan p. 108; Howes C205; Rader 618
Chapter VI is entitled: A Tramp to California
in 1852.

617 CARTWRIGHT, PETER

AUTOBIOGRAPHY OF PETER CARTWRIGHT, THE
BACKWOODS PREACHER . . . NEW – YORK: PUB-
LISHED BY CARLTON & PORTER, 1856.

[1]–525, [526 blank, 527–28 advertisements].
18.6 x 12.3 cm. Portrait. Blue cloth, embossed
design on sides, title in gilt on backstrip.

Ref.: Buck 186; Dobie p. 65; Howes C208a;
Hubach p. 60; Sabin 11160 see

Cartwright was one of the most famous of the
nineteenth century Methodist circuit-riders.

618 CARVALHO, SOLOMON N.

INCIDENTS OF TRAVEL AND ADVENTURE IN THE
FAR WEST: WITH COL. FREMONT'S LAST EXPEDITION
ACROSS THE ROCKY MOUNTAINS: INCLUDING
THREE MONTHS' RESIDENCE IN UTAH, AND A
PERILOUS TRIP ACROSS THE GREAT AMERICAN
DESERT, TO THE PACIFIC . . . NEW YORK: DERBY &
JACKSON, 1856.

[iii]–[xvi, xvi blank], [17]–380. 19.3 x 13 cm.
Green cloth, uncut.

Ref.: Howes C213; Wagner-Camp 273;

Contrary to Wagner-Camp 273, illustrations
were not issued with this edition. The American
edition of the following year carried a frontispiece.

619 CARVALHO, SOLOMON N.

THE SAME, 1857.

[i]–[xvi, xvi blank], [17]–380, [1–4 advertise-
ments]. 18.6 x 12.5 cm. Frontispiece. Brown
cloth.

Prov.: Bookplate of John Thomas Lee.

Ref.: Bradford 799; Cowan p. 108; Edwards
p. 30; Field 249; Howes C213; Munk (Alliot)
p. 46; Sabin 11180; Smith 1547; Wagner-Camp
273 note

The first American edition was printed from
the plates used for the British edition, with title-
page changes.

620 CARVER, HARTWELL

[Caption title] MEMORIAL FOR A PRIVATE CHAR-
TER, ASKED FOR BY DR. HARTWELL CARVER AND
HIS ASSOCIATES, TO BUILD A RAILROAD FROM SOME
POINT ON THE MISSISSIPPI OR MISSOURI RIVERS, OR
FROM LAKE MICHIGAN TO THE PACIFIC OCEAN. . . .
J. & G. S. GIDEON, PRINTERS.

[1]–8. 23 x 15 cm. Unbound, uncut, unopened.

Ref.: Bancroft (*California*) VII p. 498; *Railway Economics* p. 281; Sabin 11182

The first person to propose a railway for any
portion of the Pacific coast was Hartwell Carver
. . . [he spent] 40 years of his life and $23,000 of
his own money endeavoring to float the project.
He had for his reward in 1869 a free pass over a
railway to the Pacific!—Bancroft.

Dated on page 8: Washington, D.C., January, 1849.

621 CARVER, HARTWELL

PROPOSAL FOR A CHARTER TO BUILD A RAILROAD
FROM LAKE MICHIGAN TO THE PACIFIC OCEAN . . .
WASHINGTON: PRINTED BY J. AND G. S. GIDEON,
1847.

[1]–38, [39–40 blank]. 22.7 x 14.6 cm. Yellow
printed wrappers with title on front wrapper
within decorative border and with Table of
Contents on back wrapper.

Ref.: Cowan p. 108; Howes C214; *Railway
Economics* p. 281

Carver includes criticisms of Whitney's and
Wilkes' plans for transcontinental railroads.

622 CARVER, JONATHAN

TRAVELS THROUGH THE INTERIOR PARTS OF NORTH
AMERICA, IN THE YEARS 1766, 1767, AND 1768 . . .
LONDON: PRINTED FOR C. DILLY, M DCC LXXXI.*

[*]2, A–C4, A2–4, b8, A–Ll8, Mm–Nn4, Oo2.
[i–iv, iv blank], [1–24], [i]–xvi, [17]–[564].
20.7 x 12.7 cm. Four illustrations and two maps
listed, all colored, and one portrait and one
colored plate unlisted. Map: A / New Map / of /
North / America, / From the / Latest Discoveries / 1778. / [swelled rule] / Engrav'd for
Carvers / Travels. / 33 x 35.8 cm. Scale: about
260 miles to one inch. Map: A Plan / of Captain
Carvers Travels / in the interior Parts of / North
America / in 1766 and 1767. / 26.6 x 34.2 cm.
No scale given. Full contemporary polished calf,
green leather label on backstrip.

Prov.: The Littlehales bookplate.

Ref.: Bradford 801; Fenton p. 56; Field 251;
Howes C215; Pilling (*Alg.*) 68; Sabin 11184;
Vail 670

This Third Edition is generally considered the
best contemporary edition.

Editions: London, 1778, 1779, 1780. Dublin,
1779.

623 CARVER, WILLIAM F.

LIFE OF DR. WM. F. CARVER, OF CALIFORNIA,
CHAMPION RIFLESHOT OF THE WORLD. BEING AN
INTERESTING AND TRUTHFUL STORY OF HIS CAP-
TURE BY THE INDIANS WHEN A CHILD, AND ROMAN-

TIC LIFE AMONG THE SAVAGES FOR A PERIOD OF SIX-TEEN YEARS. TO WHICH IS APPENDED, RECORD OF HIS REMARKABLE EXHIBITIONS OF SKILL WITH A RIFLE . . . BOSTON: PRESS OF ROCKWELL AND CHURCHILL, 1878.

[i]–iv, [5]–177, [178 blank]. 18.3 x 12 cm. Buff pictorial wrappers with title on front wrapper. In a gray buckram case.

Ref.: Howes C215a

A curious and fascinating work. Carver published it for publicity purposes and included a number of undocumented episodes. Raymond W. Thorp, whose biography of Carver, *Spirit Gun of the West* . . . , was published at Glendale, California, in 1957, either did not know of the present work (which is excessively scarce) or decided to ignore it.

Laid in are an Autograph Letter, signed by Colonel C. D. Randolph ("Buckskin Bill") and an Autograph Postcard, signed by Dr. Richard J. Tanner ("Diamond Dick").

624 [CASS, LEWIS]

FRANCE, ITS KING, COURT, AND GOVERNMENT. NEW-YORK: WILEY & PUTNAM, 1840.

[i]–vi, [7]–191, [192 blank]. 21.7 x 13.7 cm. Frontispiece. Plum cloth, blind embossed panels on sides.

Prov.: Inscribed on front endleaf: For Wm Fitch / With the regards of / Lew Cass /.

Ref.:

Inserted at the back is an Autograph Letter, signed, by Henry Ledyard, 1840 August 6, Paris, American Legation, to D. W. Fitch, regarding the presentation of the book at the request of the author. Ledyard was Cass' son-in-law.

625 CASTANARES, MANUEL

COLECCION DE DOCUMENTOS RELATIVOS AL DEPARTAMENTO DE CALIFORNIAS. MEXICO: IMPRENTA DE LA VOZ DEL PUEBLO, 1845.*

[1]–70, [71–2 blank]. 24.8 x 15 cm. Stabbed, printed pink back wrapper, apparently removed from bound volume. Title-leaf in facsimile or type-facsimile, lacks front wrapper.

Prov.: Signature on page [3]: De Raf^{le} Sanchez — /.

Ref.: Bancroft (*California*) IV, pp. 412–18; Barrett 467; Cowan p. 110; Gaer p. 51; Hanna-Powell p. 29; Howes C224; Sabin 11376

Contains much information on the missions, the Pious Fund, the Russians in California, and the first published account of gold in California [in the Los Angeles area].—Hanna-Powell

626 CASTANEDA DE NAGERA, PEDRO DE

VOYAGES, RELATIONS ET MEMOIRES ORIGINAUX POUR SERVIR A L'HISTOIRE DE LA DECOUVERTE DE L'AMERIQUE, PUBLIES POUR LA PREMIERE FOIS EN FRANCAIS, PAR H. TERNAUX-COMPANS. RELATION DU VOYAGE DE CIBOLA, ENTREPRIS EN 1540. INEDIT. PARIS: ARTHUS BERTRAND, M. DCCC XXXVIII.*

[i–iv], [I]–XVI, [1]–392. 22 x 14 cm. Green printed wrappers, with title on front wrapper, advertisement on verso of back wrapper, uncut. In a green cloth case.

Ref.: Howes C224a; Rader 624; Raines pp. 44–5; Sabin 11379; Streit III 1586; Wagner (*SS*) 5 note

Comprises Volume 9 of the series of voyages published by Ternaux-Compans.

627 CASWALL, HENRY

THE CITY OF THE MORMONS; OR, THREE DAYS AT NAUVOO, IN 1842 . . . LONDON: PRINTED FOR J. G. F. & J. RIVINGTON, 1843.

[i–iv], [1]–87, [88 colophon]. 16 x 10.2 cm. Frontispiece. Stiff tan printed wrappers with title on front wrapper, advertisements on back wrapper. In a brown cloth case.

Ref.: Bradford 817; Buck 370; Howes C234; Sabin 11476; Woodward 35

Editions: London, 1842.

628 CATECHISM

[Caption title] CATECHISM . . .

[1]–4. 12.8 x 7.7 cm. Bound with Number 1278.

Ref.: Hargrett (*Oklahoma*) 55; Pilling 671

Printed at Park Hill, probably in 1843. Text in Sequoyan. The version described by Hargrett comprises 32 numbered questions and answers. The present copy comprises 33, not 31 as Hargrett states in his note to Hargrett (*Oklahoma*) 21.

Editions: Park Hill, 1838.

629 CATLIN, A. P.

RANCHO "RIO DE LOS AMERICANOS," GRANTED TO WILLIAM A. LEIDESDORFF, BY GOVERNOR MICHELTORENA; FINALLY CONFIRMED TO THE EXECUTORS OF JOSEPH L. FOLSOM, DECEASED. SURVEYED BY SURVEYOR GENERAL JOHN G. HAYS, AND APPROVED BY THE U.S. DISTRICT COURT FOR THE NORTHERN DISTRICT OF CALIFORNIA, 25TH JUNE, 1862. STATEMENT OF THE TITLE, AND PROCEEDINGS UNDER IT TO THE CONFIRMATION; AND OF THE PROCEEDINGS HAD IN THE CONTROVERSY RESPECTING THE LOCATION AND SURVEY—CONTAINING, IN A CONDENSED FORM ALL THAT IS MATERIAL BEARING UPON THE QUESTION OF LOCA-

TION. BY A. P. CATLIN, OF COUNSEL FOR CLAIM-
ANTS.

[i]–iv, [1]–71, [72 blank]. 22.7 x 14.4 cm. Map:
Rancho del Paso / Rio de los Americanos. /
30.4 x 45.2 cm. Scale: about two leagues to
3 11/16 inches. Tan printed wrappers, with title
on front wrapper.
   Ref.: Cowan p. 362; Greenwood 1624
   Printed at San Francisco by B. F. Sterett in
1862.

630   CATLIN, GEORGE

DIE INDIANER NORD-AMERIKAS UND DIE WAHREND
EINES ACHTJAHRIGEN AUFENTHALTS UNTER DER
WILDESTEN IHRER STAMME ERLEHTEN ABENTEUER
UND SCHICKSALE VON G. CATLIN . . . BRUSSELS
AND LEIPZIG: CARL MUQUARDT, [1846–] 1848.

[i]–x, 1–382, [383 list of plates], [384 blank].
25.1 x 17 cm. 24 colored plates. Contemporary
black boards, red calf back and corners, green
edges.
   Ref.: Howes C243; Sabin 11539
   First German Edition. The text is a translation of *Letters and Notes* . . .

631   CATTERMOLE, E. G.

FAMOUS FRONTIERSMEN, PIONEERS AND SCOUTS;
THE VANGUARDS OF AMERICAN CIVILIZATION. TWO
CENTURIES OF THE ROMANCE OF AMERICAN HIS-
TORY. A THRILLING NARRATIVE OF THE LIVES AND
MARVELOUS EXPLOITS OF THE MOST RENOWNED
HEROES, TRAPPERS, EXPLORERS, ADVENTURERS,
SCOUTS AND INDIAN FIGHTERS . . . CHICAGO: THE
COBURN & NEWMAN PUBLISHING COMPANY, 1883.

[i]–xvi, [17]–540, [541–44 advertisements]. 18.6 x
12.8 cm. 70 illustrations listed. Green pictorial
cloth.
   Ref.: Cowan p. 111 see; Howes C245; Rader
639
   Includes sketches of frontiersmen from Boone
and Girty to Custer and Crook.

632   CENTENNIAL (Georgetown, Colorado), THE

[Newspaper] 1876. THE CENTENNIAL. VOL. I.
GEORGETOWN, COLO., JAN., 1876. No. 1. . . .

[1–4]. 29.3 x 20.8 cm. Unbound.
   Ref.: McMurtrie & Allen (*Colorado*) pp. 98,
271
   The Centennial was published by Jesse S.
Randall in Printers' Alley, near Miners' Assay
Office and boasted "Circulation—1,000 copies
occasionally." Issues for January and February,
1876, only are known.

633   CENTRAL OVERLAND, CALIFOR-NIA AND PIKE'S PEAK EXPRESS CO., THE

[Broadside] FOR PIKE'S PEAK, HO! DAILY U.S.
MAIL LINE THROUGH TO DENVER CITY IN 6 1–2
DAYS! THE CENTRAL OVERLAND, CALIFORNIA AND
PIKE'S PEAK EXPRESS CO. FORMERLY JONES, RUS-
SELL & CO. ARE NOW RUNNING A DAILY LINE OF
COACHES FROM ST. JOSEPH TO DENVER CITY. FOR
FURTHER PARTICULARS APPLY AT OFFICE AT THE
PATEE HOUSE, ST. JOSEPH, MO. WEST JOB ROOMS,
SECOND STREET, OPPOSITE THE POST OFFICE, ST.
JOSEPH, MO.

Broadside, 36.9 x 18.4 cm. Text, 32.7 x 15 cm.
   Ref.:
   Printed in 1860.

634   CENTRAL   PACIFIC   RAILROAD COMPANY

[Broadside] CENTRAL PACIFIC RAILROAD EXCUR-
SION SUNDAY, JULY 15TH, 1866, TO ALTA . . .
CONDUCTOR WILL CHARGE FULL FARE ON THE
TRAIN FOR ALL PERSONS NOT PROVIDED WITH EX-
CURSION TICKETS. C. CROCKER, SUPERINTENDENT.

Broadside, 22.5 x 15.3 cm. Text, 19 x 10.9 cm.
   Ref.:
   Probably printed at San Francisco.

635   CENTRAL   PACIFIC   RAILROAD COMPANY

THE PACIFIC RAILROAD. A DEFENSE AGAINST ITS
ENEMIES, WITH REPORT OF THE SUPERVISORS OF
PLACER COUNTY, AND REPORT OF MR. MONTANYA,
MADE TO THE SUPERVISORS OF THE CITY AND
COUNTY OF SAN FRANCISCO. DECEMBER, 1864.

[1]–35, [36 blank]. 21.4 x 13.2 cm. Bound with
The Great Dutch Flat Swindle!! in red sheepskin,
gilt. Rebacked.
   Ref.: Cowan p. 512; *Railway Economics* p. 290
   The pamphlet was printed in San Francisco
in 1864.

636   CENTRAL UNIVERSITY, Iowa

FIRST ANNUAL REPORT OF EXECUTIVE COMMITTEE,
AND PROCEEDINGS OF THE ANNUAL MEETING OF
THE BOARD OF TRUSTEES OF THE CENTRAL UNIVER-
SITY OF IOWA, HELD JUNE 1ST & 2D A.D. 1854 . . .
KEOKUK, IOWA: PRINTED AT THE DAILY WHIG
BOOK AND JOB OFFICE, 1854.

[1]–16. 22 x 14.5 cm. Gray printed wrappers,
with title on front wrapper. Lacks back wrapper.
   Ref.: AII (*Iowa*) 63; Moffit 148 see
   Moffit describes an edition published at Oskaloosa.

637 CENTURY ILLUSTRATED MONTH-LY MAGAZINE, THE

[Extracts from] THE CENTURY ILLUSTRATED MONTHLY MAGAZINE. NOVEMBER, 1890, TO APRIL, 1891. VOLS. XLI–XLIII, NEW SERIES VOLS. XIX–XXI. NEW YORK: THE CENTURY CO., 1890–91.

Extracts, as listed below. Illustrated. Octavo, bound together in brown half morocco.

The collection comprises the following materials:

BIDWELL, JOHN: The First Emigrant Train to California. Vol. XIX, pages 106–130.

SHINN, CHARLES H.: Californiana. Pages 130–31.

EDITORS, THE: The Making of California. Page 151.

BIDWELL, JOHN: Life in California before the Gold Discovery. Pages 163–83.

VALLEJO, GUADALUPE: Ranch and Mission Days in Alta California. Pages 183–92.

CALIFORNIANA: [two notes] pages 192–93:
Higuera, Prudencia: Trading with the Americans.
Pratt, Julius H.: The Date of the Discovery of the Yosemite.

SHINN, CHARLES H.: Pioneer Spanish Families in California. Pages 377–89.

DOYLE, JOHN T.: The Missions of Alta California. Pages 389–402.

CALIFORNIANA: [five notes] pages 467–70:
Castro, Maria A.: A California Lion and a Pirate.
Briones, Brigida: A Carnival Ball at Monterey in 1829.
Sibrian, Amalia: A Spanish Girl's Journey from Monterey to Los Angeles.
Briones, Brigida: A Glimpse of Domestic Life in 1827.
Sutter, John A.: A Letter from General Sutter.

BIDWELL, JOHN: Frémont in the Conquest of California. Pages 518–25.

HITTELL, JOHN S.: The Discovery of Gold in California. Pages 526–36.

CALIFORNIANA: [two notes] pages 537–39:
Gillespie, Charles B.: Marshall's Own Account of the Gold Discovery.
Kemble, E. C.: Confirming the Gold Discovery.

BOURKE, JOHN G.: General Crook in the Indian Country. Pages 643–60.

FREMONT, JESSIE B.: Résumé of Frémont's Expeditions. Pages 759–71.

MC GEHEE, MICAJAH: Rough Times in Rough Places. Pages 771–80.

CALIFORNIANA: [two notes] pages 780–87:
Royce, Josiah: Montgomery and Frémont: New Documents on the Bear Flag Affair.

Marshall, J. F. B.: Three Gold Dust Stories.

PRATT, JULIUS H.: To California by Panama in '49. Pages 901–17.

FREMONT, JOHN C.: The Conquest of California. Pages 917–28.

CALIFORNIANA: [three notes] pages 928–31:
Buchanan, James: The Official Policy for the Acquisition of California.
Ferris, A. C.: Hardships of the Isthmus in '49.
Doyle, John T.: Spanish Jealousy of Vancouver.

WAITE, E. G.: Pioneer Mining in California. Vol. XX, pages 127–41.

GILLESPIE, CHARLES B.: A Miner's Sunday in Coloma. Pages 259–69.

CALIFORNIANA: [two notes] pages 269–70:
Burgess, Hubert: Anecdotes of the Mines.
Pratt, Julius H.: The Date of the Discovery of the Yosemite.

MURPHY, VIRGINIA REED: Across the Plains in the Donner Party (1846). Pages 409–26.

CALIFORNIANA: [two notes] pages 477–78:
Ferris, A. C.: Arrival of Overland Trains in California in '49.
Editor, The: A Fourth Survivor of the Gold Discovery Party.

FARWELL, WILLARD B.: Cape Horn and Coöperative Mining in '49. Pages 579–94.

FERRIS, A. C.: To California in 1849 through Mexico. Pages 666–79.

BALDWIN, JR., ROGER S.: Tarrying in Nicaragua. Pages 911–31.

COLEMAN, WILLIAM T.: San Francisco Vigilance Committees. Vol. XXI, pages 133–50.

SHERMAN, WILLIAM T.: Sherman and the San Francisco Vigilantes. Pages 296–309.

PALMER, JOHN W.: Pioneer Days in San Francisco. Pages 541–60.

638 CHAMBERS, JOHN

AUTOBIOGRAPHY . . . EDITED BY JOHN CARL PARISH. IOWA CITY: STATE HISTORICAL SOCIETY OF IOWA, 1908.*

[i]–[xiv, xiv blank], [1]–49, [50 blank]. 26.5 x 17.5 cm. Three illustrations listed. Red buckram, gilt top, uncut.

Ref.: Howes C271; Mott (*Iowa*) p. 85
Limited to 400 copies.

639 CHAMBERS, JULIUS

THE MISSISSIPPI RIVER AND ITS WONDERFUL VALLEY . . . NEW YORK: G. P. PUTNAM'S SONS, 1910.

[i]–xvi, [1]–308, [1–7 advertisements, 8 blank]. 23.9 x 16.6 cm. 80 illustrations and maps listed. Dark blue pictorial cloth, gilt top, uncut.

Ref.: Rader 650

640 CHAMBERS, MARGARET W.

REMINISENCES[!] . . .

[1]–48. 13.8 x 10.2 cm. Maroon limp leather, stamped in gilt on front cover: Reminisences[!] /, outer corners rounded.

Ref.: Howes C272; Smith 1616

On verso of title-page: Written 1894 / Printed 1903 /.

Mrs. Chambers crossed the Plains in 1851 with her three brothers. She celebrated her eighteenth birthday en route cooking for a family of eight. She reached Portland in 1851 and was employed by the Reverend Mr. Lyman. In October of 1852, she arrived at Chambers' Prairies, Puget Sound, where she settled. The work is important both for the author's description of her overland trip and for her reminiscences of the Indian Wars of 1855–66.—EDG

641 CHAMBERS, WILLIAM & ROBERT, *Editors*

CHAMBERS'S JOURNAL OF POPULAR LITERATURE SCIENCE AND ARTS . . . VOLUME IV, NOS. 79–104. JULY–DECEMBER 1855. LONDON: W. AND R. CHAMBERS, MDCCCLVI.

[iii]–viii, [1]–416. 25.4 x 16.8 cm. Plum cloth.

Ref.: Wagner-Camp 257

The issues for December 1, 8, 15, 22, 29 contain an account of an overland trip in 1849 under the heading: Journey from New Orleans to California. Wagner-Camp states this is L. Dow's letter from Mormon Station, Carson Valley, November 25, 1851.

642 CHAMPLAIN, SAMUEL DE

LES VOYAGES DE LA NOVVELLE FRANCE OCCIDENTALE, DICTE CANADA . . . A PARIS: CHEZ CLAVDE COLLET . . . M. DC. XXX II. . . .

[A]–B⁸, A–PP⁴, QQ², A–Pp⁴, Qq³, A⁴, [A]–G⁴, A–B⁴, C². [1]–16, 1–308, 1–310, 1–8, [1]–54, [1–2 blank], 1–20. 23 x 16 cm. Six copperplates, two woodcuts in text, and folding map: Carte de la nouuelle france, augmentée depuis la / derniere, seruant a la nauigation faicte en son vray / Meridien, par le Sᶠ de Champlain Capitaine pour le Roy en la Marine; lequel depuis l'an 1603 jusques en l'année / 1629; a descouuert plusieurs costes, terres, lacs, riuieres, / et Nations de sauuages, par cy deuant incognués, comme / il se voit en ses relations quil a faict Imprimer en 1632. / ou il se voit cette marque ⊞ ce sont habitations / qu'ont faict les françois. / [right of centre:] Faicte l'an 1632 par le Sieur de Champlain / 51.2 x 85.6 cm. Scale: about 23 leagues to one inch. Old French mottled calf, gilt.

Prov.: Brinley-Leiter copy, with book label of the former.

Ref.: JCB III pp. 239–40; Church 420; Field 268; Greenly (*Michigan*) 4; Harrisse 50; Jones 236; Sabin 11839; Streit II 2493

Of all the editions of Champlain, this is the only complete one, the First Part being almost a literal reprint of the other voyages . . . This work gives us the first accurate account we have of the life, habits, and warfare of the Indians in the interior of the present state of New York.—Church

This copy does not contain the passage on page 27 said to have been offensive to Cardinal Richelieu.

643 CHAMPNESS, W.

[Caption title] TO CARIBOO AND BACK. AN EMIGRANT'S JOURNEY TO THE GOLD-FIELDS IN BRITISH COLUMBIA.* I.—ENGLAND TO PANAMA. . . .

203–8, 215–20, 231–34, 245–50, [257]–60 (pages 208, 220, 245 do not carry above title). 26.7 x 18.1 cm. Illustrated. Extracts bound together in blue cloth.

BOUND WITH:

[Caption title] MY ADVENTURES IN THE FAR WEST. CHAPTER I. . . .

11–14, 31–32, 45–48, 59–62, 77–80, 91–94, 107–10, 121–24, 139–44, 155–58, 171–72, 187–90, 205–06, 221–22, 235–38, 249–52 (pages 14, 45, 48, 59, 62, 80, 91, 94, 107, 121, 139, 144, 155, 190, 238, 252 do not carry above title). Illustrated.

Ref.:

Two sets of extracts from *The Leisure Hour*, London, 1865. The second account may have been by J. S. Lee, since the caption under a map within the text reads as follows: Map to Illustrate Adventures in California and Oregon, / By J. S. Lee, Esq. /

644 CHANDLER, E. W., & H. CHANDLER

AUTOGRAPH LETTER, SIGNED. 1845 July 2, Keosauqua, Iowa. Three pages, folio. To John P. Capron, Mashfield, Vermont.

645 CHANDLER, R. W.

[Map] MAP / OF THE / UNITED STATES' / LEAD MINES / ON THE / UPPER MISSISSIPPI RIVER. / DRAWN & PUBLISHED BY / R. W. CHANDLER OF GALENA. / 1829. / EBᴿ MARTIN ENGRAVER / CINCINNATI. / [within lower border:] COPY RIGHT SECURED. /

Map, 37.7 x 44.4 cm. Scale: about 11 miles to one inch.

Ref.:

646 CHANDLESS, WILLIAM

A VISIT TO SALT LAKE; BEING A JOURNEY ACROSS THE PLAINS AND A RESIDENCE IN THE MORMON SETTLEMENTS AT UTAH . . . LONDON: SMITH, ELDER AND CO., 1857.

[i]–xii, [1]–346, [1]–16 advertisements. 19.7 x 12.5 cm. Map: Map / Shewing the / Author's Route. / [centre, below neatline:] Published by Smith, Elder & Cº, 65, Cornhill. London, 1857, / [lower right:] Standidge & Cº, Lith. Old Jewry, London. / 16.2 x 28.7 cm. No scale given. Dark yellow cloth, blind embossed panels on sides, title in gilt on backstrip, uncut.

Ref.: Bradford 844; Cowan p. 113; Howes C286; Wagner-Camp 287

The advertisements in the present copy are dated April, 1857. The book is more common with advertisements dated December, 1858.—EDG

647 CHAPMAN, J. BUTLER

HISTORY OF KANSAS: AND EMIGRANT'S GUIDE. A DESCRIPTION GEOGRAPHICAL AND TOPOGRAPHICAL—ALSO, CLIMATE, SOIL, PRODUCTIONS AND COMPARATIVE VALUE WITH THE OTHER STATES AND TERRITORIES, INCLUDING ITS POLITICAL HISTORY, OFFICERS—CANDIDATES—EMIGRANT COLONIES—ELECTION, ABOLITION, SQUATTER AND PROSLAVERY CONTENTIONS AND INQUISITIONS; WITH THE PROSPECTS OF THE TERRITORY FOR FREEDOM OR SLAVERY. ALL COMPILED FROM A THREE MONTH'S TRAVEL THROUGH THE TERRITORY IN 1854 . . . AKRON: TEESDALE, ELKINS & CO., 1855.

[1]–116. 17.6 x 13.2 cm. Tan printed wrappers with title on front wrapper. In a red cloth case.

Ref.: Dolbee, C. (*Kansas Historical Quarterly*, Vol. VIII, No. 3); Howes C293; Wagner-Camp 252

Only Volume I was published. None of the four known copies contains the map. Miss Dolbee's article contains a full discussion of the author and his work.

648 CHAPMAN, SAMUEL D.

HISTORY OF TAMA COUNTY, IOWA. ITS CITIES, TOWNS AND VILLAGES WITH EARLY REMINISCENCES, PERSONAL INCIDENTS AND ANECDOTES, AND A COMPLETE BUSINESS DIRECTORY OF THE COUNTY . . . PRINTED AT THE TOLEDO TIMES OFFICE, 1879.

[5]–296. 21.2 x 14 cm. Green cloth, title in gilt on front cover and backstrip.

Ref.: Howes C296; Mott (*Iowa*) p. 45 Published at Toledo, Iowa.

649 CHARLESS, JOSEPH

[Wrapper title] NO. I. CHARLESS' MISSOURI & ILLINOIS MAGAZINE ALMANAC, FOR 1818 . . . ST. LOUIS, MRI. TER.: PRINTED AND SOLD BY JOSEPH CHARLESS.

C–E⁶. [25?–60?]. 19.5 x 12 cm. White printed wrappers with title on front wrapper, advertisements on verso of back wrapper. Lacks all leaves before leaf C, page [24?].

Ref.: AII (*Missouri*) 14

The AII (*Missouri*) collation of the MoHi copy calls for 62 pages with a query, and the copy is described as lacking four leaves. It is a little difficult to reconcile the collations, unless either the first or last gathering consisted of eight instead of six leaves of which one was a blank. In the present copy, page [60?] carries Finis at the foot.

650 CHARLEVOIX, PIERRE FRANCOIS XAVIER DE

HISTOIRE ET DESCRIPTION GENERALE DE LA NOUVELLE FRANCE, AVEC LE JOURNAL HISTORIQUE D'UN VOYAGE FAIT PAR ORDRE DU ROI DANS L'AMERIQUE SEPTENTRIONALE . . . PARIS: CHEZ PIERRE-FRANCOIS GIFFART . . . M. DCC. XLIV.

[¶]², *², *⁴, a–h⁴, b–c⁴, d¹, A–OOoo⁴. [*]², a⁴, e⁴, A–Cccc⁴, Ddddd³, a–g⁴. [*]², a–b⁴, c², a⁴, b³, A–Yyy⁴. [1–8], [i]–viij, i–[lxiv], ix–xxvj, [1]–664. [1–4], i–[xvi], [1]–582, [1]–56. [1–2], [i]–[xx], i–xiv, [1]–543, [544 blank]. (Volume 1: leaves L and Bbbiij are cancels, pages 355 and 455 mispaginated 354 and 454; Volume 2: leaves A and Qqqij are cancels, page 215 is mispaginated 189.) 25 x 19.2 cm. 22 plates and 28 maps. Map: Carte de / L'Amerique Septentrionale / Pour servir à l'Histoire de la Nouvelle / France. / Dressée par N. B. Ing. du Roy, et Hydrog. de la Marine. / 1743. / [lower right:] Dheulland Sculp. / 28 x 35.8 cm. Scale: about 120 French Leagues to one inch. Map: Carte / de l'Accadie / Dressée sur les Manuscrits au Dépost / des Cartes et Plans de la Marine. / Par N. B. Ingʳ et Hyd. de la Marine. / 1744. / 20.3 x 22.1 cm. Scale: about 13 1/2 French Leagues to one inch. Map: Carte des Costes de la Floride / Françoise / Suivant les premieres découvertes. Dressée par N. Bellin Ingʳ de la Marine. / [in left margin:] 39. / 20.7 x 14.5 cm. Scale: about 22 French Leagues to one inch. Map: Carte / de la Riviere de Richelieu / et du / Lac Champlain, / Dressée sur les Manuscrits / du Dépost des / Cartes, Plans, et Journˣ de la Marine / Par N. B. Ingʳ de la M. / 1744. / [lower right:] Desbruslins sculpˢ / [left margin:] 7. / 30.5 x 13.7 cm. Scale: about 3 3/4 French Leagues to one inch. Map: Carte de / LIsle de Montreal / et de ses Environs / Dressée sur les Manuscrits du Depost des Cartes Plans / et Journaux de la Marine. / Par N. Bellin Ingénieur et Hidrographe de la Marine. / 1744. / [lower right:] Dheulland Sculp / [left margin:] 17. / 24.6 x 30.4 cm. Scale: about 1 French League to one inch. Map: Carte de / l'Isle de Terre-neuve / Dressée par N. B. Ingenieur au Dépôt / des Cartes et Plans de la Marine. / 1744. / [three-line note] / [lower right:] Dheulland Sculp. / [left margin:] 21. / 28.6 x 36.5 cm. Scale: 14 French Leagues to one inch. Map: Carte des / Bayes, Rades et Port / de Plaisance / dans l'Isle de Terre Neuve / Dressée sur les Manuscrits au Dépôt / des Cartes, Plans et Journaux de la Marine / Par N. B. Ingénieur du Roy et de la Marine, / 1744. / [lower right:] Dheulland Sculp. / [left margin:] 2. / 19.6 x 28.4 cm. Scale: 750 toises to one inch. Map: Carte / de la Partie Orientale / de la Nouvelle France / ou du Canada / Dédiée / A Monseigneur le Comte de Maurepas / Ministre et Secretaire d'Etat, / Commandeur des Ordres du Roy. / Par N. Bellin Ingénieur de la Marine 1744. / [lower right:] Desbruslins Sculpsit /. 40.2 x 56 cm. Scale: about 22 French Leagues to one inch. Map: Carte de la / Baye de Hudson / Par N. Bellin Ingenieur de la Marine 1744. / [lower right:] Desbruslins Sculpsit / [left margin:] 3. / 21 x 29.1 cm. Scale: about 40 French Leagues to one inch. Map: Carte du Fonds de la Baye de Hudson / que les Anglois appellent Baye James. Par N. Bellin Ing^r de la Marine 1744. / [lower right:] Desbruslins Sculpsit / [left margin:] 38. / 19.7 x 14.2 cm. Scale: about 15 1/2 French Leagues to one inch. Map: Carte de / La Louisiane / Cours du Mississipi[!] et / Pais Voisins / Dediée à M. le Comte de Maurepas, Ministre et / Secretaire d'Etat Commander des Ordres / du Roy. / Par N. Bellin Ingenieur de la Marine. 1744. / [lower left:] Dheulland Sculp / [left margin:] 38 [?] / 39.6 x 55.9 cm. Scale: about 33 French Leagues to one inch. Map: Plan du / Port Royal / dans l'Accadie / Appellé aujourd'. par les Anglois / Annapolis Royale / Par N. B. Ing. de la M. / 1744. / Echelles / [lower left:] Dheulland Sculp / [left margin:] 4. / 19.4 x 28.1 cm. Scale: about 900 toises to one inch. Map: Plan du Port de la Haive / Situé à la Côte d'Accadie / . . . / Par N. B. Ing. de la M. 1744. / [lower left:] Dheulland Sculp. / [left margin:] 5. / 19.8 x 28.2 cm. Scale: 1/4 French League to one inch. Map: Plan de la Baye de Chedabouctou / aujourd'hui / Havre de Milfort / Par N. B. Ingénieur de la Marine 1744. / [lower right:] Dheulland Sculpsit / [left margin:] 6. / 19.9 x 28.3 cm. Scale: about 3/8 French marine League to one inch. Map: Carte de /

L'Isle Royale / Dressée par N. Bellin / Ingenieur de la Marine / 1744. / [left margin:] 18. / 22.5 x 26.6 cm. Scale: about 6 French Leagues to one inch. Map: Plan du Port et Ville de Louisbourg dans l'Isle Royale. P. N. B. Ing. de la M. 1744. / [three lines] [lower right:] Dheulland Sculpsit / [left margin:] 8. / 19.8 x 28.1 cm. Scale: 110 toises to one inch. Map: Plan du Port Dauphin / et de sa Rade / Avec l'Entrée de Labrador. / Par N. B. Ing. au D. de la M. / 1744. / [left margin:] 9. / Inset: Fort Projetté pour défendre l'Entreé[!] du Port Dauphin. / 9.2 x 11.1 cm. Scale: about 98 toises to one inch. 19.9 x 28.4 cm. Scale: about 1100 toises to one inch. Map: Plan de la Nouvelle Orleans Sur les Manuscrits du Dépôt des Cartes de la Marine. Par N. B. Ing^r de la M. 1744. / [6 lines] / [lower right:] Dheulland sculpsit / [left margin:] 10. / 19.5 x 27.9 cm. Scale: about 65 toises to one inch. Map: Carte de l'Ocean Occidental et Partie de l'Amérique Septentrionale Dressée pour l'intelligence du Journal du Voyage, / Que le R. P. de Charlevoix de la Compagnie de Jesus a fait en 1720. au Canada, à la Louisiane, & à St Domingue. Par N. Bellin Ingénieur de la Marine 1744. / [one line] / [lower right:] Desbruslins sculpsit / [left margin:] 19. / 24.5 x 37.5 cm. No scale given. Map: Carte du Cours / de la Riviere du Saguenay / appellée par les Sauvages / Pitchitaouichetz / Dressée sur les Manuscrits du Dépost / des Cartes, et Plans de la Marine. / 1744. / Par N. Bellin Ingénieur de la Marine. / [lower right:] Dheulland Sculp. / [left margin:] 11. / 19.9 x 28.6 cm. Scale: 3 French Leagues to one inch. Map: Carte de / l'Isle d'Orleans / et du Passage de la Traverse / dans le Fleuve St Laurent / Dressée sur les Manuscrits du Dépôt des Cartes / Plans et Journaux de la Marine. / Par N. Bellin Ing. et Hidrographe de la Marine. / 1744. / [lower right:] Dheulland Sculp. / [left margin:] 12. / 19.1 x 27.6 cm. Scale: about 1 1/8 French marine Leagues to one inch. Map: Plan du Bassin de / Quebec / et de ses Environs / Par N. B. Ingénieur de la Marine. 1744. / [lower right:] Dheulland Sculp. / [left margin:] 13. / 19.8 x 28.1 cm. Scale: about 430 toises to one inch. Map: Plan de la Ville de / Quebec / [25 lines] / [lower right:] Dheulland sculp. / [left margin:] 14. / 19.5 x 29.7 cm. Scale: about 90 toises to one inch. Map: Carte / des Lacs du Canada / Dressée sur les Manuscrits du Depost / des Cartes, Plans et Journaux de la Marine / et sur le Journal du RP. de Charlevoix. / Par N. Bellin Ingenieur et Hydrographe / de la Marine 1744. / 28.9 x 44.3 cm. Scale: about 22 French Leagues to one inch. Map: Carte du Detroit / Entre le Lac Superieur et / le Lac Huron, / avec le Sault Sainte Marie et le Poste de / Michilli-makinac, / Dressé[!] sur les Manuscrits du Dé-pôt des / Cartes et Plans de la Marine / 1744. / Par N. B. Ingénieur de la / Marine. / [lower right:] Desbruslins Sculpsit / [left margin:] 37. / 21.3 x 15.9 cm. Scale: about 4 3/4 French Leagues to one inch. Map: Carte des Em-bouchures du / Mississipi / Sur les Manuscrits du Dépôt des Cartes et Plans de la Marine. / Par N. B. Ing^r de la Marine. / 1744. / [lower left:] Dheulland Sculp / [left margin:] 15. / 19.9 x 28.4 cm. Scale: about 300 toises to one inch. Map: Partie de / La Coste de la Louisiane et de la Floride / depuis le Mississipi Jus qua[!] St Marc d'Apalache / Dressée sur les Manuscrits du Depost des Plans de la Marine / Par N. B. Ing^r du Roy et de la Marine / 1744. / [left margin:] 34. / 20.2 x 43 cm. Scale about 8 French Leagues to one inch. Map: Plan de la / Baye de Pansa-cola[!] / Par N. B. Ingénieur de la Marine. / 1744. / [lower left:] Dheulland Sculp / [left mar-gin:] 16. / 19.7 x 28.1 cm. Scale: about 1900 toises to one inch. Three volumes, contem-porary polished calf, gilt backstrips, yellow edges.

    Ref.: Clark I 59; Field 282; Greenly (*Michi-gan*) 11; Howes C307; Raines p. 49; Sabin 12135; Staton & Tremaine 4697

Widely read at the time of publication, Charlevoix's *Histoire* is one of the best works of the period about the New World.

651 CHARLEVOIX, PIERRE FRANCOIS-XAVIER DE

JOURNAL OF A VOYAGE TO NORTH-AMERICA . . . LONDON: PRINTED FOR R. AND J. DODSLEY, IN PALL-MALL, M DCC LXI.

A^4, B–Aa^8. A^4, B–Cc^8, Dd^4. [i]–viii, [1]–382, [383–84 blank]. [i]–viii, [1]–380, [382–84 adver-tisements], [385–406 Index], [407–08 blank]. 20.8 x 12.6 cm. Map: A Map of the Western Ocean and Part of North America. / Intended to Illustrate the Voyage made by F. Charlevoix the Jesuit in 1720, to Canada, Louisiana, & St Domingo. / [one line] / [upper right:] Frontis-piece to Vol. I / [lower left:] T. Kitchin Sculp. / 23.5 x 37 cm. Scale: about 125 leagues to one inch. Two volumes, contemporary full polished calf, red leather labels, yellow edges.

    Ref.: Clark I 60; Field 283; Greenly (*Michigan*) 11; Howes C308; Hubach p. 11; Sabin 12139; Staton & Tremaine 190; Streit III 1423

Father Charlevoix created one of the most interesting of all eighteenth century travel books in his *Journal*, of which this is the first English translation.

652 CHASE, CHARLES M.

THE EDITOR'S RUN IN NEW MEXICO AND COLORADO. EMBRACING TWENTY-EIGHT LETTERS ON STOCK RAISING, AGRICULTURE, TERRITORIAL HISTORY, GAME, SOCIETY, GROWING TOWNS, PRICES, PROS-PECTS, &C . . . LYNDON, VERMONT.

[1]–233, [234–36 advertisements]. 22.6 x 14.7 cm. Frontispiece and illustrations in text, unlisted. Gray printed wrappers with title on front wrap-per, advertisements on verso of front and recto and verso of back wrapper. In a red cloth case.

    Ref.: Adams (*Ramp. Herd*) 450; Howes C315; Rader 666; Saunders 3957

Copyrighted 1882. Printed at Montpelier, Vermont, by the Argus and Patriot Steam Book and Job Printing House.

653 CHASE, PHILANDER

AN ADDRESS, DELIVERED AT SAINT JAMES' CHURCH, CHICAGO . . . JUNE 3, 1839 . . . [CHICAGO:] PRINTED AT THE OFFICE OF THE CHICAGO AMERI-CAN, 1839.

[1]–11, [12 blank]. 22 x 14.5 cm. Tan printed wrappers with title on front wrapper. In a green cloth case.

    Ref.: Byrd 443; McMurtrie (*Chicago*) 21

654 CHASE, PHILANDER

BISHOP CHASE'S ADDRESS AND OTHER SERVICES, AT THE LAYING OF THE CORNER STONE OF THE CHAPEL AND SCHOOL-HOUSE OF JUBILEE COLLEGE, ILLINOIS, ON THE THIRD DAY OF APRIL, 1839. PEORIA: PRINTED BY S. H. DAVIS, 1839.

[1]–12. 20.7 x 13.4 cm. Removed from bound volume, unbound. In large red cloth case stamped: Bishop Chase. Jubilee College.

    Ref.: Byrd 444; McMurtrie (*Peoria*) 4

655 CHASE, PHILANDER

BISHOP CHASE'S ADDRESS, AT THE CLOSE OF THE CONVENTION OF THE PROTESTANT EPISCOPAL CHURCH, IN CINCINNATI, OHIO, OCTOBER 16, A.D. 1850. PHILADELPHIA: KING & BAIRD.

[1]–16. 21.1 x 13.5 cm. Removed from bound volume, unbound. In large red cloth case stamped: Bishop Chase. Jubilee College.

    Ref.: Sabin 12194

656 CHASE, PHILANDER

BISHOP CHASE'S ADDRESS DELIVERED BEFORE THE CONVENTION OF THE PROTESTANT EPISCOPAL CHURCH, SPRINGFIELD, ILLINOIS, JUNE 16TH, 1845. SAINT LOUIS: PRINTED BY DANIEL DAVIES, 1845.

[i–ii blank], [1]–27, [28–32 blank]. 22.5 x 14.1 cm. View of Jubilee College. Buff printed wrap-pers, with title as above on front wrapper within decorative border. In large red case stamped: Bishop Chase. Jubilee College.

Ref.: AII (*Missouri*) 433; Sabin 12190

A second copy of this pamphlet accompanies the Protestant Episcopal Church (Illinois): *Journal of the Ninth Annual Convention . . .*

657 CHASE, PHILANDER

[Caption title] BISHOP CHASE'S ADDRESS TO THE CONVENTION OF THE PROT. EPIS. CHURCH, ILLINOIS, IN JUBILEE CHAPEL, JUNE 7, 1841. . . .

[1]–14, [15 blank, 16 price]. 22.2 x 12.3 cm. Removed from bound volume, unbound. In a red cloth case stamped: Bishop Chase Pamphlets.

Ref.: Sabin 12194

The edition of this address which appeared as an appendix to the Protestant Episcopal Church in the U.S.A. (Illinois): *Journal of the Sixth Annual Convention . . .* is identical except for the caption title and the price on the last page.

658 CHASE, PHILANDER

BISHOP CHASE'S ANSWER TO BISHOP WHITTINGHAM'S 'PROTEST.'

[1]–8. 20.7 x 13.3 cm. Removed from bound volume, unbound. In large red cloth case stamped: Bishop Chase. Jubilee College.

Ref.: Byrd 1678

No place of printing given.

The pamphlet carries a letter from Bishop Chase to the Archbishop of Canterbury dated Jubilee College, Illinois, U.S., April 19, 1851. There are also included two letters to Chase from Lord Kenyon, a letter from an unnamed British clergyman, and "Some closing Remarks" by Chase.

659 CHASE, PHILANDER

BISHOP CHASE'S PASTORAL LETTER TO HIS DIOCESE OF ILLINOIS . . . MAY 14, A.D. 1837. PEORIA: PRINTED AT THE REGISTER OFFICE, 1837.

[1]–25, [26–8 blank]. 21 x 13.1 cm. Sewn, removed from bound volume, unbound. In large red cloth case stamped: Bishop Chase. Jubilee College.

Ref.: Byrd 310; McMurtrie (*Peoria*) 2

660 CHASE, PHILANDER

[Wrapper title] DEFENCE OF KENYON COLLEGE . . . COLUMBUS, OHIO: OLMSTED & BAILHACHE, 1831.

[1]–72. 22.4 x 14.2 cm. Gray printed wrappers with title on front wrapper. In large red case stamped: Bishop Chase. Jubilee College.

Ref.: Sabin 12191

The caption title on page [1] reads: Bishop

Chase's Defence / against / The Slanders / of the / Rev. G. M. West. / [double rule] / . . .

661 CHASE, PHILANDER

LETTER OF BISHOP CHASE TO THE MEMBERS OF THE PROTESTANT EPISCOPAL CHURCH, IN THE CITY OF CHICAGO.

[1]–[8], [1]–7, [8 blank]. 20.7 x 13.4 cm. Removed from bound volume, unbound. In large red case stamped: Bishop Chase. Jubilee College.

Ref.: Byrd 1679

The first letter is dated Chicago, May 19, A.D. 1851. The second part, which bears the imprint of the Chicago Democrat Steam Presses on page [1], is headed: Address of the Wardens and Vestrymen of Grace Church, Chicago, to the Protestant Episcopal Church in the Diocese of Illinois.

662 CHASE, PHILANDER

A PLEA FOR THE WEST . . . BOSTON: SAMUEL H. PARKER, 1827.

[1]–15, [16 blank]. 23 x 15.3 cm. Sewn, uncut, unopened. In large red box stamped: Bishop Chase. Jubilee College.

Prov.: Inscribed by the recipient on the title-page: Wm Jenks / From the R̲ᵗ Rev̲ᵈ / Bp. Chase. / Laid in is a presentation note, one page, 19.7 x 12.6 cm. No place, no date. With Bishop Chase's most / respectful compliments / Hancock House /.

Ref.: Sabin 12192

663 CHASE, PHILANDER

[Wrapper title] . . . REMINISCENCES OF BISHOP CHASE. PEORIA, ILL.: S. M. DAVIS, 1841.

[1]–120. 121–240. 241–480. [481]–731. [733]–876. 22.5 x 14 cm. Seven parts in five numbers, brown printed wrappers, with title on front wrappers, errata on verso of front wrapper of first part. In a dark red cloth case.

Ref.: Byrd 613, 614, 698; Clark II 141; Howes C319; McMurtrie (*Peoria*) 5, 6; Sabin 12193

In the *Peoria and Northwestern Gazetteer* for December 17, 1841, the statement is made that Bishop Chase's *Reminiscences* is "now in course of publication" and that "all would have been taken if edition had been 10,000 instead of 1500" indicating that the first two numbers were published in an edition of 1500 copies.—EDG

Parts 5–7, issued in two numbers, carry the following New York imprint: New York: / R. Craighead, Printer, 112 Fulton Street. / [dash] / 1843. / Nos. 5 & 6. 1843. / [within thick and thin and thin rule borders].

664 CHASE, SAMUEL

[Wrapper title] MALIGNITY EXPOSED; OR, A VINDI-
CATION OF BISHOP CHASE AGAINST THE MALICIOUS
ACCUSATIONS OF AN ANONYMOUS PAMPHLET
PRINTED IN ANN-STREET, NEW-YORK . . . PEORIA:
S. H. DAVIS, 1847.

[1]–40. 23.2 x 14.5 cm. Brown printed wrappers
with title on front wrapper. Lacks back wrapper.
In red cloth case stamped: Bishop Chase Pam-
phlets.
 Ref.: Byrd 1165; McMurtrie (*Peoria*) 22;
Sabin 12208
 The dedication appears on the inside front
wrapper. The "anonymous pamphlet" was *A
Plain Statement for the Consideration of the
Friends, of the Protestant Episcopal Church* . . .
New York, 1846.

665 CHASE, SAMUEL

THE PERPETUITY AND IDENTITY OF THE THREEFOLD
PRIESTHOOD. A SERMON, PREACHED IN THE CHAPEL
OF JUBILEE COLLEGE . . . PEORIA: WM. H. AND
S. G. BUTLER, 1843.*

[1]–36. 18.3 x 11.6 cm. Removed from bound
volume, unbound. In red cloth case stamped:
Bishop Chase Pamphlets.
 Ref.: Byrd 770; McMurtrie (*Peoria*) 12

666 CHASE, SAMUEL

[Caption title] REVIEW OF JUBILEE COLLEGE . . .
CHRISTMAS, 1843 . . .

[1]–34, [35–6 blank]. 19 x 11.6 cm. Old plain
wrappers. In red cloth case stamped: Bishop
Chase Pamphlets.
 Prov.: Chicago Historical Society copy.
 Ref.: Byrd 771; McMurtrie (*Peoria*) 13;
Sabin 12208
 The imprint appears on page 34: S. H. Davis,
Printer, Peoria. / The Society's perforated
stamps appear in the front wrapper and in pages
19–20.

667 CHASE, SAMUEL

[Wrapper title] REVIEW OF JUBILEE COLLEGE . . .
CHRISTMAS, 1843.

[i]–iv, [5]–32, [1–4 advertisements]. 16.7 x 11.3
cm. Two folding frontispieces, view of Jubilee
College. Gray printed wrappers with title on
front wrapper, dedication on verso of front
wrapper, prospectus of Jubilee College on recto
and verso of back wrapper. In red cloth case
stamped: Bishop Chase Pamphlets.
 Ref.: Byrd 771 see; McMurtrie (*Peoria*) 13
see; Sabin 12208
 Pages [i]–iv comprise: Bishop Chase's Letter
to his Absent / Friends / Dated New York, 12th
of July, 1844. / The advertisements at the back

are for books published by Alexander V. Blake,
77 Fulton Street, New York.
 Editions: [Peoria, 1843].

668 CHASTELLUX, FRANCOIS JEAN, MARQUIS DE

VOYAGES . . . EN AMERIQUE. 1785.

[A]–O⁸, P². [1]–228. 25 x 13.3 cm. Plain gray
wrappers, uncut. In a cloth case.
 Prov.: Bookplate of Nicolao de Nobili. Press-
mark on verso of title-leaf: 3:10 /.
 Ref.: Howes C324; Monaghan 404; Sabin
12226
 A brilliant copy of the unauthorized Paris edition. Chastellux had twenty-four to twenty-
seven copies of his journal printed on the press
of the French fleet off Newport in 1781. Then
he allowed extracts of a later journal to appear
in a periodical published at Gotha over several
years, but not in chronological order. These extracts were collected and printed in a 191-page
volume at Cassell. The present edition was probably printed at Paris.

669 CHEADLE, WALTER B.

CHEADLE'S JOURNAL OF TRIP ACROSS CANADA
1862–1863 . . . OTTAWA, CANADA: GRAPHIC PUB-
LISHERS LIMITED, 1931.*

[1]–311, [312 blank]. 19.7 x 12.4 cm. Illustrated.
Maroon limp fabrikoid.
 Ref.: Wagner-Camp 420 note
 Cheadle's *Journal* was the basis for Milton
and Cheadle: *The Northwest Passage by Land*,
London, 1865.

670 CHEROKEE NATION. Laws, Statutes, etc.

LAWS OF THE CHEROKEE NATION . . . TAHLEQUAH,
C. N.: CHEROKEE ADVOCATE OFFICE, 1852.*

[1]–179, [1]–248. 18 x 12 cm. Marbled boards,
calf backstrip and corners. Lacks back endleaf.
 Prov.: Inscribed in pencil on front endleaf:
To W H Kromegay / from Mary F Bell / In
memory of / Hoolie Bell /.
 Ref.: Hargrett (*Oklahoma*) 152; Hargrett
(*Bibliography*) 18; Rader 710
 This is perhaps the most important single vol-
ume in the fields of Cherokee law and history.—
Hargrett (*Bibliography*)
 Pages [118] comprise: Constitution / of / the
Cherok[!] Nation: / formed by a Convention of
Delegates / from the several districts, / at New
Echota, / July, 1827. /
 The second part carries a separate title-page:
The / Constitution and Laws / of the / Cherokee
Nation: / passed at / Tahlequah, Cherokee Na-

tion, / 1839–51. / [double rule] / Tahlequah. Cherokee Nation: / 1852. /

671 [CHESTERFIELD, PHILIP DORMER STANHOPE, 4TH EARL OF]

AN APOLOGY FOR A LATE RESIGNATION . . . LONDON: PRINTED FOR JOHN FREEMAN [1748].

[A]–E⁴, F³. [1]–46. 19.4 x 11.7 cm. Bound with Number 3115. (Leaf F4 missing, probably a blank.)
   Ref.:
Lord Marchmont was co-author of this defensive pamphlet.

672 CHETLAIN, AUGUSTUS L.

RECOLLECTIONS OF SEVENTY YEARS . . . GALENA: THE GAZETTE PUBLISHING COMPANY, 1899.

[1]–304. 21.1 x 14.4 cm. Portrait. Green cloth.
   Prov.: Inscribed on recto of frontispiece: To / Mrs Emma Sandieson and her / affectionate and devoted son Montague, / with cordial esteem and best wishes / The author / Galena Ill April 1900 /.
   Ref.:
A very interesting book, with much on early Galena, the Civil War, Grant, Sherman, Utah in 1867, and early Chicago.—EDG

673 CHEW, BEVERLY

AUTOGRAPH LETTER, SIGNED. 1798 November 7, New Castle, Delaware. One page, 34.4 x 20.8 cm. To Philip Nolan.

Announcing his departure on a voyage to Bilbao. One passage reads as follows: "Respecting the connexion we have so long contemplated you will then find my wishes for it undiminished, and will be able to make it much more advantageous *on my part* than when I last saw you." The letter is accompanied by a duplicate copy on two pages, with an additional paragraph stating that three copies of the letter were despatched.

674 CHEYENNE CLUB

BY-LAWS, ARTICLES OF INCORPORATION AND HOUSE RULES, WITH LIST OF OFFICERS AND MEMBERS OF THE CHEYENNE CLUB. CLUB HOUSE, 17TH ST., COR. WARREN AVENUE. 1888.

[1]–36. 16.9 x 13 cm. Semi-limp maroon leather, red edges.
   Ref.:
Printed at Cheyenne, Wyoming, 1888. The Cheyenne Club was the informal headquarters of the Wyoming cattle barons.

675 CHICAGO

CHICAGO. A STRANGERS' AND TOURISTS' GUIDE TO THE CITY OF CHICAGO, CONTAINING REMINIS-CENCES OF CHICAGO IN THE EARLY DAY . . . CHICAGO: RELIG. PHILO. PUB. ASSOCIATION, 1866.

[1]–129, [130 blank, 131–50 advertisements]. (Two leaves of advertisements on yellow paper precede the frontispiece.) 15.2 x 9.5 cm. 23 illustrations, unlisted, and a map: Map of / Chicago / 1865. / Published by Edᵂ Mendel. / Chicago. / [3 lines] / Lith. by Ed Mendel Chicago / 38 x 25.2 cm. No scale given. Plum cloth, title in gilt on front cover within blind fillet borders, advertisements on yellow printed endpapers.
   Ref.: AII (*Chicago*) 1031; Howes C365

676 CHICAGO. Charter

CHARTER OF THE CITY OF CHICAGO, AND AMENDMENTS. WITH RULES OF COUNCIL AND ORDINANCES. CHICAGO: PRINTED AT THE DEMOCRAT OFFICE, 1849.

[1]–116. 21.2 x 13.7 cm. Old marbled board sides, new calf backstrip.
   Prov.: Inscribed on title-page: B. S. Morse's /.
   Ref.: Byrd 1426; Howes C364; McMurtrie (*Chicago*) 170
McMurtrie's collation shows a typographical error; 16 p. instead of 116.

677 CHICAGO. Public Works, Board of

[Broadsheet] SIDEWALK NOTICE. OFFICE OF THE BOARD OF PUBLIC WORKS, STREET DEPARTMENT, CHICAGO, 187 . . .

Broadsheet, 17.5 x 21.6 cm.
   Ref.:
Filled in in pencil to Isaac N. Arnold and dated April 11, 1873. Signed in facsimile at lower right by the Secretary of the Board of Public Works, F. H. Bailey. The verso bears extracts from the City Charter relating to sidewalks.
   Tipped into ILLINOIS AND MICHIGAN CANAL: *Complete List of Lots and Lands . . . 1850.*

678 CHICAGO. Sewerage Commissioners, Board of

REPORT AND PLAN OF SEWERAGE FOR THE CITY OF CHICAGO, ILLINOIS, ADOPTED BY THE BOARD OF SEWERAGE COMMISSIONERS DECEMBER 31, 1855. CHICAGO: PRINTED AT THE OFFICE OF CHARLES SCOTT, 1855.

[1]–22. Bound with related materials in contemporary half black calf.
   Ref.: AII (*Chicago*) 120; Byrd 2239; Sabin 12653
See under ILLINOIS CENTRAL RAILROAD COMPANY.

679 CHICAGO. MAYOR (R. B. Mason)

[Broadside] PROCLAMATION! IN CONSEQUENCE OF THE GREAT CALAMITY THAT HAS BEFALLEN OUR CITY, AND FOR THE PRESERVATION OF GOOD ORDER, IT IS ORDERED BY THE MAYOR AND COMMON COUNCIL OF CHICAGO, THAT NO LIQUOR BE SOLD IN ANY SALOON UNTIL FURTHER ORDERS. THE BOARD OF POLICE ARE CHARGED WITH THE EXECUTION OF THIS ORDER. R. B. MASON, MAYOR. CHICAGO, OCT. 9, 1871.

Broadside, 9.5 x 19.7 cm. Text, 8 x 19 cm.
Ref.:

680 CHICAGO. MAYOR (R. B. Mason)

[Broadside] PROCLAMATION! THE PRESERVATION OF THE GOOD ORDER AND PEACE OF THE CITY IS HEREBY ENTRUSTED TO LIEUT. GENERAL P. H. SHERIDAN, U.S. ARMY. THE POLICE WILL ACT IN CONJUNCTION WITH THE LIEUT. GENERAL IN THE PRESERVATION OF THE PEACE AND QUIET OF THE CITY, AND THE SUPERINTENDENT OF POLICE WILL CONSULT WITH HIM TO THAT END. THE INTENT HEREOF BEING TO PRESERVE THE PEACE OF THE CITY, WITHOUT INTERFERING WITH THE FUNCTIONS OF THE CITY GOVERNMENT. GIVEN UNDER MY HAND THIS 11TH DAY OF OCTOBER, 1871. R. B. MASON, MAYOR.

Broadside, 16.8 x 14.3 cm. Text, 14.9 x 11 cm.
Ref.:

681 CHICAGO ACADEMY OF SCIENCES

TRANSACTIONS OF THE CHICAGO ACADEMY OF SCIENCES. CHICAGO: PUBLISHED BY THE ACADEMY, 1867–1869.

[i]–[xii, xii blank], [1]–337, [338 blank]. [i]–viii, [1]–23, [24 blank]. 27.8 x 18.7 cm. Portrait, two maps, and 33 plates (some colored). (Plates numbered 1–19, 21–34.) Two volumes bound together, black cloth, black leather corners and backstrip, title in gilt on backstrip.
Ref.: AII (*Chicago*) 1149, 1473; Howes C375; Meisel III pp. 256–60; Sabin 12618

The first volume, pages 133–226, contains Robert Kennicott's journal (extracts) with a *Memoir* to him. Kennicott was a founder of the Academy. He had made a trip to the Red River country in 1857 and two years later went to British and Arctic America for the Smithsonian Institution as far as Fort Yukon. In 1865 he surveyed a route for a telegraph line for Western Union in Alaska and on the Yukon River. He died at Fort Nulato, Alaska, in 1866.

682 CHICAGO, BURLINGTON & QUINCY RAILROAD

THE BROKEN BOW COUNTRY IN CENTRAL AND WESTERN NEBRASKA, AND HOW TO GET THERE.

WITH A SECTIONAL MAP OF NEBRASKA, SHOWING TOWNS AND RAILWAY LINES, COMPLETED AND IN COURSE OF CONSTRUCTION, ON AUGUST 1ST, 1886. PUBLISHED BY "BURLINGTON ROUTE," AUGUST, 1886. OMAHA, NEBRASKA. LINCOLN, NEB.: JOURNAL COMPANY, STATE PRINTERS, 1886.

[1]–[18]. 21.9 x 14.6 cm. Map: Map of / Nebraska / Published by the / Burlington Route. / 1886 / Compiled from Official / Records of the Government / and Rail Road Offices. / Scale 12 Miles to 1 Inch / [diagrammatic scale] / F. Hirschfeld, C. E. / 58.4 x 100.5 cm. Scale as above. Orange printed wrappers with title on front wrapper, advertisement on verso of front wrapper, small map of the Burlington Route on verso of back wrapper.
Ref.:

683 CHICAGO COLORADO COLONY

CHICAGO COLORADO COLONY. CONSTITUTION AND BY-LAWS, WITH COMPREHENSIVE CHAPTERS, ON AGRICULTURE, IRRIGATION, CLIMATE . . . LONGMONT, COLORADO. JULY 1ST, 1871. DENVER: ROCKY MOUNTAIN NEWS PRINTING HOUSE, 1871.

[1]–29, [30 blank, 31–32 advertisements]. 22 x 13.9 cm. Light blue printed wrappers with title on front wrapper, advertisements on verso of front and recto and verso of back wrapper.
Ref.: McMurtrie & Allen (*Colorado*) 131; Wilcox p. 24

Although the *Sentinel* was being printed at Longmont, this pamphlet was produced in Denver.

684 CHICAGO COLORADO COLONY

CHICAGO COLORADO COLONY PRELIMINARY ORGANIZATION. CONSTITUTION AND BY-LAWS WITH COMPREHENSIVE CHAPTERS ON AGRICULTURE, IRRIGATION, CLIMATE, THE NEW TOWN OF LONGMONT, SCHOOLS, SOCIETIES, CHURCHES, ETC., ETC. CHICAGO: REPUBLICAN PRINT, 1871.

[1]–26, [27–8 advertisements]. 19.7 x 11.4 cm. Map: [two maps on one sheet; map at left:] Map of the / Kansas Pacific & Denver Pacific Railways, / Showing Land for Sale by the / National Land Company. / 17.3 x 31 cm. No scale given. [Map at right:] Atlantic Ocean / to / Kansas & Colorado. / Drawn by D. Mc.Caffrey & E. Frank McLoughlin. / [lower right:] Eng^d by Fisk, Russell & Ames. / 17.3 x 13.5 cm. No scale given. Whole map size: 17.3 x 44.5 cm. Stitched, unbound.
Ref.:

An edition printed in Denver, 1871, is listed in McMurtrie & Allen (*Colorado*) 131 and in Wilcox page 24.

685 CHICAGO DEMOCRAT

[Newspaper] CHICAGO DEMOCRAT.—EXTRA. CHICAGO, MARCH 25, 1835. AN ACT FOR THE CONSTRUCTION, OF THE ILLINOIS AND MICHIGAN CANAL. . . .

[1–4]. 32.5 x 19.4 cm. Unbound.
Ref.:

The first issue of the paper was printed in November, 1833, and it was continued as a weekly until January, 1835. There was only one issue in January after which publication was suspended, except for the March 25 issue, until a supply of newsprint was received in May or June. An explanation of the suspension (with an appeal for subscribers) appears on page [4].

686 CHICAGO EVENING POST

[Newspaper] CHICAGO EVENING POST. EXTRA. CHICAGO, TUESDAY, OCT. 10, 1871. THE EVENING POST WILL BE ISSUED THIS AFTERNOON, AT 95 & 97 WEST RANDOLPH ST. AND REGULARLY THEREAFTER, FROM OUR YESTERDAY'S EDITIOU[!]. CHICAGO IN FLAMES. AN ALL-NIGHT CARNIVAL OF THE FIRE FIEND! . . .

[1–4]. (Pages [2–3] blank.) 38.4 x 27.2 cm. Unbound.
Ref.:

687 CHICAGO MAGAZINE

[Pictorial wrapper title] MARCH [–AUGUST], 1857. VOL. 1. NO. 1 [–5]. CHICAGO MAGAZINE. THE WEST AS IT IS; ILLUSTRATED. CHICAGO: JOHN GAGER & CO. FOR CHICAGO MECHANICS' INSTITUTE. 1857.

[i–viii], [1]–96. [i–iv], [97]–[188], [1–8 advertisements]. [189]–276, [1–8 advertisements]. [277]–372, [1–4 advertisements]. [373]–451, [452, 1–8 advertisements]. 28 full-page plates at the front of each part, numerous other text and full-page illustrations included in pagination. Green pictorial wrappers, some minor variations in settings, advertisements on versos of front and rectos and versos of back wrappers, uncut. Part 4 unopened. In a green cloth case.
Ref.: Sabin 12625

688 CHICAGO AND NORTHWESTERN RAILROAD COMPANY

[Broadsheet] SEE THE OTHER SIDE. TO THE BLACK HILLS RATE BULLETIN NO. 15. ALWAYS IN THE ADVANCE WITH RELIABLE INFORMATION, AND WITH VALUABLE POINTS FOR PROSPECTIVE GOLD SEEKERS IN THE BLACK HILLS OF DAKOTA AND WYOMING, WE ARE ENABLED TO ANNOUNCE THE FOLLOWING RATES VIA THE OLD RELIABLE CHICAGO & NORTH-WESTERN RAILWAY, AND ITS CONNECTIONS . . . MAP OF THE CHICAGO & NORTHWESTERN TO THE GOLD HILLS. [Map, 16 x 30.4 cm. No scale given.] AS SOON AS FURTHER RELIABLE INFORMATION IN REGARD TO RATES AND ROUTES SHALL BE OBTAINED, BULLETIN NO. 16 WILL BE ISSUED. APRIL 10, 1878. . . . [Page 2:] . . . ALL ABOUT THE BLACK HILLS AND ROUTES THERETO VIA THE CHICAGO & NORTH-WESTERN RAILWAY. . . . RAND McNALLY & CO., PRINTERS, ENGRAVERS AND ELECTROTYPERS, 77 AND 79 MADISON STREET, CHICAGO. . . .

Broadsheet, 55 x 19.5 cm. Text arranged in vertical columns to be folded to 19.5 x 11.3 cm.
Ref.:

689 CHICAGO AND NORTHWESTERN RAILWAY

[Broadsheet] 1877. CORRECT TIME CARDS OF THE CHICAGO AND NORTHWESTERN RAILWAY IN EFFECT APRIL 18TH, 1877. COMPRISING THE TRANSCONTINENTAL ROUTE, . . .

Broadsheet, 19 x 102.2 cm. Map on page [2]: New Map / of the / Chicago and North-Western / Railway / and its Connections /. 18 x 89.4 cm. No scale given.
Ref.:
Printed by Rand, McNally & Co.

690 CHICAGO AND NORTHWESTERN RAILWAY

[Broadside] IF YOU ARE BOUND TO GO TO THE GOLD FIELDS OF THE BLACK HILLS OF DAKOTA YOU MUST BUY YOUR TICKETS VIA THE CHICAGO AND NORTH WESTERN RAILWAY. WE OWN THE BEST ROUTES TO ALL POINTS YOU WOULD GO TO, TO START ON THE WAGON ROUTE TO THE HILLS. THIS MAP SHOWS OUR ROUTES. [Map of routes, 16 x 30.2 cm.] . . . FORM X RAND, MC NALLY & CO., PRINTERS, CHICAGO.

Broadside, 60.5 x 18 cm. Text, 58.5 x 16.9 cm. Printed on yellow paper.
Ref.:
Printed in 1877 or 1878.

691 CHICAGO TIMES, THE

[Newspaper] THE CHICAGO TIMES. VOLUME 17. WEDNESDAY MORNING, OCTOBER 18, 1871. NUMBER 309. THE FIRE. A RESUME OF THE GREAT CALAMITY. DETAILED ACCOUNT OF ITS ORIGIN PROGRESS . . .

[1–4]. 78.3 x 56.3 cm. Unbound.
Ref.:

Most of the paper is devoted to a recapitulation of the events of the Great Fire.

692 CHIDLAW, BENJAMIN W.

YR AMERICAN, YR HWN SYDD YN CYNNWYS NODAU AR DAITH O DDYFFRYN OHIO I GYMRU, GOLWG AR DALAETH OHIO . . . LLANRWST: ARGRAFFWYD, GAN JOHN JONES, 1840.

[1]–48. 19 x 11 cm. Green printed wrappers, with title on front wrapper uncut, unopened.

Ref.: Quarterly of Hist. and Phil. Soc. of Ohio, Vol. VI, pages 1–41.

The text comprises short descriptive paragraphs about cities and areas, principally in Ohio, preceded by a general description of the country and an account of travels from Wales.

693 CHIHUAHUA (Mexican State)

CONSTITUCION POLITICA DEL ESTADO LIBRE DE CHIHUAHUA SANCIONADA POR SU CONGRESO CONSTITUYENTE EN 7 DE DICIEMBRE DE 1825. IMPRESA EN CHIHUAHUA EN 1826. EN LA OFICINA DEL GOBIERNO A CARGO DE FRANCISCO CARRASCO.

[1]–32. 18.5 x 12.4 cm. White printed wrappers, with pattern of printer's ornaments, flowers, and letters.

Ref.:
Signed at the end: José de Urquidi. / José María Ponce de Leon. / Secretario. /

Apparently the second printing of the *Constitucion*, the first having been issued in an undated edition of 1825. (See Clagett p. 28.)

694 CHILD, ANDREW

OVERLAND ROUTE TO CALIFORNIA, DESCRIPTION OF THE ROUTE, VIA COUNCIL BLUFFS, IOWA; KEEPING THE NORTH SIDE OF THE PLATTE RIVER, FOR THE WHOLE OF THE DISTANCE, LYING NEAR THAT STREAM; THENCE OVER THE SOUTH PASS, VIA THE GREAT SUBLETTE AND BEAR RIVER CUT-OFFS, AND THE TRUCKIE RIVER ROAD, OVER THE SIERRA NEVADA, TO SACRAMENTO VALLEY . . . MILWAUKEE: DAILY SENTINEL STEAM POWER PRESS, 1852.

[I]–VIII, [9]–61, [62 blank]. 13 x 8 cm. Original maroon leather with label, 5.1 x 7.6 cm., on front cover. In maroon half morocco case.

Ref.: AII (*Wisconsin*) 189; Cowan p. 116; Howes C378; Wagner-Camp 209

The Preface comprises a letter from the author to his brother, dated from Nevada City, December 10, 1850, in which the author states: "The following pages, which I send you, I have copied with much care from a daily record kept of the road and trip, and its correctness I will vouch for. The absence of any reliable guidebook, was a source of great inconvenience to the emigration of last season . . ."

Andrew Child accompanied the Upper Mississippi Ox Company overland in 1850, with eighty-seven people and thirty-two wagons. He

was one of a few members of the company who split off at Fort Laramie under the leadership of Vance L. Davidson. Most of them were from Illinois, Iowa, and Wisconsin. The Milwaukee *Daily Sentinel* noticed the publication of Child's guide on April 5, 1852. Two years later, the same newspaper recorded the marriage of Child to Miss Alice J. Lowell. By 1855, Child had settled at Delafield, Wisconsin, where he was active as a fruit grower.—EDG

695 CHILDREN ON THE PLAINS, THE

THE CHILDREN ON THE PLAINS. BY AUNT FRIENDLY . . . NEW YORK: ROBERT CARTER & BROTHERS, 1864.

[1]–192. 15.2 x 9.7 cm. Frontispiece. Green embossed cloth, gilt back. Lacks front endleaf.

Ref.: Wagner-Camp 425 note

Wagner-Camp lists only a London, 1865, edition under 425—for no easily discernible reason.

The work has been ascribed to Mrs. Sarah S. Baker.

696 CHITTENDEN, HIRAM M.

THE AMERICAN FUR TRADE OF THE FAR WEST. A HISTORY OF THE PIONEER TRADING POSTS AND EARLY FUR COMPANIES OF THE MISSOURI VALLEY AND THE ROCKY MOUNTAINS AND OF THE OVERLAND COMMERCE WITH SANTA FE. . . . NEW YORK: FRANCIS P. HARPER, 1902.*

[i]–[xvi, xvi blank], [1]–482. [i]–[x, x blank], [483]–892. [i]–iv], [893]–1029, [1030 blank]. 23.3 x 14.4 cm. Ten illustrations listed. Three volumes, dark green cloth.

Ref.: Howes C390; Munk (Alliot) p. 49; Rader 770; Saunders 2814; Smith 1721

Sixty years after publication, this is still the great work on the subject.

697 CHITTENDEN, HIRAM M.

HISTORY OF EARLY STEAMBOAT NAVIGATION ON THE MISSOURI RIVER. LIFE AND ADVENTURES OF JOSEPH LA BARGE . . . NEW YORK: FRANCIS P. HARPER, 1903.*

[i]–xiv, [1]–248. [i–viii, viii blank], [249]–461, [462 blank]. 22.5 x 16 cm. 15 illustrations and one map listed. Two volumes, dark blue ribbed cloth, fore and lower edges uncut.

Ref.: Cuthbertson & Ewers p. 104; Howes C391; Mott (*Iowa*) p. 64

Limited to 950 copies.

698 [CHIVINGTON, JOHN M.]

TO THE PEOPLE OF COLORADO. SYNOPSIS OF THE SAND CREEK INVESTIGATION. DENVER, COLORADO, JUNE 1865.

[1]–8. 19.9 x 13.5 cm. Removed from bound volume, unbound.

Ref.: McMurtrie & Allen (*Colorado*) 56; Sabin 12855; Wagner-Camp 413

The first part of a seventeen-page defense by Chivington of his actions at the Sand Creek Massacre.

699 CHORIS, LOUIS

VOYAGE PITTORESQUE AUTOUR DU MONDE, AVEC DES PORTRAITS DE SAUVAGES D'AMERIQUE, D'ASIE, D'AFRIQUE, ET DES ILES DU GRAND OCEAN . . . PARIS, DE L'IMPRIMERIE DE FIRMIN DIDOT, 1822.

[1–4], [I–VI], [1]–17, [18 blank], [3]–20, [1]–10, [1]–3, [4 blank], [1]–24, [1]–22, [1]–28, [1]–19, [20 blank], [1]–6, [1–4]. 43 x 27 cm. 104 plates and three maps. Map (two on one sheet): Plan / du Groupe des Iles / Rumanzoff, / . . . 17.3 x 23 cm. Scale: about 40 miles to one inch. [2]: Carte / des / Iles Radack / et Ralik. / 22.6 x 16.4 cm. No scale given. Map: Carte / du / Grand Océan / Pour servir au Voyage de M. O. / de Kotzebue autour du Monde. / de 1815 à 1818. / [lower left:] Gravé à Paris, par Ambroise Tardieu, Graveur du Dépôt Général de la Marine. / 52 x 44.8 cm. No scale given. Red boards with red straight grain calf backstrip, gilt.

Prov.: Bookplate of le Comte de Waronzow-Daschkaw and with his book stamp at the foot of the title-page.

Ref.: Cowan p. 123; Howell 51; Howes C397; Rader 815; Sabin 12884

One of the more spectacular productions of the early nineteenth century relating to the Northwest Coast.

700 CHORPENNING, GEORGE

[Wrapper title] THE CASE OF GEORGE CHORPENNING VS. THE UNITED STATES. A BRIEF HISTORY OF THE FACTS BY THE CLAIMANT. WASHINGTON, D.C., MAY 1, 1874. M'GILL & WITHEROW, PRINTERS AND STEREOTYPERS, WASHINGTON, D.C.

[1]–56. 21.6 x 14.4 cm. Blue printed wrappers with title on front wrapper; removed from bound volume. In a red cloth case of Chorpenning pamphlets.

Prov.: Signature on front wrapper: J. Niles /.

Ref.: Howes C398

Signed at the end: Geo. Chorpenning, / Claimant. / Washington, D.C., May 1, 1874. The Niles whose signature appears on the wrapper was Jason Niles, congressman from Mississippi.

George Chorpenning held three contracts with the Post Office Department for running mail between California and Salt Lake City from May 1, 1851, and June 30, 1862. At the time of the first contract, no white man had crossed that expanse of country in the winter, a distance of 910 miles. Chorpenning, in the years of his contract, lost at the hands of the Indians sixteen men, 300 horses and mules, and other property. His claims for compensation were before Congress for many years, and although he was awarded damages of $443,000 in December, 1870, by the Postmaster General, Congress by joint resolution having authorized and directed that official to investigate, adjust, and settle Chorpenning's claims, he never received any compensation.—EDG

701 CHORPENNING, GEORGE

[Cover title] THE CLAIMS OF GEORGE CHORPENNING AGAINST THE UNITED STATES.

[i]–[iv, iv blank], [i]–[iv, iv blank], [1]–80, [1]–103, [104 blank]. 23 x 14.5 cm. Green printed boards, black cloth backstrip.

Prov.: Inscribed on front endleaf: Compliments. / Geo. Chorpenning. / [flourishes] /.

Ref.: Howes C398

Published in Washington, D.C., 1889. Signed and dated on page 80: George Chorpenning, / Claimant. / John McDonald, / of Counsel. / January, 1889. /

702 [CHORPENNING, GEORGE]

[Caption title] MEMORANDA OF ITEMS CLAIMED AND AMOUNTS ALLOWED AND DISALLOWED BY P. M. GENERAL CRESWELL, AND OF EXTRA SERVICES PERFORMED AFTER NOVEMBER 1ST, 1856. . . .

[1]–7, [8 blank]. 23.1 x 14.4 cm. Sewn, unbound, removed from bound volume. In red cloth box with other Chorpenning pamphlets.

Ref.:

Signed on page 7: George Chorpenning, / Claimant. / John McDonald, / Of Counsel. / Although undated, the leaflet was printed at Washington in 1889. There are references to the preceding item, *The Claims of George Chorpenning . . .* [1889].

703 CHORPENNING, GEORGE

[Wrapper title] PETITION OF GEORGE CHORPENNING. PRINTED BY W. H. MOORE . . .

[1]–7, [8 blank]. 21.5 x 14 cm. Gray printed wrappers with title on front wrapper. In red cloth box with other Chorpenning pamphlets.

Ref.:

Signed and dated at the end: George Chorpenning. / Washington City, Feb., 1870. /

704 CHOUTEAU, AUGUSTE

FRAGMENT OF COL. AUGUSTE CHOUTEAU'S NAR-
RATIVE OF THE SETTLEMENT OF ST. LOUIS . . . ST.
LOUIS: GEORGE KNAPP & CO., 1858.

[1]–10, [11–12 blank]. 22.5 x 14.7 cm. Tan
printed wrappers with title on front wrapper.

Prov.: Note in pencil at top of front wrapper:
Gift of Col. Twitchell. / Rubber stamp on same
of Museum of New Mexico, Santa Fé.

Ref.:

705 CHRISTIAN BANKER

[Newspaper] CHRISTIAN BANKER. SETH PAINE,
JOHN M. HOLMES, EDITORS . . . PUBLISHED
WEEKLY. VOLUME I. CHICAGO, WEDNESDAY JANU-
ARY 5 [12, 19], 1853. NUMBER 1 [–3]. . . .

[1–4]. [1–4]. [1–4]. 30.1 x 23.9 cm. Three issues,
unbound.

Ref.:

Some of the articles are clearly libelous;
others are slightly temperate.

706 CHRISTY, WILLIAM, *Defendant*

PROCEEDINGS IN THE CASE OF THE UNITED STATES
VERSUS WILLIAM CHRISTY, ON THE CHARGE OF
HAVING SET ON FOOT A MILITARY EXPEDITION, IN
NEW-ORLEANS, AGAINST THE TERRITORY OF MEXICO
IN NOVEMBER, 1835; CONTAINING THE EVIDENCE
TAKEN ON THE EXAMINATION BEFORE JUDGE
RAWLE, AND OTHER DOCUMENTS CONNECTED WITH
THE ACCUSATION. NEW-ORLEANS: PRINTED BY
BENJAMIN LEVY, MDCCCXXXVI.

[1]–55, [56 blank]. 21.2 x 13.5 cm. Blue wrappers. Lacks front wrapper. In a blue half morocco case.

Ref.: Howes C403; Sabin 12956; Streeter
1188

707 CHURCH OF JESUS CHRIST OF LAT-TER-DAY SAINTS

A BOOK OF COMMANDMENTS, FOR THE GOVERN-
MENT OF THE CHURCH OF CHRIST, ORGANIZED AC-
CORDING TO LAW, ON THE 6TH OF APRIL, 1830.
ZION: PUBLISHED BY W. W. PHELPS & CO., 1833.

[1]–160. 12.5 x 7.1 cm. Contemporary red calf.
Lacks endleaves.

Prov.: The Herbert S. Auerbach copy. Also
see below.

Ref.: AII (*Missouri*) 136; Howes S622; Sabin
50729; Woodward 17

The title-page appears in two forms, with and
without a decorative border. Note that in the
present copy, at least, the title-page without a
border is a conjugate of the last leaf of the first
gathering.

A Book of Commandments, which is better

known as *The Book of Doctrine and Covenants*,
comprises the first versions of the rules for
church government and the revelations given to
Joseph Smith. These are the only rules and
revelations which escaped destruction when a
mob wrecked the Mormon printing office at Independence, Missouri (Zion to the Mormons), in
1833.

On the verso of the title-leaf there are two
manuscript notes: A. S. Gilbert / died the
twenty ninth / day of June in the year / of our
Lord one thousand / eigh[!] hundred and
thirty / *four* /. In another hand: This Manuscript
of / this Book was— / —Stolen from the Mob /
in Jackson Co. Mo. / by Mary E. Rollins / 14
Years old *in* / 1832 /. There is also a newspaper
clipping mounted on the inner back cover.

708 CHURCH OF JESUS CHRIST OF LAT-TER-DAY SAINTS

THE BOOK OF MORMON . . . KIRTLAND, OHIO:
PRINTED BY O. COWDERY & CO. FOR P. P. PRATT
AND J. GOODSON, 1837.

[i]–vi, [7]–[621], [622 blank]. (Pages [i–ii] blank.)
14.5 x 8.3 cm. Light brown tree sheepskin, with
brown leather label on backstrip lettered in gilt.

Prov.: Herbert S. Auerbach copy.

Ref.: Howes S623; Sabin 83039; Woodward
231

Second Edition. Some typographical errors in
the first edition were corrected, a few changes
were made, and Pratt and Goodson, for whom
the work was printed, wrote a new preface.

709 CHURCH OF JESUS CHRIST OF LAT-TER-DAY SAINTS

THE BOOK OF MORMON . . . NAUVOO, ILL: PRINTED
BY ROBINSON AND SMITH, 1840.

[1]–[573], [574–76 blank], [i]–vii, [viii blank].
14.9 x 9.4 cm. Brown mottled sheepskin, black
leather label on backstrip, lettered in gilt, gray
sprinkled edges.

Prov.: Signature in pencil on front endleaf:
Capt. J. Miner /.

Ref.: Howes S623; Sabin 83040; Woodward
232

Although the imprint is Nauvoo, the work
was printed and bound at Cincinnati. However,
as Sabin points out, the index used in the first
edition (pages i–vii) was revised and the new
index printed at Nauvoo. The present copy carries the Nauvoo printing of the index. There is
another arrangement of the last few leaves of
text in which page [572] is blank and pages [573–
74] carry the text which is here found on pages
[572–73].

710 CHURCH OF JESUS CHRIST OF LATTER-DAY SAINTS

THE BOOK OF MORMON ... NAUVOO, ILLINOIS: PRINTED BY JOSEPH SMITH, 1842.

[1]–[573], [574 blank]. (Pages [1–2] blank.) 14.3 x 9.5 cm. Sheepskin, gilt border on sides, gilt backstrip, black leather label with title in gilt on backstrip, lightly sprinkled red edges.

Prov.: Herbert S. Auerbach copy. Manuscript notes in pencil in an unidentified hand on blank leaves at back.

Ref.: Howes S623; Sabin 83042; Woodward 233

Note that Jr. does not follow Smith's name in this edition.

711 CHURCH OF JESUS CHRIST OF LATTER-DAY SAINTS

DOCTRINES AND COVENANTS OF THE CHURCH OF THE LATTER DAY SAINTS: CAREFULLY SELECTED FROM THE REVELATIONS OF GOD, AND COMPILED BY JOSEPH SMITH JUNIOR ... KIRTLAND, OHIO: PRINTED BY F. G. WILLIAMS & CO., 1835.

[i]–iv, [5]–257, [258 blank], i–xxv, [xxvi blank]. 15 x 10.3 cm. Mottled sheepskin, brown leather label, title in gilt.

Ref.: Howes S624; Sabin 83152; Woodward 240

712 CHURCH OF JESUS CHRIST OF LATTER-DAY SAINTS

THE DOCTRINE AND COVENANTS OF THE CHURCH OF JESUS CHRIST OF LATTER DAY SAINTS; CAREFULLY SELECTED FROM THE REVELATIONS OF GOD ... NAUVOO, ILL.: PRINTED BY JOHN TAYLOR, [dash] 1844.

[1]–448. (Pages [1–2] blank.) 15 x 9 cm. Sheepskin, title in gilt on backstrip.

Prov.: Signature on title-page: Edward W Hatch /. Also bookplate of Edward W. Hatch. Old manuscript notes in unidentified hand on preliminary blank leaves and inside back cover.

Ref.: Howes S624; Sabin 83153

713 CHURCH OF JESUS CHRIST OF LATTER-DAY SAINTS

THE DOCTRINE AND COVENANTS OF THE CHURCH OF JESUS CHRIST OF LATTER DAY SAINTS ... NAUVOO, ILL.: PRINTED BY JOHN TAYLOR, 1845.

[1]–448. (Pages [1–2] blank.) 15 x 9.5 cm. Maroon leather, gilt border on sides, gilt backstrip, title in gilt on backstrip.

Ref.: Howes S624; Sabin 83154

714 CHURCH OF JESUS CHRIST OF LATTER-DAY SAINTS

THE DOCTRINE AND COVENANTS OF THE CHURCH OF JESUS CHRIST OF LATTER DAY SAINTS ... NAUVOO, ILL.: PRINTED BY JOHN TAYLOR, 1846.

[1]–448. (Pages [1–2] blank.) 14.8 x 8.8 cm. Sheepskin, title in gilt on backstrip.

Prov.: Herbert S. Auerbach copy.

Ref.: Howes S624; Sabin 83156

715 CHURCH OF JESUS CHRIST OF LATTER-DAY SAINTS

[Caption title] GENERAL EPISTLE FROM THE COUNCIL OF THE TWELVE APOSTLES, TO THE CHURCH OF JESUS CHRIST OF LATTER DAY SAINTS ABROAD, DISPERSED THROUGHOUT THE EARTH GREETINGS: ...

[1]–8. 24.5 x 15.7 cm. Uncut, unopened. In a dark blue half morocco case.

Ref.: AII (*Nebraska*) 1; Golder (*March of the Mormon Battalion*) pp. 239–45; McMurtrie (*The General Epistle of the Latter Day Saints*); Streeter (*Americana—Beginnings*) 65; Wagner-Camp 160

Streeter's arguments in favor of St. Louis as the place of printing, rather than Winter Quarters, Nebraska, are conclusive.

This Epistle of Brigham Young's is one of the great documents of Mormon history ... — Streeter

716 CHURCH OF JESUS CHRIST OF LATTER-DAY SAINTS

[Broadside] G. S. L. CITY. JAN. 20. 1849. [at left:] NO. [at right:] 2.00C GOOD TO   OR BEARER. TWO DOLLARS ON DEMAND. 2.00C CLERK.

Broadside, 5 x 9.6 cm. Text, 3.3 x 8.8 cm.

Ref.: McMurtrie (*Utah*) 2; Streeter (*Americana—Beginnings*) 69 note

Embossed with blind seal. All of the type used except the numerals in line 5 are swash characters. One of the earliest pieces of printing at Salt Lake City.

Signed by Brigham Young and countersigned by Thomas Bullock and Heber C. Kimball.

717 CHURCH OF JESUS CHRIST OF LATTER-DAY SAINTS

THE SAME, except 3.000 and three dollars. Same signatures, same type, same embossed seal.

718 CHURCH OF JESUS CHRIST OF LATTER-DAY SAINTS. Sheffield Conference.

REPORT OF THE SHEFFIELD QUARTERLY CONFERENCE, HELD ... DECEMBER 23D, 1849 ...

[1]–8. Bound with Number 3346.

Ref.:

Imprint at foot of page 8: [dotted rule] / T. Potter, Printer, Barker Pool, Sheffield. /

719 CHURCH OF JESUS CHRIST OF LAT-TER-DAY SAINTS. Sheffield Conference.

REPORT OF THE SHEFFIELD CONFERENCE . . . HELD . . . MAY 19TH, 1850.

[1]–8. Bound with Number 3346.
>*Ref.:*
>Imprint at foot of page 8: [rule] / T. Potter, Printer, 4, Barker Pool, Sheffield. /

720 CHURCH OF JESUS CHRIST OF LAT-TER-DAY SAINTS. Sheffield Conference.

REPORT OF THE SHEFFIELD CONFERENCE . . . HELD . . . NOVEMBER 24TH, 1850. SHEFFIELD: STEPHEN NEW, 1850.

[1]–12. Bound with Number 3346.
>*Ref.:*

721 CHURCH OF JESUS CHRIST OF LAT-TER-DAY SAINTS. Sheffield Conference.

[Caption title] REPORT OF THE SHEFFIELD CONFERENCE . . . HELD . . . ON THE EIGHTH DAY OF JUNE, 1851.

[1]–12. Bound with Number 3346.
>*Ref.:*
>Imprint at foot of page 12: Stephen New, Printer, 14, Waingate, Sheffield. /

722 CHURCHILL, FRANKLIN H.

SKETCH OF THE LIFE OF BVT. BRIG. GEN. SYLVESTER CHURCHILL . . . NEW YORK: WILLIS MC DONALD & CO., PRINTERS, 1888.

[i]–vi, [1]–201, [202 blank]. 23 x 14.9 cm. Tan semi-limp cloth.
>*Ref.:* Howes C407
>Active in Florida and Mexican wars.—Howes

723 CINCINNATI LITERARY GAZETTE

THE CINCINNATI LITERARY GAZETTE. VOL. I. JANU-ARY TO JUNE, 1824 . . . CINCINNATI: PUBLISHED BY JOHN P. FOOTE, 1824.

[i–ii], [1]–208. (Pages 52–3 mispaginated 53–4.) [1]–208. (Pages 83, 98, 107, 130 mispaginated 82, 89, 017, 131.) 27.5 x 22.8 cm. Two volumes bound together, contemporary gray boards, calf back and corners. Second title-leaf not present.
>*Ref.:* Rusk I, p. 162; Sabin 13079
>. . . *The Cincinnati Literary Gazette* (1824–1825) was perhaps the earliest to enjoy any degree of success, and even this paper was continued beyond its first year only in the face of financial disaster. The *Gazette* had a number of Western contributors of some importance . . .
>—Rusk
>Of special interest is a series of letters by JR regarding travel in Ohio, particularly along the Ohio River. Several articles signed B. describe

the Indians of Texas and there are essays by Rafinesque including one with vocabularies of the Pawnee, Shoshone, and Mandan languages.

The periodical was continued beyond the present issues to August, 1825.

724 CINCINNATI WEEKLY GAZETTE

[Newspaper] CINCINNATI WEEKLY GAZETTE. VOL. LXVIII. CINCINNATI, THURSDAY, AUGUST 11, 1859. NO. VIII.

[1–4]. 78.7 x 62.1 cm. Unbound.
>*Ref.:*
>Under the heading: Map of the Pike's Peak Gold Regions. / there are a four-column map and two and one-half columns of descriptive matter. The description of the map reads as follows: The above map, prepared and engraved expressly for the Gazette, gives an accurate view of the Gold Fields of Western Kansas and Nebraska, and the intervening country to the Missouri river, comprising more valuable information than many of the blanket-sized lithographs of that region. The portion delineating the "Pike's Peak" country, was drawn by Messrs. J. M. Sheafer and W. S. Foster, two thoroughly competent Civil Engineers, residing in Denver City, and personally familiar with the various localities represented. It exhibits the positions of the famous Gregory Diggings, the other points where mining is now carried on, the mountain streams, peaks and parks, the towns established, and all other points of interest in the Gold Region up to the present time.

725 CITY OF WINONA AND SOUTHERN MINNESOTA

CITY OF WINONA AND SOUTHERN MINNESOTA: A SKETCH OF THEIR GROWTH AND PROSPECTS, WITH GENERAL INFORMATION FOR THE EMIGRANT, ME-CHANIC, FARMER AND CAPITALIST . . . WINONA, MIN. PRINTED AT THE REPUBLICAN OFFICE, 1858.

[1]–36. 22 x 13.5 cm. Green printed wrappers with title on front wrapper, advertisements on verso of front and recto and verso of back wrapper.
>*Ref.:* AII (*Minnesota*) 231; Bradford 3534; Howes W570

726 CLAPP, JOHN T.

A JOURNAL OF TRAVELS TO AND FROM CALIFORNIA, WITH FULL DETAILS OF THE HARDSHIPS AND PRIVA-TIONS; ALSO A DESCRIPTION OF THE COUNTRY, MINES, CITIES, TOWNS, &C . . . KALAMAZOO: GEO. A. FITCH & CO., 1851.

[1]–67, [68 blank]. 19.6 x 12.5 cm. Yellow printed wrappers, with title on front wrapper,

illustrations on verso of back wrapper. In a green half morocco case.

Ref.: Howes C424; Matthews p. 324; Wagner-Camp 197

Clapp's Journal comprises a day by day account from the time he left Kalamazoo on March 6, 1850. He drove with several companions from Niles, Michigan, to Council Bluffs where he joined the Lake County Company of Illinois commanded by John G. Ragan. The Company started from Council Bluffs on May 4 and arrived in Sacramento on July 28. A list of the members of the Company, including the names and residences of seventy-one persons, is given. Late in November of the same year, Clapp returned to Michigan by way of Panama.—EDG

727 CLAPPE, LOUISE AMELIA KNAPP SMITH

CALIFORNIA IN 1851 [–1852]. THE LETTERS OF DAME SHIRLEY . . . SAN FRANCISCO: THE GRABHORN PRESS, 1933.*

[i]–[xx, xx blank], 1–[148]. [i]–[xx, xx blank], 1–[150]. 21.9 x 15 cm. Vignettes unlisted, map. Two volumes, gray printed boards, blue cloth backstrips, fore and lower edges uncut.

Ref.: Heller & Magee 178, 179; Howes C427

Limited to 500 sets. Rare Americana Series, Nos. 5–6.

728 CLARINDA (Iowa) HERALD

[Broadside] CLARINDA HERALD EXTRA. CLARINDA, IOWA, JANUARY 30, 1886 . . .

Broadside, 30.2 x 22.6 cm. Text, 24.5 x 17.5 cm.

Ref.:

Contains a report of the disastrous fire which destroyed four buildings, including the hotel, on the night of January 29–30, 1886.

729 CLARK, AUSTIN S.

1852–1865. REMINISCENCES OF TRAVEL . . .

[1]–54. 23.2 x 14.2 cm. Portrait. Dark purple embossed boards, with title in gilt on front cover.

Ref.: Howes C429

The author reached California in 1852, locating at Coloma. After spending thirteen years in California mines, he made his way to Idaho, where he says he taught the first school in Owyhee County.—EDG

The work has been erroneously attributed to F. A. Isbell, whose memoirs were also printed by S. J. Stewart, Middleton, Connecticut, about 1871. In format, binding, etc., the two works look very much alike, Howes suggests *ca* 1865 as the date.

730 [CLARK, BENNETT C.]

DIARY OF A JOURNEY FROM MISSOURI TO CALIFORNIA IN 1849. EDITED BY RALPH P. BIEBER . . . REPRINTED BY THE STATE HISTORICAL SOCIETY OF MISSOURI FROM THE MISSOURI HISTORICAL REVIEW, VOLUME 23, NO. 1 (OCTOBER, 1928). COLUMBIA, 1928.

[1]–43, [44 blank]. Portrait. Brown printed wrappers with short title on front wrapper.

Ref.: Morgan (Pritchard) p. 183

731 CLARK, CHARLES M.

A TRIP TO PIKE'S PEAK AND NOTES BY THE WAY, WITH NUMEROUS ILLUSTRATIONS . . . CHICAGO: S. P. ROUNDS' STEAM BOOK AND JOB PRINTING HOUSE, 1861.

[i–iv], [vi]–vii, [viii Illustrations], [ix blank], [1]–134, [135 errata, 136 blank]. 21 x 12.8 cm. Frontispiece and 17 woodcuts on tinted leaves. Black cloth, title in gilt on front cover, blind embossed corner ornaments.

Ref.: AII (*Chicago*) 548; Howes C430; Jones 1435; Wagner-Camp 372; Wilcox p. 24

One of the best of the few contemporary accounts of the Pike's Peak gold rush, Clark's work contains a fine series of early views of Denver and other western cities.—EDG

732 CLARK, DANIEL

PROOFS OF THE CORRUPTION OF GEN. JAMES WILKINSON, AND OF HIS CONNEXION WITH AARON BURR, WITH A FULL REFUTATION OF HIS SLANDEROUS ALLEGATIONS IN RELATION TO THE CHARACTER OF THE PRINCIPAL WITNESS AGAINST HIM . . . PHILADELPHIA: WM. HALL, JUN. & GEO. W. PIERE, PRINTERS, 1809.

[*]2, A–S4, T2, 1–254. [i–iv], [3]–150, 1–199, [200 blank]. 23.2 x 14.7 cm. Gray boards, tan paper back, with contemporary manuscript label, uncut, mostly unopened.

Ref.: Howes C431; Jones 731; Rader 830; Sabin 13265; Shaw & Shoemaker 17221

Clark, who was thoroughly involved with both Burr and Wilkinson, was one of the wealthiest men in New Orleans during the first quarter of the nineteenth century. He turned on both of his associates, when they were in trouble. The present work, which is rather untrustworthy, was quite effective as anti-Wilkinson propaganda.

733 CLARK, FRANCIS D.

1846–1882. THE FIRST REGIMENT OF NEW YORK VOLUNTEERS COMMANDED BY COL. JONATHAN D. STEVENSON, IN THE MEXICAN WAR. NAMES OF THE MEMBERS OF THE REGIMENT DURING ITS TERM OF SERVICE IN UPPER AND LOWER CALI-

FORNIA, 1847–1848, WITH A RECORD OF ALL KNOWN SURVIVORS ON THE 15TH DAY OF APRIL, 1882, AND THOSE KNOWN TO HAVE DECEASED, WITH OTHER MATTERS OF INTEREST PERTAINING TO THE ORGANIZATION AND SERVICE OF THE REGIMENT . . . NEW YORK: GEO. S. EVANS & CO., 1882.

[1]–94, [1]–16. 23 x 14.5 cm. Two portraits. Brown cloth, title and decorative bands stamped in gilt on front cover, gilt decorative bands on backstrip and back cover, gilt edges.

Prov.: Inscribed on blank leaf at front: To / Gen'l H. G. Gibson, U S A. / With the Compliments of / Francis D. Clark. / N Y Sept 18, 1883. /

Ref.: Cowan p. 126; Howes C432

The sixteen-page Appendix is dated August 1st, 1883.

734   CLARK, GEORGE R.

COL. GEORGE ROGERS CLARK'S SKETCH OF HIS CAMPAIGN IN THE ILLINOIS IN 1778–9 WITH AN INTRODUCTION BY HON. HENRY PIRTLE, OF LOUISVILLE . . . CINCINNATI: ROBERT CLARKE & CO., 1869.

[i]–[viii, viii blank], [1]–119, [120 blank]. 23.1 x 15.8 cm. Portrait. Dark green cloth.

Ref.: Buck 31; Field 325; Howes C433; Sabin 13287

735   CLARK, ISAAC

CLARKS'S [!] MISCELLANY, IN PROSE AND VERSE . . . NASHVILLE, (TEN.): PRINTED FOR THE AUTHOR, BY T. G. BRADFORD, 1812.

[*]⁸, A–[P]⁴. (Gatherings K and P unsigned.) [i]–xvi, [9]–120. (Pagination of 115 inverted.) 12.8 x 7.5 cm. Calf, title stamped in blind on tan leather label on backstrip.

Ref.: AII (*Tennessee*) 107; Howes C435; Sabin 13299; Shaw & Shoemaker 25076

Describes trips to various parts of the country, from Alabama to Illinois.—Howes

736   CLARK, JOHN A.

GLEANINGS BY THE WAY . . . PHILADELPHIA: W. J. & J. K. SIMON, 1842.

[i]–[vi, vi blank], [7]–352. 18.9 x 11.4 cm. Brown cloth, blind embossed sides, backstrip with gilt title.

Ref.: Buck 310; Clark III 144; Howes C440; Hubach p. 85; Woodward 39

Clark's work contains considerable material on the Mormons in addition to his travels in the Middle West.—EDG

737   [CLARK, JOHN A., CYRUS SMALLING, E. G. LEE, & OTHERS]

THE MORMONS, OR, KNAVERY EXPOSED. GIVING AN ACCOUNT OF THE DISCOVERY OF THE GOLDEN PLATES; THE TRANSLATION AND VARIOUS TRICKS RESORTED TO—THE PROCEEDINGS AT KIRTLAND—BUILDING A TEMPLE—ESTABLISHMENT OF A BANK, A CORRECT SPECIMEN OF ITS NOTES, OF WHICH TWO HUNDRED THOUSAND DOLLARS WORTH HAVE BEEN PALMED OFF UPON THE COMMUNITY—THE MANNER IN WHICH THE COMMUNITY OF FRANKFORD, PA., RID THEMSELVES OF THE MORMONS . . . THE WHOLE BEING DESIGNED AS A CAUTION TO THE IGNORANT AND UNSUSPECTING AGAINST ONE OF THE MOST BAREFACED AND BLASPHEMOUS DEVICES WHICH HAS EVER BEEN WITNESSED. AFFORDING A LAMENTABLE EXHIBITION OF THE CREDULITY AND WEAKNESS OF HUMAN NATURE, IN SO READILY ALLOWING ITSELF TO BE MADE THE DUPE OF ARTFUL AND DESIGNING KNAVES. FRANKFORD, PA.: PUBLISHED BY E. G. LEE, 1841.

[1]–24. 21.5 x 14 cm. Sewn, removed from a bound volume.

Ref.: Howes M815; Sabin 50761

The pamphlet comprises an account of Joseph Smith's career by John A. Clark (pages 5–12), details of financial chicanery at Kirtland by Cyrus Smalling (pages 12–15), and descriptions by E. G. Lee and others of Lee's appearance at a Mormon meeting in Frankford, Pennsylvania, which broke up in a riot.

738   CLARK, MARTIN V. B., *Chairman*

THE 'CENTENNIAL' SKETCH OF CLAY COUNTY, NEBRASKA . . . SUTTON, NEBRASKA: E. H. WHITE, PUBLISHER, 1876.

[i–ii], [1]–22. 24.1 x 15.8 cm. Blue printed wrappers with title on front wrapper.

Ref.: AII (*Nebraska*) 397; Howes C444

The printer's imprint appears on the verso of the title-leaf: [double rule] / Printed at the Office of the / Clay Co. Globe, / Published every Friday. / E. H. White, Editor & Proprietor. / Sutton Nebraska. / [double rule] /.

739   [CLARK, ORTON S.]

CLAY ALLISON OF THE WASHITA: FIRST A COW MAN AND THEN AN EXTINGUISHER OF BAD MEN. RECOLLECTIONS OF COLORADO, NEW MEXICO, AND THE TEXAS PANHANDLE. REMINISCENCES OF A '79ER. 1920.

[1]–38, three loose leaves. 23.1 x 12.6 cm. Tan printed wrappers with title on front wrapper.

Ref.: Adams 202; Howes C445; Rader 832

The three supplementary leaves are inserted at the back. The first is headed: Insert No. 1, Page 33. The second is headed: Insert No. 3, Page 34. The third insert is mounted on the inner back cover. There is a typed copyright notice inside the front cover: Copyright applied for / O. S. Clark Attica Ind / 1920 /.

The pamphlet was printed in Attica, Indiana.

740 [CLARK, ORTON S.]

THE SAME.

[1–2], [5]–135, [136 blank]. 22.9 x 15.2 cm. Illustrations, unlisted. Brown printed wrappers bound into cowskin (with fur).

Prov.: Inscribed on the title-page: Your Friend / O. S. Clark /, and by Charles A. Siringo: With consent of the Author, / Mr. Clark, I am sending this / little book to my friend Mr. / Frank Caldwell of Austin, / Texas. / Sincerely / Chas. A. Siringo /.

Ref.: Adams 203; Howes C445; Rader 832 note

Adams states that most of the extensive additional material was supplied by other writers. This edition was issued in 1922 at Attica, Indiana.

741 CLARK, ORTON S.

ADDENDUM TO "THE LIFE OF BILLIE DIXON."

[1–8]. 19.3 x 12 cm. Unbound leaflet.

Signed on the title-page: O. S. Clark. / Attica. / Ind. / Neither place nor date of printing is given. Inserted at back of BARDE, F. S.: *Life and Adventures of "Billy" Dixon* . . . [1914], Number 183.

742 CLARK, STERLING B. F.

HOW MANY MILES FROM ST. JOE? THE LOG OF STERLING B. F. CLARK, A FORTY-NINER . . . SAN FRANCISCO: PRIVATELY PRINTED, 1929.*

[i]–xii, [1]–56, [57 blank, 58 colophon]. (Small erratum slip inserted at end.) 19.9 x 12.8 cm. Six illustrations listed. Marbled boards, red cloth backstrip, printed label on front cover, fore and lower edges uncut.

Ref.: Cowan p. 127; Matthews p. 314; Morgan (Pritchard) p. 183

Printed in a limited edition by Taylor and Taylor for Senator James D. Phelan.

743 CLARK, WILLIAM

AUTOGRAPH MANUSCRIPT ACCOUNT BOOK, May 25, 1825, to June 14, 1828. 68 leaves, 22.2 x 14 cm., bound in original gray boards, sheep backstrip and corners. Binding repaired. In a black half morocco case.

Prov.: Former owners: William Clark, George Rogers Hancock Clark, Mrs. Julia Clark Voorhis. Sold at auction by G. A. Baker & Co., 1941.

The volume comprises financial records kept by William Clark between 1825 and 1828, almost entirely in his hand. Of the sixty-eight leaves, there are records on 132 pages plus both inner endpapers. Of prime importance is the record by Clark inscribed on the front cover, given here in full:

Men on Lewis & Clarks Trip
Capt. Lewis   Dead
Odoway   Dead
N. Pryor   at Fort Smith
Rd. Windser   on Sangamah Ills.
G. Shannon   Lexington Ky.
R. Fields   near Louisville
Wm. Bratten   near Greenville Ohio
F. Labieche   St. Louis
R. Frazier   on Gasconade
Ch. Floyd   Dead
P. Gass   Dead
J. Collins   do.
J. Colter   do.
P. Cruzate   Killed
J. Fields   do.
S. Goodrich   deadead[!]
G. Gibson   Deadead[!]
T. P. Howard
H. Hall
H. McNeal   dead
J. Shields   do.
J. Potts   Killed
J. B. Le Page   dead
J. Thomson   Killed
Wm. Warner   Vir
P. Wiser   Killed
Whitehouse
Warpenton
Newman

[Second column:]
Alr. Willard   Mo
Geo. Drulard   Killed
Toust Chartono   Mandans
Se car ja we au   Dead
Tousant Charbon in Wertenburgh, Gy.

Dr. Donald D. Jackson, whose edition of Clark's correspondence was published in 1962, has studied the manuscript twice. He has concluded that "Clark was the only person who could have drawn up such a roster at this time and included the present status of the expedition members; yet the roster is only as reliable as Clark's information could make it. He is incorrect, for example, in listing Gass as dead. We may expect him to have the most reliable information about those members of the party who were still in the West."

Dr. Jackson's comments on Sacagáwea are particularly illuminating: "The notation that Sacagáwea was dead by 1825–1828 is the most interesting piece of intelligence that Clark presents here, because it tends to contradict a popular belief. Sacagáwea was never acclaimed as a real heroine by the American public until she was, in a sense, rediscovered by Eva Emery Dye in 1902. Then the task of elevating her to an even loftier position in history was assumed by Grace Raymond Hebard, who wrote *Sacajawea, a guide and interpreter of the Lewis and Clark expedition, with an account of the travels of Toussaint Charbonneau, and of Jean Baptiste, the expedition papoose* (Glendale, Calif., 1933). Mrs. Hebard believed that Sacagáwea had survived the rigors of her youth and was the very old Shoshoni woman of the same name who lived, until late in the nineteenth century, in the Wind River country of Wyoming. Other historians have been inclined to suspect that Sacagáwea may have died on the upper Missouri in 1812, in view of trader John Luttig's journal entry of 20 Dec.: 'this Evening the Wife of Charbonneau a Snake Squaw, died of a putrid fever she was a good and the best Woman in the fort, agd abt 25 years she left a fine infant girl.' But, since Charbonneau had at least two wives, both Shoshoni, the matter has remained in doubt . . .

"Although Clark's notation here is not conclusive, it cannot be dismissed lightly. We are hardly justified in saying, 'If Clark is wrong about Gass, then perhaps he is also wrong about Sacagáwea,' for the cases are different. Gass had gone back to Virginia and severed his contacts with the West, but Sacagáwea, her husband Charbonneau, and her children were Clark's concern for many years after the expedition. He cared about them and felt a kind of responsibility for them. It is difficult to believe that he could have been wrong about Sacagáwea's death."

However, Clark was in error in his last entry, for it was Jean Baptiste Charbonneau who visited Württemberg, Germany, in the entourage of Paul Wilhelm Friedrich, Herzog von Württemberg. Prince Paul took the boy with him when he returned to Germany and brought him back to St. Louis in 1829. Dale Morgan suggests that Charbonneau had only two children, Jean Baptiste and Lizette, and that Jean Baptiste was sometimes referred to as Toussaint, his father's name.

744 CLARK, WILLIAM

AUTOGRAPH LETTER, SIGNED (draft). 1811 December 18, St. Louis. One page, 24.9 x 19.7 cm. To Captain H. Heald, Chicago.

An interesting letter, in which Clark asked Heald to prevent attacks on the Osage Indians and reported Harrison's success over the Prophet.

745 CLARKE, ADELE

OLD MONTREAL. JOHN CLARKE: HIS ADVENTURES, FRIENDS AND FAMILY . . . MONTREAL: THE HERALD PUBLISHING COMPANY, 1906.

[1]–47, [48 blank]. 25.4 x 17 cm. Five plates listed. Red cloth.

Ref.: Howes C450

Clarke was a partner in the Astor Fur Co. and had charge of the 1811 Expedition to Oregon in the 'Beaver'—remaining there 'till Astoria was abandoned to the British N.W. Fur Co. in 1813 . . . the rest of his life was spent with the Hudson's Bay Co.—Howes, inscription in book.

746 CLARKE, ASA BEMENT

TRAVELS IN MEXICO AND CALIFORNIA: COMPRISING A JOURNAL OF A TOUR FROM BRAZOS SANTIAGO, THROUGH CENTRAL MEXICO, BY WAY OF MONTEREY, CHIHUAHUA, THE COUNTRY OF THE APACHES AND THE RIVER GILA, TO THE MINING DISTRICTS OF CALIFORNIA . . . BOSTON: WRIGHT & HASTY, 1852.

[1]–138, [139–44 blank]. 19 x 11.2 cm. White printed wrappers with title on front wrapper.

Ref.: Cowan p. 128; Edwards p. 35; Howes C451; Jones 1275; Sabin 13393; Wagner-Camp 210

Clarke, who was born in Conway, Massachusetts, and died in Independence, Iowa, sailed from New York, January 29, 1849, as a member of the Hampden Mining Company. He reached the mining districts of California, via Central Mexico, Arizona, the Gila River, and Los Angeles, about the first of August. He engaged in the mining enterprise until December, when he went to San Francisco for the winter. "After spending a considerable portion of 1850 in Mercantile Business in Sacramento and Marysville," he wrote, "I arrived home in March 1851."—EDG

747 CLAVIJERO, FRANCISCO JAVIER

STORIA DELLA CALIFORNIA . . . IN VENEZIA: APPRESSO MODESTO FENZO, MDCCLXXXIX.*

A–Q⁸, R¹⁰, [S]¹. [1]–276, [277 errata, 278 blank]. A–M⁸, N¹⁰, [O]¹. [1]–212, [213 errata, 214 blank]. 18.9 x 12.5 cm. Map: Carta / della / California / suo Golfo / e Contracoste della / Nuova Spagna / [lower left:] Da D. Raimondo Tarros Delineata 1788 / [lower right:] J. Zambelli Sculp. / 36.5 x 19.8 cm. No scale given. Two volumes bound together in old light brown half sheep, brown decorated paper sides, with red and green labels on backstrip, yellow edges.

Prov.: Bookplate of Francesco Carafa, Duke of Forli and Count of Policastro. Manuscript numerals at top of backstrip: 1120. Shelf-mark on inner front cover: II 3 /.

Ref.: Barrett 527; Bradford 939; Cowan p. 129; Howes C465; Leclerc 846; Sabin 13524; Streit III 1113; Uriarte II 3668; Wagner (*Cart. of NW Coast*) 716; Wagner (*SS*) 172

One of the source books for the history of missions in Lower California. The map was developed from the Konsag map of 1757.

748 CLAY, JOHN

MY LIFE ON THE RANGE . . . CHICAGO: PRIVATELY PRINTED.*

[i–viii, viii blank], 1–[366], [367 colophon, 368 blank]. 23 x 15.2 cm. 17 illustrations. Green cloth, gilt top, uncut.

Ref.: Adams 205; Adams (*Ramp. Herd*) 475; Dobie pp. 98–9; Howes C470; Jennewein 153; Malone p. 2; Rader 841

Published in 1924. One of the best books on ranching.

749 CLAY, JOHN

OLD DAYS RECALLED . . . CHICAGO, 1915. [1]–56.

22.4 x 15.4 cm. Seven illustrations. Dark blue cloth, gilt top, uncut.

Ref.:

750 CLAY, JOHN, JR.

NEW WORLD NOTES: BEING AN ACCOUNT OF JOURNEYINGS AND SOJOURNINGS IN AMERICA AND CANADA . . . KELSO: J. & J. H. RUTHERFURD, 1875.

[i]–[viii, viii blank], [1]–200, [1]–4 advertisements. 17 x 11 cm. Portrait and one plate. Purple cloth. Worn, backstrip faded.

Ref.: Adams (*Ramp. Herd*) 477; Howes C471

Contains chapters on Illinois, Chicago, Iowa, Nebraska, the gold mines in Colorado, etc.

751 CLAYTON, WILLIAM

THE LATTER-DAY SAINTS' EMIGRANTS' GUIDE: BEING A TABLE OF DISTANCES . . . ST. LOUIS: MO. REPUBLICAN STEAM POWER PRESS, 1848.

[1]–24. 18.5 x 11.5 cm. Contemporary medium blue wrappers. In a green half morocco case.

Prov.: Marginal notes in an unidentified hand on pages 12, 13, 14, 17.

Ref.: AII (*Missouri*) 557; Howes C475; Jones 1166; Roberts, B. H. (*Comprehensive History of the Church of Jesus Christ of Latter Day Saints* . . . Salt Lake City, 1930) III pp. 547–72; Sabin 13580; Wagner-Camp 147

For the route covered, Clayton's guide was the best itinerary of the time. The author accompanied the pioneer band to Salt Lake in 1847 as the clerk or historian. He kept a careful record and description of the route and also kept a diary for himself and another for Heber Kimball. Shortly after he reached Salt Lake, he decided to use his materials for a guide book. He returned to Winter Quarters on October 21, 1847, and set about preparing a manuscript for the press. The Preface is dated March 13, 1848.

Clayton's guide book was used extensively by successive waves of Mormon emigrants. John D. Lee, who accompanied the 1848 migration, mentions using the Clayton work. Lorenzo Snow had the pamphlet with him, for several of his place names are identical with Clayton's.

Tipped in at the back is a Letter, signed, by Brigham Young, 1853 August 31, Salt Lake City, to Captain W. H. Hooper.

752 CLAYTON, WILLIAM

ANOTHER COPY.

19.1 x 11.5 cm. Full contemporary sheep, with name stamped in gilt on front cover: P. P. Pratt /.

Prov.: Name of Parley P. Pratt stamped on front cover. Inscribed inside front cover, in pencil: Mr Kathonis Pratt /.

Bound in at the end is a filler of lined notepaper (five leaves have been cut out) on one page of which is a four-line stanza of verse. Laid in is a document signed by William Duggins witnessed by William Clayton.

753 CLEAR CREEK COUNTY (Colorado) MINING CERTIFICATE

[Broadsheet] REPUBLICAN PRINT, DENVER. TERRITORY OF COLORADO, COUNTY OF CLEAR CREEK. KNOW ALL MEN BY THESE PRESENTS, THAT THE OWNER BY PRE-EMPTION, OF . . .

Broadsheet. 12.5 x 19.7 cm. Unbound.

Ref.:

Printed and manuscript docket on verso, recorded May 13, 1862. Claim No. 4 Westerly, Falcose Lode, Idaho District. Similar to McMurtrie & Allen (*Colorado*) 27.

754 CLELAND, ROBERT G.

THE CATTLE ON A THOUSAND HILLS. SOUTHERN CALIFORNIA, 1850–1870 . . . SAN MARINO, CALIFORNIA: THE HUNTINGTON LIBRARY, 1941.

[i]–xiv, [1]–327, [328 blank]. 22.7 x 15.2 cm. Two illustrations and two maps listed. Green buckram. In dust jacket.

Ref.: Adams 210; Adams (*Ramp. Herd*) 485; Barrett 528; Dobie p. 99; Edwards p. 36; Howes C477

755 [CLEMENS, JEREMIAH]

BERNARD LILE; AN HISTORICAL ROMANCE, EMBRAC-
ING THE PERIODS OF THE TEXAS REVOLUTION. AND
THE MEXICAN WAR. PHILADELPHIA: J. B. LIPPIN-
COTT & CO., 1856.

[iii]–xii, [13]–287, [288 blank]. 18.4 x 10.8 cm.
Green cloth, blind embossed sides, gilt title on
backstrip.

Ref.: Sabin 13617; Wright II 543

The author was a United States Senator from
Alabama. Another issue carries the author's
name on the title-page.

756 CLEMENS, JEREMIAH

MUSTANG GRAY; A ROMANCE . . . PHILADELPHIA:
J. B. LIPPINCOTT & CO., 1858.

[i]–[viii, viii blank], [13]–296, 1–40 advertisements. 18.7 x 12 cm. Brown cloth, blind embossed sides, gilt title on backstrip.

Prov.: Signature on inner front cover:
M. C. A. Lawrence / Dec 12, 1857 / [flourish] /.
Bookplate of Susan M. Lawrence.

Ref.: Sabin 13620; Wright II 544

Note that the inscription on inner front cover
is dated 1857, although the title-page bears the
date 1858.

Exploits of Mabry Gray during the Texas
Revolution.—Wright II

757 CLEMENS, ORION

CITY OF KEOKUK IN 1856 . . . A VIEW OF THE CITY
. . . ALSO, A SKETCH OF THE BLACK HAWK WAR,
AND HISTORY OF THE HALF BREED TRACT . . .
KEOKUK: PRINTED BY O. CLEMENS, 1856.

[1]–44. 22.5 x 15 cm. Buff printed wrappers with
title on front wrapper, verso of back wrapper
used for mailing address, with Keokuk postmark.

Prov.: Addressed on back wrapper to D. R.
Leland Esq / (Care T. C. Leland) / New York
City /.

Ref.: Bradford 953; Field 328; Howes C478;
Moffit 217; Mott (*Iowa*) pp. 56–7; Sabin 13622

The text is the same as *Keokuk Directory for
1856–7* and is evidently the printing referred to
by the author in the preface: For convenience of
mailing, the names are omitted in the pamphlet
edition.

Inserted between pages 24 and 25 is an eight-
page Northern Cross Rail Road schedule,
printed on yellow paper. See Number 3034.

758 CLEMENS, ORION

THE SAME . . . FOR 1856–7 . . .

[1]–112, 1–41 advertisements, [42 blank].
21.4 x 14 cm. Tan printed boards, black cloth
backstrip, paper label, 3.9 x 2 cm., on backstrip,
advertisements on front and back covers. Label
defective.

Ref.: Howes C479; Moffit 250

First Keokuk directory. The longer version
with the directory of residents.

759 CLEMENS, ORION

KEOKUK DIRECTORY AND BUSINESS MIRROR FOR
THE YEAR 1857, CONTAINING A GENERAL DIREC-
TORY OF THE CITIZENS . . . KEOKUK: PRINTED BY
O. CLEMENS, 1857.

[1]–186. 22 x 14 cm. Plan: Edward Kilbourne's /
First Addition to / Keokuk, —Iowa. / [5 lines] /
11.1 x 22 cm. No scale given. Buff printed
boards, with one-line title at top of front cover
followed by advertisements, advertisements on
back cover.

Ref.: Moffit 316

Mounted on the inside front cover is a small
broadside, 3.9 x 11 cm., headed: Correction. /
followed by six lines of text. Tipped in on the
front endleaf is an advertisement printed on
salmon paper offering the two printing presses of
the author for sale. This advertisement has also
been noted in the IaHi copy. One advertisement
inserted is a folding sheet.

760 CLEMENS, SAMUEL L.

ADVENTURES OF HUCKLEBERRY FINN (TOM SAW-
YER'S COMRADE) . . . NEW YORK: CHARLES L.
WEBSTER AND COMPANY, 1885.

[1]–366. 21.4 x 16.7 cm. Illustrations listed. Dark
green pictorial cloth.

Ref.: Blanck 3415

Title leaf is a cancel, copyright notice dated
1884. On page [13] "Him and another Man" is
listed as 88. Page 57, line 11 up reads "with the
was." Page 283 is a cancel. Page 155 is mispaginated 15. There is no signature on page 161.
The final blank leaf has been excised: a pair of
leaves has been tipped to the original stub,
bound in, and the second leaf pasted down under
the back end paper. The sculptor's name appears on the finished edge of the shoulder in
the frontispiece and the Heliotype Printing Co.
imprint is used.

761 CLEMENS, SAMUEL L.

MARK TWAIN'S AUTOBIOGRAPHY . . . INTRODUC-
TION BY ALBERT BIGELOW PAINE . . . NEW YORK:
HARPER & BROTHERS. 1924.

[i]–xvi, [1]–368. [i]–[viii, viii blank], 1–365, [366–
67 advertisements, 368 blank]. 23.5 x 15.8 cm.
Illustrations unlisted. Two volumes, dark blue
cloth, gilt tops, uncut.

Ref.: Blanck 3537
Blanck's Variant A.

762 CLEMENS, SAMUEL L.

ROUGHING IT . . . BY MARK TWAIN. HARTFORD, CONNECTICUT: AMERICAN PUBLISHING COMPANY, 1872.

[i]–xviii, [19]–591, [592 advertisement]. 22 x 14.3 cm. 300 illustrations listed. Black cloth, gilt vignette and blind embossed borders on front cover, publisher's monogram and embossed border in blind on back cover, title in gilt on backstrip.

Ref.: Blanck 3337; Howes C481
Page 242 is in Blanck's A state. The imprint is as quoted by Blanck.
Editions: London, 1872.

763 CLEMENTS, JAMES I.

THE KLONDYKE . . . A COMPLETE GUIDE TO THE GOLD FIELDS . . . LOS ANGELES, CAL.: B. R. BAUMGARDT & CO., 1897.

[1]–98, [99–100 advertisements], [101–03 blank], [104 map]. 19.4 x 13 cm. 19 illustrations listed. Yellow printed wrapper with title on front wrapper. In a yellow cloth case.

Ref.: Howes C484; Smith 1814; Wickersham 3903

764 CLEVELAND, RICHARD J.

A NARRATIVE OF VOYAGES AND COMMERCIAL ENTERPRISES . . . CAMBRIDGE: PUBLISHED BY JOHN OWEN, 1842.

[i]–xvi, [1]–249, [250 blank]. 19.6 x 12.2 cm. Two volumes, black cloth, printed paper labels on backstrips.

Ref.: Barrett 530; Cowan p. 131 note; Howes C485; Sabin 13635
Cleveland visited California in 1803. He caused some trouble at San Diego.

765 CLEVELAND, COLUMBUS & CINCINNATI RAILROAD COMPANY, THE CLEVELAND AND TOLEDO RAILROAD COMPANY, ET AL., THE, Defendants

[Caption title] IN THE CIRCUIT COURT OF THE U.S. FOR THE NORTHERN DISTRICT OF OHIO. HENRY HOLMES, JULIUS C. SHELDON ET AL., VS. THE CLEVELAND, COLUMBUS & CINCINNATI RAILROAD COMPANY, THE CLEVELAND AND TOLEDO RAILROAD COMPANY ET AL. IN CHANCERY IN CIRCUIT COURT OF THE UNITED STATES FOR THE NORTHERN DISTRICT OF OHIO. . . .

[1]–26. Bound with related materials in contemporary black half calf.

Ref.:
See under ILLINOIS CENTRAL RAILROAD COMPANY.

Imprint at foot of page [1]: [rule] / Gideon, Printer, 511 Ninth st., Washington, D.C. /

766 CLEVELAND LAND COMPANY

[Broadside] CLEVELAND LAND COMPANY. THIS CERTIFIES, THAT   IS THE OWNER OF ONE SHARE OF CAPITAL STOCK IN THE CLEVELAND LAND COMPANY . . . CLEVELAND, NEBRASKA TERRITORY . . .

Broadside, 12.6 x 20.4 cm. Text, 11.8 x 19.1 cm.
Ref.:
Printed at Brownville or Omaha, Nebraska, dated partly in manuscript 1858.

767 CLINTON HERALD, THE

[Newspaper] THE CLINTON HERALD. C. E. LEONARD, PUBLISHER . . . VOLUME 1. CLINTON, CLINTON COUNTY, IOWA, THURSDAY, DECEMBER 18, 1856. NUMBER 1. . . .

Newspaper, [1–4]. 55.2 x 39.6 cm. Unbound.
Ref.:
Contains a sketch of the history of Clinton, which was then little more than a year old.

768 CLYMAN, JAMES

AUTOGRAPH MANUSCRIPT OF Memorandum & Diary of J Clyman. 1840–1841. Twenty-five pages, 17.4 x 14.5 cm. Gray paper over wooden boards, calf backstrip.

The manuscript entries by Clyman are for the first few days of 1840 and comprise speculative remarks on various subjects. Included are comments on his experiences in the Rocky Mountains and the Black Hills. According to his notes, Clyman was trading in furs in the Rockies between 1823 and 1827. There is one long, good passage about buffaloes.

The volume was used later by Hiram I. Ross, who was in partnership with Clyman in 1836, as an account book (85 pages and the back endleaf) from 1848 to 1862. Nearly all of the Ross entries are in pencil. Part of the time, Ross operated a sawmill near Milwaukee.

769 CLYMAN, JAMES

JAMES CLYMAN, AMERICAN FRONTIERSMAN, 1792–1881. THE ADVENTURES OF A TRAPPER AND COVERED WAGON EMIGRANT . . . SAN FRANCISCO: CALIFORNIA HISTORICAL SOCIETY, 1928.*

[1]–[251], [252 blank]. (Pages [1–2] blank.) 25.6 x 17.2 cm. Six illustrations and maps listed. Blue cloth.

Ref.: Cowan p. 132; Howes C81; Rader 849; Smith 1826

770 COAHUILA AND TEXAS (Mexican State)

[Broadside] GOBIERNO SUPREMO. DEL ESTADO DEL COAHUILA Y TEJAS EL GOBERNADOR DEL ESTADO LIBRE DE CUAHUILA[!] Y TEJAS A TODOS SUS HABITANTES SABED: QUE EL CONGRESO DEL MISMO ESTADO HA DECRETADO LO QUE SIGUE. DECRETO NUMERO 187. - . . . DADO EN LA CIUDAD DE LEONA VICARIO A 16. DE ABRIL DE 1832 . . . SANTIAGO DEL VALLE, SECRETARIO.

Broadside, 30.6 x 21 cm. Text, 20.5 x 17.5 cm.
Ref.:
Decree 187 establishes a yearly fair for products of the state. Printed at Leona Vicario.

771 COAHUILA AND TEXAS (Mexican State)

[Broadside] GOBIERNO SUPREMO DEL ESTADO LIBRE DE COAHUILA Y TEJAS. EL GOBERNADOR DEL ESTADO DE COAHUILA Y TEJAS A TODOS SUS HABITANTES, SABED: QUE EL CONGRESO DEL MISMO ESTADO HA DECRETADO LO SIGUIENTE. DECRETO NUMERO 110 . . . DADO EN LA CIUDAD DE LEONA VICARIO A 8 DE ENERO DE 1830 . . . SANTIAGO DEL VALLE, SECRETARIO.

Broadside, 31 x 20.9 cm. Text, 25.6 x 15.5 cm.
Ref.:
Decree 110 supplements Decree 108, both relating to the establishment of military reserves in the state.

772 COAHUILA AND TEXAS (Mexican State)

[Broadside] GOBIERNO SUPREMO DEL ESTADO DE COAHUILA Y TEJAS EL VICE GOBERNADOR DEL ESTADO DE COAHUILA Y TEJAS EN EJERCICIO DEL SUPREMO PODER EJECUTIVO A TODOS SUS HABITANTES SABED: QUE EL CONGRESO DEL MISMO ESTADO HA DECRETADO LO SIGUIENTE: ,, EL CONGRESO CONSTITUCIONAL DEL ESTADO LIBRE INDEPENDIENTE Y SOBERANO DE COAHUILA Y TEJAS HA TENIDO A BIEN DECRETAR . . . DADO EN LA CIUDAD DE LEONA-VICARIO A 6 DE ENRO DE 1833 . . . SANTIAGO DEL VALLE, SECRETARIO.

Broadside, 30.5 x 20.5 cm. Text, 21 x 16 cm.
Ref.:
Official support for the presidency of Manuel Gomez Pedraza.

773 COAHUILA AND TEXAS (Mexican State). Comision de Puntos Constitucionales

[Broadside] DICTAMEN DE LA COMISION DE PUNTOS CONSTITUCIONALES. HONORABLE CONGRESO. LA COMISION DE PUNTOS CONSTITUCIONALES A CUYO ECSAMEN PASO LA ATENTA CARTA . . . CIUDAD DE LEONA VICARIO, 1830. IMPRESO EN LA OFICINA DEL SUPREMO GOBIERNO DE ESTE ESTADO EN PALACIO, A CARGO DEL CIUDADANO JOSE MANUEL BANGS.

Broadside, 42.1 x 31 cm. Text, 32.3 x 23 cm.
Ref.:
Relates to the establishment of a military reserve in Coahuila y Texas. The broadside is a report of the commission established to consider the matter.

774 COAHUILA AND TEXAS (Mexican State). Congreso Constituyente

[Caption title] EL GOBERNADOR INTERINO NOMBRADO POR EL SOBERANO CONGRESO DE ESTE ESTADO A TODOS LOS QUE LAS PRESENTES VIEREN, SABED: QUE EL MISMO CONGRESO HA DECRETADO LO QUE SIGUE. NUMERO 23. . . . SALTILLO 27 DE MAYO DE 1826 . . . JUAN ANTONIO PADILLA, SECRETARIO.

[1], [2–4 blank]. 30.5 x 21 cm. Unbound leaflet.
Ref.: Kimball 23; Streeter 707 note
Printed at Saltillo, this decree of amnesty in the José Maria Letona affair returned the liberties denied by Decrees 21 and 22. Kimball, as Streeter points out, misdated this document March 27.

775 COAHUILA AND TEXAS (Mexican State). Constitution

CONSTITUCION POLITICA DEL ESTADO LIBRO DE COAHUILA Y TEJAS, SANCIONADA POR SU CONGRESO CONSTITUYENT EN 11 DE MARZO DE 1827. REIMPRESA PAR ORDEN DEL H. CONGRESO, FECHA 27 DE FEBRERO DE 1829. CIUDADA DE LEONA VICARIO IMPRENTA DEL GOBIERNO DEL ESTADO, A CARGO DE J. M. BANGS.

[1]–82, [83–5 index, 86 blank]. 13.3 x 9.3 cm. Tan printed wrappers, with title on front wrapper. In a green half morocco case.
Ref.: Clagett p. 36; Clements Library (*Texas*) 8; Howes C504; Kimball p. [313]; Robles (*Coahuila y Texas*) p. 339; Robles (*La Primera Imprenta*) p. 71; Streeter 708B
Editions: [Saltillo, 1826]. Mexico, 1827.

776 COALE, CHARLES B.

THE LIFE AND ADVENTURES OF WILBURN WATERS, THE FAMOUS HUNTER AND TRAPPER OF WHITE TOP MOUNTAIN; EMBRACING EARLY HISTORY OF SOUTHWESTERN VIRGINIA . . . RICHMOND: G. W. GARY & CO., 1878.

[iii]–xiv, [xv–xvi blank], [17]–265, [266 blank], [267–80 blank]. 19.7 x 13.5 cm. Black cloth, beveled edges. Worn, lacks blank leaf before title.
Ref.: Clark (*New South*) I 48; Howes C507; Summers, L. P.: *Annals of Southwestern Virginia*, Abingdon, 1929, pp. 1516–1635

The series of sketches had appeared previously in the *Abingdon Virginian*, of which the author was editor. The text is reprinted in the Summers volume noted above.

Neither Howes nor the Library of Congress catalogue card mentions the leaf preceding the title, but from the evidence in the present copy, it must have existed.

777 [COBBETT, WILLIAM]

A PROSPECT FROM THE CONGRESS-GALLERY, DURING THE SESSION, BEGUN DECEMBER 7, 1795. CONTAINING THE PRESIDENT'S SPEECH . . . BY PETER PORCUPINE. PHILADELPHIA: PUBLISHED BY THOMAS BRADFORD, 1796.

A–H^4, I^2. [i]–iv, [1]–68. Bound with Number 3867.
> *Ref.:* Evans 30229; Sabin 14010
Number One of Cobbett's *Political Censor*.

778 COBBETT, WILLIAM

A YEAR'S RESIDENCE IN THE UNITED STATES OF AMERICA . . . NEW-YORK: PRINTED FOR THE AUTHOR, 1818–19.

[1]–11^6, 12$^{[2]}$. [13]^4, 14–26^6, 27^4. 28^8, 29–37^6, 38^4. (12 2, [13]1, [28]1 blank.) [1]–134. [135]–304. [305]–432. 19 x 11.5 cm. Three volumes, tan printed boards with natural linen backstrips, with titles on front covers, uncut.
> *Ref.:* Buck 112; Howes C525; Matthews p. 231; Sabin 14021
The first part was copyrighted in 1818 and the second the following year. The third part is uncopyrighted.

779 COBURN, WALLACE D.

RHYMES FROM A ROUND-UP CAMP . . . 1899.

[1–6], 9–138. 16.8 x 12.7 cm. Eight illustrations by Charles M. Russell listed. Pictorial limp morocco, fore and lower edges uncut.
> *Prov.:* Inscribed on page [1]: Compliments / of the Author / Oct 10—1900. / [in pencil:] Malta Montana / I hope we will be blest / in this dear land of the / west. /
> *Ref.:*
Place of publication is Great Falls, Montana.

780 COCHRAN, MRS. M. A.

POSIE; OR, FROM REVEILLE TO RETREAT. AN ARMY STORY . . . CINCINNATI: THE ROBERT CLARKE COMPANY, 1896.

[1]–194. 17.5 x 11 cm. 13 illustrations listed. Light brown pictorial cloth.
> *Ref.:* Howes C527

Nearly half of the book deals with Army life in Arizona after the Civil War.

781 CODDING, I.

[Wrapper title] MODERN INFIDELITY PRACTICALLY CONSIDERED. AN ADDRESS, DELIVERED BEFORE A MASS CONVENTION OF ABOLITIONISTS, AT SOUTHPORT, ON THE 27TH JANUARY, 1847 . . . WAUKESHA: PRINTED AT THE OFFICE OF THE AMERICAN FREEMAN, 1848.

[1]–16. 20 x 13 cm. Removed from bound volume, unbound.
> *Ref.:*
According to McMurtrie (*Wisconsin*), page 74, the *American Freeman* moved to Milwaukee in May, 1848, from Waukesha. The press disseminated all kinds of anti-slavery materials, but this seems to be the only survivor, other than the newspaper.—EDG
No other copy has been located.

782 CODY, WILLIAM F.

AUTOGRAPH LETTER, SIGNED. 1887 February 15, New York. One page, 21.3 x 14.1 cm. Mounted. To Edwin A. Havers.

Inviting the recipient to call "and spend an evening with me and my people behind the scenes."

783 CODY, WILLIAM F.

[Caption title] DIETZ OPERA HOUSE, OAKLAND, ONE NIGHT ONLY WEDNESDAY, JUNE 13TH, 1877 . . . THE RENOWNED HISTORICAL CELEBRITIES, BUFFALO BILL AND CAPTAIN JACK (HON. W. F. CODY.) (J. W. CRAWFORD.) . . . IN THE REALISTIC WESTERN DRAMA, WRITTEN ESPECIALLY FOR BUFFALO BILL, IN 5 ACTS, ENTITLED LIFE ON THE BORDER . . . FRANCK & VALENTINE, PRINTERS . . . SAN FRANCISCO.

[1–4]. 22.7 x 15 cm. Unbound leaflet.
> *Ref.:*
Page [4] carries an eleven stanza poem, "Custer's Death," signed: Jack Crawford.

784 CODY, WILLIAM F.

BUFFALO BILL'S WILD WEST AND CONGRESS OF ROUGH RIDERS OF THE WORLD . . . CHICAGO, ILL. —1893 . . . THE BLAKELY PRINTING COMPANY, CHICAGO.

[1]–64. 23.8 x 18.4 cm. Illustrated. Pictorial wrappers. In a blue cloth case.
> *Ref.:*
An imprint appears on page 64: Copyrighted by / Cody and Salsbury, / Chicago, Ill., 1893. /
In his best years as a showman, Cody had few rivals.

785 CODY, WILLIAM F.

[Wrapper title] BUFFALO BILL'S WILD WEST. AMER-
ICA'S NATIONAL ENTERTAINMENT. CALHOUN
PRINT. CO. LED BY THE FAMED SCOUT AND GUIDE.
BUFFALO BILL (HON. W. F. CODY). CAPT. A. H.
BOGARDUS, CHAMPION WING SHOT OF THE WORLD.
MAJOR FRANK NORTH, THE PILOT OF THE PRAIRIE.
"OKLAHOMA" PAYNE, THE PROGRESSIVE PIONEER.
"BUCK" TAYLOR, KING OF THE COW-BOYS. "CON"
GRONER, THE COW-BOY SHERIFF OF THE PLATTE. A
HOST OF WESTERN CELEBRITIES; A CAMP OF CHEY-
ENNE, ARAPPAHOE, SIOUX, AND PAWNEE INDIANS;
A GROUP OF MEXICAN VAQUEROS; ROUND-UP
OF WESTERN COW-BOYS; COMPANY OF PRAIRIE
SCOUTS; A HERD OF WILD BUFFALOS; A CORRAL
OF INDIAN PONIES; A BAND OF MOUNTAIN ELK; A
DROVE OF TEXAS STEERS; PACK-TRAIN OF MEXICAN
BURROS; MOUNTAIN LIONS, COYOTTES, DEER, AN-
TELOPE, MOUNTAIN SHEEP, ETC. ARTISTICALLY
BLENDING, LIFE-LIKE, VIVID, AND THRILLING PIC-
TURES OF WESTERN LIFE. W. F. CODY, NATE SALS-
BURY, & A. H. BOGARDUS, PROPRIETORS. JOHN M.
BURKE, GENERAL MANAGER. FOR PARTICULARS,
DATE, AND DESCRIPTION, SEE POSTERS, SMALL
BILLS, AND NEWSPAPERS. THE CALHOUN PRINTING
COMPANY, HARTFORD, CONN.

[1–32, including covers]. 24.8 x 17.2 cm. Illustrated. Printed self wrappers, with title as above
on front wrapper, text on verso of front wrapper,
text and illustration on recto of back wrapper,
and illustration on verso of back wrapper.
   Ref.:
   The "Salutatory" on the inside front cover is
dated North Platte, Neb., March 1, 1884.
   In 1883, Buffalo Bill teamed up with Dr.
Carver; the following year he joined with Nate
Salsbury for the first of many successful seasons
of the Wild West Show.

786 CODY, WILLIAM F.

THE LIFE OF HON. WILLIAM F. CODY . . . AN AUTO-
BIOGRAPHY. HARTFORD, CONN: FRANK E. BLISS.

[i]–xvi, [17]–365, [366 blank]. 20.9 x 14.2 cm.
80 illustrations listed. Dark red cloth.
   Ref.: Howes C531; Jennewein 75; Rader 859;
Smith 1849
   Copyrighted 1879.
   According to a letter by A. D. Worthington
of Hartford, to Richard I. Dodge, March 10,
1884, only three or four thousand of these books
were sold.

787 CODY, WILLIAM F.

[Photograph] ORIGINAL PHOTOGRAPH, group,
William F. Cody, "Pawnee Bill," and "Buffalo"
Jones. "Pawnee Bill" seated centre, Cody at his
right and Jones at his left, latter two standing.

14 x 9.7 cm. on card mount 16.5 x 10.8 cm.,
mount with printed name of photographer:
Tessford / 373 Fifth Avenue / New York /.
   Two inscriptions on verso of card. Buffalo
Bill / "   " Jones / "Pawnee Bill" / [wavy
line] 3/2/39 / To / Mr. Hugh B. Tabb— / I arranged for having / this photo taken in 1910 and
was / present at the time. / The / handwriting
above line is that / of "Pawnee Bill," who is
seated / in picture. / This photo is rare—not /
many *if any* originals like this / being in existence—Please / accept it with my sincerest / well
wishes / Frank Winch / Los Angeles Calif. /

788 CODY, WILLIAM F.

TRUE TALES OF THE PLAINS . . . NEW YORK: EMPIRE
BOOK COMPANY, 1908.

[i–iv], 1–259, [260 blank]. 19.2 x 13 cm. 16 plates
unlisted. Green pictorial cloth.
   Prov.: Presentation copy inscribed on front
fly-leaf: With the compliments / of the Author /
W. F. Cody / "Buffalo Bill" / To / G. W. Zorn /
Jan 30th / 1909 /.
   Ref.: Howes C532
   First Edition.

789 CODY, WILLIAM F.

THE SAME; with different imprint. New York /
Cupples & Leon Company / 1908 /.

[i–iv], 1–259, [260–65 advertisements, 266
blank]. 18.8 x 13 cm. Gray pictorial wrappers.
In a yellow cloth case.
   Ref.: Howes C532; Rader 861
   Second Edition.

790 COE, CHARLES H.

JUGGLING A ROPE, LARIAT ROPING AND SPINNING,
KNOTS AND SPLICES. ALSO THE TRUTH ABOUT TOM
HORN . . . PENDLETON, ORE.: HAMLEY & CO., 1927.*

[1]–114. 19.1 x 13.2 cm. Illustrations unlisted.
Blue cloth.
   Ref.: Adams 224; Adams (*Ramp. Herd*) 497;
Dobie p. 106; Howes C533
   Contains a defense of Tom Horn.

791 COFFEEN, HENRY A.

. . . VERMILION COUNTY, HISTORICAL, STATISTI-
CAL, AND DESCRIPTIVE. A HANDBOOK . . . DAN-
VILLE, ILL.

[1]–116. 18.1 x 11.2 cm. Map: Map of Vermilion
County, Ill. [reading up left side:] Drawn by
Edward Oakes. / [reading down right side:] Published by H. A. Coffeen. / 15.2 x 8.9 cm. No
scale given. Blue cloth with title in gilt on front
cover.
   Ref.: Bradford 969; Buck 1104; Howes C536

Published late in 1870 or early in 1871. Page 116 carries a note that 2000 copies were printed by Messrs. Sherman & Co., of Philadelphia.

792 COFFIN, ADDISON

LIFE AND TRAVELS OF ADDISON COFFIN . . . CLEVE-LAND: WILLIAM G. HUBBARD, 1897.

[1]–570, [571 advertisement, 572 blank]. (Pages [1–2] blank.) 18.8 x 12.9 cm. Two portraits. Green cloth, title in gilt on backstrip.

Ref.:

Addison lived for some time in Iowa. His travels included many through the West including two overland journeys in the Eighties and Nineties.—EDG

793 COFFIN, CHARLES C.

THE SEAT OF EMPIRE . . . BOSTON: FIELDS, OSGOOD, & CO., 1870.

[i]–viii, 1–232, [1–11 advertisements, 12 blank]. 17.7 x 11.6 cm. Folding map, five unlisted plates. Green cloth.

Ref.: Jones 1526; Smith 1859

Normally, Coffin used the name Carleton for his publications.

794 COFFIN, GEORGE

A PIONEER VOYAGE TO CALIFORNIA AND ROUND THE WORLD, 1849 TO 1852 . . . *

[1]–235, [236 blank]. 22.2 x 14.9 cm. 14 illustrations, unlisted. Mustard cloth, title in gilt on backstrip.

Prov.: Inscribed on front endleaf: Mr. B. R. Atwood / Compliments of / Gorham B. Coffin / Chicago Oct 1. 1908 /.

Ref.: Cowan p. 133; Howes (1954) 2070

Copyrighted Chicago, 1908. Gorham B. Coffin was a son of the author.

795 COIT, DANIEL W.

THE DRAWINGS AND LETTERS OF DANIEL WADS-WORTH COIT . . . EDITED . . . BY EDITH M. COUL-TER. [SAN FRANCISCO]: BOOK CLUB OF CALIFORNIA, 1937.

[i]–[xiv, xiv blank], [1]–31, [32 blank], [33–48, 48 blank]. 33.7 x 22.8 cm. Eight collotype plates. Blue boards, cream buckram backstrip, printed paper labels on front cover and backstrip, fore and lower edges uncut.

Ref.: Heller & Magee 276

Limited to 325 copies printed at the Grabhorn Press.

796 COKE, HENRY J.

A RIDE OVER THE ROCKY MOUNTAINS TO OREGON AND CALIFORNIA. WITH A GLANCE AT SOME OF THE TROPICAL ISLANDS, INCLUDING THE WEST INDIES

AND THE SANDWICH ISLES . . . LONDON: RICHARD BENTLEY, 1852.

[i]–x, [1]–388, [389–90], [1–16 advertisements]. 22.1 x 14.1 cm. Frontispiece portrait. Brown cloth, marbled. Top of backstrip chipped away.

Prov.: Presentation copy, inscribed on the front fly-leaf: Mʳ Faulkner / from the Author /.

Ref.: Cowan p. 134; Field 340; Howell 56; Howes C548; Matthews p. 314; Sabin 14240; Wagner-Camp 211

Contains a day-by-day journal of a trip across the plains in 1850.

797 COKE, HENRY J.

TRACKS OF A ROLLING STONE . . . LONDON: SMITH, ELDER, & CO., 1905.

[i–vi (v–vi fly-title)], [1]–349, [350 blank]. 20.1 x 13.5 cm. Portrait. Red cloth.

Prov.: Presentation copy, inscribed on the front fly-leaf: To / Sir Frederick Macmillan / with the author's / kind regards— /.

Ref.: Howes C549; Wagner-Camp 211 note

Contains considerable additional material relating to his western experiences and his overland trip of 1850.

798 COLBURN, J. G. W.

THE LIFE OF SILE DOTY, THE MOST NOTED THIEF AND DARING BURGLAR OF HIS TIME . . . TOLEDO, O.: BLADE PRINTING & PAPER COMPANY, 1880.

[1]–269, [270 blank]. 21.9 x 14.5 cm. Illustrations unlisted. Brown embossed cloth, title in gilt on backstrip.

Ref.: Adams 226; Howes C556

A predatory profession, practised chiefly in Michigan, Indiana and Ohio, and told of with gusto by the old rogue at seventy-five; his horrified family succeeded in destroying many copies. —Howes

799 COLE, CORNELIUS

MEMOIRS OF CORNELIUS COLE, EX-SENATOR OF THE UNITED STATES FROM CALIFORNIA. NEW YORK: McLOUGHLIN BROTHERS, 1908.*

[i]–x, 1–354. 23 x 17.2 cm. Portrait. Blue cloth, printed paper label on backstrip, gilt top, uncut, unopened.

Ref.: Adams 228; Cowan p. 134; Howes C565

800 COLE, GEORGE E.

EARLY OREGON. JOTTINGS OF PERSONAL RECOLLEC-TIONS OF A PIONEER OF 1850.*

[1]–95, [96 blank]. 19 x 13.3 cm. Portrait. Red cloth.

Ref.: Howell 57; Smith 1879

Copyrighted 1905. Printed in Spokane.

801 COLE, GILBERT L.

IN THE EARLY DAYS ALONG THE OVERLAND TRAIL IN NEBRASKA TERRITORY, IN 1852 . . . KANSAS CITY: FRANKLIN HUDSON PUBLISHING COMPANY.*

[iii]–[xii], 13–125, [126 blank]. 16.8 x 12 cm. Portrait. Gray cloth.

Ref.: Howes (1954) 2102; Rader 867

Copyrighted 1905. Contains a narrative of a trip from Michigan to California by a party of twenty-four in 1852.

802 COLEMAN, ROBERT J.

LIFE AND MINISTERIAL LABORS OF ELD. R. J. COLEMAN . . . LITTLE ROCK ARK.: ARKANSAS BAPTIST PRINT, 1894.

[i–viii, viii blank], [1]–[81], [82 blank]. 15.9 x 11 cm. Portrait. Maroon blind embossed wrappers with title in gilt on front wrapper.

Ref.: Howes C570

This little book deals with early conditions in Arkansas. While in Little Rock, in 1940, I spoke to Mr. Allsop about it. He told me he did not have a copy and had never heard of the book.—EDG

803 COLESON, ANN

MISS COLESON'S NARRATIVE OF HER CAPTIVITY AMONG THE SIOUX INDIANS! . . . IN MINNESOTA. PHILADELPHIA: PUBLISHED BY BARCLAY & CO., 1864.

[17]–28, 33–46, 53–58, 63–70. 23.9 x 14.7 cm. Four illustrations. Colored pictorial wrappers, with title on front cover, another illustration from the text on the verso of the back wrapper. In a red cloth case.

Ref.: Ayer 49; Fields 343; Howes C575; Sabin 14335

Although the date 1866 appears in the copyright notice and on the front wrapper, the title-page is dated 1864. The ICN (Ayer) copy is copyrighted 1865, the title-page is dated 1864, and the front wrapper (bound in) is dated 1866. The text, including the erratic pagination is the same. The present copy is complete, the collation being quite clearly [1]–3⁸.

Thomas M. McDade's article on the Barclay firm in the *Pennsylvania Magazine of History and Biography*, Volume LXXX, Number 4, 1956, describes the activities of a sensational publisher. He concludes that most of Barclay's productions were fiction in the guise of personal narrative and that nearly everything from the shop must be viewed with suspicion.

804 COLLAMER, J.

SPEECH OF MR. J. COLLAMER, OF VERMONT, DELIVERED IN THE HOUSE OF REPRESENTATIVES . . . ON THE CONSTITUTIONAL VALIDITY OF THE ACT OF CONGRESS REQUIRING THE ELECTION OF REPRESENTATIVES . . . FEBRUARY 8, 1844. WASHINGTON: PRINTED BY GALES AND SEATON, 1844.

[1]–13, [14 blank]. Bound with Number 1084.

Ref.: Sabin 14360

805 COLLIERY ENGINEERING COMPANY, THE, *Publishers*

PLACER MINING: A HAND-BOOK FOR KLONDIKE AND OTHER MINERS AND PROSPECTORS WITH INTRODUCTORY CHAPTERS REGARDING THE RECENT GOLD DISCOVERIES IN THE YUKON VALLEY, THE ROUTES TO THE GOLD FIELDS, OUTFIT REQUIRED, AND MINING REGULATIONS OF ALASKA AND THE CANADIAN YUKON . . . SCRANTON, PA.: THE COLLIERY ENGINEER COMPANY, 1897.

[i]–vi, [1]–146. 18.5 x 12.5 cm. Illustrations unlisted, folding map. Map: The Colliery Engineer Company's Map of the Yukon Valley, Showing Routes to the Gold Fields. / 30 x 50.5 cm. No scale given. *Inset:* Enlarged Map of Klondike Mining District. / [rule] / 14.6 x 15.1 cm. No scale given. *Inset:* Enlarged Map of / [underline] / Chilkoot, / [underline] / Chilkat and / [underline] / White Pass Routes / [underline] / 10.2 x 10.2 cm. No scale given. Gray pictorial cloth with title on front wrapper.

Ref.: Smith 8177; Wickersham 3905

Advertisements on inner covers.

806 COLLINS, CHARLES, *Compiler*

COLLINS' OMAHA DIRECTORY. EMBRACING A GENERAL RESIDENT AND BUSINESS DIRECTORY OF THE CITIZENS, AND AN APPENDIX CONTAINING A GREAT VARIETY OF HISTORICAL DATA, STATISTICS AND FACTS . . . JUNE, 1866.

[i–ii], [1]–80, [97]–204. (Page [i] blank, [ii] advertisement.) 19.8 x 12.1 cm. Tan printed boards, black leather backstrip, with title on front cover, with advertisements below and on inner covers.

Ref.: AII (*Nebraska*) 93; Howes C588; Sabin 57261

The compiler's preface is dated from Omaha, June, 1866. There is no indication that the omitted pages 81–96 were ever included, and there is no reference to them in the Index. Inserted between pages 160 and 161 is an unnumbered orange sheet carrying advertisements of the *Nebraska Republican*.

This first Omaha directory is unusually interesting. It contains about fifty pages of historical matter on the early history of Nebraska and Omaha. There is also a section headed "Route to the West" (five pages) which contains much on the new route to Montana and includes a table of distances. There is also a post office directory for the state of Kansas and the territories of Nebraska, Colorado, Nevada, Dakota, Idaho, Montana, New Mexico, Washington, and Utah. —EDG

807 COLLINS, DENNIS

THE INDIANS' LAST FIGHT; OR, THE DULL KNIFE RAID . . . *

[1]–326. (Pages [1–2] blank.) 22.9 x 15 cm. Seven illustrations, unlisted. Green cloth, title in black on front cover and backstrip.

Ref.: Adams 232; Howes C590; Rader 871

Published at Girard, Kansas, in 1915 by the Press of The Appeal to Reason.

808 COLLINS, HUBERT E.

WARPATH & CATTLE TRAIL . . . NEW YORK: WILLIAM MORROW, 1928.*

[i]–[xxii, xxii blank], 1–296. 23.4 x 15.9 cm. Ten illustrations. Green cloth, fore and lower edges uncut.

Prov.: Inscribed by the author on the recto of the frontispiece: Inscribed for / Mr Geo M. Morton / by / the Author / Hubert E Collins— / July 31, 1929. / [underline] /.

Ref.: Adams 233; Adams (*Ramp. Herd*) 506; Dobie p. 99; Howes C592; Rader 872

Re Southwestern Indians and cattlemen.

809 COLLINS, JOHN S.

ACROSS THE PLAINS IN '64. INCIDENTS OF EARLY DAYS WEST OF THE MISSOURI RIVER . . . OMAHA, NEBRASKA: NATIONAL PRINTING COMPANY, 1904.

[1]–151, [152 blank]. 19.4 x 13.1 cm. Facsimile. Green pictorial cloth, with title in gilt and black on front cover and in gilt on backstrip.

Prov.: Inscribed on front endleaf: For / Dr. A F. Jonas / From / John S. Collins / June 25/05 /. Manuscript corrections by the author on pages 14 and 53.

Ref.: Howes C594

The author went overland to Virginia City, Montana, in 1864. He spent the decade 1872 to 1882 as a Post Trader at Fort Laramie.—EDG

810 COLLINS, JOHN S.

THE SAME.

[i–ii], [1]–151, [152 blank], [1]–152. 19.4 x 13.1 cm. 12 illustrations listed. Green pictorial cloth as above.

Ref.: Howes C594

Second Edition. According to a note on page [1] of the second part, the edition was published in 1911.

A note on the recto of the frontispiece reads: *June 23rd* 1911 Received / this book (by express)

from / John Morrison / & / John W. Collins Executors of / John S. Collins estate / B. M. Webster /.

811 COLLYER, ROBERT

A MAN IN EARNEST: LIFE OF A. H. CONANT . . . BOSTON: HORACE B. FULLER, 1868.

[1]–230, [3]–8, 11–13 advertisements, [14 blank]. 17.5 x 11.3 cm. Maroon cloth, blind fillets on sides, title in gilt on backstrip.

Ref.: Buck 256A; Nicholson p. 161; Sabin 14465

Collyer's work, based on Conant's papers, contains much on preaching in Illinois. Conant became chaplain of the 19th Illinois Regiment in 1861 and served with the regiment until his death in 1863.—EDG

812 COLNETT, JAMES

A VOYAGE TO THE SOUTH ATLANTIC AND ROUND CAPE HORN INTO THE PACIFIC OCEAN, FOR THE PURPOSE OF EXTENDING THE SPERMACETI WHALE FISHERIES, AND OTHER OBJECTS OF COMMERCE . . . LONDON: PRINTED FOR THE AUTHOR, 1798.

[*]4, a–b4, c1, A–Y4, Z2. [i]–iv, [iii]–vi, [i]–xviii, [1]–179, [180 blank]. 31.3 x 24.8 cm. Three plates, two folding charts and four folding plans. Map: A / Chart / Shewing the Track / [swelled rule] of the [swelled rule] / Ship Rattler / from Rio Janeiro / Round Cape Horn, to the Coast of / California, / By / Capt. James Colnett, / [swelled rule] of the [swelled rule] / Royal Navy, / 1793-1794. / [lower centre:] Engraved by T. Foot. / [lower centre below neat line:] London. Published January 1st 1793, by A. Arrowsmith, Charles Street, Soho. / 56 x 37.5 cm. No scale indicated. With small flap of extension in right margin, 9 x 5.3 cm. Map: Plan / of the / Islands / Felix and Ambrose / [swelled rule] by [swelled rule] / Capt. James Colnett, / of the / Royal Navy. / 1793. / [lower centre:] [as in preceding map] / [lower centre below neat line:] [as in preceding map] 36.2 x 50.1 cm. No scale given. Map: Chart / [swelled rule] of the [swelled rule] / Galapagos, / Surveyed / in the Merchant-Ship Rattler, and Drawn / By / Capt: James Colnett, / [swelled rule] of the [swelled rule] / Royal Navy. / in 1793 1794. / [lower centre:] Engraved by T. Foot, Weston Place, / St Pancras. / [centre below neat line:] London: Published 1st January 1798, by A: Arrowsmith, Charles Street, Soho. / 76.1 x 56.9 cm. No scale given. Map: Plan / [swelled rule] of the [swelled rule] / Island / Cocos / Surveyed and Drawn by / Capt. James Colnett / [swelled rule] of the [swelled rule] / Royal Navy, / 1793. [lower centre:] [as in first map above] / [lower centre be-

low neat line:] [as in first map above except A: and Soho Square] / 36.4 x 49.9 cm. No scale given. Map: Plan / of the Anchoring Place / at the Island / Quibo / By / Capt: James Colnett. / [swelled rule] of the [swelled rule] / Royal Navy. / [swelled rule] / 1794. / [lower centre:] [as in first map above] / [lower centre below neat line:] [as in first map above except Soho Square.] 37.3 x 51.2 cm. Scale: 3 1/5 miles to one inch. Map: Plan / of the / Islands / [swelled rule] of [swelled rule] / Revillagigedo, / [swelled rule] by [swelled rule] / Capt. James Colnett, / of the / Royal Navy. / 1793. / [lower centre:] [as in first map above] / [lower centre below neat line:] [as in preceding map] / 36 x 50.1 cm. No scale given. *Inset:* Rocka Partida / 12.6 x 10.6 cm. Scale: 25 fathoms to one inch. Gray boards, white paper backstrip, contemporary manuscript label, uncut.

Ref.: Bancroft (*NW Coast*) I, pp. 210–23; Cowan (1914) p. 52; Howell 59; Howes C604; Sabin 14546; Smith 741; Wagner (*Cart of NW Coast*) p. 207 *et seq.*

A highly important work regarding the West Coast and the Nootka Sound area.

813 COLONIZATION SOCIETY OF THE STATE OF IOWA

THE ANNUAL REPORT OF THE COLONIZATION SOCIETY OF THE STATE OF IOWA, WITH THE PROCEEDINGS OF THE SECOND ANNIVERSARY, IN THE CAPITOL, JANUARY 23, 1857. IOWA CITY: SYLVESTER, HARRISON & BROTHER.

[1]–16. 21.5 x 14 cm. Gray printed wrappers with title on front wrapper.

Ref.: Moffit 277; Mott (*Iowa*) p. 57
Published in 1857.

814 COLORADO BRAND BOOK

COLORADO BRAND BOOK AND STOCKGROWERS AND BREEDERS READY REFERENCE WITH INDEX OF BRANDS AND INDEX OF OWNERS, CONTAINING ALL STOCK BRANDS ON RECORD IN THE OFFICE OF SECRETARY OF STATE OF COLORADO. DENVER, COLO.: S. H. STANDART.

[i]–[vi], [1]–[319], [320 advertisement]. 18.7 x 10.1 cm. Limp red leather with wallet flap; advertisements on inner covers and fly-leaves, additional page of advertisement before title-page, verso blank.

Ref.: Adams (*Ramp. Herd*) 511; Howes S870
Copyrighted 1887. Pages [318–19]: table of Distances by Rail from Denver.

815 COLORADO AND CALIFORNIA WAGON ROAD COMPANY

[Broadside printed in red] TERRITORY OF COLORADO. COLORADO AND CALIFORNIA WAGON ROAD

CO. CAPITOL STOCK, $50,000 SHARES, $10.00 EACH. THIS IS TO CERTIFY, THAT IS THE OWNER OF SHARES . . . IN WITNESS WHEREOF, THE PRESIDENT AND SECRETARY HAVE HEREUNTO AFFIXED THEIR SIGNATURES . . . REGISTER PRINT, CENTRAL.

Broadside, 16.8 x 25 cm. Text, 14 x 21.1 cm.

Ref.:
Mounted over the ornament incorporating the word Stamp is a five-cent Internal Revenue Stamp, uncancelled.

Dated in part print, part manuscript 1866.

816 COLORADO CATTLE GROWERS' ASSOCIATION

[Caption title] ARTICLES OF ASSOCIATION OF THE COLORADO CATTLE GROWERS ASSOCIATION, AS AMENDED. . . .

[1–4]. 21.6 x 13.9 cm. Unbound leaflet.
Ref.:
There is no indication of place of printing or date. After 1884, probably Denver.

817 COLORADO CATTLE GROWERS ASSOCIATION

BRANDS BELONGING TO THE COLORADO CATTLE GROWERS ASSOCIATION . . . CHICAGO: THE J. M. W. JONES STATIONERY & PRINTING CO.

[i]–viii, [1]–61, [62 blank]. 16 x 10.1 cm. Tan sheepskin, red edges.

Prov.: Inscribed on front cover: N.° 1 / Tenney Bros / Fort Collins / Colo /.

Ref.: Howes C605
Published in Chicago in 1884.

818 COLORADO CATTLE GROWERS ASSOCIATION

SECOND COPY: Signature on front fly-leaf: Henry E Brennan / Greeley, / Colo. / June 1905. / [underline] /.

819 COLORADO CATTLE GROWERS' ASSOCIATION

SUPPLEMENTARY BRANDS FOR 1885, BELONGING TO THE COLORADO CATTLE GROWERS' ASSOCIATION . . . DENVER, COLORADO: THE COLLIER & CLEAVELAND LITH. CO.

[1]–[94]. 16 x 10.3 cm. Sheepskin, red edges.

Prov.: Inscribed on front cover: N.° 2 / Tenney Bros / Fort Collins / Colo /. Some manuscript notes in text.

Ref.: Howes C605
The Tenney Bros. brands are included in this Supplement on page 37.

820 COLORADO MINER, THE

[Newspaper] THE COLORADO MINER. VOLUME III. GEORGETOWN, COLORADO, THURSDAY, NOVEMBER 25, 1869. NUMBER 27. . . .

[1–4]. 65.1 x 44.8 cm. Unbound.

The editors and proprietors were A. W. Barnard and M. E. Ward. This issue contains information about mining activities in Colorado.

821 COLORADO TERRITORY. ADJU-
TANT GENERAL'S OFFICE (Hal Sayr)

BIENNIAL REPORT OF THE ADJUTANT-GENERAL OF
THE TERRITORY OF COLORADO . . . CENTRAL CITY:
PRINTED BY D. C. COLLIER, 1870.

[1]–19, [20 blank]. 23 x 14.5 cm. Yellow printed wrappers with title on front wrapper.

Ref.: McMurtrie & Allen (*Colorado*) 111

822 COLORADO TERRITORY. GOVER-
NOR (John Evans)

[Caption title] GOVERNOR EVAN'S[!] CORRE-
SPONDENCE IN RELATION TO THE INDIAN WAR. . . .

[1]–8. 19.9 x 13.3 cm. Unbound, removed from bound volume.

Ref.:

A hitherto unnoted pamphlet relating to the Chivington affair, the work seems to have been printed at Denver in 1865.

823 COLORADO TERRITORY. GOVER-
NOR (John Evans)

GOVERNOR'S MESSAGE, DELIVERED TO THE LEGISA-
TIVE[!] ASSEMBLY OF COLORADO: IN JOINT SESSION
AT GOLDEN CITY, WEDNESDAY, FEBRUARY 3, 1864.
PRINTED AT THE OFFICE OF THE COMMONWEALTH,
DENVER.

[i–ii], [1]–9, [10 blank]. 19.8 x 14 cm. Rebound in blue half morocco.

Ref.: McMurtrie & Allen (*Colorado*) 41 see
This is not the printing described by McMurtrie & Allen.

824 COLORADO TERRITORY. GOVER-
NOR (John Evans)

[Caption title] REPLY OF GOVERNOR EVANS . . . TO
. . . THE REPORT OF "THE COMMITTEE ON THE CON-
DUCT OF THE WAR," . . . DENVER, AUG. 6TH,
1865 . . .

[1]–16, [1]–[5], [6 blank]. 19.9 x 13.5 cm. Unbound, removed from bound volume.

Ref.: McMurtrie & Allen (*Colorado*) 58;
Howes E224; Wagner-Camp 415
The pamphlet contains also a report of a council with the Indians and an appendix describing the captivity of Mrs. Ewbank.

825 COLORADO TERRITORY. GOVER-
NOR (John Evans)

ANOTHER COPY. On somewhat thinner paper.

826 COLQUHOUN, JAMES

THE EARLY HISTORY OF THE CLIFTON-MORENCI
DISTRICT . . . LONDON AND BECCLES: PRINTED FOR

PRIVATE CIRCULATION BY WILLIAM CLOWES AND
SONS, LIMITED.

[i–vi, vi blank], 1–85, [86 colophon]. 17.2 x 10.9 cm. Bright red cloth.

Prov.: Inscribed on front fly-leaf: To / Sir Cecil / L. Budd. / With the Compliments / Of His Friend, / The Author. / Tunbridge Wells— [bracket] / 4 June, 1935 /.

Ref.:

Colquhoun's work describes the establishment and the formative years of the Longfellow Copper Mining Company by Henry Lesinsky and his associates. The work is undated, but on page 63 there is a reference to Charles Nicholson as being "now" Publicity Agent for President Roosevelt.

827 COLT, MIRIAM D.

WENT TO KANSAS; BEING A THRILLING ACCOUNT
OF AN ILL-FATED EXPEDITION . . . WATERTOWN:
PRINTED BY L. INGALLS & CO., 1862.*

[i]–[xii, xii blank], [13]–294. 19.1 x 11.8 cm. Dark gray cloth, blind embossed sides, title in gilt on backstrip.

Prov.: Signature on inner back cover: Dewitt Miller / Forest Glen / Maryland. /
Ref.: Howes C616; Rader 875

828 COLTON, CALVIN

MANUAL FOR EMIGRANTS TO AMERICA . . . LON-
DON: F. WESTLEY AND A. H. DAVIS, 1832.

[i]–x, [1]–203, [204 colophon]. (Page vi mis-
paginated viii.) 15.1 x 9.1 cm. Dark green smooth cloth, printed white paper label, 3.2 x 1.5 cm., on backstrip, uncut.

Ref.: Buck 239; Howes (1954) 2157; Sabin 14779
Four of the chapters deal with the Mississippi River Valley.

829 COLTON, GEORGE W.

[Map] G. WOOLWORTH COLTON'S / TOWNSHIP
MAP OF / THE STATE OF / IOWA, / 1863. / DRAWN,
ENGRAVED & PUBLISHED BY / G. WOOLWORTH
COLTON 18 BEEKMAN ST. / NEW YORK. / MILLS &
COMPANY, DES MOINES IOWA / RUFUS BLANCHARD,
CHICAGO, ILL. / [at lower centre:] ENTERED AC-
CORDING TO ACT OF CONGRESS, IN THE YEAR 1862,
BY G. WOOLWORTH COLTON, IN THE CLERKS OF-
FICE OF THE DISTRICT COURT OF THE UNITED
STATES FOR THE SOUTHERN DISTRICT OF NEW
YORK /

Map, 45.5 x 60 cm. Scale: 16 miles to one inch. Folded into green cloth covers, 14.8 x 9.3 cm., with title stamped in gilt on front cover, publishers' advertisements inside front cover.

Ref.:
Editions: New York, 1862.

830 COLTON, GEORGE W.

[Map] G. WOOLWORTH COLTON'S / TOWNSHIP MAP OF / THE STATE OF / IOWA, / DRAWN, ENGRAVED AND PUBLISHED BY / G. W. & C. B. COLTON & CO. 172 WILLIAM ST. NEW YORK. / 1869. / [lower centre:] ENTERED ACCORDING TO ACT OF CONGRESS, IN THE YEAR 1862, BY G. WOOLWORTH COLTON, IN THE CLERKS OFFICE OF THE DISTRICT COURT OF THE UNITED STATES FOR THE SOUTHERN DISTRICT OF NEW YORK /

Map, 44.2 x 56.7 cm. Scale: about 16 miles to one inch. Folded into black cloth covers, 14.5 x 9.1 cm., with title stamped on front cover in gilt, advertisements of the publisher inside front cover.

Ref.:

There are numerous changes from the 1863 version, particularly in the west.

831 COLTON, GEORGE W., & C. B.

[Map] MAP OF THE / SILVER MINES / OF / NEVADA / COMPILED, ENGRAVED AND / PUBLISHED BY G. W. & C. B. COLTON / 172 WILLIAM ST. N.Y. / 1865. / [at lower right:] ENTERED ACCORDING TO ACT OF CONGRESS IN THE YEAR 1865 BY G. W. & C. B. COLTON, IN THE CLERKS OFFICE OF THE DISTRICT COURT OF THE UNITED STATES FOR THE SOUTHERN DISTRICT OF NEW YORK. /

Map, 32.2 x 34.2 cm. Scale: 19 miles to one inch. Folded into black cloth covers, 14.5 x 9.4 cm., with title stamped in gilt on front cover, publishers' advertisements inside front cover.

Ref.: Phillips (*Maps*) p. 461

832 COLTON, JOSEPH H.

[Map] COLTON'S, / TOWNSHIP MAP, / OF THE STATE OF / IOWA / COMPILED FROM THE UNITED STATES SURVEYS, / & OTHER AUTHENTIC SOURCES; / PUBLISHED BY J. H. COLTON, / NO. 86 CEDAR ST. NEW YORK, / 1854. / [at lower left:] ENTERED ACCORDING TO ACT OF CONGRESS, IN THE YEAR 1851, BY J. H. COLTON, IN THE CLERKS OFFICE OF THE DIST. COURT, FOR THE SOUTH.ⁿ DIST. OF NEW YORK. /

Map, 62 x 73.1 cm. Scale: about 15 miles to one inch. Folded into red cloth covers, 14.5 x 9 cm., same in blind on back cover.

Ref.:

833 COLTON, JOSEPH H.

GUIDE FOR THE TERRITORY OF IOWA, WITH A CORRECT MAP, SHOWING THE TOWNSHIP SURVEYS, &C. &C. NEW YORK: PUBLISHED BY J. H. COLTON. 1839.

[1]–[6]. 10.6 x 7.1 cm. Folding map: Map / of the Surveyed Part / of / Iowa / New York, / Published by J. H. Colton, / 1839. / [at lower right:] Engraved & Printed by Stiles, Sherman & Smith, N.Y. / [at lower centre:] Entered according to Act of Congress in the year 1839 by J. H. Colton, in the Clerks office of the District court of the southern district of N. York / Scale: about 13 miles to an inch. 41.7 x 27.9 cm. Green cloth, with title stamped in gilt on front cover. In a dark blue morocco solander case, by Lakeside Press.

Prov.: Bookplate of C. G. Littell.

Ref.: Mott (*Iowa*) p. 57

One of the important (and scarce) early guides to Iowa.

834 COLTON, JOSEPH H.

THE SAME . . . 1840.

[1]–7, [8 colophon]. 11.5 x 7.3 cm. Folding map attached to inside front cover: Map / of the Surveyed part / of / Iowa / New York, / Published by J. H. Colton. / 1840. / [at lower centre:] Entered according to Act of Congress in the year 1839 by J. H. Colton, in the Clerks office of the District court of the Southern district of N. York /. 42 x 27.8 cm. Scale: about 13 miles to one inch. Black cloth, with title stamped in gilt on front cover. In a red cloth case.

Ref.: Mott (*Iowa*) p. 57

Two newspaper clippings have been pasted to a blank leaf preceding the title-page.

835 COLTON, JOSEPH H.

[Map] MAP OF THE / UNITED STATES / THE BRITISH PROVINCES / MEXICO &C. / SHOWING THE ROUTES OF THE U.S. MAIL / STEAM PACKETS TO CALIFORNIA, / AND A PLAN OF THE GOLD REGION. / [thin and thick rules] / PUBLISHED BY J. H. COLTON, / 86 CEDAR Sᵀ. NEW YORK. / 1849. / DRAWN & ENGRAVED BY J. M. ATWOOD, NEW YORK / ENTERED ACCORDING TO ACT OF CONGRESS, IN THE YEAR 1848, BY J. H. COLTON IN THE CLERKS OFFICE OF THE DISTRICT COURT OF THE SOUTHERN DISTRICT OF NEW YORK. / PRINTED AT ACKERMAN'S ROOMS, 120 FULTON ST. N.Y. / *Inset:* [Route] From New York to San / Francisco via Cape Horn / 17,000 miles / Via Panama 5.900 m. / 17.4 x 8.6 cm. No scale indicated. *Inset:* Map of the / Gold Region. / California. / 12.4 x 7.1 cm. No scale indicated. *Insets:* Engraved Table of Distances and a view of Pyramid Lake.

Map, 45.5 x 61 cm. Scale: about 300 miles to one inch. Folded into brown cloth covers, 13.5 x 8.5 cm., with printed paper label on front cover.

Ref.: Phillips (*Maps*) p. 900; Wheat (*Gold Region*) 70; Wheat (*Transmississippi*) 591

Attached to the inside front cover is: [Caption title] Particulars / of / Routes, Distances,

Fares, &c., / To Accompany / Colton's Map of California / and the Gold Region. / Collected from Official Documents. / [wavy rule] / ... [1]–11, [12 blank]. 13.1 x 8.2 cm.

The map was also used in *California and its Gold Regions with a Geographical and Topographical View of the Country* ... By Fayette Robinson, New York, 1849.

836 COLTON, JOSEPH H.

[Map] NEBRASKA AND KANSAS. / [at foot:] PUB-LISHED BY J. H. COLTON & CO. N.º 172 WILLIAM S.ᵀ NEW YORK, 1857. / *Inset:* Territory / acquired from / Mexico / by the Gadsden Treaty /. 11.4 x 28.9 cm. Scale: 65 miles to one inch. *Inset:* [County map of Nebraska, Kansas, and parts of Iowa and Missouri]. 32.9 x 18.6 cm. No scale given.

Map, 69.7 x 50 cm. Scale: about 60 miles to one inch. Folded into brown cloth covers, 14.6 x 8.9 cm., with title in gilt stamped on front cover and in blind on back cover, advertisements inside front cover.

Ref.: Phillips (*Maps*) p. 459

837 COLTON, JOSEPH H.

[Map] NORTH AMERICA. / [at foot:] PUBLISHED BY J. H. COLTON & CO. N.º 172 WILLIAM S.ᵀ NEW YORK, 1857. / [at lower left:] ENTERED ACCORD-ING TO ACT OF CONGRESS, IN THE YEAR 1855, BY J. H. COLTON, IN THE CLERKS OFFICE OF THE DIS-TRICT COURT OF THE SOUTHERN DISTRICT OF NEW YORK. / *Inset:* Hawaiian Group / or / Sandwich Islands. / 11.1 x 7.2 cm. Scale: 60 miles to one inch. *Insets:* Six vignettes, *viz.:* Falls of St. Anthony, Vancouver(?), Pyramid Lake, Cen-tral America, Arctic View, and Niagara Falls. Also two tables.

Map, 65.7 x 61.6 cm. Scale: about 225 miles to one inch. Folded into red cloth, 14.6 x 9 cm., with title in gilt stamped on front cover, pub-lisher's advertisements inside front cover.

Ref.:

838 COLTON, JOSEPH H.

THE STATE OF INDIANA DELINEATED: GEOGRAPHI-CAL, HISTORICAL, STATISTICAL & COMMERCIAL, AND A BRIEF VIEW OF THE INTERNAL IMPROVE-MENTS ... NEW-YORK: PUBLISHED BY J. H. COL-TON, 1838.

[1]–92, [93 advertisements, 94 blank]. 15 x 9.5 cm. Folding map: Colton's / New Map of / In-diana, Reduced from his Large Map / Exhibiting the / Boundaries of Counties, Township Sur-veys, / Location of Cities, Towns, Villages, Post Offices, / Canals, Rail Roads & Other / Internal Improvements. / [decorative line] / New-York, /

Published by J. H. Colton. / 1838. / [below neat line:] Entered according to Act of Congress in the year 1838, by J. H. Colton, in the Clerk's Office of the District Court of the Southern Dis-trict of New York. [space] Engraved by S. Stiles, Sherman & Smith. / 38.2 x 30 cm. Scale: 20 miles to one inch. Blue boards, brown roan black, with printed white paper label on front cover, 3.8 x 6.9 cm. In a cloth case with morocco back.

Prov.: C. G. Littell bookplate in folding case.
Ref.: Bradford 1005; Howes C622; Phillips (*Maps*) p. 334

839 COLTON, WALTER

THREE YEARS IN CALIFORNIA ... NEW YORK: A. S. BARNES & CO., 1850.

[1]–456. 18.5 x 12.3 cm. Six portraits listed, map, facsimile and plates unlisted. Black cloth, gilt vignette on front cover, blind embossed borders, title in gilt on backstrip, advertisements on end-sheets.

Ref.: Blumann & Thomas 2089; Cowan p. 137; Field 346; Howes C625; Jones 1234; Matthews p. 301; Sabin 14800

In later states of the work, the plates were omitted.

840 COLUMBUS (Ohio). COMMITTEE OF CITIZENS

REPORT ON THE TERRITORY OF OREGON, BY A COM-MITTEE APPOINTED AT A MEETING OF THE CITIZENS OF COLUMBUS, TO COLLECT INFORMATION IN RELA-TION THERETO. COLUMBUS, O.: PRINTED AT THE OFFICE OF THE OHIO STATESMAN, 1843.

[1]–21, [22 blank]. 21.7 x 14.5 cm. Map: Map / of the / Territory / of / Oregon /. [lower right:] Eng.ᵈ by F. H. Wheeler. / 13.2 x 12.1 cm. No scale given. White on black. Removed from bound volume, unbound. In a blue half morocco case.

Prov.: With C. G. Littell bookplate.
Ref.: Smith 1921

Schemes to promote emigration to Oregon flowered in many places, including Columbus, Ohio. This one contains Samuel Medary's re-port.

841 COLVILLE, SAMUEL

THE SACRAMENTO DIRECTORY, FOR THE YEAR 1853–54, EMBRACING A GENERAL DIRECTORY OF CITIZENS ... WITH A HISTORY OF SACRAMENTO, WRITTEN BY DR. JOHN F. MORSE ... SACRAMENTO: PRINTED AT THE UNION OFFICE, 1853.

[i–iv], [1]–40, [1–2], [1]–110, 1–14. 22.9 x 14.6 cm. Pale green printed boards, black roan backstrip, advertisements on front and back and inner covers.

Ref.: AII (*California*) 264; Blumann & Thomas 2481; Cowan p. 171; Greenwood 403; Howes C633

842 COLVILLE, SAMUEL

SAMUEL COLVILLE'S CITY DIRECTORY, OF SACRAMENTO, FOR THE YEAR 1854-5 . . . SAN FRANCISCO: MONSON & VALENTINE, 1854.

[1]-16, [1-4 on yellow paper], [17]-116, [1-64 advertisements on colored paper]. 22.2 x 14.2 cm. Green printed boards, black leather backstrip, advertisements on back and front and inner covers.

Ref.: AII (*California*) 354; Blumann & Thomas 2481; Cowan p. 171; Greenwood 495; Howes C633

843 COLVILLE, SAMUEL

COLVILLE'S SACRAMENTO DIRECTORY VOLUME VI. FOR THE YEAR COMMENCING MAY, 1856. . . . SAN FRANCISCO: PRINTED BY MONSON, VALENTINE & CO., 1856.

[i]-xxxix, [xl advertisement], [1]-140, [1-8 advertisements]. 22.5 x 14.5 cm. Gray printed boards, black roan backstrip, advertisements on both covers and page of advertisement mounted on inner covers.

Ref.: Blumann & Thomas 2481; Greenwood 730

844 COLVOCORESSES, GEORGE M.

FOUR YEARS IN A GOVERNMENT EXPLORING EXPEDITION; TO THE ISLAND OF MADEIRA—CAPE VERD ISLANDS—BRAZIL—COAST OF PATAGONIA—PERU . . . SANDWICH ISLANDS—NORTHWEST COAST OF AMERICA—OREGON—CALIFORNIA—EAST INDIES . . . NEW YORK: CORNISH, LAMPORT & CO., 1852.

[1]-371, [372 blank], [373-75 advertisements, 376 blank]. 18.5 x 12.2 cm. Illustrations unlisted. Blue cloth.

Ref.: Cowan p. 138; Howes C635; Rader 878

The author accompanied the Wilkes Expedition. His journal is an important source for the overland journey from California to Oregon.

845 COMPARATIVE, CHRONOLOGICAL STATEMENT . . .

[Caption title] COMPARATIVE CHRONOLOGICAL STATEMENT OF THE EVENTS CONNECTED WITH THE RIGHTS OF GREAT BRITAIN AND THE CLAIMS OF THE UNITED STATES TO THE OREGON TERRITORY . . .

[1]-15, [16 colophon]. 17.8 x 11.9 cm. Sewn, unbound.

Prov.: Signature on page [1]: J. E. Swinburne /.

Ref.: Smith 1941

The London imprint of the publisher, James Wyld, appears on page [16]. The pamphlet was probably printed in 1845.

846 CONARD, HOWARD L.

"UNCLE DICK" WOOTTON, THE PIONEER FRONTIERSMAN OF THE ROCKY MOUNTAIN REGION . . . CHICAGO: W. E. DIBBLE & CO., 1890.

[I]-VIII, [9]-472, 473-[474] advertisements. Pages [I-II] blank. 22.8 x 15 cm. 31 illustrations listed. Brown pictorial cloth.

Prov.: Inscribed on recto of frontispiece: Compliments of the Author / Howard L Conard /.

Ref.: Cuthbertson & Ewers p. 135; Dobie p. 72; Howes C659; Jones 1659; Rader 881; Saunders 2828

In his ability to recreate in ample detail the scenes of his past life consists the great charm, as well as the chief historical value of the book. —Quaife

847 CONARD, HOWARD L.

ANOTHER COPY. Original full brown morocco, blind borders on sides, gilt title on backstrip, gilt edges.

Prov.: Bookplate of John Thomas Lee.

Apparently a binding issued by the publisher.

848 CONGREGATIONAL CHURCHES IN ILLINOIS. GENERAL ASSOCIATION

CONSTITUTION, ARTICLES OF FAITH, STANDING RULES, AND GENERAL PRINCIPLES OF CHURCH POLITY OF THE GENERAL CONGREGATIONAL ASSOCIATION OF ILLINOIS. GALESBURG, ILL.: "INTELLIGENCER" PRINT, 1848.

[1]-12. 16.7 x 10.8 cm. Yellow printed wrappers with title on front wrapper.

Ref.: Byrd 1315

849 CONGREGATIONAL CHURCHES IN IOWA. GENERAL ASSOCIATION

[Caption title] MINUTES OF THE GENERAL ASSOCIATION OF IOWA, AT THEIR SESSION IN DAVENPORT, JUNE, 1854 . . .

[1]-12. 22.7 x 14 cm. Yellow printed wrappers with title on front wrapper.

Ref.: AII (*Iowa*) 64

Although Moffit had stated under his note for the Minutes of 1849 that "neither place nor date of publication could be ascertained," the compilers of AII (*Iowa*) decided to list it as an Iowa imprint.

850 CONNELLEY, WILLIAM E.

QUANTRILL AND THE BORDER WARS . . . CEDAR RAPIDS, IOWA: THE TORCH PRESS, 1910.*

[1]–542. 24.1 x 15.3 cm. 72 illustrations and seven maps listed. Red buckram, fore and lower edges uncut, unopened.

Ref.: Adams 237; Howes C689; Rader 894

851 CONNELLEY, WILLIAM E.

WAR WITH MEXICO, 1846–1847. DONIPHAN'S EXPEDITION AND THE CONQUEST OF NEW MEXICO AND CALIFORNIA . . . PORTRAITS, MAPS, AND ILLUSTRATIONS . . . TOPEKA: PUBLISHED BY THE AUTHOR, 1907.*

[i]–[xvi, xvi blank], [1]–670. 22.2 x 15 cm. 66 illustrations and maps listed. Gray pictorial cloth.

Ref.: Cowan p. 139; Howes C688; Munk (Alliot) p. 54; Saunders 2829

Includes a reprint of Hughes' work on the Doniphan Expedition, with notes.

852 CONNELLEY, WILLIAM E.

WILD BILL AND HIS ERA: THE LIFE & ADVENTURES OF JAMES BUTLER HICKOK . . . NEW YORK: THE PRESS OF THE PIONEERS, 1933.

[1–2], [i]–[xiv, xiv blank], 1–229, [230 blank]. 23.4 x 15.8 cm. 12 illustrations listed. Red buckram.

Ref.: Adams 238; Dobie pp. 141–42; Howes C690; Rader 896

Limited to 200 copies.

853 CONNOLLY, A. P.

A THRILLING NARRATIVE OF THE MINNESOTA MASSACRE AND THE SIOUX WAR OF 1862–63 . . . CHICAGO: A. P. CONNOLLY.

[1]–273, [274 blank]. 19.2 x 13.2 cm. Illustrations unlisted. Red cloth.

Ref.:

Copyrighted 1896. Laid in is a colored portrait of a Civil War officer, published by the author and signed by him on the verso.

854 CONOVER, GEORGE W.

SIXTY YEARS IN SOUTHWEST OKLAHOMA . . . ANDARKO, OKLAHOMA: N. T. PLUMMER, BOOK AND JOB PRINTER, 1927.*

[1–6], [i]–[iv, iv blank], [1]–130. 19.2 x 13 cm. 23 illustrations, unlisted. Blue cloth.

Ref.: Adams (*Ramp. Herd*) 565; Rader 899

855 CONQUEST OF SANTA FE, THE

THE CONQUEST OF SANTA FE AND SUBJUGATION OF NEW MEXICO, BY THE MILITARY FORCES OF THE UNITED STATES . . . AND A HISTORY OF COLONEL DONIPHAN'S CAMPAIGN IN CHIHUAHUA . . . PHILADELPHIA: H. PACKER & CO., 1847.

[1]–48. 23.5 x 14.9 cm. Brown printed wrappers with title on front wrapper. In a red cloth folder.

Ref.: Howes S102; Rader 900; Sabin 15888; Wagner-Camp 129

According to Wagner-Camp this is a scissors and paste job, but some interesting newspaper accounts are included.

856 CONVENTION OF DELEGATES FOR THE PROMOTION OF INTERNAL IMPROVEMENTS WITHIN . . . MISSOURI

PROCEEDINGS OF A CONVENTION OF DELEGATES, FOR THE PROMOTION OF INTERNAL IMPROVEMENTS WITHIN THE STATE OF MISSOURI, HELD AT THE CITY OF ST. LOUIS, ON THE TWENTIETH DAY OF APRIL, 1836. ST. LOUIS: PRINTED BY CHARLES KEEMLE, 1836.

[1]–30, [31–2 blank]. 22.7 x 14.3 cm. Unbound, removed from bound volume.

Ref.: AII (*Missouri*) 177; Howes M669

The original owner, James S. Rollins, was a delegate from Boone County. The printer was secretary to the Convention. The convention was the first movement toward constructing a Missouri railroad.

857 CONVENTION HELD AT CARTHAGE, HANCOCK COUNTY, ILLINOIS

[Caption title] THE PROCEEDINGS OF A CONVENTION, HELD AT CARTHAGE, IN HANCOCK COUNTY, ILL., ON TUESDAY AND WEDNESDAY, OCTOBER 1ST AND 2D, 1845. PUBLISHED BY ORDER OF THE CONVENTION, UNDER THE SUPERINTENDANCE OF THE MILITARY COMMITTEE OF QUINCY, ILL. . . .

[1]–9, [10 blank]. 20.8 x 13.5 cm. Rebound in gray boards, leather label on backstrip.

Prov.: Perforated stamp of Chicago Historical Society through first two leaves, release of Society mounted on blank leaf following text.

Ref.: Byrd 942

The imprint appears at the foot of the second column on page 9: [rule] / Printed at the Quincy Whig Book and Job Office. /

The Convention was called in protest against the Mormons. Extra-legal activities were planned to control Mormon depredators.

858 CONVENTION TO CONSIDER THE OPENING OF THE INDIAN TERRITORY

PROCEEDINGS OF THE CONVENTION TO CONSIDER THE OPENING OF THE INDIAN TERRITORY, HELD AT KANSAS CITY, MO. FEBRUARY, 1888. KANSAS CITY, MO.: PRESS OF RAMSAY, MILLETT & HUDSON, 1888.

[1]–80. 22.5 x 14.5 cm. Tan printed wrappers with title on front wrapper.

Ref.: Howes I25; Rader 904

859 CONYERS, JOSIAH B.

A BRIEF HISTORY OF THE LEADING CAUSES OF THE HANCOCK MOB, IN THE YEAR 1846 . . . SAINT LOUIS: PRINTED FOR THE AUTHOR BY CATHCART & PRESCOTT, 1846.

[1]–[84]. 18.8 x 11.8 cm. Printed yellow wrappers with title on front wrapper, advertisement on verso of back wrapper. Small part of pages 81–2 supplied.

Ref.: AII (*Missouri*) 476; Howes C725; Sabin 16227

860 COOK, DARIUS B.

SIX MONTHS AMONG INDIANS, WOLVES AND OTHER WILD ANIMALS, IN THE FORESTS OF ALLEGAN COUNTY, MICH., IN THE WINTER OF 1839 AND 1840 . . . NILES, MICHIGAN: PRINTED AND PUBLISHED BY THE AUTHOR, 1889.

[i–iv], [1]–101, [102 blank]. 19.5 x 13.5 cm. Four plates including one printed in red and nineteen text illustrations. Pink printed wrappers, with title on front wrapper.

Ref.: Greenly (*Michigan*) 121; Howes C727

A rough job, but containing some narratives unrecorded elsewhere—and possibly imaginary. The stories are said (by the author) to have been recorded in his diaries. The ICN (Ayer) copy, which is rebound, includes a front wrapper of a much brighter color. The inserted plate opposite page 48 is printed in sepia instead of red.

861 COOK, DAVID J.

HANDS UP; OR, TWENTY YEARS OF DETECTIVE LIFE IN THE MOUNTAINS AND ON THE PLAINS . . . DENVER: REPUBLICAN PUBLISHING COMPANY, 1882.

[1]–285, [286 blank]. 22.9 x 15.9 cm. Portrait and 31 plates, the latter signed by A. P. Proctor, Engraver, Denver. Printed pictorial wrappers with title on front wrapper. In a red cloth case.

Ref.: Adams 241; Howes C728; Rader 905 see; Wilcox p. 32

So far, this is the only copy in original wrappers located. The volume is copyrighted by D. J. Cook. Cook was superintendent of the Rocky Mountain Detective Association.

Laid in is a typewritten note by Edward Eberstadt: This book was written by Thos. F. Dawson, Director of the Colorado Historical Society. Dawson was killed in the automobile accident which occurred in Denver during Harding's visit.

Mr. Dawson told me also, that the reason both this work and his "Ute Massacre" were so rare, was because the copies were used to make paper wadding for cartridges during the Indian Campaign.

862 COOK, DAVID J.

HANDS UP; OR, THIRTY-FIVE YEARS OF DETECTIVE LIFE IN THE MOUNTAINS AND ON THE PLAINS . . . DENVER: THE W. F. ROBINSON PRINTING CO., 1897.

[i–ii], [1]–442. 22.5 x 15 cm. 40 illustrations listed. Dark blue cloth. Front hinge repaired, portion supplied.

Prov.: Signature in pencil on front fly-leaf: T. J. Carr /. Also some annotations by Carr in text.

Ref.: Adams 241; Howes C728; Rader 905; Wilcox p. 32

According to the title-page, the work was compiled by John W. Cook. See preceding note.

Tipped to the inner front cover and both sides of the front fly-leaf are clipped letterheads in which Thomas Jefferson Carr's name appears. Also pasted in are three newspaper obituaries and editorials. Tipped to the verso of the illustration opposite page 354 is an original photograph of Buffalo Bill, signed, and with an undeciphered line of manuscript along the top edge.

Thomas J. Carr was associated with the Rocky Mountain Detective Association for many years. At various times, he was also chief of police at Cheyenne, sheriff of Laramie County, and United States Marshall for Wyoming. He is often mentioned in the book by name.

Editions: Denver, 1882.

863 COOK, JAMES H.

FIFTY YEARS ON THE OLD FRONTIER AS COWBOY, HUNTER, GUIDE, SCOUT, AND RANCHMAN . . . NEW HAVEN: YALE UNIVERSITY PRESS, MDCCCCXXIII.*

[i]–[xx, xx blank], [1]–291, [292 colophon]. 23.5 x 15.2 cm. 46 illustrations listed. Blue cloth.

Ref.: Adams 242; Adams (*Ramp. Herd*) 569; Dobie p. 100; Malone p. 3; Rader 907; Saunders 2833; Smith 2008

864 COOK, JOHN R.

THE BORDER AND THE BUFFALO: AN UNTOLD STORY OF THE SOUTHWEST PLAINS . . . TOPEKA, KANSAS: CRANE & COMPANY, 1907.

[i]–xii, 1–[352]. (Page [i] blank, page [ii] frontispiece.) 22.8 x 15.1 cm. 18 illustrations listed. Yellow pictorial cloth.

Ref.: Adams 245; Dobie p. 159; Howes C730; Rader 909; Saunders 2836

Border warfare between Missouri and Kansas and the slaughter of the buffalo are the principal subjects.

Laid in is a four-page leaflet: [caption title]

Address. To the Hunters After the Ninety Days' Scout . . . This twenty-seven stanza "poem" may have been written by Cook.

865 COOK, JOSEPH W.

DIARY AND LETTERS . . . ARRANGED BY THE RT. REV. N. S. THOMAS . . . LARAMIE, WYOMING: THE LARAMIE REPUBLICAN COMPANY, 1919.

[1]–137, [138 blank]. 19.1 x 12.9 cm. Portrait. Gray printed wrappers. In a gray cloth case.

Ref.: Howes C730a

866 COOK COUNTY, ILLINOIS. County Commissioners' Court

[Broadside] NOTICE IS HEREBY GIVEN, THAT ON MON-DAY . . . NEXT, AT THE HOUSE OF   IN PRECINCT, IN THE COUNTY OF COOK, AN ELECTION WILL BE HELD . . . DATED AT CHICAGO, IN SAID COUNTY OF COOK . . . IN THE YEAR OF OUR LORD ONE THOUSAND EIGHT HUNDRED AND THIRTY- . . . CLERK OF THE COUNTY COMMISSIONERS' COURT . . .

Broadside, 31.4 x 20.1 cm. Text, 16.7 x 17.5 cm.

Ref.: Byrd 268a

Dated partly in manuscript: April 16, 1836.

The officers to be elected were a justice of the peace and two constables.

Accompanied by a manuscript: Poll Book of an Election held in Thornton . . . /

867 COOK & SARGENT, DAVENPORT, IOWA

PRAIRIE VERSUS BUSH. IOWA AS AN EMIGRATION FIELD. CHEAP FARMING LANDS, ON LINES OF RAIL-ROAD. DAVENPORT, IOWA: COOK & SARGENT, 1859.

[1]–24. 21.2 x 13.7 cm. Map: Railway / Guide / to / Iowa Lands / For Sale by / Cook & Sar-gent. / Davenport Iowa. / J. H. Bufford's Lith. / [below border:] For Sale at Iowa Land Office, (Cook & Sargent's Agency) Toronto Canada West. / Yellow printed wrappers with title on front wrapper. In a blue cloth case.

Ref.: Howes C732

Pages 8–12 carry "Iowa through Canadian Spectacle. Memoranda of a trip to Iowa, June, 1859," by Mr. Charles Clarke, Reeve of Elora, C.W.

Although a double imprint appears on both title-page and front wrapper, the pamphlet was probably printed at Toronto rather than Daven-port, Iowa.

868 COOKE, LUCY R.

CROSSING THE PLAINS IN 1852. NARRATIVE OF A TRIP FROM IOWA TO "THE LAND OF GOLD," AS TOLD IN LETTERS WRITTEN DURING THE JOURNEY . . . MODESTO, CALIFORNIA: 1923.

[1]–94, [95–6 blank]. 19.1 x 13.4 cm. Two por-traits. Maroon printed wrappers with title on front wrapper in gilt.

Ref.: Howes C737

Composed almost entirely of letters written by Mrs. Cooke to her sister in 1852 and 1853, the narrative is a vivid account of an overland trip, events along the way, her nine-months stay in Salt Lake City, and an amusing proposal made by a Mormon Elder.—EDG

869 COOKE, PHILIP ST. GEORGE

THE CONQUEST OF NEW MEXICO AND CALIFORNIA; AN HISTORICAL AND PERSONAL NARRATIVE . . . NEW YORK: G. P. PUTNAM'S SONS, 1878.

[i]–[vi, vi blank], 1–307, [308 blank]. 18.5 x 12.6 cm. Map: Sketch / of part of the march & wagon road of Lt. Colonel Cooke, from Santa Fe to the Pacific Ocean 1846–7 / (From a point on Grande River, (near which the road should cross,) to the Pimo Villages, down the Gila River.) / [lower left:] Engraved for Cooke's "Conquest of Mexico." / [lower right:] G. P. Putnam's Sons, New York. / 21.8 x 42.8 cm. No scale given. Green cloth, black stamped bands on front cover, same in blind on back cover, title in gilt on backstrip.

Ref.: Bradford 1055; Cowan p. 142; Ed-wards pp. 38–9; Howes C738; Munk (Alliot) p. 54; Rader 912; Saunders 2837; Wheat (*Trans-mississippi*) 505 see

Cooke assumed command of the Mormon Battalion at Santa Fé and marched it to Califor-nia. His opinion of the Battalion was poor at first, but in nine months he worked it into a satisfactory force of which he was proud. The present work is really a sequel to his *Scenes and Adventures . . .* 1857; it is based in part on his *Journal . . .* [1849] in which a version of the map had also previously appeared.

870 COOKE, PHILIP ST. GEORGE

[Caption title] . . . A COPY OF THE OFFICIAL JOUR-NAL OF LIEUTENANT COLONEL PHILIP ST. GEORGE COOKE, FROM SANTA FE TO SAN DIEGO, &C. . . .

[1]–85, [86–8 blank]. 24.8 x 15.1 cm. Rebound in new red cloth, uncut.

Ref.: Cowan p. 142; Howes C739; Matthews p. 293; Munk (Alliot) p. 54; Wagner-Camp 165

30th Congress, Special Session, Senate, Executive Document No. 2, Serial 547. [Wash-ington, 1849.]

871 COOKE, PHILIP ST. GEORGE

SCENES AND ADVENTURES IN THE ARMY: OR RO-MANCE OF MILITARY LIFE . . . PHILADELPHIA: LINDSAY & BLAKISTON, 1857.

[i]–xii, [13]–432. 18.6 x 12.4 cm. Red cloth, blind embossed borders with monogram in centres on sides, title in gilt on backstrip.

Ref.: Clark III 24; Field 359; Howes C740; Rader 914; Sabin 16339; Wagner-Camp 288

As a personal narrative of adventures with the 2nd Dragoons, *Scenes and Adventures in the Army* is an outstanding account of life in the far west. Much of the time, Cooke was guiding and protecting travelers on the Santa Fé trail, from 1829 to 1845.

872 COOKE, PHILIP ST. GEORGE

THE SAME.

18.4 x 12 cm. Full green morocco, blind panels on sides, title on backstrip in gilt, gilt edges.

Prov.: Inscribed on front endleaf: Mʳˢ Helen N. Hammond / from her friend / P. Sᵗ George C. /

One of a few copies bound for presentation. Laid in is a carte-de-visite photograph of the author, signed.

873 COOKE, PHILIP ST. GEORGE

THE SAME. Philadelphia: Lindsay & Blakiston, 1859.

[i]–xii, [13]–432. Gray cloth, blind embossed borders on sides, title in gilt on backstrip.

Second Edition. The new title-page raises Cooke's rank from Lieutenant Colonel to Colonel.

874 COOKE & CO., D. B., Chicago

[Map] D. B. COOKE & CO'S / RAILWAY / GUIDE / FOR / ILLINOIS / SHEWING ALL THE / STATIONS / WITH THEIR RESPECTIVE DISTANCES / CONNECTING WITH / CHICAGO [space] ENTERED ACCORDING TO ACT OF CONGRESS IN THE YEAR 1854 / PUB. BY D. B. COOKE & Cᵒ, CHICAGO / JAN: '55. / *Inset:* Rail-Road / connections. / 13.3 x 14.5 cm. No scale given.

Map, 68.5 x 52 cm. No scale given. Folded into blue cloth covers, 13.5 x 9 cm., with title stamped in gilt on front cover: D. B. Cooke & Co's / Railway Map / [vignette of a train] / Illinois. /, advertisements inside front cover.

Ref.:

An index of railroads appears in the left margin and an index of towns in the right.

875 [COOLEY, DEWITT C.]

TRI-ENNIAL MESSAGE OF THE GOVERNOR OF THE SOVEREIGNS, OF MINNESOTA. DELIVERED TO THEIR REPRESENTATIVES ASSEMBLED IN THE THIRD HOUSE, FEBRUARY 8TH, 1860. 100,000 COPIES NOT ORDERED PRINTED IN ALL THE LANGUAGES. SAINT PAUL: PRINTED AT THE EXPENSE OF THE SOVEREIGNS, 1860.

[1]–12. 21.8 x 14.1 cm. Sewn, unbound.

Ref.: AII (*Minnesota*) 293

A copy in the Minnesota Historical Society is signed by Cooley. The pamphlet contains a satire on Governor Ramsey's annual message to the Legislature.

876 COOLIDGE, LOUIS A.

KLONDIKE AND THE YUKON COUNTRY A DESCRIPTION OF OUR ALASKAN LAND OF GOLD FROM THE LATEST OFFICIAL AND SCIENTIFIC SOURCES AND PERSONAL OBSERVATION . . . PHILADELPHIA: HENRY ALTEMUS, 1897.

[1]–213, [214 blank], [1–15 advertisements, 16 blank]. 17.2 x 11.6 cm. 18 plates and a folding map, unlisted. Yellow printed wrappers. In a brown cloth case.

Ref.: Howes C743; Smith 2014; Wickersham 3907

877 COPLEY, JOHN M.

A SKETCH OF THE BATTLE OF FRANKLIN, TENN.; WITH REMINISCENCES OF CAMP DOUGLAS . . . AUSTIN, TEXAS: EUGENE VON BOECKMANN, 1893.

[1]–206. 17 x 12.4 cm. Four illustrations, unlisted. Red cloth, gilt vignette on front cover, title in black on backstrip.

Ref.: Coulter 93; Howes C765; Nicholson 167

878 CORNER, WILLIAM, *Editor*

SAN ANTONIO DE BEXAR: A GUIDE AND HISTORY . . . ILLUSTRATED. SAN ANTONIO: BAINBRIDGE & CORNER, CHRISTMAS, 1890.

[i]–[viii, viii blank], [1]–166, [1–27 advertisements, 28 blank]. 25.4 x 16.8 cm. 17 illustrations listed and numerous unlisted illustrations. Red cloth, gilt title on front cover and backstrip.

Ref.: Bradford 1076; Howes C778; Raines p. 55

Includes an historical sketch written in 1872 by Sidney Lanier, extracts from Mrs. M. A. Maverick's memoirs, and interviews with old settlers.

879 CORNEY, PETER

VOYAGES IN THE NORTHERN PACIFIC. NARRATIVE OF SEVERAL TRADING VOYAGES FROM 1813 TO 1818, BETWEEN THE NORTHWEST COAST OF AMERICA, THE HAWAIIAN ISLANDS AND CHINA, WITH A DESCRIPTION OF THE RUSSIAN ESTABLISHMENTS ON THE NORTHWEST COAST . . . HONOLULU, H.I.: THOS. G. THRUM, PUBLISHER, 1896.*

[i]–[xii, xii blank], [1]–138, [i]–v Index, [vi advertisement]. 19.7 x 12 cm. Rebound in blue half morocco, gilt top, uncut.

Ref.: Cowan p. 143; Howes C779

First separate printing of the Corney narrative. The sections relating to California, Oregon, and American-Russian relations are quite interesting.

880 CORNWALL, BRUCE

LIFE SKETCH OF PIERRE BARLOW CORNWALL . . . SAN FRANCISCO: A. M. ROBERTSON, 1906.*

[i–x, x blank], 1–87, [88 blank]. 21.5 x 14 cm. Six portraits listed and one unlisted. Black half leather, gilt top, uncut.

Prov.: The Phillips bookplate.

Ref.: Cowan p. 143; Howes C780

Included is a narrative of an overland journey in 1848 to California via Carson Pass. On the verso of the title-leaf: Printed for Private Distribution. /

881 CORNWALLIS, KINAHAN

THE NEW EL DORADO; OR, BRITISH COLUMBIA . . . LONDON: THOMAS CAUTLEY NEWBY, 1858.

[i]–xxviii, [1]–405, [406–08 advertisements]. 19.3 x 12.1 cm. Frontispiece and folding map: Map of / British Columbia / and / Vancouver Island / Denoting the Gold and Coal Districts. / Scale of English Miles / [diagrammatic scale; about 85 English miles to one inch] / [at lower right:] Stannard & Dixon, Lith. Poland Str. / 17.5 x 24.3 cm. Red cloth, uncut.

Ref.: Sabin 16819; Smith 2043; Staton & Tremaine 3802

Contains a personal narrative of the Fraser River gold rush.

882 CORONELLI, MARCO VINCENZO

[Map] LE NOUVEAU / MEXIQUE / APPELE AUSSI / NOUVELLE GRENADE ET / MARATA, / AVEC PARTIE DE CALIFORNIE, / SELON LES MEMOIRES LES PLUS NOUVEAUX. / PAR LE PERE CORONELLI COSMOGRAPHE DE LA SS^ME. REPUBLIQUE DE VENISE / CORRIGEE ET AUGMENTEE PAR LE S^R TILLEMON / A PARIS. / CHEZ J. B. NOLIN SUR LE QUAY DE L'HORLOGE, A L'ENSEIGNE DE LA / PLACE DES VICTOIRES VERS LE PONT-NEUF / AVEC PRIVILEGE DU ROY. / 168[!] / *

Map, 45.4 x 59.5 cm. (plate mark). Scale: about 25 French leagues to one inch.

Ref.: Wheat (*Transmississippi*) 66

Father Coronelli (1650–1718) was born in Venice. He became General of the Franciscan Order and one of the most eminent geographers of his time, producing more than 400 maps and 50 globes. This particular map was probably published approximately 1685.—Wheat

883 CORTAMBERT, LOUIS

VOYAGE AU PAYS DES OSAGES. UN TOUR EN SICILE . . . PARIS: CHEZ ARTHUS-BERTRAND, M DCCC XXXVII.

[1]–94. 21.8 x 13.9 cm. Yellow printed wrappers with title on front wrapper, small vignette and wide border on back wrapper, title reading up on backstrip, uncut, unopened. In a green buckram case.

Ref.: Clark III 26; Howes C792; Rader 932; Sabin 16928; Wagner-Camp 65

A remarkably fine copy. Sabin calls for 96 pages, but this is apparently an error.

884 COSTANSO, MIGUEL

DIARIO HISTORICO DE LOS VIAGES DE MAR, Y TIERRA HECHOS AL NORTE DE LA CALIFORNIA . . . DE ORDEN DEL EXCMO. SR. VIRREY, EN LA IMPRENTA DEL SUPERIOR GOBIERNA.*

A–O², P¹. [i–ii], [1]–56. 28.9 x 19.1 cm. Brown levant morocco, blind tooled borders and panels on sides, title in gilt on backstrip, gilt edges, by Rivière. Part of title-leaf supplied in facsimile.

Ref.: Bradford 1078; Cowan p. 144; Hanna-Powell pp. 15, 16, 20, 24; Howes C795; Jones 535; Medina (*Mexico*) 5363; Sabin 17019; Streeter (*Americana—Beginnings*) 74; Wagner (*Cart. of NW Coast*) p. 164; Wagner (*SS*) 149; Zamorano Eighty 22

Signed and dated at the end: Mexico, y Octubre 24, de 1770. / D. Miguel Costansó. / Printed at Mexico City, 1770.

This account of the first exploration of California is the first book relating exclusively to that state . . . —Streeter (*Americana—Beginnings*)

The present copy has been exhibited at the Pierpont Morgan Library.

885 COUES, ELLIOTT

IN MEMORIAM. SERGEANT CHARLES FLOYD. REPORT . . . BY ELLIOTT COUES . . . SIOUX CITY: PRESS OF PERKINS BROS. COMPANY, 1897.*

[1]–[4], 1–58, [59–60 blank]. 21.8 x 14.9 cm. Facsimile and plan. Gray printed wrappers.

Prov.: Inscribed on title-page: Col. R. T. Durrett, / compliments of / Elliott Coues. /

Ref.:

886 COULTER, JOHN

ADVENTURES ON THE WESTERN COAST OF SOUTH AMERICA, AND THE INTERIOR OF CALIFORNIA . . . LONDON: LONGMAN, BROWN, GREEN, AND LONGMANS, 1847.

[i]–xiv, [1]–288, [1]–32 advertisements dated October, 1847. (Pages [i–ii] blank.) [i]–xii, [1]–278, [1]–2 advertisements. 19.7 x 12 cm. Two volumes, blue cloth, blind embossed borders on sides, title stamped in gilt on backstrips, uncut.

Ref.: Cowan p. 145; Howes C802; Sabin 17143

This is a continuation of the author's *Adventures in the Pacific . . . 1845.*

887 COUNCIL BLUFFS, IOWA

[Broadsheet] COUNCIL BLUFFS, IOWA. THIS IS THE SEAT OF JUSTICE OF POTTAWATTAMIE COUNTY. IT IS SITUATED ON THE EAST BANK OF THE MISSOURI RIVER, AND HAS A POPULATION OF 12,000. IT IS THE WESTERN TERMINUS OF THE FOLLOWING RAILROADS: . . .

Broadsheet, 25.1 x 19.8 cm. Unbound.

Ref.:

At the foot of page [2], left: Printed by Bluff City Job Office, Council Bluffs. / The broadsheet is signed on page [2], lower right: A. V. Larimer, Attorney, / Jno. H. Keatley, Attorney, / W. H. M. Pusey, Banker. /

888 [COURTNEY, T. E.]

POMAREDE'S ORIGINAL PANORAMA OF THE MISSISSIPPI RIVER.

[1]–84, [85–6 blank]. 20.5 x 13.6 cm. Pictorial title-page and eight plates. Yellow printed wrappers with title on front wrapper, advertisement on recto of back wrapper, table of distances on verso of back wrapper. Removed from bound volume, roughly restitched.

Ref.: AII (*Missouri*) 640; Howes C807

Title on front wrapper dated: St. Louis, 1850.

The AII (*Missouri*) and Howes descriptions do not mention a pictorial title-page. Howes described two editions, New York and St. Louis, 1849 and 1850, respectively, but he does not describe an undated edition. "I examined the OCHP copy in May, 1946, and find it exactly the same as the above copy."—EDG

Editions: New York, 1849.

889 COUTANT, CHARLES G.

THE HISTORY OF WYOMING FROM THE EARLIEST KNOWN DISCOVERIES . . . LARAMIE, WYOMING: CHAPLIN, SPAFFORD & MATHISON, 1899.

[i]–xxiv, [17]–712. 22.6 x 15 cm. 78 illustrations listed. Brown half morocco, mottled green edges.

Ref.: Howes C810; Jones 1683; Malone p. 3

Only the first volume was published.

890 COUTANT, CHARLES G.

INDEX TO THE HISTORY OF WYOMING . . . PREPARED BY THE HISTORICAL RECORDS SURVEY . . . CHEYENNE, WYOMING: WYOMING STATE LIBRARY, 1941.

[1]–45 leaves (rectos only used). 21.5 x 14 cm. Green wrappers, black cloth backstrip, stapled.

Ref.: Howes C810

Typed copy, mimeographed.

891 [COX, JAMES, *Editor*]

HISTORICAL AND BIOGRAPHICAL RECORD OF THE CATTLE INDUSTRY AND THE CATTLEMEN OF TEXAS AND ADJACENT TERRITORY. SAINT LOUIS: PUBLISHED BY WOODWARD & TIERNAN PRINTING CO., 1895.

[1]–743, [744 blank]. 30.7 x 23.1 cm. 247 illustrations listed. Black leather, blind and gilt stamped sides, title on front cover and backstrip, marbled edges.

Ref.: Adams (*Ramp. Herd*) 593; Dobie p. 100; Howes C820; Rader 1891; Saunders 2846

An important book on the history of the cattle industry . . . —Adams

892 COX, JOHN E.

FIVE YEARS IN THE UNITED STATES ARMY. REMINISCENCES AND RECORDS OF AN EX-REGULAR . . . OWENSVILLE, IND.: GENERAL BAPTIST PUBLISHING HOUSE, 1892.

[i–ii], [1]–171, [172 blank]. 19.3 x 12.5 cm. Frontispiece and vignettes in text. Mottled blue printed wrappers with title printed in black over pink vignette. In a red cloth case.

Ref.: Howes C821

Three of Cox's five years in the Army were spent in Wyoming and Montana, 1875–77.

893 COX, ROSS

ADVENTURES ON THE COLUMBIA RIVER, INCLUDING THE NARRATIVE OF A RESIDENCE OF SIX YEARS ON THE WESTERN SIDE OF THE ROCKY MOUNTAINS, AMONG VARIOUS TRIBES OF INDIANS HITHERTO UNKNOWN: TOGETHER WITH A JOURNEY ACROSS THE AMERICAN CONTINENT . . . LONDON: HENRY COLBURN AND RICHARD BENTLEY, 1831.

[i]–xxiv, [1]–368. [i]–viii, [1]–400. 22.6 x 14.1 cm. Two volumes, blue boards, gray paper backs, printed white paper labels, uncut. In a red cloth case.

Ref.: Bradford 1097; Field 376; Howes C822; Jones 915; Sabin 17267; Smith 2078; Wagner-Camp 43

Although Cox arrived in Oregon in 1812 via Hawaii, his return East in 1817 was overland through Canada.

894 COX, SANFORD C.

RECOLLECTIONS OF THE EARLY SETTLEMENT OF THE WABASH VALLEY . . . LAFAYETTE: COURIER STEAM BOOK AND JOB PRINTING HOUSE, 1860.

[1]–160. 21.7 x 14.3 cm. Dark blue cloth, blind embossed sides, gilt title on front cover.

Ref.: Bradford 1098; Howes C823; Jones 1423; Sabin 17272

895 [COXE, TENCH]

AN ENQUIRY INTO THE PRINCIPLES ON WHICH A COMMERCIAL SYSTEM FOR THE UNITED STATES OF AMERICA SHOULD BE FOUNDED . . . [PHILADELPHIA:] ROBERT AITKEN, M.DCC.LXXXVII.

A–F⁴, G². [1]–52. Bound with Number 3867. Inscription torn from title-leaf.

Ref.: Evans 20306; Sabin 17295

896 [COXE, TENCH]

THOUGHTS ON THE SUBJECT OF NAVAL POWER IN THE UNITED STATES OF AMERICA; AND ON CERTAIN MEANS OF ENCOURAGING AND PROTECTING THEIR COMMERCE AND MANUFACTURES. PHILADELPHIA, PRINTED IN THE YEAR 1806.

[A]–D⁴, E². [1]–35, [36 blank]. Bound with Number 3289.

Ref.: Sabin 17306, 95727; Shaw & Shoemaker 10223

897 COYNER, DAVID H.

THE LOST TRAPPERS; A COLLECTION OF INTERESTING SCENES AND EVENTS IN THE ROCKY MOUNTAINS; TOGETHER WITH A SHORT DESCRIPTION OF CALIFORNIA: ALSO, SOME ACCOUNT OF THE FUR TRADE . . . CINCINNATI: J. A. & U. P. JAMES, 1847.

[i]–[xvi, xvi blank], 17–255, 256 blank, [257–63 advertisements, 264 blank]. 18.7 x 11.6 cm. Brown cloth, blind embossed sides, title in gilt on backstrip.

Ref.: Cowan p. 149; Cuthbertson & Ewers p. 116; Dobie p. 72; Field 380; Howes C836; Jones 1144; Rader 948; Sabin 17319; Wagner-Camp 130

Howes and Wagner-Camp suggest doubt about the veracity of the author (the "lost trappers" were from the Lewis and Clark Expedition). Some statements in the work are demonstrably untrue, but there are sections which may be proven authentic.

898 COZZENS, SAMUEL W.

THE MARVELOUS COUNTRY; OR, THREE YEARS IN ARIZONA AND NEW MEXICO, THE APACHES' HOME . . . ILLUSTRATED . . . BOSTON: SHEPARD AND GILL, 1873.

[1]–532. 22.4 x 14.7 cm. 100 illustrations listed. Dark orange pictorial cloth.

Ref.: Bradford 1104; Howes C838; Jones 1562; Munk (Alliot) p. 57; Rader 950

899 CRADLEBAUGH, JOHN

[Caption title] UTAH AND THE MORMONS. SPEECH OF HON. JOHN CRADLEBAUGH, OF NEVADA, ON THE ADMISSION OF UTAH AS A STATE. DELIVERED IN THE HOUSE OF REPRESENTATIVES, FEBRUARY 7, 1863. . . .

[1]–67, [68 blank]. 22.8 x 14.5 cm. Sewn, removed from bound volume.

Ref.: Howes C840; Sabin 17331; Woodward 46

Printed at Washington, D.C., in 1863.

The Appendix contains much important information on the Mountain Meadows Massacre. —EDG

900 CRAIG, JOHN R.

RANCHING WITH LORDS AND COMMONS . . . FACTS AND CONDITIONS RELATING TO THE CATTLE INDUSTRY IN THE NORTH-WEST TERRITORIES OF CANADA . . . TORONTO: PRINTED FOR THE AUTHOR BY WILLIAM BRIGGS.

[i]–[viii, viii blank], 9–293, [294 blank]. 18.8 x 12.8 cm. 17 illustrations listed. Green pictorial cloth. Lacks front flyleaf.

Ref.: Adams (*Ramp. Herd*) 598; Dobie pp. 100–01; Howes C842

Published in 1903. This is the story of the Oxley Ranch from the managers' side. See also A. Stavely Hill: *From Home to Home.*

901 CRAIG, LULU A.

GLIMPSES OF SUNSHINE AND SHADE IN THE FAR NORTH . . . CINCINNATI: THE EDITOR PUBLISHING CO., 1900.

[i]–[x, x blank], 1–123, [124 blank]. 21.6 x 14.5 cm. 14 illustrations, some in color. Light blue cloth.

Ref.: Smith 2087; Wickersham 2312

Smith's description calls for a map, but when he rechecked two copies in the University of Washington and Seattle Public Libraries, he found no map present and believes the description is in error.

902 CRAIG, NEVILLE B.

THE HISTORY OF PITTSBURGH, WITH A BRIEF NOTICE OF ITS FACILITIES OF COMMUNICATION, AND OTHER ADVANTAGES FOR COMMERCIAL AND MANUFACTURING PURPOSES . . . PITTSBURGH: PUBLISHED BY JOHN H. MELLOR . . . 1851.

[i]–xiv, [15]–312. 18.7 x 11.4 cm. Three folding maps: Map: Braddock's Route / A.D. 1755. / Drawn by Middleton / Scale 12 miles to an inch. / 15.7 x 23.1 cm. Map: Map / of / Pittsburgh, / Allegheny, / Birmingham & Manchester. / Lith. by Schuckman & Haunlein /. 14.1 x 18 cm. No scale given. Map: [Map of the Vicinity of Pittsburgh.] [Below neat line:] Schuckman & Haunlein lith. / 15.5 x 16.9 cm. No scale given. Black cloth.

Ref.: Bradford 1109; Howes C844; Sabin 17363

The best history of Pittsburgh to the time of

publication. Craig was editor of *The Olden Time.*

The first map differs from the ICN (Ayer) copy in that the phrase Gillespie Sc. Pitts'g / does not appear in lower right corner and the Potomac River is interrupted between Sideling Hill and Great Cacapon River. The paper is white with a slightly soft finish instead of hard-finished and faintly blue-gray.

903 CRAKES, JR., SYLVESTER

FIVE YEARS A CAPTIVE AMONG THE BLACK-FEET INDIANS; OR, A THRILLING NARRATIVE OF THE ADVENTURES, PERILS, AND SUFFERING ENDURED BY JOHN DIXON AND HIS COMPANIONS, AMONG THE SAVAGES OF THE NORTHWEST TERRITORY OF NORTH AMERICA . . . COLUMBUS: OSGOOD & PEARCE, 1858.

[i]–vi, [7]–224. 17.7 x 11.3 cm. Six illustrations. Blue cloth, blind embossed sides, title in gilt on backstrip.

Ref.: Ayer (*Supp.*) 37; Howes C850; Wagner-Camp 299

There is suspicion that this is a romance based on a captivity which occurred considerably later than 1806.

904 CRAM, GEORGE F.

[Map] CRAM'S / SECTIONAL MAP / OF / COLORADO / DRAWN & ENGRAVED FROM THE LATEST GOVERNMENT SURVEYS. / BY / GEORGE F. CRAM. / PROPRIETOR OF THE / WESTERN MAP DEPOT. / 55 W. LAKE ST. CHICAGO. / ILL, / 1873. / [lower right corner:] ENTERED ACCORDING TO ACT OF CONGRESS IN THE YEAR 1872, BY G. F. CRAM, IN THE OFFICE OF THE LIBRARIAN OF CONGRESS, AT WASHINGTON. /

Map, 73.3 x 92.8 cm. No scale given. Folded into black cloth covers, 13.7 x 9 cm., gilt stamped on front cover: New / Sectional Map / of / Colorado / [decorative rule] / Published by / Geo. F. Cram. / [within blind embossed panel], advertisement on inner front cover.

Ref.:

905 CRAM, GEORGE F., *Publisher*

[Wrapper title] NEW OFFICIAL MAP OF ALASKA AND THE KLONDIKE GOLD FIELDS. THE NEW "ELDORADO." NEW YORK: GEORGE F. CRAM, 1897.

[1]–28, [29–32 maps]. 16.5 x 10.8 cm. Four full page maps and one folding map: Map of / Alaska / Copyright Secured 1897 by / Geo. F. Cram, / Engraver and Publisher, / 415 Dearborn St., Chicago, - - - - Illinois. / 30.3 x 50.7 cm. Scale: about 110 miles to one inch. Text in outer left margin. Yellow printed wrappers with title on

front wrapper, advertisement on verso of back wrapper.

Ref.:

906 [CRAM, THOMAS J.]

[Caption title] . . . HARBOR AT DUBUQUE . . . A COPY OF THE REPORT OF THE SURVEY OF THE HARBOR AT THE TOWN OF DUBUQUE . . .

[1]–9, [10 blank]. 23.4 x 15.3 cm. Folding map: Harbour of Dubuque, / Exhibiting the Outlines of the Various Plans for the Improvement / Described and Estimated for in the Report. / 1844. / T J Cram / Capt. T. E. / [flourish] / St Louis / 24 Dec. 1844 /. 56 x 122.3 cm. Scale: 450 feet to an inch. Stabbed, unbound, uncut.

Ref.:

28th Congress, 2nd Session, House, Document No. 57, Serial 441. [Washington, 1845.]

Imprint at foot of page [1]: [rule] / Blair & Rives, printers. /

907 CRAM, THOMAS J.

[Caption title] . . . TOPOGRAPHICAL MEMOIR OF THE DEPARTMENT OF THE PACIFIC . . . THE TOPOGRAPHICAL MEMOIR AND REPORT OF CAPTAIN T. J. CRAM, RELATIVE TO THE TERRITORIES OF OREGON AND WASHINGTON, IN THE MILITARY DEPARTMENT OF THE PACIFIC . . .

[1]–126, [127–28 blank]. 24.2 x 15.1 cm. Stabbed, unbound, uncut, unopened.

Ref.: Howes C853

35th Congress, 2nd Session, House, Executive Document No. 114, Serial 1014. [Washington, 1859.]

908 CRANE, ALICE R.

SMILES AND TEARS FROM THE KLONDYKE . . . NEW YORK: DOXEY'S, AT THE SIGN OF THE LARK.

[1]–203, [204 blank]. 18.6 x 12.7 cm. Eight illustrations listed. Gray pictorial cloth.

Ref.: Smith 2095; Wickersham 4302

Copyrighted 1901.

909 CRANE, GEORGE B.

A LIFE HISTORY . . . WITH COMMENTS ON A VARIETY OF TOPICS . . . SAN JOSE: MERCURY PRINT, 1886.

[i–ii], [1–2 blank], [iii]–[xiv], [3]–243, [244 blank]. 19.2 x 13.7 cm. Rebound in contemporary blue half calf, gilt edges. Rebacked, preserving original backstrip.

Prov.: Inscribed on preliminary blank leaf in indelible pencil: Miss Mildred Howar / Morrisson / Your father waives his / claim to this copy of my / Autobiography in be-/half of his daughter / The beautiful finish / with which he has graced / the unbound leaves that I / gave him justly entitles / him to the Book, but / parental affection dom-/ [following on verso:] inates the sentiment of ownership, and yet a / false conception of the at-/tributes of the Almighty may / cause a Superstitionist / to forget that he has a / daughter as illustrated / by the cruel example / of the Biblical Jeptha / The above is the auto-/graph with the respects of / G B Crane M D / St- Helena Cal Nov 1896 /.

Ref.: Cowan p. 149; Howes C860

Some copies are found with a portrait on the front endpaper. The reminiscences include adventures throughout the United States from New York to California.

910 CRANE, JAMES M.

THE PAST, THE PRESENT AND THE FUTURE OF THE PACIFIC . . . SAN FRANCISCO, CAL.: PRINTED BY STERETT & CO., 1856.*

[1]–79, [80 blank]. 21.3 x 13.5 cm. Rebound in old marbled boards, calf backstrip, leather label, sprinkled edges.

Ref.: Cowan p. 149; Howes C861

911 CRAWFORD, CHARLES H.

SCENES OF EARLIER DAYS IN CROSSING THE PLAINS TO OREGON, AND EXPERIENCES OF WESTERN LIFE . . . PETALUMA, CAL.: J. T. STUDDERT, 1898.

[i–vi], [1]–186. 20.3 x 14.4 cm. Illustrations unlisted. Black cloth, red leather backstrip.

Ref.: Cowan p. 149; Howes C870; Smith 2098

Crawford crossed the plains in 1851. He recounts also adventures at the Powder River mines as a prospector and miner.

912 CRAWFORD, LEWIS F.

REKINDLING CAMP FIRES. THE EXPLOITS OF BEN ARNOLD (CONNOR), (WA-SI-CU TAM-A-HE-CA) . . . BISMARCK, NORTH DAKOTA: CAPITAL BOOK CO.

[i–iv], [1]–324. 21.8 x 14.6 cm. 14 illustrations listed, pictorial endpapers. Dark blue half morocco, gilt top, uncut.

Ref.: Adams 262; Adams (*Ramp. Herd*) 607; Dobie p. 101; Howes C872; Jennewein 95; Rader 959; Smith 2100

Limited to 100 copies signed by the author. Copyrighted 1926.

913 CRAWFORD, MEDOREM

[Caption title] . . . A COPY OF THE REPORT AND JOURNAL OF CAPTAIN MEDOREM CRAWFORD, COMMANDING THE EMIGRANT ESCORT TO OREGON AND WASHINGTON TERRITORY IN THE YEAR 1862 . . .*

[1]–14. 22.5 x 14.5 cm. Rebound in new red cloth.

Ref.: Howes C874; Wagner-Camp 386

37th Congress, 3rd Session, Senate, Executive Document No. 17, Serial 1149. [Washington: Government Printing Office, 1863.]

914 CRAWFORD, MEDOREM

. . . JOURNAL OF MEDOREM CRAWFORD. AN ACCOUNT OF HIS TRIP ACROSS THE PLAINS WITH THE OREGON PIONEERS OF 1842 . . . EUGENE, OREGON: STAR JOB OFFICE, 1897.*

[1]–26. 23.1 x 15.4 cm. Stapled, unbound.

Ref.: Howes C874; Smith 2102

First separate printing. The journal had been issued in 1863 as a Government Document.

Editions: Washington, 1863.

915 CREMONY, JOHN C.

LIFE AMONG THE APACHES . . . SAN FRANCISCO: A. ROMAN & COMPANY, 1868.

[1]–322. 18.3 x 11.2 cm. Green cloth, gilt title on backstrip.

Prov.: Inscribed by author on front endleaf: Wirt Davis, U.S.A. / Ft. Huachuca, A. T. /

Ref.: Edwards p. 45; Howes C879; Munk (Alliot) p. 58; Rader 977; Raines p. 57; Saunders 716; Wagner-Camp 234 note

A cavalry officer's adventures in Arizona, New Mexico, and Texas told with dash and a fine sense of humor.

916 CRESCENT CITY (Iowa) ORACLE

[Newspaper] CRESCENT CITY ORACLE. VOL. 1. . . . NO. 2. L. O. LITTLEFIELD—EDITOR & PUBLISHER. —CRESCENT CITY, POTTAWATAMIE COUNTY, IOWA, FRIDAY MORNING, FEBRUARY 27, 1857 . . .

Newspaper, [1–4]. 47.6 x 31.4 cm. Unbound.

Ref.:

917 CRESCENT CITY (Iowa) ORACLE

[Broadside] NEW-YEAR'S ADDRESS, TO THE READERS OF THE CRESCENT CITY ORACLE, FROM THE MAN IN THE MOON . . .

Broadside, 31.5 x 24.8 cm. Text, 28.3 x 21 cm. Printed on pink paper.

The *Address* is dated Jan. 1, 1858. /

918 CRESCENT CITY & YREKA PLANK AND TURNPIKE ROAD

REPORT OF THE ENGINEER ON THE SURVEY OF THE CRESCENT CITY & YREKA PLANK AND TURNPIKE ROAD. CRESCENT CITY, CAL.: PRINTED AT THE OFFICE OF THE CRESCENT CITY HERALD, 1854.

[1]–7, [8 blank]. 22.6 x 15 cm. Unbound, folded, uncut.

Ref.:

The report is signed at the end: T. P. Robinson, Engineer, / Crescent City, Nov. 16, 1854. /

Although Dawson's Book Shop listed this in Part III of their *The West and the Pacific* (item 748), it is not noted in the new bibliography of California Imprints by Greenwood.

919   CRESWELL, JOHN A. J.

[Caption title] NO. 3. INTER-OCEAN CAMPAIGN DOCUMENTS. NO. 3. THE POSTAL SERVICE. SPEECH OF POSTMASTER GENERAL CRESWELL, AT JACKSON, MICHIGAN, AUGUST 1, 1872 ... THE CHORPENNING CASE—THE COST AND EXTENT OF THE U.S. MAIL SERVICE ...

[1]–7, [8 blank]. 22.2 x 14.4 cm. Unbound, removed from bound volume. With other Chorpenning materials in a red cloth box.
Ref.:
Printed in Chicago in 1872. An advertisement for the Inter-Ocean, 16 Congress St., Chicago, Ill. appears on page 7.

920   CREUZBAUR, ROBERT

[Map] J. DE CORDOVA'S / MAP / OF THE / STATE / OF / TEXAS / COMPILED FROM THE RECORDS OF THE / GENERAL LAND OFFICE OF THE STATE, BY / ROBERT CREUZBAUR, / HOUSTON. / 1849. / WITHOUT MY SIGNATURE ALL COPIES OF THIS MAP HAVE / BEEN FRAUDULENTLY OBTAINED / [in manuscript: J De Cordova /] / [at left of cartouche:] ENGRAVED BY J. M. ATWOOD, NEW YORK. / [lower centre:] ENTERED ACCORDING TO ACT OF CONGRESS ON THE 28TH DAY OF JULY 1848 BY J. DE CORDOVA, IN THE CLERK'S OFFICE OF THE UNITED STATES DISTRICT COURT FOR THE DISTRICT OF TEXAS. *Inset:* [Boundaries of the state, within oval]. 23.9 x 28.9 cm. Scale: 145 miles to one inch.

Map, 83.3 x 76.6 cm. Scale: 10 miles to one inch. Folded into brown stamped roan folder, 15.8 x 10.5 cm., with title in gilt on front cover.
Ref.: Phillips (*Maps*) p. 844
Laid in is a letter from Anson Jones to R. J. Walker, July 16, 1847, relating to publication of the map.

921   CREUZBAUR, ROBERT

ROUTE FROM THE GULF OF MEXICO AND THE LOWER MISSISSIPPI VALLEY TO CALIFORNIA AND THE PACIFIC OCEAN, ILLUSTRATED BY A GENERAL MAP AND SECTIONAL MAPS: WITH DIRECTIONS TO TRAVELLERS ... NEW YORK: PUBLISHED BY H. LONG & BROTHER, 1849.

[1]–40, [41], [42 blank]. 18.2 x 11 cm. Black ribbed cloth, blind embossed corners, title in gilt on front cover.
Ref.: Clark III 294; Cowan p. 149; Howes C881; Rader 978; Sabin 17492; Wagner-Camp 166
An excellent guide. Lacks the six maps.

922   CRITCHELL, ROBERT S.

RECOLLECTIONS OF A FIRE INSURANCE MAN INCLUDING HIS EXPERIENCES IN U.S. NAVY (MISSISSIPPI SQUADRON) DURING THE CIVIL WAR ... CHICAGO: A. C. McCLURG & CO., 1909.*

[1]–164. 19.3 x 13.2 cm. Five illustrations, unlisted. Dark blue cloth.
Ref.:

923   CROCKER & CO., H. S.

NOVEMBER. NO. 27. RAILROAD GAZETTEER. FOR GRATUITOUS DISTRIBUTION ON RAILWAYS, STEAMERS AND STAGES. PUBLISHED MONTHLY BY H. S. CROCKER & CO. ... SACRAMENTO.

[1]–82 only. (Lacks [83–96].) 16.5 x 10.7 cm. Woodcuts in text, unlisted. Yellow printed wrappers with title on front wrapper, advertisements on verso of front and recto and verso of back wrapper.
Ref.:
The date 1871 appears in the imprint on the front wrapper.
Inserted before the title-page is a dark yellow printed slip headed: New Arrangement. / [diamond rule] / ...

924   CROGHAN, GEORGE

JOURNAL OF COL. GEORGE CROGHAN, WHO WAS SENT, AFTER THE PEACE OF 1763, ... TO EXPLORE THE COUNTRY ADJACENT TO THE OHIO RIVER, AND TO CONCILIATE THE INDIAN NATIONS ... FROM FEATHERSTONHAUGH: AM. MONTHLY JOURNAL OF GEOLOGY, DECEMBER 1831.*

[1]–38. 21.6 x 15.1 cm. Rebound in red half morocco, gilt.
Ref.: Howes C902
Reprinted at Burlington, New Jersey, in 1875.

925   CROIX, CARLOS FRANCISCO DE

INSTRUCCION PARA FORMAR UNA LINEA O CORDON DE QUINCE PRESIDIOS SOBRE LAS FRONTERAS DE LAS PROVINCIAS INTERNAS DE ESTE REINO DE NUEVA-ESPANA ... ANO DE 1771 ... EN MEXICO EN LA IMPRENTA DEL BR. D. JOSEPH ANTONIO DE HOGAL ...

[*]¹, A–V². [i–ii], 1–80. 28 x 19.8 cm. Bound with Number 9.
Ref.: Medina (*Mexico*) 5439; Wagner (*SS*) 154
Signed and dated at the end: Dado en Mé-/xico á diez y ocho de Julio de mil setecien-/tos setenta y uno. / El Marques de Croix. / [paraph] /.

926 CROIX, CARLOS FRANCISCO DE

ORDENANZAS DE LA REAL RENTA DE LA POLVORA ... REIMPRESAS EN MEXICO: EN LA IMPRENTA NUEVA MADRILENA DEL NUEVO REZADO, DE LOS HEREDEROS DEL LIC. DON JOSE JAUREGUI, 1787.

[*]¹, A–T². [i–ii], 1–73, [74 blank]. 28 x 19.8 cm. Bound with Number 9.

Ref.: Medina (*Mexico*) 7708

927 CROOK, GEORGE

PHOTOGRAPH, seated, nearly full length, facing slightly to his right, in uniform, high hat, beard braided. Printed in sepia. 14.6 x 9.8 cm. Mounted on yellow stiff card, 16.5 x 10.8 cm.

Photographer's name printed on verso: [on decorated standard and ribbon] D. S. Mitchell / Photographer, / Eddy Street / Cheyenne / Wyo. /

Also on verso, apparently in Crook's hand: George Crook / Brig. Gen. U.S.A. / And in a later hand: Brig. Gen'l Crook was Commander / of the Dept. of the Platte at / Omaha from 1875 to 1882 / Succeeded by Sheridan Aug 8—1882 /.

Accompanying the photograph is correspondence with Martin Schmitt who used a copy of this photograph from the National Archives for the dust jacket of his edition of Crook's autobiography. Schmitt surmises the photograph was taken by Morrow rather than Mitchell.

928 CROOK, GEORGE

[Wrapper title] ANNUAL REPORT OF BRIGADIER GENERAL GEORGE CROOK, U.S. ARMY. COMMANDING DEPARTMENT OF ARIZONA. 1883.

[1]–43, [44 blank]. 19 x 12.5 cm. Rebound in blue buckram, black leather label on backstrip. Original gray printed front wrapper bound in.

Ref.: Bancroft (*Arizona*) pp. 569–73; Howes C913

Dated: Headquarters Department of Arizona, / Whipple Barracks, Prescott, September 27, 1883. / Probably printed at Prescott.

Contains considerable information about the troubles with Geronimo and the Chiricahua Apaches. Signed in manuscript on page 17 by S. Roberts.

929 CROOK, GEORGE

[Wrapper title] ANNUAL REPORT OF BRIGADIER GENERAL GEORGE CROOK, U.S. ARMY. COMMANDING DEPARTMENT OF ARIZONA. 1885.

[i–ii], [1]–41, [42–44 blank], [iii–iv]. (Pages [i–ii] and [iii–iv] blank.) 18.8 x 12.2 cm. Gray printed wrappers with title as above on front wrapper.

Ref.: Howes C914

Dated: Headquarters Department of Arizona, / in the Field, / Fort Bowie, A. T., September 9, 1885. / Probably printed at Los Angeles.

Devoted almost exclusively to the affairs of the Chiricahua Apaches and their leaders, including Geronimo.

930 [CROOK, GEORGE]

[Typewritten copy] HEADQUARTERS DEPARTMENT OF ARIZONA, IN THE FIELD, FORT BOWIE, A. T., APRIL 10TH, 1886. ADJUTANT GENERAL, DIVISION OF THE PACIFIC, PRESIDIO OF SAN FRANCISCO, CAL. SIR:—I HAVE THE HONOR TO SUBMIT THE FOLLOWING REPORT OF THE OPERATIONS OF THE TROOPS UNDER MY COMMAND IN THE PURSUIT OF HOSTILE CHIRICAHUAS ...

Nine pages, 32.7 x 20.2 cm. Stapled at top edges.

A stirring account of the chase and capture of Geronimo and his later escape.

This is a copy sent to General Grierson by Crook, corrected in manuscript, but unsigned.

931 CROOK, GEORGE

[Wrapper title] RESUME OF OPERATIONS AGAINST APACHE INDIANS, 1882 TO 1886 ... 1886.

[1]–25, [26–8 blank]. 19.8 x 12.4 cm. Gray printed wrappers with title on front wrapper.

Ref.:

No place of printing is given, probably Santa Fé.

An uncommonly interesting account dealing principally with the fight against Geronimo and the successful quieting of the Apaches.

932 CROSBY, J. O.

[Map] MAP / OF / THE COUNTY / OF / CLAYTON / IOWA. / SCALE OF 2 MILES TO AN INCH / [diagrammatic scale] / LITH. BY J. SAGE & SONS, BUFFALO, N.Y. / [at lower left:] ENTERED ACCORDING TO CIRCUMSTANCES, BY J. O. CROSBY AT GARNAVILLO, IN THE YEAR 1857. /

Map 41.1 x 50.5 cm. Scale: Two miles to one inch. Folded into black cloth covers, 17.6 x 11.1 cm., with title stamped in gilt on front cover: Map / of / Clayton County. /

Ref.:

Below the bottom neat line there are ten columns of four lines each under the heading: Abstract from the Census of Clayton County for the Year 1856. In the upper right corner, there is an advertisement for J. O. Crosby's services as Attorney at Law in Garnavillo. There are manuscript notes on the face of the map in an unidentified hand.

933 CROSS, FRED J.

THE FREE LANDS OF DAKOTA; A DESCRIPTION OF THE COUNTRY; THE CLIMATE; THE BEAUTIFUL VALLEYS, AND THE OCEAN-LIKE PRAIRIES; THE CROPS; THE LAND LAWS, AND THE INDUCEMENTS OFFERED TO IMMIGRANTS . . . YANKTON, DAKOTA: BOWEN & KINGSBURY, 1876.

[1]–[32]. 22.1 x 14.2 cm. Rebound in green half morocco.

Ref.: Adams (*Ramp. Herd*) 617; Allen (*Dakota*) 131; Bradford 1138; Howes C918

There are several pages on the Black Hills and valuable suggestions to settlers. No wrappers appear to have been issued for this work, the title-page having served that purpose.

934 CROSS, FRED J.

INFORMATION FOR PERSONS SEEKING A HOME IN THE WEST. DAKOTA TERRITORY AS IT IS . . . SIOUX FALLS, DAKOTA: M'DONALD & SHERMAN, 1875.

[1]–[48]. 20.6 x 13.8 cm. Stabbed, unbound.

Ref.: Adams (*Ramp. Herd*) 616; Allen (*Dakota*) 120; Howes C919

935 CROSS, OSBORNE, *Defendant*

PROCEEDINGS OF A GENERAL COURT MARTIAL FOR THE TRIAL OF MAJOR OSBORNE CROSS . . . WASHINGTON: PRINTED BY HENRY POLKINHORN, 1860.

[1]–98. 22 x 14.3 cm. Tan printed wrappers with title on front wrapper.

Ref.:

Major Cross published the proceedings for his friends.

936 CROZIER, ROBERT H.

THE CONFEDERATE SPY: A STORY OF THE WAR OF 1861 . . . GALLATIN, TENN.: R. B. HARMON, 1866.

[1]–406. 18.8 x 11.9 cm. Brown cloth, blind fillet borders on sides, gilt title on backstrip.

Prov.: Large F stamped on front endpaper.

Ref.: Howes C935; Wright II 667

The Confederate Spy has often been called the first Confederate novel.

937 CRUMPTON, HEZEKIAH J. & WASHBURN B.

THE ADVENTURES OF TWO ALABAMA BOYS . . . PART ONE: THE ADVENTURES OF DR. H. J. CRUMPTON . . . IN HIS EFFORTS TO REACH THE GOLD FIELDS IN 1849. PART TWO: THE ADVENTURES OF REV. W. B. CRUMPTON, GOING TO AND RETURNING FROM CALIFORNIA . . . PART THREE: TO CALIFORNIA AND BACK AFTER A LAPSE OF FORTY YEARS. MONTGOMERY, ALA.: THE PARAGON PRESS, 1912.

[1]–238. 18.1 x 12.7 cm. Three plates. Dark red cloth.

Ref.: Howes C937

The overland trip occurred in 1849 and was via Fort Smith and the southern route.

938 CULBERTSON, ALEXANDER

AUTOGRAPH LETTER, SIGNED. 1856 June 9, Sioux City, Steamer Robert Campbell. Three pages, 20 x 13.2 cm. To his daughter, Julia Roberts.

Announcing that instead of returning home, he is setting off on another expedition to the Mountains.

939 CULBERTSON, ALEXANDER

AUTOGRAPH LETTER, SIGNED. 1875 September 4, Fort Belknap, Montana Territory. Three pages, 24.8 x 19.6 cm. To George H. Roberts.

An affectionate letter to his son-in-law about family matters, but containing an interesting passage about depredations by the Indians.

940 CULIACAN (Occidente Province), MEXICO. AYUNTAMIENTO

[Caption title] REPRESENTACION QUE EL ILUSTRE AYUNTAMIENTO DE CULIACAN. LLEVA AL ESCMO. SR. GOBERNADOR DEL ESTADO, PARA QUE NO PERMITA LA REUNION ESTRAORDINARIA DE LA LEGISLATURA DEL MISMO. . . .

[1–4]. 30.7 x 21.2 cm. Unbound, uncut.

Ref.:

Imprint at foot of page [4]: Imprenta del Gobierno Supremo de Occidente. / Año de 1829. / The president of the Ayuntamiento was José Ignacio Verdugo.

The *Representacion* is a protest of the City Council against a session of the legislature in which Occidente might be divided.

941 CULLEY, JOHN H.

CATTLE, HORSES & MEN OF THE WESTERN RANGE . . . LOS ANGELES: THE WARD RITCHIE PRESS.

[i]–xvi, [1]–337, [338 blank]. 22.8 x 15 cm. 12 illustrations. Brown cloth.

Ref.: Adams 272; Adams (*Ramp. Herd*) 623; Dobie p. 101; Howes C942; Saunders 3995

Copyrighted 1940. The frontispiece is signed by the author.

942 CUMBERLAND PRESBYTERIAN CHURCH IN THE UNITED STATES

THE CONSTITUTION OF THE CUMBERLAND PRESBYTERIAN CHURCH, IN THE UNITED STATES OF AMERICA: CONTAINING THE CONFESSION OF FAITH, A CATECHISM, THE GOVERNMENT AND DISCIPLINE, AND THE DIRECTORY FOR THE WORSHIP OF GOD . . . NASHVILLE, T.: PRINTED BY M. & J. NORVELL, 1815.

[A]³, B–V⁴, W¹. (W1 may have been printed as A4.) 15.6 x 9.3. cm. Brown mottled sheep, green leather label.

Ref.: AII (*Tennessee*) 157; McMurtrie (*Tennessee*) 118

The publishers mentioned on the title-page were Finis Ewing and Hugh Kirkpatrick. Neither is listed as a printer, but Ewing's name appears in AII (*Tennessee*) as author of a volume of sermons. According to Minutes of the Cumberland Synod dated October 7, 1813, and April 8–9, 1814, the cost was to be 37 1/2 cents per copy bound.

There is said to have been a Russellville edition of 1813, but a copy has not been located. There was a later (1821) Russellville edition. It seems unlikely that there was an 1813 edition in view of the dates given in the Minutes. It is quite likely that the 1813 edition is a ghost.

943 CUMBERLAND PRESBYTERIAN CHURCH IN THE UNITED STATES

THE CONSTITUTION OF THE CUMBERLAND PRESBYTERIAN CHURCH, IN THE UNITED STATES OF AMERICA: CONTAINING THE CONFESSION OF FAITH, A CATECHISM, THE GOVERNMENT AND DISCIPLINE, AND THE DIRECTORY FOR THE WORSHIP OF GOD. RATIFIED AND ADOPTED BY THE SYNOD OF CUMBERLAND, HELD AT SUGG'S CREEK, IN TENNESSEE STATE, APRIL THE 5TH, 1814 . . . RUSSELLVILLE: PRINTED BY CHARLES RHEA, 1821.

[i–iv], [1]–[140]. 17.4 x 11 cm. Calf, black leather label.

Ref.: AII (*Tennessee*) 157 note
Editions: See preceding note.

944 CUMING, FORTESCUE

SKETCHES OF A TOUR TO THE WESTERN COUNTRY, THROUGH THE STATES OF OHIO AND KENTUCKY; A VOYAGE DOWN THE OHIO AND MISSISSIPPI RIVERS, AND A TRIP THROUGH THE MISSISSIPPI TERRITORY, AND PART OF WEST FLORIDA . . . PITTSBURGH: PRINTED & PUBLISHED BY CRAMER, SPEAR & EICHBAUM, 1810.

[A]⁴, B–2S⁶, 2T². [i]–viii, [9]–24, 28, 26–504. 19.8 x 11.7 cm. Unbound, uncut, mostly unopened. Resewn and some leaves reinforced at hinge, gatherings E–M supplied from a cut copy. In a green cloth case.

Ref.: Buck 71; Howes C947; Jones 739; Sabin 17890; Thomson 286

This is one of the most interesting works relating to the West.—Thomson. The Appendix contains contributions by Loskiel, Forsyth, Hildreth, Badger, Heckewelder, and others.

Page 25 is mispaginated 28 as is the ICN copy. The ICN (Ayer) copy, however, is correctly paginated.

945 CUMING, THOMAS B.

FUNERAL SERVICES. THE FUNERAL OF HON. T. B. CUMING WILL TAKE PLACE AT THE CAPITOL BUILDING THIS AFTERNOON AT 2 O'CLOCK. REV. MR. WATSON WILL OFFICIATE. THE FRIENDS OF THE DECEASED ARE REQUESTED TO BE PRESENT. OMAHA, N. T., MARCH 24TH, 1858.

[1–4 (2–4 blank)]. 15.5 x 10 cm. Unbound.
Ref.:
Cuming was Territorial Governor of Nebraska.

946 [CUMINGS, SAMUEL]

JAMES' TRAVELERS COMPANION: BEING A COMPLETE GUIDE THROUGH THE WEST AND SOUTH, TO THE GULF OF MEXICO AND THE PACIFIC, VIA THE RAILROADS, LAKES, RIVERS, CANALS, ETC., WITH HISTORICAL NOTES, STATISTICAL TABLES, AND A VAST AMOUNT OF GENERAL INFORMATION . . . CINCINNATI: PUBLISHED BY J. A. & U. P. JAMES, 1853.

[i]–x, [9]–193, [194 blank]. 14.8 x 9.3 cm. Text illustrations and maps unlisted.

BOUND WITH:

JAMES' RAIL ROAD AND ROUTE BOOK FOR THE WESTERN AND SOUTHERN STATES. COMPILED BY J. GRISWOLD. CINCINNATI: J. A. & U. P. JAMES, 1853.

[i]–[xii], [9]–67, [68 blank], [69–80 advertisements]. Two volumes bound together, blue cloth, title within blind embossed pictorial frame on covers, gilt title on backstrip.

Ref.: Buck 484; Clark III 358; Howes C948; Rader 2362; Sabin 28885, 35714, 35715

Cumings' work had been based on Cramer, as noted in the next item. *James' Travelers Companion* was developed from Cumings; in 1851 an earlier edition of the present work without the second title had appeared under the name Stephen L. Massey. In the present edition, the two works were published together, although there are separate title-pages and separate pagination.

947 CUMINGS, SAMUEL

THE WESTERN NAVIGATOR; CONTAINING CHARTS OF THE OHIO RIVER, IN ITS WHOLE EXTENT, AND OF THE MISSISSIPPI RIVER . . . PHILADELPHIA: PUBLISHED BY E. LITTELL, 1822.

[1–2], 33 engraved charts on 27 plates. [1]–4, [1]–[238], [239–40 blank]. Volume I: 41.3 x 27.3 cm. Volume II: 22.7 x 13.7 cm. The maps are numbered Ohio Nos. 1–15, Mississippi Nos. 1–

15, and Mississippi 1–3 From Mouth of Missouri. Each of the Ohio maps is a separate double page spread. The Mississippi series is fifteen on ten double page spreads. The second Mississippi series is three double page spreads. Each sheet carries the publisher's imprint at the foot: Published by E. Littell, Nº 88, Chesnut Sᵗ Philadᵃ / and the cartographer's name: H. S. Tanner Sc. / There are insets on Ohio Nos. 8, 10, 11 (two), 12 (two), 13 (two), 14 (three), and 15 (three), and on Mississippi Nos. 1, 2, 3, 5, 6, 7, 8, and 14. Two volumes, folio and octavo, original tan boards with titles on front covers and advertisements on back covers, calf backstrips.

Prov.: Bookplate of William A. Phillips.

Ref.: Bay 332; Buley I, pp. 3, 432–33, II, p. 642; Howes C948; Rader 995; Sabin 17902; Thomson 287, 288

Based without credit on Cramer's *Navigator*. There were several later editions under different titles.

948 CUMMINS, JAMES R.

JIM CUMMINS' BOOK . . . THE LIFE STORY OF THE JAMES AND YOUNGER GANG AND . . . THE OPERATIONS OF QUANTRELL'S GUERILLAS . . . DENVER: THE REED PUBLISHING COMPANY, 1903.

[i]–xv, 16–191, [192 advertisement]. 19.3 x 13.2 cm. 22 illustrations listed. Red pictorial cloth.

Ref.: Adams 273; Howes C951; Rader 996

He had been written about so much in Wild West fiction, and in real life was such a meek-looking man, that when he tried several times to give himself up after the breakup of the James gang, no one would believe him. He was never brought to trial.—Adams

949 CUMMINS, SARAH J.

AUTOBIOGRAPHY AND REMINISCENCES . . . LA GRANDE, OREGON: LA GRANDE PRINTING CO.

[1]–63, [64 blank]. 20.1 x 14.9 cm. Portrait. Gray printed wrappers.

Ref.: Howell 70; Howes C952; Hubach p. 100; Smith 2151

Copyrighted 1914. The author crossed the Plains in 1852. There were several reprints made later in Walla Walla.

950 CUMMINS, SARAH J.

AUTOBIOGRAPHY AND REMINISCENCES . . .

[1]–61, [62–4 blank]. 20.3 x 14.2 cm. Portrait. Gray printed wrappers.

Ref.: Howes C952; Smith 2153

Copyrighted 1914, but reprinted later. The present copy bears the following imprint on the verso of the back wrapper: [rule] / Walla Walla Bulletin / [rule] / [ornament] /.

951 CUNNINGHAM, EUGENE

TRIGGERNOMETRY: A GALLERY OF GUNFIGHTERS . . . FOREWORD BY EUGENE M. RHODES . . . NEW YORK: THE PRESS OF THE PIONEERS, 1934.

[i]–[xx, xx blank], 1–441, [442 blank]. 22.8 x 15.7 cm. 21 illustrations listed. Dark blue buckram.

Ref.: Adams 275; Dobie p. 141; Howes C954; Rader 1000

952 CUNYNGHAME, SIR ARTHUR AUGUSTUS THURLOW

A GLIMPSE AT THE GREAT WESTERN REPUBLIC . . . LONDON: RICHARD BENTLEY, 1852.

[1–4 advertisements], [i–iv, iv blank], [1]–152. 17 x 10.6 cm. Light orange pictorial boards, with title on front cover, advertisements on back cover; rebacked with cloth.

Ref.: Buck 460; Howes C958; Clark III 458; Sabin 17979

The author's hunting experiences and descriptions of scenes make good reading.

Editions: London, 1851.

953 CURLEY, EDWIN A.

GLITTERING GOLD. THE TRUE STORY OF THE BLACK HILLS . . . CHICAGO: PUBLISHED BY THE AUTHOR, 1876.

[i]–iv, [5]–128, [i]–xii, [1–4 (page [4] pasted to inner back wrapper)]. 19.3 x 13.6 cm. Illustrated, map: The / Cheyenne Mountains / —or— / Black Hills, / And their Surroundings, / Compiled by / Edwin A. Curley, / And corrected from Governmental and / the most authentic mining sources, / up to August 1st, 1875. / [below neat line:] Drawn and Engraved by Sears Bros., 48 Exchange Building, Chicago, under direction of the Author and Compiler; Printed by H. S. Tiffany, Chicago. / 16.3 x 22.3 cm. Scale: 21 miles to one inch. Half of verso of map mounted on inner front wrapper. Map: Map / of the / Black Hills / Gold Fields, / And the Best Route / to Reach Them. / 9.1 x 20 cm. No scale given. On recto of final leaf, verso mounted on inner back wrapper. Pictorial wrappers, with title on front wrapper, advertisements on back wrapper. In a red cloth case.

Ref.: Howes C959; Jennewein 81

954 CURTIS, GEORGE W.

LOTUS-EATING: A SUMMER BOOK . . . NEW YORK: HARPER & BROTHERS, 1854.

[1]–206, [207–10 blank]. 18.6 x 12.6 cm. Black cloth, embossed borders on sides, title on backstrip.

Prov.: Inscribed on front fly-leaf: Presented to the Post Library / of Fort C. F. Smith M. T. / by H. M. Matthews M. D. / Sp'cl Agt. Ind Peace Com. / Sept 13ᵗʰ 1867 /. Mounted on the inside front cover is a manuscript bookplate: Post Library / Fort C. F. Smith, / M. T. / N°. 1. / From the Templeton Papers.

Ref.: Blanck 4263 see

Editions: London, 1852; New York, 1852.

955 CURTIS, HARVEY

SECESSION CONSIDERED AS A MEANS OF REFORMA-
TION. A SERMON, PREACHED IN THE FIRST PRESBY-
TERIAN CHURCH, CHICAGO, ILLINOIS, JULY 13TH,
1851 . . . CHICAGO: PRINTED BY R. L. & C. L.
WILSON, 1851.

[1]–20. 20.7 x 12.2 cm. Tan printed wrappers with title on front wrapper.

Prov.: Addressed on back wrapper: Rev B. Manley D. D. / Tuscaloosa / Abᵃ /. Stamped in red: Paid /.

Ref.: AII (*Chicago*) 11; Byrd 1695

956 CURTIS, NEWTON M.

THE PRAIRIE GUIDE; OR, THE ROSE OF THE RIO
GRANDE. A TALE OF THE MEXICAN WAR . . . NEW
YORK: WILLIAM BROTHERS.

[1]–96. 25.4 x 16.2 cm. Pale yellow printed wrappers with title on front wrapper, advertisement on verso of back wrapper.

Ref.: Clements Library (*Texas*) 31; Raines p. 124; Wright I 805

The wrapper title shows 1847 in the imprint.

Despite the title-page, the Mexican War is only a faint background for the dashing hero's pursuit of the wealthy and beautiful girl. Of course, there is an abduction, a betrayal, a capture, an imprisonment, and a rescue, but the hero and heroine survive to "live happily ever after."

957 CURTISS, DANIEL S.

WESTERN PORTRAITURE AND EMIGRANTS' GUIDE: A
DESCRIPTION OF WISCONSIN, ILLINOIS, AND IOWA;
WITH REMARKS ON MINNESOTA, AND OTHER TERRI-
TORIES . . . NEW YORK: PUBLISHED BY J. H. COL-
TON, 1852.

[i]–xxx, [31]–351, [352 blank], 1–18 advertise-
ments. 18.3 x 11.9 cm. Map: Township Map / of the / States / of / Indiana, Illinois, / Wisconsin, Iowa, / Missouri & Minnesota. / Published by J. H. Colton / N° 86 Cedar Sᵗ New York / 1852 / 50.8 x 46.9 cm. No scale given. Green cloth, blind embossed borders on sides, title in gilt on backstrip.

Prov.: Inscribed in pencil on front endpaper: Miss Mary Rise— / With Compliments / of the Author. / 1859. / Signature in pencil on verso of map: Mrs E. W. Judd /.

Ref.: Buck 473; Howes C967; Sabin 18069

Buck calls this "one of the best descriptive books of the period."

958 CUSHING, S. W.

WILD OATS SOWINGS; OR, THE AUTOBIOGRAPHY OF
AN ADVENTURER . . . NEW-YORK: PUBLISHED BY
DANIEL FANSHAW, 1857.

[1]–483, [484 blank]. 18.9 x 11.8 cm. Four plates, unlisted. Blue-gray cloth, blind embossed sides, gilt title on backstrip.

Ref.: Clark III 30; Howes C974; Raines pp. 59–60; Sabin 18121

The author was correct in describing himself as an adventurer; he had a fantastic career which included soldiering at San Jacinto and a stint as a sailor in the Texas Navy.

959 CUSTER, ELIZABETH B.

"BOOTS AND SADDLES"; OR, LIFE IN DAKOTA WITH
GENERAL CUSTER . . . NEW YORK: HARPER &
BROTHERS, 1885.

[1]–312. 18.5 x 12.2 cm. Brown pictorial cloth, title in gilt on front cover and backstrip.

Ref.: Howes C980; Jennewein 53; Jones 1632; Malone p. 3; Rader 1010; Smith 2183

Neither portrait nor map was issued with the first printing.

960 CUSTER, ELIZABETH B.

THE SAME. With frontispiece portrait and small map.

The portrait and map were issued with later printings.

961 CUSTER, GEORGE A.

MY LIFE ON THE PLAINS. OR, PERSONAL EXPERI-
ENCES WITH THE INDIANS . . . NEW YORK: SHEL-
DON AND COMPANY, 1874.

[1]–256. (Pages [1–2] blank.) 22.6 x 14.7 cm. Eight illustrations. Green cloth, gilt and black stamping on front cover including title and blind stamping on back cover.

Ref.: Howes C981; Jones 1566; Rader 1011; Smith 2188

962 CUSTER, FORT, MONTANA

[A COLLECTION OF TWENTY-TWO BLUEPRINT PHO-
TOGRAPHS OF SCENES IN AND NEAR FORT CUSTER,
MONTANA, ABOUT 1896.] Mounted on eleven sheets of stiff paper, 11.9 x 16.8 cm.

The collection comprises the following materials:

Eight photographs mounted on one sheet.

Group of Indians seated behind windbreak. 5.5 x 14 cm.

Indian camp, with ten tepees. 5.6 x 14.8 cm.

View of railroad bridge near camp. 5 x 12.1 cm.

Indian camp, with four tepees. 9.2 x 8.5 cm.

Three barnyard scenes. 5.5 x 6.1 cm., 4.7 x 2.8 cm., 4 x 4.4 cm.

Indian. 2.7 x 1.8 cm.

Fern frond, dated in manuscript in the photograph: May 14, 1896. 11.8 x 16.7 cm.

Five photographs mounted on one sheet.
Barnyard scene. 11.4 x 9.5 cm.
Indians dancing. 7 x 13.7 cm.
Horses on bank of stream. 7.4 x 12.5 cm.
Cow. 7 x 3.7 cm.
Horses and wagon. 5 x 5.7 cm.

Two Indian tepees. 11.9 x 16.7 cm.

Two photographs mounted on one sheet.
Two Indians in dance costume. 11 x 7 cm.
Indian in dance costume. 9.9 x 3.6 cm.

View of Indian camp across the water. 9.8 x 15.7 cm.

View of bend in river, dam, factory, pump house, from a bluff. 11.3 x 15.5 cm.

Two photographs mounted on one sheet.
Two Indian tepees, women working in foreground. 9.3 x 7.8 cm.
Two Indian tepees. 9.3 x 7.8 cm.

Cow before log cabin (or barn). 3.6 x 4.8 cm.

Manuscript note: Finis. / Fort Custer, / Montana. / W. C. S. / E. E. P. S. / 11.9 x 16.8 cm. *Photograph.*

Manuscript list of titles, probably designed for this series of photographs. 11.9 x 16.8 cm. *Photograph.*

The series of photographs bears no captions; those given above have been supplied.

963 [CUTLER, JERVIS]

A TOPOGRAPHICAL DESCRIPTION OF THE STATE OF OHIO, INDIANA TERRITORY, AND LOUISIANA. COMPREHENDING THE OHIO AND MISSISSIPPI RIVERS . . . AND A CONCISE ACCOUNT OF THE INDIAN TRIBES WEST OF THE MISSISSIPPI. TO WHICH IS ADDED, AN INTERESTING JOURNAL OF MR. CHAS. LE RAYE, WHILE A CAPTIVE WITH THE SIOUX NATION, ON THE WATERS OF THE MISSOURI RIVER . . . BOSTON: PUBLISHED BY CHARLES WILLIAMS, 1812.

1–18⁴, 19². [i]–[vi, vi blank], [7]–219, [220 blank]. 17.3 x 10.2 cm. Five engraved plates after drawings by the author. Buff boards, calf backstrip.
Ref.: Ayer 56; Bradford 1165; Buck 77; Field 395; Howes C984; Jones 752; Rader 1015; Sabin 18170; Thomson 298; Wagner-Camp 10

The view of Cincinnati used as a frontispiece is said to be the first engraved view of the city.

The plates are on rather thick paper. An extraordinarily fine copy.

Pages 149–52 are inverted and in reverse order.

964 [CUTLER, JERVIS]

ANOTHER COPY. Contemporary mottled sheepskin, new calf backstrip and red leather label.

The plates appear on thinner paper than in the preceding copy.

965 CUTTS, JAMES M.

THE CONQUEST OF CALIFORNIA AND NEW MEXICO, BY THE FORCES OF THE UNITED STATES, IN THE YEARS 1846 & 1847 . . . PHILADELPHIA: PUBLISHED BY CAREY & HART, 1847.

[1]–264. 18.6 x 11.5 cm. Engraved frontispiece, title-page, and four maps and plans included in the text. Black cloth, blind embossed sides, title in gilt on backstrip.
Ref.: Bradford 1169; Cowan p. 154; Edwards p. 46; Howes C989; Jones 1145; Munk (Alliot) p. 60; Rader 1016; Sabin 18208; Saunders 2861; Wagner-Camp 131

D

966 DABNEY, OWEN P.

TRUE STORY OF THE LOST SHACKLE; OR, SEVEN YEARS WITH THE INDIANS . . .

[i–vi], [1]–98. 19.1 x 13.1 cm. Illustrations unlisted. Blue pictorial wrappers with title on front wrapper.
Ref.: Ayer (*Supp.*) 38; Howes (1954) 2527; Rader 1017; Smith 2200

Copyrighted 1897. Published in Salem, Oregon. Laid in is a pictorial postcard, printed in green, bearing a poem by Dabney: Your Sweetheart and Mine / . . . Hood River, Oregon, U.S.A.

967 DACUS, JOSEPH A.

ILLUSTRATED LIVES AND ADVENTURES OF FRANK AND JESSE JAMES AND THE YOUNGER BROTHERS, THE NOTED WESTERN OUTLAWS . . . NEW YORK AND ST. LOUIS: N. D. THOMPSON & COMPANY, 1882.

[i]–xviii, [13]–[520]. 18 x 12.2 cm. 64 illustrations listed. Rebound in brown half levant morocco, gilt backstrip.
Ref.: Howes D6

Extra-illustrated with a card, signed in pencil, by Frank James, nine original photographs of members of the gangs, etc., five engraved portraits, and three newspaper articles.

Editions: St. Louis, 1880, 1881. Cincinnati, 1881. Etc.

968 DAGGETT, THOMAS F.

BILLY LEROY, THE COLORADO BANDIT; OR, THE KING OF AMERICAN HIGHWAYMEN! . . . NEW YORK: PUBLISHED BY RICHARD K. FOX.

[1]–66, [67–76]. (Page [1] blank, [22] frontispiece.) 44.2 x 16.1 cm. Frontispiece and 22 full-page plates. Yellow printed wrappers with title on front wrapper, advertisements on verso of front wrapper and recto and verso of back wrapper.

Ref.: Adams 280; Dykes 15; Howes D8

Originally written about a Colorado bandit, *Billy LeRoy* was advertised in the *National Police Gazette* as a life of Billy the Kid. Some of the New Mexico episodes resemble events in the life of the Kid—but not closely. Dykes lists two earlier editions of this work, but seems to have been unable to locate copies. The only copy of the present edition he found is in the Library of Congress.

Editions: New York, 1881, 1881 (publication presumed from newspaper advertisements).

969 DAILY CHICAGO AMERICAN

[Newspaper] DAILY CHICAGO AMERICAN. VOL. I. FRIDAY, JUNE 7 [SATURDAY, JUNE 15], 1839. NO. 52, [59] . . .*

[1–4]. [1–4]. 46.2 x 19.7 cm. Two issues, unbound.

Ref.:

William Stuart was the editor and publisher.

970 DAILY COLORADO TIMES, THE (Central City)

[Newspaper] THE DAILY COLORADO TIMES. VOLUME I. CENTRAL CITY, COLORADO, SATURDAY, MAY 18, 1867. NUMBER 140 . . .

[1–4]. 55.4 x 41 cm. Unbound.

Ref.: McMurtrie & Allen (*Colorado*) p. 235

Henry Garbanati and O. J. Goldbrick were the editors. The newspaper was begun at Black Hawk in December, 1866, transferred to Central City in April of the next year, and discontinued under this title by January of 1868. McMurtrie & Allen list no copies of this issue.

971 DAILY GAZETTE (Galena, Illinois)

[Broadside newspaper] DAILY GAZETTE—EXTRA. GALENA, OCTOBER 10TH, 3 O'CLOCK. GREAT CHICAGO FIRE. THE FIRE OUT! . . .

Broadside newspaper, 38.8 x 14 cm. Text, 35.8 x 11.1 cm.

Ref.:

Published in 1871.

972 DAILY MINING JOURNAL, THE (Black Hawk, Colorado)

[Newspaper] THE DAILY MINING JOURNAL. VOLUME III. BLACK HAWK, COLORADO, SATURDAY, JANUARY 13, 1866. NUMBER 34 . . .

[1–4]. 55.1 x 40.2 cm. Unbound.

Ref.: McMurtrie & Allen (*Colorado*) p. 225

Ovando J. Hollister was the editor and publisher at this time. (See also item 1937.) McMurtrie & Allen located only one other copy of the January 13, 1866 issue.

973 DAILY SNORT (Brownville, Nebraska Territory)

[Newspaper] DAILY SNORT. BROWNVILLE, N. T. JAN. 21, 1859. LANGDON & GOFF EDITORS AND PROPRIETORS . . .

[1–4]. 11.3 x 7.4 cm. Unbound.

Ref.:

Possibly this is the only issue of the *Daily Snort*. It may have been occasioned by a shortage of paper (mentioned in the text) at one of the four regular papers published at Brownville, Nebraska Territory. It is a good example of frontier newspaper humor.

974 DAILY TELEGRAPH, THE (Omaha, Nebraska Territory)

[Newspaper] THE DAILY TELEGRAPH. OMAHA, N. T. . . . COUNCIL BLUFFS. VOLUME 1. WEDNESDAY MORNING, FEBRUARY, 20. 1861. NUMBER 64 . . .

[1–2]. 32.5 x 25.5 cm. Unbound.

Ref.:

Henry Z. Curtis was the editor-proprietor. The paper was published simultaneously at Omaha and Council Bluffs. This issue contains the Inaugural Address of Jefferson Davis.

975 DAKOTA TERRITORY. Board of Immigration

[Map] MAP OF DAKOTA. / DRAWN FROM OFFICIAL PLATS OF SURVEYS IN THE SURVEYOR GENERAL'S OFFICE, MARCH 1ST, 1876, BY A. W. BARBER, FOR THE BOARD OF IMMIGRATION. / [lower left:] RAND, MC NALLY & CO., / MAP ENGRAVERS, CHICAGO. / [below neat line:] PAMPHLETS GIVING FULL INFORMATION FURNISHED FREE, BY ADDRESSING FRED. J. CROSS, SUPERINTENDENT OF IMMIGRATION, YANKTON, DAKOTA. /

Map, 40 x 35.5 cm. Scale: 30 miles to one inch. Printed on pink paper.

Ref.:

There are several manuscript notations on the face of the map, the inscription: Col. Wm. Wood U. S. Army / appears at the foot of the map, and on the verso there is: Mrs. Wm. H. Wood /.

The pamphlets mentioned in the last line of the description above are in the Graff Collection, items 933–34.

976 DAKOTA TERRITORY. COMMIS-SIONER OF IMMIGRATION (Frank H. Hagerty)

1889. THE TERRITORY OF DAKOTA: THE STATE OF NORTH DAKOTA; THE STATE OF SOUTH DAKOTA; AN OFFICIAL STATISTICAL, HISTORICAL AND POLITICAL ABSTRACT . . . ABERDEEN, S. D.: DAILY NEWS PRINT, 1889.

[1]–119, [120 blank], [1]–90, [1]–102. 22 x 14.7 cm. Black cloth.

Ref.: Allen (*Dakota*) 683; Howes H14
The three parts were also issued separately.
This publication, the last to be issued by this as a territorial office, contains much general and statistical matter, gathered with difficulty owing to the small fund given for the purpose.—Introduction

977 DAKOTA TERRITORY. GOVERNOR (Andrew J. Faulk)

SIXTH ANNUAL SESSION. FIRST ANNUAL MESSAGE . . . TO THE LEGISLATIVE ASSEMBLY, OF THE TERRITORY OF DAKOTA. DELIVERED, DECEMBER 1866. YANKTON, DAKOTA TERRITORY: GEO. W. KINGSBURY, 1866.

[1]–13, [14–16 blank]. 23.2 x 13.6 cm. Gray printed wrappers with title on front wrapper, partly unopened.

Ref.: Allen (*Dakota*) 36; Sabin 18297

978 DAKOTA TERRITORY. GOVERNOR (Andrew J. Faulk)

SEVENTH ANNUAL SESSION. SECOND ANNUAL MESSAGE . . . TO THE LEGISLATIVE ASSEMBLY OF THE TERRITORY OF DAKOTA. DELIVERED, DECEMBER 1867. YANKTON, DAKOTA TERRITORY: GEO. W. KINGSBURY, 1867.

[1]–20. 22.3 x 13.5 cm. Green printed wrappers with title on front wrapper.

Ref.: Allen (*Dakota*) 51
Contains the earliest known printed reference to the separation of Laramie and Carter counties from Dakota Territory to form the new Territory of Wyoming.—Allen

979 DAKOTA TERRITORY. GOVERNOR (Andrew J. Faulk)

EIGHTH ANNUAL SESSION. THIRD ANNUAL MESSAGE TO THE LEGISLATIVE ASSEMBLY OF THE TERRITORY OF DAKOTA. DELIVERED, DECEMBER 1868. YANKTON, DAKOTA TERRITORY: GEO. W. KINGSBURY, 1868.

[1]–14, [15–16 blank]. 22.2 x 12.7 cm. Yellow printed wrappers, with title on front wrapper.
Ref.: Allen (*Dakota*) 58; Sabin 18297

980 DAKOTA TERRITORY. GOVERNOR (Andrew J. Faulk)

[Broadside] PROCLAMATION! TO THE PEOPLE OF DAKOTA TERRITORY: THE UNDERSIGNED, GOVERNOR OF SAID TERRITORY, IS INSTRUCTED BY A CIRCULAR LETTER, FROM LIEUT-GEN'L W. T. SHERMAN, COMMANDING THIS MILITARY DIVISION, THAT IF DAKOTA WILL ORGANIZE A BATTALIAN OF MOUNTED MEN, READY TO BE CALLED INTO THE SERVICE OF THE UNITED STATES, IT WILL BE CALLED FOR BY THE DEPARTMENT COMMANDER, GEN'L TERRY, . . . A. J. FAULK. EXECUTIVE OFFICE, YANKTON, D. T., JULY 10, 1876.

Broadside, 31.7 x 19.5 cm. Text, 25.8 x 17 cm.
Ref.: Allen (*Dakota*) 52
There is an autograph manuscript note on the verso, in pencil, in an unidentified hand relating to Indian affairs in Dakota.

981 DAKOTA TERRITORY. GOVERNOR (Andrew J. Faulk)

[Caption title] TERRITORY OF DAKOTA. BY THE GOVERNOR. A PROCLAMATION . . . A. J. FAULK. ATTEST: S. L. SPINK, SECRETARY.

[1–4]. (Pages [2–3] blank.) 24.6 x 19 cm. Unbound.

Ref.: Allen (*Dakota*) 59
Thanksgiving Day proclamation for November 26, 1868.

982 DAKOTA TERRITORY. GOVERNOR (William Jayne)

SECOND ANNUAL MESSAGE OF GOVERNOR WILLIAM JAYNE, DELIVERED TO THE LEGISLATIVE ASSEMBLY OF DAKOTA TERRITORY, IN JOINT CONVENTION, ON THURSDAY, DECEMBER 18, 1862. YANKTON, DAKOTA TERRITORY: KINGSBURY & ZIEBACH, 1862.

[1]–8. 22.8 x 13.5 cm. Unbound, unopened.

Ref.: Allen (*Dakota*) 3
The second pamphlet printed in Dakota. Devoted entirely to Indian affairs and protection for the people of the Territory.

983 DAKOTA TERRITORY. GOVERNOR (Arthur C. Mellette)

[Broadside] PROCLAMATION. TERRITORY OF DAKOTA, EXECUTIVE DEPARTMENT. THE PRESIDENT OF THE UNITED STATES HAS SET APART TUESDAY, THE 30TH OF APRIL, 1889, THE SAME BEING THE FIRST CENTENNIAL DAY OF THE INAUGURATION OF GEORGE WASHINGTON . . . BISMARCK, THE CAPITAL, ON THIS EIGHTEENTH DAY OF APRIL, IN THE YEAR OF OUR LORD ONE THOUSAND EIGHT HUN-

DRED AND EIGHTY-NINE. ARTHUR C. MELLETTE, GOVERNOR. L. B. RICHARDSON, SECRETARY.

Broadside, 15.7 x 6.9 cm. Text, 12.3 x 5.4 cm.

Ref.: Allen (*Dakota*) 689

Seemingly printed from type taken from the columns of a newspaper.—Allen

984 DAKOTA TERRITORY. GOVERNOR (Nehemiah G. Ordway)

MESSAGE . . . TO THE LEGISLATIVE ASSEMBLY, FOURTEENTH SESSION, JANUARY, 1881. YANKTON: BOWEN AND KINGSBURY, 1881.

[1]–32. 21.3 x 14.6 cm. Tan printed wrappers, with title on front wrapper.

Ref.: Allen (*Dakota*) 202

Tipped in before page [3] is a slip, 3.9 x 9 cm.: Compliments of / N. G. Ordway /.

This is Ordway's first biennial message.

985 DAKOTA TERRITORY. GOVERNOR (John L. Pennington)

[Caption title] CIRCULAR TO THE FARMERS, MANU-FACTURERS AND MINERS OF DAKOTA TERRITORY. YANKTON, AUG. 20, 1877. . . .

[1–4]. (Pages [2–3] blank.) 27.8 x 21.5 cm. Unbound.

Ref.:

Page [1] is a call for materials to form an exhibition of Dakota products for the National Immigration Bureau in Philadelphia signed by Governor Pennington and I. E. West. Page [4] is a circular advertising the Bureau signed by Lee Crandall.

986 DAKOTA TERRITORY. LEGISLA-TIVE ASSEMBLY

MANUAL FOR THE USE OF THE LEGISLATIVE ASSEM-BLY OF THE TERRITORY OF DAKOTA, FOR THE YEAR 1866-7 . . . YANKTON, DAKOTA TERRITORY: GEO. W. KINGSBURY, 1866.

[1]–47, [48 blank]. 22.3 x 13.2 cm. Green wrappers with title on front wrapper.

Ref.: Allen (*Dakota*) 39

Inserted facing page 24 is a broadside headed: Amendments to the Organic Act. / [decorative rule] / [40 lines] / 18.3 x 11 cm.

The only copy located.

987 DAKOTA. CONSTITUTIONAL CONVENTION

[Wrapper title] DAKOTA CONSTITUTIONAL CON-VENTION, SIOUX FALLS. RULES, ORDER OF BUSINESS AND STANDING COMMITTEES. SEPTEMBER, 1883. SIOUX FALLS, DAK.: DAILY PRESS NEWS, 1883.

[1–4]. 22.9 x 14.7 cm. White printed wrappers with title on front wrapper.

Ref.: Allen (*Dakota*) 252

988 DAKOTA TAWAXITKU KIN

[Caption title] DAKOTA TAWAXITKU KIN; OR, THE DAKOTA FRIEND. PUBLISHED MONTHLY BY THE DAKOTA MISSION.—G. H. POND, EDITOR. VOL. II. ST. PAUL, MINNESOTA TERRITORY, JANUARY 1 [–AUGUST], 1852. NO. I [–VIII] . . .

Eight numbers, each [1–4]. 40.5 x 27.6 cm. Illustrated. Eight leaflets, unbound.

Ref.: Butler (*Dakota*) 65; Pilling 3029; Pond, S. W., Jr.: *Two Volunteer Missionaries* . . . Boston [1893], p. 206; Sabin 18286

The first two pages of most numbers are printed in the Santee Dakota language and the last two pages in English. The leaflets were printed at the Office of the Minnesota Democrat.

No. VIII contains the following note: The Dakota Mission deem it unadvisable, while the Indians are so unsettled, to continue the Friend.

Pond misdates the last issue as August, 1851.

989 DAKOTA TERRITORIAL AGRICUL-TURAL SOCIETY

[Broadside] DAKOTA TERRITORIAL AGRICULTURAL SOCIETY. SECRETARY'S OFFICE, YANKTON, AUG. 17, 1877 . . . THE DAKOTA TERRITORIAL AGRICUL-TURAL SOCIETY HAVE DECIDED UPON HOLDING THEIR ANNUAL EXHIBITION . . . ON THE 3D, 4TH AND 5TH DAYS OF OCTOBER, 1877 . . . VERY RE-SPECTFULLY YOURS, SECRETARY.

Broadside, 26.7 x 20.3 cm. Text, 20.6 x 16 cm.

Ref.: Allen (*Dakota*) 144

The only copy located.

990 DAKOTAH (*pseudonym*)

[Broadside] SAINT PAUL, M. T., DECEMBER 15, 1851. SIR: WE HAVE JUST RECEIVED THE LAST RE-PORT OF THE HON. L. LEE, COMMISSIONER OF IN-DIAN AFFAIRS AT WASHINGTON CITY, . . . DAKO-TAH.

Broadside, 41 x 27 cm. Text, 36 x 26.8 cm.

Prov.: Rubber stamp on verso: M Y Johnson 12/1921 /. Formerly in the collections of the Chicago Historical Society.

Ref.:

The text comprises an attack on the Indian policy of the Federal Government.

991 DALLAM, JAMES W.

THE LONE STAR: A TALE OF TEXAS; FOUNDED UPON INCIDENTS IN THE HISTORY OF TEXAS . . . NEW YORK: E. FERRETT & CO., 1845.

[1]–95, [96 blank]. 24.5 x 15.1 cm. Tan printed wrappers with title on front wrapper, advertise-ments on verso of front and recto and verso of back wrapper. Label removed from imprint on front wrapper.

Ref.: Rader 1045; Raines p. 60; Streeter 1578; Wright I 818

992 DALLY, NATHAN

TRACKS AND TRAILS; OR, INCIDENTS IN THE LIFE OF A MINNESOTA TERRITORIAL PIONEER . . . WALKER, MINN.: THE CASS COUNTY PIONEER.

[i–vi, vi blank], [1]–138, [139 map, 140 blank]. 22.4 x 15.1 cm. 12 illustrations listed, unlisted map. Light brown wrappers. In a red cloth case.

Ref.: Howes D31

Copyrighted 1931. Contains material on steamboating on Leech Lake in north-central Minnesota.

993 DALTON, KIT

UNDER THE BLACK FLAG . . . A CONFEDERATE SOLDIER, A GUERRILLA CAPTAIN UNDER THE FEARLESS LEADER QUANTRELL, AND A BORDER OUTLAW FOR SEVENTEEN YEARS . . .

[1]–252. 19.3 x 13.5 cm. Illustrations unlisted. White pictorial wrappers, advertisement on recto of back wrapper.

Ref.: Adams 286; Rader 1048

At foot of frontispiece (which is dated 1910): Copyright Applied for / Lockard Publishing Company / Memphis, Tenn. / The work was published in 1914.

994 DAMON, SAMUEL C.

A TRIP FROM THE SANDWICH ISLANDS TO LOWER OREGON AND UPPER CALIFORNIA; OR, THIRTY LEAVES SELECTED FROM "OUR LOG-BOOK." . . . HONOLULU, OAHU, H. I.: PRINTED AT THE POLYNESIAN OFFICE, 1849.

[i–ii], [41]–44, [49]–51, 57–60, [65]–68, [73]–75, [81]–84, [89]–91. 29 x 23.2 cm. Rebound in half brown calf.

Ref.: Cowan p. 155; Howes D44; Matthews p. 315

The author's vivid descriptions cover Northwest United States from the Columbia River to San Francisco. The volume comprises a contemporary title-page and pertinent leaves from the periodical *The Friend* (of which the author was editor), volume 7, numbers 6–12.

995 DANA, C. W.

THE GARDEN OF THE WORLD, OR THE GREAT WEST; ITS HISTORY, ITS WEALTH, ITS NATURAL ADVANTAGES, AND ITS FUTURE. ALSO, COMPRISING A COMPLETE GUIDE TO EMIGRANTS . . . BOSTON: WENTWORTH AND COMPANY, 1856.

[1]–[8, 8 blank], [13]–396. 18.1 x 12.1 cm. Plum cloth.

Ref.: Buck 564; Cowan p. 155; Howes (1954)

2571; Rader 1051; Smith 2244; Wagner-Camp 279a

The note in Wagner-Camp 279a gives an erroneous description of the contents. Buck 564 is better.

996 DANA, EDMUND

A DESCRIPTION OF THE BOUNTY LANDS IN THE STATE OF ILLINOIS: ALSO, THE PRINCIPAL ROADS AND ROUTES, BY LAND AND WATER, THROUGH THE TERRITORY OF THE UNITED STATES; EXTENDING FROM THE PROVINCE OF NEW-BRUNSWIC[!], IN NOVA SCOTIA, TO THE PACIFIC OCEAN . . . CINCINNATI: LOOKER, REYNOLDS & CO., 1819.

[A]–I⁶. [1]–108. 19.8 x 11.5 cm. Map: Map / of / The Military / Bounty Lands / in the State of / Illinois, / from actual survey, / By Edmund Dana & John McDonald, / who surveyed the Land. / Gridley Sc. / 53.3 x 34.3 cm. Scale: 9 3/4 miles to one inch. Gray boards, uncut.

Ref.: AII (*Ohio*) 474; Buck 135; Howes D46; Jones 807; Rusk II 138; Sabin 18407; Thomson 305

Copies with the map are very uncommon. The second part carries its own title-page on page [49]: Description / of the / Principal / Roads and Routes, / by Land and Water, / through the Territory of the United States . . . 1819. /

997 DANA, EDMUND

GEOGRAPHICAL SKETCHES ON THE WESTERN COUNTRY: DESIGNED FOR EMIGRANTS AND SETTLERS: BEING THE RESULT OF EXTENSIVE RESEARCHES AND REMARKS . . . CINCINNATI: LOOKER, REYNOLDS & CO., 1819.

A–Bb⁶. [i]–iv, [5]–312. 18.2 x 11.4 cm. Grayblue printed boards with title on front cover and advertisement on back cover, uncut. In orange cloth case.

Ref.: AII (*Ohio*) 475; Bradford 1183; Buck 136; Howes D47; Sabin 18408; Thomson 306

Thomson claims the work was prepared for the press by Reuben Kidder, since Dana was an "uneducated man."

998 DANA, RICHARD H., JR.

TWO YEARS BEFORE THE MAST . . . NEW-YORK: HARPER & BROTHERS, 1840.

[1]–483, [484 blank]. 15.2 x 9.3 cm. Coarse black cloth, title in gilt on backstrip. Lacks blank leaf at back. In a blue cloth case.

Ref.: Blanck 4434A; Cowan p. 156; Howes D49; Sabin 18448

The generally accepted earlier printing, with the dotted i in the copyright notice and the type undamaged in the headline on page 9.

999 DANENHOWER, WILLIAM W., *Publisher*

DANENHOWER'S CHICAGO CITY DIRECTORY, FOR 1851; CONTAINING AN ALPHABETICAL LIST OF THE MECHANICS AND BUSINESS MEN WITH THEIR SEVERAL PLACES OF RESIDENCE; ALSO, BRIEF NOTICES OF THE RELIGIOUS, LITERARY AND BENEVOLENT ASSOCIATIONS OF THE CITY, MILITARY, FIRE DEPARTMENT, ETC., ETC., ETC., ETC. CHICAGO: PUBLISHED BY W. W. DANENHOWER, 1851.

[i advertisements, ii blank], [1]–264. 17.7 x 11.2 cm. Green printed boards, new red leather backstrip, title on front cover, advertisement on back cover, advertisement mounted on inner front cover. Lacks map.

Ref.: AII (*Chicago*) 8; Byrd 1696

The introduction is dated from Chicago, December, 1850. The imprint of Jas. J. Langdon as printer appears on the verso of the title-page.

1000 [DANIELS, ARTHUR M.]

A JOURNAL OF SIBLEY'S INDIAN EXPEDITION, DURING THE SUMMER OF 1863, AND RECORD OF THE TROOPS EMPLOYED . . . WINONA, MINN.: PRINTED AT THE REPUBLICAN OFFICE, 1864.

[1]–52. 21.3 x 14.7 cm. Buff printed wrappers with title on front wrapper, advertisement on verso of back wrapper. In a blue cloth case.

Prov.: U.S. Geological Survey copy with rubber stamp on front cover and title-page partially removed.

Ref.: AII (*Minnesota*) 541; Howes D56; Sabin 80821

Both the preface and the list of errata are signed by Daniels, the latter as Q. M. Dep't. Fort Ridgely, December, 1863. AII (*Minnesota*) calls for 53 pages, probably because the second numeral of the pagination on page 52 is smudged and looks like a 3.

Pages [5]–19 comprise a day-by-day journal kept by Daniels.

1001 DANIELS, WILLIAM M.

[Wrapper title] A CORRECT ACCOUNT OF THE MURDER OF GENERALS JOSEPH AND HYRUM SMITH, AT CARTHAGE, ON THE 17TH DAY OF JUNE, 1844 . . . NAUVOO, ILL.: PUBLISHED BY JOHN TAYLOR, 1845.

[1]–24. 22.6 x 14.2 cm. Woodcut on page 7 and two woodcuts inserted between pages 14 and 15. Buff printed wrappers with title on front wrapper. Marginal repairs, corner of final leaf, not affecting text, supplied.

Ref.: Byrd 948; Howes D57; McDade 878; Woodward 48

Editions: Nauvoo, 1845 (no plates).

1002 DANIELS, WILLIAM M.

[Wrapper title] . . . THE SAME.

[1]–24. 21 x 12.5 cm. Woodcut on page 7 and two woodcuts between pages 14 and 15. Rebound in red half morocco, with original printed yellow wrappers bound in.

Prov.: Huntington duplicate, with stamp on verso of back fly-leaf.

Ref.: Byrd 948; Howes D57; McDade 878; Woodward 48

The wrapper differs from the preceding copy. There is a three-line copyright notice above the title and the paper used for the wrapper is a thin sheet, bright yellow. The preceding copy is in thick, coarse buff paper wrappers. The text is identical in both copies; the two plates are reversed.

1003 DARBY, JOHN F.

PERSONAL RECOLLECTIONS . . . RELATING TO THE HISTORY OF ST. LOUIS . . . ST. LOUIS: G. I. JONES AND COMPANY, 1880.

[i–iv, iv blank], [1]–480. 20.4 x 14 cm. Portrait. Green cloth, gilt top.

Ref.: Bradford 1189; Howes D60

Limited to 500 copies.

An intensely interesting and important book of reminiscences by a lawyer and mayor of St. Louis. His stories of legal battles in the early courts of the section remind one of Linder's book treating the same period in Illinois history. —EDG

1004 DARLINGTON, MARY C.

FORT PITT AND LETTERS FROM THE FRONTIER. PITTSBURGH: J. R. WELDIN & CO., 1892.

[1]–312. 28 x 21.4 cm. Six plates on Japan paper. Green cloth, printed white paper label.

Ref.: Howes D70

Limited to 100 copies.

1005 DAUBENY, CHARLES G. B.

JOURNAL OF A TOUR THROUGH THE UNITED STATES, AND IN CANADA, MADE DURING THE YEARS 1837–38 . . . OXFORD: PRINTED BY T. COMBE, M.DCCC.XLIII.*

[i]–vi, [1]–231, [232 blank]. 17.6 x 10.6 cm. Map: Map / of the / United States, / and of the / Canadas. / English Miles. / [diagrammatic scale: about 200 miles to one inch] / 17.8 x 23.7 cm. Blue-gray cloth, title in gilt on backstrip, marbled edges.

Prov.: Inscribed on title-page: To the British & Foreign Institute / presented / by the / Author / [double underline] /. Bookplate removed, Bookplate of Joseph S. Treacher.

Ref.: Buck 323; Clark III 149; Howes D77; Hubach p. 86; Matthews pp. 278–79; Sabin 18662

One hundred copies printed.

1006 DAUGHTERS OF TEMPERANCE
(Muscatine, Iowa)

[Broadside] [SEAL OF BLOOMINGTON UNION NO. 1, DAUGHTERS OF TEMPERANCE, MUSCATINE, IOWA, FEB. 4, 1850.]

Broadside, 19.5 x 25.2 cm. Text, 5.2 cm. diameter.

Ref.:

The lettering within the seal is as given above in white on black ground, enclosing a robed female figure trampling a snake on a rock and simultaneously pouring from a jug of wine, holding a staff surmounted by a liberty cap in the other hand; rising or setting sun in background.

1007 DAVENPORT, B. M.

RESOURCES OF NEBRASKA. A BRIEF ACCOUNT . . . AND OTHER IMPORTANT INFORMATION TO IMMIGRANTS AND OTHERS WHO DESIGN LOCATING IN THE WEST . . . NEBRASKA CITY, NEBRASKA: NEBRASKA PRESS PRINTING OFFICE, 1869.

[1]–[21], [22–4 advertisements]. 20.7 x 14.9 cm. Green printed wrappers with title on front wrapper, advertisements on verso of front and recto and verso of back wrapper.

Ref.: AII (*Nebraska*) 142; Howes D82

The author was a real estate dealer and, although he slightly exaggerated the values of the land he was selling, he knew the country he described from personal experience.

1008 DAVENPORT, GEORGE & MARGARET

DOCUMENT, SIGNED BY GEORGE DAVENPORT AND MARGARET DAVENPORT. 1841 October 29, Scott County, Iowa. One page, 38.9 x 31.2 cm.

Printed and manuscript deed conveying 80 60/100 acres of land in Iowa to Antoine Le Claire in consideration of $1500. The land later became part of the city of Davenport, Iowa. The document is signed also by L. E. Johnson as witness and as Justice of the Peace.

Both of the Davenport signatures are in the handwriting of George Davenport. According to a docket on the verso, the deed was recorded on November 5, 1841, in Book B of Deeds, page 25. The docket is signed: Jno O Evans /.

The printed form may be an unrecorded Iowa imprint, although there is no indication of place or printer on the face of the document. Enclosed in a plastic, sealed envelope and laid in a green buckram case.

1009 DAVENPORT AND IOWA CITY RAIL ROAD COMPANY

[Caption title] DAVENPORT & IOWA CITY RAILROAD. ENGINEER'S REPORT. TO LE GRAND BYINGTON AND OTHERS, DIRECTORS OF THE DAVENPORT AND IOWA CITY RAIL ROAD COMPANY: . . .

[1]–7, [8 blank]. 23.2 x 15.8 cm. Map: [Buffalo to Council Bluffs, St. Louis to Toronto]. 20.2 x 44.8 cm. (paper size). No scale given. Unbound, unopened, uncut.

Ref.:

Signed on page 7: Richard P. Morgan. / The Report is undated and there is no place of printing given. The date is probably 1850 or 1851. The style of printing suggests Chicago rather than the work of an Iowa printer.

1010 [DAVENPORT, IOWA] CITIZENS' ASSOCIATION

1874. DAVENPORT. MANUFACTURING FACILITIES AND BUSINESS WANTS. DAVENPORT, SCOTT COUNTY, IOWA . . . PUBLISHED BY THE CITIZENS' ASSOCIATION. DAVENPORT: GAZETTE COMPANY, 1874.

[1]–32. 22.6 x 14.5 cm. Map: Map of / Davenport / [flourish] showing its [flourish] / Transportation Facilities / [flourish] by Rail and River [flourish] / [decorative rule] / [lower right:] Rice, Sc—Davenport, Ia. / 19.9 x 27.5 cm. No scale given. Printed in white on green. Map: [title within flourishes] Map of / Davenport / and Vicinity / With Coal Fields / [lower right:] Rice, Sc.—Davenport, Ia. / 19.9 x 27.4 cm. No scale given. Printed in white on green. Tan printed wrappers with title on front wrapper, advertisement of Citizens' Association on verso of back wrapper.

Ref.:

1011 DAVENPORT [Iowa] GAS LIGHT & COKE COMPANY

[Wrapper title] STATEMENT OF THE DAVENPORT GAS LIGHT & COKE COMPANY IN REGARD TO LATE ADVANCE IN PRICE OF GAS, ETC., WITH CORRESPONDENCE RELATIVE THERETO. DAVENPORT: POWER PRESS OF THE DAILY GAZETTE, 1857.

[1]–8. 22.6 x 14.5 cm. Pink printed wrappers with title on front wrapper.

Ref.:

Signed on page 6: Geo. L. Davenport, / Pres't of Davenport Gas Light and Coke Co. /

1012 DAVID, ROBERT B.

MALCOLM CAMPBELL, SHERIFF . . . OF THE PLATTE VALLEY, AND OF THE FAMOUS JOHNSON COUNTY INVASION OF 1892. CASPER, WYOMING: WYOMINGANA, INC.

[1]–[366]. 19.3 x 13.3 cm. 20 plates. Blue cloth.
  Ref.: Howes D85; Malone p. 3
  Copyrighted 1932. Laid in is a series of notes
and three letters by R. A. Clevenger of Omaha,
Nebraska, relating to Malcolm Campbell. The
letters are not complimentary and dispute some
of the author's statements about his subject.
  For a different view of the Johnson County
"War" see Mercer: *Banditti of the Plains* . . .
[1894].

1013 [DAVIES, HENRY E.]

TEN DAYS ON THE PLAINS . . . NEW YORK: PRINTED
BY CROCKER & CO.
  [1–6], [9]–68. 23.5 x 15.6 cm. 18 mounted photographs of which 15 are portraits, and a folding
map. Map: Map / Showing Trail of / General
Sheridan's / Great Buffalo Hunt. / Sept. & Oct.
1871. / Crocker & Co. Stationers, 444 Broome
St. N.Y. / Scale. / [diagrammatic scale: 20 miles
to one inch] / Drawn in Engineer Office / Hd.
Qrs. Mil. Div. of the Missouri / Capt. Corps of
Engineers, U.S.A. / Distances. / [given for each
of ten days] / Total 194 Miles. / 31.8 x 58.4 cm.
Red glazed boards, black cloth backstrip title in
gilt.
  Ref.: Howes D97
  Published in 1872.
  This book, written by Gen. Henry E. Davies,
is an account of Sheridan's famous buffalo hunt
on the Plains during the fall of 1871. General
Sheridan and his guests left Chicago September
20th and the party separated there October 5th,
1871. The volume includes photographs of the
party and their guide across the plains—"the
far-famed Buffalo Bill."—EDG
  The photographs were not included in all
copies. The first of them is signed by Julien T.
Davies.

1014 DAVIS, CARLYLE C.

OLDEN TIMES IN COLORADO . . . LOS ANGELES: THE
PHILLIPS PUBLISHING COMPANY, 1916.
  [i–xvi], 1–448. 23.5 x 16 cm. 47 plates and one
map unlisted. Dark green limp morocco, gilt,
gilt top, uncut.
  Ref.: Howes D105; Wilcox p. 36
  De Luxe Edition, signed by the author.

1015 DAVIS, GARRETT

[Caption title] EXTRACT FROM THE SPEECH OF MR.
GARRET[!] DAVIS, OF KENTUCKY, EXHIBITING THE
EXPENDITURES OF MR. VAN BUREN'S ADMINISTRA-
TIONS . . . APRIL 5, 1844 . . .
  [1]–8. Bound with Number 1084.
  Ref.: Sabin 18818
  Printed in Washington in 1844.

1016 DAVIS, GARRETT

[Caption title] . . . REPORT OF THE MINORITY . . .
MR. GARRETT DAVIS . . . MADE THE FOLLOWING
REPORT . . .
  [1]–16. Bound with Number 1084.
  Ref.:
  28th Congress, 1st Session, House, Report
No. 60 [*bis*]. Serial 445. [Washington, 1844.]

1017 DAVIS, GEORGE T. M.

AUTOBIOGRAPHY OF THE LATE COL. GEO. T. M.
DAVIS, CAPTAIN AND AID-DE-CAMP, SCOTT'S ARMY
OF INVASION (MEXICO) . . . NEW YORK, 1891.
  [1]–395, [396 blank]. (Pages [1–2] blank.)
18.2 x 12.2 cm. Dark blue cloth, title in gilt on
front cover, author's name on backstrip.
  Prov.: Printed slip on front endleaf: Compli-
ments of the legal representatives of Col. Davis, /
Mrs. Ellen D. Cady, / . . . / Mrs. Susan Train
Gulager, / . . . / Inscribed on front endleaf:
For / Dr Charles Lee— / April / 91. /
  Ref.: Howes D113; Hubach p. 75
  Contains material about the Mormons in Il-
linois, the Lovejoy murder, the War Depart-
ment, and the Civil War, as well as the Mexican
War.

1018 DAVIS, HENRY T.

SOLITARY PLACES MADE GLAD: BEING OBSERVA-
TIONS AND EXPERIENCES FOR THIRTY-TWO YEARS
IN NEBRASKA; WITH SKETCHES AND INCIDENTS
TOUCHING THE DISCOVERY, EARLY SETTLEMENT,
AND DEVELOPMENT OF THE STATE . . . CINCIN-
NATI: PRINTED FOR THE AUTHOR BY CRANSTON &
STOWE, 1890.
  [1]–422. 18.2 x 12 cm. Portrait. Brown cloth.
  Ref.: Howes D114
  A fine copy of an interesting account of early
Nebraska settlements. Contains an account of
the author's trip across the plains in the spring of
1850 from South Bend, Indiana, to Weaverville,
California.—EDG

1019 DAVIS, W. B.

[Broadside] A NEW WAY TO ACQUIRE CUBA. MR.
EDITOR:—I ASK LEAVE TO PRESENT THE SUBJECT OF
CUBA AND A PACIFIC RAIL ROAD . . . RESPECT-
FULLY, W. B. DAVIS. WILMINGTON, N. C., APRIL
18, 1859.
  Broadside, 46 x 20.3 cm. Text, 38.7 x 13.1 cm.
  Ref.:
  Davis advocated the building of a railroad
from the Atlantic across the isthmus of Florida
to the mouth of the Arkansas River, thus saving
our commerce between Texas and the Atlantic
seaboard from the guns of Spain in Cuba. The
price of Cuba would thus be reduced, or Spain
would live in peace as our neighbor.—EDG

1020   DAVIS, WILLIAM H.

SIXTY YEARS IN CALIFORNIA: A HISTORY OF EVENTS
AND LIFE IN CALIFORNIA; PERSONAL, POLITICAL
AND MILITARY . . . SAN FRANCISCO: A. J. LEARY,
1889.*

[i]–xxii, [1]–639, [640 blank]. 21.4 x 14.4 cm.
Dark red cloth, marbled edges.

  Ref.: Adams (*Ramp. Herd*) 659; Barrett 647;
Blumann & Thomas 67; Bradford 1234; Cowan
pp. 160–61; Howes D136; Zamorano Eighty 27

1021   DAVIS, WILLIAM W. H.

EL GRINGO; OR, NEW MEXICO AND HER PEOPLE . . .
NEW YORK: HARPER & BROTHERS, 1857.

[i]–xii, [13]–432. 19.5 x 12.6 cm. 13 illustrations
listed. Blue-gray cloth, blind embossed sides,
gilt title on backstrip.

  Ref.: Dobie p. 76; Howes D139; Munk (Alliot) p. 63; Rader 1073; Raines p. 64; Saunders
4013

1022   DAVIS, WILLIAM W. H.

THE SPANIARD IN NEW MEXICO . . . DOYLESTOWN,
PA., 1888.

[1]–21, [22–4 blank]. 22.5 x 14.2 cm. Pale salmon
printed wrappers with title on front wrapper. In
brown cloth case.

  Prov.: Inscribed on front cover: Compliments of / W. W. H. Davis, / Doylestown, Pa. /
June 30: 1890. /

  Ref.: Munk (Alliot) p. 63; Rader 1074;
Saunders 3357

  Separate from the American Historical Association *Journal*.

1023   DAVIS, WILLIAM W. H.

THE SPANISH CONQUEST OF NEW MEXICO . . .
DOYLESTOWN, PA., 1869.

[i]–[xvi, xvi blank], [17]–438. 23.7 x 14.7 cm.
Portrait and map: Map of / New Mexico, /
showing the routes of Niza, / Coronado, Ruiz,
and Espejo. / Drawn according to the original
boundaries established by Congress. / 35.3 x
49.7 cm. No scale indicated. Green cloth, top
edges uncut.

  Prov.: Signed on front endleaf: Maj. Gen.
H. G. Sickel / [flourish] /.

  Ref.: Howes D141; Munk (Alliot) p. 63;
Rader 1075; Raines p. 65; Saunders 2488

1024   DAVIS, WINFIELD J.

. . . HISTORY OF POLITICAL CONVENTIONS IN CALI-
FORNIA, 1849–1892 . . . SACRAMENTO, 1893.

[i–vi], [1]–711, [712 blank]. 22.2 x 14.7 cm.
Brown cloth.

  Ref.: Cowan p. 161; Howes D142; Zamorano
Eighty 28

  Inserted before page [1] is a small errata slip,
7.5 x 14.7 cm. Davis was state historian of California.

1025   DAWSON, CHARLES

PIONEER TALES OF THE OREGON TRAIL AND OF JEF-
FERSON COUNTY . . . TOPEKA: CRANE & COMPANY,
1912.*

[i]–[xvi, xvi blank], 1–488. 22.9 x 14.9 cm. 80 illustrations listed. Printed yellow cloth.

  Ref.: Adams 291; Howes D150; Smith 2336

  Although the last line on page 488 reads: The
End of Vol. I. /, a second volume was not published.

1026   DAWSON, MOSES

A HISTORICAL NARRATIVE OF THE CIVIL AND MILI-
TARY SERVICES OF MAJOR-GENERAL WILLIAM H.
HARRISON, AND A VINDICATION OF HIS CHARACTER
AND CONDUCT AS A STATESMAN, A CITIZEN, AND A
SOLDIER . . . CINCINNATI: PRINTED BY M. DAW-
SON, AT THE ADVERTISER OFFICE, 1824.

[i]–viii, 1–464, [465–72]. 22.7 x 13.7 cm. Blue
boards, tan paper back, with printed white paper
label, 5.3 x 3.8 cm. Binding chipped, pages 137–
38 mended. In a green half morocco case.

  Ref.: Buley I, p. 61, II, pp. 555, 644; Howes
D158; Sabin 18956

  Not only the principal contemporary authority on Harrison, but also one of the most exhaustive and dependable sources on events of the war
of 1812 in the western country, Tecumseh's up-
rising, etc.—Howes

  The errata slip, 8.8 x 12.4 cm., inserted at the
back differs from the example in the ICN (Ayer)
copy since the present copy carries twenty-four
lines and the Ayer copy fifteen only.

1027   DAWSON, NICHOLAS

CALIFORNIA IN '41. TEXAS IN '51. MEMOIRS . . .

[1]–119, [120 blank]. 16.6 x 10.8 cm. Purple
cloth, title in gilt on front cover, beveled covers,
sprinkled edges. In a red cloth case.

  Ref.: Adams (*Ramp. Herd*) 661; Cowan p.
161; Howes D159; Rader 1084

  One of about fifty copies printed at Austin,
Texas, in 1901. On page 101 the date January,
1901, is mentioned.

  Dawson was a member of the first (1841) immigrant train to California as was General Bidwell. He stayed in California until 1843, when he
returned East via San Blas, Mexico City, Vera
Cruz, and New Orleans. In March, 1849, he went
overland to California again, from Sherman,
Texas, via El Paso and the southern route, ar-

riving at the Mariposa Diggings about November 1. He returned to his home in Arkansas via Panama in May, 1851, and the same year settled near Austin, Texas, where he continued to live for the next fifty years or more.—EDG

The present copy contains corrections by Dawson's daughter in manuscript. It was secured from one of Dawson's sons.

1028 DAWSON, THOMAS F., & F. J. V. SKIFF

THE UTE WAR: A HISTORY OF THE WHITE RIVER MASSACRE AND THE PRIVATIONS AND HARDSHIPS OF THE CAPTIVE WHITE WOMEN AMONG THE HOSTILES ON GRAND RIVER . . . 1879. PRINTED BY HERMAN BECKURTS, PROPRIETOR, DENVER, COLORADO: THE TRIBUNE PUBLISHING HOUSE, 1879.

[1]–192. 22.6 x 14.5 cm. Illustrations unlisted. Gray printed wrappers with title on front wrapper. In a red cloth case.
Prov.: Inscribed on title-page: E. B. Morgan copy / in pencil. Rubber stamp of State Historical and Natural History Society on front wrapper and title-page.
Ref.: Ayer (*Supp.*) 42; Howes D161; Jones 1601; Wilcox p. 37

The authors of this scarce work were the editors of the *Denver Tribune.* Pages [185]–192 carry advertisements.

1029 DAY, LUELLA

THE TRAGEDY OF THE KLONDIKE . . . THE TRUE FACTS OF WHAT TOOK PLACE IN THE GOLD-FIELDS UNDER BRITISH RULE . . . NEW YORK, 1906.*

[1–4], [i–ii, ii blank], 5–181, [182 blank]. 18.7 x 13.1 cm. Illustrations unlisted. Blue cloth, fore and lower edges uncut.
Ref.: Smith 2346; Wickersham 4307

Above the place of publication on the title-page appears a rubber-stamped line: Luella Day Publishing Co., /.

1030 DEADWOOD, DAKOTA TERRITORY. Board of Trade

[Wrapper title] THE BLACK HILLS OF DAKOTA, 1881. DEADWOOD, D. T.: "DAILY PIONEER," BOOK AND JOB OFFICE.

[1]–44, [45–54 advertisements]. 20.7 x 13.4 cm. Tan printed wrappers with title on front wrapper, cut of miners on verso of back wrapper.
Prov.: Rubber stamps and manuscript notes of Department of Agriculture Library on front wrapper and page [3].
Ref.: Allen (*Dakota*) 210

Published in 1881. Pages [25]–44 carry: Lecture Delivered / —by— / Edwin Van Cise, / —on the— / Resources of the Black Hills. /

1031 DEADWOOD, DAKOTA TERRITORY. CHARTER

AN ACT TO INCORPORATE THE CITY OF DEADWOOD, DAKOTA TERRITORY. DEADWOOD: EVENING PRESS PUBLISHING COMPANY, 1881.

[1]–27, [28 blank]. 21.3 x 14.9 cm. Blue glazed wrappers with title in gilt on front wrapper.
Ref.: Allen (*Dakota*) 211

1032 DEARBORN, HENRY A. S.

LETTERS ON THE INTERNAL IMPROVEMENTS AND COMMERCE OF THE WEST . . . BOSTON: DUTTON AND WENTWORTH, 1839.

[1]–119, [120 errata]. 24 x 14.3 cm. Blue printed wrappers with title on front wrapper. In a blue cloth case.
Ref.: Buck 331; Howes D176; Sabin 19076

The edition published in Boston by Lewis in the same year comprises only 75 pages. The present edition seems to be a privately printed edition.
Editions: Boston: Lewis, 1839.

1033 DEARBORN, R. H.

AUTOGRAPH MANUSCRIPT RECEIPT, SIGNED. 1863 April 1, Umpqua County, Oregon. One page, 16.5 x 19.8 cm.

Receipt by Loren L. Williams' successor in the county clerkship for money turned in by Williams. Inserted in Manuscript Journals of Loren L. Williams, Volume III.

1034 DEATON, L. B.

ELEVEN MONTHS OF EXILE LIFE IN SOUTHERN ILLINOIS . . . CHICAGO: PRINTED FOR THE AUTHOR, 1862.

[i]–[vi], [7]–128. 21.2 x 14.1 cm. Rebound in brown cloth, dark brown morocco backstrip. Portion of title-leaf supplied, including three letters of imprint.
Ref.: Howes D180

The author, an itinerant Methodist minister, left his Tennessee home accompanied by his son at the outbreak of the Civil War to enlist in the Union Army in Illinois. Rejected because of his hearing, he spent many months traveling in six southern Illinois counties preaching and attending religious meetings. He had numerous troubles with Confederate sympathizers. A splendid picture of life at that time in Illinois.—EDG

1035 DE BARTHE, JOE

THE LIFE AND ADVENTURES OF FRANK GROUARD, CHIEF OF SCOUTS, U.S.A. . . . ST. JOSEPH, MO.: COMBE PRINTING COMPANY.*

[i]–xii, [13]–545, [546 blank]. 22.2 x 14.7 cm. 68 illustrations, unlisted. Red pictorial cloth, title on front cover and backstrip.

Ref.: Adams 294; Howes D183; Jennewein 70; Jones 1669; Rader 1090

Copyrighted 1894.

1036   DE CORDOVA, JACOB

THE TEXAS IMMIGRANT AND TRAVELLER'S GUIDE BOOK . . . AUSTIN: DE CORDOVA & FRAZIER, 1856.

[1]–103, [104 blank]. 17.7 x 11.3 cm. Black cloth, blind embossed sides with title in gilt on front cover.

Ref.: Bradford 1263 note; Howes D202; Rader 1099; Raines p. 65; Winkler 686

1037   DEFOURI, JAMES H.

HISTORICAL SKETCH OF THE CATHOLIC CHURCH IN NEW MEXICO . . . SAN FRANCISCO, CAL.: McCORMICK BROS., 1887.

[1]–164, [165–66 blank]. 18.7 x 13.1 cm. Rebound in new blue wrappers with part of original front wrapper mounted.

Ref.: Howes D218; Saunders 4018

1038   DE GROOT, HENRY

BRITISH COLUMBIA; ITS CONDITION AND PROSPECTS, SOIL, CLIMATE, AND MINERAL RESOURCES, CONSIDERED . . . SAN FRANCISCO: PRINTED AT THE ALTA CALIFORNIA JOB OFFICE, 1859.

[1]–24. 24.6 x 16 cm. Tan printed wrappers with title on front wrapper.

Ref.: Greenwood 1072; Smith 2372

Originally published in the *Daily Alta California*, the pamphlet seems to have been run off from the newspaper setting.

1039   DE LACY, WALTER

[Map] MAP / OF THE / TERRITORY OF MONTANA / WITH PORTIONS OF THE ADJOINING TERRITORIES / [decorative rule] / SHOWING THE GULCH OR PLACER DIGGINGS ACTUALLY WORKED, AND DISTRICTS / WHERE QUARTZ (GOLD & SILVER) LODGES[!] HAVE BEEN DISCOVERED, TO JANUARY 1ˢᵀ 1865 / [three lines] / DRAWN BY W. W. DE LACY FOR THE USE OF / THE FIRST LEGISLATURE OF MONTANA / [decorative rule] / JUL. HUTAWA / LITHᴿ N⁰ 65 CHESTNUT ST. ST. LOUIS MO. / [diagrammatic scale: 24 miles to one inch] /.

Map, 54.8 x 75.3 cm. Scale as above.

Ref.: Phillips (*Maps*) p. 447; Wagner-Camp 424 note

There were at least four variants of this map, two with the imprint of Hauser (one dated, one undated), one with the Friedenwald imprint, and one with the Hutawa imprint.

1040   DE LACY, WALTER W.

[Map] MAP / OF THE / TERRITORY / OF / MONTANA / WITH PORTIONS OF THE / ADJOINING TERRITORIES / COMPILED AND DRAWN BY W. W. DE LACY / OF THE SURVEYOR GENERAL'S OFFICE / HELENA, M. T. / SCALE OF MILES / [diagrammatic scale: 20 miles to one inch] / 1870. / [at right of cartouche:] ENGRAVED PRINTED AND / PUBLISHED BY G. W. & C. B. COLTON & C⁰. / NO. 172 WILLIAM Sᵀ. / NEW YORK. / [at upper right:] ENTERED ACCORDING TO ACT OF CONGRESS, IN THE YEAR 1870 BY W. W. DE LACY, / IN THE OFFICE OF THE LIBRARIAN OF CONGRESS, AT WASHINGTON. / *Inset:* Map of the / Northwestern Portion / of the / United States / Entered according to Act of Congress in the year 1870 by W: W: De Lacy in the Office of the Librarian of Congress, at Washington. / 17.6 x 44.5 cm. Scale: about 115 miles to one inch.

Map, 71.6 x 104.7 cm. Scale: 20 miles to one inch. Folded into black cloth covers, 15.2 x 9.7 cm., with title stamped in gilt on front cover: Map of / Montana. / [decorative rule] / G. W. & C. B. Colton & Co. /, publishers' advertisements inside front cover.

Ref.: Phillips (*Maps*) p. 448

1041   DELANEY, MATILDA J. S.

A SURVIVOR'S RECOLLECTIONS OF THE WHITMAN MASSACRE . . . SPOKANE, WASHINGTON: ESTHER REED CHAPTER, DAUGHTERS OF THE AMERICAN REVOLUTION.*

[1]–46. 22.7 x 14.7 cm. Two illustrations. Printed white wrappers. In a blue cloth case.

Ref.: Howes D229; Smith 2377

Copyrighted 1920.

1042   DELANO, ALONZO

LIFE ON THE PLAINS AND AMONG THE DIGGINGS; BEING SCENES AND ADVENTURES OF AN OVERLAND JOURNEY TO CALIFORNIA: WITH PARTICULAR INCIDENTS OF THE ROUTE, MISTAKES AND SUFFERINGS OF THE EMIGRANTS, THE INDIAN TRIBES, THE PRESENT AND FUTURE OF THE GREAT WEST . . . AUBURN: MILLER, ORTON & MULLIGAN, 1854.

[i]–[xii, xii blank], [13]–384. 19 x 12.5 cm. Black cloth, title stamped in gilt on backstrip.

Prov.: Inscribed on front fly-leaf: E. P. Christy / June 1856 /. And the following note in pencil: Sensibly written. Interesting / in detail. Alltogether[!] first rate /.

Ref.: Blumann & Thomas 2230; Bradford 1281; Cowan p. 163; Howes D230; Matthews p. 315; Rader 1104; Sabin 19348; Wagner-Camp 238

Wagner considered this one of the most interesting of all California books.

1043 DELANO, ALONZO

OLD BLOCK'S SKETCH-BOOK; OR, TALES OF CALIFORNIA LIFE . . . SACRAMENTO: JAMES ANTHONY & CO., 1856.

[i–ii], [I]–[IV], [1]–[79], [80 blank], [81 advertisement, 82 blank]. 22.5 x 14.4 cm. 15 illustrations by Nahl, included in pagination. Pink printed wrappers with title on front wrapper, advertisement on verso of back wrapper.

Ref.: Blumann & Thomas 2232; Cowan p. 163; Howes D230; Zamorano Eighty 29

Both author and illustrator are characteristically Californian, and few volumes have a truer flavor of the Mother Lode than this result of their combined efforts.—Zamorano

Note that in the copyright notice reproduced in Zamorano Eighty line 2 starts under the "a" in according while the EDG copy starts under the third "e" of Entered. The imprint is set farther left in the Zamorano copy.

1044 [DELAVAN, JAMES]

NOTES ON CALIFORNIA AND THE PLACERS: HOW TO GET THERE, AND WHAT TO DO AFTERWARDS . . . NEW-YORK: H. LONG & BROTHER, 1850.

[1]–128. 23.8 x 14.6 cm. Two lithographic views. Salmon printed wrappers with title on front wrapper, advertisements on verso of front and recto and verso of back wrapper, uncut.

Ref.: Cowan p. 164; Hanna-Powell p. 26; Howes D237; Jones 1236; Sabin 10036

Henry R. Wagner included this among his twenty rarest and most important books about California. It contains a candid account of life in the California mines in 1849. Delavan was one of the Feather River Party of that year and was highly successful. The work is based on a carefully kept diary.

1045 DEMOCRATIC COMMITTEE OF JOHNSON COUNTY, IOWA, THE

[Broadside] TO THE SOLDIERS OF IOWA, AND ESPECIALLY THOSE FROM JOHNSON COUNTY. SOLDIERS: —THE OLD DEMOCRATIC PARTY ASKS YOUR VOTES . . . BY ORDER OF THE DEMOCRATIC COMMITTEE, OF JOHNSON CO., IOWA.

Broadside, 33.1 x 25.5 cm. Text, 27.3 x 23.5 cm.
Ref.:
The broadside contains a letter from General J. M. Tuttle, to the citizens of Iowa, dated from Keosauqua, August 13, 1863, in which the general attacks Lincoln's war policy.

1046 DEMOCRATIC PARTY. Illinois

[Broadside] DEMOCRATIC MEETING! AT A PUBLIC MEETING OF DEMOCRATS, HOLDEN ACCORDING TO PREVIOUS NOTICE AT THE SCHOOLHOUSE IN LA SALLE, ON THE 27TH OF JUNE, A. D. 1843 . . . PREAMBLE AND RESOLUTIONS . . .

Broadside, 26.7 x 26.7 cm. Text, 24.7 x 23.8 cm. In a blue cloth case.
Ref.: Byrd 778
The report of a meeting in opposition to the candidacy of John Wentworth and in support of Dr. Richard Murphy.
The only copy located.

1047 DEMOCRATIC PARTY. Illinois

[Caption title] PROCEEDINGS OF A GREAT DEMOCRATIC MEETING, HELD IN CHICAGO JUNE 7, 1843 . . .

[1]–8. 26.1 x 18 cm. Sewn, uncut. In a blue cloth case.
Ref.: Byrd 779; McMurtrie (*Chicago*) 57
The meeting was called in opposition to the candidacy of John Wentworth and for the purpose of promoting the cause of Dr. Richard Murphy.
The only copy located.

1048 DEMOCRATIC PARTY. Illinois

PROTEST OF THE DELEGATES WHO WITHDREW FROM THE DEMOCRATIC CONGRESSIONAL CONVENTION, HELD AT JULIET[!] ON THE 18TH OF MAY, AND THE PROCEEDINGS OF A DEMOCRATIC MEETING, HELD AT THE COURT HOUSE IN JULIET ON THE 20TH OF MAY, 1842. JULIET, ILL.: SIGNAL PRESS, 1843.

[1]–8. 24 x 16.3 cm. Unbound.
Ref.: Byrd 777
The only copy located.

1049 DENISON, D. B.

AUTOGRAPH NOTE, SIGNED. 1873 November 25, Lawrence, Kansas. One page, 10 x 19.5 cm. To Loren L. Williams.

Inserted in Manuscript Journals of Loren L. Williams, Volume IV.

1050 DENISON, E. S.

E. S. DENISON'S YOSEMITE VIEWS. SAM MILLER, AGENT. 2 NEW MONT'G. ST. SAN FRANCISCO.

[1–103, 104 blank]. 22.6 x 14.8 cm. Two maps, 50 full-page views and numerous vignettes, unlisted. Rebound in brown contemporary cloth, with colored pictorial wrappers bound in, title lettered in gilt on backstrip.
Ref.: Blumann & Thomas 1885; Howes D252

Published in 1881. Wrapper title: Yosemite / and the Big Trees / of California / Tourist Ticket Agency / 2 Montgomery St. / Co. Market St. / San Francisco. / [below border:] Lith. H. S. Crocker & Co. S. F.

1051 DENMARK (Iowa) ACADEMY

CATALOGUE OF THE TRUSTEES, TEACHERS, AND STUDENTS, OF DENMARK ACADEMY, FOR THE YEAR ENDING AUGUST 15TH, 1853. FORT MADISON: PRINTED AT THE EVANGELIST BOOK AND JOB OFFICE, 1853.

[1]–16. 21.4 x 13.7 cm. Yellow printed wrappers with title on front wrapper.

Prov.: Back wrapper used as mailing address: Denmark Iowa / Aug 16 / Dr H Jewett / Dayton / Ohio / [short rule] / paid / [short rule] / 2c /.

Ref.: Moffit 123

1052 DENMARK (Iowa) ACADEMY

CATALOGUE OF THE TRUSTEES, TEACHERS AND STUDENTS, OF DENMARK ACADEMY. FOR THE YEAR ENDING JULY 18, 1854 . . . BURLINGTON: TELEGRAPH PRINTING COMPANY, MDCCCLIV.

[1]–14, [15–16 blank]. 22.1 x 13.9 cm. Pale green printed wrappers with title on front wrapper.

Prov.: On inner back wrapper: Jewett / Dayton, / Ohio. / [upper right corner:] one-cent stamp, post office canceled in light red: Denmark, Iowa, Jul 10. / Circular cancel.

Ref.: Moffit 149

1053 DENNY, ARTHUR A.

PIONEER DAYS ON PUGET SOUND . . . SEATTLE, W. T.: C. B. BAGLEY, 1888.

[1]–83, [84 blank]. 16.8 x 11.8 cm. Brown cloth.

Ref.: Howes D253a; Smith 2408

Privately printed by the author. Many copies are believed to have been destroyed in the Seattle fire of 1889. Errata slip, 5.2 x 9.2 cm., tipped in before page 83.

Deservedly prized as an authoritative source upon the early history of Seattle and Puget Sound . . . —*Washington Historical Quarterly*

1054 DENVER PACIFIC RAILWAY & TELEGRAPH COMPANY

FIRST ANNUAL REPORT OF THE OFFICERS OF THE DENVER PACIFIC RAILWAY & TELEGRAPH CO. TO THE STOCKHOLDERS . . . CHICAGO: RAND, MCNALLY & CO., 1869.

[1]–32. 22.2 x 14.3 cm. Two maps: Denver / Colorado, / Showing the / Location of Depot Grounds & / the Right of Way / of the / Denver Pacific Railway / Through the City / 1868 / Scale 1000 Ft to the Inch. / Chicago Lithographing Co. / 36.1 x 43 cm. Scale as above. Map: Denver Pacific Railway / Map / Showing the / Final Location / with / Prospective Connections / Compiled from Rail Road & Govt Surveys / F. M. Case Chief Engr. / Scale, 9 Miles to the Inch.

1868 Chicago Lithographing Co. / 49.8 x 39.3 cm. Scale as above. Cream printed wrappers with title on front wrapper.

Ref.: Railway Economics p. 309 see

1055 DENVER VILLA PARK ASSOCIATION

ARTICLES OF INCORPORATION AND BY LAWS OF THE DENVER VILLA PARK ASSOCIATION . . . DENVER, COL.: THE DENVER TRIBUNE ASSOCIATION PRINT, 1872.

[1]–12. 14.6 x 9.4 cm. Blue printed wrappers with title on front wrapper.

Ref.:

1056 DEPESTRE, JULIAN

AFFIDAVIT, SIGNED. 1807 October 1, Richmond, Virginia. Four pages, 33.5 x 20.6 cm. Silked.

From the eleventh of August to the second or third of September, 1806, Depestre accompanied Aaron Burr on travels through Pennsylvania, Virginia, and Ohio. In this affidavit he declared that during that time he heard no evidence that Burr was plotting anything against the United States.

The first part of the document comprises Depestre's statement; this is followed by a series of questions on cross examination by Burr with Depestre's answers. The whole is signed and is followed by a six-line attestation by E. Carrington that Depestre appeared before him and swore to the truth of the document.

1057 [DE PEYSTER, ARENT SCHUYLER]

MISCELLANIES . . . DUMFRIES: PRINTED AT THE DUMFRIES AND GALLOWAY COURIER OFFICE, 1813.

[1]–35⁴. [1]–59, 55, 61–85, 80, 87–226, 218, 228–77, [278–80 blank]. 27.5 x 21.5 cm. Tan boards, gray-green paper back, with printed white paper label, uncut. Label probably supplied.

Prov.: Presentation copy from the author, inscribed on leaf facing title-page: To / The Revᵈ Doctor Hamilton / From / The Author. / Herschel V. Jones copy.

Ref.: Buley II, p. 558; Clements Library (*Michigan*) 48; Howes D263; Jones 763; Pilling (*Alg.*) 112; Rusk I, pp. 343–44; Sabin 19622; Thomson 323

Without too much insistence on the point, we may, perhaps trace the tradition of Indian lore in Western frontier verse back to the days of the British officer Depeyster, who, while stationed on service at Detroit, at Michilimackinac, and on the shores of Lake Michigan, from about 1776 to 1785, amused himself and his companions with rimes, years later gathered into a volume for publication in Scotland.—Rusk

There are manuscript corrections in the Graff copy on pages [3], 8, 11, 20, 21, 24, 48, 51, 54, 59, 60, 64, 65, 69, 70, 71, 76, 80, 81, 85, 86, 93, 94, 105, 108, 109, 117, 119, 125, 135, 140, 152, 159, 170, 209, 211, and 221. There are similar manuscript corrections in the Ayer copy except for those on pages 50, 64, 105, 135, and 211. It is interesting to note that in the Graff copy the corrections on the additional pages are in a different handwriting.

1058 DERBY, EDWARD G. G. S. STANLEY, 14TH EARL OF

JOURNAL OF A TOUR IN AMERICA, 1824–1825 . . . PRIVATELY PRINTED, 1930.

[i–vi], 1–[343], [344 blank]. 22.5 x 15.6 cm. Four maps and one facsimile. Half dark orange morocco, gilt top, uncut.

Ref.: Howes S878

Limited to fifty copies, signed on the limitation leaf: D. /

Printed in London.

This rather unfriendly observer . . . travelled through Ohio and Kentucky, by river to Natchez and Louisiana and by horseback through the deep south to Charleston.—Howes. The author, who made the tour as a young man, was thrice Prime Minister of Great Britain.

1059 DERBY, GEORGE H.

[Caption title] . . . A RECONNOISSANCE[!] OF THE GULF OF CALIFORNIA AND THE COLORADO RIVER BY LIEUTENANT DERBY . . .

[1]–28. 25 x 15.9 cm. Folding map: Reconnaissance / of the / Colorado River / made by order of / Maj. Gen. P. F. Smith, / com'd'g Pacific Division. / by / Geo. H. Derby, Lt. U. S. Top^l Eng^{rs} / Dec. 1850. / Drawn by Lieut. Derby. / Scale of miles / [diagram] / 56.2 x 27.5 cm. Scale: about four miles to an inch. Stabbed, unbound, uncut, unopened.

Ref.: Farquhar (*Colorado River*) 15; Munk (Alliot) p. 64; Wheat (*Transmississippi*) 668

32nd Congress, 1st Session, Senate, Executive Document No. 81, Serial 620. [Washington, 1852.]

The first reconnaissance of the Colorado River. Derby's fame lies in his writings as John Phoenix and Squibob.

1060 DESCRIPTION OF THE TOWN OF LAWRENCE (Iowa)

DESCRIPTION OF THE TOWN OF LAWRENCE, VAN BUREN COUNTY, IN THE DES MOINES VALLEY, IOWA: ITS HYDRAULIC POWER AND MANUFACTURING FACILITIES. KEOKUK: J. B. HOWELL & COMPANY, 1856.

[1]–11, [12 blank]. 20.9 x 13.6 cm. Yellow printed wrappers with title on front wrapper printed in green. Lacks back wrapper.

Ref.: Moffit 223; Sabin 39387

1061 DESERET. Constitutional Convention, 1849

CONSTITUTION OF THE STATE OF DESERET, WITH THE JOURNAL OF THE CONVENTION WHICH FORMED IT, AND THE PROCEEDINGS OF THE LEGISLATURE CONSEQUENT THEREON . . . KANESVILLE: PUBLISHED BY ORSON HYDE, 1849.

[1]–16. 22.7 x 14.1 cm. Stitched, unbound. In a brown half morocco case.

Ref.: Howes M813; Jones 1195; Moffit 55; Sabin 98219; Streeter (*Americana—Beginnings*) 70

The Deseret *Constitution* was the first attempt of the Mormons to establish a civil government after they reached Utah. In 1849 there was no operating printing press in Utah large enough to print the pamphlet, and Kanesville (later Council Bluffs), Iowa, was the nearest convenient town with a press.

1062 DESERET NEWS (Salt Lake City)

[Caption title] DESERET NEWS,—EXTRA. GREAT SALT LAKE CITY, U. T., SEPTEMBER 14, 1852. MINUTES OF CONFERENCE. A SPECIAL CONFERENCE OF THE ELDERS OF THE CHURCH OF JESUS CHRIST OF LATTER-DAY-SAINTS, ASSEMBLED IN THE TABERNACLE, GREAT SALT LAKE CITY, AUGUST 28TH, 1852, 10 O'CLOCK, A. M., PURSUANT TO PUBLIC NOTICES . . .

[1]–48. 21.9 x 14.6 cm. Stabbed, uncut, mostly unopened.

Ref.:

Pages 27–48 comprise two discourses by Brigham Young, August 8 and 15, 1852.

1063 DE SHIELDS, JAMES T.

BORDER WARS OF TEXAS . . . CONFLICT WAGED BETWEEN SAVAGE INDIAN TRIBES AND THE PIONEER SETTLERS OF TEXAS . . . TIOGA: THE HERALD COMPANY, 1912.

[1]–400. 22 x 14.4 cm. 40 illustrations listed. Decorated gray cloth.

Ref.: Howes D277; Rader 1125

1064 DE SHIELDS, JAMES T.

CYNTHIA ANN PARKER. THE STORY OF HER CAPTURE AT THE MASSACRE OF THE INMATES OF PARKER'S FORT; OF HER QUARTER OF A CENTURY SPENT AMONG THE COMANCHES, AS THE WIFE OF THE WAR CHIEF, PETA NOCONA; AND OF HER RECAPTURE AT THE BATTLE OF PEASE RIVER, BY CAP-

TAIN L. S. ROSS, OF THE TEXIAN RANGERS . . . ST. LOUIS: PRINTED FOR THE AUTHOR, 1886.*

[I]–[VIII, VIII blank], [9]–80. 17.8 x 13.2 cm. Four illustrations, unlisted. Dark green cloth, blind embossed bands and gilt title and vignette on front cover.

Ref.: Ayer 63; Dobie p. 33; Howes D278; Rader 1126; Raines p. 67

1065 DESILVER, CHARLES

[Map] A NEW MAP OF / THE / STATE OF IOWA / PUBLISHED BY / CHARLES DESILVER, / Nº 253 MARKET STREET PHILADELPHIA. / 1856. / SCALE OF MILES. / [diagrammatic scale: 30 miles to one inch] / [at lower right:] ENTERED ACCORDING TO ACT OF CONGRESS IN THE YEAR 1850, BY THOMAS, COWPERTHWAIT & CO. IN THE CLERK'S OFFICE OF THE DISTRICT COURT OF THE EASTERN DISTRICT OF PENNSYLVANIA. /

Map, 34.1 x 40.8 cm. Scale: 30 miles to one inch. Folded into green leather covers, 12.7 x 8 cm., with title stamped in gilt on front cover.

Ref.:
Mounted on inside front cover is a broadside: Population of Iowa, / By Counties, in 1850. / . . .

1066 DES MOINES NAVIGATION AND RAILROAD COMPANY

[Caption title] REPORT OF THE DEMOINE[!] RIVER IMPROVEMENT AND NAVIGATION COMPANY. OTTUMWA, NOV. 15, 1856 . . .

[1]–48. 21.7 x 14.7 cm. Stabbed, unbound.
Ref.:

1067 DE SOTO, NEBRASKA, BANK OF

BANK NOTE FOR ONE DOLLAR, ISSUED BY THE BANK OF DE SOTO, NEBRASKA. SIGNED BY M. FORMAN AND W. WILLIAMS. DATED JUNE 2ND, 1862. Numbered B No. 219. Engraved by Baldwin, Bald, & Cousland, New York.

1068 DESOTO (Nebraska) PILOT

[Newspaper] DESOTO PILOT. Z. JACKSON, PUBLISHER . . . VOLUME I. DESOTO, NEBRASKA, TUESDAY, MARCH 23, 1858. NUMBER 4 . . .

[1–4]. 53.5 x 35.7 cm. About half of second leaf missing.
Ref.:
Contains a long Sut Lovingood yarn.

1069 DES SULLES, ALBERT

AN ARIZONA RANGER. A STORY OF THE SOUTHWESTERN SOLITUDE . . . NEW YORK: BROADWAY PUBLISHING CO., 1906.

[i–iv, iv blank], [1]–241, [242 blank, 243–52 advertisements]. 18.2 x 12.3 cm. Two illustrations. Dark red buckram.

Ref.: Munk (Alliot) p. 65
Des Sulles knew his Arizona, but whether his adventures were factual or fiction is yet to be decided.

1070 DETROIT TRIBUNE, THE

[Broadside] [FROM THE DETROIT TRIBUNE. JANUARY 16TH.] RIPARIAN RIGHTS ON THE DETROIT RIVER . . .

Broadside, 47.5 x 23.2 cm. Text, 44.2 x 17 cm. Tipped to an inserted blank leaf and bound with related materials in contemporary black half calf.
Ref.:
Undated, but 1860.
See under ILLINOIS CENTRAL RAILROAD COMPANY.

1071 DEVOL, GEORGE H.

FORTY YEARS A GAMBLER ON THE MISSISSIPPI . . . FIRST EDITION . . . CINCINNATI: DEVOL & HAINES, 1887.

[i]–viii, [9]–300. 21.2 x 13.7 cm. Five illustrations. Maroon cloth.
Ref.: Howes D295

1072 DEWEES, FRANCIS P.

[Caption title] THE CASE OF GEORGE CHORPENNING. ARGUMENT BEFORE COMMITTEE ON THE JUDICIARY, H. OF R., 46TH CONGRESS. THE JURISDICTION OF THE COMMITTEE—THE LEGAL EFFECT OF THE ADJUSTMENT MADE BY POSTMASTER GENERAL CRESSWELL[!] PURSUANT TO THE JOINT RESOLUTION OF 15TH JULY, 1870 . . .

[1]–12. 21.5 x 14.5 cm. Unbound, removed from bound volume. In box with other Chorpenning materials.
Ref.:
Dewees signed himself "Of Counsel for Claimant" on page 12.

1073 DEWEES, WILLIAM B.

LETTERS FROM AN EARLY SETTLER OF TEXAS . . . LOUISVILLE, KY.: MORTON & GRISWOLD, 1852.

[i]–viii, [9]–312, [1–8] advertisements. 19 x 11.7 cm. Black cloth, blind embossed sides, gilt title on backstrip.

Ref.: Bradford 1311; Howes D299; Rader 1131; Raines p. 57; Sabin 19842
Only 250 copies were printed. Raines suggests that the material applying to Dewees' own adventures is valuable, but that the compiler (Clara Cardelle) lost her way in Texas history. Dewees traveled from Nashville to Arkansas in 1819 and describes buffalo hunting, the general countryside, history, etc.

1074 DEWEY, SQUIRE P.

THE BONANZA MINES OF NEVADA. GROSS FRAUDS IN THE MANAGEMENT EXPOSED. REPLY OF S. P. DEWEY TO THE MISREPRESENTATIONS OF THE BONANZA FIRM IN THEIR LIBELOUS PUBLICATION OF MAY 25TH, 1878.

[1]–78, [79–80 blank]. 22.3 x 14.4 cm. Two diagrams. Gray printed wrappers, with title on front wrapper. Lacks back wrapper.

Ref.: Cowan p. 168; Howes D302 see

Printed in San Francisco in 1878.

1075 DEWEY, SQUIRE P.

THE BONANZA MINES AND THE BONANZA KINGS OF CALIFORNIA. THEIR 5 YEARS REIGN: 1875–1879 . . .

[i–vi], [3]–87, [88 blank]. 22 x 14.4 cm. Two diagrams. Contemporary black roan, title in gilt on front cover.

Prov.: Inscribed on front fly-leaf: Hon. Hugh McCullough /. This was probably intended for Hugh McCulloch, Secretary of the Treasury under Lincoln and Johnson.

Ref.: Cowan p. 168; Howes D302

The new material starts on page 71, otherwise the text of the pamphlet is that of the preceding item. The pamphlet was printed in San Francisco in 1880.

1076 DE WOLFF, J. H.

PAWNEE BILL (MAJOR GORDON W. LILLIE): HIS EXPERIENCES AND ADVENTURES ON THE WESTERN PLAINS; OR, FROM THE SADDLE OF A "COWBOY AND RANGER" TO THE CHAIR OF A "BANK PRESIDENT" . . . PUBLISHED BY PAWNEE BILL'S HISTORIC WILD WEST COMPANY, 1902.*

[1]–108. ([1] blank, [2] frontispiece.) 23 x 15.1 cm. 21 illustrations unlisted. Blue pictorial boards.

Ref.: Adams 303; Howes D311; Rader 1134

Uncopyrighted, the little volume was used as an advertisement for the Wild West show.

1077 DEXTER, A. HERSEY

EARLY DAYS IN CALIFORNIA . . . 1886.

[1]–214. (Pages [1–2] blank.) 19.7 x 15.1 cm. Blue cloth, title and vignette in gilt on front cover, title in gilt on backstrip.

Ref.: Cowan p. 168; Howes D312

The following imprint appears on the verso of the title-leaf: Denver, Colorado: / Tribune-Republican Press. / 1886. /

1078 DICKENSON, LUELLA

REMINISCENCES OF A TRIP ACROSS THE PLAINS IN 1846 AND EARLY DAYS IN CALIFORNIA . . . SAN FRANCISCO: THE WHITAKER & RAY COMPANY, 1904.*

[1]–117, [118 vignette]. 18.7 x 12.5 cm. Illustrations unlisted. Blue pictorial cloth, fore and lower edges uncut.

Ref.: Blumann & Thomas 4937; Cowan p. 168; Howes D318

Mrs. Dickenson's husband left Independence, Missouri on May 1, 1846, at the age of fifteen. His father, G. D. Dickenson, was Captain of the company. Their party crossed into the Truckee Valley just ahead of the ill-fated Donner and Reed party.—EDG

1079 DICKERSON, PHILIP J.

[Wrapper title] HISTORY OF THE OSAGE NATION, ITS PEOPLE, RESOURCES AND PROSPECTS . . . BY PHILIP DICKERSON, M. A.*

[1]–[146] including wrappers. 23.4 x 15.7 cm. Illustrations unlisted. Blue printed wrappers with title on front wrapper, illustrations on recto of front and recto and verso of back wrapper. In a gray buckram case.

Ref.: Howes D321; Rader 1137

Published at Pawhuska in 1906.

1080 DICKERSON, PHILIP J.

[Wrapper title] HISTORY OF TULSA, I. T. HER NATURAL ADVANTAGES OF LOCATION, CLIMATE, FERTILE SOIL, ETC. A RAILROAD CENTRE OF THE CREEK, CHEROKEE, AND OSAGE NATIONS . . . 1903.

[1]–36. 19 x 13.6 cm. Pink printed wrappers with title on front wrapper, advertisements on recto of front and recto and verso of back wrapper.

Ref.: Howes D322

Printed at Tulsa. The text appears on the rectos only, advertisements on the versos.

1081 DICKINSON, JONATHAN

GOD'S PROTECTING PROVIDENCE . . . EVIDENCED IN THE REMARKABLE DELIVERANCE OF ROBERT BARROW, WITH DIVERS OTHER PERSONS, FROM THE DEVOURING WAVES OF THE SEA; AMONGST WHICH THEY SUFFERED SHIPWRACK[!]; AND ALSO, FROM THE CRUEL DEVOURING JAWS OF THE INHUMANE CANIBALS OF FLORIDA . . . LONDON: T. SOWLE, 1700.

[A]–F⁸, G², A⁴. [i–x], 1–89, [90 blank], [91–98: Books Printed and Sold by T. Sowle in White-Hart-Court in Gracious-street and at the Bible in Leaden-Hall-Street, 1699.] 17.5 x 11 cm. Old mottled calf.

Prov.: Book label of John Horne and Eliza Glaisyer. Signatures of: Susanna Caroline (?) / 8 mo 10 1819 / and J. H. & E. Glaisyer / on title-page. On page [90] the following: Mary / Sicth / J Harry /.

Ref.: Andrews: *Jonathan Dickinson's Journal,*

New Haven, 1945; Ayer 65; Howes D317; Jones 368; Sabin 20015

Andrews describes two states of the 1700 edition, the first containing 89 pages, the second 85 and the latter containing eight unnumbered pages of advertisements at the back. The present copy has the title-page of the first state, 89 pages of text, and eight unnumbered pages of advertisements. The 1699 edition is present in the ICN (Ayer) collection, as are both states of the 1700 edition, and thirteen other editions. The present copy adds a variant to the pair of 1700-edition states.

1082 DICKSON, ALBERT J., *Editor*

COVERED WAGON DAYS. A JOURNEY ACROSS THE PLAINS IN THE SIXTIES, AND PIONEER DAYS IN THE NORTHWEST . . . CLEVELAND: THE ARTHUR H. CLARK COMPANY, 1929.*

[1]–287, [288 blank]. 24 x 16 cm. 20 illustrations and one map listed. Blue ribbed cloth, gilt top, uncut.

Ref.: Smith 2445

1083 DIETZ, ARTHUR A.

MAD RUSH FOR GOLD IN FROZEN NORTH . . . LOS ANGELES: TIMES-MIRROR PRINTING AND BINDING HOUSE, 1914.

[1]–281, [282 blank]. 19.6 x 13.5 cm. Illustrations unlisted. Blue pictorial cloth.

Prov.: Inscribed on front fly-leaf: Arthur A. Dietz / [flourish] / July 1917 /. Also signed on same leaf: Tricia D Kenson. /

Ref.: Smith 2453; Wickersham 4310

1084 DILLINGHAM, PAUL

[Caption title] SPEECH OF MR. DILLINGHAM, OF VERMONT, ON THE RIGHT OF THE GENERAL MEMBERS ELECTED BY GENERAL TICKET TO RETAIN THEIR SEATS. DELIVERED IN THE HOUSE OF REPRESENTATIVES, FEBRUARY 7, 1844 . . .

[1]–8. 22.7 x 14.1 cm.

BOUND WITH:

WISE, HENRY A.: [Caption title] Opinions of Hon. Henry A. Wise, upon the Conduct and Character of James K. Polk . . . [1]–8.

BOUND WITH:

DAVIS, GARRETT: [Caption title] Report of the Minority . . . Mr. Garrett Davis . . . Made the Following Report . . . [1]–16.

BOUND WITH:

COLLAMER, J.: Speech of Mr. J. Collamer, of Vermont, Delivered in the House of Representatives . . . on the Constitutional Validity of the Act of Congress Requiring the Election of Representatives . . . February 8, 1844. Washington:

Printed by Gales and Seaton, 1844. [1]–13, [14 blank].

BOUND WITH:

WHITE, JOHN: [Caption title] Speech of the Hon. John White, of Kentucky, in Defence of Mr. Clay . . . Delivered in the House of Representatives . . . April 23, 1844 . . . [1]–8.

BOUND WITH:

HARDIN, J. J.: Speech of Mr. J. J. Hardin, of Illinois, Reviewing the Principles of James K. Polk & the Leaders of Modern Democracy . . . June 3, 1844 . . . Washington: Printed by J. & G. S. Gideon, 1844. [1]–16. (Pages 13–16 misbound between 4 and 5.)

BOUND WITH:

WEBSTER, DANIEL: Speech of Mr. Webster, in the Senate, in Reply to Mr. Calhoun's Speech . . . Delivered on the 16th of February, 1833. Washington: Printed by Gales and Seaton, 1833. [1]–48.

BOUND WITH:

OGLE, A. J.: [Caption title] Remarks of Mr. Ogle, of Pennsylvania, on the Civil and Diplomatic Appropriation Bill . . . April 14, 1840 . . . 1–32.

BOUND WITH:

STEWART, ANDREW: [Caption title] Speech of Mr. Stewart, of Pennsylvania, in Favor of Western Improvements . . . January 16, 1844 . . . [1]–16.

BOUND WITH:

GIDDINGS, JOSHUA R.: Speech of Mr. Giddings, of Ohio, upon the Proposition of Mr. Johnson, of Tennessee, to Reduce the Army to the Basis of 1821 . . . June 3, 1842. Washington: Printed at the National Intelligencer Office, 1842. [1]–19, [20 blank].

BOUND WITH:

GIDDINGS, JOSHUA R.: [Caption title] Speech of Mr. Giddings, of Ohio, on his Motion to Reconsider the Vote Taken upon the Final Passage of the "Bill for the Relief of Owners of Slaves lost on Board the Comet and Encomium." . . . February 13, 1843 . . . [1]–8.

BOUND WITH:

HOLMES, JOHN: [Caption title] Speech of Mr. Holmes, of Maine, on the Annual Appropriation Bill . . . April 9th, 10th, and 11th, 1832 . . . [1]–24.

BOUND WITH:

HARDIN, J. J.: [Caption title] Speech of Mr. J. J. Hardin, of Illinois, Reviewing the Public Life & Political Principles of Mr. Van Buren . . . March 21, 1844 . . . [1]–32.

BOUND WITH:

RAYNER, N.: [Caption title] Speech of Mr. N. Rayner, of N. Carolina, on the Sub-Treasury . . . June 22, 1840 . . . [1]–32.

BOUND WITH:

WHITE, JOHN: [Caption title] Speech of Mr. White, of Kentucky, . . . June 5, 1840 . . . in Opposition to the Sub-Treasury Bill . . . [1]–48.

BOUND WITH:

DAVIS, GARRETT: [Caption title] Extract from the Speech of Mr. Garret[!] Davis, of Kentucky, Exhibiting the Expenditures of Mr. Van Buren's Administrations . . . April 5, 1844 . . . [1]–8.

BOUND WITH:

MCDUFFEE, JOHN: [Caption title] Statistical Information on Canals and Railroads. By John McDuffee, Esq. . . . [1]–8.

BOUND WITH:

SMITH, JOSEPH: General Smith's Views of the Powers and Policy of the Government of the United States. John Taylor, Printer: Nauvoo, Illinois. 1844. [1]–12.

BOUND WITH:

MOREHEAD, JAMES T.: Report of the Committee on Retrenchment of the Senate of the United States, Made by Hon. James T. Morehead . . . on the 15th of June, 1844 . . . Washington: Printed by Gales and Seaton, 1844. [1]–6, [7–8 blank], [1]–448.

Nineteen pamphlets bound together in contemporary marbled boards, gray cloth backstrip.

Prov.: Inscribed on front endleaf: E P Walton Jr / H. A. Huse / (of Mrs. E. P. Walton) / March 15, 1898. /

The Joseph Smith pamphlet has been removed from the bound volume; see Number 3856.

1085 DIMSDALE, THOMAS J.

[Broadside] NOW COMPLETED AND FOR SALE! AN IMPARTIAL AND CORRECT HISTORY OF THE VIGILANTES OF MONTANA TERRITORY! COMPRISING A FULL ACCOUNT OF THE CHASE, CAPTURE, TRIAL, AND EXECUTION OF PLUMMER'S GREAT BAND OF ROAD AGENTS! SINGLE COPIES, OR BY THE WHOLESALE, CAN BE SECURED OF D. W. TILTON & CO., AT THE CITY BOOK STORE, VIRGINIA CITY, AND AT THEIR OFFICE ON BRIDGE STREET, HELENA, MONTANA. A LIBERAL REDUCTION MADE ON LARGE ORDERS! SEND IN YOUR ORDERS IMMEDIATELY! AS A LIMITED EDITION HAS BEEN PRINTED. PRICE, PER COPY, IN DUST, -- $2 00 GREENBACKS, ------- $2 25.

Broadside, 73.5 x 53.3 cm. Text, 65.9 x 48.6 cm. Mounted on cloth.

Ref.:

Printed in red and blue.

1086 DIMSDALE, THOMAS J.

THE VIGILANTES OF MONTANA, OR POPULAR JUSTICE IN THE ROCKY MOUNTAINS . . . VIRGINIA CITY, M. T.: MONTANA POST PRESS, 1866.

[i]–iv, [5]–228, [229–32 advertisements]. 16.5 x 12.1 cm. Gray printed wrappers with title on front wrapper, title on backstrip, advertisements on recto of front and recto and verso of back wrapper. Backstrip supplied. In a gray cloth case.

Prov.: Inscribed in pencil on verso of title-page: To- G D / from Q P Schults / who brought it from / Montana in 1868 / [flourish] /. There is also an erased note below the text on page 228.

Ref.: Adams 308; Bradford 1334; Howes D345; Jones 1620; McMurtrie (*Montana*) 2; Smith 2457

The first edition is known in three forms, the variations occurring in the advertisements at the end and on the wrappers. The present copy appears to be the earliest variety. Later versions show fancier borders on the front wrapper and a different setting of the title. The third variant is without advertisements following the text and without advertisements on inner wrappers.

1087 DIMSDALE, THOMAS J.

THE SAME.

[i]–iv, [5]–228. 17 x 12.5 cm. Yellow printed wrappers with title on front wrapper, advertisement on verso of back wrapper, title on backstrip. In a green cloth case.

Prov.: Inscribed in pencil on inside front wrapper: This most wonderful chapter in criminal / history is strictly true in every particular. I have / have[!] personally conversed with Langford, Hauser, / W. F. Sanders & others who had personal knowledge / of most of the events / W. R. Marshall /. There was a William R. Marshall who was governor of Minnesota. Manuscript notes in the same hand on pages 106–7, 116, 167, 91, 47.

The advertisement on the back wrapper differs from the preceding copy. A small rectangular label, 1.3 x 4.7 cm., has been removed from the top of the front wrapper and remounted above the imprint to cover manuscript numerals 4220 and a rule. The label reads: Presented by / J. Fletcher Williams, / St. Paul, Minn. /

1088 DIMSDALE, THOMAS J.

THE SAME . . . SECOND EDITION. VIRGINIA CITY, M.T.: D. W. TILTON, 1882.

[1]–241, [242 blank]. 17.1 x 12.2 cm. Gray printed wrappers. In a gray cloth case.

Ref.: Howes D345

1089 DIMSDALE, THOMAS J.

THE SAME . . . FOURTH EDITION. HELENA, MONT.

[1]–290. 22.6 x 14.8 cm. Illustrations unlisted. Green cloth.

Ref.: Howes D345

Edited by A. J. Noyes, published in 1915.

1090 DIOMEDI, ALEXANDER

[Caption title] SKETCHES OF MODERN INDIAN LIFE . . .

[1]–79, [80 blank]. 22.9 x 15 cm. Gray wrappers. In a green cloth case.

Ref.: Howes D347; Smith 2467

The narrative describing the author's life among Indians in Idaho, Montana, Oregon, and Washington was written in 1879, according to the preface, but there is no clue given as to date or place of publication. Howes suggests Woodstock, Maryland, 1894.

1091 DISTURNELL, JOHN,

THE EMIGRANT'S GUIDE TO NEW MEXICO, CALIFORNIA AND OREGON . . . NEW YORK: PUBLISHED BY J. DISTURNELL, 1849.

[1]–80. 14.7 x 9.3 cm. Map: Map of / California, / New Mexico / and Adjacent Countries / Showing the Gold Regions &c. / [thin and thick rules] / New York. / Published by J. Disturnell. / 1849. / Printed at Ackerman's rooms, 120 Fulton St N. Y. / 74 x 51.6 cm. Scale: 75 miles to one inch. *Inset:* Routes from / Vera Cruz & Alvarado to / Mexico. / 12.1 x 31.4 cm. Scale: 20 miles to one inch. Also, two inset profiles. Blue cloth, gilt stamped on front cover and in blind on back cover. In a blue cloth case.

Ref.: Cowan pp. 175–76; Howes D351; Jones 1196; Munk (Alliot) p. 66; Rader 1145; Sabin 20325; Wheat (*Gold Region*) 81; Wheat (*Transmississippi*) 605

This edition with the Disturnell map instead of one by Colton is thought to be preferable.

1092 DISTURNELL, JOHN

[Map] MAPA / DE LOS / ESTADOS UNIDOS / DE / MEJICO, / SEGUN LO ORGANIZADO Y DEFINIDO POR LAS VARIAS / ACTAS DEL CONGRESO DE DICHA REPUBLICA: Y / CONSTRUIDO POR LAS MEJORES AUTORIDADES. / LO PUBLICAN J. DISTURNELL, 102 BROADWAY. / NUEVA YORK. / 1847. / SCALE OF ENGLISH MILES. / [diagrammatic scale; about 70 miles to one inch] REVISED EDITION. / *Inset:* Map / Showing the Battle Grounds / of the 8th and 9th May 1846. / By / J. H. Eaton 3d Infy / 7.5 x 10.7 cm. (irregular shape). Scale: 7 miles to one inch. *Inset:* Plan of / Monterey / and its / Environs. / 9.8 x 9.3 cm. (irregular shape). No scale indi-

cated. *Inset:* Tampico / and its / Environs. / 5.8 x 10.2 cm. (irregular shape). No scale indicated. *Inset:* Chart / of the / Bay of Vera Cruz. / Drawn by order of V Admiral Baudin. / 8.7 x 12 cm. (irregular shape). No scale indicated. *Inset:* Carta de los Caminos &c. desde / Vera Cruz y Alvarado a / Méjico. / 12.3 x 32 cm. Scale: about 18 miles to one inch. *Inset:* Two insets of Tabla de Distancias and two inset profiles, Mexico to Vera Cruz and Mexico to Acapulco.

Map, 74.5 x 103.7 cm. Scale: about 70 miles to one inch. Remounted on cloth, folded into new blue cloth folder, with original smaller covers mounted on front and back, broadside mounted inside front cover: Statistics of the Republic of Mexico, 13.6 x 8.3 cm., printed on blue paper.

Ref.: Martin, Laurence: *Disturnell's Map* . . . Washington, 1937; Phillips (*Maps*) p. 410

The Revised Edition of Disturnell's map was used for the treaty to determine the border between Mexico and the United States.

1093 DISTURNELL, JOHN

TOURIST'S GUIDE TO THE UPPER MISSISSIPPI RIVER: GIVING ALL THE RAILROAD AND STEAMBOAT ROUTES DIVERGING FROM CHICAGO, MILWAUKEE, AND DUBUQUE, TOWARD ST. PAUL, AND THE FALLS OF ST. ANTHONY . . . NEW YORK: PUBLISHED BY THE AMERICAN NEWS COMPANY, 1866.

[1]–84, [85–100 advertisements]. 16.1 x 12.4 cm. Illustrations unlisted. Map: Map of the / Lake Region / and / Upper Mississippi River / [lower right:] Lith. of Cooper & Stone 100 Nassau St. N. Y. / 38.6 x 64.8 cm. Scale: about 55 miles to one inch. Green limp cloth, blind border on sides, title in gilt on front cover.

Ref.: Buck 654; Howes D354; Sabin 20325

1094 DISTURNELL, JOHN

THE TRAVELLER'S GUIDE THROUGH THE STATE OF ILLINOIS. CONTAINING INFORMATION OF IMPORTANCE TO THE TRAVELLER AND EMIGRANT . . . NEW YORK: PUBLISHED BY J. DISTURNELL, MDCCCXXXVIII.

[1]–16. 12.3 x 8.2 cm. Map: Map of / Illinois / 1838. / Scale of Statute Miles. / [diagrammatic scale: about 22 miles to one inch] / Scale of Geographic Miles. / [diagrammatic scale: 19 miles to one inch] / [lower left:] Drawn by J. H. Young. [centre:] New York. Published by J. Disturnell. [right:] Engraved by J. H. Young & E. Yeager. / 47.3 x 32.8 cm. Scale as indicated. *Inset:* Map of the / Lead Mine Region, / east of the / Mississippi River. / Scale of Miles. / [diagrammatic scale: about 16 miles to one inch] / 10.1 x 13.2 cm. Scale as indicated. Text, protected by green back wrapper which is also used for back end-

paper, bound into black cloth covers, title in gilt on front cover. Map laid in. Map repaired, mounted.
Ref.:

1095 DIVINE, ROBERT M.

TWO HUNDRED AND FORTY AUTOGRAPH LETTERS, SIGNED, BY ROBERT M. DIVINE. 1891 February 10 to 1898 September 20. Various places. 438 pages, various sizes. To E. T. David, and others.

This excellent series of letters is mounted in a copy of *Shapleigh's General Hardware Catalog No. 250* . . . The letters are numbered in blue pencil 1–255; two of the numbers are filled by photographs, several numbers were skipped, and letters for two numbers have been removed from the volume.

The series comprises reports of the daily operation of a Wyoming ranch, accounts, tallies, etc. Most of the time, Divine worked for the CK Ranch near Casper, Wyoming. The CK Ranch was one of four ranches which made up the J. M. Carey & Bro. outfit, the headquarters of which was at Inez (later Careyhurst), Wyoming. E. T. David was the manager, Divine was foreman of the CK Ranch.

The letters contain a good deal of material about cattle rustlers (including an encounter with the Hole-in-the-Wall gang), court trials, round-ups, and the day-to-day management of a large ranch. Divine's early life was spent as a rancher in Arkansas; he was about fifty-five years old when he found work with the CK Ranch and he was then supporting a wife and sixteen children.

1096 DIXON, JOSEPH

[Extract] [caption title] . . . TOPOGRAPHICAL MEMOIR OF THE COMMAND AGAINST THE SNAKE INDIANS, UNDER MAJOR E. STEEN, UNITED STATES DRAGOONS, IN THE SUMMER OF 1860, BY BREVET SECOND LIEUTENANT JOSEPH DIXON, UNITED STATES TOPOGRAPHICAL ENGINEERS. . .

527–569 [570 blank]. 22.4 x 14.4 cm. Map: Map / Showing the Routes travelled by the / Command of Maj^r E. Steen, U. S. Drag^s / against the Snake Indians in 1860 / by / Lieut Joseph Dixon U. S. Top^l Eng^{rs} / from explarations[!] and surveys made by him / while attached to this Command. / drawn under the direction / of / Capt. G. Thom. U. S. Top^l Eng^{rs} / Scale 750,000 / [diagrammatic scale: 12 miles to one inch] / Legend / [ten lines] / [upper right:] Sen. Ex. Doc. N° 1–37th Cong. 2^d Sess. / [lower right:] Lith. of J. Bien 180 Broadway New York / 60.1 x 85.3 cm. Scale as above. Rebound in new red cloth.

Ref.: Wagner-Camp 356; Wheat (*Transmississippi*) 1016

The report by Lieutenant Dixon occupies pages 528–40. The extract is from 37th Congress, 2nd Session, Senate Document 1, Vol. 2, Serial 1118, Report of the Secretary of War. [Washington: Government Printing Office, 1861.]

Pages 541–69 comprise short reports on explorations of the Yellowstone and Missouri and on military roads in the far Northwest and the Southwest by J. W. Macomb, W. F. Raynolds, A. A. Humphreys, John Pope, Howard Stansbury, Geo. Thom, and John Mullan. The Mullan reports (pages 549–69) are Appendix XVII. / United States Military Road Expedition from Fort Walla-Walla to / Fort Benton, W. T., by Lieutenant John Mullan, 2d Artillery. / Apparently missed by Wagner-Camp.

1097 DOANE, GUSTAVUS C.

. . . THE REPORT OF LIEUTENANT GUSTAVUS C. DOANE UPON THE SO-CALLED YELLOWSTONE EXPEDITION OF 1870 . . .

[1]–40. 22.9 x 14.8 cm. Blue printed wrappers with title on front wrapper. In a brown cloth case.

Ref.: Howes D371; National Parks (*Yellowstone*) p. 29

41st Congress, 3rd Session, Senate, Executive Document No. 51, Serial 1440. [Washington: Government Printing Office, 1873.]

Possibly an offprint for private circulation, with a special printed wrapper. Imprint on front wrapper: Washington: Government Printing Office, 1873.

1098 DOBBS, ARTHUR

AN ACCOUNT OF THE COUNTRIES ADJOINING TO HUDSON'S BAY, IN THE NORTH-WEST PART OF AMERICA . . . LONDON: PRINTED FOR J. ROBINSON, M DCC XLIV.

[A]^2, A–Ee^4. [1–2], [i–ii], 1–211, [212 blank], two blank leaves. 29.1 x 22.7 cm. Folding map: A / New Map of Part of / North America / From the Latitude of 40 to 68 Degrees. / Including the late discoveries made on / the Furnace Bomb Ketch in 1742. / And the Western Rivers & Lakes falling into / Nelson River in Hudson's Bay, as described / by Joseph La France a French Canadese / Indian, who Travaled[!] thro those Countries / and Lakes for 3 Years from 1739 / to 1742— /. 32.5 x 47.2 cm. No scale given. Contemporary full crimson calf, wide gilt tooled borders on sides, inner borders gilt, gilt backstrip, gilt edges. Skilfully rebacked.

Prov.: Bookplates of William Harrison and J. C. MacCoy.

Ref.: Field 433; Howes D373; Sabin 20404; Smith 2483; Staton & Tremaine 193; Wagner (*Cart. of NW Coast*) p. 158

Large paper copy.

Dobbs compiled his work from many sources (he had not visited Hudson's Bay), some of which had not been published. He was actively engaged in an attempt to break the monopoly held by the Hudson's Bay Company. It was largely at the insistence of Dobbs that the Christopher Middleton expedition (two ships) set out in 1741. In the present work, he criticized Middleton because he had failed to explore two or three inlets and suggested that Middleton was thereby favoring the interests of the Hudson's Bay Company. See Wagner's notes regarding the maps used by Dobbs.

1099   DOBIE, J. FRANK

. . . THE LONGHORNS . . . ILLUSTRATED BY TOM LEA. BOSTON: LITTLE, BROWN AND COMPANY, 1941.

[i]–[xxiv, xxiv blank], [1]–388, leaf inserted after viii. 22 x 15 cm. Illustrations unlisted. Full leather, fore and lower edges uncut. In board slip case.

Ref.: Adams (*Ramp. Herd*) 694; Daniel 9; Dobie p. 151; Howes D375

Limited to 265 copies signed by the author and the artist.

1100   DOBIE, J. FRANK

THE MUSTANGS . . . ILLUSTRATED BY CHARLES BANKS WILSON. BOSTON: LITTLE, BROWN AND COMPANY.*

[i]–[xviii, xviii blank], [1]–376. 21.3 x 14.3 cm. Illustrations unlisted. Blue and tan cloth, blue top. In dust jacket.

Ref.: Adams (*Ramp. Herd*) 696; Daniel 14; Dobie p. 151

Copyrighted 1952.

1101   DOCKHAM, C. AUGUSTINE

MILWAUKEE BUSINESS DIRECTORY, FOR THE YEAR 1858 . . . MILWAUKEE: DAILY WISCONSIN STEAM PRESS, 1858.

[1]–64, [1]–31, [32 blank]. 15.9 x 10.1 cm. Maroon cloth, blind embossed borders on sides, title in gilt on front cover, advertisements on endpapers.

Ref.: AII (*Wisconsin*) 538

Pages [1]–28 of the second section carry "Business Cards." AII (*Wisconsin*) gives the collation for the second part only and does not list the first.

1102   DODD, BETHUEL

AUTOGRAPH LETTER, SIGNED. 1848 January 4, St. Louis. Two pages, 23.8 x 19 cm. To William S. Williams.

An interesting letter to Old Bill Williams, in which the writer regrets missing him in St. Louis. He speaks also of planning a trip to Salt Lake.

Following the letter and preceding a postscript is a sight draft for forty-five dollars drawn on Thomas Smith by Bethuel Dodd in favor of Bill Williams. The postscript mentions Peg[leg] Smith as being at Bent's Fort.

1103   DODGE, AUGUSTUS C.

SPEECH OF MR. A. C. DODGE, OF IOWA, ON THE BILL ESTABLISHING THE BOUNDARY LINE BETWEEN MISSOURI AND IOWA, IN REPLY TO MR. EDWARDS OF MISSOURI. DELIVERED IN THE HOUSE OF REPRESENTATIVES, JULY 20, 1842. WASHINGTON: PRINTED AT THE GLOBE OFFICE, 1842.

[1]–8. 25.2 x 14.9 cm. Unbound, uncut.
Ref.:

1104   DODGE, FREDERICK P.

[Broadside] TO-NIGHT. PYGMALION AND GALATEA . . . PYGMALION, AN ATHENIAN SCULPTOR, FREDERICK PAULDING . . .

Broadside, 16.5 x 11.2 cm. Text, 13.2 x 8.8 cm.
Ref.:

Paulding was the son of Richard Irving Dodge. No place or date of performance or printing given.

1105   DODGE, GRENVILLE M.

THE BATTLE OF ATLANTA AND OTHER CAMPAIGNS . . . COUNCIL BLUFFS, IOWA: THE MONARCH PRINTING COMPANY, 1910.*

[1]–183, [184 blank]. 22.7 x 15.3 cm. 18 illustrations listed. Green cloth, title on front cover.

Ref.: Nicholson p. 243

Some of the essays relate to Indian campaigns and the Civil War in the West.

1106   DODGE, GRENVILLE M.

BIOGRAPHICAL SKETCH OF JAMES BRIDGER MOUNTAINEER, TRAPPER AND GUIDE . . . NEW YORK: UNZ & COMPANY, 1905.*

[1]–27, [28 blank]. 22.3 x 15.1 cm. Three illustrations, unlisted. Tan printed wrappers bound into gray boards with yellow cloth backstrip.

Ref.: Howes D392; Jones 1695 see; Smith 2492

Editions: Kansas City [1905].

1107 DODGE, GRENVILLE M.

HOW WE BUILT THE UNION PACIFIC RAILWAY AND OTHER RAILWAY PAPERS AND ADDRESSES . . .

[1]–171, [172–76 blank]. 22.9 x 15.2 cm. 30 illustrations listed. Gray-green printed wrappers, bound into gray boards with yellow cloth backstrip.

Prov.: Printed slip (7.6 x 15.2 cm.) tipped in before page [1]: Compliments / of / General Grenville M. Dodge /.

Ref.: Howes D393; Malone p. 3; Mott (*Iowa*) p. 65; Nicholson p. 242; *Railway Economics* p. 298 see

Facing the title-page is the printer's imprint: The Monarch Printing Co. / Council Bluffs / Iowa /. Probably printed in 1908.

1108 DODGE, GRENVILLE M.

THE INDIAN CAMPAIGN OF WINTER OF 1864–65 . . . READ TO THE COLORADO COMMANDERY OF THE LOYAL LEGION OF THE UNITED STATES AT DENVER, APRIL 21, 1907.*

[1]–[21], [22 blank]. 22.4 x 15.1 cm. Gray printed wrappers bound into gray boards with yellow cloth backstrip.

Ref.: Rader 1168

Printed in Denver, 1907.

1109 DODGE, GRENVILLE M.

PAPER READ BEFORE THE SOCIETY OF THE ARMY OF THE TENNESSEE . . . SEPT. 15, 1888 . . . NEW YORK: UNZ & CO., 1899.

[1]–50, [51–2 blank]. 22.7 x 14.9 cm. Four illustrations listed. Green printed wrappers bound into gray boards with yellow cloth backstrip.

Ref.:

An account of the building of the first transcontinental railroad.

1110 DODGE, RICHARD IRVING

THE PAPERS OF RICHARD IRVING DODGE, 1875–1905.

The collection comprises the following materials:

Autograph Manuscript Diary, May 6 to October 19, 1875. Six volumes, 729 pages, 11.6 x 8 cm. and 14.6 x 9 cm. Written in pencil in pocket scratch pads.

The diary comprises day-by-day accounts of exploratory operations in the Black Hills.

Autograph Manuscript Diary, October 31, 1876, to January 8, 1877. Four volumes, 490 pages, 18.2 x 11.7 cm. and 12.3 x 8.5 cm. Written in pencil in pocket scratch pads.

The diary covers the Powder River Winter Campaign with General Crook.

Autograph Manuscript Diary, September 18, 1878, to May 25, 1880. Seven volumes, 756 pages, 16.8 x 9.2 cm. Written in pencil in pocket notebooks.

The diaries include accounts of the Cheyenne Campaign of 1878, turkey hunting, military life, etc.

Autograph Manuscript Diary, September 1 to December 18, 1880. One volume, 63 pages, 16.8 x 9.2 cm. Written in pencil in a pocket notebook.

The Ute Campaign of 1880.

Autograph Manuscript Diaries, June 23 to September 28, 1883. Two volumes, 170 pages, 14.3 x 8.2 cm. Written in pencil in notebooks.

A vivid account of a trip with General Sherman.

Autograph Manuscript: Indian Boys and Girls. / 44 pages, 20.2 x 13.2 cm. Incomplete.

Autograph Manuscript: Rail Road Towns- /. 16 pages, 20.4 x 12.6 cm.

Autograph Manuscript, untitled. 21 pages, 20.2 x 13.2 cm. Incomplete.

Seventy-nine Autograph Letters, Documents, Manuscripts, etc., by and to Richard I. Dodge, 1879 to 1905, by the following writers:

Baird, Spencer	Paulding, Frederick
Beeson, B. A.	Perry, Alex. J.
Blunt, P. E.	Pope, John
Bussey, William	Putnam's Sons, G. P.
Dawes, H. L.	Rideing, William H.
Dodge, Julia	Sharp, Alex
Dodge, Richard I.	Sherman, William T.
Duane, —	Smiley, Joseph B.
Gilmore, Q. A.	Spofford, A. R.
Glenn, Annie	Stephens, Edward
Glenn, R. B.	Tupper, I. B. I.
Kilpatrick, R. L.	Whipple, William D.
McKeeber, C.	Woodhull, R. F.
Mallery, Garrick	Worthington, A. D.

Seven printed broadsides and pamphlets, described under numbers 1104, 1115, 1378, 4319, 4320, 4323, 4324.

Ninety-four photographs of Dodge, Mrs. Dodge, members of their family and friends.

Richard Irving Dodge, Army officer and author, was a North Carolinian who was graduated from West Point in 1848. His career in the Army, with the exception of the Civil War years, was almost wholly in the West. The manuscripts and letters described above contain a vivid picture of Army life during the last quarter of the nineteenth century. Most of the material is unpublished.

1111 DODGE, RICHARD IRVING

THE BLACK HILLS. A MINUTE DESCRIPTION OF THE ROUTES, SCENERY, SOIL, CLIMATE, TIMBER, GOLD, GEOLOGY, ZOOLOGY, ETC. . . . NEW YORK: JAMES MILLER, 1876.

[1]–151, [152 blank], [153–56 advertisements]. 18.5 x 12.3 cm. 14 illustrations and a map listed. Map: The / Black Hills / of the / Cheyenne / Map of Explorations and Surveys / made under the direction of / Lieut. Colonel R. I. Dodge, 23ᵈ U. S. Infantry, / 1875. [lower right:] American Photo-Lithographic Co. N. Y. (Osborne's Process) / 50.5 x 35.9 cm. Scale: about nine miles to one inch. Rust cloth, black borders on sides, title in gilt on backstrip.
Ref.: Bradford 1345; Howes D401; Jennewein 59

1112 DODGE, RICHARD IRVING

THE HUNTING GROUNDS OF THE GREAT WEST. A DESCRIPTION OF THE PLAINS, GAME, AND INDIANS OF THE GREAT NORTH AMERICAN DESERT . . . LONDON: CHATTO & WINDUS, 1877.

[i]–[lviii, lviii blank], [1]–440. 21.3 x 13.5 cm. 20 illustrations and a map. Map: Map of the Western States and Territories of the United States / Showing the existing Indian Reservations and the Buffalo range in 1830 and 1876. / [lower centre:] London, Chatto & Windus. / [lower right:] Edᵂ Weller, Litho. / 21.5 x 31.5 cm. No scale given. Contemporary red levant morocco, gilt sides, gilt backstrip, inner borders gilt, gilt edges, by Hammond.
Prov.: Inscribed on blank leaf at front: To / Frederick Paulding Dodge / from his affectionate / Father / The Author / New York / Jan.y. 27ᵗʰ 1877. /
Ref.: Dobie p. 151; Howes D404; Rader 1170
First English Edition. Presentation binding.

1113 DODGE, RICHARD IRVING

THE SAME . . . SECOND EDITION . . .

[i]–[lviii, lviii blank], [1]–448. 22 x 14.2 cm. Red pictorial cloth, title in gilt on backstrip, uncut.
Ref.: Howes D404
According to Howes, there was also an English edition of 1878.

1114 DODGE, RICHARD IRVING

OUR WILD INDIANS: THIRTY-THREE YEARS' PERSONAL EXPERIENCE AMONG THE RED MEN OF THE GREAT WEST . . . HARTFORD: A. D. WORTHINGTON AND COMPANY, 1882.

[i]–[xl, xl blank], 29–653, [654 blank]. 22.1 x 14.4 cm. 25 illustrations listed. Maroon pictorial cloth, title in gilt on backstrip and front cover.

Ref.: Howes D403; Rader 1172; Saunders 2143

1115 DODGE, RICHARD IRVING

[Caption title] A STANDARD SUPERB WORK OF GREAT VALUE AND INTEREST. THIRTY-THREE YEARS' PERSONAL EXPERIENCE AMONG OUR WILD INDIANS . . .

[1–4]. 29.9 x 22.5 cm. Unbound leaflet.
Ref.:
Advertisement for Dodge's book, published by A. D. Worthington in 1882.

1116 DOLLAR MONTHLY, THE

[Caption title] THE DOLLAR MONTHLY AND OLD-SETTLERS' MEMORIAL. VOL. 1 [–3]. HAMILTON, ILLINOIS,—MAY 1, 1873 [–DECEMBER, 1875]. NO. 1 [–8, 1–12, 1–12] . . .

[1–128]. [1–202]. [1–202]. 37.4 x 27 cm. Three volumes, roughly bound in original printed wrappers. First volume lacks front wrapper.
Ref.:
Edited and published by Thomas Gregg. Contains a good deal of material about the Mormons in Missouri and Illinois as well as numerous articles of general reminiscences.
For related periodicals see under DOLLAR RURAL MESSENGER and THE RURAL MESSENGER.

1117 DOLLAR RURAL MESSENGER

[Caption title] DOLLAR RURAL MESSENGER. FOR THE HOME OF THE PEOPLE. VOL. 4 - - - NO. 4. HAMILTON, ILL. - - - KEOKUK, IOWA. APRIL, 1876 . . .

[49]–64. 37.4 x 27 cm. Unbound.
Ref.:
A continuation of Thomas Gregg's THE DOLLAR MONTHLY.

1118 DOLLARD, ROBERT

RECOLLECTIONS OF THE CIVIL WAR AND GOING WEST TO GROW UP WITH THE COUNTRY . . . SCOTLAND, SOUTH DAKOTA: PUBLISHED BY THE AUTHOR, 1906.*

[i–vi, inserted errata leaf, vii–viii], [5]–296. 21.7 x 14.5 cm. Six portraits. Blue cloth, red sprinkled edges.
Ref.: Howes D406
Among the author's "recollections" are experiences in Texas, the Northwest, and the Dakotas.

1119 DOMENECH, EMMANUEL H. D.

JOURNAL D'UN MISSIONNAIRE AU TEXAS ET AU MEXIQUE . . . 1846–1852. PARIS: LIBRAIRIE DE GAUME FRERES, 1857.

[I]–XII, 1–477, [478 blank, 479 erratum, 480 blank]. 20.8 x 12.4 cm. Map: Carte du Texas /

pour les / Missions et Voyages / de / l'Abbé Em. Domenech / dressée d'après / les Documents Officiels topographiques / et les travaux de J. Cordova. / Paris, Février, 1857. / [decorative rule] / [lower left:] Gravée chez Erhard rue Bonaparte 42. / [lower centre:] Paris Gaume frères, Editeurs 4 rue Cassette. / [lower right:] Paris, Imp. Bineteau rue Antoine Dubois, 6. / 44.2 x 35.6 cm. Scale: about 40 miles to one inch. Contemporary mottled calf, maroon leather label, backstrip gilt, marbled edges.

Ref.: Howes D408; Rader 1175; Raines p. 69; Sabin 20549

1120 DOMENECH, EMMANUEL H. D.

MISSIONARY ADVENTURES IN TEXAS AND MEXICO. A PERSONAL NARRATIVE OF SIX YEARS' SOJOURN IN THOSE REGIONS . . . LONDON: LONGMAN, BROWN, GREEN, LONGMANS, AND ROBERTS, 1858.

[i]–[xvi, xvi blank], [1]–366, [1–2 advertisements]. 21.7 x 13.8 cm. Map: Map of / Texas / illustrating the / Missions & Journeys / of / the Abbé Em. Domenech. / [lower centre:] London, Longman & Co. / [lower right:] Engraved by Edwᵈ Weller, Duke Strᵗ Bloomsbury. / 44 x 34.8 cm. Scale: 40 miles to one inch. Red cloth, blind embossed sides, gilt title on backstrip, uncut, unopened.

Ref.: Bradford 1350; Dobie pp. 40, 66; Field 443; Howes D408; Rader 1176; Raines pp. 69–70; Sabin 20553

1121 DOMENECH, EMMANUEL H. D.

SEVEN YEARS' RESIDENCE IN THE GREAT DESERTS OF NORTH AMERICA . . . LONDON: LONGMAN, GREEN, LONGMAN, AND ROBERTS, 1860.

[i]–xiv, [1]–445, [446 colophon], [447–48 advertisements]. [i]–xii, [1]–465, [466 colophon], [467–68 advertisements]. 21.8 x 13.8 cm. 58 illustrations and a map: Map Drawn / to illustrate the travels / & from the Documents of / the Abbe Domenech / showing / the actual situation / of the / Indian Tribes / of / North America / and the road described / by the author / P. Bineteau geographer del / 1860 / [lower left:] Gravé chez Erhard 42 R. Bonaparte / [lower right:] Imp Bineteau R. Antoine Dubois 6. / 44.2 x 35.6 cm. Scale: about 40 miles to one inch. Two volumes, brown cloth, blind embossed sides, title in gilt on backstrips, uncut.

Ref.: Howes D410; Rader 1177; Raines p. 70; Sabin 20554; Wagner-Camp 356a

1122 DONALD, JAY

OUTLAWS OF THE BORDER. A COMPLETE AND AUTHENTIC HISTORY OF THE LIVES OF FRANK AND JESSE JAMES THE YOUNGER BROTHERS, AND THEIR ROBBER COMPANIONS, INCLUDING QUANTRELL AND HIS NOTED GUERILLAS, THE GREATEST BANDITS THE WORLD HAS EVER KNOWN . . . PHILADELPHIA, PA.: DOUGLASS BROS., 1882.

[i]–[x], 11–520. 18.5 x 12 cm. 40 illustrations listed. Blue pictorial cloth, title in gilt on backstrip.

Ref.: Adams 318; Howes D415

The title-leaf is a cancel and is somewhat smaller than the text size.

1123 DONAN, PATRICK

THE LAND OF GOLDEN GRAIN. NORTH DAKOTA. THE LAKE-GEMMED, BREEZE-SWEPT EMPIRE OF THE NEW NORTHWEST . . . CHICAGO, ILL.: PUBLISHED BY CHARLES R. BRODIX, 1883.

[i–xviii advertisements], [3]–70, [71–96 advertisements]. 21.3 x 14.4 cm. Unbound, removed from bound volume.

Ref.:

Adams (*Ramp. Herd*), Rader, and Smith describe other promotional works by Donan, but do not mention this one.

1124 DONIPHAN, ALEXANDER W., & STERLING PRICE

ORIGINAL STEEL PLATE ENGRAVED WITH PORTRAITS OF DONIPHAN AND PRICE. As used in the U. P. James bound editions of Hughes, John T.: *Doniphan's Expedition* . . . Cincinnati, 1848. 20.6 x 28.2 cm.

1125 DONNEL, WILLIAM M.

PIONEERS OF MARION COUNTY, CONSISTING OF A GENERAL HISTORY OF THE COUNTY FROM ITS EARLIEST SETTLEMENT TO THE PRESENT DATE. ALSO, THE . . . HISTORY OF EACH TOWNSHIP, INCLUDING BRIEF BIOGRAPHICAL SKETCHES OF SOME OF THE MORE PROMINENT EARLY SETTLERS . . . DES MOINES, IOWA: REPUBLICAN STEAM PRINTING HOUSE, 1872.

[1]–346, [347 advertisements, 348 blank]. 21 x 14 cm. Dark green cloth, title in gilt on backstrip.

Ref.: Cook p. 143; Howes D425

This Marion County is in Iowa.

1126 DONNELLY, IGNATIUS

MINNESOTA. ADDRESS DELIVERED AT THE BROADWAY HOUSE, NEW-YORK, ON 27TH MARCH, 1857 . . . NEW-YORK: FOLGER & TURNER, 1857.

[1]–13, [14 blank]. 20.5 x 13.3 cm. Unbound, inserted in gray boards, gray cloth backstrip, typed label.

Ref.: Bradford 1359; Sabin 20602

Both Bradford and Sabin call for 15 pages.

1127 DONNELLY, IGNATIUS

NININGER CITY . . . 1856. PHILADELPHIA: DUROSS, PRINTER.

[1]–32. 22.3 x 14.8 cm. Map: Map / of / Minnesota / Herline & Hensel, Lith. / Philᵃ / [lower centre:] Engraved expressly for the Nininger Pamphlet. / 22.9 x 24.4 cm. Scale: about 18 miles to one inch. Pink printed wrappers with title on front wrapper within decorative border. In a brown cloth folder.

Prov.: Folder stamped with monogram ACL.

Ref.: Bradford 1358; Howes D426; Jones 1349

The author was later Lt. Governor of Minnesota. Howes calls for two maps, but there is no evidence that a second ever accompanied the present copy.

1128 DONNER MISCELLANY

DONNER MISCELLANY. 41 DIARIES AND DOCUMENTS EDITED BY CARROLL D. HALL. SAN FRANCISCO: THE BOOK CLUB OF CALIFORNIA, 1947.

[i–ii], [1]–97, [98 blank]. 25.2 x 16.5 cm. Illustrations unlisted. Decorated neutral cloth, green cloth backstrip, fore and lower edges uncut.

Ref.:

Limited to 350 copies.

1129 DONOHO, MILFORD H.

CIRCLE-DOT: A TRUE STORY OF COWBOY LIFE FORTY YEARS AGO . . . TOPEKA: CRANE & COMPANY, 1907.*

[1]–256. 19.3 x 13 cm. Frontispiece. Red cloth.

Ref.: Adams 320; Adams (*Ramp. Herd*) 716; Howes D427; Rader 1184

1130 DORAN, THOMAS

[Map] MAP OF / MOLINE / ROCK ISLAND CO. / ILLINOIS / SURVEYED, DRAWN & PUBLISHED BY / THO.ˢ DORAN / 1857 / POPULATION, 2,900 / SCALE, 300 FEET TO AN INCH / SKETCHES BY H. C. FORD, ESQᴿ LITH. OF FRIEND & AUB, 80 WALNUT ST. PHILA. / COLORED & MOUNTED BY R. L. BARNES, / HARTS BUILDING / 6.ᵀᴴ ABOVE CHESTNUT / PHILADELPHIA. /

Map, 103.7 x 114.7 cm. Scale as above. Folded into green cloth covers, 18.8 x 12.5 cm., blind embossed borders, title in gilt on front cover: Map of Moline / Rock Island Co. / Illinois /.

Ref.:

In left and right margins there are fifteen views of residences and factories and a list of subscribers.

1131 DOSCH, HENRY E.

[Wrapper title] VIGILANTE DAYS AT VIRGINIA CITY . . . PORTLAND, OREGON: PUBLISHED BY FRED LOCKLEY.

[1]–19, [20 blank]. 22.5 x 15 cm. Tan printed wrappers with title on front wrapper, bound into gray boards, yellow cloth backstrip.

Ref.: Cowan p. 178; Smith 2535

The imprint on the back wrapper carries the date 1924.

1132 DOUBLEDAY, CHARLES W.

REMINISCENCES OF THE "FILIBUSTER" WAR IN NICARAGUA . . . NEW YORK: G. P. PUTNAM'S SONS, 1886.

[i]–[x, x blank], 1–225, [226 blank, 227–28 advertisements]. 19 x 12.6 cm. Map. Brown cloth.

Prov.: Presentation copy from the author to A. A. Lipscomb.

Ref.: Howes D430

A first-hand narrative.

1133 DOUGLAS, DAVID

JOURNAL KEPT BY DAVID DOUGLAS DURING HIS TRAVELS IN NORTH AMERICA 1823–1827 . . . LONDON: WILLIAM WESLEY & SON, 1914.*

[i–viii, viii blank], [1]–364. 24.7 x 15.3 cm. Frontispiece. Gray-blue buckram.

Ref.: Howes D435; Matthews p. 248; Staton & Tremaine 1432; Wagner-Camp 60 note

Limited to 500 copies.

1134 DOUGLAS, STEPHEN A.

[READ AND CIRCULATE.] SPEECH OF HON. STEPHEN A. DOUGLAS, ON THE "MEASURES OF ADJUSTMENT," DELIVERED IN THE CITY HALL, CHICAGO, OCTOBER 23, 1850. CHICAGO: DEMOCRATIC ARGUS BOOK AND JOB PRINTING OFFICE, 1850.

[1]–16. 22.2 x 14.4 cm. Pale pink printed wrappers with title on front wrapper, advertisement on back wrapper.

Ref.: Byrd 1559; McMurtrie (*Chicago*) 209; Sabin 29693 see

This was a *Democratic Argus Extra*.

1135 DOUGLAS COUNTY, OREGON

FIVE PRINTED AND MANUSCRIPT COUNTY WARRANTS, SIGNED by James Walton (1) or E. A. Lathrop (4). 1862 April 8 to 1866 May 23, Roseburg, Oregon. Each one page, about 9 x 20 cm.

Printed in San Francisco. Made out to Samuel Cole, J. T. Hinkle, E. A. Lathrop, and C. S. Rice. Inserted in Manuscript Journals of Loren L. Williams, Volume II.

1136 DOW, PEGGY

VICISSITUDES; OR, THE JOURNEY OF LIFE . . . SECOND EDITION, CORRECTED AND ENLARGED BY THE AUTHOR. PHILADELPHIA: PRINTED BY JOSEPH RAKESTRAW, 1815.

[A]–Y⁸,⁴. [1]–264. 12.5 x 7.2 cm. Contemporary mottled sheep.

Ref.: Howes D442; Sellers, Charles: *Lorenzo Dow*, New York, 1928; Shaw & Shoemaker 34593

Describes one of the most amazing trips ever made by a woman; down the Ohio from Wheeling to Natchez on the Mississippi thence overland through the hostile Creek country to the Georgia settlements, Carolina and Virginia . . . Peggy Dow was the wife of the great Methodist itinerant preacher Lorenzo Dow.—Howes

Editions: New York, 1814.

1137 DOW, PEGGY

VICISSITUDES IN THE WILDERNESS; EXEMPLIFIED, IN THE JOURNAL OF PEGGY DOW . . . FIFTH EDITION. NORWICH, CONN.: PRINTED BY WILLIAM FAULKNER, 1833.

[1]–214, [215–16 blank]. 17.6 x 11.7 cm. Woodcut portraits of Peggy and Lorenzo Dow. Black cloth, white printed label on backstrip.

Ref.: De Renne I, pp. 431–32; Howes D442; Sabin 20759

First Complete Edition. This is the first edition with this title and the first with these portraits.

Editions: New York, 1814. Philadelphia, 1815.

1138 DOWELL, BENJAMIN F.

AUTOGRAPH LETTER, SIGNED, by B. F. Dowell. 1888 August 14, Jacksonville, Ore. Two pages, 32 x 20.3 cm. To Twogood. Re his claims. Accompanied by five pages (33 x 20.2 cm.) of questions, typed carbon copy.

1139 DOWELL, BENJAMIN F.

THE PETITION OF B. F. DOWELL AND OTHERS, ASKING PAY FOR TWO COMPANIES OF OREGON VOLUNTEERS . . . JACKSONVILLE, OREGON: OREGON SENTINEL OFFICE PRINT, 1869.

[1]–14, [15–16 blank]. 23.4 x 15.7 cm. Buff printed wrappers with title on front wrapper. In a maroon half morocco case.

Prov.: Bookplate of C. G. Littell.
Ref.: McMurtrie (*Oregon*) 516; Smith 2544

1140 DOWELL, BENJAMIN F.

[Broadside] TO THE OREGON INDIAN WAR CLAIMANTS. THE OREGON INDIAN WAR DEBTS OF 1854 ARE NOW BEING PAID . . . B. F. DOWELL.

Broadside, 20 x 13.8 cm. Text, 17.4 x 11.6 cm.
Ref.:
Probably printed by the *Oregon Sentinel* at Jacksonville in 1874. See Smith 1018 for letters and briefs mentioned in the text of the broadside.

1141 DOWN, ROBERT H.

A HISTORY OF THE SILVERTON COUNTRY . . . PORTLAND, OREGON: THE BERNCLIFF PRESS, 1926.*

[i–viii, viii blank], 1–258. Frontispiece and map. 21.9 x 14.5 cm. Blue cloth.
Prov.: Signature on fly-leaf: Robt H. Down /.
Ref.: Howes D445; Smith 2545
Contains an overland narrative.

1142 DOWNEY, JOSEPH T.

. . . FILINGS FROM AN OLD SAW. REMINISCENCES OF SAN FRANCISCO AND CALIFORNIA'S CONQUEST . . . SAN FRANCISCO: JOHN HOWELL, MCMLVI.*

[i–viii, viii blank], 1–170, [171 colophon, 172 blank]. 23.4 x 16 cm. Portrait. Green cloth.
Ref.:
Limited to 750 copies.

1143 DOWNIE, WILLIAM

HUNTING FOR GOLD. REMINISCENCES OF PERSONAL EXPERIENCE AND RESEARCH IN THE EARLY DAYS OF THE PACIFIC COAST FROM ALASKA TO PANAMA . . . SAN FRANCISCO, CAL.: THE CALIFORNIA PUBLISHING CO., 1893.

[1]–407, [408 blank]. 22.2 x 14.6 cm. 71 illustrations listed. Red cloth, title in gilt on front cover and backstrip.
Ref.: Blumann & Thomas 4443; Cowan p. 179; Howes D448

1144 DOWSE, THOMAS

[Wrapper title] THE NEW NORTHWEST. MONTANA. FORT BENTON; ITS PAST, PRESENT AND FUTURE . . . CHICAGO, ILL.: COMMERCIAL ADVERTISER CO., 1879.

[1]–22, [23–4 blank]. 26.4 x 20 cm. Illustrations unlisted. Light blue wrappers, with title on front wrapper, advertisement of Chicago & Northwest-Railway Company on verso of front and recto and verso of back wrappers.
Ref.: Adams (*Ramp. Herd*) 724; Howes D452; Smith 1553

1145 DOY, JOHN

THE NARRATIVE OF JOHN DOY, OF LAWRENCE, KANSAS . . . NEW YORK: THOMAS HOLMAN, 1860.

[1]–132. 18.3 x 12.6 cm. Tan printed wrappers with title on front wrapper, advertisements on verso of front and recto and verso of back wrapper. In a dark blue cloth case.
Ref.: Bradford 1376; Howes D453; Rader 1216
John Brown, Kansas settling, abolitionism, etc.

Editions: Boston, 1860.

1146 DOYLE, JOHN T.

MEMORANDUM AS TO THE DISCOVERY OF THE BAY OF SAN FRANCISCO . . . READ BEFORE THE AMERICAN ANTIQUARIAN SOCIETY . . . OCTOBER 21, 1873 . . . SAN FRANCISCO: REPRINTED BY BACON & COMPANY, 1889.

[1]–18. 22.7 x 14.8 cm. Map. Orange printed wrappers, with title on front cover.

Prov.: Inscribed on front wrapper: [name erased] / Compts of / Jno T Doyle / [flourish] /.

Ref.: Bradford 1379 see; Cowan p. 181

Editions: Worcester, 1874.

1147 DRANNAN, WILLIAM F.

THIRTY-ONE YEARS ON THE PLAINS AND IN THE MOUNTAINS; OR, THE LAST VOICE FROM THE PLAINS . . . CHICAGO: RHODES & McCLURE PUBLISHING COMPANY, 1899.

[5]–586, [587–95 advertisements, 596 blank]. 19.2 x 13.2 cm. 73 illustrations unlisted. Green cloth stamped in silver.

Ref.: Adams 325; Howes D482; Smith 2568

The author's veracity has been questioned effectively by W. N. Bate and others.

1148 DRANNAN, WILLIAM F.

CAPT. W. F. DRANNAN, CHIEF OF SCOUTS, AS PILOT TO EMIGRANT AND GOVERNMENT TRAINS, ACROSS THE PLAINS OF THE WILD WEST OF FIFTY YEARS AGO . . . CHICAGO: RHODES & McCLURE PUBLISHING CO., 1910.*

[11]–407, [408–12 advertisements]. 19.2 x 13.4 cm. 11 illustrations listed. Green cloth, stamped in silver.

Ref.: Howes D483; Rader 1226; Smith 2566 see

1149 DRAPER, ELIAS J.

AN AUTOBIOGRAPHY OF ELIAS JOHNSON DRAPER, A PIONEER OF CALIFORNIA, CONTAINING SOME THRILLING INCIDENTS RELATIVE TO CROSSING THE PLAINS BY OX TEAM, AND SOME VERY INTERESTING PARTICULARS OF LIFE IN CALIFORNIA IN THE EARLY DAYS . . . FRESNO, CALIFORNIA: EVENING DEMOCRAT PRINT, 1904.

[1–2], 7–76. 20.9 x 13.4 cm. Portrait. Black limp cloth, title in gilt on front cover.

Ref.: Cowan p. 183; Howes D484

Includes an account of the author's overland journey. A blank leaf at the end is headed in manuscript, in pencil: Annex / followed by notes concerning the author's ancestry.

1150 DREW, CHARLES S.

[Caption title] . . . COMMUNICATION FROM C. S. DREW, LATE ADJUTANT OF THE SECOND REGIMENT OF THE OREGON MOUNTED VOLUNTEERS, GIVING AN ACCOUNT OF THE ORIGIN AND EARLY PROSECUTION OF THE INDIAN WAR IN OREGON . . .

[1]–48. 24.3 x 15.2 cm. Red buckram, with morocco corners and backstrip, mostly unopened.

Ref.: Howes D497

36th Congress, 1st Session, Senate, Miscellaneous Document No. 59, Serial 1036. [Washington, 1860.]

1151 DREW, CHARLES S.

ANOTHER COPY. 24.1 x 15.5 cm. Stabbed, unbound, uncut, unopened.

1152 DREW, CHARLES S.

OFFICIAL REPORT OF THE OWYHEE RECONNOISSANCE, MADE BY LIEUT. COLONEL C. S. DREW, 1ST OREGON CAVALRY, IN THE SUMMER OF 1864 . . . JACKSONVILLE, OREGON: OREGON SENTINEL PRINTING OFFICE, 1865.

[i–ii, ii blank], [1]–[32]. 21.1 x 14 cm. Yellow printed wrappers with title on front wrapper. In a blue cloth folder.

Prov.: Inscribed on front wrapper: Hon. J. W. Nesmith, / U. S. Senate, / Compliments of / C. S. Drew /.

Ref.: Howes D498; McMurtrie (*Oregon*) 301; Wagner-Camp 429

According to Bancroft (Oregon; Vol. II, page 503 footnote), the reconnaissance was chiefly topographical. Drew's account had appeared between January 28 and March 11, 1865, in the Jacksonville *Sentinel*.

1153 DRIGGS, GEORGE W.

OPENING OF THE MISSISSIPPI; OR, TWO YEARS' CAMPAIGNING IN THE SOUTH-WEST. A RECORD OF THE CAMPAIGNS, SIEGES, ACTIONS AND MARCHES IN WHICH THE 8TH WISCONSIN VOLUNTEERS HAVE PARTICIPATED . . . MADISON, WIS.: WM. J. PARK & CO., 1864.

[i]–vi, [7]–[150]. 20.4 x 13.3 cm. Blue cloth, blind embossed sides, title in gilt on front cover.

Ref.: Howes D502; Coulter 133; Nicholson p. 249

. . . a remarkably interesting and valuable commentary on the country and its people. The writing is somewhat humorous and 'smart,' but there is little bias or bitterness.—Coulter

1154 DRIPS, JOSEPH H.

THREE YEARS AMONG THE INDIANS IN DAKOTA . . . KIMBALL. SOUTH DAKOTA: BRULE INDEX, 1894.

[i–viii], [1]–139, [140–44 blank]. (Pages [i–ii], [iv–vi] blank.) 18.9 x 14.6 cm. Four portraits. Pink printed wrappers with title on front wrapper. In a black cloth case.

Ref.: Howes D505

Drips gives a personal account of the campaigns under General Sully, 1863–65, on the Missouri, in the Dakotas, and in Idaho. The work is signed and dated at the end: J. H. Drips, / Malone, Iowa / October 1, 1894. /

1155 DROWN, SIMEON DE W.

DROWN'S RECORD AND HISTORICAL VIEW OF PEORIA, FROM THE DISCOVERY BY THE FRENCH JESUIT MISSIONARIES, IN THE SEVENTEENTH CENTURY, TO THE PRESENT TIME . . . TO WHICH IS ADDED A BUSINESS DIRECTORY OF THE CITY . . . PEORIA, ILL.: PRINTED BY E. O. WOODCOCK, MAIN STREET. 1850.

[1]–164, [165–208 advertisements]. 18.2 x 11.5 cm. Three full-page illustrations and 32 cuts in the text. Green printed boards, black cloth backstrip, title on front cover, advertisements on back cover.

Ref.: Bradford 1419; Byrd 1698; Howes D509; McMurtrie (*Peoria*) 31; Sabin 26965

On page 122, the author states the work was completed March 5, 1851.

1156 DROWN, SIMEON DE W.

THE PEORIA DIRECTORY, FOR 1844: CONTAINING AN ACCOUNT OF THE EARLY DISCOVERY OF THE COUNTRY, WITH A HISTORY OF THE TOWN, DOWN TO THE PRESENT TIME . . . PEORIA: PRINTED FOR THE AUTHOR, 1844.

[1]–124. 18.9 x 11.1 cm. Illustrations and maps in text, folding map of Peoria (fragment only). Yellow printed boards, brown cloth backstrip, with title on front cover, advertisements on back cover.

Ref.: Byrd 857; Howes D508; McMurtrie (*Peoria*) 16; Sabin 60833; Wirick 119

Peoria's first history and first directory.

1157 DROWN, SIMEON DE W.

[Wrapper title] PEORIA RECORD AND ADVERTISER: FOR AUGUST, 1856. PEORIA: PRINTED BY S. DE WITT DROWN, 1856.

[i–vi advertisements], [1]–24, [vii–xii advertisements]. 21.7 x 14.1 cm. Two illustrations. Orange printed wrappers with title on front wrapper.

Prov.: Inscribed on front wrapper: Hon Robt Rantoul / Beverly Mass /.

Ref.: Byrd 2428

An August number is not listed by McMurtrie (*Peoria*), but No. 5, March 4, 1850, and March, 1857, are listed.

1158 DRUMHELLER, DANIEL M.

"UNCLE DAN" DRUMHELLER TELLS THRILLS OF WESTERN TRAILS IN 1854 . . . SPOKANE, WASHING-TON: INLAND-AMERICAN PRINTING COMPANY, 1925.

[I]–[XII, XII blank], 1–131, [132 blank]. 19 x 13 cm. Two portraits. Gray cloth.

Ref.: Cowan p. 185; Howes D511; Smith 2585

1159 DUBOIS, H. A.

[Broadside] $1000 REWARD!! THE ABOVE REWARD WILL BE PAID BY ME FOR THE CONVICTION AND SUMMARY PUNISHMENT OF THE PARTY OR PARTIES WHO, ON THE NIGHT OF THE 13TH OF MARCH, 1867, STOLE TWO PRIVATE HORSES AND ONE GOVERNMENT MULE FROM THE STABLE, NEAR THE POST HOSPITAL, AT FORT UNION, N. M. . . . H. A. DUBOIS, ASSISTANT SURGEON, U. S. A. POST AND DEPOT HOSPITAL, FORT UNION, N. M. MARCH 15, 1867.

Broadside, 20.5 x 31.9 cm. Text, 21.6 x 25.9 cm. Printed on light yellow paper.

Ref.:

1160 DUBUQUE, IOWA. First Ward School

[Broadside] PROGRAMME FIRST WARD SCHOOL FRIDAY DEC. 23RD. 1870 . . .

Broadside, 18 x 10.5 cm. Text, 14.5 x 8.1 cm. Bound with eight works by Orestes A. Brownson, Jr., contemporary marbled boards, light red scored calf backstrip.

Ref.:

1161 DUBUQUE AND PACIFIC RAILROAD COMPANY

[Manuscript] (COPY) STATEMENT OF ASSETS & LIABILITIES OF THE DUB & PAC R R^D CO. NOV. 1, 1857. . . Two pages, 32.2 x 19.9 cm.

Signed at the end (but not in his hand): J. P. Farley Prest / D & P R R Compy /. At the time of the report the assets amounted to $3,638,200. and the liabilities to $2,148,200.

1162 DUBUQUE AND PACIFIC RAILROAD COMPANY

STATE OF IOWA. REPORT OF THE DUBUQUE & PACIFIC RAILROAD COMPANY. JANUARY 1ST, 1858. DUBUQUE: W. A. ADAMS, 1858.

[1]–45, [46–8 blank]. 21.4 x 14 cm. Map: Map of the / Dubuque and Pacific R. R. / and / The Great Iowa Coal Field / [below border at left:] Lith. Hopkins & Co 128 Main St Dubuque, Iowa. / 22.4 x 37 cm. No scale given. Pale green printed wrappers with title on front wrapper.

Ref.: Howes D532; Moffit 354; *Railway Economics* p. 205

The first report is unsigned. The treasurer's, superintendent's, and chief engineer's reports are signed by C. H. Booth, D. H. Dotterer, and B. B. Provoost respectively.

1163 DUBUQUE EMIGRANT ASSOCIATION

NORTHERN IOWA. BY A PIONEER. CONTAINING VALUABLE INFORMATION FOR EMIGRANTS. DUBUQUE: NONPAREIL JOB PRINTING AND PUBLISHING HOUSE, 1858.

[1]–40. 21.3 x 13.8 cm. Illustrations unlisted. Yellow printed wrappers with title on front wrapper.

Ref.: Howes I72; Jones 1398; Moffit 360; Mott (*Iowa*) p. 58; Sabin 35029

There were at least four printings, apparently all in the same year.

1164 DUDEN, GOTTFRIED

BERICHT UBER EINE REISE NACH DEN WESTLICHEN STAATEN NORDAMERIKA'S UND EINEM MEHRJAHRIGEN AUFENTHALT AM MISSOURI (IN DEN JAHREN 1824, 25, 26 UND 1827), IN BEZUG AUF AUSWANDERUNG UND UEBERVOLKERUNG . . . STAATEN UND DESSEN BEDEUTUNG FUR DIE HAUSLICHE UND POLITISCHE LAGE DER EUROPAER, DARSTELLT A) IN EINER SAMMLUNG VON BRIEFEN, B) IN EINER BESONDEREN ABHANDLUNG UBER DEN POLITISCHEN ZUSTAND DER NORDAMERIKANISCHEN FREISTAATEN, UND C) IN EINEM RATHGEBENDEN NACHTRAGE FUR AUSWANDERNDE DEUTSCHE ACKERWIRTHE UND DIEJENIGEN, WELSCHE AUF HANDELSTUNTERNEHMUNGEN DENKEN, VON ELBERFELD: BEI SAM. LUCAS, 1829.

[I]–XVI, [1]–348. 21 x 13 cm. Green pulled paste paper, green paper label on backstrip with title in manuscript.

Ref.: Buck 188; Clark II 19; Howes D534; Hubach p. 61 *et seq.;* Sabin 21073

His rose-colored descriptions of life on the frontier are credited with attracting thousands of his fellow-countrymen to Missouri and neighboring Illinois. He seems to have been quite honest but too enthusiastic and eloquent.— Clark

1165 DUDEN, GOTTFRIED

THE SAME . . . BONN: EDUARD WEBER, 1834.

[1–4], [I]–LVIII, [1]–404. 21 x 13.9 cm. Map: Charte / vom Missouri-/Staate / mit Andeutung der angrenzenden / Länder / nach Lucas. / [lower right:] Lithogr. v. Dunst & Comp. Bonn. / 24.1 x 18.6 cm. Scale: about 40 miles to one inch. Tan printed wrappers with title on front wrapper, advertisement on back wrapper, uncut, mostly unopened. Gray paper pasted over backstrip and inner wrapper edges.

Ref.: Buck 188; Clark II 19; Howes D534; Hubach p. 61; Sabin 21073

Second Edition.

Editions: Elberfeld, 1829.

1166 DUDLEY, WILLIAM L.

GRAND FORKS AND NORTH DAKOTA MANUAL FOR 1885. CONTAINS A COMPLETE CITY AND BUSINESS DIRECTORY OF GRAND FORKS. HISTORICAL, GEOGRAPHICAL, DESCRIPTIVE, BIOGRAPHICAL AND BUSINESS SKETCHES . . . GRAND FORKS: PLAINDEALER BOOK AND JOB ROOMS, 1885.

[1]–146. (Page [1] pasted to inner front cover.) 18.7 x 11.9 cm. Five mounted photographs, four full-page illustrations, illustrations in text, and two maps. Map on inner front cover and recto of front endleaf: Map of the Central Portion / —of the— / City of Grand Forks / Dakota. / [Scale 1000 feet to one inch.] / 21.9 x 16.3 cm. Scale as above. Map on verso of front endleaf: Map / of the St. Paul, / Minneapolis / and Manitoba / and Connections. / 11 x 15 cm. No scale given. Brown cloth, title in gilt on front cover.

Ref.: Allen (*Dakota*) 373; Howes D537

Inserted after the first illustration is a small manuscript slip inscribed: Mrs. W$^{m.}$ Thorne. / Hastings, Minn. / Dakota Co. / It is difficult to determine whether this is an advertisement or a mark of ownership. Several of the photographs show points of interest marked in red ink. Advertisements interspersed throughout.

1167 DUFF, JOSEPH

[Broadside] TRAVELLER'S GUIDE. A MAP OF THE OHIO AND MISSISSIPPI RIVERS. EXTENDING FROM PITTSBURGH TO THE GULF OF MEXICO . . . CINCINNATI: PUBLISHED BY GEORGE CONCLIN, 1844 . . .

Broadside map, 60.2 x 23.4 cm., folded. Folded into pink board covers, 12 x 8 cm.

Ref.:

The woodcut map is a schematic plan of the Ohio from Pittsburgh to the Mississippi, from the Illinois to the Ohio, and from New Madrid to the Gulf of Mexico. Mileages between towns and cumulative mileages from Pittsburgh are recorded in a table in the left column.

1168 DUFFIELD, GEORGE C.

MEMORIES OF FRONTIER IOWA . . . DES MOINES: BISHARD BROTHERS, 1906.

[i–iv], 1–54. 22 x 14.8 cm. Nine illustrations listed. Dark red cloth.

Ref.: Howes D541; Mott (*Iowa*) p. 85

Limited to 25 copies bound in cloth, of an edition of 250. According to Mott, written by Edgar R. Harlan.

1169 DUFLOT DE MOFRAS, EUGENE

EXPLORATION DU TERRITOIRE DE L'OREGON, DES CALIFORNIES ET DE LA MER VERMEILLE, EXECUTEE PENDANT LES ANNEES 1840, 1841 ET 1842 . . . PARIS: ARTHUS BERTRAND, 1844.

[i]–xii, [1–4 Avertissement, 4 blank], [1]–524. [i–iv], [1]–514. [i–iv], 17 LEAVES (one double) of maps, plans, and plates, numbered 2–26. Four plates and tables in each of the first two volumes and 26 plates and maps in the Atlas, all listed. Map: Carte / de la Côte de l'Amérique / sur l'Océan Pacifique Septentrional / comprenant / le Territoire de l'Orégon, / les Californies, la Mer Vermeille, / Partie des Territoires de la Compagnie de la Baie Hudson, / et de l'Amérique Russe. / Dressée / par Mr Duflot de Mofras, Attaché à la Légation de France à Mexico; / Pour servir à l'intelligence de son Voyage d'exploration / Publié par l'ordre du Roi, / sous les Auspices / de M^r le Maréchal Duc de Dalmatie, / Président du Conseil des Ministres / et de / M^r le Ministre des Affaires Etrangères. / Paris, 1844. / Le plan gravé par Jacobs. L'écriture gravée par Hacq. / [lower centre:] Publié par Arthus Bertrand. / 90.8 x 57.6 cm. Scale: one to 5,555,555. Map: Carte / de l'Océan Pacifique / au Nord de l'Equateur. / [upper left:] Voyage de Mr Duflot de Mofras. / [upper right:] N° 2. / [lower left:] Publié par Arthus Bertrand. / [lower right:] Gravé par S. Jacobs. / 29 x 39.5 cm. No scale given. Map: Isthme / de / Tehantepec / [upper left:] [same as preceding] / [upper right:] N° 3. / [lower centre:] Publié par Arthus Bertrand. / 31.2 x 25.5 cm. No scale given. Profile in right margin. Two maps on one sheet: Plan du Fort del Manzanillo / dans le Territoire de Colima. / [upper left:] [same as preceding] / [upper right:] N° 5. / 17.9 x 23.3 cm. Scale: about 3 1/3 kilometres to one inch. [2]: Plan du Port / d'Acapulco / sur la côte occidentale / du Mexique. / [upper right:] N° 4. / [lower centre:] Publié par Arthus Bertrand. / 17.9 x 23.3 cm. Scale: about 1 1/5 kilometres to one inch. Two maps on one sheet: Plan / de Mazatlan / [upper left:] [same as No. 5.] / [upper right:] N° 7. / 18.2 x 23.7 cm. Scale: 2 kilometres to one inch. [2]: Plan / de San Blas / [upper right:] N° 6. / [lower centre:] [same as No. 4] / 18.8 x 23.7 cm. Scale: 1.9 kilometres to one inch. Two maps on one sheet: Plan / du Port / de Guaymas / sur la Mer Vermeille. / [upper left:] [same as No. 7] / [upper right:] N° 9. / 23 x 17.8 cm. Scale: 2.5 kilometres to one inch. [2]: Plan / de la Baie de la Paz / et du Port / de Pichilingue / [upper right:] N° 8. / 23.1 x 17.8 cm. Scale: 2.4 kilometres to one inch. [lower centre:] [same as No. 4] / Two maps on one sheet: Plan / de l'Embouchure / du Rio Colorado / dans la Mer Vermeille. / [upper left:] [same as No. 5.] / [upper right:] N° 10. [lower centre:] [same as No. 4] / 23.1 x 17.9 cm. Scale: 7 kilometres to one inch. [2]: Plan / du

Port de S. Diego / situé sur la côte septentrionale / de la Californie. / [upper right:] N° 11. / 23.1 x 17.9 cm. Scale: 3.66 kilometres to one inch. Two maps on one sheet: Mouillage / de San Pedro / [upper left:] [same as No. 5] / [upper right:] N° 12. / [lower centre:] [same as No. 4] / 23.2 x 18 cm. Scale: 1.5 kilometres to one inch. [2]: Mouillage / de la Mission / de Sta Barbara / [upper right:] N° 13. / 23.2 x 18 cm. Scale: .75 kilometres to one inch. Two maps on one sheet: Plan / du Port et de la Baie / de Monte-Rey / situé sur la Côte Sept^le de la Californie. / [upper left:] [same as No. 5] / [upper right:] N° 14. / [lower centre:] [same as No. 4] / 23.1 x 17.8 cm. Scale: six kilometres to one inch. [2]: Baie de la Trinidad / [upper right:] N° 15. / 23.1 x 17.8 cm. Scale: one kilometre to one inch. Map: Port / de San Francisco / dans la Haute Californie. / [upper left:] [same as No. 5] / [upper right:] N° 16. / [lower left:] Publié par Arthus Bertrand. / [lower right:] Gravé par S. Jacobs. / 44 x 25.9 cm. No scale given. *Inset:* Entrée du Port / de San Francisco / et des mouillages del Sausalito / et de la Yerba Buena. / 13.2 x 25.9 cm. Scale: about 1.8 kilometres to one inch. Map: Carte Détaillée / du / Mouillage du Fort Ross / et du / Port de la Bodega ou Romanzoff / dans la Nouvelle Californie, / occupés par les Russes. / [upper left:] [same as No. 5] / [upper right:] N° 17. / [lower centre:] [same as No. 4] /. 55.5 x 40.6 cm. No scale given. Map: Carte / du Rio Colombia / depuis son Embouchure jusqu'au Fort Vancouver, / à 17 Myriamtres de la Mer. / [upper left:] [same as No. 5] / [upper right:] N° 18. / [lower centre:] [same as No. 4]. 22.7 x 40.7 cm. Scale: eight kilometres to one inch. Two maps on one sheet: Port / de Quadra / ou / de la Découverte. / [upper left:] [same as No. 5] / [upper right:] N° 19. / [lower centre:] [same as No. 4] /. 23.2 x 17.8 cm. Scale: two marine miles to one inch. [2]: Plan / du Port de Nutka / Cala de los Amigos. / [upper right:] N° 20. / 23.2 x 17.8 cm. Scale: about 110 metres to one inch. Two maps on one sheet: Plan / du / Port Sulgrave. / [upper left:] [same as No. 5] / [upper right:] N° 22. / 17.9 x 23.3 cm. Scale: one kilometre to one inch. [2]: Plan du Port / de la / Nouvelle Archangel / dans l'Ile de Sitka / Capitale / des Etablissements de l'Amérique Russe. / [upper right:] N° 21. / [lower centre:] [same as No. 4] /. 17.9 x 23.3 cm. Scale: about 175 metres to one inch. Nos. 23–26: views and illustrations. Two volumes of text and one Atlas, blue printed wrappers, with titles on front wrappers, uncut, text unopened. In octavo and large folio red cloth cases.

Prov.: Laid in the first volume is a folded

sheet carrying the following inscription: à / Edwin de Comte de Blacas / avec / les plus sincère compliments / M /.

Ref.: Bradford 3642; Cowan p. 186; Hanna-Powell p. 25; Howell 92; Howes D542; Sabin 21144; Smith 2597; Streit III 2299; Zamorano Eighty 30

One of the great books of the West Coast in extraordinarily fine condition.

1170 DUGGINS, WILLIAM

DOCUMENT SIGNED. 1857 April 9, Salt Lake City, Utah Territory. One page, 33 x 20.1 cm.

A manuscript and printed bond to pay William H. Hooper $100.00. Signed as witness by William Clayton.

1171 DULUC, ANDREW

DOCUMENT SIGNED. 1810 July 13, New Orleans. One page, 28 x 16.3 cm.

Printed and manuscript shipping receipt, in favor of George Black, for seventeen bales of cotton sent to Norfolk, Virginia. There are two copies of the receipt on the same sheet, each filled in and signed by Andrew Duluc.

1172 DUMAS, ALEXANDRE

LE CAPITAINE PAUL . . . BRUXELLES: C. HOCH-HAUSEN ET FOURNES, 1838.

[i]–x, [11]–269, [270 blank]. 15 x 9.5 cm. Contemporary marbled boards, black calf backstrip and corners, marbled edges.

Ref.:

The only French edition cited by Sabin is Paris, 1862.

1173 DUMONT DE MONTIGNY, JEAN FRANCOIS BENJAMIN

MEMOIRES HISTORIQUES SUR LA LOUISIANE, CON-TENANT CE QUI Y EST ARRIVE DE PLUS MEMORABLE DEPUIS L'ANNEE 1687. JUSQU'A PRESENT . . . PARIS: CHEZ CL. J. B. BAUCHE, M. DCC. LIII.

[*]¹, a⁶, A–L¹². [1–4], j–x, [1]–261, [262–64 blank]. (Page 199 mispaginated Iive, 249 mispaginated 254.) [*]², A–N¹², O⁴, P¹⁰. [i–iv], [1]–338, [339–40 blank]. (Pages 293, 313, and 317 mispaginated 295, ix, and x.) 15.8 x 9.4 cm. Four plates and a map in the first volume, two plates and three plans in the second. Map: Carte / de la / Louisiane. / [upper right:] Tom 1 pag. 1. / [lower right:] Dressé et Gravé par Chambon. / 17.9 x 15.1 cm. No scale given. Plan: Plan de la Nouvelle Orleans Capitale de la Louisiane / [upper right:] Tom 11 Pag 51 / 11.8 x 15.1 cm. Scale: about 133 toises to one inch. Plan: Plan de la Concession de M. Le Blanc

et associes aux Yazoux / [upper right:] Tom II. Pag 85 / 11.7 x 15.1 cm. No scale given. Plan: Plan / de Fort Rozalie / des Natchez avec / ses Environs. / [upper right:] Tom II. Pag 94 / 11.8 x 15 cm. No scale given. Two volumes contemporary full mottled calf, gilt tooled backstrips, leather labels, red edges.

Ref.: Bradford 687; Field 463; Howes L250; Rader 1233; Sabin 9605

The unpublished manuscript of this account of Louisiana from the death of La Salle to 1740 from which Abbé Le Mascrier took the present work is in ICN (Ayer). The original manuscript, which differs greatly from this version, is described in *Mid-America*, Vol. XIX, No. 1, 1937, pages 31–47, in an article by Father Jean Delanglez.

1174 DUNBAR, WILLIAM

AUTOGRAPH LETTER, SIGNED. No place, no date. One page and postscript (one-third page), 20.5 x 12.2 cm. To Philip Nolan.

The postscript reads as follows: "For God sake, if you can, come & see us tomorrow, I want to show you what I have written to Jefferson. I have endeavoured to make it appear probable, that with the help of your symbolical language of the west, we may be able to discypher the hieroglyphicks of the East."

Tipped in Dunbar, W.: *Life, Letters and Papers* . . . 1930.

1175 DUNBAR, WILLIAM

LIFE, LETTERS AND PAPERS OF WILLIAM DUNBAR OF ELGIN, MORAYSHIRE, SCOTLAND, AND NATCHEZ, MISSISSIPPI . . . COMPILED . . . BY MRS. DUNBAR ROWLAND . . . JACKSON, MISSISSIPPI: PRESS OF THE MISSISSIPPI HISTORICAL SOCIETY, 1930.

[i–vi, vi blank], 1–26, [26a, 26b], 27–410. 23.4 x 15.5 cm. Illustrations unlisted. Green ribbed cloth.

Prov.: Inscribed on front fly-leaf: From Mrs. Dunbar Rowland / To / Mr. Jas. H Bruns / With best wishes /.

Ref.:

Autograph Letter, signed by William Dunbar tipped to half-title.

1176 DUNBAUGH, JACOB

AUTOGRAPH LETTER, SIGNED. 1807 April, Baton Rouge. Two pages, 25.6 x 20.2 cm. Silked. To Daniel Bissell.

Dunbaugh was a sergeant at Fort Massac, where Bissell was captain in command. Bissell ordered Dunbaugh to join Burr "as a Spy against Colº Burr." Dunbaugh was detected and in this letter reported that he had had to confess that Bissell wanted to "know what Burrs mening Was to take Someny men Down the River With him."

1177 DUNDAS, J. H.

[Caption title] NEMAHA COUNTY . . .

[1]–220. 19.4 x 13.5 cm. Black cloth.

Prov.: The inner front cover and front fly-leaf bear the rubber stamp of Wendell A. Dundas and one signature in pencil. W. A. Dundas is stamped in numerous places throughout the volume, including the top of page [1].

Ref.:

Probably published in Auburn, Nebraska, 1902. The following passage is found on page 220: Having condensed a review of the events in Nemaha county for the past forty years into these pages I now dedicate this volume to the readers of the *Granger.* J. H. Dundas, Auburn, Nebraska, June 21, 1902.

1178 DUNDASS, SAMUEL R.

JOURNAL OF SAMUEL RUTHERFORD DUNDASS . . . INCLUDING HIS ENTIRE ROUTE TO CALIFORNIA, AS A MEMBER OF THE STEUBENVILLE COMPANY BOUND FOR SAN FRANCISCO, IN THE YEAR 1849. STEUBEN-VILLE, O.: PRINTED AT CONN'S JOB OFFICE, 1857.

[1]–60. 19.1 x 12.5 cm. White printed wrappers with title on front wrapper.

Ref.: Cowan pp. 187–88; Howes D566; Hubach p. 110; Jones 1370; Matthews p. 316; Morgan (Pritchard) p. 185; Wagner-Camp 290

Dundass died in Buffalo, of typhoid fever, on his way home from California in October, 1850. His *Journal* was published posthumously.

1179 DUNHAM, E. ALLENE TAYLOR

[Wrapper title] ACROSS THE PLAINS IN A COVERED WAGON . . .

[1]–20. 22.1 x 15 cm. Gray printed wrappers with title on front wrapper.

Ref.:

Neither place nor date of publication has been determined. Possibly Milton, Iowa, certainly during the 1920's.

Page 1: The following narrative is written with a view of telling . . . my experiences when a girl of travelling overland from New Hartford, Iowa to San Jose, California in 1864 . . . leaving our Iowa home the second of May, 1864, it was the middle of October before our trip was ended . . . This narrative was written after we had returned to Iowa to again make our home near the place where we started on that long, and at that time perilous journey across the plains . . .

1180 DUNIWAY, ABIGAIL J.

CAPTAIN GRAY'S COMPANY; OR, CROSSING THE PLAINS AND LIVING IN OREGON . . . PORTLAND, OREGON: PRINTED AND PUBLISHED BY S. J. MC-CORMICK, 1859.

[i]–[vi, vi blank], [7]–342. 18.1 x 11 cm. Plum cloth, blind embossed sides, title in gilt on back-strip.

Ref.: Cowan p. 75; Howes D568; Jones 1408; McMurtrie (*Oregon*) 165; Smith 2636; Wagner-Camp 323

This first literary work written and printed in Oregon is fiction based on the author's personal experiences crossing the plains in 1852. The story is set in 1850 in the form of journal entries.

1181 DUNN, JACOB P., JR.

MASSACRES OF THE MOUNTAINS. A HISTORY OF THE INDIAN WARS OF THE FAR WEST . . . NEW YORK: HARPER & BROTHERS, 1886.

[i]–[x, x blank], [1]–784. (Pages [i–ii] blank.) 21.3 x 14.1 cm. 170 illustrations listed. Map: Map of the / Indian Reservations / within the / United States / [decorative rule] / 1884. / [lower right:] Fisk & Co. Engr's N. Y. / 18.3 x 27.7 cm. Scale: about 225 miles to one inch. *Inset:* [Northwest corner of the Indian Territory]. 2.5 x 2.6 cm. No scale given. The illustrations include some page-size maps. Green pictorial cloth, title in gilt on front cover and backstrip.

Ref.: Howes D575; Munk (Alliot) p. 69; Rader 1239; Saunders 2872; Smith 2647

Best single volume covering the subject.— Howes

1182 DUNN, JOHN

HISTORY OF THE OREGON TERRITORY AND BRITISH NORTH-AMERICAN FUR TRADE; WITH AN ACCOUNT OF THE HABITS AND CUSTOMS OF THE PRINCIPAL NATIVE TRIBES ON THE NORTHERN CONTINENT . . . LONDON: EDWARDS AND HUGHES, 1844.

[i]–viii, [1]–359, [360 blank]. 22.1 x 14 cm. Folding map: A Map of the Oregon / Territory. / [lower centre:] Drawn on Stone by J. Traxton 13, Cross St Hatton Garden. / 44.1 x 32.9 cm. No scale indicated. Green cloth. In a green cloth case.

Ref.: Bradford 1443; Field 466; Howes D577; Smith 2649; Wagner-Camp 106

The author's personal experiences comprise almost a history of the Hudson's Bay Company in the Northwest.

1183 DUNRAVEN, W. T. WINDHAM-QUIN, 4TH EARL OF

THE GREAT DIVIDE: TRAVELS IN THE UPPER YEL-LOWSTONE IN THE SUMMER OF 1874 . . . NEW

YORK: SCRIBNER, WELFORD, AND ARMSTRONG, 1876.

[i]–[xx, xx blank], [1]–377, [378 colophon, 379 British publisher's device, 380 blank]. 22 x 14.1 cm. 15 illustrations and two maps listed. Red pictorial cloth.

Ref.: Jones 1582; Smith 2658

1184   DUPONT, SAMUEL F.

EXTRACTS FROM PRIVATE JOURNAL-LETTERS OF CAPTAIN S. F. DUPONT, WHILE IN COMMAND OF THE CYANE, DURING THE WAR WITH MEXICO, 1846–1848 . . . WILMINGTON, DEL.: FERRIS BROS., 1885.

[i–vi], [1]–444. 22.4 x 14.4 cm. Dark brown half morocco, marbled and sprinkled edges.

Ref.: Barrett 744; Howes D588

One of possibly fewer than fifty copies of a privately printed edition. This important book on the naval actions during the war with Mexico is valuable because of the information relative to Frémont's conduct. It is, unfortunately, relatively unknown.

1185   DURKIN, JAMES A.

THE AUTO BANDITS OF CHICAGO . . . CHICAGO: PUBLISHED BY CHARLES C. THOMPSON CO.

[1]–190, [191 advertisements, 192 blank]. 18.8 x 13.1 cm. Colored pictorial wrappers with title on front wrapper, advertisement on recto and verso of back wrapper. In a red cloth case.

Ref.:

Copyrighted 1913. A remarkably fine copy.

1186   DURRIE, DANIEL S.

[Wrapper title] THE EARLY OUTPOSTS OF WISCONSIN. GREEN BAY FOR TWO HUNDRED YEARS, 1639–1839. ANNALS OF PRAIRIE DU CHIEN . . .

[1]–15, [16 blank]. 22.9 x 15.3 cm. Lavender printed wrappers with title on front wrapper.

Ref.:

Neither place nor date of publication indicated, but probably Madison, Wisconsin, about 1872.

1187   DUVAL, JOHN C.

THE ADVENTURES OF BIG-FOOT WALLACE, THE TEXAS RANGER AND HUNTER . . . PHILADELPHIA: CLAXTON, REMSEN & HAFFELFINGER, 1871.

[i]–xii, 13–291, [292 blank]. 19 x 12 cm. Eight illustrations, unlisted. Green cloth, gilt title on backstrip.

Ref.: Dobie p. 55; Howes D602; Raines pp. 73–4

Duval served as a Texas Ranger with Bigfoot Wallace, who was in the Meier Expedition. His narrative of Bigfoot's *Adventures* is the rollickiest and most flavorsome that any American frontiersman has yet inspired. The tiresome thumping on the hero theme present in many biographies of frontiersmen is entirely absent.—Dobie

1188   DUVAL, JOHN C.

EARLY TIMES IN TEXAS . . . AUSTIN, TEXAS: H. P. N. GAMMEL & CO., 1892.

[i]–viii, [9]–135, [136 blank], [1]–253, [254 blank]. 19.1 x 13 cm. Dark green cloth, gilt title on front cover and backstrip.

Ref.: Dobie p. 55; Howes D603; Rader 1248; Raines p. 74

The first section comprises "Early Times in Texas, or the Adventures of Jack Dobell" while the second part consists of "The Young Explorers" and an appendix. The first section is the story of Duval's adventures during the Goliad Massacre and his escape from the Mexicans.

1189   DWINELLE, JOHN W.

THE COLONIAL HISTORY OF THE CITY OF SAN FRANCISCO: BEING A NARRATIVE ARGUMENT IN THE CIRCUIT COURT OF THE UNITED STATES FOR THE STATE OF CALIFORNIA, FOR FOUR SQUARE LEAGUES OF LAND CLAIMED BY THAT CITY AND CONFIRMED TO IT BY THAT COURT. THIRD EDITION . . . SAN FRANCISCO: PRINTED BY TOWNE & BACON, 1866.

[i]–iv, [unpaginated leaf of errata], [v]–[x, x blank], [unpaginated blank leaf], [xi]–[xlvi, xlvi blank], [1]–[35], [36 blank], [1]–106, [1]–365, [366 blank], 363–[370], [367]–391, [392 blank]. 22.1 x 14.3 cm. Three lithographed plates, one single-page map, and one double-page map. Contemporary half maroon leather, marbled sides, gilt title on backstrip, sprinkled edges.

Prov.: Inscribed on blank leaf at front: T. C. Van Ness / [underline] / San Francisco / Feby 22^d 1873 / [underline] / From F. McC. / [wavy underline] /. The donor was Frank McCoppin.

Ref.: Bradford 1474; Cowan p. 189; Howes D614; Sabin 21573; Zamorano Eighty 32

There is a small slip (7.7 x 14.3 cm.), listing three additional entries, preceding page xlv, and before page 365 there is a slip, 13.6 x 14.3, headed: No. CLXXI-Bis. /.

The collation of this copy follows that of the fourth edition, although Third Edition appears on the title-page. It seems probable that the additional text of the fourth edition was inserted in a small part of the third edition before the fourth was ready for distribution. The last two of the inserted leaves are about 2 cm. shorter than the rest of the text.

1190 DYE, JOB F.

RECOLLECTIONS OF A PIONEER, 1830–1852: ROCKY MOUNTAINS, NEW MEXICO, CALIFORNIA . . . LOS ANGELES: GLEN DAWSON, 1951.

[i–viii, viii blank], 1–80, [81 blank, 82 colophon]. 18.3 x 12.6 cm. Portrait. Blue cloth.

Ref.:

Limited to 200 copies. Early California Travels Series II.

1191 DYER, IDA M. CASEY

"FORT RENO;" OR, PICTURESQUE "CHEYENNE AND ARRAPAHOE ARMY LIFE," BEFORE THE OPENING OF "OKLAHOMA" . . . NEW YORK: G. W. DILLINGHAM, MDCCCXCVI.

[1]–216. 18.5 x 12.4 cm. Ten illustrations, unlisted. Blue cloth, decoration on sides in black, name of author gilt, title on backstrip in gilt.

Ref.: Howes D619; Rader 1250

The author's husband, Oklahoma City's first mayor, resented certain allusions to his conduct and succeeded in destroying many copies.—Howes

Tipped in at the front is a newspaper clipping regarding the second divorce of Colonel and Mrs. Dyer.

1192 DYER, J. E.

[Wrapper title] DAKOTA: THE OBSERVATIONS OF A TENDERFOOT. 1884.

[1]–129, [130–44 advertisements]. 23.1 x 15.3 cm. Three plates, five illustrations in text, and ten maps. Map: [Township map of parts of seven Dakota counties] [lower right:] H. B. Stranahan & Co. Cleveland. O and S^t. Paul. Minn. / 59.8 x 15.9 cm. No scale given. Map: Map of Binghampton. / 12.2 x 10.9 cm. (includes legend). No scale given. Map: Map of the Town of Elliott. / 15.1 x 11.4 cm. (includes legend). No scale given. Map: Map of the Town of Brockway. / 13.2 x 11.5 cm. (includes legends). No scale given. Map: Map of Sargent. / 17 x 8.2 cm. (includes legend). No scale given. Map: Map of the Town of Newark. / 13.3 x 11.6 cm. (includes legend). No scale given. Map: Map of / Britton, / Day County, / Dakota. / 1884. / Scale 300 Feet to one Inch. / [lower right:] H. B. Stranahan Map Publisher St Paul Minn. / 13 x 11.4 cm. Scale as above. Map: Map / —) of the (— / Dakota & Great Southern / Railway. / Rand, McNally & Co., Engr's, Chicago. / 53.3 x 37.2 cm. No scale given. Map: Map of / Detroit, / Brown County, / Dakota. / 1884. / Scale 200 feet to one inch. / [lower right:] H. B. Stranahan & Co. Cleveland O. & St Paul Minn. / 15.5 x 11.6 cm. Scale as above. Map: Map of Dunbar. / 10 x 11.6 cm. (includes legend). Scale: 200 feet

to one inch. Gray printed wrappers with title on front wrapper, bands at top and bottom run across backstrip and back wrapper; in centre of back wrapper: Fargo Republican / Steam Printing House. / Fargo, D. T. In a black half morocco case.

Ref.: Allen (*Dakota*) 299; Howes D621

1193 DYER, JOHN L.

THE SNOW-SHOE ITINERANT. AN AUTOBIOGRAPHY . . . CINCINNATI: PUBLISHED FOR THE AUTHOR BY CRANSTON & STOWE, 1890.*

[1]–362. 18.8 x 12.2 cm. Illustrations unlisted. Brown cloth, title in gilt on backstrip.

Ref.: Howes D622

The author's experiences in the Rocky Mountains were fascinating.

E

1194 EAGLEMANN, CHARLES F.

THE UNITED STATES ALMANACK, FOR THE YEAR OF OUR LORD 1857 . . . PHILADELPHIA: PUBLISHED BY WILLIAM G. MENTZ.

[A]^1, [B]^{16}, [C]^8. [1]–[34], 37–52. 18.7 x 15.5 cm. Green printed wrappers with title on front wrapper: The / Prairie / Almanac. / [cut] / 1857. / Published by / Rathbun & Orton, / Booksellers and Stationers, / East side Brady St., below 3d, / Davenport, Iowa. / [double rule] / Luse & Co., Job Printers and Book-Binders—LeClaire Hall, Davenport. / [within decorative border]; advertisements on recto of front and recto and verso of back wrapper.

Ref.:

Pages [3]–[34] appear to have been printed in Philadelphia, while pages [1–2 (2 blank)], 37–52, and the wrappers were printed in Davenport. Pages [35–36] are not present and were apparently skipped in pagination. Page [1] is a catalogue of books published by Rathbun & Orton and pages 37–52 carry advertisements for Davenport merchants.

1195 EARLE, THOMAS, *Compiler*

THE LIFE, TRAVELS AND OPINIONS OF BENJAMIN LUNDY, INCLUDING HIS JOURNEYS TO TEXAS AND MEXICO; WITH A SKETCH OF COTEMPORARY[!] EVENTS, AND A NOTICE OF THE REVOLUTION IN HAYTI . . . PHILADELPHIA: PUBLISHED BY WILLIAM D. PARRISH, 1847.

[1]–316. (Pages [1–4] blank.) 18.6 x 11.4 cm. Portrait and map. Map: California, / Texas, / Mexico, / and part of the / United States. / Compiled from the latest and best Authorities. /

21.6 x 25.4 cm. Scale: 200 miles to one inch. Black cloth, blind embossed sides.

Ref.: Clark III 66; Howes E10; Matthews pp. 255–56; Rader 2264; Wagner-Camp 108 note

The title-leaf in this copy is on a stub.

1196 EARLY SETTLEMENT OF JOHNSON COUNTY, [IOWA]

[Caption title] EARLY SETTLEMENT OF JOHNSON COUNTY. CHAPTER I.—PIONEER DAYS . . .

[1]–46. 26.2 x 16.8 cm. Unbound. In blue-green cloth case with Iowa City Republican Leaflets.

Ref.:

The text ends in the middle of a sentence on page 46. It is identical with the last portion of Iowa City Republican Leaflets. Apparently incomplete and probably all published. Place and date of publication not given.

1197 EAST DUBUQUE, ILLINOIS

[Map] [Plan of Dunleith (later East Dubuque), Illinois.]

Map, 31.8 x 39.1 cm. (border). No scale given. Cut into panels, 15.9 x 9.7 cm., and mounted on cloth.

Ref.:

There are manuscript figures and sketch of a building on the verso.

1198 EAST TENNESSEE BIBLE SOCIETY

[Caption title] SECOND REPORT OF THE DIRECTORS OF THE E. TENNESSEE BIBLE SOCIETY. PRESENTED AT THE ANNUAL MEETING, 30th APRIL, 1817 . . .

[A]⁴. [1]–8. 22.5 x 13.5 cm. Unbound leaflet.

Ref.:

On page 8 below a wavy rule and against a right-hand brace is the imprint: Heiskell & Brown, Printers, / Knoxville, Tenn. / The date is obviously 1817. Probably a unique copy.

1199 EASTMAN, EDWIN

SEVEN AND NINE YEARS AMONG THE CAMANCHES AND APACHES. AN AUTOBIOGRAPHY.

[i–ii], [1]–73, [73]–219. (Even numbers on rectos, pages 74–219.) 18 x 12.3 cm. Illustrations unlisted. Orange cloth.

Ref.: Ayer 90 see; Rader 1265

A revolting fictitious story written to advertise Dr. Clark Johnson's Indian blood syrup, and made up mainly of descriptions of Indian life and customs, some of which are cribbed, with considerable garbling from Catlin.—G. P. Garrison in Ayer 90

Inserted at the end is a slip, 8.9 x 11.3 cm., by the publisher on yellow paper, regarding a proposed second edition.

There are two dated editions of 309 pages published at Jersey City. The present edition seems to be earlier, but neither place nor date is apparent.

1200 EASTMAN, S.

[Map] MAP / OF / NEBRASKA / AND / KANSAS TERRITORIES. / SHOWING THE LOCATION OF INDIAN RESERVES, ACCORDING TO THE / TREATIES OF 1854. / COMPILED BY S. EASTMAN, CAPTAIN U. S. A. / FROM ACTUAL SURVEYS. / 1854. / P. S. DUVAL & CO. STEAM LITH. PRESS PHIL.ᵃ / [double rule] / NOTES FROM INDIAN TREATIES MADE IN 1854. / [38 lines of text] / SCALE OF 20 MILES TO 1 INCH. / [diagrammatic scale] / PUBLISHED BY LIPPINCOTT, GRAMBO & CO. / PHILADELPHIA, PA. / [lower left:] ENTERED ACCORDING TO ACT OF CONGRESS, IN THE YEAR 1854 BY LIPPINCOTT, GRAMBO & CO., IN THE CLERK'S OFFICE OF THE DISTRICT COURT OF THE EASTERN DISTRICT OF PENNSYLVANIA. /

Map, 61 x 90.5 cm. Scale: 20 miles to one inch. Folded into brown cloth covers, 14.7 x 9.3 cm., with printed paper label on front cover.

Ref.: Phillips (*Maps*) p. 459

1201 EASTMAN, ZEBINA

NORTH-WESTERN LIBERTY ALMANAC, FOR 1846 . . . CHICAGO, ILL.: EASTMAN & DAVIDSON, PUBLISHERS.

[i–vi advertisements], [1]–32, [33–8 advertisements]. 19.2 x 12 cm. Stitched, unbound. Lacks wrappers.

Ref.: McMurtrie (*Chicago*) 80

McMurtrie's collation is slightly different, with only four pages of advertisements at the front and four at the back.

1202 EASTWICK, MORRIS & CO., Seattle

[Map] MAP OF / SOUTH EASTERN / WASHINGTON TERRITORY, / COMPILED FROM OFFICIAL SURVEYS / AND PUBLISHED BY / EASTWICK, MORRIS & CO. / CIVIL & MINING ENGINEERS. / 1878 / SEATTLE, WASH. TER. / DRAWN BY / JOHN HANSON, / WITH / EASTWICK, MORRIS & CO. / SEATTLE, / W. T. / [lower left:] ENTERED ACCORDING TO ACT OF CONGRESS IN THE YEAR 1878 BY EASTWICK, MORRIS & CO. IN THE OFFICE OF THE LIBRARIAN OF CONGRESS AT WASHINGTON / [lower right:] LITH. BY A. M. ASKEVOLD, ASHLAND BLOCK CHICAGO /

Map, 67 x 90.9 cm. Scale: 6 miles to one inch. Folded into black cloth covers, 16.5 x 11.4 cm., with title stamped in gilt on front cover.

Prov.: Inscribed on inner front cover: Compliments / Hanson. / And in same hand on verso of map: E. T. Scovills (last letter crossed through) /. Also inscribed on inner front cover in another hand: E. T. Scovill / Asst. Engr. N. P. R. R. / Spokane Falls, W. T. / Feb. 1880 / [flourish] /.

Ref.: Phillips (*Maps*) p. 998

1203 EASY CATECHISM FOR FREE HOME-SEEKERS IN DAKOTA

[Wrapper title] EASY CATECHISM FOR FREE HOME-SEEKERS IN DAKOTA.

[1]–[8]. 20 x 15.5 cm. Map: [Map of the Chicago, Milwaukee & St. Paul Railway lines from Chicago to Deadwood.] 20 x 15.5 cm. (page size). No scale given. Self wrappers, printed on yellow paper.

Ref.:

On page [8] there is a calendar for the year 1885. In the margins of the same page, a rubber stamp of: S. D. McNeal. / Hoskins, Dak. / and words stamped: Homestead. / Preemption. / For Free Lands. / Tree Claim. /

1204 ECKHOFF, EMIL A., & PAUL RIECKER

[Map] OFFICIAL MAP / OF THE / TERRITORY OF / ARIZONA / COMPILED FROM SURVEYS, RECONNAISSANCES / AND OTHER SOURCES / BY E. A. ECKHOFF / AND P. RIECKER, / CIVIL ENGINEERS. / 1880. / [at left of cartouche:] [seal of state] / OFFICIAL MAP OF THE TERRITORY / OF ARIZONA. / J. C. FREMONT / GOVERNOR. / [lower left:] DRAWN BY ECKHOFF & RIECKER. / [lower centre:] ENTERED ACCORDING TO ACT OF CONGRESS IN THE YEAR 1879, BY EMIL ECKHOFF AND PAUL RIECKER, IN THE OFFICE OF THE LIBRARIAN OF CONGRESS AT WASHINGTON, D. C. / [11 lines of notes] / [lower right:] THE GRAPHIC CO. PHOTO-LITH. 39 & 41 PARK PLACE, N. Y. /

Map, 93.8 x 72 cm. (sheet size), 80.3 x 66.6 cm. (neat line). Scale: about 14 miles to one inch. Folded into black cloth covers, 20.8 x 11.8 cm., with title in gilt on front cover, with broadside (17.9 x 9.5 cm.) Table of Distances / inside front cover.

Prov.: From the Grierson Papers.

Ref.: Munk (Alliot) p. 81; Phillips (*Maps*) p. 123

The broadside inside the front cover reads: Table of Distances / to accompany Official Map. / [41 lines] /; within decorative border. On the verso of the map is the rubber stamp of W. B. Walkup & Co., Framers, Map and Chart Mounters, 540 Clay Street, San Francisco.

1205 ECLECTIC REVIEW, THE

[Caption title] THE ECLECTIC REVIEW, FOR FEBRUARY, 1816. ART. I. TRAVELS TO THE SOURCE OF THE MISSOURI RIVER, AND ACROSS THE AMERICAN CONTINENT TO THE PACIFIC OCEAN. . . .

[105]–208. 21.1 x 13.1 cm. New green wrappers.
Ref.:

Pages [105]–132 carry an unsigned review of the first two editions of the Lewis & Clark narrative.

1206 EDMUNDS, A. C.

PEN SKETCHES OF NEBRASKANS WITH PHOTOGRAPHS . . . LINCOLN, NEBRASKA: R. & J. WILBUR, 1871.

[1]–[511], [521 blank]. 19 x 13 cm. 20 mounted photographs. Orange cloth.

Ref.: Howes E46

According to a note by the author on page 504, fifty copies were issued with a frontispiece differing slightly from the regular edition. In the present copy, there are two portraits in the left border of the frontispiece.

1207 EDMUNDS, A. C.

THE SAME. Green cloth.

The two portraits are not present in the left border of the frontispiece. Several of the individual portraits inserted in the text differ from the similar photographs in the other copy.

1208 EDWARD, DAVID B.

THE HISTORY OF TEXAS; OR, THE EMIGRANT'S, FARMER'S, AND POLITICIAN'S GUIDE TO THE CHARACTER, CLIMATE, SOIL AND PRODUCTIONS OF THAT COUNTRY: GEOGRAPHICALLY ARRANGED FROM PERSONAL OBSERVATION AND EXPERIENCE . . . CINCINNATI: J. A. JAMES & CO., 1836.

[i]–xii, 13–336. 18 x 11 cm. Map: Map of / Texas, / Containing the Latest / Grants & Discoveries / By E. F. Lee. / Published by J. A. James & Co. / Cincinnati / 1836. / Doolittle & Munson. / [lower right:] Entered according to Act of Congress, in the year 1836, by J. A. James & Cº in the Clerks Office of the District Court of Ohio. 31 x 21.4 cm. Scale: 75 miles to one inch. Blue cloth, yellow printed label, 5.8 x 2.7 cm., on backstrip. Rebacked, preserving original back; label may have been supplied.

Ref.: Bradford 1511; Clark III 35; Howes E48; Rader 1279; Raines p. 74; Sabin 21886; Streeter 1199

As a Preceptor of Gonzales Seminary and resident of Texas, Edward was well equipped to record his observations accurately.

This contemporary history by Edward, notwithstanding some idiosyncrasies of the author, is one of the essential Texas books.—Streeter

1209 EDWARDS, CYRUS

AN ADDRESS DELIVERED AT THE STATE HOUSE, IN VANDALIA, ON THE SUBJECT OF FORMING A STATE COLONIZATION SOCIETY, AUXILIARY TO THE AMERICAN COLONIZATION SOCIETY . . . JACKSONVILLE: PRINTED BY JAMES G. EDWARDS, 1831.

[1]–22. 21.7 x 14.1 cm. Unbound, removed from bound volume.

Ref.: Byrd 110

A newspaper, of which no copy has been found, was established in Jacksonville in 1830 and another was started at the end of the following year. This appears to be the earliest pamphlet printed at Jacksonville.

1210 EDWARDS, FRANK S.

A CAMPAIGN IN NEW MEXICO WITH COLONEL DONIPHAN . . . PHILADELPHIA: CAREY AND HART, 1847.

[i]–xvi, [17]–184, [185–86 blank], [1–22 advertisements]. 18.4 x 13 cm. Map: Map / Showing / Col. A. W. Doniphan's / Route through the States of / New Mexico, Chihuahua / and Coahuila. / [lower right:] Lith. of Thoˢ Sinclair, 79, Sᵒ Third St. Philadᵃ / [lower centre:] Entered according to act of Congress in the Year 1847 by Carey & Hart, in the Clerks office of the District court of the eastern District of Pennsylᵃ / 38.8 x 22.8 cm. No scale indicated. Pale yellow printed wrappers, with title on front cover, errata on verso of front wrapper and advertisements on recto and verso of back wrapper. In a tan cloth case.

Ref.: Howes E52; Hubach p. 103; Jones 1146; Rader 1282; Raines p. 75 see; Saunders 2874; Sabin 21920; Wagner-Camp 132

1211 EDWARDS, FRANK S.

THE SAME. LONDON: JAMES S. HODSON, 1848.

[1–4], [i]–iv, [1]–134, [135–36 advertisements]. 18.8 x 22.3 cm. Map: Map / Shewing / Col. A. W. Doniphan's / Route through the States of / New Mexico, Chihuahua / and / Coahuila. / [lower centre:] London, Published by J. S. Hodson, 2 Cliffords Inn Passage, April 10, 1848. / 38.2 x 32.6 cm. No scale given. Green cloth, blind embossed borders on sides, gilt title on front cover.

Ref.: Howes E52; Munk (Alliot) p. 81; Raines p. 75; Wagner-Camp 132

1212 EDWARDS, J. C.

SPEECH OF MR. J. C. EDWARDS, OF MISSOURI, IN RELATION TO THE TERRITORY IN DISPUTE BETWEEN THE STATE OF MISSOURI AND THE UNITED STATES, AND TO THE TRUE LOCATION OF THE BOUNDARY BETWEEN MISSOURI AND IOWA, DELIVERED IN THE HOUSE OF REPRESENTATIVES, JULY 20, 1842. WASHINGTON: PRINTED BY GALES AND SEATON, 1843.

[1]–20. 22 x 17.1 cm. Unbound, removed from bound volume.

Ref.:

1213 EDWARDS, JOHN N.

NOTED GUERILLAS; OR, THE WARFARE OF THE BORDER. BEING A HISTORY OF THE LIVES AND ADVENTURES OF QUANTRELL, BILL ANDERSON, GEORGE TODD, DAVE POOLE, FLETCHER TAYLOR, PEYTON LONG, OLL SHEPHERD, ARCH CLEMENTS, JOHN MAUPIN, TUCK AND WOOT HILL, WM. GREGG, THOMAS MAUPIN, THE JAMES BROTHERS, THE YOUNGER BROTHERS, ARTHUR McCOY, AND NUMEROUS OTHER WELL KNOWN GUERILLAS OF THE WEST . . . ST. LOUIS: BRYAN, BRAND & COMPANY, 1877.

[v]–[xii, xii blank], [13]–488, [489–90 advertisements]. 21 x 14.3 cm. 26 illustrations listed. Brown cloth, title in black on front cover, in gilt on backstrip.

Ref.: Adams 344; Howes E53; Nicholson p. 267; Rader 1283

Adams suggests that while the author tried to tell the truth, his sources of information were faulty.

1214 EDWARDS, JOHN N.

SHELBY'S EXPEDITION TO MEXICO. AN UNWRITTEN LEAF OF THE WAR . . . KANSAS CITY: KANSAS CITY TIMES STEAM BOOK AND JOB PRINTING HOUSE, 1872.

[1]–139, [140 blank]. 23 x 14.9 cm. Red cloth, gilt title on front cover. Advertisements on inner covers.

Prov.: Inscribed in pencil on blank leaf at front: Presented to ticket / 2697 by the Kansas City / Times / M. Mumford(?) / Aug 31—76 /.

Ref.: Howes E55

Said to have been the first book bound in Kansas City.

1215 EDWARDS, JOSEPH L.

CENTENNIAL HISTORY OF PAWNEE COUNTY, NEBRASKA . . . PAWNEE CITY, NEBRASKA: REPUBLICAN PRINT.

[1]–50. (Pages [1–2] blank.) 23 x 15 cm. Blue printed wrappers with title on front wrapper, illustration on verso of back wrapper.

Ref.: AII (*Nebraska*) 402; Howes E60

Published in 1876.

1216 EDWARDS, PHILIP L.

CALIFORNIA IN 1837. DIARY OF COL. PHILIP L. EDWARDS CONTAINING AN ACCOUNT OF A TRIP TO THE PACIFIC COAST , , , SACRAMENTO: A. J. JOHNSTON & CO., 1890.

[1]–47, [48 blank]. 16 x 11.5 cm. Brown cloth with title in gilt on front cover.

Ref.: Adams (*Ramp. Herd*) 747; Bancroft (*California*) Vol. IV, p. 85; Cowan p. 192; Howes E66; Matthews p. 279; Wagner-Camp 48 note

Edwards tells the story of the company of about fifteen men who left the Willamette Valley in Oregon to drive a herd of cattle from California to the American Missionary Establishment in Oregon. The diary ends four days after they crossed the Shasta River on the return trip.

First published in *Themis*, Volume II, September 13–27, 1890, under the title "California in 1837."

1217 EDWARDS, SAMUEL E.

THE OHIO HUNTER: OR, A BRIEF SKETCH OF THE FRONTIER LIFE OF SAMUEL E. EDWARDS, THE GREAT BEAR AND DEER HUNTER OF THE STATE OF OHIO. BATTLE CREEK, MICH.: REVIEW AND HERALD STEAM PRESS PRINT, 1866.*

[1]–240. 17 x 10.5 cm. Portrait and vignettes. Plum cloth, blind panels embossed on sides, gilt lettered back.

Ref.: Bay pp. 324, 345; Clements Library (*Michigan*) 93; Howes E70; Jones 1493; Thomson 367

The Ohio Hunter is endlessly fascinating, for while some of the episodes are close to fancy, most of them are probably based on fact, if not wholly accurate. Many of Edwards' adventures occurred in Michigan.

1218 EELLS, MYRON

HISTORY OF THE CONGREGATIONAL ASSOCIATION OF OREGON, AND WASHINGTON TERRITORY; THE HOME MISSIONARY SOCIETY OF OREGON AND ADJOINING TERRITORIES; ND[!] THE NORTHWESTERN ASSOCIATION OF CONGREGATIONAL MINISTERS . . . PORTLAND, OREGON: PUBLISHING HOUSE OF HIMES THE PRINTER, 1881.

[1]–124. 21.5 x 14.3 cm. White printed wrappers with short title on front wrapper.

Ref.: Howes (1954) 3233; Smith 2758
Howes calls for a table which is not present.

1219 EELLS, MYRON

HYMNS IN THE CHINOOK JARGON LANGUAGE . . . PORTLAND, OREGON: DAVID STEELE, 1889.

[1]–40. 14.4 x 10.2 cm. Pink wrappers with title on front wrapper.

Ref.: Butler (*Chinook*) 20; Smith 1760
Editions: Portland, 1878.

1220 EGAN, J. H.

AUTOGRAPH LETTER, SIGNED. 1873 March 1, Portland, Oregon. Three pages, 20.4 x 12.5 cm. To Loren L. Williams.

Inserted in Manuscript Journals of Loren L. Williams, Volume IV.

1221 EGAN, WILLIAM M.

PIONEERING THE WEST, 1846 TO 1878 . . . EDITED . . . BY WM. M. EGAN . . . RICHMOND, UTAH: HOWARD R. EGAN ESTATE, 1917.

[1]–302, [303 illustration, 304 blank]. 19.4 x 13.2 cm. 54 illustrations listed. Black cloth, stamped in gilt down backstrip.

Ref.: Howes E76; Jones 1733; Smith 2771
Copies in black cloth are of the original binding; copies in brown cloth were bound later.
Index . . . 1942 laid in.

1222 EGAN, WILLIAM M.

[Wrapper title] INDEX TO "PIONEERING THE WEST." MAJOR HOWARD EGAN (DIARY). UTAH STATE HISTORICAL SOCIETY, 1942.

[1–12]. 19 x 12 cm. White printed wrappers with title on front cover.

Ref.: Howes E76
Laid in a copy of the book.

1223 EGGLESTON, EDWARD

THE HOOSIER SCHOOL-MASTER. A NOVEL . . . NEW YORK: ORANGE JUDD AND COMPANY.

[1]–226, [227–28 advertisements]. 19.5 x 12.3 cm. Twelve full-page and seventeen text illustrations. Dark green cloth.

Ref.: Johnson (Blanck) p. 161
Published in 1871. Page 71, line 3, shows the reading "is our" instead of "was out." The full-page illustrations are listed as: (*Tinted*), instead of: (*Page*).

1224 [EGMONT, JOHN PERCEVAL, 2ND EARL OF]

AN EXAMINATION OF THE PRINCIPLES, AND AN ENQUIRY INTO THE CONDUCT, OF THE TWO B*****RS; IN REGARD TO THE ESTABLISHMENT OF THEIR PROSECUTION OF THE WAR, 'TILL THE SIGNING OF THE PRELIMINARIES . . . LONDON: PRINTED FOR A. PRICE, M.DCC.XLIX.

[*]², [A]–K⁴. [i–iv, iv blank], [1]–79, [80 blank]. 19.4 x 11.7 cm. Bound with Number 3315.
Ref.:
The two brothers of the title were the Duke of Newcastle and Henry Pelham.

1225 EHRENBERG, HERMANN

[Map] MAP / OF THE / GADSDEN PURCHASE / SONORA / AND PORTIONS OF / NEW MEXICO CHIHUAHUA & CALIFORNIA / BY / HERMAN EHRENBERG C. E. / FROM HIS PRIVATE NOTES AND THOSE OF COLONEL GRAY / MAJ: HEINTZELMAN, LIEUT: PARKS[!] AND OTHERS. / THE YAQUI, MAYO AND FUERTE VALLEYS ARE BY A. FLEURY MILLITARY[!] ENG: / OF SONORA / [diagrammatic scale: 32 miles to one inch] / SCALE OF STATUTE MILES. / [thick and thin rules] / 1858. / MIDDLETON, STROBRIDGE & CO. LITHOGRAPHERS, CINCINNATI O. / [below border:] ENTERED ACCORDING TO ACT OF CONGRESS IN THE YEAR 1858 BY HERMAN EHRENBERG IN THE CLERKS OFFICE OF THE SOUTHERN DISTRICT OF OHIO. /

Map, 61.7 x 62.2 cm. Scale as above. Folded into brown cloth covers, 14.3 x 9.6 cm., with white printed label, 8 x 7.8 cm., on front cover.

Prov.: Signed in pencil on inside front cover: Herman Ehrenberg / Tubac N. M. / [rule] / [following in ink:] to / J. Adelberg / San Francisco / 1860. / On the front cover, below the first word: No 18 /.

Ref.: Phillips (*Maps*) p. 291; Wheat (*Transmississippi*) 941

1226 EHRENBERG, HERMANN

FAHRTEN UND SCHICKSALE EINES DEUTSCHEN IN TEXAS . . . LEIPZIG: VERLAG VON OTTO WIGAND, 1845.

[I]–IV, 1–258, [259–60 advertisements]. 22.8 x 13.8 cm. Contemporary (?) plain blue wrappers, uncut, unopened. In a blue cloth case.

Ref.: see item 1228

Third edition of *Texas und seine Revolution.*

1227 EHRENBERG, HERMANN

DER FREIHEITSKAMPF IN TEXAS IM JAHRE 1836 . . . LEIPZIG: VERLAG VON OTTO WIGAND, 1844.*

[i–ii], [I]–IV, 1–293, [294 colophon]. 12.8 x 8.4 cm. Contemporary mottled boards, cloth corners, red leather backstrip.

Ref.: see item 1228

Second edition of *Texas und seine Revolution.*

1228 EHRENBERG, HERMANN

TEXAS UND SEINE REVOLUTION . . . LEIPZIG: OTTO WIGAN, 1843.

[i]–iv, 1–258, [259–60 advertisements]. 21.1 x 13.4 cm. Contemporary yellow boards with wrappers mounted on sides and backstrip.

Prov.: Bookstamps on title-page and mounted arms on backstrip of the Erbgrossherzogs von Hessen.

Ref.: Clements Library (*Texas*) 25; Howes E83; Jones 1069; Rader 1285; Raines p. 75; Sabin 22072; Streeter 1454

The author founded the town of Ehrenberg, Arizona. He was a gifted explorer, map maker and surveyor in the Southwest during the 1840's to '60's. Accompanying Fannin during the Texas Revolution, he barely escaped the massacre. Later he went to Oregon and California and then returned to the Southwest, where he was killed by Indians in 1866.

1229 ELDERKIN, JAMES D.

BIOGRAPHICAL SKETCHES AND ANECDOTES OF A SOLDIER OF THREE WARS . . . THE FLORIDA, THE MEXICAN WAR AND THE GREAT REBELLION . . . DETROIT, MICHIGAN, 1899.*

[i–iv], [1]–202. 17 x 13 cm. Four illustrations, unlisted. Light blue pictorial boards, blue cloth backstrip.

Ref.: Howes E86

1230 ELLICOTT, ANDREW

THE JOURNAL OF ANDREW ELLICOTT . . . DURING PART OF THE YEAR 1796, THE YEARS 1797, 1798, 1799, AND PART OF THE YEAR 1800: FOR DETERMINING THE BOUNDARY BETWEEN THE UNITED STATES AND THE POSSESSIONS OF HIS CATHOLIC MAJESTY IN AMERICA . . . PHILADELPHIA: PRINTED BY BUDD & BARTRAM, 1803.

a⁴, B–Pp⁴, Qq², a², b–t⁴, u², [x]¹. [i]–[viii, viii blank], [1]–232, 232–99, [1]–151, [152 blank], [153 errata, 154 blank]. (Two pages are numbered 232; 232–99 show even numbers on rectos.) 27.4 x 21.5 cm. Fourteen maps: Map: [Map of the Ohio River from Pittsburg to Cincinnati] [upper left:] Plate A. / [lower right:] Lawson sc. / [lower left:] A Ellicott del. / 30.9 x 46.2 cm. (plate mark). No scale given. Map: [Map of the Ohio River from Cincinnati to the Mississippi] [upper left:] Plate B. / [lower left:] A Ellicott. del. / [lower right:] Lawson sc. / 32.4 x 46.1 cm. (plate mark). No scale given. Map: [Map of the Mississippi River from the Ohio to the Arkansas Rivers] [upper right:] Plate C. / [lower left:] And^W Ellicott del. / [lower right:] Jones sc. / 38.8 x 23.3 cm. (plate mark). No scale given. Map: [Map of the Mississippi River from the Arkansas River to below Fort Adams] [upper right:] Plate D. / [lower right:] And^W Ellicott del. Jones sc. / 38.8 x 32.3 cm. (plate mark). No scale given. Map: Southern Boundary of the United States / [upper right:] Plate E. / [lower left:] And. Ellicott del. / [lower right:] Alex^r Lawson sc. / 29 x 53.5 cm. (plate mark). No scale given. Diagram: [Method of observing Arcturus] [upper right:] N.º 1. / [lower right:] Engrav'd by B. Jones. / 31.7 x 34 cm. Map: [Portion of the Mississippi River] [upper centre:] N.º 2. / [lower centre:] Lawson sc. / 21.1 x 42.2 cm. (neat line). Scale: partly one mile to one inch and partly one-half mile to one inch. Map: [Boundary line, in part] [upper centre:] N.º 3. / [lower centre:] Alex.ʳ Lawson sc. / 28.9 x 14.3 cm. (plate mark). No scale given. Map: [Boundary line, continuation] [upper centre:] N.º 4. / [lower centre:] Lawson sc. / 29.1 x 24.3 cm. (plate mark). No scale given. Map: [Boundary line, continuation] [upper centre:] N.º 5. / 34.4 x 20.4 cm. (plate mark). No scale given. Inset: Fig. G. / 7.9 x 19 cm. (neat line). Scale: 500 perches to one inch. Map: [Boundary line, continuation] [upper centre:] N.º 6. / [lower left:] C. de Krafft, del. / [lower right:] Lawson. sc. / 28.7 x 35.6 cm. (plate mark). No scale given. Map: [Part of the Chatohochee River] [upper centre:] N.º 7 / [lower left:] C. de Krafft del. / [lower right:] Lawson sc. / 32 x 23.2 cm. No scale given. Inset: Fig. E. / 12.7 x 14 cm. (neat line). Scale: 1350 feet to one inch. Map: [Part of St. Mary's River] [upper centre:] N.º 8. / 34.2 x 17 cm. (plate mark). No scale given. Inset: Fig. F. / 7.7 x 7.6 cm. (neat line). Blue boards, tan paper backstrip, printed white paper label, 3.1 x 4.1 cm., uncut. New backstrip.

Ref.: Buck 50; Clark II 89; Howes E94; Hubach p. 35; Matthews p. 191; Rader 1295; Sabin 22216; Shaw & Shoemaker 4147

One of the great United States surveys.

1231   ELLIOT, JAMES

THE POETICAL AND MISCELLANEOUS WORKS OF JAMES ELLIOT . . . GREENFIELD, MASSACHUSETTS: PRINTED BY THOMAS DICKMAN, M,DCC,XCVIII.

[A]–Y⁶. [i]–vi, [7]–[276]. 16.4 x 9.7 cm. Contemporary full calf, red leather label on backstrip.

Ref.: Brinley 6847; Evans 33669; Howes E97; Jones 661; Matthews p. 183; Sabin 22230

The Brinley Catalogue and Howes state that 300 copies were printed.

The author enlisted on July 12, 1793 and until the following May he was on recruiting duty. His journal of military experiences covers the period April 2, 1794 to August 23, 1796, and occupies pages 109–82. The work also contains elegies on Harmar's and St. Clair's defeats. Elliot was present at Greeneville and includes a poem on Wayne's victory at Fallen Timbers. He was later a Member of Congress, attended the state legislature, and held various local offices.

1232   ELLIOTT, CHARLES

INDIAN MISSIONARY REMINISCENCES, PRINCIPALLY OF THE WYANDOT NATION . . . NEW YORK: PUBLISHED BY T. MASON AND G. LANE, 1837.*

[1]–216. (Pages [1–2] blank.) 13.2 x 8.2 cm. Marbled boards, black roan backstrip and corners. Lacks frontispiece.

Ref.: Howes E104

The volume includes a journal kept by Elliott while a missionary at Upper Sandusky in 1822. Elliott's experiences "convinced him that it was wise to convert first and civilize later." The *Reminiscences* is "a work calculated not so much for secular inquiries as for theologians . . . in much of his writing he appears to be the fanatic rather than the philosopher."—DAB

1233   ELLIOTT, CHARLES

THE SAME with imprint: New-York: Published by Lane & Scott, 1850.

[1]–216. (Pages [1–2] blank.) 14.7 x 9.5 cm. Light brown cloth.

Ref.: Howes E104; Rader 1296

The plates of the 1837 edition were used for this second printing. It is interesting to note that the ICN (Ayer) copy is bound in reddish cloth with the same design embossed in blind on the sides, but with different lettering on the backstrip.

Editions: New York, 1837.

1234   ELLIOTT, CHARLES

SOUTH-WESTERN METHODISM. A HISTORY OF THE M. E. CHURCH IN THE SOUTH-WEST FROM 1844 TO 1864 . . . CINCINNATI: PUBLISHED BY POE & HITCHCOCK, 1868.

[1]–469, [470 blank]. 18.9 x 12.1 cm. Portrait. Dark brown cloth, gilt emblems on front cover, title in gilt on backstrip.

Ref.: Howes E106; Rader 1297

1235   ELLIOTT, DAVID S.

LAST RAID OF THE DALTONS. A RELIABLE RECITAL OF THE BATTLE WITH THE BANDITS AT COFFEYVILLE, KANSAS, OCTOBER 5, 1892 . . . COFFEYVILLE, KANSAS: COFFEYVILLE JOURNAL PRINT, 1892.

[1]–[72]. (Page [1] blank, portrait on verso.) 19.2 x 13.5 cm. Illustrations unlisted. Terra cotta pictorial wrappers with title on front wrapper.

Prov.: Inscribed in pencil on page [1]: Coffeyville, Kansas / April 18, 1894. / Presented to D M Pepper / by the author / [flourish] /.

Ref.: Adams 347; Howes E107

This exceedingly rare little book is an accurate account of this battle written . . . immediately after the raid when details were fresh.— Adams

1236 ELLIOTT, RICHARD S.

NOTES TAKEN IN SIXTY YEARS . . . ST. LOUIS: R. P. STUDLEY & CO., 1883.

[i–iv], [1]–336. 21.7 x 14.5 cm. Portrait. Green cloth, blind embossed sides, gilt title on backstrip.

Prov.: Inscribed on front blank leaf: Robert Gordon Esq. C. E. / with respects of / The Author /.

Ref.: Bradford 1634; Howes E111

Elliott was an Indian agent at Council Bluffs in the thirties and went on Doniphan's Expedition in 1846. According to Howes, the portrait is not found in later editions.

1237 [ELLIS, EDWARD S.]

ON THE PLAINS; OR, THE RACE FOR LIFE. A STORY OF ADVENTURE AMONG THE BLACK HILLS. NEW-YORK: SINCLAIR TOUSEY.

[1]–62, [63–4 advertisements]. 23.3 x 14.7 cm. Yellow printed pictorial wrappers printed in black and orange, with title on front wrapper, advertisement on verso of back wrapper.

Ref.: Johannsen I p. 129; Wagner-Camp 386a

On the Plains was originally two stories published under the pseudonym Latham C. Carleton, *The Hunters* and *The Trappers' Retreat*. Earlier printings under the title *On the Plains* have entirely different pictorial wrappers and bear the Tousey name on title-page and wrapper. The American News Company was formed by combining the Tousey firm and Dexter, Hamilton & Co. on February 1, 1864. Numbers 4 and 5 of *American Tales* carry Tousey's name on the title-page and the new firm name on the wrapper.

1238 ELLISON, J. R.

AUTOGRAPH MANUSCRIPT DOCUMENT, SIGNED. 1872 April 16, Hall of Umpqua Lodge No. 37, I. O. O. F. One page, 16.5 x 18.9 cm.

Resolution of thanks to Loren L. Williams. Inserted in Manuscript Journals of Loren L. Williams, Volume IV.

1239 ELLSWORTH, EPHRAIM E.

MANUAL OF ARMS FOR LIGHT INFANTRY, ADAPTED TO THE RIFLED MUSKET, WITH, OR WITHOUT, THE PRIMING ATTACHMENT, ARRANGED FOR THE U. S. ZOUAVE CADETS, GOVERNOR'S GUARD OF ILLINOIS . . .

[1]–110, [111–12 blank], [1]–[40], [1]–40. 13.5 x 9.1 cm. Black cloth, blind embossed borders on sides, title in gilt on front cover.

Prov.: Inscribed on front endleaf; in pencil: Reynolds / Deer Park / Ills /.

Ref.:

The latest date mentioned in the text is August 20, 1860.

The second section carries a separate title-page: U. S. Zouave Cadets, / Governor's Guard. / [decorative rule] / Organization, / Drill and Uniforms, / same as / Zouaves & Chasseurs d'Vincennes / of the French Army. / [vignette] / Armory: / Cadets' Assembly Rooms, / Corner of State and Randolph Sts., / Chicago. / [decorative rule] / Drill every Evening, except Sunday. / The title-page of the third section reads: General Regulations / of the / Illinois State Troops. / [rule] / Plan of Organization / of / Skeleton Regiments. / [rule] / Scott & Company, Printers. /

1240 ELLSWORTH, EPHRAIM E.

MANUAL OF ARMS FOR LIGHT INFANTRY . . . CHICAGO: P. T. SHERLOCK, 112 DEARBORN STREET. 1861.

[1]–192. 13.4 x 9.2 cm. Purple cloth, blind embossed borders on sides, title in gilt on front cover.

Ref.: AII (*Chicago*) 550

A later edition was issued in Philadelphia in 1862.

Editions: [Chicago, no date.]

1241 ELLSWORTH, HENRY W.

VALLEY OF THE UPPER WABASH, INDIANA, WITH HINTS ON ITS AGRICULTURAL ADVANTAGES: PLAN OF A DWELLING, ESTIMATES OF CULTIVATION, AND NOTICES OF LABOR-SAVING MACHINES . . . NEW YORK: PUBLISHED BY PRATT, ROBINSON, AND CO., 1838.

[i]–xii, [1]–175, [176 blank]. 20.9 x 13.4 cm. Three illustrations and a map. Map: Mitchell's / Map of the / United States; / Showing the / Principal Travelling, Turnpike and Common Roads; / on which are given the / Distances in Miles from One Place to Another; / also, the Courses of the Canals & Rail Roads / Throughout the Country, Carefully Compiled from the / Best Authorities. / Philadelphia: Published by S. Augustus Mitchell. / 1838 / Sold by Mitchell & Hinman / [rule] / N⁰ 6 North Fifth Street. / [lower left:] Entered according to Act of Congress, in the year 1835, by S. Augustus Mitchell, in the Clerks office of the district court, of the eastern district of Pennsylvania. / 47.4 x 59.8 cm. Scale: about 73 miles to one inch. *Insets:* Eight insets, each about 8.5 x 6.5 cm., of Environs of Niagara Falls, Baltimore and Washington, Charleston, Hartford and New Haven, Albany, Boston, New York, and Philadelphia. No scales given. Contemporary dark blue velvet, gilt rule borders on sides, blind embossed panels

in centres, new pink leather label on backstrip, gilt edges.

Prov.: Signature on blank leaf at front: H W. Ellsworth / [flourish] /. Bookplates of Anson Phelps Stokes and Rev. Anson Phelps Stokes.

Ref.: Buck 324; Bradford 1558; Howes E128; Jones 1009; Sabin 22346

The author's copy, specially bound. The copy is about one-half inch taller than regular copies. There are several manuscript corrections and marginal notes in the hand of the author.

1242 ELLSWORTH & PACIFIC RAILROAD COMPANY

THE ELLSWORTH & PACIFIC RAILROAD. SOME FACTS AND INFORMATION AS TO THE ROUTES . . . AND THE COUNTRY THROUGH WHICH IT WOULD PASS . . . LEAVENWORTH, KANSAS: PRINTED AT THE BULLETIN OFFICE.

[1]–30, [31–2 blank]. 20.9 x 13.5 cm. Sewn, removed from bound volume, remnants of green wrappers along backstrip.

Ref.: AII (*Kansas*) 621; Howes E131; *Railway Economics* p. 207

Dated on page [3]: Ellsworth, Kansas, Jan. 26, 1868. /

1243 ELY, ELISHA

A DIRECTORY FOR THE VILLAGE OF ROCHESTER, CONTAINING THE NAMES, RESIDENCE AND OCCUPATIONS OF ALL MALE INHABITANTS OVER FIFTEEN YEARS OF AGE, IN SAID VILLAGE, ON THE FIRST OF JANUARY, 1827. TO WHICH IS ADDED, A SKETCH OF THE HISTORY OF THE VILLAGE, FROM 1812 TO 1827. ROCHESTER: PUBLISHED BY ELISHA ELY, 1827.

[1]–[142], [1–14 advertisements]. 17.4 x 10.5 cm. Folding map: Map / of / Rochester / By / E. Johnson / . . . / Eng. by Rawden, Clark & Cᵒ Albʸ / 21.8 x 16.1 cm. Scale: 20 chains to one inch. Yellow printed boards, sheepskin back, with title on front cover, advertisement on back cover.

Ref.: Howes E134; Sabin 72340

The first Rochester directory. Also, the first history of Rochester. For a separate edition of the history, see under Jesse Hawley. The advertisements following the text are dated March, March 1, or March 20, 1827. Histories of Monroe County and Rochester occupy pages 71–89.

1244 ELY, ELISHA D.

THE ELY AND WEARE FAMILIES, PIONEERS OF MICHIGAN AND IOWA . . . CEDAR RAPIDS: PRIVATELY PRINTED BY THE TORCH PRESS, 1926.

[1]–93, [94 blank]. 23.8 x 15.8 cm. Three illustrations, unlisted. Red buckram, fore and lower edges uncut.

Ref.:

The work is not a formal genealogy, but anecdotal in character. Most of the stories concern Allegan County, Michigan, and Cedar Rapids, Iowa.

1245 [EMERSON, CHARLES L.]

RISE AND PROGRESS OF MINNESOTA TERRITORY. INCLUDING A STATEMENT OF THE BUSINESS PROSPERITY OF SAINT PAUL; AND INFORMATION IN REGARD TO THE DIFFERENT COUNTIES, CITIES, TOWNS, AND VILLAGES IN THE TERRITORY, ETC., ETC., ETC. SAINT PAUL: PUBLISHED BY C. L. EMERSON, 1855.

I–IV advertisements, [i–iv, iv blank], [1]–64. 25 x 17 cm. Green printed wrappers with title on front wrapper, advertisements on verso of front and recto and verso of back wrapper. Backstrip and part of back wrapper supplied. In a dark terra cotta cloth case.

Ref.: AII (*Minnesota*) 84; Howes E138; Jones 1329; Sabin 49306

Pages [56]–64 carry advertisements.

1246 EMIGRANT'S GUIDE, THE, . . . 1818

THE EMIGRANT'S GUIDE; OR, POCKET GEOGRAPHY OF THE WESTERN STATES AND TERRITORIES, CONTAINING A DESCRIPTION OF THE SEVERAL CITIES, TOWNS, RIVERS, ANTIQUITIES, POPULATION, MANUFACTORIES, PRICES OF LAND, SOIL, PRODUCTIONS, AND EXPORTS . . . CINCINNATI: PUBLISHED BY PHILLIPS & SPEER, 1818.

[i]–iv, [5]–266. 13.9 x 8.5 cm. Old calf.

Prov.: Signature on inside front cover: Henry F Hunter /, and on facing page: John H /. Embossed stamp of Chicago Historical Society in title-leaf, duplicate stamp on verso.

Ref.: Buck 114; Clark II 200; Howes E141; Sabin 22480

1247 EMIGRANTS' GUIDE, THE, . . . 1857

THE EMIGRANTS' GUIDE TO IOWA, WISCONSIN, AND MINNESOTA, CONTAINING A DISCRIPTION[!] OF ALL THE TOWNS ON THE MISSISSIPPI RIVER AND ITS TRIBUTARIES, FROM DUBUQUE TO ITS HEAD WATERS; ALSO, ALL THE PRINCIPAL TOWNS IN MINNESOTA . . . SAINT PAUL: PRINTED AT THE MINNESOTIAN OFFICE, 1857.

[1]–182, [183–84 Index], [1–8 advertisements]. 14.4 x 10.5 cm. Blue printed wrappers with title on front wrapper. In a red cloth case.

Ref.: AII (*Minnesota*) 129; Howes I69

1248 EMMERT, D. B.

WICHITA CITY DIRECTORY AND IMMIGRANT'S GUIDE. 1878. CONTAINING A LIST OF THE INHABITANTS . . . ALSO, HISTORICAL SKETCHES OF CITY AND COUNTY . . . KANSAS CITY, MO.: TIERNAN & WAINWRIGHT, 1878.

[1]–144, [145–46 blank]. (Pages [1]–8 printed on tan paper, page [1] pasted to inner front cover.) 22.3 x 14.5 cm. Three mounted photographs, each attached to linen stub. Pink printed boards, black leather backstrip, short title and two advertisements on front cover.

Prov.: Printed presentation slip inserted, from the Mayor and Councilmen of Wichita.

Ref.: Howes E143

1249 EMORY, WILLIAM H.

. . . NOTES OF A MILITARY RECONNOISSANCE, FROM FORT LEAVENWORTH, IN MISSOURI, TO SAN DIEGO, IN CALIFORNIA, INCLUDING PART OF THE ARKANSAS, DEL NORTE, AND GILA RIVERS . . . MADE IN 1846–7 . . . WASHINGTON: WENDELL AND VAN BENTHUYSEN, 1848.

[1]–614. 21.8 x 13.7 cm. 64 plates, three plans, two small maps and one large map, unlisted. Map: Sketch of the Passage / of the / Rio San Gabriel / Upper California / by the / Americans, discomfiting / the opposing Mexican Forces / January 8ᵗʰ 1847. / 13.4 x 22.3 cm. (paper size). No scale given. Map: Sketch of the Battle / of / Los Angeles / Upper California / Fought / between the Americans / and Mexicans / Janʸ 9ᵗʰ 1847. / 13.4 x 22.3 cm. (paper size). No scale given. Map: Sketch / of the / Actions / Fought at / San Pasqual / in / Upper California / Between the Americans / and Mexicans / Dec. 6ᵗʰ & / 7ᵗʰ 1846. / 22.3 x 13.4 cm. (paper size). No scale given. Map: Map / of the / Territory of New Mexico, / made by order of / Brig. Gen. S. W. Kearny, / under instructions from / Lieut. W. H. Emory, U. S. T. E. / by / Lieut's J. W. Abert and W. G. Peck, U. S. T. E. / 1856–7. / 63.3 x 49.5 cm. Scale: ten miles to one inch. [Note in upper left corner:] . . . This map is connected with the map of Senate Document, Nº 438, / 2ⁿᵈ Session, 29ᵗʰ Congress. / Map: Sketch / of part of the march & wagon road of Lt. Colonel Cooke, / from Santa Fe to the Pacific Ocean, 1846–7. / [2 lines] / Lithʸ of P. S. Duval, Philᵃ / 29.4 x 57 cm. No scale given. Map: Military Reconnaissance / of the / Arkansas Rio Del Norte and Rio Gila / By / W. H. Emory, Lieut. Top. Engʳˢ / Assisted from Fort Leavenworth to Santa Fé by Lieutˢ J. W. Abert and W. G. Peck, and from / Santa Fé to San Diego and the Pacific by Lieuᵗ W. H. Warner

and Mr. Norman Bestor, / Made in 1846–7, with the advance guard of the "Army of the West". / Under Command of / Brig. Gen. Stephⁿ Kearny / Constructed under the orders of / Col. J. J. Abert / Ch. Corps Top. Engʳˢ / 1847 / Drawn by Joseph Welch. / Engraved on stone by E. Weber & Co. Baltimore / 75.8 x 164.8 cm. Scale: 24 miles to one inch. Dark brown cloth, printed white paper label, 6.1 x 4.2 cm., on backstrip.

Ref.: Bradford 1576; Cowan p. 195; Edwards p. 54; Field 500; Howes E145; Hubach p. 103; Munk (Alliot) p. 73; Sabin 22536; Saunders 2883; Wagner-Camp 148; Wheat (*Transmississippi*) 544

30th Congress, 1st Session, House, Executive Document No. 41, Serial 517.

All of the plates carry the Graham imprint except those opposite pages 93, 158, 468, and 470. There is no title on the plate opposite page 93. There are no imprints on the three maps opposite pages 108, 119, 120.

Howes calls for 64 plates and 6 maps and plans. Wagner-Camp calls for 64 plates, 3 plans, two maps, and a large map.

The last map described above was not issued with all copies of the book and in the present instance is separate from the volume. It has been mounted on linen. There is a rubber-stamp on the verso releasing it from the collections of the Royal College of Surgeons of England. This appears on a sheet of gray paper attached to one corner of the verso.

1250 ENGELHARDT, ZEPHIRIN [CHARLES ANTHONY]

THE FRANCISCANS IN CALIFORNIA . . . HARBOR SPRINGS, MICHIGAN: PRINTED AND PUBLISHED AT THE HOLY CHILDHOOD INDIAN SCHOOL, 1897.

[1–4], I–XVI, 1–[517], [518 blank]. (Some irregularity in pagination.) 24.4 x 16.1 cm. 51 illustrations listed and one map. Orange wrappers, uncut.

Ref.: Blumann & Thomas 4949; Cowan p. 196; Howes E152; Streit III 2929

1251 [ENGLISH, MARY K. J.]

PRAIRIE SKETCHES; OR, FUGITIVE RECOLLECTIONS OF AN ARMY GIRL OF 1899. WYOMING SAGEBRUSH.*

[1]–76. 21.5 x 13.9 cm. 19 illustrations, unlisted. Green printed wrappers with title on front wrapper.

Ref.: Howes (1954) 3323

Howes suggests Denver as a place of publication and Library of Congress suggests 1899 as the date.

1252 ENOS, A. A.

[Wrapper title] ACROSS THE PLAINS IN 1850.

[i–iv], [1–56]. 24 x 16.3 cm. Brown printed wrappers, 28.6 x 18.1 cm., with title on front wrapper, overlapping fold, stapled, punched, tied with black silk ribbon. In a red cloth folder.

Prov.: Inscribed: Compliments of / A. F. Enos, / 3426 Oceola St., / Denver, Col. /

Ref.: Howes E160

Published at Stanton, Nebraska, about 1905. According to the dedication, signed by A. F. Enos, the articles were written by A. A. Enos at the age of eighty-two and were first published in the younger Enos' paper, the *Stanton Picket*.

Enos left La Porte, Indiana, March 18, 1850, and reached Hangtown (Placerville), California, on July 25. In addition to the overland trip, the author describes life in the mines.

1253 ENSIGN & THAYER, New York

ENSIGN & THAYER'S TRAVELLERS' GUIDE THROUGH THE STATES OF OHIO, MICHIGAN, INDIANA, ILLINOIS, MISSOURI, IOWA, AND WISCONSIN; WITH RAILROAD, CANAL, STAGE, AND STEAMBOAT ROUTES . . . NEW YORK: PUBLISHED BY HORACE THAYER & CO., 1852.

[1]–33, [34 blank, 35–6 advertisements]. 13.6 x 8.5 cm. Folding map: Map of the / Western States / By J. M. Atwood. / [upper right:] Published by / Horace Thayer & Co. / Nº 50 Ann St. New York / 1852. / [6 lines of references] / Drawn & Engraved by J. M. Atwood, N. York. / [lower centre:] Entered according to Act of Congress in the year 1848 by Ensign's & Thayer in the Clerks office of the District Court for the Southern District of New York. / [within wide borders which incorporate views of four cities in the corners]. 54.8 x 69.7 cm. Scale: 40 miles to one inch. Black leather, with title stamped in gilt on front and in blind on back cover. The pamphlet, attached only at the inner front hinge, is supplied with a marbled paper back wrapper.

Ref.: Buck 347 see; Howes E165

Published, and reissued several times, originally as *Phelps & Ensign's Traveller's Guide . . .* New York, 1839.

1254 ENSIGN, BRIDGMAN & FANNING, New York

ENSIGN, BRIDGMAN & FANNING'S LAKE AND RIVER GUIDE; BEING A TRAVELER'S COMPANION TO THE CITIES, TOWNS, AND VILLAGES ON THE WESTERN WATERS OF THE UNITED STATES . . . NEW YORK: ENSIGN, BRIDGMAN & FANNING, 1856.

[3]–[144], [145–46 blank]. 15.1 x 9.8 cm. 24 illustrations listed and one map. Map: Great Western Rivers. / [five strips, each 52.1 x 7.7 cm.,

Missouri River, Ohio River, and three of the Mississippi River], 55.8 x 40.9 cm. (page size). No scale given. Blue printed boards, with title on front cover.

Ref.: Buck 572; Howes E164; Sabin 22662 see

1255 ERMATINGER, EDWARD

[Caption title] . . . EDWARD ERMATINGER'S YORK FACTORY EXPRESS JOURNAL, BEING A RECORD OF JOURNEYS MADE BETWEEN FORT VANCOUVER AND HUDSON BAY IN THE YEARS 1827–1828 . . .

67–132. 24.5 x 16 cm. Portrait and folding map. Rebound in contemporary half maroon calf, sprinkled edges.

Ref.: Wagner-Camp 140 note

Extract from *Royal Society of Canada, Proceedings and Transactions*, Section II, Volume 6, 1912.

1256 ERNST, FERDINAND

WAARNEMINGEN OP EENE REIZE DOOR DE BINNENLANDEN DER VEREENIGDE STATEN VAN NOORD-AMERIKA, IN HET JAAR 1819 . . .

A–C^8, D^3. [1]–54. [*]^1, D–F^8. [i–ii], [49]–96. 23 x 13.1 cm. Two volumes, gray wrappers, uncut. In a red cloth case.

Prov.: Manuscript note inside front cover: Kuiper /. Bookplate of C. G. Littell.

Ref.: Buck 1819; Howes E170

Published at Amsterdam in 1821. Ernst's *Bemerkungen auf einer Reise durch das Innere der Vereinigten Staaten von Nord-Amerika im Jahre 1819 . . .* had been published at Hildesheim in 1820. The present two parts are the first two sections (all published?) of the Dutch translation. The second title-page is almost identical with the first. A catchword: Rei-/ on the last page of each part suggests a longer work.

1257 ERWIN, MILO

THE HISTORY OF WILLIAMSON COUNTY, ILLINOIS. FROM THE EARLIEST TIMES, DOWN TO THE PRESENT . . . MARION, ILLINOIS, 1876.

[i]–viii, [1]–186. 16.4 x 10.8 cm. Buff printed wrappers with title on front wrapper. In a red cloth case.

Ref.: Buck 1143; Howes E173

1258 ESCUDERO, JOSE A. DE

NOTICIAS ESTADISTICAS DEL ESTADO DE CHIHUAHUA . . . MEXICO: POR JUAN OJEDA, 1834.

[1]–[260]. (Pages 256–60 mispaginated 156–60.) 20.1 x 15 cm. Pale lavender printed wrappers, with title on front wrapper. Lacks back wrapper. In a red cloth case.

Ref.: Howes E176; Palau 81652; Sabin 22844

A careful statistical summary of the resources of the old state of Chihuahua.

Editions: Mexico, 1834.

1259   ESPEJO, ANTONIO DE

HISTOIRE DES TERRES NOUUELLEMENT DESCOUUERTES . . . PARIS, CHEZ LA VEFUE NICOLAS ROFFET, M.D.LXXXVI.

[A]–B⁴, C, D1–2, C2–3, D3, C4, D4, D, C1–2, D2–3, C3, D4, C4, E–F4. [1]–17, 26, 25, 19–19, 28, 27, 20–21, 30, 29, 22–23, 32, 31, 24–25, 18, 17, 26–27, 20, 19, 28–29, 22, 21, 30–31, 24, 23, 32–46, 46, [48]. 15.4 x 9.8 cm. Rebound in dark red crushed levant morocco Jansenist, gilt inner dentelles, gilt edges, by Riviere. Some pagination and sidenotes bled.

Prov.: Bookplate of J. C. MacCoy.

Ref.: Palau 82371; Wagner (*SS*) 8a

A unique variant (of three known copies) in which the inner formes of gatherings C and D were reversed, this French edition was corrected by pasting two half sheets together so that the proper formes matched. Mr. MacCoy had these pasted sheets separated. The type for both inner and outer formes of gatherings C and D was reset. The other two copies located (Ayer and Lenox, the former being a Lenox duplicate) are identical. In resetting, approximately one hundred changes in spelling, contractions, abbreviations, etc., were made.

The text had appeared first in Spanish in the Madrid edition of González de Mendoza's *Historia* . . . printed by Querino Gerardo Flamenco in 1586, which was followed by a Madrid edition by Pedro Madrigal the following year. In the meantime, the Espejo account alone was published in Spanish in Paris at the instance of Richard Hakluyt in 1586. During the same year, this French version translated by Basanier appeared.

Editions: see above.

1260   ESPINOSA, ISIDRO FELIX DE

EL PEREGRINO SEPTENTRIONAL ATLANTE: DELINEADO EN LA EXEMPLARISSIMA VIDE DEL VENERABLE PADRE F. ANTONIO MARGIL . . . EN MEXICO POR JOSEPH BERNARDO DE HOGAL . . . ANO DE 1737.

[*]¹, ¶–¶¶¶¶⁴, W², A–L11⁴, Mmm². [i–xxxviii], [1]–456, [457–60 Index]. 19.9 x 14.6 cm. Copperplate portrait, woodcut head and tail pieces. Limp vellum with pattern of rules on covers and title on backstrip in manuscript.

Ref.: Howes E184; Jones 444; Medina (*Mexico*) 3461; Palau 82703; Streit III 403; Wagner (*SS*) 102

The present copy agrees with the title-page as transcribed by Medina and differs slightly from the facsimile given by Wagner, i.e. line 10 reads Santo in Wagner and Sto. in the present copy, and line 4 up reads Con Licencia . . . in Wagner and Impressa con Licencia . . . in the present copy.

The references to St. Uriel on pages 426–27 are crossed out in manuscript.

1261   ESPINOSA, ISIDRO FELIX DE

NUEVAS EMPRESSAS DEL PEREGRINO AMERICANO SEPTENTRIONAL ATLANTE, DESCUBIERTAS EN LO QUE HIZO QUANDO VIVIA, Y AUN DESPUES DE SU MUERTE HA MANIFESTADO EL V. P. F. ANTONIO MARGIL DE JESUS . . . IMPRESSAS EN MEXICO, EN LA IMPRENTA REAL DEL SUPERIOR GOBIERNO, Y DEL NUEVO REZADO, DE DONA MARIA DE RIVERA . . . ANO 1747.

¶–¶¶¶⁴, A–E4, F³. [i–xxiv], [1]–46. 20.3 x 14.6 cm. Limp vellum, remnants of leather ties.

Prov.: Inscribed on front endleaf: S E Illsso de Th Jṗh de Villar conLicencia / —de suo Prelados— /. Signature on title-page: Th. Pablo Jṗh de Villar [paraph] /. Rubber stamp of Alejandro Ruiz on same page. Inscribed on blank leaf at back: ad mayorem dei Gloriam / soi de Doña Josefa Aguilar / [paraph] /.

Ref.: Howes E183; Jones 464; Medina (*Mexico*) 3825; Palau 82705; Sabin 22898; Streit III 527; Wagner (*SS*) 119

This is a supplement to the preceding item.

1262   ESPINOSA Y TELLO, JOSE

RELACION DEL VIAGE HECHO POR LAS GOLETAS SUTIL Y MEXICANA EN EL ANO DE 1792 PARA RECONOCER EL ESTRACJO DE FUCA . . . MADRID EN LA IMPRENTA REAL ANO DE 1802.

*–**⁴, a–x⁴, A–Z⁴, AA¹. [1–16], [i]–clxviii, [1]–185, [186 blank]. 22 x 16 cm. Five plates, three portraits and nine maps, in a separate atlas, with title-page: Atlas / para el Viage de las Goletas / Sutil y Mexicana / al Reconocimiento / del Estrecha de Juan de Fuca / en 1792, / Publicado en 1802. / [*]². [1–4]. 31.1 x 20.8 cm. Map: Número 1º / Carta Esferica / de los Reconocimientos hechos en la Costa N. O. / de America / en 1791, y 92. por las Goletas / Sutíl y Mexicana, / y otros Buques de S.M. / [lower left:] Cordano lo Grabo / [lower right:] Morata lo escribío. / 48.2 x 36.9 cm. No scale given. Map: Numº 2 / Carta Esférica / de los Reconocimientos hechos en la Costa N. O. / de América / en 1791. y 92. por las Goletas sutíl y Mexicana / y otros Buques de S. M. / [lower left:] Cordano lo Grabo /. 47.4 x 35.6 cm. No scale given. Map: Numero 3. / Continuacion / de los reconocimientos hechos / en la Costa No. de America / por los Buques de S. M. / en varias Campañas /

desde 1774 á 1792 / [lower left:] Cardano Scul / [lower right:] Morata esc. / 36.3 x 47.1 cm. No scale given. Map: Num⁰ 4. / Carta / de los reconocimientos / hechoes en 1602. / por el Capitan / Sebastian Vizcayno / Formada por los Planos / que hizo èl mismo / durante su comision / [lower left:] Cardano lo grabo /. 36.1 x 35 cm. Scale: 19 maritime leagues to one inch. Map: Num⁰ 5⁰ / Plano del Puerto / de S. Diego / en la Costa Setent^l de Californ^g / Levantado por el 2⁰ Piloto de la / Armada D. Juan Pantoja. / Año 1782. / [lower left:] Cardano lo grabó / [lower right:] Morata lo escr. / 21.7 x 17.6 cm. Scale: about 2 maritime miles to one inch. Map: Plano del Puerto / y Bahia / de Monte Rey / situado en la Costa de Californ^g / Frabasado[!] / à bordo de las Corvetas / Descubierta y Atrevida. / Año 1791. / [lower left:] Cordano lo grabó / [upper left:] Num⁰ 6. / [lower right:] Morata lo escribió /. 23.7 x 17.7 cm. Scale: about 3 1/3 maritime miles to one inch. Map: Plano / de la Cala / de los Amigos. / Situada / en la parte Ocidental / de la entrada de Nutka / Año 1791. / [upper left:] Num⁰ 7. / [lower left:] Cardano lo grabó / [lower right:] Morata lo esc⁰ / 25.1 x 17.6 cm. Scale: 3 1/2 maritime miles to one inch. Map: Plano / del Puerto / de Mulgrave / Frabasado[!] / á bordo de las Corvetas / Descubierta y Atrevida / de la Marina Real / Año 1791. / [upper left:] Num⁰ 8. / [lower left:] Cardano lo grabó / [lower right:] Morata lo esc⁰ / 17.5 x 25.1 cm. Scale: about 5 miles to one inch. Map: Num⁰ 9. / Plano / del Puerto del / Desengaño / Trabasado / de Orden del Rey / en 1791. / [lower left:] J. Cardano f^t / 22.5 x 18.8 cm. Scale: about one maritime mile to one inch. Two volumes, original marbled wrappers, uncut. Each volume in a board and cloth case.

Prov.: Bookplates of A. Pinart.

Ref.: Howes G18; Jones 686–88 (3 copies); Medina (*BHA*) 5934; Palau 82853–54; Sabin 69221; Smith 2887

The important account of the exploration of the Far Northwest coast by the Spanish.

1263 ESQUISSE DE LA SITUATION . . .

ESQUISSE DE LA SITUATION POLITIQUE ET CIVILE DE LA LOUISIANE, DEPUIS LE 30 NOVEMBRE 1803, JUSQU'AU 1er, OCTOBRE 1804 . . . NOUVELLE-ORLEANS: DE L'IMPRIMERIE DU TELEGRAPHE, 1804.

[A]⁸, B–C⁴, D⁷. [1–2], [i]–iv, [7]–46. (Lacks final blank?). 19.3 x 12.1 cm. Rebound in blue half morocco, uncut.

Ref.: Howes L514; McMurtrie (*New Orleans*) 69

The first several pages contain a fascinating pair of descriptions of the surrender of Louisiana

by the Spanish to the French and by the latter to the United States at New Orleans. The anonymous work is a clear and well-argued exposition of the difficulties involved in the transfer of a large territory from one country to another, with especial emphasis on the problems of bilingual living.

1264 ESTRACTO DE NOTICIAS

[Caption title] . . . ESTRACTO DE NOTICIAS DEL PUERTO DE MONTERREY, DE LA MISSION, Y PRESIDIO QUE SE HAN ESTABLECIDO EN EL CON LA DENOMENACION DE SAN CARLOS, Y DEL SUCESSO DE LAS DOS EXPEDICIONES DE MAR, Y TIERRA QUE A ESTE FIN SE DESPACHARON EN EL ANO PROXIMO ANTERIOR DE 1769 . . .*

[1–5, 6 blank.] 27.9 x 19.9 cm. Tipped into marbled wrappers. In a red half morocco case.

Prov.: Henry R. Wagner and Herschel V. Jones copy.

Ref.: Cowan p. 199; Jones 538; Medina (*Mexico*) 5330; Palau 84307; Wagner (*SS*) 150

Dated at the end: Mexico 16. de Agosto de 1770. / Con Licencia y Orden, del Ex^{mô} Señor Virrey. / En la Imprenta del Superior Govierno.

The earliest printed account of the Spanish occupation of Northern California, and of Portolá's expedition to Monterrey and San Francisco.—Eames

1265 ESTRELLA, JOSE MANUEL, TOMAS ESCALANTE, & JESUS GAXIOLA

INFORME DADO A LAS CAMARAS GENERALES DE LA FEDERACION . . . COSALA: A CARGO DE J. FELIPE GOMEZ. ANO DE 1827.

[*]², [1]–5⁴, 6². ([*] is wrap-around of first and last leaves.) [1]–22, [i]–xxiv, [xxv–xxvi blank]. 19.8 x 15 cm. Stabbed, unbound.

Ref.: Howes I31; Palau 119496

First book printed at Cosalá. Sonora and Sinaloa had been combined to form the province of Occidente. Delegate Estrella and his friends wanted the state split into its old parts.

1266 ETHELL, HENRY C.

THE RISE AND PROGRESS OF CIVILIZATION IN THE HAIRY NATION. A COMPARATIVE TOPICAL REVIEW OF THE STAGES OF PROGRESS IN THE BRIEF HISTORY OF DAVIS COUNTY, IOWA . . . BLOOMFIELD, IOWA: H. C. ETHELL, 1883.

[i]–viii, 9–144. 19.1 x 13 cm. Blue cloth, blind embossed borders on sides, title in gilt on front cover.

Ref.: Howes E208; Mott (*Iowa*) p. 46

Amusingly written.

1267 EVANS, ELWOOD

[Wrapper title] PUGET SOUND: ITS PAST, PRESENT AND FUTURE. AN ADDRESS DELIVERED . . . AT PORT TOWNSEND, WASHINGTON TERRITORY, JANUARY 5TH, 1869 . . . OLYMPIA, WASHINGTON TERRITORY, 1869.

[1]–16. 22.6 x 14.4 cm. Yellow printed wrappers with title on front wrapper.

Ref.: AII (*Washington*) 131; Sabin 23146; Smith 2925

Numerous manuscript corrections of typographical errors throughout.

1268 EVANS, ELWOOD

WASHINGTON TERRITORY: HER PAST, HER PRESENT AND THE ELEMENTS OF WEALTH WHICH ENSURE HER FUTURE. ADDRESS DELIVERED AT THE CENTENNIAL EXPOSITION, PHILADELPHIA, SEPT. 2, 1876 . . . OLYMPIA: C. B. BAGLEY, 1877.

[1]–51, [52 blank]. 22.7 x 14.5 cm. Salmon printed wrappers with title on front wrapper.

Prov.: Inscribed at the top of the front wrapper: Sam. Wilkeson, Esq / With the kindest regards of / Elwood Evans /.

Ref.: Howes E218; Smith 2930

Published by order of the territorial Legislative Assembly.

1269 EVANS, ESTWICK

A PEDESTRIOUS TOUR, OF FOUR THOUSAND MILES, THROUGH THE WESTERN STATES AND TERRITORIES, DURING THE WINTER AND SPRING OF 1818 . . . CONCORD, N.H.: PRINTED BY JOSEPH C. SPEAR, 1819.

[1]–21⁶, 22⁴. [1]–256, [257–60 blank]. 18.4–19.2 x 11.9–12 cm. Woodcut frontispiece. Tan printed boards, with title on front cover, uncut. In a blue cloth case.

Ref.: Bradford 1591; Buck 115; Clark II 201; Clements Library (*Michigan*) 54; Field 509; Howes E220; Hubach p. 51; Rader 1314; Sabin 23148; Thomson 382

The second copyright leaf is pasted to the verso of the title-leaf. This appears to be one of the thin paper copies; some have been reported on thick paper.

Evans' work is the best description we have of the places he visited and the conditions he found in 1818. His route took him (on foot) as far as Detroit, from which town he backtracked to Pittsburgh. He then followed the line of the Ohio and Mississippi Rivers to New Orleans and eventually returned to New England by sea. Evans apparently had no other purpose for the trip than pleasure and experience. His comments on people, scenes, customs, manners, etc., personal as they are, are entertaining and illuminating. He was an intelligent observer.

1270 EVANS, LEWIS

GEOGRAPHICAL, HISTORICAL, POLITICAL, PHILOSOPHICAL AND MECHANICAL ESSAYS . . . PHILADELPHIA: PRINTED BY B. FRANKLIN, AND D. HALL, MDCCLV.

[*]², A–D⁴. [i]–iv, 1–32. 23.5 x 17.7 cm.

BOUND WITH:

GEOGRAPHICAL, HISTORICAL, POLITICAL, PHILOSOPHICAL AND MECHANICAL ESSAYS. NUMBER II. . . . . PHILADELPHIA: PRINTED FOR THE AUTHOR . . . MDCCLVI.

[A]–L². [1]–42, [43 advertisement, 44 blank]. Two volumes bound together in old blue boards, new calf backstrip and corners, red leather label, yellow edges.

Ref.: Church 1003; Evans 7412; Hildeburn 1412; Howes E226, E227; Sabin 23175; Thomson 384

Inserted between the two parts is a manuscript leaf bearing an extract regarding Evans from Smith: *History of New York* . . .

1271 EVENING JOURNAL (Chicago)

[Broadside] EVENING JOURNAL—EXTRA. CHICAGO, MONDAY, OCTOBER 9, 1871. THE GREAT CALAMITY OF THE AGE! CHICAGO IN ASHES!! HUNDREDS OF MILLIONS OF DOLLARS' WORTH OF PROPERTY DESTROYED. THE SOUTH, THE NORTH AND A PORTION OF THE WEST DIVISIONS OF THE CITY IN RUINS . . . THERE WILL BE A MEETING OF THE DIRECTORS OF THE CHICAGO BOARD OF TRADE AT 51 AND 53 CANAL ST. TO-MORROW, 10TH, AT 10 O'CLOCK. J. W. PRESTON, PRESIDENT.

Broadside, 34.3 x 23.8 cm. Text, 30 x 17 cm.

Prov.: Dr. Otto F. Schmidt copy.

Ref.:

Printed by the Interior Printing Company, 15 & 18 Canal Street.

1272 EVENING POST, THE (Chicago)

[Newspaper] THE EVENING POST. SATURDAY, NOVEMBER 25, 1871. SUPPLEMENT . . .

Broadsheet newspaper, 71 x 53.4 cm.

Ref.:

On the second page there is a reprint of the newspaper for Monday, Evening, October 9, 1871, reporting the great Chicago fire.

1273 EVENTFUL NARRATIVES . . .

EVENTFUL NARRATIVES, THE THIRTEENTH BOOK OF THE FAITH-PROMOTING SERIES. DESIGNED FOR THE INSTRUCTION AND ENCOURAGEMENT OF YOUNG

LATTER-DAY SAINTS. SALT LAKE CITY, UTAH: JUVENILE INSTRUCTOR OFFICE, 1887.

[I]–[VIII, VIII blank], [9]–98, [99–100 advertisements]. 18.1 x 11.7 cm. Brown cloth, title in gilt on front cover.

Ref.:

The volume contains "Leaving Home" by Robert Avedon (pages [9]–49), "A Boy's Love: A Man's Devotion" by an anonymous writer (pages 49–76), and "A Trip to Carson Valley" by O. B. Huntington (pages 77–98).

1274 EVERETT, HORACE

[Caption title] . . . REGULATING THE INDIAN DEPARTMENT . . . MR. H. EVERETT, FROM THE COMMITTEE ON INDIAN AFFAIRS, MADE THE FOLLOWING REPORT: . . .

[1]–131, [132 blank]. 25.5 x 15.5 cm. Map: Map / of the / Western / Territory / &c. / 43.1 x 45.3 cm. Scale: 50 miles to one inch. Rebound in new red cloth, uncut.

Ref.: Sabin 23282

23rd Congress, 1st Session, House, Report No. 474, Serial 263. [Washington, 1834.]

Contains considerable important material about trade with the Indians of the Far West.

Page [1], lower left corner: [short rule] / [Gales & Seaton, print.] /

1275 EVERETT HOUSE, Chicago

[Caption title] EVERETT HOUSE. BRYON A. BALDWIN & CO., PROPRIETORS. COR. CLARK AND VAN BUREN STREETS . . .

[1]–4]. 21 x 14.1 cm. Unbound.

Ref.:

Page [2] carries the Annual Thanksgiving Dinner menu for November 24, 1870. Page [3] is a wine list. Page [4] is headed: Amusements.

1276 EVERHART, J. F.

QUINCY CITY DIRECTORY, FOR 1855-6. QUINCY, ILLINOIS: GIBSON & MORRISON, 1855.

[1]–143, [144 blank]. 15.8 x 10.4 cm. Brown cloth, yellow paper label, 5 x 6.4 cm., glazed, apparently printed in gold.

Ref.: Byrd 2267; Howes E236

Contains an historical sketch. Pages 57–137 are advertisements.

1277 EVERTS, TRUMAN C.

THIRTY-SEVEN DAYS OF PERIL. A NARRATIVE OF THE EARLY DAYS OF THE YELLOWSTONE . . . SAN FRANCISCO, 1923.*

[i–viii, viii blank], [1]–57, [58 colophon]. 20.8 x 13.8 cm. Frontispiece and vignette by Joseph Sinel. Gray boards, cloth backstrip, printed paper label.

Ref.: Heller & Magee 53

Printed by Edwin and Robert Grabhorn and James McDonald. The author was a member of the Washburn Party of 1870 who became lost from his companions and suffered considerable hardship. Everts' account had appeared in *Scribner's Monthly*, Volume III, November, 1871, pages [1]–17.

1278 EVIL OF INTOXICATING LIQUOR, THE

. . . THE EVIL OF INTOXICATING LIQUOR, AND THE REMEDY. SECOND EDITION. PARK HILL: MISSION PRESS, 1844.

[1]–24. 12.8 x 7.7 cm. Hargrett (*Oklahoma*) 71; Pilling 1249

BOUND WITH:

[Two temperance hymns, entirely in Sequoyan]

[1]–4]. Hargrett (*Oklahoma*) 71

BOUND WITH:

[Caption title] MISCELLANEOUS PIECES.

[1]–24. Hargrett (*Oklahoma*) 70; Pilling 2597

BOUND WITH:

THE DAIRYMAN'S DAUGHTER: BY REV. LEGH RICHMOND . . . BOB THE SAILOR BOY. BY REV. G. C. SMITH . . . PARK HILL: MISSION PRESS, 1847.

[i–iv], [1]–67, [68 blank]. Hargrett (*Oklahoma*) 113

BOUND WITH:

POOR SARAH . . . 1843.

[1]–18, [19–20 blank]. Hargrett (*Oklahoma*) 59

BOUND WITH:

THE SWISS PEASANT. BY REV. CESAR MALAN, OF GENEVA . . . PARK HILL: MISSION PRESS, 1848.

[1]–24. Hargrett (*Oklahoma*) 127

BOUND WITH:

[Caption title] A TREATISE ON MARRIAGE . . .

[1]–20. Hargrett (*Oklahoma*) 60; Pilling 3888

BOUND WITH:

[Caption title] CATECHISM . . .

[1]–4. Hargrett (*Oklahoma*) 55; Pilling 671

Eight pamphlets bound together, black limp cloth.

Ref.: Hargrett (*Oklahoma*) 71, 71, 70, 113, 59, 127, 60, 55; Pilling 1249, 2597, 3888, 671

Text in Sequoyan.

Editions: (*The Evil of Intoxicating Liquor*) Park Hill, 1838

1279 EWELL, THOMAS T.

A HISTORY OF HOOD COUNTY TEXAS, FROM ITS EARLIEST SETTLEMENT TO THE PRESENT, TOGETHER WITH BIOGRAPHICAL SKETCHES OF MANY LEADING

MEN AND WOMEN AMONG THE EARLY SETTLERS . . .
ALSO A SKETCH OF THE HISTORY OF SOMERVELL
COUNTY . . . GRANBURY, TEXAS: PUBLISHDD[!] BY
THE GRANBURY NEWS, 1895.

[i–iv], [1]–161, [162–68]. (Four pages of advertisements on pink paper inserted after pages [iv]
and 64 and two pages after pages 76 and 128.)
21.8 x 14.2 cm. Black cloth, gilt title on front
cover.

Ref.: Adams (*Ramp. Herd*) 779; Howes E239
Advertisements on inner covers.

1280 EXTRAIT DU JOURNAL . . .

EXTRAIT DU JOURNAL D'UN OFFICIER DE LA
MARINE DE L'ESCADRE DE M. LE COMTE D'ESTAING.
1782.

[A]–Q³. [1]–126. (Lacks blank leaf at end.)
19.8 x 11.9 cm. Engraved portrait. Mottled calf,
gilt back, red leather label.

Ref.: Howes E198; Monaghan 646; Sabin
23033

Three editions appeared the same year consisting of 126, 158, and 94 pages. There are portraits present in the first two listed, but they are
not identical.

The unidentified author [possibly Captain
Walsh, the Chevalier O'Connor] is highly critical
of the conduct of his superior.—Howes

F

1281 FAIRFIELD, ASA M.

FAIRFIELD'S PIONEER HISTORY OF LASSEN COUNTY,
CALIFORNIA: CONTAINING EVERYTHING THAT CAN
BE LEARNED ABOUT IT FROM THE BEGINNING OF
THE WORLD TO THE YEAR OF OUR LORD 1870 . . .
SAN FRANCISCO: PUBLISHED FOR THE AUTHOR BY
H. S. CROCKER COMPANY.*

[i]–xxii, [1]–506, [507 colophon, 508 blank].
21.5 x 14.2 cm. Four illustrations and one map
listed. Red cloth, gilt, gilt top.

Ref.: Adams 355; Blumann & Thomas 1115;
Cowan p. 201; Howes F11
Copyrighted 1916.

1282 FAITHFUL PICTURE . . .

FAITHFUL PICTURE OF THE POLITICAL SITUATION
OF NEW ORLEANS, AT THE CLOSE OF THE LAST AND
THE BEGINNING OF THE PRESENT YEAR, 1807. BOS-
TON: RE-PRINTED FROM THE NEW-ORLEANS EDI-
TION, 1808.*

[A]–F⁴. (Signature D failed to print.) [1]–48.
20.4 x 12.8 cm. Removed from binding, sewn,
unbound.

Ref.: Howes W677; Sabin 53325; Shaw &
Shoemaker 14981

The authorship of this pamphlet is in doubt
It has been attributed to James Workman and to
Edward Livingston.

1283 FALCONER, THOMAS

ON THE DISCOVERY OF THE MISSISSIPPI, AND ON THE
SOUTH-WESTERN, OREGON, AND NORTH-WESTERN
BOUNDARY OF THE UNITED STATES . . . LONDON:
SAMUEL CLARKE, 1844.

[i]–iv, [5]–96, [1]–99, [100 errata]. 19 x 11.5 cm.
Folding map: North America / Published under
the Superintendance of the Society for the / Dif-
fusion of Useful Knowledge / [at foot:] London
Chaˢ Knight & Cᵒ 22, Ludgate Street. 127
[lower right:] Engraved by J. & C. Walker.
38.1 x 31.3 cm. Scale: about 350 English miles to
one inch. Rebound in black half morocco,
marbled board sides, marbled edges.

Prov.: Author's copy, with manuscript corrections in text and signature on verso of front fly-
leaf: Tho Falconer D H. R. / Decʳ 14– 1844– /.

Ref.: Bradford 1610; Howell 98; Howes F16;
Rader 1328; Sabin 23726

In addition to a careful consideration of the
rights of Great Britain to Oregon, Falconer produced the first translation into English of
LaSalle's report and of Tonty's *Mémoire*, 1693.

Editions: Same, without map.

1284 FANNING, EDMUND

VOYAGES ROUND THE WORLD; WITH SELECTED
SKETCHES OF VOYAGES TO THE SOUTH SEAS, NORTH
AND SOUTH PACIFIC OCEANS, CHINA, ETC., PER-
FORMED UNDER THE COMMAND OF THE AUTHOR . . .
NEW YORK: COLLINS & HANNAY, M DCCC XXXIII.

[i]–xii, [13]–499, [500 blank]. 22.8 x 14.1 cm.
Five lithographed plates. Tan boards, new green
cloth backstrip, original paper label, 4.4 x 4 cm.

Ref.: Howes F27; Sabin 23780

Fanning's expedition was the first sponsored
by the United States government.

1285 FANNING, EDMUND

VOYAGES TO THE SOUTH SEAS, INDIAN AND PA-
CIFIC OCEANS, CHINA SEA, NORTH-WEST COAST . . .
BETWEEN THE YEARS 1830–1837. ALSO, THE ORI-
GIN, AUTHORIZATION, AND PROGRESS OF THE FIRST
AMERICAN NATIONAL SOUTH SEA EXPLORING EX-
PEDITION . . . NEW-YORK: WILLIAM H. VERMILYE,
1838.

[i]–xii, [13]–324. 18.7 x 11.8 cm. Frontispiece.
Black cloth.

Prov.: Inscribed in ink at top of fly-leaf: from
Capt Fanning /, and in pencil: Presented by the
author with his / respects to Messrˢ Bloodgood
& / Vanschaick as a friendly token. /

Ref.: Howes F28; Sabin 23781

Although much of the material is repeated, this work differs from Fanning's earlier publication, *Voyages Round the World* . . . New York, 1833.

There is an excellent account of the destruction of the "Tonquin," Astor's ship, in Nootka Sound.

Editions: Four editions, same place, same date.

1286 FARGO, FRANK F.

[Caption title] A FULL AND AUTHENTIC ACCOUNT OF THE MURDER OF JAMES KING, OF WM. . . . . BY JAMES P. CASEY, AND THE EXECUTION OF JAMES P. CASEY AND CHARLES CORA, BY THE VIGILANCE COMMITTEE . . .

[1]–24. 22.8 x 14.7 cm. Yellow printed wrappers with title on front wrapper, advertisement on verso of back wrapper. In a dark blue cloth case.

Ref.: Blumann & Thomas 3100; Cowan p. 202; Greenwood 679; Howes F31; McDade 557; Sabin 23798

A famous and exciting murder case.

1287 FARIA, FRANCISCO XAVIER DE

VIDA. Y HEROYCAS VIRTUDES DEL V^BLE. PADRE PEDRO DE VELASCO, PROVINCIAL, QUE FUE, DE LA COMPANIA DE JESUS, DE NUEVA-ESPANA . . . CON LICENCIA EN MEXICO: EN LA IMPRENTA DE DONA MARIA DE RIBERA. EN EL EMPEDRADILLO. ANO DE 1753.

[i–xiv], [1]–64, 57–170. (Pages 9–16 printed in following order: 9, 14, 15, 12, 13, 10, 11, 16; pages 65–178 mispaginated 57–170.) 20.1 x 15.1 cm. Limp vellum, manuscript title on backstrip.

Prov.: Signature on title-page: Jesus Guayardo /. Rubber stamp of a college at Puebla on pages 1, 107, and 170.

Ref.: Carayon 2663; Howes F33; Jones 474; Medina (*Mexico*) 4116; Streit III 599; Wagner (*SS*) 127

Father Velasco's years in Sinaloa as a missionary spanned a period of deep unrest among the Indians.

1288 FARISH, T. E.

CENTRAL AND SOUTHWESTERN ARIZONA: THE GARDEN OF AMERICA . . . 1889.

[i–ii], [1]–48. 19.8 x 13.2 cm. Illustrations unlisted. Gray printed wrappers with title on front wrapper, note on back wrapper.

Prov.: Rubber stamps of J. A. Black, Commissioner of Immigration, and of the Arizona Pioneers' Historical Society.

Ref.: AII (*Arizona*) 138; Howes F35; Munk (Alliot) p. 75

Published at Phoenix, Arizona.

Editions: [Tucson, 1889].

1289 FARMER, JOHN

THE EMIGRANTS' GUIDE; OR, POCKET GAZETTEER OF THE SURVEYED PART OF MICHIGAN . . . ALBANY: PRINTED BY B. D. PACKARD AND CO., 1830.

[1]–32. 12 x 8 cm. Folded map: Map / of the / Territories / of / Michigan / and Ouisconsin [pointing hand] {pronounced Wisconsin / On a scale of 30 Geographical Miles to an inch / By John Farmer / of Detroit / 1830 / Engraved by Rawdon Clark & Co. Albany N.Y. / Entered according to Act of Congress in the Clerk's Office of the Circuit & District Court of Detroit in the Territory of Michigan by John Farmer on the 11th day of May 1829 /. 50 x 29.6 cm. Scale as above. Mounted on silk. Brown leather folder, 13.8 x 8.2 cm., title stamped in gilt on front cover. In a cloth case.

Prov.: Bookplate of C. G. Littell.

Ref.: Howes F40; Karpinski 107; Phillips (*Maps*) p. 424; Sabin 23821

First Edition of the text. There was a second edition the same year. According to Karpinski, this was the third Farmer map and the first with both Michigan and Wisconsin.

1290 FARMER, JOHN

[Map] MAP / OF THE / TERRITORIES / OF / MICHIGAN / AND / OUISCONSIN [pointing hand] {PRONOUNCED WISCONSIN / ON A SCALE OF 30 GEOGRAPHICAL MILES TO AN INCH / BY JOHN FARMER / OF DETROIT / 1836. / ENGRAVED BY RAWDON CLARK & CO ALBANY, N.Y. / ENTERED ACCORDING TO ACT OF CONGRESS IN THE CLERK'S OFFICE OF THE DISTRICT COURT OF THE SOUTHERN DISTRICT OF NEW YORK BY J. H. COLTON & C^O ON THE 9TH NOV^R. 1835. / *Inset:* Map / of Part of / Ste Marie River / from actual Survey /. 8.7 x 15.3 cm. Scale: 8 miles to one inch.

Map, 51.5 x 83.9 cm. Scale as above. Folded into green roan covers, 14.5 x 9 cm., title stamped in gilt on front cover.

Ref.:

Advertisements of J. H. Colton & Co. on inner front cover.

1291 FARNAM, HENRY W.

AUTOGRAPH MANUSCRIPT NOTE SIGNED. 1922 November 19, New Haven, Connecticut. One page, 14 x 21.7 cm. To Mr. A. N. Harbert.

Covering the gift of a copy of a daguerreotype portrait of Henry Farnam. Accompanied by the portrait. Both letter and portrait laid in the following item.

1292 FARNAM, HENRY W.

HENRY FARNAM.

[1]–136, [137 colophon, 138 blank]. 20.2 x 13.2 cm. Portrait. Cream printed parchment paper wrappers with title on front wrapper, gilt top, uncut.

Ref.: Howes F45

Limited to 100 copies. Dated on page 6: New Haven, July 1889. Imprint in colophon: Press of Tuttle, Morehouse & Taylor, New Haven /.

Laid in is an Autograph Manuscript Note, signed, by the author. 1922 November 19, New Haven, Connecticut.

Farnam was chief engineer of the Mississippi and Missouri Railroad Company.

1293 FARNHAM, THOMAS J.

TRAVELS IN THE CALIFORNIAS, AND SCENES IN THE PACIFIC OCEAN . . . NEW YORK: PUBLISHED BY SAXTON & MILES, 1844.

[i]–iv, [5]–416. 21.6 x 13.2 cm. Frontispiece and folding map: Map of / The Californias / By T. J. Farnham. / Scale of Miles / [diagrammatic scale; 53 miles to one inch] / [at lower left:] Entered according to Act of Congress in the year 1845, by Thomas J Farnham in the Clerk's Office of the Southern District of New York. / 35.2 x 27.5 cm. Scale as above. Green cloth.

Ref.: Barrett 829; Bradford 1628; Cowan p. 203; Edwards p. 57; Howes F49; Sabin 23871; Wagner-Camp 107

The success of Farnham's earlier work encouraged him to write this sequel. It seems to have been issued first in four parts.

1294 FARNHAM, THOMAS J.

TRAVELS IN THE GREAT WESTERN PRAIRIES, THE ANAHUAC AND ROCKY MOUNTAINS, AND IN THE OREGON TERRITORY . . . POUGHKEEPSIE: KILLEY AND LOSSING, 1841.

[1]–197, [198 blank]. 17.9 x 11.3 cm. Gray ribbed cloth, printed paper label on backstrip.

Ref.: Howes F50; Jones 1044; Smith 2999; Wagner-Camp 85

A good work which received much popularity.

1295 FARNHAM, THOMAS J.

THE SAME . . . LONDON: RICHARD BENTLEY, 1843.

[i]–[xxiv, xxiv blank], [1]–297, [298 blank, 299–300 advertisements]. [i]–viii, [1]–315, [316 blank]. 20 x 12.5 cm. Two volumes, plum cloth, uncut.

Ref.: Field 524; Howes F50; Rader 1340 note; Sabin 23872; Smith 3003

Howes considers this the best edition.

Editions: Poughkeepsie, 1841, 1843. New York, 1843.

1296 FARNSWORTH, OLIVER, *Publisher*

THE CINCINNATI DIRECTORY, CONTAINING THE NAMES, PROFESSION AND OCCUPATION OF THE INHABITANTS OF THE TOWN, ALPHABETICALLY ARRANGED . . . PUBLISHED BY OLIVER FARNSWORTH, 1819.

[A]–N⁶. [i]–x, [11]–85, 73, 87–155, [156]. 19.5 x 12.5 cm. Folding map: Plan / of / Cincinnati, / Including / All the late Additions & Subdivisions, / Engraved for / Oliver Farnsworth, / 1819. / Scale 800 feet to an inch. / [below border:] T. Sharpless del. Lat. 39.° 6′30′. Long. 7.° 24′45″ W. from Washington City. E. G. Gridley sc. / 36.8 x 42.4 cm. Scale as above. Printed gray wrappers, with title on front wrapper, advertisements on verso of back wrapper, uncut. In a blue cloth case.

Ref.: AII (*Ohio*) 466; Buley II p. 349; Howes F51; Jones 806; Sabin 13085; Rusk II p. 50; Thomson 196; Wilkie 608

The first Cincinnati Directory. Farnsworth also published the *Freeman's Almanac*.

1297 FARRELL, NED E.

COLORADO, THE ROCKY MOUNTAIN GEM, AS IT IS IN 1868. A GAZETTEER AND HAND-BOOK OF COLORADO . . . INFORMATION FOR THE FARMER, MECHANIC, MINER, LABORER, CAPITALIST OR TOURIST . . . CHICAGO: PUBLISHED BY THE WESTERN NEWS COMPANY, 1868.

[i]–viii, [9]–72. 18.5 x 11.3 cm. Map printed on pink paper: Union Pacific / Railroad / and Connections. / Main Line. / [lower right:] Eng'd by Fisk & Russell. N York /. 12.4 x 19.6 cm. No scale given. Advertisement for Union Pacific Railroad on recto. Removed from bound volume, unbound.

Ref.: AII (*Chicago*) 1352; Adams (*Ramp. Herd*) 788; Bradford 1634; Howes F53; Sabin 23889; Wilcox p. 43

AII (*Chicago*) calls for two maps, but Howes for one only.

1298 FARWELL, JOHN V.

SOME RECOLLECTIONS . . . A BRIEF DESCRIPTION OF HIS EARLY LIFE AND BUSINESS REMINISCENCES. CHICAGO: R. R. DONNELLEY & SONS COMPANY, 1911.*

[1]–230. 16.3 x 10.8 cm. Illustrations unlisted. Dark green cloth, gilt top, uncut.

Ref.:

A Chicago business career with Texas connections.

1299 FAULCONER, M. A.

QUESTIONS ON THE HOLY SCRIPTURES, DESIGNED FOR THE USE OF SCHOLARS IN THE LATTER DAY SAINTS' SUNDAY SCHOOLS . . . PLANO, ILL, PUBLISHED BY THE REORGANIZED CHURCH OF JESUS CHRIST OF LATTER DAY SAINTS, 1869.

[1–2], [i]–[iv, iv blank], [7]–152. 15.3 x 10.5 cm. Black cloth, red leather backstrip.

Ref.: Woodward 67

Laid in are two copies of: [caption title] *No. 38. The Inspired Translation of the Holy Scriptures* . . . Lamoni: Iowa: Reorganized Church of Jesus Christ, n.d.

1300 FAUX, WILLIAM

MEMORABLE DAYS IN AMERICA: BEING A JOURNAL OF A TOUR TO THE UNITED STATES, PRINCIPALLY UNDERTAKEN TO ASCERTAIN, BY POSITIVE EVIDENCE, THE CONDITION AND PROBABLE PROSPECTS OF BRITISH EMIGRANTS; INCLUDING ACCOUNTS OF MR. BIRKBECK'S SETTLEMENT IN THE ILLINOIS: AND INTENDED TO SHEW MEN THE THINGS AS THEY ARE IN AMERICA . . . LONDON: PRINTED FOR W. SIMPKIN AND R. MARSHALL, 1823.

[i]–xvi, [1]–488. 22 x 13.9 cm. Frontispiece. Gray boards, white printed label on backstrip, 5.1 x 3.8 cm., uncut. In a brown half morocco case.

Ref.: Buck 139; Clark II 202; Howes F60; Hubach pp. 52–3; Matthews p. 234; Sabin 23933

Faux concluded that the United States was not suitable for British farmers, but he found some admirable aspects of American life. The controversies aroused on both sides of the Atlantic by the book were more bitter than the book.

1301 FEARON, HENRY B.

SKETCHES OF AMERICA. A NARRATIVE OF A JOURNEY OF FIVE THOUSAND MILES THROUGH THE EASTERN AND WESTERN STATES OF AMERICA; CONTAINED IN EIGHT REPORTS ADDRESSED TO THE THIRTY-NINE ENGLISH FAMILIES BY WHOM THE AUTHOR WAS DEPUTED, IN JUNE 1817, TO ASCERTAIN WHETHER ANY, AND WHAT PART OF THE UNITED STATES WOULD BE SUITABLE FOR THEIR RESIDENCE. WITH REMARKS ON MR. BIRKBECK'S "NOTES" AND "LETTERS." . . . LONDON: PRINTED FOR LONGMAN, HURST, REES, ORME, AND BROWN, 1818.

A⁴, B–FF⁸, GG⁷. [i]–[viii], [1]–462. 21.5 x 13.9 cm. Gray boards, tan paper backstrip, white printed label on backstrip, 3.7 x 3 cm., uncut.

Ref.: Buck 98; Clark II 22; Howes F65; Hubach p. 49; Thomson 406

The chief value of the work lies in the information Fearon gathered about the problems of making a living in the United States. In general he agreed with William Faux.

1302 FEENAN, MARTIN J.

AUTOGRAPH MANUSCRIPT ACCOUNT OF THE SULLY CAMPAIGNS, 1863–1865.

59 pages, 27.7 x 21.3 cm. With other Feenan Papers.

Feenan's account of the Sully Campaigns was written in 1920 as a history of the 6th Iowa Cavalry, Co. M, of which he was Quarter Master Sergeant. It is based on "memorandum notes of the march and lay of country; not every day, but when [I] could find time and disposition, these I kept and correspondence with members of my company, this with letters sent my people home . . ." It is a good account from the non-commissioned officer's point of view.

Accompanying the manuscript are miscellaneous manuscripts and letters by Feenan, broadsides, photographs, and memoranda, including forty-five pages of manuscript.

1303 FELL, SARAH

THREADS OF ALASKAN GOLD . . .

[1]–34 numbered LEAVES. 23 x 15.1 cm. Illustrations unlisted. Black pictorial wrappers printed in gold, bound along top edge, with three punched holes, tied with metallic gold cord. In a dark blue cloth case.

Ref.: Smith 3028 see

Copyrighted 1904; probably printed in Omaha.

This courageous and energetic woman left Seattle in the spring of 1897 and made her entry into Alaska at Skagway. The seven weeks it took to cover the portage of forty miles to Lake Bennett were days of horror and hardship. From Lake Bennett she sledded down the Yukon until the ice rotted, then traveled by boat through White Horse Rapids and Miles Canyon, and after surmounting many dangers finally reached Dawson City. At this camp, among many other activities, she became a dressmaker to some of the female entertainers, otherwise known as "chippies." She left Dawson for Nome and gives a good description of that maelstrom. Becoming tired of life in mining camps, she returned to the United States.—EDG

1304 FELLOWES, W. DORSET

AUTOGRAPH MANUSCRIPT NOTE. No date, no place. Two pages, 20.7 x 13.1 cm.

Regarding his association with Augustin de Iturbide. Bound in Iturbide: *A Statement of Some of the Principal Events* . . . 1824.

1305 FERGUSON, CHARLES D.

THE EXPERIENCES OF A FORTY-NINER DURING THIRTY-FOUR YEARS' RESIDENCE IN CALIFORNIA AND AUSTRALIA . . . EDITED BY FREDERICK T. WALLACE. CLEVELAND, OHIO: THE WILLIAMS PUBLISHING COMPANY, 1888.

[I]–XVIII, 9–507, [508 blank]. 21.8 x 14.5 cm. Illustrations unlisted. Dark brown cloth, decorative bands in black on front cover and backstrip, title in gilt on same.

Ref.: Blumann & Thomas 2198 note; Cowan p. 206

1306 FERGUSSON, DAVID

[Caption title] . . . A COPY OF A REPORT OF MAJOR D. FERGUSSON ON THE COUNTRY, ITS RESOURCES, AND THE ROUTE BETWEEN TUCSON AND LOBOS BAY . . .

[1]–22. 22.9 x 14.1 cm. Three maps. Map: Sketch of / Lobos Bay / Drawn under the Direction of / Maj D. Fergusson / 1st Cav. Cal. Vols. / by J. B. Mills. / [upper right:] Senate Ex. Doc. Nº 1.—Special Session, 1863. / [lower left:] Lith of J. Bien, 24 Vesey St. N. Y. / 24.2 x 36.4 cm. No scale given. Map: [Practicable railroad routes across lower New Mexico, Arizona, and California]. [upper right:] Senate Ex. Doc. Nº 1.—Special Session, 1863. / [lower left:] Lith. of J. Bien, 24 Vesey St. N Y. / 16.1 x 35.9 cm. No scale given. Map: [Bay of Lobos]. [upper right:] Senate Ex. Doc. Nº 1—Special Session, 1863. / [lower left:] Lith. of J. Bien, 24 Vesey Street. N. Y. / 51.6 x 73.1 cm. Scale: 500 metres to one inch. Rebound in new red cloth.

Ref.: Howes F87; Munk (Alliot) p. 76; Sabin 24103; Wagner-Camp 387; Wheat (*Transmississippi*) 1042

37th Congress, Special Session, Senate, Executive Document No. 1, Serial 1082. [Washington: Government Printing Office, 1863.]

1307 FERNANDEZ DURO, CESAREO

DON DIEGO DE PENALOSA Y SU DESCUBRIMIENTO DEL REINO DE QUIVIRA . . . MADRID: IMPRENTA Y FUNDICION DE MANUEL TELLO, 1882.

[1]–160. 28.1 x 20.3 cm. Pink printed wrappers with title on front wrapper, advertisements on recto and verso of back wrapper. In a cloth case.

Ref.: Howes D595; Raines p. 73

Fernandez Duro here refutes the account of Nicolas de Freytas.

1308 FERRIS, MRS. BENJAMIN G.

THE MORMONS AT HOME; WITH SOME INCIDENTS OF TRAVEL FROM MISSOURI TO CALIFORNIA, 1852–3. IN A SERIES OF LETTERS . . . NEW YORK: DIX & EDWARDS, 1856.

[i]–viii, 1–299, [300 blank, 301–04 advertisements]. 18.4 x 12 cm. Plum cloth, blind embossed sides, gilt backstrip.

Ref.: Bradford 1652; Cowan p. 207; Howes F99; Sabin 24186; Wagner-Camp 274; Woodward 70

1309 FERRIS, JACOB

THE STATES AND TERRITORIES OF THE GREAT WEST; INCLUDING OHIO, INDIANA, ILLINOIS, MISSOURI, MICHIGAN, WISCONSIN, IOWA, MINESOTA[!], KANSAS, AND NEBRASKA . . . NEW YORK: MILLER, ORTON, AND MULLIGAN, 1856.

[i]–xii, [13]–352, [353–56 advertisements]. 19 x 12.4 cm. 12 illustrations and a map, unlisted. Map: A new Map of the / Great West / Published by / Miller, Orton & Mulligan, / New York and Auburn. / E. F. Beadle, / Buffalo. / Lith. Warren & Buell, Buffalo / 37 x 64 cm. Scale: 75 miles to one inch. Black cloth, blind embossed borders on sides with gilt vignette on front cover and same in blind on back cover, title in gilt on backstrip, advertisements on front endpapers.

Ref.: Bradford 1654; Buck 565

1310 FERSLEW, WILLIAM C. L. E.

FERSLEW'S KANE COUNTY GAZETTEER, DIRECTORY, AND BUSINESS ADVERTISER, 1857 . . . GENEVA, ILL: PUBLISHED BY FERSLEW & CO., 1857.

[xi]–[xviii, xviii blank], [19]–28, [i–ii], 49–198, [199 advertisement, 200 blank]. 17.9 x 10.6 cm. Black cloth, blind embossed sides, title in gilt on front cover; advertisements on endsheets.

Prov.: Perforated stamps of Iowa Historical Society in title-leaf; accompanied by letter of release from the Society.

Ref.: Byrd 2645; Howes F102

The earliest Kane County history and directory listed by Buck is 1859.

1311 FERSLEW, WILLIAM C. L. E.

GAGER & CO.'S ROCKFORD CITY REGISTER AND ANNUAL ADVERTISER. 1857. NUMBER ONE. ROCKFORD, 1857.

[1]–[16], [25]–136. 17.3 x 10.9 cm. One illustration. Tan printed boards with title on front cover, advertisements on back cover. Rebacked with new black leather.

Prov.: Manuscript lettering on front cover: Wm Hulin / Dec. 1856. / and with his signature on the front endleaf in pencil. Signature inside front cover: O. F. Barbeau. / Rockford, / Ill. /

Ref.: Byrd 2646; Howes F103

William Hulin wrote the history of Rockford for this work.

1312 FETTERMAN, WILLIAM J.

AUTOGRAPH LETTER, SIGNED. 1866 November 26, Fort Phillip[!] Kearney. To Dr. Charles Terry. Three pages, 24.8 x 19.7 cm.

A fine letter, with the original envelope. Introducing Captain Jackson and giving news of the journey to Fort Phil Kearney, encounters with the Indians, chasing hostile Indians, the incompetency of Colonel Carrington, etc. Less than a month after this letter was written, Captain Fetterman led eighty men to death in the famous Fetterman Massacre near Fort Phil Kearney.

1313 FIELD, MR. & MRS.

MR. AND MRS. FIELD'S COMPLIMENTS, AND REQUEST THE PLEASURE OF YOUR COMPANY, ON TUESDAY EVENING NEXT, AT 7 O'CLOCK. LITTLE ROCK, NOV. 15, 1838.

[1–4]. 19.5 x 12.5 cm. Unbound.
Ref.:
Pages [2–3] are blank; addressed in manuscript on page [4]: Mr. Turner / of Cranfull (?).

1314 FIELD, JOSEPH E.

THREE YEARS IN TEXAS. INCLUDING A VIEW OF THE TEXAN REVOLUTION, AND AN ACCOUNT OF THE PRINCIPAL BATTLES, TOGETHER WITH DESCRIPTIONS OF THE SOIL, COMMERCIAL AND AGRICULTURAL ADVANTAGES, &C. . . . BOSTON: ABEL TOMPKINS, 1836.

[i]–iv, [5]–47, [48 blank]. 19.3 x 11.8 cm. Blue printed wrappers with title on front wrapper. In a maroon half morocco case.
Ref.: Bradford 1665; Clark III 157; Clements Library (*Texas*) 14; Howes F114; Jones 980; Raines p. 81; Sabin 24283; Streeter 1202A

One of the few survivors of Colonel Fannin's command, Dr. Field describes his experiences with the Texan army, why he was not killed in the Goliad Massacre, and how he escaped from the Mexican soldiery.

1315 FIELD, STEPHEN J.

PERSONAL REMINISCENCES OF EARLY DAYS IN CALIFORNIA WITH OTHER SKETCHES . . . PRINTED FOR A FEW FRIENDS. NOT PUBLISHED.

[i]–[vi, vi blank], [1]–248. 21.5 x 14.2 cm. Red cloth.
Ref.: Bradford 1666; Cowan p. 208; Howes F117
Copyrighted 1880, printed in San Francisco.

1316 FIELD, STEPHEN J.

PERSONAL REMINISCENCES OF EARLY DAYS IN CALIFORNIA, WITH OTHER SKETCHES . . . TO WHICH IS ADDED THE STORY OF HIS ATTEMPTED ASSASSINATION BY A FORMER ASSOCIATE ON THE SUPREME BENCH OF THE STATE. BY HON. GEORGE C. GORHAM. PRINTED FOR A FEW FRIENDS. NOT PUBLISHED.

[i]–vi, [1]–406. 19.5 x 13 cm. Contemporary red half morocco, red sprinkled edges.
Prov.: Inscribed on front fly-leaf: T. J. Coffey— / With the compliments of / Stephen J. Field. /
Ref.: Bradford 1666; Cowan p. 209; Howes F117
Copyrighted 1893, printed in Washington, D.C.

1317 FIELDING, HARRIET C.

THE ANCESTORS AND DESCENDANTS OF ISAAC ALDEN AND IRENE SMITH HIS WIFE (1599–1903) . . .*

[1]–144. 22.7 x 15.1 cm. Illustrations unlisted. Blue cloth.
Ref.:
Copyrighted 1903, printed at East Orange, New Jersey. Contains an account of Wyllis Alden's overland journey to Oregon in 1851, pages 45–9.

1318 FIGUEROA, JOSE

AUTOGRAPH LETTER SIGNED José Figueroa. 1834 September 27, Los Angeles. Two pages, 21 x 15.3 cm. To Don Maximiliano G. Vallejo.

Relating to local military matters and to family affairs.

1319 FIGUEROA, JOSE

MANIFIESTO[!] A LA REPUBLICA MEJICANA . . . SOBRE SU CONDUCTA Y LA DE LOS SENORES D. JOSE MARIA DE HIJAR Y D. JOSE MARIA PADRES, COMO DIRECTORES DE COLONIZACION EN 1834 Y 1835. MONTERREY: IMPRENTA DEL C. AGUSTIN V. ZAMORANO, 1835.

[i–iv], [1]–[184]. 14.9 x 10.4 cm. Original plain yellow wrappers. Lower right corners discolored, part of backstrip missing. In a green morocco slip case.
Ref.: Cowan p. 210; Greenwood 9; Howes F122; Sabin 24322
Zamorano was California's first printer. This is the first substantial book printed in California. In it, Figueroa defended and explained his administration as "Comandante General y Gefe Politico de la Alta California."

1320 FIGUEROA, JOSE

THE MANIFESTO, WHICH THE GENERAL OF BRIGADE . . . MAKES TO THE MEXICAN REPUBLIC, IN REGARD TO HIS CONDUCT AND THAT OF THE SNRS. D. JOSE MARIA DE HIJARS AND D. JOSE MARIA PADRES, AS DIRECTORS OF COLONIZATION IN 1833 AND 1834.

MONTEREY: 1835. PRINTING OFFICE OF CITIZEN AGUSTIN V. ZAMORANO. PRINTED AT THE SAN FRANCISCO HERALD OFFICE: 1855.

[1]–[105], [106 blank]. 21.1 x 13.3 cm. Contemporary dark blue calf, gilt title on front cover, borders on sides, and bands on backstrip, sprinkled edges.

Ref.: Cowan p. 210; Greenwood 562; Howes F122; Jones 1330; Sabin 24322, 98728; Zamorano Eighty 37 see

The dedication, preceding the title-page, reads in part: T[!] THE / Californians . . .

It was the most ambitious attempt at colonization made during the Mexican régime and brought to California many families who afterward took a prominent part in the development of the province.—Wagner

1321 FILISOLA, VICENTE

EVACUATION OF TEXAS. TRANSLATION OF THE REPRESENTATION ADDRESSED TO THE SUPREME GOVERNMENT BY GEN. VICENTE FILISOLA, IN DEFENCE OF HIS HONOR, AND EXPLANATION OF HIS OPERATIONS AS COMMANDER-IN-CHIEF OF THE ARMY AGAINST TEXAS. COLUMBIA: PRINTED BY G. & T. H. BORDEN, 1837.

[1–4, 3–4 blank], [i]–iv, [3]–68. 19.6 x 12.5 cm. Rebound in half calf.

Ref.: Clements Library (*Texas*) 17; Howes F127; Rader 1379; Raines p. 82; Sabin 24323; Streeter 191

Filisola wrote this vindication of his actions only four months after the Battle of San Jacinto. The "Documents" on pages 37–68 are as important as his account of Santa Ana's failure. The Spanish version of the work had appeared in Mexico City the preceding year. The translation was made by George L. Hammeken and the English version was printed by order of the Texas House of Representatives.

1322 FILLEY, WILLIAM

LIFE AND ADVENTURES OF WILLIAM FILLEY, WHO WAS STOLEN FROM HIS HOME IN JACKSON, MICH., BY THE INDIANS, AUGUST 3D, 1837, AND HIS SAFE RETURN FROM CAPTIVITY, OCTOBER 19, 1866 . . . CHICAGO: FILLEY & BALLARD, 1867.

[i]–vi, [7]–112. (Illustrations on yellow paper are included in pagination.) 22.7 x 14.6 cm. Illustrations unlisted. Pale green printed wrappers. In a brown board case.

Ref.: Ayer 34, 98; Field 535; Howes F128; Sabin 24328

Editions: Chicago: Fergus, 1867.

1323 FILSON, JOHN

THE DISCOVERY, SETTLEMENT AND PRESENT STATE OF KENTUCKE . . . THE ADVENTURES OF COL. DANIEL BOON . . . WILMINGTON: PRINTED BY JAMES ADAMS, 1784.

[A]–P⁴. [1]–118, [119–20 blank]. 21.5 x 13.1 cm. Folding map, removed from volume, not originally with this copy; This Map / of / Kentucke, / Drawn from actual Observations, / is inscribed with the most perfect respect / to the Honorable the Congress of the / United States of America; and / to his Excellᵞ George Washington / late Commander in Chief of their / Army. By their / Humble Servant, / John Filson. / [lower centre:] Philadᵃ Engrav'd by Henry D. Pursell, & Printed by T. Rook, for the Author 1784. / 50.4 x 45.4 cm. (neat line). 52.2 x 47.2 cm. (plate mark). 55.5 x 48.2 cm. (paper size). Scale: Ten miles to one inch. Gray paper over thin wooden boards, white paper backstrip with contemporary manuscript title, uncut. Some wear, some chipping. In a brown morocco solander case.

Ref.: Brinley 4590, 8462; Church 1202; Evans 18467; Field 536; Howes F129; Jones 586; Sabin 24336; Thruston (*Filson Club Hist. Quart.*, Jan. 1934) pp. 1–38; Vail 694

The first edition of one of the most notable American books of the eighteenth century. It contains many stories about Daniel Boone and other pioneers in printed form for the first time.

The map is Martin's Stage III, a unique copy. Stages I and II are each known in one copy only, the first being in the Deering Collection and the second in the Library of Congress.

1324 FILSON, JOHN

LIFE AND ADVENTURES OF COLONEL DANIEL BOON . . . PROVIDENCE: PRINTED BY H. TRUMBULL, 1824.

[1]–36. 18.1 to 19.5 x 11.2 to 12 cm. Portrait. Old marbled boards, calf back, uncut.

Ref.: Evans 19514; Howes T369; Jillson (*RKB*) pp. 5, 19; Trumbull (*Books Printed in Conn.*) 38; Streeter (*Americana—Beginnings*) 45; Vail 743

The first edition, Norwich, 1786, is known in three copies only. The pamphlet was derived from the Appendix to Filson's *Kentucke* probably by the publisher John Trumbull. Additional material was probably also supplied by him and the later publisher Henry Trumbull. It is, as Thomas W. Streeter has remarked, "an Americana classic." It is also, as Mr. Streeter has pointed out, an early American sporting book and contains the first printing of the Frances Scott captivity in book form.

Editions: See above.

1325 FINERTY, JOHN P.

WAR-PATH AND BIVOUAC; OR, THE CONQUEST OF
THE SIOUX, A NARRATIVE OF STIRRING PERSONAL
EXPERIENCES AND ADVENTURES IN THE BIG HORN
AND YELLOWSTONE EXPEDITION OF 1876, AND IN
THE CAMPAIGN ON THE BRITISH BORDER, IN 1879
. . . CHICAGO.

[i]–[xxii, xxii blank], 25–460. 20 x 14 cm. 18 illustrations and a map, unlisted. Map: U. S. Service
Map / —of the— / Seat of War. / Scale of
Miles. / [diagrammatic scale: 31 miles to one
inch] / 34.5 x 24.4 cm. Bright blue pictorial
cloth, designs in black on front cover, in blind
on back, title in gilt on front cover and backstrip, marbled edges.

Ref.: Howes F136; Jennewein 62; Rader
1384; Smith 3064

Copyrighted 1890, apparently published by
the author.

1326 FIRST NATIONAL BANK, Valley City, North Dakota

[Wrapper title] BRIGHT, BEAUTIFUL, BOUNTEOUS
BARNES THE BANNER COUNTY OF NORTH DAKOTA.
1882. VALLEY CITY DAILY TIMES PRINT.

[1]–[26], [27–32 advertisements]. 19.5 x 13.5 cm.
Three illustrations and six vignettes. Printed
pale green wrappers with title on front wrapper,
advertisement on verso of back wrapper.

Ref.: Allen (*Dakota*) 235

Probably published by the First National
Bank. The bank's advertisement appears on the
verso of the back wrapper.

1327 [FISH, REEDER McC.]

THE GRIM CHIEFTAIN OF KANSAS, AND OTHER
FREE-STATE MEN IN THEIR STRUGGLES AGAINST
SLAVERY. SOME POLITICAL SEANCES, INCIDENTS,
INSIDE POLITICAL VIEWS AND MOVEMENTS IN THEIR
CAREER . . . CHERRYVALE, KANSAS: CLARION BOOK
& JOB PRINT, 1885.

[1]–145, [146 blank]. 13 x 8.9 cm. Yellow printed
wrappers, with title on front wrapper.

Ref.: Howes F149

Wendell Holmes Stephenson in his *The Political Career of General James H. Lane* . . . Topeka, 1930, calls this work "totally unreliable in
facts." Regardless of this appraisal, I found the
book fascinating.—EDG

Lane was, to say the least, a controversial figure; many of his actions could be criticized.
Still, he had his defenders and Fish was one of
them.

1328 FISHER, EZRA

CORRESPONDENCE . . . EDITED BY SARAH FISHER
HENDERSON, NELLIE EDITH LATOURETTE, KENNETH
SCOTT LATOURETTE.*

[1]–487, [488 blank]. 23.7 x 15.6 cm. New black
buckram, green top. Lacks Index, pages 489–92.

Ref.: Howes F150a

Published in 1919; place of publication unde-
termined. Relates mostly to early Oregon Baptist
missions.

1329 FISHER, GEORGE

MEMORIALS OF GEORGE FISHER, LATE SECRETARY TO
THE EXPEDITION OF GEN. JOSE ANTONIO MEXIA,
AGAINST TAMPICO, IN NOVEMBER, 1835. PRESENTED
TO THE FOURTH AND FIFTH CONGRESSES OF THE
REPUBLIC OF TEXAS, PRAYING FOR RELIEF IN FAVOR
OF THE MEMBERS OF THE SAID EXPEDITION. HOUS-
TON: PRINTED AT THE TELEGRAPH OFFICE, 1840.

[1]–87, [88 blank]. 21.9 x 13.7 cm. Contemporary brown cloth.

Prov.: Inscribed on the inner front cover: To
the Hon Jeremiah S. Black / of Pennsylvania /
Attorney General U. S. A. / With the Respects
of / Geo. Fisher / Washington, D. C. / May
1850. / And with manuscript note by Fisher on
front endleaf: Index to special Reading / [rule] /
[16 lines] /.

Ref.: Clements Library (*Texas*) 22; Howes
F151; Jones 1035; Raines p. 82; Sabin 24460;
Streeter 384

Inserted before the *Memorials* . . . is: [cap-
tion title] George Fisher, / Secretary and Translator to the California Land Commission, / . . .
[1]–6. A reprint from Livingston, John: *Portraits of Eminent Americans now Living* . . . New
York, 1853–54, Volume III, pages 441–46.

Inserted after the *Memorials* . . . is: [caption
title] The Madisonian. / [rule] / Washington
City, D. C., February 5th, 1844. / [rule] / Published by John B. Jones. / [wavy rule] / Correspondence of the Madisonian. / Houston,
(Texas,) January 2d, 1844. / . . . [1]–[8, 8 blank].
Pages [1]–3 are notes regarding the annexation
of Texas, page [4] is blank, pages [5]–7 comprise
a reprint: [caption title] The Panama Echo. /
[rule] / Saturday Morning, June 1, 1850. /
[rule] / E. A. Theller, Editor and Publisher. /
[double rule] / . . . , page [8] is blank.

Mexia's expedition against Tampico, described in the *Memorials*, was the first armed
effort by Texans against Mexico.

1330 FISHER, ORCENETH

SKETCHES OF TEXAS IN 1840; DESIGNED TO AN-
SWER, IN A BRIEF WAY, THE NUMEROUS ENQUIRIES
RESPECTING THE NEW REPUBLIC . . . SPRINGFIELD,
ILL.: WALTERS & WEBER, 1841.

[i]–viii, [9]–64. 23.8 x 9.4 cm. Contemporary
green marbled boards, black leather backstrip.
In a green half morocco case.

Ref.: Howes F152; Rader 1394; Raines p. 82; Streeter 1376

Fisher spent two years in Texas before publishing this work. It contains some sound counsel about the advantages and disadvantages of living in Texas.

1331   FISHER, WILLIAM

AN INTERESTING ACCOUNT OF THE VOYAGES AND TRAVELS OF CAPTAINS LEWIS AND CLARKE, IN THE YEARS 1804–5, & 6 . . . BALTIMORE: PRINTED AND PUBLISHED BY P. MAURO, 1813.*

A–X⁶, Y⁴. [i]–[xii], [13]–266, [267–68 blank]. 17 x 10.3 cm. Two portraits and three plates. Contemporary sheep, red morocco label on backstrip. Worn, foxed.
Ref.: Bradford 1684; Howes F153a; Rader 1397; Sabin 24508; Wagner-Camp 8 note

This is the last of the so-called "Counterfeit Editions." Some copies carry two portraits and four plates.
Editions: Philadelphia, 1812. Baltimore, 1812.

1332   FISK, JAMES L.

[Caption title] . . . EXPEDITION FROM FORT ABERCROMBIE TO FORT BENTON . . . REPORT OF CAPTAIN J. L. FISK, OF THE EXPEDITION TO ESCORT EMIGRANTS FROM FORT ABERCROMBIE TO FORT BENTON, &C. . . .

[1]–36. 22.5 x 14.4 cm. Rebound in new red cloth.
Ref.: Howes F154; Wagner-Camp 388

37th Congress, 3rd Session, House, Executive Document No. 80, Serial 1164. [Washington: Government Printing Office, 1863.]

The copy of this work in the Minnesota Historical Society has a map inserted, the same map which appears in Fisk: *Idaho: Her Gold Fields, and the Routes to Them* . . . 1863. Page 2, line 21, of the present work mentions a map submitted with the report and recommended for publication. It was probably not published with the report. The copy of the map in MnHi has no indication of printing for Congress on the face.

A reduced photostat of the map has been laid in this copy.

1333   FISK, JAMES L.

[Caption title] . . . EXPEDITION OF CAPTAIN FISK TO THE ROCKY MOUNTAINS . . . REPORT OF CAPTAIN FISK OF HIS LATE EXPEDITION TO THE ROCKY MOUNTAINS AND IDAHO . . .*

[1]–39, [40 blank]. 22.5 x 14.5 cm. Rebound in new red cloth.
Ref.: Howes F154a; Sabin 24526 see; Wagner-Camp 399

38th Congress, 1st Session, House, Executive Document No. 45, Serial 1189. [Washington: Government Printing Office, 1864.]

Wagner-Camp lists the Senate version in preference to the House printing. However, the House ordered the report printed on March 3, 1864, and the Senate did not follow with its order until March 15. There were two separate printings of the report (unlike many other simultaneous printings by House and Senate) since the Senate version reported by Wagner-Camp consists of 38 pages.

1334   FISK, JAMES L.

IDAHO: HER GOLD FIELDS, AND THE ROUTES TO THEM. A HAND-BOOK FOR EMIGRANTS . . . NEW-YORK: JOHN A. GRAY, 1863.

[i]–iv, [5]–99, [100–04 blank]. 14.9 x 9.6 cm. Map: Map Illustrative of Report of Capt. Fisk / of the Expedition from Ft. Abercrombie to Ft. Benton Made in the Summer of 1862. / [lower left:] Jos. F. Gedney, Lith. Washington. / 19.3 x 39.7 cm. Scale: 80 miles to one inch. Gray printed wrappers with title on front wrapper. In a green half morocco case.
Ref.: Howes F155; Wagner-Camp 389

The Introduction is dated April, 1863. The first part contains a description of the country, routes, letter from a miner, equipment needed, etc. Pages 25–99 carry the report printed by Congress March 2, 1863.

1335   FISK, JAMES L.

[Map] MAP SHOWING PROPOSED MILITARY & EMIGRANT ROADS TO THE GOLD FIELDS OF / MONTANA OR EAST IDAHO / BY CAP.ᵀ JA.ˢ L. FISK A. Q. M. U. S. VOL.ˢ 1864. /

Map, 37.5 x 73.5 cm. No scale given.
Ref.:

The map defines Iowa, Minnesota, Nebraska, Dakota, the Montana Gold Fields, and Idaho. The present state of Wyoming is "Transferred to Dakota." Captain Fisk's 1862–63 route is shown and far to the south is the road he proposed for the 1864 expedition. Actually, the route pursued was somewhat north of the proposed route, going through Fort Rice. About 155 miles west of Fort Rice, the expedition was attacked by Sioux Indians and the party was forced back to Fort Rice where the expedition was abandoned for the year.—EDG

1336   [FISKE, J.]

A VISIT TO TEXAS: BEING THE JOURNAL OF A TRAVELLER THROUGH THOSE PARTS MOST INTERESTING TO AMERICAN SETTLERS. WITH DESCRIPTIONS OF SCENERY, HABITS, &C. &C. NEW YORK: GOODRICH & WILEY, 1834.

[i]–iv, [9]–264, [265–68]. 18.3 x 11 cm. Four engravings by J. T. Hammond. Map: Map / of the State of / Coahuila / -and- / Texas. / W. Hooker Sculp! / 25.7 x 33.2 cm. Scale: 90 miles to one inch. Dark gray cloth, gilt title on backstrip.

Ref.: Bradford 5374; Clark III 114; Jones 962; Phillips p. 388; Rader 3547; Raines p. 210; Sabin 95133; Streeter 1155

The name of the author is pencilled on the title-page. Clark suggests Colonel Morris or Dr. M. Fiske. It is usually entered under title.

1337 [FISKE, J.]

THE SAME . . . WITH AN APPENDIX, CONTAINING A SKETCH OF THE LATE WAR. NEW-YORK: VAN NOSTRAND AND DWIGHT. MOBILE:—WOODRUFF, FISKE, AND M'GUIRE. 1836.

[i]–[xii, xii blank], [1]–262. 14.6 x 9 cm. Green cloth, blind embossed sides, gilt title on backstrip.

Ref.: see above
Editions: New York, 1834.

1338 FITCH, FRANKLIN Y.

THE THE[!] LIFE, TRAVELS AND ADVENTURES OF AN AMERICAN WANDERER: A TRUTHFUL NARRATIVE OF EVENTS IN THE LIFE OF ALONZO P. DEMILT . . . NEW YORK: JOHN W. LOVELL COMPANY.*

[i–ii], [1–2], [iii]–viii, [9]–228, [1]–[48] advertisements. (Pages [1–2] carry a list of illustrations on recto, verso blank, an inserted leaf.) 18.9 x 12.2 cm. 12 illustrations listed. Light brown pictorial cloth, title on front cover in black and gilt and in gilt on backstrip.

Ref.: Cowan p. 213; Howes F156
Copyrighted 1883.
Almost too good for the movies.

1339 FITCH & CO., THOMAS, *Publishers*

DIRECTORY OF THE CITY OF PLACERVILLE AND TOWNS OF UPPER PLACERVILLE, EL DORADO, GEORGETOWN, AND COLOMA, CONTAINING A HISTORY OF THESE PLACES, NAMES OF THEIR INHABITANTS, AND EVERYTHING APPERTAINING TO A COMPLETE DIRECTORY. TOGETHER WITH A BUSINESS DIRECTORY . . . PLACERVILLE REPUBLICAN PRINTING OFFICE, 1862.

[1]–128. 18 x 11.4 cm. Pale green printed boards, brown leather backstrip, with title on front cover, advertisement on back cover, both printed in brown.

Ref.: Blumann & Thomas 808; Cowan p. 171; Howes F159
Inserted slip, 7.8 x 10.1 cm., before front endleaf headed: Explanation. / The Placerville section occupies pages [1]–[68], Upper Placerville,

pages [69]–82, El Dorado pages [83]–[97], Georgetown, pages [99]–115, Coloma pages [117]–128. A history of each town is included.

1340 FITHIAN, WILLIAM

[Wrapper title] . . . THE GREAT TORNADO, OF THE NORTHWEST, SABBATH, JUNE 3, 1860 . . . IOWA CITY: WM. CRUM, 1860.

[1]–12. 22 x 14.3 cm. Pale yellow printed wrappers with title on front wrapper.

Ref.: Moffit 479
Editions: Iowa City [1860].

1341 FITZGERRELL, J. J.

[Wrapper title] ADDRESS DELIVERED . . . AT SANTA FE, N. M., ON DECORATION DAY, MAY 30, 1885, ON THE OCCASION OF THE UNVEILING OF THE "KIT" CARSON MONUMENT, ERECTED BY THE GRAND ARMY OF THE REPUBLIC . . . LAS VEGAS, NEW MEXICO: J. A. CARRUTH, 1885.

[1]–8. 22.1 x 14.8 cm. Green printed wrappers with title on front wrapper and diagram of monument on verso of back wrapper.

Ref.:

1342 FITZ-JAMES, ZILLA

ZILLA FITZ JAMES, THE FEMALE BANDIT OF THE SOUTH-WEST; OR, THE HORRIBLE, MYSTERIOUS, AND AWFUL DISCLOSURES IN THE LIFE OF THE CREOLE MURDRESS[!], ZILLA FITZ JAMES, PARAMOUR AND ACCOMPLICE OF GREEN H. LONG, THE TREBLE MURDERER, FOR THE SPACE OF SIX YEARS. AN AUTOBIOGRAPHICAL NARRATIVE, EDITED BY REV. A. RICHARDS. LITTLE ROCK, ARK.: PUBLISHED BY A. R. ORTON, 1852.

[1]–[32]. (Page [1] blank, [2] portrait, [32] illustration.) 22.1 x 14.4 cm. Four illustrations. Pink printed wrappers with title on front wrapper, illustration on page 28 repeated on verso of back wrapper.

Ref.: Adams 829; Allen (*Arkansas*) 211; Howes F166; Rader 1403; Sabin 24621

Allen suggests this may have been printed at Buffalo or some other New York place. Since there was a New York edition without date and with the same collation, this is likely.

1343 FITZMAURICE, JOHN W.

"THE SHANTY BOY;" OR, LIFE IN A LUMBER CAMP . . . CHEBOYGAN, MICH., 1889.

[i–iv advertisements], [1]–246, [1–8 advertisements]. 23.4 x 15.3 cm. Blue printed wrappers with title on front wrapper, advertisements on verso of front and recto and verso of back wrapper. In a blue cloth case.

Prov.: Signature in pencil on front wrapper: W. B. Webb /. A. H. Greenly copy.

Ref.: Greenly (*Michigan*) 104; Howes F167

The author reached Michigan in 1865 and lived among the lumberjacks long enough to write the best narrative of the industry.

1344 [FITZPATRICK, THOMAS]

[Extract] [Executive Documents . . . during the First Session of the Thirtieth Congress . . . Washington: Printed by Wendell and Van Benthuysen, 1847.]

723–1310, [1]–249, [250 blank]. 22.4 x 14.5 cm. Blue marbled boards, calf backstrip and corners. Worn, broken, incomplete.

Ref.: Wagner-Camp 133

30th Congress, 1st Session, Senate, Executive Document No. 1, Serial 503.

Page [237] carries the half-title: [double rule] / Appendix to the Report / of the / Commissioner of Indian Affairs. / [double rule] /. Pages 238–49 comprise a letter by Thomas Fitzpatrick, Indian Agent, Upper Platte and Arkansas, containing his account of experiences with Capt. Love's party, the attack on Hayden's party, and his interviews with Cheyenne and Arapahoe chiefs.

1345 [FLAGG, EDMUND T.]

THE FAR WEST; OR, A TOUR BEYOND THE MOUNTAINS. EMBRACING OUTLINES OF WESTERN LIFE AND SCENERY; SKETCHES OF THE PRAIRIES, RIVERS, ANCIENT MOUNDS, EARLY SETTLEMENTS OF THE FRENCH, ETC., ETC. . . . NEW-YORK: PUBLISHED BY HARPER & BROTHERS, 1838.

[i]–xvi, [13]–263, [264 blank]. [i]–[xii, xii blank], [9]–241, [242 blank]. 18.8 x 11.3 cm. Two volumes, brown embossed cloth, white printed labels on backstrips, 6.3 x 2.1 cm. Lacks front endleaf in first volume.

Ref.: Buck 299; Clark III 158; Howes F169; Hubach p. 83; Sabin 24651; Thomson 419

Most of the text appeared originally in the *Louisville Journal*. The sections on Illinois and Missouri are especially valuable.

1346 FLANIGAN, J. H.

MORMONISM TRIUMPHANT! TRUTH VINDICATED, LIES REFUTED, THE DEVIL MAD, AND PRIESTCRAFT IN DANGER!!! . . . BEING A REPLY TO PALMER'S INTERNAL EVIDENCE AGAINST THE BOOK OF MORMON . . . LIVERPOOL: PRINTED BY R. JAMES, 1849.

[1]–32. Bound with Number 3346.

Ref.: Howes F171; Sabin 24674

1347 FLEMING, G. A.

CALIFORNIA: ITS PAST HISTORY; ITS PRESENT POSITION; ITS FUTURE PROSPECTS: CONTAINING A HISTORY OF THE COUNTRY FROM ITS COLONIZATION BY THE SPANIARDS TO THE PRESENT TIME . . . LONDON: PRINTED FOR THE PROPRIETORS, 1850.

[i]–viii, [1]–270. (Engraved title-page included in pagination.) 22.2 x 13.8 cm. Two colored illustrations, colored map and colored engraved title-page. Reddish cloth, blind embossed sides, uncut.

Ref.: Bradford 732; Cowan p. 93; Howes F178; Sabin 9973

G. A. Fleming is the author, according to a presentation copy owned by B. E. Waters. This particularly interesting account is sometimes found with nine plates instead of the present three.

1348 FLETCHER, ALICE C.

[Wrapper title] HISTORICAL SKETCH OF THE OMAHA TRIBE OF INDIANS IN NEBRASKA . . . WASHINGTON: JUDD & DETWEILER, 1885.

[1]–12. 23.6 x 15.1 cm. 11 illustrations and a map. Gray printed wrappers with title on front wrapper.

Ref.: Rader 1410

1349 FLETCHER, CHARLES H.

1776. 1876. JEFFERSON COUNTY, IOWA. CENTENNIAL HISTORY . . . FAIRFIELD, IOWA: PRINTED AT THE LEDGER OFFICE, 1876.

[1]–[36]. 22.9 x 15.3 cm. Gray printed wrappers with title on front wrapper. In a red cloth folder.

Ref.: Bradford 1696; Howes F187; Mott (*Iowa*) p. 47

1350 FLETCHER, DANIEL C.

REMINISCENCES OF CALIFORNIA AND THE CIVIL WAR . . . AYER, MASS.: PRESS OF HUNTLEY S. TURNER, 1894.

[1]–196. 21.8 x 14.5 cm. Portrait. Dark red cloth, title in gilt on backstrip.

Ref.: Cowan p. 214; Howes F188

1351 FLINT, JAMES

LETTERS FROM AMERICA, CONTAINING OBSERVATIONS ON THE CLIMATE AND AGRICULTURE OF THE WESTERN STATES, THE MANNERS OF THE PEOPLE, THE PROSPECTS OF EMIGRANTS, &C. &C. . . . EDINBURGH: PRINTED FOR W. & C. TAIT, 1822.

[i]–viii, [1]–330. [331–32 advertisements]. 21.8 x 14 cm. Gray boards, printed white paper label on backstrip, 4.7 x 2.5 cm., uncut. In a marbled board case, green inner cloth wrapper.

Prov.: Inscribed on front endleaf: To George H. Walker Esquire.— / With the Author's respectful compliments / Edinburgh / 7th October 1822 [bracket] /. In the same hand on inner front cover: 5 High Terrace, Edinburgh. / and on the front cover: George Henry Walker, Esquire, / at Miss Drake's / 128 Pine Street.— / Philadelphia.— /

Ref.: Bradford 1699; Buck 131; Clark II 25; Howes F198; Hubach p. 52; Sabin 24780; Thomson 420

Somewhat critical but, on the whole, as might be suspected from the quotation by Alexander Hamilton on the title-page, favorable.

1352 FLINT, TIMOTHY

BIOGRAPHICAL MEMOIR OF DANIEL BOONE, THE FIRST SETTLER OF KENTUCKY. INTERSPERSED WITH INCIDENTS IN THE EARLY ANNALS OF THE COUNTRY . . . CINCINNATI: N. & G. GUILFORD & CO., 1833.

[i]–viii, [9]–267, [268 blank]. 16.3 x 10.4 cm. Portrait. Blue boards, purple cloth backstrip, white printed label on backstrip, 3.8 x 1.6 cm.

Prov.: Bookplate of Bibliothèque du Chateau d'Oberhofen. Signature, partially erased chemically, on front endpaper: Albert Jn Nourt (?) /.

Ref.: Howes F199; Sabin 24784

1353 FLINT, TIMOTHY

A CONDENSED GEOGRAPHY AND HISTORY OF THE WESTERN STATES; OR, THE MISSISSIPPI VALLEY . . . CINCINNATI: PUBLISHED BY E. H. FLINT, 1828.

[1]–592. [1]–520. 20.9 x 13.3 cm. Two volumes, rebound in red half levant morocco, gilt backstrips, gilt tops.

Prov.: Bookplates of Edward Everett. Book label removed.

Ref.: Buck 211; Howes F200; Rader 1417; Sabin 24786; Thomson 422

Errata slip, 9.9 x 12.4 cm., in first volume.

1354 FLINT, TIMOTHY

FRANCIS BERRIAN; OR, THE MEXICAN PATRIOT . . . BOSTON: CUMMINGS, HILLIARD, AND COMPANY, 1826.

[i]–iv, [5]–299, [300 blank]. [1]–185, [186 blank]. 19.1 x 11.7 cm. Two volumes, tan boards, white printed labels on backstrips, 5.4 x 2.3 cm., uncut.

Ref.: Jones 1045; Sabin 24787; Streeter 1091; Wright I 958

1355 [FLINT, TIMOTHY]

GEORGE MASON, THE YOUNG BACKWOODSMAN; OR, 'DON'T GIVE UP THE SHIP.' A STORY OF THE MISSISSIPPI. BOSTON: HILLIARD, GRAY, LITTLE, AND WILKINS, 1829.

[1]–167, [168 blank]. 19.1 x 12 cm. Tan boards, brown cloth backstrip, white printed label on backstrip, 2.6 x 1.3 cm., uncut.

Ref.: Sabin 24788; Wright I 961

1356 FLINT, TIMOTHY

THE HISTORY AND GEOGRAPHY OF THE MISSISSIPPI VALLEY. TO WHICH IS APPENDED A CONDENSED PHYSICAL GEOGRAPHY OF THE ATLANTIC UNITED STATES, AND THE WHOLE AMERICAN CONTINENT . . . CINCINNATI: E. H. FLINT AND L. R. LINCOLN, 1832.

[i]–xvi, [17]–464. [1]–276. 20.9 x 13.3 cm. Two volumes bound together, contemporary tree calf, red leather label on backstrip.

Ref.: Bradford 1703a; Buck 211 note; Howes F200; Sabin 24789; Thomson 423

The text of the second volume had not appeared previously.

1357 FLINT, TIMOTHY

JOURNAL OF THE REV. TIMOTHY FLINT, FROM THE RED RIVER, TO THE OUACHITTA OR WASHITA, IN LOUISIANA, IN 1835. FROM WALDIE'S SELECT CIRCULATING LIBRARY.

[1]–31, [32 blank]. 16.2 x 10.7 cm. Contemporary blue wrappers. In a half morocco case.

Ref.: Howes F202; Jones 982; Rader 1419

This journal as well as the journey itself is not mentioned by Kirkpatrick in his life of Flint (Cleveland, 1911).—EDG

Separates of the journal were printed at Alexandria, Louisiana, Philadelphia, and Cincinnati. The present copy appears to be the Cincinnati printing.

1358 FLINT, TIMOTHY

THE LOST CHILD . . . BOSTON: PUTNAM & HUNT, PIERCE & WILLIAMS, AND WAIT, GREENE & CO., 1830.

[1]–121, [122 blank]. 15 x 9.1 cm. Gray boards, sheepskin backstrip.

Ref.: Howes F203

Adventures of Henry Howe, stolen from his Arkansas home and found five years later in New Orleans.—Howes

1359 FLINT, TIMOTHY

RECOLLECTIONS OF THE LAST TEN YEARS, PASSED IN OCCASIONAL RESIDENCES AND JOURNEYINGS IN THE VALLEY OF THE MISSISSIPPI, FROM PITTSBURG AND THE MISSOURI TO THE GULF OF MEXICO, AND FROM FLORIDA TO THE SPANISH FRONTIER . . . BOSTON: CUMMINGS, HILLIARD, AND COMPANY, 1826.

[i–ii], [1]–395, [396 blank]. 24.4 x 14.5 cm. Tan boards, white printed label on backstrip, 7.1 x 3 cm., uncut.

Ref.: Bradford 1702; Buck 93; Clark II 26; Howes F204; Hubach pp. 47–8; Jones 874; Rader 1420; Sabin 24794; Thomson 421

1360 [FLINT, TIMOTHY]

THE SHOSHONEE VALLEY; A ROMANCE . . . CINCIN-
NATI: PUBLISHED BY E. H. FLINT, 1830.

[i]–[vi, vi blank], [7]–323, [324 blank]. [1]–264.
18.9 x 11.1 cm. Two volumes, tan boards, green
cloth backstrips, printed white labels on backstrips, 3.2 x 2 cm., uncut.

Ref.: Smith 3167; Wright I 963

A romance with an Oregon locale.

1361 FLORENCE, NEBRASKA

[Broadsheet] PRINTED BY J. E. JOHNSON. ORACLE
OFFICE, CRESCENT CITY. THIS INDENTURE, MADE
. . . IN THE YEAR OF OUR LORD ONE THOUSAND
EIGHT HUNDRED AND FIFTY-SEVEN, WITNESSETH:
. . . LEVI HARSH MAYOR OF THE CITY OF FLOR-
ENCE. . . .

Broadsheet, 32.1 x 20 cm.

Ref.:

Signed also by H. Veeder as Notary Public,
with embossed seal. Docketed on verso, partly
in print and partly in manuscript. The sale was
made to William Reeves and the cost of the lot
was $2.50.

1362 FLORENCE (Nebraska) LAND COM-
PANY

[Broadside in three columns] [PRINTED AT THE
SEMI-WEEKLY BUGLE OFFICE, COUNCIL BLUFFS,
IOWA.] $100. NO. FLORENCE LAND COMPANY. THIS
IS TO CERTIFY, THAT . . .

Broadside, 14.8 x 18.6 cm. Text, 9.1 x 16.8 cm.
Repaired with plastic tape.

Ref.:

The certificate for $100, in favor of Thomas
Henshall, is signed by J. B. Stutsman as president and James C. Mitchell as Secretary. On the
verso are manuscript assignments of the certificate from Henshall to Mitchell and by the
latter to William H. Hervey, dated August 13,
1855, and July 10, 1856.

1363 FLORIDA. Governor (W. D. Moseley)

[Broadside] TO THE INHABITANTS OCCUPYING THE
FRONTIER OF THE INDIAN COUNTRY. I DEEM IT AD-
VISABLE TO ADOPT THIS PUBLIC MODE OF INFORM-
ING YOU THAT I HAVE VISITED THIS REGION OF
COUNTRY, UNDER ORDERS FROM THE EXECUTIVE,
FOR THE PURPOSE OF MUSTERING INTO THE SERVICE
A CORPS OF MOUNTED VOLUNTEERS FOR THE DE-
FENCE OF THE FRONTIER . . . G. W. HUTCHINS, AID
DE CAMP TO HIS EXCELLENCY W. D. MOSELEY, GOV-
ERNOR OF FLORIDA. ST. AUGUSTINE, JULY 31, 1849.

Broadside, 26.4 x 16.4 cm. Text, 17.2 x 14.7 cm.

Ref.:

The report refers to raising a corps of one
hundred mounted men to control the Indian dis-

turbances. It also contains the results of Lieutenant Garland's military expedition to Pease
Creek. The trading house had been found
burned and the bones of Payne and Wheeden
had been collected and buried.

1364 FLORIDAS. (Revolutionary Government)

REPORT OF THE COMMITTEE APPOINTED TO FRAME
THE PLAN OF PROVISIONAL GOVERNMENT FOR THE
REPUBLIC OF FLORIDAS. P. GUAL, CHAIRMAN,
V. PAZOS. M. MURDEN . . . FERNANDINA DECEMBER
9TH. OF 1817, FIRST OF THE INDEPENDENCE OF
FLORIDAS.

[A]⁴. [1]–7, [8 blank]. 24.5 x 14.3 cm. Unbound,
uncut. In a cloth box, morocco back.

Ref.: Jones 785; McMurtrie (*Florida*) p. 8;
Streeter (*Americana—Beginnings*) 35

The short-lived attempt to establish Florida
as a republic is peculiarly interesting because the
plan of government showed such dependence on
the theories of the founders of the United States.
The present pamphlet is the third piece printed
in Florida.

1365 FLORY, JACOB S.

THRILLING ECHOES FROM THE WILD FRONTIER. IN-
TERESTING PERSONAL REMINISCENCES OF THE AU-
THOR . . . CHICAGO: RHODES & McCLURE PUB-
LISHING COMPANY, 1893.

[1–6], 17–248, [249–50 advertisements]. 18.7 x
13.2 cm. Illustrations unlisted. Red cloth.

Ref.: Adams (*Ramp. Herd*) 814; Howes F216

1366 FLOWER, RICHARD

LETTERS FROM LEXINGTON AND THE ILLINOIS, CON-
TAINING A BRIEF ACCOUNT OF THE ENGLISH SETTLE-
MENT IN THE LATTER TERRITORY, AND A REFUTA-
TION OF THE MISREPRESENTATIONS OF MR. COB-
BETT . . . LONDON: PRINTED BY C. TEULON, 1819.

[i–iv], [5]–32. 20 x 12.8 cm. Three-quarter blue
levant morocco, by Sangorski & Sutcliffe.

Prov.: Inscribed on title-page: J. C. Hob-
house, Esqʳᵉ / With B. Flower's Respec[ts] /.
Word crossed out after With in second line.

Ref.: Bradford 1715; Buck 140; Howes F219;
Jones 809; Sabin 24910

The *Letters* is a glowing description of the
English settlement in Illinois urging emigration
from England, and an interesting account of
Kentucky and its people.—EDG

1367 FLOWER, RICHARD

LETTERS FROM THE ILLINOIS, 1820. 1821. CON-
TAINING AN ACCOUNT OF THE ENGLISH SETTLE-
MENT AT ALBION . . . WITH A LETTER FROM M.
BIRKBECK . . . LONDON: PRINTED FOR JAMES RIDG-
WAY, 1822.

[i]–[xii, xii blank], [9]–76. 22.5 x 14 cm. Blue wrappers, uncut. In a brown half morocco case.

Ref.: Bradford 1715; Buck 165; Howes F220; Jones 839; Sabin 24911

1368 FLOYD, CHARLES

THE NEW FOUND JOURNAL OF CHARLES FLOYD, A SERGEANT UNDER CAPTAINS LEWIS AND CLARK. BY JAMES DAVIE BUTLER. FROM PROCEEDINGS OF THE AMERICAN ANTIQUARIAN SOCIETY . . . APRIL 25, 1894. WORCESTER, MASSACHUSETTS: PRESS OF CHARLES HAMILTON, 1894.

[1]–30. 25 x 14.8 cm. Green printed wrappers bound into brown half morocco.

Ref.: Howes B1055; Hubach pp. 39–40; Matthews p. 205

The manuscript is in the Wisconsin Historical Society.

1369 FOLEY, THADDEUS J.

MEMORIES OF THE OLD WEST . . .

[1]–54, [55–6 blank]. 17.2 x 12.1 cm. Gray wrappers.

Ref.: Adams (*Ramp. Herd*) 817

The latest date in the text is June 25, 1927. No place of printing is indicated.

Stories of early days, 1869–1883, near North Platte and Grand Island, Nebraska.—EDG

1370 FOLSOM, DAVID E.

THE FOLSOM-COOK EXPLORATION OF THE UPPER YELLOWSTONE IN THE YEAR 1869 . . . WITH A PREFACE BY NATHANIEL P. LANGFORD. ST. PAUL, MINN., 1894.

[1]–22, [23–24 blank]. 23.3 x 15.2 cm. Gray printed wrappers. In a green cloth case.

Prov.: Inscribed on the title-page: Presented to L. W. Bahney by D. E. Folsom / August 3rd 1910 /.

Ref.: National Parks (*Yellowstone*) p. 34; Smith 3172

Five hundred copies of this edition were printed. The text had appeared previously in the *Western Monthly*, Chicago, July, 1870.

Langford, the author of the preface, was an experienced explorer who had accompanied James Fisk on his expedition from Fort Abercrombie to Fort Benton in 1862. He traces the history of the various explorations in this region and credits the Folsom-Cook expedition with arousing interest which led to the establishment of the National Park.—EDG

1371 FOLSOM, G.

[Broadside] FOR SALE! THE FOLLOWING LAND IN MAHASKA COUNTY: N. W. 1–4 S. E. 1–4 S. 22, T. 77, R. 14. ENQUIRE OF G. FOLSOM. IOWA CITY, JUNE 30, 1854.

Broadside, 15.2 x 18.7 cm. Text, 13.2 x 16.3 cm.
Ref.:
Mahaska County is in Iowa.

1372 [FOLSOM, GEORGE F.]

MEXICO IN 1842: A DESCRIPTION OF THE COUNTRY, ITS NATURAL AND POLITICAL FEATURES; WITH A SKETCH OF ITS HISTORY, BROUGHT DOWN TO THE PRESENT YEAR. TO WHICH IS ADDED, AN ACCOUNT OF TEXAS AND YUCATAN; AND OF THE SANTA FE EXPEDITION . . . NEW YORK: CHARLES J. FOLSOM, 1842.

[1]–256. 15 x 9.2 cm. Map: Mexico and Texas / in 1842. / Published by C. J. Folsom, Nọ 40 Fulton St. cor. Pearl, / New-York. / [swelled rule] / Entered according to Act of Congress in the year 1842, by C. J. Folsom, in the Clerks Office of the District Court of the Southern District of New-York. / [rule] / Lith. of G. W. Lewis, cor. Beckman & Nassau St. N.Y. / 22.8 x 25.5 cm. Scale: 215 miles to one inch. Black cloth, blind embossed borders on sides, gilt title on backstrip.

Prov.: Bookplate of Daniel Webster on inner back cover.

Ref.: Howes F226; Rader 1423; Raines p. 83; Sabin 24968; Streeter 1413; Wagner-Camp 91

The work is sometimes attributed to the publisher, Charles J. Folsom, but see the next item.

1373 [FOLSOM, GEORGE F.]

ANOTHER COPY. Embossed sides differ from preceding, but title on backstrip is identical. Following note appears on front endleaf in pencil: Benjamin Ela / presented by Geo. Folsom Esq / The Author. /

The narrative of the Texan Santa Fé Expedition is the work of Franklin Combs.

1374 FONTENELLE BANK (Bellevue, Nebraska)

BANK NOTE FOR THREE DOLLARS, ISSUED BY THE FONTENELLE BANK OF BELLEVUE, NEBRASKA. 1856 September 8. Signed by John J. Town and John Weare. Numbered A 5132. Canceled with holes.

1375 FONTENELLE BANK (Bellevue, Nebraska)

BANK NOTE FOR FIVE DOLLARS, ISSUED BY THE FONTENELLE BANK OF BELLEVUE, NEBRASKA. 1856 September 8. Signed by John J. Town and John Weare. Numbered B No. 2706. Canceled with holes.

Each of the above engraved by Danforth, Wright & Co., New York & Philadelphia. Mounted on yellow paper.

1376 FOOTE, HENRY S.

TEXAS AND THE TEXANS; OR, ADVANCE OF THE ANGLO-AMERICANS TO THE SOUTH-WEST; INCLUDING A HISTORY OF LEADING EVENTS IN MEXICO, FROM THE CONQUEST BY FERNANDO CORTES TO THE TERMINATION OF THE TEXAN REVOLUTION . . . PHILADELPHIA: THOMAS, COWPERTHWAIT & CO., 1841.*

[i]–viii, 13–314. [i]–[vi, vi blank], 7–403, [404 blank]. 18.4 x 11.5 cm. Map: A / New Map of / Texas, / with the Contiguous / American & Mexican States / By J. H. Young. / Philadelphia: / Published by S. Augustus Mitchell. / 1842 / Entered according to Act of Congress in the year 1835 by S. Augustus Mitchell in the Clerks office of the district court of the eastern district of Pennsylvania. / [left of cartouche:] Sold by / Thomas, Cowperthwait & Co. / N⁰ 253 Market Street, / [lower centre:] Engraved by J. H. Young / 31.4 x 38 cm. Scale: 75 miles to one inch. Two volumes, green cloth, blind embossed sides, gilt titles on backstrips, with large star at foot.

Ref.: Bradford 1725; Howes F238; Rader 1425; Raines p. 84; Sabin 25019; Streeter 1377

A third volume was announced but never published. There is some doubt that the map was issued originally with the work, since it is dated 1842. Possibly, as Howes suggests, the map was intended for the third volume and, unused, was inserted in the first volume of remaining copies, when plans for the third volume were abandoned.

1377 FORBES, ALEXANDER

CALIFORNIA: A HISTORY OF UPPER AND LOWER CALIFORNIA FROM THEIR FIRST DISCOVERY TO THE PRESENT TIME . . . LONDON: SMITH, ELDER AND CO., 1839.

[i]–xvi, [1]–352. 22 x 14.1 cm. Ten illustrations and a map listed. Map: The Coasts of / Guatimala and Mexico, from / Panama to Cape Mendocino; / with the Principal Harbours in / California. / 1839. / [lower centre:] London, Smith, Elder & Cº 1839. / [lower right:] John Arrowsmith. / 37 x 49.5 cm. No scale given. *Inset:* Sketch / of / Port Bodega, / by / Captⁿ John Hall. / 11.8 x 8.8 cm. Scale: about two miles to one inch. *Inset:* Harbour / of / San Francisco, / By Captⁿ Beechey, R. N. / 9.8 x 12.2 cm. Scale: about four miles to one inch. *Inset:* Sketch of Puerto de S. Diego by / Captⁿ John Hall. / 10.2 x 14.4 cm. Scale: about 2 1/2 inches to one mile. *Inset:* Sketch of / Monterrey Harbour, / by / Captⁿ John Hall. / 10.2 x 8.6 cm. Scale: about 4 miles to one inch. *Inset:* Sketch of / Sᵗ Barbara Harbour, / by / Captⁿ John Hall. /

5.9 x 8.9 cm. Scale: about 1 1/8 miles to one inch. *Inset:* Sketch of / Port S. Gabriel, or S. Pedro / by / Captⁿ John Hall. / 8.3 x 7.5 cm. Scale: about 2 1/2 miles to one inch. Plum cloth, blind embossed sides, title in gilt on backstrip, uncut, unopened.

Ref.: Barrett 866; Blumann & Thomas 4959; Bradford 1728; Cowan p. 217; Field 550; Howes F242; Jones 1023; Sabin 25035

Inserted before page 339 is a slip, 6.2 x 11 cm., headed: Note to Page 339. /

The first English book to relate exclusively to California.—Cowan.

1378 FORCE, MANNING F.

[Caption title] RESPONSE OF JUDGE M. F. FORCE TO THE TOAST, "THE ARMY AND NAVY," AT THE GRANT BANQUET IN CINCINNATI, DECEMBER 11, 1879 . . .

[1]–3, [4 blank]. 20.2 x 12.6 cm. Unbound.

Ref.:

Probably published at Cincinnati in 1879. In Richard I. Dodge Papers.

1379 FORD, HENRY A.

THE HISTORY OF PUTNAM AND MARSHALL COUNTIES; EMBRACING AN ACCOUNT OF THE SETTLEMENT, EARLY PROGRESS, AND FORMATION OF BUREAU AND STARK COUNTIES . . . LACON, ILL.: PUBLISHED FOR THE AUTHOR, 1860.

[i]–[viii], [1]–160. 15 x 10 cm. Black cloth with black glazed paper label, printed in gold, 5.2 x 9.4 cm., on front cover.

Ref.: Bradford 1733; Buck 719, 969, 1036, 1084; Howes F249

1380 FORD, THOMAS

A HISTORY OF ILLINOIS, FROM ITS COMMENCEMENT AS A STATE IN 1818 TO 1847. CONTAINING A FULL ACCOUNT OF THE BLACK HAWK WAR, THE RISE, PROGRESS, AND FALL OF MORMONISM, THE ALTON AND LOVEJOY RIOTS, AND OTHER IMPORTANT AND INTERESTING EVENTS . . . CHICAGO: PUBLISHED BY S. C. GRIGGS & CO., 1854.

[i]–[xviii], [19]–447, [448 blank], [1–6 advertisements]. (Pages [i–ii, viii] blank.) 19.4 x 12.3 cm. Plum cloth, blind panels on sides.

Ref.: AII (*Chicago*) 91; Bradford 1337; Howes F254; Jones 1314; Sabin 25070

1381 FORSYTH, GEORGE A.

THE STORY OF A SOLDIER . . . NEW YORK: D. APPLETON AND COMPANY, 1900.*

[i]–[xvi, xvi blank], [1]–389, [390 blank], [391–400 advertisements]. 18.7 x 12.4 cm. Six illustrations listed. Beige cloth.

Ref.: Howes F270; Munk (Alliot) p. 81; Rader 1442

Accounts of frontier fighting, Middle West to West.

1382 FORSYTH, GEORGE A.

THRILLING DAYS IN ARMY LIFE . . . NEW YORK: HARPER & BROTHERS, 1900.

[i–vi, vi blank], [1]–[197], [198 blank], [199–200 advertisements]. 19 x 12.7 cm. 16 illustrations listed. Yellow pictorial cloth.

Ref.: Howes F271; Munk (Alliot) p. 81; Rader 1443

Adventures in the West and in the Civil War.

1383 FORSYTH, JAMES W.

. . . REPORT OF AN EXPEDITION UP THE YELLOW-STONE RIVER, MADE IN 1875 . . . UNDER THE ORDERS OF LIEUTENANT-GENERAL P. H. SHERIDAN . . . WASHINGTON: GOVERNMENT PRINTING OFFICE, 1875.

[1]–17, [18 blank]. 24.7 x 14.7 cm. Four illustrations, one sketch map, and one folding map, unlisted: Sketch of the / Yellowstone River / From the mouth of Powder River to / the head of navigation. / To accompany a report of Lt. Col. J. W. Forsyth / Mil. Sec. To Lieut. Gen. P. H. Sheridan U.S.A. / Drawn by 2nd Lt. Richard E. Thompson 6th Infty. / 61.9 x 70.1 cm. Scale: about 20 miles to an inch. Table of Distances in upper left corner. Gray printed wrappers, with title as above on front wrapper within thick and thin rules, uncut.

Ref.: Howes F272; Wheat (*Transmississippi*) 1253

Lieutenant Colonel E. D. Grant was associated with Forsyth on this expedition.

1384 FORSYTH, THOMAS

AUTOGRAPH LETTER, SIGNED. 1824 April 9, Peoria. Two pages, 32.3 x 19.7 cm. To William Clark.

Forsyth reports on arranging a meeting with Indian chiefs in the neighborhood, in this letter, and complains of the difficulty Federal agents had preventing the sale of liquor to Indians by traders and unlicensed individuals.

1385 FORT COLLINS AGRICULTURAL COLONY OF COLORADO

[Caption title] CIRCULAR NO. 1. PROSPECTUS OF THE FORT COLLINS AGRICULTURAL COLONY OF COLO. LOCATED AT FORT COLLINS, LARIMER COUNTY, COLORADO. PRINCIPAL OFFICE, FORT COLLINS, COLO. . . .

[1–4]. 26.7 x 20.3 cm. Unbound.

Ref.: McMurtrie & Allen (*Colorado*) 157 see

At the foot of page [4], the leaflet is dated: Fort Collins, Colorado, January 20, 1873. McMurtrie & Allen describe a copy (unlocated) dated December 5, 1872. Since there was no press in Fort Collins in 1873, the leaflet was probably printed at Denver.

1386 FOSDICK, HARRY M.

[Map] PLAN OF THE / CITIES OF / DENVER, AURARIA AND HIGHLAND / JEFFERSON TERR. / [scroll] 1859 [scroll] / PUBLISHED BY H. M. FOSDICK & L. N. TAPPAN, / DENVER. / [5 lines] / MEISEL BRO'S. LITH BOSTON. /

Map, 55.1 x 70.1 cm. Scale: 800 feet to one inch. Folded into cloth covers, 15.2 x 10.2 cm., title in gilt on front cover within embossed ornaments: Maps of / Denver, Auraria / and / Highland. / *Ref.:*

This is the first map of Denver. It was the subject of a long search by the Government, but remained undiscovered until 1897. In that year, a clerk in the U. S. Land Office, acting under instructions from Washington, finally located the map in the vaults of the Land Office in Denver and the rediscovery was announced on July 23.—EDG

There are several manuscript notations on the face of the map which seem to relate to original owners of tracts later incorporated into the city.

1387 FOSTER, GEORGE G.

THE GOLD REGIONS OF CALIFORNIA: BEING A SUCCINCT DESCRIPTION . . . INCLUDING A CAREFULLY PREPARED ACCOUNT OF THE GOLD REGIONS OF THAT FORTUNATE COUNTRY . . . NEW YORK: DEWITT & DAVENPORT, 1848.

[i]–[viii, viii blank], [9]–80, [2 pages of advertisements], [81 advertisement, 82 blank], [1]–[4] advertisements, [1–2, 1]–2 advertisements. 23.5 x 15.2 cm. Map: [California from below Los Angeles to above San Francisco]. 18.3 x 11.1 cm. No scale given. White printed wrappers with title on front wrapper printed in gold: The / Gold Mines / of / California. / And also / A Geographical, Topographical and Historical / View of that Country, / From Official Documents and Authentic Sources, / with / A Map of the Country, / and Particularly of the / Gold Region; / [short rule] / Edited by G. G. Foster, Esq. / [short rule] / Price Twenty-Five Cents. / [wavy rule] / New-York; / Published by DeWitt & Davenport, / Tribune Buildings. / [within decorative border], advertisements in gold on verso of back wrapper, uncut. Removed from bound volume.

Prov.: Bookplate of Robert E. Cowan. Date 1848 in manuscript twice on front wrapper.

Ref.: Barrett 871; Blumann & Thomas 4963; Bradford 1746; Cowan p. 219; Howes F287; Sabin 25225; Wheat (*Gold Region*) 39; Wheat (*Gold Rush*) 77

In an 1849 edition, another map was used.

Editions: New York, 1848. (*The Gold Mines* . . .)

1388 [FOSTER, JAMES]

THE CAPITULATION; OR, A HISTORY OF THE EXPEDITION CONDUCTED BY WILLIAM HULL, BRIGADIER-GENERAL OF THE NORTH-WESTERN ARMY. BY AN OHIO VOLUNTEER . . . CHILLICOTHE: PRINTED BY JAMES BARNES, 1812.

[A]–G⁶. [1]–78, [i]–[vi]. 16.9 x 10.2 cm. New boards, cloth back.

Prov.: Signature on inner margin of title-page: B. Van Cleve's /.

Ref.: AII (*Ohio*) 154; Howes F288; Quaife, Milo M.: *War on Detroit*, Chicago, 1940, pp. xix–xxvi, 179–320; Rusk II, p. 130; Sabin 33641; Shaw & Shoemaker 25447; Thomson 431

The author was captured at Detroit, and in this work gives an account of his imprisonment, and the principal events of that unfortunate campaign. It relates entirely to the campaign of the Army in Ohio and the Northwest, and is throughout, very severe on General Hull.— Thomson

The volume was removed from a bound volume. Preceding the title-leaf is a contemporary leaf on which are listed five titles including *The Capitulation*. The list seems to be in the handwriting of B. Van Cleve.

Quaife discusses the problem of the authorship in detail in his *War on Detroit*.

1389 FOSTER, JAMES S.

OUTLINES OF HISTORY OF THE TERRITORY OF DAKOTA, AND EMIGRANT'S GUIDE TO THE FREE LANDS OF THE NORTHWEST . . . GIVING RELIABLE INFORMATION TO EMIGRANTS, WHERE TO LOCATE, THE BEST WAY TO GO, WHAT TO CARRY, WHEN TO START AND WHERE TO BUY WHAT MAY BE NEEDED IN THEIR NEW HOMES . . . YANKTON, DAKOTA TERRITORY: M'INTYRE & FOSTER, 1870.

[1]–127, [128 blank]. 22.8 x 13.4 cm. Map: Chapman's / Sectional Map / of the Surveyed Part of / Dakota / Compiled from the United States Surveys / and other authentic Sources. / Published by / Silas Chapman, / 1869. / Milwaukee, Wisconsin. / Lith. by L. Lipman, Milwaukee, Wis. / [top right:] Entered according to Act of Congress in the Year 1864 by Silas Chapman in the Clerks Office of the District Court of the State of Wisconsin. / 70.5 x 44 cm. (including border). No scale given. *Inset:* Dakota in Miniature. / 12 x 12.4 cm. No scale given. *Inset:* [Part of Canada—Pembina.] 7 x 13 cm. No scale given. Green printed wrappers with title on front wrapper, copyright notice on verso of front wrapper, advertisements on recto and verso of back wrapper. In a green cloth case.

Prov.: Inscribed on front wrapper: Steamer Miner /. Rubber stamp of F. B. Riggs on front wrapper and title-page.

Ref.: Allen (*Dakota*) 77; Bradford 1748; Howes F289

Advertisements by local merchants occupy pages 106–25.

1390 FOSTER, ROXANNA C.

. . . THE FOSTER FAMILY: CALIFORNIA PIONEERS. FIRST OVERLAND TRIP . . . 1849; SECOND OVERLAND TRIP, 1852; THIRD OVERLAND TRIP, 1853; FOURTH TRIP (VIA PANAMA) 1857.

[1]–285, [286 blank]. 19.4 x 13.5 cm. Illustrations unlisted. Brown fabrikoid, embossed.

Ref.: Howes F292

Printed at Santa Barbara and copyrighted in 1925. Edited by Lucy A. Foster Sexton.

Editions: San José, 1889.

1391 FOU SIN, CHOU YEE, COON YOU, & OTHERS

MURDER OF M. V. B. GRISWOLD, BY FIVE CHINESE ASSASSINS; TOGETHER WITH THE LIFE OF GRISWOLD, AND THE STATEMENTS OF FOU SIN, CHOU YEE AND COON YOU, CONVICTED, AND SENTENCED TO BE HUNG AT JACKSON, APRIL 16, 1858 . . . JACKSON: T. A. SPRINGER & CO., 1858.

[1]–32. 21.5 x 15 cm. Three portraits in the text· Pink printed wrappers with title on front wrapper, advertisements on verso of back wrapper, uncut. In a blue cloth case, leather labels.

Ref.: Cowan p. 251; McDade 395

Martin Van Buren Griswold was an adventurer, born in Saratoga County, New York, in 1817, who crossed the continent overland twice (returning once by way of Mexico), visited Hawaii, mined successfully for gold in California, and settled down in Jackson, California. There, while defending the safe of his employer, in 1858, he was murdered during a robbery. It may have been the first murder by Chinese in California.

1392 FOUNTAIN COLONY OF COLORADO (Colorado Springs)

[Caption title] CIRCULAR NO. 1. PROSPECTUS OF THE FOUNTAIN COLONY OF COLORADO, LOCATED AT COLORADO SPRINGS, COLORADO . . .

[1–4, 4 blank]. 21.5 x 13.9 cm. Unbound.
Ref.: McMurtrie & Allen (*Colorado*) 138
Printed in Denver in 1871.
McMurtrie is in error: there are only three pages of text. The imprint appears on page [3]: [dotted rule] / Denver Tribune Print. /

1393 FOUNTAIN COLONY OF COLORADO (Colorado Springs)

[Broadside] OUR NEW SARATOGA. COLORADO SPRINGS AND LA FONT. ANOTHER MAMMOTH COLONY ENTERPRISE . . .

Broadside, 42.2 x 15.7 cm. Text, 38 x 12.5 cm.
Ref.:
Neither place nor date of publication given, but probably 1871.
"The new town will be called Colorado Springs." The company is called Fountaine Colony in the text.

1394 FOUNTAIN COLONY OF COLORADO (Colorado Springs)

[Broadside] VILLA LA FONT. THE FOUNTAINE COLONY OF COLORADO—A MAMMOTH ENTERPRISE—COLORADO SPRINGS PURCHASED AND A CITY TO BE LAID OUT—ONE OF THE MOST ENTICING SPOTS IN COLORADO—FULL DESCRIPTIONS . . . (FROM ROCKY MOUNTAIN NEWS, JUNE 23RD, 1871.)

Broadside, 61.3 x 13.2 cm. Text, 56.1 x 11.2 cm.
Ref.:
Neither place nor date of publication given, but probably 1871.

1395 FOWLER, SMITH W.

AUTOBIOGRAPHICAL SKETCH . . . MANISTEE MICH.: TIMES AND STANDARD STEAM POWER PRINT, 1877.

[i–iv], 1–37, [38 blank], [1]–61, [62 blank]. (Pages [5–16] of second section unpaginated.) 19 x 13.8 cm. Portrait. Dark green cloth.
Ref.: Howes F301
There were two issues of this work of which this is the second, with the cancel title-leaf (18.3 x 12.7 cm.) and with the additional material listed on the title-page bound in at the end. There is a separate title-page for the second part: The Soldiers' Voting Bill . . . Manistee, Mich.: Times and Standard Steam Power Print, 1876.
In 1846, Fowler joined a party in Pittsburgh bound for the Upper Missouri. Later he spent some time in Savannah, Mo., and followed this with a hunting expedition to the Rocky Mountains, where he was within sight of Pike's Peak. He returned East and settled at Iowa Point, below Council Bluffs. Much of the present volume deals with his Civil War experiences.

1396 FOX, EDGAR B., & W. T. DUDLEY

HISTORY AND DIRECTORY OF GREEN LAKE AND WAUSHARA COUNTIES, AND THE CITY OF RIPON, CONTAINING HISTORICAL SKETCHES . . . BERLIN, WIS.: COURANT BOOK AND JOB OFFICE, 1869.

[1–4 advertisements], [5]–144. 21.3 x 13.7 cm. Frontispiece on yellow paper. Tan printed boards with blue leather backstrip and corners, title on front cover, advertisements on back cover, advertisements on blue paper on inside covers.
Prov.: Rubber stamp of Ripon College on front cover and title-page, library numerals on title-page and verso.
Ref.: AII (*Wisconsin*) 726; Howes F303

1397 FRANCE. SOVEREIGNS, 1715–1774 (Louis XV)

[Caption title] ARREST DU CONSEIL D'ESTAT DU ROY, CONCERNANT LA RETROCESSION FAITE A SA MAJESTE PAR LA COMPAGNIE DES INDES, DE LA CONCESSION DE LA LOUISIANE & DU PAYS DES ILINOIS. DU 23. JANVIER 1731. EXTRAIT DES REGISTRES DU CONSEI L D'ESTAT. . . .

[1–4, 4 blank]. 25.5 x 19.5 cm. Unbound.
Prov.: From Dr. Otto Schmidt's Collection.
Ref.: Wroth (*Acts*) 1209
With manuscript attestation on page [3] by Solier.
Printed at Paris at the Imprimerie Royale in 1731.

1398 FRANCHERE, GABRIEL

AUTOGRAPH LETTER, SIGNED. 1851 April 15, New York. Three pages, 27 x 21 cm. To Narcisse Cyr.

Reasons for refusing a subscription to a religious journal. Laid in the second copy of Franchère's *Narrative* . . . 1854.

1399 FRANCHERE, GABRIEL

AUTOGRAPH LETTER, SIGNED. 1853 April 16, New York. One page, 24.5 x 25.2 cm. To François Benoit.

Regarding the collection of a debt for Benoit by Franchère. Laid in Franchère's *Relation d'un Voyage* . . . 1820.

1400 FRANCHERE, GABRIEL

NARRATIVE OF A VOYAGE TO THE NORTHWEST COAST OF AMERICA IN THE YEARS 1811, 1812, 1813, AND 1814; OR, THE FIRST AMERICAN SETTLEMENT ON THE PACIFIC . . . NEW YORK: REDFIELD, 1854.

[1]–376, [1–8 advertisements]. 18.6 x 12.5 cm. Three plates. Brown cloth.
Prov.: Gurdon S. Hubbard's copy, signed

twice by him and with his long manuscript note regarding his acquaintanceship with the author and his loss of a presentation copy from the author in the Chicago Fire.

Ref.: Bradford 1759; Cowan p. 90; Field 558; Howell 105; Howes F310; Jones 1315; Sabin 25432; Smith 3244; Staton & Tremaine 985; Wagner-Camp 16

To this translation of the original work, the author contributed new material in the form of a Preface to the Second Edition, an additional chapter in which he alludes to the many changes that had occurred to the scenes which he had long ago visited and described, and an Appendix in which he gives an account of some of the persons who left Astoria before and after its transfer to the British.—EDG

Franchère's *Narrative* is one of the sources of Irving's *Astoria*. He went to the Northwest on the "Tonquin" and returned overland.

1401 FRANCHERE, GABRIEL
ANOTHER COPY.

Slate gray cloth, blind embossed sides, back stamped in gilt.
Ref.: as above.
The final leaf of advertisements differs from the other copy.

Laid in is an Autograph Letter signed by Franchère. 1851 April 15.

1402 FRANCHERE, GABRIEL
RELATION D'UN VOYAGE A LA COTE DU NORD-OUEST . . . DANS LES ANNEES 1810, 11, 12, 13, ET 14 . . . MONTREAL: DE L'IMPRIMERIE DE C. B. PASTEUR, 1820.

[1]–284. 21 x 12.8 cm. Contemporary tree calf. Rebacked preserving original label.
Prov.: Inscribed in pencil inside front cover: Presented to R Crooks Esq / by / his affectionate and / Humble Servt / The Author /. Manuscript corrections and explanatory notes, in ink, throughout the text in the hand of the author.
Ref.: Cowan p. 90; Howell 107; Howes F310; Sabin 25431; Smith 3245; Staton & Tremaine 984; Wagner-Camp 16

Laid in is an Autograph Letter, signed. 1853 April 16.

1403 FRANCIS, FRANCIS, JR.
SADDLE AND MOCASSIN . . . LONDON: CHAPMAN AND HALL, 1887.

[i]–[xii, xii blank], [1]–322, [323–24 advertisements], [1]–[40] advertisements. 20.3 x 14 cm. Yellow cloth, title and decorations in black and red on front cover, gilt on backstrip, uncut, unopened.

Ref.: Adams (*Ramp. Herd*) 836; Howes F313; Munk (Alliot) p. 82; Rader 1462

The author was one of a sizable number of Englishmen living in the Southwest in the Eighties.

1404 FRANCIS, SIMEON
DOCUMENT, SIGNED. 1866 July 16, Fort Vancouver, W. T. One page, 25.4 x 19.8 cm.

Receipt in favor of Loren L. Williams. Inserted in Manuscript Journals of Loren L. Williams, Volume IV.

1405 FRANKLIN, BENJAMIN
THE PRIVATE LIFE OF THE LATE BENJAMIN FRANKLIN . . . LONDON: PRINTED FOR J. PARSONS, 1793.

[A]–X8, Y2. [i]–xvi, [1]–191, 92, [193]–248, 251, 250–324. 20.4 x 12.5 cm. Contemporary calf, red leather label. Lacks half-title.
Prov.: Bookplate of Nicholas Roch.
Ref.: Ford 386; Howes F323; Sabin 25573

A wretched re-translation from the Paris edition . . . with a continuation by the English editor . . . of interest as the first version of Franklin's autobiography which appeared in English . . . —Ford

1406 FRANKLIN, JOHN
NARRATIVE OF A JOURNEY TO THE SHORES OF THE POLAR SEA, IN THE YEARS 1819, 20, 21, AND 22 . . . LONDON: JOHN MURRAY, MDCCCXXIII.

[i]–xvi, [1]–768, [1]–8 advertisements. 28.2 x 22.3 cm. 30 plates and four maps listed. Marbled boards, green cloth backstrip, printed white paper label, 6.7 x 5.7 cm., uncut.
Ref.: Field 560; Sabin 25623; Staton & Tremaine 1248; Wagner-Camp 23
Errata slip, 6.3 x 22.3 cm. before page [1].

1407 FRANKLIN, SIR JOHN
NARRATIVE OF A SECOND EXPEDITION TO THE SHORES OF THE POLAR SEA, IN THE YEARS 1825, 1826, AND 1827 . . . LONDON: JOHN MURRAY, MDCCCXXVIII.

[i]–xxiv, [1]–320, [i]–clvii, [clviii colophon, clix errata, clx blank]. 28.3 x 21.6 cm. 31 plates and six maps listed. Light red cloth, white printed label, 6.8 x 5.3 cm., uncut.
Ref.: Field 561; Sabin 26228; Staton & Tremaine 1434

Tipped in at the front is a broadside from the publisher: Prospectus / of a Series of / North American Views / . . . 27.4 x 21 cm.

1408 FRANKS, J. M.
SEVENTY YEARS IN TEXAS. MEMORIES OF THE PIONEER DAYS, INDIAN DEPREDATIONS AND THE

NORTHWEST CATTLE TRAIL . . . GATESVILLE, TEXAS: 1924.

[1]–[134], [135–36 blank]. 23.4 x 15.2 cm. Portrait. Pale yellow printed wrappers.

Ref.: Adams 839; Adams (*Ramp. Herd*) 839; Howes F339; Rader 1466

1409 FRAZEE, GEORGE

FUGITIVE SLAVE CASE. DISTRICT COURT OF THE UNITED STATES FOR THE SOUTHERN DIVISION OF IOWA. BURLINGTON, JUNE TERM, 1850. RUEL DAGGS, VS. ELIHU FRAZIER, ET ALS. TRESPASS ON THE CASE . . . BURLINGTON: PRINTED BY MORGAN & M'KENNY, 1850.

[1]–40. 21.6 x 13.7 cm. Green printed wrappers with title on front wrapper.

Ref.: Moffit 73; Sabin 26127

1410 FREE STATE PARTY, KANSAS TERRITORY. (Topeka) 1857

AN ADDRESS TO THE PEOPLE OF THE UNITED STATES, AND OF KANSAS TERRITORY, BY THE FREE STATE TOPEKA CONVENTION, HELD MARCH 10, 1857. LEAVENWORTH CITY: PRINTED AT THE LEAVENWORTH TIMES OFFICE, 1857.

[1]–18. 19.6 x 13.1 cm. Cream printed wrappers with title on front wrapper.

Prov.: Henry E. Huntington duplicate, with stamp.

Ref.: AII (*Kansas*) 100; Sabin 37016

The outrages of the Kansas-Missouri Border War are set forth in considerable and gory detail in this famous declaration of independence. It is a miserable record of ruffianism, deceit, perjury, and treason.—EDG

1411 FREEMAN, GEORGE D.

MIDNIGHT AND NOONDAY; OR, DARK DEEDS UNRAVELED. GIVING TWENTY YEARS EXPERIENCE ON THE FRONTIER; ALSO THE MURDER OF PAT. HENNESEY, AND THE HANGING OF TOM. SMITH, AT RYLAND'S FORD, AND FACTS CONCERNING THE TALBERT RAID ON CALDWELL. ALSO THE DEATH DEALING CAREER OF McCARTY AND INCIDENTS HAPPENING IN AND AROUND CALDWELL, KANSAS, FROM 1871 UNTIL 1890. CALDWELL, KANSAS, 1890.

[1]–405, [406 blank]. 19.4 x 13.2 cm. Four plates, unlisted. Blue printed boards, brown cloth backstrip, with title on front cover.

Ref.: Adams 383; Adams (*Ramp. Herd*) 843; Dobie p. 121; Howes F353; Rader 1472

1412 [FREEMAN, JAMES W.], *Editor*

PROSE AND POETRY OF THE LIVE STOCK INDUSTRY OF THE UNITED STATES. WITH OUTLINES OF THE ORIGIN AND ANCIENT HISTORY OF OUR LIVE STOCK ANIMALS . . . DENVER: PUBLISHED BY THE NATIONAL LIVE STOCK HISTORICAL ASSOCIATION.

[1]–757, [758 blank]. (Pages [1–2] blank.) 27 x 19.8 cm. 367 illustrations listed. Black leather, blind panels on sides, title in gilt on front cover and backstrip, gilt top.

Prov.: Name of original owner stamped in gilt on front cover: F. M. Woods /.

Ref.: Adams 384; Adams (*Ramp. Herd*) 844; Dobie p. 114; Howes P636

Published in 1905. Biographies of big cowmen and history based on genuine research. The richest in matter of all the hundred-dollar-and-up rare books in its field.—Dobie

The introduction, signed by James W. Freeman, states that the "historical sections of this volume were written by Jerome C. Smiley, of Denver, Colorado, . . . " Only the first volume (of three planned) was published.

1413 FREEMASONS. ILLINOIS. Grand Lodge

PROCEEDINGS OF THE GRAND LODGE OF ANCIENT FREE AND ACCEPTED MASONS, OF THE STATE OF ILLINOIS, AT ITS EIGHTH ANNUAL COMMUNICATION, HELD IN THE CITY OF QUINCY, OCTOBER, A. L. 5847, A. D. 1847 . . . PEORIA: S. H. DAVIS, 1847.

[1]–120. 21.6 x 13.2 cm. Unbound, removed from bound volume.

Ref.: Byrd 1180; McMurtrie (*Peoria*) 23

1414 FREEMASONS. INDIAN TERRITORY.

[Wrapper title] CONSTITUTION AND BY-LAWS, OF THE M. E. GRAND ROYAL ARCH CHAPTER OF INDIAN TERRITORY ALSO THE BY-LAWS, FOR THE GOVERNMENT OF SUBORDINATE CHAPTERS, IN INDIAN TERRITORY. ATOKA, I. T.: INDIAN CITIZEN PUB CO.

[1]–[27], [28 blank]. 15.6 x 9.9 cm. Pink printed wrappers, with title as above on front wrapper.

Ref.:

Printed 1890–99.

1415 FREEMASONS. IOWA. Grand Lodge

THE BOOK OF CONSTITUTIONS, AND THE CONSTITUTION, BY-LAWS, AND GENERAL REGULATIONS OF THE GRAND LODGE OF IOWA: TO WHICH ARE ADDED A COLLECTION OF MASONIC FORMS. BURLINGTON: PRINTED BY MORGAN & M'KENNY, 1851.

[I]–VI, [7]–185, [186 blank]. 18.4 x 11.1 cm.

BOUND WITH:

CONSTITUTION AND BY-LAWS OF THE GRAND LODGE OF IOWA. ALSO, THE STANDING REGULATIONS. BURLINGTON: MORGAN & M'KENNY, 1851.

[1]–20. Two volumes bound together, contemporary black straight grained calf, blind roll

border on sides, title in gilt on front cover, gilt fillets on backstrip.

Ref.: Moffit 86

The two parts were also issued separately.

1416 FREEMASONS. IOWA. Grand Lodge. (Library)

[Caption title] CATALOGUE OF BOOKS AND PERI-ODICALS CONTAINED IN THE LIBRARY OF THE GRAND LODGE OF IOWA, JUNE 6TH, 1854. BY T. S. PARVIN, G. LIBRARIAN . . .

[1]–16. 22.4 x 12.9 cm. Unbound, unopened.

Prov.: Embossed stamps of T. S. Parvin on pages [1] and [9]. Manuscript numerals in red on page [9]: 25145 /.

Ref.: AII (*Iowa*) 70

Pages [9]–16 comprise a report by the librarian which also appeared in the *Proceedings* for the year, but the catalogue of books was not included.

1417 FREEMASONS. KANSAS. Ancient York Masons. (Wyandotte Lodge, No. 3)

BY-LAWS OF WYANDOTT[!] LODGE, NO. 3, OF FREE AND ACCEPTED ANCIENT YORK MASONS, ADOPTED, DECEMBER 11TH, A. D. 1857, A. L. 5857. WYAN-DOTT, K. T.: PRINTED BY S. D. MACDONALD, 1858.

[1]–16. 15.3 x 10.3 cm. Plain buff wrappers. Roughly opened.

Ref.: AII (*Kansas*) 162

This is the first printing of a pamphlet in Wyandotte, K.T., better known today as Kansas City, Kansas.

1418 FREEMASONS. MINNESOTA. St. Paul Lodge, No. 1

BY-LAWS OF ST. PAUL LODGE, NO. 1, OF FREE AND ACCEPTED MASONS; AND OF THE GRAND LODGE OF OHIO. ADOPTED, 1849. ST. PAUL: PRINTED BY J. A. AITKENSIDE, 1849.

[1]–36. 17.9 x 10.9 cm. Salmon printed wrappers with title on front wrapper; Account of the organization of the Lodge on verso of front wrapper and Funeral Dirge on recto of back wrapper. Repairs to title-leaf and others, inscription washed from title-page.

Ref.: AII (*Minnesota*) 1

One of the first Minnesota imprints.

1419 FREEMASONS. MISSOURI. Boonville R. A. Chapter No. 3

[Caption title] BY LAWS OF BOONVILLE R. A. CHAP-TER NO. 3 . . .

[1]–8. 17.4 x 10.3 cm. Contemporary marbled wrappers.

Ref.:

Imprint on page 8: Van Nortwick, Printer, / Register Office, Boonville, 1844. /

1420 FREEMASONS. MISSOURI. Clarksville Lodge No. 17

THE BY-LAWS OF CLARKSVILLE LODGE NO. 17, OF FREE AND ACCEPTED MASONS. BOWLING-GREEN: MISSOURI JOURNAL PRINTING OFFICE.

[1]–14, [15–6 blank]. 18.7 x 12.2 cm. Stabbed, unbound.

Ref.:

Undated, but about 1837.

1421 FREEMASONS. MISSOURI. Palmyra Lodge No. 18

THE BY-LAWS OF PALMYRA LODGE. NO. 18. OF FREE AND ACCEPTED ANCIENT MASONS. PALMYRA, MO.: B. F. HAYDEN, 1837.

[1]–14, [15–6 blank]. 17.5 x 12.4 cm. Stabbed, unbound.

Ref.: AII (*Missouri*) 195; Rusk II p. 94

1422 FREEMASONS. MISSOURI. St. Louis Lodge No. 1

BY-LAWS OF ST. LOUIS LODGE, NO. I, (AS AMENDED,) JANUARY, A. L. 5835—A. D. 1835. ST. LOUIS: C. KEEMLE, 1835.

[1]–8. 18.3 x 11.9 cm. Stitched, unbound.

Ref.:

1423 FREEMASONS. SCOTTISH RITE. Guthrie, Oklahoma

[Caption title] GUTHRIE LODGE OF PERFECTION, NO. 1. TO THE VENERABLE MASTER, THE WARDENS AND BRETHREN . . .

[1–2]. 24.2 x 15.2 cm. Unbound broadsheet.

Ref.:

Printed at Guthrie, Oklahoma, after 1899 and before 1910.

1424 FREJES, FRANCISCO

HISTORIA BREVE DE LA CONQUISTA DE LOS ESTADOS INDEPENDIENTES DEL IMPERIO MEJICANO . . . MEJI-CO: IMPRESO POR J. OJEDA, 1839.

[I]–VIII, 1–302, [303–04 Index]. 15 x 10.2 cm. Contemporary mottled calf, red leather label.

Ref.: Barrett 884; Cowan pp. 221–22; Howes F359; Sabin 25825 see

Contains much on the history, geography, Indians, and conquest of Coahuila, Texas, Sonora, and Sinaloa, and on their colonization.—EDG

Editions: Zacatecas, 1838.

1425 FREMONT, JESSIE BENTON

AUTOGRAPH LETTER, SIGNED. No date, New York. Four pages, 20.3 x 12.7 cm. To Colonel Christopher Carson.

A remarkable letter recalling with affection and pleasure the past experiences between Carson, General and Mrs. Frémont, and Thomas Hart Benton.

When I bought this from Edward Eberstadt, I told him this would be more interesting if it were a letter from Carson to Mrs. Frémont. See under Carson, Christopher.—EDG

1426 FREMONT, JESSIE BENTON

THE WILL AND THE WAY STORIES . . . BOSTON: D. LOTHROP COMPANY.

[3]–182, [183 blank, 184–91 advertisements, 192 blank]. (Pages [3–4] blank.) 17.7 x 11.7 cm. Portrait and one diagram. Blue cloth, gilt title on front cover and backstrip.
Ref.:
Copyrighted 1891.

1427 FREMONT, JESSIE BENTON

A YEAR OF AMERICAN TRAVEL . . . NEW YORK: HARPER & BROTHERS, 1878.

[1]–4 advertisements, [5]–190, [191–92 advertisements]. 11.9 x 8 cm. Green cloth, title printed on front cover in red and black.
Ref.: Howes F363; Rader 1477
Included in the work are three letters by the author's husband describing his last expedition.

1428 FREMONT, JOHN C.

DAGUERREOTYPE PORTRAIT. Miniature, bust length with head turned slightly to subject's right. 3.9 x 3.3 cm., in ornate gold colored frame. Printed card inserted in back: Maj.-General John C. Fremont. / [short rule] / Abbott & Co., 143 Nas-/sau St. N.Y. / [within decorative frame].

1429 FREMONT, JOHN C.

. . . GEOGRAPHICAL MEMOIR UPON UPPER CALIFORNIA . . . WASHINGTON: WENDELL AND VAN BENTHUYSEN, 1848.

[1]–67, [68 blank]. 22.8 x 14.7 cm. Folding map laid in: Map of / Oregon and Upper California / From the Surveys of / John Charles Fremont / And other Authorities / [rule] / Drawn by Charles Preuss / Under the Order of the / Senate of the United States / Washington City 1848 / [rule] / Scale 1:3,000000 / Lith.ʸ by E. Weber & Co. Balto. / 83.6 x 66.8 cm. *Inset:* [at top, within neat line] Profile of the traveling route from the South Pass of the Rocky Mountains to the Bay of San Francisco /. 4 x 62 cm. Blue printed wrappers, with title on front wrapper.
Ref.: Cowan p. 223; Howes F366; Munk (Alliot) p. 83; Sabin 25837; Wagner-Camp 150;

Wheat (*Gold Rush*) 58; Wheat (*Transmississippi*) 559
30th Congress, 1st Session, Senate, Miscellaneous Document No. 148, Serial 511.

1430 FREMONT, JOHN C.

[Caption title] . . . LETTER OF J. C. FREMONT TO THE EDITORS OF THE NATIONAL INTELLIGENCER, COMMUNICATING SOME GENERAL RESULTS OF A RECENT WINTER EXPEDITION ACROSS THE ROCKY MOUNTAINS, FOR THE SURVEY OF A ROUTE FOR A RAILROAD TO THE PACIFIC . . .

[1]–7, [8 blank]. 22.6 x 14.2 cm. Rebound in new red cloth.
Ref.: Wagner-Camp 239
33rd Congress, 1st Session, Senate, Miscellaneous Document No. 67, Serial 705. [Washington, 1854.]

1431 FREMONT, JOHN C.

[Map] MAP OF / OREGON AND UPPER CALIFORNIA / FROM THE SURVEYS OF / JOHN CHARLES FREMONT / AND OTHER AUTHORITIES / [rule] / DRAWN BY CHARLES PREUSS / UNDER THE ORDER OF THE / SENATE OF THE UNITED STATES / WASHINGTON CITY 1848 / [rule] / SCALE 1:3,000000 / LITH.ʸ BY E. WEBER & CO. BALTO. / *Inset:* [at top, below neat line:] PROFILE OF THE TRAVELING ROUTE FROM THE SOUTH PASS OF THE ROCKY MOUNTAINS TO THE BAY OF SAN FRANCISCO / 4. x 62. cm.

Map, 83.6 x 66.8 cm. Scale as above. Folded and sealed into original paper mailing wrapper.
Prov.: Inscribed on front of envelope: Pub Doc Free Wm P Hale / U S S ⸗ ⸗ Fremonts Map / + /.
Ref.: Phillips (*Maps*) p. 462; Wagner-Camp 150; Wheat (*Gold Region*) 40; Wheat (*Transmississippi*) 559
Because of the note by Senator Hale, the presumption is that the map is present and is identical with the copy enclosed with Senate Miscellaneous Document No. 148, 30th Congress, 1st Session.

1432 FREMONT, JOHN C.

[Caption title] . . . MESSAGE OF THE PRESIDENT OF THE UNITED STATES, COMMUNICATING THE PROCEEDINGS OF THE COURT MARTIAL IN THE TRIAL OF LIEUTENANT COLONEL FREMONT . . .

[1]–447, [448 blank]. 22.7 x 15.3 cm. Stabbed, unbound, uncut, unopened. In maroon cloth case.
Ref.: Cowan p. 222; Sabin 25840
30th Congress, 1st Session, Senate, Executive Document No. 33, Serial 507. [Washington, 1848.]

1433 FREMONT, JOHN C.

NARRATIVE OF THE EXPLORING EXPEDITION TO THE ROCKY MOUNTAINS, IN THE YEAR 1842; AND TO OREGON AND NORTH CALIFORNIA, IN THE YEARS 1843–44 . . . SYRACUSE: PUBLISHED BY HALL & DICKSON, 1847.

[1]–427, [428 blank], [1]–4 advertisements. 19.5 x 12.8 cm. Woodcuts and folding map: Map / of / Oregon, California, / New Mexico, N. W. Texas, / & / the proposed Territory of / Ne-Bras-Ka. / By / Rufus B. Sage. / [multiple rule bar] / 1846. / F. Michelin's Lith 111, Nassau St / N. Y. / 44.6 x 60.4 cm. No scale indicated. Black cloth.

Ref.: Howes F370; Wagner-Camp 115 note; Wheat (*Gold Region*) 30; Wheat (*Transmississippi*) 527

One of the revised editions of his two narratives.

1434 FREMONT, JOHN C.
ANOTHER COPY.

1435 FREMONT, JOHN C.

OREGON AND CALIFORNIA. THE EXPLORING EXPEDITION TO THE ROCKY MOUNTAINS, OREGON AND CALIFORNIA . . . BUFFALO: GEO. H. DERBY AND CO., 1851.

[1]–456. 18.5 x 12.1 cm. Illustrations and two portraits unlisted. Blue cloth.

Ref.: Smith 3360

One of the numerous editions designed for emigrants.

Editions: Buffalo, 1849.

1436 FREMONT, JOHN C.

REPORT OF THE EXPLORING EXPEDITION TO THE ROCKY MOUNTAINS IN THE YEAR 1842, AND TO OREGON AND NORTH CALIFORNIA IN THE YEARS 1843–'44 . . . WASHINGTON: GALES AND SEATON, 1845.

[1]–693, [694–96 blank]. 23.8 x 15.1 cm. 22 plates and five maps, unlisted. Map: Map / of an / Exploring Expedition / to the / Rocky Mountains in the Year 1842 / and to / Oregon & North California in the Years 1843–44 / by / Brevet Capt. J. C. Frémont of the Corps of Topographical Engineers / Under the orders of / Col. J. J. Abert, Chief of the Topographical Bureau. / 76.6 x 130.4 cm. No scale given. Across the top of the map is a Profile of the route. Map: [Route from Muddy Fork to Beer Spring] [left centre:] Lith. by E. Weber & Co. Baltimore / [lower right:] Scale, 4 1/2 Miles to an Inch. / 49 x 24.5 cm. (page size). Scale as above. Map: Beer Springs. / Scale, One Mile to an Inch. /

[lower right:] Lith by E Weber & Co. / 24.4 x 15.4 cm. (page size). Scale as above. Map: The Great Salt-Lake. / [at foot:] Scale 1:1000000. / 25.7 x 16.5 cm. (page size). Scale as above. Map: [Route from Salmon Trout River to Sacramento River] Scale Five Miles to one Inch / Lith. by E. Weber & Co Baltimore, Md. / 23.9 x 64 cm. (page size). Scale as above. Stabbed, uncut, mostly unopened. In a red cloth case.

Ref.: Bradford 1785; Cowan pp. 223–24; Edwards pp. 62–3; Field 565; Howes F370; Munk (Alliot) p. 83; Sabin 25845; Wagner-Camp 115; Wheat (*Transmississippi*) 497; Wheat (*Gold Region*) 21

Frémont's work had a powerful effect on the routes chosen by the gold-seekers in 1849–50.

Laid in is a leaf from an unidentified book inscribed by Mrs. Frémont: From Mrs. Frémont to / Jacob Dodson / for his faithful Services to the Col. / Washington City, / October 1847. /

1437 FREMONT, JOHN C.

A REPORT ON AN EXPLORATION OF THE COUNTRY LYING BETWEEN THE MISSOURI RIVER AND THE ROCKY MOUNTAINS, ON THE LINE OF THE KANSAS AND GREAT PLATTE RIVERS . . . WASHINGTON: PRINTED BY ORDER OF THE UNITED STATES' SENATE, 1843.

[3]–207, [208 blank]. 22.2 x 14.4 cm. Six lithographed plates and a map. Map: Map / to Illustrate an Exploration of the country, / lying between the Missouri River and the Rocky Mountains, on the line of the / Nebraska and Platte River. / By Lieu^t J. C. Fremont, of the Corps of Topographical Engineers. / $\frac{1}{1000000}$ / The stars indicate astronomical positions / E. Weber & Co. Lith^g / 35.2 x 82.9 cm. Scale as above. Gray printed wrappers with title on front wrapper. In a green cloth case.

Ref.: Bradford 1784; Howes F371; Sabin 25843; Wagner-Camp 95; Wheat (*Transmississippi*) 464

Frémont's report of his first expedition appeared as Senate Document 243, 27th Congress, 3rd Session, Serial 416.

1438 FRENCH, D'ARCY A.

ENGLISH GRAMMAR SIMPLIFIED: IN WHICH IT IS CLEARLY PROVED THAT IN THE GRAMMARS MOST COMMONLY USED IN OUR SCHOOLS, THE PRINCIPLES, IN THE MOST IMPORTANT CONSTRUCTIONS, ARE GROSSLY ERRONEOUS AND DEFECTIVE . . . GALENA: W. C. E. THOMAS, MDCCCXLVI.

[1]–48. 18.4 x 11.2 cm. Blue wrappers, with hole punched through upper left corner through which is an old knotted tape.

Ref.: Byrd 1057

1439 [FRENCH, JAMES S. (?)]

SKETCHES AND ECCENTRICITIES OF COL. DAVID CROCKETT, OF WEST TENNESSEE . . . NEW-YORK: PRINTED AND PUBLISHED BY J. & J. HARPER, 1833.

[i]–[viii, viii blank], 9–209, [210 blank], [1–6 advertisements], [1]–14 advertisements, [1–10 advertisements]. 19.6 x 11.5 cm. Old gray paper newly applied to original boards, new salmon backstrip, original printed label, 4.3 x 1.9 cm., on backstrip, uncut.

Ref.: Howes C898; Rader 992

The first edition of this spurious biography appeared the same year in Cincinnati. The work is attributed to James S. French; it was issued without the authorization of Crockett.

1440 FRENCH, LEIGH H.

SEWARD'S LAND OF GOLD. FIVE SEASONS EXPERIENCE WITH THE GOLD SEEKERS IN NORTHWESTERN ALASKA . . . NEW YORK: MONTROSS, CLARKE & EMMONS, PUBLISHERS.*

[1–6], i–[xiv, xiv blank], 1–101, [102 blank]. 21.3 x 15 cm. Illustrations unlisted. Red cloth.

Ref.: Smith 3371; Wickersham 1515

The date 1904 appears in the text on page 101; published the following year.

1441 FRENCH, WILLIAM

SOME RECOLLECTIONS OF A WESTERN RANCHMAN. NEW MEXICO 1883–1899 . . . LONDON: METHUEN & CO. LTD.*

[i]–[viii, viii blank], 1–283, [284 colophon], [1]–8 advertisements. 22 x 14 cm. Red cloth, fore and lower edges uncut.

Ref.: Adams (*Ramp. Herd*) 847; Coulter 176; Howes F375

First published in 1927, according to note on verso of title-leaf.

1442 FREWEN, MORETON

MELTON MOWBRAY AND OTHER MEMORIES . . . LONDON: HERBERT JENKINS LIMITED, MCMXXIV.*

[i]–[xii, xii blank], [1]–311, [312 blank]. 21 x 14 cm. 16 illustrations listed. Light green cloth.

Ref.: Adams (*Ramp. Herd*) 850; Howes F380

The author's interesting and important reminiscences of the cattle industry in Wyoming include an account of his unsuccessful ranch in Wyoming along the Powder River.

1443 FRIEND, THE

THE FRIEND: A SEMI-MONTHLY JOURNAL, DEVOTED TO TEMPERANCE, MARINE AND GENERAL INTELLIGENCE . . . HONOLULU, OAHU, H. I.: CHARLES EDWIN HITCHCOCK, PRINTER. 1846.*

[i–ii] [1]–192. 28.6 x 22.6 cm. Rebound in brown half calf.

Ref.: Cowan p. 155; Howes D44; Hussey, J. A., in Calif. Hist. Soc. *Quarterly*, XVI, pp. 209–15

This is Volume IV, Numbers 1–24, January 1 to December 15, 1846, of *The Friend*, edited by Samuel C. Damon. It contains on pages [153]–55, [161]–62, [169]–70, and [177]–78 a series of three letters (the first is divided into two parts) dated from Yerba Buena, San Francisco Bay, June 10, June 24, and June 25, 1846. They are signed: The Farthest West /. The author has been identified by John A. Hussey as Washington Allon Bartlett.

The letters describe conditions in California generally and contain some important information about the "Bear Flag Revolt."

1444 FRIEND, THE

THE SAME . . . HONOLULU, OAHU, H. I.: PRINTED AT THE POLYNESIAN OFFICE, 1848 [–1849].

[i–ii], [1]–96. [i–ii], [1]–48, [i–ii], [49]–96. 29 x 23.2 cm. Two volumes, contemporary pink boards, maroon leather backstrip. Volume VII, Number 2 present in duplicate.

Ref.: Cowan p. 155; Howes D44; Matthews p. 315

Volumes VI and VII complete. Volume VII, Numbers 6–12, contain the first printing of Samuel C. Damon's "A Trip from the Sandwich Islands to Lower Oregon and Upper California . . ." with the separate title-page before No. 6 as described in this catalogue under the author's name, item 994.

1445 FRINK, MARGARET A.

JOURNAL OF THE ADVENTURES OF A PARTY OF CALIFORNIA GOLD-SEEKERS UNDER THE GUIDANCE OF MR. LEDYARD FRINK DURING A JOURNEY ACROSS THE PLAINS FROM MARTINSVILLE, INDIANA, TO SACRAMENTO, CALIFORNIA, FROM MARCH 30, 1850, TO SEPTEMBER 7, 1850 . . .*

[1]–131, [132 blank]. 18 x 22.3 cm. Two portraits. Brown cloth.

Ref.: Cowan p. 225; Howes F388; Matthews p. 325

Howes F388 gives [Oakland, 1897] as place and date of publication, apparently derived from the Preface. Compiled from Mrs. Frink's diary.

1446 FRIZZELL, LODISA

ACROSS THE PLAINS TO CALIFORNIA IN 1852 . . . EDITED . . . BY VICTOR HUGO PALTSITS . . . NEW YORK PUBLIC LIBRARY, 1915.*

[1]–30. 25.4 x 17.7 cm. Four plates, unlisted. Brown printed wrappers, with title on front wrapper, imprint on back wrapper.

Ref.: Cowan p. 225; Howes (1954) 3824; Jones 1728; Matthews p. 333

1447 FROEBEL, JULIUS

AUS AMERIKA. LEIPZIG: VERLAGSBUCHHANDLUNG VON J. J. WEBER, 1857 [–1858].

[I]–XVI, [1]–550, [551 blank, 552 colophon]. [I]–XVI, [1]–615, [616 Berichtigungen]. 17.9 x 11.5 cm. Two volumes, yellow wrappers, with title on front wrappers, uncut. In green cloth case.

Ref.: Clark III 316; Cowan p. 225; Howes F390; Rader 1491; Raines p. 85; Sabin 25988; Wagner-Camp 292

Describes several trips over the Santa Fé Trail and a journey from Tucson and the Gila to Los Angeles.—Howes

1448 FROEBEL, JULIUS

SEVEN YEARS' TRAVEL IN CENTRAL AMERICA, NORTHERN MEXICO, AND THE FAR WEST OF THE UNITED STATES . . . LONDON: RICHARD BENTLEY, M.DCCC.LIX.

[i]–[xvi, xvi blank], [1]–587, [588 blank]. 21.1 x 13.4 cm. Eight illustrations listed, figures in text. Purple cloth, blind embossed sides, with part of front cover gilt, gilt title on backstrip, gilt edges. Front endleaf supplied.

Ref.: Clark III 316; Howes F390; Munk (Alliot) p. 84; Raines p. 85; Sabin 25992; Wagner-Camp 292

Translation of the author's *Aus Amerika.*

1449 FROISETH, B. A. M.

[Map] MAP / OF THE / TERRITORY / OF / UTAH. / [below map:] ENTERED ACCORDING TO ACT OF CONGRESS, IN THE YEAR 1870 BY / B. A. M. FROISETH, / IN THE CLERKS OFFICE OF THE DISTRICT COURT OF THE U. S. FOR THE 3.$^{\underline{D}}$ DIST. OF UTAH. / [rule] / AM. PHOTO-LITHOGRAPHIC CO. N. Y. (OSBORNE'S PROCESS.) / [Map on same sheet:] GREAT SALT LAKE VALLEY / [below map:] [copyright same as above except date 1869 and spelling Clerk's]. [Map on same sheet:] PLAT / OF / SALT LAKE CITY / UTAH. / [below map:] [copyright same as above]. [Portrait on same sheet:] [Portrait of Brigham Young, signed]. [Within double rule borders.]

Maps and portrait, 38 x 31.5 cm. Scale: 72 miles to one inch for first map, 20 miles to one inch for second map, scale not given for third map. Folded into brown cloth covers, 13.3 x 8.4 cm., with title stamped in gilt on front cover: Maps / of / Utah Territory, / Great Salt Lake Valley / and / Salt Lake City, / with / Portrait and Autograph / of / Brigham Young. / Published by / Scandanavinsk Post, N. Y. /

Ref.: Phillips (*Maps*) p. 948

1450 FRONTIER GUARDIAN, THE

[Newspaper] THE FRONTIER GUARDIAN. BY ORSON HYDE. KANESVILLE, IOWA, FRIDAY MORNING, APRIL 18 [–MAY 16–30], 1851. VOLUME III.—NUMBER 6 [–8, 9] . . .

Three issues, each [1–4]. 57.8 x 41.5 cm. Unbound.

Ref.: Moffit in *Iowa Journal*, Vol. 36, No. 2, p. 182; Smith, W. W. p. 284

The printer of this Mormon newspaper was John Gooch, Jr., the editor was Orson Hyde.

1451 FRONTIER SCOUT

[Newspaper; reprints] FRONTIER SCOUT. WINEGAR & GOODWIN, PUBLISHERS. LIBERTY AND UNION. CO. I 30TH WIS. VOLS., PROPRIETORS. VOL. 1. FORT UNION, D. T., JULY 14 [–27], 1864. No. 2 [–3] . . .

Two issues, each [1–4]. 32.4 x 20 cm. Unbound.

Ref.:

According to Usher L. Burdick of South Dakota, there were only three numbers printed, but the Minnesota Historical Society has recorded issues for July 29[!] and August 17, in the *Union List of Newspapers.* The August 17 issue is probably 1865. Both of the present issues are marked, in pencil, reprint.

1452 FRONTIER SCOUT

[Newspaper] FRONTIER SCOUT. CAPT. E. G. ADAMS, EDITOR. LIBERTY AND UNION. LIEUT. C. H. CHAMPNEY, PUBLISHER. FORT RICE, D. T., JUNE 29, 1865 [AUGUST 10, 24, 31, SEPTEMBER 7, 14, OCTOBER 12]. NO. 3 [9, 11, 12, 13, 14, 15] . . .

Seven issues, each [1–4]. 30.5 to 32.3 x 19.6 to 19.9 cm.

Ref.: Allen (*Dakota*) 33 note

Most of the issues are printed on blue-lined notepaper. Among the original articles are "March of the 1st Vol. Infantry to Fort Rice, D. T.," "Through the Rebellion," "Devil's Lake," and "Indian Village at Fort Berthold."

1453 FROST, AARON

DAHO SPRINGS; ITS MINES AND MINERAL WATERS. GEORGETOWN, COLORADO: GEORGETOWN COURIER STEAM PRINTING HOUSE AND BLANK BOOK MANUFACTORY, 1880.

[1]–40. 22.9 x 15.2 cm. Two maps included in pagination. Salmon printed wrappers with title on front wrapper.

Ref.: Wilcox p. 46

Contains a short history of the early settlement of Idaho Springs.

1454 FROST, DONALD McK.

NOTES ON GENERAL ASHLEY, THE OVERLAND TRAIL, AND SOUTH PASS . . . WORCESTER, MASSACHUSETTS: AMERICAN ANTIQUARIAN SOCIETY, 1945.

[1]–159, [160 blank]. 28.8 x 20.2 cm. Map. Green paste paper boards, red buckram backstrip, gilt top, uncut.

Prov.: Inscribed on the front fly-leaf: For: / Everett D. Graff / from his friend / Donald McKay Frost /.

Ref.: Howes F392; Malone p. 26

Limited to 50 copies on Utopian Paper. Reprinted from the *Proceedings of the American Antiquarian Society* for October, 1944.

1455 FROST, GRIFFIN

CAMP AND PRISON JOURNAL . . . QUINCY, ILLINOIS: 1867.

[i]–[viii, viii blank], [1]–303, [304 blank], [305–06 advertisements]. 19.9 x 13.7 cm. Dark brown cloth, blind embossed sides, title in gilt on backstrip.

Ref.: Howes F393; Nicholson p. 297; Sabin 26020

"All but 100 copies burned."—Howes. However, a letter by the author quoted by Parke-Bernet Galleries, Inc. states that of 700 copies printed all but fifty were destroyed.

The work was designed to show that Union prisons were just as bad as Confederate prisons.

1456 FRY, E. A.

[Wrapper title] . . . DESCRIPTIVE PAMPHLET OF KNOX COUNTY, NEB. WITH ACCURATE MAP. NIOBRARA, NEBRASKA: SANTEE & HILL, 1883.

[1–24], 14 leaves of advertisements on colored paper interspersed. 20.3 x 13.1 cm. Gray printed wrappers with title on front wrapper, advertisements on verso of front and recto of back wrapper.

Ref.:

There is no map present in this copy nor is there evidence that a map was issued with this copy. So far, no other copy for comparison has been located. The author was proprietor of the *Creighton Pioneer*. The *Knox County News* was published by Santee & Hill.

1457 FRY, FREDERICK

FRY'S TRAVELER'S GUIDE, AND DESCRIPTIVE JOURNAL OF THE GREAT NORTH-WESTERN TERRITORIES OF THE UNITED STATES OF AMERICA; COMPRISING THE TERRITORIES OF IDAHO, WASHINGTON, MONTANA, AND THE STATE OF OREGON, WITH SKETCHES OF COLORADO, UTAH, NEBRASKA, AND BRITISH AMERICA . . . CINCINNATI: PUBLISHED FOR THE AUTHOR, 1865.

[i–]vi, 7–264, [1–24 advertisements]. 18.2 x 11.9 cm. Black cloth, blind embossed borders on sides, title in gilt on backstrip.

Prov.: Inscribed in pencil on front endleaf: C. D. Nichols / Compliments of the Author / Fred^k Fry. /

Ref.: Bradford 1805; Howes F398; Jones 1480; Sabin 26095; Smith 3380; Wagner-Camp 416

Earliest accounts of the Idaho and Montana mines, visited in 1862 and 1864.—Howes

1458 FRY, JAMES B.

ARMY SACRIFICES; OR, BRIEFS FROM OFFICIAL PIGEON-HOLES. . . . EXPERIENCES OF THE REGULAR ARMY OF THE UNITED STATES ON THE INDIAN FRONTIER . . . NEW YORK: D. VAN NOSTRAND, 1879.

[i–iv, iv blank], 1–254, [255–56 advertisements]. 16.6 x 11 cm. Red cloth, title in gilt on front cover and backstrip, decorations in black on front cover and in blind on back.

Ref.: Cowan p. 227; Howes F399; Munk (Alliot) p. 84; Rader 1503

Contains chapters on the Fetterman Massacre, Forsyth's Fight, the Grattan Massacre, and the Canby Massacre, etc.

1459 FULKERSON, H. S.

RANDOM RECOLLECTIONS OF EARLY DAYS IN MISSISSIPPI . . . VICKSBURG, MISSISSIPPI: VICKSBURG PRINTING AND PUBLISHING COMPANY, 1885.

[1]–158. 19.4 x 12.8 cm. Printed white wrappers with title on front wrapper. In a yellow cloth case.

Ref.: Howes F403

1460 FULLER, EMELINE L.

[Wrapper title] LEFT BY THE INDIANS. STORY OF MY LIFE . . .*

[i–ii, ii blank], [1]–40, [iii–iv blank]. 12.9 x 9.8 cm. Three illustrations (two with three portraits each and a single portrait). Pale blue printed wrappers with title on front wrapper. In a red half morocco case.

Ref.: Howes F407; Rader 1504; Smith 3386

Page [1] bears the following: Copyrighted 1892, / By Librarian of Congress. / Price, 25 Cents. / [lower left:] Hawk-Eye Steam Print, / Mt. Vernon, Iowa. /

Only account by a survivor of the sufferings of the 1860 Utter-Myers emigrating party of fifty-four members, all but fifteen of whom perished from hunger or were killed by Indians on the Snake river in Idaho. Among overland disasters, equalled in horror only by that of the

Donner party; cannibalism was resorted to in both cases.—Howes

Laid in is an Autograph Letter signed by Geraldine Hughes, 1936 May 22, Mount Vernon, Iowa. Three pages, 27.7 x 21.3 cm. To Edward Eberstadt. Stating that her father, James Hughes, wrote the pamphlet for Mrs. Fuller.

1461 FULLER, EMELINE L.

THE SAME. Pale green printed wrappers with title on front wrapper.*

Enlarged facsimile of the original except that the wrapper title has been used also as a title-page on page [1], the original text from page [1] transferred to page [2], and a fuller title used for the front wrapper.

Publisher's note inside front wrapper: Reissued in an Edition / of 200 Copies / by / Edward Eberstadt / 55 West 42nd Street / New York City / 1936 /.

1462 FULTON, ALEXANDER R.

THE RED MEN OF IOWA: BEING A HISTORY OF THE VARIOUS ABORIGINAL TRIBES WHOSE HOMES WERE IN IOWA . . . DES MOINES: MILLS & COMPANY, 1882.

[1]–559, [560 blank]. 22.5 x 15.2 cm. 26 illustrations listed. Brown cloth, brown leather backstrip and corners, title in gilt on front cover and backstrip, marbled edges.
    Ref.: Howes F411; Mott (*Iowa*) p. 66

1463 FULTON, AMBROSE C.

A LIFE'S VOYAGE A DIARY OF A SAILOR ON SEA AND LAND, JOTTED DOWN DURING A SEVENTY-YEARS' VOYAGE . . . NEW YORK: PUBLISHED BY THE AUTHOR, 1898.

[i]–[viii, viii blank], [1]–555, [556 blank]. 19.6 x 14.5 cm. 15 illustrations listed. Blue cloth, title in gilt on backstrip.
    Ref.: Howes F413; Mott (*Iowa*) p. 85; Rader 1509
    Iowa, Hawaii, the Seven Seas, etc.

1464 FULTON, AMBROSE C.

[Wrapper title] A PORTION OF A LIFE'S VOYAGE. AMBROSE C. FULTON'S TALK TO THE SCOTT COUNTY PIONEER SETTLERS' ASSOCIATION . . . DAVENPORT, IOWA: THE OSBORN-SKELLEY CO., 1902.

[i–ii blank], [1]–144, [145–46 blank]. 22.8 x 15 cm. Red printed wrappers with title on front wrapper.
    Ref.:

1465 FULTON, FRANCES I. SIMS

TO AND THROUGH NEBRASKA. BY A PENNSYLVANIA GIRL . . . LINCOLN, NEBRASKA: JOURNAL COMPANY, 1884.

[1]–273, [274 blank]. 17.4 x 12.1 cm. Blue cloth
    Ref.: Howes F414

1466 FURNAS, ROBERT W.

NEBRASKA. HER RESOURCES, ADVANTAGES, ADVANCEMENT AND PROMISES . . . ALSO THE SCHOOL LAND LAWS . . . LINCOLN, NEB.: JOURNAL COMPANY, 1885.

[1]–48. 21.7 x 14.8 cm. Stitched, unbound.
    Ref.:

1467 FURNAS & SONS, Brownville, Nebraska

[Caption title] INSTRUCTIONS FOR TRANSPLANTING AND CULTIVATING FRUIT TREES. BY FURNAS & SONS, FURNAS NURSERIES, BROWNVILLE, NEBRASKA . . .

[1]–4. 23 x 15.6 cm. Unbound.
    Ref.: AII (*Nebraska*) 169
    AII (*Nebraska*) supplies imprint: Brownville; Advertiser Print, 1870(?).

1468 FURNAS COUNTY HERALD, Beaver City, Nebraska

[Newspaper] FURNAS COUNTY HERALD. BEAVER CITY NEB. OCT. 14 . . .

[1–4]. 13.8 x 10.3 cm. Unbound.
    Ref.:
    Volume I, Number 1. Probably the first printing in Furnas County, 1873 or 1874. "If the cheese box had been large our press would not have been small."

1469 FURTHER REPORT, A . . .

A FURTHER REPORT FROM THE COMMITTEE OF SECRECY, APPOINTED TO ENQUIRE INTO THE CONDUCT OF ROBERT, EARL OF ORFORD . . . DELIVERED THE 30TH OF JUNE 1742. LONDON: PRINTED FOR T. LEECH, 1742.

[A]–Q4, R2. [1]–132. Large folding table inserted after Q4. 19.4 x 11.7 cm. Bound with Number 3315.
    Ref.:
    The secret committee of Parliament comprised twenty-one members of whom nineteen were politically opposed to Walpole. Their second report was no more successful than the first.

G

1470 GAGE, THOMAS

THE ENGLISH-AMERICAN HIS TRAVAIL BY SEA AND LAND: OR, A NEW SURVEY OF THE WEST-INDIA'S . . . LONDON: PRINTED BY R. COTES, 1648.

[A]5, B–T6, V8. [i–x], 1–220, [221–32 Contents]. (Lacks initial blank.) (Page 22 misnumbered 23 and 131 misnumbered 113.) 28.2 x 17.4 cm. Contemporary paneled calf, blind tooled panels enclosing sprinkled bands, dark red morocco label lettered in gilt.

Prov.: Bookplate of Carroll Mercer.

Ref.: Field 584; Jones 262; Palau 96480; Sabin 26298; Wing G109

Gage was an Englishman who lived for many years as a Dominican Friar in the Spanish parts of Central and South America and the Caribees. Much of the material presented appears here in English for the first time, but some of it was taken from Thomas Nicholas' translation of Gómara. Gage later joined the Church of England and, for a time in the days of Cromwell's ascendancy, was the centre of a politico-religio controversy. He died in Jamaica.

1471 GAGE, THOMAS

A NEW SURVEY OF THE WEST-INDIA'S: OR, THE ENGLISH AMERICAN HIS TRAVAIL BY SEA AND LAND . . . LONDON: PRINTED BY E. COTES, M. DC. LV.

[A]⁵, B–T⁶, V⁸. [i–x], 1–220, [221–32 Contents]. (Lacks initial blank.) 27.7 x 18.6 cm. Four engraved maps, page size: Americae / Descrip. / [2] The / Ylandes / of the / West Indies /. [3] Hispania / Nova /. [4] Terra Firma / et / Novum Regnum / Granatense / et Popaian. / Contemporary calf, blind fillets on sides, brown morocco label on back. Rebacked.

Prov.: Bookplate of John Newsham of Chadshunt.

Ref.: Palau 96480; Raines p. 87; Sabin 2629; Wing G113

Second Edition.

Editions: London, 1648.

1472 GALE, GEORGE

UPPER MISSISSIPPI; OR, HISTORICAL SKETCHES OF THE MOUND-BUILDERS, THE INDIAN TRIBES, AND THE PROGRESS OF CIVILIZATION IN THE NORTHWEST; FROM A. D. 1600 TO THE PRESENT TIME . . . CHICAGO: CLARKE AND COMPANY, 1867.

[i]–[viii, viii blank], [9]–460. 18.6 x 12 cm. 13 illustrations and four maps, unlisted. Green cloth, blind fillets on sides, title in gilt on backstrip.

Ref.: AII (*Chicago*) 1198; Howes G14; Rader 1518; Sabin 26357

1473 GALENA AND CHICAGO UNION RAILROAD COMPANY

. . . REPORT OF WILLIAM B. OGDEN, ESQ., PRESIDENT OF THE COMPANY; TOGETHER WITH REPORTS OF THE ENGINEER, SECRETARY, AND TREASURER, READ AT THE ANNUAL MEETING OF THE STOCKHOLDERS, APRIL 5, 1848. CHICAGO: STEWART, WHEELER & ELLIS, 1848.

[1–2], [i–ii], [3]–23, [24 blank]. (Pages [i–ii] are inserted leaf.) Blue printed wrappers with title on front wrapper.

Ref.: Buck 428; Byrd 1326; Howes G17; McMurtrie (*Chicago*) 150; *Railway Economics* p. 311; Sabin 26363

The engineer's report is signed and dated: John Van Nortwick, / Chief Engineer. / Chicago, April 5th, 1848. /

1474 GALENA AND CHICAGO UNION RAILROAD COMPANY

SECOND ANNUAL REPORT . . . READ AT THE ANNUAL MEETING OF THE STOCKHOLDERS, APRIL 5, 1849. CHICAGO: H. K. DAVIS, 1849.

[1–2], [i–ii], [3]–20, [21–2 Appendix]. (Pages [i–ii] inserted leaf, inverted and reversed.) 22.6 x 14.4 cm. Yellow printed wrappers with title on front wrapper.

Ref.: Buck 428; Byrd 1445; Howes G17; McMurtrie (*Chicago*) 180; *Railway Economics* p. 311; Sabin 26363

The report of the chief engineer occupies pages [9]–17 and is signed by John Van Nortwick.

1475 GALENA AND CHICAGO UNION RAILROAD COMPANY

ANOTHER COPY. Same, but without Appendix, pages [21–2].

1476 GALENA AND CHICAGO UNION RAILROAD COMPANY

THIRD ANNUAL REPORT . . . READ AT THE ANNUAL MEETING OF THE STOCKHOLDERS, JUNE 5, 1850. CHICAGO: W. J. PATTERSON, 1850.

[1]–8, [1]–16. 22.3 x 14.1 cm. Gray printed wrappers with title on front wrapper.

Ref.: Buck 428; Byrd 1573; Howes G17; McMurtrie (*Chicago*) 214–214a; *Railway Economics* p. 311; Sabin 26363

The second part, with separate pagination, contains the reports of the engineer and secretary-treasurer, each with half-title.

1477 GALENA AND CHICAGO UNION RAILROAD COMPANY

FOURTH ANNUAL REPORT . . . READ AT THE ANNUAL MEETING OF THE STOCKHOLDERS, JUNE 4, 1851. CHICAGO: PRINTED AT THE DEMOCRAT OFFICE, 1851.

[1]–28. 22.1 x 14.1 cm. Yellow printed wrappers with title on front wrapper.

Ref.: AII (*Chicago*) 13; Buck 428; Byrd 1703; *Railway Economics* p. 311; Sabin 26363

The engineer's report by John Nortwick[!] appears on pages [7]–19.

1478 GALENA AND CHICAGO UNION RAILROAD COMPANY

. . . SIXTH ANNUAL REPORT, READ AT THE ANNUAL MEETING OF THE STOCKHOLDERS, JUNE 1, 1853. CHICAGO: PRINTED AT THE DEMOCRAT OFFICE, 1853.

[1]–32. 21.2 x 14 cm. Map: Map / Showing the / Galena & Chicago Union Rail Road / and its connections. / Mendel & Atwood, Lith. 170 Lake St. Chicago / 30.6 x 76.6 cm. No scale given. Removed from bound volume, unbound.

Ref.: AII (*Chicago*) 59; Buck 428; Byrd 1965; *Railway Economics* p. 311; Sabin 26363

The engineer's report signed by John Van Nortwick occupies pages [7]–12. Pages [24]–32 carry the charter and amendments. AII (*Chicago*) does not mention the map.

1479 GALENA AND CHICAGO UNION RAILROAD COMPANY

. . . SEVENTH ANNUAL REPORT. CHICAGO: DAILY DEMOCRAT BOOK AND JOB PRINTING OFFICE, 1854.

[1]–[18]. 22.5 x 14.1 cm. Map: Galena and Chicago Union Rail Road / the / only Rail-Road Route / [map, an oval enclosed in thin and thick rule borders] / from Chicago through / Northern Illinois to Wisconsin / Iowa and Minnesota / Lith by H. Acheson 130 & 132 Lake St. Chicago /. 51 x 60.5 cm. (including borders). No scale given. Buff printed wrappers with title in full on front wrapper.

Ref.: AII (*Chicago*) 92; Buck 428; Byrd 2114; *Railway Economics* p. 311; Sabin 26363

The engineer's report by John Van Nortwick occupies pages [9]–11.

1480 GALENA AND CHICAGO UNION RAILROAD COMPANY

EIGHTH ANNUAL REPORT . . . JUNE 6TH, 1855. CHICAGO: R. L. & C. L. WILSON & CO., 1855.

[1]–32. 22.7 x 14.6 cm. Blue printed wrappers with title on front wrapper within decorative border.

Ref.: AII (*Chicago*) 142; Buck 428; Byrd 2276; *Railway Economics* p. 311; Sabin 26363

The engineer's report by John P. Ilsley occupies pages [11]–21.

Laid in is a printed statement, broadside: Office of Galena and Chicago Union R. R. Co., / Chicago, July 13, 1855 . . .

1481 GALENA AND CHICAGO UNION RAILROAD COMPANY

[Broadside] OFFICE OF GALENA AND CHICAGO UNION R. R. CO., CHICAGO, JULY 13, 1855 SIR: — . . . W. M. Larrabee, Sec'y.

Broadside, 23.8 x 15.5 cm. Text, 11.2 x 10.8 cm.

Ref.: Byrd 2278

Regarding delay in publication of a report. Laid in the *Eighth Annual Report* of the Galena and Chicago Union Railroad . . . 1855.

1482 GALENA AND CHICAGO UNION RAILROAD COMPANY

DOCUMENTS SUBMITTED TO THE STOCKHOLDERS OF THE GALENA & CHICAGO UNION RAILROAD COMPANY BY THE BOARD OF DIRECTORS, JULY 22ND, 1858, IN RELATION TO THE LEASING OF THE CHICAGO, FULTON & MISSISSIPPI RAILROAD BRIDGE, AT FULTON, TO BE ACTED UPON BY THE STOCKHOLDERS AT A SPECIAL MEETING TO BE HELD AT CHICAGO, OCTOBER 6TH, 1858. CHICAGO: PRESS AND TRIBUNE BOOK AND JOB STEAM PRINTING HOUSE, 1858.

[1]–[56]. 22.6 x 14.4 cm. Cream printed wrappers with title on front wrapper.

Ref.: AII (*Chicago*) 324; Byrd 2908; *Railway Economics* p. 210

The report of the engineer of the Bridge Company has a special title-page on page [41], the text being an integral part of the pamphlet.

1483 GALENA AND CHICAGO UNION RAILROAD COMPANY

REPORT OF THE SURVEY OF THE ROUTE OF THE GALENA AND CHICAGO UNION RAIL ROAD, BY RICHARD P. MORGAN, ENGINEER, TOGETHER WITH THE ORIGINAL CHARTER OF THE COMPANY, AND AMENDMENTS THERETO. CHICAGO: DAILY TRIBUNE PRINT, 1847.

[1]–28. 21.2 x 13 cm. Map: [Map of the route of the Galena and Chicago Union Railroad] [lower left:] R. N. White, Sc. Chicago. / 18.5 x 41 cm. No scale given. Tan printed wrappers with title as above on front wrapper within decorative border.

Prov.: Charles F. Gunther copy, with the Chicago Historical Society embossed stamp in the title-leaf and the release stamp on the verso of the title-leaf.

Ref.: Buck 428; Byrd 1185; Howes M806; McMurtrie (*Chicago*) 116; *Railway Economics* p. 210; Sabin 26363 note, 50673

1484 GALENA (Illinois) CITY DIRECTORY, THE . . .

. . . THE GALENA CITY DIRECTORY, CONTAINING ALSO ADVERTISEMENTS OF THE PRINCIPAL MERCHANTS AND OTHERS, AND LIST OF SOCIETIES, &C. IN THE CITY OF GALENA . . . GALENA: H. H. HOUGHTON & CO., PUBLISHERS, 1854.

[1]–128. 20.9 x 13.7 cm. Blue printed boards with title on front cover, advertisements on back cover, and on front endpaper.

Prov.: Signature in pencil on title-page: Almira M. Fowler / [underline] /. Inscribed on verso of blank leaf facing title-page: Wm. A. Richards, / Cheyenne / Wyo. / 1895. / Presented to the / City of Galena / by Alice / Richards McCreery / 1925. / Mr. Richards went to school in Galena / in 1865. This book / was given to him by / Almira Fowler, / daughter of Dr. Fowler / of Galena. /

Ref.: Byrd 2100; Sabin 26362

1485 GALENA (Illinois) CITY DIRECTORY

GALENA CITY DIRECTORY . . . GALENA: BOOK AND JOB OFFICE OF W. W. HUNTINGTON, 1858.

[1]–139, [140 blank]. 15.9 x 10.6 cm. Orange printed boards, red roan backstrip, with title on front cover, advertisement on back cover.

Ref.: Byrd 2893; Howes G16

"Historical Sketch of the Upper Mississippi, Galena, and the Lead Trade" occupies pages [121]–139.

1486 GALLAGHER, W. D.

AUTOGRAPH LETTER, SIGNED. 1857 January 8, Pewee Valley, Kentucky. Six pages, 21 x 13.2 cm. To Governor John White Geary of Kansas.

An interesting letter on local matters. Contains a remark that Edwin Bryant, the author of *What I Saw in California* . . . was then living near Gallagher, about sixteen miles from Louisville.

1487 GALLAND, ISAAC

[Wrapper title] CHRONICLES OF THE NORTH AMERICAN SAVAGES: CONTAINING SKETCHES OF THEIR ANCIENT AND MODERN HISTORY . . . TOGETHER WITH TOPOGRAPHICAL SKETCHES OF THE COUNTRY WEST OF THE MISSISSIPPI AND NORTH OF THE MISSOURI RIVERS. VOL. I. MAY, 1835. NO. 1 . . . PUBLISHED MONTHLY BY T. H. SHREVE & CO., CINCINNATI.

[1]–16. 20.4 x 14.1 cm. Light blue printed wrappers with title on front wrapper, advertisement on verso of back wrapper; stabbed.

Ref.: Field 308; Pilling 798

Only five numbers in eighty pages were issued of this ambitious project. Field had a complete set as does the Library of Congress and WHi, but of four other sets reported by the *Union Catalog* none had Part 1.

1488 GALLAND, ISAAC

GALLAND'S IOWA EMIGRANT: CONTAINING A MAP, AND GENERAL DESCRIPTIONS OF IOWA TERRITORY. CHILLICOTHE: PRINTED BY WM. C. JONES, 1840.

[1]–32. 21.8 x 12.7 cm. Map: Galland's / Map / of / Iowa / Compiled from the latest / Authorities / By I. Galland / 1840 / [thick and thin rules] / Scale 30 Miles to an Inch / Engraved by J. G. Darby, Akron Ohio. / Entered according to Act of Congress, in the Year 1840, by Isaac Galland, in the Clerk's Office of the District Court of the District of Ohio. / 63 x 48.7 cm. Scale as above. Gray boards, brown cloth backstrip. In a cloth case.

Ref.: *Annals of Iowa* Vol. XII, No. 7, Jan., 1921; Bradford 1825; Howes G22; Mott (*Iowa*) pp. 58–9 see; Sabin 26383

The work was reprinted in *Annals of Iowa* in 1921 with a good sketch of the author's life and a summary of litigation in reference to the Half Breed Tract by B. L. Wicks. The work was reprinted separately at Iowa City in 1950.

1489 GALLAND, ISAAC

VILLAINY EXPOSED! BEING A MINORITY REPORT OF THE BOARD OF TRUSTEES OF THE DESMOINES LAND ASSOCIATION. ALIAS "THE NEW YORK COMPANY." . . .

[1]–[75], [76 blank]. 21.5 x 14 cm. Old yellow wrappers. In a gray cloth case.

Ref.: Howes G23

Kilbourne's *Strictures* . . . , a reply to the above pamphlet, is dated 1850. Presumably *Villainy Exposed!* was published in 1849 or 1850. So far, the place of printing has eluded us; it may have been Keokuk, Fort Madison, Dubuque, Burlington, Davenport, or Muscatine, if it was printed in Iowa.

1490 GALLATIN, EDWARD L.

WHAT LIFE HAS TAUGHT ME . . . DENVER: JNO. FREDERIC, PRINTER.

[i–ii], [1]–215, [216 blank]. 22.4 x 14.2 cm. Portrait. Black cloth.

Prov.: Several manuscript corrections in the text by the author. Inscribed on a front fly-leaf: To, Prof. Francis W. Cragin / "*My New Made friend*" / Hopeing[!] that he may not / see all the mistakes of my / crudeness in Book making, / and take me as I mean, / not, with a learned eye / of criticism / E. L. Gallatin /. And in another hand: (Denver, 1903.) /

Ref.: Howes G32; Wilcox p. 47

Published in 1900.

Gallatin is remembered as the maker of the western Gallatin saddle. Included in his volume of reminiscences is an account of a trip from Denver to Virginia City, Montana, in 1864.

1491 GALLAWAY, WILLIAM C.

AUTOGRAPH LETTER, SIGNED. 1872 February 15, West Point, Nebraska. Two pages, 20.1 x 12.7 cm. To Messrs. Bowen, Hunt and Winslow.

Regarding arrangements for shipping and selling wheat to cover a note due.

The letter is written on a printed letterhead of the writer, comprising four pages. Page [4] is headed: Leading Business Houses / of / West Point, Nebraska. / [double rule] / [three columns]. The two outer columns list the business firms and the centre column carries a description of West Point.

1492 GALT, JOHN M.

POLITICAL ESSAYS.

[1]–38, [39–40 blank]. 21.6 x 13.8 cm. Glazed cream printed wrappers with title as above on front wrapper between thick and thin and thin and thick rules.

Ref.: Howes G51; Sabin 26460

The pamphlet was printed at Williamsburg, Virginia, in 1852. It comprises: The Annexation of Texas. / Part I. /, pages [3]–11, Part II, pages 12–20, and: The Future of Democracy. /, pages 21–38. The first two parts are signed: G. / and are dated April 10, 1844, and April 26, 1844, respectively; the third part is signed: A Voice from Virginia. / Williamsburg, Va., Nov., 1852. /

1493 GALVAO, ANTONIO

THE DISCOVERIES OF THE WORLD FROM THEIR FIRST ORIGINALL UNTO THE YEERE OF OUR LORD 1555 ... LONDON: G. BISHOP, 1601.

[A]–O⁴. [i–xii], 1–97, [98 blank]. 17.4 x 13 cm. Contemporary calf, red sprinkled edges. Rebacked, lower portion of final leaf (blank) torn off, trimmed close, touching some headlines.

Prov.: Signatures inside front cover and on verso of last leaf: Hen Ch Howard / and J S H / Howard / Howard /.

Ref.: Church 323; JCB II, pt. 1, p. 9; Sabin 26469; STC 11543

First English Edition.

The worke, though small in bulke, containeth so much rare and profitable matter as I know not where to seeke the like, within so narrow and streite a compasse.—Hakluyt (Preface)

Editions: [Lisbon, 1563.]

1494 GALVESTON BAY AND TEXAS LAND COMPANY

ADDRESS TO THE READER OF THE DOCUMENTS RELATING TO THE GALVESTON BAY & TEXAS LAND COMPANY, WHICH ARE CONTAINED IN THE APPENDIX. NEW-YORK: PRINTED BY G. F. HOPKINS & SON, JANUARY 1, 1831.

[1]–[38], [39–40 blank]. 22.9 x 14.9 cm. Stabbed, unbound.

Ref.: Howes S1137; Rader 1521; Sabin 26474; Streeter 1123

Prov.: Inscribed on title-page: B Lindsey Sr / Editor of the Mercury / New Bedford / Massachusetts /, and at the foot of the page: From C S Swift- /.

The Appendix, compiled by William H. Sumner, is not present.

1495 GALVESTON BAY AND TEXAS LAND COMPANY

[Broadside] THE GALVESTON BAY AND TEXAS LAND COMPANY. NOTICE. THE ANNUAL MEETING OF THE SHAREHOLDERS OF THE GALVESTON BAY AND TEXAS LAND COMPANY ... WILL BE HELD AT ... THE CITY OF NEW YORK, ON THE FIRST MONDAY OF NOVEMBER NEXT ... DATED AT NEW YORK, THE 15TH DAY OF AUGUST, 1835 ... SECRETARY.

Broadside, 24.4 x 20.5 cm. Text, 6.2 x 13.1 cm.

Ref.:

Manuscript address and stamped postmark on verso: Mr. Duncan P. Campbell / New York /.

1496 GALVESTON BAY AND TEXAS LAND COMPANY

[Broadside] ... GALVESTON BAY AND TEXAS LAND COMPANY. THIS CERTIFIES, THAT ... ENTITLED TO SHARE IN THE ESTATE AND FUNDS OF THE GALVESTON BAY AND TEXAS LAND COMPANY ... DATED IN THE CITY OF NEW-YORK, THE ... YEAR OF OUR LORD ONE THOUSAND EIGHT HUNDRED AND ... TRUSTEES ... G. F. HOPKINS & SON, PRINTERS.

Broadside, 13.7 x 16.6 cm. Text, 13 x 15.4 cm.

Ref.:

There are two manuscript notes on the verso, each signed by W. H. Willson, relating to a dividend and to the acreage of each share.

1497 GALVESTON BAY AND TEXAS LAND COMPANY

[Broadside] GALVESTON BAY & TEXAS LAND COMPANY ... THIS CERTIFIES ... THAT THE SUBSCRIBERS AS THE TRUSTEES AND ATTORNEYS OF LORENZO DE ZAVALA, JOSEPH VEHLEIN AND DAVID G. BURNET, HAVE GIVEN AND DO HEREBY GIVE ... ONE SITIO, OF LAND ... NEW YORK 16. OCTOBER 1830 ...

Broadside, 31.3 x 19.9 cm. Text, 29.5 x 18.1 cm.

Ref.:

Endorsed on verso: Rodman Moulton /.

See Streeter 1117 for a similar certificate, but for one *labor* of land (177 $\frac{136}{1000}$ acres). Streeter notes that the Company's 1835 map refers to scrip for both *sitio* and *labor*.

1498 GALVEZ, BERNARDO DE

[Caption title] . . . INSTRUCCION FORMADA EN VIRTUD DE REAL ORDEN DE S. M., QUE SE DIRIGE AL SENOR COMANDANTE GENERAL DE PROVINCIAS INTERNAS DON JACOBO UGARTE Y LOYOLA PARA GOBIERNO Y PUNTUAL OBSERVANCIA DE ESTE SUPERIOR GEFE Y DE SUS IMMEDIATOS SUBALTERNOS . . .

A–P². 1–60. 28 x 19.8 cm. Bound with Number 9.

Ref.: Medina (*Mexico*) 7636; Wagner (*SS*) 167a

Signed at the end: México 26 de Agosto de 1784. = / El Conde de Galvez. /

Parts of the *Instruccion* relate to New Mexico, Texas, and Coahuila.

1499 GALVEZ, JOSE DE

ORDENANZAS DE LA REAL RENTA DE LOS NAYPES . . . REIMPRESAS EN MEXICO: EN LA IMPRENTA NUEVA MADRILENA DE DON FELIPE DE ZUNIGA Y ONTIVEROS, ANO DE 1777.

[*]¹, [A]–G². [i–ii], 1–27, [28 blank]. 28 x 19.8 cm. Bound with Number 9.

Ref.: Medina (*Mexico*) 6017

1500 GAMBLE, A.

AUTOGRAPH LETTER, SIGNED. 1826 January 10, St. Louis. One page, 31.4 x 19.8 cm. To Thomas Mather. In Mather Papers.

Enquiring about his plans for joining Sibley in the West. Gamble was secretary of the Santa Fé Road Commission.

1501 GAMBLE, ROBERT J.

THE RIGHT OF THE PEOPLE OF THE TERRITORY TO FORM A STATE GOVERNMENT AND THEIR RELATIONS TO THE FEDERAL GOVERNMENT. ORATION . . . AT YANKTON, DAKOTA, JULY 4TH, 1888. YANKTON: PRESS AND DAKOTAIAN PRINT. 1888.

[1]–11, [12 blank]. 23.5 x 15.5 cm. Illustration on page [2]. Stabbed, unbound.

Ref.: Allen (*Dakota*) 636

1502 [GANILH, ANTHONY]

AMBROSIO DE LETINEZ; OR, THE FIRST TEXIAN NOVEL, EMBRACING A DESCRIPTION OF THE COUNTRIES BORDERING ON THE RIO BRAVO, WITH INCIDENTS OF THE WAR OF INDEPENDENCE. BY A. T. MYRTHE . . . NEW-YORK: PUBLISHED BY CHARLES FRANCIS & CO., 1842.

[i]–viii, [9]–202. [1]–192. 18.8 x 11.7 cm. Two volumes, gray boards, plum cloth backs, printed paper labels, 4.5 x 1.6 cm.

Ref.: Howes G55; Rader 1525 note; Raines

p. 154; Sabin 51651; Streeter 1414; Wright I 1018

Editions: New York, 1838 (*Mexico versus Texas*).

1503 [GANILH, ANTHONY]

MEXICO VERSUS TEXAS, A DESCRIPTIVE NOVEL, MOST OF THE CHARACTERS OF WHICH CONSIST OF LIVING PERSONS. BY A TEXIAN. PHILADELPHIA: N. SIEGFRIED, PRINTER, 1838.

[i]–viii, [9]–348. 18.4 x 11.3 cm. Brown cloth, paper label, 4.2 x 2.4 cm.

Ref.: Clements Library (*Texas*) 19; Howes G55; NYPL *Bull.* Feb., 1937, p. 91; Rader 1525; Sabin 95143, 51651; Streeter 1310; Wright I 1017

First Edition. The hero of this longwinded novel of coincidence is Ambrosio de Letinez, whose mother was Mexican and whose father was a Marylander. The child is reared by his maternal relatives and years later finds himself (now an army captain) fighting Texans. During a skirmish, he rescues a beautiful American maiden from a band of Indians. Then he saves the girl's father from the Goliad Massacre. After a separation, the Mexican captain and the American beauty meet again and discover, by a final odd coincidence, that they are cousins; so they are married.

1504 GARCIA, BARTHOLOME

MANUAL PARA ADMINISTRAR LOS SANTOS SACRAMENTOS DE PENITENCIA, EUCHARISTIA, EXTREMAUNCION, Y MATRIMONIO . . . IMPRESSO . . . EN LA IMPRENTA DE LOS HEREDEROS DE DONA MARIA DE RIVERA, ANO DE 1760.

[*]⁴, **², **¹, A⁴, B–M², N–O⁴, P–S², T⁴. [i–xvi], 1–88, [89–90 blank]. 19.3 x 14.5 cm. Rebound in mottled purple boards with purple morocco backstrip, gilt, sprinkled edges.

Prov.: Bookplate of Joaquin Garcia Icazbalceta.

Ref.: Icazbalceta 32; Medina (*Mexico*) 4621; Rader 1531; Sabin 26560; Streit III 739; Wagner (*SS*) 139

Sabin notes two versions of the imprint, the other being without mention of "los Herederos de Doña Marìa de Rivera." Printed, of course, in Mexico City.

1505 GARDINER, JOHN

[Map] MAP / -OF THE- / BOUNTY LANDS / IN / ILLINOIS TERRITORY / -BY- / JOHN GARDINER / CHIEF CLERK / GEN⸢ᴸ LAND OFFICE / [scroll] / ENTERED ACCORDING TO ACT OF CONGRESS / BY JOHN GARDINER. / DISTRICT OF COLUMBIA / [lower right:] C. SCHWARZ SC: WASH⸢ᴺ /

Map, 47 x 37.7 cm. Scale not given. Unbound, folded to 9.5 x 22 cm.

Prov.: Inscribed on verso: Nº 12 / Archibald Hugh / [underline] /.

Ref.: Phillips (*Maps*) p. 326

At lower left, form for description of land filled in, with manuscript note and signature of John Gardiner. This is the first separate map listed by Phillips for Illinois; he supplies the date 1812–1818.

1506 GARLAND, HAMLIN

BOY LIFE ON THE PRAIRIE. REVISED EDITION . . . NEW YORK: THE MACMILLAN COMPANY, 1908.

[i]–x, 1–423, [424 blank], [425–26 advertisements]. 18.8 x 12.7 cm. Yellow cloth.

Prov.: Inscribed on half-title: for Mrs Walters / from her "star border" / Hamlin Garland /" /. Signed on page [vii]. Manuscript notes in pencil on inside front cover suggest plans for a condensed, expurgated version.

Ref.: Johnson (Blanck) p. 201

Editions: New York, 1899.

1507 GARLAND, HAMLIN

A DAUGHTER OF THE MIDDLE BORDER . . . NEW YORK: THE MACMILLAN COMPANY, 1921.

[i]–[xvi, xvi blank], 1–405, [406 blank]. 19 x 13 cm. Eight illustrations listed. Black pictorial cloth, fore and lower edges roughly trimmed.

Prov.: Inscribed on front endleaf: With the best wishes / of the Writer / Hamlin Garland / " / New York City / 1924. / Inscribed on half-title: This is Vol. II / of / A Son of the Middle Border / Hamlin Garland / " /.

Ref.: Johnson (Blanck) p. 201

1508 GARLAND, HAMLIN

MAIN-TRAVELLED ROADS. SIX MISSISSIPPI VALLEY STORIES . . . BOSTON: ARENA PUBLISHING COMPANY, 1891.

[1]–260. 19.2 x 13.3 cm. Cream printed wrappers with title on front wrapper in blue and red, advertisements on inside of wrappers, uncut. Strip of heavy paper pasted to verso of title-leaf and recto of back wrapper.

Ref.: Johnson (Blanck) p. 200

On pages [4–5] there are three original watercolor vignettes, unsigned.

1509 GARLAND, HAMLIN

THE SAME. [1]–260, [261–64 advertisements]. 19.5 x 13 cm. Portrait. Maroon cloth, title in gilt on front cover and backstrip.

Ref.: Johnson (Blanck) p. 200

The preliminaries are arranged differently from the copy in wrappers: title, copyright notice on verso; Contents, verso blank; dedication, verso blank; Acknowledgement, note on verso.

1510 GARLAND, HAMLIN

A PIONEER MOTHER . . . CHICAGO: THE BOOKFELLOWS, 1922.*

[1]–21, [22 blank]. 20.6 x 14 cm. Tan printed wrappers, uncut. In a red cloth case.

Ref.: Johnson (Blanck) p. 202

Limited to 500 copies.

1511 GARLAND, HAMLIN

A SON OF THE MIDDLE BORDER . . . NEW YORK: THE MACMILLAN COMPANY, 1923.

[i]–[x, x blank], 1–467, [468 blank]. 19 x 12.9 cm. Six illustrations listed. Black pictorial cloth, fore and lower edges uncut.

Prov.: Inscribed on front endleaf: A Son of a Middle Border / is an autobiographic / account of the pioneer / experiences of several / families. The author / is but the annalist. / Hamlin Garland / New York City / 1924 / [double underline] /.

Ref.: Johnson (Blanck) p. 201

Editions: New York, 1917.

1512 GARRARD, LEWIS H.

MEMOIR OF CHARLOTTE CHAMBERS . . . PHILADELPHIA: PRINTED FOR THE AUTHOR, 1856.

[i]–[xii, xii blank], [i]–lx, [1]–135, [136 blank]. 20.9 x 15.1 cm. Brown cloth, blind embossed sides, gilt title on backstrip. In a brown cloth case.

Prov.: Inscribed in pencil on front endleaf: To / Mrs. Maj Biddle / With compliments of / Lew H. Garrard / Paris '56 /. With bookplate of Neva and C. Guy Littell.

Ref.: Howes G69; Thomson 440

Consists largely of letters, relating to the early settlement of southern Ohio, written by Mrs. Chambers from her Cincinnati home, 1797–1821.—Howes

1513 GARRARD, LEWIS H.

WAH-TO-YAH, AND THE TAOS TRAIL; OR, PRAIRIE TRAVEL AND SCALP DANCES . . . CINCINNATI: PUBLISHED BY H. W. DERBY & CO., 1850.

[i]–[viii, viii blank], [1]–349, [350 blank]. (Page 269 mispaginated 26.) 18.4 x 12.5 cm. Black cloth, blind embossed sides, title in gilt on backstrip. Bookplate removed from inner front cover.

Ref.: Howes G70; Jones 1239; Rader 1538; Sabin 26687; Wagner-Camp 182

An important Southwest book by a perceptive observer and a thoroughly captivating writer. Edward Eberstadt often recommended this work as the first book that collectors should read about the Southwest.

1514 GARRETT, LEWIS

RECOLLECTIONS OF THE WEST . . . NASHVILLE: PRINTED AT THE WESTERN METHODIST OFFICE, 1834.

[i]–iv, [5]–240. 12.1 x 7.2 cm. Yellow printed boards, calf backstrip, with title on front cover. In a tan cloth case.

Ref.: AII (*Tennessee*) 535; Howes G72; Rusk I p. 48 note; Sabin 26698

This is an excessively rare book and an important one. In addition to general descriptions of frontier life in Kentucky and Tennessee there are good reports of the Battle of Nickajack and Lieutenant Snoddie's battle, both written by the Rev. James Orwin.—EDG

1515 GARRETT, PATRICK F.

THE AUTHENTIC LIFE OF BILLY, THE KID, THE NOTED DESPERADO OF THE SOUTHWEST, WHOSE DEEDS OF DARING AND BLOOD MADE HIS NAME A TERROR IN NEW MEXICO, ARIZONA AND NORTHERN MEXICO . . . SANTA FE, NEW MEXICO: NEW MEXICAN PRINTING AND PUBLISHING CO., 1882.

[1]–137, [138 blank]. (Pages 113–128 mispaginated 121–136.) 21.6 x 14.2 cm. Six illustrations. Blue pictorial wrappers with title on front cover, portrait on verso of back wrapper, advertisements on recto. In a blue half morocco case.

Ref.: Adams 407; Dykes 13; Howes G73; Jones 1621; Rader 1541; Saunders 2916

An errata slip, 2.8 x 13.5 cm., is tipped to the foot of page 121.

To one degree or another, all books about Billy the Kid are controversial; Garrett's work is no exception. Still, it ranks as one of the key accounts. William A. Keleher, in *The Fabulous Frontier*, claims that Garrett's companion Marshall Ashmun Upson wrote the book for Garrett.

1516 GASS, PATRICK

A JOURNAL OF THE VOYAGES AND TRAVELS OF A CORPS OF DISCOVERY, UNDER THE COMMAND OF CAPT. LEWIS AND CAPT. CLARKE[!] . . . PITTSBURGH, PRINTED BY ZADOK CRAMER, 1807.

A–Y⁶. [i]–[x], [11]–262, [263–64 blank]. 17.1 x 10.1 cm. Contemporary marbled boards, sheep back. Lacks front fly-leaf.

Ref.: Bradford 1841; Howes G77; Jones 717; Matthews p. 206; Sabin 26741; Smith 3465; Wagner-Camp 6

1517 GASS, PATRICK

THE SAME . . . LONDON: RE-PRINTED FOR J. G. BUDD, 1808.

[*]⁸, [A]², B–BB⁸. 5–8, [1]–4, 13–16, 9–12 advertisements dated on page [1] March, 1815, [i]–iv, [1]–381, [382 blank], [383–84 advertisements]. 22.5 x 14.1 cm. Gray boards with white paper backstrip, printed paper label, 9 x 4 cm., uncut. In a red cloth case.

Ref.: Bradford 1841; Field 595; Howes G77; Sabin 26741; Smith 3466; Staton & Tremaine 791; Wagner-Camp 6

1518 GASS, PATRICK

THE SAME . . . PHILADELPHIA: PRINTED FOR MATHEW CAREY, 1810.

A–Y⁶. (Lacks final leaf, a blank.) [i]–[x], [11]–262. 17.1 x 10.6 cm. Six plates. Rebound in green half morocco, gilt top.

Ref.: Bradford 1841; Howes G77; Sabin 26741; Smith 3467; Wagner-Camp 6

1519 GASS, PATRICK

VOYAGE DES CAPITAINES LEWIS ET CLARKE . . . PARIS: CHEZ ARTHUS-BERTRAND, 1810.

[*]⁸, [**]¹, 1–27⁸, 28⁶. [i]–xviii, [1]–443, [444 blank]. 19.4 x 12.1 cm. Folding map: Carte / Pour servir au Voyages / des Cap^es Lewis et Clarke, / à l'Océan Pacifique. / [lower left:] Gravé par J. B. Tardieu. / 24.1 x 19.5 cm. No scale given. Contemporary marbled boards, calf backstrip and corners, backstrip gilt, red leather label, red edges.

Prov.: Inscribed on a fly-leaf in pencil: To Everett / from / Zoë /.

Ref.: Bradford 1842; Howes G77; Sabin 26742; Smith 3470; Wagner-Camp 6

1520 GASS, PATRICK

JOURNAL OF THE VOYAGES AND TRAVELS OF A CORPS OF DISCOVERY, UNDER THE COMMAND OF CAPT. LEWIS AND CAPT. CLARKE . . . PHILADELPHIA: PRINTED FOR MATHEW CAREY, 1811.

A–Y⁶. [i]–[x], [11]–262, [263–64 blank]. 17.1 x 10.2 cm. Six plates. Contemporary mottled calf, red leather label on backstrip.

Ref.: Bradford 1841; Howes G77; Sabin 26741; Smith 3468; Wagner-Camp 6

1521 GASS, PATRICK

THE SAME . . . PHILADELPHIA: PRINTED FOR MATHEW CAREY, 1812.

A–Y⁶. [i]–x, [11]–262, [263–64 blank]. 17.6 x 10.5 cm. Six plates and folding map: Louisiana. / 19.2 x 14.5 cm. No scale given. Contemporary calf, red leather label on backstrip, stamped in gilt. Part of front fly-leaf torn off.

Ref.: Bradford 1841; Field 597; Howes G77; Sabin 26741; Wagner-Camp 6

1522 GASS, PATRICK

THE SAME . . . DAYTON: PUBLISHED BY ELLS, CLAFLIN, & CO., 1847.

[i]–viii, [9]–238, [239–40 advertisements]. 17.6 x 10.8 cm. 15 illustrations and two portraits. Contemporary mottled calf, red leather label on backstrip stamped in gilt.

Ref.: Bradford 1841; Sabin 26741; Smith 3469; Wagner-Camp 6

1523 GATEWOOD, CHARLES B.

[Caption title] LIEUTENANT CHARLES B. GATE-WOOD . . . AND THE SURRENDER OF GERONIMO. (COMPILED BY MAJOR C. B. GATEWOOD . . .) COPYRIGHTED, 1929 . . .

[1–2 blank], 3–19, [20 blank]. 23.3 x 15.5 cm. Stapled into white printed wrappers, with typed label.

Ref.:
Extract from *Proceedings of the Annual Meeting and Dinner of the Order of Indian Wars of the United States* . . . 1929.

1524 GAUSE, HARRY T.

A DETAILED DESCRIPTION OF THE SCENES AND INCI-DENTS CONNECTED WITH A TRIP THROUGH THE MOUNTAINS AND PARKS OF COLORADO, AS ACCOM-PLISHED BY H. B. B. STAPLER, AND HARRY T. GAUSE. JULY 21—AUGUST 20, 1871.

[i]–xii, [13]–205, [206 blank]. 19 x 13.9 cm. Green cloth.

Prov.: Printed presentation leaf (pages [iii–iv]) filled in to Lillie Kline and signed by Harry T. Gause.

Ref.: Howes G83; Wilcox p. 49
Published at Wilmington, Delaware, 1871.

1525 GAY, FREDERICK A.

[Wrapper title] . . . SKETCHES OF CALIFORNIA. AN ACCOUNT OF THE LIFE, MANNERS AND CUSTOMS OF THE INHABITANTS . . . ALSO INTERESTING INFOR-MATION IN RELATION TO THE CANCHALAGUA, A CALIFORNIA PLANT OF RARE MEDICINAL VIRTUES.

[1]–16. 21.8 x 13.7 cm. Yellow printed wrappers with title on front wrapper, advertisements on verso of front and recto and verso of back wrapper. In a green cloth case.

Ref.: Cowan pp. 230–31
Cowan states the pamphlet was printed in New York in 1848.
Said to be the first work printed wherein the attention of the world was directed to a natural product of California.—EDG

1526 GAYARRE, CHARLES E. A.

[Wrapper title] A SKETCH OF GENERAL JACKSON: BY HIMSELF. NEW ORLEANS: PRINTED BY E. C. WHARTON, 1857.

[1]–21, [22–4 blank]. 21.2 x 13.3 cm. Cream printed wrappers with title on front wrapper.

Ref.: Sabin 26797 note

1527 GAYLORD, JOHN

[Broadside] THE PETTICOAT CHIEF . . . PLANO, ILL., MAY 19, 1865.

Broadside, 24 x 20.1 cm. Text. 19.3 x 14.5 cm.
The subject is, of course, Jefferson Davis, the style "poetical."

1528 GAZETA DE MEXICO

[Caption title] NUM. 14. 105. GAZETA DE MEXICO. DESDE PRIMERO, HASTA FIN DE HENERO DE 1729 . . .*

O–B⁴. 105–200. 19.2 x 14.3 cm. Rebound in new yellow pulled paste paper, blue paper label.

Ref.:
Complete for the year 1729, issued monthly. Included among the entries are news items from Zacatecas and Florida.

1529 GAZETTE, THE

[Newspaper] THE GAZETTE. VOL. 1.] MONTEREY, MEXICO JAN. 1, 1848. [NO. XXVII . . .

[1–4]. 32.2 x 22 cm. Unbound.

Ref.:
The Gazette was one of the amateur newspapers issued by the troops during the Mexican War.

1530 GAZLAY, DAVID M.

GAZLAY'S SAN FRANCISCO BUSINESS DIRECTORY FOR 1861 . . . SAN FRANCISCO: COMMERCIAL BOOK AND JOB STEAM PRESSES.

[1a]–32a, [33]–184, [185a–188a], 1b–[48b]. (Pages [1a, 48b] attached to inner front and back covers, seven sets of four colored leaves inserted as additional "a" leaves, numerous mispaginations.) Map: Map / of the City of / San Francisco / Published by / Britton & Rey / Lithographers. / Montgomery St. Cor. of Comml Sts / San Francisco. / 33 x 38.5 cm. Scale: about 500 varas to one inch. Advertisement on verso. Black cloth, gilt stamped with title and advertisements.

Ref.: Blumann & Thomas 3968; Greenwood 1539
All a and b pages carry advertisements. The collation in Greenwood differs somewhat: 179. [47] p.

1531 [GEARY, EDWARD R.]

[Caption title] . . . DEPREDATIONS AND MASSACRE BY THE SNAKE RIVER INDIANS . . . A REPORT OF THE COMMISSIONER OF INDIAN AFFAIRS RELATIVE TO THE INDIAN DEPREDATIONS COMMITTED IN THE

STATE OF OREGON AND TERRITORY OF WASHINGTON, AND THE MASSACRE OF EMIGRANTS BY THE SNAKE RIVER INDIANS . . .

[1]–16. 22.3 x 14.4 cm. Rebound in new red cloth.
Ref.: Wagner-Camp 373
36th Congress, 2nd Session, House, Executive Document No. 46, Serial 1049. [Washington, 1861.]

1532 GEBOW, JOSEPH A.

A VOCABULARY OF THE SNAKE OR SHOSHONE DIALECT. G. S. L. CITY, U. T.: PRINTED AT THE OFFICE OF THE "VALLEY TAN," 1859.

[1]–16. Title-leaf: 20.9 x 12.7 cm. Text: 22.3 x 12.7 cm. Stabbed, unbound, uncut.
Ref.:
This is apparently the first imprint from Salt Lake City issued by a Gentile press. It is the earliest edition of the Gebow *Vocabulary.*

1533 GEBOW, JOSEPH A.

A VOCABULARY OF THE SNAKE, OR, SHO-SHO-NAY DIALECT . . . GREEN RIVER CITY, WG. TER.: FREEMAN & BRO., 1868.

[1]–24. 19.8 x 13 cm. Blue-green printed wrappers with title on front wrapper. Repaired, wrappers silked. In a tan cloth case.
Prov.: Inscribed on front wrapper by J. E. Johnson: This puff (?) pamphlet pub. by / ["P]ress on Wheels," to be resur/[r]ected as Frontier Phoenix / [a]t Brigham City Utah /.
Ref.: AII (*Wyoming*) 2; Butler (*Shoshone*) 2; McMurtrie (*Wyoming*) p. 48; Pilling 1487
The inscription on the front wrapper is slightly erroneous. Freeman's press became the *Frontier Index.*
Laid in is an Autograph Letter signed by J. E. Johnson. 1870 February 21, St. George, Utah. Two pages, 23 x 14.2 cm. to H. B. Dawson. Regarding the present pamphlet.

1534 [GEFFS, IRVIN]

THE FIRST EIGHT MONTHS OF OKLAHOMA CITY. BY BUNKY. OKLAHOMA CITY: THE McMASTER PRINTING COMPANY, 1890.

[1]–110, [111–12 blank]. 21.6 x 14.8 cm. Tan printed wrappers with title on front wrapper.
Ref.: Foreman p. 257; Hargrett (*Oklahoma*) 709; Howes G93
The name of the author is variously given as Goffe, Jeffs, Jeff, and Geffs. The last is probably correct.

1535 GEM, A

A GEM. "THE CITY OF THE PLAINS." ABILENE. THE CENTRE OF THE "GOLDEN BELT." BURLINGTON, IOWA: BURDETTE COMPANY, 1887.

[1]–[64]. 15.3 x 11.1 cm. Buff printed wrappers with title on front wrapper, text on verso of front and recto of back wrapper, advertisement on verso of back wrapper.
Ref.:

1536 GEMMELL, JOHN

[Map] CHICAGO / LITH. & PUBLISHED BY / JOHN GEMMELL, / 132 LAKE STREET. / [decorative rule] / 1858. /

Map, 32.7 x 27 cm. Scale: 1/2 mile to one inch.
Ref.:
A manuscript note at the top reads: City limits have extended about one mile on each side since this map was issued. / On the face of the map, one spot is marked x and another 2; these are accompanied by manuscript notes: 2 office / x B's boarding House /.

1537 GENERAL SHERIDAN'S SQUAW SPY . . .

GENERAL SHERIDAN'S SQUAW SPY AND MRS. CLARA BLYNN'S CAPTIVITY AMONG THE WILD INDIANS OF THE PRAIRIES. A THRILLING NARRATIVE OF THE DARING EXPLOITS AND HAIR-BREADTH ESCAPES OF VIROQUA, THE BETROTHED BRIDE OF MENOTI, A YOUNG CHIEF OF THE OSAGE TRIBE OF WILD INDIANS OF THE PRAIRIES; AND HER VALUABLE SERVICES TO THE WHITES . . . CAPTURE, SUFFERINGS AND DEATH OF THE LOVELY MRS. CLARA BLYNN AND HER LITTLE BOY WILLIE, WHO WERE TAKEN PRISONERS AT SAND CREEK BY THE FEROCIOUS KIOWAH CHIEF, SANTANA, AND BRUTALLY MURDERED BY HIM, WITHIN SIGHT OF THE DRAGOONS SENT BY GENERAL SHERIDAN TO RESCUE THEM. THIS NARRATIVE WILL BRING TEARS TO EVERY EYE. PHILADELPHIA: PUBLISHED BY THE CO-OPERATIVE PUBLISHING HOUSE, 1869.

[17]–78, [79 portrait], [80 blank], [81–2 advertisements]. 23 x 14.5 cm. Five illustrations, unlisted. Colored pictorial wrappers with title on front wrapper, advertisement on verso of back wrapper. In a board case.
Ref.: Ayer 59a; Howes S398
"Two utterly incredible narratives."—Howes. A German edition issued by the same publisher is in the Ayer Collection.
"Ugh! she my white squaw! She make me mad! Me kill her and papoose too!" said the savage chief, fiercely. "You infernal red demon!" exclaimed Gen'l Sheridan, "I'll hang you at daylight tomorrow! I'll teach you to murder innocent women and children!"

1538 GENTLEMAN'S MAGAZINE

THE GENTLEMAN'S MAGAZINE: AND HISTORICAL CHRONICLE. FOR THE YEAR MDCCXC. VOLUME LX. PART THE FIRST . . . LONDON: PRINTED BY JOHN NICHOLS, 1790.

[i]–iv, [1]–[596]. 21 x 13 cm. Illustrations unlisted. Contemporary sprinkled calf backstrip, vellum corners, marbled sides. Worn.

Prov.: Bookplate of Charles Clarke.

Ref.: Wagner: *Peter Pond* . . . [New Haven] 1955, pages 19, 86–96

Pages 197–99 carry: Extract of a Letter from *****, / of Quebec, to a Friend in London. / (See our Plate I.) / Sir, Quebec, Nov. 7, 1789. / . . . The letter is part of a letter from Isaac Ogden to his father, David Ogden, regarding geographical intelligence received from Peter Pond. A copy of the original letter is printed by Wagner.

In the same issue, there is: A Map shewing the communication of the Lakes / and the Rivers between Lake Superior and Slave Lake / in North America. / [upper right:] Gent. Mag. March 1790 . . . p. 197. / 19.7 x 22.8 cm. No scale given. Wagner states of this map: reputed to have been drawn by Pond but more likely to have been drawn from one of Pond's maps.

1539 GEORGE, ISAAC

HEROES AND INCIDENTS OF THE MEXICAN WAR, CONTAINING DONIPHAN'S EXPEDITION . . . GREENS-BURG, PENNSYLVANIA: REVIEW PUBLISHING CO., OCT. 1903.

[1]–296. 19.3 x 13.3 cm. Six plates, unlisted. Dark blue cloth.

Ref.: Howes G108

1540 GEORGIA HISTORICAL SOCIETY

COLLECTIONS OF THE GEORGIA HISTORICAL SO-CIETY. VOLUME III. PART I . . . SAVANNAH: PRINTED FOR THE SOCIETY, MDCCCXLVIII.

[1]–88. 23.7 x 15 cm. Printed cream wrappers.

Ref.: Field 668; Howes H318; Pound, M. B.: *Benjamin Hawkins—Indian Agent* (Athens, Ga., 1851); Sabin 30947; Swanton p. 81 *et passim*

This self-styled Volume III, Part I, of the Georgia Historical Society Collections contains Benjamin Hawkins: "A Sketch of the Creek Country." It was issued at the expense of W. B. Hodgson who signed the section on the Creek Confederacy. It should be considered as an "extra" in the series of the Society, the correct Volume III having been published in 1873.

The prefatory material is poor stuff, but the text of Hawkins' work is highly valuable for he had served for more than thirty years (1785–1816) as an employee of the federal government in its dealings with the Indian tribes. Swanton quotes Hawkins extensively.

1541 GERSTAECKER, FRIEDRICH W. C.

SCENES DE LA VIE CALIFORNIENNE . . . GENEVE: IMPRIMERIE DE JULES-G^{ME} FICK, 1859.

[1]–[261], [262 blank, 263 advertisement, 264 blank]. 22.3 x 14.4 cm. Illustrations unlisted. Bright blue cloth, sides embossed in blind, title stamped in gilt on backstrip, uncut.

Prov.: Bookplate of Robert E. Cowan.

Ref.: Blumann & Thomas 5180; Cowan p. 234; Howes G135; Jones 1409; Sabin 27188

The six illustrations are mounted India paper impressions. The German edition appeared as *Californische Skizzen* . . . in 1856.

1542 GERSTAECKER, FRIEDRICH W. C.

WILD SPORTS IN THE FAR WEST . . . TRANSLATED . . . BY HARRISON WEIR. LONDON: GEO. ROUT-LEDGE & CO., 1854.

[i]–[xii, xii blank], [1]–396. 17.8 x 11 cm. Eight illustrations, unlisted. Contemporary green half calf, dark red leather label, sprinkled edges.

Ref.: Howes G142; Rader 1575; Sabin 27191; Smith 3516

1543 GIBBINS, THOMAS

[Broadside] SALE OF LOTS IN SABINA CITY TEXAS, ON SATURDAY NEXT, AT 10 O'CLOCK A. M. AND 6 O'CLOCK P. M. AT THE AUCTION ROOM OF T. GIB-BINS . . . THOMAS GIBBINS, AUCTIONEER. PORTS-MOUTH, DEC. 14, 1840.

Broadside, 41 x 28.2 cm. Text, 32 x 21 cm.

Ref.:

1544 GIBBONS, JAMES J.

NOTES OF A MISSIONARY PRIEST IN THE ROCKY MOUNTAINS . . . NEW YORK: CHRISTIAN PRESS AS-SOCIATION PUBLISHING COMPANY.

[1]–194. 18.3 x 12 cm. Illustrations unlisted. Green pictorial cloth.

Ref.: Wilcox p. 49

Copyrighted 1898.

Editions: [Chicago] 1898.

1545 GIBBS, ADDISON C.

PRINTED AND MANUSCRIPT DOCUMENT, SIGNED. 1865 March 4, Salem, Oregon. One page, 43.5 x 35 cm.

Commission of Loren L. Williams as Captain in the First Regiment of the Oregon Infantry. Signed also by James E. May and Cyrus A. Head. Inserted in Manuscript Journals of Loren L. Williams, Volume III.

1546 GIBSON, J. WATT

RECOLLECTIONS OF A PIONEER . . .*

[1]–216. 18.7 x 12.3 cm. Portrait. Red cloth.
Ref.: Cowan p. 235; Howes G154; Rader 1578; Smith 3539

Published at St. Joseph, Missouri, 1912.

Gibson made three overland trips, the first being in 1849, when he stayed two years adventuring and mining.

1547 GIBSON, THOMAS

RULES OF PRACTICE OF THE SUPREME COURT AND THE DISTRICT COURT OF THE TERRITORY OF COLORADO, IN LAW AND EQUITY . . . DENVER, COLORADO TERRITORY: REPUBLICAN AND HERALD OFFICE, 1861.

[1]–36. 21.5 x 14 cm. Unbound, removed from bound volume.
Ref.: McMurtrie & Allen (*Colorado*) 22

Several sections of the text have been crossed out, as though this were a working or proof copy. McMurtrie & Allen (*Colorado*) list only a copy in the CoHi which lacks the first four pages.

1548 GIDDINGS, JOSHUA R.

[Caption title] SPEECH OF MR. GIDDINGS, OF OHIO, ON HIS MOTION TO RECONSIDER THE VOTE TAKEN UPON THE FINAL PASSAGE OF THE "BILL FOR THE RELIEF OF OWNERS OF SLAVES LOST ON BOARD THE COMET AND ENCOMIUM." . . . FEBRUARY 13, 1843 . . .

[1]–8. Bound with Number 1084.
Ref.: Sabin 27329
Printed in Washington in 1843.

1549 GIDDINGS, JOSHUA R.

SPEECH OF MR. GIDDINGS, OF OHIO, UPON THE PROPOSITION OF MR. JOHNSON, OF TENNESSEE, TO REDUCE THE ARMY TO THE BASIS OF 1821 . . . JUNE 3, 1842. WASHINGTON: PRINTED AT THE NATIONAL INTELLIGENCER OFFICE, 1842.

[1]–19, [20 blank]. Bound with Number 1084.
Ref.:

1550 GIFT, GEORGE W.

[Wrapper title] SOMETHING ABOUT CALIFORNIA: BEING A DESCRIPTION OF ITS CLIMATE, HEALTH, WEALTH AND RESOURCES, COMPRESSED INTO SMALL COMPASS. MARIN COUNTY: ITS INDUSTRIES, ROADS, APPEARANCE, HEALTH AND POPULATION . . . SAN RAFAEL: PUBLISHED BY THE SAN RAFAEL HERALD, 1875.

[1]–32. 22.4 x 14 cm. Pale salmon wrappers bound into contemporary black cloth, title in gilt on front cover. Lacks back wrapper.

Prov.: Inscribed on front endleaf: Compliments of Ed. Herald. /
Ref.: Blumann & Thomas 1018; Cowan p. 236 see

The editor of the San Rafael *Herald* was John Hittell. Cowan describes a Memphis, 1874, work which may be an earlier edition of this one.

1551 GILLEM, ALVAN C.

[Caption title] REPORT OF COLONEL ALVAN C. GILLEM, 1ST CAVALRY. MODOC WAR, 1873. BENICIA BARRACKS, CAL., JUNE 1, 1874 . . .

[1]–24. 19.2 x 12.6 cm. Unbound. In blue cloth folder.
Ref.: Howes G175
Printed at Benicia Barracks.

Signed at the end on page 24: Alvan C. Gillem, / Colonel 1st Cavalry, / Commander of the late Modoc Expedition, including District of the Lakes. /

Reprinted in 44th Congress, Special Session, Senate, Executive Document No. 1, 1877, Serial 1719.

1552 GILLESPIE, G. L.

[Map] SHEET NO. 3, WESTERN TERRITORIES, / PREPARED BY MAJOR G. L. GILLESPIE, CORPS OF ENG'RS, BVT. LT. COL. U S. A. / JANUARY, 1876. / [lower right:] PUBLISHED BY AUTHORITY OF THE HON. THE SECRETARY OF WAR, / IN THE OFFICE OF THE CHIEF OF ENGINEERS, U. S. ARMY. /

Map, 75.7 x 49.2 cm. Scale: 31.565 miles to one inch. Folded and inserted in Lawton Scrapbook.
Ref.:

Stamped with date of issue in lower right corner: Nov. 9, 1876. Accompanying a letter by Lawton describing, Mackenzie's fight with the Cheyennes at Willow Creek, November 25, 1876. The route of march and location of the battle are marked in manuscript.

1553 GILLETT, JAMES B.

SIX YEARS WITH THE TEXAS RANGERS, 1875 TO 1881 . . . AUSTIN: VAN BOECKMANN-JONES CO.*

[1]–332. 18.6 x 13 cm. Eight illustrations listed. Dark green cloth.
Ref.: Adams 417; Dobie pp. 59–60; Howes G177; Rader 1591

Copyrighted 1921. I regard Gillett as the strongest and straightest of all ranger narrators. He combined in his nature wild restlessness and loyal gentleness. He wrote in sunlight.—Dobie

1554 GILLIAM, ALBERT M.

TRAVELS OVER THE TABLE LANDS AND CORDILLERAS OF MEXICO. DURING THE YEARS 1843 AND 44; INCLUDING A DESCRIPTION OF CALIFORNIA,

THE PRINCIPAL CITIES AND MINING DISTRICTS OF THAT REPUBLIC, AND THE BIOGRAPHIES OF ITURBIDE AND SANTA ANNA . . . PHILADELPHIA: JOHN W. MOORE, 1846.

[i]–[xvi, xvi blank], [17]–455, [456 blank], [i]–viii advertisements. 22.6 x 14.1 cm. Twelve illustrations and maps, unlisted. Map: Map of / Gilliam's Travels / in / Mexico / Including Texas and Part / of the / United States. / [lower right:] Lith. of T. Sinclair 79 S⁰ 3ʳᵈ Sᵗ Philadelphia. / 49.1 x 47.1 cm. No scale indicated. Map: Map / of the / Valley of Mexico / [decorative rule] / Lith of Sinclair. Philᵃ / 20.6 x 18.9 cm. No scale indicated. Map: Map / of / Oregon / Upper & Lower California, / with Part of British-America, / the United States / and / Mexico. / [lower left:] Lith. of T. Sinclair, Philadelphia. / 45.1 x 42.9 cm. No scale indicated. Black cloth, blind embossed sides, gilt title on backstrip.

Ref.: Barrett 975; Bradford 1894; Cowan p. 238; Howes G179; Munk (Alliot) p. 87; Raines p. 94; Sabin 27412

Gilliam was the first United States consul at San Francisco, although he did not take up his position. His work contains considerable material about Oregon, California, Texas, the Texas Revolution, the annexation of Texas, etc.

1555 GILMAN, JAMES B.

[Broadside] TEXAN UNIVERSAL PILLS. PREPARED AFTER A CAREFUL PERSONAL EXAMINATION OF THE DISEASES INCIDENT TO THIS CLIMATE, AND WITH A PARTICULAR REFERENCE TO THE HEALTH, COMFORT, AND HAPPINESS OF THE CITIZENS OF THIS REPUBLIC: BY JAMES B. GILMAN . . . HOUSTON, 1838. THESE PILLS CAN ALWAYS BE OBTAINED OF THE REGULAR APPOINTED AGENTS, AT—GALVESTON, HARRISBURG, HOUSTON, VELASCO, QUINTONIA, BRAZORIA, COLUMBIA, RICHMOND, SAN FELIPE, WASHINGTON, BASTROP, MATAGORDA, &C.

Broadside, 32.3 x 18.5 cm. Text, 28.2 x 13.6 cm.

Ref.: Streeter 233

Also one unopened box of such pills. On top of box is printed: Texan Universal Pills / Good at all times / Price 4 Bitts /. On one side: Particularly adapted to the Climate of Texas /. On other side: Vegetable Pills Prepared by Jas B. Gilman /. Wooden box covered with paper, except bottom.

Mrs. Landauer's copy in the New-York Historical Society is also accompanied by a pill box.

1556 GILPIN, WILLIAM

THE CENTRAL GOLD REGION, THE GRAIN, PASTORAL, AND GOLD REGIONS OF NORTH AMERICA. WITH SOME NEW VIEWS OF ITS PHYSICAL GEOGRAPHY; AND OBSERVATIONS ON THE PACIFIC RAILROAD . . . PHILADELPHIA: SOWER, BARNES & CO., 1860.

[i]–xii, 13–194. 22.6 x 14.1 cm. Six folding maps: Gilpin's / Hydrographic Map of / North America / Sower, Barnes & Cᵒ / Philᵃ / [lower left:] Lith of T. S. Wagner 38 Hudson Sᵗ Philᵃ / 20.2 x 26.7 cm. No scale given. (2) Hydrographic Map / of the / Mountain Formation / of / North America. / [three lines same as map 1]. 28.5 x 20.1 cm. No scale given. (3) Map / of the / World / Exhibiting the Isothermal Zodiac . . . / [3 lines] / Sower, Barnes & Cᵒ / Philᵃ / 19.7 x 38.2 cm. No scale given. (4) Map of the Gold and Silver Region / of Pike's Peak, Sierras San Juan and La Plata. / [at foot:] Sower, Barnes, & Cᵒ / Philᵃ / 28.5 x 25.2 cm. No scale given. (5) Map / of / the South Pass of / North America. / Sower, Barnes, & Cᵒ / Philᵃ / [lower right:] Thoˢ S. Wagner lith, 38 Hudson st. Philadᵃ / 16 x 19.7 cm. No scale given. (6) Map / of the Basin / of the / Mississippi / Sower, Barnes, & Cᵒ / Philᵃ / Lith. of T. S. Wagner 38 Hudson Sᵗ Philᵃ / 20.1 x 31.8 cm. No scale given. Black cloth.

Prov.: Inscribed on front fly-leaf: Hon: Thomas Corwin. / Compliments of / William Gilpin. / March 2.nd 1861. /

Ref.: Howes G192; Munk (Alliot) p. 87; Sabin 27468; Smith 3594; Wagner-Camp 358; Wheat (*Transmississippi*) 1010, 1011

Gilpin crossed the plains the first time to Oregon in 1843. He held some curious ideas which are set out in the present volume.

1557 GILPIN, WILLIAM

SPOKEN AT THE "BRITISH ASSOCIATION OF SCIENCE," LIVERPOOL, SEPTR. 26TH, 1870. NOTES ON COLORADO; AND ITS INSCRIPTION IN THE PHYSICAL GEOGRAPHY OF THE NORTH AMERICAN CONTINENT . . .

[1]–52. 17.8 x 11.9 cm. Buff printed wrappers with title on front wrapper.

Ref.: Bradford 1902; Howes G194; Wilcox p. 50

Published in 1871. On verso of title-page is the following imprint: London: / Printed by Witherby and Co., Middle Row Place, Holborn. /

The front wrapper bears the following printed note: From the Author, on his leaving England March, 1871.

1558 GILPIN COUNTY (Colorado) MINING CERTIFICATE

[Broadsheet] REGISTER PRINT, CENTRAL. TERRITORY OF COLORADO, COUNTY OF GILPIN. KNOW ALL MEN BY THESE PRESENTS, THAT I, AM THE OWNER, . . . WITNESS: . . .

[1–2]. 12.8 x 19.5 cm. Unbound.

Ref.:

Claim No. 6, East, Seger Lode, Gregory District. Printed and manuscript docket on verso dated October 14, 1864. Cancelled sepia Internal Revenue stamp.

The following similar documents are signed variously by Nelson Plumb, Jno. Kip, Jas. H. Reed, Bela S. Buell, S. J. Lorah, F. I. Carr, Jno. R. Cleaveland, W. W. Tiffany, and others. The claims lie in Gregory District (Seger Lode), Russell Gulch, Pleasant Valley (Elephant Lode), Illinois Central District (Ulyses[!] Lode and Great Western Lode), Russell District (Ord, Brooklyn, New York City & County, and Sidney Lodes), Enterprise District (De Soto Lode).

1559 GILPIN COUNTY (Colorado) MINING CERTIFICATE

ANOTHER COPY, recorded same date. Claim No. 7, East, Seger Lode, Gregory District.

1560 GILPIN COUNTY (Colorado) MINING CERTIFICATE

ANOTHER COPY, recorded March 7, 1865 (year changed in manuscript). Claim No. 9, East, Elephant Lode, Russell Gulch, Pleasant Valley.

1561 GILPIN COUNTY (Colorado) MINING CERTIFICATE

ANOTHER COPY, recorded May 25, 1865 (year printed). Claims Nos. 12, 13, 14, West, Ulyses[!] Lode, Illinois Central District.

1562 GILPIN COUNTY (Colorado) MINING CERTIFICATE

ANOTHER COPY, recorded June 8, 1865. Claim No. 5, East, Great Eastern Lode, Illinois Central District.

1563 GILPIN COUNTY (Colorado) MINING CERTIFICATE

ANOTHER COPY, recorded July 3, 1865. Claims Nos. 6, 7, East, Ord Lode, Russell District.

1564 GILPIN COUNTY (Colorado) MINING CERTIFICATE

ANOTHER COPY, recorded July 5, 1865. Claim No. 8, East, De Soto Lode, Enterprise District.

1565 GILPIN COUNTY (Colorado) MINING CERTIFICATE

ANOTHER COPY, recorded August 10, 1865. Claim No. 4, East, Sidney Lode, Gregory District.

1566 GILPIN COUNTY (Colorado) MINING CERTIFICATE

ANOTHER COPY, recorded November 3, 1865. Claims Nos. 6, 7, West, Brooklyn Lode, Gregory District.

1567 GILPIN COUNTY (Colorado) MINING CERTIFICATE

ANOTHER COPY, recorded same date, numeral in date supplied in manuscript. Claims Nos. 3, 4, 5, 6, 7, 8, East, Brooklyn Lode, Gregory District.

1568 GILPIN COUNTY (Colorado) MINING CERTIFICATE

ANOTHER COPY, same as preceding. Claims Nos. 4, 5, 6, 7, West, New York City and County Lode, Gregory District.

1569 GILPIN COUNTY (Colorado) MINING CERTIFICATE

ANOTHER COPY, same as preceding. Claims Nos. 1, 2, 3, 4, 5, 6, 7, 8, East, New York City and County Lode, Gregory District.

These are not identical with McMurtrie & Allen (*Colorado*) 27.

1570 GIVEN, ABRAHAM

OVERLAND TRIP TO CALIFORNIA IN 1850 . . . FRANKFORT, INDIANA.

[1–24]. 21.7 x 14.4 cm. Light brown printed wrappers with title on front wrapper.

Ref.: Howes G199

The pamphlet was printed about 1900. On the last page there is the following note: Mr. Given wrote this account of his trip to California at the request of his daughter, Mrs. Geo. T. Dinwiddie. Mr. Given died December 1st, 1895.

1571 GLASS, E. L. N.

THE HISTORY OF THE TENTH CAVALRY: 1866–1921.

[1]–[145], [146–47 blank, 148 colophon]. 22.4 x 17.2 cm. Illustrations unlisted. Black stamped keratol.

Ref.:

Printed by the Acme Printing Co. at Tucson, Arizona, 1921.

1572 GLEN, JULIA V.

JOHN LYLE AND LYLE FARM. 1925.

[1]–[24]. 21.6 x 14.8 cm. 16 illustrations unlisted. Blue cloth.

Ref.:

Place of printing not indicated.

John Lyle made the overland trip to Oregon in 1845 and immediately upon his arrival in Oregon opened a school—the first in Polk County. The following year it was noticed as Jefferson Institute in the *Oregon Spectator* for February 5, 1846. Lyle was later clerk of the Provisional Court and of the District Court. He died in 1862 while at the mines in Eastern Oregon.—EDG

1573 GLENWOOD, IOWA

GRAND CHRISTMAS BALL. AT THE COURT HOUSE IN GLENWOOD, THURSDAY EVENING, DECEMBER 23, 1858. MR. YOURSELF AND LADY ARE RESPECTFULLY INVITED TO ATTEND A "CHRISTMAS BALL," TO BE GIVEN AT THE COURT HOUSE, IN GLENWOOD, ON THURSDAY EVENING, DECEMBER 23, 1858 . . . REFRESHMENTS WILL BE SERVED IN THE HALL, AT 11 O'CLOCK.

[1–4]. (Pages [2–3] blank.) 8 x 11.5 cm. Unbound.
Ref.:

1574 GLENWOOD COUNTY (Iowa). Board of Supervisors

LAWS GOVERNING THE BOARD OF SUPERVISORS. GLENWOOD: ERA PRINT, 1863.

[1–8]. 18 x 12.7 cm. Unbound, uncut, unopened. Badly worn.
Ref.:

1575 GLISAN, RODNEY

JOURNAL OF ARMY LIFE . . . SAN FRANCISCO: A. L. BANCROFT AND COMPANY, 1874.

[i]–[xii, xii blank], [1]–511, [512 blank]. 22 x 14.3 cm. 21 illustrations and a printed table, unlisted. Green pictorial cloth, title in gilt on front cover and backstrip.
Prov.: Inscribed on front endleaf: To Gen! R. B. Marcy, U. S. Army, / with the regards and compliments of / R Glisan / Feb.y 1875. /
Ref.: Cowan p. 239; Howell 118; Howes G209; Matthews 325; Munk (Alliot) p. 88; Rader 1609; Smith 3611
Marginal notes in pencil seem to be by Marcy. Glisan served in Oklahoma, Washington, and Oregon among other areas.

1576 GOBLE, BENJAMIN

NARRATIVE OF INCIDENTS IN THE LIFE OF AN ILLINOIS PIONEER . . . MOLINE, ILL.: KENNEDY, STEAM BOOK AND JOB PRINTER, 1881.

[1]–35, [36 blank]. 20.5 x 14.7 cm. Green cloth, blind fillets on sides, title in gilt on front cover.
Ref.: Howes G213
Some copies have a portrait of the author mounted on the verso of the title-page.
Goble was born in 1813 in Compton's Fort, Illinois, near Vincennes, Indiana. In 1829 the family removed to Galena and from thence to Moline, where the Gobles were among the earliest settlers. In 1869, Goble crossed Iowa with horse and wagon and explored eastern Nebraska. A very interesting pioneer narrative and a rare one.—EDG

1577 GOFF, LYMAN B.

AN 1862 TRIP TO THE WEST.

[1]–158. 17.7 x 12.6 cm. Ten illustrations. Brown limp morocco, gilt top.
Ref.: Howes G221
Printed at the Pawtucket Boys' Club Press, Pawtucket, R.I., 1926. The author's experiences, told mainly in contemporary letters, included his presence at Fort Abercrombie during the Sioux outbreak.

1578 GOLDEN CITY (Colorado) ASSOCIATION

[Broadside] GOLDEN CITY ASSOCIATION. SHARE NO , THIS IS TO CERTIFY THAT IS THE OWNER . . . ISSUED BY AUTHORITY OF SAID ASSOCIATION, AT THEIR OFFICE IN GOLDEN CITY, THIS THIRTY-FIRST DAY OF MARCH, A. D. EIGHTEEN HUNDRED AND SIXTY . . .

Broadside, 12 x 19.3 cm. Text, 7.5 x 14.8 cm.
Ref.:
Assigned twice and recorded (in manuscript) on the verso, signed by McCleery, Macdonald, and William Davidson.
No place of printing given.

1579 GOLDEN CITY (Colorado) ASSOCIATION

ANOTHER COPY. Share No. 1052. To J. H. Wall and J. F. Kirby.

1580 GOLDEN CITY (Colorado) ASSOCIATION

ANOTHER COPY. Share No. 1029. To J. H. Wall and J. F. Kirby.

1581 GOLDSMITH, OLIVER

OVERLAND IN FORTY-NINE. THE RECOLLECTIONS OF A WOLVERINE RANGER AFTER A LAPSE OF FORTY-SEVEN YEARS . . . DETROIT, MICHIGAN: PUBLISHED BY THE AUTHOR, 1896.

[1]–148. 19 x 13.4 cm. Nine illustrations, unlisted. Yellow glazed boards, tan cloth backstrip, title in red on front cover.
Prov.: Inscribed on verso of front endleaf: To / Ellwood T House / With Compliments of / The Author / Oliver Goldsmith /.
Ref.: Cowan p. 241; Howes G228; Morgan (Pritchard) p. 195 see
The "Wolverine Rangers" went to California via the South Pass in 1849. Goldsmith's narrative supplements the James Pratt letters.

1582 [GONZALEZ DE MENDOZA, JUAN]

THE HISTORIE OF THE GREAT AND MIGHTIE KINGDOME OF CHINA, AND THE SITUATION THEREOF . . .

TRANSLATED OUT OF SPANISH BY R. PARKE . . .
LONDON. PRINTED BY I. WOLFE FOR EDWARD
WHITE . . . 1588.

¶[4], A–Bb[8], Cc[6]. [i–viii], [1]–410, [411–12 blank].
19.3 x 14.5 cm. Contemporary limp vellum,
some edges uncut. Part of backstrip torn away.

Prov.: Inscribed on title-page: Tho Cavendish
Gift / to ffr mylls / ffr mylls his book /. Initials
MC / on leaf before title, signature M. Webb /
on front endleaf, armorial bookplate inside front
cover, numbered 53, numerals 11 on front endleaf and title-page, pencil underlinings and marginal notes throughout, several manuscript notes
in ink, note on page [441]: ane excelent medi-
sine / for any wound in any beast / [15 lines] /.

Ref.: JCB I 378; Church 134; Sabin 27783;
STC 12003; Streit IV 2000; Wagner (*SS*) 7jj

Pages 323–40 carry the Espejo account of his
travels in New Mexico. There is a manuscript
reference to Sir Francis Bacon on page 171.

1583   GOODHUE, JAMES M.

STRUCK A LEAD. AN HISTORICAL TALE OF THE
UPPER LEAD REGION . . . CHICAGO: JOSEPH COVER,
JR., PUBLISHER, 1883.

[1]–115, [116 blank]. 22.4 x 13.4 cm. Dark mustard cloth, title in black on front cover, gilt
vignette.

Ref.:

1584   GOODLANDER, CHARLES W.

MEMOIRS AND RECOLLECTIONS . . . OF THE EARLY
DAYS OF FORT SCOTT . . . FORT SCOTT, KANSAS:
MONITOR PRINTING CO., 1900.

[1]–[147], [148 blank]. 16 x 10.5 cm. 30 illustrations, unlisted. Dark red cloth, gilt title and advertisement on front cover, gilt vignette on back
cover.

Prov.: Inscribed on front endleaf: Compliments / of / The Goodlander /.

Ref.: Howes G240; Jones 1687; Rader 1623
note

Editions: Fort Scott, 1899.

1585   GOODMAN, THOMAS M.

A THRILLING RECORD: FOUNDED ON FACTS AND
OBSERVATIONS OBTAINED DURING TEN DAYS' EX-
PERIENCE WITH COLONEL WILLIAM T. ANDERSON,
(THE NOTORIOUS GUERRILLA CHIEFTAIN,) . . . ED-
ITED AND PREPARED FOR THE PRESS BY CAPT.
HARRY A. HOUSTON. DES MOINES, IOWA: MILLS &
CO., 1868.

[1]–66, [67–72 blank]. 17.6 x 11.2 cm. Vignettes
in text. Green printed wrappers with title on
front wrapper. In a red cloth case.

Ref.: Howes G241

Goodman was one of the few Federal soldiers

who escaped the Centralia massacre. After his
discharge from the Army, he returned to Hawleyville and remained there for a number of
years. He then removed to Clarinda, where he
pursued his trade as a blacksmith. He finally
went to California where he died about 1900.
H. H. Scott, whose name is written in several
places in the pamphlet, I knew well as a boy in
Clarinda. He was a brilliant lawyer. In September, 1957, I had a pleasant visit with his widow,
aged 91, who was still living in Clarinda.—EDG

1586   GOODRICH & SOMERS, Saint Paul, Minnesota

SAINT PAUL CITY DIRECTORY. FOR 1856–7. SAINT
PAUL: GOODRICH & SOMERS, PRINTERS, 1857.

[i]–viii, [1]–[196]. 18.2 x 11.1 cm. Map, lacking
except for a fragment. Tan printed boards, red
leather backstrip, with title on front cover, advertisements on back cover, inner covers, and
endleaves, title in gilt on backstrip.

Ref.: AII (*Minnesota*) 175; Howes S40
First directory of Saint Paul.

1587   GOODWIN, CHARLES C.

AS I REMEMBER THEM . . . SALT LAKE CITY, UTAH:
SALT LAKE COMMERCIAL CLUB, 1913.

[i–ii], [1]–360. 21.9 x 14.1 cm. Portrait. Dark red
morocco, gilt borders, gilt backstrip, gilt edges.

Ref.: Cowan p. 242
Limited to 100 copies of the Edition de Luxe.

1588   GOODWIN, CHARLES C.

THE COMSTOCK CLUB . . . SALT LAKE CITY, UTAH:
TRIBUNE JOB PRINTING COMPANY, 1891.

[i–viii, viii blank], [1]–288. 21.9 x 14.6 cm. Illustrations unlisted. Bright blue leather, gilt, gilt
top.

Prov.: Inscribed on front fly-leaf: Mrs J Lippman / With Kindest Wishes / from / Your Sincere friend / C C Goodwin / [flourish] / Jan
21" 1892 /.

Ref.:
Probably a presentation binding.

1589   GOODWIN, CHARLES C.

POEMS . . . MARYSVILLE: PRINTED AT THE HERALD
OFFICE, 1857.

[1]–[200]. 15.6 x 10.3 cm. Blue cloth, title in gilt
on backstrip. Worn.

Ref.: Cowan p. 242; Greenwood 828
The author also wrote *The Comstock Club.*

1590   GORDON, ELEANOR E.

A LITTLE BIT OF A LONG STORY FOR THE CHILDREN:
JOHN ROBERT, ALICE MARY, LOVETA PEARL,
ELEANOR SUSANNAH . . . 1934 . . .

[1–14], [15–6 blank]. 17.5 x 11.7 cm. Gray printed wrappers.
Ref.:
Probably printed at Humboldt, Iowa. Pioneer reminiscences.

1591 GORDON, ELEANOR E.

THE SECOND CHAPTER OF A LONG STORY . . . 1935.
[1–14, 15–6 blank]. (Pages [1–2] blank.) 17.4 x 11.7 cm. Gray printed wrappers.
Ref.:
Probably printed at Humboldt, Iowa.

1592 GORDON, J. R.

[Caption title] TO THE VOTERS OF BROWN COUNTY. I HAD PROMISED MYSELF THE PLEASURE OF MEETING YOU . . .
[1]–15, [16 blank]. 21 x 13.8 cm. Removed from bound volume, unbound. Rubber stamped pagination, 321–38.
Ref.: Byrd 2918
Neither place nor date of printing is apparent. However, the political attack on King Kerly is signed on page 15: J. R. Gordon. / Mt. Sterling, Ills., October 18th, 1858. /

1593 GORDON, SAMUEL

RECOLLECTIONS OF OLD MILESTOWN . . . MILES CITY, MONTANA, 1918.
[i–ii], [1]–[46]. 22.5 x 15 cm. 18 plates. Gray printed wrappers. In a blue cloth case.
Prov.: Signature on front wrapper: Lewis F. Crawford /.
Ref.: Howes G255; Smith 3688
Lewis F. Crawford wrote *Rekindling Camp Fires* [1926].

1594 [GORDON-MILLER, WILLIAM F.]

RECOLLECTIONS OF THE UNITED STATES ARMY. A SERIES OF THRILLING TALES AND SKETCHES . . . BOSTON: JAMES MUNROE AND COMPANY, 1845.
[i]–[xii], [1]–167, [168 blank]. (Page [i] blank, [ii] frontispiece.) 16 x 10.1 cm. Eight illustrations listed. Dark brown cloth, blind embossed sides, title in gilt on backstrip.
Ref.: Howes G257
At the solicitation of many of his friends, civil and military, the author, contrary to his former intention, has consented to throw these Tales and Sketches before the public, in the form of a book.—Preface

1595 [GORRELL, JOSEPH R.]

[Wrapper title] AFTER FORTY YEARS
[1]–39, [40 blank]. 21.6 x 14.8 cm. Portrait and three illustrations. Dark blue wrappers with title as above on front wrapper.
Ref.: Howes G264

Probably printed at Newton, Iowa, about 1906. Includes accounts of adventures in the Southwest and California.

1596 GOSPEL REFLECTOR, THE

THE GOSPEL REFLECTOR, IN WHICH THE DOCTRINE OF THE CHURCH OF JESUS CHRIST OF LATTER-DAY SAINTS IS SET FORTH AND SCRIPTURE EVIDENCE ADDUCED TO ESTABLISH IT . . . PHILADELPHIA: BROWN, BICKING & GUILBERT, 1841.
[i–iv, iv blank], [1]–316. 22.5 x 14 cm. Brown cloth, blind embossed sides, title in gilt on backstrip.
Ref.: Smith, W. W. p. 282; Woodward 78
Comprises the original twelve parts of the first (and last) year of publication, January 1 to June 15, 1841.

1597 GOSS, C. CHAUCER

BELLEVUE, LARIMER AND SAINT MARY, THEIR HISTORY, LOCATION, DESCRIPTION AND ADVANTAGES . . . BELLEVUE, NEBRASKA: PUBLISHED BY JOHN Q. GOSS, 1859.
[1]–48. 16.6 x 11.1 cm. Map: Map, / describing the Country about the mouth of / the Platte River, with a portion of the great Platte Valley, / Nebraska Territory. / by C. Chaucer Goss. / 15 x 26 cm. No scale given. Yellow printed wrappers with title on front wrapper, advertisements on verso of back wrapper. The final leaf may have been supplied from another copy. In a red cloth case.
Ref.: AII (*Nebraska*) 36; Howes G267
Although this is listed in AII (*Nebraska*) it was probably printed in Chicago. Note the Chicago printer's advertisement on the back wrapper.

1598 [GOSSAGE, JOSEPH B.]

THE QUEST OF ST. BRENDAN . . . 1888.
[1]–43, [44 blank]. (Blank leaf before [1] and after [44].) 18.9 x 14 cm. White printed wrappers, uncut, unopened.
Prov.: Inscribed on front wrapper: Eugene Field, Esqr. / with compliments of / the Writer. / — /.
Ref.: Allen (*Dakota*) 637
The author was publisher of the *Black Hills Journal* at Rapid City. His copyright notice dated from Rapid City in 1888 appears on the verso of the title-page.

1599 GOTTFREDSON, PETER

HISTORY OF INDIAN DEPREDATIONS IN UTAH . . .
[i]–352. 18.7 x 13 cm. Illustrations unlisted. Blue pictorial cloth.

Ref.:

Copyrighted 1919. Printed at Salt Lake City, Utah.

Laid in is: Index to "Depredations in Utah" . . . 1942.

1600 [GOTTFREDSON, PETER]

[Wrapper title] INDEX TO "INDIAN DEPREDATIONS IN UTAH" (PETER GOTTFREDSON). UTAH STATE HISTORICAL SOCIETY, 1942.

[1–28], [27–8 blank]. 18.7 x 13 cm. White printed wrappers.

Ref.:

Laid in Gottfredson: *History of Indian Depredations in Utah* . . . [1919].

1601 GOUGHNOUR, EMANUEL

ACROSS THE PLAINS IN "49" . . .

[i–vi], [1]–[54], [55–6 blank]. (Pages [i–iv] blank.) 16.6 x 10.9 cm. Portrait and one plate. Black leather, lettered in gilt on front cover, blind borders on sides, purple edges, rounded corners. In a red cloth folder.

Prov.: Inscribed in pencil inside front cover: [?]. A. Roberts / Soldiers Home / Columbus Falls / Mont /.

Ref.: Howes G271

Printed at Libertyville or Ottumwa, Iowa, in 1910–11. According to a letter described in the Holliday Catalogue, written by Alberta Goughnour Sell in 1938, only six copies of this work were printed for the Goughnour children.

Goughnour crossed the plains via Fort Laramie and South Pass. His descriptions of mining in California are especially interesting.

1602 GOULD, EMERSON W.

FIFTY YEARS ON THE MISSISSIPPI; OR, GOULD'S HISTORY OF RIVER NAVIGATION . . . SAINT LOUIS: NIXON-JONES PRINTING CO., 1889.

[i]–[xvi, xvi blank], [1]–749, [750 blank, 751 errata, 752 blank]. 22.9 x 14.7 cm. Illustrations unlisted. Green cloth.

Ref.: Howes G273; Rader 1639

1603 GOULDER, WILLIAM A.

REMINISCENCES. INCIDENTS IN THE LIFE OF A PIONEER IN OREGON AND IDAHO . . . BOISE, IDAHO: TIMOTHY REGAN, 1909.*

[1]–376. 18.7 x 13.2 cm. Portrait. Dark blue cloth, gilt top, uncut.

Ref.: Howes G277; Smith 3707

Goulder started west with Benton and Robidoux in 1844. His later adventures in Oregon and Idaho are rather interesting.

1604 GOVE, JESSE A.

THE UTAH EXPEDITION, 1857–1858. LETTERS OF CAPT. JESSE A. GOVE . . . EDITED BY OTIS G. HAMMOND . . . CONCORD, NEW HAMPSHIRE: NEW HAMPSHIRE HISTORICAL SOCIETY, 1928.

[1]–442. 27.9 x 20.4 cm. Five illustrations and illustrations in text. Gray boards, green cloth backstrip, printed paper label, fore and lower edges uncut.

Ref.: Howes G279; Matthews p. 346

Limited to 50 copies on Large Paper.

1605 GOWANLOCK, THERESA, & THERESA DELANEY

TWO MONTHS IN THE CAMP OF BIG BEAR . . . PARKDALE: TIMES OFFICE, 1885.

[1]–9⁸, [10]². [i–iv], [1]–[136], [137–39 advertisements, 140 blank]. 18.2 x 12 cm. 14 illustrations listed. Red cloth.

Ref.: Ayer (*Supp.*) 60; Peel 602

Mrs. Gowanlock and Mrs. Delaney were the sole survivors of the massacre at Frog Lake on the North Saskatchewan in 1885. The two parts are bound in one volume, as issued.

Two copies (one in green cloth and one in dark plum) in the Ayer Collection differ from the present copy. They are probably an earlier printing. The Ayer copies collate as follows: [1]–8⁸, [9]⁸⁻¹. [1]–[136], 139–40, [141–44 advertisements]. (Leaf [9]5 torn out.) In the Ayer copies the signatures appear at the lower left corner; in the Graff copy at the lower right.

1606 GOWER & CO., JAMES H., Iowa City, Iowa

[Broadsheet] . . . JAMES H. GOWER AND JAS. OTIS GOWER, IOWA CITY, IOWA . . . GOWERS' LAND AGENCY, IOWA CITY, IOWA . . . CHARLE W. GOWER, GREENVILLE, MAINE. . . .

Broadsheet, 25.1 x 20.8 cm. Unbound. Printed on blue note paper.

Ref.:

Printed by Sylvester Harrison & Brother, Iowa City, in 1855.

Advertising real estate services.

1607 GRAHAM, FREDERICK U.

NOTES OF A SPORTING EXPEDITION IN THE FAR WEST OF CANADA 1847 . . . LONDON: PRINTED FOR PRIVATE CIRCULATION ONLY, 1898.

[i–viii], [1]–120. 32.4 x 25.1 cm. Seven illustrations and six maps listed. Polished calf, gilt, gilt top, uncut.

Prov.: Inscribed on half-title: Everard Hambro / from / Jane Hermione Graham / [underline] /. Unidentified armorial bookplate.

Ref.:

1608 GRAHAM, JAMES D.

ANNUAL REPORT . . . ON THE IMPROVEMENT OF THE HARBORS OF LAKES MICHIGAN, ST. CLAIR, ERIE, ONTARIO, AND CHAMPLAIN ACCOMPANYING THE DOCUMENTS SENT TO THE 35TH CONGRESS, AT ITS SECOND SESSION . . . WASHINGTON: 1859.

[1]–96. Bound with related materials in contemporary black half calf.

Ref.:

See under ILLINOIS CENTRAL RAILROAD COMPANY.

1609 GRAHAM, JAMES D.

[Caption title] . . . THE REPORT OF LIEUTENANT COLONEL GRAHAM ON THE SUBJECT OF THE BOUNDARY LINE BETWEEN THE UNITED STATES AND MEXICO . . .

[1]–250, [251–52 blank]. 22.4 x 14.3 cm. Two folding maps and one folding Barometric Profile. Map: Mexican Boundary. / Sketch A. / Referred to in Colonel Graham's Report to the Hon: / The Secretary of the Interior, of August 16th 1851. / To face page 178 of Senate Ex. Doc. 121, / 32nd Congress, 1st Session. / [lower right:] P. S. Duval & Co's Steam Lith Pr. Philad^a / 13.2 x 47.3 cm. Scale: 10 miles to an inch. Map: Mexican Boundary / B. / Extract from the / Treaty Map of Disturnell / of 1847. / Referred to in Col: Graham's Report to the Hon: / the Secretary of the Interior of Augst 16th 1851. / To face page 179, Senate Ex: Doc: 121, / 32^d Congress, 1st Session. / P. S. Duval & Co's Lith^y Philad^a. / 22.9 x 39.3 cm. Scale: about 70 miles to an inch. Purplish cloth, blind borders on sides, with title in gilt on front cover.

Ref.: Howes G286; Munk (Alliot) p. 89; Raines p. 96; Wagner-Camp 212

32nd Congress, 1st Session, Senate, Executive Document No. 121, Serial 627. [Washington, 1853.]

1610 GRAHAM, MARTHA MORGAN

THE POLYGAMIST'S VICTIM: OR, THE LIFE EXPERIENCES OF THE AUTHOR DURING A SIX YEARS' RESIDENCE AMONG THE MORMON SAINTS . . . SAN FRANCISCO: WOMEN'S UNION PRINTING OFFICE, 1872.

[1]–72. 19.6 x 12.7 cm. Buff printed wrappers with title on front wrapper. In a blue cloth case.

Ref.: Cowan p. 245; Howes G289

Mrs. Graham, having been deserted by her first husband who had joined the Mormons, married Jesse Morgan in 1849. They left St. Joseph for California via Winter Quarters and arrived in Salt Lake City too late to complete the trip to California that year. Morgan may have been a Mormon, although, if he was, he was rather unenthusiastic about the Church. In de-

fiance of Brigham Young's Second General Epistle requiring Mormons to stay in the Salt Lake City area and raise grains, the Morgans left for California on April 22, 1850, and arrived at Pleasant Valley, California, on July 4. They went from there to Sacramento where they operated the Oak Grove House. On August 14, 1850, Jesse Morgan was killed during a squatter's riot. Shortly thereafter, the Widow Morgan returned to the States via Panama, Havana, and New Orleans. She went again to California by way of the Isthmus, arriving on February 4, 1854. Soon thereafter, she married Graham, but "I had known he was what is called a fast man . . ." and she shortly informed Mr. Graham, "our destinies are separate." About 1862, Mrs. Graham lost the use of her left hand and to help support herself, she edited and published Jesse Morgan's journal of his overland trip. There were 1000 copies printed of the first edition which she peddled from door to door, and she indicates there was a second edition or printing. The later (1875) *Life of Martha Morgan* is textually identical with *The Polygamist's Victim.*—EDG

1611 [GRAHAM, R., JOSHUA PILCHER, & OTHERS]

[Caption title] . . . MR. BENTON, FROM THE COMMITTEE ON INDIAN AFFAIRS, COMMUNICATED THE FOLLOWING DOCUMENTS: . . .

[1]–20. 22.5 x 14.3 cm. Rebound in new red cloth.

Ref.:

18th Congress, 1st Session, Senate, Document No. 56, Serial 91. [Washington, 1824.]

The text comprises principally the evidence of R. Graham and Joshua Pilcher relative to military posts on the upper Missouri River, treaties with the Indians, Indian agencies, and the fur trade.

1612 GRANDFORT, MARIE FONTENAY DE

THE NEW WORLD . . . NEW ORLEANS: PUBLISHED AND PRINTED BY SHERMAN, WHARTON & CO., 1855.

[1]–[145], [146 blank]. 22 x 14 cm. Black cloth, leather label on backstrip.

Ref.: Clark III 322; Howes G196; Monaghan 768b

This little book is a classic of parody and abuse.—Monaghan

1613 GRANGER, GIDEON

AUTOGRAPH DOCUMENT, SIGNED. 1806 October 14, Springfield. Three pages, 33.1 x 18.8 cm. Silked.

An affidavit reporting conversations with William Ely regarding Aaron Burr's plans to separate the Western Territories from the United States. The conversations involved General William Eaton, James Wilkinson, and a number of other associates of Burr. Following Granger's affidavit there is a certificate (in Granger's hand) signed by Matthew Thompson in which he states that the account of the conversation is reported correctly. This is dated October 15, 1806, and is followed by a confirmatory statement written and signed by William Eaton dated October 16.

The fourth page carries a further statement by Gideon Granger, signed, dated October 16, 1806, containing further information about Eaton's attempts to inform the President of Burr's plans. It is this statement particularly to which Eaton referred in his note.

1614 GRANGER, L. C.

[Caption title] REMINISCENCES OF THE TRIAL OF F. A. SPRAGUE AND OTHERS UNDER INDICTMENT FOR THE MURDER OF T. W. MORE . . . PUBLISHED BY REQUEST OF PROSECUTION . . .

[1]–27, [28 blank]. 22.1 x 13.6 cm. Sewn, unbound.

> *Ref.:* Cowan p. 245

The latest date mentioned in the text is November 15, 1878. The trials occurred in Ventura County, California. The pamphlet appears to have been printed from type set for a newspaper article.

On page [28] there is the following statement in manuscript: We have read the Contents of the within / pamphlet and know it contains the truth / — — /. The statement is followed by signatures of nine citizens including two attorneys for the prosecution and the sheriff who made the arrest.

1615 GRANT, J. M.

[Caption title] THREE LETTERS TO THE NEW YORK HERALD, FROM J. M. GRANT, OF UTAH. LETTER I. [FROM THE HERALD OF MARCH 9, 1852.] LETTER OF THE MAYOR OF GREAT SALT LAKE CITY. . . .

[1]–64. Bound with Number 3346.

> *Ref.:* Sabin 28305; Woodward 79

No place of printing or date of publication indicated.

1616 GRANT COUNTY, NEW MEXICO

[Wrapper title] GRANT COUNTY, NEW MEXICO, AND HER MINERAL PROSPECTS . . . DENVER, COLO.: THE TRIBUNE PUBLISHING COMPANY, 1881.

[1]–17, [18 blank]. 22.6 x 14.9 cm. Map: Map / of / Grant Co. / New Mexico. / [lower left:] Mills Eng Co Denver. / 27 x 13 cm. No scale given. Pink printed wrappers with title on front wrapper.

> *Ref.:*

1617 [GRASS VALLEY] DISTRICT, Colorado

[Broadside] MINING DISTRICT. I HEREBY CERTIFY THAT   IS THE OWNER OF ONE HUNDRED FEET IN LENGTH BY FIFTY FEET IN WIDTH ON THE QUARTZ LODE . . . GIVEN UNDER MY HAND THIS DAY OF A. D. 1861. RECORDER . . . 'HERALD' PRINT, DENVER.

Broadside, 10.3 x 19.7 cm. Text, 9.5 x 17.4 cm.

> *Ref.:* McMurtrie & Allen (*Colorado*) 18

"Grass Valley" is written in before the first printed words. "Good for Nothing" is supplied as the name of the lode. The certificate was made out to James Hamilton and the Recorder was William Jack. Endorsed on verso by James Hamilton.

McMurtrie states this form was used in the Empire Mining District.

1618 GRAVES, H. A.

ANDREW JACKSON POTTER, THE NOTED PARSON OF THE TEXAN FRONTIER. SIX YEARS OF INDIAN WARFARE IN NEW MEXICO AND ARIZONA . . . NASHVILLE: SOUTHERN METHODIST PUBLISHING HOUSE, 1883.

[1]–471, [472 blank]. 18.2 x 12.1 cm. Portrait. Brown cloth, blind embossed sides, gilt title on backstrip.

> *Ref.:* Howes G321; Raines p. 97

Although the biography of a parson, Graves' volume covers a good deal of non-religious material, including Potter's experiences as a teamster, soldier, etc., from the 1840's to after the Civil War.

Editions: Nashville, 1881, 1882.

1619 GRAVES, PEYTON S.

A SERMON, DELIVERED BEFORE COLUMBUS LODGE, NO. 6, JUNE 24, A. L. 5825 . . . PRINTED AT THE "NATCHEZ NEWSPAPER" OFFICE.

[i–ii], [1]–14. 22.5 x 13.5 cm. Original plain blue wrappers, stabbed.

> *Ref.:*

No other copy has been located. Published in 1825.

1620 GRAVES, RICHARD S.

OKLAHOMA OUTLAWS. A GRAPHIC HISTORY OF THE EARLY DAYS IN OKLAHOMA; THE BANDITS WHO TERRORIZED THE FIRST SETTLERS AND THE MARSHALS WHO FOUGHT THEM TO EXTINCTION . . .

[i–iv], [1]–131, [132 printer's device]. 17.7 x 11.6 cm. Illustrations unlisted. Red printed wrappers with short title and sketches on front wrapper and photograph on back wrapper.

> *Ref.:* Adams 428; Howes G322; Rader 1650

Printed at Oklahoma City. On page 12 the

date of writing is given as 1915. The pamphlet was prepared as publicity for the motion picture "The Passing of the Oklahoma Outlaws." The photographs of dead bandits are rather gruesome.

1621 GRAVES, S. H.

ON THE "WHITE PASS" PAY-ROLL . . . CHICAGO, 1908.

[i]–[viii, viii blank], 9–258. 19.6 x 12.6 cm. 16 illustrations listed. Semi-limp black morocco, gilt top, uncut.

Ref.: Howes G322; *Railway Economics* p. 153; Smith 3751; Wickersham 5495

An uncommon original binding.

1622 GRAVES, S. H.

ANOTHER COPY. Dark blue ribbed cloth, gilt and colors, gilt top, uncut.

1623 GRAVIER, GABRIEL

AUTOGRAPH LETTER, SIGNED. 1874 December 23, Rouen. One page, 20.7 x 13.5 cm. To M. Defrémery.

Laid in Gravier, Gabriel: *Découvertes et Établissements de Cavelier de la Salle* . . . 1870.

1624 GRAVIER, GABRIEL

DECOUVERTES ET ETABLISSEMENTS DE CAVELIER DE LA SALLE DE ROUEN DANS L'AMERIQUE DU NORD . . . ROUEN: LEON DESHAYS . . . 1870.

[I]–[XII], 1–[412]. 22.4 x 15.9 cm. Illustrations and maps unlisted.

BOUND WITH:

CAVELIER DE LA SALLE DE ROUEN . . . PARIS: MAISONNEUVE ET Cᴱ, EDITEURS, 1871.

[i–iv], [1]–123, [124 blank]. Portrait. Two volumes bound together, marbled boards, blue morocco backstrip, gilt.

Prov.: Inscribed on each half-title: A Monsieur Defrémery, de l'Institut de France, / hommage respectueux. / Gabriel Gravier /.

Ref.: Howes G325; Sabin 28358

The second work bound in is unnoted by either Howes or Sabin.

Laid in is an Autograph Letter, signed by the author. 1874 December 23, Rouen. One page, 20.7 x 13.5 cm. To M. Defrémery.

Editions: Paris, 1870.

1625 GRAY, ANDREW B.

[Caption title] . . . A REPORT AND MAP OF A. B. GRAY, RELATIVE TO THE MEXICAN BOUNDARY . . .

[1]–50. 22.5 x 14.3 cm. Two maps. Map: That Part of / Disturnell's Treaty Map / in the Vicinity of the Rio Grande / and Southern Boundary of New-Mexico / as referred to by U. S. Sur-

veyor, / in Communication to Commissioner, / July 25 1851. / [double rule] / [8 lines] / [rule] / Ackerman Lith 379 Broadway N. Y. / [upper right:] Senate Ex 55. 33ᵈ Congress 2ᵈ Session / 22 x 27.5 cm. Scale: about 70 miles to one inch. Map: Map / of the Portion of the Boundary / between the / United States and Mexico, / from the / Pacific Coast to the Junction of the Gila / and Colorado Rivers, / Surveyed under the Direction / of / Hon. John B. Weller U. S. Commissioner; / and the / Rio Gila / from near its Intersection, / with the / Southern Boundary of New Mexico, / Surveyed under the Direction / of / John R. Bartlett Esq. U. S. Commissioner; / All in accordance with the decision of the Joint Commⁿ / and / conformably to the Treaty of Guad. Hidalgo; / Showing also / the Limits of the Territory aquired[!] under the Treaty / negotiated by the Hon. James Gadsden, U. S. Minister / at the City of Mexico, 1854. / From Explorations and Surveys / made / by, and under the direction of Andrew B. Gray / as authorized to be added by the Resolution of the U. S. Senate, / February 19ᵗʰ–1855. / [short swelled rule] / Vide accompanying Report, Senate Ex. Doc. No. 55. 33ʳᵈ–Congress 2ⁿᵈ–Session. / [short rule] / Ackerman Lith. 379 Broadway N. Y. / [upper right:] Senate Ex. 55. 33ᵈ Congress 2ᵈ Session /. 54.6 x 124.7 cm. Scale: 16 miles to one inch. *Inset:* Sketch / of the / Port of San Diego / Surveyed by the U. S. Boundary Commission / in 1849 and 1850. / Hon. John B. Weller U. S. Commissioner. / A. B. Gray, U. S. Surveyor. / Chˢ J. Whiting, Principal Assistant. / 20.8 x 17.1 cm. Scale: about 2 1/2 miles to one inch. Rebound in new red cloth.

Ref.: Howes G330; Munk (Alliot) p. 90; Sabin 28376; Wagner-Camp 254; Wheat (*Transmississippi*) 820*, 821*, 839, 840

33rd Congress, 2nd Session, Senate, Executive Document No. 55, Serial 752. [Washington, 1855.]

1626 GRAY, ANDREW B.

SOUTHERN PACIFIC RAILROAD. SURVEY OF A ROUTE FOR THE SOUTHERN PACIFIC R. R., ON THE 32ND PARALLEL . . . CINCINNATI, O.: WRIGHTSON & CO.'S ("RAILROAD RECORD.") PRINT, 1856.

[1]–110. 21.2 x 13.9 cm. 33 plates and three maps. Map: Preliminary Map / To Accompany Report of A. B. Gray / of the Route of the / Texas Western Railroad / now changed to / Southern Pacific Railroad / Compiled from Explorations by A. B. Gray and Others. / 1856. / Scale of Statute Miles / [diagrammatic scale: 50 miles to one inch] / Middleton, Wallace & Co. Lithogrⁿ, Cincinnati, Ohio. / 61.7 x 96 cm. Map:

The World. Illustrating / the Course of Trade from / Europe to Asia across the / Continent of America. / [lower centre:] Middleton, Wallace & C° Lith^{rs} Cin. O. / 14.3 x 25.3 cm. No scale given. Map: Port of San Diego / Surveyed / by the U. S. Boundary Commission / in 1849–'50 / Hon. J. B. Weller, U. S. Commissioner / A. B. Gray, U. S. Surveyor / Ch^g J. Whiting Principal Assistant / [double rule] / Scale of Statute Miles / [diagrammatic scale: 3 3/4 miles to one inch] / [lower right:] Lith. of J. Bien, 107 Fulton St N.Y. / 16.8 x 11.2 cm. Board sides, black skiver backstrip and corners, front cover stamped in gilt. In a black cloth case.

Ref.: Clements Library (*Texas*) 38; Howes G331; Munk (Alliot) p. 90; Rader 1661; *Railway Economics* p. 272; Raines pp. 97–8; Sabin 28375; Wagner-Camp 275; Wheat (*Transmississippi*) 893

Errata slip, 8.4 x 13.1 cm., before page [5].

This second edition of the survey is preferred to the first, since it contains the fine drawings by Charles Schuchard (a Texan) which add much to the importance of the work. The Texas Western Railroad was a link in one of the three first railroad lines to the Pacific, the Southern Pacific System.

1627 [GRAY, FRANK S.]

"FOR LOVE & BEARS." A DESCRIPTION OF A RECENT HUNTING TRIP WITH A ROMANTIC FINALE . . . BY "JAMES DALY" . . . CHICAGO: FRANK S. GRAY, 1886.

1, 3–139, [140–45 advertisements] LEAVES. 25.4 x 19 cm. Illustrations in text, mounted photograph inserted. Tan printed pictorial wrappers, stapled along top edge, vignette on verso of front and verso of back wrappers, advertisement on recto of back wrapper.

Ref.: Howes D41

A hunting trip in northern Idaho and Oregon during the 1880's provides the background for this curious production.—EDG

The title-page is a facsimile of a manuscript, the text is a facsimile of typewritten matter.

1628 GRAY, JOHN W.

THE LIFE OF JOSEPH BISHOP, THE CELEBRATED OLD PIONEER IN THE FIRST SETTLEMENTS OF MIDDLE TENNESSEE . . . NASHVILLE, TENN.: PUBLISHED BY THE AUTHOR, 1858.

[1]–236, [237 blank, 238–40 advertisements]. 18.1 x 11.8 cm. Black cloth.

Ref.: Howes G338

An amusing and well-done narrative, except for Gray's moralizing. Most of the work is in the form of a dictated autobiography. Gray added the last three chapters.

1629 GRAY, MARTHA

[Broadsheet] MEMORIAL OF MARTHA GRAY, OF BOSTON, WIDOW OF CAPTAIN ROBERT GRAY . . . Broadsheet, 22.8 x 14.5 cm. Removed from bound volume, unbound.

Ref.:

29th Congress, 1st Session, House, Document No. 172, Serial 485. [Washington, 1846.]

1630 GRAY, WILLIAM H.

A HISTORY OF OREGON, 1792–1849, DRAWN FROM PERSONAL OBSERVATION AND AUTHENTIC INFORMATION . . . PORTLAND, OREGON: HARRIS & HOLMAN, 1870.

[1]–624. 22.6 x 14.6 cm. Frontispiece. Black cloth.

Ref.: Bradford 1965; Howell 119; Howes G342; Sabin 28416; Smith 3756

According to Howes, the work is undependable and biased, but, as a product of a pioneer of 1838, cannot be ignored. There is a small errata slip, 7.5 x 14.4 cm., on yellow paper inserted after page 624.

1631 GRAY, WILLIAM H.

THE SAME . . . SAN FRANCISCO: H. H. BANCROFT & CO., 1870.

[i–iv], [1]–707, [708 blank]. (Pages [i–ii] blank.) 27 x 19.7 cm. 21 illustrations, unlisted. Dark blue levant morocco, elaborately gilt tooled, with onlays of red, blue, gray and white morocco borders and coats of arms, doublures of red levant morocco gilt tooled and onlaid with white morocco sprays of roses, cream watered silk endleaves, gilt edges.

Prov.: Lettered in gilt on front cover: Presentation in Memory of W. H. Gray by his Daughter Mrs Caroline A. Kamm.

Ref.: Howes G342; Smith 3758

Although the last date mentioned in the text is 1923, the work may not have been printed until 1925. In addition to the *History*, the volume contains Gray's Journal, a biographical and genealogical sketch and a biographical and genealogical sketch of Jacob Kamm.

1632 GREAT DUTCH FLAT SWINDLE, THE . . .

[Caption title] THE GREAT DUTCH FLAT SWINDLE!! THE CITY OF SAN FRANCISCO DEMANDS JUSTICE! THE MATTER IN CONTROVERSY, AND THE PRESENT STATE OF THE QUESTION. AN ADDRESS TO THE BOARD OF SUPERVISORS, OFFICERS AND PEOPLE OF SAN FRANCISCO: . . .

[1]–[132]. 21.4 x 13.7 cm.

BOUND WITH:

THE PACIFIC RAILROAD. A DEFENSE AGAINST ITS

ENEMIES, WITH REPORT OF THE SUPERVISORS OF PLACER COUNTY, AND REPORT OF MR. MONTANYA, MADE TO THE SUPERVISORS OF THE CITY AND COUNTY OF SAN FRANCISCO. DECEMBER, 1864.

[1]–35, [36 blank]. 21.4 x 13.2 cm. Two volumes bound together, red sheepskin, gilt. Rebacked.

Prov.: Signature on front leaf: E. B. Crocker /.

Ref.: Cowan p. 188 and p. 512 respectively; *Railway Economics* p. 290 (second title)

The first piece was printed in 1864, probably in San Francisco. The fifteen-page appendix is not present. *Railway Economics* p. 291 lists a variant edition. The second piece was printed at San Francisco in 1864.

1633 GREAT WESTERN ALMANAC, THE

THE GREAT WESTERN ALMANAC FOR 1843 PUBLISHED AND SOLD BY JOS. Mc DOWELL, 37 MARKET STREET, PHILADELPHIA.

[1]–[36]. 19.6 x 16 cm. Illustrations unlisted. Removed from bound volume, partially sewn.

Ref.: Wagner-Camp 28 see

Pages 13, 15, 17, 19, 21, and 23 carry an article captioned: From the Louisville Literary News-Letter. / History of a Western Trapper. / By Edmund Flagg. / . . .

This is the famous story of the fight between Hugh Glass and the grizzly bear and of Glass's subsequent adventures. It was printed first in the *Literary News-Letter* of which Flagg was editor, Volume I, No. 41, September 7, 1839. It was reprinted in the *Peoria Register and Northwestern Gazette* for October 19, 1839, and in the *Dubuque Iowa News* for November 2, 1839. Earlier versions of the tale had appeared in the *Port Folio*, March, 1825, the *Missouri Intelligencer*, June, 1825, and the *St. Louis Beacon*, December 2 and 9, 1830 and January 13 and February 17, 1831. Cooke's version of the story appears to have been based on the *St. Louis Beacon* version.—EDG

1634 GREELEY, HORACE

AUTOGRAPH LETTER, SIGNED. 1864 August 1, New York. Two pages, 20.2 x 12.6 cm. To O. D. Cose.

Relating to publication of a book and payment of royalties. Laid in Greeley's *An Overland Journey* . . . 1860.

1635 GREELEY, HORACE

AN OVERLAND JOURNEY, FROM NEW YORK TO SAN FRANCISCO, IN THE SUMMER OF 1859 . . . NEW YORK: C. M. SAXTON, BARKER & CO., 1860.

[1]–386, [1]–10 advertisements. 18.8 x 12.5 cm. Light brown cloth, title in gilt on backstrip.

Ref.: Cowan p. 247; Howes G355; Sabin 28490; Wagner-Camp 359

Laid in is an Autograph Letter, signed by Greeley. 1864 August 1, New York. Regarding payment of royalties on the book.

1636 GREEN, CHARLES R.

GREEN'S HISTORICAL SERIES. EARLY DAYS IN KANSAS ALONG THE SANTA FE TRAIL, IN THE COUNTIES OF DOUGLAS, FRANKLIN, SHAWNEE, OSAGE AND LYON . . . OLATHE, KANSAS: CHARLES R. GREEN, 1912[–1913].*

[1–3], I–V, 3–151, [152 blank]. [1–5], I–V, [1–114], 93–96, [115–22]. [i–iv], 1–68, [69 advertisement, 70 blank]. 20.8 x 15 cm. Three volumes, tan marbled boards with title overprinted on front cover, manuscript labels on backstrips.

Ref.: Jones 1716, 1718; Rader 1665

A strange, amateur production. Numerous pagination irregularities. There were five volumes published, 1912–14.

1637 GREEN, J. S.

SUBSTANCE OF AN ARGUMENT, MADE BY J. S. GREEN, OF MO., BEFORE THE SUPREME COURT, U.S., IN THE CASE CONCERNING THE BOUNDARY LINE, BETWEEN THE STATE OF MISSOURI AND THE STATE OF IOWA. ST. LOUIS: PRINTED AT THE UNION JOB OFFICE, 1849.

[1]–30, [31–2 blank]. 22.7 x 14.5 cm. Tan printed wrappers with title on front wrapper.

Prov.: Stamp of Chicago Historical Society on front wrapper, cancelled.

Ref.: AII (*Missouri*) 599

Below the author's name on the front wrapper there is the following manuscript note: Hes dead—was a latter day Bourbon /. Under this note, in pencil, is the following comment: Fine. We / need more such / E /.

1638 GREEN, JONATHAN H.

GAMBLING UNMASKED! OR THE PERSONAL EXPERIENCE OF J. H. GREEN, THE REFORMED GAMBLER; DESIGNED AS A WARNING TO THE YOUNG MEN OF THIS COUNTRY . . . PHILADELPHIA: G. B. ZIEBER & CO., 1847.

[1–2], [i–ii], [3]–312. 17.5 x 10.8 cm. Illustrations unlisted. Rebound in dark blue morocco, gilt, with a cornucopia spilling out gambling equipment in the centre of each cover, gilt edges.

Ref.: Howes G365; Sabin 28535 note

Green made a good thing out of being a reformed gambler. The earliest version of his work appeared in 1843 and in the following year the present title appeared for the first time. The 1847 edition is considerably enlarged.

Editions: New York, 1843. New York or Philadelphia, 1844.

1639 GREEN, JONATHAN H.

THE LIFE, TRIAL, DEATH, AND CONFESSION OF SAM-
UEL H. CALHOUN, THE SOLDIER-MURDERER . . .
CINCINNATI: PUBLISHED BY THE AUTHOR, 1862.

[i]–xiv, 15–96. 16.3 x 10.6 cm. Two portraits.
Dark brown cloth, blind embossed sides, gilt
title on backstrip.

Ref.: Howes G366; McDade 152; Sabin
28536; Wagner-Camp 381a

Calhoun was a Texas Ranger under McCulloch in 1857, was captured by Indians, and lived
a highly adventurous life.

1640 GREEN, NELSON W.

FIFTEEN YEARS' RESIDENCE WITH THE MORMONS.
WITH STARTLING DISCLOSURES OF THE MYSTERIES
OF POLYGAMY . . . CHICAGO: PHOENIX PUBLISH-
ING COMPANY, 1876.

[i]–xvi, 17–472. (Pages [i–ii] blank.) 18.3 x 12.1
cm. Three illustrations, unlisted. Dark orange
cloth.

Ref.: Howes (1954) 4241; Wagner-Camp 300;
Woodward 82

As for the heroine, Mary Ettie V. Smith, one
cannot read her story and believe she was entirely without blame.—EDG

Editions: New York, 1858, 1859, 1860. Hartford, 1870, 1872.

1641 GREEN, ROWAN

COLORADO COUNTY, TEXAS: ITS HEALTH, CLIMATE,
SOIL, ADVANTAGES AND RESOURCES . . . COLUM-
BUS, TEXAS: PRINTED AT THE OFFICE OF THE COLO-
RADO CITIZEN, 1877.

[1]–18, [19–32 advertisements]. 21.5 x 14 cm.
Gray printed wrappers with title on front wrapper.

Ref.: Carroll p. 33

1642 [GREEN, SAMUEL B.]

[Wrapper title] A PAMPHLET ON EQUAL RIGHTS
AND PRIVILEGES. TO THE PEOPLE OF THE UNITED
STATES. ANDREW COUNTY, MISSOURI. ST. JOSEPH,
MO.: PRINTED AT THE CYCLE OFFICE, 1856.

[1]–24. 21.6 x 14 cm. Blue printed wrappers with
title on front wrapper.

Ref.: Howes G370

Green supported the rights of slaveholders to
their property. Sabin 28558 lists a later edition
only.

1643 GREEN, THOMAS J.

JOURNAL OF THE TEXIAN EXPEDITION AGAINST
MIER; SUBSEQUENT IMPRISONMENT OF THE AU-
THOR; HIS SUFFERINGS, AND FINAL ESCAPE FROM
THE CASTLE OF PEROTE , , , NEW-YORK: HARPER &
BROTHERS, 1845.

[i]–[xvi, xvi blank], [17]–487, [488 blank]. (Pages
[i–ii] blank.) 23.1 x 14.8 cm. 13 illustrations
listed including map: Plan of Mier, / The Texian
Camp / and Attack on the City, / December 25th
& 26th 1842. / [lower centre:] Harper & Brothers,
New York. / [lower right:] Eng^{d} by W. Kemble,
N. Y. / 13.3 x 25.2 cm. No scale given. Dark
olive cloth, blind embossed sides, gilt title on
backstrip.

Ref.: Bradford 1984; Dobie p. 55; Howes
G371; Jones 1104; Rader 1670; Raines p. 98;
Sabin 28562

Green's is one of the most exciting accounts
of the tragic affair of the Texian Expedition. As
a participant Green was able to write a vivid and
terrifying tale. He was particularly bitter toward
Sam Houston and believed Houston was responsible for the deaths of those Americans shot as
brigands.

1644 GREEN, THOMAS J.

LETTER FROM GENERAL THOMAS J. GREEN, OF CALI-
FORNIA, TO HON. ROBERT J. WALKER, UPON THE
SUBJECT OF PACIFIC RAILROAD. SEPTEMBER 19,
1853. NEW-YORK: SIBELLS & NAIGNE, 1853.

[1]–12. 21.7 x 13.8 cm. Yellow printed wrappers
with title on front wrapper. In a brown cloth
case.

Ref.: Railway Economics p. 282

A recapitulation of the principal reasons for
building a transcontinental railroad with the
financial assistance of the Federal Government.

1645 GREEN, THOMAS M.

THE SPANISH CONSPIRACY. A REVIEW OF EARLY
SPANISH MOVEMENTS IN THE SOUTH-WEST. CON-
TAINING PROOFS OF THE INTRIGUES OF JAMES
WILKINSON AND JOHN BROWN; OF THE COMPLIC-
ITY THEREWITH OF JUDGES SEBASTIAN, WALLACE,
AND INNES . . . CINCINNATI: ROBERT CLARKE &
CO., 1891.

[i]–viii, 9–406, [407 errata, 408 blank]. 23.1 x 15.2
cm. Dark green cloth.

Ref.: Howes G374; Rader 1672; Raines p. 99

1646 GREENE, DUANE M.

LADIES AND OFFICERS OF THE UNITED STATES
ARMY; OR, AMERICAN ARISTOCRACY. A SKETCH OF
THE SOCIAL LIFE AND CHARACTER OF THE ARMY
. . . CHICAGO: CENTRAL PUBLISHING COMPANY,
1880.

[1]–222. 16.7 x 12.5 cm. Dark orange cloth, blind
embossed front cover, title in gilt on front cover
and backstrip.

Ref.:

In Mr. Greene's opinion, the Army was the
haunt of alcoholics and morons at the mercy of
scheming women (wives).

1647 GREENE, JEREMIAH E.

THE SANTA FE TRADE: ITS ROUTE AND CHARACTER ... READ ... THE AMERICAN ANTIQUARIAN SOCIETY ... WORCESTER, MASSACHUSETTS: PRESS OF CHARLES HAMILTON, 1893.

[1]–20. 25.5 x 15.2 cm. Green printed wrappers with title on front wrapper, uncut.

Ref.: Munk (Alliot) p. 90; Rader 1675; Saunders 2926

1648 GREENE, JOHN P.

FACTS RELATIVE TO THE EXPULSION OF THE MORMONS OR LATTER DAY SAINTS, FROM THE STATE OF MISSOURI, UNDER THE "EXTERMINATING ORDER." CINCINNATI: PRINTED BY R. P. BROOKS, 1839.

[i–iv], [5]–43, [44 blank]. 21.4 x 13.8 cm. Buff printed wrappers with title on front wrapper. In a brown cloth case.

Prov.: Inscribed in pencil at the head of the title-page: Please read & return / Respectfully / O. Pratt /. Bookplate of Guy C. Littell.

Ref.: Bradford 1988; Howes G382; Sabin 28606; Woodward 84

The author, a cousin of Brigham Young, was present during the events described. The inscription on the title-page is by Orson Pratt.

1649 GREENE, MARY

LIFE, THREE SERMONS, SOME OF THE MISCELLANEOUS WRITINGS OF REV. JESSE GREENE ... LEXINGTON, MO: PATTERSON & JULIAN, 1852.

[1]–280. 18.2 x 11 cm. Portrait. Black cloth, blind embossed sides, title in gilt on backstrip.

Ref.: Howes G381

Greene was an itinerant Methodist minister whose adventures started during the War of 1812 and whose travels included Alabama, Arkansas, Missouri, and Tennessee. He worked for long periods among the Indians.

1650 GREENE, MAX.

THE KANZAS REGION: FOREST, PRAIRIE, DESERT, MOUNTAIN, VALE, AND RIVER ... NEW YORK: FOWLER AND WELLS, 1856.

[i]–viii, [9]–[168], [173]–192, [1]–4 advertisements, [1]–4 advertisements, [1]–4 advertisements. 18.8 x 12 cm. Map: [Kansas] / [lower right:] Acrography, J. H. Colton & Co New York. / 8.4 x 14.8 cm. No scale given. Map: East / Kanzas. / 14 x 8.4 cm. No scale given. Pale green printed wrappers with title on front cover, advertisements on verso of back wrapper. In a brown cloth case.

Ref.: Bradford 1989; Howes G383; Rader 1677; Sabin 28607; Wagner-Camp 276

1651 GREENHOW, ROBERT

AUTOGRAPH LETTER, SIGNED. 1845 May 28, Washington, D. C. Four pages, 25 x 20.3 cm. To the New York *Tribune*.

A fine letter in which the author defends himself from being classed with other writers on Oregon such as Farnham and Falconer. He also traces the history of the writing of his book.

1652 GREENHOW, ROBERT

THE HISTORY OF OREGON AND CALIFORNIA, AND THE OTHER TERRITORIES ON THE NORTH-WEST COAST OF NORTH AMERICA; ACCOMPANIED BY A GEOGRAPHICAL VIEW AND MAP OF THOSE COUNTRIES, AND A NUMBER OF DOCUMENTS AS PROOFS AND ILLUSTRATIONS OF THE HISTORY ... BOSTON: CHARLES C. LITTLE AND JAMES BROWN, 1844.

[i]–[xx, xx blank], 1–482. 22.6 x 14.7 cm. Map: Map of the / Western & Middle Portions of / North America, / to illustrate / the History of California, Oregon, and the other Countries / on the / North-West Coast of America / By / Robert Greenhow. / Compiled from the best Authorities by Robert Greenhow. / Drawn by George H. Ringgold, Engraved by E. F. Woodward Philadª / [below neatline:] Copy-right secured according to Law. / 57.9 x 65.5 cm. No scale given. Blue wrappers with tan paper backstrip, uncut, almost entirely unopened. Lacks front wrapper. In a blue cloth case.

Ref.: Bradford 1992; Cowan p. 249; Howes G389; Sabin 28362; Smith 3842; Wheat (*Transmississippi*) 481

The 1844 edition is revised and extended from the earlier editions and contains a new map.

Editions: Washington, Philadelphia, and New York, 1840.

1653 GREENHOW, ROBERT

... MEMOIR, HISTORICAL, AND POLITICAL, ON THE NORTHWEST COAST OF NORTH AMERICA, AND THE ADJACENT TERRITORIES; ILLUSTRATED BY A MAP AND A GEOGRAPHICAL VIEW OF THOSE COUNTRIES ... WASHINGTON: BLAIR AND RIVES, 1840.*

[i]–[xii], [1]–228. 22.9 x 14.5 cm. Folding map: The / North-West-Coast / of / North America / and / adjacent Territories / Compiled from the best authorities under the direction / of Robert Greenhow to accompany his Memoir on the North-/west Coast Published by order of the Senate of the United / States drawn by David H. Burr. / Note. The names of places on the border of the Map show their respective Latitudes. / 40.7 x 53.8 cm. No scale given. *Inset:* The / North Pacific Ocean / and the / adjacent Coasts and Islands. 13.2 x 25.7 cm. No scale given. *Inset:* Fac-simile of a Medal struck at Boston in

1787 on occasion of the departure of the vessels / Columbia and Washington for the North West Coast of America, taken from one / of the original Medals, deposited by the Hon: C. Cushing, in the Library of the Department / of State of the United States. / 6.7 x 11 cm. Old green half calf.

Ref.: Cowan p. 249; Howes G389; Sabin 28633; Smith 3848; Staton & Tremaine 2369

26th Congress, 1st Session, Senate Document No. 174, Serial 378.

1654 GREENHOW, ROSE O'N.

MY IMPRISONMENT AND THE FIRST YEAR OF ABOLITION RULE AT WASHINGTON . . . LONDON: RICHARD BENTLEY, 1863.

[i]–x, [1]–352, [353–54 advertisements]. 19.8 x 12.3 cm. Portrait. Bright blue cloth, blind embossed borders on sides, title in gilt on front cover and backstrip, uncut.

Ref.: Howes G390; Nicholson p. 331

1655 GREGG, ASA

PERSONAL RECOLLECTIONS OF THE EARLY SETTLEMENT OF WAPSINONOC TOWNSHIP AND THE MURDER OF ATWOOD BY THE INDIANS. WITH A FULL AND COMPLETE DIRECTORY OF TOWNSHIP AND TOWN OF WEST LIBERTY . . . WEST LIBERTY, IOWA: GEORGE TRUMBO, PUBLISHER.

[1]–[41], [42 blank]. 19.4 x 12.2 cm. Blue glazed printed wrappers with title on front wrapper.

Prov.: Inscribed in pencil on verso of front wrapper: Given to Jessie Chase / by the Author / Mch 23– 1894. /

Ref.: Howes G400; Jones 1577; Mott (*Iowa*) p. 47

The Directory occupies the last fourteen pages and includes the dates of arrival of the individuals; none of the dates is later than 1876 so the work was probably printed that year or the next.

1656 GREGG, JOSIAH

AUTOGRAPH LETTER, SIGNED. 1844 December 31, Washington, D. C. One page, 28.5 x 23.3 cm. To John Bigelow.

Regarding changes and additions for a projected second edition of *Commerce of the Prairies.* Laid in the so-called "Second Edition," Volume II . . . 1845.

1657 GREGG, JOSIAH

AUTOGRAPH LETTER, SIGNED. 1846 September 18, San Antonio de Bexar. Four pages, 26.9 x 20.6 cm. To John Bigelow.

A very interesting letter regarding plans for an expedition under General Wool to Chihuahua and a description of the attack on Presidio

del Rio Grande under General Harney. The letter has been printed in an article by Ralph E. Twitchell in *Publications* of the New Mexico Historical Society, No. 26, pages 18–20.

Laid in Gregg's *Scenes and Incidents in the Western Prairies . . . 1856.*

1658 GREGG, JOSIAH

AUTOGRAPH LETTER, SIGNED. 1847 August 3, Pittsburgh. Two pages, 26.8 x 20.9 cm. To John Bigelow.

Laid in Bigelow's copy of Gregg: *Commerce of the Prairies . . . 1844,* of which he was editor. The present letter relates entirely to the publication of the work, especially to the difficulties Gregg and Bigelow had run into with the publisher, Henry G. Langley. Plans for future editions of the work with another publisher are mentioned and Gregg concludes the letter with mention of his plan to return to Saltillo, Mexico.

1659 GREGG, JOSIAH

COMMERCE OF THE PRAIRIES: OR THE JOURNAL OF A SANTA FE TRADER, DURING EIGHT EXPEDITIONS ACROSS THE GREAT WESTERN PRAIRIES, AND A RESIDENCE OF NEARLY NINE YEARS IN NORTHERN MEXICO . . . NEW-YORK: HENRY G. LANGLEY, M DCCC XLIV.

[i]–xvi, [17]–320. [i]–viii, [9]–318, [319–22 blank]. 18.8 x 11.5 cm. Six plates and two maps. Map: A / Map of the / Indian Territory / Northern Texas / and / New Mexico / Showing the / Great Western Prairies / by / Josiah Gregg / [lower right:] Entered according to the Act of Congress in the year 1844 by Sidney E. Morse and Samuel Breese in the Clerks Office of the Southern District of New York. / 31 x 38 cm. No scale given. Map: Map of the Interior of Northern Mexico. / 14.4 x 9 cm. No scale given. Two volumes, black cloth, blind embossed borders on sides, gilt vignettes on front covers, title in gilt on backstrip, gilt edges. In a blue keratol case.

Prov.: Inscribed in first volume: John Bigelow, Esq. / with the sincerest regards of / His Friend, / Josiah Gregg. /

Ref.: Bay pp. 367, 371–72; Bradford 1996; Clark III 172 see; Dobie pp. 75–6; Howes G401; Jones 1087; Munk (Alliot) p. 91; Rader 1684; Raines p. 99; Sabin 28712; Wagner-Camp 108; Wheat (*Transmississippi*) 482

A brilliant copy, presented to the editor by the author. One of a few copies (for presentation?) with gilt edges.

Laid in is an Autograph Letter by the author. 1847 August 3.

1660 GREGG, JOSIAH

THE SAME.

[i]–xvi, [17]–323, [324 blank], [1]–24 advertisements. [i]–viii, [9]–327, [328 blank]. 18.5 x 11 cm. Six plates and one map, illustrations in text, and large folding map: A / Map of the / Indian Territory / Northern Texas / and / New Mexico / Showing the / Great Western Prairies / by / Josiah Gregg / [lower left:] Entered according to Act of Congress in the year 1844 by Sidney E. Morse and Samuel Breese in the Clerks Office of the Southern District of New York /. Two volumes, brown cloth, blind embossed sides with gilt vignette on each front cover, similar blind design on back covers, gilt titles and vignettes on backstrips.

Ref.: see above

Second Edition, with the prefatory note, the glossary, and the index. The map is not always present.

The map is apparently a proof copy in the first state, with manuscript corrections in the hand of the author. The ICN (Ayer) copy of the first edition contains a map to which changes have been made, including at least four changes indicated in the present example. Note particularly at right centre, two towns below Fayetteville and above the line of mountains have been omitted.

1661 GREGG, JOSIAH

THE SAME.

Two volumes, plum cloth, blind embossed borders on sides, gilt vignette on front covers, backstrips gilt.

Second State of the large map showing revisions in the plate indicated in the "proof" copy.

The embossed borders on the covers differ from the preceding copy.

1662 GREGG, JOSIAH

THE SAME . . . SECOND EDITION. NEW YORK: J. & H. G. LANGLEY, 1845.

[i]–xvi, [17]–320. [i]–viii, [9]–318. (Pages [i–ii], Vol. I, blank.) 18.8 x 11.7 cm. Six plates and one map, illustrations in text. Two volumes, black cloth, blind embossed sides, gilt title on backstrips.

Ref.: see above

The title-page of the second volume is dated M DCCC XLIV and is identical with the title-page of the First Edition. The binding differs from the first edition. The preface for the second edition and the glossary at the end of the first volume are not present. No changes seem to have been made in the text.

Laid in is an Autograph Letter, signed, by the author. 1844 December 31.

1663 GREGG, JOSIAH

SCENES AND INCIDENTS IN THE WESTERN PRAIRIES: DURING EIGHT EXPEDITIONS, AND INCLUDING A RESIDENCE OF NEARLY NINE YEARS IN NORTHERN MEXICO . . . PHILADELPHIA: J. W. MOORE, 1856.

[i]–xvi, [17]–320, [321–24 blank], [i]–viii, [9]–318. (Pages [i–ii] of first part blank.) 18.8 x 11.6 cm. Four plates and one map inserted, illustrations in text. Black cloth, blind embossed sides, title in gilt on backstrip.

Prov.: Inscribed on front endleaf: D. A. Pettibone / Book / Aug A D 1857 / Bridgeport Center /. With bookplate of John Thomas Lee.

Ref.: see above

Reprinted from the plates of the 1845 edition of *Commerce of the Prairies*, with minor corrections. The plates are the same, but the frontispieces are omitted as are also the preface, glossary, and index.

With an Autograph Letter, signed, by the author laid in. 1846 September 18.

1664 GREGG, STELLA D.

AUTOGRAPH LETTER, SIGNED. 1906 November 26, Carthage, Illinois. Three pages, 20.1 x 12.5 cm. To Luther A. Brewer.

Offering to supply a copy of her father's book, *The Prophet of Palmyra*, and containing information about her father's early career in Iowa as a newspaper publisher, post-carrier, etc. Laid in Gregg: *The Prophet of Palmyra* . . . 1890.

1665 GREGG, THOMAS

HISTORY OF HANCOCK COUNTY, ILLINOIS, TOGETHER WITH AN OUTLINE HISTORY OF THE STATE, AND A DIGEST OF STATE LAWS . . . CHICAGO: CHAS. C. CHAPMAN & CO., 1880.

[1–6], [17]–1036. 24.2 x 16.7 cm. Map and 72 illustrations listed. Map: Map of / Hancock Co. / Illinois. / 24.2 x 31.4 cm. No scale given. Black cloth, red leather corners and backstrip, title in gilt on front cover and backstrip.

Ref.: Buck 833; Howes G403

Contains a long and good section on the Mormons in Illinois.

1666 GREGG, THOMAS

THE PROPHET OF PALMYRA. MORMONISM REVIEWED AND EXAMINED IN THE LIFE, CHARACTER, AND CAREER OF ITS FOUNDER . . . TOGETHER WITH A COMPLETE HISTORY OF THE MORMON ERA IN ILLINOIS . . . NEW YORK: JOHN B. ALDEN, 1890.

[iii]–[xvi, xvi blank], [1]–552. 18.4 x 11.8 cm. 11 plates listed and an explanatory leaf with the final plate. Blue cloth, title and border stamped in black on front cover, title in gilt on backstrip.

Ref.: Bradford 1998; Howes G404

Laid in is an Autograph Letter, signed by Stella D. Gregg. 1906 November 26. Also laid in are two copies of a broadside and a copy of a broadsheet advertising the work.

1667 GREGORY GOLD MINING COMPANY

PROSPECTUS, GEOLOGICAL SURVEY AND REPORT OF THE GREGORY GOLD MINING COMPANY, GREGORY DISTRICT, COLORADO TERRITORY. NEW YORK: 1863.

[1]–36. 23.7 x 14.6 cm. Four lithographed plates. Pink glazed printed wrappers with title on front wrapper, errata on recto of back wrapper, one illustration repeated on verso of back wrapper.

Ref.:

1668 GREGORY (Colorado) MINING DISTRICT

[Broadside] COLORADO TERRITORY. MINING DISTRICT. BE IT KNOWN THAT IS THE OWNER BY PRE-EMPTION OF . . . ON . . . LODE . . . GIVEN UNDER MY HAND IN SAID DISTRICT THIS DAY OF A. D. 1861. RECORDER. PRESIDENT. ROCKY MOUNTAIN HERALD, JOB PRINTING ESTABLISHMENT, DENVER.

Broadside, 10.7 x 19.9 cm. Text, 9.6 x 17.5 cm.

Ref.:

Endorsed on verso and recorded April 2, 1861. This certificate is similar to the Jackson Mining District, Kansas Territory, certificate.

Filled in in manuscript for "Gregory" Mining District, Kip lode, in favor of W. Packard. Jno. Storms was the Recorder and A. H. Clements the President.

1669 GRIERSON, BENJAMIN H.

PHOTOGRAPH, bust-length, facing three-quarters to subject's left, in colonel's uniform. Photograph, 8.7 x 5.5 cm. Mount, 10.1 x 6.1 cm.

Signed at foot, on mount: B H Grierson / Col 6th Ills Cav /. Grierson was colonel of the 6th Illinois Cavalry from April to December of 1862.

1670 GRIERSON, BENJAMIN H.

[Wrapper title] SPECIAL REPORT OF COLONEL B. H. GRIERSON . . . WITH REFERENCE TO REMOVAL OF INTRUDERS FROM THE JICARILLA INDIAN RESERVATION. OCTOBER, 1887.

[1]–6. 19.8 x 12.6 cm. Dark salmon printed wrappers with title on front wrapper.

Prov.: Slip, 5 x 10.9 cm., tipped to front wrapper: With compliments of / General Grierson. /

Ref.:

Printed at Santa Fé.

Dated: Headquarters District of New Mexico, / Santa Fé, N. M., October 17, 1887. /

1671 GRIERSON, BENJAMIN H.

[Wrapper title] ANNUAL REPORT OF COLONEL B. H. GRIERSON . . . COMMANDING DISTRICT OF NEW MEXICO. 1887. [ornament].

[1]–8, [1]–8, [1]–6, [1]–6, [1]–5, [1]–2, [3 blank]. 19.4 x 12.9 cm. Green printed wrappers with title on front wrapper.

Ref.: Howes G415

Printed at Santa Fé. Dated: Headquarters District of New Mexico, / Santa Fé, N. M., September 10th, 1887. /

Contains a schedule of engagements with the Indians within the District.

1672 GRIERSON, BENJAMIN H.

[Cover title] ANNUAL REPORT OF COLONEL B. H. GRIERSON . . . COMMANDING DISTRICT OF NEW MEXICO. 1888.

[1]–7, [8 blank], [1]–8, [1]–4, [1]–2, [1]–4, [1]–2. 20.7 x 13.4 cm. Blueprint map: Sketch Map / of present Navajo Res: and proposed extension /. 11.5 x 18.1 cm. No scale given. Black cloth, with title stamped in gilt on front cover as above.

Prov.: From the Grierson Papers.

Ref.: Howes G416

Abstracts A–E are present.

Probably printed at Los Angeles. The report was made for the District of New Mexico to the Department of Arizona, the headquarters of which were in Los Angeles.

1673 GRIERSON, BENJAMIN H.

[Cover title] ANNUAL REPORT OF COLONEL B. H. GRIERSON . . . COMMANDING DEPARTMENT OF ARIZONA. 1889.

[i–ii], [1]–32, [33 blank], [34 maps explanatory of text]. 19.9 x 12.8 cm. Nine blueprint maps, eight of which are listed, and a view. Each map numbered: Nro. 1 [–9]. Map: Sketch Map / of present Navajo Res. and proposed Extension / 11.2 x 8.1 cm. No scale given. With matching page of text in blueprint. Map: [Fort McDowell Reservation]. 38.4 x 12.2 cm. (page size). No scale given. Map: [Fort Apache Reservation], 12.7 x 33.8 cm. (page size). No scale given. Map: [Fort Bowie Reservation], 15.2 x 15 cm. (map size). No scale given. Map: [Fort Selden Reservation]. 19.9 x 16.8 cm. (page size). No scale given. View: Cerro Roblero, / Looking South from Fort Selden. / Distance 2 Miles; Elevation 1655.' / Elevation above Sea 5676.' / 10.1 x 16.5 cm. Map: Point Loma Military Reservation. / 16.7 x 9.1 cm. No scale given. Map: San Pedro Mil. Reservation and Surroundings. / 9 x 16.5 cm. Scale: 5/8 miles to one inch. Brown cloth with title stamped in gilt on front cover.

Prov.: Inscribed on front endleaf: For Mr & Mrs Yates / with Compliments of / B H. Grierson / Brig. Gen¹ U. S. A. / Retired. /

Ref.: Howes G417

Probably printed at Los Angeles.

1674 GRIERSON, BENJAMIN H.

REPORT OF BRIGADIER GENERAL B. H. GRIERSON . . . COMPRISING A SUMMARY OF EVENTS, DEPARTMENT OF ARIZONA. FROM SEPTEMBER 1ST, 1889, TO JULY 1ST, 1890.

[i–ii], [1]–[34], [1]–21, [22 blank], [1]–8. 20 x 13 cm. Three maps, blueprints. Map: Map N° I. / Lines & Stations / of / Heliograph System Dept. of Arizona / 17.1 x 23 cm. Scale: 45 miles to one inch. Map: N° II. / [San Pedro Reservation and proposed extension]. 17 x 21.6 cm. Scale: 5/8 mile to one inch. Map: Map N° III. / [North Island and peninsula, San Diego]. 16.6 x 21.5 cm. Scale: about 5/8 mile to one inch. Brown cloth, title stamped in gilt on front cover.

Prov.: From the Grierson Papers, but without identification.

Ref.: Howes G418

Probably printed at Los Angeles.

1675 [GRIERSON, BENJAMIN H.]

BRIEF SKETCH OF GENERAL GRIERSON'S SERVICES . . . FROM RECORDS FILED IN WAR DEPARTMENT, 1861 TO 1884.

[i–ii], [1]–9, [10 blank]. 21.3 x 13.7 cm. Glued, unbound.

Ref.:

Printed at Washington, D. C., although attested (in manuscript) by J. S. Morrison and dated Fort Davis, Texas, March 10th, 1885.

1676 GRIFFITH & CO., Lawrence, Kansas

THE KANSAS RURAL HOME AND FARM ADVERTISER. PUBLISHED BY GRIFFITH & CO., REAL ESTATE AGENTS, LAWRENCE, KANSAS. IF YOU WANT TO BUY OR SELL LAND IN KANSAS, CORRESPOND WITH GRIFFITH & CO. LAWRENCE: KANSAS TRIBUNE AND JOB PRINTING HOUSE, 1876.

[1]–39, [40 advertisement]. 20.5 x 13.5 cm. Buff printed wrappers with title on front wrapper, illustrations on verso of front and back wrappers.

Ref.:

According to the text on page [3], an issue of the work was published in July and the present is a "second appearance."

1677 GRIFFITHS, D. JR.

TWO YEARS RESIDENCE IN THE NEW SETTLEMENTS OF OHIO, NORTH AMERICA: WITH DIRECTIONS TO EMIGRANTS . . . LONDON: WESTLEY AND DAVIS, 1835.

[i]–[viii], [9]–197, [198 blank]. 18.4 x 10.8 cm. Frontispiece. Green cloth, printed white paper label, 4.3 x 1.4 cm.

Ref.: Bay p. 339; Howes G427; Jones 969; Sabin 28833; Thomson 466

The whole work is given to an account of the New Settlements on the Western Reserve, and pointing them out as the most eligible for English emigrants.—Thomson

1678 GRINNELL, JOSEPH

GOLD HUNTING IN ALASKA . . . ELGIN, ILL.: DAVID C. COOK PUBLISHING COMPANY.*

[1]–96. 20.3 x 16.5 cm. Illustrations unlisted. Red marbled boards, green cloth backstrip and corners.

Ref.: Smith 3904; Wickersham 31

Copyrighted 1901. According to the title-page, "Dedicated to disappointed gold-hunters the world over."

1679 [GRINNELL, JOSIAH B.]

THE HOME OF THE BADGERS; OR, A SKETCH OF THE EARLY HISTORY OF WISCONSIN, WITH A SERIES OF FAMILIAR LETTERS AND REMARKS ON TERRITORIAL CHARACTER AND CHARACTERISTICS, ETC . . . MILWAUKIE[!]: PUBLISHED BY WILSHIRE & CO., 1845.

[1]–36. 18.1 x 11.7 cm. Tan printed wrappers with title on front wrapper, additional text on verso of front and recto and verso of back wrappers.

Ref.: AII (*Wisconsin*) 241; Howes G434; Legler 14; McMurtrie (*Wisconsin*) 219

The printer's imprint appears on the verso of the title-page: [rule] / Am. Freeman Print. / Although the title-page imprint is given as Milwaukee, Am. Freeman Print was operating in Prairieville (now Waukesha).

The pamphlet comprises Grinnell's correspondence to the New York *Tribune* in 1844. Grinnell was later the founder of Grinnell, Iowa, and of Grinnell College.

1680 GRINNELL, JOSIAH B.

MEN AND EVENTS OF FORTY YEARS. AUTOBIOGRAPHICAL REMINISCENCES OF AN ACTIVE CAREER FROM 1850 TO 1890 . . . BOSTON: D. LOTHROP COMPANY.

[iii]–xvi, [1]–426. 21.7 x 15.4 cm. Six illustrations, unlisted. Dark red cloth, leather label, gilt top, uncut.

Prov.: Inscribed on front fly-leaf: Rev. J. A. Earl / from his friend / Mrs J. B. Grinnell / In grateful remembrance of / his labors for souls in Grinnell / Feb–March 1906.

Ref.:

Copyrighted 1891. On page 39 there is a description of Grinnell's famous pamphlet, *The Home of the Badger* which was printed by the Territory to induce emigration.

1681 GRISWOLD, WAYNE

KANSAS HER RESOURCES AND DEVELOPMENTS; OR, THE KANSAS PILOT GIVING A DIRECT ROAD TO HOMES FOR EVERYBODY . . . CINCINNATI: ROBERT CLARKE & CO., 1871.

[i]–iv, [1–2], [v]–vi, [9]–95, [96 blank]. 23.4 x 15.1 cm. Vignettes in text. Yellow printed wrappers with title on front wrapper, advertisements on verso of front and recto and verso of back wrapper.

Ref.: Howes G439; Rader 1706

1682 GRUND, FRANCIS J.

HANDBUCH UND WEGWEISER FUR AUSWANDERER NACH DEN VEREINIGTEN STAATEN VON NORD-AMERIKA UND TEXAS . . . OHIO, MICHIGAN, IN-DIANA, ILLINOIS UND MISSOURI UND IN DEN TERRI-TORIEN WISCONSIN UND IOWA . . . STUTTGART UND TUBINGEN. J. G. COTTA'SCHER VERLAG. 1846.

[I]–IV, [1]–278. 19.7 x 12.8 cm. Map: Weg-weiser / durch die Staaten / Ohio, Michigan, Indiana, Illinois, & Missouri; / u. die Terri-torien / Wisconsin & Iowa. / Nach den letzten Vermessungen der Vereinigten Staaten in Graf-schaften getheilt. / [rule] / Stuttgart, / J. G. Cotta'sche Verlagsbuchhandlung. 1843. / 46.6 x 59.5 cm. Scale: 35 miles to one inch. Light green printed wrappers with short title on front wrapper, bound into half red levant morocco, gilt top, uncut.

Ref.: Buck 372; Howes G451; Raines p. 101
Editions: Stuttgart, 1843.

1683 GUEMES PACHECO, JUAN VICENTE DE

ORDENANZA PARA LA FORMACION DE LOS AUTOS DE VISITAS Y PADRONES, Y TASAS DE TRIBUTARIOS DE N. E. . . . EN MEXICO: POR LOS HEREDEROS DE DON FELIPE DE ZUNIGA Y ONTIVEROS, 1793.

[*]², 4², 3², 4², 5², 6². [1–ii], 1–22. 28 x 19.8 cm. Bound with Number 9.

Ref.: Medina (*Mexico*) 8279(?)

1684 GUEMES PACHECO, JUAN VICENTE DE

REGLAMENTO PARA LOS MERCADOS DE MEXICO . . . MEXICO: POR DON FELIPE DE ZUNIGA Y ONTIVEROS, 1791.

[A–C]². (Second and third leaves are signed 2 and 3 respectively.) [i–ii], 1–10. 28 x 19.8 cm. Bound with Number 9.

Ref.: Medina (*Mexico*) 8098

The regulations were directed principally to the merchants in the famous Plaza del Volador.

1685 GUIDE FOR EMIGRANTS TO MINNESOTA, A

A GUIDE FOR EMIGRANTS TO MINNESOTA, BY A TOURIST. SAINT PAUL: GOODRICH, SOMERS & CO., 1857.

[1]–[24]. 18.1 x 11.3 cm. Map: Map / showing the position / of the / Rum River Valley / relative to the / Mississippi / St. Croix & Superior. / 13.8 x 8.9 cm. No scale given. Green printed wrappers with title on front wrapper, advertisement on verso of back wrapper.

Ref.: AII (*Minnesota*) 133; Howes M642; Sabin 49250

Promotional pamphlet, probably distributed by R. F. Slaughter whose advertisement appears on verso of back wrapper.

1686 GUIDE TO THE CITY OF CHICAGO, A

A GUIDE TO THE CITY OF CHICAGO: ITS PUBLIC BUILDINGS, PLACES OF AMUSEMENT, COMMER-CIAL, BENEVOLENT, AND RELIGIOUS INSTITUTIONS; CHURCHES, HOTELS, RAILROADS, ETC., ETC . . . CHICAGO: T. ELWOOD ZELL & CO., 1868.

[i]–[viii, viii blank], 9–108. 15.4 x 9.8 cm. 11 unlisted illustrations and a map. Map: Map of / Chicago / 1867 / Published by Edᵂ Mendel. / Chicago. / [3 lines] / Lith. by Ed Mendel Chi-cago / 38 x 25.2 cm. No scale given. Plum cloth, blind fillet borders on sides, title in gilt on front cover and in blind on back cover.

Ref.: AII (*Chicago*) 1303; Howes C368; Sabin 12655

The collation in AII (*Chicago*), Howes, and Sabin call for twenty-four plates and 196 pages.

1687 GUIDE TO THE CITY OF CHICAGO, A

THE SAME.

[1 recto of endpaper], 2–8 advertisements on yellow paper, [9]–197, [198 verso of back end-paper, final three leaves on gray paper]. 15.3 x 9.7 cm. 14 lithographed illustrations and 12 inserted lithographed advertisements. Purple cloth, blind fillet borders on sides, title in gilt on front cover and in blind on back cover.

Ref.: AII (*Chicago*) 1303; Howes C368; Sabin 12655

The text of the two editions appears to be identical except for pagination. The present version contains a large number of advertisements interspersed.

There is no hyphen at the end of line 6 on the title-page.

1688   GUNN, LEWIS C., & ELIZABETH LE BRETON GUNN

RECORDS OF A CALIFORNIA FAMILY. JOURNALS AND LETTERS . . . EDITED BY ANNIE LEE MARSTON. SAN DIEGO, CALIFORNIA, MCMXXVIII.

[i–x, x blank], [1]–[281], [281 blank, 283 colophon, 284 blank]. 22.9 x 15.2 cm. 16 illustrations listed. Blue boards, blue cloth backstrip, fore and lower edges uncut.

Ref.: Cowan p. 254; Howes M324

Limited to 350 copies. Includes a day-by-day journal of Gunn's trip on horseback across Mexico on his way to the gold fields and Elizabeth Gunn's contemporary account of her trip around the Horn to California.—EDG

1689   GUNN, OTIS B.

AUTOGRAPH LETTER, SIGNED. 1865 June 26, Atchison, Kansas. Three pages, 20.4 x 12.8 cm. To Colonel William Osborn.

Regarding proposals of Mr. Whitney to start a "Machine" (apparently some kind of farm machinery), the scarcity of workmen, the difficulties of finding the right kind of cattle, progress of the railroad, etc. Laid in Gunn: *New Map and Hand-Book of Kansas* . . . 1859.

1690   GUNN, OTIS B.

NEW MAP AND HAND-BOOK OF KANSAS & THE GOLD MINES . . . WITH DESCRIPTION OF ALL THE ROUTES TO THE NEW GOLD MINES, OUTFITS FOR MINERS, AND A VARIETY OF OTHER USEFUL INFORMATION . . . PITTSBURGH: PRINTED BY W. S. HAVEN, 1859.

[i]–iv, [5]–71, [72 blank]. 15.1 x 9.3 cm. Map: Gunn's / New / Map of Kansas / and the / Gold Mines / Embracing all the Public Surveys up to the 6th / Principal Meridian. / Compiled from the Original Field Notes by / O. B. Gunn. / Wyandott, K. T. / 1859. / [4 lines] / January, 10. 1859. Ward B. Burnett, / Surveyor General Kansas and Nebraska. / [lower right:] Entered according to Act of Congress in the Year 1859, / by Otis B. Gunn in the Clerk's Office of the first District / Court of the Territory of Kansas. / Wm Schuchman, lith. Pittsburgh, Pa. / 65.3 x 71.3 cm. Scale not given. *Inset:* Routes / from

the / Missouri River / to the / Kansas Gold Mines. / 12.1 x 37.5 cm. No scale given. Black cloth stamped in gilt on front cover and in blind on back cover: Gunn's Map / and / Hand Book / of / Kansas / and the / Gold Mines. / Salmon wrappers, plain front wrapper pasted down, back wrapper with cut of Wm. Schuchman's establishment on verso of back wrapper. In a red cloth case.

Ref.: Hafen 5; Howes G461; Sabin 29282; Wagner-Camp 327; Wheat (*Transmississippi*) 976

Laid in is an Autograph Letter, signed by the author, 1865 June 26. The little book has been reprinted by Dr. Mumey in facsimile with notes by Hafen.

1691   GUNN, OTIS B., & DAVID T. MITCHELL

[Map] GUNN & MITCHELL'S / NEW / MAP OF KANSAS / AND THE / GOLD MINES / EMBRACING ALL THE PUBLIC SURVEYS UP TO 1861. / COMPILED FROM THE ORIGINAL FIELD NOTES BY / O. B. GUNN & D. T. MITCHELL. / LECOMPTON, K. T. / 1861. / [lower right:] ENTERED ACCORDING TO ACT OF CONGRESS IN THE YEAR 1860, BY / GUNN & MITCHELL IN THE CLERK'S OFFICE OF THE FIRST DISTRICT OF THE TERRITORY OF KANSAS. / W$^{M.}$ SCHUCHMAN, LITH. PITTSBURGH, PA. / *Inset:* Routes / from the / Missouri River / to the / Kansas Gold Mines. / [lower left:] Wm Schuchman lith. Pittsburgh, Pa. / 12.3 x 36.4 cm. No scale given.

Map, 66.8 x 68 cm. No scale given. Folded into brown cloth covers, 15.8 x 9.8 cm., title stamped in silver on front cover and in blind on back.

Ref.: Howes G461

Above the cartouche on the left side there is a small vignette of an Indian. In the upper left corner there is a note on the population of Kansas. Advertisements on inner front cover.

1692   GUNN, OTIS B., & DAVID T. MITCHELL

THE SAME, except line 6, 1864; line 10, 1864; lower right in copyright notice, 1862; lithographer's name omitted from inset; three small vignettes at left side of map.

Folded into plum cloth covers, 14.3 x 9 cm., title stamped in gilt on front cover. Advertisements on inner front cover.

Ref.: Howes G461

1693   GUNNISON, J. W., & WILLIAM GILPIN

GUIDE TO THE KANSAS GOLD MINES AT PIKE'S PEAK, DESCRIBING THE ROUTES, CAMPING PLACES, TOOLS, OUTFITS, &C. FROM NOTES OF CAPT. J. W. GUNNI-

SON, TOPOGRAPHICAL ENGINEER. ALSO, AN ADDRESS ON THE NEW GOLD MINES, DELIVERED AT KANSAS CITY, BY COL. WM. GILPIN, OF INDEPENDENCE, MO. ACCOMPANIED BY A MAP OF THE ROUTES FROM EASTERN KANSAS TO THE MINES. CINCINNATI, OHIO: PUBLISHED BY E. MENDENHALL, 1859.

[i–ii blank], [1]–40, [41–44 advertisements]. 14.6 x 9.5 cm. Map: Map of Kansas / with Route from / Kansas City / to the / Gold Mines / [lower left:] Litho: by Middleton Strobridge & Co: Cin: O / [lower right:] Entered according to act of Congress in the Year 1859 by E: Mendenhall in the Clerks office of the District Court of the Southern District of Ohio /. 24 x 58.3 cm. No scale given. Green paper backstrip, sewn into brown embossed cloth folder with title on front cover in gilt: Guide / to the / Kansas / Gold Mines /, publisher's advertisement on inner front cover, map mounted on inner back cover. Map silked. In a brown half morocco case.

Ref.: Hafen 6; Howes G462; Wagner-Camp 328; Wheat (*Transmississippi*) 977; Wilcox p. 52

The compiler of this rare guide book has not been identified. Gunnison had been killed by Indians in 1853, and his notes were used for part of the route. Gilpin, an enthusiast for any part of the West, was accustomed to seeing his words used for publicity.

Wagner-Camp lists a copy in the University of Kansas City Library. It is not an original edition, but the Mumey facsimile of 1952.

1694 GUNNISON, JOHN W.

THE MORMONS; OR, LATTER-DAY SAINTS, IN THE VALLEY OF THE GREAT SALT LAKE: A HISTORY OF THEIR RISE AND PROGRESS, PECULIAR DOCTRINES, PRESENT CONDITION, AND PROSPECTS, DERIVED FROM PERSONAL OBSERVATION, DURING A RESIDENCE AMONG THEM . . . PHILADELPHIA: LIPPINCOTT, GRAMBO & CO., 1852.

[i]–[x, x blank], 13–168. 18.7 x 11.5 cm. Frontispiece and two cuts in text. Bright dark blue cloth, blind embossed sides, title in gilt on backstrip.

Prov.: Signatures and notes by William H. Allen on title-page and blank leaves at front.

Ref.: Howes G463; Wagner-Camp 213; Woodward 85

1695 GUTHRIE, ABELARD

[Broadside] TO THE PEOPLE OF NEBRASKA TERRITORY. CITIZENS: AN INTERSTIN[!] PERIOD IN OUR TERRITORIAL HISTORY DAWNS UPON US, AND EXHORTS US TO ANOTHER STRUGGLE FOR RIGHT AND LAW. . . . ABELARD GUTHRIE. SEPT. 6, 1853.

Broadside, 63.3 x 32.5 cm. Text, 52.8 x 26.1 cm.
Ref.:

Abelard Guthrie was elected a delegate to Congress from Nebraska Territory on October 12, 1852. On July 28, 1853, he was again nominated by a convention held at Wyandotte. Through the machinations of the Indian Commissioner, he was defeated at the election held on November 8, and the Rev. Thomas Johnson was the successful candidate, although a Hadley Johnson pulled more votes at the polling place at Sarpy's Point. Both the Johnsons and Guthrie were in Washington during the session of 1853–54. The present broadside by Guthrie was his bid to the electors prior to the election. My guess is this broadside was printed at Parkville, Missouri, by the *Industrial Luminary*. Governor Walker states in his *Journals* that the *Proceedings of the Nebraska Territorial Convention* was printed at Parkville during that summer and it seems a more likely place for the printing of Guthrie's broadside than Liberty or St. Joseph. McMurtrie agreed with me.—EDG

No other copy of the broadside has been located.

1696 GUZMAN, JOSE MARIA

BREVE NOTICIA . . . DEL ACTUAL ESTADO DEL TERRITORIO DE LA ALTA CALIFORNIA, Y MEDIOS QUE PROPONE PARA LA ILUSTRACION Y COMERCIO EN QUEL PAIS . . . MEXICO: IMPRENTA DE LA AGUILA, 1833.

[i], [2]–8, [9 blank]. 19.7 x 13.3 cm. Large folding table. Rebound in plain old, white wrappers.

Ref.: Cowan p. 254; Hanna-Powell p. 25; Palau 111800; Wagner (in *Quarterly* of the Historical Society of Southern California Vol. X, No. 1)

Wagner considered the Guzman one of the twenty rarest and most important California books.

1697 GWIN, WILLIAM McK.

SPEECHES OF MR. GWIN, OF CALIFORNIA, ON THE NATIONAL RAILROAD BILL—HOMESTEAD BILL—CIVIL FUND BILL—CALIFORNIA INDIAN WAR DEBT—APPOINTMENT OF JUDGE FOR THE NORTHERN, DISTRICT OF CALIFORNIA—AND THE BILL TO CREATE A LINE OF STEAMSHIPS FROM CALIFORNIA, VIA THE SANDWICH ISLAND, TO CHINA. DELIVERED IN THE SENATE OF THE UNITED STATES, DEC. 12, 1853. WASHINGTON: PRINTED AT THE CONGRESSIONAL GLOBE OFFICE, 1853.

[1]–13, [14 blank]. 22.4 x 14.9 cm. Removed from bound volume, unbound. In a green cloth case.

Ref.: Wagner-Camp 223

Contains the journal of F. X. Aubry from Tejon Pass to the Rio del Norte, July 10–Sept. 10, 1853. Aubry's journal was first printed in the *Santa Fé Gazette*, Sept. 24, 1853, "reprinted in the *San Francisco Herald*, Dec. 5, 1853, and again in *Western Journal & Civilian*, St. Louis, 1854 (Vol. II, pages 84–96)."

H

1698 HABERSHAM, ROBERT A.

[Map] J. K. GILL & CO.S MAP OF WASHINGTON TER. PORTLAND O:N 1878 / SHOWING ALL SURVEYS MADE PREVIOUS TO JANUARY 1.ST 1878. COMPILED BY ROBT. A. HABERSHAM, CIVIL ENGINEER. / [lower left:] ENTERED ACCORDING TO ACT OF CONGRESS IN THE YEAR 1878 BY J. K. GILL & CO. IN THE OFFICE OF THE LIBRARIAN OF CONGRESS AT WASHINGTON / [lower right:] LITH. BY A. M. ASKEVOLD, ASHLAND BLOCK, CHICAGO. /

Map, 46.1 x 70 cm. (First two lines of title are above neat line.) Scale: 15 miles to one inch. Folded into black cloth covers, 15.1 x 9.5 cm., with title stamped in gilt on front cover.

Prov.: Signature in blue pencil inside front cover: E. T. Scovill / June 1879 / [flourish] /.

Ref.: Phillips (*Maps*) p. 998

1699 HADDEN, JAMES

WASHINGTON'S EXPEDITIONS (1753–1754) AND BRADDOCK'S EXPEDITION (1755), WITH HISTORY OF TOM FAUSETT, THE SLAYER OF GENERAL EDWARD BRADDOCK . . . UNIONTOWN, PA.

[1]–139, [140–44 blank]. 18.2 x 10.7 cm. 18 illustrations listed. Dark red cloth.

Ref.:
Copyrighted 1910.

1700 HADDOCK, WILLIAM J.

AUTOGRAPH LETTER, SIGNED. N.d., n.p. One page, 21.6 x 17.3 cm. To "Dear Sir." Written in pencil.

Regarding two numbers of "the American Ivy pamphlet" and sending his correspondent a photograph. The letter and photograph are laid in Haddock: *A Reminiscence . . .* 1901.

1701 HADDOCK, WILLIAM J.

A REMINISCENCE. THE PRAIRIES OF IOWA AND OTHER NOTES . . . IOWA CITY: PRINTED FOR PRIVATE CIRCULATION—50 COPIES, DECEMBER, 1901.

[i–iv, iv blank], [1]–[71], [72 blank]. 27.2 x 21.3 cm. Gray printed wrappers. In gray buckram case.

Ref.: Howes see H7; Mott p. 85
Laid in is an Autograph Letter signed by Haddock. No place, no date.
Editions: Iowa City, 1851 (Probably a ghost).

1702 HAILEY, JOHN

THE HISTORY OF IDAHO . . . BOISE, IDAHO: PRESS OF SYMS-YORK COMPANY, MCMX.*

[i–x, x blank], [1]–[400]. 22.9 x 15 cm. Portrait. Red cloth.

Ref.: Adams (*Ramp. Herd*) 956; Howes H16; Smith 3963

1703 HAINES, ELIJAH M.

HISTORICAL AND STATISTICAL SKETCHES, OF LAKE COUNTY, STATE OF ILLINOIS . . . WAUKEGAN, ILL.: PUBLISHED BY E. G. HOWE, 1852.

[1]–6, [i–ii errata], [7]–112. 15 x 10 cm. Frontispiece: View of Wakegan[!], Ill. Taken in 1847. / 18 x 34.2 cm. Pale yellow printed wrappers with title on front wrapper, additional line below border: Geer's Print, Waukegan. /

Ref.: Buck 890; Bradford 2033; Byrd 1974; Howes H20; Sabin 29554
The first history of an Illinois county.

1704 HAINES, ELIJAH M.

ANOTHER COPY. Gray printed wrappers.*

1705 HAINES, ELIJAH M.

[SCRAP BOOK containing clippings by and about Elijah M. Haines relating to early Chicago and Illinois history.]

1–100. 28.8 x 22.3 cm. Brown cloth, stamped in black.

Ref.:
The mounted clippings are all from Chicago and Illinois papers.

Pages 1–11: articles regarding Haines as Speaker of the House.
Pages 12–73: 48 articles from *The Sunday Times*, 1874(?)–1876 under the heading "By-Gone Days."
Pages 73–100: articles regarding early Chicago and Illinois history, 1879–1882.

1706 HAIR, JAMES T.

GAZETTEER OF MADISON COUNTY, CONTAINING HISTORICAL AND DESCRIPTIVE SKETCHES OF ALTON CITY, UPPER ALTON, EDWARDSVILLE, COLLINSVILLE, HIGHLAND, TROY, MONTICELLO, MARINE, BETHALTO, AND OTHER TOWNS . . . A DIRECTORY OF THE ALTONS, AND A LIST OF THE NAMES, OCCUPATION AND RESIDENCE ADDRESS OF THE MERCHANTS, MANUFACTURERS AND FARMERS, OF THE

TOWNSHIPS AND VILLAGES OF THE COUNTY. AL-
TON, ILLINOIS: COMPILED AND PUBLISHED BY
JAMES T. HAIR, 1866.

[1–4], [9]–292, [i advertisement, ii blank].
20.6 x 14.4 cm. One plate. Plum cloth, black calf
backstrip.

Ref.: Buck 957; Howes H23

Tipped in after page 91 is a leaf, 14.3 x 14.2
cm., headed: Officers and Committees of the
Common Council for 1866–7. [Elected since the
printing of this portion of the book.] . . .

Tipped in at the end is a leaf, 7.3 x 12.9 cm.,
headed: Notice—All persons who can, . . .
make any corrections or additions to this work,
are requested to communicate the same to any
of the following persons . . .

1707 HAIR, JAMES T.

IOWA STATE GAZETTEER EMBRACING DESCRIPTIVE
AND HISTORICAL SKETCHES . . . HISTORY OF THE
STATE . . . A SHIPPER'S GUIDE AND A CLASSIFIED
BUSINESS DIRECTORY OF THE MANUFACTURERS,
MERCHANTS, PROFESSIONAL AND TRADESMEN OF
IOWA, TOGETHER WITH THEIR BUSINESS ADDRESS
. . . CHICAGO: PUBLISHED BY BAILEY & HAIR, 1865.

[1]–76, [1]–722. (Page [1] of first section pasted
down as endpaper.) 22.8 x 14.7 cm. 18 illustrations listed. Dark brown cloth, title on backstrip, boxed advertisements in gilt on covers and
backstrip, advertisements on back endpapers.

Ref.: AII (*Chicago*) 943; Bradford 2035;
Howes H24; Sabin 29561

An important collection of data. Advertisements interspersed throughout are not included
in the pagination.

1708 HALE, EDWARD E.

AUTOGRAPH LETTER, SIGNED. 1876 April 10, New
Orleans. Three pages, 20.2 x 12.6 cm. To Mr.
Miner.

A fine letter asking for permission to borrow
a portrait of Philip Nolan to be photographed
and used for an engraving. Tipped into Hale:
Philip Nolan's Friends . . . 1877.

1709 HALE, EDWARD E.

KANZAS AND NEBRASKA: THE HISTORY, GEO-
GRAPHICAL AND PHYSICAL CHARACTERISTICS, AND
POLITICAL POSITION OF THOSE TERRITORIES; AN AC-
COUNT OF THE EMIGRANT AID COMPANIES, AND
DIRECTIONS TO EMIGRANTS . . . BOSTON: PHILLIPS,
SAMPSON AND COMPANY, 1854.

[I]–VIII, [9]–256, [257–60 advertisements].
19.1 x 12.1 cm. Map: Map of / Kanzas & Nebraska / From the Original Surveys. / Drawn &

Engraved for Hale's History. / Boston. Published by Phillips, Sampson & Co. / 1854. /
[lower centre:] W. C. Sharp. Lith. 251 Washⁿ
St. Boston. / 17.2 x 19 cm. No scale given. Dark
green cloth, blind embossed borders on sides,
title in gilt on backstrip.

Ref.: Bradford 2037; Howes (1954) 4371;
Kansas Historical Quarterly, Vol. II, No. 2,
May, 1933, article by Cora Dolbee: "The First
Book on Kansas"; Sabin 29624

1710 [HALE, EDWARD E.]

THE MAN WITHOUT A COUNTRY. BOSTON: TICKNOR
AND FIELDS, 1865.*

[1]–23, [24 blank]. 16.8 x 10.6 cm. Pink printed
wrappers with title on front wrapper, advertisements on verso of front and recto and verso of
back wrapper. Restabbed.

Ref.: Sabin 29627

Some copies are known with a small errata
slip before the title-page, but it is not present in
this copy.

1711 HALE, EDWARD E.

. . . THE MAN WITHOUT A COUNTRY . . . NEW
YORK: THE OUTLOOK COMPANY, 1902.

[1–2], [i]–xxxiv, [1]–97, [98 blank]. 21 x 13.8 cm.
Portrait. Limp vellum, gilt title on backstrip,
red silk ties, uncut. In a board case (broken).

Ref.:

Limited to 80 copies of which this is Copy 35,
signed by the author on his eightieth birthday,
April 3, 1902.

1712 HALE, EDWARD E.

MEMORIES OF A HUNDRED YEARS . . . NEW YORK:
THE MACMILLAN COMPANY, 1902.

[i]–xiv, [1]–318. [i]–ix, [x blank], [1]–321, [322
blank], [1–2 advertisements]. 20.2 x 13.6 cm. Illustrations listed. Two volumes, decorated gray
cloth, gilt tops, uncut.

Ref.:

1713 HALE, EDWARD E.

PHILIP NOLAN'S FRIENDS: A STORY OF THE CHANGE
OF WESTERN EMPIRE . . . NEW YORK: SCRIBNER,
ARMSTRONG, AND COMPANY, 1877.

[1]–395, [396 blank, 397–402 advertisements].
18.3 x 12 cm. Five illustrations listed. Brown
cloth, title in black on front cover and in black
and gilt on backstrip.

Ref.: Rader 1726; Raines p. 102

Tipped in before the initial blank leaf is an
Autograph Letter, signed, by the author, 1876
April 10.

1714 HALE, EDWARD E.

WORCESTER, MASS., FEB. 13, 1855. SIR:—THE
WORCESTER COUNTY KANZAS LEAGUE,—LIKE ALL
OTHER ORGANIZATIONS FOR FORWARDING EMI-
GRANTS TO KANZAS, . . .

[1–3], [4 blank]. 20.7 x 17.2 cm. Unbound.
Ref.:
Signed on page [3]: For the W. Co. Kanzas
League, / Edward E. Hale. / W. W. Rice, Secre-
tary. /

1715 HALE, IRVING

[Caption title] BIOGRAPHIC SKETCH OF BRIGADIER
GENERAL IRVING HALE . . .

[1–4]. 28 x 21.5 cm. White printed wrappers with
title on front cover.
Ref.:
Signature on inside back wrapper: Mary
King Hale /. Neither place nor date of publica-
tion is indicated.

1716 HALE, JOHN

CALIFORNIA AS IT IS; BEING A DESCRIPTION OF A
TOUR BY THE OVERLAND ROUTE AND SOUTH PASS
OF THE ROCKY MOUNTAINS . . . ROCHESTER:
PRINTED FOR THE AUTHOR, 1851.

[1]–40. 19.8 x 12 cm. Buff printed wrappers with
title on front wrapper and inverted on recto of
back wrapper. In a green half morocco case.
Ref.: Howes H31; Morgan (Pritchard) pp.
187–88; Wagner-Camp 198a
If, by publishing this work, I shall succeed in
persuading even a few of my fellow-citizens to
remain in a civilized country, who would otherwise be induced to emigrate to California, my
object will in a measure have been accomplished
and my labors and experience prove not alto-
gether useless.—Hale

1717 HALE, JOHN P.

[Cover title] DANIEL BOONE. SOME FACTS AND INCI-
DENTS NOT HITHERTO PUBLISHED . . . CHARLES-
TON, W. VA.: LEWIS BAKER & CO.

[1]–10, 13, 12–18. 22.3 x 14.9 cm. Pinkish-gray
printed wrappers.
Prov.: Note in pencil on page 15 by the au-
thor: A slight error here corrected in Trans Al-
legheny Pioneers H /.
Ref.:
Published before 1886, when the author's
Trans Allegheny Pioneers was issued.
An attempt, partially successful, to set some
of the records straight in the Boone myth.

1718 HALEY, J. EVETTS

THE XIT RANCH OF TEXAS AND THE EARLY DAYS OF
THE LLANO ESTACADO . . . CHICAGO: THE LAKE-
SIDE PRESS, 1929.

[i]–xvi, 1–261, [262 blank, 263 colophon, 264
blank]. 22.9 x 15.2 cm. 64 illustrations listed.
Green cloth, gilt top.
Prov.: Inscribed on the front fly-leaf: To my
friend / E. B. Sayles, / With all good wishes, /
J. Evetts Haley. /
Ref.: Adams (*Ramp. Herd*) 969; Howes H39;
Rader 1731
The work was suppressed by court injunction
and was, until recently, rather scarce.

1719 HALEY, J. EVETTS
ANOTHER COPY. Uninscribed.

1720 HALF-BREED ASSOCIATION

[Broadside] NOTICE IS HEREBY GIVEN TO ALL THE
SETTLERS WHO RESIDE UPON THE HALF-BREED
TRACT AND HOLD NO DECREE TITLE BY PURCHASE,
THAT THE BOARD OF DIRECTORS OF THE "HALF-
BREED ASSOCIATION" WILL MEET AT THE HOUSE OF
RICHARD BROWN, ESQ., IN MONTROSE TOWNSHIP
ON SATURDAY, THE 14TH OF SEPTEMBER, FOR THE
PURPOSE OF ELECTING DIRECTORS . . . KEOKUK,
AUGUST 23, 1850. GARRY LEWIS, SECRETARY OF
THE BOARD.

Broadside, 23.3 x 30.2 cm. Text, 18 x 25.9 cm.
Prov.: Inscribed on verso: Garry Lewis /
1850 / [underline] /.
Ref.:

1721 HALL, A. J.

[Wrapper title] . . . WESTWARD THE STAR OF EM-
PIRE TAKES ITS WAY. JUDICIOUS ADVERTISING, A
HIGHWAY TO WEALTH. EARLY & AUTHENTIC. 1857.
HISTORY OF OMAHA. 1870 . . . OMAHA DAILY RE-
PUBLICAN STEAM PRINTING HOUSE.

[1]–64, four interspersed advertisement leaves,
unpaginated. 22.9 x 15.2 cm. Gray printed
wrappers with title on front wrapper, advertisements on verso of front and recto and verso of
back wrappers.
Ref.: AII (*Nebraska*) 170; Howes H44
Published at Omaha in 1870. The title is set in
elaborate curved and rectilinear panels with
curlicues, etc.
Pages [57]–64 comprise: Address / by / Hon.
George W. Frost, / Delivered at the / Nebraska
State Fair, / At Nebraska City, Thursday, September 30th, 1869. /

1722 HALL, B. M.

THE LIFE OF REV. JOHN CLARK . . . NEW-YORK:
PUBLISHED BY CARLTON & PORTER, 1856.

[1]–276, [1–12 advertisements]. 18.3 x 12.2 cm. Portrait. Brown cloth, blind embossed sides, gilt title on backstrip.

Ref.: Howes H45

Clark was a missionary to Indians in Wisconsin, Michigan, and New York; later he went to Texas and still later was stationed in the Chicago area. Apparently he was a contentious individual.

1723 [HALL, BAYNARD R.]

THE NEW PURCHASE: OR, SEVEN AND A HALF YEARS IN THE FAR WEST. BY ROBERT CARLTON, ESQ. . . . NEW-YORK: D. APPLETON & CO., M DCCC XLIII.

[i]–xii, [1]–300. [i]–viii, [1]–316. Two volumes bound together, contemporary half calf, sprinkled edges. Part of blank leaf at front torn away.

Ref.: Blanck 6908; Howes H48; Hubach p. 60; Sabin 29728

The Far West was Indiana.

1724 HALL, EDWARD H.

THE GREAT WEST: EMIGRANTS', SETTLERS', & TRAVELLERS' GUIDE AND HAND-BOOK TO THE STATES OF CALIFORNIA AND OREGON, AND THE TERRITORIES OF NEBRASKA, UTAH, COLORADO, IDAHO, MONTANA, NEVADA, AND WASHINGTON . . . NEW YORK: PUBLISHED AND FOR SALE AT THE TRIBUNE OFFICE, 1864.

[i]–iv, [5]–89, [90–92 blank]. 18.6 x 11.2 cm. Folding map: [Northern States of the United States]. 13.5 x 36.1 cm. No scale given. Pink printed wrappers. In a brown cloth case.

Ref.: Buck 655 see; Cowan p. 258; Howes H55; Jones 1472; Munk (Alliot) p. 94; Rader 1735; Sabin 29758; Smith 2983; Wagner-Camp 400

1725 HALL, EDWARD H.

THE GREAT WEST: TRAVELLERS', MINERS', AND EMIGRANTS' GUIDE AND HAND-BOOK TO THE WESTERN, NORTH-WESTERN, AND PACIFIC STATES AND TERRITORIES . . . NEW YORK: D. APPLETON AND COMPANY, 1865.

[i–iv advertisements], [1]–198, [199–208 advertisements]. 17.2 x 11 cm. Folding map: Map of the Great West. / 23 x 36.5 cm. No scale given. Pictorial wrappers. In a green cloth case.

Ref.: see above

1726 HALL, EDWARD H.

THE GREAT WEST: RAILROAD, STEAMBOAT, AND STAGE GUIDE AND HAND-BOOK, FOR TRAVELLERS, MINERS, AND EMIGRANTS TO THE WESTERN, NORTH-WESTERN, AND PACIFIC STATES AND TERRITORIES . . . NEW YORK: D. APPLETON AND COMPANY.

[i blank, ii advertisements], 1–6 advertisements, [1]–181, [182 blank], [183–91, 192 blank]. 17 x 11 cm. Folding map: Map of the Great West. / 23 x 36.5 cm. No scale given. Green cloth.

Ref.: see above

Copyrighted 1866.

1727 HALL, EDWARD H.

THE NORTHERN COUNTIES GAZETTEER AND DIRECTORY, FOR 1855–6: A COMPLETE AND PERFECT GUIDE TO NORTHERN ILLINOIS . . . CHICAGO: ROBERT FERGUS, 1855.

[i]–[viii], [17]–[160]. 22.4 x 14.5 cm. Tan printed boards, gray cloth backstrip, gilt, advertisements on pink endleaves.

BOUND WITH:

1855–6. THE CHICAGO CITY DIRECTORY AND BUSINESS ADVERTISER . . . CHICAGO: ROBERT FERGUS, 1855.

[i–ii], [xv]–xxxii, [1]–[4], [1]–208, 1–128, [i, lithographed advertisement, verso blank]. Lacks map.

Ref.: AII (*Chicago*) 131, 149; Bradford 2049; Buck 544; Byrd 2286, 2288; Howes H57; Sabin 12641, 29760

The collations do not agree with AII (*Chicago*), Byrd, or Sabin. The works were probably issued in various forms.

1728 HALL, EDWARD H.

HALL'S BUSINESS DIRECTORY OF CHICAGO . . . CHICAGO: HALL & COMPANY, 1856.

[1–6 advertisements on pink paper], [i]–xii, [1]–94, [95–6 fly-title with verso blank], 1–50 advertisements. 14.2 x 8.8 cm. Black embossed cloth with title in gilt on front cover, printed green label on back cover.

Ref.: AII (*Chicago*) 185; Byrd 2453; Sabin 12641

The collation in AII (*Chicago*) calls for 94 pages only and does not mention the advertisements present in the Graff copy. Byrd does not mention pages [95–6]. There were four other directories printed in Chicago for 1856.

1729 HALL & CO., EDWARD H.

HALL & CO.'S CHICAGO CITY DIRECTORY, AND BUSINESS ADVERTISER. FOR 1854–'55 . . . CHICAGO: R. FERGUS.

[1–4 advertisements], [i]–iv, [1]–315, [316 blank], [1–25, 26 blank], [1–25, 26 blank], [1–2], [1]–28, [1–8 advertisements]. 18.9 x 12.3 cm. Green cloth, blind embossed borders on sides, title in gilt on front cover, advertisements on endpapers and endleaves.

Ref.: AII (*Chicago*) 83; Byrd 2123; Sabin 12641

There are fourteen pages of interspersed advertisements not included in the pagination above. There is also a slip, 13.9 x 10.5 cm., tipped to the final page 28.

1730   HALL, ELISHA I.

[OBSERVATIONS AND DOCUMENTS, RELATIVE TO A CALUMNY, CIRCULATED BY JOHN BROWN . . . TO THE PREJUDICE OF ELISHA I. HALL . . .]

[*]¹, A–F⁴. [1]–47, [48 blank]. 20.1 x 12.6 cm. Removed from binding, unbound. Lacks title-leaf and final blank.

Prov.: Inscribed on page [3]: after four lines of manuscript crossed out / Jnº W. Overton /. On page 47: Thos Overton /. On page [48]: Bay of Biscay / John Brown / Jesse Searcy / Thos Overton /. Writing on last page seems to be in one hand.

Ref.: Sabin 29765

Published in 1802. Title as above from Library of Congress card. See above under JAMES BROWN.

1731   HALL, JAMES

AN ADDRESS DELIVERED BEFORE THE ANTIQUARIAN AND HISTORICAL SOCIETY OF ILLINOIS, AT ITS SECOND ANNUAL MEETING, IN DECEMBER, 1828 . . . VANDALIA: PRINTED BY ROBERT BLACKWELL, 1829.

[1]–20. 15.5 x 10.5 cm. Rebound in contemporary blue wrappers. In a brown half morocco case.

Ref.: Blanck 6921; Byrd 89

Sabin lists a first annual meeting, but not a second. Blanck and Byrd list both.

1732   HALL, JAMES

THE HARPE'S HEAD; A LEGEND OF KENTUCKY . . . PHILADELPHIA: KEY & BIDDLE, 1833.

[v]–viii, [9]–256, 1–36 advertisements. 17 x 10.5 cm. Light red cloth, white printed paper label, 4.2 x 2.5 cm.

Ref.: Bay pp. 242–43; Blanck 6929; Howes H72; Sabin 29786; Thomson 484; Wright I 1097

The Harpe's Head was reprinted in *Legends of the West*, 1869.

1733   HALL, JAMES

LEGENDS OF THE WEST . . . PHILADELPHIA: PUBLISHED BY HARRISON HALL, 1832.

[i–viii, viii blank], [1]–265, [266 colophon, 267 advertisement, 268 blank]. 19 x 11.3 cm. Plum cloth, white printed paper label on backstrip, 3.5 x 2.2 cm., uncut.

Ref.: Blanck 6927; Howes H73; Jones 926; Sabin 29787; Thomson 481; Wright I 1098

1734   HALL, JAMES

LETTERS FROM THE WEST; CONTAINING SKETCHES OF SCENERY, MANNERS, AND CUSTOMS; AND ANECDOTES CONNECTED WITH THE FIRST SETTLEMENTS OF THE WESTERN SECTIONS OF THE UNITED STATES. LONDON: HENRY COLBURN, 1828.

[i]–vi, [1]–385, [386 advertisements]. 21.9 x 13.8 cm. Light brown boards, green cloth backstrip, white printed label, 5.3 x 3.2 cm., on backstrip, uncut.

Ref.: Blanck 6919; Howes H74; Jones 898; Rader 1741; Sabin 29789; Thomson 208

Portions of the work had appeared in *The Portfolio* between July, 1821, and May of the following year.

1735   HALL, JAMES

NOTES ON THE WESTERN STATES; CONTAINING DESCRIPTIVE SKETCHES OF THEIR SOIL, CLIMATE, RESOURCES AND SCENERY . . . PHILADELPHIA: HARRISON HALL, 1838.

[i]–[xxiv, xxiv blank], 13–304. 18.8 x 11.8 cm. Plum cloth, title in gilt on backstrip.

Prov.: Bookplate of B. F. Prince.

Ref.: Blanck 6943; Bradford 2060; Buck 300; Clark III 49; Howes H79; Jones 1010; Sabin 29791; Thomson 490

A slightly extended edition of *Statistics of the West* . . . 1836.

1736   HALL, JAMES

THE ROMANCE OF WESTERN HISTORY: OR, SKETCHES OF HISTORY, LIFE AND MANNERS, IN THE WEST . . . CINCINNATI: APPLEGATE & COMPANY, 1857.

[1]–420, [1–12 advertisements]. (Page 4 paginated iv.) 19 x 12 cm. Portrait. Purple cloth, blind embossed borders and panels on sides, title in gilt on backstrip.

Ref.: Blanck 6955; Howes H79; Jones 1374; Rader 1742; Sabin 29792; Thomson 495

Most of the material included in this work had appeared in print previously.

1737   HALL, JAMES

SKETCHES OF HISTORY, LIFE, AND MANNERS, IN THE WEST . . . PHILADELPHIA: HARRISON HALL, 1835.

[1]–4, [3]–[283], [284 blank]. [i]–viii, [13]–276. 17.6 x 10.6 cm. Frontispiece in first volume. Two volumes, plum embossed cloth, title in gilt on backstrips.

Ref.: Bay pp. 342–43; Blanck 6939; Howes H78; Jones 970; Rader 1743; Sabin 29793; Thomson 487

This is an extended edition of a work which had appeared a year earlier in one volume.

1738 HALL, JAMES

THE SOLDIER'S BRIDE AND OTHER TALES . . . PHILA-DELPHIA: KEY AND BIDDLE, 1833.

[9]–272. 18 x 10.5 cm. Dark green cloth, printed white paper label (fragments only) on backstrip.
Ref.: Blanck 6928; Sabin 29800; Thomson 482; Wright I 1100

1739 HALL, JAMES

STATISTICS OF THE WEST, AT THE CLOSE OF THE YEAR 1836 . . . CINCINNATI: PUBLISHED BY J. A. JAMES & CO., 1836.

[i]–xviii, 13–284, [285–86 advertisements]. 18.5 x 10.8 cm. Green cloth, title in gilt on backstrip.
Ref.: Blanck 6941; Buck 300; Clark III 49; Howes H79; Rader 1744; Sabin 29795; Thomson 489
Blanck describes two printings differing in pagination of the preliminaries, but neither matches the present copy, since the initial unpaged leaf is not present.

1740 HALL, JAMES

THE WESTERN READER; A SERIES OF USEFUL LESSONS, DESIGNED TO SUCCEED COREY AND FAIRBANK'S ELEMENTARY READER . . . CINCINNATI: COREY AND FAIRBANK, 1833.

[i]–viii, 9–216. (Pages [i] blank, [ii] frontispiece.) 17.8 x 10.2 cm. Four woodcut illustrations. Blue printed boards with calf backstrip, title on front cover, advertisements on back cover.
Ref.: Blanck 6930
The date 1834 on the front cover is hardly surprising, since the preface is dated December, 1833.

1741 HALL, JAMES, *Editor*

THE WESTERN SOUVENIR, A CHRISTMAS AND NEW YEAR'S GIFT FOR 1829. CINCINNATI: PUBLISHED BY N. AND G. GUILFORD.

[I]–IX, 10–324. 14.2 x 9 cm. Seven illustrations listed, including engraved title-page and decorative presentation leaf on vellum. Green silk moiré, title in gilt on backstrip, gilt edges.
Ref.: Blanck 6920; Howes H81; Sabin 29799; Thomson 479
The first Annual published in the West.

1742 HALL, SHARLOT M.

[Wrapper title] FIRST CITIZEN OF PRESCOTT: PAULINE WEAVER, TRAPPER AND MOUNTAIN MAN . . . WITH INTRODUCTION BY ALPHEUS H. FAVOUR.

[1]–28. 21.4 x 13.9 cm. Portrait and one plate. Blue printed wrappers with title on front wrapper.
Ref.: Edwards p. 69
Published at Prescott, Arizona, in 1929.

1743 HALL, THOMAS W.

RECOLLECTIONS OF A GRANDFATHER.

[1]–48. 19 x 12.2 cm. Gray cloth.
Ref.: Cowan p. 259; Howes H87
Howes gives place and date of publication as [Oak Park, Ill., *ca.* 1895]. The prefatory note is signed from Oak Park and the author's death-date, 1895, is mentioned.
Hall tells a charming story of boyhood on a farm in Ohio, residence in Madison, Wisconsin, in 1847, and an overland trip to California in 1849. The five pages of overland narrative and adventure in California are exceptionally interesting. Hall brought considerable gold dust back to his family, but the vicissitudes of life left him stranded at seventy.

1744 HALL, WILLIAM M.

SPEECH . . . IN SUPPORT OF HIS RESOLUTIONS, WHICH PASSED UNANIMOUSLY, IN FAVOR OF A NATIONAL R. ROAD TO THE PACIFIC, ON THE PLAN OF GEO. WILKES, DELIVERED AT THE GREAT RIVER AND HARBOR CONVENTION, AT CHICAGO, ILL., IN THE COMMITTEE OF THE WHOLE, JULY 7, 1847. CHICAGO: JOURNAL OFFICE PRINT, 1847.

[1]–22, [23–4 blank]. 21.5 x 12.2 cm. Removed from bound volume, unbound.
Ref.: Byrd 1190; Howes H91; McMurtrie (*Chicago*) 117; Sabin 29862

1745 HALL & SMITH, Chicago

HALL & SMITH'S CHICAGO CITY DIRECTORY, FOR 1853–'54: CONTAINING A FULL ALPHABETICAL LIST OF CITIZENS, WITH THEIR PLACES OF BUSINESS, &C . . . CHICAGO: ROBERT FERGUS, 1853.

[1–6 (5–6 blank)], [i]–xii, [1]–[260]. 19.8 x 12.4 cm. Map: Map / of the / City of / Chicago. / Published by / A H & C. Burley. 1853 / 34.8 x 26.8 cm. No scale given. Tan printed boards with black leather backstrip, advertisements on covers, title in gilt on backstrip. Name erased from front cover.
Prov.: Signature on title-page: E. B. Myers /. Note on page [1]: Purchased from E. B. Myers / Summer of 1887 for / which paid $5⁰⁰ / L J McCormick / [short underline] /.
Ref.: AII (*Chicago*) 54; Byrd 1975; Sabin 12641

1746 [HALL-WOOD, MARY C. F.]

SANTA BARBARA AS IT IS . . . SANTA BARBARA, CAL.: INDEPENDENT PUBLISHING CO.

[1]–101, [102 blank]. 22.7 x 15 cm. Pink printed wrappers with title on front wrapper and with advertisements on recto and verso of back wrapper.

Ref.: Blumann & Thomas 4210; Howes H93
Copyrighted 1884.

Inserted following page [102] is a broadside table headed: Record of Temperature at Santa Barbara, Cal. / Latitude, 34° 26′; Longitude, 119° 43′. Height above the Sea, 30 feet. / From January 1, 1883 to January 1, 1884, By Geo. P. Tebbetts. / [double rule] / . . . 28.4 x 21.5 cm.

1747 HALLER, GRANVILLE O.

THE DISMISSAL OF MAJOR GRANVILLE O. HALLER, OF THE REGULAR ARMY, OF THE UNITED STATES BY ORDER OF THE SECRETARY OF WAR, IN SPECIAL ORDERS, NO. 331, OF JULY 25TH, 1863. ALSO, A BRIEF MEMOIR OF HIS MILITARY SERVICES, AND A FEW OBSERVATIONS. PATERSON, N.J. PRINTED AT THE DAILY GUARDIAN OFFICE, 1863.

[1–2], [i–ii], [3]–84. 22.5 x 14.5 cm. Buff printed wrappers with title on front wrapper.

Ref.: Howes H95; Nicholson p. 349; Sabin 29886; Smith 4004

Contains material on Indian fighting in Oregon and Washington. Pages [i–ii] are a leaf of errata, verso blank. In some copies, line 7 ends with a comma on front wrapper.

1748 HALSEY, JOHN J.

A HISTORY OF LAKE COUNTY ILLINOIS . . . ROY S. BATES PUBLISHER, 1912.

[i]–xvi, 1–872. 26.5 x 19.5 cm. Two maps unlisted. Black leather, gilt.

Ref.: Buck 895; Howes H101

Printed in Chicago, published in Philadelphia. The authors listed are John J. Halsey, Frank R. Grover, Jesse Lowe Smith, Ellsworth J. Hill, and Henry Kelso Coale. Buck calls this "the best history of an Illinois County which has yet appeared."

1749 HAMBLETON, CHALKLEY J.

A GOLD HUNTER'S EXPERIENCE . . . CHICAGO: PRINTED FOR PRIVATE CIRCULATION, 1898.

[i–ii], [1]–116, [117 colophon, 118 blank]. 18 x 11 cm. Green cloth, gilt top, uncut.

Prov.: Inscribed on front fly-leaf: Compliments of / C. J. Hambleton / 95 Clark St. / Chicago. /

Ref.: Howes H105; Wilcox p. 55

The text comprises the story of an expedition to Pike's Peak in search of gold.

Laid in is an original pencil sketch of a pioneer scene, unfortunately unidentified, inscribed: From our front window looking North /. 12.5 x 20.1 cm.

1750 HAMBLOCK, MARY ELLEN

[Broadside] IN MEMORIAM. MARY ELLEN HAMBLOCK . . . NOTRE DAME, MISSION DOLORES, JAN. 21, 1874.

Broadside, 19 x 8.4 cm. Text, 18.3 x 6 cm.

Inserted in Manuscript Journals of Loren L. Williams, Volume IV.

1751 HAMILTON, B. B.

HISTORICAL SKETCH OF JERSEY COUNTY, ILLINOIS. DELIVERED AT JERSEYVILLE, JULY 4, 1876 . . . JACKSONVILLE, ILL.: COURIER STEAM PRINTING HOUSE, 1876.

[1]–36. 21.5 x 14.2 cm. Gray printed wrappers, with title on front wrapper. Removed from bound volume.

Ref.: Buck 862; Howes H126

1752 HAMILTON, H. W.

RURAL SKETCHES OF MINNESOTA, THE EL DORADO OF THE NORTHWEST . . . TOGETHER WITH A SERIES OF LETTERS UPON NORTHERN WISCONSIN . . . MILAN, OHIO: C. WAGGONER, 1850.

[1]–40. 21.5 x 14.1 cm. Pale blue printed wrappers, with title on front wrapper. In brown cloth folder.

Ref.: Howes H127; Sabin 30012

1753 HAMILTON, HENRY S.

REMINISCENCES OF A VETERAN . . . CONCORD, N.H.: REPUBLICAN PRESS ASSOCIATION, 1897.

[i–iv, iv blank], [1]–180. 17.7 x 13 cm. Four illustrations and several vignettes, unlisted. Green cloth, title in gilt on front cover and backstrip, gilt top.

Ref.: Howes H128; Nicholson p. 351

The author was at Fort Snelling in 1855–56 and at Fort Leavenworth in 1857. His descriptions of the Spirit Lake Massacre and the 1857 march across the plains after the Mormons are both good.—EDG

1754 HAMILTON, JAMES W.

MANUSCRIPT DOCUMENT, SIGNED. 1860 December 15, Trail Creek District [Colorado Territory]. One page, 6.5 x 20 cm.

Claim No. 12 on the Ogdensburgh Lode. Notation of recording on verso.

1755 HAMILTON, JAMES W.

MANUSCRIPT DOCUMENT, SIGNED. 1860 December 15, Trail Creek District [Colorado Territory]. One page, 5.9 x 20 cm.

Claim No. 5 on the Yankey John Lode. Notation of recording on verso.

1756 HAMILTON, JAMES W.

MANUSCRIPT DOCUMENT, SIGNED. 1860 December 29, Trail Creek District [Colorado Territory]. One page, 5 x 20 cm.

Claim No. 2 on the Tennal Lode. Notation of recording on verso.

1757 HAMILTON, WILLIAM, & SAMUEL M. IRVIN

AN IOWAY GRAMMAR, ILLUSTRATING THE PRINCIPLES OF THE LANGUAGE USED BY THE IOWAY, OTOE AND MISSOURI INDIANS . . . IOWAY AND SAC MISSION PRESS, 1848.

[I]–[XIV], [9]–152. 14.8 x 9.5 cm. Old green plain wrappers (probably not original). The preliminary blank leaves have been re-arranged.
   Ref.: Butler (*Iowa*) 2; Pilling 1654; Sabin 30041

1758 [HAMILTON, WILLIAM, & SAMUEL M. IRVIN]

ORIGINAL HYMNS IN THE IOWAY LANGUAGE . . IOWAY AND SAC MISSION PRESS, INDIAN TERRITORY, 1843.

[1]–62. 14.3 x 9.6 cm. Green printed boards with title in the Iowa Indian language on front cover, English title on back cover.
   Prov.: Signature of William Hamilton on fly-leaf.
   Ref.: Barnes: Notes on Imprints from Highland (*Kansas Historical Quarterly*, Vol. VIII, 1939, p. 141); McMurtrie (*Pioneer Press*); Pilling 1653; Sabin 30040
   An edition of 125 copies was printed in 1844, although the title-page is dated the preceding year. The printing was completed between February and September, according to diary notes by Samuel M. Irvin.

1759 HAMILTON, WILLIAM T.

MY SIXTY YEARS ON THE PLAINS; TRAPPING, TRADING, AND INDIAN FIGHTING . . . NEW YORK: FOREST AND STREAM PUBLISHING CO., 1905.

[1]–244. 20.6 x 14.3 cm. Six illustrations by Russell and two photographic portraits, listed. Red cloth.
   Prov.: Inscribed on front fly-leaf: On August 11 - 1947 I visited Hamilton's / grave and monument in the Cemetery at / Columbus, Mon-

tana—the Monument was evidently put up by the town. / Everett D. Graff / I visited this cemetery with Wright Howes of Chicago / and Dudley White of Columbus. /
   Ref.: Dobie p. 72; Howes H139; Rader 1755; Smith 4019
   Bill Hamilton was noted for his ability as a sign-talker. He also tells some mighty fine stories.

1760 HAMMOND, ISAAC B.

REMINISCENCES OF FRONTIER LIFE . . . PORTLAND, OREGON, 1904.*

[1]–[135], [136 blank]. 20.2 x 15 cm. 13 illustrations listed. Gray printed wrappers.
   Ref.: Howes H142; Smith 4024
   Contains a narrative of a trip across the Plains in '65.—EDG

1761 [HAMMOND, JOHN]

JOHN HAMMOND. DIED MAY 28, 1889, AT HIS HOME, CROWN POINT, N.Y. BORN AUGUST 17, 1827, AT CROWN POINT, IN THE OLD HOUSE, NOW STANDING, NEXT WEST OF HIS LATE RESIDENCE. CHICAGO: P. F. PETTIBONE & CO., 1890.

[1]–90. 22.5 x 18.2 cm. Three portraits. Original black leather, with lettering in silver on front cover.
   Ref.: Howes H147
   This memorial volume includes an account of Hammond's overland trip to California by the southern route in 1849. I have personally known quite well three of the grandsons of the author . . . The family as I knew them had no copies of this book.—EDG
   ICN has a series of newspaper clippings from an unidentified paper (Chicago?) which contains more material than is present in the book and includes a second section on Hammond's experiences in California written by Robert Eliot.

1762 HAMMOND, JOHN H.

TYPEWRITTEN LETTER, SIGNED. 1926 September 17, Lookout Hill, Gloucester, Mass. One page, 19.9 x 14.7 cm. To Frederick S. Dellenbaugh.

   Relating to Burnham: *Scouting on Two Continents* . . . 1926 for which Hammond had written a three-page foreword. Tipped into the book.

1763 HANBURY, DAVID T.

SPORT AND TRAVEL IN THE NORTHLAND OF CANADA . . . LONDON: EDWARD ARNOLD, 1904.*

[i]–xxxii, [1]–312, [1]–8 advertisements. 22.2 x 14.4 cm. Illustrations listed. Blue cloth, uncut.
   Ref.:

1764 HANCE, C. H.

REMINISCENCES OF ONE WHO SUFFERED IN THE LOST CAUSE DEDICATED TO RELATIVES AND FRIENDS.

[1]–37, [38–40 blank, 41 colophon, 42 blank]. 24 x 15.8 cm. Portrait. Tan printed wrappers. Silk cord stabbed and tied at front.

Prov.: Inscribed on front wrapper: With Compliments of / Writer /. Frontispiece portrait inscribed: very truly yours / C H Hance /.

Ref.: Howes H150

The colophon reads: Kingsley, Mason & Collins Co., Los Angeles /. Howes suggests 1915. Laid in is a carte-de-visite photograph (circa 1863) of a Confederate officer, possibly the author. Printed in sepia, 9.1 x 5.4 cm., mounted on stiff card, 10 x 6 cm.

1765 HANCOCK, WILLIAM

AN EMIGRANT'S FIVE YEARS IN THE FREE STATES OF AMERICA . . . LONDON: T. CAUTLEY NEWBY, 1860.

[i–vi], [1]–321, [322 blank]. 18.6 x 11.9 cm. One illustration and a map, unlisted. Map: Map / of the / Free States / of / N. America. / Shewing the Railways. / 1859. / [lower left:] Drawn by W. Hancock. / [lower right:] / Stannard & Dixon Lith^{rs} / 28.6 x 57.6 cm. No scale given. Red cloth, blind embossed borders on sides, title in gilt within gilt frame on front cover, gilt title on backstrip, gilt edges.

Prov.: Mounted on front endleaf is a printed and manuscript certificate awarding the volume to Master W. Wilkey of the Commercial Road Academy, Colchester, as a prize for General Progress.

Ref.: Buck 533; Howes H153; Rader 1762; Sabin 30192

1766 HANCOCK COUNTY [ILLINOIS] DEMOCRAT

[Broadside newspaper] HANCOCK COUNTY DEMOCRAT[!]—EXTRA. CARTHAGE, MAY 16TH, 1868. THE PRESIDENT ACQUITED[!] THE RADICAL, NEGRO-THEIVING[!] PARTY GONE UP . . .

Broadside, 27.6 x 8 cm. Text, 19.1 x 5.7 cm. Unbound.

Ref.:

Proof copy, before revision, with manuscript changes in the margins, in pencil. The broadside refers to the impeachment of President Johnson.

1767 HAND BOOK OF FILLMORE COUNTY, NEBRASKA

[Wrapper title] HAND BOOK OF FILLMORE COUNTY NEBRASKA.

[1]–36. 22.7 x 14.9 cm. Illustrations unlisted. White printed wrappers, with title on front wrapper, views on verso of front and verso of back wrapper, and advertisement on recto of back wrapper.

Ref.:

Caption title, page [1]: Fillmore County Hand-Book. /

Place of printing and date are not given, although 1883 occurs as the latest immediately apparent date, on page 2.

1768 HAND BOOK OF WOODSON COUNTY, KANSAS

[Wrapper title] HAND BOOK OF WOODSON COUNTY, KANSAS.

[1]–20. 22.4 x 15.4 cm. Three illustrations in pamphlet, one on back wrapper. Lavender printed wrappers with title on front wrapper, cut on verso of back wrapper, advertisement on verso of front wrapper.

Ref.:

Printed in two columns, the caption heading on page [1] is as follows: [thick and thin rules] / Southern Kansas! / [rule] / Editorial Notes From the Beautiful Ne-/osho and Verdigris Valleys. / . . . No place of printing is indicated. The latest date found in the text is 1882.

On the verso of the front wrapper is an advertisement for Gem City Business College, Quincy, Illinois, with a specimen of off-hand flourishing by J. A. Wesco.

1769 HANDLY, JAMES

THE RESOURCES OF MADISON COUNTY, MONTANA . . .

[1]–[61], [62–4 blank]. 22.9 x 14.6 cm. Pale cream printed wrappers, with title on front wrapper.

Prov.: Rubber stamp of U. S. Geological Survey Library, surcharged with Exchange stamp.

Ref.: Howes H155; McMurtrie (*Montana*) 135; Smith 4032

Printer's imprint on verso of title-page: Francis & Valentine, / Steam Book, Job and Poster Printing Establishment, / 517 Clay Street, San Francisco /. The prefatory note is dated Virginia City, M.T., April 2d, 1872. Pages of advertisements interspersed through text.

The pamphlet describes routes to the mines and includes a business directory.

1770 HANNIBAL AND ST. JOSEPH RAILROAD

[Broadside] 1859. NEW AND SHORT ROUTE OPEN TO THE. 1859. GOLD REGIONS. PIKE'S PEAK AND CHERRY CREEK . . . MAP OF THE HANNIBAL & S.^{T} JOSEPH R. R. AND ITS CONNECTIONS . . . AND ALL PARTS OF KANSAS AND NEBRASKA! HANNIBAL AND S.^{T} JOSEPH RAILROAD IS NOW OPEN TO THE MIS-

SOURI RIVER . . . GEO. C. RAND & AVERY, PRINT-ERS, 3 CORNHILL, BOSTON . . .

Broadside, 50.5 x 31.8 cm. Text, 48.4 x 28.8 cm. Printed on pink paper.

Ref.: Hafen 2 see; Wagner-Camp 325 see

Contains a map (7.4 x 15.4 cm.) of the Hannibal & St. Joseph Railroad "now open to the Missouri River," route distances with notes as to wood, water, and grass along the way, and condition and crossings of streams from St. Joseph to the Gold Region. Contains also various excerpts from newspapers relative to Colorado Gold Fields. Latest date is February 8.—EDG

This is not the same text as that used by the same publishers in Wagner-Camp 325 and Hafen (*Pike's Peak*) 2.

1771 HANS, FRED M.

THE GREAT SIOUX NATION . . . A COMPLETE HISTORY OF INDIAN LIFE AND WARFARE IN AMERICA . . . CHICAGO: M. A. DONOHUE AND COMPANY PUBLISHERS.

[1]–575, [576 blank]. 24.5 x 14.5 cm. Illustrations listed. Red cloth, pictorial panel mounted on front cover.

Ref.: Howes H166; Rader 1769

Copyrighted 1907. Hans was involved in the negotiations leading to the surrender of Sitting Bull in 1879.

1772 HANSON, JOSEPH M.

THE CONQUEST OF THE MISSOURI, BEING THE STORY OF THE LIFE AND EXPLOITS OF CAPTAIN GRANT MARSH . . . CHICAGO: A. C. McCLURG & CO., 1909.*

[i]–xiv, [1]–458. 20.4 x 14 cm. Map and 36 illustrations listed. Green pictorial cloth, fore and lower edges uncut.

Prov.: Bookplate of C. G. Littell.

Ref.: Howes H177; Smith 4050

1773 HANSON, JOSEPH M.

WITH SULLY INTO THE SIOUX LAND . . . CHICAGO: A. C. McCLURG & CO., 1910.

[i–ii], [1]–407, [408 blank]. 20.2 x 13.4 cm. Five illustrations listed. Brown pictorial cloth, title on front cover and backstrip in white.

Ref.:

1774 HARBERT, ALBERT N., *Editor*

PROCEEDINGS OF THE HISTORICAL SOCIETY OF LINN COUNTY, IOWA. CEDAR RAPIDS, IOWA: PUBLISHED BY THE SOCIETY, 1905 [–1907].

[1]–176. [1]–276. 19.4 x 13.5 cm. Illustrations unlisted. Two volumes bound together in half brown levant morocco, gilt back, gilt top.

1775 HARBISON, MASSY (WHITE)

A NARRATIVE OF THE SUFFERINGS OF MASSY HARBISON, FROM INDIAN BARBARITY, GIVING AN ACCOUNT OF HER CAPTIVITY, THE MURDER OF HER TWO CHILDREN, HER ESCAPE, WITH AN INFANT AT HER BREAST . . . DURING THE YEARS, 1790, '91, '92, '93, '94 . . . PITTSBURGH: PRINTED BY S. ENGLES, 1825.

[i]–vi, [7]–66, [67–8 blank]. 16.8 x 10 cm. Stabbed, unbound. In a red half morocco case.

Ref.: Ayer 335; Howes H179; Sabin 30291; Thomson 502

First Separate Edition. Massy's story had been told with others in John Winter's collection of narratives which had been published in 1792–93, 1793, 1794, and 1808–11.

Important narrative on the Ohio-Pennsylvania frontier, with account of St. Clair's defeat.—Howes

1776 HARBOR AND RIVER CONVENTION, CHICAGO, 1847

PROCEEDINGS OF THE HARBOR AND RIVER CONVENTION, HELD AT CHICAGO, JULY FIFTH, 1847 . . . CHICAGO: PRINTED BY R. L. WILSON, 1847.

[1]–79, [80 blank]. 20.1 x 12.2 cm. Yellow printed wrappers with title on front wrapper.

Ref.: Byrd 1193; Howes C371; McMurtrie (*Chicago*) 118; Sabin 12634

The . . . Convention of 1847 was the first great gathering to put Chicago "on the map" as the rallying point for the whole northwest.—McMurtrie

1777 HARDIN, JOHN J.

SPEECH OF MR. J. J. HARDIN, OF ILLINOIS, REVIEWING THE PRINCIPLES OF JAMES K. POLK & THE LEADERS OF MODERN DEMOCRACY . . . JUNE 3, 1844 . . . WASHINGTON: PRINTED BY J. & G. S. GIDEON, 1844.

[1]–16. (Pages 13–16 misbound between 4 and 5.) Bound with Number 1084.

Ref.:

1778 HARDIN, JOHN J.

[Caption title] SPEECH OF MR. J. J. HARDIN, OF ILLINOIS, REVIEWING THE PUBLIC LIFE & POLITICAL PRINCIPLES OF MR. VAN BUREN . . . MARCH 21, 1844 . . .

[1]–32. Bound with Number 1084.

Ref.: Sabin 30328

Printed at Washington in 1844.

1779 [HARDIN, JOHN J.]

[Wrapper title] OBSEQUIES OF COL. JOHN J. HARDIN, AT JACKSONVILLE, ILLINOIS, JULY 14, 1847.

1–24. 21 x 12.5 cm. White printed wrappers.

Prov.: Inscribed on front wrapper by a son of Col. Hardin: This pamphlet is an / exact copy from the / account of the Funeral of / Col. Hardin printed in the / Morgan Journal, Jacksonville / July 17ᵗʰ 1847. / An old copy of the Journal / of the above date was shown / to me by Mr P. Selby at / Springfield, Feb. 10, 1880. /
Ref.:
Caption title on page 1: Reception and Burial of the Remains / of Col. John J. Hardin. / [decorative rule] / . . .

1780 HARDIN, JOHN W.

THE LIFE OF JOHN WESLEY HARDIN, FROM THE ORIGINAL MANUSCRIPT, AS WRITTEN BY HIMSELF. SEGUIN, TEXAS: PUBLISHED BY SMITH & MOORE, 1896.

[1]–144. 18.5 x 12.8 cm. Portrait of Hardin, vignette of his brother, four illustrations, one of which is repeated on verso of back wrapper. Gray printed wrappers with title on front wrapper and illustration on verso of back wrapper. In a green cloth case.

Ref.: Adams 452; Howes H188; Rader 1773

The present copy carries a cut above the text on page [3] mistitled John Wesley Hardin. Facing page [3] is an inserted leaf with a portrait titled John Wesley Hardin. /, and the note in the lower left corner: The picture on the opposite page is that of / Joe Hardin, brother of John Wesley. /

The first few copies of the original edition released by the printers have the portrait of Joe Hardin, John's brother, for the frontispiece instead of one of John Wesley Hardin. The book is carefully written; in fact, so well written that it seems to have come from the pen of someone not so illiterate as Hardin. It was probably ghost written, but whoever the writer, he was careful of his names and dates. He tells of his life up to his death, and his death is discussed in an appendix, with a quotation from the *El Paso Herald* of August 20, 1895.—Adams

Burton Rascoe, in his biography of Belle Starr, claims Hardin was almost illiterate. However, Howes points out that Hardin passed his bar examination and practised law in Texas—not, however, a difficult feat at that time.

Richard M. Brown, after reading Hardin's letters to his family and friends, when he was in prison, concludes that "the letters are written in the same strong, vigorous, and literate prose that distinguishes the book."

1781 HARDING, BENJAMIN

A TOUR THROUGH THE WESTERN COUNTRY, A. D. 1818 & 1819 . . . NEW-LONDON: PRINTED BY SAMUEL GREEN, 1819.

[1]–2⁵ [or [1]¹⁰]. [i–ii half title], [1]–17, [18 blank]. 22.5 x 12.9 cm. Stabbed, unbound, uncut. In a red cloth case.
Prov.: Dahlinger copy.
Ref.: Buck 129; Howes H189; Sabin 30331; Thomson 504
Half-title reads: Harding's Tour. /

1782 HARDINGE, BELLE BOYD

BELLE BOYD, IN CAMP AND PRISON . . . LONDON: SAUNDERS, OTLEY, AND CO., 1865.

[i]–[xii, xii blank], [1]–291, [292 blank]. [i]–[xvi, xvi blank], [1]–280. 19.5 x 12 cm. Portrait. Two volumes, blue cloth, blind embossed panels on sides, titles in gilt on backstrips, uncut.
Ref.: Howes H190; Nicholson p. 357; Sabin 30338

1783 HARLAN, JACOB W.

CALIFORNIA '46 TO '88 . . . SAN FRANCISCO: THE BANCROFT COMPANY, 1888.

[1]–242. 21.8 x 14.9 cm. Portrait. Red cloth, title stamped in gilt on front cover with black bands and black ornament, title stamped in gilt on backstrip.
Ref.: Cowan pp. 264–65; Howes H198

Harlan went overland with the Boggs-Moran party in 1846 and immediately joined Frémont's battalion. He returned East via Panama in 1852 and made a second overland crossing (with 118 head of cattle) the following year. He resettled in California and continued to live there.

1784 HARLOW, NEAL

THE MAPS OF SAN FRANCISCO BAY FROM THE SPANISH DISCOVERY IN 1769 TO THE AMERICAN OCCUPATION . . . SAN FRANCISCO: THE BOOK CLUB OF CALIFORNIA, 1950.

[i]–xii, [1]–140, [141 colophon, 142 blank]. 31.3 x 22.8 cm. 39 maps, mostly folding. Patterned red and black boards, red morocco back, fore and lower edges uncut.
Ref.: Howes H202; Magee 501

Limited to 375 copies printed at the Grabhorn Press.

1785 HARMAN, S. W.

HELL ON THE BORDER; HE HANGED EIGHTY-EIGHT MEN. A HISTORY OF THE GREAT UNITED STATES CRIMINAL COURT AT FORT SMITH, ARKANSAS, AND OF CRIME AND CRIMINALS IN THE INDIAN TERRITORY . . . FORT SMITH, ARK.: THE PHOENIX PUBLISHING COMPANY.

[I]–[XIV, XIV blank], [1]–720. 22 x 14.4 cm. 45 illustrations listed. Light green printed wrappers, with title on front wrapper. In a dark green cloth case.

Ref.: Adams 458; Howes H203; Rader 1780
Copyrighted 1898.

An important source book,—all the statistical part of the book, the biographical sketches of those connected with the court and the transcriptions from the Court records, were the work of C. P. Sterns and are said to be scrupulously accurate. The same cannot be said of all the narratives written by Harman. These are only fairly reliable where he secures his information from Court records or local newspapers and are completely unreliable otherwise.—EDG

1786 HARMON, DANIEL W.

A JOURNAL OF VOYAGES AND TRAVELS IN THE INTERIOUR[!] OF NORTH AMERICA, BETWEEN THE 47TH AND 58TH DEGREES OF NORTH LATITUDE, EXTENDING FROM MONTREAL NEARLY TO THE PACIFIC OCEAN . . . ANDOVER: PRINTED BY FLAGG AND GOULD, 1820.

[1]–54⁴. [i]–xxiii, [xxiv blank], [25]–432. 22.5 x 14 cm. Portrait and map. Map: Map / of the / Interior / of / North America. / Engraved for Harmon's Journal. / Annin & Smith Sc. / Boston. / 19.4 x 47.5 cm. No scale given. Gray boards with old tan paper backstrip, apparently supplied, uncut. Manuscript label on backstrip. In a green cloth case.

Prov.: Bookplate of Worcester County Atheneum. Library stamp of American Antiquarian Society on title-page. Signature of Wilberforce Eames on front endleaf.

Ref.: Field 656; Howes H205; Hubach p. 36; Jones 823; Matthews p. 197; Rader 1781; Sabin 30404; Staton & Tremaine 1171; Wagner-Camp 17

The errata slip, 8.9 x 10 cm., is mounted on the inside back cover.

Editor Daniel Haskell took some liberties with the narrative and the moral and religious undertone woven into it are hardly consistent with life on the Indian frontier. An important book in spite of Mr. Haskell.—Howes

1787 HARNEY, WILLIAM S.

OFFICIAL CORRESPONDENCE OF BRIG. GEN. W. S. HARNEY . . . AND FIRST LT. GEO. IHRIE . . . WITH THE U. S. WAR DEPARTMENT, AND SUBSEQUENT PERSONAL CORRESPONDENCE.

[1]–16. 23.8 x 15 cm. Unbound, uncut.

Ref.: Sabin 30409

Published, apparently, at Washington in 1861. Harney does not appear in a favorable light in this exchange. In the Reavis biography, the reprimand given Harney in this affair is described as the result of earlier antagonisms between Harney and Winfield Scott.

1788 HARPER'S NEW MONTHLY MAGAZINE

[HARPER'S NEW MONTHLY MAGAZINE, VOL. VII, NO. 29, VOL. VIII, NO. 47, VOL. XXV, NO. 148. 1853, 1854, 1862.]

Three articles extracted from issues of the magazine as above, pages 306–34, [577]–96, 447–66. 23.7 x 15.3 cm. Illustrated. New dark blue cloth.

Ref.: Wagner-Camp 222

These three articles by George Douglas Brewerton are headed as follows: A Ride with Kit Carson through the Great American Desert and the Rocky Mountains. Incidents of Travel in New Mexico. In the Buffalo Country.

1789 HARRIS, BRANSON L.

SOME RECOLLECTIONS OF MY BOYHOOD . . . ISSUED ON HIS NINETY-FIRST BIRTHDAY.*

[i–ii], 1–70. 19.2 x 13 cm. Portrait. Dark green cloth.

Ref.: Howes H223

Printed in Indianapolis in 1908.

An interesting account of early Indiana where the author lived. He was born in Wayne County in 1817.—EDG

1790 HARRIS, CAROLINE

HISTORY OF THE CAPTIVITY AND PROVIDENTIAL RELEASE THEREFROM OF MRS. CAROLINE HARRIS, [AND] MRS. CLARISSA PLUMMER . . . NEW YORK: PERRY AND COOKE, PUBLISHERS, 1838.

[1]–[24]. 24 x 15.1 cm. Frontispiece and title-page vignette. Plain pink wrappers. In a brown cloth case.

Ref.: Ayer 209; Howes H224; Rader 1794; Sabin 30466; Streeter 1312; Wagner-Camp 71

The Caroline Harris and Clarissa Plummer narratives have every appearance of being fiction . . . —Streeter. The work has often been confused with captivity narratives of Rachel Plummer, and Mrs. Horn and Mrs. Harris. Streeter neatly sorted the narratives and described them under his numbers 1312, 1320, 1347, and 1525.

1791 HARRIS, FRANK

[Caption title] HISTORY OF WASHINGTON COUNTY CHAPTER 1 . . .

[1]–74. [see note.] 22.2 x 15 cm. Portrait. Stapled, unbound.

Ref.: Adams (*Ramp. Herd*) 999

Pages [1–3] blank, [4] Preface, [i–ii inserted portrait, verso blank], [5] Biography of Judge Frank Harris, [6] blank, 7–74 text. Pages 61–71 carry a History of Adams County. Pages 71–74 a Pioneer Honor Roll. On page 71 the date 1941 occurs. Place of printing is unmentioned. Possibly Weiser, Idaho.

Mounted on page [1] is a green paper label with typed title as follows: History of Washington County / By / Judge Frank Harris /.

1792 HARRIS, JOEL C.

UNCLE REMUS AND HIS FRIENDS. OLD PLANTATION STORIES, SONGS, AND BALLADS WITH SKETCHES OF NEGRO CHARACTER . . . BOSTON: HOUGHTON, MIFFLIN AND COMPANY, 1892.

[1–2], [i]–[xviii, xviii blank], [1]–357, [358–60 blank]. 19.1 x 12.4 cm. 12 illustrations listed. Gray-green pictorial cloth, title in gilt and black on front cover and backstrip.

Ref.: Blanck 7125

1793 HARRIS, JOEL C.

UNCLE REMUS HIS SONGS AND SAYINGS . . . NEW YORK: D. APPLETON AND COMPANY, 1881.

[1]–231, [232 blank], [233–40 advertisements]. 18.9 x 12.5 cm. Eight illustrations and vignettes in text, unlisted. Mustard pictorial cloth, front cover stamped in gilt and black, title in gilt on backstrip.

Ref.: Blanck 7100

With "presumptive" instead of the later "presumptuous" in last line, page 9, and without mention of the book in the advertisements at the back.

1794 HARRIS, N. SAYRE

JOURNAL OF A TOUR IN THE "INDIAN TERRITORY," PERFORMED BY ORDER OF THE DOMESTIC COMMITTEE OF THE BOARD OF MISSIONS OF THE PROTESTANT EPISCOPAL CHURCH, IN THE SPRING OF 1844 . . . NEW YORK: PUBLISHED FOR THE DOMESTIC COMMITTEE OF THE BOARD OF MISSIONS, 1844.

[i–iv, iv blank], [1]–74, [75–76 blank]. 22.6 x 14.6 cm. Three maps. Map: Outline Map / of / Indian Localities / in 1833. / [swelled rule] / in Vol. 2 [preceding three words crossed out heavily in manuscript] see Map of / Localities in 1840. / since all the tribes have / been removed from the States, / W. of the Mississippi. / [swelled rule] / [lower left:] G. Catlin. / [lower right:] Tosswill & C⁰ sc. / 22.1 x 36 cm. No scale given. Map: Aboriginal America / East of the / Mississippi. / [lower centre:] G. Hayward Lithʳ 1 Platt Sᵗ N. Y. / 16 x 10.7 cm. No scale given. Map: U. States' Indian Frontier in 1840, / Shewing the Positions of the Tribes that have been removed west of the Mississippi. / [lower left:] G. Catlin / [lower right:] Tosswill & C⁰ sc. / 21.7 x 13.2 cm. No scale given. Removed from bound volume, unbound, remnant of yellow wrappers on backstrip. In a red cloth case.

Prov.: Inscribed at top of title-page: E Allen / from the Author /, and in the same hand below line 10: Rev N. Sayre Harris /.

Ref.: Clark III 177; Howes H230; Rader 2743; Sabin 30491; Wagner-Camp 109; Wheat (*Transmississippi*) 453–55

1795 HARRIS, SARAH H.

AN UNWRITTEN CHAPTER OF SALT LAKE: 1851–1901 . . . NEW YORK: PRINTED PRIVATELY, 1901.*

[1]–89, [90 blank]. 17.9 x 12.2 cm. Green cloth, gilt, gilt top, uncut.

Ref.: Howes H231

The author was the wife of the first Secretary and Treasurer of the Territory, Broughton D. Harris. Her volume includes (1) record of trip across the plains to Salt Lake, (2) experiences in Utah, July to September, 1851, (3) return trip across the plains.—EDG

1796 HARRIS, WILLIAM

MORMONISM PORTRAYED; ITS ERRORS AND ABSURDITIES EXPOSED, AND THE SPIRIT AND DESIGNS OF ITS AUTHORS MADE MANIFEST . . . WARSAW, ILL.: SHARP & GAMBLE, 1841.

[1]–64. 20.3 x 13.2 cm. Removed from a bound volume, unbound, uncut. In blue solander case.

Ref.: Byrd 628; Howes H237

This is an inflammatory book and marks the beginning of the belligerent anti-Mormon spirit that developed in Illinois and was to reach its climax in 1844–45.—Byrd

1797 HARRIS, WILLIAM R.

THE CATHOLIC CHURCH IN UTAH . . . A REVIEW OF SPANISH AND MISSIONARY EXPLORATIONS . . . SALT LAKE CITY: PUBLISHED BY THE INTERMOUNTAIN CATHOLIC PRESS.*

[1–8], [i]–[iv, iv blank], [i]–[vi, vi blank], [1]–350. 24.2 x 17.3 cm. Map and illustrations unlisted. Green cloth.

Ref.: Howes H238

Copyrighted 1909. According to Howes, this work contains the first English translation of Escalante's account of his Utah discoveries.

1798 HARRIS, WILLIAM T.

REMARKS MADE DURING A TOUR THROUGH THE UNITED STATES OF AMERICA, IN THE YEARS 1817, 1818, AND 1819 . . . LIVERPOOL: PRINTED BY HENRY FISHER.

[*]¹, [A]–I⁴, K¹. [1]–74. 22.1 x 13.6 cm. Rebound in three-quarter brown morocco, gilt top.

Ref.: Buck 117; Clark II 39; Howes H239; Hubach p. 52; Jones 830 (1821 edn.); Sabin 30533; Thomson 511 (1821 edn.)

Signed and dated at the end: W.T.H. / Liverpool, Wednesday Noon, / 1st Sept. 1819. / [rule] / Printed by H. Fisher, Caxton Press, Liverpool. /

The first leaf is a half-title (mounted): [thick and thin rules] / Remarks / Made during a / Tour through the United States / of / America, / in the Years / 1817, 1818, and 1819. / [thin and thick rules] /.

Harris' "Remarks" are more favorable than those of most British travelers through Kentucky, Ohio, Indiana, and Illinois.

1799 HARRISON, E. J.

THE THRILLING, STARTLING AND WONDERFUL NARRATIVE OF LIEUTENANT HARRISON, WHO WAS TAKEN PRISONER AT GOLIAD, TEXAS, IN 1836, AND ONLY ESCAPED THE TREACHEROUS MURDER OF HIS COMPANIONS BY THE INHUMAN MEXICANS, TO BE TRANSFERRED TO A PUNISHMENT WORSE THAN DEATH, NAMELY, THE MINES OF MEXICO . . . CINCINNATI: PUBLISHED BY THE AUTHOR, 1848.

[1]–30, [31–2 blank]. (Pages [1–2] blank.) 19 x 13.3 cm. Illustration in text unlisted. Buff wrappers, with title on front cover. In a brown cloth case.

Ref.: Beinecke's facsimile, 1957; Clements Library (*Texas*) 34; Howes H241; Jones 1173; Rader 1799

On the verso of the title-page is a copyright notice in favor of Chas. P. Vorse dated 1847.

This is Harrison's account of his escape from the Goliad Massacre, his recapture by the Mexicans, and his confinement and treatment in unspecified mines of Mexico. In escaping Harrison overpowered a brutal overseer and used his clothes as a disguise. He then wandered about in Mexico until he stumbled onto Colonel Doniphan's men on their way from California to join General Taylor near Buena Vista.

The H. V. Jones copy differs from the Graff and Beinecke copies in that the cut on the front wrapper is inverted. The Beinecke copy belonged earlier to W. J. Holliday.

1800 HARRISON, F., Jr.

[Map:] MAP / OF THE MOUTH / CHICAGO RIVER ILLINOIS / WITH THE PLAN OF THE PROPOSED PIERS FOR IMPROVING / THE / HARBOUR / DRAWN BY F HARRISON JUN.ᴿ ASSIS.ᵀ / CIVIL ENGINEER / [lower right corner:] FEBY 24ᵀᴴ 1830. Wᴹ HOWARD, / U. S. CIVIL AGT. /

Map, 38.3 x 49.1 cm. Scale: 50 yards to one inch. Laminated. Bound with related materials in contemporary half black calf.

Ref.:

See under ILLINOIS CENTRAL RAILROAD COMPANY.

1801 HART, JOHN A., & Others

HISTORY OF PIONEER DAYS IN TEXAS AND OKLAHOMA . . .

[i–iv], [1]–271, [272 blank]. 15.5 x 11.7 cm. Portraits unlisted. Red cloth. Endpapers present, but unattached.

Ref.: Howes H258; Rader 1805

Place and date of printing are not given, but probably Guthrie, 1908 or 1909. The latest date mentioned in the text (page 220) is 1908. That date is probably present in the 249-page edition which Howes dates [1906].

1802 HART, JOHN A., & Others

PIONEER DAYS IN THE SOUTHWEST FROM 1850 TO 1879 . . . GUTHRIE, OKLA.: THE STATE CAPITAL COMPANY, 1909.

[i]–[vi, vi blank], [7]–320. 19.7 x 13.5 cm. 16 plates. Gray pictorial cloth.

Ref.: Howes H258

The Introduction is signed by Emanuel Dubbs. Charles Goodknight, John Hart, and others supplied material relating to frontier life for this work.

1803 HART, JOHN A., & Others

THE SAME.

[i]–[vi, vi blank], [7]–320. 19 x 13.6 cm. 20 plates. Gray pictorial cloth.

Ref.: Howes H258

Following the Introduction, there is an additional paragraph headed: Note by the Writer, E. Dubbs: /

The text from the lower third of page 281 to 320 has been reset.

1804 HARTE, FRANCIS BRET

AUTOGRAPH LETTER, SIGNED. 1870 September 30, San Francisco. To J. W. Bliss. Three pages, 20.3 x 12.8 cm.

Offering, on the author's behalf, Stephen Powers' *Afoot and Alone* for publication. Harte praises the manuscript highly. Laid in Powers: *Afoot and Alone* . . . Hartford, Conn., 1872.

1805 HARTE, FRANCIS BRET

THE LUCK OF ROARING CAMP, AND OTHER SKETCHES . . . BOSTON: FIELDS, OSGOOD, & CO., 1870.

[1]–[viii], [1]–[239], [240 blank]. 17.8 x 11.3 cm. Terra cotta cloth, blind embossed borders on sides, title in gilt on backstrip. In a brown half morocco slip case.

Ref.: Blanck 7246; Sabin 30650

First Edition.

1806 HARTHILL, ALEXANDER

THE RIVER MISSISSIPPI, FROM ST. PAUL TO NEW ORLEANS, ILLUSTRATED AND DESCRIBED . . . NEW YORK: ALEX. HARTHILL AND COMPANY.

[i–ii], [1]–[118]. 22.8 x 14.1 cm. 42 illustrations listed, 30 charts unlisted. Tan printed wrappers bound into new black cloth. Title on front wrapper, advertisements on verso and on recto and verso of back wrapper.

Ref.: Buck 607; Howes H263
Published in 1859, undated.

1807 HARTLEY, W. M.

[Map:] HARTLEY'S / MAP OF / ARIZONA / FROM OFFICIAL DOCUMENTS. / SCALE OF MILES / [diagrammatic scale: 25 miles to one inch] / OFFICE 32 PINE ST. N. Y. / [lower right:] DRAWN & ENG. BY J. C. SMITH N. Y. /

Map, 76.7 x 91.3 cm. Scale as above. Folded into green cloth folder, 15.9 x 10 cm., blind embossed corner ornaments, title in gilt on front cover.

Ref.: Munk (Alliot) p. 203
The map is undated, but in the Munk Collection, there is a copy presented by Hartley to President Lincoln.

1808 HARTMANN, H.

[Map:] MAP / SHOWING / PROPOSED RESERVATION FOR THE JICARILLA APACHES / IN / NEW MEXICO. / BOUNDARY OF NEW MEXICO AND COLORADO / [lower right:] COMPILED FROM OFFICIAL SOURCES / BY / H. HARTMANN / SANTA FE, N. M. JANUARY 1887. C. E. / SCALE: 160 CHAINS TO ONE INCH. /

Map, 50.2 x 33.5 cm. Scale as above.
Prov.: From the Grierson Papers.
Ref.:
Blueprint map.

1809 HARVEY, AUGUSTUS F.

[Map:] A NEW MAP / OF THE / PRINCIPAL ROUTES / TO THE GOLD REGION OF / COLORADO TERRITORY / DRAWN BY AUG. F. HARVEY / 1862 / CIVIL ENGINEER / [lower right:] JUL^S HUTAWA / LITHOGRAPHIC / MAP PUBLISHING OFFICE / CHESTNUT ST. 65 BETW. 3RD & 4TH STS. / N.E. COR. OF ALLEY / ST. LOUIS, MISSOURI /

Map, 54.5 x 88.5 cm. No scale given. Framed.
Ref.:
Bordered with columns at each side and broad bands of fine black lines at top and bottom on which are superimposed the business cards of 18 business firms of Nebraska City, N.T.

Augustus F. Harvey was editor of the *Nebraska City News* from October 19, 1861 to Aug.

25, 1865, and was the author of *Sketches of the Early Days of Nebraska City, Nebraska Territory, 1854–1860.* St. Louis, 1871.—EDG

1810 HARVEY, AUGUSTUS F.

SKETCHES OF THE EARLY DAYS OF NEBRASKA CITY, NEBRASKA TERRITORY. 1854–1860 . . . SAINT LOUIS: WESTERN INSURANCE REVIEW BOOK AND JOB PRINTING HOUSE, 1871.

[1]–30, [31–32 blank]. 16.9 x 12.7 cm. Brown cloth with title in gilt on front cover.

Ref.: Howes H274
Copyright notice on a slip, 2.5 x 8.5 cm., mounted on verso of title-leaf.
A grand tale and I believe authentic.—EDG
Harvey (known also as "Ajax") wrote *Nebraska as it Is; a Description of the Soil, Climate, Productions, Mineral and Agricultural Resources of the State of Nebraska* . . . Lincoln: "Statesman" Print. Office, 1869.

1811 HARWOOD, THOMAS

HISTORY OF NEW MEXICO SPANISH AND ENGLISH MISSIONS OF THE METHODIST EPISCOPAL CHURCH FROM 1850 TO 1910 . . . ALBUQUERQUE, NEW MEXICO: EL ABOGADO PRESS, 1908.*

[i–viii], 1–376. [I]–XVI, 1–[451], 452 advertisement]. (Pages [I]–II blank.) 17.6 x 12 cm. Nine illustrations. Two volumes, first volume in red cloth, second in blue.

Ref.: Howes H276; Saunders 68
Printed by Indian students at the Mission press.

1812 HASKINS, C. W.

THE ARGONAUTS OF CALIFORNIA, BEING THE REMINISCENCES OF SCENES AND INCIDENTS THAT OCCURRED IN CALIFORNIA IN EARLY MINING DAYS . . . NEW YORK: PUBLISHED FOR THE AUTHOR, 1890.

[1–4], [i–ii], [5]–501, [502 blank]. 23.5 x 17.1 cm. 118 illustrations listed. Yellow pictorial cloth.

Ref.: Blumann & Thomas 4983; Bradford 2149; Cowan p. 269; Howes H283
Especially valuable because of the list of names of pioneers before 1850.

1813 HASSLER, EDGAR W.

OLD WESTMORELAND: A HISTORY OF WESTERN PENNSYLVANIA DURING THE REVOLUTION . . . PITTSBURG: J. R. WELDIN & CO., 1900.

[1]–4, i–vi, 5–200. 22.6 x 14.9 cm. Dark green cloth.
Ref.: Howes H286

1814 HASTINGS, FRANK S.

A RANCHMAN'S RECOLLECTIONS. AN AUTOBIOGRAPHY IN WHICH UNFAMILIAR FACTS BEARING UPON

THE ORIGIN OF THE CATTLE INDUSTRY IN THE SOUTHWEST AND OF THE AMERICAN PACKING BUSINESS ARE STATED ... CHICAGO: THE BREEDER'S GAZETTE, 1921.

[i]–[xiv, xiv blank], 1–235, [236 blank]. 19.1 x 13.4 cm. 14 illustrations listed. Tan pictorial cloth, brown top, uncut.

Ref.: Adams (*Ramp. Herd*) 1009; Howes H287; Rader 1819

A very interesting and informative book on the Texas cattle business.—EDG

1815 HASTINGS, LANSFORD W.

THE EMIGRANTS' GUIDE, TO OREGON AND CALIFORNIA, CONTAINING SCENES AND INCIDENTS OF A PARTY OF OREGON EMIGRANTS; A DESCRIPTION OF OREGON; SCENES AND INCIDENTS OF A PARTY OF CALIFORNIA EMIGRANTS; AND A DESCRIPTION OF CALIFORNIA; WITH A DESCRIPTION OF THE DIFFERENT ROUTES TO THOSE COUNTRIES; AND ALL NECESSARY INFORMATION RELATIVE TO THE EQUIPMENT, SUPPLIES, AND THE METHOD OF TRAVELING ... CINCINNATI: PUBLISHED BY GEORGE CONCLIN, 1845.

[1]–152. 22.3 x 14.3 cm. Tan wrappers, with title on the front wrapper, advertisement on verso of back wrapper. In a red half morocco case.

Prov.: See below.

Ref.: Bradford 2153; Cowan p. 105; Hanna-Powell p. 25; Howes H288; Jones 1105; Sabin 30824; Smith 4148; Wagner-Camp 116; Zamorano Eighty 41

As the earliest important guide, Hastings' work was "avidly read and the suggestions closely followed."

This is the Jones copy and item 462 in the Littell sale. It is the only fine copy in wrappers I have seen.—EDG

1816 HASWELL, ANTHONY

MEMOIRS AND ADVENTURES OF CAPTAIN MATTHEW PHELPS ... PARTICULARLY IN TWO VOYAGES, FROM CONNECTICUT TO THE RIVER MISSISSIPPI, FROM DECEMBER 1773 TO OCTOBER 1780 ... COMPILED FROM THE ORIGINAL JOURNAL AND MINUTES KEPT BY MR. PHELPS, DURING HIS VOYAGES AND ADVENTURES, AND REVISED AND CORRECTED ACCORDING TO HIS PRESENT RECOLLECTION ... BENNINGTON, VERMONT: FROM THE PRESS OF ANTHONY HASWELL, 1802.

[A]², B⁶, C⁴, D–Z⁶. (L3 missigned K2.) [i]–iv, [5]–210, 1–63, [64–66], [I]–XII. 17 x 10.5 cm. Original mottled calf, with red leather label.

Prov.: J. E. Hill / stamped twice in purple ink inside front cover. On front endleaf: John Johns / His book. / bought july 30 1851. / This may be the famous "Pen-printer of Vermont."

Ref.: Bay p. 331; Bradford 2155; Clark I 287; Gilman 203; Howes H300; Hubach p. 26; Jones 289; Sabin 30829

In spite of the moralizing and some very bad verse composed by Phelps, the *Memoirs* is one of the most fascinating and harrowing narratives of the early nineteenth century. Phelps and his family were members of a party led by Phineas Lyman to settle on the Yazoo River. Their adventures were tragic and it is no wonder Phelps returned to New England as soon as he could make it.

1817 HATHAWAY, JOSHUA, Jr.

[Map:] CHICAGO / WITH THE / SCHOOL SECTION / WABANSIA / AND / KINZIE'S ADDITIONS. / COMPILED FROM THE FOUR ORIGINAL SURVEYS AS FILED IN THE / COOK COUNTY / CLERK'S OFFICE. / BY JOSHUA HATHAWAY JR. /

Map, 71.3 x 50 cm. Scale: about 400 feet to one inch. Folded into green leather folder. Mounted and laminated. In a green cloth case.

Prov.: Inscribed on inner front cover: To Mr Samuel George / From S. C. Turges(?) / [flourishes] /

Ref.: Chicago History, Vol. III, No. 3, Spring, 1952

The first published map of Chicago. A notice in the *Chicago Democrat* of June 18, 1834, notes a map for sale. Although the Hathaway map is not named, the *Democrat's* description of a map showing the "School Section, Wabansia and Kinzie's Addition" is exactly that of the Hathaway legend and does not seem to refer to the somewhat later map of J. S. Wright which bears the imprint date of 1834.—EDG

1818 HATHEWAY, O. P., & J. H. TAYLOR

CHICAGO CITY DIRECTORY, AND ANNUAL ADVERTISER, FOR 1849–50 ... CHICAGO: JAS. J. LANGDON, 1849.

[1]–264. 18.4 x 11.5 cm. Yellow printed boards, red roan back, with title on front cover, advertisements on verso of front and recto and verso of back covers.

Ref.: Howes H303; Byrd 1450; McMurtrie (*Chicago*) 173

1819 HATSUTARO

[KAIGWAI IBUN; AMERIKA SHINWA. Strange Informations from the Other Side of the Sea; or, The New Story of America.]

[1–50]. [1–40]. [1–42]. [1–37]. [1–32]. (In first volume, pages [1] and [50] are mounted on inner wrappers; in fourth volume, page [37] is mounted on inner back wrapper.) 25 x 17.9 cm. Map, 13 double page and 26 single page colored woodcuts; paper for woodcuts differs from text. Map in two sections: [Route of Hatsutarō and Kensuke]. 17.9 x 12.4 and 18 x 12.4 cm. No scale given. Five volumes, light brown striped wrappers, printed paper labels, 18.5 x 2.9 cm. In brown paper case, red leather label.

Ref.: Brown (*Block Printing & Book Illustration in Japan*) p. 216; Sakamaki (*Japan and the United States*) pp. 75–6; Toda (*Descriptive Catalogue . . . Ryerson Library*) p. 441

Published in Japan in 1854.

One of the most interesting and amusing accounts of castaway Japanese sailors. The original party consisted of thirteen men who were picked up by a Spanish ship in 1841, after drifting for four months, and taken to Baja California. Nine of the men found work in San José and the other four stayed aboard the Spanish ship. Two of the nine men, Hatsutarō and Kensuke, went to Mazatlán where they found an American ship, the *Abigail Smith*, bound for China. They reached Nagasaki aboard a Chinese ship on January 2, 1844. The account is a good one and the illustrations of Mexican scenes are very attractive.

1820 HAUPT, HERMAN

THE YELLOWSTONE NATIONAL PARK . . . A COMPLETE GUIDE TO AND DESCRIPTION OF THE WONDROUS YELLOWSTONE REGION . . . NEW YORK: J. M. STODDART, 1883.

[1]–190, [191–92 blank], [1–12 lined pages headed Tourist's Memoranda], [1–7 advertisements on yellow paper, 8 blank]. 17.5 x 10.4 cm. Folding map and 14 listed plates. Pictorial gray cloth, with wallet flap.

Ref.: Bradford 2160; National Parks (*Yellowstone*) p. 43; Russell p. 99

1821 HAVERLY, CHARLES E.

KLONDYKE AND FORTUNE. THE EXPERIENCE OF A MINER WHO HAS ACQUIRED A FORTUNE IN THE YUKON VALLEY . . . LONDON: SOUTHWOOD, SMITH & CO.*

[1–4], [i]–iv, [1]–135, [136 colophon]. 18.6 x 12.1 cm. Red printed limp boards, dark red leather back. In red cloth case.

Prov.: Inscribed on title-page: With the Compliments of / The Author / Imre Kiralfy Esq / [underline] /.

Ref.: Howes H310; Smith 4159; Wickersham 3929

Howes and Wickersham give date of publication as 1898.

According to a note in pencil on inner front cover, the recipient, Kiralfy, was the organizer of the White City Expedition.

1822 HAWES, A. G.

A HISTORICAL SKETCH AND REVIEW OF THE BUSINESS OF THE CITY OF LEAVENWORTH, KANSAS TERRITORY . . . LEAVENWORTH CITY: PRINTED AT THE "JOURNAL" BOOK AND JOB OFFICE, 1857.

[1]–32. 20.6 x 12.9 cm. Yellow printed wrappers, with title on front wrapper. In red cloth folder.

Ref.: AII (*Kansas*) 102; Howes H311; Jones 1375; Rader 1824

Preceding title-page and following final page is a leaf of yellow paper bearing advertisements.

1823 HAWES, GEORGE W.

ILLINOIS STATE GAZETTEER AND BUSINESS DIRECTORY, FOR 1858 AND 1859 . . . CHICAGO, ILLINOIS.

[i]–xxxvi, [1]–444. 22 x 14 cm. Brown printed boards, black leather backstrip with title in gilt on backstrip, advertisements on covers and on endpapers.

Prov.: Signature on title-page and following leaf: James L Young /, also on inner front cover and on page [i]. Rubber stamp of Chicago Historical Society twice on title-page and with two rubber stamps: Withdrawn / From the C. H. S. / Library numerals on title-page crossed out.

Ref.: AII (*Chicago*) 333; Byrd 2923; Howes H313

Printed in 1858.

1824 HAWES, GEORGE W., & CO.

MISSOURI STATE GAZETTEER, SHIPPERS' GUIDE, AND BUSINESS DIRECTORY FOR 1865 . . . INDIANAPOLIS: GEO. W. HAWES & CO., 1865.

[i]–xxxvi, [1]–418, [3]–112. (Page [1] pasted to inside front cover.) 22.5 x 14.3 cm. Illustrations and maps, portrait of publisher on verso of title-page. New tan boards, brown morocco backstrip, gilt advertisements, advertisement on fore edge.

Ref.: Howes H314; Sabin 49623

Villard's *The Past and Present of the Pike's Peak Gold Regions* (pages [3]–112) is bound in without title-page following the text.

There is a broadsheet advertisement following page 418: North Missouri / Railroad. / [decorative rule] / The only all rail route / from St. Louis to / St. Joseph, Atchison, / Savannah & Weston, / [43 lines] / [Republican Print.] / On verso: Map of the / North Missouri / Railway & Connections. / See Appleton's Railway Guide. / 15.3 x 22.2 cm. No scale given. Advertisements in margins. Both sides printed in red and blue. Silked.

1825 HAWK-EYE PIONEER ASSOCIATION

CONSTITUTION OF THE HAWK-EYE PIONEER ASSOCIATION, OF DES MOINES COUNTY, IOWA. WITH A

FULL REPORT OF THE PROCEEDINGS OF ITS FIRST ANNUAL FESTIVAL, CELEBRATED JUNE 2D, A. D. 1858. BURLINGTON: THOMPSON & SHEWARD, BOOK AND JOB PRINTERS, 1858.

[1]–54. 22.2 x 14.3 cm. Dark orange wrappers, with title on front wrapper.

Ref.: Moffit 375; Mott (*Iowa*) p. 68; Sabin 19764

1826 HAWKEYE PIONEER AND OLD SETTLERS ASSOCIATION

CONSTITUTION OF THE HAWKEYE PIONEER AND OLD SETTLERS ASSOCIATION, OF DES MOINES COUNTY, IOWA. ORGANIZED SEPTEMBER 7TH, 1881. TO WHICH IS APPENDED A LIST OF THE MEMBERS (INCLUDING THOSE OF THE OLD "HAWKEYE PIONEER ASSOCIATION" AND OF THE "BENTON PIONEER ASSOCIATION"), GIVING THE DATE OF THE FIRST SETTLEMENT OF EACH IN IOWA, AS SHOWN BY THE RECORDS. COMPILED BY E. C. BLACKMAR, SECRETARY . . . BURLINGTON, IOWA: ACRES, BLACKMAR & CO., PRINTERS, 1882.

[1]–22. Gray printed wrappers with list of officers on back wrapper and title on front wrapper. Bound with number 1825 in light green buckram.
Ref.:

1827 HAWKINS, JOHN P.

MEMORANDA CONCERNING SOME BRANCHES OF THE HAWKINS FAMILY AND CONNECTIONS . . .

[1]–137, [138 blank]. 22.9 x 15.3 cm. 17 illustrations unlisted. Dark red cloth, title in gilt on front cover.
Prov.: Signature of Helen P. Robison on inner front cover. Tipped to front endleaf is a slip signed by the author. Laid in is printed card: Compliments of / Gen. John P. Hawkins / 1408 N. Penn St. Indianapolis, Ind. / 3.8 x 8.2 cm.
Ref.: Howes H320
Published in Indianapolis, 1913.

Contains General Hawkins' reminiscences. He was graduated from West Point in June 1852, stationed at Fort Kearney for two years, at Fort Ridgeley, Minn. for three years, and at Fort Randall and Fort Abercrombie. He includes accounts of the Civil War, the Modoc War, etc. A scarce book.—EDG

1828 HAWLEY, ZERAH

A JOURNAL OF A TOUR THROUGH CONNECTICUT, MASSACHUSETTS, NEW-YORK, THE NORTH PART OF PENNSYLVANIA AND OHIO, INCLUDING A YEAR'S RESIDENCE IN THAT PART OF THE STATE OF OHIO, STYLED NEW CONNECTICUT, OR WESTERN RESERVE . . . NEW-HAVEN: PRINTED BY S. CONVERSE, 1822.*

[1]–158. 16 x 10 cm. Rebound in half red morocco, gilt top, uncut. Last blank leaf missing.
Ref.: Howes H333; Jones 841; Rusk I pp. 76, 120; Sabin 30988; Thomson 530

In the 1820's there were exaggerated accounts of the "Paradise" of Ohio. Hawley, as Rusk points out, was more realistic. His account is accurate, factual, and veers away from panegyrics. *The Cincinnati Literary Gazette*, Vol. II, No. 4, contains an interesting unfavorable review of the work.

1829 HAY, JOHN

LETTERS OF JOHN HAY AND EXTRACTS FROM DIARY . . . WASHINGTON: PRINTED BUT NOT PUBLISHED, 1908.

[1–2], i–xxii, 1–393, [394 blank]. [i–ii], 1–368. [i–ii], 1–350. 24.4 x 16 cm. Three volumes, blue buckram, printed white paper labels on backstrips, uncut, partly unopened.
Ref.: Howes H335

1830 HAYDEN, FERDINAND V.

THE YELLOWSTONE NATIONAL PARK, AND THE MOUNTAIN REGIONS OF PORTIONS OF IDAHO, NEVADA, COLORADO AND UTAH . . . ILLUSTRATED BY CHROMOLITHOGRAPHIC REPRODUCTIONS OF WATER-COLOR SKETCHES, BY THOMAS MORAN . . . BOSTON: L. PRANG AND COMPANY, 1876.

[I]–[VI, VI blank], 1–48. 54 x 43.5 cm. Two maps and 15 colored plates, listed. Dark green cloth, dark green morocco corners and backstrip, brass clasps, gilt edges.
Ref.: Howes H338; National Parks (*Yellowstone*) p. 44; Russell p. 100

1831 HAYES, AUGUSTUS A.

NEW COLORADO AND THE SANTA FE TRAIL . . . ILLUSTRATED. LONDON: C. KEGAN PAUL & CO., 1881.

[1]–200. (Page [3] blank, page [4] map.) 22.5 x 15.9 cm. 61 illustrations and a map listed. Red pictorial cloth.
Ref.: Rader 1833 see; Saunders 2944 see; Wilcox p. 58 see

The essays had appeared previously in *Harper's* and the *International Review*.
Editions: New York, 1880.

1832 HAYNE, M. H. E.

THE PIONEERS OF THE KLONDYKE; BEING AN ACCOUNT OF TWO YEARS POLICE SERVICE IN THE YUKON . . . RECORDED BY H. WEST TAYLOR . . . LONDON: SAMPSON LOW, MARSTON AND COMPANY, 1897.*

[i]–[xvi], [1]–184. 18.5 x 12 cm. 17 illustrations listed. Red cloth.
Ref.: Smith 4258; Wickersham 4333

1833 HAZEN, REUBEN W.

HISTORY OF THE PAWNEE INDIANS . . . [FREMONT, NEBRASKA:] FREMONT TRIBUNE, 1893.

[1]–80. 17.2 x 12.7 cm. Illustrations and vignettes unlisted. Pictorial gray cloth.

Ref.: Howes H371; Rader 1836

Includes some interesting Nebraska local history. "Early Days in Nebraska" is by James H. Peters. The history of the Pawnee war is by Hazen, a participant.

1834 HAZEN, WILLIAM B.

OUR BARREN LANDS. THE INTERIOR OF THE UNITED STATES WEST OF THE 100TH MERIDIAN, AND EAST OF THE SIERRA NEVADAS . . . CINCINNATI: ROBERT CLARKE & COMPANY, PRINTERS, 1875.*

[1]–53, [54–56 blank]. 23.5 x 15.4 cm. Original printed blue wrappers, with title on front cover within thick and thin rule borders.

Prov.: Inscribed in pencil on front wrapper: With Compliments of Gen'l Hazen /.

Ref.: Howes H372

In this and another pamphlet of eighteen pages published at St. Paul the same year, *Some corrections of "Life on the Plains,"* Hazen could see no economic possibilities in the northern interior.—Howes

1835 [HEALD, HENRY]

[Caption title] A WESTERN TOUR, IN A SERIES OF LETTERS WRITTEN DURING A JOURNEY THROUGH PENNSYLVANIA, OHIO, INDIANA, AND INTO THE STATES OF ILLINOIS AND KENTUCKY . . .

[1]–91, [92 blank]. 19.8 x 11.7 cm. Stabbed. Remnants of wrappers (probably later). Top margin of first leaf and parts of three letters supplied. In red morocco case.

Prov.: See below.

Ref.: Howes H377; Jones 811

Imprint at end: [thick and thin rules] / J. Wilson, Printer, No. 105, Market Street, Wilmington. / [thin and thick rules]. / Printed either in 1819 or 1820. The fifteen letters occupy pages [1]–89 and the "Apology" pages 90–91.

There were three copies of this narrative discovered in the hands of a descendant of Henry Heald about twenty years ago. One of these was sold to Shea and disposed of in the sale of his library in 1937 to the Pittsburgh Historical Society. Another copy was sold to Jones and this is the copy in my collection. The other copy of this narrative went into the New York Public Library. It is unlikely that another copy of this narrative will ever turn up.—EDG

1836 HEAP, GWINN H.

AUTOGRAPH LETTER, SIGNED. 1861 June 8, Powhatan . . . off S.W. Pass. Miss. River. To George F. Emmons. Four pages, 24.8 x 19.6 cm.

A good Civil War letter regarding the naval end and including remarks on the projected attack on Pensacola. Laid in Heap: *Central Route . . .* 1854.

1837 HEAP, GWINN H.

CENTRAL ROUTE TO THE PACIFIC, FROM THE VALLEY OF THE MISSISSIPPI TO CALIFORNIA: JOURNAL OF THE EXPEDITION OF E. F. BEALE . . . AND GWINN HARRIS HEAP, FROM MISSOURI TO CALIFORNIA, IN 1853 . . . PHILADELPHIA: LIPPINCOTT, GRAMBO, AND CO., 1854.

[1]–136, 1–16. 22.7 x 14.5 cm. 13 tinted lithographic plates listed and one map. Map: Map / of the / Central Route / from the / Valley of the / Mississippi to California. / Compiled & Drawn by G. H. Heap. / [double rule] / Note. The Route from the mouth of Huerfano R. to Las Vegas de Santa Clara is / from notes kept by G. H. Heap during the Expedition of Superintendent Beale from / Westport M^{r1} to California in the year 1853. / The remainder is from surveys of J. C. Frémont and others. / [diagrammatic scale: 50 miles to one inch] / Statute Miles. / [lower right:] P. S. Duval & Co's Steam lith. Press, Philad^{a} / 18.8 x 88.8 cm. Scale: 50 miles to one inch. Dark gray cloth, advertisements on endpapers.

Prov.: Inscribed in pencil on the first blank leaf: To M^{r}s Thornton / from her affectionate nephew / G H. Heap /. Also inscribed in pencil: And from Mrs. Thornton / to G. F. E[mmons]. 1856. /

Ref.: Cowan p. 273; Howes H378; *Railway Economics* p. 283; Sabin 31175; Saunders 2947; Wagner-Camp 235; Wheat (*Transmississippi*) 808

Pasted down on the inner front cover is the face of an envelope addressed by Heap to George F. Emmons. Laid in is an Autograph Letter, signed by Heap to Emmons and an Autograph Letter, signed by F. H. Rogers.

Some of the areas explored are here described for the first time.

1838 HEARD, ISAAC V. D.

HISTORY OF THE SIOUX WAR AND MASSACRES OF 1862 AND 1863 . . . NEW YORK: HARPER & BROTHERS, 1863.

[i]–[xii, xii blank], [13]–354, [1]–2 advertisements. 19 x 12.4 cm. 33 illustrations. Dark blue cloth.

Ref.: Field 675; Howes H378a; Rader 1838; Sabin 31178

1839 HEARD, ISAAC V. D.
THE SAME, 1865.

Prov.: Inscribed on recto of frontispiece: W. D. Kirk / From I. V. D. Heard / Feb 11, 1890 / St Paul / [underline] /. Also on front flyleaf in pencil: To E from E /.

1840 HEARNE, SAMUEL
A JOURNEY FROM PRINCE OF WALES'S FORT IN HUDSON'S BAY, TO THE NORTHERN OCEAN . . . IN THE YEARS 1769, 1770, 1771, & 1772 . . . LONDON: PRINTED FOR A. STRAHAN AND T. CADELL, 1795.

[A]², a–e⁴, B–3M⁴, 3N². [i]–xliv, [1]–458, [459–60]. 30 x 23.8 cm. Four engraved plates and five maps: Map: A Map / exhibiting Mʳ Hearne's Tracks in his / two Journies for the discovery of the / Copper Mine River, / in the Years 1770, 1771 and 1772; / [short swelled rule] under the direction of the [short swelled rule] / Hudson's Bay Company. / [swelled rule] / [at foot, below border:] London Published Janʸ 1ˢᵗ 1795, by Cadell & Davies Strand. / [lower right corner:] Engraved by S. J. Neele 352, Strand. / 53.5 x 65.5 cm. No scale given. Map: A / Plan / of the / Copper-Mine River, / Surveyed by / Samuel Hearne / July. 1771. / [upper left corner:] Plate III / [upper right corner:] To face Page 164 / [lower centre:] London, Published Janʸ 1ˢᵗ 1795, by Cadell & Davies, Strand. / 20.3 x 44.8 cm. Scale: about 2 1/8 English sea miles to one inch. Map: A Plan of / Albany River / in Hudson's Bay. / Latitude, 52ʺ 12ʺ 0 North. / Longitude 82ʺ 40ʺ 0 W. from London. / by, S. H. 1774. / [swelled rule] / [upper left:] Plate VI / [upper right:] At the end / [lower centre:] London, Published Janʸ 1ˢᵗ 1795, by Cadell & Davies, Strand. / [lower right:] S. J. Neele sculpᵗ 362 Strand. / 27.4 x 35.6 cm. Scale: about 1 7/8 miles to one inch. Map: Plan / of / Moos River, / [swelled rule] in [swelled rule] / Hudsons Bay, North America. / Lat. 53° N. Lon. 83° W. from London. / by S. H. 1774. / [upper left:] Plate VII / [upper right:] At the end / [lower centre:] London Published Janʸ 1ˢᵗ 1795, by Cadell & Davies, Strand. / [lower right:] Neele sculpᵗ 352 Strand. / 25.5 x 45 cm. Scale: 1 1/4 miles to one inch. Map: Plan / of / Slude River, / Lat. 52ʺ 15′ N, Lon. 83ʺ 20′ W. / by S. H. / [upper left:] Plate VIII / [upper right:] At the end / [lower centre:] London Published Janʸ 1ˢᵗ 1794, by Cadell & Davies, Strand. / [lower right:] Neele Sculpᵗ 352, Strand /. 35.5 x 27.4 cm. Scale: 1 1/2 miles to one inch. Half blue polished calf, marbled board sides, gilt back, red leather label, gilt top.

Ref.: Field 676; Sabin 31181; Smith 4283; Staton & Tremaine 445; Wagner-Camp 7, 9 (notes)

Published posthumously, Hearne having died in 1792. The manuscript is said to have been found at Fort Albany, when Lapérouse captured the fort. When the fort was re-surrendered, Lapérouse insisted the manuscript should be published. It is the best eighteenth century account of the northern reaches of the Hudson's Bay area by a careful observer. The work is of considerable importance in the study of the Indians and their manners and customs in the Hudson's Bay region.

1841 HEART, JONATHAN
JOURNAL OF CAPT. JONATHAN HEART . . . SEVENTH OF SEPTEMBER, TO THE TWELFTH OF OCTOBER, 1785 . . . THE DICKINSON-HARMAR CORRESPONDENCE OF 1784–5 . . . [EDITED BY] CONSUL WILLSHIRE BUTTERFIELD . . . ALBANY, N.Y.: JOEL MUNSELL'S SONS, 1885.

[i]–[xvi, xvi blank], [1]–94. 22 x 18 cm. Tan printed wrappers, uncut. In a yellow cloth case.

Ref.: Howes H379; Matthews p. 168
Limited to 150 copies.

1842 HEBERT, FRANK
40 YEARS PROSPECTING AND MINING IN THE BLACK HILLS OF SOUTH DAKOTA . . .

[i–viii], [1]–199, [200 blank]. 20.5 x 13.9 cm. Seven illustrations listed. Green cloth.

Ref.: Adams 470; Howes H385; Jennewein 100

Published at Rapid City, South Dakota, by the Rapid City Daily Journal. Copyrighted 1921.

1843 HECKE, J. VALENTIN
REISE DURCH DIE VEREINIGTEN STAATEN VON NORD-AMERIKA IN DEN JAHREN 1818 UND 1819 . . . BERLIN: IN COMMISSION BEI H. PH. PETRI, 1820 [–21].

[I]–[X], [1]–228. [I]–XVI, [1]–326, [327–28 advertisements]. 19.8 x 11.8 cm. Colored frontispiece. Two volumes bound together in brown half calf, yellow leather label on backstrip.

Ref.: Buck 130; Clark II, 205; Howes H388; Sabin 31202; Streeter 1078

This book is, nevertheless, interesting reading, if only because of the author's gullibility, speculative thoughts and invalid conclusions.—Clark

One of the earliest books (if not the first) in which German colonization of Texas is urged strongly.

1844 HECKENDORN & WILSON, *Compilers*

MINERS & BUSINESS MEN'S DIRECTORY. FOR THE YEAR COMMENCING JANUARY 1ST, 1856. EMBRACING A GENERAL DIRECTORY OF THE CITIZENS OF TUOLUMNE, AND PORTIONS OF CALAVERAS, STANISLAUS AND SAN JOAQUIN COUNTIES. TOGETHER WITH THE MINING LAWS OF EACH DISTRICT, A DESCRIPTION OF THE DIFFERENT CAMPS . . . COLUMBIA: PRINTED AT THE CLIPPER OFFICE, 1856.

[i–viii (i.e., [i–iv] advertisements, [v] title-page, [vi] blank, [vii] illustration, [viii] blank)], [1]–104. 23 x 14 cm. One illustration. Sheep. Rebacked with calf to match.

Prov.: Rubber stamp releasing volume from Mercantile Library Association at head of title-page. Rubber stamp of same library on page [1].

Ref.: Blumann & Thomas 4726; Cowan p. 174; Greenwood 693; Howes H389; Sabin 97445

For each area there is a short historical section. An important feature of this volume is the series of mining laws, most of which are printed here for the first and only time.

Page [9]: . . . Mining Laws of Columbia District. /

Pages [54]–55: . . . Mining Laws of Jamestown District. /

Pages [60]–61: . . . Mining Laws of Shaw's Flat. /

Pages [65]–66: . . . Mining Laws of Springfield / District. /

Page [72]: . . . By-Laws of Gold Springs Mining / District. /

Page 76: Mining Laws of Saw Mill Flat. /

Pages 77–78: . . . Brown's Flat Mining Laws. /

Pages 79–80: . . . Mining Laws of Tuttletown. /

Page 80: . . . Mining Laws of Jackass Gulch. /

Pages 81–82: . . . Mining Laws of Montezuma District. /

Page 83: . . . Mining Laws of Chinese Camp. /

Page 86: . . . Mining Laws of Jacksonville. /

Page 87: . . . Mining Laws of Poverty Hill, Yorktown / and Chili Camp. /

Page 91: . . . Mining Laws of Garote. /

Pages 93–94: . . . Mining Laws of La Grange. /

Especially important are the lists of miners and business men in the various camps, towns, districts, etc.

1845 HELENA (Montana) THEATRE

[Broadside] HELENA THEATRE! WOOD STREET . . . J. S. POTTER. THE MANAGEMENT MOST RESPECTFULLY ANNOUNCES THAT THEY HAVE EFFECTED AN ENGAGEMENT WITH THE TALENTED AND POPULAR WALTER BRAY'S DRAMATIC AND CONCERT TROUPE! BY GENERAL DESIRE THE BEAUTIFUL DRAMA OF ANDY BLAKE WILL BE PRESENTED . . . MONDAY EVENING, JULY 16TH, 1866 . . . ADMISSION, . . . $2.00. "RADIATOR" PRINT, HELENA, MON. TER.

Broadside, 61 x 22.7 cm. Text, 56.7 x 17.4 cm.

Ref.:

Among the performers was Ned Ward, "The Excellent Gymnast and Eccentric Ethiopian Comedian."

1846 HELENA'S SOCIAL SUPREMACY . . .

HELENA'S SOCIAL SUPREMACY . . . HELENA, MONTANA, MDCCCXCIV.

[1]–48. 16.5 x 11.2 cm. Illustrations unlisted. Yellow printed wrappers, with title on front wrapper, cartoon on verso of back wrapper.

Ref.: Smith 4318

Although the imprint is given as Helena, this pamphlet was probably not printed there. It is an attack on Helena during the fight over the location of the Montana state capitol. It was published by the adherents of Anaconda. Humorous advertisements on pages 46–48.

1847 HELM, MARY S.

SCRAPS OF EARLY TEXAS HISTORY . . . AUSTIN, TEXAS: PRINTED FOR THE AUTHOR AT THE OFFICE OF B. R. WARNER & CO., 1884.

[1–2], [i]–iv, [3]–[199], [200 blank]. 21.1 x 13.7 cm. Maroon cloth, blind embossed borders on sides, enclosing gilt title on front cover.

Ref.: Howes H399; Rader 1846

Contains field notes of Elias R. Wightman, one of the first surveyors working in Texas under Stephen A. Austin. The gilt-stamped title on the front cover reads: Scraps from Early Texas History . . .

1848 HELPER, HINTON R.

THE LAND OF GOLD . . . BALTIMORE: PUBLISHED FOR THE AUTHOR, BY HENRY TAYLOR, 1855.

[i]–xii, [13]–300. 19 x 11.3 cm. Gray cloth, sides blind embossed, title stamped in gilt on backstrip.

Ref.: Bradford 2222; Cowan p. 274; Howes H401; Sabin 31272

An entertaining book. One chapter is closed with the charming remark that "It is my unbiased opinion that California can and does furnish the best bad things that are obtainable in America." Seventy-five years have wrought no visible change.—Cowan

1849 HEMENWAY, MOSES

THE MANUFACTURER'S, FARMER'S, & MECHANIC'S GUIDE; BEING A COMPILATION OF THE MOST VALUABLE RECEIPTS, FOR MANUFACTURERS, AGRICULTURISTS, AND MECHANICS . . . PITTSBURGH: PRINTED FOR the COMPILER, 1822.

[1]–[179], [180 blank]. 14.3 x 8.6 cm. Tan boards, paper back.

Prov.: Bookplate of Charles Norton Ewing.

Ref.:

1850 HENDERSON, GEORGE D.

[Wrapper title] ADDRESS ON THE DEATH OF GEN. NATHANIEL LYON. DELIVERED AT MANHATTAN, KANSAS, SEPTEMBER 26TH, 1861 . . . LEAVENWORTH: PRINTED AT THE DAILY CONSERVATIVE BOOK AND JOB PRINTING OFFICE.

[1]–8. 22 x 14.1 cm. Bright yellow printed wrappers, with title on front wrapper.

Ref.: AII (*Kansas*) 284; Sabin 31311

Lyon was one of the first national heroes of the Civil War. He had been in large part responsible for the fact that Missouri remained out of the Confederacy. Much of his active army career was lived out in "Bleeding Kansas."

1851 HENDERSON, JOHN G.

EARLY HISTORY OF THE "SANGAMON COUNTRY;" BEING NOTES ON THE FIRST SETTLEMENTS IN THE TERRITORY NOW COMPRISED WITHIN THE LIMITS OF MORGAN, SCOTT AND CASS COUNTIES . . . DAVENPORT, IOWA: DAY, EGBERT, & FIDLAR, 1873.

[i]–v, [vi blank], [7]–33, [34 blank]. (Errata slip, 7.4 x 13.9 cm., before p. 33.) 21 x 13.9 cm. Removed from bound volume, unbound.

Ref.: Buck 732; Howes H409

Illinois history.

1852 HENDERSON, THOMAS

AN EASY SYSTEM OF THE GEOGRAPHY OF THE WORLD; BY WAY OF QUESTION AND ANSWER, PRINCIPALLY DESIGNED FOR SCHOOLS . . . LEXINGTON, KY.: PRINTED BY THOMAS T. SKILLMAN, 1813.

[A]–S⁶. (G1 unsigned, Q3 missigned p2.) [1]–213, [214–16 blank]. 17 x 10 cm. Original or contemporary calf, skiver label. Lacks front endleaf.

Prov.: W. J. Holliday copy.

Ref.: AII (*Kentucky*) 460; Howes H410; Shaw & Shoemaker 28730

Appendix devoted chiefly to the Mississippi Valley and the Old Northwest.—Howes

1853 HENDRY, ANTHONY

[Wrapper title] . . . YORK FACTORY TO THE BLACKFEET COUNTRY. THE JOURNAL OF ANTHONY HENDRY, 1754–55. EDITED BY LAWRENCE J. BURPEE . . . OTTAWA: PRINTED FOR THE AUTHOR BY THE ROYAL SOCIETY OF CANADA, 1908.

307–364. 24.8 x 16.3 cm. Five illustrations, one sketch map, one folding map. Olive-green wrappers.

Prov.: Inscribed on front cover: With the editor's / Compliments / ——— /.

Ref.:

1854 HENDRY, J. E., & C. S. FELL, *Compilers*

RESIDENCE AND BUSINESS DIRECTORY OF BILLINGS, MONTANA . . . ALSO A HISTORY OF BILLINGS AND OF YELLOWSTONE CO. . . . MINNEAPOLIS: REYNOLDS & HAMMOND, PRINTERS, 1883.

[1]–96. (Page [1] blank, page [2] portrait of Frederick Billings.) 21.1 x 14.3 cm. Portrait and two illustrations. Gray printed boards, black cloth backstrip, advertisements on front and back covers, with title in centre of front cover.

Prov.: Signature on front cover: J. Breuchaud / June 1883 /. Breuchaud is listed in the work as County Treasurer.

Ref.: Howes H411

1855 HENN, WILLIAMS & CO.

[Map] A / SECTIONAL MAP / OF / IOWA / COMPILED FROM THE / OFFICIAL SURVEYS OF THE UNITED STATES / AND THE / PUBLIC RECORDS OF THE STATE & COUNTIES / AND FROM / PERSONAL RECONNOïSSANCE. / [three columns, column 1:] BY / HENN WILLIAMS & C°. / OF FAIRFIELD, IOWA. / [column 2:] 1857. / [column 3:] PUBLISHED BY / KEEN & LEE, / CHICAGO, ILLINOIS. / [above cartouche, slightly to right, within flourishes:] ENGRAVED BY / THEODORE LEONHARDT / UNDER THE DIRECTION OF / J. L. HAZZARD. / [below preceding, within flourishes:] PRINTED, MOUNTED & COLORED / BY / CHARLES DESILVER, PUBLISHER / NO. 251 MARKET STREET, / PHILADELPHIA / [lower left:] ENTERED ACCORDING TO ACT OF CONGRESS BY KEEN & LEE, IN THE YEAR 1857, IN THE CLERKS OFFICE OF THE DISTRICT COURT OF ILLINOIS. /

Map, 131 x 165.5 cm. (decorative border). No scale given. Laid in maroon roan covers, with wallet flap, gilt lettered on flap: Henn Williams & Co. / Sectional Map / of Iowa / Keen & Lee / Chicago / 1857 /.

Ref.: Phillips (*Maps*) p. 337

Printed advertisement inside front cover for Keen & Lee.

Editions: Burlington, Iowa, 1851. Fairfield, Iowa, 1854.

1856 HENN, WILLIAMS & CO.

[Map:] A TOWNSHIP MAP / OF THE STATE OF / IOWA / [decorative rule] / COMPILED FROM THE UNITED STATES SURVEYS AND PERSONAL / RECONNAISSANCE SHOWING THE STREAMS, ROADS, TOWNS, / COUNTY SEATS, WORKS OF INTERNAL IMPROVEMENT, &C. &C. / BY HENN, WILLIAMS & CO.

FAIRFIELD, IOWA. / [decorative rule] / J. F. ABRAHAMS, PUBLISHER, BURLINGTON, IOWA / AND BY R. L. BARNES, PHILADELPHIA, / N.E. CORNER OF 7.ᵀᴴ & MARKET STS. / 1851. / [swelled rule] / FRIEND & AUB LITH. PHIL.ᴬ / [centre, above neat line:] ENTERED, ACCORDING TO AN ACT OF CONGRESS, IN THE YEAR 1851, BY R. L. BARNES IN THE CLERKS OFFICE OF THE DISTRICT COURT OF PA. / Map, 47.3 x 79.6 cm. No scale given.

Ref.:

Advertisement of Henn, Williams & Co. as land agents in upper right corner, also advertising card of J. F. Abrahams. A few manuscript notes in ink on the western part of the map and in the left margin.

1857 HENN, WILLIAMS & CO.

[Map] A TOWNSHIP MAP / OF THE STATE OF / IOWA / COMPILED FROM THE UNITED STATES SURVEYS, OFFICIAL INFORMATION AND / PERSONAL RECONNAISSANCE; SHOWING THE STREAMS, ROADS, TOWNS, POST OFFICES, / COUNTY SEATS, WORKS OF INTERNAL IMPROVEMENT, &C &C. / PUBLISHED BY HENN, WILLIAMS & CO. FAIRFIELD, IOWA / AND BY R. L. BARNES, PHILADELPHIA, / N.°. 6 SOUTH 7.ᵀᴴ STREET / 1855. / LITH OF FRIEND & AUB, PHIL.ᴬ / ENTERED, ACCORDING TO ACT OF CONGRESS, IN THE YEAR 1854, BY R. L. BARNES IN THE CLERK'S OFFICE OF THE EASTERN DISTRICT-COURT OF PENN.ᴬ /

Map, 52.8 x 86.4 cm. No scale given. Folded into black cloth covers, 14.7 x 9.5 cm., in gilt on front cover: Henn. Williams & Co.ᵃ / Township Map / of / Iowa /.

Ref.: Phillips (*Maps*) p. 337

Publishers' advertisements (as land dealers) in upper left corner.

Editions: Burlington, Iowa, 1851.

1858 HENNEPIN, LOUIS

DESCRIPTION DE LA LOUISIANE, NOUVELLEMENT DECOUVERTE AU SUD'OUEST DE LA NOUVELLE FRANCE, A PARIS: CHEZ LA VEUVE SEBASTIEN HURE', M. DC. LXXXIII.

ã⁶, A⁸, B⁴, C–Cc^alternately 8 and 4, A⁸, B⁴, C [missigned B¹⁻², corrected C³⁻⁴]⁸, D–H^alternately 4 and 8, I⁶. [Heading and pagination on 223 imperfectly printed. Ornament on p. 63 of Pt II incomplete, signature Eiiij missigned Biiij.] [i–xii], [1]–312, [1]–107, [108 blank]. Folding map: Carte / de la / Nouuelle France / et de la / Louisiane / Nouuellement decouuerte / dediée / Au Roy / l'An 1683. / Par le Reuerend Pere / Louis Hennepin / Missionaire Recollect / et Notaire Apostolique— / [lower left of cartouche:] N. Guerard. / [lower left:] Roussel scripsit. / 29 x 47.1 cm. No scale given. Contemporary full

red levant morocco, triple gilt fillets on sides, with arms of Louis-Auguste de Bourbon, duc de Maine, (son of Louis XIV and la marquise de Montespan) on covers, gilt over marbled edges. In brown leather case.

Ref.: Bradford 2233; Greenly (*Michigan*) 8; Harrisse 150; Howes H415; Jones 330; Paltsits pp. xlix–1; Rader 1851; Sabin 31347; Staton & Tremaine 81; Streit II 2721

The 107 pages of text at the end are headed with a caption title: Les Moeurs / des Sauvages. / [rule] / . . .

1859 HENNEPIN, LOUIS

THE SAME . . . A PARIS, CHEZ AMABLE AUROY, RUE SAINT SAINT[!] JACQUES A L'IMAGE S. JEROME, ATTENANT LA FONTAINE S. SEVERIN. M. DC. L. XXXVIII.*

ã⁶, A–Cc^alternately 8 and 4, A–H^alternately 8 and 4, I⁶. [i–xii], [1]–312, [1]–107, [108 blank]. 15.4 x 8.6 cm. Folding map: as in the First Edition, but a facsimile. Contemporary calf, gilt backstrip, leather label.

Ref.: see preceding.

At the end of the printer's license (page [xii]): Acheve' d'imprimer pour le secon. / 1 de fois, le 10. Mars 1688. / [rule] / De l'Imprimerie de Laurent / Rondet. / The errors in the signatures, gathering C, have been corrected.

1860 HENNEPIN, LOUIS

A DESCRIPTION OF LOUISIANA . . . TRANSLATED FROM THE EDITION OF 1683 . . . BY JOHN GILMARY SHEA . . . NEW YORK: JOHN G. SHEA, 1880.

[1]–40, 41*–56*, [41]–407, [408 blank]. 25.5 x 15.1 cm. Map and facsimile. Gray wrappers, printed gray paper label on backstrip, uncut. In a gray cloth case.

Ref.: Bradford 2251; Howes H415; Rader 1852; Streit III 2712

Some of the additional material appears here for the first time in English.

1861 HENNEPIN, LOUIS

A DISCOVERY OF A LARGE, RICH, AND PLENTIFUL COUNTRY, IN THE NORTH AMERICA; EXTENDING ABOVE 4000 LEAGUES . . . LONDON: PRINTED FOR W. BOREHAM.

[A]², B–E⁴. [i–iv], [1]–22, [23–24 advertisements]. 18.7 x 11.4 cm. Rebound in full mottled polished calf, gilt fillets on sides, gilt corner ornaments, gilt backstrip, red leather label on backstrip, gilt dentelles, by Riviere.

Ref.: Bradford 2250; Paltsits p. lvi; Sabin 31373

This is an abridgment, published in 1720, of Hennepin's *Nouvelle Decouverte . . .* 1697.

1862 HENNEPIN, LOUIS

A NEW DISCOVERY OF A VAST COUNTRY IN AMER-
ICA, EXTENDING ABOVE FOUR THOUSAND MILES,
BETWEEN NEW FRANCE AND NEW MEXICO . . .
LONDON: PRINTED FOR M. BENTLEY, J. TONSON,
H. BONWICK, T. GOODWIN, AND S. MANSHIP, 1698.

A⁸, a⁴, B–T⁸, V⁶, Aa⁶, Bb–Ee⁸, *ee², Ff–Nn⁸,
Oo⁴, [*]¹, X–Z⁸, Aa². [i]–xxiv, [1]–299, [300
blank], [i]–xvi, [1]–178, [301–02 half-title, verso
blank], 303–55, [356 blank]. [Mispaginations:
95 & 94 transposed, 102 and 103 for 202 and
203, 109 and 107 for 206 and 207; Part II: inserted *ee, (45, 46), (47, 48), 81 for 91, 141 for
131. Chapter heading for XXIII misnumbered
XXII.] 18.5 x 11.5 cm. Six folding plates and
two folding maps. Map: A Map / of a Large
Country / Newly Discovered / in the / Northern
America / Situated between / New Mexico / And
the Frozen Sea / together with the Course of the
Great River / Meschasipi / Dedicated to his
Maᵗʸ· / William III / King of Great Britain / By
Father / Lewis Hennepin / Missionary Recollect
and / Apostolic Notary. / 36.6 x 42.7 cm. Scale:
about 200 miles to one inch. Map: A Map / of a
New World / between New Mexico / And the
Frozen Sea / Newly Discovered by Father /
Lewis Hennepin / Missionary Recollect and Native / of Aht in Hainault / Dedicated to his Majesty / of / Great Britain / William III. /
26.6 x 43.6 cm. No scale given. *Inset:* Land of
Iesso / 5.3 x 7.6 cm. No scale given. Contemporary sprinkled calf, blind fillets on sides and
backstrip, red sprinkled edges.

Ref.: Church 772; Field 685; Greenly (*Michigan*) 8 note; Harrisse 181; Howes H416; Jones
364; Paltsits pp. lix–lxi; Sabin 31371

This is the "Bon" edition described by Paltsits. The Continuation, printed with smaller type,
is an insert between page [300] and the half-title
of "An Account of several New Discoveries in
America." The Church copy, following the order
of signatures, has the Continuation at the end of
Part I, after page [356].

1863 HENNEPIN, LOUIS

NOUVEAU VOYAGE D'UN PAIS PLUS GRAND QUE
L'EUROPE AVEC LES REFLECTIONS DES ENTERPRISES
DU SIEUR DE LA SALLE, SUR LES MINES DE ST.
BARBE, &C . . . A UTRECHT: CHEZ ANTOINE SCHOU-
TEN, MARCHAND LIBRAIRE, 1698.

*_**12, ***11, A–Q¹², R⁴. [i–lxx], [1]–389, [390–
92 blank]. 15.3 x 9 cm. One map and three
plates. Map: Carte / d'un nouueau / Monde, /
entre le nouueau / Mexique, / et la Mer Gla-
cialle / Novellement decouvert par le / R. P.

Louis de Hennepin / Missionaire Recollect,
natif d'Aht / en Hainaut / dediee' a sa Majeste' /
Britanique, le Roy / Guilaume Troisieme /
[lower left:] Gasp: Bouttats fecit / 28.7 x 46.3
cm. No scale given. *Inset:* Terre de Iesso. /
4.9 x 7.5 cm. No scale given. Original marbled
boards (limp), with new brown paper backstrip,
contemporary manuscript label on backstrip,
uncut. In a brown half morocco case.

Prov.: Bookplate of J. C. MacCoy.

Ref.: Bradford 2237; Church 774 note; Harrisse 177; Howes H417; Paltsits pp. lvi–lviii;
Sabin 31351; Staton & Tremaine 84; Streit II
2775

1864 HENNEPIN, LOUIS

NOUVELLE DECOUVERTE D'UN TRES GRAND PAYS
SITUE DANS L'AMERIQUE, ENTRE LE NOUVEAU
MEXIQUE, ET LA MER GLACIALE . . . A UTRECHT:
CHEZ GUILLAUME BROEDELET, MDCXCVII.

*_***12, A–N¹², O*⁴⁺¹, O–X¹², Y¹ (Q4 missigned
Q7, R6 missigned R8). [i]–lxxii, [1]–506 (with 10
pages, each paginated *313, between pages 312
and 313). 16 x 10 cm. Engraved frontispiece,
(leaf *1 and conjugate of *12), two plates and
two folding maps. Map: Carte / d'un tres
grand / Pays / entre le / Nouveau Mexique / et
la / Mer Glaciale / Dediée a / Guillaume IIIᵉ /
Roy de la Grand Brettagne / Par le R. P. / Louis
de Hennepin / Mission: Recol: et Not: Apost: /
Chez G. Broedelet / a Utreght / [in cartouche:]
I. V. Varea del. et fecit / 42.9 x 51.8 cm. Scale:
about 115 lieues to one inch. *Inset:* Terre de
Iesso. / 9.8 x 16. cm. No scale given. Map:
Carte / d'un tres grand Pais / Nouvellement
découvert / dans / l'Amerique Septentrionale /
entre le / Nouveau Mexique et la / Mer Glaciale / avec le Cours du Grand Fleuve / Meschasipi / Dediée a / Guillaume IIIᵉ / Roy de la
Grand Brettagne / Par le R. P. / Louis de Hennepin / Mission: Recoll: et Not: Apost: / Chez
G. Broedelet / a Utreght. / 37.2 x 43.8 cm. Scale:
about 62.5 lieues to one inch. Original mottled
boards, uncut, manuscript paper label on backstrip. In a brown half morocco case.

Prov.: Bookplate of Giovanni Rossi of Venice. MacCoy copy with bookplate.

Ref.: Bradford 2235; JCB II 1513; Church
762; Harrisse 175; Howes H416; Paltsits lii–liv;
Sabin '31349; Staton & Tremaine 83; Streit II
2773

Engraved title-page preceding printed title:
Nouvelle Decouverte / d'un tres grand / Pays /
Situé dans l'Amerique / Par R. P. Lovis de
Hennepin / a Utrec / Chez Guiliaume Broede-
let. /

1865 HENNESSEY, A. L., & H. F. TYLER,
Compilers

A COMPLETE CITY DIRECTORY OF LA SALLE AND PERU . . . LA SALLE, ILLINOIS: PRINTED BY A. L. HENNESSEY, 1876.

[i], [1]–150, [151 blank]. (Rectos carry even numbers.) 19.2 x 13.2 cm. Printed green boards with short title and advertisement on front cover, advertisement on back cover, blue cloth backstrip.
Ref.:

1866 HENRY, ALEXANDER

TRAVELS AND ADVENTURES IN CANADA AND THE INDIAN TERRITORIES, BETWEEN THE YEARS 1760 AND 1776 . . . NEW-YORK: PRINTED AND PUBLISHED BY I. RILEY, 1809.

[1]–41⁴, [42]². [i]–[viii], [1]–330, [331 errata], [332 blank]. 23 x 14.4 cm. Portrait. Gray boards, white paper back, white printed label, 3.4 x 2.7 cm., uncut, mostly unopened. In dark red cloth case.
Ref.: Field 686; Howes H420; Jones 732; Sabin 31383; Staton & Tremaine 484; Wagner-Camp 7

Authentic narrative of fur-trading among Indians of the upper lakes. A miraculous escape from massacre during Pontiac's war, captivity, etc.—Howes

1867 HENRY, JAMES P.

RESOURCES OF THE STATE OF ARKANSAS, WITH DESCRIPTION OF COUNTIES, RAILROADS, MINES, AND THE CITY OF LITTLE ROCK . . . SECOND EDITION . . . LITTLE ROCK: PRICE & M'CLURE, 1872.

[1]–[168]. 19.8 x 13.2 cm. Map: Rail-Road & County map / of the / State of Arkansas. / Accompanying James P. Henry's pamphlet / on the Resources of the State of Arkansas. / [decorative rule] / Scale, 36 Miles to the Inch. / [decorative rule] / Sanford Robinson, Del. / [decorative rule] / [lower right:] Henry Seibert & Bros. Ledger Building, Cor. Williams & Spruce St N. Y. / 22.6 x 22 cm. (inner neat line). Scale as above. Printed yellow wrappers, with title on front wrapper, advertisements on verso of front and recto and verso of back wrapper, sprinkled edges. Removed from bound volume, new backstrip supplied. In a yellow cloth case.
Ref.: Allen (*Arkansas*) 652

There had been an earlier edition of the same year with only 134 pages of text and no map. In the present copy there is no phrase: —Price 50 cents / following Second Edition. / on the front wrapper. Pages [167–68] carry additional text, not advertisements.
Editions: Little Rock, 1872.

1868 HENRY, STUART O.

CONQUERING OUR GREAT AMERICAN PLAINS . . . NEW YORK: E. P. DUTTON & CO.*

[i]-xvi, [1]–395, [396 blank]. 20.7 x 13.8 cm. Eight illustrations listed. Green cloth, yellow top, uncut.
Ref.: Adams 475; Howes H427; Rader 1854
Copyrighted 1930.

The author lived in Abilene, Kansas, from 1868 and wrote from personal knowledge and reliable records. He tore Emerson Hough apart for historical inaccuracies and dislodged Wild Bill Hickok from his pedestal.—EDG

1869 HENSHAW, DAVID

LETTERS ON THE INTERNAL IMPROVEMENTS AND COMMERCE OF THE WEST . . . BOSTON: DUTTON AND WENTWORTH, 1839.

[1]–29, [30–32 blank]. 23.4 x 14.3 cm. Printed blue wrappers, with title on front wrapper.
Ref.: Buck 325; Howes (1954) 4762; Sabin 31422

The last letter, from Peoria, details intended improvements in Illinois.

1870 HERNDON, SARAH RAYMOND

DAYS ON THE ROAD CROSSING THE PLAINS IN 1865 . . . NEW YORK: BURR PRINTING HOUSE, 1902.*

[i]-xvi, [1]–270. 17.9 x 12.4 cm. Portrait. Brown cloth.
Ref.: Howes H439; Smith 4371

The work had appeared previously as a series of letters in the *Rocky Mountain Husbandman*. The author was a member of the Hardinbrooke ox-train.

1871 HERNDON, WILLIAM H., & JESSE W. WEIK

HERNDON'S LINCOLN. THE TRUE STORY OF A GREAT LIFE . . . CHICAGO: BELFORD, CLARKE & COMPANY.

[i]-xx, 1–199, [200–04 advertisements]. [200]–418, [419–24 advertisements]. [419]–638, [639–42 advertisements]. 63 illustrations unlisted. Three volumes, blue cloth, gilt facsimile of Lincoln's signature on front covers, titles on backstrips, gilt tops.
Ref.: Howes H440; Monaghan 1049
Copyrighted 1889.

1872 HESPERIAN, THE

THE HESPERIAN; OR, WESTERN MONTHLY MAGAZINE. EDITED BY WILLIAM D. GALLAGHER AND OTWAY CURRY . . . COLUMBUS, OHIO: PUBLISHED BY JOHN D. NICHOLS. 1828 [–1829].

[1–4], [7]–500, [I]–II. [i]–iv, [5]–500. [i]–iv, [9]–500. 22.8 x 15.3 cm. Three volumes, third volume in contemporary half russia, first two volumes bound in calf to match.

Ref.: Gregory p. 1204; Sabin 31615; Thomson 547

The title in the second volume was changed to: The Hesperian; / A Monthly / Miscellany of General Literature, / Original and Select. / Curry's name was dropped as co-editor. The third volume follows the second, except that the place of publication is given as Cincinnati.

Each of the volumes consists of six numbers. Among the original contributions are the following:

"Ohio in Eighteen Hundred Thirty Eight," signed W. D. G. [William D. Gallagher.] Vol. I, Nos. 1–3.

"Notes on Texas," signed R. Vol. I, Nos. 5–6; Vol. II, Nos. 1–6.

"Recollections of a Tour through the Territory of Wisconsin Six Years Since," unsigned. Vol. II, No. 4.

"Hunting Sports of the West," unsigned. Vol. II, No. 6.

"Scenes on the Mississippi. By the Author of 'Tales from the Queen City.'" Vol. III, No. 3.

1873 HESSE, NICHOLAS

DAS WESTLICHE NORDAMERIKA, IN BESONDERER BEZIEHUNG AUF DIE DEUTSCHEN EINWANDERER IN IHREN LANDWIRTHSCHAFTLICHEN, HANDELS- UND GEWERBVERHALTNISSEN . . . PADERBORN: BEI JOSEPH WESENER, 1838.

[i–viii, viii blank], [I]–XIV, [1]–244. 20.3–20.6 x 13.6–12.2 cm. Map: Deutsches Sogen. / West-Falen / Settle-ment im / Missouri-Staate am / Osage [lettering disposed around windrose] [lower right:] Stdr. v. P. Herle, & C°. in Paderborn. / *Inset:* C [Settlement on Maria Creek] 16 x 9.8 cm. No scale given. *Inset:* B [Section grid on Maria Creek] 16 x 9.8 cm. No scale given. *Inset:* D [View of a log cabin] 8.5 x 12.5 cm. 33.8 x 43.3 cm. No scale given. Tan printed wrappers, with title on front wrapper, uncut. In a blue cloth case.

Ref.: Howes H446; Hubach pp. 80–81

Containing some information about Arkansas and Texas, the book deals principally with Missouri. Hesse was not encouraged by his American adventure.

1874 HEUSTIS, DANIEL D.

A NARRATIVE OF THE ADVENTURES AND SUFFERINGS OF CAPTAIN DANIEL D. HEUSTIS AND HIS COMPANIONS, IN CANADA AND VAN DIEMAN'S LAND, DURING A LONG CAPTIVITY; WITH TRAVELS IN CALIFORNIA, AND VOYAGES AT SEA. BOSTON: PUBLISHED FOR REDDING & CO., 1847.

[i]–vi, [7]–168. 19.3 x 12.3 cm. Frontispiece. Yellow printed wrappers with title on front wrapper. In blue board case.

Ref.: Cowan p. 277; Howes H449; Sabin 31627 see; Staton & Tremaine 2718

1875 HEWITT, RANDALL H.

ACROSS THE PLAINS AND OVER THE DIVIDE. A MULE TRAIN JOURNEY FROM EAST TO WEST IN 1862 . . . NEW YORK: BROADWAY PUBLISHING CO.

[1–6], i–[iv, iv blank], [1]–521, [522 blank], [1–12 advertisements]. 18.6 x 12.8 cm. Illustrations unlisted. Green pictorial cloth, printed paper label on front cover, fore and lower edges uncut.

Prov.: Inscribed on front fly-leaf: To Mr. Sam T. Clover / Editor News / With compliments of / The Author / Randall H. Hewitt / Los Angeles, Calif. / Nov. 21, '06 / .

Ref.: Howes H457; Smith 4393; Wagner-Camp 391 note

Copyrighted 1906. Third Edition of the famous work which had appeared in 1863 as *Notes by the Way.*

Editions: Olympia, 1863, 1872.

1876 HEWITT, RANDALL H.

NOTES BY THE WAY. MEMORANDA OF A JOURNEY ACROSS THE PLAINS, FROM DUNDEE, ILL., TO OLYMPIA, W. T. MAY 7, TO NOVEMBER 3, 1862 . . . OLYMPIA: PRINTED AT THE OFFICE OF THE WASHINGTON STANDARD, 1863.

[1]–58, [59–60 blank]. 22.1 x 15.3 cm. Yellow printed wrappers with title on front wrapper. In a green cloth case.

Prov.: With bookplate of Randall H. Hewitt tipped to front cover and with pencil notes by the author throughout. Laid in is a typewritten statement signed by Emily E. Hewitt, a granddaughter of the author, stating that this was her grandfather's copy and was used by him for preparation of the later edition *Across the Plains* . . . [1906].

Ref.: AII (*Washington*) 64; Howes H457; Smith 4394; Wagner-Camp 391

One of the best Oregon Trail narratives.

1877 HIBERNICUS . . .

HIBERNICUS; OR, MEMOIRS OF AN IRISHMAN, NOW IN AMERICA . . . PITTSBURGH: PRINTED FOR THE AUTHOR BY CRAMER & SPEER, 1828.

[i]–vi, [7]–251, [252 blank]. 18.5 x 12 cm. Blue boards, white paper backstrip, uncut.

Prov.: Bookplate of D. L. Davis.

Ref.: Howes H462; Sabin 31688

An interesting autobiography, in a gruesome way, which may be largely truthful.

1878 HICKMAN, GEORGE

HISTORY OF MARSHALL COUNTY, DAKOTA. ITS TOPOGRAPHY AND NATURAL HISTORY, AND SKETCHES OF PIONEER SETTLERS . . . BRITTON, DAK.: J. W. BANBURY, PUBLISHER, 1886.

[1]–50, [51 illustration, 52 blank, 53–72 advertisements]. 23.2 x 15.4 cm. Illustrations unlisted. Gray printed wrappers, with title on front wrapper, advertisements on verso of back wrapper.

Prov.: Rubber stamps of James D. Brown and of D. Jay Collver, passenger agents, of Cleveland, on front wrapper.

Ref.: Adams (*Ramp. Herd*) 1030; Allen (*Dakota*) 457; Howes H464

Contains innumerable details of early Marshall County settlements and settlers. The advertisements are all of businesses in Britton or in Langford.—Allen

1879 HICKMAN, WILLIAM A.

BRIGHAM'S DESTROYING ANGEL: BEING THE LIFE, CONFESSION, AND STARTLING DISCLOSURES OF THE NOTORIOUS BILL HICKMAN, THE DANITE CHIEF OF UTAH . . . NEW YORK: GEO. A. CROFUTT, 1872.

[i]–[viii], [9]–219, [220–24 advertisements]. (Pages [i–ii] blank.) 16.8 x 12.3 cm. Illustrations unlisted. Brick cloth, gilt vignette and black ornaments on front cover, gilt and black backstrip.

Prov.: Signed under frontispiece: Wm A Hickman / [flourish] / April 27—1.72— /.

Ref.: Howes H465; Woodward 90

1880 HICKOK, JAMES B.

ORIGINAL PHOTOGRAPH OF JAMES B. HICKOK. Seated, full face turned very slightly to his right. Printed in sepia, 9 x 5.4 cm. Mounted on stiff card 9.6 x 6.2 cm., lower corners clipped. Printed on verso of card: Chas. T. Smith, / photographer, / Topeka, Kan.

1881 HICKS, E. W.

HISTORY OF KENDALL COUNTY ILLINOIS, FROM THE EARLIEST DISCOVERIES TO THE PRESENT TIME . . . AURORA, ILL.: KNICKERBOCKER & HODDER, 1877.

[I]–VIII, [9]–438. (Pages [I–II] blank.) 18.8 x 12.5 cm. Frontispiece. Brown cloth, sides stamped with black borders, title in gilt on backstrip.

Ref.: Bradford 2285; Buck 882

1882 HIGGINSON & GOLDSWORTHY, Silver City, Nevada

[Map] MAP OF / VIRGINIA, GOLD HILL, DEVILS GATE, AMERICAN FLAT, / GOLD & SILVER / MINING DISTRICTS. / STATE OF NEVADA. / HIGGINSON & GOLDSWORTHY, / SILVER & MINING ENGINEERS.

SILVER CITY, NEVADA. / SCALE 10 CHAINS TO THE INCH / [diagrammatic scale] / PUBLISHED AT THE / PACIFIC MAP DEPOT / BY A. GENSOUL BOOKSELLER & STATIONER, / 511 MONTGOMERY S.T SAN FRANCISCO CAL. / [lower centre:] L. NAGEL PRINT; ENTERED ACCORDING TO ACT OF CONGRESS IN THE YEAR 1865 BY HIGGINSON & GOLDSWORTHY, IN THE CLERKS OFFICE OF THE DISTRICT COURT OF THE NORTHERN DISTRICT OF THE STATE OF CALIFORNIA. W. VALLANCE GRAY, LITH; S. F. /

Map, 66.4 x 92.5 cm. Scale: 40 chains to one inch. Folded into black cloth covers, 15.6 x 10.1 cm., with title stamped in gilt on front cover: Map of / Virginia, Gold Hill, / American Flat / and / Devil's Gate / Mining Districts, / Nevada. / Advertisement of A. Gensoul inside front cover.

Ref.:

1883 HILDEBRAND, SAMUEL S.

AUTOBIOGRAPHY OF SAMUEL S. HILDEBRAND, THE RENOWNED MISSOURI "BUSHWHACKER" AND UNCONQUERABLE ROB ROY OF AMERICA; BEING HIS COMPLETE CONFESSION RECENTLY MADE TO THE WRITERS, AND CAREFULLY COMPILED BY JAMES W. EVANS AND A. WENDALL KEITH, M. D. . . . JEFFERSON CITY, MO.: STATE TIMES BOOK AND JOB PRINTING HOUSE, 1870.

[1]–312. (Pagination includes plates.) 18.4 x 11.5 cm. Eight illustrations listed. Black cloth, blind fillet borders on sides, title in gilt on backstrip.

Ref.: Adams 353; Howes H470; Rader 1873; Sabin 31761

1884 HILDEBRAND, SAMUEL S.

THE SAME, in original blue printed wrappers with title on front wrapper: Autobiography of Sam. S. Hildebrand, the Renowned Missouri "Bushwhacker" and Unconquerable Rob Roy of America being his Complete Confession, together with all the Facts Connected with his History. [decorative rule] St. Louis, Mo. Edw. C. Junge, Book and Job Printer. 1877. [Within decorative border.]

1885 [HILDRETH, JAMES (?)]

DRAGOON CAMPAIGNS TO THE ROCKY MOUNTAINS; BEING A HISTORY OF THE ENLISTMENT, ORGANIZATION, AND FIRST CAMPAIGNS OF THE REGIMENT OF UNITED STATES DRAGOONS . . . NEW-YORK: WILEY & LONG, 1836.

[1]–288. 19.2 x 11.6 cm. Brown cloth, title stamped in gilt on backstrip.

Ref.: Field 692; Howes H471; Jones 983; Rader 1874; Sabin 31769; Wagner-Camp 59

First active service of this newly organized

regiment, commanded by Col. Dodge; from St. Louis to Ft. Gibson and the Pawnee villages . . . —Howes

1886   HILL, ALEXANDER S.

FROM HOME TO HOME: AUTUMN WANDERINGS IN THE NORTH-WEST IN THE YEARS 1881, 1882, 1883, 1884 . . . LONDON: LAMPSON LOW, MARSTON, SEARLE, & RIVINGTON, 1885.

[i]–[x], [1]–432, [1]–32 advertisements. 21.8 x 14.4 cm. 34 illustrations and two folding maps listed. Dark blue pictorial cloth.
   Ref.: Adams (*Ramp. Herd*) 1033; Howes H479; Smith 4456
   For another view of the operation of Hill's great cattle establishment, see Craig, John R.

1887   HILL, EMMA SHEPARD

A DANGEROUS CROSSING AND WHAT HAPPENED ON THE OTHER SIDE . . . DENVER, 1924.

i–viii, [1]–206, [207–08 blank]. 18.3 x 13.2 cm. Three plates and small chapter heads. Green cloth, pictorial end-papers.
   Ref.: Howes H481; Wilcox p. 59
   Editions: Denver, [1914].

1888   HILL, J. L.

THE END OF THE CATTLE TRAIL . . . 337 EAST THIRD STREET, LONG BEACH, CAL.: GEO. W. MOYLE PUBLISHING CO.*

[1]–120. 22 x 14.8 cm. Illustrations unlisted. Gray printed wrappers.
   Ref.: Adams (*Ramp. Herd*) 1035; Cowan p. 280; Rader 1881
   Published between 1905 and 1910.
   A very interesting history by one who spent his life in the business.—EDG

1889   HILLHOUSE, WILLIAM

AUTOGRAPH MANUSCRIPT of "Incidents and Experiences" and "In Iowa," / from 1840 to 1844. /

128 pages, 20.3 x 16.6 cm. Red cloth with black and blind borders on sides, rounded corners, ruled paper, manuscript paper label (as above) on front cover. Mounted on inner front cover is a pencil drawing, 10.9 x 16.2 cm., of the: St. Louis & New Orleans Packet. 1864— / In Government Service. W. Hillhouse Master /. Numerous newspaper clippings mounted or tipped to back endleaves and last few leaves.
   Captain William Hillhouse came to Burlington in 1840, having ridden there on a horse from Chillicothe, Ohio, in eleven days. His experiences as an Indian trader (1840–42) are of the utmost interest and importance. He was well acquainted with Keokuk and the other Sac and Fox chiefs, accompanying them on their annual buffalo hunts and living with them. This is a very interesting account of conditions existing at that time. Of special importance are descriptions of a buffalo hunt in 1842 in eastern and central Iowa (30 head killed in one afternoon), the Indian payment and treaty of September 1842 (the treaty by which the Federal Government obtained the remaining portion of Iowa lands giving Indians until 1845 to vacate), and the Indians meeting for a treaty at Neutral Grounds.—EDG
   There are several stories of Indian experiences which are fairly vivid. At the end is a short section on the author's steamboating, including Government service during the Civil War.

1890   [HIMMELWRIGHT, ABRAHAM L. A.]

IN THE HEART OF THE BITTER-ROOT MOUNTAINS. THE STORY OF "THE CARLIN HUNTING PARTY" SEPTEMBER–DECEMBER, 1893. BY HECLAWA. ILLUSTRATED. NEW YORK: G. P. PUTNAM'S SONS, 1895.

[i]–xx, [xxi–xxii fly-title, verso blank], 1–259, [260 blank]. 18.8 x 13 cm. Illustrations listed. Green buckram.
   Ref.: Smith 4484

1891   [HINCHCLIFFE, JOHN]

HISTORICAL REVIEW OF BELLEVILLE, ILLINOIS, FROM EARLY TIMES TO THE PRESENT, WITH A GLANCE AT ITS BUSINESS, PRESENT AND PROSPECTIVE. BELLEVILLE, ILL.: G. A. HARVEY, 1870.

[1]–80. 23.3 x 14.8 cm. Pale green printed wrappers with title on front wrapper and advertisements on verso of front and recto and verso of back wrapper. In a gray cloth case.
   Ref.: Howes H499
   Inserted at the front is a large folding advertisement sheet.

1892   HIND, HENRY Y.

NARRATIVE OF THE CANADIAN RED RIVER EXPLORING EXPEDITION OF 1857 AND OF THE ASSINIBOINE AND SASKATCHEWAN EXPLORING EXPEDITION OF 1858 . . . LONDON: LONGMAN, GREEN, LONGMAN, AND ROBERTS, 1860.

[i]–xx, [1]–494, [495–96 advertisements], [1]–24 advertisements. [i]–xvi, [1]–472. 22.1 x 14.1 cm. 20 plates, three plans and one profile. Two volumes, purple cloth, uncut. Advertisements on inner covers.
   Ref.: Sabin 31934; Staton & Tremaine 3820; Wagner-Camp 361

1893   HIND, HENRY Y.

NORTH-WEST TERRITORY. REPORTS OF PROGRESS; TOGETHER WITH A PRELIMINARY AND GENERAL REPORT ON THE ASSINIBOINE AND SASKATCHEWAN

EXPLORING EXPEDITION . . . TORONTO: PRINTED BY JOHN LOVELL, 1859.

[i]–xii, [1]–[201], [202 colophon], 2 plates, each with unpaginated leaf of explanation, 4 folding maps. 33.2 x 25 cm. Plates and maps as follows: facing pages 36 (folding map), 56 (folding map, colored), 86 (woodcut view), [165] (folding map, colored), 170 (folding diagram, colored), text illustrations throughout. Also two plates after text and four folding maps. Gray cloth, sheep back, paper label on front cover: North-West Territory. / [decorative rule] / Report / on the / Assiniboine and Saskatchewan / Exploring Expedition; / by / Henry Youle Hind, M.A. / [within thick and thin rules].

Ref.: Sabin 31937; Staton & Tremaine 3912; Wagner-Camp 330

1894 HIND, HENRY Y.

. . . REPORT ON A TOPOGRAPHICAL & GEOLOGICAL EXPLORATION OF THE CANOE ROUTE BETWEEN FORT WILLIAM, LAKE SUPERIOR, AND FORT GARRY, RED RIVER; AND ALSO OF THE VALLEY OF RED RIVER, NORTH OF THE 49TH PARALLEL, DURING THE SUMMER OF 1857 . . . TORONTO: PRINTED BY STEWART DERBISHIRE & GEORGE DESBARATS, 1858.

[1–16]. 24.3 x 15.7 cm.

BOUND WITH:

. . . REPORT ON THE EXPLORATION OF THE COUNTRY BETWEEN LAKE SUPERIOR AND THE RED RIVER SETTLEMENT . . . TORONTO: JOHN LOVELL, PRINTER, 1858.

[1–248]. Map: Plan / Shewing the Proposed Route from / Lake Superior to Red River Settlement / Compiled from Messrs Dawson & Napier.^{s} Maps / [diagrammatic scale: 8 1/2 miles to one inch] / T. Devine, Surveyor Branch West. / Crown Lands Department / Toronto 29th May 1858 / Andrew Russell / Assistant Commissioner. / [low at left:] Maclear & Co. Lith.^{s} Toronto. / 87.3 x 146.7 cm. Scale as indicated. *Two insets.* Map: Map / of Part of the Valley of / Red River / North of the 49th Parallel / to Accompany / A / Report / on the Canadian Red River Exploring Expedition. / By / H. Y. Hind. / Eng.^{d} by Maclear & Co Toronto. / [diagrammatic scale] / Scale 4 miles to an inch. / 17 *Insets.* [lower left:] J Fleming del /. 36.3 x 80.8 cm. Scale as above. Two volumes bound together, new half calf, green cloth sides, red and blue leather labels on sides.

Ref.: Sabin 31938 note; Staton & Tremaine 3736 (title 1); Wagner-Camp 301 and 331 notes

Wagner-Camp describes a printing of the first part owned by Thomas W. Streeter in which there are only fourteen pages. It seems probable that the second leaf in that copy is missing.

Of the second part, Wagner-Camp 331 appears to be a later printing. The 1858 edition (except in French) is not mentioned. The maps described by Wagner-Camp are not those of the present copy. This second part consists of letters and reports by the principal members of the expedition, George Gladman (the leader), S. J. Dawson, W. H. Napier, and H. Y. Hind.

1895 HINDMAN, DAVID R.

THE WAY TO MY GOLDEN WEDDING . . . ST. JOSEPH, MO.: PRINTED BY AMERICAN PRINTING CO., 1908.*

[i–viii], 1–200. (Pages [i–ii] blank.) 17 x 11 cm. Four portraits and one illustration on four plates. Green cloth.

Prov.: Signature on page [i]: Richard L. Hindman /. On blank following text, in pencil: Lee Hindman / Downers Grove / [underline] /.

Ref.: Howes H501

Stamped in gilt at the foot of the front cover: Gift Edition / February Twenty Third / 1908. /

Contains an account of a trip in 1846 from Western Pennsylvania to Rushville, Illinois, and in the Spring of 1849 from the latter place to California overland. Pages 10–67 give a splendid description of overland travel. They went through Missouri and Iowa to Fort Kearney, thence to Fort Laramie and South Pass and, via Hudspeth's Cut-off, to the headwaters of the Humboldt, and to Weaverville which the party reached September 21st. The trip was made by ox-team without the loss of a man and the loss of two oxen only.—EDG

1896 HINES, GUSTAVUS

LIFE ON THE PLAINS OF THE PACIFIC. OREGON: ITS HISTORY, CONDITION AND PROSPECTS . . . BUFFALO: GEO. H. DERBY AND COMPANY, 1852.

[i]–viii, [9]–437, [438 blank, 439–56 advertisements]. 19.4 x 12.4 cm. Portrait. Black cloth.

Ref.: Howes H505 see; Sabin 31953 see; Smith 4489

Hines was an early arrival in Oregon (1840); he tells much of value about the pioneer days.

Editions: Buffalo, 1850, 1851. Other editions.

1897 HINES, H. K.

AT SEA AND IN PORT; OR, LIFE AND EXPERIENCES OF WILLIAM S. FLETCHER, FOR THIRTY YEARS SEAMAN'S MISSIONARY IN PORTLAND, OREGON . . . PORTLAND, OREGON: THE J. K. GILL COMPANY, 1898.

[1]–251, [252 blank]. 19 x 13.6 cm. Portrait. Red cloth.

Prov.: Inscribed on recto of frontispiece: Miss Antoinette P. Jones / Falmouth, Mass. / With

Christian Regards of / Wᵐ S. Fletcher, / Portland, Oregon / July 1, 1899 /.

Ref.: Smith 4501

1898 HINKLE, JAMES F.

EARLY DAYS OF A COWBOY ON THE PECOS . . . ROSWELL, N.M., 1937.

[1]–35, [36 blank]. 17.8 x 12.7 cm. Illustrations unlisted. White printed wrappers, with title on front wrapper.

Ref.: Adams (*Ramp. Herd*) 1041; Howes H507

Limited to 35 copies, according to information received from the author's widow through Herbert Brayer.

1899 HINMAN, CHARLES G.

A COLLECTION OF TEN AUTOGRAPH LETTERS, SIGNED, as listed below, to Mrs. Sarah H. Hinman or to Charles Hinman. 1849 May 3, St. Joseph, Missouri, to 1850 February 17, California.

1849 May 3, St. Joseph, Missouri. To Mrs. Hinman. Four pages, 31.1 x 19.8 cm.

1849 May 8, St. Joseph, Missouri. To Mrs. Hinman. Three pages, 31.1 x 19.8 cm.

1849 May 27, Fort Childs. To Charles Hinman. Four pages, 25 x 20 cm.

1849 June 7, [within 170 miles of Fort Laramie]. To Mrs. Hinman. Two pages, 25 x 20 cm.

1849 June 17, Fort Laramie. To Mrs. Hinman. Four pages, 25 x 20 cm.

1849 July 20, City of the Lakes [Salt Lake City]. To Mrs. Hinman. Four pages, 24.7 x 19.8 cm.

1849 October 7, Readings Diggins. To Mrs. Hinman. Four pages, 24.7 x 19.8 cm.

1849, October 18, Sacrimento[!] City. To Mrs. Hinman. Two pages, 24.7 x 18.6 cm.

1850 January 16, California [fifty miles from Sacramento]. To Mrs. Hinman. Four pages, 25.3 x 19.8 cm.

1850 February 17, California. To Mrs. Hinman. Four pages, 25.1 x 19.7 cm.

Each of the letters, except the eighth, carries an address leaf, most of which show postmarks.

A very interesting collection with numerous details about overland travel. Especially important are remarks about the prevalence of cholera, prices of goods, availability of forage, deaths on the route, names of the company, etc., etc. Hinman was a member of the Groveland Belle company.

Hinman's diary is in the Denver Public Library. Both the diary and letters are described in Morgan's edition of the Pritchard Diary, page 188.

The collection of letters was published in 1960 by EDG.

1900 HINMAN, CHARLES G.

A COLLECTION OF MISCELLANEOUS LETTERS, DOCUMENTS, ETC. by and relating to various members of the Hinman family and their friends. Sixty-one pieces.

1901 HINMAN, CHARLES G.

"A PRETTY FAIR VIEW OF THE ELIPHENT" . . . EDITED BY COLTON STORM. CHICAGO: PRINTED FOR EVERETT D. GRAFF BY GORDON MARTIN, 1960.

[i–iv, i and iv blank], 1–45, [46 blank, 47 limitation notice, 48 blank]. 16.5 x 10.8 cm. Frontispiece. Gray-green cloth backstrip, gray decorated paper sides, printed white paper label on backstrip.

Ref.:

Limited to 200 copies. An overland narrative in ten letters, 1849.

1902 HISTOIRE DE LA CONQUESTE . . .

HISTOIRE DE LA CONQUESTE DE LA FLORIDE, PAR LES ESPAGNOLS, SOUS FERDINAND DE SOTO. ECRITE EN PORTUGAIS PAR UN GENTIL-HOMME DE LA VILLE D'ELVAS . . . PARIS: CHEZ DENYS THIERRY, M. DC. LXXXV.

[ã]⁸, ẽ⁴, A–Z^alternately 8 and 4, Aa—Bb⁴, Cc². [i–xxiv], 1–300. 16.3 x 9 cm. Contemporary or early calf, gilt back, red leather label.

Ref.: JCB 1324; Robertson (*Relaçam Verdadeira*) II, p. 397; Sabin 24864; Vail 3; Winsor II, pp. 288–89

There are two imprints, of which this is the first listed by Sabin.

The author was probably one of the eight Portuguese listed in the second chapter, but he has not been identified. Certainly he was an eyewitness.

For a complete discussion of the work see the Robertson work noted above.

1903 HISTORICAL, DESCRIPTIVE . . . DIRECTORY, A

A HISTORICAL, DESCRIPTIVE AND COMMERCIAL DIRECTORY OF OWYHEE COUNTY, IDAHO. JANUARY, 1898. SILVER CITY, IDAHO: PRESS OF THE OWYHEE AVALANCHE, MDCCCXCVIII.

[1]–140, [1–16 advertisements], [1–2 blank], [i]–iv index. 22.7 x 15.3 cm. Illustrations listed. Blue cloth.

Ref.: Howes O173; Smith 7764

1904 HISTORICAL SKETCH . . .

HISTORICAL SKETCH OF ST. ANTHONY AND MINNEAPOLIS, WITH STATISTICS OF BUSINESS AND CAPITAL, FROM THEIR FIRST SETTLEMENT, TO NOVEMBER, 1855. PRINTED AT THE ST. ANTHONY EXPRESS OFFICE, 1855.

[1]–24. 20.5 x 15.1 cm. Stabbed, uncut. In red cloth folder. Tear in title-leaf clumsily mended.
Ref.: AII (*Minnesota*) 88; Howes S21; Sabin 32081

1905 HISTORY OF ALMA, NEBRASKA...

HISTORY OF ALMA, NEBRASKA, HARLAN COUNTY ... FROM 1870 TO 1906.

[1]–76, [77–78 blank]. 22.5 x 16.4 cm. Illustrations unlisted. Printed gray-green wrappers, with title on front wrapper printed in colors.
Ref.:
Probably printed at Alma in 1906.

1906 HISTORY OF DIXON AND LEE COUNTY...

HISTORY OF DIXON AND LEE COUNTY, CHRONOLOGICAL RECORD, SHOWING THE CURRENT EVENTS AND MANY INTERESTING REMINISCENCES IN THE HISTORY OF DIXON AND LEE COUNTY, FROM THE EARLIEST WHITE SETTLEMENT TO THE PRESENT. HISTORICAL AND DESCRIPTIVE SKETCH OF DIXON ... BIOGRAPHY OF FATHER DIXON ... A FULL LIST OF SOLDIERS THAT LEFT DIXON FOR THE WAR OF THE REBELLION, ETC ... DIXON, ILLINOIS: DIXON TELEGRAPH PRINT, 1880.

[1]–32, 25–52, 55–6, 53–4, 55–78. (Pages 25–32 repeated in this copy, 55–6 and 53–4 transposed in printing, 78 mispaginated 66.) 21.7 x 14.6 cm. Four illustrations (two folding plates) and a map: Pinckney's Map of Lee County, Illinois. / 15.2 x 24.9 cm. No scale given. Pale green printed wrappers with title on front wrapper, list of contents on verso of front wrapper. In a gray buckram case.
Ref.: Buck 910; Howes D369
The second history of Lee county, according to Buck.

1907 HISTORY OF SOUTHEASTERN DAKOTA...

HISTORY OF SOUTHEASTERN DAKOTA; ITS SETTLEMENT AND GROWTH, GEOLOGICAL AND PHYSICAL FEATURES—COUNTIES, CITIES, TOWNS, AND VILLAGES—INCIDENTS OF PIONEER LIFE—BIOGRAPHICAL SKETCHES OF THE PIONEERS AND BUSINESS MEN, WITH A BRIEF OUTLINE HISTORY OF THE TERRITORY IN GENERAL ... SIOUX CITY, IOWA: WESTERN PUBLISHING COMPANY, 1881.*

[1]–392, [393–400 advertisements]. But: [1]–256, [257–90 advertisements], [305 advertisement], 306–92, [393–400 advertisements]. 22.1 x 14.8 cm. Plum cloth.
Ref.: Howes D14

1908 HITCHCOCK, ETHAN A.

FIFTY YEARS IN CAMP AND FIELD. DIARY OF MAJOR-GENERAL ETHAN ALLEN HITCHCOCK, U.S.A. ... NEW YORK: G. P. PUTNAM'S SONS, 1909.*

[i]–xv, [xvi blank], 1–514. 23.8 x 16 cm. Portrait. Green cloth, gilt top, uncut.
Ref.: Howes H539; Rader 1898
Hitchcock was an amazing man—educated, able, honest, industrious, conscientious, and patriotic in the highest degree. His estimates of the public men of his era, most of whom he knew well, are enlightening and interesting.—EDG

1909 HITCHCOCK, FRANK

A TRUE ACCOUNT OF THE CAPTURE OF FRANK RANDE "THE NOTED OUTLAW" ... EDITED BY JOHN W. KIMSEY ... PEORIA, ILLINOIS: J. W. FRANKS & SONS, 1897.

[1]–159, [160 blank]. 19.1 x 13 cm. 11 illustrations unlisted. Pale green printed boards, red cloth backstrip.
Ref.: Adams 480
Bloodcurdling. The illustrations are "real primitive."

1910 HITTELL, JOHN S.

THE PROSPECTS OF VALLEJO; OR, EVIDENCE THAT VALLEJO WILL BECOME A GREAT CITY ... VALLEJO: CHRONICLE STEAM PRINTING HOUSE, 1871.

[1]–50, [51]–62, 51–56. 22.3 x 14.6 cm. Purple printed wrappers, with title on front wrapper, advertisements on recto and verso of back wrapper.
Ref.: Blumann & Thomas 4523; Cowan p. 284; Howes H540
The original text ended with page 50 (pages 51–56 are advertisements), but inserted after page 50 is a gathering of six leaves captioned: Vallejo in November 1871. / [decorative rule] / A Sequel to the Prospects of Vallejo. / [thick and thin rules] / ... Cowan describes a map with this section which is not present.

1911 HITTELL, JOHN S.

YOSEMITE: ITS WONDERS AND ITS BEAUTIES ... SAN FRANCISCO: H. H. BANCROFT & COMPANY, 1868.

[1]–59, [60 blank], [1–3 advertisements, 4 blank]. 18.4 x 11.3 cm. 20 original photographs, listed, by Edward J. Muybridge and a map. Map: Yosemite / Valley. / [lower right:] Lith. Britton & Rey. S.F. / 17.6 x 20.3 cm. Scale: about 1 1/2 miles to one inch. Green cloth, with title stamped in gilt on front cover.
Ref.: Cowan p. 284; Farquhar 8; Howes H542; Sabin 32274

The photographer was the famous Muybridge who made the first "motion pictures." The first Yosemite guide book.

1912 HITTELL, THEODORE H.

THE ADVENTURES OF JAMES CAPEN ADAMS, MOUNTAINEER AND GRIZZLY BEAR HUNTER, OF CALIFORNIA . . . SAN FRANCISCO: TOWNE AND BACON, 1860.

[1]–378. 18.7 x 12 cm. 12 illustrations listed, by Charles Nahl. Brown cloth, embossed borders on sides, title stamped in gilt on backstrip.

Ref.: Cowan p. 284; Greenwood 1274; Howes H543; Jones 1426; Sabin 32274 see; Wagner-Camp 348

Probably the most popular work of its time issued in California.—Cowan

1913 HOBART, CHAUNCEY

RECOLLECTIONS OF MY LIFE. FIFTY YEARS OF ITINERANCY IN THE NORTHWEST . . . RED WING: RED WING PRINTING CO. 1885.

[1]–409, [410 blank]. 19.2 x 12.6 cm. Portrait. Dark red cloth.

Prov.: Inscribed in pencil on first blank leaf: Presented / to / John Williamson D. D. / by / The Author / [flourish] /.

Ref.: Howes H548

Inserted before the first page of text is a small errata slip, 8.8 x 12.3 cm.

John Williamson, the recipient, was a noted missionary among the Sioux.

1914 HOBBS, JAMES

WILD LIFE IN THE FAR WEST; PERSONAL ADVENTURES OF A BORDER MOUNTAIN MAN. COMPRISING HUNTING AND TRAPPING ADVENTURES WITH KIT CARSON AND OTHERS; CAPTIVITY AND LIFE AMONG THE COMANCHES; SERVICES UNDER DONIPHAN IN THE WAR WITH MEXICO, AND IN THE MEXICAN WAR AGAINST THE FRENCH; DESPERATE COMBATS WITH APACHES, GRIZZLY BEARS, ETC., ETC. HARTFORD: WILEY, WATERMAN & EATON. 1872.

[1]–488. 20.6 x 13.6 cm. 33 illustrations listed. Green cloth, sprinkled edges. Lacks front flyleaf.

Ref.: Adams 483; Barrett 1215 note; Dobie pp. 86–7; Howes H550; Rader 1901; Saunders 2956; Smith 4531 see

As an associate of Kit Carson, James Kirker and other mountain men of the Southwest, Hobbs had good stories to tell.

1915 HOBSON, GEORGE C., *Editor*

GEMS OF THOUGHT AND HISTORY OF SHOSHONE COUNTY . . . COMPILED AND EDITED BY GEORGE

C. HOBSON . . . KELLOGG, [IDAHO]: EVENING NEWS PRESS, 1940.

[1]–84, [85–86 blank]. 22.7 x 15.2 cm. Illustrations unlisted. Black wrappers printed in silver, with title on front wrapper, advertisements on verso of front and recto of back wrapper.

Ref.: Smith 4533

Advertisements of local merchants at foot of each page of text.

1916 HOEHNE, FRIEDRICH

WAHN UND UEBERZENGUNG. REISE . . . NACH NORDAMERIKA UND TEXAS IN DEN JAHREN 1839, 1840 UND 1841 . . . WEIMAR: WILHELM HOFFMANN, 1844.

[1–4], [I]–VI, [1]–435, [436–38 advertisements]. 15.2 x 10.8 cm. Seven maps, plans and illustrations, unlisted. Map: [Ohio River at Louisville.] [top centre:] 145 /. 12 x 8.4 cm. No scale given. Map: Plan / von / Philadelphia /. [top centre:] 270. / 10 x 8.7 cm. No scale given. Contemporary mottled black boards, yellow paper label on backstrip with manuscript title.

Prov.: Bookplate of K. Hahn.

Ref.: Buck 337; Clark III 180; Howes H565; Sabin 32375; Streeter 1505

1917 HOFFMAN, CHARLES F.

AUTOGRAPH LETTER, SIGNED. [1836] May 4, New York. Four pages, 25.5 x 20.1 cm. To Lieutenant [Albert M.] Lea.

A fine letter concerning the publication of his *Winter in the West* . . . 1835. Also about publishing Lea's book on Iowa and Wisconsin.

1918 [HOFFMAN, CHARLES F.]

A WINTER IN THE WEST . . . NEW-YORK: PUBLISHED BY HARPER & BROTHERS, 1835.

[i–iv, iv blank], [1]–337, [338–40 blank]. [i–iv, iv blank], [1]–346, [347–48 blank]. 18 x 10.8 cm. Two volumes, contemporary dark blue polished calf, blind and gilt borders on sides, blind and gilt backs.

Prov.: Inscribed on blank leaf at front of first volume: Washington Irving Esq. / With the sincere respect / and affectionate re-/gard of the Author /. Note on front endleaf: Bot. at E. Romayne's / Vendue—1841 / By / Andrew D Archer /. Similar note on endleaf of second volume. Note on endpaper of second volume Presented to the / Mt[?] Sem Library / N° 73 /. Signature on front endleaf of second volume: Washington Irving /.

Ref.: Blanck 8521; Bradford 2336; Buck 274; Clark II 55; Howes H568; Sabin 32389

285

1919 HOFFMAN, OGDEN

REPORTS OF LAND CASES DETERMINED IN THE UNITED STATES DISTRICT COURT FOR THE NORTHERN DISTRICT OF CALIFORNIA. JUNE TERM, 1853 TO JUNE TERM, 1858, INCLUSIVE . . . SAN FRANCISCO: NUMA HUBERT, PUBLISHER, 1862.

[i]–[viii, viii blank], [9]–458, [1]–146. 22.8 x 14.5 cm. Original full calf, red and black leather labels. Worn and chipped.

Ref.: Cowan p. 287; Greenwood 1654; Howes H569

Volume One was the only volume published.

1920 [HOFFMAN, PHIL]

ROUSTABOUT'S HISTORY OF MAHASKA COUNTY . . . BY ROUSTABOUT.

[1]–[103], [104 blank]. 17.8 x 10.2 cm. Gray cloth.

Ref.: Mott (*Iowa*) p. 48

Apparently published at Oskaloosa, Iowa. About 1917?

1921 HOFFMAN, S. B.

HOFFMAN'S QUINCY COMMERCIAL DIRECTORY FURNISHING THE NAME AND ADDRESS OF THE PRINCIPAL MERCHANTS, MANUFACTURERS, RAILROADS, BANKING HOUSES, SCHOOLS, CITY OFFICERS, STEAM BOATS, STAGES, &C. . . . QUINCY, ILLINOIS: HOFFMAN & BROTHER.

[1]–164. 15 x 10.6 cm. Yellow printed wrappers, with title on front wrapper, advertisement on verso of back wrapper. In a yellow cloth case.

Ref.: Byrd 2291

Front wrapper dated 1855.

Contains a short history of the town.

1922 [HOGAN, JOHN]

THOUGHTS ABOUT THE CITY OF ST. LOUIS, HER COMMERCE AND MANUFACTURES, RAILROADS, &C. . . . ST. LOUIS, MO.: REPUBLICAN STEAM PRESS PRINT, 1854.*

[1]–[80]. 23.1 x 15 cm. 17 plates, including panoramic view 15.5 x 134.6 cm. Yellow printed wrappers, with title on front wrapper, advertisement on verso of back wrapper, Table of contents on verso of front wrapper, Addenda on recto of back wrapper but each is covered by mounted leaf of text paper. In a blue buckram case.

Ref.: Howes H572; Sabin 32420

Fascinating lithographs.

1923 HOGAN, JOHN J.

ON THE MISSION IN MISSOURI. 1857–1868 . . . KANSAS CITY, MO.: JOHN A. HEILMANN, 1892.*

[1]–205, [ccvi]–ccxi, [ccxii blank]. (Page ccxi mispaginated ccxxxi.) 17.8 x 12.1 cm. Gray cloth, title in gilt on front cover and backstrip.

Ref.: Howes H573

1924 HOGANE, JAMES T., & H. LAMBACH

[MAP] MAP / OF THE CITY OF / DAVENPORT / AND ITS / SUBURBS, / SCOTT COUNTY, IOWA. / [decorative rule] / COMPILED FROM ORIGINAL SURVEYS / BY / JAMES T. HOGANE & H. LAMBACH / LATE DEPUTY C? SURVEYOR. [space] CIV. ENGINEER & SURVEYOR. / 1857. / LITH. OF ED. MENDEL, CHICAGO, ILL. / [No scale given.]

Map, 121.5 x 156.4 cm. Folded into black cloth covers, 19.5 x 12.8 cm., gilt stamped on front cover: Map / of / Davenport. /

Ref.: Byrd 2669

Tinted lithographed vignettes in the border comprise the following sixteen subjects: residences of Geo. L. Sargent, J. Lambrite, Hiram Price and John F. Dillon (one view), J. T. Hogane, Ebenezer Cook, H. S. Finley, Antoine Le Claire, G. C. R. Mitchell, and J. M. D. Burrows. Also Iowa College, Ladies' College, Mississippi Bridge, the Le Claire Block, Geo. L. Davenport's Block, the Burrows Block, and a large colored view (mounted) of Davenport.

1925 HOLBROOK, JOHN C.

[Wrapper title] OUR COUNTRY'S CRISIS: A DISCOURSE DELIVERED IN DUBUQUE, IOWA, . . . JULY 6, 1856 . . . DUBUQUE REPUBLICAN OFFICE.

[1]–12. 23.9 x 14.5 cm. Buff printed wrappers with title on front wrapper.

Ref.: Moffit 238

Printed in Dubuque apparently in 1856.

1926 HOLDITCH, ROBERT

THE EMIGRANT'S GUIDE TO THE UNITED STATES OF AMERICA . . . LONDON: PRINTED FOR WILLIAM HONE, 1818.

[A]², B–Q⁴, R². [i]–iv, [1]–[124], [1–4 advertisements]. 22.1 x 13.6 cm. Contemporary marbled boards, roan corners and back, uncut, unopened.

Ref.: Buck 119; Howes H584; Rusk I, p. 129; Sabin 32485

1927 HOLLADAY, BENJAMIN

AUTOGRAPH NOTE, SIGNED. 1864 September 29, Kearney Station. One page, 22.7 x 18.4 cm. To Agents of The Overland Stage Line.

Pass signed by Holladay as "Proprietor" issued to Colonel Livingston, 1st Reg. Nebraska Vol. [or Vet.?] Cav. Commanding Eastern Sub District, between Julesburg and Thompson's Station "until otherwise ordered."

1928 HOLLADAY, BENJAMIN

SPOLIATIONS COMMITTED BY INDIANS ON PROPERTY OF BENJAMIN HOLLADAY WHILST CARRYING THE UNITED STATES MAILS . . . MEMORIAL, PROOFS, AND REFERENCE TO PRECEDENTS. NEW YORK: CHARLES VOGT, 1872.

[1]–59, [60 blank]. 22.9 x 14.7 cm. Buff printed wrappers, with title on front wrapper. Lacks back wrapper. In a blue cloth case.

Ref.: Jones 1553; Rader 1910

1929 HOLLADAY OVERLAND MAIL & EXPRESS CO.

[Printed envelope] (21.) / THE / HOLLADAY / OVERLAND MAIL & EXPRESS CO. / C. O. D. / EXPRESS FORWARDERS. / COLLECT ON DELIVERY OF GOODS / [31 lines] / SLOTE & JANES, STATIONERS, 93 FULTON ST., N.Y. / [within thick and thin rule borders].

22.3 x 9.7 cm. Printed in red on yellow paper.

Ref.:

Across the face of the envelope, in Bela S. Buell's hand: Deeds & Power of Atty for / Bela S. Buell / [underline] /.

1930 HOLLAND BROTHERS, Chicago

HOLLAND'S OTTAWA CITY DIRECTORY. FOR 1869–70, CONTAINING A COMPLETE LIST OF ALL RESIDENTS IN THE CITY ALSO A CLASSIFIED BUSINESS DIRECTORY, WITH THE NAMES AND ADDRESS OF THE MERCHANTS, MANUFACTURERS, PROFESSIONAL MEN, &C., IN THE CITY. CHICAGO: WESTERN PUBLISHING COMPANY.

[1]–190, [33]–40, 191–96, 41–90. 22.3 x 14.3 cm. Brown cloth, advertisements stamped in gilt on front cover and in blind on back cover, title and advertisement in gilt on backstrip.

Ref.:

The separately paginated section at the back is headed with a title-page on page [33]: Internal Revenue Guide / and / Tax Payers' Adviser. / With Corrections to November 1868. /

The yellow endpapers at the front bear advertisements; there are also two inserted leaves of advertisements on yellow paper before the title-page.

Holland Brothers was a patent medicine firm operating from Chicago.

1931 HOLLANDERS IN JOWA, DE

DE HOLLANDERS IN JOWA. BRIEVEN UIT PELLA, VAN EEN GELDERSCHMAN. TE ARNHEM: BIJ D. A. THIEME, 1858.*

[III]–[XXIV], [25]–189, [190 blank]. 17.7 x 11.2 cm. Large folding colored frontispiece and one tinted illustration. Contemporary marbled boards, black cloth back and corners, title in gilt on backstrip.

Ref.: Howes I71; Mott (*Iowa*) p. 67; Sabin 32520

The author was a native of Gelderland in The Netherlands.

1932 HOLLEY, FRANCES CHAMBERLAIN

ONCE THEIR HOME; OR, OUR LEGACY FROM THE DAHKOTAHS. HISTORICAL, BIOGRAPHICAL, AND INCIDENTAL . . . CHICAGO: DONOHUE & HENNEBERRY, 1891.

[i]–vi, [7]–419, [420 blank], [i]–v index, [vi blank] 21.9 x 14.5 cm. 32 illustrations listed and one unlisted portrait. Dark blue cloth, marbled edges.

Ref.: Bradford 2346; Howes H592; Jennewein 168

Editions: Chicago, 1890.

1933 HOLLEY, GEORGE W.

AN ADDRESS, DELIVERED BEFORE THE UNION AGRICULTURAL SOCIETY, AT JULIET, ILLINOIS, JULY 8, 1840 . . . CHICAGO: PRINTED AT THE AMERICAN OFFICE, 1840.

[1]–12. 20.5 x 12.2 cm. Removed from bound volume, unbound.

Ref.: Byrd 524; McMurtrie (*Chicago*) 31a

Note Juliet for Joliet. The town of Romeo is only a few miles away.

1934 HOLLEY, MARY AUSTIN

TEXAS. OBSERVATIONS, HISTORICAL, GEOGRAPHICAL AND DESCRIPTIVE, IN A SERIES OF LETTERS, WRITTEN DURING A VISIT TO AUSTIN'S COLONY . . . IN THE AUTUMN OF 1831 . . . BALTIMORE: ARMSTRONG & PLASKITT. 1833.

[1]–167, [168 blank]. 17.7 x 11 cm. Map: Map / of the State of / Coahuila / [swelled rule] and [swelled rule] / Texas. / W. Hooker Sculp[t] / Scale of Miles. / [diagrammatic scale: 90 miles to one inch] / 26.4 x 33.7 cm. Scale as above. Red cloth, short title in gilt on front cover.

Ref.: Bradford 2348; Howes H593; Jones 935; Rader 1912; Raines p. 116; Sabin 32528; Streeter 1135

The author was Stephen F. Austin's cousin. The present series of letters was written to promote colonization.

1935 HOLLEY, MARY AUSTIN

THE SAME. LEXINGTON, KY: J. CLARKE & CO. 1836.

[1–2], [i]–viii, [1]–410. 17.8 x 11 cm. Map: Map / of the State of / Coahuila / —and— / Texas. / W. Hooker Sculp[t] / Scale of Miles. / [diagrammatic scale: 90 miles to one inch] / 26.3 x 33.6 cm. Scale as above. Blue cloth, gilt title on backstrip.

Ref.: Clements Library (*Texas*) 15; Howes H593; Jones 984; Rader 1911; Raines p. 116; Sabin 32528; Streeter 1207

In addition to Mrs. Holley's account of society and manners in Texas, there are Stephen F. Austin's *Address* at Louisville in 1836, the Mexican Constitution, and the "Constitution of the Republic of Texas."

The map is identical with the version which appeared in the first edition, 1833. It is an earlier state of the map which appears (colored) in J. Fiske: *A Visit to Texas . . .* New York, 1834. The map, then, was probably a remainder from the first edition rather than a new printing.

Editions: Baltimore, 1833.

1936 HOLLIDAY, GEORGE H.

ON THE PLAINS IN '65 . . . TWELVE MONTHS IN THE VOLUNTEER CAVALRY SERVICE, AMONG THE INDIANS OF NEBRASKA, COLORADO, DAKOTA, WYOMING, AND MONTANA . . . ENTERED ACCORDING TO THE ACT OF CONGRESS IN THE LIBRARIAN'S OFFICE, AT WASHINGTON, D. C., IN THE YEAR 1883.

[1]–97, [98 blank]. 21.1 x 14.6 cm. Eight illustrations, unlisted. Orange pictorial wrappers, with title on front wrapper. In a black cloth case.

Ref.: Howes H596

Probably printed at Wheeling, West Virginia. An extremely interesting story.—EDG

1937 HOLLISTER, OVANDO J.

HISTORY OF THE FIRST REGIMENT OF COLORADO VOLUNTEERS . . . DENVER, C.T.: THOS. GIBSON & CO., 1863.

[1]–178, [179–80 blank]. 19.1 x 12.7 cm. Yellow printed wrappers, with title on front wrapper, advertisement on verso of back wrapper. In orange half morocco case.

Ref.: Howes H601; McMurtrie & Allen (*Colorado*) 39; Nicholson p. 384; Wagner-Camp 392; Wilcox p. 61

Leading authority on early Colorado Indian wars and rarest book printed in this state.—Howes

1938 HOLLISTER, OVANDO J.

ANOTHER COPY.

[1]–178. 18.8 x 12.5 cm. Rebound in black calf.
Ref.: As above

1939 HOLLISTER, URIAH S.

[Pictorial title-page] THE NAVAJO AND HIS BLANKET . . . DENVER, COLO.: 1903.*

[1]–144. (Pages [1–2] blank.) 24.2 x 18.5 cm. Ten colored plates and 25 illustrations listed. Red cloth, small cut mounted on front cover.

Ref.: Howes H603; Munk (Alliot) p. 107; Saunders 1014

1940 HOLMES, JOHN

[Caption title] SPEECH OF MR. HOLMES. OF MAINE, ON THE ANNUAL APPROPRIATION BILL . . . APRIL 9TH, 10TH, AND 11TH, 1832 . . .

[1]–24. Bound with Number 1084.
Ref.: Sabin 32611
Printed at Washington after January, 1834.

1941 HOLMES, JOSEPH T.

QUINCY IN 1857. OR FACTS AND FIGURES EXHIBITING ITS ADVANTAGES, RESOURCES, MANUFACTURES AND COMMERCE . . . QUINCY, ILL.: HERALD BOOK AND JOB PRINTING ESTABLISHMENT, 1857.

[1]–69, [70 blank]. 15.5 x 9.9 cm. Green cloth, blind embossed borders on sides, title in gilt on front cover.

Ref.: Byrd 2670; Howes H612; Sabin 32615
Contains a short historical sketch of Quincy.

1942 HOLMES, REUBEN

. . . GLIMPSES OF THE PAST. THE FIVE SCALPS . . . ST. LOUIS: JEFFERSON MEMORIAL, 1938.

[1]–54, [55–56 blank]. 24.2 x 16.6 cm. Printed self wrappers, with title on page [1].

Ref.:
The story revolves about Edward Rose whose "colorful life finally came to an end sometime during the winter of 1832–1833, when he was killed by a war party of Arikara Indians, while in company of Hugh Glass, and a man named Menard. The murder took place on the Yellowstone River, below Big Horn."—EDG

1943 HOLMES & SWEETLAND

A DESCRIPTIVE SKETCH OF THE SPIRIT LAKE REGION . . . CHICAGO: THE J. M. W. JONES STATIONERY AND PRINTING CO., 1885.

[1]–42, [43–46 advertisements and map]. 19.3 x 13.6 cm. Illustrations, vignettes, and map included in pagination. Map: Map / of the / Iowa Route / Burlington, Cedar Rapids & Northern / Railway / and Connections. / 12.5 x 19 cm. No scale given. Printed pictorial wrappers, in color, with title on front wrapper, verso of back wrapper: Spirit Lake / Region /.

Ref.:
Issued by the Passenger Department of the Burlington, Cedar Rapids & Northern Railway.

1944 HOLT, GEORGE L.

[Map] HOLT'S NEW MAP / OF / WYOMING. / COMPILED BY PERMISSION FROM OFFICIAL RECORDS IN U. S. LAND OFFICE. / PUBLISHED BY G. L. HOLT, CHEYENNE, WYO. / FRANK & FRED. BOND, DRAFTSMEN. SCALE OF MILES 12 TO AN INCH / [diagrammatic scale] / 1885. / [lower left:] ENGRAVED & PRINTED BY G. W. & C. B. COLTON & CO. NEW YORK.

/ [lower right:] ENTERED ACCORDING TO ACT OF CONGRESS, IN THE YEAR 1883 BY GEO. L. HOLT, IN THE OFFICE OF THE LIBRARIAN OF CONGRESS AT WASHINGTON, D.C. / [vignettes in upper corners].

Map, 72.3 x 79.5 cm. Scale: 12 miles to one inch. Mounted on linen and folded, unbound.

Ref.: Phillips (*Maps*) p. 1128 see *Editions*: Cheyenne, 1883.

1945 HOLT, GEORGE L.

THE SAME. 1886.

Map, 72.3 x 79.5 cm. Scale: 12 miles to one inch. Folded into brown cloth covers, 16.5 x 11.7 cm., with title stamped in gilt on front cover: Holt's / New Map of / Wyoming / Published by / Geo. L. Holt / Cheyenne /, publisher's advertisements inside front cover.

Ref.:

The 1886 edition differs slightly from the 1885 in that Albany County is increased in size and shape. At the right, between 43° and 44°, 9 S.P. has been changed to 10 S.P. Mining districts, ranches, telegraph routes, etc., are all listed.

1946 HOLTON, AMOS

THE CASE OF MRS. CLARA H. PIKE, WIDOW OF GEN. Z. MONTGOMERY PIKE, NOW PENDING BEFORE THE U. S. CONGRESS . . . HER PETITION, PRAYING COMPENSATION FOR EXTRAORDINARY SERVICES, RENDERED BY HER LATE HUSBAND . . . WASHINGTON: T. BARNARD, PRINTER. 1846.

[1]–16. 23.9 x 15.1 cm. Stabbed, unbound, uncut.

Prov.: Inscribed on title-page: Henry R. Schoolcraft, Esquire / with the respectful compliments of / Amos Holton. / Rubber stamps and duplicate stamp of U. S. Geological Survey Library on title-page.

Ref.: Wagner-Camp 9 note

1947 [HOOKER, SIR WILLIAM J.]

COMPANION TO THE BOTANICAL MAGAZINE; BEING A JOURNAL CONTAINING SUCH INTERESTING BOTANICAL INFORMATION, AS DOES NOT COME WITHIN THE PRESCRIBED LIMITS OF THE MAGAZINE; WITH OCCASIONAL FIGURES . . . LONDON: PRINTED BY EDWARD COUCHMAN, 1835 [–36].

[1]–384. [1]–[384]. 25.4 x 15.6 cm. Three portraits and 32 plates, mostly colored. Two volumes, black cloth, uncut.

Prov.: Bookplate of Lord Chief Justice Wilde in Vol. I, and of Lord Truro in Vol. II.

Ref.: Howes H624; Wagner-Camp 60

The second volume contains the first printing of Hooker's: "A Brief Memoir of the Life of Mr. David Douglas . . ." pages 79–182.

1948 HOPEWELL, MENRA

LEGENDS OF THE MISSOURI AND MISSISSIPPI . . . LONDON: WARD, LOCK, AND TYLER, WARWICK HOUSE, PATERNOSTER ROW.

[i]–vi, [7]–506. (Including frontispiece as [i–ii].) 16 x 10.3 cm. Four illustrations unlisted. Green cloth, blind fillet borders on sides, title in gilt on backstrip, gilt edges.

Ref.: Howes H628; Johannsen II p. 146

Stories of Indians, Peter Griffin, Père Marquette, De Soto, Blackbird, Pontiac, Jack Pierce, etc. Part fiction, part distorted fact. No date given, but about 1874.

Editions: London, [1862–63].

1949 HOPKINS, GERARD T.

A MISSION TO THE INDIANS, FROM THE INDIAN COMMITTEE OF BALTIMORE YEARLY MEETING, TO FORT WAYNE, IN 1804 . . . PHILADELPHIA: T. ELLWOOD ZELL, 1862.

[1]–198. 15.2 x 9.8 cm. Three text illustrations. Rebound in half red morocco, gilt top. Some corners supplied, lacks final blank leaf.

Ref.: Field 718; Howes T545; Jones 1448; Sabin 32917; Thomson 605

There are several manuscript corrections in the text probably in the hand of the editor, Martha E. Tyson.

Privately printed and never sold. Hopkins' visit to the Miamis and Pottawatomies is interesting and important, but no more so than the additional material by George Ellicott, in the same mission, found in the appendix.—Howes

The work had appeared first in *Friend's Intelligencer*.

1950 HOPKINS, SARAH WINNEMUCCA

LIFE AMONG THE PIUTES: THEIR WRONGS AND CLAIMS . . . BOSTON: CUPPLES, UPHAM & CO., 1883.

[1]–268. 18.4 x 12.1 cm. Green cloth.

Prov.: Signed on fly-leaf: Sarah Winnemucca Hopkins / Feb 23 1884 /.

Ref.: Rader 1927; Smith 4618

It is the first outbreak of the American Indian in human literature and has a single aim—to tell the truth.—Mrs. Mann, the editor

1951 HOPKINS & MILLARD, Fremont, Nebraska

A. P. HOPKINS. ALFRED MILLARD. HOPKINS & MILLARD, BANKERS. CORNER MAIN AND SIXTH STREETS, FREMONT,—NEBRASKA.

[1–4]. 16.2 x 12.8 cm. Unbound leaflet.

Ref.:

Text on pages [2–3], [4] blank. Printed at

Fremont, Nebraska. Announcement of change of name from Alfred Millard to Hopkins & Millard. Dated September 1, 1879.

1952 HORN, HOSEA B.

HORN'S OVERLAND GUIDE, FROM THE U. S. INDIAN SUB-AGENCY, COUNCIL BLUFFS, ON THE MISSOURI RIVER, TO THE CITY OF SACRAMENTO, IN CALIFORNIA; CONTAINING A TABLE OF DISTANCES, AND SHOWING ALL THE RIVERS, CREEKS, LAKES, SPRINGS, MOUNTAINS, HILLS, CAMPING-PLACES, AND OTHER PROMINENT OBJECTS . . . NEW YORK: PUBLISHED BY J. H. COLTON, 1852.

[i]–iv, [5]–78, 1–18 J. H. Colton Catalogue. 15.2 x 9.6 cm. Folding map: Map / to Illustrate / Horn's Overland Guide / to / California and Oregon. / Published by J. H. Colton, / Nº 86, Cedar Street, / New York. / 1852. / 32.8 x 50.4 cm. No scale given. Routes marked in dark red. Brown cloth, blind embossed sides, title in gilt on front cover with "Horn's" slanted: Horn's / Overland Guide / to / California /.

Prov.: Signature on title-page: George W Martin July 13th /. Numerous pencil notes. Inside front cover: 1852 / Dubuque Apr 9th / Jeremiah Getwins / Book, and Guide / to California / Over Land Rout /. Other notes by Martin, including dates and places, corrections in text, etc. Rubber stamp inside front cover: Lewis N. Martin, / Massey, / Hill Co. Texas. /

Ref.: Cowan p. 114; Howes H641; Jones 1278; Sabin 33021; Wagner-Camp 214; Wheat (*Transmississippi*) 715

This is the first issue of the *Guide*. On page 5 under "Certificates" no newspaper notices appear as they do in later issues. The date 1852 is on the title-page. On page 68 there appears the advertisement of the Council Bluffs Agency Ferry, which appears on page [84] of later issues. The present copy was carried across the plains in 1853 and contains many notes and corrections in pencil, unquestionably by the owner who made the notes as he covered the route across the plains.—EDG

Best handbook for the central route available at the time. The first issue has no newspaper comments on page eight.—Howes

1953 HORN, HOSEA B.

THE SAME.
Blue cloth.
A brilliant, untouched copy.

1954 HORN, HOSEA B.

THE SAME.
[i]–iv, [5]–[84], [1–18 advertisements]. 15.4 x 9.7 cm. Folding map. Same as above. Original plum cloth, blind embossed sides, title in gilt on front cover: Horn's / Overland Guide / to / California /. "Horn's" is upright.
Ref.: As above
Second Issue.

1955 HORN, HOSEA B.

A PRACTICAL GUIDE FOR JUSTICES OF THE PEACE AND CONSTABLES: CONTAINING A COMPREHENSIVE COLLECTION OF JUDICIAL AND MISCELLANEOUS FORMS, ADAPTED TO THE LAWS OF THE STATE OF IOWA . . . KEOKUK, IOWA: PRINTED AT THE DISPATCH OFFICE, 1854.

[i]–iv, [5]–162, [I]–IV Index. 19.1 x 11.2 cm. Calf, red leather label on backstrip.
Prov.: Each leaf embossed with notarial seal of D. B. Lamberson and with paper impressions of embossed seal pasted to front and back covers.
Ref.: Moffit 160

1956 HORN, HOSEA B.

ANOTHER COPY.
[i]–iv, [5]–162, [I]–IV Index. 19 x 11 cm. Original full sheepskin, rebacked with calf. In a gray cloth case.
Prov.: In pencil on front endleaf: Samuel H Chubbs / Book / followed by faint pencil notes. On inner front cover, some columns of figures. On verso of back endleaf, in ink: Couty[!] of Dallas County of Dalls[!] / July 21 / 1833 / July 21 / 182 /.

1957 HORN, TOM

LIFE OF TOM HORN GOVERNMENT SCOUT AND INTERPRETER WRITTEN BY HIMSELF . . . DENVER: THE LOUTHAN BOOK COMPANY.*

[3]–317, [318 blank]. 18.7 x 13 cm. 13 illustrations. Brown pictorial wrappers.
Ref.: Adams 497; Adams (*Ramp. Herd*) 1066; Dobie pp. 106–07; Jones 1696; Rader 1931
Copyrighted in 1904.
The volume may have been compiled by John C. Coble from notes and manuscripts left by Horn after his execution, although there are other claimants of authorship.

1958 HORNADAY, WILLIAM T.

THE EXTERMINATION OF THE AMERICAN BISON . . .
367–548. 22.3 x 14.2 cm. 22 illustrations and two maps listed. Dark green cloth.
Ref.: Rader 1932
A separate from the *Report of the National Museum*, 1887.

1959 HOSKINS, NATHAN

NOTES UPON THE WESTERN COUNTRY. CONTAINED
WITHIN THE STATES OF OHIO, INDIANA, ILLINOIS,
AND THE TERRITORY OF MICHIGAN: TAKEN ON A
TOUR THROUGH THAT COUNTRY IN THE SUMMER
OF 1832 . . . GREENFIELD: PRINTED BY JAMES P.
FOGG, 1833.

[1]–108. 20.3 x 11.9 cm. Tan wrappers, uncut. In
a maroon half morocco case.

Ref.: Bradford 2385; Buck 243; Howes
H656; Sabin 33097; Thomson 608

1960 HOSMER, JOHN A.

AUTOGRAPH MANUSCRIPT of a theatre program.
1863 December 2. One page, 19.5 x 11.2 cm.
Mounted, edges and fold worn.

The program for the Stat[e] Theatre, Season
1, Week 1, Night 1, Monday eve. Dec. 21 '63,
comprised *Richard III, Macbeth* and *Hamlet*.
The cast for each play is indicated.

Apparently this program was carried across
the Plains to Virginia City, Montana, the following year.

The titles of the plays are stamped in heavy
black ink on the verso of the sheet.

1961 HOSMER, JOHN A.

PHOTOGRAPH. Full length, turned slightly to left,
hand on back of chair. 9 x 5.5 cm. on mount
10.1 x 6.3 cm. Imprint on verso: J. A. Keenan, /
Photographer, / No. 526 South Second Street, /
Philadelphia. / Remnant of Proprietary stamp at
foot.

1962 HOSMER, JOHN A.

PHOTOGRAPH. Bust, vignette, turned slightly to
right, full face. 9.3 x 5.5 cm. on mount 10 x 6 cm.
Imprint on verso: Montana / Picture Gallery, /
Jackson St., Virginia City, M.T. / [10 lines] /
A. C. Carter, Artist. / [within thick and thin rule
borders].

Accompanied by a photostatic copy of the
first photograph with the signature John Hosmer
at the foot.

Laid in case with Hosmer: *A Trip to the
States* . . . 1867.

1963 HOSMER, JOHN A.

A TRIP TO THE STATES, BY THE WAY OF THE YEL-
LOWSTONE AND MISSOURI . . . VIRGINIA CITY,
MON. TER.: BEAVER HEAD NEWS PRINT, 1867.

[i–ii], [1]–82, [1]–12. 13.2 x 10.4 cm. Tan printed
boards, with title on front cover, red cloth backstrip. In half red morocco case.

Prov.: Inscribed on front endleaf: Fredy B.

Farwell / M. T. / Feb 16 1867 / Presented By /
A. J. Hosmer /.

Ref.: Howes H662; McMurtrie (*Montana*)
26; Smith 4649

This copy comes from Judge Hosmer's li-
brary now owned by his son in San Francisco.
Laid in are two photographs of the author.—
EDG

1964 HOTCHKISS, CHARLES F.

ON THE EBB: A FEW LOG-LINES FROM AN OLD SALT
. . . NEW HAVEN: TUTTLE, MOREHOUSE & TAYLOR,
1878.

[1]–127, [128 blank]. 18 x 13 cm. Dark orange
cloth, title and vignette stamped in gilt on front
cover, blind ornamental bands at top and foot of
covers.

Ref.: Cowan p. 292; Howes H666

Advertisement on recto of first fly-leaf. Included are twenty-five pages of reminiscences of
California in 1849.

1965 HOUGH, EMERSON

THE COVERED WAGON . . . NEW YORK: D. APPLE-
TON AND COMPANY, MCMXXII.*

[i–viii, viii blank], 1–[379], [380 blank]. 18.7 x
12.4 cm. Frontispiece. Red cloth, title stamped
in black on front cover and backstrip.

Ref.: Blanck 9359; Rader 1940; Smith 4656

First Edition, with (1) at end of text.

1966 HOUGH, EMERSON

NORTH OF 36 . . . NEW YORK: D. APPLETON AND
COMPANY, 1923.

[i]–[x, x blank], 1–429, [430 blank], [431–37 advertisements, 438 blank]. 18.6 x 12.2 cm. Four
illustrations listed. Green cloth, title stamped in
gilt on front cover and backstrip. In dust jacket.

Ref.: Blanck 9362; Dobie pp. 107–08; Rader
1941

Second printing, with (2) following text on
page 429. According to Dobie, the Appendix of
Stuart Henry: *Conquering Our Great American
Plains* contains strictures on the use of history by
Hough.

1967 HOUGH, EMERSON

THE STORY OF THE COWBOY . . . NEW YORK: D. AP-
PLETON AND COMPANY, 1897.

[i]–[xii], 1–349, [350 blank], [351–56 advertise-
ments]. 18.7 x 12.5 cm. Ten illustrations listed.
Tan cloth, front cover and backstrip with title
stamped in black and silver.

Ref.: Adams 500; Adams (*Ramp. Herd*) 1043;
Blanck 9315; Dobie p. 107; Howes H673; Munk
(*Alliot*) p. 109; Rader 1944; Smith 4669

1968 HOUGH, EMERSON

THE STORY OF THE OUTLAW. A STUDY OF THE WESTERN DESPERADO . . . NEW YORK: THE OUTING PUBLISHING COMPANY, 1907.

[i]–xiv, 1–401, [402 blank]. 18.3 x 12.4 cm. 18 illustrations listed. Pictorial brown boards, brown cloth backstrip.

Ref.: Adams 501; Blanck 9326; Dobie p. 141; Howes H674; Munk (Alliot) p. 109; Rader 1945; Smith 4071

With the printer's rules at top of page v.

1969 HOUGH, EMERSON

THE WAY TO THE WEST AND THE LIVES OF THREE EARLY AMERICANS BOONE—CROCKETT—CARSON . . . INDIANAPOLIS: THE BOBBS-MERRILL COMPANY, [1903].*

[i–vi, vi blank], 1–446. 18.6 x 12.6 cm. Six illustrations unlisted. Gray pictorial cloth, title in gilt on front cover and backstrip.

Ref.: Blanck 9319; Munk (Alliot) p. 109

1970 HOUGH, FRANKLIN B., *Editor*

DIARY OF THE SIEGE OF DETROIT IN THE WAR WITH PONTIAC. ALSO A NARRATIVE OF THE PRINCIPAL EVENTS OF THE SIEGE, BY MAJOR ROBERT ROGERS; A PLAN FOR CONDUCTING INDIAN AFFAIRS, BY COLONEL BRADSTREET; AND OTHER AUTHENTICK DOCUMENTS, NEVER BEFORE PRINTED. EDITED WITH NOTES BY FRANKLIN B. HOUGH. ALBANY, N.Y.: J. MUNSELL, M.D.CCC.LX.

[1–2], [1]–[xxiv, xxiv blank], [1–2], [1]–304. 21.5 x 17.8 cm. Green cloth, gilt top, uncut.

Ref.: Bradford 2402; Howes H675; Matthews p. 64; Sabin 19788; Thomson 611

Munsell's Historical Series, No. IV.

1971 HOUGHTON, ELIZA P. DONNER

THE EXPEDITION OF THE DONNER PARTY AND ITS TRAGIC FATE . . . CHICAGO: A. C. McCLURG & CO., 1911.*

[i]–[xxiii], [xxiv blank], 1–[375], [376 blank]. 20.8 x 13.8 cm. 56 illustrations listed. Light brown cloth, fore and lower edges uncut.

Ref.:

1972 HOUSE, E.

AN AUTHENTIC AND THRILLING NARRATIVE OF THE CAPTIVITY OF MRS. HORN, AND HER TWO CHILDREN, WITH MRS. HARRIS, BY THE CAMANCHE INDIANS, AND THE MURDER OF THEIR HUSBANDS AND TRAVELING COMPANIONS . . . CINCINNATI: PUBLISHED BY THE AUTHOR.

[1]–32. 22.5 x 14.9 cm. Salmon printed wrappers with title on front wrapper, advertisements on other wrapper surfaces. In a brown cloth case.

Ref.: AII (*Missouri*) 244 see; Ayer 135; Field 716; Howes H642; Sabin 33024 see; Streeter 1347 see; Wagner 74 note

Copyrighted 1851.

The introduction by E. House and some further observations on the Comanches are omitted from this edition.

Editions: St. Louis, 1839.

1973 HOUSE, E.

A NARRATIVE OF THE CAPTIVITY OF MRS. HORN, AND HER TWO CHILDREN, WITH MRS. HARRIS, BY THE CAMANCHE INDIANS, AFTER THEY HAD MURDERED THEIR HUSBANDS AND TRAVELLING COMPANIONS . . . ST. LOUIS: C. KEEMLE, PRINTER, 1839.

[1]–60. 18.2 x 11.6 cm. Buff printed paper over blue boards, tan cloth backstrip, with title on front cover: A / Narrative / of [the] / Captivity / of / Mrs. Horn, / And her Two Children, / with that of / Mrs. Harris, / by the / Camanche Indians, / And who was ransomed by the American Traders, / and brought by them from Santa Fé to New / Franklin, Mo., in the fall of 1838. / [decorative rule] / Written by E. House. / [decorative rule] / St. Louis: / C. Keemle, Printer, 22 Olive Street. / 1839. / [within decorative border], advertisement on verso of back cover. Unprinted parts of both front and back covers mostly eaten away by cockroaches. In a brown cloth case.

Ref.: AII (*Missouri*) 244; Ayer 134; Field 715; Howes H642; Sabin 33024; Streeter 1347; Wagner-Camp 74

Mrs. Horn's engrossing tale was dictated to E. House. The Horns were English. They immigrated first to New York and then decided to join Dr. Beales' colony on the Rio Grande in Texas. After a short stay in an unpleasant situation, the family determined to return to England and set out in a company of eleven persons. The Comanches attacked them, killing all except Mrs. Horn, her two sons and their friend Mrs. Harris. After two years of extreme hardship, both of the women were ransomed by Santa Fé traders. Mrs. Horn was uncertain of the fate of her two sons at the time of writing her account; she believed the younger may have died and was fairly certain the elder had survived.

The back cover bears a "Notice" stating that Mrs. Horn is still at Workman's brother's house, and naming other persons who could attest the truth of the narrative.

1974 HOUSEWORTH, HENRY

FEDERURBIAN; OR, UNITED STATES LESSONS: INTENDED TO PROMOTE LEARNING AND A KNOWLEDGE OF REPUBLICAN PRINCIPLES, IN THE MINDS OF

OUR YOUTH . . . PHILOMATH, IND.: PUBLISHED BY THE AUTHOR, 1839.

[A], B, D, F, H, J, L, N, P, R, T each in six. Verso of last leaf of each gathering signed A, C, E, G, I, K, M, O, Q, S. [i]–iv, [5]–144. 16.1 x 10.6 cm. Blue-gray boards, cloth back. Lacks part of front endleaf.

Ref.: Buley II p. 376; Byrd & Peckham 799; Walker 248

First known printing in Philomath, Indiana. The work was listed for copyright twice, April 12, 1837 and April 6, 1839.

1975 HOUSTON, SAM

DOCUMENTS OF MAJOR GEN. SAM. HOUSTON, COMMANDER IN CHIEF OF THE TEXIAN ARMY, TO HIS EXCELLENCY DAVID G. BURNET, PRESIDENT OF THE REPUBLIC OF TEXAS; CONTAINING A DETAILED ACCOUNT OF THE BATTLE OF SAN JACINTO . . . NEW ORLEANS: JOHN COX & CO., 1836.

[1]–18, [19 errata, 20 blank]. 21.2 x 13.8 cm. Contemporary blue wrappers, stabbed. With manuscript title on front cover: Battle of / San Jacinto /. On back cover: San Jacinto / List /.

Prov.: Signature on title-page: Anson Jones /. Inscribed on page [20]: Presented to / Anson Jones / by Sam¹ Ralph / Jan: 1848 /. Some manuscript notes in text in pencil.

Ref.: Sabin 94961; Streeter 1239

. . . the first edition in book form of Houston's report on the battle of San Jacinto, is one of the great Texas books.—Streeter

Anson Jones (if he needs identifying) was the last president of the Republic of Texas.

1976 HOUSTOUN, MATILDA C.

HESPEROS: OR, TRAVELS IN THE WEST . . . LONDON: JOHN W. PARKER, M DCCC L.

[i]–viii, [1]–293, [294 colophon]. [i]–viii, [1]–279, [280 colophon], [1–8 advertisements]. 19.8 x 12.2 cm. Two volumes, smooth brown cloth, original printed white paper labels, 5.5 x 2.8 cm.: [rule] / Hesperos: / or / Travels / in / The West. / [rule] / Mrs. Houstoun. / [rule] / Vol. I [–II]. / [short rule] / 14s. / [rule] /, uncut.

Ref.: Buck 452; Howes H692; Rader 1950; Sabin 33200; Thomson 612

1977 HOWARD, FREDERICK P., & GEORGE BARNETT

THE BRITISH COLUMBIAN AND VICTORIA GUIDE AND DIRECTORY, FOR 1863 . . . VICTORIA, V. I.: OFFICE OF THE BRITISH COLUMBIAN AND VICTORIA DIRECTORY, 1863.

3–46, [1–2], [47]–216. 22.1 x 14.5 cm. Printed boards, black leather back, with short title on front cover; rest of cover, back cover, and inner covers carry advertisements.

Ref.:

The volume was printed in San Francisco by Towne & Bacon.

There are important articles on "Cariboo," pages 199–203; "The Peace River Mines," pages 204–05; and "The Territory of Sticken," pages 206–08.

1978 HOWARD, J. W.

THE UNION PACIFIC RAILROAD FROM OMAHA TO PROMONTORY . . . OMAHA: BARKALOW BROS. & CO., 1869.

[1]–12. 20.7 x 14 cm. Folding woodcut map: Union Pacific / Railroad / and / Connections / [lower left corner:] Engraved by Fisk & Russell New York /. 23.1 x 43.8 cm. (neat line). 30.2 x 50.4 cm. (paper size); advertisements in margins. On verso of map: advertisements and Condensed Time Table, 1869. Pale cream printed wrapper, with title on front wrapper. Removed from bound volume; lacks back wrapper.

Ref.:

1979 HOWARD, JACOB M.

[Caption title] TRANSCONTINENTAL, MEMPHIS, AND EL PASO RAILROAD. SPEECH OF HON. JACOB M. HOWARD, OF MICHIGAN, IN THE SENATE OF THE UNITED STATES, JUNE 22 AND 23, 1870 . . .

[1]–16. 22.6 x 14.8 cm. Stabbed, unbound.

Ref.:

Howard takes General Frémont apart for his share in the flimflamming of French citizens to secure funds for the above railroad.—EDG

1980 HOWARD, OLIVER O.

ANNUAL REPORT . . . DEPARTMENT OF THE COLUMBIA. (NON-TREATY NEZ-PERCE CAMPAIGN.) JANUARY 26, 1878. FORT VANCOUVER, W. T.: HEADQUARTERS DEPARTMENT OF THE COLUMBIA, 1879.

[1]–61, [62 blank]. 17.8 x 11.5 cm.

Ref.: Howes H707

BOUND WITH:

APPENDIX TO SUPPLEMENTARY REPORT (NON-TREATY NEZ-PERCE CAMPAIGN) . . . OFFICERS AND ENLISTED MEN SPECIALLY COMMENDED FOR GALLANTRY OR FOR OTHER MERITORIOUS CONDUCT IN CONNECTION WITH THE CAMPAIGN AGAINST HOSTILE NON-TREATY NEZ-PERCE INDIANS. PORTLAND, OREGON: ASSISTANT ADJUTANT GENERAL'S OFFICE, 1878.

[i–ii], [1]–13, [14 blank]. (Pages 5–12 misbound.)

Ref.:

BOUND WITH:

REPORT . . . DEPARTMENT OF THE COLUMBIA. OC-
TOBER 15, 1878. FORT VANCOUVER, W. T.: ASSIST-
ANT ADJUTANT GENERAL'S OFFICE, 1879.

[1]–53, [54 blank].
Ref.: Howes H713

BOUND WITH:

[Caption title] HEADQUARTERS DEPARTMENT OF
THE COLUMBIA, IN THE FIELD, FORT VANCOUVER,
W. T., OCTOBER 4, 1878. GENERAL FIELD ORDERS,
NO. 9 . . . [foot of page 2:] BY COMMAND OF
BRIGADIER-GENERAL HOWARD: EDWIN C. MASON.
MAJOR 21ST INFANTRY, ACTING ASSISTANT INSPEC-
TOR GENERAL.

Broadsheet, [1]–2.
Ref.:

BOUND WITH:

[Caption title] DEPARTMENT OF THE COLUMBIA.
ROSTER OF TROOPS IN THE FIELD, OPERATING
AGAINST HOSTILE INDIANS, COMMANDED BY BRIGA-
DIER-GENERAL O. O. HOWARD, U. S. ARMY . . .

[1]–4.
Ref.:
Dated on page 4: August 10, 1877.

BOUND WITH:

REPORT . . . DEPARTMENT OF THE COLUMBIA, SEP-
TEMBER 10, 1879. VANCOUVER BARRACKS, W. T.:
HEADQUARTERS DEPARTMENT OF THE COLUMBIA,
1879.

[1]–[26].
Ref.: Howes H712
Six pieces bound together, contemporary half
brown morocco, black cloth sides, titles in gilt
on black leather label on front cover, title in gilt
on backstrip, with name of owner at base, red
sprinkled edges.
Prov.: Stamped in gilt at foot of backstrip:
Col. E. C. Mason. / Part of his signature appears
on the first title-page.
Ref.: See above
Colonel Mason was on General Howard's
staff.
The first report is a reprint, so noted on the
title-page.

1981 HOWARD, OLIVER O.

MY LIFE AND EXPERIENCES AMONG OUR HOSTILE
INDIANS. A RECORD OF PERSONAL OBSERVATIONS,
ADVENTURES, AND CAMPAIGNS AMONG THE IN-
DIANS OF THE GREAT WEST . . . HARTFORD, CONN.:
A. D. WORTHINGTON & COMPANY.*

[1]–570. 22.1 x 14.3 cm. 46 plates listed, including ten in color. Dark blue cloth, blind embossed
front cover with facsimile signature in gilt, title
in gilt on backstrip, sprinkled edges.

Ref.: Howes H710; Munk (Alliot) p. 109;
Rader 1955 see; Saunders 2967; Smith 4699
Copyrighted 1907.

1982 HOWARD, OLIVER O.

NEZ PERCE JOSEPH. AN ACCOUNT OF HIS ANCES-
TORS, HIS LANDS, HIS CONFEDERATES, HIS ENEMIES,
HIS MURDERS, HIS WAR, HIS PURSUIT AND CAP-
TURE . . . BOSTON: LEE AND SHEPARD, 1881.

[1–2], [i]–xii, 1–274. 19.8 x 13.5 cm. Two portraits and two maps unlisted. Map: Map of the /
Grande Ronde / Wallowa and Imnaha Country. / [rule] / H. Chandler, Eng., Buffalo. /
16.2 x 9.6 cm. No scale given. Map: Map to illustrate Gen'l Howard's Nez-Percé Campaign.
1877. / 11.8 x 28.1 cm. No scale given. Blue
cloth, blind embossed sides, title in gilt on backstrip.
Ref.: Howes H711; Jones 1611; Rader 1956;
Smith 4700

1983 HOWARD, OLIVER O.

REPORT . . . DEPARTMENT OF THE COLUMBIA. SEP-
TEMBER 10, 1879. VANCOUVER BARRACKS, W. T.:
HEADQUARTERS DEPARTMENT OF THE COLUMBIA,
1879.

[1]–[26]. 19.5 x 12.5 cm. Pink printed wrappers,
with title on front wrapper, bound into red half
morocco. Lacks back wrapper.
Ref.: Howes H712
The Appendix on page [26] reads in part: My
Annual Report indicated a failure in the main
object of the expedition against the Sheep-eaters
and renegades located between the little Salmon
and Snake rivers. Now it is reversed, and the
expedition has handsomely been completed by
Lieutenant Farrow and his scouts . . . [they] deserve special mention for gallantry, energy, and
perseverance, resulting in success. There is not a
rougher or more difficult country for campaigning in America. Please add this to my report . . .
See also Number 45.

1984 HOWBERT, IRVING

THE INDIANS OF THE PIKE'S PEAK REGION, INCLUD-
ING AN ACCOUNT OF THE BATTLE OF SAND CREEK,
AND OF OCCURRENCES IN EL PASO COUNTY, COLO-
RADO, DURING THE WAR WITH THE CHEYENNES
AND ARAPAHOES, IN 1864 AND 1868 . . . NEW
YORK: THE KNICKERBOCKER PRESS, 1914.*

[i]–x, 1–230. 20.6 x 13.8 cm. Four illustrations
listed. Blue ribbed cloth, gilt top, uncut.
Ref.: Howes H715; Rader 1958; Wilcox p.
62

1985 HOWE, EBER D.

MORMONISM UNVAILED: OR, A FAITHFUL ACCOUNT OF THAT SINGULAR IMPOSITION AND DELUSION, FROM ITS RISE TO THE PRESENT TIME. WITH SKETCHES OF THE CHARACTERS OF ITS PROPAGATORS, AND A FULL DETAIL OF THE MANNER IN WHICH THE FAMOUS GOLDEN BIBLE WAS BROUGHT BEFORE THE WORLD . . . PAINESVILLE: PRINTED AND PUBLISHED BY THE AUTHOR, 1834.

[i]–[x, x blank], [11]–290. 17.9 x 10.4 cm. Frontispiece. Purple cloth.

Ref.: Howes H717; Sabin 33290; Woodward 99

First elaborate critique of this sect, the first to exploit the Spaulding manuscript, and the best contemporary account of Mormon activities in Ohio.—Howes

1986 HOWE, FRANCES R.

THE STORY OF A FRENCH HOMESTEAD IN THE OLD NORTHWEST . . . COLUMBUS, O.: PRESS OF NITSCHKE BROS., 1907.

[1–2], [5]–165, [166–68 blank]. 19.6 x 13.1 cm. Two folding maps. Map: Map Nº 4. / Colonies / during the / Revolutionary War. / By Russell Hinman C.E. / [lower left:] Eclectic U. S. Hist Map No. 4 Chap. XIV–XIX. / (142) / [lower right:] (143) /. 15.8 x 20.3 cm. Scale: about 150 miles to one inch. *Inset:* Arnold's Expedition / against Quebec / Scale: about 200 miles to one inch. 4.9 x 3.4 cm. *Inset:* Map of Boston / & Environs / 4.9 x 4.5 cm. Scale: about 4 miles to one inch. Map: Map Nº 6. / War of 1812. / By Russell Hinman C. E. / [lower left:] Eclectic U. S. History Map No. 6. Chaps. XXIV–XXV. / (228) / [lower right:] (229) /. 15.9 x 20.2 cm. Scale: about 225 miles to one inch. *Inset:* Operations about / Washington. / 6.4 x 4.1 cm. Scale: about 85 miles to one inch. *Inset:* Operations / about / Niagara. / 6.4 x 3.7 cm. (neat line). Scale: about 11 miles to one inch. Blue cloth, with title in gilt on front cover and on backstrip.

Ref.: Howes H718

Most of the edition deliberately burned by the eccentric authoress.—Howes

1987 HOWE, MARCUS A. D.

THE LIFE AND LABORS OF BISHOP HARE, APOSTLE TO THE SIOUX . . . NEW YORK: STURGIS & WALTON COMPANY, 1911.

[i–x, x blank], [1]–417, [418 blank]. 21.3 x 14.3 cm. Eight illustrations listed. Green cloth, gilt top, uncut.

Ref.: Rader 1962

1988 [HOWELLS, WILLIAM D.]

LIVES AND SPEECHES OF ABRAHAM LINCOLN AND HANNIBAL HAMLIN. COLUMBUS, O.: FOLLETT, FOSTER & CO., 1860.

[1]–[8, 8 blank], [ix]–[xvi, xvi blank], 17–170. Buff printed wrappers with title on front wrapper, advertisement on verso of front wrapper headed: 20,416 Sold! /, Publisher's Announcement. / on recto of back wrapper, and view of: The Republican Wigwam at Chicago. / on verso of back wrapper. In a tan cloth case.

Ref.: Blanck 9538; Howes H735; Monaghan (*Lincoln*) 43; Sabin 33354; Wessen "Campaign Lives of Abraham Lincoln" in *Papers in Illinois History* 1937, No. 9

According to Howes only MWA and Graff have copies of this state.

1989 HOWISON, NEIL M.

[Caption title] . . . REPORT OF LIEUT. NEIL M. HOWISON, UNITED STATES NAVY, TO THE COMMANDER OF THE PACIFIC SQUADRON; BEING THE RESULT OF AN EXAMINATION IN THE YEAR 1846 OF THE COAST, HARBORS, RIVERS, SOIL, PRODUCTIONS, CLIMATE, AND POPULATION OF THE TERRITORY OF OREGON . . .

[1]–36. 25 x 15.5 cm. Stabbed, unbound, uncut, unopened.

Ref.: Howell 141; Howes H738; Sabin 33368

30th Congress, 1st Session, House, Miscellaneous Document No. 29, Serial 523. [Washington, 1848.]

Imprint at foot of page [1]: [rule] / Tippin & Streeper, printers. /

1990 HOWISON, NEIL M.

THE SAME.

BOUND WITH:

[Caption title] . . . MEMORIAL OF J. QUINN THORNTON, PRAYING THE ESTABLISHMENT OF A TERRITORIAL GOVERNMENT IN OREGON, AND FOR APPROPRIATIONS FOR VARIOUS PURPOSES . . .

[1]–24. 22.5 x 14.5 cm.

30th Congress, 1st Session, Senate, Miscellaneous Document No. 143, Serial 511. [Washington, 1848.]

BOUND WITH:

[Caption title] . . . OREGON. MEMORIAL OF THE LEGISLATIVE ASSEMBLY OF OREGON TERRITORY, RELATIVE TO THEIR PRESENT SITUATION AND WANTS . . .

[1]–26.

30th Congress, 1st Session, House, Miscellaneous Document No. 98, Serial 523. [Washington, 1848.]

Three volumes bound together, red marbled boards, black cloth backstrip.

Ref.: Howes H738, T223, O107

The printer's imprint appears on each page [1], lower left corner: [short rule] / Tippin & Streeper, printers. /

Bound in before the first item is a special title-page printed at the Grabhorn Press: Oregon Tracts / Report of Neil M. Howison / Memorial of / J. Quinn Thornton / and the Legislative Assembly / of Oregon Territory / [vignette] / Washington: 30th Congress / 1848 /.

The third piece is an important Whitman massacre document.

1991 [HOWLAND, MRS. E. P.]

A TALE OF HOME AND WAR BY E. P. H. PORTLAND, MAINE: BROWN THURSTON & COMPANY, 1888.

[1]–200. (Pages [1–2] blank.) 18.6 x 11.7 cm. Portrait. Dark red cloth, blind embossed borders on sides, title in gilt on front cover.

Ref.: Howes H741

Initials on title-page filled out in ink.

Experiences of the family of missionary Worcester Willey among the Cherokees of the Indian Territory during the Civil War.—Howes

1992 HOWLETT, WILLIAM J.

LIFE OF THE RIGHT REVEREND JOSEPH P. MACHEBEUF, D.D. . . . PUEBLO, COLORADO, 1908.*

[1]–419, [420 blank]. 22.5 x 15 cm. Illustrations unlisted. Lavender cloth.

Ref.: Howes H743

Used by Willa Cather for her *Death Comes to the Archbishop.*—EDG

1993 HUBBARD, GURDON S.

AUTOGRAPH LETTER, SIGNED. 1835 June 23, Chicago. To Thomas Mather or Edmund Roberts. Three pages, 24.2 x 19.9 cm.

A fine letter regarding the sale of lots in Chicago, apparently jointly owned by the three men.

1994 HUBBARD, GURDON S.

AUTOGRAPH LETTER, SIGNED. 1884 March 14. Green Cove Springs, Florida. To Miss Anna M. Holt. Four pages, 24.8 x 19.7 cm.

A charming letter describing his visit to Green Cove Springs. With original envelope.

1995 HUBBARD, GURDON S.

AUTOGRAPH LETTER, UNFINISHED. 1885 March 17. Chicago. To Miss Mary Greene. Three pages, 20.4 x 12.7 cm.

Regarding his early years in Chicago.

1996 HUBBARD, GURDON S.

AUTOGRAPH MANUSCRIPT, fragment, in pencil. Two pages, 24.8 x 19.5 cm.

Details of his first year as an employee of the American Fur Company.

1997 HUBBARD, GURDON S.

INCIDENTS AND EVENTS . . . COLLECTED FROM PERSONAL NARRATIONS AND OTHER SOURCES, AND ARRANGED BY HIS NEPHEW, HENRY E. HAMILTON. 1888.

[i–ii], [1]–189, [190 blank]. 21.8 x 15.3 cm. Portrait. Black cloth, gilt fillet border on front cover, title in gilt on front cover, name in gilt on backstrip.

Prov.: Inscribed on blank leaf at front: Mr & Mrs Watkins — / with kind regard / from Mrs Hubbard. /

Ref.: Buck 132; Howes H749

Laid in are an Autograph Letter, signed (1884 March 14), an unfinished letter (1885 March 17), and an Autograph Manuscript fragment, in pencil.

Incidents and events of early Chicago. An important chronicle.

1998 HUBBARD, MARY ANN

FAMILY MEMORIES PRINTED FOR PRIVATE CIRCULATION, 1912.*

[i]–[viii, viii blank], 1–146. 17 x 10.4 cm. Portrait and one plate unlisted. Dark green cloth, gilt top, uncut.

Ref.:

Mary Ann Hubbard was the widow of Gurdon Saltonstall Hubbard. She came to Chicago in 1836.—EDG

1999 HUDSON, C. F.

THE IMPERATIVE NATURE OF DUTY. A DISCOURSE DELIVERED . . . MAY 30, 1852 . . . CHICAGO: FULTON & CO., PRINTERS, 1853.

[i]–iv, [5]–19, [20 blank]. 22.9 x 14.4 cm. Pale blue printed wrappers with title on front wrapper.

Prov.: Rubber stamp of Historical & Philosophical Society of Ohio on front cover and numerals 252. Manuscript numerals on same cover in red ink: 4740 /.

Ref.: AII (*Chicago*) 63; Byrd 1980

2000 HUFFMAN, LATON A.

ORIGINAL PHOTOGRAPHS, as below:

[Portrait of Two Moons]. Tinted. Photographer's name, copyright symbol and date 1913 in plate. 25.7 x 24 cm. Printed in sepia. Reproduced in *The Frontier Years*, page 225.

After the Chase. L. A. Huffman. Photo. / 25.3 x 20.3 cm. *The Frontier Years*, page 72.

Buffalo Family Big Dry Creek. Montana L. A. Huffman Photo /. 20.3 x 25.3 cm.

Two Moons Family on Rosebud River / [In plate:] 3 Huffman, Photo. Miles City, Mont. / 25.9 x 20.8 cm. Page size: 29.3 x 23.3 cm. Printed in sepia.

#383—"Jerk-line twelve" on the old freight road, Neg. Print & copyright by L. A. Huffman Milestown 1883. / 22.6 x 27.9 cm. Printed in sepia. *The Frontier Years*, page 175.

[In plate:] #176 The Round-up Breaking Camp, Negative, Print and Copyright by L. A. Huffman Miles C Mont 04. / 23.9 x 27.9 cm.

Noon Camp on Big Dry River Montana 1905 L. A. Huffman Photo /. 20.2 x 35.6 cm.

Mountain Sheep /. Photographer's name, copyright symbol and date 1913 in plate. 23.4 x 36.2 cm. Paper size: 25.2 x 40.4 cm. Printed in sepia.

Buffalo near Smoky Butte North Montana 1883 L. A. Huffman Photo /. [In plate:] 107B /. 25.4 x 50.7 cm. Printed in sepia. *The Frontier Years*, page 51, where the title is given: "Buffalo Grazing in the Big Open, North Montana, 1880."

[Another view of Buffalo grazing in the Big Open.] 25.4 x 49.3 cm. *The Frontier Years*, page 62. [In the plate:] 106B /.

Most of these photographs have been touched up in the plate. Those which appear in *The Frontier Years* seem to have been reproduced from the original negatives and the present series for over-the-counter sale. Captions are in hand of Huffman.

2001 HUGHES, F. W.

[Wrapper title] THE CASE OF GEORGE CHORPEN-NING. ARGUMENT BY F. W. HUGHES, BEFORE THE JUDICIARY COMMITTEE OF THE HOUSE OF REPRE-SENTATIVES, WASHINGTON, D.C., MARCH, 1880. L. G. STEPHENS & SON, PRINTERS . . .

[1]–67, [68 blank]. 21.6 x 14.1 cm. Gray printed wrappers with title on front wrapper. With other Chorpenning materials in a red cloth case.

Ref.: Howes C399

Signed on page 67: F. W. Hughes, / Of Counsel for Claimant. / Printed in Washington, 1880.

The earliest overland mail and pony express operations.—Howes

2002 HUGHES, GERALDINE

AUTOGRAPH LETTER, SIGNED. 1936 May 22, Mount Vernon, Iowa. To Edward Eberstadt.

A very interesting letter about Emeline Fuller's *Left by the Indians* . . . [1892]. Miss Hughes

states that she has a copy of the pamphlet, but lacking the wrappers. She also states that her father, James Hughes, an evangelist, wrote the story for Mrs. Fuller.

Laid in the copy of Mrs. Fuller's work.

2003 HUGHES, JOHN T.

CALIFORNIA: ITS HISTORY, POPULATION, CLIMATE, SOIL, PRODUCTIONS, AND HARBORS. FROM SIR GEORGE SIMPSON'S "OVERLAND JOURNEY ROUND THE WORLD." AN ACCOUNT OF THE REVOLUTION IN CALIFORNIA, AND CONQUEST OF THE COUNTRY BY THE UNITED STATES, 1846-7. BY JOHN T. HUGHES . . . CINCINNATI: PUBLISHED BY J. A. & U. P. JAMES, 1848.

[1]–105, [106 blank]. 20.1 x 12.3 cm. Brown printed wrappers, with title on front wrapper: [See Palmer, Joel: *Journal* . . .].

Ref.: Bradford 2456 see; Cowan p. 295; Howes H768; Jones 1175; Sabin 33595

Bound and issued with Palmer's *Journal of Travels over the Rocky Mountains, to the Mouth of the Columbia River* . . . Cincinnati . . . 1847 [7 written over in manuscript: 8].

2004 HUGHES, JOHN T.

DONIPHAN'S EXPEDITION; CONTAINING AN AC-COUNT OF THE CONQUEST OF NEW MEXICO; GEN-ERAL KEARNEY'S OVERLAND EXPEDITION TO CALI-FORNIA; DONIPHAN'S CAMPAIGN AGAINST THE NAVAJOS; HIS UNPARALLELED MARCH UPON CHI-HUAHUA AND DURANGO; AND THE OPERATIONS OF GENERAL PRICE AT SANTA FE . . . CINCINNATI: PUBLISHED BY J. A. & U. P. JAMES, 1847.

[i]–viii, [9]–144. 23.9 x 14.9 cm. Frontispiece, illustrations and three plans. Brown printed wrappers, with title on front wrapper, title on back-strip reading down: Doniphan's Expedition. /, advertisements on verso of front and recto and verso of back wrapper. In a brown cloth case.

Ref.: Bradford 2457 see; Cowan p. 295; Edwards p. 80; Howes H769; Jones 1151; Munk (Alliot) p. 111; Rader 1970; Sabin 33596; Saunders 2972 see; Wagner-Camp 134

The expeditions of Doniphan and Kearny were later used as the basis for the United States claim to Arizona and New Mexico. Eventually the matter was settled by the Gadsden Purchase.

2005 HUGHES, JOHN T.

THE SAME . . . CINCINNATI: PUBLISHED BY J. A. & U. P. JAMES, 1848.

[i]–xii, 13–407, [408 blank]. 19 x 11.7 cm. Two portraits, illustrations and maps in text, folded map: A / New Map / of / Mexico, / California & Oregon. / Published by / J. A. & U. P. James, / Cincinnati. / 1848. / *Inset:* [Yucatan] 8.2 x 8 cm.

No scale indicated. 32.2 x 23.7 cm. No scale indicated. Dark brown cloth, blind embossed borders on sides, vignettes in centres, gilt on front blind on back, gilt title on backstrip.

Ref.: Bradford 2457; Cowan p. 295; Edwards p. 80; Howes H769; Jones 1176; Rader 1970; Sabin 33596; Saunders 2972

Although Howes states the portrait of Price appears with copies which carry a list of illustrations, there is no list of illustrations in this copy and the portrait of Price is present.

Editions: Cincinnati, 1847; 1848.

2006 HUGHES, JOHN T.

THE SAME . . . CINCINNATI: U. P. JAMES.

[i]–viii, 9–144. (Page [i] blank, page [ii] frontispiece.) 23.3 x 14.6 cm. 13 illustrations and maps listed. Printed salmon wrappers, with title on front wrapper, advertisements on verso of front and recto and verso of back wrapper, title reading down on backstrip: Doniphan's Expedition. /, uncut, unopened. In a green cloth case.

Ref.: Howes H769; Munk (Alliot) p. 111; Rader 1970 see; Sabin 33596; Saunders 2972 see; Wagner-Camp 134

Editions: Cincinnati, 1847; 1848; 1848 (cloth).

2007 [HUGHES, W. E.]

THE JOURNAL OF A GRANDFATHER.

[1]–139, [140 blank]. 21.6 x 15 cm. 15 illustrations listed. Brown boards, tan cloth backstrip, gilt top, uncut.

Ref.:

Privately printed at St. Louis. Copyrighted 1912. The author signs himself: W. E. H. Gramp.

2008 HUMASON, W. L.

FROM THE ATLANTIC SURF TO THE GOLDEN GATE . . . HARTFORD: PRESS OF WM. C. HUTCHINGS. 1869.

[1]–56. 24 x 16.2 cm. Black leather, gilt stamped panels on sides, title in gilt on front cover, gilt edges.

Ref.: Cowan pp. 295–96; Howes H785; Sabin 33685; Woodward 100

By rail across the country.

2009 HUMBOLDT, ALEXANDER VON

ATLAS GEOGRAPHIQUE ET PHYSIQUE DU ROYAUME DU LA NOUVELLE-ESPAGNE . . . PARIS: CHEZ F. SCHOELL, 1811.

[i–iv], [1]–4. 47.4 x 32.1 cm. 20 maps and charts as follows: Map: Carte Générale / du Royaume de la Nouvelle Espagne / depuis le Parallele de 16° jusqu'au Parallele de 38° (Latitude Nord) / Dressée / Sur des Observations Astronomiques et sur l'ensemble des Matériaux / qui existoient à Mexico, au commencement de l'année 1804. / Par Alexandre de Humboldt. / L^g Aubert Scripsit. / [upper right:] I. / 47.7 x 68.6 cm. No scale given. Map: [Same as preceding, lower half, without title]. [upper right:] I. (bis) / [lower left:] Dessiné à Mexico par l'Auteur en 1804, perfectionné par le mê[me], par MM. Friesen, Oltmanns et Thulier 1809. / [lower right:] Gravé par Barriere—et l'Ecriture par L. Aubert pere, à Paris. / 51.7 x 69 cm. No scale given. Map: Carte / du Mexique / et des Pays Limitrophes / Situés au Nord et à l'Est / Dressée / d'après la Grande Carte de la Nouvelle-Espagne / de Mr A. de Humboldt / et d'autres Matériaux / par / J. B. Poirson. / 1811. / [upper right:] 2. / [lower left:] Gravé par Barriere. [lower centre:] Se trouve à Paris chez F. Schoell, Libraire. / [lower right:] et l'écriture par L. Aubert. / 42.5 x 72.8 cm. No scale given. Map: Carte / de la Vallée de Mexico / et des Montagnes Voisines / esquissée sur les Lieux en 1804, / par Don Louis Martin / redigée et corrigée en 1807 / d'après les opérations Trigonométriques de Don Joaquin Velasquez / et d'après les observations Astronomiques et les mesures Barométriques / de Mr de Humboldt par Jabbo Oltmanns. / [upper right:] 3. / [lower left:] Dessiné par G. Grossmann, terminé par F. Friesen à Berlin 1807 et par A. Humboldt à Paris 1808. / [lower right:] Gravé par Barriere—et l'Ecriture par L. Aubert pere. / 38.9 x 45.8 cm. No scale given. Map: [Eight numbered maps on one sheet] [upper right:] 4. / [lower left:] Dessinés par J. B. Poirson. / [lower right:] Gravé par Barriere—et l'écriture par L. Aubert. / [lower centre:] Points de partage et Communications projettées / entre le Grand Océan et l'Océan Atlantique. / [ornamental rule] / I. Rivière de la Paix et Tacoutché Tessé. II. Rio del Norte et Rio Colorado. III. Rio Huallaga et Rio Huanuco. IV. Golfe de S. Georges et Estero de Aysen. / V. Rio de Huasacualco et Rio Chimalpa. VI. Lac de Nicaragua. VII. Isthme de Panama. VIII. Ravin de la Raspadura et Embarcadero de Naipi. / Measurements: I–IV, 10.6 x 7 cm. V, 16.4 x 16.5 cm. VI–VIII, 10.5 x 9 cm. No scales given. Map: Carte Réduite / de la Route d'Acapulco à Mexico, / Dressée sur des Observations Astronomiques et sur un nivellement Barométrique / par A. de Humboldt. / [upper right:] 5. / [lower left:] Dessiné par A. de Humboldt, à Berlin 1807. / [lower right:] Gravé par Barriere et l'Ecriture par L. Aubert. / 39.2 x 19.2 cm. No scale given. Map: [three maps on one sheet] Route de Chihuahua à Santa Fe. / 8. / [lower left:] Dessiné et redigé par F, Friesen, à Berlin 1807. / 42 x 12.7 cm. No scale given. Route de

Durango à Chihuahua. / 7. / [lower left: same as preceding] 25.8 x 12.5 cm. No scale given. Route de Mexico à Durango. / 6. / [lower left: same as preceding] 34.8 x 12.7 cm. No scale given. [below all three maps:] Carte de la Route qui mène depuis la Capitale de la Nouvelle Espagne / jusqu'à S. Fe du Nouveau Mexique. / Dressée sur les Journaux de Don Pedro de Rivera et en partie sur les Observations Astronomiques de Mr de Humboldt. / [above right of title:] Gravé par Barriere, et l'Ecriture par L. Aubert, directeur du dit Ouvrage. / Map: Carte réduite de la Partie orientale de la Nouvelle Espagne / depuis le Plateau de la ville de Mexico jusqu'au Port de la Veracruz. / Dressée sur les opérations Géodesiques de Don Miguel Costanzo et de D^n D^{go} Garcia Conde, Officiers au service de sa Majesté Catholique / sur les Observations Astronomiques et le Nivellement Barométrique de Mr de Humboldt. / [upper right:] 9. / [lower left:] Dessinée d'après l'esquise de Mr de Humboldt par F. Friesen, à Berlin 1807. / [lower right:] Le Plan gravé par Barriere et l'Ecriture par L. Aubert, directeur du dit ouv^e à Paris. / 21.3 x 62.6 cm. No scale given. Map: Carte des Fausses Positions / de Mexico, Acapulco, Veracruz et du Pic d'Orizaba. / [upper right:] 10. / [lower left:] Dessiné par A. de Humboldt à Mexico 1804. / [lower right:] Gravé par L. Aubert. / 18.7 x 31.7 cm. No scale given. Map: Plan du Port de Veracruz, / Dressé par Don Bernardo de Orta, Capitaine de Vaisseau au service de Sa Majesté Catholique. / [upper left:] 11. / [lower left:] F. Bauza f. a Madrid. (copié et diminué de moitié par F. Wittich 1807.) d'après le Plan publié par le Deposito hydrograffico de Madrid. / [lower right:] Le Plan gravé par Barriere et l'Ecriture par L. Aubert, directeur, Paris. / 21.5 x 28.4 cm. Scale: un Mille marin de 950 Toises. Nos. 12–15, profiles. Nos. 16–17, views. Map: Plan du Port d'Acapulco / Dressé par les Officiers de la Marine Royale de S. M. C. embarqués sur / les Corvettes la Descubierta et l'Atrevida l'année 1791. / [upper right:] 18. / [lower left:] Gravé par Barriere. / [lower centre:] Dessiné à Madrid au Dépôt Hydrographique. l'Ecriture par L. Aubert. / 17.1 x 18.3 cm. No scale given. Map: Carte des diverses Routes par lesquelles les richesses métalliques refluent d'un Continent à l'autre. / [upper right:] 19. / Dessiné par J. B. Poirson d'après une esquisse de Mr de Humboldt. / [lower right:] Gravé par L. Aubert. / [upper left:] Vol. II. p. 660. / [upper centre:] I. / 16.3 x 29.7 cm. No scale given. Four graphs on same sheet. No. 20, two tables. Each map and chart cut and carefully mounted on cotton cloth,

folded and fitted into a blue morocco folding box, 34.5 x 26 cm.

Ref.: Howes H786; Palau 116974; Sabin 33756; Wheat (*Transmississippi*) 272*, 274*, 275*, 302*, 304*, 305*

The *Atlas* is usually found with the quarto edition of *Essai Politique sur le Royaume de la Nouvelle-Espagne . . . 1811.*

2010 HUMBOLDT, ALEXANDER

ESSAI POLITIQUE SUR LE ROYAUME DE LA NOUVELLE-ESPAGNE . . . A PARIS: CHEZ F. SCHOELL, 1811.

[1–12, 12 blank], [i]–[iv, iv blank], 1–456. [i–iv, iv blank], 1–514. [i–iv, iv blank], 1–[420]. [i–iv, iv blank], 1–[565], [566 blank], [567–68 advertisement]. [i–iv, iv blank], 1–350, [351–52 advertisement]. 20.5 x 12.8 cm. Table and map in Vol. II: Carte / du Mexique / et des Pays Limitrophes / Situé au Nord et à l'Est / Dressée / d'après la Grande Carte de la Nouvelle-Espagne / de Mr A. de Humboldt / et d'autres Matériaux / par / J. B. Poirson. / 1811. / [upper right:] 2. / [lower left:] Gravé par Barriere. / [lower centre:] Se trouve à Paris chez F. Schoell, Libraire. / [lower right:] et l'écriture par L. Aubert. / 42.4 x 73.3 cm. No scale given. Five volumes, contemporary full tree calf, gilt, yellow edges. Rebacked preserving original labels.

Ref.: Howes H786; Palau 116975; Raines p. 121; Sabin 33713; Wheat (*Transmississippi*) 275*, 305*

Issued the same year as the quarto edition.

2011 HUMFREVILLE, JAMES LEE

TWENTY YEARS AMONG OUR SAVAGE INDIANS. A RECORD OF PERSONAL EXPERIENCES, OBSERVATIONS, AND ADVENTURES AMONG THE INDIANS OF THE WILD WEST . . . HARTFORD, CONN.: THE HARTFORD PUBLISHING COMPANY, 1897.

[i]–xlviii, [49]–64, 49–674. 22.2 x 14.5 cm. Ten plates in color, 243 illustrations listed, including 29 full-page plates. Dark red pictorial cloth.

Ref.: Howes H790; Rader 1976; Saunders 2974; Smith 4811

2012 HUNT, GEORGE W.

A HISTORY OF THE HUNT FAMILY . . . SETTLEMENT IN OREGON; MINING EXPERIENCES IN CALIFORNIA IN 1849; INCIDENTS OF PIONEER LIFE AND ADVENTURES AMONG THE INDIAN TRIBES OF THE NORTHWEST . . . BOSTON: PRESS OF McDONALD, GILL & CO., 1890.*

[1]–79, [80 blank]. 16.6 x 10.4 cm. Blue cloth, title in gilt on front cover, edges of binding beveled.

Ref.: Cowan p. 297; Howes H802; Smith 4814.

Contains a short account of an overland trip to Oregon.

2013   HUNT, JAMES H.

MORMONISM: EMBRACING THE ORIGIN, RISE AND PROGRESS OF THE SECT, WITH AN EXAMINATION OF THE BOOK OF MORMON; ALSO, THEIR TROUBLES IN MISSOURI, AND FINAL EXPULSION FROM THE STATE . . . WITH AN APPENDIX, GIVING AN ACCOUNT OF THE LATE DISTURBANCES IN ILLINOIS, WHICH RESULTED IN THE DEATH OF JOSEPH AND HYRUM SMITH. BY G. W. WESTBROOK. ST. LOUIS: PRINTED BY USTICK & DAVIES, 1844.

[i]–[vi, vi blank], [5]–304, [3]–36, [i errata, ii blank]. 18.5 x 10.5 cm. Black cloth.

Ref.: AII (*Missouri*) 408; Howes H805; Woodward 101

The errata leaf is slightly smaller than the text leaves. The Appendix was also issued as a separate title, with wrappers. See Paullin Sale 2162.

2014   HUNT, JOHN W.

AUTOGRAPH LETTER, SIGNED. 1800 April 13, Lexington. Two pages, 26.2 x 21.9 cm. To Philip Nolan. The letter is badly chewed affecting some text.

An interesting request for the payment of a bond of $1,994 which Nolan owed J. W. Hunt and A. Hunt. The determination of the amount due had been settled for Nolan in Philadelphia by General Wilkinson.

2015   HUNT, MEMUCAN

[Caption title] GEN. HUNT'S LETTER TO SENATOR SAM HOUSTON . . .

[1]–11, [12 blank]. 19.7 x 12.9 cm. Sewn into plain gray modern wrappers.

Ref.: Sabin 33882; Winkler 99

Winkler suggests [Austin: Printed by William H. Cushney ? 1849.]

A wide-ranging attack on Sam Houston with reflections on his "ambition, vindictiveness, and selfishness," his "shifts and subterfuges," "his weapons of attack," etc.

2016   HUNT, NANCY A.

BY OX-TEAM TO CALIFORNIA . . .*

[1]–[16]. 24.5 x 16.7 cm. Illustrations in text. Self-wrappers, included in pagination; imprint on verso of back wrapper.

Ref.: Cowan p. 297

Back wrapper: From / Overland Monthly / April, 1916 /. Edited by Rockwell D. Hunt.

2017   HUNT, RICHARD S., & JESSE F. RANDEL

GUIDE TO THE REPUBLIC OF TEXAS: CONSISTING OF A BRIEF OUTLINE OF THE HISTORY OF ITS SETTLEMENT; A GENERAL VIEW OF THE SURFACE OF THE COUNTRY; ITS CLIMATE, SOIL, PRODUCTIONS; RIVERS, COUNTIES, TOWN, AND INTERNAL IMPROVEMENTS; THE COLONIZATION AND LAND LAWS; LISTS OF COURTS AND JUDICIAL OFFICERS; TARIFF AND PORTS OF ENTRY &C. . . . NEW YORK: PUBLISHED BY J. H. COLTON, 1839.*

[i–iv blank], [1]–63, [64], [65 advertisements], [66–8 blank]. 14.5 x 9.3 cm. Folding map: Map [star] of / Texas, / Compiled from Surveys on record in the / General Land Office of the Republic, / to the year 1839, by / Richard S. Hunt and Jesse F. Randel. / [decorative rule] / New York, Published by J. H. Colton / Engraved by Stiles, Sherman & Smith. New York. / [lower left:] Entered according to Act of Congress in the year 1839, by J. H. Colton, in the Clerks Office of the District Court of the Southern District of New York. / *Inset:* Map of the Rio Grande / and the / Country west to the Pacific. / 21.9 x 26.9 cm. No scale given. 80.1 x 61.1 cm. Scale: 20 miles to one inch. Green embossed cloth, with title on front cover: Guide / to / Texas / with a / Map / Published by / J. H. Colton / 1839 /.

Ref.: Bradford 2469; Howes H809; Rader 1980; Raines p. 122; Sabin 33887 see; Streeter 1348

. . . the first general guide to Texas . . . The map is important.—Streeter

2018   HUNTER, GEORGE

REMINISCENCES OF AN OLD TIMER. A RECITAL OF THE ACTUAL EVENTS, INCIDENTS, TRIALS, HARDSHIPS, VICISSITUDES, ADVENTURES, PERILS, AND ESCAPES OF A PIONEER, HUNTER, MINER AND SCOUT OF THE PACIFIC NORTHWEST . . . SAN FRANCISCO: H. S. CROCKER AND COMPANY, 1887.

[i]–xxv, [xxvi blank], 1–454. 19.6 x 13.6 cm. 16 illustrations listed. Red pictorial cloth.

Prov.: Rubber stamp at top of title-page: Donated to the / Springfield Public Library / by / Fred R. Waters /. Pocket removed from inside back cover.

Ref.: Cowan p. 298; Howes H811; Smith 4891

2019   HUNTER, JOHN D.

MANNERS AND CUSTOMS OF SEVERAL INDIAN TRIBES LOCATED WEST OF THE MISSISSIPPI; INCLUDING SOME ACCOUNT OF THE SOIL, CLIMATE, AND VEGETABLE PRODUCTIONS, AND THE INDIAN MATERIA MEDICA: TO WHICH IS PREFIXED THE HISTORY OF

THE AUTHOR'S LIFE DURING A RESIDENCE OF SEVERAL YEARS AMONG THEM . . . PHILADELPHIA: PRINTED AND PUBLISHED FOR THE AUTHOR, BY J. MAXWELL, 1823.

[i]–viii, [9]–402. 21.6 x 13.3 cm. Contemporary sheepskin, rebacked with brown levant morocco, new red and black leather labels, red edges. New endpapers, corners repaired.

Ref.: Ayer 141; Field 743; Howes H813; Rader 1982; Sabin 33920; Smith 4822; Wagner-Camp 24

2020 HUNTER, JOHN M., *Editor*

THE TRAIL DRIVERS OF TEXAS . . .

[1]–498, [499 colophon, 500 blank]. [i–ii], [1]–496, [497 advertisement, 498 blank]. 22.4 x 15.5 cm. Many portraits and illustrations. Two volumes, pictorial cloth, Vol. I in blue and Vol. II in green.

Ref.: Adams 528; Adams (*Ramp. Herd*) 1103; Howes H816; Rader 1988

Published at San Antonio in 1920 and 1923.

In spite of the crudeness of the two volumes, they are perhaps the most important single contribution to the history of cattle driving on the western trails.—Adams

2021 HUNTINGTON, WILLIAM

ADVOCATES FOR DEVILS REFUTED. AND THEIR HOPE OF THE DAMNED DEMOLISHED: OR, AN EVERLASTING TASK FOR WINCHESTER AND ALL HIS CONFEDERATES . . . CHARLESTON: REPUBLISHED FOR C. S. MORTON, OF CHARLESTON, ILLINOIS, BY JACOB I. BROWN, 1845.

[1]–40. 22.3 x 14 cm. Contemporary tan wrappers, partly unopened.

Ref.: Byrd 961

Probably unique. See Byrd's excellent note.

Editions: London, 1794; and many others.

2022 [HUNTLEY, SIR HENRY V.]

CALIFORNIA: ITS GOLD AND ITS INHABITANTS . . . LONDON: THOMAS CAUTLEY NEWBY, 1856.

[i]–iv, [1]–303, [304 blank]. [i–ii], [1]–286. 18.9 x 11.7 cm. Two volumes, half red calf, gilt.

Ref.: Bradford 2479; Cowan p. 199; Howes H825; Jones 1352; Sabin 33981

Howes states there was only a small edition of this first printing.

2023 HUNTON, JOHN

JOHN HUNTON'S DIARY . . . ECHOES FROM 1875 (WITH GLIMPSES AT 1873) [Vol. 2:] 1876–'77 . . .*

[i–ii], 1–[136]. [i–iv], [1]–[292]. 15.1 x 10.3 cm. Illustrations and maps unlisted. Two volumes, brown flocked paper.

Ref.: Adams (*Ramp. Herd*) 1106

Printed at Lingle, Wyoming. Copyrighted, 1956 and 1959.

Limited to 1500 copies, signed by the editor, L. G. (Pat) Flanery. Volume 1 is copy 67 and Volume 2 is copy 884. A third volume (in ICN) was published in 1960.

2024 HUSTON, GEORGE

MEMORIES OF EIGHTY YEARS BY GEORGE HUSTON.*

[i–viii], 1–153, [154 blank]. 18.4 x 13.2 cm. Portrait. Bright blue cloth.

Prov.: Mounted on the front endleaf is a presentation card from Mrs. N. Huston Banks, the author's daughter.

Ref.: Bay p. 375; Howes H842

Distributed by the family of the author. The imprint: Sun Print, / Morganfield, Ky. / 1904. / appears on the verso of the title-leaf.

The work deals with the author's boyhood in Kentucky, 1825–40, his law school days at Harvard, etc.

2025 HUTAWA, EDWARD & JULIUS

[Map] MAP / OF THAT PART OF THE / STATE OF MISSOURI / WHICH LIES ON THE LEFT BANK OF THE MISSOURI RIVER AND / WEST OF THE FORMER WEST BOUNDARY OF THE STATE, / CALLED / PLATTE COUNTRY / [decorative rule] / [11 lines of text] / RESPECTFULLY DEDICATED / [5 lines] / BY THE DRAFTSMEN / EDWARD & JULIUS HUTAWA / [double rule] / PUBLISHED BY / EDWARD HUTAWA / LITHOGRAPHER, / NO. 7, S. THIRD ST. BETWEEN MARKET & WALNUT, / S$_\text{T}$ LOUIS, M$_\text{O}$ / J. ERWIN'S SCRIP ET SC. / [at left:] MAP ENG$^\text{D}$ BY JULIUS HUTAWA. [at centre:] ENTERED ON THE 27$^\text{TH}$ JULY 1842 ACCORDING TO AN ACT OF CONGRESS RESPECTING COPY RIGHTS BY EDWARD HUTAWA IN THE CLERK'S OFFICE OF THE U. S. DIST$^\text{R}$ COURT OF MISSOURI. / Map, 63.1 x 42.9 cm.

Scale: 5 miles to one inch. Folded into blue boards with brown cloth back, 14.7 x 11.3 cm., with printed paper label: Sectional Map / of the / Platte Country / Missouri. /

Ref.: Phillips (*Maps*) 715

2026 HUTAWA, JULIUS

[Map] MAP / OF / MEXICO / & / CALIFORNIA / COMPILED FROM THE LATEST AUTHORITIES / BY JUL$^\text{S}$ HUTAWA / LITH$^\text{R}$ SECOND ST. 45 ST. LOUIS, MO. / 2$^\text{ND}$ EDITION / 1863. / *Inset:* Vicinity / of / Mexico /. 11.7 x 12.2 cm. No scale given. Map, 59.1 x 48 cm. No scale given.

Folded into yellow board covers, 13.7 x 8.9 cm., with title printed on front cover: Hutawa's / Traveling Map / of / Mexico / and / California. /

[within double rule borders with corner ornaments].

Ref.:

The first edition of this map was considerably earlier, probably about 1846. The line: 2.nd Edition / has been lithographed over a partially erased line which read: St. Louis, Mo. / The words: New Mexico / were stamped in later. The northern Oregon border is set at 42°, but a new colored border above 48° has been added. Particularly interesting is the number of routes west traced on the map; most of them are accurate. The locations given in New Mexico are very full.

2027 HUTCHINGS, JAMES M.

[Broadside] HUTCHINGS' CALIFORNIA SCENES.— METHODS OF MINING. [twelve vignettes, each with printed caption] [at right, vertical rule, column of names:] NAMES OF MINING LOCALITIES [64 names]. ENTERED ACCORDING TO ACT OF CONGRESS, IN THE YEAR 1855, BY JAMES M. HUTCHINGS, IN THE CLERK'S OFFICE OF THE U. S. DISTRICT COURT OF CALIFORNIA ADDRESS J F. LARRABEE. SAN FRANCISCO. PRINTED BY HANNA & CO.

Broadside, 27 x 21.2 cm. Text, 26 x 20 cm. Printed on pale blue paper, ruled in blue on verso. Two names cut from list at right.

Ref.: AII (*California*) 425; Greenwood, Appendix A, 75

Four of the vignettes are signed in the cut by C. Nahl and T. C. Boyd. A former owner probably considered the two names excised vulgar.

2028 HUTCHINGS, JAMES M.

[Broadside] THE MINER'S TEN COMMANDMENTS. [244 lines in three columns] [within borders of 11 woodcut scenes] [below woodcuts at foot:] SUN PRINT, SAN FRANCISCO. ENTERED ACCORDING TO ACT OF CONGRESS, IN THE YEAR 1853, BY JAMES M. HUTCHINGS, IN THE CLERK'S OFFICE OF THE U. S. DISTRICT COURT FOR THE NORTHERN DISTRICT OF CALIFORNIA. ORDERS PRE PAID[!], ADDRESSED "BOX H, PLACERVILLE, EL DORADO CO., CAL."

Broadside, 28.6 x 23.4 cm. Text, 27.5 x 22.1 cm. Printed on blue notepaper, ruled in blue on verso.

Ref.: AII (*California*) 248; Greenwood, Appendix A, 44

One of the woodcuts is signed in the cut H. Eastman Del., another is signed Eastman, and two are signed Anthony & Baker.

2029 HUTCHINS, THOMAS

A TOPOGRAPHICAL DESCRIPTION OF VIRGINIA, PENNSYLVANIA, MARYLAND, AND NORTH CAROLINA, COMPREHENDING THE RIVERS OHIO, KENHAWA, SIOTO, CHEROKEE, WABASH, ILLINOIS, MISSISIPPI[!], &C. . . . LONDON: PRINTED FOR THE AUTHOR, AND SOLD BY J. ALMON, M DCC LXXVIII.

[A]², B–I⁴, K². [1–2], [i]–ii, [1]–[68]. 19.6 x 11.6 cm. Two folding maps, a folding table, and a large separate map: Map: A Plan / of the Several Villages in the / Illinois Country, / with Part of the / River Mississippi &c. / by / Thos Hutchins. / 18.3 x 12.6 cm. Scale: 10 miles to one inch. Imprint trimmed from foot of map. Map: A Plan of the / Rapids, / in the River Ohio, / by / Thos Hutchins. / [below neat line:] London. Published according to Act of Parliament Novemb.^r ẙ 1.st 1778 by Thos Hutchins. J. Cheevers sculp.^t / 14.5 x 18.4 cm. Scale: 800 yards to one inch. Table: A / Table of Distances / between / Fort Pitt, / and the Mouth / of the / River Ohio / [below neat line:] London, Published according to Act of Parliament Novemb.^r 1.st 1778 by Thos Hutchins. / 15.4 x 30.3 cm. Map: A / New Map / of the Western Parts of / Virginia, Pennsylvania, / Maryland and North Carolina; / Comprehending the River Ohio, and all the Rivers, which fall into it; / Part of the River Mississippi, the Whole of the / Illinois River, / Lake Erie; Part of the Lakes Huron, / Michigan &c. / And all the Country bordering on these / Lakes and Rivers. / By Thos Hutchins. / Captain in the 60 Regiment of Foot. / London, Published according to Act of Parliament Novemb.^r. / ẙ 1.st 1778 by T. Hutchins. / 89.8 x 109 cm. No scale given. Rebound in green half morocco, gilt top. Enclosed in dark blue buckram case, 45.5 x 28 cm.

Prov.: Ex-library copy. Embossed stamp pressed out of title-leaf, rubber stamped numerals erased from foot of page [i], numerals 750 stamped on third plan, faint pencil numbers on page [i].

Ref.: Bradford 2500; Buck 14; Buley I, pp. 11, 546; Fenton p. 60; Field 744; Howes H846; Sabin 34054; Thomson 625

First State of the text, with the errata list on the last page and with the errors uncorrected.

Valuable source for the western country during the late British period, written by the first— and only—official geographer of the United States, the originator of our range system of land surveys.—Howes

2030 [HUTCHINSON, ELLIOT ST. M.]

TWO YEARS A COW BOY AND LIFE ON THE PRAIRIE, AMONG THE INDIANS, AND BACKWOODS OF AMERICA. BY BUNNY. LONDON: THE LONDON LITERARY SOCIETY, 1887.

[1]–128. 18 x 11.9 cm. Rebound in red cloth.

Ref.: Adams (*Ramp. Herd*) 353

The author was a migrant worker in the Far West spending part of his time as a swineherd, a miner, a laborer, and hunter, and with one spell as a cow puncher. It seems to be one of the earliest books on the experiences of a cowhand. It was, according to the prefatory note, inspired by the visit of Buffalo Bill to England. The author mentions few dates, places or names of companions, yet a careful reading of the work leaves one with the impression that most (if not all) the episodes described were part of the author's experience.

Bound in is a copy of Sir Walter Scott: *Kenilworth* . . . London: J. Dicks, no date. [1]–160. Vignettes in text.

2031 HUTCHINSON, K. M.

A MEMOIR OF ABIJAH HUTCHINSON, A SOLDIER OF THE REVOLUTION . . . ROCHESTER: WILLIAM ALLING, PRINTER, 1843.

[i]–iv, [5]–22. 18.9 x 11.3 cm. Rebound in half olive morocco. Original front wrapper bound in.

Prov.: Otis Library, Norwich, Conn. label on verso of wrapper, embossed stamp of library on title-page and several other pages of volume.

Ref.: Howes H849; Sabin 34066

Contains an account of Abijah Hutchinson's captivity by Indians.

2032 HUTCHINSON, WILLIAM H.

A NOTEBOOK OF THE OLD WEST . . . CHICO, CALIF.; BOB HURST.

[1]–122. 23.3 x 15.7 cm. Blue-green printed wrappers. In a blue cloth case.

Prov.: Signed on the dedication page by the author: W H Hutchinson / January, 1948. /

Ref.: Adams 531

Copyrighted 1947.

2033 HUTCHISON, J. R.

REMINISCENCES, SKETCHES AND ADDRESSES SELECTED FROM MY PAPERS DURING A MINISTRY OF FORTY-FIVE YEARS IN MISSISSIPPI, LOUISIANA AND TEXAS . . . HOUSTON, TEXAS: E. H. CUSHING, 1874.

[i]–vi, [7]–262. (Pages [i–ii] blank.) 18.3 x 11.5 cm. Dark orange cloth, gilt title on backstrip.

Ref.: Howes H856; Raines p. 123

Second issue, enlarged.

Interesting material relating to the Presbyterians in Texas, etc.

2034 HYATT, H. S.

MANUFACTURING, AGRICULTURAL AND INDUSTRIAL RESOURCES OF IOWA WITH RELIABLE INFORMATION TO CAPITALISTS SEEKING THE BEST FIELDS FOR INVESTMENTS . . . DES MOINES, IOWA: REPUBLICAN STEAM PRINTING HOUSE, 1872.

[1]–155, [156–60 advertisements]. 21.5 x 14.5 cm. Small maps on text pages, folding map at front: Map of / Iowa / Engraved expressly / for /

Iowa Progress. / [lower right corner:] Baker Co /. 15.8 x 22.3 cm. No scale given. Green printed wrappers, with title on front wrapper, advertisements on verso of front and recto and verso of back wrapper.

Ref.: Bradford 2521

2035 HYATT, THADDEUS

THE PRAYER OF THADDEUS HYATT TO JAMES BUCHANAN, PRESIDENT OF THE UNITED STATES, IN BEHALF OF KANSAS, ASKING FOR A POSTPONEMENT OF ALL THE LAND SALES IN THAT TERRITORY, AND FOR OTHER RELIEF . . . WASHINGTON: HENRY POLKINHORN, PRINTER, 1860.

[1–2], [unpaginated, inserted leaf], [3]–68. 21.6 x 14.2 cm. Removed from original binding, sewn, unbound.

Ref.: Rader 1995; Sabin 34114

The inserted leaf after the title-leaf, is slightly shorter, measuring 21.1 cm.

2036 HYDE, S. C.

HISTORICAL SKETCH OF LYON COUNTY, IOWA, AND A DESCRIPTION OF THE COUNTRY AND ITS RESOURCES . . . SIOUX CITY, IOWA: PERKINS BROS., 1873.

[1]–40. 18.6 x 12.7 cm. Map: Map of / Lyon County, / Iowa. / Drawn by S. C. Hyde. / from Government Surveys 1873. / 14.8 x 28.9 cm. No scale given. Blue printed wrappers with title on front wrapper. In a blue cloth folder.

Ref.: Cook p. 142; Howes H863; Mott (*Iowa*) p. 48

Editions: Lemars, Iowa, 1872.

2037 HYER, JOSEPH K., & WILLIAM S. STARRING

[Caption title] DICTIONARY OF THE SIOUX LANGUAGE . . .

[1–31] [32 blank]. 19.8 x 13.6 cm. White printed wrappers with title on front cover: Lahcotah. / [decorative rule] /. Wide brass staples. Verso of front wrapper: Rules for Pronunciation. / [7 lines].

Ref.: AII (*Wyoming*) 1; Butler (*Dakota*) 85; McMurtrie (*Wyoming*) pp. 10, 44, 46

McMurtrie suggests this may have been printed at Camp Douglas, Utah.

Note at foot of page [31]: Compiled with the aid of Charles Guerreu / Indian Interpreter, by Lieuts. J. K. Hyer and / W. S. Starring, U. S. A. and is as complete as / a perfect knowledge of the Lahcotah Lan-/guage can make it. / Fort Laramie, Dakota. / December, 1866. /

The Ayer copy contains a note by J. C. Pilling stating that his copy came from General Starring who thought only fifty copies were printed.

2038 HYNES, W. F.

SOLDIERS OF THE FRONTIER . . .

[1]–208. 22.9 x 15 cm. Five illustrations unlisted. Maroon cloth, title stamped in gilt on front cover and backstrip. Lacks front endleaf.

Ref.:

Copyrighted 1943. Place of publication not indicated.

From May, 1866, to May, 1869, Hynes served at Fort Caspar, Dakotah Territory and at Fort Laramie.—EDG

I

2039 ICARIAN COMMUNITY, *Nauvoo, Illinois*

CHARTER AND BY-LAWS OF THE ICARIAN COMMUNITY. NAUVOO, ILL.: ICARIAN PRINTING ESTABLISHMENT, 1857.

[1]⁸, [2]⁴, 3⁴⁺¹. [1]–33, [34 blank]. 19.8 x 13.3 cm. White printed wrappers with title on front wrapper.

Prov.: Stamp of U. S. Geological Survey Library and cancellation stamp on title-page. C. G. Littell bookplate.

Ref.: Byrd 2671

The Icarian Community, founded by Etienne Cabet and his followers was one of the most interesting of the communistic establishments in the United States during the nineteenth century.

2040 ICARIAN COMMUNITY, *Nauvoo, Illinois*

[Collection of newspaper clippings mounted in a report of the Iowa Library Commission for 1915.]

[1]–36. 21.6 x 14.4 cm. Red cloth, red edges.

Prov.: Oval rubber stamp of Edward F. Carter, Keokuk, Iowa, on front endleaf.

Ref.:

The text, through page 31 is covered, or partly covered, by a series of newspaper clippings mounted, as follows:

Communism / [short rule] / History of the Experiment / at Nauvoo of the Icar-/ian Settlement. / . . . /. Eight articles mounted on 20 pages. In pencil at head of first article: Rustler / Mch. 6, 1917 /.

About the Icarians [within rule box] /. Article mounted on two pages, signed at end, C. P. Dadant. / Hamilton, Ill., Dec. 29, 1916. /

Short untitled article, unsigned, mounted on one page.

[Vignette] Voyage into Icaria /. Article

mounted on four pages, unsigned. At head of first page: [ ]'s Golden (50th) Anniversary Edition, November 14, 1923 /.

The Icarian / Community / at Nauvoo / [short rule] / By C. P. Dadant /. Article mounted on four pages. Note in pencil at head of first column: Hamilton / Press / Oct. 2, 1924 /.

Laid in is a news article from the *Chicago Daily News*, July 24, 1942, headed: Old Illinois Houses / By John Drury /. With illustration.

Laid in are the following manuscripts:

Manuscript Document. Samuel M Griffith / vs / The Icarian Community /. 1835, April 11, Lee County, Iowa. 11 pages, 30.6 x 20 cm. The replication of the plaintiff, prepared and signed by J. M. Beck for the firm Miller & Beck.

Mr. Griffith had instituted a charge of trespass against the Icarian Community. Among the present papers is a manuscript copy of the Charter of the Icarian Community. Docket by S. A. James.

Manuscript Document. Samuel Griffith / vs / The Icarian Community /. 1835 November 5, Lee County, Iowa. One page, 30.6 x 20 cm.

Notice regarding taking of depositions in Montrose. Acceptance of notice signed by Jno. S. Hamilton.

Autograph Letter, signed by J. F. Powell. 1861 March 26, Quincy Adams Co., Iowa. One page, 30.3 x 18.9 cm. To J. M. Beck. Regarding ownership of property by The Icarian Community under the rights of a Trust Deed.

Laid in is *Constitution of The Icarian Community . . .* Nauvoo, 1854. See item 2041.

2041 ICARIAN COMMUNITY, *Nauvoo, Illinois*

CONSTITUTION OF THE ICARIAN COMMUNITY, ADOPTED UNANIMOUSLY ON THE 21 OF FEBRUARY 1850; REVISED, DISCUSSED AND ADOPTED ANEW UNANIMOUSLY ON THE 4 OF MAY 1851. NAUVOO, ILL.: ICARIAN PRINTING ESTABLISHMENT, 1854.

[1]–23, [24 blank]. 20.1 x 23.9 cm. Stabbed, uncut. Last leaf torn, soiled.

Ref.: Byrd 2130

This pamphlet is laid in a scrapbook containing newspaper clippings about the Community. The scrapbook is described in this catalogue as item 2040.

2042 IDAHO. Boise County. District Court

[PRINTED AND MANUSCRIPT LEGAL FORM summoning John Howe to answer the complaint of M. Brown.] 1864 September 13, Idaho City. 2 pages, 31.5 x 20 cm.

The summons, printed by the Boise News Print, was filled in by John C. Henley, Clerk of the District Court, and docketed by him on the verso. On the verso there is also an autograph manuscript affidavit by Charles Wilson on behalf of S. Pinkham, Sheriff, certifying delivery of the summons.

It is interesting to note the cost of serving the summons was $14.00. The account is detailed on the verso.

2043 IDAHO. Commissioner of Immigration, Labor and Statistics (T. C. Egleston)

[Wrapper title] BOISE COUNTY, IDAHO. RESOURCES AGRICULTURAL AND MINERAL . . . BOISE, IDAHO, 1903.
[1]–8. 22.6 x 10.2 cm. Gray printed wrappers.
Ref.:
In the text, there are four corrections in ink.

2044 IDAHO. Constitution

[Wrapper title] CONSTITUTION OF THE STATE OF IDAHO. ADOPTED IN CONVENTION AT BOISE CITY, AUGUST 6, 1889. BOISE CITY, IDAHO: THE STATESMAN PRINTING CO., 1889.
[1]–42. 23.4 x 15.2 cm. Printed green wrappers, with title on front wrapper.
Ref.: AII (*Idaho*) 158

2045 IDAHO. Constitution

CONSTITUTION OF THE STATE OF IDAHO AND THE ACT PROVIDING FOR THE ADMISSION OF THE STATE . . . BOISE CITY, IDAHO: THE STATESMAN PRINTING CO., 1891.
[1]–59, [60–64 blank]. 21.2 x 14.2 cm. Tan printed wrappers, with title on front wrapper.
Ref.:

2046 IDAHO (TERRITORY). Governor (George L. Shoup)

[Broadside] PROCLAMATION. WHEREAS, ON THE SECOND DAY OF APRIL, HON. E. A. STEVENSON, GOVERNOR OF IDAHO, ISSUED A PROCLAMATION TO THE PEOPLE OF THE TERRITORY, RECOMMENDING THEM TO TAKE THE NECESSARY STEPS, PRELIMINARY TO ASKING FOR ADMISSION INTO THE UNION AS A STATE . . . [50 lines] IN TESTIMONY WHEREOF, I HAVE HEREUNTO SET MY HAND . . . DONE AT THE CITY OF BOISE, . . . THIS 2ND DAY OF OCTOBER, IN THE YEAR OF OUR LORD ONE THOUSAND, EIGHT HUNDRED AND EIGHTY-NINE, . . . [2 lines] GEORGE L. SHOUP. BY THE GOVERNOR: E. J. CURTIS, SECRETARY OF IDAHO.
Broadside, 31.5 x 21.5 cm. Text, 26.2 x 15.1 cm.
Ref.:

2047 IDAHO (TERRITORY). Prison Commissioner (Ephraim Smith)

REPORT OF THE TERRITORIAL PRISON COMMISSIONER . . .

[1]–8. 23.2 x 14.7 cm. Stabbed, unbound.
Ref.: AII (*Idaho*) 24
Bound with: Second Annual Report of the Territorial Treasurer . . . Boise City, 1865.
Printed by Jas. S. Reynolds & Co. at Boise City in 1865. See item 2048.

2048 IDAHO (TERRITORY). Treasurer (Ephraim Smith)

SECOND ANNUAL REPORT OF THE TERRITORIAL TREASURER OF IDAHO TERRITORY . . . BOISE CITY: JAS. S. REYNOLDS & CO., 1865.
[1]–4. 23.2 x 14.7 cm. Stabbed, unbound.
Ref.: AII (*Idaho*) 26
Bound with: [thick and thin rules] / Report / of the / Territorial / Prison Commissioner. / [rule] / Ephraim Smith, Commissioner. / [thin and thick rules] /, dated at Boise City, December 5th, 1865. 8 pages.
The three copies listed by AII (*Idaho*) have a wrapper title as follows: Messages and Documents / -of- / Third Session / -of- / the Idaho Legislature. / 1865–'66. / Boise City: / Jas. S. Reynolds & Co., Territorial Printers. / [rule] / 1865.
There is no evidence of wrappers issued with this copy.

2049 IDAHO CITY AND GRAHAM STAGE LINE

[Broadside] IDAHO CITY AND GRAHAM STAGE LINE. J. C. GARDDET, PRO. LEAVES IDAHO CITY AT 6 O'CLOCK ON MONDAY AND FRIDAY MORNINGS. LEAVES GRAHAM THURSDAY AND SATURDAY MORNINGS AT 6 O'CLOCK. STAGES CARRY PASSENGERS AND LIGHT FREIGHT. FARE, ONE WAY, $7.00. STAGE OFFICE AT POSTOFFICE, IDAHO CITY.
Broadside, 31.8 x 23.2 cm. Text, 28 x 21 cm.
Ref.:
Printed after 1864, since until then Idaho City had been called Bannock.

In this copy, the word Thursday has been crossed out and the word Tuesday supplied in manuscript. Later, a printed slip, 1.4 x 5.3 cm., with the word Tuesday printed on it was pasted over the original printing and the manuscript change. Graham was on the north fork of the Boise River.

2050 IDAHO MINING DISTRICT, *Colorado*

[Broadside] DENVER MOUNTAINEER PRINT. [in manuscript: Idaho] MINING DISTRICT. BE IT KNOWN, THAT [in manuscript: J. W. Hamilton] IS THE OWNER OF [in manuscript: Quartz] MINING CLAIM [two lines] GIVEN UNDER MY HAND AT [in manuscript: Idaho] THE [in manuscript: 15th] DAY OF [in manuscript: April] A. D. 1861. [in manuscript: W Spruance] RECORDER. DEPUTY.

Broadside, 7.7 x 20.6 cm. Text, 6.6 x 18.8 cm. Blue paper.
Ref.:
Endorsed by J. W. Hamilton on verso. Claim No. 5 westerly, Virago Lode.

2051 IDAHO MINING DISTRICT, *Colorado*

[Broadside] SOUTH CLEAR CREEK, DENVER MOUN-TAINEER PRINT. IDAHO MINING DISTRICT, THIS IS TO CERTIFY, THAT [in manuscript: J. W. Hamilton] IS ENTITLED BY PRE-EMPTION . . . [one line] . . . [in manuscript: Decr 15 1861] [in manuscript: W Spruance] RECORDER. [in manuscript: W. E. Sisty] President.
Broadside, 8.3 x 19.3 cm. Text, 6.6 x 16.7 cm.
Ref.:
Not endorsed by Hamilton on verso. Claim No. 6 N East, December Lode.

2052 IDAHO MINING DISTRICT, *Colorado*

ANOTHER COPY. Endorsed by Hamilton. Claim No. 3 N. E. Boomarang Lode. Dated November 11, 1861.

2053 IDAHO MINING DISTRICT, *Colorado*

ANOTHER COPY. Not signed by Sisty. Claim No. 4 Westerly Kangaroo Lode. November 19, 1861.

2054 IDAHO PIONEERS, HISTORICAL SOCIETY OF

CONSTITUTION, BY-LAWS AND PROSPECTUS OF THE HISTORICAL SOCIETY OF IDAHO PIONEERS . . . BOISE CITY, IDAHO: MILTON KELLY, 1881.
[1]–13, [14–16 blank]. 14.8 x 10.7 cm. Yellow printed wrappers, with title on front wrapper, within decorative borders.
Ref.: AII (*Idaho*) 118
Two words rubber stamped (inverted) in lower quarter of front wrapper: Defendant. Where /.

2055 IDAHO PRINTING

A COLLECTION OF 73 CARDS PRINTED IN IDAHO TERRITORY, 1867–1887.
73 cards, about 6 x 9 cm., various colors.
The collection comprises advertisements, labels, tickets, etc., probably all printed at Idaho City by one printing house. The pieces are described below, giving category, sponsor, place and date of event, and nature of event.
Advertisement: Adolph Ballot. Idaho City, n.d. Watchmaker.
Advertisement: M. M. Chipman. Idaho City, n.d. Druggist.
Advertisement: Fashion Restaurant. Centreville, n.d. Clothier.
Advertisement: C. S. Kingsley. Idaho City, n.d. Hardware.

Advertisement: D. G. Strong. Idaho City, n.d. Preaching schedule.
Label: J. B. & C. H. Atkins. Idaho City, n.d. Castor Oil.
Label: T. J. Sutton. Atlanta, I. T., n.d. Unused druggist's label.
Membership Card: Fenian Brotherhood, John Mitchel Circle. Granite Creek, 1868. Unused.
Pass: B. & F. Toll Road. N.p., 186—. 3 passes on one card, unused.
Pass: Same. Another variety, unused.
Ticket: Anonymous. N.p., 1876. "T T" Ball.
Ticket: Anonymous. N.p., n.d. Raffle ticket for house, lot, etc.
Ticket: Anonymous. Warm Springs, March 17, 1880. Social Dance.
Ticket: A. F. & A. M., Idaho Lodge No. 35. N.p., September 26, 1867. Bartholomew's Great Western Circus.
Ticket: Apollo Minstrels. N. p., n.d. Admission.
Ticket: Beard Farm. N.p., n.d. Raffle ticket.
Ticket: Bed Rock Shaft Company. Idaho City, September 3, 1869. Grand Ball.
Ticket: J. G. Bohen. [Idaho City] April 3, 1868. Complimentary Ball.
Ticket: Mrs. Bright. Idaho City, July 4, 1877. Grand Ball.
Ticket: Mrs. Jonas W. Brown. N.p., September 27, 1867. Raffle ticket for ten oil paintings by Mrs. Brown.
Ticket: Chow Lee. N.p., n.d. Two checks on one ticket, unspecified.
Ticket: John Cody. N.p., October 25, 1867. Grand Opening Ball.
Ticket: Mr. & Mrs. Wm. Cole. N.p., August 8, 1868. Benefit raffle.
Ticket: Frank Cooper. Warm Springs, July 4, 1873. Fourth of July Celebration Ball.
Ticket: Frank Cooper. Warm Springs, February 6, 1879. Ball.
Ticket: Frank Cooper. Hot Springs, October 27, 1880. Grand Social Ball.
Ticket: O. J. Daly. Quartzburg, February 17, 1887. Grand Ball.
Ticket: Eagle Bakery. N.p., n.d. Three tickets on one card, each for a loaf of bread.
Ticket: Mrs. Wm. Fagan. Miner's Brewery, September 19, n.y. Raffle for real estate and personal property.
Ticket: Fenian Brotherhood, Idaho Circle. Idaho City, February 22, 1869. Washington's Birthday Ball.
Ticket: Freemasons. Centreville, June 24, 1870. Masonic Ball.
Ticket: Mrs. French. Idaho City, March 16, 1877. St. Patrick's Ball.
Ticket: Michael Garraty. Pioneer City, October 30, 1874. Hallow-Een Ball.

Ticket: Idaho City Public School. Idaho City, n.d. Literary & Musical Entertainment.

Ticket: Same, but a different setting.

Ticket: Idaho City Theatricals. Idaho City, n.d. Theatre performance.

Ticket: Idaho Juvenile Amateur Histrionic Troupe. Idaho City, August 4, 1868. Theatrical Performance.

Ticket: Independent Champions of the Red Cross. Idaho City, August 21, n.y. Calico Ball.

Ticket: Independent Order of Good Templars. Idaho City, November 14, 1867. Grand Ball.

Ticket: Same. Idaho City, February 21, 1868. Washington Anniversary Ball.

Ticket: Same. Granite Creek, August 21, 1868. Grand Ball.

Ticket: Same. Idaho City, September 11, 1868. Grand Ball.

Ticket: Same. Centreville, December 25, 1868. Christmas Ball.

Ticket: Same, Boise Lodge No. 2. Idaho City, March 9, 1871. Ball.

Ticket: Independent Order of Odd Fellows. Idaho City, April 26, 1869. Grand Anniversary Ball.

Ticket: Same, Lodge No. 1. [Idaho City] April 26, 1870. Grand Anniversary Ball.

Ticket: Same, Covenant Lodge No. 6. Placerville, March 8, 1871. Grand Ball.

Ticket: Same. N.p., January 1, 1877. Odd Fellows' Ball.

Ticket: Same, Covenant Lodge No. 1. Placerville, October 2, 1877. Dedication Ball.

Ticket: Mr. John Kelley and Wife. Idaho City, February 10, 1880. Testimonial.

Ticket: Ladies of Idaho City. Idaho City, February 22, 1871. Washington Birth Day Ball.

Ticket: Lisle Lester (Mrs. L. P. Higbee). N.p., n.d. Dramatic Readings.

Ticket: Mrs. Friedrich Linstadt. [Idaho City] March 2, n.y. Charity Ball.

Ticket: Mat. Luney. Idaho City, January 8, 1868. Grand Anniversary Ball (The Battle of New Orleans).

Ticket: Same. Idaho City, January 15, 1868. Grand Ball.

Ticket: McGregor's Hall. [Idaho City] November 5, 1868. Social Ball.

Ticket: Martin & Johnson's Fire-Proof Cellar. Idaho City, August 25, 1867. Raffle.

Ticket: "Meffert's Day!" Centreville, January 21, 1876. Grand Ball.

Ticket: J. C. Mills. Garden Valley, n.d. Grand Ball.

Ticket: Frank Money. N.p., n.d. Round trip ticket to Warm Springs.

Ticket: Oaon Chaon & C. N.p., n.d. Scrip, four on one ticket, ten cents each.

Ticket: Poujade & Barthes. [Idaho City] February 3, 1869. Grand Ball.

Ticket: Mrs. A. D. Saunders. Idaho City, July 1, 1871. Raffle.

Ticket: Annie Smith. [Idaho City] May 4, 1868. Fancy Ball.

Ticket: Southern Relief Fund. N.p., May 15, 1867. Grand Ball.

Ticket: Star Ranch. N.p., n.d. Ball.

Ticket: Mrs. Steckels. Placerville, December 21, 1876. Grand Ball.

Ticket: Thomas Thebo. Granite City, August 7, 1868. Grand Ball.

Ticket: Warm Springs Pavilion. Warm Springs, August 7, 1867. Grand Opening Ball.

Ticket: Same. August 29, 1867. Grand Ball.

Ticket: Weekly Soirees, Patrons of the. [Idaho City], February 26, 1869. Complimentary Ball for Benefit of John F. Welton.

Ticket: Welton & Doh. N.p., n.d. Admission to Dancing Academy.

Ticket: Yan Wah. N.p., n.d. Scrip, 4 on one card, each ten cents.

2056 [IDAHO] STOCK BOARD, DISTRICT NO. 6

BY-LAWS OF STOCK BOARD, DISTRICT NO. 6. ADOPTED FOR THE BETTER OBSERVANCE OF THE RIGHTS OF STOCKOWNERS AT THE ANNUAL ROUND-UP. IDAHO STATESMAN PRINT, 1880.

[1]–[7], [8 blank]. 9.7 x 6.2 cm. White printed wrappers with title on front wrapper.

Prov.: Inscribed on front cover: Compliments of / Sam D. Riggs /.

Ref.: AII (*Idaho*) 115

The *Idaho Statesman* was printed at Boise.

AII (*Idaho*) mentions a copy in the possession of S. D. Riggs; this may be the copy. The present copy differs somewhat from the AII (*Idaho*) description. There are only seven pages of text— not eight—and the size of the original is as given above, not 14.5 x 10 cm.

There is a blank leaf before the title-leaf and and one after the final leaf of text.

2057 IDAHO STOCK GROWERS' ASSOCIATION, CENTRAL

MARKS AND BRANDS OF THE CENTRAL IDAHO STOCK GROWERS' ASSOCIATION . . . [BOISE CITY:] STATESMAN PRINT, 1885.

[1]–28, [29–30 blank]. 13.8 x 9.7 cm. Gray printed wrappers with title on front wrapper.

Ref.: Howes I3

Apparently the first Idaho brand book.

2058 IDAHO TRI-WEEKLY STATESMAN

[Newspaper] IDAHO TRI-WEEKLY STATESMAN. VOL. III. BOISE CITY, I. T., SATURDAY, JANUARY 19, 1867. NO. 78 . . .

[1–4]. 40.7 x 30.2 cm. Unbound.

Ref.:

The present issue contains a full column signed Don Loui of Owyhee Correspondence, dated from Silver City, January 15, 1867. There is also a column signed Matthew Maypole dated from Portland, January 7, 1867.

2059 IDE, SIMEON

A BIOGRAPHICAL SKETCH OF THE LIFE OF WILLIAM B. IDE: WITH A MINUTE AND INTERESTING ACCOUNT OF ONE OF THE LARGEST EMIGRATING COMPANIES, (3000 MILES OVER LAND), FROM THE EAST TO THE PACIFIC COAST. AND WHAT IS CLAIMED AS THE MOST AUTHENTIC AND RELIABLE ACCOUNT OF "THE VIRTUAL CONQUEST OF CALIFORNIA, IN JUNE, 1846, BY THE BEAR FLAG PARTY," AS GIVEN BY ITS LEADER, THE LATE HON. WILLIAM BROWN IDE. PUBLISHED FOR THE SUBSCRIBERS.

[i–ii], [1]–[240]. 16.6 x 11 cm. Gray cloth, title in gilt on front cover, between bands and ornaments in black: The Conquest of / California / by the / Bear Flag Party / Organized and Led by / William B. Ide. / In a brown half morocco case.

Prov.: Inscribed in pencil on a preliminary blank leaf: To Edwin Edgerton, Esq. / To read— and then / Send his son in Calif'a / From his old Friend / Simeon Ide. / Now of Claremont, N H. /

Ref.: Blumann & Thomas 4583; Cowan p. 301; Howes I4; Jones 1606; Zamorano Eighty 45

Published at Claremont, New Hampshire, in 1880.

William Ide was leader of the Bear Flag movement at Sonoma, and has often been referred to as the "President" of California. He was a man of high ideals and integrity. This little book is source material, and the only volume published thus far that deals exclusively with this incident of California history. Ide died in California in 1852. The book was set in type by hand by Simeon Ide, William's brother, when he was 86 years old. The edition was small and copies are now extremely rare.—Zamorano Eighty

2060 IGLEHART, N. P. & Co., Chicago

[Map] N. P. IGLEHART & Cᵒˢ. / MAP / OF / THE CITY / OF / CHICAGO / COOK Cᵒ. ILLINOIS. / PUBLISHED BY / H. ACHESON / LITH BY H ACHENSON [!], 130 LAKE ST / (COR LAKE & CLARK, CHICAGO) / INDEX / [118 lines] / [upper left:] N. P. IGLEHART & Cᵒˢ / REAL ESTATE DEALERS / & / STOCK BROKERS / CHICAGO / [lower centre:] ENTERED ACCORDING TO ACT OF CONGRESS IN THE YEAR 1854, BY H ACHESON /

Map, 51 x 41.2 cm. No scale given. Unbound. Mounted.

Ref.: Byrd 2038

Removed from J. A. Wills' copy of a collection of pamphlets relating to the Bates vs. Illinois Central case.

Same as the Rees & Kerfoot map, except that the Iglehart name has been added to the list under Public Buildings and the location marked on the map. Also appears with other imprints.

2061 IKIN, ARTHUR

TEXAS: ITS HISTORY, TOPOGRAPHY, AGRICULTURE, COMMERCE, AND GENERAL STATISTICS. TO WHICH IS ADDED, A COPY OF THE TREATY OF COMMERCE ENTERED INTO BY THE REPUBLIC OF TEXAS AND GREAT BRITAIN . . . LONDON: SHERWOOD, GILBERT, AND PIPER, 1841.*

[i]–[viii], [1]–100. 14.1 x 9 cm. Folding map: Map of / Texas / [lower left:] Drawn by A. Ikin. / [lower centre:] Sherwood & Cᵒ Paternoster Row / J. & C. Walker Litho. / 20.5 x 23.4 cm. No scale given. Plum cloth, with title in gilt on front cover: Texas /.

Ref.: Bradford 2530; Clark III 184; Clements Library (*Texas*) 23; Howes I6; Rader 2000; Raines p. 123; Sabin 34194; Streeter 1384

The author of this little guide book to Texas was "Texian Consul" in Great Britain. He explains in a prefatory note that the people of Texas prefer to describe themselves as Texians instead of Texans.

2062 ILES, ELIJAH

SKETCHES OF EARLY LIFE AND TIMES IN KENTUCKY, MISSOURI AND ILLINOIS . . . SPRINGFIELD, ILL.: SPRINGFIELD PRINTING CO., 1883.

[1]–64. 21.3 x 14.5 cm. Photographic portrait. Brown cloth, blind embossed borders on sides, gilt title on front cover.

Ref.: Howes I7

The portrait, which is a photograph, doesn't ordinarily appear in the book.—EDG

2063 ILLINOIS. CONSTITUTIONAL CONVENTION, 1847

ILLINOIS CONSTITUTIONAL CONVENTION. CONSTITUTION OF THE STATE OF ILLINOIS, ADOPTED . . . JUNE 7, 1847 . . . SPRINGFIELD: LANPHIER & WALKER, 1847.

[1]–39, [40 blank]. 25 x 17.2 cm. Stabbed, unbound, uncut, mostly unopened.

Prov.: Inscribed on title-page: Hon. Caleb Cushing, / Newbury Port / from C Choate / La Harpe Ill /.

Ref.: Byrd 1195

2064 ILLINOIS. COOK COUNTY. Summons
[Broadside] STATE OF ILLINOIS, [in manuscript: Cook] COUNTY. SS. [SUMMON.] B. M'CARY—PRINTER, BEARDSTOWN, ILLINOIS. THE PEOPLE OF THE STATE OF ILLINOIS. TO ANY CONSTABLE OF SAID COUNTY—GREETING: [eight lines].

Broadside, 11 x 19.5 cm. Text, 9.6 x 16.3 cm.

Ref.:

The summons is filled in in manuscript. It was issued by John Blackstone on June 7, 1831 (?), on the complaint of Cornelius C. Van Horn against Jediah Woolley and Henry Watkins. The document is docketed on the verso by Abraham Francis (and also in another hand) with a record of costs of serving the summons.

2065 ILLINOIS. GOVERNOR (Ninian Edwards)

ILLINOIS INTELLIGENCER—EXTRA. AN ADDRESS, DELIVERED BY NINIAN EDWARDS, GOVERNOR OF THE STATE OF ILLINOIS, TO BOTH HOUSES OF THE LEGISLATURE. DECEMBER 7, 1830. PRINTED BY ORDER OF THE LEGISLATURE. VANDALIA: PRINTED BY ROBERT BLACKWELL, 1830.

[1]–37, [38–40 blank]. 22.2 x 14.3 cm. Removed from bound volume, unbound.

Ref.:

Pages 23 and 25 carry the same text. The reading sequence is pages 22, 24, 25. But there is no text missing.

2066 ILLINOIS. GOVERNOR (Ninian Edwards)

ILLINOIS-INTELLIGENCER—EXTRA. VANDALIA, JANUARY 3, 1829. MESSAGE, FROM THE GOVERNOR OF ILLINOIS, TO THE GENERAL ASSEMBLY, AT THE DECEMBER SESSION, 1828. VANDALIA: PRINTED BY ROBERT BLACKWELL, 1828[!].

[1]–25, [26 blank]. 22.3 x 14.3 cm. Removed from bound volume, unbound.

Ref.: Byrd 93

Signed and dated on page 25: Ninian Edwards. / December 2d, 1828. / The *Message* appeared in *Illinois Intelligencer*, December 6, 1828. AII (*Missouri*) describes an edition printed at St. Louis; Charless & Paschall, 1829, and locates one copy (ICHi). See number 2067.

2067 ILLINOIS. GOVERNOR (Ninian Edwards)

MESSAGE FROM GOVERNOR EDWARDS, TO THE LEGISLATURE OF THE STATE OF ILLINOIS, AT THE COMMENCEMENT OF THE SESSION IN DECEMBER, 1828. ST. LOUIS: CHARLESS & PASCHALL, 1829.

A–B⁶, C². [1]–28. 19.7 x 12.1 cm. Stabbed, uncut, partly unopened.

Prov.: Several manuscript corrections in an unidentified hand in the text.

Ref.: AII (*Missouri*) 104; Byrd 93 see

There was an edition printed at Vandalia dated 1828.

2068 ILLINOIS. GOVERNOR'S TROOPS. (Volunteers)

[Broadside] INSULT TO THE GOVERNOR! IN PUBLISHING THE FOLLOWING PROCEEDINGS OF THE OFFICERS AND MEN BELONGING TO THE DETACHMENT OF VOLUNTEERS NOW AT NAUVOO, IT IS DUE TO THE RESPECTABLE PORTION OF THE ANTI-MORMON PARTY TO SAY, THAT IT IS BELIEVED, THEY HAD NOTHING TO DO IN THE MATTER. . . . [5 lines] [167 lines in three columns] ALL THE PRINTERS IN THE STATE ARE RESPECTFULLY INVITED TO PUBLISH THESE PROCEEDINGS, AS A MERE ACT OF JUSTICE, TO A MAN WHO HAS BEEN MUCH AND UNDESERVEDLY PERSECUTED, MERELY FOR THE CONSCIENTIOUS DISCHARGE OF HIS DUTY.

Broadside, 35.7 x 28.1 cm. Text, 27.3 x 23.4 cm. Trimmed at top edge. Mounted on cloth.

Ref.: Byrd 1079

Neither place nor date is indicated. Probably Nauvoo, 1846.

The meeting was held on November 7, 1846. Resolutions were adopted in defense of Governor Ford and strong language was thrown at the Mormons.

2069 ILLINOIS. Laws, Statutes, etc.

[Broadside] AN ACT, FOR THE CONSTRUCTION OF THE ILLINOIS AND MICHIGAN CANAL. [5 columns, 123 lines each except for 122 in Column 1] [end of Column 5:] DONE AT VANDALIA, THE 15TH DAY OF JANUARY, A.D. 1836. A. P. FIELD, SECRETARY OF STATE. [centered below text:] T. O. DAVIS, PRINTER, CHICAGO.

Broadside, 53.5 x 43.4 cm. Text 47.1 x 29.6 cm. Laid in blue cloth folder, brown morocco back.

Ref.: Byrd 274; McMurtrie (*Chicago*) 10

No other copy known.

2070 ILLINOIS. Laws, Statutes, etc.

AN ACT TO INCORPORATE THE CITY OF CHICAGO. CHICAGO: PRINTED AT THE OFFICE OF THE DEMOCRAT, 1837.

[1]–23, [24 blank]. 24 x 16.4 cm. Pinned, uncut, unopened in part. In red cloth case.

Ref.: Byrd 312; Howes C361; McMurtrie (*Chicago*) 8

On December 9th a Committee of five met

the city's Board of Trustees and presented their draft of a City Charter. After some discussion and amendment, it was approved for presentation to the Citizens, and 500 copies were ordered to be printed. It was adopted at a public meeting on January 23, 1837, and was forwarded to Springfield. The Charter was passed by the Legislature, and approved March 4th, 1837, but it had been printed following the meeting on Dec. 9 (1836) and prior to approval by the Legislature on March 4th. Both the Streeter and Chicago Historical Society copies bear notice of the March 4th approval, hence were printed subsequent to that approval.

2071 ILLINOIS. Laws, Statutes, etc.

[Caption title] AN ACT TO INCORPORATE THE TOWN OF LITTLE FORT, LAKE COUNTY, ILLINOIS . . .

[1]–12. 19 x 11.4 cm. Plain gray wrappers. In a red cloth case.

Ref.: Byrd 1473; McMurtrie (*Chicago*) 193

Published in 1849. Imprint at the foot of page [1]: [broken rule] / Chicago Democrat Print. / Little Fort is now Waukegan.

2072 ILLINOIS. SUPREME COURT

REPORTS OF CASES ARGUED AND DETERMINED IN THE SUPREME COURT OF THE STATE OF ILLINOIS. BY J. YOUNG SCAMMON, COUNSELLOR AT LAW . . . CHICAGO: STEPHEN F. GALE, 1840 [–1844]. [imprints vary, see below].

[i]–xxiv, [1]–624. [i]–xviii, [1]–663, [664 blank]. [i]–xv [xvi blank], [1]–682. [i]–xviii, [xix–xx blank], [1]–649. [650–52 blank]. 21.7 x 13.8 cm. Four volumes, contemporary calf. Volume 2 rebound, other volumes rebacked.

Ref.: Byrd 530, 790, 864; McMurtrie (*Chicago*) 32, 60, 73; Sabin 77443

The slip, 5 x 13.8 cm., is present in the first volume, before the title-page, explaining the loss of all but twenty copies in a bindery fire. The second volume was printed in Boston. The third and fourth volumes carry the additional imprint of Augustus H. Burley of Galena.

2073 ILLINOIS. SUPREME COURT

REPORTS OF CASES ARGUED AND DETERMINED IN THE SUPREME COURT OF THE STATE OF ILLINOIS. BY J. YOUNG SCAMMON, COUNSELLOR AT LAW. VOLUME I. CHICAGO: STEPHEN F. GALE, 106, LAKE STREET. 1840.

[i]–xxiv, [1]–624, 68 LEAVES (see below). 21.9 x 14.2 cm. Original gray-green boards, calf backstrip, red leather label.

Ref.: As above

The only copy known with Index. The sixty-eight leaves following the text are page proofs of

an unpublished Index. They comprise pages 633–704, printed for the most part on one side of a leaf, extensively corrected in manuscript. The Index starts with the heading Appeal and ends with Process. Apparently only this much of the proof sheets survived the fire which destroyed most of the edition in the bindery. The explanation slip is present in this copy preceding the title-page.

2074 ILLINOIS AND MICHIGAN CANAL

COMPLETE LIST OF THE LOTS AND LANDS CONVEYED TO THE TRUSTEES OF THE ILLINOIS AND MICHIGAN CANAL, SHOWING SIZE OF LOTS, APPRAISAL, SALES IN SEPT. 1848, AND MAY, 1849, NAMES OF PURCHASERS, &C. COMPILED BY ORDER OF THE BOARD, FEBRUARY, 1850. CHICAGO: PRINTED AT THE DEMOCRAT OFFICE, 1850.

[i]–xvi, [1]–151, [152 blank]. 23 x 14.4 cm. Blue printed wrappers, with title on front wrapper. In blue cloth case.

Prov.: Presentation copy from Isaac N. Arnold to the Chicago Historical Society, inscribed on title-page: Chicago Historical / Society / from / Isaac N. Arnold /. Bookplate of Thomas Dumody on front wrapper.

Ref.: Byrd 1586; McMurtrie (*Chicago*) 136

Tipped in is a printed broadsheet form: Sidewalk Notice. / [decorative rule] / Office of the Board of Public Works, / Street Department, / Chicago, [dotted rule] 187. / This is filled in to J. N. Arnold and dated April 11th, 1873, in pencil. 17.5 x 21.6 cm. Facsimile signature at lower right: F. H. Bailey / Secretary Board of Public Works. /

2075 ILLINOIS AND MICHIGAN CANAL

[Broadside] LIST OF LOTS AND LANDS IN AND ABOUT CHICAGO, TO BE OFFERED AT PUBLIC SALE BY THE CANAL TRUSTEES, IN CHICAGO, ON THE 9TH OF MAY, 1853; AND ALSO A LIKE LIST OF THE UNSOLD LOTS IN THE TOWN OF LA SALLE, TO BE OFFERED IN THAT PLACE ON THE 13TH INST. THE UNSOLD LOTS IN OTHER TOWNS ALONG THE CANAL, AS WELL AS THE LANDS, ARE NOT HERE LISTED, BUT WILL BE OFFERED IN CHICAGO ON THE 9TH, WITH THE OTHER PROPERTY. THE ORIGINAL VALUATION IS OMITTED, INASMUCH AS IT IS EXPECTED THAT THOSE OLD FIGURES, MADE FIVE YEARS AGO, WILL HAVE LITTLE INFLUENCE ON THE PRICE THE PROPERTY SHOULD NOW BRING. [decorative rule] [476 lines in five columns]

Broadside, 45.7 x 33.2 cm. Text, 38.1 x 29.3 cm.

Ref.: Byrd 1992

Numerous additions in pencil in an unidentified hand, names of purchasers and prices paid, etc. "Newbury" purchased one lot.

2076 ILLINOIS, ANTIQUARIAN AND HISTORICAL SOCIETY OF

PROCEEDINGS OF THE ANTIQUARIAN AND HISTORICAL SOCIETY OF ILLINOIS, AT ITS FIRST SESSION, IN DECEMBER 1827: WITH AN ADDRESS, DELIVERED BY THE HON. JAMES HALL, PRESIDENT OF THE SOCIETY . . . EDWARDSVILLE: PRINTED BY BOBERT[!] K. FLEMING, AT THE OFFICE OF THE ILLINOIS CORRECTOR. 1828.

[1]–22, [23–4 blank]. 16.4 x 10.4 cm. Stabbed, unbound, uncut, unopened. In a brown half morocco case labeled: Illinois / Historical / Society / Hall / 1828 /.

Ref.: Blanck 6918; Byrd 79; Sabin 34310

2077 ILLINOIS, ANTIQUARIAN AND HISTORICAL SOCIETY OF

[Broadside] VANDALIA, AUGUST 1ST, 1828. SIR: ACCOMPANYING THIS LETTER, YOU WILL RECEIVE A COPY OF THE PROCEEDINGS OF THE ANTIQUARIAN AND HISTORICAL SOCIETY OF ILLINOIS . . . [ten lines] JAMES WHITLOCK, SECRETARY.

Broadside, 25 x 20.1 cm. Text, 6.3 x 14.4 cm.
Ref.: Byrd 80
Laid in brown half morocco case labeled: Illinois / Historical / Society / Hall / 1828 /.

2078 ILLINOIS ANTI-SLAVERY SOCIETY

ALTON OBSERVER.—EXTRA. PROCEEDINGS OF THE ILL. ANTI-SLAVERY CONVENTION. HELD AT UPPER ALTON ON THE TWENTY-SIXTH, TWENTY-SEVENTH, AND TWENTY-EIGHTH OCTOBER, 1837. ALTON: PARKS AND BREATH, 1838.

[1]–36. 19.4 x 12.2 cm. Rebound in red marbled boards, red straight-grain calf backstrip and corners, gilt top, uncut.
Ref.: Byrd 391

2079 ILLINOIS CENTRAL RAILROAD COMPANY

[Caption title] THE ILLINOIS CENTRAL RAILROAD COMPANY IS NOW PREPARED TO SELL OVER TWO MILLIONS OF ACRES OF SELECTED PRAIRIE, FARM AND WOOD LANDS! IN TRACTS OF FORTY ACRES OR UPWARDS, TO SUIT PURCHASERS, ON LONG CREDITS AND AT LOW RATES OF INTEREST . . .

[1–4]. 35.3 x 25 cm. Unbound leaflet.
Ref.: Byrd 2300
At the foot of page [1]: Office of the Company, No. 52 Michigan Avenue, Chicago. / Charles M. Du Puy, Jr., / Land Agent Ill. Cent. R.R. Co. / For Interesting Letters from Illinois Farmers, see following Pages. / Letters from Illinois farmers printed on pages [2] and [4] are dated between January and September, 1855.

2080 ILLINOIS CENTRAL RAILROAD COMPANY

[Map] MAP / OF / ILLINOIS CENTRAL RAILROAD COMPANY'S / DEPOT GROUNDS & BUILDINGS / IN / CHICAGO, ILL^S / SHOWING POSITION & DIMENSIONS OF PASSENGER, FREIGHT & GRAIN / HOUSES, TRACKS, BASINS, PROTECTION CRIB WORK &.^{C} / [3 lines] / COMPILED IN PART FROM MAP MADE UNDER THE DIRECTION OF BREVET LIEUT. COL. / J. D. GRAHAM U. S. TOP^L ENG^{RS} / AND / FROM SURVEYS OF R. B. MASON / CHIEF ENGINEER / ILL.^{S} CENT^L R. R. / [lower left:] LITH. OF E^D MENDEL, 170 LAKE ST CHICAGO. / SCALE 1200 FEET TO 1 INCH. / [decorative rule] / [7 lines] /

Map 65.7 x 45.2 cm. Scale as above. Bound with related materials in contemporary black half calf.
Ref.:
See under ILLINOIS CENTRAL RAILROAD COMPANY.
No date is mentioned.

2081 ILLINOIS CENTRAL RAILROAD COMPANY

[Wrapper title] SECTIONAL MAPS, SHOWING 2,500,000 ACRES FARM AND WOOD LANDS, OF THE ILLINOIS CENTRAL RAIL ROAD COMPANY, IN ALL PARTS OF THE STATE OF ILLINOIS, WITH THE LINE OF THEIR RAIL ROAD, AND OTHER INTERSECTING RAIL ROADS. THE SHADED SECTIONS SHOW THE LANDS OF THE COMPANY. OFFICE, UP TO THE FIRST OF MAY, NO. 84 LAKE STREET, (UP STAIRS,)—AFTER THAT DATE,—AT NO. 52 MICHIGAN AVENUE, CHICAGO, ILLINOIS.

Blank leaf, 34 plates, blank leaf. 23.2 x 14 cm. 30 numbered maps, one preliminary map, and one map lettered A. Two maps are folded. Brown printed wrappers, with title on front wrapper. Lower outer corner of front wrapper and blank leaf defective.
Ref.: Byrd 2467
Published in 1855 or 1856.

2082 ILLINOIS CENTRAL RAILROAD COMPANY

UNITED STATES OF AMERICA. DOCUMENTS RELATING TO THE ORGANIZATION OF THE ILLINOIS CENTRAL RAILROAD COMPANY . . . NEW-YORK: G SCOTT ROE, 1855.

[1]–[73], [74 blank]. 22.5 x 13.7 cm. Bound with eleven other pamphlets, broadsides, etc. in contemporary black half calf.
Ref.: Howes I8 see
The collection relates to the suit by George C. Bates against the Illinois Central Railroad and was gathered by J. A. Willis. Two maps of Chicago (the Wright map of 1834 and the Iglehart

map of 1854) have been removed from the volume. The volume now comprises the following materials, each of which is described under the headings given:

ILLINOIS CENTRAL RAILROAD COMPANY, Defendant

[Caption title] United States Circuit Court . . . George C. Bates, vs. Ill. Central Rail Road Co. Ejectment . . .

ILLINOIS CENTRAL RAILROAD COMPANY, Defendant

Report of the Evidence in the Case of Geo. C. Bates vs. Ill. Central R. R. Co. . . . Chicago: Daily Evening Journal Office, 1859.

MCLEAN, JOHN

[Broadside] Remarks of Judge McLean, at the Former Trial. [62 lines].

ILLINOIS CENTRAL RAILROAD COMPANY, Defendant

[Caption title] September Term, A. D. 1859. Circuit Court . . . for the Northern District of Illinois. George C. Bates v. The Illinois Central Railroad Co. Argument . . .

CLEVELAND, COLUMBUS & CINCINNATI RAILROAD COMPANY, THE CLEVELAND AND TOLEDO RAILROAD COMPANY ET AL., THE, Defendants

[Caption title] In the Circuit Court of the U. S. for the Northern District of Ohio. Henry Holmes, Julius C. Sheldon et al., vs. The Cleveland, Columbus & Cincinnati Railroad Company, The Cleveland and Toledo Railroad Company et al. . . . [imprint at foot of page:] Gideon, Printer . . . Washington, D. C.

BENSON, HENRY E., Defendant

[Caption title] Charles A. Lorman, vs. Henry E. Benson. In the Circuit Court for the County of Wayne. To the Hon. the Justices of the Supreme Court of the State of Michigan: Case Reserved . . .

BENSON, HENRY E., Defendant

[Caption title] Supreme Court—State of Michigan. Charles E. Lorman vs. Henry E. Benson . . .

DETROIT TRIBUNE, THE

[Broadside] [From *The Detroit Tribune*, January 16th.] Riparian Rights on the Detroit River . . . [1860].

MONTHLY LAW REPORTER, THE

The Monthly Law Reporter. January, 1860. Riparian and Littoral Rights . . . [Extract.]

GRAHAM, J. D.

Annual Report of Brevet Lieut. Col. J. D. Graham, Major of U. S. Topographical Engineers, on the Improvement of the Harbors of Lakes Michigan, St. Clair, Erie, Ontario, and Champlain . . . Washington: 1859.

CHICAGO. Board of Sewerage Commissioners

Report and Plan of Sewerage for the City of Chicago, Illinois, Adopted by the Board of Sewerage Commissioners December 31, 1855. Chicago: Charles Scott, 1855.

The volume also contains the following insertions:

[Manuscript copy of map:] U. S. Government Map of [Chicago] 1818. Copied from a map in the Topographical Bureau. Inserted before first title-page.

[Manuscript copy of map:] Map of the mouth of Chicago River Illinois with the plan of the proposed piers for improving the Harbour Drawn by F. Harrison . . . Feby 24th 1830 . . . Inserted before first title-page.

ILLINOIS CENTRAL RAILROAD COMPANY

[Map:] Map of Illinois Central Railroad Company's Depot Grounds & Buildings in Chicago . . . Compiled . . . from Map . . . of Brevet Lieut. Col. J. D. Graham . . . and from Surveys of R. B. Mason . . . Inserted after first title-page.

Newspaper clipping inserted between second and third pamphlets. Six newspaper clippings inserted after the first broadside. [Map:] Plan N° 1. Chicago Sewerage . . . Inserted before last pamphlet, probably designed to accompany pamphlet.

2083 ILLINOIS CENTRAL RAILROAD COMPANY, Defendant

REPORT OF THE EVIDENCE IN THE CASE OF GEO. C. BATES VS. ILL. CENTRAL R. R. CO. IN THE UNITED STATES CIRCUIT COURT, FOR THE NORTHERN DISTRICT OF ILLINOIS. HON. JOHN MCLEAN, PRESIDING JUDGE, HON. THOMAS DRUMMOND, ASSOCIATE JUDGE. OCTOBER TERM. GEO. C. BATES, VS. ILL. CENTRAL R. R. CO., EJECTMENT. MESSRS. N. C. MCLEAN, J. A. WILLS, E. C. LARNED, T. HOYNE, S. A. GOODWIN, FOR PLAINTIFF. MESSRS. JAS. F. JOY, J. M. DOUGLAS, D. STUART, C. BECKWITH, FOR DEFENDANTS. R. R. HITT, REPORTER. CHICAGO: DAILY EVENING JOURNAL OFFICE, 1859.

[i]–iv, [1]–263, [264 blank]. 22.5 x 13.7 cm. Bound with related materials in contemporary black half calf.

Ref.: AII (*Chicago*) 358

See under ILLINOIS CENTRAL RAILROAD COMPANY.

2084 ILLINOIS CENTRAL RAILROAD COMPANY, Defendant

[Caption title] SEPTEMBER TERM, A. D. 1859. CIRCUIT COURT OF THE UNITED STATES FOR THE

NORTHERN DISTRICT OF ILLINOIS. GEORGE C. BATES V. THE ILLINOIS CENTRAL RAILROAD CO. ARGUMENT. . . .

[1]–77, [78 blank]. Bound with related materials in contemporary black half calf.

Ref.: AII (*Chicago*) 358(?)

Manuscript corrections and notes throughout text, two sheets of manuscript notes inserted between pages 56–7, newspaper clippings inserted before page [1] and between pages 76–7.

See under ILLINOIS CENTRAL RAILROAD COMPANY.

2085 ILLINOIS CENTRAL RAILROAD COMPANY, Defendant

[Caption title] UNITED STATES CIRCUIT COURT, FOR THE NORTHERN DISTRICT OF ILLINOIS. HON. JOHN McLEAN AND HON. THOMAS DRUMMOND. GEORGE C. BATES, VS. ILL. CENTRAL RAIL ROAD CO. EJECTMENT. FIRST DAY—MONDAY, SEPTEMBER 28, 1858. . . .

[1]–130, [131 Index, 132 blank]. (Last leaf bound before title-leaf.) 22.5 x 13.7 cm. Bound with related materials in contemporary black half calf.

Ref.:

See under ILLINOIS CENTRAL RAILROAD COMPANY

Probably printed in Chicago.

2086 ILLINOIS COLLEGE

CATALOGUE OF THE OFFICERS AND STUDENTS OF ILLINOIS COLLEGE. FOR THE YEAR ENDING JUNE, MDCCCXLVI. BURLINGTON, IOWA: PRINTED AT THE HAWK-EYE OFFICE, 1846.

[1]–16. 18.9 x 11.7 cm. Yellow printed wrappers, with title on front wrapper.

Ref.: Moffit 24

2087 ILLINOIS COLLEGE

[Caption title] DESCRIPTION OF JACKSONVILLE AND OF THE PLOT OF LANDS HERETO ANNEXED, AND NOW OFFERED FOR SALE IN BEHALF OF ILLINOIS COLLEGE . . .

[1]–12. 21.3 x 13 cm. Folding map on tissue paper: A Plat of Lands / Belonging to the Trustees of / Illinois College /. 46.5 x 37.9 cm. No scale given. *Inset:* [Township map of part of Cass County near Jacksonville]. 11.4 x 10 cm. No scale given. *Inset:* [Map of College lands southwest of Jacksonville]. 9 x 14.6 cm. No scale given. Green printed wrappers, with title on front wrapper, advertisement on verso of front wrapper.

Prov.: Manuscript note in unidentified hand on back wrapper: Appeal & / off Lots for / [rule] / Sale Oct 1835— /.

Ref.:

On the inside front wrapper, there is a long advertising statement about the sale of the lots signed by Nathaniel Coffin, Agent for the Trustees of Illinois College. The note is dated as from New York, October, without year. The meeting at which Coffin was appointed was held August 15, 1836 (see page 9). Printed in New York, presumably.

2088 ILLINOIS EDUCATION CONVENTION

[PERIODICAL.] PROCEEDINGS OF THE ILLINOIS EDUCATIONAL CONVENTION: HELD IN THE STATE HOUSE AT VANDALIA, DECEMBER 5TH AND 6TH, 1834, WITH AN ADDRESS TO THE PEOPLE OF ILLINOIS, AND A MEMORIAL TO THE LEGISLATURE, ON COMMON SCHOOLS. ROCK-SPRING, ILLINOIS: PRINTED AT THE PIONEER OFFICE, 1834.

[1]–11, [12 blank]. 21.3 x 15.3 cm. Stabbed, unbound, uncut, partially unopened.

Ref.: Byrd 179

Among the delegates from Sangamon County was A. Lincoln esq. Stephen A. Douglass[!], delegate from Morgan County was Secretary *pro tem.*

2089 ILLINOIS MONTHLY MAGAZINE

ILLINOIS MONTHLY MAGAZINE. VOL. I. VANDALIA: PRINTED BY ROBERT BLACKWELL, 1831.

WITH:

THE ILLINOIS MONTHLY MAGAZINE. VOLUME II. CINCINNATI: PUBLISHED BY COREY AND FAIRBANK, 1832.

WITH:

THE WESTERN MONTHLY MAGAZINE, A CONTINUATION OF THE ILLINOIS MONTHLY MAGAZINE, VOL. I [–IV]. CINCINNATI: PUBLISHED BY COREY & FAIRBANK [-TAYLOR & TRACY], 1833 [–35].

WITH:

SEPARATE ISSUES OF VOLUMES 5–6 AS BELOW.

[i–ii], [i]–ii, [1]–576. October, 1830—September, 1831.

[i–iv], [1]–572. October, 1831—September, 1832.

[i–vi, vi blank], [1]–600. January–December, 1833.

[i–ii], [1]–670. January–December, 1834.

[i–ii], [2]–4, 6–[400]. January–June, 1835.

[1]–[426]. July–December, 1835.

Four illustrations, Volume III, February, October, December, Vol. V, May. Five volumes, uniformly bound in contemporary half calf, gilt, green leather labels on backstrips, sprinkled edges. Thirteen separate parts, wrappers or unbound; see below.

Prov.: Contemporary bookplates of William A. Porter and signatures of May Porter.

Ref.: Byrd 89 see; Mott (*Amer. Mag.*) I, pp. 595–96; Sabin 34261

Complete run of the first five volumes of this notable monthly magazine edited by James Hall. The individual numbers varied from 48 to 60 pages per month. There were no numbers issued between September, 1832 and January, 1833. In Volume IV (Volume II of second series), pages 409–16 are present in duplicate.

Volumes V and VI of *Western Monthly Magazine* are present in the following monthly parts:

Volume V:

No. 1. January, 1836. Pages [1]–64.
   Removed from binding.
No. 2. February,   [65]–128.
   Same as preceding.
No. 3. March,   [131]–194.
   Same as preceding.
No. 4. April,   [195]–258.
   Lacks green wrappers.
No. 5. May,   [259]–322.
   Removed from bound
   volume.
No. 6. June,   [323]–386.
   Same as preceding.
No. 8. August,   [447]–506.
   Same as preceding.
No. 9. September,   [507]–566.
   Original brown printed
   front wrapper.

New Series. Vol. I:

No. 1. February, 1837. Pages [5]–76.
   Original brown printed
   wrappers, but re-
   moved from bound
   volume.
No. 1. Another copy. Same.
No. 2. March, 1837. Pages [77]–148.
   Same as preceding.
No. 3. April,   [149]–220.
   Original printed wrap-
   pers.
No. 4. May,   [201]–08,
                          229–292.
   Removed from bound
   volume.

2090   ILLINOIS WOMAN'S KANSAS AID AND LIBERTY ASSOCIATION

CONSTITUTION AND BY-LAWS OF THE ILLINOIS WOMAN'S KANSAS AID AND LIBERTY ASSOCIATION. ORGANIZED JUNE 10, 1856. CHICAGO: DAILY TRIBUNE BOOK AND JOB OFFICE, 1856.

[1]–11. [12 blank]. 11.5 x 7.8 cm. Buff printed wrappers, with title on front wrapper. On back wrapper: Form of Collector's Credentials. / [short rule] / [6 lines] / [within rule border].

Ref.: Byrd 2479

2091   IMLAY, GILBERT

A TOPOGRAPHICAL DESCRIPTION OF THE WESTERN TERRITORY OF NORTH AMERICA . . . LONDON: PRINTED FOR J. DEBRETT, 1797.

A⁶, B–Rr⁸, Ss¹. [i]–xii, [1]–[626]. (A1 supplied, SsZ [blank] not present.) 21.9 x 13.5 cm. Map: A Map of / The Western Part of / the Territories belonging / to the / United States / of / America. / Drawn from the best Authorities. / [swelled rule] / Engraved for Imlay's Topographical Description of / that Country. / [lower centre:] Published June 1ˢᵗ 1795, by J. Debrett, Piccadilly, London. / [lower right:] T. Conder Sculpᵗ / 35.3 x 33.3 cm. Scale: about 100 miles to one inch. Map: A Plan of / The Rapids / of the / Ohio. / [upper centre:] Engraved for Imlay's American Topography. / [lower right:] T. Conder Sculpᵗ / [lower centre:] Published Febʸ 1ˢᵗ 1793, by J. Debrett, Piccadilly, London. / 15.2 x 18.4 cm. Scale: about 750 yards to one inch. Map: A Map of / The State of / Kentucky, / from Actual Survey / by Elihu Barker / of Philadelphia. / [upper centre:] Engraved for Imlay's American Topography. / [lower right:] T. Conder Sculpᵗ / [lower centre:] London, Published June 1ˢᵗ 1795, by J. Debrett, Piccadilly. / 33.8 x 74.6 cm. Scale: 15 miles to one inch. Map: A Map of the / Tennassee[!] Government, / formerly part of / North Carolina, taken chiefly from Surveys / by Geneˡ D. Smith & others. / [upper centre:] Engraved for Imlay's American Topography. / [lower right:] T. Conder Sculpᵗ / [lower centre:] London, Published June 1ˢᵗ 1795, by J. Debrett, Piccadilly. / 16.2 x 40.7 cm. Scale not given. Blue boards, new tan paper backstrip, new white printed label, uncut.

Ref.: Bradford 2574; Buck 43; Clark II 41; Howes I12; Rader 2003; Sabin 34356; Thomson 632

The third and best edition of Imlay. Considered one of the more important books of the period about the country west of the Alleghenies.

2092   IMMIGRANTS' GUIDE TO MINNESOTA, THE

THE IMMIGRANTS' GUIDE TO MINNESOTA IN 1856. BY AN OLD RESIDENT. ST. ANTHONY: W. W. WALES, 1856.

[i]–viii, [9]–116, [117–127 advertisements, 128 blank]. (Page [i] blank, page [ii] frontispiece.) 18.7 x 11.4 cm. Three illustrations and map,

Map: Lake Minnetonka and Vicinity. / 8.1 x 13.8 cm. No scale given. Yellow pictorial wrappers with title on front wrapper, title on backstrip reading down, advertisement on verso of back wrapper. In green cloth case.

Ref.: Howes M644; Sabin 34366

On verso of the title-leaf there is a copyright notice in favor of Ivison & Phinney. Below at left: Stereotyped by / Thomas B. Smith, / 82 & 84 Beekman Street. / At right: Printed by / Daniel Adee, / 211 Center Street. *Ergo*, printed in New York.

2093 IMPARTIAL APPEAL, AN

AN IMPARTIAL APPEAL TO THE REASON, INTEREST AND PATRIOTISM, OF THE PEOPLE OF ILLINOIS, ON THE INJURIOUS EFFECTS OF SLAVE LABOUR. 1824.

[1]–16. 19.4 x 11.6 cm. Stabbed, uncut.

Ref.: Sabin 81996

Probably printed in Philadelphia. The London edition described by Sabin notes the imprint: Philadelphia Printed; London Reprinted . . .

In the "Sketch of Edward Coles, etc." by E. B. Washburne, Chicago, 1882, there is printed correspondence between Governor Coles and Robert Vaux of Philadelphia which indicates pretty clearly that the original edition of this pamphlet was printed in Philadelphia at the expense of Vaux and friends and sent to Governor Coles via St. Louis. At least one other and possibly two other pamphlets were printed in Philadelphia and sent out. Two thousand copies of each were requested by Governor Coles and it was thought wise to leave out the place of printing. In his letter to Morris Birkbeck of Jan. 29, 1824, Governor Coles writes of reprinting a large edition of Birkbeck's pamphlet at Edwardsville and possibly these Philadelphia pamphlets may have been reprinted at Edwardsville or elsewhere, but I have no information that they were.—EDG

2094 IMPERIAL ATLANTIC AND PACIFIC RAILROAD

[Caption title] IMPERIAL ATLANTIC AND PACIFIC RAILROAD . . .

[1]–4. 21.1 x 13.4 cm. Removed from bound volume, unbound.

Ref.:

Imprint at foot of page 4: London: Trelawny Saunders, / Colonial Publisher, 6, Charing Cross, / May, 1851. /

Comments on a visit to England by Asa Whitney.

2095 IMPROVEMENT OF THE MISSISSIPPI RIVER, THE

[Wrapper title] THE IMPROVEMENT OF THE MISSISSIPPI RIVER. STATEMENT MADE TO CONGRESS BY THE RIVER INTEREST. CLINTON, IOWA: AGE WATER POWER PRINT, 1881.

[1]–36. 22.6 x 14.4 cm. Yellow printed wrappers with title on front wrapper.

Ref.:

2096 INCIDENTS AND SKETCHES

INCIDENTS AND SKETCHES CONNECTED WITH THE EARLY HISTORY AND SETTLEMENT OF THE WEST . . . CINCINNATI: J. A. & U. P. JAMES, 1854.

[1]–72. 25.2 x 17 cm. Illustrations listed on page [4]. Green printed wrappers, with title on front wrapper, advertisements on verso of front and recto and verso of back wrapper.

Ref.: Field 748; Howes I19; Sabin 34426 see; Thomson 635 see

Contains contributions by John Mason Peck and others.

Editions: Cincinnati, [1847], 1853.

2097 INDEPENDENT DISTRICT. Colorado

[Broadside] MINING CLAIM CERTIFICATE. INDEPENDENT DISTRICT. KNOW ALL MEN BY THESE PRESENTS, THAT I [in manuscript: J Mellen] CLAIM BY PRE-EMPTION, . . . [three lines] GIVEN UNDER MY HAND AT GAMBLE GULCH, IN SAID DISTRICT, THIS [in manuscript: 15th] DAY OF [in manuscript: March] A. D., 1861. [in manuscript: W B Osborn] RECORDER. DEPUTY. PRESIDENT. [below border, centre:] HERALD PRINT, DENVER.

Broadside, 13.9 x 21.2 cm. Text, 11 x 18.9 cm.

Ref.:

Endorsed by Mellen on verso. Claim No. 9 East, McQueen Lode.

2098 INDEPENDENT ORDER OF ODD FELLOWS (Illinois)

CONSTITUTION, BY-LAWS, AND RULES OF ORDER OF DUANE LODGE, NO. 11, I. O. O. F. CHICAGO: ROBERT FERGUS, 1848.

[1]–[52]. 14.6 x 8.6 cm. Gray-green plain wrappers.

Ref.: Byrd 1363

2099 INDEPENDENT ORDER OF ODD FELLOWS (Oregon)

[Broadside] IN MEMORIAM. TO THE N. G., V. G., OFFICERS AND MEMBERS OF PHILETARIAN LODGE NO 8, I. O. O. F.; SIRS AND BROTHERS: [61 lines].

Broadside, 25.1 x 13.5 cm. Text, 23 x 5.5 cm.

Ref.:

Memorial resolutions on the death of Loren L. Williams. [At foot, in manuscript:] Roseburg Or. April 2ᵈ 1881 /. Inserted in Manuscript Journals of Loren L. Williams, Volume I.

2100 INDEPENDENT ORDER OF RECHABITES

THE REGULATIONS AND GENERAL LAWS TO BE OBSERVED BY THE MEMBERS OF THE INDEPENDENT ORDER OF RECHABITES, IN NORTH AMERICA. ADOPTED SEPT. 19, 1845, AMENDED AUG. 27, 1846. CHICAGO: PRINTED AT 128 COR. OF LAKE & CLARK STS., 1847.

[i]–iv, [1–2], 11–[36]. (Pages 3–10 missing.) 14.7 x 9.6 cm. Pink plain wrappers.

Ref.: Byrd 1238; McMurtrie (*Chicago*) 124

Only copy located. The missing pages were never present in this copy.

2101 INDEX TO MAP OF THE COPPER MINES . . .

INDEX TO MAP OF THE COPPER MINES OF CALAVERAS COUNTY, CALIFORNIA. STOCKTON: PRINTED AT THE INDEPENDENT BOOK AND JOB PRINTING ESTABLISHMENT. 1864.

[1]–10, [i]–vi. 23 x 14.4 cm. Yellow printed wrappers with title on front wrapper. Lacks back wrapper. In a red cloth case.

Ref.:
Note on front wrapper in pencil: Keep this book / Do not destroy /.

A copy of the map for which this *Index* was designed has not been located.

2102 INDIAN BATTLES, MURDERS . . .

INDIAN BATTLES, MURDERS, SEIGES[!] AND FORAYS IN THE SOUTH-WEST . . . NASHVILLE TENN.: PUBLISHED BY WALES & ROBERTS.

[1]–100. 22 x 12.2 cm. Rebound in brown half morocco. In a cloth slip case.

Prov.: Bookplate of C. G. Littell.

Ref.: Howes W30; Sabin 34461

Copyrighted 1853. Sabin reports an edition with the date 1853 on the title-page. The title-page ends with a comma.

The anonymous compiler gathered some of the more exciting narratives of pioneer days in the Old Northwest from the less frequently told episodes.

2103 INDIAN TERRITORY. General Council

JOURNAL OF THE SIXTH ANNUAL SESSION OF THE GENERAL COUNCIL OF THE INDIAN TERRITORY . . . AT OKMULGEE, INDIAN TERRITORY, FROM THE 3D TO THE 15TH (INCLUSIVE) OF MAY, 1875 . . . LAWRENCE, KANSAS: REPUBLICAN JOURNAL STEAM PRINTING ESTABLISHMENT, 1875.

[1]–114. 20.4 x 14 cm. Green printed wrappers, with title on front wrapper. In green cloth slip case.

Ref.: AII (*Kansas*) 1350; Hargrett (*Bibliography*) 201

The Appendix, pages [73]–97, contains reports of committees; pages [99]–114 is the Constitution of the Indian Territory with the Declaration of Rights.

2104 INDIAN TERRITORY. International Council of Indians

[Wrapper title] PROCEEDINGS OF THE INTERNATIONAL COUNCIL OF INDIANS OF THE INDIAN TERRITORY HELD AT EUFAULA, INDIAN TERRITORY, JUNE 6, 7, 8, AND 9, 1887 . . . EUFAULA: INDIAN JOURNAL STEAM PRINT, 1887.

[1]–7, [8 blank]. 22 x 14.3 cm. Violet printed wrappers, with title on front wrapper.

Ref.: Foreman p. 183; Hargrett (*Oklahoma*) 603

Signed in manuscript on page 7 by S. H. Benge as President and G. W. Grayson as Clerk.

2105 INDIANA TERRITORY. SUNDRY INHABITANTS OF THE COUNTIES OF RANDOLPH AND ST. CLAIR

MEMORIAL OF SUNDRY INHABITANTS OF THE COUNTIES OF RANDOLPH AND ST. CLAIR, IN THE INDIANA TERRITORY. JANUARY 17, 1806 . . . CITY OF WASHINGTON: A. & G. WAY, 1806.

[1]–12. 20.1 x 12.5 cm. Rebound in very dark green levant morocco, gilt top.

Prov.: Chicago Historical Society copy, with perforation through title-leaf, rubber stamp and accession number on verso of title-leaf, typed note, signed in manuscript with initials M S [Margaret Scriven] releasing book.

Ref.:
9th Congress, 1st Session. Executive Document.

A petition to divide the territory north of the Ohio River into smaller territories leading toward statehood.

2106 INGALLS, ELEAZER S.

JOURNAL OF A TRIP TO CALIFORNIA, BY THE OVERLAND ROUTE ACROSS THE PLAINS IN 1850–51 . . . WAUKEGAN: TOBEY & CO., 1852.

[1]–51, [52–54 advertisements of merchants, etc. in Antioch, Lake County, Illinois]. 21.2 x 13.6 cm. Yellow printed wrappers with title on front wrapper, advertisement on back wrapper. In a red half morocco case.

Ref.: Byrd 1861; Cowan p. 303; Howes I34; Wagner-Camp 215

2107 [INGALLS, RUFUS]

[Extract] [caption title] . . . REPORT . . . WASH-INGTON CITY, D. C., NOVEMBER 22, 1855. . . .

151 (end of preceding report), 152–168. 22.6 x 14.2 cm. Rebound in new red cloth.

Ref.: Wagner-Camp 256

Extract from Report of the Secretary of War, 34th Congress, 1st Session, Senate Executive Document No. 1, Part 2, Serial 811. It also appeared in House of Representatives Executive Documents, Serial 841.

Two letters of Rufus Ingalls (November 22, 1855 and August 25, 1855) both addressed to Major General Thomas S. Jesup. Contains an account of a trip with Colonel Steptoe from Fort Leavenworth to Salt Lake between June 1 and August 31, 1854.

2108 INGHAM, HARVEY

THE ALGONA BEE. A STORY OF NEWSPAPER BEGIN-NINGS.

[1–84, (1 blank)]. 22.7 x 14.3 cm. Numerous illustrations, unlisted. Maroon cloth, title in gilt on front cover.

Prov.: Inscribed on title-page: Compliments / Harvey Ingham /. Signature in pencil on front endleaf: Laura A. Smith. /

Ref.:

Des Moines, 1922, which date is in the text twice.

2109 INGHAM, HARVEY

FATHER TAYLOR. A STORY OF MISSIONARY BEGIN-NINGS.

[1–64 (1 and 64 blank)]. 22.3 x 15.1 cm. Numerous illustrations, unlisted. Purple cloth, title in gilt on front cover.

Prov.: Inscribed on title-page: To Geo. F. Henry with / the compliments and / good wishes of / Harvey Ingham /.

Ref.:

Probably Des Moines, 1924, since the date is mentioned as the present on page [61].

2110 INGHAM, HARVEY

THE NORTHERN BORDER BRIGADE. A STORY OF MILITARY BEGINNINGS.

[1–98 (1 and 98 blank)]. 22.9 x 14.5 cm. Numerous illustrations, unlisted. Blue cloth, title in gilt on front cover.

Prov.: Inscribed on title-page: To George T. Henry with / good wishes for a / 1926 Merry Christmas / Harvey Ingham /.

Ref.: Howes I42

Howes supplies place and date: Des Moines, 1926. Contains, among other pieces, the Journal of Lewis H. Smith on the Wagon Road from Niobrara to Virginia City.

2111 INGHAM, HARVEY

TEN YEARS ON THE IOWA FRONTIER . . . IN THE FIFTIES.

[1–92]. 23 x 15.2 cm. Illustrations unlisted. Brown cloth, title in gilt on front cover.

Ref.: Howes I43; Mott (*Iowa*) p. 86

Howes supplies place and date: Des Moines, 1915, but Mott says 1919. An inscription on the inner front cover and the front blank leaf carries the date October 15, 1919.

2112 [INGRAHAM, EDWARD D.]

A SKETCH OF THE EVENTS WHICH PRECEDED THE CAPTURE OF WASHINGTON, BY THE BRITISH, ON THE TWENTY-FOURTH OF AUGUST, 1814 . . . PHIL-ADELPHIA: CAREY AND HART, 1849.

[i]–iv, [1]–66, [67–8 blank]. 22.9 x 14 cm. Folding map: Sketch / of the / March of the British Army / under Genl Ross. / From the 19th to the 29th August. / 1814. / [short rule] / From a Sketch by D. Evans, / L^t 3^d Dr^{ns} Dy. As^t Q^r Mas^t Genl / *Inset:* Sketch / of the Engagement on the / 24th of August 1814 between / the British and American / Forces. / [lower centre:] Military Depot Quarter Mas^r. Genl Office Horse Guards Oct. 10th 1817. / 24.2 x 24.5 cm. Scale: 1.4 mile to one inch. [lower left corner:] J. Wyld / [lower right corner:] T. Sinclairs. lith Phila. / 46.5 x 34.5 cm. Scale: about 2 1/2 miles to one inch. Contemporary half green morocco, marbled board sides, red top.

Prov.: Presentation copy, inscribed on the front endleaf: For Major Pringle / Who commanded a company of / Grenadiers under Genl Ross in the / attack upon Washington— / From his friend Major Genl Steuart of Balto / Who commanded a company / of Infantry in the 5 Regt / under Genl Winder— / Baltimore 4 March 1853 /. Beneath the above, apparently in the hand of Major Pringle, is the following: 1814 [at end of penultimate line] / I saw Genl Steuart / in Stockholm / in 1857—and we / talked over the / events of our / Friendly meeting / at the action / before Baltimore / when Steuart / was married / He prided him / self much on / being an Ast aid / [?] at Stock. / There are also some textual corrections in an unidentified hand and there are marginal notes and comments by Pringle on pages 14, 15, 16, 29, 30–55 and [67–8].

Ref.: Howes I48; Sabin 34772

An extraordinary association copy. The extensive annotations by Pringle, some of which are signed or carry his initials, correct or comment on the text. There are also three full pages of manuscript at the end with acute criticisms of the conduct of Sir E. Pakenham at the Battle of

New Orleans, including detailed descriptions of two "very gross blunders."

2113 INGRAHAM, JOSEPH H.

THE SUNNY SOUTH; OR, THE SOUTHERNER AT HOME, EMBRACING FIVE YEARS' EXPERIENCE OF A NORTHERN GOVERNESS IN THE LAND OF THE SUGAR AND THE COTTON . . . PHILADELPHIA: G. G. EVANS, 1860.

[1]–526, [1]–18 advertisements. 18.5 x 12.1 cm. Dark green embossed cloth, sides in blind, title in gilt on backstrip.

Ref.: Clark III p. 54; Howes I50; Sabin 34776

Detailed portrayal of life on tobacco, cotton and sugar plantations in ante-bellum Mississippi.—Howes

2114 INGRAHAM, JOSEPH H.

THE TEXAN RANGER; OR, THE MAID OF MATAMORAS. A TALE OF THE MEXICAN WAR . . . BOSTON: HENRY L. WILLIAMS, 1846.

[3]–90. 23.5 x 15 cm. Woodcut illustration, repeated on front cover. Printed pictorial wrappers, with title on front wrapper, advertisement on verso of back wrapper, uncut.

Ref.: Clements Library (*Texas*) 28; Raines p. 124; Wright I 1356

By the time the end of this novel is reached, it is impossible to say which is more confused, the reader or the author. But even more fascinating than the convolutions of the plot is the language of the author. Here is a sample in which a Mexican colonel's horse is described:

He was impetuous and restless, as if ready each moment to dash forward, 'as if he smelt the battle afar off, the thunder of the captains and the shouting,' and wished to say among the trumpets, 'a-ha! a-ha!'

Although the pamphlet starts on page [3], there is apparently no missing leaf; the first gathering is complete.

2115 INMAN, HENRY

STORIES OF THE OLD SANTA FE TRAIL . . . KANSAS CITY, MO.: RAMSEY, MILLETT & HUDSON, 1881.

[i–viii], [1]–287, [288 blank]. 17.1 x 12.1 cm. Illustrations unlisted. Green pictorial cloth, gilt title on backstrip. Inner hinges repaired.

Ref.: Howes I58; Munk (Alliot) p. 114; Rader 2024

Some of Inman's stories stem from a vivid imagination rather than sober fact.

There is another edition of the same imprint consisting of 291 pages. The text on pages 283, line 1, to 287, line 4, is omitted in the present volume but present in the 291-page edition. The latter [at least in the ICN (Ayer) copy] is not as well printed and shows numerous broken letters. In the 287-page edition, there is an error in the Contents listing (312 for 212) which is corrected in the 291-page edition. It is probable that the 287-page edition precedes the 291-page edition.

2116 INMAN, HENRY

TALES OF THE TRAIL. SHORT STORIES OF WESTERN LIFE . . . TOPEKA: CRANE & COMPANY, 1898.

[1]–viii, 1–280. (Pages [i–ii] blank.) 18.7 x 12.6 cm. 24 illustrations listed. Yellow pictorial cloth, yellow edges.

Ref.: Howes I58; Rader 2025

Four of the chapters had appeared in *Stories of the Old Santa Fe Trail*, Kansas City, 1881.

2117 INMAN, HENRY, & WILLIAM F. CODY

THE GREAT SALT LAKE TRAIL . . . NEW YORK: THE MACMILLAN COMPANY, 1898.*

[i]–[xiv, xiv blank], 1–529, [530–31 advertisements, 532 blank]. 22 x 14.8 cm. Eight illustrations and one map listed. Green pictorial cloth, gilt top.

Ref.: Adams 538; Bradford 2605; Dobie p. 79; Howes I55; Smith 4924

Howes lists blue and brown bindings only.

2118 INQUIRY INTO THE PRESENT STATE, AN

AN INQUIRY INTO THE PRESENT STATE OF THE FOREIGN RELATIONS OF THE UNION, AS AFFECTED BY THE LATE MEASURES OF ADMINISTRATION . . . PHILADELPHIA: SAMUEL F. BRADFORD, 1806.

[A]–Z⁴. [1]–183, [184 blank]. Bound with Number 3289.

Ref.: Sabin 34815; Shaw & Shoemaker 10615

2119 INSPECTOR OF STEAMBOATS FOR THE PORT OF ST. LOUIS

[Broadside] PROPOSED CERTIFICATE OF INSPECTION. BE IT KNOWN THAT I, ——— ——— INSPECTOR OF STEAMBOATS FOR THE PORT OF ST. LOUIS, HAVE THIS DAY THOROUGHLY INSPECTED THE BOILERS, ENGINES AND MACHINERY OF THE STEAMBOAT SARANAC, AND FIND THAT HER BOILERS ARE IN GOOD CONDITION . . . [26 lines] THAT THE OWNERS, CAPTAIN AND ENGINEER HAVE ENTERED INTO THE PROPER BONDS, IN THE SUM OF FIVE HUNDRED DOLLARS, TO THE BENEFIT OF ANY PASSENGER PROSECUTING THE SAME IN CASE OF ANY NEGLIGENCE OR VIOLATION OF THE CONDITIONS OF THIS PERMIT. INSPECTOR. CHICAGO DEMOCRAT PRINT.

Broadside, 34 x 26.5 cm. Text, 29 x 22.6 cm.
Ref.:
Manuscript corrections in lines 11 and 16.
Probably printed about 1850.

2120   IOWA. AUDITOR

BIENNIAL REPORT OF THE AUDITOR OF STATE . . .
FOR THE YEARS 1849–'50 . . . IOWA CITY: PALMER
& PAUL, 1850.

[1]–3⁴, 4⁸. (However, printed and folded as
three gatherings, octavo, quarto, octavo.) [1]–36,
[37–40 blank]. 24.1 x 15.3 cm. Stabbed, uncut,
unopened.
Ref.: Steele p. 7
The office of Auditor of State was created by
act of the Second Legislative Assembly, January
7, 1840. Its first report was issued the same year.
According to Miss Steele, reports before 1857
were irregular.

2121   IOWA. CITIZENS

[Broadside] A GREAT MASS CONVENTION, COM-
POSED OF DELEGATES FROM FOURTEEN COUNTIES,
HELD AT OTTUMWA, WAPELLO COUNTY, IOWA, ON
THE 13TH FEBRUARY 1852, BY THE FRIENDS OF THE
LAFAYETTE AND MISSOURI RIVER RAIL ROAD. [133
and 128 lines in two columns] WM. H. WALLACE,
PRESIDENT. W. H. BRUMFIELD, J. H. M'KENNY,
SECRETARIES.

Broadside, 48.9 x 14.9 cm. Text, 39.6 x 11.9 cm.
Ref.:
The convention was called to arouse enthusiasm for a railroad from Burlington to the
mouth of the Platte.

2122   IOWA. COMMITTEE OF CITIZENS

A DESCRIPTION OF CENTRAL IOWA: WITH ESPECIAL
REFERENCE TO POLK COUNTY AND DES MOINES, THE
STATE CAPITAL; TOGETHER WITH EIGHT ADJACENT
COUNTIES . . . DES MOINES, IOWA: PRINTED AT THE
IOWA STATE JOURNAL OFFICE, 1858.

[1]–32. 18.8 x 12.5 cm. Pink printed wrappers,
with title on front wrapper, advertisements on
verso of back wrapper.
Ref.: Howes I68; Moffit 347; Sabin 34984
On page 32 there is a section headed: The
Discoveries of Gold.

2123   IOWA. CONSTITUTION

CONSTITUTION DES STAATES IOWA . . . DUBUQUE:
GEDRUCKT BEI B. HANF, 1851.

[1]–[29], [30–2 blank]. 18.4 x 12.5 cm. Pale salmon printed wrappers with title on front wrapper.
Ref.:

2124   IOWA. CONSTITUTION

CONSTITUTION FOR THE STATE OF IOWA, ADOPTED
IN CONVENTION, NOV. 1, 1844. IOWA CITY:
PRINTED BY JESSE WILLIAMS, 1844.

[1]–18, 23–24. 22.7 x 14 cm. Removed from
bound volume, unbound. Lacks two leaves,
pages 19–22.
Ref.: Steele p. 13

2125   IOWA. CONSTITUTION

[Caption title] . . . CONSTITUTION OF THE STATE
OF IOWA, ADOPTED IN CONVENTION, NOVEMBER 1,
1844 . . .

[1]–15, [16 blank]. 22.8 x 14.4 cm. Removed
from bound volume, unbound.
Ref.:
28th Congress, 2nd Session, House, Document No. 5, Serial 463. [Washington, 1844.]

2126   IOWA. CONSTITUTION

[Caption title] . . . CONSTITUTION OF THE STATE
OF IOWA, ADOPTED IN CONVENTION, NOVEMBER 1,
1844 . . .

[1]–21, [22–4 blank]. 22.9 x 16 cm. Stabbed,
unbound, uncut, partially unopened.
Ref.:
28th Congress, 2nd Session, House, Document No. 77, Serial 465. [Washington, 1845.]
Document No. 77 contains three pages of
additional material relating to abstracts of the
vote of the people May 1, 1844, and a census of
the number of inhabitants of Iowa Territory,
not found in House Document No. 5.

2127   IOWA. CONSTITUTIONAL CON-
VENTION

JOURNAL OF THE CONSTITUTIONAL CONVENTION OF
THE STATE OF IOWA, IN SESSION AT IOWA CITY,
FROM THE NINETEENTH DAY OF JANUARY, A. D.,
ONE THOUSAND EIGHT HUNDRED AND FIFTY-
SEVEN, TO THE FIFTH DAY OF MARCH OF THE SAME
YEAR, INCLUSIVE. MUSCATINE: PRINTED BY JOHN
MAHIN, 1857.

[1]–406, [407–08 blank]. 21.6 x 14.3 cm. New
plain tan wrappers. In a brown cloth case.
Ref.: Sabin 34983; Steele p. 13

2128   IOWA. COURTS. Sixth Judicial Dis-
trict

RULES OF PRACTICE IN THE SIXTH JUDICIAL DIS-
TRICT OF THE STATE OF IOWA. KNOXVILLE:
PRINTED BY E. G. STANFIELD, 1859

[1]–16. 19.6 x 12.5 cm. Blue printed wrappers
with title on front wrapper.
Ref.:
Tipped to inside back cover is an errata slip,
2.6 x 8.5 cm., four lines of corrections.

2129 IOWA. GENERAL ASSEMBLY. House. Select Committee to Investigate Alleged Frauds in the Location of the Capitol

REPORT OF THE SPECIAL COMMITTEE APPOINTED BY THE HOUSE OF REPRESENTATIVES, OF THE SEVENTH GENERAL ASSEMBLY, TO INVESTIGATE ALLEGED FRAUDS IN THE LOCATION OF THE CAPITOL. DES MOINES, IOWA: J. TEESDALE, 1858.

[1]–79, [80 blank]. 21.8 x 14.3 cm. Tan printed wrappers with title on front wrapper.
Ref.:

2130 IOWA. GOVERNOR (James Clarke)

[Caption title] GOVERNOR'S MESSAGE. GENTLEMEN OF THE COUNCIL AND OF THE HOUSE OF REPRESENTATIVES: . . .

[1]–8. 22.9 x 14.1 cm. Removed from bound volume, unbound.
Ref.:
Dated on page eight: December 3, 1845.

2131 IOWA. IMMIGRATION, BOARD OF

IOWA: THE HOME FOR IMMIGRANTS, BEING A TREATISE ON THE RESOURCES OF IOWA, AND GIVING USEFUL INFORMATION WITH REGARD TO THE STATE, FOR THE BENEFIT OF IMMIGRANTS AND OTHERS . . . DES MOINES: MILLS & CO., 1870.

[1]–96. 22.8 x 14.6 cm. Gray printed wrappers, with title on front wrapper. In red cloth case.
Ref.: Bradford 2615; Sabin 35011; Steele p. 28

2132 IOWA. JOHNSON COUNTY. Old Settlers Association

PROCEEDINGS OF THE JOHNSON COUNTY OLD SETTLERS ASSOCIATION FROM 1866 TO 1899.

[1]–149, [150–52 blank]. 23.2 x 14.8 cm. Gray printed wrappers with title on front wrapper. In a black cloth case.
Ref.:
Covers reunions through the thirty-first in 1897. No place or date of publication indicated.

2133 IOWA. JOHNSON COUNTY. Old Settlers Association

[Wrapper title] THIRTY-FIFTH ANNUAL REUNION OF THE OLD SETTLERS OF JOHNSON COUNTY, AUGUST 22, 1901. IOWA CITIZEN PUBLISHING COMPANY, 1901.

[1]–36 (including wrappers). 23.2 x 15 cm. White printed wrappers, with title on front wrapper.
Ref.:

2134 IOWA. JOHNSON COUNTY. Old Settlers Association

[Wrapper title] THIRTY-SIXTH ANNUAL REUNION OF THE OLD SETTLERS OF JOHNSON COUNTY, AUGUST 21ST, 1902. IOWA CITY, IOWA, 1902.

[1]–[36] (including wrappers). (Pages [35–6] blank.) 23 x 15.3 cm. White printed wrappers, with title on front wrapper.
Ref.:

2135 IOWA. JOHNSON COUNTY. Old Settlers Association

[Wrapper title] THIRTY-SEVENTH ANNUAL REUNION OF THE OLD SETTLERS OF JOHNSON COUNTY, AUGUST 20TH, 1903.

[1]–[32] (including wrappers). (Pages [30–2] blank.) 22.9 x 15.5 cm. White printed wrappers, with title on front wrapper.
Ref.:

2136 IOWA. JOHNSON COUNTY CITIZENS. (Committee to Prepare an Address)

AN ADDRESS TO THE PEOPLE OF THE STATE OF IOWA, AND A MEMORIAL TO THE CONGRESS OF THE UNITED STATES FOR A GRANT OF LAND FOR THE COUNCIL BLUFFS AND DAVENPORT RAIL ROAD. IOWA CITY: PRINTED AT THE REPORTER OFFICE, 1849.

[1]–7, [8 blank]. 20.8 x 15.9 cm. Unbound leaflet.
Ref.: AII (*Iowa*) 27
Both the address and the memorial were reported out for the committee by Governor Robert Lucas.

2137 IOWA. PUBLIC WORKS, BOARD OF

BIENNIAL REPORT OF THE BOARD OF PUBLIC WORKS OF THE STATE OF IOWA. READ . . . ON THE SEVENTH DAY OF DECEMBER, 1850. IOWA CITY: PALMER & PAUL, 1850.

[1]–77, [78–80 blank]. 24.4 x 15.2 cm. Stabbed, uncut, unopened.
Ref.: Steele p. 41
The Board of Public Works was created by act of the First General Assembly, February 24, 1847. Its first report was made in 1848 and its second in 1850. The Board was abolished February 5, 1851, to be succeeded by the Des Moines River Improvement.

The signatures run [1]–10, but the volume is printed and folded in five octavo gatherings.

2138 IOWA. STATE HISTORICAL SOCIETY

CONSTITUTION OF THE STATE HISTORICAL SOCIETY OF IOWA ADOPTED AT IOWA CITY, FEBRUARY 7, 1857. PRINTED BY JEROME & DUNCAN. FEB. 22TH[!], 1861.

[1]–14, [15–16 blank]. 14.5 x 9.3 cm. Tan printed boards, with title on front cover.

Prov.: Signature of T. S. Parvin at head of front wrapper and note by him on back wrapper.

Ref.:

Jerome and Duncan operated at Iowa City.

2139 IOWA. SUPREME COURT

[Wrapper title] DECISION OF THE SUPREME COURT, OF THE STATE OF IOWA, IN THE CASE OF LAWRENCE SCOTT VS. IRA BABCOCK . . . 1850, FORT MADISON: PRINTED AT THE STATESMAN OFFICE, 1852.

[1]–13, [14–16 blank]. 23.9 x 15.6 cm. Yellow printed wrappers with title on front wrapper.

Ref.:

Earliest known printed decision of the Iowa Supreme Court, antedating by four years the earliest decision recorded in Moffit.—EDG

2140 IOWA. SUPREME COURT

SUPREME COURT OF IOWA, FIRST JUDICIAL DISTRICT. IN THE CASES OF HUGH T. REID VS. JAS. WRIGHT, AND JOHN M. YOUNG VS. HUGH T. REID. PETITION AND ARGUMENT FOR REHEARING, BY J. C. HALL AND HENRY W. STARR, ATTORNEYS FOR REID. BURLINGTON: PRINTED BY MORGAN & M'KENNY, 1850.

[1]–35, [36 blank]. 21.7 x 13.8 cm. Salmon printed wrappers, with title as above on front wrapper.

Ref.:

2141 IOWA. UNIVERSITY

CIRCULAR OF THE STATE UNIVERSITY OF IOWA, LOCATED AT IOWA CITY, IOWA. PUBLISHED BY THE UNIVERSITY. 1856.

[1]–16. 23.2 x 14.6 cm. White glazed printed wrappers, with title on front wrapper. Removed from bound volume. Lacks back wrapper.

Ref.: Steele p. 54

2142 IOWA. UNIVERSITY

REPORT OF THE JOINT COMMITTEE TO WHOM WAS REFERRED THE COMMUNICATION OF THE BOARD OF TRUSTEES OF THE STATE UNIVERSITY, TO THE GENERAL ASSEMBLY OF IOWA. IOWA CITY: D. A. MAHONY & J. B. DORR, 1855.

[1]–40. 19.5 x 12.9 cm. Stabbed, unbound.

Ref.: Steele p. 54

2143 IOWA TERRITORY. GOVERNOR (John Chambers)

GOVERNOR'S MESSAGE, TO BOTH HOUSES OF THE LEGISLATIVE ASSEMBLY OF THE TERRITORY OF IOWA, DELIVERED ON THE 8TH DAY OF DECEMBER, A. D. 1841.

[1]–8. 23 x 15.6 cm. Unbound leaflet, unopened in part.

Ref.:

Fitzpatrick, in his bibliography of the Iowa Territorial Documents, states: "The Governors Messages were ordered printed in comparatively large editions; and yet not one copy is now known to be preserved where it would naturally be expected." The Journal of the Council of the fourth legislative assembly of the Territory of Iowa begun and held at Iowa City, on the sixth day of December 1841 was printed by Jno. B. Russell at Bloomington and in the body of the Journal is found Governor Chambers' annual message. Fitzpatrick does not list this separate printing.—EDG

2144 IOWA TERRITORY. GOVERNOR (John Chambers)

[Caption title] GOVERNOR'S MESSAGE, DELIVERED MAY 8, 1845. FELLOW CITIZENS OF THE COUNCIL, AND OF THE HOUSE OF REPRESENTATIVES: . . .

[1]–8. 22.6 x 14.1 cm. Removed from bound volume, unbound, uncut and partly unopened.

Ref.: Steele p. 19

Contains also a letter to the Governor of Missouri regarding the boundary between Iowa and Missouri.

2145 IOWA TERRITORY. LEGISLATIVE ASSEMBLY

[Broadside] MEMORIAL IN REGARD TO THE OF[!] THE[!] RESERVED MINERAL LANDS, DRAWN BY THE HON. D. S. WILSON, OF DUBUQUE COUNTY, AND PASSED THE IOWA LEGISLATURE ON THE 17TH DEC. TO THE HONORABLE THE SENATE AND HOUSE OF REPRESENTATIVES IN CONGRESS ASSEMBLED: YOUR MEMORIALISTS, THE LEGISLATURE OF IOWA . . . [2 columns, 123 and 111 lines].

Broadside, 49.2 x 15.5 cm. Text, 40 x 11.6 cm.

Ref.: Fitzpatrick p. 38 see

Relates to change in laws regarding sale of lands without mineral rights.

In this copy the words "of the" in line 2 have been crossed out.

Fitzpatrick's *Bibliography of Iowa Territorial Documents*, p. 38, reports "ordered printed 240 copies of Mr. Wilson's report in regard to the sale of reserved mineral lands.—H.J. 8:43; December 12, 1845." This memorial dated Dec. 17th [1845] is not mentioned and may be unknown except in this copy.—EDG

2146 IOWA TERRITORY. SECRETARY OF THE TERRITORY (James Clarke)

COMMUNICATION FROM THE SECRETARY OF THE TERRITORY, MADE IN COMPLIANCE WITH A RESOLUTION OF THE HOUSE OF REPRESENTATIVES, ON THE SUBJECT OF THE LIABILITIES OF THE TERRITORY . . . BURLINGTON: J. H. M'KENNY, 1840.

[1]–6, [7–8 blank]. 23.2 x 16 cm. Unbound leaflet.

Ref.: Fitzpatrick p. 25

Signed on page 6: James Clarke, / Secretary of the Territory. / The Legislature ordered 200 copies printed.

2147 IOWA TERRITORY. SUPREME COURT

REPORTS OF THE DECISIONS OF THE SUPREME COURT OF IOWA, FROM THE ORGANIZATION OF THE TERRITORY IN JULY, 1838, TO DECEMBER, 1839, INCLUSIVE . . . BY WM. J. A. BRADFORD, REPORTER TO THE SUPREME COURT. GALENA: PRINTED BY WM. C. TAYLOR, 1840.

[1]–16, [1–iv], 17–20. 25.4 x 14.8 cm. Stabbed, plain tan wrappers, uncut.

Ref.: Byrd 536; Steele p. 55

The four pages misbound between pages 16 and 17 comprise a list of cases and an index.

2148 IOWA TERRITORY. SUPREME COURT

REPORTS OF THE DECISIONS OF THE SUPREME COURT OF IOWA. CASES ARGUED AND DECIDED AT THE JULY TERM, 1840 . . . BY WM. J. A. BRADFORD, REPORTER TO THE SUPREME COURT. IOWA CITY: PRINTED BY HUGHES & WILLIAMS, 1843.

[i]–iv, [5]–75, [76–78 blank]. 21.4 x 14.3 cm. Rebound in green morocco backstrip, green cloth sides.

Ref.: Fitzpatrick, p. 25; Steele p. 55

On the verso of the title leaf there is a list of the judges at the time of the decisions.

2149 IOWA TERRITORY. SUPREME COURT

REPORTS OF THE DECISIONS OF THE SUPREME COURT OF THE TERRITORY OF IOWA. CASES ARGUED AND DECIDED AT THE JULY TERM, 1841 . . . BY WM. J. A. BRADFORD, REPORTER TO THE SUPREME COURT. IOWA CITY: PRINTED BY VAN ANTWERP & HUGHES, 1841.

[i]–iv, [5]–62, [63–4 blank]. 21.4 x 14.3 cm. Rebound in blue morocco backstrip, blue cloth sides.

Ref.: Fitzpatrick p. 24; Steele p. 55

On the verso of the title leaf there is a list of the judges making the decisions.

Probably the first Iowa City imprint other than newspapers.

2150 IOWA TERRITORY. SUPREME COURT

IN THE SUPREME COURT OF IOWA. HIRAM BARNEY, PETITIONER VS. JONATHAN McCARTY, ET. AL., DEFENDANTS. AN APPEAL FROM LEE COUNTY, IOWA. ARGUMENT OF H. SCOTT HOWELL, SOLICITOR FOR HIRAM BARNEY, APPELLANT.

[i–ii], [1]–9, [10 blank]. 22.4 x 14.4 cm. Removed from bound volume, unbound.

Ref.:

The suit in question was started in January, 1859. The pamphlet was printed in 1859 or 1860, probably at Des Moines.

2151 IOWA CENTRAL AIR LINE RAILROAD COMPANY

FIRST ANNUAL REPORT OF THE PRESIDENT AND DIRECTORS TO THE STOCKHOLDERS OF THE IOWA CENTRAL AIR LINE RAILROAD COMPANY, AND EXHIBITS AND DOCUMENTS RELATING THERETO. JUNE 2D, 1858. CHICAGO: DAILY PRESS & TRIBUNE PRINTING ESTABLISHMENT, 1858.

[i–viii (vii–viii blank)], [1]–102, [103–04 blank]. 21.2 x 14.5 cm. Two maps on one sheet: Map of Iowa / Showing / the Line of the / Iowa Central / Air Line Rail Road / and the Boundaries / of its / Landgrant. / 25.5 x 40 cm. No scale given. Map: Map / of the / Iowa Central / Air Line Rail Road / Showing its / Eastern & Projected Western / Connections. / [lower centre:] Lith. of Ed. Mendel, Chicago, Ill. / 14.9 x 40 cm. No scale given. Buff printed wrappers with title on front wrapper.

Ref.: AII (*Chicago*) 335; Byrd 2951; Wheat (*Gold Rush*) 311; Wheat (*Transmississippi*) 949

2152 IOWA CITY. BOARD OF TRADE

SKETCH OF JOHNSON COUNTY, IOWA, WITH A REVIEW OF ITS EARLY HISTORY AND SUBSEQUENT DEVELOPMENT, ITS EDUCATIONAL, MANUFACTURING, AGRICULTURAL, AND OTHER INTERESTS. PUBLISHED BY IOWA CITY BOARD OF TRADE. IOWA CITY: REPUBLICAN STEAM PRINTING AND PUBLISHING COMPANY, NOVEMBER, 1880.

[1]–23, [24 blank]. 23 x 15.3 cm. Gray-blue printed wrappers, with short title on front wrapper.

Prov.: Embossed stamp of Iowa Masonic Library, / Cedar Rapids. / on title-page. Location symbol on verso of title-page in pencil.

Ref.:

2153 IOWA CITY REPUBLICAN LEAF-LETS

[Caption title] EARLY IOWA. THE IOWA CITY RE-PUBLICAN LEAFLET—NO. 1 [–18]. SEPTEMBER 15, 1880 [–JUNE 15, 1881] . . .

[1]–90. 26.2 x 16.8 cm. Unbound, uncut. In a blue-green cloth case.

Ref.:

The text stops in the middle of a sentence at the foot of page 90, but this seems to be all printed. Accompanying the leaflets is the same text for the last portion of the leaflet (pages [47]–90) with the caption title: *Early Settlement of Johnson County.* The text is also incomplete, as above. According to W. J. Petersen, the copy belonging to the State Historical Society of Iowa is identical with this one.

2154 IOWA CITY STANDARD, THE

[Newspaper] THE IOWA CITY STANDARD . . . VOL. 1. IOWA CITY, I. T., FRIDAY, OCTOBER 22, 1841. NO. 47. IN THIS PAPER THE ORDERS, LAWS, RESOLVES AND PUBLIC TREATIES OF THE UNITED STATES ARE PUBLISHED BY AUTHORITY . . .

Newspaper, [1–4]. 51.5 x 40.2 cm. Six columns.

Ref.:

Edited by William Crum.

2155 IOWA RAILROAD LAND COMPANY

CHOICE IOWA FARMING LANDS. 1,000,000 ACRES, FOR SALE AT LOW PRICES ON CREDIT OR FOR CASH, BY THE IOWA RAILROAD LAND COMPANY, IN TRACTS TO SUIT PURCHASERS. CEDAR RAPIDS, IOWA, 1870.

[1]–[64]. 22.9 x 14.8 cm. 27 illustrations of Bridges' Ready-Made Houses, full-page map, and one illustration on recto of back wrapper. Map: Outline Map / of / Iowa / showing location of / lands belonging to the / Iowa Rail Road Land Company. / [lower left:] Chicago Lithographing Co. / 11.9 x 20.5 cm. No scale given. Lavender printed wrappers, with title as above on front wrapper.

Ref.: AII (*Chicago*) 1711; *Railway Economics* p. 216 see

Laid in is a broadside form: If you wish a copy of the Iowa Rail Road Company's Pamphlet . . . / [5 lines] /. 11.9 x 20.4 cm.

The following imprint appears at the foot of the front wrapper: Horton & Leonard, Printers, 108 and 110 Randolph Street, Chicago. /

2156 IOWA WESTERN RAILROAD COMPANY

REPORT OF THE ENGINEER OF THE IOWA WESTERN RAILROAD: (MADE NOV. 27, 1851.) WITH AN AP-PENDIX CONTAINING THE GENERAL INCORPORATION ACT OF IOWA, THE ARTICLES OF ASSOCIATION OF THE I. W. R. R. COMPANY, THE ACT OF THE GEN. ASSEMBLY GRANTING THE RIGHT OF WAY, &C. &C. . . . MUSCATINE: PRINTED BY H. D. LA. COSSITT, 1851.

[1]–20. 21.7 x 13.5 cm. Green printed wrappers with title on front wrapper, list of officers on verso of back wrapper.

Ref.:

2157 IRVING, JOHN T., JR.

INDIAN SKETCHES, TAKEN DURING AN EXPEDITION TO THE PAWNEE TRIBES . . . PHILADELPHIA: CAREY, LEA AND BLANCHARD, 1835.

[1]–4, [9]–272. [1–2], [5]–296. 18.8 x 11.4 cm. Two volumes, green cloth, stamped in gilt on backstrips.

Ref.: Field 764; Howes I79; Hubach p. 75; Jones 973; Rader 2026; Sabin 35116; Wagner-Camp 55

2158 IRVING, WASHINGTON

ASTORIA; OR, ANECDOTES OF AN ENTERPRISE BEYOND THE ROCKY MOUNTAINS . . . PHILADELPHIA: CAREY, LEA, & BLANCHARD, 1836.

[1]–6, [vii]–xii, [13]–285, [286 blank]. [i]–viii, [9]–279, [280 blank], [281–88 advertisements]. 21.6 x 13.7 cm. Folding map: Sketch / of / the Routes of / Hunt & Stuart. / 24.3 x 45.4 cm. No scale given. Two volumes, plum cloth, title in gilt on backstrips.

Ref.: Bradford 2623; Howes I81; Langfeld & Blackburn p. 35; Sabin 35130; Smith 5023; Wagner-Camp 61; Wheat (*Transmississippi*) 419

Langfeld & Blackburn do not mention plum cloth. The present copy carries the map in Volume I, a printed copyright notice on the verso of the first title-page, and the signature 1 on page 5.

2159 IRVING, WASHINGTON

THE CRAYON MISCELLANY . . . PHILADELPHIA: CAREY, LEA, & BLANCHARD, 1835.

[i]–[xvi, xvi blank], [17]–274, [275–76 blank], [1–24 advertisements]. 18.1 x 11.1 cm. Green cloth, printed white paper label on backstrip: The / Crayon / Miscellany. / [short rule] / A / Tour / of the / Prairies. / By the Author of / The / Sketch Book. / [thick and thin and thin and thick rules at top and bottom]

Ref.: Howes I86; Langfeld & Blackburn page 33; Rader 2029; Sabin 35139; Wagner-Camp 56

First issue of the label.

2160 IRVING, WASHINGTON

THE ROCKY MOUNTAINS; OR, SCENES, INCIDENTS, AND ADVENTURES IN THE FAR WEST . . . PHILADELPHIA: CAREY, LEA, & BLANCHARD, 1837.

[1]–[10, 10 blank], [xi]–xvi, [17]–248. [i]–[viii, viii blank], [9]–248. 19.1 x 11.3 cm. Folding map in each volume: A / Map / of the / Sources of the / Colorado & Big Salt Lake, / Platte, Yellow-Stone, Muscle-Shell, / Missouri; & Salmon & Snake Rivers, / branches of the / Columbia River. / Eng^d by S Stiles. New-York. / 41.6 x 39.2 cm. Scale: about 23 miles to one inch. Map: Map / of the / Territory West of the / Rocky Mountains. / Eng^d by S. Stiles. 43.6 x 41.6 cm. Scale: 50 miles to one inch. Two volumes, blue cloth, printed white paper labels on backstrips.

Ref.: Howes I85; Langfeld & Blackburn pp. 36–7; Rader 2028; Sabin 35195; Smith 5046; Wagner-Camp 67

In each volume, there is an endpaper front and back and a fly-leaf front and back; there are no advertisements, as required by Langfeld and Blackburn.

2161 IRVING, WASHINGTON

UN TOUR DANS LES PRAIRIES A L'OUEST DES ETATS-UNIS, . . . TOURS: R. PORNIN ET CIE, 1845.

[i–iv], 1–296. 17.4 x 10.5 cm. Three engraved plates and engraved title-page: Un Tour / dans les Prairies / à l'Ouest des Etats-Unis, / Traduit de l'Anglais de Washington-Irving[!], / Par Ernest W.*** / [vignette] / Je criai à Beatte de ne point tirer, il était trop tard! / Tours, / R. Pornin et Cie. Imp-Libraires. / Black cloth, blind and gilt panels on sides, gilt back.

Ref.: Howes I86; Langfeld & Blackburn p. 76; Rader 2029 note; Sabin 35143

Stamped beneath the imprint on the printed title-page is the following: New-York / Roe Lockwood & Son / American and Foreign Books. 411 Broadway /.

2162 ISBELL, F. A.

1852–1870. MINING AND HUNTING IN THE FAR WEST . . .

[1]–41, [42 blank]. 23 x 14.4 cm. Portrait. Dark purple embossed boards with title on front cover in gilt.

Refs.: Howes I87

Imprint on verso of title-leaf: J. S. Stewart, Printer and Bookbinder, Middletown, Conn. Probably printed in 1870 or 1871.

Mining and hunting, chiefly the latter, in California and Idaho.

Note similarity of format between this and Clark, Austin S.: *Reminiscences* . . .

2163 ITURBIDE, AUGUSTIN DE

[Print, lithograph:] [title in circular form] AUGUSTIN, 1ST CONSTITUTIONAL EMPEROR OF MEXICO. 1822. / D. DIGHTON FOR W. BULLOCK, FROM AN ORIGINAL DRAWING IN THE / POSSESSION OF GEN^L WAVILL. / PRINTED BY C. HULLMANDEL. / 29.4 x 20.8 cm. (page size). Folded.

Bound in Iturbide: *A Statement of Some of the Principal Events* . . . 1824.

2164 ITURBIDE, AUGUSTIN DE

SIGNATURE, clipped. 7.2 x 10 cm.

Bound in Iturbide: *A Statement of Some of the Principal Events* . . . 1824.

2165 ITURBIDE, AUGUSTIN DE

SEAL, red wax, 3.5 x 3. cm., set in mount.

Bound in Iturbide: *A Statement of Some of the Principal Events* . . . 1824.

2166 ITURBIDE, AUGUSTIN DE

A STATEMENT OF SOME OF THE PRINCIPAL EVENTS IN THE PUBLIC LIFE OF AUGUSTIN DE ITURBIDE, WRITTEN BY HIMSELF . . . LONDON: JOHN MURRAY, MDCCCXXIV.

[i]–[xxiv, xxiv blank], [1]–157, [158 blank]. 20.7 x 13.1 cm. Contemporary full polished calf, blind and gilt borders, gilt backstrip, large green leather label on front cover, marbled edges.

Prov.: Inscribed on front fly-leaf: W. D. Fellowes Esqr / With the compliments / of the Translator /. With an Autograph Letter, signed, by Michael J. Quin, the translator, presenting the copy to Fellowes. With the bookplate and leather label of Dorset Fellowes.

Ref.: Palau 122182; Sabin 35296

Extra-illustrated by W. Dorset Fellowes with numerous newspaper clippings mounted on blank pages and the following manuscript materials: Autograph Manuscript Note by Fellowes regarding his own association with Iturbide, 2 pages; Autograph Letter, signed, by Lord Torrington, 3 pages; Autograph Letter, signed, by Lord Torrington, 3 pages; Autograph Manuscript Copy by Fellowes of a newspaper article, 2 pages; Autograph Letter, signed, by Michael J. Quin, 3 pages, with Fellowes' reply on fourth page; Autograph Letter, signed, by Michael J. Quin, 3 pages, with note by Fellowes on fourth page; Clipped signature of George Canning; Autograph Letter, signed, by Michael J. Quin, 2 pages; [Print, lithograph:] Augustin, 1st Constitutional Emperor of Mexico, 1822. / D. Dighton for W. Bullock, from an original Drawing in the / Possession of Genl Wavill. / Printed by C. Hullmandel. /; Seal of Iturbide, in sunken mount; One line of manuscript and signature of Iturbide; Clipped signature of A. de Iturbide, son of the Emperor; Autograph Letter, signed, by Vicomte Rocafuerte, 2 pages; Autograph Letter, signed, by Vicomte Rocafuerte, 2 pages, with Autograph Note, signed, by Torrington on second page; Autograph Letter, signed in the third person, by Vicomte Rocafuerte, one page, with Autograph Manuscript Note, signed, by Fellowes on verso; Calling card of General Paroissien; Calling card of Domingo B. y Briceño; several marginal manuscript notes by Fellowes; notes on the seal and Iturbide signatures by Quin.

2167 ITURBIDE, AUGUSTIN DE, the Younger

SIGNATURE, clipped. 1.5 x 10.5 cm.

Bound in Iturbide: *A Statement of Some of the Principal Events* . . . 1824.

2168 IVINS, VIRGINIA WILCOX

PEN PICTURES OF EARLY WESTERN DAYS . . . COPYRIGHTED 1905.

[1]–157, [158 blank]. (Pages [1–2] blank.) 22.1 x 14.6 cm. Five illustrations and a series of illuminated initials, unlisted. Green cloth, title in gilt on front cover.

Ref.: Cowan p. 306; Howes I93

Reminiscences of Iowa and a trip overland to California in 1853. Printed at Keokuk.

2169 IVINS, VIRGINIA WILCOX

ANOTHER COPY. Inscribed by the author.

2170 IVINS, VIRGINIA WILCOX

YESTERDAYS. REMINISCENSES[!] OF LONG AGO . . .*

[1]–107, [108 blank]. 20.1 x 13.6 cm. Four illustrations and a series of illuminated initials, unlisted. Dark blue cloth, title in gilt on front cover.

Ref.: Howes I94

Reminiscences of early life in Iowa. Howes supplies place and date as [Keokuk, 1908].

2171 IVINS, VIRGINIA WILCOX

THE SAME . . . COPYRIGHTED 1908.

[3]–160. 21.4 x 14.4 cm. Five illustrations and a series of illuminated initials, unlisted. Red cloth, with title in gilt on front cover.

Ref.: Howes I93

Rewritten and with much additional material. Printed at Keokuk.

J

2172 JACK, JOHN H.

AUTOGRAPH DOCUMENT, SIGNED. 1860 August 3, Shirt tail District, [Colorado Territory]. One page, 10.1 x 18.4 cm.

Certificate of James W. Hamilton's claim No. 8 in the Jack Lode. Docket on verso.

There is a manuscript note under Shirt tail District as follows: Now Idaho /.

2173 JACK, O. G.

A BRIEF HISTORY OF MUSCATINE; GIVING ITS LOCATION, EARLY SETTLEMENT, TRADE, MANUFACTURES, FINE RESIDENCES, BUSINESS HOUSES, ETC., TOGETHER WITH MANY ACCIDENTS AND INCIDENTS . . . MUSCATINE, IOWA: JOURNAL BOOK AND JOB PRINTING HOUSE, 1870.*

[1]–80. 21.1 x 14 cm. Blue printed wrappers, with title on front wrapper, advertisements on verso of front and recto and verso of back wrapper.

Ref.: Howes J2

Inserted at back is a yellow slip (7.7 x 12.5 cm.) headed Erratum. A smaller green slip has been removed.

2174 JACKSON, A. P., & E. C. COLE

OKLAHOMA! POLITICALLY AND TOPOGRAPHICALLY DESCRIBED. HISTORY AND GUIDE TO THE INDIAN TERRITORY. BIOGRAPHICAL SKETCHES OF CAPT. DAVID L. PAYNE, W. L. COUCH, WM. H. OSBORN, AND OTHERS . . . KANSAS CITY, MO.: RAMSEY, MILLETT & HUDSON.

[1]–150, [151–52 advertisements]. 18.9 x 13.1 cm. 28 illustrations and numerous vignettes, unlisted, and map: [Oklahoma] / [lower left:] Ramsey, Millett & Hudson. Engr's. K. C. / 31 x 42 cm. No scale given. Tan pictorial wrappers, with title on front wrapper, advertisements on verso of front and recto of back wrapper. In a red cloth case.

Ref.: Bradford 2626a; Howes J3; Rader 2032

Copyrighted on wrapper 1885.

2175 JACKSON, HENRY

[Map] MAP OF KANSAS / WITH PARTS OF NEIGHBORING STATES AND TERRITORIES. / PREPARED BY ORDER OF MAJ. GEN. J. M. SCHOFIELD U. S. A. / COMPILED UNDER DIRECTION OF 1ST LIEUT. HENRY JACKSON, 7TH U. S. CAVALRY, MARCH 1870. / [lower left corner:] PHOTO LITH BY EZRA A. COOK & CO. CHICAGO. [lower right corner:] DRAWN BY ADO HUNNIUS. /

Map, 54.5 x 81.6 cm. (map only) Printed on linen. Scale: 20 miles to one inch.

Prov.: In upper right corner; Geo Robinson / Asst [balance illegible] /. From Grierson Papers.
Ref.:

2176 JACKSON, JOSEPH H.

THE ADVENTURES AND EXPERIENCE OF JOSEPH H. JACKSON: DISCLOSING THE DEPTHS OF MORMON VILLANY[!] PRACTICED IN NAUVOO. WARSAW: PRINTED FOR THE PUBLISHER, 1846.

[1]–36. 18.3 x 11 cm. Yellow printed wrappers with title on front wrapper. Back wrapper supplied.
Ref.: Byrd 1080; Howes J24
Editions: Warsaw, 1844.

2177 JACKSON, JOSEPH H.

A NARRATIVE OF THE ADVENTURES AND EXPERIENCE OF JOSEPH H. JACKSON, IN NAUVOO, DISCLOSING THE DEPTHS OF MORMON VILLAINY. WARSAW, ILLINOIS, AUGUST, 1844.

[1]–32. 20.7 x 13.8 cm. Tan printed wrappers with title on front wrapper. In a brown cloth case.
Ref.: Byrd 870; Howes J24; Sabin 35443

2178 JACKSON, WILLIAM A.

[Map] MAP / OF THE / MINING DISTRICT / OF / CALIFORNIA / BY / WM. A. JACKSON. / PUBLISHED BY LAMBERT & LANE / 69 WALL ST. NEW YORK. / [below border:] ENTERED ACCORDING TO ACT OF CONGRESS IN THE YEAR 1851 BY LAMBERT & LANE IN THE CLERKS OFFICE OF THE DISTRICT COURT OF THE SOUTHERN DISTRICT OF NEW YORK. /

Map, 58.4 x 49.1 cm. No scale given. Folded into maroon cloth covers, 15 x 9.5 cm., with title stamped in gilt on front cover.
Ref.: Phillips (*Maps*) p. 185; Wheat (*Gold Rush*) 196

Accompanying the map and bound in the folder is the following pamphlet: Appendix / to / Jackson's Map / of the / Mining Districts of California, / bringing down / all the Discoveries since 1849, / to the present time, / of the placers and all descriptions of / vein mines, to which so much atten-/tion is at this time directed. / -Also,- / the new towns built and located, / with the boundaries of the counties, and the seats / of justice in each. / [short rule] / Second Edition, Revised and Enlarged. / [rule] / New-York: / Lambert & Lane, 69 Wall-Street. / [short rule] / 1851. / Pages [1]–16, [17–18 blank]. 14.6 x 9.6 cm.
Editions: New York, 1850.

2179 JACKSON, WILLIAM A.

[Map, facsimile] MAP / OF THE / MINING DISTRICT / -OF- / CALIFORNIA, / -BY- / W.^{M} A. JACK-

SON. / [rule] / [lower left:] ENTERED ACCORDING TO ACT OF CONGRESS IN THE YEAR 1850 BY THEODORE A. MUDGE IN THE CLERK'S OFFICE OF THE DISTRICT COURT OF THE SOUTHERN DISTRICT OF NEW YORK [lower right:] LAMBERT & LANE'S LITH. N.^{O} 69 WALL ST. N.Y. /

Folding map, 44 x 44 cm. No scale given. Folded into red cloth covers, 15.4 x 9.3 cm., lettered on front cover: 1850 / Jackson's Map of / California / With Appendix / [vignette] /.
Ref.: Heller & Magee 258; Wheat (*Gold Rush*) 161 note

Reprint of San Francisco, 1936. Accompanying the map and bound in with it is: [wrapper title] Appendix / to / Jackson's Map / of the / Mining District / of / California. / [1–12].

The "Appendix" was reproduced from a copy owned by John Howell and the map from Thomas W. Norris' collection, both were for Mr. Norris, December, 1936. Printed at the Grabhorn Press.

2180 JACKSON, W. H. & S. A. LONG

THE TEXAS STOCK DIRECTORY; OR, BOOK OF MARKS AND BRANDS . . . SAN ANTONIO: PRINTED AT THE HERALD OFFICE, 1865.

[i–ii], [1]–402, [1]–50 advertisements. (Page [i] blank, [ii] To Stockraisers: /.) 15.9 x 11 cm. Frontispiece and one illustration, both on yellow paper. Salmon printed boards, brown cloth back, with title on front cover, calendar for 1866 mounted on inner front cover.
Prov.: Signature on title-page: Th. Koester / [underline] /.
Ref.: Adams (*Ramp. Herd*) 1142; Howes J28; Raines p. 125

Th. Koester, the original owner, is listed on page 147. Some copies appear in gray boards. Many errors corrected by hand according to Adams. Page 266 follows 268, p. 370 is unfoliated. A supplement was issued in 1866.

2181 JACKSON, WILLIAM H., & CO.

NINE ORIGINAL PHOTOGRAPHS OF SCENES ON THE PIKE'S PEAK TOLL ROAD, 1888.

Photographs: 18.8 x 23.9 cm. Mounts: 20.2 x 25.3 cm. Nine photographs, loose, each mounted on dark brown cardboard, gilt edges, versos gray, each stamped with: W. H. Jackson & Co., -Photographs of- / Rocky [ornament] Mountain [ornament] Scenery, / Denver, Colorado. /

The series comprises the following photographs:

3400—Pike's Peak Toll Road. The Start from Cascade. W.H.J. & Co /

3402—Toll Gate—Pike's Peak Wagon Road. W.H.J. & Cº /

3404—Signal Sta. Summit of Pike's Peak. "Press Excursion," Seᴾ 6ᵗʰ 1888 W.H.J. & Cº /

3405—The Toll Gate—Pike's Peak Carriage Road. W.H.J. & Cº /

3406—Pike's Peak Carriage Road—Near the Toll Gate. W.H.J. & Cº /

3407—Pike's Peak Carriage Road, Near the Toll Gate / W.H.J. & Cº /

3408—The "W." Pike's Peak Carriage Road. W.H.J. & Cº /

3411—Rocks by the Road Side—Pike's Peak Carriage Road—W.H.J. & Cº /

3412—Grand View—Pike's Peak Carriage Road. W.H.J. & Cº /

2182 JACKSON (Kansas Territory) MINING DISTRICT

[Broadside] KANSAS TERRITORY, / JACKSON DISTRICT JACKSON / MINING DISTRICT. / BE IT KNOWN THAT [in manuscript: J W Hamilton] / IS THE OWNER, BY PREEMPTION, OF [in manuscript: Quartz] MINING CLAIM NO. [in manuscript: 6] . . . GIVEN UNDER MY HAND IN JACKSON DISTRICT THIS [in manuscript: 31ˢᵀ] DAY / OF [in manuscript: January] A. D. 1861. / [in manuscript: W. B. Lawrence] RECORDER. PRESIDENT. [below border at centre:] ROCKY MOUNTAIN HERALD PRINT. /

Broadside, 10.4 x 20.1 cm. Text, 9.5 x 17.5 cm.
Ref.:
Endorsed in manuscript on verso.
Applies to General Scott Lode in Jackson District. Claim No. 6.

2183 JACOB, JOHN G.

THE LIFE AND TIMES OF PATRICK GASS, NOW THE SOLE SURVIVOR OF THE OVERLAND EXPEDITION TO THE PACIFIC, UNDER LEWIS AND CLARK, IN 1804–5–6 . . . WELLSBURG, VA.: JACOB & SMITH, 1859.*

[i]–viii, [9]–280. 18 x 11.9 cm. Four plates and two vignettes. Dark brown cloth.
Ref.: Howes J31; Jones 1411; Smith 5081; Thomson 639; Wagner-Camp 6 note

2184 JACOB, JOHN J.

AUTOGRAPH LETTER SIGNED. 1826 March 13. Cumberland. One page, 24.7 x 19.4 cm. To Michael Cresap and Michael Cresap, Jr.

Relating to the author's *Biographical Sketch . . . of Capt. Michael Cresap . . .* 1826. The recipients are asked to secure depositions from Captain George Cox and John Caldwell. Jacob states he will delay publication of his book until they are in his hands. He also mentions certificates from Mr. Machen and Squire Lane. The requested depositions were not published.

2185 JACOB, JOHN J.

A BIOGRAPHICAL SKETCH OF THE LIFE OF THE LATE CAPT. MICHAEL CRESAP. CUMBERLAND, MD.: PRINTED FOR THE AUTHOR, BY J. M. BUCHANAN, 1826.

A⁸, B⁴, C–I⁶, K⁸. (Bound as an 18mo, A and B signed on last leaf of gatherings.) [1]–[124]. 16.9 x 10.5 cm. Marbled boards, sheepskin corners and back, title lettered in gilt on back.
Prov.: Inscribed on the title-page: Neville B. Craig / Presented by / T C Atkinson Esq. / Bookplate of Isaac Craig inside front cover partly covering booklabel of Mechanics' Circulating Library dated Cumberland, 1841. In an unidentified hand, on the front endleaf: The Cresap Family from / the Allegany Mountains / to the top of the Alps / The Cresap family from the / "Allegany m /. On the next blank leaf: The Cresap Family from / the Allegany mountains / to the top of the Alps /.
Ref.: Field 769; Howes J32; Sabin 35488; Thomson 640
Jacob's *Biographical Sketch* contains a violent attack on Jefferson's treatment of Cresap. Lawrence Wroth points out in his sensible biographical sketch in DAB that Jefferson did suppress facts in his discussion of the Cresap case.
Laid in is an Autograph Letter signed by Jacob to Michael Cresap and Michael Cresap, Jr. asking for depositions from Captain George Cox and John Caldwell for use in the book. The depositions were not included in the work.

2186 JACOB, UDNEY H.

AN EXTRACT, FROM A MANUSCRIPT ENTITLED THE PEACE MAKER; OR, THE DOCTRINES OF THE MILLENIUM: BEING A TREATISE ON RELIGION AND JURISPRUDENCE. OR A NEW SYSTEM OF RELIGION AND POLITICKS . . . NAUVOO, ILL.: J. SMITH, PRINTER. 1842.

[1]–37, [38–40 blank]. 19.8 x 13.1 cm. Stabbed, unbound. Worn, outer corners clipped off, not affecting text.
Prov.: Inscribed on title-page: George Lamb his / Book Bought Nauvoo / Illinoise[!] /. And in pencil on same page: George Lambs / Property /. Auerbach copy.
Ref.: Byrd 717; Howes J34
Jacob's pamphlet was a crucial step in Joseph Smith's campaign to popularize plural marriages among the Mormons. Smith may have inspired the work although he later denounced it.

2187 JACOBS, BELA

A VOICE FROM THE WEST. REV. BELA JACOBS' RE-
PORT OF HIS TOUR IN THE WESTERN STATES, PER-
FORMED IN THE SPRING AND SUMMER OF 1833 . . .
BOSTON: J. HOWE, 1833.

[1]–[28]. 21.6 x 13.4 cm. Removed from bound
volume, unbound.

Ref.: Buck 259; Howes J36; Rusk II p. 115;
Sabin 35497

The "Western States" at that time were
Ohio, Indiana, Illinois, etc.

Small rubber stamp on title-page reading:
Sabin's bibl. No. followed by the number in
pencil: 34597 / but this is repeating Sabin's
typographical error for 35497.

2188 JAMES, EDWIN

ACCOUNT OF AN EXPEDITION FROM PITTSBURGH TO
THE ROCKY MOUNTAINS, PERFORMED IN THE YEARS
1819 AND '20 . . . UNDER THE COMMAND OF MA-
JOR STEPHEN H. LONG . . . PHILADELPHIA: H. C.
CAREY AND I. LEA, 1823.

[i–iv], [1]–[8], [1]–503, [504 blank]. [i–vi, vi
blank], [1]–442, [i]–xcviii. 24.5 x 15 cm. Two
volumes, original gray boards, rebacked with
with darker gray paper, with original printed
paper labels, 4.7 x 3.4 cm.: Major Long's / Expedition / to the / Rocky Mountains. / Vol.
I [–II]. /, uncut. In a red cloth case.

Ref.: Bradford 2637; Field 772 (1830 edn.);
Howes J41; Jones 852 (1830 edn.); Rader 2046;
Sabin 35682; Wagner-Camp 25

Notable government expedition [commanded
by Maj. Stephen H. Long], supplementing earlier discoveries of Pike and of Lewis and Clark,
and pronouncing the plains region as nothing
but a desert, incapable of cultivation! The atlas
volume of the original edition is dated 1822.—
Howes

In the second volume, the last portion carries
a separate title-page on page [i]: Astronomical
and Meteorological / Records, / and / Vocabularies of Indian Languages, / Taken on the / Expedition for Exploring / the / Mississippi and its
Western Waters, / under the Command of Major S. H. Long, / of the United States' Topographical Engineers, / in 1819 and 1820. / [dia-
mond rule] / Philadelphia: / 1822. /

ACCOMPANIED BY:

ACCOUNT OF AN EXPEDITION FROM PITTSBURGH TO
THE ROCKY MOUNTAINS PERFORMED IN THE YEARS
1819–20 . . . MAPS AND PLATES. PHILADELPHIA:
H. C. CAREY AND I. LEA, 1822.

[i–iv], two double-page maps, eight plates (one
colored), and two "Vertical Sections" on one
double-page plate. 30.1 x 24 cm. Map: Country / drained by the / Mississippi / Eastern Section. / ͏[rule] / Scale of Miles / [diagrammatic
scale: 75 miles to one inch]. *Inset:* Country / of
the / Mississippi / below the 33ᵈ deg. N. Lat. /
[rule] / Scale of Miles. / [diagrammatic scale:
about 100 miles to one inch] / 8.4 x 9.5 cm. Scale
as above. *Inset:* Profile or Vertical Section of the
Country / on the Parallel of Latitude 38 degrees
North. / 4.6 x 26.3 cm. [lower left:] Drawn by
S. H. Long Maj. T. Engineers. / [centre:] For the
Expedition to the Rocky Mountains Vol. I. /
[lower right:] Engrav'd by Young & Delleker. /
41.6 x 26.9 cm. Scale as above. Map: Country /
drained by the / Mississippi / Western Section. /
[rule] / Scale of Miles. / [diagrammatic scale: 75
miles to one inch] / *Inset:* Profile or Vertical
Section of the Country / on the Parallel of Latitude 38 degrees North. / 4.7 x 26.5 cm. [lower
left:] Drawn by S. H. Long Maj. T. Engineers. /
[centre:] For the Expedition to the Rocky
Mountains Vol. II. / [right:] Engrav'd by Young
& Delleker. / 41.6 x 27 cm. Scale as above.
Original brown boards, lighter brown paper
backstrip, printed paper label on front cover:
5.8 x 11 cm.: Maps and Plates / for / Major
Long's Expedition / to the / Rocky Mountains. /
[within decorative border].

2189 JAMES, EDWIN

A NARRATIVE OF THE CAPTIVITY AND ADVENTURES
OF JOHN TANNER, (U. S. INTERPRETER AT THE
SAUT[!] DE STE. MARIE,) DURING THIRTY YEARS
RESIDENCE AMONG THE INDIANS IN THE INTERIOR
OF NORTH AMERICA . . . NEW-YORK: G. & C. H.
CARVILL, 1830.

[1]–426. 23.5 x 14.8 cm. Portrait. Tan boards,
green cloth backstrip, white printed paper label,
6.1 x 3.4 cm., on backstrip: [thick and thin
rules] / Tanner's / Narrative / of / Thirty
Years' / Residence / Among / The Indians / of /
North America. / [thin and thick rules] /, uncut.

Ref.: Ayer 290; Butler (*Chippewa*) 148; Field
772; Howes J42; Jones 911; Sabin 35684; Wagner-Camp 40

2190 JAMES, JASON W.

MEMORIES AND VIEWPOINTS . . . ROSWELL, NEW
MEXICO: PRIVATELY PRINTED, 1928.

[1]–183, [184 blank]. 18.3 x 12.4 cm. Gray cloth.

Prov.: Inscribed on front endleaf: To H M.
Sender / With the Compliments / and best
wishes of the / Author / Jason W. James / Camp
Wood Tex. / April 28ᵗʰ 1933 / My Nintieth[!]
birth / day. / Jarvies (?) Beach (?) /.

Ref.: Howes J46

Buffalo hunting; ranching on the Rio
Grande; with Johnston's Utah expedition in
1858, etc.—Howes

2191 JAMES, JESSE E.

JESSE JAMES, MY FATHER . . . PUBLISHED AND DIS-
TRIBUTED BY JESSE JAMES, JR. . . . KANSAS CITY,
MO. INDEPENDENCE, MISSOURI: THE SENTINEL
PRINTING CO., 1899.

[1]–194. 19 X 13 cm. Four portraits. White
printed wrappers, with title on front wrapper,
advertisement of author's loan business on verso
of back wrapper, title down backstrip. In a light
brown buckram case.

Prov.: Inscribed inside front cover: For /
Frank R. Billingslea / From A. B. Macdonald /
The Author / Kansas City, Mo / Sept 7, 1931 /.

Ref.: Adams 560; Howes J48; Rader 2059

Macdonald was an oldtime newspaper writer
in Kansas City and may have ghost-written the
pamphlet.

2192 JAMES, JOHN

MY EXPERIENCE WITH INDIANS . . . AUSTIN: GAM-
MEL'S BOOK STORE.*

[1]–147, [148 blank]. 18.9 x 13.2 cm. 22 illustrations, unlisted. Black cloth.

Ref.: Rader 2060
Copyrighted 1925.

2193 JAMES, THOMAS

THREE YEARS AMONG THE INDIANS AND MEXI-
CANS . . . WATERLOO, ILL.: PRINTED AT THE OF-
FICE OF THE "WAR EAGLE," 1846.

[i–iv], [1]–130, [131–32 blank]. (Pages [i–ii]
blank.) 22.4 x 14.5 cm. Yellow wrappers. In blue
half morocco case.

Ref.: Byrd 1082; Howes J49; Jones 1125;
Rader 2065; Wagner-Camp 121

One of the earliest narratives of the fur-trade;
covering experiences on the upper Missouri in
1809, and an expedition to Santa Fé, in 1821.
Written from James' dictation by Nathan Niles,
who, resenting local newspaper criticism, destroyed nearly all copies.—Howes

The first copy of James' work to turn up
came into the collection of the Missouri Historical Society, St. Louis, Missouri, in 1909 or 1910.
Realizing the importance and rarity of the
James narrative, this Society issued a reprint in
1916 under the able editorship of Walter B.
Douglas.

In the preface to the reprint Mr. Douglas
stated that during the six or seven years between
the time of acquiring the original edition and
publishing the reprint, the Society made a careful search, but the only other copy of the Waterloo edition they could hear of was sold in Philadelphia in 1912 and they could never discover
the buyer.

In April 1936 I was in St. Louis on business
and during the late afternoon I stepped into
Hyke's Book Store at 1019 Locust Street. I had
never met Mr. Hyke before but I told him about
my interest in books and pamphlets relating to
the west, and asked him what he had of interest.
Somewhat facetiously, I asked him if he had a
copy of the James book. Hyke, assuming I was
referring to the 1916 reprint, apologized because
he didn't happen to have a copy. But I said, "I
am interested in the original edition." Where-
upon he almost floored me by going to a filing
case and bringing forth a parcel, which, when
opened, proved to be a copy of the Waterloo
edition. This copy lacked the final leaf and had
been left with him for sale a few days before by
a man from up near Springfield, Illinois. Of
course I bought the copy, imperfect as it was,
secured a photostat of the last leaf through the
kindness of the Missouri Historical Society, and
had the copy fixed up. But I was never happy
with it. I urged Hyke to keep his eyes open and
find a complete and perfect copy for me, never
having any real hope of his finding one. Much to
my surprise I received a letter from him in December of that same year, telling me he had located a fine copy with the original plain yellow
wrappers, in a college library. The copy had only
been discovered by the institution's librarian
two weeks before, and Hyke wasn't at all sure
they would sell it. Later correspondence developed the fact that this copy was in the possession
of St. Louis University, a Jesuit institution
founded in 1818 as a Latin Academy, and the
repository of Father de Smet's letter-books and
papers,—a fact that had considerable bearing
later on their decision to sell the James book. I
went down to St. Louis in June 1937 and Hyke
and I went out to see the book and to talk to
Father Reignet, the Librarian. They had not yet
decided to sell. Finally in October of that year,
Hyke wrote me that Father Reignet "was now
authorized to sell—he is now working on the
Father de Smet collection and is anxious to get
money for that purpose." Again I went to St.
Louis and Hyke and I went out to the University to be greeted by the news that Father Reignet was "in retreat" and couldn't be seen. We
got word to him through one of the priests, and
finally he appeared and we consummated the
purchase of the book. That is the end of the
story, except that Hyke told one of his newspaper friends "in confidence" about the transac-
tion and the *St. Louis Post Dispatch* the following Sunday carried the story. One or two of the
Chicago papers copied some of it, and as a result
some of my friends were curious to see the vol-

ume, and I think they thought I was crazy to pay such a high price for the little pamphlet.

I turned the defective copy over to a dealer, who of course had no trouble in disposing of it.

Wright Howes and I made two visits to the old town of Waterloo, Illinois, where this book was printed. It had a population of about 2500 and is a short drive south of St. Louis. The first visit was in 1940 and we went to the public library to talk to the librarian about the James book. We soon learned that almost everybody in Waterloo had heard about it. A copy had turned up in Waterloo some fifteen to twenty years before in a basketful of old books which some junkman in town bought for 50¢. This copy was disposed of to Dr. Rosenbach, the famed antiquarian bookseller, at a fancy price, so many people in Waterloo were on the lookout for the book. As far as I know no other copy has ever been found around Waterloo. I was there again in 1942, but learned nothing new.

Early in 1952 Mr. Charles van Ravenswaay of the Missouri Historical Society wrote me that they had found in a library given to them about that time another copy of the James book bound in with some other pamphlets. They, of course, still had the copy which they secured in 1909 or 1910 and were giving some consideration to disposing of this second copy. They promised me first chance at it in case they decided to sell. I must plead guilty to the fact that I didn't tell Mr. van Ravenswaay that I already had a copy of the book, and I corresponded with him throughout the year, finally buying the duplicate on December 23, 1952, and turning it over to my friend, W. J. Holliday, an outstanding collector of western Americana, who then lived in Tucson and who was very glad to secure a copy of the book.—EDG

2194 JAMES, WILL S.

27 YEARS A MAVRICK[!]; OR, LIFE ON A TEXAS RANGE . . . CHICAGO: DONOHUE & HENNEBERRY.

[i–ii (i blank, ii frontispiece)], [1]–6, 9–213, [214 blank]. 19 x 13.4 cm. 25 illustrations included in pagination. Printed pink wrappers.

Prov.: Inscribed on recto of frontispiece: To C. S. Stobie / Compliments of / The Author / Will S. James /.

Ref.: Adams (*Ramp. Herd*) 1159; Howes J51; Rader 2067 note

Copyrighted 1893.

. . . the reason is that I prefer to spell it as designated in the title and if that is not sufficient, I am at a loss how to apologize for the change . . . *Preface.*

Editions: Chicago, 1893 (with a different title).

2195 JAMISON, JAMES C.

WITH WALKER IN NICARAGUA; OR, REMINISCENCES OF AN OFFICER OF THE AMERICAN PHALANX . . . COLUMBIA, MO.: E. W. STEPHENS PUBLISHING COMPANY, 1909.*

[1]–181, [182 blank]. 19.8 x 13.3 cm. Three illustrations listed. Brown cloth.

Ref.: Cowan p. 309; Howes J57; Rader 2073

Best eye-witness account of Walker's bid for empire, by one of his most dependable officers.— Howes

Mounted on the inner front cover is a printed collection of notices of the book. Across the Dedication, there is pasted a yellow clipping bearing Joaquin Miller's poem "In Men Whom Men Condemn." And mounted on the inner back cover is Kipling's "If."

2196 JAMISON, MATTHEW H.

RECOLLECTIONS OF PIONEER AND ARMY LIFE . . . KANSAS CITY : HUDSON PRESS.*

[1–4, 4 blank], [i]–iv, 7–363, [364 blank]. 22.2 x 14.6 cm. Portrait, vignettes in text. Green cloth, blind insignia on front cover, title in gilt on backstrip.

Prov.: Signed in pencil on front endleaf: R. C. Jamison / Duluth / Minn. /

Ref.: Howes J58

Copyrighted 1911.

Includes an overland trip to Oregon and a trip to Pike's Peak, the former in the 1840's and the latter in 1860.

2197 JAQUES, JOHN

[Caption title] [No. 1.] SALVATION: A DIALOGUE BETWEEN ELDER BROWNSON AND MR. WHITBY . . .

[1]–8. Bound with Number 3346.

Ref.:

2198 JAQUES, JOHN

THE SAME. NO. 2.

[1]–8.

Imprint at foot of each page 8: Liverpool: / Published by S. W. Richards, 15, Wilton Street. / London: / For sale at the L. D. Saints' Book and Millenial Star Depôt, 35, Jewin Street, City, / and by Agents and all Booksellers throughout Great Britain and Ireland. / [rule] / Printed for the Publisher, by R. James, 39, South Castle Street, Liverpool. /

2199 JARMAN, W.

U. S. A. UNCLE SAM'S ABSCESS; OR, HELL UPON EARTH FOR U. S. UNCLE SAM . . . EXETER, ENGLAND: PRINTED AT H. LEDUC'S STEAM PRINTING WORKS, 1884.

[3]–194. 18.3 x 12.2 cm. White printed wrappers.
Ref.:
The printer may have considered the front wrapper as pages [1–2].

2200 JARVIS, NATHAN S.

[Caption title] AN ARMY SURGEON'S NOTES OF FRONTIER SERVICE, 1833–48 . . .

[1]–8. [1]–12. [1]–[12]. [1]–[12]. [1]–[20]. [1]–16. 23.3 x 15.5 cm. Illustrations and maps. Six extracts in series bound together, contemporary red half leather. Rebacked.

Prov.: Inscribed on front endleaf: Macrae Sykes / Compliments of / Capt. N. S. Jarvis U. S. A. / Jan. 15ᵗʰ 1908. /

Ref.: Howes J67

Reprints (with revised pagination) from *Journal of the Military Service Institution*, Volumes XXXIX–XL, July–August, September–October, November–December, 1906, March–April, May–June, July–August, 1907. The caption titles vary slightly. The last two parts appear under a general heading: Types and Traditions of the Old Army.

The service described occurred at Fort Snelling, Florida, and Mexico.

2201 JEFFERSON, THOMAS

MEMOIRS, CORRESPONDENCE, AND PRIVATE PAPERS . . . EDITED BY THOMAS JEFFERSON RANDOLPH . . . LONDON: HENRY COLBURN AND RICHARD BENTLEY, 1829.

[i]–[xi], [xii blank], [1]–464. [i–iv], [1]–496. [i–iv], [1]–521, [522 blank]. [i–iv], [1]–552. Frontispiece portrait and facsimile. Four volumes, gray boards, printed paper labels, uncut.

Ref.: Sabin 35892

2202 [JEFFERSON, THOMAS]

OBSERVATIONS SUR LA VIRGINIE . . . PAR M. J***. PARIS: CHEZ BARROIS, 1786.

[*]², [a]⁴, A–Aa⁸, Bb⁴, [**]². [1–4], [i]–viii, [1]–[391], [392 blank], [i–iv]. (Pages 18, 388–90 mispaginated 20, 288, 289, 290.) 21.4 x 13.6 cm. Folding map: A Map of the country between Albemarle Sound and Lake Erie, comprehending the whole of Virginia, Maryland, Delaware and Pennsylvania, with part of / several other of the United States of America. ——— Engraved for the Notes on Virginia. / . . . [lower right corner:] Engraved by S. J. Neele Nº 352 Strand. London. 64.2 x 62.2 cm. (plate mark). Scale: 20 miles to one inch. Gray wrappers, white paper label with manuscript title on backstrip, uncut. In a cloth case, leather label.

Ref.: Bradford 2646; Howes J78; Sabin 35895; Vail 746

An amazingly fine copy. The first French Edi-

tion, translated by André Morellet. Thick paper copy.

2203 [JEFFREY, J. K.]

THE TERRITORY OF WYOMING ITS HISTORY, SOIL, CLIMATE, RESOURCES, ETC. LARAMIE CITY: DAILY SENTINEL PRINT, DECEMBER 1874.

[1]–[84]. 22.4 x 14.4 cm. Mauve printed wrappers with title on front wrapper. Matching back wrapper supplied. In a black cloth case.

Prov.: With the Neva and Guy Littell bookplate.

Ref.: Adams (*Ramp. Herd*) 1166; AII (*Wyoming*) 15; Howes J85

The first book printed at Laramie.

The final page shows a list of Territorial Officers among whom J. K. Jeffrey is listed as Commissioner of Immigration. Pages 49–83: "letters taken from the *London Field* . . . from the graphic pen of Mr. E. A. Curley, one of the special correspondents of that paper in America . . ."

2204 [JEFFREY, J. K.]

ANOTHER COPY.

Brilliant, perfect copy. In a red cloth case.

2205 JENKINS, JAMES

AUTOBIOGRAPHY OF JAMES JENKINS, WRITTEN FOR HIS GRANDCHILDREN . . . OSHKOSH, WISCONSIN: THE HICKS PRINTING COMPANY, 1889.

[1]–110. (Pages [1–2, 4, 6] blank). 23.1 x 15.5 cm. Dark blue cloth, black bands top and bottom of front cover, lettered in gilt at centre. Front flyleaf removed.

Ref.: Howes J93

Includes accounts of trading voyages along the California coast, in the thirties.—Howes

I secured this book from a descendant of the author through a friend who belonged to the same church in Oshkosh and who worked a long time to prevail on this elderly woman to give it up.—EDG

2206 JENKINS, JEFF.

THE NORTHERN TIER; OR, LIFE AMONG THE HOMESTEAD SETTLERS . . . TOPEKA, KANSAS: GEO. W. MARTIN, 1880.

[1]–205, [206 blank]. 17.7 x 13.7 cm. Bright blue cloth, blind embossed sides, title in gilt on backstrip.

Prov.: Signed on first blank leaf at front: Robert Misell. / [underline] /. Inscribed on second blank leaf at front: Compliments / of / The Author / E. J. Jenkins /.

Ref.: Bradford 2668; Howes J94

Early days in Kansas by a resident of Concordia.

2207 JENNEY, WALTER P.

THE MINERAL WEALTH, CLIMATE AND RAIN-FALL, AND NATURAL RESOURCES OF THE BLACK HILLS OF DAKOTA . . . WASHINGTON: GOVERNMENT PRINTING OFFICE, 1876.

[i–ii], [1]–71, [72 blank]. 23.4 x 15 cm. Map: Department of the Interior. / [rule] / U.S. Geological and Geographical Survey / of the / Black Hills. / W. P. Jenney, E.M. Geologist in charge. / H. Newton, E.M. Ass^t Geologist. / H. P. Tuttle, Astronomer. / V. T. McGillycuddy, Topographer. / Preliminary Map / 1875. / Scale 8 miles = 1 inch /. 40.5 x 45.4 cm. Tan printed wrappers, with title as above on front wrapper within thick and thin rule borders.
Prov.: Embossed stamp of Columbia College Library through first three leaves, stamped number 55788 on front wrapper, embossed stamp of library on map.
Ref.: Adams (*Ramp. Herd*) 1170; Jennewein 57

2208 JENNINGS, NAPOLEON A.

A TEXAS RANGER . . . NEW YORK: CHARLES SCRIBNER'S SONS, 1899.

[i]–[xii, xii blank], 1–321, [322 blank]. 18.5 x 12.4 cm. Tan pictorial cloth.
Ref.: Adams 570; Clements Library (*Texas*) 50; Dobie p. 60; Howes J100; Rader 2086

For more than a century the Texas Rangers added color and drama to Texas life. Jennings' book is a readable account of his life as a Ranger in the late 1870's.

2209 JEWELL, M. H., *Compiler*

JEWELL'S FIRST ANNUAL DIRECTORY OF THE CITY OF BISMARCK, DAKOTA . . . BISMARCK, D.T.: M. H. JEWELL, 1879.

11–74, 79–120. 17.7 x 12.2 cm. Photograph pasted inside front cover: Bird's-eye View of the City of Bismarck, photographed for this work, by O. S. Goff. / Green printed boards with title on front cover, black cloth back-strip, advertisements on inner and outer back covers.
Ref.: Allen (*Dakota*) 167; Howes J110
Pages 27–29 contain a history of the Black Hills gold excitement. Lacks pages [5]–10, inserted leaf after page 40, and pages 121–44. Allen describes this as "Another issue."

2210 JEWELL, M. H., *Compiler*

ANOTHER COPY.

[1]–40, [i–ii], 41–144. Same.
Complete copy. Pages [1–2] are advertisements. Pages [i–ii] are a continuation of the text on page 40 and are an inserted leaf.

The Bird's-eye View on the inside front cover differs slightly from the first copy, but not of bibliographical importance.

2211 JEWETT, WILLIAM C.

[Advertisement] SAN FRANCISCO, FEBRUARY 1.ST 1849. THE UNDERSIGNED HAVING ESTABLISHED A COMMERCIAL COMMISSION HOUSE AT NEW YORK AND SAN FRANCISCO UNDER THE FIRM OF JEWETT & CO. NEW YORK, & WILLIAM CORNELL JEWETT, SAN FRANCISCO, RESPECTFULLY SOLICITS CONSIGNMENTS & GENERAL BUSINESS FROM HIS FRIENDS. THE USUAL CHARGES WILL BE MADE & THE INTERESTS OF CONSIGNEES FAITHFULLY ATTENDED TO . . . [signed in manuscript:] W^{M} CORNELL JEWETT, SAN FRANCISCO.

[1]–[2–4 blank]. 27 x 21 cm. Unbound leaflet.
Ref.:
The third page has been used for an Autograph Letter signed by Jewett. 1849 February 6, Panama City. One page, 27 x 21 cm. To John M. Read. Relating his arrival at Panama and intention to leave for San Francisco. The fourth page has been used for the address. The printed page was undoubtedly prepared at Panama.
Laid in folder with *Campbell & Hoogs' Directory of San Francisco*.

2212 JOCKNICK, SIDNEY

EARLY DAYS ON THE WESTERN SLOPE OF COLORADO AND CAMPFIRE CHATS WITH OTTO MEARS THE PATHFINDER FROM 1870 TO 1883 . . . DENVER, COLO.: THE CARSON-HARPER CO., MCMXIII.*

[1]–384. 19.4 x 13.4 cm. 25 illustrations listed. Green cloth.
Prov.: Inscribed on the inner front cover: Compliment / of / Otto Mears /. Also signed by Mears are the two portraits of him.
Ref.: Adams 572; Adams (*Ramp. Herd*) 1173; Howes J115; Wilcox p. 65
The leaf of typed text between pages 322 and 323 is not present in this copy. It often appears.

2213 JOHNSON, ADAM R.

THE PARTISAN RANGERS OF THE CONFEDERATE STATES ARMY . . . LOUISVILLE, KENTUCKY: GEO. G. FETTER COMPANY, 1904.*

[i]–[xiv, xiv blank], 1–476. 22.2 x 14.9 cm. 65 illustrations listed. Dark red cloth, title in gilt on front cover and backstrip.
Ref.: Coulter 257; Howes J122
The story of a very brave and daring man. His Indian warfare experiences in Texas in the late 1850's, when he was connected with the Butterfield Stage outfit and also when as a surveyor he surveyed much virgin territory, are al-

most beyond belief. The same or more can be said of his Civil War service in Kentucky as a Partisan Ranger.—EDG

In many details the narrative must be accepted with caution, as it was written many years after the war, apparently from memory but from some official military documents.— Coulter

2214 JOHNSON, CHARLES B.

LETTERS FROM NORTH AMERICA . . . PHILADEL-PHIA: PRINTED FOR HALL, 1821.

[i]–xii, [13]–185, [186 blank], 7–12 advertisements. 14.9 x 9.4 cm. Gray boards, lighter gray paper backstrip supplied, new white printed paper label, uncut.

Ref.: Buck 145; Howes J128; Sabin 36199

The text contains an attack on Birkbeck and plans for a British colony in Illinois. Johnson favored British settlements in Pennsylvania.

Howes calls for a map which is not present. *Editions:* Philadelphia, 1819. London, 1820.

2215 JOHNSON, DON CARLOS

A BRIEF HISTORY OF SPRINGVILLE, UTAH, FROM ITS FIRST SETTLEMENT SEPTEMBER 18, 1850, TO THE 18TH DAY OF SEPTEMBER, 1900 . . . SPRINGVILLE: PRINTED BY WILLIAM F. GIBSON, SEPTEMBER, 1900.

[i–vi, vi blank], [1]–[125], [126 blank]. 22.5 x 15.5 cm. Illustrations unlisted. Green printed wrappers. In green cloth case.

Prov.: Inscribed on recto of frontispiece: Presented by / Don C Johnson / Springville, Utah / 5–2–'27 /.

Ref.: Howes J130

The errata, printed in red, appear on page [125].

2216 JOHNSON, EDWIN F.

RAILROAD TO THE PACIFIC. NORTHERN ROUTE. ITS GENERAL CHARACTER, RELATIVE MERITS, ETC. . . . NEW YORK: RAILROAD JOURNAL JOB PRINTING OFFICE, 1854.

[i]–iv, [5]–166. 22.5 x 14.4 cm. Eight plates, a profile and two maps. Map: Nº 2. / Sketch /of the Routes traversed by / Lewis and Clark / between the waters of the / Missouri and Columbia, / in 1805 and 1806. / [decorative rule] / Routes indicated by the dotted lines. / [lower centre:] Lith. of E. C. Kellogg & Co., Hartford, Conn. / 20.7 x 28.5 cm. No scale given. Map: Map / of the / Proposed Northern Route for a / Railroad to the / Pacific, / by Edwin F. Johnson, C. E. / 1853. / Scale in Statute Miles. / [diagrammatic scale: about 105 miles to an inch] / Lith. of E. C. Kellogg & Co., Hartford, Conn. / [lower centre:] Entered according to Act of Congress, in the year 1853, by Edwin F. Johnson, in the Clerk's office of the District Court of Connecticut. / 52 x 82 cm. Scale: about 105 miles to one inch. Buff wrappers, with title as above on front wrapper within decorative border. In yellow cloth case.

Ref.: Howes J133; *Railway Economics* p. 244; Sabin 36207; Smith 5237; Wagner-Camp 223 note; Wheat (*Transmississippi*) 811

Although noted as second edition on the title-page, this is the first in book form, the work having appeared previously in a periodical. It contains a good summary of ideas about the Northern Route.

2217 JOHNSON, J. E.

AUTOGRAPH LETTER, SIGNED. 1870 February 21, St. George, Utah. Two pages, 23 x 14.2 cm. To H. B. Dawson.

Regarding the second edition of Gebow: *A Vocabulary of the Snake, or, Sho-Sho-Nay Dialect . . . 1868.*

2218 JOHNSON, JAMES H.

A PLAIN STATEMENT OF FACTS, CONNECTED WITH THE CONCEPTION, NUTRITION, PROGRESS AND ABORTION, OF THE ST. LOUIS HOTEL FOR INVALIDS . . . ST. LOUIS: PRINTED AT THE OFFICE OF THE POST AND MYSTIC FAMILY, 1848.

[1]–14. [15–16 blank]. 21.6 x 13.6 cm. Stabbed, unbound.

Ref.:

2219 JOHNSON, JOHN

AUTOGRAPH LETTER, SIGNED. 1809 April 12, Garrison Belle Vue [i.e., Fort Madison, Iowa]. Three pages, 25.5 x 20.6 cm. To William Clark.

Plans for the extension of the fort to a larger establishment, farming, experiences with the Indians—including a possible attempt to attack the fort patterned on the successful attack on Fort Michilimackinac during the so-called "Pontiac Rebellion," etc.

2220 JOHNSON, LAURA WINTHROP

EIGHT HUNDRED MILES IN AN AMBULANCE . . . PHILADELPHIA: J. B. LIPPINCOTT COMPANY, 1889.

[1]–131, [132 blank]. 17.6 x 11.4 cm. Olive cloth, title in gilt on front cover and backstrip.

Ref.: Howes J141

An important, first-hand account by a perceptive writer. The excursionists started from Cheyenne to visit forts and Indian agencies in Wyoming Territory in 1874.

2221 JOHNSON, OVERTON, & WILLIAM H. WINTER

ROUTE ACROSS THE ROCKY MOUNTAINS, WITH A DESCRIPTION OF OREGON AND CALIFORNIA; THEIR GEOGRAPHICAL FEATURES, THEIR RESOURCES, SOIL, CLIMATE, PRODUCTIONS, &C., &C. . . . LAFAYETTE IND: JOHN B. SEMANS, 1846.

[i]–viii, [9]–152. 20.4 x 13.2 cm. Pale green boards, blue cloth back, with printed pale yellow paper label, 8 x 57 mm., on backstrip; [reading up:] Description of Oregon / and California. / In blue half morocco slip case.

Ref.: Bradford 2705; Cowan p. 315; Howes J142; Jones 1126; Sabin 36260; Wagner-Camp 122

In the *Indiana Quarterly for Bookmen* for April, 1946, R. E. Banta published an interesting article giving all available information about the two authors, both of whom attended Wabash College at Crawfordsville, Indiana. Johnson, whom he says did most of the writing, died in Indiana on Feb. 15, 1849 while Winter went to California again in April, 1849, returned to Indiana in late 1850 or early 1851, and a year or so later left a third time for California in which state he died in July or August, 1879. He lived between Sonoma and Napa until 1875 when he built a house in Fall River.

On page [26], line 3 of the chapter heading, the letters Ri of River are turned to read Я.ver. Page 36, line 13, there is a vertical slug before Fort. Page 57, the signature appears as follows: individuals . . . instead of: different individuals
8   8
. . .

In the ICN copy River appears correctly, there is no vertical slug on page 36, and the signature on page 57 is between the two words.

2222 JOHNSON, RICHARD W.

A SOLDIER'S REMINISCENCES IN PEACE AND WAR . . . PHILADELPHIA: J. B. LIPPINCOTT COMPANY, 1886.

[1]–428. 22.7 x 14.9 cm. Two illustrations. Green cloth, title in gilt on backstrip.

Ref.: Coulter 261; Nicholson p. 427

Johnson describes service in the West (principally Texas) before the Civil War, including several famous forts, experiences during the Civil War, and life in Minnesota after the War.

2223 JOHNSON, THEODORE T.

SIGHTS IN THE GOLD REGION, AND SCENES BY THE WAY . . . NEW YORK: BAKER AND SCRIBNER, 1849.

[i]–xii, 1–278. 18.5 x 11.5 cm. Dark gray-blue cloth, embossed sides, title stamped in gilt on backstrip.

Ref.: Bradford 2714; Cowan p. 315; Howes J154; Jones 1206; Sabin 36328; Smith 5296

2224 JOHNSON, THEODORE T.

THE SAME.

NEW YORK: BAKER AND SCRIBNER, 1850.

[i]–xii, 1–324. 18.2 x 11.9 cm. Illustrations and folding map unlisted. Map: Map of the / Gold Region / From actual survey / by direction of Co., Jones. / 1849. / [lower centre:] Copy Right secured. / [lower right:] Lith. by T. Sinclair Philadª / 17.5 x 15.2 cm. Scale: about 28 miles to one inch. Red cloth, gilt stamped vignette and blind borders on front cover, all blind on back cover, gilt backstrip with title, red sprinkled edges.

Ref.: as above and see Wagner-Camp 183 note

Second edition. The map is uncolored. An Appendix by Thurston (contrary to Wagner-Camp) did not appear until the third edition.

2225 JOHNSON, THEODORE T.

THE SAME.

PHILADELPHIA: LIPPINCOTT, GRAMBO & CO., 1851.

[i]–xii, 1–348, 1–24 advertisements. 18.3 x 11.4 cm. Illustrations and map unlisted, as in preceding. Green cloth, blind embossed borders on sides, title stamped in gilt on backstrip.

Ref.: as above and see Wagner-Camp 183 note

The third and best edition. With the important Appendix by Samuel R. Thurston. The map is colored.

2226 JOHNSTON, CHARLES

A NARRATIVE OF THE INCIDENTS ATTENDING THE CAPTURE, DETENTION AND RANSOM OF CHARLES JOHNSTON . . . IN THE YEAR 1790 . . . NEW YORK: PRINTED BY J. & J. HARPER, 1827.

[i]–vi, 7–264. 19.3 x 11.6 cm. Salmon boards pink cloth back, printed white paper label (4.5 x 3.4 cm.): [thick and thin rules] / Johnston's / Indian / Narrative. / [thin and thick rules] /, uncut and unopened.

Ref.: Ayer 165; Field 784; Howes J158; Jones 884; Sabin 36355; Thomson 650

2227 JOHNSTON, JOSEPH E.

NARRATIVE OF MILITARY OPERATIONS, DIRECTED, DURING THE LATE WAR BETWEEN THE STATES, BY JOSEPH E. JOHNSTON, GENERAL, C. S. A. ILLUSTRATED BY STEEL-PLATES AND MAPS. NEW YORK: D. APPLETON AND COMPANY, 549 AND 551 BROADWAY. 1874.

[1]–602, [603–08 advertisements]. 23.1 x 14.7 cm. 21 illustrations and maps listed. Dark yellow pictorial cloth. Worn, waterstained.

Prov.: Signed on inside front cover: Jefferson Davis /. Signed on page 61: Varina A. Davis /. Annotated in pencil by Jefferson Davis throughout. See below.

Ref.: De Renne p. 746; Freeman pp. 22–3; Howes J167; Nicholson p. 429

Numerous passages in the work are ticked or marked in pencil and in thirteen instances there are marginal notes by Davis in which he disagrees with the text. On the verso of the last blank leaf, there are several lines of references to disputed passages. Davis probably used this copy of the book in preparing his own work for publication.

Laid in is a printed memorial tribute to Johnston by Livingston Mims.

2228 JOHNSTON, JOSEPH E., W. F. SMITH, AND OTHERS

... REPORTS OF THE SECRETARY OF WAR, WITH RECONNAISSANCES OF ROUTES FROM SAN ANTONIO TO EL PASO, BY BREVET LT. COL. J. E. JOHNSTON; LIEUTENANT W. F. SMITH; LIEUTENANT F. T. BRYAN; LIEUTENANT N. H. MICHLER; AND CAPTAIN S. G. FRENCH, OF Q'RMASTER'S DEP'T. ALSO, THE REPORT OF CAPT. R. B. MARCY'S ROUTE FROM FORT SMITH TO SANTA FE; AND THE REPORT OF LIEUT. J. H. SIMPSON OF AN EXPEDITION INTO THE NAVAJO COUNTRY; AND THE REPORT OF LIEUTENANT W. H. C. WHITING'S RECONNAISSANCES OF THE WESTERN FRONTIER OF TEXAS ... WASHINGTON: PRINTED AT THE UNION OFFICE, 1850.

[1]–250. 22.4 x 14.2 cm. Two maps and 72 plates, unlisted. (No. 49 in duplicate.) Map: Reconnoissances / of Routes / from / San Antonio de Bexar / El Paso del Norte, / &c. &c. / by / Bvt. Lt. Col. J. E. Johnston, T. Eng.ᵣˢ / Lt. W. F. Smith, / Lt. F. T. Bryan, / Lt. N. H. Michler. / 1849. / Including the Reconnoissance of / Lt. W. H. C. Whiting, U. S. Eng.ᵣˢ / 1849. / [upper right:] Senate Ex: Doc: 1ˢᵗ Sess. 31ˢᵗ Cong: Nᵒ 64. / [lower left:] P. S. Duval's Lith. Steam Press Phil.ᵃ / 62.4 x 93.2 cm. Scale: about 20 miles to one inch. Map: Map / of the Route pursued in 1849 by the U. S. Troops, / under the command of / Bvt. Lieut. Col. Jno. M. Washington, Governor of New Mexico, / in an expedition against the Navajos Indians, / By / James M. Simpson, 1ˢᵗ Lieut. T. Eng.ʳˢ / Assisted by Mr. Edw. M. Kern. / [double rule] / Constructed under the general orders of / Col. J. J. Abert, Chief Top.ˡ Eng.ʳˢ / Drawn by Edward M. Kern. / Santa Fe, N. M. 1849. / [upper left:] Senate Ex. doc. 1ˢᵗ Sess. 31ˢᵗ Cong. Nᵒ 64. / [lower left:] P. S.

Duval's Steam Lith. Press, Philad.ᵃ / 51.6 x 70.2 cm. Scale: 10 miles to one inch. Under heading: Notes. / there are 22 lines of text. Black cloth, blind embossed sides, title in gilt on backstrip.

Ref.: Bradford 2724; Howes J170; Munk (Alliot) p. 119; Raines p. 128; Sabin 36377; Wagner-Camp 184; Wheat (*Transmississippi*) 677

31st Congress, 1st Session, Senate, Executive Document No. 64, Serial 562.

Plates 65–7 were printed by Ackerman, the balance by Duval.

The expanded text of the Simpson report appeared two years later.

2229 JOHNSTON, WILLIAM G.

EXPERIENCES OF A FORTY-NINER, BY WM. G. JOHNSTON, A MEMBER OF THE WAGON TRAIN FIRST TO ENTER CALIFORNIA IN THE MEMORABLE YEAR 1849 ... PITTSBURGH, MDCCCXCII.

[1]–390. 22.2 x 14.6 cm. 13 illustrations listed, one listed and one unlisted map. The inserted illustration is a portrait of the author in 1891. Map: [Route of the author from Independence to Sacramento] / [lower right:] Stewart Johnston Del., 1893. / 22.1 x 82 cm. No scale given. Blueprint map inserted after last page of text. Green cloth, gilt date 1849 within decorative diamond on front cover, title in gilt on backstrip, edges of covers beveled.

Ref.: Cowan p. 316; Howes J173; Jones 1666; Matthews p. 316; Morgan (Pritchard) p. 189

Laid in the present copy is a printed notice, 20.4 x 12.8 cm., about the portrait and map to be added to the volume. The notice is dated in manuscript Nov 6, 1893 /

Dale Morgan uses the volume extensively in his edition of the Pritchard Diary.

2230 JOLY DE ST. VALIER

HISTOIRE RAISONEE DES OPERATIONS MILITAIRES ET POLITIQUES DE LA DERNIERE GUERRE ... LIEGE, CHEZ LES PRINCIPAUX LIBRAIRES DE L'EUROPE, M.DCC.LXXXIII.

[*]⁶, A–O⁸, P⁶, A⁴, B¹. [i]–xii, [1]–236, [1]–10. 19.5 x 12 cm. Contemporary or original mottled calf, gilt back leather label.

Ref.: Howes J182; Sabin 36428

Pages 9 and 10 of the Supplement are a different setting of type than the ICN copy. Page 10, line 4 begins "ser d'eux"; in the ICN copy it begins "d'eux." The leaf was reset, but there are no other changes, except the omission of a period after "Supplément" in the headline.

The author was more interested in naval operations than military.

2231 JONES, ABNER D.

ILLINOIS AND THE WEST. WITH A TOWNSHIP MAP, CONTAINING THE LATEST SURVEYS AND IMPROVEMENTS . . . BOSTON: WEEKS, JORDAN AND COMPANY, 1838.

[v]–[xii, xii blank], [13]–[256]. 15.8 x 9.1 cm. Map: Illinois; / Exhibiting the / Latest Surveys / and / Improvements. / 1838. / Eddy's Lithography. Graphic Court, Boston. / [lower centre:] Entered according to Act of Congress in the year 1838 by A. D. Jones in the Clerks Office of the District Court of Massachusetts. / Pub^d by Weeks, Jordan & Co Boston. / 36.7 x 30.2 cm. Scale: 28 miles to one inch. Plum embossed cloth, title in gilt on front cover.

Ref.: Bradford 2727; Buck 326; Howes J184; Hubach p. 88; Jones 1013; Sabin 36449

This volume of the author's personal adventures when he was prospecting in Illinois contains also much about education, agriculture, etc. in Illinois.

2232 JONES, ANSON

AUTOGRAPH LETTER, SIGNED. 1847 July 16, Barrington, Washington County, Texas. Two pages, 24.7 x 20 cm. To R. J. Walker.

A fine letter by the last President of the Republic of Texas introducing J. De Cordova. "He takes on to the North for publication the new Map of Texas, made out from authentic data at the General Land Office of the State . . ."

Laid in Robert Creuzbaur's map of Texas published by De Cordova.

2233 JONES, CHARLES J.

BUFFALO JONES' FORTY YEARS OF ADVENTURE. A VOLUME OF FACTS GATHERED FROM EXPERIENCE . . . TOPEKA, KANSAS: CRANE & COMPANY, 1899.

[i]–xii, 1–469, [470 blank]. 22.6 x 15.7 cm. 43 illustrations, unlisted. Gray pictorial cloth.

Ref.: Howes I54

Considerably more accurate than some other works touched by Henry Inman.

2234 [JONES, DANIEL W.]

FORTY YEARS AMONG THE INDIANS. A TRUE YET THRILLING NARRATIVE OF THE AUTHOR'S EXPERIENCES AMONG THE NATIVES. SALT LAKE CITY, UTAH: JUVENILE INSTRUCTOR OFFICE, 1890.

[i]–[xvi, xvi blank], [17]–400. (Pages [i–ii] blank.) 22 x 14.7 cm. Black cloth, title stamped in gilt on front cover and backstrip, blind panels on sides.

Ref.: Howes J207; Munk (Alliot) p. 120; Rader 2112; Saunders 2992

The portrait was not included with this copy.

2235 JONES, DAVID

A JOURNAL OF TWO VISITS MADE TO SOME NATIONS OF INDIANS ON THE WEST SIDE OF THE RIVER OHIO, IN THE YEARS 1772 AND 1773 . . . BURLINGTON: PRINTED AND SOLD BY ISAAC COLLINS, M.DCC.LXXIV.

[A]–M⁴. [i]–iv, [5]–[96]. 18.7 x 11 cm. Rebound in brown polished morocco, by Riviere. Last leaf supplied from another copy. In a cloth case.

Prov.: C. G. Littell copy.

Ref.: Evans 13356; Howes J208; Sabin 36487; Vail 631

The author was a missionary to the Delawares and Shawnees, 1772–1773 and gives an excellent account of their manners and customs. He travelled part of the way with George Rogers Clark and was an army chaplain under General Anthony Wayne from 1794 until peace was declared with the Indians.—Vail

Copies: Vail lists ICN, MH, MHi, MWA, PHC, PPiU, PPL-R, RPJCB, WHi, Deering, Graff. But MHi states it has never owned a copy, the MWA copy (which was imperfect) has been missing since 1947, and both the PHC and WHi copies are also reported missing. To the above list should be added CtY (imperfect) and Goodspeed.

2236 JONES, HENRIETTA C.

SKETCHES FROM REAL LIFE . . .

[1]–239, [240 blank]. 22.3 x 14 cm. Portrait. Blue cloth, title stamped in gilt on front cover and backstrip.

Ref.: Howes J215

Printed by O. E. Hungerford, Watertown, N.Y. The introduction is dated from Berlin, N.Y., June 1, 1897. The author signs herself at this point: Henrietta Spink, Walker, Clark, Jones.

The author settled in Barry, Illinois (near Hannibal, Mo.) in 1840. She gives a good picture of life and conditions of that period. Her husband went overland to California in 1849 and spent seven years there in the mines and elsewhere. Many of his letters describing the overland trip and California life are reproduced. After her husband's death in 1856, the author taught school in St. Louis and kept a diary that is also reproduced.—EDG

2237 [JONES, J.]

THE WEST POINT CADET; OR, THE YOUNG OFFICER'S BRIDE. A ROMANCE OF REAL LIFE. BY HARRY HAZEL. . . BOSTON: PUBLISHED BY F. GLEASON, 1845.

[5]–100. 25. x 16.2 cm. Five illustrations included in pagination. Printed, colored pictorial

wrappers, with title on front wrapper, advertisement on verso of back.

Ref.:
A lurid tale of the Seminole Campaign.

2238 JONES, J. W. C.

THE ELKHORN VALLEY; ITS CLIMATE, SOIL, SURFACE, WATER, TIMBER, GRASSES, PRODUCTS, PEOPLE, AND INDUSTRIAL RESOURCES; OR A TWO MONTH'S TALK, WALK, AND DRIVE, IN THE COUNTIES OF CUMING, STANTON, MADISON, ANTELOPE, WAYNE AND PIERCE, NEBRASKA . . . WEST POINT, NEB.: REPUBLICAN JOB OFFICE PRINT, 1880.

[1–60]. 21.6 x 14.6 cm. Map: Map of the / Elkhorn Valley, / Nebraska. / [three lines] [preceding six lines in rule box] / Lithographed by A. Gast & Co's New Process St. Louis. / 45.8 x 67.5 cm. No scale given. *Inset:* Map of / Nebraska / 17.6 x 39.1 cm. No scale given. Pink printed wrappers, with title on front wrapper, Garden Valley / —of— / Nebraska. / [short rule] / West Point, Neb. / Republican Job Office Print. / 1880. / [within decorative border which includes following phrases: (at top:) Best Government Lands. / (right side reading down:) Choicest Private Land. / (bottom:) Healthful Climate, Pure Water, Fertile Soil], advertisements on verso of front and recto of back wrapper, verso of back wrapper: Twenty Reasons / Why You Should Settle / —in the— / Elkhorn Valley. /

Ref.: Howes J217

2239 JONES, JAMES

PRACTICAL FORMS OF WRITS, PROCESSES, &C. SELECTED FROM THE MOST APPROVED PRECEDENTS AND ADAPTED TO THE LAWS OF THE STATE OF ILLINOIS NOW IN FORCE . . . GALENA: PRINTED AND PUBLISHED BY THE AUTHOR, 1830.

[1]–164, [165 blank], [166 errata], [1]–52, [1]–10. 17.9 x 10.3 cm. Tan boards, with calf backstrip and corners, red leather label.

Prov.: Frank Stevens's copy, without identification.

Ref.: Byrd 104

2240 JONES, JOHN B.

A REBEL WAR CLERK'S DIARY AT THE CONFEDERATE STATES CAPITAL . . . PHILADELPHIA: J. B. LIPPINCOTT & CO., 1866.

[i]–xii, 13–392. [1–2], 3–480. 20.5 x 13.1 cm. Two volumes, brown cloth, blind embossed fillets on sides, gilt title on backstrips.

Prov.: Signed inside front covers: V. Jefferson Davis, / Beauvoir House, / 1890. / And with autograph manuscript notes in the same hand on pages 133, 134, 141, 145, 153, 193, 212, 285, 336,

339, 355, and 453 of Vol. II. Some further passages underlined.

Ref.: De Renne p. 685; Freeman pp. 43–8; Howes J220; Nicholson p. 434; Sabin 36531

The comments by Mrs. Davis are most interesting, comprising principally objections to the text.

2241 JONES, JOHN B.

WILD WESTERN SCENES; A NARRATIVE OF ADVENTURES IN THE WESTERN WILDERNESS, FORTY YEARS AGO; WHEREIN THE CONDUCT OF DANIEL BOONE, THE GREAT AMERICAN PIONEER, IS PARTICULARLY DESCRIBED . . . NEW YORK: SAMUEL COLMAN, 1841.

[Part 1:] [5]–44; [2:] 45–84; [3:] 85–124; [4:] 125–164; [5:] 165–204; [6:] 205–[248], [i–iv]. 23.4 to 22.3 x 14.5 to 14.3 cm. Six woodcuts in the text. Printed green (Part 1) and pink (Parts 2–6) wrappers, with title on front wrappers. Each verso of front wrapper carries copyright notice. Rectos of back wrappers headed "Advertisement." state that publication is simultaneous in Baltimore, New York, Philadelphia, and Boston and that the work will be issued in six or seven parts. Advertisements on verso of back wrappers, uncut. In a brown cloth slip case.

Ref.: Bay p. 350; Howes J221; Rader 2117; Sabin 36535 see

There was a slight historical basis for this piece of fiction.

2242 JONES, JOHN PAUL

MEMOIRES DE PAUL JONES . . . PARIS: CHEZ LOUIS AN VI. 1798.

[a]⁸, b⁴, A–V alternately 8 and 4, X². [i–iv], [i]–[xx], [1]–244. 15.6 x 8.6 cm. Engraved portrait. Gray-green paste paper wrappers, with manuscript white paper label on back. Wrappers are lined with waste from prospectus for *La Revue Britannique*.

Ref.: Howes J228; Sabin 36559; Seitz p. 182.

Seitz states that a translation of this work appeared in *Niles Register* for 1812, and that it is a narrative made up from the manuscript "Journal for the King" presented by Jones to Louis XVI. Benoit-André, who is described in the title as translator, was, for a time, secretary to Jones.

2243 JONES, JOHN W.

AUTOGRAPH MANUSCRIPT JOURNAL: Across the Plains. / My trip from Faribault, Minn., to Oregon, via, / Saskatchewan route, British America— / Account of the country, our / Sufferings and trials, &c. / 128 pages, 27 x 21.9 cm. Original half black roan, green marbled sides. Badly worn.

The journal was commenced July 20, 1858, a few miles west of Faribault, Minnesota, and closed at The Dalles, April 29, 1859. In between are careful and interesting accounts of daily events on the route which included St. Paul, Pembina, Fort Garry, the Red River Settlements, Fort Ellice, Fort Carlton, Fort Pitt, Fort Edmonton, the Rocky Mountains, Clark's Fork of the Columbia, Colville Valley, and The Dalles. It was a difficult and gruelling trip, yet the account is filled with humor and good sense from beginning to end.

Mounted inside the front cover there is a pencil and wash drawing (circular, 18 cm. diameter) of an elaborate house, labeled in pencil: Sketch—J. W. Jones. / On the front endleaf there is mounted a label, within a decorative manuscript border, as follows: My Trip / Across the Plains, via: St. Paul, Red River, Saskatchewan River, / Kootonais Pass, Colville, / During 1858 and '59. / On the verso of the same leaf are mounted six newspaper clippings about the calligraphic work of the author who was then Chief Clerk in the County Recorder's office. Facing these clippings is an incomplete pencil sketch, with the legend: Ich Dien. / On the verso appears: J. W. Jones / Portland, / Oregon. / in fancy lettering. Tipped in preceding the first page of text is a map: Statistical Map / of the / United States / of America / Scale of English Statute Miles. / [diagrammatic scale: about 120 miles to one inch] / [17 lines] / July 1864 / U. S. Treasury Department / Washington, D. C. / [lower right:] Bowen &. Cº lith. Phila. / 37.4 x 49 cm. Scale as above. Jones's track drawn in red ink. Following the text, there are thirteen woodcut views along the way, clipped from printed journals; five of the views carry captions in Jones's hand.

Following the journal proper, which is concluded on page 119, there are four pages of Remarks about the trip, four pages of legends and a Chinese Oath, and one page on which are listed tribes of Indians met on the journey. Laid in are two manuscript poems by Jones, one on a small octavo sheet, two pages, and the other on a leaf torn from the volume; the first is in pencil, the second in ink.

The present journal is a copy of a lost original. Jones states that his original journal, which had been written in pencil, had nearly been obliterated. There are a few obvious changes in the manuscript, two or three comments inserted after the events recorded, and some errors of transcription, but on the whole this seems to be very much as written at the time of the events.

During the whole journey, Jones met only two outstanding characters. He met them both on the same day at Fort Pitt. They were Captains Palliser and Blakiston.

Small parts of the Journal were published in Oregon.

2244 JONES, JOHN WESLEY

[Broadside ticket] JONES' PANTOSCOPE OF CALIFORNIA, THE PLAINS AND SALT LAKE, NOW EXHIBITING AT HOPE CHAPEL, NO. 718 BROADWAY, - - - - NEW YORK. ADMIT ONE.

Broadside ticket, 4.2 x 6.7 cm. Text, 3.6 x 5.9 cm. Printed on green card.

Ref.:

Laid in case with Phillips: *Amusing and Thrilling Adventures . . .* 1854.

2245 JONES, JOHN WESLEY

[Photograph] PORTRAIT OF JOHN WESLEY JONES three-quarters turned to his left, bust length, vignette type. 14.5 x 10 cm. Mount, 16.3 x 10.3 cm., maroon board, stamped in gilt at foot: Richardson Bros., Brooklyn, L. I. Gilt edges.

Laid in case with Phillips' *Amusing and Thrilling Adventures . . .* 1854.

2246 JONES, JONATHAN H.

A CONDENSED HISTORY OF THE APACHE AND COMANCHE INDIAN TRIBES FOR AMUSEMENTS AND GENERAL KNOWLEDGE. PREPARED FROM THE GENERAL CONVERSATION OF HERMAN LEHMANN, WILLIE LEHMANN, MRS. MINA KEYSER, MRS. A. J. BUCHMEYER AND OTHERS . . . SAN ANTONIO, TEXAS: JOHNSON BROS. PRINTING CO., 1899.

[1]–235, [236 blank]. (Pages [1–2] blank.) 2.5 x 13.4 cm. Frontispiece and 27 illustrations. Dark blue cloth, blind embossed sides, with vignette in gilt on front cover, gilt title on backstrip.

Ref.: Howes J232; Rader 2122

Interesting reminiscences of the captivity of Herman and Willie Lehmann, with a flavor of authenticity.

2247 JONES, LLOYD

LIFE AND ADVENTURES OF HARRY TRACY "THE MODERN DICK TURPIN" . . . CHICAGO: JEWETT & LINDROOTH, 1902.

[1]–[124]. 19.5 x 13.3 cm. Three illustrations, unlisted. Yellow cloth, title stamped in black and white on front cover and black on backstrip.

Prov.: Inscribed on front endleaf: Compliments of / Lloyd Jones / R. 703—218 La Salle St / Just to make / Fred Jordan *uneasy* / [underline] /.

Ref.:

2248 JONES, THOMAS A.

J. WILKES BOOTH: AN ACCOUNT OF HIS SOJOURN IN SOUTHERN MARYLAND AFTER THE ASSASSINATION OF ABRAHAM LINCOLN, HIS PASSAGE ACROSS THE POTOMAC, AND HIS DEATH IN VIRGINIA . . . CHICAGO: LAIRD & LEE, 1893.

[1]–126. 18.8 x 12.8 cm. Illustrations unlisted. Maroon cloth, title in gilt on front cover and backstrip.

Ref.: Howes J241

Written by the man who sheltered and attended Booth and Herold during one week and who conducted them to the Potomac and provided a boat to enable them to cross the river.

2249 JONES, THOMAS L.

FROM THE GOLD MINE TO THE PULPIT. THE STORY OF THE REV. T. L. JONES . . . CINCINNATI: PRINTED FOR THE AUTHOR BY JENNINGS AND PYE.*

[1]–169, [170 blank]. 18.8 x 12.4 cm. Illustrations unlisted. Gray pictorial cloth, gilt top, uncut.

Ref.: Smith 5335

Copyrighted 1904.

A good picture of frontier conditions in the Pacific Northwest.

2250 JONES, WILLARD, & EZEKIEL BOYLAND

DOCUMENT, SIGNED. 1838 January 15. McHenry County, Illinois. One page, 24.7 x 19.4 cm.

Jones and Boyland, land commissioners "acting under authority and in behalf of the settlers of the Abingdon Association", establish Elijah M. Haines "in his right to all the land within the following boundaries . . ." On the verso, the following:—152— / E Middlebrook Haines / Certificate / Registered March 11th 1839 / Jared Cage Clk /.

Laid in Abingdon Association of Settlers: *Constitution & By-Laws* . . . [1836].

2251 JOUTEL, HENRI

JOURNAL HISTORIQUE DU DERNIER VOYAGE QUE FEU M. DE LA SALE FIT DANS LE GOLFE DE MEXIQUE, POUR TROUVER L'EMBOUCHURE, & LE COURS DE LA RIVIERE DE MISSICIPI . . . A PARIS: CHEZ ESTIENNE ROBINOT, MDCCXIII.

ã12, ẽ4, ẽ1, A–Q12, R1. [i]–xxxiv, 1–386. 16.7 x 9.3 cm. Map: Carte Nouvelle / de la Louisiane, et de la Riviere / de Missisipi, découverte par / feu Mr de la Salle, es années 1681. / et 1686. dans l'Amérique Septentri-/onale, et de plusieurs autres Rivieres, / jusqu'icy jnconnües, qui tom-/ bent dans la Baye de St Loüis. / Dressée par le

Sr Joutel, / qui étoit de ce Voyage. / 1713. / 35.6 x 39.1 cm. No scale given. *Inset:* [In upper left corner:] View of Niagara Falls. Contemporary calf, gilt tooled backstrip, red leather label on backstrip, red mottled edges.

Prov.: Unidentified paraph on title-page. Bookplate of L. Emile Grothé. Dahlinger Sale.

Ref.: Bradford 2765; Church 855; Clark I 14; Howes J266; Jones 394; Rader 2129; Sabin 36760; Wagner (*SS*) 79

2252 JOUTEL, HENRI

A JOURNAL OF THE LAST VOYAGE PERFORM'D BY MONSR. DE LA SALE, TO THE GULPH OF MEXICO, TO FIND OUT THE MOUTH OF THE MISSISIPI RIVER . . . LONDON: PRINTED FOR A. BELL, 1714.

A8, a8, B–O8. [1–2], [i]–[xxx, p. xxx advertisement], 1–[210]. 20.5 x 13.1 cm. Map: A New Map / of the Country of Louisiana / and of ỹ River Missisipi in North / America discouer'd by Mons. de la Salle in ỹ Years 1682 and 1686. as allso of / Several other Rivers, before un / known and Falling into ỹ / Bay of St Lewis By the / Sr Joutel, who perform'd / that Voyage. / 1713. / 35.9 x 38.8 cm. No scale given. View of Niagara Falls in upper left corner, reversed from French map, as are animals, ships, etc. Plain gray wrappers, uncut, almost entirely unopened. In a maroon morocco solander case.

Prov.: Bookplate of J. C. MacCoy.

Ref.: Bradford 2767; Church 859; Clark I14; Field 808; Howes J266; Jones 399; Rader 2129; Sabin 36762; Wagner (*SS*) 79 (a)

A miraculously fine copy.

2253 JOUTEL, HENRI

JOURNAL OF LA SALLE'S LAST VOYAGE . . . NOTES BY MELVILLE B. ANDERSON. [CHICAGO:] THE CAXTON CLUB, MDCCCXCVI.

[i–xii], [i]–[xxx], 1–229, [230 blank], [231 colophon, 232–34 blank]. 23.1 x 14.9 cm. Facsimile and folding map. Gray boards, vellum back, uncut, mostly unopened. In white board slip case.

Ref.: Howes J266

Limited to 206 copies.

2254 JOYCE, JOHN A.

A CHECKERED LIFE . . . CHICAGO: S. P. ROUNDS, JR., 1883.

[1]–318, [319 vignette, 320 blank]. (Pages [1–2] blank, [3] blank, [4] portrait.) 19.5 x 13.1 cm. Portrait and facsimiles unlisted. Yellow cloth, decorated in black.

Ref.: Cowan p. 319

2255 [JUDAH, THEODORE D.]

REPORT OF THE CHIEF ENGINEER ON THE PRELIMINARY SURVEY AND COST OF CONSTRUCTION OF THE CENTRAL PACIFIC RAILROAD, OF CALIFORNIA, ACROSS THE SIERRA NEVADA MOUNTAINS, FROM SACRAMENTO TO THE EASTERN BOUNDARY OF CALIFORNIA. SACRAMENTO, OCTOBER 1, 1861.

[1]–36. 23.1 x 14.6 cm. Map: [Map of the United States from Michigan to the Pacific Ocean, from Oklahoma to Canada, showing line of projected railroad through the Sierra Nevada.] 53.8 x 116.4 cm. Scale: about 50 miles to an inch. Light yellow printed wrappers, with title on front wrapper.
Prov.: Inscribed at top of front wrapper: Hon A. Johnson / Respects of T. D. Judah /.
Ref.: Greenwood 1438; Howes J269; *Railway Economics* p. 290; Sabin 36830
The map is not mentioned in the references noted above.

2256 [JUDAH, THEODORE D.]

REPORT OF THE CHIEF ENGINEER ON THE PRELIMINARY SURVEY, COST OF CONSTRUCTION, AND ESTIMATED REVENUE, OF THE CENTRAL PACIFIC RAILROAD OF CALIFORNIA, ACROSS THE SIERRA NEVADA MOUNTAINS, FROM SACRAMENTO TO THE EASTERN BOUNDARY OF CALIFORNIA. OCTOBER 22, 1862. SACRAMENTO: H. S. CROCKER & CO.'S PRINT, 1862.

[1]–56. 22.7 x 14.4 cm. Dark blue printed wrappers, with title on front wrapper, list of errata on recto of back wrapper. In a brown cloth case.
Ref.: Cowan p. 508; Greenwood 1627; Howes J269; *Railway Economics* p. 290
There is no evidence that a map was included with this copy, yet EDG has a back wrapper of the pamphlet with the proper errata printed on green paper. Attached is a copy of the War Department's map of the Territory and Military Department of Utah . . . 1860 [revised to January, 1862].

2257 JUDD, A. N.

CAMPAIGNING AGAINST THE SIOUX . . . BEING EXTRACTS FROM A DIARY KEPT DURING ONE OF THREE EXPEDITIONS PARTICIPATED IN BY THE AUTHOR AGAINST THE SIOUX, UNDER GENERAL ALFRED SULLY IN 1863-4-5 . . .

[1]–45, [46 blank], [47 colophon, 48 blank]. 25.5 x 17.2 cm. Illustrations unlisted. Pictorial cream wrappers, tied with lilac cord. In a dark blue morocco case.
Ref.: Howes J271; Rader 2133
Limited to 40 copies. Colophon: [rule] / Press of the Daily Pajaronian / Watsonville, California / July, 1906 / [rule] /.

2258 JUDGES AND CRIMINALS . . .

JUDGES AND CRIMINALS: SHADOWS OF THE PAST. HISTORY OF THE VIGILANCE COMMITTEE OF SAN FRANCISCO, CAL. WITH THE NAMES OF ITS OFFICERS. SAN FRANCISCO: PRINTED FOR THE AUTHOR. 1858.

[1]–100. 18.3 x 11.5 cm. Blue printed wrappers, with title on front wrapper. In a blue morocco case.
Prov.: Signed on front cover: E. J. M. McHenry / 1858 /.
Ref.: Cowan pp. 319–20; Greenwood 956; Hanna-Powell p. 23; Howes J334; Sabin 76048(?)
This work would appear to have been written by one who was not a member of the committee. The author is not known, but a copy, that formerly existed in the Mercantile Library in San Francisco, bore a contemporary manuscript note in which the authorship was ascribed to Dr. Henry M. Gray.—Cowan
This was picked by Cowan as one of twenty most important and rarest books relating to California history.—EDG

2259 JUDSON, PHOEBE GOODELL

A PIONEER'S SEARCH FOR AN IDEAL HOME . . . BELLINGHAM, WASHINGTON, 1925.*

[1]–[314]. (Pages [1–2] blank.] 19.6 x 13.3 cm. Frontispiece. Green cloth, stamped in silver.
Ref.: Howes J274; Smith 5373
Overland to Puget Sound in 1853.

2260 JUNCTION CITY [Oregon] CHURCH

[Broadside] GRAND DRAMATIC AND MUSICAL CONCERT! BENEFIT OF JUNCTION CITY CHURCH. [25 lines] TO BE GIVEN AT SMITH, BRASSFIELD & CO'S HALL. JUNCTION CITY, SATURDAY EVENING, DEC. 23, 1876. [3 lines] ED. HOUSTON, MANAGER.

Broadside, 29.4 x 19.4 cm. Text, 23.8 x 18.5 cm.
Ref.:
No place of printing given. Inserted in Manuscript Journals of Loren L. Williams, Volume V.

K

2261 KALBFUS, JOSEPH H.

DR. KALBFUS' BOOK. A SPORTSMAN'S EXPERIENCES AND IMPRESSIONS EAST AND WEST . . .

[i–viii], [1]–342. 20.7 x 13.4 cm. Frontispiece. Green cloth.
Ref.: Adams 583
Copyrighted 1926. Published at Altoona, Pennsylvania.
Pasted to inside front cover is a Letter signed

by Joseph H. Kalbfus. 1913 April 15, Harrisburg. To Mr. McGraw. Regarding game laws of Pennsylvania.

2262 KANE, PAUL

WANDERINGS OF AN ARTIST AMONG THE INDIANS OF NORTH AMERICA FROM CANADA TO VANCOUVER'S ISLAND AND OREGON THROUGH THE HUDSON'S BAY COMPANY'S TERRITORY AND BACK AGAIN . . . LONDON: LONGMAN, BROWN, GREEN, LONGMANS, AND ROBERTS, 1859.

[i]–[xviii], [1]–[463], [464 colophon]. 22.3 x 14.2 cm. Eight colored plates and 13 woodcuts, folding map: Map to Illustrate / Mr Kane's Travels / in the / Territory / of the / Hudson's Bay Company / [lower centre:] London, Longman & Co. [lower right:] Engraved by Edwd Weller, Duke Street, Bloomsbury. / 20.2 x 59.2 cm. Scale: about 145 British miles to one inch. Light brown cloth, advertisements on inner covers.
Ref.: Field 811; Howes K7; Hubach p. 104; Jones 1412; Sabin 37007; Smith 5392; Staton & Tremaine 2911; Wagner-Camp 333
Excellent impressions of the fine plates. The text is based on the author's journal put into narrative form.

2263 KANE, THOMAS L.

THE MORMONS. A DISCOURSE DELIVERED . . . MARCH 26, 1850 . . . PHILADELPHIA: KING & BAIRD, PRINTERS, 1850.

[1]–84. 23.3 x 14.5 cm. Dark gray printed wrappers, with title on front and back wrappers. In a red cloth case.
Ref.: Bradford 2775; Howes K8; Sabin 37011 see; Wagner-Camp 185; Woodward 114
Most sympathetic Gentile appraisal of Mormon conduct. Kane describes their trek to Utah in which he participated.—Howes

2264 KANE, THOMAS L.

THE SAME.

[1]–84. Bound with Number 3346.

2265 KANE, THOMAS L.

THE SAME.*

[1]–92. 23.3 x 14.3 cm. Dark printed gray wrappers, with title on front and back wrappers.
Page [85] is headed: Postscript to the Second Edition. Wagner-Camp states that the Latin quotation does not appear on the title-page in the second edition. Yet it is present in this copy —with an error in the last word.
Editions: Philadelphia, 1850 (84 pages).

2266 KANSAS. ADJUTANT GENERAL'S OFFICE

OFFICIAL. MILITARY HISTORY OF KANSAS REGIMENTS DURING THE WAR FOR THE SUPPRESSION OF THE GREAT REBELLION. LEAVENWORTH: W. S. BURKE, 1870.

[1]–453, [454 blank], [i–ii], [454]–464, [465 blank] [466], [467 blank]. (Rectos carry even numbers after p. [ii].) 21.1 x 13.7 cm. Sheep.
Prov.: Printed and manuscript presentation slip from David Whittaker, Adjutant General, tipped in at end paper.
Ref.: AII (*Kansas*) 771; Howes B986; Nicholson p. 620
There is a half-title inserted after page [454] for the Appendix.
Compiled by J. B. McAfee from material collected by Adjutant General T. J. Anderson and originally published as an appendix to v. 2 of the [special] Report of the Adjutant General for 1861–1865, Leavenworth, 1867.—DLC

2267 KANSAS. CONSTITUTION

[Caption title] CONSTITUTION OF THE STATE OF KANSAS; ADOPTED AT WYANDOT, JULY 19, '59 . . .

[1]–16. 21.2 x 15 cm. Stitched, unbound.
Ref.: AII (*Kansas*) 215; Sabin 37024
Printed in 1859, probably at Wyandotte.

2268 KANSAS. CONSTITUTION

[Broadside] KANSAS STATE CONSTITUTION. CONSTITUTION OF THE STATE OF KANSAS. ADOPTED AT WYANDOTT, JULY 29, 1859 . . . DONE IN CONVENTION AT WYANDOTT, THIS 29TH DAY OF JULY A. D. 1859. JAMES M. WINCHELL, PRESIDENT OF THE KANSAS CONSTITUTIONAL CONVENTION AND DELEGATE FROM OSAGE COUNTY . . .

Broadside, 47.5 x 41 cm. Text, 42.5 x 35.9 cm.
Prov.: Manuscript note in pencil on verso: Hon Andrew Johnson /. Manuscript note in ink: Constitution of Kansas— / To be examined at son[!] future time /.
Ref.: Hawley & Farley 52
Mounted on verso is a small yellow sticker, 2.2 x 7.2 cm.: Printed at, and forwarded from / State Register Office, / Leavenworth, Kansas. /

2269 KANSAS. SENATE

INDIAN RAID OF 1878. THE REPORT OF COMMISSION APPOINTED IN PURSUANCE OF THE PROVISIONS OF SENATE JOINT RESOLUTION NO. 1, RELATING TO LOSSES SUSTAINED BY CITIZENS OF KANSAS BY THE INVASION OF INDIANS DURING THE YEAR 1878. TOPEKA, KANSAS: GEO. W. MARTIN, 1879.

[1]–58. 21.8 x 14.3 cm. Purple printed wrappers, with title as above on front wrapper.
Ref.:

2270 KANSAS TERRITORY. BOARD OF COMMISSIONERS FOR THE INVESTIGATION OF ELECTION FRAUDS

REPORT OF THE BOARD OF COMMISSIONERS FOR THE INVESTIGATION OF ELECTION FRAUDS . . . LEAVENWORTH CITY, K.T.: C. H. MCLAUGHLIN, 1858.

[1]–142, [143 errata, 144 blank]. 16.6 x 12.8 cm. Plain blue wrappers.

Ref.: AII (*Kansas*) 175; Howes A49

Report to Governor Denver concerning voting on the acceptance of the Lecompton Constitution [forbidding slavery], doomed to failure by armed bands of pro-slave ruffians.—Howes

2271 KANSAS TERRITORY. CONSTITUTIONAL CONVENTION, WYANDOTTE, 1859

[Broadside] LIST OF MEMBERS OF THE CONSTITUTIONAL CONVENTION, ASSEMBLED AT WYANDOTTE, KANSAS, JULY 5TH, 1859 . . .

Broadside, 35.2 x 21.6 cm. Text, 18 x 19.4 cm.
Ref.: AII (*Kansas*) 217
Printed in blue-green.

2272 KANSAS TERRITORY. GOVERNOR (S. Medary)

[Caption title] VETO MESSAGE OF GOVERNOR MEDARY, ON THE BILL PROHIBITING SLAVERY IN KANSAS. EXECUTIVE OFFICE, K. T., FEBRUARY 20, 1860. TO THE HONORABLE, THE HOUSE OF REPRESENTATIVES . . .

[1]–16. 22.5 x 14.2 cm. Removed from bound volume, unbound.
Ref.: AII (*Kansas*) 251; Sabin 37035
Apparently printed at Lawrence, Kansas, since the text refers to "The *Republican*, of this place . . ."

2273 KANSAS CENTRAL RAILWAY

STATEMENT OF THE CONDITION AND RESOURCES OF THE KANSAS CENTRAL RAILWAY NARROW GAUGE FROM LEAVENWORTH, KANSAS, TO DENVER, COLORADO. LEAVENWORTH: PRINTED AT THE OFFICE OF THE KANSAS FARMER, 1871.

[1]–19, [20 blank]. 21.3 x 13.7 cm. Folding map: Map of the / Kansas Central / Railway / and its Connections. / 31.4 x 60.5 cm. No scale given. Bright blue wrappers, title printed in gold and black.
Ref.: Hawley & Farley 240

2274 KANSAS MANUFACTURING COMPANY

1776. 1876. THE CENTENNIAL EXHIBITION. KANSAS WAGON. MANUFACTURED BY KANSAS MANUFACTURING CO. LEAVENWORTH, KANSAS. C. J. SMITH & CO., PRINTERS, LEAVENWORTH.

[1–4]. 20.1 x 13.2 cm. Fold along upper edge, unbound.
Ref.:
Text printed in red and blue, principally red.

2275 KANSAS PACIFIC RAILWAY COMPANY

GUIDE MAP OF THE BEST AND SHORTEST CATTLE TRAIL TO THE KANSAS PACIFIC RAILWAY: WITH A CONCISE AND ACCURATE DESCRIPTION OF THE ROUTE: SHOWING DISTANCES, STREAMS, CROSSINGS, CAMPING GROUNDS, WOOD AND WATER, SUPPLY STORES, ETC. FROM THE RED RIVER CROSSING TO ELLIS, RUSSELL, ELLSWORTH, BROOKVILLE, SALINA, SOLOMON, AND ABILENE. COPY RIGHT SECURED BY THE KANSAS PACIFIC RAILWAY COMPANY.

[1]–21, [22–24 blank]. 16.1 x 10.9 cm. Map: Kansas Pacific Railway / The / Best and Shortest / Cattle Trail / from / Texas. / [lower centre:] K. C. Lith Cº Kansas City Mº / 53.2 x 37.6 cm. No scale given. Stiff blue printed wrappers, with title on front wrapper. In blue cloth slip case.
Ref.: Adams (*Ramp. Herd*) 1256; Clements Library (*Texas*) 44; Rader 2139
The introductory text is signed on page 11 by the General Freight Agent, T. F. Oakes, G.F.A.
The printer's trademark appears on the verso of the title-leaf: Ramsey, / Millett & Hudson / Steam Printers / Book Binders / and / Engravers / Kansas City / Mo /
About the time this guide map was issued, Texas began to assume its preëminence as a source of American food, particularly of beef. Moving cattle from grazing lands in Texas to rail transportation terminals was an annual job. The map indicates some of the popular trails from Texas to Kansas.

2276 KANSAS PACIFIC RAILWAY COMPANY

SILVER-SEEKING IN THE SAN JUAN MINES. LOCATION OF THE SILVER REGION—HOW TO GET THERE—WHAT YOU WANT, AND COST OF OUTFIT—HOW TO LOCATE YOUR CLAIM, TOGETHER WITH THE MINING LAWS OF COLORADO AND ACTS OF CONGRESS RELATING THERETO. KANSAS CITY, MO: JOURNAL OF COMMERCE PRINTING AND PUBLISHING HOUSE. 1877.

[1]-66. 21.3 x 14.5 cm. Folding map: A Geographically Correct Map / of the / Kansas Pacific Railway, / Showing the only Direct Route to Denver and all the Popular / Rocky Mountain Resorts. / Also, to the / Black Hills Country / And the famous San Juan Mines in Colorado. / [lower left corner:] Woodward, Tiernan & Hale, Map Engr's. St. Louis. / 29.8 x 64.3 cm.

No scale given. Silver foil mounted on paper wrappers, with title as above on front wrapper, advertisements on verso of front and recto and verso of back wrapper.

Ref.:

2277 KAUTZ, AUGUST V.

[Wrapper title] ANNUAL REPORT . . . DEPARTMENT OF ARIZONA, FOR THE YEAR ENDING AUGUST 31, 1875. PRESCOTT: 1875.

[1]–12. 20 x 12.6 cm. White printed wrappers with title on front wrapper.

Ref.:

Printed at Prescott.

Dated: Headquarters Department of Arizona, / Prescott, August 31, 1875. /

An interesting report with special attention to the Hualpai Indians and the Indians of the San Carlos Agency.

2278 KAUTZ, AUGUST V.

[Wrapper title] ANNUAL REPORT . . . DEPARTMENT OF ARIZONA, FOR YEAR 1875–76. PRESCOTT: 1876.

[1]–14. 19.2 x 12 cm. White printed wrappers with title on front wrapper.

Ref.:

Dated: Headquarters Department of Arizona, / Prescott, A. T., Sept. 15th, 1876. / Printed at Prescott.

Contains sections on the Indians, Indian Scouts, the Border, Posts, etc.

2279 KAUTZ, AUGUST V.

[Wrapper title] ANNUAL REPORT . . . DEPARTMENT OF ARIZONA FOR YEAR 1876–77. PRESCOTT: 1877.

[1]–22, [23–4 blank]. 19.1 x 12.4 cm. White printed wrappers with title on front wrapper. Part of front wrapper supplied, but not affecting text except border, upper part of back wrapper cut off.

Ref.:

Dated: Headquarters Department of Arizona, / Prescott, A. T., August 15, 1877. / Printed at Prescott.

Contains considerable material on the interference of civilians with military control of the Indians, particularly by the Governor of the Territory.

2280 KEATING, WILLIAM H.

NARRATIVE OF AN EXPEDITION TO THE SOURCE OF ST. PETER'S RIVER, LAKE WINNEPEEK, LAKE OF THE WOODS, &C. &C. PERFORMED IN THE YEAR 1823 . . . PHILADELPHIA: H. C. CAREY & I. LEA, 1824.

[i]–[xiv], [9]–439, [440 blank]. [i]–vi, [5]–459, [460 blank]. 23 x 14.5 cm. Map and 15 plates listed. Folding map: Map / of the / Country / Embracing the Route / of the Expedition of 1823 / commanded by Major S. H. Long. / [lower right:] J. H. Young Sc. / 25.9 x 52.8 cm. No scale given. Two volumes, tan boards, buff backstrips, with printed paper labels, uncut. In board wrappers.

Prov.: Signature on each front cover: DeWitt Clinton /. Braislin copy, item 1087.

Ref.: Bradford 2789; Howes K20; Hubach p. 59; Sabin 37137

2281 KEELER, WILLIAM J.

[Map] NATIONAL MAP / OF THE / TERRITORY OF THE UNITED STATES / FROM THE / MISSISSIPPI RIVER TO THE PACIFIC OCEAN. / MADE BY AUTHORITY OF THE HON. O. H. BROWNING SECRETARY OF THE INTERIOR. / IN THE OFFICE OF THE INDIAN BUREAU CHIEFLY FOR GOVERNMENT PURPOSES UNDER THE DIRECTION OF THE / HON. N. G. TAYLOR COMMIS.R OF INDIAN AFFAIRS & HON. CHARLES E. MIX CHIEF CLERK OF THE INDIAN BUREAU; / COMPILED FROM AUTHORIZED EXPLORATIONS OF PACIFIC RAIL ROAD ROUTES, / PUBLIC SURVEYS, AND OTHER RELIABLE DATA FROM THE / DEPARTMENTS OF THE GOVERNMENT AT WASHINGTON, D. C. / BY / W. J. KEELER, CIVIL ENGINEER. / 1867. / [left below cartouche:] N. DU BOIS / DRAUGHTSMAN. / [right below cartouche:] J. F. GEDNEY, / LITHOGRAPHER, ENGRAVER / & / PLATE PRINTER, / WASHINGTON, D. C. / [centre, below cartouche:] SCALE 36 MILES TO AN INCH. / [diagrammatic scale] / ENTERED ACCORDING TO ACT OF CONGRESS IN THE YEAR 1867 BY W.M.J. KEELER IN THE CLERKS OFFICE OF THE DISTRICT COURT OF THE DISTRICT OF COLUMBIA. /

120.9 x 146.4 cm. Scale: 36 miles to one inch. Mounted on linen and folded into original brown cloth covers with title in gilt on front cover.

Prov.: Inscribed on inside front cover: Hon Cha[s] Upson / House of Rep[s] / With Compliments of / [rubber stamped name:] N. G. Taylor / Comm[r] Indian Affairs /.

Ref.: Howes K22; Munk (Alliot) p. 121; Phillips (*Maps*) p. 916

Howes calls for a page of text which is not present.

2282 KEILY, P. T., *Compiler*

[Caption title] PIERRE CITY DIRECTORY. JULY, 1883 . . .

[1]–44. 18.8 x 13.4 cm. Gray printed wrappers, with advertisements and title on front wrapper. Two rivets through inner margin.

Ref.: Allen (*Dakota*) 277; Howes K28

The *Directory* lists Folsom as editor and Haines as business manager of the Pierre *Daily and Weekly Signal*. Most of the versos are occupied by advertisements.

2283 KEIM, DE BENNEVILLE RANDOLPH

SHERIDAN'S TROOPERS ON THE BORDERS . . . PHILADELPHIA: CLAXTON, REMSEN & HAFFELFINGER, 1870.

[1]–4, V–VIII, 9–308. 19 x 12 cm. Eight illustrations unlisted. Green cloth, blind fillet borders on sides, gilt title on backstrip. Lacks front endleaf.

Ref.: Field 813; Howes K31; Rader 2151; Sabin 37172

2284 KELLER, GEORGE

A TRIP ACROSS THE PLAINS, AND LIFE IN CALIFORNIA; EMBRACING A DESCRIPTION OF THE OVERLAND ROUTE; ITS NATURAL CURIOSITIES, RIVERS, LAKES, SPRINGS, MOUNTAINS, INDIAN TRIBES, &C. &C.; THE GOLD MINES OF CALIFORNIA: ITS CLIMATE, SOIL, PRODUCTIONS, ANIMALS, &C. . . . A GUIDE OF THE ROUTE FROM THE MISSOURI RIVER TO THE PACIFIC OCEAN . . .

[i]–vi, [7]–58, [59–60 blank]. 18 x 11.4 cm. Tan printed wrappers, with title on front wrapper. In a red half morocco case.

Ref.: Cowan pp. 323–24; Howes K41; Sabin 37250; Wagner-Camp 199

Imprint on verso of title-page: [rule] / [wavy rule] / White's Press—Massillon, 1851. / [wavy rule] / [rule] /. Very rare. Wessen surmises the pamphlet may never have been distributed, since in August of 1851 a severe fire destroyed all the buildings on the north side of a square on Main Street.—EDG

2285 KELLEY, HALL J.

THE AMERICAN INSTRUCTOR, SECOND BOOK. DESIGNED FOR THE COMMON SCHOOLS IN AMERICA . . . CONCORD, N. H.: PUBLISHED BY ISAAC HILL, 1826.

[1]–168. (Page [1] blank, page [2] frontispiece.) 16.8 x 9.5 cm. Frontispiece and ten illustrations in the text. Blue board sides, calf backstrip.

Prov.: Bookplate of Donald McKay Frost.
Ref.:

2286 KELLEY, HALL J.

A GENERAL CIRCULAR TO ALL PERSONS OF GOOD CHARACTER, WHO WISH TO EMIGRATE TO THE OREGON TERRITORY, EMBRACING SOME ACCOUNT OF THE CHARACTER AND ADVANTAGES OF THE COUNTRY; THE RIGHT AND THE MEANS AND OPERA-

TIONS BY WHICH IT IS TO BE SETTLED; —AND ALL NECESSARY DIRECTIONS FOR BECOMING AN EMIGRANT . . . CHARLESTOWN: PRINTED BY WILLIAM W. WHEILDON, 1831.

[1]–[28]. 23.4 x 14.7 cm. Tan printed wrappers, with title on front wrapper. In maroon cloth case.

Ref.: Bradford 2795; Howell 160; Howes K43; Jones 919; Sabin 37260; Smith 5428

Published also as an appendix to the second edition of Kelley's *A Geographical Sketch of that Part of North America, called Oregon* . . . Boston [1831].

Laid in is a certificate, No. 79, partially filled out and cancelled.

Page [28] carries a woodcut map and a list of agents "where this Manual may be had."

2287 KELLEY, HALL J.

A GEOGRAPHICAL SKETCH OF THAT PART OF NORTH AMERICA, CALLED OREGON . . . BOSTON: PRINTED AND PUBLISHED BY J. HOWE, 1830.

[1]–80. 23.8 x 15.1 cm. Folding map: Map / of / Oregon. / Pendleton's Lithography, Boston. / Drawn by H. J. Kelley 1830. / 29.7 x 33.5 cm. No scale given. Blue printed wrappers, with title on front wrapper. In a blue half morocco case.

Ref.: Bradford 2800; Howell 161; Howes K44; Jones 906; Sabin 37261; Smith 5430; Wheat (*Transmississippi*) 395

2288 KELLEY, HALL J.

THE SAME. BOSTON: PRINTED AND PUBLISHED BY J. HOWE.

[1]–80, [1]–[28]. 22.6 x 13.7 cm. Folding map, as in first edition. Page [28] carries a map of the proposed layout of the settlement. Green boards, tan paper backstrip. Backstrip supplied. In brown half morocco case.

Ref.: Bradford 2800; Howes K44; Sabin 37261

The appendix carries a separate title-page: A / General Circular / to all / Persons of Good Character, / who wish to Emigrate/ to the / Oregon Territory, / embracing some Account of the Character and / Advantages of the Country; the right / and the Means and Operations by / which it is to be Settled; — / and / all Necessary Directions for becoming / an Emigrant. / [rule] / Hall J. Kelley, General Agent. / [rule] / By Order of the American Society for Encouraging / the Settlement of the Oregon Territory. / Instituted in Boston, A. D. 1829. / [decorative rule] / Charlestown: / Printed by William W. Wheildon. / R. P. & C. Williams—Boston. / 1831. /

Editions: Boston, 1830.

2289 KELLEY, HALL J.

HISTORY OF THE COLONIZATION OF THE OREGON TERRITORY . . . SPRINGFIELD, MASS.: PRINTED FOR THE AUTHOR BY G. W. WILSON, 1849.

[1]–12, 5–8, 17–18, [1–10]. 21.6 x 12.5 cm. Rebound in old blue wrappers. In a red half morocco case.

Ref.: Bradford 2799 see; Sabin 37263

At least one copy contains 26 pages, but the pamphlet was never published and few copies now exist. Possibly some were distributed containing less material than others. The corrections on page 12 may be by Kelley himself. The footnotes are not reproduced in the Powell reprint; apparently the copy Powell worked from lacked them.

2290 KELLEY, HALL J.

A HISTORY OF THE SETTLEMENT OF OREGON AND THE INTERIOR OF UPPER CALIFORNIA; AND OF PERSECUTIONS AND APPLICATIONS OF FORTY YEARS' CONTINUANCE, ENDURED BY THE AUTHOR . . . SPRINGFIELD, MASS: UNION PRINTING COMPANY, 1868.

[i]–[xviii, xviii blank], [1]–7, [8 blank], [1]–128. 22.2 x 14.5 cm. Gray printed wrappers with title on front wrapper. In a blue half morocco case.

Ref.: Bradford 2797; Cowan p. 324; Howes K45; Sabin 37262; Smith 5433

Probably the rarest of the Kelley pamphlets. —EDG

2291 KELLEY, HALL J.

A NARRATIVE OF EVENTS AND DIFFICULTIES IN THE COLONIZATION OF OREGON, AND THE SETTLEMENT OF CALIFORNIA; AND, ALSO, A HISTORY OF CLAIMS OF AMERICAN CITIZENS TO LANDS ON QUADRA'S ISLAND; TOGETHER WITH AN ACCOUNT OF THE TROUBLES AND TRIBULATIONS ENDURED BETWEEN THE YEARS 1824 AND 1852, BY THE WRITER . . . BOSTON: PRINTED BY THURSTON, TORRY & EMERSON, 1852.

[1]–92. 22.8 x 14.4 cm. Gray printed wrappers with title on front wrapper. In a dark green half morocco case.

Ref.: Bradford 2798; Howes K46; Sabin 37263; Smith 5434

Manuscript note in pencil on front wrapper by Edward Eberstadt: Probably the finest copy in existence / Superlatively rare /.

2292 KELLEY, WILLIAM D.

. . . THE NEW NORTHWEST: AN ADDRESS . . . ON THE NORTHERN PACIFIC RAILWAY, IN ITS RELATIONS TO THE NORTHWESTERN SECTION OF THE UNITED STATES, AND TO THE INDUSTRIAL AND COMMERCIAL INTERESTS OF THE NATION.

[1]–32. 23.9 x 16.7 cm. Buff printed wrappers, with title on front wrapper, map on verso of back wrapper.

Ref.: Jones 1542; Smith 5436

Published at Philadelphia in 1871. Pages [31]–32 carry an article: Climate and Resources of Montana. / [decorative rule] / By B. F. Potts, / Governor of Montana Territory. / [decorative rule] /.

2293 KELLOGG, GEORGE J.

[Wrapper title] NARATIVE[!] OF GEO. J. KELLOGG FROM 1849 TO 1915 AND SOME HISTORY OF WISCONSIN SINCE 1835.

[1]–[36]. 22.3 x 9.6 cm. Portrait. Cream printed wrappers. In brown cloth case.

Ref.: Howes K48

At the end of the text: Geo. J. Kellogg. / Alvin, Texas, Dec. 4, 1914. /

Includes day by day contemporary journal of trip across the plains to California in 1849 and life at the mines. Evidently printed originally in the *Janesville Gazette* and reprinted in a small edition for distribution to friends.—EDG

2294 KELLOGG, HARRIET

LIFE OF MRS. EMILY J. HARWOOD . . . ALBUQUERQUE, NEW MEXICO: EL ABOGADO PRESS, 1903.

[i–vi], I–XXVIII, [1]–152, [150]–[385]. (Even pagination on rectos from [150] to end.) 17.4 x 11.6 cm. Illustrations, some included in pagination. Green cloth, gilt. Lacks front endleaf.

Ref.: Howes K49

Printed by Indian students at the Mission press.

2295 KELLOGG, MERRITT G.

NOTES CONCERNING THE KELLOGG'S . . . BATTLE CREEK, MICHIGAN, 1927.

[1]–116. 23 x 15.3 cm. Frontispiece portrait. White printed wrappers with title on front wrapper.

Ref.: Carson, Gerald: *Cornflake Crusade* (New York, 1957) p. 37 et seq.; Howes K54

The early part of this book relates to pioneer conditions and life near Battle Creek, Michigan during the years 1840 and later. Pages 53–116 contain an account of a trip overland from Battle Creek to Marysville, California in 1859.—EDG

Laid in: Smith Kellogg / [ornament] / [within triple rule border]. [1–8] ([1] title, [2] blank, [3–5] text], [6–8 blank]). 22.8 x 14.9 cm.

2296 KELLY, FANNY

NARRATIVE OF MY CAPTIVITY AMONG THE SIOUX INDIANS . . . WITH A BRIEF ACCOUNT OF GENERAL SULLY'S INDIAN EXPEDITION IN 1864, BEARING UPON EVENTS OCCURRING IN MY CAPTIVITY. CINCINNATI: WILSTACH, BALDWIN & CO., 1871.

[i]–x, 11–285, [286 blank]. 19.4 x 12.4 cm. 12 illustrations. Purple cloth.
Ref.: Howes K62; Rader 2153

2297 KELLY, FANNY

[Broadside] TO THE SENATORS AND MEMBERS OF THE HOUSE OF REPRESENTATIVES OF CONGRESS: YOUR MEMORIALIST, MRS. FANNIE[!] KELLY, A CITIZEN OF THE UNITED STATES, AND RESIDING IN THE STATE OF KANSAS, RESPECTFULLY PETITIONING YOUR HONORABLE BODIES, REPRESENTS . . . YOUR MEMORIALIST ASKS SOME COMPENSATION IN SUCH SUM AS MAY SEEM METE, AND SHE WILL, AS IN DUTY BOUND, EVER PRAY. FANNIE KELLY.

Broadside, 35.6 x 21.6 cm. Text, 25.4 x 16.8 cm.
Ref.:
Probably printed in Washington and probably in 1870.

Mrs. Kelly's memorial prays for relief on the grounds she had saved Fort Sully from massacre, and other services.

In her book, Mrs. Kelly states her husband died July 28th, 1867. She mentions a trip to Sheridan and Fort Hays the following spring (1868). Evidently she left Kansas for Wyoming in the fall of 1868 or the spring of 1869, probably the latter. She says she stayed in Wyoming one year and then started for Washington, D. C. to present a claim to the Government. There she saw President Grant and Congress appropriated for her the sum of $5000 for valuable services rendered the Government. Thus the broadside is dated not later than 1870.—EDG

2298 KELLY, WILLIAM

AN EXCURSION TO CALIFORNIA OVER THE PRAIRIE, ROCKY MOUNTAINS, AND GREAT SIERRA NEVADA. WITH A STROLL THROUGH THE DIGGINGS AND RANCHES OF THAT COUNTRY . . . LONDON: CHAPMAN AND HALL, MDCCCLI.

[i]–x, [1]–342. [i]–viii, [1]–334, [335–36 advertisements]. 19.7 x 12.2 cm. Two volumes, bright green cloth, embossed design on sides, title stamped in gilt on backstrip, uncut.
Ref.: Blumann & Thomas 5025; Bradford 2807; Buck 453; Cowan pp. 325–26; Howes K68; Sabin 37321; Wagner-Camp 200

According to Buck, most of Kelly's comments were unfavorable.

2299 KEMBLE, FRANCES ANNE (MRS. PIERCE BUTLER)

JOURNAL OF A RESIDENCE ON A GEORGIAN PLANTATION IN 1838–1839 . . . LONDON: LONGMAN, GREEN, LONGMAN, ROBERTS, & GREEN, 1863.

[i–viii, viii blank], [1]–434, [435–36 blank], [1]–32 advertisements dated on p. 32 January, 1863. 19.6 x 12 cm. Brown embossed cloth, title in gilt on backstrip, uncut.
Ref.: Clark III 187; De Renne pp. 655–56; Howes K70; Sabin 37329

Fannie Kemble's first *Journal*, critical of some American customs, created considerable trouble. The second *Journal*, for 1838–39, the author suppressed until 1863, at which time she believed it might influence the British reading public against the Confederacy.

2300 KEMPKER, JOHN F.

[Wrapper title] THE CATHOLIC CHURCH IN COUNCIL BLUFFS, IOWA . . . LACONA, IOWA, 1904.

[1]–18. 22.4 x 15.3 cm. Light blue printed wrappers with title as above on front wrapper, imprint on verso of back wrapper: Ledger Printing House, / Lacona, Iowa. /, uncut.
Prov.: Inscribed on front cover: Rev. John F. Kempker. / [flourish] /.
Ref.: Mott (*Iowa*) p. 70

2301 KEMPKER, JOHN F.

HISTORY OF THE CATHOLIC CHURCH IN IOWA . . . IOWA CITY, IOWA: REPUBLICAN PUBLISHING COMPANY, 1887.

[1]–64. 22.3 x 14.6 cm. Chartreuse printed wrappers with title on front wrapper.
Prov.: Inscribed on front wrapper: Rev. John F. Kempker. / [flourish] /. Rubber stamp partially erased from back wrapper.
Ref.: Mott (*Iowa*) p. 70; Streit III 2785

2302 KEMPKER, JOHN F.

VERY REVEREND J. A. M. PELAMOURGUES, FIRST PASTOR OF ST. ANTHONY'S CHURCH, DAVENPORT, IOWA . . . WINTERSET, IOWA, 1901.

[1]–12. 20 x 15.5 cm. Portrait and two illustrations in text. Pale green printed wrappers with title on front wrapper.
Prov.: Inscribed on front wrapper: [rule] / Rev. John F. Kempker. / [flourish] /.
Ref.:
Imprint on verso of back wrapper: Madisonian Print. / Winterset, Ia. /

2303 KENDALL, AMOS

AUTOBIOGRAPHY OF AMOS KENDALL. EDITED BY . . . WILLIAM STICKNEY. BOSTON: LEE AND SHEPARD, 1872.

[i]–[x, x blank], 1–700. 23.3 x 14.6 cm. Three illustrations and a facsimile. Brown cloth.

Prov.: Inscribed on title-page: Hon. C. W. Kendall— / with compliments of / Wᵐ Stickney. / Dec 1874. /

Ref.: Howes K72

2304 KENDALL, GEORGE W.

NARRATIVE OF THE TEXAN SANTA FE EXPEDITION, COMPRISING A DESCRIPTION OF A TOUR THROUGH TEXAS, AND ACROSS THE GREAT SOUTHWESTERN PRAIRIES, THE CAMANCHE AND CAYGUA HUNTING-GROUNDS, WITH AN ACCOUNT OF THE SUFFERINGS FROM WANT OF FOOD, LOSSES FROM HOSTILE INDIANS, AND FINAL CAPTURE OF THE TEXANS, AND THEIR MARCH, AS PRISONERS, TO THE CITY OF MEXICO . . . NEW-YORK: HARPER AND BROTHERS, 1844.

[1–2], [i]–xii, [13]–405, [406 blank]. [i]–xii, [13]–406. 19.9 x 12.9 cm. Five plates and a map. Map: Texas / and Part of / Mexico & the United States, / showing the Route of / The First Santa Fé Expedition, / Drawn & Engᵈ by W. Kemble N. York. / [below border:] Harper & Brothers, New York. / 40.3 x 29.3 cm. No scale indicated. Two volumes, plum cloth, blind embossed sides, gilt title on backstrips.

Prov.: Tipped to front endleaf is a slip, 11.8 x 14.1 cm., inscribed: To Chas. Lever, Esq. / with the compliments of one who, / while confined in the gloomy / hospital of San Lararo, Mexico, / beguiled many weary hours of / imprisonment by perusing and / re-perusing his inimitable *"Charles / "O'Malley."* / Geo. Wilkins Kendall / [broken underline] / New Orleans, La. Jan. 1844. / Bookplate of Richard Nevill.

Ref.: Bradford 2809; Clark III 188; Dobie p. 56; Field 818; Howes K75; Jones 1089; Munk (Alliot) p. 122; Rader 2157; Raines p. 131; Sabin 37360; Saunders 2998; Wagner-Camp 110; Wheat (*Transmississippi*) 483

2305 KENDALL, GEORGE W.

ANOTHER COPY. Black cloth.

Prov.: Inscribed on front endleaf: To Chas. Obermayer / with respects of / Geo. Wilkins Kendall / [broken underline] /.

2306 KENDALL, GEORGE W.

THE SAME. NEW YORK: HARPER & BROTHERS, 1856.

[i]–xviii, [13]–452. [i]–xiii, [xiv blank], [11]–442. 19.4 x 12.4 cm. Three plates and map in first volume, two plates in second. Map same as preceding. Two volumes, black cloth, blind embossed borders on sides, gilt title on backstrips.

Prov.: Thomas Falconer's copy with signature, photograph, notes, and corrections in text. Several bookplates of John Egerton Falconer.

Ref.: Bradford 2809 note; Clark III 188 note; Howes K75; Wagner-Camp 110 note

Pages 438–51 of the first volume contain part of Falconer's diary relating to events after Kendall left the main command.

Inserted between pages [ii–iii] of first volume are two blank leaves of stiff paper on which have been mounted newspaper clippings relating to the death of Kendall.

Editions: New York, 1844, 1846, 1847, 1850, 1857; London, 1844, 1845, 1847.

2307 KENNEDY, JOHN, *Compiler*

IOWA CITY DIRECTORY AND ADVERTISER, FOR 1857. CONTAINING A HISTORY OF THE CITY AND COUNTY . . . IOWA CITY: A. G. TUCKER & CO.

[1]–34, [1]–46, 47 (inside of back cover). 17.3 x 11 cm. Yellow printed boards, with title on front cover.

Ref.: Howes K85; Moffit 309

First Directory of Iowa City. The first 34 pages are advertisements, as are pages 46–47.

2308 KENNEDY, WILLIAM

TEXAS: THE RISE, PROGRESS, AND PROSPECTS OF THE REPUBLIC OF TEXAS . . . LONDON: R. HASTINGS, 1841.

[i]–lii, [1]–378. [i]–vi, [1]–548. 22.4 x 14 cm. Two folding and two full-page maps: Map: Map of / Texas, / compiled from / Surveys recorded in the Land Office of Texas, / and other Official Surveys, / By / John Arrowsmith. / Soho Square, London. / [lower centre:] London. Pubᵈ 17 April, 1841. by John Arrowsmith, 10 Soho Square. 59.1 x 49.7 cm. Scale: about 42 miles to one inch. / *Inset:* Plan of / Galveston Bay / from a MS. / 12.7 x 19 cm. No scale given. *Inset:* [Western Part of United States, Texas, and Mexico] 15 x 13 cm. No scale given. Map: [Chart of Matagorda Bay]. 11.5 x 18.3 cm. Scale: about 1 1/3 miles to one inch. Map: Aranzas Bay, / as Surveyed by / Captⁿ Monroe / of the "Amos Wright." / [lower left:] C. F. Cheffins, litho. Southampton Bᵈᵍˢ Holborn. / 19.1 x 11.5 cm. Scale: three miles to one inch. Map: A / Map of the Republic / of / Texas / and the / Adjacent Territories, / Indicating the Grants of Land / Conceded under the Empresario System / of / Mexico. / 31.4 x 38 cm. Scale: about 75 miles to one inch. Two volumes, green cloth, blind embossed sides, gilt title on backstrips, uncut.

Prov.: Inscribed on title-page of first volume: To / W. D. Cooley Esq. / With the Author's Best Respects / [underline] /.

Ref.: Bradford 2814; Clark III 189; Howes K92; Rader 2159; Raines pp. 132–33; Sabin 37440; Streeter 1385

Paints a favorable picture of Texas, and may have hastened English recognition of her independence.—Howes

2309 KENTUCKY. CITIZENS

[Broadside] AT A MEETING OF THE CITIZENS OF FRANKLIN, AT THE STATE HOUSE IN FRANKFORT, ON FRIDAY THE 24TH OF JULY, 1807, FOR THE PURPOSE OF TAKING INTO CONSIDERATION THE DEPREDATIONS, INSULTS, AND OUTRAGES COMMITTED BY BRITISH SUBJECTS, ON THE PROPERTY, RIGHTS, AND PERSONS OF AMERICAN CITIZENS . . . THE COMMITTEE APPOINTED FOR THE PURPOSE, REPORTED, THAT HAVING HAD THE SEVERAL SUBJECTS REFERRED TO THEM, UNDER THEIR DELIBERATION— HAVING HEARD THE RECITAL OF THE LATE UNPROVOKED AND PIRATICAL ATTACK MADE UPON THE UNITED STATES' FRIGATE, THE CHESAPEAK, OF THIRTY SIX GUNS, . . . BY THE BRITISH SHIP OF WAR, THE LEOPARD OF FIFTY GUNS, . . . THEREFORE, RESOLVED, UNANIMOUSLY, . . . SIGNED BY ORDER OF THE MEETING, CHRISTOPHER GREENUP, CHAIRMAN. TESTE. WILLIAM TRIGG, SECRETARY.

Broadside, 37 x 20 cm. Text, 30.5 x 11 cm. Left margin mutilated, text intact.
Ref.:
Printed at Frankfort in 1807.

2310 KENYON, WILLIAM A.

MISCELLANEOUS POEMS, TO WHICH ARE ADDED WRITINGS IN PROSE, ON VARIOUS SUBJECTS . . . CHICAGO: PRINTED BY JAS. CAMPBELL & CO., 1845.
[1]–208. (Page 192 mispaginated 19.) 14.1 x 18.8 cm. Blind embossed gray cloth, with black skiver label on backstrip lettered in gilt.
Ref.: Byrd 976; McMurtrie (*Chicago*) 86

2311 KEOKUK, IOWA. Ordinances, etc.

THE REVISED ORDINANCES OF THE CITY OF KEOKUK, REVISED AND DIGESTED BY THE CITY COUNCIL, DURING THE SUMMER OF 1851. WITH THE CONSTITUTION OF THE STATE OF IOWA, AND THE CITY CHARTER, INCLUDING THE STATE LAWS CONCERNING VAGRANTS, AND THE SALE OF INTOXICATING LIQUORS. KEOKUK: PRINTED AT THE WHIG OFFICE, 1851.
[1]–108. 22.7 x 13.8 cm. Sheep.
Ref.: Moffit 91

2312 KEPHEART TRAGEDY, THE

THE KEPHEART TRAGEDY: BEING A COMPLETE HISTORY OF THE MURDER OF A WOMAN AND TWO CHILDREN, IN WAPELLO COUNTY, IOWA; THE ARREST, ABDUCTION FROM JAIL AND EXECUTION OF THE MURDERER BY THE PEOPLE. TO WHICH IS ADDED A SKETCH OF THE CAREER OF KEPHEART. MUSCATINE: PUBLISHED BY THE AUTHOR, 1860.
[1]–23, [24 blank]. 21.5 x 13.6 cm. Yellow printed wrappers with title on front wrapper. Lacks back wrapper.
Ref.:

2313 KERR, LEWIS

AN EXPOSITION OF THE CRIMINAL LAWS OF THE TERRITORY OF ORLEANS . . . NEW-ORLEANS: PRINTED BY JOHN MOWRY, 1806.
A6, B–Y4. [i]–xii, [1]–134, [i]–xxxiv. (Page xvii mispaginated xvi.) 18.9 x 12.5 cm. Rebound in contemporary calf, blind borders on sides, red and green leather labels on backstrip. In a yellow cloth slip case.
Prov.: Thomas Jefferson's copy with his manuscript T. before the printed signature I and his manuscript I. after the printed signature T.
Ref.: McMurtrie (*Louisiana*) 56; Sabin 37629; Shaw & Shoemaker 10675

Miss Sowerby described two copies of the French translation as being in the Jefferson library, but did not mention the English version. McMurtrie (*New Orleans*) 87 is an edition with both English and French texts, the French printed by Jean Renard and the English probably by Bradford & Anderson.

The Library of Congress copy of this work contains an additional page, an apology for an inadvertent error in the Appendix. The leaf, obviously printed later than the text, is not present in this copy.

2314 KERSHAW, W. L.

HISTORY OF PAGE COUNTY, IOWA. ALSO BIOGRAPHICAL SKETCHES OF SOME PROMINENT CITIZENS OF THE COUNTY . . . CHICAGO: THE S. J. CLARKE PUBLISHING CO., 1909.
[1]–478, [479–481], [482 blank]. [1]–[608]. (In each volume, pages [1–2] blank.) 26.1 x 18.2 cm. Illustrations listed in first volume, not in second. Two volumes, half leather, gilt edges.
Ref.: Cook p. 145

2315 KEYES, ERASMUS D.

FIFTY YEARS' OBSERVATION OF MEN AND EVENTS CIVIL AND MILITARY . . . NEW YORK: CHARLES SCRIBNER'S SONS, 1884.
[i]–vii, [viii blank], 1–515, [516 blank, 517–20 advertisements]. 18.9 x 12.7 cm. Dark gray cloth.
Ref.: Blumann & Thomas 3242; Cowan p. 328; Howes K115; Rader 2164

The best picture of General Scott. Keyes was his aide for many years and gives an intimate picture of him, also remarks on life in California in 1849 and Indian campaigns on the Pacific Coast.—EDG

2316 KILBOURNE, DAVID W.

INAUGURAL ADDRESS . . . DELIVERED AT CONCERT HALL, APRIL 10, 1855 . . . KEOKUK: GATE CITY PRINT, 1855.

[1]–20. 22.7 x 14 cm. Gray printed wrappers, with title on front wrapper.

Ref.: Moffit 200

Kilbourne superintended the laying out of Keokuk in 1837 and his mayoral address contains much interesting information about its early history.—EDG

2317 KILBOURNE, DAVID W.

THE SAME.

Bound into Gaylord binder, gray boards, gray cloth backstrip.

2318 KILBOURNE, DAVID W.

[Broadside] NOTICE. WHEREAS WE ARE THE OWNERS IN FEE SIMPLE, OF ABOUT 800 LOTS, IN THE TOWN OF KEOKUK, AND ABOUT 50,000 ACRES OF LAND IN THE HALF BREED SAC AND FOX RESERVATION, IN LEE COUNTY, IOWA TERRITORY; . . . WE OFFER TO SELL PART OF OUR LOTS . . . TOGETHER WITH THIRTY OR FORTY THOUSAND ACRES OF THE ABOVE FARMING LANDS, SITUATED IN DIFFERENT PARTS OF THE RESERVATION, IN LOTS AND PARCELS TO SUIT PURCHASERS. MARSH, LEE & DELAVAN. TRUSTEES. BY D. W. KILBOURNE, THEIR ATTORNEY IN FACT . . . D. W. KILBOURNE. KEOKUK, LEE COUNTY, IOWA TERRITORY, MAY 16, 1846.

Broadside, 30.7 x 25.1 cm. Text, 25.7 x 19.5 cm.
Ref.:
Probably printed at Fort Madison.

2319 KILBOURNE, DAVID W.

STRICTURES, ON DR. I. GALLAND'S PAMPHLET, ENTITLED, "VILLAINY EXPOSED," WITH SOME ACCOUNT OF HIS TRANSACTIONS IN LANDS OF THE SAC AND FOX RESERVATION, ETC., IN LEE COUNTY, IOWA . . . FORT MADISON: PRINTED AT THE STATESMAN OFFICE, 1850.

[1]–24. 18.4 x 13.3 cm. Stabbed, uncut. In brown cloth case.

Ref.: Howes K131; Moffit 77

Dr. Galland's pamphlet is present in the Graff collection, item 1489.

2320 KIMBALL, A. S.

DOCUMENT, SIGNED, by A. S. Kimball. 1886 September 16, Whipple Barracks, Prescott, A. T. To the Assistant Adjutant General, Department of Arizona. Twenty-eight pages, 26.9 x 19.8 cm.

Annual Report of the Chief Quartermaster. Accompanied by printed enclosures (2), one of which is incomplete.

2321 KIMBALL, CHARLES P.

THE SAN FRANCISCO CITY DIRECTORY, BY CHARLES P. KIMBALL. SEPTEMBER 1, 1850. SAN FRANCISCO. JOURNAL OF COMMERCE PRESS, 1850.

[1]–136. 14 x 9.4 cm. Yellow printed wrappers with title on front wrapper, advertisements on verso of back wrapper. Wrappers defective, name torn from front wrapper. In a green half morocco case.

Prov.: Bookplate of John Francis Neylan.

Ref.: AII (*California*) 142; Blumann & Thomas 3956; Cowan p. 172–73; Greenwood 236; Howes K134; Sabin 76092; Wagner (*California Imprints*) 86

First real directory of this city, preceded only by two business directories.—Howes

2322 KIMBALL, CHARLES P.

THE SAME.*

[1]–139 [140 blank]. 14.4 x 10.2 cm. Red cloth. Advertisements on inner covers.

Ref.: Greenwood 236 note; Howes K134

One of two reprints published about 1870 or 1890.

2323 KIMBALL, HEBER C.

JOURNAL OF HEBER C. KIMBALL . . . GIVING AN ACCOUNT OF HIS MISSION TO GREAT BRITAIN . . . BY R. B. THOMPSON. NAUVOO, ILL.: PRINTED BY ROBINSON AND SMITH, 1840.

[i]–viii, [9]–60. 16.6 x 10 cm. Rebound in full polished calf, gilt fillet borders on sides, gilt backstrip, brown leather labels, gilt edges, by Riviere.

Ref.: Byrd 558; Howes T202; Jones 1036; Sabin 95525

Robert Blaskel Thompson was the secretary of Joseph Smith, Sr., and also a member of the committee appointed by the fugitives to petition Illinois for the incorporation of Nauvoo.

2324 KIMBALL, MARIA BRACE

MY EIGHTY YEARS . . . PRIVATELY PRINTED, MCMXXXIV.

[1]–103 [104 blank]. 20.2 x 13.2 cm. Three plates. Blue boards, blue cloth backstrip.

Ref.: Howes K136

Printed at Boston by the Thomas Todd Company. A charming story of an intelligent woman's experiences, especially interesting because of the section dealing with Army frontier life in the Southwest.

2325 KIMBALL, MARIA BRACE

A SOLDIER-DOCTOR OF OUR ARMY: JAMES P. KIMBALL . . . BOSTON: HOUGHTON MIFFLIN COMPANY, 1917.

[i]–[xiv, xiv blank], [1]–192, [193 blank, 194 colophon]. 18.8 x 12.8 cm. Blue cloth, title in gilt on front cover and backstrip, decoration on front cover in red and white. In dust jacket.

Prov.: Inscribed on front endleaf: Compliments of the Author. /

Ref.: Howes K137

Much of Kimball's life was spent at Army posts in the West.

2326 KING, CHARLES

CAMPAIGNING WITH CROOK AND STORIES OF ARMY LIFE . . . NEW YORK: HARPER & BROTHERS, 1890.

[i]–[x, x blank], [1]–295, [296 blank], [297–304 advertisements]. 18.4 x 12.3 cm. Ten illustrations listed. Dark blue pictorial cloth, title in gilt on front cover and backstrip.

Ref.: Saunders 3000; Smith 5487

According to *Army and Navy Journal*, October 11, 1890, p. 107, this issue was called in by the publishers at the demand of Reuben D. Davenport . . . who claimed certain statements in Chapter 25 (15, actually) were libellous. The volume was re-issued in 1891 under an 1890 date line and a retraction was published. See *The Westerners* (N.Y.) Vol. 2 No. 4, p. 84.—note on front endleaf by EDG.

2327 KING, CHARLES

THE FIFTH CAVALRY IN THE SIOUX WAR OF 1876. CAMPAIGNING WITH CROOK . . . MILWAUKEE, WIS.: PRINTED BY THE SENTINEL COMPANY, 1880.

[i–viii, viii blank], [1]–[134], [135–36 blank]. 23.4 x 15 cm. Buff printed wrappers, with title on front wrapper. In brown cloth case.

Prov.: Inscribed on front wrapper: Gen! David Atwood, / compliments of The Author / [flourish] /.

Ref.: Howes K147; Jones 1607

2328 KING, CHARLES

TRIALS OF A STAFF-OFFICER . . . PHILADELPHIA: L. R. HAMSERSLY & CO., 1891.*

[1]–214, [215–22 advertisements]. 19 x 13.2 cm. Olive-green cloth, title in gilt on front cover and backstrip.

Ref.:

2329 KING, CLARENCE

MOUNTAINEERING IN THE SIERRA NEVADA . . . LONDON: SAMPSON LOW, MARSTON, LOW, & SEARLE, 1874.

[i]–[viii, viii blank], [1]–308. 17.6 x 11.8 cm. Frontispiece and two maps, unlisted. Blue cloth, gilt, black and blind, gilt edges.

Ref.: Cowan p. 328; Farquhar (*Yosemite*) 12e; Howes K148

Editions: Boston, 1872, 1874. London, 1872.

2330 KING, J. H. T.

A BRIEF ACCOUNT OF THE SUFFERINGS OF A DETACHMENT OF UNITED STATES CAVALRY FROM DEPRIVATION OF WATER DURING A PERIOD OF EIGHTY SIX HOURS WHILE SCOUTING ON THE STAKED PLAINS OF TEXAS. FORT DAVIS, TEXAS: CHAS. KRULL, POST PRINTER.

[1]–7, [8 blank]. 20.4 x 12.7 cm. Unbound.

Prov.: Inscribed at foot of title-page: Compliments of / Lieut. Chas. S. Cooper / U. S. A. /

Ref.:

The report is dated at the end Sept., 1877. The donor was second in command of the party. An appalling incident of extraordinary courage.

2331 KING, RICHARD

THE FRANKLIN EXPEDITION FROM FIRST TO LAST . . . LONDON: JOHN CHURCHILL, 1855.

[i]–xxxviii, [3]–280. 18.7 x 11.2 cm. Illustrations unlisted. Half calf, red sprinkled edges.

Prov.: Inscribed on title-page: G. S. Steinman Esqʳ / F. S. A. / with the Kind Regards / of the Author / Richard. King. / [dash] /. Bookplate of Marcus Steinman Kemmis.

Ref.: Smith 5493; Staton & Tremaine 3571

Bound in at the end after the volume collated above are pages 29–112 of what are described in a pencil note on the first page: Appendix to Dʳ K's Letter to / the Duke of Newcastle / published in 1860 & of which / he presented me a copy. / There is also bound in an eight-page leaflet headed: The Franklin Expedition / from / First to Last. / By / Dr. King, M.D. / [rule] / Publisher: John Churchill, New Burlington Street. / [diamond rule] / Tabular Form of Contents. / The leaflet contains press notices dated 1860.

Both Smith and Staton & Tremaine call for 224 pages.

2332 KING, RICHARD

NARRATIVE OF A JOURNEY TO THE SHORES OF THE ARCTIC OCEAN, IN 1833, 1834, AND 1835; UNDER THE COMMAND OF CAPT. BACK, R. N. . . . . LONDON: RICHARD BENTLEY, 1836.*

[i]–[xvi, xvi blank], [1]–312. [i]–viii, [1]–321, [322 colophon]. 18.5 x 11.6 cm. Illustrations unlisted. Two volumes, contemporary citron calf, red sprinkled edges.

Prov.: With bookplates of Radcliffe College,

Oxford, surcharged with duplicate stamp of the Bodleian Library.

Ref.: Field 831; Sabin 37831; Smith 5494; Staton & Tremaine 1899; Wagner-Camp 62

An account of the George Back expedition.

2333 KINGMAN, HENRY

THE TRAVELS AND ADVENTURES OF HENRY KINGMAN IN SEARCH OF COLORADO AND CALIFORNIA GOLD, 1859–1865 . . . DELAVAN, MORRIS COUNTY, KANSAS, 1917.*

[i–ii], 1–68. 22.1 x 15.4 cm. Illustrations unlisted. Gray printed wrappers, matching backstrip.

Ref.: Howes K159

Printed at Herington Sun Press, Herington, Kansas, 1917.

2334 KINGMAN, JOHN

LETTERS, WRITTEN BY JOHN KINGMAN, WHILE ON A TOUR TO ILLINOIS AND WISCONSIN, IN THE SUMMER OF 1838. HINGHAM: JEDIDIAH FARMER, PRINTER, 1842.

[1]–48. 18.5 x 11.6 cm. Blue printed wrappers with title on front wrapper: Journal / of / A Tour to the West, / by John Kingman, / in a Series of Letters. / On verso of back wrapper: [rule] / Tour to the West, / in 1838. / [rule] / Both within borders of type ornaments. In green cloth case.

Ref.: Bradford 2857; Buck 327; Howes K160; Sabin 37868

2335 KINGSBURY, GAINES P.

[Caption title] . . . A REPORT OF THE EXPEDITION OF THE DRAGOONS, UNDER THE COMMAND OF COLONEL HENRY DODGE, TO THE ROCKY MOUNTAINS, DURING THE SUMMER OF 1835, &C. . . .

[1]–38, [39–40 blank]. 22.7 x 14.1 cm. Two maps. Map: Map / Showing the Lands / assigned to / Emigrant Indians / West of / Arkansas & Missouri / [lower right:] A / 47.2 x 45.1 cm. Scale: 40 miles to one inch. Map: [Similar to preceding, untitled] [upper right:] B / 49.4 x 86.6 cm. Scale: 20 miles to one inch. Light blue printed wrappers, with short title on front wrapper, uncut. In a blue cloth case.

Ref.: Howes K161; Jones 985; Matthews p. 274; Sabin 20497; Wagner-Camp 63

24th Congress, 1st Session, Senate, Document No. 209, Serial 281. [Washington, 1836.]

This copy is a remarkably fine one, with the two maps (uncolored) and with the original wrappers.

The present document is missing in the ICN set of Government Documents, as it is in most sets (according to *Monthly Catalogue of U. S. Public Documents*, No. 178, October, 1909, pages 144–45) but the material is present in 24th Congress, 1st Session, House, Executive Document No. 181, Serial 289. The two maps in the latter printing are colored.

Printer's imprint at foot of page [1]: [short rule] / Gales & Seaton, print.] /

2336 KINGSFORD, WILLIAM

IMPRESSIONS OF THE WEST AND SOUTH. DURING A SIX WEEKS' HOLIDAY . . . TORONTO: A. H. ARMOUR & CO., 1858.

[1]–83, [84 blank]. 20.9 x 13.6 cm. Dark gray-blue cloth, blind embossed borders on sides, title in gilt on front cover.

Ref.: Buck 579; Clark III 472; Howes K164; Sabin 37886

The book is brief and often superficial, but for a study of New Orleans, Charleston, and Mississippi River travel conditions, it should not be overlooked.—Clark

2337 KINGSLEY, CALVIN S.

THE CALVIN S. KINGSLEY PAPERS comprising fifty-three manuscripts, letters, documents, receipts, etc. Various places (principally Portland, Oregon), 1850–1881.

The Papers cover Kingsley's experiences, business, religious, and social affairs. Included is a Pocket Diary for 1860 which contains some financial records, numerous deeds, property exchanges, etc.

2338 KINZIE, JULIETTE A. McGILL

[Broadside] AN IMPORTANT WORK ON THE NORTH-WEST. WAU-BUN, THE "EARLY DAY" IN THE NORTH-WEST. BY MRS. JOHN H. KINZIE, OF CHICAGO. 1 VOL. 8VO., 500 PAGES, WITH ILLUSTRATIONS ON STONE. PRICE, $2.25. DERBY & JACKSON, PUBLISHERS, 119 NASSAU STREET, NEW YORK.

Broadside, 48.9 x 61 cm. Text, 45.1 x 55.8 cm.

Ref.:

2339 [KINZIE, JULIETTE A. McGILL]

NARRATIVE OF THE MASSACRE AT CHICAGO, AUGUST 15, 1812, AND OF SOME PRECEDING EVENTS. CHICAGO, ILL.: PRINTED BY ELLIS & FERGUS, 1844.

[1]–34. 22.4 x 14.7 cm. Map: Chicago, in 1812. / 10.3 x 18.9 cm. No scale given. Blue printed wrappers, with title on front wrapper. In a full blue morocco solander case.

Prov.: Herschel V. Jones copy.

Ref.: Bradford 2863; Byrd 872; Field 832; Howes K170; Jones 1090; McMurtrie (*Chicago*) 75; Sabin 37940

2340   KINZIE, JULIETTE A. McGILL

WAU-BUN, THE "EARLY DAY" IN THE NORTH-WEST . . . NEW YORK: PUBLISHED BY DERBY & JACKSON, 1856.

[i]–xii, 13–498. 22.4 x 14.6 cm. Six lithographed views, unlisted. Bright blue cloth, blind embossed designs on sides, backstrip gilt with title.

Ref.: Ayer 175; Bradford 2864; Buck 230; Field 883; Howes K171; Hubach p. 19; Sabin 37941

There is a charming pencil sketch on page [iv].

2341   KIP, LAWRENCE

ARMY LIFE ON THE PACIFIC; A JOURNAL OF THE EXPEDITION AGAINST THE NORTHERN INDIANS, THE TRIBES OF THE COEUR D'ALENES, SPOKANS, AND PELOUZES, IN THE SUMMER OF 1858 . . . NEW YORK: REDFIELD, 1859.

[i]–vi, [7]–144. 18.5 x 12.4 cm. Brown cloth, blind fillets on sides, title in gilt on backstrip.

Ref.: Cowan (1914) pp. 130–31; Field 837; Howell 165; Howes K172; Jones 1413; Sabin 37944; Smith 5519

Best account, by a participant, of the 1858 campaign against the northwestern tribes.— Howes

2342   KIP, LAWRENCE

THE INDIAN COUNCIL IN THE VALLEY OF THE WALLA-WALLA. 1855 . . . SAN FRANCISCO: WHITTON, TOWNE & CO., 1855.

[1]–32. 21.8 x 14.4 cm. Pink printed wrappers with title on front wrapper. Removed from bound volume, lacks backstrip. In a dark red half morocco case.

Prov.: Inscribed on front wrapper: Hon Hamilton Fish / with regards of / W. Ingraham Kip / [flourish] /.

Ref.: AII (*Calif.*) 431; Cowan (1914) p. 131; Field 836; Greenwood 573; Howell 166; Howes K173; Jones 1335; Sabin 37945; Smith 5521

Only twenty-five copies of this source book of Oregon history were printed.

2343   [KIP, LEONARD]

CALIFORNIA SKETCHES, WITH RECOLLECTIONS OF THE GOLD MINES. ALBANY: ERASTUS H. PEASE & CO., 1850.

[1]–57, [58–60 blank]. 20.8 x 12.4 cm. White printed wrappers, with title on front wrapper, advertisements on verso of front and recto and verso of back wrapper, uncut.

Ref.: Cowan p. 331; Howes K174; Sabin 37946; Vail (*Gold Fever*) p. 252; Wheat (*Gold Rush*) 119

An informative and valuable work. Sabin gives Munsell as the publisher.

2344   KIP, WILLIAM I.

THE EARLY DAYS OF MY EPISCOPATE . . . NEW YORK: THOMAS WHITTAKER, 1892.

[i]–x, [1]–263, [264 blank], [265–78 advertisements]. 18.6 x 12.6 cm. Portrait. Dark red cloth, gilt stamped title on front cover and backstrip.

Prov.: Inscribed on title-page: Mr. & Mrs. Frederick Stahl / From / Bp. Kip & Mrs. Lanier— /.

Ref.: Blumann & Thomas 5027; Cowan p. 332

Personal and local history from Bishop Kip's arrival in California in 1853 to 1860 are treated here.

2345   KIP, WILLIAM I.

THE EARLY JESUIT MISSIONS IN NORTH AMERICA; COMPILED AND TRANSLATED FROM THE LETTERS OF THE FRENCH JESUITS, WITH NOTES. BY THE REV. WILLIAM INGRAHAM KIP . . . NEW YORK: WILEY AND PUTNAM, 1846.

[i]–[xviii, xviii blank], [1]–135, [136 blank]. [i–vi, vi blank], [139]–321, [322 blank], [i]–[iv], [xiii]–xiv, xxix–xxxii, [1–4] advertisements. 19 x 12.7 cm. Two volumes, white printed wrappers, with title on front wrappers, advertisements on verso of front and recto and verso of back wrappers, uncut. In a green cloth case.

Ref.: Field 834; Howes K176; Rader 2179; Sabin 37949; Streit III 2330

An English translation of selections from the "Jesuit Relations."

2346   KIRK, ROBERT C.

TWELVE MONTHS IN KLONDIKE . . . LONDON: WILLIAM HEINEMANN, 1899.

[i]–xii, [1]–273, [274 colophon]. 18.3 x 12.2 cm. 100 illustrations listed, map. Gray cloth.

Ref.: Smith 5549; Wickersham 4343

2347   KIRTLAND   SAFETY   SOCIETY   BANK, THE

[Broadside] NO. [in manuscript: 705] A. THE KIRTLAND SAFETY SOCIETY BANK WILL PAY FIVE DOLLARS ON DEMAND TO [in manuscript: O P Good] OR BEARER KIRTLAND OHIO [in manuscript: 10 Feb] 18 [in manuscript: 37]. [in manuscript: J Smith Jr]. CASH.R [in manuscript: S. Rigdon] PRES.T UNDERWOOD BALD SPENCER & HUFTY, N. YORK & PHILAD.A

Broadside, 7.6 x 17.4 cm. Text size, 7.2 x 17.1 cm.

Ref.:

Signed on face, to right of left column: J. McConnel /.

2348 KNAPP, N. M.

HISTORICAL SKETCH OF SCOTT COUNTY, ILLINOIS
. . . ALSO RESPONSE TO A TOAST, BY JOHN MOSES.
DELIVERED AT WINCHESTER, ILLINOIS, JULY 4TH,
1876. WINCHESTER, ILL.: TIMES JOB PRINTING
HOUSE, 1876.

[1]–36. 20.7 x 14.3 cm. Gray printed wrappers,
with title on front wrapper.

Ref.: Buck 1076; Howes K209

**2349 KNICKERBOCKER, OR NEW-YORK
MONTHLY MAGAZINE, THE**

[Wrapper title] VOL. 58. NO. 680. AUGUST 1861.
THE KNICKERBOCKER, OR NEW-YORK MONTHLY
MAGAZINE. NEW-YORK: J. R. GILMORE.

[97]–188, 1–4 advertisements. 23.6 x 15.2 cm.
Dark yellow printed wrappers, with title on front
wrapper, contents on verso of front wrapper,
advertisements on verso of back wrapper.

Ref.: Wagner-Camp 369 see

Pages 115–128 comprise: To Pike's Peak and
Denver. / [short rule] / By Thomas W. Knox. /
[short rule] / . . .

2350 KNOX & M'KEE (Wheeling, Virginia)

[Caption title] TRANSPORTATION TO THE WEST.
WHEELING, MAY 20, 1834. AS FREQUENT INQUIRIES
ARE MADE RESPECTING THE TRANSPORTATION OF
GOODS FROM THE EAST TO THE WEST, VIA BALTI-
MORE AND WHEELING, THE UNDERSIGNED TAKE
THIS METHOD OF SUGGESTING TO THEIR CORRE-
SPONDENTS SOME GENERAL REMARKS . . . KNOX &
M'KEE, COMMISSION & FORWARDING MERCHANTS,
WHEELING, VA.

[1–4]. (Pages [2–4] blank.) 24.9 x 20.1 cm. Unbound leaflet.

Ref.:

An advertising leaflet intended to take business away from Pittsburgh. Knox & M'Kee offered six-day service between Baltimore and
Wheeling, with regular service between the latter
point and the interior of Ohio and down the
Ohio River.

Imprint at foot: Times Press, Wheeling, /

2351 KOCH, ALBRECHT K.

REISE DURCH EINEN THEIL DER VEREINGTEN
STAATEN VON NORDAMERIKA IN DEN JAHREN 1844
BIS 1846 . . . DRESDEN: ARNOLDISCHE BUCH-
HANDLUNG, 1847.

[i–iv], [1]–162. 21.7 x 13.7 cm. Two plates, one
colored. Green marbled boards, red label on
backstrip.

Ref.: Buck 391; Clark III 340; Howes K234;
Sabin 39198

Experiences of a geologist along the Ohio and
Mississippi Rivers.

2352 KOEHLER, CARL

BRIEFE AUS AMERIKA FUR DEUTSCHE AUSWAN-
DERER . . . DARMSTADT: VERLAG VON GUSTAV
GEORG LANGE, 1852.

[i]–iv, [1]–234. 17.4 x 11.5 cm. Five engraved illustrations. Pale green printed boards, with title
on front cover, vignette from title-page on verso
of back cover, title, reading down, on backstrip
in two panels. In a green cloth case.

Prov.: Bookplate of C. G. Littell.

Ref.: Buck 495; Howes K239; Sabin 38220
see

Pages 205–34 deal with California. Buck
probably never saw the first edition of this work
as his collation is wrong and he does not locate
any copies except of the 2nd or 3rd editions. On
page 12, Buck refers to this work as one of the
rarest and little known books of value in the bibliography.—EDG

2353 KOERNER, GUSTAVE

MEMOIRS OF GUSTAVE KOERNER 1809–1896 . . .
EDITED BY THOMAS J. McCORMACK . . . CEDAR
RAPIDS, IOWA: THE TORCH PRESS, 1909.*

[i]–[xv, xvi blank], [1]–628. [i]–xii, [1]–768.
23.7 x 16 cm. Portrait. Two volumes, red ribbed
cloth, gilt tops, uncut.

Ref.: Buck 270; Howes K243

Much of the work deals with the author's
relations with Abraham Lincoln.

2354 KOHL, JOHANN G.

KITCHI-GAMI. WANDERINGS ROUND LAKE SU-
PERIOR . . . LONDON: CHAPMAN AND HALL, 1860.

[i]–xii, [1]–428, [1]–32 advertisements. 22.1 x
14.4 cm. 16 illustrations, unlisted. Black cloth.

Ref.: Field 842; Howes K247; Sabin 38215;
Staton & Tremaine 3573

Editions: Bremen, 1859 (original German edition).

2355 KONSAG, FERNANDO

[Caption title] CARTA DEL P. FERNANDO CONSAG
DE LA COMPANIA DE JESUS, VISITADOR DE LAS MIS-
SIONES DE CALIFORNIAS, A LOS PADRES SUPERIORES
DE ESTA PROVINCIA DE NUEVA-ESPANA. . . .

A–E⁴, F². [1]–43, [44 blank]. 20.1 x 14.7 cm.
Sewn, unbound.

Ref.: Barrett 1396; Cowan p. 140; Howes
K250; Medina (*Mexico*) 3886; Streit III 540;
Wagner (*SS*) 120

The work is dated at the end: San Ignacio, y
Octubre I. de 1748. It was printed at Mexico
City.

Konsag (or Consag), a Jesuit of Hungarian
origin, spent many years in Baja California and
played an active part in the exploration of the

Colorado-Gila country. He and Ugarte proved finally that no strait separated the Californias from the mainland. This discovery opened the way for development of the overland routes and assured future permanent settlements.—EDG

2356 KOTZEBUE, OTTO VON

A VOYAGE OF DISCOVERY, INTO THE SOUTH SEA AND BEERING'S STRAITS, FOR THE PURPOSE OF EXPLORING A NORTHEAST PASSAGE, UNDERTAKEN IN THE YEARS 1815-1818 . . . LONDON: PRINTED FOR LONGMAN, HURST, REES, ORME, AND BROWN, 1821.

[i]–[xvi, xvi blank], [1]–358. [i–iv], [1]–433, [434 colophon]. [i–iv], [1]–442. 20.9 x 13.5 cm. Eight colored plates, one uncolored plate and seven maps, listed. Map: Chart / from the 14th to the 16th Degree of / South Latitude & from the 138th to the 149th Degree of West Longitude, / from Greenwich, / Shewing the Course taken by / The Rurick; / the Direction and Strength of the Current & the Declination of the Needle. / [swelled rule] April, 1816. [swelled rule] / [lower centre:] London, Published by Longman & Co Octr 8th 1821. / [lower right:] Sid^y Hall, Sculp^t / 16.6 x 50.9 cm. No scale given. Map: Chart / of / Beering's Straits / on / Mercator's Projection. / August 1816. / [lower centre, as in preceding] / [lower right:] Engraved by Sid^y Hall, Bury Str^t Blooms[bury] / 32.8 x 38.4 cm. No scale given. Map: Plan / of the Group called / Romanzoff's Islands, / the middle of which is 9° 26' 47'' North Lat. / and 189° 57$^{''}$ 13'' West Long. / of Greenwich. / Declination of the Needle 11° 38 1/2'. East. / January 1817. / [lower centre: as in preceding] / [lower right:] Sid^y Hall, Sculp^t / 37.3 x 51 cm. Scale: about 1 1/2 geographical miles to one inch. Map: Chart of the Islands / of / Radack and Ralick, / on Mercator's Projection. / November: 1817. / [lower centre: as in preceding] / [lower right:] Sid^y Hall, Scu[lp^t] / 26.4 x 20.8 cm. No scale given. Three maps on one sheet: Chart of the / Caroline Islands, / [swelled rule] after [swelled rule] / I. A. Cantova. / Lettres Edifiantes, T. 18. P. 188. / [lower centre: as in preceding] / [lower right:] Sid^y Hall, Sculp^t / 10.3 x 18.5 cm. No scale given. Chart of the / Caroline Islands, / [swelled rule] after [swelled rule] / Don Luis de Torres. / [lower centre and lower right: as in preceding] / 10.4 x 18.6 cm. No scale given. Chart of the / Caroline Islands, / after the / Statement of Edock. / [lower centre and lower right: as in preceding] / 9.1 x 18.6 cm. No scale given. Three volumes, contemporary red straight grain calf, gilt backs, marbled edges.

Prov.: Signature of George Wyndham dated 1829 on first two title-pages, initials G. W.

stamped in gilt at foot of each backstrip, Egremont bookplate in each volume.

Ref.: Cowan p. 335; Howes K258; Jones 832; Sabin 38291; Staton & Tremaine 1142; Wickersham 6196

One of the great early nineteenth-century voyages of discovery. Published in Russian at St. Petersburg in 1821–23, and in German at Weimar in 1821.

2357 KOTZEBUE SOUND MINING AND TRADING CO., THE

[Broadside] FOR ALASKA GOLD FIELDS. THE KOTZEBUE SOUND MINING AND TRADING CO. WILL DISPATCH THE FAST SAILING BARK J. A. FALKENBURG UNDER COMMAND OF CAPT. P. H. COOK, THE WELL-KNOWN ARCTIC WHALER. ON MAY 10, 1898 DIRECT TO KOTZEBUE SOUND . . . LYNDE & HOUGH CO. 40 CALIFORNIA ST., SAN FRANCISCO GENERAL AGENTS AND TICKET OFFICE ADDRESS ALL COMMUNICATIONS TO A. H. HERRIMAN, 201 FRONT ST., SAN FRANCISCO, CAL. GENERAL MANAGER J. G. MCCALL & CO., TICKET AGENTS, 46 OR 636 MARKET STREET.

Broadside, 66.2 x 25.2 cm. Text, 62 x 22.1 cm.

Ref.:

Text printed in red, blue, green, and brown.

2358 KRUSENSHTERN, IVAN FEDOROVICH

VOYAGE ROUND THE WORLD, IN THE YEARS 1803, 1804, 1805, & 1806 . . . LONDON: PRINTED BY C. ROWORTH, 1813.

a^6, b–d^4, B-RR^4, S^1. [i]–[viii, viii blank], [1–4], [ix]–xxxii, [1]–314. [a]^1, b^4, B-3E^4, 3F^2. [i–x, x blank], [1]–404. 26.4 x 20.5 cm. Two colored plates and a map. Map: Chart / of / The Northwest Part of the / Great Ocean, / Drawn / By D. F. Sotzmann 1811. / [swelled rule] Reduced [swelled rule] / from Cap^n Krusenstern's / Original Chart. / [lower right:] Neele sc. Strand. / 24.5 x 33 cm. No scale given. Two volumes, contemporary full tree calf, backs gilt, leather labels, sprinkled edges.

Ref.: Howes K271; Sabin 38331; Wickersham 6234

The Russian edition of this fine account was published at St. Petersburg in 1809–14, but the English translation was from the German edition, St. Petersburg, 1810–14.

2359 KURZ, RUDOLPH F.

. . . JOURNAL . . . AN ACCOUNT OF HIS EXPERIENCES AMONG FUR TRADERS AND AMERICAN INDIANS ON THE MISSISSIPPI AND THE UPPER MISSOURI RIVERS DURING THE YEARS 1846 TO 1852. TRANS-

LATED BY MYRTIS JARRELL . . . WASHINGTON: GOVERNMENT PRINTING OFFICE, 1937.*

[i]–ix, [x blank], 1–382. 23.2 x 14.9 cm. 48 plates, unlisted. Green printed wrappers.

Ref.: Dobie p. 87; Howes K281; Matthews pp. 308–09

Bureau of Ethnology Bulletin 115.

2360 KUYKENDALL, WILLIAM L.

FRONTIER DAYS: A TRUE NARRATIVE OF STRIKING EVENTS ON THE WESTERN FRONTIER. J. M. & H. L. KUYKENDALL, PUBLISHERS, 1917.*

[i]–[xii, xii blank], [1]–251, [252 blank]. 18.5 x 12.4 cm. Portrait. Light green cloth.

Ref.: Adams 600; Howes K284; Jennewein 111

Probably printed at Denver. A pencil note on the inside front cover reads: Only 500 printed.

L

2361 LACHAPELLE, ALFRED DE, *Editor*

LE COMTE DE RAOUSSET-BOULBON ET L'EXPEDITION DE LA SONORE: CORRESPONDENCE, SOUVENIRS ET OEUVRES INEDITES . . . PARIS: E. DENTU, 1859.*

[i–ii], [1]–[319], [320 blank]. 17.5 x 11 cm. Portrait and map: Carte / de la Sonore / et de la / Basse Californie / dressée par / A. Buillemin / d'après les documents communiqués par / A. De Lachapelle / 1859. / [lower left:] Gravée chez Avril f^{res} rue des Bernardins, 18. / [centre:] E. Dentu, Editeur, Palais Royal. / [right:] Lith. Kaeppelin, à Paris. / 25.5 x 21.5 cm. Scale: about 85 miles to one inch. Rebound in red mottled boards, maroon morocco back, sprinkled edges.

Refs.: Cowan p. 339; Howes L6; Monaghan 1352 note

The audacious dream of the conquest of Sonora and the mines of Arizona extinguished only by two ill-starred expeditions and a final firing squad.—Howes

2362 LADUE, JOSEPH

KLONDYKE FACTS, BEING A COMPLETE GUIDE BOOK TO THE GOLD REGIONS OF THE GREAT CANADIAN NORTHWEST TERRITORIES AND ALASKA . . . NEW YORK: AMERICAN TECHNICAL BOOK CO.

[1]–205, [206 advertisements]. 18.2 x 12.5 cm. Maps and illustrations unlisted. Green cloth. In a green cloth case.

Ref.: Howes L13; Smith 5637; Wickersham 3942

Copyrighted 1897.

Editions: Montreal, 1897.

2363 [LA GRANGE DE CHESSIEUX, GILBERT ARNAUD FRANCOIS SIMON DE]

[Caption title] [1] ME'MOIRE SUR LE PAYS & LA MER SITUES A L'OUEST DU CANADA. PAR M. D. L. G. D. C. . . .

A^{12}. 1–24. 15.9 x 9.6 cm. Rebound in gray boards, black skiver label.

Prov.: Bookplate of the Marquis de Bassano.

Ref.: Leclerc 736

Imprint at foot of page 24: Extrait du Mercure de France, Mai 1754. /

Relates to the controversy over the discoveries of Admiral de Fonte. A footnote on page 1 states that the memoir was contributed by Mm. de l'Isle and Buache.

2364 LAHONTAN, LOUIS ARMAND DE LOM D'ARCE, BARON DE

NEW VOYAGES TO NORTH-AMERICA. CONTAINING AN ACCOUNT OF THE SEVERAL NATIONS OF THAT VAST CONTINENT . . . LONDON: PRINTED FOR H. BONWICKE, 1703.

A^8, a^4, B–S^8, T^4. [*]^1, Aa–Vv^8. [i–xxiv], 1–280. [i–ii], 1–302, [303 advertisement, 304 blank], [305–17 Index, 318 blank, 319–320 blank]. 18.8 x 11.4 cm. 22 plates and maps. Map: [Map of the Great Lakes Region] [upper left:] Vol. I. Title-page / 10.6 x 16.7 cm. Scale: 55 leagues to one inch. Map: A General Map of / New France / Com, call'd Canada. / [upper right:] Vol. I. p. I.A. / 21.8 x 33.4 cm. Scale: about 170 miles to one inch. Map: New-/Found / Land. / [upper left:] H. Moll Fecit. / [rule] / Vol. I. p. 225. / 16 x 10.8 cm. Scale: 60 miles to one inch. Map: A Map drawn upon Stag-skins by ẙ Gnacsitares who gave / me to know ẙ Latitudes of all ẙ places mark'd in it, by pointing to ẙ respective places of ẙ heavens that one or t'other corresponded to; / for by this means I could adjust ẙ Lat: to half a Degree or little / more; having first receṽ'd from 'em a computation of ẙ distances / in Tazous each of wĩch I compute to be 3 Long French Leagues. / [Second title at right of preceding:] A Map of ẙ Long River and of some others / that fall into that small part of ẙ Great River / of Missisipi wich[!] is here laid down. / [five lines of text] / [upper left: Vol. I. p. I. B. / 22 x 33.8 cm. (platemark). Scale: about 56 leagues to one inch. Two inset illustrations above map. Two volumes contemporary mottled calf, gilt backstrips, red leather labels on backstrips, mottled red edges. In a brown cloth case.

Prov.: Bookplates of Robert Massingberd, dated 1781.

Ref.: Clark I 111; Field 852; Greenly (*Lahon-*

tan) pp. 17–20; Greenly (*Michigan*) 9(a); Howes L25; Hubach p. 11; Paltsits pp. lx–lxii; Sabin 38644; Wheat (*Transmississippi*) 87

Page 279 in the second volume is mispaginated 276. No frontispiece in Volume II, as in some copies.

2365 LAHONTAN, LOUIS ARMAND DE LOM D'ARCE, BARON DE

NOUVEAUX VOYAGES DE MR. LE BARON DE LAHONTAN, DANS L'AMERIQUE SEPTENTRIONALE . . . A LA HAYE: CHEZ LES FRERES L'HONORE, M. DCCIII. [Title-page of second volume:] MEMOIRES DE L'AMERIQUE SEPTENTRIONALE, OU LA SUITE DES VOYAGES DE MR. LE BARON DE LAHONTAN . . . A LA HAYE, CHEZ LES FRERES L'HONORE, M. DCCIII. *11, A–L12, M8. A–I12, K10. [i–xxii], 1–279, [280 blank]. [1]–[236]. 16 x 9 cm. Two frontispieces (repeated in second volume), and twenty-four plates and maps. Map: Carte Generale / de Canada. / Dediée au Roy de Danemark Par / son tres humble et tres obeissant et tres / fidele serviteur Lahontan / 41.2 x 54.8 cm. Scale: about 30 lieues to one inch. Map: Carte que les Gnacsitares ont dessiné sur / des peaux de cerfs m'ayant fait conoistre a 30 minutes prés les latitudes / de tous les lieux qui y sont marqués, en me montrant la partie du ciel / vers laquelle gisent les uns et les autres, apres m'en auoir donné les / distances par tazouz, qui sont trois grandes lieues de France selon ma supputation / [Second title at right of preceding:] Carte de la Riviere Longue et de quelques autres / qui se dechargent dans la grand fleuve de Missisipi[!], en le petit espace de ce fleuve / marqué sur cette carte / [four lines of text] / 27.7 x 65.7 cm. (platemark). Scale: about 30 lieuves to one inch. Map: Carte Generale de Canada a Petit Point / 8.8 x 3.9 cm. Scale: about 65 lieuves to one inch. Two volumes, contemporary calf, gilt tooled backstrips, red leather labels on backstrips, red mottled edges.

Prov.: Bookplates of le Comte de Salaberry.
Ref.: Clark I 111; Greenly (*Lahontan*) pp. 12–13; Greenly (*Michigan*) 9(a); Howes L25; Hubach p. 11; Paltsits pp. liv–lv; Sabin 38635; Staton & Tremaine 104; Wheat (*Transmississippi*) 86

The first issue.

The *Supplement* is not present.

2366 LAHONTAN, LOUIS ARMAND DE LOM D'ARCE, BARON DE

THE SAME.
*12, A–L12, M8. A–K12. [i–xxiv], 1–279, [280 blank]. [1]–[248], [249–50 blank]. 16 x 9.1 cm. Two volumes, contemporary calf, gilt tooled

backstrips, red leather labels on backstrips, red mottled edges.
Ref.: as above

Second printing. Signature D3 printed in small cap.

2367 LAIRD, EGERTON K.

A TRIP TO THE YELLOWSTONE NATIONAL PARK IN 1884 . . . BIRKENHEAD: WILLMER BROTHERS & CO., 1885.
[1]–30, [31–32 blank]. 21.3 x 13.6 cm. Light blue-green printed wrappers, with title on front wrapper.
Prov.: Inscribed on title-page: Rev. N. Herz / with the respect / of the Author / ———— /.
Ref.:

2368 LAKE COUNTY LEADER

[Newspaper] LAKE COUNTY LEADER. VOL. 3. MADISON, D.T., MARCH 19, 1881. NO. 43 . . .
[1–4]. (Pages [2–3] blank.) 24.3 x 18.1 cm. Unbound. Printed on linen.
Ref.:
On page [1], second column, there is the following: —Neither paper nor fuel this week. On page [4], third column, there is the following explanation: The Leader this week is printed on seven different colors of tissue paper, on linen pocket handkerchiefs, cotton cloth, silk neckties, shingles and antelope skins.

The peculiar form of the paper was the result of a great storm which had swept across the Dakotas during the previous week. Madison was temporarily cut off from the rest of the world.

2369 LAMB, E. J.

MEMORIES OF THE PAST AND THOUGHTS OF THE FUTURE. AUTOBIOGRAPHY OF REV. E. J. LAMB . . . PRESS OF UNITED BRETHREN PUBLISHING HOUSE, 1906.
[i]–xii, 13–257, [258 blank]. 18.7 x 13 cm. Five illustrations unlisted. Green cloth.
Ref.: Howes L35
Published at South Bend, Indiana. Reminiscences of Kansas, Colorado, and Iowa in the middle of the nineteenth century.

2370 LAMBOURNE, ALFRED

THE OLD JOURNEY. REMINISCENCES OF PIONEER DAYS . . . GEO. Q. CANNON & SONS CO.
[1]–53, [54 blank]. 20 x 14 cm. 18 illustrations listed. Yellow and buff buckram, gilt top, uncut.
Ref.: Howell 174; Howes L43
Published at Salt Lake City, copyrighted 1892–1897. This is a re-issue in much smaller

format of *An Old Sketch-Book*, 1892. It was reprinted in 1897 on the occasion of the fiftieth anniversary of the great Mormon trek west and an edition of 500 copies is said to have been distributed to the living pioneers of that journey.

Editions: Boston [1892].

2371 LAMBOURNE, ALFRED

AN OLD SKETCH-BOOK . . . BOSTON: SAMUEL E. CASSINO.

[1–78, 78 blank]. 39.9 x 30.1 cm. 18 plates printed on thin Japan paper mounted on stiff paper. Tan cloth, brown leather backstrip.

Ref.: Howes L43
Published in 1892.

Scenes along the Mormon trail to Utah. Laid in is a four-page folder of lined paper with the following inscription on the first page: Frank J. Cannon / This Volume "An Old Sketch-Book, / Published for *Private* Circulation. / With Compliments of the / Season / from the Author /.

2372 LAMBOURNE, ALFRED

PICTURES OF AN INLAND SEA . . . THE DESERET NEWS PUBLISHERS.

[1]–150. 19.8 x 13.2 cm. Seven illustrations listed. Yellow and buff buckram, gilt top, uncut.
Ref.:
Published at Salt Lake City, without date.

For an account of Lambourne, see Dale L. Morgan: *The Great Salt Lake*, pages 338–47.

2373 LAMBOURNE, ALFRED

SCENIC UTAH: PEN AND PENCIL . . . NEW YORK: J. DEWING PUBLISHING CO., 1891.

[i]–[vi, vi blank], [1–50]. 40.1 x 30.1 cm. 20 plates. White cloth, black leather backstrip, title in gilt on front cover and backstrip.
Prov.: Inscribed on blank leaf at front: Mrs. Emily S. Richards, / with Compliments of / Alfred Lambourne / June 1897. /
Ref.: Howes L44

Text appears on rectos only. Each plate is preceded by a thin leaf bearing the plate number, not included in pagination.

2374 LAMON, WARD H.

THE LIFE OF ABRAHAM LINCOLN; FROM HIS BIRTH TO HIS INAUGURATION AS PRESIDENT . . . BOSTON: JAMES R. OSGOOD AND COMPANY, 1872.

[i]–[xvi, xvi blank], 1–547, [548 blank]. 23.4 x 15.4 cm. 16 illustrations listed. Green cloth, beveled edges, title in gilt on front cover and backstrip.
Ref.: Howes L46; Monaghan 926

2375 LAMON, WARD H.

RECOLLECTIONS OF ABRAHAM LINCOLN, 1847–1865 . . . CHICAGO: A. C. McCLURG AND COMPANY, 1895.

[i]–xvi, [9]–276, [277–80 advertisements]. 18.8 x 12.2 cm. Illustrations and facsimiles unlisted. Light blue cloth, front cover and backstrip stamped with dark blue designs and title in gilt.
Ref.: Monaghan 1168

2376 LAMSON, WARD

[Broadside] LAND WARRANTS. A CONSTANT SUPPLY AND WARRANTED GENUINE, FOR SALE AT THE VERY LOWEST RATE FOR CASH, OR ON TIME, IF WANTED AT THE SHOE STORE OF R. S. ADAMS, BY WARD LAMSON. A MAP OF UNENTERED LANDS IN THE COUNTIES OF DES MOINES, LOUISA AND LEE, CORRECTED TRI-WEEKLY, WILL BE KEPT FOR THE ACCOMMODATION OF PARTIES PURCHASING WARRANTS . . . WARD LAMSON. BURLINGTON, DECEMBER 7, 1848.

Broadside, 24.4 x 31.5 cm. Text, 16.1 x 24.5 cm.
Ref.:

2377 LANCASTER, COLUMBIA

[Caption title] CITIZENS OF WASHINGTON TERRITORY . . .

[1]–32. [1]: 24 x 15.4 cm. Folded, unbound, uncut, unopened.
Ref.:
Lancaster was delegate from Washington Territory in 1854. The present document comprises the reports of debates in Congress relating to measures in which his constituents were interested. The summary is dated at the end: Columbia Lancaster. / Washington City, November 25, 1854. /

2378 LANDER, FREDERICK W.

[Caption title] . . . ADDITIONAL ESTIMATE FOR FORT KEARNEY, SOUTH PASS, AND HONEY LAKE WAGON ROAD. LETTER FROM THE ACTING SECRETARY OF THE INTERIOR, TRANSMITTING A COMMUNICATION FROM COLONEL LANDER IN REGARD TO THE FORT KEARNEY, SOUTH PASS AND HONEY LAKE WAGON ROAD . . .

[1]–27, [28 blank]. 22.1 x 14.3 cm.

BOUND WITH:

[Caption title] . . . MAPS AND REPORTS OF THE FORT KEARNEY, SOUTH PASS, AND HONEY LAKE WAGON ROAD. LETTER FROM THE ACTING SECRETARY OF THE INTERIOR, TRANSMITTING REPORTS AND MAPS OF THE FORT KEARNEY, SOUTH PASS, AND HONEY LAKE WAGON ROAD . . .

[1]–39, [40 blank]. Two volumes bound together in red cloth.

Ref.: Howes L58; Wagner-Camp 376

36th Congress, 2nd Session, House, Executive Documents Nos. 63, 64, Serial 1100. [Washington, 1861.]

The maps mentioned as appended to the report were not published. According to Wagner-Camp, 250 copies of the second piece were printed.

2379 LANE, JOSEPH

[Caption title] LETTER OF HON. JOSEPH LANE, TO THE PEOPLE OF OREGON. WASHINGTON, D. C., JANUARY 12TH, 1859 . . .

[1]–8. 22.5 x 14.5 cm. Unbound, newly stapled.

Ref.: Smith 5678

A reply to a communication in the *Oregon Statesman*, of August 3, 1858, over the signature "Metropolis" charging Lane with the defeat of the admission bill in the House of Representatives and imputing to him corrupt motives.— EDG

2380 LANE, JOSEPH, & ISAAC I. STEVENS

SPEECHES OF HON. JOSEPH LANE, OF OREGON, AND HON. ISAAC I. STEVENS, OF WASHINGTON, ON PAYMENT OF THE OREGON AND WASHINGTON INDIAN WAR DEBT. DELIVERED IN THE HOUSE OF REPRESENTATIVES, MAY 13, 1858. WASHINGTON: PRINTED BY LEMUEL TOWERS, 1858.

[1]–16. 22 x 14.1 cm. Removed from bound volume, unbound.

Ref.: Smith (1921) 2097

2381 LANE, LYDIA SPENCER

I MARRIED A SOLDIER; OR, OLD DAYS IN THE OLD ARMY . . . PHILADELPHIA: J. B. LIPPINCOTT COMPANY, 1893.

[1]–214. 17.8 x 11.6 cm. Gray pictorial cloth, with title in blue on front cover and backstrip, gilt top, uncut.

Ref.: Howes L68

First Edition. A very interesting account of Army life at western and southwestern Army posts in Texas, New Mexico, Colorado, and Arizona prior to and immediately after the Civil War.—EDG

2382 LANE, LYDIA SPENCER

THE SAME . . . 1910.

[1]–214. 18.3 x 11.5 cm. Blue pictorial cloth, front cover stamped in gilt, title in gilt on backstrip.

Ref.: Howes L68

Second Edition.

2383 LANE, SAMUEL A.

FIFTY YEARS AND OVER OF AKRON AND SUMMIT COUNTY . . . AKRON, OHIO: BEACON JOB DEPARTMENT, 1892.

[i–ii], 1105–40. 25.4 x 17 cm. Marbled boards, red morocco back.

Ref.: Bradford 2905

Chapter LV of the above title, extracted and bound with the original title-page. Included in the chapter are Lane's account of his trip overland to California in 1850 and a list of 350 names of Akron men who crossed the plains between 1849 and 1852.

2384 LANE, WALTER P.

THE ADVENTURES AND RECOLLECTIONS OF GENERAL WALTER P. LANE, A SAN JACINTO VETERAN. CONTAINING SKETCHES OF THE TEXIAN, MEXICAN, AND LATE WARS, WITH SEVERAL INDIAN FIGHTS THROWN IN. MARSHALL, TEXAS: TRI-WEEKLY HERALD JOB PRINT, 1887.

[i–vi], [1]–114. (Page [i] errata, [2–4] blank, portrait between [2–3].) 17.2 x 11.5 cm. Portrait. Red printed wrappers, with title on front wrapper. In a red cloth case.

Ref.: Howes L69; Rader 2198; Raines p. 136

Contains some exciting and unusual personal accounts, especially the "Indian fights thrown in."

2385 [LANG, HERBERT O., *Editor*(?)]

A HISTORY OF TUOLUMNE COUNTY CALIFORNIA . . . SAN FRANCISCO: PUBLISHED BY B. F. ALLEY, 1882.

[1–2], [i]–[xii, xii blank], [1]–509, [510 blank], [1]–48. 20.8 x 14 cm. 11 portraits. Calf, red and black skiver labels on backstrip, speckled edges.

Ref.: Blumann & Thomas 4712 see; Cowan p. 646; Howes L71

The preface is signed H. O. L., possibly Herbert O. Lang. Mark Twain's portrait and a sketch of his life appear on pages 47–8 of the Appendix.

2386 LANG, JOHN D., & SAMUEL TAYLOR, JR.

REPORT OF A VISIT TO SOME OF THE TRIBES OF INDIANS, LOCATED WEST OF THE MISSISSIPPI RIVER . . . NEW-YORK: PRESS OF M. DAY & CO., 1843.

[1]–34, [35–6 blank]. 21.6 x 14 cm. Tan printed wrappers with title on front wrapper. In a brown cloth folder.

Ref.: Field 855; Howes L72; Jones 1073; Sabin 38868; Wagner-Camp 96

The contents are identical with the Providence, 1843, 47-page edition. The only difference I can detect is page 19, third paragraph, where the first sentence in the Providence edition is made the last sentence of the preceding paragraph, where it belongs. Hence I conclude this is a correction and the New York edition may be the first.—EDG

2387 LANG, JOHN D., & SAMUEL TAY-LOR, JR.

THE SAME. PROVIDENCE: PRINTED BY KNOWLES AND VOSE, 1843.

[1]–47, [48 blank]. 23 x 14.2 cm. Tan printed wrappers, with title on front wrapper. In a blue cloth case.

Ref.: Field 855 see; Howes L72; Hubach p. 95; Jones 1073 see; Rader 2199; Sabin 38868; Wagner-Camp 96
Editions: New York, 1843.

2388 LANG, WILLIAM W.

A PAPER ON THE RESOURCES AND CAPABILITIES OF TEXAS, READ BY COL. WILLIAM W. LANG, BEFORE THE FARMER'S CLUB OF THE AMERICAN INSTITUTE, COOPER UNION, NEW YORK, MARCH 8TH, 1881 . . .

[1]–[62]. 23 x 15.1 cm. Frontispiece, included in pagination. Buff printed wrappers, with title on front wrapper and advertisement on verso of back wrapper. Lacks map.

Ref.: Howes L74; Raines p. 137
Published at Austin, Texas, in 1881.

2389 LANGFORD, NATHANIEL P.

DIARY OF THE WASHBURN EXPEDITION TO THE YEL-LOWSTONE AND FIREHOLE RIVERS IN THE YEAR 1870 . . .

[i]–[xxxii], [1]–122. 20 x 13.8 cm. Illustrations unlisted. Dark blue pictorial cloth, gilt top.

Ref.: Jones 1704; National Parks (*Yellowstone*) p. 53 see

Copyrighted 1905. Below the author's name on the title-page, there is the following rubber-stamp: Published only by / J. E. Haynes / Selby at Virginia / St. Paul, Minnesota /.

2390 LANGFORD, NATHANIEL P.

VIGILANTE DAYS AND WAYS: THE PIONEERS OF THE ROCKIES, THE MAKERS AND MAKING OF MONTANA, IDAHO, OREGON, WASHINGTON, AND WYOMING . . . BOSTON: J. G. CUPPLES CO., 1890.

[i]–xxvi, [1]–426. [i]–[xvi, xvi blank], [1]–485, [486 colophon, 487–92 advertisements]. 18.8 x 12.5 cm. 18 illustrations listed. Two volumes, brown morocco, gilt, gilt edges.

Prov.: Inscribed by the author on the blank leaf preceding half-title: Clara / from / Nathaniel. / April 8ᵗʰ 1890. /

Ref.: Bradford 2909; Cowan (1914) pp. 134–35; Howes L78; Jones 1661; Smith 5682
The author married Emma Wheaton of Northfield, Minn. in 1876. She died soon afterward and Langford married her sister, Clara Wheaton, in 1884. This copy was presented by the author to his wife.

2391 LANGSDORFF, GEORG HEIN-RICH, FREIHERR VON

VOYAGES AND TRAVELS IN VARIOUS PARTS OF THE WORLD, DURING THE YEARS 1803, 1804, 1805, 1806, AND 1807 . . . LONDON: PRINTED FOR HENRY COLBURN, 1813–14.

[a]–c⁴, B–AAA⁴. [i]–[xxiv, xxiv blank], [1]–[368]. [A]–Ddd⁴. [i–viii], [1]–[392]. 28 x 22 cm. 21 engraved plates and a map, listed. Map: Map / of the / World / Illustrating the Voyages / [swelled rule] and Travels of [swelled rule] / G. H. Von Langsdorff / [lower centre:] London, Published Febʸ 1ˢᵗ 1814, by Henry Colburn, Conduit Street. / [lower right:] Thomson & Hall, sculpᵗ 14, Bury Strᵗ Bloomsbʸ / 24.1 x 39 cm. Scale: 2500 versts to one inch. Two volumes blue gray boards, rebacked with brown cloth, uncut. Inner hinges supported with cloth.

Prov.: J. W. Holliday copy.

Ref.: Cowan p. 383; Howes L81; Sabin 38896; Wickersham 6245
This expedition visited San Francisco in 1806 . . . The Russian chamberlain Rézanof, came with the expedition, and while at the Presidio met Concepción Argiiello . . . whence is derived the well-known romance.—Cowan

Published first in German at Frankfort in 1812.

2392 LANGWORTHY, FRANKLIN

SCENERY OF THE PLAINS, MOUNTAINS AND MINES; OR, A DIARY KEPT UPON THE OVERLAND ROUTE TO CALIFORNIA, BY WAY OF THE GREAT SALT LAKE . . . IN THE YEARS 1850, '51, '52 AND '53 . . . OGDENS-BURGH: PUBLISHED BY J. C. SPRAGUE, 1855.

[i]–vi, [7]–324. 20.1 x 12 cm. Black cloth, blind embossed sides, title in gilt on backstrip.

Ref.: Blumann & Thomas 5033; Cowan p. 383; Howes L84; Jones 1336; Rader 2201; Sabin 38904; Wagner-Camp 258

2393 LANGWORTHY, LUCIUS H.

DUBUQUE: ITS HISTORY, MINES, INDIAN LEGENDS, ETC., IN TWO LECTURES, DELIVERED BEFORE THE DUBUQUE LITERARY INSTITUTE, DECEMBER 18TH, 1854, AND FEBRUARY 26TH, 1855 . . . DUBUQUE: PUBLISHED BY THE INSTITUTE.

[1]–82. 22.1 x 13.6 cm. Pink printed wrappers, with title on front wrapper.

Ref.: Bradford 2910; Howes L85; Moffit 201; Mott (*Iowa*) p. 49; Sabin 38906
Printed in 1855.
Reminiscences of a pioneer who arrived at the Dubuque lead mines in 1827.

2394 LANGWORTHY, LUCIUS H.

ANOTHER COPY. Red ribbed cloth.

2395 [LANIER, JAMES F. D.]

SKETCH OF THE LIFE OF J. F. D. LANIER. (PRINTED FOR THE USE OF HIS FAMILY ONLY.) NEW YORK, 1871.

[1]–62. 21.6 x 14 cm. Photographic portrait, mounted, as frontispiece. Brown cloth, blind embossed borders on sides.

Ref.:

In 1824, Lanier was appointed assistant clerk of the House of Representatives of Indiana at Corydon. He was an early settler in the state, having arrived in Madison in 1817. In 1833, he chartered the State Bank of Indiana which had a successful career. During the Civil War, he preserved the credit of the state by paying interest on state bonds when disloyal elements among state officials refused to pay.—EDG

2396 LANNING, C. M.

A GRAMMAR AND VOCABULARY OF THE BLACKFOOT LANGUAGE, BEING A CONCISE AND COMPREHENSIVE GRAMMAR FOR THE USE OF THE LEARNER, TO WHICH IS ADDED AN EXHAUSTIVE VOCABULARY . . . COMPILED BY C. M. LANNING FROM ORIGINAL TRANSLATIONS BY JOSEPH KIPP AND W. S. GLADSTON, JR. FORT BENTON, PUBLISHED BY THE AUTHOR.*

[i]–iv, [5]–143, [144 blank]. (Two-page Errata slip between pages ii and iii.) 14.6 x 11.5 cm. Gray-green printed boards with dark brown cloth back, with title on front cover, advertisement on back cover.

Prov.: Inscribed in pencil on front fly-leaf: To Everett Graff Esq / from / The Blackhearted / Blackfoot / Ed Eberstadt /.

Ref.: Butler (*Blackfoot*) 11; Pilling 2198; Pilling (*Alg.*) p. 296; Smith 5692

The errata list is printed on dark violet paper. There are two unnumbered pages of dark violet paper at the end with advertisements of C. M. Lanning, Manufacturer; outside back cover also used for same.

2397 LA PEROUSE, JEAN FRANCOIS DE GALAUP, COMTE DE

THE VOYAGE OF LA PEROUSE ROUND THE WORLD, IN THE YEARS 1785, 1786, 1787, AND 1788 . . . LONDON: PRINTED FOR JOHN STOCKDALE, 1798.

A⁸, A*², a–1⁸, m², B–T⁸, U. [1–20], [i]–cxc, [1]–290. A⁴, B–Ee⁸, Ff⁵, a–h⁴, (A)–(G)⁸, (H)⁴. [i]–viii, [1]–442, [1]–64, [1]–119, [120 advertisements]. 20.8 x 12.8 cm. 51 illustrations and maps listed. Map: Chart / of a great part of the / Great Pacific / Ocean, / to the East & South East of / New Guinea. / Shewing the Track of the Spanish Frigate / la Princesa commanded by / Don

Franc⁰ Antonio Maurelle / in 1781. / [lower centre:] London Published, August 27, 1798, by I. Stockdale, Piccadilly. / 18.1 x 22.5 cm. No scale given. Map: A / Chart of the World / exhibiting the Track of / M. de LaPérouse / and the Route of / M. Lesseps / across the Continent. / [lower centre:] Published July 20ᵗʰ 1798. by J. Stockdale Piccadilly. / [lower right:] J. Allen Sculpᵗ / 35.8 x 61.5 cm. No scale given. Map: A Chart / of the / North-West Coast / of / America / [lower centre:] Publish'd July 20ᵗʰ 1798. by J. Stockdale. / 18.7 x 11.1 cm. No scale given. Map: Plan of / Port des Français / on the North West Coast of / America, / In Latitude 58° 37′ North & Longitude / 139° 50′ West of Paris. / [short swelled rule] / Publish'd July 20ᵗʰ 1798. by / J. Stockdale / 11.4 x 17.9 cm. No scale given. Map: Chart / of / the Discoveries in / the Seas of / Chican and Tartary / from / Manilla to Avatscha Bay / [swelled rule] / Publishd[!] July 20, 1798. By J. Stockdale. / 24.1 x 20.8 cm. No scale given. Map: Part / of the / Island of / Maouna. / 8.9 x 9.9 cm. Scale: about 3 1/2 marine miles to one inch. *On same sheet:* Plan / of the Creek / Du Massacre. / 8.3 x 9.9 cm. Scale: 75 toises to one inch. [lower centre, below centre, below lower map:] Publish'd July 20ᵗʰ 1798. by J. Stockdale. / 16.8 x 9.9 cm. Scales as above. Map: Plan / and Views of / Easter Isle, / on the same Scale / [four profile views] / [lower right:] Neele sc / [lower centre:] Published August 29, 1798, by I. Stockdale, Piccadilly. / 17.2 x 10.1 cm. Scale: about 6 1/2 miles to one inch. Two volumes, contemporary marbled calf, gilt backs, sprinkled edges.

Ref.: Allen, E. W.: "Jean François Galaup de Lapérouse; A Check List" in *California Historical Society Quarterly*, Vol. 20, 1941, pp. 47–64; Barrett 1437; Howes L93; Sabin 38964; Zamorano Eighty 49 note

Both Allen and Howes list the Stockdale edition as the first in English. The French version had appeared in Paris in 1797.

2398 LAPHAM, INCREASE A.

A GEOGRAPHICAL AND TOPOGRAPHICAL DESCRIPTION OF WISCONSIN . . . MILWAUKEE, WISCONSIN: PUBLISHED BY P. C. HALE, 1844.

[i]–iv, [5]–[256]. 15.6 x 10.6 cm. Map: Wisconsin / Southern Part / [lower left:] Entered according to Act of Congress in the year 1844 by Sidney E. Morse and Samuel Breese in the Clerks Office of the Southern District of New York. / 30 x 38.5 cm. Scale: about 12 miles to one inch. Black, vertically ribbed cloth, black leather label on backstrip.

Ref.: AII (*Wisconsin*) 205; Bradford 2917; Howes L97; Sabin 38979
First bound book printed in Milwaukee.—Howes

2399 LARIMER, SARAH LUSE

THE CAPTURE AND ESCAPE; OR, LIFE AMONG THE SIOUX . . . PHILADELPHIA: CLAXTON, REMSEN & HAFFELFINGER, 1870.

[i]–xii, 13–252. 18.5 x 11.7 cm. Portrait and one plate. Blue cloth. Worn, lacks three plates.

Ref.: Ayer 179; Field 859; Howes L101; Sabin 39033

2400 LARIMER, WILLIAM H. H.

REMINISCENCES OF GENERAL WILLIAM LARIMER AND OF HIS SON WILLIAM H. H. LARIMER TWO OF THE FOUNDERS OF DENVER CITY. COMPILED . . . BY HERMAN S. DAVIS . . . LANCASTER, PA.: THE NEW ERA PRINTING COMPANY, 1918.*

[1–2], 5–194, 194A–194B, 195–199, 199A–199H, 200–256. 23.4 x 16 cm. Six plates, five portraits, two facsimiles, and a folding genealogical table. Black limp leather, gilt top, uncut.

Prov.: Inscribed on blank leaf: To my friend / Frederic A. Godcharles / with best wishes / W. L. Mellon. / April 11ᵗʰ 1928. / Regiven by W. L. Mellon to S. E. Hackett for EDG.

Ref.: Howes L102; Wilcox p. 69

2401 LARIMER COUNTY (Colorado) STOCK GROWERS' ASSOCIATION

STOCK BRANDS PUBLISHED BY THE LARIMER COUNTY STOCK GROWERS' ASSOCIATION. FORT COLLINS, COLO.: THE COURIER BOOK AND JOB PRINT, 1885.

[1]–36, [37–52 blank (different paper)], [53 Index, 54 blank]. 16.5 x 10.2 cm. Sheepskin, red edges.

Prov.: Inscribed on front cover: Tenney Bro's / Larimer Co. / Brands /.

Ref.: Howes L103
The Tenney Bros. brands are listed on page 12.

2402 LA ROCHE, FRANK

EN ROUTE TO THE KLONDIKE: A SERIES OF PHOTOGRAPHIC VIEWS OF THE PICTURESQUE LAND OF GOLD AND GLACIERS PHOTOGRAPHED BY F. LA ROCHE . . . NEW YORK: W. B. CONKEY COMPANY.

[1–144]. 19.1 x 27 cm. Seven maps on one sheet and 143 photographic illustrations. Black cloth, black leather backstrip and corners, gray sprinkled edges.

Ref.: Smith 5698; Wickersham see 3947
Each of the illustrations is copyrighted 1897.

2403 LAROCQUE, FRANCOIS ANTOINE

. . . JOURNAL OF LAROCQUE FROM THE ASSINIBOINE TO THE YELLOWSTONE 1805 . . . EDITED . . . BY L. J. BURPEE, . . . OTTAWA: GOVERNMENT PRINTING BUREAU, 1910.*

[i–ii], [1]–82. 24.8 x 16.7 cm. Gray printed wrappers, with title on front wrapper. In a dark blue cloth case.

Ref.: Howes L107; Matthews p. 209
A map is mentioned on page 7, but it seems to have been unpublished.

2404 LARPENTEUR, CHARLES

FORTY YEARS A FUR TRADER ON THE UPPER MISSOURI . . . 1833–1872 . . . EDITED . . . BY ELLIOTT COUES . . . NEW YORK: FRANCIS P. HARPER, 1898.

[i]–xxvii, [xxviii blank], [1]–236, inserted leaf of advertisements, recto only used. [i]–[ix], [x blank], 237–473, [474 blank], inserted leaf of advertisements, recto only used. 22.6 x 15.8 cm. 12 illustrations and six maps listed. Two volumes, blue ribbed cloth, fore and lower edges uncut.

Ref.: Cuthbertson & Ewers p. 109; Howes C800; Hubach p. 77; Rader 2204; Smith 5700
Limited to 950 copies.

2405 LA SALLE, NICOLAS DE

RELATION OF THE DISCOVERY OF THE MISSISSIPPI RIVER . . . THE TRANSLATION DONE BY MELVILLE B. ANDERSON. CHICAGO: THE CAXTON CLUB, 1898.

[i–viii], [1]–69, [70 blank, 71 colophon, 72 blank]. 23.2 x 14.2 cm. Gray boards, vellum back, uncut. Board slip case.

Ref.: Howes L109
Limited to 266 copies.

2406 LA SALLE, ROBERT, CAVALIER DE

RELATION OF THE DISCOVERIES AND VOYAGES OF CAVELIER DE LA SALLE FROM 1679 TO 1681 . . . THE TRANSLATION DONE BY MELVILLE B. ANDERSON. CHICAGO: THE CAXTON CLUB, 1901.

[i]–[viii, viii blank], [1]–299, [300 blank, 301 colophon, 302 blank]. 23.2 x 15 cm. Blue boards, vellum back.

Ref.: Howes L110; Hubach p. 10; Rader 2205
Limited to 224 copies.

2407 LASLEY, M. E. A.

[Caption title] HOUSE ON WHEELS! THE FAMILY RESIDENCE OF A MAN AND FAMILY FROM THE STATE OF WASHINGTON. REASONS FOR LEADING THIS MODE OF LIFE . . .

[1]–16. 15.2 x 10 cm.

BOUND WITH:

[Caption title] SKETCH FROM LIFE'S BOOK OF THE
HOUSE ON WHEELS . . .

[1–4]. 15.1 x 11 cm. Contemporary light blue
wrappers. Much worn.

SEWN WITH:

[Caption title] COPYRIGHTED 1898, BY M. E. A.
LASLEY. SKETCHES FROM LIFE'S BOOK OF THE
HOUSE ON WHEELS . . .

[1]–16. 14.5 x 11.7 cm. Three parts in buff wrappers, printed with narrative advertisement for
Sweet, Orr & Co. on wrappers.

Ref.: Howes L112 see

The three parts were apparently printed in
different places at various times.

There are several manuscript notes, for instance, in the upper margin of the first part, page
[1]: 273. St Louis Mo. / Bot. Dec. 25, 1896
11.45 AM. / at S.E. Cor. vacant lot former site /
John Kaufmann's steam flouring / Mill. /

Lasley published a larger volume describing
his family's experiences, *Across America, in the
only House on Wheels* . . . New York, 1898.

Laid in is a printed photograph on a card of
the Lasley family before their home, 10.2 x 13.8
cm. Inscribed under the view: 12-12-99. 4.10
P.M. from Vi.L. / see p. 283 & 504. /

2408   LATHAM, DR. HENRY

TRANS-MISSOURI STOCK RAISING: THE PASTURE
LANDS OF NORTH AMERICA . . . OMAHA, NEBRAS-
KA: DAILY HERALD STEAM PRINTING HOUSE, 1871.

[1]–88. 21.6 x 14.7 cm. Printed pink wrappers,
title on front wrapper, map on verso of back
wrapper: Map / of the / Union Pacific / Railroad / and its / Connections. / 10.9 x 19.1 cm.
No scale given. In a green cloth case.

Ref.: Adams (*Ramp. Herd*) 1309; AII (*Nebraska*) 226; Howes L118

Includes the earliest general survey of the
cattle industry.

AII (*Nebraska*) mentions maps and tables.
Correspondence with institutions, with one exception, disclosed no tables except those in the
text. Only two copies with a folding map were
located at American Antiquarian and Library
Company of Philadelphia. In each of these
copies, the verso of the front cover contains text
and the folding map is entitled: Map of the Land
Grants & Connections of the Union Pacific
Railroad 1037 Miles of Road, 12,000,000 Acres
of land. 1871. Eng. by Chas. Shober, Chicago
Ill. 7 3/8 x 28 1/4 inches. This same map is included in *Guide to the Union Pacific Railroad
Lands* . . . 1873. I think my copy and other
copies not containing the map and with verso of

front wrapper blank are the original issues.—
EDG

Laid in case with: *Guide to the Union Pacific
Railroad Lands* . . . 1873.

2409   LATHROP, GEORGE

[Wrapper title] MEMOIRS OF A PIONEER . . . COM-
PLIMENTS OF THE LUSK HERALD, LUSK, WYOMING*

1–[34]. 15.8 x 8.2 cm. Green printed wrappers,
with title on front wrapper.

Ref.: Howes L119

Published about 1917.

George Lathrop was one of the early cattle
and stage drivers of the West. He died in 1917
and Luke Voorhees, proprietor of stage routes,
finished the narrative from notes given him by
Lathrop.—EDG

2410   LATHROP, GEORGE

SOME PIONEER RECOLLECTIONS . . . AND A STATE-
MENT MADE BY JOHN SINCLAIR RELATIVE TO THE
RESCUE OF THE DONNER PARTY; ALSO AN EXTRACT
FROM A LETTER WRITTEN BY GEO. McKINSTRY WITH
REFERENCE TO THE RESCUE OF THE DONNER PARTY;
TOGETHER WITH PERSONAL RECOLLECTIONS OF
PIONEER LIFE BY LUKE VOORHEES. PHILADELPHIA:
GEORGE W. JACOBS & CO., 1927.

[1]–32, [33–34 blank], [1]–75, [76 blank].
22.8 x 15 cm. Portrait. Green cloth, title in gilt
on back, paper label on front cover.

Ref.: Cowan p. 385; Howes L119, V142;
Smith 5707

The second part has a separate title-page:
Personal / Recollections / of / Pioneer Life / on
the / Mountains and Plains / of / The Great
West / [ornament] / By Luke Voorhees / The
Voorhees had been published in Cheyenne
[1920], an earlier version of the Lathrop about
1917.

2411   LATIMER, JOHN

AUTOGRAPH LETTER, SIGNED. 1811 October 9,
Chicago. Three pages, 25.2 x 20.2 cm. To William Clark.

A fascinating letter about the situation of the
Indians near Chicago, their attitude toward the
whites, and their intentions. Captain N. Heald
is mentioned as the commanding officer at Chicago. Note is made of news from Fort Wayne
that Harrison was to have left on the twentieth
of September to march against the Prophet.

2412   LATROBE, BENJAMIN H.

THE JOURNAL OF LATROBE . . . 1796 TO 1820 . . .
WITH AN INTRODUCTION BY J. H. B. LATROBE. NEW
YORK: D. APPLETON, 1905.*

[i]–xlii, 1–269, [270 blank]. 22.6 x 15.5 cm. 26 plates, 5 text illustrations. Orange cloth, gilt top, uncut.

Ref.: Howes L126; Matthews p. 191

Latrobe revised Dr. Thornton's plans for the Capitol at Washington.

2413 LATROBE, CHARLES J.

THE RAMBLER IN NORTH AMERICA: MDCCCXXXII.–MDCCCXXXIII . . . LONDON: R. B. SEELEY AND W. BURNSIDE, MDCCCXXXV.

[i]–[xii, xii blank], [1]–321, [322 blank], [323 advertisement, 324 blank]. [i]–viii, [1]–336. 19.5 x 12.2 cm. Map: The / United States / of / America. / [lower centre:] Published Feby 1. 1836, by R. B. Seeley & W. Burnside, 72, Fleet Street. / 24.6 x 28.8 cm. Scale: about 140 miles to an inch. Two volumes, dark green embossed cloth, title in gilt on backstrip, uncut.

Ref.: Buck 250; Clark III 62; Field 894; Howes L127; Hubach p. 76; Rader 2206; Sabin 39222; Wagner-Camp 57

Latrobe was a travelling companion of Washington Irving and Henry L. Ellsworth in the West.

2414 LATTA, ROBERT R.

REMINISCENCES OF PIONEER LIFE . . . KANSAS CITY, MO.: FRANKLIN HUDSON PUBLISHING CO., 1912.*

[1]–186. 20 x 13 cm. Gray pictorial cloth.

Ref.: Howes L130; Mott (*Iowa*) p. 86

Covers early life in Iowa, Nebraska, the Ozarks, etc.

2415 LATTER-DAY SAINTS' MILLENIAL STAR, THE

THE LATTER-DAY SAINTS' MILLENIAL STAR. VOLUME XI–XII . . . LIVERPOOL: EDITED AND PUBLISHED BY ORSON PRATT, MDCCCXLIX–MDCCCL.

[1–iv], [1]–380. [i]–iv, [1]–380. 21.4 x 13.8 cm. Two volumes bound together, contemporary half calf, gilt.

Ref.: Sabin 39230; Wagner-Camp 171

Contains: Interesting Items Concerning the Journeying of the Latter-/Day Saints from the City of Nauvoo, until their Location / in the Valley of the Great Salt Lake. / (Extracted from the Private Journal of Orson Pratt.) / Volume XI, pages 362–63, 369–70; Volume XII, pages [1]–4, [17]–19, [33]–35, [49]–50, [65]–68, [81]–83, [97]–100, [113]–15, [129]–31, [145]–47, [161]–66, [177]–80.

2416 LAW, JOHN

ADDRESS DELIVERED BEFORE THE VINCENNES HISTORICAL AND ANTIQUARIAN SOCIETY, FEBRUARY 22, 1839 . . . LOUISVILLE, KY.: PRENTICE AND WEISSINGER, PRINTERS, 1839.

[1]–48. 22.5 x 14.2 cm. Folding map: Lac Superieur / et autres lieux ou sont / les Missions des Pères de / la Compagnie de Iesus com-/ prises sous le nom / D'Outaouacs / . . . Drawn on stone by Thomas Campbell. / Louisville, June 1839. / Printed by C. R. Milne. / [decorative rule] / 34.5 x 47.5 cm. No scale indicated. Printed blue wrappers with title on front wrapper. In half morocco case.

Prov.: The Herschel V. Jones copy.

Ref.: Howes L152; Sabin 39316

In this history of the early settlement of the Vincennes area, there are letters by George Rogers Clark and extracts from the journal of the capture of Vincennes kept by Major Bowman.

2417 LAWRENCE, R. S.

BUYER'S BOOK OF MEMORANDUMS, FOR THE WESTERN TRADE, CONTAINING CITY, COUNTY AND STATE OFFICERS, MEMBERS OF THE BOARD OF TRADE, TRADE REPORTS, MASONIC, ODD FELLOWS AND CHURCH DIRECTORY, MEMORANDA, ETC . . . SAINT JOSEPH, MO.: F. M. POSEGATE'S STEAM BOOK AND JOB PRINTING HOUSE, 1870.

[1]–40, [41–60 ruled pages, horizontal lines in blue, vertical lines in red]. 16.7 x 10.2 cm. Cream printed wrappers, with advertisements on recto and verso of front and recto and verso of back wrappers and with short title in center of front wrapper.

Ref.:

Miscellaneous scribblings on pages [1] and several blank leaves at back.

2418 LAWRENCE MASSACRE, THE

[Caption title] THE LAWRENCE MASSACRE BY A BAND OF MISSOURI RUFFIANS UNDER QUANTRELL, AUGUST 21, 1863. INTRODUCTION. . . .

[1]–36, [37–40 advertisements]. 15.6 x 8.8 cm. Contemporary plain gray wrappers.

Ref.:

Probably printed in Lawrence, Kansas, in 1884. An advertisement by Anson Storm is dated 1884 on page [39].

2419 LAWTON, HENRY W.

[Caption title] REPORT . . . EN ROUTE TO FORT MARION, FLORIDA, SEPTEMBER 9, 1886 . . . I HAVE THE HONOR TO SUBMIT THE FOLLOWING REPORT OF OPERATIONS AGAINST GERONIMO'S AND NATCHEZ'S BANDS OF HOSTILE INDIANS . . .

[1]–9, [10 blank]. 19.8 x 13 cm. White printed wrappers, with title on front wrapper. Lacks back wrapper.

Printed at Albuquerque.

The captor of Geromino reports. See his important comment on General Leonard Wood's actions in this Campaign.

In Lawton Scrap Book.

2420 LAWTON, HENRY W.

[SCRAPBOOK RELATING TO THE CAREER OF MAJOR-GENERAL HENRY WARE LAWTON COMPILED BY ROBERT G. CARTER.] 166 pages, 29.1 x 23.7 cm., bound in full leather, gilt stamped borders.

Mounted on the 166 pages and tipped to them are hundreds of newspaper clippings, magazine articles, etc. relating to Lawton. Also tipped in are the following manuscript and printed separate pieces:

Index to Lawton Scrap-Book. 7 pages, 4to. Manuscript by R. G. Carter.

Photograph: Portrait of Lawton, full length, civilian clothing. 14.4 x 10 cm. mounted on card 16.4 x 10.7 cm. Fly's Gallery, Tombstone, A.T. /

Broadsheet: Military Order of the Loyal Legion / of the / United States, / Commandery of the District of Columbia. / [at left:] Circular No. 30. / Series of 1899. / Whole No. 228. / [vertical bracket connecting preceding three lines] / [at right:] Headquarters, City of Washington, / December 19, 1899. / [short thick rule] / In Memoriam / Companion / Henry Ware Lawton / [within wide rule border] 20 x 12.7 cm. Verso carries concise account of Lawton's career. See item 2553.

Manuscript: Autograph Letter, signed by Lawton. 1874 Jan. 19, Fort Clark, Tex. To Carter. Two pages, 8vo.

Pamphlet: In Memoriam / [short thick rule] / Funeral Oration / at Obsequies of / Major General Henry Wm. Lawton, / U. S. Volunteers, / by / Professor M. Woolsey Stryker, / D. D., LL.D. / Church of the Covenant, / February 9, 1900. / Washington City. / [1]–11, [12 blank]. 24.4 x 15.8 cm. Cream printed wrappers. See item 4018.

Manuscript: ALS, by Lawton. 1874 Dec. 17, Camp on Fresh Water Fork Brazos River, Tex. Three pages, 4to. To Carter.

Photograph: [Monument erected to the memory of Lieut. Charles L. Hudson]. 7.8 x 7.7 cm. On card 8.8 x 8.7 cm. Photographer's name at left: H. L. Bingham. / Apparently half of a stereoptic photograph. With long manuscript note about the monument by Carter.

Manuscript: ALS by Lawton. 1876 Aug. 20, Cheyenne, W. T. Two pages, 4to. To Carter. Mentions Red Cloud.

Manuscript: AL by Lawton (signature cut out). 1876 Oct. 15, Camp Robinson, Neb. Eleven pages, 4to. To Carter.

Manuscript: ALS by Lawton. 1876 Nov. 29, Camp on Crazy Woman Fork. Six pages, 4to. To Carter. Fine description of Mackenzie's fight with the Cheyennes at Willow Creek, Nov. 25, 1876.

Map: Sheet No. 3, Western Territories, / Prepared by Major G. L. Gillespie, Corps of Eng'rs, Bvt.Lt.Col. U. S. A. / January, 1876. / [lower right:] Published by authority of The Hon. the Secretary of War, / in the Office of the Chief of Engineers, U. S. Army. / 75.7 x 49.2 cm. Scale: 31.565 miles to one inch. In lower right corner, rubber stamped date of issue, Nov. 9, 1876. The route of the march and the location of the battle described in the preceding letter (in which this map was enclosed) are marked in manuscript. See item 1555.

Manuscript: ALS by Lawton. 1876 Dec. 4, Laramie. Two pages, 4to. To Carter.

Manuscript: ALS by Lawton. 1877 May 20, Camp Robinson, Neb. Four pages, 8vo. To Carter.

Manuscript: ALS by Lawton. 1877 Aug. 17, Fort Sill, I.T. Four pages, 4to. To Carter.

Broadside: Regt'l Band, Fourth Cavalry. / [decorative rule] / Programme / -for- / Retreat, at Fort Sill, I. T., / Tuesday, August 21, 1877. / [thick and thin rules] / [six lines] / [double rule] / P. Th. Held, / Chief Musician. / [within thick and thin rule borders]. 13.1 x 10.7 cm. Text, 11.8 x 8.5 cm. See item 4280.

Broadside: Regt'l Band, Fourth Cavalry. / [decorative rule] / Programme / -for- / Retreat, at Fort Sill, I. T., / Monday, August 20, 1877. / [thick and thin rules] / [8 lines] / [double rule] / P. Th. Held, / Chief Musician. / [within thick and thin rules] /. 13.3 x 10.5 cm. Text, 11.9 x 8.6 cm. See item 4279.

Manuscript: ALS by Lawton. 1877 Sept. 16, Fort Sill, I. T. Two pages, 4to. To Carter.

Broadside: Regimental Band, Fourth Cavalry. / [decorative rule] / Programme / -for- / Retreat at Fort Sill, I. T., / Thursday, August 23, 1877. / (Promenade Concert and Serenade, Wednesday and Satur-/day evenings.) / [thick and thin rules] / [six lines] / [double rule] / P. Th. Held, / Chief Musician. / [within thick and thin rule border]. 12.7 x 10.9 cm. Text, 11.9 x 8.7 cm. See item 4281.

Broadside: Regimental Band, Fourth Cavalry./ [decorative rule] / Programme / -for- / Retreat at Fort Sill, I. T., / Friday, August 24, 1877. / (Promenade Concert and Serenade, Wednesday and Satur-/day evenings.) / [thick and thin rules] /.[5 lines] / [double rule] / P. Th. Held, / Chief Musician. / [within thick and thin rule border] /. 15.1 x 10.9 cm. Text, 12 x 6.7 cm. With manuscript notes by Lawton at head and foot. See item 4282.

Manuscript: ALS by Lawton. 1878 May 27, Fort Clark, Tex. Two pages, 8vo. To Carter.

Manuscript: ALS by Lawton. 1879 Sept. 4, Fort Elliott, Tex. Three pages, 8vo. To Carter.

Map: [seal of Engineers Corps] / Map of Colorado / Prepared in the Office of the / Chief of Engineers U. S. A. / 1879. / 60.5 x 59.2 cm. Scale: about 25 miles to one inch. See item 4311.

Manuscript: ANS by Lawton. N.d., n.p. One page, oblong 8vo. To Carter.

Manuscript: TLS by John Kendrick Bangs. 1900 Jan. 2, New York. To Carter. One page, 8vo. Refusing to publish an account of Lawton's capture of Geronimo. See item 156.

Manuscript: Manuscript Telegram from Colliers' Magazine. 1900 Jan. 12, New York. To Carter. Accepting his article about Lawton and Geronimo.

Pamphlet: [Wrapper title] / [double rule] / Report / -of- / Captain H. W. Lawton, / 4th Cavalry. / [rule] / 1886. / [rule] /. [1]–9, [10 blank]. 19.8 x 13 cm. White printed wrappers. Lacks back wrapper. Manuscript note on front cover: Sent to me by Lawton /. See item 2419.

Manuscript: ALS by Lawton. 1886 Oct. 31, Fort Huachuca, A.T. Three pages, 4to. To Carter. Re his capture of Geronimo.

Pamphlet: [Wrapper title] [double rule] / Annual Report / of / Brigadier General Nelson A. Miles, / U. S. Army. / Commanding / Department of Arizona. / [rule] / 1886. / [rule] / [double rule] / [1]–22. 19.5 x 12.5 cm. Gray printed wrappers with title as above on front wrapper. Lacks back wrapper. See item 2785.

Manuscript: ALS by Lawton. 1886 Nov. 16, Fort Huachuca. Three pages, 4to. To Carter.

Pamphlet: [Caption title] Report / -of- / Assistant Surgeon Leonard Wood, / U. S. Army. / [short rule] / Fort Bowie, A. T., September 8, 1886. / To Brigadier General N. A. Miles, U. S. A., / Albuquerque, New Mexico. / . . . [1]–7, [8 blank]. 19.6 x 12.9 cm. White printed wrappers with title on front wrapper. Inscribed by Carter on front wrapper: Sent to me by Lawton. / See item 4735.

Pamphlet: [Caption title] Engineer Office, Headquarters Department of Arizona. / Whipple Barracks, Prescott, September 25, 1886. / The Assistant Adjutant General, / Department of Arizona. / . . . [Signed at end by E. J. Spencer, 1st Lieut. of Engineers] [1]–4. 20 x 12.8 cm. White printed wrappers with title on front

wrapper. Inscribed on front wrapper by Carter: Sent to me by Lawton /. See item 3928.

Manuscript: ALS by Lawton. 1887 July 4, Huachuca, A. T. One page, 4to. To Carter.

Manuscript: ALS by Lawton. 1887 Aug. 18, Fort Myer, Va. Three pages, 4to. To Carter.

Manuscript: ALS by Lawton. 1887 Aug. 20, Fort Myer, Va. Two pages, 4to. To Carter.

Manuscript: ANS by Lawton. N.p., n.d. One page, small 8vo. To Carter.

Manuscript: TLS by Lawton. 1887 Nov. 27, Fort Myer, Va. One page, 4to. To Carter.

Manuscript: ALS by Lawton. 1890 March 17, Washington, D. C. One page, 8vo. To Carter.

Manuscript: Typed Letter by Mary C. Lawton. 1900 June 22, Louisville, Ky. One page, 4to. To Carter. From Lawton's widow.

Manuscript: ALS by Lawton. 1889 Jan. 19, Deadwood, Dak. T. Two pages, 8vo. To Carter.

Manuscript: ALS (copy) by Lawton. 1898 Aug. 5, Santiago de Cuba. One page, 4to. To Carter.

Manuscript: TLS by Mrs. Lawton. 1899 May 3, Manila. Three pages, 4to. To Carter.

Manuscript: TLS by Mrs. Lawton. 1899 June 30, Manila. Two pages, 4to. To Carter.

Manuscript: ALS by Mrs. Lawton. 1897 June 8, Washington, D. C. Three pages, 8vo. To Carter.

Manuscript: ALS by Mrs. Lawton (in pencil). Sunday afternoon, 1899. One page, 4to. To Tod Carter (son of R. G. Carter).

Manuscript: Typed Manuscript by Lawton. 1899 June 6, Manila. 43 pages, 4to. Report to the Adjutant General, Department of the Pacific & Eighth Army Corps.

Throughout the many pages of the volume are annotations by Carter regarding the newspaper and magazine articles. In some cases, statements are disputed, in others, confirmed.

2421 LAZELL, FREDERICK J.

DOWN THE CEDAR RIVER. AN ACCOUNT OF A LITTLE VOYAGE FROM VINTON TO CEDAR RAPIDS . . . CEDAR RAPIDS, IOWA: THE TORCH PRESS, NINETEEN EIGHT.

[1–8]. 24.1 x 15.9 cm. Cream printed wrappers, uncut.

Ref.: Mott (*Iowa*) p. 71

2422 LAZELL, FREDERICK J.

SOME AUTUMN DAYS IN IOWA . . . CEDAR RAPIDS, IOWA: THE IOWAY CLUB, NINETEEN HUNDRED SIX.

[1]–33, [34 blank]. 23.3 x 15.1 cm. Gray boards, green cloth backstrip, title stamped in gilt on front cover and backstrip, gilt top, uncut.

Ref.:

Limited to 75 copies.

2423 LEA, ALBERT M.

NOTES ON WISCONSIN TERRITORY, WITH A MAP . . .
PHILADELPHIA: HENRY S. TANNER, 1836.

[i]–vi, [7]–53, [54 blank]. 15.2 x 9.5 cm. Folding map: Map of Part of the / Wisconsin Territory / Compiled from Tanner's Map of U States, from Survey's of Public Lands and Indian Boundaries, from personal / reconnoissance, and from original information derived from explorers and traders.— / [thin and thick rules] / Scale of 16 Miles to 1 Inch / [diagrammatic scale] / A. M. Lea, of Tenn / 2d Lt. Dragoons / [below border:] On Stone by G. Kramm / [right:] Lehman, & Duval Lith^rs Phila^a / 55.8 x 46.9 cm. Scale as above. Blue printed limp boards, with title on front cover: Notes / on / the Wisconsin Territory; / particularly with Reference to / the Iowa District, / or / Black Hawk Purchase. / [rule] / By / Lieutenant Albert M. Lea, / United States Dragoons. / [rule] / With the Act for Establishing the Territorial / Government of Wisconsin, / and an Accurate Map of the District. / [double rule] / Philadelphia: / H. S. Tanner—Shakspeare[!] Buildings. / [short rule] / 1836. / [within decorative border], advertisements on verso of back cover. In a brown half morocco case.

Ref.: Bradford 2949; Howes L161; Hubach p. 83; Jones 986; Mott (Iowa) p. 59; Sabin 39482

I bought a fine copy lacking the map from the Smith Book Co. of Cincinnati and several years later found the right map in Plumbe's *Sketches* on the shelves of Edward Eberstadt in New York. Eberstadt was disgusted to find his copy of Plumbe had the wrong map and gladly sold the map to me which enabled me to complete my defective copy.—EDG

2424 LEA, ALBERT M.

A PACIFIC RAILWAY . . .

[1]–16. 23.3 x 15 cm. Pink printed wrappers, with title on front wrapper.

Ref.: Railway Economics p. 283

Without imprint. The pamphlet is signed and dated at the end: Albert M. Lea, Civil Engineer. / Knoxville, Tenn., Oct. 15, 1858. /

Relates to the Rio Grande, Mexican, and Pacific Railroad Company.

2425 LEA, ALBERT M.

ANOTHER COPY.
Lacks wrappers.

2426 LEA, ALBERT M.

[Broadside] [PUBLISHED, IN SUBSTANCE, IN THE "NATIONAL INTELLIGENCER," SEPTEMBER, 1859.] THE GULF OF MEXICO: WITH SPECIAL REFERENCE TO ITS NORTHWEST ANGLE, THE MONSOON, AND THE GULF STREAM . . . A. M. LEA. CORPUS CHRISTI, TEXAS, SEPT. 6, 1859.

Broadside, 35.1 x 21.5 cm. Text, 27.2 x 17.3 cm.
Ref.:
Relates to the Rio Grande, Mexican, and Pacific Railroad.

2427 LEACH, ADONIRAM J.

EARLY DAY STORIES. THE OVERLAND TRAIL, ANIMALS AND BIRDS THAT LIVED HERE, HUNTING STORIES, LOOKING BACKWARD . . .*

[1]–244. (Pages [1–2] blank.) 19.3 x 13.2 cm. Illustrations unlisted. Brown cloth. In dust jacket.
Ref.: Howes L162a; Smith 5779
Imprint on verso of title-leaf: Press of / Huse Publishing Co., / Norfolk, Neb. / The Prefatory is dated from Oakdale, Nebraska, March 13, 1916.

2428 LEACH, ADONIRAM J.

A HISTORY OF ANTELOPE COUNTY NEBRASKA FROM ITS FIRST SETTLEMENT IN 1868 TO THE CLOSE OF THE YEAR 1883 . . . DECEMBER, 1909.*

[i–vi, vi blank], 1–262. 20.1 x 14.2 cm. Olive-green cloth, gilt top, uncut.
Ref.: Howes L163
The imprint of the Lakeside Press, Chicago, appears on the verso of the title-leaf. The Introduction is dated from Oakdale, Nebraska.

2429 LEACH, FRANK A.

RECOLLECTIONS OF A NEWSPAPERMAN. A RECORD OF LIFE AND EVENTS IN CALIFORNIA . . . SAN FRANCISCO: SAMUEL LEVINSON, MCMXVII.

[i–x, xi–xii fly-title, verso blank], 1–416. 22.7 x 15.2 cm. 16 illustrations listed. Red cloth.
Ref.: Blumann & Thomas 5193; Cowan p. 386

2430 LEAVENWORTH COUNTY, KANSAS. (Citizens)

[Broadside] TO THE PEOPLE OF LEAVENWORTH COUNTY: WE, THE UNDERSIGNED RESIDENTS OF SAID COUNTY, ACTUATED, WE HOPE, BY SENTIMENTS OF PATRIOTISM, SUBMIT TO THE PEOPLE FOR THEIR CONSIDERATION, THE FOLLOWING VIEW RESPECTING THE ISSUE BEFORE THEM, AND CALL UPON THEM, SHOULD IT MEET THE APPROVAL OF THEIR DELIBERATE JUDGMENT, TO SUPPORT AT THE COMING ELECTION FOR MEMBERS OF THE CONSTITUTIONAL CONVENTION, PERSONS PLEDGED TO CARRY IT OUT . . . JUNE 3D, 1857.

Broadside, 47.3 x 21.3 cm. Text, 44.1 x 13.4 cm.
Ref.: AII (Kansas) 145

Undoubtedly printed at Leavenworth. John A. Halderman and the 52 others signing the broadside were pro-slavery men. They presented ten candidates for the Lecompton Constitutional Convention.

There were two printings of this broadside, apparently with identical text, but set up differently.

2431   LE CLAIRE, ANTOINE, GEORGE DAVENPORT, & OTHERS

MANUSCRIPT DOCUMENT signed by Antoine Le Claire, George Davenport, William Gordon, P. G. Hambaugh, L. S. Colton, and Alexander W. McGregor, and for James May by George Davenport and Thomas F. Smith by Antoine Le Claire. 1836 February 23, no place. Two pages, 25 x 19.6 cm. and one page 10.8 by 19.5 cm., the latter attached to the lower margin of page [2] with sealing wax.

These are the Articles of Agreement by which the city of Davenport, Iowa, was established. The eight founders agreed to purchase the property from Antoine Le Claire, lay the lots out, and sell them off as of May 1, 1836. Le Claire retained an eighth interest in the property as his share, the others paying $1750 for their seven shares.

In the margin to the left of the signatures there is a short deed signed by A. W. McGregor transferring his share to Stanton Sholes. The deed bears Sholes' signature and also that of Elnathan C. Gavit as witness.

Accompanying the document is the original docketed wrapper. The manuscript is encased in a sealed plastic envelope and laid in a green buckram folding box with the 1841 deed from Davenport to Le Claire.

In the *Memoirs and Memories* of Judge G. C. R. Mitchell, published in 1915, on page 51, there is the following passage: At the home of Colonel George Davenport, Government Island, a meeting was held February 23, 1836, to found the town of Davenport. At this meeting six of the eight original owners were present, among them were Antoine Le Claire and Colonel Davenport. Judge Mitchell was present, though his signature does not appear on the document, which was executed in his fine clear handwriting. Drawing up this document was probably one of the first acts of his professional career in Davenport. The original is still in existence, in the possession of Mr. Louis A. Le Claire, nephew of Antoine Le Claire.

There are several changes and emendations in the body of the document.

2432   LE CLERCQ, CHRETIEN

NOUVELLE RELATION DE LA GASPESIE . . . PARIS: CHEZ AMABLE AUROY, M. DC. XCI.

[ã8, ẽ4, ĩ2, A–Zz alternately in 8 and 4, Aaa8, Bbb2. [i–xxviii], 1–572. 15.8 x 9.3 cm. Contemporary full brown calf, gilt backstrip.

Prov.: Bookplate of J. C. MacCoy.

Ref.: JCB II 1415; Church 717; Field 902; Harrisse 170; Sabin 39649; Streit II 2750

Important for the descriptions of French experiences in Canada.

2433   LE CLERCQ, CHRETIEN

PREMIER ETABLISSEMENT DE LA FOY DANS LA NOUVELLE FRANCE . . . PARIS: CHEZ AMABLE AUROY, M DC. CXI.

ã8, ẽ2, A–Zzalternately 8 and 4, Aaa4. [*]1, [**]4, A8, B2, C–Ppalternately 8 and 4, Qq1. [i–xx], [1]–559, [560 blank]. [i–x], [1]–458 [i.e., 454]. (Volume 1: page 65 mispaginated 69; 95, 9; 235, 245; 268, 286; 312, 313; 313, 315; 316, 16; 319, 316; 363, 393; 382, 302; 447, 44; 486, 496; 495, 49; 525, 527. Volume 2: page 152 mispaginated 52; 189, 186; 221, 22; 315, 31; 338, 38; 410, 408; 411, 409; 414, 412; 415, 413; 418, 416; 419, 417; 422, 420; 423, 420; 426, 424; 427, 423; 441, 445; 453, 457; 454, 458.) 15.5 x 9 cm. Map: Carte / Generalle de la / Nouvelle / France / ou est compris / la Louisiane / Gaspesie / et le Nouueau Mezique / auec les Isles / Antilles [flourish] / Dressé sur les memoires / les plus nouueaux / 1691 / [lower left:] I. Rouillard, delineauit / [lower right:] L. Boudan Sculp. / 33.5 x 48.4 cm. Scale: about 67 French Leagues to one inch. Two volumes, contemporary brown calf, gilt backstrips, sprinkled red edges.

Prov.: Contemporary signature on each title-page: Constantine /. Signature in pencil on front fly-leaf of first volume: Ch. Edward Pratt /. Nine-line note in pencil on same leaf signed: TWS[treeter] Oct 30 1944/.

Ref.: JCB II 1413; Church 718; Field 903; Harrisse 169; Sabin 39650; Streeter (*Americana—Beginnings*) 38; Streit II 2749; Wagner (*SS*) 61a

The present copy is one of the early printings with the collation as given above. The title begins *Premier Establissement* instead of *Etablissement;* the Privilege is dated April 20; the engraved map is present; leaf A1 in the second volume is not a cancel and shows the reading "Chapitre I;" the "Table des Chapitres" is present in the second volume. The catalogue of books, however, is not present in the second volume.

2434 LE DUC, WILLIAM G.

MINNESOTA YEAR BOOK FOR 1851 . . . ST. PAUL, MINNESOTA TERRITORY.

[1]–51 [52 blank], [1–10 advertisements], [1–10 blank]. 18.3 x 12.1 cm. Buff printed wrappers, with title on front wrapper, advertisements on verso of front and recto and verso of back wrappers. In brown cloth folder.

2435 LE DUC, WILLIAM G.

THE SAME.

[1]–51, [52 blank], [1–10 advertisements], [1–6 blank, but with four additional leaves of advertising attached to the blank leaves and a leaf of errata tipped to inner back cover]. Folding map: Map of / Minnesota. / Scale of Miles. / [diagrammatic scale: 40 miles to one inch/ [Eng^d by W. Kemble, N. York. / [below border:] Harper & Brothers, New York. / 29.4 x 41.6 cm. Scale as above. Buff printed boards, with title as above, advertisement on verso of back cover, black leather backstrip.

Ref.: AII (*Minnesota*) 33; Bradford 2957; Howes L179; Sabin 39689

AII (*Minnesota*) 33 states that "Advertising pages at end of book differ" and that DLC and MnHi lack maps. In both issues, the preface is dated St. Paul, Feb. 4, 1851, and the ten pages of advertisements are dated St. Paul, February, 1851. The additional advertising pages in the second copy are dated April and May, 1851, all being from St. Paul except one from St. Anthony and one from Stillwater.

No evidence of map issued with wrapper copy.

2436 LE DUC, WILLIAM G.

MINNESOTA YEAR BOOK FOR 1852 . . . ST. PAUL, MINNESOTA TERRITORY.

[1]¹⁰⁺¹, 3–5¹², 6¹²⁺¹. Pages [1–2 front endpaper], [3 blank], [4 frontispiece], [5 title-page], [6 blank], [7 Preface] [8 blank] [9 Eclipses . . .], [10 blank], [11–22 almanack], [17]–98 text, [1–12 advertisements], [blank leaf], [13–14 back endpaper]. 18.4 x 11.3 cm. Frontispiece, woodcut: Traverse des Sioux. Tan printed boards, sheep back, title on front cover. In blue half morocco case.

Ref.: AII (*Minnesota*) 49; Bradford 2957; Howes L179; Jones 1280; Sabin 39689

2437 LE DUC & ROHRER, *Publishers*

THE MINNESOTA YEAR BOOK FOR 1853. ST. PAUL, MINNESOTA: PUBLISHED ANNUALLY BY LE DUC & ROHRER.

[1]–37, [38–54 advertisements], [55–6 blank]. 18.8 x 11.9 cm. Map: Map of / Minnesota / Ter-

ritory / 1853. / Scale of Miles / [diagrammatic scale: about 65 miles to one inch.] / 20.4 x 25.7 cm. Scale as above. Buff printed wrappers, with title on front wrapper, advertisements on verso of front and recto and verso of back wrapper.

Ref.: AII (*Minnesota*) 63; Howes 5998; Sabin 39689

2438 LEE, BENJAMIN F.

[Wrapper title] THE STORY OF MY LIFE . . .

[i–iv], [1]–49, [50–2 blank]. 22.7 x 15.2 cm. Two portraits on one sheet mounted on page [iii]. Dark gray-green printed wrappers with title as above, side-sewn through three punched holes with red and cream cord, tassels (one missing), uncut.

Prov.: Inscribed on page [i]: F. W. Cragin, / from the author, B F Lee / June 10, 1908. /

Ref.: Howes L191

A crudely printed piece, probably run off at Paonia, Colorado, in 1907.

Inserted are two manuscript slips; one on page [iv] is a Preface dated June 1907 and the other is an addition to page 38. Numerous manuscript corrections and changes in the text.

The author went overland to Colorado in 1865 and the volume is principally of Colorado interest.

2439 LEE, CHARLES H.

THE LONG AGO: AN ANECDOTAL HISTORY OF PIONEER DAYS IN THE RED RIVER VALLEY OF THE NORTH. WALHALLA, NORTH DAK.: SEMI-WEEKLY MOUNTAINEER PRINT, 1898.

[i–ii], [1]–76. 23.4 x 15.4 cm. Illustration. Gray-green printed wrappers.

Prov.: Signature of Florence H. Davis on front wrapper.

Ref.: Howes L195

Enclosed with pamphlet is a letter from Florence H. Davis, librarian of the State Historical Society of North Dakota, whose copy this was. Mrs. Davis, who came from Walhalla, knew the author.—EDG

2440 LEE, DANIEL, & JOSEPH H. FROST

TEN YEARS IN OREGON . . . NEW-YORK: PUBLISHED FOR THE AUTHORS, 1844.

[1]–344. 18.5 x 11.4 cm. Folding map: A Sketch of the Columbia River, and adjacent / Country. / 20.6 x 16.5 cm. No scale given. Black cloth.

Ref.: Bradford 2959; Field 904; Howell 185; Howes L197; Sabin 39724; Smith 5800; Wagner-Camp 111

Contains an account of Wyeth's journey to Oregon, April to September, 1834.

2441 LEE, JOHN D.

MORMONISM UNVEILED; OR, THE LIFE AND CONFES-
SIONS OF THE LATE MORMON BISHOP, JOHN D. LEE;
(WRITTEN BY HIMSELF) EMBRACING A HISTORY OF
MORMONISM FROM ITS INCEPTION DOWN TO THE
PRESENT TIME . . . ALSO THE TRUE HISTORY OF THE
HORRIBLE BUTCHERY KNOWN AS THE MOUNTAIN
MEADOWS MASSACRE . . . ST. LOUIS, MO.: BRYAN,
BRAND & CO., 1877.

[iii]–xiv, [15]–390, [391 advertisement, 392
blank]. 21 x 14.2 cm. 13 illustrations unlisted.
Bright green cloth, title stamped in gilt on front
cover and backstrip, decorative border in black
on front cover and in blind on back.

Ref.: Howes L209

2442 LEE, L. P., *Editor*

HISTORY OF THE SPIRIT LAKE MASSACRE! 8TH
MARCH, 1857, AND OF MISS ABIGAIL GARDINER'S
THREE MONTH'S CAPTIVITY AMONG THE INDIANS.
ACCORDING TO HER OWN ACCOUNT . . . NEW
BRITAIN, CT.: L. P. LEE, PUBLISHER, 1857.

[1]–[48]. 23 x 14.8 cm. Vignettes in text. Cream
printed wrappers, with title on front wrapper.
In a red cloth case.

Ref.: Ayer 181; Howes L210

More properly, the captive's name was
Abigail Gardner, later Mrs. Abbie Sharp.

MacKinlay Cantor's *Spirit Lake . . .* 1961 is
based in part on this.

2443 LEE, L. W.

AUTOBIOGRAPHY OF A PIONEER . . . VALLEY VIEW,
TEXAS, AUGUST 10TH, 1914.

[1–19, 20 blank]. 17.2 x 12.4 cm. Brown printed
wrappers, with title on front wrapper.

Ref.:

Lee went overland to the California gold-
fields in 1850 taking four months for the trip from
Missouri to Sacramento. He returned to Missouri overland with pack mules in 1852, and in
1857 went across again as captain of a train and
driving a herd of cattle through. He stayed in
California until 1859, disposing of his cattle to
good advantage, and returned via Panama. He
moved to Texas in 1869 and laid out the town of
Valley View in 1873.—EDG

2444 LEE, NELSON

THREE YEARS AMONG THE CAMANCHES, THE NAR-
RATIVE OF NELSON LEE, THE TEXAN RANGER, CON-
TAINING A DETAILED ACCOUNT OF HIS CAPTIVITY
AMONG THE INDIANS, HIS SINGULAR ESCAPE
THROUGH THE INSTRUMENTALITY OF HIS WATCH,
AND FULLY ILLUSTRATING INDIAN LIFE AS IT IS ON
THE WAR PATH AND IN THE CAMP. ALBANY:
BAKER TAYLOR, 1859.

[i]–xii, [13]–224, [225–28 blank]. 18.7 x 12.2 cm.
Portrait on verso of front wrapper. Green pictorial wrappers, with title on front wrapper. In
a blue half morocco case.

Ref.: Ayer 182; Dobie p. 34; Field 905;
Howes L212; Jones 1414; Rader 2215; Sabin
39778; Wagner-Camp 334

The added pictorial title-page is probably the
portrait Howes refers to. The printed title is not
identical with the wrapper title.

2445 LEE COUNTY, IOWA. Sheriff (Braxton W. Gillock)

[Broadside] $150 REWARD. WHEREAS A ROBBERY
WAS COMMITTED IN THE VICINITY OF THE TOWN OF
FORT MADISON, ON THE 22D INST., . . . BRAXTON
W. GILLOCK, SHERIFF OF LEE CO. IOWA. DATED
FORT MADISON, APRIL 23D, 1840.

Broadside on blue paper, 25 x 30.6 cm. Text,
22 x 25.7 cm.

Ref.:

A manuscript note at the foot of the broadside reads: caught /. The broadside is addressed
in manuscript on the verso: Warsaw / Postmaster / Warsaw Ills. / P. M / Warsaw / Post
Master / Warsaw /. There are also a few words
in another hand: B Belmont W / y of To those
many / These are /.

2446 LEE TRIAL, THE

THE LEE TRIAL! AN EXPOSE OF THE MOUNTAIN
MEADOWS MASSACRE, BEING A CONDENSED REPORT
OF THE PRISONER'S STATEMENT, TESTIMONY OF
WITNESSES, CHARGE OF THE JUDGE, ARGUMENTS OF
COUNSEL, AND OPINIONS OF THE PRESS UPON THE
TRIAL. SALT LAKE CITY, UTAH: TRIBUNE PRINTING
COMPANY, 1875.*

[1]–64. 21 x 14.2 cm. Removed from bound volume, unbound.

Prov.: Rubber stamp of U.S. Geological Survey Library on title-page surcharged with Ex-
changed stamp.

Ref.: Howes L208; Woodward 126

Copyrighted by George F. Prescott.

2447 LEEPER, DAVID R.

THE ARGONAUTS OF 'FORTY-NINE. SOME RECOLLEC-
TIONS OF THE PLAINS AND THE DIGGINGS . . .
SOUTH BEND, INDIANA: J. B. STOLL & COMPANY,
1894.

[1]–146, [I]–XVI. 22 x 14.8 cm. Illustrations unlisted. Brown cloth, title stamped in gilt on front
cover and backstrip, decorative border stamped
in black on front cover and in blind on back.

Ref.: Cowan p. 388; Howes L226; Jones 1671

Inserted after the last page of text is a small
(4.5 x 13.8 cm.) errata slip.

2448 LEESON, MICHAEL A.

HISTORY OF MONTANA. 1739–1885. A HISTORY OF ITS DISCOVERY AND SETTLEMENT . . . HISTORIES OF COUNTIES, CITIES, VILLAGES AND MINING CAMPS; ALSO, PERSONAL REMINISCENCES . . . CHICAGO: WARNER, BEERS & COMPANY, 1885.

[1]–1367, [1368 blank]. 26.4 x 19.8 cm. Illustrations and map listed. Dark red half morocco, marbled edges.

Ref.: Adams (*Ramp. Herd*) 1322; Howes L228; Smith 5812

2449 LEGARD, ALLAYNE B.

COLORADO . . . LONDON: CHAPMAN AND HALL, 1872.

[i–iv, iv blank], [1]–170. 19.1 x 12.4 cm. Green cloth, uncut.

Prov.: Inscribed inside front cover: Price 2ˢ/6 / ———— / M. F. Dunnawey Esq. / Royal Engineers / Your attention is particularly / directed to the preface. / J. D. L. / ———— /

Ref.: Bradford 2967; Howes L233; Jones 1555; Wilcox p. 70

The writer of this Journal would remind those to whom it is sent, that it is printed entirely for private circulation. He would also request those possessing copies, not to part with them, as for obvious reasons, he would not like the book to get into the hands of those with whom he is not acquainted.—Preface

The author, reporting his personal experiences, is frank and critical about cattle and sheep ranches in Colorado.

2450 LEIGH, FRANCES BUTLER

TEN YEARS ON A GEORGIA PLANTATION SINCE THE WAR . . . LONDON: RICHARD BENTLEY & SON, 1883.

[i]–[xii, xii blank], [1]–347, [348 blank]. 22 x 14.1 cm. Dark purple-red cloth, gilt vignette on front cover, gilt title on backstrip.

Ref.: Clark (*New South*) I 131; De Renne p. 820; Howes L241

Mrs. Leigh was the daughter of Fanny Kemble.

2451 LEIGH, WILLIAM R.

THE WESTERN PONY . . . NEW YORK, HUNTINGTON PRESS.

[1]–[117], [118 blank]. 31.3 x 23.4 cm. Six colored plates (reproduced by Max Jaffe) and 18 illustrations listed. Light red cloth, title in gilt on backstrip, silhouette of horse's head in gilt on black skiver label on backstrip, gilt top, uncut.

Ref.: Adams (*Ramp. Herd*) 1325; Dobie p. 134; Howes L242

Published in 1933. Limited to 100 copies. With an extra copy, signed, of one of the colored plates laid in.

2452 LEISHER, J. J.

THE DECLINE AND FALL OF SAMUEL SAWBONES, M.D. ON THE KLONDIKE. BY HIS NEXT BEST FRIEND. NEW YORK: THE NEELY COMPANY.

[1–2], [i]–[vi, vi blank], [7]–197, [198 blank]. 19 x 13 cm. Illustrations unlisted. Gray pictorial cloth, fore and lower edges uncut.

Ref.: Smith 5818; Wickersham 4346

Copyrighted 1900. Klondike humor, according to the experts.

2453 LELAND, CHARLES G.

THE UNION PACIFIC RAILWAY, EASTERN DIVISION; OR, THREE THOUSAND MILES IN A RAILWAY CAR . . . PHILADELPHIA: RINGWALT & BROWN, STEAM-POWER BOOK AND JOB PRINTERS, 1867.

[1]–95, [96 blank]. 22.6 x 14.9 cm. Light brown printed wrappers, with title on front wrapper within decorative borders.

Ref.: Howes L246; *Railway Economics* p. 298; Sabin 39964

2454 LENOX, EDWARD H.

OVERLAND TO OREGON IN THE TRACKS OF LEWIS AND CLARKE . . . EDITED BY ROBERT WHITAKER . . . OAKLAND, CALIFORNIA: 1904.

[i]–[x, x blank], 1–69, [70 blank]. 25.1 x 14.4 cm. Illustrations unlisted. Black pictorial cloth.

Ref.: Howell 186; Howes L255a; Smith 5859

Not autographed. Bound in at the front is an extra set of endpapers.

2455 LEONA VICARIO (Mexican State). AYUNTAMIENTO

[Broadside] LISTA GENERAL DE LOS CIUDADANOS QUE CONFORME AL ARTICULO SEPTIMO DE LA LEY DE 14 DE OCTUBRE DE 1828, DEBEN SERBIR DE JURADOS EN LOS DENUNCIOS QUE SE HAGAN SOBRE ABUSOS QUE SE COMETEN EN LA LIBERTAD DE IMPRENTA . . . SALA DE SESIONES DEL ILUSTRE AYUNTAMIENTO DE LEONA VICARIO ENERO 30 DE 1830 . . . IMPRESO EN LA OFICINA DEL SUPREMO GOBIERNO EN PALACIO, A CARGO DEL C. JOSE MANUEL BANGS.

Broadside, 43 x 31 cm. Text, 40.4 x 23.5 cm. Uncut.

Ref.:

The list comprises the names of those citizens eligible for jury duty in cases of censorship.

On verso, in manuscript: Copia de su original / Inacio de Arizpe Tomas de la Vega / Pedro del Valle / Martin Alcala /. Each with paraph.

2456 LEONARD, A. & CO., Burlington, Iowa

A CATALOGUE OF FRUIT TREES & SHRUBBERY TO BE HAD AT THE PLANK ROAD NURSERIES OF A. LEONARD & CO. SEPTEMBER, 1852. BURLINGTON: PRINTED AT THE HAWK-EYE OFFICE, 1852.

[1]–12. 16.2 x 11.3 cm. Tan printed wrappers, with title on front wrapper.

Ref.: Moffit 107

2457 LEONARD, ABNER

THE MODE OF BAPTISM: A LETTER TO REV. G. J. JOHNSON, PASTOR OF THE FIRST BAPTIST CHURCH, IN BURLINGTON, IOWA . . . BURLINGTON: THE TELEGRAPH PRINTING COMPANY, 1854.

[1]–9, [10 blank]. 22 x 13.5 cm. Buff printed wrappers, with title on front wrapper.

Ref.:

2458 LEONARD, CHARLES C.

THE HISTORY OF PITHOLE BY "CROCUS," (CHAS. C. LEONARD.) . . . PITHOLE CITY, PA.: MORTON, LONGWELL & CO., 1867.

[1]–106, [1–8 advertisements]. 17.5 x 12 cm. Six illustrations. Patterned plum cloth. Blank leaf torn out before title-leaf.

Ref.: Howes L257; Sabin 40095

Early times in the oil region. Pithole had, during its boom, 16,000 people; it exists no more.— Howes. In addition to descriptions and history of the area there is considerable "oil field humor."

2459 LEONARD, H. L. W.

OREGON TERRITORY: CONTAINING A BRIEF, BUT AUTHENTIC ACCOUNT OF SPANISH, ENGLISH, RUSSIAN, AND AMERICAN DISCOVERIES ON THE NORTH-WEST COAST OF AMERICA . . . CLEVELAND: YOUNG-LOVE'S STEAM PRESS, 1846.

[i]–iv, [5]–88. 17.4 x 11.2 cm. Buff printed wrappers with title on front wrapper, title reading down on backstrip: History of Oregon. /, itinerary from Missouri to Oregon on verso of back wrapper. (The wrappers were probably pinkish beige originally, now faded to buff.) In a brown half morocco case.

Ref.: Howes L261; Wagner-Camp 122a

The first copy of this work to come to my knowledge was owned by Goodspeed in 1928 or 1929 and was sold to Eberstadt for the Coe Collection. In 1945 a second copy turned up and was sold by Eberstadt to T. W. Streeter. My copy, the third one, was bought by Wessen from an Ohio library. The contents of the book are quite disappointing.—EDG

2460 LEONARD, S. L.

[Broadside] TO THE SETTLERS OF THE COUNTIES OF PLATTE BUCHANAN AND HOLT, I HAVE SELECTED ABOUT ONE HUNDRED AND SIXTY THOUSAND ACRES OF LAND FOR THE STATE . . . YOUR FELLOW-CITIZEN, S. L. LEONARD. PLATTE CITY, MARCH 22, 1844.

Broadside, 55.1 x 41.3 cm. Text, 40 x 35 cm.

Ref.:

Leonard, Commissioner on the part of the State, answers "objections urged to the validity of the selections made for the State," questions the actions of the Register and Receiver at Plattsburgh and the Commissioner of the General Land Office, and assures the settlers that they may "rest contented as far as the right of the State [of Nebraska] is concerned."—EDG

In the heading, the word *and* has been crossed out in manuscript and in the following line *Andrew and* have been inserted in manuscript.

2461 LEONARD, ZENAS

NARRATIVE OF THE ADVENTURES OF ZENAS LEONARD, A NATIVE OF CLEARFIELD COUNTY, PA. WHO SPENT FIVE YEARS IN TRAPPING FOR FURS, TRADING WITH THE INDIANS, &C. &C., OF THE ROCKY MOUNTAINS . . . CLEARFIELD, PA.: PRINTED AND PUBLISHED BY D. W. MOORE, 1839.

[i]–iv, [1]–87, [88 blank]. 22.7 x 15.3 cm. Original marbled boards, maroon roan back and corners. In a red cloth case.

Prov.: With the name Gibbon on the title-page and with the bookplate of Laura R. Gibbon.

Ref.: Blumann & Thomas 1902; Cowan p. 389; Dobie p. 73; Farquhar (*Yosemite*) 1a; Howes L264; Hubach p. 70; Jones 1025; Rader 2217; Wagner-Camp 75

Leonard's *Narrative* is a classic of the Rocky Mountain fur trade. It is not only a pleasure to read, but comprises an accurate account of personal experience.

This copy was secured from the granddaughter of Laura R. Gibbon after more than fifteen years of negotiations. Mrs. Gibbon was the daughter of Leonard Gifford, the publisher of the *Smithland* (Kentucky) *Bee*, who was shot one afternoon while walking with his seven-year-old daughter Laura. The episode was the basis for James Lane Allen's *Aftermath*, New York, 1896.—EDG

2462 LE PAGE DU PRATZ, ANTOINE SIMON

HISTOIRE DE LA LOUISIANE, CONTENANT LA DE-COUVERTE DE CE VASTE PAYS . . . UN VOYAGE DANS LES TERRES . . . DEUX VOYAGES DANS LE NORD DU

NOUVEAU MEXIQUE . . . PARIS: CHEZ DE BURE L'AINE, M.DCC.LVIII.

[a]⁸, A–P¹². [a]², A–S¹², T⁵. [a]², A–T¹². [i]–xvj, [1]–358, [359 errata, 360 blank]. (Leaves B1 and G5 cancels, page 322 mispaginated 323.) [i–iv], [1]–441, [442 blank]. (Leaf B5 is a cancel, pages 194–95 mispaginated 195–96; 200, 190; 201, 191; 202, 122; 203, 123; 204, 104; 206, 106; 208, 108; 209–64, 207–62.) [i–iv], [1]–451, [452–54 approbation and privilege, 455–56 blank]. (Pages 430–31 mispaginated 431, 430.) 16.9 x 9.6 cm. 39 plates, two maps and a plan. Map: Carte /de la Louisiane / Colonie Française / avec le Cours du Fleuve S.ᵗ Louis, / les Rivieres Adjacentes, / les Nations des Naturels, les Etablissem⁸ Français, / et les Mines. / Par l'Auteur de l'Histoire / de cette Province / 1757. / [upper left:] To. 1. Pag. 138. / 25.6 x 34.2 cm. No scale given. Map: [Mouth of the Mississippi River.] [upper right:] To. 1. Pag. 139 /. 14.3 x 17.9 cm. No scale given. Plan: Nouvelle Orleans Capitale de la Louisiane /. [upper right:] T. 2. p. 202 /. 12.9 x 18.7 cm. Scale: about 130 toises to one inch. Three volumes, yellow-brown pulled paste papers, orange manuscript labels on backstrips.

Ref.: Clark I 75; Howes L266; Rader 2219; Raines p. 73; Sabin 40122

Le Page du Pratz lived in Louisiana for about sixteen years; he acquired much information and misinformation about the colony. His descriptions of the native inhabitants are valuable. He includes a short account of the expedition of Louis de St. Denis to New Mexico in 1715.

2463 LE PAGE DU PRATZ, ANTOINE SIMON

THE HISTORY OF LOUISIANA; OR, OF THE WESTERN PARTS OF VIRGINIA AND CAROLINA . . . LONDON: PRINTED FOR T. BECKET AND P. A. DE HONDT, MDCCLXIII.

[*]². a–b¹²⁺¹, a⁴, B–Q¹². [*]², A², B–M¹², N⁴. [1–4], [i]–1, i–vii, [vii advertisement], 1–368. [i–viii], 1–272. 16.8 x 10.2 cm. Two maps. Map: A / Map of / Louisiana, / with the course of the / Missisipi[!], / and the adjacent Rivers, / the Nations of the Natives, / the French Establishments / and the Mines; / By the Author of ẙ History of / that Colony. / 1757. / 25.1 x 33.9 cm. No scale given. Map: [Mouth of the Mississippi River.] 14.5 x 17.5 cm. No scale given. Two volumes, contemporary full calf.

Prov.: Stephen Tempest bookplate.

Ref.: as above

The translator took a good many liberties with the original.

2464 LESTER, CHARLES E.

SAM HOUSTON AND HIS REPUBLIC . . . NEW YORK: BURGESS, STRINGER & CO., 1846.

[1]–208. 23.7 x 14.5 cm. Portrait of Houston. Printed buff wrappers, with title on front wrapper, advertisement on verso of back wrapper. Bound into red half morocco.

Ref.: Howes L271; Rader 2221; Sabin 40229

2465 LESTER, JOHN C., & D. L. WILSON

KU KLUX KLAN. ITS ORIGIN, GROWTH AND DISBANDMENT . . . NASHVILLE, TENN.: WHEELER, OSBORN & DUCKWORTH MANUFACTURING CO., 1884.

[1]–117 [118 blank]. 14.2 x 9.3 cm. Gray printed wrappers, with title on front wrapper; rebacked. In a gray buckram case.

Ref.: Howes L272

Lester was one of the ten founding fathers of this order.—Howes

2466 LETTER FROM A GERMAN DOCTOR, A

A LETTER FROM A GERMAN DOCTOR OF THE UNIVERSITY OF STRASBURG, TO A PROTESTANT GENTLEMAN. ST. LOUIS: PRINTED BY CHARLES KEEMLE, 1828.

[1]–31. [32 blank]. 22.8 x 14 cm. Black boards, black cloth back.

Ref.:

2467 LETTRE ECRITE PAR UN FRANCOIS EMIGRANT . . .

[Caption title] LETTRE ECRITE PAR UN FRANCOIS EMIGRANT SUR LES TERRES DE LA COMPAGNIE DU SCIOTO, A SON AMI A PARIS. A NEW-YORK, LE 23 MAI 1790 . . .

A⁸, B⁶. [1]–27, [28 blank]. 18.4 x 11.5 cm. Rebound in red morocco, by Elizabeth Greenhill.

Ref.: Howes L216; Monaghan 973; Vail 809-A

Probably printed in Paris in 1790.

The unidentified author was on his way to the Scioto when he wrote this letter exposing some of the fraudulent claims of the Compagnie du Scioto.

2468 LETTRES EDIFIANTES ET CURIEUSES . . .

LETTRES EDIFIANTES ET CURIEUSES, ECRITES DES MISSIONS ETRANGERES, PAR QUELQUES MISSIONNAIRES DE LA COMPAGNIE DE JESUS. XI. RECUEIL. A PARIS: CHEZ NICOLAS LE CLERC, MDCCXV.

a¹², A–S¹², T². [i–xxiv], [1]–[436]. 15.2 x 9.6 cm. Map: [Map of the Philippine Islands]. [upper left:] p. 74. / 12.8 x 16.5 cm. Scale: about 5 leagues (?) to one inch. Original vellum, orange sprinkled edges.

Ref.: Howes L299; Sabin 40697; Streit I 750, 805

Contains Father Marest's letter from Kaskaskia, November 9, 1712. This is Volume XI of a 34-volume set of Jesuit letters.

2469 [LETTS, JOHN M.]

CALIFORNIA ILLUSTRATED: INCLUDING A DESCRIPTION OF THE PANAMA AND NICARAGUA ROUTES . . . NEW YORK: WILLIAM HOLDREDGE, 1852.

[1]–[viii, viii blank], [9]–224. 22.6 x 14.8 cm. 48 lithographed plates with tinted grounds. Dark blue cloth, blind embossed sides with gilt vignette of miner on front cover and same in blind on back, title and miner vignette stamped in gilt on backstrip.

Ref.: Bradford 2979 see; Cowan p. 390; Howes L300; Jones 1281 see; Sabin 40722 see

There was another printing of the same year, apparently later, in which the author's name appears on the title-page. Some copies vary in number of plates; both Cowan and Howes call for 48.

2470 LEVENS, HENRY C., & NATHANIEL M. DRAKE

A HISTORY OF COOPER COUNTY, MISSOURI, FROM THE FIRST VISIT BY WHITE MEN, IN FEBRUARY, 1804, TO THE 5TH DAY OF JULY, 1876 . . . ST. LOUIS: PERRIN & SMITH, 1876.

[i]–x, [11]–231, [232 blank, 233 errata, 234 blank]. 22.4 x 15.1 cm. Gray printed boards, green cloth backstrip.

Ref.: Bradford 2980a; Howes L302

Interspersed throughout the volume are small advertising sheets for Boonville merchants.

2471 LEWIS, ALFRED H.

WOLFVILLE . . . NEW YORK: FREDERICK A. STOKES COMPANY.

[i–xii, xii blank], [1]–337, [338 blank]. 18.8 x 12.5 cm. 18 illustrations listed. Red pictorial cloth, with title on front cover and backstrip in black.

Ref.: Dobie p. 110
Copyrighted 1897.

"The Old Cattleman," who tells all the Wolfville stories, is a substantial and flavorsome creation.—Dobie

2472 LEWIS, ALFRED H.

WOLFVILLE DAYS . . . NEW YORK: FREDERICK A. STOKES COMPANY.*

[i]–[xii, xii blank], [1]–311, [312 blank]. 18.4x 12.5 cm. Frontispiece. Red pictorial cloth, title on front cover and backstrip in gilt.

Ref.: Dobie p. 110
Copyrighted 1902.

2473 LEWIS, ALFRED H.

WOLFVILLE NIGHTS . . . NEW YORK: FREDERICK A. STOKES COMPANY.*

[i–vi, vi blank], [1]–326. 18.5 x 12.3 cm. Frontispiece. Dark gray pictorial cloth, title stamped in gilt on front cover and backstrip.

Ref.: Dobie p. 110
Copyrighted 1902.

2474 LEWIS, HENRY

DAS ILLUSTRIRTE MISSISSIPPITHAL . . . DUSSELDORF, ARNZ & COMP.

[1]–431, [432 blank]. 26 x 18.7 cm. Pictorial title-page reading: Der Mississippi. / [Large vignette] / Düsseldorf. / Verlag des lithogr. Jnstituts von Arnz & Cº /. One illustration and 78 colored plates (one folding). Rebound in half green morocco, gilt backstrip, marbled edges.

Ref.: Bay pp. 328, 389; Buck 589; Howes L312; Jones 1376; Rader 2227; Sabin 40807

Das Mississippithal is one of a half-dozen great and rare illustrated books relating to North America. It was issued originally in twenty parts, the first three of which were also published in an English version of the text. In the present copy the plates before pages [73], 77, 85, 99, 109 (two plates), 121, 145, 147, [175], 197, 387 carry English titles only while the others show German only or German and English.

2475 [LEWIS, JOHN W.]

[Wrapper title] THE FIVE CENT WIDE AWAKE LIBRARY . . . VOL. I. NEW YORK, AUGUST 29, 1881 . . . THE TRUE LIFE OF BILLY THE KID.

[1]–[16]. 29.3 x 20.9 cm. Unbound.

Ref.: Adams 618; Dykes 6

The caption title on page 2 reads: . . . / The True Life of Billy the Kid. / [short rule] / By Don Jenardo. / [short rule] / . . .

According to Dykes, this was "on thousands of newstands about six weeks after the killing of the Kid." It precedes the more famous biography of Pat Garrett.

2476 LEWIS, JOHN W.

THE SAME, in slightly reduced facsimile, with additional text by Jefferson C. Dykes, a checklist of Billy the Kid books, and signed on page 2 by Dykes. The format differs slightly.

2477 LEWIS, MERIWETHER, & WILLIAM CLARK

HISTORY OF THE EXPEDITION UNDER THE COMMAND OF CAPTAINS LEWIS AND CLARK . . . BY PAUL ALLEN . . . PHILADELPHIA: PUBLISHED BY BRADFORD AND INSKEEP, 1814.

[a]–c⁴, d², B–3O⁴ [3O4 blank]. [A]⁶, B–3U⁴, 3X²
[A1 blank]. [i]–xxviii, [1]–470. [i]–ix, [x blank],
[1]–522. 22.1 x 14.2 cm. Five single-page maps,
one folding map. Folding map: A / Map of /
Lewis and Clark's Track, / Across the Western
Portion of / North America / From the / Missis-
sippi to the Pacific Ocean; / By Order of the
Executive / of the / United States. / In 1804. 5 &
6. / Copied by Samuel Lewis from the / Original
Drawing of Wᵐ Clark. / Samˡ Harrison fcᵗ /
30.1 x 70 cm. No scale given. Two volumes, tan
printed boards, with title on front covers, advertisements on back covers, title on backstrips,
uncut. In two brown half morocco cases.
Prov.: Signature on inside front cover of Vol.
I: John Peirce /
Ref.: Bradford 2995; Church 1309; Field 928;
Howes L317; Jones 771; Paltsits p. lxxvii; Sabin
825, 40829; Smith 5894; Sowerby 4168;
Wagner-Camp 13

First authorized and complete account of the
most important western exploration and the
first of many overland narratives to follow. Less
than 2000 copies printed of the original edition.—Howes

2478   LEWIS, MERIWETHER, & WILLIAM
CLARK
THE SAME.

Two volumes, contemporary (original) mottled calf, gilt and blind borders on sides, gilt
backstrips, marbled edges. Rebacked preserving
most of original backstrips.
Prov.: Thomas Jefferson's copy with the manuscript T. before the signature I and J. before the
signature T in each volume. William Clark's
copy with his signature on the initial blank leaf
in Volume II; W. Clark's property / at the head
of page 100 in the first volume; manuscript initials: W. C. / above the signature on the first
blank leaf in second volume; Wᵐ Clark / on
second title-page; Genˡ William Clark's property / in outer margin of plate facing page 31 of
second volume (as above); W. Clark's property / at the head of page 100 of second volume.
Julia Clark's copy with signature: Julia Clark /
on each title-page. There are also two marginal
notes which may be in Thomas Jefferson's hand
in Volume I, pages 18 and 463. On page 291,
there is a manuscript note in pencil which may
be in the hand of William Clark: A Salute in
honor of the day /.
Ref.: as above
According to Miss Sowerby, Jefferson received two copies of the work bound in calf and
eleven in boards. This is undoubtedly the copy
sent by Jefferson to Clark, although a covering
letter has not yet been located.

Julia Clark was the wife of William Clark.
Their third son and fourth child was George
Rogers Hancock Clark (1816–1858). He inher-
ited the volumes and his eldest child, Julia
Clark, received them. She later married a man
by the name of Voorhis and they had a daughter, Eleanor Glasgow Voorhis. The so-called
Voorhis material was used by Thwaites for his
1904 edition of the Journals and parts of it were
sold years later by G. A. Baker & Co., Max
Hartzoff's auction house in New York. The
present copy of the *History* came into the hands
of W. J. Holliday at whose sale it was offered in
1954. The fact of Jefferson's ownership was not
mentioned.

2479   LEWIS, MERIWETHER, & WILLIAM
CLARK
THE TRAVELS OF CAPTS. LEWIS & CLARKE . . . LON-
DON: PRINTED FOR LONGMAN, HURST, REES, AND
ORME, 1809.

[A]⁴⁺¹, B–U⁸, X², Y¹. [i]–ix, [x blank], [1]–309,
[310 blank]. (Page 38 mispaginated 83.) 22.5 x
14.2 cm. Folding map: Map / of the Country
Inhabited by the / Western Tribes of Indians. /
[lower right:] Neele sc Strand. / [lower centre:]
Published Sepʳ 12ᵗʰ 1809, by Longman & Cᵒ
Pater-noster Row. / 24.4 x 19.7 cm. No scale
given. Gray boards, white paper backstrip, with
printed paper label, 3.7 x 3 cm., on backstrip.
Ref.: as above.

This edition contains some documents not
published in any other edition . . . —Sabin

2480   LEWIS, MERIWETHER, & WILLIAM
CLARK
TRAVELS TO THE SOURCE OF THE MISSOURI RIVER
. . . LONDON: PRINTED FOR LONGMAN, HURST,
REES, ORME, AND BROWN, 1814.

a², b–c⁴, d², B–4P⁴. [i]–xxiv, [1]–663, [664 adver-
tisements]. (Page 323 mispaginated 223.) 28.5 x
21.1 cm. Folding map and five other maps on
three plates. Folding map: A / Map of / Lewis
and Clark's Track / Across the Western Portion
of / North America, / from the / Mississippi to
the Pacific Ocean, / By Order of the Executive
of / The United States / in 1804, 5 & 6. / Copied
by Samuel Lewis from the Original Drawing of
Wᵐ Clark. / [below border:] London Published
April 28ᵗʰ 1814 by Longman, Hurst, Rees,
Orme, & Brown, Paternoster Row. / [lower
right:] Neele. sculp. 352. Strand /. 29.8 x 67.8
cm. No scale given. Two maps on one page:
Map: Ancient / Fortification / on the / Missouri. / [upper right:] Page 47 / 10 x 17.2 cm.
No scale given. Map: Great Falls / of / Columbia River. / [upper right:] Page 364 / [lower

right:] Neele sc. Strand. / [lower centre:] Published April 28th 1814 by Longman & Co Paternoster Row. / 10.1 x 17.3 cm. No scale given. Map: Great Falls of the Missouri. / [upper right:] Page 191 / [lower right and lower centre, as in preceding.] Two maps on one page: Map: Lower Falls / of / The Columbia. / [upper right:] Page 379 /. 10 x 17.4 cm. No scale given. Map: Mouth / of / Columbia River. / [upper right:] Page 398 / [lower right and centre, as in preceding.] 10 x 17.4 cm. No scale given. Gray boards, original printed label on backstrip, 4 x 4.8 cm.: [thick and thin rules] / Lewis and Clarke's / Travels / across the / American Continent. / [thin and thick rules] /, uncut. In a red half morocco case.

Ref.: as above

2481 LEWIS, MERIWETHER, & WILLIAM CLARK

TRAVELS TO THE SOURCE OF THE MISSOURI RIVER ... THE AMERICAN CONTINENT TO THE PACIFIC OCEAN. PERFORMED BY ORDER OF THE GOVERNMENT OF THE UNITED STATES, IN THE YEARS 1804, 1805, AND 1806. BY CAPTAINS LEWIS AND CLARKE PUBLISHED FROM THE OFFICIAL REPORT, AND ILLUSTRATED BY A MAP OF THE ROUTE, AND OTHER MAPS. A NEW EDITION, LONDON: PRINTED FOR LONGMAN, HURST, REES, ORME, AND BROWN, 1815.

A^8, a^6, B–CC^8, DD^4, EE^2. a^6, B–EE^8, FF^1. A^6, B–BB^8, CC^4. [i]–xxvi, [xxvii–xxviii Directions for placing the Maps], [1]–411, [412 blank]. [i]–xii, [1]–434. [i]–xii, [1]–394. 21.8 x 13.2 cm. Folding map and two small maps in Vol. I, three small maps in Vol. II. Folding map: A / Map of / Lewis and Clark's Track / Across the Western Portion of / North America, / from the / Mississippi to the Pacific Ocean, / By Order of the Executive of / The United States / in 1804, 5 & 6. / Copied by Samuel Lewis from the Original Drawing by Wm Clark. / [below border:] London Published April 28th 1814 by Longman, Hurst, Rees, Orme & Brown, Paternoster Row. / [right corner:] Neele. Sculp. 352. Strand /. 29.7 x 68.2 cm. Scale: about 500 yards to one inch. Map: Ancient / Fortification / on the / Missouri. / [upper right:] Page 47 / 10 x 17.5 cm. No scale given. Map: Great Falls of the Missouri. / [lower centre:] Published April 28th 1814 by Longman & Co Paternoster Row. / [upper right:] Page 191 / [lower right:] Neele sc. Strand. / 17.6 x 10 cm. No scale given. Map: Great Falls / of / Columbia River. / [upper right:] Page 364 / [lower centre:] as above [lower right:] as above. 10.1 x 17.2 cm. No scale given. Map: Lower Falls / of / the Columbia. / [upper right:] Page 379 / 10 x 17.6 cm. No scale given. Map: Mouth / of / Columbia River. /

[upper right:] page 398 / [lower centre and lower right as above]. 10.2 x 17.6 cm. No scale given. Three volumes, blue boards, new gray paper backstrips with printed paper labels, 5 x 3.3 cm. (each mounted and partly defective).

Ref.: as above

2482 LEWIS, MERIWETHER, & WILLIAM CLARK

HISTORY OF THE EXPEDITION UNDER THE COMMAND OF CAPTAINS LEWIS AND CLARKE, TO THE SOURCES OF THE MISSOURI ... PHILADELPHIA: PUBLISHED BY BRADFORD AND INSKEEP, 1817.

[A]^6, B–C^4, D^2, b^4, D3–4, E–4H^4. [A]1, b^4, c^2, [A]2–4, B–4M^4, 4N^2. [i–ii], [1–2], [i]–xxvii, [xxviii blank], [1–8, 8 blank], [1]–588. [1–2], [i]–xii, [3]–643, [644 blank]. 21.5 x 12.7 cm. Folding map and six plates and maps. Folding map: A / Map of / Lewis and Clark's / Track Across the Western Portion of / North America / from the / Mississippi to the Pacific Ocean: / By Order of the Executive of the United States / in 1804 5 & 6 / Copied by Samuel Lewis from the / Original Drawing of W^m, Clark. / 15.3 x 34.9 cm. No scale given. Map: [Indian] Fortification [opposite Bon Homme Island]. 17.7 x 10.8 cm. No scale given. Map: The Falls and Portage. / 17.8 x 10.3 cm. No scale given. Map: Great Falls of / Columbia River / 17.6 x 10.2 cm. No scale given. Map: The Great Shoot or / Rapid ... / 17.5 x 10.2 cm. No scale given. Map: [Mouth of Columbia River] 17.7 x 10.3 cm. No scale given. Plate and all maps tinted by hand. Two volumes, contemporary full diced calf, gilt Greek key borders on sides, gilt panels on backstrips, marbled edges.

Ref.: as above

2483 LEWIS, MERIWETHER, & WILLIAM CLARK

HISTORY OF THE EXPEDITION UNDER THE COMMAND OF CAPTAINS LEWIS AND CLARKE ... ACROSS THE ROCKY MOUNTAINS, AND DOWN THE RIVER COLUMBIA TO THE PACIFIC OCEAN: PERFORMED DURING THE YEARS 1804, 1805, 1806, BY ORDER OF THE GOVERNMENT OF THE UNITED STATES. REVISED ... BY ARCHIBALD M'VICKAR. NEW-YORK: HARPER AND BROTHERS, 1842.

[i]–vi, [i]–li, [52]–371, [372 advertisement]. [i]–x, [9]–395, [396 advertisement]. 15.2 x 9.5 cm. Folding map as frontispiece: Map of / Lewis and Clark's, / Track across the Western Portion of / North America, / from the / Mississippi to the Pacific Ocean; / By Order of the Executive of the United States. / in 1804. 5 & 6. / [lower right:] Drawn & Engraved by W. G. Evans N.York. / 15.2 x 34.5 cm. No scale given. Illus-

trations facing (Vol. I) pages 87 (map), 223, 234 (map). Vol. II, 64, 79, 92 (all maps). Two volumes, black cloth, gilt on backstrips as follows: [within frame] The / Family / Library / N° 154 [-155] / [below frame] Lewis / and / Clarke / Vol. 1 [-2]. /

Ref.: as above

2484 LEWIS, MERIWETHER, & WILLIAM CLARK

HISTORY OF THE EXPEDITION UNDER THE COMMAND OF LEWIS AND CLARK, . . . [Edited by] ELLIOTT COUES . . . NEW YORK: FRANCIS P. HARPER, 1893.

[1–2], [i]–cxxxii, [1]–352. [i]–vi, 353–820. [i]–vi, 821–1298. [i]–v, [vi blank], eight maps, two tables. 25.7 x 16.3 cm. Four illustrations, eight maps, two tables listed. Four volumes, gray boards, white cloth backs, printed paper labels, uncut.

Ref.: as above
Limited to 200 sets on Large Paper.

2485 LEWIS, MERIWETHER, & WILLIAM CLARK

ORIGINAL JOURNALS OF THE LEWIS AND CLARK EXPEDITION 1804–1806 . . . TOGETHER WITH MANUSCRIPT MATERIAL OF LEWIS AND CLARK FROM OTHER SOURCES, INCLUDING NOTEBOOKS, LETTERS, MAPS, ETC., AND THE JOURNALS OF CHARLES FLOYD AND JOSEPH WHITEHOUSE NOW FOR THE FIRST TIME . . . EDITED . . . REUBEN GOLD THWAITES . . . NEW YORK: DODD, MEAD & COMPANY 1904 [-1905].

Vol. I, Pt. 1: [iii]–xciii, [xciv blank], [1]–120. Pt. 2: [i–x (x blank)], 121–374. Vol. II, Pt. 1: [i–x (x blank)], [1]–177, [178 blank]. Pt. 2: [i–viii, (viii blank)], [177]–386. Vol. III, Pt. 1: [i]–x, [1]–140. Pt. 2: [i]–viii, 141–363, [364 blank]. Vol. IV, Pt. 1: [i]–x, [1]–179, [180 blank]. Pt. 2: [i]–vii, [viii blank], [179]–372. Vol. V, Pt. 1: [i–x], [1]–182. Pt. 2: [i]–vii, [viii blank], 183–395, [396 blank]. Vol. VI, Pt. 1: [i–x (x blank)], [1]–136. Pt. 2: [i]–viii (viii blank)], 137–280. Vol. VII, Pt. 1: [i]–xi, [xii blank], [1]–256. Pt. 2: [i]–ix, [x blank], 257–534. 31.1 x 23 cm.

WITH: ATLAS ACCOMPANYING THE ORIGINAL JOURNALS OF THE LEWIS AND CLARK EXPEDITION 1804–1806 BEING FACSIMILE REPRODUCTIONS . . . NEW YORK: DODD, MEAD & COMPANY, 1905.

[i]–xvi, 54 maps. 219 illustrations listed, some present in duplicate (colored), and 54 maps, all listed. 15 volumes, original tan buckram, white buckram backs, gilt, colored labels on front covers (one lacking on Vol. VIII), gilt tops, uncut.

Ref.: as above
Limited to 50 sets printed on Imperial Japan Vellum.

2486 LEWIS, WILLIAM S.

THE STORY OF EARLY DAYS IN THE BIG BEND COUNTRY: BREAKING TRAILS, RUSH OF MINERS, COMING OF CATTLEMEN, MAKING HOMES, PIONEER HARDSHIPS . . . SPOKANE, WASH.: W. D. ALLEN, 1926.*

[i]–35, [36 blank]. 24.5 x 17.2 cm. Frontispiece and illustration facing page [36], both printed in green. Gray printed wrappers.

Prov.: Inscribed on verso of title-page: Mr Fred Lockley / Compliments of / William S Lewis / Spokane W Aug 24, 1926 /.

Ref.: Howes L326; Smith 5921
Limited to 100 copies.

2487 [L'HERITIER, LOUIS FRANCOIS]

LE CHAMP-D'ASILE, TABLEAU TOPOGRAPHIQUE ET HISTORIQUE DU TEXAS . . . PARIS: LADVOCAT, LIBRAIRE, 1819.

[*]⁴, [*]⁴, *⁴, 1–15⁸, 16⁴. (Leaf 11 7 is a cancel.) [i]–viii, [i]–xvi, [1]–247, [248 blank]. 19.8 x 12.5 cm. Folding map: Le Champ-d'Asile / ou / Carte des Etablissements / fondés dans l'Amérique Septentrionale / par les Réfugiés Français / d'abord au Texas, et actuellem⁷ au Tombechbé. / Dessinée par Ladvocat / d'après les Matériaux qui ont été envoyés / par un des principaux Colons. / Mars 1819. / [lower centre:] à Paris, chez Ladvocat Libraire Editeur des Fastes de la Gloire, Galerie de Bois Palais Royal, N° 197. / [lower left:] Gravé par B. Tardieu. / [lower right:] T. Pelicier scr. / 28.3 x 44 cm. Scale: 55 leagues to one inch.

BOUND WITH:

LE TEXAS, OU NOTICE HISTORIQUE SUR LE CHAMP D'ASILE . . . A PARIS: CHEZ BEGUIN, JUIN 1819.

[*]⁴⁺¹, 1–8⁸, 9⁴. [i]–viii, [i]–ix, [x blank], [11]–135, [136 blank]. Folding frontispiece with leaf of descriptive letter press.

BOUND WITH:

L'HEROINE DU TEXAS, OU VOYAGE DE MADAME *** AUX ETATS-UNIS ET AU MEXIQUE . . . A PARIS: CHEZ PLANCHER, 1819.

[*]⁴, 1–6⁸, 7⁷ (probably lacks blank leaf). [1]–118. Frontispiece. Three volumes bound together, contemporary boards, leather back.

Prov.: Signature on front endleaf: Guibert peintre. / Bookplate of Emile Miguet.

Ref.: Clements Library (*Texas*) 6; Howes L329 (*Champ-d'Asile*), H270 (*Texas*), T126 (*L'Héroine*); Rader 1807; Raines p. 102, 109; Sabin 23581, 30706, 95072; Streeter 1072B, 1069, 1068

The first eight pages of *Le Champ-d'Asile* comprise the preliminaries of the first edition, and the next eight those of the second edition. The title-pages are identical through the sixth line, then: Productions de cette contrée; des Réfugiés français; des Notices sur ses / principaux fondateurs; des Extraits de leurs / proclamations et autres actes publics: suivi de / Lettres écrites par de Colons à quelques-uns de / leurs compatriotes. / (Publié au profit des Réfugiés.) / Balance of title-page identical.

The map, which did not appear until the second edition, is bound preceding the title-page of the first edition.

On the verso of the half-title of *Le Texas* . . . there are the manuscript signatures of the publisher and authors authenticating the edition, Béguin, Hartmann and Uillard.

The author of the third title has not been identified.

2488 LIBRARY OF AMERICAN HISTORY

LIBRARY OF AMERICAN HISTORY; CONTAINING BIOGRAPHICAL SKETCHES, OF WASHINGTON, ADAMS, PAUL JONES, FULTON, SMITH, CLARKE, SHELBY, PUTNAM, BRANT, KING PHILIP, AND MANY OTHER DISTINGUISHED CHARACTERS . . . CINCINNATI: U. P. JAMES.

[i]–x, 11–640. 25.6 x 17.3 cm. Illustrations listed. Dark brown cloth, blind sides, gilt lettering on backstrip.

Ref.: Sabin 40953

Copyrighted 1851.

Contains the Obadiah Oakley narrative. See under Oakley.

2489 LIDELL, JOHN

DOCUMENT, SIGNED. 1807 April 28, New York. One page, 17.2 x 27.2 cm. Printed and manuscript citizenship paper of Michael McDonogh.

2490 LIFE AND PUBLIC SERVICES OF HON. ABRAHAM LINCOLN . . .

THE WIDE-AWAKE EDITION. THE LIFE AND PUBLIC SERVICES OF HON. ABRAHAM LINCOLN, OF ILLINOIS, AND HON. HANNIBAL HAMLIN, OF MAINE. BOSTON: THAYER & ELDRIDGE, 1860.

[1]–320. 18.9 x 12 cm. Two portraits. Brown cloth, blind embossed borders on sides, title in gilt on backstrip.

Prov.: Inscribed in pencil on front endleaf: Mrs. E. Shelton / Petealuma [!] Cal / Sonoma County /.

Ref.: Monaghan (*Lincoln*) 89; Sabin 41198

Laid in is an original campaign ribbon, 20.4 x 5.2 cm., printed on white silk: [vignette of American eagle and shield] / Republican / Standard / Bearers. / [mounted oval portrait of Lincoln] / Abraham / Lincoln. / [mounted oval portrait of Hamlin] / Hannibal / Hamlin. / [flourish] / Photographs by Briggs, / Galesburg, Ill. /

2491 [LILLIE, GORDON W.]

[Pictorial wrapper title] SOUVENIR. PAWNEE BILL'S HISTORIC WILD WEST.

1–28. 23.5 x 14.9 cm. Illustrated. Pictorial colored wrappers.

Ref.:

No place or date of publication given. One press notice dated 1890. Lacks two leaves at end.

2492 LINCE GONZALEZ, JOSE ANTONIO

REGLAMENTO, U ORDENANZAS DE ENSAYADORES, FORMADAS EN VIRTUD DE LO MANDADO POR EL EXCMO. SENOR DON MATIAS DE GALVEZ . . . MEXICO, POR DON FELIPE DE ZUNIGA Y ONTIVEROS, 1789.

[A]–[X]². [i–ii], 1–[82]. 28 x 19.8 cm. Bound with Number 9.

Ref.: Medina (*Mexico*) 7888

Pertains to regulations and ordinances for assayers, particularly in the *Provincias Internas*.

2493 LINCOLN, ABRAHAM

[Photograph] PORTRAIT, oval, 18.8 x 13.1 cm., half length, facing to his left. Unbearded type. Mounted. Photograph by S. M. Fassett, Chicago, 1859. In a red cloth case.

Said to be considered by Mrs. Lincoln as the finest photograph.

2494 LINCOLN, ABRAHAM

[Caption title] SPEECH OF THE HON. ABRAM [!] LINCOLN, IN REPLY TO JUDGE DOUGLAS, DELIVERED IN REPRESENTATIVES' HALL, SPRINGFIELD, JUNE 26TH, 1857 . . .

[1]–7, [8 blank]. 29.9 x 20.5 cm. Unbound, unopened, uncut.

Ref.: Byrd 2715; Monaghan (*Lincoln*) 9; Sabin 41162

Printed at Springfield in 1857.

2495 LINCOLN, ABRAHAM, & STEPHEN A. DOUGLAS

POLITICAL DEBATES BETWEEN HON. ABRAHAM LINCOLN AND HON. STEPHEN A. DOUGLAS, IN THE CELEBRATED CAMPAIGN OF 1858, IN ILLINOIS . . . COLUMBUS: FOLLETT, FOSTER AND COMPANY, 1860.

[i]–[viii, vi–viii blank], [1] 268. 23.2 x 15.5 cm. Brown cloth, blind embossed sides, title in gilt on backstrip.

Prov.: Inscribed on inside front cover: D. W. Gage / Bought April 30 / / 60 /.

Ref.: Howes L338; Monaghan (*Lincoln*) 69; Sabin 41156

No line above publisher's imprint on verso of title-leaf, numeral 2 not present at foot of page 13, without advertisements.

377

2496 LINCOLN, Nebraska. Board of Trade

[Wrapper title] NEBRASKA. ITS CHEAP LANDS, HOMESTEADS, ETC., ETC. ALSO A BRIEF DESCRIPTION OF LINCOLN, THE CAPITAL OF THE STATE . . . LINCOLN: RANDALL & SMAILS, 1870.

[1]–8. 18.4 x 12.4 cm. Map on pages [4–5]: A Sketch of / Southern Nebraska / [lower left:] W. D. Baker, Chicago. West'n Agent for Fisk & Russell, N. York. / 14.3 x 12.3 cm. No scale given. Yellow printed wrappers with title on front wrapper, advertisement on verso of back wrapper.

Ref.: AII (*Nebraska*) 172

2497 LINCOLN, Nebraska. Ordinances.

THE REVISED ORDINANCES OF THE CITY OF LINCOLN, IN FORCE APRIL 1ST, 1871 . . . LINCOLN: GERE & BROWNLEE, 1871.

[1]–64. 22.2 x 14.4 cm. Green printed wrappers, with title on front wrapper.

Ref.: AII (*Nebraska*) 228

2498 LINDER, USHER F.

REMINISCENCES OF THE EARLY BENCH AND BAR OF ILLINOIS . . . CHICAGO: THE CHICAGO LEGAL NEWS COMPANY, 1879.

[1]–406. 19.5 x 12.8 cm. Brick red cloth, gilt and black stamping on front cover and backstrip, blind stamping on back cover.

Ref.:

Contains some Lincoln material.

2499 LINDERMAN, FRANK B.

INDIAN WHY STORIES. SPARKS FROM WAR EAGLE'S LODGE-FIRE . . . NEW YORK: CHARLES SCRIBNER'S SONS, 1915.

[i]–xvi, [1]–236. 20.1 x 15.4 cm. Eight illustrations in color by Charles M. Russell listed, and with marginal decorations unlisted. Red cloth, paper label on front cover with illustration by Russell in color, fore and lower edges uncut.

Ref.: Smith 3954

2500 LINFORTH, JAMES

[Caption title] THE REV. C. W. LAWRENCE'S "FEW WORDS FROM A PASTOR TO HIS PEOPLE ON THE SUBJECT OF THE LATTER-DAY SAINTS." REPLIED TO AND REFUTED BY JAMES LINFORTH . . .

[1]–8. Bound with Number 3346.

Imprint at foot of page 8: Printed by J. Sadler, 16, Moorfields, Liverpool. /

2501 LINFORTH, JAMES

ROUTE FROM LIVERPOOL TO GREAT SALT LAKE VALLEY. ILLUSTRATED WITH STEEL ENGRAVINGS AND WOOD CUTS FROM SKETCHES MADE BY FREDERICK PIERCY . . . LIVERPOOL: PUBLISHED BY FRANKLIN D. RICHARDS, MDCCCLV,

[i]–viii, [1]–120. 30.5 x 24.2 cm. Nine woodcuts, 30 plates, folding map. Map: Utah, / And the Overland Routes to it, / from the Missouri River: / Published with / "Route from Liverpool to G. S. L. Valley" / By / F. D. Richards: Liverpool. / 1855. / 29.3 x 47.5 cm. Scale: 110 miles to one inch. Contemporary red morocco, gilt borders on sides, gilt back, gilt edges.

Prov.: Inscribed on fly-leaf: Presented to President Heber C. Kimball / by / Fred. Piercy, / and / James Linforth. / Liverpool May, 17, 1856. / [double rule] /, all in hand of Linforth except Piercy's signature.

Ref.: Howes L359; Jones 1337; Sabin 41325; Wagner-Camp 259; Wheat (*Transmississippi*) 858

A fine and beautiful book. The map is in the rare state with the thirteen counties in Utah colored by hand.

2502 LINGENFELTER, L.

HISTORY OF FREMONT COUNTY, IOWA . . . INTENDED TO GIVE A CORRECT HISTORY OF THE EARLY SETTLEMENT OF THE COUNTY, ITS ORGANIZATION—GROWTH AND DEVELOPMENT—ITS EDUCATIONAL AND SOCIAL ADVANTAGES, AND THE MANY FACILITIES IT POSSESSES FOR BECOMING THE MOST DESIRABLE PLACE TO LIVE IN OF ANY IN THE WEST. SCENES AND INCIDENTS OF EARLY LIFE. ST. JOSEPH, MO.: STEAM PRINTING COMPANY, 1877.

[1]–28. 24.1 x 17.3 cm. Stabbed, unbound.

Ref.: Howes L360

An edition of this work printed at Hamburg, Iowa, without date and comprising 62 pages, 5 x 4 inches, is in the Minnesota Historical Society.

2503 LINN, JOHN J.

REMINISCENCES OF FIFTY YEARS IN TEXAS . . . NEW YORK: D. & J. SADLIER & CO., 1883.

[1]–369, [370 blank]. 18.1 x 12 cm. Two portraits and two plates; one of the latter mislabeled: The Alamo / has been corrected by an overlay to: Goliad /. Plum cloth, blind embossed sides, gilt title on backstrip.

Ref.: Bradford 3019; Dobie p. 57; Howes L363; Raines p. 139

With the errata slip, 11 x 10.3 cm., tipped to page 369.

This privately printed narrative relates largely to the fight for the independence of Texas.

2504 LINTOT, BERNARD

AUTOGRAPH LETTER, SIGNED. 1798 December 1, Laurel Hill, Natchez. Two pages, 26 x 20.3 cm. To Mr. Hubert Rowell.

A description of the death of his daughter Nancy, written to his son-in-law. Lintot was a substantial merchant of Natchez whose daughter Frances married Philip Nolan in 1799.

The third page is blank; the fourth carries the address of the recipient and his docket.

2505 LINTOT, F.

AUTOGRAPH LETTER, SIGNED. No year, November 3, Natchez. Two pages, 19.9 x 12.5 cm.

The writer was probably Frances Lintot who, in 1799, married Philip Nolan. The letter may have been addressed to Nolan. Family chit-chat comprises most of the letter, but the following paragraph occurs: General Wilkinson is just arrived from above.

2506 LISIANSKII, IURII FEDOROVICH

A VOYAGE ROUND THE WORLD, IN THE YEARS 1803, 4, 5, & 6 . . . London: Printed for John Booth, 1814.

[a]–c⁴, B–3C⁴, 3D². [i]–[xxiv], [1]–388. 27.8 x 21.8 cm. Portrait, three engraved plates, two colored engravings, and eight maps. Map: Chart / of the / World / Shewing the Track of the Neva / in the Years 1803 4. 5. 6. / [lower left:] Engraved under the Direction of Mᵣ Arrowsmith / [lower centre:] London Published by John Booth Duke Street Portland Place March 1ˢᵗ 1814. / 24.2 x 45.3 cm. No scale given. Map: Harbour of / Sᵗ Catherine. / [swelled rule] / 1804. / [lower left:] Engᵈ under the direction of Mᵣ Arrowsmith. / [lower centre:] London: Published by John Booth, Duke Street, Portland Place, March 1ˢᵗ 1814. / [lower right:] Surveyed by Captain Lisiansky. / 25.3 x 19.4 cm. Scale: about 2 3/4 miles to one inch. Map: Washington Islands / 1804. / Inset: B. Tayohaia / 12.6 x 9.6 cm. Scale: about 3/8 mile to one inch. Inset: B. Jegawe / 12.6 x 9.6 cm. Scale: about 3/16 mile to one inch. [lower left, centre, and right as in preceding map:] 25.3 x 19.4 cm. No scale given. Map: Harbour of Sᵗ Paul. / 1805. / [lower left, centre, and right as above] 25.3 x 38.8 cm. Scale: 1 mile to one inch. Map: Island of Cadiack, / with its Environs / 1805. / [lower left, centre and right as above] 25.4 x 19.5 cm. No scale given. Map: Chart / of the Coast from / Behrings Bay to Sea Otter Bay, / with different Settlements / of the Natives. / [lower left, centre, and right as above] 25.3 x 19.5 cm. No scale given. Map: Sitca or Norfolk Sound / Surveyed / By Captⁿ Lisiansky / 1805. / [lower left and centre same as above]. 38.7 x 25.4 cm. Scale: about 1 2/3 miles to one inch. Map: Lisiansky's Isle / 1805. / [lower left, centre, and

right as above]. 19.4 x 25.3 cm. Scale: about 1/2 mile to one inch. Full contemporary red straight grain calf, gilt borders on sides, gilt back with cypher AS five times, green leather label, gilt edges.

Prov.: From library of Albert, Duke of Saxe-Gotha (1738–1822).

Ref.: Howes L372; Sabin 41416; Wickersham 6261

Highly important work on Sitka, Kodiak and other parts of the northwest coast. The author, commanding the "Neva," accompanied the great Russian expedition under Krusenstern.—Howes

Editions: St. Petersburg, 1812.

2507 L'ISLE, GUILLAUME DE

[Map] CARTE DE LA LOUISIANE ET DU COURS DU MISSISSIPI DRESSEE SUR UN GRAND NOMBRE DE MEMOIRES ENTR'AUTRES SUR CEURX DE Mᴿ LE MAIRE PAR GUILLᴹᴱ DE L'ISLE DE L'ACADEMIE Rᴸᴱ DES SCIENCES. / [lower centre:] A AMSTERDAM / CHEZ JEAN COVENS ET CORNEILLE MORTIER / GEOGRAPHES. /

Map, 45.2 x 60.2 cm. (plate mark); 43.7 x 59.4 cm. (neat line). Scale: 30 leagues to one inch.

Ref.: Karpinski L1 see; Phillips (*Maps*) p. 367; Wheat (*Transmississippi*) 99 see

This is a reprint of the 1718 edition by De L'Isle with a new imprint.

2508 LITTELL, WILLIAM

FESTOONS OF FANCY . . . IN VERSE AND PROSE . . . LOUISVILLE: PRESS OF WILLIAM FARQUAR, 1814.

[*]¹, A–I⁶, J–P⁶. [i–ii], [1]–180. 16.7 x 10.2 cm. Original or contemporary mottled sheep, gilt back, red leather label. Two blank leaves before title-leaf supplied.

Ref.: AII (*Kentucky*) 507; Howes L378; Jillson p. 52

The first humorous book produced West of the Alleghanies.—Howes

This is the *first* work of American Humour.—F. J. Meine, as quoted by Jillson

2509 LITTLE, JAMES A.

BIOGRAPHICAL SKETCH OF FERAMORZ LITTLE, WRITTEN UNDER THE PATRONAGE OF HIS FAMILY, BY HIS BROTHER . . . SALT LAKE CITY, UTAH: JUVENILE INSTRUCTOR OFFICE, 1890.

[i]–viii, [9]–191, [192 blank]. 22.7 x 15 cm. Black leather, title stamped in gilt on front cover and backstrip, blind borders on sides, gilt edges.

Ref.: Howes L381

Between 1851 and 1853, Little ran the overland mail from Laramie to Salt Lake City.

2510 LITTLE, JAMES A.

FROM KIRTLAND TO SALT LAKE CITY . . . SALT LAKE CITY, UTAH: PRINTED AT THE JUVENILE INSTRUCTOR OFFICE, 1890.

[i]–viii, [9]–260. 21.9 x 14.5 cm. Illustrations unlisted. Dark red cloth, title stamped in gilt on front cover and backstrip, blind borders on sides.

Ref.: Bradford 3022; Howes L382; Hubach p. 71

Contains a good overland narrative to Salt Lake City.

2511 LITTLE, JAMES A.

JACOB HAMBLIN, A NARRATIVE OF HIS PERSONAL EXPERIENCE, AS A FRONTIERSMAN, MISSIONARY TO THE INDIANS AND EXPLORER . . . PERILOUS SITUATIONS AND REMARKABLE ESCAPES. FIFTH BOOK OF THE FAITH-PROMOTING SERIES, BY JAMES A. LITTLE . . . SALT LAKE CITY, UTAH: JUVENILE INSTRUCTOR OFFICE, 1881.

[i]–viii, [9]–140, [141]–144 advertisement. 17.3 x 11.5 cm. Blue cloth, blind borders on sides, title stamped in gilt on front cover, sprinkled edges.

Ref.: Howes L383; Hubach p. 54; Munk (Alliot) p. 132; Wagner-Camp 354 note

The Wagner-Camp reference is to the Hamblin *Journal* in manuscript. Mentions the Mountain Meadow massacre, page 46. Hubach p. 54 gives the date as 1861, an error.

2512 LITTLE, JAMES A.

WHAT I SAW ON THE OLD SANTA FE TRAIL. CARAVANS OF PRAIRIE SCHOONERS. FORTY WAGONS, FIVE-HUNDRED OXEN. MILLIONS OF BUFFALOES. THOUSANDS OF WILD HORSES . . . A CONDENSED STORY OF FRONTIER LIFE HALF A CENTURY AGO . . . PLAINFIELD, INDIANA: THE FRIENDS PRESS.

[i]–ii], [1]–127, [128 blank]. 19.2 x 13.3 cm. Three portraits. Black printed wrappers, printed in yellow with title on front cover. In a dark blue cloth case.

Ref.: Howes L384; Rader 2240

Copyrighted 1904.

2513 LITTLE FORT PORCUPINE [Illinois] AND DEMOCRATIC BANNER

[Broadside] PROSPECTUS FOR THE "LITTLE FORT PORCUPINE AND DEMOCRATIC BANNER." COMMENCING MARCH 4, 1845. THE "PORCUPINE"WILL BE DEVOTED TO THE SUPPORT OF DEMOCRATIC PRINCIPLES, AND THE PARTY IN POWER, STATE AND NATIONAL . . . A. B. WYNKOOP, PROPRIETOR. N. W FULLER, PUBLISHER. SUBSCRIBERS' NAMES WHERE TAKEN.

Broadside, 31.7 x 20 cm. Text, 6.8 x 16.2 cm.

Ref.: Byrd 979

Issued at Little Fort, Lake County, later Waukegan. Ample space has been left below the text for names and addresses.

2514 LIVINGSTON, JOHN

[Caption title] GEORGE FISHER, SECRETARY AND TRANSLATOR TO THE CALIFORNIA LAND COMMISSION, . . .

[1]–6. 21.9 x 13.7 cm. Bound in Fisher, George: *Memorials* . . . Houston, 1840.

Ref.:

A reprint from Livingston's *Portraits of Eminent Americans now Living* . . . New York, 1853–54, Volume III, pages 441–46.

2515 LIVINGSTON, ROBERT R.

TWENTY-THREE LETTERS AND DOCUMENTS from the Papers of Colonel Robert R. Livingston, 1st Nebraska Cavalry. 1864 October 18 to 1865 November 23, various posts in Nebraska Territory. 50 pages, quarto and folio.

Signed by the following: Bowen, William R.; Gillespie, John; Gillette, Lee P.; Laycock, Fred B.; Livingston, Robert R.; McDonald, F. A.; McKittrick, J. L.; Majors, Thomas F.; Mitchel, Robert B.; Morse, S. W.; Murphy, John S.; North, Frank; Northrop, William H.; Porter, Charles F.; Strong, Charles; Thompson, Charles; Wilcox, John.

2516 LOBENSTINE, WILLIAM C.

EXTRACTS FROM THE DIARY OF WILLIAM C. LOBENSTINE DECEMBER 31, 1851–1858. BIOGRAPHICAL SKETCH BY BELLE W. LOBENSTINE. PRINTED PRIVATELY, 1920.*

[i–xvi], [1]–101, [102 blank]. 22.4 x 15 cm. Portrait and illustrations. Brown boards, printed paper label on front cover, yellow cloth backstrip, fore and lower edges uncut.

Prov.: With the engraved calling card of Mrs. Lobenstine pasted down inside front cover.

Ref.: Cowan p. 394; Howes L410; Matthews p. 330

Probably printed in New York.

Describes his 1851 overland trip to California and life in the mines.—Howes

2517 LOCKARD, FRANK M.

BLACK KETTLE . . . GOODLAND, KANSAS: R. G. WOLFE, PUBLISHER.*

[1]–40. 18.8 x 13.4 cm. Illustrations unlisted. Gray printed wrappers.

Ref.: Adams (*Ramp. Herd*) 1340

No date of printing given.

Black Kettle was the name given a famous wild horse on the Kansas plains in the 1870's.

This little pamphlet describes the author's adventures while trying to capture the noted steed. —EDG

2518 LOCKLEY, FRED

[Wrapper title] TO OREGON BY OX-TEAM IN '47. THE STORY OF THE COMING OF THE HUNT FAMILY TO THE OREGON COUNTRY AND THE EXPERIENCES OF G. W. HUNT IN THE GOLD DIGGINGS OF CALIFORNIA IN 1849 . . . PORTLAND: FRED LOCKLEY.*

[1]–[16]. 22.8 x 15.2 cm. Dark blue printed wrappers. In an orange cloth case.

Prov.: Inscribed on front wrapper: For Dr Wm C Braislin / with Best Wishes / of the author / Fred Lockley /.

Ref.: Hubach p. 105; Smith 6000

2519 LOCKMAN, JOHN

TRAVELS OF THE JESUITS, INTO VARIOUS PARTS OF THE WORLD: PARTICULARLY CHINA AND THE EAST-INDIES . . . PRINTED FOR T. PIETY, 1762.

[*]⁴, A⁸, a⁴, B–Hh⁸, Ii⁴, A–C⁴. [A]¹, a², B–Ii⁸, Kk⁶, A–B⁴, C². [1–2], [i]–vi, [i]–[xxii], [1–2], [1]–487, [488 blank], [1]–24. [i–vi], [1]–507, [508 advertisement], [1–20, 20 blank]. 20 x 12 cm. One plate and five maps unlisted. Map: A / Map / of the / Malabar / and / Cormandel / Coasts. / E. Bowen Sculp. [upper right:] Vol. I, pag. I. / 30.3 x 28.6 cm. Scale: about 14 German miles to one inch. Map: Passage by land to California / Discover'd by Father Eusebius / Francis Kino a Jesuit; / between the years 1698, & / 1701: / containing likewise the / New Missions of the Jesuits. / [upper right:] Vol. I. pag. 395. / [lower right centre:] E. Bowen, Sc. / 22 x 19.3 cm. Scale: about 22 leagues to one inch. Map: A Map of / Terra del Fuego: / and of the Straits of / Magellan, & Le Maire; / with the new Islands / of Anycan and / Beauchéne. / [upper right:] Vol II. p. 34. / [lower right:] E. Bowen sculp. / 12.8 x 24.9 cm. Scale: about 23 leagues to one inch. Map: Nangasak call'd by the Chinese Tchangk / [upper right:] Vol. II. pag. 192. / [lower right:] E. Bowen Sculp. / 13.4 x 23 cm. Scale: one league to 3 1/8 inches. Map: Mission / of the / Moxos, or / Moxes: / Settled by the / Jesuits in / Peru. / [upper right:] Vol. II. pag. 437 / [lower right:] E. Bowen Sculp. / 18 x 12.7 cm. Scale not given. Two volumes, contemporary marbled board sides, sprinkled calf backstrips, new red and black labels, red sprinkled edges.

Prov.: Bookplate of Henry Home, Lord Kames, in each volume.

Ref.: Barrett 1499 note; Cowan p. 394 note; Howes L414; Streit I 998; Wagner (*SS*) p. 311
Published at London.

Although abridged, Lockman's translation introduced an adequate account of the Jesuit missionaries to the English reading public.
Editions: London, 1743.

2520 LOCKWOOD, JAMES D.

LIFE AND ADVENTURES OF A DRUMMER BOY; OR, SEVEN YEARS A SOLDIER . . . ALBANY, N.Y.: PUBLISHED BY JOHN SKINNER, 1893.

[1]–191, [192 blank]. 19.4 x 13.3 cm. Frontispiece. Cream pictorial cloth, stamped in black, title in gilt on backstrip.

Ref.: Howes L418; Nicholson p. 477

After the close of the Civil War, Lockwood re-enlisted and, marching from Fort Leavenworth to Fort Kearney, was assigned to the 18th U. S. Infantry under Col. Henry B. Carrington. He marched with Carrington to Fort Philip Kearney and from there went to Fort C. F. Smith and was one of the less than 200 men who built the latter fort.

He was stationed there during the two years of its existence. He participated in the "Hayfield fight." He also tells of Beckwourth's death among the Crows. But the work is of little value. —EDG

2521 LOCKWOOD, RUFUS A.

THE VIGILANCE COMMITTEE OF SAN FRANCISCO. METCALF VS. ARGENTI ET AL. SPEECHES OF R. A. LOCKWOOD, ESQ. SAN FRANCISCO, CAL., MDCCCLII.

[1]–[48]. 21 x 13.8 cm. Removed from bound volume, unbound.

Ref.: AII (*California*) 200; Blumann & Thomas 3276; Cowan pp. 394–95; Greenwood 333; Howes L420; Sabin 41752

Peter Metcalf was a drayman employed during the fire of June 22, 1851, to remove four loads of furniture and goods from the house of Felix Argenti's doxy. After the fire, Metcalf was accused of stealing some of the properties and Argenti and a companion searched Metcalf's house unsuccessfully. Argenti and his "great and good friend" appealed to the Committee of Vigilance and a second and more vigorous search was made, equally unsuccessful. In retaliation, Metcalf resorted to the courts. The first trial ended unsatisfactorily and Metcalf secured a change of venue to Santa Clara where, in a jury trial, he won nominal damages.

The two speeches in the present pamphlet were those delivered by Lockwood at the trials. They are directed less at attacking Argenti and supporting Metcalf than at the Vigilance Committee. They are scathing denunciations of the Committee and its actions. As EDG notes, considering the time at which the trials took place, Lockwood "must be rated a very brave man."

2522 [LOGAN, STEPHEN T.]

MEMORIALS OF THE LIFE AND CHARACTER OF STEPHEN T. LOGAN. SPRINGFIELD, ILL.: H. W. ROKKER, 1882.

[i–ii], [1]–87, [88 blank]. 20.4 x 14.5 cm. Engraved portrait facing title. Dark plum cloth, blind embossed borders on sides, title on front cover in gilt.

Prov.: Inscribed on front blank leaf: Presented to Hon. E. A. Storrs / by — M Hay /. Hay was Logan's son-in-law. Logan was one of Lincoln's law partners.

Ref.: Howes L435

2523 LOMAS, THOMAS J.

RECOLLECTIONS OF A BUSY LIFE.

[1]–220. (Pages [1–4] blank.) 17.8 x 12.9 cm. Portraits, two on one plate. Blue cloth, gilt edges.

Ref.: Howes L436

Published at Cresco, Iowa, about 1923.

Describes a trip to California by the overland route in the spring of 1864 written about sixty years later.—EDG

2524 [LONG, GREEN H.]

THE ARCH FIEND: THE LIFE, CONFESSION, AND EXECUTION OF GREEN H. LONG, THE ARCH FIEND AMONG DESPERADOES. LITTLE ROCK, ARK.: PUBLISHED BY A. R. ORTON, 1852.

[1]–[32]. (Page [1] blank, page [2] portrait, page [32] illustration.) 22.2 x 14.8 cm. Four illustrations. Yellow printed wrappers with title on front wrapper, illustration on page [32] repeated on verso of back wrapper.

Ref.: Adams 630 see; Allen (*Arkansas*) 214; Howes L440

Allen suggests that this was printed in Buffalo or some other New York town. He is probably correct, although the imprint Little Rock is on the front wrapper. See also the life of Zilla Fitz-James which Green claimed she wrote and sent him from Mexico. The author was probably either A. R. Orton or Dr. A. Richards, described as the editor of the Zilla Fitz-James piece. Adams describes an 1851 edition, but reproduces the 1852 title-page.

2525 LONG, J. V.

REPORT OF THE FIRST GENERAL FESTIVAL OF THE RENOWNED MORMON BATTALION, WHICH CAME OFF ON TUESDAY AND WEDNESDAY, FEB. 6 AND 7, 1855, IN THE SOCIAL HALL, G. S. L. CITY, PRINTED AT THE DESERET NEWS OFFICE, 1855.

[1]–39, [40 blank]. 19.3 x 12.9 cm. Unbound. Remnants of gray wrapper.

Ref.: Howes L442

Published at Salt Lake City.

2526 LONG, J. V.

THE SAME. ST. LOUIS: PRINTED AT THE ST. LOUIS LUMINARY OFFICE, 1855.

[1]–36. 19.3 x 13.2 cm. Plain white wrappers.

Ref.: Howes L442 see

Editions: Salt Lake City, 1855.

2527 LONG, JOHN

VOYAGES AND TRAVELS OF AN INDIAN INTERPRETER TRADER, DESCRIBING THE MANNERS AND CUSTOMS OF THE NORTH AMERICAN INDIANS; WITH AN ACCOUNT OF THE POSTS SITUATED ON THE RIVER SAINT LAWRENCE, LAKE ONTARIO, &C . . . LONDON: PRINTED FOR THE AUTHOR, M,DCC,XCI.

[*]¹, [**]², A–Pp⁴. [1–2], [i]–[x, x blank], [1]–295, [296 blank]. 29.3 x 23 cm. Map: Sketch / of the / Western Countries / of / Canada / 1791. / 20.7 x 30.1 cm. Scale: 90 miles to one inch. Gray boards, new tan paper back, new printed white paper label, uncut. Rebacked.

Prov.: Presentation copy from Sir James Winter Lake (one of the subscribers) to C. Gower, and with the latter's signature and note.

Ref.: Butler (*Algonkin*) 28, (*Chippewa*) 128, 150; Field 946; Howes L443; Hubach p. 27; Jones 619; Pilling 2311; Rader 2249; Sabin 41878; Smith 6073; Staton & Tremaine 597

An excellent account of the customs and manners of the Indians among whom the author lived as a representative of the Hudson's Bay Company. There are 112 pages of Indian vocabularies at the back of the volume.

2528 LONG, STEPHEN H.

VOYAGE IN A SIX-OARED SKIFF TO THE FALLS OF SAINT ANTHONY IN 1817 . . . PHILADELPHIA: HENRY R. ASHMEAD, PRINTER, 1860.

[1]–[88]. 21.7 x 14.1 cm. Map: Sketch / of the / Mississippi River, / between / Prairie du Chien and the / Falls of St. Anthony, / Illustrative of / Major Long's Expedition of 1817. / [short rule] / Scale 1—1,000,000. / [short rule] / Compiled from Major Long's Field Notes. / Corrected by the U. S. Land Surveys. / [lower right:] [Compiled by A. J. Hill, 1860.] / 20.7 x 11.6 cm. Scale: as above. Gray printed wrappers. In a blue cloth case.

Ref.: Buck 100; Field 950; Howes L445; Sabin 41888

2529 [LONGSTREET, AUGUSTUS B.]

MASTER WILLIAM MITTEN: OR, A YOUTH OF BRILLIANT TALENTS, WHO WAS RUINED BY BAD LUCK . . . MACON, GA.: BURKE, BOYKIN & COMPANY 1864.

[1]–239, [240 blank]. 21.9 x 13.3 cm. White printed wrappers, stabbed, with title on front wrapper, advertisements on verso of back wrapper. In a cloth case.

Ref.:

An exceptionally fine copy.

2530 LONGSWORTH, BASIL N.

DIARY OF BASIL NELSON LONGSWORTH MARCH 15, 1853 TO JANUARY 22, 1854 COVERING THE PERIOD OF HIS MIGRATION FROM OHIO TO OREGON. DENVER, COLORADO: BY D. E. HARRINGTON, 1927.*

[1]–43 [44 blank]. 21.3 x 14 cm. Red printed wrappers with title on front wrapper. Mounted on the front wrapper is a slip of cover paper, 3.8 x 7.9 cm., on which is printed the following: Over the Oregon Trail /.

Ref.: Howes L458; Smith 6091

Mounted on the inner back wrapper is a printed Index, fifty lines plus heading.

This is a detailed day by day contemporary diary—a real overland.—EDG

2531 LOOMIS, AUGUSTUS W.

SCENES IN THE INDIAN COUNTRY . . . PHILADELPHIA: PRESBYTERIAN BOARD OF PUBLICATION.

[1]–283, [283 blank]. 14.8 x 9.5 cm. Three illustrations unlisted. Brown cloth, blind embossed sides, title in gilt on backstrip.

Prov.: Inscribed on the front endleaf: Rev. P. V. Veeder / With kind regards of / A. W. Loomis /.

Ref.: Field 1358; Howes L461; Rader 2250

Copyrighted 1859.

The author spent about a year among the Creek Indians along the Arkansas River. He traveled through this country and writes interestingly of his experiences and with a minimum of theological cant. Fort Coffee, Fort Gibson, Tallagassee Mission, Kowetah Mission were visited and described. The conditions under which the Indians lived, including the scourge of whisky, receive full attention.—EDG

2532 LOOMIS, CHESTER A.

[Wrapper title] A JOURNEY ON HORSEBACK THROUGH THE GREAT WEST, IN 1825 . . . VISITING ALLEGANY TOWNS, OLEAN, WARREN, FRANKLIN, PITTSBURG, NEW LISBON, ELYRIA, NORFOLK, COLUMBUS, ZANESVILLE, VERMILLION, KASKASKIA, VANDALIA, SANDUSKY, AND MANY OTHER PLACES. BATH, N.Y.: PLAINDEALER PRESS.*

[1–27], [28 blank]. 18.7 x 14.4 cm. Self wrappers, with title on front wrapper.

Ref.: Boggess pp. 225–26; Buck 194; Howes L462; Hubach p. 62

Apparently printed from a newspaper set-

ting. No date of publication indicated but before 1908. The *Plaindealer* (Bath) was started in 1883 and ran to 1930 at least.

Boggess (1908) describes two editions, but I think he is confused, having used a copy without the wrappers. The caption title on page [1] reads: The Notes of a Journey / to the Great West in 1825 - - - / By Chester Loomis, of Rush-/ville, Ontario Co., N.Y. / - - - / . . .

2533 LOOMIS, H.

AUTOGRAPH LETTER, SIGNED. 1830 December 6, from Kaskaskia, Randolph County, Illinois. Three pages, 30.5 x 19.1 cm. Address on fourth page. To William Kimball.

A fine letter describing the country and its possibilities. Accompanied by typed transcripts.

2534 LORD, ELIZABETH LAUGHLIN

REMINISCENCES OF EASTERN OREGON . . . PORTLAND, OREGON: THE IRWIN-HODSON CO., 1903.

[1]–155, [156 blank]. 20.5 x 14.7 cm. 14 illustrations unlisted. Dark olive cloth.

Ref.: Howes L468; Smith 6110

Includes a narrative of a trip over the Oregon Trail in 1850.

2535 LORD & PETERS (Oakland, California)

PRINTED AND MANUSCRIPT RECEIPT. 1863 July 10, Oakland, California. One page, 6.5 x 18.7 cm.

Printed at San Francisco. Inserted in Manuscript Journals of Loren L. Williams, Volume III.

2536 LOUGHBOROUGH, JOHN

THE PACIFIC TELEGRAPH AND RAILWAY. AN EXAMINATION OF ALL THE PROJECTS FOR THE CONSTRUCTION OF THESE WORKS, WITH THE PROPOSITION FOR HARMONIZING ALL SECTIONS AND PARTIES OF THE UNION, AND RENDERING THESE GREAT WORKS TRULY NATIONAL IN THEIR CHARACTER . . . SAINT LOUIS: PRINTED BY CHARLES & HAMMOND, 1849.

[1]–80. 22.8 x 14.3 cm. Two folding maps. Map: Map / of the / Position of our Continent as compared with Europe and Africa on / one side and Asia on the other, placing us in the centre. Europe / 3000 from us with a population of 250,000,000 and Asia on / the other side about 5000 miles from us with a population of more / than 700,000,000. The Rail Road across our continent will make us / the centre and thoroughfare for both. / [in border at foot:] Julius Hutawa Lith.ʳ Second St 45 St. Louis Mo /. 32 x 52.5 cm. No scale given. Map: Map / and Profile Sections / showing the / Railroads / of the United

States, / the several projected Railways to the Pacific, and their Connections, / exhibiting the lines of the States, and the natural features of the / Country, from the Mississippi to the Pacific. / From the latest official authorities, furnished from the Office of the / Topographical Bureau at Washington. / Drawn and Lithographed by / Julius Hutawa, / to accompany J. Loughborough project for a / Pacific Railway Laid before the / St. Louis Convention Octth[!] 15 1849 / 52.4 x 83.6 cm. No scale given. *Insets:* Five profiles in upper part of sheet. Blue morocco backstrip, cloth sides.

 Ref.: AII (*Missouri*) 605; Cowan p. 397; Howes L489; *Railway Economics* p. 283; Sabin 42167; Wheat (*Transmississippi*) 261

 The first map is a re-drawing of the first map in Whitney, Asa: *A Project for a Railroad to the Pacific* . . . New York, 1849.

 There are two states, one, as in the Graff, and the other with a preliminary 20 pages, then [5]–80, two folding maps.

 AII (*Missouri*) gives the author's name as Joleur Loughborough.

2537 LOUISIANA PROVINCE. Intendant (Martin Navarro)

[Broadside] LETTRE AUX HABITANTS DE LA PROVINCE DE LA LOUISIANE. DU 29 AOUST 1780. MESSIEURS, APRES AVOIR RENDU COMPTE A SA MAJESTE DE L'OURAGAN DESASTREUX, QUI A TANT AFFLIGE CETTE PROVINCE LE 18 DU MOIS D'AOUST DE L'ANNEE PRECEDENTE 1779 . . . MARTIN NAVARRO.
Broadside, 32.7 x 20.6 cm. Text, 25.3 x 15.2 cm.

 Ref.: Gayarré (*Hist. of Louisiana*, N.Y., 1845) III, p. 151–52; McMurtrie (*Louisiana*) Supp. 12

 Gayarré says this circular letter was printed by the King's printer, Antoine Boudousquié. The letter of consolation by Navarro was written after two disastrous hurricanes had struck Louisiana within a short time of one another.

2538 LOUISIANA PROVINCE. Intendant (Martin Navarro)

[Broadside] CARTA A LOS HABITANTES DE LA PROVINCIA DE LA LUISIANA. DE 29 DE AGOSTO DE 1780. MUI SENORES MIOS: HAVIENDO DADO QUENTA A SU MAJESTAD DEL URACAN ACAECIDO EN ESTA PROVINCIA EL 18 DE AGOSTO DEL ANO PROXIMO PASADA DE 1779 . . . MARTIN NAVARRO.
Broadside, 32.5 x 20.6 cm. Text, 21.6 x 15.2 cm.

 Ref.: McMurtrie (*Louisiana*) Supp. 13

 The Spanish version of the preceding item.

2539 LOUISIANA TERRITORY. Governor (W. C. C. Claiborne)

[Caption title] (CIRCULAR.) NEW-ORLEANS, JUNE 16TH 1808. SIR, THE ENCLOSED GENERAL ORDER

WILL I HOPE BE FAITHFULLY EXECUTED . . . I AM SIR, VERY RESPECTFULLY YOUR HUMBLE SERVANT, [in manuscript: Wm C. C. Claiborne] . . .
[1–4]. (Pages [1] and [4] blank.) 24.3 x 19.7 cm. Unbound leaflet.

 Ref.:

 Page [3] carries the text of page [2] in French. It is not signed in manuscript by Claiborne.

 The General Order which this circular accompanied was the establishment of a state militia.

2540 LOUISIANA TERRITORY. Laws, Statutes, etc.

THE LAWS OF THE TERRITORY OF LOUISIANA. COMPRISING ALL THOSE WHICH ARE NOW ACTUALLY IN FORCE WITHIN THE SAME. ST. LOUIS, (L.): PRINTED BY JOSEPH CHARLESS, 1808.
[A]–Hhh⁴, I¹. [1]–[434]. 21.2 x 12.9 cm. Rebound in tan cloth, calf backstrip with red and black leather labels.

 Ref.: AII (*Missouri*) 1; BSA *Papers* Vol. 52, No. 4, pp. 306–09; Howes L504; Sabin 42246; Shaw & Shoemaker 15451

 First book printed west of the Mississippi River. David Kaser (in BSA *Papers*) has shown that pages 349–71 were printed off as a separate pamphlet in December, 1808, (although no copy is extant) and that a Masonic oration may have been printed before the Laws appeared. Although the title-page is dated 1808, a certificate appears on page 373 dated April 29, 1809. Thus the volume was probably not published until May, 1809. A further evidence that the volume was in process of printing over a long period of time is the variety of paper used from gathering to gathering. It is still the first substantial book printed west of the Mississippi.

2541 LOUISIANA. Governor (W. C. C. Claiborne)

[Broadside] MILITIA GENERAL ORDERS HEAD QUARTERS NEW-ORLEANS, DECEMBER 25TH, 1813. GENERAL FLOURNOY, COMMANDING THE REGULAR TROOPS, WITHIN THE SEVENTH MILITARY DISTRICT, HAS UNDER A SPECIAL AUTHORITY, VESTED IN HIM, BY THE PRESIDENT OF THE U. STATES, CALLED UPON THE EXECUTIVE OF LOUISIANA, FOR AN AUXILIARY MILITIA FORCE, TO BE CONTINUED IN THE SERVICE OF THE U. STATES FOR SIX MONTHS . . . HEAD QUARTERS, NEW ORLEANS, DECEMBER 26, 1813. IN CONSEQUENCE OF THE REQUISITION UNDER THE AUTHORITY OF THE PRESIDENT OF THE UNITED STATES, AS ANNOUNCED IN THE GENERAL ORDERS OF YESTERDAY, THE MILITIA FORCE, HOLDEN IN READINESS FOR SERVICE UNDER THE AUTHORITY OF THE STATE, AND IN CONFORMITY TO THE GENERAL ORDERS OF THE 8TH OF JULY AND 6TH OF SEPTEM-

BER LAST, ARE HEREBY RELEASED AND DISCHARGED
—EXCEPTING ONLY THE ST. CHARLES . . . BY OR-
DER OF HIS EXCELLENCY, WM. C. C. CLAIBORNE,
GOVERNOR AND COMMANDER IN CHIEF. A. LANEU-
VILLE, COL. AND ADJT GEN.

Broadside, 36.7 x 31.2 cm. Text, 31.3 x 17 cm.
Ref.:
In manuscript in margin at foot: True Copy
A. La Neuville / Adj^t Genl /

2542 LOUISIANA. Governor (William C. C.
Claiborne)

[Broadsheet] TO HIS EXCELLENCY THE GOVERNOR
OF THE STATE OF LOUISIANA AND COMMANDER IN
CHIEF OF THE MILITIA. THE UNDERSIGNED MEMBERS
OF THE GENERAL ASSEMBLY SEEING WITH REGRET
THE RESISTANCE MADE BY THE OFFICERS ATTACHED
TO THE FIRST MILITIA BRIGADE, TO THE REQUISI-
TION MADE BY THE PRESIDENT OF THE UNITED
STATES . . . NEW ORLEANS, 24TH JANUARY, 1814.
PHILEMON THOMAS . . .

Broadsheet, 31.4 x 21 cm.
Ref.:
The verso contains Governor Claiborne's re-
ply headed: New Orleans, February 4, 1814. /
Gentlemen, / [43 lines] William C. C. Claiborne.

2543 LOUISIANA. Governor (W. C. C. Claiborne)

[Broadside] MILITIA GENERAL ORDERS. HEAD
QUARTERS, NEW-ORLEANS, AUGUST, 6, 1814. IN A
LETTER FROM THE HON THE SECRETARY AT WAR,
UNDER DATE OF THE 4TH ULTIMO, THE GOVERNOR
OF LOUISIANA HAS RECEIVED THE ORDERS OF THE
PRESIDENT OF THE U. STATES, TO ORGANIZE AND
HOLD IN READINESS FOR IMMEDIATE SERVICE, A
CORPS OF A THOUSAND MILITIA INFANTRY . . . IN
CASE OF INVASION, THE WHOLE MILITIA, WILL BE
ORDERED TO FRONT THE ENEMY.—IF OUR HOMES
AND FIRE SIDES ARE MENACED, UNION, ZEAL AND
MUTUAL CONFIDENCE SHOULD WARM EVERY HEART
AND STRENGTHEN EVERY ARM. BY ORDER OF HIS
EXCELLENCY WILLIAM C. C. CLAIBORNE, GOV.
AND COMMANDER IN CHIEF. A. LANEUVILLE, AD-
JUTANT GENERAL.

Broadside, 34.6 x 13.4 cm. Text, 32.3 x 11.4 cm.
Ref.:
Inscribed on verso: Genl Orders / of the Gov-
ernor / of Louisiana / for calling into / service
the proportion / of militia from / that State
S——— /

2544 LOUISIANA. Governor (W. C. C. Claiborne)

ANOTHER COPY. 35 x 13.7 cm. Text, 32.4 x 11.3
cm. In a cloth folding case.

2545 LOUISIANA. Governor (W. C. C. Claiborne)

[Broadside] (PAR AUTHORITE.) ORDRES GENERAUX
DE MILICE. QUARTIERS-GENERAUX, A LA NOUVELLE-
ORLEANS, 6 AVRIL 1814. PAR UNE LETTRE DE
L'HONORABLE SECRETAIRE DE LA GUERRE, DATEE
DU 4 DU MOIS DERNIER, LE GOUVERNEUR DE LA
LOUISIANE A RECU, DU PRESIDENT DES ETATS-UNIS,
L'ORDRE D'ORGANISER ET DE TENIR PRET A ENTRER
EN ACTIVITE UN CORPS DE MILICE DE MILLE
HOMMES . . . EN CAS D'INVASION TOUTE LA MILICE
SERA APPELEE A FAIRE FACE A L'ENNEMI, SI NOS
FOYERS SONT MENACES. QUE L'UNION, LE ZELE ET
LA CONFIANCE MNTEUELLE[!] ECHAUFFENT TOUS
LES COEURS ET DONNENT DE LA VIGUEUR A TOUS
LES BRAS. PAR ORDRE DE SON EXCELLENCE WILLIAM
C. C. CLAIBORNE, GOUVERNEUR ET COMMANDANT
EN CHEF. A. LANEUVILLE, ADJUTANT-GENERAL[!]

Broadside, 31.5 x 21.8 cm. Text, 21.3 x 18 cm.
Ref.:
The text is the French version of the General
Orders dated August 6, 1814. The present broad-
side is misdated.

2546 LOUISIANA. Governor (W. C. C. Claiborne)

[Broadside] MILITIA GENERAL ORDERS. HEAD
QUARTERS, NEW-ORLEANS, SEPTEMBER 5, 1814.
MAJOR GENERAL JACKSON, ACTING UNDER THE
AUTHORITY OF THE PRESISIDENT[!], HAVING DE-
MANDED THE IMMEDIATE SERVICE IN THE FIELD OF
THE WHOLE CORPS OF LOUISIANA MILITIA, DI-
RECTED TO BE HOLDEN IN READINESS FOR SERVICE
UNDER THE GENERAL ORDERS OF THE 6TH ULTIMO,
THE GOVERNOR AND COMMANDER IN CHIEF DI-
RECTS THAT THE OFFICERS, NON-COMMISSIONED OF-
FICERS AND PRIVATES, DRAWN FROM THE 1ST, 2D,
3D, 4TH AND 5TH REGIMENTS UNDER THE ORDERS
AFORESAID, RENDEZVOUS IN NEW ORLEANS ON
SATURDAY THE 10TH INSTANT, AT 10 O'CLOCK
A.M. . . . THE TIME OF RENDEZVOUS FOR DETACH-
MENTS, DRAWN FROM THE MORE DISTANT COUN-
TIES, WILL BE FIXED IN AFTER ORDERS. WM. C. C.
CLAIBORNE, GOV. & COMMANDER IN CHIEF. AFTER
GENERAL ORDERS, H. Q. N. ORLEANS, SEPT. 5,
1814 . . . BY ORDER OF HIS EXCELLENCY WM. C C
CLAIBORNE, GOV. & COMD. IN CHIEF. A. LANU-
VILLE[!] ADJUTANT GENERAL. BY ANOTHER GEN-
ERAL ORDER, THE DETACHMENT DRAWN FROM THE
6TH 7TH 8TH & 9TH REGIMENT ARE ORDERED TO
RENDEZVOUS AT THE MAGAZINE BARRACKS . . . ON
SATURDAY THE 24TH INSTANT.

Broadside, 24 x 19.7 cm. Text, 19.5 x 11.4 cm·
Ref.:

2547 LOUISIANA. Governor (W. C. C. Claiborne)

[Broadside] HEAD QUARTERS. PARISH OF IBERVILLE, SEPTEMBER 8TH, 1816. MILITIA GENERAL ORDERS. THE GOVERNOR AND COMMANDER IN CHIEF NOTICES WITH REGRET, THE NEGLECT AND INATTENTION OF THE SEVERAL CORPS TO THE MILITIA DUTY, AND THE CONSEQUENT DISORGANIZATION IN WHICH THEY HAVE FALLEN . . . (SIGNED) WILLIAM C. C. CLAIBORNE. ADJUTANT GENERAL'S OFFICE, NEW-ORLEANS, SEPT. 13, 1816. THE ABOVE IS A TRUE COPY OF THE ORIGINAL ON FILE IN THIS OFFICE. [in manuscript: Alex^dr. la Neuville Adj^t Genl].

Broadside, 31.4 x 22 cm. Text, 26.5 x 18.4 cm.
Ref.:

2548 LOUNSBERRY, CLEMENT A.

EARLY HISTORY OF NORTH DAKOTA . . . WASHINGTON, D.C.: LIBERTY PRESS, 1919.

[i]–xv, [xvi blank], 1–645, [646 blank]. 26.1 x 18.5 cm. Illustrations listed. Green cloth, gilt, marbled edges.
Ref.: Howes L516

2549 LOVEJOY, HORATIO

[Wrapper title] HORATIO LOVEJOY'S TERRIBLE NEW YEAR EVE.

3–20. 18.1 x 12.3 cm. Buff wrappers, with title on front wrapper.
Ref.:
Probably printed in Whiteside County, 1864 or 1865. Horatio Lovejoy's "terrible New Year Eve" occurred in 1863, when Horatio and Amelia Lovejoy arranged to go to Morrison, Illinois, for a sleigh ride. They reached Morrison and started for home, which was in Kingsbury Grove in the western part of Whiteside County, about 3 p.m. They became lost in a snow storm and as a result Amelia died and Horatio lost both feet and both hands. By selling this little book, "he seeks to assist his Mother and himself to live."—EDG

2550 LOWE, PERCIVAL G.

FIVE YEARS A DRAGOON ('49 TO '54), AND OTHER ADVENTURES ON THE GREAT PLAINS . . . KANSAS CITY, MO.: THE FRANKLIN HUDSON PUBLISHING CO., 1906.*

[i–ii], [1]–[418]. 19.1 x 13.3 cm. 46 illustrations, vignettes, etc., unlisted. Yellow pictorial cloth, title on front cover and backstrip, sprinkled edges.
Ref.: Howes L526; Rader 2255

2551 LOWELL, DANIEL W., & CO.

MAP OF THE NEZ PERCES AND SALMON RIVER GOLD MINES IN WASHINGTON TERRITORY . . . SAN FRANCISCO: PRINTED BY WHITTON, WATERS & CO., 1862.

[1]–[24]. 14.5 x 10 cm. Folding map: Map of / Nez Perces and Salmon River Mines, / Washington Territory. / [below border:] Entered according to Act of Congress in the year 1862 by Daniel W. Louell[!] & Co. in the Clerks Office of the U. S. District Court of the North Dist. of Cal^a / 37.6 x 62.1 cm. Scale: 24 miles to one inch. Blue limp cloth, with title on front cover. In blue cloth case.
Ref.: Greenwood 1666; Howes L527; Jones 1452; Smith 6125; Wagner-Camp 383; Wheat (*Transmississippi*) 1047
Pages 22–[24] carry regional advertisements.

2552 [LOWTHER, THOMAS D.]

MEMORIALS OF THE OLD CHICAGO LIBRARY, FORMERLY YOUNG MEN'S ASSOCIATION, AND OF THE ADVENT OF THE NEW . . . CHICAGO: JOHN K. SCULLY, PRINTER, 1878.

[1]–4, [i–ii], [5]–138. 22.5 x 14.4 cm. Contemporary half tan calf, gilt back, brown leather label on backstrip, marbled edges. Original printed gray front wrapper bound in.
Prov.: Signed on title-page: By / T. D. Lowther. / With marginal annotations and corrections, notes, etc., throughout by the compiler. Inserted is one page of manuscript addition. On verso of front endleaf is following note: A Copy of this Book was / deposited under the Corner-/-Stone of the New Public Library, 30th Novr 1893. /
Ref.:
Fascinating.

2553 LOYAL LEGION OF THE UNITED STATES, MILITARY ORDER OF THE (Commandery of the District of Columbia)

CIRCULAR NO. 30. SERIES OF 1899. WHOLE NO. 228. HEADQUARTERS, CITY OF WASHINGTON, DECEMBER 19, 1899. IN MEMORIAM. COMPANION HENRY WARE LAWTON.

[1–2]. 20 x 12.7 cm. Mounted in Lawton Scrapbook.
Ref.:
Page [2] carries a concise account of Lawton's career.

2554 LUCAS, CORYDON L.

THE MILTON LOTT TRAGEDY. A HISTORY OF THE FIRST WHITE DEATH IN BOONE COUNTY, AND THE EVENTS WHICH LEAD UP TO THE DARK TRAGEDY AND THE PLACING OF THE MONUMENT IN MEMORY

OF THIS HISTORIC EVENT . . . MADRID, IOWA: PUB-
LISHED UNDER THE AUSPICES OF THE MADRID HIS-
TORICAL SOCIETY.*

[i–ii blank, iii–iv], [1]–24. 21 x 14.2 cm. Two
illustrations. Gray printed wrappers, new black
cloth backstrip.

    Ref.: Howes L545; Mott (*Iowa*) p. 71

Apparently published in 1906. The monument was dedicated on December 18, 1905, as
noted on page 8.

2555   LUCAS, ROBERT

PRINTED AND MANUSCRIPT DOCUMENT, SIGNED.
1840 July 2. Burlington, Iowa. 20.1 x 31.5 cm.

Appointment of Alexander J. Majors as Captain in the state militia. Signed also by Ver
Planck Van Antwerp.

2556   LUKE DARRELL . . .

LUKE DARRELL, THE CHICAGO NEWSBOY. CHI-
CAGO: TOMLINSON BROTHERS. 1866.

[i]–x, 11–377, [378 blank]. 16 x 10.6 cm. Six illustrations, unlisted. Black cloth, title in gilt on
backstrip.

    Ref.:

A later edition, 1867, is listed in AII (*Chicago*)
1226. One other copy of the 1866 has been
noted; see *Antiquarian Bookman*, 12/10/49, p.
1383.

2557   LUKENS, MATILDA BARNS

THE INLAND PASSAGE. A JOURNAL OF A TRIP TO
ALASKA . . . 1889.

[i–vi, vi blank], [1]–84. 14.8 x 11.7 cm. Dark
brown cloth, gilt edges.

    Prov.: Inscribed on front fly-leaf: Emma N.
Garrett / from / Mrs M. B. Lukens /. Inscribed
(inverted) on back fly-leaf: Emma N. Garrett, /
165 W. Cheltin Ave, / Germantown. /

    Ref.: Smith 6143

A privately printed journal without place of
publication indicated.

2558   LUSE, H. H.

AUTOGRAPH LETTER, SIGNED. 1873 April 28, San
Francisco. Two pages, 20.4 x 12.8 cm. To Loren
L. Williams.

Ordering a map. Williams noted on the letter
that the map had been supplied, twenty dollars
charged, and the bill paid. Inserted in Manuscript Journals of Loren L. Williams, Volume
IV.

2559   LUTHERAN CHURCH IN MIS-
SOURI, OHIO, ETC.

DRITTER SYNODALBERICHT DER DEUTSCHEN EVAN-
GELISCH-LUTHERISCHEN SYNODE VON MISSOURI,
OHIO UND ANDERN STAATEN VOM JAHRE 1849.
CHICAGO, ILL. GEDRUCKT BEI R. HOFFGEN, 1849.

[A]¹, [B]⁴, *⁴, [large dot]⁴, [C]². [i–ii], [1]–27,
[28 blank]. 24.5 x 16.5 cm. Stabbed and pasted
into old plain green-gray wrappers, with remnants of earlier wrappers pasted along inner
edges of inner wrappers. Pencil notes and scribblings on front.

    Ref.: Byrd 1441; McMurtrie (*Chicago*) 178

McMurtrie transcribes the second line:
Synodal-Bericht / and makes the third line above
the first word of the next line. This may mean
two settings of the title-leaf, or it may be simply
McMurtrie.

2560   LYFORD, C. P.

BRIGHAM YOUNG'S RECORD OF BLOOD! OR THE
NECESSITY FOR THAT FAMOUS "BIBLE AND RE-
VOLVER." . . . A LECTURE DELIVERED IN THE FIRST
M. E. CHURCH, SALT LAKE CITY, JAN. 23D, 1876 . . .
PUBLISHED IN SALT LAKE DAILY TRIBUNE, JAN
25TH, 1876, AND ROCKY MOUNTAIN CHRISTIAN
ADVOCATE, FEB. 1ST, 1876.

[1]–[16]. 20.5 x 13.6 cm. Stitched, unbound.

    Prov.: Library stamp of U. S. Geological
Survey Library on title-page surcharged with an
exchange stamp.

    Ref.:

Probably printed at Salt Lake City in 1876.

2561   LYFORD, WILLIAM G.

THE WESTERN ADDRESS DIRECTORY: CONTAINING
THE CARDS OF MERCHANTS, MANUFACTURERS, AND
OTHER BUSINESS MEN, IN PITTSBURGH, (PA.) DAY-
TON, (O.) WHEELING, (VA.) CINCINNATI, (O.)
ZANESVILLE, (O.) MADISON, (IND.) PORTSMOUTH,
(O.) LOUISVILLE, (K.) ST. LOUIS, (MO.) TOGETHER
WITH HISTORICAL, TOPOGRAPHICAL & STATISTICAL
SKETCHES, (FOR THE YEAR 1837,) OF THOSE CITIES,
AND TOWNS IN THE MISSISSIPPI VALLEY. INTENDED
AS A GUIDE TO TRAVELLERS . . . BALTIMORE:
PRINTED BY JOS. ROBINSON, 1837.

[1]–468. 17.5 x 10.5 cm. Brown cloth, printed
white paper label on backstrip, 7.5 x 3 cm.

    Ref.: Clark III 200; Howes L576; Sabin
42767; Thomson 737

The advertisements and business cards are
printed on colored paper.

2562   LYKKEJAEGER, HANS

LUCK OF A WANDERING DANE . . . PHILADELPHIA,
PA.: MATLACK & HARVEY, 1885.

[3]–130. 20.1 x 13.3 cm. Humorous illustrations
in text. Black cloth, title stamped in gilt on backstrip, red edges.

    Ref.: Cowan p. 400; Howes S572

California and adventures in the west.

2563 LYMAN, O., & C. C. A. STRIBLEN

[Caption title] FIRST ANNUAL EXHIBIT, SHOWING THE NUMBER OF BUILDINGS ERECTED AND IMPROVEMENTS MADE, THEIR COST, &C., IN THE CITY OF KEOKUK, IOWA, FOR THE YEAR 1857 . . .

[1–4]. 48.1 x 31.8 cm. Unbound leaflet.
Ref.: Moffit 386
Probably printed at Keokuk in 1858.

2564 [LYNCH, JAMES K.]

WITH STEVENSON TO CALIFORNIA, 1846.

[1]–65, [66 blank]. 20 x 13.4 cm. Dark blue cloth, title stamped in gilt on front cover, uncut.
Prov.: Inscribed on a front blank leaf: F. R. Fulton / from / James K Lynch / Jan 24.th 1898. /
Ref.: Cowan p. 401; Howes L583
Limited to 100 copies.
The prefatory note is signed from Tierra Redonda, San Luis Obispo County, July, 1896. No place of publication or printing is indicated.
Personal narrative of the Conquest and the Gold Rush.—Howes

2565 LYNCH, JEREMIAH

A SENATOR OF THE FIFTIES: DAVID C. BRODERICK OF CALIFORNIA . . . SAN FRANCISCO: A. M. ROBERTSON, 1911.

[i–xii, xii blank], 1–246. 19.3 x 12.3 cm. 15 illustrations listed. Dark red cloth, fore and lower edges uncut.
Prov.: Inscribed on front fly-leaf: To / [underline] / Everett D. Graff. / From / [underline] / Orie / Sept. - 15 - 1932 / I knew the author very / well. Lived at the / Bohemian Club. Looked / after their Library. / Worked hard on this book / and his facts are authentic / He was a crank on facts. / Orie. /
Ref.: Cowan p. 401

2566 LYONS, W. F.

BRIGADIER-GENERAL THOMAS FRANCIS MEAGHER: HIS POLITICAL AND MILITARY CAREER; WITH SELECTIONS FROM HIS SPEECHES AND WRITINGS . . . NEW YORK: D. & J. SADLIER & CO., 1870.

[i]–vi, [7]–357, [358 blank]. 18.1 x 11.3 cm. Portrait. Brown cloth, vignette stamped in gilt on front cover and in blind on back, title in gilt on backstrip.
Prov.: Inscribed on the first blank leaf: To my Son / I. I. Carbery on / attaining his majority June 25th / 1870. — / Remember to keep bright in / your mind the story of Ireland / and should God send the opportunity / during your life and that you / can aid by voice or means the / great struggle which is but / postponed then I charge you / in your manhood to act as / becometh your

race, / Your affec Father / Jas P. Carbery / Cincinnati O. /
Ref.: Howes (1954) 6390; Nicholson p. 488; Smith 6169
Immediately after the Civil War, in which he served, Meagher was appointed Secretary of the Territory of Montana by Andrew Johnson. Meagher later served as Acting Governor, also.

2567 LYONS CITY, IOWA

LYONS CITY, IOWA; ITS POSITION AND RESOURCES AND ITS NATURAL ADVANTAGES. LYONS CITY: HAWES & STOW, MIRROR OFFICE, 1858.

[1]–26. (Lacks [27–32].) 21.3 x 13.6 cm. Eight woodcut plates, and one in text. Sewn, removed from bound volume, unbound.
Ref.: Moffit 837
The copy described by Moffit has 32 pages, the final four probably advertisements. The Streeter copy has wrappers with same title on front wrapper and advertisements on back wrapper.

M

2568 McAFEE, ROBERT B.

HISTORY OF THE LATE WAR IN THE WESTERN COUNTRY . . . LEXINGTON: WORSLEY & SMITH, 1816.

[A]^8, B–I, L–P, R–2P, 2R–3P, 3R–3U^4. [i]–viii, [1]–534, [535–36]. 21.5 x 13.8 cm. Gray boards, printed white paper label, uncut, partly unopened. Label defective. In a clear plastic case.
Prov.: Penciled signature on title-page: E. T. Thorp Martin. Red stamp of New-York Historical Society on title-page, released as a duplicate, "Sold to B & W."
Ref.: AII (*Kentucky*) 612; Bay pp. 323, 325; Buley II, pp. 550, 554; Howes M9; Jones 781; Rader 2270; Rusk II, pp. 243, 247–48; Sabin 42929; Thomson 738
No other copy in this condition has been located.
According to AII (*Kentucky*) the work was written by McAfee and revised by James Buchanan.

2569 [McBRIDE, JAMES]

NAVAL BIOGRAPHY, CONSISTING OF MEMOIRS OF THE MOST DISTINGUISHED OFFICERS OF THE AMERICAN NAVY; TO WHICH IS ANNEXED THE LIFE OF GENERAL PIKE. CINCINNATI: PRINTED AND PUBLISHED BY MORGAN, WILLIAMS, & CO., JUNE 1815.

[i]–[viii, viii blank], [1]–296. 16.9 x 9.5 cm. Rebound in gray half morocco.
Ref.: AII (*Ohio*) 263; Howes M17

2570 MacCABE, JULIUS P. B.

DIRECTORY OF THE CITY OF DETROIT, WITH ITS ENVIRONS, AND REGISTER OF MICHIGAN FOR THE YEAR 1837 . . . DETROIT: PRINTED BY WILLIAM HARSHA, 1837.

[1–40 advertisements], [41 blank], [42], [1]–[115], [116 blank]. 19.5 x 12 cm. Engraved advertisement of C. Piquette on page [42]. Gray printed boards, black cloth back, title on front cover, advertisements on back cover.
Ref.: AII (*Michigan*) 328; Clements Library (*Michigan*) 68; Greenly 76; Howes M22

A sign that a city had come of age in the eighteenth or nineteenth century was the appearance of its first directory. Detroit was old, in 1837, when the earliest directory was delivered to subscribers. The first number lists families which were prominent during the French and British regimes and which, more than 125 years later, are still closely associated with Detroit.

2571 MacCABE, JULIUS P. B.

DIRECTORY OF THE CITY OF MILWAUKEE, FOR THE YEARS 1847–'48, CONTAINING AN EPITOMIZED HISTORY OF MILWAUKEE, WITH A COPY OF ITS CITY CHARTER . . . MILWAUKEE: PRINTED BY WILSON & KING, 1847.

[1]–148, [1]–92 advertisements. 17.7 x 11.4 cm. Tan printed boards with title on front cover and advertisement on back cover, advertisement mounted on inner front cover. New sheepskin back, rebound, new endpapers.
Prov.: Signature on leaf preceding title-page [lower part of leaf torn off]: H. N. Conant / Milwaukee Ap¹ 10 /. Conant's advertisement appears on page 23 of the advertising section.
Ref.: AII (*Wisconsin*) 350; Howes M24; Legler 29; McMurtrie (*Wisconsin*) 271; Sabin 29154

First Milwaukee directory.

2572 McCAIN, CHARLES W.

HISTORY OF THE S.S. "BEAVER" BEING A GRAPHIC AND VIVID SKETCH OF THIS NOTED PIONEER STEAMER AND HER ROMANTIC CRUISE FOR OVER HALF A CENTURY ON THE PLACID ISLAND-DOTTED WATERS OF THE NORTH PACIFIC.—ALSO CONTAINING—A DESCRIPTION OF THE HUDSON'S BAY COMPANY FROM ITS FORMATION IN 1670, DOWN TO THE PRESENT TIME. BIOGRAPHY OF CAPTAIN McNEILL. THE NARRATIVE OF A FRASER RIVER PROSPECTOR OF 1859 . . . VANCOUVER, B.C., 1894.

[1]–99, [100 blank]. 15.9 x 12.3 cm. Six illustrations, unlisted. Blue cloth.
Ref.: Howes M26; Smith 6206

2573 McCALL, GEORGE A.

[Caption title] . . . COLONEL McCALL'S REPORTS IN RELATION TO NEW MEXICO . . .

[1]–23, [24 blank]. 22.6 x 14.5 cm. Rebound in new red cloth.
Ref.: Howes M31; Munk (Alliot) p. 138; Saunders 3020; Wagner-Camp 201

31st Congress, 2nd Session, Senate, Executive Document No. 26, Serial 589. [Washington, 1851.]

The work contains a good description of New Mexico in 1849–50.

2574 McCALL, GEORGE A.

LETTERS FROM THE FRONTIERS. WRITTEN DURING A PERIOD OF THIRTY YEARS' SERVICE IN THE ARMY OF THE UNITED STATES . . . PHILADELPHIA: J. B. LIPPINCOTT & CO., 1868.

[i]–x, 11–539, [540 blank]. 20.5 x 13.3 cm. Red cloth, title in gilt on backstrip, uncut.
Ref.: Clark III 68; Howes M30; Munk (Alliot) p. 138; Rader 2273; Sabin 42970; Wagner-Camp 201 note

A fascinating account of Army service on the frontiers of Florida in the 1820's, the Black Hawk War, Tennessee in the 1830's, Arkansas, the Mexican War, and after that Santa Fé. In 1853 he resigned his commission as Lieutenant Colonel due to ill health. During the Civil War he returned to military service in the Volunteers as Major General of Pennsylvania Volunteers. He wrote charmingly of his horses, dogs, hunting, and the military life. The work is a classic of its period.—EDG

2575 McCALLA, WILLIAM L.

ADVENTURES IN TEXAS, CHIEFLY IN THE SPRING AND SUMMER OF 1840 . . . PHILADELPHIA: PRINTED FOR THE AUTHOR, 1841.

[1]–8, [13]–199, [200 blank]. 14.9 x 9.4 cm. Black cloth, blind embossed boards, gilt title on front cover.
Ref.: Howes M34; Rader 2275; Raines p. 142; Sabin 42979; Streeter 1387

The author, a Presbyterian clergyman, was favorably impressed by Texas.

2576 McCLURE, ALEXANDER K.

THREE THOUSAND MILES THROUGH THE ROCKY MOUNTAINS . . . PHILADELPHIA: J. B. LIPPINCOTT & CO., 1869.

[1]–456. 18.7 x 11.8 cm. Frontispiece. Brown cloth, title stamped in gilt on backstrip.
Ref.: Adams 646; Howes M49; Smith 6231

Both Howes and Smith list three plates.

2577 McCOID, MOSES A.

JOHN WILLIAMSON OF HARDSCRABBLE . . . CHI-
CAGO: M. A. DONOHUE & COMPANY.

[1]–341, [342 blank]. 19 x 13.4 cm. Ten illustrations listed. Red cloth, title in gilt on front cover
and backstrip.

Prov.: E. R. Harlan's copy, with autograph
manuscript note, two pages, in pencil by him at
the end. Pasted down on inner front cover is a
slip signed by the author.

Ref.:
Copyrighted 1902.
Concerned principally with the early years of
Jefferson County, Iowa.

2578 McCONKEY, HARRIET E. BISHOP

DAKOTA WAR WHOOP; OR, INDIAN MASSACRES AND
WAR IN MINNESOTA . . . SAINT PAUL: PUBLISHED
BY D. D. MERRILL, 1863.

[i]–[viii, viii blank], [13]–304. 18.8 x 12.3 cm.
Six portraits including a mounted photograph of
General Sibley as frontispiece. Black cloth.

Ref.: AII (*Minnesota*) 487; Bradford 3131;
Howes M58; Sabin 43085

2579 McCONNELL, H. H.

FIVE YEARS A CAVALRYMAN; OR, SKETCHES OF
REGULAR ARMY LIFE ON THE TEXAS FRONTIER,
TWENTY ODD YEARS AGO . . . JACKSBORO, TEXAS:
J. N. ROGERS & CO., PRINTERS, 1889.

[i]–[x, x blank], [11]–319, [320 blank]. 18.8 x
12.5 cm. Light brown cloth, blind fillet bands on
covers, title in gilt on front cover and backstrip,
and in blind on back cover.

Ref.: Adams (*Ramp. Herd*) 1380; Dobie p.
52; Howes M59; Rader 2280; Raines p. 142
Printed on "Brooks Brothers pink" paper.

2580 McCONNELL, WILLIAM J.

EARLY HISTORY OF IDAHO . . . CALDWELL, IDAHO:
THE CAXTON PRINTERS, MCMXIII.*

[1]–420. (Pages [1–2] blank.) 22.5 x 14.5 cm.
Olive green cloth.

Ref.: Howes M62; Smith 6242

2581 McCORKLE, JOHN

THREE YEARS WITH QUANTRELL[!]. A TRUE STORY
. . . WRITTEN BY O. S. BARTON. ARMSTRONG, MO.:
ARMSTRONG HERALD PRINT.

[1]–157, [158 blank]. 23.1 x 15.5 cm. 11 illustrations, unlisted. Maroon semi-limp wrappers,
title printed in gold on front wrapper, wallet
edges.

Ref.: Adams 76; Howes M63
Published about 1914.

2582 McCORMICK, ANDREW P.

SCOTCH-IRISH IN IRELAND AND IN AMERICA, AS
SHOWN IN SKETCHES OF THE PIONEER SCOTCH-
IRISH FAMILIES McCORMICK, STEVENSON, McKENZIE
AND BELL, IN NORTH CAROLINA, KENTUCKY, MIS-
SOURI AND TEXAS . . . 1897.

[i–iv], [1]–174, [175–76 blank], [1]–[73], [74
blank]. 23.1 x 15.1 cm. Light brown cloth, blind
embossed bands on covers, gilt title on backstrip. In a natural linen case.

Prov.: Inscribed on verso of front endleaf:
To / Mr Leander J. McCormick / With the
Compliments of / Andrew Phelps McCormick /
June 14. 1897 /.

Ref.: Vandale 108
Probably published at Chicago.
Contains considerable Texas material includ-
ing personal narratives.

2583 McCORMICK, RICHARD C.

ARIZONA: ITS RESOURCES AND PROSPECTS. A LET-
TER TO THE EDITOR OF THE NEW YORK TRIBUNE,
(REPRINTED FROM THAT JOURNAL OF JUNE 26TH,
1865.) . . . NEW YORK: D. VAN NOSTRAND, 1865.

[1]–22, [23–24 blank]. 23.3 x 14.8 cm. Map:
General Outline / Map / of Arizona. / A. Brown
& Co. 65 Liberty St. N.Y. / 22.6 x 29.1 cm. No
scale given. Buff printed wrappers, with title on
front wrapper.

Ref.: Bradford 3134; Howes M65; Munk
(Alliot) p. 140; Sabin 43101

2584 McCORMICK, S. J.

THE PORTLAND DIRECTORY, FOR THE YEAR 1863:
EMBRACING A GENERAL DIRECTORY OF CITIZENS, A
BUSINESS DIRECTORY, AND OTHER STATISTICAL IN-
FORMATION RELATIVE TO THE PROGRESS AND
PRESENT CONDITION OF THE CITY. PORTLAND,
OREGON: S. J. McCORMICK, COMPILER AND PUB-
LISHER, 1863.

[1]–133, [134–36 blank]. 22.5 x 14.5 cm. Tan
boards, red (now neutral) cloth backstrip, with
title on front and back cover and with advertisements. Advertisements on front and back inner
covers.

Ref.: Howes P493; McMurtrie (*Oregon*) 256
The first Portland Directory.

2585 [McCOY, ISAAC]

[Caption title] ADDRESS TO PHILANTHROPISTS IN
THE UNITED STATES, GENERALLY, AND TO CHRIS-
TIANS IN PARTICULAR, ON THE CONDITIONS AND
PROSPECTS OF THE AMERICAN INDIANS . . .

[1]–8. 21 x 12.9 cm. Sewn, unbound.

Prov.: Inscribed on page [1]: Hon. N. Sils-
bee / With the respects / of the author /.

Ref.: Sabin 43109

Signed and dated on p. 8: Isaac McCoy. / Surveyor's Camp, Neosho river, / Indian Territory, Dec. 1, 1831. / [preceding two lines joined by bracket]. No place of printing is indicated.

2586 McCOY, ISAAC

NO. 2. THE ANNUAL REGISTER OF INDIAN AFFAIRS WITHIN THE INDIAN (OR WESTERN) TERRITORY. SHAWANOE BAPTIST MISSION, IND. TER.: J. MEEKER, PRINTER, 1836.

[1]–88. 23.5 x 14.5 cm. Blue-gray wrappers with title on front wrapper, editorial note on recto and verso of back wrapper. Wrappers silked. In a dark blue cloth case.

Prov.: At top of front wrapper: Hon. Thomas Lee H of Repres. / Washington D.C. /

Ref.: Field 983; Howes M67; McMurtrie & Allen (*Meeker*) 41; Sabin 43111

In December, 1845, the second number of the Annual Register of Indian Affairs was published, and the expense defrayed by the board [of missions].—McCoy: *History of Baptist Indian Missions*, p. 492. See also Meeker *Journal*, April 21 and August 5, 1835.

2587 McCOY, ISAAC

NO. 3. THE ANNUAL REGISTER OF INDIAN AFFAIRS WITHIN THE INDIAN (OR WESTERN) TERRITORY . . . SHAWANOE BAPTIST MISSION, IND. TER.: J. G. PRATT, PRINTER, 1837.

[1]–81, [82–4 blank]. 23.6 x 14.3 cm. Blue-gray printed wrappers, with title on front wrapper, notice regarding Benevolent Exploring Expedition. / on back wrapper, uncut. In a blue cloth case.

Prov.: At top of front wrapper: Hon. Wm Buchanan / U.S. Senate / Washington / D.C. /

Ref.: Field 983; Howes M67; McMurtrie & Allen (*Meeker*) 58; Sabin 43111

No more issues of the *Annual Register* were printed at the Shawanoe Baptist Mission; No. 4 was printed at Washington by Peter Force.

2588 McCOY, ISAAC

. . . NO. 4. THE ANNUAL REGISTER OF INDIAN AFFAIRS WITHIN THE INDIAN TERRITORY . . . WASHINGTON: PRINTED BY PETER FORCE, 1838.

[i]–[96]. 22.5 x 14.1 cm. Yellow printed wrappers, with title on front wrapper. In a blue cloth case.

Ref.: Howes M67; Sabin 43111 note

2589 McCOY, ISAAC

HISTORY OF BAPTIST INDIAN MISSIONS; EMBRACING REMARKS ON THE FORMER AND PRESENT CONDITION OF THE ABORIGINAL TRIBES; THEIR SETTLEMENT WITHIN THE INDIAN TERRITORY, AND THEIR FUTURE PROSPECTS . . . WASHINGTON: WILLIAM M. MORRISON, 1840.

[i–viii], [1]–611, [612 blank]. 21.6 x 13.5 cm. Rebound in contemporary half calf, dark red leather label, marbled edges.

Ref.: Clark III 69; Field 982; Howes M68; Rader 2285; Sabin 43112

McCoy's devotion to the Indians inspired a remarkable appreciation of their customs and characteristics.

2590 McCOY, ISAAC

[Wrapper title] . . . PERIODICAL ACCOUNT OF BAPTIST MISSIONS WITHIN THE INDIAN TERRITORY FOR THE YEAR ENDING DECEMBER 31, 1836 . . . SHAWANOE BAPTIST MISSION HOUSE, INDIAN TERRITORY: PUBLISHED BY ISAAC M'COY, 1837.

[1]–52. 23.7 x 14.4 cm. Blue printed wrappers, with title on front wrapper, verso of front wrapper with note explaining delay of publication, recto of back wrapper carries list of addresses for receipt of gifts, uncut. In a red cloth case.

Prov.: On front wrapper: Hon. Walter Coles / H. Reprs. Washington / D. C. /.

Ref.: Field 984; Howes M69; Jones 997; McMurtrie & Allen (*Meeker*) 56; Sabin 43113

2591 McCOY, ISAAC

REMARKS ON THE PRACTICABILITY OF INDIAN REFORM, EMBRACING THEIR COLONIZATION . . . BOSTON: PRINTED BY LINCOLN & EDMANDS, DECEMBER, 1827.

[1]–47, [48 blank]. 20.5 x 12.7 cm. Removed from bound volume, unbound.

Ref.: Field 985; Howes M70; Sabin 43113

Recommending reservations and education for Indians west of the Mississippi.

2592 [McCOY, ISAAC]

[Caption title] . . . REMOVE INDIANS WESTWARD.

[1]–23, [24 blank]. 22.8 x 14.2 cm. Newly stabbed, unbound. In green cloth slip case.

Ref.: Howes M71; Wagner-Camp 38

20th Congress, 2nd Session, House, Report No. 87, Serial 190. Imprint on page 23: [rule] / Gales & Seaton, Printers. /

Isaac McCoy's report, submitted by the Committee on Indian Affairs, occupies pages 5–23.

2593 [McCOY, ISAAC]

ANOTHER EDITION.

[1]–48. 23 x 14.5 cm. Stabbed, uncut, unopened. Two holes punched through inner margin.

Ref.: Howes M71; Wagner-Camp 38

20th Congress, 2nd Session, House, Report No. 87, Serial 190.

Imprint on page 48: [rule] / Gales & Seaton, / Printers to House of Reps. /

Isaac McCoy's report occupies pages 6–24 in this edition. Kennerly's and Hood's reports and the notes to accompany their map appear on pages 24–48.

2594 McCOY, JOSEPH G.

HISTORIC SKETCHES OF THE CATTLE TRADE OF THE WEST AND SOUTHWEST . . . KANSAS CITY, MO.: PUBLISHED BY RAMSEY, MILLETT & HUDSON, 1874.

[i–vi, vi blank], [1]–427, [428 blank], [1–24] advertisements. 21.8 x 14.8 cm. Illustrations (portraits & views) unlisted. Brown cloth, with head of Texas longhorn stamped on each cover, title in gilt on back cover, advertisements on inner covers.

Ref.: Adams (*Ramp. Herd*) 1385; Bay pp. 320, 398; Dobie p. 111; Howes M72; Jones 1571; Rader 2286

One of the most interesting and important books on the nineteenth-century cattle trade.

2595 McCRACKIN, JOSEPHINE (WOEMPNER) CLIFFORD

OVERLAND TALES . . . SAN FRANCISCO: A. ROMAN & CO., 1877.

[i]–[xii, xii blank], 13–383, [384 blank]. (Pages [1–2] blank.) 18.4 x 12.4 cm. Dark orange cloth, triple blind fillets on sides, title in gilt on backstrip.

Ref.: Munk (Alliot) p. 51

Includes an expedition across the Plains in the 1860's with adventures in Arizona and New Mexico.

2596 McCULLOCH, BENJAMIN

AUTOGRAPH LETTER, SIGNED. 1857 May 16, New Orleans. One page, 24.5 x 19.6 cm. To Jacob Thomson.

Declining to allow his name to be submitted to the President for an appointment as Governor of Utah.

Laid in Rose: *The Life and Services of Gen. Ben McCulloch* . . . 1888.

2597 McCULLOCH, HUGH

MEN AND MEASURES OF HALF A CENTURY . . . NEW YORK: CHARLES SCRIBNER'S SONS, 1888.

[i]–xxv, [xxvi blank], 1–542. 23.2 x 16 cm. Dark blue buckram, beveled covers.

Ref.: Nicholson p. 581 see

McCulloch was Secretary of the Treasury under Lincoln, Johnson, and Arthur.

2598 McDONALD, FRANK V.

NOTES PREPARATORY TO A BIOGRAPHY OF RICHARD HAYES McDONALD OF SAN FRANCISCO, CALIFORNIA . . . CAMBRIDGE: UNIVERSITY PRESS: JOHN WILSON AND SON, 1881.

[i]–[xxvi], 29–95, [96 blank], [1]–119, [120 blank]. 33.4 x 25.6 cm. 34 illustrations listed. Brown cloth, gilt, uncut.

Ref.: Cowan p. 406; Howes M82

Copy 1 of 150 copies printed. Only Volume I was published. It contains an overland narrative.

2599 MACDONALD, JAMES

FOOD FROM THE FAR WEST; OR, AMERICAN AGRICULTURE WITH SPECIAL REFERENCE TO THE BEEF PRODUCTION . . . LONDON: WILLIAM P. NIMMO, 1878.

[i]–xvi, [1]–331, [332 blank], 1–[4] advertisements. 19 x 12.5 cm. Orange cloth.

Ref.: Adams (*Ramp. Herd*) 1393

2600 McDONNELL, ALEXANDER

AUTOGRAPH LETTER, SIGNED. 1850 October 13, "Goodyears bar Yuba river 75 miles from the head of navigation". To Edward [McDonnell]. Four pages, 24.7 x 19.7 cm.

Regarding experiences with the Aldrich party overland to California.

2601 McDONNELL, ALEXANDER

AUTOGRAPH LETTER, SIGNED. 1850 November 25, "Rough & ready". To Edward [McDonnell]. Four pages, 25.4 x 20.1 cm.

Regarding experiences gold mining in California. In the letter is a pen and ink sketch of a riffle box and tom or, as the author calls it, "a long tome."

These two excellent letters accompany Lorenzo D. Aldrich: *A Journal . . . to California!* . . . 1851.

2602 McDOWELL, IRWIN

AUTOGRAPH LETTER, DRAFT. 1865 March 12. San Francisco. To Ulysses S. Grant. Eight pages, 25 x 22 cm.

An important letter relating to ex-Senator Gwin and his activities in Sonora, to the Naval situation in California waters, and to military affairs in California and the Southwest.

2603 McDOWELL, J.

AUTOGRAPH DOCUMENT, SIGNED. 1808 December 5, Staunton, [Va.?] One page, 18.7 x 15.3 cm. Account with Robert McKnight.

2604 McDUFFEE, JOHN

[Caption title] STATISTICAL INFORMATION ON CANALS AND RAILROADS . . .

[1]–8. Bound with Number 1084.

Ref.:

Neither place of publication nor date is indicated.

2605 McELRATH, THOMSON P.

THE YELLOWSTONE VALLEY. WHAT IT IS, WHERE IT IS, AND HOW TO GET TO IT. A HAND-BOOK FOR TOURISTS AND SETTLERS . . . ST. PAUL: THE PIONEER PRESS CO., 1880.

[1]–138, [139–42]. 18.8 x 13 cm. Illustrations unlisted, folding map: Map of the / Northern Pacific / Railroad, / and Connections. / [lower right corner:] Rand, McNally Co. Engr's, Chicago. / 13.6 x 44.7 cm. No scale indicated. Red cloth.

Ref.: Adams (*Ramp. Herd*) 1397; Howes M91; Smith 6320

One of the earliest adequate guides, written by a resident of the area.

2606 McEVOY, HENRY N.

1857. GALESBURG, MONMOUTH, KNOXVILLE AND ABINGDON DIRECTORIES. CONTAINING A FULL AND COMPLETE LIST OF THE HOUSEHOLDERS; TOGETHER WITH USEFUL INFORMATION RELATING TO EACH CITY; AND ADVERTISEMENTS OF THE PRINCIPAL BUSINESS HOUSES . . . CHICAGO: ROBERT FERGUS, 1857.

[i–iv], [1]–26, [29]–168. 18.9 x 11.4 cm. Pink printed boards, with title on front cover and advertisements on front cover and back, and on back, and on endpapers. New brown leather backstrip.

Ref.: AII (*Chicago*) 266; Byrd 2660

2607 McGAW, JAMES F.

PHILIP SEYMOUR; OR, PIONEER LIFE IN RICHLAND COUNTY, OHIO. FOUNDED ON FACTS . . . MANS-FIELD: PUBLISHED BY R. BRINKERHOFF, 1858.

[1]–40, 43–44, [41]–42, 47–48, [45]–46, 49–295, [296 vignette, 297–98 blank], [i–ii advertisements]. 20.3 x 13 cm. Three full-page plates and 22 vignettes. Brown cloth.

Ref.: Field 990; Howes M100; Sabin 43258; Thomson 753; Wright II 1616

A War of 1812 tale based in part on narratives collected by the author on his home grounds.

2608 McGEE, JOSEPH H.

STORY OF THE GRAND RIVER COUNTRY, 1821–1905. MEMOIRS OF MAJ. JOSEPH H. McGEE.*

[1–67, 68 blank]. 24.2 x 15.8 cm. Portrait. Brown printed wrappers. In a red cloth case.

Ref.: Howes M101

There is the following imprint on the verso of the title: The North Missourian Press / Gallatin, Missouri /. The volume was printed in 1909. The Preface is signed: Guy Blue / Gallatin, Missouri, Feb. 27, 1909. /

2609 McGILLIVRAY, DUNCAN

THE JOURNAL OF DUNCAN M'GILLIVRAY OF THE NORTH WEST COMPANY AT FORT GEORGE ON THE SASKATCHEWAN, 1794–5. [EDITED] BY ARTHUR S. MORTON . . . TORONTO: THE MACMILLAN COMPANY, MCMXXIX.*

[i]–lxxviii, [lxxix–lxxx blank], [1]–79, [80 blank]. 23.2 x 16 cm. Two maps. Red buckram, fore and lower edges uncut.

Ref.: Smith 6342

Limited edition for review.

2610 McGLASHAN, CHARLES F.

HISTORY OF THE DONNER PARTY. A TRAGEDY OF THE SIERRAS . . . TRUCKEE, CAL., PUBLISHED BY CROWLEY & McGLASHAN.

[1]–193, [194 blank]. 22.5 x 14.3 cm. Black embossed cloth, gilt title on backstrip. In a black half morocco case.

Prov.: W. J. Holliday copy, without identification.

Ref.: Blumann & Thomas 2208; Cowan p. 406; Howes M102; Rader 2295

Copyrighted 1879.

The ordeal of the Donner Party is one of the most memorable events in the history of overland narratives.

2611 McGOWAN, EDWARD

NARRATIVE OF EDWARD McGOWAN, INCLUDING A FULL ACCOUNT OF THE AUTHOR'S ADVENTURES AND PERILS WHILE PERSECUTED BY THE SAN FRANCISCO VIGILANCE COMMITTEE OF 1856 . . . SAN FRANCISCO: PUBLISHED BY THE AUTHOR, 1857.

[i]–viii, [9]–240. 18.8 x 11.7 cm. Seven full-page illustrations, unlisted. Buff printed wrappers with title on front wrapper. In a red cloth case.

Ref.: Adams 653; Blumann & Thomas 3287; Cowan p. 407; Howes M103; Sabin 43278; Wheat, Carl I., Calif. Hist. Soc. *Quarterly*, VI (1927), 4; Wheat (*Gold Rush*) 132

Ned McGowan, as his *Narrative* proves, and as Carl I. Wheat indicates in his continuation of the work, was a prime rascal, one of the truly colorful characters in California during the middle of the last century.

2612 MacGREGOR, JOHN

OUR BROTHERS AND COUSINS . . . LONDON: SEELEY, JACKSON, AND HALLIDAY, MDCCCLIX.

[i]–[xx, xx blank], [1]–156. 16 x 11 cm. Semi-limp green cloth, blind embossed borders on sides, title in gilt on front cover.

Ref.: Howes M105; Sabin 43290; Staton & Tremaine 3919

Tipped to the front endpaper are four pages of advertisements dated June, 1862. Numerous marginal notes in pencil throughout.

The author made a summer tour of Canada and the United States, Halifax to Niagara.

2613 McGUFFEY, WILLIAM H.

MCGUFFEY'S NEWLY REVISED THIRD READER . . . CINCINNATI: WINTHROP B. SMITH.

1–216. (Pages 1–2 advertisement.) 17.8 x 11.2 cm. Green printed boards with leather back-strip, title on front cover, advertisements on back cover.

Prov.: Signature of George M. Templeton on front flyleaf.

Ref.:

One of the innumerable reprints.

2614 McILHANY, EDWARD W.

RECOLLECTIONS OF A '49ER. A QUAINT AND THRILLING NARRATIVE OF A TRIP ACROSS THE PLAINS, AND LIFE IN THE CALIFORNIA GOLD FIELDS . . . KANSAS CITY, MISSOURI: HAILMAN PRINTING COMPANY, 1908.

[1]–212. 19.5 x 13.3 cm. Illustrations unlisted. Yellow pictorial cloth.

Ref.: Cowan p. 407; Howes M111; Hubach p. 109; Morgan (Pritchard) p. 186; Wheat (*Gold Rush*) 133

McIlhany was a member of the Charlestown Company.

2615 McILVAINE, WILLIAM, JR.

SKETCHES OF SCENERY AND NOTES OF PERSONAL ADVENTURE, IN CALIFORNIA AND MEXICO . . . PHILADELPHIA, 1850.*

[1]–44. 24.9 x 16.9 cm. Added title-page (described as plate x) and 16 plates. Purplish cloth, title in gilt on front cover, blind embossed borders on sides.

Prov.: With bookplate of George Bancroft.

Ref.: Bradford 3147; Cowan p. 408; Howes M112; Jones 1244; Rader 2297; Sabin 43328

The imprint on the verso of the title-page as follows: [rule] / E. B. Mears, Stereotyper. / Smith & Peters, Printers. / [rule] /.

2616 McINTIRE, JAMES

EARLY DAYS IN TEXAS; A TRIP TO HELL AND HEAVEN. KANSAS CITY, MO., MCINTIRE PUBLISHING COMPANY.*

[1]–229, [230 blank]. 19.4 x 13.3 cm. 16 illustrations, unlisted. Green pictorial cloth.

Ref.: Adams 655; Adams (*Ramp. Herd*) 1405; Howes M113; Rader 2298

Copyrighted 1902. The preface is signed James McIntyre, the title-page Jim McIntire, and the frontispiece portrait Jas. McIntire. An interesting rascal.

2617 MACK, ROBERT

KYLE STUART; WITH OTHER POEMS . . . VOL. 1. . . . COLUMBIA, T.: PRINTED FOR THE AUTHOR, BY FELIX K. ZOLLICOFFER. 1834.

[i]–[xvi], [1]–200. 17 x 11 cm. Old green boards, red morocco back, darker red label.

Ref.: AII (*Tennessee*) 539; Sabin 43346

All published.

2618 McKAY, ROBERT H.

LITTLE PILLS . . . BEING SOME EXPERIENCES OF A UNITED STATES ARMY MEDICAL OFFICER ON THE FRONTIER NEARLY A HALF CENTURY AGO. PITTS-BURG, KANSAS: PITTSBURG HEADLIGHT, 1918.*

[1]–127, [128 blank]. (Pages [1–2] blank.) 22 x 15.8 cm. Three illustrations, unlisted. Khaki cloth, title stamped in black on front cover.

Ref.: Howes M122; Rader 2305

Detailed pictures of life at Army posts in New Mexico, Colorado, Kansas, etc., after the Civil War.

On the title-page, in manuscript: Copyright /, probably in the hand of the author.

2619 McKEE, JAMES C.

[Wrapper title] NARRATIVE OF THE SURRENDER OF A COMMAND OF U.S. FORCES AT FORT FILLMORE, N.M. IN JULY, A.D. 1861, AT THE BREAKING OUT OF THE CIVIL WAR, BETWEEN THE NORTH AND THE SOUTH . . . PRESCOTT, A.T., MARCH, 1878.

[1]–15, [16 blank]. 20.2 x 12.7 cm. White printed wrappers, with title on front wrapper. Backstrip supplied, covers mounted on paper. In folding blue cloth box.

Prov.: Inscribed on front wrapper: To / Brig^d Genl A. H. Terry U.S.A. / with Compliments of the / Author /.

Ref.: AII (*Arizona*) see 25; Howes M125; Nicholson p. 586

Manuscript notes in pencil and some textual corrections, signed R. C. and R. Coruba.

AII (*Arizona*) 25 lists an unexamined edition of 1867 taken from Anderson Galleries catalogue 2315. This is a ghost. In the third edition,

McKee states he wrote the pamphlet in 1878, published a second edition in 1881, and the third edition in 1886.

Signed in manuscript on the last page of text, in the space left for the signature, James Cooper McKee /.

2620 McKEE, JAMES C.

[Wrapper title] THE SAME. SECOND EDITION, REVISED AND CORRECTED. NEW YORK: JANUARY, 1881.

[1]–30, [31–2 blank]. Wrappers included in pagination. 18.5 x 12.6 cm. Printed self wrappers, with title as above on page [1].

Prov.: Inscribed on front wrapper: To / Lieut. E. I. Anderson / 6th U.S. Cavalry / With the Sincere regards of the / Author / West Point / Feby 17/81 / [vertical bracket joins last two lines].

Ref.: Howes M125; Saunders 3026

The space left blank for the author's signature on page 30 is not filled in.

2621 McKEE, JAMES C.

THE SAME. BOSTON: PRINTED BY JOHN A. LOWELL & CO., 1886.

[1]–32. 28 x 22.3 cm. Two maps. Stapled, plain gray wrappers.

Ref.: Howes M125; Munk (Alliot) p.143; Nicholson p. 586; Saunders 3026

Limited to 300 copies.

In the Introductory, the author describes the history of writing and publishing the work. No mention is made of an 1867 edition.

2622 McKEE, JOHN

AUTOGRAPH LETTER, SIGNED. 1805 October 19, Chickasaws. Three pages, 25.6 x 20.6 cm. Silked. To James Wilkinson.

McKee hinted strongly in this letter that he would appreciate an appointment from Wilkinson, then Governor of Louisiana Territory.

2623 McKEE, JOHN

AUTOGRAPH LETTER, SIGNED. 1806 February 22, Chickasaw. One page, 31.9 x 21.9 cm. Silked. To James Wilkinson.

About his prospects for an appointment. The final paragraph: Has any news reached your capitol from Captains Lewis & Clark? it is rumored here that they have been killed, I hope sincerely there is nothing of it.

2624 McKEE, JOHN

AUTOGRAPH LETTER, SIGNED. 1806 December 26, Chickasaw Bluffs. One page, 25.2 x 20 cm. Silked. To James Wilkinson.

Season's greetings and encouragement for troubles ahead.

2625 McKEE, JOHN

AUTOGRAPH LETTER, SIGNED. 1807 January 25, Natchez. Two pages, 24.6 x 20.2 cm. Silked. To James Wilkinson.

McKee went to Natchez with an idea in mind that he might join Burr. In this letter he expressed his disillusionment about the scheme.

2626 McKEE, LANIER

THE LAND OF NOME. A NARRATIVE SKETCH OF THE RUSH TO OUR BERING SEA GOLDFIELDS, THE COUNTRY, ITS MINES AND ITS PEOPLE, AND THE HISTORY OF A GREAT CONSPIRACY 1900–1901 . . . NEW YORK: THE GRAFTON PRESS.

[i]–[xii, xii blank], 1–260. 18.5 x 12.7 cm. Dark blue cloth, fore and lower edges uncut.

Prov.: Inscribed on front fly-leaf: To / Francis W. Stearns, Esq. / with the Compliments of / Lanier McKee /.

Ref.: Smith 6369; Wickersham 1541

Copyrighted 1902.

2627 McKEITH, GEORGE R.

[Wrapper title] PIONEER STORIES OF THE PIONEERS OF FILLMORE AND ADJOINING COUNTIES . . . EXETER, NEBRASKA: FILLMORE COUNTY NEWS.*

[1–60]. 21.3 x 14.7 cm. Illustrations unlisted, included in pagination. Gray printed wrappers, with title on front wrapper.

Ref.:

Copyrighted 1915.

2628 McKENNEY, THOMAS L.

MEMOIRS, OFFICIAL AND PERSONAL; WITH SKETCHES OF TRAVELS AMONG THE NORTHERN AND SOUTHERN INDIANS; EMBRACING A WAR EXCURSION, AND DESCRIPTIONS OF SCENES ALONG THE WESTERN BORDERS . . . NEW YORK: PAINE AND BURGESS, 1846.

[i]–viii, [17]–340, [i]–vi, [9]–136. 23.1 x 14.6 cm. 13 illustrations, including one plate in color, all except three being by F. O. C. Darley. Two volumes in one, dark green cloth, blind panels on sides, gilt backstrip, with title on backstrip, gilt edges.

Prov.: Inscribed on the front fly-leaf: From the author, (with / his respects and best / wishes) to M^{r.s} Col^l Ja^s Watson Webb. / N. York, December 1846 /.

Ref.: Clark III 70; Howes M130; Hubach p. 63; Rader 2313; Sabin 43403

Howes calls for 12 plates, but 13 is correct.

2629 McKENNEY, WILLIAM

LETTER, SIGNED. 1825 June 3, Department of War, Office of Indian Affairs. One page, 14.5 x 19.7 cm. To Thomas Mather. In Mather Papers.

Appointment as Commissioner of the Santa Fé Road Commission.

2630 MACKENZIE, SIR ALEXANDER

VOYAGES FROM MONTREAL, ON THE RIVER ST. LAURENCE, THROUGH THE CONTINENT OF NORTH AMERICA, TO THE FROZEN AND PACIFIC OCEANS; IN THE YEARS 1789 AND 1793. WITH A PRELIMINARY ACCOUNT OF THE RISE, PROGRESS, AND PRESENT STATE OF THE FUR TRADE OF THAT COUNTRY . . . LONDON: PRINTED FOR T. CADELL, JUN. AND W. DAVIES, M.DCCC.I.

[*]², A⁴, a–q⁴, r², B–3G⁴. [1–4], [i]–viii, [i]–cxxxii, [1]–412, [413–414 errata], [415–16 blank]. 28.7 x 22.1 cm. Frontispiece portrait and three folding maps: Map: A Map of America, / between Latitudes 40 and 70 North, and Longitudes 45 and 180 West, / Exhibiting Mackenzie's Track / From Montreal to Fort Chipewyan & from thence to the North Sea / In 1789, & to the West Pacific Ocean in 1793. / [below border:] London. Published 15 Oct. 1801, by Alexander MacKenzie Nº 38 Norfolk Street Strand. / 44.1 x 77.4 cm. No scale given. Map: A Map of / Mackenzie's Track / from / Fort Chipewyan / to the / North Sea, / in 1789. / [at foot below border: imprint as above]. 59.5 x 55.8 cm. No scale given. Map: A Map of / MacKenzie's Track, / from / Fort Chipewyan / to the / Pacific Ocean / in 1793. / [below border: same imprint as above, except Norflk for Norfolk]. 55.8 x 60.1 cm. No scale given. Gray boards, with printed paper label, 3.8 x 4 cm. In a green half morocco case.

Prov.: The Herschel V. Jones copy.

Ref.: Field 967; Howes M133; Jones 682; Sabin 43414; Smith 6382; Staton & Tremaine 658; Wagner-Camp 1

Mackenzie's narrative is of consummate importance in the Literature of Transcontinental Travel. It is the first account of an ocean to ocean crossing of the North American continent. Mackenzie's account of the fur trade is of almost equal interest.

2631 MACKENZIE, ALEXANDER

THE SAME. PHILADELPHIA: PUBLISHED BY JOHN MORGAN, 1802.

[A]–Ii⁴. [1–8], [i]–viii, [i]–cxxvi, [1]–113, [114 blank]. [*]¹, Kk–3X⁴. [i–ii], [115]–392, [393–94 blank]. 23 x 13.8 cm. Frontispiece portrait and three maps. Portrait and maps identical with first edition. Two volumes, gray boards with white paper backstrips, original printed labels, 4.6 x 3.2 cm., uncut.

Ref.: Field 968; Howes M133; Sabin 43415; Smith 6383; Wagner-Camp 1

Editions: London, 1801.

2632 McKNIGHT, GEORGE S.

CALIFORNIA 49ER . . . TRAVELS FROM PERRYSBURG TO CALIFORNIA.*

[1]–[28]. 19.7 x 13.8 cm. Vignette on page [28]. Red printed wrapper with title on front wrapper.

Ref.: Howes M145

The front wrapper is dated in the upper left corner 1903. The following imprint appears at the foot of the wrapper: Published by / Capt. Geo. S. McKnight, / Perrysburg, Ohio. /

McKnight's narrative includes an overland journey via Texas to Mazatlan and from that place to San Francisco by steamer.

2633 [McKNIGHT, ROBERT]

AUTOGRAPH MANUSCRIPT, Journal from Urbana to Louisiana /. Ten pages, 6 x 10 cm. Loose leaves laid in contemporary blue paper wrappers, manuscript title on front wrapper: Day Book /.

Urbana in this case is the Urbana in Champaign County, Ohio. The author went overland, instead of by river, having crossed the Ohio at Cincinnati. The date 1811 appears in the first line.

Published in *Journal of the Illinois Historical Society*, Vol. 36, No 2, June, 1943, as an "unidentified traveler" (pages [208]–210). In the December, 1943, issue of the *Journal* EDG corrected this to "probably McKnight," page [408].

2634 McKNIGHT, ROBERT

AUTOGRAPH MANUSCRIPT DOCUMENT, SIGNED. 1810 January 30, no place. One page, 11.6 x 19.5 cm. Account of Mr. Walsh with McKnight.

2635 McKNIGHT, ROBERT

AUTOGRAPH LETTER, SIGNED. 1811 May 27, no place. One page, 33 x 19.5 cm. To James McKnight.

Regarding his financial troubles—which seem to have been constant.

2636 McKNIGHT, ROBERT, PAPERS

A COLLECTION OF TWELVE FRAGMENTS of poetry, miscellaneous manuscript notes, etc. Various sizes, oblong small 8vo to folio.

2637 McKNIGHT & BRADY

MANUSCRIPT DOCUMENT, SIGNED McKnight & Brady. 1812 May 19, St. Louis. One page, 21.5 x 19 cm. To M. McDonogh. Account for goods purchased for trade in the Southwest.

2638 McKNIGHT & BRADY

MANUSCRIPT LETTER, SIGNED McKnight & Brady. 1812 May 21, St. Louis. Two pages, 25 x 19.8 cm. To M. McDonogh. Regarding business and the Santa Fé trade.

2639 McLAUGHLIN, JAMES

MY FRIEND THE INDIAN . . . BOSTON: HOUGHTON MIFFLIN COMPANY, 1910.

[i]–[xiv, xiv blank], 1–[417], [418 colophon]. 20.8 x 14.7 cm. 16 illustrations listed; an extra-illustration inserted facing page 1. Red half morocco, gilt top, uncut.

Prov.: The provenance is puzzling. On the title-page there is the following note in pencil: M. William. Bradley. / Philadelphia. / [flourish] / [sketch of teepee with F above door] / Dan Frost / New York / N.Y. / [Below centre of title:] "The class of men selected by the Government for Indian Agents / have always been a scandal." / Col. Dodge "Our Wild Indians." (1890.) / Throughout the volume, there are critical marginal comments in the same handwriting disputing statements by the author; some of them are initialed D.F. Laid in is a trade card of S. A. Frost's Son, / Beads and all other Goods for Indian Trade, 33 Howard Street, / New York. / Dan Frost /.

Ref.: Howes M147; Rader 2317

2640 McLEAN, JOHN

NOTES OF A TWENTY-FIVE YEARS' SERVICE IN THE HUDSON'S BAY TERRITORY . . . LONDON: RICHARD BENTLEY, 1849.

[i]–xii, [13]–308. [i]–[viii blank], [9]–328. 19.5 x 12.1 cm. Two volumes, brown cloth. In a brown cloth case.

Ref.: Field 996; Smith 6418; Staton & Tremaine 2729; Wagner-Camp 169

2641 McLEAN, JOHN

[Broadside] REMARKS OF JUDGE McLEAN, AT THE FORMER TRIAL . . .

Broadside, 22.3 x 12.9 cm. Text, 16 x 9 cm. Bound with related materials in black half calf.

Ref.:

Neither place nor date is indicated, but undoubtedly printed in Chicago in 1859.

See under ILLINOIS CENTRAL RAILROAD COMPANY.

2642 McMASTER, S. W.

60 YEARS ON THE UPPER MISSISSIPPI. MY LIFE AND EXPERIENCES . . . ROCK ISLAND, ILLINOIS, 1893.

[i–iv], [1]–300. 17.9 x 12.1 cm. Maroon wrappers, with title stamped in gold on front wrapper. In a brown half levant morocco case.

Ref.: Howes M169

The printer's introduction is signed J. B. Brown and is dated from Galena, Ill., Nov. 30, 1895.

Covers a long life in Galena, Rock Island, St. Louis, Wisconsin, Illinois, Iowa, and Minnesota—all along the Mississippi River. Although the work is dated 1893 on title-page and front cover, events in 1894 are mentioned.

2643 McMECHEN, EDGAR C.

LIFE OF GOVERNOR EVANS, SECOND TERRITORIAL GOVERNOR OF COLORADO . . .

[i]–x, [1]–224. 19.4 x 13.4 cm. 16 illustrations listed. Black fabrikoid.

Ref.: Howes M170; Wilcox p. 74

Copyrighted 1924. The printer's imprint on the verso of the half-title reads: The Wahlgren Publishing Company, Denver, Colo. / Only a few copies were printed for the Evans family and their friends.

2644 McNAIR, A.

AUTOGRAPH LETTER, SIGNED. 1812 May 21, St. Louis. Three pages, 31.5 x 19.7 cm. To James Baird.

On financial matters.

2645 McNAMARA, JOHN

IN PERILS BY MINE OWN COUNTRYMEN. THREE YEARS ON THE KANSAS BORDER . . . NEW YORK: MILLER, ORTON & MULLIGAN, 1856.

[i]–viii, 9–240. 18.6 x 11.9 cm. Dark purple cloth, blind embossed sides, title in gilt on backstrip.

Ref.: Howes M175

McNamara's career in Kansas was a stormy one.

2646 McNAUGHTON, MARGARET

OVERLAND TO CARIBOO. AN EVENTFUL JOURNEY OF CANADIAN PIONEERS TO THE GOLD-FIELDS OF BRITISH COLUMBIA IN 1862 . . . TORONTO: WILLIAM BRIGGS, 1896.

[i]–[xviii, xviii blank], [19]–176. 18.2 x 12.2 cm. 41 illustrations listed. Red pictorial cloth.

Ref.: Smith 6461

2647 MACOMB, JOHN N.

... REPORT OF THE EXPLORING EXPEDITION FROM SANTA FE, NEW MEXICO, TO THE JUNCTION OF THE GRAND AND GREEN RIVERS OF THE GREAT COLORADO OF THE WEST, IN 1859 ... WASHINGTON: GOVERNMENT PRINTING OFFICE, 1876.

[i]–vii, [viii blank], [1]–152. 29.4 x 23.3 cm. 22 plates, 11 in color, listed, folding map. Brown cloth.

Ref.: Howes M179; Munk (Alliot) p. 144; Saunders 3030; Wagner-Camp 377

2648 McPHERSON, WILLIAM G.

[Newspaper articles mounted in bound volume] JOURNAL OF OVERLAND TRAVEL KEPT BY WILLIAM GREGG McPHERSON ... [typed:] ORANGE, CALIF. NEWS AUG. 6–12, 1937.

[1]–48. (Pagination 3–48 stamped in blue.) Columns of newsprint about 16 cm. on leaves 21.5 x 15.4 cm. Portrait. Blue boards, black cloth back, title stamped in gilt on backstrip.

Ref.:

Apparently prepared for distribution in this form. The text comprises one of McPherson's diaries covering his overland journey from Oregon, Ogle County, Illinois, to Downieville, California, in the spring of 1859, by way of Fort Kearney, Fort Laramie, the Sweet Water, Sublette's Cut-off, Lawson's Meadows, Honey Lake Valley, etc. The original intention was to head for Pike's Peak, but discouraging news sent the party to California instead.

2649 McREYNOLDS, ROBERT

AUTOGRAPH LETTER, SIGNED. 1895 February 4, Guthrie, Oklahoma Territory. To General Leonard Wright Colby. One page, 26.6 x 20.2 cm.

WITH:

AUTOGRAPH LETTER, SIGNED. 1895 February 12, Guthrie, Oklahoma Territory. To General Leonard Wright Colby. Two pages, 20.6 x 20.2 cm.

An uncommonly interesting pair of letters in which McReynolds offers his services and one hundred men for a campaign against Mexico. "I can promise that they will sack every Cathedral in the enemy's country and fill their haversacks with little gold Jesuses." Laid in McReynolds: *Thirty Years on the Frontier* ... 1906.

2650 McREYNOLDS, ROBERT

THIRTY YEARS ON THE FRONTIER ... COLORADO SPRINGS: EL PASO PUBLISHING CO., 1906.*

[i–viii], [1]–256. 18.5 x 12.9 cm. 11 illustrations listed. Red cloth.

Ref.: Adams 664; Adams (*Ramp. Herd*) 1423; Howes M186; Rader 2325

Laid in are two Autograph Letters, signed, by the author to General Leonard Wright Colby, February 4 and 12, 1895.

2651 McWILLIAMS, JOHN

RECOLLECTONS[!] OF JOHN McWILLIAMS HIS YOUTH EXPERIENCES IN CALIFORNIA AND THE CIVIL WAR.*

[i–vi, vi blank], 1–186. 22.8 x 15 cm. Portrait. Blue cloth, gilt top, uncut.

Ref.: Cowan p. 410; Howes M194

Printed at the Princeton University Press in 1919.

The author traveled overland to Oregon in 1849.

2652 [MADDOX, JOHN]

THE RICHMOND DIRECTORY, REGISTER AND ALMANAC, FOR THE YEAR 1819. RICHMOND: PUBLISHED BY JOHN MADDOX, 1819.

[*]², A–C⁶, [†]¹, D–G⁶. [1]–76, [1–12]. (Leaf inserted between pages 40 and 41, unsigned, printed on recto only.) Gray-blue boards, new calf back, red leather label.

Ref.: Bradford 3170; Howes M197; Shaw & Shoemaker 49292

The first Richmond directory.

2653 MADISONIAN, THE

[Caption title] THE MADISONIAN. WASHINGTON CITY, D. C., FEBRUARY 5TH, 1844. PUBLISHED BY JOHN B. JONES. CORRESPONDENCE OF THE MADISONIAN. HOUSTON, (TEXAS,) JANUARY 2D, 1844. ...

[1]–[8, 8 blank]. 21.9 x 13.7 cm. Bound in Fisher, George: *Memorials* ... Houston, 1840.

Ref.:

Pages [1]–3 comprise notes on the annexation of Texas, page [4] is blank, pages [5]–7 comprise a reprint from *The Panama Echo*, page [8] is blank.

2654 MADOX, D. T.

LATE ACCOUNT OF THE MISSOURI TERRITORY, COMPILED FROM NOTES TAKEN DURING A TOUR THROUGH THAT COUNTRY IN 1815, AND A TRANSLATION OF LETTERS FROM A DISTINGUISHED FRENCH EMIGRANT, WRITTEN IN 1817 ... PARIS KY.: PRINTED FOR THE AUTHOR, BY JOHN LYLE. 1817.

[A]–E⁶, F⁴. [i]–[x, x blank], [11]–[66], [67–8 blank]. (Page 12 mispaginated 2.) 22.5 to 23 x 14.2 to 15.3 cm. Stabbed, uncut. In a blue half morocco case.

Prov.: Inscribed on title-page: N° 2 / William

Gellibrand / [and in another hand:] Ny: Hist. Society / Shaws. / The last word probably refers to Shawnee Indians mentioned in text. Herschel V. Jones copy.

Ref.: AII (*Kentucky*) 653; Bradford 3170; Howes M206; Jones 789; Rader 2330; Sabin 49589; Shaw & Shoemaker 41329

Madox's pamphlet is one of the earliest works to give any considerable account of the parts of the Louisiana Territory south of the Missouri River.

2655   MAGAZINE OF TRAVEL

VOL. I]. JANUARY, 1857. [NO. 1. MAGAZINE OF TRAVEL; A WORK DEVOTED TO ORIGINAL TRAVELS, IN VARIOUS COUNTRIES, BOTH OF THE OLD WORLD AND THE NEW . . . DETROIT: PRINTED BY H. BARNS, 1857.

[I]–VI, [7]–528, [513]–528, [545]–576. 21.3 x 14 cm. 12 numbers bound together in contemporary marbled boards, blue cloth back and corners.

Ref.: Howes T333; Sabin 43812; Wagner-Camp 183 note

Each of the twelve numbers has a caption title including number and date. The February number is incorrectly numbered: No. 1. Page 515 is mispaginated 415. No more published.

Sketches of Border Life. / By a Civil Engineer. / running through the volume appears in the second edition (Detroit, 1858) as "Sketches of Border Life, or Incidents of a Railroad Survey across the Prairies of Iowa, by W. P. Isham." The volume also contains G. Hathaway: "Travels in the South-West."

On the title-page, Warren Isham and W. Parsons Isham are described as "Conductors" of the journal.

2656   MAGOFFIN, SUSAN SHELBY

DOWN THE SANTA FE TRAIL AND INTO MEXICO. THE DIARY OF SUSAN SHELBY MAGOFFIN 1846–1847. EDITED BY STELLA M. DRUMM . . . NEW HAVEN: YALE UNIVERSITY PRESS, MDCCCCXXVI.*

[i]–xxv, [xxvi blank], 1–294. 23.5 x 15.4 cm. Eight illustrations listed. Dark blue cloth. In dust jacket.

Ref.: Howes M211; Hubach p. 104; Matthews p. 304; Rader 2331

One of the great Santa Fé Trail diaries.

2657   MAGRUDER, ALLAN B.

POLITICAL, COMMERCIAL AND MORAL REFLECTIONS, ON THE LATE CESSION OF LOUISIANA TO THE UNITED STATES . . . LEXINGTON: PRINTED BY D. BRADFORD, 1803.

[A]–Aa^alternately 4 and 2, Bb⁴. [i]–ix, [x blank], [11]–150, [151–52 blank]. 18.3 x 11.4 cm. Calf.

Ref.: AII (*Kentucky*) 185; Howes M215; Sabin 43848; Shaw & Shoemaker 4578

One of the earliest works discussing the Louisiana Purchase.

2658   MAGUIRE, HENRY N.

[Caption title] THE LAKESIDE LIBRARY. THE PEOPLE'S EDITION OF THE BLACK HILLS AND AMERICAN WONDERLAND. CHICAGO: DONNELLEY, LOYD & CO., 1877.

[277]–312. 30.8 x 20.4 cm. 27 illustrations in text and a full-page map. Map: Map of the / Black Hills. / [below neat line:] Drawn and Engraved expressly for The Lakeside Library, from the latest Surveys and Explorations. / 25.5 x 17.5 cm. Scale: 72 miles to one inch. Bound into pale green buckram, green skiver label on backstrip.

Ref.: Bradford 3172; Howes 6599; Jennewein 39

The late Mr. Thomas E. Donnelley, then chairman of the Board of R. R. Donnelley & Sons, told me that The Lakeside Library was issued irregularly, sometimes once a week and sometimes once in three months. Almost uniformly they were reprints of standard authors. In fact, after reading a list of titles, I could find no other original work. The Lakeside Press Memorial Library does not have a copy of this work.—EDG

2659   MAGUIRE, HENRY N.

THE COMING EMPIRE. A COMPLETE AND RELIABLE TREATISE ON THE BLACK HILLS, YELLOWSTONE AND BIG HORN REGIONS . . . SIOUX CITY, IOWA: WATKINS & SMEAD, 1878.

[2]–177, [1–12 advertisements]. (Even pagination of text on rectos.) 16.5 x 12.5 cm. Seven plates, illustrations in text, and folding map. Folding map: [Map of Lawrence, Pennington, and Custer Counties and surrounding territory] Designed and Compiled / by / Samuel Scott. / Expressly for the coming Empire / Scale 10 Miles to one inch. / Copyright Secured 1878 C. F. Cram Lith, Chicago, Ill. / 41.3 x 45.4 cm. Scale as above. Maroon cloth with title in gilt on front cover.

Ref.: Howes M218; Jennewein 41; Smith 6483

The author had visited all the regions he described in this book. He reported first-hand information about the history and current conditions in the Black Hills.

2660 [MAGUIRE, HENRY N.]

NEW MAP AND GUIDE TO DAKOTA, AND THE BLACK HILLS. GIVING MINING LAWS, DESCRIPTION OF THE COUNTRY, ROUTES, SORT OF OUTFITS, ETC., ETC. CHICAGO: RAND, McNALLY & CO.

[1]–86, [87–90 advertisements]. 21.5 x 14.6 cm. Six full-page plates, illustrations in text, and two maps. Map at front: Rand, McNally & Co.'s Map / —of the— / Northern Portion / of the / Black Hills / Showing all Prominent / Gold and Silver Quartz Lodes. / Compiled from actual survey and Observation by Geo. Henckel, U. S. Deputy Surveyor. / 1877. / Copyright secured by Rand, McNally & Co., Chicago, / [Line of advertising below border.] 44.7 x 58.6 cm. (border). No scale given. Map at back: Rand, McNally & Co.'s United States Map, Showing Location of Black Hills. / [Line of advertising below map.] 31.2 x 48.5 cm. Scale: 170 miles to one inch. Yellow pictorial wrappers with title on front wrapper against a large view, advertisement on back wrapper. In a blue cloth case.

Ref.: Howes M220; Jennewein 38
Dated on front wrapper 1878.

2661 MAHAN, PHINEAS J.

[Wrapper title] REMINISCENCES OF THE WAR FOR TEXAS INDEPENDENCE. A NARATIVE[!] OF SOME OF THE THRILLING ADVENTURES, MARVELOUS ESCAPES FROM DEATH, AND TERRIBLE SUFFERINGS OF A FEW OF THOSE NOBLE SOULS WHO MADE TEXAS FREE . . .

[1]–9, [10 blank]. 21 x 13.5 cm. Blue printed wrappers, with title as above.

Ref.: Clements Library (*Texas*) 45
Published (probably at Houston, Texas) after May 3, 1875, the date of the author's death which is mentioned on page 6. Although these reminiscences, written long after the events, tell the story of cruel forced marches and brutal treatment of captives, there are some new twists. Mahan tells of the Mexican method of tying fourteen men together and marching them for five days without food, and of being threatened with execution five times, etc. He was captured near San Patricio on February 27, 1836, and spent eleven months at Matamoras. In later years, he lived in Houston where he kept bees and was a gardener.

2662 MAHIN, JOHN, *Compiler*

MUSCATINE CITY DIRECTORY AND ADVERTISER, FOR 1856: CONTAINING A HISTORY OF THE CITY AND COUNTY . . . MUSCATINE: PRINTED AT THE "ENQUIRER" OFFICE, 1856.

[1–4], [i]–xl (advertisements on pink, green gray, yellow, and white), [5]–80. 17.9 x 10.8 cm.

Gray printed boards, black roan back, with title on front cover, advertisement on back cover. New backstrip.

Prov.: Paullin copy.

Ref.: Howes M222; Moffit 253; Paullin 1616
There is an unnumbered leaf, broadside, 11.9 x 10.6 cm., inserted opposite page 33 regarding the "First Presbyterian Church—(New School)" which was not included in the text. Some marginal notes, newspaper clippings tipped in.

First history and first directory of Muscatine.

2663 MAILLARD, N. DORAN

THE HISTORY OF THE REPUBLIC OF TEXAS, FROM THE DISCOVERY OF THE COUNTRY TO THE PRESENT TIME; AND THE CAUSE OF HER SEPARATION FROM THE REPUBLIC OF MEXICO . . . LONDON: SMITH, ELDER, AND CO., 1842.

[i]–xxiv, [1]–512. 21.9 x 14.1 cm. Map: A / New Map of / Texas, / 1841. / [lower right corner:] Day & Haghe Lith^{rs} to the Queen / 41.8 x 38.2 cm. Scale: about 72 miles to one inch. Dark blue cloth, blind embossed sides, title in gilt on backstrip, uncut.

Ref.: Howes M225; Raines p. 144; Streeter 1422
Texas cut down to size—a difficult feat even in 1842.

2664 MAJORS, ALEXANDER

SEVENTY YEARS ON THE FRONTIER . . . WITH A PREFACE BY "BUFFALO BILL" (GENERAL W. F. CODY) . . . CHICAGO: RAND, McNALLY & COMPANY, 1893.

[1]–325, [326 blank, 327–28 advertisements]. 18.8 x 13.2 cm. Illustrations unlisted. Blue cloth.

Prov.: Inscribed on the recto of the frontispiece (first three lines in one hand, signature in a different hand): Presented with / Compliments / of the Author / Alexander Majors /.

Ref.: Bradford 3185; Cowan p. 412; Dobie p. 79; Edwards p. 109; Howes 6614; Malone p. 6; Munk (Alliot) p. 144; Rader 2334; Saunders 3031; Smith 6488; Wagner-Camp 359 note
Possibly a special edition for presentation, since the page size is slightly larger and the quality of paper somewhat better than other copies examined.

2665 MALAN, HENRI ABRAHAM CESAR

THE SWISS PEASANT . . . PARK HILL: MISSION PRESS, 1848.

[1]–24. 12.8 x 7.7 cm. Bound with Number 1278.

Ref.: Hargrett (*Oklahoma*) 127
Text in Sequoyan.

2666 MALLANDAINE, EDWARD

FIRST VICTORIA DIRECTORY; COMPRISING A GEN-
ERAL DIRECTORY OF CITIZENS . . . PRECEDED BY A
PREFACE AND SYNOPSIS OF THE COMMERCIAL
PROGRESS OF THE COLONIES OF VANCOUVER ISLAND
AND BRITISH COLUMBIA . . . VICTORIA, V. I.: PUB-
LISHED BY EDW. MALLANDAINE & CO., MARCH,
1860.

[1]–[54], [55–8]. (Pages [1] and [58] pasted to
covers, pages [2] and [57] advertisements, all on
green paper.) 22.6 x 14.2 cm. Printed white
boards, black leather back, advertisements on
front and back covers.

Ref.: Greenwood 1395; Smith 2354

Printed at the Commercial Printing Establishment, San Francisco. Although the title-page
states the work is illustrated, the only pictorial
matter appears in the advertisements. Pages [3]–
8 and 53–[54] are printed on pale green paper as
are pages [1–2], [57–8]; pages [55–6] are printed
on bright yellow paper.

Some copies are known with 84 pages, the
additional section being headed: San Francisco
Department.

2667 [MALTBY, WILLIAM J.]

CAPTAIN JEFF; OR, FRONTIER LIFE IN TEXAS WITH
THE TEXAS RANGERS . . . COLORADO, TEX.: WHIP-
KEY PRINTING CO. 1906.

[1]–161, [162 blank]. 20.7 x 14.5 cm. Three illustrations. Red cloth, title stamped in gilt on front
cover.

Ref.: Dobie p. 60; Howes M243; Rader 2340
see

Howes' collation calls for 166 pages. There is
also a later printing with the same date and imprint comprising 204 pages. Possibly the present
example is an earlier printing.

2668 MANDAT-GRANCEY, BARON ED-
MOND DE

LA BRECHE AUX BUFFLES . . . PARIS: LIBRAIRIE
PLON, 1889.

[I]–XVI, 1–292, 1–4 advertisements on yellow
paper, [1]–[8] advertisements on pink paper.
18.6 x 12 cm. Illustrations unlisted. White
printed wrappers with title on front wrapper,
advertisements on back wrapper. In a blue cloth
case.

Ref.: Adams 666; Adams (*Ramp. Herd*) 1436;
Dobie p. 100; Howes M245; Jennewein 156;
Monaghan 1017

There is a brief summary of Billy the Kid's
exploits in the Lincoln County War on pages
76–81.

2669 MANDAT-GRANCEY, BARON ED-
MOND DE

DANS LES MONTAGNES ROCHEUSES . . . PARIS:
LIBRAIRIE PLON, 1884.

[i–iv], [1]–[315], [316 blank]. 17.4 x 11 cm. Nine
illustrations and one folding map listed. Blue
half morocco, red leather label, red top.

Ref.: Adams 665; Adams (*Ramp. Herd*) 1435;
Dobie pp. 99–100; Howes M246; Jennewein
157; Monaghan 1012

2670 MANLY, WILLIAM L.

DEATH VALLEY IN '49 . . . SAN JOSE, CAL.: THE
PACIFIC TREE AND VINE CO., 1894.

[1]–498. 19.4 x 13.5 cm. Portrait and three illustrations, unlisted. Mustard cloth, with title and
decorative bands in black on front cover and in
blind on back cover, title in gilt on backstrip.

Ref.: Bradford 3190; Blumann & Thomas
1003; Cowan p. 412; Edwards pp. 110–11;
Howes M255; Wheat (*Gold Rush*) 136; Wheat
(*Transmississippi*) III 103, 282

Mounted on front endleaf is an original manuscript, a schematic view of part of Death Valley, in pencil, tinted, by W. L. Manly, with nine
points located and identified in a marginal note.
17.5 x 25.2 cm. Inscribed in pencil: W. L. Manly
made this map / for E. L. Williams Sept.
1897— /. Mounted on the recto of the frontispiece leaf is part of a blueprint map of Death
Valley on which is traced Manly's route.
18.4 x 11.9 cm. On the facing blank page is the
following note by Williams (in ink): .... / Indicates the Manly route as described by / himself at the office of E. L. Williams Oct. 26th
1896 / in Santa Cruz— / [and in pencil:] Map
was copied from the U. S. Gov^t survey— /
E L W has been to Death Valley and / across the
Mohave Desert— /.

Inscribed in pencil on the verso of the front
endleaf: Please / Return this Book / to / E. L.
Williams / Santa Cruz /. Inscribed on the recto
of the initial blank leaf, in pencil: E L Williams— / Purchased of the Author at / Santa
Cruz in October 1896— /

2671 MANN, DONALD

MEMORIAL OF DONALD MANN CONCERNING ABUSES
IN THE DEMOINE[!] NAVIGATION & RAILROAD COM-
PANY . . . IOWA CITY. CRUM & BOYE, 1856.

[1]–8. 22 x 14.1 cm. Folded leaflet, unbound,
unopened.
Ref.:

2672 MAP OF DAKOTA

[Map] MAP OF DAKOTA. / [at foot, left:] COPY-RIGHT, 1883, BY RAND, MCNALLY & CO., MAP PUB-LISHERS, CHICAGO. / [centre:] DAKOTA CITY. / [at right:] RAND, MCNALLY & CO., MAP PUBLISHERS AND ENGRAVERS, CHICAGO. / [seven lines of advertising] / HALE & CAMMANN, AGENTS, MITCHELL, DAKOTA. HALE & WRIGHT, PROPRIETORS OF DA-KOTA CITY TOWNSITE. /

Map, 63.5 x 48.4 cm. Page size: 71.7 x 53.2 cm.

Ref.:

The town of Dakota City was platted in May, 1883 and "had a boom that surprises everybody who visits it."

2673 MAP OF THE SOUTHERN PART OF TEXAS

[Map] MAP OF THE SOUTHERN PART OF TEXAS / [lower centre:] E. S. MESIER, LITH. NEW YORK. /

Map, 32.1 x 45.6 cm. Scale: 40 miles to one inch.

Ref.: Phillips (*Maps*) p. 843; Streeter 1137A

An early and very rare map. Streeter suggests 1833 as the date of publication.

2674 MARCY, RANDOLPH B.

BORDER REMINISCENCES . . . NEW YORK: HARPER & BROTHERS, 1872.

[i]–[xii, xii blank], [13]–396, [1]–8 advertisements. (Pages [i–ii] blank and frontispiece.) 18.8 x 12.3 cm. 17 illustrations, text and full-page, listed. Purple cloth, gilt design and fillet on front cover, blind fillets and monogram on back cover, gilt title on backstrip, beveled covers.

Ref.: Howes M275; Munk (Alliot) p. 146; Rader 2345; Sabin 44511 see; Smith 6508

Mostly humor—military, western humor.

Pasted to front blank leaf is an Autograph Letter, signed, by the author. 1872 January 18, Washington City. One page, 20.2 x 12.8 cm. To Col. J. W. Forney. Asking for three copies of the Philadelphia *Press*.

Mounted on the verso of the front endleaf is the complimentary notice about the book which appeared in the *Press*.

Marcy had a scientific mind and a high sense of values. He knew how to write and what he wrote remains informing and pleasant.—Dobie

Editions: New York, 1871 (noted only by Howes and Sabin).

2675 MARCY, RANDOLPH B.

. . . EXPLORATION OF THE RED RIVER OF LOUISIANA, IN THE YEAR 1852; BY RANDOLPH B. MARCY, . . . ASSISTED BY GEORGE B. MCCLELLAN, . . . WITH REPORTS ON THE NATURAL HISTORY OF THE COUNTRY, AND NUMEROUS ILLUSTRATIONS. WASHINGTON: ROBERT ARMSTRONG, PUBLIC PRINTER, 1853.

[i]–[xvi, xvi blank], [1]–320. 21.8 x 13.9 cm. 65 illustrations and a map, listed. Map: Map / of the / Country between the Frontiers / of / Arkansas and New Mexico / embracing the section explored in 1849. 50. 51. & 52, / By / Capt R. B. Marcy 5th U. S. Infy / under orders from the / War Department. / Also a continuation of the emigrant road from Fort Smith and Fulton / down the Valley of the Gila. / [thick, thin, thin rules] / Ackerman Lith 379 Broadway N. Y. / 69.3 x 150.5 cm. Scale: 25 miles to one inch. Map (unlisted): Map / of the / Country upon Red-River / Explored in 1852 / By / Capt R. B. Marcy 5th U. S. Infy / Assisted by / Bvt. Capt G. B. McClellan U. S. Engs / under orders from the Head Quarters / of the / U. S. Army. / [decorative rule] / Ackerman Lith 379 Broadway N Y /. 41 x 86.3 cm. Scale: ten miles to one inch. Brown cloth, blind embossed sides, title in gilt on backstrip. Map bound into original green cloth atlas (23 x 14.4 cm.) blind embossed sides, title in gilt on front cover.

Ref.: Clark III 354; Howes M276; Rader 2346; Sabin 44512; Wagner-Camp 226

32nd Congress, 2nd Session, Senate, Executive Document No. 54, Serial 666.

All plates carry the imprint of Ackerman except Palaeontology Plate III (which is without title), Zoology Plates IV–IX, XII, and XIV. Geology Plate II was not published, nor was Plate XVIII of Botany.

2676 MARCY, RANDOLPH B.

THE PRAIRIE TRAVELER. A HAND-BOOK FOR OVER-LAND EXPEDITIONS . . . NEW YORK: HARPER & BROTHERS, 1859.

[i]–[xiv, xiv blank], [15]–340. (Pages [i–ii] blank.) 16.6 x 10.6 cm. 30 illustrations and one folding map listed. Folding map: Sketch / Of the / Different Roads / Embraced in the Itineraries. / 23.2 x 27.8 cm. Scale: about 280 miles to one inch. Black cloth, blind embossed sides, title stamped in gilt on backstrip.

Prov.: Inscribed on page [i]: With the respects / of the Author / R. B. Marcy /.

Ref.: Cowan p. 414; Howes M279; Munk (Alliot) p. 146; Rader 2347; Sabin 44514; Smith 6509

2677 MARCY, RANDOLPH B.

THE SAME . . . EDITED (WITH NOTES) BY RICHARD F. BURTON . . . LONDON: TRUEBNER AND CO., 1863.

[i]–[viii], [xi]–xvi, [1]–251, [252 blank], [1]–24 advertisements dated August, 1882. 18.2 x 12 cm. 13 illustrations and a folding map listed. Folding map: Itineraries / described in Capt. Marcy's / Prairie Traveler, / Edited by Capt. R.

Burton. / [lower left:] Engr^{yd} by G. W. Sharp, Wine Or^{ne} C^t E. C. / [lower right:] Drawn by E. G. Ravenstein, F. R. G. S. / 14.1 x 19.6 cm. Scale: About 300 miles to one inch. *Inset:* The Gold Region / near / Pikes Peak /. 4.6 x 3.3 cm. Scale: 60 miles to one inch. Black cloth, blind embossed borders on sides, gilt-stamped back.

Ref.: see preceding

2678 MARCY, RANDOLPH B.

[Caption title] . . . THE REPORT AND MAPS OF CAPTAIN MARCY OF HIS EXPLORATIONS OF THE BIG WITCHITA AND HEAD WATERS OF THE BRAZOS RIVERS . . .

[1]–48. 22.4 x 14.3 cm. Map: Map of / the / Country / upon the / Brazos and Big Witchita Rivers / Explored in 1854 / Capt. R. B. Marcy 5th U. S. Inf^y / Embracing the Lands appropriated by the State / of Texas for the use of the Indians / Drawn by Capt Marcy. / [upper right:] Senate Ex. Doc. N° 60 1 Sess: 34 Cong: / [lower right:] P. S. Duval & Co. Lith. Press. Phil. / 64.8 x 79.3 cm. Scale: eight miles to one inch. Rebound in red cloth.

Ref.: Howes M277; Wagner-Camp 278

34th Congress, 1st Session, Senate, Executive Document No. 60, Serial 821. [Washington, 1856.]

2679 MARCY, RANDOLPH B.

THIRTY YEARS OF ARMY LIFE ON THE BORDER . . . NEW YORK: HARPER & BROTHERS, 1866.

[v]–xvi, [17]–442. 21.4 x 14.1 cm. 13 full-page plates and three illustrations in text, all included in pagination, unlisted. Brown cloth, gilt design on front cover, blind monogram on back cover, title in gilt on backstrip, beveled covers, uncut.

Prov.: Bookplate of David I. Hudnut pasted over cancelled bookplate of Soldiers' Library, Boston Public Library.

Ref.: Dobie p. 155; Howes M280; Munk (Alliot) p. 146; Rader 2348; Sabin 44516; Smith 6511

2680 MARGRY, PIERRE, *Editor*

[Wrapper title] . . . MEMOIRES ET DOCUMENTS . . . DECOUVERTES ET ETABLISSEMENTS DES FRANCAIS DANS L'OUEST ET DANS LE SUD DE L'AMERIQUE SEPTENTRIONALE (1614–1698) . . . PARIS: MAISON-NEUVE ET CIE M DCCC LXXIX [–M DCCC LXXXVIII].

Vol. 1: [1–4], [I]–XXXII, [1]–618, [619 colophon, 620 blank]. Vol. 2: [I–IV], [1]–619, [620 colophon]. Vol. 3: [I–IV], [1]–656. Vol. 4: [1–4], [I]–LXXII, [1]–653, [654 blank]. Vol. 5: [I]–CLX, [1]–[699], [700 colophon]. Vol. 6: [1–4], [I]–XIX, [XX blank], [1]–759, [760 colophon]. 25 x 15.9 cm. Six volumes, printed green wrappers, uncut.

Prov.: Wrapper of Vol. 5: à son vaillant et excellent / ami hommage / d'un camarade las Mais / non abattu / Pierre Margry. / Wrapper of Vol. 6: à mon ancien Et excellent ami / Pierre Margry: /.

Ref.: Howes M283; Palau 151549; Rader 2349; Raines p. 146; Streit III 2705

Streit lists the contents of each volume.

Editions: Paris: Jouast, 1876–86.

2681 MARIGNY, BERNARD

REFLEXIONS SUR LA CAMPAGNE DU GENERAL ANDRE JACKSON, EN LOUISIANE, EN 1814 ET 1815 . . . NOUVELLE-ORLEANS: IMPRIMERIE DE J. L. SOLLEE, 1848.

[1]–[52]. 22.2 x 13.5 cm. Violet wrappers.

Prov.: Manuscript note on front cover: Dr Frank Perret Esq / by / Bernard Marigny / né a la N^{lle} Orleans en 1785 / mort en 1869 a 84 ans / [short rule] / [short rule] /

Ref.: Howes M285

A translation of this pamphlet by Grace King appeared in the *Louisiana Historical Quarterly*, Vol. 6, pp. 61–85, January, 1923.

2682 MARLOW, GEORGE & CHARLES

LIFE OF THE MARLOWS AS RELATED BY THEMSELVES. OURAY, COLO.: PLAINDEALER PRINT.

[1]–[182]. 19.1 x 13.5 cm. Five illustrations. Pink printed wrappers. In a red cloth case.

Ref.: Adams 668; Howes M295

Copyrighted 1892 by George and Charles Marlow.

Of five brothers, only the two authors lived to tell their fantastic tale.

2683 MARMADUKE, MEREDITH M.

[Wrapper title] JOURNAL . . . OF A TRIP FROM FRANKLIN, MISSOURI TO SANTA FE, NEW MEXICO IN 1824. REPRINTED FROM THE MISSOURI INTELLIGENCER . . . COLUMBIA, MISSOURI, 1911.

[1]–10. 23.1 x 15.4 cm. Gray printed wrappers, with title on front cover.

Ref.: Hubach pp. 60–1; Matthews p. 248

Caption title as follows: Missouri / Historical Review. / [double rule] / Vol. 6. October, 1911. No. 1. / [double rule] / Santa Fe Trail. / . . .

The author was a governor of Missouri.

2684 MARQUIS, THOMAS B.

MEMOIRS OF A WHITE CROW INDIAN (THOMAS H. LEFORGE) . . . NEW YORK: THE CENTURY CO.

[i–x (x blank)], [1]–356. 18.6 x 12.8 cm. Eight illustrations listed. Pictorial yellow cloth.

Ref.:

Copyrighted 1928.

2685 MARRYAT, FRANCIS S.

MOUNTAINS AND MOLEHILLS; OR, RECOLLECTIONS OF A BURNT JOURNAL . . . LONDON: LONGMAN, BROWN, GREEN, AND LONGMANS, 1855.

[i]–[xii], [1]–443, [444 blank], [1]–24 advertisements. 22 x 14 cm. Eight colored plates and 18 woodcuts. Embossed salmon cloth, uncut.

Ref.: Adams (*Ramp. Herd*) 1445; Blumann & Thomas 5198; Cowan p. 416; Howes M299; Sabin 44695; Wheat (*Gold Rush*) 137

Experiences in the Rocky Mountains and the California gold regions.

2686 MARRYAT, FREDERICK

THE TRAVELS AND ROMANTIC ADVENTURES OF MONSIEUR VIOLET, AMONG THE SNAKE INDIANS AND WILD TRIBES OF THE GREAT WESTERN PRAIRIES . . . LONDON: LONGMAN, BROWN, GREEN, & LONGMANS, 1843.

[i]–viii, [1]–312. [i–iv], [1]–299, [300 colophon]. [i–iv], [1]–318, [319 colophon, 320 blank]. 19.7 x 12.2 cm. Folding map: [Land of the Shoshones.] [lower right:] W. Lake, lith, 170, Fleet St. / 17.2 x 29.7 cm. No scale given. Three volumes, red cloth, sides with blind embossed borders and vignettes, title stamped in gilt on backstrips, uncut, mostly unopened.

Ref.: Cowan p. 416; Howes M302; Rader 2352; Sabin 44698; Wagner-Camp 97

The title-leaves are cancels, but the half-titles and map are present.

These incredible adventures of an imaginary Frenchman were derived from many sources.

2687 MARSH, CHARLES W.

RECOLLECTIONS, 1837–1910 . . . CHICAGO: FARM IMPLEMENT NEWS COMPANY, 1910.*

[i]–xv, [xvi blank], [1]–299, [300 blank]. (Pages [i–ii] blank.) 20.1 x 14.1 cm. Illustrations listed. Green cloth, gilt top, uncut.

Ref.:

Pioneering, farming, and manufacturing reapers in Illinois. With his brother, Marsh invented the first practicable hand binding reaper.

2688 MARSH, JAMES B.

FOUR YEARS IN THE ROCKIES; OR, THE ADVENTURES OF ISAAC P. ROSE, OF SHENANGO TOWNSHIP, LAWRENCE COUNTY, PENNSYLVANIA . . . NEW CASTLE, PA.: PRINTED BY W. B. THOMAS, 1884.

[1]–262. 19.1 x 13 cm. Portrait. Blue cloth, with type ornament borders and ornaments in black, title in black on front cover.

Ref.: Howes M306; Smith 6536; Wagner-Camp 75 see

The account of Rose's adventures supplements the stories of the Wyeth expedition and of the early fur trade days. Rose was captured by Indians, but escaped.

2689 MARSHALL, ANN J.

THE AUTOBIOGRAPHY OF MRS. A. J. MARSHALL, AGE, 84 YEARS. PINE BLUFF, ARKANSAS: ADAMS-WILSON PRINTING COMPANY, 1897.

[1]–232. 18.4 x 12.7 cm. Dark green cloth, title in gilt on front cover, decorative gilt bands, red edges.

Ref.: Howes M309

Mrs. Marshall was a missionary teacher among the Cherokees and Creeks from 1846.

2690 MARSHALL, JOHN

MANUSCRIPT DOCUMENT, SIGNED: J Marshall Ch. Just. of the US. / 1807 October 20, Virginia District. One page, 31.6 x 21 cm.

Acknowledgement of the appearance of Aaron Burr, Luther Martin, and John Cummins for the purpose of setting bail for their appearance in court.

The document reads as follows: United states of America—Virginia district to wit, / Be it remembered that on this twentieth day of / October in the year one Thousand eight hundred seven & / in the thirty second year of the Independence of the United / states Aaron Burr and Luther Martin & John Cummins / personally appeared before me John Marshall chief / Justice of the United states and acknowledged themselves / to be severally indebted to the United states as follows— / the said Aaron Burr in the sum of Three Thousand / dollars and the said Luther Martin & John Cummins / in the sum of One thousand five hundred dollars— / each of their respective goods & chattels lands and / tenements to be levied & to the use of the said United / states rendered—Yet upon this condition that if the / said Aaron Burr shall make his personal appearance / before the court of the United states for the seventh circuit / and district of Ohio at Chilicothe on the first day of the / next stated term or session thereof then & there to be / tried for a Misdemeanor against the United states in / beginning or seting[!] on foot or preparing or providing / the means of a military expedition or enterprize against Mexico a Province in North America of the King of / Spain with whom the United states were & are at peace & shall not depart thence without the leave of the said / court or until discharged by due course of law then / the foregoing recognizance to be void else to remain / in full force & virtue— / acknowledged before me / J Marshall Ch. Just. of the US. /

404

On page [4]: The U States / vs / Aaron Burr / [vertical flourish connecting three lines] / Recognizance / for appearance / in Ohio /. On same page, at right angles, in centre: United states 25th / vs / Burr / [vertical flourish opposite vs] / recogniz:ce for / app. ce in Ohio. / [double underline] /

On the first page, the last two lines are in the hand of John Marshall.

Burr and Blennerhasset were indicted in January, 1808, at Chillicothe, Ohio, but the charges against them were not pressed.

2691 MARSHALL, WILLIAM I.

ACQUISITION OF OREGON AND THE LONG SUPPRESSED EVIDENCE ABOUT MARCUS WHITMAN . . . COPYRIGHT 1905 BY WILLIAM I. MARSHALL. ALL RIGHTS RESERVED.*

[i–ii], [1]–450. [1]–368. 22.9 x 15.1 cm. Portrait. Two volumes, green cloth, uncut.
Ref.: Howes M322; Smith 6556
Printed at Seattle, 1911.

An attempt, based on the research of twenty-five years, to expose the myth that Whitman saved Oregon.

Editions: [Seattle, 1905].

2692 MARTIN, CHARLES I.

HISTORY OF DOOR COUNTY, WISCONSIN, TOGETHER WITH BIOGRAPHIES OF NEARLY SEVEN HUNDRED FAMILIES, AND MENTION OF 4,000 PERSONS . . . STURGEON BAY, WIS: EXPOSITOR JOB PRINT, 1881.

[I]–[X, X blank], [1]–136. (Pages 100 1/2 and 100 3/4 printed on yellow paper inserted after page 100.) 17.1 x 11.6 cm. Portrait. Gray printed boards with title on front cover, brown cloth backstrip, advertisement on recto of back endleaf. In a red cloth case.
Ref.: Howes M327

2693 MARTIN, DON JOSE

MEMORIAL AND PROPOSALS OF SENOR DON JOSE MARTIN ON THE CALIFORNIAS, MEXICO, MDCCCXXII. TRANSLATED INTO ENGLISH WITH AN INTRODUCTION BY HENRY R. WAGNER. 1945.

[i]–xxiv, [xxv colophon, xxvi blank]. 28.5 x 18.8 cm. Decorated green and yellow boards, green cloth back, printed paper label.
Ref.: Magee & Magee 410
Limited to 250 copies printed at the Grabhorn Press.

2694 MARTINEZ, ANTONIO JOSE

ESPOSICION QUE EL PRESBITERO ANTONIO JOSE MARTINEZ CURA DE TAOS EN NUEVO MEXICO, DIRIJE AL GOBIERNO DEL EXMO. SOR. GENERAL D. ANTONIO LOPEZ DE SANTA—ANNA. PROPONIENDO LA CIVILISACION DE LAS NACIONES BARBARAS QUE SON AL CONTORNO DEL DEPARTAMENTO DE NUEVO—MEXICO. TAOS: IMPRENTA DEL MISMO A CARGO DE J. M. B., 1843.

[1–12]. 19.6 x 15.8 cm. Stabbed and rebound into old blue wrappers. In a brown cloth case.
Ref.: AII (*New Mexico*) 21; Wagner (*New Mexico*) 22
Both AII (*New Mexico*) and Wagner call for 14 pages, but this appears complete in 12.

2695 MARTINEZ CARO, RAMON

VERDADERA IDEA DE LA PRIMERA CAMPANA DE TEJAS Y SUCESOS OCCURIDOS DESPUES DE LA ACCION DE SAN JACINTO . . . MEXICO: IMPRENTA DE SANTIAGO PEREZ, 1837.

[I]–VII, [VIII blank], [1]–162. 20.1 x 12.7 cm. Modern Mexican tree calf, red leather label, with original printed wrappers bound in.
Prov.: Collection of General Guajardo, Mexico City, with his stamp (twice) on the wrapper.
Ref.: Clements Library (*Texas*) 16; Gómez & González 357; Howes C155; Jones 999; NYPL *Bull.* Feb., 1937, p. 86; Rader 592; Raines p. 44; Sabin 10950; Streeter 923

To Texans struggling for independence, General Antonio López de Santa Anna was a *bête noir*. He was held responsible for both of the tragedies of 1836—the Fall of the Alamo and the Goliad Massacre—but his defeat at San Jacinto by inferior numbers of Texans under Sam Houston relieved some of the pain. The present book was written by Santa Anna's secretary. It is remarkably well documented and includes the general's own report to the Ministry of War.

2696 MARTINEZ CARO, RAMON

ANOTHER COPY.

Half sheepskin. Original front wrapper bound in.

2697 MARVIN, FREDERIC R.

THE YUKON OVERLAND. THE GOLD-DIGGER'S HAND-BOOK . . . CINCINNATI, OHIO: THE EDITOR PUBLISHING COMPANY, 1898.

[I]–XII, 13–170, [171–74 advertisements]. 16.1 x 12.3 cm. Illustrations unlisted, folding map. Orange printed wrappers. Front wrapper damaged affecting some text. In a red cloth case.
Ref.: Howes M357; Smith 6574
Describes the route overland from Spokane. Contains a Chinook vocabulary, pages 149–70.

2698 MARYSVILLE AND BENICIA NATIONAL RAIL ROAD

REPORT OF THE ENGINEERS ON THE SURVEY OF THE MARYSVILLE AND BENICIA NATIONAL RAIL ROAD. MARYSVILLE: PRINTED AT THE OFFICE OF THE CALIFORNIA EXPRESS, 1853.

[1]–29, [30–32 blank]. 25 x 14.8 cm. Green printed wrappers, with title on front wrapper, stabbed.
Ref.: AII (California) 253; Cowan, p. 510; Greenwood 393

2699 MASON, JOHN

AUTOGRAPH LETTER, SIGNED. 1812 August 11 [Washington]. One page, 24.6 x 19.4 cm. To William Clark.
Sending a shoemaker to take measurements for seven pair of half boots for six Indian chiefs and their orator.

2700 MASON, RICHARD L.

NARRATIVE OF RICHARD LEE MASON IN THE PIONEER WEST, 1819. NEW YORK CITY: CHAS. FRED. HEARTMAN.

[1]–74. 23 x 16 cm. Boards, printed paper label, fore and lower edges uncut.
Ref.: Howes M372
Published in 1915. Limited to 160 copies. Heartman's Historical Series, No. 6.

2701 MASSACHUSETTS. Legislature

AUTOGRAPH MANUSCRIPT RESOLUTION. [1846].

One page, 31.5 x 20.2 cm.
Copy of a resolution regarding the admission of Texas to the United States. "Resolved, That Massachusetts hereby refuses to acknowledge the act of the government of the United States, authorizing the admission of Texas, . . ."

2702 MASSACHUSETTS EMIGRANT AID COMPANY

NEBRASKA AND KANSAS. REPORT OF THE COMMITTEE OF THE MASSACHUSETTS EMIGRANT AID CO. WITH THE ACT OF INCORPORATION, AND OTHER DOCUMENTS. BOSTON: PUBLISHED FOR THE MASSACHUSETTS EMIGRANT AID CO., 1854.

[1]–32. 19.4 x 12.4 cm. Stabbed, unbound.
Ref.: Sabin 52198; Wagner-Camp 243a
Contains a series of letters by Dr. Charles Robinson of Fitchburg originally printed in the Worcester Spy. These letters include excerpts from his diary kept on his trip through Kansas in 1849 and comprise a day by day account of an overland trip across Kansas in 1849.—EDG

2703 MASSACHUSETTS STATE TEXAS COMMITTEE

[Broadside] CIRCULAR. BOSTON, NOVEMBER 3, 1845. DEAR SIR— . . . ELIZUR WRIGHT, JR., SECRETARY OF THE ANTI-TEXAS COMMITTEE, 10 COURT STREET.

Broadside, 24.6 x 19.8 cm. Text, 17.1 x 16.9 cm.
Ref.: Streeter 1590
The broadside is a protest against the admission of Texas as a slave state. It contains a request for signatures to petitions and a plea for readers to solicit signatures. Fifty thousand signatures were sent to Congress in December, 1845.

2704 MASSACHUSETTS STATE TEXAS COMMITTEE

[Caption title] HOW TO SETTLE THE TEXAS QUESTION. DIRECTIONS . . .

[1]–[12] 18.5 x 10.9 cm. Stitched, unbound.
Ref.: Sabin 45092; Streeter 1593
Published in Boston, 1845. The Massachusetts State Texas Committee was formed to act against the admission of Texas as a slave state. The first page of the present pamphlet is a series of ten instructions on how to proceed. Pages 2–10 comprise an Address: / to the Friends of Free Institutions in Massachu-/setts and other Free States. / It is signed by Charles Francis Adams, William Lloyd Garrison, Wendell Phillips and thirty-six other residents of Boston and its suburbs. Pages 11 and [12] comprise a printed form of remonstrance addressed: To the Honorable Senate and House of Representatives of the / United States in Congress Assembled. /

The meeting at which the committee was appointed was held in Cambridge, October 21, 1845. Copies of the pamphlet were distributed by Elizur Wright, Boston.

See Brauer, K. J.: "The Massachusetts State Texas Committee," in The Journal of American History, Vol. LI, No. 2 (September, 1964), pp. 214–31.

2705 MASSON, LOUIS FRANCOIS RODRIGUE

LES BOURGEOIS DE LA COMPAGNIE DU NORD-OUEST RECITS DE VOYAGES, LETTRES ET RAPPORTS INEDITS RELATIFS AU NORD-OUEST CANADIEN . . . QUEBEC: DE L'IMPRIMERIE GENERALE A. COTE ET CIE, 1889 [–1890].*

[i]–[x, x blank], [1]–154, [1]–[415], [416 blank]. [i]–vi, [1]–499, [500 blank]. 23.5 x 17 cm. Folding map: Map / -of the- / North West Territories / [below border:] Drawn by Gustave Rinfret /. 42.4 x 71.1 cm. Scale: about 100 miles

to one inch. Two volumes, brown half morocco, gilt tops, uncut, partly unopened.

Ref.: Howes M385; Smith 6956; Wagner-Camp 7 note

Included in the text are several valuable journals and accounts of early traders among the Indians not only in the far Northwest but in the Great Lakes and Rocky Mountain regions.

2706 MASTERS, EDGAR L.

SPOON RIVER ANTHOLOGY . . . NEW YORK: THE MACMILLAN COMPANY, 1915.*

[i]–[xviii, xviii blank], 1–248, [249–54 advertisements]. 18.6 x 12.6 cm. Blue pictorial cloth, front cover and backstrip stamped with black, title on front cover and backstrip in gilt, fore and lower edges uncut.

Ref.: Johnson (Blanck) p. 352

First Edition. First state: measures 7/8 inch across top of covers.

2707 MATHER, THOMAS, PAPERS

A COLLECTION OF LETTERS, A MAP, AND A DIARY, BY AND TO THOMAS MATHER, one of the three commissioners of the Santa Fé Road Commission established in 1825.

The collection comprises the following materials:

Manuscript Letter by James Barbour (copy). 1825 March 16, Department of War. Three pages, 24.7 x 19.8 cm. To Benjamin H. Reeves, George C. Sibley, and Pierre Menard. Instructions to the Commissioners regarding keeping of accounts.

Manuscript Letter by James Barbour (copy). Same as preceding, but with three-line postscript relating to Thomas Mather as successor to Pierre Menard. With original cover.

Letter, signed by William L. McKenney. 1825 June 3, Department of War, Office of Indian Affairs. One page, 24.5 x 19.7 cm. To Thomas Mather. Appointment as a Commissioner of the Santa Fé Road Commission.

Letter, signed by C. Van de Venter. 1825 June 4, Department of War. One page, 24.5 x 19.8 cm. To Thomas Mather. Covering letter for his appointment as Commissioner.

Autograph Letter, signed by Thomas Mather. 1825 July 16, Fort Osage. Three pages, 24.8 x 20.3 cm. To Miss H. G. Lamb. Regarding his journey to Fort Osage from Kaskaskia.

Autograph Letter, signed by Thomas Mather. 1825 [i.e., 1826] January 4, Vandalia. One page, 24.9 x 20.1 cm. To his wife. According to the last few lines of the letter, this is the first letter to Mrs. Mather as his wife. She was the Miss Lamb

to whom the preceding letter was written. Mather had been sent by Sibley and Reeves to Washington with originals of the Indian treaties concluded en route. He mentions the fact he is on his way to Washington in the letter.

Autograph Letter, signed by A. Gamble. 1826 January 10, St. Louis. One page, 31.4 x 19.8 cm. To Thomas Mather. Enquiring about his plans for joining Sibley in the West. Gamble was secretary of the Commission.

Copies of two letters and an extract from a third, as follows: Manuscript Letter from George C. Sibley. 1826 May 20, Valley of Taos, New Mexico. Two pages, 31.9 x 19.5 cm. To Benjamin Reeves and Thomas Mather. Re political situation and possibility of completing the survey. Manuscript Letter from Joel R. Poinsett. 1825 December 31, Mexico City. One page, 31.9 x 19.5 cm. To George C. Sibley. Re chances of completing the survey. Manuscript Letter from Sibley (extract). 1826 March 5, Santa Fé. Two pages, 31.9 x 19.5 cm. To Poinsett. Reply to preceding.

Manuscript ". . . list of articles that I think it will be proper for Cols. Reeves and Mather to bring out with them to Santa Fee . . ." (copy). 1826 February 7, Santa Fé. Two pages, 31.1 x 18.9 cm. The list was sent by Sibley. Manuscript Letter from Sibley (copy). 1826 February 14, San Fernando, Taos. Two pages, 31.1 x 18.9 cm. To Reeves and Mather. Regarding accounts of the Commission. Manuscript Letter by Sibley (copy). 1826 February 15, San Fernando. Two pages, 31.1 x 18.9 cm. To Reeves and Mather. Re business of the Commission. Manuscript Letter by Sibley (copy). 1826 February 16, San Fernando. One page, 31.1 x 18.9 cm. To Reeves and Mather. Introducing Paul Ballio.

Autograph Letter, signed by Joseph C. Brown. 1826 October 30, St. Louis. Two pages, 31 x 20 cm. To Thomas Mather. Regarding return of Sibley from Santa Fé and other business of the Commission. Brown was the official surveyor of the Commission.

Autograph Letter, signed by Benjamin H. Reeves. 1826 November 5, Fayette, Mo. Two pages, 19.5 x 16 cm. To Mather. Re a meeting of the Commissioners to prepare for a report.

Autograph Letter, signed by Benjamin H. Reeves. 1826 November 19, Fayette, Mo. Three pages, 19.7 x 16 cm. To Mather. Re meeting of the Commissioners.

Autograph Letter, signed by George C. Sibley. 1827 May 10, Fort Osage. Three pages, 14.9 x 19.8 cm. To Mather. Details of his plans for his survey of the Santa Fé Road in 1827.

Autograph Letter, signed by George C. Sibley. 1828 April 1, St. Charles. One page, 14.9 x 20 cm. To Mather. About finances of the Commission.

Manuscript Map (in an unidentified hand) of the route from the western U. S. border to Taos. 26.5 x 43.2 cm. (page size). 20 x 32.6 cm. (neat line). No scale given.

Autograph Manuscript, signed W. H. M., dated June 1886. 28 pages, 21.1 x 16 cm. A long biographical sketch of Mrs. Thomas Mather, probably written by a nephew. There is considerable material about Thomas Mather in the sketch.

Autograph Manuscript Diaries of Thomas Mather, July 16, 1825 to September 19, 1825. Two volumes, 14.4 x 9.8 cm., 44 pages, 49 pages; first volume sewn, unbound, second volume in blue paper wrappers. The first volume apparently lacks an initial leaf at the front and a leaf at the back. Typewritten transcript accompanies the diaries. The front cover of the second volume bears the following: Thomas Math[er] / No. 2 / [underline] /.

Autograph Manuscript: Thomas Mathers / Accounts / With the Mexican / Road Commissioners /. Ten pages, 16 x 9.6 cm. bound in original blue paper wrappers.

2708 MATHEWS, ALFRED E.

GEMS OF ROCKY MOUNTAIN SCENERY, CONTAINING VIEWS ALONG AND NEAR THE UNION PACIFIC RAILROAD . . . NEW-YORK: PUBLISHED BY THE AUTHOR, 1869.

[1–46]. 33.1 x 26.1 cm. 20 lithographic plates. Purple cloth, blind stamped borders on sides, title stamped in gilt on front cover.

Ref.: Howes M411; Sabin 46823

The text to accompany the plates is printed on the versos of the leaves facing the plates.

2709 MATHEWS, ALFRED E.

PENCIL SKETCHES OF COLORADO, ITS CITIES, PRINCIPAL TOWNS AND MOUNTAIN SCENERY . . . 1866.

[1–16]. 33.5 x 47.7 cm. 24 lithographic plates of which four sheets contain four views each and four sheets contain two views each. Brown cloth, gilt title on front cover.

Ref.: Howes M413

Published in New York.

2710 MATHEWS, ALFRED E.

PENCIL SKETCHES OF MONTANA . . . NEW-YORK: PUBLISHED BY THE AUTHOR, 1868.

[1–6], [63]–95, [96 blank]. (Page 91 mispaginated 19.) 32.9 x 25.7 cm. 31 numbered plates (except number 22 which is unnumbered). Blue cloth, blind stamped corner ornaments and borders, title stamped in gilt on front cover.

Prov.: Inscribed on blank leaf at front: Presented to Louis McLane, Esqr., by the author, / Alfred E. Mathews. /

Ref.: Howes M414; Smith 6603

The thirty-one plates comprise pages [7–62] preceding the text.

2711 MATHEWS, EDWARD J.

CROSSING THE PLAINS . . . IN '59. PRIVATELY PRINTED.*

[1]–91, [92 blank]. 17.2 x 11 cm. Rough blue cloth, with printed paper label on front cover.

Prov.: Inscribed on back fly-leaf (inverted): Dearest Sidney- / Heres the fine / record of father's / early adventures / I have had the diary / printed that his grand-/children & theirs may / keep something of his golden / spirit / Afftly / Roscoe / May 31 /.

Ref.: Howes M415

The party left Iowa City April 7th, 1859, for Pike's Peak, but became discouraged by the reports heard along the way and changed the destination to California. At Salt Lake City, which they reached July 28th, they decided to sell their cattle and buy passage the balance of the way. They left Salt Lake City on August 10th with Read to whom Mathews paid $50.00 for transport to Sacramento. They stopped at Carson for a few days and went from there to Virginia City where Mathews made money building and clerking. By June, 1860, he could have sold out for $45,000, but Indian troubles brought about a collapse of values and he became disgusted and left for Esmerelda in October.

Library of Congress supplies date [1930?]. No place of publication given.

2712 [MATHISON, JOHN, *Editor and Publisher*]

. . . SEQUEL TO THE COUNSEL FOR EMIGRANTS, CONTAINING INTERESTING INFORMATION FROM NUMEROUS SOURCES; WITH ORIGINAL LETTERS FROM CANADA AND THE UNITED STATES . . . ABERDEEN: JOHN MATHISON, 1843.

[1]–72. 18.2 x 11.5 cm. Folding map: Canada / and / Part of / the / United States / [below border] Published by John Mathison, Broad Street Aberdeen. / 27.4 x 43.6 cm. Scale: about 48 miles to one inch. Tan printed wrappers with title on front wrapper.

Ref.: Howes S294

2713 MATSON, NEHEMIAH

FRENCH AND INDIANS OF ILLINOIS RIVER . . . PRINCETON, ILL.: REPUBLICAN JOB PRINTING ESTABLISHMENT, 1874.

[5]–260. 17.1 x 11.8 cm. Blue cloth, blind embossed borders on sides, title in gilt on backstrip.

Prov.: Bookplate of T. H. Haseltine. Signature and manuscript marginal notes by J. F. Steward, in pencil.

Ref.: Howes M419

Steward was the author of *Lost Maramech and Earliest Chicago*.

2714 MATSON, NEHEMIAH

THE SAME, except: Second Edition.

[5]–270. (Pages [13–4] blank.) 17.9 x 11.9 cm. Blue cloth, borders embossed in blind on covers (differing from first edition), title in gilt on backstrip.

Prov.: Inscribed in pencil by the author on front endleaf: Henry L Boies / compliments of the author /.

Ref.: Howes M419

Inserted before the title-page is a mounted original photograph of the author, signed on the mount.

The Introduction in the first edition is dated April 18, 1874, and in the second edition September 1, 1874.

2715 MATSON, NEHEMIAH

[Map] MAP / OF / BUREAU COUNTY / ILLINOIS / POPULATION 23,692 / DRAWN & PUBLISHED / BY / N. MATSON / 1858. / LITH. OF ED. MENDEL CHICAGO ILL. / ENTERED ACCORDING TO ACT OF CONGRESS IN THE YEAR 1857 BY N. MATSON IN THE NORTHERN DISTRICT OF ILLINOIS / *Insets:* [VIEWS OF THREE BUILDINGS AT THE FOOT AND SIX SMALL VIGNETTES AT RIGHT.]

Map, 80.7 x 109 cm. Scale not given. Folded into black cloth covers, 17.1 x 12 cm., with title stamped in gilt on front cover.

Ref.: Buck 720 note; Howes M418 note

There is a small circular photograph pasted to the left of the cartouche, possibly a portrait of Matson.

Editions: Chicago, 1857.

2716 MATSON, NEHEMIAH

MAP OF BUREAU COUNTY, ILLINOIS, WITH SKETCHES OF ITS EARLY SETTLEMENT . . . CHICAGO: GEORGE H. FERGUS, 1867.

[1]–88. 19 x 19.8 cm. Eight plates and 26 township maps, unlisted. Rebound in black cloth, blind embossed borders on sides, newly lettered in gilt on front cover.

Ref.: Bradford 3409; Buck 721; Howes M418; Sabin 46876

2717 MATSON, NEHEMIAH

MEMORIES OF SHAUBENA. WITH INCIDENTS RELATING TO THE EARLY SETTLEMENT OF THE WEST . . . CHICAGO: D. B. COOKE & CO., 1878.

[9]–269, [270 blank]. 19.4 x 13.3 cm. 13 illustrations listed. Brown embossed cloth, blind fillets on sides, title in gilt on backstrip.

Prov.: Inscribed in pencil on blank leaf at front: G S Hubbard / Compliments of the author / Presented to my friend / Miss Caroline McIlvaine / Jany 21, 1932 / H. R. Hamilton /. With several long marginal annotations by Hubbard (a Chicago pioneer) in the first part of the text.

Ref.: Bradford 3411; Howes M420

2718 MATSON, NEHEMIAH

PIONEERS OF ILLINOIS, CONTAINING A SERIES OF SKETCHES RELATING TO EVENTS THAT OCCURRED PREVIOUS TO 1813 . . . CHICAGO: KNIGHT & LEONARD, 1882.

[9]–306. 19.2 x 13.3 cm. Portrait. Blue cloth, embossed with decorative designs in black on covers, gilt title on backstrip.

Ref.: Bradford 3412; Howes M421

2719 MATSON, NEHEMIAH

REMINISCENCES OF BUREAU COUNTY . . . PRINCETON, ILLINOIS: REPUBLICAN BOOK AND JOB OFFICE, 1872.

[7]–406. 19.7 x 13.4 cm. 15 illustrations listed, one repeated as frontispiece. Embossed black cloth, fillets and oval in blind on covers, title in gilt on backstrip.

Ref.: Bradford 3410; Buck 721; Howes M422

2720 MATTHEWS, LEONARD

A LONG LIFE IN REVIEW.

[i]–[viii, viii blank], 1–178. 17 x 10.6 cm. Illustrations unlisted. Dark green cloth, gilt top.

Ref.:

On page [iii] is the following note: Privately Printed / with the author's permission / in anticipation of his / 100th birthday, / December 17th, 1928 / [decorative rule] / [within thick and thin rule borders].

In this earlier edition, the frontispiece appears between pages [ii] and [iii].

There is no place of printing nor date of printing indicated, but the Introduction is dated from St. Louis and the frontispiece is dated December 17th, 1927.

Contains an overland narrative and an account of adventures in California. Matthews returned via Panama.

2721 MATTHEWS, LEONARD

THE SAME.

[i–viii, viii blank], 1–[182]. 17 x 10.6 cm. Illustrations unlisted. Dark red cloth.

Ref.:

On page [iii] is the following note: Privately Printed / with the author's permission / in anticipation of his / 100th anniversary / December 17th, 1928 / Second Edition / [decorative rule] / [within thick and thin rule borders].

Chapter 11 of the first edition and chapter 12 are reversed. The excerpt from the St. Louis *Globe-Democrat* (pages 174–77) is omitted and an Index added at the end. Numerous changes were made in this second edition.

2722 MATTHEWS, WILLIAM B.

THE SETTLER'S MAP AND GUIDE BOOK. OKLAHOMA. A BRIEF REVIEW OF THE HISTORY . . . WASHINGTON, D. C.: WM. H. LEPLEY, 1889.

[1]–66. 23.6 x 15 cm. Map: Oklahoma / and / Indian Territories / Scale of Miles / [diagrammatic scale: about 25 miles to one inch.] / Prepared for Wᵐ B. Matthews, / Land and Mining Attorney / Washington D.C. / [lower right:] N. Peters. Photo-Lithographer. Washington, D. C. / 17.4 x 53.7 cm. Scale as above. Light gray wrappers, with title on front wrapper, advertisements on verso of front and recto of back wrapper. In a brown cloth case.

Ref.: Adams (*Ramp. Herd*) 1455; Bradford 3415; Howes M428; Rader 2368 note

The inserted slip before the title-page commending the pamphlet is present in this copy. Howes reports it for the second edition, with appendix.

2723 MATTSON, HANS

REMINISCENCES. THE STORY OF AN EMIGRANT . . . SAINT PAUL: D. D. MERRILL COMPANY, 1891.

[i–iv], 1–314. 21.2 x 15 cm. Illustrations unlisted. Dark red cloth.

Ref.:

Although most of the volume deals with the author's experiences in the consular service of the United States, there are included pioneer adventures in Wisconsin and Minnesota among the Norwegian emigrants.

2724 MAURY, DABNEY H.

RECOLLECTIONS OF A VIRGINIAN IN THE MEXICAN, INDIAN, AND CIVIL WARS . . . NEW YORK: CHARLES SCRIBNER'S SONS, 1894.

[i]–[xii, xii blank], 1–279, [280 colophon]. 20.2 x 13.4 cm. Portrait. Gray pictorial cloth, title in blue on front cover and in gilt on backstrip.

Prov.: Signed in pencil on front endleaf and recto of frontispiece: P R Stetson / Reading / Pa - /.

Ref.: Howes M440; Rader 2369; Raines p. 148; Saunders 3041

First Edition.

2725 MAURY, DABNEY H.

THE SAME, except line 7 on title-page reads: Third Edition /.

Prov.: Inscribed in pencil on front endleaf by Edward Eberstadt.

2726 MAURY, DABNEY H.

THE SAME. London: Sampson Low, Marston & Company, 1894. Red cloth.

Ref.: Howes M440; Munk (Alliot) p. 149

2727 MAVERICK, MARY A.

MEMOIRS . . . EDITED BY RENA MAVERICK GREEN . . . SAN ANTONIO, TEXAS: ALAMO PRINTING CO., 1921.*

[1]–136. 22.9 x 15 cm. 16 illustrations, unlisted. Cream printed wrappers.

Ref.: Adams (*Ramp. Herd*) 1460; Howes M443

The Appendix contains notes on the origin of the word "Maverick."

2728 MAXWELL, WILLIAM A.

CROSSING THE PLAINS. DAYS OF '57 . . .*

[i–viii], 1–179, [180 blank]. 17.2 x 12.7 cm. 19 illustrations listed. Brown printed wrappers with title on front cover in gold. In a green cloth case.

Ref.: Cowan p. 420; Howes (1954) 6808

Copyrighted 1915. Printed at San Francisco by the Sunset Publishing House.

2729 MAY, JOHN

JOURNAL AND LETTERS OF COL. JOHN MAY, OF BOSTON RELATIVE TO TWO JOURNEYS TO THE OHIO COUNTRY IN 1788 AND '89 . . . CINCINNATI: ROBERT CLARKE & CO., 1873.*

[1]–160. 23.5 x 16 cm. Green cloth, gilt top, uncut.

Ref.: Clarke II 44; Howes M450; Sabin 47070; Thomson 804

2730 MAYER, BRANTZ

TAH-GAH-JUTE; OR, LOGAN AND CAPTAIN MICHAEL CRESAP . . . DELIVERED IN BALTIMORE, BEFORE THE MARYLAND HISTORICAL SOCIETY, ON ITS SIXTH ANNIVERSARY, 9 MAY, 1851.

[1]–86, [87 erratum, 88 blank]. 22.7 x 14.4 cm. Printed cream wrappers, with short title on front wrapper. Back wrapper roughly repaired. Enclosed in Gaylord binder.

Prov.: Inscribed on wrapper: Hon Caleb Cushing, / with the Compliments of / Brantz Mayer: /. Note removed chemically from front wrapper: Bought of L. Godwin / 78 Leonard St. N.W. / [word obliterated] Brigd Command/. Bookplate of Charles Morton Ewing.

Ref.: Field 1039; Howes M451; Sabin 47104; Thomson 805

See also under Jefferson and John J. Jacob.

Appears also with imprint: Baltimore: John Murphy & Co., 1851.

2731 [M A Z Z U C H E L L I, S A M U E L CHARLES]

MEMOIRS HISTORICAL AND EDIFYING OF A MISSION-ARY APOSTOLIC OF THE ORDER OF SAINT DOMINIC AMONG VARIOUS INDIAN TRIBES AND AMONG CATHOLICS AND PROTESTANTS IN THE UNITED STATES OF AMERICA . . . CHICAGO: PRESS OF W. F. HALL PRINTING COMPANY, 1915.

[i]–xx, [1–2], [xxi–xxvi], [1]–375, [376 blank]. 22.1 x 15.3 cm. Large folding map and two smaller maps, portrait and one illustration. Green cloth sides, black leather backstrip and corners, gilt top.

Ref.: Howes M457; Hubach p. 66; Mott (*Iowa*) p. 86; Streit III 2302 note

2732 [M A Z Z U C H E L L I, S A M U E L CHARLES]

MEMORIE ISTORICHE ED EDIFICANTI D'UN MIS-SIONARIO APOSTOLICO DELL'ORDINE DEI PREDICA-TORI FRA VARIE TRIBU DI SELVAGGI E FRA I CAT-TOLICI E PROTESTANTI NEGLI STATI-UNITI D'AME-RICA. MILANO: COI TIPI DELLA DITTA BONIARDI-POGLIANI, 1844. /

[1]–364. 21 x 13.7 cm. Frontispiece and two maps: Map: Geografia dei luoghi delle missioni nei territorj di Wisconsin e di Michigan negli Stati Uniti d'Ame-/rica, ad illustrare il prime libro delle Memorie istoriche ed edificanti, giusta la conoscenza che 3 avevasi di quei Paesi prima dell'anno 1835. / 21. x 32.6 cm. (page size). No scale given. Map: Carta Geografica / delle Diocesi delle Citta Vescovili / negli Stati Uniti / d'America / 1844 / [lower centre:] Milano Prem.ª Litog.ª Pagani /. 37.7 x 42.5 cm. Scale: about 1 3/4 Milanese degrees of longitude to one inch. Contemporary mottled boards with brown leather backstrip, gilt, sprinkled edges.

Ref.: Howes M457; Hubach p. 66; Sabin 47208; Streit III 2302

Lacks a third map.

2733 MEAGHER, THOMAS F.

LECTURES . . . TOGETHER WITH HIS MESSAGES, SPEECHES, &C. TO WHICH IS ADDED THE EULOGY OF RICHARD O'GORMAN, ESQ., DELIVERED AT COOPER INSTITUTE, NEW YORK. VIRGINIA CITY, M. T.: BRUCE & WRIGHT, 1876.

[1]–104. 19.8 x 11.3 cm. Green cloth with title on front cover. Lacks front endleaf.

Ref.: Howes M464; McMurtrie (*Montana*) 27; Smith 6645

Apparently preceded only by Dimsdale and possibly Hosmer among non-documentary imprints of Montana.

2734 MEARES, JOHN

VOYAGES MADE IN THE YEARS 1788 AND 1789, FROM CHINA TO THE NORTH WEST COAST OF AMER-ICA. TO WHICH ARE PREFIXED, AN INTRODUCTORY NARRATIVE OF A VOYAGE PERFORMED IN 1786, FROM BENGAL, IN THE SHIP NOOTKA; OBSERVA-TIONS ON THE PROBABLE EXISTENCE OF A NORTH WEST PASSAGE; AND SOME ACCOUNT OF THE TRADE BETWEEN THE NORTH WEST COAST OF AMERICA AND CHINA; AND THE LATTER COUNTRY AND GREAT BRITAIN . . . LONDON: PRINTED AT THE LOGO-GRAPHIC PRESS, M.DCCXC.

[*]^4, d^4, c^2, A–Zz^4, 3A^2, a–1^2, A–H^4. [i]–[xx], [i]–[xcvi]. [1]–372, [373–480]. 28.2 x 22.5 cm. 26 plates and maps. Map: A Chart of the Northern Pacific Ocean, Containing the N. E. Coast of Asia & N. W. Coast of America, Explored in 1778 & 1779, by Captain Cook, and further Explored in 1788 & 1789, by John Meares. / [lower left:] J. Haywood, del. N° 3 St Martin's Church Yard / [centre:] Published Novr 18, 1790, by J. Walter, N° 169 Piccadilly. [lower right:] Palmer, sculp. / 43.2 x 58.3 cm. No scale given. Map: A Chart / of the Interior Part of / North America / Demonstrating the very great probability / [swelled rule] of an [swelled rule] / Inland Navi-gation / from Hudsons Bay / [short swelled rule] to the [short swelled rule] / West Coast / [lower left:] J. Haywood. del^t St Martin's Church Yard. / [lower right:] Woodman & Mutlow, Sculp^t Russel Court. / 25 x 46.4 cm. No scale given. Map: Chart / of the N. W. Coast of America and N. E. Coast of Asia, ex-plored in the Years 1778, & 1779, / by Captn Cook; / and further explored, in 1788, and 1789. / [lower left:] J. Haywood, del. N° 3 St Martins Church Yard. / 43 x 62.2 cm. No scale given. Map: Sketch of / Friendly Cove / [swelled rule] in [swelled rule] / Nootka Sound, / taken by / Mr Wedgborough / [lower centre:] En-graved by T. Foot. / 23.5 x 18.8 cm. No scale given. Map: A Sketch / of / Port Cox / in the / District / of / Wicananish. / Engraved by T. Foot. / 23.7 x 18.9 cm. Scale: about 1 1/2 miles to one inch. Map: A Plan / of / Port Effingham / [swelled rule] in [swelled rule] / Berkley's

Sound. / 18.7 x 23.4 cm. No scale given. Map: A View / [swelled rule] of [swelled rule] / Otter Sound. / [lower left] Engraved by T. Foot. / 23.9 x 19 cm. No scale given. Map: A Plan / of / Sea Otter Harbour / and / S⁺ Patricks Bay, / taken by / Cap⁺ James Hanna / [lower centre:] Foot Sculp⁺ / 23.7 x 18.9 cm. Scale: about two miles to one inch. Map: A View / [swelled rule] of [swelled rule] / Port Meares. / . . . / Engraved by T. Foot. / 23.8 x 18.7 cm. No scale given. Map: A Sketch / of / Raft-Cove, / taken by Mʳ Funter, Master of the / North West American. / . . . / [swelled rule] Engraved by T. Foot. / 24.2 x 19.4 cm. Scale: about 1 1/8 miles to one inch. Full contemporary tree calf, gilt borders, gilt back, red morocco label. In a brown cloth case.

Ref.: Eberstadt Catalogue 119, 83; Howes M469; Sabin 47260; Smith 6690; Staton & Tremaine 612

The British based their claim to Oregon in large measure on Meares' voyage to and exploration of the Northwest Coast.

Most of plates are printed in sepia, nearly all the original tissue guards are present.

2735 MEARES, JOHN

VOYAGES DE LA CHINE A LA COTE NORD-OUEST D'AMERIQUE . . . A PARIS: CHEZ F. BUISSON, AN 3ᴱ. DE LA REPUBLIQUE.

a⁸, b⁴, A–Aa⁸, Bb⁴. [a]², A–Aa⁸, Bb¹. [a]², A–Z⁸, Aa². [i]–xxiv, [1]–391, [392 blank]. [i–iv], [1]–386. [i–ii], [1]–[372]. 19.1 x 12.1 cm. Atlas, described below. Three volumes, contemporary tree calf, gilt, gilt edges.

Prov.: Bookplates of le Comte Frédéric de Pourtales.

Ref.: Howes M469; Sabin 47262; Smith 6688

2736 MEARES, JOHN

[Atlas] COLLECTION DE CARTES GEOGRAPHIQUES, VUES, MARINES, PLANS ET PORTRAITS, RELATIFS AUX VOYAGES DU CAPITAINE J. MEARES . . . A PARIS: CHEZ F. BUISSON, AN 3ᴱ DE LA REPUBLIQUE.

[i–iv]. 28.4 x 20.8 cm. Plate I: Le Capitaine Jean Meares. / II. Carte de la Mer Pacifique du Nord, contenant la Côte Nord-Est d'Asie et la Côte Nord-Ouest d'Amérique reconnues en 1778. et 79. par le Capⁿᵉ Cook, et plus particulierement encore en 1788. et 89. par le Capⁿᵉ Jean Meares. / 42.2 x 56.5 cm. No scale given. III: Isles Bashee. IV: [Profiles of three islands]. V: [Six profiles of landfalls]. VI: Carte / de la Partie Intérieure de / l'Amérique Septentrionale / Ou est démontrée la trés grande Probabilité d'une / Navigation Intérieure / Depuis / la Baye d'Hudson /

Jusq'à la / Côte Nord-Ouest. / 24.9 x 45.7 cm. No scale given. VII: Entrée des Détroits de Jean de Fuca. VIII: Plan / du / Port la Loutre de Mer / et / de la Baye de S⁺ Patrice; / Dressé par le Capitaine Jacques Hanna. / Latitude Nord, 50 dég. 41 min. / Longitude Est de Greenwich, 231 dég. 24 min. / 23.4 x 18.8 cm. Scale: about two miles to one inch. IX: Vue de la Ville de Macao. X: Vüe de l'Entrée du Bocca Tigris, / Conduisant à Canton. / XI: Pic de Lantao, / Près de l'entrée du Bocca Tigris, / . . . XII: Vue de l'ile Tiger, située sur le Bocca Tigris, / et nommée Tailoc Tow par les Chinois. / XIII: Tianna, Prince d'Atooi, / l'une des Îles Sandwich. / XIV: Vües de la Terre dans les Îles Philippines, au Sud de Manilla. / XV: Winée, Naturelle d'Owhyée, / l'une des Îles Sandwich. / XVI: [Five profiles of the Sandwich Islands.] XVII: Vue du Rocher la Femme de Loth, / . . . / et Femme de Loth. / . . . Two views on one plate. XVIII: Esquisse / de l'Anse des Amis / dans / l'Entrée de Nootka. / 23.1 x 18.5 cm. No scale given. XIX: Callicum et Maquilla, / Chefs de l'entrée de Nootka. / XX: Carte / De la Côte N.O. d'Amérique et de la Côte N. E. d'Asie reconnues en 1778 et 79. / Par le Capitaine Cook. / et plue particulierement encore en 1788. et 89. par le Capⁿᵉ / J. Meares. / 42 x 61 cm. No scale given. XXI: Esquisse / du / Port Cox / dans le / District / de / Wocananish. / 13.3 x 18.6 cm. Scale: about one and one-half miles to one inch. XXII: Pays de la Nouvelle Albion, / Situé par 45 dégrés de latitude Nord. / . . . XXIII: Plan / du Port / Effingham / dans l'Entrée de Berkley, / Situé par les 49 dég. de Latitude Nord, / Et les 223 dégrés 48 minutes de Longitude / Est de Greenwich. / 18.5 x 22.9 cm. No scale given. XXIV: [Three profiles of the Nootka Sound area.] XXV: Vüe / du / Port Meares / Situé par les 54 deg. 51 minutes de Latitude Nord, / et les 227 degres 54 minutes de Longitude Est de / Greenwich. / 23.1 x 18.4 cm. No scale given. XXVI: Le Vaisseau la Côte Nord-Oüest d'Amérique, / . . . XXVII: Vüe / de l'Entrée / de la / Loutre. / Elle gît / Par les 55 dégrés 45 Minutes de Latitude Nord, / et les 226 dégrés 30 Minutes de Longitude Est / de Greenwich. / 33.5 x 18.8 cm. No scale given. XXVIII: Esquisse / de / l'Anse du Radeau / Dressée par M. Funter Maitre du Vaisseau / la Côte Nord-Ouest d'Amérique. / Latitude Nord, 50 dégrés 35 min. / Longitude Est de Greenwich, / 231 dégrés 55 min. / 33.5 x 18.9 cm. Scale: about 1 1/5 miles to one inch. Plate number in upper left corner of each plate: Pl. I, etc. Original brown paste paper boards with mottled calf backstrip, gilt.

Prov.: Bookplate of le Comte Frédéric de Pourtales.
Ref.: As above

2737 MEDICAL REPOSITORY, THE

THE MEDICAL REPOSITORY, AND REVIEW OF AMERICAN PUBLICATIONS ON MEDICINE, SURGERY, AND THE AUXILIARY BRANCHES OF SCIENCE . . . NEWYORK: PRINTED AND SOLD BY T. & J. SWORDS, 1803 [–1807].

[a]–b⁴, B–P⁴, Q², R–3Q⁴, R². [i]–[xvi, xvi blank], [1]–[482]. 20.2 x 12.5 cm. [a]², b⁴, A–2D⁴, 2E², 2F–3K⁴. [i]–xii, [1]–[440], [1–4 advertisement]. [a]², b⁴, A–3L⁴, 3M². [i]–xii, [1]–[459], [460 blank]. [a]⁴, b², A–P⁴, Q², R–3L⁴, 3M¹. [Followed by four stubs: missing text?] [i]–xii, [1]–454. [a]², b⁴, A–3L⁴. [i]–xi, [xii blank], [1]–456. Four engraved plates. Five volumes (First Hexade, Volume VI, Second Hexade, Volumes I–IV), contemporary marbled boards with calf backstrips and corners, fourth volume in full mottled calf.
Ref.: Wagner-Camp 9 note
Contains considerable material relating to Western explorations. There are a few pieces of interest in earlier volumes, but the important accounts start with Vol. VI of the First Hexade, 1803.
The periodical is complete in 23 volumes, 1797–1824.

2738 MEEKER, BRADLEY B.

OVERLAND MAIL ROUTE FROM LAKE SUPERIOR TO PUGET'S SOUND, PROPOSED AND CONSIDERED, IN A LETTER TO THE POSTMASTER GENERAL . . . 1858.

[1]–16. 23.7 x 14.6 cm. Stabbed, unbound. In a gray cloth case.
Ref.: AII (*Minnesota*) 192
There is no indication of place of printing or of printer. AII (*Minnesota*) claims the pamphlet, but it seems unlikely from the quality of printing that it was printed west of Washington, D. C.

2739 MEEKER, BRADLEY B.

A PLAN FOR THE SPEEDY CONSTRUCTION OF A PACIFIC RAILROAD, WITH THE DRAFT OF A BILL . . . ST. LOUIS: GEORGE KNAPP & CO., 1860.

[1]–15, [16 blank]. 23.2 x 15.8 cm. Stitched, unbound.
Ref.: Sabin 47372
Laid in is: [caption title] A Bill / For the purpose of aiding in the construction of a line of railroad across that / portion of the public domain lying between the Mississippi river and the / eastern boundary of the State of California. / . . . [1]–5, [6 blank]. 31.2 x 19.6 cm. Un-

bound, second leaf tipped in; folded into four sections.
Prov.: Inscribed on page [6]: Rail Road / J. C. Burch /
Ref.:
Laid in is: [caption title] House of Representatives, / Washington City, Jan. 28, 1860. / Sir: Herewith please find enclosed copy of a Me-/ morial for a "Pacific Rail Road," . . . [1–4]. 20.1 x 12.7 cm. Unbound leaflet.
Ref.:
Signed in manuscript Jno C Burch / and addressed: Hon A Johnson / U S.S. /

2740 MEEKER, EZRA

WASHINGTON TERRITORY WEST OF THE CASCADE MOUNTAINS, CONTAINING A DESCRIPTION OF PUGET SOUND, AND RIVERS EMPTYING INTO IT . . . OLYMPIA, W. T.: PRINTED AT THE TRANSCRIPT OFFICE, 1870.

[1]–52, [I]–[XXIV]. 20.5 x 13.5 cm. Green printed wrappers, title on front wrapper, contents on verso of front wrapper, advertisements on inner and outer back wrapper. Rebacked. In a black cloth case.
Ref.: AII (*Washington*) 142; Howes M478; Sabin 47373; Smith 6715
Laid in is a broadside prospectus for the book.

2741 MEEKER, EZRA

[Broadside] NEW BOOK. WASHINGTON TERRITORY WEST OF THE CASCADE MOUNTAINS. CONTENTS: . . . ADDRESS, E. MEEKER, OLYMPIA, WASHINGTON TERRITORY.

Broadside, 20.2 x 11.4 cm. Text, 17.5 x 9 cm.
Ref.: AII (*Washington*) 141
Laid in the author's *Washington Territory . . .* Olympia, 1870.

2742 MEEKER, JOSEPHINE

THE UTE MASSACRE! BRAVE MISS MEEKER'S CAPTIVITY! HER OWN ACCOUNT OF IT. ALSO, THE NARRATIVES OF HER MOTHER AND MRS. PRICE . . . PHILADELPHIA, PA.: PUBLISHED BY THE OLD FRANKLIN PUBLISHING HOUSE, 1879.

[1]–[64]. 23.2 x 14.7 cm. Six illustrations included in pagination, three of which carry additional titles in German. Pink pictorial wrappers with title on front wrapper, advertisements on verso of back wrapper. In a blue half morocco case.
Ref.: Ayer (*Supp.*) 42 see; Howes U36
Thomas F. Dawson's *The Ute War . . .* 1879, carried the narrative of the Meeker captivity first.

2743 MELINE, JAMES F.

TWO THOUSAND MILES ON HORSEBACK. SANTA FE AND BACK. A SUMMER TOUR THROUGH KANSAS, NEBRASKA, COLORADO, AND NEW MEXICO, IN THE YEAR 1866 . . . NEW YORK: PUBLISHED BY HURD AND HOUGHTON, 1868.

[i]–x, [1]–317, [318 blank]. 18 x 11.8 cm. Map: Route Map, to accompany Colonel Meline's / "Two Thousand Miles on Horseback." / [lower left:] Endicott & Co. 59 Beekman St. New York. / 30 x 43 cm. No scale given. Maroon cloth, blind fillets on sides, title in gilt on backstrip.

Ref.: Dellenbaugh, p. 710; Howes M488; Rader 2376; Sabin 47427; Saunders 3048

A fascinating work. Meline went up the Platte to Fort McPherson, on to Denver, south via Raton Pass to Santa Fé and Albuquerque, and returned to Fort Leavenworth mostly by way of the Santa Fé Trail.

Editions: New York, 1867.

2744 MELISH, JOHN

[Map] [vignette] / MAP / OF THE / UNITED STATES / WITH THE CONTIGUOUS / BRITISH & SPANISH POSSESSIONS / COMPILED FROM THE LATEST & BEST AUTHORITIES / BY / JOHN MELISH / ENGRAVED BY J. VALLANCE & H. S. TANNER. / [short swelled rule] / ENTERED ACCORDING TO ACT OF CONGRESS THE 6ᵀᴴ DAY OF JUNE 1816. / PUBLISHED BY JOHN MELISH PHILADELPHIA. / *Inset:* WEST INDIES. / 12.3 x 23.7 cm. No scale given.

Map, 88.1 x 142.6 cm. Scale: 60 miles to one inch. Cut into forty panels, 22.8 x 14.6 cm., mounted on cloth, edges bound with blue ribbon, two panels backed with marbled paper, inserted in new board slip case, calf backstrip and calf edges.

Ref.: Karpinski 37

The earliest edition noted by Phillips is 1818.

2745 MELISH, JOHN

[Map] [vignette] / MAP / OF THE / UNITED STATES / WITH THE CONTIGUOUS / BRITISH & SPANISH POSSESSIONS / COMPILED FROM THE LATEST & BEST AUTHORITIES / BY / JOHN MELISH / ENGRAVED BY J. VALLANCE & H. S. TANNER. / [short swelled rule] / ENTERED ACCORDING TO ACT OF CONGRESS THE 16ᵀᴴ DAY OF JUNE 1820. / PUBLISHED BY JOHN MELISH PHILADELPHIA. / [short swelled rule] / IMPROVED TO 1822. / [short swelled rule] / *Inset:* WEST INDIES. / 15.5 x 26 cm. No scale given.

Map, 108.2 x 142.4 cm. Scale: 60 miles to one inch. Folded and mounted, cut into fifty panels, 22 x 14.5 cm., mounted on cloth, edges bound with green silk ribbon, two panels backed with marbled paper.

Ref.: Karpinski 71 note

2746 MELISH, JOHN

TRAVELS THROUGH THE UNITED STATES OF AMERICA, IN THE YEARS 1806 & 1807, AND 1809. 1810, & 1811; INCLUDING AN ACCOUNT OF PASSAGES BETWIXT AMERICA & BRITAIN . . . LONDON: REPRINTED FOR LONGMAN, HURST, REES, ORME, & BROWNE, 1818.

1–814. [i]–[xxiv, xxiv blank], [25]–648. 21.1 x 13.2 cm. Map: View of the Country / round / Pittsburg /. 16.1 x 10.1 cm. No scale given. Map: Kentucky /. 18.4 x 35.9 cm. Scale: 30 miles to one inch. Map: Ohio /. 23.2 x 23.2 cm. Scale: about 30 miles to one inch. Map: Falls of Ohio / [lower right] T. Badge sc. / 15.2 x 10.1 cm. No scale given. View: General View of the Falls of Niagara /. 10.3 x 17.5 cm. Map: View of the Country / round the / Falls of Niagara /. 16.6 x 10.1 cm. Scale: about 7 miles to one inch. View: View of Lake George. / 10.1 x 17.5 cm. Map: View of the Country / round / Zanesville /. 15.8 x 10.3 cm. Scale: two miles to one inch. Contemporary full pink calf, blind fillets on sides, gilt and blind backstrip, edges sprinkled.

Ref.: Buck 74; Clark II 159; Howes M496; Sabin 47436

Editions: Philadelphia, 1812, 1815, 1818.

2747 MELLON, THOMAS

THOMAS MELLON AND HIS TIMES . . . PITTSBURGH: WM. G. JOHNSTON & CO., 1885.

[i–ii], [1]–648, [i]–viii. 22.8 x 14 cm. Five illustrations, unlisted. Brown cloth.

Prov.: Inscribed on first blank leaf: Presented / to / J M Shields Esq / On account of my / long and intimate / association with his / father / Thos Mellon /. Bookplates of J. M. Shields, William Shields, and Edwin Stanton Fickes. Newspaper clippings pasted in, marginal notes.

Ref.: Howes M499

A work important to the history of Pittsburgh and western Pennsylvania.

2748 MELODY, GEORGE H. C.

NOTICE SUR LES INDIENS IOWAYS, ET SUR LE NUAGE BLANC . . . PARIS: IMPRIMERIE DE WITTERSHEIM, 1845.

[1]–24. 19.2 x 12 cm. Eight full-page woodcuts after Catlin. Pink printed wrappers with title on front wrapper and one illustration repeated on back. In a red half morocco case.

Prov.: Joseph G. Shea copy.

Ref.: Howes M500; Sabin 47467

Especially important because of the lists of names of Indians.

2749 MEMORIAL FOR A NORMAL SETTLEMENT

[Broadside] MEMORIAL FOR A NORMAL SETTLEMENT. AS IT APPEARS FROM SOME OF THE CONGRESSIONAL REPORTS THAT MISAPPREHENSION EXISTS WITH RESPECT TO THE OBJECT AS WELL AS THE NATURE OF OUR APPLICATION, WE MAY BE ALLOWED TO TRESPASS A LITTLE FURTHER ON PUBLIC ATTENTION IN EXPLAINING WHAT IS MEANT BY—A NORMAL SETTLEMENT. WE MEAN A SETTLEMENT WHICH IS LAID OUT IN ACCORDANCE WITH THE LAWS OF HUMAN NATURE IN HEALTHFUL ACTION . . . WE THEREFORE REQUEST PERMISSIEN[!] TO LOCATE 12,000 ACRES IN A BODY FOR A NORMAL SETTLEMENT. SIGNED IN BE-HALF OF THE MEMORALISTS[!] WILLIAM REES, SECRETARY. KEOKUK, IOWA, FEB., 20TH, 1854.

Broadside, 31.1 x 20.5 cm. Text, 22 x 15 cm.
Ref.:
In the same year, William Rees published his *Description of the City of Keokuk . . .*
No other copy of the broadside has been located.

2750 MERCER, ASA S.

THE BANDITTI OF THE PLAINS; OR, THE CATTLEMEN'S INVASION OF WYOMING IN 1892 . . .

[Four blank leaves], [i–ii (i advertisement, verso blank)], [1]–139, [140 blank], [three blank leaves]. 20.7 x 13.9 cm. 12 illustrations, both full-page and in the text. Black cloth. In a blue cloth case.
Prov.: Inscribed, inverted, on the verso of the last blank leaf: Compliments of / A S Mercer /.
Ref.: Adams 679; Adams (*Ramp. Herd*) 1474; Howes M522; Jones 1673; Smith 6735
The Preface is dated Cheyenne, Wyoming, February 20, 1894. The work was probably published at Cheyenne in that year.
An exposé which nearly cost the author his life, and one of the few copies that have escaped destruction by interested people.
Laid in the cloth case which holds the book is an original photograph of participants in the Johnson County War taken at Fort D. A. Russell in front of Warehouse 54. Photo: 15 x 20.3 cm. Mount: 17.6 x 22.7 cm. Mounted on thick cardboard printed in gold: Kirkland Cheyenne, Wyo. / The photograph was published in David, Robert B.: *Malcolm Campbell, Sheriff . . .* Casper, Wyo.: Wyomingana, Inc., [1932].
Accompanying the photograph is a typed list identifying all of the individuals except one.

2751 MERCER, ASA S.

BIG HORN COUNTY, WYOMING. THE GEM OF THE ROCKIES . . . HYATTVILLE, WYOMING: A. S. MERCER.

[1]–[116]. 18 x 12 cm. Illustrations unlisted. White pictorial wrappers. In a blue cloth case.
Ref.: Adams (*Ramp. Herd*) 1475; Howes M523; Smith 6739
The following appears on the verso of the title-leaf: Copyright, 1906 by A. S. Mercer / [below, at left within printer's mark:] W. B. Conkey Company, Chicago. / The Hammond Press. /

2752 MERCER, ASA S.

THE MATERIAL RESOURCES OF MARION COUNTY, OREGON; WITH A COMPLETE BUSINESS DIRECTORY . . . SALEM, OREGON: E. M. WAITE, BOOK AND JOB PRINTER, 1876.

[i–iv], [1]–80. 20.8 x 13.8 cm. Folding map: [Township map of surveyed areas in western Oregon]. 21.2 x 41.1 cm. Scale: 20 miles to one inch. Two-page table headed Weather Record, / on pages [ii–iii]. Salmon printed wrappers, with short title on front wrapper and advertisements on all wrapper surfaces.
Prov.: Rubber stamp and Exchange stamp of U.S. Geological Survey on title-page, former on page 27.
Ref.: Adams (*Ramp. Herd*) 1477; Howes M524; Smith 6742
The text is interspersed with advertisements.

2753 MERCER, ASA S.

THE PIONEER . . . CHICAGO: PRINTED AND BOUND BY THE HENNEBERRY COMPANY.

[1]–47, [48 blank]. (Pages [1–2] blank.) 17.9 x 11.8 cm. Green cloth, title in gilt on front cover.
Ref.: Smith 6743
Copyrighted 1913.

2754 MERCER, ASA S.

WASHINGTON TERRITORY. THE GREAT NORTHWEST, HER MATERIAL RESOURCES, AND CLAIMS TO EMIGRATION. A PLAIN STATEMENT OF THINGS AS THEY EXIST . . . UTICA, N.Y.: L. C. CHILDS, 1865.

[1]–38, [39–40 blank] 23.1 x 14.2 cm. Salmon printed wrappers with title on front wrapper. In a blue half morocco case.
Ref.: Adams (*Ramp. Herd*) 1478; Bradford 3450; Howell 215; Howes M526; Sabin 47899; Smith 6745
Mercer, a pioneer leader, was first president of the University of Washington.

2755 MERKLEY, CHRISTOPHER

BIOGRAPHY OF CHRISTOPHER MERKLEY. WRITTEN BY HIMSELF. SALT LAKE CITY: J. H. PARRY & COMPANY, 1887.

[1]–46, [47–8 blank]. 17.8 x 11.8 cm. Pink printed wrappers, with title on front wrapper, advertisements on verso of back wrapper.

Ref.: Howes M537

A Mormon's experiences in Missouri, Illinois, and farther west.

2756 MERRICK, GEORGE B.

OLD TIMES ON THE UPPER MISSISSIPPI . . . CLEVELAND, OHIO: THE ARTHUR H. CLARK COMPANY, 1909.

[1]–323, [324 blank]. (Pages [1–2] blank.) 24 x 15.8 cm. 25 illustrations and maps listed. Blue ribbed cloth, gilt top, uncut.

Ref.: Howes M539

2757 MERRILL, D. D., *Publisher*

THE NORTHERN ROUTE TO IDAHO: AND THE PACIFIC OCEAN. SAINT PAUL, MINN.: PUBLISHED BY D. D. MERRILL. BOOK SELLER AND STATIONER.

[1]–8. 14.8 x 9.3 cm. Folding map: Minnesota Route / the shortest and best to the / Idaho Gold Mines. / Compiled by C. A. F. Morris. / [5 lines of distances] / Lith. by Louis Buechner, St Paul. / Published by D. D. Merrill, St Paul. / [below border at left:] Entered according to Act of Congress in the year 1864 by D. D. Merrill in the Clerks Office of the District Court of the 2^d District of Minnesota. / 44.3 x 105.9 cm. No scale given. Brown cloth, 15.8 x 10 cm., with title stamped in gilt on front cover.

Ref.: AII (*Minnesota*) 577; Dunbar: *History of Travel in America*, Vol. IV, "The Rubber Stamp Map"; Jones 1473; Wagner-Camp 401

The imprint on page 8 reads as follows: Printed by D. Ramaley, Saint Paul, Minn. In later impressions of the map, there were changes made either in manuscript or by rubber stamp. The present copy is in the original state.

2758 MERRILL, ORIN S.

"MYSTERIOUS SCOTT," THE MONTE CRISTO OF DEATH VALLEY AND TRACKS OF A TENDERFOOT . . . CHICAGO, ORIN S. MERRILL.

[1]–[211], [212 blank], [213–19 advertisements, 220 blank]. 19.1 x 13.1 cm. Map and illustrations unlisted. Yellow printed wrappers with title and pictorial design on front wrapper. In a red cloth case.

Ref.: Blumann & Thomas 1006; Edwards p. 116

Published in 1906. More important than stories about "Death Valley Scotty" are descriptive passages about earlier days of Death Valley.

2759 MERRILL, WILLIAM E.

[Map] KANSAS / WITH PARTS OF NEIGHBORING STATES AND TERRITORIES. / 2ND EDITION—WITH CORRECTIONS BY LT. JACKSON, 7TH CAV. ACT.

CHIEF ENGR. DEPT. MO. / OCT. 1868. / BVT. MAJ. GEN. A. A. HUMPHREYS, CHIEF OF ENGINEERS. COMPILED UNDER DIRECTION OF BVT. COL. W.^{M} E. MERRILL, MAJ. ENGRS. ST. LOUIS, MAY 1868. / [lower left corner:] JOHN GAST & CO. LITH., COR. 3rd & OLIVE STS. ST. LOUIS, MO. /

Map, 52.7 x 89.2 cm. printed on cotton. Scale: about 20 miles to an inch. Part of edge tipped to maroon cloth covers, ostrich skin backstrip.

Ref.:

The measurements do not include title above neat line or line and scale below.

On verso of map is stamped in red a large "R" and the numerals 41$^{\underline{2}}$. Two paper labels are mounted on the sheet; one, label of Boott Cotton Mills and the other label of Lowell Bleachery Finish.

2760 MERRITT, W.

[Wrapper title] ANNUAL REPORT . . . DEPARTMENT OF THE MISSOURI, 1889.

[1]–6, [7–8 blank]. 19.7 x 12.5 cm. Blue-gray printed wrappers, with title as above on front wrapper.

Ref.:

Dated: Headquarters Department of the Missouri, / Fort Leavenworth, Kansas, September 12, 1889. /

Describes the opening of Oklahoma to white settlers, April 22, 1889.

2761 MERRYWEATHER, F.

FROM ENGLAND TO CALIFORNIA . . . LIFE AMONG THE MORMONS AND INDIANS . . . SACRAMENTO CITY, CAL.: J. A. WILSON, PUBLISHER.

[1]–146. 18.7 x 11.3 cm. Sewn. Front wrapper and pages [1]–6, 142–146 supplied in photostat.

Ref.:

The copy used for the photostat is the Bancroft Library copy.

Copyrighted in 1868 by F. Merryweather, M.D.

2762 MESSITER, CHARLES A.

SPORT AND ADVENTURES AMONG THE NORTH-AMERICAN INDIANS . . . LONDON: R. H. PORTER, 1890.*

[i]–[xviii, xviii blank], [1]–368. 21.8 x 14 cm. Nine illustrations listed. Green pictorial cloth.

Ref.: Howes M558; Rader 2387

2763 METHODIST EPISCOPAL CHURCH, SOUTH

MINUTES OF THE SEVENTH SESSION OF THE MONTANA ANNUAL CONFERENCE, METHODIST EPISCOPAL CHURCH, SOUTH, HELD AT STEVENSVILLE, MON-

TANA, AUGUST 21–25, 1884. TOGETHER WITH A BRIEF HISTORY OF THE M. E. CHURCH, SOUTH, IN MONTANA FROM 1864 TO 1884, AND A SKETCH OF THE HISTORY AND RESOURCES OF MONTANA TERRITORY. BY EDWIN J. STANLEY. KANSAS CITY: PRESS OF RAMSEY, MILLETT & HUDSON, 1884.

[1]–106, 107–16 advertisements. 22 x 14.3 cm. Black cloth.

Ref.:

See also under Stanley, Edwin J.

2764 METHVIN, JOHN J.

ANDELE; OR, THE MEXICAN-KIOWA CAPTIVE. A STORY OF REAL LIFE AMONG THE INDIANS . . . LOUISVILLE, KY.: PENTECOSTAL HERALD PRESS, 1899.

[1]–184. 18.8 x 12.9 cm. Nine illustrations, unlisted. Gray cloth, stamped in black.

Ref.: Ayer (*Supp.*) 85; Howes M562; Rader 2388

The captivity of Andrés Martinez.

Editions: Louisville, 1899.

2765 MEXICO. Commission to Investigate the Northern Frontier

REPORTS OF THE COMMITTEE OF INVESTIGATION SENT IN 1873 BY THE MEXICAN GOVERNMENT TO THE FRONTIER OF TEXAS. TRANSLATED FROM THE OFFICIAL EDITION MADE IN MEXICO. NEW YORK: BAKER & GODWIN, 1875.

[i]–viii, [3]–443, [444 blank]. 22.5 x 14.6 cm. Three maps: A / Map of the / Indian Territory / Northern Texas / and / New Mexico / Showing the / reat[!] Western Prairies / by / Josiah Gregg / [lower left:] Entered according to Act of Congress in the year 1844 by Sidney F. Morse and Samuel Breese in the Clerks Office of the Southern District of New York. / [lower centre, below neat line:] [three-line note in Spanish] /. 30.8 x 37.9 cm. Scale: about 60 miles to one inch. Map: Copiado del Mapa de S. Mc. L. Staples, en 1828; del Mapa de Nigra de San Martin en cuanto á las dis-/tancias respectivas, y de la Carta general de la República Mexicana de García Cubas; . . . / . . . / Dibujado y extractado de los documentos y datos dichos, por F. L. Mier.—Monterey, Diciembre de 1873. / [below neat line; three lines in Spanish] /. 39 x 25.6 cm. No scale given. Map: Mapa del Rio Grande / desde su Desembocadura en el Golfo hasta San Vicente, Presidion Antíguo. / [4 lines] / Monterey, Diciembre de 1873. / M. J. Martinez, / Ingeniero Topógrafo. / 81 x 71.8 cm. Scale: 20 kilometers to one inch. Buff printed wrappers, brown cloth back, title on front wrapper.

Ref.:

Members of the Commission were Emilio Velasco, Ygnacio Galindo, and Antonio Garcia Carrillo, with Augustin Silicio as secretary. The second part is signed by Galindo, Carillo and Siliceo[!] with Francisco Valdés Gomez as secretary.

2766 MEXICO. Constitution

CONSTITUCION FEDERAL DE LOS ESTADOS UNIDOS MEXICANOS, SANCIONADA POR EL CONGRESO GENERAL CONSTITUYENTE, EL 4 DE OCTUBRE DE 1824. IMPRENTA DEL SUPREMO GOBIERNO DE LOS ESTADOS-UNIDOS MEXICANOS, EN PALACIO.

[*]², 1–7², [8]¹. [i–iv], 1–[30]. 29 x 20.6 cm. Stabbed, bound into blue paste paper wrappers. Laid into blue board folder, calf back, red leather label on front cover.

Ref.: Sabin 48379

Published in 1824. On pages [iv] and 28, the printed signature of Juan Guzman is followed by a manuscript paraph.

Probably only a very small number printed for distribution to the members of the government.

2767 MEXICO. Constitution

CONSTITUCION FEDERAL DE LOS ESTADOS UNIDOS MEXICANOS, SANCIONADA POR EL CONGRESO GENERAL CONSTITUYENTE, EL 4. DE OCTUBRE DE 1824. IMPRENTA DEL SUPREMO GOBIERNO DE LOS ESTADOS-UNIDOS MEXICANOS, EN PALACIO.

[1–4], [I]–XVIII, [1]–62, [63–5 Index, 66 blank], I–III, [IV blank], [1]–12. 13.7 x 8.8 cm. One plate.

Ref.: Sabin 48379

BOUND WITH:

CONSTITUCION POLITICA DEL ESTADO LIBRE DE XALISCO SANCIONADA POR SU CONGRESO CONSTITUYENTE EN 18 DE NOVIEMBRE DE 1824. GUADALAJARA. IMPRENTA DEL C. URBANO SANROMAN, 1824.

[1]–80. 13.7 x 8.8 cm.

Ref.: Clagett p. 68

BOUND WITH:

REGLAMENTO INSTRUCCTIVO PARA EL GOBIERNO ECONOMICO-POLITICO DEL ESTADO LIBRE DE JALISCO. GUADALAJARA: IMPRENTA DEL C. URBANO SANROMAN, 1825.

[1]–58, [59 index, 60 blank]. 13.7 x 8.8 cm.

Ref.:

BOUND WITH:

REGLAMENTO PARA LA ADMINISTRACION DE JUSTICIA EN EL ELESTADO[!] LIBRE DE JALISCO. GUADALAJARA: IMPRENTA DEL C. URBANO SANROMAN, 1825.

[1]–44, [45–46 index], [47–8 blank] 13.7 x 8.8
cm.
Ref.: Clagett p. 73
Four volumes bound together in contemporary half black roan brown marbled board sides, red leather label on backstrip lettered in gilt, gilt edges.

The twelve pages at the end of the first volume carry a separate title-page as follows: Acta / Constitutiva / de la Federacion / Mexicana / [vignette] / [vignette] / 12 /.

2768 MEXICO. Constitution

COLECCION DE CONSTITUCIONES DE LOS ESTADOS UNIDOS MEXICANO. MEXICO : IMPRENTA DE GALVAN, 1828.

[i–iv], XV–XX, 1–473, [474 errata], [I]–XIV index. [i–ii], [1]–469, [470 errata], [I]–XI, index, [XII blank]. [i–ii], [1]–484, [I]–XII index. 14.4 x 10.2 cm. Engraved plate in first volume. Three volumes, full contemporary mottled calf, leather labels on backstrips.
Ref.: Clagett p. 47, 68, etc.; Sabin 48349; Streeter Part II p. xix
The sections dealing with Chihuahua, Coahuila y Tejas, and the Mexican federal constitution all appear in the first volume.

2769 MEXICO. Constitution

[THE CONSTITUTION OF] MEXICA[N UNITED STATES.] CHILLI[COTHE:] PRINTED BY R. [KERCHEVAL,] 1829.
[1]–26. 18.6 x 12.3 cm.
BOUND WITH:
THE CONSTITUTION OF CUAHUILA AND TEXAS. CHILLICOTHE: PRINTED BY R. KERCHEVAL. 1829.
[1]–34. Contemporary gray wrappers with tan paper back. Lacks most of title-leaf of first part as indicated above.
Ref.: Clements Library (*Texas*) 9; Howes C504; Sabin 94943; Streeter 1106, 1109
The Kercheval edition seems to be the second edition in English. As with the only other copy we have located, the two pieces are bound together. They were probably issued in this fashion.
Editions: Tuscumbia, 1825; Natchez, 1826.

2770 MEXICO. Laws

[Caption title] SECRETARIA DE GUERRA Y MARINA SECCION 2.ᴬ EL ECSMO. SR. PRESIDENTE DE LOS ESTADOS UNIDOS MEXICANOS SE HA SERVIDO DIRIGIRME EL DECRETO QUE SIGUE. EL PRESIDENTE DE LOS ESTADOS UNIDOS MEXICANOS A LOS HABITANTES DE LA REPUBLICA, SABED: QUE EL CONGRESO GENERAL HA DECRETADO LO SIGUIENTE . . .

[1–12]. 29.5 x 20.3 cm. Two folded tables. Plain white wrappers.
Ref.: Streeter 714
These laws were passed by Congress on March 21, 1826. They provide for presidial companies in the Eastern and Western Internal States and the territory of New Mexico. Dated and signed at the end: Por tanto mando se imprima, publique y circule, y se le de / el debido cumplimiento. Palacio del gobierno federal en México á / 21 de Marzo de 1826. — Guadalupe Victoria. — A D. Manuel Gomez Pe-/draza. / Y lo comunico á V. para su intel—gencia y cumplimiento en la / parte que le toca. / Dios y libertad, México 21 de Marzo de 1826. / Gomez Pedraza. /

2771 MEXICO. Laws

[Broadside] ESTADO QUE MANIFIESTA LA FUERZA QUE DEBEN TENER LAS SEIS COMPANIAS QUE SE CONSIDERAN NECESARIAS PARA LA GUARNICION DE LOS TERRITORIOS DE LA ALTA Y BAJA CALIFORNIA, CON ESPRESION DE LOS HABERES Y GRATIFICACIONES QUE DEBERAN DISFRUTAR . . . NOTA. LAS GRATIFICACIONES SENALADAS A LAS COMPANIAS SON PER INDEMNIZACION DE LAS QUE GOZAN EN EL INTERIOR LAS TROPAS PERMANENTES, Y EN CONSECUENCIA DE LO QUE EN EL PARTICULAR PREVIENE EL REGLAMENTO DEL ANO DE 1781.—PACHECO.— F. MARTINEZ. ES COPIA MEXICO 8 DE MAYO DE 1828.—CORREGIDO.—BASCONCELCOS. F. CASTRO.

Broadside, 43.4 x 31.5 cm. Text, 37 x 24.8 cm.
Ref.:
Budget for military forces in California in San Francisco, Monterrey, Santa Barbara, San Diego, Fronteras, and Loreto. The *Reglamento* mentioned in the text was published in 1784. See number 9.

2772 MEXICO. LEGACION. United States

CORRESPONDENCIA QUE HA MEDIADO ENTRE LA LEGACION EXTRAORDINARIA DE MEXICO Y EL DEPARTAMENTO DE ESTADO DE LOS ESTADOS-UNIDOS, SOBRE EL PASO DEL SABINA POR LAS TROPAS QUE MANDABA EL GENERAL GAINES. MEXICO : REIMPRESO POR JOSE M. F. DE LARA, 1837.

[i]–xxix, [xxx blank], [1]–122. 19.1 x 11.6 cm. Rebound in half black cloth, mottled board sides.
Ref.: Howes G6; Raines p. 95; Sabin 16908; Streeter 1220A
The correspondence relates to the Gorostiza affair. Apparently there was no map with this edition.
Editions: Philadelphia, 1836.

2773 MEXICO. Real Audiencia

NUEVAS INSTRUCCIONES PARA EL JUZGADO DE BIENES DE DIFUNTOS DE LA REAL AUDIENCIA DE MEXICO . . . MEXICO: POR DON MARIANO DE ZUNIGA Y ONTIVEROS, 1805.

[1]–5², 6¹. [i–ii], 1–20. 28 x 19.8 cm. Bound with Number 9.

Ref.: Medina (*Mexico*) 9773

Signed in manuscript at the end: José Mª de Castra / [paraph] /.

2774 MEXICO. Treaty

[Caption title] PRIMERA SECRETARIA DE ESTADO. DEPARTAMENTO DEL ESTERIOR. EL ESCMO. SR. PRESIDENTE INTERINO DE LOS ESTADO UNIDOS MEXICANOS SE HA SERVIDO DIRIGIRME EL DECRETO QUE SIGUE. EL VICE-PRESIDENTE DE LOS ESTADOS UNIDOS MEXICANOS, EN EJERCICIO DEL SUPREMO PODER EJECUTIVO, A TODOS LOS QUE LAS PRESENTES VIEREN, SABED: QUE HABIENDOSE CONCLUIDO Y FIRMADO EN ESTA CAPITAL EL DIA ONCE DE ABRIL DEL PRESENTE ANO, UN TRATADO DE AMISTAD, COMERCIO Y NAVEGACION ENTRE LOS ESTADOS UNIDOS MEXICANOS Y LOS ESTADOS UNIDOS DE AMERICA, POR MEDIO DE PLENIPOTENCIARIOS DE AMBOS GOBIERNOS AUTORIZADOS DEBIDA Y RESPEC-TIVAMENTE PARA ESTE EFECTO, CUYO TRATADO ES EN LA FORMA Y TENOR SIGUIENTE: . . .

[1]–21, [22 blank]. 29.2 x 20.7 cm. Stabbed. Last leaf trimmed at foot.

Ref.: Streeter 1103B see

Published at Mexico City, December 1, 1832. With a manuscript paraph of Francisco Fagoaga on page 21. The text of the treaty is present in both Spanish and English. Streeter describes another edition, but does not mention this one.

2775 MEXICO. Treaty

TRATADO DE PAZ, AMISTAD, LIMITES Y ARREGLO DEFINITIVO ENTRE LA REPUBLICA MEXICANA Y LOS ESTADOS-UNIDOS DE AMERICA, FIRMADO EN GUADALUPE HIDALGO EL 2 DE FEBRERO DE 1848, CON LAS MODIFICACIONES CON QUE HA SIDO APROBADO POR EL SENADO, Y RATIFICADO POR EL PRESIDENTE DE LOS ESTADOS-UNIDOS. QUERETARO: IMPRENTA DE J. M. LARA, 1848.

[1]–28. 22.6 x 15.4 cm.

BOUND WITH:

ESPOSICION DIRIGIDA AL SUPREMO GOBIERNO POR LOS COMISIONADOS QUE FIRMARON EL TRATADO DE PAZ CON LOS ESTADOS-UNIDOS. QUEREARO[!]: IMPRENTA DE JOSE M. LARA, 1848.

[1]–27, [28 blank]. Buff printed wrappers with title on front wrapper, decorative border and centre ornament on verso of back wrapper.

Ref.: Howes M565

2776 MEYER, C., & H. VON MINDEN

[Map] MAP / OF / MINNESOTA / COMPILED FROM THE / UNITED STATES SURVEYS / BY C. MEYER & H. V. MINDEN / Sᵀ PAUL, M. T. 1856. / ENGRᴰ BY FRIEND & AUB LITH.ᴿˢ 80, WALNUT Sᵀ PHILDAᴬ / EXPLANATION. / [6 lines] / FOR SALE WHOLESALE AT BERNHEIMER, BROTHERS, Nᵒ 199, BROADWAY, NEW-YORK / ARNOLD, NUSBAUM & NIRDLINGER, Nᵒ 51, NORTH 3ᴿᴰ Sᵀ PHILAᴬ / & C. MEYER & H. V. MINDEN, Sᵀ PAUL, MINNESOTA. / ENTERED ACCORD-ING TO ACT OF CONGRESS, IN THE YEAR 1856 BY C. MEYER & H. V. MINDEN, IN THE CLERK'S OFFICE / OF THE UNITED STATES DISTRICT COURT FOR THE SECOND JUDICIAL DISTRICT, TERRITORY OF MINNE-SOTA. / *Inset:* Map of / Sᵗ Paul / Capital of / Minnesota /. 12.6 x 13.2 cm. No scale given.

Map, 76.3 x 54.8 cm. No scale given. Folded into black cloth, 14 x 9.5 cm., green printed paper label on front cover.

Ref.:

2777 MEYER, GEORGE

AUTOBIOGRAPHY . . . ACROSS THE PLAINS WITH AN OX TEAM IN 1849. HIS SUCCESS IN THE GOLD FIELDS OF CALIFORNIA. SHENANDOAH, IOWA: THE OPEN DOOR, 1908.

[1]–[29], [30–32 blank]. (Pages [1–2] blank.) 19.9 x 13.8 cm. Two portraits, on recto and verso of frontispiece leaf. Tan printed wrappers with title on front wrapper. In a red cloth folder.

Ref.: Howes M573

The party, a small one, went by way of the South Pass and eventually mined near Coloma for a year. Meyer returned by ship, via the Isthmus, to New York.

2778 MEYERS, AUGUSTUS

TEN YEARS IN THE RANKS U. S. ARMY . . . NEW YORK: THE STIRLING PRESS, 1914.*

[i–vi, vi blank], 1–356. 21.4 x 14.3 cm. Blue-gray cloth, title in gilt on front cover and backstrip, large white Maltese Cross on front cover, gilt top.

Prov.: Inscribed on front endleaf: A. Stirling Smith Esq. / Compliments of / Augustus Meyers / January 15 / 1915 /.

Ref.: Howes M574

First Issue, with gilt top.

Includes sketches of campaigning on the Nebraska-Dakota frontier between 1855 and 1860.

2779 MICHAUX, ANDRE

JOURNAL . . . 1787–1796 . . . AMERICAN PHILO-SOPHICAL SOCIETY, VOL. XXVI, NO. 129.

[i–iv], [1]–145, [146 blank]. 23.1 x 14.8 cm. Cream printed wrappers with cream cloth backstrip, title on front wrapper. In a red cloth case.

Prov.: C. G. Littell bookplate.

Ref.: Buck 44; Clark II 45; Howes M578; Hubach p. 34 see; Matthews p. 184

This separate printing with French text and notes in English was issued in 1889 at Philadelphia.

2780 MICHAUX, FRANCOIS ANDRE

TRAVELS TO THE WESTWARD OF THE ALLEGANY MOUNTAINS, IN THE STATES OF THE OHIO, KENTUCKY, AND TENNESSEE, AND RETURN TO CHARLESTOWN, THROUGH THE UPPER CAROLINAS . . . UNDERTAKEN IN THE YEAR X, 1802 . . . LONDON: PRINTED BY W. FLINT, 1805.

A–Z⁸. [i]–xvi, [1]–350, [351–52 advertisements]. 21.7 x 13.2 cm. Map: Map / of the / Southern, Western & Middle / Provinces / of the / United States. / [lower right:] Neele, sc. 352. Strand. / [lower centre:] London Publish'd Janʸ 1ˢᵗ 1805 by J. Mawman Poultry. / 35 x 49.2 cm. Scale: 75 miles to one inch. Gray boards, new tan paper backstrip, original white printed paper label, 4.5 x 3.6 cm. (incomplete), uncut.

Ref.: Bradford 3461; Clark II 106; Howes M579; Hubach p. 38; Meisel III 365–66; Monaghan 1063; Sabin 48704; Thomson 822

2781 MICHAUX, FRANCOIS ANDRE

VOYAGE A L'OUEST DES MONTS ALLEGHANYS, DANS LES ETATS DE L'OHIO, DU KENTUCKY ET DU TENNESSEE, ET RETOUR A CHARLESTON PAR LES HAUTES-CAROLINES . . . ENTREPRIS PENDANT L'AN X–1802 . . . A PARIS: CHEZ LEVRAULT, SCHOELL ET COMPAGNIE, AN XII—1804.

[*]², a³, A–T⁸, V⁴. (F, F5, R7 are cancels.) [1–4], [i]–vj, [1]–312. 21.5 x 13.6 cm. Folding map: Carte / des Etats du Centre, de / l'Ouest et du Sud / des / Etats-Unis. / Dessinée par Dupuis fils / An XII.—1804. / [lower left:] Glot S. / 35.8 x 50.2 cm. No scale given. Purplish-brown wrappers, uncut, mostly unopened, printed white paper label (4 x 3 cm.) on backstrip: Voyage / a l'Ouest / des Monts / Alleghanys. / 1804 / [within double rule border]. Label worn. In a brown cloth case.

Ref.: Bradford 3464; Clark II 106; Howes M579; Hubach p. 38; Meisel III 365; Monaghan 1064; Sabin 48703; Thomson 821

The cancels are present in three copies examined. Copies printed on fine and thick paper, as is the present copy, contain an Avertissement of six pages following the title-leaf, and there is an accent in Tennessée, line 5 of title.

2782 MICHIGAN TERRITORY. Legislative Council

[Caption title] . . . MICHIGAN—LEGISLATURE—SOUTHERN BOUNDARY. MEMORIAL OF THE LEGISLATIVE COUNCIL OF MICHIGAN, EXPRESSIVE OF THE VIEWS ENTERTAINED BY THEM ON THE SUBJECT OF THE SOUTHERN BOUNDARY OF THAT TERRITORY . . .

[1]–13, [14 blank]. (First leaf loose; p. 9 (leaf 5) signed 2.) 22.7 x 14.3 cm. Removed from binding, unbound.

Ref.:

23rd Congress, 1st Session, House, Document No. 302, Serial 257. [Washington, 1834.]

Signed at end: John McDonell, President of the Legislative Council. Attest: John Norvell, Secretary.

Printer's imprint on page [1] lower left: Gales & Seaton, Print. /

2783 [MICHLER, NATHANIEL H.]

[Caption title] . . . ROUTES FROM THE WESTERN BOUNDARY OF ARKANSAS TO SANTA FE AND THE VALLEY OF THE RIO GRANDE. LETTER FROM THE SECRETARY OF WAR . . . MAY 16, 1850 . . .

[1]–12. 24 x 15.5 cm. Stabbed, unbound, uncut, unopened.

Ref.: Wagner-Camp 186-A

31st Congress, 1st Session, House, Executive Document No. 67, Serial 562. [Washington, 1850.]

Comprises principally a report by Lieutenant Michler of the country between the Red River and the Rio Pecos.

2784 MIDDLETON, JOHN W.

HISTORY OF THE REGULATORS AND MODERATORS AND THE SHELBY COUNTY WAR IN 1841 AND 1842, IN THE REPUBLIC OF TEXAS, WITH FACTS AND INCIDENTS IN THE EARLY HISTORY OF THE REPUBLIC AND STATE, FROM 1837 TO THE ANNEXATION . . . FORT WORTH, TEXAS: LOVING PUBLISHING COMPANY, 1883.

[1]–40. 19.9 x 13.9 cm. Buff printed wrappers, with title on front wrapper. In green half morocco case.

Ref.: Adams 680; Clements Library (*Texas*) 46; Howes M588; Rader 2392; Raines p. 149

The Regulators were Texan settlers organized to fight frontier lawlessness. The Moderators were also Texan settlers, but they were organized to combat the harsher Regulators. The two groups often fought bitterly, as witness the Shelby County War, here described. The author was an active Regulator.

2785 MILES, NELSON A.

[Wrapper title] ANNUAL REPORT . . . DEPART-
MENT OF ARIZONA. 1886.

[1]–22. 19.5 x 12.5 cm. Blue-gray printed wrap-
pers with title on front wrapper. Lacks back
wrapper.
Ref.:
Printed at Albuquerque.
Signed at end: Nelson A. Miles, / Brigadier
General, U. S. Army, / Commanding Depart-
ment of Arizona. /
Chiefly the report of operations against Ge-
ronimo's and Natchez's bands of hostile In-
dians. General Miles includes reports by Captain
Lawton, Lieutenant Leonard Wood (Assistant
Surgeon), E. J. Spencer, and others who took
part in the campaign.
In Lawton Scrap-book.

2786 MILES, NELSON A.

[Wrapper title] ANNUAL REPORT . . . DEPART-
MENT OF ARIZONA, 1887.

[1]–10, [1]–7, [1]–3, [blank leaf]. 19.4 x 12.3 cm.
White printed wrappers with title on front
wrapper.
Prov.: With slip tipped to top of front wrap-
per, 5 x 12.2 cm.: Compliments of / Brigadier
General Nelson A. Miles, U. S. A. / Head-
quarters Department of Arizona, / Los Angeles,
Cal., January 12, 1888. /
Ref.:
The report is dated Headquarters Depart-
ment of Arizona, / Los Angeles, Cal., September
3, 1887. / Printed at Los Angeles.
Most of the material relates to the Indians on
the San Carlos Reservation.

2787 MILES, NELSON A.

[Wrapper title] ANNUAL REPORT . . . DEPART-
MENT OF ARIZONA, 1888.

[1]–40. 19.5 x 13.3 cm. Gray printed wrappers
with title on front wrapper.
Ref.: Howes M594
Printed at Los Angeles.
Dated: Headquarters Department of Ari-
zona, / Los Angeles, Cal., September 8, 1888. /
Contains detailed reports of engagements
with the Indians.

2788 MILES, NELSON A.

ANNUAL REPORT . . . SAN FRANCISCO, CAL.: AS-
SISTANT ADJUTANT GENERAL'S OFFICE, DIVISION OF
THE PACIFIC, 1889.

[1]–14, [15–16 blank], [1]–74. 23.5 x 15.2 cm.
Gray printed wrappers with title on front wrapper.

Prov.: Signed by the author on front cover
with line above and line below in hand of a secretary: With the compliments of / [signature of]
Nelson A. Miles / Brig. Gen'l, U. S. A. /
Ref.: Howes M593

2789 MILES, NELSON A.

PERSONAL RECOLLECTIONS AND OBSERVATIONS . . .
EMBRACING A BRIEF VIEW OF THE CIVIL WAR; OR,
FROM NEW ENGLAND TO THE GOLDEN GATE AND
THE STORY OF HIS INDIAN CAMPAIGNS . . . CHI-
CAGO: WERNER COMPANY, 1896.

[i]–[viii, viii blank], 1–590. 24.4 x 18.5 cm. 203
illustrations listed. Full black leather, gilt and
blind stamping on front cover, title in gilt on
front cover and backstrip, gilt edges.
Ref.: Howes M595; Munk (Alliot) p. 152;
Nicholson p. 514; Rader 2397; Saunders 3051;
Smith 6791
The earlier issue, with "General" on the
frontispiece instead of the later "Maj. Gen."

2790 MILES, W. H., JOHN BRATT, & Others

EARLY HISTORY AND REMINISCENCE, OF FRONTIER
COUNTY, NEB. MAYWOOD, NEBRASKA: PUBLISHED
BY N. H. BOGUE, 1894.

[i–ii], [1]–39, [40 blank]. 19.2 x 12.9 cm. Cream
pictorial stiff wrappers, with title on front cover,
red cloth backstrip.
Ref.: Howes M596
Largely written by John Bratt, whose other
and later book on this country is well known.

2791 MILES, WILLIAM

JOURNAL OF THE SUFFERINGS AND HARDSHIPS OF
CAPT. PARKER H. FRENCH'S OVERLAND EXPEDITION
TO CALIFORNIA, WHICH LEFT NEW YORK CITY,
MAY 13TH, 1850, AND ARRIVED AT SAN FRAN-
CISCO, DEC. 14 . . . CHAMBERSBURG: PRINTED AT
THE VALLEY SPIRIT OFFICE, 1851.

[1]–24. 20.4 x 12.4 cm. Tan wrappers. In blue
cloth case.
Ref.: Cowan p. 429; Howes M597; Jones
1265; Matthews p. 327; Wagner-Camp 202
The copy described by Wagner-Camp has a
green printed wrapper, apparently with title as
above.
French's party went by sea to New Orleans
and then overland to San Diego, etc.

**2792 MILFORT, JEAN ANTOINE LE
CLERC, KNOWN AS GENERAL**

MEMOIRE; OU, COUP D'OEIL RAPIDE SUR MES DIF-
FERENS VOYAGES ET MON SEJOUR DANS LA NATION
CRECK . . . A PARIS: DE L'IMPRIMERIE DE GIGUET
ET MICHAUD, AN XI.—(1802.)

[*]⁴, 1–20⁸, 21⁴. [1]–4, [1]–331, [332 errata].
(Page 79 mispaginated 99.) 19 x 12 cm. Rebound
in tan half morocco, gilt back, gilt top.

Ref.: Field 1065; Howes M599; Jones 693;
Monaghan 1073; Sabin 48949

For a critical discussion of the author and his
Mémoire see the Lakeside Classics edition (1956)
edited with a long introduction by John Francis
McDermott.

2793 MILLAR, J. H.

[Map] IOWA CITY / AND ITS ENVIRONS. / [decora-
tive rule] / COMPILED AND DRAWN BY / J. H.
MILLAR / OF THE FIRM BRYAN & MILLAR, PANORA,
GUTHRIE CO. IOWA. / ILLUSTRATIONS BY G. H.
YEWEL / 1854. / W. SCHUCHMAN LITH. 3ᴰ ST.
PITTSBURGH. /

Map, 63.6 x 85.2 cm. Scale: 400 feet to an inch.
Within neat line, at left and right are twelve
views and one trade card, lithographed. Unbound, folded.

Ref.:

2794 MILLER, ANDREW

NEW STATES AND TERRITORIES, OR THE OHIO,
INDIANA, ILLINOIS, MICHIGAN, NORTH-WESTERN,
MISSOURI, LOUISIANA, MISSISIPPI[!] AND ALABAMA,
IN THEIR REAL CHARACTERS, IN 1818 . . . 1819.

A–D¹². [1]–96. 12.7 x 6.8 cm. Folding table:
Map Table of the State of Ohio. / 21.6 x 24.8 cm.
Old marbled paper with new mottled calf back-
strip. In a blue board case.

Ref.: Bradford 3484; Buck 124; Howes
M608; Jones 814; Sabin 49008; Thomson 826

Believed to have been printed at Keene, New
Hampshire. The attribution of place appears to
stem from Obadiah Rich. A very interesting production. Miller counts thirty printing offices in
twenty-two Ohio towns. Not bad! AII locates
printing in only twenty-six towns before 1820.

The Map Table in the Ayer copy differs
somewhat and, if it was not entirely reset, was in
part reset. For instance, in the Note, the error
13,000 is corrected to 1,300. Different ornaments are used for the direction sign, etc. The
text seems to be the same, except page 94,
where the last numeral is dropped in the Ayer
copy.

2795 MILLER, BENJAMIN S.

RANCH LIFE IN SOUTHERN KANSAS AND THE INDIAN
TERRITORY AS TOLD BY A NOVICE . . . NEW YORK:
FLESS & RIDGE PRINTING COMPANY, 1896.

[1]–[164]. 20.3 x 14.2 cm. Portrait. Tan printed
wrappers with title on front wrapper. Title down
backstrip. In a brown buckram case.

Ref.: Adams 681; Adams (*Ramp. Herd*) 1485;
Howes M602

Deals mainly with ranching in the Cherokee
Strip.

2796 MILLER, ELIJAH

THE HISTORY OF PAGE COUNTY, IOWA, FROM THE
EARLIEST SETTLEMENT, IN 1843, TO THE FIRST CEN-
TENNIAL OF AMERICAN INDEPENDENCE, JULY 4,
1876 . . . CLARINDA, IOWA: HERALD BOOK AND
JOB OFFICE, 1876.

[1]–98, 98 1/4, 98 1/2, 99, [100–116 advertise-
ments]. 17.1 x 10.3 cm. Original limp black
cloth. Folding map: [Page County]. 15.1 x 18.6
cm. No scale given.

Prov.: Signature in pencil on inner front
cover: H. H. Scott / Clarinda / Ia / Aug 23 /
1912— /.

Ref.: Cook p. 145; Howes M603; Mott (*Iowa*)
p. 49; Peterson p. 54

A very interesting little book to me as I was
born in Clarinda, Page County, August 7,
1885.—EDG

2797 MILLER, ELIJAH

ANOTHER COPY.* Lacks front endleaf.

2798 MILLER, F. L.

[Map] MAP / OF THE / COEUR-D'-ALENE / MINES /
AND VICINITY. / IDAHO TERRITORY. / [decorative
rule] / CAREFULLY COMPILED BY F. L. MILLER,
CIVIL ENGINEER, FROM OFFICIAL MAPS OF / THE
U. S. ARMY, THE U. S. LAND SURVEYS, THE NORTH-
ERN PACIFIC / R. R. CO., AND DATA OF RECENT EX-
PLORATIONS. / [decorative rule] / SCALE—FOUR
MILES TO ONE INCH. / [decorative rule] / 1884. /
ENTERED ACCORDING TO ACT OF CONGRESS IN THE
YEAR 1884, BY F. L. MILLER, IN THE / OFFICE OF THE
LIBRARIAN OF CONGRESS AT WASHINGTON. / IN-
DEX. / [two columns of 12 lines each] / [at lower
right:] WALLING-LITH-PORTLAND-OR. /

Map, 42.4 x 57 cm. Scale: four miles to one inch.
Folded into black cloth covers, 15.7 x 10 cm.,
with title stamped in gilt on front cover.

Prov.: Inscribed on verso of map, in indelible pencil: Mr T. Merry / [underline] / Compliments / of / F. L. Miller /.

Ref.:

Folded and pasted to inside front cover is a
broadside: [pointing hand] Guide [pointing
hand] / to the / Great Coeur d'Alene Gold
Field. / [thick and thin rule] / [69 lines] / [rule] /
All orders sent to F. L. Miller, Land Department, N. P. R. R., Portland, Or. / [rule] / D. C.
Ireland & Co., Printers, 110 Front Street, Portland, Or. / 33.1 x 15.4 cm. Text, 29.2 x 12.6 cm.
With two manuscript corrections in text.

2799 MILLER, GEORGE

[Caption title] CORRESPONDENCE OF BISHOP GEORGE MILLER WITH THE NORTHERN ISLANDER FROM HIS FIRST ACQUAINTANCE WITH MORMONISM UP TO NEAR THE CLOSE OF HIS LIFE. WRITTEN BY HIMSELF IN THE YEAR 1855. . . .

[1]–50. 21.6 x 14.7 cm. Tan printed wrappers, with short title on front wrapper: Correspondence / of / Bishop George Miller /.

Ref.: Howes M605; Morgan II 85

There is no clue as to where or when this was published. Morgan suggests it was printed in 1916 at Burlington, Wis. In his opinion this pamphlet is of extreme interest and importance.

The letters are enlightening as to conditions in and around Nauvoo from 1838 until after Joseph Smith's murder. The author was a man of daring and full of energy. He describes scenes as they appeared to him without fear or favor. He was not a follower of Brigham Young.

2800 MILLER, WILLIAM H.

THE HISTORY OF KANSAS CITY, TOGETHER WITH A SKETCH OF THE COMMERCIAL RESOURCES OF THE COUNTRY WITH WHICH IT IS SURROUNDED . . . KANSAS CITY: BIRDSALL & MILLER, 1881.

[I]–VI, [5]–264. 24.3 x 16.5 cm. 17 full-page illustrations and numerous vignettes, unlisted. Map: Map of / Kansas City / and / Suburban Towns. / S.F.Scott & Co. / Real Estate / and Loan Brokers. / Ramsey, Millett and Hudson /. 29.7 x 37.5 cm. No scale given. Dark green cloth, blind embossed sides, title in gilt on backstrip.

Ref.: Adams (*Ramp. Herd*) 1495; Howes M619; Rader 2403

2801 MILLER & CO., *Lithographers*

[Map] GENEVA / WAYNE COUNTY, / IOWAY DISTRICT WISCONSIN TERRITORY. / [thin and thick rules] SITUATED UPON THE WEST BANK OF THE MISSISSIPPI RIVER, . . . / [10 lines] / SCALE 20 RODS TO AN INCH. / MILLER & C^{O.'S} LITH. 15 BROAD ST. NEW YORK. / *Inset:* Parts / of the States / Wisconsin, Illinois / & Missouri / from the latest Authorities. / 34.7 x 20 cm. No scale given. *Inset:* Geneva / and / Adjacent Country / Scale 8 Miles to an Inch. / 19 x 20.8 cm. Scale as above.

Map, 46.4 x 61.3 cm. Scales as given in text. Printed on tissue paper.

Ref.:

No other copy of this map has been located.

2802 MILLISON & HEIL, *Publishers*

TOPEKA CITY DIRECTORY, AND BUSINESS MIRROR, FOR 1868–69 . . . TOPEKA: D. G. MILLISON & CO., 1868.

[i–ii], [xix]–xxvi, [25]–145, [146 blank]. (Page xxiv mispaginated xxvi.) 21.2 x 13.6 cm. Tan printed boards, roan back, with short title and advertisements on covers.

Ref.: AII (*Kansas*) 670; Howes M622

The two copies described in AII (*Kansas*) are in wrappers.

Apparently the first Topeka Directory.

2803 MILLS, ANSON

BIG HORN EXPEDITION, AUGUST 15 TO SEPTEMBER 30, 1874 . . .

[1]–15, [16 blank]. 23 x 14.9 cm. Folding map following title-leaf: Map of route of / Big Horn / Expedition / August 15 to September 30. / 1874. / Companies / "B" and "D" 2^d Cav., "F", "H" and "M" 3^d Cav., "H", 4th / Infy and D 13th Infy. / Commanded by / Capt Anson Mills, 3^d Cav. / Drawn by C. Page, Pvt Co "M", 3^d Cav. / 37.3 x 29.7 cm. Scale: 20 miles to an inch. Tan printed wrappers, with title on front wrapper.

Ref.:

No place or date of printing indicated, but before 1924.

2804 MILLS, ANSON

MY STORY . . . WASHINGTON, D.C.: PRESS OF BYRON S. ADAMS, 1918.

[1]–412. 20.7 x 14.3 cm. Numerous illustrations included in pagination, 96 listed. Black cloth, gilt, bible corners, gilt edges.

Prov.: Inscribed and signed on page [1]: [first line printed:] Compliments of the Author to / his friend / W. M. Camp / Anson Mills /.

Ref.: Howes M623

Howes calls for an errata slip, not present in this copy.

2805 MILLS, ROBERT

[Caption title] . . . MEMORIAL OF ROBERT MILLS, SUBMITTING A NEW PLAN OF ROADWAY . . .

[1]–27, [28 blank]. 22.9 x 14.7 cm. Folding map: [Map of the United States, with railroads finished, unfinished, and proposed.] [lower right corner:] Drawn and Engraved by O. H. Throop Washington, D. C. / 24.3 x 39.3 cm. No scale given. Removed from bound volume, unbound.

Ref.: Howes M626; Sabin 49118 note

29th Congress, 1st Session, House, Document No. 173, Serial 485. [Washington, 1846.]

Imprint at foot of page [1]: [rule] / Ritchie & Heiss, print. /

2806 MILLS, SAMUEL J., & DANIEL SMITH

REPORT OF A MISSIONARY TOUR THROUGH THAT PART OF THE UNITED STATES WHICH LIES WEST OF

THE ALLEGANY MOUNTAINS; PERFORMED UNDER THE DIRECTION OF THE MASSACHUSETTS MISSIONARY SOCIETY . . . ANDOVER: PRINTED BY FLAGG AND GOULD, 1815.

[1]–8⁴. [1]–64. 24 x 14.5 cm. Mauve printed wrappers, with title on front wrapper, advertisements on recto and verso of back wrapper, uncut.

Ref.: Buck 86; Howes M629; Sabin 49122

The tour was by wagon from Philadelphia to Pittsburgh, and on through Ohio, Indiana, Illinois, and Missouri eastward to Louisville, Kentucky, and from thence by keel boat to Natchez and New Orleans.

2807 MILLS, WILLIAM W.

FORTY YEARS AT EL PASO, 1858–1898 . . .*

[1]–166. (Pages [1–2] blank.) 19.4 x 13 cm. Portrait. Red cloth.

Ref.: Howes M633; Rader 2405

Copyrighted 1901. The author's prefatory note: A Warning. / is dated from El Paso, November, 1901. The author was a brother of General Anson Mills.

2808 MILTON, WILLIAM WENTWORTH FITZWILLIAM, VISCOUNT, & WALTER B. CHEADLE

AN EXPEDITION ACROSS THE ROCKY MOUNTAINS INTO BRITISH COLUMBIA, BY THE YELLOW HEAD OR LEATHER PASS . . . PRINTED FOR PRIVATE CIRCULATION. LONDON: PRINTED BY PETTER AND GALPIN.

[1]–37, [38–40 blank]. 21.2 x 14.1 cm. Blue printed wrappers, with title on front wrapper. In a brown cloth case.

Ref.: Jones 1482; Wagner-Camp 420 see

A preliminary report published in 1865.

2809 MILTON, WILLIAM WENTWORTH FITZWILLIAM, VISCOUNT, & WALTER B. CHEADLE

THE NORTH-WEST PASSAGE BY LAND. BEING THE NARRATIVE OF AN EXPEDITION FROM ATLANTIC TO PACIFIC, UNDERTAKEN WITH THE VIEW OF EXPLORING A ROUTE ACROSS THE CONTINENT TO BRITISH COLUMBIA THROUGH BRITISH TERRITORY, BY ONE OF THE NORTHERN PASSES IN THE ROCKY MOUNTAINS . . . LONDON: CASSELL, PETTER, AND GALPIN.

[i]–xviiii, [1]–397, [398 colophon]. 21.9 x 14 cm. 23 illustrations and two maps listed. Map: The Western Portion of / British North America, / Showing the Route followed by / Lord Milton & Dʳ Cheadle, / from the Saskatchewan to British Columbia / 1863–4. / [lower right:] J. Arrowsmith. / [lower centre:] London: Cassell, Petter & Galpin—Belle Sauvage Yard. / 21.4 x 34.8

cm. No scale given. Map: General Map of / British North America, / Showing the Route of / Lord Milton & Dʳ Cheadle. / in 1862–3. / [lower right:] J. Arrowsmith. / [lower centre:] London: Cassell, Petter & Galpin—Belle Sauvage Yard. / 20.6 x 30.4 cm. No scale given. Blue cloth, uncut.

Ref.: Sabin 24631; Smith 6844; Staton & Tremaine 4340; Wagner-Camp 420

Published in 1865. Although Viscount Milton's name takes preference on the title-page, Dr. Cheadle wrote most of the book from his own journal.

2810 MILWAUKEE, Wisconsin Territory. Board of Trustees

REPORT OF A COMMITTEE APPOINTED BY THE TRUSTEES OF THE TOWN OF MILWAUKEE, RELATIVE TO THE COMMERCE OF THAT TOWN, AND THE NAVIGATION OF LAKE MICHIGAN. PUBLISHED BY ORDER OF THE BOARD OF TRUSTEES. MILWAUKEE, W.T., PRINTED AT THE COURIER OFFICE.

[1]–12. 22.8 x 14.1 cm. Sewn, uncut.

Ref.: AII (*Wisconsin*) 124; Sabin 49163

The letter of transmittal is signed on page 4: I. A. Lapham, / F. Randall. / Milwaukee, February 17, 1842. /

2811 MILWAUKEE. *Directory*

DIRECTORY OF THE CITY OF MILWAUKEE, FOR THE YEARS 1848–49, WITH A SKETCH OF THE CITY . . . A LIST OF ITS CITIZENS AND PUBLIC OFFICERS, AND OTHER INTERESTING INFORMATION. MILWAUKEE: PUBLISHED BY RUFUS KING, 1848.

[1]–204. 20.3 x 12.2 cm. Map: Map of / Milwaukee / Population / in 1835 none / in 1843 6068, / in 1847 14,061! / By I. A. Lapham. / 1848. / [lower right:] Eng. by Sherman & Smith N. Y. / 60.4 x 51.5 cm. Scale: 660 feet to one inch. Dark yellow printed boards with title as above on front cover, advertisement on back cover, broadside advertisement on inner front cover, dark green leather backstrip.

Ref.: AII (*Wisconsin*) 406; Howes M637

The second Milwaukee directory.

2812 MIMS, LIVINGSTON

[Caption title] TRIBUTE TO GEN. JOS. E. JOHNSTON, FROM THE ADDRESS OF MAJOR LIVINGSTON MIMS, DELIVERED BEFORE THE SOUTHEASTERN TARIFF ASSOCIATION, AT THEIR ANNUAL MEETING, IN WASHINGTON CITY, MARCH 25TH, 1891 . . .

[1–4]. 22 x 14.5 cm. Unbound.

Ref.:

The text appears on pages [1] and [3] within thick rule borders crossed at the corners.

Laid in Johnston: *Narrative of Military Operations . . .* 1874.

2813 MINERS' OWN BOOK, THE

THE MINERS' OWN BOOK, CONTAINING CORRECT IL-
LUSTRATIONS AND DESCRIPTIONS OF THE VARIOUS
MODES OF CALIFORNIA MINING, INCLUDING ALL
THE IMPROVEMENTS INTRODUCED FROM THE EARLI-
EST DAY TO THE PRESENT TIME. SAN FRANCISCO:
PUBLISHED BY HUTCHINGS & ROSENFIELD, 1858.

[1]–32. 23.2 x 14.6 cm. Illustrations, unlisted, by
Charles Nahl. Tan printed wrappers with title on
front wrapper, advertisement on verso of front
wrapper. Lacks back wrapper. In a green cloth
case.

Ref.: Cowan p. 431; Greenwood 967; Howes
M639

The woodcut on page 23 is not inverted.

2814 MINNESOTA. Governor, 1860–1863 (Alexander Ramsey)

MESSAGE OF GOVERNOR RAMSEY TO THE LEGISLA-
TURE OF MINNESOTA. DELIVERED AT THE EXTRA
SESSION, SEPTEMBER 9, 1862 . . . SAINT PAUL:
WM. R. MARSHALL, STATE PRINTER. 1862.

[1]–24. 21.7 x 14.2 cm. Green printed wrappers,
with title on front wrapper. In a gray half morocco case.

Ref.: AII (*Minnesota*) 436; Jones 1453; Sabin
49267

On the Sioux War.

2815 MINNESOTA. Laws, Statutes, etc.

. . . AN ACT TO ENABLE CITIZENS OF MINNESOTA
ENGAGED IN THE NAVAL OR MILITARY SERVICE TO
VOTE AT ELECTIONS . . . SAINT PAUL: WM. R.
MARSHALL, STATE PRINTER, 1862.

[1]–7, [8 blank]. 21.9 x 13.5 cm. Green printed
wrappers, with title on front wrapper.

Ref.:

2816 MINNESOTA. Laws, Statutes, etc.

. . . AN ACT TO ESTABLISH THE STATE LAND OFFICE,
AND FOR OTHER PURPOSES. APPROVED MARCH 10,
1862. SAINT PAUL: WILLIAM B. MARSHALL, INCI-
DENTAL PRINTER, 1862.

[1]⁴, 2³, [4]². [1]–17, [18 blank]. 22.2 x 13.8 cm.
Pink printed wrappers, with title on front wrapper.

Ref.:

2817 MINNESOTA. Laws, Statutes, etc.

AN ACT TO PROVIDE FOR TOWNSHIP ORGANIZA-
TION, IN THE STATE OF MINNESOTA. WITH FORMS
REQUIRED BY THE ACT, AND NOTES OF DECISIONS,
AS PREPARED BY THE ATTORNEY GENERAL . . .
SAINT PAUL: EARLE S. GOODRICH, STATE PRINTER,
1858.

[i]–viii, [3]–95, [96 blank]. 21.8 x 14.3 cm. Green
printed wrappers, with title on front wrapper,
statement on verso of back wrapper headed:
Circular. / [diamond rule] /.

Ref.: AII (*Minnesota*) 207; Sabin 49234

In 1938, according to AII, the MnHi copy
was not available.

2818 MINNESOTA. Laws, Statutes, etc.

[Wrapper title] LAWS RELATING TO TOWN AND
COUNTY ORGANIZATION, AND GENERAL ELECTIONS.
PUBLISHED BY AUTHORITY OF THE LEGISLATURE OF
MINNESOTA. 1860.

[3]–[44], [45–46 blank], [inserted leaf, verso
blank]. 22.3 x 14.4 cm. Blue printed wrappers,
with title on front wrapper.

Ref.:

Printed at Saint Paul.

2819 MINNESOTA. Legislature. House. Select Committee on Overland Route to Oregon

LEGISLATURE OF MINNESOTA. REPORT FROM A SE-
LECT COMMITTEE OF THE HOUSE OF REPRESENTA-
TIVES, ON THE OVERLAND EMIGRATION ROUTE
FROM MINNESOTA TO BRITISH OREGON. WITH AN
APPENDIX. 500 COPIES ORDERED PRINTED FOR
H. OF R. SAINT PAUL: EARLE S. GOODRICH, STATE
PRINTER, PIONEER AND DEMOCRAT OFFICE, 1858.

[1]–100. 22.7 x 14.3 cm. Gray printed wrappers,
with title on recto of front and verso of back
wrappers. In a blue half morocco case.

Ref.: AII (*Minnesota*) 211; Sabin 49301;
Wagner-Camp 304

The Report occupies pages [3]–6. The Appendix contains the following material:

I. Proceedings of Public Meetings Held at St.
Paul, Minnesota, on the first, / seventh, tenth
and seventeenth days of July, A.D. 1858. /
Pages [9]–38.

II. Particulars of the Gold Discovery on Frazer
and Thompson Rivers, / and of Emigration
Thither. / . . . Pages 39–47. [Extracts from the
London *Times* and the Sacramento *Union*.]

III. Geographical Description of Minnesota
North of Latitude Forty-six. / [From a communication by J. W. Taylor, to the St. Paul Advertiser of January 31, 1857.] Pages 47–53.

IV. Routes through Minnesota to the Navi-
gable Waters of the Red / River of the North. /
[Contains a day-by-day diary of a canoe voyage
to Pembina by E. A. C. Hatch.] Pages 53–63.

V. Climatology of Minnesota. / [Excerpt from a
report by D. C. Shepard.] Pages 63–68.

VI. Climatology of the Saskatchewan District and of British Oregon. [Excerpt from a report in Blodgett's *Climatology* . . .] Pages 69–72.

VII. Memoir of the Selkirk Settlement on the Red River of the North, / with Notices of the Manners and Life of the Settlers. / [By J. A. Wheelock.] Pages 73–90.

VIII. A Visit to the Red River Settlement. [From an address by Alexander Ramsey.] Pages 90–97.

IX. Proceedings of a Public Meeting Held at St. Anthony on the twelfth / of July, 1958. / Pages 98–100. [Describes a Minnesota Legislature House report.]

2820 MINNESOTA. Legislature. House.
THE SAME.

[3]–98. 21.4 x 13.8 cm. Rebound in plain tan wrappers.
Ref.:
Contents as follows:

Report of the Committee of the House of Representatives. Pages 3–6.
Appendix No. I. Pages [7]–36.
Appendix No. II. Pages 37–45.
Appendix No. III. Pages 45–51.
Appendix No. IV. Pages 51–61.
Appendix No. V. Pages 61–66.
Appendix No. VI. Pages 67–70.
Appendix No. VII. Pages 71–88.
Appendix No. VIII. Pages 88–95.
Appendix No. IX. Pages 96–98.

Wagner-Camp 304 describes the report of a Select Committee of the Minnesota House of Representatives, item 2819 above. This is another edition of that report, lacking title-page and possibly lacking original wrappers. The pagination differs in that the half-title leaf before the Appendices and labeled "Appendix" (paged [7–8]) is not present and in consequence the total pages are 98 instead of 100. This may be the Senate edition, as the same type was used for both. No record exists of this variation.

2821 MINNESOTA TERRITORY. Legislative Assembly. Council

RULES FOR THE GOVERNMENT OF THE COUNCIL OF MINNESOTA TERRITORY, AND JOINT RULES OF THE COUNCIL AND HOUSE, ADOPTED AT A SESSION OF THE LEGISLATURE, COMMENCED SEPTEMBER 3, 1849. SAINT PAUL: JAMES M. GOODHUE, PRINTER, 1849.

[1]–15, [16 blank]. 17.8 x 11.7 cm. Stabbed. There may have been buff wrappers at one time, but the evidence is not clear.
Ref.: AII (*Minnesota*) 11

2822 MINNESOTA HISTORICAL SOCIETY

ANNALS OF THE MINNESOTA HISTORICAL SOCIETY, FOR THE YEAR A. D., 1850–1. COMPRISING AN ADDRESS BY THE PRESIDENT, THE ANNUAL REPORT OF THE SECRETARY, TWO PAPERS BY REV. S. R. RIGGS, ONE ON THE "DESTINY OF THE INDIAN TRIBES," THE OTHER ON THE "DAKOTA LANGUAGE," AND LASTLY "A MEMOIR OF THE HISTORY AND PHYSICAL GEOGRAPHY OF MNNESOTA[!], &C., &C., &C. ST. PAUL: D. A. ROBERTSON, PRINTER, 1851.

[1]–184. 23 x 15.5 cm. Stabbed, uncut, unopened.
Ref.: AII (*Minnesota*) 32; Howes M641; Sabin 49274

There were four volumes issued, 1850–53. As Howes writes: The Society's activities went into eclipse in 1856; on resumption of operations sixteen years later, the above material was reissued as Volume I of their *Collections*.

2823 MINNESOTA HISTORICAL SOCIETY

ANNALS OF THE MINNESOTA HISTORICAL SOCIETY: 1852; CONTAINING THE ANNUAL ADDRESS, BY J. H. SIMPSON, FIRST LIEUT. CORPS U. S. TOPOGRAPHICAL ENGINEERS; AND OTHER PAPERS . . . ST. PAUL: OWENS & MOORE, PRINTERS.

[1]–64. 25.1 x 15 cm. Yellow printed wrappers, with title on front wrapper.
Ref.: AII (*Minnesota*) 47; Howes M641; Sabin 49274

2824 MINNESOTA HISTORICAL SOCIETY

ANNALS OF THE MINNESOTA HISTORICAL SOCIETY, FOR EIGHTEEN HUNDRED AND FIFTY-THREE. NUMBER IV. SAINT PAUL: OWENS & MOORE, PRINTERS, 1853.

[1]–72. 25.2 x 17 cm. Salmon printed wrappers, with title on front wrapper.
Ref.: AII (*Minnesota*) 62; Howes M641; Sabin 49274

2825 MINOR, JOHN

MANUSCRIPT DOCUMENT SIGNED BY JOHN MINOR AS ATTORNEY IN FACT FOR STEPHEN MINOR. 1800 APRIL 7. TWO PAGES, 32.4 x 20 cm.

Bill of sale by Stephen Minor to Philip Nolan of a Negro slave named Ceazar. Witnessed by William Kennoe and Snelling Wooley. On the second page, the sale is registered by William Kennoe, same date. Page 3 is blank, page 4 is docketed: Bill of Sale / of / Ceazar / [flourish].

2826 MISCELLANEOUS PIECES

[Caption title] MISCELLANEOUS PIECES.

[1]–24. 12.8 x 7.7 cm. Bound with Number 1278.
Ref.: Hargrett (*Oklahoma*) 70; Pilling 2597
Printed at Park Hill: Mission Press, 1844. A temperance tract. Text in Sequoyan.

2827 MISSIONARY HERALD, THE

THE MISSIONARY HERALD: CONTAINING THE PROCEEDINGS AT LARGE OF THE AMERICAN BOARD OF COMMISSIONERS FOR FOREIGN MISSIONS, WITH A GENERAL VIEW OF OTHER BENEVOLENT OPERATIONS. FOR THE YEAR 1835 [–1838]. VOL. XXXI [–XXXIV] . . . BOSTON: PRINTED BY CROCKER AND BREWSTER.*

[i–ii], 1–480, [iii–viii]. [i–ii] 1–480, [iii–viii]. [i–ii], 1–512, [iii–viii]. [i–ii], 1–488, [iii–viii]. 23.1 x 14 cm. Woodcuts, portrait, and two maps, unlisted. Four volumes, contemporary marbled boards, calf backs and corners.
Ref.: Wagner-Camp 54, 64, 68, 70
Contains reports and extracts by John Dunbar, Samuel Parker, and Henry Harmon Spaulding.

2828 MISSISSIPPI AND MISSOURI RAIL-ROAD COMPANY

LAWS OF THE STATE OF IOWA IN RELATION TO CORPORATIONS FOR RAIL ROAD PURPOSES, AND ARTICLES OF INCORPORATION OF THE MISSISSIPPI AND MISSOURI RAILROAD COMPANY. DAVENPORT: SANDERS & DAVIS, PRINTERS, 1853.

[1]–24. 18 x 11.4 cm. Stabbed.
Ref.:
Comprises only the material described on the title-page.

2829 MISSISSIPPI AND MISSOURI RAIL-ROAD COMPANY

THE SAME.

[1]–28. 21 x 13.9 cm. Old green wrappers.
Ref.:
Issued after the stockholders meeting on June 9, 1853. It contains the Amendments adopted at that meeting, a "Public Notice" dated July 1, 1853, and a list of the officers of the company, pages 21–27.
Editions: Davenport, 1853 (24 pages).

2830 MISSOURI. Constitution

. . . CONSTITUTION OF THE STATE OF MISSOURI. NOVEMBER 14, 1820. WASHINGTON: PRINTED BY GALES & SEATON, 1820.

[1]–25, [26 blank]. 21.2 x 13.8 cm. Rebound in blue half calf, uncut.

Ref.: Sabin 49585
16th Congress, 2nd Session, Senate, Document No. 1, Serial 42.

2831 MISSOURI. Laws, Statutes, etc.

[Broadsheet] AN ACT INCORPORATING A COMPANY TO MAKE A McADAMIZED TURNPIKE ROAD, FROM THE TOWN OF CALEDONIA, IN WASHINGTON COUNTY, TO THE MISSISSIPPI RIVER . . . APPROVED, MARCH 16TH 1835. STATE OF MISSOURI. I HAVE COMPARED THE FOREGOING ACT WITH THE ORIGINAL ROLL NOW ON FILE IN THE OFFICE OF SECRETARY OF STATE, AFORESAID, AND HAVE CORRECTED THE SAME THEREBY. IN TESTIMONY WHEREOF, I HAVE HEREUNTO SET MY HAND AND AFFIXED THE SEAL OF MY OFFICE, THE SIXTEENTH DAY OF MARCH, A.D. 1835. JOHN C. EDWARDS, SECRETARY OF STATE. (PRINTED AT THE ARGUS OFFICE, ST. LOUIS, MO.)

Broadsheet, 33 x 20.2 cm.
Ref.:

2832 MISSOURI. Laws, Statutes, etc.

AN ACT TO AMEND AND REDUCE INTO ONE THE SEVERAL ACTS OF THE GENERAL ASSEMBLY FOR REGULATING THE MILITIA OF THIS STATE. APPROVED, JANUARY 11, 1822. ST. CHARLES: PRINTED BY ROBERT M'CLOUD, PRINTER TO THE STATE, 1822.

[1]–51, [52 blank]. 23.6 x 15.5 cm. Stabbed, unbound, uncut, unopened. In a blue half morocco case.
Ref.:

2833 MISSOURI. Secretary of State (James L. Minor)

DOCUMENT CONTAINING THE CORRESPONDENCE, ORDERS, &C. IN RELATION TO THE DISTURBANCES WITH THE MORMONS; AND THE EVIDENCE GIVEN BEFORE THE HON. AUSTIN A. KING, JUDGE OF THE FIFTH JUDICIAL CIRCUIT OF THE STATE OF MISSOURI, AT THE COURTHOUSE IN RICHMOND, IN A CRIMINAL COURT OF INQUIRY, BEGUN NOVEMBER 12, 1838, ON THE TRIAL OF JOSEPH SMITH, JR., AND OTHERS, FOR HIGH TREASON AND OTHER CRIMES AGAINST THE STATE . . . FAYETTE, MISSOURI: PRINTED AT THE BOON'S LICK DEMOCRAT, 1841.

[i–iv], [1]–163, [164 blank]. 21.8 x 14.3 cm. Half black morocco, gray cloth sides. Last two leaves mended by Donnelley, some text in upper right corner supplied.
Ref.: AII (*Missouri*) 310; Woodward 55
2000 copies were ordered printed under direction of the Secretary of State.
AII (*Missouri*) is in error (collation 162 pp.); collation above is correct.

2834 MISSOURI, SUNDRY INHABITANTS OF . . .

. . . PETITION OF SUNDRY INHABITANTS OF THE STATE OF MISSOURI, UPON THE SUBJECT OF A COMMUNICATION BETWEEN THE SAID STATE AND THE INTERNAL PROVINCES OF MEXICO, WITH A LETTER FROM ALPHONSO WETMORE, UPON THE SAME SUBJECT . . . WASHINGTON: PRINTED BY GALES & SEATON, 1825.

[1]–8. 22.2 x 14.2 cm. Removed from bound volume, unbound. In a brown cloth case.

Ref.: Wagner-Camp 30

18th Congress, 2nd Session, House, Document No. 79, Serial 116.

2835 MITCHELL, DAVID T.

[Map] MITCHELL'S / SECTIONAL MAP OF KANSAS, / COMPILED FROM THE FIELD NOTES IN THE SURVEYOR GENERALS OFFICE BY, / DAVID T. MITCHELL. / U. S. SURVEYOR AND LAND AGENT. / LECOMPTON KANSAS. / SHOWING THE U. S. SURVEY UP TO 1859. / SCALE 9 MILES TO ONE INCH. / MIDDLETON, STROBRIDGE & CO. LITH. CIN. O. / ENTERED ACCORDING TO ACT OF CONGRESS IN THE YEAR 1859 BY D. T. MITCHELL IN THE CLERKS OFFICE OF THE SOUTHERN DISTRICT OF OHIO. /

Map, 61 x 71.3 cm. Scale: 9 miles to one inch· Folded into black cloth, 14.7 x 9 cm., title stamped in gilt on front cover.

Ref.: Phillips (*Maps*) p. 346

Advertisements on inner front cover.

2836 MITCHELL, JAMES C., R. B. PEGRAM, & Others

MANUSCRIPT DOCUMENT SIGNED BY JAMES C. MITCHELL, R. B. PEGRAM & CO., THOS. J. MCMAHON, AND OTHERS. 1854 May 19, Council Bluff City. Two pages, 32.3 x 10.2 cm., riveted.

The Articles of Agreement for the establishment of the town of Florence, Nebraska. There were twelve proprietors, some of whom signed by proxy. The document is docketed: Winter Quarters / Article of Agreement /.

Accompanying the manuscript is a portion of a manuscript headed: A Plat of the lands Claimed by the Nebraska Winter Quarters or Florence Company . . . [description of the claim] as appears on the Lithographed Plat of said Town . . . [list of proprietors]. Docketed on verso with record of filing claim.

2837 MITCHELL, JOSEPH

THE MISSIONARY PIONEER; OR, A BRIEF MEMOIR OF THE LIFE, LABOURS, AND DEATH OF JOHN STEWART, (MAN OF COLOUR,) FOUNDER, UNDER GOD OF THE MISSION AMONG THE WYANDOTTS AT UPPER SANDUSKY, OHIO. NEW-YORK, PRINTED BY J. C. TOTTEN, 1827.*

1–8⁶. [i]–viii, [9]–96. 14.5 x 9.1 cm. Tan boards, black leather back, gilt fillets on backstrip. Lacks front and back endleaves and blank at front and back.

Ref.: Howes M680; Sabin 49704

2838 MITCHELL, SAMUEL A.

[Broadside] A CONCISE VIEW OF THE NUMBER, RESOURCES, AND INDUSTRY OF THE AMERICAN PEOPLE, IN THE YEAR 1840 . . . ENTERED, ACCORDING TO THE ACT OF CONGRESS, IN THE YEAR 1842, BY S. AUGUSTUS MITCHELL, IN THE CLERK'S OFFICE OF THE DISTRICT COURT OF THE EASTERN DISTRICT OF PENNSYLVANIA.

Broadside, 65.1 x 58.8 cm. Text, 63.4 x 86.7 cm. With: Map: Mitchell's / National Map of the / American Republic / or / United States of North America. / Together with Maps / of the Vicinities / of Thirty-two of the Principal Cities and Towns / in the Union. / Published by S. Augustus Mitchell Philadelphia, / No. 8 1/2 South [ornament] 1843 [ornament] Seventh Street. / Drawn by J. H. Young. Engraved by J. H. Brightly. / [lower centre: copyright notice as above] / *Inset:* Map of the / North-Eastern Boundary / of the United States. / According to the Treaty of 1842. / 10.2 x 9.6 cm. *Inset:* Map of / the / Southern Part / of / Florida. / 10 x 6.6 cm. *Insets:* three printed tables. 62.1 x 85.9 cm. Scale: 52 miles to one inch. Folded into original dark green straight-grain calf, 18.3 x 11 cm., with title on front cover and designs on back cover in gilt.

Ref.: Phillips (*Maps*) p. 896

The earliest similar map listed by Phillips was issued in 1843.

Surrounding the text of the broadside is a border composed of plans of thirty-two cities, 8.2 x 9 cm., each enclosed within a decorative frame.

2839 MITCHELL, SAMUEL A.

DESCRIPTION OF OREGON AND CALIFORNIA, EMBRACING AN ACCOUNT OF THE GOLD REGIONS; TO WHICH IS ADDED, AN APPENDIX, CONTAINING DESCRIPTIONS OF VARIOUS KINDS OF GOLD, AND METHODS OF TESTING ITS GENUINENESS . . . PHILADELPHIA: THOMAS, COWPERTHWAIT & CO., 1849.

[1]–76. 12.8 x 8 cm. Map: A / New Map of / Texas Oregon / and / California / with the Regions Adjoining. / Compiled / from the most recent authorities. / Philadelphia / Published by / Thomas Cowperthwait & Cᵒ / Market Sᵗ Nᵒ 253. / [double rule] 1849 [double rule] / [below border:] Entered according to Act of Congress in the year 1845 by H. N. Burroughs in the

clerks office of the District Court of the eastern district of Pennsylvania. 53 x 49.2 cm. No scale. *Inset:* Map of the / Maritime / and Overland Routes / to California. / 12 x 11.7 cm. No scale. *Inset:* Map of the / Gold / and Quicksilver / District / of / California. / 6.7 x 5.5 cm. No scale. Original embossed green leather, with title in gilt on front cover. In a black cloth case.

Ref.: Cowan pp. 433–34; Howes M687; Sabin 19712; Smith 6889; Wheat (*Gold Rush*) 143; Wheat (*Gold Region*) 108; Wheat (*Transmississippi*) 629 see

Editions: Philadelphia, 1845, 1846, 1849.

2840 MITCHELL, SAMUEL A.

ILLINOIS IN 1837; A SKETCH DESCRIPTIVE OF THE SITUATION, BOUNDARIES, FACE OF THE COUNTRY . . . ALSO, SUGGESTIONS TO EMIGRANTS, SKETCHES OF THE COUNTIES, CITIES, AND PRINCIPAL TOWNS IN THE STATE . . . PHILADELPHIA: PUBLISHED BY S. AUGUSTUS MITCHELL, 1837.

[i]–viii, 9–141, [142 advertisement]. (Pages iii & v paginated 3 & 5.) 22.3 x 13.8 cm. Map: Mitchell's / Map of / Illinois / Exhibiting its / Internal Improvements, / Counties, Towns, Roads, &c. / Philadelphia: / Published by S. A. Mitchell. / 1837 / Scale of Miles. / [diagrammatic scale: about 29 miles to one inch] / [lower right:] Engraved by J. H. Young / [lower left:] Entered according to Act of Congress in the year 1837 by S. A. Mitchell in the Clerks office of the District Court of the Eastern District of Pennsylvania /. 38.3 x 31.9 cm. Scale as above. Limp tan printed boards, with title on front cover: Illinois / In 1837: / With a Map. / [within decorative borders], four thin and thick rules on backstrip. Parts of backstrip eaten away. In a light brown cloth case.

Ref.: Buck 313; Howes M689; Sabin 32460

The error in line 6 (Animalas instead of Animals) of the title-page was corrected for later printings.

2841 MITCHELL, SAMUEL A.

[Map] A / NEW MAP OF / TEXAS OREGON / AND / CALIFORNIA / WITH THE REGIONS ADJOINING. / COMPILED / FROM THE MOST RECENT AUTHORITIES. / PHILADELPHIA / PUBLISHED BY S. AUGUSTUS MITCHELL / N.E. CORNER OF MARKET & SEVENTH STREETS. / [double rule] 1846 [double rule] / [lower left corner:] EXPLANATION. / [six lines] / EMIGRANT ROUTE FROM MISSOURI TO OREGON. / [seventeen lines] / SCALE OF STATUTE MILES. / [diagrammatic scale: 105 miles to one inch] / SCALE OF GEOGRAPHIC MILES. / [diagrammatic scale: 70 miles to one inch] / ENTERED ACCORDING TO ACT OF CONGRESS IN THE YEAR 1845 BY H. N.

BURROUGHS IN THE CLERKS OFFICE OF THE DISTRICT COURT OF THE EASTERN DISTRICT OF PENNSYLVANIA. /

Map, 56.4 x 52.1 cm. Scale as above. Folded into original black roan stamped folder, 13.4 x 8.2 cm., with title in gilt on front cover.

Ref.: Howes 7044; Wheat (*Gold Region*) 29; Wheat (*Transmississippi*) 520

Bound in the same folder and preceding the map, is Accompaniment / to / Mitchell's New Map / of / Texas, Oregon, / and California, / with / the Regions Adjoining / [diamond rule] / Philadelphia: / S. Augustus Mitchell, / N. E. Cor. Market and Seventh Sts. / 1846. / [1]–38, 29–46 advertisements, [47–8 blank]. 12.3 x 7.6 cm. Plain blue wrappers, with front wrapper and front fly-leaf laid down on inner front cover.

Howes mentions a 34-page edition first, but Wheat does not describe it at all.

In the Upper California portion, Fremont is carefully followed, while further north Wilkes is followed. The boundary (to be) with Mexico is imperfectly shown but Texas appears with the magnified boundaries, including Santa Fé, of 1844 *Emory*. The various claims to Oregon appear. The *Accompaniment* is of particular interest, containing perhaps the clearest statement of Oregon and California facts that came out of the period just prior to the settlement of the former's boundaries and the inclusion of the latter in the United States.—Wheat (*Transmississippi*)

2842 MITCHELL, W. H.

DAKOTA COUNTY. ITS PAST AND PRESENT, GEOGRAPHICAL, STATISTICAL AND HISTORICAL, TOGETHER WITH A GENERAL VIEW OF THE STATE . . . MINNEAPOLIS: TRIBUNE PRINTING COMPANY, 1868.

[i]–vi, [1]–[162], [163–78 advertisements]. 18.6 x 12.5 cm. Illustrations unlisted. Gray printed wrappers, with title on front wrapper, advertisements on verso of front and recto and verso of back wrapper. In a red cloth case.

Ref.: Howes M691; Sabin 49734

First history of the second Minnesota settlement.—Howes

2843 MITCHELL, W. H., & U. CURTIS

AN HISTORICAL SKETCH OF DODGE COUNTY, MINNESOTA, CONTAINING FULL GEOGRAPHIC AND STATISTIC INFORMATION . . . ROCHESTER, MINN.: FEDERAL UNION BOOK AND JOB PRINTING OFFICE, 1870.

[i]–vi, [7]–124, [125 errata, 126–36 advertisements]. 18 x 12.3 cm. Light gray printed wrappers. In a brown board case.

Ref.: Howes M696; Sabin 49733

2844 MITCHELL, W. H., & J. H. STEVENS

GEOGRAPHICAL AND STATISTICAL HISTORY OF THE COUNTY OF HENNEPIN, EMBRACING LEADING INCIDENTS IN PIONEER LIFE . . . MINNEAPOLIS: RUSSELL AND BELFOY, PRINTERS, 1869.

[1]–149, [150–74 advertisements, 175 errata, 176 blank]. 17.2 x 11 cm. Gray printed wrappers, with title on front wrapper, advertisements on verso of front and recto and verso of back wrapper. In a dark blue cloth case.

Ref.: Howes M692

First history of the first Minnesota settlement.—Howes

2845 MITCHELL COUNTY (Texas) IMMIGRATION SOCIETY

HAND-BOOK OF THE MITCHELL COUNTY IMMIGRATION SOCIETY. HEADQUARTERS: COLORADO CITY, TEX. OFFICE: FRONTING DEPOT AND RAILROAD. CONTAINING DESCRIPTIONS OF MITCHELL, SCURRY, BORDEN, GARZA, KENT, DICKENS, FLOYD, LUBBOCK, LYNN, DAWSON, TERRY, CROSBY AND HALE COUNTIES IN NORTHWESTERN TEXAS, ALL BEING CONTIGUOUS TO AND READILY REACHED FROM THEIR TRADE CENTER, COLORADO CITY, MITCHELL COUNTY, TEXAS. THIS HAND-BOOK SENT FREE ON APPLICATION TO SECRETARY.

[1]–21, [22–32 advertisements]. 22 x 14.3 cm. Yellow printed wrappers with title on front wrapper, advertisements on recto of back wrapper.

Ref.:

Latest date in the text is 1888.

2846 MITCHELL'S CAVALIER

[Newspaper] MITCHELL'S CAVALIER. WE GO WHERE "REBS." AWAIT US. VOL. 1. FAYETTEVILLE, SATURDAY, JULY 25, 1863. NO. 1 . . .

[1–4]. 41.3 x 19.1 cm. Unbound.

Ref.:

Carries on the first page a long Synopsis of the March of the First / Cavalry Division from Triune / to Decherd. /

2847 MIX, GEORGE A.

REPORT GIVEN BY COL. GEO. A. MIX, DUBUQUE, OF THE EXPLORATION OF THE PROPOSED ROUTE OF THE DUBUQUE & PACIFIC RAILROAD! DUBUQUE: PRINTED AT THE DAILY TRIBUNE OFFICE, MAIN STREET, 1855.

[1]–8. 21.8 x 13.6 cm. Blue printed wrappers, with title on front wrapper. Lower margin of second leaf cut off.

Ref.: Moffit 185; Sabin 21042

Moffit lists under Dubuque & Pacific Railroad.

2848 MOELLER, JOACHIM VAN

AUF NACH ALASKA . . . CHARLOTTENBURG: VERLAG VON FRIEDRICH CHIEL, 1897.

[1]–[205], [206–07 advertisements, 208 colophon]. 22.3 x 14.4 cm. 58 illustrations and decorations and one map listed. Light green printed boards, green cloth back.

Prov.: Rubber stamp booklabel on title-page: Bibliothek / Museum f. / Länder- u. Völkerkunde / Linden-Museum / Stuttgart /. And with duplicate stamp.

Ref.: Howes M710; Smith 6907; Wickersham 6451

2849 MOELLHAUSEN, BALDUIN

DIARY OF A JOURNEY FROM THE MISSISSIPPI TO THE COASTS OF THE PACIFIC WITH A UNITED STATES EXPEDITION . . . LONDON: LONGMAN, BROWN, GREEN, LONGMANS, & ROBERTS, 1858.

[i]–[xxxii, xxxii blank], [1]–352. [i]–[xii, xii blank], [1]–397, [398 colophon], [399–400 advertisements]. Map, 11 colored plates, and 12 woodcuts listed. Map: Map / Illustrating / Baldwin Möllhausen's Travels / from the / Mississippi to the Coast of the Pacific, / in the Years 1853–1854. / [lower right:] Engraved by Edwᵈ Weller, Duke Strᵗ Bloomsbury / [lower centre:] London, Longman & Co. / 19.5 x 44.6 cm. Scale: about 100 miles to one inch. *Inset:* Section from Fᵗ Smith to the Pacific Ocean. / 3.4 x 43.3 cm. Scale: Vertical scale, 1:150,000. Two volumes, blue cloth, gilt edges.

Ref.: Howes M713; Rader 2418; Sabin 49915; Wagner-Camp 305; Wheat (*Transmississippi*) 956

For the original German version see number 2851.

2850 MOELLHAUSEN, BALDUIN

REISEN IN DIE FELSENGEBIRGE NORD-AMERIKAS BIS ZUM HOCH-PLATEAU VON NEU-MEXICO . . . LEIPZIG, OTTO BURFURST.

[i]–xvi, 1–455, [456 advertisements]. [i]–[x], 1–406. 22.1 x 15.3 cm. 13 colored plates and one map listed. Map: Karte der Völkerwanderung im Colorado-Gebiete / nebst Angabe der Route der Colorado-Expedition zu Möllhausen's "Reisen in die Felsengebirge Nord-Amerikas". / [3 lines of explanation below map]. 14.1 x 21.5 cm. No scale indicated. Two volumes, maroon cloth, marbled edges.

Ref.: Howes M712; Rader 2419; Sabin 49913; Wagner-Camp 362; Wheat (*Transmississippi*) 1032

The probable date of publication is 1860. Laid in is a photograph of an original drawing by Möllhausen which, according to a manuscript note on the verso by EDG, was taken at Stuttgart by Charles L. Camp. As yet untranslated into English, this is an account of the Ives-Newberry expedition.

2851 MOELLHAUSEN, BALDUIN

TAGEBUCH EINER REISE VOM MISSISSIPPI NACH DEN KUSTEN DER SUDSEE . . . LEIPZIG: HERMANN MENDELSSOHN, 1858.

[1–12], [i]–[xvi, xvi blank], [1]–[496]. 30.4 x 23.6 cm. 13 illustrations listed and one map. Map: Karte / zu / Balduin Möllhausen's Reise / vom Mississippi nach der Küste der Südsee / im Jahre 1853–1854. / Entworfen und gezeichnet / von / Dr. Henry Lange. / [lower centre] F. A. Brockhaus' Geogr.-artist. Anstalt, Leipzig. / Verlag von Hermann Mendelssohn. / 20.6 x 44.6 cm. Scale: about 100 English miles to one inch. *Inset:* [Kansas and vicinity]. 7.3 x 11 cm. Scale: about 200 miles to one inch. Dark green cloth, blind panels on sides, title in gilt on front cover and backstrip.

Ref.: Howes M713; Rader 2420; Sabin 49914; Smith 6909; Wagner-Camp 305; Wheat (*Transmississippi*) 955

Experiences and observations of the author while with the Whipple expedition, of which his is the best account.—Howes

2852 MOFFAT, JAMES D.

HISTORICAL SKETCH OF WASHINGTON AND JEFFERSON COLLEGE . . . WASHINGTON, PA., 1890.

[1]–29, [30 blank]. 23.2 x 14.7 cm. Buff printed wrappers, with title on front wrapper.

Ref.:

2853 MOFFETTE, JOSEPH F.

THE TERRITORIES OF KANSAS AND NEBRASKA: BEING AN ACCOUNT OF THEIR GEOGRAPHY, RESOURCES, AND SETTLEMENTS . . . NEW YORK: J. H. COLTON AND COMPANY, 1855.

[1]–84, 1–36 advertisements. 14.9 x 9.3 cm. Map: Nebraska / and / Kanzas[!]. / Published by J. H. Colton & Co. Nº 172 William Sᵗ New York. / 1855 / Scale of Miles. / [diagrammatic scale: 75 miles to one inch] / Entered according to Act of Congress in the year 1855 by J. H. Colton & Co. in the Clerks Office of the District Court of the United States for the Southern District of New York. / 31.7 x 40.2 cm. (including border). Scale as above. Map: Nebraska / and / Kanzas[!] / Published by J. H. Colton & C: Nº 172 William Sᵗ / New York / 1855. / [lower centre:] Drawn & Engraved by / J. H. Colton & Cº / Nº 172 William Sᵗ New York / 1855. / Entered according to Act of Congress in the year 1855 by J. H. Colton & Co. in the Clerks Office

of the District Court of the United States for the Southern District of New York / 46.8 x 29 cm. (including border). No scale given. Blue cloth, blind embossed borders on sides, title in gilt on front and in blind on back cover.

Ref.: Bradford 3641; Howes M716; Rader 2415; Sabin 49834; Wagner-Camp 260

Some of the information was secured from Peter Sarpy, one of the pioneer traders on the upper Missouri.—Howes

2854 MOFFETTE, JOSEPH F.

THE SAME . . . 1856.

[1]–84, 1–24 advertisements. 14.7 x 9.1 cm. Two folding maps: as in 1855 edition except second map dated 1856. Red stamped cloth, gilt on front and in blind on back.

Ref.: Howes M716; Wagner-Camp 260

2855 MOLL, HERMAN

[Map] A NEW MAP OF THE NORTH PARTS OF / AMERICA CLAIMED BY FRANCE / UNDER Ẏᴱ NAMES OF LOUISIANA, MISSISSIPPI, CANADA AND / NEW FRANCE WITH Ẏᴱ ADJOYNING TERRITORIES OF ENGLAND AND SPAIN. / A GREAT PART OF THIS MAP IS TAKEN FROM Ẏᴱ ORIGINAL DRAUGHTS OF Mᴿ BLACKMORE, THE INGENIOUS Mᴿ / BERISFORD NOW RESIDING IN CAROLINA, CAPᵀ NAIRN AND OTHERS NEVER BEFORE PUBLISHE'D, THE SOUTH WEST PART OF / LOUISIANA IS DONE AFTER A FRENCH MAP PUBLISHED AT PARIS IN 1718. AND WE GIVE YOU HERE THE DIVISION OR / BOUNDS ACCORDING TO THAT MAP, WHICH BOUNDS BEGIN 30 MILES S. WEST FROM CHARLES TOWN IN CAROLINA / AND RUN ON TO Ẏᴱ INDIAN FORT SASQUESAHANOK 30 MILES WEST OF PHILADELPHIA &C. / NB THE FRENCH DIVISIONS ARE INSERTED ON PURPOSE, THAT THOSE NOBLE-MEN, GENTLEMEN, MERCHANTS &C. WHO / ARE INTERESTED IN OUR PLANTATIONS IN THOSE PARTS, MAY OBSERVE WHETHER THEY AGREE WITH THEIR PROPERTIES, OR / DO NOT JUSTLY DESERVE Ẏᴱ NAME OF INCROACHMENTS; AND THIS IS Ẏᴱ MORE TO BE OBSERVED, BECAUSE THEY DO THER-/EBY COMPREHEND WITHIN THEIR LIMITS Ẏᴱ CHARAKEYS AND IROQUOIS, BY MUCH Ẏᴱ MOST POWERFULL OF / ALL Ẏᴱ NEIGHBOURING INDIAN NATIONS, THE OLD FRIENDS AND ALLIES OF THE ENGLISH, WHO EVER ESTEEMED THEM / TO BE THE BULWARK AND SECURITY OF ALL THEIR PLANTATIONS IN NORTH AMERICA. / THE PROJECTION OF THIS MAP IS CALL'D MERCATOR'S, AND IT IS LAID DOWN ACCORDING / TO THE NEWEST AND MOST EXACT OBSERVATIONS BY H. MOLL GEOGRAPHER, 1720. / *Inset:* The Harbour of / Annapolis Royal / 10.4 x 17.1 cm. Scale: 2 1/2 miles to one inch. *Inset:* A Map of ẏᵉ Mouth / of Mississippi and / Mobile Rivers &c. / 12.2 x 17.1 cm. Scale: 10 English leagues to one mile. *Inset:* [View] The Indian Fort Sasquesahanok / 12 x 15.9 cm.

Map, 60.7 x 100.8 cm. Scale: 72 miles to one inch.

Ref.: Phillips 567

2856 MONROE, ADOLPHUS F.

THE LIFE AND WRITINGS OF ADOLPHUS F. MONROE, WHO WAS HUNG BY A BLOOD-THIRSTY MOB IN CHARLESTON, ILL., ON THE 15TH DAY OF FEBRUARY, 1856, FOR KILLING HIS FATHER-IN-LAW, NATHAN ELLINGTON, ESQ., IN SELF-DEFENSE. CINCINNATI: PRINTED FOR THE PUBLISHER, 1857.

[7]–118. 22.5 x 14.7 cm. Frontispiece. Dark brown cloth, blind embossed borders on sides, title in gilt on front cover.

Ref.: McDade 696; Sabin 50010

Quite an interesting case and a good account (including a lynching) of what may have been a miscarriage of justice.

2857 MONTAGUE, E. J.

A DIRECTORY, BUSINESS MIRROR, AND HISTORICAL SKETCHES OF RANDOLPH COUNTY . . . WITH A CONDENSED SKETCH OF KASKASKIA AND PRAIRIE DU ROCHER, COMMENCING WITH THEIR INDIAN HISTORY . . . ALSO, A CONDENSED SKETCH OF RANDOLPH COUNTY . . . ALTON, ILL.: COURIER STEAM BOOK AND JOB PRINTING HOUSE, 1859.

[1]–246. (Inserted before page [1]: 2 leaves printed on pink paper, advertisements on pages [2–3].) 18 x 11.7 cm. Cream printed boards with title on front cover, advertisement on back cover. Rebacked with red morocco.

Prov.: Inscribed on front cover and front endleaf: Joseph Cox / 200 Court St / Cincinnati / O /. Endleaf slightly different. Bookplate of Dr. Otto L. Schmidt.

Ref.: Bradford 3649; Buck 1041; Howes M730; Sabin 50048

Numerous advertisements throughout, included in pagination.

2858 MONTANA. Agriculture, Labor and Industry, Department of (Division of Publicity)

[Wrapper title] CARRYING ON FOR 50 YEARS WITH THE COURAGE OF CUSTER . . . PRINTED AND CIRCULATED BY AUTHORITY OF THE STATE OF MONTANA HELENA [1926].

[1–8]. 22.8 x 15.3 cm. Ten illustrations and map, including portrait on front wrapper, unlisted. Self-wrapped, with title on page [1].

Ref.:

Laid in Ostrander: *After 60 Years . . .* [1925].

2859 MONTANA. Stock Commissioners, Board of

REPORT OF THE BOARD OF STOCK COMMISSIONERS OF THE STATE OF MONTANA. REPORT OF THE STATE VETERINARIAN. ANNUAL REPORT OF THE STATE RECORDER OF MARKS AND BRANDS FOR THE YEAR 1889. HELENA, MONT.: JOURNAL PUBLISHING CO., 1890.

[1]–157, [158 blank]. 22 x 14.5 cm. Green printed wrappers with title on front wrapper.

Ref.: Adams (*Ramp. Herd*) 1557

Montana became a state in 1889. These reports are the first issued as state reports. The report of the State Recorder contains many brands and marks for cattle.

2860 MONTANA TERRITORY. Assembly

COUNCIL JOURNAL OF THE FIRST LEGISLATIVE ASSEMBLY OF MONTANA TERRITORY, CONVENED AT BANNACK, DECEMBER 12, 1864. VIRGINIA CITY, MONTANA: D. W. TILTON & CO., 1866.

[1]–304. 22.5 x 14.1 cm. Printed gray wrappers. In a brown cloth case.

Ref.: McMurtrie (*Montana*) 130

McMurtrie states this was printed in Maine.

2861 MONTANA TERRITORY. Vigilance Committee

[Broadside] NOTICE! TO ALL, WHOM IT MAY CONCERN. WHEREAS, DIVERS FOUL CRIMES AND OUTRAGES AGAINST THE PERSONS AND PROPERTY OF THE CITIZENS OF MONTANA, HAVE BEEN LATELY COMMITTED, AND, WHEREAS, THE POWER OF HE[!] CIVIL AUTHORITIES, THOUGH EXERTED TO ITS FULLEST EXTENT, IS FREQUENTLY INSUFFICIENT TO PREVENT THEIR COMMISSION, AND TO PUNISH THE PERPETRATORS THEREOF, NOW THIS IS TO WARN AND NOTIFY ALL WHOM IT MAY CONCERN, THAT THE VIGILANCE COMMITTEE COMPOSED OF THE CITIZENS OF THE TERRITORY, HAVE DETERMINED TO TAKE THESE MATTERS INTO THEIR OWN HANDS, AND TO INFLICT SUMMARY PUNISHMENT UPON ANY AND ALL MALEFACTORS, IN EVERY CASE WHERE THE CIVIL AUTHORITIES ARE UNABLE TO ENFORCE THE PROPER PENALTY OF THE LAW . . . THIS NOTICE WILL NOT BE REPEATED, BUT WILL REMAIN IN FULL FORCE AND EFFECT FROM THIS DATE. BY ORDER OF THE VIGILANCE COMMITTEE. SEPTEMBER 19TH, 1865.

Broadside, 40.5 x 29.8 cm. Text, 36.1 x 24.5 cm.

Ref.:

2862 MONTANA TERRITORY. Auditor and Treasurer

ANNUAL REPORT OF THE AUDITOR AND TREASURER OF THE TERRITORY OF MONTANA, FOR THE FISCAL YEAR 1886, TOGETHER WITH AN APPENDIX CON-

TAINING A RECORD OF MARKS AND BRANDS. HELENA, M. T.: FISK BROS., PRINTERS AND BINDERS, 1887.

[1]–244. 20.7 x 13.7 cm. Folded, unbound.
Ref.:
The Appendix contains data on the cattle industry and a collection of brands and marks used in Montana.

2863 MONTANA TERRITORY. Deer Lodge County Recorder's Office

[Broadside] TERRITORY OF MONTANA. DEER LODGE COUNTY RECORDER'S OFFICE, SILVER BOW CITY, [in manuscript: July 15th] 186 [in manuscript: 5] I HEREBY CERTIFY, THAT [in manuscript: Jasaphine Sowers] HAS RECORDED CLAIM NO. [in manuscript: (2) two East] FROM DISCOVERY, ON THE [in manuscript: Kit Clayton] LODE, [in manuscript: 200] FEET, LOCATED IN DEER LODGE COUNTY. RECORDED IN BOOK [in manuscript: "D"], PAGE [in manuscript: 65] [in manuscript: C, E, Irvine] COUNTY RECORDER. MONTANA "POST" PRINT.

Broadside, 6.7 x 7.5 cm. Text, 6.6 x 7.4 cm.
Ref.:
Publication of the *Montana Post* was started by John Buchanan (with Marion M. Manner as printer) on August 27, 1864.

2864 MONTANA TERRITORY. Governor (Green Clay Smith)

[Wrapper title] MESSAGE OF HON. GREEN CLAY SMITH, GOVERNOR OF MONTANA, TO THE FOURTH LEGISLATIVE ASSEMBLY AT VIRGINIA CITY, M.T., NOV. 4TH, 1867. D. W. TILTON & CO., 1867.

[1]–22. 20.8 x 13.4 cm. Orange printed wrappers with title as above on front wrapper.
Ref.: McMurtrie (*Montana*) 29
Contains also the annual reports of the Auditor, the Superintendent of Public Instruction, and the Surveyor-General of the Territory for the year 1866–67. There are also reports from Professors A. K. Eaton and G. C. Swallow in response to Governor Smith's request for their views on the natural resources of Montana, and a letter from Professor Augustus Steitz regretting that circumstances prevented him from complying fully with the governor's request.

2865 MONTANA TERRITORY. Laws, Statutes, etc.

[Wrapper title] ORGANIC ACT OF MONTANA TERRITORY. VIRGINIA CITY: D. W. TILTON & CO., 1867. [within double rule borders]

[1]–11, [12 blank]. 21 x 13.4 cm. Orange printed wrappers with title on front wrapper.
Ref.: McMurtrie (*Montana*) 33

2866 MONTANA TERRITORY. Mining Bureau

PROSPECTUS OF THE MINING BUREAU OF MONTANA . . . VIRGINIA CITY, M.T.: PRINTED AT THE OFFICE OF THE "MONTANA POST," 1866.

[1]–14, [15 cut], [16 blank]. (Pages [1–2] blank.) 17.7 x 15.5 cm. Woodcut: Tunnel in Summit District. Pink printed wrappers with title on front wrapper, additional text on verso of back wrapper.
Ref.: McMurtrie (*Montana*) 21

2867 MONTANA . . .

[Wrapper title] MONTANA. A CONCISE DESCRIPTION OF THE CLIMATE, SOIL, GRAZING LANDS, AGRICULTURAL AND MINERAL PRODUCTIONS OF THE COUNTRY ADJACENT AND TRIBUTARY TO THE NORTHERN PACIFIC RAILROAD. PUBLISHED FOR THE USE OF PERSONS SEEKING INFORMATION CONCERNING THIS GREAT NEW LAND. HELENA, MONTANA: FISK BROS., BOOK AND JOB PRINTERS, 1882. Another copy, without map, is inadvertently entered as number 3037 below.

[1]–16. 19.5 x 12.5 cm. Gray printed wrappers, with title on front wrapper and with advertisements on verso of front wrapper and recto and verso of back wrapper.
Ref.:

2868 MONTANA DEMOCRAT

[Newspaper] THE MONTANA DEMOCRAT. JOHN P. BRUCE, PUBLISHER . . . VOL. 1. VIRGINIA CITY, MONTANA TERRITORY, THURSDAY, MARCH 15, 1866. NO. 18 . . .

[1–4]. 55.8 x 40.7 cm. Unbound.
Ref.:
The editor at this time was John P. Bruce. Most of the front page is occupied by a printing of: Joint Rules / of Council and House, / Adopted at the / Second Session of the Montana Legislature. /

2869 MONTANA PIONEERS, SOCIETY OF

SOCIETY OF MONTANA PIONEERS CONSTITUTION, MEMBERS, AND OFFICERS . . . VOLUME I MDCCCXCIX.

[i–iv], xiii–xxxii, 33–262. 25.4 x 17.8 cm. Illustrations unlisted. Green cloth, gilt.
Ref.:
Probably printed at Helena, Mont.

2870 MONTANA, HISTORICAL SOCIETY OF

[Caption title] THE HISTORICAL SOCIETY OF MONTANA . . .

[1]–[8]. 22.9 x 15.4 cm. Unbound.
Ref.: McMurtrie (*Montana*) 87

Prospectus for the Society. Page [8] carries a list of the officers of the Society for 1874. This does not seem to be present in the copy described by McMurtrie.

Probably printed in Helena.

2871 MONTANA POST, THE

[Newspaper] THE MONTANA POST. A NEWSPAPER, DEVOTED TO THE MINERAL, AGRICULTURAL AND COMMERCIAL INTEREST OF MONTANA TERRITORY. VOL. 4, NO. 27. VIRGINIA CITY, MONTANA, SATURDAY, MARCH 28. WHOLE NO. 188 . . .

[1]–8. 53.1 x 35.6 cm. Unbound, unopened.

Ref.: McMurtrie (*Montana*) p. 10

In the first column on page [1], the publisher announces suspension of the newspaper. It had been established on August 27, 1864. At this point, the paper was sold by the publisher, D. W. Tilton & Co., to Ben. R. Dittes, who intended to move the publishing office to Helena and continue issuing the paper about April 15.

2872 MONTANA STOCK GROWERS' ASSOCIATION

BRAND BOOK OF THE MONTANA STOCK GROWERS' ASSOCIATION FOR 1886. FIRST EDITION. PUBLISHED BY THE MONTANA STOCK GROWERS' ASSOCIATION. CHICAGO: THE J. M. W. JONES STATIONERY AND PRINTING COMPANY, 1886.

[1]–213, [214–16 blank], [i–xvi ruled blank paper]. 18.3 x 10.5 cm. Red leather with side flap, pencil holder inside flap.

Ref.: Howes 731a

Preceding the title-page there is an engraved title mounted on the front endleaf: Brand Book / [ornament] of the [ornament] / Montana / [vignette within decorative frame] / Stock Growers [on ruled ground with decorative sides] / Association / [ornament] for [ornament] / 1885 and 86 / [ornament] / First Edition / Published by the / Montana Stock Growers' Association. / [following six lines in decorative box:] The / Homer Lee Bank Note / Company. N. Y. / Engravers and Lithographers of Bonds / Stock Certificates &c; For Stock Companies. / Estimates Given and Correspondence Invited. / Printed on the verso of the preceding and mounted against the endleaf is an advertisement of the bank note company.

Mounted on the inside front cover is a card: Compliments of / R. B. Harrison, / . . .

Although both Adams and Howes describe an edition thought to have been printed in Helena a year earlier, we have been unable to locate a copy of such an edition.

2873 MONTGOMERY, CORA [MRS. WILLIAM LESLIE CAZNEAU]

EAGLE PASS; OR, LIFE ON THE BORDER . . . NEW YORK: GEORGE P. PUTNAM & CO., MDCCCLII.

[i]–viii, [9]–188, [1]–2 advertisements, [1]–2 advertisements. 18.4 x 12.4 cm. Pale salmon printed wrappers, with advertisements on inner front wrapper (pasted down) and on verso of back wrapper, title on front wrapper. In a buff cloth case.

Ref.: Howes C215; Sabin 50132

2874 MONTHLY ANTHOLOGY AND BOSTON REVIEW, THE

[Wrapper title] MONTHLY ANTHOLOGY AND BOSTON REVIEW. FOR APRIL [JUNE–JULY], 1807. VOL. IV.—NO. IV [VI, VII] . . . BOSTON: PUBLISHED BY MUNROE & FRANCIS.

X–Dd⁴, D⁴. [169]–224, 25–32. Nn–Tt⁴, E⁴. [289]–344, 33–40. Uu–3B⁴, F⁴. [345]–400, 41–48. 23.1 x 14.5 cm. Three parts, gray printed wrappers with title on front wrappers, advertisements on all other wrapper surfaces, uncut.

Prov.: Inscribed on each front wrapper: Hon S Van Renssalaer /. Rubber stamp of W. B. Van Rensselaer on each first page.

Ref.: Sabin 50167

In each of the three parts there is an appendix with running heads: American State Papers. / These sections are separately paginated. Page 25 is headed: . . . / An Account of a Voyage / Up the Mississippi river, from St. Louis to its source; made / under the orders of the War Department, by Lieut. Pike, of / the United States army, in the years 1805 and 1806. Com-/piled from Mr. Pike's journal. / . . . The account is complete except for the final number, consisting of pages 49–52. The Newberry set of *The Monthly Anthology* is complete.

2875 MONTHLY LAW REPORTER, THE

[Caption title] THE MONTHLY LAW REPORTER. JANUARY, 1860. RIPARIAN AND LITTORAL RIGHTS . . .

[514]–23. Printed on one side of each leaf only and with blank pages pasted together. Bound with related materials in contemporary black half calf.

Ref.:

At foot of page [514]: Vol. XXII.—No. IX. 33 /.

See under ILLINOIS CENTRAL RAILROAD COMPANY.

2876 MONTHLY RECORDER, THE

[Caption title] THE MONTHLY RECORDER, FOR JULY, 1813. FOR THE RECORDER. BIOGRAPHICAL

MEMOIR OF THE LATE BRIGADIER-GENERAL ZEBU-
LON MONTGOMERY PIKE. . . .

Ee–Mm⁴. [221]–284. 21.9 x 14.1 cm. Stipple portrait of Pike, colored by hand. Old maroon
glazed wrappers.

Ref.:

The Monthly Recorder ran for five months,
April through August, 1813. It was written by
William Dunlap and others. The Newberry copy
(which lacks one portrait) has a title-page reading as follows: A Record, / Literary and Political, / of Five Months / in the Year 1813. / [short
decorative rule] / By William Dunlap / and
others. / [thick and thin rules] / Printed for the
Proprietor, by David Carlisle. / [A]², B–Uu⁴.
[1]–348. (Pages [1–2] blank.) Four portraits
(should be five).

Accompanying the present pamphlet is a
duplicate copy (trimmed) of the portrait.

2877 MOODY, DANIEL W.

THE LIFE OF A ROVER 1865 TO 1926 . . .*

[i–iv], [1]–116, [117–118 blank, 119–121 advertisements, 122–124 blank] 22.2 x 14.9 cm. Folding map and illustrations unlisted. Brown
printed wrappers.

Ref.: Rader 2428; Smith 6978

Facing title-page: Copyrighted by D. W.
Moody, 1926 / All rights reserved / Price / Paper
Cover Edition . . . 50c / Library Edition . . .
$1.00 /. Printed in Chicago.

Dan was in a lot of the right places at just the
right times. As to what basis of fact exists for the
events recorded, I have no idea.—EDG

2878 MOORE, D. N., & McCABE MOORE

PROCEEDINGS OF THE CENTENNIAL REUNION OF
THE MOORE FAMILY, HELD AT BELLEVILLE, ILL.,
MAY 31 AND JUNE 1, 1882 . . . ST. LOUIS, MO:
A. R. FLEMING, PRINTER, 1882.

[1]–82. 21.1 x 13.7 cm. Black cloth, blind embossed borders on covers, gilt title on front
cover.

Ref.:

2879 MOORE, EDWARD

FABLES FOR THE LADIES . . . LEXINGTON: PRINTED
BY DOWNING & PHILLIPS, 1815.

[*]⁴, A–C¹², D⁸. [1]–94. 12.7 x 7 cm. Soft gray
boards. Worn, back mostly missing, part of
front endleaf torn away.

Ref.:

Originally published in London in 1744 under
the title *Fables for the Female Sex.* Not listed in
AII (*Kentucky*). Downing & Phillips printed two
other books in 1815 but are otherwise unknown.

Editions: London, 1744. Philadelphia, 1787.
Exeter, N.H., 1794. Haverhill, Mass., 1805.

2880 MOORE, FRANCIS, JR.

MAP AND DESCRIPTION OF TEXAS, CONTAINING
SKETCHES OF ITS HISTORY . . . PHILADELPHIA:
H. TANNER, JUNR., 1840.

[1]–143, [144 blank, 145 errata, 146–48 blank].
14.6 x 9.3 cm. Eight engraved plates and a map.
Map: Genˡ Austins / Map / of / Texas / With
Parts of the Adjoining States / Compiled by
Stephen F. Austin / Published by H. S. Tanner
Philadelphia / [4 lines of text] / 1840. / Scale of
Miles. / [diagrammatic scale: about 25 miles to
one inch] / Engraved by John & Wm. W. Warr
Philadᵃ / [lower left:] Entered according to Act
of Congress, in the year 1840, in the Clerks Office
of the Eastern District of Pennsylvania. / 73.5 x
59.8 cm. Scale as above. Very dark brown cloth,
blind embossed fillet borders and corner ornaments, title in gilt on front cover.

Ref.: Bradford 3666; Howes M764; Raines p.
151; Sabin 50353; Streeter 1363

The binder's name appears in embossed
border.

The Ayer copy (1840) has an entirely different
map, is without plates and errata leaf, has no
pagination on page iv, is correctly paginated on
33, and is bound as Streeter 1363.

2881 MOORE, H. L.

[Caption title] AN INDIAN CAMPAIGN . . .

[1]–13, [14 blank]. 22.3 x 14.8 cm. Stapled.

Ref.:

Neither place nor date of publication is
given. The campaign was carried out in the
winter of 1868–69 against Satanta and Lone
Wolf. Moore commanded the Nineteenth Kansas cavalry.

2882 MOORE, J. M.

THE WEST.

[i–viii], [1]–[149], [150 blank]. 23.4 x 15 cm. Six
plates and one facsimile. Blue fabrikoid.

Ref.:

Copyrighted 1935 by the Wichita Printing
Company.

2883 MOORE, NATHANIEL F.

. . . DIARY: A TRIP FROM NEW YORK TO THE FALLS
OF ST. ANTHONY IN 1845. EDITED BY STANLEY
PARGELLIS AND RUTH LAPHAM BUTLER. CHICAGO:
PUBLISHED FOR THE NEWBERRY LIBRARY BY THE
UNIVERSITY OF CHICAGO PRESS, 1946.

[i]–xviii, [1]–[102]. (Pages [i–ii] blank.) 20.3 x
13.3 cm. Eight illustrations listed, maps on endpapers. Brown cloth. In dust jacket.

Prov.: Signed by the editors on the title-page.
Ref.:

2884 MOORE, S. A.

[Wrapper title] HISTORY OF DAVIS COUNTY, IOWA, READ AT BLOOMFIELD, JULY 4, 1876 . . . BLOOM-FIELD, IOWA: MOORE & ETHELL, 1876.

[1]–24. 22.9 x 15.1 cm. Gray wrappers with title on front cover as above.

Ref.: Cook p. 134; Mott (*Iowa*) p. 50

On page 2, the author acknowledges his indebtedness to Hosea B. Horn for information received and help in writing.

2885 MOOSO, JOSIAH

THE LIFE AND TRAVELS OF JOSIAH MOOSO. A LIFE ON THE FRONTIER AMONG INDIANS AND SPANIARDS, NOT SEEING THE FACE OF A WHITE WOMAN FOR FIFTEEN YEARS . . . WINFIELD, KANSAS: TELEGRAM PRINT, 1888.

[1]–400. 18.8 x 12.9 cm. Portrait. Blue cloth.

Ref.: Ayer (*Supp.*) 86; Cowan p. 440; Howes M784; Jones 1647; Rader 2440

Includes an account of his overland trip to Oregon and California.

2886 MOREHEAD, JAMES T.

REPORT OF THE COMMITTEE ON RETRENCHMENT OF THE SENATE OF THE UNITED STATES, MADE BY HON. JAMES T. MOREHEAD . . . ON THE 15TH OF JUNE, 1844 . . . WASHINGTON: PRINTED BY GALES AND SEATON, 1844.

[1]–6, [7–8 blank], [1]–448. Bound with Number 1084.

Ref.:

28th Congress, 1st Session, Senate, Document No. 399.

2887 MORGAN, DICK T.

MORGAN'S MANUAL OF THE U. S. HOMESTEAD AND TOWNSITE LAWS . . . GUTHRIE, OK.: STATE CAPITAL PRINTING CO., 1893.

[1]–[146], [147–48 advertisements]. 15 x 11 cm. Pages [145–46] are a cancel leaf, inserted on a stub, with six illustrative vignettes. Buff printed wrappers with title on front wrapper, advertisements on verso of front and recto and verso of back wrapper.

Ref.:

2888 MORGAN, GEORGE H.

ANNUAL STATEMENT OF THE TRADE AND COMMERCE OF ST. LOUIS FOR THE YEAR 1865. REPORTED TO THE UNION MERCHANTS' EXCHANGE . . . SAINT LOUIS: R. P. STUDLEY AND CO., 1866.

[1]–116, [i]–xv, [xvi blank]. 20.6 x 13.7 cm. Bound with Number 1084.

Ref.: Sabin 75335

The second section is a list of members of the Union Merchants' Exchange.

2889 MORGAN, P. A.

[Broadside] BALLAD OF LOVE'S INDEPENDENCE . . . SERGT. P. A. MORGAN, CO. E., 1ST U. S. V. INF.

Broadside, 19.7 x 12.3 cm. Text, 13.2 x 11.6 cm.

Ref.: Allen (*Dakota*) 33

Very crude verse, crudely printed, undoubtedly on the press used for printing the *Frontier Scout*, a little newspaper published by the soldiers at Fort Rice in 1864 and 1865.

Fort Rice, established in 1864 and abandoned in 1879, was located on the west bank of the Missouri River, some twenty-five or thirty miles below the present city of Bismarck.—Allen

2890 MORGAN, P. A.

[Broadside] POETRY FOR THE TIMES . . . P. A. MORGAN, CO. E, 1ST U. S. V. INF.

Broadside, 18.7 x 14.8 cm. Text, 11.7 x 5.6 cm. Printed on vertically ruled paper.

Ref.: Allen (*Dakota*) 34

See preceding broadside by Morgan.

2891 MORGENSTJERNEN

MORGENSTJERNEN. ET HISTORISK-BIOGRAFISK MAANEDSSKRIFT . . . SALT LAKE CITY, UTAH: TRYKT HOS, ,DESERET NEWS COMPANY,' 1882 [–1885].

[i]–iv, [1]–188. [i]–iv, [1]–188. [i]–viii, [1]–376. [i–ii], [1]–[190]. 23.5 x 15.3 cm. Illustrations unlisted. Four volumes bound together in contemporary sheepskin, black leather labels.

Ref.:

Edited and published by Andrew Jenson.

The work was continued in English, after the first four volumes, as *The Historical Record*.

2892 MORGENSTJERNEN (continued as THE HISTORICAL RECORD)

. . . THE HISTORICAL RECORD, (CONTINUATION OF "MORGENSTJERNEN") A MONTHLY PERIODICAL, DEVOTED EXCLUSIVELY TO HISTORICAL, BIOGRAPHICAL, CHRONOLOGICAL AND STATISTICAL MATTERS. VOLUME FIVE [–SIX]. SALT LAKE CITY, UTAH, 1886.

[i–iv, iv blank], [1]–120. [i]–iv, [121]–352. 23.5 x 15.6 cm. Illustrations not listed. Two volumes bound together black half leather.

Ref.:

THE SAME. Volumes 7–8. 1888–1889.

[i–iv, iv blank], [353–684]. [i–iv, iv blank], [685]–[1012 Memorandum].

THE SAME. Volume Nine. 1890.
[i–iv, iv blank], [1]–124. 23.4 x 15.5 cm.

BOUND WITH:

SUPPLEMENT TO THE "HISTORICAL RECORD." CHURCH CHRONOLOGY: OR A RECORD OF IMPORTANT EVENTS CONNECTED WITH THE HISTORY OF THE CHURCH OF JESUS CHRIST OF LATTER-DAY SAINTS, AND THE TERRITORY OF UTAH. COMPILED BY ANDREW JENSON. SALT LAKE CITY, UTAH: 1886.
[1–4], [i]–xx, [1]–112.

BOUND WITH:

SUPPLEMENT TO THE "HISTORICAL RECORD." A CHRONOLOGY OF IMPORTANT EVENTS OF THE YEAR 1885. COMPILED BY ANDREW JENSON . . . SALT LAKE CITY, UTAH: 1887.
[1–2], [i]–vi, [1]–24.

BOUND WITH:

THE SAME FOR 1886. SALT LAKE CITY, UTAH: 1887.
[i]–viii, [1]–24.

BOUND WITH:

THE SAME FOR 1887. SALT LAKE CITY, UTAH: 1887.
[i]–viii, [1]–23, [24 blank]. Contemporary black half calf.

2893 MORLEY, JAMES H.
JAMES HENRY MORLEY: 1824–1889. A MEMORIAL. CAMBRIDGE: PRINTED AT THE RIVERSIDE PRESS, 1891.
[1]–61, [62 blank]. 20.2 x 14.4 cm. Portrait. Dark blue cloth.
   Ref.:
   From May, 1862 until August, 1865, Morley was prospecting in the Northwest. He went by boat from St. Louis to Fort Benton and then by trail to the gold fields. Extracts from his diary appear on pages 28–39.

2894 MORRELL, Z. N.
FLOWERS AND FRUITS IN THE WILDERNESS; OR, FORTY-SIX YEARS IN TEXAS, AND TWO WINTERS IN HONDURAS . . . ST. LOUIS: COMMERCIAL PRINTING COMPANY, 1882.
[i]–xviii, 19–412. 19 x 12.4 cm. Portrait. Dark blue cloth, blind embossed sides, title in gilt on backstrip.
   Ref.: Howes M819; Raines p. 153
   According to a note on page [viii] this third edition contains additional material.
   Editions: Boston, 1872, 1873.

2895 MORRILL, CHARLES H.
THE MORRILLS AND REMINISCENCES . . . CHICAGO: UNIVERSITY PUBLISHING CO.*
[i]–iv], 1–160. 19.5 x 13.5 cm. 47 illustrations listed and one folding chart. Dark blue cloth, gilt top, uncut.

   Ref.:
   Copyrighted 1918. Contains reminiscences of early Nebraska, Buffalo Bill, etc.

2896 MORRILL, EDMUND N.
HISTORY AND STATISTICS OF BROWN CO., KANSAS, FROM ITS EARLIEST SETTLEMENT TO THE PRESENT TIME . . . HIAWATHA, KANSAS: KANSAS HERALD BOOK, NEWS AND JOB OFFICE, JULY 4TH, 1876.
[1]–82, [83–4 blank]. 21.7 x 14.6 cm. Yellow printed wrappers, with title on front wrapper. Portion of front wrapper restored, including part of border and all of last line of imprint. In a tan cloth case.
   Ref.: AII (*Kansas*) 1537; Howes M820

2897 MORRILL, J. E.
[Broadside] MERRICK COUNTY . . . J. E. MORRILL, LEAKE & REED.
Broadside, 25.7 x 20.4 cm. Text, 22.8 x 13.4 cm.
   Ref.:
   The broadside describes Merrick County, Nebraska, and the town of Chapman. Probably printed in 1870.
   On the verso is a letter written by H. J. Whiton, dated: Chapman Nebraskey, March 25th '70. On the face of the broadside, Whiton made the following comment: This is spread on purty thick /. With original stamped envelope.

2898 MORRIS, C.
AUTOGRAPH DOCUMENT, SIGNED. 1807 September 11, Staunton [Va.?] One page, 8.8 x 19.4 cm. Receipt to Robert McKnight.

2899 MORRIS, MAURICE O'C.
RAMBLES IN THE ROCKY MOUNTAINS: WITH A VISIT TO THE GOLD FIELDS OF COLORADO . . . LONDON: SMITH, ELDER AND CO., 1864.
[i]–viii, 1–264. 19.5 x 12.5 cm. Green cloth, fore and lower edges uncut.
   Ref.: Bradford 3694; Howes M831; Sabin 50853; Wagner-Camp 403

2900 MORRIS, THOMAS
AUTOGRAPH LETTER, SIGNED. 1765 August 29, Detroit. To Mrs. Van Schaack. Two pages, 18.7 x 15.7 cm. With part of address leaf, but lacking address.
   An amusing letter to the wife of a friend.
   Laid in Morris: *Miscellanies* . . . 1791.

2901 MORRIS, THOMAS
MISCELLANIES IN PROSE AND VERSE . . . LONDON: JAMES RIDGWAY, 1791.
[A]–Aa⁴. [1–2], [i]–vi, [1]–64, [67]–181, [182–83 blank, 184–85 advertisements, 186 blank]. (Page

74 mispaginated 76.) 20.5 x 12.7 cm. Stipple portrait. Contemporary marbled boards, new calf back, red leather label.

Prov.: Signature on half-title crossed out: Amasa Jones / Jany—1791/. Signature on title-page: Henry Jones.' /. Manuscript correction, last line, page 95.

Ref.: Clements Library (*Michigan*) 31; Howes M833; Jones 620; Sabin 50876; Thomson 854; Vail 880

Captain Morris came to America with the British Army in 1758. He fought at Louisbourg, Quebec, Havana, and elsewhere. He was stationed for a time at Mackinac. Much of the material in his *Miscellanies* was written in Michigan. The volume also contains an expanded version of his *Journal*, a manuscript copy of which may be seen in the Gage Papers at the Clements Library.

In 1764, the British set out to punish the Indians for the troubles stirred up by Pontiac. One of the minor, but exciting episodes of that expedition was the attempt of Captain Morris to carry a message from Colonel John Bradstreet to the French commandant at Fort Chartres, in the Illinois country. His *Journal* records his travels from Cedar Point, Ohio, to the site of today's Fort Wayne—his farthest point west—and his retreat to Detroit.

2902   MORRIS, THOMAS A.

MISCELLANY: CONSISTING OF ESSAYS, BIOGRAPHICAL SKETCHES, AND NOTES OF TRAVEL . . . CINCINNATI: PUBLISHED BY L. SWORMSTEDT & J. H. POWER, 1852.

[1]–390. 18.2 x 11.5 cm. Portrait. Blue-grey cloth, blind embossed sides, gilt title on backstrip.

Ref.: Clark III 214; Howes M832; Sabin 50878

Includes a 46-page account of a trip through Missouri and Arkansas to Austin, Texas, in 1841–2; also an 1844 trip to Tallequah.— Howes. Sixty-seven pages are devoted to the St. Louis–Austin trip.

2903   MORRISON, JAMES & JESSE

AUTOGRAPH LETTER, SIGNED James & Jesse Morrison, in the hand of one or the other. 1812 May 6, St. Charles. Two pages, 32.1 x 19.1 cm. To Baptiste LaLande.

An accounting of monies due the Morrisons from LaLande and with an urgent request that the bearer, Robert McKnight, be paid. The account started in 1804, and amounted to $1787.90.

Reproduced in *The Colorado Magazine*, Vol. xxiv, No. 5, Sept. 1947.

2904   MORRISON, JAMES & JESSE

AUTOGRAPH MANUSCRIPT NOTE, SIGNED by James or Jesse Morrison. No place, no date. To Robert McKnight. Request to pay $2.50 for a pair of shoes.

2905   [MORRISON, N. B.]

A BRIEF DESCRIPTION OF FORT DODGE, IOWA . . . BEING AN ANSWER TO LETTERS OF INQUIRY ON THE SUBJECT. FORT DODGE: PRINTED BY A. S. WHITE, 1858.

[i–ii], [1]–16. (Page [i] blank, [ii] advertisement.) 19.7 x 13.6 cm. Folding map: [two maps on one sheet] Map of the Dubuque and Pacific Rail Road and / its Connections. / [lower left:] Lith. by J. H. Colton & Cº 172 William St. N.Y. / 7 x 21.7 cm. No scale given. Map: [Iowa] / [lower left:] Engraved & Printed / by / J. H. Colton & Co / 172 William St. N. York. / 14.9 x 22.2 cm. No scale given. White printed wrappers, with title on front wrapper, verso of back wrapper carries advertisement for the Fort Dodge *Sentinel*.

Prov.:

Ref.: Moffit 337

The map follows the first leaf. Advertisements on pages 11–16.

2906   MORRISON, WILLIAM

HORRIBLE AND AWFUL DEVELOPMENTS FROM THE CONFESSION OF WILLIAM MORRISON. THE ROCKY MOUNTAIN TRAPPER: GIVING A TRUE AND FAITHFUL ACCOUNT OF HIS MURDERS AND DEPREDATIONS . . . PHILADELPHIA: PUBLISHED BY E. E. BARCLAY, 1853.

[1]–32. 22.2 x 14.5 cm. Frontispiece and one illustration, unlisted. Blue printed wrappers; removed from bound volume. In a blue cloth case.

Ref.: Howes M838; Wagner-Camp 227
Sheer horror.

Editions: Philadelphia, 1852.

2907   MORSE, CHARLES W.

[Map] MORSE'S / CEROGRAPHIC MAP OF / IOWA. / PUBLISHED BY RUFUS BLANCHARD, / 52 LA SALLE ST., CHICAGO, ILL. / [rule] / ENTERED, ACCORDING TO ACT OF CONGRESS, IN THE YEAR 1856, BY CHARLES W. MORSE, IN THE CLERK'S OFFICE OF THE DISTRICT / COURT OF THE UNITED STATES, FOR THE SOUTHERN DISTRICT OF NEW YORK. / SCALE OF MILES / [diagrammatic scale: 14 miles to one inch] /.

Map, 59.5 x 79 cm. Scale as above. Folded into green cloth covers, 15 x 9.5 cm., with title stamped in gilt on front cover, advertisements on inner front cover.

Ref.:

438

2908 MORSE, JEDIDIAH

A REPORT TO THE SECRETARY OF WAR . . . ON IN-
DIAN AFFAIRS, COMPRISING A NARRATIVE OF A
TOUR PERFORMED IN THE SUMMER OF 1820 . . .
FOR THE PURPOSE OF ASCERTAINING . . . THE AC-
TUAL STATE OF THE INDIAN TRIBES IN OUR COUN-
TRY . . . NEW-HAVEN: PUBLISHED BY DAVIS &
FORCE . . . 1822.

[1]–96, [1]–400. 21.7 x 14 cm. Portrait and folding map: United States. / [lower right:] A. Dog-
gett Sc. N. Haven. / 25.1 x 42.2 cm. No scale
indicated. Gray boards, buff paper backstrip
with early manuscript label, uncut. In a blue
cloth case.

Prov.: Rubber stamped name: E. A. Andrews. / on front and back covers, a preliminary
blank leaf, and on the title-page. Bookplate of
the Athenaeum of the New Haven Young
Ladies' Institute, with note of presentation by
Professor Andrews.

Ref.: Howes M843; Sabin 50945; Wagner-
Camp 25 note

The errata slip called for by Howes is not
present in this copy, nor is there evidence it was
ever present.

2909 MORSE, JOHN F., & SAMUEL COL-VILLE

ILLUSTRATED HISTORICAL SKETCHES OF CALIFOR-
NIA . . . TOGETHER WITH A MORE AMPLE HISTORY
OF SACRAMENTO VALLEY AND CITY, AND BIO-
GRAPHICAL REFERENCES TO PROMINENT INDIVID-
UALS . . . SACRAMENTO: PRINTED FOR THE PUB-
LISHER AT THE DEMOCRATIC STATE JOURNAL OF-
FICE, 1854.

[i]–iv, [5]–46, [1]–8. 21.8 x 14.4 cm. Frontispiece
view, portrait, and one vignette in text. Removed from bound volume, pink printed wrappers with title on front wrapper, note to the public, list of contents, and advertisement on back
wrapper. Backstrip supplied with two strips of
cloth.

Ref.: Blumann & Thomas 2394; Cowan p.
444; Greenwood 482; Howes M844

Relates principally to missions in California.
Also contains a substantial sketch of the life of
John A. Sutter. No other numbers of the pro-
jected series were issued.

2910 MORSMAN, EDGAR M., JR.

E M MORSMAN.

[1]–[16]. 26.2 x 18.7 cm. Brown cloth.

Prov.: Inscribed on the title-page: This book
presented to me, December 3^d, 1950, by Joseph /
J. Morsman, a son of Edgar Martin Morsman.
I have / known Joe since 1909 or over forty
years, he having married / a sister of my brother
Walter's wife. As a boy in Clarinda I / remember
hearing stories of Cap. Morsman who lived in
Clarinda / in the early days. Cap. and Westel
Morsman are the same person. / E. D. G. / The
dedication on page 3, which is dated December
1st, 1942, is signed in manuscript by Edgar M.
Morsman, Jr.

Ref.:

Included is a letter from Virginia City, M.T.,
January 20, 1865, giving a great deal of informa-
tion as to the route and conditions overland.
Also included is a letter from E. M. Morsman to
John S. Collins in regard to the latter's book
Across the Plains in '64.

The printed, gummed label of the Omaha
Printing Co. appears on the inner back cover.

2911 MORTON, CYRUS

AUTOBIOGRAPHY OF CYRUS MORTON. OMAHA,
NEB.: THE DOUGLAS PRINTING CO., 1895.

[1]–46, [47–8 blank]. 23 x 15.4 cm. Portrait.
White glazed wrappers, with author's signature
on front wrapper between gold head and foot
bands.

Ref.:

2912 MORTON, JULIUS S.

[Wrapper title] ADDRESS . . . DELIVERED AT THE
FIRST ANNUAL FAIR OF THE TERRITORIAL BOARD OF
AGRICULTURE, HELD AT NEBRASKA CITY, ON THE
21ST, 22ND & 23RD DAYS OF SEPTEMBER, 1859.
OMAHA CITY: ROBERTSON & CLARK, PRINTERS,
1860.

[1]–10. 23.8 x 15.4 cm. Light blue printed wrappers, with title on front wrapper.

Ref.: AII (*Nebraska*) 53

AII (*Nebraska*) lists only one imperfect copy,
without wrappers and without title-page.

2913 MORTON, JULIUS S.

A COMMEMORATIVE PAMPHLET: IT RELATES TO
JULY 4TH, 1876, AT NEBRASKA CITY, OTOE
COUNTY, NEBRASKA, AND CONTAINS THE NAMES
AND POSITIONS OF ALL THE OFFICERS OF THE DAY,
THE PROGRAMME OF EXERCISES, AND AN ORATION,
BY J. STERLING MORTON. CHICAGO: J. M. W. JONES,
1876.

[1]–38, [39–40 blank]. 22.3 x 14.8 cm. Gray
printed wrappers with title on front wrapper.

Ref.:

2914 MOSELEY, HENRY N.

OREGON: ITS RESOURCES, CLIMATE, PEOPLE, AND
PRODUCTIONS . . . LONDON: EDWARD STANFORD,
1878.

[1]–125, [126 blank]. 16.7 x 13.8 cm. Map: A /
Map of / Oregon / [lower right:] Stanford's

Geog¹ Estab.ᵗ / [centre, below neat line:] London: Edward Stanford, 55, Charing Cross. / 18.1 x 21.8 cm. Scale: about 50 miles to an inch. Green cloth.

Ref.: Bradford 3717; Smith 7102

2915 [MOTT, M. H.]

HISTORY OF THE REGULATORS OF NORTHERN INDIANA . . . INDIANAPOLIS: INDIANAPOLIS JOURNAL COMPANY, 1859.

[1]–67, [68 blank]. 22.7 x 14.6 cm. Printed yellow wrappers with title on front wrapper, advertisements on verso of back wrapper.

Prov.: Label of J. Francis Ruggles, "Ye-Bibliopoloexperto," a bookseller of Bronson, Michigan.

Ref.: Greenly 98; Howes M860

The Regulators were interested in keeping the law and punishing law breakers.

2916 MOTTO OF JUBILEE COLLEGE, THE

[Cover title] THE MOTTO OF JUBILEE COLLEGE . . . VOL. 2. JUNE 20, 1851. NO. 3. JUBILEE COLLEGE: PRINTED AT THE JUBILEE PRESS. 1851.

[75]–96. 20.7 x 13.4 cm. Pale yellow printed wrappers, removed from bound volume. Lacks back wrapper. In red cloth case stamped: Bishop Chase. Jubilee College.

Ref.:

Jubilee College was an Episcopalian school founded by Bishop Philander Chase.

2917 MOTTO OF JUBILEE COLLEGE, THE

[Caption title] . . . LITERARY NOTICES. THE MOTTO OF JUBILEE COLLEGE, &C. VOL. I, NO. 7. MAY 22, 1849. AN ARTICLE SIGNED G. L. IN THE BOSTON ADVERTISER, OF JULY 12TH, 1849. AN ARTICLE SIGNED P. IN THE CALENDAR, PUBLISHED AT HARTFORD, JUNE 30TH, 1849 . . .

[469 blank], 470–76. 21 x 13.3 cm. Removed from bound volume, unbound. In red cloth case stamped: Bishop Chase Pamphlets.

Ref.:

This is an extract from a monthly journal published in 1849 attacking rather scornfully an article which had appeared in the Jubilee College magazine, *The Motto.*

2918 MOUNTAIN BUGLE, THE

[Prospectus] [broadside] THE MOUNTAIN BUGLE, EDITED BY ELLA A. CHAPPEL; WILL BE PUBLISHED WEEKLY AT COUNCIL BLUFF AGENCY, THE PROSPECTIVE CAPITOL OF NEBRASKA TERRITORY . . . EDITORS COPYING THIS PROSPECTUS, AND SENDING A PAPER MARKED TO DU BUQUE, (IF SENT BEFORE THE 1ST OF MARCH,) AFTER THAT TIME TO COUNCIL BLUFF AGENCY, NEBRASKA TERRITORY, WILL BE ENTITLED TO AN EXCHANGE. DU BUQUE, DEC. 25, 1849. ELLA A. CHAPPEL.

Broadside, 24.6 x 19.8 cm. Text: 14.5 x 15.3 cm.

Ref.:

The Mountain Bugle may never have materialized. *The Annals of Iowa*, IX (1871) page 677, University of Iowa *Extension Bulletin* No. 175, July 1, 1927, page 90, and *History of Pottawattamie County*, Chicago, 1883, page 39, note the establishment of *The Bugle* at Council Bluffs in 1850 by A. W. Babbitt. Neither *The Mountain Bugle* nor Ella A. Chappel is mentioned.

2919 MOURELLE, FRANCISCO ANTONIO

JOURNAL OF A VOYAGE IN 1775. TO EXPLORE THE COAST OF AMERICA, NORTHWARD OF CALIFORNIA, BY THE SECOND PILOT OF THE FLEET, DON FRANCISCO ANTONIO MAURELLE[!], IN THE KING'S SCHOONER, CALLED THE SONORA, AND COMMANDED BY DON JUAN FRANCISCO DE LA BODEGA.

A, a⁴, A2, B–H⁴, I–K². [i]–[x, x blank], [3]–67, [68 blank]. 26.7 x 20.7 cm. Map: [West coast of North America]. 23.6 x 17.6 cm. No scale given. Contemporary marbled boards, calf corners and backstrip, leather label on backstrip.

Prov.: Bookplate of W. C. Mylne.

Ref.: Cowan p. 420 see; Howes M438; Sabin 46951; Wagner (*SS*) 164

Printed at London in 1780 or 1781.

Included in Daines Barrington: *Miscellanies* . . . 1781 with different signatures and pagination. In the present copy, the signature A appears at the foot of the title page.

2920 MOWRY, SYLVESTER

ARIZONA AND SONORA: THE GEOGRAPHY, HISTORY, AND RESOURCES OF THE SILVER REGION OF NORTH AMERICA . . . NEW YORK: HARPER & BROTHERS, 1864.

[i]–xiv, [15]–251, [252 blank]. (Pages [i–ii] blank.) 19.2 x 12.2 cm. Black cloth, blind embossed sides, with publishers' initials in centres, title in gilt on backstrip.

Prov.: Inscribed on front blank leaf: Miss Lucy Gwin[?] / with the sincere regards / of her friend / The Author / [underline] / New York Hotel / Feby 22ⁿᵈ 1865– /

Ref.: Bradford 3737; Howes M869; Munk (Alliot) p. 158; Sabin 51210

Editions: Washington, 1859, San Francisco, 1863.

2921 MOWRY, SYLVESTER

THE GEOGRAPHY AND RESOURCES OF ARIZONA & SONORA: AN ADDRESS BEFORE THE AMERICAN GEOGRAPHICAL & STATISTICAL SOCIETY . . . NEW-

YORK, FEBRUARY 3, 1859. WASHINGTON: HENRY POLKINHORN, PRINTER, 1859.*

[1]–48. 21.4 x 14 cm. Yellow printed wrappers with title on front wrapper. Removed from bound volume, lacks back wrapper and back-strip.

Prov.: Inscribed on front cover: H. Danby Seymour Esq / M. P. / Compliments of / Sylvester Mowry /.

Ref.: Bradford 3735; Howes M869; Munk (Alliot) p. 158; Sabin 51211; Wagner-Camp 336

Parts of this address had appeared previously in the author's *Memoir . . . 1857*. The errata slip mentioned by Howes is not present.

2922 MOWRY, SYLVESTER

MEMOIR OF THE PROPOSED TERRITORY OF ARIZONA . . . WASHINGTON: HENRY POLKINHORN, PRINTER, 1857.

[1]–30, [31–32 blank]. 22.4 x 14.2 cm. Map: Map of Proposed Arizona Territory / From explorations by A. B. Gray & others, to accompany memoirs by Lieut. Mowry / U. S. Army, Delegate elect. / [centre, below neat line:] Middleton Wallace & Cº Lithoˢ Cin. / 16.8 x 36.3 cm. No scale given. Some manuscript additions. Buff printed wrappers with title on front wrapper.

Ref.: Bradford 3734; Howes M870; Jones 1378; Munk (Alliot) p. 158; Sabin 51212; Streeter (*Americana—Beginnings*) 62; Wagner-Camp 293

This seems to be the first book relating wholly to Arizona.—Streeter

The map was prepared for and should be present in copies of the pamphlet. Manuscript additions appear on several copies of the map.

2923 MOWRY, SYLVESTER

THE MINES OF THE WEST. SHALL THE GOVERNMENT SEIZE THEM? THE MINING STATES. HOW SHALL THEY BE TAXED? . . . NEW YORK: G. E. CURRIE, 1864.

[1]–16. 22.1 x 14.3 cm. Stitched, unbound.

Ref.:

The letters were originally published in the *New York World*, April 25, 1864, and in the following month in the *New York Herald*.

2924 MOWRY, WILLIAM A.

[Broadside] IN-RE MY ARMY LIFE AND THE FORT PHIL KEARNEY MASSACRE . . . WILLIAM A. MOWRY.

Broadside, 17.9 x 12.6 cm. Text, 16.4 x 9.3 cm.

Ref.:

Laid in Carrington, Frances C.: *My Army Life and the Fort Phil. Kearney Massacre . . .* Philadelphia, 1910. The letter is dated from Oak Bluffs, Martha's Vineyard, Mass., June 29, 1910.

2925 MUDGE, ZACHARIAH A.

THE MISSIONARY TEACHER: A MEMOIR OF CYRUS SHEPARD, EMBRACING A BRIEF SKETCH OF THE EARLY HISTORY OF THE OREGON MISSION . . . NEW-YORK: PUBLISHED BY LANE & TIPPETT, 1848.

[1]–221, [222 blank], [223–34 advertisements]. 14.7 x 9.6 cm. Seven plates unlisted. Black cloth.

Ref.: Howes M873; Smith 7131

First Edition. The copy reported by Smith is without date on the title-page. Howes considers the undated edition later than the dated 1848 edition.

"We take pleasure in acknowledging our indebtedness to Charles Wilkes, Esq., U. S. Navy, for the privilege of copying the cuts found in this volume, from the fourth volume of the United States Exploring Expedition."—Preface, page 6.

Shepard was with the Wyeth Expedition of 1834.

2926 [MUDGE, ZACHARIAH A. (?)]

SKETCHES OF MISSION LIFE AMONG THE INDIANS OF OREGON. NEW-YORK: PUBLISHED BY CARLTON & PORTER.

[1]–229, [230 blank], [231–34 advertisements.] (Pages [1–2] blank.) 14.5 x 9.5 cm. Five illustrations. Blue-purple cloth, embossed sides, gilt backstrip, with title. Lacks front fly-leaf.

Ref.: Howes P230; Smith 7132

Copyrighted 1854.

Jason Lee's experiences are recounted in this work.

2927 MULFORD, AMI F.

FIGHTING INDIANS IN THE 7TH U. S. CAV. CUSTER'S FAVORITE REGIMENT . . . CORNING, N. Y.: PRINTED AND FOR SALE BY LEE & A. F. MULFORD, 1878.

[1]–[223], [224 blank]. 14.3 x 11 cm. Printed wrappers, light green printed cartoons, title overprinted in red on front wrapper, printed pattern continues on inside of wrappers. Gray cloth folding case.

Ref.: Howes M880a; Smith 7149

2928 MULFORD, AMI F.

FIGHTING INDIANS IN THE 7TH UNITED STATES CAVALRY, CUSTER'S FAVORITE REGIMENT . . . CORNING, N.Y.: PUBLISHED BY PAUL LINDSLEY MULFORD.*

[1]–[156]. 23.6 x 14.7 cm. Brown wrappers, with short title on front wrapper, stapled, punched and tied with yellow cord.

Ref.: Howes M880a see; Smith 7149

Page [156]: Second Edition / Revised by A. F. Mulford / 1879. /

Editions: Corning, 1878.

2929 MULFORD, PRENTICE

... PRENTICE MULFORD'S STORY: LIFE BY LAND AND SEA ... NEW YORK: F. J. NEEDHAM, PUBLISHER, 1889.

[i]–iv, [5]–299, [300 blank]. 19.3 x 13.2 cm. Dark red cloth, stamped with title on front cover with gilt, and on backstrip.

Prov.: Bookplate of Joseph Gregg Layne, historian and editor of the Quarterly of the Historical Society of Southern California.

Ref.: Blumann & Thomas 5206; Cowan p. 447; Howes M882

Mulford arrived in California in 1856, remaining for sixteen years. His charming story is chiefly of this picturesque period.

2930 MULHOLLAND, JAMES

AN ADDRESS TO AMERICANS: A POEM IN BLANK VERSE, ... INTENDED AS A BRIEF EXPOSURE OF THE CRUELTIES AND WRONGS, WHICH THE CHURCH HAS LATELY EXPERIENCED IN THE STATE OF MISSOURI ... NAUVOO: PRINTED BY E. ROBINSON, 1841.

[1]–11, [12 blank]. 18.8 x 10.7 cm. Gray printed wrappers, with title on front wrapper.

Ref.: Byrd 648

Published posthumously, according to preface on verso of title-leaf, which is signed and dated: R. B. Thompson. / Nauvoo, January 1, 1841.

2931 MULHOLLAND, JAMES

THE SAME ... BATAVIA: PRINTED BY D. D. WAITE, 1844.

[3]–15, [16–18 blank]. 21.6 x 14.9 cm. Stabbed, unbound.

Ref.:
Editions: Nauvoo, 1841.

2932 MULLAN, JOHN

REPORT ON THE CONSTRUCTION OF A MILITARY ROAD FROM FORT WALLA-WALLA TO FORT BENTON ... WASHINGTON: GOVERNMENT PRINTING OFFICE, 1863.

[i–ii, ii blank], [1]–[365], [366 blank]. 22.6 x 14.1 cm. Ten colored plates, four maps, unlisted. Map: Map / of the Mountain Section / of the / F^t Walla Walla & F^t Benton Military Wagon Road / from Coeur d'Alene Lake to the Dearborn River / Washington Territory / constructed under direction of the War Department / by Capt. John Mullan, U. S. Army / surveyed & drawn by Theodore Kolecki C. E. / 1859–1863. / Scale of 1:300000. / Scale of Statute Miles. / [diagrammatic scale: five miles to one inch] / Lith. of J. Bien, 24 Vesey St. N. Y. / [upper right:] Sen. Ex. Doc. N° 43—37th Cong. 3rd Sess. / 53.1 x 125.9 cm. Scale as above. Map:

War Dept. / Office Explorations and Surveys. / [rule] / Map of / Military Reconnaissance / from / Fort Taylor to the Coeur d'Alene Mission, / Washington Territory; / made under direction of Capt. A. A. Humphreys, U. S. Top^l Eng^r,/by Lieut. John Mullan, U. S. Army,/assisted by / Theodore Kolecki and Gustavus Sohon, Civil Eng^{rs}, / while attached to the Military Expedition under / Col. Geo. Wright, 9th Infantry, in / 1858. / Scale.—1:3000,000. / [diagrammatic scale: about 5 miles to one inch] / [upper right:] Senate Ex. Doc. N°43—47th[!] Cong. 3^d Sess. / [lower right:] Lith. of J. Bien, 24 Vesey St. N. Y.] 55 x 51.2 cm. Scale as above. Map: War Dept. / Office Explorations and Surveys. / [rule] / Map of / Military Reconnaissance / from / Fort Dalles, Oregon, via Fort Wallah-Wallah, / to / Fort Taylor, Washington Territory; / made under direction of Capt. A. A. Humphreys, U. S. Top^l Eng^{rs}, / by Lieut. John Mullan, U. S. Army, / assisted by / Theodore Kolecki and Gustavus Sohon, Civil Eng^{rs}, / while attached to the Military Expedition under / Col. Geo. Wright, 9th Infantry, in / 1858. / Scale.—1:300,000. / [upper right.] Senate Ex. Doc. N° 43-47th[!] Cong. 3^d Sess. / [lower right:] Lith. of J. Bien, 24 Vesey St. N. Y. / 54 x 90.1 cm. Scale: about 5 miles to one inch. Map: War Department. / Map of / Military Road from / Fort Walla Walla on the Columbia / to Fort Benton on the Missouri. / made under direction of Topl. Bureau / by Captain John Mullan U. S. Army / prepared by E. Freyhold from / field notes from 1858–1863; / Scale of 1/1,000,000 / Scale of Statute Miles / [diagrammatic scale: 16 miles to one inch] / [5 lines] / Lith. of J. Bien, 24 Vesey Street, New York / [upper right:] Senate Ex. Doc. N° 43—37th Cong^r 3^d Sess. / 44.5 x 85.5 cm. Scale as above. Plum cloth, blind embossed sides, title in gilt on backstrip.

Ref.: Howes M884; Sabin 51275; Wagner-Camp 393

2933 MULLAN, JOHN

MINERS AND TRAVELERS' GUIDE TO OREGON, WASHINGTON, IDAHO, MONTANA, WYOMING, AND COLORADO. VIA THE MISSOURI AND COLUMBIA RIVERS ... NEW YORK: PUBLISHED BY WM. M. FRANKLIN, 1865.

[1]–153, [154 blank]. 18.6 x 12.2 cm. Folding map: General Map / of the / Northern Pacific States and Territories / Belonging to the United States / and of / British Columbia, / Extending from / Lake Superior to the Pacific Ocean / and between Latitude 39° and 53° North. / Exhibiting Mail Routes, Gold Mines, / and Including the Most Recent Surveys / of the / Topographi-

cal Bureau. / Prepared by / Captain John Mullan / Late Superintendant of Northern Pacific / Military Wagon Road. / & Commissioner Northern Pacific Rail Road. / Drawn by Edward Freyhold T. E. / Lithographed by J. Bien, 24 Vesey St.. N.Y. / 59.7 x 97.1 cm. No scale given. Black cloth.

Prov.: Bookplate of Frederick W. Skiff.

Ref.: Bradford 3745; Howes M885; Sabin 51274; Smith 7153; Wagner-Camp 418

2934 MUNSON, A. D., *Editor*

THE MINNESOTA MESSENGER, CONTAINING SKETCHES OF THE RISE AND PROGRESS OF MINNESOTA . . . SAINT PAUL, M.T.: A. D. MUNSON, EDITOR AND PUBLISHER, 1855.

[1]-78, [79-80 blank] 21.6 x 14.1 cm. Blue printed wrappers, with title on front wrapper, verso of front and recto and verso of back advertisements on other wrapper. In red cloth case.

Ref.: AII (*Minnesota*) 92; Howes M648; Sabin 49283

Advertising matter interspersed throughout, on all versos, pages 8-70. On the verso of the title-leaf, the copyright is in favor of A. D. Munson. At the foot of the page: [rule] / Saint Paul, N.T.: / Printed at the Minnesotian Office. / [short rule] / 1855. / [rule] /

2935 MURPHY, J. W.

OUTLAWS OF THE FOX RIVER COUNTRY. STORY OF THE WHITEFORD AND SPENCER TRAGEDIES, THE ASSASSINATION OF JUDGE RICHARDSON, THE EXECUTION OF JOHN BAIRD, AND THE MOBBING OF W. J. YOUNG . . . HANNIBAL, MO.: HANNIBAL PRINTING COMPANY. 1882.

[1]-138, [139-44 blank]. 20.9 x 14.1 cm. Seven illustrations, unlisted. Yellow pictorial wrappers, with title on front wrapper. In yellow cloth case.

Ref.: Adams 717; Howes M907

Lurid narrative of midwestern crime, comparable to Bonney's classic *Banditti of the Prairies.*—Howes

2936 MURPHY, JOHN M., & —— HARNED

PUGET SOUND BUSINESS DIRECTORY, AND GUIDE TO WASHINGTON TERRITORY, 1872, COMPRISING A CORRECT HISTORY OF WASHINGTON TERRITORY . . . OLYMPIA, MURPHY & HARNED, COMPILERS AND PUBLISHERS.

[1]-[72], [1-116]. 22.2 x 14 cm. Tan printed boards, with black roan back, title in centre of front cover, advertisements above, below, and outside border, advertisements on back cover and both inner covers.

Ref.: AII (*Washington*) 160; Howes M910
Copyrighted 1872.

In two parts, the first being descriptive and historical, the second the directory. Each part has a title-page as above, but the second title-leaf does not carry the preface on the verso. Three leaves of different paper carrying five pages of advertisements are inserted. A section on Portland, Oregon, occupies the last 21 pages.

2937 MURRAY, ALEXANDER H.

. . . JOURNAL DU YUKON 1847-48 . . . EDITE PAR L. J. BURPEE . . . OTTAWA: IMPRIMERIE NATIONALE, 1910.

[1]-138. 24.4 x 16.4 cm. Illustrations unlisted. Contemporary maroon half calf.

Ref.: Howes M911

Murray's was the first detailed account of the Yukon.

Editions: No place, 1848; Ottawa, 1910 (in English).

2938 MURRAY, CHARLES A.

TRAVELS IN NORTH AMERICA DURING THE YEARS 1834, 1835, & 1836. INCLUDING A SUMMER RESIDENCE WITH THE PAWNEE TRIBE OF INDIANS, IN THE REMOTE PRAIRIES OF THE MISSOURI . . . LONDON: RICHARD BENTLEY, 1839.

[i]-xvi, [1]-473, [474 blank]. [i]-[xii, xii blank], [1]-372. 22.6 x 14.5 cm. Two frontispieces. Two volumes, brown cloth, uncut.

Ref.: Field 1111; Howes M913; Rader 2460; Sabin 51490; Wagner-Camp 77

The section dealing with Murray's stay among the Pawnees is especially valuable.

Although Wagner-Camp mentions two plates in addition to the frontispieces, the latter are the only illustrations found in the work.

2939 MURRAY, CHARLES A.

THE PRAIRIE-BIRD . . . LONDON: RICHARD BENTLEY, 1844.

[i]-iv, [1]-336. [i-ii], [1]-352. [i-ii], [1]-372. 19.1 x 11.4 cm. Three volumes, full green levant morocco, triple gilt fillets on sides, gilt backs, gilt edges, by Hayday.

Ref.: Sabin 51489; Wagner-Camp 112

2940 MURRAY, LOIS L.

INCIDENTS OF FRONTIER LIFE . . . WRITTEN FROM PERSONAL EXPERIENCE . . . IN THE YEAR 1878. GOSHEN, INDIANA: EV. UNITED MENNONITE PUBLISHING HOUSE, 1880.

[i]-x, [11]-274. 19.3 x 13.2 cm. Portrait. Maroon cloth, blind borders on sides, title in gilt on backstrip.

Ref.: Howes M918

Narrative of eighteen years of life in Kansas.—Howes

2941 MUTZ, OTTO

THE STOCKMAN'S BRAND BOOK; HOLT, ROCK, AND BOYD COUNTIES. AINSWORTH, NEBRASKA: WESTERN RANCHER PRINT, 1904.

[1]–72, [73–100]. 16 x 9.5 cm. Black cloth.
 Ref.: Adams (*Ramp. Herd*) 1593

There is a calendar for 1904 inside the front cover and another for 1903 inside the back cover. Pages [73–6] carry advertisements, [77–84] are blank forms for additions, [85–99] is an Index, and [100] is an advertisement.

2942 MYERS, FRANK

SOLDIERING IN DAKOTA, AMONG THE INDIANS, IN 1863–4–5 . . . HURON, DAKOTA: HURONITE PRINTING HOUSE, 1888.

[1]–60. 20.5 x 14.6 cm. Reddish brown printed wrappers, with title on front wrapper. In red cloth case.
 Ref.: Allen (*Dakota*) 648; Howes M929

N

2943 [NAHL, CHARLES]

[Broadside] WAY-SIDE SCENES IN CALIFORNIA . . . Broadside, 27.3 x 21.7 cm. Four woodcuts surrounding text. Text, 26.1 x 20.2 cm.
 Ref.:

One of the woodcuts is signed in the cut by Charles Nahl and all four of the cuts carry the names of Anthony & Baker Sc.

This broadside is similar to a pair issued by James M. Hutchings. Neither place of publication nor date is present. Probably issued about 1855.

2944 NAPTON, WILLIAM B.

OVER THE SANTA FE TRAIL, 1857 . . . KANSAS CITY, MO.: FRANKLIN HUDSON PUBLISHING CO., 1905.

[1]–99, [100 blank]. 17.2 x 12.7 cm. Ten illustrations, unlisted. Gray pictorial wrappers. In brown cloth case.
 Prov.: Inscribed on title-page: Missouri Hist Society / from / W. B. Napton /. With Historical Society stamp erased from front wrapper.
 Ref.: Howes N9

Pages [73]–99 comprise: Lewis & Clark's Route Retraveled. / The Upper Missouri in 1858. / [rule] / By / W. B. Napton. / [rule] / . . .

2945 NASATIR, ABRAHAM P.

BEFORE LEWIS AND CLARK. DOCUMENTS ILLUSTRATING THE HISTORY OF THE MISSOURI, 1785–

1804. EDITED . . . BY A. P. NASATIR . . . ST. LOUIS: ST. LOUIS HISTORICAL DOCUMENTS FOUNDATION, 1952.*

[i]–xv, [xvi blank], [xvii–xviii fly-title, verso blank], 1–375, [376 blank]. [i–x], [xi–xii fly-title, verso blank], 376–853, [854 blank]. 22.8 x 15.3 cm. Nine illustrations and maps listed. Two volumes, gray-green cloth. In dust jackets.
 Ref.: Wagner-Camp 3 note

2946 NASON, DANIEL

AUTOGRAPH MANUSCRIPT of A Journal of a Tour from Boston to Savannah. 108 pages, 16.3 x 11 cm. Original wrappers.

The manuscript is dated 1848. See following number for the printed version.

2947 [NASON, DANIEL]

A JOURNAL OF A TOUR FROM BOSTON AND SAVANNAH, THENCE TO HAVANA, IN THE ISLAND OF CUBA, WITH OCCASIONAL NOTES DURING A SHORT RESIDENCE IN EACH PLACE: THENCE TO NEW ORLEANS AND SEVERAL WESTERN CITIES, WITH REFERENCES DESIGNED FOR MY OWN PRIVATE USE . . . CAMBRIDGE: PRINTED FOR THE AUTHOR, 1849.

[1]–114. 15.5 x 9.5 cm. Black cloth.
 Ref.: Clark III 369; Howes N19; Sabin 51881

2948 NATIONAL ATLAS AND TUESDAY MORNING MAIL, THE

[Caption title] THE NATIONAL ATLAS AND TUESDAY MORNING MAIL . . . VOL. I. PHILADELPHIA, TUESDAY, NOVEMBER 1 [8, 15, 22, 29, DECEMBER 6], 1836. NO. 14 [–19] . . .

[209]–304. 29.2 x 22.2 cm. Two maps. Spain / and / Portugal. / [lower centre:] Published for the National Atlas by S. C. Atkinson. / [lower right:] B. Jones sc. / 24.5 x 39.4 cm. No scale given. Map: Europe / [lower centre:] Published for the National Atlas by S. C. Atkinson. / 24.3 x 28.7 cm. No scale given. Six issues bound together in gray boards with brown leather backstrip.
 Ref.: A. Hanna (*The Rocky Mountain Letters of Robert Campbell . . . 1955*)

The editor and publisher was Samuel C. Atkinson.

Five letters (numbered I to V) appear on pages 219–20, [225]–226, 253, 266–67, and 299. They were written by Robert Campbell to his brother in Philadelphia and appeared in print here for the first time. They were reprinted in 1955 from the only other known file by Frederick W. Beinecke, edited by Archibald Hanna and with an introduction by Charles Eberstadt.

2949 NATIONAL DEMOCRATIC PARTY. Texas

PROCEEDINGS OF THE MASS MEETING OF THE NATIONAL DEMOCRACY OF TEXAS. GEN. SAM HOUSTON FOR THE PRESIDENCY. HIS INAUGURAL ADDRESS. AUSTIN: PRINTED AT THE SOUTHERN INTELLIGENCER BOOK OFFICE, 1860.

[1]–24. 31.8 x 13.6 cm. Removed from bound volume, unbound.

Prov.: Inscribed in pencil on title-page is: Hon Andrew Johnson. Also, in ink, the following: Andrew Johnson / [flourish] / Send this to my room / Andrew Johnson Esq / James C. Jones of Mem / phis Tennessee— / On page 24 appears the name Andrew Johnson twice.

Ref.: Clements Library (*Texas*) 41; Winkler 1321

2950 NATIONAL GREENBACK PARTY. Nebraska. State Central Committee

[Caption title] INDEPENDENT STATE CONVENTION. THE ELECTORS OF THE INDEPENDENT GREENBACK PARTY OF THE STATE OF NEBRASKA, ARE REQUESTED TO SEND DELEGATES FROM THE SEVERAL COUNTIES, TO MEET IN STATE CONVENTION AT LINCOLN, ON TUESDAY THE 26TH OF SEPTEMBER, 1876 . . .

[1–4]. 22.9 x 15.2 cm. Unbound leaflet.
Ref.:
At foot of page [4]: Beach, Printer, Lincoln. /

2951 NATIONAL INTELLIGENCER

[Newspaper] NATIONAL INTELLIGENCER. VOL. XLII. WASHINGTON: THURSDAY [& TUESDAY], MAY 27 [& NOVEMBER 9], 1841. NO. 6029 [& 7000] . . .

Two issues, each [1–4]. 60 x 46.5 cm. Removed from binding, unbound.

Ref.: Wagner-Camp 85 note; Wagner-Camp 86 note

The earlier issue contains a long article headed "A Letter from Oregon." which is signed by Francis Fletcher, Amos Cook, Joseph Holman, Robert Shortess, and R. L. Kilbourn, controverting some of the statements made by Obadiah Oakly about the Farnham expedition. Oakly's journal had appeared in the *Peoria Register and North-Western Gazetteer*, issues of December 1839 and January 1841 (present in the Graff Collection), and an interview with Oakly in the same paper had appeared on November 9, 1839, and in the *National Intelligencer*, November 23, 1839. The present letter was directed against the interview; it was later printed in the Peoria paper.

In the later issue there is a long, unsigned article under the heading: Santa Fe and the Far west. / ——— / From the Evansville (Indiana) Journal. / This is an earlier printing than the account described by Wagner-Camp from *Niles' Register* for December 8, 1841. The account covers the arrangements for and the trip from Vincennes to Santa Fé on the road to California. Reprinted by Dawson. Dale Morgan believes the author was John McClure, according to Wagner-Camp.

2952 NATIONAL SHIP-CANAL CONVENTION. Chicago, 1863

PROCEEDINGS OF THE NATIONAL SHIP-CANAL CONVENTION, HELD AT THE CITY OF CHICAGO, JUNE 2 AND 3, 1863. CHICAGO: TRIBUNE COMPANY'S BOOK AND JOB PRINTING OFFICE, 1863.

[1]–248. 22.4 x 14.2 cm. Tan printed wrappers, with title on front wrapper. In a blue cloth case.

Ref.: AII (*Chicago*) 735; Howes C372; Sabin 12638

"Memorial to the President and Congress of the United States" occupies pages [227]–246.

The "Memorial" was also issued separately, same press, same year, 24 pages. Sabin 12635; AII (*Chicago*) 734.

2953 NAUVOO, ILLINOIS

THE CITY CHARTER: LAWS, ORDINANCES, AND ACTS OF THE CITY COUNCIL OF THE CITY OF NAUVOO. AND ALSO, THE ORDINANCES OF THE NAUVOO LEGION: FROM THE COMMENCEMENT OF THE CITY TO THIS DATE. NAUVOO, ILL.: JOSEPH SMITH, PRINTER, 1842.

[1]–8. 22.9 x 13.1 cm. Stabbed, unbound.
Ref.: Byrd 725

The work was issued in three forms. Harvard has a slightly different setting paginated [9]–14, and there was a thirty-two page edition with additional material. The present work contains only the Charter, while the larger work contains all the material mentioned on the title-page.

2954 NAVIGATOR, THE

THE NAVIGATOR: CONTAINING DIRECTIONS FOR NAVIGATING THE MONONGAHELA, OHIO, AND ALLEGHANY, MISSISSIPPI RIVERS . . . PITTSBURGH, PUBLISHED BY ZADOK CRAMER, 1808.

[*]², [**]¹, A⁸, B⁴, C–M⁶, N⁴. [1–4], [i–ii], [5]–156. 17.5 x 10.5 cm. 28 woodcuts in the text. Tan boards, roan back, gilt fillets on backstrip.

Ref.: Bradford 1112 note; Buck 59 note; Clark II 192–93 notes; Howes C855; Sabin 17385; Thomson 282 note; Wagner-Camp 4 note

Contains a rough summary of the discoveries of Lewis and Clark.

Editions: No copies of first two editions known. Pittsburgh, 1802, 1804, 1806.

2955 NEBRASKA. Commissioners to Locate the Seat of Government of the State of Nebraska.

REPORT OF COMMISSIONERS TO LOCATE THE SEAT OF GOVERNMENT OF THE STATE OF NEBRASKA. OMAHA, NEB.: PRINTED BY ST. A. D. BALCOMBE, STATE PRINTER, 1869.

[1]–42, [43–4 blank]. 21.4 x 14.3 cm. Lavender printed wrappers, with title on front wrapper. Lacks back wrapper.
Ref.:
The choices were Lancaster or Ashland. Lancaster was chosen on the second vote and renamed Lincoln.

2956 NEBRASKA. Legislative Assembly

[Broadsheet] MEMORIAL AND JOINT RESOLUTION RELATIVE TO THE INDIAN POLICY. TO THE HONORABLE, THE SENALE[!] AND HOUSE OF REPRESENTATIVES OF THE UNITED STATES, IN CONGRESS ASSEMBLED: YOUR MEMORIALISTS, THE LEGISLATIVE ASSEMBLY OF THE STATE OF NEBRASKA, RESPECTFULLY REPRESENT TO YOUR HONORABLE BODIES THAT THE MATERIAL INTEREST AND PROGRESS OF OUR STATE, IN COMMON WITH THOSE OF SEVERAL OTHER STATES AND TERRITORIES WEST OF THE MISSISSIPPI RIVER, ARE RETARDED BY THE LONG CONTINUED AND INCREASING INDIAN HOSTILITIES ON OUR WESTERN BORDER. WE REPRESENT TO YOU THE UNVARNISHED AND UNPALATABLE TRUTH THAT AT NO POINT FROM THE NORTHERN BOUNDARY OF TEXAS TO THE BRITISH POSSESSIONS CAN EITHER TRADE OR TRAVEL BE PROSECUTED FROM THE WESTERN SETTLEMENTS TO THE ROCKY MOUNTAINS, WITHOUT IMMINENT DANGER TO LIFE AND PROPERTY . . . APPROVED, JUNE 20, 1867.

Broadsheet, 24.6 x 19.5 cm.
Ref.:
The Legislative Assembly took a tough line against the Indians.

2957 NEBRASKA TERRITORY. Acting Governor (Thomas B. Cuming)

[Wrapper title] ANNUAL MESSAGE TO THE LEGISLATIVE ASSEMBLY OF NEBRASKA: DELIVERED BY THOMAS B. CUMING . . . DEC. 9TH, 1857. OMAHA CITY, N.T.: ROBERT W. FURNAS, TERRITORIAL PRINTER, 1857.

[1]–8. 24.5 x 14.8 cm. Yellow printed wrappers, with title on front wrapper, stabbed, uncut. In a red cloth case.
Ref.:

2958 NEBRASKA TERRITORY. Council

JOURNAL OF THE COUNCIL, AT THE FIRST REGULAR SESSION OF THE GENERAL ASSEMBLY, OF THE TERRITORY OF NEBRASKA, BEGUN AND HELD AT OMAHA CITY, COMMENCING . . . SIXTEENTH DAY OF JANUARY, A. D. 1855, AND ENDING ON THE SIXTEENTH DAY OF MARCH, A. D. 1855. OMAHA CITY: SHERMAN & STRICKLAND, PRINTERS, 1855.*

[1]–157, [158–60 blank]. (Pages [1–4] blank.) 23.2 x 14.4 cm. Gray-brown printed wrappers, with title on front wrapper. In a brown buckram case.
Ref.: Sabin 52190

2959 NEBRASKA TERRITORY. Council

THE RULES OF THE COUNCIL OF THE TERRITORY OF NEBRASKA. OMAHA CITY: SHERMAN & STRICKLAND, PRINTERS, 1855–'56.

[1]–6, [7–8 blank]. 22.5 x 14.3 cm. Buff wrappers. Strip torn from outer edge of front wrapper, hole through back wrapper and final blank leaf.
Prov.: Signature of James C. Mitchell on front cover, title-page, and page [7], the latter two dated January 15, 1856.
Ref.:

2960 NEBRASKA TERRITORY. General Assembly

[Broadside] TO THE PEOPLE OF NEBRASKA. FELLOW CITIZENS:— THE GENERAL ASSEMBLY OF NEBRASKA TERRITORY ARE NO LONGER ABLE TO DISCHARGE THEIR LEGITIMATE FUNCTIONS AT THE OMAHA SEAT OF GOVERNMENT. . . . FLORENCE, JANUARY 9, 1858. JAMES H. DECKER, SPEAKER OF THE HOUSE OF REPRESENTATIVES . . .

Broadside, 35.3 x 18.4 cm. Text, 27.3 x 11.7 cm.
Ref.:
In the fight over the location of the permanent capitol of Nebraska, a majority of the Territorial Legislature left the temporary capitol at Omaha and set themselves up in Florence, where they stayed for forty days. This was a protest against the actions of the minority who favored Omaha as the location for a permanent capitol.—EDG

2961 NEBRASKA TERRITORY. Governor (Samuel W. Black)

MESSAGE OF SAMUEL W. BLACK . . . ON THE BILL FOR AN "ACT TO PROHIBIT SLAVERY." DELIVERED . . . JANUARY 9, 1860. OMAHA CITY: ROBERTSON & CLARK, PRINTERS, 1860.

[1]–8. 25.3 x 16.4 cm. Unbound leaflet, unopened.
Ref.:

2962 NEBRASKA TERRITORY. Governor (Samuel W. Black)

[Cover title] VETO MESSAGES OF HON. SAMUEL W. BLACK . . . ON THE BILLS TO PROHIBIT SLAVERY, PASSED AT THE SESSIONS OF 1860 & 1861. OMAHA, N. T.: E. D. WEBSTER, PUBLIC PRINTER, 1861.

[1]–15, [16 blank]. 21.8 x 14.9 cm. Yellow printed wrappers, with title on front wrapper.
Prov.: Inscribed on front wrapper: Hon [undeciphered name] / with the respects of / Sam¹ W Black /.
Ref.:

2963 NEBRASKA TERRITORY. Governor (Mark W. Izard)

ANNUAL MESSAGE OF MARK W. IZARD, GOVERNOR OF THE TERRITORY OF NEBRASKA . . . DECEMBER 18, 1855. OMAHA CITY: SHERMAN & STRICKLAND, PRINTERS. 1855.

[1]–12, [13–14 blank]. 22.5 x 14.5 cm. Removed from bound volume, unbound.
Ref.: Sabin 52195
No evidence of wrappers.

2964 NEBRASKA TERRITORY. Laws, Statutes, etc.

TERRITORY OF NEBRASKA. LAWS, RESOLUTIONS AND MEMORIALS, PASSED AT THE REGULAR SESSION OF THE FIRST GENERAL ASSEMBLY OF THE TERRITORY OF NEBRASKA, CONVENED AT OMAHA CITY, ON THE 16TH DAY OF JANUARY, ANNO DOMINI, 1855 . . . OMAHA CITY, N.T.: SHERMAN & STRICKLAND, TERRITORIAL PRINTERS, 1855.

[1]–517, [518–20 blank]. (Pages [1–4] blank.) 21.5 x 14.4 cm. Light brown printed wrappers, with title on front wrapper, on verso of back wrapper: Joint Resolution, / Providing for the Printing of the Laws of the / Present Session. / [15 lines] / Approved, March 15, 1855. /
Prov.: Signature on front wrapper: Daniel Gantt / Dan: Gantt /. Leather label of E. H. Westerfield on front wrapper.
Ref.: Sabin 52193
A leaf of errata is mounted on a blank leaf at the back of the volume.

2965 NEBRASKA TERRITORY. Second Judicial District

THE COURT GUIDE, FOR THE SECOND JUDICIAL DISTRICT, NEBRASKA TERRITORY. APPROVED BY HON. EDWARD R. HARDEN, ASSOCIATE JUSTICE OF THE SUPREME COURT, NEBRASKA TERRITORY, JULY 28TH, 1856. BROWNVILLE, N.T.: NEBRASKA ADVERTISER PRINT, 1856.

[1]–8. 17.9 x 10.8 cm. Unbound leaflet, unopened.
Ref.:

2966 NEBRASKA TERRITORY. Territorial Warrant

[Broadside] . . . TERRITORIAL WARRANT. OFFICE OF TERRITORIAL AUDITOR, OMAHA, [in manuscript: June 19th] 186 [1 in manuscript]. TO [in manuscript: W W Wyman] TREASURER NEBRASKA TERRITORY, PLEASE PAY TO . . . ADVERTISER PRINT, BROWNVILLE, NEBRASKA. TERRITORIAL AUDITOR.

Broadside, 11.6 x 19.2 cm. Text, 11.3 x 18.9 cm.
Ref.:
An order to pay William F. Kiter $14 for binding for the librarian, signed by R. C. Jordan and dated as above. Endorsed on verso by Kiter, but payment denied on August 7, 1861 "for want of funds." The warrant was apparently discounted by Clarke & Bro. and was paid (with interest) on February 7, 1862.

2967 NEBRASKA ADVERTISER, THE (Brownville, Nebraska)

[Newspaper] THE NEBRASKA ADVERTISER.—EXTRA. BROWNVILLE, NEBRASKA, OCTOBER 1, 1872 . . .

Broadsheet, 49.7 x 32.7 cm. Unbound.
Ref.:
This special issue is a staunch defense of the Republican ticket, including General Grant for President and Robert W. Furnas for Governor of Nebraska.

2968 NEBRASKA ADVERTISER, [THE] (Brownville, Nebraska)

[Newspaper, broadside] NEBRASKA ADVERTISER. —EXTRA. LET THE PEOPLE HAVE LIGHT. LET THE PEOPLE HAVE LIGHT!!! MORTON'S RECORD! . . .

Broadside, 38 x 22.9 cm. Text, 30.7 x 17.7 cm.
Ref.:
The Extra comprises a vigorous attack on J. Sterling Morton. It was printed in Brownville in 1860.

2969 NEBRASKA CITY, Nebraska. Citizens' Committee

[Broadside] AN APPEAL TO THE PEOPLE OF OTOE AND ADJOINING COUNTIES. CHICAGO, THE COMMERCIAL HEART OF THE NORTH-WEST, HAS BEEN CONSUMED BY FIRE. HER PLACES OF BUSINESS, THE HOMES OF HER PEOPLE, HER NEWSPAPERS, HER SCHOOLS AND HER CHURCHES ARE LEVELLED IN A COMMON DESOLATION.—MORE THAN A HUNDRED THOUSAND HUMAN BEINGS ARE TO-DAY SHELTERLESS AND FOODLESS AMIDST THE RUINS OF THEIR INDUSTRIES . . . WORDS OF EXHORTATION TO BE LIBERAL, TO BE GENEROUS, TO EXERCISE CHARITY,

FROM US, ARE UTTERLY NEEDLESS. THE UNDER-SIGNED WERE APPOINTED BY A PUBLIC MEETING OF THE CITIZENS OF NEBRASKA CITY HELD ON TUES-DAY EVENING, OCT. 10TH, A COMMITTEE TO MAKƎ[!] TO YOU THIS APPEAL . . . J. STERLING MORTON, J. D. KERR, H. A. GUILD. COMMITTEE. NEBRASKA CITY, OCT. 11TH, 1871.

Broadside, 25.3 x 19.9 cm. Text, 21.3 x 17.2 cm.
Ref.:

2970 NEBRASKA—INDIAN TREATIES— AND THE RIGHTS OF CITIZENS . . .

[Caption title] NEBRASKA—INDIAN TREATIES—AND THE RIGHTS OF CITIZENS. FROM THE MISSOURI DEMOCRAT. THE GOVERNMENT AND THE INDIANS. INDEPENDENCE, MO., JULY 24, 1844 . . .

[1]–8. 24.8 x 15.5 cm. Unbound folder, top edges unopened.
Prov.: Signature on page [1]: Joel Walker Esq / Kansas City /
Ref.:
The text consists of two letters to the Editor of the *Missouri Democrat*, signed "Justice to All."

2971 NEBRASKA NATIONAL GUARD

REPORT OF BRIG. GEN'L. L. W. COLBY, COMMAND-ING THE NEBRASKA NATIONAL GUARD IN THE IN-DIAN CAMPAIGN OF 1890–91 TO THE ADJUTANT GENERAL, N. N. G. LINCOLN, NEB.: CALHOUN & WOODRUFF, PRINTERS, 1891.

[1]–23, [24 blank]. 22.5 x 15 cm. Folding map: Map Showing / Positions of Nebraska / State Troops / in—Indian Campaigns / of the / Win-ter of 1890–91. / [lower right:] Rand, McNally & Co., Engravers, Chicago. / 20.5 x 32.5 cm. No scale given. Green printed wrappers, with title on front wrapper.
Ref.:

2972 NEBRASKA SUNDAY SCHOOL AS-SOCIATION

TENTH CONVENTION OF THE NEBRASKA SUNDAY SCHOOL ASSOCIATION, AT OMAHA, JUNE 5, 6, 7, 1877.

[1]–40, I–XIII, [XIV blank], [XV–XVI adver-tisements]. 21.6 x 14.7 cm. Buff printed wrap-pers, with title on front wrapper, advertisements on verso of front and recto and verso of back wrapper.
Ref.:
According to the front wrapper, the pamphlet was printed at Fremont by the Herald Print.

2973 NEBRASKA WINTER QUARTERS COMPANY

[Broadside] KNOW ALL MEN BY THESE PRESENTS, THAT THE NEBRASKA WINTER QUARTERS COM-PANY, FOR AND IN CONSIDERATION OF [in manu-script: seventy one] DOLLARS, TO THEM IN HAND PAID BY [in manuscript: William Keef] . . . HAVE SOLD . . . THAT CERTAIN LOT . . . IN THE TOWN OF FLORENCE, NEBRASKA TERRITORY . . . [in manuscript: twentieth] DAY OF [in manu-script: October] A. D. 185 [in manuscript: 4]. ATTEST [in manuscript: James C. Mitchell] SEC. [in manuscript: S. B. Stutsman] PRES.

Broadside, 14.5 x 18.5 cm. Text, 12.3 x 17.1 cm.
Ref.:
Docketed in manuscript on verso and signed by James C. Mitchell.

2974 NEILL, EDWARD D.

DAHKOTAH LAND AND DAHKOTAH LIFE. WITH THE HISTORY OF THE FUR TRADERS OF THE EXTREME NORTHWEST DURING THE FRENCH AND BRITISH DOMINIONS . . . PHILADELPHIA: J. B. LIPPINCOTT & CO., 1859.

[i–iv], 49–239, [240 blank], [1]–4 advertisement. 21.5 x 13.8 cm. Contemporary marbled boards, dark green morocco back.
Prov.: Presentation copy from the author in-scribed on the title-page: M. Pierre Margry / with the compliments [of] / Ed^W D. Ne[ill] /. Tipped in before the first page of text is a small leaf: By the Courtesy of / Hon E. B. Wash-burne / En. Ex. & Min. Plen. U. S. of America / for / M. Pierre Margry / 11 Rue du Mount Thabor / Paris / France /. The preceding is in the author's hand; beneath is the rubber stamp of Mr. Washburne. Several marginal notes, some in the hand of the author and some in the hand of the recipient.
Ref.: Howes N35; Sabin 52281
Issued separately from the larger *History of Minnesota*, with new title leaf and leaf of ex-planation.

2975 NEILL, EDWARD D.

MICHAL; OR, FASHIONABLE DANCING, AN UNDIG-NIFIED AMUSEMENT FOR A CHRISTIAN . . . SAINT PAUL: FOR SALE BY COMBS & BRO., 1859.

[i–ii blank], [1]–18. 18.3 x 11.7 cm. Pale printed green wrappers, with title on front wrapper.
Ref.: AII (*Minnesota*) 260
The copy described by AII (*Minnesota*) ap-parently does not carry the date in the imprint on the title-page.

2976 NEILL, EDWARD D., & JOHN OGDEN

ADDRESSES DELIVERED AT THE OPENING OF THE STATE NORMAL SCHOOL, WINONA, MINNESOTA . . . SAINT PAUL: PIONEER PUBLISHING COMPANY, 1860.

[1]–55, [56 blank]. 22 x 14.4 cm. Gray-green printed wrappers, with title on front wrapper.
Ref.: AII (*Minnesota*) 340

2977 NELSON AND SONS, T. (London), *Publishers*

NELSON'S PICTORIAL GUIDE-BOOKS. SALT LAKE CITY, WITH A SKETCH OF THE ROUTE OF THE CENTRAL PACIFIC RAILROAD . . . LONDON: T. NELSON AND SONS.

[1]–31, [32] blank. 10.4 x 16.7 cm. Unbound. Inserted in Manuscript Journals of Loren L. Williams, Volume IV.

The illustrations by Savage have been removed from the pamphlet and scattered through the Manuscript Journals, Volume IV.

2978 NEMAHA VALLEY JOURNAL

[Newspaper] NEMAHA VALLEY JOURNAL. A WEEKLY NEWSPAPER, OF HISTORY, POLITICS, LITERATURE, SCIENCE, ART, AGRICULTURE, MECHANICS, COMMERCE, AND GENERAL INTELLIGENCE. BY S. BELDEN. NEMAHA CITY, N. T., MARCH 5, 1858. NUMBER 16 . . .

[1]–4]. 61 x 47 cm. Unbound.
Ref.:
Edited by S. Belden.
Contains a long editorial on Non-Intervention.

2979 [NENTUIG, JUAN]

RUDO ENSAYO, TENTATIVA DE UNA PREVENCIONAL DESCRIPCION GEOGRAPHICA DE LA PROVINCIA DE SONORA . . . SAN AUGUSTIN DE LA FLORIDA, ANO DE 1863.

[i]–x, [1]–208. 21.6 x 17.6 cm. Gray printed wrappers with title on front wrapper, uncut, unopened. In a gray buckram case.
Ref.: Field 1430; Howes S578; Sabin 73899
Limited to 160 copies. Printed in Albany, New York. Edited by Buckingham Smith.

The author, according to A. F. Pradeau in *Mid-America*, XXXV (April, 1953), pages 81–90, was Father Juan Nentuig, who completed his manuscript in 1762. The "rough essay" contains a good deal of fascinating information about the Indians of Arizona and New Mexico.

2980 NEVADA. Governor (H. G. Blasdel)

SECOND INAUGURAL ADDRESS OF H. G. BLASDEL . . . DELIVERED JANUARY 8TH, 1867, BEFORE THE SENATE AND ASSEMBLY, IN JOINT CONVENTION. ALSO FIRST BIENNIAL MESSAGE. DELIVERED TO THE LEGISLATURE, JANUARY 10TH, 1867. CARSON CITY: J. E. ECKLEY, STATE PRINTER, 1867.

[1]–22. 22.6 x 14.6 cm. Blue-gray printed wrappers, with title on front wrapper.
Prov.: At foot of front wrapper: With Compliments of / H. G. Blasdel /.
Ref.: AII (*Nevada*) 94

2981 NEVADA. House of Representatives (Speaker elect) (R. D. Ferguson)

INTRODUCTORY ADDRESS OF THE HON. R. D. FERGUSON . . . DELIVERED JANUARY 7TH, 1867. CARSON CITY: J. E. ECKLEY, STATE PRINTER, 1867.

[1]–7, [8 blank]. 22.5 x 14.4 cm. Gray printed wrappers with title on front wrapper.
Prov.: In pencil at top of front wrapper: With the Compliments of / R D Ferguson /.
Ref.:

2982 NEVADA. Laws, Statutes, etc.

[Caption title] NEVADA STATE MINING LAW. AN ACT CONCERNING THE LOCATION AND POSSESSION OF MINING CLAIMS . . .

[1]–7, [8 blank]. 22.3 x 13.7 cm. Unbound, removed from bound volume.
Ref.:
Imprint at foot of second column, page 7: Printed by J. D. Fairchild & Co., / Daily Reese River Reveille Office. / Austin, Nevada. /

Apparently the first separate printing of this notable law. The Senate Committee on Mines and Mining Interests reported on the Act on February 23, 1866 [AII (*Nevada*) 81] and the Legislature adjourned on March first. The present Act was passed.

Nevada's mining laws, because of the effectiveness of Senator William M. Stewart's arguments, exerted a considerable effect on Federal mining laws after 1866.

2983 NEVADA TERRITORY. Governor (James W. Nye)

SECOND ANNUAL MESSAGE . . . TO THE LEGISLATURE OF NEVADA TERRITORY, NOVEMBER 13, 1862. CARSON CITY: J. T. GOODMAN & CO., 1862.

[1]–48. 21.1 x 15.4 cm. Salmon back wrapper, uncut, mostly unopened. Front wrapper lacking.
Ref.: AII (*Nevada*) 5
The place of publication is probably fictitious, since Goodman was a Virginia City printer.

2984 NEVADA TERRITORY. Governor (James W. Nye)

[Broadside] THANKSGIVING PROCLAMATION. EXECUTIVE DEPARTMENT, CARSON CITY, NEVADA TERRITORY, NOVEMBER 17TH, 1863 . . . I, JAMES W. NYE, GOVERNOR OF THE TERRITORY OF NEVADA, DO HEREBY APPOINT THURSDAY, THE 26TH DAY OF NOVEMBER INSTANT, AS A DAY OF PUBLIC THANKSGIVING . . . IN WITNESS WHEREOF, I HAVE HEREUNTO SET MY HAND, AND CAUSED THE GREAT SEAL OF THE TERRITORY TO BE AFFIXED, THE DAY AND YEAR ABOVE WRITTEN. JAMES W. NYE. SEAL ATTEST: ORION CLEMENS, SECRETARY OF NEVADA TERRITORY.

Broadside, 35.4 x 43.1 cm. Text, 26 x 36 cm.
Ref.:

2985 NEVADA COUNTY [California] DIRECTORY . . .

NEVADA COUNTY DIRECTORY, FOR 1871–72 . . . COMPILED AND PUBLISHED BY COUNTY DIRECTORY PUBLISHING COMPANY. SACRAMENTO: H. S. CROCKER & CO., 1871.

[i]–xvi, 1–[304]. ([i] and [304] pasted to inner covers.) 21.6 x 14.2 cm. One inserted plate, illustrations in many advertisements. Gray boards, leather backstrip, boards with advertisements on sides.
Ref.: Blumann & Thomas 2226

The text is completed on page 285, the balance and the first eight leaves are advertisements.

2986 NEVINS, ALLAN

FREMONT: THE WEST'S GREATEST ADVENTURER . . . NEW YORK: HARPER & BROTHERS, MCMXXVIII.*

[i]–ix, [x blank, xi–xii fly-title, verso blank], 1–344 (errata slip before page 1). [i]–viii, [ix–x fly-title, verso blank], 345–738. 23.7 x 15.8 cm. 64 illustrations listed. Two volumes, dark blue cloth, gray tops, uncut.
Ref.: Howes N64

2987 NEW ENGLAND COLONY OF IOWA

[Broadside] NEW ENGLAND COLONY OF IOWA! THIS COLONY, CONSISTING OF PERSONS FROM THE NEW ENGLAND STATES, IS LOCATED IN THE SOUTHERN PART OF ADAIR AND THE NORTHEASTERN PART OF ADAMS COUNTIES, IN THE TOWN OF NEVIN . . . THE PRICES OF LOTS AND THE CONDITIONS OF SALE CAN BE LEARNED FROM SOLOMON BROWN, ESQ., ON THE GROUND. APRIL 15, 1856.

Broadside, 30.8 x 25.3 cm. Text, 27.1 x 19.3 cm.
Ref.:
No place of publication is listed.
Penciled note at head: 2 miles north of my land /.

2988 NEW GOLD FIELD!, THE

[Broadside] THE NEW GOLD FIELD! THE BIG HORN COUNTRY LOOMING UP! AN EXPEDITION GOING IN APRIL, 1877. AN OUTFITTING POINT WITHIN 150 MILES! THE BEST ROUTE, ETC, VIA RAWLINS, WYOMING TERRITORY! . . . HERALD STEAM PRINTING HOUSE, OMAHA.

Broadside, 31.5 x 23.3 cm. Text, 25.2 x 19.2 cm.
Ref.:
Possibly printed late in 1876, but probably early in 1877. An expedition to the Big Horn Country is announced for April 1–10, 1877, leaving from Rawlins.

2989 NEW MEXICO (Department). Gobernador (Manuel Armijo)

[Broadside] EL GOBERNADOR CONSTITUCIONAL Y COMANDANTE PRINCIPAL DEL DEPARTAMENTO DE NUEVO MEJICO, A SUS HABITANTES . . . SANTA FE MARZO 6 DE 1839. MANUEL ARMIJO. NUEVO-MEJICO. IMPRENTA DEL CURA DE TAOS A CARGO DE J. M. BACA.

Broadside, 29.9 x 19.7 cm. Text, 26.2 x 13.5 cm. Bound into full dark red leather.
Ref.: AII (*New Mexico*) 13; Wagner (*New Mexico*) 13

The Governor calls on the New Mexicans to save their dear country from the attacks of their enemy, in this case, France, with which country hostilities had just begun.—Wagner

This may be the Wagner copy, although Wagner does not list a copy for himself in his list but only the Streeter copy.

2990 NEW MEXICO TERRITORY. Bureau of Immigration

THE RESOURCES OF NEW MEXICO. PREPARED UNDER THE AUSPICES OF THE BUREAU OF IMMIGRATION, FOR THE TERRITORIAL FAIR, TO BE HELD AT ALBUQUERQUE, N.M., OCTOBER 3D TO 8TH, 1881. SANTA FE, N.M.: NEW MEXICAN BOOK AND JOB PRINTING DEPARTMENT, 1881.

[1]–64. (Pink errata slip tipped to page 60, 2.8 x 12.6 cm.) 22.6 x 14.5 cm. Buff printed wrappers, with title on front wrapper, advertisements on verso of front and recto and verso of back wrapper.
Prov.: Inscribed on front wrapper: Compliments of / Max Frost / Adj. Gen. N.M. /
Ref.:

2991 NEW MEXICO TERRITORY. Bureau of Immigration

TAOS COUNTY. REPORT TO THE BUREAU OF IMMIGRATION OF NEW MEXICO, BY THEO. C. CAMP, COMMISSIONER OF IMMIGRATION. SANTA FE, N.M.: NEW MEXICAN BOOK AND JOB PRINTING DEPARTMENT, 1881.

[1]–11, [12 blank]. 22 x 15.2 cm. Sewn, unbound.
Ref.:
Signed on page 11: Theo. C. Camp, / Commissioner. / Territory of New Mexico, / Fernandez de Taos, Taos County. / September, 1881, / [last three lines to left of vertical bracket].

2992 NEW MEXICO TERRITORY. Committee of Citizens of Santa Fé

[Broadside] AVISO. LOS CIUDADANOS DEL CONDADO DE SANTA-FE, ESTAN CONVIVADOS PARA CONCURRIR A UNA JUNTA PUBLICA EN EL PATIO DE LA CASA DE LA CORTE, EL SAVADO 20 DEL CORRIENTE A LAS DIES DE LA MANANA, CON EL FIN DE TRATAR SOBRE LOS MEDIOS DE FORMAR UNA CONSTITUCION DE ESTADO, Y PETICIONAR AL GOBERNADOR SC[!] SIRVA DESPACHAR UN ACTO CONVIDANDO A UNA CONVENCION PARA LLENAR DICHO OBGETO . . . SANTA FE ABRIL 13, DE 1850.
Broadside, 15.2 x 19.8 cm. Text, 10.5 x 15 cm.
Ref.:
See English version next.

2993 NEW MEXICO TERRITORY. Committee of Citizens of Santa Fé

[Broadside] NOTICE. THE CITIZENS OF THE COUNTY OF SANTA FE ARE REQUESTED TO ATTEND A PUBLIC MEETING TO BE HELD AT THE COURT HOUSE, ON SATURDAY, THE 20TH INST., AT 10 O'CLOCK, A. M., FOR THE PURPOSE OF PASSING RESOLUTIONS IN FAVOR OF A STATE FORM OF GOVERNMENT, AND REQUESTING THE GOVERNOR OF THE TERRITORY TO CALL A CONVENTION TO FORM A STATE CONSTITUTION . . . SANTA FE, APRIL 13TH, 1850.
Broadside, 15.4 x 18.6 cm. Text, 11.2 x 15 cm.
Ref.:
For Spanish version, see preceding item.

2994 NEW MEXICO TERRITORY. Constitution, 1850

[Caption title] CONSTITUCION DEL ESTADO DE NUEVE MEJICO . . .
[1]–19, [20 blank]. 18.5 x 10.5 cm. Stabbed, unbound. Edges trimmed.
Ref.: AII (*New Mexico*) 41; McMurtrie (*New Mexico*) 33
The convention was concluded May 25, 1850. The pamphlet was printed at Santa Fé, undoubtedly the same year.

2995 NEW MEXICO TERRITORY. Constitutional Convention, 1849

[Caption title] JOURNAL OF THE CONVENTION OF THE TERRITORY OF NEW MEXICO . . .
[1]–12. 19.4 x 13.6 cm. Stabbed, unbound, uncut.

Ref.: AII (*New Mexico*) 38
Printed at Santa Fé by Davies & Jones (?) 1849, according to AII (*New Mexico*).
The Convention was in session from September 24–26, 1849. A delegate to Congress was elected and "the President appointed a committee of five to report the basis of a Constitution for the government of the Territory, and instructions for the consideration of the Delegate to Congress, which was unanimously adopted."—EDG
Signed at the end, on page 12: Antonio José Martinez, President. / James H. Quinn, Secretary. /

2996 NEW MEXICO TERRITORY. Governor (Albino Perez)

[Broadside] HACE ALGUNOS DIAS QUE ESTABA POR DECIDIRME A . . . DIOS Y LIBERTAD. SANTA FE 3 DE AGOSTO DE 1835. ALBINO PEREZ.
Broadside, 20.9 x 15.5 cm. Text, 22.4 x 9.4 cm. In a dark red cloth folder.
Prov.: Manuscript inscription in lower margin: S͂r D. Juan Man̅ Vigil /.
Ref.:
Apparently unique.
This printed summons was addressed to the "Señores principales del Territorio" asking them to meet at Santa Fé on August 15, 1835. Glen Dawson suggests that the broadside was issued to the territorial deputation, but this was a group of only four to six men and would be hardly worth printing a summons for.
Wagner states that the press was moved some time between June 26 and November 24 from Santa Fé to Taos. The present broadside narrows this gap to August 3 and November 24.

2997 NEW MEXICO TERRITORY. Governor (James S. Calhoun)

[Broadside] TO THE PUBLIC. IT IS HEREBY ANNOUNCED THAT NO INTERREGNUM WILL TAKE PLACE IN THE OFFICE OF GOVERNOR OF THIS TERRITORY. IF GOVERNOR CALHOUN SHOULD BE OBLIGED TO LEAVE FOR THE STATES BEFORE THE ARRIVAL OF THE HON. SECRETARY OF THE TERRITORY, THE MILITARY AUTHORITY OF THIS DEPARTMENT WILL SO FAR TAKE CHARGE OF THE EXECUTIVE OFFICE AS TO MAKE THE PRESERVATION OF LAW AND ORDER, ABSOLUTELY CERTAIN. GIVEN AT SANTA FE, THIS 21ST DAY OF APRIL, 1852. J. S. CALHOUN, GOVERNOR OF THE TERRITORY OF NEW MEXICO. E. V. SUMNER, BREVET COL. U. S. A. COMMANDING 9TH MIL. DEPARTMENT.
Broadside, 28.3 x 33.6 cm. Text, 14.4 x 25.4 cm.
Ref.:
Not listed in this form in AII (*New Mexico*).

There is said to be a copy in the National Archives with a Spanish translation at the foot of the broadside.

2998   NEW MEXICO TERRITORY. Governor (Henry Connelly)

[Caption title] PROCLAMATION BY THE GOVERNOR. WHEREAS THIS TERRITORY IS NOW INVADED BY AN ARMED FORCE FROM THE STATE OF TEXAS WHICH HAS TAKEN POSSESSION OF TWO FORTS WITHIN THE LIMITS OF THE TERRITORY, HAS SEIZED AND APPROPRIATED TO ITS OWN USE OTHER PROPERTY OF THE GENERAL GOVERNMENT AND HAS ESTABLISHED MILITARY RULE OVER THE PART ALREADY INVADED; . . . DONE AT SANTA FE THIS 9TH DAY OF SEPTEMBER IN THE YEAR EIGHTEEN HUNDRED AND SIXTY ONE. BY THE GOVERNOR, HENRY CONNELLY. M. A. OTERO, SECRETARY OF NEW MEXICO.

[1–4]. 21.5 x 13.3 cm. Unbound, folded leaflet.
   Ref.: AII (*New Mexico*) 149
   Text on page one, only. For version in Spanish, see following item. The proclamation calls out the militia to repel the invaders from Texas.

2999   NEW MEXICO TERRITORY. Governor (Henry Connelly)

[Caption title] PROCLAMACION DEL GOBERNADOR. POR CUANTO, ESTE TERRITORIO SE HALLA INVADIDO POR UNA FUERZA ARMADA DEL ESTADO DE TEXAS, QUE SE HA POSESIONADO DE DOS FUERTES DENTRO DE LOS LIMITES DEL TERRITORIO, APODERADOSE Y APROPIADOSE PARA SU PROPIO USO OTRAS PROPIEDADES DEL GOBIERNO GENERAL, Y HA ESTABLECIDO DOMINIO MILITAR SOBRE LAS PARTES INVADIDAS, Y : . . . DADA EN SANTA FE HOY DIA 9 DE SEPTIEMBRE DEL ANO DE MIL OCHOCIENTOS SESENTA Y UNO. POR EL GOBERNADOR. ENRIQUE CONNELLY. MIGUEL A. OTERO, SECRETARIO DE NUEVO MEJICO.

[1–4]. 21.4 x 13.3 cm. Unbound, folded leaflet.
   Ref.:
   For English version, see preceding item. Text on page [1] only.

3000   NEW MEXICO TERRITORY. Governor (Civil and Military) (John Munroe)

[Broadside] PROCLAMATION. WHEREAS, THE PEOPLE OF NEW MEXICO, BY THEIR DELEGATES IN CONVENTION ASSEMBLED, DID, ON THE 25TH DAY OF MAY, FRAME A STATE CONSTITUTION FOR THE TERRITORY OF NEW MEXICO, AND REQUEST THE PRESENT CIVIL AND MILITARY GOVERNOR OF THIS TERRITORY TO ISSUE A PROCLAMATION FOR ELECTIONS, FOR THE PURPOSE OF SUBMITTING THE SAME TO THE PEOPLE, AND FOR THE PURPOSE OF ELECTING SUCH OFFICERS AS ARE PROVIDED TO BE SO ELECTED IN SAID CONSTITUTION : THEREFORE, I, JOHN MUNROE, CIVIL AND MILITARY GOVERNOR OF THE TERRITORY OF NEW MEXICO, DO HEREBY DIRECT THAT THE QUALIFIED ELECTORS SHALL ASSEMBLE AT THE PRECINCTS OF THEIR RESPECTIVE COUNTIES ON THURSDAY, THE 20TH DAY OF JUNE NEXT, BETWEEN THE RISING AND SETTING OF THE SUN, TO VOTE ON A SEPARATE BALLOT *for* OR *against* THE CONSTITUTION AS FRAMED BY THE CONVENTION . . . GIVEN UNDER MY HAND AT THE GOVERNMENT HOUSE, CITY OF SANTA FE, THIS 28TH DAY OF MAY, A.D., 1850. JOHN MUNROE, CIVIL AND MILITARY GOVERNOR TERRITORY OF NEW MEXICO.

Broadside, 32 x 21.4 cm. Text, 20 x 15 cm.
   Ref.: AII (*New Mexico*) 45
   For a version of this broadside in Spanish, see next item.

3001   NEW MEXICO TERRITORY. Governor (Civil and Military) (John Munroe)

[Broadside] PROCLAMACION. POR CUANTO QUE EL PUEBLO DE NUEVO-MEJICO POR SUS DELEGADOS EN CONVENCION REUNIDA HICIERON UNA CONSTITUCION DE ESTADO POR EL TERRITORIO DE NUEVO-MEJICO, Y PETICIONARON AL PRESENTE GOBERNADOR CIVIL Y MILITAR DE ESTE TERRITORIO A ESPEDIR UNA PROCLAMACION PARA ELECCIONES CON EL FIN DE SOMETER LA MISMA AL PUEBLO, Y CON EL INTENTO DE ELEGIR TALES OFICIALES QUE ESTAN PRECAVIDOS DE SER ELEGIDOS EN DICHA CONSTITUCION . . . DADO BAJO DE MI FIRMA EN LA CASA DE GOBIERNO, CIUDAD DE SANTA FE EL DIA 28, DE MAYO A. D. 1850. JOHN MUNROE, GOBERNADOR CIVIL Y MILITAR DEL TERRITORIO DE N. M.

Broadside, 21.9 x 21.5 cm. Text, 19.2 x 15 cm.
   Ref.: AII (*New Mexico*) 44
   Text is that of AII (*New Mexico*) 45, but in Spanish. Note that AII (*New Mexico*) 44 shows an inverted m in line 4 up; in the present copy, the m is correct.

3002   NEW MEXICO TERRITORY. Governor (Civil and Military) John Munroe

[Broadside] A LOS INDIOS DE PUEBLO DE NUEVO MEJICO . . . DADO BAJO MI FIRMA EN LA CASA DE GOBIERNO DE LA CIUDAD DE SANTA FE ESTE DIA 6, DE JUNIO DEL ANO DE NUESTRO SENOR DE 1850. JOHN MUNROE. GOBERNADOR CIVIL Y MILITAR, DEL TERRITORIO DE N.-MEJICO.

Broadside, 20.2 x 25.4 cm. Text, 8.3 x 14.9 cm.
   Ref.: AII (*New Mexico*) 46
   Indians are advised that voting is not a compulsory obligation, and that no government officials are authorized to influence any exercise of the privilege they may choose to accept.—AII (*New Mexico*)

3003 NEW MEXICO TERRITORY. Governor (Civil and Military) (John Munroe)

[Broadside] SANTA FE, NUEVO MEJICO, JUNIO 25 DE 1850. A LOS CACIQUES GOBERNADORCILLOS Y OTRAS AUTORIDADES DE LOS PUEBLOS DE INDIOS DEL TERRITORIO DE N. MEJICO . . . JOHN MUNROE, GOBERNADOR CIVIL Y MILITAR DE NUEVO MEJICO. JAMES S. CALHOUN, AGENTE DE LOS INDIOS.

Broadside, 25.5 x 20 cm. Text, 9.8 x 15 cm.

Ref.: AII (*New Mexico*) 47

Indians are assured of protection under the new constitution, to their persons and their property.—AII (*New Mexico*)

3004 NEW MEXICO TERRITORY. Governor (Military). (John Munroe)

[Broadside] AL PERFECTO DEL CANDADO DE [three lines in manuscript: Santa Fe,—San Miguel del Bado, Santa Anna—Bernalillo, Valencia, Rio Arriva—Taos] SENOR:—POR CUANTO: DOS DOCUMENTOS FIRMADOS "MANUEL ALVAREZ, VICE-GOBERNADOR DEL ESTADO DE NUEVO MEJICO," DIRIGIDOS AL PERFECTO DEL CANDADO DE SANTA FE, UNO SIGNIFICA SER UNA PROCLAMACION PARA TENER ELECCIONES, . . . DADO BAJO MI FIRMA EN LA SECRETARIA DEL TERRITORIO, ESTE VEINTE Y TRES DIA DE JULIO, ANO DE MIL OCHO CIENTOS Y CINCUENTA. [in manuscript: Signed Donaisano Vigil.]

Broadside, 25.1 x 19.4 cm. Text, 11.2 x 14.6 cm.

Ref.: AII (*New Mexico*) 48

Form of notice to the effect that laws passed in the name of the Legislature of the State of New Mexico and documents signed by Manuel Alvarez, vice-gobernador del Estado de Nuevo-Mejico are invalid, and that the territorial government must continue to function until New Mexico can be admitted to statehood.—AII (*New Mexico*)

Apparently the New Mexico Historical Society copy is unsigned.

3005 NEW MEXICO TERRITORY. Governor (William A. Pile)

[Broadside] [Column 1:] PROCLAMATION. WHEREAS R. B. MITCHELL, GOVERNOR OF THE TERRITORY OF NEW MEXICO, DID ON THE 2ND DAY OF AUGUST EIGHTEEN HUNDRED AND SIXTY NINE ISSUE HIS PROCLAMATION DECLARING THE NAVAJOE TRIBE OF INDIANS OUTLAWS; AND . . . NOW, THEREFORE, I, WILLIAM A. PILE, GOVERNOR OF THE TERRITORY OF NEW MEXICO, DO ISSUE THIS MY PROCLAMATION MODIFYING SO MUCH OF THE SAID PROCLAMATION AS REFERS TO THE NAVAJOE INDIANS, SO THAT ONLY MARAUDING BANDS, KNOWN TO BE COMMITTING DEPREDATIONS SHALL BE CONSIDERED AND TREATED AS HOSTILE . . . THIS 8TH DAY OF SEP-TEMBER A. D. 1869. WM. A. PILE, GOVERNOR. BY THE GOVERNOR. H. H. HEATH, SECY. TERRITORY. PROCLAMACION . . .

Broadside, 22.4 x 15.5 cm. Text, 15.4 x 12.5 cm.

Ref.: AII (*New Mexico*) 214

The second column, headed: Proclamacion. / is a Spanish version of the English text in the first column.

3006 NEW MEXICO CATTLE GROWERS' ASSOCIATION, CENTRAL

BRAND BOOK OF THE CENTRAL NEW MEXICO CATTLE GROWERS' ASSOCIATION WITH BY-LAWS AND LIST OF MEMBERS. APRIL 1, 1885. LAS VEGAS: NEW MEXICO STOCK GROWER, 1885.

[1]–64, 65–92 advertisements. 16.9 x 9.2 cm. Calf with calf flap over fore edge, manuscript lettering on back cover. Two lines on back cover scratched off, blank leaf torn out.

Ref.:

Tipped to page 76 is a small broadside, 6.4 x 8.7 cm., headed: Special Notice! / Signed at the foot: S. T. Butler.

3007 NEW SOCIETY, A . . .

A NEW SOCIETY, FOR THE BENEFIT OF INDIANS, ORGANIZED AT THE CITY OF WASHINGTON, FEBRUARY, 1822.

[1]–15, [16 blank]. 21.1 x 13.2 cm. Removed from bound volume, unbound.

Prov.: Inscribed at top of title-page in hand of Jedidiah Morse: Dr S.L.Mitchell L L D &c /. In another hand: N° 5. /

Ref.:

Inserted between pages 8 and 9 are two copies of a four-page prospectus for Jedidiah Morse's *A Report to the Secretary of War . . . On Indian Affairs . . . 1822.*

Among the members of the American Society for Promoting the Civilization and General Improvement of the Indian Tribes within the United States, Dr. Mitchell is listed as a "Special Correspondent." Page 11 is a Circular signed by Jedidiah Morse; it is addressed in manuscript to Dr. Mitchell with the following note in Morse's hand: A full Communication is requested fr[om] Dr M. to lay before the Society at their An[nual] Meeting— /.

3008 NEW YORK HERALD, THE

[Newspaper] THE NEW YORK HERALD. WHOLE NO. 8846. MORNING EDITION—TUESDAY, NOVEMBER 27, 1860 . . .

[1]–12. 58.8 x 40.5 cm. Unbound.

Ref.:

The final column of the first page is headed:

The Great West. / [wavy rule] / The Commerce of the Great / Plains of North America. [wavy rule] / The Past and Present Condition of the / Great Overland Traffic with New / Mexico, and Pike's Peak / Gold Regions and Utah. / [wavy rule] / Location of the Traffic—Its Ways / and Means. / [wavy rule] / The Overland Routes. / [wavy rule] / Freighting Life on the Great Prairies. / The Immense Government and Private Trans-/portation Business Across the Plains, &c., &c., &c. / The article occupies about nine and one-half columns on pages [1]–3.

3009 NEWELL, C.

LIFE AMONG THE SIOUX INDIANS . . . NEW YORK: NEW YORK POPULAR PUBLISHING CO.

[1]–13, [14–16 advertisements]. 16.5 x 10.7 cm. Pictorial wrappers, colored, with title against woodcut portrait of the author on front wrapper, woodcut of fight with Indians (Custer's "Last Stand") on back wrapper, on pink ground.

Ref.:
Published about 1890–1900.

3010 NEWELL, CHESTER

HISTORY OF THE REVOLUTION IN TEXAS, PARTICULARLY OF THE WAR OF 1835 & '36; TOGETHER WITH THE LATEST GEOGRAPHICAL, TOPOGRAPHICAL, AND STATISTICAL ACCOUNTS OF THE COUNTRY, FROM THE MOST AUTHENTIC SOURCES . . . NEW-YORK: PUBLISHED BY WILEY & PUTNAM, 1838.

[i]–x, [xi–xii blank], [1]–215, [216 blank]. 18.1 x 11 cm. Map: Texas, / 1838. / [lower right:] Lith. by Baker, 8 Wall St. N. Y. / 20.3 x 31.2 cm. Scale: 75 miles to one inch. Printed on tissue paper. Dark brown cloth, blind embossed sides, title in gilt on backstrip.

Ref.: Howes N115; Rader 2479; Raines p. 154; Sabin 54948; Streeter 1318

Streeter describes two issues of the book and two of the map. The present copy carries the dedication on page [iii], and the map is dated.

3011 NEWHALL, JOHN B.

THE BRITISH EMIGRANTS' "HAND BOOK," AND GUIDE TO THE NEW STATES OF AMERICA, PARTICULARLY ILLINOIS, IOWA, AND WISCONSIN . . . LONDON: PRINTED AND PUBLISHED FOR THE AUTHOR, BY T. STUTTER, 1844.

[i]–xi, [xii blank], [13]–[100]. 17.8 x 10.9 cm. Yellow-green printed wrappers, with title on front wrapper.

Ref.: Buck 388; Howes N117; Mott (*Iowa*) p. 59; Sabin 54996

3012 NEWHALL, JOHN B.

A GLIMPSE OF IOWA IN 1846; OR, THE EMIGRANT'S GUIDE, AND STATE DIRECTORY . . . BURLINGTON, IOWA: W. D. SKILLMAN, PUBLISHER, 1846. KEEMLE & FIELD, PRINTERS, ST. LOUIS, MO.

[i]–[viii], [9]–106, [107–12 Advertisement Directory]. 18.1 x 11 cm. Gray printed wrappers, with title on front wrapper, verso of back wrapper carries advertisements. In maroon cloth case.

Ref.: AII (*Iowa*) 18; AII (*Missouri*) 484; Howes N118; Mott (*Iowa*) p. 59; Sabin 54997

3013 NEWHALL, JOHN B.

[Map] NEWHALL'S / OUTLINE / MAP / OF / IOWA, / EXHIBITING ALL THE NEW / COUNTIES, CHIEF TOWNS, ROADS, &C. / BY / J. B. NEWHALL / AUTHOR OF SKETCHES OF IOWA / BURLINGTON / 1848 / [lower left:] ENGRAVED BY R. I. CAMPBELL, ST. LOUIS. MO. [lower right:] PUBLISHED BY J. F. ABRAHAMS, BURLINGTON. / [centre] ENTERED ACCORDING TO ACT OF CONGRESS, IN THE YEAR 1848, BY J. B. NEWHALL, IN THE CLERK'S OFFICE, OF THE FIRST JUDICIAL DISTRICT OF THE STATE OF IOWA. / Map, 37.3 x 53.5 cm. No scale given. Folded and bound into dark green or blue board covers. In a blue half morocco case.

Prov.: Inside front cover: Christian Amis / Burlington / Iowa / October / 5th 1848 / [flourish] /.

Ref.: Moffit 42

The map is engraved, the text and border printed. Map surrounded by printed text, with caption title as follows: Newhall's New Map of Iowa, for 1848, with Descriptive Notes. / Designed especially for the use of Emigrants and Travelers and as a Chart of reference invaluable to every Citizen of the State. / By J. B. Newhall, Author of "Sketches of Iowa." &c. / . . . / [lower left corner:] (Third Edition.) / [lower right corner:] (Burlington Hawk-Eye Print.) /

3014 NEWHALL, JOHN B.

THE SAME. (With slight differences in title.) Map, 27 x 37.1 cm. No scale given.

Ref.: Moffit 41

The map proper bears the title: Newhall's / Outline / Map / of / Iowa, / Exhibiting all the New / Counties, Chief Towns, Roads, &c. / By / J. B. Newhall, / Author of Sketches of Iowa / Burlington / 1848. / [below neat line, lower corner, right:] Published by J. F. Abrahams Burlington / [left:] Engraved by R. I. Campbell St Louis Mo / [centre:] Entered according to Act of Congress in the year 1848 by J. B. Newhall in the Clerks Office of the first Judicial District of the State of Iowa /.

Text within decorative border, at sides and below map in seven columns. A New Map of

Iowa, For 1848–9 With Descriptive Notes. / Designed for the use of Emigrants and Travelers, and as a Chart of reference invaluable to every citizen of the State. / By J. B. Newhall, Author of "Sketches in Iowa" &c. / [right corner below rule:] (Fourth Edition.) / Valley Whig. Print. Keosauqua /.

3015 NEWHALL, JOHN B.

SKETCHES OF IOWA; OR, THE EMIGRANT'S GUIDE . . . NEW-YORK: PUBLISHED BY J. H. COLTON, 1841.

[1]–252. 14.9 x 9.5 cm. Folding colored map attached to back cover: Newhall's / Map / of / Iowa / Compiled from the United States Surveys, / Exhibiting the boundaries of Counties, Township-/lines, Ranges, Prairies and Timber Lands; / The location of Cities, Towns, Indian Villages, / Post and Steam Boat Routs[!] &c. / By J. B. Newhall, Burlington, Iowa. / Published by / J. H. Colton, New-York. / 1841. / [vignette] / [in lower border:] Entered according to Act of Congress, in the year 1841, by John B. Newhall, in the Clerk's Office of the District Court of the Southern District of New York. / [at right:] Eng'd. by Sherman & Smith, N.Y. 49.2 x 39 cm. Scale: 12 miles to one inch. *Inset:* The / Territory of Iowa / Exhibiting the Country between the / Mississippi & Missouri Rivers / and the / British Possessions. 14 x 14.3 cm. No scale given. At the left of the title is the Surveyor General's certificate of the accuracy of the map, dated Dubuque, Iowa, Augt 3rd 1840. Also at the left of the map is a table of population and other statistics and a Table of Distances. Green cloth, blind embossed borders on sides, title in gilt on front cover: Newhall's / Sketches of / Iowa / with a / Map / [rule] / Published by / J. H. Colton / 1841 /.

Ref.: Howes N119; Mott (*Iowa*) p. 59; Sabin 54998

See note on Newhall by Jean P. Black in *The Palimpsest*, October, 1944, Vol. XXV, No. 10, pp. 289–97.

3016 NEWMARK, HARRIS

SIXTY YEARS IN SOUTHERN CALIFORNIA 1853–1913 . . . EDITED BY MAURICE H. NEWMARK, MARCO R. NEWMARK . . . NEW YORK: THE KNICKERBOCKER PRESS, 1916.*

[i]–[xxx, xxx blank], 1–688. 22.5 x 15.2 cm. 150 illustrations listed. Dark red cloth, gilt top, uncut. In dust jacket.

Ref.: Cowan 454; Howes N123

3017 NEWSOME, EDMUND

EXPERIENCE IN THE WAR OF THE GREAT REBELLION . . . SECOND EDITION . . . CARBONDALE, ILL.: EDMUND NEWSOME, 1880.

[i–ii], [1]–297, [298 advertisement]. 14 x 10.7 cm. Rebound in black cloth.

Ref.: Coulter 340; Nicholson p. 596

This narrative is of considerable value as its author was interested in the country and people he saw on his travels and took pains to record his observations.—Coulter

Editions: Carbondale, 1879.

3018 NEWSOME, EDMUND

HISTORICAL SKETCHES OF JACKSON COUNTY, ILLINOIS . . . SECOND EDITION. CARBONDALE, ILL.: E. NEWSOME, 1894.

[i–iv], [1]–233, [234 blank]. 14.4 x 10 cm. Illustrations and map unlisted. Fragment (13.5 x 8 cm.) only of folded map present. White printed boards, with title on front cover. Worn, remnants of blue cloth backstrip on sides, but all worn away on backstrip, amateur repairs.

Ref.: Buck 855; Howes N125

Contains "Sketches Of the early settlement of Jackson County, Ill." by Ben. Boone, pages 25–75.

Editions: Carbondale, 1879, 1882.

3019 NEWSON, THOMAS M.

THRILLING SCENES AMONG THE INDIANS. WITH A GRAPHIC DESCRIPTION OF CUSTER'S LAST FIGHT WITH SITTING BULL . . . CHICAGO: BELFORD, CLARKE & CO., 1884.

[1]–241, [242 blank]. 17.8 x 12.2 cm. Eight illustrations listed. Brown cloth, title stamped in black on front cover and gilt on backstrip.

Ref.: Howes N127; Rader 2482

3020 NEWTON, JOHN M.

MEMOIRS OF JOHN MARSHALL NEWTON. COPYRIGHT 1913 BY JOHN M. STEVENSON.

[i–viii], [1]–91, [92 blank]. 22.5 x 15 cm. Seven illustrations and maps unlisted. Black printed wrappers with title on front wrapper in yellow.

Prov.: Inscribed on page [i]: Eliza S. Lane / from her Brother / John M. Stevenson / Jany 23—1913 /.

Ref.: Howes N130

The preliminaries are disposed as follows: [i blank], [ii] title, [iii] portrait, [iv–v blank], [vi] portrait, [vii] view, [viii blank].

Published at Cambridge, N. Y.

The author died December 9, 1897. The narrative was completed by Ellen Huldah Newton and published in 1913 by the author's brother-in-law John M. Stevenson. At the end is an account of Newton's later life by his daughter. He was librarian of the Historical and Philosophical Society of Ohio at Cincinnati and Curator from

1868 until his death. This is a good narrative covering his trip overland to California in 1850 and his life there during two years.—EDG

3021 NICELY, WILSON S.

THE GREAT SOUTHWEST; OR, PLAIN GUIDE FOR EMIGRANTS AND CAPITALISTS, EMBRACING A DESCRIPTION OF THE STATES OF MISSOURI AND KANSAS . . . ST. LOUIS: R. P. STUDLEY & CO., 1867.

[1]–115, [116–24 advertisements]. 18.6 x 11.5 cm. Map: New Map / Of the States of / Missouri and Kansas / Compiled from United States Surveys, / and other Sources, / By / Wilson Nicely. / R. P. Studley & Co., / Printers, / Lithographers / And Stationers. / S. W. Cor. Main and Olive Sts., St. Louis, Mo. / Scale / 18 miles to one inch. / [lower left corner: advertisement for Connecticut Mutual Life Insurance Co.] 45.3 x 70.4 cm. Scale as above. Brown cloth, title in gilt on front cover.

Ref.: Howes N134; Rader 2484; Sabin 55165

Pages 60–105 give an account of Nicely's travels and residence in this country over a two year period. His visit via horseback to the Cherokee Neutral Lands, as well as his camping trip to Arkansas, is informative and interesting giving a picture of conditions there soon after the close of the Civil War.—EDG

3022 NICOLLET, JOSEPH N.

. . . REPORT INTENDED TO ILLUSTRATE A MAP OF THE HYDROGRAPHICAL BASIN OF THE UPPER MISSISSIPPI RIVER . . . WASHINGTON: BLAIR AND RIVES, 1843.

[1]–170. 22.7 x 14.6 cm. Map: Hydrographical Basin / of the / Upper Mississippi River / From Astronomical and Barometrical Observations Surveys and Information / by J. N. Nicollet. / in the Years 1836, 37, 38, 39, and 40; assisted in / 1838, 39 & 40, by Lieut. J. C. Fremont, of the Corps of / Topographical Engineers / under the superintendence of the Bureau of the Corps of Topographical Engineers / and authorized by / The War Department / [thick and thin rule] / Reduced and compiled under the direction of / Col. J. J. Abert / in the Bureau of the Corps of Top^l Eng^{rs} / by Lieut. W. H. Emory / from the Map published in 1842 and from / other authorities in / 1843. / [double rule] / Published by order of the U. S. Senate. / W. J. Stone Sc. / [lower left:] Mountains Engraved by E. F. Woodward Phil^a / 93.1 x 77.9 cm. Scale: about 19 miles to one inch. Sheepskin, dark red leather label on backstrip.

Ref.: Buck 339; Howes N152; Sabin 55257; Wagner-Camp 98

26th Congress, 2nd Session, Senate, Document No. 237, Serial 380.

3023 NOBLE, D. J.

[Broadside] THE NOBLE PLOW. IN OFFERING THIS CULTIVATOR TO THE PUBLIC, WE FEEL CONFIDENT THAT IT WILL PROVE ITSELF TO BE ALL THAT WE CLAIM FOR IT . . . THE ABOVE COMPRISES THE ENTIRE LIST OF PURCHASERS OF THE NOBLE PLOW. THESE MEN ALL PURCHASED WITH A GUARANTEE, GIVING PERMISSION TO RETURN THE PLOW IF NOT SATISFACTORY; NOT ONE OF WHOM, HOWEVER, HAS RETURNED THE ARTICLE, NOR EVEN HINTED A SINGLE OBJECTION . . . D. J. NOBLE. NEW BOSTON ILL. FEB., 12TH, 1866.

Broadside, 33.9 x 16.3 cm. Text, 30 x 13 cm.
Ref.:

3024 NOBLES, WILLIAM H.

SPEECH OF THE HON. WM. H. NOBLES, TOGETHER WITH OTHER DOCUMENTS, RELATIVE TO AN EMIGRANT ROUTE TO CALIFORNIA AND OREGON, THROUGH MINNESOTA TERRITORY . . . SAINT PAUL: OLMSTED & BROWN, TERRITORIAL PRINTERS, 1854.

[1]–13, [14–16 blank]. 23.1 x 16.5 cm. Buff printed wrappers, with title on front wrapper. In a brown half morocco case.

Ref.: AII (*Minnesota*) 77; Sabin 55390; Wagner-Camp 241

"House of Representatives, February 16, 1854 . . . Mr. McKusick offered the following resolution: *Resolved*, That one thousand copies of the proceedings of the meeting . . . relative to an emigrant route to California, and the speech of Mr Nobles' as printed for the Council, be printed for this House, five hundred of which copies to be circulated by Mr. Nobles, on his way to Washington City, which motion prevailed."

There was another edition, which Wagner-Camp lists first, "Printed by order of the Council."

3025 NOLAN, PHILIP

AUTOGRAPH LETTER (retained copy) signed with initials. No date, no place. Two pages, 23.2 x 19.1 cm. Stained, large hole affecting text. To Mr. Newman.

A strange letter, written apparently to a deserter in an attempt to induce the return of the recipient to the Army. Retained copy, with numerous changes.

3026 NOLTE, VINCENT

FIFTY YEARS IN BOTH HEMISPHERES; OR, REMINISCENCES OF THE LIFE OF A FORMER MERCHANT . . . NEW YORK: REDFIELD, 1854.

[i]–xxii, [11]–484. 18 x 12.3 cm. Rebound in half dark blue levant morocco, gilt, gilt top, by The Lakeside Press.

Prov.: Bookplate of Neva and Guy Littell.

Ref.: Howes N169; Sabin 55412

3027 NORRIS, JAMES W.

GENERAL DIRECTORY AND BUSINESS ADVERTISER OF THE CITY OF CHICAGO, FOR THE YEAR 1844; TOGETHER WITH A HISTORICAL SKETCH AND STATISTICAL ACCOUNT, TO THE PRESENT TIME . . . CHICAGO: ELLIS & FERGUS, 1844.

[1–2], [i]–iv, [5]–116. 19.4 x 11.5 cm. Pink printed wrappers bound into old marbled wrappers, red cloth back, manuscript label on front wrapper, advertisements on verso of front and recto and verso of back wrapper.

Prov.: See notes below.

Ref.: Byrd 886; Howes N185; McMurtrie (*Chicago*) 69

Pages [1–2] carry advertisements on pink paper, possibly the same as those mentioned by McMurtrie as being present in the Streeter copy in cloth, but not present in wrappered copies.

There are numerous notes, additions, changes, corrections, etc., in pencil throughout. These are probably in the hand of Robert Fergus and may have been made when he was preparing his Directory of 1839. The copy was secured from a granddaughter of Fergus.

The wrapper bearing the manuscript label reads as follows: property of O. Sherman / Chicago City / Directory / 1844. /

The signature Orin Sherman appears at the top of the front printed wrapper.

3028 NORRIS, JAMES W.

A BUSINESS ADVERTISER AND GENERAL DIRECTORY OF THE CITY OF CHICAGO, FOR THE YEAR 1845–6, TOGETHER WITH A HISTORICAL AND STATISTICAL ACCOUNT . . . CHICAGO: J. CAMPBELL & CO. PUBLISHERS, 1845.

[1–14], [13]–[157], [158–168 advertisements on colored paper]. 19.3 x 11.2 cm. Folding frontispiece and illustrations. Pink printed wrappers (lacks front wrapper), advertisements on recto and verso of back wrapper. Plain front wrapper supplied.

Prov.: Chicago Historical Society copy with perforated title-leaf and other markings.

Ref.: Byrd 986; Howes N183; McMurtrie (*Chicago*) 83; Sabin 12639

The unpaginated leaves at the front carry the title-page, preface, woodcuts and descriptions and advertisements. The unpaginated leaves at the back carry a page of addenda and errata and eleven pages of advertisements.

3029 NORRIS, JAMES W.

THE SAME.

[1–8], [1–4 on pink paper], [9–10], [13]–[160], [1–10 advertisements on white, pink, brown, tan, and pink paper]. Title-leaf, map, three pages of woodcuts of churches on text paper, churches and advertisements on white paper, two churches and advertisements on pink paper, Preface, text, Addenda, advertisements on white, pink, brown, tan, and pink paper. 19.3 x 10.8 cm. Rebound in brown half morocco.

Prov.: Signature on title-page: Orin Sherman. / There are also manuscript notes, changes and corrections, etc., probably in the hand of Robert Fergus.

Ref.: Byrd 986; Howes N183; McMurtrie (*Chicago*) 83; Sabin 12639

Copy 1 is arranged slightly differently: folding frontispiece, title-leaf, Preface, map, three pages of churches on text paper, two churches and advertisements on yellow paper, one leaf of churches and advertisements, text to page 156, Addenda, advertisement on verso, twelve pages of advertisements on white, green, pink, blue, tan, and pink paper.

The last leaf of advertisement in each case may be the back wrapper.

3030 NORRIS, JAMES W.

NORRIS' CHICAGO DIRECTORY. FOR 1848–9 . . . CHICAGO, PUBLISHED BY NORRIS & TAYLOR, 1848.

[1]–132, 1–28 advertisements. 19 x 12 cm. Salmon printed boards with black leather backstrip, with title on front cover; advertisement on verso of back cover.

Ref.: Byrd 1362; Howes N183; McMurtrie (*Chicago*) 143

3031 NORRIS, JAMES W., & G. W. GARDINER, Chicago, Illinois

ILLINOIS ANNUAL REGISTER, AND WESTERN BUSINESS DIRECTORY . . . CHICAGO: GEER & WILSON, PRINTERS, 1847.

[1]–120, [1]–36, [1–12]. 19.8 x 12.3 cm. Blue printed wrappers, with title on front wrapper, advertisement on verso of back wrapper.

Prov.: Chicago Historical Society duplicate, with stamp, markings, etc.

Ref.: Byrd 1231; Howes N186; McMurtrie (*Chicago*) 119

The second part has a separate title-page.

The Almanac (the unpaginated twelve pages at the end) is listed in the Table of Contents as beginning on page 37.

3032 NORTH MISSOURI RAILROAD COMPANY

REPORT OF THE BOARD OF DIRECTORS OF THE NORTH MISSOURI RAILROAD COMPANY TO THE STOCKHOLDERS, MADE FIRST MONDAY OF APRIL, 1866.

[1]–114. 20.6 x 13.7 cm. Map: G. Woolworth Colton's County & Township Railroad Map of the States of / Missouri, Iowa, Illinois and Wisconsin / Published by G. W. & C. B. Colton & Co No. 172. William St. New York 1866. / North Missouri Rail Road Map / Showing their connections & Proposed Branches. / [lower left:] Entered according to Act of Congress in the year 1865 by G. W. & C. B. Colton, in the Clerks Office of the District Court of the United States for the Southern District of New York. / 76 x 67.4 cm. Scale: 20 miles to one inch.

Ref.:
Neither place nor date of printing is given on the title-page. Probably St. Louis, 1866.

3033 NORTHEND, CHARLES

DICTATION EXERCISES . . . NEW YORK: A. S. BARNES & CO., 1855.

[i]–iv, [5]–[119], [120 blank]. 18.3 x 11.6 cm. Pink printed boards, brown leather backstrip, title on front cover. Figured cotton cover sewn onto cover, contemporary.

Prov.: Signature of George M. Templeton three times.

Ref.:
A schoolbook from Templeton's Canonsburg days.

3034 NORTHERN CROSS RAIL ROAD

[Wrapper title] TRAVELERS' GUIDE, TO THE NORTH AND EAST. TRAINS RUN INTO 'UNION DEPOT,' CHICAGO . . . QUINCY: PRINTED AT THE "WHIG" BOOK AND JOB OFFICE, 1856.

[1]–8, (including wrappers). 13.7 x 8.9 cm. Stitched. Printed on yellow paper.

Ref.: Byrd 2510
Inserted between pages 24 and 25 of Clemens, Orion: *City of Keokuk in 1856* . . . Keokuk: O. Clemens, 1856.

Stations and distances are given for the Northern Cross Rail Road between Quincy and Galesburg, for the Chicago & Burlington Rail Road from Cameron to Chicago, and for various other Illinois lines including the Chicago & Rock Island, Illinois Central, and Chicago & Galena Union. Quincy to New York is described as a forty-four-hour journey.

3035 NORTHERN CROSS RAIL ROAD COMPANY

REPORT OF AN EXPERIMENTAL SURVEY OF THAT PORTION OF THE NORTHERN CROSS RAILROAD EXTENDING FROM QUINCY TO MEREDOSIA, BY WM. P. WHITTLE AND JAS. J. SHIPMAN. QUINCY: PRINTED BY ORDER OF THE BOARD OF DIRECTORS, 1850.

[1]–35, [36 blank]. 21.8 x 14 cm. Removed from bound volume, unbound.

Ref.: Byrd 1608
The printer's imprint appears on the verso of the title-leaf: [wavy rule] / Woods' Print, Quincy, Ill.: /.

3036 NORTHERN NEW MEXICO STOCK GROWERS' ASSOCIATION

BRAND BOOK OF THE NORTHERN NEW MEXICO STOCK GROWERS' ASSOCIATION, BY-LAWS AND LIST OF MEMBERS. JULY 1, 1884. RATON, N.M.: THE RATON COMET PRINT, 1884.

[1]–80, 81–95 advertisements, [96 blank]. 16.7 x 9.7 cm. Cream cloth, with wallet flap, red edges.

Prov.: Signature in pencil inside front cover: Chas Wilcox /. Rubber stamp on fly-leaf: The Field and Farm, / Denver, Colorado. /

Ref.:

3037 NORTHERN PACIFIC RAILROAD

[Wrapper title] MONTANA. A CONCISE DESCRIPTION OF THE CLIMATE, SOIL, GRAZING LANDS, AGRICULTURAL AND MINERAL PRODUCTIONS OF THE COUNTRY ADJACENT AND TRIBUTARY TO THE NORTHERN PACIFIC RAILROAD. PUBLISHED FOR THE USE OF PERSONS SEEKING INFORMATION CONCERNING THIS GREAT NEW LAND. HELENA, MONTANA: FISK BROS., 1882. For a copy with map, see number 2867 above.

[1]–16. 19.3 x 12.4 cm. Folding map preceding text: Map of Montana, Showing Line of Northern Pacific Railroad through the Territory. / [preceding above map; following in lower left:] Montana / Compiled from the latest / Official Records and other Sources by / Jacob Medary / References / [5 lines] / 1882 /. Copyright, 1881, by James Monteith /. [lower right:] Russell & Struthers, Eng's N.Y. / 33 x 50.9 cm. (page size). Scale: about 40 miles to one inch. Gray printed wrappers, with title on front wrapper, advertisements on verso of front and recto and verso of back wrapper.

Ref.:

3038 NORTH-WESTERN JOURNAL, THE

[Caption title] THE NORTH-WESTERN JOURNAL. VOL. I. MARCH [–APRIL], 1850. NO. 1 [–2] . . .

[1]–60. [61–116. 20 x 13.3 cm. Removed from bound volume, sewn.

Ref.:

The magazine ran only to three numbers, the May issue being the last. All three numbers are in the Wisconsin Historical Society. These first two numbers contain the papers read at the first annual meeting of the Society at Madison, on January 15, 1850.

3039 NORTH WESTERN MINING COMPANY

ACTS OF INCORPORATION, ORGANIZATION, AND BY-LAWS OF THE NORTH WESTERN MINING COMPANY, TEXAS. CHARTERED BY TWO GENERAL ACTS OF THE REPUBLIC OF TEXAS. 1846.

[1]–17, [18 blank]. 17.7 x 12.1 cm. Rebound in red calf.

Prov.: On page [18] there is a manuscript note by E. L. R. Wheelock: The undersigned has / Negotiated a Capital / of $50.000 per annum / for 5 years based upon / the hypothecation of / the Companies Lands / &c / E L R Wheelock / Agent &c /.

Ref.: Clements Library (*Texas*) 29; Winkler 11

The place of printing has not been determined.

The Remarks on page 17 are signed by E.L.R.Wheelock, D[irector]. N.W.M.C. and Agent.

On page 16, there is a certificate of authenticity by S. W. Kellogg, Sec'y N.W.Mining Co. under date "Office of the North Western Mining Company, Robertson County, Texas, May, 1846."

3040 NORTH-WESTERN REVIEW, THE

[Caption title] THE NORTH-WESTERN REVIEW AND COMMERCIAL AND REAL ESTATE REPORTER. VOL. I. JUNE, 1857 [–APRIL, 1858]. NO. 1 [–11] . . .

[1]–64. [1]–62. [1]–[64]. [1]–64. [1]–64. [1]–62. [1]–62. [1]–62. [1]–62. [1]–62. [1]–[64]. 20.6 x 12.7 cm. Eleven parts bound together in contemporary blue boards, calf backstrip.

Prov.: Inscribed in pencil on the front end-leaf: Compliments [underlined] / of / H. H. Belding / To / The Mayor & City / Council of Keokuk /.

Ref.: Sabin 55853

The editor of this journal was H. H. Belding. It was published at Keokuk, Iowa. Only eleven numbers were published, according to W. Gregory: *Union List of Serials* (New York: H. W. Wilson, 1943) page 2036.

3041 NORTON, HARRY J.

WONDER-LAND ILLUSTRATED; OR, HORSEBACK RIDES THROUGH THE YELLOWSTONE NATIONAL PARK . . . VIRGINIA CITY, MONTANA: HARRY J. NORTON.

[1]–132. 18.7 x 11.6 cm. Folding map and illustrations unlisted. Buff printed wrappers with title and pictorial design on front wrapper. In an olive green cloth case.

Ref.: Howes N205; McMurtrie (*Montana*) 81

The work is copyrighted 1873 and the prefatory note on the verso of the title-leaf is dated the same year. Probably printed at Virginia City. The spelling Montaña is used on the title-page.

Pages 113–32 comprise business directories for Virginia City, Helena, Deer Lodge, Bozeman, and a section of miscellaneous advertisements.

In his introduction, the author says these letters were originally written for the Virginia City *Montanian* and are published without revision.

3042 NORTON, LEWIS A.

LIFE AND ADVENTURES OF COL. L. A. NORTON . . . OAKLAND, CAL.: PACIFIC PRESS PUBLISHING HOUSE, 1887.

[i]–viii, [9]–492. 19.5 x 14 cm. Portrait. Dark brown cloth, title stamped on front cover in gilt, decorative bands on front cover in black, and on backstrip and back cover in blind.

Ref.: Cowan p. 457; Howes N210

The author was a veteran of the Mexican War. His accounts of early days in Placerville and elsewhere are in the vein of the old pioneer—generally interesting, and sometimes slightly but not offensively coarse.—Cowan. Norton was also involved in the Canadian Rebellion of 1837. He crossed the plains in 1848.

3043 NORTON, LEWIS A.

THE RESTORATION: A METRICAL ROMANCE OF CANADA . . . CHICAGO: PUBLISHED IN THE ARGUS OFFICE, 1851.

[i]–xii, [13]–180. (Page [i] blank, page [ii] frontispiece.) 14.8 x 9.5 cm. Portrait. Black embossed cloth, with title in gilt on front cover.

Ref.: AII (*Chicago*) 20; Byrd 1749

The front endleaf may have been removed, although the volume looks as though it were issued without the endleaf.

3044 NOTICE SUR LE TERRITOIRE . . .

NOTICE SUR LE TERRITOIRE ET SUR LA MISSION DE L'OREGON, SUIVIE DE QUELQUES LETTRES DES SOEURS DE NOTRE-DAME ETABLIES A SAINT PAUL DU WALLAMETTE. BRUXELLES: BUREAU DE PUBLICATION DE LA BIBLIOTHEQUE D'EDUCATION, 1847.

[1]–180. 18.1 x 11.4 cm. Double-page map: Carte / de la / Province Ecclésiastique / de / l'Orégon. / [rule] / [5 lines] / [lower centre:] Etablissement de D. Raes, Rue de la Fourche, 36, Bruxelles. / 20.1 x 15.3 cm. Scale: 80 lieues communes to an inch. Gray printed wrappers with title on front wrapper, uncut. In gray cloth case.
Ref.: Howes O109; Sabin 55988(?); Smith 7483

3045 NOTT, MANFORD A.

ACROSS THE PLAINS IN '54 . . .*

[i–iv], [1]–232. 19.4 x 14 cm. Light brown wrappers, with title on front wrapper. In light red buckram case.
Ref.: Cowan p. 457; Howes N213
Printed at San Francisco by Chase & Roe in 1905 (?).
Contains the sequel, *The Captive Maidens* . . ., pages [135]–232.
Editions: [San Francisco, n.d.] 132 pages.

3046 NOURSE, CHARLES C.

AUTOBIOGRAPHY . . . CONTAINING THE INCIDENTS OF MORE THAN FIFTY YEARS' PRACTICE AT THE BAR IN THE STATE OF IOWA. PRIVATELY PRINTED, MCMXI.

[1]–235, [236 blank]. 24 x 15.8 cm. Gray wrappers, uncut.
Ref.:

3047 NOURSE, CHARLES C.

IOWA AND THE CENTENNIAL. THE STATE ADDRESS DELIVERED . . . AT PHILADELPHIA . . . SEPTEMBER, 7, 1876. DES MOINES: IOWA STATE REGISTER PRINT, 1876.

[1]–42. [43–44 blank]. 22.8 x 14.9 cm. Green printed wrappers, with title on front wrapper.
Ref.:

3048 NOURSE, D. H.

1891. THE TIN CENTRE OF AMERICA. HILL CITY AND THE GREAT HARNEY PEAK REGION OF THE BLACK HILLS. A COMPREHENSIVE REVIEW . . . HILL CITY, S. D.: TIN MINER PRINT, 1891.

[i–iv], [1]–[44]. 18.1 x 13.6 cm. Six illustrations including a frontispiece printed in green. White printed wrappers with title on front wrapper, advertisement on verso of back wrapper.
Ref.:
Pages [i–ii] and [29–44] are advertising pages.

3049 NOWLIN, WILLIAM

THE BARK COVERED HOUSE; OR, BACK IN THE WOODS AGAIN; BEING A GRAPHIC AND THRILLING DESCRIPTION OF REAL PIONEER LIFE IN THE WIL-DERNESS OF MICHIGAN . . . DETROIT: PRINTED FOR THE AUTHOR, 1876.

[i–iv blank], [v]–[xvi, xvi blank], [17]–250. 19.1 x 13 cm. Six plates and two vignettes. Plum cloth, decorated in black, gilt and in blind.
Ref.: Bay p. 328; Buley I, p. 146; Clements Library (*Michigan*) 94; Howes N217
A consistently interesting account of pioneer life, Nowlin's little book has long been a classic in its field.

3050 NOYES, ALVA J.

IN THE LAND OF CHINOOK; OR, THE STORY OF BLAINE COUNTY . . . HELENA, MONT., STATE PUBLISHING CO.*

[1]–152. 22.9 x 15.1 cm. Illustrations unlisted. Blue cloth.
Ref.: Howes N218; Smith 7487
Copyrighted 1917.

3051 NOYES, ALVA J.

THE STORY OF AJAX. LIFE IN THE BIG HOLE BASIN . . . HELENA, MONTANA: STATE PUBLISHING COMPANY, 1914.

[i]–[viii, viii blank], [1]–158. 23.2 x 15.1 cm. 13 illustrations listed. Dark green cloth.
Prov.: Inscribed on blank leaf at front: Yours truly / A. J. Noyes / (Ajax) / Sept / 3rd 1914 /.
Ref.: Howes N219; Smith 7488

3052 NUMBER OF MISCELLANEOUS LETTERS, A

A NUMBER OF MISCELLANEOUS LETTERS FROM A FATHER TO HIS CHILDREN . . . SOUTH HANOVER, IA.: PRINTED AND PUBLISHED BY JAMES MORROW, 1838.

[1]–102, [103–04]. 18.7 x 11 cm. Black cloth, red roan back.
Ref.: Byrd & Peckham 755
Unlike the earlier *A Series of Miscellaneous Letters* (which see), the contents of the present second series is entirely theological.

3053 NUNES CABECA DE VACA, ALVAR

. . . RELATION ET NAUFRAGES D'ALVAR NUNEZ CABECA DE VACA . . . PARIS: ARTHUS BERTRAND, M. DCCC XXXVII.

[i–iv], [1]–8, [1]–302. 22.3 x 14.2 cm. Pink wrappers, printed paper label on backstrip, uncut, unopened. In a red cloth case.
Ref.: Wagner (*SS*) 1 note

3054 NUNES CABECA DE VACA, ALVAR

RELATION THAT ALVAR NUNEZ CABECA DE VACA GAVE OF WHAT BEFEL THE ARMAMENT IN THE INDIAS . . . PRINTED FROM THE BUCKINGHAM SMITH TRANSLATION OF 1871.

[i–x], [1]–[124]. 31.4 x 22.2 cm. Decorations in color by Valenti Angelo. Cream boards, fore and lower edges uncut. In cloth slip case.

Ref.: Heller & Magee

Limited to 300 copies printed at the Grabhorn Press in 1929. Signed by Edwin Grabhorn.

3055 NUTTALL, THOMAS

A JOURNAL OF TRAVELS INTO THE ARKANSA TERRITORY, DURING THE YEAR 1819 . . . PHILADELPHIA: PRINTED AND PUBLISHED BY THOS. H. PALMER, 1821.

[1]⁴, 1², 3–27⁴. [i]–xii, [9]–296. 22.9 x 14 cm. Five engraved plates, each with tissue guard, and a folding map. Map: A Map of the / Arkansas River, / intended to illustrate the Travels of / Tho⁸ Nuttall; Constructed from his original manuscripts by / H. S. Tanner. / [lower right:] Engraved by H. S. Tanner. / 24.7 x 49.5 cm. Scale: about 20 miles to one inch. Gray boards, with paper label, 3.2 x 2.3 cm., on backstrip, uncut. Label somewhat defective. In a brown cloth case.

Ref.: Bradford 4035; Buck 124a; Clark II 48; Field 1145; Howes N229; Jones 834; Rader 2494; Sabin 56348; Wagner-Camp 20

There is considerable information about the Cherokee, Osage, and Chickasaw Indians.

3056 NYE-STARR, KATE

A SELF-SUSTAINING WOMAN; OR, THE EXPERIENCE OF SEVENTY-TWO YEARS . . . CHICAGO: ILLINOIS PRINTING AND BINDING CO., 1888.

[1]–161, [162 blank]. (Pages [1–2] blank.) 17.3 x 12.3 cm. Portrait. Red cloth, title stamped in gilt on front cover, border in black, same border on back cover in blind.

Ref.: Howes N232

The author was the sister of Governor Nye of Nevada. In 1862, she and her family left Niagara, N.Y., via Buffalo to Chicago. From Chicago via Rock Island R.R. to Brooklyn, Iowa, then the terminus of the railroad. From there via "mules and canvas covered wagon" to Council Bluff, arriving July 1st. Thence to Salt Lake City where she met Porter Rockwell and Brigham Young and then to Carson City where she lived in the same house occupied by the Clemens boys.—EDG

3057 NYSTEL, OLE T.

LOST AND FOUND; OR, THREE MONTHS WITH THE WILD INDIANS A BRIEF SKETCH OF THE LIFE OF OLE T. NYSTEL, EMBRACING HIS EXPERIENCE WHILE IN CAPTIVITY TO THE COMANCHES, AND SUBSEQUENT LIBERATION FROM THEM . . . DALLAS, TEXAS: WILMANS BROS., 1888.

[1]–26. 20.8 x 12.4 cm. Yellow printed wrappers (slightly glazed paper), with title on front wrapper.

Ref.: Howes N233

On a printed slip, 12.6 x 12.4 cm., tipped in at the front is a list of thirteen citizens of Bosque County, Texas, who certify that they believe the facts given by Nystel to be true.

O

3058 OAK GROVE CITY COMPANY, Oak Grove, Nebraska Territory

[Broadside] ONE SHARE. 1280 ACRES. NO. [in manuscript: 422–] THIS ENTITLES [in manuscript: W.H.Bassett] TO ONE SHARE IN OAK GROVE CITY, EACH SHARE BEING ONE FOUR HUNDRED & EIGHTIETH PART OF THE LANDS, TOWN SITE, AND LOTS CLAIMED BY THE OAK GROVE CITY COMPANY . . . OAK GROVE CITY, NEBRASKA TERRITORY, 1856. "TIMES" PRINT, GLENWOOD, IOWA.

Broadside, 12.5 x 20.2 cm. Text, 10.8 x 17.3 cm.

Ref.:

Signed by H. P. Bennet and William Street. Dated Nov. 3, 1856. Made out to W.H.Bassett. Printed in reddish-brown. Signature of W.H. Bassett on verso.

3059 OAKLY, OBADIAH

EXPEDITION TO OREGON . . . REPRINTED FROM THE PEORIA REGISTER. NEW YORK, 1914.*

[1]–19, [20 blank]. 22.2 x 14.9 cm. Gray printed wrappers, with title on front wrapper.

Ref.: Wagner-Camp 85

The account appeared first in the *Peoria Register and North-Western Gazetteer* December 14, 21, 28, 1839, and January 4, 1840. An interview with Oakly had appeared in the November 9, 1839 issue of the same. It was reprinted in the *National Intelligencer*, November 23, 1839, and in the *Library of American History* (Cincinnati, ca. 1840).

3060 OATMAN, OLIVE

[Broadside] FIVE YEARS AMONG WILD SAVAGES. THE RENOWNED APACHEE CAPTIVE MISS OLIVE OATMAN. THIS DISTINGUISHED LADY . . . WILL LECTURE AT . . . SUBJECT: "HER LIFE, ADVENTURES AND SUFFERINGS AMONG THE APACHEE & MOHAVE INDIANS." . . . BLADE PRINT, TOLEDO, OHIO.

Broadside, 47.5 x 16.4 cm. Text, 45.5 x 14.6 cm.

Ref.: Sabin 92742 see

The spaces for the place and time of the lecture have not been filled in in the present copy. At the foot of the broadside is a series of press notices, the latest of which is dated November 9, 1859. Sabin describes a different broadside.

Laid in Stratton: *Life Among the Indians* . . . 1857.

3061 O'BRYAN, WILLIAM

A NARRATIVE OF TRAVELS IN THE UNITED STATES OF AMERICA, WITH SOME ACCOUNT OF AMERICAN MANNERS AND POLITY, AND ADVICE TO EMIGRANTS AND TRAVELLERS GOING TO THAT INTERESTING COUNTRY . . . DEVON: PUBLISHED FOR THE AUTHOR, 1836.

[i]–[xii, xii blank], [13]–419, [420 blank]. 18 x 11 cm. One illustration, two vignettes, with portrait laid in. Dark blue cloth.

Ref.: Howes O6; Hubach p. 70; Sabin 56436

The author founded the religious sect known as the Bryanites. In the present volume he describes his travels in Pennsylvania, Ohio, and Kentucky. Most of the edition is said to have been destroyed in a printing house fire.

The portrait, which is laid in and trimmed close, is identical with the example found in the ICN copy and presumably identical with the copy described by DLC.

3062 OCCIDENTE, MEXICO

ARTICULOS BAJO LOS CUALES SE HA CELEBRADO LA CONTRARA ENTRE EL SUPREMO GOBIERNO DEL ESTADO DE OCCIDENTE, Y EL SR. D. JOSE ANTONIO HERRERA, APODERADO DEL SR. D. RICARDO EXTER DE LA COMPAGNIA INGLESA PARA HABILITACION DE MINAS, ACUNAR Y CAMBIAR POR SU CUENTA LAS PLATAS, ORO Y COBRE QUE SE LE PRESENTEN EN LA CASA DE MONEDA DEL ESTADO . . . FUERTE: IMPRENTA DEL ESTADO LIBRE DE OCCIDENTE, 1825.

[i–ii, ii blank], 1–8, [9–10 blank]. 20.5 x 15 cm. Folded, unbound.

Ref.:

The mint provided for in this document was not completed.

3063 OCCIDENTE, MEXICO

[Broadside] DISCURSO PRONUNCIADO POR EL CIUDADANO DIPUTADO DEL ESTADO DE OCCIDENTE, TENIENTE, CORONEL CARLO CRUZ DE ECHEVERRIA, EN LA SESION DEL 6 DE JUNIO DE 1828. SENOR. DESDE EL MOMENTO QUE TUVE EL HONOR DE SER ELECTO REPRESENTANTE POR EL DEPARTAMENTO DE ARISPE, EN ESTA LEGISLATURA, FUE EL ASUNTO DE DIVISION EL PRIMERO DE QUE ME OCUPE; Y DESDE LUEGO CREI DE MI DEBER ECSAMINAR EN ESTA PARTE A AQUELLOS SUGETOS QUE EN MI CONCEPTO POSEIAN BUENOS SENTIMIENTOS EN FAVOR DE LA FELICIDAD DE ESTADO . . . CARLOS CRUZ DE ECHEVERRIA. IMPRENTA DEL SUPREMO GOBIERNO DEL ESTADO DE OCCIDENTE.

Broadside, 31.5 x 21.6 cm. Text, 22.2 x 13.1 cm.

Ref.:

Printed at Concepción de Alamos.

Carlos Cruz de Echeverria, as representative for Arizpe, protested the division of the state of Occidente into the Territory of the Californias, and the states of Sonora and Sinaloa.

3064 OCCIDENTE, MEXICO

MANIFIESTO QUE A LOS PUEBLOS DE SU ESTADO DIRIJE EL CONGRESO DE OCCIDENTE, SOBRE LA CONDUCTA POLITICA DEL CIUDADANO FRANCISCO IRIARTE, EN EL TIEMPO QUE OBTUVO EL GOBIERNO DEL MISMO ESTADO. ESTADO DE OCCIDENTE: CONCEPCION DE ALAMOS IMPRENTA DEL SUPREMO GOBIERNO, 1829.

[*]¹, [1–3]², a–e², f¹, [*]¹. [1]–32, [33–34 blank]. 28 x 18.2 cm. Sewn, but first and last leaves (conjugates) a wraparound.

Ref.:

Included with this manifesto about the political conduct of Francisco Iriarte is a series of documents (pages 15–32) relating to the various steps by which Iriarte was removed from his office as Vice-Governor and declared ineligible for re-election. The episode was part of the struggle over the divisions of Occidente.

The present manifesto is signed on page 14: Concepcion de Alamos 21 de Enero de 1829. = Demetrio / Soto, diputado Presidente, = Ignacio Arriola, diputado srio. = Fran-/cisco Delgado, diputado srio. /

3065 OCCIDENTE, MEXICO. Congreso

[Broadsheet] MANIFIESTO DEL HONORABLE CONGRESO, A LOS HABITANTES DEL ESTADO SENORENSES: AL PRESENTAROS EL CONGRESO DEL ESTADO EL CODIGO SAGRADO DE VUESTRAS LIBERTADES, SE HA CREIDO EN EL DEBER DE DIRIGIROS LA PALABRA PARA ANUNCIAROS CON SENCILLEZ, QUE SOLO UN RESPETO SANTO Y RELIGIOSO A VUESTRA VOLUNTAD PUDO OBLIGARLO A EMPRENDER ESA GRANDE OBRA QUE SIRVIENDO DE BASE INDESTRUCTIBLE AL GRANDIOSO EDIFICIO DE VUESTRA SOCIEDAD, DEBIERA CON FIARSE A MANOS MAS DIESTRAS, QUE LLEVARAN A SU TERMINO LA PERFECION DE VUESTROS VOTOS: . . . FUERTE 31 DE OCTUBRE DE 1825. MANUEL ESCALANTE Y ARVIZU. PRESIDENTE. JOSE FRANCISCO VELASCO, DIPUTADO SRIO. ANTONIO FERNANDEZ ROXO, DIPUTADO SRIO. FUERTE 1825. IMPRENTA DEL GOBIERNO DEL ESTADO LIBRE DE OCCIDENTE, A CARGO DEL CIUDADANO JOSE FELIPE GOMEZ.

Broadsheet, 28.8 x 19.7 cm.

Ref.:

Statement from the Congress presenting a code of laws protecting the liberties of the citizens of Occidente.

3066 OCCIDENTE, MEXICO. Gobernador
(José Maria Gaxiola)

[Broadsheet] EL GOBERNADOR DEL ESTADO DE OCCIDENTE A SUS HABITANTES CONCIUDADANOS: ESTA ES LA SEGUNDA VEZ QUE OS DIRIJO LA PALABRA IMPELIDO DE UNA CAUSA QUE NOS ES COMUN . . . CONCEPCION DE ALAMOS CAPITAL DEL ESTADO DE OCCIDENTE OCTUBRE 5 DE 1828. JOSE MARIA GAXIOLA.

Broadsheet, 30.5 x 20.8 cm.
Ref.:
Printed at Concepción de Alamos.

In this proclamation, Governor Gaxiola recommends that Occidente shall take no decisive stand for or against General Santa Ana and suggests that the people of the state remain calm, and seek only Independence, Federation, Liberty, or Death.

3067 O'CONNOR, HENRY

HISTORY OF THE FIRST REGIMENT OF IOWA VOLUNTEERS . . . MUSCATINE: PRINTED AT THE FAUST FIRST PREMIUM PRINTING HOUSE, 1862.

[1]–24. 21.8 x 14 cm. Orange printed wrappers with title on front wrapper.
Ref.:
O'Connor was a Private in Company "A."

3068 OCTAGON SETTLEMENT COMPANY, THE

[Broadside] THE OCTAGON PLAN OF SETTLEMENT, ORIGINATED BY HENRY S. CLUBB . . . NEW YORK: PUBLISHED BY FOWLERS & WELLS.

Broadside, 56.5 x 43.2 cm. Text, 50 x 38.4 cm. Folded and tipped to maroon cloth covers, 15 x 9.6 cm., blind embossed and with white printed paper label on front cover.
Ref.:
The printer's name appears as Fowlers on the broadside and on the front cover, but in the pamphlet on the Octagon Settlement Company, the printer's name is given as Fowler.

Published after 1865.

3069 OCTAGON SETTLEMENT COMPANY, THE

THE OCTAGON SETTLEMENT COMPANY, KANZAS, CONTAINING FULL INFORMATION FOR INQUIRERS. NEW YORK: PUBLISHED FOR THE COMPANY BY FOWLER & WELLS.

[1]–14, [stub of 15–16]. 21.8 x 13.8 cm. White printed wrappers with title on front wrapper. Removed from bound volume.
Ref.:
The missing pages [15–16] may have been blank since page 14 could be the final page of text.

The pamphlet is undated. Published after 1865.

There is a map of the settlement on the front wrapper.

3070 O'DONOVAN, JEREMIAH

A BRIEF ACCOUNT OF THE AUTHOR'S INTERVIEW WITH HIS COUNTRYMEN, AND OF THE PARTS OF THE EMERALD ISLE WHENCE THEY EMIGRATED. TOGETHER WITH A DIRECT REFERENCE TO THEIR PRESENT LOCATION IN THE LAND OF THEIR ADOPTION, DURING HIS TRAVELS THROUGH VARIOUS STATES OF THE UNION IN 1854 AND 1855 . . . PITTSBURGH, PA.: PUBLISHED BY THE AUTHOR, 1864.

[1]–382. 18.1 x 11.3 cm. Blue marbled boards, dark blue leather back, title in gilt on backstrip.
Ref.: Buck 436; Howes O24; Hubach p. 106

O'Donovan went as far west as the Mississippi (St. Louis to Galena), but spent most of his time in the Old Northwest.

3071 O'FALLON, BENJAMIN, WILLIAM GORDON, & OTHERS

. . . DOCUMENTS ACCOMPANYING THE MESSAGE OF THE PRESIDENT OF THE UNITED STATES, TO BOTH HOUSES, AT THE COMMENCEMENT OF THE FIRST SESSION OF THE EIGHTEENTH CONGRESS . . . WASHINGTON: PRINTED BY GALES & SEATON, 1823.

[1]–109, [110 blank]. 22.2 x 13.5 cm. 20 folding tables and charts inserted. Nineteenth century marbled boards with sheep corners and backstrip, black leather label on backstrip.
Ref.: Howes D385; Wagner-Camp 22

18th Congress, 1st Session, Senate, Document No. 2, Serial 89.

Contains correspondence relative to the Hostilities with the Arickaree Indians, Document L, pages 55–108. Letters and reports by Benjamin O'Fallon, William Gordon, and William H. Ashley are included.

3072 O'FERRALL, SIMON A.

A RAMBLE OF SIX THOUSAND MILES THROUGH THE UNITED STATES OF AMERICA . . . LONDON: PUBLISHED BY EFFINGHAM WILSON, 1832.

[i]–xii, [1]–360. 22.2 x 14.2 cm. Frontispiece. Gray boards, green cloth backstrip, white printed paper label, 5.7 x 3 cm., uncut.
Ref.: Buck 245; Clark III 80; Howes F83; Hubach p. 69; Sabin 24161

The author's real name was O'Ferrall, although he uses Ferrall on the title page.

O'Ferrall came to his country as a visitor looking for novelty. "As the Americans always allowed me to act as I thought proper, and even to laugh at such of their habits as I thought singular, I am by no means inclined to take exception to them."

3073 OFFICERS OF THE WAR OF 1812

[Caption title] BOUNTY LANDS TO THE REGULAR AND VOLUNTEER OFFICERS OF THE WAR OF 1812. AT AN ADJOURNED MEETING OF THE OFFICERS OF THE WAR OF 1812, HELD IN THE CITY OF WASHINGTON ON THE 6TH OF APRIL, 1850, . . .

[1]–12. 22.2 x 14.5 cm. Stabbed, unbound.
Ref.:
Signed at the end: C.S.Todd, Chairman. / John G. Camp, Secretary. /

3074 OFFICIAL GUIDE TO THE KLONDYKE, THE

THE OFFICIAL GUIDE TO THE KLONDYKE COUNTRY AND THE GOLD FIELDS OF ALASKA WITH THE OFFICIAL MAPS . . . CHICAGO: W. B. CONKEY COMPANY, 1898.

[13]–296. 19.4 x 13.6 cm. Seven maps and 38 illustrations listed. Pictorial wrappers with title on front wrapper, advertisements on verso of front and recto and verso of back wrapper.
Ref.: Howes K205; Smith 7533; Wickersham 3906
The seven maps are all printed on both sides of one sheet inserted at the front. The front wrapper is dated 1897.
Editions: Chicago, 1897.

3075 OGDEN, GEORGE W.

LETTERS FROM THE WEST, COMPRISING A TOUR THROUGH THE WESTERN COUNTRY, AND A RESIDENCE OF TWO SUMMERS IN THE STATES OF OHIO AND KENTUCKY: ORIGINALLY WRITTEN IN LETTERS TO A BROTHER . . . NEW-BEDFORD: PUBLISHED BY MELCHER & ROGERS, 1823.*

[i]–iv, [5]–126. 17.1 x 10.4 cm. Polished green calf, gilt, gilt top.
Ref.: Buck 172; Clark II 224; Howes O35; Jones 853; Sabin 56806; Thomson 881

3076 [OGDEN, PETER S.]

TRAITS OF AMERICAN-INDIAN LIFE AND CHARACTER . . . LONDON: SMITH, ELDER AND CO., 1853.
[i]–[xv], [xvi blank], [1]–218, [219 colophon, 220 blank], [1]–16 advertisements dated April, 1853. 19.8 x 12 cm. Reddish brown cloth, blind embossed borders on sides, title in gilt on backstrip, uncut.
Ref.: Field 1562; Howes F139; Smith 7539; Staton & Tremaine 2218
The work has been attributed also to Duncan Finlayson. Library of Congress attributes it to Ogden. Staton & Tremaine enter it under title.

3077 OGDEN HOUSE, Council Bluffs, Iowa

[Broadside] COMPLIMENTARY, OGDEN HOUSE OPENING AND RECEPTION. COUNCIL BLUFFS, IOWA, DEC. 22ND 1869. B. F. MONTGOMERY, SEC'Y. GEN. G.M.DODGE, CHAIR,N TO

Broadside, 7.6 x 12 cm., on stiff card.
Ref.:
Engraved. In manuscript on verso: G M Dodge / Chn /.

3078 OGDEN HOUSE, Council Bluffs, Iowa

1869. [monogram OH] 1876. GRAND FORMAL OPENING OF THE NEW OGDEN HOUSE, COUNCIL BLUFFS, IOWA, THURSDAY EVENING, NOVEMBER 16, 1876. YOURSELF AND LADIES ARE CORDIALLY INVITED. TICKETS, ADMITTING GENTLEMAN AND LADIES, 5.00. GEORGE T. PHELPS, PROPRIETOR. FRANK H. POINDEXTER, MANAGER. NONPAREIL STEAM PRINT.

[1–4]. 16.7 x 14.4 cm. Unbound folded leaflet, enclosed in envelope with view of Ogden House on large flap, printed in gold.
Prov.: Addressed on face of envelope: Gustavus S. Lawrence Esq /.
Ref.:

3079 OGLE, A. J., of Pennsylvania

[Caption title] REMARKS OF MR. OGLE, OF PENNSYLVANIA, ON THE CIVIL AND DIPLOMATIC APPROPRIATION BILL . . . APRIL 14, 1840 . . .
1–32. Bound with Number 1084.
Ref.: Sabin 56841
Printed at Washington in 1840.

3080 O'HANLON, JOHN

LIFE AND SCENERY IN MISSOURI. REMINISCENCES OF A MISSIONARY PRIEST . . . DUBLIN: JAMES DUFFY & CO., LTD., 1890.
[i]–xii, [1]–292, [293–96 advertisements]. 14.7 x 9.3 cm. Dark green cloth, single fillets on sides, gilt harp on front cover, gilt title on backstrip.
Ref.: Howes O46; Rader 2501

3081 OHIO [Colorado] MINING DISTRICT

[Broadside] NO. [in manuscript: Three] OHIO MINING DISTRICT, COLORADO TERRITORY. BE IT KNOWN, THAT [in manuscript: Jas. W. Hamilton] HAS RECORDED [in manuscript: one] MINING CLAIM . . . GIVEN UNDER MY HAND AT MY OFFICE, THIS [in manuscript: Twenty-ninth] DAY OF [in manuscript: May] A. D., 1861. [in manuscript: Thomas Harper] RECORDER. [in manuscript: J. Paul Gwinn] DEPUTY.

Broadside, 11.5 x 17.4 cm. Text, 9.9 x 16.1 cm.
Ref.:
Claim No. 3 West, Young Lode.

3082 OKLAHOMA. INFORMATION FOR CONGRESS.

OKLAHOMA. INFORMATION FOR CONGRESS. TOWN-SITE FRAUDS. DON'T LEGALIZE TOWN ACTS, NOR GIVE THEM ANY FORCE: COPIES OF ORDINANCES, JUDGEMENTS[!] AND RECORDS. OKLAHOMA CITY DAILY TIMES PRINT. 1889.

[i–ii, ii blank], [1]–19, [20 blank]. 20.8 x 14.9 cm. Stitched, unbound.

Ref.: Foreman p. 257; Hargrett (*Oklahoma*) 660

3083 OKLAHOMA WAR-CHIEF

[Broadside] OKLAHOMA WAR-CHIEF. THE OKLA-HOMA WAR-CHIEF WILL RESUME PUBLICATION, AS A BREEZY NEWSPAPER, SATURDAY, APRIL 16TH, 1884 . . . ADDRESS W. F. GORDON, (FOR THE PRESENT) ARKANSAS CITY, KANSAS.

Broadside, 7.4 x 20.3 cm. Text, 5.5 x 19 cm. Lower edge unevenly cut.

Ref.:

3084 OLD, ROBERT O.

COLORADO: UNITED STATES, AMERICA. ITS HIS-TORY, GEOGRAPHY, AND MINING . . . LONDON: PUBLISHED UNDER THE AUSPICES OF THE BRITISH AND COLORADO MINING BUREAU.

[1]–64. 20 x 13.2 cm. Folded map: Map of / Colorado / Territory / United States / Pub: by the / British & Colorado Mining / Bureau.—London. / 17.5 x 22.1 cm. No scale given. Removed from bound volume, unbound.

Ref.: Howes O58; Sabin 57110; Wilcox p. 64
Published in 1869.

3085 OLD SETTLERS' ASSOCIATION OF MINNESOTA

A SKETCH OF THE ORGANIZATION, OBJECTS AND MEMBERSHIP OF THE OLD SETTLERS' ASSOCIATION OF MINNESOTA; . . . SAINT PAUL: RAMALEY, CHANEY & CO., 1872.

[1]–29, [30–32 blank]. 21 x 14.4 cm. Lavender printed wrappers, with title on front wrapper, list of officers on verso of back wrapper.

Prov.: Inscribed in pencil down fore-edge margin of front wrapper: Hist. and Phil. Soc. of O. / from Capt. Wm McK. Heath. / Numerals 3312 in red at top of front cover.

Ref.:

3086 OLD SETTLERS OF MUSCATINE, Iowa

[Caption title] OLD SETTLERS' ANNIVERSARY. PICNIC AND EXCURSION TO THE MOUTH OF PINE CREEK—LIST OF THE EXCURSIONISTS—SPEECHES, &C . . .

[1]–7, [8 blank]. 24.1 x 15.5 cm. Unbound leaflet.

Prov.: Rubber stamp of T.S.Parvin on page [1]: Sep. 14, 1886.

Ref.:

Neither place nor date of publication is indicated. Probably printed at Muscatine, certainly in late 1886.

3087 OLD SETTLERS OF MUSCATINE, Iowa

[Caption title] OLD SETTLER'S CELEBRATION OF IOWA'S SEMI-CENTENNIAL HELD JULY 4TH, 1888, IN COURT HOUSE SQUARE, MUSCATINE,—IOWA . . .*

[1–6], [7–8 blank]. 24.1 x 15.5 cm. Unbound, folded leaflet, unopened.

Ref.:

Neither place nor date indicated, but probably Muscatine, 1888.

3088 OLD SETTLERS OF MUSCATINE, Iowa

[Caption title] OLD SETTLERS' REUNION, HELD AT THE FAIR GROUNDS, MUSCATINE, IOWA, TUESDAY, AUGUST 30, 1898 . . .*

[1]–8. 24 x 15.8 cm. Unbound, folded leaflet, unopened.

Ref.:

Contains a history of the Old Settlers of Muscatine. Probably printed at Muscatine.

3089 OLDEN TIME, THE

THE OLDEN TIME; A MONTHLY PUBLICATION, DEVOTED TO THE PRESERVATION OF DOCUMENTS AND OTHER AUTHENTIC INFORMATION IN RELATION TO THE EARLY EXPLORATIONS, AND THE SETTLEMENT AND IMPROVEMENT OF THE COUNTRY AROUND THE HEAD OF THE OHIO . . . PITTSBURGH: PRINTED BY DUMARS & CO., 1846 [–1848].

[i]–viii, [1]–576. (Pages 301 and 381 mispaginated 381 and 181.] [i]–iv, [1]–572. (Pages 111, 201, 233, 239, 508 mispaginated 11, 20, 23, 236, and o8. Four leaves misbound as follows: 443–44, 441–42, 447–48, 445–46.) 22.7 x 14.2 cm. Folding plate, plan in text, and map: Braddock's Route / A. D. 1755. / Drawn by Middleton / [below neat line, at right:] Gillespie Sc. Pitts'g / 15.6 x 23.5 cm. Scale: 12 miles to one inch. Folding plate bound at page 288 instead of after [336]. Two volumes, rebound in marbled boards, calf backs, black skiver labels.

Ref.: Bay p. 397; Field 381; Howes C846; Sabin 17365; Thomson 892

An invaluable work. "The first edition is seldom found complete with the final number, many copies having been confiscated at the printer's on a creditor's writ."—Howes. Edited by Neville B. Craig.

3090 OLDROYD, OSBURN H.

THE ASSASSINATION OF ABRAHAM LINCOLN . . .
WASHINGTON, D. C.: O. H. OLDROYD, MDCCCCI.

i]–xviii, [1]–305, [306 blank], [307–08 advertisements]. 19.7 x 13.1 cm. 82 illustrations and one map listed. Olive-green cloth.
Prov.: Bookplate of C.G.Littell.
Ref.:

3091 OLIPHANT, LAURENCE

MINNESOTA AND THE FAR WEST . . . EDINBURGH:
WILLIAM BLACKWOOD AND SONS, MDCCCLV.

[i]–[xiv], [1]–306, [1]–16 advertisements. 22.1 x 14.1 cm. 16 illustrations and folding map listed. Map: Map / of the / North-Western Provinces of America / including / Minnesota. / By W. & A. K. Johnston, Edinburgh. / English Miles / [diagrammatic scale: about 85 miles to an inch] /. 20.3 x 26.8 cm. Tan cloth, blind panels on side, gilt vignette in centre of front cover, same in blind on back cover, gilt on backstrip, uncut.
Prov.: Embossed crest through title-leaf and following leaf: lion rampant holding sword, within garter lettered Desperadum /.
Ref.: Howes O64; Sabin 57183

3092 [OLIVER, JOHN W.]

GUIDE TO THE NEW GOLD REGION OF WESTERN KANSAS AND NEBRASKA, WITH TABLE OF DISTANCES AND AN ACCURATE MAP. NEW-YORK: JOHN W. OLIVER, STEAM JOB PRINTER, 1859.

[1]–32. 14.5 x 11.5 cm. Map: Map of Routes to the / Gold Region of Western Kansas / Compiled from / Maps of the United States, / and / Berthoud's Map of the U.S. Surveys, / of Territories West of the / Missouri River / 1859 /. [lower centre:] Lith. of J. W. Oliver 43 Ann St. N.Y. / [lower right:] Fr. Heppenheimer / 15.2 x 81.6 cm. No scale given. Cream printed wrappers with title on front wrapper, woodcut on verso of back wrapper: View of Pike's Peak. / In a brown morocco-backed folding box.
Ref.: Hafen 9; Howes O69; Sabin 29210; Wagner-Camp 337; Wilcox p. 85

3093 OLIVER, WILLIAM

EIGHT MONTHS IN ILLINOIS; WITH INFORMATION TO EMIGRANTS . . . NEWCASTLE UPON TYNE: PRINTED BY WILLIAM ANDREW MITCHELL, MDCCCXLIII.

[1–6], [I]–IV, [1]–141, [142 colophon]. 19.2 x 10.2 cm. Blue cloth, title in gilt on backstrip, uncut. In a green cloth case.
Ref.: Bay p. 333; Buck 375; Clark II 219; Howes O71; Jones 1078; Sabin 57214

3094 OLMSTED, FREDERICK L.

THE COTTON KINGDOM: A TRAVELLER'S OBSERVATIONS ON COTTON AND SLAVERY IN THE AMERICAN SLAVE STATES . . . NEW YORK: PUBLISHED BY MASON BROTHERS, 1861.

[i]–viii, [1]–376. [i]–iv, [1]–404. 18.6 x 12.5 cm. Map: A Map of / The Cotton Kingdom / and its Dependencies / in America. / [13 lines] / Fred. Law Olmsted. / [lower left:] D. McLellan Lith. 26 Spruce St N. Y. [lower right:] New York—Mason Brothers. / 24.1 x 43 cm. No scale given. Two volumes, brown embossed cloth, title in gilt on backstrips.
Ref.: Clark III 481–82 see; De Renne p. 636; Howes O76; Sabin 572401[!] [i.e., 57240]

3095 OLMSTED, FREDERICK L.

A JOURNEY IN THE BACK COUNTRY . . . NEW YORK: MASON BROTHERS, 1860.

[i]–xvi, [11]–492. 18.4 x 12.6 cm. Dark blue embossed cloth, title in gilt on backstrip.
Ref.: Clark III 481; Howes O77; Sabin 57241
Half-title reads: Our Slave States. / III. /
. . . one of the most important observers of Southern life in the ante bellum period.—Clark

3096 OLMSTED, FREDERICK L.

A JOURNEY IN THE SEABOARD SLAVE STATES, WITH REMARKS ON THEIR ECONOMY . . . NEW YORK: DIX & EDWARDS, 1856.

[iii]–[xvi], [1]–[724]. 19.5 x 12.8 cm. Green embossed cloth, title in gilt on backstrip, uncut.
Ref.: Clark III 482; De Renne pp. 580–81; Howes O78; Sabin 57242
The half-title reads: Our Slave States. / This is the first of three volumes with this general title. In the present instance, the same title is used on the backstrip.

3097 OLMSTED, FREDERICK L.

A JOURNEY THROUGH TEXAS . . . NEW YORK: DIX, EDWARDS & CO., 1857.

[1–2], [i]–xxxiv, [1]–516. 18.7 x 12.7 cm. Frontispiece and map. Map / of Part of the State of / Texas. / Prepared by J. H. Colton & Co. / New York. / 18.7 x 22.8 cm. No scale given. Brown cloth, blind embossed sides, gilt title on backstrip, advertisements on endpapers.
Ref.: Clark III 481–82 see; Howes O79; Rader 2549; Raines p. 159; Sabin 57243
Half-title reads: Our Slave States. / II. /
No better book yet written of travels in Texas; and by an intelligent student of our industrial system.—Raines

3098 OLMSTED, JOHN

A TRIP TO CALIFORNIA IN 1868 . . . NEW YORK: TROW'S PRINTING AND BOOKBINDING COMPANY, 1880.*

[i]–vi, [7]–131, [132 blank]. 16.8 x 11 cm. Blue cloth, title stamped in gilt on front cover.

Ref.: Cowan, p. 463; Howes O80

Uncopyrighted, issued for private circulation.

3099 OLSHAUSEN, THEODOR

DER STAAT IOWA; GEOGRAPHISCH UND STA- TISTISCH . . . KIEL: AKADEMISCHE BUCHHAND- LUNG, 1855.*

[I]–X, [1]–201, [202 blank]. 23 x 14 cm. Map: Karte des Staates Iowa / nach den besten Hülfsmitteln bearbeitet von / Th. Olshausen. / [lower centre:] Kiel, Akademische Buchhand- lung / 1855. / [lower right:] Lith. Anst. von H. Cordts, Altona / 27.6 x 43.3 cm. No scale given. Light printed green wrappers with title on front wrapper, publisher's notice inside front cover and advertisements on recto and verso of back wrapper, uncut, mostly unopened.

Prov.: Rubber stamp of S. R. Steinmetz, / Amsterdam. / on title-page, verso of map, and on page 201.

Ref.: Howes O82; Rader 2551 see; Sabin 57256 see

Facing the title-page above is a general title for the series projected: Das / Mississippi-Thal / und die einzelnen Staaten des Mississippi-Thals / geographisch und statistisch / beschrieben / von / Theodor Olshausen, / in St. Louis im Staate Missouri. / [rule] / Band II. 2te Hälfte. / Der Staat Iowa. / Mit 1 colorirten Karte. / [rule] / Kiel, / Akademische Buchhandlung. / 1855. / Only three parts in two volumes were issued.

3100 OMAHA CITY

[Map] OMAHA CITY / NEBRASKA TERRITORY / [up- per right:] ENOS LOWE / JAMES A. JACKSON / SAMUEL S. BAYLISS & Co / PROPRIETORS / [lower right:] E. ROLYN LITHOGR. N. 2. ST. N° 42 ST. LOUIS M^{o} /

Map, 69.2 x 61.9 cm. No scale given.

Ref.:

3101 OMAHA DAILY NEBRASKIAN

[Newspaper] OMAHA DAILY NEBRASKIAN. VOLUME 2. OMAHA, NEBRASKA, TUESDAY [–WEDNESDAY] MORNING, MARCH 31 [APRIL 1], 1863. NUMBER 104 [–105] . . .

Two issues, each [1–4]. 32.5 x 25 cm. Two issues, unbound.

Ref.:

The publisher and proprietor was M. H. Clark and the editor was M. W. Reynolds.

Contains "Sketch of a Trip from Omaha to Salmon River" by Daniel McLaughlin. Published by EDG in 1954.

3102 OMAHA DAILY NEBRASKIAN

[Newspaper] OMAHA DAILY NEBRASKIAN. VOL- UME 2. OMAHA, NEBRASKA, WEDNESDAY MORNING, SEPTEMBER 2, 1863. NUMBER 229 . . .

[1–4]. 33 x 25.3 cm. Unbound.

Ref.:

In addition to Civil War news, this issue of the paper contains: Statement / Made by / Judge Cyrus Tator / From the Scaffold upon which he was / Executed, Aug. 28th, 1863, for the / Murder of Issac H. Neff! /.

3103 OMAHA GYMNASIUM CLUB

ARTICLES OF INCORPORATION OF THE OMAHA GYM- NASIUM CLUB. ADOPTED MARCH 21, 1878. OMAHA, NEB.: REPUBLICAN BOOK AND JOB PRINTING HOUSE, 1878.

[1]–[12]. 13.3 x 8.5 cm. Pink printed wrappers, with title on front wrapper. Pencil score on back cover.

Ref.:

Tipped to the inside front wrapper is a small card, with manuscript note as follows: Compli- ments of A. Cane / For Woodford Contest / Friday Eve, 8 P.M. / (Present at door) Admit two. /

3104 OMAHA HIGH SCHOOL

OMAHA HIGH SCHOOL, CLASS OF '76 GRADUATING EXERCISES, IN THE AUDITORIUM OF THE HIGH SCHOOL BUILDING, THURSDAY EVENING, JUNE 22, 1876. EXERCISES TO COMMENCE AT 7:30 O'CLOCK. C. F. CATLIN, PRINTER, OMAHA.

[1–4]. 16.8 x 10.6 cm. Unbound, folded leaflet.

Ref.: AII (*Nebraska*) 426

With duplicate of pages [3–4].

Text printed in red and black.

3105 OMAHA HIGH SCHOOL LITERARY & DEBATING SOCIETY

[Broadside] SECOND ANNIVERSARY OF THE HIGH SCHOOL LITERARY & DEBATING SOCIETY, FRIDAY EVENING, NOV. 27, 1874 . . . G. W. GRAY, PRINTER, OMAHA.

Broadside, 17.6 x 11 cm. Text, 14.2 x 10.2 cm.

Ref.:

Programme.

3106 OMAHA HIGH SCHOOL LITERARY SOCIETY

HIGH SCHOOL LITERARY SOCIETY. CLOSING EX-
ERCISES. FRIDAY EVENING, JUNE 25, 1875. G. W.
GRAY, PRINTER, OMAHA.

[1–4]. 17.9 x 10.2 cm. Unbound, folded leaflet.
Ref.:
Title on page [1], programme on page [3],
others blank.

3107 OMAHA, NEBRASKA

NOTE FOR ONE DOLLAR, issued by the City of
Omaha, Nebraska. Signed by H. C. Anderson
and Jesse Lowe. Dated October, 1857. Numbered A No. 4987. Engraved by Wellstood, Hay
& Whiting, New York. 7.2 x 18.2 cm.

3108 OMAHA, NEBRASKA

NOTE FOR THREE DOLLARS, issued by the City of
Omaha, Nebraska. Signed by H. C. Anderson
and Jesse Lowe. Dated November 15, 1857.
Numbered No. 5351 A. Engraved by Wellstood,
Hay & Whiting, New York. 7.2 x 18.2 cm.

3109 OMAHA, NEBRASKA

NOTE FOR FIVE DOLLARS, issued by the City of
Omaha, Nebraska. Signed by H. C. Anderson
and Jesse Lowe. Dated December 1, 1857. Numbered No. 5790 A. Engraved by Wellstood, Hay
& Whiting, New York. 7.2 x 18.2 cm.

3110 OMAHA NEBRASKIAN, THE

[Newspaper] THE OMAHA NEBRASKIAN . . . VOL-
UME 3. OMAHA, NEBRASKA, WEDNESDAY MORNING,
JUNE 24, 1857. NUMBER 22 . . .

[1–4]. 66.6 x 51.2 cm. Unbound.
Ref.:
The editor was T. H. Robertson. Contains a
long article on the Dakota country.

3111 OMAHA PUBLIC SCHOOLS

[Caption title] ANNIVERSARY EXERCISES OF THE
OMAHA PUBLIC SCHOOLS, JUNE 1873 . . .

[1–4]. 18.4 x 12.7 cm. Unbound, folded leaflet.
Ref.: AII (*Nebraska*) 315

3112 ONDERDONK, JAMES L.

IDAHO: FACTS AND STATISTICS CONCERNING ITS
MINING, FARMING, STOCK-RAISING, LUMBERING,
AND OTHER RESOURCES AND INDUSTRIES . . . SAN
FRANCISCO, CAL.: A. L. BANCROFT & COMPANY,
1885.

[1]–150, [151–52 blank]. 22.3 x 14.6 cm. Buff
pictorial wrappers, with title on front wrapper,
publisher's imprint on back cover. In a blue
cloth case.
Prov.: C. G. Littell copy, with bookplate.
Ref.: Adams (*Ramp. Herd*) 1717; Howes O92;
Smith 7589

3113 O'NEILL, JOHN

NORTHERN NEBRASKA AS A HOME FOR IMMIGRANTS,
CONTAINING A GENERAL DESCRIPTION OF THE
STATE, SKETCHES OF NORTHERN NEBRASKA COUN-
TIES, AND ANSWERS TO CORRESPONDENCE OF IN-
TENDING IMMIGRANTS . . . SIOUX CITY, IOWA:
SIOUX CITY TIMES PRINT, 1875.

[1]–108. 21.4 x 14.5 cm. Map: Map of the State
of / Nebraska / By / J. H. Noteware / State Superintendent of Immigration / Omaha Neb^r
1875. / Approved by the State Board of Immigration / [three lines] / Entered according to Act
of Congress, in the year 1873 by G. W. & C. B.
Colton & Co. in the Clerks Office of the District
Court of the United States, for the Eastern District of New York. / [lower centre:] Prepared by
G. W. & C. B. Colton & Co 172 William Street
New York. / 39 x 66 cm. Scale: 18 miles to one
inch. *Inset:* Map showing the Railroad Routes
between / the Seaboard and Nebraska. /
6.3 x 50.7 cm. Scale: 100 miles to one inch. Pale
green wrappers, with title on front wrapper, advertisements on recto of front and recto and
verso of back wrapper.
Prov.: Embossed stamp of Kansas State Library removed from title-leaf and second leaf.
Ref.: Adams (*Ramp. Herd*) 1719; Howes O97
Account of the Platte River and Black Hills
Country, written from investigations made while
seeking a site for an Irish colony.—Howes

3114 ONSTOT, THOMAS G.

PIONEERS OF MENARD AND MASON COUNTIES,
MADE UP OF PERSONAL REMINISCENCES OF AN
EARLY LIFE IN MENARD COUNTY, WHICH WE
GATHERED IN A SALEM LIFE FROM 1830 TO 1840,
AND A PETERSBURG LIFE FROM 1840 TO 1850; IN-
CLUDING PERSONAL REMINISCENCES OF ABRAHAM
LINCOLN AND PETER CARTRIGHT . . . FOREST CITY,
ILLINOIS: PUBLISHED BY T. G. ONSTOT, 1902.

[3]–400. 22 x 14.8 cm. Ten illustrations listed.
Blue cloth, blind embossed panels on front
cover, title stamped in white on front cover and
backstrip.
Ref.: Bradford 4098; Buck 979, 985; Howes
O100
Almost the entire edition burned.—Howes

3115 OPPOSITION NOT FACTION . . .

OPPOSITION NOT FACTION: OR, THE RECTITUDE OF
THE PRESENT PARLIAMENTARY OPPOSITION TO THE
PRESENT EXPENSIVE MEASURES, JUSTIFIED BY REA-
SON AND FACTS . . . LONDON: PRINTED FOR
M. COOPER, 1743.

[A]–H^4. [1]–63, [64 blank]. 19.4 x 11.7 cm.
Bound with five other contemporary pamphlets
in marbled boards and sheepskin backstrip.

Prov.: Bookplate of John Hales Calcraft.

Written in reply to Lord Egmont's *Faction Detected* . . . London, 1743.

Bound with the following:

[CHESTERFIELD, PHILIP DORMER STANHOPE, 4TH EARL OF]. An Apology for a Late Resignation . . . London: John Freeman [1748].

VERAX, *pseud.* An Expostulatory Epistle to the Welch[!] Knight . . . London: J. Robinson, 1745.

[EGMONT, JOHN PERCEVAL, 2ND EARL OF]. An Examination of the Principles, and an Enquiry into the Conduct, of the Two B*****rs . . . London: A. Price, 1749.

FURTHER REPORT, A . . . A Further Report from the Committee of Secrecy, Appointed to Enquire into the Conduct of Robert, Earl of Orford . . . London: T. Leech, 1742.

WASHINGTON, GEORGE. The Journal of Major George Washington . . . London: T. Jefferys, 1754.

3116 ORDWAY, JOHN

. . . THE JOURNALS OF CAPTAIN MERIWETHER LEWIS AND SERGEANT JOHN ORDWAY . . . 1803–1806. EDITED . . . BY MILO M. QUAIFE. MADISON: STATE HISTORICAL SOCIETY OF WISCONSIN, 1916.

[1]–444. 24 x 17 cm. 13 illustrations listed. Blue buckram.

Ref.:

3117 ORDWAY'S RECORD

[Newspaper] ORDWAY'S RECORD. VOL. I. SIOUX FALLS, D. T., SEPTEMBER, 1881. NO. 1 . . .

[1–4]. 45.6 x 30.3 cm. Unbound.

Ref.:

An anti-Ordway publication giving utterance to various accusations and charges against Ordway's political record and conduct.—EDG

3118 OREGON. Adjutant General (Cyrus A. Reed)

REPORT OF THE ADJUTANT GENERAL OF THE STATE OF OREGON, FOR THE YEARS 1865–6. SALEM, OREGON: HENRY L. PITTOCK, STATE PRINTER, 1866.

[1]–353, [354 blank]. 22.1 x 13.8 cm. Marbled boards, black roan back.

Prov.: Inscribed on verso of back endleaf: Compliments of / Cyrus A. Reed / Adjt Genl of / Oregon /.

Ref.: McMurtrie (*Oregon*) 348; Sabin 57569

Errata slip, 8.9 x 13 cm., tipped in at the end. Small (4.2 x 6.3 cm.) label on inside front cover: From / H. P. Cramer & Co.'s / Book Bindery / —and— / Blank Book Manufactory. / Portland, Oregon. / [within decorative border] /.

3119 OREGON. Governor (Lafayette F. Grover)

REPORT OF GOVERNOR GROVER TO GENERAL SCHOFIELD ON THE MODOC WAR, AND REPORTS OF MAJ. GEN. JOHN F. MILLER AND GENERAL JOHN E. ROSS, TO THE GOVERNOR. ALSO LETTER OF THE GOVERNOR TO THE SECRETARY OF THE INTERIOR ON THE WALLOWA VALLEY INDIAN QUESTION. SALEM, OREGON: MART. V. BROWN, STATE PRINTER, 1874.

[1]–68. 20.6 x 13.3 cm. Removed from bound volume, unbound.

Ref.:

3120 OREGON. State Board of Immigration

OREGON AS IT IS. PUBLISHED FOR GRATUITOUS DISTRIBUTION, BY THE STATE BOARD OF IMMIGRATION. A BRIEF DESCRIPTION OF THE STATE, CONTAINING ACCURATE AND TRUSTWORTHY INFORMATION FOR THOSE SEEKING NEW HOMES IN A MILD AND HEALTHFUL CLIMATE, OR THE BEST FIELDS FOR INVESTMENT OF CAPITAL. PORTLAND, NOV., 1885.

[1]–64. 20.5 x 14.6 cm. Tan printed wrappers, with title on front wrapper, newspaper Directory on recto of back wrapper, listing 75 newspapers and magazines, text on verso front wrapper. In red cloth case.

Ref.:

Adams (*Ramp. Herd*) describes an 1887 edition of 112 pages.

3121 OREGON TERRITORY. Commissioner to Collect the Laws and Archives of Oregon

THE OREGON ARCHIVES: INCLUDING THE JOURNALS, GOVERNORS' MESSAGES AND PUBLIC PAPERS OF OREGON, FROM THE EARLIEST ATTEMPT ON THE PART OF THE PEOPLE TO FORM A GOVERNMENT, DOWN TO, AND INCLUSIVE OF THE SESSION OF THE TERRITORIAL LEGISLATURE, HELD IN THE YEAR 1849 . . . SALEM: ASAHEL BUSH, PUBLIC PRINTER, 1853.

[1]–[335], [336 blank]. 21.8 x 14 cm. Buff printed front wrapper with title on front wrapper, bound into half red morocco.

Prov.: James Wickersham's copy with bookplate. Presentation copy from Elwood Evans to Robert Newell on front wrapper: o–o, No. 3. / Hon Robert Newell / with fraternal regards of / Elwood Evans / [underline] / [at left:] E. Evans. / Signature on title page: Elwood Evans /

Ref.: Howell 122; Howes G447; Jones 1300; McMurtrie (*Oregon*) 73; Sabin 57558

Page [334]: Note—The law creating the office of commissioner to collect the "Oregon Archives" and prepare the same for publication, made provision for including therein the Journals of the Legislative Assembly of Oregon, of the session begun and held in 1849; but, by joint resolution of the said assembly, held in the winter of 1853-4, just previous to the completion of this work, the journals of 1849 were ordered to be printed in pamphlet form, by themselves, and, consequently, will not be found in this volume, as by the title indicated. L. F. G., Commissioner.

3122 OREGON TERRITORY. Legislative Assembly

CORRESPONDENCE AND OFFICIAL PROCEEDINGS RELATING TO THE EXPEDITIONS AGAINST THE INDIANS . . . SALEM, OREGON: ASAHEL BUSH, TERRITORIAL PRINTER, 1855.

[1]–68. 20.8 x 14.6 cm. Removed from bound volume, unbound. Remnants of cream wrappers on backstrip.

Ref.: McMurtrie (*Oregon*) 91

4000 copies were ordered printed by the House.

3123 OREGON TERRITORY. Militia (Board of Enrollment)

[Broadside] INSTRUCTIONS TO ENROLLING OFFICERS. BOARD OF ENROLLMENT, HEADQUARTERS, PROVOST MARSHAL . . .

Broadside, 33 x 19.1 cm. Text, 30.6 x 16 cm.

Ref.:

Filled in in manuscript for the 1st District, Oregon, September 21, 1863, addressed to L. L. Williams, and signed at the end by two members of the Board, Julius M. Keeler and Joseph W. Drew. Inserted in Manuscript Journals of Loren L. Williams, Volume III.

3124 OREGON CONVENTION, Cincinnati, Ohio

APPENDIX TO SENATE JOURNAL. PROCEEDINGS OF THE OREGON CONVENTION, HELD IN CINCINNATI ON THE THIRD, FOURTH AND FIFTH DAYS OF JULY, 1843 . . .

[1]–45, [46 blank]. 22.1 x 16 cm. Stabbed, unbound, uncut.

Ref.:

This is one of the more prominent evidences of agitation over the boundary of Oregon with Canada.

Published in Cincinnati in 1844.

3125 OREGON CENTRAL MILITARY ROAD COMPANY

REPORT OF THE RECENT SURVEYS AND PROGRESS OF CONSTRUCTION OF THE OREGON CENTRAL MILITARY ROAD. MADE BY B. J. PENGRA, SUPERINTENDENT. EUGENE CITY, OREGON: NOVEMBER 29, 1865.

[1]–63, [64 blank]. 21.6 x 15.4 cm. Stabbed, uncut, unbound. In blue cloth case.

Ref.: Howes P200; McMurtrie (*Oregon*) 319; Smith 7634

George N. Belknap, the Oregon bibliographer, reports that the pamphlet was printed in 1866 by A. L. Stinson at the Statesman Office in Salem.

3126 OREGON SPECTATOR

[Newspaper] OREGON SPECTATOR. VOL. I. OREGON CITY, (OREGON TER.) THURSDAY, SEPTEMBER 3, 1846. NO. 16 . . .

[1–4]. 41.1 x 18 cm. Unbound.

Ref.:

The editor and proprietor was J. Fleming.

3127 OREGONIAN, THE

[Caption title] THE OREGONIAN, AND INDIAN'S ADVOCATE. VOL. I. OCTOBER, 1838 [–AUGUST, 1839] NO. 1 [–11] . . .

[1]–352. 22.8 x 13.8 cm. Folding map: Map / of / Oregon Territory / by / Samuel Parker. / 1838. / Copy right secured. / [lower right:] Eng^d by M. M. Peabody. Utica, N. Y. / 34.5 x 58.8 cm. Scale: 130 miles to one inch. Contemporary marbled boards with leather backstrip and corners. In a red half morocco slip case.

Ref.: Howes O118; Jones 1015; Sabin 57575; Wagner-Camp 72

Published at Boston. The map was also used in Samuel Parker: *Journal of an Exploring Tour beyond the Rocky Mountains . . .* 1838 which is reviewed in Part 3.

3128 O'REILLY, HARRINGTON

FIFTY YEARS ON THE TRAIL. A TRUE STORY OF WESTERN LIFE . . . LONDON: CHATTO & WINDUS, 1889.

[i]–xvi, [1]–381, [382 blank, 383 ornament, 384 blank]. 18.4 x 14 cm. Illustrations by Paul Frénzeny unlisted. Cream pictorial wrappers with title in brown on front wrapper and pictorial designs on backstrip and back wrapper. In a blue cloth case.

Ref.: Adams 740; Adams (*Ramp. Herd*) 1721; Howes O120; Smith 7734

Life story of Johnny Nelson [John Y. Nelson], white renegade with the Sioux, adopted by Spotted Tail, married to Red Cloud's sister, army scout, trapper and colossal liar.—Howes

3129 ORLEANS TERRITORY

THE MILITIA LAWS OF THE TERRITORY OF ORLEANS . . . NEW-ORLEANS: PRINTED BY JOHN DACQUENY, 1811.

[*]^1, A–B^8, C^{6+1}, D^6, E–[F]^6. [F6 blank], [i–ii], [1]–[34], [iii–iv], 35–69, [70–72 blank]. (Pages [i], [34], and [iii] blank.) 17.5 x 10.4 cm. Brown pulled paste paper wrappers, stabbed.

Ref.:

The Militia Laws were issued at the direction of Governor William C. C. Claiborne. The French translation is headed by a title-page on page [35] as follows: Lois / de la / Milice / du / Territoire d'Orleans. / [double rule] / Par Autorite'. / [double rule] / Nouvelle-Orleans: / Imprime' par John Dacqueny, / Imprimeur des Lois des Etats-Unis. / [short dotted rule] / 1811. / On page [ii] the heading reads: Head Quarters, New-Orleans, May 22, 8111[!]. /

3130 ORLEANS TERRITORY. Governor (W. C. C. Claiborne)

[Caption title] (CIRCULAR.) NEW ORLEANS, JUNE 16TH 1808. SIR, THE ENCLOSED GENERAL ORDERS WILL I HOPE BE FAITHFULLY EXECUTED . . .

[1–4]. 24.3 x 19.9 cm. Unbound leaflet.

Ref.: Carter, C. E.: *Territorial Papers of the U.S.* IX (1940), pp. 793–95; McMurtrie (*Louisiana*) 59

First page in English, text on pages 2 and 3 in English and French. English text signed in manuscript by William C. C. Claiborne.

Relates to military duty. It may have been printed by Bradford & Anderson, printers to the Territory for at least part of the year 1808.

3131 ORR, NELSON M.

THE CITY OF STOCKTON; ITS POSITION, CLIMATE, COMMERCE, RESOURCES, ETC. TOGETHER WITH A BRIEF SKETCH OF THE GREAT SAN JOAQUIN BASIN OF CALIFORNIA, OF WHICH STOCKTON IS THE NATURAL BUSINESS CENTER . . . STOCKTON, CAL.: "INDEPENDENT" PRINT, 1874.

[1]–58, 59–64 advertisements. 21.7 x 14.3 cm. Gray printed wrappers, with title on front wrapper.

Ref.: Blumann & Thomas 4046; Cowan p. 465; Howes O126

3132 ORTEGA, JOSE

APOSTOLICOS AFANES DE LA COMPANA DE JESUS . . . BARCELONA: POR PABLO NADAL IMPRESSOR, 1754.

∫4, ∫∫2, A–Lll4, Mmm2+1. [i–xii], [1]–452, [453–59 index, 460 blank], [461 errata, 462 blank]. 20.3 x 14.7 cm. Contemporary vellum with manuscript title on backstrip.

Prov.: Inscribed on title page: Compº pr el Dⁿ Jose de Lezana pª el Coleg. Caroli / ho Año de 74 /.

Ref.: Howes O127; Jones 477; Medina (*BHA*) 3651; Sabin 57680; Streit III 624; Wagner (*SS*) 128

Includes much on the movements and discoveries of the missionary priests Kino and Konsag in Arizona and California.—Howes

3133 OSGOOD, ERNEST S.

THE DAY OF THE CATTLEMAN . . . MINNEAPOLIS: THE UNIVERSITY OF MINNESOTA PRESS, 1929.

[i]–[xiii], [xiv blank], [1]–283, [284 blank]. (Frontispiece in pagination.) 23.6 x 16 cm. 15 illustrations and maps listed, pictorial endpapers. Tan buckram, fore and lower edges uncut.

Ref.: Adams 742; Adams (*Ramp. Herd*) 1739; Howes O130; Rader 2559; Smith 7742

Significant study into the expansion of the range cattle industry into the northern plains, from the late sixties to the early nineties.—Howes

3134 OSTRANDER, ALSON B.

AFTER 60 YEARS. SEQUEL TO A STORY OF THE PLAINS.*

[1]–120. 22.8 x 15 cm. Numerous illustrations, unlisted. Red pictorial cloth, with onset view printed in blue.

Prov.: Inscribed on front endleaf: Yours very Truly / A. B. Ostrander /.

Ref.:

Printed at Seattle, Washington, by the Gateway Printing Company. Copyrighted 1925.

3135 OSTRANDER, ALSON B.

AN ARMY BOY OF THE SIXTIES: A STORY OF THE PLAINS . . . YONKERS-ON-HUDSON, NEW YORK: WORLD BOOK COMPANY, 1924.*

[i]–[xii], 1–272. 19.5 x 13.3 cm. Illustrations unlisted. Gray pictorial boards, gray cloth backstrip.

Ref.:

Although Ostrander entered the Army in 1864, when he was fifteen years old, most of the book is devoted to army life in the Far West.

3136 OTERO, MIGUEL ANTONIO

MY LIFE ON THE FRONTIER 1864–1882 . . . NEW YORK: THE PRESS OF THE PIONEERS INCORPORATED, 1935.*

WITH:

MY LIFE ON THE FRONTIER 1882–1897 . . . ALBUQUERQUE: THE UNIVERSITY OF NEW MEXICO PRESS.

[i–xiv (xiv blank)], 1–293, [294 blank]. 23 x 15.2 cm. [1–2], [i]–[xv], [xvi blank], 1–306. 24 illustrations listed. Two volumes, first in tan cloth, second in tan buckram. Each with dust jacket.

Ref.: Adams 743; Howes O141; Rader 2561; Saunders 3068

First volume limited to 750 copies, signed by the author. Second volume (published 1939) limited to 400 copies.

3137 OTERO, MIGUEL ANTONIO

[Caption title] TEXAS VOLUNTEER REGIMENT. SPEECH OF HON. M. A. OTERO OF NEW MEXICO, IN THE HOUSE OF REPRESENTATIVES, APRIL 18, 1860 . . .

[1]–16. 24.5 x 15.4 cm. Unbound, folded, uncut, unopened. In a brown cloth case.

Ref.:

The printer's imprint at the foot of the first page reads: H. Polkinhorn, printer, Washington /.

3138 OUR GREAT INDIAN WAR . . .

OUR GREAT INDIAN WAR. THE MIRACULOUS LIVES OF MUSTANG BILL (MR. WM. RHODES DECKER) AND MISS MARION FANNIN. THE BRAVE INDIAN FIGHTER AMONG THE HOSTILE SIOUX. THE CUSTER EXPEDITION AND MASSACRE . . . PHILADELPHIA: BARCLAY & CO.

[17]–[80]. 23.7 x 14.7 cm. Seven illustrations, unlisted. Pictorial pale green wrappers, with title on front wrapper, illustration on verso of back wrapper. In a blue board case.

Prov.: Inscribed in pencil on front cover: To Everett from Ed / with affectionate / Regards / [rule] / Edw Eberstadt /.

Ref.: Howes D194

Copyrighted 1876.

The captions under the illustrations carry legends in both English and German.

3139 OUR WHOLE UNION . . .

[Broadside newspaper] OUR WHOLE UNION; OR, THE MISSOURI REGISTER. PUBLISHED AT MACON CITY, MO, BY THE PRINTERS OF THE 1ST REG. IOWA VOLUNTEERS. OUR WHOLE UNION. PUBLISHED FOR ONCE ONLY AT MACON CITY MISSOURI, BY A SQUAD OF IOWA VOL'RS . . .

Broadside, 60.7 x 45.4 cm. Text, 53.9 x 39.6 cm. Printed in blue.

Ref.:

The editor was Franc B. Wilkie. His appointment was made by Special Order No. 1, which is printed in the second column. The paper was established because the regiment had captured a "Secession printing office." The paper is also announced as the last issue.

3140 OVERLAND DAILY STAGE LINE

TABLE OF DISTANCES OF THE OVERLAND DAILY STAGE LINE, FROM ATCHISON, KANSAS, TO GREAT SALT LAKE CITY, THE ROUTE PASSING THROUGH DENVER CITY, THENCE BY THE CHEROKEE TRAIL ALONG THE CACHE LA POUDRE RIVER, THROUGH LARAMIE PLAINS, BY FORT HALLECK AND MEDICINE BOW MOUNTAINS, BRIDGER'S PASS AND FORT BRIDGER, TO GREAT SALT LAKE CITY. BEN HOLLA-DAY, PROPRIETOR, NO. 88 WALL STREET, NEW YORK. NEW YORK: SLOTE & JANES, STATIONERS, 1863.

[1–4]. 12.2 x 8.4 cm. Unbound leaflet. Laid in green cloth case labeled: Overland Stage Line Schedule. Circa 1860. /

Ref.:

Laid in is a yellow card headed: Overland Mail Co., for which see number 3142.

3141 OVERLAND JOURNEY TO THE PACIFIC OCEAN FORTY YEARS AGO

[Caption title] 390 AMERICAN REGISTER AND MAGAZINE . . . AN OVERLAND JOURNEY TO THE PACIFIC OCEAN FORTY YEARS AGO . . .

390–396. 21.7 x 14 cm. Extract, unbound. In a green cloth case.

Ref.: Wagner-Camp 180, 193

Extract from *Stryker's American Register and Magazine*, Volume 4, July, 1850.

This recounts the expedition of Hunt, Crooks, Miller, McClellan, McKenzie, and about sixty men who left St. Louis in March, 1811, for the Pacific Ocean.

Laid in folder with Carleton: "The Overland Journey to California."

3142 OVERLAND MAIL COMPANY

[Broadsheet] OVERLAND MAIL CO. FROM SALT LAKE CITY TO VIRGINIA, NEV.—STATIONS AND DISTANCES . . .

Broadsheet card 6.2 x 11.1 cm. Unbound, yellow card, laid in green cloth case labeled: Overland Stage Line Schedule. Circa 1860. /

Ref.:

On the verso is a schedule: Pioneer Stage Company. / From Virginia, Nev., to Sacramento, Cal.—Stations and Distances. / (Connecting with Overland Mail Co.) / [rule] / [22 lines] / H. S. Rumfield, / Agent O. M. Co. / [lower left:] Salt Lake City, January 1st, 1866. / [within rule border].

3143 OVERLAND MAIL COMPANY

[Broadside] [in manuscript: 1,000.] [in manuscript: S L C Dec 14] 18 [in manuscript: 63] RECEIVED OF [in manuscript: H. J. Rumfield] SUP'T OF THE OVERLAND MAIL COMPANY, [in manuscript: One Thousand long dash] DOLLARS FOR [in manuscript: Grain a/c] [in manuscript: T. W. Olerbeck] NO. [in manuscript: Clk for B. Young.] R. C. ROOT, ANTHONY & CO., 16 NASSAU ST., N. Y. OVERLAND MAIL COMPANY.

Broadside, 9.3 x 7.3 cm. Text, 8.3 x 6.1 cm.

Ref.:

Docketed in red on face: C. B. / [underline] / 195 / [underline] /.

3144 OVERLAND STAGE LINE

[Caption title] OFFICE OF THE OVERLAND STAGE LINE, 186. THE OVERLAND MAIL, BETWEEN ATCHISON (KANSAS), AND PLACERVILLE, (CAL.,) VIA DENVER CITY, GREAT SALT LAKE CITY AND CARSON, LEAVES ATCHISON (KANSAS), AND PLACERVILLE, (CAL.) DAILY, THROUGH IN 17 OR 20 DAYS . . .

[1–4]. 20.6 x 13.7 cm. Unbound leaflet. In green cloth case.

Ref.:

Comprises rates of fares and general information, baggage, meals, stopovers, etc. The inner pages are a table of distances. Atchison to Placerville was $200.

3145 OVERLAND TRACTION ENGINE COMPANY

OVERLAND TRACTION ENGINE COMPANY. TRANSPORTATION BY STEAM FROM MISSOURI RIVER TO THE ROCKY MOUNTAINS. REPORTS OF A. P. ROBINSON, ESQ., CIVIL ENGINEER, AND EDW. WARNER, ESQ., CIVIL ENGINEER. BOSTON: WRIGHT & POTTER, PRINTERS, 1865.

[1]–61, [62 blank]. 28 x 18 cm. Two frontispieces and folding map. Map: [Strip map, Nebraska City to Camp No. 5] [lower left:] Lith. by L. Prang & Co. Boston. / 21 x 61.8 cm. (page size). No scale given. Tan printed wrapper with title on front wrapper.

Prov.: Charles Deane's copy.

Ref.: Sabin 57977

The report was circulated privately.

3146 [OVERTON, JOHN]

A VINDICATION OF THE MEASURES OF THE PRESIDENT AND HIS COMMANDING GENERALS, IN THE COMMENCEMENT & TERMINATION OF THE SEMINOLE WAR . . . NASHVILLE, T.: PRINTED BY TUNSTALL & NOWELL.

[A]–P⁴, Q¹. [1]–119, [120 blank], [121 errata, 122 blank]. 22.1 x 14 cm. Rebound in red half morocco, gilt top, uncut. Some marginal repairs.

Prov.: Inscribed on title-page: For James Loague Esq. / ———— / Sam.¹ K. Overton. / [and in another hand:] Presented to the Lex. Liby by / J. Logue. / On page [3]: Presented to the Lex. Library / by Jas. Logue /.

Ref.: AII (*Tennessee*) 211, Field 1163; Howes O158; Sabin 57981

Defends Jackson's Florida invasion as attacked in Chairman Abner Lacock's *Report of the Select Committee of the Senate.*—Howes. Howes gives date [1819].

The errata leaf is not described in AII (*Tennessee*). There are some interesting textual dif-ferences between the present copy and the ICN (Ayer) copy.

Location	Graff Copy	ICN(Ayer) Copy
P. 45, line last:	Vattel	Vatt l
P. 47, line last:	Marshall's	arMshall's
P. 61, line 3 up:	Doyle	oyle
P. 64, line 2 up:	N o.	No.
P. 88, line 2 up:	Lacoc k 's	Lacock 's
P. 97:		44-line errata pasted down.

Editions: Washington, 1819.

3147 OVIEDO Y VALDEZ, GONZALO FERNANDEZ DE

HISTORIA GENERAL Y NATURAL DE LAS INDIAS, ISLAS Y TIERRAFIRME DEL MAR OCEANO, MADRID: IMPRENTA DE LAS REAL ACADEMIA DE LA HISTORIA, 1851 [1852, 1853, 1855].*

[I]–CXII, 1–632, [633 errata, 634 blank]. [I]–VII, [VIII blank], 1–[512], [513 errata, 514 blank]. [I]–VIII, 1–[652], [653 errata, 654 blank]. [I]–VIII, 1–[620], [621 errata, 622 blank]. 32.4 x 22 cm. 14 engraved plates and maps bound in at ends of volumes. Four volumes, green printed wrappers with title on front wrappers, bound in half black morocco, uncut.

Prov.: Bookplate of Henry R. Wagner in Volume I.

Ref.: Howes O159; Sabin 57990; Streit III 1665

The fourth volume (comprising Part III of the original work) had not been previously printed.

3148 OWEN, JOHN

THE JOURNALS AND LETTERS OF MAJOR JOHN OWEN, PIONEER OF THE NORTHWEST, 1850–1871 . . . NEW YORK: EDWARD EBERSTADT, 1927.

[i]–xx, 1–346. [i–iv], 1–367, [368 blank]. 28.2 x 18.8 cm. Plates and maps listed. Two volumes, blue boards, vellum paper backs, gilt tops, uncut, unopened.

Prov.: Inscription on first fly-leaf in pencil: To my good friend / Everett D. Graff / Collector and scholar par excellence / whose unending quest / for the sources / of / Western History / has led him along all the / Trails and Cut-offs pioneered / by John Owen / Edw Eberstadt /.

Ref.: Howes O163; Smith 7762

Limited to 50 sets on Large Paper. An unnumbered copy.

3149 [OWEN, ROBERT D.(?)]

BIOGRAPHY OF JOSEPH LANE . . . WASHINGTON: PRINTED AT THE CONGRESSIONAL GLOBE OFFICE, 1852.

[1]–40. 22.3 x 14.5 cm. Stabbed, unbound.

Ref.: Howes L65; Smith 10870; Wagner-Camp 216

There are two approximately simultaneous editions, of which Howes lists this first. Wagner-Camp describes the other edition (By a Westerner) first and then states it is possible the other edition is earlier.

Authorship has been ascribed to Robert Dale Owen.—Howes

3150 OWEN PUBLISHING COMPANY, Davenport, Iowa

OWEN'S GAZETTEER AND DIRECTORY OF JACKSON COUNTY, IOWA, CONTAINING A HISTORY OF THE COUNTY . . . DAVENPORT, IOWA: OWEN PUBLISHING COMPANY, 1878.*

[1]–[308]. (Pages [1] and [308] pasted down on inner covers.) 22.6 x 15 cm. Black cloth, black leather backstrip, with title in gilt on backstrip, marbled edges.

Ref.: Cook p. 139; Howes O169

Advertisements on various colors of paper interspersed throughout.

3151 OXLEY, THOMAS J.

A COLLECTION OF FIVE AUTOGRAPH LETTERS, signed, by Thomas J. Oxley, as described below. 1850 August 27, Crescent City, California, to 1853 September 12, Columbia, California. To members of his family.

1850 August 27, Crescent City, California. Four pages, 24.7 x 19.3 cm. To his aunt. Describing his overland journey and arrival in California, scenes and activities in and around Crescent City and Sacramento.

1850 November 27, Washington, South Yuba River, California. Four pages, 25.1 x 19.8 cm. To his mother, sister and brother. Disillusions and disappointments of California, the ability "to get by," "golden crows always fly in foreign lands," etc.

1851 June 15, Nevada City, California. Four pages, 24.3 x 19.2 cm. To his aunt and uncle, Dr. & Mrs. J. H. Oliver. Difficulties and delights of living in California—"Gold mining from beginning to end is a perfect gambling business."

1852 August 12, Columbia, California. Two pages, 25.3 x 19.9 cm. To his aunt and uncle, as above. Descriptions of his medical practice in Columbia—five dollars for a house call and fifty to one hundred dollars for an operation.

1853 September 12, Columbia, California. To Dr. J. H. Oliver. Three pages, 18.6 x 12.3 cm. Regarding medical practice in California, reporting that his practice netted $12,000 per year

(not all collectable), and that mining ventures were risky.

Dr. Oxley tells little in his letters of his political aspirations and achievements. He was, particularly after 1855, heavily involved in California politics. He had been a Whig and later became a Know-nothing leader and member of the state legislature. In 1857, he joined Henry A. Crabb in the ill-fated filibustering expedition into Sonora as surgeon-general. He was among those who lost their lives before the Mexican firing squads at Caborca. Accompanying the series of Oxley letters is an Autograph Letter, signed by J. M. Vansycke. 1857 May 15, San Francisco. Five pages, 25 x 19.8 cm. To A. W. Francisco. The Vansycke letter describes and comments on the Crabb expedition and mentions Oxley as a member of the party. The recipient was a newspaper man on the Cincinnati *Daily Enquirer.*

P

3152 PACIFIC, THE

[Newspaper] THE PACIFIC. REV. J. W. DOUGLAS . . . PROPRIETOR. VOL. I. SAN FRANCISCO, CALIFORNIA, FRIDAY, JULY 30, 1852. NO. 50 THE PACIFIC, A RELIGIOUS AND FAMILY NEWSPAPER, IS PUBLISHED EVERY FRIDAY . . .

[197]–200. 59.5 x 45.3 cm. Unbound.

Ref.:

Edited by the proprietor.

3153 PACIFIC CITY, Iowa

[Broadside] PACIFIC CITY WAS LAID OUT IN MAY, 1857; SOON AFTER THE FIRST HOUSE WAS COMMENCED . . . JEHU JOHN, ELIDA, WINNEBAGO COUNTY, ILL.

Broadside, 24.9 x 19.6 cm. Text, 19 x 16.5 cm.

Ref.:

Several manuscript corrections and changes in text. Docketed on verso: Jehu John / Circular / ——— /

In 1859, Luke Tierney's Pikes Peak Guide was published in Pacific City at the Herald Office, A. Thomson, printer. Perhaps the *Herald* was successor to the *Pacific City Enterprise* mentioned in this broadside. Pacific City has disappeared. I visited its site near the present Pacific Junction in 1955, and nothing remains of this mushroom town. The railroad, the bridge over the river, the drop in river traffic all caused its end. The 1845 *Iowa Gazetteer* only mentions the post office.—EDG

3154 PACIFIC NEWS, THE

[Newspaper] THE PACIFIC NEWS. FOR THE STEAMER CALIFORNIA OF APRIL 1ST, 1850. THE PACIFIC NEWS, IS PUBLISHED EVERY MORNING, (SUNDAY EXCEPTED) BY FAULKNER & ALLEN. KEARNY ST., BETWEEN PACIFIC AND JACKSON. . . .

[1–4]. 55.3 x 37 cm. Unbound.
Ref.:
Edited by J. Winchester.

3155 PACIFIC RAILROAD

[Map] MAP OF THE / PACIFIC RAILROAD. / [rule] / WESTERN P. R. R. . . . / CENTRAL P. R. R. . . . / UNION P. R. R. . . . / [three lines] / SAN FRANCISCO TO NEW YORK, 3,287 MILES. THROUGH TIME, 7 DAYS. /

Map, 15 x 62.7 cm. No scale given.
Probably printed in San Francisco. No date indicated. On the verso are advertisements of A. L. Bancroft & Co., D. Hicks & Co., Joseph Winterburn & Co., and others. Inserted in Manuscript Journals of Loren L. Williams, Volume IV.

3156 PACIFIC RAILROAD CONVENTION

PROCEEDINGS OF A PACIFIC RAILROAD CONVENTION, AT LACON, ILLINOIS; WITH THE ADDRESS OF COL. SAMUEL R. CURTIS. CINCINNATI: PRINTED BY JOHN D. THORPE, 1853.

[1]–16. 22.5 x 14.6 cm. Buff printed wrappers with title on front wrapper. In a blue cloth case.
Ref.: Sabin 58089
The Convention was called to promote a railway to the Pacific. Colonel Curtis urged the Platte Valley and South Pass route, "at much length," according to the pamphlet.

3157 PACKARD, WELLMAN & GREENBERRY LARISON

EARLY MIGRATION TO CALIFORNIA, 1849–1850 . . . BLOOMINGTON, ILLINOIS, 1928.*

[i–viii], 1–23, [24 blank]. (Pages [1–2] blank.) 22.4 x 15 cm. Brown wrappers, with title on front wrapper. In a brown cloth case.
Ref.: Howes P6
Limited to 30 copies.

3158 PADDOCK, BUCKLEY B.

[Wrapper title] EARLY DAYS IN FORT WORTH MUCH OF WHICH I SAW AND PART OF WHICH I WAS . . .

[1]–33, [34–35 blank, 36 colophon]. 22.4 x 14.9 cm. Tan printed wrappers, with title on front wrapper and illustration on verso.
Ref.: Carroll p. 141; Howes P7
The colophon on page [36]: Press / Texas Printing Co. / The pamphlet was printed at Fort Worth about 1906.

3159 [PAGE, FREDERICK B.]

PRAIRIEDOM: RAMBLES AND SCRAMBLES IN TEXAS OR NEW ESTREMADURA. BY A SOUTHRON . . . NEW YORK: PAINE & BURGESS, 1845.

[1–2], [i]–vi, [9]–166, [1–2 blank], [3]–18. 17.9 x 11.5 cm. Map: Mexico. / Scale. / [diagrammatic scale: about 240 miles to one inch] / 23.7 x 20 cm. (including border). Scale as above. *Inset:* Texas / Miles. / [diagrammatic scale: about 135 miles to one inch] / 10.4 x 8.7 cm. Green cloth, blind embossed sides, title in gilt on backstrip.
Ref.: Howes P9; Rader 2568; Raines p. 167; Sabin 88599, 93969 note; Streeter 1604
Howes distinguishes between two editions, one with Suthron and the other with Southron on title-page.

3160 PAGE COUNTY DEMOCRAT

[Newspaper] PAGE COUNTY DEMOCRAT. N. C. RIDENOUR, EDITOR . . . VOL. XVII. CLARINDA, IOWA, THURSDAY, OCTOBER 9, 1884. NO. 4 . . .

[1–4]. 66 x 50.9 cm.
Ref.:

3161 PAGES, PIERRE MARIE F., VICOMTE DE

VOYAGES AUTOUR DU MONDE, ET VERS LES DEUX POLES, PAR TERRE ET PAR MER, PENDANT LES ANNEES 1767, 1768, 1769, 1770, 1771, 1773, 1774 & 1776 . . . A PARIS: CHEZ MOUTARD, M. DCC. LXXXII.

[1]–432. [1]–272. 19 x 12 cm. Ten maps and plates bound at end of second volume. Map: Carte Reduite du Globe Terrestre / Pour servir aux Trois Voyages autour du Monde et vers les deux Poles, faits par M. de Pages, Chevalier de l'Ordre Royal et Militaire de S. Louis, Capitaine des Vaisseaux / du Roi, et Correspondant de l'Académie Royale des Sciences, Dressée d'après toutes les nouvelles découvertes, par le S. Seguin, Ingénieur Géographe du Roi, en 1782. / [upper right:] Pl. 1. / [lower left:] Benard Direxit / [lower right:] J. B. L. Aubert Scripsit. / 27 x 33.7 cm. No scale given. Map: Carte d'une Partie de l'Amérique / Septentrionale, / qui contient partie de la N^{le} Espagne, / et de la Louisiane. / Pour servir aux Voyages au Tour du Monde et vers / les deux Pôles, faits par M. de Pagès, Chevalier de / l'Ordre Royal et Militaire de St Louis, Capitaine des / Vaisseaux du Roi, et Correspondant de l'Académie / Royale des Sciences. / [upper right:] Voyages de Mr de Pagès Pl. 2. / [lower right:] Benard direxit. / 31.8 x 42.5 cm. Map: Carte d'une Partie des Côtes de l'Inde, /

depuis Bombay jus'qu'a Surate, avec le Détail / des Habitations de cette Côte / Pour servir aux Voyages au Tour du Monde et vers les deux / Pôles, faits par M. de Pagès, Chevalier de l'Ordre Royal et / Militaire de St Louis, Capitaine des Vaisseaux du Roi, et / Correspondant de l'Académie Royale des Sciences. / Remarques / ... / [upper right:] Voyages de Mr de Pagès. Pl. 3. / [lower right:] Benard direxit. / 23.8 x 40.6 cm. No scale given. Map: Carte d'une Partie de l'Asie, / depuis la Mer Méditerranée jusqu'au Golfe de Cambaye / dans la Mer de l'Inde. / Pour servir aux Voyages au Tour du Monde et vers les deux Pôles, faits par / M. de Pagès, Chevalier de l'Ordre Royal et Militaire de St Louis, Capitaine / des Vaisseaux du Roi, et Correspondant de l'Académie Royale des Sciences. / Remarques / ... / [upper right:] Voyages de Mr de Pagès. Pl. 4 / [lower right:] Benard direxit. / 23.7 x 40.1 cm. No scale given. Map: Carte / d'une Partie de la Syrie et de la / Palestine, / Pour servir aux Voyages au Tour du Monde et vers les deaux / Poles, faits par M. de Pagès, Chevalier de l'Ordre Royal, et Mi-/-litaire de St Louis, Capitaine des Vaisseaux du Roi, et Corres-/-pondant de l'Academie Royale des Sciences. / ... / [upper right:] Voyagès[!] de Mr de Pagès. Pl. 5. / [lower right:] Benard direxit. / 24.2 x 38.5 cm. No scale given. Map: Carte Reduite d'une Partie des Côtes des Isles Australes, Pour servir aux Voyages au Tour du Monde et vers les deux Pôles, faits par / M. de Pagès, Chevalier de l'Ordre Royal et Militaire de St Louis, Capitaine des Vaisseaux du Roi, et Correspondant de l'Académie Royale des Sciences. / [nine inset views and small maps] [upper right:] Voyages de Mr de Pagès. Pl. 6 / [lower right:] Benard direxit. / 24.6 x 40.5 cm. No scale given. Map: Carte du Spits-Berg, / et Partie de la Côte de Galles Hans-Kes / au Nouveau Groenland. / Pour servir aux Voyages au Tour du Monde et vers / les deux Pôles, faits par M. de Pagès, Chevalier de / l'Ordre Royal et Militaire de St Louis, Capitaine des / Vaisseaux de Roi, et Correspondant de l'Académie / Royale des Sciences. / [two inset maps and four inset views] / [upper right:] Voyages de Mr de Pagés[!]. Pl. 7 / [lower right:] Benard direxit. / 32.1 x 46.4 cm. No scale given. Two volumes, contemporary mottled calf, gilt backs, red morocco labels, red edges.
Ref.: Howes P13; Sabin 58168; Wagner (*SS*) 165

The author is supposed to have made an overland journey through Texas in 1767, but Wagner inclined to the notion that the "journey" was compiled in Paris and never took place.

3162   PAGETT & STINCHCOMB

[Wrapper title] A DESCRIPTIVE REVIEW OF CASS COUNTY, NEBRASKA, SHOWING THE RESOURCES, CLIMATE, WATER, TIMBER, GRAINS, GRASSES, TOWNS AND PEOPLE. A GENERAL LETTER OF INFORMATION FOR PARTIES SEEKING HOMES IN THE WEST ... OMAHA, NEB.: PRINTED AT THE DAILY REPUBLICAN OFFICE, 1879.

[1]–36. 22.4 x 15.1 cm. One vignette in text, repeated on back wrapper. Light blue printed wrappers, with title on front wrapper as above, advertisements on verso of front and recto of back, vignette on verso of back wrapper.
Prov.: Rubber stamp at head of page [1]: With Compliments of / Daniel H. Wheeler, / Plattsmouth, Neb. /
Ref.:
The text includes a directory of the several towns in Cass County. Pagett & Stinchcomb were "Immigration Agents."

3163   PAINE, THOMAS

PUBLIC GOOD, BEING AN EXAMINATION INTO THE CLAIM OF VIRGINIA TO THE VACANT WESTERN TERRITORY ... LONDON: PRINTED BY W. T. SHERWIN, 1817.

[A]–B^8, C^2. [1]–35, [36 blank]. 22 x 14 cm. Unbound, inserted into Gaylord binder, uncut.
Ref.: Howes P30; Sabin 58238; Vail 668
A defense of the government's claim to unsettled lands against that of individual states, especially Virginia.—Vail
Editions: Philadelphia, 1780. Albany [1780?].

3164   [PAINTER, HENRY M.]

BRIEF NARRATIVE OF INCIDENTS IN THE WAR IN MISSOURI, AND OF THE PERSONAL EXPERIENCE OF ONE WHO HAS SUFFERED. BOSTON: PRESS OF THE DAILY COURIER, 1863.

[1]–28. 23.2 x 14.5 cm. Salmon printed wrappers, with title as above on front wrapper within thick and thin rule borders.
Ref.: Bradford 4135; Howes P35; Nicholson p. 631; Sabin 58258

3165   PAINTER, ORRIN C.

WILLIAM PAINTER AND HIS FATHER, DR. EDWARD PAINTER. SKETCHES AND REMINISCENCES ... BALTIMORE: THE ARUNDEL PRESS, 1914.

[1]–[153], [154 blank]. 30.8 x 23.4 cm. Numerous illustrations throughout, unlisted. Dark red cloth, title in gilt on front cover, gilt top.
Ref.: Howes P36
Contains considerable material relating to Dr. Edward Painter and his experiences among the Omaha Indians in Nebraska. There is also a pair of essays by Emilie Painter Jackson describ-

ing her life among the Omahas. A number of excellent photographs are reproduced.

Dr. Painter's daughter married William H. Jackson. About 40 pages are devoted to Jackson's photography and painting.

3166 PALLADINO, LAWRENCE B.

INDIAN AND WHITE IN THE NORTHWEST; OR, A HISTORY OF CATHOLICITY IN MONTANA . . . BALTIMORE: JOHN MURPHY & COMPANY, 1894.

[1–2], [i]–xxv, [xxvi blank], 1–411, [412 blank]. 22.7 x 15.1 cm. Illustrations listed, folding map. Blue cloth.

Ref.: Howes P40; Smith 7852; Streit III 2894

3167 PALLISER, JOHN

EXPLORATION—BRITISH NORTH AMERICA. PAPERS RELATIVE TO THE EXPLORATION BY CAPTAIN PALLISER OF THAT PORTION OF BRITISH NORTH AMERICA WHICH LIES BETWEEN THE NORTHERN BRANCH OF THE RIVER SASKATCHEWAN AND THE FRONTIER OF THE UNITED STATES; AND BETWEEN THE RED RIVER AND ROCKY MOUNTAINS . . . LONDON: PRINTED BY GEORGE EDWARD EYRE AND WILLIAM SPOTTISWOODE, 1859.

[1]–64. 32.1 x 20.4 cm. Twelve maps on eight sheets, one folding. Map: British North American Exploring Expedition. / [rule] / Country Between / the Red River Settlement / and / the Rocky Mountains; / Showing the Various Routes of the Expedition, / under the Command of / Captn John Palliser. / 1857 & 1858. / [rule] / [at foot right:] John Arrowsmith, Litho. 1859. / 30 x 80 cm. Scale: about 33 miles to one inch.

BOUND WITH:

EXPLORATION—BRITISH NORTH AMERICA. FURTHER PAPERS RELATIVE TO THE EXPLORATION BY THE EXPEDITION UNDER CAPTAIN PALLISER OF THAT PORTION OF BRITISH NORTH AMERICA WHICH LIES BETWEEN THE NORTHERN BRANCH OF THE RIVER SASKATCHEWAN AND THE FRONTIER OF THE UNITED STATES; AND BETWEEN THE RED RIVER AND THE ROCKY MOUNTAINS, AND THENCE TO THE PACIFIC OCEAN . . . LONDON: 1860.

[1]–75, [76 blank]. Three folding maps: Saskatchewan River & Rocky Mountains. / [rule] / Routes of the / British North American Expedition, / under Command of / Captn John Palliser, / 1858–1859 / James Hector, / 1860. / [lower right:] John Arrowsmith, 1860. / [rule] / 40.6 x 51.7 cm. No scale given. Map: Sketch Map / showing the Routes / of / Cap^{tn} Palliser & Mr Sullivan / during 1859. / [rule] / [lower right:] J. W. Sullivan / [below neat line:] John Arrowsmith, Litho. 1860. / 28 x 49.4 cm. Scale: about 8 miles to one inch. Map: The / Kootanie

and Boundary / Passes / of the / Rocky Mountains. / Explored in 1858 by / Lieutenant (now Captain) Blakiston, / Royal Artillery. / [lower right:] as in preceding. 26.6 x 40 cm. Scale: 8 1/2 miles to one inch. Includes two supplementary sections.

BOUND WITH:

EXPLORATION.—BRITISH NORTH AMERICAN. THE JOURNALS, DETAILED REPORTS, AND OBSERVATIONS RELATIVE TO THE EXPLORATION, BY CAPTAIN PALLISER, OF THAT PORTION OF BRITISH NORTH AMERICA, WHICH, IN LATITUDE, LIES BETWEEN THE BRITISH BOUNDARY LINE AND THE HEIGHT OF LAND OR WATERSHED OF THE NORTHERN OR FROZEN OCEAN RESPECTIVELY, AND IN LONGITUDE, BETWEEN THE WESTERN SHORE OF LAKE SUPERIOR AND THE PACIFIC OCEAN DURING THE YEARS 1857, 1858, 1859, AND 1860 . . . LONDON: PRINTED BY GEORGE EDWARD EYRE AND WILLIAM SPOTTISWOODE, 1863.

[1]–[326], [327-28 blank], [1–3 index, 4 blank]. Five folding maps. Three volumes bound together in three-quarter morocco.

Ref.: Howes P42; Sabin 58332; Staton & Tremaine 3928, 4002, 4264; Wagner-Camp 358; Wheat (*Transmississippi*) 1011a, 1082

The Index and maps in the third part were published in 1865.

3168 PALLISER, JOHN

SOLITARY RAMBLES AND ADVENTURES OF A HUNTER IN THE PRAIRIES . . . LONDON: JOHN MURRAY, 1853.

[i]–[vi (vi blank)], [1]–326, [327–28 advertisements]. 19 x 12.5 cm. Eight illustrations listed including pictorial title-page. Gray speckled cloth, gilt vignette on front cover, gilt backstrip, uncut.

Ref.: Howes P43; Rader 2578, Sabin 58333; Smith 7856

The pictorial title-page reads as follows: The / Hunter in the Prairies. / [large vignette] / Ishmah / "He had by this time overcome all his prejudices against his white master." / London: John Murray, Albemarle Street. /

3169 PALMER, FREDERICK

IN THE KLONDYKE, INCLUDING AN ACCOUNT OF A WINTER'S JOURNEY TO DAWSON . . . NEW YORK: CHARLES SCRIBNER'S SONS, 1899.

[i]–x, [xi–xii fly-title], 1–218, [219–20 advertisements]. 18.7 x 12.1 cm. 28 illustrations listed. Pictorial brown cloth with title on front cover and backstrip.

Ref.: Wickersham 4394

3170 PALMER, H. E.

THE POWDER RIVER EXPEDITION, 1865. A PAPER READ BEFORE THE NEBRASKA COMMANDERY OF THE MILITARY ORDER OF THE LOYAL LEGION OF THE UNITED STATES, FEBRUARY 2, 1887 . . . OMAHA: THE REPUBLICAN COMPANY, 1887.

[1]–59, [60 blank]. 22.3 x 14.9 cm. Gray printed wrappers with title on front wrapper. In a brown half morocco case.

Prov.: Rubber stamp of New-York Society Library on front wrapper, page [2] and page [60], stamp on front wrapper overstamped: Withdrawn /.

Ref.: Howes P46

This is the original printing of an important narrative of the 1865 Powder River Expedition. It was reprinted in Vol 11 *Transactions and Reports* of the Nebraska State Historical Society, 1887. The last fifteen pages are omitted. A revised issue, with some added material, was printed in 1902 in *Civil War Sketches and Incidents. Papers read by Companions of the Commandery of the State of Nebraska, Military Order of the Loyal Legion of the United States.*—EDG

3171 PALMER, JOEL

JOURNAL OF TRAVELS OVER THE ROCKY MOUNTAINS, TO THE MOUTH OF THE COLUMBIA RIVER; MADE DURING THE YEARS 1845 AND 1846 . . . CINCINNATI: J. A. & U. P. JAMES, 1847.

[i]–iv, 9–189, [190 blank]. Leaf, 6 x 10.5 cm., of "Corrections." tipped in after page 188. 21 x 11.6 cm. Brown printed wrappers with title on front wrapper, backstrip reading down, advertisements on verso of back wrapper, uncut. In maroon half morocco case.

Ref.: Cowan (1914) p. 168; Howes P54; Sabin 58358; Smith 7866; Wagner-Camp 136

The errata slip reads as follows: Corrections. / On page 31, line 7 from the bottom, for "sandy" read "grassy." / " " 121, for "The company own from six to eight mills / above the fort," read "The grist mill stands six miles, and / the saw mill eight miles, above the fort." /

Most reliable of the early guides to Oregon; in addition, the best narrative by a participant in the overland migration of 1845, which more than doubled the population of Oregon.—Howes

3172 PALMER, JOEL

THE SAME.

In a dark brown folding case, half morocco.

Without the slip of Corrections. Two changes were made in manuscript in pencil, probably in the hand of the author.

3173 PALMER, JOEL

THE SAME . . . 1847 [7 overprinted with 8].

[i]–viii, 9–189, [190–92 blank], [1]–105, [106 blank, 107–08 advertisements]. 20.1 x 12.3 cm. Light printed brown wrappers with title on front wrapper, title on backstrip reading down, advertisements on verso of front and recto and verso of back wrapper. In a green cloth case.

Ref.: Field 1165; Howes P54; Jones 1157; Sabin 58358; Smith 7866; Wagner-Camp 136

In this edition the corrections listed on the slip in the first edition have been made. The wrapper is undated.

The second section of the volume is introduced by the following title-page: California: / its / History, Population, Climate, Soil, / Productions, and Harbors. / From / Sir George Simpson's / "Overland Journey Round the World." / [short rule] / An Account of / The Revolution in California, / and Conquest of the Country by the United States, / 1846–7. / By John T. Hughes, A. B., / Author of "Doniphan's Expedition." Cincinnati: / Published by J. A. & U. P. James. / ::::::::::: / 1848. /

3174 PALMER, JOHN M.

PERSONAL RECOLLECTIONS . . . CINCINNATI: THE ROBERT CLARKE COMPANY, 1901.*

[i]–[xvii], [xviii blank], 1–631, [632 blank]. 23.5 x 15.4 cm. Ten illustrations listed. Dark red ribbed cloth, gilt top.

Ref.:

3175 PALMER, LYMAN L.

HISTORICAL SKETCH OF RIO VISTA, CAL. AND REMINISCENT SKETCHES FORTY YEARS AGO . . . PUBLISHED BY THE RIVER NEWS, RIO VISTA, CAL.

[i–ii], 1–63, [64 blank]. 20.6 x 14.4 cm. Portrait. Gray printed wrappers.

Ref.: Blumann & Thomas 4514 see

Dated on page 63: Gainesville, Florida, February 20, 1914. Blumann & Thomas describe an edition dated 1914 with 68 pages.

3176 PALMER, WILLIAM J.

LETTERS, 1853–1858 . . . PHILADELPHIA, 1906.*

[1–2], [i]–v, [6]–128, slip headed Addendum. 22.5 x 15.4 cm. Illustrations unlisted. Olive-green cloth, beveled covers, gilt top, uncut.

Ref.:

Not copyrighted, privately printed.

3177 PALMER, WILLIAM J.

REPORT OF SURVEYS ACROSS THE CONTINENT, IN 1867–'68, ON THE THIRTY-FIFTH AND THIRTY-SECOND PARALLELS, FOR A ROUTE EXTENDING THE

KANSAS PACIFIC RAILWAY TO THE PACIFIC OCEAN AT SAN FRANCISCO AND SAN DIEGO . . . PHILADELPHIA: W. B. SELHEIMER, PRINTER, 1869.

[1]–6, [i–ii], 7–250. 23.2 x 14.6 cm. 20 photographic plates, folding map, unlisted. Map: Map / of the Route of the / Southern Continental R. R. / with connections from Kansas City Mo. Ft. Smith Ark. / and / Shreveport La. / giving a general View of the Recent / Surveys of the / Kansas Pacific Railway Co, / across the Continent / Made in 1867 & 1868. / under the direction of / Gen. Wm J. Palmer. / On the Routes of the 32nd and 35th Parallels. / Scale 60 miles to an inch. [diagrammatic scale] / J. F. Gedney Lith, Washington, D. C. / 75.7 x 95.3 cm. Scale as above. Profile: General Profile / of the / Union Pacific Railway. E. D. / or / Kansas Pacific Rail Road. / From / St. Louis to San Francisco. / W. H. Greenwood, / Chief Engineer / of Survey on 35th Parallel. / Wm J. Palmer. / Manager of Survey's / [lower right:] J. F. Gedney, Lith. Washington D. C. / 14.9 x 15.2 cm. Gray printed wrappers with title on front wrapper. In light blue cloth case.

Prov.: Manuscript note at top of front wrapper: Hon Jas. F. Wilson /.

Ref.: Howes P54; *Railway Economics* p. 218; Sabin 58383

Wilson was senator from Iowa and a member of the Pacific Railway Commission.

3178 PALOU, FRANCISCO

LIFE OF VEN. PADRE JUNIPERO SERRA . . . TRANSLATED BY VERY REV. J. ADAM. SAN FRANCISCO: P. E. DOUGHERTY & CO., 1884.

[1]–156. 19.1 x 13.2 cm. Portrait. Black cloth, title stamped in gilt on front cover.

Ref.: Cowan p. 471–72; Howes P56

Inserted after the title-leaf is a small slip, 6.1 x 13 cm., with copyright notice. Facing last page of text is another small slip, 6.2 x 12.2 cm., of errata.

3179 PALOU, FRANCISCO

RELACION HISTORICA DE LA VIDA Y APOSTOLICAS TAREAS DEL VENERABLE PADRE FRAY JUNIPERO SERRA, Y DE LAS MISIONES QUE FUNDO EN LA CALIFORNIA SEPTENTRIONAL, Y NUEVOS ESTABLECIMIENTOS DE MONTEREY . . . IMPRESA EN MEXICO: EN LA IMPRENTA DE DON FELIPE DE ZUNIGA Y ONTIVEROS, 1787.

[a]^4, $*^2$, $*^4$, [b]^4, [1]–43^4. [i–xxviii], 1–344. 20.1 x 14.8 cm. Portrait of Serra and two maps. Folding map: Californias: An-/tigua y Nueva / Notas. / En èsta Carta no se escrib^n los nombr^s / de tod^s las Yslas, P^{tos} Rios, y demàs, p^r ser / hecha p^a solo demostrar lo q^e andubo, y Mi-/

sion^s q^e fundó en la Nvã. Calif^a el V. P. Fr. Junipero Sèrra, Presid^{te} de èllas. / La long^d es arreglada al meridiano de / S. Blas. / Diego Froncoso sc. Mex^{co} / a^o 1787. / 25.8 x 34.5 cm. Scale not given. Map between pages 101–02: Plan del Gran Puerto de San / Francisco descubierto, y demarcado por el / Alferez graduado de Fragata de la Real / Armada, D^n Jose de Cañizares primer Piloto / del Departamento de San Blas, Situado en / la Costa Occidental de la California al Norte de la Linea, en el / Mar Asiatico en Latitud Norte 37 g^s 44. minutos, y grav^{o}do por / Manuel Villavicencio Añ.de 1781. / Escala de nueve leguas Francesas. / [diagrammatic scale: about six leagues to one inch] / 16.8 x 11.9 cm. Scale: as above. Vellum with title in manuscript on backstrip.

Prov.: The volume is branded on the top edge: ⊙ . Early shelf mark on backstrip: [painted white surface outlined in red:] H / VI. / 39 / 72 /.

Ref.: Cowan p. 472; Howes P56; Jones 607; Medina (*Mexico*) 7731; Sabin 58392; Streit III 1094; Wagner (*SS*) 168; Wheat (*Transmississippi*) 208; Zamorano Eighty 59

The second map is the first printed map of the Bay of San Francisco, of which there is only one other copy known according to Wagner. This map is dated 1781. Evidently it was printed much earlier than the book, which bears the imprint of 1787. The only other copy of the map, however, also appears in a copy of this book. This copy of the map formerly belonged to Mr. Douglas Watson and was in a different copy of the book.—EDG

An autograph signature of Paloú is mounted on the fly-leaf facing page [1].

3180 PANCOAST, CHARLES E.

A QUAKER FORTY-NINER . . . EDITED BY ANNA PASCHALL HANNUM . . . PHILADELPHIA: UNIVERSITY OF PENNSYLVANIA PRESS, 1930.*

[i]–xv, [xvi blank], 1–402. 22.7 x 15.3 cm. 15 illustrations, map on endpapers listed. Dark brown cloth, plum top, uncut.

Ref.: Cowan p. 473

3181 PANTON, JAMES H.

[Wrapper title] RAMBLES IN THE NORTH WEST; ACROSS THE PRAIRIES AND IN THE PASSES OF THE ROCKY MOUNTAINS . . . GUELPH, ONT.: MERCURY STEAM PRINTING HOUSE, 1885.

[1]–20. 22.3 x 14.7 cm. Gray printed wrappers, with title on front wrapper.

Prov.: At top of wrapper: With compliments of the writer /.

Ref.: Smith 7873

3182 PARISOT, PIERRE F.

THE REMINISCENCES OF A TEXAS MISSIONARY . . .
SAN ANTONIO, TEXAS: PRESS OF JOHNSON BROS.
PRINTING CO., 1899.

[1]–227, [i]–v, [1–6 advertisements]. 19 x 13.6
cm. Portrait. Glazed mauve printed wrappers,
with title on front wrapper. In red cloth folder.

Ref.: Howes P67; Rader 2587

The text ends on page 227 the verso of which
is page [i] of the Contents, which is designated
Index.

3183 PARKER, AMOS A.

TRIP TO THE WEST AND TEXAS. COMPRISING A
JOURNEY OF EIGHT THOUSAND MILES, THROUGH
NEW-YORK, MICHIGAN, ILLINOIS, MISSOURI, LOUISI-
ANA AND TEXAS, IN THE AUTUMN AND WINTER OF
1834–5 . . . CONCORD, N. H.: PRINTED AND PUB-
LISHED BY WHITE & FISHER, 1835.

[1]–276. 19.3 x 11.5 cm. Two illustrations, unlisted. Brown cloth, brown leather label.

Ref.: Buck 276; Howes P74; Rader 2588;
Raines p. 161; Rusk II pp. 120–21; Sabin 58643;
Streeter 1172

A friendly traveler.

3184 PARKER, AMOS A.

THE SAME . . . CONCORD, N. H.: PUBLISHED BY
WILLIAM WHITE, 1836.

[i]–iv, [5]–380. 17.9 x 10.5 cm. Two plates, unlisted, and one map: Texas / Scale. / [diagram-
matic scale: about 80 miles to one inch] / 19.1 x
15.5 cm. Scale as above. Green cloth, blind embossed sides, title in gilt on backstrip, with word
Independence lettered on flag inverted.

Ref.: as above

The second and better edition. The map is not
found in all copies.

3185 PARKER, B. G.

RECOLLECTIONS OF THE MOUNTAIN MEADOW MAS-
SACRE, BEING AN ACCOUNT OF THE AWFUL ATROC-
ITY AND REVEALING SOME FACTS NEVER BEFORE
MADE PUBLIC . . . PLANO, CAL.: FRED. W. REED,
AMERICAN PRINTER, 1901.

[i], [1]–31. (Rectos show even pagination, versos
odd.) 14.8 x 9.6 cm. Portrait. Tan wrappers,
stapled, with title on front wrapper.

Ref.: Howes P75

3186 PARKER, JAMES

THE OLD ARMY. MEMORIES, 1872–1918 . . . DOR-
RANCE & COMPANY.*

[1]–454. 20.2 x 13.3 cm. 24 illustrations listed.
Dark blue cloth. In dust jacket.

Ref.:

Copyrighted 1929, New York.

Very interesting account of frontier Indian
warfare and life at the forts in the Southwest and
West during the 70's and 80's. He gives a fine
account of the Geronimo Campaign, and his
appreciation of General Mackenzie as an Indian
fighter is excellent.—EDG

3187 PARKER, JAMES W.

THE RACHEL PLUMMER NARRATIVE . . . COPY-
RIGHT, 1926.

[1]–118. 22.1 x 14.5 cm. Three portraits. Green
printed wrappers.

Ref.: Ayer 221 see; Howes P80 see; Wagner-
Camp 113 see

In this reprint, the Parker narrative and description of Texas end on page 88, and the
Plummer Narrative, with special title-page,
dated 1839, occupies pages [89]–118. Wagner-
Camp calls this an inaccurate reprint.

3188 PARKER, NATHAN H.

THE IOWA HANDBOOK, FOR 1857 . . . BOSTON:
PUBLISHED BY JOHN P. JEWETT & CO., 1857.

[i]–viii, 9–188. 18.5 x 12.5 cm. Map: Iowa /
[upper left centre:] Corrections Furnished by
N. H. Parker / [lower left:] Entered according to
Act of Congress in the year 1855 by J. H.
Colton & Co. in the Clerks Office of the District
Court for the Southern District of New York. /
[lower centre:] Published by J. H. Colton & Co.
Nº 172 William St New York. / Scale of Miles. /
[diagrammatic scale: about 23 miles to one
inch]. 32.5 x 39.8 cm. (including border). Scale
as above. Black cloth, title in gilt on front cover
and backstrip, in blind on back cover.

Ref.: Howes P83; Mott (*Iowa*) p. 60

Editions: Chicago, 1855, 1856. Boston, 1856.

3189 PARKER, NATHAN H.

THE MINNESOTA HANDBOOK, FOR 1856–7 . . .
BOSTON: JOHN P. JEWETT AND COMPANY,
M DCCC LVII.

[i]–viii, [9]–159, [160 advertisement]. 18.4 x 12.4
cm. Folding map: Minnesota / Published by
J. H. Colton & Co. Nº 172 William St New
York / 1857. / Scale of Miles / [diagrammatic
scale: about 42 miles to one inch] / Entered according to Act of Congress in the Year 1855 by
J. H. Colton & Co. in the Clerks Office of the
District Court of the United States for the
Southern District of New York / 32.5 x 39.5 cm.
(including border). Scale as above. Brown cloth,
gilt title on front cover within decorative diamond.

Ref.: Howes P85

The final page is paginated in lower left:
(148). Possibly it was prepared for page 148, but
the Appendix which starts on that page was inserted instead.

3190 PARKER, NATHAN H.

[Map] PARKER'S / SECTIONAL & GEOLOGICAL / MAP OF / IOWA / EXHIBITING HER IRON LEAD COPPER COAL / AND OTHER / GEOLOGICAL RESOURCES / AND ALL /RAIL ROADS/ COMPLETED, IN PROGRESS, AND PROJECTED / COMPILED FROM THE U. S. SURVEYS AND OTHER OFFICIAL RECORDS / BY NATHAN H. PARKER / AUTHOR OF "IOWA AS IT IS" / CLINTON I? / 1856 / J. H. COLTON & C? 172 WILLIAM S͟T NEW YORK / KEEN & LEE, CHICAGO, ILL. / [?] SCHEDLER ENGR. / SCALE OF 8 MILES TO 1 INCH. / [diagrammatic scale] / ENTERED ACCORDING TO ACT OF CONGRESS IN THE YEAR 1856 BY N. H. PARKER IN THE CLERKS OFFICE FOR THE DISTRICT OF IOWA. / [left of cartouche:] A. M. BAILEY / DRAUGHTSMAN / [*Inset:*] MAP / SHOWING THE CONNECTIONS / BETWEEN THE / IOWA AND EASTERN / RAILROADS / 22.8 x 19.7 cm. No scale given.

Map, 81.2 x 117.6 cm. Folded into brown embossed cloth covers, 15.8 x 10.4 cm., with title in gilt on front cover and blind on back cover.

Ref.:

Advertising imprints of Parker, Dole & Co. (bankers) and various others appear in open areas on the map.

3191 PARKER, NATHAN H., & D. H. HUYETT

THE ILLUSTRATED MINERS' HAND-BOOK AND GUIDE TO PIKE'S PEAK, WITH A NEW AND RELIABLE MAP, SHOWING ALL THE ROUTES, AND THE GOLD REGIONS OF WESTERN KANSAS AND NEBRASKA . . . ST. LOUIS, 1859.

[1]–75, [76–112]. 14.9 x 10.5 cm. Six plates and two folding maps. Map: New Map / of the / Pikes Peak / Gold Region. / Showing all the routes from the / Mississippi & Missouri Rivers, and the Out-/fitting Points. / [decorative rule] / Published by / Parker & Huyett, / S͟t Louis, M? 1859. / [decorative rule] / Drawn by A. M. Bailey C. E. / Lith. of A. Janicke & Co. 3͟d St. opposite the new Custom House St. Louis. / [in border:] Entered according to the act of Congress in the year 1859 by Parker & Huyett in Clerks Office of the District Court of the U. S. for the District of Missouri /. 31.8 x 60.4 cm. No scale given. Map: [St. Louis, Alton and Chicago Railroad, with connecting lines in the St. Louis and Chicago areas]. 16.3 x 12.2 cm. No scale given. Accompanies advertisement of company. Green cloth, with title in gilt on front cover and in blind on back: Parker & Huyett's / New / Illustrated / Miners' Hand Book / and Guide to / [ornament] / Pike's Peak. /, embossed borders in blind.

Ref.: Bradford 4182a; Eberstadt (in *Book-*

men's Holiday (New York, 1943) p. 40; Hafen pp. 261–69; Howes P82; Wagner-Camp 339

3192 PARKER, SAMUEL

JOURNAL OF AN EXPLORING TOUR BEYOND THE ROCKY MOUNTAINS, UNDER THE DIRECTION OF THE A. B. C. F. M. PERFORMED IN THE YEARS 1835, '36, AND '37 . . . ITHACA, N.Y.: PUBLISHED BY THE AUTHOR, 1838.

[i]–xii, [13]–371, [372 blank]. 18.8 x 12 cm. Folding map and one plate. Map: Map / of / Oregon Territory. / By / Samuel Parker. / 1838. / Copy right secured. / [lower right:] Eng͟d by M. M. Peabody. Utica N.Y. / 35.6 x 56.4 cm. Scale: 60 miles to one inch. Blue embossed cloth, printed green paper label (4.6 x 2.8 cm.) on backstrip.

Ref.: Bradford 4183; Howes P89; Rader 2600; Sabin 58729; Smith 7893; Wagner-Camp 70

Parker accompanied a fur-trading party, in 1835, from Council Bluffs to Walla Walla.— Howes. The map is the earliest map of the Oregon interior with a pretense to accuracy.

3193 PARKER, SAMUEL

THE SAME, 1842.

[i]–xvi, [17]–408. 19.4 x 12.1 cm. Folding map and one plate. Map as in preceding. Black cloth, sides embossed in blind, title in gilt on backstrip.

Revised. Some changes on map.

3194 PARKER, SAMUEL

THE SAME. 1844.

[i]–xvi, [17]–416. 19.4 x 12.2 cm. Illustrations and map as in preceding. Black cloth, blind embossed sides, title in gilt on backstrip.

3195 PARKER, SAMUEL

THE SAME. AUBURN, 1846.

[i]–xvi, [17]–422, [1]–6 advertisements. 18.6 x 11.2 cm. Illustrations and map as in preceding. Dark brown cloth, blind embossed sides, title in gilt on backstrip.

3196 PARKER, WILLIAM B.

NOTES TAKEN DURING THE EXPEDITION COMMANDED BY CAPT. R. B. MARCY, U. S. A., THROUGH UNEXPLORED TEXAS, IN THE SUMMER AND FALL OF 1854 . . . PHILADELPHIA: HAYES & ZELL, 1856.

[i]–xii, [9]–242, [1]–6 advertisements. 18.5 x 12.4 cm. Brown cloth, publishers' names on sides in blind, title in gilt on backstrip.

Ref.: Bradford 4186; Howes P91; Rader 2602; Raines p. 162; Sabin 58775; Wagner-Camp 279

Especially valuable for the northwest part of Texas.

3197 PARKER, WILLIAM T.

PERSONAL EXPERIENCES AMONG OUR NORTH AMER-
ICAN INDIANS FROM 1867 TO 1885 . . . NORTHAMP-
TON, MASS., 1913.

[1]–232. 23.5 x 15.7 cm.

BOUND WITH:

PERSONAL EXPERIENCES AMONG OUR NORTH AMER-
ICAN INDIANS. SUPPLEMENT . . . NORTHAMPTON,
MASSACHUSETTS, 1918.

[1]–46. Extra-illustrated as below. Rebound in
contemporary black half morocco, title in gilt on
front cover and backstrip, uncut.

Prov.: Author's copy, with manuscript notes
and signatures, and with extra-illustrations,
bookplate, etc.

Ref.: Howes P94; Rader 2605

A fascinating copy. The author's copy extensively extra-illustrated as follows:

Bookplate inside front cover.

[Broadside] For God and Country / [short
rule] / [46 lines] / William Thornton Parker,
M. D., / Indian War Veteran, U. S. Army. /
Northampton, Massachusetts / November 2nd,
1922 /. 22.7 x 14.1 cm. Text 15.8 x 8.3 cm.

Signature on front endleaf.

Military Testimonials / of / William Thornton Parker, M. D. / United States Army / 1866–
1884 / [rule] / Northampton, Massachusetts /
A. D. 1915 /. [1–4]. 21.5 x 14 cm.

[Caption title] [vignette] / The Manliness of
The Christian / Soldier / . . . [1–4, 4 blank].
20.4 x 15.3 cm. Dated at end Northampton,
Mass. / March, 1925 /.

Two photographs, Army & Navy Union
Drum Corps and Captain Thornton Parker Fife
Drum and Bugle Corps. 18.7 x 13.6 cm. and
18.3 x 13.1 cm.

Manuscript dedication: To The Men Who
Blazed The Trail / [10 lines]

Portrait of George A. Custer, issued June 21,
1921, in commemoration of his death, dated
from Hardin, Montana. 15.3 x 11.4 cm.

Manuscript dedication: To The / [3 lines] /
Army of The United States /.

Manuscript paragraph, 12 lines, mounted.
16.5 x 13.5 cm.

[Broadsheet prospectus] New England / Indian War Veterans / . . . / of / Abraham Parker's Family / . . . 22.5 x 15 cm. Incomplete?

[Caption title] Rooms of the Essex Institute. /
Salem, Mass., Nov. 8, 1890. / [rule] / The Free-
Lecture Course . . . [1–4, 2 & 4 blank]. Includes
announcement of lecture by Parker.

Manuscript, five lines of verse, initialed by
Parker. 4.7 x 12.8 cm. Mounted.

Personal Experiences / . . . / Northampton,
Mass. / A. D. 1913 / [1]–8. 20.4 x 13.7 cm.

Prospectus and press notices of the book, manuscript quotation, 3 lines, on page 3.

[Caption title] The old Indian War Veterans
who served / in the Sixties and Seventies. / By /
William Thornton Parker, M. D. / . . . [1–4, 4
blank]. 23.2 x 15.1 cm. Dated on page [3]; December 23, 1924. Two copies; one cut down.

[Prospectus of] Annals of Old Fort Cummings / New Mexico 1867–8 / . . . [1–4, 4
blank]. Printed in red. 21.5 x 13.5 cm.

[Broadside] [two rules] / Dear Doctor: / I am
making a study of Midwifery among our Abo-
rigines. . . . / [14 lines] / W. Thornton Parker,
M. D., / M. M. S. S., / Late Surgeon U. S. Indian Service. / 22 x 16.7 cm. Text, 19.2 x 15.1
cm.

[Broadside] Names of Honor and Affection
given to / Mrs. W. Thornton Parker, by the /
Chippewa Indians at White Earth / Indian Reservation, Minnesota / [rule] / [23 lines] /
W. Thornton Parker, M. D. / [4 lines] / Northampton, Mass. / December 1924 /. 22.9 x 14.2
cm. Text, 16.8 x 9.5 cm.

Second copy of preceding, cut down,
mounted.

[Caption title] Leaflet 96 / [vignette] / What
Will You Do for Jesus? / [1–4]. 16 x 10 cm.
Signed by Parker and dated at end June, 1912.

[Caption title] A Soldier's Plea For Justice /
An Indian War Veteran's Experiences in / Kansas and New Mexico during the / Indian Wars of
1867–1868 / by / William Thornton Parker,
M. D. / . . . [1–4]. 22.7 x 15.1 cm. Dated on
page [4] February 2nd, 1925. Second copy, line
6: William Thornon[!] Parkr[!], M. D. / Paper
differs: 21.7 x 14.2 cm.

[Prospectus] [broadsheet] Personal Experiences / . . . 20.1 x 13.8 cm. Issued after November 1, 1918. Includes advertisement for *Supplement* and press notices.

[Broadside] W. Thornton Parker, M. D.,
Univ. Ludovic-/Maximilian, Munich, 1873 /
[rule] / [27 lines] / Northampton, Massachusetts. / Dated on page [3] February 22, 1914.
17 x 12.3 cm. Text, 12.4 x 8.4 cm.

[Broadside] [vignette of Indian] / National
Indian War Veterans, U. S. Army. / "The men
who never showed 'the white feather.' " / [8
lines] / Printed by Comrade Captain W. Thornton Parker, M. D. / Member National Committee N. I. W. V., U. S. A. / A. D. 1914. / [printed
in red]. 26 x 21 cm. Text, 18.7 x 15.2 cm.

31 illustrations interspersed. Numerous newspaper clippings pasted in. Numerous manuscript
notes, in addition to those described above, inserted. Laid in is an Autograph Manuscript
Note, signed Elizabeth R. Parker. No date,
Northampton, Massachusetts. One page, 17.8 x

15.6 cm. In pencil. As follows: These Bound Books of Dr. / Parker's Writings are to / go to the Pynchon / Memorial Building to / be placed in the Drawers / of the old Secretary or on the Shelves if they / care for them / Elizabeth R. Parker /.

3198 PARKHURST, JACOB

SKETCHES OF THE LIFE AND ADVENTURES OF JACOB PARKHURST; WRITTEN WITH HIS OWN HAND WHEN ABOUT THREE SCORE AND TEN YEARS OF AGE . . . NEWCASTLE IND.: JOHN W. GRUPPS[!], PRINTER, "COURIER" OFFICE, 1842.

[1]–28. 16.5 x 12 cm. Half brown morocco, by Riviere. Title-leaf and some margins repaired.

Ref.: Byrd & Peckham 1003; Howes P95

Parkhurst joined Harmar for the Ohio campaign of 1790, but did not march north with him from Cincinnati. Later, he had several narrow escapes from Indians along the shores of the Ohio.

In a copy reported by Robert G. Hayman, the printer's name is correctly spelled: Grubbs. Examination of the present copy under ultraviolet light shows that the imprint has been supplied in printed "facsimile."

3199 PARKHURST, JACOB

THE SAME.

[i–ii], [1]–55, [56 blank]. 13.5 x 10 cm. Frontispiece portrait of the author. Yellow printed wrappers mounted on linen.

Ref.: Howes P95

On verso of title-page: This book was originally published in 1842 / —reproduced in 1893 *ver batim et literatim.* / Mort Edwards, / Knightstown, Ind. /

This reprint has become quite scarce. In 1940 I did not find a copy of it in the Indiana State Library at Indianapolis nor in the Knightstown Public Library. The Henry County Historical Society at Newcastle, Indiana, had a copy but possibly imperfect as they reported it as having 54 pages.—EDG

3200 PARKINSON, T. D.

[Map] MAP / OF THE / COMSTOCK LODE / AND THE / WASHOE MINING CLAIMS / IN / STOREY & LYON COUNTIES, / NEVADA. / COMPILED FROM OFFICIAL SURVEYS / AND OTHER RELIABLE DATA BY / T. D. PARKINSON, C. E. / SCALE, 1000 FEET TO THE INCH. / ENTERED ACCORDING TO ACT OF CONGRESS IN THE YEAR 1875 BY T. D. PARKINSON IN THE OFFICE OF THE LIBRARIAN OF CONGRESS AT WASHINGTON, D. C. / G. T. BROWN & CO. LITH. 540 CLAY ST. S. F.

Map, 60.8 x 77 cm. Scale: 1000 feet to an inch. Brown cloth covers, 17.5 x 11.5 cm., with title in gilt on front cover.

Ref.: Phillips (*Maps*) p. 245

Tipped to the inside front cover is a broadsheet, 16.6 x 10.6 cm., headed: List of Mineral Claims Shown upon / Parkinson's Map of the Comstock Lode. / The map includes, at the top: Longitudinal Section of the Comstock Lode /. 13.5 x 77 cm.

3201 PARKMAN, FRANCIS

THE CALIFORNIA AND OREGON TRAIL . . . LONDON: JOHN CHAPMAN, 1849.

[3]–448, 3–6, [1]–24, both advertisements. 18.8 x 12.5 cm. Tinted frontispiece and facing pictorial title-page. Light blue cloth, blind embossed sides, printed white paper label, 4.4 x 3.2 cm., on backstrip. Lacks front fly-leaf.

Ref.: Howes P97; Johnson (Blanck) p. 409; *New Colophon*, 1950, pp. 279–85; Sabin 58801

First English edition. The first section of advertisements is for Putnam and the second for Chapman, the latter dated March, 1849. Note that instead of a gilt stamped title on the spine there is a printed paper label. There is no note on the frontispiece; the type on pages [436–]7 is perfect.

3202 PARKMAN, FRANCIS

THE OREGON TRAIL . . . ILLUSTRATED BY FREDERIC REMINGTON. BOSTON: LITTLE, BROWN, AND COMPANY, 1892.

[i]–xvi, 1–411, [412 blank]. 21.7 x 14.8 cm. Illustrated by Frederic Remington with full-page plates, illustrations in the text, and decorations. Full original decorated calf, gilt top, uncut. In original printed dust jacket.

Ref.: Howes P97; Johnson (Blanck) p. 427

3203 PARR, LOUISE LINCOLN

SKETCH OF THE LIFE OF "DICK" PARR IN THE FAR WEST. GREAT ROUGH RIDER OF THE WESTERN PLAINS, GENERAL PHIL SHERIDAN'S PRIVATE CHIEF OF SCOUTS, INDIAN INTERPRETER AND GUIDE DURING THAT GALLANT COMMANDER'S INDIAN CAMPAIGN, 1868–9 . . .

[1]–62. 18.8 x 12.4 cm. Nine illustrations, unlisted. White pictorial wrappers, with title on front wrapper. In a red cloth folder.

Ref.: Howes P103

"Dick" Parr was Cephas W. Parr.

Published in New York in 1901.

Although the pamphlet was copyrighted in 1900, it contains a letter to Parr from General Sheridan's brother, Colonel M. V. Sheridan, dated Governor's Island, March 27th, 1901.

3204 PARSONS, GEORGE F.

THE LIFE AND ADVENTURES OF JAMES W. MAR-
SHALL, THE DISCOVERER OF GOLD IN CALIFOR-
NIA . . . SACRAMENTO: PUBLISHED BY JAMES W.
MARSHALL AND W. BURKE, 1870.

[1]–188. 16.7 x 11.6 cm. Portrait. Pale gray
printed wrappers with title on front wrapper,
printer's monogram on verso of back wrapper.
In a blue cloth case.

Ref.: Blumann & Thomas 806; Cowan p.
475; Howes P105; Jones 1534; Sabin 58882

Eberstadt points out that copies in cloth have
the three stab-holes which were used for the
copies in wrappers and are probably later than
the wrappered copies.

The tragedy with Marshall as with Sutter was
that the consequences of his discovery were too
much for him. Up to the moment of the find he
had every prospect of becoming a substantial
citizen in the new territory. . . . Certainly the
account that this little book gives of his ensuing
years may be interpreted to show a delusion of
persecution. But if the wrongs were fancied, if it
was only a broken mind that made Marshall feel
he was being driven from his claims and hunted
like one accursed, his tragedy is the greater.—
G. Ezra Dane, in the 1935 reprint.

3205 PARSONS, WILLIAM B.

THE GOLD MINES OF WESTERN KANSAS; BEING A
COMPLETE DESCRIPTION OF THE NEWLY DISCOV-
ERED GOLD MINES, DIFFERENT ROUTES, CAMPING
PLACES, TOOLS & OUTFITS; AND CONTAINING EV-
ERYTHING IMPORTANT FOR THE EMIGRANT AND
MINER TO KNOW . . . LAWRENCE, KANSAS:
PRINTED FOR THE AUTHOR, 1858.

[1]–45, [46–8 advertisements]. 18.9 x 11.8 cm·
Green printed wrappers with title on front wrapper, advertisement on verso of back wrapper. In
a gray half morocco case.

Ref.: AII (*Kansas*) 205; Hafen p. 147; Howes
P110; Sabin 58923; Wagner-Camp 305b; Wilcox
p. 87 see

First edition of the first Pike's Peak Gold
Mines guide book. The work was published in
December of 1858 and a second edition (see next
item) was to be ready in February of the next
year.

The Library of Congress copy (which is in
printed blue wrappers) is the only other copy
known to date. The Wagner-Camp collation is in
error. Hafen reprinted the fuller, second, edition.

3206 PARSONS, WILLIAM B.

NEW AND ENLARGED EDITION. THE NEW GOLD
MINES OF WESTERN KANSAS: BEING A COMPLETE

DESCRIPTION OF THE NEWLY DISCOVERED GOLD
MINES . . . CINCINNATI, OHIO: GEO. S. BLANCHARD,
1859.

[1]–63, [64–72 advertisements]. 18.2 x 12 cm.
Yellow printed wrappers with title on front
wrapper, advertisements on verso of front and
recto and verso of back wrapper.

Ref.: Hafen p. 147; Howes P110; Rader
2617; Sabin 58923; Wagner-Camp 340; Wilcox
p. 87

The second edition.

3207 PARVIN, THEODORE S.

REPORT ON THE CLIMATE OF IOWA: EMBRACING
THE RESULT OF THE METEOROLOGICAL RECORDS OF
THE YEAR 1856, AT MUSCATINE, IOWA, WITH A
SYNOPSIS OF THE RECORDS OF THE SEVEN YEARS
FROM 1850 TO 1856, INCLUSIVE . . . MUSCATINE:
PRINTED BY RAYMOND, FOOTE & CO., 1857.

[1]–12. 20.7 x 13.6 cm. Stabbed, unbound.

Ref.: Moffit 326

3208 PATRIOTA NEO-MEXICANO, EL

[Broadside] PROSPECTO. CON LA DURA CRUZ DE
LA FIRME OPOSICION, VENCEREMOS CUALQUIERA
FALSEDAD Y CORRUPCION. EL PATRIOTA NEO-
MEXICANO. ORGANO DE LAS POBLACIONES HISPANO-
AMERICANAS, SITUADAS AL SUD-OESTE DE LA GRAN
REPUBLICA OCCIDENTAL, PUBLICADO POR LA
"ASOCIACION PATRIOTICA DE NUEVO MEXICO." . . .
PARA MAS INFORMACION DIRIJANSE A LA "ASOCIA-
CION PATRIOTICA DE NUEVO MEXICO." LAS VEGAS,
N.M.

Broadside, 30.3 x 21.5 cm. Text, 27 x 15.3 cm.

Ref.:

The broadside is printed in three columns, the
first being quoted above and reading up. The
second and third columns describe the intentions of the publishers, i.e. strong support for the
party of H. Greeley, "compuesto de los Republi-
canos mas liberales y Demócratas mas pro-
gresivos."

The newspaper seems not to have been published, and no other reference to this broadside
has been found. It was probably printed in the
late 1860's or early 1870's.

According to Douglas McMurtrie, the first
newspaper printed in Las Vegas was *The Advertiser*, May 1870.

3209 PATTERSON, A. W.

HISTORY OF THE BACKWOODS; OR, THE REGION OF
THE OHIO . . . PITTSBURGH: PUBLISHED BY THE
AUTHOR, 1843.

[1–2], [i]–x, [5]–311, [312 blank]. 21.5 x 13.4 cm.
(Page 295 mispaginated 265.) Map: Map/of the/
Backwoods / in / 1764. / Engraved Pittsburgh

1843. / 21.4 x 27.5 cm. No scale given. Black cloth. Lacks front endleaf.

Ref.: Field 1168; Howes P118; Jones 1081; Sabin 59132; Thomson 911

The events detailed, relate principally to the Western part of Pennsylvania, in the neighborhood of Fort Pitt, but it contains some valuable information, in regard to the Indians and early settlements in Ohio.—Thomson

3210 PATTERSON, D. C.

[Wrapper title] 1776. 1876. CENTENNIAL HISTORY AND DIRECTORY OF LA PORTE CITY, BLACKHAWK COUNTY, IOWA. CONTAINING A HISTORICAL SKETCH OF LA PORTE CITY FROM ITS SETTLEMENT UP TO THE PRESENT DAY . . . LA PORTE CITY, IOWA: PROGRESS PRINT, 1876.

[1–26]. 23.2 x 14.7 cm. Light blue printed wrappers, with title on front wrapper, advertisements on verso of front and recto and verso of back wrapper. In a blue cloth folder.

Ref.: Howes P119

Versos of leaves through page [18] carry advertisements.

3211 PATTERSON, LAWSON B.

TWELVE YEARS IN THE MINES OF CALIFORNIA; EMBRACING A GENERAL VIEW OF THE GOLD REGION, WITH PRACTICAL OBSERVATIONS ON HILL, PLACER, AND QUARTZ DIGGINGS; AND NOTES ON THE ORIGIN OF GOLD DEPOSITS . . . CAMBRIDGE: PRINTED BY MILES AND DILLINGHAM, 1862.

[1]–108. 17.2 x 11.3 cm. Black cloth, title stamped in gilt on front cover.

Ref.: Bradford 4212; Cowan pp. 475–76; Howes P121; Sabin 59140

3212 PATTERSON, R., & LAMBDIN, Pittsburgh

CATALOGUE OF BOOKS, IN THE DIFFERENT DEPARTMENTS OF LITERATURE, FOR SALE BY R. PATTERSON & LAMBDIN, BOOKSELLERS & STATIONERS . . . PITTSBURGH: PRINTED BY BUTLER & LAMBDIN, 1818.

A⁶, [B]⁴, A–F⁶. [i–xx], [1]–72. 17.7 x 10.6 cm. New boards, printed paper label.

Ref.:

No other copy of this catalogue has been located. Catalogues for 1811 and 1815 are known.

3213 PATTERSON, ROBERT M.

A FUNERAL DISCOURSE, DELIVERED, NOV. 5TH. 1848, ON OCCASION OF THE DEATH OF ROBERT STUART, ESQ., WHO DIED SUDDENLY AT CHICAGO, ON THE 29TH OF OCT., 1848. DETROIT: HARSHA & WILLCOX, 1849.

[1]–27, [28 blank]. 22.2 x 14.1 cm. Pale yellow printed wrappers with title on front cover.

Prov.: Numerals and stamps of Historical and Philosophical Society of Ohio on front wrapper and with penciled note by Wessen.

Ref.: AII (*Michigan*) 824

Robert Stuart was an agent of the North West Fur Company, an associate of Astor, Ramsay, Crooks, and others. In later life he lived in Detroit.

3214 PATTERSON, ROBERT W.

EARLY SOCIETY IN SOUTHERN ILLINOIS. A LECTURE, READ BEFORE THE CHICAGO HISTORICAL SOCIETY, OCTOBER 19, 1880 . . . CHICAGO: FERGUS PRINTING COMPANY, 1881.

[i–ii blank], [1]–34. 23.5 x 15.5 cm. Gray printed wrappers, with title on front wrapper.

Ref.: Bradford 4213

3215 PATTERSON, WILLIAM D.

[Map] MAP / —OF THE— / CARIBOO & OMINECA / GOLD FIELDS / AND / THE ROUTES THERETO / COMPILED & DRAWN FROM RELIABLE AUTHORITIES / BY / WM D PATTERSON C E / LITH F. W. GREEN C E / 37 x 51 cm. No scale given. *Inset:* [Fraser River from New Westminster to below Fort Alexander]. 24.5 x 12 cm. No scale given.

Yellow printed boards, 14.5 x 9.5 cm., green cloth back, with title on front cover, advertisement on back cover.

Ref.:

Tipped in at the front is a broadside, 25.4 x 25.3 cm., text, 21.3 x 21.2 cm., headed: Distance Tables and Miscellaneous Information. / [rule] / [48 lines of text, mostly in tabular form]. Also bound in facing inner front cover is a page of advertisements, verso blank. Advertisements on both inner covers.

3216 PATTIE, JAMES O.

THE PERSONAL NARRATIVE OF JAMES O. PATTIE, OF KENTUCKY, DURING AN EXPEDITION FROM SAINT LOUIS, THROUGH THE VAST REGIONS BETWEEN THAT PLACE AND THE PACIFIC OCEAN, AND THENCE BACK THROUGH THE CITY OF MEXICO TO VERA CRUZ, DURING JOURNEYINGS OF SIX YEARS . . . CINCINNATI: PRINTED AND PUBLISHED BY JOHN H. WOOD, 1831.

[i]–xi, [xii blank], [13]–300. (Page 251 mispaginated 151.) 19.8 x 12 cm. Five plates engraved by W. Woodruff of Cincinnati. Original tree sheep, red leather label.

Ref.: Cowan p. 476; Howes P123; Jones 920; Rader 2619; Wagner-Camp 45

Pages 225–288 contain an account of Dr. Willard's tour entitled "Inland Trade with New

Mexico." Pages 289–291 contain the "Downfall of the Fredonian Republic." Both pieces had appeared in Flint's *Western Monthly Review*.

Second overland journey to California, first over the route taken, with adventures incredible had they not been substantiated by later investigations.—Howes

3217 PATTIE, JAMES O.

THE SAME. CINCINNATI: PUBLISHED BY E. H. FLINT, 1833.

[i]–xi, [xii blank], [13]–300. (Page 251 mispaginated 151.) 19.6 x 11.9 cm. Five plates, engraved by W. Woodruff of Cincinnati. Original full tree sheep, with citron leather label.

Ref.: Bradford 4214; Cowan p. 476; Field 1186; Howes P123; Jones 937; Rader 2619; Sabin 59150; Wagner-Camp 45

Copyrighted 1833 by John H. Wood.

Wagner-Camp notes four variants of the copyright in the 1833 edition, of which he lists this second.

3218 PAUL WILHELM, HERZOG VON WURTTEMBERG

ERSTE REISE NACH DEM NORDLICHEN AMERIKA IN DEN JAHREN 1822 BIS 1824 ... STUTTGART: VERLAG DER J. G. COTTA'SCHEN BUCHHANDLUNG, 1835.

[i]–vi, [1]–394, [395–96 errata]. 23 x 14 cm. Folding map: Louisiana. / Scale / [diagrammatic scale: about 27 miles to one inch] / [lower left:] Herzog Pauls v. Württemberg Reise nach Amerika / [centre:] Verlag der J. G. Cotta'schen Buchhandlung. / 31.3 x 34.6 cm. Scale as above. Gray marbled boards, original leather label on backstrip, with title.

Ref.: Buck 184; Howes P130; Rader 2621; Sabin 59182; Wagner-Camp 58

A translation of this work is found in the *South Dakota Historical Society Collections*, Vol. XIX, 1938.

The map is copied from an American or British original.

Editions: Mergentheim, 1828.

3219 PAULISON, C. M. K.

ARIZONA. THE WONDERFUL COUNTRY. TUCSON ITS METROPOLIS. A COMPREHENSIVE REVIEW OF THE PAST PROGRESS, PRESENT CONDITION AND FUTURE PROSPECTS OF THE TERRITORY OF ARIZONA ... TUCSON, A. T.: PRINTED AT THE OFFICE OF THE ARIZONA STAR, 1881.

[1]–31, [32 blank]. 21.7 x 14 cm. Sewn, removed from bound volume.

Ref.: AII (*Arizona*) 64; Howes P137; Munk (Alliot) p. 175

3220 PAXTON, JOHN A.

THE ST. LOUIS DIRECTORY AND REGISTER ... TOGETHER WITH DESCRIPTIVE NOTES ON ST. LOUIS ... ST. LOUIS: PRINTED FOR THE PUBLISHER, 1821.

[i–iv advertisements], [1–100, 101–102 blank]. 18.8 x 11.1 cm. Blue printed boards (text almost wholly lost). Later brown leather backstrip, new endpapers.

Ref.: AII (*Missouri*) 46; Howes P148

The first directory printed west of the Mississippi.

3221 PAYNE, DAVID L.

[Business card] D. L. PAYNE, OKLAHOMA, PRESIDENT, PAYNE OKLAHOMA COLONY CO. INDIAN TERRITORY. Calling card. 4.9 x 9.4 cm.

3222 PAYNE, DAVID L.

[Broadside] LAST CHANCE FOR CHEAP HOMES! HEADQ'RS OF THE SOUTHWEST COLONIZATION ASSOCIATION, WICHITA, KANSAS, JANUARY 1, 1880. MY DEAR SIR: ... FOR ANY INFORMATION ADDRESS THE PRESIDENT OR SECRETARY, LOCK BOX 194, WICHITA, KANSAS. D. L. PAYNE, PRESIDENT. W. C. GLENN, SECRETARY. W. B. HUTCHISON, PRINTER, WICHITA, KANSAS.

Broadside, 32.2 x 23.9 cm. Text, 27.8 x 17.8 cm.

Ref.:

One of Payne's schemes to seize control of lands in the Indian Territory.

3223 PAYNE, DAVID L.

[Broadside] OKLAHOMA COLONY! A COLONY HAS BEEN ORGANIZED FOR THE PURPOSE OF OPENING UP AND SETTLING THIS BEAUTIFUL COUNTRY ... CAPT. D. L. PAYNE, THE FAMOUS OKLAHOMA AGITATOR, WILL LECTURE UPON THIS SUBJECT TONIGHT! ...

Broadside, 10.1 x 14 cm. Text, 8 x 11.7 cm.

Ref.:

Issued in 1882 or 1883, probably at Wichita, Kansas, which was the headquarters of Captain Payne, the organizer of the colony.

3224 PAYNE, DAVID L.

[Broadside] ON TO OKLAHOMA! AN OPPORTUNITY IS NOW OFFERED TO EVERY PERSON DESIROUS OF SECURING A HOME UPON GOVERNMENT LANDS, ... CAPT. D. L. PAYNE, WHO HAS LONG BEEN AGITATING THE QUESTION OF THE SETTLEMENT OF THIS COUNTRY WILL LECTURE ...

Broadside, 10 x 14.4 cm. Text, 8 x 10.8 cm.

Ref.:

Issued in 1882 or 1883, probably at Wichita, Kansas.

3225 PAYNE, DAVID L.

[Ticket] PAYNE'S LECTURE ON OKLAHOMA. ADMIT ONE. Ticket, printed on green cardboard, 4.9 x 9.2 cm.

3226 PAYNE, DAVID L.

[Caption title] TO OUR OKLAHOMA COLONISTS. THOSE WHO WISH A HOME IN THAT BEAUTIFUL COUNTRY . . .

[1–4]. 21.9 x 14.6 cm. Unbound leaflet.
Ref.:
Signed at the end (above a nine-line note): D. L. Payne, Pres. / W. H. Osburn, Secretary. / Wichita, Kansas, June 8, 1882, (Box 184) /.

3227 PEARESON, PHILIP E.

SKETCH OF THE LIFE OF JUDGE EDWIN WALLER, TOGETHER WITH SOME OF THE MORE IMPORTANT EVENTS OF THE EARLY TEXAS REVOLUTION, IN WHICH HE PARTICIPATED, SUCH AS THE BATTLE OF VELASCO, AND INCIDENTS LEADING THERETO, AND FOLLOWING . . . GALVESTON: PRINTED AT THE "NEWS" STEAM BOOK AND JOB ESTABLISHMENT, 1874.

[1]–25, [26–8 blank]. 22.2 x 14.2 cm. Lavender printed wrappers, with title on front wrapper. In green cloth case.
Ref.: Howes P158; Raines pp. 162–63

3228 PEARSE, JAMES

A NARRATIVE OF THE LIFE OF JAMES PEARSE . . . RUTLAND: PRINTED BY WILLIAM FAY, FOR THE AUTHOR, 1825.

[i]–vi, [7]–144. 17.5 x 11 cm. Gray boards, sheep back. Worn.
Ref.: Clark II 51; Howes P160; Jones 869; Rader 2626; Sabin 59438
A good narrative, especially the second part. —Howes. Middle West, the South and New York state.

3229 PEASE & COLE

COMPLETE GUIDE TO THE GOLD DISTRICTS OF KANSAS & NEBRASKA CONTAINING VALUABLE INFORMATION WITH REGARD TO ROUTES, DISTANCES, ETC., ETC. . . . CHICAGO, ILL.: WM. H. RAND, PRINTER, 1859.

[1]–20. 16.3 x 10.7 cm. Folding map: Map / of the / Routes to / The Gold Regions / in Western / Kansas & Nebraska / from latest Observations of / government Officers / By / Pease & Cole / Chicago, Ill. / Entered in the Clerks Office of the U. S. District Court for the Northern District of Illinois January 1859 by Pease & Cole, according to Act of Congress respecting Copyrights / [lower right:] Lith. Chas. Shober 109 Lake St. Chicago / 42.3 x 42 cm. No scale

given. Maroon cloth, lettered on front cover in gilt. In a red cloth case.
Ref.: AII (*Chicago*) 425; Hafen p. 86; Howes P167; Wagner-Camp 341; Wilcox p. 88

3230 PEASE & TAYLOR (Cheyenne, Wyoming)

[Trade card] PEASE & TAYLOR, WHOLESALE AND RETAIL DEALERS IN GROCERIES AND PROVISIONS, GREEN AND DRIED FRUITS, VEGETABLES, RANCH BUTTER, TEAS, SUGARS, SPICES, CANNED GOODS, ETC. FERGUSON STREET, MARBLE FRONT BLOCK, CHEYENNE, WYO.

Broadsheet, 6.3 x 10.4 cm.
Ref.:
On the verso is a: Table of Distances from / Cheyenne / to the / Black Hills. / [decorative rule] / [28 lines: 25 entries and a three-line note] /. The distances given cover the route from Cheyenne to Custer City.
Probably printed in Cheyenne after August 10, 1875 (date of laying out of Custer City), but before a permanent road was established.

3231 [PECK, JOHN M.]

"FATHER CLARK;" OR, THE PIONEER PREACHER. SKETCHES AND INCIDENTS OF REV. JOHN CLARK . . . NEW YORK: SHELDON, LAMPORT & BLACKMAN, 1855.

[i]–viii, [9]–287, [288 blank]. 16.5 x 10.4 cm. Frontispiece. Purple cloth, blind embossed borders on sides with title in gilt on front cover and in blind on back, title in gilt on backstrip.
Ref.: Howes P169; Sabin 59482

3232 PECK, JOHN M.

A GAZETTEER OF ILLINOIS, IN THREE PARTS: CONTAINING A GENERAL VIEW OF THE STATE, A GENERAL VIEW OF EACH COUNTY; AND A PARTICULAR DESCRIPTION OF EACH TOWN, SETTLEMENT, STREAM, PRAIRIE, BOTTOM, BLUFF, ETC. . . . JACKSONVILLE: PUBLISHED BY R. GOUDY, 1834.

[i]–viii, [1]–376. 14.9 x 10.1 cm. Mottled sheepskin, black leather label on backstrip.
Ref.: Bradford 4232; Buck 278; Byrd 191; Howes P170; Sabin 59483
Peck was well-equipped to compile a gazetteer of Illinois, for he had traveled over most of the state. His descriptions and observations are almost entirely drawn from personal experience.

3233 PECK, JOHN M.

THE SAME . . . PHILADELPHIA: GRIGG & ELLIOT, 1837.

[i]–[xii, xii blank], [1]–328. 14.7 x 9.5 cm. Purple cloth, embossed in blind with all-over leafy pat-

tern, original green printed paper label, 3.8 x 6.2 cm., on front cover.

Editions: Jacksonville, 1834, 1834.

3234 PECK, JOHN M.

A GUIDE FOR EMIGRANTS, CONTAINING SKETCHES OF ILLINOIS, MISSOURI, AND THE ADJACENT PARTS . . . BOSTON: LINCOLN AND EDMANDS, 1831.

[1]–336. 14.5 x 8.8 cm. Map: Western States. / Scale / [diagrammatic scale: about 100 miles to one inch.] / Published by Lincoln & Edmands, Boston. / H. Morse Sc. / 14.9 x 18.7 cm. Scale as above. Smooth green cloth, printed paper label on backstrip, 3.4 x 2.5 cm.

Ref.: Buck 236; Clark III 86; Howes P171

3235 PECK, JOHN M.

A NEW GUIDE FOR EMIGRANTS TO THE WEST . . . OF OHIO, INDIANA, ILLINOIS, MISSOURI, MICHIGAN, WITH THE TERRITORIES OF WISCONSIN AND ARKANSAS, AND THE ADJACENT PARTS . . . BOSTON: GOULD, KENDALL & LINCOLN, 1836.

[i]–[viii, viii blank], [v]–x, [11]–374, [1]–6 advertisements. 15.7 x 9.4 cm. Green cloth, blind embossed sides, with name of binder, B. Bradley, incorporated in design, title in gilt on backstrip.

Ref.: Bradford 4234a; Buck 236; Clark III 86; Howes P171; Sabin 59485

Editions: Boston, 1831, 1835.

3236 PECK, JOHN M.

THE SAME . . . 1837.

[i]–[xiv, xiv blank], [15]–381, [382 blank], [383–84 advertisements]. 15.6 x 9.2 cm. Green cloth, blind embossed panels on sides, title in gilt on backstrip.

3237 PECK, JOHN M.

THE TRAVELER'S DIRECTORY FOR ILLINOIS; CONTAINING ACCURATE SKETCHES OF THE STATE . . . NEW-YORK: PUBLISHED BY J. H. COLTON, 1839.

[1]–219, [220 advertisement]. 14.9 x 9.6 cm. Map: Map / of the State of / Illinois / Compiled / from the / United States Surveys, / exhibiting the / Sections, / with / Internal improvements, distances between / Towns, Villages, Post Offices &c. / by / J. M. Peck & John Messinger[!], / [rule] / Published by J. H. Colton, New York. / 1840. / [diagrammatic scale: 12 miles to one inch] / Scale of Miles / Entered according to Act of Congress, in the year 1840, by J. H. Colton, in the Clerk's Office of the District Court of the Southern District / of New York. / *Inset:* Map of the / Lead Region / 15.3 x 15.1 cm. Scale: 24 miles to one inch. *Inset:* Vicinity / of / Chicago /. 11.4 x 10.6 cm. 8 miles to one inch. *Inset:* Vicinity / of / Alton & S^t

Louis. / 15.4 x 14.8 cm. Scale: 6 miles to one inch. [Lower centre:] Engraved by Stiles, Sherman & Smith. / 85.1 x 59.8 cm. Scale: 12 miles to one inch. Dark brown ribbed cloth, blind embossed panels on sides, title in gilt on front cover.

Ref.: Buck 341; Howes P172; Sabin 59486

According to Buck, *The Traveler's Directory* "embodies much of the same material as his *Gazetteer of Illinois*." Note that on page 219, the text is signed by Peck under the date Feb. 13, 1840, although title is dated 1839.

3238 PECK, JOHN M., & JOHN MESSENGER

[Map] A / NEW MAP / OF / ILLINOIS / AND PART OF THE / WISCONSIN TERRITORY / BY J. M. PECK & J. MESSENGER. / CINCINNATI / PUBLISHED BY DOOLITTLE & MUNSON. / [lower centre:] ENTERED ACCORDING TO ACT OF CONGRESS IN THE YEAR 1835 BY J. M. PECK IN THE CLERKS OFFICE OF THE DISTRICT COURT OF ILLINOIS. /

Map, 46.8 x 32 cm. Scale not given. Folded into brown leather covers, 12.1 x 7.8 cm., with gilt borders and with gilt title on front cover. Front cover loose.

Ref.:

In lower right corner: Engraved by Doolittle & Munson Cincinnati Ohio. / Above this is a small vignette captioned: Illinois College. /

This precedes by four years the sectional map of Illinois in Peck: *The Traveler's Directory* . . . 1839. It is the first such map of Illinois.

3239 PECK, S. L.

HISTORY OF IRA, VERMONT . . . TO WHICH IS ADDED THE AUTHORS EARLY EXPERIENCES UPON THE PLAINS AND THE ROCKIES OF THE GREAT WEST DURING THE YEARS 1866–1867 . . . RUTLAND, VT.: THE TUTTLE COMPANY, 1926.*

[1]–83, [84 blank]. 22.9 x 15.4 cm. Illustrations unlisted. Green cloth.

Ref.:

3240 PEERY, EDWARD T.

SELECT HYMNS WITH THEIR TRANSLATIONS, IN THE DELAWARE LANGUAGE ON THE OPPOSITE PAGE . . . INDIAN MANUAL LABOR SCHOOL, 1846.

[1–4], 5–84. [Pages 18–19 imperfect?] 16.3 x 10.6 cm. Mottled sheepskin.

Ref.: McMurtrie & Allen (*Meeker*) 78 see

Rev. Edward T. Peery . . . was sent in 1832 to the Shawnee Mission (Methodist) and served in various fields and in different relations. For a time he was Superintendent of the Indian Manual Labor School, and was also presiding elder. He subsequently settled near Kansas City, where he died and was buried in 1864.—*Life of Rev. L. B. Stateler* by E. J. Stanley, Nashville, 1907, page 128. This may be the hymnal referred to by McMurtrie & Allen under No. 78 as having been printed by J. G. Pratt at Stockbridge. No other printing at the Indian Manual Labor School at Shawanoe (Shawnee) before 1855 has been noted.

3241 PEIRCE, PARKER I.

THE ADVENTURES OF ANTELOPE BILL IN THE INDIAN WAR OF 1862. BY PARKER I. PIERCE[!].

[1]–[244]. 17.2 x 11.1 cm. Pink pictorial wrappers. In a red cloth case.

Ref.: Howes P180

Signed on page 6: Parker I. Peirce. Marshall, Lyon County, Minn. At the end of the volume, page [244]: Copyright 1898.

No place of publication apparent, probably Marshall, Minnesota.

3242 PENA Y REYES, JUAN ANTONIO DE LA

DERROTERO DE LA EXPEDICION EN LA PROVINCIA DE LOS TEXAS, NUEVO REYNO DE PHILIPINAS . . . CON LICENCIA EN MEXICO: EN LA IMPRENTA NUEVA PLANTINIANA DE JUAN FRANCISCO DE ORTEGA BONILLA, 1722.

A–N², [O]¹. [i], 1–29 LEAVES. 28.3 x 20 cm. Four engraved folding plans and one folding manuscript map. Titles and text printed on verso of engraved maps. Manuscript map: [Isla de Culebra and Costa Azia la Veracruz] 42.5 x 31 cm. (paper size). Watercolor and ink. Twenty-line manuscript note on verso: Carta de la Bahia del Espiritu S^{to} . . . Map: [Plan del Presidio de N. S. Del Pilar, de los Adays, en la Frõtera de los Texas . . .] [lower centre:] Sylverio Sculp. Mex. / 27.9 x 39.3 cm. Scale: 13 baras to one inch. Map: [Plan del Presidio de N. S. de los Dolores . . .] [lower centre:] Sylverio, F. / 27.3 x 38.1 cm. Scale: 11 varas to one inch. Map: [Plan del Presidio de San Antonio de Bejar . . .] [lower left:] Sylverio scul. / 28.3 x 40.8 cm. (paper size). Scale: 14 baras to one inch. Map: [Presidio de N. S. de Loreto en la Bahia del Espiritu Santo . . .] [lower right:] Sylverio f. / 38.4 x 27.4 cm. Scale: 16 varas to one inch. Each map contains plants, trees, animals, etc., in the margins. Full new tree calf, green morocco label. In a red half morocco case.

Prov.: The Herschel V. Jones copy.

Ref.: Clements Library (*Texas*) 4; Howes P195; Jones 414; Medina (*Mexico*) 2689; Sabin 59626; Streeter (*Americana—Beginnings*) 56; Wagner (*SS*) 83

The Spanish expedition of the Marqués de San Miguel de Aguayo to secure control of Texas is described in Peña's *Derrotero*. Several Spanish missions had been forced to retreat to San Antonio by the French and the Indians. The Aguayo expedition (1720–1722) retrieved the Spanish position. This is generally considered the first book relating wholly to Texas.

According to a manuscript note on the verso of the manuscript map, the information was supplied by Aguayo himself. One other copy (of seven known) contains this manuscript map.

3243 PENDLETON, NATHANIEL G.

[Caption title] . . . MILITARY POSTS—COUNCIL BLUFFS TO THE PACIFIC OCEAN . . . MR. PENDLETON, OF OHIO, FROM THE COMMITTEE ON MILITARY AFFAIRS, MADE THE FOLLOWING REPORT: . . .

[1]–78, [79–80 blank]. 24.9 x 16.4 cm. Map: Map / of the / United States / Territory of Oregon / West of the Rocky Mountains. / Exhibiting the various Trading Depots or Forts / occupied by the British Hudson Bay Company con-/nected with the Western and northwestern Fur Trade. / [short swelled rule] / Compiled in the Bureau of Topographical / Engineers from the latest authorities, under / the direction of Col. J. J. Abert by / Wash: Hood. / 1838. / M. H. Stansbury del. / [short rule] / W. J. Stone Sc. Wash^n / 44.1 x 51.8 cm. Scale: about 20 statute miles to one inch. Stabbed, unbound, uncut. In a green cloth case.

Ref.: Howes P199; Wagner-Camp 100; Wheat (*Transmississippi*) 434

27th Congress, 3rd Session, House, Report No. 31, Serial 426. [Washington, 1843.]

3244 [PENGRA, B. J. & H. CUMMINS]

[Wrapper title] OREGON BRANCH OF THE PACIFIC RAILROAD. WASHINGTON, D. C.: McGILL & WITHEROW, PRINTERS & STEREOTYPERS.

[1]–19, [20 blank]. 22.6 x 14.7 cm. Reddish printed wrappers with title on front wrapper.

Ref.: Howes P200; *Railway Economics* p. 284

Signed and dated at the end (page 19): P[!]. J. Pengra, / Late Surveyor General of Oregon. / H. Cummins. / Washington City, D. C., April 28, 1868.

Details the advantages of speedy construction of the Oregon branch of the Pacific railway.

3245 PEOPLE'S REFORM LEAGUE. Nebraska

[Broadside] "COME, BROTHERS, AROUSE!" A MASS MEETING OF THE CITIZENS AND TAX-PAYERS OF OTOE COUNTY WILL BE HELD AT THE COURT HOUSE AT NEBRASKA CITY, SATURDAY, SEPTEMBER 17, 1870. AT 12 O'CLOCK NOON, FOR THE PURPOSE OF

CONSIDERING THE PRESENT CONDITION OF OUR COUNTY AFFAIRS AND OF NOMINATING A FULL PEOPLE'S REFORM TICKET FOR ALL COUNTY OFFICES, TO BE FILLED IN THE OCTOBER ELECTION, 1870. COME ONE, COME ALL! . . . NEBRASKA CITY, SEPTEMBER, 1870. BY ORDER OF THE PEOPLE'S REFORM LEAGUE, H. C. WOLPH . . .

Broadside, 51.1 x 22 cm. Text, 46.1 x 17.1 cm.

Ref.:

Contemporary manuscript note on verso: Gov Butler will speak at Tecumseh / on next Tuesday sharp at 2 o'clock / — / Will be at Ponca next Monday /.

3246 PEOPLE'S REFORM LEAGUE. Nebraska

[Broadside] READ AND PONDER! THE PEOPLE'S REFORM TICKET, FOR ALL STATE AND COUNTY OFFICES, TO BE FILLED IN THE OCTOBER ELECTION, 1870 . . . EXECUTIVE COMN,T-TEE[!].

Broadside, 46 x 29 cm. Text, 35.7 x 22 cm.

Ref.:

The text of the call for the September 17 mass meeting is here reprinted, followed by the names placed in nomination at the meeting, and the resolutions adopted. The last paragraph appeals to the citizens of Otoe County "to elect the above ticket, by such an overwhelming majority, as shall satisfy the world, that we are in earnest."

3247 PEORIA REGISTER AND NORTH-WESTERN GAZETTEER

[Newspaper] PEORIA REGISTER AND NORTH-WESTERN GAZETTEER. VOL. III. PEORIA, ILLINOIS . . . SATURDAY, JUNE 29, 1839. NO. 13. [–VOL. VII. PEORIA, ILLINOIS . . . FRIDAY, SEPTEMBER 15, 1843. NO. 24.] . . .

Each issue [1–4] except as noted below. 57.7 x 44 cm. Unbound.

Ref.:

Comprises the following numbers:

Vol. III, No. 13, June 29, 1839; No. 15, July 13; No. 17, July 17; No. 20, August 17; No. 21, August 24; No. 32, November 9; No. 37, December 14; No. 39, December 28; No. 40, January 4, 1840 (Contains list of state legislature, including A. Lincoln); No. 41, January 11; No. 42, January 18; No. 43, January 25; No. 45, February 8; No. 48, February 29; No. 51, March 21; No. 52, March 28

Vol. IV, No. 2, April 10, 1840; No. 13, June 26; No. 15, July 10; No. 22, August 28; No. 25, September 18; No. 27, October 2; No. 29, October 16; No. 31, October 30; No. 33, November 13; No. 34, November 24; No. 35, November

27; No. 36, December 4; No. 37, December 11; No. 38, December 18; No. 39, December 25; No. 41, January 8, 1841; No. 43, January 22 (Complete in two pages); No. 44, January 29; No. 45, February 5; No. 46, February 12; No. 47, February 19; No. 49, March 5; No. 50, March 12; No. 51, March 19; No. 52, March 26

Vol. V, No. 1, April 2, 1841; No. 2, April 9; No. 5, April 30; No. 6, May 7; No. 7, May 14; No. 8, May 21; No. 10, June 4; No. 11, June 11; No. 12, June; No. 13, June 25; No. 15, July 9; No. 17, July 23; No. 18, July 30; No. 20, August 13; No. 21, August 20; No. 22, August 27; No. 23, September 3; No. 24, September 10; No. 26, September 24; No. 27, October 1; No. 28, October 8; No. 30, October 22; No. 31, October 29; No. 32, November 5; No. 34, November 19; No. 35, November 26; No. 36, December 3; No. 38, December 17; No. 39, December 24; No. 41, January 7, 1842; No. 44, January 28; No. 45, February 4; No. 46, February 11; No. 47, February 18; No. 48, February 25; No. 49, March 4; No. 50, March 11; No. 51, March 18; No. 52, March 25

Vol. VI, No. 2, April 8, 1842; No. 3, April 15; No. 4, April 22; No. 5, April 29; No. 6, May 6; No. 7, May 13; No. 8, May 20; No. 9, May 27; No. 10, June 3; No. 11, June 10; No. 12, June 17; No. 15, July 8; No. 17, July 22; No. 16, July 15; No. 19, August 5; No. 20, August 12; No. 21, August 19; No. 22, August 26; No. 23, September 2; No. 24, September 9; No. 26, September 23; No. 27, September 30; No. 28, October 7; No. 29, October 14; No. 31, October 28; No. 32, November 4; No. 33, November 11; No. 34, November 18; No. 35, November 25; No. 37, December 9; No. 38, December 16; No. 39, December 23; No. 41, January 8, 1843; No. 42, January 13; No. 43, January 20; No. 44, January 27; No. 47, February 17; No. 48, February 24; No. 49, March 3; No. 52, March 24

Vol. VII, No. 1, April 7, 1843 (Name changed to *Peoria Register*); No. 2, April 14; No. 4, April 28; No. 6, May 12; No. 7, May 19; No. 8, May 26; No. 9, June 2; No. 10, June 9; No. 10[!], June 16; No. 12, June 23; No. 13, June 30; No. 14, July 7; No. 17, July 28; No. 18, August 4; No. 19, August 11; No. 21, August 25; No. 24, September 15.

One hundred and thirty-seven numbers, mostly complete, but from a few numbers articles, advertisements, or columns have been excised.

Vol. III, No. 13, June 29, 1839, contains a letter from Thomas J. Farnham from Elm Grove, Shawnee Territory, dated June 1, 1839, describing his trip across Illinois and giving the names of his party. Vol. III, No. 32, November 9, 1839, contains a full-page article describing the trip of Obadiah Oakly, reprinted in the *National Intelligencer* for November 23, 1839, and in New York in 1914. Vol. III, No. 37, December 14, 1839, No. 39, December 28, and No. 40, January 4, 1840, contain Oakly's own account of his trip to the mountains. (No. 38, December 21, also contains an installment, but is missing from this run.) Vol. V, No. 13, June 25, 1841, contains a quote from the *National Intelligencer* comprising a letter signed by Francis Fletcher, Joseph Holman, R. L. Kilburn, Amos Cook, and Robert Shortess stating they had read the Oakly story in the *National Intelligencer* for November 23, 1839, as repeated from the *Peoria Register*, and that they deny the accuracy of Oakly's account in many particulars. Their letter is dated from Wallamet, Oregon territory, Sept. 3, 1840. It appeared first in the *National Intelligencer* for May 27, 1841.

3248   PERKINS, D. A. W.

HISTORY OF OSCEOLA COUNTY, IOWA. FROM ITS ORGANIZATION TO THE PRESENT TIME . . . SIOUX FALLS, SO. DAK.: BROWN & SAENGER, PRINTERS AND BINDERS, 1892.*

[1]–[296]. 22.2 x 14.5 cm. Illustrations unlisted. Dark red cloth, title in gilt on backstrip.

Ref.: Cook p. 145

3249   PERKINS, JAMES H.

THE MEMOIR AND WRITINGS . . . CINCINNATI: TRUEMAN & SPOFFORD, 1851.

[i]–xii, [1]–527, [528 blank]. [i]–[viii, viii blank], [1]–502. 19.2 x 11.8 cm. Portrait. Two volumes, dark brown cloth, blind embossed decorative panels on sides, titles in gilt on backstrip.

Ref.: Howes P232; Sabin 60956

Lawyer, newspaper editor, minister, Perkins spent most of his adult life in Cincinnati and vicinity. Several of the historical sketches from his pen deal with the old Northwest Territory.

3250   PERON, FRANCOIS

MEMOIRES DU CAPITAINE PERON, SUR SES VOYAGES AUX COTES D'AFRIQUE, EN ARABIE, A L'ILE D'AMSTERDAM, AUX ILES D'ANJOUAN ET DE MAYOTTE, AUX COTES NORD-OUEST DE L'AMERIQUE, AUX ILES SANDWICH, A LA CHINE, ETC. . . . PARIS: BRISSOT-THIVARS, LIBRAIRE, 1824.

[i–iv], I–[VI], 1–359, [360 blank]. [i–iv], 1–336. 21.5 x 13.5 cm. Six lithographed views and maps: Map: Plan de l'Ile d'Amsterdam, Mer Pacifique. / [above neat line:] N.°. 1. Memoires du Capitaine Péron. Tome Ier Page 170 / [below neat line, right:] Lith. de G. Engelmann / 21.8 x 17 cm. Scale: 8562 French feet to one inch. [View of seals and penguins]. Opposite page 182. [View] Lion marin ou Eléphant de mer . . . Opposite page 192. Map: Carte / D'un partie de la Côte N. O. / de l'Amérique, depuis le Détroit de Juan de Fucas, jusqu'à la pointe / aux Brisans au sud de Nootka. / [decorative rule] / [above neat line:] N.º 4 Mémoires du Capitaine Péron Longitude Orientale du Paris. Tome 1er Page 293. / [lower right:] Lith. de G. Engelmann. / Map: Carte, / de l'Embouchure Septentrionale / du Canal de la Reine Charlotte, / Côte N. O. de l'Amérique depuis / la pointe Rose, dans l'Ile de / la Reine Charlotte, jusqu'à / l'entrée de Bokerelle par / 55.º 18! de Lat. Nord. / [above neat line:] N.º 5. Memoires du Capitaine Péron. Longitude Orientale de Paris. Tome 2ème Page 29. / [lower right:] Lith. de G. Engelmann. / 16.5 x 21.2 cm. No scale given. Map: Carte, / du Port du Bokerelle, Côte N. O. de / l'Amérique *nec plus ultrà* de notre navigation / au Nord. . . . / [7 lines] / [above neat line:] N.º 6. Mémoires du Capitaine Péron. Longitude Orientale de Paris. Tome 2ème Page 59. / [lower right:] Lith. de G. Engelmann. / 21.3 x 18.8 cm. No scale given. Two volumes, light blue printed wrappers with title on front wrappers, advertisements on verso of back wrappers, inner wrappers strengthened by printed waste sheets, uncut. Rebacked with old paper.

Ref.: Howes P240; Monaghan 1174; Sabin 61001

Péron was chief officer on the "Otter" under Captain Ebenezer Dorr. The "Otter" was possibly the first American vessel to sail in California water. There is some doubt on the part of bibliographers that Péron existed, the idea being that M. Bénard compiled the work from numerous sources. However, see Henry R. Wagner's account in *California Historical Society Quarterly*, Vol. I, No. 2, pages 173–77.

3251   [PERREAU, JEAN ANDRE]

LETTRES ILLINOISES, PAR J. A. P. AUTEUR DE CLARISSE. A. LONDRES, ET SE TROUVE A PARIS, CHEZ MERLIN, M. DCC. LXXII.

A–V⁸, X⁴. [1]–[327], [328 blank]. 15.9 x 9.9 cm. Contemporary green vellum, red leather label on backstrip, red edges.

Ref.: Sabin 61007

The noble savage wins the French beauty. There are several cancelled leaves, identical with Ayer copy.

3252 PERRIE, GEORGE W.

BUCKSKIN MOSE; OR, LIFE FROM THE LAKES TO THE PACIFIC, AS ACTOR, CIRCUS-RIDER, DETECTIVE, RANGER, GOLD-DIGGER, INDIAN SCOUT, AND GUIDE . . . NEW YORK: HENRY L. HINTON, PUBLISHER, 1873.

[1]–285, [286 blank, 287–88 advertisements]. (Page [1] is blank, advertisement on page [2].) 18.7 x 12.3 cm. 12 illustrations listed. Green cloth, borders and lettering on sides and backstrip in black.

Ref.: Howes P242

Busy man—out to make a buck.

3253 PERRIN DU LAC, FRANCOIS

TRAVELS THROUGH THE TWO LOUISIANAS, AND AMONG THE SAVAGE NATIONS OF THE MISSOURI . . . IN 1801, 1802, & 1803 . . . LONDON: PRINTED FOR RICHARD PHILLIPS, 1807.

A–N⁴, O². [1]–[108]. 20.5 x 12.5 cm. Rebound in new brown half levant morocco, title in gilt up backstrip.

Portions omitted (from a sense of delicacy on the part of the translator) prevent this from being usable.

3254 PERRIN DU LAC, FRANCOIS MARIE

VOYAGE DANS LES DEUX LOUISIANES, ET CHEZ LES NATIONS SAUVAGES DU MISSOURI . . . EN 1801, 1802 ET 1803 . . . A LYON: CHEZ BRUYSET AINE ET BUYNAND, AN XIII—1805.

a⁸, A–Gg⁸. [1–6], [i]–x, [1]–479, [480 blank]. 20.7 x 13.6 cm. Plate: Mamoth tel qu'il existe au / Musaeum à Philadelphie /. Map: Carte / du Missouri / Levée ou Rectifiée dans toute son / Etendue. / Par F⁹ⁱˢ Perrin du Lac / l'An 1802. / 45.1 x 58 cm. No scale given. Pink wrappers, manuscript title on backstrip, uncut. In a blue cloth case.

Ref.: Bradford 4369; Buck 61; Clark II 52, 114; Field 1204; Howes P244; Monaghan 1176; Rader 2647; Sabin 61012

Perrin du Lac's is a puzzling work; it deserves a critical examination. Howes calls for the Lyon edition on bluish paper, but this is on a creamy white and rather thick paper.

Editions: Paris, 1805.

3255 PERRINE, HENRY E.

A TRUE STORY OF SOME EVENTFUL YEARS IN GRANDPA'S LIFE . . .

[i]–xii, [1]–303, [304 blank]. 21.2 x 14.2 cm. Frontispiece and plan. Maroon cloth, blind borders on sides, title in gilt on backstrip.

Prov.: Presentation copy from the author to his sister: For / Sarah M. Hall / from her brother / Henry E. Perrine / Buffalo Oct 29 1886 /.

Ref.: Cowan p. 480; Howes P245

The preface is dated: Buffalo, N. Y., November, 1885. Printed in Buffalo in 1885, with imprint on verso of title-page: [ornament] / [rule] Press of E. H. Hutchinson / Buffalo, N. Y. / [rule] / [ornament] /.

Account of experiences with the Seminole Indians in Florida, and a trip to California in 1849. Also letters from the author's father from the Illinois country in 1819.—EDG

The frontispiece is a view of Dr. Perrine's house and the wharf on Indian Key. The plan is a groundplan of Indian Key in 1840, with descriptive letterpress on verso.

3256 PERROT, NICOLAS

MEMOIRE SUR LES MOEURS, COUSTUMES ET RELIGION DES SAUVAGES DE L'AMERIQUE SEPTENTRIONALE . . . LEIPZIG: LIBRAIRIE A. FRANCK, ALBERT L. HEROLD, 1864.

[I]–VIII, [I]–XLIII, [XLIV blank], 1–341, [342 colophon]. 28.7 x 23.2 cm. Green buckram, uncut.

Ref.: Howes P246; Sabin 61022; Staton & Tremaine 130

Large Paper Copy.

General title-page faces title above: Bibliotheca / Americana / Collection d'Ouvrages / inédits ou rares / sur L'Amérique. / [globe] / Leipzig & Paris, / Librairie A. Franck / Albert L. Herold. / 1864. / [lines 1, 3, 4, 5, 6, 9 printed in red]

Perrot's manuscript was written about 1700 and remained unpublished until 1864. Especially valuable for accounts of midwestern explorations and Indians.

3257 PERRY, JOHN A.

THRILLING ADVENTURES OF A NEW ENGLANDER. TRAVELS, SCENES AND SUFFERINGS IN CUBA, MEXICO AND CALIFORNIA . . . BOSTON: REDDING & CO., 1853.

[1]–96. 21.9 x 13.6 cm. Illustrations in text. Cream pictorial wrappers, with title on front wrapper. In a maroon half morocco case.

Ref.: Cowan p. 480; Howes P247a; Wagner-Camp 229

The best parts deal with California.

3258 PERRY, OLIVER H.

HUNTING EXPEDITIONS OF OLIVER HAZARD PERRY OF CLEVELAND VERBATIM FROM HIS DIARIES, EMBELLISHED WITH TAILPIECES ENGRAVED ABOUT 1800 BY DR. ALEXANDER ANDERSON AND OTHERS

AND PRINTED FROM THE ORIGINAL WOOD. CLEVE-
LAND: FOR PRIVATE DISTRIBUTION, 1899.

[i]–viii, [1]–246, [247–48]. 23.1 x 15 cm. Portrait, two plates, and 22 woodcuts in text. Gray-
green cloth, uncut.

Prov.: Inscribed on front endleaf in pencil:
David Douglas from / D Sage by request of Col
Payne a / nephew of the author— / N. Y. Jan^y
30 1901 /. And on half-title, also in pencil: from
Dean Sage / circa 1901 /.

Ref.: Howes P250

Limited to 100 copies.

Contemporary accounts, here first printed, of
hunting expeditions in Ohio and Michigan, 1836
to 1855.—Howes

3259 PERRYS & YOUNG, & MALCOLM CLARK

[Broadside] LOOK OUT! FOR A SALE OF VALUABLE
TOWN LOTS AT THE TOWN OF ELIZABETHTOWN,
ANDREW COUNTY, MO, ON TUESDAY, APRIL 15,
1851. ELIZABETHTOWN IS SITUATED IMMEDIATELY
ON THE MISSOURI RIVER, ABOUT SIXTEEN MILES
ABOVE ST. JOSEPH . . . AS A PLACE OF RENDEZVOUS
FOR THE EMIGRANTS TO CALIFORNIA OR OREGON,
NO POINT POSSESSES GREATER ADVANTAGES IN
POINT OF LOCATION . . . PERRYS & YOUNG. MAL-
COLM CLARK. MARCH 1, 1851. WESTON REPORTER
PRINT.

Broadside, 45.7 x 30.5 cm. Text, 29.5 x 13.8 cm.
Ref.:

3260 PETERS, DE WITT C.

THE LIFE AND ADVENTURES OF KIT CARSON, THE
NESTOR OF THE ROCKY MOUNTAINS, FROM FACTS
NARRATED BY HIMSELF . . . NEW YORK: W. R. C.
CLARK & CO., M DCCC LVIII.

[1–4], [i]–xii, 13–534, [1]–[6] advertisements.
22.2 x 14.1 cm. Ten illustrations. Contemporary
half calf, gilt back, marbled edges.

Prov.: Inscribed in pencil on front blank: To /
Hugh Campbell Jr / From his beloved / Father /
Robert Campbell / March 15. 1859 / St Louis.
Mo. /

Ref.: Cowan p. 481 see; Field 1207 see;
Howes P256; Munk (Alliot) p. 177 see; Rader
2649; Sabin 61190; Wagner-Camp 306

Hugh Campbell died August 9, 1931, in his
84th year so he was approximately 11 years of
age when this youthful script was penned. His
father was the famous fur trader and partner of
William Sublette and friend of Kit Carson. Robert had thirteen children only three of whom
lived beyond the age of seven—James Alexander
who died in 1890, Hugh who died in 1931, and
Hazlett who died in 1938. This book came from

the Hazlett Campbell sale of house furnishings,
etc. Wright Howes bought this book at the sale
and sold it to Holliday.—EDG

3261 PETERS, DE WITT C.

ANOTHER COPY. Light brown cloth.

3262 PETTIJOHN, JONAS

AUTOBIOGRAPHY, FAMILY HISTORY AND VARIOUS
REMINISCENCES OF THE LIFE OF JONAS PETTIJOHN,
AMONG THE SIOUX OR DAKOTA INDIANS. HIS
ESCAPE DURING THE MASSACRE OF AUGUST, 1862.
CAUSES THAT LED TO THE MASSACRE . . . CLAY
CENTER, KANSAS: DISPATCH PRINTING HOUSE,
1890.*

[1]–104. 18 x 13 cm. Blue cloth with title on
cover. Lacks back endleaf.

Ref.: Howes P268

3263 PETTIS, GEORGE H.

FRONTIER SERVICE DURING THE REBELLION; OR, A
HISTORY OF COMPANY K, FIRST INFANTRY, CALI-
FORNIA VOLUNTEERS . . . PROVIDENCE: PUBLISHED
BY THE SOCIETY, 1885.

[1]–54. 20.3 x 15.6 cm. Pale brick printed wrappers, with title on front wrapper, uncut. In a
dark red cloth case.

Ref.: Howes P269; Munk (Alliot) p. 178;
Nicholson p. 645

Preceding the title-page there is a general title
as follows: Personal Narratives / of Events in
the / War of the Rebellion, / Being Papers Read
before the / Rhode Island Soldiers and Sailors /
Historical Society. / [short rule] / Third Series.—
No. 14. / [short rule] / Providence: / Published
by the Society. / 1885. / Inserted before the general title is an erratum slip, 6.5 x 2.1 cm.

3264 PETTIS, GEORGE H.

KIT CARSON'S FIGHT WITH THE COMANCHE AND
KIOWA INDIANS, AT THE ADOBE WALLS, ON THE
CANADIAN RIVER, NOVEMBER 25TH, 1864 . . .
PROVIDENCE: SIDNEY S. RIDER, 1878.

[1]–44. 20.5 x 16.2 cm. Pale gray printed wrappers, with title on front wrapper, uncut. In a
dark blue cloth case.

Ref.: Howes P270; Rader 2656; Saunders
3093

Preceding the title-page as above is a general
title-page for the series as follows: Personal Narratives / of the / Battles of the Rebellion, /
being / Papers Read before the / Rhode Island
Soldiers and Sailors / Historical Society. / No.
5. / "Quaeque ipse miserrima vidi, / Et quorum
pars magna fui." / Providence: / Sidney S.
Rider. / 1878. /

3265 PEYTON, JOHN L.

THE ADVENTURES OF MY GRANDFATHER. . . . LON-
DON: JOHN WILSON, MDCCCLXVII.

[i]–x, [1]–249, [250 blank], [1–4 advertisements
and press notices]. 21.4 x 14 cm. Maroon cloth,
blind embossed borders on sides, gilt title on
backstrip.

Prov.: Inscribed on front endleaf: John
Fradgley Esq.ʳ / With the respects / of the Author. / London January 1868. / And with the
book label of the recipient.

Ref.: Howes P275; Sabin 61320

John R. Peyton's adventures included capture by the Spanish, imprisonment at Santa Fé
in 1774, and a return overland to Saint Louis.

3266 PEYTON, JOHN L.

OVER THE ALLEGHANIES AND ACROSS THE PRAIRIES.
PERSONAL RECOLLECTIONS OF THE FAR WEST ONE
AND TWENTY YEARS AGO . . . LONDON: SIMPKIN,
MARSHALL AND CO., MDCCCLXIX.

[i]–xvi, [1]–377, [378 blank], [1–2 advertise-
ments]. 19 x 12.4 cm. Maroon cloth, blind embossed covers, title in gilt on backstrip.

Ref.: Buck 438; Clark III 381; Howes P280;
Sabin 61323

The work is both contemporary and historical, for he injects much of the history of the
region and many personalities encountered.—
Clark

3267 PEYTON, JOHN L.

A STATISTICAL VIEW OF THE STATE OF ILLINOIS; TO
WHICH IS APPENDED AN ARTICLE UPON THE CITY
OF CHICAGO . . . CHICAGO: SPAULDING & TOBEY,
PRINTERS, 1855.

[1]–48. (Page 48 mispaginated 40.) 17.8 x 12.1
cm. Rebound in gray boards, leather label.
Trimmed very close at top and bottom.

Ref.: AII (*Chicago*) 156; Buck 525; Byrd
2339; Howes P281; Sabin 61324

The text appeared originally in issues of
Hunt's Merchants' Magazine, New York.

Page [3] is headed: Advertisement. / Page [4]
is blank.

3268 PHELPS, H., & BELA S. SQUIRE, JR.

[Broadside] TRAVELLERS GUIDE & EMIGRANTS DI-
RECTORY, THROUGH THE STATES OF OHIO, ILLINOIS,
INDIANA AND MICHIGAN . . . ENTERED ACCORDING
TO ACT OF CONGRESS, IN THE CLERKS OFFICE OF THE
SOUTHERN DISTRICT OF THE STATE OF NEW-YORK
IN THE YEAR 1836, BY H. PHELPS & B. S. SQUIRE,
JUN.

Broadside, 56 x 45.2 cm. Text, including border,
55.1 x 44.1 cm. Folding map: Map / of / Illinois / with a Plan of / Chicago / Scale of Miles /

[diagrammatic scale] / Published by B. S.
Squire Jr. / New-York / 1836 / [lower left:]
Eng.ᵈ by J. T. Hammond N. York / [lower
right:] Entered according to Act of Congress on
the 1.ˢᵗ day of Dec.ʳ in the year 1835 by Bela S.
Squire J.ʳ in the Clerks office of the District Court
of the Southern District of New York /. 44.8 x
31.6 cm. Scale: about 21 miles to an inch. *Inset:*
Chicago /. 15 x 8.9 cm. No scale given. Broadside folded and pasted to inner front cover and
map folded and pasted to inner back cover,
black leather, 13 x 7.9 cm., with title in gilt on
front cover.

Ref.: Buck 303a

Buck locates only one copy which he described and which also contained the Illinois
map.

3269 PHELPS, HUMPHREY

PHELPS'S TRAVELLERS' GUIDE THROUGH THE
UNITED STATES . . . NEW-YORK: PUBLISHED BY
ENSIGNS[!] & THAYER, 1849.

[i–ii], 1–70. 14 x 8.6 cm. Folding map: Phelps's /
National Map / of the / United states, / A /
Travellers Guide. / Embracing the Principal Rail
Roads, Canals, / Steam Boat & Stage Routes, /
throughout the / Union. / [decorative rule] /
New York, / Published by / Ensign & Thayer, /
50 Ann Street / 1849. / [short rule] / Drawn &
Engraved by J. M. Atwood N. Y. / Entered according to Act of Congress in the year 1849 by
Ensign & Thayer, in the Clerks office of the District Court of the Southern District of New
York. / 44.1 x 57.4 cm. plus border 3.8 cm. on
each side. Scale: 75 miles to an inch. *Inset:* Map
of / Oregon, California / & Texas. / 13.3 x 15.4
cm. *Inset:* N. Part of Maine. / 2.8 x 2.8 cm. *Inset:* Southern / part of / Florida. / 6 x 3.8 cm.
Border composed of forty-three vignettes, including portraits of presidents, seals of states,
etc. Red leather, with design and title in gilt on
front cover, and in blind on back cover. Back
and backstrip of pamphlet protected by marbled
paper cover.

Ref.: Howes P291; Moffit p. 60

Editions: New York, 1847, 1848.

3270 PHELPS, JOSHUA

ZION, THE PERFECTION OF BEAUTY; OR, THE TRUTH,
ORDER AND SPIRIT OF THE PRESBYTERIAN CHURCH,
BRIEFLY CONSIDERED. A SERMON PREACHED . . . AT
OSKALOOSA, THURSDAY, OCT. 11, 1855 . . . DU-
BUQUE: W. A. ADAMS, PUBLISHER, 1856.

[1]–72. 14.1 x 9.6 cm. Brown embossed cloth,
with title in gilt on front cover: Zion. / The /
Perfection / of / Beauty. /

Prov.: Inscribed on the front endleaf: Miss

Alice M Brainerd / With the kind regards / Of the Author / [double underline and one "] /.

Ref.: Moffit 255

Dr. Phelps was president of Alexander College.

3271 [PHELPS, WILLIAM D.]

FORE AND AFT; OR, LEAVES FROM THE LIFE OF AN OLD SAILOR. BOSTON: NICHOLS & HALL, 1871.*

[i]–vi, 7–359, [360 blank]. 17.4 x 11.5 cm. Illustrations unlisted. Dark orange cloth, title stamped in gilt on front cover and backstrip.

Ref.: Cowan p. 482; Howes P290; Sabin 61399

The author, William D. Phelps, came to California in 1840, as master of the Boston ship "Alert." He was actively engaged in the "Commodore Jones war," as he calls it, and his various narratives are of much importance, although occasionally presenting minor inaccuracies. His chapter on "The Hudson's bay company" is one of the few sources of information regarding the operations of this great corporation in California.—Cowan

Only a few copies had been issued when fire destroyed the plates.—Howes

3272 [PHILIPS, GEORGE]

TRAVELS IN NORTH AMERICA. DUBLIN: PRINTED BY BRETT SMITH, 1824.

[1]–180. 13.6 x 8.5 cm. Five woodcut plates. Contemporary speckled calf.

Ref.: Howes P305; Sabin 62456

Contains a summary of the Lewis & Clark Expedition in the form of personal adventure.

Editions: Dublin, 1822.

3273 [PHILLIPS, GEORGE S.]

AMUSING AND THRILLING ADVENTURES OF A CALIFORNIA ARTIST, WHILE DAGUERREOTYPING A CONTINENT, AMID BURNING DESERTS, SAVAGES, AND PERPETUAL SNOWS AND A POETICAL COMPANION TO THE PANTOSCOPE OF CALIFORNIA, NEBRASKA & KANSAS, SALT LAKE & THE MORMONS . . . BOSTON: PUBLISHED FOR THE AUTHOR, 1854.

[1]–92, [93–96 blank]. 18.2 x 11.3 cm. Illustrated, four woodcuts in text. Reddish printed wrappers, with title on front wrapper, advertisements on verso of front and recto and verso of back wrapper. In a red cloth case.

Ref.: Howes P315; Sabin 20342; Wagner-Camp 240

Part 2 (pages [51]–87) has a special pictorial title-page: Part II. / [rule] / A Poetical Companion / of / [vignette] / Jones' Pantoscope / of / California, Nebraska, Utah, and the Mormons. /

Photograph of J. Wesley Jones and ticket of admission to Jones' Pantoscope laid in.

See *Journal of the Illinois State Historical Society*, December, 1943, for an article by Clarence P. McClelland on "The Education of Females in Illinois," where is found considerable information about J. Wesley Jones. Together with his younger brother, William P. Jones, he founded the Northwestern Female College in Evanston in 1855 and his brother became president. J. Wesley Jones at that time was owner of an investment business in Brooklyn and donated money to build an imposing four-storey building for the college. McClelland also states that J. Wesley Jones made considerable money in the California gold rush.—EDG

"John Ross Dix" (who is noted on the title-page as the author) was George Spencer Phillips, a journalist and writer who died in Brooklyn Nov. 7, 1865.

3274 PHILLIPS, GEORGE S.

THE SAME.

Lacks back wrapper. In a green cloth case.

3275 PHILLIPS, SEMIRA A.

AUTOGRAPH LETTER, SIGNED. 1905 November 6, Oskaloosa. One page, 15.7 x 12.5 cm. To Luther A. Brewer.

Regarding the purchase of a copy of the writer's book. Brewer was one of Iowa's great book collectors. Laid in a copy of *Proud Mahaska . . .* 1900.

3276 PHILLIPS, SEMIRA A.

PROUD MAHASKA. 1843–1900 . . . OSKALOOSA, IOWA: HERALD PRINT, 1900.

[9]–383, [384 blank]. 22 x 14.5 cm. Two portraits. Brown and beige cloth, title in gilt on backstrip.

Ref.: Cook p. 142; Moffit p. 51

Laid in is an Autograph Letter, signed by the author. 1905 November 6.

3277 PIATT, GUY X., *Editor*

THE STORY OF BUTTE. BUTTE, MONTANA: PRESS OF THE STANDARD MANUFACTURING & PRINTING CO.

[1]–[96]. 24.1 x 32.5 cm. Numerous illustrations in text, unlisted. Tan printed wrappers, with title on front wrapper, advertisements on verso of front and recto and verso of back wrapper.

Prov.: Inscribed on page [4]: Gift of Cin. Public Library / June 1, 1934 / Rubber stamp of library inside front cover, stamp of Historical and Philosophical Society of Ohio on front cover, location symbol on front cover.

Ref.:

Copyrighted 1897.

The pamphlet was issued as a special number of *The Butte Bystander*.

3278 PICKARD, SAMUEL

AUTOBIOGRAPHY OF A PIONEER . . . AND SOME AC-
COUNT OF THE LABORS OF ELDER JACOB KNAPP . . .
EDITED BY O. T. CONGER . . . CHICAGO: CHURCH &
GOODMAN, 1866.

[i]–xii, [13]–403, [404 blank]. 18.4 x 12 cm.
Seven illustrations, unlisted. Brown cloth, blind
fillets on sides, gilt vignette on front cover, initials in blind on back cover, title in gilt on backstrip. Lacks front endleaf.

Ref.: AII (*Chicago*) 1101; Howes C677;
Sabin 62617

3279 PICOLO, FRANCISCO MARIA

INFORME DEL ESTADO DE LA NUEVA CHRISTIANDAD
DE CALIFORNIA, QUE PIDIO POR AUTO, LA REAL
AUDIENCIA DE GUADALAXARA[!], OBEDECIENDO A
LA REAL CEDULA DE N. REY Y SENOR, D. PHELIPE V.
FECHA EN MADRID, A 17. DE JULIO, DE 1701 . . .

A–C¹, D², 3¹, 3¹, 3¹. [1]–16. 28.6 x 19.8 cm. Full
new black morocco, gilt borders, title in gilt on
front cover and backstrip.

Ref.: Beristain II p. 478; Medina (Mexico)
2083; Picolo (Ed. by Burrus) *Informe* . . . 1962,
pp. 26–7; Streit III 21; Wagner (*SS*) 74

Second edition.

One of the earliest accounts of Jesuit missions
in California. Wagner points out that Picolo's
account is much better known in translation and
suggests that the original edition has always been
rare.

Wagner accepts Beristain's assignment of
printing to Carrascoso of Mexico City in 1702.
The Ayer copy is the first edition.

Editions: [Mexico City, 1702.]

3280 PIERCE, GEORGE F.

INCIDENTS OF WESTERN TRAVEL: IN A SERIES OF
LETTERS . . . EDITED BY THOMAS O. SUMMERS, D. D.
NASHVILLE, TENN.: PUBLISHED BY E. STEVENSON &
F. A. OWNE, 1857.

[i]–x, [11]–249, [250 blank]. 18 x 11.8 cm. Portrait—most amusing. Gray cloth, blind embossed sides, title in gilt on backstrip.

Ref.: Bradford 4405; Clark III 487; Buck
557; Howes P353; Rader 2669; Sabin 62718

Pierce was a bishop of the Methodist Episcopal Church, South. His tour took him west from
Georgia to the Plains and back through Texas
and Louisiana in 1855–56.

3281 PIERCE, W. H.

THIRTEEN YEARS OF TRAVEL AND EXPLORATION IN
ALASKA . . . EDITED BY PROF. AND MRS. J. H. CAR-
RUTH . . . LAWRENCE, KANSAS: JOURNAL PUB-
LISHING COMPANY, 1890.

[i]–[viii], [9]–224. 19.1 x 13 cm. Illustrations
unlisted. Original buff printed wrappers with
title on front wrapper. In light brown cloth case.

Ref.: Howes P357; Wickersham 2784

Pierce . . . drove the first tunnel at Treadwell
mines.—Wickersham

3282 PIERCE, W. H.

THE SAME.

18.3 x 12.3 cm. Dark green cloth, with title in
gilt on front cover.

Prov.: Charles L. Camp's copy, with signature and note in pencil inside front cover and
with several marginal notes throughout.

Camp's note inside front cover: This is one of
the first, if not *the* first, / account of gold discoveries / in the Yukon. /

3283 PIKE, ALBERT

AN ADDRESS DELIVERED . . . TO THE YOUNG
LADIES OF THE TULIP FEMALE SEMINARY, AND
CADETS OF THE ARKANSAS MILITARY INSTITUTE: AT
TULIP, ON THE 4TH JUNE, 1852. LITTLE ROCK: WM.
E. WOODRUFF, PRINTER, 1852.

[1]–31, [32 blank]. 21.5 x 13.2 cm. Removed
from bound volume, sewn.

Ref.: Allen (*Arkansas*) 216; Boyden, William:
Bibliography of . . . Alfred Pike (Washington,
1921) p. 31

3284 PIKE, ALBERT

LETTER OF ALBERT PIKE TO THE CHOCTAW PEOPLE.
WASHINGTON: CUNNINGHAM & McINTOSH, PRINT-
ERS. 1872.

[1]–25, [1]–14, [15 blank]. 21.9 x 14.2 cm. Rose
printed wrappers with title on front wrapper.

Ref.: Howes P362

The second section, in which rectos are paginated with even numbers, is an Appendix.

3285 PIKE, ALBERT

PROSE SKETCHES AND POEMS, WRITTEN IN THE
WESTERN COUNTRY . . . BOSTON: LIGHT & HOR-
TON, 1834.

[i]–viii, [9]–200. 18.9 x 11.6 cm. Brown cloth,
brown leather label on backstrip. In a brown
half morocco case.

Prov.: Presentation copy inscribed on front
endleaf: C E Rice Esqr / from his friend / The
Author / [rule] / Little Rock Jan 22 1834 /.

Inscribed on title-page: S. I Kellogg / [flourish] / Sheldon F. Kellogg. / Clifton / Nov. 14. 1858. /

Ref.: Field 1219; Howes P365; Jones 959; Rader 2670; Sabin 62815; Wagner-Camp 50

The preface is dated: Ark. Territory, 1st May, 1833.

Includes a graphic 80-page narrative of a trip over the southwestern prairies to Santa Fé, made by Aaron Lewis, in 1831. Pike's own narrative covers his trip to Santa Fé the same year, trapping adventures in the Comanche country and Colorado and return to Arkansas in 1832.— Howes

3286 PIKE, JAMES

THE SCOUT AND RANGER: BEING THE PERSONAL ADVENTURES OF CORPORAL PIKE, OF THE FOURTH OHIO CAVALRY. AS A TEXAS RANGER . . . CINCINNATI: J. R. HAWLEY & CO., 1865.

[i]–[xii, xii blank], 19–394, [395 errata], [396 blank]. 20.2 x 14 cm. 25 illustrations, unlisted. Smooth black cloth, embossed borders and monograms in blind on sides, title in plain block gilt letters on backstrip.

Ref.: Howes P369; Rader 2671; Raines p. 165; Sabin 62816

The earliest form with the errata uncorrected, and with simple stamping on the binding. The woodcuts in a later edition vary considerably.

3287 PIKE, WARBURTON

THROUGH THE SUBARCTIC FOREST. A RECORD OF A CANOE JOURNEY FROM FORT WRANGEL TO THE PELLY LAKES AND DOWN THE YUKON RIVER TO THE BEHRING SEA . . . LONDON: EDWARD ARNOLD, 1896.

[i]–[xv], [xvi blank], [1]–295, [296 blank], [1]–32 advertisements. 22 x 14.2 cm. 19 illustrations and maps listed. Brown pictorial cloth, uncut.

Ref.: Wickersham 2785

3288 PIKE, WARBURTON

THE BARREN GROUNDS OF NORTHERN CANADA . . . LONDON: MACMILLAN AND CO., 1892.

[i]–[xii, xii blank], small slip (Corrigendum), [1]–300, 1–55 advertisements, [56 blank]. 22.3 x 14.2 cm. Two maps listed. Green cloth, uncut.

Ref.: Wickersham 2785a

The purpose of the journey was to determine the habits of the musk-ox and the habits of the Indians who hunted them.

3289 PIKE, ZEBULON M. [?]

AN ACCOUNT OF A VOYAGE UP THE MISSISSIPPI RIVER, FROM ST. LOUIS TO ITS SOURCE; MADE UNDER THE ORDERS OF THE WAR DEPARTMENT, BY LIEUT. PIKE, OF THE UNITED STATES ARMY, IN THE YEARS 1805 AND 1806. COMPILED FROM MR. PIKE'S JOURNAL.

[A]–H⁴, I². [1]–68. 20.4 x 12.9 cm. Map: Map / of the Mississippi River. From its / Source to the Mouth of the Missouri: / Laid down from the notes of Lieut⁺ Z. M. Pike, by Anthony Nau. / Reduced, and corrected by the Astronomical Observations of Mʳ Thompson at its source; / and of Captⁿ M. Lewis, where it receives the water of the Missouri. / [short diamond rule] / By Nichˢ King. [short diamond rule] / [decorative rule] / Engraved by Francis Shallus, Philadelphia. / 23.3 x 76.5 cm. Scale: 25 miles to one inch. Repaired and mounted on cloth.

BOUND WITH:

[STEPHEN, JAMES]. The Dangers of the Country . . . Philadelphia: Printed for Samuel F. Bradford, 1807.

BOUND WITH:

An Inquiry into the Present State of the Foreign Relations of the Union . . . Philadelphia: Samuel F. Bradford, 1806.

BOUND WITH:

[COXE, TENCH]. Thoughts on the Subject of Naval Power. Philadelphia, printed in the year 1806.

BOUND WITH:

POPKIN, JOHN S. A Sermon, Preached May 4, 1806 . . . Newburyport: Printed for Angier March, 1806.

BOUND WITH:

BRADSTREET, NATHAN. A Discourse, Delivered at Hopkington . . . Amherst: Printed by Joseph Cushing, June—1807.

Six pamphlets bound together, contemporary marbled boards, calf corners and backstrip, red leather label: Fugitive /, and numbered in centre of backstrip: 43 /.

Prov.: Signatures on inner front cover: Wᵐ Plumer's / Sam Plumer. / Inscribed on recto of front endleaf: The Fugitive / Volume 43. / Collected by William Plumer / for his own use. / January 22ᵈ 1808. / On verso of same leaf is a list, 17 lines, in manuscript headed: Contents of this Volume. / [underline] / . . . In Plumer's hand, at the top of each title-page appear the numbers 373 through 378. On the first title-page, also in Plumer's hand is the following: From President Jefferson / to / William Plumer /. Plumer has noted the author of the second pamphlet, on the tltle-page, as Dr. James Stevens, and has identified the third pamphlet as having been written by Hon. Gouverneur Morris. The half-title of the fifth pamphlet bears the signature: john levitt /. Plumer has inscribed the last pamphlet on the title-page as follows: From James Wilson / to William Plum[er] /. Several manuscript notes appear in Plumer's hand recording where the pamphlets were reviewed.

Ref.: 1st: Coues, E.: *The Expeditions of . . . Pike* (New York, 1895), I, xxxii–v; Howes P372; Rader 2673; Sabin 62835; Wagner-Camp 9 (notes)

The first pamphlet was probably written by Nicholas King and follows closely Pike's journal. King's name appears on the map (which is not always present with the pamphlet) and there is a copy of the text in the Library of Congress wholly in King's handwriting. It is described in the DLC Iowa Centennial Exhibition catalogue, item 74. According to EDG, Wilberforce Eames had a copy of the pamphlet with a letter of presentation by Henry Dearborn, dated March 9, 1807, in which the map is mentioned. Some surviving copies of the pamphlet lack the last two leaves of text and, indeed, the copy used for the reprint in the *Boston Anthology and Review . . . 1807,* lacked the final two leaves.

3290 PIKE, ZEBULON M.

AN ACCOUNT OF EXPEDITIONS TO THE SOURCES OF THE MISSISSIPPI, AND THROUGH THE WESTERN PARTS OF LOUISIANA, TO THE SOURCES OF THE ARKANSAW, KANS, LA PLATTE, AND PIERRE JUAN, RIVERS; PERFORMED . . . DURING THE YEARS 1805, 1806, AND 1807 . . . PHILADELPHIA: PUBLISHED BY C. & A. CONRAD, & CO., 1810.

[*]⁴, A–N⁴, O1, [5 unsigned leaves], O2–4, P–Mm⁴, [1 unsigned leaf], 1–26⁴. [1–8, 8 blank], [1]–105, [106 blank], [1–10], [107]–277, [278–80 blank], [281–82], [1]–[66], [folding table], [1]–52, [folding table], 53–[54, 54 blank], [1]–87, [88 blank]. 22.5 x 13.6 cm. Portrait frontispiece. Accompanied by Atlas of maps, charts, etc. Map: Falls of St Anthony / 11.2 x 20.1 cm. No scale given. Map: Map / of the Mississippi River from its / Source to the Mouth of the Missouri: / Laid down from the notes of Lieut^t Z. M. Pike, by Anthony Nau. / Reduced, and corrected by the Astronomical Observations of Mr Thompson at its source; / and of Captn M. Lewis, where it receives the waters of the Missouri. / [open diamond rule] By Nich^s King. [open diamond rule] / [ornamental rule] / Engraved by Francis Shallus, Philadelphia. / 23.5 x 76.4 cm. Scale: about 25 miles to one inch. Map: The / First Part / of Captn Pike's / Chart / of the Internal Part of / Louisiana / [short swelled rule] / See

Plate 2^d & References. / [lower left:] Plate I. / [lower centre:] Reduced and laid down on a Scale of 40 miles to the Inch. / By Anthony Nau. / 43.9 x 44.8 cm. Scale as above. Map: A / Chart / of the / Internal Part / of / Louisiana, / Including all the hitherto unexplored Countries, / lying between the River La Platte of the Missouri / on the N: and the Red River on the S: the / Mississippi East and the Mountains of Mexico / West; with a Part of New Mexico & the Province / of Texas, by Z. M. Pike Captn U. S. I. / [lower left:] Plate II /. 44.8 x 39.1 cm. Scale presumably same as preceding map. Map: A Map / of / The Internal Provinces / of / New Spain. / The Outlines are from the Sketches of, but corrected and / improved by Captain Zebulon M. Pike, who was / conducted through that Country, in the Year 1807, by / Order of the Commandant General of those Provinces. / 45 x 46.3 cm. Scale: about 75 miles to one inch. Map: A / Sketch / of the / Vice Royalty / Exhibiting / the several Provinces and its / Approximation to the / Internal Provinces / of / New Spain. / 32.7 x 41 cm. Scale: 50 miles to one inch. Two volumes, text in original gray boards, tan paper backstrip, printed white paper label, 3.8 x 4.1 cm., uncut. Atlas in original tan boards, sprinkled calf backstrip, printed white paper label, 4.7 x 5.4 cm.

Ref.: Bradford 4415; Braislin 1474; Brinley 4512; Field 1217; Howes P373; Jefferson (Sowerby) 4169; Jones 743; Sabin 62936; Wagner-Camp 9

First government exploration of the Southwest.—Howes

Alexander von Humboldt to Thomas Jefferson, 1811 December 20: . . . Mr. Arrowsmith in London has stolen my large map of Mexico, and Mr. Pike has taken, rather ungraciously, my report which he undoubtedly obtained in Washington with the copy of this map, and besides, he also extracted from it all the names . . . I don't find my name in his book and a quick glance at Mr. Pike's map may prove to you from where he got it.

Thomas Jefferson to Alexander von Humboldt, 1813 December 6: . . . That their Arrowsmith should have stolen your map of Mexico, was in the piratical spirit of his country. But I should be sincerely sorry if our Pike has made an ungenerous use of your candid communication here . . . Whatever he did was on a principle of enlarging knolege and not for filthy shillings and pence of which he made none from that book. . . . I am sorry he omitted even to acknowledge the source of his information. it has been an oversight, and not at all in the spirit of his generous nature . . . Quoted by Helmut de Terra: "Alexander von Humboldt's Correspondence with Jefferson, Madison, and Gallatin" in *Proceedings of the American Philosophical Society*, Volume 103, Number 6, December 15, 1959, pages 792, 794.

3291 PIKE, ZEBULON M.

THE SAME.

Contemporary or original mottled calf (rebacked) and old marbled (over printed text) boards, new mottled calf backstrip and corners.

3292 PIKE, ZEBULON M.

EXPLORATORY TRAVELS THROUGH THE WESTERN TERRITORIES OF NORTH AMERICA: COMPRISING A VOYAGE FROM ST. LOUIS, ON THE MISSISSIPPI, TO THE SOURCE OF THAT RIVER, AND A JOURNEY THROUGH THE INTERIOR OF LOUISIANA, AND THE NORTH-EASTERN PROVINCES OF NEW SPAIN. PERFORMED IN THE YEARS 1805, 1806, 1807 . . . LONDON: PRINTED FOR LONGMAN, HURST, REES, ORME, AND BROWN, 1811.

[a]², b¹, B–3I⁴, 3K². [i]–xx, [1]–436. 28.4 x 22.4 cm. Two maps. Map: Map / of the Interior of / Louisiana, / with a part of / New Mexico, / By / Z. M. Pike—Captⁿ U. S. I. / [upper left:] to face Title Page. / [lower centre:] Published by Longman & Cᵒ Janʸ 1811 /. 25.9 x 35.2 cm. Scale: 150 miles to one inch. Map: Map / of the Mississippi River, from its / Source to the Mouth of the Missouri. / Laid down from the Notes of Lieutᵗ Z. M. Pike, by Anthony Nau; / Corrected by the Astronomical Observations of Mᵣ Thompson at its source; / and of Captⁿ M. Lewis, where it receives the waters of the Missouri. / [upper right:] to face Page 1. / [lower centre:] Published by Longman & Cᵒ Janʸ 1811. / 12.6 x 23.6 cm. Scale: about 80 miles to one inch. Gray-green boards, with white printed paper label (5.3 x 4.2 cm.) on backstrip, uncut. Label defective. In a blue half morocco case.
Ref.: See above
This London edition was edited by Thomas Rees.

3293 PILGRIM, THOMAS

LIVE BOYS IN THE BLACK HILLS; OR, THE YOUNG TEXAN GOLD HUNTERS . . . GIVEN IN LETTERS TO ARTHUR MORECAMP . . . BOSTON: LEE AND SHEPARD, PUBLISHERS.

[1–2], [i]–x, [11]–363, [364 blank], [365–66 advertisement]. (Pages [1–2] advertisements.) 17.1 x 12.2 cm. Illustrations unlisted. Mustard cloth, printed in black and gold.
Ref.: Adams (*Ramp. Herd*) 1572; Jennewein 275; Howes M789; Raines p. 165
Copyrighted 1880.

3294 [PILGRIM, THOMAS]

LIVE BOYS; OR, CHARLEY AND NASHO IN TEXAS. A NARRATIVE RELATING TO TWO BOYS OF FOURTEEN, ONE A TEXAN, THE OTHER A MEXICAN; SHOWING THEIR LIFE ON THE GREAT TEXAS CATTLE TRAIL, AND THEIR ADVENTURES IN THE INDIAN TERRITORY, KANSAS AND NORTHERN TEXAS . . . BY ARTHUR MORECAMP . . . BOSTON: LEE AND SHEPARD, PUBLISHERS.

[1–2], [i–x], [11]–308, [309–18 advertisements]. (Pages [1–2] blank) 17.1 x 12.2 cm. Illustrations unlisted. Mustard cloth, printed in black and gold.
Ref.: Adams (*Ramp. Herd*) 1572; Dobie p. 113; Howes M790; Raines p. 165
Copyrighted 1878.
Howes calls this the "earliest authentic, though fictionized, cowboy narrative."

3295 PINKHAM, E.

[Broadside] PASTURE! I WILL TAKE A LIMITED NUMBER OF HORSES TO PASTURE . . . E. PINKHAM, BOISE CITY, I.T., MAY 28TH, 1888.

Broadside, 23.3 x 16. Text, 17.3 x 12 cm.
Ref.:
Probably printed in Boise.

3296 PINO, PEDRO BAUTISTA

EXPOSICION SUCINTA Y SENCILLA DE LA PROVINCIA DEL NUEVO MEXICO . . . CADIZ: IMPRENTA DEL ESTADO-MAYOR-GENERAL, 1812.

[A]–F⁴, [G]². [1]–48, [49–51 index, 52 blank]· 19 x 13 cm. Half red morocco, red edges.
Ref.: Howes P383; Jones 756; Sabin 62979; Saunders 2606
Pino's detailed account of New Mexico is the best extant for 1801–22. The work was probably composed by Juan López Cancelada.

3297 PINO, PEDRO BAUTISTA, ANTONIO BARREIRO, & JOSE AGUSTIN DE ESCUDERO

NOTICIAS HISTORICAS Y ESTADISTICAS DE LA ANTIGUA PROVINCIA DEL NUEVO-MEXICO . . . ADICIONADAS POR EL LIC. D. ANTONIO BARREIRO EN 1839[!]; Y ULTIMAMENTE ANOTADAS POR EL LIC. DON JOSE AGUSTIN DE ESCUDERO . . . MEXICO: IMPRENTA DE LARA, 1849.

[1–2], [I]–IV, [1]–98, [99–102 index]. 21.5 x 14.6 cm. Map: Rutas / de la Caravanas que pasan / de los E. U. de Norte América / a la República Mexicana. / 29.8 x 37 cm. Scale: 60 miles to one inch. *Inset:* Continuacion del camina al interior de Méjico. / 14 x 8.8 cm. No scale given. Green printed wrappers, with title on front wrapper, ornament and decorative border on verso of back wrapper. In a red cloth case.

Ref.: Howes P383; Sabin 62980; Saunders 2607

For a translation and discussion of this work, see Quivira Society Publication, Vol. XI, *Three New Mexico Chronicles* . . . Translated with Introduction and Notes by H. B. Carroll and J. V. Haggard, Albuquerque, 1942.

3298 PIONEER AND PERSONAL REMINISCENCES

PIONEER AND PERSONAL REMINISCENCES. MARSHALLTOWN, IA.: MARSHALL PRINTING COMPANY, 1893.

[1]–105, [106–08 blank]. 22.7 x 15 cm. Pale green wrappers, with title on front wrapper.

Ref.: Howes C866

A series of reminiscences by various authors culled from newspapers.

3299 PIONEER SETTLERS' ASSOCIATION (Louisa County, Iowa)

CONSTITUTION AND BY-LAWS OF THE PIONEER SETTLERS' ASSOCIATION OF LOUISA COUNTY, IOWA, WITH THE PROCEEDINGS OF THE FIRST AND SECOND ANNUAL FESTIVALS. WAPELLO, IOWA: JOHN JENKINS, PRINTER, 1860.

[i–iv], [1]–8. 22.1 x 14.7 cm. Yellow printed wrappers with title on front wrapper, uncut.

Ref.: Moffit 506

Contains historical sketches and some anecdotes.

3300 PIONEER SETTLERS' ASSOCIATION (Louisa County, Iowa)

PROCEEDINGS OF THE PIONEER SETTLERS' ASSOCIATION, OF LOUISA COUNTY, IOWA, AT THE THIRD ANNUAL FESTIVAL. FEBRUARY 22D, 1861. WAPELLO, IOWA: WM. KEACH, PRINTER, 1861.

[1]–14, [15–16 blank]. 22.3 x 14.6 cm. Light gray printed wrappers with title on front wrapper, uncut, unopened.

Ref.:

Sketches and anecdotes of early history of the county.

3301 PIONEER SETTLERS' ASSOCIATION (Scott County, Iowa)

PROCEEDINGS OF THE PIONEER SETTLERS' ASSOCIATION, OF SCOTT COUNTY, IOWA, WITH A FULL REPORT OF THE SECOND FESTIVAL. DAVENPORT, IOWA: PUBLISHING HOUSE OF LUSE, LANE & CO., 1859.

[1]–[31], 32 blank, inserted yellow leaf, [1]–[18]. 22.7 x 14.5 cm. Pink printed wrappers, with title on front wrapper.

Ref.: Moffit 452

Page [1] of the second part: Organization and Proceedings / of the / Young Pioneer Settlers' Association / of / Scott County, Iowa, / with a / Full Report of the First Festival. / [rule] / 1859. / [rule] / Davenport, Iowa: / Publishing House of Luse, Lane & Co. / 1859. / The inserted yellow leaf preceding the title-page is a wrapper, yet it seems to have been issued without a conjugate. The second part was originally bound in this copy. Not described by Moffit.

3302 PITTMAN, PHILIP

THE PRESENT STATE OF THE EUROPEAN SETTLEMENTS ON THE MISSISIPPI[!]; WITH A GEOGRAPHICAL DESCRIPTION OF THAT RIVER . . . LONDON: PRINTED FOR J. NOURSE, MDCCLXX.

[i]–viii, [1]–99, [100 blank]. 26.3 x 20 cm. Map: A Plan / of / Mobile / [lower left:] Thos Kitchin Sculpsit. / 14.8 x 45 cm. Scale: 400 feet to one inch. Map: A Draught of the / River Missisippi[!] / from the Balise up to Fort Chartres. / 3 / 48.7 x 40.9 cm. Scale: 9 miles to one inch. Map: A Draught of the River Missisippi[!] / from the Balise up to Fort Chartres / 2 / 51.1 x 40.5 cm. Scale: 9 miles to one inch. Map: A Draught of the / River Missisippi[!] / [lower left:] Thos Kitchin Sculpsit. / 46 x 40.3 cm. Scale: 9 miles to one inch. Map: Plan of New Orleans. NB. No plan yet Published like this, being its present State. / [lower left:] 600 f^t. to an Inch. / [lower right:] Thos Kitchin Sculp. / 31.1 x 28.9 cm. Scale as above. Map: Draught of the / R. Ibbeville[!] / Being a short communication / from the Sea to the first of the / English Settlements on the Missisippi[!] / Scale, french League to 1 inch. / [lower right:] Thos Kitchin Sculp. / 52.5 x 23 cm. Scale: as above. Map: Plan of Fort Rosalia. / [lower right:] Thos Kitchin Sculp. / 22.5 x 18.5 cm. Scale: 250 feet to one inch. Map: A Plan / of / Cascaskies / [lower left:] Thos Kitchin Sculpsit / 25.5 x 47.6 cm. Scale: 400 feet to one inch. Original full calf. Front cover loose.

Ref.: Bradford 4421; Buck 6; Clark II 53; Howes P396; Sabin 63103

Extra-illustrated with a colored lithograph: The Escape of Deerfoot the Indian Runner from the Chippeways. / Signed in plate: Concanen & Lee / 61 /. [lower left:] Concanen & Lee, Lith. / [lower right:] Stannard & Dixon, Imp. / 31.2 x 23.5 cm. [curved top edge].

3303 PLAIN STATEMENT, A . . . 1846

A PLAIN STATEMENT FOR THE CONSIDERATION OF THE FRIENDS, OF THE PROTESTANT EPISCOPAL CHURCH, IN THE DIOCESE OF ILLINOIS, THE RT. REV.

PHILANDER CHASE, D. D. BISHOP. DRAWN UP SOME YEARS AGO, BUT MOST PROPER FOR THE PRESENT TIME; BY ONE WHO NOW RESTS FROM HIS LABORS. WITH NOTES BY OBSERVER. NEW YORK: TURNER & LAWRENCE, 1846.

[1]–[16]. 21 x 14 cm. Removed from bound volume, unbound, fore edges uncut. Repaired, part of last leaf supplied. In large red box stamped: Bishop Chase. Jubilee College.

Ref.:

Bishop Chase was not the author. It is an anonymous attack to which Samuel Chase replied in *Malignity Exposed . . .* 1847.

3304   PLATT, P. L., & N. SLATER

THE TRAVELERS' GUIDE ACROSS THE PLAINS, UPON THE OVERLAND ROUTE TO CALIFORNIA SHOWING DISTANCES FROM POINT TO POINT, ACCURATELY MENSURED[!] BY ROADOMETER . . . CHICAGO: PRINTED AT THE DAILY JOURNAL OFFICE, 1852.

[i]–[vi, vi blank], [7]–64. 14.5 x 10.2 cm. Folding map, untitled: [Independence, Mo. to the Pacific Ocean, from slightly south of San Francisco to the Columbia River]. [lower centre:] R. N. White. Sc. English Prairie. Ill. / [below plate:] four lines of errata. 9.9 x 22.5 cm. Yellow printed wrappers with title on front wrapper. In a brown half morocco folding case.

Ref.: Byrd 1879; Howes P417; Wagner-Camp 242; Wheat (*Transmississippi*) 760

The only known perfect copy. Streeter's copy lacks eighteen pages, including title-page, and the Nebenzahl-Howell copy lacked nearly all of the map.

3305   PLEASANTS, WILLIAM J.

TWICE ACROSS THE PLAINS, 1849 . . . 1856 . . . SAN FRANCISCO: PRESS OF WALTER N. BRUNT CO.: 1906.

[1]–160. 17 x 12.5 cm. Ten plates and two portraits. Green pictorial cloth. In a blue cloth case.

Prov.: Signature: Ansel P. Pleasants / on inside front cover.

Ref.: Cowan p. 494; Howes P421; Morgan (Pritchard) p. 183; Rader 2684

Note in pencil on title-page: Entire edition destroyed in fire of 1906 /.

3306   PLUMBE, JOHN

[Caption title] . . . IOWA TERRITORY. ITS PRESENT CONDITION AND PROSPECTIVE INCREASE. BY JOHN PLUMBE, JR. . . .

285–290. 25.9 x 17.9 cm. Inserted into gray board folder, cloth back, typed paper label on front cover.

Ref.:

Extract from *The Family Magazine*, 1840.

3307   PLUMBE, JOHN

[Map] MAP / OF THE SURVEYED PART / OF / IOWA TERRITORY, / FROM THE OFFICIAL PLATS; / DEFINING ALL THE TOWNSHIPS & COUNTIES; AND BEING THE / ONLY MAP YET PUBLISHED, EXHIBITING THE LOCATION / OF / IOWA CITY / THE PERMANENT SEAT OF GOVERNEMENT[!] OF THE TERRITORY, / AS ESTABLISHED BY THE COMMISSIONERS 4TH MAY, 1839. / ST. LOUIS: COMPILED AND PUBLISHED BY / JOHN PLUMBE JUNR / OF SINIPEE, WISCONSIN. / [lower right:] LITH. OF E. DUPRE S^{T} LOUIS MO. /

Map, 49.8 x 41 cm. Scale: nine miles to an inch. Folded into dark green leather folder, 13.7 x 9.3 cm., stamped in gilt on front cover: Iowa /, with trade card, 6.2 x 9.7 cm., of E. Dupré inside front cover. Map silked.

Ref.:

There are manuscript additions and changes in the map. The outlines of counties are colored. The engraving appears to be identical with the maps which appear in Plumbe's book. Apparently hitherto unknown as a separate.

3308   PLUMBE, JOHN

[Caption title] MEMORIAL AGAINST MR. ASA WHITNEY'S RAILROAD SCHEME. TO THE HONORABLE THE SENATE AND HOUSE OF REPRESENTATIVES OF THE UNITED STATES IN CONGRESS ASSEMBLED: . . . BUELL & BLANCHARD, PRINTERS.

[1]–48. 22.2 x 14.4 cm. Stabbed, unbound. In a blue half morocco case.

Ref.: Howes P425; *Railway Economics* p. 284; Sabin 63443

Dated on page 44, December, 1850, and with a postscript on page 49 dated Washington City, February, 1851. Imprint of Buell & Blanchard on page [1].

Plumbe's *Memorial* was in opposition to Whitney's plan for a railroad to Oregon.

3309   PLUMBE, JOHN

SKETCHES OF IOWA AND WISCONSIN, TAKEN DURING A RESIDENCE OF THREE YEARS IN THOSE TERRITORIES . . . ST. LOUIS: CHAMBERS, HARRIS & KNAPP, 1839.

[i–ii], [1–4, 4 blank], [5]–103, [104 blank]. 19.1 x 11.3 cm. Folding map: Map / of the Surveyed Part / of / Iowa Territory, / from the Official Plats; / Defining all the Townships & Counties; and being the / only Map yet published, exhibiting the location / of / Iowa City / the permanent Seat of Governement[!] of the Territory, / as established by the Commissioners 4th May, 1839. / St Louis: compiled and published by / John Plumbe, Junr / of Sinipee, Wisconsin. / [decorative rule] / [at foot, left:] Scale 9 Miles to an Inch. / [right:] Lith. of E. Dupré

S⁺ Louis Mo. / 49.6 x 39.8 cm. Scale as above. Tan printed boards, with brown cloth back, title on front cover, advertisement on back cover. Red morocco pull off case.

Prov.: Presentation copy inscribed on title-page: Gen. W. R. Smith / With the best Respects of / his obd⁺ Ser⁺. / the Author / [flourish]. Pencilled note on fly-leaf: I knew the Author, and his Father / and family, residing at Phillipsburg /, Centre Co. Penn⁴ W. R. Smith /.

Ref.: AII (*Missouri*) 250; Bradford 4430; Howes P426; Jones 1028; Mott (*Iowa*) p. 60; Sabin 63444

Born in Wales, Plumbe became a resident of Dubuque in the spring of 1835. In 1837 he commenced advocating a project for a railroad to the Pacific in the New York and Boston press. In 1838 he convened in Dubuque a large public meeting to consider this subject. In 1849 he visited California via the overland route. In 1855 he returned to Dubuque disheartened, having exhausted his financial resources, and in May, 1857, at Dubuque he committed suicide.—EDG

3310 PLUMMER, CLARISSA

NARRATIVE OF THE CAPTIVITY AND EXTREME SUFFERINGS OF MRS. CLARISSA PLUMMER, WIFE OF THE LATE MR. JAMES PLUMMER, OF FRANKLIN COUNTY, STATE OF NEW-YORK; WHO, WITH MRS. CAROLINE HARRIS, WIFE OF THE LATE MR. RICHARD HARRIS, WERE, IN THE SPRING OF 1835, WITH THEIR UNFORTUNATE FAMILIES, SURPRISED AND TAKEN PRISONERS BY A PART OF THE CAMANCHE TRIBE OF INDIANS . . . NEW-YORK: PERRY AND COOKE, PUBLISHERS. 1838.

[1]–[24]. (Page [1] blank, page [2] frontispiece.) 23.5 x 15.6 cm. Frontispiece. Green wrappers. In a brown half morocco case.

Ref.: Ayer 209; Field 1223; Howes P427; Jones 1018; Rader 2686; Raines p. 166; Sabin 63462, 30466 see; Streeter 1320; Wagner-Camp 71

On the verso of page 23 is a Certificate from one Ebenezer C. Elfort, a native of Georgia, who, while in Santa Fé in the fall of 1837, learned that the Indians had two white women as prisoners and went to the Indians and redeemed them, the white women, that is.

3311 POINSETT, JOEL R.

MANUSCRIPT LETTER (Copy). 1825 December 31, Mexico City.

One page, 31.9 x 19.5 cm. To George C. Sibley. In Mather Papers.

Regarding chances of completing the survey of the Santa Fé Road Commission.

3312 POLITICAL CABINET, THE

[Caption title] THE POLITICAL CABINET . . .

A–M⁴. [1]–96. A–K⁴. [1]–80. 21.4 x 12.7 cm. Two volumes bound together in red half morocco.

Ref.: Howes P436; Paltsits p. lxiv; Sabin 40826; Wagner-Camp 6a

As recommended by the publisher, these two sets of appendices to Volumes III and IV of the *Monthly Anthology* . . . Boston, 1806–07, have been removed from the periodical and bound separately. The first part contains a reprinting of a good deal of Jefferson's Message of February 19, 1806, and other related documents dealing with the Lewis and Clark expedition. The second part contains a letter from Clark dated from Saint Louis, September 23, 1806. Pike's narrative of his expedition up the Mississippi River to its source is also present.

Each of the twenty-two appendices comprised eight pages.

3313 POND, SAMUEL W., JR.

TWO VOLUNTEER MISSIONARIES AMONG THE DAKOTAS; OR, THE STORY OF THE LABORS OF SAMUEL W. AND GIDEON H. POND . . . BOSTON: CONGREGATIONAL SUNDAY-SCHOOL AND PUBLISHING SOCIETY.

[i]–xii, 7–278. 18.6 x 12.1 cm. Ten illustrations. Gray cloth title in black on backstrip and front cover.

Ref.:
Copyrighted 1893.

3314 PONTING, TOM C.

LIFE OF TOM CANDY PONTING.

[1]–102. 19 x 11.9 cm. Two portraits. Cream printed wrappers, with title on front wrapper in gilt: Tom Candy Ponting's / Life /, on back wrapper: the Review Press, Decatur, Ill. / In a brown cloth case.

Ref.: Adams (*Ramp. Herd*) 1815; Howes P469

The reprint of the Ponting book made in 1952 by the Branding Iron Press, Evanston, Illinois, was made from this copy. In the introduction to the reprint, Herbert O. Brayer states this pamphlet was published in June, 1907, in an edition of 25 copies. In the following year a further 25 copies were printed from the still standing type. This second printing was identical with the first printing with the sole exception that twelve copies of the second printing were bound in black cloth. The copy above described is of the first printing in all probability as it belonged to Miss

Mabel Jacobs, to whom Ponting dictated the book. According to Brayer it is her writing that appears in several places in this copy. In preparing for the reprint, Brayer was able to locate only four copies of the original in various public depositories and five copies in private collections in the U. S. A., one in Canada, and one in Great Britain. These plus seven copies in the hands of descendants of the author make a total of eighteen recorded copies of the original edition.— EDG

3315   POOLE, DEWITT C.

AMONG THE SIOUX OF DAKOTA: EIGHTEEN MONTHS EXPERIENCE AS AN INDIAN AGENT . . . NEW YORK: D. VAN NOSTRAND, 1881.

[1]–235, [236 blank]. 18 x 12.3 cm. Brown cloth sides stamped in black, gilt and black title on backstrip.

Prov.: Inscribed on front fly-leaf: R. Clay Wood U.S.A. / From The Author. / N.Y. City / Nov. 1. 81. / [last two lines joined by vertical wavy scrawl at right].

Ref.: Howes P470

Author was Indian Agent at the Whetstone Indian Reservation in the 'sixties and a prominent figure in military events on the Dakota-Wyoming-Montana frontier.—Howes

3316   POOR SARAH . . .

POOR SARAH . . . 1843.

[1]–18, [19–20 blank]. 12.8 x 7.7 cm. Bound with Number 1278.

Ref.: Hargrett (*Oklahoma*) 59

Printed at Park Hill in 1843. Text in Sequoyan.

Editions: New Echota, 1833.

3317   POORE, BEN P.

THE CONSPIRACY TRIAL FOR THE MURDER OF THE PRESIDENT, AND THE ATTEMPT TO OVERTHROW THE GOVERNMENT BY THE ASSASSINATION OF ITS PRINCIPAL OFFICERS . . . BOSTON: J. E. TILTON AND COMPANY, 1865 [–1866].

[1]–480. [1]–552, [553–54 blank]. [1]–552, [553–54 blank]. 19 x 12.4 cm. Three volumes, maroon cloth, title in gilt on backstrip.

Ref.: Howes P475; Monaghan 676; Sabin 41181

Dr. Otto Eisenschiml says only a dozen copies of Volume III escaped the fire which burned the printing establishment where it was printed. —EDG

3318   POPE, D. H.

[Letterpaper] J. D. POPE, LATE OF ATLANTA, GA. D. H. POPE, LATE OF ALBANY, GA. J. D. & D. H. POPE, ATTORNEYS AT LAW, WILL PRACTICE IN THE STATE AND FEDERAL COURTS OF TEXAS. SHERMAN, TEXAS. 1873.

[1]–[4]. 21.6 x 14 cm. Unbound leaflet.

Ref.:

Pages [2]–[4] comprise text beginning as follows: Written for the Albany (Ga.) News, by D. H. Pope, and printed in / circular form (by the Sherman, Texas, Democrat) as an answer to the many / inquiries made of us from Georgia and elsewhere. / J. D. & D. H. Pope. / June, 1873. / Sherman and Grayson County. / [diamond rule] / . . .

3319   POPE, JOHN

A TOUR THROUGH THE SOUTHERN AND WESTERN TERRITORIES OF THE UNITED STATES OF NORTH-AMERICA; THE SPANISH DOMINIONS ON THE RIVER MISSISSIPPI, AND THE FLORIDAS; THE COUNTRIES OF THE CREEK NATIONS; AND MANY UNINHABITED PARTS . . . . RICHMOND: PRINTED BY JOHN DIXON, M,DCC,XCII.

A⁸, B–M⁴, N². [i]–iv, [5]–105, [106 blank, 107 errata, 108 blank]. 20.1 x 13 cm. Newly bound in contemporary gray wrappers, uncut. In brown full morocco case by Lakeside Press.

Ref.: Clark II 54; Evans 24705; Howes P476; Jones 629; Pilling (*Muskhogean*) 71; Sabin 64109; Vail 920

Of seven copies located, four are complete with the full 108 pages. This important early narrative of travel was reprinted in 1888 from the copy now in ICN (Ayer) which runs only through page 104.

3320   POPE, JOHN

[Caption title] . . . THE REPORT OF AN EXPLORATION OF THE TERRITORY OF MINNESOTA, BY BREVET CAPTAIN POPE . . .

[1]–56. 23.1 x 14.8 cm. Folding map: Map / of the / Territory of Minnesota / Exhibiting the / Route of the Expedition to the Red River of the North, in the Summer of / 1849/ By Captⁿ John Pope, Corps Top. Engʳ. / [thick and thin rules] / Drawn by P. S. Morawski / [rule] / Scale / . . . 67.4 x 55.8 cm. Scale: 20 miles to one inch. Unbound, pasted into Gaylord Binder, uncut, unopened.

Ref.: Howes P479

31st Congress, 1st Session, Senate, Executive Document No. 42, Serial 558. [Washington, 1850.]

3321 POPKIN, JOHN S.

A SERMON, PREACHED MAY 4, 1806, THE LAST TIME OF ASSEMBLING IN THE OLD MEETING-HOUSE, IN THE FIRST PARISH IN NEWBURY . . . NEWBURY-PORT: PRINTED FOR ANGIER MARCH, 1806.

[A]–I⁴. [1]–71, [72 blank]. Bound with Number 3289.

Ref.: Sabin 64138; Shaw & Shoemaker 11189–90 see

Page [1] is a half-title reading: [decorative rule] / Two Sermons, / on Quitting the Old, / and Entering the New Meeting House, / in the First Parish in Newbury. / By John Snelling Popkin, A. M. / [decorative rule] /. Page [25] carries the title-page for the second sermon, preached September 17, 1806. Pages [57]–71 are an Appendix comprising historical data.

3322 POPPLE, HENRY

[Map] A MAP / OF THE BRITISH EMPIRE IN / AMERICA / WITH THE FRENCH AND SPANISH / SETTLEMENTS ADJACENT THERETO. / BY HENRY POPPLE. / C. LEMPRIERE INV & DEL. B. BARON SCULP. / [lower right:] LONDON ENGRAV'D BY WILL.ᴹ HENRY TOMS 1733. /

Fifteen double-page and five single-page maps bound together. 53.3 x 38.5 cm. Marbled boards, calf back, uncut. In a red cloth folder.

Ref.: Phillips p. 569; Howes P481; Sabin 64140

The key map is present, with title same as above but without last line and with W. H. Toms Sculp. / in lower right corner. Mounted inside front cover are the original prospectus and the contents leaf, the latter headed: The Contents of each Sheet of the Twenty Plates of / Mr. Popple's Map of America. / [39 lines]. 28.1 x 21.1 cm.

3323 PORT FOLIO, THE

[Caption title] THE PORT FOLIO. Nº V. PHILADELPHIA, AUGUST 1, 1807. NEW ADVERTISEMENTS. PROSPECTUS OF LEWIS AND CLARK'S TOUR TO THE PACIFICK OCEAN . . .

[1]–4. 21.7 x 13.6 cm. Unbound, removed from a bound volume. In a black cloth case.

Ref.: Thwaites I xxxvii, VII 363–66

The text is nearly identical with the prospectus issued by Meriwether Lewis and reprinted in Volume VII of the Thwaites edition, except that the original was dated June 3ᵈ 1807 and the present is dated August 1, 1807. Thwaites states that the original appeared in two forms, octavo and quarto and that only three copies of the original printing are known, all in the possession of Mrs. Julia Clark Voorhis and her daughter.

3324 PORTER, BURTON B.

ONE OF THE PEOPLE . . . PUBLISHED BY THE AUTHOR.*

[i]–[vii, viii blank], 1–382. 18.5 x 12.4 cm. Portrait. Green ribbed cloth.

Ref.: Cowan p. 496.

Copyrighted 1907. The place of publication is not given. The prefatory note is dated from Colton, California, October, 1906.

The author reached California in 1863 (via Panama) and spent some time in the gold fields.

3325 PORTER, LAVINIA HONEYMAN

BY OX TEAM TO CALIFORNIA. A NARRATIVE OF CROSSING THE PLAINS IN 1860 . . . OAKLAND, CAL.: OAKLAND ENQUIRER PUB. CO., NINETEEN HUNDRED AND TEN.

[i]–[xii, xii blank], [1]–139, [140 blank]. 23.5 x 15.7 cm. Olive buckram, title printed in pale green on front cover and on backstrip, fore and lower edges uncut.

Prov.: Inscribed on front endleaf: Ada B. Sloat / Sister of the Author / of this Book. / Tipped to the same leaf is a calling card of the author inscribed in pencil: To Lottie dear I / wish it were some thing / better, but with them / loving Christmas / Greetings /. Stamped on same leaf is: Library of A. D. Trunkey /.

Ref.: Cowan 496; Howes P488

Limited to fifty copies. Tipped to leaf opposite the title-page is an original photograph of the author, 9.6 x 9 cm., signed by the author in full.

3326 PORTLAND, OREGON. Board of Statistics, Immigration and Labor Exchange

OREGON, ITS ADVANTAGES AS AN AGRICULTURAL AND COMMERCIAL STATE . . . PORTLAND, OREGON: A. G. WALLING, BOOK AND JOB PRINTER, 1870.

[1]–62, [63–64 blank]. 22.2 x 13.5 cm. Pale green printed wrappers with title on front wrapper, list of Board on back wrapper.

Prov.: Stamp of Minnesota Historical Society and their number 6547 partially erased from front wrapper.

Ref.: McMurtrie (*Oregon*) 593

The Board was a Portland organization rather than a state board. The pamphlet urges settlement and development of the state.

3327 PORTLAND, OREGON. Board of Statistics, Immigration, and Labor Exchange

READ AND CIRCULATE. OREGON: ITS RESOURCES, SOIL, CLIMATE, PRODUCTIONS . . . JACKSONVILLE, OREGON: OREGON SENTINEL OFFICE PRINT, 1871,

[1]–12. 22.9 x 14.6 cm. Unbound, leaves tipped together.

Ref.: Smith 7666
Editions: Portland, 1869.

3328 [POST, CHARLES C.]

TEN YEARS A COWBOY. CHICAGO: RHODES & McCLURE PUBLISHING COMPANY, 1888.

[1–20], 17–471, [472–78 advertisements]. 19.2 x 13 cm. Illustrations unlisted, some used twice. Dark red pictorial cloth, with black and gilt stamping.

Ref.: Adams (*Ramp. Herd*) 1819; Howes P500 see

The 1888 edition is not listed by Howes who starts with 1886. Post's name does not appear as author.

Editions: Chicago, 1886, 1887.

3329 [POST, CHARLES C.]

PHIL. JOHNSON'S LIFE ON THE PLAINS . . . CHICAGO: RHODES & McCLURE PUBLISHING COMPANY, 1888.

[1–8], 17–358, [359–60 advertisements]. 18.4 x 13.2 cm. Illustrations on pages [2–8]. Semi-limp dark red cloth, stamped in black on backstrip and front cover.

Ref.: Adams (*Ramp. Herd*) 1181; Howes P500

Identical with the first 358 pages of Charles C. Post's *Ten Years a Cowboy . . .* 1886.

3330 POST, CHRISTIAN F.

THE SECOND JOURNAL OF CHRISTIAN FREDERICK POST . . . LONDON: PRINTED FOR J. WILKIE, M DCC LIX.

A–D⁸, E². [i]–[vi, vi blank], [7]–67, [68 blank]. 21 x 13 cm. Rebound in blue half morocco, uncut.

Ref.: JCB (*In Retrospect*) 82; Field 1233; Howes P501; Rusk I p. 40; Sabin 64453; Thomson 939; Vail 534; Wroth (*American Bookshelf*) pp. 104–06

The first journal covered the period July 15 to September 20, 1758, and the second October 25 of the same year to January 10, 1759.

Post's *Second Journal* carries on the narrative of his *Journal* appended to Charles Thomson's *Enquiry into the Alienation of the Delaware and Shawanese Indians*, London 1759. Both journals seem to have been published at the instigation of Benjamin Franklin. They relate in language, moving because of its simplicity, the bold, tireless and successful effort of a Moravian mission-

ary to detach from the French the allegiance of the Ohio Indians in the period between Braddock's defeat and General Forbes's capture of Fort Duquesne in 1758. As the result of Post's labors the Ohio Valley came into the hands of the English, one of the strategic successes which brought to an end the French empire in America.—JCB (*In Retrospect*)

3331 POST, TRUMAN A.

TRUMAN MARCELLUS POST, D. D. A BIOGRAPHY, PERSONAL AND LITERARY . . . BOSTON: CONGREGATIONAL SUNDAY-SCHOOL AND PUBLISHING SOCIETY.

[i]–[xvi, xvi blank], [1]–507, [508 blank]. 20.8 x 14 cm. Ten illustrations unlisted. Dark blue smooth cloth, beveled edges, title in gilt on backstrip.

Prov.: Inscribed on front endleaf: For Col J. F. How / with kindest / regards of / his friend / T. A. Post / St Louis / July 15ᵗʰ 1892 /. Book label of James F. How inside front cover.

Ref.: Buck 268
Copyrighted 1891.

Presbyterian and Congregational minister in Missouri (St. Louis) and Illinois. Post observed the troubles of the Mormons in both Illinois and Iowa.

3332 POSTON, CHARLES D.

SPEECH OF HON. CHARLES D. POSTON, OF ARIZONA, ON INDIAN AFFAIRS. DELIVERED IN THE HOUSE OF REPRESENTATIVES, THURSDAY, MARCH 2, 1865. NEW YORK: EDMUND JONES & CO., PRINTERS, 1865.

[1]–20. 22.8 x 14.6 cm. Stitched.

Ref.: Munk (Alliot) p. 180; Sabin 64569; Wagner-Camp 422

Issued both with and without wrappers. No evidence of wrappers on the present copy.

3333 POTTER, THEODORE E.

THE AUTOBIOGRAPHY OF THEODORE EDGAR POTTER.*

[i]–[xii, xii blank], 1–228. 20.8 x 13.3 cm. Three portraits. Dark blue cloth.

Ref.: Cowan p. 497; Howes P514
Copyrighted 1913. Printed by The Rumford Press, Concord, N. H.

The author gives us his experiences in an interesting and readable style. He arrived in California [overland] in 1852, and remained here until he enlisted in Walker's filibustering expedition in Nicaragua, arriving at the scene of action at the very end of Walker's career in that country.—Cowan

3334 POWELL, H. M. T.

THE SANTA FE TRAIL TO CALIFORNIA, 1849–1852. THE JOURNAL AND DRAWINGS OF H. M. T. POWELL . . . SAN FRANCISCO: THE BOOK CLUB OF CALIFORNIA.

[i–xvi, xvi blank], [1]–272. 34.1 x 23.7 cm. 18 illustrations and maps listed and numerous unlisted facsimile decorations. Tan buckram, brown morocco backstrip, blind lettered, fore and lower edges uncut.

Ref.: Howes P525; Rader 2716

Limited to 300 copies printed at the Grabhorn Press in 1931.

Laid in is an original leaf of drawings by Powell comprising two sketches reproduced on pages [vii] and [ix]. 23.3 x 18.8 cm. Pencil and pen and ink.

3335 POWELL, JOHN W.

CANYONS OF THE COLORADO . . . MEADVILLE, PA.: FLOOD & VINCENT M DCCC XCV.*

[1–2], [i]–xiv, [15]–400, [401 advertisement of Santa Fé Railroad, 402 blank]. 28.8 x 21.8 cm. Illustrations listed. Half brown morocco, gilt, gilt top.

Ref.: Farquhar (*Colorado River*) 43; Howes P527

First complete narrative; his earlier reports were largely devoted to scientific data.—Howes

3336 [POWELL, JOHN W.]

EXPLORATION OF THE COLORADO RIVER OF THE WEST AND ITS TRIBUTARIES. EXPLORED IN 1869, 1870, 1871, AND 1872 . . . WASHINGTON: GOVERNMENT PRINTING OFFICE, 1875.

[1–4], [i]–xi, [xii blank], [1]–291, [292 blank]. 29.2 x 23.2 cm. 80 illustrations, folding map and profile. Brick red cloth.

Ref.: Farquhar (*Colorado River*) 42; Howes P528; Munk (Alliot) p. 180; Sabin 64753

3337 POWER, JOHN C.

HISTORY OF THE EARLY SETTLERS OF SANGAMON COUNTY, ILLINOIS . . . SPRINGFIELD, ILL.: EDWIN A. WILSON & CO., 1876.

[1]–[798]. 23.7 x 17.2 cm. Portraits and map, unlisted. Brick cloth, pictorial borders and vignette on front cover in black and gilt, blind stamped border on back cover, title in gilt on backstrip, red edges.

Ref.: Buck 1063; Howes P532; Sabin 64771

Contains Lincoln material. Also an account of the Donner Party and George McKinstry's day-by-day journal.

3338 POWER, THOMAS

AUTOGRAPH LETTER, SIGNED: Power. 1806 December 6. New Orleans. To Stephen Minor. Four pages, 25.2 x 20.3 cm.

An interesting letter by one of the witnesses in the trial of Aaron Burr. Power had been a Spanish agent and was alleged to have paid Wilkinson $9000 on behalf of Governor Carondelet. The present letter deals principally with the purchase of two islands by Power and his associates. One passage regarding a "mad dog" may refer to Wilkinson who is also mentioned on the fourth page, in a postscript.

Laid in Wilkinson's *Memoirs*, Vol. II, 1811.

3339 POWERS, STEPHEN

AFOOT AND ALONE; A WALK FROM SEA TO SEA BY THE SOUTHERN ROUTE. ADVENTURES AND OBSERVATIONS IN SOUTHERN CALIFORNIA, NEW MEXICO, ARIZONA, TEXAS, ETC. . . . HARTFORD, CONN.: COLUMBIAN BOOK COMPANY, 1872.

[v]–xvi, [17]–327, [328 blank], [329 advertisement, 330 blank]. (Pages [v–vi] blank.) 20 x 12.7 cm. 29 illustrations listed. Green half morocco, red edges.

Prov.: Possibly the publisher's copy or, at least, someone closely associated with him.

Ref.: Cowan p. 498; Howes P537; Munk (Alliot) p. 181; Sabin 64804; Saunders 3106; Zamorano Eighty 61

The author, a distinguished ethnologist, journeyed from Raleigh to San Francisco, a distance of 3,556 miles. Although occasionally overdone, his descriptions are entertaining and frequently amusing.—Cowan

Laid in is an Autograph Letter, signed, by Bret Harte. San Francisco, September 30, 1870. To J. W. Bliss. Three pages, 20.3 x 12.8 cm. The letter offers, on behalf of Stephen Powers, the manuscript of his *Afoot and Alone* for publication. Harte praises the manuscript highly.

Pasted down on the recto of the first fly-leaf is the original pencil and wash drawing for the vignette used on the front cover of the cloth-bound edition.

3340 POWHOCCO CITY COMPANY, Powhocco City, Nebraska Territory

[Broadside] POWHOCCO CITY COMPANY. Nº 229 480 SHARES. THIS CERTIFICATE ENTITLES   TO ONE SHARE IN THE POWHOCCO CITY COMPANY . . . POWHOCCO CITY, N. T. A. D. 1856.

Broadside, 10.1 x 18.7 cm. Text, 8.8 x 17 cm.

Ref.:

Signed by J. W. Coolidge and J. Garside. Dated No. 3, 1856. Made out to W. H. Bassett.

Printed in blue. Signature of W. H. Bassett on verso.

Powhocco City was located in Sanders County, apparently plotted but never "created."

3341 POWNALL, THOMAS

A TOPOGRAPHICAL DESCRIPTION OF SUCH PARTS OF NORTH AMERICA AS ARE CONTAINED IN THE (ANNEXED) MAP OF THE MIDDLE BRITISH COLONIES, &C. IN NORTH AMERICA . . . LONDON: PRINTED FOR J. ALMON, MDCCLXXVI.*

[a]², b¹, A–L², M¹, A–D². [i]–vi, [1]–46, [1]–16. 44 x 26.3 cm. Map: A Map of the / Middle British Colonies in North America. First Published by Mᵣ Lewis Evans, of Philadelphia, in 1755; / and since corrected and improved, as also extended, / with the Addition of New England, and bordering Parts of Canada; / from Actual Surveys now lying at the Board of Trade. / By T. Pownall MP. / With a Topographical Description of such Parts of North America / as are contained in this Map. / Printed & Published according to Act of Parliament for J. Almon in Piccadilly, London. / March 25ᵗʰ 1776. / [lower left corner, outside cartouche:] Engraved by Jaˢ Turner in Philadelphia. Insets: Evans' acknowledgement "To the Honourable Thomas Pownall, Esqᵣ", "A Sketch of the remaining Part of Ohio R. & c.", and a "Table of Travelling Distances." 49.5 x 84 cm. (neat line). 57 x 97 cm. (paper size). No scale given. Rebound in dark blue half morocco, gilt top.
Ref.: Buck 28a; Howes P543; Sabin 64935; Vail 651

Large paper copy. The text includes the first printings of the Harry Gordon and Christopher Gist journals. There were two printings of 1000 copies each.

3342 PRAIRIE ROSE, THE

[Caption title] THE PRAIRIE ROSE: A MONTHLY MISCELLANY FOR YOUNG PEOPLE . . . BY J. W. A'NEALS & CO . . . VOLUME 1. WARSAW, ILLINOIS, MARCH, 1848. NUMBER 1 . . .

[1]–8. 27.2 x 19.8 cm. Green printed wrappers with title on front wrapper and advertisement on verso of back wrapper.
Ref.:
Contains a summary from Peck's "forthcoming 'History of Illinois.'"

3343 PRATT, DANIEL D.

ADDRESS AT THE CELEBRATION OF THE ANNIVERSARY OF Sᵀ· JOHN THE BAPTIST, BEFORE THE MEMBERS OF LOGAN CHAPTER AND TIPTON LODGE, JUNE 24TH, 1839 AT LOGANSPORT, INDIANA . . .

LOGANSPORT: PRINTED AT THE HERALD OFFICE, 1839.

[1]–21, [22–4 blank]. 21 to 19.7 x 13 cm. Removed from bound volume, uncut.
Ref.: Byrd & Peckham 818

3344 PRATT, JOHN J., & BELA S. BUELL

[Map] MAP / OF THE / GOLD REGIONS / IN THE / VICINITY OF CENTRAL CITY / GILPIN COUNTY, COLORADO TERRITORY / FROM ACTUAL SURVEY BY / JOHN J. PRATT AND BELA S. BUELL / CIVIL ENGINEERS AND SURVEYORS CENTRAL CITY 1862. / [diagrammatic scale: 500 feet to one inch] / SCALE OF 500′ TO ONE INCH. / ENTERED ACCORDING TO ACT OF CONGRESS IN THE YEAR 1862 BY Wᴹ H. REASE, / IN THE CLERKS OFFICE OF THE DISTRICT COURT OF THE EASTERN DISTRICT OF PENNSYLVANIA / [at foot centre:] LITH. & PRINTED BY W. H. REASE, N.E. COR. 4ᵀᴴ & CHESTNUT ST. PHILᴬ / [lower right:] J. E. DILLINGHAM DEL. / Inset map: Map / of / Colorado Territory / compiled from the latest official / and different private maps & Surveys, / by / F. G. Ebert, Engineer & Surveyor. / 38 x 52.3 cm. Scale: 18 miles to one inch. Insets: see below.

Map, 131.5 x 160.7 cm. Scale: 500 feet to one inch. Maroon cloth covers, lettered in gold on front and in blind on back: B.S.Buell's / Map of / Colorado Terʸ /
Ref.: Wagner-Camp 342; Wheat (*Transmississippi*) 1049

The mining districts have been indicated in contemporary manuscript. Dr. Nolie Mumey in his book *Pioneer Denver* . . . 1948, reproduced twenty-two of the twenty-seven views in the margins of this map. From a copy in the Denver Public Library he reproduces one view, "Black Hawk Point," not shown on this map. Regarding the map Mumey says "The maps are so rare that a single copy has not been found." His reproductions were made from lithographs which were sold separately. There are five views on this map which Mumey never saw, but three of these he had seen noticed in contemporary newspapers.—EDG

The vignettes surrounding the map are as follows (across top, left to right): Colorado Republican & Herald Office / 5ᵗʰ Street West Denver. / 10.6 x 12.7 cm.

Castle Rock from the South. / On Plumb Creek between Colorado & Denver City. / 10.2 x 18.2 cm.

"Camp—Weld." C. T. / [at right:] Dillingham del. / Oval shape, 10.5 x 21.9 cm.

Pikes Peak. / 11.9 x 18.8 cm.

View in Bear Creek Valley. Co. Ter. / [lower left:] F. M. Case. / 11.8 x 18.2 cm.

Mountains near Canon City / Showing the Stratified Rocks over lying the Igneons. / 11.8 x 18.2 cm.

Down left side:

Res. R. E. Whitsett / Curtis St East Denver / 9.8 x 9.4 cm. Woolworth & Moffatt Book Store [flourish] / Larimer St. near E St. E. D. / 10.7 x 10.6 cm.

Overland Stage Line / Blake St. / 9.2 x 11.7 cm.

G. F. Givens / Cor. Ferry, & 5th Streets, West Denver. / 9.3 x 11.5 cm.

El Paso House / Colorado City, Base of Pikes Peak. / 9.2 x 11.8 cm.

Rocky Mountain Brewery / Brewery Block, Highland. / Solomon Endlieh & Good, Proprietors. / 7.8 x 11.9 cm.

R. E. Whitsett Office / Cor. Larimer & G St. E. D. / 9.4 x 13.4 cm.

Down right side:

Broadwell House / J. M. Broadwell Prop.^{r} / Cor Larimer & G. St. E. D. / 8.5 x 12.1 cm.

Overland Stage Co. Office / Central City. C.T. / 10.9 x 8.4 cm.

A. C. Hunt & Co. / 5th St near Ferry W D /. 10 x 9.6 cm.

Kershaw & Co's. Ice House. / Kershaw & Co. Proprietors /. 7.3 x 10.7 cm.

Tappan & Co / Branch Store in Colorado City. / 8.8 x 10.9 cm.

Bank & Mint, Clark, Bruber & Co / Cor McGaa & G St E. D. / 9.8 x 8.8 cm.

Rocky Mountain News / News Printing C^o Press. / 9.4 x 10.5 cm.

Upper right corner, below top row, left to right: The Red Rocks at Colorado City. / 13.9 x 18.4 cm.

Central City. Col'o. Ter. / [lower left:] Dillingham, del. / 17.5 x 38.7 cm.

Across lower edge, left to right:

U. S. Post Office / Central City Col. Ter. / 11.4 x 9.9 cm.

G. W. Claytons Store. / Cor. Larimer & F St E. D. / 11.1 x 11.4 cm.

Brick Block / Ferry St W D /. 9.5 x 14.5 cm.

A. J. & J. M. Van Deren's Quartz Mill. / Nevada Col' May 1862. / 10.8 x 15.8 cm.

Denver City Col. Ter. / [lower left:] Lith & Printed by W. H. Rease, N. E. Cor. 4th & Chestnut St. Phil^a / [lower right:] J. E. Dillingham. De. / 11.3 x 75.8 cm.

3345 PRATT, JULIUS H.

REMINISCENCES, PERSONAL AND OTHERWISE . . . PRIVATELY PRINTED, 1910.*

[i–x, x blank], 1–287, [288 blank]. 20.2 x 13.8 cm. Nine illustrations listed. Dark blue cloth. Bookplate removed, rubber stamped words "Recreation Center" on page [ix].

Ref.: Cowan p. 499; Howes P554

Pages 34–99 carry "The Argonauts of 'Forty-Nine' " which had appeared in *The Century Magazine*, April, 1891, under the title "To California by Panama in '49." The present version is "with some corrections" according to a footnote on page 34. Place of printing in California not given.

3346 PRATT, ORSON

A SERIES OF PAMPHLETS BY ORSON PRATT, ONE OF THE TWELVE APOSTLES OF THE CHURCH OF JESUS CHRIST OF LATTER-DAY SAINTS . . . LIVERPOOL: PUBLISHED BY FRANKLIN D. RICHARDS, 1851.

[i]–iv, [1]–16, [1]–8, [1]–8, [1]–8, [1]–16, [1]–16, [1]–24, [1]–96, [1]–16, [1]–32, [1]–16, [i–ii], [1]–46, [i–ii], [1]–49 [50 blank]. 20.2 x 13.5 cm. Three portraits and one folding plate.

Ref.: Sabin 64962

BOUND WITH:

FLANIGAN, J. H.: Mormonism Triumphant! . . . Liverpool, 1849. [1]–32.

BOUND WITH:

LINFORTH, JAMES: [Caption title] The Rev. C. W. Lawrence's "Few Words from a Pastor to his People on the Subject of the Latter-Day Saints." [1]–8.

BOUND WITH:

SNOW, LORENZO: . . . An Explanation of the First Principles of the Doctrine of the Church of Jesus Christ of Latter-Day Saints . . . London, 1851. [1]–8.

BOUND WITH:

SPENCER, ORSON: [Caption title] Patriarchal Order, or Plurality of Wives! . . . [1]–16.

BOUND WITH:

BELL, J. F.: [Caption title] A Reply to the Bare-Faced Falsehoods and Misrepresentations of Mr. John Theobald . . . [1]–8.

BOUND WITH:

JAQUES, JOHN: [Caption title] [No. 1.] Salvation: A Dialogue between Elder Brownson and Mr. Whitby . . . [1]–8.

THE SAME. No. 2. [1]–8.

BOUND WITH:

TAYLOR, JOHN: The Government of God . . . Liverpool, MDCCCLII. [i]–viii, [1]–118.

BOUND WITH:

PIERCY, FRED: Steel engraved portrait of F. D. Richards. Signed in plate Fred Piercy 1852. With facsimile of the signature of the subject in lower margin.

BOUND WITH:

SMITH, JOSEPH: The Pearl of Great Price . . . Liverpool, 1851. [i]–viii, [1]–56. Three illustrations.

BOUND WITH:

BROWN, BENJAMIN: Testimonies for the Truth: A Record of Manifestations of the Power of God . . . Liverpool, 1853. [1]–32.

BOUND WITH:

WANDELL, C. W.: History of the Persecutions!! Endured by the Church of Jesus Christ of Latter Day Saints, in America . . . Sydney. [1]–64.

BOUND WITH:

[PRATT, PARLEY P:] [Caption title] Proclamation! to the People of the Coasts and Islands of the Pacific; of Every Nation, Kindred and Tongue. [1]–16.

BOUND WITH:

SNOW, LORENZO: The Italian Mission, London, 1851. [1]–28.

BOUND WITH:

SNOW, ERASTUS: One Year in Scandinavia: Results of the Gospel in Denmark and Sweden . . . Liverpool, 1851. [1]–24.

BOUND WITH:

SPENCER, ORSON: The Prussian Mission of the Church of Jesus Christ of Latter-Day Saints . . . Liverpool, 1853. [1]–16.

BOUND WITH:

SNOW, ZERUBBABEL: . . . Opinion . . . Upon the Official Course of His Excellency Gov. Brigham Young . . . Liverpool, 1852. [1]–24.

BOUND WITH:

GRANT, J. M.: [Caption title] Three Letters to the New York Herald . . . [1]–64.

BOUND WITH:

KANE, THOMAS L.: The Mormons. Philadelphia, 1850. [1]–84.

BOUND WITH:

CHURCH OF JESUS CHRIST OF LATTER-DAY SAINTS: Report of the Sheffield Quarterly Conference, Held . . . December 23d, 1849 . . . [1]–8.

BOUND WITH:

CHURCH OF JESUS CHRIST OF LATTER-DAY SAINTS: Report of the Sheffield Conference . . . Held . . . November 24th, 1850 . . . Sheffield, 1850. [1]–12.

BOUND WITH:

CHURCH OF JESUS CHRIST OF LATTER-DAY SAINTS: Report of the Sheffield Conference . . . Held May 19th, 1850 . . . [1]–8.

BOUND WITH:

CHURCH OF JESUS CHRIST OF LATTER-DAY SAINTS: Report of the Sheffield Conference . . . Held . . . on the Eighth Day of June, 1851 . . . [1]–12.

BOUND WITH:

[SMITH, JOSEPH:] A Dialogue between Josh.[!] Smith & the Devil. [1]–16.

Inserted after the third series of pamphlets by Orson Pratt is the following: [Caption title] Exclusive Salvation, / by / John Jaques, / Elder in the Church of Jesus Christ of Latter-day Saints. / [rule] / . . . [1]–8.

The last two sections of *A Series of Pamphlets* . . . carry the following title-pages (each preceded by a portrait): Report / of / Three Nights' / Public Discussion / in / Bolton, / between / William Gibson, H. P., / Presiding Elder of the Manchester Conference of the Church / of Jesus Christ of / Latter-day Saints, / and the / Rev. Woodville Woodman, / Minister of the / New Jerusalem Church. / [rule] / Reported by G. D. Watt. / [rule] / Liverpool: / Published by Franklin D. Richards, 15, Wilton Street, / and for Sale by Agents throughout Great Britain and Ireland. / 1851. / The second title-page: Three Nights' / Public Discussion / between the / Revds. C. W. Cleeve, James Robertson, and Philip Cater, / and / Elder John Taylor, / of the / Church of Jesus of Latter-day Saints, / at Boulogne-sur-Mer, France. / Chairman, Rev. K. Groves, M. A., / Assisted by / Charles Townley, LL.D., and Mr. Luddy. / [rule] / Also a / Reply / to the / Rev. K. Groves, M. A., & Charles Townley, LL.D. / Price Eightpence each. / Liverpool: / Published by John Taylor, / and for Sale by O. Pratt, at 15, Wilton Street, and by Agents throughout / Great Britain in Boulogne. / 1850. /

Twenty-four pieces bound together, half calf, black leather label on backstrip: Pratt's / Pamphlets / &C. /.

Prov.: H. Roper. / stamped in gilt at foot of backstrip.

Ref.:

This volume also contained a copy of the *Constitution of Deseret* which was removed and sold.

509

3347 [PRATT, PARLEY P.]

A DIALOGUE BETWEEN JOSH.[!] SMITH & THE DEVIL.

[1]–16. Bound with Number 3346.

Ref.:

Neither imprint nor date is given. However, this appears to be a British printing—probably Liverpool.

Chad Flake of the University of Utah, one of that band of noble souls who has started a Mormon bibliography, tells us that Pratt claimed authorship of this work in his autobiography.

3348 PRATT, PARLEY P.

LATE PERSECUTION OF THE CHURCH OF JESUS CHRIST, OF LATTER DAY SAINTS . . . NEW YORK: J. W. HARRISON, PRINTER, 1840.

[i]–xx, [21]–214. 14.6 x 9 cm. Black cloth, with title on backstrip. Pages 83–4 torn affecting text, pages 215–[16 (blank)] missing.

Ref.: Howes P558; Sabin 64966; Woodward 195

3349 [PRATT, PARLEY P.]

[Caption title] PROCLAMATION! TO THE PEOPLE OF THE COASTS AND ISLANDS OF THE PACIFIC; OF EVERY NATION, KINDRED AND TONGUE. BY AN APOSTLE OF JESUS CHRIST. PUBLISHED FOR THE AUTHOR, BY C. W. WANDELL, MINISTER OF THE GOSPEL . . .

[1]–16. Bound with Number 3346.

Ref.:

Signed on page 16: P. P. Pratt, / President of the Pacific Mission of the / Church of Jesus Christ of Latter Day Saints. / [rule] / William Baker, Printer, Hibernian Press, King-Street. /

3350 PRATT, PARLEY P.

A VOICE OF WARNING AND INSTRUCTION TO ALL PEOPLE, OR AN INTRODUCTION TO THE FAITH AND DOCTRINE OF THE CHURCH OF JESUS CHRIST, OF LATTER DAY SAINTS . . . NAUVOO: PRINTED BY JOHN TAYLOR, 1844.

[i]–x, [11]–79, 281–84, [285 blank]. (Page 281 on verso of 279.) 12.3 x 7.7 cm. Brown marbled boards, brown cloth back.

Ref.: Byrd 892; Sabin 64972

With five lines of quotations on the title-page, not fifteen.

Editions: New York, 1837, 1839.

3351 PRATT, PARLEY P.

THE SAME.

Brown cloth, stamped on backstrip. Bound inverted, worn, lacks fly-leaf at front, part of endpaper missing.

3352 PRESBYTERIAN AND CONGREGATIONAL CONVENTION, Chicago, 1847

MINUTES OF THE PRESBYTERIAN AND CONGREGATIONAL CONVENTION, HELD AT CHICAGO, ILLINOIS, JUNE 17, 1847. CHICAGO, ILL.: DAILY TRIBUNE PRINT, 1847.

[1]–41, [42–44 blank]. 15.6 x 10.7 cm. Plain yellow wrappers.

Ref.: Byrd 1235; McMurtrie (*Chicago*) 123; Sabin 12659

3353 PRESBYTERIAN CHURCH IN THE U. S. A. Iowa

1839. THE 1889. SEMI-CENTENNIAL CELEBRATION OF THE ORGANIZATION OF THE PRESBYTERIAN CHURCH, IN YELLOW SPRING TOWNSHIP, HELD AT KOSSUTH, DES MOINES COUNTY, IOWA. AUGUST 24, 1889. MEDIAPOLIS, IOWA: J. W. & S. C. MERRILL, PRINTERS, 1890.

[1]–68. 20.7 x 14.5 cm. Blue printed wrappers, with title on front wrapper within decorative frame.

Ref.:

Some marginal marks and annotations in an unidentified hand.

3354 PRESBYTERIAN CHURCH IN THE U. S. A. New Mexico. Laguna Mission

[Caption title] PRESBYTERIAN BOARD OF HOME MISSIONS, AND FRIENDS OF THE LAGUNA MISSION. DEAR FRIENDS: IN ORDER TO GIVE YOU A FAIRER VIEW OF OUR FIELD, . . .

[1]–20. 14.3 x 10.6 cm. Stabbed, unbound.

Ref.:

Signed on page 20: John Menaul. / Third Annual Report of the / Laguna Mission. / Laguna. Valencia Co. / New Mexico. / March 1st, 1879. / Printed at the Laguna Mission Press.

3355 PRESBYTERIAN CHURCH IN U. S. A. New Mexico. Santa Fé Presbytery

[Caption title] NEW MEXICO AND ITS CLAIMS, BRIEFLY PRESENTED BY THE COMMISSIONER FROM THE PRESBYTERY OF SANTA FE TO THE GENERAL ASSEMBLY OF 1881 . . .

[1]–24. 13.1 x 9.6 cm. Sewn, uncut, unopened.

Ref.:

Signed on page 24: John Menaul. / Laguna Mission Press. / Laguna, New Mexico. / May 2nd 1881. /

Printed at the Laguna Mission Press.

3356 PRESCOTT, WILLIAM H.

HISTORY OF THE CONQUEST OF MEXICO, WITH A PRELIMINARY VIEW OF THE ANCIENT MEXICAN CIVILIZATION, AND THE LIFE OF THE CONQUEROR, HERNANDO CORTES . . . NEW YORK: HARPER AND BROTHERS, M DCCC XLIII.

[i]–xxxiv, 1–488. [i]–xviii, 1–480. [iii]–[xviii, xviii blank], 1–524. 23.3 x 14.7 cm. Three portraits, two maps, facsimile signature. Three volumes, black embossed cloth, with gilt back including coat of arms of Cortés mentioned in list of illustrations, top edges uncut. Lacks half-title of third volume. In a black cloth case.

Prov.: Inscribed on front endleaf of Volume I: To Mr Roux de Rochelle— / from his Obliged & Obed^t Ser't, / W^m. H. Prescott / Boston, Feby. 10, 1844. / With signature on each inner front cover of G. H. Williamson and on inner back cover of last volume. With rubber-stamped monogram GW on front endleaf of Volume I and title-page of Volume II.

Ref.: Sabin 65262

The third half-title is often missing.

3357 PRESCOTT, WILLIAM H.

HISTORY OF THE CONQUEST OF PERU, WITH A PRELIMINARY VIEW OF THE CIVILIZATION OF THE INCAS . . . NEW YORK: HARPER AND BROTHERS, M DCCC XLVII.

[i]–xl, [1]–527, [528 blank]. [i]–[xx, xx blank], [1]–547, [548 blank]. 23.6 x 15 cm. Two portraits, map, and facsimile signature. Two volumes, dark green embossed cloth, gilt back, stamped with arms of Pizarro mentioned in note on illustrations in Volume I, top edge uncut. In a black cloth case.

Ref.: Sabin 65272

3358 PRESENT ADVANTAGES, THE . . .

THE PRESENT ADVANTAGES AND FUTURE PROSPECTS OF THE CITY OF FREEPORT, ILL., INCLUDING A COMPLETE STRANGERS' GUIDE TO ALL THE PUBLIC OFFICES, CHURCHES, HOTELS, BANKING-HOUSES, ETC. IN THE CITY. FREEPORT: PUBLISHED BY BOSS & BURROWS, 1857.

[1]–48. 17.8 x 11.4 cm. Folded map before title-leaf: Map / of the / Present & Prospective / Rail-Road Connections / of the City / of / Freeport, Illinois / Published by / Boss & Burrows / Freeport. / J. Gemmell. / Chicago. / 19.8 x 29.5 cm. No scale given. Gray printed wrappers, with title on front wrapper, advertisements on verso of front and recto and verso of back wrapper, black cloth backstrip.

Ref.: Byrd 2763; Sabin 65303

3359 PRESENT STATE OF . . . LOUISIANA, THE

THE PRESENT STATE OF THE COUNTRY AND INHABITANTS, EUROPEANS AND INDIANS, OF LOUISIANA, ON THE NORTH CONTINENT OF AMERICA. BY AN OFFICER AT NEW ORLEANS TO HIS FRIEND AT PARIS . . . LONDON: PRINTED FOR J. MILLAN, 1744.

[A]^1, B–G^4, H^3, [I]^2. [1]–55, [56–60 advertisements]. 19.5 x 12.1 cm. Contemporary mottled calf, gilt edges. Rebacked.

Ref.: JCB III 773; Howes L509; Jones 455; Sabin 42283; Vail 429

Louisiana as used in the title refers to the Ohio-Mississippi Valley from the Gulf of Mexico to the Canadian border. The original French manuscript was part of the loot from a French ship captured by Captain Aylmer of H. M. S. Portmahon. The authorship has been ascribed to Jean-P. Gougon de Grondel.

3360 PREUSS, CHARLES

[Map, seven sections] TOPOGRAPHICAL MAP / OF THE / ROAD FROM MISSOURI TO OREGON / COMMENCING AT THE MOUTH OF THE KANSAS IN THE MISSOURI RIVER / AND ENDING AT THE MOUTH OF THE WALLAH WALLAH IN THE COLUMBIA / [rule] / IN VII SECTIONS / [rule] / SECTION I [–VII] / FROM THE FIELD NOTES AND JOURNAL OF CAPT. J. C. FREMONT / AND FROM SKETCHES AND NOTES MADE ON THE GROUND BY HIS ASSISTANT CHARLES PREUSS / COMPILED BY CHARLES PREUSS, 1846 / BY ORDER OF THE SENATE OF THE UNITED STATES / [rule] / SCALE—10 MILES TO THE INCH. / [rule] / LITHOGR. BY E. WEBER & CO. BALTIMORE. /

Map, in seven sections, each 40.1 x 66.3 cm. (page size). Contemporary green paper backstrip along right edge.

Ref.: Wagner-Camp 115 note; Wheat (*Transmississippi*) 523

An extraordinary map by a master cartographer. Inscribed on the verso of the sixth map: Road from Missouri to Oregon /.

3361 PRICE, GEORGE F.

ACROSS THE CONTINENT WITH THE FIFTH CAVALRY . . . NEW YORK: D. VAN NOSTRAND, PUBLISHER, 1883.

[1]–[706]. 22.8 x 14.5 cm. Four portraits. Blue pictorial cloth, title in gilt on backstrip.

Prov.: Inscribed on front blank leaf: To the President of the United States / Chester A. Arthur / Commander-in-chief of the Army & Navy, / with the highest respect of / Geo. F. Price / Capt 5th Cav. / June 6th 1883. /

Ref.: Howes P582; Munk (Alliot) p. 181; Nicholson p. 669; Rader 2735

3362 PRICE, SIR ROSE LAMBART

A SUMMER ON THE ROCKIES . . . LONDON: SAMPSON LOW, MARSTON & COMPANY, LTD., 1898.*

[i]–x, [1]–279, [280 colophon]. 19 x 12.5 cm. Two illustrations and map listed. Red cloth, with title on front cover and backstrip in gilt, uncut, unopened.

Ref.: Adams (*Ramp. Herd*) 1841; Howes P587

3363 PRINCE, L. BRADFORD

HISTORICAL SKETCHES OF NEW MEXICO FROM THE EARLIEST RECORDS TO THE AMERICAN OCCUPATION . . . NEW YORK: LEGGAT BROTHERS, 1883.

[1]–327, [328 blank]. 19.5 x 13.1 cm. Dark green cloth, blind embossed sides, with title in blind on front cover, gilt on backstrip.

Ref.: Bradford 4492; Howes P611; Rader 2738; Saunders 2610

Printed in Kansas City, also carries Kansas City imprint.

3364 PRINCE, L. BRADFORD

[Caption title] NEW MEXICO. ITS RESOURCES AND BUSINESS OPPORTUNITIES. CHIEF JUSTICE PRINCE'S LETTER TO THE TRIBUNE . . .

[1]–4. 24.1 x 15 cm. Unbound leaflet.

Ref.:

The prefatory note is dated from Santa Fé, Nov. 12, 1879. The letter which follows is dated New Mexico, Aug. 29, 1879. No place of printing is indicated.

3365 PROCEEDINGS OF THE FRIENDS . . .

[Wrapper title] PROCEEDINGS OF THE FRIENDS OF A RAIL-ROAD TO SAN FRANCISCO, AT THEIR PUBLIC MEETING, HELD AT THE U. S. HOTEL, IN BOSTON, APRIL 19, 1849. INCLUDING AN ADDRESS TO THE PEOPLE OF THE U. STATES; SHOWING THAT, P. P. F. DEGRAND'S PLAN IS THE ONLY ONE, AS YET PROPOSED, WHICH WILL SECURE PROMPTLY AND CERTAINLY, AND BY A SINGLE ACT OF LEGISLATION, THE CONSTRUCTION OF A RAIL-ROAD TO CALIFORNIA, IN THE SHORTEST TIME ALLOWED BY ITS PHYSICAL OBSTACLES . . . BOSTON: DUTTON AND WENTWORTH, PRINTERS 1849.

[1]–24. 23.5 x 14.6 cm. Pink printed front wrapper with title (back wrapper lacking), bound into red cloth.

Ref.: Railway Economics p. 284
Editions: Boston, 1849, 1849.

3366 PROPOSED CATHEDRAL IN ILLINOIS, THE, . . .

[Caption title] THE PROPOSED CATHEDRAL IN ILLINOIS. A FEW DAYS SINCE, WE RECEIVED THROUGH THE MAIL A PAMPHLET . . .

[1]–8. 20.8 x 13.4 cm. Removed from bound volume, unbound.

Ref.:

No place or date of publication indicated. Probably Chicago, 1853.

Accompanies Whitehouse: *Address* . . . New York, 1854.

3367 PROSCH, CHARLES

REMINISCENCES OF WASHINGTON TERRITORY. SCENES, INCIDENTS AND REFLECTIONS OF THE PIONEER PERIOD ON PUGET SOUND . . . SEATTLE, WASHINGTON, 1904.

[3]–128. 21.8 x 15.1 cm. Portrait and two views. Red cloth.

Prov.: Inscribed on front fly-leaf in indelible pencil: To / Hon. Thomas Burke, / A token of the esteem of / Chas. Prosch. /

Ref.: Howes P633; Smith 8383

3368 PROSCH, THOMAS W.

DAVID S. MAYNARD AND CATHERINE T. MAYNARD. BIOGRAPHIES OF TWO OF THE OREGON IMMIGRANTS OF 1850 . . . SEATTLE: LOWMAN & HANFORD STATIONERY & PRINTING CO., 1906.*

[1]–80. 22.9 x 15.2 cm. Two portraits and facsimile. Gray printed wrappers, with title on front wrapper.

Ref.: Howes P634; Smith 8385

3369 PROTESTANT EPISCOPAL CHURCH. Dakota

JOURNAL OF THE PROCEEDINGS OF THE EIGHTH ANNUAL CONVOCATION OF THE PROTESTANT EPISCOPAL CHURCH. IN THE TERRITORY OF DAKOTA, ASSEMBLED IN CHRIST CHURCH, YANKTON, SEPTEMBER 7TH, 8TH AND 9TH, 1877. YANKTON, DAKOTA: BOWEN & KINGSBURY, PRINTERS AND BINDERS, 1877.

[1]–16. 22.2 x 14.9 cm. Folding table at end, 13 x 33.8 cm. Blue printed wrappers, with title on front wrapper.

Ref.: Allen (*Dakota*) 149

3370 PROTESTANT EPISCOPAL CHURCH. Illinois

CONSTITUTION AND CANONS OF THE DIOCESE OF ILLINOIS. JUBILEE COLLEGE: PRINTED AT THE JUBILEE PRESS, 1847.

[1]–15, [16 blank]. 19.7 x 13 cm. Removed from bound volume, unbound. In box marked: Bishop Chase Pamphlets.

Ref.: Byrd 1236

3371 PROTESTANT EPISCOPAL CHURCH. Illinois

THE CONSTITUTION AND CANONS OF THE PROTESTANT EPISCOPAL CHURCH, IN THE DIOCESE OF ILLINOIS. ADOPTED AT THE CONVENTION HELD IN ST. PAUL'S CHURCH, PEORIA, 21ST, 22ND AND 23RD OCTOBER, 1857. CHICAGO: CHAS. SCOTT & CO., BOOK AND JOB PRINTERS, 1857.

[1]–40. 21.1 x 13.5 cm. Removed from bound volume, unbound.

Ref.: AII (*Chicago*) 279; Byrd 2764

3372 PROTESTANT EPISCOPAL CHURCH. Illinois

JOURNAL OF THE SECOND ANNUAL CONVENTION, OF THE CLERGY AND LAITY OF THE PROTESTANT EPISCOPAL CHURCH, IN THE DIOCESE OF ILLINOIS, HELD IN TRINITY CHURCH, JACKSONVILLE, ON THE 16TH AND 17TH MAY, 1836. SPRINGFIELD, ILLINOIS: PRINTED AT THE JOURNAL OFFICE.

[1]–14, [15–16]. 21.1 x 13.1 cm. Blue wrappers. Laid in case marked: Bishop Chase. Jubilee College.

Ref.: Byrd 289; Sabin 66165

The Right Rev. Jackson Kemper, D. D., Missionary Bishop, presided at the convention, since Bishop Chase was in England on a mission.

3373 PROTESTANT EPISCOPAL CHURCH. Illinois

JOURNAL OF THE THIRD ANNUAL CONVENTION OF THE PROTESTANT EPISCOPAL CHURCH, IN THE DIOCESE OF ILLINOIS, HELD IN SPRINGFIELD, MAY 15TH AND 16TH, 1837. PEORIA: S. H. DAVIS, PRINTER, 1837.

[1]–16. 20.5 x 13.4 cm. Tan printed wrappers, with title on front wrapper, notice on verso of back wrapper. Laid in case labeled: Bishop Chase. Jubilee College.

Ref.: Byrd 344; McMurtrie (*Peoria*) 3

Bishop Chase's letter of April 3, 1835 from Gilead, M. T. accepting the episcopate of Illinois occurs on page 3. Bishop Chase's first address to his diocese, delivered at Springfield, May 15, 1837, occupies pages [5]–12.

3374 PROTESTANT EPISCOPAL CHURCH. Illinois

JOURNAL OF THE FOURTH ANNUAL CONVENTION OF THE PROTESTANT EPISCOPAL CHURCH, OF THE DIOCESE OF ILLINOIS, HELD IN RUSHVILLE, ON THE 4TH AND 5TH JUNE, 1838. PRINTED AT THE QUINCY WHIG OFFICE, 1838.

[1]–31, [32 Erata[!]]. 19.6 x 13 cm. Sewn, removed from bound volume. In box marked: Bishop Chase Pamphlets.

Ref.: Byrd 413

Bishop Chase's address to the convention occupies pages 4–11. The Appendix, pages 21–31, contains Rules of Order, Constitution, and Canons of the Diocese of Illinois.

3375 PROTESTANT EPISCOPAL CHURCH. Illinois

A JOURNAL OF THE FIFTH ANNUAL CONVENTION, OF THE PROTESTANT EPISCOPAL CHURCH, OF THE DIOCESE OF ILLINOIS, HELD IN CHICAGO, THIRD AND FOURTH OF JUNE, 1839. PRINTED AT THE OFFICE OF THE CHICAGO AMERICAN, 1839.

[1]–21, [22–24 blank]. 20.5 x 13.1 cm. Sewn, removed from bound volume, unbound. In box marked: Bishop Chase Pamphlets.

Ref.: Byrd 481; McMurtrie (*Chicago*) 25

3376 PROTESTANT EPISCOPAL CHURCH. Illinois

JOURNAL OF THE SIXTH ANNUAL CONVENTION OF THE PROTESTANT EPISCOPAL CHURCH OF THE DIOCESE OF ILLINOIS, HELD IN THE CHAPEL OF JUBILEE COLLEGE, ON THE SEVENTH AND EIGHTH OF JUNE, 1841 . . . PEORIA: S. H. DAVIS, PRINTER, 1841.

[1]–12, [1]–14 Appendix, [15–16 blank]. 23.5 x 15.1 cm. Stabbed, unbound. Laid in box marked: Bishop Chase Pamphlets.

Ref.: Byrd 653

The fourteen pages at the end have a caption title: Appendix. / [thick and thin rules] / Bishop Chase's Address / in Jubilee Chapel, June 7, 1841.

The Address was also issued separately. The Graff copy has been extracted from a bound volume and may have had a title-page or wrapper title—as it stands the caption title is: "Bishop Chase's Address / to the / Convention of the Prot. Epis. Church, Illinois, / in Jubilee Chapel, June 7, 1841. / . . . 14 p., [1] p. (or wrappers) with [Price 12 1/2 cents.]" on verso.—McMurtrie (1943)

3377 PROTESTANT EPISCOPAL CHURCH. Illinois

JOURNAL OF THE SEVENTH ANNUAL CONVENTION OF THE PROTESTANT EPISCOPAL CHURCH IN THE DIOCESE OF ILLINOIS, HELD IN RUSHVILLE, SCHUYLER COUNTY, ON THE SIXTH AND SEVENTH OF JUNE, 1842. PEORIA: S. H. DAVIS, PRINTER, 1842.

[1]–16. 19.6 x 12.9 cm. Removed from bound volume, unbound. Last line of page [3] bled in trimming. In box marked: Bishop Chase Pamphlets.

Ref.: Byrd 727; McMurtrie (*Peoria*) 9

Bishop Chase's address to the convention occurs on pages [7]–10.

**3378 PROTESTANT EPISCOPAL
CHURCH.** Illinois

JOURNAL OF THE EIGHTH ANNUAL CONVENTION OF
THE PROTESTANT EPISCOPAL CHURCH IN THE DIO-
CESE OF ILLINOIS, HELD IN QUINCY, ADAMS
COUNTY, ON THE FOURTH OF JUNE, 1843. PEORIA:
WILLIAM H. BUTLER, PRINTER, 1843.

[1]–20. 21 x 13.3 cm. Removed from bound volume, unbound. In box marked: Bishop Chase
Pamphlets.

Ref.: Byrd 811; McMurtrie (*Peoria*) 15

**3379 PROTESTANT EPISCOPAL
CHURCH.** Illinois

JOURNAL OF THE NINTH ANNUAL CONVENTION OF
THE PROTESTANT EPISCOPAL CHURCH IN THE DIO-
CESE OF ILLINOIS, HELD IN SPRINGFIELD, SANGA-
MON COUNTY, ON THE SIXTEENTH AND SEVEN-
TEENTH OF JUNE, 1845 . . . PEORIA: S. H. DAVIS,
PRINTER, 1845.

[1]–27, [28 blank]. 20.7 x 13.8 cm. Frontispiece:
Design for Jubilee College /. Removed from
bound volume, unbound. In case marked: Bishop Chase Pamphlets.

Ref.: Byrd 988; McMurtrie (*Peoria*) 17

The 27 pages at the end have a special title-
page: Bishop Chase's / Address / Delivered /
before the Convention / of the / Protestant Episcopal Church, / Springfield, Illinois, / June 16th,
1845. / [short thick and thin rules] / Saint
Louis: / Printed by Daniel Davies. / Corner of
Main and Olive streets. / . . . . . / 1845. / 19.6 x
13 cm. Removed from bound volume, unbound.

The address was also issued as a separate.
Page 9 of the *Journal:* On motion, resolved, that
the secretary cause to be printed 300 copies of
the Journal, to be distributed as usual, and 500
copies of the Bishop's address, extra, to be
placed at his disposal.

**3380 PROTESTANT EPISCOPAL
CHURCH.** Illinois

JOURNAL OF THE TENTH ANNUAL CONVENTION OF
THE PROTESTANT EPISCOPAL CHURCH, OF THE DIO-
CESE OF ILLINOIS, HELD IN GALENA, JO DAVIESS
COUNTY, ON THE TWENTY-SECOND AND TWENTY-
THIRD OF JUNE, 1846. ALTON: PRINTED AT THE
"TELEGRAPH" OFFICE, 1846.*

[1]–16, [1]–15, [16 blank]. 19.6 x 13 cm. Removed from bound volume, unbound. Remnants of yellow wrappers. In case marked: Bishop Chase Pamphlets.

Ref.: Byrd 1109

Bishop Chase's address occupies Appendix
C, the 15 pages at the end.

**3381 PROTESTANT EPISCOPAL
CHURCH.** Illinois

JOURNAL OF THE ELEVENTH ANNUAL CONVENTION
OF THE PROTESTANT EPISCOPAL CHURCH, IN THE
DIOCESE OF ILLINOIS, HELD IN ALTON, MADISON
COUNTY, ON THE TWENTY-FIRST AND TWENTY-
SECOND OF JUNE, 1847. JUBILEE COLLEGE: PRINTED
AT THE JUBILEE PRESS. 1847.*

[1]–[48]. 19.6 x 13 cm. Removed from bound
volume, unbound. Trace of original lavender
wrappers. In box marked: Bishop Chase Pamphlets.

Ref.: Byrd 1237

Bishop Chase's Address occupies the Appendix A, pages [22]–40.

**3382 PROTESTANT EPISCOPAL
CHURCH.** Illinois

JOURNAL OF THE TWELFTH ANNUAL CONVENTION
OF THE PROTESTANT EPISCOPAL CHURCH, IN THE
DIOCESE OF ILLINOIS, HELD IN JACKSONVILLE, ON
THE NINETEENTH AND TWENTIETH OF JUNE, 1848.
JUBILEE COLLEGE: PRINTED AT THE JUBILEE PRESS,
1848.*

[1]–24. 19.6 x 13 cm. Removed from bound volume, unbound. Traces of original pink wrappers. In box marked: Bishop Chase Pamphlets.

Ref.: Byrd 1365

Bishop Chase's Address to the convention
appears as Appendix A, pages [11]–13.

**3383 PROTESTANT EPISCOPAL
CHURCH.** Illinois

JOURNAL OF THE THIRTEENTH ANNUAL CONVEN-
TION OF THE PROTESTANT EPISCOPAL CHURCH, IN
THE DIOCESE OF ILLINOIS, HELD IN CHICAGO, ON
THE SEVENTEENTH & EIGHTEENTH OF JUNE, 1850.
JUBILEE COLLEGE: PRINTED AT THE JUBILEE PRESS,
1850.*

[1]–11, [12 blank]. [1]–36. 19.6 x 13 cm. Removed from bound volume, unbound. In box
marked: Bishop Chase Pamphlets.

Ref.: Byrd 1616

Bishop Chase's address to the convention appears on pages [1]–21 of the second part.

**3384 PROTESTANT EPISCOPAL
CHURCH.** Illinois

JOURNAL OF THE FOURTEENTH ANNUAL CONVEN-
TION OF THE PROTESTANT EPISCOPAL CHURCH, IN
THE DIOCESE OF ILLINOIS, HELD IN QUINCY, ON THE
SIXTEENTH DAY OF JUNE, 1851. JUBILEE COLLEGE:
PRINTED AT THE JUBILEE PRESS, 1851.

[1]–40. 19.7 x 13.1 cm. Removed from bound
volume, unbound. In box marked: Bishop Chase
Pamphlets.

Ref.: Byrd 1756

Bishop Chase's address to the convention occurs on pages 9–27.

3385 PROTESTANT EPISCOPAL CHURCH. Illinois

ANOTHER COPY.*

20.7 x 13.4 cm. Remnants of salmon wrappers.

3386 PROTESTANT EPISCOPAL CHURCH. Illinois

JOURNAL OF THE FIFTEENTH ANNUAL CONVENTION OF THE PROTESTANT EPISCOPAL CHURCH, IN THE DIOCESE OF ILLINOIS, HELD IN PEKIN, TAZEWELL COUNTY, ON THE TWENTY-FIRST DAY OF JUNE, 1852. JUBILEE COLLEGE: PRINTED AT THE JUBILEE PRESS, 1852.

[1]–28. 19.7 x 13.1 cm. Removed from bound volume, unbound. In box marked: Bishop Chase Pamphlets.

Ref.: Byrd 1880

Bishop Chase's Address to the convention occurs on pages 5–8. It was read by the Assistant Bishop Whitehouse.

3387 PROTESTANT EPISCOPAL CHURCH. Illinois

JOURNAL OF A SPECIAL CONVENTION IN LIEU OF THE SEVENTEENTH ANNUAL CONVENTION OF THE PROTESTANT EPISCOPAL CHURCH, IN THE DIOCESE OF ILLINOIS, HELD IN TRINITY CHURCH, CHICAGO, ON THE TWENTY-FIFTH, SIXTH, AND SEVENTH DAYS OF OCTOBER, 1854. PEORIA: PRINTED BY BENJAMIN FOSTER, 1854.

[1]–42, folding table. 20.2 x 12.5 cm. Removed from binding, unbound. In box marked: Bishop Chase Pamphlets.

Ref.: Byrd 2169; McMurtrie (*Peoria*) 43

3388 PROTESTANT EPISCOPAL CHURCH. Illinois

JOURNAL OF THE THIRTY-FOURTH ANNUAL CONVENTION OF THE DIOCESE OF ILLINOIS, HELD IN THE CATHEDRAL CHURCH OF SS. PETER AND PAUL, CHICAGO, SEPT. 12TH, 13TH, 14TH AND 15TH, A. D. 1871. PUBLISHED BY ORDER OF THE CONVENTION. 1872.*

[1]–58, [1]–[60], [61–2 blank]. 21 x 14.4 cm. Mauve front wrapper. Removed from bound volume, unbound. With notice on front wrapper: In consequence of the destruction by fire of / the partly printed Journal of 1871, the reprint-/ing of the same was deferred to the present / date. / In box marked: Bishop Chase Pamphlets.

Ref.:

The second part carries a separate title-page: Twentieth / Annual Address / of / Henry J. Whitehouse, / Bishop of Illinois, / Read in the Cathedral, Chicago, at the Thirty-Fourth / Annual Convention of the Diocese. / [decorative rule] / 1871. / [decorative rule] / Published by Order of the Convention. /

Each part bears on the verso of its title-page the following imprint: [rule] / Culver, Page, Hoyne & Co., Printers. / Chicago. / [rule] /.

3389 PROTESTANT EPISCOPAL CHURCH. Illinois

JOURNAL OF THE THIRTY-FIFTH ANNUAL CONVENTION OF THE DIOCESE OF ILLINOIS, HELD IN THE CATHEDRAL CHURCH OF SS. PETER AND PAUL, CHICAGO, SEPT. 10TH, 11TH AND 12TH, A. D. 1872. PUBLISHED BY ORDER OF THE CONVENTION. 1872.*

[1]–97, [98 blank]. 20.9 x 14.6 cm. Mauve front wrapper. Removed from bound volume, unbound. In box marked: Bishop Chase Pamphlets.

Ref.:

Second part carries separate title-page: Twenty-First / Annual Address / of / Henry J. Whitehouse, / Bishop of Illinois, / Read in the Cathedral, Chicago, at the Thirty-Fifth / Annual Convention of the Diocese. / [decorative rule] / 1872. / [decorative rule] / Published by Order of the Convention. /

Each title-page bears on the verso the following imprint: [rule] / Culver, Page, Hoyne & Co., Printers. / Chicago. / [rule] /.

3390 PROTESTANT EPISCOPAL CHURCH. Illinois

SPECIAL CONVENTION OF THE PROTESTANT EPISCOPAL CHURCH IN ILLINOIS, FOR THE ELECTION OF AN ASSISTANT BISHOP, HELD AT PEKIN, ILLINOIS, MONDAY, SEPTEMBER 8, 1851. CHICAGO: PUBLISHED FOR THE REPORTERS. 1851.

[1]–12. 19.2 x 12.4 cm. Removed from bound volume, unbound. In box marked: Bishop Chase Pamphlets.

Ref.: Byrd 1758

An anti-Chase report of a brisk session at which Henry John Whitehouse was elected assistant bishop.

3391 PROTESTANT EPISCOPAL CHURCH. Iowa

JOURNAL OF THE FIRST ANNUAL CONVENTION OF THE PROTESTANT EPISCOPAL CHURCH IN THE DIOCESE OF IOWA, HELD IN DAVENPORT, MAY 31ST., A. D. 1854. DUBUQUE, IOWA: ADAMS & HACKLEY'S PUBLISHING OFFICE, 1854.

[1]–19, [20 blank]. 20 x 12.5 cm. Unbound, removed from binding. Remnants of blue wrappers along backstrip, burned along outer margin.

Ref.: Moffit 170

3392 PROTESTANT EPISCOPAL CHURCH. Iowa

JOURNAL OF THE PROCEEDINGS OF THE SECOND AN-
NUAL CONVENTION OF THE PROTESTANT EPISCOPAL
CHURCH, IN THE DIOCESE OF IOWA, HELD IN CHRIST
CHURCH, BURLINGTON, MAY 30TH, AND 31ST,
1855. BURLINGTON: PRINTED FOR THE CONVEN-
TION, 1855.

[1]–62, [63–64 blank]. 19.7 x 12.7 cm. Removed
from bound volume, unbound. Fore edge
scorched.

Ref.: Moffit 206

3393 PROTESTANT EPISCOPAL CHURCH. Iowa

JOURNAL OF THE PROCEEDINGS OF THE THIRD
ANNUAL CONVENTION OF THE PROTESTANT EPISCO-
PAL CHURCH IN THE DIOCESE OF IOWA, HELD IN ST.
JOHN'S CHURCH, DUBUQUE, MAY 28TH AND 29TH,
1856. BURLINGTON: HAWK-EYE BOOK AND JOB
OFFICE PRINT, 1856.

[1]–72. 20.5 x 13 cm. Removed from bound volume, unbound.

Ref.: Moffit 257

3394 PROTESTANT EPISCOPAL CHURCH. Niobrara

[Wrapper title] SECOND ANNUAL REPORT OF THE
INDIAN COMMISSION. FIRST ANNUAL REPORT OF THE
MISSIONARY BISHOP OF NIOBRARA. THE REPORT OF
THE SPECIAL COMMITTEE ON THE TWO REPORTS.

[1]–[17], [18 blank], [1]–11, [1]–3. 23.2 x 14.8
cm. White printed wrappers, with title as above
on front wrapper.

Ref.:

The second listed report (which is first in the
pamphlet) is signed at the end by William H.
Hare, and is dated September 30, 1873. Probably
printed in New York in 1873.

3395 PROTESTANT EPISCOPAL CHURCH. Niobrara

ELEVENTH ANNUAL REPORT OF THE MISSIONARY
BISHOP OF NIOBRARA.

[i–ii], [1]–[17], [18 blank]. 21.1 x 14.1 cm. Eight
illustrations, as follows: Facing pages [1]: Bear
Dance, / Collotype reproduction from Catlin.
2: Pine Ridge Mission. / (Missionary District of
Niobrara.) Lithograph in color. 4: St. Paul's
Boarding School for Boys. / Woodcut. 6: St.
Mary's Boarding School, / Santee Reserve. /
Mounted photograph, original. 8: St. John
Boarding School, / Cheyenne River Reserve. /
Collotype reproduction of photograph. 10:
Hope Boarding School, / Springfield. / Mounted
photograph, original. 12: Choir of Church of the

Holy Fellowship, / Yankton Reserve. / Mounted
photograph, original. 14: Native Clergy and
Candidates. / Collotype reproduction of photograph. Removed from bound volume, unbound.

Ref.:

Bishop Hare signed the report from Yankton,
August, 1883. It may have been printed there,
although neither place nor date of publication is
given.

3396 PROTESTANT EPISCOPAL CHURCH. Ohio

JOURNALS OF THE CONVENTION, OF THE PROTES-
TANT EPISCOPAL CHURCH IN THE STATE OF OHIO,
BEGUN AND HELD AT WORTHINGTON, JUNE 3,
A. D. 1818; AND CONTINUED BY ADJOURNMENTS
TO FIFTH OF SAID MONTH. COLUMBUS: P. H. OLM-
STED, PRINTER, 1818.

[1]–18, [19–20 blank]. 18 x 10.5 cm. Rebound in
black cloth, uncut. In box marked: Bishop
Chase Pamphlets.

Ref.: AII (*Ohio*) 437; Sabin 56939

Signed on page 18: Philander Chase, Prest. /
Charles Hammond, Sec'ry. /

3397 PROTESTANT EPISCOPAL CHURCH. Oregon & Washington

PROCEEDINGS OF THE SECOND CONVOCATION OF
THE CLERGY AND LAITY OF THE PROTESTANT EPIS-
COPAL CHURCH OF OREGON AND WASHINGTON
TERRITORIES. PORTLAND: PRINTED BY THOS. J.
DRYER, 1854.*

[1]–12. 20.4 x 12.9 cm. Blue printed wrappers,
with title on front wrapper.

Ref.: McMurtrie (*Oregon*) 74

3398 PROTESTANT EPISCOPAL CHURCH. Texas

JOURNAL OF THE TENTH ANNUAL CONVENTION OF
THE PROTESTANT EPISCOPAL CHURCH, IN THE DIO-
CESE OF TEXAS, HELD IN TRINITY CHURCH, GAL-
VESTON, MAY 5TH AND 6TH, 1859. SAN ANTONIO,
TEXAS: PRINTED AT THE HERALD OFFICE, 1859.

[1]–52. 22 x 13.7 cm. Green printed wrappers,
with title on front wrapper, recto of back wrapper: Form of a / Certificate of Appointment . . .

Ref.: Winkler 1200

Winkler calls for title on cover.

3399 PUCKETT, JAMES L. & ELLEN

HISTORY OF OKLAHOMA AND INDIAN TERRITORY
AND HOMESEEKEKERS'[!] GUIDE . . . VINITA,
OKLAHOMA: CHIEFTAIN PUBLISHING COMPANY,
1906.*

[1]–[151], [152 blank]. (Pages [1–2] blank.)
22 x 14.6 cm. Eight illustrations listed, included

in pagination. Pale green printed wrappers with portrait on recto of front and verso of back wrapper. In a green cloth case.

Ref.: Adams (*Ramp. Herd*) 1844; Foreman p. 53; Howes P645

3400 PUELLES, JOSE MARIA DE JESUS

INFORME QUE SE DIO AL EXCMO. SR. PRESIDENTE DE LA REPUBLICA MEJICANA, SOBRE LIMITES DE LA PROVINCIA DE TEJAS. CON LA DE LA LUISIANA. ZACATECAS: 1828. IMPRENTA DEL SUPREMO GOBIERNO, A CARGO DEL C. PEDRO PINA.

[1]–5⁴, 6². [I]–III, [IV blank], 1–38. 19.2 x 13.2 cm. Full new tree calf, morocco label, gilt, gilt edges.

Ref.: Howes P646; Streeter 734

Father Puelles had helped the commissioners who established the boundary between Texas and Louisiana in 1807–12. This report was compiled at the request of the President of Mexico from his original notes.

The TxU copy carries a leaf of errata not present in this copy. As in the Streeter copy, corrections have been made in manuscript in the text.

3401 PUMPELLY, RAPHAEL

MY REMINISCENCES . . . NEW YORK: HENRY HOLT AND COMPANY, 1918.*

[i]–[xiii, xiv blank], [1]–438. [i]–[xi, xii blank], [1–2], 439–844. 21.7 x 14.5 cm. 93 illustrations and maps listed. Two volumes, ribbed cloth, gilt tops, uncut. In dust jackets and board case.

Prov.: Bookplates of Frederick K. Tinkham, Grand Rapids. Tipped in Vol. I is a slip: Frederick K. Tinkham / with compliments / of / Raphael Pumpelly / April 19ᵗʰ 1922 /.

Ref.: Howes P650

In his early years, Pumpelly managed a mine in Arizona; later, as an economic geologist, he traveled and worked in Japan, China, Siberia, Wisconsin, Michigan, the Rockies, Mexico, and New Hampshire.

3402 PURCELL, POLLY JANE

[Caption title] AUTOBIOGRAPHY AND REMINISCENCES OF A PIONEER . . .

Seven leaves, printed on rectos only. 24 x 12.7 cm. Text punched with two holes in top margin, light green paper back wrapper folded over at top edge and tied through holes with pink ribbon.

Ref.:

Undated, no place of publication or printer indicated.

Polly ferried across the Missouri River at St. Joseph in April, 1846. She writes an interesting account of her trip and early pioneer experiences in Oregon.—EDG

Signed on last page: Mrs. Polly Jane Purcell, / Freewater, Oregon. /

3403 PURPLE, EDWIN R.

IN MEMORIAM. EDWIN R. PURPLE. BORN, 1831. DIED, 1879. NEW YORK: PRIVATELY PRINTED, 1881.

[1]–12. 26.8 x 2.4 cm. Blue cloth, uncut.

Ref.: Cowan p. 504

Limited to 125 copies.

Purple went to California in 1850 via the Isthmus. After stays in San Francisco and Sacramento he made a trading tour across the Sierra Nevada range to meet the incoming emigration. Returning, he mined at Carson's Creek and Murphy's Camp in Calaveras County. In 1861 he left Los Angeles for Salt Lake City in charge of 130 horses, 18 stages, and 30 men as agent for the Butterfield Overland Mail Company. An abstract of his account of his trip is given.—EDG

3404 PURVIANCE, LEVI

THE BIOGRAPHY OF ELDER DAVID PURVIANCE, WITH HIS MEMOIRS . . . DAYTON: PUBLISHED FOR THE AUTHOR BY B. F. & G. W. ELLS, 1848.

[i]–viii, [9]–304. (Pages [i] blank, [ii] frontispiece.) 18.2 x 12 cm. Portrait. Rebound in contemporary blue straight-grain calf, title in gilt on backstrip.

Ref.: Bay p. 376; Clark II 163; Howes P654; Sabin 66730

There is enough social history to make it a significant item for the study of Kentucky and Ohio.—Clark

Q

3405 QUATREFAGES, CHARLES DE

AUTOGRAPH MANUSCRIPT, SIGNED, of "Notice sur les Indians Ioways et Ojibways qui se sont montés à Paris en 1849"

26 pages, small quarto (20 x 15.3 cm.), each leaf hinged to stub and bound in marbled boards, dark olive polished calf back.

The manuscript is preceded by a leaf on which appears the following: Entreé / [underline] / Juillet 1847 / [double underline] / Societé d'Ethnologie /. Signed on the last page: C De Quatrefages / 16 Xbre 1849 /. With the bookplate of E. T. Hamy.

3406 QUID NUNC, THE

[Newspaper] THE QUID NUNC. D. S. GRISWOLD, EDITOR . . . ELLIS, FERGUS & CO., PROPRIETORS. VOL. I.—NO. 29. CHICAGO, ILL., WEDNESDAY, JULY 27, 1842 . . .

[1–4]. 41.5 x 29.4 cm. Unbound.
Ref.:
The printer's imprint appears at the foot of the last column on page [4]: Ellis & Fergus, / Book and Job Printers, / Saloon Buildings, Clarke Street. /

The first column on the first page is a prospectus for the paper. It was designed to avoid political quarrels and was apparently too tame for Chicago, since it ran for only a year.

3407 QUIGG, LEMUEL E.

[Wrapper title] LIBRARY OF TRIBUNE EXTRAS. VOL. I. AUGUST, 1889. NO. 8. NEW EMPIRES IN THE NORTHWEST . . . THE TRIBUNE ASSOCIATION, NEW-YORK.

[1]–84. 25.5 x 17.2 cm. Blue printed wrappers, with title on front wrapper, Table of Contents. / on verso of front wrapper, and advertisement on verso of back wrapper.
Ref.: Howes Q14; Smith 8457

3408 QUIGG, MATTHEW

ATCHISON CITY DIRECTORY, AND BUSINESS MIRROR FOR 1865 . . .*

[1]–126. 20.3 x 13.4 cm. Removed from bound volume, sewn, unbound. Lacks pages 5–8.
Ref.: AII (*Kansas*) 439; Howes Q15
Howes gives [Atchison 1864?] as place and date of publication.

3409 QUIN, MICHAEL J.

AUTOGRAPH LETTER, SIGNED. 1824 January 23. Three pages, 8vo. To W. Dorset Fellowes.
With Fellowes' reply on the fourth page.

3410 QUIN, MICHAEL J.

AUTOGRAPH LETTER, SIGNED. 1824 January 27. Three pages, 8vo. To W. Dorset Fellowes.
With manuscript note by Fellowes about Quin on the fourth page.

3411 QUIN, MICHAEL J.

AUTOGRAPH LETTER, SIGNED. No date, Wednesday. Two pages, 8vo. To W. Dorset Fellowes.
Presenting a copy of Iturbide: *A Statement of Some of the Principal Events . . .* 1824 to Fellowes.
The three letters are bound in a copy of the book.

3412 QUIN, SMITH & VAN ZANDT

[Map] THE / TERRITORY / OF / NEBRASKA / EMBRACING THE PUBLIC SURVEYS / UP TO THE SUMMER OF 1858 / COMPILED & DRAWN IN THE SURVEYOR GENERAL'S OFFICE / FROM ORIGINAL NOTES. / BY / QUIN, SMITH & VAN ZANDT. / SCALE: FIVE MILES TO ONE INCH. / [certificate, directional arrow, and diagram] / LEOPOLD GAST & BROTHER LITH / SECOND CARONDELET AVE. BETWEEN LAFAYETTE & GEIER AVE[s]. / ST. LOUIS, MO. / [lower right:] ENTERED IN THE CLERKS OFFICE OF THE U. S. DISTRICT COURT OF MISSOURI JULY 1857 BY QUIN, SMITH & VAN ZANDT ACCORDING TO ACT OF CONGRESS RESPECTING COPY RIGHTS. /

Map, 87.6 x 56.2 cm. Scale: five miles to one inch. Brown cloth covers, 16.7 x 10.8 cm., with printed paper label, 4.9 x 7.1 cm., on front cover.
Prov.: See below.
Ref.:
Laid in is a printed and manuscript document, signed by G. H. Nixon, Register, dated at Land Office, Brownville, Nebraska, September 6, 1858. A certificate of a claim filed by Joseph B. Wesley under the Pre-emption law of 1841. Inside the front cover there is the signature: Joseph B Wesley / Nebraska City / May 10th 1859 /. In the upper left corner, in pencil, the following note: April 3 1858 / [rule] / returned May 3 1859 /. Also in pencil, below the signature: Went to Nebraska April 3. / 58 / Returned home May 3, / 1859 /.
On the face of the map, two locations are marked in pencil.
Editions: St. Louis, 1857.

3413 [QUINER, EDWARD B.]

CITY OF WATERTOWN, WISCONSIN: ITS MANUFACTURING & RAIL ROAD ADVANTAGES, AND BUSINESS STATISTICS. WATERTOWN: PUBLISHED BY ORDER OF CITY COUNCIL, 1856.

[1]–24. 18.4 x 11 cm. Map: Map / of / Wisconsin / showing / The City of Watertown / and its Rail Road Connections / 1856 / [lower right:] H. Seifert, Milwaukee /. 20 x 28.5 cm. No scale given. *Inset map:* City / of Watertown / showing its Water Power / 7.5 x 5.9 cm. No scale given. Dark yellow printed wrappers, with title on front wrapper, verso of front wrapper headed: Business Register /, recto of back wrapper is repeat of recto of front wrapper, verso same as verso of front wrapper.
Ref.: AII (*Wisconsin 1855–58*) 217; Howes Q19; Sabin 67300
AII makes no mention of the map, but it is mentioned on page 10. AII calls for "Advertisements printed on both sides of back paper cover."

The mayor, Wm. Chappell, was perhaps the chief factor in getting the city to publish this pamphlet. It was intended for eastern capitalists to buy Railroad bonds, issued by the city. E. B. Quiner . . . was the compiler.—AII

R

3414   RADFORD, B. J.

HISTORY OF WOODFORD COUNTY. GIVING A BRIEF ACCOUNT OF ITS SETTLEMENT, ORGANIZATION, PHYSICAL CHARACTERISTICS AND PROGRESS . . . PEORIA, ILLS.: W. T. DOWDALL, PRINTER, 1877.

[1]–78. 20.5 x 13.5 cm. Black cloth, title in gilt on front cover.

Ref.: Howes R3

The earliest history of Woodford County listed by Buck is 1878.

3415   RAE, JOHN

NARRATIVE OF AN EXPEDITION TO THE SHORES OF THE ARCTIC SEA IN 1846 AND 1847 . . . LONDON: T. & W. BOONE, 1850.

[i]–viii, [1]–[248]. 22 x 14 cm. Two maps: Discoveries of the / Honble Hudson's Bay Co^s Arctic Expedition, / to the North of Repulse Bay; / Conducted by John Rae Esq^e 1846 & 1847; / Shewing in connection, the Discoveries made by / Parry, Ross, Back, / & the Honble Company's Expedition Conducted by / Dease & Simpson 1838–1839. / Adjusted & Drawn by / John Arrowsmith / [below border:] London, Pub^d Jany 1st 1848, by John Arrowsmith, 10 Soho Square. 48.5 x 60.6 cm. Scale: 23 miles to one inch. Map [two maps on one sheet]: Northern America / 20.2 x 29.9 cm. No scale given. Map: Discoveries / of the / Honble Hudson's Bay Company's / Arctic Expeditions / between / 1839 & 1851. / [lower centre:] John Arrowsmith / 8.1 x 29.9 cm. Scale: about 50 miles to one inch. Green cloth, blind embossed panels on sides, title in gilt on backstrip, uncut. In a green cloth case.

Ref.: Field 1253; Sabin 67428; Smith 4864; Staton & Tremaine 2868; Wagner-Camp 137

3416   RAHT, CARLYSLE G.

THE ROMANCE OF DAVIS MOUNTAINS AND BIG BEND COUNTRY . . . EL PASO: THE RAHTBOOKS COMPANY.*

[i–vi], 1–381, [382 blank]. 19.4 x 13.3 cm. Double-page map and thirteen plates. Dark blue pictorial cloth.

Ref.: Howes R16; Rader 2752

Copyrighted 1919. A history of the region between the Pecos and the Rio Grande.—Howes

3417   RAMBLER, THE

THE RAMBLER; OR, A TOUR THROUGH VIRGINIA, TENNESSEE, ALABAMA, MISSISSIPPI AND LOUISIANA . . . ANNAPOLIS: PRINTED BY J. GREEN, 1828.

[i]–iv, [5]–41, [42]. 19.3 to 18.5 x 11.5 cm. Gray boards, uncut. Part of front endleaf torn off. In a green cloth case.

Ref.: Clark II 230; Howes R22; Sabin 67617

The author of this apperceptive view of the South has not been identified. He was born, according to the text, in Charles County, Maryland, on January 22, 1801.

3418   RAMSEY, ALEXANDER

DAGUERREOTYPE PORTRAIT. Waist length, seated, nearly full face, tinted. Oval, 6.5 x 5.2 cm. (frame opening), in a black embossed leather plush-lined case, 9.5 x 8.1 cm.

Alexander Ramsey was the first Territorial Governor of Minnesota.

3419   RAND, McNALLY & CO.

RAND, McNALLY & CO.'S INDEXED MAP OF DAKOTA SHOWING THE RAILROADS IN THE TERRITORY, AND THE EXPRESS COMPANY DOING BUSINESS OVER EACH . . . CHICAGO: RAND, McNALLY & CO.

[1]–[11], [12 blank]. 14.7 x 8.3 cm. Folded map, colored, headed above neat line: Rand, McNally & Co.'s Dakota. / [lower left:] Rand, McNally & Co., Relief Plate Map Engravers, Chicago. / 52.4 x 47 cm. No scale given. Pamphlet in self wrappers, sewn, loose in green cloth cover; map attached to recto of back cover, advertisements on verso of front cover.

Ref.: Phillips (*Maps*) p. 258

Published in 1881.

3420   RAND, McNALLY & CO.

RAND, McNALLY & CO.'S NEW MAP AND GUIDE TO THE BLACK HILLS OF DAKOTA. CHICAGO: RAND, McNALLY & CO., 1875.

[1]–32. 16 x 9.3 cm. Two illustrations in text, two views pasted inside front and back covers, and a folding map. Folding map: Rand, McNally & Co.'s New Map of the Black Hills. / [at foot left:] Copyright Secured. [centre:] Rand, McNally & Co., Printers, Engravers and Publishers, Chicago. / 43.8 x 47.7 cm. No scale given. Illustration verso of front cover: View of Table Rock, Sioux Falls, / 65 Miles North of Elk Point. / Illustration verso of back cover: View of Sioux Falls, D.T., / 65 Miles North of Elk Point. / Yellow printed boards, with title on front cover, advertisement on verso of back cover, brown cloth backstrip.

Ref.: Howes B491; Phillips (*Maps*) p. 134

3421 RANDOLPH, C. D.

AUTOGRAPH LETTER, SIGNED. 1939 June 17. Davenport, Iowa. To Peter Decker. Two pages, 24.8 x 20.1 cm.

Regarding Dr. William F. Carver, "Idaho Bill," "Pawnee Bill," and "Diamond Dick." Colonel Randolph's sobriquet was "Buckskin Bill." He also described himself "Poet of the Plains."

Laid in Carver: *The Life of Dr. Wm. F. Carver . . . 1878.*

3422 RAPIDS CONVENTION, Burlington, Iowa

PROCEEDINGS OF THE RAPIDS CONVENTION, HELD AT BURLINGTON, IOWA, ON THE 23D AND 24TH OF OCTOBER, 1851. BURLINGTON, IOWA: PRINTED BY MORGAN & McKENNY, 1852.

[1]–24. 21.4 x 12.9 cm. Old (but not original) buff wrappers. Remnants of green wrappers.

Ref.: Moffit 112

The Convention was called for delegates from Illinois, Missouri, Wisconsin, and Iowa to consider ways of encouraging trade and settlement of the Upper Mississippi Valley, especially by furthering navigation on the Mississippi.

3423 RAVOUX, AUGUSTIN

THE LABORS OF MGR. A. RAVOUX AMONG THE SIOUX OR DAKOTA INDIANS. FROM THE FALL OF THE YEAR 1841 TO THE SPRING OF 1844.

[i–ii], [1]–10. 23.1 x 15.5 cm. Stapled.

Ref.:

Imprint on verso of title-page: St. Paul, Minn.: / Pioneer Press Company, / Printers. / 1897 /. Note on page [1]: The following article appeared in the St. Paul Pioneer Press, Mar. 7, 1897.

3424 RAVOUX, AUGUSTIN

[Extract] MISSIONARY EXCURSION IN IOWA.—NO. I. THE FOLLOWING INTERESTING LETTERS WERE WRITTEN IN FRENCH, BY THE REV. A. RAVOUX, TO THE RIGHT REV. DR. LORAS, BISHOP OF DUBUQUE, WHO KINDLY FURNISHED THEM FOR THIS MAGAZINE. . . .

[19]–25. 24.3 x 15.4 cm.

BOUND WITH:

MISSIONARY EXCURSION IN IOWA.—NO. II.

[84]–87. Two extracts bound together in yellow wrappers with printed strip label on front cover.

Ref.:

The two extracts appeared in Volume 7 of *The United States Catholic Magazine and Monthly Review . . .* Edited by Rev. Charles I. White . . . Baltimore: John Murphy, 1848, in the issues for January and February, 1848.

3425 RAVOUX, AUGUSTIN

REMINISCENCES, MEMOIRS AND LECTURES . . . ST. PAUL, MINN.: BROWN, TREACY & CO., 1890.

[i]–x, [1]–223, [224 blank]. 24.9 x 17 cm. Mounted photograph of the author as frontispiece, two woodcut portraits. Pale blue printed limp boards, with title between two decorative bands, brown cloth backstrip.

Ref.: Howes R75

Ravoux came to Minnesota in 1840; as missionary to the Sioux from 1840 to 1876 his operations covered the vast region between Dubuque and Ft. Pierre.—Howes

3426 RAWLINGS, THOMAS

EMIGRATION, WITH SPECIAL REFERENCE TO MINNESOTA, U. S., AND BRITISH COLUMBIA . . . LONDON: CLAYTON & CO.

[1]–24. 19.8 x 13.2 cm. Light yellow printed wrappers, with title on front wrapper. Lacks back wrapper.

Prov.: Rubber stamp of Chicago Historical Society, 1885, on title-page and book label of Historical Society of Minnesota on verso of front wrapper. Numeral 9 in ink on title-page and on front wrapper.

Ref.:

Dated from London, February 20, 1864.

3427 RAWSON, ALLEN A.

MONOGRAPH OF ALLEN ABEL RAWSON, M. D. AND EARLY DAYS OF ADAMS COUNTY, IOWA. RED OAK, IOWA: THE THOS. D. MURPHY COMPANY, 1900.

[1]–[62]. 18.9 x 13.4 cm. 26 illustrations listed. Dark blue cloth, title in gilt on front cover within gilt rule border.

Ref.: Mott (*Iowa*) p. 86

3428 RAYNER, N.

[Caption title] SPEECH OF MR. N. RAYNER, OF N. CAROLINA, ON THE SUB-TREASURY BILL . . . JUNE 22, 1840 . . .

[1]–32. Bound with Number 1084.

Ref.: Sabin 68121

Printed at Washington in 1840.

3429 RAYNOLDS, WILLIAM F.

REPORT ON THE EXPLORATION OF THE YELLOWSTONE RIVER . . . WASHINGTON: GOVERNMENT PRINTING OFFICE, 1868.

[i–ii, ii blank], [1]–174. 22.3 x 14.4 cm. Map: U. S. War Department. / [short rule] / Yellowstone and Missouri Rivers / and their Tributaries. / explored by / Capt. W. F. Raynolds Top⟦l⟧ Eng⟦rs⟧ / and / 1⟦st⟧ Lieut. H. E. Maynadier

10th Inf^y Assistant. / 1859–60. / To accompany a report to the Bureau of Engineers. / 1867. / Scale 1/1200000 / [diagrammatic scale: about 20 miles to one inch.] / Engraved in the Engineer Bureau War Dep^t / [seal of the Bureau] /. 68.5 x 106 cm. Scale as above. Green cloth, title in gilt on front cover.

Ref.: Howes R88; Phillips (*Maps*) p. 1130; Wheat (*Transmississippi*) 1012

40th Congress, 1st Session, Senate, Executive Document 77.

3430 READ, BENJAMIN M.

ILLUSTRATED HISTORY OF NEW MEXICO . . . TRANS-LATED . . . BY ELEUTERIO BACCE . . . COPYRIGHT, 1912, BY BENJAMIN M. READ . . .*

[1]–812. 25.1 x 16.5 cm. 113 illustrations listed. Purple cloth.

Prov.: Signature on verso of title-page: C. A. Rising /. Also rubber stamp of author's name on same page.

Ref.: Howes R90; Rader 2765; Saunders 4545

Limited to 500 copies. Published at Santa Fé. The Spanish original was published in 1911. Errata slip (17 x 12.3 cm.) laid in. Twelve corrections appear on the slip.

3431 READ, GEORGE W.

A PIONEER OF 1850: GEORGE WILLIS READ, 1819–1880. THE RECORD OF A JOURNEY OVERLAND FROM INDEPENDENCE, MISSOURI, TO HANGTOWN (PLACERVILLE), CALIFORNIA, IN THE SPRING OF 1850 . . . EDITED BY GEORGIA WILLIS READ. BOSTON: LITTLE, BROWN, AND COMPANY, 1927.*

[i]–xxvi, [1]–185, [186 blank]. 21.8 x 14.7 cm. 21 illustrations and one map listed. Blue cloth, fore and lower edges uncut.

Ref.: Cowan p. 523; Howes (1954) 8420; Rader 2766

First publication of one of the best overland diaries.—Howes

3432 READ, J. A. & D. F., *Illustrators*

[Pictorial title] JOURNEY TO THE GOLD DIGGINS[!] BY JEREMIAH SADDLEBAGS. ILLUSTRATED BY J. A & D. F. READ . . . CINCINNATI: U. P. JAMES, 1849.*

[1]–63, [64 blank]. 13.5 x 22.5 cm. 112 illustrations on 62 pages. Yellow printed wrappers with title as above on front wrapper, advertisement on verso of back wrapper.

Ref.: Cowan p. 523; Howes R92

An amusing series of caricatures recounting adventures on the way to California via Panama and return overland. Wreden's reprint was made from this copy.

3433 READING, PIERSON B.

AUTOGRAPH LETTER, SIGNED. 1847 July 10, New Helvetia. Two pages, 25 x 19.7 cm. To R. M. Sherman.

Order for tools in preparation for building a certain famous sawmill. Reading was willing to hold himself responsible for payment of the tools. A list of the required tools follows the letter and is signed by Reading.

Reading was the founder of the famous Readings Diggings. His memoirs appear in the *Quarterly* of the Society of California Pioneers, Volume VII, No. 3, September, 1930. He crossed the plains in 1843.

R. M. Sherman is listed in Kimball's *San Francisco Directory* for 1850 as a Horse keeper.

3434 REAGAN, JOHN H.

MEMOIRS WITH SPECIAL REFERENCE TO SECESSION AND THE CIVIL WAR . . . EDITED BY WALTER FLAVIUS McCALEB . . . NEW YORK: THE NEALE PUBLISHING COMPANY, 1906.*

[1]–351, [352 blank]. 22.1 x 14.8 cm. Four illustrations listed. Gray buckram, gray fillet on front cover enclosing title and seal in gilt, title in gilt on backstrip.

Ref.: Howes R100

Contains material relative to The Peters' Colony in Texas, the "Hexcombe War," etc. Reagan was Postmaster-General of the Confederacy.

3435 REAVIS, LOGAN U.

THE LIFE AND MILITARY SERVICES OF GEN. WILLIAM SELBY HARNEY . . . SAINT LOUIS: BRYAN, BRAND & CO., 1878.

[i]–xvii, 18–477, [478 blank]. 21.1 x 14.3 cm. 29 illustrations, unlisted. Bright blue cloth, title in gilt and black on front cover and backstrip.

Ref.: Howes R102; Nicholson p. 696; Rader 2770

A long and interesting life, much of which was spent in the Far West.—EDG

3436 REDMOND, PAT. H.

HISTORY OF QUINCY, AND ITS MEN OF MARK; OR, FACTS AND FIGURES EXHIBITING ITS ADVANTAGES AND RESOURCES, MANUFACTURES AND COMMERCE . . . QUINCY: HEIRS & RUSSELL, 1869.

[1]–302. 16.7 x 12 cm. Dark blue embossed cloth, title in gilt on front cover.

Ref.: Bradford 4565; Howes R117; Sabin 68522

3437 REDPATH, JAMES, & RICHARD J. HINTON

HAND-BOOK TO KANSAS TERRITORY AND THE ROCKY MOUNTAINS' GOLD REGION . . . NEW YORK: J. H. COLTON, 1859.

[1, advertisement, 2 blank], [i]–vi, [7]–177, [178–184 advertisements (182–83 blank)]. 14.6 x 9.4 cm. Two maps on one sheet: Kansas / and / Nebraska. / Published by J. H. Colton & Cº Nº 172 William Sᵗ New York. / 1859. / Scale of Miles: 18 to an Inch. / [diagrammatic scale] / [lower left:] Entered according to Act of Congress in the Year 1858 by J. H. Colton & Cº in the Clerks Office of the District Court of the United States for the Southern District of New York. / 44 x 37.2 cm. Nebraska / and / Kanzas[!]. / showing Pikes Peak and the Gold Region. / Published by J. H. Colton & Cⁿ, 172, William St, New York. / Scale of Miles. / [diagrammatic scale: 80 miles to one inch] / Entered according to Act of Congress in the year 1855 by J. H. Colton & Co. in the Clerks Office of the District Court of the United States for the Southern District of New York. / 19.6 x 37.2 cm. Map at back: Military Map / of Parts of / Kansas, Nebraska and Dakota / By / Lieut. G. K. Warren, Top. Eng.ʳˢ / from the Explorations made by him in 1855 56 & 57. / Exhibiting also Routes reconnouered[!] and Surveyed / by various other Government Officeʳˢ. / J. H. Colton, Nº 172 William St. New York. / Scale of Miles. / 1:1,200000. / [diagrammatic scale: about 29 miles to one inch] / 44.8 x 80.5 cm. Red cloth, blind panels on sides, title in gilt on front cover and in blind on back cover.

Ref.: Hafen 14; Howes R120; Rader 2773; Sabin 68526; Wagner-Camp 343

The present copy has a leaf of advertisement (verso blank) preceding the title-page; the Sibley tent advertisement appears on page [178]; page [179], Grover & Baker's advertisement for sewing machines; page [180], Toledo, Wabash & Great Western Railroad Lines; page [181], Grand Trunk Railroad; page [182], blank; page [183], blank; page [184], Terre Haute, Alton and St. Louis Railroad Line. There are advertisements for pages [182–83] in some copies.

3438 REED, ISAAC

THE CHRISTIAN TRAVELLER . . . NEW-YORK: PRINTED BY J. & J. HARPER, 1828.

[1]–242, [i, errata, ii blank; 13.1 x 9.5 cm.]. 15.8 x 10.1 cm. Tan board sides, brown cloth backstrip, white paper label, 5.5 x 2 cm., uncut. Lacks fly-leaves.

Ref.: Clark II 56

Reed covered about eighteen thousand miles in nine years; many of his observations about Virginia, Kentucky, Indiana, and Ohio are illuminating.

3439 REED, ISAAC

THE YOUTH'S BOOK . . . INDIANAPOLIS: STACY AND WILLIAMS—PRINT, 1840.

[i]–[vi], [7]–230. 15.7 x 10.7 cm. Marbled boards, red leather back, gilt.

Ref.: Buley I pp. 32–3, II pp. 424, 430–31, 432, 438; Byrd & Peckham 879; Howes R126 note

Part IV contains "Extracts from the Christian Traveller, published in New York, by the Rev. Isaac D. Reed, 1828."

3440 REED, JULIUS A.

REMINISCENCES OF EARLY CONGREGATIONALISM IN IOWA . . . GRINNELL, IOWA: PRINTED AT THE HERALD OFFICE, 1885.

[1]–18. 21.3 x 14.3 cm. Tan printed wrappers, with short title on front wrapper.

Ref.: Mott (*Iowa*) p. 86

The address was delivered at the joint meeting of Denmark and Des Moines River Associations, held at Fairfield, Sept. 25, 1883, and was published by request in *Congregational Iowa*.

3441 REES, WILLIAM

DESCRIPTION OF THE CITY OF KEOKUK, LEE COUNTY IOWA . . . KEOKUK DISPATCH PRINT, 1854.

[1]–24, [i–iv advertisements]. 22.5 x 15 cm. Yellow printed wrappers, with title on front wrapper. In a red cloth case.

Prov.: Paullin copy.

Ref.: Howes R139; Moffit 172

With original cord hanger at upper left corner. Contains also a Directory of Keokuk.

3442 REES, WILLIAM

THE MISSISSIPPI BRIDGE CITIES, DAVENPORT, ROCK ISLAND AND MOLINE, DESCRIBING THE LOCAL COMMERCIAL AND MANUFACTURING RELATIONS OF THIS POINT, ANNEXED IS A BRIEF DESCRIPTION OF THE STATE OF IOWA . . . PUBLISHED AND FOR SALE BY H. A. PORTER & BROTHER . . . ROCK ISLAND; W. H. HOLMES & CO. . . . DAVENPORT; RICHARDS & ALLEN . . . MOLINE; APPLEGATE & CO. . . . . CINCINNATI, 1854.

[i–iv advertisements on green paper], [1]–[32]. 22.4 x 14.7 cm. Frontispiece on page [ii]. Yellow printed wrappers, with title on front wrapper, advertisements on recto and verso of back wrapper.

Ref.: Bradford 4572; Byrd 2171; Howes R140; Sabin 68647

Possibly printed in Cincinnati.

3443 REES, WILLIAM

[Wrapper title] REES' DESCRIPTION OF KEOKUK, THE "GATE CITY," LEE COUNTY; IOWA . . . KEOKUK: PRINTED AT THE OFFICE OF THE "KEOKUK DAILY & WEEKLY TIMES," 1855 . . .

[i–iv], [1]–22, [1–2], [17]–23, [24 advertisement]. 22.8 x 15.6 cm. Cream printed wrappers with title on front wrapper, advertisements on verso of front and recto and verso of back wrapper. Original cord hanger through upper left corner.

Ref.: Bradford 4573; Howes R139; Moffit 207; Sabin 68648

The section at the end, pages [17]–23 comprises the "Sixth Annual Circular and Announcement of the Medical Department of the Iowa State University, located in the City of Keokuk, Iowa." Business cards in lower third of nearly every page.

3444 REES & KERFOOT, Chicago

[Map] REES & KERFOOT'S / MAP / OF / THE CITY / OF / CHICAGO / COOK C⁰ ILLINOIS. / PUBLISHED BY / H. ACHESON / LITH BY H. ACHENSON[!], 130 LAKE ST / (COR LAKE & CLARK, CHICAGO) /

Map, 50 x 40.5 cm. No scale given.

Ref.: Byrd 2038

At top of map, above neat line, Rees & Kerfoot / Real Estate & / Stock Brokers, / 48 / Clark Street / Chicago /. Below neat line and border: Entered according to Act of Congress in the year 1854 by H Acheson /.

This is the same as the N. P. Iglehart & Co map, except that Iglehart is neither listed among the Public Buildings nor located on the map.

3445 REES & RUCKER, Chicago

[Map] MAP / OF / CHICAGO AND VICINITY / COMPILED BY / REES & RUCKER / LAND AGENTS. / DRAWN BY Wᴹ CLOGHER. / 1849 / SCALE: 1000 FEET TO ONE INCH. / JULˢ HUTAWA LITHᴿ / MAP PUBLISHING OFFICE N. SECOND ST. 45 ST. LOUIS MO /*

Map, 111.1 x 82.2 cm. Scale as above. Cut into 48 panels, 18.8 x 10.8 cm., mounted on cloth, two panels backed with blue embossed glazed paper.

Prov.: Rubber stamp of Chicago Historical Society with manuscript number 15449 above. In upper right corner: No. 112, "Chicago maps," and with same repeated on verso. Bookplate removed from verso.

Ref.:

3446 REEVES, BENJAMIN H.

AUTOGRAPH LETTER, SIGNED. 1826 November 5, Fayette, Missouri. Two pages, 19.5 x 16 cm. To Thomas Mather. In Mather papers.

Regarding a meeting of the Santa Fé Road Commissioners to prepare a report.

3447 REEVES, BENJAMIN H.

AUTOGRAPH LETTER, SIGNED. 1826 November 19, Fayette, Missouri. Three pages, 19.7 x 16 cm. To Thomas Mather. In Mather Papers.

More about a meeting of the Commissioners.

3448 REGAN, JOHN

THE EMIGRANT'S GUIDE TO THE WESTERN STATES OF AMERICA; OR, BACKWOODS AND PRAIRIES: CONTAINING A COMPLETE STATEMENT OF THE ADVANTAGES AND CAPACITIES OF THE PRAIRIE LANDS— FULL INSTRUCTIONS FOR EMIGRANTS IN FITTING OUT; AND IN SELECTING, PURCHASING, AND SETTLING ON, LAND . . . EDINBURGH: OLIVER & BOYD.

[i]–[xiv], [9]–408. 17 x 10.5 cm. Illustrations, unlisted. Green cloth, blind embossed sides, title in gilt on backstrip, uncut.

Ref.: Bradford 4574; Buck 376; Clark III 228; Howes R143; Sabin 68798

Published in 1852 (?).

Called Second Edition because the text had been printed previously in the *Ayrshire Advertiser*. Sabin gives the date 1842 for the first edition, but this is an error, since Regan arrived in New Orleans in 1842. A letter written in December, 1851, is quoted in the text and a letter received the same month is mentioned.

3449 REID, J. M.

SKETCHES AND ANECDOTES OF THE OLD SETTLERS, AND NEW COMERS, THE MORMON BANDITS AND DANITE BAND . . . KEOKUK, IOWA: R. B. OGDEN, PUBLISHER, 1876.

[1]–177, [178 blank], [1–16 advertisements]. 22.8 x 15 cm. Illustrations unlisted. Pink printed wrappers, with title on front wrapper, advertisements on verso of front and recto and verso of back wrapper. In a brown cloth case.

Ref.: Howes R168; Mott (*Iowa*) p. 86

Copyrighted 1876.

One of the liveliest, spiciest books of anecdotes of pioneer days in Iowa.—Mott

3450 REID, JOHN C.

REID'S TRAMP; OR, A JOURNAL OF THE INCIDENTS OF TEN MONTHS TRAVEL THROUGH TEXAS, NEW MEXICO, ARIZONA, SONORA, AND CALIFORNIA . . . SELMA, ALABAMA: PRINTED AT THE BOOK AND JOB OFFICE OF JOHN HARDY & CO., 1858.

[1]–237, [238 blank]. 20.7 x 13 cm. Blue cloth, blind embossed sides, title in gilt on backstrip. In a brown half morocco pulloff case.

Ref.: Clark III 490; Cowan p. 528; Howes R172; Jones 1401; Rader 2776; Raines p. 172; Wagner-Camp 307

3451 REID, SAMUEL C.

THE SCOUTING EXPEDITIONS OF McCULLOCH'S TEXAS RANGERS; OR, THE SUMMER AND FALL CAMPAIGN OF THE ARMY OF THE UNITED STATES IN MEXICO—1846 . . . PHILADELPHIA: G. B. ZIEBER AND CO., 1848.

[1]–251, [252 blank]. 18.5 x 11.5 cm. 12 illustrations and a two-page map, unlisted. Black cloth, blind embossed sides, title in gilt on backstrip.

Prov.: Inscribed on page 3: To Miss Mary Moore— / with the regards of the / Author. / April. 1855. / [underline] /.

Ref.: Dobie p. 60; Howes R175; Raines p. 172; Sabin 69088

3452 REID, T. MAYNE

THE ENGLISH FAMILY ROBINSON. THE DESERT HOME; OR THE ADVENTURES OF A LOST FAMILY IN THE WILDERNESS . . . BOSTON: TICKNOR, REED, AND FIELDS, M DCCC LII.

[1]–411, [412 blank], [1]–4 advertisements. 16.6 x 10.7 cm. 12 illustrations listed. Green cloth, blind embossed sides, title in gilt on backstrip.

Ref.: Sabin 69039
First American edition.
Editions: London, 1851.

3453 REID, T. MAYNE

THE HEADLESS HORSEMAN: A STRANGE TALE OF TEXAS . . . LONDON: CHAPMAN & HALL.

[i]–iv, [1]–240. [i]–iv, 241–470. 21.7 x 14.1 cm. 20 illustrations. Two volumes, original red pictorial cloth, uncut.

Ref.: Sabin 69049
Published 1866.
Editions: London, 1865–66.

3454 REISTER, J. T.

SKETCHES OF COLORADO. VALUABLE INFORMATION, OBTAINED FROM PERSONAL OBSERVATIONS OF THIS NEW ELDORADO . . . MACON, MO.: EXAMINER PRINTING COMPANY, 1876.

[1]–62, [63–64 blank]. (Pages [1–2] blank.) 14.3 x 10.1 cm. Glazed yellow wrappers, with title on front wrapper, advertisement on verso of back wrapper. In red cloth case.

Ref.: Howes R183; Wilcox p. 94

3455 REMINGTON, FREDERIC

CROOKED TRAILS . . . NEW YORK: HARPER & BROTHERS, 1898.

[i]–[viii, viii blank], 1–[151], [152 blank]. 22.2 x 14.8 cm. 49 illustrations listed. Yellow pictorial cloth.

Ref.: Adams (*Ramp. Herd*) 1877; Dobie p. 115; Howes R203; Johnson (Blanck) p. 426

3456 REMINGTON, FREDERIC

ANOTHER COPY. The same, except imprint reads: London and New York /, size is 22.6 x 15.3 cm., and binding is mauve pictorial cloth, gilt top, uncut.

3457 REMINGTON, FREDERIC

DRAWINGS . . . NEW YORK: R. H. RUSSELL, MDCCCXCVII.

[i–vi, vi blank]. 29.3 x 44.3 cm. 61 illustrations. Printed pictorial boards, tan buckram backstrip, gilt top.

Ref.: Howes R205; Johnson (Blanck) p. 426

3458 REMINGTON, FREDERIC

PONY TRACKS . . . NEW YORK: HARPER & BROTHERS, 1895.

[i]–[x, x blank], 1–269, [270 blank, 271 advertisement, 272 blank]. 22.2 x 14.9 cm. 70 illustrations listed. Light brown pictorial cloth.

Ref.: Adams (*Ramp. Herd*) 1878; Dobie 114; Howes R107; Johnson (Blanck) p. 426

3459 REMSBURG, GEORGE J.

AN OLD KANSAS INDIAN TOWN ON THE MISSOURI . . . PLYMOUTH, IOWA, G. A. CHANDLER, PRINTER.

[i–ii], [1]–11, [12 blank]. 21.4 x 14.1 cm. One plate. Salmon printed wrappers.

Prov.: Inscribed at top of title-page: Compliments of / Geo J Remsburg / [underline] / Porterville, Calif. /

Ref.:
Published about 1919.

3460 [REMSBURG, JOHN E. & GEORGE J.]

[Caption title] CHARLIE REYNOLDS . . .

[1–40]. 22.8 x 15.3 cm. Stapled, glazed tan limp wrappers.

Ref.: Howes R209

Offprints of twenty articles which appeared in the *Weekly Kansan*, Potter, Kansas, 1914–15. Each of the twenty parts comprises two pages, all of the articles being numbered except I and XII.

3461 REMY, JULES, & JULIUS BRENCHLEY

A JOURNEY TO GREAT-SALT-LAKE CITY . . . WITH A SKETCH OF THE HISTORY, RELIGION, AND CUSTOMS OF THE MORMONS . . . LONDON: W. JEFFS, MDCCCLXI.

[1–2], [i]–[cxxxii, cxxxii blank], [1]–508. [i]–[viii, viii blank], [1]–605, [606 colophon]. 25 x 157.

cm. Ten illustrations and a folding map: Carte dressée pour l'intelligence du voyage au Pays des Mormons, de Mr Jules Remy. / Map designed to accompany the Journey to Mormon Land. / [lower right:] Lemaitre sculp. / [lower left:] Vuillemin del. / 16.9 x 44.9 cm. Scale: about 190 English miles to an inch. Title outside neat line. Two volumes, blue cloth, blind embossed panels on sides, gilt vignettes on front covers, titles in gilt on backstrips, uncut.

Prov.: Inscribed on half-title of first volume: William Balston Esqr / With Mr Brenchley's Compt^s /.

Ref.: Bradford 4585; Howes R210; Monaghan 1220; Sabin 69594; Wagner-Camp 364

3462   RENICK, WILLIAM

MEMOIRS, CORRESPONDENCE AND REMINISCENCES . . . CIRCLEVILLE, OHIO: UNION-HERALD BOOK AND JOB PRINTING HOUSE, 1880.

[i–vi (vi blank)], [1]–115, [116 blank]. 22.6 x 15 cm. Portrait. Reddish brown cloth, title in gilt within blind design on front cover.

Ref.: Adams (*Ramp. Herd*) 1879; Howes R211

Inserted before page 115 is a small erratum slip, 3.9 x 13.7 cm.

Comprises reprints of various contributions to newspapers and other publications about the history of cattle raising in Ohio. Renick relates that his father, in the winter of 1804–05, fed a lot of cattle and sent them to Baltimore the next spring, the first fat cattle to cross the Alleghany Mountains. Also he tells of his own purchase of about 1,200 head of cattle in the winter of 1853–54 in Texas, and how they were brought to Illinois in the spring and summer of 1854, the first drove of cattle ever brought north from Texas.—EDG

3463   RENINGER, J. E.

GUIDE BOOK ON KIOWA, COMANCHE, AND APACHE RESERVATION . . . BURLINGAME, KANSAS: J. E. RENINGER, AUTHOR AND PUBLISHER.

[i–ii blank], [1]–50. 16.2 x 10.1 cm. Map on salmon paper: J. E. Reninger, / Author and Publisher of / . . . Guide Book on Kiowa . . . / Comanche and Apache Reservation. / With Sectional Map / Burlingame, Kansas, / Scale of Miles / [diagrammatic scale: ten miles to one inch] /. 31.4 x 22.6 cm. Scale as above. *Inset:* Diagram of Corner Stones /. 11 x 10.5 cm. Light green printed wrappers with title on front wrapper.

Ref.:
Copyrighted 1901.

3464   RENO, MARCUS A., *Defendant*

THE OFFICIAL RECORD OF A COURT OF INQUIRY CONVENED AT CHICAGO, ILLINOIS, JANUARY 13, 1879, BY THE PRESIDENT OF THE UNITED STATES UPON THE REQUEST OF MAJOR MARCUS A. RENO, 7TH U. S. CAVALRY TO INVESTIGATE HIS CONDUCT AT THE BATTLE OF THE LITTLE BIG HORN, JUNE 25–26, 1876. WITH AN INTRODUCTORY CHAPTER BY COL. W. A. GRAHAM . . . PACIFIC PALISADES, CALIF.: W. A. GRAHAM, 1951.

[1–4], I–XIII, [XIV blank], 1–351 LEAVES. [I–IV (IV blank)], 1–575 LEAVES. 32.5 x 21.5 cm. Two volumes, brown buckram.

Ref.: Dustin 605

Printed on recto of each leaf, versos blank. Direct Liquid Duplication of typewritten copy. Limited to 125 copies.

Title of Volume II: Proceedings of / A / Court of Inquiry / in the Case of / Major Marcus A. Reno / —— / Concerning his Conduct / At the / Battle of the Little Big Horn River / June 25–26, 1876. / Volume II / —— / Q. Q. 979 /.

3465   REORGANIZED CHURCH OF JESUS CHRIST OF LATTER-DAY SAINTS

[Caption title] MEMORIAL TO CONGRESS FROM A COMMITTEE OF THE REORGANIZED CHURCH OF JESUS CHRIST OF LATTER DAY SAINTS, ON THE CLAIMS AND FAITH OF THE CHURCH. PRINTED AT THE TRUE LATTER DAY SAINTS' HERALD STEAM BOOK OFFICE, PLANO, ILLINOIS . . .

[1]–8. 26.6 x 17.9 cm. Unbound, partly unopened, uncut.

Ref.:
Dated at the end: 11th day of April, 1870 . . .

A Memorial in opposition to polygamy praying that the Reorganized Church be recognized as *the* Church of Jesus Christ of Latter-Day Saints.

3466   REORGANIZED CHURCH OF JESUS CHRIST OF LATTER-DAY SAINTS

[Caption title] NO. 38. THE INSPIRED TRANSLATION OF THE HOLY SCRIPTURES. PUBLISHED BY THE REORGANIZED CHURCH OF JESUS CHRIST, AT LAMONI, IOWA . . .

[1]–4. 18.6 x 12.7 cm. Unbound.

Ref.:
Undated and uncopyrighted. The preliminary text on page [1] is signed W. W. Blair and page 4 is signed with initials of the same. Laid in Faulconer, M. A.: *Questions on the Holy Scriptures* . . . 1869.

3467   REORGANIZED CHURCH OF JESUS CHRIST OF LATTER-DAY SAINTS

ANOTHER COPY.

3468 REPUBLICAN PARTY. De Kalb County, Illinois

[Broadside] THE PUBLIC RECORD OF GENERAL FARNSWORTH . . .

Broadside, 45.5 x 30.3 cm. Text, 38.7 x 23.3 cm.
Ref.:
Since the broadside relates to the Campaign of 1868, the date of publication is clear enough, but no place of publication is mentioned. Possibly De Kalb?

The second section of the broadside supports Reuben Ellwood as De Kalb County's second choice in the congressional race.

3469 REPUBLICAN PARTY. Oregon

[Broadside] NATIONAL REPUBLICAN TICKET. 1872.

Broadside, 21.6 x 8 cm. Text, 20.9 x 7.7 cm. Printed in blue.

Possibly printed at Roseburg, Oregon. Includes a vignette portrait of U. S. Grant. Inserted in Manuscript Journals of Loren L. Williams, Volume IV.

3470 REPUBLICAN PARTY. Oregon

[Broadside] REPUBLICAN TICKET . . . CLERK. L. L. WILLIAMS . . .

Broadside, 23.4 x 7.7 cm. Text, 19.6 x 6 cm.

For the July, 1872, election. Probably printed at Roseburg, Oregon. Inserted in Manuscript Journals of Loren L. Williams, Volume IV.

3471 REPUBLICAN PARTY. Oregon

[Broadside] REPUBLICAN TICKET . . . FOR COUNTY CLERK, L. L. WILLIAMS . . .

Broadside, 20.2 x 6.5 cm. Text, 14.7 x 5.5 cm.

Probably printed at Roseburg, Oregon, in 1876. Inserted in Manuscript Journals of Loren L. Williams, Volume V.

3472 RETAIL HARDWARE, IMPLEMENT, AND VEHICLE DEALERS ASSOCIATION

[Wrapper title] CONSTITUTION AND BY-LAWS OF THE RETAIL HARDWARE, IMPLEMENT AND VEHICLE DEALERS ASSOCIATION, OF THE INDIAN TERRITORY. POTEAU, I. T.: NEWS PRINT.

[1]–8. 14.1 x 8.5 cm. Self wrappers.
Ref.:
The Association was established in 1900.

3473 REVERE, JOSEPH W.

KEEL AND SADDLE: A RETROSPECT OF FORTY YEARS OF MILITARY AND NAVAL SERVICE . . . BOSTON: JAMES R. OSGOOD AND COMPANY, 1872.

[i]–[xiv, xiv blank], 1–360. 18.9 x 12.1 cm. Brown cloth, vignette stamped on front cover in gilt and on back in blind, title stamped in gilt on backstrip.

Ref.: Cowan p. 530; Howes (1954) 8548; Nicholson p. 700; Sabin 70179

3474 REVERE, JOSEPH W.

A TOUR OF DUTY IN CALIFORNIA; INCLUDING A DESCRIPTION OF THE GOLD REGION: AND AN ACCOUNT OF THE VOYAGE AROUND CAPE HORN; WITH NOTICES OF LOWER CALIFORNIA, THE GULF AND PACIFIC COASTS, AND THE PRINCIPAL EVENTS ATTENDING THE CONQUEST OF THE CALIFORNIAS . . . NEW YORK: C. S. FRANCIS & CO., 1849.

[1–4], [i–ii], 3, IV–[VIII, VIII blank], [1]–305, [306 blank], 1–2, 6–7, 10, 14 advertisements. 19 x 11.7 cm. Six illustrations unlisted, folding map. Map: Harbour of San Francisco / California. / Sketched from Beechey's survey. / By Joseph W. Revere U. S. N. / Published by C. S. Francis & C⁰ N. York. / [lower left:] Lith of Wᵐ· Endicott & C⁰· N. York. / [lower centre:] Copyright secured according to law. / 29.9 x 25.2 cm. Scale: about six miles to one inch. Very dark brown cloth, embossed panels on sides, title stamped in gilt on backstrip.

Ref.: Blumann & Thomas 5088; Bradford 4587; Cowan p. 530; Howes R222; Sabin 70182

Description of the gold fields and authoritative particulars on the California conquest.—Howes

3475 REVERE, JOSEPH W.

ANOTHER COPY.

18.5 x 11.7 cm. Dark gray cloth, blind embossed sides, title stamped in gilt on backstrip, embossed designs differ from other copy.

Prov.: Bookplate of John Thomas Lee. Numerous penciled notes in margins by John Wesley Jones, the note on page 70 being signed.

For the third time I have changed my copy of this work. My present copy comes from the collection of John Thomas Lee who procured it from a relative of John Wesley Jones, the well-known California daguerreotypist and trader. This copy doubtless belonged to him at one time and contains numerous penciled notes of caustic comment in his hand, one on page 70 being signed.—EDG

3476 REVISTA OFICIAL, LA

[Broadsheet] ALCANCE AL NUMERO 31 DE LA REVISTA OFICIAL. EXTRAORDINARIO DE HOY VENIDO DEL NUEVO MEXICO, SOBRE INVASION DE TEJANOS EN EL MISMO DEPARTAMFNTO[!] CHIHUAHUA JUEVES 20 DE JULIO DE 1843 . . . CHIHUAHUA: IMPRENTA DEL GOBIERNO A CARGO DE CAYETANO TAMOS, 1843.

Broadsheet, 30.4 x 19.9 cm. Text, 25.5 x 16 cm.
Ref.:

An undescribed separate broadsheet announcing the Texan invasion of New Mexico in 1843 under Colonel Snively. The broadsheet is an excellent example of inflammatory propaganda designed to arouse the countryside for the defense of New Mexico and Chihuahua.

See Streeter 991 for a related broadside.

3477 REYNOLDS, JOHN

"THE BALM OF GILEAD." AN INQUIRY INTO THE RIGHT OF AMERICAN SLAVERY . . . BELLEVILLE, ILLINOIS: JULY 1860.

[1]–48. 21.1 x 14.1 cm. Removed from bound volume, yellow wrappers, with title on front wrapper. Lacks back wrapper. In a red cloth case.

Prov.: Inscription of front wrapper: W. C. Flagg / from the Author /.

Ref.: Howes R234; Sabin 70419

3478 REYNOLDS, JOHN

FRIENDSHIP'S OFFERING. A SKETCH OF THE LIFE OF DR. JOHN MASON PECK . . . BELLEVILLE, ILLINOIS: "ADVOCATE" BOOK AND JOB OFFICE, PRINT, 1858.

[1]–34, [35–6 blank]. 21.7 x 13.6 cm. Glazed yellow wrappers, with title on front wrapper. In black cloth case.

Ref.: Byrd 3046; Howes R235

3479 REYNOLDS, JOHN

MY OWN TIMES, EMBRACING ALSO, THE HISTORY OF MY LIFE . . . 1855.

[1]–600, [i]–xxiii, [xxiv colophon]. 17.5 x 11.2 cm. Portrait. Black cloth, blind embossed sides, backstrip blind embossed and with title in gilt.

Prov.: Inscribed on blank leaf at front, in pencil: I present this / book to my friend / Dr Staap with / the esteem and / respect of the / author / John Reynolds / 1st July 1864– /

Ref.: Buck 57; Byrd 2343; Howes R236; Sabin 70420

Published at Belleville, Illinois.

The most interesting sketch of Governor Reynolds which I have found is in *Adam W. Snyder in Illinois History, 1817–1842* by John Francis Snyder M.O. Springfield, 1903.—EDG

3480 REYNOLDS, JOHN

THE PIONEER HISTORY OF ILLINOIS, CONTAINING THE DISCOVERY, IN 1673, AND THE HISTORY OF THE COUNTRY TO THE YEAR EIGHTEEN HUNDRED AND EIGHTEEN . . . BELLEVILLE, ILL.: PUBLISHED BY N. A. RANDALL, 1852.

[1]–348. 18.5 x 11.2 cm. Dark blue-gray cloth, title in gilt on backstrip.

Ref.: Bradford 4593; Byrd 1882; Howes R237; Sabin 70421

3481 REYNOLDS, JOHN

SKETCHES OF THE COUNTRY, ON THE NORTHERN ROUTE FROM BELLEVILLE, ILLINOIS, TO THE CITY OF NEW YORK, AND BACK BY THE OHIO VALLEY; TOGETHER WITH A GLANCE AT THE CRYSTAL PALACE . . . BELLEVILLE: PRINTED BY J. A. WILLIS, 1854.

[1]–264. 17.3 x 11.1 cm. Maroon embossed cloth, title in gilt on backstrip.

Prov.: Inscribed in pencil on front endleaf: with my respects / I present this book / to my friend The / Revd J. M. Peck / 15th Sept, 1854 / John Reynolds /. Signed on inner front cover in pencil: Mary A. Smith / Rock Spring / Ill / May 12. 1858 /. John M. Peck's daughter Mary married a Mr. Smith of Rock Spring. However, Mary Smith was also the name of a servant in the Peck household.

Ref.: Buck 510; Byrd 3173; Howes R238; Sabin 70422

"Contains detailed historical and descriptive notes of places along the route . . . The first chapter was reprinted with the title: *Belleville in January, 1854* . . . N. p., n. d., 12 pages."—Buck

3482 REYNOLDS, JOHN

ANOTHER COPY.

Prov.: Initials on inside front cover: B R /. Inscribed in pencil on front endleaf: E M Haines / Bought at St. Louis / by order to / Wilson & Father / old book dealers / March 12th 1870 /.

3483 RICE, G. JAY

[Map] / RICE'S / SECTIONAL MAP OF / DAKOTA / TERRITORY. / DRAUGHTED BY FRED STURNEGK. / DRAUGHTSMAN Q. M. DEPT. OF DAKOTA. / PUBLISHED BY THE ST. PAUL LITHOG & ENG CO. / 1872 / ST. PAUL MINNESOTA. / SCALE 15 MILES TO ONE INCH / [lower right corner:] ENTERED ACCORDING TO ACT OF CONGRESS IN THE YEAR 1872 BY G. JAY RICE IN THE OFFICE OF THE LIBRARIAN OF CONGRESS, AT WASHINGTON. /

Map, 86.6 x 68.6 cm. Scale as above. Folded into original blank cloth covers, 15.2 x 9.7 cm.

Ref.:

3484 RICE, H. D.

[Wrapper title] REMINISCENCES . . . (READ BEFORE THE CONGREGATIONAL PIONEER SOCIETY OF TOPEKA.)

[1]–14. 20.5 x 14.4 cm. Salmon printed wrappers, with title on front wrapper.

Ref.:

No place or date of publication indicated.

The last date mentioned in the pamphlet is 1872 and the year is referred to as considerably in the past.

3485   RICE, J. M., & J. B. FOSTER, *Compilers*

[Wrapper title] THE ALTURAS MINING REPORTER AND KEY TO THE MAMMOTH CABINET OF ORES, COLLECTED FOR EXHIBITION IN EASTERN CITIES, BY THE CAMAS PRAIRIE AND WOOD RIVER COLONIZATION CO. OF ALTURAS COUNTY, IDAHO . . . OMAHA, NEB.: HERALD PRINTING AND ELECTROTYPING HOUSE, 1883.

[1]–56. 22.8 x 15.5 cm. Gray printed wrappers, with title on front wrapper.
Ref.:
Pages 51–56 carry business directories for Bellevue, Hailey, Ketchum, and Bullion.

3486   RICE, MARTIN

RURAL RHYMES, AND TALKS AND TALES OF OLDEN TIMES . . . KANSAS CITY: RAMSEY, MILLETT & HUDSON, 1882.

[i]–[viii], [1]–392. 19.5 x 13.1 cm. Portrait. Brown cloth, title in gilt on front cover and backstrip, blind stamped ornaments on front and back covers.
Ref.:
Second edition. The humor and the rhymes leave much to be desired; some of the historical sketches are informative. Mostly rural Missouri and Civil War.
Editions: Kansas City, 1877.

3487   RICHARDS, F. D.

STEEL ENGRAVED PORTRAIT OF F. D. RICHARDS. Signed in plate by Fred Piercy / 1852. / With facsimile of the signature of the subject in the lower margin.
Bound with Number 3346.

3488   [RICHARDS, ROBERT, *Pseudonym*]

THE CALIFORNIAN CRUSOE; OR, THE LOST TREASURE FOUND. A TALE OF MORMONISM. LONDON: JOHN HENRY PARKER, M DCCC LIV.

[i]–iv, [1]–162. 16.6 x 10.9 cm. Frontispiece. Purple cloth, embossed panels on sides, title in gilt on backstrip.
Ref.: Cowan p. 531; Howes R250; Wagner-Camp 243
Completely fictitious, even to the pseudonym. —Howes
Wagner-Camp states the first issue should have only the London imprint; the present copy has both London and New York.

3489   RICHARDSON, A. L.

TO SILVER CITY AND RETURN. THE ADVENTURES OF A PARTY OF BOSTON GENTLEMEN IN NEW MEXICO . . . BOSTON: PRESS OF ROCKWELL AND CHURCHILL, 1889.

[1]–55, [56 blank]. 24.5 x 17.6 cm. Nine illustrations unlisted. Orange printed wrappers, with title on front wrapper. In a brown cloth case.
Ref.:

3490   RICHARDSON, ALBERT D.

LETTER, SIGNED. 1866 May 9, New York. Two pages, 20 x 12.6 cm. To George H. Roberts, Jr.
Thanking the recipient for sending a painting from Alexander Culbertson, and stating that a life of Culbertson is planned for publication.

3491   RICHARDSON, ALBERT D.

OUR NEW STATES AND TERRITORIES, BEING NOTES OF A RECENT TOUR OF OBSERVATION THROUGH COLORADO, UTAH, IDAHO, NEVADA, OREGON, MONTANA, WASHINGTON TERRITORY AND CALIFORNIA . . . NEW YORK: BEADLE AND COMPANY.

[2]–80, [81–82 blank]. 22.1 x 14.3 cm. 45 illustrations listed. Yellow printed wrappers, with title on front wrapper, advertisements on verso of front and recto and verso of back wrapper.
Ref.: Cowan p. 532; Howes R253; Sabin 70983; Smith 8646
Copyrighted 1866.

3492   RICHARDSON, SIR JOHN

AUTOGRAPH LETTER, SIGNED. 1853 February 11. Haslar Hospital, Gosport. Three Pages, 18.2 x 11.4 cm. To Dr. Booth.
Thanking the recipient for courtesies paid his wife. Laid in Richardson: *Arctic Searching Expedition* . . . 1851.

3493   RICHARDSON, SIR JOHN

ARCTIC SEARCHING EXPEDITION: A JOURNAL OF A BOAT-VOYAGE THROUGH RUPERT'S LAND AND THE ARCTIC SEA, IN SEARCH OF THE DISCOVERY SHIPS UNDER COMMAND OF SIR JOHN FRANKLIN . . . LONDON: LONGMAN, BROWN, GREEN, AND LONGMANS, 1851.

[i]–viii, [1]–413, [414 colophon]. [i]–vii, [viii blank], [1]–426. 21.9 x 14 cm. Ten colored plates, eight woodcuts and diagrams listed, and one folding map: Map: British / North America / [lower right:] S. Hall. Sculp^{t} / [lower center:] London, Longman & Co / 41.5 x 50.3 cm. Scale: about 24 miles to an inch. Two volumes, brown cloth, with title in gilt on backstrips, uncut.
Ref.: Sabin 71025; Staton & Tremaine 3029
Autograph letter signed by the author laid in.

3494 RICHARDSON, R. H.

"ASLEEP IN JESUS." A FUNERAL DISCOURSE, PREACHED ON OCCASION OF THE DEATH OF MRS. GEO. A. GIBBS, NOVEMBER 4, A. D. 1849. CHICAGO: JAS. J. LANGDON, 1849.

[I]–XXI, [XXII–XXIV blank]. 18.7 x 12.3 cm. Cream wrappers, with title on front wrapper.

Ref.: Byrd 1495; McMurtrie (*Chicago*) 189

3495 RICHARDSON, R. L.

REPORT OF THE VISIT OF THE BRITISH ASSOCIATION TO THE CANADIAN NORTH-WEST . . . WINNIPEG, MANITOBA: McINTYRE BROS., 1884.

[1]–48. 21.8 x 14.6 cm. Green printed wrappers, with title on front wrapper, advertisements on verso of front and recto and verso of back wrapper.

Ref.:

3496 RICHARDSON, WILLIAM H.

JOURNAL OF WILLIAM H. RICHARDSON, A PRIVATE SOLDIER IN COL. DONIPHAN'S COMMAND. BALTIMORE: PRINTED BY JOS. ROBINSON, 1847.

[1]–84. 18.7 x 11.2 cm. Rebound in half red morocco, marbled board sides.

Ref.: Clements Library (*Texas*) 33; Cowan p. 532; Howes R262; Sabin 71093; Wagner-Camp 137

The journal describes Richardson's personal adventures during the Doniphan Expedition and covers the entire period August, 1846, to July, 1847.

3497 RICHMOND, C. W., & H. F. VALLETTE

A HISTORY OF THE COUNTY OF DU PAGE, ILLINOIS; CONTAINING AN ACCOUNT OF ITS EARLY SETTLEMENT AND PRESENT ADVANTAGES, A SEPARATE HISTORY OF THE SEVERAL TOWNS . . . CHICAGO: STEAM PRESSES OF SCRIPPS, BROSS & SPEARS, 1857.

[i]–iv, [5]–205, [206 blank], 207–12 advertisements. 17.5 x 11 cm. One woodcut illustration. Black cloth, blind embossed sides, title in gilt on backstrip.

Prov.: Bookplate of Dr. Otto L. Schmidt.

Ref.: AII (*Chicago*) 281; Buck 788; Byrd 2781; Howes R263

The first Du Page County history.

3498 RICHMOND, LEGH

THE DAIRYMAN'S DAUGHTER . . . BOB THE SAILOR BOY. BY REV. G. C. SMITH . . . PARK HILL: MISSION PRESS, 1847.

[i–iv], [1]–67, [68 blank]. 12.8 x 7.7 cm. Bound with Number 1278.

Ref.: Hargrett (*Oklahoma*) 113

Text in Sequoyan.

3499 RICHTHOFEN, WALTER, BARON VON

CATTLE-RAISING ON THE PLAINS OF NORTH AMERICA . . . NEW YORK: D. APPLETON AND COMPANY, 1885.

[1]–102, [103–08 advertisements]. 17.5 x 12 cm. Green cloth stamped in gilt and red, with title on front cover.

Ref.: Adams (*Ramp. Herd*) 1892; Howes R273; Rader 2786

The Baron was a leading cattleman of Colorado and father of Germany's famous flyer.—Howes

3500 RICKETTS, WILLIAM P.

50 YEARS IN THE SADDLE . . . SHERIDAN, WYOMING: STAR PUBLISHING COMPANY, 1942.

[i–xii], [1]–198. 22.7 x 25.3 cm. Frontispiece, map and three illustrations. Green cloth.

Ref.: Adams (*Ramp. Herd*) 1893; Howes R275

3501 [RICKMAN, JOHN]

AN AUTHENTIC NARRATIVE OF A VOYAGE TO THE PACIFIC OCEAN: PERFORMED BY CAPTAIN COOK, AND CAPTAIN CLERKE. IN HIS BRITTANIC MAJESTY'S SHIPS, THE RESOLUTION, AND DISCOVERY, IN THE YEARS, 1776, 1777, 1778, 1779, AND 1780 . . . PHILADELPHIA: PRINTED AND SOLD BY ROBERT BELL, M, DCC, LXXXIII.

A[1], B–M[4], N[3], O–Ff[4]. [i–ii]. [9]–96, 99–[230], [231–32 advertisements]. (2 in 125 inverted.) 19.8 x 12 cm. Two volumes bound together, full calf, red leather label on backstrip.

Prov.: Contemporary signature on title-page: Robert Coleman /. Bookplate of John Thomas Lee.

Ref.: Evans 17921; Holmes 38 note; Howes R276; Mitchell Library p. 67; Sabin 16244; Smith 1987

As Lawrence Wroth has pointed out, Rickman's journal and map were something more than the models for John Ledyard's book brought out in Hartford in 1783. The Ledyard map is a precise copy of the Rickman map present in the London 1781 first edition and his book contains nothing of importance beyond what he copied from Rickman. Consequently, we may say this Philadelphia edition of Rickman is the first American book dealing with the West Coast explorations, and with Cook's third and last voyage.—EDG

3502 [RICKMAN, JOHN]

JOURNAL OF CAPTAIN COOK'S LAST VOYAGE TO THE PACIFIC OCEAN . . . PERFORMED IN THE YEARS 1776, 1777, 1778, 1779 . . . LONDON: PRINTED FOR E. NEWBERRY, M DCC LXXXI.

[A]², B–C⁸, D¹²⁻¹, E–Ee⁸, Ff². [i–iv], [i]–xlvi, [1]–396. (Mispagination: v instead of iv, iv for vi, 22 for 225, 331 for 231, 381 for 393, 378 for 394, 379 for 395, and 388 for 396. The 1 of 221 is widely separated from 22.) 20.7 x 12.6 cm. Five engraved plates and one map. Map: Chart / shewing the Tracks / of the Ships employed in / Cap:ᵗ Cook's / last Voyage to the / Pacific Ocean; / in the Years, / 1776, 1777, 1778, 1779. / 35.5 x 34.3 cm. No scale given. Contemporary half sprinkled calf, marbled board sides, green leather label on backstrip, yellow edges.
Ref.: Holmes 38; Howes R276; John Carter Brown Library *Annual Report*, 19, pp. 18–19; Mitchell Library p. 67; Smith 1993

Copies vary in mispagination. ICN (Ayer) copy shows page iv correct and 221 has not begun to separate. The Ayer copy shows two entries in the list of errata on page [iv] while the present copy shows six entries.

3503 RIDEING, WILLIAM H.

. . . A-SADDLE IN THE WILD WEST. A GLIMPSE OF TRAVEL AMONG THE MOUNTAINS, LAVA BEDS, SAND DESERTS, ADOBE TOWNS, INDIAN RESERVATIONS, AND ANCIENT PUEBLOS OF SOUTHERN COLORADO, NEW MEXICO, AND ARIZONA . . . NEW YORK: D. APPLETON AND COMPANY, 1879.

[1]–165, [166 blank], [1]–4 advertisements, [1–6] advertisements. 16.2 x 10.5 cm. Light orange cloth, beveled covers.
Ref.: Adams (*Ramp. Herd*) 1895; Munk (Alliot) p. 189; Saunders 3124

Rideing accompanied Lieutenant George M. Wheeler on his survey, during a two-year period, acting as a newspaper correspondent. He traveled 4000 miles a-saddle in New Mexico, Arizona, Southern Colorado, Nevada, and Eastern California.—EDG

3504 RIDGE, JOHN R.

POEMS . . . SAN FRANCISCO: HENRY PAYOT & COMPANY, PUBLISHERS, 1868.

[1]–137, [138 vignette]. 17.6 x 11.5 cm. Portrait. Green cloth, title stamped in gilt on front cover and backstrip.
Ref.: Cowan p. 533

Ridge was a Cherokee Indian, who was for many years on the editorial staff of the San Francisco *Alta*.

3505 RIGGS, STEPHEN R., & GIDEON H. POND

THE DAKOTA FIRST READING BOOK . . . CINCINNATI: KENDALL AND HENRY, PRINTERS, 1839.

[1]–[40]. 14.1 x 9.5 cm. Six illustrations in text.
BOUND WITH:
THE HISTORY OF JOSEPH, IN THE LANGUAGE OF THE DAKOTA OR SIOUX INDIANS . . . CINCINNATI: KENDALL AND HENRY, PRINTERS, 1839.

[1]–56. Three illustrations in text. Two works bound together, contemporary plum cloth.
Ref.: Pilling 3297, 3033; Sabin 71326, 63995

Each work has a second title [page 31]: Dakota / [large cut with base at fore edge of page] / Oyawa Wowapi. / Otokahe kin. / [short rule] / 1839. / And: Josep / Oyakapi Kin. / [cut] / Maza on Kagapi. / Cincinnati, Ohio. / 1839. /

The first gift to the Graff Collection, from Louis H. Silver.

3506 [RILEY, BENNET]

[Caption title] . . . MESSAGE FROM THE PRESIDENT OF THE UNITED STATES . . . RELATING TO THE PROTECTION OF THE TRADE BETWEEN MISSOURI AND MEXICO . . .

[1]–9, [10 blank]. 22 x 14.1 cm. Rebound in new red cloth.
Ref.: Wagner-Camp 41

21st Congress, 1st Session, Senate, Document No. 46, Serial 192. [Washington, 1830.]

Major Bennet Riley's report occupies pages 2–9.

3507 RINFRET, RAOUL

LE YOKON ET SON OR . . . MONTREAL: IMPRIMERIE DU "CULTIVATEUR," L. J. TARTE & FRERE, PROP.

[1]–[93], [94–6 blank]. 17.4 x 11 cm. Illustrations unlisted. Buff printed boards (limp) with red cloth back, title on front cover, advertisements on inner covers and outer back cover.
Ref.: Howes R301; Smith 8681; Wickersham 4403a
Published in 1898.
Editions: Montreal [1898].

3508 RIO GRANDE AND TEXAS LAND COMPANY

[Caption title] RIO GRANDE AND TEXAS LAND COMPANY. INFORMATION TO THE EMIGRANT WHO IS DESIROUS OF SETTLING IN GRANTS NOW COLONIZING BY THE RIO GRANDE AND TEXAS LAND COMPANY . . .

[1]–8. 24.5 x 15 cm. Stabbed, uncut. In a green cloth case.
Ref.: Streeter 1146A

No place or date of publication; probably New York, 1834. Signed on page 8: Charles Edwards, / Counsellor at Law, and Secretary to the Rio Grande and Texas Land Company, / 53, Wallstreet, New York. /

Contains extracts from letters and the press dated 1833 and 1834. The latest date found is October 22, 1834.

3509   RIO GRANDE, MEXICAN, AND PA-CIFIC RAILROAD COMPANY

CHARTER OF THE RIO GRANDE, MEXICAN, AND PA-CIFIC RAILROAD COMPANY . . . CAMBRIDGE: PRESS OF JOHN WILSON AND SON, 1871.

[1]–34, [35–36 blank]. 23.6 x 15 cm. Buff printed wrappers, with title on front wrapper.

Prov.: Manuscript note on front wrapper: No. 1. / (*No. 3–* is on page 22. of this) /. On page [23]: *No. 3.*

Ref.:

3510   RIO GRANDE, MEXICAN, AND PA-CIFIC RAILROAD COMPANY

[Broadside] MEMORANDUM. ELEMENTS OF VALUE OF THE PRIVILEGES POSSESSED BY THE RIO GRANDE, MEXICAN, AND PACIFIC RAILROAD COMPANY . . .

Broadside, 25 x 19.5 cm. Text, 19 x 15.3 cm.

Prov.: Manuscript note at top: No. 2. / Manuscript note on verso: No. 2. / Memoranda of / Value of Privileges / Rio Grande. Mexican & Pac. Rway. Co /. Also: No. 2. /

Ref.:

3511   RIO GRANDE, MEXICAN, AND PA-CIFIC RAILROAD COMPANY

[Caption title] MEMORIAL OF THE RIO GRANDE, MEXICAN AND PACIFIC RAILROAD COMPANY. TO THE SENATE OF THE UNITED STATES: . . .

[1]–8. 24.4 x 14.8 cm. Folded sheet, uncut, un-opened.

Ref.:

Signed on page 8 by Luke Lea as president of the railroad, dated Washington, February 8, 1860. With note in manuscript inserted above date line: John L Hayes / Secretary /. Manuscript note on page [1]: No. 3. /

3512   RIO GRANDE, MEXICAN, AND PA-CIFIC RAILROAD COMPANY

ANOTHER COPY.

Uncut, unopened. With folded map laid in: Map / Illustrating the advantages / of the / Central Transit Route / through Mexico / to the / Pacific Ocean. / [decorative rule] / Prepared by J. B. Moore, C.E. / 1860. / [lower left corner:] Bowen & Co. Lith. Philada. / 41.3 x 49.8 cm. No scale given.

3513   RITCH, WILLIAM G.

ILLUSTRATED NEW MEXICO . . . PUBLISHED BY THE BUREAU OF IMMIGRATION. SANTA FE, NEW MEXICO: NEW MEXICAN PRINTING & PUBLISHING[!] CO., 1883.

[i]–[xviii], [19]–[141], [142–44 blank]. 21.6 x 14.6 cm. Two folded maps, one folded panoramic view, and numerous illustrations. Gray printed wrappers, with short title on front wrapper, vignette on verso of back wrapper.

Ref.: Adams (*Ramp. Herd*) 1910; Saunders 4563 see

Third edition.

3514   RITTENHOUSE, RUFUS

BOYHOOD LIFE IN IOWA FORTY YEARS AGO . . . DUBUQUE, IOWA: CHAS. B. DORR, BOOK AND JOB PRINTER, 1880.

[1]–23. [24 blank]. 19.5 x 12.6 cm. Woodcuts in text, unlisted. Gray printed wrappers, with title on front wrapper. In red cloth folding case.

Ref.: Howes R319; Mott (*Iowa*) p. 87

3515   RITTENHOUSE, RUFUS

ANOTHER COPY.

3516   ROBB, JOHN S.

GREAT AMERICAN PRIZE ROMANCE. KAAM; OR, DAYLIGHT. THE ARAPAHOE HALF-BREED, A TALE OF THE ROCKY MOUNTAINS . . . BOSTON: "STAR SPAN-GLED BANNER" OFFICE, 1847.

[3]–37, 38–42 advertisements. 25.3 x 17 cm. Yellow printed wrappers with title on front wrapper, advertisement on verso of back wrapper, uncut. In a blue cloth case.

Ref.: Wagner-Camp 138; Wright I 2125

The author won a prize of $150 for this half-bred tale.

3517   ROBBINS, PROSPERT K.

AUTOGRAPH MANUSCRIPT PROMISSORY NOTE, SIGNED. 1812 January 30, No place. One page, 8.3 x 18.4 cm. A ninety-day note to Robert McKnight.

3518   ROBERTS, LOU CONWAY

A WOMAN'S REMINISCENCES OF SIX YEARS IN CAMP WITH THE TEXAS RANGERS . . . AUSTIN, TEXAS: PRESS OF VON BOECKMANN-JONES CO.*

[1]–64. 23.1 x 15.3 cm. Illustrations unlisted. Blue printed wrappers.

Ref.: Adams 845; Howes R340

Dated at the end: Austin, Texas, / September 13, 1928. /

3519 ROBERTS, LOUISA J.

BIOGRAPHICAL SKETCH OF LOUISA J. ROBERTS WITH EXTRACTS FROM HER JOURNAL AND SELECTIONS FROM HER WRITINGS . . . PHILADELPHIA: PRESS OF ALFRED J. FERRIS, 1895.

[1]–286. (Pages [1–2] blank.) 18.7 x 11.3 cm. Two illustrations. Blue cloth, gilt top.

Ref.:

Nebraska and Dakota Indian Reservation pioneer reminiscences.—EDG

3520 ROBERTS, MORLEY

THE WESTERN AVERNUS; OR, TOIL AND TRAVEL IN FURTHER NORTH AMERICA . . . LONDON: SMITH, ELDER, & CO., 1887.*

[i–vii], [viii blank], [1]–307, [308 blank, 309–12 advertisements]. 20.2 x 13.3 cm. Folding map, colored. Gray-green cloth, uncut.

Ref.: Adams (*Ramp. Herd*) 1919; Smith 8695

3521 ROBERTS, WILLIAM M.

SPECIAL REPORT OF A RECONNOISSANCE OF THE ROUTE FOR THE NORTHERN PACIFIC RAILROAD BETWEEN LAKE SUPERIOR AND PUGET SOUND, VIA THE COLUMBIA RIVER, MADE IN 1869 . . .

[1]–51, [52 blank, 53–56 advertisements of Jay Cooke & Co.]. 20.9 x 13.7 cm. Removed from bound volume, unbound.

Ref.: Howes R349; *Railway Economics* p. 243; Smith 8699

Published in Philadelphia in 1869. Sponsored by Jay Cooke & Company.

3522 ROBIDOUX, ORRAL M.

MEMORIAL TO THE ROBIDOUX BROTHERS: A HISTORY OF THE ROBIDOUXS IN AMERICA . . . KANSAS CITY, MISSOURI: PRINTED BY SMITH-GRIEVES COMPANY, 1924.*

[1]–311, [312 blank]. 23.5 x 15.1 cm. Illustrations unlisted. Dark blue fabrikoid.

Ref.: Howes R360

3523 ROBIN, ABBE

NOUVEAU VOYAGE DANS L'AMERIQUE SEPTENTRIONALE, EN L'ANNEE 1781 . . . A PHILADELPHIE: CHEZ MOUTARD, M. DCC. LXXXII.

a6, A–N8, O7. (First leaf blank.) [i]–[x, x blank], [1]–222. 21.4 x 13.7 cm. Contemporary marbled boards, red morocco back, gilt top, uncut.

Ref.: Clark I 298; Howes R361; Monaghan 1241; Sabin 72032

The account given of the activities of the French under Rochambeau is one of the best we have.

Mounted on the verso of the back endleaf is a long manuscript note in French about the contents of the volume and facing the manuscript note is mounted a second note dated March 26, 1805, regarding M. de St. Victor, who is mentioned on page 73.

3524 ROBIN, CLAUDE C.

VOYAGES DANS L'INTERIEUR DE LA LOUISIANE, DE LA FLORIDE OCCIDENTALE, ET DANS LES ISLES DE LA MARTINIQUE ET DE SAINT-DOMINGUE, PENDANT LES ANNEES 1802, 1803, 1804, 1805 ET 1806 . . . A PARIS: CHEZ F. BUISSON, 1807.

[*]2, a6, A–X8, Y5. [*]2, A–Hh8, Ii7. [*]6, A–T8, V4, a4, X–Ll8, Mm4. [1–4], [i]–xij, [1]–346. [i–iv], [1]–511, [512 blank]. [i]–xij, [1]–551, [552 blank]. 19.9 x 12.5 cm. Portrait, folding plan, and folding map. Map: Carte / des / Deux Florides / et de / la Louisiane Inférieure, / Dressée pour les Voyages de Mr Robin, / dans les Années 1802, 1803, 1804, 1805 et 1806, / par J. B. Poirson Ingénieur Géographe. / [upper left:] Tome II. / [upper right:] Page 512. / [lower left:] Gravé par J. B. Tardieu, Rue et Porte St Jacques, N° 157. / 40.7 x 67.3 cm. Scale: about 50 miles to one inch. Three volumes bound in two, contemporary or original brown and yellow marbled boards, red paper labels stamped in gilt, sprinkled edges. Volumes I–II are bound together.

Ref.: Howes R362; Monaghan 1247; Sabin 72039

Robin was present at the ceremonies held in New Orleans and at Natchitoches for the surrender of the Louisiana Territory to the United States. (For another description of this ceremony, see *Esquisse de la Situation Politique et Civile de la Louisiane* . . . 1804.) His descriptions of Louisiana and large sections of Florida and Texas are excellent. Most of the third volume deals with flora of Florida.

3525 [ROBINSON, ALFRED]

LIFE IN CALIFORNIA: DURING A RESIDENCE OF SEVERAL YEARS IN THAT TERRITORY . . . NEW YORK: PUBLISHED BY WILEY & PUTNAM, 1846.

[i]–[xiv, xiv blank], [1]–341, [342 blank]. 19 x 11.5 cm. Nine illustrations listed. Black cloth, blind embossed sides, title in gilt on backstrip.

Ref.: Blumann & Thomas 5091; Cowan p. 536–7; Howes R363; Sabin 72048

The Spanish manuscript mentioned on the title-page runs from page [227]–341. There is a separate title-page: Chinigchinich; A Historical Account of the Origin, Customs, and Traditions, of the Indians at the Missionary Establishment of St. Juan Capistrano, Alta California . . . By the Reverend Father Friar Geronimo

Bascana . . . New York: Published by Wiley & Putnam, 1846.

Useful authority on the period covered and the first account of California in English by a resident. The author came to the province in 1829 and married into the prominent De Guerra family.—Howes

3526 ROBINSON, BENAIAH

NO. 1. TO BE CONTINUED ANNUALLY. THE ILLINOIS FARMER'S ALMANAC AND REPOSITORY OF USEFUL KNOWLEDGE, FOR THE YEAR 1835 . . . CALCULATED FOR THE STATE OF ILLINOIS . . . JACKSONVILLE: PUBLISHED AND SOLD BY R. GOUDY.

[1–24]. 17.2 x 10.5 cm. Stabbed, unbound.
  Ref.: Byrd 159
On the last page appears the note: Just published, by R. Goudy, / A Gazetteer of Illinois, / by J. M. Peck, of Rockspring. / . . . Peck's *Gazetteer* is dated 1834.

3527 ROBINSON, FAYETTE

CALIFORNIA AND ITS GOLD REGIONS; WITH A GEOGRAPHICAL AND TOPOGRAPHICAL VIEW OF THE COUNTRY . . . NEW YORK: STRINGER & TOWNSEND, 1849.

[1]–137, [138 blank], [139–44 advertisements]. 20.5 x 14.2 cm. Map: Map of the / United States / The British Provinces / Mexico &c. / Showing the Routes of the U. S. Mail / Steam Packets to California, / and a Plan of the Gold Region. / [thin and thick rules] / Published by J. H. Colton, / 86 Cedar S.t New York. / 1849. / Drawn & Engraved by J. M. Atwood, New York / Entered according to Act of Congress, in the year 1849, by J. H. Colton, in the clerks office of the District Court of the Southern District of New York. / 45.3 x 63.2 cm. (border line). Scale: about 225 miles to one inch. *Inset:* Table of Distances. *Inset:* [Route around Cape Horn]. 17.3 x 8.6 cm. No scale given. *Inset:* Map of the / Gold Region. / California. / 12.2 x 7.5 cm. Scale: 60 miles to one inch. *Inset:* Pyramid Lake, Upper California. Yellow printed wrappers, with title on front wrapper, advertisements on verso of back wrapper, uncut, partly unopened.
  Ref.: Cowan p. 537; Howes R366; Jones 1215; Sabin 76202; Wheat (*Gold Rush*) 168

3528 ROBINSON, GEORGE T.

[Map] MAP / OF THE / MILITARY DISTRICT, / KANSAS AND THE TERRITORIES. / MAJ. G. M. DODGE. COMMANDING. / 1866. / EXECUTED UNDER THE DIRECTION OF / MAJ. GEO. T. ROBINSON. CHF. ENGR. / DRAWN BY T. H. WILLIAMS. / SCALE. / [diagrammatic scale: about 30 miles to one inch.] / [upper right corner:] R. STEVENSON & CO., / PHOTOGRAPH ROOMS, / 48 DELAWARE STREET, / LEAVENWORTH, — KANSAS. /

Map, 67.2 x 97.3 cm. Scale as above. Cut into panels 17.2 x 13.8 cm. and mounted on linen, folded to 18 x 14.5 cm.
  Ref.:
Reproduced by a photographic process from an engraved original. Colored by hand.

3529 ROBINSON, GEORGE T.

[Manuscript map] SURVEYS OF ROADS / BETWEEN FORT GIBSON & F.T ARBUCKLE, I. T. / MADE AUGUST– 1867, BY— / GEO. T. ROBINSON / CAPT. 10.TH. U. S. CAVALRY / [flourish] /.

Manuscript map on tracing cloth, 29.7 x 55 cm.
  Ref.:
From the Grierson Papers.

3530 ROBINSON, JACOB S.

SKETCHES OF THE GREAT WEST. A JOURNAL OF THE SANTA-FE EXPEDITION, UNDER COL. DONIPHAN, WHICH LEFT ST. LOUIS IN JUNE, 1846 . . . PORTSMOUTH JOURNAL PRESS, 1848.

[1]–71, [72 blank]. 13.9 x 9.5 cm. Blue printed boards, black cloth backstrip, with title on front cover. Lacks front endleaf. In a red half morocco case.
  Ref.: Clements Library (*Texas*) 35; Howes R368; Rader 2802; Wagner-Camp 154
Published at Portsmouth, New Hampshire.
Robinson was a member of the Doniphan party from Portsmouth, N.H. His journal, like Richardson's, is an account of his personal exploits rather than a broad report such as Hughes gave.

3531 ROBINSON, JOSEPH W.

HISTORY OF KANSAS, AND RAILROAD AND STEAMBOAT SKETCHES . . . PHILADELPHIA: JOHN F. ROBINSON, 1857.

[1]–74, [1]–21, [22 blank]. 18.4 x 11.4 cm. Gray printed wrappers with title on front wrapper. In a brown half morocco case.
  Ref.: Bradford 4682; Howes R370; Rader 2803; Sabin 72139; Wagner-Camp 293a
The second part, entitled "Railroad and Steamboat Sketches between Philadelphia and Kansas," was also issued separately.
According to the author's Advertisement, the pamphlet is an abridgement of a four-hundred-page work. This was never issued.

3532 ROBSON, JOSEPH

AN ACCOUNT OF SIX YEARS RESIDENCE IN HUD-
SON'S-BAY, FROM 1733 TO 1738, AND 1744 TO
1747 . . . LONDON: PRINTED FOR J. PAYNE AND
J. BOUQUET, MDCCLII.

[*]¹, a³, B–F⁸, G², a–f⁸. [1–2], [i]–vi, [1]–84, [1]–
95, [96 blank]. 22.3 x 14.1 cm. Three maps on
one sheet. Map: Plate N⁰ I. / A Draught of /
Nelson & Hayes's Rivers / Latᵈ 5⁰7. 1ᵒ6. North, /
Var. 1ᵒ6. 4⁰5. Westerly. / [upper right:] To face the
Title. / [lower right:] T. Jefferys Sculp. / 16.8 x
44.7 cm. Scale: 4 miles to one inch. Map: Plate
N⁰ II. / A Draught of / Churchill River, / Latᵈ
59⁰0ᵒ6. North, / Va. 1ᵒ6. 4ᵒ6. West. / [upper right:]
To face Page 9. / 16.2 x 24.4 cm. Scale: about
1 1/4 miles to one inch. Map: Plate N⁰ III. /
Plans of York and Prince of Wales's forts /
[centre:] Fig. I. I York fort. / 10.7 x 10.4 cm.
Scale: 118 feet to one inch. *Inset:* Fig. II. /
Prince of Wales's Fort. / 12.2 x 8.5 cm. Scale:
114 feet to one inch. *Inset:* Fig. III. / Snow
Shoes. / 4.4 x 18.9 cm. [upper right:] To face
Page 30. / 17.4 x 19 cm. Plate mark for three
plates: 37.4 x 46 cm. Original yellow plain wrap-
pers, uncut, unopened. In a red cloth case.

Ref.: Field 1312; Sabin 72259; Smith 8728;
Staton & Tremaine 217

The errata appear on the verso of the title-
leaf. The second part commences with a new
title-page: Appendix. Numb. I. / [decorative
rule] / A Short / Account / of the / Discovery /
of / Hudson's Bay; / and / Of the British Proceedings there since / the Grant of the Hudson's-Bay Charter. / Together / With Remarks
upon the papers and / Evidence produced by
that Company, / in the Year 1749, before a Committee of / the Honourable House of Commons, / appointed to enquire into the State and
Con-/dition of the Countries about Hudson's-/
Bay, and the Trade carried on there. / [decora-
tive rule] /.

A remarkably fine copy. The format is peculiar; the title-page may have been printed as
the fourth leaf of gathering a, but if so, it was
removed and tipped to leaf a.

3533 ROCAFUERTE, VICOMTE

AUTOGRAPH LETTER, SIGNED. 1826 April 19. Two
pages, 4to. To Lord Torrington. With Autograph Note, Signed, by Torrington on second
page.

3534 ROCAFUERTE, VICOMTE

AUTOGRAPH LETTER, SIGNED. 1826 April 21. To
Lord Torrington. Two Pages, 12mo.

3535 ROCAFUERTE, VICOMTE

AUTOGRAPH LETTER SIGNED IN THE THIRD PERSON.
No date, Tuesday Morning. One page, 8vo. To
W. Dorset Fellows. With Autograph Manu-
script, Signed by Fellows on verso.

Bound in Iturbide: *A Statement of Some of
the Principal Events* . . . 1824.

3536 ROCK, MARION TUTTLE

ILLUSTRATED HISTORY OF OKLAHOMA, ITS OCCU-
PATION BY SPAIN AND FRANCE—ITS SALE TO THE
UNITED STATES—ITS OPENING TO SETTLEMENT IN
1889—AND THE MEETING OF THE FIRST TERRITORI-
AL LEGISLATURE . . . TOPEKA, KANSAS: C. B. HAM-
ILTON & SON, 1890.

[i]–xii, [1]–[278]. 21.7 x 14.6 cm. 105 illustrations
listed. Dark gray cloth, gilt title and decorations
on front cover, gilt title on backstrip, red edges.

Ref.: Howes R390; Rader 2810

Most of the edition was burned, according to
Howes.

3537 ROCK RIVER SEMINARY

CATALOGUE OF THE OFFICERS AND STUDENTS OF
ROCK RIVER SEMINARY, MOUNT MORRIS, ILL., FOR
THE YEAR ENDING SEPTEMBER, 1843. CHICAGO:
ELLIS & FERGUS, 1843.

[1–2], [7]–15, [16 blank]. (Page 12 misnumbered
11.) 21.7 x 13.1 cm. Plain blue wrappers. Apparently lacks pages 3–6.

Prov.: Inscribed on front wrapper as a mailing cover: Cambridge Acadʸ / Cambridge /
Wash- Co- / N-Y- /. In lower left corner, reading up: Mt. Morris Ills / Nov. 5. 1843. / [flour-
ish] / 2 sheets /. Numerals in red ink on front
wrapper: 8010 /. Formerly in Ohio Historical
and Philosophical Society. Heavy black numerals in upper left corner: 378 /.

Ref.: Byrd 813; McMurtrie (*Chicago*) 61

The only copy listed by McMurtrie is the
OCHP copy, which he describes as comprising
15 pages. Byrd also locates only this copy, but
his collation calls for only nine pages.

3538 ROCKWELL, WILLIAM S., & OTHERS

[Wrapper title] COLORADO: ITS MINERAL AND
AGRICULTURAL RESOURCES.

[1]–20. 22.3 x 14.8 cm. Buff printed wrappers
with title as above on front wrapper.

Prov.: Rubber stamp of Central Mining
Company twice on back cover. Name removed
chemically from title-page and front wrapper,
and verso of last leaf.

Ref.: Wilcox p. 97

Printed in New York in 1869, so dated on

page 20. Signed at the end: Wm. S. Rockwell, / Chairman. / Other members of the Committee were John H. Langley, S. F. Nuckolls, Edward Bliss, and Hiram A. Johnson.

Page [1]: At a social gathering of Coloradians on the evening of the 20th instant, it was proposed that five gentlemen be requested to act as a Committee to prepare a brief historical sketch of Colorado—her mines and agricultural resources, and report on Thursday evening following . . . Report having been read, on motion of D. O. D. Cass, it was ordered printed in pamphlet form for distribution, F. H. Judd, Chairman, J. Bright Smith, Secretary.

3539 ROCKY MOUNTAIN DETECTIVE ASSOCIATION

ORIGINAL BADGE OF THE ROCKY MOUNTAIN DETECTIVE ASSOCIATION.

Shield 4.7 x 4.5 cm. surmounted by eagle in low relief; total measurements 6 x 4.5 cm. Spring pin on reverse. Gold colored metal.

The obverse is engraved with a star in each upper corner, a pair of crossed revolvers between; centre, a pair of upraised hands on each side of the word UP; at foot, R. M. D. A.

3540 ROCKY MOUNTAIN GOLD REPORTER

[Newspaper] ROCKY MOUNTAIN GOLD REPORTER AND MOUNTAIN CITY HERALD. VOL. 1. MOUNTAIN CITY, JEFFERSON, AUGUST 6 [–13], 1859. NO. 1 [–2] . . .

[1–4]. [1–4]. 40.4 x 25.5 cm. Text, 33.7 x 20.8 cm. 36.6 x 24.6 cm. Text, 33.7 x 20.5 cm. Unbound.

Prov.: No. 1 is signed in pencil on page [1]: O. J. Hollister /. No. 2 is inscribed on page [1]: A. N. J. C. Posey County / Indiana /.

Ref.: McMurtrie & Allen (*Colorado*) pp. 26, 28, 279

The *Rocky Mountain Gold Reporter* was the first newspaper published at Gregory Gulch, where the first discoveries of gold in the area had been made earlier in the same year.

There are copies of Vol. 1 No. 1 in the Denver Public Library and the Colorado Historical Society, but no other copy of Vol. 1 No. 2 has been located.

3541 ROCKY MOUNTAIN MEDICAL ASSOCIATION

BY-LAWS OF THE ROCKY MOUNTAIN MEDICAL ASSOCIATION. NEW MEXICO TERRITORIAL MEDICAL SOCIETY. TRINIDAD, COL.: PRINTED BY URBANO CHACON, 1875.

[i–ii], [1]–4, [5–6 blank]. 19 x 13 cm. Unbound, folded leaflet, partly unopened.

Ref.:
The printer is listed by McMurtrie & Allen as working in Trinidad in 1875. He issued the *Colorado Pioneer.*

3542 ROCKY MOUNTAIN NEWS

[Broadside newspaper] ROCKY MOUNTAIN NEWS EXTRA.—GREELEY'S REPORT. THE MINES AND MINERS OF KANSAS AND NEBRASKA. VOL. 1. CHERRY CREEK, K. T., SATURDAY, JUNE 11, 1859. NO. 6 . . .

Broadside, 40.3 x 26.9 cm. Text, 37.8 x 23.6 cm. Unbound.

Ref.: McMurtrie & Allen (*Colorado*) pp. 34–5, 240–42

Four columns of text, 97 lines to a full column.

McMurtrie states that Colorado Historical has an issue for June 11, but he states further that two issues are dated June 11, Nos. 5 and 6. He does not indicate what number Colorado Historical has, but in the case of the Denver Public, he states that they have No. 6. In no case is anything said of the "Extra."

Greeley's report had been anxiously awaited by all of the United States. It had a powerful influence on the Pike's Peak Gold Rush.

3543 ROCKY MOUNTAIN NEWS

[Newspaper] ROCKY MOUNTAIN NEWS. THE MINES AND MINERS OF KANSAS AND NEBRASKA. VOL. 1. AURARIA AND DENVER, K. T., THURSDAY, OCTOBER 6, 1859. NO. 20 . . .

[1–4]. 55.6 x 40.5 cm. Unbound.

Ref.: McMurtrie & Allen (*Colorado*) pp. 240–41

The paper was established April 23, 1859 by William N. Byers, John L. Dailey, and Thomas Gibson. It was published irregularly at first but later appeared weekly. There was also a daily edition which was started in 1860.

3544 RODENBOUGH, THEOPHILUS F.

FROM EVERGLADE TO CANON WITH THE SECOND DRAGOONS, (SECOND UNITED STATES CAVALRY.) AN AUTHENTIC ACCOUNT OF SERVICE IN FLORIDA, MEXICO, VIRGINIA, AND THE INDIAN COUNTRY . . . NEW YORK: D. VAN NOSTRAND, 1875.

[1]–[14, 14 blank], [17]–561, [562 blank], [563–66 advertisements]. 23.8 x 17.2 cm. 25 illustrations and maps listed, including six in color. Red cloth, insignia in gilt on front cover and in blind on back cover, title in gilt on backstrip.

Ref.: Howes R395; Munk (Alliot) p. 191; Nicholson p. 711; Rader 2813; Sabin 72467

3545 RODRIGUEZ, JOSE POLICARPO

JOSE POLICARPO RODRIGUEZ, "THE OLD GUIDE"; SURVEYOR, SCOUT, HUNTER, INDIAN FIGHTER, RANCHMAN, PREACHER. HIS LIFE IN HIS OWN WORDS. NASHVILLE, TENN.; PUBLISHING HOUSE OF THE METHODIST CHURCH, SOUTH.

[1]–121, [122 blank]. 18.2 x 12.4 cm. Portrait. Gray semi-stiff printed wrapper (front only) with title on front wrapper, bound into black cloth.

Ref.: Adams (*Ramp. Herd*) 1930; Howes R399

The Introductory Note, signed on page 5 by G. B. Winton, states: This story as follows was dictated to the Rev. D. W. Carter, D. D., at odd times during the years from 1892 to 1897.

Rodriguez was with Lieutenant Whiting in Texas in 1849, when he located the road from San Antonio to El Paso, and "continued in the service for twelve years, or up to 1861, the beginning of the War."—EDG

3546 ROE, FRANCES M. A.

ARMY LETTERS FROM AN OFFICER'S WIFE, 1871–1888 . . . NEW YORK: D. APPLETON AND COMPANY, 1909.

[i]–x, 1–387, [388 blank]. 19.9 x 13.2 cm. 26 illustrations listed. Blue cloth, gilt top, uncut.

Ref.: Howes R403; Rader 2815

3547 ROE, FRANCES M. A.

ANOTHER COPY.*

3548 ROE HOUSE, Fort Madison, Iowa

[Caption title] GRAND FOURTH OF JULY BALL. SIR—YOUR COMPANY WITH LADY, IS RESPECTFULLY SOLICITED . . . MONDAY EVENING, JULY 4TH, 1859 . . .

[1], [2–4 blank except for blind embossed borders.] 16.9 x 10.6 cm. Unbound leaflet.

Ref.:

The ball was held at the Roe House, Fort Madison, Iowa.

3549 ROEMER, FERDINAND

TEXAS. MIT BESONDERER RUCKSICHT AUF DEUTSCHE AUSWANDERUNG . . . BONN: BEI ADOLPH MARCUS, 1849.

[I]–XIV, [XV errata, XVI blank], [1]–464. 22.7 x 14 cm. Folding map: Topographisch-geognostiche Karte / von / Texas / mit Zegrundelegung der geographischen Karte v. Wilson / nach eigenen Beobactungen bearbeitet / [rule] von [rule] / D͞r Ferd. Roemer. / [3 rules] / Bonn bei Adolph Marcus. / . . . [lower right:] Lith von Henry & Cohen in Bonn. / 55.5 x 48.1 cm. Scale: 50 English miles to one inch. Manila

paper wrappers with original tan printed wrapper pasted on front wrapper.

Ref.: Howes R407; Raines p. 177; Sabin 72593

Roemer here produces the first geological map of Texas.

3550 ROGERS, ANDREWS N.

[Wrapper title] COMMUNICATION RELATIVE TO THE LOCATION OF THE U. P. R. R. ACROSS THE ROCKY MOUNTAINS THROUGH COLORADO TERRITORY . . . CENTRAL CITY: COLLIER & HALL, PRINTERS, 1867.

[1]–16. 21.5 x 13.1 cm. Yellow printed wrappers with title on front wrapper.

Ref.: McMurtrie & Allen (*Colorado*) 82; Wilcox p. 97

3551 ROGERS, FORDYCE H.

AUTOGRAPH LETTER, SIGNED. 1861 July 9. Detroit. To George F. Emmons. Two pages, 24.8 x 19.6 cm.

An application to his cousin for help in securing an appointment as a naval officer. Mentions a trip to California.

Laid in Heap: *Central Route* . . . 1854.

3552 [ROGERS, GEORGE]

MEMORANDA OF THE EXPERIENCE, LABORS, AND TRAVELS OF A UNIVERSALIST PREACHER . . . CINCINNATI: JOHN A. GURLEY, PUBLISHER, 1845.

[1]–400. 19.5 x 11.9 cm. Contemporary sheepskin, red leather label on backstrip.

Ref.: Clark III 232; Howes R412

His account . . . has great value, for he gave exact statements about persons and places, and he traveled on the backroads to out-of-the-way hamlets as well as on steamboats to the larger cities.—Clark

3553 ROGERS, JUSTUS H.

COLUSA COUNTY: ITS HISTORY TRACED FROM A STATE OF NATURE THROUGH THE EARLY PERIOD OF SETTLEMENT AND DEVELOPMENT, TO THE PRESENT DAY . . . ORLAND, CALIFORNIA, 1891.

[i]–viii, 9–[474]. (Pages [1–2] blank.) 22.9 x 15.2 cm. 95 illustrations listed. Dark brown leather, blind borders on sides, gilt back, gilt edges.

Ref.: Blumann & Thomas 673; Cowan p. 539; Howes R415

Contains, pages 37–54, the first printing of General John Bidwell's autobiography, biographical sketch of William B. Ide, pages 343–45, but most important, the "Autobiography of Major Stephen Cooper" written in 1888. Major Cooper settled in Missouri in 1807. He tells of Indian troubles there in 1814, and of how, in 1822, with fourteen others, he fitted out the first Company that opened up the Santa Fé trade.

He made a trip to Texas in the 1820's overland and returning north made further trips to Santa Fé. He served in the Black Hawk War. In 1836 he was one of the Commissioners to locate the boundary between Iowa and Missouri. In 1825–1828 he acted as guide [named as pilot] to Commissioners appointed to lay out a road from St. Louis to Santa Fé. He served as Indian Agent at Council Bluffs, joined Frémont in 1845, and stayed with him until Bent's Fort was reached and went from there to Texas. He traveled overland to California in 1846, was on hand promptly after the gold discovery in 1848, and claimed Polk's message on the subject resulted from one of his letters.—EDG

3554 ROGERS, ROBERT

A CONCISE ACCOUNT OF NORTH AMERICA: CONTAINING A DESCRIPTION OF THE SEVERAL BRITISH COLONIES . . . LONDON: PRINTED FOR THE AUTHOR, M DCC LXV.

a⁴, B–Ll⁴. [i]–[viii], 1–264. 20 x 12.5 cm. Contemporary calf, red leather label.

Prov.: Henry E. Huntington Duplicate, with duplicate stamp inside back cover.

Ref.: Buck 3; Clark I 301; Field 1316; Howes R418; Sabin 72723; Staton & Tremaine 392; Vail 562

The descriptions of Indian tribes and of the little-known western country are especially valuable. Rogers may have supplied the information for the work, but it is doubtful that he put it into the present form.

Page 43 correctly paginated, catchword on page 79 is non, page 214 mispaginated 194, and page 248 is mispaginated 240.

3555 ROGERS, ROBERT

JOURNALS OF MAJOR ROBERT ROGERS: CONTAINING AN ACCOUNT OF THE SEVERAL EXCURSIONS HE MADE UNDER THE GENERALS WHO COMMANDED UPON THE CONTINENT OF NORTH AMERICA, DURING THE LATE WAR . . . LONDON: PRINTED FOR THE AUTHOR, M DCC LXV.

[A]–Hh⁴. [i]–viii, 1–236, [237–38], [1–2]. 20.7 x 12.8 cm. Contemporary calf, red leather label, sprinkled red edges.

Ref.: Clark II 58; Howes R419; Thomson 996; Sabin 72725; Staton & Tremaine 393; Vail 563

The *Journals* cover the period September, 1755 to February, 1761, during which time Rogers was active with his famous "Rogers' Rangers." A second part, intended to give an account of Rogers' visit to the Cherokee nation, announced in the Advertisements was not published.

3556 ROLAND TREVOR . . .

ROLAND TREVOR: OR, THE PILOT OF HUMAN LIFE. BEING AN AUTOBIOGRAPHY OF THE AUTHOR. SHOWING HOW TO MAKE AND LOSE A FORTUNE, AND THEN TO MAKE ANOTHER. PHILADELPHIA: LIPPINCOTT, GRAMBO, AND CO., 1853.

[i]–xvi, [13]–415, [416 blank], 1–36 advertisements. 18.9 x 11.8 cm. Black cloth, sides embossed in blind, title in gilt on backstrip. Some binding repairs.

Ref.: Raines p. 206

Possibly written by Robert Triplett. Raines lists this as Trevor being the author.

3557 ROLLINS, PHILIP A.

THE COWBOY; HIS CHARACTERISTICS, HIS EQUIPMENT, AND HIS PART IN THE DEVELOPMENT OF THE WEST . . . NEW YORK: CHARLES SCRIBNER'S SONS, 1922.

[i]–xiv, [xv fly-title, xvi blank], 1–353, [354 blank]. Dark red cloth, fore and lower edges uncut.

Prov.: Two inscriptions by the author on the front fly-leaf: To Albert Trumonti who knows / mountains and their messages / and who comes from a nation / of *men*, is expressed the hope / that this little book about men / may carry some interest / Philip Ashton Rollins / Rocky Mountain Boys Camp / Estes Park, Colorado / August 15, 1922 / [decoration] / March 30, 1932, at the home of / Everett D. Graff, a delightful host, I / discovered that this shabby volume had / found a delightful resting place. / To Mr and Mrs Graff, my warmest / thanks. / Philip Ashton Rollins /.

Ref.: Adams 855; Adams (*Ramp. Herd*) 1938; Rader 2826

3558 ROMSPERT, GEORGE W.

THE WESTERN ECHO: A DESCRIPTION OF THE WESTERN STATES AND TERRITORIES OF THE UNITED STATES . . . DAYTON, OHIO: UNITED BRETHREN PUBLISHING HOUSE, 1881.

[1]–406. (Pages [1–2] blank.) 17.7 x 11.9 cm. Six illustrations listed. Green cloth with black border on front cover and with three words in gilt, title in gilt on backstrip.

Ref.: Adams (*Ramp. Herd*) 1945; Howes R427; Munk (Alliot) p. 192; Rader 2829

3559 RONAN, PETER

HISTORICAL SKETCH OF THE FLATHEAD INDIAN NATION FROM THE YEAR 1813 TO 1890 . . . HELENA, MONTANA: THE JOURNAL PUBLISHING COMPANY.

[i–iv], [1]–[82]. 23.1 x 15.3 cm. 12 illustrations listed. Brick red cloth, title on cover and backstrip in gilt, red edges.

Ref.: Smith 8764

Copyrighted 1890. Contains an account of St. Mary's Indian Mission in the Bitter Root Valley, and a biographical sketch of Father Ravalli.

3560 ROOSEVELT, THEODORE

HUNTING TRIPS OF A RANCHMAN. SKETCHES OF A SPORT ON THE NORTHERN CATTLE PLAINS . . . NEW YORK: G. P. PUTNAM'S SONS, 1885.

[1–2], [i]–xvi, 1–318. 28 x 20.4 cm. 31 illustrations listed, also unlisted decorations and vignettes. Brown buckram, gilt, uncut.

Prov.: On the half-title: Andrew Jameson / from / Elliott Roosevelt / March 1886. /. (The inscription is in the hand of the author's brother, the dedicatee.) With the Andrew Jameson bookplate.

Ref.: Adams (*Ramp. Herd*) 1949; Howes R430; Johnson (Blanck) p. 444

The Medora Edition. Limited to 500 copies.

3561 ROOSEVELT, THEODORE

THE WILDERNESS HUNTER: AN ACCOUNT OF THE BIG GAME OF THE UNITED STATES AND ITS CHASE WITH HORSE, HOUND, AND RIFLE . . . NEW YORK: G. P. PUTNAM'S SONS.

[1 blank, 2 limitation notice], [i]–xvi, [1]–472. 27.6 x 20.4 cm. 24 illustrations listed. Cream buckram, gilt top, uncut.

Ref.: Adams (*Ramp. Herd*) 1954; Johnson (Blanck) p. 444

Limited to 200 copies on Large Paper, signed by the author, and with the plates on Japan paper.

3562 ROOT, FRANK A., & WILLIAM E. CONNELLEY

THE OVERLAND STAGE TO CALIFORNIA. PERSONAL REMINISCENCES AND AUTHENTIC HISTORY OF THE GREAT OVERLAND STAGE LINE AND PONY EXPRESS FROM THE MISSOURI RIVER TO THE PACIFIC OCEAN . . . TOPEKA, KANSAS: PUBLISHED BY THE AUTHORS, 1901.

[i]–[xviii], [1]–630, [631–32 blank, 633 advertisement, 634 blank]. 22.8 x 15.2 cm. Illustrations listed. Light brown pictorial cloth.

Prov.: Inscribed on the front endleaf: To Major J. B. Pond in recognition of / his services in connection with the / Smoky Hill Route, / Frank A. Root. / William E. Connelley / [flourish] / Topeka, Kansas, March 21, 1902 / [flourish] /. All the above except the signature of

Frank A. Root is in the hand of W. E. Connelley. With the bookplate of James B. Pond.

Ref.: Adams 861; Cowan p. 541; Howes R434

Laid in is a copy of a long and interesting letter by Root in which he disclaims Connelley's part in the writing of the book. There are also references to his own experiences crossing the plains, etc.

Laid in are two prospectuses, printed in 1901 and 1903, with press notices, etc., regarding the book and with manuscript notes in the margins by Root.

3563 ROOT, JERIEL

ANALYSIS OF THEOLOGY, LAW, RELIGION AND THE RIGHTS OF MAN . . . PEORIA: PRINTED BY BENJAMIN FOSTER, 1855.

[i]–iv, 5–72. 21 x 13.9 cm. Yellow printed wrappers, title on front wrapper.

Ref.: Byrd 2346

3564 ROOT, OMI E.

1861.—FIRST ISSUE.—1861. ROOT'S GALESBURG CITY DIRECTORY, FOR THE YEAR 1861 . . . GALESBURG, ILLINOIS, 1861.

[1]–108. 22.3 x 14.4 cm. Frontispiece. Black cloth, blind embossed borders on sides, title on front cover in gilt and on back cover in blind. Worn.

Ref.:

Patrons' names were printed in capital letters. The gimmick worked: a surprising number of names appear in capital letters.

3565 ROOT, RILEY

JOURNAL OF TRAVELS FROM ST. JOSEPHS[!] TO OREGON, WITH OBSERVATIONS OF THAT COUNTRY, TOGETHER WITH SOME DESCRIPTION OF CALIFORNIA . . . GALESBURG: GAZETTEER AND INTELLIGENCER PRINTS, 1850.

[1]–143, [144 blank]. 23 x 13.3 cm. Tan printed wrappers, buff cloth backstrip, with title on front wrapper. In a terra cotta cloth case.

Prov.: Signature in pencil on title-page: Clarissa N. Hinckley / Galesburg /. A manuscript note about the author is tipped to a front fly-leaf.

Ref.: Byrd 1621; Cowan p. 542; Howes R436; Smith 8766; Wagner-Camp 189

On a visit to Galesburg, Illinois, in October, 1951, Professor Conger told me the story of the discovery of this pamphlet. Edward Caldwell of New York City, at one time president of McGraw-Hill Co., publishers, was accumulating a fine collection of mid-western and western Americana to be presented to Knox College

Lathrop C. Harper was acting as his adviser and was selling him many of the books for the collection. A woman graduate of Knox College gave Caldwell a copy of the Root pamphlet to be included in the collection if he thought it worthy of that honor. Harper showed the pamphlet to Eberstadt, who had never heard of it, and who proceeded to trace the descendants of Riley Root. In the process, he found eighteen copies in a box in the attic of an abandoned house which had earlier been occupied by a daughter of Root. Conger and Murray (the famous book scout) later picked up three copies from family connections, one of which I bought from Morris Briggs in about 1930.—EDG

Riley Root was an excellent reporter and a careful observer, both qualities that make this book one of the top four written about the overland route to Oregon. It has a usefulness the fluffy first accounts of Oregon and California did not have. It has the charm, too, of his direct manner of writing.—Webster Jones

3566 ROOT, RILEY

[Broadside] [Two versions of the front wrapper of Root's *Journal of Travels* . . . , text as above]

Broadside, 23.9 x 30.4 cm. Text, 18.8 x 25 cm.
   Ref.:
The two versions, side-by-side, show differences only in the text of the imprints and in the decorative borders. The version on the left matches the wrapper of the Graff copy. Since the backstrip of the pamphlet is cloth and the front wrapper a single leaf, both versions of the front wrapper may have been used. But copies checked are identical with the Graff copy. The broadside is printed on bright yellow paper.

Laid in case with Root's *Journal of Travels* . . . 1850.

3567 ROOT, RILEY

MUSICAL PHILOSOPHY; COMPRISING THE TRANSPOSITION OF THE MUSICAL KEYS, IN ALL ITS VARIED FORMS, TOGETHER WITH MANY ABSTRUSE QUESTIONS RELATING TO TRANSPOSITION, AND THE NATURE AND CHANGES OF MUSICAL INTONATION . . . GALESBURG: WM. J. MOURER, BOOK AND JOB PRINTER, 1866.

[1]–20. 18.7 x 12 cm. Yellow wrappers with title on front wrapper.
   Ref.:
With several manuscript corrections in pencil, apparently in the hand of the author.

3568 ROOT, RILEY

ANOTHER COPY. Identical, except measuring 18.7 x 12.7 cm.

3569 ROOT, RILEY

[Broadside] ROOT'S MUSICAL TRANSPOSITION KEYBOARD! . . . RILEY ROOT.

Broadside, 22.8 x 30.7 cm. Text, 18.8 x 27.4 cm.
   Ref.:
Undated and without place of printing, but undoubtedly Galesburg and probably by 1866.

Laid in case with Root's *Journal of Travels* . . . 1850.

3570 RORER, DAVID

ARGUMENT IN BEHALF OF THE CITY IN THE MATTER OF ISSAC LEFFLER, CLAIMANT OF MARKET SQUARE, IN THE CITY OF BURLINGTON, IOWA . . . BURLINGTON: DAILY IOWA STATE GAZETTE, 1857.

[1]–14. 24.8 x 15.5 cm. Unbound.
   Ref.:
Contains information relative to settlers of Burlington who arrived as early as 1834.—EDG

3571 ROSARIST'S COMPANION, THE . . .

THE ROSARIST'S COMPANION; OR, MANUAL OF DEVOUT EXERCISES: . . . CHICAGO: PRINTED FOR THE PROPRIETOR, AND SOLD BY CHARLES M'DONNEL.

[i–ii], [1]–264, [265–270 blank (different paper)]. (Page [1] blank.) 12.1 x 7.9 cm. Gray cloth, front cover stamped in gilt, back in blind, title on backstrip.
   Ref.: Byrd 943; McMurtrie (*Chicago*) 82
Bishop William Quarter, whose approbation appears on the verso of the title-leaf, was the first Roman Catholic bishop of Chicago.

Printed in 1845 by Ellis & Fergus.

3572 ROSE, VICTOR M.

THE LIFE AND SERVICES OF GEN. BEN McCULLOCH . . . PHILADELPHIA: PICTORIAL BUREAU OF THE PRESS, 1888.

[i–vi, vi blank], [25]–260. 22.3 x 14.2 cm. Two portraits. Black cloth, blind embossed sides, title in gilt on backstrip.
   Ref.: Howes R443; Raines p. 178
Laid in is an Autograph Letter, signed by McCulloch.

3573 ROSE, VICTOR M.

SOME HISTORICAL FACTS IN REGARD TO THE SETTLEMENT OF VICTORIA, TEXAS; ITS PROGRESS AND PRESENT STATUS . . . LAREDO, TEXAS, DAILY TIMES PRINT.

[i–ii blank], [1]–316. 22.5 x 14.7 cm. Black limp cloth with title on front cover in gold.
   Ref.: Bradford 4705; Howes R445; Rader 2834; Raines p. 178
Dated in Preface: February 28th, 1883.

3574 ROSEBURG, OREGON. Public School

PUBLIC SCHOOL ENTERTAINMENT AT CENTRAL SCHOOL, FRIDAY EVE., JUNE 23, 1876. EXERCISES TO COMMENCE AT 8 O'CLOCK . . . GEO. H. HIMES, JOB PRINTER, 5 WASHINGTON-ST.

[1–4]. 21.6 x 14 cm.

Ref.:

Himes maintained his printing establishment in Portland. The programme may have been prepared for a Portland school, but Roseburg is a more likely place. Inserted in Manuscript Journals of Loren L. Williams, Volume V.

3575 ROSEN, PETER

PA-HA-SA-PAH; OR, THE BLACK HILLS OF SOUTH DAKOTA. A COMPLETE HISTORY OF THE GOLD AND WONDER-LAND OF THE DAKOTAS . . . ST. LOUIS: NIXON-JONES PRINTING CO., 1895.*

[i]–xiii, [xiv blank], 1–645, [646 blank], 647 advertisements, [648 blank]. 23.1 x 15.3 cm. 82 illustrations listed. Brown pictorial cloth, with title on front cover and backstrip.

Ref.: Adams 864; Howes R446a; Jennewein 125

3576 ROSS, ALEXANDER

ADVENTURES OF THE FIRST SETTLERS ON THE OREGON OR COLUMBIA RIVER: BEING A NARRATIVE OF THE EXPEDITION FITTED OUT BY JOHN JACOB ASTOR . . . LONDON: SMITH, ELDER AND CO., 1849.

[i]–[xvi], [1]–352, [1]–16 advertisements. 19.6 x 12.3 cm. Folding map: Map of / The Columbia / to illustrate / Ross's Adventures / [decorative rule] / George & Cº.ⁿ Lithography, 54 Hatton Garden / [lower centre:] Published by Smith, Elder & Cº London. / 18.7 x 25 cm. No scale given. Red cloth, blind embossed sides, title in gilt on backstrip, uncut.

Ref.: Field 1325; Howes R448; Sabin 73326; Smith 8783; Staton & Tremaine 958; Wagner-Camp 172

No colored frontispiece.

3477 ROSS, ALEXANDER

THE SAME. With colored frontispiece. 18.7 x 11.7 cm. Blue cloth, gilt edges, gilt lettered on backstrip.

3578 ROSS, ALEXANDER

THE FUR HUNTERS OF THE FAR WEST; A NARRATIVE OF ADVENTURES IN THE OREGON AND ROCKY MOUNTAINS . . . LONDON: SMITH, ELDER AND CO., 1855.

[i]–xv, [xvi blank], [1]–333, [334 blank, 335 advertisement, 336 blank.] [i]–viii, [1]–262, [263 advertisement, 264 blank]. 19.7 x 12.2 cm. Folding map and frontispieces. Map: Map of / The Oregon / to illustrate / Ross's Fur Hunters / of the Far West. / [decorative rule] / Ford & West, Lithog. 54, Hatton Garden. / [lower centre:] Published by Smith, Elder & Cº London. / 18.3 x 15 cm. No scale given. Two volumes, dark gray cloth, blind embossed sides, title in gilt on backstrips.

Ref.: Field 1326; Howes R449; Sabin 73327; Smith 8785; Staton & Tremaine 1235; Wagner-Camp 269

3579 ROSS, ALEXANDER

THE RED RIVER SETTLEMENT: ITS RISE, PROGRESS, AND PRESENT STATE . . . LONDON: SMITH, ELDER AND CO., 1856.

[i]–xvi, [1]–416. 18.4 x 12 cm. Frontispiece. Bright blue cloth, gilt, with gilt title on front cover and backstrip, gilt edges.

Ref.: Field 1327; Sabin 73328; Staton & Tremaine 3304

3580 ROSS, ALEXANDER

THE SAME.

[i]–xvi, [1]–416, [1]–16 (advertisements). 19.8 x 12.6 cm. Frontispiece. Rust cloth, blind borders, gilt lettered on backstrip.

3581 ROSS, EDMUND G.

HISTORY OF THE IMPEACHMENT OF ANDREW JOHNSON, PRESIDENT OF THE UNITED STATES, BY THE HOUSE OF REPRESENTATIVES, AND HIS TRIAL BY THE SENATE, FOR HIGH CRIMES AND MISDEMEANORS IN OFFICE, 1868 . . . 1896.

[i–iv, iv blank], [1]–180. 23.6 x 15 cm. Gray cloth, title stamped in blue on front cover.

Ref.: Howes R452

Printed at Santa Fé, New Mexico.

The author was senator from Kansas at the time of the Johnson impeachment. He was one of three Republican senators who crossed party lines to declare Johnson not guilty. During Cleveland's administration, Ross was Governor of New Mexico.

3582 ROSS, GEORGE M. VON

DER NORDAMERIKANISCHE FREISTAAT TEXAS . . . RUDOLSTADT: DRUCK UND VERLAG VON G. FROEBEL, 1851.

[i–ii], [1]–85, [86 blank]. 21.1 x 13 cm. Map: Map / of / Texas. / Compiled from surveys at the Land Office of Texas / by / K. W. Presler & W. Völker / Geometers of the Land Office of Texas. / R. Diedrich grav. / Engraving and Printing of L. Holle's Office. [at top:] Karte von Texas. / Zusammengetragen nach den Aufnahmen der Land Office von Texas, u. gezeichnet von / K. W. Presler u. W. Völker / Geometer an der Land Office v. Texas zu Austin. / Gravirt u. gedruckt im geogr. lithogr. Institut v. L. Holle. / [lower centre:] Zu dem Werke: Der nordamerikanische Freistaat Texas, nach eigener Anschauung und nach den neusten und besten Quellen geschildert von G. M. von Ross, gehörig. / 61 x 44.8 cm. Scale: about 22 English miles to one inch. Gray printed boards, with title on front cover, advertisements on back cover.

Ref.: Biesele p. 230; Howes R455; Raines p. 179; Sabin 73357

Von Ross was the translator of Wislezenus' *Memoir of a Tour to Northern Mexico* (Braunschweig, 1850).

3583 ROSS, HARVEY L.

THE EARLY PIONEERS AND PIONEER EVENTS OF THE STATE OF ILLINOIS . . . CHICAGO: EASTMAN BROTHERS, 1899.*

[i]–[xii], [1]–199, [200 blank]. 20.8 x 14 cm. Portrait. Dark red cloth, blind fillet borders on sides, title in gilt on backstrip.

Ref.: Buck 167; Howes R456

Ross knew Lincoln well and in this volume disagrees with a number of statements made earlier by Herndon.—EDG

3584 ROSS, JOHN

[Map] COURSE / OF THE / RIVER MISSISSIPPI, / FROM THE BALISE TO FORT CHARTRES; / TAKEN ON AN EXPEDITION TO THE ILLINOIS, / IN THE LATTER END OF THE YEAR 1765. / BY / LIEU.ᵀ ROSS OF THE 34ᵀᴴ REGIMENT: / IMPROVED / FROM THE SURVEYS OF THAT RIVER MADE BY THE FRENCH. / [swelled rule] / [diagrammatic scale] / BRITISH MILES 69 1/2 TO A DEGREE / [diagrammatic scale: about 19 miles to one inch.] / LONDON / PRINTED FOR ROB.ᵀ SAYER, Nº 53 IN FLEET STREET. / PUBLISHED AS THE ACT DIRECTS. 1 JUNE 1772 /.

Map, 113 x 35.7 cm. (plate mark), 111.8 x 34.2 cm. (neat line). Scale as above.

Ref.: Stevens & Tree 31

Printed number on verso: 33 /. There were three states of this map of which this is the first. The second was dated 1775 and the third 1794.

3585 ROUTE OF THE MORMON PIONEERS . . .

[Caption, lower left] MILLROY & HAYES PUBLISHERS SALT LAKE CITY, UTAH. EXPLANATION . . . JULY, 1847. ROUTE OF THE MORMON PIONEERS FROM NAUVOO TO GREAT SALT LAKE. FEB'Y, 1846. COPYRIGHT 1899, BY MILLROY & HAYES.

Map, 35.3 x 106.2 cm. (paper size). Folded into board cover, with two flaps, original khaki printed cover, 18.7 x 11.4 cm.

Ref.:

Printed in colors, the map appears in the upper portion and the scenes along the route in the lower portion. At the right of the caption is a sketch depicting the Mormon pioneers pushing handcarts.

3586 ROWBOTHAM, FRANCIS J.

A TRIP TO PRAIRIE-LAND BEING A GLANCE AT THE SHADY SIDE OF EMIGRATION . . . LONDON: SAMPSON LOW, MARSTON, SEARLE, & RIVINGTON, 1885.

[i]–xii, [1]–243, [244 colophon], [1]–32 advertisements. 18.8 x 12.5 cm. Pictorial olive cloth, with title in red on front cover, uncut.

Ref.:

3587 ROY, JOSEPH E.

[Broadside] THE FRUIT OF HOME MISSIONS. THIS HISTORY OF A CHRISTIAN CHURCH IN ONE OF OUR WESTERN . . . JOSEPH E. ROY, AGENT A.H.M.S. CHICAGO.

Broadside, 20.2 x 12.4 cm. Text, 17.6 x 9.2 cm. Light yellow paper.

Ref.:

Issued for the American Home Missionary Society and inserted in Turner: *Reminiscences of Morris . . .* 1865.

3588 ROYALL, ANNE NEWPORT

AUTOGRAPH LETTER, SIGNED. 1835 February 9. [Washington, D. C.] To Peter Force. One page, 25.1 x 20 cm.

Requesting a loan of "a few reams of paper."

3589 ROYALL, ANNE NEWPORT

AUTOGRAPH LETTER, SIGNED IN THE THIRD PERSON. 1837 March 1, [Washington, D. C.] To Hon. Gideon Lee & others [at] Mrs. Pitman's. One page, 24.8 x 19.7 cm. With address leaf.

Soliciting subscriptions to her newspaper. Mrs. Pitman's was a Washington boardinghouse.

3590 ROYALL, ANNE NEWPORT

THE BLACK BOOK; OR, A CONTINUATION OF TRAVELS, IN THE UNITED STATES . . . WASHINGTON, D. C.: PRINTED FOR THE AUTHOR, 1828 [–1829].

[1]–184, 205–328, [329 Index, 330 blank]. [1]–[396]. [1]–235, [236 blank]. 19.8 to 19.1 x 11.4 to 11.2 cm. Three volumes, rebound in contemporary blue boards, new tan paper backs, new printed labels, uncut.

Prov.: Inscribed on front cover of third volume: The Honble. / Post Master General. / Signed on title-page: M I Weller /.

Ref.: Clark III 95; Howes R481; Sabin 73818

There is no text missing from the first volume.

3591 ROYALL, ANNE NEWPORT

LETTERS FROM ALABAMA ON VARIOUS SUBJECTS . . . WASHINGTON: 1830.

[1]–165, [166 blank], [167]–232, [1]–6. 20 x 13.3 cm. Contemporary marbled boards, plum roan back and corners.

Prov.: Signature on title-page: Levi. H. Weeks / 1863 /.

Ref.: Clark III 96; Howes R482; Sabin 73820

3592 ROYALL, ANNE NEWPORT

MRS. ROYALL'S PENNSYLVANIA; OR, TRAVELS CONTINUED IN THE UNITED STATES . . . WASHINGTON: PRINTED FOR THE AUTHOR, 1829.

[1]–276. (Pages 77–8 follow 79–80.) [1]–273, [274–76 blank], [1]–24. (Pages 181–82 mispaginated 180–81.) 20 x 11 cm. Two volumes rebound in contemporary blue boards, new tan paper backs, new printed white paper labels.

Prov.: Signature on each title-page: M. I. Weller.

Ref.: Bradford 4726; Howes R484; Sabin 73821

3593 ROYALL, ANNE NEWPORT

MRS. ROYALL'S SOUTHERN TOUR; OR, SECOND SERIES OF THE BLACK BOOK . . . WASHINGTON, 1830 [–1831].

[1]–169, [170 blank], [3]–12. (Page 113 unpaginated.) [1]–148, 179–[218]. (Page 14 unpaginated, pages 149–78 omitted in pagination.) [1]–[247], [248 blank]. 22.9 to 22 x 14 to 13.1 cm. Three volumes, Vol. I in old dark brown cloth, black roan back and corners, Vols. II–III rebound in contemporary gray boards, new tan paper backs, new printed white paper labels.

Ref.: Clark III 97; Howes R483; Sabin 73822 Sabin mentions only the first two volumes.

3594 [ROYALL, ANNE NEWPORT]

SKETCHES OF HISTORY, LIFE, AND MANNERS, IN THE UNITED STATES . . . NEW-HAVEN: PRINTED FOR THE AUTHOR, 1826.

[i–iv], [13]–392. (Pages 357–58 omitted, but no text lacking.) 19.5 x 12 cm. Frontispiece. Rebound in contemporary gray boards, new tan paper back, new printed white paper labels, uncut, partly unopened.

Ref.: Clark III 98; Howes R485; Sabin 73824 The collation given by Sabin is: (6), 13–392.

3595 ROYALL, ANNE NEWPORT

THE TENNESSEAN; A NOVEL, FOUNDED ON FACTS . . . NEW-HAVEN: PRINTED FOR THE AUTHOR, 1827.

[1]–372. (Pages 248, 325–36, and 349 mispaginated 284, 315–25, and 348.) 19 x 11.8 cm. Rebound in contemporary brown boards, new tan paper backstrip, new printed white paper label, uncut.

Prov.: Bookplate of William Pierson Judson.

Ref.: Sabin 73825; Wright I 2257

3596 ROYALL, ANNE NEWPORT

[Broadside] TO THE MEMBERS OF THE TWENTY-FIRST CONGRESS . . . POSTS OF SCREENING WHITE MEN? AND TO WHAT BRANCH OF THE CAPITOL DO THE PARTIES BELONG?

Broadside, 35 x 20.8 cm. Text, 28.3 x 13.6 cm.

Prov.: Addressed on verso to: Editors of the N. Y. Courier & / Enquirer / New York City /. Inscribed on face by Mrs. Royall: From Anne Royall to Ed^s Courier & Enquirer /. In lower margin: don't drop a hint I sent the H. B I would murdered /. Followed by note in red pencil in another hand: Autograph of that mad cap Anne Royal / G S T (?) /.

Ref.:

The broadside is a general attack on the political corruption of the times and a particular libel against Matthew St. Clair Clarke.

3597 ROYCE, CHARLES C.

JOHN BIDWELL: PIONEER, STATESMAN, PHILANTHROPIST. A BIOGRAPHICAL SKETCH . . . CHICO, CALIFORNIA, 1906.

[1]–66, [1–294, 294 blank]. 25 x 16.9 cm. Numerous illustrations, unlisted. Half red morocco, green cloth sides, red edges.

Prov.: Inscribed on front blank leaf: To Mr Howell / With kindest regards / from / Eva S Kennedy / July 26, 1925. / Mrs. Kennedy was John Bidwell's daughter.

Ref.: Blumann & Thomas 641; Cowan p. 545; Howes R486; Wagner-Camp 88 note

The first part was issued separately. Part II carries the following title-page on page [1]: Addresses / Reminscences, Etc. / of / General John Bidwell / [short rule] / Compiled by C. C. Royce / [short rule] / Chico, California, 1907 / [rule border].

Laid in is an Autograph Letter, signed by John Bidwell.

3598 ROYCE, SARAH

A FRONTIER LADY. RECOLLECTIONS OF THE GOLD RUSH AND EARLY CALIFORNIA . . . NEW HAVEN: YALE UNIVERSITY PRESS, MDCCCCXXXII.*

[i]–[xv], [xvi blank], [1]–144. 20.6 x 13.8 cm. Frontispiece and map. Gray cloth, fore and lower edges uncut, unopened.

Ref.:

An account of a trip across the plains in 1849 written with the aid of her diary in 1888.—EDG

3599 ROZIER, FIRMIN A.

150TH CELEBRATION OF THE FOUNDING OF STE. GENEVIEVE. ADDRESS . . . GIVING A FULL HISTORY OF STE. GENEVIEVE, THE FIRST PERMANENT SETTLEMENT IN THE UNITED STATES WEST OF THE MISSISSIPPI RIVER. DELIVERED AT THE CITY OF STE. GENEVIEVE, MO., JULY 21, 1885.

[i–ii], [1]–19, [20 blank]. 21.6 x 14.2 cm. Removed from bound volume, unbound. Trimmed close.

Ref.: Bradford 4731; Howes R488

There may have been an imprint below the last line quoted above. Bradford gives an imprint: St. Louis: G. A. Pierrot & Son, Prs. 1885.

3600 RUDDOCK, SAMUEL A.

[Caption title] . . . NORTHWEST COAST OF AMERICA . . .

[1]–22, [23–4 blank]. 22.1 x 14.1 cm. Rebound in new red cloth.

Ref.: Wagner-Camp 31

19th Congress, 1st Session, House, Report 213, Serial 142. [Washington, 1826.]

There seems some doubt that the expedition described in this work by Samuel Adams Ruddock took place.

3601 RUGER, THOMAS H.

[Caption title] HEADQUARTERS DEPARTMENT OF CALIFORNIA, SAN FRANCISCO, CAL., OCTOBER 19, 1891. TO THE ADJUTANT GENERAL, U. S. ARMY, WASHINGTON, D. C. SIR:— I HAVE THE HONOR, IN ACCORDANCE WITH THE TELEGRAM OF THE 19TH OF SEPTEMBER LAST, FROM THE HEADQUARTERS OF THE ARMY, TO SUBMIT A REPORT AS FOLLOWS OF THE PART TAKEN BY THE TROOPS OF THE DEPARTMENT OF DAKOTA IN THE SIOUX INDIAN CAMPAIGN DURING THE LATTER PART OF 1890 AND THE EARLY PART OF THE PRESENT YEAR. . . .

[1]–28, [1]–8, [1]–11, [1]–10, [1]–8, [1]–5, [1]–6, [1]–44, [1]–44, [1]–4, [1]–12, [1]–26, [1]–3, [4 blank], [5]–[6 blank], [1]–[2 blank]. 18 x 11.9 cm. Half black morocco, lettered in gilt on backstrip.

Prov.: Rubber stamp of W. F. Drum on first page and on verso of front endleaf.

Ref.: Howes R497

The second to twelfth sections, Exhibits A–I, K–M, are followed by a leaf of attestation signed by L. A. Lovering, dated San Francisco, Cal., October 19, 1891. Tipped in at the end is a Circular No. 5 of the Headquarters, Department of Dakota, St. Paul, Minn., March 21, 1892.

The original orange front wrapper has been removed and an inserted single leaf before the final leaf (Circular No. 5) has also been removed.

In pencil at head of Exhibit "B.": This report of Chapmans, I believe / to be a fake, pure and simple, on / the face of it— /.

The reports cover the Messiah Craze, the death of Sitting Bull, and other Indian affairs.

3602 RUGG, S. M.

[Caption title] A THRILLING STORY FROM ALASKA . . .

[1–8]. 14.3 x 7.7 cm. Illustration. Unbound, panoramic fold.

Ref.:

Signed at end: S. M. Rugg, / Los angeles, Cal. / [rule] / Don't let this tract die, pass it on. / [rule] / All tracts free, as the Lord permits. / Interdenominational Free Tract Society, / 730 San Pedro St., Los Angeles, Cal. / Telephone Broadway 6639, F 2675. /

Rugg says he was born in 1834 and that at the time of writing is "nearly 79 years old." *Ergo* published about 1913.

3603 RULE, EDITH

LITTLE STORIES OF MASON CITY'S PAST, 1851–1870 . . . MASON CITY, IOWA: PRIVATELY PRINTED, NINETEEN TWENTY-EIGHT.*

[1]–103, [104 blank]. 19.6 x 13.8 cm. Frontispiece. Original floral-print cloth, printed paper label on front cover.

Ref.:

On title-page, the name Rule is crossed out and Peach supplied in manuscript.

3604 [RUNNION, JAMES B.]

OUT OF TOWN. BEING A DESCRIPTIVE, HISTORICAL AND STATISTICAL ACCOUNT OF THE SUBURBAN TOWNS AND RESIDENCES OF CHICAGO. CHICAGO: THE WESTERN NEWS COMPANY, 1869.

[i–ii], [1]–64, [1–2 advertisements]. 22.7 x 14.9 cm. Map: This Plate shows the relative position of Oak Park, Harlem and Thatcher to the City Limits. / Oak Park, 3 1/2 miles; Harlem, 4 miles; and Thatcher, 5 miles. / 12.1 x 21.2 cm. No scale given. Gray printed wrappers, with title on front wrapper, advertisements on verso of front and recto and verso of back wrapper. In a green cloth case.

Prov.: Bookplate of Neva and Guy Littell.

Ref.: Howes R503

Preceding the title-page are two pages of advertisements printed on purple paper; tipped in at the back is a two-page advertisement for the Baptist Union Theological Seminary.

3605 RUPP, ISRAEL D.

THE GEOGRAPHICAL CATECHISM OF PENNSYL-
VANIA, AND THE WESTERN STATES; DESIGNED AS A
GUIDE AND POCKET COMPANION, FOR TRAVELLERS
AND EMIGRANTS, TO PENNSYLVANIA, OHIO, IN-
DIANA, ILLINOIS, MICHIGAN AND MISSOURI . . .
HARRISBURG, PA.: PRINTED AND PUBLISHED BY
JOHN WINEBRENNER, 1836.

[i]–iv, [1]–384. 16.3 x 10.8 cm. Contemporary
full mottled calf, dark red leather label on backstrip.
 Ref.: Bradford 4742; Buck 303; Howes
R506; Sabin 74157

3606 RURAL MESSENGER, THE

THE RURAL MESSENGER. VOL. 4—NO. 6. HAM-
ILTON, ILL.—KEOKUK, IOWA. JUNE, 1876. PUB-
LISHED MONTHLY BY GREGG & BROWN . . .

[83]–96. 37.4 x 27 cm. Unbound.
 Ref.:
Continuation of *The Dollar Monthly* and
Dollar Rural Messenger.

3607 RUSK COUNTY, TEXAS

[Broadside] 1876. RUSK COUNTY TEXAS. 1877.
CHEAP HOMES FOR 10,000 FAMILIES. RUSK COUNTY
IS ONE OF THE OLDEST SETTLED COUNTIES IN THE
STATE . . .

Broadside, 43.4 x 27.8 cm. Text, 33.3 x 22.8 cm.
 Ref.:
The first part of the broadside is a description
of the county, and contains an invitation for
readers to send their queries to J. N. Still, Corresponding Secretary, Rusk County Immigration Society, Henderson, and fifteen other residents. The second part is a description of lands
for sale in the county.
 There is a marked similarity between this
broadside and one for Bell County, but in
neither is there a hint about place of publication.

3608 RUSSELL, JOHN

CLAUDINE LAVALLE; OR, THE FIRST CONVICT. THE
MORMONESS; OR, THE TRIALS OF MARY MAVERICK
. . . ALTON: COURIER STEAM PRESS PRINT, 1853.

[i–ii], [1]–89, [90–92 blank]. 21.3 x 13.1 cm.
Pink printed wrappers, with title on front wrap-
per, brass staples. Lacks back wrapper.
 Ref.: Byrd 2027
John Russell and John Mason Peck were co-
founders of Rockspring College, now Shirtleff
College, at Alton, Illinois. The first story de-
scribed incidents in the early history of St.
Charles.—EDG

3609 RUSSELL, MORRIS C.

UNCLE DUDLEY'S ODD HOURS, WESTERN SKETCHES,
INDIAN TRAIL ECHOES, STRAWS OF HUMOR . . .
LAKE CITY, MINN.: "THE HOME PRINTERY," 1904.

[1]–256 (including portrait). 24.3 x 15.6 cm. Por-
trait. Dark gray printed wrappers, with silk cord
ties, uncut. In black cloth case.
 Ref.: Howes R536
Uncommon; uncommonly uninteresting.—
Howes

3610 RUSSELL, OSBORNE

JOURNAL OF A TRAPPER; OR, NINE YEARS IN THE
ROCKY MOUNTAINS: 1834–1843 . . . COPYRIGHTED
1914.

[1]–105, [106 blank, 107–9 index, 110 blank].
21.5 x 14 cm. Blue cloth.
 Ref.: Howes R537; Jones 1741; Smith 8877;
Wagner-Camp 75 see
Limited to 100 copies. The manuscript of this
journal is in Yale University Library.
 Imprint on verso of title-leaf: Published by
Syms-York Co., Inc. / Boise, Idaho / 1914 /
From the Original Manuscript. /

3611 RUSSELL, OSBORNE

THE SAME . . . 1921.*

[i]–xviii, [5]–149, [150 blank]. 21.4 x 14.4 cm.
Dark red cloth.
 Ref.: Howes R537; Smith 8878
Limited to 100 copies published by the Syms-
York Company, Inc., Boise, Idaho. With addi-
tional material not in the first edition.

3612 RUSSELL, FORT D. A.

[Photograph] [PARTICIPANTS IN THE JOHNSON
COUNTY WAR, TAKEN IN FRONT OF WAREHOUSE 54,
FORT D. A. RUSSELL]

Photograph: 15 x 20.3 cm. Mount: 17.6 x 22.7
cm.
 Printed in gold on the mount is: Kirkland
Cheyenne, Wyo. / Accompanying the photograph is a typed list identifying all of the individuals except one. Laid in case with Mercer, Asa
S.: *The Banditti of the Plains* . . . [1894].

3613 RUXTON, GEORGE A. F.

MINIATURE PORTRAIT IN OILS ON A THIN SHEET OF
IVORY, UNSIGNED.

Half-length, full face, body turned slightly to his
right. 11.5 x 8.7 cm. In a maroon leather case
15.5 x 12.8 cm.
 Reproduced in *Ruxton of the Rockies* . . .
[1950], provenance described in same.

3614 RUXTON, GEORGE A. F.

THE RUXTON PAPERS. The collection comprises ninety pages of autograph manuscripts, notes, drafts, copies, etc., mostly relating to his travels in America, octavo to large folio, as follows:

Autograph Letter, signed. No year, May 9, no place. Three pages, small 8vo. To his mother.

Autograph Letter, signed with initials. No date, no place. Four pages, small 8vo. To his mother.

Six original pen and ink sketches on five sheets, various sizes. Includes a large self portrait.

Engraved calling card of Ruxton, with manuscript address in his hand. 3.8 x 7.7 cm.

Four photographs of Ruxton's brothers and a niece.

Photograph of the Ruxton family home, Broadoak, Brenchley, Kent. 10.3 x 18.2 cm. on card 13.4 x 20.8 cm.

Broadside: Geographical Club. / [rule] / 1.—The object is the association of Travellers to discuss / [10 lines] / G. F. Ruxton, / Army and Navy Club. / 19.5 x 11.7 cm. Text, 11.3 x 8.4 cm. Printed on blue paper.

Five newspaper clippings mounted on four pages, folio. Reviews of Ruxton's *Adventures in Mexico and the Rocky Mountains* from *Bell's Weekly Messenger*, December 11, 1847; *The Critic*, December 11, 1847; *The Economist*, December 25, 1847; *The Morning Chronicle*, December 27, 1847; and *The Morning Post*, January 1, 1848.

Accompanying the above are the following letters:

Autograph Letter, signed by John Blackwood. 1848 July 11, Edinburgh. Three pages, small 8vo. To Ruxton.

Autograph Letter, signed by Augustus Ruxton. [1848] Sept. 20, Halifax. Four pages, small 8vo. To William Ruxton. Re arrangements for burial of Ruxton.

Autograph Letter, signed by Augustus Ruxton. [1848 September 21 or 22?] Four pages, small 8vo. To Henry Ruxton. Re arrangements for burial of Ruxton.

Autograph Letter in the third person by Sir John Harvey. 1848 September 21, Halifax. To the British Consul at New York. Introducing Augustus Ruxton.

Autograph Letter, signed by Edmund A. Grattan. 1848 September 24, Boston. To the Mayor of the City of St. Louis. One page, 4to. Letter of introduction for Augustus Ruxton.

Autograph Letter, signed by William Elliott. 1848 September 25, Boston. One page, small

4to. To B. H. Cheever. Introducing Augustus Ruxton.

Autograph Letter, signed by John Blackwood. 1848 October 3, Edinburgh. Five pages, small 8vo. To Hay Ruxton. With a contemporary copy of the same.

Autograph Letter, by Hay Ruxton. 1848 October 5, Broad Oak, Brenchley, Kent. Two pages, folio. To John Blackwood. Retained copy.

Autograph Letter, signed by Richard King. 1848 October 5, London. Three pages, 8vo. To Henry Hay Ruxton.

Autograph Letter, signed by John Blackwood. 1848 October 9, Edinburgh. Three pages, small 8vo. To Henry Hay Ruxton.

Autograph Letter, signed by Richard King. 1848 October 7, London. Four pages, small 8vo. To Henry Hay Ruxton.

Autograph Letter, signed by Richard King. October 9, 1848. London. Four pages, small 8vo. To Mrs. Arthy.

Autograph Letter, signed by John Blackwood. 1848 October 28, Edinburgh. Two pages, small 8vo. To Henry Hay Ruxton.

Autograph Letter, signed by John Blackwood. 1848 October 28, Edinburgh. Two pages, small 8vo. To Henry Hay Ruxton. In the blank portions of this letter and across the face of the original is H. H. Ruxton's reply to Blackwood.

Autograph Letter, signed by Augustus Ruxton. [1848] October 31. Four pages, 4to. To his mother. Re burial of Ruxton.

Autograph Letter, signed by John Blackwood. 1848 November 2, Edinburgh. Two pages, small 8vo. To Henry Hay Ruxton.

Autograph Letter, signed by John Blackwood. 1848 December 6, Edinburgh. Three pages, small 8vo. To Henry Hay Ruxton. Re copyright of Ruxton's book.

Autograph Letter, signed by A. Cathcart. No date, no place. Pages 9–12 only, small 4to. To Augustus Ruxton. Accounting for charges against Ruxton's estate, etc.

Autograph Memorandum by Richard King. Undated. One page, small 8vo.

Autograph Letter, signed by Augustus Ruxton. No date, no place. Pages 3–5 only, small 8vo. To his mother.

Autograph Manuscript by Henry Hay Ruxton (incomplete). Four pages, folio. Beginning of a sketch of the career of G.A.F. Ruxton.

Document, signed by C. Th. Colocothoni. 1847, Mai 6, Athens. Three pages, folio. Signed by Colocothoni and others. Passport.

Document, signed by Onorfre Villaseñor. 1847 September 21, Silao. One page, folio. Visa for travel in Mexico.

Document, signed by Francisco Schneider. 1848 September 5, Mexico City. One page, small oblong 8vo. Permit to visit a Mexican market.

Document signed by Lieutenant General De Lacy Evans. 1837 June 3, San Sebastian, Spain. One page, folio. Award of the First Class of the Royal and Military Orders of St. Ferdinand and Isabel 2d.

Unidentified letter in Arabic or Turkish. Seven pages, small 4to.

Autograph Manuscript list by Mrs. Roberts, niece of Ruxton: List of MSS. / G. F. Ruxton /. No date, no place. Four pages, small 8vo. With note by E. G. Roberts dated May 16, 1948. It was from Roberts that the Porters secured this material.

Document, signed by Francisco Lopez and Ed. Fr. Moore. One page, small 4to. 1839 April 1, London. Certifying Ruxton's actions in Spain.

Three typed letters relating to acquisition of the Ruxton Papers.

3615   RUXTON, GEORGE A. F.

AUTOGRAPH MANUSCRIPT NOTEBOOK USED IN 1843.

173 pages used, plus recto of front fly-leaf and back endpaper, some leaves or pages blank. 19 x 5.3 cm. Original black leather backstrip and corners, marbled sides. Worn.

The volume comprises various notes and sketches made principally in North America. There are also a few interspersed pencil drawings. Most of the volume is written in pencil, one passage is inked over the pencil original and there are a few pages in ink.

The materials in this volume were used in *Ruxton of the Rockies* and the provenance of the volume is there described.

3616   RUXTON, GEORGE A. F.

AUTOGRAPH MANUSCRIPT NOTES AND DIARY ENTERED IN: PUNCH'S- POCKET-BOOK, FOR 1845 . . . LONDON: PUNCH OFFICE.

[1]–192. 12.4 x 8.3 cm. Folding frontispiece, engraved title-page, and six engraved plates by Leech. Brown leather, wallet flap, gilt edges.

Ruxton's entries are for January 1 to March 17 and December 11 to 31.

The materials in this volume were used in *Ruxton of the Rockies* and the provenance of the volume is there described.

3617   [RUXTON, GEORGE A. F.]

[Passport] DOCUMENT, SIGNED ABERDEEN. 1844 June 25, London. One page, 44.3 x 27.4 cm. Mostly engraved, partly in manuscript. Bound into maroon leather wallet notebook, stamped on flap: PASSPORT.

On the verso are seven visas, stamped and signed. The notebook comprises sixty pages, seven of which contain certificates of police stations in towns visited by Ruxton and the balance notes in pencil regarding his experiences in Spain. There is also a pencil sketch of Ruxton's servant Halif.

The materials in this volume were used in *Ruxton of the Rockies* and the provenance of the volume is there described.

3618   [RUXTON, GEORGE A. F.]

ISABELLA II OF SPAIN.

National Military Order of San Fernando. Enamel on gold, Maltese cross in white surmounted by green leafy sprays; in centre, an armed and robed king with flags against a yellow ground, encircled by a blue border lettered in gold: Al Merito Militar /. Reverse: same as preceding except centre shows arms of Isabella in gold against a blue ground, with dark blue border lettered in gold: El Rey y la Patria /. Accompanied by enameled pin of four swords, scabbarded in red on gold, joined at pommels. In velvet and silk lined red leather case with gilt borders.

Mentioned in *Ruxton of the Rockies* where the provenance is described.

3619   RUXTON, GEORGE A. F.

LIFE IN THE "FAR WEST." [Extracts from *Blackwood's Magazine*, October to November, 1848, pages 713–32, 17–30, [129]–144, 293–314, 429–43, 573–94. (Pages 591–94 are an obituary. This is present in duplicate as a separate, laid in.) Vols. LXIII–LXIV.]

21 x 13.3 cm.

BOUND WITH:

G. F. RUXTON, ESQ. [Extract from *United Service Magazine Advertiser*, November, 1848, pages [477]–78.]

BOUND WITH:

NOTES ON THE SOUTH-WEST COAST OF AFRICA,— BY LIEUT. RUXTON. COMMUNICATED BY COL. JACKSON, SEC. R. G. S. / [Extract from *The Nautical Magazine, and Naval Chronicle*, January, 1846, pages 4–16.]

BOUND WITH:

THE OREGON QUESTION. A GLANCE AT THE RESPECTIVE CLAIMS OF GREAT BRITAIN AND THE UNITED

STATES, TO THE TERRITORY IN DISPUTE . . . LON-
DON: JOHN OLLIVIER, 1846.

[1]–43, [44 blank].

Ref.: Howes R555; Sabin 74504

BOUND WITH:

SELF PORTRAIT, IN PENCIL. Full length, head in
profile, body three-quarters to his right, in hunting garb, knife at belt, gun in right hand, attended by dog. Signed in pencil. 18.9 x 13 cm.
The dog is identified by Ruxton as Dash.

BOUND WITH:

MANUSCRIPT BY RUXTON IN THE HAND OF HIS
MOTHER, Description of a Day on Lake Erie.
Two pages.

ORIGINAL PENCIL DRAWING, BY RUXTON, of: Tent
in Mexico /, signed, 18.8 x 12.9 cm.

ORIGINAL PENCIL DRAWING, BY RUXTON, of:
Mis-sis-a Ga / the Rattle Snake /, unsigned.
10 x 13.5 cm. Mounted on verso of preceding.

BOUND WITH:

MANUSCRIPT IN THE HAND OF RUXTON'S MOTHER:
Copy of a letter from the / Messrs Blackwood to
Hay Ruxton / on hearing of the death of his
dear Brother /. Two pages, 8vo.

MANUSCRIPT BY RUXTON IN THE HAND OF HIS
MOTHER: My 1st Successful Hunt—(By G F
Ruxton) /. Four pages. 8vo.

MANUSCRIPT BY RUXTON IN THE HAND OF HIS
MOTHER: A Short Sketch of his boyhood—
written by / G F R— /. 21 pages. 8vo.

ORIGINAL PENCIL SKETCH BY RUXTON, self portrait on horseback carrying rifle on shoulder followed by servant bearing rifle, pack and bucket.
12.3 x 17 cm.

MANUSCRIPT BY RUXTON IN THE HAND OF HIS
MOTHER: Snap Shots from the Rocky Moun-
tains / the Death of the Grizzly Bear. G F R /.
Two pages. 8vo.

MANUSCRIPT BY RUXTON IN THE HAND OF HIS
MOTHER: An Irish Sub^s Lament—G F R /. One
page, 8vo. Verse.

ORIGINAL PENCIL SKETCH BY RUXTON: Pesh-Igo—
The Split log / Decr 18—1843 /. 13.5 x 9.2 cm.
Part of the title has been inked over pencil.

ORIGINAL PEN AND INK SKETCH BY RUXTON, WITH
TITLE IN THE HAND OF HIS MOTHER: The Irish Sub
Paying his Monthly / Mess Bill /. 11.6 x 18.6 cm.

Full diced purple roan, with blind borders, lettered in gilt on front cover: George F. Ruxton,
Esqr / Member of the / Royal Geographical Society, / The Ethnological Society. / &c. &c. /
Rebacked with black leather.

The present volume was compiled as a kind of
memorial by the author's mother. In addition to
the material described above, there is a short
newspaper clipping announcing the Queen's permission to Ruxton to accept and wear a military
decoration from the Queen of Spain. There are
also included six short newspaper obituaries and
a short article about Ruxton.

The materials incorporated in this volume
were used in *Ruxton of the Rockies* and the
provenance of the volume is there described.

3620 RUXTON, GEORGE F.

ADVENTURES IN MEXICO AND THE ROCKY MOUN-
TAINS . . . LONDON: JOHN MURRAY, 1847.

[1–2 advertisement], [1]–viii, [1]–332, [1]–16 advertisements. 17.7 x 11.7 cm. Red embossed
cloth, top uncut, fore and lower edges trimmed.

Ref.: Field 1336; Howes R553; Munk (Alliot) p. 196; Sabin 74501; Saunders 3137; Wagner-Camp 139

Murray's Colonial & Home Library binding.

3621 RUXTON, GEORGE F.

ANOTHER COPY. With bookplate of John Thomas
Lee.

3622 RUXTON, GEORGE F.

THE SAME.

[i]–viii, 177–332. 17.8 x 12.3 cm. Tan printed
wrappers, with title on front wrapper, backstrip,
reading up, advertisements on verso of front and
recto and verso of back wrapper.

Issued in this form the same year as the first
edition. Part II only.

3623 RUXTON, GEORGE F.

LIFE IN THE FAR WEST . . . EDINBURGH: WILLIAM
BLACKWOOD AND SONS, M.DCCC.XLIX.

[i]–xvi, [1]–312. 18.5 x 11.9 cm. Red cloth, blind
stamped sides, gilt on backstrip, uncut.

Ref.: Howes R554; Smith 8890; Wagner-
Camp 173

3624 [RUYSDALE, PHILIP]

A PILGRIMAGE OVER THE PRAIRIES . . . LONDON:
T. CAUTLEY NEWBY, 1863.

[i–ii advertisements, iii–iv], [1]–298. [i–ii advertisements, iii–iv], [1]–313, [314 blank, 315–16 ad-
vertisements]. (313 mispaginated 261.) 19.3 x
12.2 cm. Two volumes, maroon cloth, blind embossed sides, gilt title on backstrips, uncut.

Ref.: Howes R556; Sabin 62846; Wagner-
Camp 394

A romance, incorporating an 1825 trip to the
Rockies and the Wind River Blackfeet.—Howes

Copies appear containing six plates, but none
have been included in the present copy.

3625 RYAN, JOHN G.

LIFE AND ADVENTURES OF GEN. W. A. C. RYAN, THE CUBAN MARTYR. CAPTURED ON THE STEAMER VIRGINIUS, AND MURDERED BY THE SPANIARDS AT SANTIAGO, CUBA, NOV. 4, 1873 . . . NEW YORK, 1876.

[I]–[VI], 7–256. 16.5 x 12 cm. Gray printed front wrapper and most of backstrip, with title on front wrapper. Back wrapper supplied. In a dark red cloth folder.

Ref.:

Ryan went to Montana with Captain Fisk in 1866. The work contains an interesting account of his adventures there.

3626 RYAN, WILLIAM R.

PERSONAL ADVENTURES IN UPPER AND LOWER CALIFORNIA, IN 1848–9; WITH THE AUTHOR'S EXPERIENCE AT THE MINES . . . LONDON: WILLIAM SHOBERL, 1850.

[1]–4 advertisements, [i]–[viii, viii blank], [1]–347, [348 colophon]. [i–ii], [1]–413, [414 colophon]. 19.7 x 12.4 cm. 23 illustrations listed. Two volumes, red cloth, vignettes on covers, gilt on fronts and blind on backs, blind embossed borders, title stamped in gilt on backstrips, uncut.

Ref.: Bradford 4767; Cowan p. 547; Howes R558; Sabin 74532; Wheat (*Gold Rush*) 173

The charming narrative of an artist and bohemian who left unrecorded but little that he saw. His descriptions are among the best of his time.—Cowan

3627 RYERSON, JOHN

HUDSON'S BAY; OR, A MISSIONARY TOUR IN THE TERRITORY OF THE HON. HUDSON'S BAY COMPANY . . . TORONTO: G. R. SANDERSON, 1855.

[i]–xiv, [1]–190. 17.5 x 10.5 cm. Ten plates unlisted. Gray blind stamped cloth, gilt backstrip, with title.

Ref.: Sabin 74586; Smith 8901; Staton & Tremaine 3608; Wagner-Camp 270

3628 RYUS, WILLIAM H.

THE SECOND WILLIAM PENN: A TRUE ACCOUNT OF INCIDENTS THAT HAPPENED ALONG THE OLD SANTA FE TRAIL IN THE SIXTIES . . . KANSAS CITY, MO.: PRESS OF FRANK T. RILEY PUBLISHING CO.*

[1]–176. (Pages [1–2] blank.) 19 x 13.4 cm. Nine illustrations, unlisted. Yellow pictorial cloth.

Ref.: Howes (1954) 8882; Rader 2865

Copyrighted 1913.

S

3629 SABIN, EDWIN L.

LETTER, SIGNED. 1926 May 31, La Jolla, California. To Wright Howes. One page, 17.7 x 15.2 cm.

Ordering a book. Laid in Sabin: *Kit Carson Days* . . . 1914.

3630 SABIN, EDWIN L.

KIT CARSON DAYS (1809–1868) . . . CHICAGO: A. C. McCLURG & CO., 1914.

[i]–[xvi, xvi blank], 1–669, [670 blank]. 20.1 x 14.1 cm. Illustrations listed. Brown ribbed cloth.

Ref.: Howes S1; Rader 2867

Laid in is a Letter, signed by the author. 1926 May 31.

3631 SABIN, EDWIN L.

THE SAME . . . NEW YORK: THE PRESS OF THE PIONEERS, INC., 1935.

[i]–[xiii], [xiv blank, xv–xvi fly-title (verso blank)], [1]–488. [i]–[ix], [x blank, xi–xii fly-title, (verso blank)], [489]–996, [997 colophon, 998 blank]. 22.9 x 15.2 cm. Illustrations listed. Two volumes, dark green buckram.

Ref.: Howes S1; Rader 2867; Saunders 3140

Limited to 1000 copies.

3632 SACRAMENTO THEATER

[Broadside] SACRAMENTO THEATER! . . . THIS (MONDAY) EVENING, JULY 27TH, WILL BE PRESENTED, FOR THE SECOND TIME, AN ENTIRE NEW DRAMA, IN THREE ACTS, WRITTEN BY MR. C. E. B'NGHAM[!], ENTITLED THE CAPTIVITY AND MASSACRE OF THE OATMAN FAMILY! BY THE APACHE & MOHAVE INDIANS! . . . DAILY BEE PRINT.

Broadside, 45.1 x 14.8 cm. Text, 41.8 x 12.1 cm. Printed on bright yellow paper.

Ref.:

The part of Olive Oatman was played by Miss Sophie Edwin. The date was probably 1857.

Laid in Stratton: *Life Among the Indians* . . . 1857.

3633 [SAGE, RUFUS B.]

SCENES IN THE ROCKY MOUNTAINS, AND IN OREGON, CALIFORNIA, NEW MEXICO, TEXAS, AND THE GRAND PRAIRIES; OR, NOTES BY THE WAY, DURING AN EXCURSION OF THREE YEARS . . . PHILADELPHIA: PUBLISHED BY CAREY & HART, 1846.

[i]–xii, [13]–303, [304 blank]. 18.3 x 12.2 cm. Folding map: Map / of / Oregon, California, / New Mexico, N. W. Texas, / & / the proposed Territory of / Ne-Bras-Ka. / By / Rufus B. Sage. / [thick and four thin rules] / 1846. /

F. Michelin's Lith. 111, Nassau St / N. Y. / 44.2 x 61 cm. Scale not given. Green cloth, blind embossed sides, title in gilt on backstrip. In a green half morocco case.

Ref.: Bradford 4774; Cowan pp. 548–49; Howell 274; Howes S16; Rader 2870; Raines p. 181; Sabin 74892; Saunders 3141; Smith 8923; Wagner-Camp 123; Wheat (*Gold Region*) 30; Wheat (*Transmississippi*) 527

In the present copy, the pagination is correctly placed at the outer margins on pages 77–88, 270, 271, 302.

3634 [SAGE, RUFUS B.]

THE SAME.

Cream printed wrappers with title on front cover: Price Fifty Cents. / [wavy rule] / Scenes in the / Rocky Mountains, / Oregon, California, New Mexico, / Texas and Grand Prairies: / or, / Notes by the Way During / an Excursion of Three Years: / with a Description of / the Countries Passed through. / By a New Englander. / Price 50 Cents. / Philadelphia: / Carey & Hart, 126 Chesnut Street, / For Sale by G. B. Zieber & Co., Philadelphia; W. H. Graham, New York; / Redding & Co. and Halliburton & Co., Boston; Wm. Taylor & Co. and / N. Hickman, Baltimore; Drinker & Morris and Nash & Woodhouse, / Richmond, Va.; J. W. Cook, Pittsburg; C. W. Noble, Louisville, Ky.; / C. Marshall, Lexington, Ky.; Robinson & Jones, Cincinnati; / J. C. Morgan, J. B. Steel and B. M. Norman, New Orleans, / and M. Boullemet, Mobile. / 1846. / [within wavy rule borders with corner ornaments], title on backstrip reading up: Scenes in the Rocky Mountains. /, advertisements on verso of front and recto and verso of back wrapper. In a brown half morocco case.

According to Carey & Hart's letter 1846 August 27, the first hundred copies were issued in wrappers. In their letter of 1846 September 19 there is mention of a "fine edition on calendered paper with the map."

This is a sophisticated copy. The title-leaf, map, and pages [xi]–xii have been supplied from another copy.

Enclosed in the case with the book is a copy of *The Whig Battering-Ram, or Straightout Revived*, Vol. 1, Number 5, City of Columbus, Friday, Sept. 6, 1844. Rufus B. Sage, Editor.

3635 SAGE, RUFUS B.

THE SAME . . . SECOND EDITION REVISED. PHILADELPHIA: CAREY AND HART, 1847.

[i]–xii, [13]–303, [304 blank]. 17.3 x 11.2 cm. Rebound in brown half morocco, gilt top.

Prov.: Bookplate of John Thomas Lee.

Printed from the plates of the 1846 edition. The only revision is the title-page which shows Sage as the author.—EDG

3636 SAGEAN, MATHIEU

THE ORIGINAL MANUSCRIPT ACCOUNT OF THE KINGDOM OF AACINABA . . . LONDON, PRINTED FOR THE TRANSLATOR, MDCCLV.

[*]², A–B², C¹. [i–iv], 1–10. 36 x 22.8 cm. New marbled boards, green morocco back and corners, green morocco label on front cover.

Prov.: Inscribed on blank leaf at front: To / The Rᵗ Honrᵇˡᵉ Earl of Loudon, &c, &c, &ca / My Lord / Please accept this Ensueing Account of Aca[naba] / as a Pledge of The Hereditary Respects with which I have the honour to [be?] / My Lord / Your Lordship's / most humble & most obedient Servan[t] / Quin Mackenzie / London, 31ˢᵗ of July 1755. / The last line on the title-page has been crossed out and the following inserted: (*No Money*).

Ref.: Field 1347; *The Month*, Vol. 34, Nos. 4–5, pp. 92–5; Howes S17; Sabin 74898

A curious production, this fraud is closely related to the imaginary parts of Lahontan's work. The result of the writing of the original manuscript was, as Mackenzie points out in the title, the establishment of the Mississippi Company.

3637 SAINT-AMANT, PIERRE CHARLES FOURNIER DE

VOYAGE EN CALIFORNIE, 1850–1851 . . . PARIS: CHEZ GARNIER FRERES, 1851.

[1]–48. 22 x 14.2 cm. Cream printed wrappers, with title on front wrapper, advertisement on verso of back wrapper.

Ref.: Cowan p. 549; Howes S20 note; Monaghan 1289; Sabin 74988

Saint-Amant was French consul at Sacramento.

3638 ST. CHARLES BULLETIN, THE, Cairo, Illinois

[Broadside] THE ST CHARLES BULLETIN. CAIRO, ILLINOIS FRIDAY, APRII[!] 18TH. 1874. THE ST HARLES[!] BULLETIN. O DEVOTED TO THE NEWS OF THE ST CHARLES HOTEL &C W. J. WILCOX, EDITOR ISSUED . . . DAILY. PENCIL PIOINTS.[!] . . .

Broadside, 12.9 x 10.1 cm. Text, 10.4 x 7.3 cm.

Ref.:

An amateur production.

3639 ST. CLAIR, ARTHUR

A NARRATIVE OF THE MANNER IN WHICH THE CAMPAIGN AGAINST THE INDIANS, IN THE YEAR

ONE THOUSAND SEVEN HUNDRED AND NINETY-ONE, WAS CONDUCTED . . . PHILADELPHIA: PRINTED BY JANE AITKEN, 1812.

[1]⁴, 2–4², [2N]²⁻⁴, 20–2P⁴, 2Q², A⁴, C–2M⁴, 2N. [i]–[xx, xx blank], [1–26], [1]–273, [274 blank]. 23.3 x 14.8 cm. Gray boards, tan paper back, printed paper label, uncut. In a green cloth case, morocco back.

Ref.: Buley I, pp. 13, 18, 58, 96; II, pp. 3–4; Field 1349; Howes S24; Jones 757; Sabin 75020; Thomson 1012

St. Clair's was one of the most humiliating disasters suffered by the United States Army at the hands of the Indians.

This copy contains twenty-two pages of subscribers' names and a list of errata, verso blank.

3640 [ST. JOHN, PERCY BOLINGBROKE(?)]

A HUNTER'S EXPERIENCES IN THE SOUTHERN STATES OF AMERICA BEING AN ACCOUNT OF THE NATURAL HISTORY OF THE VARIOUS QUADRUPEDS AND BIRDS WHICH ARE THE OBJECTS OF CHASE IN THOSE COUNTRIES . . . LONDON: LONGMANS, GREEN, AND CO., 1866.

[i–vi, vi blank], [1]–359, [360 blank]. 18.8 x 11.8 cm. Original dark green morocco, gilt back, lettered in gilt on front cover, marbled edges.

Prov.: Inscribed on blank leaf at front: Algernon Mercer, / Prize for "English" Subjects / Cl. iii, div. x. / J. H. / Christmas, 1872. / And with the bookplate of Algernon Mercer.

Ref.: Dobie pp. 52, 147; Howes S32; Raines p. 83

On the title-page the work is ascribed to Captain Flack.

3641 ST. JOHN, PERCY BOLINGBROKE

THE TRAPPER'S BRIDE: A TALE OF THE ROCKY MOUNTAINS. WITH THE ROSE OF OUISCONSIN. INDIAN TALES . . . LONDON: JOHN MORTIMER, 1845.

[i–viii, viii blank], [1]–166. 17 x 10.4 cm. Plum cloth, blind embossed sides, title stamped in gilt on backstrip. Lacks front endleaf, labels removed from front and back endpapers.

Ref.: Sabin 75261 see; Wagner-Camp 118

The first tale is based on Fort Bent. According to the Advertisement on page [vi] the author lived "in the wilds of America, the back woods of Texas."

This is the only copy recorded by Wagner-Camp.

3642 ST. JOSEPH, Missouri

THE ORDINANCES OF THE CITY OF ST. JOSEPH, PASSED BY THE CITY COUNCIL, IN THE YEAR 1851, WITH THE CONSTITUTIONS OF THE UNITED STATES AND THE STATE OF MISSOURI; THE VARIOUS CHARTERS OF, AND LAWS APPLICABLE TO THE TOWN AND CITY OF ST. JOSEPH . . . ST. JOSEPH: WM. RIDENBAUGH, CITY PRINTER, 1851.

[1]–187, [188 blank]. 21.8 x 13.9 cm. Brown marbled boards with sheep backstrip and corners.

Ref.:

This is the first book printed at St. Joseph. No other copy has been located.

3643 ST. JOSEPH GAZETTE

[Newspaper] ST. JOSEPH GAZETTE. BY WM. RIDENBAUGH. ST. JOSEPH, MO. WEDNESDAY, JUNE 11, 1851. VOL. VI—NO. 34 . . .

[1–4]. 59.3 x 43.2 cm. Unbound.

Ref.:

Contains on the first page a long letter by General Thomas Jefferson Sutherland to Luke Lea, Commissioner of Indian Affairs, relative to Indian depredations. Sutherland mentions the appearance of an article on the subject in *The Frontier Guardian* for May 16, 1851, which issue is present in the Graff Collection.

3644 ST. LOUIS, Missouri

[Wrapper title] REPORT OF THE CELEBRATION OF THE ANNIVERSARY OF THE FOUNDING OF ST. LOUIS, IN THE FIFTEENTH DAY OF FEBRUARY, A. D. 1847. PREPARED FOR THE MISSOURI REPUBLICAN. PRINTED BY CHAMBERS & KNAPP, 1847.

[1]–32. 14.5 x 16.9 cm. Buff printed wrappers, with title as above on front wrapper.

Ref.: AII (*Missouri*) 539; Howes P609; Sabin 75374

AII (*Missouri*) lists this under Wilson Primm, who gave the principal address.

3645 ST. LOUIS. CHAMBER OF COMMERCE

REPORT OF THE COMMITTEE APPOINTED BY THE CHAMBER OF COMMERCE TO EXAMINE THE AFFAIRS OF THE OHIO AND MISSISSIPPI RAILROAD COMPANY. ST. LOUIS: PRINTED BY USTICK, STUDLEY & CO., 1855.

[1]–94, [95–6 blank]. 20.6 x 13.7 cm. Bound with three other pamphlets in contemporary half green leather.

Ref.:

BOUND WITH:

Report of the Board of Directors of the North Missouri Railroad Company to the Stockholders, Made first Monday of April, 1866. No place, no date. [1]–114. With map.

BOUND WITH:

Annual Statement of the Trade and Commerce of St. Louis for the Year 1865 . . . by George H. Morgan . . . Saint Louis: R. P. Studley and Co., 1866. [1]–116, [i]–xv, [xvi blank].

BOUND WITH:

Geological Report of the Country along the Line of the South-Western Branch of the Pacific Railroad, State of Missouri, by G. C. Swallow . . . St. Louis: George Knapp & Co., 1859. [i]–xvii, [xviii blank], [1]–93, [94 blank, 95 errata, 96 blank]. With map.

3646 ST. LOUIS. CITIZENS

MEMORIAL OF THE CITIZENS OF ST. LOUIS, MISSOURI, TO THE CONGRESS OF THE UNITED STATES, PRAYING AN APPROPRIATION FOR REMOVING THE OBSTRUCTION TO THE NAVIGATION OF THE WESTERN RIVERS, FOR THE IMPROVEMENT OF THE ST. LOUIS HARBOR AND FOR OTHER PURPOSES. ST. LOUIS, MO. PRINTED BY CHAMBERS & KNAPP. 1844.

[1]–24. 22.5 x 15.1 cm. Blue printed wrappers, with title on front wrapper.
Ref.: AII (*Missouri*) 422; Sabin 75355

3647 ST. MARY GAZETTE, St. Mary, Iowa

[Broadside] ST. MARY GAZETTE. EXTRA. ST. MARY, IOWA, TUESDAY, JANUARY 24, 1854. IMPORTANT GOVERNMENT INSTRUCTIONS IN REGARD TO INDIAN TERRITORY . . .

Broadside, 20.7 x 14.3 cm. Text, 12.5 x 11.7 cm.
Ref.:
From text: The district of country embraced in this proposition to buy [from the Indians] is about one half of the reserved lands included within the bounds of Nebraska Territory. It is all of that country fronting on the Missouri, opposite to Iowa and that part of the State of Missouri, above the Great Nemaha.

3648 SAINT PAUL. CITIZENS

PROCEEDINGS OF A PUBLIC MEETING OF CITIZENS OF MINNESOTA, IN FAVOR OF A SEMI-WEEKLY OVERLAND MAIL FROM SAINT PAUL TO PUGET SOUND. HELD JANUARY 3, 1859. SAINT PAUL: PIONEER PRINTING COMPANY, 1859.

[1]–16. 21.3 x 14.9 cm. Buff printed wrappers, with title on front wrapper, and on verso of back wrapper.
Prov.: See below.
Ref.: AII (*Minnesota*) 271; Sabin 49297
Probably the personal copy of Aaron Goodrich. On page 9, a note in pencil signed by him: This part of my speech is not correctly / reported. / Goodrich. /

3649 SAINT PAUL BRIDGE COMPANY

CONSTITUTION AND BY-LAWS OF THE SAINT PAUL BRIDGE CO. SAINT PAUL, MIN. SAINT PAUL: MINNESOTIAN JOB PRINT, 1858.

[1]–10, [i–ii], [11]–16. 12.9 x 9.1 cm. Yellow printed wrappers, with title on front wrapper.
Ref.: AII (*Minnesota*) 230
Leaf inserted between pages 10 and [11]: An Act / To amend an Act to incorporate the Saint Paul / Bridge Company . . .

3650 SAINT PAUL PRESS, THE

[Newspaper] THE SAINT PAUL PRESS. VOLUME V. SAINT PAUL, THURSDAY [–FRIDAY], JUNE 8 [–9], 1865. NUMBER 130 [–131] . . .

Two issues, each [1–4]. 62.3 x 47.8 cm. Unbound.
Ref.:
The earlier number contains an article on page [1] regarding the Fisk Expedition to Idaho, and on page [2] a longer article on the same subject copied from the *Washington Chronicle*. The later issue contains on the first page a long advertisement for the Colony for the Yellowstone Country signed by Fisk.

3651 ST. PETER COMPANY

[Broadside] OFFICE ST. PETER COMPANY, ST. PETER NICOLLET COUNTY, M.T. JULY, 1856. THIS ELIGIBLY LOCATED AND BEAUTIFUL TOWN IS SITUATE ON THE MINNESOTA RIVER . . . ALL INQUIRIES OR COMMUNICATIONS IN REFERENCE TO THE TOWN AND SURROUNDING COUNTRY ADDRESSED TO GEORGE HEZLEP, AGENT ST. PETER COMPANY, ST. PETER, NICOLLET COUNTY, M.T., WILL BE PROMPTLY ATTENDED TO.

Broadside, 24.5 x 38.3 cm., folded to 24.5 x 19.1 cm., with fold at right. Text, 10.7 x 17 cm.
Ref.:
Following the printed text, there is a manuscript note as follows: firend[!], L. unless I write in all / of them you may think I wasted / paper in this wooden Country / yours to the end of the / work / E D Ingersoll /.

3652 SALAZAR YLARREGUI, JOSE

DATOS DE LOS TRABAJOS ASTRONOMICOS Y TOPOGRAFICOS, DISPUESTOS EN FORMA DE DIARIO. PRACTICADOS DURANTE EL ANO DE 1849 Y PRINCIPIOS DE 1850 POR LA COMISION DE LIMITES MEXICANA EN LA LINEA QUE DIVIDE ESTA REPUBLICA DE LA DE LOS ESTADOS-UNIDOS, POR EL GEOMETRA DE DICHA COMISION . . . MEXICO: IMPRENTA DE JUAN R. NAVARRO, 1850.

[I]–V, [VI blank], [7]–123, [124 blank]. 21.7 x 14.3 cm. Two folding maps: Map: Plano / de la confluencia de los rios / Gila y Colorado / y del curso de este último hasta donde lo corta la linea que divide las republicas de / [ornament] Mexico y los Estados Unidos [ornament] / [rule] / En este plano van indicadas todas las operaciones que hizo la comision mexicana para levantarlo. / Cópia del que presentó al Sr. Gral D. Pedro García-Conde, como comisario de dicha comision / el agrimensor de la misma / José Salazar Ilarregui / Año de 1850 / [short rule] / [lower right:] Lito. de Salazar. / 21.7 x 41.5 cm. Scale: about 85 yards to one inch. Map: Plano de la parte austral del puerto de S. Diego, y del terreno / comprendido entre dicha parte, el punto inicial en la costa del / Pacifico y la sesta estacion hecha en la dirrecion de la linea que / divide las repúblicas de México y de los Estados-Unidos. / En este plano van indicadas las operaciones que hizo la comision mexicana para levantarlo y para determinar con arreglo al / tratado de Guadalupe Hidalgo, el punto mas austral del referido puerto. / Cópia del que presentó al Sr. general D. Pedro García Conde, como comisario de dicha / comision, el agrimenso de la misma C. José Salazar Ilarregui. / Año de 1850. / 23.7 x 41.3 cm. No scale given. *Inset:* Cópia del plano del puerto de S. Diego en la costa selen-/trional de Californias. Levantado por el segundo piloto de / la armada D. Juan de Pantoja en el año de / 1782. / 11.5 x 7.3 cm. Scale: about 6 maritime miles to one inch. Rebound in red half morocco, gilt top.

Ref.: Barrett 2191; Howes S47; Sabin 75598; Wagner-Camp 190

Salazar's account of the Boundary Survey was published before the United States report and is the first accurate description of the country.

3653 [SALES, LUIS]

NOTICIAS DE LA PROVINCIA DE CALIFORNIAS EN TRES CARTAS . . . EN VALENCIA: POR LOS HERMANOS DE ORGA, M.DCC.XCIV.

A–F⁸, G⁴, A–F⁸, A–F⁸, G⁴. [1]–104, [1]–96, [1]–104. 14.5 x 10 cm. Two folding tables between pages 98 and 99. Vellum. Lacks front endleaf.

Ref.: Barrett 2192; Bradford 4777; Cowan p. 550; Hanna-Powell p. 16; Howes S52; Jones 647; Medina (*BHA*) 5649; Sabin 38381, 56007, 75765; Streit III 1174; Wagner (*SS*) 177

This book, which contains interesting material on the Nootka embroglio and Martinez's capture of Colnett, is said to have been suppressed. It was the only work on California written by a Dominican.—Howes

3654 [SALPOINTE, JEAN BAPTISTE]

A BRIEF SKETCH OF THE MISSION OF SAN XAVIER DE BAC, WITH A DESCRIPTION OF ITS CHURCH . . . TUCSON, A. T.: PRINTED AT THE ARIZONA STAR JOB PRINTING OFFICE, 1880.

[1]–22, [23–24 blank]. (Pages [1–2] blank.) 22 x 14.3 cm. Blue printed wrappers with title on front wrapper, uncut, partly unopened.

Ref.: AII (*Arizona*) 51; Howes S54

3655 [SALPOINTE, JEAN BAPTISTE]

THE SAME . . . SAN FRANCISCO: THOMAS' STEAM PRINTING HOUSE, 1880.

[1]–20. 23.1 x 14.6 cm. Lavender printed wrappers, with title on front wrapper.

Prov.: Inscribed on front wrapper: Compliments of Father Derachés / to Miss Fremont. / *Ref.:* Munk (Alliot) p. 196; Howes S54

3656 SALT LAKE CITY, Utah

CHARTER OF GREAT SALT LAKE CITY AND ORDINANCES AND RESOLUTIONS OF THE CITY COUNCIL, WITH CONSTITUTION OF THE UNITED STATES, AND ORGANIC ACT OF THE TERRITORY OF UTAH . . . DESERET NEWS PRINT, 1860.

[I]–XXIII, [XXIV blank], [i]–xliv, [1]–75, [1]–6, [7–8 blank]. 19.1 x 12.7 cm. Marbled boards, green leather backstrip, typed label.

Prov.: Auerbach copy.
Ref.: McMurtrie (*Utah*) 42; Sabin 75840
Printed at Salt Lake City.

3657 SALTER, WILLIAM

AUTOGRAPH LETTER, SIGNED. November 30, 1900. Burlington, Iowa. One page, 21.6 x 14 cm. To Frank E. Stevens.

Regarding sale of a copy of the writer's *The Life of Henry Dodge* and a note about the occasion on which the writer saw Black Hawk.

3658 SALTER, WILLIAM

AUTOGRAPH LETTER, SIGNED. December 6, 1900. Burlington, Iowa. One page, 21.6 x 14 cm. To Frank E. Stevens.

Regarding securing a copy of a book for the recipient.

Both letters laid in Salter: *The Life of Henry Dodge* . . . 1890.

3659 SALTER, WILLIAM

THE LIFE OF HENRY DODGE, FROM 1782 TO 1833 . . . BURLINGTON, IOWA, 1890.

[i–ii], [1]–76, [77–8 blank]. 23.5 x 15.1 cm. Portrait by George Catlin and two maps. Gray printed wrappers, bound into gray boards, black cloth backstrip.

Ref.: Mott (*Iowa*) p. 44

Several manuscript changes and corrections are in the hand of the author.

Laid in are two Autograph Letters, signed, by the author, 1900 November 30 and December 6.

3660 SALTER, WILLIAM

MEMOIRS OF JOSEPH W. PICKETT, MISSIONARY SUPERINTENDENT IN SOUTHERN IOWA AND IN THE ROCKY MOUNTAINS FOR THE AMERICAN HOME MISSIONARY SOCIETY . . . BURLINGTON, IOWA: JAMES LOVE, 1880.

[1]–150. (Pages [1–2] blank.) 18.5 x 12.2 cm. Brown cloth, blind embossed sides, title in gilt on backstrip.

Ref.: Mott (*Iowa*) p. 44

3661 SALZBACHER, JOSEPH

MEINE REISE NACH NORD-AMERIKA IM JAHRE 1842 . . . WIEN: IN COMMISSION BEI WIMMER, SCHMIDT & LEO, 1845.

[1–2], [i]–[x, x blank], [1]–68, [I]–XII, [69]–[480], [481 advertisements, 482 blank]. 21.8 x 13.7 cm. Map: Karte / der katholischen / dioecesen und deren Missionen / in / Nordamerika / nach den / neuesten geographischen / Angaben / zusamengestellt und herausgegeben / von / D^{or} Joseph Salzbacher / Comcapitular zu St: Stephan in Wien / 1845 / . . . / [below border at left:] Steindr. v. H. Engel in Wien. / [at right:] Lith. v. Hauptm. Baron Liechtenstern. / 46.4 x 52. 6 cm. Scale: about 75 miles to one inch. Marbled boards with green cloth back.

Ref.: Buck 373; Clark III 233; Howes S58

Dr. Salzbacher toured the South first and went as far west as St. Louis. Later, he traveled east via Chicago. His primary concern was an examination of Roman Catholic institutions.

3662 SAMPLE, HUGH W.

INAUGURAL ADDRESS OF HUGH W. SAMPLE, ESQ. MAYOR OF THE CITY OF KEOKUK, DELIVERED APRIL 15, 1858 . . . KEOKUK: DAILY GATE CITY PRINT, 1858.

[1]–[19], [20 blank]. 22.3 x 14.4 cm. Buff printed wrappers with title on front wrapper.

Ref.: Moffit 384

3663 SAMPLE, HUGH W.

THE SAME. Removed from bound volume, but in original wrappers. In a gray cloth case.

3664 SAN DIEGO. CHAMBER OF COMMERCE

DESCRIPTIVE, HISTORICAL, COMMERCIAL, AGRICULTURAL, AND OTHER IMPORTANT INFORMATION RELATIVE TO THE CITY OF SAN DIEGO, CALIFORNIA . . . ALSO A BUSINESS DIRECTORY OF THE CITY . . . SAN DIEGO: PRINTED AT THE OFFICE OF THE "SAN DIEGO DAILY UNION," 1874.

[1–4], [inserted, unpaginated leaf], [5]–[66]. 22 x 14.2 cm. 22 original photographs in sepia mounted with printed captions opposite title-page, and on pages [52–62]. Blue printed wrappers, with title on front wrapper, advertisements on verso of front and recto and verso of back wrapper.

Ref.: Cowan p. 551; Howes S67

On pages [53–63] there are two photographs per page, each page within double rule borders and with a rule across the middle. Pages [63–6] similarly ruled but without photographs and captions. Page [51] is blank.

3665 SAN FRANCISCO. COMMITTEE OF VIGILANCE

CONSTITUTION AND ADDRESS[!] OF THE COMMITTEE OF VIGILANCE OF SAN FRANCISCO. SAN FRANCISCO: MORNING GLOBE PRINT, 1856.

[1]–8. 22.6 x 13.5 cm. Unbound, unopened.

Ref.: Cowan p. 140; Greenwood 743

Prov.: Bookplate of Robert E. Cowan.

The embossed seal of the Committee appears on page 5.

3666 SAN FRANCISCO OVERLAND AND OCEAN MAIL LETTER

[Caption title] PUBLISHED SEMI-WEEKLY, IN TIME FOR THE OVERLAND AND OCEAN MAIL, AT THE OFFICE 134 CLAY STREET, SAN FRANCISCO, AND TO BEHAD[!] OF ALL THE BOOKSELLERS IN SAN FRANCISCO, AND AT THE MAIL STATIONS ON THE LINES OF TRAVEL. SAN FRANCISCO OVERLAND AND OCEAN MAIL LETTER. A SUMMARY OF EVENTS FROM MAIL TO MAIL, AND TRAVELLERS' GUIDE TO THE PACIFIC COAST. NO. 2. SAN FRANCISCO, SATURDAY, NOV. 20, 1858. VOL. I . . .

[1–4]. 31.8 x 19.5 cm. Punched and tied with silk ribbon. Printed on blue paper.

Ref.:

Below the border on page [1]: Printed at the Commercial Steam Book and Job Printing Establishment, 129 Sansome Street. /

Page [4] of the original is blank except for a return address, reading up: The San Francisco Overland and Ocean Mail Letter. / Saturday, November 20th, 1858. / An address in manuscript follows: Hon. I. Thompson, / Washington, / D. C. / Page [4] of the Supplement is docketed in manuscript, reading in part: Rec'd 14 Dec: '58 / W W. Bland /

Accompanying the above and bound with it is a Supplement, same caption title as above except first two lines replaced by Supplement. / [1–3], [4 blank]. Printed on blue ruled paper. Text of the Supplement deals mainly with the Almaden Mining Case.

3667 SANDERS, SUE A.

A JOURNEY TO, ON AND FROM THE "GOLDEN SHORE" . . . DELAVAN, ILL.: TIMES PRINTING OFFICE, 1887.

[1]–118. 19.4 x 13.3 cm. Dark brown cloth, title stamped in gilt on front cover.

Ref.:

Account of a six-weeks trip to California in 1886 to attend a G. A. R. Encampment in San Francisco.—EDG

3668 [SANDERSON, J. L.]

BIOGRAPHICAL SKETCH OF COL. J. L. SANDERSON, OF ST. LOUIS MO. KANSAS CITY, MO.: RAMSEY, MILLETT & HUDSON, 1880.

[1]–8. 19.6 x 12.9 cm. Frontispiece printed in blue. Green semi-limp calf, with blind decorative borders and title in gilt on front cover.

Ref.:

Inserted on the recto of the frontispiece is an oval photograph of Sanderson, with his signature beneath the portrait.

Biographical sketch of one of the founders and (in 1880) the sole owner of the famous Barlow and Sanderson's Stage Lines. Most of these enterprises started from Kansas City. After the Civil War, Barlow and Sanderson stages ran to Santa Fé and Arizona, and later, in Colorado, Canon City, Leadville, etc. were covered by the line.—EDG

3669 SANDS, FRANK

A PASTORAL PRINCE. THE HISTORY AND REMINISCENCES OF J. W. COOPER . . . SANTA BARBARA, CAL., 1893.

[I]–[XVI, XVI blank], [1]–190. (Pages [I] blank, [II] frontispiece.) 19.1 x 13.7 cm. Four portraits. Brown cloth, pictorial front cover in gilt, another scene on back cover in black, title stamped on backstrip in black.

Ref.: Cowan p. 566; Howes S90

This thrilling account of early California includes a section on the first sheep drive across the continent to California.—EDG

3670 SANFORD, HENRY S.

CORRESPONDENCE ON THE OCCASION OF THE PRESENTATION BY MAJOR-GENERAL SANFORD, UNITED STATES MINISTER RESIDENT AT THE COURT OF BRUSSELS, OF A BATTERY OF STEEL CANNON, TO THE STATE OF MINNESOTA, FOR THE USE OF THE FIRST MINNESOTA REGIMENT OF VOLUNTEERS. SAINT PAUL: OFFICE OF THE PRESS PRINTING COMPANY, 1862.

[1]–12. 21.7 x 13.7 cm. Yellow printed wrappers, with title on front wrapper.

Ref.: AII (*Minnesota*) 461

3671 SANFORD, JOHN F.

INTRODUCTORY LECTURE, DELIVERED IN THE COLLEGE OF PHYSICIANS AND SURGEONS OF THE UPPER MISSISSIPPI. SESSION OF 1849–50 . . . DAVENPORT: SANDERS & DAVIS, PRINTERS, 1849.

[1]–13, [14 advertisements, 15–16 blank]. 21.5 x 14 cm. Yellow printed wrappers with title on front wrapper.

Prov.: Inscribed on front wrapper: "Boston Med. & Surgical Journal" / With Respects of Author. /

Ref.: Moffit 63

There may be more than one printing of this, since MHi reports 14 pages, OC 13 pages, and OClM 15 pages.

3672 SANFORD, NETTIE

CENTRAL IOWA FARMS AND HERDS . . . NEWTON, IOWA: PUBLISHED FOR THE AUTHOR, 1873.

[1], i–[v], [1]–125, [126 blank]. 20 x 13.3 cm. Blue cloth, title in gilt on front cover. Lacks endleaves.

Ref.: Howes S95; Mott (*Iowa*) p. 77

The pagination of the preliminaries begins on the verso of the first leaf.

Central Iowa, according to the author, comprises the counties of Wapello, Monroe, Mahaska, Marion, Poweshiek, Jasper, Polk, Story, Marshall, Hardin, Franklin, Grundy and Cerro Gordo. Her book contains descriptions of the owners and the farms of 101 outstanding situations in this section of Iowa.—EDG

3673 SANFORD, NETTIE

HISTORY OF MARSHALL COUNTY, IOWA . . . CLINTON, IOWA: LESLIE, McALLASTER & CO., PRINTERS AND BINDERS, 1867.*

[1–2], [i]–viii, [9]–168. 18.5 x 11.5 cm. Five lithographed plates; three views and two groups of portraits. Green cloth, with gilt lettering on front cover, blind embossed corners and rule borders.

Ref.: Bradford 4802; Howes S96; Mott (*Iowa*) p. 51

Pages [153]–[158]: Marshalltown / Business Directory. / Pages 159–168: advertisements.

3674 SANFORD, NETTIE

[Wrapper title] MARSHALLTOWN AND MARSHALL COUNTY . . . 1873.

[1]–48. 17.7 x 13.8 cm. Light green printed wrappers with title on front wrapper, advertisements

on recto of front and recto and verso of back wrapper.

Ref.:

The imprint appears at the foot of page 40: Printed at "The Liberal" Book and Job Printing House, / Chas. A. Clark, Proprietor, / Newton, Jasper County, Iowa. / The final eight pages carry advertisements.

3675 SANTA FE, NEW MEXICO. AYUNTAMIENTO

[Broadside] LISTA DE LOS CIUDADANOS QUE DEDERAN COMPONER LOS JURADOS DE IMPRENTA, FORMADA POR EL AYUNTAMIENTO DE ESTA CAPITAL. . . . FISCALES. C. JOSE RAFAEL BENAVIDES ID. C. APOLONIO MONDRAGON. SANTA FE AGOSTO 14 DE 1834.—JUAN GALLEGO, PRECIDENTE.— DOMINGO FERNANDEZ, SECRETARIO. SANTA FE 1834. IMPRENTA DE RAMON ABREU A CARGO DE JESUS MARIA BACA.

Broadside, 32.8 x 10.4 cm. Text, 24.2 x 13 cm.
Ref.: AII (*New Mexico*) 3

"A list of citizens pronounced by the Ayuntamiento of Santa Fé as qualified and obligated to serve as jurors in lawsuits affecting the freedom of the press. Such a list was required by the Mexican law of October 14, 1828."—AII (*New Mexico*)

3676 SANTLEBEN, AUGUST

A TEXAS PIONEER. EARLY STAGING AND OVERLAND. FREIGHTING DAYS ON THE FRONTIERS OF TEXAS AND MEXICO . . . EDITED BY I. D. AFFLECK. NEW YORK: THE NEALE PUBLISHING COMPANY, 1910.*

[1]–321, [322 blank]. 20.2 x 13.5 cm. Lavender cloth, gilt top.
Ref.: Dobie p. 79; Howes S104

Best treatise available on freighting on Chihuahua Trail.—Dobie

3677 SARGENT, ALICE APPLEGATE

FOLLOWING THE FLAG: DIARY OF A SOLDIER'S WIFE . . . KANSAS CITY, MO.: E. B. BARNETT, PUBLISHER. 204 MANHATTAN BUILDING.

[1]–91, [92 blank]. 19.8 x 13.3 cm. Portrait. Blue pictorial cloth, with printed white paper panel mounted on front cover.
Prov.: Inscribed on half-title: Presented to John Thomas Lee / with the cordial good wishes of / Alice Applegate Sargent- / Feb- 3- 1934- /. With the John Thomas Lee bookplate.
Ref.:

The portrait is dated 1908.

In the course of her army life, the author and her husband were stationed at Fort Bidwell, California; Fort Walla Walla, Washington; Fort Huachuca, Arizona (best-loved of all their stations); Fort Logan, Colorado; Fort Wingate, New Mexico; Fort Riley, Kansas; Cuba, Manila, etc.

3678 SARGENT, GEORGE B.

LECTURE ON THE "WEST;" DELIVERED . . . AT THE TREMONT TEMPLE, BOSTON, MASS., FEBRUARY 24, 1858 . . . DAVENPORT: PUBLISHING HOUSE OF LUSE, LANE & CO., 1858.

[1]–27, [28 blank]. 22.4 x 14.5 cm. Green printed wrappers, with title on front wrapper.
Prov.: Embossed stamp of Meadville Theological School through title-leaf.
Ref.: Howes S105; Moffit 400; Sabin 76969

The author was mayor of Davenport at the time.

3679 SARGENT, GEORGE B.

NOTES ON IOWA: WITH A NEW AND BEAUTIFULLY ENGRAVED MAP, SHOWING THE STATE, COUNTY, AND TOWNSHIP LINES, PUBLIC ROADS, CONTEMPLATED RAILROADS, AND INCLUDING THE MOST RECENT SETTLEMENTS AND IMPROVEMENTS . . . NEW YORK: PUBLISHED BY BERFORD & CO., 1848.

[1]–72, [73–4 advertisement]. 13.4 x 9 cm. Map: A / New Map / of / Iowa / By / George B. Sargent. / U.S. Dept. Surveyor. / Published by Berford & Co. / New York. / 1848. / [lower left:] Entered according to Act of Congress in the year 1848 by G. B. Sargent, in the Clerk's Office of the District Court of the District of Iowa. / 49.6 x 58.5 cm. No scale given. Brown cloth, gilt title on front cover.
Ref.: Howes S106; Mott (*Iowa*) p. 61; Sabin 76970

The *Iowa Journal of History and Politics*, April, 1947, contains an account of Sargent's career as a western pioneer.

3680 SARGENT, MARTIN P.

PIONEER SKETCHES: SCENES AND INCIDENTS OF FORMER DAYS . . . ERIE, PA.: HERALD PRINTING AND PUBLISHING COMPANY, LIMITED, 1891.*

[1]–512. 19.5 x 13.2 cm. Illustrated. Brown cloth.
Ref.: Howes S108

Sargent's work contains fine accounts of the early development of the oilfields of Pennsylvania.

3681 SARINANA Y CUENCA, ISIDRO

ORACION FUNEBRE, QUE DIXO EL DOCTOR D. YSIDRO SARINANA, Y CUENCA . . . EL DIA 20. DE MARCO DE 1681 . . . EN MEXICO, POR LA VIUDA DE BERNARDO CALDERON, 1681.

[*]⁴, A², A–C², D⁴, E², F¹. [1–12 pages], 1–13 LEAVES (verso of leaf 13 blank). 19.5 x 14.4 cm. Removed from bound volume, unbound. Edges

sprinkled blue-gray, part of brand on top edges (indecipherable).

Ref.: Medina (*Mexico*) 1235; Streit II 2151; Sabin 77046; Wagner (*SS*) 54

Wagner notes that the sermon contains a list of missionaries murdered, with notices of some of the more noteworthy priests. The sermon was translated and published as Publication No. 7 of the Historical Society of New Mexico, in 1906.

3682 SATTERLEE, MARION P.

[Wrapper title] THE COURT PROCEEDINGS IN THE TRIAL OF DAKOTA INDIANS FOLLOWING THE MASSACRE IN MINNESOTA IN AUGUST 1862. MINNEAPOLIS, MINN.: SATTERLEE PRINTING CO., 1927.

[1]–[84]. 21.5 x 13.9 cm. Brown printed wrappers, with title on front wrapper.
Ref.:
The caption title on page [1] reads as follows: Notes from the Trials of Dakota Indians / following the Outbreak of 1862. /

3683 SATTERLEE, MARION P.

A DETAILED ACCOUNT OF THE MASSACRE BY THE DAKOTA INDIANS OF MINNESOTA IN 1862 . . . PUBLISHED BY MARION P. SATTERLEE, MINNEAPOLIS, MINN.

[i–iv], [1]–136. 19.6 x 12.6 cm. Gray printed wrappers.
Ref.:
The Explanatory Remarks are dated Oct. 31, 1923.

3684 SATURDAY STAR, THE, Clarinda, Iowa

[Newspaper] THE SATURDAY STAR. WEEKLY. CLARINDA, AUG. 28, 1883. NO. 1 . . .

[1–4]. 22.4 x 15.2 cm.
Ref.:
According to pencil note on page [1], date should be July 28.

3685 SATURDAY STAR, THE, Clarinda, Iowa

SAME. AUG. 25, 1883. NO. 5.

[1–4]. 22.4 x 15.1 cm.
Ref.:

3686 SAUL, JAMES

AUTOGRAPH LETTER, SIGNED. 1809 October 27, New Orleans. To William Clark. One page, 25 x 19.9 cm.

Announcing safe arrival of peltries sent by Clark and mentioning the delay in Governor Lewis' arrival.

3687 SAWYER, LORENZO

WAY SKETCHES, CONTAINING INCIDENTS OF TRAVEL ACROSS THE PLAINS FROM ST. JOSEPH TO CALIFORNIA IN 1850 WITH LETTERS DESCRIBING LIFE AND CONDITIONS IN THE GOLD REGION . . . NEW YORK: EDWARD EBERSTADT, 1926.*

[1]–125, [126 colophon]. (Pages [1–2] blank.) 25.3 x 17.3 cm. Portrait. Gray board sides, white vellum back, uncut, unopened.
Ref.: Cowan p. 570; Howes S133
Limited to 35 copies on large paper.

3688 SAWYER, LORENZO

ANOTHER COPY.

Tan boards, tan cloth backstrip. Limited to 385 copies.

3689 SCANLAND, JOHN M.

LIFE OF PAT F. GARRETT AND THE TAMING OF THE BORDER OUTLAW. A HISTORY OF THE "GUN MEN" AND OUTLAWS, AND A LIFE STORY OF THE GREATEST SHERIFF OF THE OLD SOUTHWEST . . . EL PASO, TEXAS: PRESS OF THE SOUTHWESTERN PRINTING CO.

[i–ii], [1]–42. 22.3 x 15 cm. Five illustrations. White pictorial wrappers, with title on front wrapper, portrait of Billy the Kid on back wrapper.
Prov.: Six-line rubber stamp of I. W. W. stamped on front wrapper, title-page, and several other places in pamphlet.
Ref.: Adams 885; Dykes 51; Howes S137
Copyrighted 1908.

J. J. Lipsey, Colorado Springs bookseller, in issuing a reprint of this edition in 1952 states that the original edition "has become one of the most desired, most difficult to find pieces of Southwest Americana . . . A famous bibliographer of the West, anxious to study and describe the booklet had every Americana specialist advertising for it. He never got an offer. Only two copies were located and they were not for sale."—EDG

3690 [SCANTLEBURY, THOMAS]

[Wrapper title] WANDERINGS IN MINNESOTA DURING THE INDIAN TROUBLES OF 1862. CHICAGO: F. C. S. CALHOUN, 1867.

[i–ii blank], [iii–iv], [1]–32. 21.6 x 14.5 cm. Tan printed wrappers with title on front wrapper. In green half morocco case.
Ref.: AII (*Chicago*) 1266; Howes S138; Jones 1500

On the front wrapper there is a manuscript note in an unidentified hand: Diary of Thomas Scantlebury / Cousin of Elijah M. Wray. / The same appears also at top of page [1], and on page [28]: Elijah Wray's cousin— / Thomas Scantlebury /.

3691 SCHAEFFER, LUTHER M.

SKETCHES OF TRAVELS IN SOUTH AMERICA, MEXICO AND CALIFORNIA . . . NEW-YORK: JAMES EGBERT, 1860.

[1]–247, [248 blank]. 18.3 x 12 cm. Purple cloth, embossed sides, title stamped in gilt on backstrip.

Ref.: Cowan p. 570; Sabin 77485

3692 SCHARMANN, HERMANN B.

SCHARMANN'S LANDREISE NACH CALIFORNIEN . . . 1905.

[1]–125, [126 blank]. 15.7 x 10.6 cm. Illustrations unlisted. Red cloth, lower edge uncut.

Prov.: Presentation copy, inscribed in German and signed H. B. Scharmann. Also inscribed and signed beneath the portrait frontispiece, latter dated February 22, 1908.

Ref.: Cowan pp. 570–71; Howes S149

According to the title-page, the account had been printed in the *New-Yorker Staats-Zeitung*, April 10, 17, 24, and May 1, 1852.

3693 SCHARMANN, HERMANN B.

SCHARMANN'S OVERLAND JOURNEY TO CALIFORNIA FROM THE PAGES OF A PIONEER'S DIARY . . .

[1]–114. 15.8 x 10.2 cm. Illustrations not listed. Original green cloth.

Ref.: Cowan p. 571; Howes S149

Published in New York in 1918. Limited to 50 copies.

3694 SCHMEDDING, JOSEPH

COWBOY AND INDIAN TRADER . . . CALDWELL: THE CAXTON PRINTERS, LTD., 1951.*

[1]–364. 22.8 x 15.2 cm. 42 illustrations listed, map on endpapers. Brown cloth, pictorial design on front cover. In dust jacket.

Ref.: Adams (*Ramp. Herd*) 2021

A fascinating account of recent events in Arizona's Indian country.

3695 [SCHMOELDER, B.]

THE EMIGRANT'S GUIDE TO CALIFORNIA, DESCRIBING ITS GEOGRAPHY, AGRICULTURAL AND COMMERCIAL RESOURCES . . . TO WHICH IS APPENDED THE GOVERNOR OF CALIFORNIA'S (COLONEL MASON'S) OFFICIAL DESPATCHES CONCERNING THE GOLD DISTRICTS . . . LONDON: PELHAM RICHARDSON.

[1]–65, [66 blank], [i]–[xiv, xiv blank]. 22.2 x 13.8 cm. Frontispiece (View of the Harbour of San Francisco, in Upper California.) and folding map: Map of California / and the / Country east from the Pacific. / 21.2 x 27.3 cm. No scale given. Green printed wrappers with title on front wrapper. In a brown half morocco case.

Ref.: Cowan pp. 194–95; Howes C46 (see also S173); Wagner-Camp 155 see; Wheat (*Gold Region*) 83; Wheat (*Transmississippi*) 608, 633, 637

Published about 1850.

All of this except the introduction and the appendix and the part beginning on page 60, "How to Reach California," is a translation from Schmölder. [*Neuer praktischer Wegweiser für Auswanderer nach Nord-Amerika . . .* Mainz, 1848.]—Wagner-Camp

This "valuable" map is perhaps the worst map of California that appeared during 1849.—Wheat

3696 SCHOEPF, JOHANN DAVID

TRAVELS IN THE CONFEDERATION [1783–1784] . . . PHILADELPHIA: WILLIAM J. CAMPBELL, 1911.*

[i]–x, [1]–426. [i]–iv, [1]–344. 19.3 x 13 cm. Portrait and two facsimiles. Two volumes, green cloth, uncut.

Ref.: Buck 36; Clark II 120; Howes S176

Schoepf's is one of the best accounts of travel in the newly established United States exclusive of New England.

3697 [SCHOLTE, HENRY P.]

WEGWIJZER EN RAADGEVER VOOR LANDVERHUIZERS NAAR NOORD-AMERIKA, INZONDERHEID NAAR DE WESTELIJKE STATEN: OHIO, MICHIGAN, INDIANA, ILLINOIS, MISSOURI, WISCONSIN EN JOWA. TE ZWIJNDRECHT; BIJ J. BODEN, 1846.

[i]–iv, [1]–[65], [66 blank]. 18.6 x 11.7 cm. Blue printed wrappers with title on front wrapper, advertisement on verso of back wrapper, uncut.

Ref.: Buck 408; Howes S179

Scholte, a political exile, was one of the principal founders of Pella, Iowa.

3698 SCHOOLCRAFT, HENRY R.

NARRATIVE OF AN EXPEDITION THROUGH THE UPPER MISSISSIPPI TO ITASCA LAKE, THE ACTUAL SOURCE OF THIS RIVER; EMBRACING AN EXPLORATORY TRIP THROUGH THE ST. CROIX AND BURNTWOOD (OR BROULE) RIVERS; IN 1832 . . . NEW-YORK: PUBLISHED BY HARPER & BROTHERS, 1834.

[1–2], [i]–vi, [7]–307, [308 errata]. 22.7 x 14.5 cm. Five maps. Map: Sketch of the Sources / of the / Mississippi River, / Drawn from Lieu^t Allen's observations / in 1832, to illustrate / Schoolcraft's Inland Journey / to Itasca Lake. / [swelled rule] / Le Count & Hammond S^c / 51 x 34 cm. No scale given. Map: Cass Lake / 2978 miles above the Gulf of Mexico. / 15.9 x 9.5 cm. No scale given. Map: Itasca Lake / [two-line parenthesis] the source of the Mississippi River, 3160 [two-line parenthesis] / miles from the Balize, / 16 x 9.8 cm. No scale given. Map: Leech Lake / 15.2 x 9.5 cm. No scale given. Map: St. Croix and Misacoda or Burntwood Rivers. / [lower right corner:] Drawn by James Allen U.S.A. / 45.3 x 20.6 cm. No scale given. Pink cloth, paper label (6 x 2.6 cm.) on backstrip, uncut.

Ref.: Bradford 4848; Field 1367; Howes S187; Sabin 77863

3699 SCHOOLCRAFT, HENRY R.

PERSONAL MEMOIRS OF A RESIDENCE OF THIRTY YEARS WITH THE INDIAN TRIBES ON THE AMERICAN FRONTIERS: WITH BRIEF NOTICES OF PASSING EVENTS, FACTS, AND OPINIONS, A.D. 1812 TO A.D. 1842 . . . PHILADELPHIA: LIPPINCOTT, GRAMBO AND CO., 1851.

[i]–xlviii, [17]–703, [704 blank]. 22.4 x 14.7 cm. Frontispiece portrait. Rebound in green half morocco, gilt top.

Ref.: Field 1377; Howes S190; Sabin 77870

3700 SCHOOLCRAFT, HENRY R.

SCENES AND ADVENTURES IN THE SEMI-ALPINE REGION OF THE OZARK MOUNTAINS OF MISSOURI AND ARKANSAS, WHICH WERE FIRST TRAVERSED BY DE SOTO, IN 1541 . . . PHILADELPHIA: LIPPINCOTT, GRAMBO & CO., 1853.

[i]–xii, 13–256, 1–36 advertisements. 22.3 x 14.6 cm. Three engraved plates. Dark purple cloth, blind panels on sides, backstrip gilt.

Ref.: Howes S194; Sabin 77876; Wagner-Camp see

Another edition of Schoolcraft's *A View of the Lead Mines* . . . 1819

Editions: New York, 1819; London, 1821.

3701 SCHOOLCRAFT, HENRY R.

TRAVELS IN THE CENTRAL PORTIONS OF THE MISSISSIPPI VALLEY . . . IN THE YEAR 1821 . . . NEW-YORK: PUBLISHED BY COLLINS AND HANNY, 1825.

[i]–iv, [1]–459, [460 blank]. 22.9 x 14.1 cm. Three engraved plates and two maps. Map: A Sketch of the Western Country, / Designed to illustrate the present Work. / [lower right corner:] Scoles sculp. / 22.5 x 30.2 cm. Scale: about 60 miles to an inch. Map: Geological Sketch / of the Lead Mine District of / Missouri. / embracing the Granitical Tract of / St Michael. / 20.5 x 12 cm. No scale given. Below cartouche: Scoles sculp. Colored. Gray boards, printed paper label (new), uncut.

Ref.: Bradford 4847; Field 1364; Howes S193; Rader 2892; Sabin 77880

Describes a trip, with Gen. Cass, via the Wabash and Ohio to Illinois and Missouri, returning via the Mississippi and Illinois rivers to Peoria and Chicago.—Howes

3702 SCHOOLCRAFT, HENRY R.

A VIEW OF THE LEAD MINES OF MISSOURI; INCLUDING SOME OBSERVATIONS ON THE MINERALOGY, GEOLOGY, GEOGRAPHY, ANTIQUITIES, SOIL, CLIMATE, POPULATION, AND PRODUCTIONS OF MISSOURI AND ARKANSAW, AND OTHER SECTIONS OF THE WESTERN COUNTRY . . . NEW-YORK: PUBLISHED BY CHARLES WILEY & CO., 1819.

[1]–299, [300 blank]. 23.1 x 15.2 cm. Three plates. Rebound in contemporary gray boards, printed paper label (new), uncut.

Ref.: Bradford 4845; Howes S194; Sabin 77881

3703 SCHOOLCRAFT, HENRY R., & JAMES ALLEN

[Caption title] . . . WAR DEPT. SCHOOLCRAFT AND ALLEN—EXPEDITION TO NORTHWEST INDIANS. LETTER FROM THE SECRETARY OF WAR, TRANSMITTING A MAP AND REPORT OF LIEUT. ALLEN AND H. B. SCHOOLCRAFT'S VISIT TO THE NORTHWEST INDIANS IN 1832 . . .

[1]–68. 23.7 x 14.8 cm. Folding map: Map / of the Route passed over by / an Expedition into the Indian / Country in 1832 to the Source / of the Mississippi / By / Lieut J. Allen U.S. Inf / Reduced from the original and drawn by Lieut Drayton / 39.7 x 48.1 cm. (neat line). No scale given. New gray wrappers, uncut, unopened. In blue cloth box.

Ref.: Howes A148

23rd Congress, 1st Session, House, Document No. 323, Serial 262. [Washington, 1834.]

Page [1], lower left corner: [short rule] / [Gales & Seaton, print.] /

Accompanying this is the Allen broadside, Chicago, 1835. See ALLEN, JAMES.

3704 SCHOOLCRAFT, HENRY R., & JAMES ALLEN

ANOTHER COPY. Rebound in red cloth. Without the broadside.

3705 SCHOONOVER, THOMAS J.

THE LIFE AND TIMES OF GEN'L JOHN A. SUTTER . . . SACRAMENTO: D. JOHNSTON & CO., 1895.*

[i–viii, viii blank], [1]–136. 14.4 x 10.5 cm. Portrait and woodcuts, unlisted. Brown cloth, title and vignette stamped in gilt on front cover.

Ref.: Cowan p. 572; Howes S196

3706 SCHOYER, SOLOMON

[Map] MAP / OF THE / UNITED STATES / DRAWN / FROM THE MOST APPROVED / SURVEYS [decorative rule] / PUBLISHED BY SOLOMON SCHOYER. NEW YORK / SCALE OF MILES / [diagrammatic scale] / ENGRAVED BY G. W. MERCHANT ALBANY / 1826. /

Map, 41.4 x 52 cm. Scale: about 150 miles to an inch. Folded loose into red board folders, 16 x 9.8 cm., lettered on front cover: U. States. /
Ref.:

3707 SCHULTZ, CHRISTIAN

TRAVELS ON AN INLAND VOYAGE THROUGH THE STATES OF NEW-YORK, PENNSYLVANIA, VIRGINIA, OHIO, KENTUCKY AND TENNESSEE, AND THROUGH THE TERRITORIES OF INDIANA, LOUISIANA, MISSISSIPPI AND NEW-ORLEANS; PERFORMED IN THE YEARS 1807 and 1808 . . . NEW-YORK: PRINTED BY ISAAC RILEY, 1810.

[1]–2⁴, 3², A–Cc⁴. [i]–xviii, blank leaf, [1]–207, [208 blank]. [1]⁴, A–Ee⁴. [i]–viii, [1]–224. 23.2 to 23.6 x 14 to 15 cm. Two engraved plates, portrait, and five maps: Map / of the / United States / including / Louisiana / [lower left:] C. Schultz Jun. del. / [centre:] New York Published by I Riley May 1810 / [lower right:] I Seeles sculp. / 41.7 x 47.2 cm. No scale given. Map: A Map / Of the Hudson and Mohawk Rivers; west Wood Creek, Oneida Lake, Onondaga / River, part of Lake Ontario, Niagara River, part of Lake Erie, Le Beau and French Creeks, / and the Alleghany River, Containing the Route from New York to Pittsburgh. / [lower left:] C. Schultz Jr. del. / [lower right:] P Maverick sc Newark. / 18.9 x 33.3 cm. No scale given. Plan: A Plan / of the Ruins / of the Ancient Fortifications / at Marietta; with the Probable junction of the two Rivers at the time they were erected. / [lower left:] C. Schultz Jun. del. / [lower right:] P. Maverick sculp. Newark. / 19.7 x 19.4 cm. No scale given. Map: A Map / Of the Ohio River and part / of the Mississippi, Containing the Route from Pittsburgh to St. Louis / and the Mines. / [lower left:] C. Schults Jr. del. / [lower right:] P. Maverick sc. Newark. / *Inset:* [Mississippi River from the Mouth of the Ohio to the Mouth of the Missouri] 9.9 x 5.5 cm. No scale given. 22 x 40.3 cm. No scale given. Map: A Map / of the / Mississippi River, / Containing the Route from the Mouth of the / Ohio to New-Orleans. / [lower left:] C. Schultz Jun. del. / [lower right:] P. Maverick sc⁺ Newark N. J. / Two sections on one sheet, left: 24.6 x 14 cm., right: 24.6 x 18.8 cm. No scale given. Two volumes, original marbled boards, red roan backs and corners, uncut. Worn.

Prov.: Harvard College Library copy, with bookplates removed. Inscriptions clipped from upper margins of title-pages.
Ref.: Buck 70; Howes S202; Sabin 78001; Thomson 1027

The earliest work to give a detailed account of the distances, modes of travelling, time required, and the actual risks and dangers encountered in traversing the western country.—Dunbar

3708 SCHWATKA, FREDERICK

ALONG ALASKA'S GREAT RIVER. A POPULAR ACCOUNT OF THE TRAVELS OF THE ALASKA EXPLORING EXPEDITION OF 1883, ALONG THE GREAT YUKON RIVER . . . NEW YORK: CASSELL & COMPANY, LIMITED.

[1]–360. 22.6 x 14.8 cm. 74 illustrations and maps listed. Dark green cloth, title in gilt and decorative bands in black on front cover, monogram and bands in black on back cover, title in gilt on backstrip, beveled edges, gilt top.
Prov.: Inscribed on front blank: Genˡ and Mrs J. C. Smith / With Christmas Greetings / from / Fred'k Schwatka /. Manuscript note in lower left corner in another hand: Date believed / to be 1890 /.
Ref.: Bradford 4857a; Wickersham 2793
Copyrighted 1885.

3709 SCOTT, EDWIN J.

RANDOM RECOLLECTIONS OF A LONG LIFE, 1806 TO 1876 . . . COLUMBIA, S.C.: CHARLES A. CALVO, JR., 1884.

[1–2], [i]–vi, [3]–216. 18.7 x 12.4 cm. Brown cloth, decorative bands in black on front cover and in blind on back, title in gilt on backstrip.
Ref.: Howes S220

The list of errata on the verso of the title-leaf is supplemented by a small slip, 1.4 x 7.3 cm., with two additional errata.

The author, a resident of Columbia for many years, was present when the capitol was burned by Sherman's soldiers and gives an interesting account of the catastrophe.—EDG

3710 SCOTT, JAMES

A CHECK TO ARIANISM. BEING DESIGNED AS AN ANSWER TO THE ARGUMENTS OF BARTON W. STONE . . . INDIANAPOLIS: PRINTED AT THE GAZETTE OFFICE, 1826.

[1]–[59], [60 blank]. 20.3 x 12 cm. Stabbed, unbound. Soiled, some manuscript corrections and annotations in ink, note removed chemically from last leaf.
Ref.: *Gazette* of the Grolier Club, Vol. II, No. 3, October, 1944; Byrd & Peckham 294

3711 SCOTT, JAMES L.

A JOURNAL OF A MISSIONARY TOUR THROUGH PENNSYLVANIA, OHIO, INDIANA, ILLINOIS, IOWA, WISKONSON[!] AND MICHIGAN . . . PROVIDENCE: PUBLISHED BY THE AUTHOR, 1843.

[i]–viii, [9]–203, [204 blank]. 18.2 x 11.5 cm. Black cloth, blind embossed borders on sides, gilt flower in centres, title in gilt on backstrip.

Ref.: Buck 374; Howes S226; Mott (*Iowa*) p. 67; Sabin 78280; Thomson 1030

3712 SCOTT, JOHN

THE INDIANA GAZETTEER; OR, TOPOGRAPHICAL DICTIONARY . . . CENTREVILLE: PUBLISHED AND SOLD BY JOHN SCOTT & WM. M. DOUGHTY, 1826.

[1]–143, [144 blank]. Gray-green wrappers. Small portion of backstrip missing. In a maroon cloth case.

Ref.: Bradford 4867; Buley II p. 643; Byrd & Peckham 296; Howes S230; *Ind. Quart. for Bookmen*, April 1945; Jones 877; Sabin 78304

As early as July, 1826, Scott issued a map of Indiana which he had prepared and had engraved by William Woodruff of Cincinnati . . . The *Gazetteer* was published later, probably in September.—Byrd & Peckham

3713 SCOTT, JOHN

THE SAME . . . SECOND EDITION . . . INDIANAPOLIS: PUBLISHED BY DOUGLASS AND MAGUIRE, 1833.

[i]–iv, [5]–[200]. 17.5 x 10.3 cm. Plum cloth, red leather label. In a red cloth case.

Prov.: Signature and rubber stamp of William A. Peelle on front fly-leaf. Bookplate of C. G. Littell.

Ref.: Byrd & Peckham 515; Howes S230; Sabin 78305

From the Preface: ". . . having purchased the copyright of Mr John Scott's Gazetteer, now present to the public a new edition, much enlarged and improved."

3714 [SCOTT, JOHN, of Kentucky]

ENCARNACION PRISONERS: COMPRISING AN ACCOUNT OF THE MARCH OF THE KENTUCKY CAVALRY FROM LOUISVILLE TO THE RIO GRANDE, TOGETHER WITH AN AUTHENTIC HISTORY OF THE CAPTIVITY OF THE AMERICAN PRISONERS, INCLUDING INCIDENTS AND SKETCHES OF MEN AND THINGS ON THE ROUTE IN MEXICO . . . LOUISVILLE, KY: PRENTICE AND WEISSINGER, 1848.

[1]–96. 21.3 x 13.5 cm. Stabbed, unbound, remnants of green wrappers on backstrip.

Prov.: At top of title-page: S. M. Swigert / U. S. [undeciphered letters] / West Point, / N. Y. /

Ref.: Howes S231; Sabin 78306

Among the names of the prisoners listed on page 91 is a John Swigert.

There was another edition printed at Louisville in 1848 of 123 pages.

3715 SCOTT, SIR WALTER

KENILWORTH . . . LONDON: J. DICKS, no date. Bound following Hutchinson, Elliot St. M.: *Two Years a Cow Boy* . . . London, 1887.

3716 SCOTT, WINFIELD

MEMOIRS OF LIEUT.-GENERAL SCOTT, LL.D. . . . NEW YORK: SHELDON & COMPANY, 1864.

[1–2], [i]–xxii, [1]–653, [654 blank]. 23.9 x 16.1 cm. Portrait. Green cloth, blind embossed fillet borders on sides, title in gilt on backstrip, uncut.

Prov.: Inscribed on front blank leaf: To / My dear friends— / The Hon M^r & Mrs. Hamilton Fish— / I gratefully inscribe this book. / Winfield Scott. / 1864 /.

Ref.: Howes S242; Sabin 78418

One of 250 copies issued in one volume on large paper.

3717 SCRIPPS, JOHN L.

THE UNDEVELOPED NORTHERN PORTION OF THE AMERICAN CONTINENT. A LECTURE DELIVERED IN THE COURSE BEFORE BELL'S COMMERCIAL COLLEGE FEBRUARY, 1856 . . . CHICAGO: "DEMOCRATIC PRESS" STEAM PRINTING HOUSE, 1856.

[1]–20. 22.3 x 14.4 cm. Plain buff wrappers, apparently original.

Ref.: AII (*Chicago*) 221; Byrd 2537; Howes S248; Sabin 78485

3718 [SEALSFIELD, CHARLES]

THE CABIN BOOK; OR, SKETCHES OF LIFE IN TEXAS. BY SEATSFIELD. TRANSLATED FROM THE GERMAN BY PROFESSOR C^H F^R. MERSCH. NEW YORK: J. WINCHESTER, 1844.

[i–ii], [1]–155, [156 blank]. 21.8 x 13.6 cm. Rebound in bright blue cloth.

Ref.: Howes P502; Rader 2987; Raines pp. 153–54 see; Sabin 64536; Wright I 2327

This first translation into English differs from the London translation.

3719 SEALSFIELD, CHARLES

THE CABIN BOOK: OR, NATIONAL CHARACTERISTICS. BY CHARLES SEALSFIELD. TRANSLATED FROM THE GERMAN, BY SARAH POWELL . . . LONDON: INGRAM, COOKE, & CO., MDCCCLII.

[i–vi, vi blank], [1]–296, [1–4 advertisements]. 19.3 x 12.8 cm. Seven illustrations and a vignette listed. Light red cloth, blind embossed sides, title in gilt on backstrip, uncut, mostly un-opened.

Ref.: Howes P502; Raines pp. 153–54 see; Sabin 64537

3720 [SEALSFIELD, CHARLES]

LIFE IN THE NEW WORLD; OR, SKETCHES OF AMERICAN SOCIETY . . . NEW YORK: J. WINCHESTER.

[1]–349, [350 blank]. 22.1 x 13.4 cm. Rebound in nearly contemporary half brown morocco.

Ref.: Howes P504; Rader 2900; Sabin 64545; Wright I 2330

Published in 1844.

First edition in English. The five parts were issued in seven originally and in this copy bound together.

3721 [SEALSFIELD, CHARLES]

DIE VEREINIGTEN STAATEN VON NORDAMERIKA, NACH IHREM POLITISCHEN, RELIGIOSEN UND GESELLSCHAFTLICHEN VERHALTNISSE BETRACHTET. MIT EINER REISE DURCH DEN WESTLICHEN THEIL VON PENNSYLVANIEN, OHIO, KENTUCKY, INDIANA, ILLINOIS, MISSURI[!], TENNESSEE, DAS GEBIET ARKANSAS, MISSISSIPPI[!] UND LOUISIANA . . . STUTTGART: IN DER J. G. COTTA'SCHEN BUCHHANDLUNG, 1827.

[i]–x, [1]–206. [i]–iv, [1]–247, [248 blank]. 20 x 12.2 cm. Two volumes, original yellow paste paper, manuscript labels on front covers and backstrips, uncut.

Ref.: Clark III 100 see; Howes 506; Rader 2901; Sabin 64557

3722 SEARS, W. H.

NOTES FROM A COWBOY'S DIARY . . . LAWRENCE, KANSAS.

[1–8]. 20.2 x 13.5 cm. Blue printed wrappers with title on front wrapper.

Ref.: Adams (*Ramp. Herd*) 2032

Date of publication not given. Probably about 1925.

3723 SEDGLEY, JOSEPH

OVERLAND TO CALIFORNIA IN 1849 . . . OAKLAND: BUTLER & BOWMAN, STEAM BOOK AND JOB PRINTERS, 1877.*

[1]–66. 22 x 14.8 cm. Dark gray cloth, title in gilt on front cover.

Ref.: Cowan p. 575; Howes S268; Morgan (Pritchard) p. 196

This is a day by day journal of an overland trip in 1849. The party was recruited from Massachusetts. It left Booneville, Missouri, May 8, 1849. Sedgley recorded all the graves passed on the trail so it is a rather lugubrious narrative.—EDG

3724 SEELY, O. C., *Publisher*

OKLAHOMA ILLUSTRATED. A BOOK OF PRACTICAL INFORMATION. SHOWING THE TERRITORY'S PRESENT STATUS AND FUTURE PROSPECTS . . . GUTHRIE, OKLAHOMA: THE LEADER PRINTING CO., 1894.

[i–viii], [1]–229, [230–52 advertisements]. 23.4 x 16.1 cm. Profusely illustrated in text with portraits, views, and maps. Red leather stamped in gilt on front cover with title within elaborate design. Advertisement on inner front cover.

Ref.: Howes S270

An early work in praise of Oklahoma.

3725 SELMAN, MORMON V.

[Wrapper title] DICTIONARY OF UTE INDIAN LANGUAGE . . . PROVO, UTAH: M. H. GRAHAM PRINTING CO.*

1–20. 19.9 x 10.1 cm. Tan printed wrappers, with title on front wrapper.

Ref.:

This book was probably printed during the nineties since it is not listed in Pilling's bibliography (1885). The portrait of Selman on the front wrapper shows a man in his later life. He says he spent twenty-two years with the Utes including the winter of 1879–80.—EDG

3726 SELTZER HOUSE, Seltzer Spring, Colorado

[Broadside] SELTZER SPRING. DEDICATION BALL, AT THE SELTZER HOUSE, SPRING DALE, COLO., FRIDAY, AUGUST 4TH, 1876. MR. C. E. PEASE, THE PROPRIETOR, EXTENDS A CORDIAL INVITATION TO YOURSELF AND LADIES. GOOD MUSIC. TICKETS INCLUDING SUPPER $3 . . . BOULDER NEWS, PRINT.

Broadside, 19.5 x 13.7 cm. Text, 6.1 x 10.5 cm.

Ref.:

The first dated printing in Boulder was April 3, 1876, the *Boulder Valley News*.

3727 SEMALLE, RENE DE

CONSIDERATIONS ON THE ESTABLISHMENT IN THE INDIAN TERRITORY OF A NEW STATE OF THE AMERICAN UNION . . . VERSAILLES: PRINTED BY E. AUBERT, 1876.

[1]–8. 21.1 x 13.4 cm. Blue printed wrappers, with title on front wrapper.

Prov.: Rubber stamps of U. S. Geological Survey Library on front wrapper and title-page.

Ref.: Rader 2906; Sabin 79042

3728 SEMMES, JOHN E.

JOHN H. B. LATROBE AND HIS TIMES 1803–1891 . . . BALTIMORE, MD.: THE NORMAN, REMINGTON CO.

[i]–viii, 1–601, [602 blank]. 23.7 x 15.8 cm. 39 plates listed, 19 in color. Original full dark blue morocco, gilt, gilt top, uncut, partly unopened.

Ref.:

Copyrighted 1917.

Limited to 50 special copies, signed by the author and containing three pages, folio, of the original manuscript.

3729 [SEMPLE, JAMES]

CHARTER OF THE ILLINOIS TRANSPORTATION COMPANY, WITH A DESCRIPTION OF THE PRAIRIE CAR. 1848.

[1]–20. 13.5 x 14.9 cm. Removed from bound volume, unbound. Strip torn from top of last leaf, including three lines of text.

Ref.: Byrd 1343

Material relating to the Charter occupies pages [3]–5. The balance of the pamphlet deals with the Prairie Coach.

Probably printed at Chicago, although Byrd suggests Alton.

3730 SEQUOYAH, STATE OF

[Caption title] CONSTITUTION OF THE STATE OF SEQUOYAH. PREAMBLE . . .

[1]–[68]. 25.7 x 17.5 cm. Map: State of / Sequoyah / Scale $\frac{1}{500000}$ / Approximately 8 miles to the inch / [diagrammatic scale] / [lower centre:] Aug. Gast Bank Note & Litho. / Company. / Map Publishers, / St. Louis. / 41 x 37.5 cm. Scale as above. Stapled, unbound. In a red cloth case.

Ref.: Foreman p. 50 see; Hargrett (*Bibliography*) 222; Howes S295; Rader 2011

Signed at the foot of page [68]: In testimony whereof we hereto set our hands this 14th day of / October, 1905. / P. Porter, / Chairman. / Attest: / Alex Posey, / Secretary. / Phoenix Printing Co, Muskogee, I T. [union label, printed inverted] /

Hargrett describes an earlier printing (also Muskogee, 1905) with pagination on 68 and no imprint at foot.

3731 SEQUOYAN

[TWO TEMPERANCE HYMNS IN SEQUOYAN.]

[1]–4. 12.8 x 7.7 cm. Bound with Number 1278.

Ref.: Hargrett (*Oklahoma*) 71

Apparently printed at Park Hill: Mission Press, 1844. Hargrett considers this part of *The Evil of Intoxicating Liquor . . . 1844.* Text in Sequoyan.

3732 SERIES OF MISCELLANEOUS LETTERS, A

A SERIES OF MISCELLANEOUS LETTERS, FROM A FATHER TO HIS CHILDREN . . . SOUTH HANOVER, IA.: PRINTED AND PUBLISHED BY JAMES MORROW, 1835.

[i]–iv, [5]–144. 13.7 x 9.2 cm. Pink calf, gilt back.

Ref.: Bay 396; Byrd & Peckham 598

The same anonymous author later published *A Number of Miscellaneous Letters* (see 3052). The early letters have some interesting observations on early times in Pennsylvania and Ohio, but the main part of the volume consists of dry theological discussions.

3733 SERRANO Y AGUIRRE, FRANCISCO PEREZ

EXPOSICION DE LA PROVINCIA DEL NUEVO MEXICO . . . MEXICO: OFICINA DE D. JOSE MARIA RAMOS PALOMERA, 1822.

[1]–2⁴, 3². [1]–20. 21 x 15.7 cm. Blue morocco backstrip, blue cloth sides, uncut.

Ref.:

An eloquent plea for political and social reforms in New Mexico. Among the author's suggestions were an enlarged educational system (including a Colegio Seminario at Santa Fé), and the importation of metallurgists, manufacturers, and Norteamericano families.

3734 SEVILLE, WILLIAM P.

. . . NARRATIVE OF THE MARCH OF CO. A, ENGINEERS FROM FORT LEAVENWORTH, KANSAS, TO FORT BRIDGER, UTAH, AND RETURN MAY 6 TO OCTOBER 3, 1858 . . . WASHINGTON BARRACKS, D. C.: PRESS OF THE ENGINEER SCHOOL, 1912.*

[i–iv], 1–46, [47–48 blank]. (Pages [i–ii] blank.) 22.8 x 15.2 cm. Pale blue printed glazed wrappers, with title on front wrapper.

Ref.: Howes S300

3735 SEWALL, J. S., & C. W. IDDINGS

[Map] SECTIONAL MAP / OF THE / SURVEYED PORTIONS OF MINNESOTA / AND THE / NORTH WESTERN PART OF WISCONSIN. / SCALE, TWELVE MILES TO ONE INCH. SCALE OF MILES. / [diagrammatic scale] / C. A. SWETT, ENGRAVER, / BOSTON, MASS. / [below border:] ENTERED ACCORDING TO ACT OF CONGRESS IN THE YEAR 1857, BY J. S. SEWALL, IN THE CLERK'S OFFICE OF THE DISTRICT COURT OF THE SECOND DISTRICT OF MINNESOTA. [at right:] DRAWN BY A. J. HILL. /

Map, 80.6 x 62 cm. Scale: twelve miles to an inch. Folded into black cloth covers, 15.7 x 9.7 cm., with gilt title on front cover.

Ref.: Phillips p. 433

Pasted to the inner front cover is a leaf headed: Notice. / [short rule] / [14 lines] / Published by / J. S. Sewall & C. W. Iddings, / Saint Paul, Jan. 1, 1860. /

3736 [SEYMOUR, SILAS]

INCIDENTS OF A TRIP THROUGH THE GREAT PLATTE VALLEY, TO THE ROCKY MOUNTAINS AND LARAMIE PLAINS, IN THE FALL OF 1866, WITH A SYNOPTICAL STATEMENT OF THE VARIOUS PACIFIC RAILROADS, AND AN ACCOUNT OF THE GREAT UNION PACIFIC EXCURSION TO THE ONE HUNDREDTH MERIDIAN OF LONGITUDE. NEW YORK: D. VAN NOSTRAND, 1867.

[1]–129, [130 blank]. 18.8 x 12.5 cm. Light brown cloth, with title in gilt on front cover.

Prov.: Inscribed in pencil on a preliminary blank leaf: Mr Basant / Compliments of / S Seymour / [underline] / N.Y. June 6, 1886 / [underline] /.

Ref.: Howes S315; *Railway Economics* p. 285; Sabin 79669

3737 SHANNON, PETER C.

THE STATE OF DAKOTA: HOW IT MAY BE FORMED. REPLIES TO THE PAMPHLET OF HON. HUGH J. CAMPBELL. U.S. ATTORNEY OF DAKOTA TREATING UPON THE ABOVE SUBJECT. OPINIONS OF COURTS, JURISTS AND STATESMEN, AS TO THE ADMISSION OF NEW STATES INTO THE UNION . . . YANKTON, D. T.: HERALD PRINTING HOUSE, 1883.

[1]–58. 22.3 x 14.8 cm. Gray printed wrappers with title on front wrapper.

Ref.: Allen (*Dakota*) 280

Reprinted from the columns of the Dakota Herald. The "Introductory" is signed by the Editors of the Dakota Herald.

3738 SHARLAND, GEORGE

KNAPSACK NOTES OF GEN. SHERMAN'S GRAND CAMPAIGN THROUGH THE EMPIRE STATE OF THE SOUTH . . . SPRINGFIELD, ILL.: JOHNSON & BRADFORD, 1865.

[1]–68. 20.3 x 13.5 cm. White printed wrappers, with title on front wrapper. Piece torn from front wrapper affecting one word and border. In a blue cloth case.

Ref.: Howes S329; Sabin 79773

3739 SHARP, J. L.

[Broadside] RAILROAD TERMINUS. THE STEAM FERRY-BOAT, EMMA, WILL MAKE HER REGULAR TRIPS DURING THE SEASON BETWEEN THE GLENWOOD LANDING AND THE CITY OF PLATTSMOUTH, WHERE EMIGRANTS AND THE TRAVELLING PUBLIC WILL BE ACCOMODATED WITH A SAFE AND SPEEDY PASSAGE ACROSS THE RIVER AT ALL TIMES BETWEEN THE RISING AND SETTING OF THE SUN. OUR BOAT IS SECOND TO NONE ON THE MO. RIVER, WITH FIRST CLASS ENGINEER AND PILOT, AND THE COMPANY WILL SPARE NO LABOR OR EXPENSE TO GIVE GENERAL SATISFACTION. J. L. SHARP, PRES. M. W. GREENE, SEC. [MARCH 15, 1858.

Broadside, 42.3 x 29 cm. Text, 38.3 x 26 cm.

Ref.:

This broadside was first called to my attention fifteen or twenty years ago by the late H. M. Sender, the Kansas City bookseller, who saw it in the Clarinda Public Library and tried to buy it without success. Shortly thereafter I tried to get it, but was also unsuccessful. The broadside then disappeared and I suspected it had either been destroyed or stolen. This spring (1953), at my suggestion, a search for it was inaugurated which was successful. I was then able to convince the Board of Trustees they did not have facilities for preserving items of this kind.—EDG

3740 SHAW, J. HENRY

HISTORICAL SKETCH OF CASS COUNTY, ILLINOIS: AN ORATION DELIVERED JULY 4, 1876, AT BEARDSTOWN, ILLS . . . BEARDSTOWN: PUBLISHED AT THE OFFICE OF THE "CASS COUNTY MESSENGER," 1876.

[i–ii], [1]–[54]. 21.7 x 14 cm. Pink glazed printed wrappers, with title on front wrapper printed in red. Removed from bound volume.

Ref.: Buck 734; Howes S339

3741 SHAW, JAMES

TWELVE YEARS IN AMERICA: BEING OBSERVATIONS ON THE COUNTRY, THE PEOPLE, INSTITUTIONS AND RELIGION; WITH NOTICES OF SLAVERY AND THE LATE WAR; AND FACTS AND INCIDENTS ILLUSTRATIVE OF MINISTERIAL LIFE AND LABOR IN ILLINOIS . . . LONDON: HAMILTON, ADAMS, AND CO., 1867.

[i]–xvi, [1]–440. 18.1 x 12 cm. Frontispiece and map: A Correct Map / of the / Pennsylvania Central / Rail Road / with its / Branches & Connections. / The Shortest & Quickest Route / between the East & West. / Lith of Ed. Mendel, Cor. Lake & La Salle St., Chicago. / 18.9 x 23.2 cm. No scale given. Green cloth, blind embossed borders on sides, title in gilt on backstrip.

Ref.: Buck 563; Howes S340; Sabin 79918

3742 SHAW, JOHN R.

A NARRATIVE OF THE LIFE & TRAVELS OF JOHN ROBERT SHAW, THE WELL-DIGGER, NOW RESIDENT IN LEXINGTON, KENTUCKY . . . LEXINGTON: PRINTED BY DANIEL BRADFORD, 1807.

[A]–P^6. [1]–180. 21 x 12.5 cm. Six woodcut illustrations full-page and one in text. Gray boards, printed white paper label (1.8 x 1.5 cm.), uncut.

Prov.: Bookplate of subscriber J. Clemens, and with his signature and notes on title-page, front and back covers. Bookplate of Alden Scott Boyer laid in and with a note by him on inner back cover.

Ref.: AII (*Kentucky*) 300; Howes S344; Sabin 79932

In this fascinating production, the author recounts his experiences in the British Army and with the American Army during the Revolutionary War, and his travels through many parts of the United States.

This curious autobiography of an eccentric character was the earliest original work of a literary nature produced and written west of the Alleghanies.—Howes

Two of Shaw's "eccentricities" were addiction to alcohol and belief in dowsing.

3743 SHAW, LUELLA

TRUE HISTORY OF SOME OF THE PIONEERS OF COLORADO . . . HOTCHKISS, COLORADO: W. S. COBURN, JOHN PATTERSON AND A. K. SHAW, 1909.*

[i–ii], [1]–[269], [270 blank]. 20.1 x 14.9 cm. 12 illustrations unlisted. Gray printed wrappers.

Ref.: Adams 898; Howes S347
Printed in Denver.
Contains an account of the Sand Creek Massacre.

3744 SHAW, REUBEN C.

ACROSS THE PLAINS IN FORTY-NINE . . . FARMLAND, IND.: W. C. WEST, PUBLISHER, 1896.*

[i]–viii, [9]–200. 16.2 x 11 cm. Portrait. Dark red cloth. Lacks front fly-leaf.

Ref.: Howes S349; Morgan (Pritchard) p. 180
Shaw was a member of the Granite State and California Mining and Trading Company.

3745 SHAW, WILLIAM

GOLDEN DREAMS AND WAKING REALITIES; BEING THE ADVENTURES OF A GOLD-SEEKER IN CALIFORNIA AND THE PACIFIC ISLANDS . . . LONDON: SMITH, ELDER AND CO. 1851.

[i]–xii, [1]–316, [1]–16 advertisements dated June 1851. 19.5 x 12.2 cm. Bright blue cloth, blind embossed panels on sides, title stamped in gilt on backstrip.

Ref.: Cowan p. 580; Howes S351; Sabin 79971
The keen observations vividly told by a Britisher who, like most of his class, professed to suffer from his contact with California society.—Cowan

3746 SHEA, JOHN C.

THE ONLY TRUE HISTORY OF QUANTRELL'S RAID EVER PUBLISHED. REMINISCENCES OF QUANTRELL'S RAID UPON THE CITY OF LAWRENCE, KAS. THRILLING NARRATIVES BY LIVING EYE WITNESSES . . . KANSAS CITY, MO: ISAAC P. MOORE, PRINTER AND BINDER, 1879.

[1]–27, [28 blank]. 21.9 x 14.4 cm. Dark green printed wrappers with title in gold on front wrapper.

Ref.: Howes S355
Note inside front cover: This is the only known copy / aside from that in Mr Connellys[!] library. . . . / . . .

3747 SHEAHAN, JAMES W.

[Elaborate lithographic pictorial wrappers] PART 1 [–13]. CHICAGO ILLUSTRATED 1830 . . . 1866, LITERARY DESCRIPTION BY JAMES W. SHEAHAN ESQ. ILLUSTRATIONS BY THE CHICAGO LITHOGRAPHY CO. PUBLISHED BY JEVNE & ALMINI, 152 & 154 S. CLARK ST. CHICAGO. ENTERED ACCORDING TO ACT OF CONGRESS IN 1866 BY JEVNE & ALMINI IN THE CLERKS OFFICE OF THE DISTRICT COURT FOR N. ILLINOIS . . .

[1–104]. (Leaf of text for each plate.) 29.5 x 37.5 cm. 52 lithographic plates. 13 original parts, original pictorial wrappers, with title on front wrappers and advertisements on verso of back wrappers. In a brown buckram case.

Ref.: Howes J108
A superb set in the original wrappers. The best views of pre-fire Chicago.

3748 SHEAHAN, JAMES W.

THE SAME.

[1–104] 27.7 x 35.5 cm. 52 lithographic plates. Contemporary full brown leather, beveled covers, blind stamped borders on sides, name stamped in gilt on front cover: C. J. Gilbert. /, title stamped in gilt on backstrip, gilt edges.

Prov.: C. J. Gilbert copy, with his name stamped on the front cover.
The Lake Street fire is highly colored.

3749 SHELLEY, JOSEPH

[Pictorial wrapper title] WESTERN WILDS OF AMERICA . . .

[1–20]. 26.1 x 17.7 cm. Pictorial blue wrappers, with title on front wrapper, pictorial back wrapper. In a blue cloth case.

Ref.: Howes S380
Apparently printed at Brussels in 1888.
Shelley was a Texas Ranger for five years.

3750 SHEPARD, A. K.

THE LAND OF THE AZTECS; OR, TWO YEARS IN MEXICO . . . ALBANY: WEED, PARSONS & COMPANY, 1859.

[1]–209, [210 blank]. 18.7 x 12 cm. Dark brown cloth, blind embossed sides, title in gilt on backstrip.

Ref.: Howes S385; Sabin 80162

Overland narrative, across Mexico to Monterey on horseback, thence to Nueces. At San Antonio Shepard sold his horse, and then proceeded north across Texas and the Arkansas bottoms to Little Rock.—EDG

3751 SHEPHERD, WILLIAM

PRAIRIE EXPERIENCE IN HANDLING CATTLE AND SHEEP . . . LONDON: CHAPMAN AND HALL, LIMITED, 1884.

[i–vi (vi blank)], [1]–266, [1]–32 advertisements. 21.9 x 14.1 cm. Eight illustrations and one map listed. Green pictorial cloth with title in gilt on backstrip.

Ref.: Adams (*Ramp. Herd*) 2057; Howes S389; Rader 2920

3752 SHEPLER, C. V.

LITTLE GEM BRAND BOOK (CONTINUATION OF BIG FOUR BRAND BOOK.) FOR THE SPRING WORK OF 1900. THESE BRANDS WERE ALL GATHERED NEW IN THE YEAR 1899. VOL. 1, NO. 1, 1900. CONTAINS BRANDS OF CATTLE AND HORSES OF THE RANGE DISTRICT OF NORTH AND SOUTH DAKOTA, MONTANA AND WYOMING, (WHERE THE WATER RUNS EAST) NORTHEAST COLORADO AND NEBRASKA . . . KANSAS CITY, MO.: PUBLISHED BY THE LITTLE GEM BRAND BOOK CO., 1900.

[i]–xlviii, 1–155, [156 blank], + 4 [advertisement pasted over xxxiii; two-page cancel and advertisement pasted over xlii]. 17 x 10.2 cm. Printed calf. Worn, chipped, rebacked with cloth.

Ref.: Adams (*Ramp. Herd*) 2058

Advertisements interspersed throughout text and on inner covers.

3753 SHERIDAN, PHILIP H.

RECORD OF ENGAGEMENTS WITH HOSTILE INDIANS WITHIN THE MILITARY DIVISION OF THE MISSOURI, FROM 1868 TO 1882 . . . CHICAGO: HEADQUARTERS MILITARY DIVISION OF THE MISSOURI, 1882.*

[1]–120. 22.9 x 14.7 cm. Gray printed wrappers with title on front wrapper, bound into blue half morocco, gilt backstrip, gilt top.

Prov.: Inscribed on front wrapper: Compliments of / Lt. Gen. Sheridan /.

Ref.: Howes S395; Rader 3180

Over 400 engagements are listed and described.

3754 SHERMAN, SIDNEY

DEFENCE OF GEN. SIDNEY SHERMAN, AGAINST THE CHARGES MADE BY GEN. SAM HOUSTON IN HIS SPEECH DELIVERED IN THE UNITED STATES SENATE, FEBRUARY 28TH, 1859. GALVESTON: PRINTED AT THE "NEWS" BOOK AND JOB OFFICE, 1859.

[1]–29, [30 advertisement, 31–32 blank]. 21.7 x 14.2 cm. Removed from bound volume, unbound.

Ref.: Howes S402; Raines pp. 186–87; Winkler 1208

The advertisement on page [30] for the *Texas Almanac for 1860* does not appear in all copies.

3755 SHERMAN, WILLIAM T.

AUTOGRAPH LETTER, SIGNED. 1862 December 9, Headquarters, Right Wing, College Hill. One page, 25 x 20 cm. To Ulysses S Grant.

Letter commending Colonel Grierson to Grant's notice as "the best Cavalry Officer I have yet had."

3756 SHERMAN, WILLIAM T.

AUTOGRAPH LETTER, SIGNED. 1871 June 8, Fort Gibson C[herokee] T[e]r[ritory]. Four pages, 24.9 x 19.9 cm. To General Grierson.

Signed "Sherman," the letter contains remarks on the capture of the Kiowa chief Satanta, comments on the road situation between Fort Sill and Fort Gibson, and orders Grierson and McKenzie to "lay a trap to catch some party of horse thieves in Texas, near the line, and hang every one of them / it will stop this raiding."

3757 SHERWELL, SAMUEL

OLD RECOLLECTIONS OF AN OLD BOY . . . NEW YORK: THE KNICKERBOCKER PRESS, 1923.*

[i]–ix, [x blank], [1]–271, [272 blank]. 20.3 x 13.6 cm. Frontispiece portrait. Red cloth.

Ref.: Howes S405

Medical memoirs chiefly, but includes an overland narrative to Colorado in 1863.—EDG

3758 SHERWOOD, GHOST & CO., Lincoln, Nebraska

AUTOGRAPH LETTER, SIGNED. 1869 June 29, Lincoln, Nebraska. To Hon. R. R. Livingston. One page, 24.6 x 19.4 cm., of a four-page leaflet.

The letter is a recommendation for Mr. Wymph as a surveyor.

On pages [2–3] appears the following printed material: Nebraska Central Land Agency, / Sherwood, Ghost & Co., Lincoln, —Nebraska. / Our facilities for giving correct information and for aiding the Purchaser as / well as ten thousand Homeseekers in securing the most eligible locations / induces us to present the public with a brief statement of the superior ad-/vantages of our State. / [short rule] / [32 lines on page 2] / [39 lines on page 3] / Sherwood, Ghost & Co., / Lincoln, Nebraska, /

3759 SHIELDS, GEORGE O.

THE BATTLE OF THE BIG HOLE. A HISTORY OF GEN-ERAL GIBBON'S ENGAGEMENT WITH NEZ PERCES INDIANS IN THE BIG HOLE VALLEY, MONTANA, AU-GUST 9TH, 1877 . . . CHICAGO: RAND, McNALLY & COMPANY, 1889.

[1]–120, [121–24 advertisements]. 18.7 x 12.6 cm. Seven illustrations. Full dark brown leather, title in gilt on front cover and backstrip, gilt edges.

Ref.: Howes S412; Smith 9420

Probably a presentation binding. There is no evidence that a plate has been removed from the present copy.

3760 SHINN, CHARLES H.

MINING CAMPS: A STUDY IN AMERICAN FRONTIER GOVERNMENT . . . NEW YORK: CHARLES SCRIB-NER'S SONS, 1885.*

[i]–[xii, xii blank], 1–316, [317–24] advertise-ments. 20.2 x 13 cm. Brown cloth, title stamped in gilt on backstrip.

Ref.: Adams 904; Cowan p. 584; Howes S416

In this very readable book the author has traced closely and ably the evolution of laws and methods of government as devised by those primitive American communities, particularly in California, wherein the demand for protection and justice was imperative, and established courts were few and remote.—Cowan

3761 SHINN, JONATHAN

THE MEMOIRS OF CAPT. JONATHAN SHINN. GREELEY, COLORADO: WELD COUNTY DEMOCRAT. 1890.*

[1]–88. 17.8 x 11.5 cm. Dark orange printed wrappers with title on front wrapper.

Ref.: Howes S417

Shinn fought in the Black Hawk War, drove a stage between Peoria and Galena and Peoria and Springfield during the 1830's, in 1850 operated a ferry across the Missouri River at Council Bluffs, and in 1861 went to Pike's Peak.—EDG

3762 SHIPMAN, DANIEL

FRONTIER LIFE . . . 58 YEARS IN TEXAS. CONTAIN-ING A DESCRIPTION OF THE RESCOURCES[!] AND CAPABILITIES OF THE STATE, WITH A GRAPNICAL[!] OUTLINE OF ITS HISTORY. ALSO GIVING INTEREST-ING STATISTICS, AMOUNT OF LAND DONATED BY THE STATE FOR EDUCATIONAL PURPOCES[!], ETC., TOGETHER WITH THE HISTORY AND INCIDENTS OF THE SHIPMAN FAMILY, ETC., ETC.

[i–viii], [1]–403, [404 blank]. 20.3 x 14 cm. Mounted photograph of the author as frontis-piece. Green cloth, black leather backstrip.

Ref.: Dobie p. 52; Howes S421

Published at Houston, Texas, in 1879.

One of the pioneer reminiscences that should be reprinted.—Dobie. After copy-editing, we hope.

3763 SHIRREFF, PATRICK

A TOUR THROUGH NORTH AMERICA; TOGETHER WITH A COMPREHENSIVE VIEW OF THE CANADAS AND UNITED STATES . . . EDINBURGH: PRINTED BY BALLANTYNE AND COMPANY, 1835.

[1–2], [i]–iv, [i]–[vi, vi blank], [1]–473, [474 blank]. 21.6 x 14 cm. Red moiré cloth, printed white paper label.

Ref.: Buck 263; Buley I pp. 388–89, II, pp. 486, 640; Howes S425; Sabin 80554; Staton & Tremaine 1809

Shirreff was a level-headed British farmer who was both a good judge of people and of land.—Buley

3764 [SHIRT TAIL MINING] DISTRICT

[Broadside] KANSAS TERRITORY, [in manuscript: Shirt tail] DISTRICT. BE IT KNOWN, THAT [in man-uscript: James Hamilton] IS THE OWNER . . . THIS [in manuscript: 3ᵈ] DAY OF [in manuscript: Octo-ber] A. D. 1860. [in manuscript: John H. Jack] RECORDER. PRESIDENT. DENVER MOUNTAINEER PRINT.

Broadside, 12.5 x 19.2 cm. Text, 10.9 x 18.1 cm.

Ref.:

Above the phrase Shirt tail District, in manu-script: Now Idaho /. Docket on verso: Lincoln Lode / Shirt tail Dis. / Claim No. 2 S.W. Lin-con[!] Lode.

3765 SHOSHONE. Codsiogo

ORIGINAL PHOTOGRAPH, seated Indian in cos-tume, head to waist, body full-face, head three-quarters to his right. On verso: Baker & John-ston, Photographers. At top, in manuscript: *10* Codsiogo—a Shoshone /. 16.9 x 10.7 cm. Printed in sepia, mounted on stiff card, 17.4 x 11 cm.

3766 SIBLEY, GEORGE C.

MANUSCRIPT LETTER (Copy). 1826 May 20, Val-ley of Taos, New Mexico. Two pages, 31.9 x 19.5 cm. To Benjamin Reeves and Thomas Mather. In Mather Papers.

Regarding the local political situation and the possibility of completing the survey of the Santa Fé Road Commission.

3767 SIBLEY, GEORGE C.

MANUSCRIPT LETTER (Copy of an extract). 1826 March 5, Santa Fé. Two pages, 31.9 x 19.5 cm. To Joel R. Poinsett. In Mather Papers.

Reply to Poinsett's letter of 1825 December 31 regarding chances of completing the survey.

3768 SIBLEY, GEORGE C.

MANUSCRIPT ". . . list of articles that I think it will be proper for Cols. Reeves and Mather to bring out with them to Santa Feé . . ." (copy). 1826 February 7, Santa Fé. Two pages, 31.1 x 18.9 cm. In Mather Papers.

3769 SIBLEY, GEORGE C.

MANUSCRIPT LETTER (Copy). 1826 February 14, San Fernando, Taos. Two pages, 31.1 x 18.9 cm. To Reeves and Mather. In Mather Papers.
Regarding accounts of the Commission.

3770 SIBLEY, GEORGE C.

MANUSCRIPT LETTER (Copy). 1826 February 15, San Fernando. Two pages, 31.1 x 18.9 cm. To Reeves and Mather. In Mather Papers.
Regarding business of the Commission.

3771 SIBLEY, GEORGE C.

MANUSCRIPT LETTER (Copy). 1826 February 16, San Fernando. One page, 31.1 x 18.9 cm. To Reeves and Mather. In Mather Papers.
Introducing Paul Ballio.

3772 SIBLEY, GEORGE C.

AUTOGRAPH LETTER, SIGNED. 1827 November 19, Fayette, Missouri. Three pages, 19.7 x 16 cm. To Thomas Mather. In Mather Papers.
Suggesting a meeting of the Commissioners.

3773 SIBLEY, GEORGE C.

AUTOGRAPH LETTER, SIGNED. 1827 May 10, Fort Osage. Three pages, 14.9 x 19.8 cm. To Thomas Mather. In Mather Papers.
Details of his plans for a survey of the Santa Fé Road in 1827.

3774 SIBLEY, GEORGE C.

AUTOGRAPH LETTER, SIGNED. 1828 April 1, St. Charles. One page, 14.9 x 20 cm. To Thomas Mather. In Mather Papers.
Regarding finances of the Santa Fé Road Commission for 1828.

3775 SIBLEY, HENRY H.

[Caption title] ADDRESS OF HENRY H. SIBLEY, TO THE PEOPLE OF MINNESOTA TERRITORY . . .

[1]-8. 24 x 15.3 cm. Unbound leaflet, uncut, unopened. In a brown cloth folder with two other speeches by Sibley.
Ref.:
Without imprint or date. Signed at end and dated Washington City, July 29th, 1850.

3776 SIBLEY, HENRY H.

[Caption title] THE HOMESTEAD BILL. SPEECH . . . IN THE HOUSE OF REPRESENTATIVES, APRIL 24, 1852. IN FAVOR OF FREE GRANTS OF LAND TO ACTUAL SETTLERS, AND IN OPPOSITION TO THE BILL MAKING DONATIONS OF THE PUBLIC LANDS TO SEVERAL STATES, "FOR THE RELIEF AND SUPPORT OF THE INDIGENT INSANE THEREIN." . . .

[1]-7, [8 blank]. 24 x 15.6 cm. Unbound leaflet, uncut, unopened. In brown cloth case with two other Sibley pamphlets.
Ref.: Sabin 80820
Imprint in lower left corner of first page: [rule] / Printed at the Congressional Globe Office. / The date is probably 1852.

3777 SIBLEY, HENRY H.

[Double rule] MINNESOTA TERRITORY: ITS PRESENT CONDITION AND PROSPECTS . . .

[1]-6, [7-8 blank]. 24 x 15.9 cm. Unbound leaflet, uncut, unopened. In a cloth folder with two other Sibley pamphlets.
Ref.: Sabin 80822
Imprint on page 6 [double rule] / Printed at the Globe Office, Washngton[!]. / Dated at the end from Washington City, February 20, 1852. /

3778 SIBLEY, LEWIS

MANUSCRIPT DOCUMENT. 1809 June 16, Brownsville. One page, 18.1 x 19.4 cm. List of articles sent by Jacob Bowman to J. Johnson in Sibley's boat.

3779 SIGERSON, WILLIAM, & CO., St. Louis

[Caption title] TO CATTLE OWNERS AND DEALERS. YOUR ATTENTION IS CALLED TO THE KANSAS STOCK YARDS LOCATED AT ELLSWORTH, IN ELLSWORTH COUNTY, KANSAS. THE UNDERSIGNED HAVING ESTABLISHED LARGE AND COMMODIOUS YARDS FOR THE HANDLING AND SHIPPING OF TEXAS AND INDIAN CATTLE AT ELLSWORTH, WOULD RESPECTFULLY INVITE THE ATTENTION OF DROVERS AND DEALERS TO THE FOLLOWING FACTS: . . . VERY RESPECTFULLY WM. SIGERSON & CO. ST. LOUIS, MAY 20, 1869.

[1-3], [4 blank]. 24.9 x 20.1 cm. Map on page [3]: Map / of / Kansas / [lower left:] R. P. Studler & Co. lith. St. Louis. / 17.2 x 22.2 cm. No scale given. Unbound leaflet.
Ref.:
Manuscript note on page [4]: Wᵐ Sigerson & Co / Map of Kansas /.
Ellsworth was not an important market in 1869. No figures are available for 1869 or 1870, but in 1871 and 1872 it was an important shipping point, in fact the principal shipping point

for cattle on the Kansas Pacific R.R. In 1872 between 90,000 and 100,000 cattle came to Ellsworth from Texas.—EDG

3780 SIMMONS, FLORA E.

A COMPLETE ACCOUNT OF THE JOHN MORGAN RAID THROUGH KENTUCKY, INDIANA AND OHIO, IN JULY, 1863. PUBLISHED BY FLORA E. SIMMONS, 1863.

[1]–108. 13.5 x 8.8 cm. Gray printed wrappers with title on front cover as above within thick and thin rule borders.

Prov.: Rubber stamp of Dr. Otto L. Schmidt, / Chicago. / on front wrapper.

Ref.: Howes S463; Sabin 81156

Laid in is a broadside, headed: To the Public. /

Editions: No place, 1863 (94 pages).

3781 SIMMONS, FLORA E.

[Broadside] TO THE PUBLIC. THE BEARER OF THIS, MISS FLORA E. SIMMONS, IS AN HONEST AND INDUSTRIOUS GIRL, AND IN EVERY WAY WORTHY OF YOUR PATRONAGE. SHE SUPPORTS HERSELF AND MOTHER FROM THE PROCEEDS OF HER SALES . . .

Broadside, 12 x 18.5 cm. Text, 11.4 x 17.5 cm. Portion of upper right corner restored (affecting one word).

Ref.:

Neither place nor date of publication is given. Laid in Simmons: *A Complete Account of the John Morgan Raid . . .* 1863.

3782 SIMMONS, JAMES

THE HISTORY OF GENEVA, WISCONSIN . . . PUBLISHED AT THE OFFICE OF GENEVA LAKE HERALD, 1875.

[1]–101, [102 blank]. 21 x 14.7 cm. Gray cloth, title stamped in gilt on front cover, with black decorative bands on front cover and in blind on back cover.

Ref.: Bradford 4976; Howes S464

3783 SIMONIN, LOUIS LAURENT

LE GRAND-OUEST DES ETATS-UNIS . . . LES PIONNIERS ET LES PEAUXROUGES, LES COLONS DU PACIFIQUE. PARIS: CHARPENTIER, 1869.

[1–4], [i]–iv, [iv blank], [1]–364. 17.7 x 11 cm. Two maps, one folding. Green boards with green morocco back, sprinkled edges.

Ref.: Howes S486; Monaghan 1319; Sabin 81309; Smith 9454

Simonin, a mining engineer, made this trip in 1867 with the Colorado mining man, J. P. Whitney. Also included is a six-chapter account of early California which he visited in 1858–59.—EDG

3784 SIMONTON, J.

PRINTED AND MANUSCRIPT DOCUMENT, SIGNED. Clarinda, Iowa, November 21, 1860. One page, 31.7 x 20.2 cm.

Warrant of title issued by Judge Simonton to Leander Dixon for a quarter of a quarter of a section.

Imprint at foot: Herald, Print, Clarinda, Iowa. /

Docket on verso recording entry of the deed, signed by Solomon West.

3785 SIMPSON, ALEXANDER

THE LIFE AND TRAVELS OF THOMAS SIMPSON, THE ARCTIC DISCOVERER . . . LONDON: RICHARD BENTLEY, 1845.

[i]–viii, [1]–424. 21.5 x 13.7 cm. Portrait and folding map, unlisted. Map: Map of / the Country North of / Athabasca Lake, / North America. / Traversed by the different Arctic Expeditions. / [lower centre:] London. Richard Bentley. 1845. / 20.7 x 29.5 cm. Scale: 160 miles to one inch. Red cloth, blind embossed sides, gilt title on backstrip, unopened.

Ref.: Field 1412; Sabin 81338; Smith 9457; Staton & Tremaine 2397; Wagner-Camp 101 note

3786 SIMPSON, SIR GEORGE

NARRATIVE OF A JOURNEY ROUND THE WORLD, DURING THE YEARS 1841 AND 1842 . . . LONDON: HENRY COLBURN, 1847.

[i]–[xii], [1]–438, [1]–24, advertisements. [i]–[viii (viii blank)], [1]–469, [470 blank]. 23.4 x 14.8 cm. Portrait and folding map listed. Map: Map / Shewing / the Author's Route. / [rule] / NB. The Route is described by a Dotted Line colored Red. . . . . / [lower centre:] London.— Published by H. Colburn, 13 G^t Marlborough St. 1847. [lower right:] J. Netherclift & Son Lithog. / 22 x 62.5 cm. No scale given. Two volumes, dark blue cloth, blind embossed sides, title gilt on backstrips, uncut, partly unopened.

Ref.: Cowan p. 589; Howes S495; Sabin 81343; Staton & Tremaine 2548; Wagner-Camp 140

3787 SIMPSON, SIR GEORGE

PEACE RIVER. A CANOE VOYAGE FROM HUDSON'S BAY TO PACIFIC . . . IN 1828. JOURNAL OF THE LATE CHIEF FACTOR, ARCHIBALD McDONALD . . . WHO ACCOMPANIED HIM. OTTAWA: PUBLISHED BY J. DURIE & SON. 1872.

[i]–xix, [xx blank], [1]–119, [120 blank]. 22 x 14.6 cm. Map: British / North America. / By Permission Dedicated to / The Honble Hudson's Bay Company, / Containing the latest informa-

tion which / their documents furnish / By their Obedient Servant / J. Arrowsmith. / Leggo & C⁰ Steam-lith. Montreal 1832. / Copied from original, & with latest additions. / 47.1 x 60.9 cm. No scale given. Pale green printed wrappers with title on front wrapper. In a green cloth case.

Ref.: Smith 6284

Laid in is a calligraphic specimen by Malcolm McLeod dated July 20, 1838, 18.8 x 24.3 cm.

Tipped in before the title-page is a fifteen-line errata slip, 7.6 x 13.7 cm.

3788 SIMPSON, HENRY I.

THE EMIGRANT'S GUIDE TO THE GOLD MINES. THREE WEEKS IN THE GOLD MINES, OR ADVENTURES WITH THE GOLD DIGGERS OF CALIFORNIA IN AUGUST, 1848 . . . NEW YORK: JOYCE AND CO., 1848.

[1]–30, [31–2 advertisements]. 24.1 x 15 cm. Three vignettes in text, vignette on title-page (repeated on front wrapper), and large cut on verso of front wrapper. Map: Map of / California / and the Routes to reach it / 27.1 x 26 cm. Scale: about 200 miles to one inch. *Inset:* [Map of the Americas showing sea route to San Francisco] 14 x 10.5 cm. (irregular shape). No scale given. Light brown printed wrappers with title on front wrapper, cut on verso, advertisements on recto and verso of back, uncut.

Ref.: Cowan pp. 589–90; Howes S497; Vail (*Gold Fever*) p. 251; Wheat (*Gold Rush*) 189; Wheat (*Gold Region*) 57

Simpson, alleged member of Stevenson's Regiment of New York Volunteers, claimed to have spent three weeks in the gold region. This very early pamphlet (32 pages) contains his "personal narrative" of the experience, together with a sketchy "Description of California" for the edification of prospective goldseekers.—Wheat

According to the front wrapper, the pamphlet was sold for eighteen cents with the map, or twelve and one-half cents without the map.

3789 SIMPSON, JAMES H.

JOURNAL OF A MILITARY RECONNAISSANCE, FROM SANTA FE, NEW MEXICO, TO THE NAVAJO COUNTRY . . . PHILADELPHIA: LIPPINCOTT, CRAMBO AND CO., 1852.

[1]–140, 1–27, [28 blank], 9–12 advertisements. 22.4 x 14.1 cm. 75 illustrations, 27 in color, listed. And a map, listed. Map: Map / of the Route pursued in 1849 by the U. S. Troops, / under the command of / Bvt. Lieut. Col. Jno. M. Washington, Governor of New Mexico, / in an expedition against the Navajos Indians, / By / James M. Simpson, 1ˢᵗ Lieut. T. Engʳˢ / As-

sisted by Mr. Edw. M. Kern. / [double rule] / Constructed under the general orders of / Col. J. J. Abert, Chief Topˡ Engʳˢ / Drawn by Edward M. Kern. / Santa Fe, N. M. 1849. / [lower left:] J. G. Shoemaker, engr. / [below cartouche:] P. S. Duval's Steam Lith. Press. Philadᵃ / 51.6 x 70.2 cm. Scale: 10 miles to one inch. Notes consist of 24 lines. Green cloth, blind embossed sides, title in gilt on backstrip.

Ref.: Field 1413; Howes S498; Rader 2924; Sabin 81353; Wagner-Camp 218; Wheat (*Transmississippi*) 641

First separate edition. Howes and Wagner-Camp call for 72 plates of which 34 are colored. Confusion probably arises because two plates are in two and three parts respectively. All plates carry the Duval imprint. Three plates 2, 21, 39 were not issued.

3790 SIMPSON, JAMES H.

[Caption title] . . . REPORT FROM THE SECRETARY OF WAR, COMMUNICATING . . . THE REPORT AND MAP OF THE ROUTE FROM FORT SMITH, ARKANSAS, TO SANTA FE, NEW MEXICO, MADE BY LIEUTENANT SIMPSON . . .

[1]–25, [26 blank]. 22.2 x 14.5 cm. Map: Map / of route pursued by U. S. Troops, from Fort Smith, Arkansas, to Santa Fe, New Mexico / via / South Side of Canadian River, / in the year 1849. / Whilst serving as an Escort to a party of California Emigrants. / Escort commanded and Location and Construction of Road directed by / Cap. R. B. Marcy, 5ᵗʰ Infʸ assisted as far as Topofke Creek by Byᵗ[!] Cap. F. T. Dent, 5ᵗʰ Infʸ / 1ˢᵗ Lieut. James H. Simpson, U. S. T. Engʳˢ / assisted as far as Topofke Creek, by Cap. Dent, and all the way through by Mr. Thoˢ A. P. Champlin. / projected & drawn by / Lᵗ Simpson, assisted by Mʳ E. M. Kern, and Mʳ Champlin. / [decorative rule] / . . . [lower centre:] P. S. Duval's Steam Lith press Phil. / 31 x 48.1 cm. Scale: 10 miles to one inch. [Horizontal cut across centre] Map: Map, N⁰ 2. / Showing a Continuation of Details of Fort Smith and Santa Fé Route / from Old Fort Holmes to Mounds near 100 1/2 degree of Longitude / By / 1ˢᵗ Lieut. J. H. Simpson Corpˢ Topˡ Engʳ / 1849, / [10 lines] / Lith by E. Weber & C⁰, Balto. / [upper right:] Senate Executive Doc. N⁰ 12, 1ˢᵗ Session 31. Congress / 27.6 x 49.5 cm. Scale: 10 miles to one inch. Map: Map, N⁰3, / Showing continuation of details of Fort Smith and Santa Fé Route, from / Mounds near the 100 1/2 degree of W. Longitude to Tucumcari Creek. / by / 1st Lieut: J. H. Simpson Corps of Top: Engⁿ / 1849 / [6 lines] / P. S. Duval's Steam Lith. Press. Philᵃ / 31.3 x 51.2 cm. Scale: 10 miles to one

inch. Map: Map, N⁰ 4. / Showing Continuation of Fort Smith and Santa Fé Route, / from Tucumcari Creek to Santa Fé. / By / 1ˢᵗ Lieut. J. H. Simpson Corps Topᴸ Engʳˢ / 1849. / [7 lines] / Exploration and survey terminated at / Santa Fé June 28ᵗʰ 1849. / Lith. by E. Weber & Cᵒ Balto. / [upper right:] Senate Executive Doc. N⁰ 12, 1ˢᵗ Session 31. Congress. / 17.8 x 49.8 cm. Scale: 10 miles to one inch. Rebound in new red cloth.

Ref.: Howes S500; Wagner-Camp 192; Wheat (*Transmississippi*) 640

31st Congress, 1st Session, Senate, Executive Document No. 12, Serial 554. [Washington, 1850.]

3791 SIMPSON, JAMES H.

. . . REPORT OF EXPLORATIONS ACROSS THE GREAT BASIN OF THE TERRITORY OF UTAH FOR A DIRECT WAGON-ROUTE FROM CAMP FLOYD TO GENOA, IN CARSON VALLEY, IN 1859 . . . WASHINGTON: GOVERNMENT PRINTING OFFICE, 1876.*

[1]–518. (Errata slip, 22 x 17.3 cm., tipped to page [7].) 29.6 x 23.3 cm. 25 plates and maps listed. Map: Map of Route / of / Father Escalante / From Santa Fé to Lake Utah / and back / by way of Oraybe, Zuñi & Acoma / 1776–7. / [upper left:] Explorations of Capt. J. H. Simpson, T. E. U. S. A. in 1859. / [upper right:] Plate G. / 22.1 x 24.2 cm. No scale given. Map: Map of / Wagon Routes / in Utah Territory / Explored & opened by / Capt. J. H. Simpson Topl. Engrs. U. S. A. / Assisted by / Lieuts. J. L. K. Smith and H. S. Putnam Topl. Engrs. U. S. A. / and Mr. Henry Engelmann / in 1858–59 / by authority of / Hon. John B. Floyd Sec. of War / and under Instructions from / Bvt. Brig. Gen. A. S. Johnston U. S. A. / Comdg. Dept. of Utah. / Drawn by J. P. Mechlin. / Scale 1/1,000,000. / Scale of Statute Miles. / [diagrammatic scale: about 16 miles to one inch] / [upper right:] Explorations of Capt. J. H. Simpson, T. E. U. S. A. in 1859. / [lower right:] Facsimile Reproduction by The Graphic Co. 39 & 41 Park Place, N. Y. / 66.4 x 121.5 cm. Scale as above. Green cloth.

Ref.: Bradford 4984; Howes S501; Sabin 81355; Wagner-Camp 345; Wheat (*Transmississippi*) 999

Edward M. Kern's diary of Frémont's 1845–46 explorations appears here for the first time, pages 474–86. The publication of the report in 1861 was prevented by the Civil War.

3792 SIMPSON, JAMES H.

[Caption title] . . . REPORT OF THE SECRETARY OF WAR, COMMUNICATING . . . CAPTAIN SIMPSON'S

REPORT AND MAP OF WAGON ROAD ROUTES IN UTAH TERRITORY . . .

[1]–84. 24.5 x 15.3 cm. Map: Preliminary / Map / of / Routes Reconnoitred and Opened / in the / Territory of Utah / by / Captain J. H. Simpson, Corps of Topographical Engineers, / in the Fall of 1858. / under the Orders of / Bvt. Brigadier General A. S. Johnston, Commanding / The Department of Utah. / [upper right:] 35ᵗʰ Cong. 2ⁿᵈ Session Senate Ex. Doc. N⁰ 40. / [lower centre:] Lith. of J. Bien, 60 Fulton Street N. Y. / 76.1 x 111.9 cm. Scale: five miles to one inch. Rebound in new red cloth, map in pocket attached to back endpaper, uncut, mostly unopened.

Ref.: Howes S499; Sabin 81354; Wagner-Camp 345

35th Congress, 2nd Session, Senate, Executive Document No. 40, Serial 984. [Washington, 1859.]

3793 SIMPSON, JAMES H.

THE SHORTEST ROUTE TO CALIFORNIA ILLUSTRATED BY A HISTORY OF EXPLORATIONS OF THE GREAT BASIN OF UTAH WITH ITS TOPOGRAPHICAL AND GEOLOGICAL CHARACTER AND SOME ACCOUNT OF THE INDIAN TRIBES . . . PHILADELPHIA: J. B. LIPPINCOTT & CO., 1869.

[1]–58, [59–60 blank]. 20.7 x 13.5 cm. Folding map: Explorations / of / Capt. J. H. Simpson, / Corps of Topˡ Engrˢ U.S.A. in 1859. / Across the Great Basin of Utah / [lower right:] T. Sinclair, lith. Philada. / 22.3 x 43.1 cm. No scale given. Salmon printed wrappers with title on front cover. In a red cloth case.

Prov.: Inscribed on the title-page: To Hon James Harlan / with the respects of the / Author /.

Ref.: Howes S504; Rader 2925; Sabin 81358

3794 SIMPSON, THOMAS

NARRATIVE OF THE DISCOVERIES ON THE NORTH COAST OF AMERICA; EFFECTED BY THE OFFICERS OF THE HUDSON'S BAY COMPANY DURING THE YEARS 1836–39 . . . LONDON: RICHARD BENTLEY, 1843.

[i]–xix, [xx blank], [1]–419, [420 colophon]. 22.1 x 14 cm. Two folding maps in pocket in front cover: Map of / the Arctic Coast of / America / from Return Reef to Point Barrow / explored by / Messʳˢ P. W. Dease & T. Simpson / under the direction of / The Honᵇˡᵉ Hudson's Bay Company / 1837. / [lower right:] John Arrowsmith. / 11.5 x 19.4 cm. No scale given. Map: Northern America / [lower centre:] London, Richard Bently, New Burlington Sᵗ 1843. [lower right:] John Arrowsmith. / 31 x 32.7 cm. (plate mark). Scale: about 170 miles to

one inch. *Inset:* Discoveries / of the / Honble Hudson's Bay Company's Arctic Expedition / in / 1838 & 1839. / 8.1 x 29.7 cm. Scale: 50 miles to one inch. Brown cloth, blind embossed covers, gilt title on backstrip, uncut.

Ref.: Field 1411; Sabin 81374; Smith 9470; Staton & Tremaine 2315; Wagner-Camp 101; Wickersham 2804

3795 SIMS, J. MARION

THE STORY OF MY LIFE . . . NEW YORK: D. APPLETON AND COMPANY, 1884.

[1]–471, [472 blank], [473–80 advertisements]. 19 x 12.5 cm. Light brown cloth, title stamped in gilt on backstrip.

Ref.: Howes S509

An interesting and important medical autobiography.—EDG

3796 SIOUX. Rain-in-the-Face

ORIGINAL PHOTOGRAPH, seated Indian, full face, body turned slightly to his right, buckskin shirt, cloth vest, beads, furs, etc. Lettered in print at foot: 542. Rain-in-the-Face. Slayer of General Custer. / Printed in sepia, mounted on stiff card. Print, 13.3 x 9.6 cm. Card, 16.5 x 10.8 cm.

Ref.: Hodge II 353

Hodge describes Rain-in-the-Face as a Hunkpapa and as a Sioux warrior and chief. Born about 1835; died Sept. 14, 1905.

3797 SIOUX. Sitting Bull (Tatanka Yotanka)

PHOTOGRAPH, seated Indian in white shirt, pipe across knees, faced slightly to his right, oval shape. In print, at foot, (Ta-ton-ka-i-yo-ton-ka,) "Sitting Bull" / The Sioux Chief in command at the Custer Massacre. / Below print, on card: Copyright applied for. Printed in sepia, mounted on stiff card. Print, 15 x 10.2 cm. Card, 16.6 x 10.8 cm.

Ref.: Hodge II 583

On verso: Photographs and Stereoscopic Views / ---of--- / "Sitting Bull" and Camp, / . . . W. R. Cross, / Photographer and Publisher, / Niobrara, Nebraska. / . . .

Hodge describes Sitting Bull as a Hunkpapa Teton Sioux and states he was born in 1834 and was killed on December 15, 1890.

3798 SIOUX. Struck-by-the-Ree (Palaneapape)

ORIGINAL PHOTOGRAPH, seated Indian in heavy clothing, deerstalker cap, crucifix on chest, seated in rocker, cane against right knee. Printed in sepia, mounted on stiff card. Print, 14.7 x 10.2 cm. Card, 16.4 x 10.8 cm.

Ref.: Hodge II 644–45

Inscribed in manuscript on back: "*Strike The Ree.*" / Chief of the Sioux / Died June, 1888. / Aged 109 years /.

Hodge describes Struck-by-the-Ree as a Yankton Sioux and gives his birthdate as Aug. 30, 1804 and his death date as July 29, 1888.

3799 SIOUX CITY DIRECTORY

GENERAL DIRECTORY OF SIOUX CITY . . . 1880–81. SIOUX CITY, IOWA: DAILY JOURNAL BOOK AND JOB PRINTING HOUSE, 1880.

[1]–85, [86 blank]. (Page 85 mispaginated 84.) 21.6 x 13.7 cm. Pink printed boards, red leather backstrip, advertisements on covers and endpapers.

Ref.:

3800 SIOUX CITY & ST. PAUL RAILROAD

NORTHWESTERN IOWA AND ITS RESOURCES . . . GIVING VALUABLE INFORMATION TO THOSE SEEKING HOMES OR DESIRING A RELIABLE DESCRIPTION OF THE COUNTRY . . . SIOUX CITY, IOWA: GEORGE D. PERKINS, BOOK AND JOB PRINTER, 1876.

[1]–16. 21.5 x 13.6 cm. Map: [title within flourishes] Map / of the North Western Part of / Iowa. / Showing the / Land Grant / of the / Sioux City and St Paul R. R. / Scale 6 Miles to one Inch. / Lithographed and printed by Rice & Co., St. Paul. / 40.8 x 38.8 cm. Scale as above. Dark yellow wrappers, with title on front wrapper, two lines on verso of back wrapper.

Ref.:

On the title-page, this version is called a New Edition. Earlier editions have not been found.

3801 SIRINGO, CHARLES A.

AUTOGRAPH LETTER, SIGNED, in pencil. 1926 April 1, Hollywood, California. Two pages, 27.8 x 21.3 cm. To C. V. Ritter.

Regarding books available and prices. Written on the verso of a letter by C. V. Ritter. Laid in Siringo, Charles A.: *A Texas Cowboy* . . . [1886].

3802 SIRINGO, CHARLES A.

A COWBOY DETECTIVE; A TRUE STORY OF TWENTY-TWO YEARS WITH A WORLD-FAMOUS DETECTIVE AGENCY GIVING THE INSIDE FACTS OF THE BLOODY COEUR D'ALENE LABOR RIOTS, AND THE MANY UPS AND DOWNS OF THE AUTHOR THROUGHOUT THE UNITED STATES, BRITISH COLUMBIA AND OLD MEXICO . . . CHICAGO: W. B. CONKEY COMPANY, 1912.

[1]–519, [520 blank]. 19 x 13.3 cm. 20 illustrations listed. Light blue-gray cloth.

Ref.: Adams 911; Adams (*Ramp. Herd*) 2072; Dobie p. 119; Dykes 63; Howes S515

3803 SIRINGO, CHARLES A.

A LONE STAR COWBOY; BEING FIFTY YEARS EXPERIENCE IN THE SADDLE AS COWBOY, DETECTIVE AND NEW MEXICO RANGER, ON EVERY COW TRIAL IN THE WOOLY OLD WEST . . . SANTA FE, NEW MEXICO, 1919.

[i–viii], [1]–291, [292 advertisement]. 19.6 x 13.6 cm. 15 illustrations listed. Stapled and bound into dark red cloth. In dust jacket.

Prov.: Inscribed on fly-leaf: To Mr. Gilbert E. Morton, / who has crossed many / of the cow-trails mentioned / in this Volume. / With good wishes / from the Author, / Chas. A. Siringo / Hollywood, Calif. / Oct. 10ᵗʰ 1925. /

Ref.: Adams 914; Adams (*Ramp. Herd*) 2074; Dobie p. 119; Dykes 73; Howes S518

3804 SIRINGO, CHARLES A.

A TEXAS COW BOY; OR, FIFTEEN YEARS ON THE HURRICANE DECK OF A SPANISH PONY . . . CHICAGO, ILLINOIS: M. UMBDENSTOCK & CO., PUBLISHERS, 1885.

[i]–xii, [13]–316. 19.6 x 13.3 cm. Four illustrations, including colored title-page and colored frontispiece included in pagination. Dark green pictorial cloth, with title in gilt on front cover, backstrip plain.

Prov.: Signature on preliminary leaf: C S. Finch /. On the same leaf: Regards of the author /. This may be in the hand of Siringo.

Ref.: Adams 917; Adams (*Ramp. Herd*) 2077; Clements Library (*Texas*) 48; Dobie p. 119; Dykes 17; Howes S518

This "stove up" cowboy, as he describes himself, recorded his life story when about thirty years old. His memories were, therefore, fresh. In strongly cowboy language, he has given a vivid picture of Texas ranch life.

3805 SIRINGO, CHARLES A.

THE SAME . . . CHICAGO, ILL.: SIRINGO & DOBSON, PUBLISHERS, 1886.

[i]–xii, [13]–347, [348 blank]. 19.4 x 13.2 cm. 11 illustrations. Dark red pictorial cloth with title on front cover and on backstrip.

Ref.:

3806 SIRINGO, CHARLES A.

THE SAME . . . CHICAGO: THE EAGLE PUBLISHING CO., 1890.

[i]–xii, [13]–347, [348 blank, 349–50 advertisements, 351–52 blank]. 11 illustrations including one in color. Dark green cloth, gilt.

3807 SIRINGO, CHARLES A.

THE SAME . . . CHICAGO AND NEW YORK: RAND, MCNALLY & COMPANY. PUBLISHERS.

[i–iii advertisements, iv frontispiece], [1]–347, [348–50 advertisements]. (Advertisements on page [8].) 18.7 x 12.5 cm. Frontispiece and one plate. Pictorial wrappers, with title on front wrapper, advertisements on verso of front and recto and verso of back wrapper. In a green cloth case.

Retains Siringo copyright of 1886, although printed later. No. 56 in the Globe Library.

Laid in is an Autograph Letter, signed in pencil by the author. 1926 April 1, Hollywood, California.

3808 SIRINGO, CHARLES A.

TWO EVIL ISMS: PINKERTONISM AND ANARCHISM . . . CHICAGO, ILL.: BY CHAS. A SIRINGO, 1915.*

[i–iv], 1–109, [110 advertisements]. 19.3 x 13.3 cm. Two-page frontispiece. Printed pictorial wrappers.

Ref.: Adams 918; Dykes 68; Howes S519

3809 SITGREAVES, LORENZO

. . . REPORT OF AN EXPEDITION DOWN THE ZUNI AND COLORADO RIVERS . . . WASHINGTON: ROBERT ARMSTRONG, PUBLIC PRINTER, 1853.

[1]–198. 22.3 x 14.1 cm. 78 plates, incorrectly listed, and a map. Map: Reconnaissance / of the / Zuñi, Little Colorado / and / Colorado Rivers. / Made in 1851 under the direction of / Col. J. J. Abert, Chief of Corps Topographical Engineeʳˢ / by / Bvt. Capt. L. Sitgreaves, T. E. / Assisted by / Lieut. J. G. Parke, T. E. and Mʳ M. H. Kern. / Drawn by R. H. Kern. / 1852. / [swelled rule] / Gila River from a reconnaissance by Maj. Emory Topographical Engʳˢ / Colorado River below Camp Yuma from a reconnaissance by Lᵗ Derby Topographical Engʳˢ / Ackerman Lith: 379 Broadway N. Y. / . . . / 67 x 120.3 cm. Scale: ten miles to one inch. Black cloth, blind embossed sides, title in gilt on backstrip.

Ref.: Field 1414; Howes S521; Munk (Alliot) p. 202; Sabin 81472; Wagner-Camp 230

32nd Congress, 2nd Session, Senate, Executive Document No. 59, Serial 668.

The illustrations do not follow the list in all particulars and Wagner-Camp has confused the matter.

In the section titled Landscapes, etc., plates 14–20 are misnumbered 15–[21], plate 21 is unnumbered, and plates 22–3 are misnumbered 23–4. The section headed Birds; plate 2 was not issued. In the section titled Reptiles, plate 10a is misnumbered 10 and plate 12 is misnumbered XIII. In the final section headed Plants, there is an unlisted plate XXI.

3810 SKINNER, A. A.

AUTOGRAPH LETTER, SIGNED. 1865 January 10, Eugene City, Oregon. One page, 24.8 x 19.9 cm. To Jesse Applegate.

Inserted in Manuscript Journals of Loren L. Williams, Volume III.

3811 SKINNER, JAMES

SKETCHES OF PIONEER LIFE . . . QUINCY, ILLINOIS: THE JOHN HALL PRINTING CO., 1917.

[i]–[viii, viii blank], [1]–430. 19.3 x 13.6 cm. Five portraits unlisted. Green cloth, title stamped in yellow on front cover and backstrip.

Ref.:

The author was a most active man; his adventures took place in Illinois, Missouri, Kansas, California, Texas, and a few other places. He was married three times.

3812 SKINNER, MARK

AN ADDRESS, DELIVERED BEFORE THE NEW ENGLAND SOCIETY, OF CHICAGO, ILLINOIS, DECEMBER 22, 1847 . . . CHICAGO, ILL.: CHICAGO DEMOCRAT BOOK AND JOB ESTABLISHMENT, 1848.

[1]–30, [31–2 blank]. 20.4 x 12 cm. Rebound in green buckram.

Ref.: Byrd 1376; McMurtrie (*Chicago*) 192(?); Sabin 81618

Mark Skinner was an old friend of Walter L. Newberry and was an original trustee of his estate.

3813 SLACUM, WILLIAM A.

[Caption title] . . . MEMORIAL OF WILLIAM A. SLACUM, PRAYING COMPENSATION FOR HIS SERVICES IN OBTAINING INFORMATION IN RELATION TO THE SETTLEMENTS ON THE OREGON RIVER . . .

[1]–31, [32 blank]. 22.7 x 14.8 cm. Removed from bound volume, unbound. In a green cloth case.

Ref.:

25th Congress, 2nd Session, Senate, Document No. 24, Serial 314. [Washington, 1838.] Printer's imprint at foot of page [1]: [short rule] / Blair & Rives, printers. /

A fascinating early account of Oregon, particularly of the Willamette Settlement.

3814 SLATER, NELSON

FRUITS OF MORMONISM; OR, A FAIR AND CANDID STATEMENT OF FACTS ILLUSTRATIVE OF MORMON PRINCIPLES, MORMON POLICY, AND MORMON CHARACTER . . . COLOMA, CAL.: HARMON & SPRINGER, 1851.

[i–ii], [1]–[94]. 16.7 x 12.2 cm. Black cloth. In a black cloth case.

Prov.: Slip pasted to inside front cover inscribed as follows: With Respects of / the Author— / Written in the spring / of 1851— /.

Ref.: AII (*California*) 181; Cowan p. 591; Greenwood 301; Howes S542; Jones 1268; Wagner (*California Imprints*) 137; Wagner-Camp 205

Blanket arraignment of Utah Mormons. One of the earliest English books printed in California.—Howes

3815 SLOAN, WALTER B.

HISTORY OF KANSAS AND NEBRASKA: DESCRIBING SOIL, CLIMATE, RIVERS, PRAIRIES, MOUNDS, FORESTS, MINERALS, ROADS, CITIES, VILLAGES, INHABITANTS, AND OTHER SUBJECTS RELATING TO THAT REGION . . . GALESBURG, ILL.: BOISHEL, KUHN & CO., 1857.

[1–4], [9]–80. 19.2 x 12.1 cm. Folding map: Map / of / Kansas & Nebraska / Redrawn from official sources with emendations / Ed. Mendel Lith. Chicago / 22.3 x 17 cm. No scale given. Green printed wrappers, with title on front wrapper, advertisements on verso of front and recto and verso of back wrapper. In a black cloth case.

Ref.: Byrd 2349; Howes S557; Jones 1343 (Chicago ed.); Rader 2929 (Chicago ed.); Wagner-Camp 271 (Chicago, 1855 ed.)

No other copy with the Galesburg imprint located.

Verso of front and recto of back wrapper: Latest Information / for / Emigrants to Kansas. / Continued on back wrapper and upper third of verso of back wrapper, balance of latter with advertisement of publisher.

Editions: Chicago, 1855.

3816 SLOAN, WALTER B.

SLOAN'S ALMANAC AND TRAVELER'S GUIDE FOR 1851 . . . CHICAGO: PUBLISHED BY W. B. SLOAN.

[1]–32. 18.3 x 12.3 cm. Stitched, unbound.

Ref.: Byrd 1515–1516 see; McMurtrie (*Chicago*) 198 note

There were at least two editions published with imprints of Chicago printers, but this was probably printed at Buffalo, New York.

3817 SMALLEY, EUGENE V.

HISTORY OF THE NORTHERN PACIFIC RAILROAD . . . NEW YORK: G. P. PUTNAM'S SONS, 1883.

[i]–xxii, [3]–437 [438 blank]. 23.4 x 17 cm. Folding profile and large folding map, latter in pocket at back, five other maps. Map: Map of the Northern Pacific Railroad, its Branches and Allied Lines. / [lower right:] Julius Bien & Co. Lith. / 31.4 x 71.2 cm. Scale: 80 miles to an inch. Brown cloth, gilt monogram on front cover, gilt title on backstrip.

Ref.: Howes S561; *Railway Economics* p. 244
Tipped in before the title-page is a small slip with printed text: Advance Copy. / [short rule] / With the Compliments of / The Northern Pacific Railroad Company. /

The forty-eight plates called for by Howes are not present in this copy; perhaps they were not issued with the advance copies.

3818 SMART, STEPHEN F.

COLORADO TOURIST AND ILLUSTRATED GUIDE VIA THE "GOLDEN BELT ROUTE," THE GREAT WHEAT AND CORN PRODUCING REGION EXTENDING FROM THE MISSOURI RIVER THROUGH CENTRAL KANSAS AND COLORADO (WHICH IS TRAVERSED BY THE KANSAS PACIFIC RAILWAY) TO THE ROCKY MOUNTAIN RESORTS . . . KANSAS CITY: RAMSEY, MILLETT & HUDSON, 1879.

[1]–72. 27.2 x 20.2 cm. Illustrations unlisted. Map: A Geographically Correct map of / Kansas & Colorado, / Showing Principal Cities & Towns, / Including the Famous Health & Pleasure Resorts of the Rocky Mountains, / Reached by the / Kansas Pacific Railway. / The / "Golden Belt Route." 24.5 x 63.1 cm. No scale given. Printed pictorial wrappers, with title on front wrapper, illustration on verso of back wrapper. In a brown board case.

Ref.: Bradford 5003; Howes S563

3819 SMART, STEPHEN F.

LEADVILLE, TEN MILE EAGLE RIVER, ELK MOUNTAIN, TIN CUP AND ALL OTHER NOTED COLORADO MINING CAMPS, ILLUSTRATED, WITH ACCURATE MAP OF THE LEADVILLE DISTRICT, AND KANSAS AND COLORADO, TOGETHER WITH U. S. AND STATE MINING LAWS, AND RULES OF THE NATIONAL LAND DEPARTMENT . . . KANSAS CITY, MO.: RAMSEY, MILLETT & HUDSON, 1879.

[1]–56. 22.6 x 14.8 cm. Illustrations and two folding maps unlisted. Map: Map of the / Leadville Silver Mines and Claims, / Corrected to Date. / 35.3 x 45.7 cm. (page size). No scale given. *Inset:* This Map of the most Direct Route from the Missouri River to Leadville / and all other important cities, Health and Pleasure Resorts of / Colorado, was furnished by the Kansas Pacific Railway. / 7.2 x 19.7 cm. No scale given. Map: A Geographically Correct Map of / Kansas & Colorado, / Showing Principal Cities & Towns, / Including the Famous Health & Pleasure Resorts of the Rocky Mountains, / Reached by the / Kansas Pacific Railway. / The / "Golden Belt Route." 24.3 x 63.6 cm. No scale given. Gray printed wrappers with title on front cover, advertisements on verso of front and recto of back wrapper, cut on verso of back wrapper. In a red half morocco slip case.

Ref.: Bradford 5002; Howes S562; Sabin 82236 see

3820 SMEDLEY, WILLIAM

ACROSS THE PLAINS IN '62 . . .

[i–ii], [1]–56. 20.4 x 14.2 cm. Illustrations unlisted. Gray printed boards, brown cloth back.

Prov.: Inscribed on half-title: Fraternally Yours / W$^{\underline{m}}$ Smedley / 6–15–'16 /

Ref.: Howes S566
Published in Denver in 1916.

Laid in is a menu of the dinner in honor of the author in 1916 by the Colorado State Dental Association.

3821 SMET, PIERRE JEAN DE

CINQUANTE NOUVELLES LETTRES . . . PARIS: H. CASTERMAN, EDITEUR, 1858.

[I]–[X, X blank], [1]–502, [503 errata, 504 colophon]. 17.8 x 11.3 cm. Black cloth, blind embossed sides, title in gilt on backstrip.

Ref.: Howes D281; Pilling (*Alg.*) pp. 468, 573; Sabin 82260; Smith 9537; Streit III 2456; Wagner-Camp 308

3822 [SMET, PIERRE JEAN DE]

THE INDIAN MISSIONS IN THE UNITED STATES OF AMERICA, UNDER THE CARE OF THE MISSOURI PROVINCE OF THE SOCIETY OF JESUS. PHILADELPHIA: KING AND BAIRD, PRINTERS, 1841.

[1]–34. 17.7 x 11.4 cm. Rebound into old blue plain wrappers. In a black half morocco case.

Ref.: Howes D282; Sabin 82261; Streit III 2284; Wagner-Camp 87
This pamphlet comprises a report on the Indian missions by Father P. J. Verhaegen, an extract from a pastoral letter by the Archbishop of Baltimore and the bishops of the Church in Provincial Council, an extract from a long letter by Father Pierre Jean De Smet, and a complete letter by De Smet. In each of the latter cases, the author is given as De Smedt.

3823 SMET, PIERRE JEAN DE

LETTERS AND SKETCHES: WITH A NARRATIVE OF A YEAR'S RESIDENCE AMONG THE INDIAN TRIBES OF THE ROCKY MOUNTAINS . . . PHILADELPHIA: PUBLISHED BY M. FITHIAN, 1843.

[i]–[xii], [13]–252. (Pages [i–ii] blank). 18.7 x 11.4 cm. Lithographic plates: symbolic frontispiece, ten scenes, and a large folding allegorical plate. Brown cloth with blind bands on sides including the binder's name, brown leather label on backstrip lettered in gilt.

Ref.: Field 1423; Howes D283; Jones 1081; Pilling (*Sal.*) p. 61; Sabin 82262; Smith 9538; Streit III 2294; Wagner-Camp 102

3824 SMET, PIERRE JEAN DE

LIFE, LETTERS AND TRAVELS OF FATHER PIERRE-JEAN DE SMET, S.J. 1801–1873 . . . NEW YORK: FRANCIS P. HARPER, 1905.*

[i]–xv, [xvi blank], [1]–402. [i]–vii, [viii blank], 403–794. [i]–vi, 795–1211, [1212 blank]. [i]–vi, 1213–1624. 23.8 x 15.3 cm. 17 illustrations and maps listed. Four volumes, green ribbed cloth, uncut.

Ref.: Howes C392; Smith 9545; Streit III 3195

Editions: New York, 1904.

3825 SMET, PIERRE JEAN DE

[Pictorial title-page] MISSIEN VAN DEN OREGON EN REIZEN NAER DE ROTSBERGEN EN DE BRONNEN DER COLUMBIA DER ATHABASCA EN SASCATSHAWIN, IN 1845–46 . . . GENT: BOEK-EN STEENDRUKKERY VAN W.^{WE} VANDER SCHELDEN, 1849.

[V]–[XVI, XVI blank], [17]–425, [426 blank]. 19.4 x 11.5 cm. Lithographed frontispiece and title-page and 14 illustrations, three maps. Map: Nieuwe Kaert / des grondgebieds / van den / Oregon / gemaekt door / P.-J. De Smet, / van de Societeit Jesu. / —1846.— / [lower left:] Gand, imp. & lith. Ve Vander Schelden, rue Basse. / [lower right:] E. Vande Steene. / 20.4 x 27.1 cm. No scale given. Text in French. Map: Bronnen der Colombia, / door P.-J. De Smet. / [lower left and lower right as in preceding except Ed. Vande Steene.] 13.1 x 20.4 cm. No scale given. Text in French. Map: Bronnen der Rivier Tète-Plate, / Gemaekt door P.-J. De Smet. / 1846. / [lower left and lower right as in preceding] / 13 x 20.2 cm. No scale given. Text in French. Green printed wrappers, with title on front wrapper, advertisement on verso of back wrapper, uncut, unopened.

Ref.: Howes D286; Jones 1218; Pilling (*Sal.*) p. 63; Sabin 82264; Smith 9546; Streit III 2355

3826 SMET, PIERRE JEAN DE

MISSIONS DE L'OREGON ET VOYAGES DANS LES MONTAGNES ROCHEUSES EN 1845 ET 1846 . . . PARIS: LIBRAIRIE DE POUSSIELGUE-RUSAND, 1848.

[1–4], [i]–ii, [7]–408. 18.8 x 8.9 cm. Frontispiece, pictorial title-page, and 12 illustrations, all lithographed on tinted grounds. Buff printed wrappers with title on front wrapper, advertisements on verso of back wrapper, uncut.

Prov.: Signature on half-title: Jules Remy / [flourish] /.

Ref.: Field 1425; Howes D286; Sabin 82266; Smith 9549; Streit III 2348

There was an undated edition printed at Gand which may have preceded this.

3827 SMET, PIERRE JEAN DE

[Pictorial title-page] MISSIONS DE L'OREGON ET VOYAGES AUX MONTAGNES ROCHEUSES AUX SOURCES DE LA COLOMBIE, DE L'ATHABASCA ET DU SASCATSHAWIN, EN 1845–46 . . . GAND: IMPR. & LITH. DE V.^E VANDER SCHELDEN, EDITEUR.

[1–4], [I]–[X, X blank], [7]–389, [390 blank]. 18.9 x 11.5 cm. Frontispiece, 14 illustrations and three maps. Map: Nouvelle Carte / du Territoire / de / l'Orégon, / dressée par le R. P. / de Smet, / de la Compagnie de Jésus. / [rule] 1846. [rule] /. [lower left:] Gand, imp. & lith. de Ve Vander Schelden, rue Basse. / [lower right:] E. Vande Steene. / 20.4 x 27 cm. No scale given. Map: Nouvelle Carte / des / Sources du Fleuve Colombia, / dressée par R. P. De Smet, de la Compagnie de Jésus.–1846. / [lower left:] Gand, imp. & lith. de Ve Vander Schelden, rue Basse. / [lower right:] Ed. Vande Steene. / 13.1 x 20.5 cm. No scale given. Map: Nouvelle Carte / des / Sources de la Rivière Tète-Plate, / dressée par le R. P. De Smet, de la Compagnie de Jesus. / 1846. / [lower left and lower right, as in preceding map] /. 13 x 20.5 cm. No scale given. Blue printed wrappers with title on front wrapper, advertisement on verso of back wrapper within decorative border, uncut, unopened.

Ref.: Howes D286; Jones 1184; Pilling (*Sal.*) p. 63; Sabin 82265; Smith 9547; Streit III 2347

May precede the Paris edition.

3828 SMET, PIERRE JEAN DE

NEW INDIAN SKETCHES . . . NEW YORK: D. & J. SADLIER & CO., 1863.

[1]–175, [176 blank]. 15.5 x 10 cm. Frontispiece and one plate. Brown cloth, embossed sides, title in gilt on backstrip with blind decorative bands.

Ref.: Field 1427; Howes D285; Jones 1419 (undated); Pilling (*Sal.*) p. 64; Sabin 82267; Smith 9550; Streit III 2504; Wagner-Camp 395

3829 SMET, PIERRE JEAN DE

OREGON MISSIONS AND TRAVELS OVER THE ROCKY MOUNTAINS, IN 1845–46 . . . NEW-YORK: PUBLISHED BY EDWARD DUNIGAN, M DCCC XLVII.

[v]–xii, [13]–[412]. 17 x 11 cm. Lithographed frontispiece, title-page, 12 plates (all on tinted grounds) and a folding map. Map: Oregon / Territory. / 1846. / 20.4 x 25.6 cm. No scale given. Gray-blue embossed cloth with title on backstrip.

Ref.: Cowan (1914) p. 217; Field 1424; Howes D286; Jones 1159; Pilling (*Alg.*) p. 467; Sabin 82268; Smith 9556; Streit III 2339; Wagner-Camp 141

3830 SMET, PIERRE JEAN DE

VOYAGE AU GRAND-DESERT, EN 1851 . . . BRU-
XELLES: IMPRIMERIE DE J. VANDEREYDT, 1853.

[1]–36, [1]–71, [72 blank]. 14.5 x 9.7 cm. Rebound in blue morocco with red leather label on
backstrip, marbled edges.

Ref.: Howes D287; Pilling (*Alg.*) p. 573;
Sabin 82271; Streit III 2397

The title-page of the second part is identical
with that of the first part, except for inserted
three lines.

3831 SMET, PIERRE JEAN DE

VOYAGES AUX MONTAGNES ROCHEUSES, ET UNE
ANNEE DE SEJOUR CHEZ LES TRIBUS INDIENNES DU
VASTE TERRITOIRE DE L'OREGON, DEPENDANT DES
ETATS-UNIS D'AMERIQUE . . . MALINES: P. J. HA-
NICQ, IMPRIMEUR, 1844.

[1–2], [i]–vi, [1]–304. 17.2 x 11 cm. Frontispiece
portrait, 19 plates, and a map. Map: [Northwest
United States and southwest Canada] [lower
left:] Etablissement Géographique de Bruxelles. / 30.5 x 39.4 cm. No scale given. Contemporary red boards, red leather backstrip, gilt,
fore and lower edges uncut.

Ref.: Howes D288; Sabin 82272; Smith 9566;
Streit III 2305; Wagner-Camp 102

First French Edition.

3832 SMET, PIERRE JEAN DE

WESTERN MISSIONS AND MISSIONARIES: A SERIES OF
LETTERS . . . NEW YORK: JAMES B. KIRKER, 1863.

[3]–8, [7]–532, [533–40 advertisements]. (Pages
[3–4] blank.) 18.5 x 12.1 cm. Portrait. Brown
embossed cloth, title in gilt on backstrip.

Prov.: Inscribed on front endleaf: Presented
to Mr Henry Belen / with the consideration &
respect / of his obedient servant / P. J. De Smet
S.J. / [flourish] / St Louis Feb: 20/66. / [under-
line] /.

Ref.: Field 1426; Howes D289; Pilling (*Alg.*)
p. 573; Sabin 82277; Smith 9568; Streit III 2505

Although copyrighted 1859, the book was not
issued until 1863, due to the failure of the
original publisher.

3833 SMET, PIERRE JEAN DE

THE SAME . . . NEW YORK: T. W. STRONG.

[3]–8, [7]–532. (Pages [3–4] blank.) 18 x 12.4 cm.
Blue cloth, publisher's device (Dunigan & Bro.)
blind embossed on sides, title in gilt on backstrip.

Prov.: Inscribed on front endleaf: Presented
to / Miss Elizabeth Heidemann, / with my best
respects. / P. J. De Smet, S. J. / [flourish] /.

Ref.: Howes D289; Pilling (*Alg.*) p. 574;
Sabin 82277; Smith 9569; Streit III 2588
Editions: New York: J. Kirker, 1863.

3834 SMITH, ABNER C.

A RANDOM HISTORICAL SKETCH. OF MEEKER COUN-
TY, MINNESOTA. FROM ITS FIRST SETTLEMENT, TO
JULY 4TH, 1876 . . . LITCHFIELD, MINN.: BELFOY &
JOUBERT, PUBLISHERS, 1877.

[i–iv], [1]–160, [161 errata, 162 blank]. 16.5 x
12.2 cm. Folding map: Map of Meeker County
Minn. / Entered according to Act of Congress in
the year 1877 by Henry L. Smith in the Office of
the Librarian at Washington D.C. / By Henry L.
Smith, / Chicago, / 1876 Ill. / Scale = 7/24
inch = One Mile /. 25.3 x 20.3 cm. Scale as
above. Black plain cloth.

Ref.: Bradford 5004; Howes S569

3835 SMITH, B. M., & A. J. HILL

[Map] MAP OF THE CEDED PART / OF / DAKOTA
TERRITORY / SHOWING ALSO PORTIONS OF / MIN-
NESOTA, IOWA & NEBRASKA. / COMPILED BY B. M.
SMITH AND A. J. HILL. 1861. / [below border,
centre:] ENTERED ACCORDING TO ACT OF CON-
GRESS, IN THE YEAR 1861 BY B. M. SMITH AND A. J.
HILL, IN THE CLERK'S OFFICE OF THE DISTRICT
COURT FOR THE DISTRICT OF MINNESOTA. [right:]
LITH. BY LOUIS BUECHNER SAINT PAUL, MINNE-
SOTA /

Map, 43.2 x 56.7 cm. Scale: 16 miles to one
inch.

Ref.: Phillips (*Maps*) p. 257

Mounted on the verso is a broadside on green
paper, 15.1 x 9.2 cm. (Text, 13 x 7.5 cm.): Map
of the Ceded Part of / Dakota Territory, &c. /
Size 17 by 22 inches. Scale 15 78–100 miles to 1
inch. / Price, colored in pocket form, $1.00.
Colored in sheet, 75 cts. / Sheet uncolored, 50
cts. / [short rule] / Second Edition.—1863. /
Prospectus. / [26 lines] / St. Paul, Minn., June
15, 1863. /

3836 SMITH, CHARLES W.

JOURNAL OF A TRIP TO CALIFORNIA ACROSS THE
CONTINENT FROM WESTON, MO., TO WEBER CREEK,
CAL. IN THE SUMMER OF 1850 . . . EDITED . . . BY
R. W. G. VAIL . . . NEW YORK: THE CADMUS BOOK
SHOP.*

[1]–79, [80 blank]. 19.6 x 13.5 cm. Dark red
cloth.

Ref.:
The Introduction is dated March 20, 1920.

3837 SMITH, D. N., *Publisher*

NEW MAP. GOLD IN THE BLACK HILLS, WITH EX-
PLANATORY NOTES AND EXTRACTS FROM OFFICIAL

REPORTS, WITH LAWS APPENDED UPON THE SUBJECT OF MINES AND MINING. BURLINGTON, IOWA: PUBLISHED BY D. N. SMITH, 1876.

[1]-40. 17 x 11.3 cm. Map: Black Hills Map / Including / Nebraska and Part of Dakota / Wyoming Colorado and Kansas. / Published by / D. N. Smith / Burlington Iowa March 1876. / [lower right:] Chas. Shober & Co. Prop^s Chicago Litho. Co. / 41.8 x 77.1 cm. (border). No scale given. Black cloth, embossed sides, title in gilt on front cover, advertisement mounted inside front cover. Pamphlet bound into marbled wrappers, the front wrapper being mounted on inside front cover. In a blue half morocco case.

Prov.: W. J. Holliday copy.

Ref.: Howes S585; Phillips (*Maps*) p. 144

3838 SMITH, D. P.

[Wrapper title] D. P. SMITH'S POCKET MAP AND WRITE-UP OF THE KIOWA, COMANCHE AND APACHE RESERVATION ... CHICKASHA, IND. TER.: D. P. SMITH, 1894.

[i–ii], [1]-54, [55 blank, 56–70 advertisements]. 17.9 x 11.2 cm. Map: Map / of the / Kiowa, / Comanche, / and / Apache / Reservation. / Compiled from U. S. Surveys, / Personal Knowledge and other / Sources by / D. P. Smith, C. E. / Scale, 4 Miles to 1 Inch. / [diagrammatic scale] / ... 59.7 x 74 cm. Scale as above. Pink printed wrappers with title on front wrapper, advertisements on verso of front wrapper and verso of back wrapper.

Ref.:

3839 SMITH, DANIEL

A SHORT DESCRIPTION OF THE TENNASSEE[!] GOVERNMENT; OR, THE TERRITORY OF THE UNITED STATES SOUTH OF THE RIVER OHIO, TO ACCOMPANY AND EXPLAIN A MAP OF THAT COUNTRY. PHILADELPHIA: PRINTED BY MATHEW CAREY, 1793.

[A]–B^4, C^2. [1]-20. 27 x 12.3 cm. Map: A / Map of The / Tennassee[!] Government / formerly Part of / North Carolina / taken Chiefly from Surveys by / Gen^1 D. Smith, & others / J. T. Scott sculp. / 13.9 x 51.6 cm. Scale: 22 miles to one inch. Trimmed from upper margin (above neat line) but leaving remnants of descenders was the following: Engraved for Careys American Edition of Guthries Geography improved /. ICN(Ayer) owns a separate of the map, but in a later state, with additional information. Rebound in full dark brown morocco. In a brown cloth case.

Prov.: C. F. Heartman and C. G. Littell bookplates.

Ref.: Evans 26168; Howes S587; Jones 640; Sabin 82420; Vail 955

Howes and Vail state the map was not issued with the pamphlet. Eberstadt (Cat. 113, item 398) described this copy as the only copy known with the map. Vail describes the MH copy as having this map inserted.

Smith's *Short Description* was the first account of the Tennessee territory.

3840 SMITH, DANIEL

A SHORT DESCRIPTION OF THE STATE OF TENNESSEE, LATELY CALLED THE TERRITORY OF THE UNITED STATES, SOUTH OF THE RIVER OHIO ... PHILADELPHIA: PRINTED FOR MATHEW CAREY, 1796.

A–C^6, D^4. [1]-44. 16.3 x 10.2 cm. Original or contemporary marbled boards, leather back. Worn. In a half morocco case.

Editions: Philadelphia, 1793.

3841 SMITH, DAVID

AUTOGRAPH LETTER, SIGNED. 1915 June 23, Paw Paw, Illinois. To Frank E. Stevens. One page, 20.1 x 12.9 cm.

Regarding materials supplied for his book and stating he will send a copy of the completed work to the Chicago Historical Society. Tipped in the writer's *Recollections of David Smith*, [1915].

3842 SMITH, DAVID

RECOLLECTIONS OF DAVID SMITH.

[1]-[93], [94 blank]. 23 x 15.1 cm. 18 illustrations listed. Cream buckram, title in black on front cover.

Ref.:

The introduction on page [7] is dated Paw Paw, Ill., February 4, 1915. The volume was probably printed at Dixon.

Tipped to the front endleaf is an Autograph Letter, signed, from the author. 1915, June 23, Paw Paw, Illinois.

3843 SMITH, EDWARD

ACCOUNT OF A JOURNEY THROUGH NORTH-EASTERN TEXAS, UNDERTAKEN IN 1849, FOR THE PURPOSES OF EMIGRATION ... LONDON: HAMILTON, ADAMS, & CO., 1849.

[i]–vi, [5]-188. 18.3 x 10.7 cm. Two folding maps; Map of Texas. / [lower right centre:] R. B. Moody & Co. Lith 12, Cannon St. Birm^n / 22.1 x 33.3 cm. Scale: 20 miles to one inch. Map: Part of North Eastern Texas shewing the Route of the Inspectors / [lower right:] R. B. Moody & Co. Lith 12, Cannon St. Birm.^{m} / 22.1 x 33.3 cm. Scale: 20 miles to one inch.

Green cloth, blind bands on sides, gilt title on backstrip. In green half morocco case.

Prov.: Rubber stamp on lower edge and on slip case: B. A. McKinney Collection /.

Ref.: Bradford 5018; Clark III 411; Howes S589; Paullin 2781; Rader 2939; Raines p. 190, see; Sabin 82444

An attempt to attract British emigrants to Texas.

3844 SMITH, EMMA, *Compiler*

A COLLECTION OF SACRED HYMNS FOR THE CHURCH OF JESUS CHRIST OF LATTER DAY SAINTS . . . NAUVOO, ILL.: PRINTED BY E. ROBINSON, 1841.

[i]–iv, [5]–351, [352 blank]. 10.2 x 6.4 cm. Sheep, title in blind on backstrip.

Ref.: Byrd 661

Editions: Independence, Mo., 1832. Kirtland, Ohio, 1835.

3845 [SMITH, GEORGE W.]

INCIDENTS OF TRAVEL, FROM THE PENCIL NOTES OF THE AUTHOR, A BOOK IN FIVE PARTS: . . . THE LIFE OF JOHN PROCTOR . . . A JOURNAL OF TRAVELS AFTER HIM IN 1852 . . . A TOUR TO WASHINGTON CITY, AFTER HIS PENSION, IN 1852 . . . THE FACTS IN HIS PENSION CLAIM . . . STRICTURES ON THE CASE BY AN EXPERIENCED JUDGE . . . INDIANAPOLIS: PRINTED FOR GEORGE W. SMITH, 1855.

[1]–118, [119–20 blank]. 20.7 x 13.4 cm. Stabbed. Stained. In a blue cloth case.

Ref.: Howes S598

Although an earlier edition (1852) is hinted at in the Preface, no copy has been found, nor has any other record of such an edition been located.

3846 [SMITH, GEORGE W.]

ANOTHER COPY.

3847 SMITH, HENRY

RECOLLECTIONS AND REFLECTIONS OF AN OLD ITINERANT . . . NEW YORK: PUBLISHED BY LANE & TIPPETT, 1848.

[1]–352. 17.6 x 11 cm. Portrait. Brown cloth, blind embossed borders on sides, title in gilt on backstrip.

Ref.: Howes S601

Chiefly Ohio, Indiana, and Kentucky.

3848 [SMITH, ISAAC B.]

SKETCHES OF THE EARLY SETTLEMENT AND PRESENT ADVANTAGES OF PRINCETON, INCLUDING VALUABLE STATISTICS, ETC. . . . PRINCETON, ILL.: PUBLISHED BY ISAAC B. SMITH, 1857.

[1]–[54], [55]–96. (Pages [1]–16 duplicated.) 19.2 x 11.5 cm. Frontispiece and two illustra-

tions. Yellow printed wrappers, with title on front wrapper, advertisements on verso of front and recto and verso of back wrapper.

Ref.: AII (*Chicago*) 284; Byrd 2792; Howes S603

The imprint on the verso of the title-leaf reads: [broken rule] / C. Scott, Printer and Binder, / Chicago, Ill. /

The "Business Directory" occupies pages [55]–96.

3849 SMITH, JAMES

AN ACCOUNT OF THE REMARKABLE OCCURRENCES IN THE LIFE AND TRAVELS OF COL. JAMES SMITH . . . LEXINGTON: PRINTED BY JOHN BRADFORD, 1799.

[A]², B–L⁴, M². [1]–88. 21.2 x 13.3 cm. Rebound in full red levant morocco, gilt tooled, with inlaid bands of black morocco à la Grolier, green levant morocco doublures, gilt tooled, gilt edges, uncut, by David, finished by Renard. In a brown morocco solander case.

Prov.: Bookplate of William L. Clements. H.V. Jones copy.

Ref.: Ayer 266; AII (*Kentucky*) 122; Church 1287; Field 1438; Howes S606; Jones 672; Sabin 82763; Thomson 1055; Vail 1216

First Edition of one of the most historically valuable of captivities. He was a captive at Fort Duquesne in 1755 and witnessed the Indians' preparations for and celebration after the Braddock defeat. He was a captive and adopted Indian on the Ohio until 1759 when he escaped while at Montreal and spent a useful life as frontiersman in Pennsylvania and Kentucky.— Vail

3850 SMITH, JAMES

A TREATISE, ON THE MODE AND MANNER OF INDIAN WAR, THEIR TACTICS, DISCIPLINE AND ENCAMPMENTS . . . PARIS, KENTUCKY: PRINTED BY JOEL R. LYLE, 1812.

[*]², A–N². [i], [1]–59. (Starting with page [1] odd pages appear on versos, even on rectos.) 23 x 14.5 cm. Two plans set with type. Rebound in contemporary gray wrappers, uncut. Leaves [*]1–2, L2, and N1–2 supplied in facsimile on old paper. In a red cloth case.

Ref.: AII (*Kentucky*) 438; Ayer 269; Jillson (*Smith*) p. 29; Howes S607; Sabin 82771; Vail 1217

The *Treatise* was designed as a kind of basic manual on the way to fight Indians and win the War of 1812. Vail points out that while much of the work is derived from Smith's famous *Account* of his captivity, there is additional material.

3851 SMITH, JOHN

ORIGINAL PENCIL DRAWING of a barroom murder, signed. 24.7 x 19.6 cm.

Dated at top: Fort D. A. Russell. Wyoming Territory. / December 11th A. D. 1877. /

Laid in Apple, Charles: *Cheyenne Directory* . . . 1895.

3852 SMITH, JOHN C.

THE WESTERN TOURIST AND EMIGRANT'S GUIDE THROUGH THE STATES OF OHIO, MICHIGAN, INDIANA, ILLINOIS, MISSOURI, IOWA, AND WISCONSIN, AND THE TERRITORIES OF MINESOTA[!], MISSOURI, AND NEBRASKA . . . NEW YORK: PUBLISHED BY J. H. COLTON, 1853.

[1]–89, [90 blank], 1–[24] advertisements. 14.9 x 9.5 cm. Map: Guide / through / Ohio, Michigan, Indiana, Illinois, / Missouri, Wisconsin & Iowa. / Showing the Township lines of the / United States Surveys, / Location of Cities, Towns, Villages, Post Hamlets, Canals, Rail and Stage Roads. / By J. Calvin Smith. / New York. / Published by J. H. Colton, 86 Cedar St. / [dash] 1853 [dash] / [scale] / Scale of Miles. / [lower centre:] D. McLellan, Print. 26 Spruce St. N.Y. / [lower right:] Engraved by S. Stiles, Sherman & Smith / [inset view] / 52.4 x 66 cm. (including wide border). Scale: 35 miles to one inch. Brown cloth, gilt pictorial frame and title on front cover, same on back cover in blind.

Ref.: Howes S615

3853 SMITH, JOHN C.

THE WESTERN TOURIST AND EMIGRANT'S GUIDE, WITH A COMPENDIOUS GAZETTEER OF THE STATES OF OHIO, MICHIGAN, INDIANA, ILLINOIS, AND MISSOURI, AND THE TERRITORIES OF WISCONSIN, AND IOWA . . . NEW-YORK: PUBLISHED BY J. H. COLTON, 1839.

[i]–vi, [7]–180. 15.1 x 9.3 cm. Map: Guide / through / Ohio, Michigan, Indiana, Illinois, / Missouri, Wisconsin & Iowa. / Showing the Township lines of the / United States Surveys, / Location of Cities. Towns. Villages. Post Hamlets. Canals. Rail and Stage Roads. / By J. Calvin Smith. / New York. / Published by J. H. Colton, 124 Broadway. / [rule] 1839. [rule] / [diagrammatic scale: 35 miles to one inch] / Scale of Miles. / [lower right:] Engraved by J. Stiles, Sherman & Smith / [lower centre:] Entered according to Act of Congress in the year 1840 by J. C. Smith in the Clerk's office of the District Court of the Southern district of New York. / 50.3 x 61.8 cm. (neat line including wide border). Scale as above. Dark blue cloth, blind embossed borders on sides, title in gilt on front cover. Lacks front endleaf.

Ref.: Buck 348; Howes S615; Sabin 82931

3854 SMITH, JOHN C.

THE SAME . . . 1840.

[i]–vi, [7]–180. 14.9 x 9.5 cm. Map: Same as preceding except for changed address and date 1840. Black cloth, blind embossed borders on sides, title in gilt on front cover.

Editions: New York, 1839.

3855 SMITH, JOSEPH

[TIMES AND SEASONS—EXTRA.] GENERAL JOSEPH SMITH'S APPEAL TO THE GREEN MOUNTAIN BOYS, DECEMBER, 1843. NAUVOO, ILL.: TAYLOR AND WOODRUFF, PRINTERS, 1843.

[1]–7, [8 blank]. 23.2 x 14.8 cm. Stabbed, unbound.

Ref.: Byrd 818; Sabin 83241

Since Vermont was his birthplace, Joseph Smith here appeals to the famed "Green Mountain Boys" to support him in his troubles with Missouri.

3856 SMITH, JOSEPH

GENERAL SMITH'S VIEWS OF THE POWERS AND POLICY OF THE GOVERNMENT OF THE UNITED STATES. NAUVOO, ILLINOIS: JOHN TAYLOR, PRINTER, 1844.

[1]–12. Sewn, unbound.

Ref.: Byrd 897; Sabin 83242

3857 SMITH, JOSEPH

THE PEARL OF GREAT PRICE: BEING A CHOICE SELECTION FROM THE REVELATIONS, TRANSLATIONS, AND NARRATIONS OF JOSEPH SMITH, FIRST PROPHET, SEER, AND REVELATOR TO THE CHURCH OF JESUS CHRIST OF LATTER-DAY SAINTS. LIVERPOOL: PUBLISHED BY F. D. RICHARDS, 1851.

[i]–viii, [1]–56. Three illustrations. Bound with Number 3346.

Ref.: Howes S628; Sabin 83258; Woodward 243

3858 SMITH, JOSEPH

THE VOICE OF TRUTH, CONTAINING GENERAL JOSEPH SMITH'S CORRESPONDENCE WITH, GEN. JAMES ARLINGTON BENNETT; APPEAL TO THE GREEN MOUNTAIN BOYS; CORRESPONDENCE WITH JOHN C. CALHOUN, ESQ.; VIEWS OF THE POWERS AND POLICY OF THE GOVERNMENT OF THE UNITED STATES; PACIFIC INNUENDO, AND GOV. FORD'S LETTER; A FRIENDLY HINT TO MISSOURI, AND A FEW WORDS OF CONSOLATION FOR THE "GLOBE"; ALSO, CORRESPONDENCE WITH THE HON. HENRY CLAY. NAUVOO, ILL.: PRINTED BY JOHN TAYLOR, 1844.

[1]–64. 21.1 x 13.7 cm. Removed from bound volume, unbound. Fragment of yellow wrapper.

Ref.: Byrd 899; Howes S629; Sabin 83288

3859 SMITH, JOSEPH, *Trial*

EVIDENCE TAKEN ON THE TRIAL OF MR. SMITH, BE-
FORE THE MUNICIPAL COURT OF NAUVOO, ON
SATURDAY, JULY 1, 1843. RESPECTING THE LATE
PERSECUTION OF THE LATTER DAY SAINTS, IN THE
STATE OF MISSOURI, NORTH AMERICA. NAUVOO:
PRINTED BY TAYLOR AND WOODRUFF.

[i–ii], [1]–38. 23.2 x 13.8 cm. Stabbed, unbound,
uncut.

Ref.: Byrd 781; Sabin 83240; Howes S626
The setting is that of the *Times and Seasons*
(1843) printing with an added title-page and
new pagination.

3860 SMITH, LUCY

BIOGRAPHICAL SKETCHES OF JOSEPH SMITH THE
PROPHET, AND HIS PROGENITORS FOR MANY GEN-
ERATIONS . . . LIVERPOOL: PUBLISHED FOR ORSON
PRATT BY S. W. RICHARDS, 1853.

[i]–xii, [13]–[297], [298 colophon]. (Initial
blank? missing). 15.1 x 9.3 cm. Portrait. Contemporary black leather, gilt and blind stamped
design on covers, gilt title on backstrip, gilt
edges.

Prov.: With signature on front blank leaf:
Mr Daniel Spence /. Spence was mayor of
Nauvoo after Smith's death.

Ref.: Howes S637; Woodward 252

3861 SMITH, LUCY

THE SAME.

Dark brown morocco, gilt panels on sides, gilt
backstrip, gilt edges.

Prov.: Inscribed in an unidentified hand: Presented to / D J. Thompson / 1856. / By a
friend. /
Portrait not present.

3862 SMITH, MARY

AN AFFECTING NARRATIVE OF THE CAPTIVITY AND
SUFFERINGS OF MRS. MARY SMITH WHO WITH HER
HUSBAND AND THREE DAUGHTERS, WERE TAKEN
PRISONERS BY THE INDIANS, IN AUGUST LAST
(1814) AND AFTER ENDURING THE MOST CRUEL
HARDSHIPS AND TORTURE OF MIND FOR SIXTY DAYS
(IN WHICH TIME SHE WITNESSED THE TRAGICAL
DEATH OF HER HUSBAND AND HELPLESS CHILDREN)
WAS FORTUNATELY RESCUED FROM THE MERCILESS
HANDS OF THE SAVAGES BY A DETACHED PARTY
FROM THE ARMY OF THE BRAVE GENERAL JACKSON.
NOW COMMANDING AT NEW-ORLEANS. PROVI-
DENCE, (R. I.), PRINTED BY L. SCOTT.

[A–B]⁶. [1]–24. 16.6 x 10.8 cm. Three woodcuts on pages 6, 9, 11. Unbound, removed from
bound volume. Lacks folding frontispiece.

Ref.: Howes S638; Jones 777 see; Sabin
83535
One of the scarcer captivities.

3863 SMITH, MARY

THE SAME.

[A–B]⁶. [1]–24. 19.4 x 10.9 cm. Folding colored
frontispiece. Plain gray wrappers enclosing blue
wrappers, stabbed. Worn, frontispiece mended
by sewing.

Ref.: Howes S638; Jones 777 see; Sabin
83538
Published the same year as the first edition.

3864 [SMITH (?), RICHARD P.]

COL. CROCKETT'S EXPLOITS AND ADVENTURES IN
TEXAS: WHEREIN IS CONTAINED A FULL ACCOUNT
OF HIS JOURNEY FROM TENNESSEE TO THE RED
RIVER AND NATCHITOCHES, AND THENCE ACROSS
TEXAS TO SAN ANTONIO; INCLUDING HIS MANY
HAIR-BREADTH ESCAPES; TOGETHER WITH A TOPO-
GRAPHICAL, HISTORICAL, AND POLITICAL VIEW OF
TEXAS . . . LONDON: R. KENNETT, 1837.

[i]–[viii, viii blank], [1]–152. 19 x 11.1 cm. Gray
boards, printed white label, 4.3 x 1.8 cm., on
backstrip: [thick and thin rules] / Crockett's /
Exploits / and / Adventures / in / Texas. /
[rule] / Price 5s. 6d. / [rule] / J. Kennett, / London. / [thin and thick rules] /, uncut.

Ref.: Howes S654; Rader 985 note; Raines
p. 57; Sabin 17566, 83778; Streeter 1192E
Editions: Philadelphia, 1836, 1837.

3865 SMITH, SIDNEY

THE SETTLER'S NEW HOME; OR, THE EMIGRANT'S
LOCATION, BEING A GUIDE TO EMIGRANTS IN THE
SELECTION OF A SETTLEMENT, AND THE PRELIMI-
NARY DETAILS OF THE VOYAGE . . . LONDON:
JOHN KENDRICK, 1849.

[i–ii], [1]–106, [107–14 advertisements]. 16.7 x
10.5 cm. Yellow printed wrappers, with title on
front wrapper, list of contents and advertisements on verso of front wrapper, advertisements
on recto and verso of back wrapper.

Ref.: Buck 455; Clark III 414; Howes S669;
Sabin 84224
Among areas urged for emigrants is Califor-
nia.

Editions: There were at least four other editions or printings in 1849.

**3866 [SMITH, THOMAS BUCKINGHAM,
Compiler]**

COLECCION DE VARIOS DOCUMENTOS PARA LA
HISTORIA DE LA FLORIDA Y TIERRAS ADYACENTES
. . . LONDON: TRUBNER.

[i–viii], [1]–208. 31.7 x 23 cm. Frontispiece. Pale green wrappers, new tan paper back, uncut. Chipped.

Prov.: Mason Collection, Champaign Public Library.

Ref.: Howes S576; Sabin 84379

Limited to 500 copies. Published in 1857.

3867 [SMITH, WILLIAM] 1727–1803

AN ACCOUNT OF THE PROCEEDINGS OF THE ILINOIS[!] AND OUABACHE LAND COMPANIES, IN PURSUANCE OF THEIR PURCHASES MADE OF THE INDEPENDENT NATIVES, JULY 5TH, 1773, AND 18TH OCTOBER, 1775. PHILADELPHIA: PRINTED BY WILLIAM YOUNG, 1796.

[*]², A⁴, b⁷, B–G⁴. (Probably lacks blank b4). [i–xvi], [1]–55, [56 blank]. 22.4 x 11.5 cm.

BOUND WITH:

[COBBETT, WILLIAM:] A Prospect from the Congress-Gallery . . . Philadelphia, 1796. [i]–iv, [1]–68.

BOUND WITH:

[BORDLEY, JOHN B.:] [Sketches on Rotation of Crops . . . Philadelphia, 1796.] [1]–76, [77–8 blank]. Lacks title-leaf.

BOUND WITH:

BELKNAP, JEREMY: A Discourse, Intended to Commemorate the Discovery of America . . . Boston, 1792. [1]–132, [133–34 advertisements], [135–36 blank].

BOUND WITH:

[COXE, TENCH:] An Enquiry into the Principles on which a Commercial System . . . Should be Founded . . . [Philadelphia,] 1787. [1]–52.

BOUND WITH:

UNITED STATES. President (John Adams): Message . . . April 3d, 1798. Philadelphia: 1798. [1]–60.

Six pamphlets bound together in marbled boards, later oilcloth backstrip.

Ref.: Evans 30618; Howes S684; Sabin 84577

Sabin lists two printings of the first pamphlet with the same imprint, without describing differences. The pamphlet is usually accompanied by a series of documents (of which there are also two printings) not included with this copy.

3868 SMITH, WILLIAM L. G.

FIFTY YEARS OF PUBLIC LIFE. THE LIFE AND TIMES OF LEWIS CASS . . . NEW YORK: DERBY & JACKSON, 1856.

[i]–xii, [13]–781, [782 blank]. 22.7 x 14.2 cm. Portrait. Black cloth.

Ref.: Howes S714

3869 SMITH, WILLIAM R.

OBSERVATIONS ON THE WISCONSIN TERRITORY; CHIEFLY THAT PART CALLED THE "WISCONSIN LAND DISTRICT." WITH A MAP, EXHIBITING THE SETTLED PARTS OF THE TERRITORY, AS LAID OFF IN COUNTIES BY ACT OF THE LEGISLATURE IN 1837. PHILADELPHIA: E. L. CAREY & A. HART, 1838.

[i]–viii, [1]–134. 18.2 x 11.1 cm. Map: Map / of the Settled Part / of / Wisconsin Territory / Compiled from / The Latest Authorities / Philadelphia: Published by / Hinman & Dutton N⁰ 6 North Fifth Street. / 1838 / [lower right:] Engraved by J. H. Young / [lower left:] Entered according to Act of Congress in the year 1837, by Hinman & Dutton, in the Clerk's office of the District Court of the eastern district of Pennsylvania. / 55.1 x 43.7 cm. Scale: 19 miles to one inch. *Inset:* The / Entire Territory of / Wisconsin / as / Established by Act of Congress. / April 10. 1836. / 18.2 x 25 cm. No scale given. Red cloth, printed white paper label, .6 x 2.5 cm., on backstrip; [reading up:] Wisconsin. /.

Ref.: Bradford 5111; Howes S721; Sabin 84865

3870 SMITH & DU MOULIN, *Compilers*

CHICAGO BUSINESS DIRECTORY AND COMMERCIAL ADVERTISER, 1859 . . . CHICAGO, ILL.: S. C. GRIGGS & CO.

[i]–x, advertisement], [1]–260, i–xxxviii, [1–4]. 20 x 12.5 cm. Light blue printed boards, dark brown cloth backstrip with title in gilt, advertisements on covers, advertisements on endpapers.

Ref.: AII (*Chicago*) 305; Byrd 3057; Sabin 12641

Lithographed advertisement inserted before title-page.

3871 SMITHER, GEORGE

AUTOGRAPH LETTER, SIGNED. 1859 April 18, Fillmore, Andrew County, Mo. Two pages, 30.3 x 18.9 cm. To his mother.

Fine anecdotal letter of the start of a trip across the Plains.

3872 SMITHWICK, NOAH

THE EVOLUTION OF A STATE; OR, RECOLLECTIONS OF OLD TEXAS DAYS . . . AUSTIN, TEXAS: GAMMEL BOOK COMPANY.

[i–ii], [1]–354. 19.2 x 13.1 cm. Eight illustrations. Red pictorial cloth.

Ref.: Bradford 5116; Howes S726; Rader 2948; Sabin 85099

Copyrighted 1900.

3873 SMYTHE, HENRY

HISTORICAL SKETCH OF PARKER COUNTY AND WEATHERFORD, TEXAS . . . ST. LOUIS: LOUIS C. LAVAT, BOOK AND JOB PRINTER, 1877.

[i]–xvi, [i]–vii, [viii blank], [1]–476. (Pages [i]–xvi advertisements.) 18.5 x 11.5 cm. Plum cloth, blind embossed sides, title in gilt on backstrip.

Ref.: Bradford 5121; Carroll p. 121; Howes S734; Raines pp. 191–92; Sabin 85356

Pages [443]–459: [Caption title] Directory / -of- / Weatherford. / [rule] / July 1, 1877. / [rule] / . . .

Contains an account of General Sherman's tour of inspection during the months of April, May and June, 1871, taken from the manuscript journal kept by Inspector-General R. B. Marcy, with a full account of the Indian chiefs Big Tree and Satanta.—EDG

3874 [SNELLING, WILLIAM J.]

TALES OF THE NORTHWEST; OR, SKETCHES OF IN-DIAN LIFE AND CHARACTER . . . BOSTON: HIL-LIARD, GRAY, LITTLE, AND WILKINS, M DCCC XXX.

[i]–viii, [1]–228. 16.2 x 9.9 cm. Light red cloth, printed paper label, 4 x 2 cm., on backstrip, uncut.

Ref.: Howes S738; Sabin 85428; Wright I 2477

Most of the *Tales* deal with the "Dacotahs" of Minnesota and the Dakotas.

3875 [SNELLING, WILLIAM J.]

TALES OF TRAVELS WEST OF THE MISSISSIPPI. BY SOLOMON BELL . . . BOSTON: GRAY AND BOWEN, 1830.

[i]–xvi, 1–162. 14.8 x 9.3 cm. Illustrations un-listed. Yellow boards, red cloth back, brown leather label.

Ref.: Howes S739; Sabin 85429

This was Snelling's first book, the earliest juvenile on the Far West. The author's father was Josiah Snelling after whom Fort Snelling was named. He was, at one time, a fur trader in the far west.

3876 SNOW, ERASTUS

ONE YEAR IN SCANDINAVIA: RESULTS OF THE GOS-PEL IN DENMARK AND SWEDEN . . . LIVERPOOL: PUBLISHED BY F. D. RICHARDS, 1851.

[1]–24. Bound with Number 3346.

Ref.: Sabin 85510

The Mormons in Scandinavia.

3877 SNOW, LORENZO

THE ITALIAN MISSION . . . LONDON: PRINTED BY W. AUBREY, 1851.

[1]–28. Bound with Number 3346.

Ref.: Sabin 85526

The Mormons in Italy.

3878 SNOW, LORENZO

. . . THE ONLY WAY TO BE SAVED . . . AN EXPLANA-TION OF THE FIRST PRINCIPLES OF THE DOCTRINE OF THE CHURCH OF JESUS CHRIST OF LATTER-DAY SAINTS . . . LONDON: PRINTED BY W. BOWDEN, 1851.

[1]–8. Bound with Number 3346.

Ref.: Sabin 85527

3879 SNOW, ZERUBBABEL

LATTER-DAY SAINTS IN UTAH. OPINION OF THE HON. Z. SNOW, JUDGE OF THE SUPREME COURT OF THE UNITED STATES FOR THE TERRITORY OF UTAH, UPON THE OFFICIAL COURSE OF HIS EXCELLENCY GOV. BRIGHAM YOUNG . . . LIVERPOOL: F. D. RICHARDS, 1852.

[1]–24. Bound with Number 3346.

Ref.: Sabin 85564

3880 SNYDER, JOHN F.

AUTOGRAPH LETTER, SIGNED. 1907 May 9, Vir-ginia, Ill. One page, 30.6 x 24.3 cm. To Merton J. Clay.

Regarding two books which Snyder had pub-lished.

Tipped into his *Captain John Baptiste Saucier* . . . 1901.

3881 SNYDER, JOHN F.

ADAM W. SNYDER, AND HIS PERIOD IN ILLINOIS HISTORY 1817–1842 . . . SPRINGFIELD, ILLINOIS: THE H. W. ROKKER CO., PRINTERS AND BINDERS, 1903.

[1]–[394]. 19 x 13.1 cm. Two portraits, unlisted. Tan cloth, pictorial design on front cover in black incorporating title, title in black on back-strip.

Prov.: Inscribed on inside front cover: Sup-pressed Edition / [underline] / Dr. W. F. Boya-kin, / with high regards of / his sincere friend of / other days, / J. F. Snyder, M. D. / Virginia, Ills. /

Ref.: Howes S745

3882 SNYDER, JOHN F.

THE SAME . . . VIRGINIA, ILL.: E. NEEDHAM, 1906.

[1]–437, [438 blank]. 18.8 x 13.3 cm. Seven por-traits, unlisted. Tan cloth, printed in black, title on front cover and on backstrip.

Prov.: Inscribed on inside front cover: Hon. Joseph E. Paden, / with sincere regards / of / Dr. J. F. Snyder. / Virginia, / Ills. / March 24th 1910. /

Ref.: Howes S745
Editions: Springfield, 1903.

3883 SNYDER, JOHN F.

CAPTAIN JOHN BAPTISTE SAUCIER AT FORT CHARTRES IN THE ILLINOIS, 1751–1763 . . . PEORIA, ILL.: SMITH & SCHAEFER, PRINTERS, 1901.

[1]–93, [94 blank]. 17.3 x 9.3 cm. Plan of Fort Chartres. Black cloth, with title in gilt on front cover.

Ref.: Howes S746

Tipped in is an Autograph Letter, signed by the author, 1907 May 9, Virginia, Ill.

3884 SOCIETE DE GEOGRAPHIE

[Wrapper title] BULLETIN DE LA SOCIETE DE GEOGRAPHIE . . . DEUXIEME SERIE. TOME III. N° 17.—MAI. PARIS: CHEZ ARTHUSBERTRAND, 1835.

[298]–368. 22.5 x 14.4 cm. Blue printed wrappers, uncut, mostly unopened.

Ref.: Wagner-Camp 52

Contains, pages 316–22, Antonio Armijo: Itinéraire / du Nord-Mexico à la Haute-Californie, / Parcouru en 1829 et 1830 par soixante Mexicains. /

The diary had appeared in *Registro Oficial del Gobierno de los Estados-Unidos, Mexicanos,* for June, 1830. It is translated and described in Hafen's *Old Spanish Trail* . . . Glendale, Calif., 1954, pages 158–165. The latter work contains references to other appearances.

3885 SOCIETY FOR THE PROPAGATION OF THE FAITH

ANNALS OF THE PROPAGATION OF THE FAITH COMPILED FOR THE PROVINCE OF QUEBEC. VOL. 1.—NO. 1. [–NO. 13.] THREE-RIVERS: PUBLISHED FOR THE INSTITUTION.

[1]–416. Various sizes, 21.2 x 13.7 cm. to 19.1 x 12.7 cm. Thirteen parts, green wrappers with title on front wrappers, text on verso of back wrapper. One wrapper in buff rather than green. In a green cloth case.

Ref.:

The parts were published in February and October, 1877 to 1883; each consisted of 32 pages.

3886 SOCIETY FOR THE PROPAGATION OF THE FAITH

NOTICE SUR LES MISSIONS DU DIOCESE DE QUEBEC, QUI SONT SECOURUES PAR L'ASSOCIATION DE LA PROPAGATION DE LA FOI. JANVIER, 1839. NO. 1. [–MAI, 1874. NO. 21.] QUEBEC: DE L'IMPRIMERIE DE FRECHETTE & CIE.

1—[i]–[vi, vi blank], [1]–77, [78 blank]. 1839. 2—[i]–xii, [1]–71, [72 blank]. 1840. 3—[i]–xii, [1]–100. 1841. 4—[1–2], [i]–[x, x blank], [1]–92.

1842. 5—[i]–xii, ix–xii [text repeated], [1]–136. Folding plate. 1843. 6—[i]–[xviii, xviii blank], [3]–156. 1845. 7—[i]–xii, [xiii–xiv blank], [1]–129, [130 blank]. 1847. 8—[i]–xvi, [1]–105, [106 blank]. 1849. 9—[i]–xvi, [1]–128. Large folding map. 1851. 10—[i]–xx, [1]–140. 1853. 11—[i]–xx, [1]–164. 1855. 12—[i]–[xxii, xxii blank], [1]–105, [106 blank]. (Page iv mispaginated 4.) 1857. 13—[i]–xiv, [15]–144. 1859. 14—[i]–xviii, [19]–192. Uncut. 1861. 15—[1]–185, [186 blank]. 1863. 16—[1]–127, [128 blank]. 1864. 17—[i]–[xxiv, xxiv blank], [1]–152. 1866. 18—[i]–[xxxii, xxxii blank], [1]–120. (Errata slip before title-page.) 1868. 19—[i]–xxxvi, [1]–118, [119–20 blank]. 1870. 20—[i]–xxxi, [2]–137, [138 blank]. 1872. 21—[i]–xxxiv, [1]–108, [109–10 blank]. 1874. Various sizes, 21 x 13.5 cm. to 17.5 x 11 cm. Folding plate and folding map. Twenty-one volumes, printed wrappers, with titles on front wrappers, each varying slightly. In three half morocco slip cases.

Ref.:

An invaluable source of information about Canadian frontier living.

3887 SOCIETY FOR THE PROPAGATION OF THE FAITH

RAPPORT DE L'ASSOCIATION DE LA PROPAGATION DE LA FOI, ETABLIE A MONTREAL . . . MAI, 1839.—NO. 1. [–QUARANTE-TROISIEME NUMERO.] MONTREAL: A VENDRE POUR LE PROFIT DE L'ASSOCIATION DE LA PROPAGATION DE LA FOI, AU MAGAZIN DE C. P. LEPROHON.

1—[1]–57, [58 blank]. 1839. 2—[1]–92. 1840. 3—[i]–ii, [1]–[63], [64 blank]. 1841. (No title-page.) 4—[1]–[83], [84 blank]. 1842. (No title-page.) [5]—[1]–[52]. [1849] Caption title: Mission de la Baie d'Hudson. / [short rule] / Lettre du R. P. Laverlochère / à Mgr. l'Evêque de Bytown. / . . . 6—[1]–[64]. 1850. [7]—[1]–76. 1851. [8]—[1]–108. 1852. [9]—[1]–63, [64 blank]. 1853. [10]—[i]–iv, [1]–160. 1855. [11]—[i]–viii, [1]–101, [102–04 blank]. 1859. [12]—[i]–[xii, xii blank], [1]–164. 1860. [13]—[i]–xxiv, [1]–129, [130 blank]. 1861. Numbered 11. [14]—[i]–[xxiv, xxiv blank], [1]–127, [128 blank]. 1864. Numbered 12. [15]—[i]–[xx, xx blank], [1]–95, [96 blank]. 1866. Numbered 13. [16]—[1]–146. Title-page: Esquisse / sur le / Nord-Ouest de l'Amerique / par / Mgr. Taché, Évêque de St. Boniface, 1868. / [decorative rule] / Montreal / Typographie du Nouveau Monde / 23, Rue St. Vincent. / [short rule] / 1869. / (Imprint differs on front wrapper; recto of back wrapper carries title as above within decorative border.) [17]—[1]–48. Janvier, 1871.

Numbered 15. [18]—[1]-48. Mai, 1871. Numbered 16. [19]—[1]-48. Septembre, 1871. Numbered 17. [20]—[1]-47, [48 blank]. Janvier, 1872. Numbered 18. [21]—[1]-32. Février, 1872. Numbered 19. [22]—[1]-32. Avril, 1872. Numbered 20. [23]—[1]-31, [32 blank]. Juin, 1872. Numbered 21. [24]—[1]-32. Août, 1872. Numbered 22. [25]—[1]-32. Octobre, 1872. Numbered 23. [26]—[1]-32. Decembre, 1872. Numbered 24. [27]—[1]-32. Février, 1873. Numbered 25. [28]—[1]-32. Juin, 1873. Numbered 26. [29]—[1]-32. Septembre, 1873. Numbered 27. [30]—[1]-64. Février, 1874. Numbered 28. Title changed to: Annales / de la / Propagation de la Foi / pour le Diocèse de Montreal . . . [31]—[65]-127, [128 blank]. Juin, 1874. Numbered 29. [32]—[129]-160. Septembre, 1874. Numbered 30. [33]—[161]-192. Novembre, 1874. Numbered 31. [34]—[1]-32. Janvier, 1875. Numbered 32. [35]—[33]-68. Mars, 1875. Numbered 33. [36]—[69]-104. Mai, 1875. Numbered 34. [37]—[105]-136. Juillet, 1875. Numbered 35. [38]—[136]-167, [168 blank]. Septembre, 1875. Numbered 36. [39]—[169]-200. Novembre, 1875. Numbered 37. [40]—[1]-40. Février, 1876. Numbered 38. [41]—[41]-72. Avril, 1876. Numbered 39. [42]—[73]-104. Juin, 1876. Numbered 40. [43]—[105]-136. Août, 1876. Numbered 41. [44]—[137]-168. Octobre, 1876. Numbered 42. [45]—[169]-200. Decembre, 1876. Numbered 43. Various sizes, 21.3 x 13.6 cm. to 23.2 x 15.1 cm. Forty-five parts, printed wrappers in several colors, some parts uncut. In a dark blue cloth box with inner cloth folders.

Ref.:

3888 SOLA, A. E. IRONMONGER

KLONDYKE: TRUTH AND FACTS OF THE NEW EL DORADO . . . LONDON: THE MINING AND GEOGRAPHICAL INSTITUTE.*

[i–x], [1]-102. 27.1 x 18.5 cm. 26 plates and three maps listed. Green cloth, with title in gilt on front cover and on backstrip reading up.

Ref.: Howes S749; Smith 9646; Wickersham 4414

The introduction is dated December 1st, 1897.

Pages [i], 93–102 carry advertisements; page [ii] carries a colophon.

3889 SOLMS-BRAUNFELS, CARL, PRINZ ZU

TEXAS. GESCHILDERT IN BEZIEHUNG AUF SEINE GEOGRAPHISCHEN, SOCIALEN UND UEBRIGEN VERHALTNISSE MIT BESONDERER RUCKSICHT AUF DIE DEUTSCHE COLONISATION . . . FRANKFURT AM MAIN: JOHANN DAVID SAUERLANDER'S VERLAG, 1846.

[I]–X, 1–134. 20.5 x 13.3 cm. Map: Map / of the northwestern Part / of / Texas / received from the general Land Office / in 1845. / [thin and thick rules] / Frankfurt a. M. / J. D. Sauerlaender's Verlag. / [lower right:] Lith. u. gedr. im geogr. Institut von M. Frommann in Darmstadt. / 40.6 x 51.1 cm. No scale given. Map: Karte / von / Texas / entworsen nach den Vermessungen / der / General-Land-Office der Republic / Frankfurt a / M / J. D. Sauerländer's Verlag / [lower centre:] Geogr. & Lith. Anstalt von Eduard Foltz-Eberlein Frankfurt a / M. / 46.8 x 40.1 cm. No scale given. [*Inset:*] [Mexico and the central part of the United States] 14.6 x 11.3 cm. Map: Situations-Plan der Stadt / Neu-Braunfels / und der dabei angekausten Ländereien. / [rule] / Nach der Aufnahme des Mayor Hays gefertigt / von Carl Prinz zu Solms. / 19.4 x 31.8 cm. Scale: about 1200 veras to one inch. Map: Plan / von / Friedrichsburg / Vereins Colonie / am Piedernales / Texas / [double rule] / 1846. / [double rule] / 19.3 x 32.1 cm. No scale given. Original mottled black boards. Rebacked.

Ref.: Clark III 241; Howes S751; Sabin 86505

The prince was one of the leading colonizers of German nationals in Texas.

3890 SOMERS, W. H.

[Wrapper title] CENTENNIAL HISTORY OF GAGE COUNTY, NEBRASKA . . . BEATRICE, NEBRASKA: EXPRESS BOOK AND JOB PRINTING HOUSE, 1876.

[1]-18. 22.5 x 14.9 cm. Gray wrappers with title on front wrapper, cuts on recto and verso of back wrapper.

Ref.:

3891 SONORA, MEXICO

[Broadside] ESCMO. SR. = PUESTA EN CONOCIMIENTO DEL HONORABLE CONGRESO LA INSTANCIA QUE V. E. NOS ACOMPANO CON NOTA DE 14 DEL CORRIENTE RELATIVA A MANIFESTAR LA GRAVEDAD DE LOS MALES QUO LO AQUEJAN, IMPULSADO POR LO MISMO A RENUNCIAR EL GOBIERNO QUE ES A SU CARGO; S. SOB. EN SESION DE AYER SE SERVIO RESOLVER DIGAMOS A V. E. QUE CONVENCIDO DE LOS PODEROSOS MOTIVOS QUE LO HACEN SEPARARSE DEL ENCARGO CON QUE LOS PUEBLOS DISTINGUIERON SUS VIRTUDES Y MERECIMIENTOS LE QUEDA ADMITIDA LA INDICADA RENUNCIA QUE HACE V. E. DEL EJECUTIVO DEL ESTADO. = PONEMOSLO EN CONOCIMIENTO DE V. E. PARA LOS EFECTOS CONSIGUIENTES REITERANDOLE LAS CONSIDERACIONES Y RESPETO DE NUESTRO PARTICULAR APRECIO. = DIOS Y LEY ALAMOS 25 DE MAYO DE 1830. = JESUS SERRANO, DIPUTADO SRIO. = TOMAS HERRAN, DIPUTADO SRIO. = ESCMO. SR.

GOBERNADOR DEL ESTADO. ES COPIA. ALAMOS MAYO 26 DE 1830. = ESCUDERO.

Broadside, 29.1 x 20.2 cm. Text, 15.9 x 13.8 cm.
Ref.:
Official acceptance of the resignation of the Governor of Sonora for reasons of health.

3892 SONORA EXPLORING AND MINING COMPANY

[Caption title] FIRST ANNUAL REPORT OF THE SONORA EXPLORING AND MINING COMPANY, MADE TO THE STOCKHOLDERS, MARCH 16, 1857 . . .

[1–4]. (Pages [1] and [4] blank.) 27.6 x 21.7 cm. Unbound leaflet, removed from bound volume, part of inner margins cut away.
Ref.: Munk (Alliot) p. 245; Sabin 86974 note
The place of publication is not given, probably Cincinnati.

The report contains an account of the first exploring party sent out by the company under Colonel Charles D. Poston.

3893 SONORA EXPLORING AND MINING COMPANY

REPORT OF FREDERICK BRUNCKOW, GEOLOGIST, MINERALOGIST, AND MINING ENGINEER, TO A COMMITTEE OF THE STOCKHOLDERS OF THE SONORA EXPLORING & MINING CO. UPON THE HISTORY, RESOURCES, AND PROSPECTS OF THE COMPANY IN ARIZONA . . . CINCINNATI: RAILROAD RECORD, PRINT, 1859.

[I]–IV, [5]–47, [48 blank]. 22.7 x 14.9 cm. Frontispiece, The Heintzelman Mine, at Cerro Colorado, near Tubac, Arizona. Map, facing page [21]: Map of / Arizona / or the / Gadsden Purchase / with the Position / of its / Silver Mines / as now worked / 1859. / [lower centre:] Middleton, Strobridge & Cº Cin / 12.1 x 18.9 cm. No scale given. Blue printed wrappers, with title on front wrapper, vignette and decorative border on verso of back wrapper.
Ref.: Howes B895; Munk (Alliot) p. 40; Wagner-Camp 280 see

3894 SONORA EXPLORING AND MINING COMPANY

SONORA—AND THE VALUE OF ITS SILVER MINES. REPORT OF THE SONORA EXPLORING AND MINING CO., MADE TO THE STOCKHOLDERS. DECEMBER, 1856. CINCINNATI: RAILROAD RECORD PRINT, 1856.

[1]–44. 21.3 x 13.6 cm. Four lithographed plates, tinted, and two maps. Map: Tubac / Head Quarters "Sonora Exploring & Mining Cº" / For description of Country see Col. Gray's Rail Road Report. / 18.7 x 24.3 cm. No scale given.

Map: Map of the Mineral Regions / on the proposed Southern Pacific Rail Road through Gadsden purchase. / [lower centre:] Middleton, Wallace & Cº Lithoˢ Cin. / 16.8 x 36.4 cm. No scale given. Removed from bound volume, unbound.
Ref.: Howes S763; Munk (Alliot) p. 245; Wagner-Camp 280
There were two states of the pamphlet, one with 44 pages and two maps and another with 43 pages and four maps. Howes suggests the 44-page state is earlier.

3895 SONS OF TEMPERANCE. Illinois. Elgin Division, No. 127

CONSTITUTION, BY-LAWS, AND RULES OF ORDER OF ELGIN DIVISION, NO. 127, OF THE SONS OF TEMPERANCE; LOCATED IN ELGIN, KANE CO., ILL. CHICAGO: PRINTED BY R. L. WILSON, DAILY JOURNAL OFFICE, 1848.

[1]–45, [46–48 advertisements]. (Pages 13, 27–28, 32, 40–44, 46–48 unpaginated.) 13.4 x 8.4 cm. Yellow wrappers. Lacks back wrapper. Partly unopened.
Ref.: Byrd 1379; McMurtrie (*Chicago*) 163
The only copy located by McMurtrie and by Byrd.

3896 SONS OF TEMPERANCE. Illinois. Prairie Division, No. 8

CONSTITUTION, AND BY-LAWS, OF PRAIRIE DIVISION NO. 8. OF THE SONS OF TEMPERANCE; LOCATED IN CHICAGO, ILLINOIS . . . CHICAGO: DAILY TRIBUNE PRINT, 1848.

[1]–35, [36 blank]. 14.1 x 8.4 cm. Brown wrappers.
Ref.: Byrd 1383; McMurtrie (*Chicago*) 165
The only copy located by McMurtrie and by Byrd.

3897 SORENSON, ALFRED R.

EARLY HISTORY OF OMAHA; OR, WALKS AND TALKS AMONG THE OLD SETTLERS: A SERIES OF SKETCHES IN THE SHAPE OF A CONNECTED NARRATIVE OF THE EVENTS AND INCIDENTS OF EARLY TIMES IN OMAHA, TOGETHER WITH A BRIEF MENTION OF THE MOST IMPORTANT EVENTS OF LATER YEARS . . . OMAHA: PRINTED AT THE OFFICE OF THE DAILY BEE, 1876.

[i–iv], [1]–226, [227]–248 advertisements. 21.8 x 14.7 cm. 20 illustrations listed. Red cloth, title in gilt on front cover.
Ref.: Howes S765; Sabin 87143
Tipped to the inside front cover is a newspaper clipping about the publication of the book. Accompanying the volume is a collection of clippings, apparently from Sorenson's newspaper relating to local news.

3898 SORENSON, ALFRED R.

"HANDS UP!" OR, THE HISTORY OF A CRIME. THE GREAT UNION PACIFIC EXPRESS ROBBERY . . . OMAHA, NEB.: PUBLISHED BY BARKALOW BROS., 1877.

[i–viii (viii blank)], 11–139, [140 blank], [141–44 advertisements]. 16.8 x 12.8 cm. Five plates, listed. Tan printed wrappers with title on front wrapper, advertisements on verso of front and recto and verso of back wrapper. In a blue cloth case.

Prov.: Presentation copy, inscribed, inverted, on front wrapper. Compliments Al. Sorenson, / City Editor Omaha Bee /.

Ref.: Adams 932; Howes S766

3899 SORIN, MATTHEW

THE INFLUENCE OF RELIGION ON CIVIL GOVERNMENT: BEING THE SUBSTANCE OF A DISCOURSE, DELIVERED IN GALENA . . . RED WING, MINN. TER., 1854.

[1]–36. 21 x 14.1 cm. Removed from bound volume, sewn.

Ref.: AII (*Minnesota*) 81

An anti-Roman Catholic discourse.

3900 [SORIN, T. R.]

HAND-BOOK OF TUCSON AND SURROUNDINGS EMBRACING STATISTICS OF THE MINERAL FIELDS OF SOUTHERN ARIZONA . . . TUCSON, A. T.: CITIZEN PRINT, 1880.

I–IV advertisements, [1]–40, V–VIII advertisements, 41–44 Directory, IX–XII advertisements, [1–12 including inserted leaf on gray paper, advertisements]. 18.6 x 12.7 cm. Map: Map of Southeastern Arizona, / Circular lines represent 25, 50, 75 and 100 miles distance, air line. [Entered According to Law in the Office of the Librarian of Congress.] / [lower right corner:] A. Zeese & Co., Map Eng., Chicago. / 34.7 x 23.6 cm. Scale: about 80 miles to one inch. Map: Tombstone Town Plat. / 13.4 x 20.6 cm. No scale given. Printed in two colors. Gray printed wrappers with title on front wrapper. In a brown cloth case.

Ref.: Munk (Alliot) 205; AII (*Arizona*) 52

3901 SOULE, FRANK, JOHN H. GIHON, & JAMES NISBET

THE ANNALS OF SAN FRANCISCO; CONTAINING A SUMMARY OF THE HISTORY OF THE FIRST DISCOVERY, SETTLEMENT, PROGRESS, AND PRESENT CONDITION OF CALIFORNIA, AND A COMPLETE HISTORY OF ALL THE IMPORTANT EVENTS CONNECTED WITH ITS GREAT CITY . . . NEW YORK: D. APPLETON & COMPANY, M.DCCC.LV.*

[1]–824. 22.5 x 14.3 cm. 150 illustrations listed. Folding map: General Map / Showing the Countries Explored & Surveyed / by the / United States & Mexican / Boundary Commission / in the Years 1850, 51, 52 & 53. / Under the direction of / John R. Bartlett. / U. S. Commissioner. / [lower left:] J. H. Colton & Cº Nº 172. William Sᵗ. New York. / 38.8 x 49.1 cm. Scale: about 105 miles to one inch. Contemporary half red morocco, gilt top.

Prov.: Manuscript-lettered name on blank leaf at front within flourished frame: C. H. Farwell. /

Ref.: Cowan p. 601; Howes S769; Sabin 87268; Zamorano Eighty 70

3902 SOUTH BOULDER DISTRICT, Colorado

[Broadside] SOUTH BOULDER. MINING CLAIM CERTIFICATE. SOUTH BOULDER DISTRICT. KNOW ALL MEN BY THESE PRESENTS, THAT I, [in manuscript: Thomas Forbush] CLAIMS BY PRE-EMPTION, NO . . . GIVEN UNDER MY HAND AT SOUTH BOULDER, IN SAID DISTRICT, THIS [in manuscript: 6ᵗʰ] DAY OF [in manuscript: Nov″] A. D. 1861 [in manuscript: R. P. Chambers] RECORDER. SAMUEL MAN [crossed out and name supplied in manuscript above caret: Jno. McKnight] PRESIDENT. DEPUTY. CLAIMS HELD AS REAL ESTATE. REPUBLICAN AND HERALD PRINT.

Broadside, 12.3 x 19.8 cm. Text, 11.4 x 18.6 cm.

Ref.: McMurtrie & Allen (*Colorado*) 20

Identical with McMurtrie & Allen's entry except /, Denver / does not appear in last line of present copy.

Endorsed by Forbush on verso. Claim No. 1 East, Locus[!] Township Lode.

3903 SOUTH DAKOTA. Commissioner of Immigration

1890. FAKTISKE OPLYSNINGER OM SYD DAKOTA. EN OFFICIEL ENCYKLOPEDI INDEHOLDENDE NYTTIGE OPLYSNINGER FOR NYBGGERE, LANDSOGERE OG KAPITALISTER, MED HENSYN TIL JORDBUND, KLIMA, PRODUKTIONER, FORDELE OG UDVIKLING, LANDBRUG, FABRIKDRIFT, HANDEL OG BJAERGVAERKSDRIFT . . . BROOKINGS, S. D.: SYD DAKOTA EKKO'S TRYKKERI, 1890.

[1]–47, [48 blank], [I]–IV. 22.3 x 14.9 cm. Gray-green printed wrappers, with title on front wrapper, notes on recto and verso of back wrapper.

Ref.:

A translation of F. H. Hagerty: *A Dictionary of Dakota* . . . [1889].

3904 SOUTH DAKOTA. Legislature. (Committee)

[Broadside] AN APPEAL. PIERRE, FEBRUARY 21, 1890. THE SENATE AND HOUSE OF REPRESENTATIVES HAVE PASSED WITH PRACTICAL UNANIMITY, AFTER A FULL INVESTIGATION AND UNDERSTANDING OF THE SITUATION, THE FOLLOWING JOINT RESOLUTION . . . A. C. MELLETTE, COMMITTEE

Broadside, 17.9 x 21.6 cm. Text, 19.2 x 18.4 cm.
Ref.:
An appeal for money and seed grains to supply residents of the state suffering from severe drought.

3905 SOUTHERN COLORADO . . .

SOUTHERN COLORADO. HISTORICAL AND DESCRIPTIVE OF FREMONT AND CUSTER COUNTIES WITH THEIR PRINCIPAL TOWNS. CANON CITY, AND OTHER TOWNS, FREMONT COUNTY. ROSITA, SILVER CLIFF, ULA, AND WEST MOUNTAIN VALLEY, CUSTER COUNTY . . . CANON CITY: BY BINCKLEY & HARTWELL, 1879.*

[1]–134. 23.1 x 15.3 cm. Illustrations unlisted. Buff boards, brown cloth backstrip, with title on front cover, advertisement on back cover.
Ref.: Wilcox p. 105
Advertisements on inner covers. Pages 121–34 carry advertisements.
The imprint of Rand, McNally & Co., Chicago, appears on the front cover.

3906 SOUTH-WESTERN BRAND BOOK!

SOUTH-WESTERN BRAND BOOK! CONTAINING THE MARKS AND BRANDS! OF THE CATTLE AND HORSE RAISERS OF SOUTH-WESTERN KANSAS, THE INDIAN TERRITORY AND THE PANHANDLE OF TEXAS. FOR THE ROUND-UP OF 1883. PUBLISHED BY MEDICINE-LODGE CRESSET: BARBOUR COUNTY INDEX: 1883.

[1]–84. 15.5 x 8.8 cm. Calf.
Ref.: Adams (*Ramp. Herd*) 2124; Howes S793
Pages 69–73 carry the Cherokee Strip / Live Stock Association / The / Charter and By-Laws of Association, / Adopted at / Cherokee Strip Meeting, / Held at / Caldwell, Kas., March 6, 7 & 8, 1883. /

3907 SOWELL, ANDREW J.

EARLY SETTLERS AND INDIAN FIGHTERS OF SOUTH-WEST TEXAS . . . AUSTIN, TEXAS: BEN C. JONES & CO., 1900.

[i]–viii, [1]–844. 23.3 x 14.8 cm. 12 plates and numerous illustrations in text. Red cloth, sprinkled edges.
Ref.: Carroll p. 177; Howes S797; Rader 2957

3908 SOWELL, ANDREW J.

HISTORY OF FORT BEND COUNTY, CONTAINING BIOGRAPHICAL SKETCHES OF MANY NOTED CHARACTERS . . . HOUSTON, TEXAS: W. H. COYLE & CO., 1904.

[1–2], [i]–ii, [v]–xii, [1]–373, [374 blank]. 21.9 x 14.5 cm. Two portraits. Red cloth.
Ref.: Adams 933; Carroll p. 57; Howes S798
Fewer than 100 copies were printed.

3909 SOWELL, ANDREW J.

RANGERS AND PIONEERS OF TEXAS. WITH A CONCISE ACCOUNT OF THE EARLY SETTLEMENTS, HARDSHIPS, MASSACRES, BATTLES, AND WARS, BY WHICH TEXAS WAS RESCUED FROM THE RULE OF THE SAVAGE AND CONSECRATED TO THE EMPIRE OF CIVILIZATION . . . SAN ANTONIO, TEXAS: SHEPARD BROS. & CO., 1884.

[i–ii], [1]–411, [412 blank]. 18.3 x 12.3 cm. Illustrations in text, unlisted. Brown cloth, blind embossed sides, gilt vignette on front cover, title in gilt on backstrip.
Ref.: Howes S801; Raines p. 194

3910 SPAIN. Laws, Statutes, etc. Charles III

PRAGMATICA SANCION DE SU MAGESTAD, EN FUERZA DE LEY, POR LA QUAL SE PROHIBE LA INTRODUCION Y USO EN ESTOS REYNOS DE LOS TEGIDOS DE ALGODON . . . EN MADRID: EN LA OFICINA DE DON ANTONIO SANZ, 1771.

A^6. [i–ii], [1]–6 LEAVES, verso of folio 6 blank. 28 x 19.8 cm. Bound with Number 9.
Ref.: Palau 235637

3911 SPAIN. Laws, Statutes, etc. Charles III

REAL DECRETO EN QUE S. M. HA RESUELTO AMPLIAR LA CONCESION DEL COMERCIO LIBRE, CONTENIDA EN DECRETO DE 16. DE OCTUBRE DE 1765 . . . EN MADRID: POR JUAN DE SAN MARTIN, ANO de 1778.

[A–B]^2. [i–ii], [1]–3 LEAVES. 28 x 19.8 cm. Bound with Number 9.
Ref.: Palau 251081

3912 SPAIN, Laws, Statutes, etc. Charles III

REGLAMENTO, E INSTRUCCION PARA LOS PRESIDIOS QUE SE HAN DE FORMAR EN LA LINEA DE FRONTERA DE LA NUEVA ESPANA. RESUELTO POR EL REY N. S. EN CEDULA DE 10. DE SETIEMBRE DE 1772 . . . MADRID: POR JUAN DE SAN MARTIN, 1772.

[*]^1, A–P^4, Q^1. [i–ii, ii blank], [1]–122. 20.2 x 14.6 cm. Rebound in limp vellum.
Ref.: Cowan p. 526; Jones 546; Medina 4564; Sabin 56262; Wagner (*SS*) 159
Wagner's copy carried a leaf following the title-leaf with the king's arms.

3913   SPAIN. Laws, Statutes, etc. Charles III

THE SAME. MEXICO: REIMPRESO EN LA OFICINA DE LA GUILA, 1834.

[1]–7², 8¹. [1]–30. 30 x 20.4 cm. Rebound in marbled boards, black morocco backstrip.

Ref.: Medina 4564; Sabin 56262; Streeter 706B; Wagner (*SS*) 159 see

3914   SPAIN. Laws, Statutes, etc. Charles III

[Caption title] . . . SUPERINTENDENCIA Y JUZGADO PRIVATIVO DEL RAMO DEL PAPEL SELLADO. MEXICO 30. DE JUNIO DE 1785. DECLARASE QUE TODOS LOS GOBERNADORES, CORREGIDORES, ALCALDES MAYORES Y DEMAS JUSTICIAS Y ESCRIBANOS DEL DISTRITO DE ESTA REAL AUDIENCIA, CONCLUIDO EL BIENIO DEBEN DEVOLVER PRECISAMENTE A LA TESORERIA GENERAL DEL RAMO, EN LOS TRES MESES PRIMEROS DEL SIGUIENTE, TODO EL PAPEL SELLADO QUE LES HUBIERE SOBRADO; . . .

[A]². [1–4]. 28 x 19.8 cm. Bound with Number 9.
Ref.:
The latest date in the text is August 3, 1785, at which time 500 copies of the document were ordered printed, apparently at Mexico City.

3915   SPAIN. Laws, Statutes, etc. Charles IV

[Caption title] EL REY. CON REAL ORDEN DE PRIMERO DE DICIEMBRE PROXIMO PASADO REMITI A MI CONSEJO DE INDIAS, PARA SU CUMPLIMIENTO EN LA PARTE QUE CORRESPONDE, COPIA DEL REAL DECRETO QUE ME HE SERVIDO EXPEDIR CON FECHA DE VEINTE Y OCHO DE NOVIEMBRE ULTIMO, Y DE LA INSTRUCCION QUE ACOMPANA, RELATIVO A LA VENTA DE LOS BIENES DE OBRAS PIAS EN MIS REYNOS DE LAS INDIAS E ISLAS FILIPINAS; CUYO TENOR, EL DE LA CITADA INSTRUCCION, Y DE LOS QUATRO FORMULARIOS QUE EN ELLA SE EXPRESAN, SON LOS SIGUIENTES: . . .

[1]–7². 1–28. 28 x 19.8 cm. Bound with Number 9.
Ref.:
Relates to the establishment of and regulations for *Juntas Superiores* and *Juntas Subalternas* as determined by the King and the Council of the Indies.
Dated at the end: Madrid 23 de Enero de 1805. = Exmô. Señor. = Antonio Porcel. = Se-/ñor Virrey de Nueva España. / Es Copia. México   de Julio de 1805. / Ximenez. /
Manuscript paraph in right margin of page 1.

3916   SPAIN. Laws, Statutes, etc. Charles IV

[Caption title] EL SENOR PRINCIPE DE LA PAZ ME DICE LO QUE SIGUE EN OFICIO DE 29. DE DICIEMBRE ULTIMO . . .

a⁶. [1–12, 12 blank]. 28 x 19.8 cm. Bound with Number 9.
Ref.:
Final paragraph: Lo translado á V. de Real órden para su / complimiento en la parte que la toca. Dios / guarde á V. muchos años. San Lorenzo 3 de / Enero de 1796. /
Regarding complaints of the Spanish directed to Lord Bute on the subject of seizure of ships, and the replies of the British.

3917   SPALDING, CHARLES C.

ANNALS OF THE CITY OF KANSAS: EMBRACING FULL DETAILS OF THE TRADE AND COMMERCE OF THE GREAT WESTERN PLAINS . . . KANSAS CITY: VAN HORN & ABEEL'S PRINTING HOUSE, 1858.

[1]–111, [112 blank]. 22.1 x 13.9 cm. Seven plates, on buff paper, unlisted. Pale blue printed wrappers, with title on front wrapper. Possibly removed from binding, backstrip and wrappers repaired. In a green half morocco case.

Ref.: Bradford 5145; Howes S805; Jones 1403; Sabin 88862; Wagner-Camp 309
MWA copy is the only other located copy in wrappers.

3918   SPALDING, CHARLES C.

THE SAME.

Maroon cloth, blind embossed borders, title in gilt on front cover. In a maroon half morocco case.

3919   SPALDING, HENRY H.

AUTOGRAPH NOTE, SIGNED. 1843 January 9, Clear Water, Oregon. To John McLaughlin, Fort Vancouver. One page, 10 x 19.7 cm.
An order to pay fifty-five dollars and twenty-five cents to A. I. Smith.

3920   SPALDING, HENRY H.

AUTOGRAPH MANUSCRIPT DOCUMENT, SIGNED. 1848 February 22. One page, 22.8 x 20.2 cm.
Record of a land claim in Tualoty County, Oregon. With certificate of entry (five lines) signed by Thomas Magruder, Recorder.

3921   SPANISH BAR DISTRICT MINING LAWS

REVISED LAWS OF SPANISH BAR DISTRICT, IDAHO TERRITORY. ADOPTED BY THE MINERS, JANUARY 22, 1861. CITY OF DENVER: DAILY MOUNTAINEER BOOK AND JOB OFFICE, 1861.

[1]–12. 22.1 x 14.6 cm. Pink printed wrappers, with title on front wrapper.
Ref.: McMurtrie & Allen (*Colorado*) 12

3922 SPARKS, CHARLES H.

HISTORY OF WINNESHIEK COUNTY, WITH BIO-
GRAPHICAL SKETCHES OF ITS EMINENT MEN . . .
DECORAH, IOWA: JAS. ALEX LEONARD.

[i]–xii, [1]–156, [1–11 advertisements, 12 blank].
22.2 x 14.6 cm. Black cloth, blind fillet borders
on sides, title in gilt on front cover.

Ref.: Cook p. 151

Copyrighted 1877. The volume was printed at
Milwaukee by Riverside Printing House.

This earliest Winneshiek County history begins in 1842, when the Mission to the Winne-
bagoes was founded. Fort Crawford at Prairie
Du Chien was near by and contributed Indian
traders who founded "Sodom and Gomorrah."
There is a full history and description of Fort
Atkinson which was established in 1840. After
the removal of the Indians in 1848, the need for
the fort ceased.—EDG

3923 SPARKS, JARED

THE LIFE OF JOHN LEDYARD, THE AMERICAN TRAV-
ELLER; COMPRISING SELECTIONS FROM HIS JOUR-
NALS AND CORRESPONDENCE . . . CAMBRIDGE:
PUBLISHED BY HILLIARD AND BROWN, 1828.

[i]–xii, 1–325. (Seven pages of advertisements
preceding half-title.) 23.5 x 14.7 cm. Gray
boards, gray cloth back, printed paper label,
uncut. Bookplate removed.

Ref.: Howes S818; Sabin 88991

Ledyard accompanied Cook on his third
voyage.

3924 SPARKS, WILLIAM H.

THE MEMORIES OF FIFTY YEARS . . . WITH SCENES
AND INCIDENTS OCCURRING DURING A LONG LIFE
OF OBSERVATION CHIEFLY SPENT IN THE SOUTH-
WEST . . . PHILADELPHIA: CLAXTON, REMSEN &
HAFFELFINGER, 1870.

[i]–xii, 13–489, [490 blank]. 20.5 x 13.6 cm.
Green cloth, blind embossed fillet on sides, title
in gilt on backstrip.

Ref.: Howes S819; Sabin 89015

The author's Southwest was east of the Mississippi River; somewhat more than half of the
book deals with Georgia and the Southeast.

3925 SPEARMAN, FRANK H.

WHISPERING SMITH . . . NEW YORK: CHARLES
SCRIBNER'S SONS, 1906.*

[i]–[xi], [xii blank], 1–421, [422 blank, 423–24
advertisements]. 18.8 x 12.7 cm. Four illustrations by N. C. Wyeth listed. Red cloth, pictorial
cover.

Ref.:

3926 SPEARS, JOHN R.

ILLUSTRATED SKETCHES OF DEATH VALLEY AND
OTHER BORAX DESERTS OF THE PACIFIC COAST . . .
CHICAGO: RAND, McNALLY & COMPANY, 1892.

[1]–226, [227–32 advertisements]. 18.7 x 12.7
cm. 57 illustrations listed. Brown cloth, title
stamped in gilt on front cover and backstrip.

Ref.: Cowan p. 604; Howes S821; Munk
(Alliot) p. 206

3927 SPEED, JOSHUA F.

REMINISCENCES OF ABRAHAM LINCOLN AND NOTES
OF A VISIT TO CALIFORNIA. TWO LECTURES . . .
LOUISVILLE, KY.: PRINTED BY JOHN P. MORTON
AND COMPANY, 1884.

[1]–67, [68 blank]. 20.2 x 13.3 cm. Brown cloth,
beveled edges, title in gilt on front cover and
backstrip.

Ref.: Howes S826; Monaghan 1005

3928 [SPENCER, E. J.]

[Caption title] ENGINEER OFFICE, HEADQUARTERS
DEPARTMENT OF ARIZONA. WHIPPLE BARRACKS,
PRESCOTT, SEPTEMBER 25, 1886. THE ASSISTANT
ADJUTANT GENERAL, DEPARTMENT OF ARIZONA.
SIR: I HAVE THE HONOR TO SUBMIT HEREWITH A
MAP OF THE FIELD OPERATIONS AGAINST THE HOS-
TILE BANDS OF CHIRICAHUA INDIANS UNDER
NATCHEZ AND GERONIMO. UPON THIS MAP WILL BE
FOUND THE HOSTILES TRAIL AS FOLLOWED BY THE
VARIOUS COMMANDS IN THE DEPARTMENT; THE
HELIOGRAPH SYSTEM OF COMMUNICATION AS ES-
TABLISHED IN NEW MEXICO . . . AND IN ARIZONA
. . . ; THE LOCATION OF MILITARY POSTS AND
CAMPS, AND OF THE VARIOUS ENGAGEMENTS OF
THE UNITED STATES AND MEXICAN TROOPS WITH
THE HOSTILES. . . .

[1]–4. 20 x 12.8 cm. White printed wrappers
with title on front wrapper. In Lawton Scrap-
book.

Prov.: Inscribed on front wrapper: Sent to
me by Lawton /.

Ref.:

Where is the map? Possibly unpublished.

3929 SPENCER, JOHN W.

REMINISCENCES OF PIONEER LIFE IN THE MISSISSIPPI
VALLEY . . . DAVENPORT: GRIGGS, WATSON, &
DAY, PRINTERS, 1872.

[i]–[vi, vi blank], [7]–73, [74 blank]. 21.6 x 14.7
cm. Original photograph of the author, mounted,
as frontispiece. Green cloth, title in gilt on front
cover.

Ref.: Buck 166; Howes S834

Especially important for his view of the Black Hawk War—he being sympathetic toward Black Hawk.—EDG

3930 SPENCER, OLIVER M.

INDIAN CAPTIVITY. A TRUE NARRATIVE OF THE CAPTURE OF THE REV. O. M. SPENCER, BY THE INDIANS, IN THE NEIGHBORHOOD OF CINCINNATI . . . WASHINGTON, PA.: G. W. BRICE, PRINTER, 1835.

[1]–56. 21.6 x 13.7 cm. Pictorial gray wrappers, with large woodcut on front wrapper with base at inner edge. Backstrip repaired. Bound into brown boards, calf backstrip and corners.
Ref.: Howes S835; Sabin 89367; Thomson 1086
Editions: New York, 1835.

3931 SPENCER, ORSON

[Caption title] PATRIARCHAL ORDER, OR PLURALITY OF WIVES! . . .

[1]–16. Bound with Number 3346.
Ref.: Sabin 89372; Woodward 259
Imprint at foot of page 16: Liverpool: / S.W. Richards, 15, Wilton Street. / [rule] / Printed for the Publisher by R. James, 39, South Castle Street. /

3932 SPENCER, ORSON

THE PRUSSIAN MISSION OF THE CHURCH OF JESUS CHRIST OF LATTER-DAY SAINTS . . . LIVERPOOL: S. W. RICHARDS, 1853.

[1]–16. Bound with Number 3346.
Ref.: Sabin 89373
The Mormons in Germany.

3933 SPENCER, THOMAS

NARRATIVE OF THE EVENTS ATTENDING THE MASSACRE OF PART OF THE CREW BELONGING TO THE WHALESHIP TRITON, OF NEW-BEDFORD, BY THE NATIVES OF SYDENHAM'S ISLAND . . . HONOLULU, OAHU: E. A. ROCKWELL, PRINTER, 1848.

[1]–17, [18 blank]. 21.2 x 13.9 cm. Removed from bound volume, unbound.
Ref.: Sabin 89389

3934 SPOONER, WALTER W.

THE BACK-WOODSMEN; OR, TALES OF THE BORDERS A COLLECTION OF HISTORICAL AND AUTHENTIC ACCOUNTS OF EARLY ADVENTURE AMONG THE INDIANS . . . CINCINNATI: W. E. DIBBLE & CO., 1883.

[i]–[xvi, xvi blank], 17–608. (Pages [i–ii] blank.) 22.5 x 14.7 cm. 26 illustrations listed. Brown morocco backstrip and corners, marbled edges.
Ref.: Howes S841; Rader 2964
Contains a long account of Robert McClellan and his adventures on the plains.—EDG

3935 SPRINGFIELD (Massachusetts) GAZETTE

[Newspaper] SPRINGFIELD GAZETTE. SPRINGFIELD, (MASS.)—PRINTED BY L. BRIGGS, FOR THE PROPRIETORS.—WILLIAM HYDE, EDITOR. VOL. I. WEDNESDAY, SEPTEMBER 28, 1831. NO. 3 . . .

Newspaper, [1–4]. 52.8 x 39.2 cm.
Ref.:
Page [3] column 6 carries advertisement headed: Interesting to the Oregon / Emigrants. / . . . H. J. Kelley, Gen. Agent. / [79 lines].
Kelley was General Agent of the "American Society" incorporated in Massachusetts by Special Act, June 20, 1831. This advertisement antedates the General Circular by almost six months.

3936 SPROAT, GILBERT M.

SCENES AND STUDIES OF SAVAGE LIFE . . . LONDON: SMITH, ELDER AND CO., 1868.

[i]–xii, [1]–317, [318 colophon, 319–320 advertisements]. 18.8 x 12.3 cm. Lithographed frontispiece. Green cloth, blind fillets on sides, title gilt on backstrip.
Ref.: Butler (*Aht*) 1; Howes S858; Pilling 3716; Sabin 89910
Contains an account of the "Boston" massacre at Nootka in 1803.

3937 SPURR, JOSIAH E.

THROUGH THE YUKON GOLD DIGGINGS. A NARRATIVE OF PERSONAL TRAVEL . . . BOSTON: EASTERN PUBLISHING COMPANY, 1900.*

[1]–276. 20 x 13.4 cm. 25 illustrations listed. Light brown pictorial cloth.
Prov.: Signed on the front fly-leaf: J. E. Spurr / [underline] / .
Ref.: Smith 9796; Wickersham 4417

3938 STACEY, JOHN F.

TO ALASKA FOR GOLD. AS TOLD BY JOHN F. STACEY, SO. ASHBURNHAM, MASS. TO HIS DAUGHTER MRS. JOHN A. DAVIS, WORCESTER, MASS.

[1]–[70], [71–72 blank]. (Pages [1–2] blank.) 22.6 x 15.2 cm. Illustrations unlisted. Brown printed wrappers, with title on front wrapper.
Ref.:
Without imprint or date.

3939 STAFFORD, MALLIE

THE MARCH OF EMPIRE THROUGH THREE DECADES. EMBRACING SKETCHES OF CALIFORNIA HISTORY; EARLY TIMES AND SCENES; LIFE IN THE MINES; TRAVELS BY LAND AND SEA BEFORE THE ERA OF RAILROADS; THE EAST DURING THE YEARS OF THE CIVIL WAR; LIFE IN THE BORDER STATES; CROSSING

THE PLAINS WITH OX TEAMS; CROSSING THE PLAINS ON THE TRANSCONTINENTAL RAILWAY; PROGRESS AND IMPROVEMENT OF THE GOLDEN STATE; RESOURCES; ETC., ETC. . . . SAN FRANCISCO: GEO. SPAULDING & CO., 1884.

[1]–189, [190 blank]. 17.5 x 11.6 cm. Portrait. Brown cloth, title and decorative bands stamped in black on front cover, decorative bands in blind on back cover.

Ref.: Cowan, p. 606; Howes S864

Mrs. Stafford later went with her husband to Colorado.

3940 [STAMBAUGH, SAMUEL C.]

A STATEMENT AND EXPLANATION OF THE ORIGIN AND PRESENT CONDITION OF THE CLAIM OF PELAGIE FERRIBAULT, A HALF-BREED WOMAN OF THE SIOUX TRIBE, FOR THE VALUE OF AN ISLAND AT THE CONFLUENCE OF ST. PETERS AND MISSISSIPPI RIVERS, RESERVED TO HER BY THE SIOUX CHIEFS FROM A TRACT OF LAND CONVEYED TO THE UNITED STATES FOR MILITARY PURPOSES, AT THE ESTABLISHMENT OF FORT SNELLING, AUG. 9, 1820 . . . WASHINGTON: PRINTED AT THE UNION OFFICE, 1856.

[1]–36. 23.2 x 15 cm. Stabbed, unbound, uncut. Roughly opened.

Prov.: Inscribed at top of title-page: Respects of S. C. Stambaugh /.

Ref.:

3941 STANFORD, LELAND, and Others, *Defendants*

[Wrapper title] SUPERIOR COURT, SONOMA COUNTY, STATE OF CALIFORNIA. ELLEN COLTON VS. LELAND STANFORD ET AL. LETTERS OF C. P. HUNTINGTON, CHARLES CROCKER, ETC.

[1]–226. 25.6 x 17.2 cm. Gray-green printed wrappers with title on front wrapper.

Ref.:

These are the letters, cold, callous, profane, and cynical which influenced the popular conception of Collis Porter Huntington and his associates. Some names, indicated by long dashes in the text, have been supplied in manuscript.

Neither place nor date of publication is given. The case reached the Supreme Court of California in 1889. The present document was probably printed during that year.

3942 STANLEY, CLARK

THE LIFE AND ADVENTURES OF THE AMERICAN COW-BOY . . . PUBLISHED BY CLARK STANLEY, 1897.*

[1]–50. 22.8 x 15.3 cm. 15 illustrations. Pictorial green wrappers, printed in red and blue, advertisements on verso of front and recto and verso of back wrapper.

Ref.: Adams (*Ramp. Herd*) 2147; Howes S875; Rader 2971

Pages 39–[50] and wrappers carry advertisements for Clark Stanley's Snake Oil Liniment. The author claims he was known as the "Rattle Snake King."

Probably printed at Providence, Rhode Island.

3943 STANLEY, D. S.

[Wrapper title] ANNUAL REPORT OF BRIGADIER GENERAL D. S. STANLEY, U. S. ARMY, COMMANDING DEPARTMENT OF TEXAS. 1886.

[1]–4; [1]–[2 blank]; [1]–[2 blank]; [1]–7, [8 blank]; [1]–[2 blank]; [1]–11, [12 blank]; [1]–3, [4 blank]; [1]–5, [6 blank]; [1]–15, [16 blank]; [17 blank]; [1]–2; [1]–[2 blank]; [1]–2; [1]–[2 blank]; [1]–15, [16 blank]; [1]–6. 20.5 x 13 cm. Buff printed wrappers with title on front wrapper. Sections loose in wrappers, unbound.

Ref.: Howes S876

3944 STANLEY, EDWIN J.

RAMBLES IN WONDERLAND; OR, UP THE YELLOWSTONE, AND AMONG THE GEYSERS AND OTHER CURIOSITIES OF THE NATIONAL PARK . . . NEW YORK: D. APPLETON AND COMPANY, 1878.

[i]–[x (x blank)], [7]–179, [180 blank, 181–90 advertisement]. 19.8 x 13 cm. Folding map and 12 illustrations listed. Blue cloth with decorative design in black on front cover and title in gilt, title in gilt on backstrip.

Ref.: Howes S880

Contains personal narratives of the survivors of the Radersburg party who fell into hands of the Nez Perces in 1877.

3945 STANLEY, EDWIN J.

LIFE OF REV. L. B. STATELER; OR, SIXTY-FIVE YEARS ON THE FRONTIER CONTAINING INCIDENTS, ANECDOTES, AND SKETCHES OF METHODIST HISTORY IN THE WEST AND NORTHWEST . . . NASHVILLE, TENN.: PUBLISHING HOUSE OF THE M. E. CHURCH, SOUTH, 1907.*

[i]–xviii, [xviii blank], 1–356, [357 advertisement, 358 blank]. 18.6 x 13.2 cm. Illustrations unlisted. Light blue pictorial cloth.

Ref.: Howes S879; Smith 9807

3946 STANLEY, HENRY M.

MY EARLY TRAVELS AND ADVENTURES IN AMERICA AND ASIA . . . LONDON: SAMPSON LOW, MARSTON AND COMPANY LIMITED, 1895.

[i]–[xxii, xxii blank], [1]–301, [302 colophon]. [i]–[x, x blank], [1]–424. 17.5 x 12 cm. Two portraits and two maps: Map Showing the Route / of the / Hancock & Sherman Indian / Cam-

paigns, 1867. / English Miles. / [diagrammatic scale: about 100 miles to one inch.] / [lower right:] George Philip & Son. 12, Fleet St. London [lower half of line cut off] / 16.2 x 26.5 cm. Map: Map / Illustrating the Author's Route / from / The Suez Canal / to / Zanzibar & Ujiji / [lower right:] G. Philip & Son, London & Liverpool. / [lower centre:] London, Sampson, Low, Marston & Company, Limited. / 22.6 x 21.4 cm. No scale given. Two volumes, green cloth, title in gilt on backstrips.

Ref.:

"Dr. Livingston, I presume."

3947 STANSBURY, HOWARD

. . . EXPLORATION AND SURVEY OF THE VALLEY OF THE GREAT SALT LAKE OF UTAH, INCLUDING A RECONNOISSANCE OF A NEW ROUTE THROUGH THE ROCKY MOUNTAINS . . . PHILADELPHIA: LIPPINCOTT, GRAMBO & CO., 1852.

[1]–487, [488 blank]. 21.9 x 14.4 cm. Three maps, 34 tinted lithographs, and 23 black and white plates, listed. Map: Fac simile / of a part of a map of / North America / corrected from the observations / communicated to the Royal Society / at London and the Royal Academy / at Paris. / by John Senex E R. S. 1710. / 15.3 x 23.6 cm. No scale given. Map: Map / of the / Great Salt Lake / and / Adjacent Country / in the / Territory of Utah. / Surveyed in 1849 and 1850, / under the orders of / Col. J. J. Abert, Chief of the Topographical Bureau, / by / Capt. Howard Stansbury of the Corps of Topographical Engineers / aided by / Lieut. J. W. Gunnison Corps Topographical Engineers / and / Albert Carrington. / Drawn by Lieut. Gunnison and Charles Preuss. / [swelled rule] / Ackerman Lith 379 Broadway N. Y. / 109.5 x 76.4 cm. Scale: 4 miles to one inch. Map: Map / of a Reconnoissance between / Fort Leavenworth / on the Missouri River, and the / Great Salt Lake / in the / Territory of Utah, / made in 1849 and 1850 / under the orders of / Col. J. J. Abert, Chief of the Topographical Bureau, / by / Capt. Howard Stansbury of the Corps of Topographical Engineers, / aided by / Lieut. J. W. Gunnison Corps Topographical Engineers, / and / Albert Carrington. / The adjacent country laid down from the latest and most authentic data. / Drawn by Lieut. Gunnison and Charles Preuss. / Ackerman Lith. 379 Broadway N. Y. / 72 x 171.2 cm. Scale: about 15 miles to one inch. Purple cloth, blind embossed sides, title in gilt on backstrip, accompanied by atlas (23.3 x 15.2 cm.) containing two large maps, plum cloth, blind embossed borders, title in gilt on front cover.

Prov.: Inscribed on inner front cover: Baron Gerault / with Compliments of / Col. Abert /.

Ref.: Bradford 5173; Field 1490; Howes S884; Sabin 90372; Wagner-Camp 219; Wheat (*Transmississippi*) 764, 765

31st Congress, Special Session, Senate, Executive Document No. 3, Serial 547.

The printer's imprint on page 487 reads: [rule] / Stereotyped by L. Johnson & Co. / Philadelphia. /

3948 STANTON, IRVING W.

SIXTY YEARS IN COLORADO REMINISCENCES AND REFLECTIONS OF A PIONEER OF 1860 . . . DENVER, COLORADO, 1922.*

[5]–320. 20.4 x 13.3 cm. Portrait. Dark red cloth.

Ref.: Howes S887

3949 STAPP, WILLIAM P.

THE PRISONERS OF PEROTE: CONTAINING A JOURNAL KEPT BY THE AUTHOR, WHO WAS CAPTURED BY THE MEXICANS, AT MIER, DECEMBER 25, 1842, AND RELEASED FROM PEROTE, MAY 16, 1844 . . . PHILADELPHIA: G. B. ZIEBER AND COMPANY, 1845.

[i]–[xii, xii blank], [13]–164, [165–68 advertisements]. 18.8 x 11.5 cm. Buff printed wrappers with title on front wrapper, advertisements on verso of front and recto and verso of back wrapper. In a dark blue cloth case.

Ref.: Clements Library (*Texas*) 27; Dobie p. 58; Howes S891; Raines p. 194; Sabin 90483; Streeter 1610

The author was a member of Colonel W. S. Fisher's party which was defeated by the Mexicans at Mier in 1842. The better part of the book is the author's account of his long march to Mexico City and his imprisonment in the castle of Perote. He was released after nearly two years through the intervention of his uncle, General Milton Stapp.

3950 STARING, GEORGE B.

1883–84. HELENA DIRECTORY. A COMPLETE, RELIABLE BUSINESS AND RESIDENCE DIRECTORY. TOGETHER WITH A BRIEF HISTORY OF MONTANA AND CITY OF HELENA . . . HELENA: GEO. E. BOOS & CO., PRINTERS, 1884.

[1]–116. (Advertisements, not included in pagination, on inside front cover, recto and verso of front endleaf, and recto of back endleaf.) 20.5 x 14 cm. Buff printed boards with red leather backstrip, with title on front cover, advertisement on lower half of front cover, rule border, advertisement in gilt reading up leather on front cover, title in gilt reading up backstrip: Helena Directory, 1884. /, advertisements on back cover.

Prov.: Signature on title-page: R. B. Harrison /. Russell B. Harrison is listed in the directory as Superintendent of the United States Assay Office.

Ref.: Howes S893

A history of Montana occupies pages [3]–42. This includes excerpts from Granville Stuart's article on Verendrye published in the *Montana Historical Collections*, Vol. 1, 1876, and also an article by the same author on the gold discoveries in Montana which I have not seen elsewhere. Some excerpts are printed from W. A. Clark's Centennial Address at the Philadelphia Exhibition in 1876. This latter in its entirety is printed in Vol. 2, *Montana Historical Collections*, 1896. A history of Helena occupies pages 43–52.—EDG

3951   [STARR, EMMET]

CHEROKEES "WEST." 1794 TO 1839. CLAREMORE, OKLAHOMA: EMMET STARR, 1910.

[3]–164. 22.7 x 15.2 cm. Light blue cloth, title stamped in black on front cover.

Ref.: Howes S898; Rader 2973

Virtually a reprint of Cephas Washburn: *Reminiscences of the Indians . . .* [1869].

3952   STARR, HENRY

[Wrapper title] THRILLING EVENTS. LIFE OF HENRY STARR . . . TULSA, OKLA.: R. D. GORDON, 1914.

[1]–[51], [52 blank]. 19.7 x 11.9 cm. Pink printed wrappers, with title on front wrapper. In a brown cloth case.

Ref.: Adams 952; Howes S901

The pages are numbered consecutively, but the text is badly jumbled. Apparently complete.

3953   STATISTICAL HISTORY OF CLEAR CREEK COUNTY, COLORADO . . .

[Wrapper title] STATISTICAL HISTORY OF CLEAR CREEK COUNTY, COLORADO, FROM 1859 TO 1881, INCLUSIVE . . . "MINER" PRINT. GEORGETOWN.

[1]–8. 20.8 x 13.6 cm. Map: Map / of / Clear Creek County, / Colo. / Scale one inch to three miles. / [lower left:] Ernest. Le Neve Foster, M.E. / Georgetown Colo. / [lower right:] Mills Eng. Co. Denver /. 17.7 x 14.5 cm. Scale: three miles to an inch. Gray printed wrappers, with title on front wrapper.

Ref.: Wilcox p. 107

Published in 1881.

3954   STEAMER PACIFIC NEWS

[Newspaper] STEAMER PACIFIC NEWS. FOR THE STEAMER TENNESSEE, NOVEMBER 15TH. WEEKLY PACIFIC NEWS. MONDAY MORNING, NON[!]. 11, 1850. J. WINCHESTER, EDITOR. H. L. WINANTS AND C. M. BLAKE, ASSISTANTS . . .

[1–4]. 58 x 41.5 cm. Unbound.

Ref.:

Large woodcut portrait of Jenny Lind on first page.

3955   STEBBINS, CHARLES M.

THE NEW AND TRUE RELIGION . . . HARTSDALE, N. Y.: CHARLES M. STEBBINS, 1897.

[i–ii], [1]–423, [424 blank]. 19.4 x 13.5 cm. Gray cloth, stamped with black bands and arabesque on front cover, title gilt on backstrip.

Ref.:

According to the preface the first edition was published in the summer of 1896. Stebbins freighted between Kansas points and Denver, particularly between Atchison, Kansas, and Denver, with a wholesale grocery business in Denver, during the Civil War. He went across the plains in 1864.—EDG

3956   STEED, THOMAS

[Wrapper title] THE LIFE OF THOMAS STEED FROM HIS OWN DIARY, 1826–1910.*

[1]–43, [44 blank]. 22.8 x 15.3 cm. Green printed wrappers.

Ref.: Howes S915

No place or date of publication. Probably Salt Lake City, 1935.

Steed reached Nauvoo from England on April 13th, 1844. He remained in the vicinity of Nauvoo and at Keokuk, Iowa, until the spring of 1850, when with his family and relations he crossed the plains to Salt Lake City arriving there August 28. They settled at Farmington about eighteen miles from the City. This account of his life is based to some extent on his journals.—EDG

3957   STEEDMAN, CHARLES J.

BUCKING THE SAGEBRUSH; OR, THE OREGON TRAIL IN THE SEVENTIES . . . NEW YORK: G. P. PUTNAM'S SONS, 1904.*

[i]–ix, [x blank], 1–270. 20.6 x 14 cm. 12 illustrations, including nine by Charles M. Russell, numerous small sketches by Russell and one map. Yellow pictorial buckram, gilt top, uncut.

Ref.: Howes S916; Smith 9832

3958   STEELE, ELIZA R.

A SUMMER JOURNEY IN THE WEST . . . NEW YORK: JOHN S. TAYLOR, AND CO., 1841.

[7]–278. 18.4 x 11.4 cm. Engraved title-page with vignette. Blue cloth, embossed design on covers in blind, gilt vignette in centre of each cover, title in gilt on backstrip.

Ref.: Buck 355; Howes S919; Sabin 91116; Thompson 1101

3959 STEELE, JAMES

OLD CALIFORNIAN DAYS . . . CHICAGO: BELFORD-CLARKE CO., 1889.

[i]–viii, [9]–227, [228 blank]. (Page [i] blank, [ii] frontispiece.) 18.5 x 12.5 cm. 41 illustrations listed. Gray cloth, title stamped in gilt on front cover and backstrip.

Ref.: Bradford 5198; Cowan p. 612; Howes (1954) 9797

3960 STEELE, JAMES W.

FRONTIER ARMY SKETCHES . . . CHICAGO: JANSEN, McCLURG & COMPANY, 1883.

[1]–329, [330 blank], [331–36 advertisements]. 18.9 x 12.6 cm. Green-gray pictorial cloth, with title on front cover and backstrip.

Prov.: Inscribed on first blank leaf: W. F. White Esq; / G. P. & T. A. / A gentleman who / has long since commended / himself to a world / of humbug / by knowing what he professes / to know, and doing well all / he pretends to do, remaining / all the time the "prince of / Good Fellows; / With the compliments / of / The Author. /

Ref.: Howes S922

Six stories from the earlier edition (*The Sons of the Border* . . . 1873) have been omitted and six new stories added.

3961 STEELE, JAMES W.

THE SONS OF THE BORDER. SKETCHES OF THE LIFE AND PEOPLE OF THE FAR FRONTIER . . . TOPEKA, KANSAS: COMMONWEALTH PRINTING COMPANY, 1873.

[1]–260. 21.4 x 13.9 cm. Green cloth, black fillets and gilt vignette on front cover, title in gilt on backstrip.

Ref.: Howes S922; Sabin 91122; Wright II 2353

Contains six stories omitted from the second edition (*Frontier Army Sketches*). Steele also wrote under the pseudonym Deane Monahan.

3962 STEELE, JOHN

AUTOGRAPH LETTER, SIGNED. 1851 March 31, Sacramento. To Miss Loretta Steele. Three pages, 31.3 x 20 cm. Portion of third page missing.

Contains an account of exploration for gold on the Feather River. Laid in his *Across the Plains in 1850* . . . 1930.

3963 STEELE, JOHN

AUTOGRAPH LETTER, SIGNED. 1852 November 6, Rio las Americanos. Addressed at head "My dear Sister" but addressed on fourth page: Mr Edward L Steele . . . Three pages, 21 x 13.3 cm.

A fine letter regarding his experiences in the gold mines of California. Laid in his *In Camp and Cabin* . . . 1901.

3964 STEELE, JOHN

IN CAMP AND CABIN. MINING LIFE AND ADVENTURE, IN CALIFORNIA DURING 1850 AND LATER . . . LODI, WIS.: PUBLISHED BY J. STEELE, 1901.

[i–iv], [1]–81, [82–4 blank]. (Pages [i–ii] blank.) 22.8 x 15.2 cm. Green printed wrappers, with title on front wrapper, uncut. In a red half morocco case.

Ref.: Cowan p. 612; Howes S924

Laid in are typed notes about Steele by John Thomas Lee, a newspaper clipping by the uncle of the author, three portraits of the author, etc. All the material was used in preparation for the Caxton Club edition of *Across the Plains in 1850* . . .

Also laid in is an Autograph Letter, signed by the author, 1852 November 6, Rio de las Americanos. To his sister.

3965 STEELE, JOHN

THE TRAVELER'S COMPANION THROUGH THE GREAT INTERIOR. A GUIDE FOR THE ROAD TO CALIFORNIA, BY THE SOUTH PASS IN THE ROCKY MOUNTAINS, AND SUBLETT'S AND HEADPATH'S CUT OFFS . . . GALENA: POWER PRESS OF H. H. HOUGHTON & CO. . . . 1854.

[I]–V, [6]–54, [55–56 blank]. (Page 15 mispaginated 51.) 14.2 x 9.6 cm. Pink printed wrappers, with title on front wrapper. In a black half morocco case.

Ref.: Byrd 2188; Cowan p. 612; Howes S925; Sabin 91127; Wagner-Camp 244

3966 [STEELE, OLIVER G.]

STEELE'S WESTERN GUIDE BOOK, AND EMIGRANT'S DIRECTORY; CONTAINING DIFFERENT ROUTES THROUGH THE STATES OF NEW YORK, OHIO, INDIANA, ILLINOIS, MICHIGAN, WISCONSIN, IOWA, MINESOTA[!], ETC., ETC. . . . BUFFALO: OLIVER G. STEELE, 1849.

[1]–72. 14.5 x 9.5 cm. Two folding maps: Map of / Michigan, Ohio, Indiana, / Illinois, Missouri, Wisconsin / & Iowa. / With the Indian Country west of the Mississippi. / Exhibiting the Base, Meridian and Township Lines / According to the U. S. Surveys / by S. W. Higgins Topographer of the Geological Survey of Michigan / and U. S. Dep. Surveyor. / O. G. Steele. / Buffalo, N.Y. / Entered according to Act of Congress in the year 1846 by O. G. Steele in the Clerks / Office of the District Court of the Northern District of New York. / Engraved by J. M. Atwood, N. York. / 38.1 x 51.6 cm. No

scale given. Map: Map of / Routes / to / California and Oregon. / Lith. of Hall & Mooney, Buffalo. / 10.7 x 24.1 cm. No scale given. Green cloth, with title on cover.

Ref.: Buck 253; Howes S927; Sabin 91143

Contains an appendix giving Oregon and California routes.

Editions: Buffalo, 1832, 1834, 1835, 1836, 1839, 1843, 1846, 1847 etc.

3967 [STEELE, OLIVER G.]

THE TRAVELLER'S DIRECTORY, AND EMIGRANT'S GUIDE; CONTAINING GENERAL DESCRIPTIONS OF DIFFERENT ROUTES THROUGH THE STATES OF NEW-YORK, OHIO, INDIANA, ILLINOIS, AND THE TERRITORY OF MICHIGAN . . . BUFFALO: PUBLISHED BY STEELE & FAXON, 1832.

[1]–82, [1]–2 Contents. 13.9 x 9.2 cm. Green boards, brown cloth back, printed paper label, 3.5 x 7.9 cm.

Ref.: Buck 253; Howes S927; Sabin 91144

3968 STEELE, R. J., JAMES P. BULL, & F. I. HOUSTON

DIRECTORY OF THE COUNTY OF PLACER, FOR THE YEAR 1861: CONTAINING A HISTORY OF THE COUNTY, AND OF THE DIFFERENT TOWNS IN THE COUNTY . . . SAN FRANCISCO: PRINTED FOR THE PUBLISHERS, BY CHARLES F. ROBBINS, 1861.

[i]–vi, [7]–208. 22.5 x 14.5 cm. Buff printed boards with red leather backstrip, title on front cover; advertisement on back cover.

Ref.: Blumann & Thomas 2327; Howes P402; Sabin 91146

Advertisements interspersed throughout, but included in pagination.

3969 STEINECK, W. E.

[Wrapper title] PRACTICAL GUIDE FOR THE PROSPECTOR AND MINER, WITH MAP OF ROUTE TO THUNDER MOUNTAIN. COMPLETE MINING LAWS . . . BOISE, IDAHO: THE STATESMAN PRINT.

1–48. 15.2 x 8.2 cm. Folding map: Map / of the / Roads and Trails / from Railways to / Thunder Mountain / Compiled for / The Evening Capital News / By E.B. True / U.S. Dept. Min. Surv. / Felloes & Faust, Eng. / Portland, Or. / [three lines of advertisements in right margin]. 29.8 x 45.3 cm. (paper size). No scale given. Yellow printed wrappers, with title on front wrapper, advertisements on verso of front and recto and verso of back wrapper.

Ref.:

The date 1899 appears several places in the text; otherwise the volume is undated.

3970 STEINERT, W.

NORDAMERIKA VORZUGLICH TEXAS IM JAHRE 1849 . . . BERLIN: K. M. KRUGER'S VERLAGSHANDLUNG, 1850.

[i]–[viii, viii blank], 1–280. 18.3 x 11.7 cm. Contemporary marbled boards, manuscript label on backstrip.

Ref.: Howes S933; Raines p. 194; Sabin 91208

Howes and Sabin give the collation [6] 280 [1]. In the copies examined, the leaf headed Inhalt was probably bound after page 280 instead of as pages [vii–viii].

3971 [STEPHEN, JAMES]

THE DANGERS OF THE COUNTRY . . . PHILADELPHIA: PRINTED FOR SAMUEL F. BRADFORD, 1807.

[A]², B–T⁴. [i–iv, iv blank], [1]–142, [143–44 blank]. Bound with Number 3289.

Ref.: Sabin 18487; Shaw & Shoemaker 13643

Editions: London, 1807, 1807. Charleston, 1807.

3972 STEPHENS, LORENZO D.

LIFE SKETCHES OF A JAYHAWKER OF '49 . . . NINETEEN SIXTEEN.*

[1]–68. (Pages [1–2] blank.) 23.3 x 15.3 cm. Illustrations unlisted. Brown printed wrappers. In a blue cloth case.

Ref.: Blumann & Thomas 1017; Cowan p. 613; Howes S941

Limited to 300 copies, published at San José, California. The author was with Manly in Death Valley.

3973 STERNE, LOUIS

SEVENTY YEARS OF AN ACTIVE LIFE . . . LONDON: PRINTED FOR PRIVATE DISTRIBUTION ONLY, MCMXII.

[i–iv], [1]–191, [192 blank]. 21.9 x 14.2 cm. Frontispiece portrait. Full green morocco, gilt.

Prov.: Inscribed by the author on the first blank leaf: To Mr & Mrs Donald / amour from / L Stern / Nov 9ᵗʰ 12 /.

Ref.: Howes S950

As a young man Stern adventured with Ben McCullough in Texas and Utah in the '50's. His reminiscences include many interviews with Lincoln who sent him to Europe on a secret mission to prevent building of a blockade runner in the Baltic.—EDG

3974 STEVENS, HAZARD

THE LIFE OF ISAAC INGALLS STEVENS . . . BOSTON: HOUGHTON, MIFFLIN AND COMPANY, 1900.

[i]–[xxi], [xxii blank], [1]–480, [481 blank, 482 colophon]. [i]–xx, [1]–530, [531 blank, 532 colo-

phon]. 23 x 15.2 cm. 39 illustrations and 18 maps listed. Two volumes, dark blue ribbed cloth, gilt tops, uncut.

Ref.: Smith 9885

Contains much on pioneer Oregon.

3975 [STEVENS, HIRAM B.]

[Caption title] HO, FOR SOUTHERN DAKOTA! AND THE BLACK HILLS! UNCLE SAM'S FARM IS GROWING SMALLER EVERY DAY. THE ARMY AND NAVY COLONY HAVE LOCATED IN SOUTHERN DAKOTA ON THE ROUTE TO AND NEAR THE BLACK HILLS . . .

[1]–14, [15 blank, 16 notice]. 20 x 13.7 cm. Map: Map of the Chicago & North-Western R'y,— The Great Trans-Continental Route. / This is the Best Route to Sioux City and Yankton. / 16.6 x 30.7 cm. No scale given. Stitched.

Prov.: Rubber stamp of Chicago Historical Society on page [1].

Ref.:

Printed in Chicago in 1875? Signed on page 14: H. B. Stevens, Agent, / 125 S. Clark St., Room 48, Chicago. /

The notice on the last page reads: H. B. Stevens, / Removed to / 126 Washington St. Room 60 Chicago. /

3976 STEVENS, ISAAC I.

ADDRESS ON THE NORTHWEST, BEFORE THE AMERICAN GEOGRAPHICAL AND STATISTICAL SOCIETY, DELIVERED AT NEW YORK, DECEMBER 2, 1858 . . . WASHINGTON: G. S. GIDEON, PRINTER, 1858.

[1]–56. 22.3 x 14.5 cm. Gray printed wrappers with title on front wrapper. In a red cloth case.

Prov.: Inscribed on front wrapper: Hon. A. Johnson / with the respects / of the Author /. Note on back wrapper: Send this to my room / A. Johnson /.

Ref.: Howes S960; Sabin 91521; Smith 9888; Wagner-Camp 310

In this *Address*, Stevens summarizes his Pacific Railroad Surveys.

3977 STEVENS, ISAAC I.

A CIRCULAR LETTER TO EMIGRANTS DESIROUS OF LOCATING IN WASHINGTON TERRITORY . . . WASHINGTON: GEORGE S. GIDEON, PRINTER, 1858.

[1]–21, [22 blank]. 22.3 x 14.2 cm. Stabbed, unbound. In a blue cloth case.

Ref.: Howes S963; Jones 1404; Sabin 91523; Wagner-Camp 311

3978 STEVENS, ISAAC I.

PACIFIC RAILROAD—NORTHERN ROUTE. LETTER OF HON. ISAAC I. STEVENS . . . TO THE RAILROAD CONVENTION OF WASHINGTON AND OREGON, CALLED TO MEET AT VANCOUVER, W. T., MAY 20, 1860. WASHINGTON: THOMAS MCGILL, PRINTER, 1860.

[1]–24. 22.8 x 14.6 cm. Pale yellow printed wrappers, with title on front wrapper.

Ref.: *Railway Economics* p. 244; Sabin 91526

3979 STEVENS, ISAAC I.

[Caption title] PACIFIC RAILROAD. SPEECH OF HON. ISAAC I. STEVENS, OF WASHINGTON TERRITORY, IN THE HOUSE OF REPRESENTATIVES, MAY 25, 1858 . . .

[1]–7, [8 blank]. 21.5 x 14.1 cm. Removed from bound volume, unbound.

Ref.: *Railway Economics* p. 285; Sabin 91525

Printed at the Congressional Globe Office, Washington, in 1858.

3980 STEVENS, ISAAC I.

SPEECH . . . ON THE WASHINGTON AND OREGON WAR CLAIMS. DELIVERED IN THE HOUSE OF REPRESENTATIVES OF THE UNITED STATES. MAY 31, 1858. WASHINGTON: PRINTED BY LEMUEL TOWERS. 1858.

[1]–16. 21.9 x 14.2 cm. Removed from bound volume, unbound.

Ref.: Sabin 91529; Smith (1921) 3850

3981 STEVENS, ISAAC I.

VINDICATION OF GOVERNOR STEVENS, FOR PROCLAIMING AND ENFORCING MARTIAL LAW IN PIERCE COUNTY, W. T. MAY 10, 1856.

[1]–8. 22.5 x 15.2 cm. Folded, unbound.

Prov.: Signature on title-page: E M Meeker /

Ref.: AII (*Washington*) 21; Sabin 91530

Printed at Olympia, W. T.

A fascinating case, resulting from the encouragement of Indians by a few whites to engage in war against other whites.

3982 [STEVENS, WILLIAM H.]

FIELD NOTES, CROSSING THE PRAIRIES AND PLAINS FROM ATCHISON, KANSAS, TO DENVER, THROUGH THE MINERAL REGION OF COLORADO TERRITORY. PHILADELPHIA: J. B. CHANDLER, PRINTER, 1865.

[1]–21, [22–4 blank]. 22.5 x 14.6 cm. Pink printed wrappers, with title on front wrapper. In a dark red cloth case.

Prov.: Inscribed on front wrapper: F. L. Lasier / from Wᵐ H. Stevens / Phila. / [underline] /.

Ref.: Howes S972; Wagner-Camp 423; Wilcox p. 107

A very interesting series of notes compiled from personal observation. Examples of mining laws are included, especially those of the South Park mining district.

3983 STEVENSON, JONATHAN D.

MEMORIAL AND PETITION OF COL. J. D. STEVENSON OF CALIFORNIA. SAN FRANCISCO: J. R. BRODIE & CO., 1886.

[1]–16, 16a–16j, 17–89, [90 blank]. (Pages [1–2] blank.) 25.2 x 17.6 cm. Frontispiece portrait and three colored plates. Gray printed wrappers with title on front wrapper.

Prov.: Presentation copy to S. B. Maxey, with printed and manuscript inscription on front wrapper.

Ref.: Cowan p. 614; Howes S979

This petition for a pension for services in the Mexican war throws light upon the operations of the petitioner's famous New York regiment. —Howes

3984 STEWART, ANDREW

[Caption title] SPEECH OF MR. STEWART, OF PENN-SYLVANIA, IN FAVOR OF WESTERN IMPROVEMENTS . . . JANUARY 16, 1844 . . .

[1]–16. Bound with Number 1084.

Ref.: Sabin 91643

Printed at Washington in 1844.

3985 STEWART, CATHERINE

NEW HOMES IN THE WEST . . . NASHVILLE: CAMERON AND FALL, M DCCC XLIII.

[i]–iv, [5]–198. 17 x 11 cm. Black cloth, black skiver label.

Ref.: AII (*Tennessee*) 90; Buck 308; Clements Library (*Michigan*) 78; Howes S982; Sabin 91650

This little volume is on the way to become a midwestern classic. It contains a narrative of nearly twelve years' residence and travel in our part of the country, and is filled with acute observations and fine descriptions. For some time the author lived among the Pottawatomies near St. Joseph, Michigan. The volume also contains some verses of pioneer interest.

3986 [STEWART, SIR WILLIAM DRUMMOND]

ALTOWAN; OR, INCIDENTS OF LIFE AND ADVENTURE IN THE ROCKY MOUNTAINS . . . NEW YORK: HARPER & BROTHERS, 1846.

[1–2], [i]–xxix, [xxx blank], [25]–255, [256 blank]. [1]–240. 18.8 x 11.7 cm. Two volumes, brown cloth, embossed sides with vignette in gilt on front covers, backstrips with gilt title.

Ref.: Howes S991; Sabin 91392; Smith 9911; Wagner-Camp 125

There is some question about the authorship. The story is based on Drummond Stewart's sporting adventures in the Far West, but it may have been written by the editor, J. Watson Webb. Alex S. Webb, as reported in Sabin, said that "Stuart[!] . . . wrote Altowan . . ."

3987 [STEWART, SIR WILLIAM DRUMMOND]

EDWARD WARREN . . . LONDON: G. WALKER, 1854.

[A]², B–2A⁸. [*]¹, 2B–2Z⁸, 3A². [1–2], [i]–ii, [3]–368. [i–ii], 369–724. 21.4 x 13.5 cm. Half calf, red edges. In a brown cloth case.

Prov.: Presentation copy, inscribed on front blank leaf: To / Mrs Bigoe Williams / from Sir W. Drummond / Stuart. Bart. / Xmas 1869. / Numerous manuscript corrections by the author.

Ref.: Howes S991; Jones 1322; Wagner-Camp 245

A mid-Victorian novel, the scenes of which are laid in London and the Rocky Mountains in the '30's. The author speaks of himself in the third person on page 162 n.—EDG

There is a copy in the Archives of Scotland, Edinburgh, with an inscription by William Fraser in which he states that Stewart told him the book was written in the Rocky Mountains.

3988 STEWART, WILLIAM F.

LAST OF THE FILLIBUSTERS[!]; OR, RECOLLECTIONS OF THE SIEGE OF RIVAS . . . SACRAMENTO: HENRY SHIPLEY AND COMPANY, 1857.

[1]–85, [86 blank]. 21.8 x 14.6 cm. Pale pink pictorial wrappers, with title on front wrapper. In a brown half morocco case.

Ref.: Cowan p. 615; Greenwood 883; Howes S993; Jones 1383; Sabin 91711

The author was a captain in the Red Star Guards in the filibustering activities of William Walker in Nicaragua. He left California a supporter of Walker, but wound up a bitter opponent. His account is especially interesting because it contains information about the movements of the surrendered troops after Walker and his staff left Nicaragua.

3989 STIFF, EDWARD

THE TEXAN EMIGRANT: BEING A NARRATION OF THE ADVENTURES OF THE AUTHOR IN TEXAS . . . CINCINNATI: PUBLISHED BY GEORGE CONCLIN, 1840.

[i]–[vi, vi blank], [7]–367, [368 advertisement]. 19.3 x 12.5 cm. Two illustrations and map unlisted: Texas / Cincinnati / Published by George Conclin. / [lower right:] Doolittle & Munson Engravers. Cincinnati. / 23.7 x 29 cm. No scale given. Red cloth, title in gilt on backstrip.

Ref.: Bradford 5210; Howes S998; Rader 2983; Raines pp. 195–96; Sabin 91727

One of the most objective accounts of Texas affairs issued in the days of the Republic, written largely from personal knowledge.—Howes

3990 [STILLMAN, LEVI, & ERASTUS BENTON]

EXPOSE OF THE DOINGS OF THE CONGREGATIONAL CHURCH, IN MENDON, ADAMS COUNTY, ILLINOIS; IN RELATION TO THE EXCOMMUNICATION OF THE SUBSCRIBERS. QUINCY: PRINTED BY BARTLETT & SULLIVAN, 1839.

[1]–14, [15–16 blank]. 20.9 x 14.1 cm. Stabbed, unbound. Laid in old blue wrappers.

Ref.: Byrd 484

Signed on page 14: Levi Stillman, / Erastus Benton. /

3991 [STINSON, H. C., & W. N. CARTER, *Compilers*]

ARIZONA. A COMPREHENSIVE REVIEW . . . 1891.

[1]–144. 31.4 x 24.5 cm. Numerous illustrations, unlisted. Pictorial wrappers bound into red buckram. Wrappers frayed and silked.

Prov.: Bookplate of Frederick Webb Hodge.

Ref.: Howes S1009; Munk (Alliott) p. 209

Printed in Los Angeles.

3992 STOBO, ROBERT

MEMOIRS OF MAJOR ROBERT STOBO, OF THE VIRGINIA REGIMENT . . . PITTSBURGH: PUBLISHED BY JOHN S. DAVIDSON, 1854.

[iii]–vi, [ix]–xii, [13]–92. 14.1 x 9 cm. Plan: Fort Duquesne, 1754. / By Robert Stobo. / [at foot:] Wᵐ. Schuchman, lith. Pittsb. / 29 x 43.4 cm. No scale indicated. Dark blue cloth.

Ref.: Field 382; Howes S1015; Sabin 91869

Reprinted from the first edition, London, 1800, with additions and notes by Neville B. Craig. Howes and Sabin suggest that the two editions were printed from different manuscripts. The ICN and ICN (Ayer) copies are found in different cloth bindings. The paper used for the maps in the latter copies is somewhat harder than the paper in the present copy.

3993 STOCKING, MOSES

[Caption title] HISTORY OF SAUNDERS COUNTY, NEBRASKA . . .

[1]–41, [42 blank]. 21.1 x 13.6 cm. Rebound in old plain yellow wrappers, stabbed. Remnants of an original yellow wrapper pasted to page [1].

Ref.: Howes S1018

Printed at Wahoo, Nebraska (?) in 1876.

Signed and dated on page 41: Moses Stocking. / Wahoo, Nebraska, August, 1876. /

3994 STODDARD, AMOS

SKETCHES, HISTORICAL AND DESCRIPTIVE, OF LOUISIANA . . . PHILADELPHIA: PUBLISHED BY MATHEW CAREY, 1812.

[A]–3Q⁴. [i]–viii, [1]–172, 175–488, [488–90 blank]. 23.5 x 15 cm. Gray boards, white printed label, 2.5 x 3 cm., on backstrip. Label mostly defective. In a green case.

Ref.: Bradford 5238; Clark II 168; Field 1505; Howes S1021; Rader 2984; Raines p. 196; Sabin 91928

Pages 173–74 were omitted from pagination; there is no text missing.

3995 STONE, ARTHUR L.

FOLLOWING OLD TRAILS . . . MISSOULA, MONTANA: MORTON JOHN ELROD, 1913.*

[1]–304. 22.8 x 15 cm. 23 illustrations listed, included in pagination. Dark red cloth.

Ref.: Howes S1027

Pioneer experiences in Montana.

3996 STONE, ELIZABETH ARNOLD

UINTA COUNTY; ITS PLACE IN HISTORY . . .*

[1]–276. 22.6 x 15.1 cm. Illustrations unlisted. Map on endpapers. Green embossed cloth.

Prov.: Inscribed on title-page: [at top right:] No. 145 / [below text:] Sincerely yours / Elizabeth Arnold Stone /.

Ref.:

The printer's imprint appears at the foot of page 276: The Laramie Printing Company / Laramie, Wyoming / 1924 /. There is an added line in manuscript apparently in the hand of the author: Copyright Applied For. /

3997 [STORROW, SAMUEL A.]

[Caption title] BROWNVILLE, 1ST DECEMBER, 1817. TO MAJOR GENERAL BROWN. MY DEAR SIR, I BEG LEAVE TO SUBMIT TO YOU A DETAIL OF SUCH OCCURRENCES, SUBSEQUENT TO MY DEPARTURE FROM YOU, AS HAVE NOT ALREADY BEEN PRESENTED IN A DIFFERENT SHAPE. WHATEVER RELATES TO THE TOUR IS DUE TO YOURSELF, AS YOUR REQUEST WAS THE CAUSE OF IT . . .

[1]–39, [40 blank]. 23.2 x 14.9 cm. Plain blue wrappers, stabbed, uncut. In a blue half morocco case.

Prov.: Signature at top of first page: J: Sparks /. Shelfmark on front wrapper: A.110.15.4. / [underline] /. Probably the H. V. Jones copy.

Ref.: Buck 103; Howes S1046; Jones 802; Sabin 92227

Issued without a title-page.

This is Storrow's official report of a tour to Michigan and the Northwest.

3998 STORRS, AUGUSTUS

. . . ANSWERS OF AUGUSTUS STORRS, OF MISSOURI, TO CERTAIN QUERIES UPON THE ORIGIN, PRESENT

STATE, AND FUTURE PROSPECT, OF TRADE AND INTERCOURSE, BETWEEN MISSOURI AND THE INTERNAL PROVINCES OF MEXICO, PROPOUNDED BY THE HON. MR. BENTON . . . WASHINGTON: PRINTED BY GALES & SEATON, 1825.

[1]–14. 22.1 x 14.3 cm. Rebound in new red cloth.

Ref.: Wagner-Camp 29.

18th Congress, 2nd Session, Senate, Document No. 7, Serial 108.

A highly important document describing the Santa Fé Trail trade. It affected directly the phenomenal increase in trade which was described later in detail by Josiah Gregg.

3999 STRAHORN, CARRIE ADELL

FIFTEEN THOUSAND MILES BY STAGE. A WOMAN'S UNIQUE EXPERIENCE DURING THIRTY YEARS OF PATH FINDING AND PIONEERING FROM THE MISSOURI TO THE PACIFIC AND FROM ALASKA TO MEXICO . . . NEW YORK: G. P. PUTNAM'S SONS, 1911.

[i]–[xxviii, xxviii blank], 1–673, [674 blank]. 22.7 x 15.3 cm. 350 illustrations and decorations, listed. Green cloth, with pictorial panel applied to front cover, gilt top, uncut.

Ref.: Adams (*Ramp. Herd*) 2180; Howes S1054

4000 STRAHORN, ROBERT E.

THE HAND-BOOK OF WYOMING AND GUIDE TO THE BLACK HILLS AND BIG HORN REGIONS FOR CITIZEN, EMIGRANT AND TOURIST . . . CHEYENNE, WYOMING, 1877.

[i]–vi, [7]–249, [250 blank], 251–72 advertisements. 23 x 15.2 cm. 14 illustrations listed. Gray printed wrappers with title on front wrapper, advertisements on recto and verso of back wrapper. In a gray cloth case.

Ref.: Adams (*Ramp. Herd*) 2181; Bradford 5261; Howes S1055; Jennewein 91

Printed in Chicago by Knight & Leonard.

4001 STRAHORN, ROBERT E.

THE SAME.

Rust cloth, gilt lettering on front cover and backstrip, black heavy rule borders.

4002 STRANG, E. D.

A GLIMPSE AT OWATONNA AND STEELE COUNTY, MINNESOTA . . . OWATONNA, MINNESOTA: JOURNAL PRINT, 1884.

[1]–32. 22.2 x 14.9 cm. 19 woodcuts and one woodcut map, unlisted. Light green printed wrappers, with title on front wrapper, advertisements on verso of front and recto and verso of back wrapper, latter includes map.

Ref.:

Amusingly crude woodcuts.

4003 [STRANG, JAMES]

THE BOOK OF THE LAW OF THE LORD, CONSISTING OF AN INSPIRED TRANSLATION OF SOME OF THE MOST IMPORTANT PARTS OF THE LAW GIVEN TO MOSES, AND A VERY FEW ADDITIONAL COMMANDMENTS, WITH BRIEF NOTES AND REFERENCES. PRINTED BY COMMAND OF THE KING, AT THE ROYAL PRESS, SAINT JAMES, A. R. I.

[i]–viii, [9]–80, [34 blank leaves]. 19.5 x 13.4 cm. Red straight-grain morocco, gilt back, gilt frames on sides, back lettered in gilt: Law / of the / Lord /, gilt edges.

Ref.: Greenly (*Michigan*) 94; Howes S1061; Morgan 21; Sabin 92675

The "Testimony" on the verso of the title-leaf is signed in manuscript by Samuel Graham, Albert N. Hosmer, and Samuel P. Bacon.

This preliminary version of 1851, apparently issued for the use of the ministry and Saints only, must not be confused with the longer work published by Strang in 1856.

4004 [STRANG, JAMES]

THE BOOK OF THE LAW OF THE LORD . . . PRINTED BY COMMAND OF THE KING, AT THE ROYAL PRESS, SAINT JAMES, A. R. I.

[1]–8, [17]–336. (Pages [1]–8 on different, inferior paper.) 15.9 x 10.5 cm. Contemporary sheep, black leather label. Repaired.

Prov.: Bookplate of Joseph Smith, Jr., Nauvoo, Ill. With pencil inscription on front endleaf: From Sr Jannett Black / Sussex, Wis. / presented to / J Smith / Aug 1877 /. With numerous notes and underlinings throughout in the hand of Joseph Smith, Jr., the son of Joseph Smith the Prophet.

Ref.: Greenly (*Michigan*) 94 note; Howes S1061; Morgan II 31; Sabin 92678

Second edition. Morgan's variant C of the preliminary matter. Inserted at the front and at the back are eight leaves of notepaper, apparently bound in originally for notes.

Since the volume was presented to Smith in 1877, this pushes Morgan's 1878 date back a year.

4005 [STRATTON, GEORGE W. (?)]

SIEGE OF MEXICO; OR, THE CONFRERE OF MECHANICS. A MELODRAMA, IN THREE ACTS. (FOUNDED ON THE MEXICAN WAR.) . . . MILWAUKEE: 1850.

[1]–47, [48 blank]. 15.6 x 10.2 cm. Yellow printed wrappers with title on front wrapper.

Ref.: Roden, Robt. F.: *Later American Plays*, (N. Y. 1900) p. 107

Florena speaks: "No, I cannot give the signal for Alonzo's death!—he shall live!"

Roden lists *The Buccaneer* (one of the titles ascribed to the author) as by George W. Stratton.

4006 STRATTON, ROYAL B.

LIFE AMONG THE INDIANS: BEING AN INTERESTING NARRATIVE OF THE CAPTIVITY OF THE OATMAN GIRLS, AMONG THE APACHE AND MOHAVE INDIANS . . . SAN FRANCISCO: WHITTON, TOWNE & CO'S EXCELSIOR STEAM POWER PRESSES, 1857.

[i]–iv, 5–183, [184 blank]. 18.7 x 11.4 cm. Illustrated, with vignettes in text. Blue cloth, lettered in gilt on front cover. In a green cloth case.

Ref.: Ayer 283; Greenwood 884; Howes S1068; Jones 1384; Sabin 92743; Wagner-Camp 294

Laid in is a broadside: Sacramento / Theater! / [thick and thin rules] / [19 lines] / This (Monday) Evening, July 27th, / Will be presented for the second time, an entire new Drama, in three acts, / written by Mr. C. E. B'ngham[!], entitled The / Captivity and Massacre / of the / Oatman / Family! / By the / Apache & Mohave Indians! / [35 lines] / Daily Bee Print. / 45.1 x 14.8 cm. Text, 41.8 x 12.1 cm.

Also laid in is a handbill advertising a lecture by Olive Oatman. See under Oatman, Olive.

4007 STREET, FRANKLIN

CALIFORNIA IN 1850, COMPARED WITH WHAT IT WAS IN 1849, WITH A GLIMPSE AT ITS FUTURE DESTINY. ALSO A CONCISE DESCRIPTION OF THE OVERLAND ROUTE, FROM THE MISSOURI RIVER, BY THE SOUTH PASS, TO SACRAMENTO CITY . . . CINCINNATI: R. E. EDWARDS & CO., 1851.

[1]–88. (Page [1] blank, [2] frontispiece.) 17 x 11.2 cm. Three woodcuts. White printed wrappers, with title on front wrapper. Backstrip and back wrapper supplied. In brown half morocco case.

Ref.: Cowan p. 620; Howes S1071; Jones 1269; Sabin 92776; Wagner-Camp 206

4008 STRICKLAND, WILLIAM P.

HISTORY OF THE MISSIONS OF THE METHODIST EPISCOPAL CHURCH . . . CINCINNATI: PUBLISHED BY L. SWORMSTEDT & J. H. POWER, 1850.

[1]–338. 18.6 x 11.5 cm. Blue-gray cloth, blind embossed sides, gilt title on backstrip.

Ref.: Sabin 92819

Contains material relating to the Methodist church in the Far West.

4009 STRONG, CHARLES

AUTOGRAPH MANUSCRIPT, SIGNED of Journal / of / Expedition against hostile Indians / in / Southern Nebraska / Commanded by / Lieut-Col. R. H. Brown, 12th Mo. Cav. Vols. / January and February, / 1865 and [preceding two words crossed out] 1866 /. Twenty-two pages [paginated 1–23 including a blank page], 31.8 x 20.2 cm. Stabbed along top edge with pink tape. Accompanied by original envelope inscribed Record of Expedition / Commanded by Lt. Col Brown / 12th Mo. Cavalry Vol. / In Jan. & February 1866. / Enclosed in a red full morocco folder, gilt.

An interesting account of an unsuccessful attempt to punish marauding Indians along the Overland Stage Route. There were a couple of brushes with the Indians, one man and a few horses were killed, but little was accomplished.

Strong signs himself Lieutenant in Charge of Artillery. He had two bronze mountain howitzers (with crews) under his command.

4010 STRONG, CHARLES

A COLLECTION OF FIFTY-FOUR LETTERS, DOCUMENTS, REPORTS, ETC. relating to military affairs of Second Lieutenant Charles Strong, Sixth U. S. Volunteers. The collection comprises retained copies of Statements of Charges on Muster and Pay Rolls, Quarterly Returns of Ordnance and Ordnance Stores, Invoices of Stores, Receipts for Issues, Reports of Surveys, letters of commendation, Pension Papers, etc. Enclosed in a dark red cloth case, red morocco backstrip.

4011 STRONG, EZRA

[Map] THE STATES OF / OHIO / INDIANA & ILLINOIS / AND / MICHIGAN TERRITORY / FROM THE LATEST AUTHORITIES. / PUBLISHED BY EZRA STRONG NEW YORK. / 1835. /

Map, 40.7 x 51.4 cm. Scale: 35 miles to an inch. Folded and pasted to inner back cover of a light red leather folder, 12.6 x 8.2 cm., front cover with title in gilt.

Ref.:

4012 STRONG, HENRY W.

[Wrapper title] MY FRONTIER DAYS & INDIAN FIGHTS ON THE PLAINS OF TEXAS . . .

[1]–122. 22 x 15.1 cm. Portrait. Blue wrappers, red cloth backstrip.

Ref.: Adams (*Ramp. Herd*) 2189; Rader 2994

Published at Dallas, Texas, in 1926.

Laid in is a photograph of the author printed

on a stiff card. It differs from the photograph on the wrapper, but was probably made at the same time.

4013   STRONG, JAMES C.

BIOGRAPHICAL SKETCH OF JAMES CLARK STRONG . . . LOS GATOS, SANTA CLARA COUNTY, CALIFORNIA: 1910.*

[i–vi], [1]–106. 19.1 x 13.3 cm. Five illustrations listed. Red cloth, title in gilt on front cover.

Ref.: Howes S1080

A Californian of 1850, member of Washington Territory's first legislature and active in Northwestern Indian wars.—Howes

4014   STRONG, WILLIAM E.

A TRIP TO THE YELLOWSTONE NATIONAL PARK IN JULY, AUGUST, AND SEPTEMBER, 1875 . . . WASHINGTON: 1876.

[1]–143, [144 blank]. 27.1 x 20.4 cm. Seven photographs (two signed), seven illustrations, and two maps. Map: Map / of / North Western Territories. / showing route to and from / Yellowstone National Park. / Followed by Hon. W. W. Belknap, Secretary of War, / and party—July & August 1875. / Compiled under direction of Major G: L. Gillespie U. S. Engineers / Scale: 1 Inch = 50 Miles / [diagrammatic scale] 16 x 32.9 cm. Scale as above. Map: Map / of / Yellowstone National Park. / wyoming[!] Territory. / showing points of interest, visited by / Hon. W. W. Belknap, Secretary of War, / and party—July & August 1875. / [swelled rule] / Compiled under direction / of Major G. L. Gillespie, U. S. Engineers. / 33.1 x 14.7 cm. Scale: five miles to one inch. Dark brown leather, stamped in gilt and black with title in gilt on front cover.

Prov.: Bookplate of Robert E. Cowan.

Ref.: Howes S1083

4015   [STRUBBERG, FRIEDRICH ARMAND]

AMERIKANISCHE JAGD- UND REISEABENTEUER AUS MEINEM LEBEN IN DEN WESTLICHEN INDIANERGEBIETEN . . . STUTTGART: J. G. COTTA'SCHER VERLAG, 1858.

[I]–VI, [1]–460. 21.1 x 13.7 cm. 24 plates. Black cloth, with frontispiece in gilt on front cover, scene in gilt on backstrip, marbled edges.

Ref.: Barba p. 139; Clements Library (*Texas*) 40; Howes S1086; Rader 2996; Sabin 93102; Wagner-Camp 311a

This is Strubberg's first work. The scene is laid on the Leona, a tributary of the Rio Grande. The author describes in great minuteness several years of his life there. In no other work in German literature and perhaps in no other literature, has the prairie been portrayed with more skill than in this work. It was translated into English (although Strubberg is not credited with its authorship) and published in 1864 under the title of *The Backwoodsman; or, Life on the Indian Frontier*, edited by Sir C. F. Lascelles Wraxall.—EDG

4016   [STRUBBERG, FRIEDRICH ARMAND]

THE BACKWOODSMAN; OR, LIFE ON THE INDIAN FRONTIER. EDITED BY SIR C. F. LASCELLES WRAXALL, BART. LONDON: JOHN MAXWELL AND COMPANY, M DCCCLXIV.

[i]–iv, 1–428. 18.8 x 12.6 cm. 12 plates including frontispiece and pictorial title-page. Green cloth, title in gilt on front cover with gilt border and vignette, title in gilt on backstrip, uncut.

Ref.: Howes S1086; Rader 3742; Wagner-Camp 407

Strubberg's authorship is not acknowledged, although the work is a translation of his *Amerikanische Jagd- und Reiseabenteuer . . .* 1858.

4017   [STRUBBERG, FRIEDRICH ARMAND]

FRIEDRICHSBURG, DIE COLONIE DES DEUTSCHEN FURSTEN-VEREINS IN TEXAS . . . LEIPZIG: FRIEDRICH FLEISCHER, 1867.

[i–xiv], 1–[234], [235–38 advertisements]. [1–4 advertisements], [i–viii], [1–236, [237 note, 238 blank]. 18.3 x 11.4 cm. Two volumes, yellow printed front wrappers mounted on heavy buff paper.

Ref.: Barba p. 140; Howes S1088; Rader 2997; Raines p. 12

4018   STRYKER, M. WOOLSEY

IN MEMORIAM. FUNERAL ORATION AT OBSEQUIES OF MAJOR GENERAL HENRY WM. LAWTON . . . CHURCH OF THE COVENANT, FEBRUARY 9, 1900. WASHINGTON CITY.

[1]–11, [12 blank]. 24.4 x 15.8 cm. Cream printed wrappers. In Lawton Scrapbook.

Ref.:

4019   STUART, GRANVILLE

MONTANA AS IT IS; BEING A GENERAL DESCRIPTION OF ITS RESOURCES, BOTH MINERAL AND AGRICULTURAL, INCLUDING A COMPLETE DESCRIPTION OF THE FACE OF THE COUNTRY . . . NEW YORK: C. S. WESTCOTT & CO., 1865.

[1]–175, [176 blank]. 22.9 x 14.5 cm. Buff printed wrappers, with title on front wrapper. Backstrip, with manuscript title partly chipped away. In a blue cloth case.

Prov.: Inscribed by the author on the title-page: To Dr Elliott Coues. / With Compliments of / Granville Stuart /. At foot of page in Coues' hand: From the library of Elliott Coues. / With bookplate, monogram T W T or T T W (?)

Ref.: Bradford 5281; Howes S1097; Jones 1488; Wagner-Camp 424

4020   STUART, JOSEPH A.

GENEALOGICAL HISTORY OF THE DUNCAN STUART FAMILY IN AMERICA . . . CAXTON PRESS, 1894.

[i–ii blank, iii–iv], [1]–183, [184 blank]. 18.5 x 12.2 cm. Portrait, frontispiece, facsimile in text, and three small colored plates in text, several vignettes in text. Original black cloth, with title in gilt on front cover.

Ref.:
No place of publication given.

Tipped to page 55 is a small slip, 9 x 12.2 cm. Pages 71–74 are shorter than the rest of the text and may be cancels. Pages [181]–[184] are supplement.

Joseph Alonzo Stuart was also the author of *My Roving Life* . . . 1895. The present volume contains material about his life not connected with his travels.

4021   STUART, JOSEPH A.

MY ROVING LIFE. A DIARY OF TRAVELS AND ADVENTURES BY SEA AND LAND, DURING PEACE AND WAR . . . AUBURN, CAL.: 1895.*

[i–viii], [1]–203, [204 blank]. [i–viii], [1]–229, [230 blank]. (In each volume, pages [i–ii] blank.) 18.3 x 12.6 cm. 17 illustrations (one duplicate), six maps and thirty-two figures in the text. Two volumes, tan printed boards, with title on front cover, black cloth backstrips, printed white paper labels, 2.6 x 1.8 cm., on backstrips.

Ref.: Cowan p. 622; Howes S1102; Matthews p. 322; Morgan (Pritchard) p. 197

This account of the roving portion of my life is the result of a desire on the part of each of my children to possess a copy of my diaries kept during my wanderings . . . The typography and press-work have been my own work (except the press-work of the half-tones, as my little 4 x 6 press had not the requisite strength for a half-tone impression.) Now that the work is finished I am past seventy years old . . .—Preface

Morgan notes that Stuart started overland in 1849 with the "Granite State Company" which united with the "Mount Washington Company." Stuart's diary is used as 118 on Morgan's chart.

4022   STUDER, HERMANN

AUSWANDERUNG NACH HOCH-TEXAS . . . ZURICH: DRUCK AND VERLAG VON ORELL, FUSSLI & COMP., 1855.

[1]–32. 18.6 x 11.8 cm. Rebound in marbled boards, with white printed label on backstrip.

Ref.: Howes S1106

This is part of the German edition of Victor Considerant: *Au Texas* . . . 1854. Orell, Füssli & Comp. were publishers of Fourierist literature.

4023   STULLKEN, G.

MY EXPERIENCES ON THE PLAINS . . . WICHITA, KANSAS: THE GRIT PRINTERY, 1913.

[1]–36, [37–8 blank]. (Pages [37–8] conjugate of frontispiece portrait.) 20.2 x 12.9 cm. Portrait. Tan printed wrappers, with title on front wrapper. In a red cloth case.

Ref.: Howes S1108

4024   STURTEVANT, JULIAN M.

A DISCOURSE, DELIVERED AT THE FUNERAL OF HON. JOSEPH DUNCAN, EX-GOVERNOR OF THE STATE OF ILLINOIS, JANUARY, 16, 1844 . . . JACKSONVILLE: A. V. PUTMAN, BOOK & JOB PRINTER, 1844.

[1]–16. 19.3 x 12.1 cm. Yellow printed wrappers with title on front wrapper.

Ref.: Byrd 901
Jacksonville, Illinois.

4025   SULLIVAN, SIR EDWARD R.

RAMBLES AND SCRAMBLES IN NORTH AND SOUTH AMERICA . . . LONDON: RICHARD BENTLEY, 1852.

[i]–viii, [9]–424. 20.2 x 13.3 cm. Green cloth, blind embossed sides, title in gilt on backstrip, uncut.

Ref.: Clark III 420; Howes S1119; Sabin 93482; Staton & Tremaine 3113

4026   SULLIVAN, JOHN H.

[Wrapper title] LIFE AND ADVENTURES OF THE GENUINE COWBOY. BY BRONCHO JOHN.

[1]–56. 18.5 x 12.9 cm. Illustrated. Gray wrappers, with title on front wrapper. Introduction on verso of front wrapper, cut on recto and verso of back wrappers. Rebacked with brown paper, wrappers defective.

Ref.: Adams (*Ramp. Herd*) 2197; Howes S1126

Copyrighted 1896 and 1900. This printing was after May 30, 1900, since a letter on page 54 carries that date. Apparently printed at Valparaiso, Indiana. Howes suggests New York. A later, 40-page edition was printed at Valparaiso.

4027 SULLIVAN, W. JOHN L.

TWELVE YEARS IN THE SADDLE FOR LAW AND OR-
DER ON THE FRONTIERS OF TEXAS . . . AUSTIN: VON
BOECKMANN-JONES CO., 1909.

[i–vi], [1]–284. 20.3 x 14 cm. 13 illustrations, 12
listed. Red pictorial cloth.

Ref.: Adams 969; Adams (*Ramp. Herd*) 2201;
Howes S1129; Rader 3007

An exceedingly scarce book on the life of a
Texas Ranger, it contains chapters on the hanging of Bill Longley, on the Bill Cook gang, feuds,
and bank robbers.—Adams

4028 SUMMERHAYES, MARTHA

VANISHED ARIZONA. RECOLLECTIONS OF MY ARMY
LIFE . . . PHILADELPHIA: PRESS OF J. B. LIPPINCOTT
COMPANY, 1908.

[1]–[270]. 19.3 x 13.4 cm. 22 illustrations listed.
Blue pictorial cloth, with title on front cover and
backstrip, gilt top, uncut.

Ref.: Howes S1132; Munk (Alliot) p. 210

One of the most readable books about
Arizona.

4029 SUMMERHAYES, MARTHA

THE SAME . . . SALEM, MASS.: THE SALEM PRESS CO.*

[1]–319, [320 blank]. (Pagination inverted on
page 319.) 18.7 x 12.7 cm. 26 illustrations listed.
Blue pictorial cloth, title on front cover and
backstrip.

Published 1911.

Editions: Philadelphia, 1908.

4030 SUMNER, CHARLES

JUSTICE TO THE LAND STATES. SPEECH OF HON.
CHARLES SUMNER . . . ON THE IOWA LAND BILL.
WASHINGTON, D. C.: BUELL & BLANCHARD, 1852.

[1]–15, [16 blank]. 24.3 x 15.7 cm. Unbound,
uncut.

Prov.: Inscribed on title-page (in two unidentified hands): From Hon Chas Sumner / Rox-
bury Athenaeum /.

Ref.: Mott (*Iowa*) p. 79; Sabin 93660

4031 SUMNER, CHARLES A.

[Wrapper title] A TRIP TO PIOCHE; BEING A SKETCH
OF RECENT FRONTIER TRAVEL . . . DELIVERED AT
DASHAWAY HALL, AUGUST 17TH, 1873. SAN FRAN-
CISCO, CAL.: BACON & COMPANY BOOK & JOB
PRINTERS.

[1]–13, [14–16 blank]. 22.3 x 14.4 cm. Purple
printed wrappers, with title as above on front
wrapper, advertisements on verso of front and
recto and verso of back wrapper.

Ref.: Cowan p. 625
Published in 1873.

4032 SURRATT, JOHN H., Trial

TRIAL OF JOHN H. SURRATT IN THE CRIMINAL
COURT FOR THE DISTRICT OF COLUMBIA, HON.
GEORGE P. FISHER, PRESIDING . . . WASHINGTON:
GOVERNMENT PRINTING OFFICE, 1867.

[i–ii], [I]–II, [3]–728. [i–ii], [I]–III, [IV blank],
729–1383, [1384 blank]. 22.3 x 14.8 cm. Two
volumes, black cloth. Poor condition.

Ref.: Monaghan 896; McDade 626

4033 SUTHERLAND, JAMES

ATCHISON CITY DIRECTORY, AND BUSINESS MIRROR,
FOR 1860–61 . . . A BUSINESS MIRROR, AND SKETCH
OF THE CITY, WITH INFORMATION IN REGARD TO
ITS VARIOUS SOCIETIES AND INSTITUTIONS, CITY,
COUNTY AND OTHER OFFICERS. INDIANAPOLIS,
IND.: JAMES SUTHERLAND.

[1]–99, [100 blank]. (Page 100 pasted to inner
back cover, pages 1–2 advertisements, [3] blank,
[4] frontispiece.) 22.1 x 14.3 cm. Map on page
13: A Map / Showing the Position of the City of
Atchison. / [lower left:] Connor & Hussey.
Eng. St. Louis Mo. / 6.9 x 11.4 cm. No scale
given. Frontispiece. Black cloth, with title on
front cover, blind embossed sides, original red
ribbon bookmark and brown tape loop for
hanging, mottled edges.

Ref.: Howes S1147; Wagner-Camp 364a

Included is much information on mail routes.
Page 9 carries a statistical statement of the transportation business between Atchison and Utah,
the Pike's Peak gold regions and other points on
the Plains. Pages 15–20 are a guide to Pike's
Peak headed: Routes and Tables of Distances to
the Pike's Peak Gold Mines. The Overland and
Pike's Peak Express and many of the large
freighting concerns of the day inserted advertisements full of interesting statements. Henry
R. Wagner never was able to secure a copy of
this *Directory*, and, until he secured my incomplete duplicate, Eberstadt had never had it (except the copy he sold me in 1940 which, too late,
he discovered was the item he had looked for
for twenty-five years).—EDG

Inserted after page 16 is an unpaged leaf on
which is mounted a small, 5.8 x 9.5 cm., lithographed tradecard for the Massassoit House.

Along inner hinge (partially concealed) in
pencil: —In liquidation of "Past Sins" E. E.
1940— /

4034 SUTHERLAND, THOMAS A.

HOWARD'S CAMPAIGN AGAINST THE NEZ PERCE
INDIANS, 1878. PORTLAND, OREGON: A. G.
WALLING, 1878.

[1]–47, [48 blank]. 21.1 x 13.6 cm. Rebound in marbled boards, calf backstrip.

Ref.: Howes S1151; Smith 10032

4035 [SUTHERLAND, WILLIAM]

THE WONDERS OF NEVADA: WHERE THEY ARE AND HOW TO GET TO THEM. A GUIDE FOR TOURISTS TO THE GREAT SILVER MINES, THE LAKES, THE TOWNS, AND THE MOUNTAINS. VIRGINIA, NEVADA: ENTERPRISE BOOK AND JOB PRINTING HOUSE, 1878.

[1]–32. 15.7 x 10.6 cm. Map: Lake Tahoe / and / Vicinity / 15.7 x 17.3 cm. No scale given. Two advertisements on verso. White printed wrappers with title on front wrapper, advertisements on verso of front and recto and verso of back wrapper.

Prov.: Rubber stamp of Chicago Historical Society on front cover.

Ref.: AII (*Nevada*) 237; Howes S1153

Sutherland was holder of the copyright and presumably the author.

4036 SUTHERLAND & McEVOY (James Sutherland and Henry N. McEvoy)

KANSAS CITY DIRECTORY, AND BUSINESS MIRROR, FOR 1859–60 . . . ST. LOUIS, MO.: SUTHERLAND & McEVOY.

[ii], iii–[x], inserted leaf, xi–xviii, 1–99. (Pages [i] and [100] pasted to inner covers, pages 97–[100] on yellow paper.) Brown cloth, with title on front cover.

Ref.: Howes S1148

The first Kansas City Directory.

Copyrighted 1859. Imprint on verso of title-leaf: Bingham & Doughty, / Printers, / Daily State Sentinel Office, / Indianapolis, Ind. / [vertical rule] [same as preceding, but line 2 reads Bookbinders. /]

4037 SUTHERLAND & McEVOY

LEAVENWORTH CITY DIRECTORY, AND BUSINESS MIRROR, FOR 1859–60 . . . ST. LOUIS, MO.: SUTHERLAND & McEVOY.

[i]–xxiv, [1]–197, [198 advertisements]. (Page [i] pasted to inner front cover.) 21.8 x 13.5 cm. Black cloth, with title on cover.

Ref.: Howes S1149; Sabin 93956

Advertising matter interspersed throughout.

4038 SUTHERLIN, F., W. WILLSON, & Others

TELEGRAM, SIGNED. 1874 April 15, Salem, Oregon. One page, 21.9 x 13.3 cm. To Loren L. Williams.

Asking Williams to stand for Secretary of State on the Independent ticket. Williams declined. Inserted in Manuscript Journals of Loren L. Williams, Volume IV.

4039 SUTLEY, ZACK T.

THE LAST FRONTIER . . . NEW YORK: THE MAC-MILLAN COMPANY, MCMXXX.*

[i]–[x], [x blank], 1–350. 21.5 x 14.6 cm. Map. Brown cloth.

Ref.: Adams 972; Adams (*Ramp. Herd*) 2204; Rader 3012

4040 SUTTER, JOHN A., Defendant

IN THE UNITED STATES DISTRICT COURT, NORTHERN DISTRICT OF CALIFORNIA. THE UNITED STATES VS. JOHN A. SUTTER. NO. 319. "NEW HELVETIA." PART OF THE TESTIMONY TAKEN IN BEHALF OF THE CLAIMANT, IN SUPPORT OF THE OFFICIAL SURVEY OF THE LAND FINALLY CONFIRMED. VOLNEY E. HOWARD AND CROCKETT & CRITTENDEN, ATTORNEYS FOR THE CLAIMANT. 1861.

[i]–iv, [5]–96. 22.8 x 14.1 cm. White printed wrappers, with title on front cover.

Ref.: Greenwood 1578

One other volume of testimony is listed by Cowan for this year and one for 1855, but not the present work.

4041 SUTTER, JOHANN AUGUST

NEW HELVETIA DIARY . . . FROM SEPTEMBER 9, 1845, TO MAY 25, 1848. SAN FRANCISCO: THE GRABHORN PRESS, 1939.*

[i]–[xxviii], 1–[146]. 30.5 x 19.4 cm. Illustrations unlisted. Decorated boards, canvas back, fore and lower edges uncut.

Ref.: Howes S1155

Limited to 950 copies.

4042 SUTTON, FRED E., & A. B. MAC-DONALD

HANDS UP! STORIES OF SIX-GUN FIGHTERS OF THE OLD WILD WEST . . . INDIANAPOLIS: THE BOBBS-MERRILL COMPANY.

[i–ii], [1]–303, [304 blank]. 21 x 14 cm. 15 illustrations listed. Green ribbed cloth, orange top, uncut.

Ref.: Adams 974; Rader 3013

The author makes some doubtful statements . . . —Adams

4043 SWALLOW, G. C.

GEOLOGICAL REPORT OF THE COUNTRY ALONG THE LINE OF THE SOUTHWESTERN BRANCH OF THE PACIFIC RAILROAD, STATE OF MISSOURI . . . ST. LOUIS: GEORGE KNAPP & CO., 1859.

[i]–xvii, [xviii blank], [1]–93, [94 blank, 95 errata, 96 blank]. 20.5 x 13.7 cm. Map: Geological Map / of / South-West Branch / Pacific Rail Road / [decorative rule] / By G. C. Swallow / State Geologist / [decorative rule] / Drawn by

G. C. Broadhead / Lith. by Schaerff & Bro. St. Louis, Mo. / 20.5 x 92 cm. (paper size). No scale given. Bound with Number 3645.

Ref.: Railway Economics p. 249

4044 SWALLY, MILTON

[Broadside] NEBRASKA CITY, N. T., JAN. 5TH, 1858. HON. THOMAS A. HENDRICKS—COMMISSIONER OF THE GENERAL LAND OFFICE: SIR:— IN CONSIDERATION THAT MY RIGHTS ARE TO BE ADJUDICATED[!] BY YOUR HONOR— I BEG LEAVE TO SUBMIT THE ACCOMPANYING BRIEF AND ASK ITS CAREFUL PERUSAL BY YOUR HONOR. FOR THE REASON THE CASE IS NEW AND NOVEL IN ITS CHARACTER, AND IS TO SETTLE THE PRETENDED CLAIMS OF MAIL CONTRACTORS ON NORTH AND SOUTH LINES WEST OF THE MISSISSIPPI RIVER, UNDER THE ACT OF THE 3D OF MARCH, 1855. RESPECTFULLY YOUR OBD'T SERV'T, MILTON SWALLY. BY ATT'Y I. L. GIBBS . . . YOUR OBEDIENT SERVANT, MILTON SWALLY. BY ATT'Y I. L. GIBBS. ALMOST EVERY QUARTER SECTION NOW CLAIMED BY NORTH AND SOUTH MAIL LINE CONTRACTORS IS ACTUALLY OCCUPIED BY "BONA FIDE" SETTLERS—MANY OF WHOM SETTLED LONG BEFORE THE CONTRACTORS PRETENDED TO CLAIM A PRE-EMPTIVE RIGHT UNDER THE ACT OF THE 3D OF MARCH, 1855.

Broadside, 47 x 35 cm. Text, 43 x 26 cm.

Ref.: AII (*Nebraska*) 32

Place of publication is not given. The latest date in the text is January 5, 1858. Probably printed at Nebraska City.

Contains much information relative to the mail routes and transportation in the early days of the Nebraska Territory.

AII (*Nebraska*) lists only this copy.

4045 SWAN, ALONZO M.

CANTON: ITS PIONEERS AND HISTORY. A CONTRIBUTION TO THE HISTORY OF FULTON COUNTY . . . CANTON, FULTON COUNTY, ILLINOIS: 1871.*

[1]–[164]. 22.1 x 14.3 cm. Brown cloth, blind fillets on sides, title in gilt on backstrip.

Ref.: Howes S1162

The author was the son of the proprietor of Canton who laid out the town in 1825.

4046 SWAN, JAMES G.

THE NORTHWEST COAST; OR, THREE YEARS' RESIDENCE IN WASHINGTON TERRITORY . . . NEW YORK: HARPER & BROTHERS, 1857.

[i]–[xvi (xvi blank)], [17]–435, [436 blank], [1–4 advertisements]. 19.4 x 12.5 cm. Map and 27 illustrations listed. Black cloth, blind embossed covers, title in gilt on backstrip.

Ref.: Bradford 5303; Howes S1164; Smith 10044

4047 SWASEY, WILLIAM F.

THE EARLY DAYS AND MEN OF CALIFORNIA . . . OAKLAND, CAL.: PACIFIC PRESS PUBLISHING COMPANY, 1891.

[i]–x, 9–406. 22.1 x 14.7 cm. Four plates. Blue pictorial cloth, with title and design stamped in gilt on front cover and title on backstrip.

Prov.: Inscribed on recto of frontispiece: With the Compliments of / W. F. Swasey / Author /.

Ref.: Bradford 5305; Cowan p. 627; Howes S1167

Capt. William F. Swasey arrived in California in 1845. He wrote easily, and his work forms a reliable picture of the men and events of the early days, more especially of San Francisco.— Cowan

4048 SWEENY, THOMAS W.

MILITARY OCCUPATION OF CALIFORNIA, 1849–53. FROM THE JOURNAL OF LIEUTENANT THOMAS W. SWEENY . . . REPRINTED FROM THE JOURNAL OF THE MILITARY SERVICE INSTITUTION, 1909.

[1]–47, [48 blank]. 24.3 x 16.6 cm. 12 illustrations unlisted. Gray printed wrappers.

Prov.: Inscribed on front cover: Sylvester Vigilante, Esq., with / kind regards of William / Sweeny. /

Ref.: Cowan p. 627; Howes S1172

4049 SWEENY, THOMAS W.

SECOND COPY. Bound into red cloth covers. Pencil note on front wrapper (in E. Eberstadt's hand): One of 25 copies /.

4050 SWENSON BROS., Stamford, Texas

[Wrapper title] THE STORY OF THE S·M·S RANCH . . . STAMFORD, TEX.

1–106, [107–08 blank]. 15.1 x 22.8 cm. Pages 1–76 and 103–06 illustrations. Pictorial wrappers.

Ref.: Adams (*Ramp. Herd*) 2269

Adams attributes this to Frank S. Hastings, manager of the ranch, but lists it under Texas.

Neither place nor date of publication is indicated.

4051 SWISHER, JAMES

HOW I KNOW; OR, SIXTEEN YEARS' EVENTFUL EXPERIENCE. AN AUTHENTIC NARRATIVE, EMBRACING A BRIEF RECORD OF SERIOUS AND SEVERE SERVICE ON THE BATTLE-FIELDS OF THE SOUTH; A DETAILED ACCOUNT OF HAZARDOUS ENTERPRISES, THRILLING ADVENTURES, NARROW ESCAPES, AND DIRE DISASTERS ON THE WESTERN FRONTIER AND IN THE

WILDS OF THE WEST; LIFE AMONG THE MORMONS, THE MINERS, AND THE INDIANS . . . CINCINNATI, OHIO: PUBLISHED BY THE AUTHOR, 1881.

[i]–x, [11]–384. 20.8 x 14.3 cm. 93 illustrations listed. Brown cloth, black embossed borders on sides, title in gilt on front cover and backstrip.

Ref.: Adams (*Ramp. Herd*) 2225; Howes S1183

Swisher crossed the Plains to Utah and then went on to California. On a later crossing his party was ambushed by Navajo Indians in New Mexico.

T

4052   TACHE, ALEXANDRE

ESQUISSE SUR LE NORD-OUEST DE L'AMERIQUE . . . MONTREAL: TYPOGRAPHIE DU NOUVEAU MONDE, 1869.

[1]–146. 21.7 x 14.1 cm. Bright orange boards stamped in black and gold, title on backstrip in gold.

Ref.: Smith 10065; Streit III 2574

This also appeared in *Missions de la Congrégation des Missionnaires*, Paris, 1888 and as part of *Rapport de l'Association de la Propagation de la Foi*, Nos. 13–14, 1869–70.

4053   TACHE, ALEXANDRE

VINGT ANNEES DE MISSIONS DANS LE NORD-OUEST DE L'AMERIQUE . . . MONTREAL: EUSEBE SENECAL, 1866.

[i]–xiii, [xiv blank], [1]–245, [246 blank]. 20.1 x 14.1 cm. Green cloth, gilt and blind embossed sides with title in gilt on backstrip.

Ref.: Smith 10069; Staton & Tremaine 4540; Streit III 2546

Oblate missionary work from 1845–66.

4054   TAFT, STEPHEN H.

AN ADDRESS DELIVERED ON THE OPENING OF HUM- BOLDT COLLEGE . . . HUMBOLDT, IOWA: PRINTED BY C. W. CALKINS & CO. [BOSTON, MASSACHU- SETTS], 1873.

[1]–23, [24 blank]. 23.4 x 14.9 cm. Lavender printed wrappers, with title on front wrapper, view on verso of back wrapper.

Prov.: Inscribed on the front wrapper: Pil- grim Society / Presented by the, / Author. / Jan 20, 1874.— /. With rubber stamp on front wrap- per and title-page: Pilgrim Hall Library, / Pamphlets, Vol. 175 /.

Ref.:

On the verso of the back wrapper there is a lithographic view of Humboldt College.

4055   TAFT, STEPHEN H.

[Wrapper title] THE HISTORY OF HUMBOLDT, IOWA. A SEMI-CENTENNIAL ADDRESS GIVEN AT HUMBOLDT, IOWA, ON THE 16TH DAY OF SEPTEM- BER, 1913 . . .

[1–24 (24 blank)]. 20.9 x 13.7 cm. Printed self wrappers.

Ref.:

Page [2]: Printed and Presented by / The Jaqua Printing Company / Humboldt, Iowa / 1934 /.

4056   TAGLIABUE & BARKER

MAP / OF THE / WHITE PINE MINES / AND THE / REGIONS ADJACENT, / WITH AN / ESSAY ON THE GEOLOGY AND VEIN SYSTEM OF THE / DISTRICT AND THE CHARACTER OF THE SUR-/ROUNDING COUN- TRY, ACCOMPANIED WITH / TABLES OF HIGHTS[!], DISTANCES, BULL-/ION PRODUCTS, ETC. / BY / TAGLIABUE & BARKER. / [rule] / SAN FRANCISCO: / FRANCIS & VALENTINE, COMMERCIAL STEAM PRINT- ING HOUSE, / 1869. /

[1]–32. 16.3 x 9.9 cm. Large folding map: Map / of / White Pine / Mining District / White Pine County / Nevada. / Drawn from Surveys by / Tagliabue & Barker / Civil Engineers & Sur- veyors. / Treasure City, 1869 / Scale 1 = 9600. / [lower centre:] G. T. Brown & Co Lith. 540 Clay St. S. F. / 99.2 x 68 cm. Scale as above. *Inset:* Geological Section / through Treasure Hill / East & West. / 9.9 x 17.8 cm. Scale: 1000 feet to one inch. *Inset:* [Eastern Part of Nevada.] 47.2 x 22 cm. No scale given. Dark gray cloth with title in silver on front cover, blind borders. Rebacked (and extended), with map cut to 42 pieces, each 17 x 10.2 cm. and mounted on cloth. In a blue half morocco case.

Ref.:

No other copy has been located.

4057   TAIT, JAMES S.

THE CATTLE-FIELDS OF THE FAR WEST: THEIR PRESENT AND FUTURE. EDINBURGH: WILLIAM BLACKWOOD & SONS, MDCCCLXXXIV.

[1]–71, [72 blank]. 20.5 x 12.9 cm. Rebound in dark blue half morocco. Some sidenotes bled.

Ref.: Adams (*Ramp. Herd*) 2228; Howes T8

The cattle business from an investor's point of view.—Adams

The author was partner in the firm Tait, Den- man & Co., cattle ranch and range brokers of New York and Edinburgh.

4058   TALCOTT, E. B.

[Map] CHICAGO / WITH THE / SEVERAL ADDI- TIONS / COMPILED FROM THE RECORDED PLATS IN THE / CLERK'S OFFICE / COOK COUNTY / ILLINOIS. /

DRAWN TO A SCALE OF 500 FEET TO THE INCH. /
P. A. MESIER'S LITH: 28 WALL S.ᵀ NEW-YORK. /
[lower left:] E. B. TALCOTT DEL.ᵀ /

Map, 57 x 95.5 cm. Scale: 500 feet to an inch.
Folded into green leather covers, 15.7 x 9.5 cm.,
with title in gilt on front cover. Mounted, folds
reinforced, tears repaired.

Ref.:

Probably printed in early 1836, as indicated
by a legend on map as follows: The lots in the
Original Town except those Marked with / the
letter S, together with lots in Fract.ˡ Section 15
will / be offered for Sale by the Canal Commissioners on / the 20.ᵗʰ of June 1836. / The Chicago
Historical Society has two copies of this map,
neither of which is in the original covers. It is
probably the third map of Chicago, preceded
only by one in 1835 and an undated map (possibly also printed in 1835). Both of these maps
are in the Chicago Historical Society.—EDG

P. A. Mesier was located at 28 Wall Street
from 1816 to 1844.

4059   [TALLACK, WILLIAM]

[Caption title] THE CALIFORNIA OVERLAND EX-
PRESS: THE LONGEST STAGE-RIDE IN THE WORLD . . .

11–15, [16 blank], 21–23, [24 blank], 43–45, [46
blank], [59 blank], 60–64. 26.2 x 17.7 cm. Illustrations unlisted. Dark red cloth.

Ref.: Wagner-Camp 425

Extracts from *The Leisure Hour*, London,
1865.

The account is of an eastbound journey
across the plains in 1860. It was reprinted later
in *Rides Out and About*, London, no date.

The original texts on the pages listed as blank
above have been covered.

4060   [TALLACK, WILLIAM]

RIDES OUT AND ABOUT. A BOOK OF TRAVELS AND
ADVENTURES. LONDON: THE RELIGIOUS TRACT SO-
CIETY.

[3]–159, [160 blank]. 17 x 11.3 cm. Illustrations
unlisted. Brown pictorial cloth, with title in
black on front cover and gilt on backstrip.

Ref.: Wagner-Camp see 425

The material appeared originally in *The
Leisure Hour*, 1865.

Wagner-Camp suggests 1864 as the date of
publication, but a more probable date is 1878.

4061   TALLENT, ANNIE D.

THE BLACK HILLS; OR, THE LAST HUNTING GROUND
OF THE DAKOTAHS. A COMPLETE HISTORY OF THE
BLACK HILLS OF DAKOTA FROM THEIR FIRST IN-
VASION IN 1864 TO THE PRESENT TIME . . . ST.
LOUIS: NIXON-JONES PRINTING CO., 1899.

[i]–xxii, 1–713, [714 blank]. 22.7 x 14.9 cm. 100
illustrations listed. Dark green cloth, with blind
embossed borders on sides and title in gilt on
front cover and backstrip.

Ref.: Howes T14; Jennewein 124

4062   TANNER, HENRY S.

MEMOIR ON THE RECENT SURVEYS, OBSERVATIONS,
AND INTERNAL IMPROVEMENTS, IN THE UNITED
STATES . . . PHILADELPHIA: PUBLISHED BY THE
AUTHOR, 1829.

[i–iv], [1]–108, [1]–8 advertisements. 17.9 x 11
cm. Red leather backstrip and corners, gilt, with
marbled board sides.

ACCOMPANIED BY:

[Map] UNITED STATES / OF / AMERICA: / BY H. S.
TANNER, 1829. / [lower left:] ENTERED ACCORD-
ING TO ACT OF CONGRESS, THE 10.ᵀʰ DAY OF JUNE,
1829, BY H. S. TANNER OF THE STATE OF PENNSYL-
VANIA. [lower centre:] PHILADELPHIA, PUBLISHED
BY H. S. TANNER. [lower right:] ENGRAVED BY
H. S. TANNER, ASSISTED BY E. B. DAWSON, W. AL-
LEN & J. KNIGHT. / 94.8 x 209 cm. Scale: 32 miles
to one inch. *Insets at left,* each approximately
11 x 13.7 cm.: ENVIRONS / OF / ALBANY. / Scale:
about 8 miles to one inch. ENVIRONS / OF / BOS-
TON. / Scale: 5 1/4 miles to one inch. ENVIRONS /
OF NEW YORK. / Scale: 5 miles to one inch. EN-
VIRONS OF / PHILADELPHIA / AND / TRENTON /.
Scale: 5 miles to one inch. ENVIRONS OF / BALTI-
MORE / AND / WASHINGTON. / Scale: about ten
miles to one inch. ENVIRONS / OF / SAVANNAH /.
Scale: 6 miles to one inch. CHARLESTON /. Scale:
about 2500 feet to one inch. NEW ORLEANS /.
Scale: about 2500 feet to one inch. Ten physical
sections, profiles, etc., various shapes and sizes.
Insets at top: OREGON / AND / MANDAN / DIS-
TRICTS. / *Inset:* OUTLET OF / OREGON RIVER /.
5 x 3 cm. Scale: 13 miles to one inch. 20.5 x 23.5
cm. (irregular shape). Scale: 32 miles to one
inch. PITTSBURG / & ENVIRONS. / 12 x 6.5 cm.
Scale: 7/8 mile to one inch. *Insets at right:* BOS-
TON /. 15 x 11.5 cm. (irregular shape). Scale:
2250 feet to one inch. NEW YORK /. 15 x 12.9 cm.
Scale: about 3250 feet to one inch. PHILADEL-
PHIA /. 15.3 x 14.6 cm. Scale: about 3250 feet to
one inch. BALTIMORE /. 12.1 x 14.7 cm. Scale:
about 2750 feet to one inch. WASHINGTON /.
11.4 x 14.7 cm. Scale: one mile to one inch.
SOUTH PART / OF / FLORIDA /. 17.4 x 14.7 cm.
Scale: about 47 miles to one inch. Three profiles
and a table of statistics.

Map cut to sixty panels, each 20.9 x 15.8 cm.,
mounted on cloth, one panel backed with marbled paper, edges bound with pale blue ribbon.
Folded into brown marbled boards with red
leather backstrip and corners, with gilt cloth ties.

Ref.: Howes T28; Sabin 94318

4063 TANNER, J. M.

A BIOGRAPHICAL SKETCH OF JAMES JENSEN . . .
SALT LAKE CITY, UTAH: THE DESERET NEWS, 1911.

[i–vi, vi blank], [1]–190. 16.9 x 12.4 cm. Six illustrations unlisted. Brown cloth.

Ref.:

Tanner gives an account of Jensen's trip across the plains from Iowa City to Salt Lake City with the hand-cart company of 1857. There is also considerable material on early life in Utah.—EDG

4064 TANNER, RICHARD J.

AUTOGRAPH POSTCARD, SIGNED. 1939 March 1, Norfolk, Nebraska. One page, 8.3 x 14 cm. To Peter Decker.

Dr. Tanner was also known as "Diamond Dick." He reports on the death and burial place of Dr. William F. Carver.

Laid in Carver: *Life of Dr. Wm. F. Carver* . . . 1878.

4065 TANNER, HALPIN & CO., *Chicago*

D. B. COOKE & CO.'S DIRECTORY OF CHICAGO FOR THE YEAR 1858 . . . CHICAGO: D. B. COOKE & CO., 1858.

[i]–xvi, [1]–496. (Numerous advertisement leaves on various colored paper inserted throughout.) 22.5 x 13.8 cm. Brown printed boards, black leather backstrip, advertisements on sides, title in gilt on backstrip.

Prov.: Inscribed on front cover: Cleveland / Cleveland and Russell /. Cleveland and Russell was a firm of builders which advertised in the present volume.

Ref.: AII (*Chicago*) 306; Byrd 3065; Sabin 12641

4066 TARASCON, LOUIS A.

LOUIS ANASTASIUS TARASCON, TO HIS FELLOW CITIZENS OF THE UNITED STATES OF AMERICA; AND, THROUGH THEIR MEDIUM, TO ALL HIS OTHER FELLOW HUMAN BEINGS ON EARTH; NOT ANY WHERE ELSE!! NEW YORK: PUBLISHED BY H. D. ROBINSON, 1837.

[1]–82. 15.2 x 9.5 cm. Marbled boards, leather back. In a brown cloth case.

Ref.: Howes T32; Jones 1004; Sabin 94384

This early project for settlement of Oregon was (according to the text) printed first at Louisville, Ky., in 1836.

This second edition, amplified from fourteen to eighty-two pages, was issued in September, 1837.

4067 TARASCON, LOUIS A.

. . . PETITION OF LEWIS[!] A. TARASCON, (AND OTHERS,) PRAYING THE OPENING OF A WAGON ROAD, FROM THE RIVER MISSOURI, NORTH OF THE RIVER KANSAS, TO THE RIVER COLUMBIA . . . WASHINGTON: PRINTED BY GALES & SEATON, 1824.

[1]–12. 22.1 x 14.5 cm. Removed from bound volume, unbound. In a blue cloth case.

Ref.:

18th Congress, 2nd Session, Senate, Document No. 2, Serial 108.

4068 TARBELL, J.

THE EMIGRANT'S GUIDE TO CALIFORNIA; GIVING A DESCRIPTION OF THE OVERLAND ROUTE, FROM THE COUNCIL BLUFFS, ON THE MISSOURI RIVER, BY THE SOUTH PASS, TO SACRAMENTO CITY . . . KEOKUK: PRINTED AT THE WHIG BOOK AND JOB OFFICE, 1853.

[1]–18. 17.2 x 11.4 cm. Blue printed wrappers, with title on front wrapper. In a brown half morocco case.

Ref.: Wagner-Camp 232a

On a visit to Keokuk, Iowa, in October, 1951, I saw Edwin Carter an ex-newspaper man. He stated he had secured a copy of this guide many years ago from the widow of Horace Ayer. H. H. Ayer appears in the 1856 Keokuk Directory and may have had some connection with Tarbell, the author of this guide. Ayer's widow told Carter she had, in a closet, a lot of old pamphlets which he could have, but Carter never got around to looking this material over. The man who was running the Chicago Book & Art Auctions, Inc. in its last days, bought the contents of the Ayer closet which included three copies of this pamphlet. He catalogued it, but before the sale, Eberstadt came to Chicago, and finding there were three copies bought them all. Carter later sold his copy to Goodspeed.—EDG

4069 TARBLE, HELEN MAR

THE STORY OF MY CAPTURE AND ESCAPE DURING THE MINNESOTA INDIAN MASSACRE OF 1862 . . . ST. PAUL: THE ABBOTT PRINTING COMPANY, 1904.*

[1]–65, [66–68 blank]. 23.3 x 15.5 cm. Portraits in text unlisted. Gray-green printed wrappers, with title on front wrapper printed in red.

Ref.: Ayer (*Supp.*) 27; Howes T34

An account of this captivity is included in Bryant: *A History of the Great Massacre* . . . 1868, with an earlier name of the author, Mrs. Helen Carrothers.

4070 TASSE, JOSEPH

LES CANADIENS DE L'OUEST . . . SECONDE [DEUX-IEME] EDITION . . . MONTREAL: CIE. D'IMPRIMERIE CANADIENNE, 1878.

[i]–xxxix, [xl blank], [1]–364. [i–iv], [1]–413, [414 blank]. 21.1 x 13.9 cm. Illustrations unlisted. Two volumes, gray cloth with embossed borders in blind, gilt vignettes on front covers, same in blind on back covers, title in gilt on backstrip.

Ref.: Howes T39; Smith 10129
Edition: Montréal, 1878.

4071 TATUM, LAWRIE

OUR RED BROTHERS AND THE PEACE POLICY OF PRESIDENT ULYSSES S. GRANT . . . PHILADELPHIA: JOHN C. WINSTON & CO., 1899.

[i]–[xx, xx blank], 21–366. 19.3 x 13.3 cm. 16 illustrations listed. Red cloth, blind fillets on sides, title in gilt on front cover and backstrip.

Ref.: Howes T42; Rader 3035
Most copies destroyed—or damaged—by fire.—Howes

4072 TAYLOR, ALEXANDER S.

DISCOVERY OF CALIFORNIA AND NORTHWEST AMERICA. THE FIRST VOYAGE TO THE COASTS OF CALIFORNIA; MADE IN THE YEARS 1542 AND 1543, BY JUAN RODRIGUEZ CABRILLO AND HIS PILOT BARTOLOME FERRELO . . . SAN FRANCISCO: PUBLISHED BY LE COUNT & STRONG, 1853.

[1]–19, [20 blank]. 24.3 x 15.9 cm. Removed from bound volume, unbound, remnants of lavender wrappers along inner margin.

Prov.: Inscribed on page [3]: To Henry W. Longfellow Esq. / with the sincere respects / of the Author, who asks in some / spare half hour, A perusal of his / little sketch /.

Ref.: Bartlett 2374; Cowan pp. 629–30; Howes T44; Sabin 94437

4073 TAYLOR, BAYARD

ELDORADO; OR, ADVENTURES IN THE PATH OF EMPIRE; COMPRISING A VOYAGE TO CALIFORNIA, VIA PANAMA . . . NEW YORK: GEORGE P. PUTNAM, 1850.

[1]–xii, 1–251, [252 blank]. [i–ii], [1]–[4, 4 blank], [iii–iv], [5]–247, [248 blank], 1–[45], [46 blank]. 19.1 x 12.6 cm. Eight illustrations listed. Two volumes, green cloth, embossed cartouche on each cover incorporating publisher's initials, title stamped in gilt on backstrips.

Ref.: Bradford 5344; Cowan p. 630; Howes T43; Rader 3037; Sabin 94440
An excellent description of the California of gold-rush days.

4074 TAYLOR, BAYARD

THE SAME . . . LONDON: RICHARD BENTLEY, 1850.

[i]–xii, 1–251, [252 blank]. [i–iv, iv blank], [1]–247, [248 blank]. 19.4 x 13 cm. Eight illustrations listed. Two volumes, dark orange cloth, blind embossed sides, title stamped in gilt on backstrips, uncut.

Issued simultaneously with the American edition from the same plates, but with a new title-page. There was also a reset London edition in the same year.

4075 TAYLOR, F.

A SKETCH OF THE MILITARY BOUNTY TRACT OF ILLINOIS: DESCRIPTIVE OF ITS UNEQUALLED FERTILITY OF SOIL—SUPERIOR INDUCEMENTS FOR AN EMIGRANT'S LOCATION . . . PHILADELPHIA: PRINTED BY I. ASHMEAD & CO., 1839.

[1]–12. 22.5 x 14.3 cm. Brown printed wrappers with title on front wrapper.

Prov.: Rubber stamp of New Jersey Historical Society on title and page [5], manuscript note on front wrapper and title.

Ref.: Jones 1031; Sabin 77835, 94454
The manuscript note on the title-page identifies the author as: Sec^y Ill Land C° /.

4076 TAYLOR, G.

A VOYAGE TO NORTH AMERICA, PERFORM'D BY G. TAYLOR, OF SHEFFIELD, IN THE YEARS 1768, AND 1769 . . . NOTTINGHAM: PRINTED BY S. CRESWELL FOR THE AUTHOR, M D CC LXXI.

[*]⁴, A–K¹², L⁴. [i–viii], 1–248. (Page 239 mispaginated 339.) 18.9 x 11 cm. Rebound in blue half morocco, uncut. Original back wrapper and two original blank leaves bound in.

Ref.: Buck 19, De Renne I, 198; Field 1533; Howes T48; Sabin 94457
This interesting work, which is probably in part fictitious, is one of the earliest English books to advocate prairie settlement.

4077 TAYLOR, HAWKINS

INAUGURAL ADDRESS OF HAWKINS TAYLOR, ESQ., MAYOR OF THE CITY OF KEOKUK. DELIVERED APRIL 13, 1857 . . . KEOKUK: DAILY GATE CITY PRINT, 1857.

[1]–8. 21.3 x 14.1 cm. Buff printed wrappers, removed from binding, with title on front wrapper. Lacks back wrapper.

Ref.: Moffit 315
A rather more optimistic speech than Sample's of the following year. The Panic of 1857 had yet to hit Keokuk, full of railroad speculation and building.—EDG

4078 TAYLOR, HAWKINS

ANOTHER COPY. Stapled into gray Gaylord binder.

4079 TAYLOR, JAMES W.

. . . NORTHWEST BRITISH AMERICA, AND ITS RELATIONS TO THE STATE OF MINNESOTA . . . A REPORT COMMUNICATED TO THE LEGISLATURE OF MINNESOTA BY GOVERNOR RAMSEY, MARCH 2D, AND ORDERED TO BE PRINTED. ST. PAUL: NEWSON, MOORE, FOSTER & COMPANY, PRINTERS, 1860.*

[1]–[42]. 22 x 14.5 cm. Map on page 4: The / Northwest, / River & Rail Road / System. / [lower right:] J. Welch Eng. S⁺ Paul. / 6.5 x 16.5 cm. No scale given. Yellow printed wrappers, removed from bound volume, with title on recto of front and verso of back wrappers. In a red cloth case.

Ref.: AII (*Minnesota*) 309; Howes T56; Wagner-Camp 365

There were at least five editions issued in 1860 and 1862. AII (*Minnesota*) calls this the earliest; Howes prefers a 54-page edition.

4080 TAYLOR, JAMES W.

THE RAILROAD SYSTEM OF THE STATE OF MINNESOTA, WITH ITS RAILROAD, TELEGRAPHIC AND POSTAL CONNECTIONS . . . REPORTED TO THE COMMON COUNCIL OF THE CITY OF ST. PAUL, MARCH 31, 1859 . . . SAINT PAUL: PIONEER PRINTING COMPANY, 1859.*

[1]–24. 22.8 x 14.7 cm. Pink printed wrappers with title on recto of front and verso of back wrappers.

Ref.: AII (*Minnesota*) 278; Howes T57

An interesting, highly optimistic report on the position of Minnesota in relation to transcontinental railroad lines, with a recapitulation of proposals in the making.

4081 TAYLOR, JOHN

MANUSCRIPT LETTER composed by John Taylor and signed by Brigham Young, Willard Richards, N. K. Whitney, and George Miller. Three pages, 32.8 x 20.1 cm. 1845 April 30, Nauvoo, Illinois. To Governor Mordecai Bartley, of Ohio. Laid in a full white leather portfolio.

An extremely interesting letter composed by John Taylor for the "committee, in behalf of the Church of Jesus Christ of Latter Day Saints at Nauvoo, Ill." The letter was designed to be sent to the governor of each state except Illinois and Missouri and the President of the United States, James K. Polk. Polk's copy differs slightly from the version for the governors. Only one governor replied, Thomas S. Drew of Arkansas.

The letter is a plea for refuge and asylum for the Saints immediately after the fact became obvious that they were to be forced out of Illinois. It is a cleverly written letter suggesting that the Far West might be a suitable place for the Saints and, while it may not have achieved the publicity for which it seems to have been designed, it may have more subtly influenced the satisfaction of the rest of the country with the projected move toward Oregon.

Copies of the letter were signed variously. B. H. Roberts: *A Comprehensive History of the Church of Jesus Christ of Latter-Day Saints . . .* Salt Lake City, 1930, Vol. II, pages 522–24, quotes part of the letter and gives a longer list of signers for the version for the governors and a different list for the copy which went to Polk.

The letter is postmarked Cincinnati, a curious feature which is explained by the postscript, in which the statement is made that the letter will be taken by special messenger to a distant post office to ensure delivery.

Mary A. Benjamin, in the *Collector* for October, 1938, attributes the letter to Brigham Young—on internal evidence. However, Roberts quotes from John Taylor's Journal (apparently a manuscript) "Engaged in writing a document to the governors of the different states. The following is a copy."

4082 TAYLOR, JOHN

THE GOVERNMENT OF GOD . . . LIVERPOOL: PUBLISHED BY S. W. RICHARDS, MDCCCLII.

[i]–viii, [1]–118. Bound with Number 3346.
   Ref.:

4083 TAYLOR, JOHN W.

JOHN W. TAYLOR'S DESCRIPTIVE PAMPHLET. NO. I. IOWA, THE "GREAT HUNTING GROUND" OF THE INDIAN; AND THE "BEAUTIFUL LAND" OF THE WHITE MAN. INFORMATION FOR IMMIGRANTS . . . DUBUQUE: DAILY TIMES BOOK AND JOB PRINTING HOUSE, 1860.

[1]–16. 21 x 13.2 cm. Frontispiece and illustration in text. Tan wrappers rebound in tan cloth, with title on front wrapper. Lacks back wrapper.
   Ref.: Moffit 510

4084 TAYLOR, JOSEPH [WILLIAM G. UNDERBRINK]

A JOURNAL OF THE ROUTE FROM FORT SMITH, ARK. TO CALIF. IN THE YEAR 1849. WITH A FULL ACCOUNT OF THE TRAIL, NECESSARY EQUIPMENT, AND MANY OTHER INTERESTING FACTS AS EXPERIENCED ON ROUTE . . . BOWLING GREEN, MO.: PRINTED BY JOB OFFICE, 1850.

[1]–15, [16 blank]. 16 x 10.2 cm. Blue printed wrappers with title on front wrapper, stabbed.

Ref.: Wagner-Camp 192b

A fraud.

4085 TAYLOR, JOSEPH H.

BEAVERS: THEIR WAYS AND OTHER SKETCHES . . . WASHBURN N. DAK.: PRINTED AND PUBLISHED BY THE AUTHOR, 1904.

[1]–132, 132–[171], 171–178, [179–80 blank], [1–4 press comments]. 20.2 x 13.5 cm. 17 illustrations listed. Green pictorial boards, red cloth back and corners.

Ref.: Howes T66

Copyrighted 1903.

The list of illustrations calls for twenty plates, those opposite pages 49, 54, and 128 are not present.

4086 TAYLOR, JOSEPH H.

THE SAME. WASHBURN, NORTH DAKOTA: PRINTED AND PUBLISHED BY THE AUTHOR, 1906.

[1]–99, [100 blank], [i–ii], [101]–132, 132–218, [219 blank], [1–4 press notices]. (Page 115 unpaginated, pages 132–218: numbers on rectos.) 20.1 x 13.9 cm. 26 plates listed. Blue cloth.

Copyrighted 1903, 1906.

In this edition, two new chapters have been added and two have been dropped, the number of chapters remaining the same.

Editions: Washburn, N.D., 1904.

4087 TAYLOR, JOSEPH H.

KALEIDOSCOPIC LIVES. A COMPANION BOOK TO FRONTIER AND INDIAN LIFE . . . WASHBURN, N. DAK.: PRINTED AND PUBLISHED BY THE AUTHOR, 1901.

[i–iv], [1], 1–113, [1–4 press comments]. (Even numbers on rectos.) 20.7 x 14 cm. Nine plates. Green printed wrappers, with title on front wrapper, vignette on verso of back wrapper. In green cloth case.

Ref.: Howes T67

Copyrighted 1896.

The fly-leaves are salmon, the text is on yellow (various shades) paper, and the press comments on pink paper.

4088 TAYLOR, JOSEPH H.

THE SAME . . . WASHBURN, N.D.: PRINTED AND PUBLISHED BY THE AUTHOR, 1902.

[i–vi], [5]–20, [20]–206, [207 ornament], [1–4 press comments]. (Pages 114–117 paginated [12]–15. Mostly even numbers on rectos.) 19.7 x 13.3 cm. 23 plates and portraits, listed. Blue cloth.

Copyrighted 1896, 1901.

The plate listed as facing page [20] is on the verso of page 19.

Editions: Washburn, N.D., 1901.

4089 TAYLOR, JOSEPH H.

SKETCHES OF FRONTIER AND INDIAN LIFE ON THE UPPER MISSOURI AND GREAT PLAINS EMBRACING THE AUTHOR'S PERSONAL RECOLLECTIONS OF NOTED FRONTIER CHARACTERS, AND SOME OBSERVATIONS OF WILD INDIAN LIFE DURING A TWENTY-FIVE YEARS' RESIDENCE IN THE TWO DAKOTAS AND OTHER TERRITORIES, BETWEEN THE YEARS 1864 AND 1889 . . . POTTSTOWN, PA.: PRINTED AND PUBLISHED BY THE AUTHOR, 1889.

[1]–200, [201 blank]. (Page 137 skipped, 144 mispaginated 134. From 138 to 200 even numbers are on rectos.) 19.5 x 13.3 cm. 12 illustrations, listed. Dark red half leather, marbled sides, title on backstrip.

Ref.: Howes T68

Some illustrations listed do not match those in the volume.

4090 TAYLOR, JOSEPH H.

THE SAME. WASHBURN, N.D.: PRINTED AND PUBLISHED BY THE AUTHOR, 1895.

[1–12], [12]–59, [59]–106, [i–ii], 107–210, [i–ii], [212]–283, [284 blank]. (Pages 213–223 mispaginated 13–23, pages 56–59 misplaced, most even pages are rectos, i.e., only 107–210 are properly paginated.) 19.7 x 13.2 cm. 26 illustrations (one in duplicate). Dark red half leather, marbled sides, lettered on backstrip: Frontier / and / Indian Life / Taylor /.

Many of the sketches of the first work are omitted and others substituted which more nearly conform to the book's title.—Preface

Editions: Pottstown, Penna., 1889.

4091 TAYLOR, JOSEPH H.

THE SAME. BISMARCK, N.D.: PRINTED AND PUBLISHED BY THE AUTHOR, 1897.

[i–vi], [1 fly title, 2 blank], [2]–59, [59]–63, [62]–106, [i–ii], [107]–170, [173]–210, [i–ii], [212]–306, [307 blank, 308–11 press notices]. (Some even numbers on rectos.) 19.5 x 13.3 cm. Illustrated. Green cloth, Indian scene and title on cover: Frontier / and Indian / Life /. Title reading down backstrip: Frontier and Indian Life. / [at foot] Taylor /.

Some materials omitted from earlier editions; some additions.

Editions: Pottstown, 1889. Washburn, N.D., 1895.

4092 TAYLOR, JOSEPH H.

TWENTY YEARS ON THE TRAP LINE. BEING A COLLECTION OF REVISED CAMP NOTES WRITTEN AT INTERVALS DURING A TWENTY YEARS EXPERIENCE IN TRAPPING . . . BISMARCK, N.D.: PRINTED AND PUBLISHED BY THE AUTHOR, 1891.*

[1]–154. 17.1 x 12.3 cm. Ten illustrations listed. Rust cloth.

Ref.: Howes T69

4093 TAYLOR, JOSEPH H.

THE SAME.

[1]–173, [174 blank]. 16.8 x 12 cm. Ten illustrations listed. Dark red half leather, marbled sides.

Although "Sioux Chief Rain in the Face" is omitted from the list of illustrations on page [9], the portrait is present opposite page 47.

4094 TAYLOR, LANDON

THE BATTLE FIELD REVIEWED. NARROW ESCAPE FROM MASSACRE BY THE INDIANS OF SPIRIT LAKE, WHEN PRESIDING ELDER OF SIOUX CITY DISTRICT. ROCKY MOUNTAIN HISTORY AND TORNADO EXPERIENCES. ALSO REMARKABLE AND AMUSING INCIDENTS, EMBRACING FORTY YEARS IN THE MINISTRY: INCLUDING FOUR YEARS IN SOUTHERN OHIO, THIRTY YEARS IN THE TERRITORY AND STATE OF IOWA, AND ONE YEAR IN VINELAND, N.J., IN 1863 . . . CHICAGO: PUBLISHED FOR THE AUTHOR, 1881.

[i]–[xxiv, xxiv blank], [1]–375, [376 blank]. 19.2 x 13.3 cm. Two portraits, unlisted. Dark brown cloth, decorative bands stamped in black on front cover and in blind on back cover, title in gilt on backstrip, motto in gilt on front cover.

Ref.: Howes T70

The title-page describes the contents adequately.

4095 TAYLOR, R. HOWE

AUTOGRAPH LETTER, SIGNED. 1878 November 11, Marshalltown, Iowa. To Mr. George S. Bowen. One page, 26 x 17 cm.

Printed heading: Mayor's Office. / [wavy rule] / Marshalltown, Iowa, ... 187 . . . /

Regarding appointment of a committee. On the verso is a printed schematic plan of the town: Plat of Business Portion of Marshalltown, Marshall Co., Iowa. /

4096 TEICHMANN, EMIL

A JOURNEY TO ALASKA IN THE YEAR 1868: BEING A DIARY . . . KENSINGTON: PRIVATELY PRINTED AT THE CAYME PRESS, 1925.

[1]–272. 20 x 16 cm. Map and illustrations unlisted. Brown cloth sides, white cloth back, brown leather label on backstrip, gilt edges.

Ref.: Howes T88; Smith 10161

Limited to 100 copies.

4097 TEMPERANCE CRUSADER

[Newspaper] TEMPERANCE CRUSADER: A CAMPAIGN PAPER DEVOTED TO THE LEGAL PROHIBITION OF THE LIQUOR TRAFFIC . . . VOLUME 1. WARSAW, ILLINOIS, MARCH 15, 1854. NUMBER 3 . . .

[1–4]. 47.4 x 33.2 cm. Unbound newspaper.

Ref.:

4098 TEMPLETON, DAVID

WATERCOLOR PORTRAIT, profile, of a young man, possibly George M. Templeton. Signed beneath the drawing: David Templeton 1820 /. 20.4 x 13.7 cm.

4099 TEMPLETON, GEORGE H.

THE DIARIES OF GEORGE H. TEMPLETON, 1862 to 1868, as described below:

1862:

Daily Pocket Remembrancer for 1862. New York: For the Trade.

84 LEAVES of which 82 pages bear entries. 12.2 x 7.6 cm. Black leather, wallet flap, pocket in back cover, marbled edges.

1863:

Pocket Diary for 1863 . . . New York: Published Annually for the Trade, 1863.

65 LEAVES of which 109 pages bear entries. 12 x 7.7 cm. Black varnished cloth, with wallet flap, marbled edges.

1864:

Pocket Diary for 1864 . . . 1864.

2 LEAVES of text and 62 LEAVES of diary of which 120 pages bear entries. 12 x 7.7 cm. Black varnished cloth, marbled edges.

1865:

Pocket Diary for 1865 . . . 1865.

2 LEAVES of text, 62 LEAVES of diary of which 93 pages bear entries. 12.2 x 7.4 cm. Black varnished cloth with wallet flap, marbled edges. Flap loose.

1866:

[Ruled blank book]

120 LEAVES of which 191 pages bear entries. 14.6 x 9.5 cm. Limp black leather with wallet flap, marbled edges.

1867:

[Ruled blank book]

48 LEAVES of which 94 pages bear entries. 16.2 x 10 cm. Limp calf.

1868:

[Ruled blank book]

54 LEAVES of which 50 pages bear entries. 18.5 x 12 cm. Unbound. Lacks covers and backstrip.

The diaries for 1866–68 have been transcribed. They cover the period of Templeton's duties at Fort C. F. Smith, from the establishment of the fort to its abandonment. A very important diary.

Included in the collection are the following photographs:

Original photograph of Templeton, full length, faced slightly to his right, in Union uniform. 9.1 x 5.8 cm., mounted on thin card 10.1 x 6.3 cm. No photographer's name given.

Original photograph of Templeton, bust length, vignette, head turned slightly to his right, in uniform. 9 x 5.8 cm., mounted on card, 10 x 6.2 cm. Photographer's name on verso: Heiss' / Gallery, / No. 1028 Chestnut Street. /

Original daguerreotype of Templeton, waist length, seated, turned three-quarters to his left, tinted. Before 1862. 5.6 x 4.7 cm. Unmounted.

Original daguerreotype of Templeton and a Mr. Jones, full face, full length, each in uniform, Templeton on right. 10.6 x 8 cm., in gold colored frame, 10.8 x 8.2 cm. Probably 1863.

Original daguerreotype group photograph of four men, including Templeton, two men standing, Templeton and another seated, Templeton in centre. 10.6 x 8 cm., in gold colored oval frame, 11 x 8.4 cm. About 1867.

Original photograph of Robert W. Webb. Three-quarter length, seated, full face. 8.8 x 5.9 cm., mounted on card 10.2 x 6.3 cm. Photographer's name on verso: J. R. Laughlin's / Photograph Rooms, / N.W. Corner of / Twelfth & Market Streets, / Philada. / [2 lines] /

The diaries are all written in pencil. The first four are signed at the front by the writer.

4100 [TEMPLETON, GEORGE M.]

SILVER PLATED DRINKING MUG. Stamped on bottom, in circle, Rogers Smith & Co. New Haven Conn. Below circle is number 39. With engraved design around mug and with name: Templeton / U. S. A. / engraved opposite handle. Height: 8.9 cm.

4101 [TEMPLETON, GEORGE M.]

THE PHOTOGRAPHIC ALBUM.

[1–4], 25 thick boards with printed frames. 23.1 x 17.2 cm. Heavily embossed leather, metal clasps, gilt and gauffered edges.
  Prov.: From the George M. Templeton Papers.
  Ref.:
Prepared and kept by Templeton or a member of his family. Comprises photographic portraits of ancestors, members of family, classmates, fraternity brothers, brother officers, and friends. Each thick leaf has a printed frame for four portraits with cut-out centre and provision for insertion of portraits at top and bottom of leaf. There are 180 photographs including a few tintypes and a few loose photographs.

4102 TENNESSEE TERRITORY. Laws, Statutes, etc.

ACTS AND ORDINANCES OF THE GOVERNOR AND JUDGES OF THE TERRITORY OF THE UNITED STATES OF AMERICA SOUTH OF THE RIVER OHIO.

[A]⁴. [i]–viii. 22 x 12.3 cm. Unbound, uncut.
  Ref.: AII (*Tennessee*) 1; Sabin 94764
Printed at Knoxville by George Roulstone in 1793.

4103 TERRELL, JOSEPH C.

REMINISCENCES OF THE EARLY DAYS OF FORT WORTH . . . FORT WORTH: TEXAS PRTG. CO., 1906.

[i–ii], [1]–101, [102 blank]. 22.1 x 14.9 cm. 12 illustrations listed. Brown cloth. Some scribbling in blue pencil in text.
  Prov.: Inscribed on front endleaf: From / Jno. C. Terrell / to / Mrs Geo W Hiett / March 15—1907 / [underline] /.
  Ref.: Howes T105; Rader 3047
The author includes an account of his 1852 trip to California.

4104 TERRY, DAVID S., Defendant

TRIAL OF DAVID S. TERRY BY THE COMMITTEE OF VIGILANCE, SAN FRANCISCO. SAN FRANCISCO: R. C. MOORE & CO., 1856.

[1]–75, [76 blank]. 23.1 x 14.5 cm. Tan printed wrappers with title on front wrapper.
  Ref.: Cowan p. 633; Greenwood 772; Howes T106; Sabin 94889
The trial of David S. Terry was one of the most notable of the Committee of Vigilance trials. Terry's career was also fascinating in the extreme.

4105 TERWECOREN, EDOUARD

COLLECTION DE PRECIS HISTORIQUES MELANGES LITTERAIRES ET SCIENTIFIQUES . . . PARIS: E. REPOS, 1853.

[3]–641, [642 blank]. 22.4 x 15 cm. Rebound in mottled boards, black leather backstrip, gilt.
  Ref.: Carayon 185; Sabin 82271; Streit I 1296, III 2397 note; Wagner-Camp 231
Comprises the 25ᵉ through 48ᵉ *Livraisons*, January 1 to December 15, 1853.
  Livraisons 40 and 44–45, pages [391]–405, and

[461]–[492], contain six letters by Father Pierre Jean De Smet which were later published as *Voyage au Grand-Désert en 1851 . . .* Brussels, 1853. The *Livraisons* are dated August 15, October 15 and November 1, 1853. The first of the three *Livraisons* is headed: 15 Août 1853 40° Livraison / [rule] / Collection de Précis Historiques / [rule] / Lettres du R. P. Pierre de Smet / Missionaire de la Compagnie de Jésus, / Au directeur des Précis Historiques, à Bruxelles. / Voyage au Grand Désert / en 1851. / [short rule] / . . .

4106 TEXAS

[Map] [NORTHWEST TEXAS; ELM FORK OF BRAZOS WEST TO SHAFTER LAKE, BLOCK CREEK NORTH TO SALT FORK OF BRAZOS]

Map, 44.4 x 92 cm.

The map is of two sheets joined. The westerly part is a very faint photograph over which parts have been worked in manuscript, both ink and pencil. Martin, Howard, and Mitchell counties are outlined. The easterly section of the map is all manuscript, ink and pencil.

The county seats are not named. For instance, Martin County was created in 1876 and organized in 1884; at the latter time, Mariensfield was changed to Stanton and named the county seat. The map is probably therefore between 1876 and 1884.

4107 TEXAS. Committee of the People of the State of Texas of the Territory between the Nueces River and the Rio Grande

[Wrapper title] AN APPEAL BY THE PEOPLE OF THE STATE OF TEXAS, OF THE TERRITORY BETWEEN THE NUECES RIVER AND THE RIO GRANDE, PREPARED BY CERTAIN CIVIL AUTHORITIES OF THAT DISTRICT, AND ADDRESSED THROUGH THE HON. SECRETARY OF STATE OF THE UNITED STATES, TO THE PRESIDENT, TO CONGRESS, AND TO THE COUNTRY, FOR PROTECTION AGAINST INCURSIONS OF THE SAVAGES OF THE STATE OF COHAHUILA, MEXICO, AND, ALSO, THE HISTORY OF A LATE MURDEROUS AND DEVASTATING RAID, WITH AFFIDAVITS OF EYE-WITNESSES TO THE ATROCIOUS CRIMES COMMITTED . . . CORPUS CHRISTI, TEXAS: FREE PRESS PRINT, 1878.

[1]–40. 20 x 13.4 cm. Green printed wrappers, with title on front wrapper. In brown cloth case.

Ref.: Howes T111

4108 TEXAS. Constitutional Convention, 1868–1869

[Wrapper title] CONSTITUTION OF THE STATE OF WEST TEXAS.

[1]–[36]. 20 x 13.1 cm. Yellow printed wrappers with title on front wrapper.

Ref.: Clements Library (*Texas*) 43; Howes T117; NYPL *Bull.* Vol. 41, p. 93

In the long Reconstruction Convention of 1868–1869, the question of dividing the state of Texas was raised. This *Constitution of West Texas* was drafted by a committee of seven at the orders of the Convention. The proposed capital of the new state was San Antonio. There is no imprint, yet the piece was probably printed at Austin, where the Convention was in progress.

4109 TEXAS. Legislature. Acts and Laws

AN ACT RELATING TO LANDS IN PETERS' COLONY. LOUISVILLE, KY.: MORTON & GRISWOLD, PRINTERS, 1852.

[1]–[16]. 15.2 x 10.2 cm. Pink printed wrappers with title on front wrapper. In a green cloth case.

Ref.: Connors, S. V.: *The Peters Colony of Texas* (Austin, 1959) especially pp. 121–35; Streeter 1461 note; *Handbook of Texas* (Austin, 1952) II pp. 366–67

The original grant for the Peters' Colony was given in 1841 and, with three later grants, was continually in dispute until the matter was settled in favor of the Colony by this act of the state legislature.

4110 TEXAS REPUBLIC. Congress. Joint Committee on Public Lands

EVIDENCE IN RELATION TO LAND TITLES, TAKEN BEFORE JOINT COMMITTEE ON PUBLIC LANDS. PRINTED BY ORDER OF THE SENATE . . .

[1]–39, [40 blank]. 20.1 x 13.2 cm. Gray cloth, red leather label on backstrip.

Ref.: Rader 3059; Sabin 94963; Streeter 408A

Published in 1840. Imprint on page [2]: [rule] / Whiting's Press, Austin. / There was another printing for the House noted by both Rader and Sabin. Streeter describes both editions.

This is the only known copy of the Senate printing, described on the title-page as consisting of 150 copies.

Relates to the so-called Eleven League Grants.

4111 TEXAS REPUBLIC. Department of State

GENERAL INSTRUCTIONS FOR THE GOVERNMENT OF THE CONSULAR AND COMMERCIAL AGENTS OF THE REPUBLIC OF TEXAS. PRINTED BY ORDER OF SECRETARY OF STATE. HOUSTON: NATIONAL BANNER OFFICE, 1838.

[1]–62, [63–4 blank]. 20.2 x 13.1 cm. Folded form. Rebound in gray cloth, red leather label on backstrip.

Ref.: Sabin 95036; Streeter 268

4112 TEXAS REPUBLIC. Laws

LAWS PASSED BY THE SIXTH CONGRESS OF THE RE-PUBLIC OF TEXAS. PUBLISHED BY AUTHORITY. AUSTIN: S. WHITING, PUBLIC PRINTER, 1842.

[1]–120, [I]–VII, [VIII blank], [I]–VIII. 20.1 x 13.1 cm. Rebound in gray cloth, red leather label on backstrip.

Ref.: Raines p. 230; Sabin 95000 note; Streeter 535

4113 TEXAS REPUBLIC. Secretary of War (A. Sidney Johnston)

ANNUAL REPORT OF THE SECRETARY OF WAR. NOVEMBER, 1839. PRINTED BY ORDER OF CONGRESS.

[1]–52. 20 x 12.9 cm. Amateur binding of old marbled boards, upper outer corners of calf, backstrip of cloth.

Prov.: Signed and annotated on inside front cover by Dr. Alex. Dienst / Temple / Texas. 1915 / [flourish] /. With marginal notes in pencil by Dr. Dienst and with two small leaves of notes laid in at the back.

Ref.: Sabin 95056; Streeter 371
Printed at Whiting's Press, 1839.

The report . . . gives a full account of the relations with the Cherokees and of the engagements beginning July 15, 1839, which resulted finally in the removal of the Cherokees from Texas.—Streeter

4114 TEXAS REPUBLIC. Supreme Court

RULES OF THE SUPREME COURT, AND OF THE DISTRICT COURTS, OF THE REPUBLIC OF TEXAS. ADOPTED BY THE SUPREME COURT, AT THE JANUARY TERM, 1840.

[1]–[14]. 19.2 x 12.2 cm. Unbound.

Ref.: Sabin 95044; Streeter 425
On page [14]: . . . Given under our hands, at the City of Austin, this 27th day of January, A.D., 1840, and of the Independence of Texas the fourth. Thomas J. Rusk, Chief Justice . . .

Printed at Austin, the Telegraph Office, in 1840. The Republic was billed for 1000 copies.

4115 TEXAS REPUBLIC. War Department

GOVERNMENT OF THE ARMY OF THE REPUBLIC OF TEXAS, PRINTED IN ACCORDANCE WITH A JOINT RESOLUTION OF CONGRESS, APPROVED JANUARY 23RD, 1839. BY ORDER OF THE SECRETARY OF WAR. HOUSTON: INTELLIGENCER OFFICE, 1839.

[i–ii], [inserted leaf, verso blank], [1]–3, [4 blank], [1]–187, [188 blank], [1]–16. 18 x 10.9 cm. Two plates, after page [188]. Rebound in red calf, gilt backstrip, green leather label, gilt top, by Oldach Co.

Ref.: Raines p. 127; Sabin 95058; Streeter 372

4116 [TEXAS ASSOCIATION]

MEMORIAL QUE VARIOS CIUDADANOS DE LOS ESTADOS-UNIDOS DE AMERICA, PRESENTAN AL GOBIERNO INDEPENDIENTE DE MEXICO. MEXICO: EN LA OFICINA DE D. ALEJANDRO VALDES, 1822.

[1]–15, [16 blank]. 19 x 13.1 cm. Unbound, leaves pasted together along inner margins.

Ref.: Sabin 95103; Streeter 692
This is apparently the earliest separately printed petition, by residents of the United States, for a grant of land for the colonization of Texas which is now known. It is dated on page 8, "á 10 de Marzo de año . . . de 1822," and signed by "N. Patteson" and sixty-nine others, residing for the most part in Davidson County, Tennessee. Ira Ingram, Sam Houston, S. C. Robertson and Robert Leftwich are among the signers.—Streeter

Contains also letters by James Wilkinson, William Carroll, John D. Bradburn, and others. Relates to the founding of the Robertson colony.

4117 TEXAS WESTERN RAILROAD COMPANY

CHARTER OF THE TEXAS WESTERN RAILROAD COMPANY, AND EXTRACTS FROM REPORTS OF COL. A. B. GRAY AND SECRETARY OF WAR, ON THE SURVEY OF ROUTE, FROM EASTERN BORDERS OF TEXAS TO CALIFORNIA. NATURE OF COUNTRY AND CLIMATE, MINERAL AND AGRICULTURAL RESOURCES, &C., &C. CINCINNATI, OHIO: PORTER, THRALL & CHAPMAN, PRINTERS, 1855.

[1]–40. 22 x 13.8 cm. Map: [Map of the southern half of the United States, Mississippi River to the Pacific]. 16.3 x 38.7 cm. No scale given. Blue printed wrappers with title on front cover. In a blue cloth case.

Ref.: Howes G329; *Railway Economics* pp. 271–72

4118 THARIN, WILLIAM C.

A DIRECTORY OF MARENGO COUNTY, FOR 1860–61 . . . A SHORT SKETCH OF THE COUNTY . . . MOBILE: FARROW & DENNETT, PRINTERS, 1861.

[1]–67, [68 blank], [69–94 advertisements]. 18.6 x 11.7 cm. Black cloth, printed paper label, 8.9 x 10.5 cm., on front cover, advertisements on endpapers.

Ref.: Howes T151
Contains a history of the early settlers, especially of the French colony in Marengo County, Alabama.

4119 THAYER, JOHN M.

CHEYENNE COUNTY, NEBRASKA THE RAPID DEVELOPMENT IF ITS GREAT AGRICULTURAL RE-

SOURCES. A LETTER TO THE "OMAHA BEE," AUGUST 25TH, 1885 . . . THE SIDNEY TELEGRAPH PRINT.

[1–4]. 21.6 x 14.9 cm. Unbound leaflet.
Ref.:
Published at Sidney, Cheyenne County, Nebraska, probably in 1885.

4120   THAYER, JOHN M.

[Caption title] REMARKS OF GEN. J. M. THAYER IN REPLY TO W. H. TAYLOR, DELIVERED IN THE LEGISLATIVE COUNCIL OF THE TERRITORY OF NEBRASKA, ON JANUARY 2D, 1861 . . .

[1]–4. 25.7 x 16.7 cm. Unbound leaflet.
Ref.:
Probably printed at Omaha in 1861.

Fascinating performance in which Thayer defends himself against an action by Taylor, President of the Legislative Council, attempting to read Thayer out of the Republican Party.

4121   [THEARD, T.]

LE MEXIQUE ET SES RICHESSES. GUIDE DES EMIGRANTS.

[1]–[40]. 19.1 x 13.3 cm. Yellow printed wrappers, with title on front wrapper as follows: Le Mexique / et ses Richesses. / [decorative rule] / Guide des Emigrants. / [vignette] / Nouvelle-Orleans, / Imprimerie Typographique de Frank E. Barclay. / [short rule] / 1862. / [within decorative border], uncut.
Ref.:
Imprint on verso of title-leaf: [wavy rule] / Nouvelle-Orleans, / Imprimerie Typographique de Frank F. Barclay, / Rue de Chartres, 195, encoignure Sainte-Anne. / [wavy rule] /.

Théard gives a great deal of information of interest to the New Orleans citizens in 1862.—EDG

4122   THEVENOT, MELCHISIDECH

RECUEIL DE VOYAGES DE MR THEVENOT . . . PARIS: CHEZ ESTIENNE MICHALLET, M. DC. LXXXI.

[a]¹, [b]⁴, ẽ⁴, A–B⁸, C⁴, D², *a*–b⁴, c², A–D⁴, [*]², a–b⁴, c², [*]⁷, A⁴, A⁸. [i–ii], [1]–16, 1–43, [44 blank], 1–[19], [20 blank and pasted to following plate], [1]–32, [i–iv, ii–iii blank], [1]–20, 1–14, 1–8, 1–16. 16.7 x 10.5 cm. 17 illustrations and maps, some in text. Map: Terre Australe / découuerte l'An 1644. / 38.4 x 57.4 cm. No scale given. Map: Carte de la decouverte / faite l'an 1663. dans l'Amerique / Septentrionale. / [lower left:] Liebaux sculp. / 16 x 39.7 cm. No scale given. Map: [La Carte de la Decouverte de la Terre d'Ielmer]. [above map:] Explication de la Carte de la Decouverte de la Terre d'Ielmer, / au de là de la Nouvelle Zemble, & des routes

pour passer par le Nort / au Japon, à la Chine, & aux Indes Orientales. / [18 lines of text] / 19.4 x 18.5 cm. No scale given. Contemporary full calf, gilt tooled backstrip, red leather label on backstrip, gilt arms on sides of the Marquis de Saint-Ange, probably Louis-Urbain Le Fèvre de Caumartin. In a brown cloth case.
Prov.: Gilt arms of Marquis de Saint-Ange, probably Louis-Urbain Le Fèvre de Caumartin on sides. Inscribed on title-page: = huzierd / [paraph] / de l'Institut / [underline] /.
Ref.: Church 672; Clark I 120 note; Greenly (*Michigan*) 6; Harrisse 147; Howes T156; JCB II 1232; Jones 320; Sabin 95332; Stevens (*Nuggets*) 2654; Streit I 683

This collection is of especial value because of its account of the discovery of the Mississippi River by Father Marquette in 1673, with the map of the river which is believed to be the earliest extant.—Church

The second map (of the Mississippi River) is usually dated 1673 (as in the Ayer copy) but there is at least one other copy known dated 1663. Lawrence C. Wroth has pointed out that in the John Carter Brown copy, the erased six is slightly visible under the correction. There may be a trace of the error in the Ayer copy—the upper tip of the 6.

There are a few differences between the Ayer and Graff copies. The first page 3 in the Ayer copy is mispaginated ẽ, whereas the Graff copy is correctly paginated. The first c2 in the Ayer copy is a free blank; the Graff copy bears text pasted to the back of a plate. In the Ayer copy, leaf [*]2 carrying errata is placed at the end of the volume.

4123   THIS PAMPHLET IS TRUE!

[Wrapper title] THIS PAMPHLET IS TRUE!! IT IS A HISTORY OF THE MANNER IN WHICH NEBRASKA BECAME A STATE, ELECTED ITS STATE OFFICERS AND FIRST U. S. SENATORS, AND ENTERED THE AMERICAN UNION. IT IS AUTHENTICATED BY TWENTY-ONE MEMBERS OF THE FIRST STATE LEGISLATURE, WHO SIGNED IT AT THE SESSION OF 1866, JULY. IT WAS NOT WRITTEN BY C. H. GERE. AND IT IS ENTIRELY DISSIMILAR FROM HIS NARRATIVE OF THE EVENTS HEREIN RECORDED. THE NEBRASKA HISTORICAL SOCIETY IS REQUESTED TO PLACE THIS AMONG ITS CONSERVED TRUTHS. 1866, OMAHA.

[1]–15, [16 blank]. 21.7 x 15.4 cm. Gray printed wrappers, with title on front wrapper.
Ref.: AII (*Nebraska*) 470
Probably printed at Omaha by the Omaha *Herald* in 1880. The account by Gere mentioned on the title was an address before the Nebraska Historical Society in January, 1880. Watkins:

Illustrated History of Nebraska (1905) attributes the pamphlet to James M. Woolworth. An edition may have been printed in 1866 (see AII (*Nebraska*) 96).

4124   THISSELL, G. W.

CROSSING THE PLAINS IN '49 . . . OAKLAND, CALIFORNIA, 1903.

[1]–176. 18 x 11.8 cm. 11 illustrations unlisted. Gray cloth.

Ref.: Cowan p. 634; Howes T160

4125   THOMAS, C., & F. V. HAYDEN

LISTS OF ELEVATIONS AND DISTANCES IN THAT PORTION OF THE UNITED STATES WEST OF THE MISSISSIPPI RIVER . . . WASHINGTON: GOVERNMENT PRINTING OFFICE, 1872.

[1]–31, [32 blank]. 18.8 x 12.6 cm. Blue printed wrappers with title on front wrapper.

Ref.:

4126   THOMAS, DAVID

TRAVELS THROUGH THE WESTERN COUNTRY IN THE SUMMER OF 1816 . . . AUBURN, (N.Y.): PRINTED BY DAVID RUMSEY, 1819.

A⁸, B–2B⁶, 2C⁴. [i–iv], [1]–320. (Lacks leaf 2B5; small errata slip, 5 x 7.9 cm., pasted to blank leaf at end.) 16.6 x 10.1 cm. Map: Vincennes District. / [rule] / [lower left:] Drawn by D. Thomas. / [lower right:] J. Ridley Sᶜ NY. / 32.8 x 21.7 cm. No scale given. Contemporary mottled sheep, red leather label lettered in gilt on backstrip. Lacks pages 309–10.

Prov.: Inscribed at top of title-page: a Present from the / Author /.

Ref.: Buck 92; Clark II 236; Howes T162; Sabin 95384; Thomson 1139

It is a work of sterling merit.—Thomson. Thomas was strongly attracted to the Wabash Valley.

4127   THOMAS, LEWIS F.

THE VALLEY OF THE MISSISSIPPI ILLUSTRATED IN A SERIES OF VIEWS . . . ST. LOUIS. MO.: PUBLISHED BY THE ARTIST, 1841.

[1]–43, [44 blank], [i, note, ii blank], [45]–60, [i–iv], [i–ii], [61]–70. 28.2 x 21.7 cm. 15 numbered plates, two unnumbered plates and one map. Contemporary pink polished calf, gilt and blind tooled borders and panels on sides, gilt backstrip, gilt edges.

Ref.: Bradford 5392a; Buck 365; Howes T178; Sabin 103972

Comprises Numbers 1 to 4 and extra number for the third part. The parts were issued in July,

August, September, and October, 1841. The impressions are somewhat better than are usually found. The plates were painted and lithographed by J. C. Wild.

4128   THOMAS, COWPERTHWAIT & CO.

[Map] MAP OF THE / STATE OF IOWA / PUBLISHED BY / THOMAS, COWPERTHWAIT & Cᵒ. Nᵒ. 253, MARKET Sᵀ / PHILADELPHIA. / SCALE OF MILES. / [diagrammatic scale] / 1851. /

Map, 32.5 x 40.3 cm. Scale: 30 miles to an inch. Black embossed leather, with gilt title on front cover. Mounted on inner back cover of folder 12.3 x 8.3 cm.

Ref.:

4129   [THOMPSON, CHARLES B.]

THE LAWS AND COVENANTS OF ISRAEL, WRITTEN TO EPHRAIM, FROM JEHOVAH, THE MIGHTY GOD OF JACOB. ALSO EPHRAIM AND BANEEMY'S PROCLAMATIONS. PREPARATION, IOWA: PRINTED AT THE BOOK AND PERIODICAL OFFICE OF ZION'S PRESBYTERY, 1857.

[i]–[viii], [9]–208. 10.2 x 7.2 cm. Dark brown calf, wallet flap, tuck-in band on front cover, title in gilt on backstrip, gilt edges.

Prov.: Bookplate of J. C. Clapp. Signature of Orrin Butts, one of the twelve apostles of Ephraim. Signature of Heman C. Smith, on a front fly-leaf and margin of page vii. Pencil note on front end paper: This book / the Ravings and / Mutterings of a / demented man / only preserved / for the absurdity / of the thing /.

Ref.: Morgan III 35

Preparation, Iowa, does not appear on present day maps. It was in Monona County, on the Missouri River between Council Bluffs and Sioux City. For an account of the Monona County Mormons, see the article of C. R. Marks in *Annals of Iowa*, 3rd series, Vol. VII, No. 5, page 321. Thompson left St. Louis with his family and a printing press on September 9, 1853, and set up the press at Preparation on November 4th of that same year.—EDG

4130   THOMPSON, DAVID

DAVID THOMPSON'S JOURNALS RELATING TO MONTANA AND ADJACENT REGIONS, 1808–1812 . . . EDITED . . . BY M. CATHERINE WHITE. MISSOULA: MONTANA STATE UNIVERSITY PRESS, 1950.*

[i]–clxi, [clxii blank], [1]–345, [346 blank]. 22.8 x 15.3 cm. Four illustrations and two maps listed. Brown cloth.

Ref.:

Limited to 500 copies.

4131 [THOMPSON, HENRY]

TEXAS. SKETCHES OF CHARACTER; MORAL & POLITICAL CONDITION OF THE REPUBLIC; THE JUDICIARY, &C. BY MILAM. PHILADELPHIA: BROWN, BICKING & GUILBERT, PRINTERS, 1839.

[3]–95, [96 blank]. 14.6 x 8.6 cm. Dark gray blind embossed cloth, black leather label on backstrip.

Ref.: Howes T195; Rader 3112; Raines p. 149; Sabin 48913, 95117; Streeter 1357

4132 THOMPSON, HUGH B.

DIRECTORY OF THE CITY OF NEVADA AND GRASS VALLEY: CONTAINING A HISTORY OF THE CITY . . . CHARLES F. ROBBINS, BOOK AND JOB PRINTER, 1861.

[1]–128. 22.2 x 14.6 cm. Tan printed boards, red roan back, advertisements on sides and on inner covers. Portion of back endleaf cut off.

Ref.: Blumann & Thomas 2254; Howes T196
Printed at San Francisco.

The second directory of Nevada and Grass Valley, the first having been issued in 1856 by Brown & Dallison.

4133 THOMPSON, JAMES H.

THE HISTORY OF THE COUNTY OF HIGHLAND, IN THE STATE OF OHIO, FROM ITS FIRST CREATION AND ORGANIZATION, TO JULY 4TH, 1876 . . . HILLSBORO, O.: PRINTED AT THE HILLSBORO GAZETTE JOB ROOM, 1878.

[1]–132. 23.1 x 15.1 cm. Yellow printed wrappers, with title within decorative borders on front wrapper.

Ref.: Bradford 5401

Contains a detailed account of the 1876 centennial celebration.

4134 THOMPSON, ROBERT A.

HISTORICAL AND DESCRIPTIVE SKETCH OF SONOMA COUNTY, CALIFORNIA . . . PHILADELPHIA: L. H. EVERTS & CO., 1877.

[1]–104, [105–19 advertisements, 120 blank]. 22.8 x 15.1 cm. Map: Map of / Sonoma County / California. / 1877. / Scale / 3 1/4 Miles to an Inch /. 41.2 x 53.6 cm. Scale as above. Inset view of Sonoma Daily and Weekly Democrat building. Mauve printed wrappers, with title on front wrapper. Removed from bound volume and rebacked. In a dark red cloth case.

Ref.: Blumann & Thomas 4537; Bradford 5408; Cowan p. 636; Howes T200

4135 THOMPSON, ROBERT A.

CONQUEST OF CALIFORNIA CAPTURE OF SONOMA BY BEAR FLAG MEN JUNE 14, 1846 RAISING THE AMERICAN FLAG IN MONTEREY BY COMMODORE JOHN D. SLOAT, JULY 7, 1846 . . . SANTA ROSA: SONOMA DEMOCRAT PUBLISHING COMPANY, 1896.

[i–iv], [1]–33, [34–6 blank]. (Pages [i–ii] blank.) 24.5 x 17.3 cm. Four plates. Light yellow printed wrappers, with title on front cover in blue.

Ref.: Blumann & Thomas 4589; Cowan p. 636; Howes T199

4136 THOMPSON, ROBERT A.

THE RUSSIAN SETTLEMENT IN CALIFORNIA KNOWN AS FORT ROSS, FOUNDED 1812, ABANDONED 1841 . . . SANTA ROSA: SONOMA DEMOCRAT PUBLISHING COMPANY, 1896.

[i–iv], [1]–34, [35–36 blank]. 26.7 x 18.3 cm. (Pages [i–ii] blank.) Plates and three cuts in text. Light orange printed wrappers, with title in red and black on front wrapper.

Ref.: Blumann & Thomas 4563; Cowan p. 637; Howes T201

The most complete account of this phase of early settlement.—Cowan

4137 THOMPSON, WADDY

RECOLLECTIONS OF MEXICO . . . NEW YORK: WILEY AND PUTNAM, 1847.

[i]–x, [1]–304. (Pages [i–ii] blank.) 19 x 12.7 cm. Dark gray-green cloth, blind embossed sides, title in gilt on backstrip. New endpapers.

Ref.: Raines p. 204; Sabin 95537
Editions: New York, 1846 (six issues).

4138 THOMPSON, WILLIAM

REMINISCENCES OF A PIONEER . . . SAN FRANCISCO, 1912.*

[i–vi], [1]–187, [188 blank]. 21.3 x 14.6 cm. Six illustrations listed. Blue cloth.

Ref.: Blumann & Thomas 1995; Cowan p. 637; Smith 10204

Thompson crossed the Plains in 1852.

4139 THOMSON, CHARLES

AN ENQUIRY INTO THE CAUSES OF THE ALIENATION OF THE DELAWARE AND SHAWANESE INDIANS FROM THE BRITISH INTEREST . . . TOGETHER WITH THE REMARKABLE JOURNAL OF CHRISTIAN FREDERICK POST . . . LONDON: PRINTED FOR J. WILKIE, MDCCLIX.

A–L8, M4. [1]–184. 20.2 x 12.5 cm. Map: A Map of the Province of / Pensylvania[!]. / intended chiefly to Illustrate the Account of the Several / Indian Purchases / made by the Proprietaries of the said Province / the Claims made by the Indians, / on lands Settled and not Purchased of them and the Tract / they now desire may be allotted for them Solely. / [lower right:] T. Jefferys sculp. / 19.1 x 25.2 cm. (neat line), 27 x 38 cm. (paper size). No scale given. Explanation of the map in right margin, printed from type. Rebound in green cloth, green morocco back.

Ref.: Church 1029; Clements Library (*Ohio*) 5; Field 1548; Howes T210; Jones 498; Rader 3119; Sabin 95562; Thomson 1145; Vail 535

Thomson's account considered the reasons for the alienation of the Indian tribes from the grasping colonial government of Pennsylvania. It was one of the most important books on relations with the Indians that had been published up to that time. Also notable was the appearance of the *Journal* of Christian Frederick Post, an intrepid Moravian missionary who almost single-handedly won over to the English side the support of the Indians along the Ohio River.— Clements Library

See also under Christian Frederick Post.

4140 THOMSON, ORIGEN

CROSSING THE PLAINS. NARRATIVE OF THE SCENES, INCIDENTS AND ADVENTURES ATTENDING THE OVERLAND JOURNEY OF THE DECATUR AND RUSH COUNTY EMIGRANTS TO THE "FAR-OFF" OREGON, IN 1852 . . . GREENSBURG, INDIANA: ORVILLE THOMSON, PRINTER, 1896.

[1]–122. 19.2 x 13.5 cm. Olive green embossed and printed boards, with title on front cover, brown edges.

Ref.: Howes T216; Matthews p. 335; Smith 10207

Comprises a day-by-day account of the Crawford Party which set out from Decatur and Rush Counties, Indiana, across the Plains to Oregon. There were about 111 members of the party, most of whom are listed in the book.

4141 THORN & CO., W., Chicago

CHICAGO IN 1860; A GLANCE AT ITS BUSINESS HOUSES . . . CHICAGO: STEAM PRESS OF THOMPSON & DAY, 1860.

[i]–xii, 13–216. 17.4 x 11.1 cm. Gray printed wrappers with title on front wrapper, advertisements on verso of front and recto of back wrapper.

Ref.: AII (*Chicago*) 455

4142 THORNTON, JESSY Q.

[Caption title] MEMORIAL OF J. QUINN THORNTON, PRAYING THE ESTABLISHMENT OF A TERRITORIAL GOVERNMENT IN OREGON, AND FOR APPROPRIATIONS FOR VARIOUS PURPOSES . . .

[1]–24. 23.6 x 15.9 cm. Stabbed, unbound, uncut, unopened.

Ref.: Howes T223

30th Congress, 1st Session, Senate, Miscellaneous Document No. 143, Serial 511. [Washington, 1848.]

Imprint at foot of page [1]: [rule] / Tippin & Streeper, printers. /

4143 THORNTON, JESSY Q.

OREGON AND CALIFORNIA IN 1848 . . . INCLUDING RECENT AND AUTHENTIC INFORMATION ON THE SUBJECT OF THE GOLD MINES OF CALIFORNIA . . . NEW YORK: HARPER & BROTHERS, 1849.

[i]–iv, [5]–6, [vii]–[x], [13]–393, [394 blank]. [i–iv blank], [v]–[xii], [13]–379, [380 blank], [1]–8 advertisements, [1]–4 advertisements. 19.7 x 12.7 cm. 12 illustrations listed and folding map: Map of / California, / Oregon, Texas, / and the Territories adjoining / with Routes &c. / Published by J. H. Colton, / N⁰ 86, Cedar Sᵗ, New York, / 1849. / Ackermans lith 120 Fulton Sᵗ N.Y. / [lower left:] Entered according to Act of Congress in the year 1849 by J. H. Colton in the Clerk's Office of the District Court for the Southern District of New York. / [lower right:] Harper and Brothers New York /. 52.6 x 46 cm. No scale given. Two volumes, black cloth, blind embossed sides, title stamped in gilt on backstrips.

Ref.: Bradford 5422; Cowan p. 638; Howes T224; Sabin 95630; Smith 10219; Wagner-Camp 174

Thornton arrived in Oregon in 1846. This work is one of the best authorities of the period, and the account he has given of the ill-fated Donner party is perhaps the most valuable in print.—Cowan

4144 THORNTON MAGISTRATES' DISTRICT, COOK COUNTY, ILLINOIS

MANUSCRIPT DOCUMENT, SIGNED by Benjamin Butterfield, John Blackstone, and Carlos Barry and attested by Henry McCulloch and Joseph Crary. One page (three sheets attached with wax wafers), 60 x 19.9 cm.

Headed: Poll Books of an Election held in THORNTON— / Magistrates district for Two Justices of peace and Two / Constables for said district at the house of John / Blackstone in said district on the Sixteenth day of May 1836 /.

Thirty-two voters are listed with their votes for the six candidates for the four offices.

Accompanies Cook County, Illinois, County Commissioners' Court.

4145 THORP, NATHAN H.

TALES OF THE CHUCK WAGON . . .

[1]–123, [124 blank]. 23.1 x 15.3 cm. Frontispiece. Brown printed wrappers. In a brown buckram case.

Ref.: Adams (*Ramp. Herd*) 2306

Published at Santa Fé in 1926.

4146 THORPE, THOMAS B.

THE HIVE OF "THE BEE-HUNTER," A REPOSITORY OF SKETCHES, INCLUDING PECULIAR AMERICAN CHARACTER, SCENERY, AND RURAL SPORTS . . . NEW-YORK: D. APPLETON AND COMPANY, M.DCCC.LIV.

[1]–312. 19.8 x 12.6 cm. Ten plates, unlisted. Green cloth, with short title and cut of Tom Owen on backstrip, blind embossed sides, top uncut.

Ref.: Howes T233

Contains practically the same material as his *The Mysteries of the Backwoods*, with several additional chapters. Some chapter headings have been changed, e.g. "Mike Fink, the Keel-Boatman" of this edition is "The Disgraced Scalp Lock" of *The Mysteries*, and the plate "Mike Fink's Great Shot" of this edition replaces Darley's "There lay, in a profound sleep, Mike Fink . . ." facing page 128 in the earlier edition.—EDG

4147 THORPE, THOMAS B.

THE MYSTERIES OF THE BACKWOODS; OR, SKETCHES OF THE SOUTHWEST . . . PHILADELPHIA: CAREY AND HART, 1846.

[1]–190. (Pages [1–2] blank.) 19 x 11.3 cm. Five illustrations by F. O. C. Darley, unlisted. Green printed wrappers with title on front wrapper, advertisements on verso of front and recto and verso of back wrapper, title on backstrip, uncut. In a blue cloth case.

Ref.: Howes T234; Sabin 95663

4148 THURSTON, JOHN H.

REMINISCENCES, SPORTING AND OTHERWISE, OF EARLY DAYS IN ROCKFORD, ILL. . . . ROCKFORD, ILL.: PRESS OF THE DAILY REPUBLICAN, 1891.

[1]–117, [118–20 blank], leaf inserted between pages [2] and [3]. 21.5 x 15.4 cm. Portrait. Pink printed wrappers, with title on front wrapper.

Ref.: Howes T252

4149 THURSTON, SAMUEL R.

[Caption title] . . . GEOGRAPHICAL STATISTICS. OREGON, ITS CLIMATE, SOIL, PRODUCTIONS, ETC. THE FOLLOWING VALUABLE LETTER OF MR. THURSTON, ADDRESSED, THROUGH THE COLUMNS OF THE NATIONAL INTELLIGENCER TO SEVERAL GENTLEMEN IN DIFFERENT PARTS OF THE UNION, WHO HAD SOUGHT INFORMATION FROM HIM, CONTAINS A MINUTE AND EXCEEDINGLY INTERESTING DESCRIPTION OF OREGON, AND THE ROUTE THITHER . . .

209–226. 21.7 x 13.9 cm. New red cloth.

Ref.: Wagner-Camp 193

Extract from Stryker's *American Register and Magazine*, for July, 1850. The Thurston letter occupies pages 210–226.

4150 THURSTON, SAMUEL R.

[Caption title] TO THE ELECTORS AND PEOPLE OF THE TERRITORY OF OREGON . . .

[1]–16. 23.9 x 15.8 cm. Folded, unbound, unopened.

Ref.: Smith (1921) 3989

Bancroft: *History of Oregon*, Vol. 2, page 118 quotes from this circular letter as a "sample of the ignorance or mendacity of the man, whichever you will."

4151 TILDEN, BRYANT P., JR.

NOTES ON THE UPPER RIO GRANDE . . . EXPLORED IN THE MONTHS OF OCTOBER AND NOVEMBER, 1846, ON BOARD THE U. S. STEAMER MAJOR BROWN . . . PHILADELPHIA: LINDSAY & BLAKISTON, 1847.*

[i]–[vi, vi blank], 7–32. 22.3 x 14.1 cm. Nine maps: A / Sketch of the / Upper Rio Grande / [decorative rule] / Explored in the months of October and November 1846 / on Board the U. S. Steamer Major Brown commanded by Capt. M. Sterling / of Pittsburgh / Under the direction of Lieu.^t Bryant P. Tilden, jr. 2.^d Reg.^t U. S. Infantry / by order of / Major General Patterson U. S. A. / commanding the 2.^d division / of the Army of occupation in Mexico. / [decorative rule] / Lith. of T. Sinclair. / [upper right:] N.º 1 / 21.3 x 37 cm. No scale given. Maps: [eight untitled detailed maps of the river, numbered in upper right N.º 2. to N.º 9. Lettered in lower right corner (except one in lower left): Lith. of T. Sinclair. / Map N.º 5 two sections on one sheet.] Various sizes. No scale given. Removed from bound volume, unbound. In a brown cloth case.

Ref.: Howes T264; Raines p. 206; Sabin 95817

4152 TILLSON, CHRISTIANA HOLMES

REMINISCENCES OF EARLY LIFE IN ILLINOIS, BY OUR MOTHER.

[i]–iv, [1]–138. 20.3 x 14.3 cm. Frontispiece and three portraits, all photographs. Brown cloth, blind rule borders on sides, name in gilt on front cover.

Ref.: Buck 155; *The Month* xxv, No. 1, October, 1953, pp. 3–6; Howes T268

Printed at Amherst, Mass. in 1872.

An intimate and valuable account of life and travels in southern Illinois, 1819–27. Tillson came to Illinois in 1819 and Mrs. Tillson in 1822. They located in Montgomery County.—Buck

4153 TILTON, D. W., & CO. Virginia City, Montana Territory

[Broadside] NOW COMPLETED AND FOR SALE! AN IMPARTIAL AND CORRECT HISTORY OF THE VIGILANTES OF MONTANA TERRITORY! COMPRISING A FULL ACCOUNT OF THE CHASE, CAPTURE, TRIAL, AND EXECUTION OF PLUMMER'S GREAT BAND OF ROAD AGENTS! . . .

Broadside, 73.5 x 53.3 cm. Text, 66 x 46.8 cm. Mounted on cloth.

Ref.: McMurtrie (*Montana*) 22;

Broadside advertising Dimsdale's *Vigilantes* . . .

4154 TIMBERLAKE, HENRY

THE MEMOIRS OF LIEUT. HENRY TIMBERLAKE (WHO ACCOMPANIED THE THREE CHEROKEE INDIANS TO ENGLAND IN THE YEAR 1762) . . . LONDON: PRINTED FOR THE AUTHOR AND SOLD BY J. RIDLEY AND C. HENDERSON, MDCCLXV.

[A]–X⁴. [i]–viii, 1–160. 18.9 x 11.6 cm. Map and engraved plate. A Draught of the / Cherokee Country, / On the West Side of the Twenty four Mountains, / commonly called Over the Hills; / Taken by Henry Timberlake, when he / was in that Country, in March 1762. / . . . / 39 x 23.7 cm. Scale: one inch to one mile. Rebound in brown half morocco, gilt top.

Prov.: Henry E. Huntington duplicate stamp inside back cover.

Ref.: De Renne I, 175; Field 1553; Howes T271; Jones 519; Rader 3135; Sabin 95836; Vail 565

Describes travels through Virginia, the Carolinas, Georgia and Tennessee; an important source on the Cherokee Nation and on the little known southern phase of the French and Indian War.—Howes

4155 TIMES (Hamburg, Iowa) EXTRA

[Broadside] TIMES EXTRA. HAMBURG, IOWA. DECEMBER 13, 1869. THE WILKERSON TRAGEDY . . . Broadside, 22.7 x 14.3 cm. Text, 15.2 x 10.5 cm.

Ref.:

A fascinating account of murder as a result of an attempted swindle in hogs.

4156 TIMES AND SEASONS

[Caption title] TIMES AND SEASONS . . . VOL. I [–VI]. COMMERCE [—CITY OF NAUVOO], ILLINOIS: NOV. 1839–1846 . . .

[1]–192. [193]–528. [577]–958. [1]–361 [i.e. 384]. [384]–767. [768]–1135. Six volumes bound in three (1–3, 4, 5–6), half calf (natural) and half sheep (green).

Prov.: Signature in pencil in first volume: Smith Tuttle, Esq / Fair Haven / Conn /. Signature in blue pencil in second volume: H. C. Smith /. Signature on front endleaf of third volume: Heman C. Smith / with pencil notations on rest of page. Signature on inner front cover: This Book belongs to / H. B. Sterrett / 104 Bowen Aven / Independence. / Jackson Co / Mo /.

Ref.: Gregory p. 2778; Woodward 276

The pagination is somewhat irregular, but no leaves are missing. In Volume IV, from page 304 to the end of Volume VI, even pagination appears on the rectos. Mr. Frederick R. Goff reports that the plate in Volume II of the DLC copy has been inserted from another work and "is not an intrinsical part of the book."

4157 TINKHAM, GEORGE H.

A HISTORY OF STOCKTON FROM ITS ORGANIZATION UP TO THE PRESENT TIME, INCLUDING A SKETCH OF SAN JOAQUIN COUNTY . . . SAN FRANCISCO: W. M. HINTON & CO., 1880.

[I]–XVI, blank leaf, [1]–397, [398 blank]. 21.8 x 13.8 cm. Photographs, engravings, etc., unlisted. Sheepskin, black skiver label on backstrip, marbled edges.

Prov.: Inscribed on front endleaf: Compliments of the / Author to / John S. Hittell / Historian. /

Ref.: Blumann & Thomas 4058; Cowan p. 640; Howes T273

4158 TITTSWORTH, W. G.

OUTSKIRT EPISODES. THE WILD AND WOOLLY WEST OF EARLY DAYS WAS A LAND OF CRIME IN MANY WAYS . . .

[1]–232, [233 poem, 234 blank]. 19.3 x 13.2 cm. Portrait on title-page. Dark red cloth. In dust jacket.

Ref.: Howes T275

Copyright, 1927, by / Jean Tittsworth / Avoca, Iowa /. The work was probably printed in Des Moines. Largely experiences in Wyoming.

4159 TIXIER, VICTOR

VOYAGE AUX PRAIRIES OSAGES, LOUISIANE ET MISSOURI, 1839–40 . . . CLERMONT-FERRAND: CHEZ PEROL, LIBRAIRE-EDITEUR, 1844.

[1]–260, [261–64 glossary and table]. 22.7 x 14 cm. Five plates after designs by the author. Buff printed wrappers with title on front wrapper, vignette and border on verso of back wrapper, uncut. In a board case.

Prov.: Presentation copy from the author: A mon vieil amis Edouard Jauffret / Temoignage de Sincère affection / Victor Tixier /.

Ref.: Clark III 250 note; Howes T276; Monaghan 1406; Rader 3139; Wagner-Camp 114

Pages [261–62] carry a "Glossaire Osage," and [263–64] a Table.

4160 TODD, AARON

THE LIFE AND CONFESSION OF AARON TODD, WHO WAS EXECUTED IN THE TOWN OF CARLVINVILLE, MACOUPIN COUNTY, ILLINOIS, ON THE SECOND DAY OF JUNE, 1840, FOR THE MURDER OF LARKIN SCOTT, JR. SPRINGFIELD, ILL.: WALTERS & WEBER, PRINTERS, 1840.

[1]–15, [16 blank]. 22.2 x 14.2 cm. New manila folders.

Ref.: Byrd 570; McDade 995

4161 TODD, JOHN

EARLY SETTLEMENT AND GROWTH OF WESTERN IOWA . . . DES MOINES: THE HISTORICAL DEPARTMENT OF IOWA, 1906.*

[1]–203, [204 blank]. 20.4 x 14.4 cm. Portrait. Dark red cloth, title in gilt on front cover and backstrip, gilt top, uncut.

Ref.: Bradford 5455; Mott (*Iowa*) p. 87

One of the best books of Iowa reminiscences. —EDG

4162 TOME, PHILIP

PIONEER LIFE; OR, THIRTY YEARS A HUNTER . . . BUFFALO: PUBLISHED FOR THE AUTHOR, 1854.

[i–ii blank], [iii]–viii, [9]–238. 19.2 x 11.3 cm. Frontispiece. Brown cloth.

Prov.: Signature on front fly-leaf: R. Brown /.

Ref.: Howes T288

Tome's association with Cornplanter was particularly interesting; his volume is an important account of pioneer life in the Old West.

4163 TONTI, HENRI DE

AN ACCOUNT OF MONSIEUR DE LA SALLE'S LAST EXPEDITION AND DISCOVERIES IN NORTH AMERICA . . . LONDON: PRINTED FOR J. TONSON, 1698.

[A]^1, P4–5, B–O^8, P1–3, P6–8, Q–R^8. [i–ii], [3–6], 1–211, [212 blank], [1–2], 7–44. (Leaves P4–5 [pages 3–6 of second part] misbound following first leaf.) 17.4 x 11.4 cm. Contemporary

red marbled sides, vellum backstrip and corners, red leather label on backstrip, uncut.

Prov.: Signature on verso of title-leaf (partially erased): Richd Fraser / Octr 21. 1736 /. Bookplate of J. C. MacCoy.

Ref.: Clark I 27 note; Greenly (*Michigan*) 7 note; Harrisse 178; Howes T294; Rader 19; Sabin 96171; Wagner (*SS*) 67a

This is a contemporary translation of *Dernières Découverte dans l'Amérique Septentrionale de M. De La Sale . . .* Paris 1697, which is attributed to Henri de Tonti. Tonti disclaimed authorship, but the work may have been written from his notes and journals.

The second part is A Relation of a Voyage Made by the Sieur de Montauban . . . on the Coasts of Guinea, In the Year 1695 . . . London: Printed in the Year 1698.

4164 TONTI, HENRI DE

DERNIERES DECOUVERTES DANS L'AMERIQUE SEPTENTRIONALE DE M. DE LA SALE . . . A PARIS: CHEZ JEAN GUIGNARD, M. DC. LXXXXVII.

[*]^2, A–Ee^8 and ^{4} alternately, Ff^8, Gg^2. [i–iv], [1]–[348], [349–54 advertisement], [355–56 blank]. 16.5 x 9.4 cm. Contemporary full calf, gilt backstrip, red leather label on backstrip, edges mottled.

Prov.: Inscribed on a blank leaf at the back: Mademoiselle destereu (?) /. On blank leaf at front: Mont que /.

Ref.: Clark I 27 note; Gagnon 3547; Greenly (*Michigan*) 7; Harrisse 174; Howes T294; JCB I 1522; Jones 361; Rader 19 note; Sabin 96172; Wagner (*SS*) 67

The earlier of two states. Pages 185–88 are present in the original form and carry the passage relating to pearls.

4165 TOPONCE, ALEXANDER

REMINISCENCES . . . 1839–1923.*

[1]–248. 17.3 x 12.8 cm. 14 illustrations unlisted. Fabrikoid, blind stamped.

Ref.: Howes T299; Smith 10262

Copyrighted 1923. Published by Mrs. Katie Toponce, Ogden, Utah.

4166 TOPPING, E. S.

THE CHRONICLES OF THE YELLOWSTONE. AN ACCURATE, COMPREHENSIVE HISTORY OF THE COUNTRY DRAINED BY THE YELLOWSTONE RIVER . . . ST. PAUL: PIONEER PRESS COMPANY, 1883.

[i]–[iv (iv blank)], [1]–[246]. 19.9 x 13.2 cm. Illustrations unlisted, folding map. Map: [Map of the Yellowstone National Park and adjacent areas] [lower right corner:] Pioneer Press Co.

Lith. St. Paul Minn. / Key to Numbers on Map. / in five columns below map. 48.3 x 48.5 cm. (paper size). No scale given. Green cloth, title in gilt on front cover, red edges.

Ref.: National Parks (*Yellowstone*) p. 74; Howes T300; Smith 10264

4167 TORNEL Y MENDIVIL, JOSE MARIA

TEJAS Y LOS ESTADOS-UNIDOS DE AMERICA, EN SUS RELACIONES CON LA REPUBLICA MEXICANA . . . MEXICO: IMPRESO POR IGNACIO CUMPLIDO, 1837.

[1]–98. 20.6 x 13.5 cm. Rebound in dark gray-blue cloth.

Ref.: Clements Library (*Texas*) 18; Howes T302; Rader 3145; Sabin 96208; Streeter 932

General Tornel, Minister Plenipotentiary to the United States from Mexico, tried to stop colonization of Texas by refusing passports to applicants in 1830. He was unsuccessful. Yet in this book, Tornel gives a fair account of Mexican-Texan relations and includes a summary of all land grants in Texas up to 1837.

4168 TORREY, EDWIN C.

EARLY DAYS IN DAKOTA . . . MINNEAPOLIS: FARNHAM PRINTING AND STATIONERY CO.*

[1]–289, [290 blank]. (Pages [1–2] blank.) 19 x 12.6 cm. Dark red cloth.

Ref.:
Dedication dated October, 1925.

4169 TORRINGTON, LORD

AUTOGRAPH LETTER, SIGNED. No place, no date. Three pages, octavo. Recipient unidentified.

4170 TORRINGTON, LORD

AUTOGRAPH LETTER, SIGNED. No place, no date. Three pages, octavo. Recipient unidentified.

Both this letter and the preceding bound in Iturbide: *A Statement of Some of the Principal Events* . . . 1824.

4171 TOTTEN, SILAS

DR. TOTTEN'S LETTER ABOUT JUBILEE COLLEGE, ADDRESSED TO A FRIEND IN HARTFORD, CONNECTICUT. DATED NOVEMBER 24, 1848.

[1]–8. 20.9 x 12.8 cm. Unbound leaflet. Removed from bound volume. Laid in case labeled Bishop Chase. Jubilee College /

Ref.: Byrd 1387
Probably printed at Jubilee College late in 1848 or early in 1849.
Signed on page 7: S. Totten /. Bishop Chase's Preface appears on page [2] and his Remarks on page 8.

4172 TOWNSEND, GEORGE A.

THE REAL LIFE OF ABRAHAM LINCOLN. A TALK WITH MR. HERNDON, HIS LATE LAW PARTNER . . . NEW YORK: PUBLICATION OFFICE, BIBLE HOUSE, 1867.

[1]–15, [16 blank]. 24.3 x 15.5 cm. Portrait. Blue printed wrappers, with title on front wrapper, uncut.

Ref.: Monaghan 895

4173 TOWNSEND, JOHN K.

NARRATIVE OF A JOURNEY ACROSS THE ROCKY MOUNTAINS, TO THE COLUMBIA RIVER, AND A VISIT TO THE SANDWICH ISLANDS, CHILI . . . PHILADELPHIA: HENRY PERKINS, 1839.

[i]–viii, [9]–352. 23.1 x 14.1 cm. Plum cloth, blind embossed on sides, backstrip with gilt title.

Ref.: Field 1558; Howes T319; Sabin 96381; Smith 10282; Wagner-Camp 79

The author accompanied Wyeth on his second expedition to Oregon in 1834.

4174 TOWNSEND, JOHN K.

SPORTING EXCURSIONS IN THE ROCKY MOUNTAINS, INCLUDING A JOURNEY TO THE COLUMBIA RIVER, AND A VISIT TO THE SANDWICH ISLANDS . . . LONDON: HENRY COLBURN, 1840.

[i]–xii, [1]–310, [311–12 advertisements]. [i]–[xii], [1]–312, [1–8] advertisements in smaller size. 20 x 12.3 cm. Two frontispieces. Two volumes, plum cloth, blind embossed sides, title in gilt on backstrip, uncut.

Ref.: Howes T319; Sabin 96383; Smith 10283; Wagner-Camp 79

Second edition of Townsend's *Narrative of a Journey across the Rocky Mountains* . . . Philadelphia, 1839.

4175 TOWNSHEND, FREDERICK T.

TEN THOUSAND MILES OF TRAVEL, SPORT, AND ADVENTURE . . . LONDON: HURST AND BLACKETT, 1869.

[i]–xiv, [1]–275, [276 blank, 277–78 fly-title,] 1–[16] advertisements. (Frontispiece included in pagination.) 22 x 14 cm. Frontispiece. Yellow cloth, blind centre panels, title in gilt on backstrip, uncut.

Ref.: Howes T322
This is a good hunting story. The U. S. Army officers gave Townshend and his companion, C. P. Kendall, a good time on the plains and in the mountains.—EDG

4176 TRAIL CREEK (Colorado) DISTRICT

[Broadside] REPUBLICAN & HERALD PRINT. TRAIL CREEK DISTRICT, COLORADO TERRITORY. BE IT KNOWN, THAT [in manuscript: J. W. Hamilton] IS THE OWNER . . . RECORDED THIS [in manuscript: 26th] DAY OF [in manuscript: November] 1861. [in manuscript: W W Ware] RECORDER. DEPUTY, CLAIMS HELD AS REAL ESTATE, UNDER THE LAWS OF THE DISTRICT.

Broadside, 8.1 x 19.8 cm. Text, 6.5 x 18.9 cm.
Ref.:
Claim No. 12 S.W. on Black Earth Lode.

4177 TRAIL CREEK (Colorado) DISTRICT

ANOTHER COPY. Claim No. 6 S.W. on Poor Man's Lode. Same date.

4178 TRAIL CREEK (Colorado) DISTRICT

ANOTHER COPY. Claim No. 10 N.E. on Fall City Lode. Same date.

4179 TRAIL CREEK (Colorado) DISTRICT

ANOTHER COPY. Claim No. 5 N.W. on Mary Knox Lode. Same date.

4180 TRAIL CREEK (Colorado) DISTRICT

ANOTHER COPY. Claim No. 11 S.W. on Canada Lode. Same date.

4181 TRAIL CREEK (Colorado) DISTRICT

ANOTHER COPY. Claim No. 8 S.W. on Glenn Lode. December 6, 1860.

4182 TRAVELER'S GUIDE TO THE NEW GOLD MINES IN KANSAS . . .

[1859 1859 TRAVELER'S GUIDE TO THE NEW GOLD MINES IN KANSAS AND NEBRASKA, WITH A DESCRIPTION OF THE SHORTEST AND MOST DIRECT ROUTE FROM CHICAGO TO PIKE'S PEAK & CHERRY CREEK GOLD MINES. POLHEMUS & DE VRIES, PRINTERS, 6 COURTLANDT ST., N. Y.]

3–4. (Lacks 1–2, 5–16.) 12.4 x 8.3 cm. Unbound fragment. Lacks pages 1–2, 5–16. Map: Map of the / Chicago, Burlington and Quincy R. R. / with its / Connections / and the / Route / to the Gold Regions. / 11.7 x 47.1 cm. No scale given.
Ref.: Hafen 15; Wagner-Camp 326
Title from a complete copy in ICN.

4183 TRAVELLER'S REGISTER, THE . . .

THE TRAVELLER'S REGISTER, AND RIVER AND ROAD GUIDE: CONTAINING A NEW AND CORRECT MAP OF THE RIVERS OF THE MISSISSIPPI VALLEY . . . CINCINNATI: ROBINSON & JONES, 1847.

[1–72]. 13.2 x 8.2 cm. Folding map: Rivers / of the / Mississippi Valley, / or / Tourist's Guide. /

Published by / Robinson & Jones. / Cincinnati. / 1847. / [at foot, in border:] Eng^d By E. O. Reed Cin^ti / [below border:] Entered according to Act of Congress, in the year 1846, by Robinson & Jones in the Clerk's Office of the District Court of Ohio. / 34.1 x 20.1 cm. No scale given. Mauve cloth.

Prov.: There are manuscript notes by Z. Allen throughout the volume in pencil, and his route is traced in blue pencil on the map.
Ref.: Howes T332
Pages [1–18] list steamboat, canal, railroad, and stage routes, pages [19–67] are an Almanac for 1847 with memorandum pages for every day of the year, and pages [68–72] carry advertisements.

Mr. Allen and his party went from New Bedford to the Falls of St. Anthony via the Ohio River and back by way of Galena, Chicago, Buffalo, etc. in 1847.

4184 TREATISE ON MARRIAGE, A

[Caption title] A TREATISE ON MARRIAGE . . .

[1]–20. 12.8 x 7.7 cm. Bound with Number 1278.
Ref.: Hargrett (*Oklahoma*) 60; Pilling 3888
Text in Sequoyan. Printed at Park Hill in 1844.
Editions: Park Hill, 1838 (no copy located).

4185 TRENY, M.

LA CALIFORNIE DEVOILEE; OU, VERITES IRRECUSABLES . . . PARIS: CHEZ TOUS LES LIBRAIRES, 1850.

[1]–60, [61–2 advertisement, 63–4 blank]. 22.3 x 14.1 cm. Vignettes. Buff printed wrappers, with title on front wrapper, vignette on verso of back wrapper.
Ref.: Cowan p. 644; Howes T347; Monaghan 1414; Sabin 96779
Editions: Paris, 1850.

4186 TRESTLE BOARD, THE

[Newspaper] THE TRESTLE BOARD . . . VOL. I. CHICAGO, APRIL, 1857. NUMBER 2 . . .

[1–8]. 47.9 x 33.2 cm. Unbound.
Ref.:
Edited and published by James J. Clarkson. *The Trestle Board* was devoted to Masonic literature.

4187 TRIAL . . . FOR THE MURDER OF JOSEPH SMITH . . .

[Caption title] TRIAL OF THE PERSONS INDICTED IN THE HANCOCK CIRCUIT COURT, FOR THE MURDER OF JOSEPH SMITH, AT THE CARTHAGE JAIL, ON THE 27TH DAY OF JUNE, 1844 . . .

[1]–32. 21 x 14.6 cm. Stabbed, unbound.

Ref.: Byrd 1001; *Chicago History*, Vol. VI, No. 9, 1962, pp. 285–86

Published at Warsaw, Illinois, in 1845. Dale Morgan located an advertisement for the pamphlet in the *Warsaw Signal*, Volume II, No. 23, August 6, 1845.

4188   TRIALS OF THE FAHRENBAUGH MURDERERS

TRIALS OF THE FAHRENBAUGH MURDERERS; IN THE TIPPECANOE CIRCUIT COURT, APRIL TERM . . . LAFAYETTE: HOWE & POMROY, PUBLISHERS, 1855.

[1]–16. 22.7 x 15.7 cm. Green printed wrappers, with title on front wrapper and short title on verso of back wrapper.

4189   TRIBUNE (Lawrence, Kansas), THE

[Broadside] BLACK BOB INDIAN LANDS. SUPPLEMENT TO THE TRIBUNE. JOHN SPEER, EDITOR. THURSDAY, JULY 21, 1870 . . . THE UNDERSIGNED THEREFORE RECOMMENDS THE PASSAGE OF THE JOINT RESOLUTION HERETO APPENDED. SIDNEY CLARKE . . .

Broadside, 52.6 x 35.4 cm. Text, 46 x 28.7 cm.

Ref.: AII (*Kansas*) 747

In the first part of the broadside, the report of Congressman Van Horn is printed in full. The second part, signed by Sidney Clarke, is the minority report.

The Tribune of Lawrence, Kansas was edited at this time by John Speer.

4190   TRIBUNE (Lawrence, Kansas), THE

[Broadsheet] THE TRIBUNE EXTRA. LAWRENCE, KANSAS: TUESDAY, AUGUST 27, 1872 REPORT ON THE CONDITION OF INDIAN AFFAIRS. IN THE INDIAN TERRITORY. ENOCH HOAG, SUPERINTENDENT INDIAN AFFAIRS: LAWRENCE, KAS., AUG. 13, 1872 . . .

Broadsheet, 71 x 50.7 cm.

Ref.:

The report occupies eight columns on the first page and two on the second; the balance of the second page consists of advertisements. Signed at the end by Cyrus Beede. An additional paragraph is also signed by Beede and is dated August 26, 1872.

This may be the only extant copy.

4191   TRIGGS, J. H.

HISTORY AND DIRECTORY OF LARAMIE CITY, WYOMING TERRITORY, COMPRISING A BRIEF HISTORY OF LARAMIE CITY FROM ITS FIRST SETTLEMENT TO THE PRESENT TIME . . . LARAMIE CITY: DAILY SENTINEL PRINT, 1875.*

[1]–91, [92–96 blank]. 22.5 x 14.5 cm. Blue printed wrappers with title on front wrapper, advertisements on verso of back wrapper. In a blue cloth case.

Ref.: AII (*Wyoming*) 23; Bradford 5479; Howes T351; Jennewein 83 note; Jones 1579

Advertisements on versos, pages 4–50 inclusive. Includes a Directory of Laramie City.

4192   TRIGGS, J. H.

HISTORY OF CHEYENNE AND NORTHERN WYOMING EMBRACING THE GOLD FIELDS OF THE BLACK HILLS, POWDER RIVER AND BIG HORN COUNTRIES . . . OMAHA, NEB.: PRINTED AT THE HERALD STEAM BOOK AND JOB PRINTING HOUSE, 1876.

[1]–144. 22.6 x 15 cm. Folding map: Map of Wyoming. / Drawn by W. M. Masi, Surveyor, etc., for J. H. Triggs' History of Cheyenne and Northern Wyoming. (See Masi's New Itinerary Map of Wyoming.) / [below border:] Copyright secured according to Act of Congress, by J. H. Triggs, 1875. / 30.1 x 38.4 cm. Scale: thirty-six miles to one inch. Blue printed wrappers, with title on front wrapper, prospectus on verso of front wrapper, advertisements on recto and verso of back wrapper. In a blue cloth case.

Ref.: AII (*Nebraska*) 443; Bradford 5480; Howes T352; Jennewein 83

Pages 132–44 carry a business directory for Cheyenne.

Some copies comprise only 143 pages.

4193   TRIGGS, J. H.

A RELIABLE AND CORRECT GUIDE TO THE BLACK HILLS, POWDER RIVER, AND BIG HORN GOLD FIELDS! FULL DESCRIPTION OF THE COUNTRY. HOW TO GET TO IT. INCLUDING A CORRECT MAP OF THE GOLD REGIONS GOLD DISCOVERIES TO FEB. 1, 1876 . . . OMAHA, NEB.: PRINTED AT THE HERALD STEAM BOOK AND JOB PRINTING HOUSE, 1876.

[1]–144. 21.9 x 14.8 cm. Folding map: Map of Wyoming. / Drawn by W. M. Masi, Surveyor, etc., for J. H. Triggs' History of Cheyenne and Northern Wyoming. (See Masi's New Itinerary Map of Wyoming.) / [below border:] Copyright secured according to Act of Congress, by J. H. Triggs, 1875. / 29.9 x 38.3 cm. Scale: 36 miles to one inch. Gray printed wrappers with title on front wrapper, advertisements on verso of front and recto and verso of back wrapper. In a blue cloth case.

Ref.: AII (*Nebraska*) 444; Howes T353

Except for the first sixteen pages, this is identical with the Triggs' *History of Cheyenne and Northern Wyoming* . . . 1876.

4194 TRIGGS, J. H.

ANOTHER COPY. Red fabrikoid.

4195 TRIPLETT, FRANK

CONQUERING THE WILDERNESS; OR, NEW PIC-
TORIAL HISTORY OF THE LIFE AND TIMES OF THE
PIONEER HEROES AND HEROINES OF AMERICA . . .
NEW YORK: N. D. THOMPSON & COMPANY, 1883.

[I]–XXXIX, [XL blank], [15]–716. 22.8 x 15 cm.
200 illustrations listed. Plum pictorial cloth.
Ref.: Adams 1015; Rader 3149

4196 TRIPLETT, FRANK

THE LIFE, TIMES AND TREACHEROUS DEATH OF
JESSE JAMES . . . CHICAGO, ILL.: J. H. CHAMBERS &
CO., 1882.

[i]–xvi, [17]–416. 18 x 11.8 cm. Illustrations unlisted. Green pictorial cloth, title in gilt on front
cover and on backstrip.
Ref.: Adams 1017; Howes T355a

4197 TRI-STATE OLD SETTLERS' AS-
SOCIATION

REPORT OF THE ORGANIZATION AND FIRST RE-
UNION OF THE TRI-STATE OLD SETTLERS' ASSOCIA-
TION, OF ILLINOIS, MISSOURI AND IOWA . . . KEO-
KUK, IOWA: TRI-STATE PRINTING CO., 1884.

[i–iv, iv blank], [1]–68. 21.6 x 14.2 cm.

BOUND WITH:

REPORT OF THE SECOND REUNION OF THE TRI-STATE
OLD SETTLERS' ASSOCIATION . . . KEOKUK, IOWA:
R. B. OGDEN & SON.

[1]–112.

BOUND WITH:

REPORT OF THE THIRD REUNION OF THE TRI-STATE
OLD SETTLERS' ASSOCIATION . . . KEOKUK, IOWA:
TRI-STATE PRINTING CO., 1887.

[1]–89, [90 blank].

BOUND WITH:

REPORT OF THE FOURTH REUNION OF THE TRI-STATE
OLD SETTLERS' ASSOCIATION . . . KEOKUK, IOWA:
PRESS OF THE GATE CITY, 1887.

[1]–84. Four volumes bound together, green contemporary board sides with original red leather
label of James C. Davis, Keokuk, Iowa, on front
cover, new calf backstrip and corners.
Prov.: Inscribed on front endleaf: Please accept this / with Compliments of / yours truly /
C. F. Davis / Keokuk Febry 18*th* 1888 /. Mr.
Davis was chairman of the Committee on Invitations each year.
Ref.:

4198 TROBRIAND, PHILIPPE REGIS
DENIS DE KEREDERN

. . . VIE MILITAIRE DANS LE DAKOTA: NOTES ET
SOUVENIRS (1867–1869). PARIS: LIBRAIRIE ANCIEN-
NE HONORE CHAMPION, 1926.*

[i]–xvi, 1–407, [408 colophon]. 25 x 16.2 cm.
Portrait. Printed wrappers, uncut, unopened.
Ref.: Howes T356

4199 TROUT, PETER L.

PROSPECTORS' MANUAL BEING A FULL AND COM-
PLETE HISTORY AND DESCRIPTION OF THE NEWLY
DISCOVERED GOLD MINES ON GRANITE CREEK, THE
CANYON OF THE TULAMEEN RIVER, AND OTHER
NEW MINERAL DISCOVERIES IN THE SIMILKAMEEN
COUNTRY . . . 1886.

[i–ii], [1]–64, with advertising leaves of blue paper interspersed throughout. 21.9 x 14.7 cm.
Two sketch maps inserted after title-page and
before page [13]. Gray-green printed wrappers,
with title on front wrapper, advertisements on
verso of front and verso of back wrapper.
Ref.: Smith 10321
Probably printed at Victoria, British Columbia.
Advertisements on blue paper appear before
pages [1], 9, 25, 33, 41, 49, and after 64. There is
a small blue slip before page 61.

4200 TROWBRIDGE, MARY E. D.

PIONEER DAYS. THE LIFE-STORY OF GERSHOM AND
ELIZABETH DAY . . . PHILADELPHIA: AMERICAN
BAPTIST PUBLICATION SOCIETY.*

[1]–160. 18.1 x 12 cm. Portrait. Green cloth.
Ref.: Howes T359
Published in 1895.
Included is a brief account of an overland
crossing in 1849. Gershom Day was killed by
Indians in 1852.

4201 TRUMAN, BENJAMIN C.

OCCIDENTAL SKETCHES . . . SAN FRANCISCO: SAN
FRANCISCO NEWS COMPANY, 1881.

[1]–212, [213 blank, 214 vignette], [215–28 ad-
vertisements]. (Pages [1–2] blank.) 17.2 x 11.5
cm. Dark purple cloth, title on front cover and
backstrip in gilt.
Ref.: Cowan p. 645; Howes T365
Pages 181–203 carry an account of Tiburcio
Vasquez; Truman later published a biography of
the bandit.

4202 TRUTH TELLER

[Newspaper] TRUTH TELLER. DEVOTED TO THE
DISSEMINATION OF TRUTH, AND THE SUPPRESSION

OF HUMBUG. EDITED BY ANN ONYMOUS. STEILA-
COOM, W. T., FEBRUARY 3 [&25], 1858. VOL. NO.
000 [sic] . . .

[1–4]. [1–4]. 45.3 x 30.4 cm. 41.2 x 30.1 cm. Two
issues, unbound.

Ref.: Meany p. 276; Oregon Hist. Soc. *Quarterly*, March, 1949, pp. 31–39

Only two numbers of this paper, which was a
defense of the actions of certain army personnel
during the affair of Leschi, were issued. August
V. Kautz, William F. Tolmie, and Frank Clark
seem to have been responsible for the paper and
Kautz probably did most of the writing. The
first number helped delay the execution of Leschi
and the second was issued after he had been
strangled.

4203 TUCKER, EPHRAIM W.

A HISTORY OF OREGON, CONTAINING A CONDENSED
ACCOUNT OF THE MOST IMPORTANT VOYAGES AND
DISCOVERIES.[!] OF THE SPANISH, AMERICAN AND
ENGLISH NAVIGATORS ON THE NORTH WEST COAST
OF AMERICA; AND OF THE DIFFERENT TREATIES
RELATIVE TO THE SAME . . . BUFFALO: PRINTED BY
A. W. WILGUS, 1844.

[i]–viii, [9]–84. 21.1 x 13.2 cm. Blue printed
wrappers with title on front wrapper, uncut.
New backstrip, repair to title-leaf.

Ref.: Bradford 5496; Howes T378; Sabin
97298; Smith 10328; Wickersham 4133

4204 TUCKER, JOSEPH C.

TO THE GOLDEN GOAL AND OTHER SKETCHES . . .
SAN FRANCISCO: WILLIAM DOXEY, 1895.

[1]–303, [304 blank]. 17.4 x 11.5 cm. Nine
plates. Tan pictorial cloth.

Ref.: Cowan p. 646; Howes T381

Fifty copies were printed for private circulation.

Tucker left New York by ship in 1848 for
California. His sketches include experiences
searching for gold, hunting, filibustering with
Walker, and a trip overland in a Butterfield
stage.

4205 [TUFTS, JAMES]

A TRACT DESCRIPTIVE OF MONTANA TERRITORY;
WITH A SKETCH OF ITS MINERAL AND AGRICUL-
TURAL RESOURCES. NEW YORK: ROBERT CRAIG-
HEAD, PRINTER, 1865.*

[1]–15, [16 blank]. 22.9 x 15.3 cm. Stapled into
plain thick manila boards, uncut, partially
unopened.

Ref.: Smith 10339

Limited to 24 copies on fine paper.

4206 TULLIDGE'S QUARTERLY MAGA-
ZINE

TULLIDGE'S QUARTERLY MAGAZINE. VOLUME I
[–THREE]. SALT LAKE CITY, UTAH: PUBLISHED BY
EDWARD W. TULLIDGE.

[i–iv], [1]–176. [177]–352. [353]–528. [529]–704.
[i–viii], [1]–[176], [1–6 advertisements]. [i–iv ad-
vertisements], [177]–376, [1–4 advertisements].
[i–iv], [377]–576, [1–6 advertisements]. [i–ii ad-
vertisements], [577]–788, [1–4 advertisements].
[i–vi], [1]–112, [1–4 advertisements]. [i–ii],
[113]–224, [1–2 advertisements]. [i–ii], [225]–
336, [1–2 advertisements]. [i–ii], [337]–512, [1–2
advertisements]. 25.9 to 24.8 x 17.3 cm. Illustrated. Three volumes in twelve original parts,
original printed wrappers.

Prov.: Laid in is a presentation inscription:
Presented to / Joseph Hall, / by his friend, /
Edward W. Tullidge. / Ogden Utah, Sept 1st,
1882. /

Ref.:

Published from 1880 to 1885. Superseded by
the *Western Galaxy*.

4207 TURNBULL, THOMAS

. . . TRAVELS FROM THE UNITED STATES ACROSS
THE PLAINS TO CALIFORNIA . . . MADISON: PUB-
LISHED FOR THE SOCIETY, 1914.*

[i–ii], 151–225, [226 blank]. 22.8 x 14.9 cm.
Sketch maps in text. Brown printed wrappers,
with title on front wrapper.

Ref.:

This detailed diary of an 1852 trip was edited
by Paxson and Thwaites. The route pursued was
the Mormon trail. This is a real overland—the
original diary is now in WHi.—EDG

A separate from the *Proceedings of the State
Historical Society of Wisconsin*, 1913, pages
151–225.

4208 [TURNER, E. B.]

[Wrapper title] REMINISCENCES OF MORRIS, AND
HISTORY OF THE CONGREGATIONAL CHURCH. A DIS-
COURSE; DELIVERED DECEMBER 4TH, 1864. CHI-
CAGO: CHURCH, GOODMAN & DONNELLEY, STEAM
BOOK AND JOB PRINTERS, 1865.

[1]–16. 21.7 x 13.8 cm. Tan printed wrappers,
with title on front wrapper.

Ref.: AII (*Chicago*) 989

Enclosed is a broadside (20.2 x 12.4 cm.) is-
sued by Joseph E. Roy as agent for the American
Home Missionary Society headed: The Fruit of
Home Missions.

4209 TURNER, FREDERICK J.

[Wrapper title] THE SIGNIFICANCE OF THE FRON-TIER IN AMERICAN HISTORY . . . MADISON: STATE HISTORICAL SOCIETY OF WISCONSIN, 1894.

[1]–34, [35–36 blank]. 24.7 x 15.8 cm. Gray printed wrappers with title on front wrapper. In a yellow cloth case.

Ref.: Grolier 96; Howes T422

4210 TURNER, JOHN

PIONEERS OF THE WEST . . . CINCINNATI: JENNINGS AND PYE.

[1]–404. 20.3 x 14 cm. Dark blue ribbed cloth.
Ref.: Howes T424
Copyrighted 1903.

4211 [TURNER, TIMOTHY G.]

TURNER'S GUIDE FROM THE LAKES TO THE ROCKY MOUNTAINS, VIA THE CLEVELAND AND TOLEDO, MICHIGAN SOUTHERN AND NORTHERN INDIANA, CHICAGO AND NORTH-WESTERN, AND UNION PA-CIFIC RAILROADS; ALSO, FROM MISSOURI VALLEY, VIA THE PACIFIC AND SIOUX CITY RAILROAD, AND THE STEAMBOATS OF THE NORTH-WEST TRANSPOR-TATION COMPANY; INCLUDING A HISTORICAL AND STATISTICAL ACCOUNT OF THE RAILROADS OF THE COUNTRY, TOWNS AND CITIES ALONG THE ROUTE . . . CHICAGO: SPALDING & LAMONTES, PRINTERS, 1868.

[1]–288. (Pages [1]–12 and [249]–288 advertise-ments.) 21.9 x 14.7 cm. Green cloth, title in gilt on backstrip, red edges.
Ref.:
The Studebaker advertisement inserted be-tween pages 4 and 5 is printed in color.

4212 [TURNER, W. S.]

NOTES BY A WANDERER FROM DEMERARA, IN THE UNITED STATES. DEMERARA: J. THOMSON; "AR-GOSY" OFFICE, 1885.

[i–iv, iv blank], [1]–126, [127–28 blank]. 20.7 x 13.8 cm. Blue printed boards, black cloth back, with title on front cover.
Ref.:
Said to be the only piece of Western Ameri-cana printed in British Guiana.

4213 TURNLEY, PARMENAS T.

AUTOGRAPH LETTER, SIGNED. 1893 June 25, High-land Park, Illinois. Three pages, 17.8 x 11.1 cm. To Dr. Piper.

Letter of presentation and explanation of his *Reminiscences* . . . [1892]. In the letter, Turnley states 250 copies were printed for private dis-tribution. Laid in the book.

4214 TURNLEY, PARMENAS T.

AUTOGRAPH LETTER, SIGNED. 1900 March 28, Highland Park, Illinois. Two pages, 25.1 x 20 cm. To Robert H. Haslam.

Regarding writing a letter to Major John Clem (possibly Clum) and other matters of reminiscence. Haslam and Turnley were associ-ates in the Army. Laid in Turnley: *Reminiscences* . . . [1892].

4215 TURNLEY, PARMENAS T.

[Wrapper title] DEW DROPS. TURNLEY'S TOWER ATTIC DEN, 1900.

Four broadsides. 21.6 x 14.2 cm. to 23.9 x 15.3 cm. Portrait. Pale green printed wrappers, punched and tied with brown cord.
Prov.: Inscribed on portrait: To Misses Lizzie and Frddie[!] Skinner / With Compli-ments / P. T. Turnley / Highland Park Ill— / July 31, 1900. /
Ref.:
The broadsides were probably issued sepa-rately also. They consist of the following: un-titled poem, 1st line reads: "How we poor mor-tals change;" "My Little Canoe," "Turnley's Epigram of the Battle of Leesburg, Va.," ". . . Turnley's Epitaph."

A duplicate copy, but a variant, is laid in Turnley: *Reminiscences* . . . [1892].

4216 TURNLEY, PARMENAS T.

PRIVATE LETTERS OF PARMENAS TAYLOR TURNLEY, (TOGETHER WITH SOME LETTERS OF HIS FATHER AND GRANDFATHER,) ON THE CHARACTER OF THE CONSTITUTIONAL GOVERNMENT OF THE UNITED STATES, AND THE ANTAGONISMS OF PURITANS TO CHRISTIANITY, &C. . . . LONDON: PRINTED BY HARRISON AND SONS, 1863.

[i]–xii, [1]–194. 22.3 x 13.9 cm. Brown cloth, blind embossed borders on sides, title in gilt on backstrip, uncut.
Ref.: Howes T428
On the verso of the title-leaf is the following note: It is desirable this should *not* reach any American Official.

The dedication is signed Cinderella Living-ston Turnley, Canton, Mississippi, April 4th, 1863.

4217 TURNLEY, PARMENAS T.

REMINISCENCES OF PARMENAS TAYLOR TURNLEY, FROM THE CRADLE TO THREE-SCORE AND TEN . . . CHICAGO, ILL.: DONOHUE & HENNEBERRY.

[i–ii], [1]–448. 19.1 x 13.1 cm. Seven illustrations unlisted. Blue cloth, blind borders and corner ornaments on sides, title in gilt on backstrip.

Prov.: Inscribed on verso of first blank leaf: To / The Racine College / Library with / Compliments of the / Author / P. T. Turnley / Highland Park Ill, / June 28. 1893 / [underline] / ※ Verba animi preferre, / et vitam impendere vero. / ※ To speak the words of the wind / and to stake one's life for the truth /. [reference marks and last two lines in red ink].

Ref.: Howes T429

Copyrighted 1892. After service in the Mexican war, this West Pointer campaigned for ten years in Nebraska, Dakota and Utah.—Howes

Tipped in at the front is an Autograph Letter, signed, 1893 June 25, Highland Park, Ill. Laid in is an Autograph Letter, signed, 1900 March 28, Highland Park, Ill. Laid in is a newspaper clipping about Turnley, with portrait. Laid in is a broadside; .... January 1st, 1892 .... / [short rule] / Turnley's Epitaph / ... By Himself ... / [short rule] / [24 lines] / [short rule] / "January 1st, 1900—Addendum—After Seven Years" / [6 lines] / [within rule border]. Text, 20.7 x 11.5 cm. Paper, 25.3 x 15.4 cm. Seven-line manuscript note on verso plus signature: P. T. Turnley /.

Tipped in after the title-page is a carbon copy of a typewritten note, 14.8 x 12 cm., regarding the difficulties of compiling the work.

4218   TURRILL, H. B.

HISTORICAL REMINISCENCES OF THE CITY OF DES MOINES ... DES MOINES, IOWA: REDHEAD & DAWSON, 1857.

[i]–viii, [9]–114, [115–44 advertisements]. 17 x 13 cm. Eight plates, including double-page frontispiece: Des Moines, Iowa / From Capitol Hill, 1857. / [lower left:] Drawn by W. R. Wheeler. / Tan printed wrappers with title on front wrapper, advertisements on verso of front and recto and verso of back wrapper. In a blue cloth folder.

Ref.: Bradford 5508; Howes T432; Moffit 333; Mott (*Iowa*) p. 52

Pages 73–84: City Charter. Pages 115–44; advertisements.

4219   TURRILL, HENRY S.

A VANISHED RACE OF ABORIGINAL FOUNDERS ... DELIVERED BEFORE THE NEW YORK SOCIETY OF THE ORDER OF THE FOUNDERS AND PATRIOTS OF AMERICA ... FEBRUARY 14, 1907. PUBLISHED BY THE SOCIETY.*

[1]–23, [24 blank]. 22.5 x 15.2 cm. White printed wrappers, with title on front wrapper.

Ref.: Rader 3160

Reminiscences of experiences among the Apaches of New Mexico and Arizona.

4220   TUTTLE, EDMUND B.

BORDER TALES AROUND THE CAMP FIRE, IN THE ROCKY MOUNTAINS ... LONDON: SAMPSON LOW, MARSTON, SEARLE & RIVINGTON, 1878.

[i]–[xviii, xviii blank], [1]–243, [244 blank], [245–47 advertisements, 248 blank]. 18.8 x 12.4 cm. Nine illustrations listed. Brown pictorial cloth, title on front cover and backstrip, uncut.

Ref.: Howes T435

These tales—including a fine account of the Fall of the Alamo—were told on a surveying expedition from Omaha to the Yellowstone country.—Howes

Editions: New York, 1878.

4221   TUTTLE, EDMUND B.

THE BOY'S BOOK ABOUT INDIANS. BEING WHAT I SAW AND HEARD FOR THREE YEARS ON THE PLAINS ... PHILADELPHIA: J. B. LIPPINCOTT & CO., 1873.

[i]–xii, 13–207, [208 blank], [209–16 advertisements]. 17.7 x 11.5 cm. Seven illustrations, unlisted. Green cloth, front cover stamped with black designs, back cover in blind, title in gilt on backstrip.

Ref.: Howes T436

The author, chaplain at several Wyoming army posts, describes Ft. Kearney, Sweetwater and Plum Creek Indian fights.—Howes

4222   TWIN LAKE MINING DISTRICT (Utah Territory)

[Broadside] [line in manuscript: on Peoria Lode Above] UTAH TERRITORY, TWIN LAKE MINING DISTRICT. BE IT KNOWN, THAT [in manuscript: E. W. Holman,] IS THE OWNER OF [in manuscript: Silver] MINING CLAIM, NO. [in manuscript: 57] ... GIVEN UNDER MY HAND, AT [in manuscript: Hamilton], IN SAID DISTRICT THIS [in manuscript: Sept], 186_ [numeral 0 supplied in manuscript] [in manuscript: C. S. Higgins] RECORDER. [in manuscript: L. W. Davis,] PRESIDENT. ROCKY MOUNTAIN NEWS PRINTING COMPANY.

Broadside, 12.4 x 19.6 cm. Text, 11 x 17 cm.

Ref.:

Assigned or endorsed on verso in manuscript·

4223   TWINING, WILLIAM

ADDRESS ON MORAL EDUCATION, BASED ON THE STUDY OF THE BIBLE AS A SCHOOL BOOK ... RISING SUN, IND.: PRINTED FOR THE ASSOCIATION, 1836.

[1]–12. 24.3 x 15 cm. Sewn, unbound.

Ref.: Byrd & Peckham 661

4224 TWOGOOD, JAMES H.

A COLLECTION OF MANUSCRIPTS, DOCUMENTS AND LETTERS BY AND TO JAMES H. TWOGOOD. 68 pages, various sizes. As detailed below.

AUTOGRAPH MANUSCRIPT, SIGNED, of: A Little Reminiscence of the First settlement / Of Southern Oregon, And the Upbuilders of Idaho / Territory— /. Twenty pages, 26.2 x 19.8 cm.

AUTOGRAPH MANUSCRIPT (fragment) of reminiscences. Eight pages (pages 4–11), 26.2 x 19.8 cm.

AUTOGRAPH DOCUMENT, SIGNED. 1888 February 23, Ada County, Idaho Territory. Eight pages, 35.6 x 21.8 cm. Includes one-page notarization by A. L. Richardson, signed.

Long, good account of an attack by Indians on Cow Creek, Oregon Territory, October 24, 1855.

AUTOGRAPH DOCUMENT (incomplete): Statement of James H. Twogood / Of Boise City Idaho, in regard to Loses[!] sustained by / Indian depredations during the Indian Wars of 1853, & 1855 & 6 /. Six pages, 31.5 x 20.3 cm. and a fragment 8.1 x 20.3 cm. Accompanied by a manuscript copy of part of an affidavit by Twogood, in pencil, one page, 31.7 x 19.7 cm.

CARBON COPY OF A TYPED LETTER (incomplete) by Twogood. 1897 November 10, Boise, Idaho. Twelve pages, 27.7 x 21.3 cm. Reminiscences and descriptions of his claims against the Federal government.

AUTOGRAPH LETTER, SIGNED, by O. L. Carter. 1888 February 16, Roseburg, Oregon. One page, 21.5 x 13.5 cm. To James H. Twogood. Regarding Twogood's claims.

AUTOGRAPH LETTER, SIGNED, by O. L. Carter. 1888 March 2, Roseburg, Ore. Two pages, 25.3 x 21 cm. To Twogood. Re his claims. Accompanied by a one-page Memorandum giving instructions.

AUTOGRAPH LETTER, SIGNED, by B. F. Dowell. 1888 August 14, Jacksonville, Ore. Two pages, 32 x 20.3 cm. To Twogood. Re his claims. Accompanied by five pages (33 x 20.2 cm.) of questions, typed carbon copy.

4225 TWOGOOD, JAMES H.

[Broadside] REMINISCENCES OF THE FIRST SETTLEMENTS OF SOUTHERN OREGON, EARLY TIMES IN IDAHO AND A FEW OF IDAHO'S PIONEERS, THE UPBUILDERS OF THE TERRITORY, WITH BRIEF REMINISCENCES OF A FEW GOOD FRIENDS OF OLDEN TIMES— FIRST GOLD DISCOVERIES NORTH OF CALIFORNIA— BY "UNCLE JIMMY TWOGOOD . . .

Broadside, 63.6 x 44.3 cm. Text, 59.9 x 40.8 cm. Fragile.

Dated at the end: August, 1910.

Included is a two-column portrait of Twogood. The text comprises a re-write of the first item listed above and some additional materials.

Accompanied by a newspaper clipping, no date, no source, comprising additional reminiscences of Twogood relating to Alexander Rossi.

4226 TYLER, DANIEL

A CONCISE HISTORY OF THE MORMON BATTALION IN THE MEXICAN WAR. 1846–1847 . . . 1881.

[1–2], [i]–viii, [9]–376. 22.1 x 14.8 cm. Dark red leather, title in gilt on backstrip, blind panels on sides, gilt edges.

Ref.: Howes T447

Printed at Salt Lake City.

Detailed narrative, by a member, of the memorable march of this organization from Council Bluffs to San Diego. Though dated 1881, internal statements indicate its actual publication in 1882.—Howes

Note similarity in binding tools to Little: *From Kirtland to Salt Lake City . . . 1891.*

4227 [TYSON, JOHN S.]

LIFE OF ELISHA TYSON, THE PHILANTHROPIST . . . BALTIMORE: PRINTED BY B. LUNDY, 1825.

[i]–vii, [viii blank], [1]–142. 16.4 x 10 cm. Portrait. Full straight-grain calf, red edges.

Prov.: Inscribed on blank leaf at front: To / George Story / from his sincere friend / Isaac Tyson Jr / [paraph] / Balt⁰ 4 Mo 3ᵈ 1846 /.

Ref.: Howes T453; Sabin 97650

Sabin's collation differs slightly: "16mo, pp. (7), verso blank, 142, and errata slip. Frontispiece portrait. Some copies have the preliminary pages numbered vii."

Describes his 1803 trip to Ohio with Gerard T. Hopkins.—Howes

4228 [TYSON, JOHN S.]

ANOTHER COPY. Gray boards, printed label. With the errata, but without the portrait.

U

4229 UDALL & HOPKINS, Chicago

UDALL & HOPKINS' CHICAGO CITY DIRECTORY, FOR 1852 & '53 . . . CHICAGO: PUBLISHED BY UDALL & HOPKINS, 1852.

[i–iv advertisements inserted before endleaf], blank leaf, [1]–294. 16.8 x 10.8 cm. Folding map: Map / of the / City of / Chicago. / Published by / A H & C. Burley. / 1852. / 33.8 x 26.6 cm. No scale given. Yellow printed boards, black roan back. With title on front cover, advertisements on back cover and both inner covers, title on backstrip.

Ref.: AII (*Chicago*) 33; Byrd 1899; Howes U1; Sabin 12641

Pages [225]–94: advertisements.

4230 UDELL, JOHN

INCIDENTS OF TRAVEL TO CALIFORNIA, ACROSS THE GREAT PLAINS; TOGETHER WITH THE RETURN TRIP THROUGH CENTRAL AMERICA AND JAMAICA . . . JEFFERSON, OHIO: PRINTED FOR THE AUTHOR, AT THE SENTINEL OFFICE, 1856.

[i]–viii, [9]–302, [303 errata, 304 blank]. 17.8 x 11.5 cm. Portrait. Black cloth, sides embossed in blind, backstrip gilt and with title.

Ref.: Cowan pp. 648–49; Howes U3; Sabin 97663; Wagner-Camp 281

The frontispiece portrait is signed by the author: Your Friend / John Udell /.

Pasted to the inside front cover is a small newspaper clipping regarding the Udell family. There are pencil notes on a blank leaf at the back; there are also corrections in pencil throughout the volume.

4231 UDELL, JOHN

JOURNAL OF JOHN UDELL, KEPT DURING A TRIP ACROSS THE PLAINS, CONTAINING AN ACCOUNT OF THE MASSACRE OF A PORTION OF HIS PARTY BY THE MOHAVE INDIANS, IN 1859 . . . JEFFERSON: ASHTABULA SENTINEL STEAM PRESS PRINT, 1868.

[1]–[48]. 22 x 14.2 cm. Portrait of Udell, on page [48]. Tan printed wrappers with title on front wrapper. In a blue half morocco case.

Ref.: Cowan p. 649; Howes U4; Jones 1513; Sabin 97663 note; Wagner-Camp 346a

See also a copy of the *Ashtabula Sentinel*, Vol. XXVIII, No. 14, Jefferson, Ohio, April 7, 1859, containing a letter from John Udell to his brothers dated Alberquerque[!], New Mexico, March 5, 1859. This letter contains details of his journey and troubles thus far including the Indian fight.—EDG

Editions: Suisun City, California, 1859.

4232 UMFREVILLE, EDWARD

THE PRESENT STATE OF HUDSON'S BAY. CONTAINING A FULL DESCRIPTION OF THAT SETTLEMENT, AND THE ADJACENT COUNTRY; AND LIKEWISE OF THE FUR TRADE . . . LONDON: PRINTED FOR CHARLES STALKER, MDCCXC.

[*]², a⁴, A–O⁴, P². [1–4], [i]–vii, [viii blank], [1]–128, 133–230, [231–32 advertisements]. 22.3 x 13.3 cm. Text: 23 x 14.5 cm. One plate and two folding tables. Original gray boards, cream paper backstrip, uncut. In blue cloth case.

Ref.: Cox II p. 163; Howes U10; JCB III,

3428; Jones 615; Sabin 97702; Staton & Tremaine 602; Stevens (*Nuggets*) 2722

A searching criticism of the Hudson's Bay Company.

4233 UMSTED, JUSTUS T.

A PLEA FOR THE PRIORITY OF DOMESTIC MISSIONS; A DISCOURSE DELIVERED BEFORE THE SYNOD OF IOWA, IN BURLINGTON, OCT. 12, 1856 . . . KEOKUK: O. CLEMENS, BOOK AND JOB PRINTER, 1856.

[1]–28. 22.2 x 14.3 cm. Sewn, removed from binding, unbound.

Ref.: Moffitt 262

4234 UNION AGRICULTURALIST, THE...

THE UNION AGRICULTURALIST AND WESTERN PRAIRIE FARMER, DEVOTED TO THE IMPROVEMENT OF WESTERN AGRICULTURE. EDITED BY THE CORRESPONDING SECRETARY. VOLUME I. CHICAGO: PUBLISHED BY THE UNION AGRICULTURAL SOCIETY, 1841.

[1]–96. 39.5 x 26.7 cm. Twelve parts bound together in black cloth.

Ref.:

Continuation of the *Union Agriculturalist*.

4235 UNION COLONY OF COLORADO

FIRST ANNUAL REPORT OF THE UNION COLONY OF COLORADO, INCLUDING A HISTORY OF THE TOWN OF GREELEY, FROM ITS DATE OF SETTLEMENT TO THE PRESENT TIME . . . NEW-YORK: GEORGE W. SOUTHWICK, 1871.

[1]–40. 22.3 x 14 cm. Pink wrappers, with title on front wrapper, advertisements on verso of front and recto and verso of back wrapper.

Ref.: Bradford 1001; Howes C68; Wilcox p. 115

Apparently the map mentioned on the title-page was not issued with the pamphlet.

Text by William E. Pabor.

4236 UNION PACIFIC RAILROAD COMPANY

[Caption title] APPENDIX NO. 1. PRELIMINARY REPORT OF ENGINEER. TO THE CHAIRMAN OF COMMITTEE UNION PACIFIC R. R. CO.: . . .

[1]–8. 23.6 x 14.6 cm. Sewn, unbound.

Prov.: Inscribed on page [1]: Proof / Compliments / Thosˢ C Durant /.

Ref.:

Thomas C. Durant was one of the principal builders of the Union Pacific Railroad. Laid in are two newspaper clippings, one dated July 19, 1881 relative to Peter Anthony Dey and the Union Pacific Railroad. The other prints two letters by Dey regarding his resignation as Chief Engineer. Peter Anthony Dey signed the present report.

4237 UNION PACIFIC RAILROAD COMPANY

[Broadsheet] DESTROY ALL PREVIOUS TIME SCHEDULES. UNION PACIFIC RAILROAD, LODGE POLE DIVISION. TIME SCHEDULE NO. 15. TO TAKE EFFECT MONDAY, OCTOBER 26, 1868, AT 3:30 O'CLOCK, A. M. FOR THE GOVERNMENT AND INFORMATION OF EMPLOYES ONLY. THE COMPANY RESERVES THE RIGHT TO VARY THEREFROM AT PLEASURE. TRAINS WILL RUN DAILY . . . H. M. HOXIE, ASS'T SUP'T. R. J. NICHOLL, ACTING DIV., SUP'T. W. SNYDER, GEN'L SUP'T. OMAHA HERALD PRINT . . .

Broadsheet, 25.8 x 34.2 cm. Unbound.
Ref.:

The second page, printed at right angles, comprises Rules and Regulations. /, and Signals. /

Not listed in AII (*Nebraska*) although a similar schedule for the Bridger Division is listed, dated December 21, 1868.

4238 UNION PACIFIC RAILROAD COMPANY

GUIDE TO THE UNION PACIFIC RAILROAD LANDS. 12,000,000 ACRES BEST FARMING, GRAZING AND MINERAL LANDS IN AMERICA, IN THE STATE OF NEBRASKA AND TERRITORIES OF COLORADO, WYOMING AND UTAH, FOR SALE BY THE UNION PACIFIC RAILROAD COMPANY, IN TRACTS TO SUIT PURCHASERS AND AT LOW PRICES . . . OMAHA, NEBRASKA: LAND DEPARTMENT: UNION PACIFIC RAILROAD BUILDING, 1872.

[i]–iv, [5]–16, inserted leaf, unpaginated, 17–48. 22.4 x 15.2 cm. Map: Map / of the / Land Grant & Connections / of the / Union Pacific Railroad / 1037 Miles of Road / 12000000 Acres of Land / 1872. / National Railway Publication Co. Phila. / [upper left of cartouche:] Thoˢ L. Kimball / General Ticket Agent / Omaha. / [upper right of cartouche:] O. F. Davis / Land Commissioner / Omaha. / 17.3 x 68.7 cm. No scale given. Map: Map of the / Land Grant / of the / Union Pacific Railroad / in Nebraska / 4,250,000 Acres / [lower left:] Entered according to Act of Congress in the year 1873 by G. W. & C. B. Colton & Co in the Office of the Librarian of Congress, at Washington. / [lower centre:] Prepared by G. W. & C. B. Colton & Cº 172 William Street New York. / 19.3 x 64.7 cm. Scale: 18 miles to one inch. Buff printed wrappers with title on front wrapper; verso of front wrapper, scale of fares for travel; advertisement on recto of back wrapper, map on verso of back wrapper: Map of the / Union Pacific / Railroad / and its / Connections. / 10.9 x 18.9 cm. No scale given. This is similar to but not identical with the map on the verso of the back wrap-

per of Latham: *Trans-Missouri Stock-Raising . . .* 1871.

Ref.: AII (*Nebraska*) 330; *Railroad Economics* p. 295

On verso of title-page: [rule] / Fifth Edition. / [rule] /.

The earliest edition reported in *Railroad Economics* is Omaha, 1870. AII (*Nebraska*) reports three editions in 1870, Nos. 193, 194, 192.

The pamphlet is inserted in the case with Latham's *Trans-Missouri Stock-Raising . . .* 1871.

4239 UNION PACIFIC RAILROAD COMPANY

[Broadside] PASSENGER TARIFF OF THE UNION PACIFIC RAIL ROAD. TO TAKE EFFECT WEDNESDAY, MAY 13TH, 1868. TABLE OF RATES. TABLE OF DISTANCES . . . INSTRUCTIONS TO CONDUCTORS . . . C. D. WHITCOMB, GENERAL TICKET AGENT. W. SNYDER, GENERAL SUPERINTENDENT. OMAHA DAILY REPUBLICAN PRINT.

Broadside, 42.3 x 71.1 cm. Text, 36 x 64.8 cm. Printed in red and blue.
Ref.:

Not listed in AII (*Nebraska*), although another version for May 4, 1868 is listed.

4240 UNION PACIFIC RAILROAD COMPANY

[Caption title] RAILWAY PIONEER. PLATTE CITY, NEB., THURSDAY, OCTOBER 25, 1866 . . .

[1–4]. 23.5 x 15.9 cm. Unbound leaflet.
Ref.:

Commemorates the "formal opening of the Unton[!] Pacific Railroad—so far as finished—for travel and the transportation of commerce . . ."

A masthead on page [2] reads: Railway Pioneer. / [decorative rule] / Camp No. 2, U.P.R.R., Buffalo Co., Neb. / Thursday, October 25, 1866. / [decorative rule].

During the stay at Platte City, a paper called *The Railway Pioneer* was printed, the type, presses, and compositors having been brought from the Republican Office at Omaha.—*The Great Union Pacific Railroad Excursion to the Hundredth Meridian from New York to Platte City . . .* Chicago, 1867.

Page [3] carries a letter dated October 26, 1866.

4241 UNION PACIFIC RAILROAD COMPANY

REPORTS OF PRELIMINARY SURVEYS FOR THE UNION PACIFIC RAILWAY, EASTERN DIVISION, FROM FORT RILEY TO DENVER CITY. SMOKY HILL ROUTE BY

GEO. T. WICKES, C.E. REPUBLICAN FORK LINE BY P. GOLAY, C.E. UNDER DIRECTION OF R. M. SHOE-MAKER, CHIEF ENGINEER. CINCINNATI: ROBERT CLARKE & CO., 1866.

[1]–27, [28–30 blank]. 22.1 x 14.5 cm. Two folding maps. Facing title-page: Map / Showing the Line of the / Union Pacific Railway, E.D. / And its Connections. / [lower right:] Ehrgott, Forbriger & Co., Lithogr⁵, Cincinnati, O. / 39.6 x 115.3 cm. No scale given. Map: Union Pacific Railway, E. D. / Surveys of the Smoky Hill Route / by / Geo. T. Wickes, C.E. / and / of the Republican Route / by / P. Golay, C.E. / R. M. Shoemaker, Chief Engr. / [triple rule] / Scale: 12 Miles to 1 Inch. / [lower right:] Ehrgott, Forbriger & Co., Lithogr⁵ Cincinnati, O. 58.3 x 131 cm. Scale as above. Buff printed wrappers, with title on front wrapper. Lacks back wrapper.

Ref.: Howes S427; *Railway Economics* p. 300; Wheat (*Transmississippi*) 1156–57

4242   UNION PACIFIC RAILROAD COMPANY

[Broadsheet] TO THE GOLD FIELDS OF THE BLACK HILLS! VIA OMAHA & SIDNEY, OR CHEYENNE. THE UNION PACIFIC R. R. OFFERS THE QUICKEST, SAFEST AND MOST RELIABLE ROUTE TO THE NEW ELDORADO! . . . THOS. L. KIMBALL, GEN'L PASSENGER AND TICKET AGENT, OMAHA, NEB. OMAHA REPUBLICAN STEAM PRINT.

Broadsheet, 51.5 x 21 cm., folded to 21 x 13 cm. Unbound. In a brown stiff paper case.

Ref.:
The verso carries a four-page sketch with caption title: The New Gold Fields. / [short rule] / Their Mineral and Agricultural Resources as Indicative of their Future / Wealth. / [short rule] / Two Million Dollars In Gold from the Black Hills Placers in the Season of / 1876—The Peculiarly Rich Characteristics of their Natural / Veins so Far as Exploited. / [short rule] / Probable Cost of Living in the Hills during the following Season—The / Indian Question— Chances for Acquiring Claims, Etc. / The Best Route. / [short rule] / . . .

The correspondence comprising the text is dated from Deadwood City, Dakota, January 14, 1877.

4243   UNION PACIFIC RAILROAD COMPANY

[Caption title] UNION PACIFIC RAILROAD. REPORT OF F. M. CASE, OF SURVEYS OF CACHE LA POUDRE & SOUTH PLATTE ROUTES, AND OTHER MOUNTAIN PASSES IN COLORADO. OMAHA, NEB. T'Y, DEC. 15, 1864 . . .

[1]–11, [12 blank]. 22.2 x 14.4 cm. Stabbed, unbound.

Ref.: Railway Economics p. 296
Signed at end: Francis M. Case, / Div. Engr. / To T. C. Durant, Esq., / Vice-Pres't U. P. R. R. Co., No. 13 William st., New York. /

Without the seven plates which accompanied it when printed as Appendix B, *Report of Thomas C. Durant . . .* New York, 1866.

4244   UNION PACIFIC RAILROAD COMPANY

UNION PACIFIC RAILROAD. REPORT OF G. M. DODGE, CHIEF ENGINEER, TO THE BOARD OF DIRECTORS, ON A BRANCH RAILROAD LINE FROM THE UNION PACIFIC RAILROAD TO IDAHO, MONTANA, OREGON, AND PUGET'S SOUND. WASHINGTON, D. C.: PHILP & SOLOMONS, 1868.

[1]–13, [14–6 blank]. 23.5 x 15.1 cm. Folding map: U. P. R. R. Map / Showing Line of Branches / from U. P. R. R. to Portland Oregon, / Puget Sound Wash, Terr, and Montana. / To Accompany Report of / G. M. Dodge. / Chief Engⁱ / 1868. / 62.6 x 75.1 cm. No scale given. Cream printed wrappers with title on front wrapper. In a green cloth case.

Ref.: Railway Economics p. 296

4245   UNION PACIFIC RAILROAD COMPANY

UNION PACIFIC RAILROAD. REPORT OF G. M. DODGE, CHIEF ENGINEER, WITH ACCOMPANYING REPORTS OF CHIEFS OF PARTIES, FOR THE YEAR 1867. WASHINGTON: GOVERNMENT PRINTING OFFICE, 1868.

[1]–85, [86–8 blank]. 23 x 14.8 cm. Light gray printed wrappers, with title on front wrapper. In a green cloth case.

Ref.: Howes D394; *Railway Economics* p. 269

4246   UNION PACIFIC RAILROAD COMPANY

[Caption title] UNION PACIFIC RAILROAD. REPORT OF JAS. A. EVANS OF EXPLORATION FROM CAMP WALBACH TO GREEN RIVER. MONTROSE, PENNA., JAN. 3, 1865 . . .

[1]–24. 22.2 x 14.2 cm. Stabbed, unbound.

Ref.: Howes E223; *Railway Economics* p. 296; Wagner-Camp 414 see
Signed at end: Jas A. Evans, / Div. Eng. / To T. C. Durant, Esq., / Vice-Pres't U. P. R. R. Co., / 13 William st., New York. /

Without the two plates and two folding maps which accompanied it when printed as Appendix A, *Report of Thomas C. Durant . . .* New York, 1866.

4247 UNION PACIFIC RAILROAD COM-
PANY

[Caption title] UNION PACIFIC RAILROAD. REPORT
OF SAMUEL B. REED, OF SURVEYS AND EXPLORA-
TIONS FROM GREEN RIVER TO GREAT SALT LAKE
CITY. JOLIET, ILLINOIS, DEC. 24, 1864 . . .

[1]–15, [16 blank]. 22.2 x 14.4 cm. Stabbed,
unbound.

> *Ref.: Railway Economics* p. 296
> Signed on page 12: Samuel B. Reed, / Divi-
sion Engineer. / To T. C. Durant, Esq., / Vice-
Pres't U.P.R.R.Co., / No. 13 William st., New
York. /
> Without the five plates and two folding maps
which accompanied it when printed as Appendix
C, *Report of Thomas C. Durant . . . N. Y.,* 1866.

4248 UNION PACIFIC RAILROAD COM-
PANY

UNION PACIFIC RAILROAD. REPORT OF THE CHIEF
ENGINEER, FOR 1866. WASHINGTON, D. C.: PHILP &
SOLOMONS, 1868.

[1]–123, [124 blank]. 23.1 x 14.9 cm. Folding
map and six plates, unlisted. Folding map:
Union Pacific Rail Road, / Map / of Surveys in /
1864, 1865 & 1866, / from / Missouri River to
Pacific Ocean. / G. M. Dodge. / Chief Eng^r /
1868 / Scale 36 miles to an Inch. / 28.6 x 145.1
cm. Scale: 36 miles to one inch. Cream printed
wrappers, with title on front wrapper. In a green
cloth case.

> *Ref.: Howes D396; Railway Economics* p. 269

4249 UNION PACIFIC RAILROAD COM-
PANY

UNION PACIFIC RAILROAD. REPORT OF THOMAS C.
DURANT, VICE-PRESIDENT AND GENERAL MAN-
AGER, TO THE BOARD OF DIRECTORS, IN RELATION
TO THE OPERATIONS OF THE ENGINEER DEPART-
MENT, AND THE CONSTRUCTION OF THE ROAD, UP
TO THE CLOSE OF THE YEAR 1865. NEW YORK:
WM. C. BRYANT & CO., PRINTERS, 1866.

[i–ii], [1]–19, [20 blank], [1]–18, [1]–23, [24
blank], [1]–18, [1]–64. 22.9 x 14.3 cm. Buff
printed wrappers, with title on front wrapper
within decorative border. In a tan cloth case.

> *Ref.: Howes D592; Railway Economics* p. 296
> Appendix A: Instructions to Division En-
> gineers, and Correspondence
> respecting Surveys, 18 pp.
> B: Report of John A. Evans, Di-
> vision Engineer, 23 pp.
> C: Report of Samuel B. Reed, Di-
> vision Engineer, 18 pp.
> D: Change of Location west of
> Omaha. 64 pp.

4250 UNION PACIFIC RAILROAD COM-
PANY

UNION PACIFIC RAILROAD. REPORT OF THOMAS C.
DURANT, VICE-PRESIDENT AND GENERAL MANAG-
ER, TO THE BOARD OF DIRECTORS, IN RELATION
TO THE SURVEYS MADE UP TO THE CLOSE OF THE
YEAR 1864. NEW YORK: WM. C. BRYANT & CO.,
PRINTERS, 1866.

[i–ii], [1]–8, [1]–24, [1]–11, [12 blank], [1]–15,
[16 blank]. 23.2 x 14.5 cm. 14 plates and four
folding maps. Map: Union Pacific Rail Road /
Survey of 1864 / Black Hills / Vicinity of Old
Camp Walbach. / Scale 800 feet to 1 inch / The
Major & Knapp Eng. Mf'g & Lith. Co. 449
Broadway N. Y. / Jas. A. Evans Div. Eng^r /
25.6 x 57.4 cm. (paper size). Scale: 800 feet to
one inch. Map: Union Pacific Rail Road / Sur-
vey of 1864 / James A. Evans Div. Eng^r / Upper
Cañon of Muddy Creek / Scale 800 feet to an
inch / The Major & Knapp Eng. Mf'g & Lith.
Co. 449 Broadway N. Y. / 18.2 x 49.5 cm. (paper
size). Scale: 800 feet to one inch. Map: Union
Pacific Rail Road / Survey of 1864 / S. B. Reed
Div. Eng^r / Weber Cañon / from its Mouth at
O to Sta. 156. / Scale 800 feet to an inch / The
Major & Knapp Eng. Mf'g & Lith. Co. 449
Broadway N.Y. / 26.5 x 54.6 cm. (paper size).
Scale: 800 feet to one inch. *Inset:* Profile of Line
from Mouth of Weber Cañon at O to Station
N° 160 Scales [bracket] Horizontal 800 feet to
inch. / Vertical 40 feet to an inch. / 14.8 x 49.3
cm. Map: Union Pacific Rail Road / Survey of
1864 / S. B. Reed Div. Eng. / Section of Weber
Cañon / Station 990 to 1150 / Scale 800 feet to
an inch. / The Major & Knapp Eng. Mf'g &
Lith. Co. 449 Broadway N.Y. / 43.8 x 59 cm.
(paper size). Scale: 800 feet to one inch. *Inset:*
Profile of Section of Weber Cañon Station 990
to 1150 Scales [bracket] Horizontal 800 feet to
an inch. / Vertical 40 feet to an inch. / 22.1 x 51.2
cm. Buff printed wrappers, with title on front
wrapper. In a yellow cloth case.

> *Ref.: Howes D593; Railway Economics* p. 296
> Appendix A: Report of James A. Evans
> B: Report of Francis M. Case
> C: Report of Samuel B. Reed.
> The three engineers' reports were printed
separately also and are present in this form in
the Graff Collection, items 4246, 4243, and 4247.

4251 UNION PACIFIC RAILROAD COM-
PANY

UNITED STATES OF AMERICA. REPORT OF THE OR-
GANIZATION AND PROCEEDINGS OF THE UNION PA-
CIFIC RAILROAD CO. NEW YORK: WM. G. BRYANT &
CO., PRINTERS, 1864.

[i–vi], [1]–58, [1]–8, [1]–8, [i]–xiv, [i]–xx, [i]–iv. 23.1 x 14.8 cm. Two folding maps. Map: Map of the / Central Portion / of the / United States / Showing the Lines of the Proposed / Pacific Railroads / 19.9 x 78.1 cm. Scale: 100 miles to one inch. Map: Union Pacific Rail Road / [double rule] / Map of Part of Colorado Territory / Showing / Survey West of Denver City / by / Francis M. Case / Civil Engineer. / 1863. / [lower left:] Scale, 120 Chains to one inch / [decorative rule] / [at foot, left:] Delineated By J. J. O'Brien C.E. [at right:] Latimer Bro⁸ & Seymour, N.Y. / 29 3 64 /. 30 x 90.4 cm. Scale as above. Buff printed wrappers with title on front wrapper. In a tan cloth case.

Prov.: Inscribed at head of front wrapper: Hon J S Morrill /.

Ref.: Howes D360; *Railway Economics* p. 296; Wheat (*Transmississippi*) 1111–12

Appendices No. 1 and No. 1a, both signed by Peter A. Dey, are printed on whiter paper than the rest of the volume and are paginated in Arabic numerals.

4252 UNION PACIFIC RAILROAD COMPANY

[Wrapper title] UNION PACIFIC RAILROAD: THE GREAT NATIONAL HIGHWAY BETWEEN THE MOUNTAINS AND THE EAST. THE DIRECT ROUTE TO COLORADO, UTAH, IDAHO, MONTANA, NEVADA, AND CALIFORNIA. OPEN FROM OMAHA TO JULESBURG. CHICAGO: HORTON & LEONARD BOOK AND JOB PRINTERS, 1867.

[1]–16. 19.5 x 13.4 cm. Folding map at back: Union Pacific / Rail Road / and Connections. / (Main Line) / [lower right:] (See Appleton's Railway Guide.) / 15 x 22.2 cm. No scale given. Green printed wrappers, with title on front wrapper, advertisements on recto and verso of back wrapper.

Prov.: In pencil on page [1]: L. Foster Morse / Feb 20–1866 left Boston / Railroad to Atchinson Kansas / Fare 50. Stage to Denver Fare $150.00 / Express Baggage 20. At Denver March 5 / Meals $1.50 each / Passengers allowed 25 pounds /. In margins on page 14, upper margin in pencil: Rail Road opened to Julesburg June—1867 / " " " " Cheyenne Nov– 1867 /. In text, in pencil: North Platte Dec 66 / (Stage from Denver to North Platte Dec– 1866–198 miles / of staging saved /. In outer margin in ink: Was a passenger on the first train to / Julesburg also to Cheyenne–the opening of / train to North Platte Nov 66 saved 298 miles of staging– / [preceding written over pencil notes] /. In lower margin, in ink: Rail Road completed to North Platte / Dec–1866 to Jules-

burg June 1867 / to Cheyenne Nov 18 1867— 23 /. Lower margin, page 15, in pencil: Nov 18–1867 /. In pencil at top of front cover: one of the first advertisements /. On back cover, in pencil: opened to Julesburg / June 23–1867 / [lower margin] To Cheyenne Nov 18 1867 /.

Ref.:

Observe transportation costs noted by former owner.

4253 UNITED STATES. ARMY. Adjutant General's Office

[Caption title] GENERAL ORDERS, NO. 19. WAR DEPARTMENT, ADJUTANT GENERAL'S OFFICE, WASHINGTON, MARCH 30, 1849 . . .

[1]–2, [3–4 blank]. 17.8 x 11.9 cm. Unbound leaflet.

Ref.:

Regarding the establishment of military posts on the Oregon route and the withdrawal of garrisons from Forts Atkinson and Crawford.

4254 UNITED STATES. ARMY. Adjutant General's Office, etc.

[A COLLECTION OF MISCELLANEOUS GENERAL ORDERS AND CIRCULARS, SEPTEMBER 22, 1856 TO OCTOBER 20, 1861]

392 leaves, variously paginated. 17.1 x 11.4 cm. Full contemporary black calf, gilt title on backstrip, name in gilt on front cover.

Prov.: Stamped in gilt on front cover: R. L. Ogden. / A. Q. M. /

Ref.:

Comprises the following:

War Department, Adjutant General's Office, Washington, General Orders Nos. 12–14, September 22–November 12, 1856. Nos. 2–3, 6–12, February 28–August 29, 1857. Nos. 1–3, 5–16, January 25–December 16, 1858. Nos. 1–18, 21, 23–28, February 14–December 31, 1859. Nos. 1–13, 15–18, 20, 22–24, January 19–December 3, 1860. Nos. 1–32, 35–38, 40–43, 45–69, January 18–August 28, 1861.

Circular. Quartermaster General's Office, Washington City, October 10, 1856.

General Orders, No. 2. Headquarters of the Army, Adjutant General's Office, Washington, March 18, 1857; No. 8, May 28, 1857; No. 10, New York, June 17, 1857.

Orders, No. 1. Headquarters, Department of the Pacific, Benicia, California, February 9; No. 5. April 1; No. 6. April 14; No. 8. San Francisco, May 28; No. 9. Portland, O. T., July 7;

No. 11. San Francisco, September 3; No. 12. October 28, 1857.

General Orders, Nos. 1–10, 12–18, 21–22, Head Quarters of the Army, New York, January 8–November 10, 1858.

Orders, No. 1. Head Quarters Department of the Pacific, San Francisco, Cal., April 16, 1858.

General Orders, No. 2, 3, 5. Head-Quarters of the Army, New York, May 16–June 28–November 10, 1859.

Orders, No. 2–4. Head Quarters Dep't of California, San Francisco, June 23–August 2, 1859.

Circular. Office of Com. Genl. of Subsistence, Washington, January 1, 1859.

General Orders, Nos. 1–12. Head-Quarters of the Army, New York, January 10–December 8, 1860.

Orders No. 1. Head Quarters Dep't of California, San Francisco, April 30, 1860; unnumbered. October 18, 1860.

General Orders, No. 4. Head-Quarters, Department of Oregon, Fort Vancouver, W. T., April 18, 1860.

General Orders, Nos. 1–2, 7, 8, 10, 12–15. Head Quarters of the Army, New York, January 21–August 17, 1861.

Orders, Nos. 5–16, 18–25, 27, 28. Head Quarters, Dep't of the Pacific, San Francisco, April 25–October 20, 1861.

Circular. Head-Quarters, Department of the Pacific. San Francisco, September 30, 1861.

The collection seems to have been gathered in California. Several Orders bear notations of dates received from Washington in California. Numerous Orders are signed in manuscript. Of exceptional interest are Orders or Circulars relating to directions for keeping journals west of the Mississippi (No. 12, April 16, 1860); regulations for uniform and dress (No. 6, March 13, 1861); garrisoning of western posts and forts (No. 2, May 16, 1859); combats with hostile Indians from September 29, 1858, to October 18, 1859 (No. 5, November 10, 1859); disposition of troops in western forts and posts (No. 6, March 12, 1860); establishment of Fort Wise (No. 8, June 30, 1860); and combats with hostile Indians, October 30, 1859, to September 18, 1860 (No. 11, November 23, 1860).

4255 UNITED STATES. ARMY. Adjutant General

[Caption title] GENERAL ORDERS, NO. 6. WAR DEPARTMENT, ADJUTANT GENERAL'S OFFICE, WASHINGTON, MARCH 12, 1860 . . .

[1]–3, [4 blank]. 18.2 x 12 cm. Unbound leaflet tipped into brown paper wrappers. In a red cloth case.
Ref.:
Court-martial of Major Osborne Cross for embezzlement.

4256 UNITED STATES. ARMY. Adjutant General's Office

[Caption title] GENERAL ORDERS, NO. 2. WAR DEPARTMENT, ADJUTANT GENERAL'S OFFICE, WASHINGTON, JANUARY 7, 1865 . . .

[1–4], folding table. 18.5 x 12 cm. Unbound.
Ref.:
Regarding clothing and cost of camp equipage. Inserted in Manuscript Journals of Loren L. Williams, Volume III.

4257 UNITED STATES. ARMY. Adjutant General's Office

[Broadside] GENERAL ORDERS, NO. 3. WAR DEPARTMENT, ADJUTANT GENERAL'S OFFICE, WASHINGTON, JANUARY 14, 1865 . . .

Broadside, 15.7 x 10.4 cm. Text, 11.7 x 8.7 cm.

Joint resolution of Congress thanking General Sherman for his march through Georgia. Inserted in Manuscript Journals of Loren L. Williams, Volume III.

4258 UNITED STATES. ARMY. Adjutant General's Office

[Broadside] GENERAL ORDERS, NO. 4, WAR DEPARTMENT, ADJUTANT GENERAL'S OFFICE, WASHINGTON, JANUARY 16, 1865 . . .

Broadside, 16.9 x 9.5 cm. Text, 15.1 x 9.3 cm.

The Secretary of War's order for mourning in memory of Edward Everett. Inserted in Manuscript Journals of Loren L. Williams, Volume III.

4259 UNITED STATES. ARMY. Adjutant General's Office

[Broadside] GENERAL ORDERS, NO. 24. WAR DEPARTMENT, ADJUTANT GENERAL'S OFFICE, WASHINGTON, FEBRUARY 21, 1865 . . .

Broadside, 18.4 x 11.5 cm. Text, 7 x 8.4 cm.
Ref.:
An order from the Secretary of War requiring a salute to the Flag once more flying over Fort Sumter. Inserted in Manuscript Journals of Loren L. Williams, Volume III.

4260 UNITED STATES. ARMY. Adjutant General's Office

[Broadside] GENERAL ORDERS, NO. 60. WAR DEPARTMENT, ADJUTANT GENERAL'S OFFICE, WASH-

INGTON, APRIL 7, 1865. RECORDS OF DISCONTIN-
UED COMMANDS . . .

Broadside, 16.7 x 11.1 cm. Text, 11 x 8.7 cm.
Inserted in Manuscript Journals of Loren L.
Williams, Volume III.

4261 UNITED STATES. ARMY. Adjutant
General's Office

[Broadside] GENERAL ORDERS, NO. 67. WAR DE-
PARTMENT, ADJUTANT GENERAL'S OFFICE, WASH-
INGTON, APRIL 16, 1865 . . .

Broadside, 18.5 x 12.4 cm. Text, 7.5 x 8.6 cm.
Announcement by General Grant of the accession of Andrew Johnson as President. Inserted in Manuscript Journals of Loren L. Williams, Volume III.

4262 UNITED STATES. ARMY. Adjutant
General's Office

[Broadside] GENERAL ORDERS, NO. 101. WAR DE-
PARTMENT, ADJUTANT GENERAL'S OFFICE, WASH-
INGTON, MAY 30, 1865. RETENTION OF ARMS BY
SOLDIERS ON BEING HONORABLY DISCHARGED
FROM SERVICE . . .

Broadside, 18.2 x 12.5 cm. Text, 8.8 x 8.6 cm.
Inserted in Manuscript Journals of Loren L.
Williams, Volume III.

4263 UNITED STATES. ARMY. Adjutant
General's Office

[Broadside] GENERAL ORDERS, NO. 108. WAR DE-
PARTMENT, ADJUTANT GENERAL'S OFFICE, WASH-
INGTON, D. C., JUNE 2, 1865 . . . U. S. GRANT . . .

Broadside, 18.4 x 12 cm. Text, 13 x 8.5 cm.
Thanks to the troops for winning the War.
Inserted in Manuscript Journals of Loren L.
Williams, Volume III.

4264 UNITED STATES. ARMY. Adjutant
General's Office

MANUSCRIPT DOCUMENT (COPY). 1865 June 15,
War Department, Adjutant General's Office,
Washington, D. C. One page, 23 x 18.3 cm.
General Order No. 114. Inserted in Manu-
script Journals of Loren L. Williams, Volume
III.

4265 UNITED STATES. ARMY. Adjutant
General's Office

MANUSCRIPT DOCUMENT (COPY). 1866 April 19,
Washington, D. C. One page, 25 x 19.8 cm.
Extract of Special Orders No. 178. Regarding
mustering out of D. W. Applegate. Inserted in
Manuscript Journals of Loren L. Williams, Vol-
ume IV.

4266 UNITED STATES. ARMY. Adjutant
General's Office

[Caption title] . . . WASHINGTON, APRIL 14, 1872.
GENERAL ORDERS NO. 3 . . .

[1–2]. Unbound.
Announcing the death of General Canby.
Laid in Bland, T. A.: *Life of Alfred B. Meacham*
. . . 1883.

4267 UNITED STATES. ARMY. Arizona,
District of

[Broadside] CUARTEL CABECERA, DISTRITO DE
ARIZONA, MESILLA, A 28 DE OCTUBRE, 1862.
ORDENES ESPECIALES, NO 67 . . . POR ORDEN
DEL CORONEL WEST. W. L. RYNERSON, TENIENTE
2° DE LA 1° INFA^A VOL^S DE CAL^A Y ACT^E ASSIST^E
AYT^E GENERAL.

Broadside, 22.8 x 17 cm. Text, 22.1 x 16 cm.
Ref.:
Printed in Mesilla, where there was a news-
paper.
The contents relate to authority to issue paper
money for use in the military district.

4268 UNITED STATES. ARMY. Arizona,
District of

[Broadside] CUARTEL GENERAL DISTRITO DE ARI-
ZONA. MESILLA, DICIEMBRE 2, DE 1862. ORDENES
GENERALES NO. 24 . . . J. R. WEST, CORONEL DEL
1° DE INFANTERIA VOLUNTARIOS DE CALIFORNIA,
COMANDANTE.

Broadside, 26.6 x 18.5 cm. Text, 26.5 x 16.8 cm
Trimmed close, last line bled.
Ref.:
Printed at Mesilla.
The contents relate to rumored plans that the
Confederate Texan troops will again invade the
valley of the Mesilla and plans to repel them.
Tucson was captured by the Federals May 25,
1862, and J. R. West was made commander of
this District Sept. 5, 1862. The District of Arizona comprised the Territory of Arizona and
that part of New Mexico south of an east-west
line drawn through Fort Thorn, and also Northwest Texas.

4269 UNITED STATES. ARMY. Arizona,
Department of

[Caption title] HEADQUARTERS DEPARTMENT OF
ARIZONA, PRESCOTT, AUGUST 2, 1870. GENERAL
ORDERS, NO. 9. THE FOLLOWING SUMMARY OF SUC-
CESSFUL OPERATIONS AGAINST THE INDIANS IN
THIS DEPARTMENT, DURING THE PAST THREE
MONTHS, IS PUBLISHED FOR GENERAL INFORMA-
TION. . . .

[1]–4. 18.3 x 12.4 cm. Unbound leaflet, removed from bound volume, inner edge rough.
Ref.:
The leaflet was printed on the Army press at Prescott.

One of the expeditions described in this leaflet covered a period of 77 days and included travel over about 500 miles.

General George Stoneman was in command in the Department of Arizona for about a year. His ideas of how to handle the Indians were in conflict with the wishes of the "ring" of Indian traders and he was unable to put his plans into practice with any success.

4270 UNITED STATES. ARMY. Arizona, Department of
[Wrapper title] DEPARTMENT OF ARIZONA, LIEU-TENANT-COLONEL GEORGE CROOK, COMMANDING ACCORDING TO HIS COMMISSION OF BREVET MAJOR-GENERAL. HEADQUARTERS, PRESCOTT, JULY 1ST, 1872.
[1–6]. 18.5 x 12.3 cm. White printed wrappers with title on front wrapper.
Ref.:
Comprises a roster of troops under Crook's command.
Printed at Prescott.

4271 UNITED STATES. ARMY. Arizona, Department of
[Wrapper title] ROSTER OF TROOPS SERVING IN THE DEPARTMENT OF ARIZONA, COMMANDED BY COLO-NEL AUGUST V. KAUTZ . . . HEADQUARTERS, PRES-COTT, A. T., SEPTEMBER, 1876.
[1–14], [15–16 blank]. 19.5 x 12.5 cm. White printed wrappers with title on front wrapper. Lacks back wrapper.
Ref.:
Printed at Prescott.

4272 UNITED STATES. ARMY. Arizona, Department of
[Caption title] WHIPPLE BARRACKS, PRESCOTT, A. T., DECEMBER 2, 1879. TO THE ASSISTANT AD-JUTANT GENERAL, DEPARTMENT OF ARIZONA, WHIPPLE BARRACKS, PRESCOTT. SIR: I HAVE THE HONOR TO REPORT THAT IN COMPLIANCE WITH SPE-CIAL ORDERS NO. 155 . . .
[1]–17, [18 blank]. 19.7 x 12.5 cm. Rebound in red cloth with red morocco backstrip.
Ref.:
Printed at Prescott.
Report by Col. W. R. Price on the difficulties between the settlers and the Maricopa and Pima Indians, with suggestions for the solution of the problem.

4273 UNITED STATES. ARMY. Arizona. Department of
[Caption title] HEADQUARTERS DEPARTMENT OF ARIZONA, WHIPPLE BARRACKS, PRESCOTT, JUNE 30, 1882. ASSISTANT ADJUTANT GENERAL, HEAD-QUARTERS MILITARY DIVISION OF THE PACIFIC, PRESIDIO OF SAN FRANCISCO, CAL. SIR: . . .
[1]–10. 19.9 x 12.5 cm. Blueprint map: Pro-posed / Reservation / for / Hualpais Indians / [lower left:] Engrs Office / Hd.Qrs. Dept of Arizona / June 25, 1882 / Carl F. Palfrey / 1st Lieut. of Engrs. / 19.5 x 12.3 cm. Scale: 24 miles to one inch. Unbound, stabbed.
Ref.:
Comprises reports by O. B. Willcox, J. W. Mason, and an extract from a report by William R. Price. On page 10 there is a copy of the Gen-eral Order No. 16 defining the limits of the Hualpai Reservation.

4274 UNITED STATES. ARMY. Arizona, Department of. (San Carlos Agency)
[Caption title] SAN CARLOS AGENCY, ARIZONA, FEBRUARY 10, 1883. MEDICAL DIRECTOR, DEPART-MENT OF ARIZONA, WHIPPLE BARRACKS, PRESCOTT, A. T. SIR: . . .
[1]–10, [11–12 blank]. 20 x 12.6 cm. Stabbed, unbound.
Ref.:
An exceedingly interesting (although some-times erroneous) report by Frederick Lloyd, A. A. Surgeon, on the "character, arms, habits, diet, clothing, habitations, occupations, etc., of the Indians residing at the San Carlos Agency."

4275 UNITED STATES. ARMY. Arkansas, District of the Upper
[Broadside] HEAD-QRS., DIST. OF THE UPPER ARKANSAS: FOR FORT RILEY, JUNE 29TH, 1865. GENERAL ORDERS, NO. 22 . . .
Broadside, 20.1 x 12.5 cm. Text, 16.3 x 8.6 cm.
Ref.:
Printed at Fort Riley.
Thirty-seven lines followed by: By Command of Brv't Brig. Gen. Ford. / Robert S. Roe, / Act. Asst. Adjt. Gen. / Official: / [wavy rule above which in manuscript: Robert S. Roe] / Act Asst. Adjt. Gen. /
Contains an account of Lieut. Richard W. Jenkins' successful defense of the mail coach between Cow Creek Station and Fort Zarah, Kansas, from an Indian attack, June 11, 1865.

4276 UNITED STATES. ARMY. Border, District of the
[Caption title] HEAD-QUARTERS DISTRICT OF THE BORDER. KANSAS CITY, MO., OCTOBER 2, 1863.

GENERAL ORDERS, NO. 16. I. IT IS THE SPECIAL DUTY OF COMMANDERS OF STATIONS IN AND ADJACENT TO THE BORDER COUNTIES OF MISSOURI TO PROTECT LOYAL PERSONS . . .

[1]–3, [4 blank]. 18.9 x 12.1 cm. Unbound leaflet, with holes punched for looseleaf binder.

Ref.:

Relates to the Missouri border troubles during the Civil War.

Issued by H. Hannahs (and signed by him in manuscript on page 3) by order of Brigadier General Ewing. Printed at Kansas City.

4277   UNITED STATES. ARMY. Border, District of the

[Caption title] HEAD-QUARTERS DISTRICT OF THE BORDER. KANSAS CITY, MO., NOVEMBER 22D, 1863. GENERAL ORDERS, NO. 21. I. ALL SCOUTS, SPIES AND DETECTIVES NOW IN THE SERVICE OF THE UNITED STATES IN THIS DISTRICT BY EMPLOYMENT FROM HEAD-QUARTERS OF THE DISTRICT OF THE BORDER, OR OF THE FRONTIER, ARE DISCHARGED THE SERVICE FROM THIS DATE. . . .

[1–2]. 19.6 x 12.3 cm. Unbound broadsheet.

Ref.:

Relative also to the seizure of property.

Issued by H. Hannahs (signed in manuscript by Cyrus Leland, Jr.) by order of Brigadier General Ewing. Printed at Kansas City.

UNITED STATES. ARMY. Bureau of the Corps of Topographical Engineers

See UNITED STATES. ARMY. Engineers, Corps of

UNITED STATES. ARMY. Bureau of Topographical Engineers

See UNITED STATES. ARMY. Engineers, Corps of

4278   UNITED STATES. ARMY. Cavalry, Tenth

[Manuscript map] MAP / OF PARTS OF / INDIAN TERRITORY, TEXAS / AND / NEW MEXICO. / COMPILED BY ORDER OF / BVT. MAJ. GENL. J. W. DAVIDSON, U. S. A. / COMMANDING FORT SILL IND. TER. / BY / 1ST LIEUT. L. H. ORLEMAN / 10TH CAVALRY. / 1875. / SCALE OF MILES: / [diagrammatic scale] / 1 INCH = 8 MILES /

Manuscript map, 70.8 x 26.7 cm. On draughtsman's cloth, in india ink.

Prov.: Inscribed at right of cartouche, in red ink: H^d Quar. Fort Sill, Ind. Ter. / February 28.th 1875 / Official Copy for the Head Quarters of the 10.th U. S. Cavalry. / L. H. Orleman / 1st Lieut. 10″ Cavalry / Acting Engineer Officer /

Ref.:

Handsome manuscript map, with numerous details carefully entered.

4279   UNITED STATES. ARMY. Cavalry, Fourth

[Broadside] REGT'L BAND, FOURTH CAVALRY. PROGRAMME FOR RETREAT, AT FORT SILL, I. T., MONDAY, AUGUST 20, 1877 . . . P. TH. HELD, CHIEF MUSICIAN.

Broadside, 13.3 x 10.5 cm. Text, 11.9 x 8.6 cm.

Ref.: Hargrett (*Oklahoma*) 393

Printed at Fort Sill.

In Lawton Scrap-book.

4280   UNITED STATES. ARMY. Cavalry, Fourth

[Broadside] REGT'L BAND, FOURTH CAVALRY. PROGRAMME FOR RETREAT, AT FORT SILL, I.T., TUESDAY, AUGUST 21, 1877 . . . P. TH. HELD, CHIEF MUSICIAN.

Broadside, 13.1 x 10.7 cm. Text, 11.8 x 8.5 cm.

Ref.: Hargrett (*Oklahoma*) 394

Printed at Fort Sill.

In Lawton Scrap-book.

4281   UNITED STATES. ARMY. Cavalry, Fourth

[Broadside] REGIMENTAL BAND, FOURTH CAVALRY. PROGRAMME FOR RETREAT AT FORT SILL, I.T., THURSDAY, AUGUST 23, 1877. (PROMENADE CONCERT AND SERENADE, WEDNESDAY AND SATURDAY EVENINGS.) . . . P. TH. HELD, CHIEF MUSICIAN.

Broadside, 12.7 x 10.9 cm. Text, 11.9 x 8.7 cm.

Ref.: Hargrett (*Oklahoma*) 395

Printed at Fort Sill.

In Lawton Scrap-book.

4282   UNITED STATES. ARMY. Cavalry, Fourth

[Broadside] REGIMENTAL BAND, FOURTH CAVALRY. PROGRAMME FOR RETREAT AT FORT SILL, I.T., FRIDAY, AUGUST 24, 1877. (PROMENADE CONCERT AND SERENADE, WEDNESDAY AND SATURDAY EVENINGS.) . . . P. TH. HELD, CHIEF MUSICIAN.

Broadside, 15.1 x 10.9 cm. Text, 12 x 6.7 cm.

Ref.: Hargrett (*Oklahoma*) 396

Printed at Fort Sill.

In Lawton Scrap-book.

In manuscript at the top and bottom of the sheet: Everybody well, regards / to family. / Send me all the music / circulars you can find / Lawton /.

4283   UNITED STATES. ARMY. Cavalry Band, Second

[Broadside] PROGRAMME OF EVENING SERENADE, AT FORT SANDERS, W. T. SATURDAY, AUGUST 30TH, 1873. FROM 8.30 TO 9.30 P.M. SECOND U.S. CAVALRY BAND . . . COMPLIMENTS OF: W. P. CLARK, ADJUTANT.

Broadside, 17 x 11.5 cm. Text, 13.2 x 8.5 cm.
Ref.:
Printed at Fort Sanders.

McMurtrie says in his *Early Printing in Wyoming* that Fort Sanders was the third point at which printing was done in Wyoming, four or five miles south of the present city of Laramie. It has been known as a printing point only because for three or four months in 1867–8 it was the seat of operations for the transitory *Frontier Index.*—EDG

4284   UNITED STATES. ARMY. Cavalry Band, Tenth

[Broadside] EVENING CONCERT. BY THE TENTH U. S. CAVALRY BAND. MONDAY OCTOBER 6, 1879 . . .

Broadside, 19.5 x 12.2 cm. Text, 11.5 x 7.9 cm.
Ref.:
Printed in gold and bronze.
Printed at Prescott, Arizona, on the Army press.

4285   UNITED STATES. ARMY. Columbia, Department of the

DOCUMENT SIGNED by W. J. Sanborn. 1865 September 20, Headquarters Department of the Columbia, Fort Vancouver, W. T. Two pages, 24.9 x 18.5 cm.
Special Orders No. 24. Inserted in Manuscript Journals of Loren L. Williams, Volume III.

4286   UNITED STATES. ARMY. Columbia, Department of the

DOCUMENT SIGNED by Charles S. Lovell. 1865 December 1, Headquarters Department of the Columbia, Fort Vancouver, W. T. One page, 17.9 x 20.1 cm.
General Orders No. 18. Inserted in Manuscript Journals of Loren L. Williams, Volume III.

4287   UNITED STATES. ARMY. Columbia, Department of the

DOCUMENT SIGNED by W. J. Sanborn. 1865 December 1, Headquarters Department of the Columbia, Fort Vancouver, W. T. One page, 17 x 20.1 cm.
Special Orders No. 63. Inserted in Manuscript Journals of Loren L. Williams, Volume III.

4288   UNITED STATES. ARMY. Columbia, Department of the

[Broadside] HEAD QUARTERS, DEPARTMENT OF THE COLUMBIA, FORT VANCOUVER, W. T., FEBRUARY 24, 1866. GENERAL ORDERS, NO. 4 . . .

Broadside, 15.4 x 11.5 cm. Text, 10.1 x 8.5 cm.
Major General Steele assumes command. Countersigned in manuscript by W. J. Sanborn. Inserted in Manuscript Journals of Loren L. Williams, Volume III.

4289   UNITED STATES. ARMY. Columbia, Department of the

DOCUMENT SIGNED by D. W. Applegate for W. J. Sanborn (copy of extract). 1866 May 1, Hd. Qrs. Department of the Columbia, Fort Vancouver, W. T. Two pages, 31.5 x 19.6 cm.
Special Orders No. 31. Regarding mustering out of Captain Loren L. Williams' troops. Inserted in Manuscript Journals of Loren L. Williams, Volume IV.

4290   UNITED STATES. ARMY. Columbia, Department of the

[Broadside] HEAD QUARTERS, DEPARTMENT OF THE COLUMBIA, PORTLAND, OREGON, JULY 11TH, 1868. GENERAL ORDERS, NO. 24. PURSUANT TO INSTRUCTIONS FROM MAJ. GEN. HALLECK . . . BREVET MAJOR. GEN. CROOK HAD A COUNCIL ON THE 30TH OF JUNE, AT CAMP HARNEY, WITH THE PRINCIPAL BANDS OF HOSTILE INDIANS INFESTING THE VICINITY OF MALHEUR RIVER, CASTLE ROCK, OWYHEE, AND STEIN'S MOUNTAINS, UNDER THEIR PRINCIPAL CHIEF, WEE-AH-WEE-WA . . . BY ORDER OF BVT. MAJ. GEN. GEO. CROOK, GEO. WILLIAMS, BREVET MAJOR, U. S. A., A. D. C. & A. A. A. G. OFFICIAL: [signed in manuscript:] GEO WILLIAMS BREVET MAJOR, U. S. A., A. D. C. & A. A. A. G.

Broadside, 19.7 x 12.3 cm. Text, 16.7 x 8.7 cm.
Ref.: McMurtrie (*Oregon*) 499a
Probably printed on an Army press at Portland.—McMurtrie
At the council, the Indians agreed to return to the vicinity of Castle Rock and remain peaceful.

4291   UNITED STATES. ARMY. Columbia, Department of the

THE STATUS OF YOUNG JOSEPH AND HIS BAND OF NEZ-PERCE INDIANS UNDER THE TREATIES BETWEEN THE UNITED STATES AND THE NEZ-PERCE TRIBE OF INDIANS, AND THE INDIAN TITLE TO LAND. PORTLAND, OREGON: ASSISTANT ADJUTANT GENERAL'S OFFICE, DEPARTMENT OF THE COLUMBIA, 1876.

[i–iv, (iv blank)], [1]–49, [50 blank]. 18.7 x 12.3 cm. Green cloth, lettered on front cover.
Ref.: Howes W626
The report was submitted on January 8, 1876, to Brigadier-General O. O. Howard, Commanding, by H. Clay Wood, Assistant Adjutant General.

UNITED STATES. ARMY. Corps of
Engineers

See UNITED STATES. ARMY. Engineers, Corps of

UNITED STATES. ARMY. Corps of
Topographical Engineers

See UNITED STATES. ARMY. Engineers, Corps of

4292 UNITED STATES. ARMY. Courts of
Inquiry. Sand Creek Massacre, 1864

[Caption title] . . . REPORT OF THE SECRETARY OF
WAR, COMMUNICATING . . . A COPY OF THE EVI-
DENCE TAKEN AT DENVER AND FORT LYON, COLO-
RADO TERRITORY, BY A MILITARY COMMISSION,
ORDERED TO INQUIRE INTO THE SAND CREEK MAS-
SACRE, NOVEMBER, 1864.

[1]–228. 22.4 x 14.2 cm. Rebound in mottled
gray and green French boards, red leather label
on backstrip.

Refs.: Howes S80

39th Congress, 2nd Session, Senate, Executive
Document No. 26, Serial 1277. [Washington:
Government Printing Office, 1867.]

4293 UNITED STATES. ARMY. Dakota,
Department of

[A COLLECTION OF GENERAL ORDERS AND CIRCU-
LARS, 1867 TO 1874 AND 1883 TO 1884, DEPART-
MENT OF DAKOTA].

Variously paged. 17 x 12.4 cm. to 19.1 x 12.3
cm. Four volumes: two volumes in cream buckram, black lettering, one volume in calf (worn),
one volume in black roan backstrip and corners.

Prov.: Duplicates from the Army War College Library. Volume for 1873–74 stamped at
foot of backstrip with name of Thomas M. Vincent, Assistant Adjutant General.

Ref.:

Comprises the following:

VOLUME I:

Index / of / Names and Subjects. / [rule] /
General Orders / Department of Dakota. /
1867. / [rule] / Saint Paul, / Pioneer Printing
Company, / 1868. / [within decorative border].
[1]–13, [14–16 blank].

Headquarters, Department of Dakota, Fort
Snelling or St. Paul; General Orders, Nos. 1–57,
January 11–December 5, 1867.

General Field Orders, No. 1, Camp near Fort
Berthold, July 4, 1867; No. 2, Camp near Fort
Berthold, July 4; No. 3, Camp near Fort Buford,
July 17, 1867; No. 4, Camp Cooke, July 26; No.
5, Fort Shaw, August 7.

Circular, Fort Snelling, February 6, 1867;
Circular, Fort Snelling, March 23, 1867.

Index / of / General Orders, / Department of
Dakota, / Brevet Major Gen. Alfred H. Terry, /

United States Army, / Commanding. / [decora-
tive rule] / St. Paul, Minn., / Assistant Adjutant
General's Office. / [short rule] / 1868. / [1]–6,
[7–8 blank].

General Orders, Nos. 1–46, 49–64, Saint
Paul, January 14–December 29, 1868.

General Field Orders, No. 1, In the Field,
Fort Rice, June 11, 1868; No. 2, In the Field,
Fort Rice, July 4.

Circular, No. 1, Saint Paul, March 13, 1868.

Index / of / General Orders, / Department of
Dakota, / 1869. / [rule] / Saint Paul: / Assistant
Adjutant General's Office, / 1870. / [within rule
border] /. [1]–12.

General Orders, Nos. 1–97, St. Paul, January
7–December 29, 1869.

Circular, St. Paul, March 3, 1869.

VOLUME II:

Index / of / General Orders, / Department of
Dakota, / 1870. / [rule] / Saint Paul. / Assistant
Adjutant General's Office, / 1871. / [rule] /. [1]–
11, [12 blank].

General Orders, Nos. 1–99, Saint Paul, January 4–December 26, 1870.

General Field Orders, No. 1, Sioux City, May
14, 1870; No. 2, Steamer "Miner," Crow Creek
Agency, May 23, 1870.

Index / of / General Orders, / Department of
Dakota, / 1871. / [rule] / St. Paul, Minn: / Assistant Adjutant General's Office. / 1872. / [rule
border]. [1]–11, [12 blank].

General Orders, Nos. 1–106, Saint Paul, January 14–December 30, 1871.

Index / of / General Orders, / Department of
Dakota, / 1872. / [rule] / St. Paul, Minn. / Assistant Adjutant General's Office. / 1873. / [rule
border]. [1]–12; inserted slip, 5.1 x 12.1 cm.,
after page [2].

General Orders, Nos. 1–81, St. Paul, January
2–December 3, 1872.

VOLUME III:

General Orders / from the / [dotted rule,
above which in manuscript: Department of Dakota.] / [decorative rule] / 18 [in manuscript:
73] /. [1–2].

Index / of / General Orders, / Department of
Dakota. / 1873. / [rule] / St. Paul, Minn. / Assistant Adjutant General's Office. / 1874. / [with-
in rule border] [below border:] [Gov't Print.] /
[1]–14.

General Orders Nos. 1–2, Saint Paul, January
2–3, 1873.

Circular, Saint Paul, January 3, 1873.

General Orders Nos. 3–94, Saint Paul, January 4–November 23, 1873.

Roster of Troops / Department of Dakota, /
Brig. Gen. Alfred H. Terry, / Commanding. /

[short rule] / Headquarters, St. Paul, Minn. / [diamond rule] / November 1, 1873. / [within decorative rule] /. [3]–20 (pages [1–2] are General Orders No. 94).

General Orders, Nos. 95–101, Saint Paul, December 4–27, 1873.

Circulars / from the / Headquarters / [dotted rule above which in manuscript: Department of Dakota.] / [decorative rule] / 18 [in manuscript: 73.] / [1–2].

Nos. 1–25, Headquarters, . . . Saint Paul, January 23–December 26, 1873.

General Orders / from the / Headquarters/ [dotted rule above which in manuscript: Department of Dakota.] / [decorative rule] / 18 [in manuscript: 74] /. [1–2].

[Double rule] / Index of General Orders. / [double rule] /. [3]–13, [14 blank].

[Double rule] / Index of Circulars. / [double rule] /. [17–22].

General Orders Nos. 1–76, St. Paul, January 13–November 1, 1874.

Roster of Troops / Department of Dakota, / Brig. Gen. Alfred H. Terry, / Commanding. / [short rule] / Headquarters, St. Paul, Minn. / [diamond rule] / November 1, 1874. / [within decorative border]. [3]–19, [20 blank]

General Orders Nos. 77–85, Saint Paul, November 6–December 26, 1874.

Circulars / from the / Headquarters, / [dotted rule above which in manuscript: Department of Dakota.] / [decorative rule] / 18 [in manuscript: 74.] / [1–2].

Nos. 1–13, Headquarters, Department of Dakota, Saint Paul, January 10–November 14, 1874.

VOLUME IV:

General Orders, / Circulars and Rosters, / Issued from / Headquarters Dep't of Dakota, / 1883. / [rule] / With Index. / Fort Snelling, Minn.: / Adjutant General's Office, Dep't of Dakota, / 1884. / [1]–9, [10–12 blank].

General Orders Nos. 1–28, Fort Snelling, January 25–December 5, 1883.

Third Annual Competition / of the / Selected Riflemen / of the / Department of Dakota. / [rule] / Programme / for / Practice, Matches and Competition. / [rule] / September, 1883. / [1]–4.

[Unnumbered circular dated July 28, 1883, regarding visits of a Committee of the Senate to the Indians of Montana and Dakota]. [1–2].

[Unnumbered circular dated September 11, 1883, regarding disbursing records]. [1], [2 blank].

Telegraphic Circular. Fort Snelling, June 19, 1883. [1], [2 blank].

[Unnumbered circular dated September 20,

1883, regarding orders in case of fire.] [1]–3, [4 blank].

Circular Nos. 1–32, Fort Snelling or Washington, January 13–December 28, 1883. (Comprise 43 Circulars including duplicated numbers).

General Orders, / Circulars and Rosters, / Issued from / Headquarters Dep't of Dakota, / 1884. / [short rule] / With Index. / Fort Snelling, Minn.: / Headquarters Department of Dakota, / 1885. / [1]–14, [15–16 blank].

General Orders Nos. 1–12, Fort Snelling, January 7–December 3, 1884.

[Unnumbered circulars or printed letters:] Washington, January 26, February 15, 21, 28, April 12, Fort Snelling, April 16, San Francisco, May 9, Fort Snelling, May 16, 19, August 1, Washington, September 2, October 20, December 9.

Circular Nos. 1–68, Fort Snelling, January 14–December 19, 1884.

Index of / General Orders, / —and— / Circulars, / Division of the Missouri, / 1884. / [1]–4.

General Orders, Nos. 1–19, Chicago, January 28–November 4, 1884.

Circular, Headquarters Division of the Missouri, Chicago, November 22, 1884. [1], [2 blank].

4294   UNITED STATES. ARMY. Dakota, Department of

[Caption title] HEADQUARTERS, DEPARTMENT OF DAKOTA, SAINT PAUL, MINN, MAY 19, 1867. GENERAL ORDERS, NO. 27 . . . THE INDIAN SCOUTS AUTHORIZED BY GENERAL ORDERS NO. 5, OF AUGUST 8TH, 1866, FROM HEADQUARTERS MILITARY DIVISION OF THE MISSISSIPPI, AND DIRECTED TO BE ORGANIZED BY SPECIAL ORDERS NO. 33, OF APRIL 3D, 1867, FROM THESE HEADQUARTERS, WILL, WHEN ORGANIZED, BE DISTRIBUTED AS FOLLOWS: . . .

[1]–2. 20.3 x 13 cm. Unbound broadsheet.

Ref.:

Issued by Ed. W. Smith by command of Brevet Major Gen. A. H. Terry.

4295   UNITED STATES. ARMY. Dakota, Department of

TABLE OF DISTANCES IN THE DEPARTMENT OF DAKOTA. COMPILED UNDER THE DIRECTION OF THE CHIEF QUARTERMASTER DEPARTMENT OF DAKOTA. ST. PAUL. MINN., JANUARY 28, 1875. WASHINGTON: GOVERNMENT PRINTING OFFICE, 1875.

[1]–28. 23.4 x 15.2 cm. Three folding tables and three folding maps. Maps numbered on versos. Map: 1. [In circle, with flourishes:] Map / of / Dakota Territory / Made under the direction of /

B. C. Card. / Bvt. Brig. General U. S. A. / Chief
Q.M. Dept. of Dakota. / Saint Paul, Minn.
1875 / [following line cut off:] F. Sturnegk
Draughtsman, Q.M.D. /, [above neat line:] Department of Dakota. / 60.8 x 52.8 cm. No scale
given. Map: 2. [In circle, with flourishes:] Map /
of / Montana Territory / Made under the direction of / B. C. Card. / Bvt. Brig. General U. S. A. /
Chief Q M. Dept. of Dakota / Saint Paul Minn.
1875 / F. Sturnegk Draughtsman, Q.M.D. /
[above neat line:] Department of Dakota / .43.9 x
70.5 cm. No scale given. Map: 3. [In circle, with
flourishes:] Map / of the State of / Minnesota /
Made under the direction of / B. C. Card. / Bvt.
Brig. General U.S.A. / Chief Q. M. Dept. of
Dakota. / Saint Paul Minn. 1875 / F. Sturnegk,
Draughtsman, Q.M.D. / [above neat line:]
Department of Dakota /. 68.8 x 51.4 cm. No
scale given. Gray printed wrappers, with title
on front wrapper.
Ref.:

4296 UNITED STATES. ARMY. Dakota,
Department of

SPECIAL ORDERS ISSUED FROM HEADQUARTERS
DEP'T OF DAKOTA. 1887. WITH INDEX. ADJUTANT
GENERALS OFFICE, DEPARTMENT OF DAKOTA.

[1]–31, [32 blank], plus variously paginated orders. 24.3 x 19.4 cm. Contemporary black half
leather, sprinkled edges, worn.
Prov.: Bookplate of Army War College Library and rubber stamps of War Department Library and Library of Congress duplicate exchange.
Ref.:
Comprises Special Orders Nos. 1–133, Saint
Paul, January 3—December 31, 1887.

4297 UNITED STATES. ARMY. Dakota,
Department of

SPECIAL ORDERS ISSUED FROM HEADQUARTERS
DEP'T OF DAKOTA. 1888. WITH INDEX. ADJUTANT
GENERAL'S OFFICE, DEPARTMENT OF DAKOTA.

[1]–23, [24 blank] plus variously paginated separate orders. 24.3 x 19.4 cm. Contemporary half
black leather, sprinkled edges.
Prov.: Bookplate of Army War College, rubber stamps of War Department Library, Inspector General's Office, Headquarters of Department of Dakota, and Library of Congress Duplicate and Exchange.
Ref.:
Comprises Special Orders Nos. 1–127, Saint
Paul, January 3–December 31, 1888.

4298 UNITED STATES. ARMY. Dakota,
Department of

GENERAL ORDERS, CIRCULARS, ANNUAL REPORT,
AND ROSTERS, ISSUED FROM HEADQUARTERS DE-
PARTMENT OF DAKOTA. 1895. ASSISTANT ADJUTANT
GENERAL'S OFFICE, DEPARTMENT OF DAKOTA.

[1]–6, [7–8 blank], plus variously paginated separate orders. 21 broadsides and pamphlets
bound together with preliminary leaves, half
black leather, marbled edges.
Prov.: Stamped in gilt at foot of backstrip:
M. V. Sheridan /.
Ref.:
Comprises General Orders Nos. 1–13, Circulars Nos. 1–4, Report, Roster of Merritt's Command, Rosters (two) of Brooke's Command for
June and October. Each of the General Orders is
signed in manuscript.

4299 UNITED STATES. ARMY. Eastern Division

[Broadside] ORDERS, NO. [in manuscript: 25]
HEAD QUARTERS, EASTERN DIVISION. CHEROKEE
AGENCY, TEN. MAY 17, 1838. MAJOR GENERAL
SCOTT, OF THE UNITED STATES' ARMY, ANNOUNCES
TO THE TROOPS ASSEMBLED AND ASSEMBLING IN
THIS COUNTRY, THAT, WITH THEM, HE HAS BEEN
CHARGED BY THE PRESIDENT TO CAUSE THE CHERO-
KEE INDIANS YET REMAINING IN NORTH CAROLINA,
GEORGIA, TENNESSEE AND ALABAMA, TO REMOVE
TO THE WEST, ACCORDING TO THE TERMS OF THE
TREATY OF 1835 . . . BY COMMAND: [in manu-
script:] Winfield Scott / W J Worth L^T Colo
Chief of staff [last two lines in manuscript].

Broadside, 34 x 24.9 cm. Text in three columns,
28.4 x 19.8 cm.
Ref.:
The broadside announces Scott's staff, di-
vides the operation into three districts, instructs
the Army to succeed by persevering acts of kindness, and gives general instructions on methods
to be used.
The broadside may have been printed locally,
since the following phrases appear in the text:
". . . to transport the prisoners, by families,
either to this place, to Ross' Landing or Gunter's
Landing . . ."

4300 UNITED STATES. ARMY. Eastern
Division

[Broadside] MAJOR GENERAL SCOTT, OF THE
UNITED STATES ARMY, SENDS TO THE CHEROKEE
PEOPLE, REMAINING IN NORTH CAROLINA, GEOR-
GIA, TENNESSEE, AND ALABAMA, THIS ADDRESS.
CHEROKEES! THE PRESIDENT OF THE UNITED STATES
HAS SENT ME, WITH A POWERFUL ARMY, TO CAUSE
YOU, IN OBEDIENCE TO THE TREATY OF 1835, TO

JOIN THAT PART OF YOUR PEOPLE WHO ALREADY ESTABLISHED IN PROSPERITY, ON THE OTHER SIDE OF THE MISSISSIPPI . . . WINFIELD SCOTT. CHEROKEE AGENCY, MAY 10, 1838.

Broadside, 24.7 x 20 cm. Text in two columns, 17.7 x 13 cm.

Ref.:

General Scott appeals as a warrior to warriors for a peaceful removal of the Cherokees to their new homes.

UNITED STATES. ARMY. Engineer Bureau

See UNITED STATES. ARMY. Engineers, Corps of

4301 UNITED STATES. ARMY. Engineers, Corps of

[Map:] U. S. GOVERNMENT / MAP OF [CHICAGO] 1818. / COPIED FROM A MAP IN / THE TOPOGRAPHICAL BUREAU. /

Map, manuscript copy, 45.8 x 30.6 cm. Scale 200 yards to one inch. Laminated. Bound with related materials in contemporary half black calf.

See under ILLINOIS CENTRAL RAILROAD COMPANY.

4302 UNITED STATES. ARMY. Engineers, Corps of

[Map] MAP OF THE / UNITED STATES / AND THEIR TERRITORIES / BETWEEN THE / MISSISSIPPI AND THE PACIFIC OCEAN; / AND OF / PART OF MEXICO. / COMPILED IN THE BUREAU OF THE CORPS OF TOPOG.ᴸ ENG.ˢ / UNDER A RESOLUTION OF THE U. S. SENATE. / FROM THE BEST AUTHORITIES WHICH COULD BE OBTAINED. / 1850. / [below cartouche:] ENGRAVED BY SHERMAN AND SMITH. NEW-YORK. /

Map, 112 x 99 cm. Scale: 50 miles to one inch. Cut and mounted on fine linen, folded into green board case with blue cloth back, cloth ties.

Prov.: Signature: John R. Bartlett / on verso.

4303 UNITED STATES. ARMY. Engineers, Corps of

[Map] U. S. WAR DEPARTMENT. / [short rule] / MAP OF THE / YELLOWSTONE AND MISSOURI RIVERS / AND THEIR TRIBUTARIES. / EXPLORED BY / CAPT. W. F. RAYNOLDS TOP.ᴸ ENG.ᴿˢ / AND / 1.ˢᵀ LIEUT. H. E. MAYNADIER 10.ᵀᴴ INF.ʸ ASSISTANT. / 1859–60. / TO ACCOMPANY A REPORT TO THE BUREAU OF TOPOGRAPHICAL ENGINEERS. / L.ᵀ COL. HARTMAN BACHE IN CHARGE. / [short rule] / SCALE 1/1200000 1 INCH = 18.94 MILES / [diagrammatic scale] / ENGRAVED IN THE ENGINEER BUREAU WAR DEP.ᵀ / [arms of Corps of Engineers] /.

Map, 68.7 x 105.3 cm. Scale as above. Cut into 40 panels, 17.6 x 10.9 cm., mounted on cloth, with two panels supported by black cloth-over-

board covers, with white printed label on front cover, 7.5 x 10.6 cm.; Montana / and / Dakota. / By / Capt. Raynolds. / [decorative rule] / Prepared for Issue in Engineer Office, M. D. Mo. / [decorative rule] / All persons into whose hands this map falls are particularly / requested to send all corrections and additions to the / Chief Engineer, Mil. Div. of the Mo., at St. Louis. / [within decorative border]. Large ink stain on face of map.

Prov.: Signature on verso: L. P. Bradley /. Inscribed in red into right of cartouche: Hd. Qr. Mil. Div. Missouri / Engineer Office / Official: / W.ᵐ E. Keemle / May 10ᵗʰ 1867 Maj. Engrs. & Bvt. Col. /

Ref.: Phillips (*Maps*) p. 1130; Wheat (*Transmississippi*) 1012 see

There are several corrections and changes on the face of the map in red ink, apparently done in the Engineer Office.

Wheat does not describe the separate publication of the map. See Number 3429 in this catalogue.

4304 UNITED STATES. ARMY. Engineers, Corps of

[Map] TERRITORY / AND / MILITARY DEPARTMENT / OF / UTAH / COMPILED IN THE / BUREAU OF TOPOGRAPH.ᴸ ENG.ᴿˢ / OF THE WAR DEPART.ᵀ / CHIEFLY FOR MILITARY PURPOSES / UNDER THE AUTHORITY OF / HON. J. B. FLOYD SEC. OF WAR / 1860 / [rule] / [lower right:] ENGRAVED BY W. H. DOUGAL /

Map, 71.5 x 104 cm. No scale given. Folded to 20.5 x 12.7 cm. and attached to green printed back wrapper of Judah's *Report . . . Central Pacific Railroad . . .* 1862.

Ref.:

The routes of the Central Pacific Railroad and the Union Pacific Railroad are drawn in in red ink.

The map has been revised to January, 1862, according to a note on the face of the map.

4305 UNITED STATES. ARMY. Engineers, Corps of

[Map] [insignia of Engineer Department] / ENGRAVED IN THE ENGINEER DEPARTMENT. / INDIAN TERRITORY / WITH PART OF THE ADJOINING STATE / OF KANSAS &C. / PREPARED FROM THE MAP OF DAN.ᴸ C. MAJOR U. S. AST.ᴿ SHOWING THE / BOUNDARIES OF THE CHOCTAW AND CHICKASAW NATIONS, THE CREEK, SEMINOLE, / AND LEASED INDIAN COUNTRY, ESTABLISHED BY AUTHORITY OF THE COMM.ᴿˢ / OF INDIAN AFFAIRS IN 1858-'59,—AND FROM LIEUT. COL. J. E. JOHNSTON'S / MAP OF THE SOUTHERN BOUNDARY OF KANSAS IN 1857. [rule] /

THE MAP OF THE CREEK COUNTRY, BY LIEUT. I. C. WOODRUFF TOP.ᴸ ENG.ᴿˢ, IN 1850–51, / ENGINEER BUREAU WAR DEP'T, / OCTOBER 1866. / [thick and thin rules] /.

Map, 47.3 x 61.4 cm. Scale: 24 miles to one inch. Map divided into 21 panels and mounted on cloth, folded into green cloth covers: 19.1 x 11.5 cm., with printed label (7.5 x 11.3 cm.) on front cover: Indian / Territory. / [decorative rule] / Engineer Bureau, M. D. / [decorative rule] / Prepared for Issue in Engineer Office, M. D. Mo. / [decorative rule] / All persons into whose hands this map falls are particularly / requested to send all corrections and additions to the / Chief Engineer, Mil Div. of the Mo., at St. Louis. / [within decorative border].

Ref.:

Inscribed at right of cartouche in red ink: Hd. Qr. Mil. Div. Missouri / Engineer Office / Official: / Wᵐ E. Hamill [?] / Maj. Engrs. & Bvt. Col. / Octr. 22ᵈ 1867 [line crossed out] / Jan. 18ᵗʰ 1868 /.

4306 UNITED STATES. ARMY. Engineers, Corps of

[Map] ENGINEER BUREAU, / WAR DEPARTMENT. / [rule] / MAP OF THE / STATES OF KANSAS AND TEXAS / AND INDIAN TERRITORY, / WITH PARTS OF THE TERRITORIES OF COLORADO AND NEW MEXICO. / FROM THE MOST RECENT OFFICIAL SURVEYS AND EXPLORATIONS / AND OTHER AUTHENTIC INFORMATION. / 1867. / SCALE 1:1,500,000 / [diagrammatic scale: 24 miles to one inch] / J. BIEN, 24 VESEY ST. N. Y. /

Map, 118.3 x 86.4 cm. Scale as above. Cut into 48 panels 20 x 11.4 cm., mounted on cloth and folded. Two outer panels attached to green cloth covers. White printed paper label, 7.9 x 11.4 cm., on front cover; badly worn, mostly indecipherable.

Ref.:

Inscribed in red ink at right of cartouche: Hd. Qrs. Mil. Div. Missouri / Engineer Office / Official: / Wᵐ E. Keemle / July 15ᵗʰ 1867 Maj. Eng'rs. & Bv't Col. / [broken rule] / Rec. at Head Quarter, Dist: of the Indian Territory / Fort Gibson, C.N. Aug 03: 1867 /.

4307 UNITED STATES. ARMY. Engineers, Corps of

[Map] OLD / TERRITORY / AND / MILITARY DEPARTMENT / OF / NEW MEXICO / COMPILED IN THE / BUREAU OF TOPOG.ᴸ ENG.ᴿˢ OF THE WAR DEP.ᵀ / CHIEFLY FOR MILITARY PURPOSES / UNDER THE AUTHORITY OF / THE / SECRETARY OF WAR / 1859 / PARTIALLY REVISED AND CORRECTED TO 1867. / [lower right corner:] ENGRAVED BY W. H. DOUGAL /.

Map, 60.3 x 87.2 cm. Scale: 24 miles to one inch. Cut to 24 panels and mounted on cloth, enclosed between dark green cloth covers, 19.9 x 13.2 cm., with printed white paper label (7.3 x 11.4 cm.) on front cover: New Mexico / and/ Arizona. / [decorative rule] / Engineer Bureau, M. D. / [decorative rule] / Prepared for Issue in Engineer Office, M. D. Mo. / [decorative rule] / All persons into whose hands this map falls are particularly / requested to send all corrections and additions to the / Chief Engineer, Mil. Div. of the Mo., at St. Louis. / [within decorative border].

Ref.:

Inscribed in manuscript in lower left corner: Hd. Qu. Mil. Div. Missouri / Engineer Office / Official: / Wᵐ E. Keemle / Maj. Engr. & Bvt. Col. / May 25 1869 /

With manuscript additions in the map.

4308 UNITED STATES. ARMY. Engineers, Corps of

[Map] ENGINEER BUREAU, / WAR DEPARTMENT, / MAP OF THE / TERRITORY OF THE UNITED STATES / FROM THE / MISSISSIPPI RIVER TO THE PACIFIC OCEAN; / ORIGINALLY PREPARED TO ACCOMPANY THE REPORTS OF THE / EXPLORATIONS FOR A PACIFIC RAILROAD ROUTE; / MADE IN ACCORDANCE WITH THE 10ᵀᴴ & 11ᵀᴴ SECTIONS OF THE ARMY APPROPRIATION, ACT OF MARCH 3ᴿ·ᴰ 1853; / COMPILED FROM AUTHORIZED EXPLORATIONS AND OTHER RELIABLE DATA BY / LIEUT. G. K. WARREN, TOP'L. ENG'RS, / IN THE OFFICE OF PACIFIC R. R. SURVEYS, WAR DEPT. UNDER THE DIRECTION OF / B'V'T. MAJ. W. H. EMORY, TOPL. ENG'RS. IN 1854. / CAPT. A. A. HUMPHREYS, TOP'L. ENG'RS. IN 1854–58. / AND PARTLY RECOMPILED AND REDRAWN UNDER THE DIRECTION / OF THE ENGINEER BUREAU IN / 1865–66–67. / SCALE OF STATUTE MILES / [diagrammatic scale: 48 miles to one inch] / 1:3,000,000 / ENGRAVED ON STONE BY JULIUS BIEN, NEW YORK. /

Map, printed on four sheets, joined in pairs, 53 x 117.6 and 54.3 x 117.6 cm. Scale as above.

Ref.:

Numerous changes and corrections in blue and red ink, including limits of some states and territories and of military districts.

This is approximately the same as the following map, although the inset of the Territory of Alaska is not present, and some dates differ.

4309 UNITED STATES. ARMY. Engineers, Corps of

[Map] [arms of Corps of Engineers] / HEAD QUARTERS CORPS OF ENGINEERS. / WAR DEPART-

MENT. / [rule] / TERRITORY OF THE UNITED STATES / FROM THE / MISSISSIPPI RIVER TO THE PACIFIC OCEAN; / ORIGINALLY PREPARED TO ACCOMPANY THE REPORTS OF THE / EXPLORATIONS FOR A PACIFIC RAILROAD ROUTE; / MADE IN ACCORDANCE WITH THE 10ᵀᴴ & 11ᵀᴴ SECTIONS OF THE ARMY APPROPRIATION, ACT OF MARCH 3ᴿ·ᴰ 1853; / COMPILED FROM AUTHORIZED EXPLORATIONS AND OTHER RELIABLE DATA BY / LIEUT. G. K. WARREN, TOP'L. ENG'RS, / IN THE OFFICE OF PACIFIC R. R. SURVEYS, WAR DEPT. UNDER THE DIRECTION OF / B'V'T. MAJ. W. H. EMORY, TOPL. ENG'RS. IN 1854. / CAPT. A. A. HUMPHREYS, TOP'L. ENG'RS. IN 1854–58. / RECOMPILED AND REDRAWN UNDER THE DIRECTION OF THE / CHIEF OF CORPS OF ENGINEERS / BY EDWARD FREYHOLD / 1865–66–67–68. / [rule] / SCALE OF STATUTE MILES. / [diagrammatic scale: 48 miles to one inch] / 1:3,000,000. / [decorative rule] / ENGRAVED & PRINTED BY JULIUS BIEN. N. Y. / *Inset:* TERRITORY OF ALASKA / CEDED BY RUSSIA TO THE UNITED STATES / 1868 / SCALE 1/9000000 / SCALE OF STATUTE MILES / [diagrammatic scale: about 145 miles to one inch] /. 32.9 x 43.9 cm. (neat line; irregular shape).

Map, 109.5 x 118.8 cm. Scale as above. Cut into 35 panels, each 22.4 x 17.4 cm., and mounted on cloth, folded and attached to full brown morocco covers, gilt, with title on front cover: Territory / of the / United States, / from the / Mississippi River / to the / Pacific Ocean. / One panel of map backed with marbled paper to match inner cover of folder. 23.7 x 18.3 cm.

Ref.: Phillips p. 904

4310   UNITED STATES. ARMY. Engineers, Corps of

[Map] SHEET N°. 2 WESTERN TERRITORIES / PREPARED BY MAJOR G. L. GILLESPIE CORPS OF ENG'RS BVT. LT. COL. U. S. A. / 1876. / [lower centre:] SCALE 1 : 2000 000; 1 INCH TO 31⁵⁶⁵ STATUTE MILES. / [diagrammatic scale: about 31 1/2 miles to one inch] / EMIL HEUBACH, DRAUGHTSMAN. / MORTON COLLINS, ENGRAVER. / [right:] PUBLISHED BY AUTHORITY OF THE HON. THE SECRETARY OF WAR / IN THE OFFICE OF THE CHIEF OF ENGINEERS. U. S. ARMY. /

Map, 63.1 x 45.8 cm. Scale as above.
Prov.: From the Grierson Papers.
Ref.:

4311   UNITED STATES. ARMY. Engineers, Corps of

[Map] [Seal of Engineers Corps] / MAP OF COLORADO / PREPARED IN THE OFFICE OF THE / CHIEF OF ENGINEERS U. S. A. / 1879. /

Map, 60.5 x 59.2 cm. Scale: about 25 miles to one inch. Folded and inserted in Lawton Scrapbook.
Ref.:

4312   UNITED STATES. ARMY. Engineers, Corps of

[Map] SOUTHWESTERN NEW MEXICO. / [lower left:] DRAWN BY W. KILP, TOP ASST. / [below neat lines, left:] OFFICE OF THE CHIEF ENGINEER, DEPARTMENT OF THE MISSOURI, 1883. / [centre:] SCALE OF MILES. / [diagrammatic scale: 7 1/2 miles to one inch] PUBLISHED BY THE OFFICE OF THE CHIEF OF ENGINEERS, U. S. A., 1883. / [right:] OFFICIAL COPY, O. M. CAITER [?] / 1ˢᵀ LIEUT. CORPS OF ENG'RS: / CH'F ENG'R, DEPT. MO. /

Map, 72.3 x 72 cm. Scale as above.
Prov.: From the Grierson Papers.
Ref.:

4313   UNITED STATES. ARMY. Engineers, Corps of

[Map] MAP OF THE / TERRITORY & DEPARTMENT / OF / ARIZONA / COMMANDED BY / BRIG. GEN. GEORGE CROOK / COMPILED & DRAWN / BY & UNDER THE DIRECTION OF / FIRST. LIEUT. T. A BINGHAM / CORPS OF ENGINEERS, / U. S. A. / 1885 / [rule] / SCALE 1:675840 / [diagrammatic scale: 11 miles to one inch.] / [lower left:] E. D. WILLIAMS & OSKAR HUBER TOP ASS·ᵀ / [lower centre:] PUBLISHED BY THE OFFICE OF THE CHIEF OF ENGINEERS, U. S. A., 1885. /

Map, 94.9 x 84.5 cm. Scale as above.
Prov.: Grierson's copy, with a few notes in blue pencil.
Ref.:

4314   UNITED STATES. ARMY. Engineers, Corps of

[Map] A PORTION OF / SOUTH EASTR'N / ARIZONA / FROM TOPOGRAPHICAL RECONNAISSANCE / FIRST LIEUT. E. J. SPENCER / CORPS OF ENGINEERS, / ASSISTED BY / E. D. WILLIAMS / OSKAR HUBER [preceding two lines joined by bracket] / TOP ASSISTANTS / DURING A PORTION OF FEBRUARY, MARCH & / APRIL 1886 / SCALE / 8 / MILES TO ONE INCH / [diagrammatic scale] /.

Map, 40.7 x 60.5 cm. Scale as above.
Ref.:

4315   UNITED STATES. ARMY. Head Quarters

[Broadside] HEAD QUARTERS OF THE ARMY, WEST POINT, N. Y., AUGUST 10, 1858. GENERAL ORDERS, NO. 19. THE GENERAL-IN-CHIEF LEARNING OF THE ARRIVAL OF THE TROOPS UNDER BREVET BRIGADIER-GENERAL JOHNSTON AT THEIR DESTINATION

IN THE SALT LAKE COUNTRY . . . BY COMMAND OF BREVET LIEUTENANT-GENERAL SCOTT. IRVIN, MC-DOWELL, ASSISTANT ADJUTANT GENERAL.

Broadside, 19.3 x 11.9 cm. Text, 15.3 x 9 cm.
Ref.:
Commendation of the troops and officers under Johnston during the winter of 1857–58.

4316   UNITED STATES. ARMY. Head Quarters

[Caption title] HEAD-QUARTERS OF THE ARMY, NEW-YORK, NOVEMBER 10, 1858. GENERAL ORDERS, NO 22. THE FOLLOWING COMBATS WITH HOSTILE INDIANS—IN WHICH THE CONDUCT OF THE TROOPS, INCLUDING VOLUNTEERS AND EMPLOYES IN THE U. S. MILITARY SERVICE, IS DESERVING OF HIGH PRAISE FOR GALLANTRY AND HARDSHIPS . . .

[1]–11, [12 blank]. 20.2 x 12.8 cm. Stitched, unbound.
Ref.:
The accounts of brushes with the Indians cover the period May 24, 1857, to October 1, 1858. The engagements took place in Arizona, Florida, Texas, New Mexico, Washington, Montana, and elsewhere.

The commendations were issued at the command of General Winfield Scott.

4317   UNITED STATES. ARMY. Head Quarters

[Caption title] HEAD-QUARTERS OF THE ARMY, NEW-YORK, NOVEMBER 10TH, 1859. GENERAL ORDERS, NO. 5. I. . THE COMBATS BETWEEN UNITED STATES TROOPS AND HOSTILE INDIANS, MENTIONED BELOW IN THE ORDER OF DATE, WITH CONJOINED GALLANT ACTS AND SOLDIER-LIKE ENDURANCE OF HARDSHIPS, HIGHLY CREDITABLE TO THE TROOPS, HAVE BEEN BROUGHT TO THE NOTICE OF THE GENERAL-IN-CHIEF . . .

[1]–8. 20 x 12.7 cm. Stitched, unbound.
Ref.:
The brief accounts cover the period September 29, 1858, to October 18, 1859. The battles and skirmishes took place principally in Arizona, New Mexico, Texas, and California.

Issued by command of General Winfield Scott.

4318   UNITED STATES. ARMY. Head Quarters

[Caption title] HEAD-QUARTERS OF THE ARMY, NEW-YORK, NOVEMBER 23, 1860. GENERAL ORDERS, NO. 11. THE HEREINAFTER-, MENTIONED COMBATS BETWEEN THE TROOPS AND HOSTILE INDIANS HAVE BEEN BROUGHT TO THE ATTENTION OF THE GENERAL-IN-CHIEF . . .

[1]–19, [20 blank]. 20.3 x 13 cm. Stitched, unbound.
Ref.:
The period covered in these commendatory reports is October 30, 1859 to September 18, 1860. The reports are divided into military departments and cover the Departments of the West, Texas, New Mexico, Utah, California, and Oregon.

The pamphlet was issued by command of General Winfield Scott.

4319   UNITED STATES. ARMY. Head Quarters

[Broadside] SPECIAL ORDERS, NO. 98. HEADQUARTERS OF THE ARMY, ADJUTANT GENERAL'S OFFICE, WASHINGTON, APRIL 29, 1881. EXTRACT.
Broadside, 26 x 20.4 cm. Text, 9 x 8.6 cm.
Order concerning Colonel Richard I. Dodge.

4320   UNITED STATES. ARMY. Head Quarters

[Broadside] SPECIAL ORDERS, NO. 140. HEADQUARTERS OF THE ARMY, ADJUTANT GENERAL'S OFFICE, WASHINGTON, JUNE 19, 1883. (EXTRACT.) . . .
Broadside, 25.4 x 20.3 cm. Text, 9.2 x 8.9 cm.
Ref.:
Order concerning Colonel Richard I. Dodge.

4321   UNITED STATES. ARMY. Infantry String Band, Fourth

MUSICAL EVENING ENTERTAINMENT. GIVEN BY THE FOURTH U. S. INFANTRY STRING BAND. AT THE POST HALL FORT BRIDGER WY. TER. DECEMBER 31 1875. FOURTH INFANTRY PRESS.

[1–4, 4 blank]. 16.8 x 11.1 cm. Unbound leaflet.
Ref.: McMurtrie, D.: *The Fourth Infantry Press at Fort Bridger* (Cheyenne, 1944)
Printed at Fort Bridger.
The musical programme included flute, cornet, violin, and zither solos.

4322   UNITED STATES. ARMY. Kansas, Department of

[Broadside] GEN. ORDER NO. 1. HEADQUARTERS DEP'T OF KAN. IN THE FIELD FORT SCOTT, KANSAS, AUGUST 12 1862. I. THE GENERAL COMMANDING THIS DEPARTMENT, HEREBY ASSUMES COMMAND IN PERSON OF THE TROOPS NOW IN THE FIELD . . . BY ORDER OF BRIG. GEN. J. G. BLUNT, THO'S, MOONLIGHT, A. A. G. AND CHIEF OF STAFF. OFFICIAL: [in manuscript: Frank Davis] A. A. G.

Broadside, 19.7 x 12.5 cm. Text, 14.5 x 10.1 cm.
Ref.:
Printed in the field.

4323 UNITED STATES. ARMY. Missouri,
Department of the

[Broadside] HEADQUARTERS DEPARTMENT OF THE
MISSOURI, ASSISTANT ADJUTANT-GENERAL'S OF-
FICE, FORT LEAVENWORTH, KANSAS, DECEMBER 24,
1880. SPECIAL ORDERS, NO. 283 . . .

Broadside, 25.4 x 20.3 cm. Text, 8.8 x 9 cm.
Ref.:
Orders relieving Colonel Richard I. Dodge of
duty.

4324 UNITED STATES. ARMY. Missouri,
Department of the

[Broadside] HEADQUARTERS DEPARTMENT OF THE
MISSOURI, ASSISTANT ADJUTANT-GENERAL'S OF-
FICE, FORT LEAVENWORTH, KANSAS, DECEMBER 16,
1880. SPECIAL ORDERS, NO. 276 . . .

Broadside, 25.4 x 20.2 cm. Text, 8.5 x 9 cm.
Ref.:
Orders for Colonel Richard I. Dodge.

4325 UNITED STATES. ARMY. Missouri,
Division of the

[Caption title] HEADQUARTERS MILITARY DIV. OF
THE MISSOURI, CHICAGO, ILLINOIS, NOVEMBER 1,
1869. BREVET MAJOR GENERAL E. D. TOWNSEND,
ADJUTANT GENERAL U. S. ARMY, WASHINGTON,
D. C. GENERAL: I HAVE THE HONOR TO SUBMIT FOR
THE INFORMATION OF . . .

[1]–4. 21.7 x 13.2 cm. Unbound folder.

ACCOMPANIED BY:

[Caption title] HEADQUARTERS MILITARY DIV. OF
THE MISSOURI, CHICAGO, ILLINOIS, NOVEMBER 1,
1869. GENERAL W. T. SHERMAN, GENERAL-IN-
CHIEF, ARMY OF THE UNITED STATES, WASHING-
TON, D. C. GENERAL: I HAVE THE HONOR TO SUB-
MIT FOR YOUR INFORMATION . . .

[1]–12. 21.6 x 13.2 cm. Two folding tables.
Stabbed, unbound. In a maroon cloth case.
Ref.:
Extremely interesting reports of engagements
with the Indians. The covering letter to General
Townsend has been signed in manuscript for
Sheridan by a secretary; the attestation by Lt.
Col. George A. Forsyth is signed personally.

Several manuscript corrections in second
part.

4326 UNITED STATES. ARMY. Missouri,
Division of the

OUTLINE DESCRIPTIONS OF THE POSTS IN THE MILI-
TARY DIVISION OF THE MISSOURI, COMMANDED BY
LIEUTENANT GENERAL P. H. SHERIDAN, ACCOM-
PANIED BY TABULAR LISTS OF INDIAN SUPERIN-
TENDENCIES, AGENCIES AND RESERVATIONS; A
SUMMARY OF CERTAIN INDIAN TREATIES, AND

TABLE OF DISTANCES. CHICAGO, ILLINOIS: HEAD-
QUARTERS MILITARY DIVISION OF THE MISSOURI,
1872.

[1]–129, [130 blank], [131 Addenda], [132
blank]. 19.2 x 12.2 cm. Folding map: Map /
showing the location of / Military Posts, Indian
Reservations, & Principal Routes / in the /
States & Territories comprising the / Military
Division of the Missouri, / Lieut. General P. H.
Sheridan, Commanding. / 1872. / [at top, above
border, left:] Engineer Office, Hd Qrs. Mil.ʸ Div.
of the Mo. Major J. W. Barlow, Chief Engineer.
[right:] With Outline Descriptions of the Posts
in the Mil. Div. of the Missouri. / [below border,
left:] Drawn by Emil Reubach, draughtsman.
[right:] Chaˢ Shober & Co. Propˢ Chicago Lith.
Co. / 27.3 x 31.5 cm. Scale: 165 miles to one
inch. Blue printed wrappers: Outline Descriptions. / [rule] / Military Division of the Missouri. / [rule] / June [1872 cut out] /. In a blue
cloth case.
Ref.: Howes S394

4327 UNITED STATES. ARMY. Missouri,
Division of the

OUTLINE DESCRIPTIONS OF THE POSTS IN THE MILI-
TARY DIVISION OF THE MISSOURI, COMMANDED BY
LIEUTENANT GENERAL P. H. SHERIDAN, ACCOM-
PANIED BY TABULAR LISTS OF INDIAN SUPERIN-
TENDENCIES, AGENCIES AND RESERVATIONS, AND A
SUMMARY OF CERTAIN INDIAN TREATIES. CHICAGO,
ILLINOIS: HEADQUARTERS MILITARY DIVISION OF
THE MISSOURI, 1876.

[1]–157, [158 blank]. 18.6 x 12.4 cm. 121 maps,
all except one, page size.

[NOTE: The Military Reservation maps are
approximately the same in form, size, etc. In the
present descriptions, titles, dates of survey, and
engineers will be given, but not size, scale, etc.
The plans of forts are approximately uniform in
size, scale, etc. In the present descriptions, only
titles will be given. Italicized words appear in
manuscript.]

Military Reservation / of / Fort Snelling. /
Minn. / Surveyed *April 13 1871* / by Capt.
D. P. Heap, C. of Engr's, / [in preceding two
lines, underlined portions (actually tiny dotted
lines) in manuscript] [lower right:] Engraved by
Vitzthum. / 17.8 x 10.1 cm. Scale: One-half mile
to one inch.

Plan / of / Fort Snelling / Minn. / 17.5 x 10.2
cm. Scale: 150 yards to one inch.

Plan / of / Fort Ripley / Minn. /

Military Reservation / of / Fort Ripley. / Minn.
[word erased and supplied in manuscript] / Surveyed *June 5 1874* / by *Capt. W. Ludlow, C. of
Engr's* /

648

Plan / of / Fort Abercrombie / D. T. /

Military Reservation / Fort Abercrombie / D. T. / Surveyed _____ 18__ / Determined by Section Survey /.

Plan / of / Fort Wadsworth / D. T. /

Military Reservation / of / Fort Wadsworth. / D. T. [in manuscript] / Surveyed *June* 1870 / by *Capt. D. P. Heap, C. of Engr's* /.

Plan / of / Fort Totten / D. T. /

Military Reservation / of / Fort Totten. / D. T. / Surveyed _____ 187— / by _____ /.

Plan / of / Fort Pembina / D. T. /

Military Reservation / of / Fort Pembina. / D. T. / Surveyed _____ 187__ / by *U. S. Land Office* /.

Plan / of / Fort Randall / D. T. /

Military Reservation / of / Fort Randall / D. T. / Surveyed *1860* / by Lt J. C. Clark, 4″ Art. /

Plan / of / Fort Sully / D. T. /

Military Reservation / of / Fort Sully. / D. T. / Surveyed _____ 187__ / by *2nd Lt J. P. Walker, 22″ Inf.* /

Plan / of / Fort Rice / D. T. /

Military Reservation / of / Fort Rice / D. T. / Surveyed September 1873 / by Capt Ludlow Corps of Eng^{rs} /.

Plan / of / Fort A. Lincoln /.

Military Reservation / of / Fort A Lincoln / Surveyed May 1873 / by Capt W. Ludlow Corps Engr^s /

Plan / of / Fort Stevenson / D. T. /

Military Reservation / of / Fort Stevenson. / D. T. / Surveyed Sept. 1870. / by Capt. D. P. Heap, C. of Engr^s /.

Plan / of / Fort Buford / D. T. /

Military Reservation / of / Fort Buford / D. T. / Surveyed July 1873 / by Capt Ludlow. Corps Eng^{rs} /

Plan / of / Fort Shaw / D. T. /

Military Reservation / of / Fort Shaw. / M. T. / Surveyed *July* 1869 / by *B. F. Marsh, U. S. Dep. Surv.* /

Plan / of / Fort Ellis / M. T. /

Military Reservation / of / Fort Ellis / M. T. / Surveyed September 1873 / by W. Y. Smith U. S. Dep^y Sur. /

Plan / of / Fort Benton / M. T. /

Military—Reservation / Fort Benton / M. T. / Surveyed _____ 1870 / by *S. V. Clevenger* /.

Military Reservation / of / Camp Baker. / M. T. / Surveyed *March* 1871 / by *T. C. Bailey, Dep. Surv.* /

Plan / of / Camp Baker / M. T. /

Plan / of / Brule Agency / D. T.

Plan / of / Cheyenne Agency / D. T. / New Post on this side of the Creek / Building commenced Septr 10.th 74. /

Plan / of / Grand River Agency / D. T. /

Plan / of / Fort Seward / D. T. /

Military Reservation / of / Fort Seward / D. T. / Surveyed July 1872 / by Capt Heap Corps of Eng.^{rs} /

Military Reservation / near / Omaha /Neb. /

Plan / of / Govm^t Corral / Omaha / Neb. /

Plan / of / Fort McPherson / Neb. /

Military Reservation / of / Fort McPherson / Neb. / Surveyed March 1870 / by _____ /.

Plan / of / North Platte Post / Neb. /

Plan / of / Sidney Barracks / Neb. /

Military Reservation / Sidney Barracks / Neb. / Surveyed October 1871 / by Capt W. A. Jones Corps Eng.^{rs} /

Military Reservation / of / Fort D. A. Russell / W. T. / Surveyed _____ 187__ / by _____ /.

Plan / of / Fort D A Russell / W. T. /

Plan / of / Cheyenne Depot / W. T. /

Plan / of / Fort Sanders / W. T. /

Military Reservation / of / Fort Sanders / W. T. / Surveyed August 1874 / by Capt Stanton, Corps Eng. /

Military Reservation / of / Fort Fred Steele / W. T. / Surveyed _____ 18 / by _____ /.

Plan / of / Fort Bridger / W. T. /

Military Reservation / of / Fort Bridger / W. T. / Surveyed October 1871 / by Capt W. A. Jones Corps Eng. /

Plan / of / Camp Brown / W. T. /

Plan / of / Camp Stambaugh / W. T. /

Military Reservation / of / Fort Laramie / W. T. / Surveyed _____ 18__ / by _____ /.

Plan / of / Fort Laramie / W. T. /

Plan / of / Fort Fetterman / W. T. /

Military Reservation / of / Fort Fetterman / W. T. / Surveyed *July* 1872 / by *Louis von Froben Ass.^t* /

Wood & Hay Reservation / of / Fort Fetterman / W. T. / Surveyed July 1872 / by Louis von Froben Assistant /.

Military Reservation / of / Camp Douglas / U. T. / Surveyed _____ 18__ / by _____ /.

Plan / of / Camp Douglas / U. T. /

Plan / of / Fort Cameron / Beaver City / Utah /.

Military Reservation / of / Fort Cameron / Utah / Surveyed May 1872 / by Capt W. A. Jones Corps of Engineers /.

Post. & Wood & Hay Reservation / of / Fort Hartsuff / Neb. / Surveyed July 1874/ by Capt Stanton Corps Eng^{rs} /

Plan / of / Fort Hartsuff / Neb. /

Plan / of / Camp Robinson / Neb. /

Plan / of / Camp Sheridan / Neb. /

Plan / of / F^t Leavenworth. / Kansas. /

Military Reservation / of / Fort Leavenworth / Kan. / Surveyed _____ 18__ / by _____ /.

Military Reservation / of / Fort Riley / Kan. / Surveyed _____ 18__ / by _____ /.

Plan / of / Fort Riley / Kan /.

Plan / of / Fort Dodge / Kan. /

Military Reservation / of / Fort Dodge / Kan. / Surveyed *March* 1868. / by Lt H. Jackson, 7" Cav /.

Plan / of / Fort Harker / Kansas. /

Plan / of / Fort Hays / Kan. /

Military Reservation / of / Fort Hays / Kan. / Surveyed *July* 1867 / by L^t *M R. Brown, C. of Engr's* /

Plan / of / Fort Larned / Kan. /

Military Reservation / of / Fort Larned / Kan. / Surveyed *Sept.* 1867 / by Lt *M. R. Brown, C. of Engr^s* /

Military Reservation / of / Fort Wallace / Kan. / Surveyed *June* 1867 / by *W. H. Greenwood, Eng'r U. P. R. R.* /

Plan / of / Fort Wallace / Kan. /

Plan / of / Fort Lyon / C. T. /

Military Reservation / of / Fort Lyon / Kan. / Surveyed *April* 1868 / by Lt H. Jackson, 7" Cav. /

Plan / of / Fort Garland /.

Military Reservation / of / Fort Garland / C. T. / Surveyed _____ 18__ / by *Capt. John Rziha, 37" Inf.* /

Plan / of / Fort Union / N. M. /

Military Reservation / of / Fort Union / N. M. / Surveyed *March* 1868 / by *J. Lambert.* /

Military Reservation / of / Fort Wingate / N. M. / Surveyed _____ 18__ / by Capt J. Rziha 37 Inftry /.

Plan / of / Fort Wingate / N. M. /

Plan / of / Fort Craig / N. M. /

Military Reservation / of / Fort Craig / N. M. / Surveyed _____ 18__ / by *Capt. John Rziha 37" Inf.* /

Military Reservation / of / Fort Stanton / N. M. / Surveyed _____ 18__ / by *Capt. John Rziha, 37" Inf.* /

Plan / of / Fort Stanton / N. M. /

Plan / of / Fort Mc Rae / N. M. /

Military Reservation / of / Fort McRae / N. M. / Surveyed _____ 18__ / by *Capt. John Rziha, 37" Inf.* /

Military Reservation / of / Fort Bayard / N. M. / Surveyed Febry. 1869 / by Capt J. Rziha *37" Inf.* /

Plan / of / Fort Bayard / N. M. /

Plan / of / Fort Cummings / N. M. /

Military Reservation / of / Fort Cummings / N. M. / Surveyed _____ 18__ / by *Capt. John Rziha, 37" Inf.* /

Plan / of / Fort Selden / N. M. /

Military Reservation / of / Fort Selden. / N. M. / Surveyed *June* 1870 / by 2nd L^t. *J. B. Mackal, C. of Eng^{rs}* /

Plan of Post / near / Santa Fe / N. M. /

Plan / of / Camp Supply / Ind. Ter. /

Plan / of / Fort Gibson / I. T. /

Military Reservation / of / Fort Gibson / I. T. / Surveyed November 1869 / by Capt Philips Corps Eng. /

Plan / of / Fort Sill / I. T. /

Military Reservation / of / Fort Sill / I. T. / Surveyed *Febry.* 1871 / by Lt Orleman 10" Cavalry /

Plan / of / Post at Austin / Tex. /

Plan / of / Fort Clark / Tex. /

Plan / of / Fort McKavett / Tex. /

Plan / of / Fort Concho / Tex. /

Plan / of / Fort Griffin / Tex. /

Plan / of / Fort Richardson / Tex. /

Plan / of / Fort Stocton / Tex. /

Plan / of / Fort Davis / Tex. /

Plan / of / Fort Brown / Tex. /

Plan / of / Ringgold Barracks / Tex. /

Plan / of / Fort Mc Intosh / Tex. /

Plan / of / Fort Duncan / Tex. /

Plan / of / Fort Quitman / Tex. /

Plan / of / Fort Bliss / Tex. /

Map / showing the location of / Military Posts, Indian Reservations & Principal Routes / in the / States & Territories comprising the / Military Division of the Missouri, / Lieut. General P. H. Sheridan, Commanding. / 1872. / [upper left:] Engineer Office, Hd Qrs Mil^y Div. of the Mo. Major J. W. Barlow, Chief Engineer. / [upper right:] With Outline Descriptions of the

Posts in the Mil Div. of the Missouri. / [lower left:] Drawn by Paul Reubach, draughtsman. / [lower right:] Cha⁵ Shober & Co Prop: Chicago Lith Co. / 27.2 x 31.4 cm. Scale: 160 miles to one inch. Purple cloth sides, brown leather backstrip and corners, marbled edges.

Ref.: Howes S394

4328 UNITED STATES. ARMY. Missouri, Division of the

[Caption title] HEADQUARTERS MIL. DIV. OF THE MISSOURI, CHICAGO, ILLINOIS, APRIL 5, 1877. GENERAL ORDERS, NO. 3. I.—TO MEET THE URGENT WANTS OF THE PUBLIC, THE FOLLOWING ROUTES CONNECTING THE MISSOURI RIVER WITH THE BLACK HILLS, HAVE BEEN SELECTED . . .

[1–2], [3–4 blank]. 20.2 x 13.2 cm. Unbound leaflet.

Ref.:
Issued by R. C. Drum by command of General Sheridan.

4329 UNITED STATES. ARMY. Missouri, Division of the

[Caption title] HEADQUARTERS MILITARY DIVISION OF THE MISSOURI, CHICAGO, ILLINOIS, SEPTEMBER 20, 1881. BRIGADIER GENERAL R. C. DRUM, ADJUTANT GENERAL UNITED STATES ARMY, WASHINGTON, D. C., GENERAL: . . .

[1]–5, [6 blank]. 27.9 x 21.5 cm. Unbound.

Ref.:
Signed at end: P. H. Sheridan, / Lieutenant General Commanding. /

This is the report of an expedition sent out "For the purpose of acquiring additional knowledge of the interesting country in and about the Big / Horn Mountains, and the valleys of the Big Horn, Grey Bull and Stinking Water, and Clark's Fork, lying west / of and between the Big Horn and main chain of the Rocky Mountains, and thence crossing the main chain / to the National Park, . . . "

4330 UNITED STATES. ARMY. Missouri, Division of the

REPORT OF LIEUT. GENERAL P. H. SHERIDAN, DATED SEPTEMBER 20, 1881, OF HIS EXPEDITION THROUGH THE BIG HORN MOUNTAINS, YELLOWSTONE NATIONAL PARK, ETC., TOGETHER WITH REPORTS OF LIEUT. COL. J. F. GREGORY, A. D. C., SURGEON W. H. FORWOOD, AND CAPT. S. C. KELLOGG, FIFTH CAVALRY. OFFICIAL COPY: R. C. DRUM, ADJUTANT-GENERAL. ADJUTANT-GENERAL'S OFFICE, DECEMBER 13, 1881. WASHINGTON: GOVERNMENT PRINTING OFFICE, 1882.

[1]–39, [40 blank]. 23.1 x 14.8 cm. Two folding maps before text: Map: [Route of march from Fort McKinney to Camas]. 27.9 x 56 cm. No scale given. Map: [Route of march from Camas to Fort Washakie]. 24.9 x 39.5 cm. No scale given. Dark blue printed wrappers, with title on front wrapper.

Ref.:

4331 UNITED STATES. ARMY. Missouri, Division of the

INDEX OF GENERAL ORDERS, AND CIRCULARS, DIVISION OF THE MISSOURI, 1884.

[1]–4, plus unpaginated General Orders, etc. Bound with General Orders for Department of Dakota, 1883–84.

Comprises the following:
General Orders, Nos. 1–19, Chicago, January 18–November 4, 1884.
Circular, Headquarters Division of the Missouri, Chicago, November 22, 1884. [1], [2 blank].

4332 UNITED STATES. ARMY. Missouri, Headquarters of the

[Caption title] HEADQUARTERS DEPARTMENT OF THE MISSOURI, ST. LOUIS, MO., JANUARY 8TH, 1865. GENERAL ORDERS, NO. 7. IT BEING THE INTENTION OF THE GENERAL COMMANDING TO EMPLOY EVERY MEANS IN HIS POWER FOR THE PURPOSE OF RIDDING THE DEPARTMENT OF BUSHWHACKERS, GUERRILLA BANDS AND REBEL EMISSARIES, AND OF RESTORING AND MAINTAINING LAW AND ORDER, HE DEEMS, IT PROPER TO MAKE KNOWN, IN ORDERS, TO THE CITIZENS OF MISSOURI, THEIR DUTY IN THE PREMISES, AND THE REQUIREMENTS THAT WILL BE EXACTED FROM THEM. . . .

[1]–3, [4 blank]. 19 x 12.3 cm. Unbound leaflet, holes punched for looseleaf binder.

Ref.:
Issued by J. W. Barnes at the command of Major General Dodge.

4333 UNITED STATES. ARMY. Nebraska, East Sub-District of

[Broadside] HEAD QUARTERS EAST SUB-DISTRICT OF NEBRASKA. OFFICE OF ASSISTANT ADJUTANT GENERAL. FORT KEARNEY, N. T., NOV. 13TH, 1865. CIRCULAR, NO. 3. I . . . . . THE ATTENTION OF POST COMMANDANTS IN THIS SUB-DISTRICT IS CALLED TO THE IMPROPRIETY OF PERMITTING STRAGGLING SOLDIERS TO REMAIN ABSENT FROM THEIR COMPANIES.—[19 lines] BY ORDER OF BREVET BRIGADIER GENERAL HEATH: WM. R. BOWEN, LIEUT. AND A. A. A. G. OFFICIAL: [in manuscript:] THEO. D GERE [underline] LIEUT. AND A. A. D. C.

Broadside, 19.8 x 12.4 cm. Text, 11.7 x 10.5 cm.

Ref.:
Printed on an Army press at Fort Kearney. Printed on blue-lined (vertically) notepaper.

4334 UNITED STATES. ARMY. Nevada, District of

[Broadsheet] GENERAL ORDERS NO. 8. HEADQUARTERS DISTRICT OF NEVADA, CAMP McGARRY, NEVADA, DEC. 31. 1866 . . .

Broadsheet, 19.4 x 11.9 cm. Unbound.
Ref.:
Printed at Fort McGarry (?).
Report and commendation signed by Brevet Colonel A. G. Brackett of engagements with the Indians during the year 1866.

4335 UNITED STATES. ARMY. New Mexico, Department of

[Caption title] HEAD QUARTERS, DEPT. OF NEW MEXICO, FORT CRAIG, N. M. MARCH 13TH 1862. GENERAL ORDERS NO. 18. I . . . . AT A GENERAL COURT MARTIAL WHICH CONVENED AT FORT CRAIG, N. M. ON THE 4TH INST. . . .

[1–6], [7–8 blank]. 20.4 x 13 cm. Stitched, unbound.
Ref.:
Printed at Fort Craig (?). Printed on blue-lined notepaper.
Series of cases acted upon under General Canby's command.

4336 UNITED STATES. ARMY. New Mexico, Department of

[Caption title] HEAD QUARTERS, DEPARTMENT OF NEW MEXICO, FORT UNION, N. M., JULY 23, 1862. GENERAL ORDERS NO. 19. IN COMMEMORATION OF THE SIGNAL VICTORIES ACHIEVED BY OUR ARMS AT GETTYSBURG AND VICKSBURG ON THE 3RD AND 4TH INSTANT—A NATIONAL SALUTE WILL BE FIRED . . . BY ORDER OF BRIGADIER GENERAL CARLETON: [in manuscript: Cyrus H De Forrest] AIDE-DE-CAMP.

[1], [2–4 blank]. 19.8 x 12.6 cm. Unbound leaflet.
Ref.:
Printed at Santa Fé.
Docketed on page [4] in manuscript.

4337 UNITED STATES. ARMY. New Mexico, Department of

[Caption title] HEAD QUARTERS, DEPARTMENT OF NEW MEXICO, SANTA FE, N. M., JULY 31ST, 1862. GENERAL ORDERS, NO. 70. AT A GENERAL COURT MARTIAL, WHICH CONVENED AT PERALTA, N. M., ON THE 2ND INSTANT . . .

[1–4]. 18.6 x 12 cm. Unbound leaflet.
Ref.:
Printed at Santa Fé.
Cases tried under the jurisdiction of General Canby.

4338 UNITED STATES. ARMY. New Mexico, Department of

[Broadside] HEAD QUARTERS, DEPT. OF NEW MEXICO, SANTA FE, N. M. SEPT. 18, 1862. GENERAL ORDERS NO. 83. THE UNDERSIGNED HEREBY RELINQUISHES THE COMMAND OF THIS DEPARTMENT TO BRIGADIER GENERAL J. H. CARLETON . . . ED. R. S. CANBY, BRIGADIER GENERAL UNITED STATES VOLS.

Broadside, 18 x 12.2 cm. Text, 5.6 x 9.7 cm.
Ref.:
Printed at Santa Fé.

4339 UNITED STATES. ARMY. New Mexico, Department of

[Caption title] HEAD QUARTERS, DEP'T OF NEW MEXICO, SANTA FE, N. M., NOV. 28, 1862. GENERAL ORDERS, NO. 99 . . . HEAD QUARTERS, DEP'T. OF NEW MEXICO, FOR UNION, N. M. DECEMBER 9, 1862. GENERAL ORDERS NO. 102 . . . HEAD QUARTERS, DEPT. OF NEW MEXICO, SANTA FE, N. M., DECEMBER 15, 1862. GENERAL ORDERS NO. 103 . . .

[1–2], [3–4 blank]. 18.4 x 12.5 cm. Unbound leaflet.
Ref.:
Printed at Santa Fé.
Three General Orders printed on one sheet. All by order of General Carleton.

4340 UNITED STATES. ARMY. New Mexico, Department of

[Caption title] HEAD QUARTERS, DEPT. OF NEW MEXICO. SANTA FE, N. M. JUNE 15TH 1863. GENERAL ORDERS NO. 15. I . . . FOR A LONG TIME PAST THE NAVAJOE INDIANS HAVE MURDERED AND ROBBED THE PEOPLE OF NEW MEXICO. . . . IT IS THEREFORE ORDERED, THAT COLONEL CHRISTOPHER CARSON, . . . PROSECUTE A VIGOROUS WAR UPON THE MEN OF THIS TRIBE . . .

[1]–2. 20.2 x 12.3 cm. Unbound broadsheet.
Ref.:
Printed at Santa Fé. Printed on blue-lined notepaper.
Issued by Ben C. Cutler by command of Brigadier General Carleton. Signed in manuscript by Cutler.
This General Order sent Carson into the field against the Navajos, established his staff, and defined the troops to be used.

4341 UNITED STATES. ARMY. New Mexico, Department of

[Caption title] DEPARTMENT GENERAL ORDERS NO. 17 . . .

[1]–7, [8 blank]. 18.6 x 12.1 cm. Stitched, unbound. Punched for looseleaf binder.
Ref.:

Printed at Santa Fé.

Dated: Head-Quarters, Department of New Mexico, / Santa Fe, N. M., June 27, 1863. / Comprises report of a General Court-Martial convened at Fort Union on June 17, 1863. Signed in manuscript by Cyrus H. De Forrest by order of General Carleton.

4342 UNITED STATES. ARMY. New Mexico, Department of

[Caption title] GENERAL ORDERS, N.º 20. HEAD-QUARTERS, DEPARTMENT OF NEW MEXICO, SANTA FE, N. M., AUGUST 11, 1863. I—A MILITARY POST . . . WILL AT ONCE BE ESTABLISHED . . . THIS POST WILL BE KNOWN AS FORT BASCOM . . .

[1]–3, [4 blank]. 19.7 x 12.7 cm. Unbound leaflet.

Ref.:

Printed at Santa Fé.

The Orders also contain extracts from two General Orders from the Secretary of War. Issued by Ben. C. Cutler (signed by him in manuscript) by order of General Carleton.

4343 UNITED STATES. ARMY. New Mexico, Department of

[Caption title] HEAD QUARTERS DEPARTMENT OF NEW MEXICO SANTA FE, N. M., OCTOBER 23, 1863. GENERAL ORDERS, NO. 27. I . . . ALL OF THE TERRITORY OF ARIZONA LYING NORTH OF THE GILA RIVER AND WEST OF THE COLORADO . . . IS HEREBY CREATED INTO A NEW MILITARY DISTRICT TO BE KNOWN AS THE "DISTRICT OF NORTHERN ARIZONA." . . .

Broadsheet, 20.1 x 12.5 cm. Unbound broadsheet.

Ref.:

Printed at Santa Fé. Printed on blue-lined notepaper.

Includes orders for the establishment of Fort Whipple, Arizona, and provides for the garrison, etc.

4344 UNITED STATES. ARMY. New Mexico, Department of

[Caption title] HEAD-QUARTERS, DEPT. OF NEW MEXICO, SANTA FE, NEW MEXICO, MARCH 25, 1864. GENERAL ORDERS NO. 8. . . . .

[1–2]. 20.1 x 12.6 cm. Unbound broadsheet.

Ref.:

Printed at Santa Fé.

Signed on page [2]: By command of Brig. General Carleton. / [signature in manuscript] Erastus W. Wood / Aide-de-Camp. /

Relates to food supplies for some seven thousand captive Indians.

4345 UNITED STATES. ARMY. New Mexico, Department of

[Caption title] CUARTELES GENERALES, DEP'TO. DE NUEVO MEJICO, SANTA FE, NUEVO MEJICO, 12 DE JULIO DE 1864. ORDENES GENERALES, NO. 22 . . .

[1–3], [4 blank]. 19 x 12 cm. Unbound leaflet, holes punched for looseleaf binder.

Ref.:

Printed at Santa Fé.

Signed on page [3]: Por orden de General Carleton: / [signature in manuscript] Ben C. Cutler. / As'te Ayd'te General. /

4346 UNITED STATES. ARMY. New Mexico, Department of

HEAD-QUARTERS, DEPARTMENT OF NEW MEXICO. SYNOPSIS OF INDIAN SCOUTS AND THEIR RESULTS, FOR THE YEAR 1864. GENERAL ORDERS, NUMBER 4. [1]–[14], [15–16 blank]. 20.8 x 12.5 cm. Folding table: Recapitulation /, attached to inner back wrapper, signed in manuscript by Erastus W. Wood. Stitched, unbound. First and last leaves loose.

Ref.:

Printed at Santa Fé.

Dated on page [3] Santa Fé, New Mexico, February 18th, 1865, and signed at the end (page 14): By command of Brigadier General Carleton: / [signature in manuscript:] Ben. C. Cutler / Assistant Adjutant General. /

A day by day record "of combats with Indians on the part of the troops, as well as on that of citizens of New Mexico and Arizona during the year 1864 . . ."

4347 UNITED STATES. ARMY. New Mexico, Department of

[Broadside] HEAD-QUARTERS, DEP'T OF NEW MEXICO, SANTA FE, NEW MEXICO, MARCH 7TH, 1865. GENERAL ORDERS, NO. 6 . . . THE TERRITORY OF ARIZONA IS RE-ANNEXED TO THE DEPARTMENT OF THE PACIFIC . . . BY COMMAND OF BRIGADIER GENERAL CARLETON: [in manuscript, Ben. C. Cutler.,] ASSISTANT ADJUTANT GENERAL.

Broadside, 19.8 x 12.8 cm. Text, 11.7 x 9.8 cm.

Ref.:

Printed at Santa Fé.

4348 UNITED STATES. ARMY. New Mexico, District of

[Wrapper title] TABLE OF DISTANCES, PUBLISHED FOR THE INFORMATION OF THE TROOPS, SERVING IN THE DISTRICT OF NEW MEXICO, WITH REMARKS AND INFORMATION NECESSARY FOR CAMPING PARTIES. ACTING ASSISTANT ADJUTANT GENERAL'S OFFICE, HEADQUARTERS DISTRICT OF NEW MEXICO, SANTA FE, N.M., JANUARY 1ST, 1878.

[1]–27, [28 blank]. 19.5 x 12.5 cm. Yellow printed wrappers with title on front wrapper. Stabbed.

Ref.: Howes N85

Printed at Santa Fé.

"... compiled by First Lieutenant C. C. Morrison, 6th Cavalry, ... and revised and extended by First Lieutenant C. A. Stedman, 9th Cavalry ..."

4349 UNITED STATES. ARMY. New Mexico, District of

[Caption title] HEADQUARTERS DISTRICT OF NEW MEXICO, FORT WINGATE, N.M., AUGUST 22, 1889. SIR: PURSUANT TO TELEGRAM DESIRING THE ANNUAL REPORT OF THE DISTRICT COMMANDER ...

[1]–13, [14 blank]. 19.2 x 12.8 cm. Removed from bound volume, unbound.

Prov.: Attached to page [1] is a printed slip (5.7 x 12.7 cm.): Compliments of / E. A. Carr, / Colonel 6th Cavalry, / Brevet major General U. S. Army. /

Ref.:

This may have been printed on an Army press at Fort Wingate.

The report is signed at the end by Colonel Carr.

Manuscript corrections of typographical errors in several places.

4350 UNITED STATES. ARMY. Oregon, District of

[Broadside] HEAD-QUARTERS, DISTRICT OF OREGON, FORT VANCOUVER, W. T. MARCH 24TH, 1865. GENERAL ORDERS, NO. 14 ... BY ORDER OF BRIGADIER-GENERAL ALVORD: W. I. SANBORN, ...

Broadside, 18.7 x 12.4 cm. Text, 10 x 8.6 cm.

Inserted in Manuscript Journals of Loren L. Williams, Volume III.

4351 UNITED STATES. ARMY. Oregon, District of

MANUSCRIPT DOCUMENT, SIGNED by E. B. White. 1865 May 1, Fort Vancouver, W. T. One page, 24.8 x 15.2 cm.

Extract from Special Order No. 96 relating to Loren L. Williams. Inserted in Manuscript Journals of Loren L. Williams, Volume III.

4352 UNITED STATES. ARMY. Pacific, Department of

[Broadside] HEAD QUARTERS DEPARTMENT OF PACIFIC, SAN FRANCISCO, CAL., MARCH 7, 1865. GENERAL ORDERS, NO. 15 ...

Broadside, 16.9 x 11.4 cm. Text, 6 x 8.9 cm.

General Alvord relieved of command. Inserted in Manuscript Journals of Loren L. Williams, Volume III.

4353 UNITED STATES. ARMY. Pacific, Department of

[Broadside] HEADQUARTERS DEPARTMENT OF PACIFIC, SAN FRANCISCO, CAL., MARCH 7, 1865. GENERAL ORDERS, NO. 28 ...

Broadside, 15.5 x 11.2 cm. Text, 5.5 x 8.7 cm.

Duties of enlisted men. Inserted in Manuscript Journals of Loren L. Williams, Volume III.

4354 UNITED STATES. ARMY. Pacific, Division of the

[Broadside] HEADQUARTERS MILITARY DIVISION OF THE PACIFIC, SAN FRANCISCO, CAL., FEBRUARY 28, 1866. GENERAL ORDERS, NO. 7 ...

Broadside, 17.8 x 11.5 cm. Text, 15.3 x 8.7 cm.

Regarding inferior quality of clothing received from the East. Countersigned by Henry A. Huntington, in manuscript. Inserted in Manuscript Journals of Loren L. Williams, Volume IV.

4355 UNITED STATES. ARMY. Pacific, Department of the

[Caption title] INTERESTING SCOUT AMONG WHITE MOUNTAIN APACHES, SOME OF WHOM SUE FOR PEACE AND A RESERVATION. HEADQUARTERS CAMP GRANT, A. T., AUGUST 20TH, 1869. ASSISTANT ADJUTANT GENERAL, DEPARTMENT OF CALIFORNIA, SIR: ...

[1]–6. 19.9 x 12.8 cm. Tipped into Gaylord binder.

Ref.:

Printed at San Francisco (?).

The scout was under command of Major John Green, 1st Cavalry, U. S. A. and the report was prepared by him. The report covers the period July 20 to August 17, 1869. Inscribed at foot of page 6: Official / John C. Sherburne / A. A. G. /

4356 UNITED STATES. ARMY. Pacific, Division of the

OUTLINE DESCRIPTIONS OF MILITARY POSTS IN THE MILITARY DIVISION OF THE PACIFIC. MAJOR-GENERAL IRVIN McDOWELL, COMMANDING. HEADQUARTERS: PRESIDIO OF SAN FRANCISCO, CAL., 1879.

[i–iv, iv blank], [1]–104. 19.8 x 12.3 cm. Folding map and 68 full-page maps. Folding map: Outline Map / of / Military Division of the Pacific, / Major General Irvin McDowell / Commanding: / [short rule] / 1878. / [short rule] / [below neat line:] To accompany "Outline description of Posts" in Military Division of the Pacific, Ed. 1878. / [lower right:] Emil EcKhoff, Top. Asst. / [upper left:] Engineer Office, Hdqr's. Mil. Div.

Pacific & Dept. California / [upper right:] Capt. John H. Coster, Eight Cav. A D. C. & A E. O. in charge. / 50.2 x 38.8 cm. Scale: 80 miles to one inch. *Inset:* Territory of Alaska / [Sketch] / [diagrammatic scale: about 450 miles to one inch] / 12.7 x 13.2 cm.

Full-page maps as follows (sizes within neat lines vary; all are lithographed except as noted below):

Camp Apache / A. T. / March / 1877. /

Military Reserve / Camp Apache / A. T. / September 1877 /.

Camp Bowie / A. T. /

Military Reserve / Camp Bowie / A. T. Jan. 1878. / [lower right:] Emil Eckhoff, Top. Asst. /

Camp Grant / A. T. /

Military Reserve / Camp Grant A. T. /

Camp Lowell / A. T. March 1877 /.

Military Reserve / Camp Lowell / A. T. / March 1877 /.

Camp McDowell / A. T. March 1877 /.

Military Reserve / Camp McDowell / A. T. March 1877 /.

Military Reserve / Camp Mojave / A. T. October 1877 /.

Camp Mojave / A. T. January 1877 /.

Military Reserve / Camp Thomas / A. T. September 1877. /

Camp Verde / A. T. August 1877 /.

Military Reserve / Camp Verde / A. T. / August 1877 /.

Fort Whipple / A. T. /

Military Reserve / Fort Whipple / A. T. / September 1877 /.

Fort Yuma / A. T. / August 1877 /.

Military Reserve / Fort Yuma / A. T. / August 1877 /.

San Diego Barracks / Cal. / July 1877. /

Location / of / San Diego Barracks / Cal. /

Yuma Depot / A. T. /

Camp John A. Rucker, A. T. / [Blueprint].

Vicinity of / Camp John A. Rucker / A. T. / [Blueprint].

Camp Huachuca / A. T. / [Blueprint].

Vicinity of / Camp Huachuca / A. T. / [Blueprint].

Camp Harney / Ogn. / August 1877. /

Military Reserve / Camp Harney / Ogn. / August 1877 /.

Fort Boise / I. T. /

Military Reserve / Fort Boise / I. T. /

Fort Canby / W. T. / October 1877 /.

Cape Disappointment / W. T. /

Fort Colville / W. T. /

Military Reserve / Fort Colville / W. T. /

Fort Klamath / Oregon /.

Military Reserve / Fort Klamath / Ogn. / [Leaf shorter than text].

Fort Lapwai / I. T. /

Military Reserve / Fort Lapwai / I. T. /

(Point Adams) / Fort Stevens / Ogn. /

Military Reserve / Point Adams / Ogn. / July 1877 /.

Fort Townsend / W. T. / July 1877 /.

Military Reserve / Fort Townsend / W. T. /

Military Reserve / Fort Vancouver / W. T. /

Fort Walla Walla / W. T. / October 1877. /

Military Reserve / Fort Walla Walla / W. T. / October 1877. /

Vancouver Arsenal / W. T. /

Vancouver Depot / W. T. /

Fort Coeur d'Alene / I. T. / July 1879 /. [Blueprint].

Military Reserve / Fort Coeur d'Alene / I. T. / [Blueprint].

Camp Howard / I. T. / [Blueprint].

Alcatraz Island / Cal. /

Camp Reynolds / Angel Island Cal. / January 1877. /

Angel Island / Cal. / January 1877 /.

Military Reserve / Benicia Arsenal Cal. / July 1877 /.

Military Reserve / Benicia Barracks Cal. / July 1877 /.

Camp Bidwell / Cal. / May 1877 /.

May 1877, / Military Reserve / Camp Bidwell Cal. /

Camp Gaston / Cal. / July 1877 /.

Military.[!] Reserve / Camp Gaston Cal. / July 1877 /.

Camp Halleck / Nev. /

Military Reserve / Camp Halleck / Nev. /

Camp McDermit / Nev. / December 1877 /.

Military Reserve / Camp McDermit Nev. / December 1877 /.

Point San Jose / Cal. / April 1877 /.

Military Reserve / Point San Jose Cal. / January 1877 /.

Presidio / Cal. /

Military Reserve / Presidio / Cal. /

Public Buildings / at / Fort Point / Cal. / [Blueprint].

Plain manila (not contemporary) wrappers. In a tan cloth case.

Ref.: Howes P2

4357 UNITED STATES. ARMY. Plains, East Sub-District of the

[Broadside] GENERAL ORDERS, NO. 10. HEAD QUARTERS, EAST SUB-DIST. OF THE PLAINS, FORT KEARNEY, N. T., MAY 24TH, 1865. I—ALL POST COMMANDANTS IN THIS SUB-DISTRICT WILL FURNISH THE MEN IN THE COMMANDS, DETAILED ON ESCORT DUTY AT THE DIFFERENT STAGE STATIONS, WITH TENTS AND COOKING UTENSILS . . . BY COMMAND OF COL. R. R. LIVINGSTON: SAM'L A. LEWIS, LIEUT. AND ACTING ASSISTANT ADJUTANT GENERAL. OFFICIAL: [in manuscript: Saml A Lewis] [in manuscript: A] ASSISTANT ADJUTANT GENERAL.

Broadside, 19.8 x 22.6 cm. Text, 14.4 x 10.2 cm.
Ref.:
Printed at Fort Kearney.
Orders to facilitate rapid deliveries of mail stages—still eminently desirable in 1967.

4358 UNITED STATES. ARMY. Plains, East Sub-District of the

[Broadside] GENERAL ORDERS, NO. 12. EAST SUB-DIST. OF THE PLAINS. FORT KEARNEY, N. T., JUNE 5TH, 1865. I—IT IS REPORTED AT THESE HEAD QUARTERS THAT THE ESCORTS TO STAGE COACHES ARE IN THE HABIT OF RUNNING THEIR HORSES . . . BY COMMAND OF COL. R. R. LIVINGSTON: SAM'L A. LEWIS. ACTING ASSISTANT ADJUTANT GENERAL. OFFICIAL: [in manuscript: S A Lewis] [in manuscript: A] ASSISTANT ADJUTANT GENERAL.

Broadside, 19.6 x 12.7 cm. Text, 17.6 x 10.3 cm.
Ref.:
Printed at Fort Kearney.
Orders for the conduct of soldiers, including prohibition of sale or purchase of intoxicating liquors.
Printed on notepaper, the verso of which is blue-lined (vertically).

4359 UNITED STATES. ARMY. Platte, Department of the

AUTOGRAPH MANUSCRIPT JOURNAL of a Scout North of Fort Kearney, June 16 to July 2, 1865. Fourteen pages, 25.4 x 16 cm. In pencil.
An interesting account of an unproductive chase after marauding Indians. The author is unidentified.
Included in the manuscript is a four-page vocabulary and phrase list of an unidentified Indian tribe, probably Sioux or Crow.

4360 UNITED STATES. ARMY. Platte, Department of the

[A COLLECTION OF GENERAL ORDERS AND CIRCULARS, 1867–1882, DEPARTMENT OF THE PLATTE.]
Variously paged. 19 x 12.5 cm. Four volumes, half leather. Worn and broken.
Prov.: Duplicates from the Army War College Library.
Ref.:
Comprises the following material:

Volume I: Department of the Platte, Omaha; General Orders, Nos. 1–13, 15–56, January 7–December 20, 1867; Circulars 2, 4–7, February 11–December 3, 1867. General Orders, Nos. 1–44, January 7–December 11, 1868; Circulars [1–5] March 11–October 1, 1868.

Volume II: Department of the Platte, Omaha; General Orders, Nos. 1–33, 35–67, January 4–December 23, 1869. General Orders, Nos. 1–47, 49–51, 53–54, January 10–December 26, 1870.

Volume III: Department of the Platte, Omaha; General Orders, Nos. 1–39, 41–76, January 2–December 28, 1871. General Orders, Nos. 1–26, January 8–December 19, 1872.

Volume IV: Department of the Platte, Omaha; General Orders, Nos. 1–19, January 3–November 27. General Orders, Nos. 1–17, 19–24, January 27–December 17, 1874. General Orders, Nos. 1–22, February 19–November 20, 1875. General Orders, Nos. 2–33, January 12–November 17, 1876. Circulars [1–7], April 20–November 29, 1876. General Orders, Nos. 1–2, 4–10, 12–27, January 15–December 29, 1877. Circulars [1–5], August 9–December 15, 1877. General Orders, Nos. 1–3, 5–12, February 12–November 6, 1878. Circulars [1–3], April 1–November 23, 1878. General Orders, Nos. 1–21, 23–30, January 7–December 31, 1879. Circulars [1–6], January 28–August 22, 1879. General Orders, Nos. 1–18, January 2–December 24, 1880. General Orders, Nos. 1–11, 13–32, January 10–December 2, 1881. Circulars [1–8], February 26–Sept. 12, 1881. General Orders, Nos. 1–29, January 11–November 28, 1882. Circulars 1–25, January 23–December 27, 1882.

The Department of the Platte had four commanders during the period covered, Generals Augur, Crook, Ord, and Howard. There are numerous references to Indian fighting in the series of General Orders as well as a great deal of information about Army organization and control.

4361 UNITED STATES. ARMY. Platte, Department of the

[Caption title] HEADQUARTERS DEPARTMENT OF THE PLATTE OMAHA, NEBRASKA, AUGUST 27TH, 1876. GENERAL ORDERS, NO. 39. THE GENERAL COMMANDING TAKES PLEASURE IN ANNOUNCING TO HIS COMMAND THE FOLLOWING DECIDED SUCCESSES ON THE PART OF TROOPS, SERVING IN THIS DEPARTMENT, AGAINST GREATLY SUPERIOR NUMBERS OF HOSTILE INDIANS. . . .

[1]–3, [4 blank]. 20.4 x 12.5 cm. Unbound leaflet.

Ref.:

Printed at Omaha.

Among the engagements noted is one against Roman Nose and his band on June 26, 1867.

4362 UNITED STATES. ARMY. Platte, Department of the. (George Crook)

[Typewritten copy] HEADQUARTERS DEPARTMENT OF ARIZONA, OMAHA, NEBRASKA, DECEMBER 27, '1886[!]. THE ADJUTANT GENERAL, U. S. ARMY, WASHINGTON, D. C. SIR:— AS THE CHIRICAHUA APACHE CAMPAIGN HAS ENDED . . . I DEEM IT PROPER TO SUBMIT THE FOLLOWING RESUME OF OPERATIONS IN ARIZONA . . .

Twenty-two pages, 32.7 x 20.2 cm. Stapled at top edges.

A most absorbing account of Crook's experiences in Arizona and including the exchange of messages between Crook and Sheridan relating to the chase after Geronimo.

Docketed on the verso of the last leaf (typewritten) [broken rule] / Copy of Report of Brigadier / General George Crook, Commanding / Department of the Platte, dated / December 27th, 1886, regarding / the Chiricahua Apache Campaign / giving a resume of operations / in Arizona and New Mexico. / [broken rule] /.

The report was printed in Omaha in 1886. It covers Crook's experiences from 1882 until his replacement by Miles in April, 1886. It is a strong defense of his policy toward the Indians, particularly in the use of Indian scouts.

Both Sheridan and Grant show up poorly in the light of their letters and telegrams.

Probably given to General Grierson by Crook, corrected in manuscript, unsigned.

4363 UNITED STATES. ARMY. Quartermaster General

ANNUAL REPORT OF THE QUARTERMASTER GENERAL, OF THE OPERATIONS OF THE QUARTERMASTER'S DEPARTMENT, FOR THE FISCAL YEAR ENDING ON THE 30TH JUNE, 1850. WASHINGTON: C. ALEXANDER, PRINTER, 1851.

[i–iv, iv blank], [1]–218. 23.2 x 14.7 cm. 36 plates, of which 35 are listed. Tan back wrapper. Lacks front wrapper.

Ref.: Howes C923; Wagner-Camp 181

Contains, pages 7–127, A report, in the form of a journal, to the Quartermaster General, of the / March of the regiment of mounted riflemen to Oregon, from May 10 / to October 5, 1849, by Major O. Cross, quartermaster United States / army. /

See page 2 for schedule of plates in 1850 and 1851 editions.

31st Congress, 2nd Session, Senate. Executive Document No. 1, Serial 587.

See also under United States. President (M. Fillmore)

4364 UNITED STATES. ARMY. Seventh Military District

[Broadside] HEAD-QUARTERS, SEVENTH MILITARY DISTRICT. NEW ORLEANS, 5TH MARCH 1815. AFTER HAVING RESISTED THE OPEN EFFORTS OF THE ENEMY, HE MUST NOT BE PERMITTED TO ACCOMPLISH BY ART AND INTRIGUE WHAT HE WAS UNABLE TO EFFECT BY THE EXERTION OF HIS MILITARY SKILL AND VETERAN PROWESS . . . ANDREW JACKSON, MAJOR-GENERAL COMMANDING. QUARTIERS-GENERAUX. SEPTIEME DISTRICT MILITAIRE. NLLE.-ORLEANS, LE 5 MARS 1815. APRES AVOIR RESISTE AUX ATAQUES OUVERTES DE L'ENNEMI . . . ANDREW JACKSON, MAJOR-GENERAL, COMMANDANT.

Broadside, 30.9 x 21.4 cm. Text, 29.8 x 12.3 cm.

Ref.:

The bi-lingual broadside was issued in an attempt to placate the Louisianans of French descent who had been offended by orders for their removal beyond Baton Rouge.

4365 UNITED STATES. ARMY. Texas, Department of

[Caption title] HEADQUARTERS DEPARTMENT OF TEXAS, (TEXAS AND LOUISIANA.) SAN ANTONIO, TEXAS, NOVEMBER 25, 1870. GENERAL ORDERS, NO. 77. THE FOLLOWING INSTRUCTIONS AND SUGGESTIONS, THE RESULT OF ACTUAL EXPERIENCE IN OUR FRONTIER SERVICE, ARE PUBLISHED FOR THE INFORMATION AND GUIDANCE OF ALL CONCERNED: . . .

[1]–10. 20.2 x 12.6 cm. Glued, unbound.

Ref.:

Printed at San Antonio.

Detailed instructions for troops leaving a post on field service, personal equipment, train equipment, etc.

Issued by H. Clay Wood by command of Colonel J. J. Reynolds.

4366 UNITED STATES. ARMY. Texas, Department of

[A COLLECTION OF GENERAL ORDERS, CIRCULARS, REPORTS, AND COURTS MARTIAL REPORTS, DEPARTMENT OF TEXAS, 1874–1882.]

Variously paged. 19 x 12.2 cm. Three volumes, half leather or unbound.

Prov.: Duplicates from the Army War College Library.

Ref.:

The collection comprises the following materials: Volume I: Department of Texas, San Antonio, General Orders, Nos. 1–11, January 30–September 4, 1874. Circulars [1–4], September 8–November 18, 1874. Memorandum, March 9, 1874. Department of Texas, San Antonio, General Orders, Nos. 1–19, January 17–December 11, 1876. Circulars [1–16], May 4–September 22, 1876. [Report of a scout by Lt.-Col. W. R. Shafter], San Antonio, January 4, 1876, 13 pages, inserted after General Orders. [Report of scouts and expeditions for the year by Brig. Gen. E. O. C. Ord], San Antonio, September 26, 1876, 8 pages, inserted after Circulars. Department of Texas, San Antonio, General Orders, Nos. 1–8, April 12–Sept. 22, 1877. Circulars [1–15], February 5–December 22, 1877. Department of Texas, San Antonio, General Orders, Nos. 1–15, January 11–December 14, 1878. Circulars 1–26, January 11–December 28, 1878. Department of Texas, San Antonio, General Orders, Nos. 1–11, January 21–Nov. 25, 1879. Circulars 1–9, 12–23, 25–43, January 8–December 26, 1879. Volume II: Index of General Court Martial Orders, Department of Texas, 1876. San Antonio, 1877, pages [i–iv]. Department of Texas, San Antonio, General Orders, Nos. 1–19, January 24–December 21, 1876 (bound in reverse order). Circulars [1–20], April 25–December 13, 1876 (bound in reverse chronological order and interfiled with General Orders). General Courts Martial Orders, Nos. 1–43, January 24–December 21, 1876 (bound in reverse order). Volume III: Department of Texas, San Antonio, General Orders, Nos. 1–24, January 9–December 13, 1882. Circulars 1–26, January 10–December 30, 1882. General Court Martial Reports, Nos. 1–42, 44–48, January 9–December 30, 1882.

4367 UNITED STATES. ARMY. Texas, Department of

HEADQUARTERS DEPARTMENT OF TEXAS, SAN ANTONIO, TEXAS, DEC. 1, 1879. BRIGADIER GENERAL E. O. C. ORD, COMMANDING. REPORT UNDER THE RESOLUTION OF THE HOUSE OF REPRESENTATIVES, DATED JUNE 25, 1879, RELATIVE TO CERTAIN INFORMATION CONNECTED WITH HIS DEPARTMENT, AND THE SECURITY AND PROTECTION OF THE TEXAS FRONTIER.

[i]–[ii–iv blank], [1]–4, [folding table], [1], [2 blank], [1]–28, [1], [2 blank], [1]–[2 blank], [3–4 blank]. 19.5 x 12.5 cm. Sewn, unbound, back supported by strip of yellow paper.

Ref.: Howes O104

Printed at San Antonio, in 1879.

Abstracts A–G are present. Includes description of each post within the department.

4368 UNITED STATES. ARMY. Texas, Department of

[Caption title] HEADQUARTERS DEPARTMENT OF TEXAS, SAN ANTONIO, TEXAS, OCTOBER 1, 1880. THE ADJUTANT GENERAL, MILITARY DIVISION OF THE MISSOURI, CHICAGO, ILLINOIS. SIR: I HAVE THE HONOR OF SUBMITTING MY ANNUAL REPORT . . .

[1]–7, [8 blank], [1]–19, [20 blank], [1]–6, [1]–16, [1], [2 blank], [1]–4, [1]–9, [10 blank], [1]–10, [1]–8, [1–2], [1]–4, [1]–3, [4 blank]. 19.7 x 12.5 cm. Stitched, back supported with yellow paper strip. Holes punched for looseleaf binder.

Ref.: Howes O103

Printed at San Antonio.

General Ord's report for 1880.

Contains the Abstracts listed, A–H, K–M. Includes a roster, movement of troops, expeditions and scouts, etc.

Corrections slip tipped to page 9 of second section, 1 x 9 cm.

UNITED STATES. ARMY. Topographical Bureau

See UNITED STATES. ARMY. Engineers, Corps of

4369 UNITED STATES. Commission appointed . . . to meet . . . Sitting Bull, 1877

REPORT OF THE COMMISSION APPOINTED . . . TO MEET THE SIOUX INDIAN CHIEF, SITTING BULL, WITH A VIEW TO AVERT HOSTILE INCURSIONS INTO THE TERRITORY OF THE UNITED STATES FROM THE DOMINION OF CANADA. WASHINGTON: GOVERNMENT PRINTING OFFICE, 1877.

[1]–12. 23 x 15 cm. Lavender printed wrappers, with title on front wrapper.

Ref.:

The report is signed at the end by the commissioners, Alfred H. Terry and A. G. Lawrence. The secretary was H. C. Corbin.

4370 UNITED STATES. Commission to the Chickasaws, Mingoes, and Choctaws, 1831

[Caption title] FRANKLIN, TEN. DEC. 30, 1831. BROTHERS OF THE CHICKASAW NATION, AT THE RE-

QUEST OF YOUR GREAT FATHER, WE LATELY TRAV-
ELLED FROM OUR HOMES TO CONFER WITH YOU ON
IMPORTANT BUSINESS . . .

[1]-12. 21.3 x 13.4 cm. Stabbed, uncut. Some
marginal ticks in ink, note on page [1].

Ref.:

An address to the Chickasaws, page 4, is
dated from Oaka Knoxabee Creek, December 6,
1831. An address to the Mingoes, Chiefs and
Head Men of the Choctaw Nation is dated from
the same place the following day, page 7. J. H.
Eaton and John Coffee were the commissioners.

4371 UNITED STATES. 8TH CONGRESS,
1ST SESSION. House (Committee of
Commerce and Manufactures)

REPORT OF THE COMMITTEE OF COMMERCE AND
MANUFACTURES, WHO WERE INSTRUCTED, BY A
RESOLUTION OF THIS HOUSE, ON THE 18TH ULT.
"TO ENQUIRE INTO THE EXPEDIENCY OF AUTHORIS-
ING THE PRESIDENT OF THE UNITED STATES, TO EM-
PLOY PERSONS TO EXPLORE SUCH PARTS OF THE
PROVINCE OF LOUISIANA, AS HE MAY DEEM
PROPER." 8TH MARCH, 1804. READ, AND ORDERED
TO BE COMMITTED TO A COMMITTEE OF THE WHOLE
HOUSE, ON WEDNESDAY NEXT.

[A]⁴. [1]-7, [8 blank]. 20.8 x 12.6 cm. Rebound
in green half morocco, gilt top, uncut.

Ref.: Paltsits p. lxxxiv

8th Congress, 1st Session, House. [Washing-
ton, 1804.]

On page 4 there is a reference to the Lewis
and Clark expedition "to attempt a passage to
the western shore of the South Sea."

4372 UNITED STATES. 10TH CONGRESS,
1ST SESSION. House

MANUSCRIPT RESOLUTION, SIGNED BY NATHANIEL
MACON. 1807 January 16, Washington. One
page, 40.3 x 25.6 cm. Silked.

Resolution of the House of Representatives
calling on the President to submit information
in his possession "touching any illegal combination of private individuals" against the safety of
the United States.

Attested by John Beckley, Clerk of the
House.

4373 UNITED STATES. 10TH CONGRESS,
1ST SESSION. Senate. (Committee . . .
[on] the Conduct of John Smith)

[Caption title] EVIDENCE REPORTED TO THE SEN-
ATE, BY THE COMMITTEE APPOINTED TO INQUIRE
INTO THE FACTS RELATING TO THE CONDUCT OF
JOHN SMITH, A SENATOR FROM THE STATE OF OHIO.
DECEMBER 21, 1807. NO. I. BILL OF INDICTMENT
FOR TREASON . . .

A–R⁴. [1]-135, [136-38 blank]. 20.4 x 12.2 cm.
Rebound in marbled boards, brown calf backstrip and corners, red leather label on front
cover.

Ref.:

10th Congress, 1st Session, Senate. [Washing-
ton, 1807.]

John Smith was involved in the Burr-Wilkinson conspiracy. An attempt to expel him from
the Senate failed, but he resigned his seat.

4374 UNITED STATES. 10TH CONGRESS,
2ND SESSION. House (Committee . . .
on . . . Compensation . . . to Captain . . .
Pike)

REPORT OF THE COMMITTEE APPOINTED ON THE
FIFTEENTH ULTIMO, TO ENQUIRE WHAT COMPENSA-
TION OUGHT TO BE MADE TO CAPTAIN ZEBULON
M. PIKE, AND HIS COMPANIONS. DECEMBER 16, 1808
. . . WASHINGTON CITY: A. & G. WAY, PRINTERS,
1808.

[A]⁸. [1]-14, [15-16 blank]. 22.8 x 14.6 cm. Rebound in gray boards, maroon leather label,
uncut.

Ref.:

10th Congress, Second Session, House.

4375 UNITED STATES. 11TH CONGRESS,
1ST SESSION. (Committee . . . Act for
Establishing Trading Houses with the
Indians)

REPORT OF THE COMMITTEE, APPOINTED TO EN-
QUIRE WHETHER ANY, AND IF ANY, WHAT ALTERA-
TIONS ARE NECESSARY TO BE MADE IN THE ACT FOR
ESTABLISHING TRADING HOUSES WITH THE IN-
DIANS, AND THE SEVERAL ACTS SUPPLEMENTARY
THERETO. APRIL 14TH, 1810 . . . WASHINGTON
CITY: PRINTED BY ROGER CHEW WEIGHTMAN,
1810.

[1]-3², 5-6². [1]-11, [12 blank], 15-22. 34 x 20.5
Cm. Stabbed, uncut. In a brown cloth case.

Ref.:

11th Congress, 1st Session, Senate.

Inserted after page [12] is a double-page table
signed 4. This is apparently treated in the pagination as two pages.

4376 UNITED STATES. 11TH CONGRESS,
2ND SESSION. House (Committee to
Inquire into the Conduct of General
Wilkinson)

REPORT OF THE COMMITTEE APPOINTED TO INQUIRE
INTO THE CONDUCT OF GENERAL WILKINSON. FEB-
RUARY 26, 1811 . . . WASHINGTON: A. AND G.
WAY, PRINTERS, 1811.

[*]⁴, 1¹, 2–73⁴. [1]–582, [583–84 blank]. 22.1 x 12.5 cm. Four folding tables. Contemporary full calf, red leather label.

Ref.: Howes W432

11th Congress, Second Session, House.

The inquiry reported in this volume failed to achieve its purpose of embarrassing President Jefferson to a disastrous point. It was one of the results of John Randolph's determined enmity toward the President and his administration.

4377   UNITED STATES. 13TH CONGRESS, 2ND SESSION. House (Committee on Claims)

[26] REPORT OF THE COMMITTEE OF CLAIMS ON THE PETITION OF KENZIE[!] & FORSYTHE. DECEMBER 31, 1813 . . . WASHINGTON: A. & G. WAY, PRINTERS, 1814.

[*]². [1]–4. (Page 4 mispaginated 3.) 20.8 x 11.9 cm. Blue buckram.

Prov.: Bookplate of Joseph T. Ryerson.

Ref.:

13th Congress, Second Session, House, Document No. 26.

Relative to a claim by Kinzie & Forsythe for compensation for whiskey, gunpowder, horse and mules lost during the Fort Dearborn Massacre.

4378   UNITED STATES. 15TH CONGRESS, 1ST SESSION. House. (Committee . . . [on the] Introduction of Slaves from Amelia Island)

[Caption title] [46] REPORT OF THE COMMITTEE TO WHOM WAS REFERRED SO MUCH OF THE PRESIDENT'S MESSAGE AS RELATES TO THE INTRODUCTION OF SLAVES FROM AMELIA ISLAND. JANUARY 10, 1818. ACCOMPANIED WITH A BILL SUPPLEMENTARY TO THE ACT, TO PROHIBIT THE IMPORTATION OF SLAVES INTO ANY PORT OR PLACE WITHIN THE JURISDICTION OF THE UNITED STATES: PASSED 2D MARCH, 1807 . . .

[1]⁴. [1]–5, [6 blank], [7], [8 blank]. 24.5 x 15 cm. Removed from bound volume, uncut.

Ref.:

15th Congress, 1st Session, House, Document No. 46, Serial 7.

Printed in Washington in 1818. Page [7] carries the following note: The first copy of this Report being incorrectly printed, is to be / cancelled, and this copy to be substituted.

4379   UNITED STATES. 16TH CONGRESS, 1ST SESSION. House (Committee on Military Affairs)

[Caption title] . . . REPORT OF THE COMMITTEE ON MILITARY AFFAIRS, IN RELATION TO THE EXPENDITURES WHICH HAVE BEEN, AND ARE LIKELY TO BE INCURRED, IN FITTING OUT AND PROSECUTING THE EXPEDITION TO THE YELLOW STONE RIVER, AND OTHER OBJECTS CONNECTED WITH THE SAID EXPEDITION; TOGETHER WITH A STATEMENT OF THE DISTRIBUTION OF THE ARMY OF THE UNITED STATES, ITS TOTAL STRENGTH, AND THE STRENGTH OF GARRISONS, &C. &C. . . .

[1]–10. 22.4 x 14.3 cm. Eight printed tables bound in. Removed from bound volume, unbound.

Ref.:

16th Congress, 1st Session, House, Report No. 24, Serial 40. [Washington, 1808.]

4380   UNITED STATES. 25TH CONGRESS, 2ND SESSION. Senate. (Select Committee . . . [on] Bill to Authorize the President to occupy the Oregon Territory)

[Caption title] . . . MR. LINN SUBMITTED THE FOLLOWING REPORT: . . . THE SELECT COMMITTEE, TO WHICH WAS REFERRED A BILL TO AUTHORIZE THE PRESIDENT OF THE UNITED STATES TO OCCUPY THE OREGON TERRITORY, SUBMIT TO THE CONSIDERATION OF THE SENATE THE FOLLOWING REPORT: . . .

[1]–23, [24 blank]. 22.2 x 14 cm. Two folding maps: Map: Map / of the / United States / Territory of Oregon / West of the Rocky Mountains, / Exhibiting the various Trading Depots or Forts / occupied by the British Hudson Bay Company, con-/-nected with the Western and northwestern Fur Trade. / [swelled rule] / Compiled in the Bureau of Topographical / Engineers, from the latest authorities, under / the direction of Col. J. J. Abert, by / Wash: Hood. / 1838. / M. H. Stansbury del. / [rule] / W. J. Stone Sc. Washⁿ / 44.4 x 52.5 cm. Scale: about 17 miles to an inch. Map: Chart / of the / Columbia River / for 90 miles from its mouth. / Drawn from several surveys in the possession of / W. A. Slacum U. S. N. / [rule] / by M. C. Ewing Civil Engineer. / 41.4 x 22.9 cm. Scale: About 5 miles to an inch. Removed from bound volume, unbound.

Ref.: Howes L364; Wheat (*Transmississippi*) 434

25th Congress, 2nd Session, Senate, Document No. 470, Serial 318. [Washington, 1838.]

Imprint at foot of page [1]: [rule] / Blair & Rives, printers. /

Contains descriptive and argumentative material about Oregon by William A. Slacum, Charles Bulfinch, and others. Lewis F. Linn was a strong supporter of action in Oregon.

4381   UNITED STATES. 25TH CONGRESS, 3RD SESSION. House (Committee on Foreign Affairs)

[Caption title] . . . TERRITORY OF OREGON . . . MR. CUSHING, FROM THE COMMITTEE ON FOREIGN

AFFAIRS, TO WHICH THE SUBJECT HAD BEEN RE-
FERRED, SUBMITTED THE FOLLOWING REPORT: . . .

[1]–51, [52 blank]. 22.2 x 14.1 cm. Extra-illustrated with a portrait of Caleb Cushing as a
frontispiece.

BOUND WITH:

[Caption title] . . . TERRITORY OF OREGON. [SUP-
PLEMENTAL REPORT.] . . .

[1]–61, [62 blank]. Map: Map / of the / United
States / Territory of Oregon / West of the Rocky
Mountains, / Exhibiting the various Trading
Depots or Forts / occupied by the British Hudson Bay Company, con-/-nected with the Western and northwestern Fur Trade. / [short swelled
rule] / Compiled in the Bureau of Topographical / Engineers, from the latest authorities, under / the direction of Col. J. J. Abert, by / Wash:
Hood. / 1838. / M. H. Stansbury del. / [short
rule] / W. J. Stone Sc. Wash^n / 44.2 x 52.1 cm.
Scale: about 17 miles to one inch. Two pieces
bound together in old gray wrappers with green
paper backstrip, manuscript title on front cover.
    Ref.:
25th Congress, 3rd Session, House, Report
No. 101, Serial 351. [Washington, 1839.]
    Printer's imprint at lower left corner of each
page [1]: [short rule] / Thomas Allen, print. /
    Contains in the first part a comprehensive
summary of the history and political significance
of Oregon. The supplement contains reports and
letters by Jason Lee, Nathaniel J. Wyeth, F. P.
Tracy, William A. Slacum, Hall J. Kelley, and
others. Also contains the Constitution of the
Oregon Provisional Emigration Society.

4382   UNITED STATES. 26TH CONGRESS,
       1ST SESSION. House. (Committee on
       Territories)

[Caption title] . . . BOUNDARY OF MISSOURI AND
IOWA . . . MR. G. DAVIS, FROM THE COMMITTEE ON
THE TERRITORIES . . . SUBMITTED THE FOLLOWING
REPORT: THE COMMITTEE, TO WHICH WERE RE-
FERRED THE MESSAGES OF THE PRESIDENT AND THE
ACCOMPANYING DOCUMENTS IN RELATION TO THE
DISPUTED BOUNDARY BETWEEN THE STATE OF MIS-
SOURI AND THE TERRITORY OF IOWA, HAVE HAD
THE MATTER UNDER CONSIDERATION, AND BEG
LEAVE TO REPORT: . . .

[1]–11, [12 blank]. 22.7 x 14.3 cm. Removed
from bound volume, unbound.
    Ref.:
26th Congress, 1st Session, House, Report
No. 2, Serial 370. [Washington, 1840.]
    Imprint at foot of page [1]: [rule] / Blair &
Rives, printers. /

4383   UNITED STATES. 27TH CONGRESS,
       3RD SESSION. House (Committee on
       Territories)

[Caption title] . . . NORTHERN BOUNDARY OF
MISSOURI . . . MR. EDWARDS, OF MISSOURI, SUB-
MITTED THE FOLLOWING RESOLUTION, WHICH WAS
AGREED TO BY THE HOUSE: RESOLVED, THAT THE
REPORT OF ALBERT M. LEA, IN REFERENCE TO THE
NORTHERN BOUNDARY OF MISSOURI, THE REPORT
OF CAPTAIN GUION AND LIEUTENANT TREMONT, IN
REFERENCE TO THE DES MOINES RIVER, AND THE
EVIDENCE IN REFERENCE TO THE NORTHERN
BOUNDARY OF MISSOURI, BE REFERRED TO THE
COMMITTEE ON TERRITORIES, AND PRINTED . . .

[1]–43, [44 blank]. 22.6 x 14.3 cm. Folding map:
Map / Showing the Disputed Boundary / of /
Missouri / and / Iowa / W. J. Stone Sc Wash. /
[lower left:] Executed under direction of the /
Commissioner on the part of the / United
States / Albert Miller Lea / Com^r for U. States. /
[lower right:] Drawn January 18th by / Geo. A.
Leakin /. 44.3 x 74.2 cm. Scale: 10 miles to one
inch. Removed from bound volume, unbound.
    Ref.:
27th Congress, 3rd Session, House, Document No. 38, Serial 420. [Washington, 1842.]
    Included in this mass of material bearing on
the disputed boundary is Albert M. Lea's report
and map.

4384   UNITED STATES. 28TH CONGRESS,
       2ND SESSION. Senate. (Documents
       1–11)

PUBLIC DOCUMENTS . . . SENATE . . . SECOND SES-
SION OF THE TWENTY-EIGHTH CONGRESS, BEGUN
. . . DECEMBER 2, 1844 . . . VOLUME I . . . WASH-
INGTON: PRINTED BY GALES AND SEATON, 1845.
[1]–48, [1]–702, [703–04 blank], [1]–[4, 4 blank],
[1]–15, [16 blank], [1]–35, [36 blank], [1]–114,
[115–16 blank], [1]–2, [1–2, 2 blank], [1–2, 2
blank], [1]–11, [12 blank]. 22.6 x 13.8 cm. Five
folded printed tables and eight maps: Map:
[The United States with acquisitions by treaties]
K /. 35.6 x 54.9 cm. No scale given. Map: B /
Sketch / of the / Public Surveys / in / Michigan /
Scale 18 miles to an inch /. 54.8 x 55.3 cm. Scale
as above. Map: Sketch / of / The Public Surveys / in / Iowa Territory / Scale 18 miles to an
inch /. 35 x 20.2 cm. Scale as above. Map: H /
Diagram / of the / State of Missouri. / W. J.
Stone Sc. Wash^n / [left centre:] Surveyor General's Office / Saint Louis Novr 1st 1844. / . . . /
Silas Reed / . . . / 44.9 x 56 cm. No scale given.
Map: [top centre:] A, (1). / [lower right:] Arkansas / Map of the Arkansas Surveying district,
shewing the extent of Public Surveys / in the said
district on the 30th Sept. 1844. [preceding two

lines bracketed against following two:] / Wm Pelham / Sur. Pub. Lands / [lower left:] W. J. Stone Sc. Wash^n / 39.4 x 47.5 cm. (paper size). No scale given. Map: A Diagram / of the / State / of / Alabama / W. J. Stone Sc. Wash. / ... / Surveyor's Office, / Florence Alabama 10 Oct. 1844. / Ja^s H. Weakley, Surveyor General / of the Public Lands in Alabama /. 57.3 x 29.8 cm. No scale given. Map: A Map / of the / Peninsula of Florida / Shewing the present field of Surveying in the / Territory / ... / Office of the Surveyor General / St. Augustine Octr 28th / [signed] V. Y. Conway / Sr General /. 45.9 x 27.5 cm. No scale given. Calf, skiver label on backstrip.

Ref.:
28th Congress, 2nd Session, Senate. Documents Nos. 1–11, Serial 449.

An exceptionally interesting volume containing, among other documents, the correspondence between the United States and Mexico relating to Texas (Snively Expedition, etc.), Reports of the Secretary of War (including Army, Topographical Engineers, Bureau of Indian Affairs, etc.), the Constitution for the State of Iowa, Reports of the Surveyors General, etc.

4385   UNITED STATES. 28TH CONGRESS, 2ND SESSION. Senate. (Committee on Private Land Claims)

[Caption title] ... MR. HENDERSON, MADE THE FOLLOWING REPORT: ... THE COMMITTEE ON PRIVATE LAND CLAIMS, TO WHOM WAS REFFERED[!] THE MEMORIAL OF PIERRE CHOUTEAU, JR., AND OTHERS, PRAYING FOR CONFIRMATION OF THEIR TITLE TO CERTAIN LANDS, KNOWN AS THE "DUBUQUE CLAIM," IN THE TERRITORY OF IOWA, HAVE CONSIDERED THE SAME, AND INSTRUCTED ME TO REPORT: ...

[1]–20. 20.5 x 14.2 cm. Removed from binding, unbound.
Ref.:
28th Congress, 2nd Session, Senate, Document No. 20, Serial 450. [Washington, 1845.]

4386   UNITED STATES. 29TH CONGRESS, 2ND SESSION. Senate. (Committee on Private Land Claims)

[Caption title] ... MR. JARNAGIN MADE THE FOLLOWING REPORT: ... THE COMMITTEE ON PRIVATE LAND CLAIMS, TO WHOM WAS REFERRED THE MEMORIAL OF THE LEGAL REPRESENTATIVES OF JULIEN DUBUQUE, DECEASED, PRAYING THE CONFIRMATION OF THEIR TITLE TO CERTAIN LANDS IN IOWA, HAVE HAD THE SAME UNDER CONSIDERATION, AND BEG LEAVE TO REPORT: ...

[1]–26. 22.3 x 14.4 cm. Removed from bound volume, unbound.
Ref.:
29th Congress, 2nd Session, Senate, Document No. 218, Serial 495. [Washington, 1847.]

4387   UNITED STATES. 35TH CONGRESS, 2ND SESSION. House

[Caption title] ... PROTECTION AFFORDED BY VOLUNTEERS OF OREGON AND WASHINGTON TERRITORIES TO OVERLAND IMMIGRANTS IN 1854 ...

[1]–61, [62 blank]. 22 x 14.5 cm. Removed from bound volume, unbound. In a light green cloth case.
Prov.: Signed on page [1]: B. F. Dowell /.
Ref.:
35th Congress, 2nd Session, House, Miscellaneous Document No. 47, Serial 1016. [Washington, 1859.]

Benjamin Franklin Dowell was a lawyer and an early settler in Oregon.

4388   UNITED STATES. 36TH CONGRESS, 2ND SESSION. Senate. (Executive Document No. 1)

INDEX TO THE EXECUTIVE DOCUMENTS ... SECOND SESSION OF THE THIRTY-SIXTH CONGRESS; AND OF THE SPECIAL SESSION. 1860–61 ... WASHINGTON: GEORGE W. BOWMAN, PRINTER. 1861.

[1]–47, [49 blank]. 22.6 x 14.5 cm.
BOUND WITH:
36TH CONGRESS, SENATE. EX. DOC. 2D SESSION. NO. 1. MESSAGE FROM THE PRESIDENT OF THE UNITED STATES TO THE TWO HOUSES OF CONGRESS ... DECEMBER 4, 1860 ... VOLUME II. WASHINGTON: GEORGE W. BOWMAN, PRINTER, 1860.

[1]–996. Original full sheepskin, black and red leather labels on backstrip. Worn.
Ref.: Wagner-Camp 377, 377A, 363
36th Congress, 2nd Session, Senate, Executive Document No. 1, Serial 1078
Comprises the Report of the Secretary of War.

Contains considerable material about the West, including operations in the Departments of the West, Texas, New Mexico, Utah, California, and Oregon.

Pages 141–45 relate to an attack on immigrants by Shoshonees or Bannocks on October 4, 1860, which was also described in Fuller's pamphlet *Left by the Indians* ... [1892].

Also contains Report of Captain J. N. Macomb, Topographical Engineers, in Charge of San Juan Expedition ... pp. 149–52.

4389 UNITED STATES. 38TH CONGRESS, 2ND SESSION. (Joint Committee on the Conduct of the War)

[Caption title] MASSACRE OF CHEYENNE INDIANS ... ON MOTION OF MR. ORTH, RESOLVED, THAT THE COMMITTEE ON THE CONDUCT OF THE WAR BE REQUIRED TO INQUIRE INTO AND REPORT ALL THE FACTS CONNECTED WITH THE LATE ATTACK OF THE THIRD REGIMENT OF COLORADO VOLUNTEERS, UNDER COLONEL CHIVINGTON, ON A VILLAGE OF THE CHEYENNE TRIBE OF INDIANS, NEAR FORT LYON ...

[I]–VI, [3]–108. 21.9 x 14.1 cm. Rebound in blue cloth.

Ref.:

38th Congress, 2nd Session, Report 142 (Part 3), Serial 1214. [Washington, 1865.]

The Sand Creek massacre.

4390 UNITED STATES. 43RD CONGRESS, 1ST SESSION. House. (Committee on the Public Lands)

[Caption title] ... GEOGRAPHICAL AND GEOLOGICAL SURVEYS WEST OF THE MISSISSIPPI ... MR. TOWNSEND, FROM THE COMMITTEE ON THE PUBLIC LANDS, SUBMITTED THE FOLLOWING REPORT: ...

[1]–91, [92 blank]. 22.7 x 14.7 cm. Stabbed, unbound.

Ref.:

43rd Congress, 1st Session, House, Report No. 612, Serial 1626. [Washington, 1874.]

4391 UNITED STATES. 44TH CONGRESS, 1ST SESSION. House. (Committee on Military Affairs)

[Caption title] ... MILITARY EXPEDITION AGAINST THE SIOUX INDIANS ...

[1]–63, [64 blank]. 22.8 x 14.6 cm. Removed from bound volume, unbound.

Ref.: Howes S512

44th Congress, 1st Session, House, Executive Document No. 184, Serial 1691. [Washington, 1876.]

Contains General Terry's report on Custer.

4392 UNITED STATES. 45TH CONGRESS, 1ST SESSION. House. (Judiciary Committee)

[Wrapper title] THE CHORPENNING CLAIM. TESTIMONY TAKEN BEFORE THE JUDICIARY COMMITTEE OF THE HOUSE OF REPRESENTATIVES OF THE FORTY-FIFTH CONGRESS. WASHINGTON, D.C., FEBRUARY 13, 1879.

[1]–18. 21.6 x 14.2 cm. Gray printed wrappers, with title on front wrapper. With other Chorpenning materials in a red cloth box.

Ref.:

Signed and dated at the end: Charles Wickliffe Beckham, / Clerk Judiciary Committee, H.R., 45th Congress. / Washington, D.C., March 4, 1879. / The evidence includes that of John A. J. Creswell, J. J. / Martin, Henry L. Dawes, George E. Spencer and C. G. Me-/grue. C.W.B. / ...

4393 UNITED STATES. Indian Affairs, Bureau of

[Caption title] THE PRESENT UTTER INEFFICIENCY OF THE INDIAN DEPARTMENT HAS OBLIGED ME TO ADOPT THE FOLLOWING RULES FOR THE GOVERNMENT OF ALL PERSONS, WHO MAY BE CONNECTED WITH THE INDIAN DEPARTMENT, IN THE TERRITORY OF NEW MEXICO ... WM. CARR LANE, SUP. IND. AFFAIRS, FOR NEW MEXICO. SANTA FE, TERRITORY OF NEW MEXICO, NOV. 2D, 1852.

[1–4]. (Pages [2–4] blank.) 24.1 x 18.8 cm. Unbound leaflet.

Ref.: AII (*New Mexico*) 70

Text appears on first page only. Paper is embossed in upper right corner: D. & J. James /. Pale blue paper.

4394 UNITED STATES. INTERIOR DEPARTMENT

[Caption title] ... WAGON ROAD FROM NIOBRARA TO VIRGINIA CITY. LETTER FROM THE SECRETARY OF THE INTERIOR ... RELATIVE TO A WAGON ROAD FROM NIOBRARA TO VIRGINIA CITY ...

[1]–32. 22.6 x 14.5 cm. Rebound in new red cloth.

Ref.:

39th Congress, 1st Session, House, Executive Document No. 58, Serial 1256. [Washington: Government Printing Office, 1866.]

4395 UNITED STATES. INTERIOR DEPARTMENT. General Land Office

[Map] MAP / OF THE / UNITED STATES / AND / TERRITORIES, / SHOWING THE EXTENT OF PUBLIC SURVEYS AND OTHER DETAILS, / CONSTRUCTED FROM / THE PLATS AND OFFICIAL SOURCES / OF THE / GENERAL LAND OFFICE, / UNDER THE DIRECTION OF THE / HON. JOS. S. WILSON, / COMMISSIONER, / BY / JOSEPH GORLINSKI, DRAUGHTSMAN, / 1867. / SCALE OF MILES / [diagrammatic scale: 60 miles to one inch] / [lower right:] JULIUS BIEN, N. Y. /

Map, 71.7 x 140.5 cm. Scale as above. Folded and mounted on cloth and pasted to green leather covers, gilt. In centre of each cover, gilt shield surmounted by General Land Office / United States of America / and above Annual Report 1868. /

Ref.: Phillips p. 916

4396   UNITED STATES. INTERIOR DE-PARTMENT. (Census Bureau)

DEPARTMENT OF THE INTERIOR, CENSUS OFFICE . . . REPORT ON INDIANS TAXED AND INDIANS NOT TAXED IN THE UNITED STATES (EXCEPT ALASKA) AT THE ELEVENTH CENSUS: 1890. WASHINGTON, D.C.: GOVERNMENT PRINTING OFFICE, 1894.

[i]–[viii, viii blank], 1–683, [684 blank]. 28.9 x 23 cm. 197 illustrations and 25 maps listed, many in color. Black cloth.

Ref.:

4397   UNITED STATES. DISTRICT COURT (Iowa)

RULES OF THE DISTRICT COURT OF THE UNITED STATES FOR THE DISTRICT OF IOWA. ADOPTED AT THE JANUARY TERM, A. D. 1848. IOWA CITY: PRINTED BY ABRAHAM H. PALMER, 1848.

[1]–28. 20.1 x 13.8 cm. New brown wrappers.

Ref.: Moffit 50

4398   UNITED STATES. NATIONAL MU-SEUM

. . . FIFTH ANNUAL REPORT OF THE BOARD OF REGENTS OF THE SMITHSONIAN INSTITUTION, TO THE SENATE AND HOUSE OF REPRESENTATIVES, SHOWING THE OPERATIONS, EXPENDITURES, AND CONDITION OF THE INSTITUTION, DURING THE YEAR 1850 . . . WASHINGTON: 1851.

[1]–325, [326–28 blank], [1]–2, [1]–5, [6–8 blank], [1]–26, [27–8 blank], [1]–15, [16 blank]. 22 x 14.4 cm. Removed from bound volume, protected by tan wrappers.

Ref.: Howes C941; Wagner-Camp 198

31st Congress, Special Session, Senate, Miscellaneous Document No. 1, Serial 547.

Included as Appendix—No. IV., pages 84–145, is Journal of an Expedition to the Mauvaises / Terres and Upper Missouri in 1850: / By Thaddeus A. Culbertson. /

4399   UNITED STATES. NATIONAL MU-SEUM

NINTH ANNUAL REPORT OF THE BOARD OF REGENTS OF THE SMITHSONIAN INSTITUTION . . . WASHINGTON: A. O. P. NICHOLSON, PUBLIC PRINTER. 1855.

[1]–463, [464 blank]. 22.3 x 14 cm. Black cloth, blind embossed sides, title in gilt on backstrip.

Ref.: Wagner-Camp 251

Contains: Diary / Of an excursion to the ruins of Abó, Quarra, and Gran Quivira, in New / Mexico, under the command of / Major James Henry Carleton, U. S. A. / Pages 296–316.

4400   UNITED STATES. POST OFFICE DE-PARTMENT

[Caption title] REPORT OF THE POSTMASTER GENERAL. POST OFFICE DEPARTMENT, DECEMBER 4, 1858. TO THE PRESIDENT OF THE UNITED STATES: . . .

[715]–862. 22.4 x 14.2 cm. New plain wrappers.

Ref.: Wagner-Camp 315

Extract from 35th Congress, 2nd Session, Senate, Executive Document No. 1, Part 4, Serial 977. [Washington, 1859.]

Pages 744–752 carry: San Antonio and San Diego Route. / Extract from a report made in March, 1858, to the Postmaster General / by the superintendent of the route from San Antonio, Texas, to San / Diego, California. / . . .

Aaron V. Brown was the postmaster general.

4401   UNITED STATES. POST OFFICE DE-PARTMENT

[Caption title] REPORT TO HON. A. V. BROWN, POSTMASTER GENERAL, ON THE UNITED STATES OVERLAND MAIL ROUTE BETWEEN SAN ANTONIO, TEXAS, AND SAN DIEGO, CALIFORNIA, BY J. C. WOOD, SUPERINTENDENT. WASHINGTON CITY, D. C., MARCH—, 1858 . . .

[1]–43, [44 blank]. 24.1 x 15.2 cm. Stabbed, unbound, uncut, unopened. Some lower outer corners crumbling. In a brown half morocco case.

Ref.: Howes W628; Wagner-Camp 315

This seems to be a private printing of a public document. See Number 4400.

4402   UNITED STATES. POST OFFICE DE-PARTMENT

[Caption title] IN THE MATTER OF GEORGE CHORPENNING, BEFORE THE POSTMASTER-GENERAL . . .

[1]–29, [30–32 blank]. 21.7 x 14.1 cm. Stabbed, unbound. With other Chorpenning pamphlets in a red cloth case.

Ref.:

The award by the Postmaster-General, John A. J. Creswell, to Chorpenning of $443,010.60.

4403   UNITED STATES. POST OFFICE DE-PARTMENT

[Map] [Seal of Post Office Department] / POST ROUTE MAP / OF THE TERRITORY OF / UTAH / WITH PARTS OF / ADJACENT STATES AND TERRITORIES / SHOWING POST OFFICES WITH THE INTERMEDIATE DISTANCES AND MAIL ROUTES / IN OPERATION ON THE 1ST OF FEBRUARY 1887. / PUBLISHED BY ORDER OF / POSTMASTER GENERAL WILLIAM F. VILAS / UNDER THE DIRECTION OF / W. L. NICHOLSON, TOPOGRAPHER P. O. DEPT / 1884. / SCALE / TEN MILES TO THE INCH (NEARLY) /

Map, cut and mounted on cloth, 104.1 x 75.4 cm. Scale as above. Maroon cloth protective panels, with printed label: Post Route Map / of the Territory of / Utah, 1884 / [date in manuscript on mounted slip; Utah / on smaller slip mounted on preceding slip].

Ref.:

There are some manuscript additions to the map. At the end of the "Explanation" the date April 1st, 1887 appears in manuscript.

4404   UNITED STATES. PRESIDENT (John Adams)

MESSAGE OF THE PRESIDENT OF THE UNITED STATES, TO BOTH HOUSES OF CONGRESS, APRIL 3D, 1798. PHILADELPHIA: PRINTED BY T. DOBSON AND J. ORMROD, 1798.

A–G⁴, H². [1]–60. Bound with Number 3867.

Ref.: Evans 34814

The *Message* contains the " X Y Z correspondence."

Editions: [Philadelphia, 1798.]

4405   UNITED STATES. PRESIDENT (Thomas Jefferson)

MESSAGE FROM THE PRESIDENT OF THE UNITED STATES TO BOTH HOUSES OF CONGRESS. 8TH NOVEMBER, 1804 . . . WASHINGTON CITY: PRINTED BY WILLIAM DUANE & SON, 1804.

[A]⁵, B³, C², B⁴, C⁴. [i–ii], [1]–8, [11]–[14], [3]–22, [23–24 blank]. 22.4 x 14.7 cm. Stabbed, unbound, uncut, unopened. In a green cloth case, green morocco back.

Ref.: Howes A401

8th Congress, 2nd Session, House.

Contains Moses Austin's *A Summary Description of the Lead Mines in Upper Louisiana. To which is Added an Estimate of their Produce for three Years Past.*

4406   UNITED STATES. PRESIDENT (Thomas Jefferson)

MESSAGE FROM THE PRESIDENT OF THE UNITED STATES, COMMUNICATING DISCOVERIES MADE IN EXPLORING THE MISSOURI, RED RIVER AND WASHITA, BY CAPTAINS LEWIS AND CLARK, DOCTOR SIBLEY, AND MR. DUNBAR; WITH A STATISTICAL ACCOUNT OF THE COUNTRIES ADJACENT. FEBRUARY 19, 1806 . . . CITY OF WASHINGTON: A. & G. WAY, PRINTERS, 1806.

[1]–22⁴, 23². [1]–[178], [179–80 blank]. 20.4 x 12.3 cm. Folding printed table after page 30, map at back. Map: Map / of the / Washita River / in / Louisiana / Engraved by Wᵐ Kneass Philad. / from the Hot Springs to the Confluence of the Red River with the / Mississippi / Laid

down from the Journal & Survey of Wᵐ Dunbar Esqʳ in the Year 1804 / by / Nicholas King. / 20 x 83.6 cm. Scale: 8 miles to one inch. Old marbled board sides, new calf backstrip and corners, green leather label. Rectos repaginated in manuscript.

Ref.: Howes L319; Rader 3358; Wagner-Camp 5

9th Congress, 1st Session, House.

4407   UNITED STATES. PRESIDENT (Thomas Jefferson)

THE SAME . . . NEW-YORK: PRINTED BY HOPKINS AND SEYMOUR, 1806.

A–Q⁴. [1]–128. 22 x 13.1 cm. Folding table between pages 24 and 25. Original gray boards, uncut. Rebacked with calf.

Prov.: Bookplate of John Jay Paul.

Ref.: Howes L319; Sabin 40824; Wagner-Camp 5 see

A reprint of the preceding number.

4408   UNITED STATES. PRESIDENT (Thomas Jefferson)

MESSAGE FROM THE PRESIDENT OF THE UNITED STATES, TRANSMITTING INFORMATION TOUCHING AN ILLEGAL COMBINATION OF PRIVATE INDIVIDUALS AGAINST THE PEACE AND SAFETY OF THE UNION, AND A MILITARY EXPEDITION PLANNED BY THEM AGAINST THE TERRITORIES OF A POWER IN AMITY WITH THE UNITED STATES . . . JANUARY 22, 1807 . . .

[1]–24⁴. [1]–16. 20.4 x 13.5 cm. Rebound in blue boards, black cloth back, blue skiver label.

Ref.:

9th Congress, 2nd Session, Senate and House. [Washington, 1807.]

The *Message* had been demanded by John Randolph, one of Jefferson's most bitter enemies, with a design to embarrass the President. It contains important letters relating to the Burr-Wilkinson conspiracy.

4409   UNITED STATES. PRESIDENT (James Monroe)

[47] MESSAGE FROM THE PRESIDENT OF THE UNITED STATES, COMMUNICATING INFORMATION OF THE TROOPS OF THE UNITED STATES HAVING TAKEN POSSESSION OF AMELIA ISLAND, IN EAST FLORIDA. JANUARY 13, 1818 . . . WASHINGTON: PRINTED BY E. DE KRAFFT, 1818.

[1]–24⁴, 3². [1]–20. 23.7 x 15.5 cm. Removed from a bound volume, uncut.

Ref.:

15th Congress, 1st Session, Senate, Document No. 47, Serial 2.

4410 UNITED STATES. PRESIDENT
(James Monroe)

[197] MESSAGE FROM THE PRESIDENT OF THE UNITED STATES, TRANSMITTING, IN COMPLIANCE WITH A RESOLUTION OF THE HOUSE OF REPRESENTATIVES, OF THE 10TH INSTANT, INFORMATION RELATIVE TO THE ARREST AND IMPRISONMENT OF CERTAIN AMERICAN CITIZENS AT SANTA FE, BY AUTHORITY OF THE GOVERNMENT OF SPAIN. APRIL, 15, 1818 . . . WASHINGTON: PRINTED BY E. DE KRAFT, 1818.

[1]–23, [24 blank]. 20.5 x 13.2 cm. Rebound in new red cloth.

Ref.: Howes S103; Wagner-Camp 15
15th Congress, 1st Session, House, Document No. 197, Serial 12.

The arrests treated in this *Message* were those of Augustus Pierre Chouteau, Julius Demun, Robert McKnight, James Baird, J. Farro, and their companies.

4411 UNITED STATES. PRESIDENT
(Andrew Jackson)

[Caption title] . . . MESSAGE FROM THE PRESIDENT OF THE UNITED STATES . . . CONCERNING THE FUR TRADE, AND INLAND TRADE TO MEXICO . . .

[1]–86, [87–8 blank]. 22.6 x 14.3 cm. Rebound in new red cloth.

Ref.: Wagner-Camp 46
22nd Congress, 1st Session, Senate, Document No. 90, Serial 213. [Washington, 1832.]

Contains a variety of letters and reports from the Far West relating to trade and the fur trade by William Clark, Joshua Pilcher, Andrew S. Hughes, William Gordon, Alphonso Wetmore, John Dougherty, Thomas Forsyth, and others.

4412 UNITED STATES. PRESIDENT
(Martin Van Buren)

[Caption title] . . . MESSAGE FROM THE PRESIDENT OF THE UNITED STATES, COMMUNICATING ADDITIONAL INFORMATION IN RELATION TO THE DISPUTED BOUNDARY LINE BETWEEN THE STATE OF MISSOURI AND TERRITORY OF IOWA . . .

[1]–20. 22.4 x 14.7 cm. Removed from bound volume, unbound.
Ref.:
26th Congress, 1st Session, Senate, Document No. 35, Serial 376. [Washington, 1840.]

Imprint at foot of page [1]: [rule] / Blair & Rives, printers. /

4413 UNITED STATES. PRESIDENT
(J. K. Polk)

. . . MESSAGE FROM THE PRESIDENT . . . DECEMBER 2, 1845 . . . WASHINGTON: PRINTED BY RITCHIE & HEISS, 1845,

[1]–893, [894 blank]. 22.9 x 14.7 cm. Tan marbled boards, calf backstrip and corners, green leather label. Hinges cracked, cover loose.

Ref.: Wagner-Camp 117
29th Congress, 1st Session, House, Executive Document No. 2, Serial 480.

Pages 210–13 comprise a "Report of a summer campaign to the Rocky mountains, &c., in 1845" in the form of a letter by Stephen W. Kearny. Pages 214–17 comprise an "Abstract of journals kept by Lt. Turner, adjutant 1st dragoons, and Lt. / Franklin, Top. Eng., during an expedition performed in the summer / of 1845, by five companies of the 1st dragoons under the command of / Colonel S. W. Kearney. /" Pages 217–20 comprise a letter from Fort Atkinson, August 23, 1845, by E. V. Sumner. Accompanying the first report is a map: Map / of the Route Pursued by the Late Expedition / under the command of Col. S. W. Kearny, U. S. 1st Dragoons. / By W. B. Franklin, Lieut. Corps Topl Engs / attached to the Expedition. / 1845. / Smith & McCleland Sc. / Washn / [upper right:] Doc. No 2 H. R. at page 210. / 1st Sess. 29th Cong. / 20.1 x 33.1 cm. (neat line). Scale: about 65 miles to one inch.

Since the reports in this volume include those of the Secretary of War, there are considerable materials relating to the West.

4414 UNITED STATES. PRESIDENT
(Zachary Taylor)

[Caption title] PUBLIC DOCUMENTS, ON THE SUBJECT OF CALIFORNIA. PRESIDENT'S SPECIAL MESSAGE. WASHINGTON, JANUARY 21, 1850. TO THE HOUSE OF REPRESENTATIVES OF THE UNITED STATES: . . .

[1]–8. 22.3 x 14.5 cm. Removed from bound volume, unbound.
Ref.:
The Message relates to the establishment of a territorial government in California and is accompanied by letters by J. M. Clayton, James Buchanan and others. Territorial governments for both California and New Mexico were treated in this Message.

There is no indication of place of printing. The general character of the printing, format, etc. suggest California rather than Washington, D. C.

Preceding the printed Message is a manuscript index (mouth-waterin', to say the least) of pamphlets apparently once bound together, including a *Constitution of California*, which see!

4415 UNITED STATES. PRESIDENT (Millard Fillmore)

. . . MESSAGE FROM THE PRESIDENT . . . DECEMBER

2, 1850 ... WASHINGTON: PRINTED FOR THE SENATE, 1850.

[1]–444, [1]–488. 22.2 x 14.2 cm. 36 plates, one of which is not listed. Marbled boards, black leather backstrip and corners. Two parts bound together.

Ref.: Howes C923; Wagner-Camp 181

31st Congress, 2nd Session, Senate, Executive Document No. 1, Serial 587.

The title-page of the second part is the same as the first, except for Part II. / above imprint. The second part comprises the Report of the Secretary of War C. M. Conrad. Pages 126–244 (illustrated) comprise a report marked A appended to the report of the Quartermaster General: A report, in the form of a journal, to the Quartermaster General, of the / march of the regiment of mounted riflemen to Oregon, from May 10 / to October 5, 1849, by Major O. Cross, quartermaster United States / army. /

There are large quantities of western material in this volume and it probably deserves a careful examination.

See also under United States. Army. Quartermaster General (T. S. Jesup)

4416 UNITED STATES. PRESIDENT
(James Buchanan)

MESSAGE OF THE PRESIDENT ... JANUARY 4, 1858 ... VOL. II. WASHINGTON: WILLIAM A. HARRIS, PRINTER, 1858.

[1]–572. 22.5 x 14.1 cm. Removed from binding, protected by tan paper wrappers.

Ref.: Wagner-Camp 286

35th Congress, 1st Session, Senate, Executive Document No. 11, Volume 2, Serial 919.

Pages 455–520 comprise a letter by Francis T. Bryan reporting his experiences on the road from Fort Riley to Bridger's Pass, a "Report on the topography of the country between Lodge Pole creek, / Cache la Poudre, and the South Platte, in connection with an explo-/ration for a road from Fort Riley to Bridger's Pass, by John Lam-/bert, topographer. /", and a "Report of a geological exploration from Fort Leavenworth to Bryan's / Pass, made in connexion with the survey of a road from Fort Riley / to Bridger's Pass, under command of Lieutenant F. T. Bryan, topo-/graphical engineer, 1856, by H. Engelmann, geologist and mining / engineer. /" The first comprises pages 455–81, the second pages 481–88, and the third pages 489–520.

Being the report of the Secretary of War, the volume contains sizable quantities of material about the West.

4417 UNITED STATES. PRESIDENT
(James Buchanan)

[Caption title] ... EXECUTION OF COLONEL CRABB AND ASSOCIATES. MESSAGE FROM THE PRESIDENT OF THE UNITED STATES, COMMUNICATING OFFICIAL INFORMATION AND CORRESPONDENCE IN RELATION TO THE EXECUTION OF COLONEL CRABB AND HIS ASSOCIATES ...

[1]–84. 22.4 x 14.4 cm. Rebound in new red cloth.

Ref.: Howes C839

35th Congress, 1st Session, House, Executive Document No. 64, Serial 930. [Washington, 1858.]

The correspondence and documents printed in this volume comprise the official record of the end of the filibustering expedition of Henry A. Crabb.

4418 UNITED STATES. PRESIDENT
(James Buchanan)

[Caption title] ... MESSAGE OF THE PRESIDENT OF THE UNITED STATES, COMMUNICATING ... INFORMATION IN RELATION TO THE MASSACRE AT MOUNTAIN MEADOWS, AND OTHER MASSACRES IN UTAH TERRITORY ...

[1]–139, [140 blank]. 22.5 x 14.6 cm. Stabbed, unbound.

Ref.: Howes M867

36th Congress, 1st Session, Senate, Executive Document No. 42, Serial 1033. [Washington, 1860.]

4419 UNITED STATES. SURVEYOR GENERAL (Wisconsin and Iowa)

[Caption title] GENERAL INSTRUCTIONS. OFFICE OF THE SURVEYOR GENERAL OF WISCONSIN AND IOWA, DUBUQUE, 18 TO DEPUTY SURVEYOR: ...

[1]–18, [i–iv blue-ruled notepaper], [19]–58. 20.7 x 13.3 cm. Plain yellow wrappers with brown cloth backstrip.

Ref.: AII (*Iowa Supp.*) 38 see

The printer's imprint appears in the lower left corner of the final page: [rule] / A. P. Wood, Printer, / Dubuque, Iowa. / The last date in the book (on the same page) is March 31, 1852, an affidavit attached to a completed survey.

AII (*Iowa*) gives a date 1851 and a collation of 80 pages.

4420 UNITED STATES. TREASURY DEPARTMENT (Secretary, A. J. Dallas)

LETTER ... EXHIBITING THE BOUNTY PAID ON THE EXPORTATION OF PICKLED FISH AND SALTED PROVISIONS ... WASHINGTON: PRINTED BY WILLIAM A. DAVIS, 1816.

[A–B]². [1–8]. Large folded table. 33.5 x 20.8 cm.
BOUND WITH:

LETTER FROM THE SECRETARY OF WAR, TRANS-
MITTING DOCUMENTS EXHIBITING THE GENERAL
EXPENSES OF THE INDIAN DEPARTMENT, EMBRACING
ANNUITIES AND PRESENTS, AND THE GENERAL AND
PARTICULAR VIEWS OF THE INDIAN TRADE . . .
WASHINGTON: PRINTED BY WILLIAM A. DAVIS,
1816.

[1]–32². [1]–128. Folded tables.
BOUND WITH:

MESSAGES FROM THE PRESIDENT OF THE UNITED
STATES TRANSMITTING A REPORT OF SECRETARY OF
THE TREASURY, RELATIVE TO THE MEASURES WHICH
HAVE BEEN TAKEN TO COMPLETE AN ACCURATE
SURVEY OF THE COAST OF THE UNITED STATES . . .
WASHINGTON: PRINTED BY WILLIAM A. DAVIS,
1816.

[1]–3². [1]–[11], [12 blank]. Folding tables.
Three documents bound together, contemporary
blue marbled boards, calf back, red leather label,
uncut.

Ref.:
14th Congress, 1st Session. Senate.

4421 UNITED STATES. TREASURY DE-
PARTMENT

REPORT OF THE SECRETARY OF THE TREASURY, IN
CONFORMITY TO THE PROVISIONS OF THE ACT OF
FIFTEENTH MAY, 1820, FOR THE RELIEF OF THE IN-
HABITANTS OF THE VILLAGE OF PEORIA, IN THE
STATE OF ILLINOIS . . . WASHINGTON: PRINTED BY
GALES & SEATON, 1821.

[1]–39, [40 blank]. 24.4 x 15.3 cm. Folded sheets,
uncut, partially unopened.

Ref.:
16th Congress, 2nd Session, Senate, Document No. 76, Serial 43.

4422 UNITED STATES. TREASURY DE-
PARTMENT

[Caption title] . . . TREAS. DEPT. LAND OFFICE AT
FAIRFIELD, IOWA. LETTER FROM THE SECRETARY OF
THE TREASURY, TRANSMITTING A COPY OF REPORT
OF THE COMMISSIONER OF THE GENERAL LAND OF-
FICE, AND ALSO OF THE REGISTER AND RECEIVER OF
THE LAND OFFICE AT FAIRFIELD, IN THE TERRITORY
OF IOWA . . .

[1]–12. 22.8 x 14.4 cm. Removed from bound
volume, unbound.

Ref.:
29th Congress, 1st Session, House, Document
No. 200, Serial 485. [Washington, 1846.]
Imprint at foot of page [1]: [rule] / Ritchie &
Hess, print. /
R. J. Walker was Secretary of the Treasury.

4423 UNITED STATES. TREASURY DE-
PARTMENT (Bureau of Statistics)

TREASURY DEPARTMENT. REPORT ON THE INTERNAL
COMMERCE OF THE UNITED STATES, BY JOSEPH
NIMMO, JR. . . . WASHINGTON: GOVERNMENT
PRINTING OFFICE, 1885.

[1]–562. 22.9 x 14.3 cm. Five folding maps.
Black cloth, title in gilt on backstrip.

Ref.: Adams (*Ramp. Herd*) 1674; Howes
N158
49th Congress, 1st Session, House, Executive
Document No. 7, Part 3, Serial 2342.

4424 UNITED STATES. TREASURY DE-
PARTMENT (Bureau of Statistics)

REPORT IN REGARD TO THE RANGE AND RANCH
CATTLE BUSINESS OF THE UNITED STATES. BY JOSEPH
NIMMO, JR., CHIEF OF THE BUREAU OF STATISTICS,
TREASURY DEPARTMENT. MAY 16, 1885. WASHING-
TON: GOVERNMENT PRINTING OFFICE. 1885.

[i]–[ix], [x blank], [1]–200, 23 x 15 cm. Folding
map. Gray printed wrappers with title within
thick and thin rule borders. In green buckram
case.

Ref.: Adams (*Ramp. Herd*) 1673 see; Howes
N158
Same as 48th Congress, 2nd Session, House,
Executive Document No. 267, Serial 2304.

4425 UNITED STATES. TREASURY DE-
PARTMENT. (Bureau of Statistics)

[Caption title] LETTER FROM THE SECRETARY OF
THE TREASURY, TRANSMITTING A REPORT FROM THE
CHIEF OF THE BUREAU OF STATISTICS . . . IN RE-
GARD TO THE RANGE AND RANCH CATTLE TRAFFIC
IN THE WESTERN STATES AND TERRITORIES . . .

[1]–200. 22.8 x 14.8 cm. Four folding maps.
Stabbed, unbound. In black half morocco
folder.

Ref.: Adams (*Ramp. Herd*) 1673; Howes
N158
48th Congress, 2nd Session, House, Executive Document No. 267, Serial 2304.

4426 UNITED STATES. TREASURY DE-
PARTMENT. (Mint)

INSTRUCTIONS FOR THE MANAGEMENT OF THE
BRANCH OF THE U. S. MINT, AT DENVER, COLORADO
TERRITORY. 1863. DENVER: PRINTED BY NEWS
PRINTING COMPANY, 1863.

[1]–8. 21.6 x 13.4 cm. Removed from bound volume, tipped into plain cream wrappers.

Ref.:
Signed on page 8: James Pollock, / Director
U. S. Mint. / Approved March 28, 1863. / S. P.
Chase. / True Copy: / H. R. Lindeman, / Direc-
tor's Clerk. /

4427 UNITED STATES. WAR DEPART-MENT.

DOCUMENTS ACCOMPANYING A BILL MAKING COMPENSATION TO MESSIEURS LEWIS AND CLARKE, AND THEIR COMPANIONS, PRESENTED THE 23D JANUARY, 1807. WASHINGTON CITY: A. & G. WAY, PRINTERS, 1807.

[1]–8, large folding table. 20.5 x 12.1 cm. Large folding table. Removed from bound volume, unbound. In a blue cloth case.

    Ref.:

9th Congress, 2nd Session, House.

The folding table is a report by Lewis of the members of his party with remarks about some of them and recommendations for suitable rewards, etc.

4428 UNITED STATES. WAR DEPART-MENT

LETTER FROM THE SECRETARY OF WAR, TRANSMITTING DOCUMENTS EXHIBITING THE GENERAL EXPENSES OF THE INDIAN DEPARTMENT, EMBRACING ANNUITIES AND PRESENTS, AND THE GENERAL AND PARTICULAR VIEWS OF THE INDIAN TRADE . . . MARCH 14, 1816 . . . WASHINGTON: PRINTED BY WILLIAM A. DAVIS, 1816.

[1]–32². [1]–128. 34 x 21.4 cm. Eight folded tables. Stabbed, uncut.

    Ref.:

14th Congress, Second Session, Senate.

Payments to the son of Sacajewea are noted.

4429 UNITED STATES. WAR DEPART-MENT

[Caption title] . . . MESSAGE FROM THE PRESIDENT OF THE UNITED STATES, IN ANSWER TO A RESOLUTION OF THE SENATE RELATIVE TO THE BRITISH ESTABLISHMENTS ON THE COLUMBIA, AND THE STATE OF THE FUR TRADE, &C. . . .

[1]–34. 22.5 x 14.2 cm. Bound into gray cloth, with early manuscript title on green paper.

    Ref.:

21st Congress, 2nd Session, Senate, Document No. 39, Serial 203.

4430 UNITED STATES. WAR DEPART-MENT

[Caption title] . . . ROAD—GREEN BAY TO PRAIRIE DU CHIEN. LETTER FROM THE SECRETARY OF WAR, TRANSMITTING ALL THE COMMUNICATIONS MADE TO THE DEPARTMENT UPON THE SUBJECT OF A ROAD BETWEEN GREEN BAY AND PRAIRIE DU CHIEN . . .

[1]–4. 24.6 x 15.3 cm. Unbound leaflet, uncut. Removed from bound volume.

    Ref.:

22nd Congress, 1st Session, House, Document No. 42, Serial 217. [Washington, 1832.]

4431 UNITED STATES. WAR DEPART-MENT

[Caption title] . . . ROAD—GREEN BAY TO PRAIRIE DU CHIEN. LETTER FROM THE SECRETARY OF WAR, TRANSMITTING FURTHER INFORMATION IN RELATION TO THE ROAD FROM GREEN BAY TO PRAIRIE DU CHIEN . . .

[1]–2. 24.9 x 14.7 cm. Unbound leaflet, removed from bound volume.

    Ref.:

22nd Congress, 1st Session, House, Document No. 83, Serial 218. [Washington, 1832.]

4432 UNITED STATES. WAR DEPART-MENT

[Caption title] . . . REPORT FROM THE SECRETARY OF WAR . . . IN RELATION TO THE PROTECTION OF THE WESTERN FRONTIER OF THE UNITED STATES . . .

[1]–19, [20 blank]. 22.7 x 14.4 cm. Two maps. Map: Map / Illustrating the plan of the defences of the / Western & North-western / Frontier, / as proposed by / The Hon: J. R. Poinsett, Sec. of War, / in his report of Dec. 30, 1837. / [decorative rule] / Compiled in the U. S. Topographical Bureau / under the direction of Col. J. J. Abert, U. S. T. E. / By W. Hood. / [upper right:] 25 Congress 2 Session / S. Nº 1. Doc. 65. / 54.6 x 39.1 cm. Scale: 50 miles to one inch. Map: Map / Illustrating the plan of the defences of the / Western & North-western / Frontier, / as proposed by / Charles Gratiot, / in his report of Oct. 31, 1837. / [decorative rule] / Compiled in the U. S. Topographical Bureau / under the direction of Col. J. J. Abert, U. S. T. E. / By W. Hood. / [upper right:] 2 Session 25 Congress / S. Nº 2 Doc. 65. / 54.5 x 38.3 cm. Scale: about 50 miles to one inch. Removed from bound volume, unbound. In a green cloth case.

    Ref.:

25th Congress, 2nd Session, Senate, Document No. 65, Serial 314. [Washington, 1838.]

Printer's imprint appears on the first page: [short rule] / Blair & Rives, printers. /

4433 UNITED STATES. WAR DEPART-MENT

[Caption title] . . . REPORT FROM THE SECRETARY OF WAR . . . IN RELATION TO THE SELECTION OF A SITE FOR A FORT ON THE WESTERN FRONTIER LINE OF ARKANSAS . . .

[1]–24. 22.3 x 14 cm. Three maps. Map: [Map of the Arkansas River at the mouth of Lees Creek.] [upper right:] 25 Congress. 2 Session / S. Doc. Nº 224. / 20 x 17.6 cm. No scale given. Maps (two on one sheet): [Part of Township map in vicinity of Fort Smith.] 20 x 17 cm. (map and margins). No scale given. [2] [Detail of area

about Fort Smith.] [upper right:] 25 Congress 2 Session / S. Doc. № 224 / 20 x 20.2 cm. (map and margins). Scale: about 1/3 mile to one inch. Two maps measure 20 x 37.5 cm. Map: [Country around Fort Gibson.] [upper right:] [as in preceding]. 20.2 x 24 cm. Scale: about 1 1/8 miles to one inch. Stapled into gray boards, black cloth backstrip, typed white paper label on front cover.

Ref.:

25th Congress, 2nd Session, Senate, Document No. 224, Serial 316. [Washington, 1838.]

Printer's imprint, lower left corner, page [1]: [short rule] / Blair & Rives, printers. /

4434 UNITED STATES. WAR DEPARTMENT

[Extract] [caption title] EX. DOC. NO. 1. 187 REPORT OF THE QUARTERMASTER GENERAL. . . .

187–244. 22.8 x 14.2 cm. Rebound in new red cloth.

Ref.: Wagner-Camp 156

Extract from 30th Congress, 1st Session, House Executive Document No. 1, Serial 514.

Most of the letters and reports deal with phases of the War with Mexico, but among the other materials in this report, No. D-6. by W. M. D. McKissack, briefly details the expeditions under Doniphan, Price, and the Mormon Battalion, pages 224–25. No. E is Thomas Swords' report of his expedition with Kearny to California, his trip to Hawaii and return, and comments on routes to California, pages 226–36. No. G is J. H. Ralston's report on possible military roads in Texas, pages 238–40.

4435 UNITED STATES. WAR DEPARTMENT

EXECUTIVE DOCUMENTS . . . DURING THE FIRST SESSION OF THE THIRTY-THIRD CONGRESS. WASHINGTON: A. O. P. NICHOLSON, PRINTER, 1854.

[1]–24, [i–ii], [1]–43, [44 blank], [1]–116, [i–ii, ii blank], [1]–4, [i]–xii, [xiii–xvi blank], [1]–599, [600 blank], [i]–xv, [xvi blank]. [1]–24, [i–viii, viii blank], 1–149, [150–52 blank], [1]–136, [1]–154, [i]–vi, index, [i]–ii errata, [1]–324. 22.7 x 14.3 cm. Atlas of fourteen maps and profiles. [1] Preliminary Sketch / of the / Northern Pacific Rail Road / Exploration and Survey / from Sᵗ Paul to Riviere des Lacs / made in 1853–4 by / I. I. Stevens / Governor of Washington Territory / Statute Miles / [diagrammatic scale: 19 1/2 miles to one inch] / [two lines] / Wagner & MᶜGuigan, Lith. Philᵃ / 68.2 x 82.6 cm. (page size). Scale as above. Profile on same sheet. [2] Preliminary Sketch / of the / Northern Pacific Rail Road / Exploration and Survey / from

Riviere des Lacs to the Rocky Mountains / made in 1853 by / I. I. Stevens / Governor of Washington Territory / Statute Miles / [diagrammatic scale: 19 1/2 miles to one inch] / [two lines] / Wagner & MᶜGuigan, Lith. Philᵃ / 66.2 x 89.7 cm. (page size). Scale as above. Profile on same sheet. [3] Preliminary Sketch / of the / Northern Pacific Rail Road / Exploration and Survey / from the Rocky Mountains to Puget Sound / made in 1853–4 by / I. I. Stevens / Governor of Washington Territory / Statute Miles / [diagrammatic scale: 19 1/2 miles to one inch] / [two lines] / Wagner & MᶜGuigan, Lith. Philᵃ /. 66.2 x 96.6 cm. (page size). Scale as above. Profile on same sheet. *Inset:* [Area near Pyramid Lake.] 8 x 15.4 cm. (map size). Scale not given. [4] Skeleton Map / Exhibiting the Route Explored by / Capᵗ J. W. Gunnison U. S. A. / 38 Parallel of North Latitude—(1853) / also that of the 41 Parallel of Latitude Explored by / Lieutenant E. G. Beskwith 3ᵈ Artʸ (1854). / Drawn by J. W. Egloffstein. / [decorative rule] / Scale at 50 m. to the Inch. / [lower right:] Lith. of Sarony & Co N. Y. / 63 x 96.2 cm. Scale as above. [5] General Profile / from Westport near the Western Border of the State of Missouri to the Sevier River [Great Basin] / 34.6 x 238.4 cm. (page size—3 sheets pasted together). Horizontal scale: 15 miles to one inch. Vertical scale: 2000 feet to one inch. [6] Map No. 1. / Reconnaissance and Survey / of a / Railway Route / from / Mississippi River / near 35ᵗʰ Parallel North Lat. / to / Pacific Ocean / Made under the Direction of the Secʳʸ of War / by / Lieut. A. W. Whipple T. Eng. / assisted by / Lieut. J. C. Ives Top. Eng. / and / A H. Campbell Civ. Eng. / 1853–4 / [fifteen lines of text] / Drawn by A. Schimmelfinnig. / Scale / 1/900,000 / [diagrammatic scale: 15 miles to one inch.] 66.8 x 202.7 cm. Scale as above. [7] Map No. 2. / [next 16 lines same as preceding except punctuation changes] / [14 lines] / Drawn by M. von Hippel / Scale / 1/900,000 / [diagrammatic scale: 15 miles to one inch] / 67 x 192.5 cm. Scale as above. [8] Profile of a Route from San Pedro on the Pacific Coast to Memphis on the Mississippi River. (via New Mexico.) / Lith. of Bien & Sterner, 90 Fulton St. N.Y. / 35 x 355.6 cm. (paper size). Vertical scale 3500 feet to one inch. No horizontal scale given. [9] Map of the / Survey of a Route for the / Pacific Railroad / near the 32ᵈ Parallel / between the Rio Grande & Red River / Made under orders of the / Hon Jef. Davis Secty. of War / by / Bvt. Capt. Jno. Pope Topogl. Engrs. assisted by Lieut. K. Garrard 1ˢᵗ Dragoons / Drawn by Theo. H Oelschlager / Scale 1/633600 / [diagrammatic scale: ten miles to one inch.] / [lower right:] D. Chillas Lith.

50. S. 3^d St. Phil^a / 82.5 x 213.3 cm. Scale as above. [10] Route of a Survey / from the Pimas Villages on the Rio-Gila / to Mesilla on the Rio-Bravo-del-Norte / with a view to determine the practicability of a Railroad / from the Mississippi to the Pacific Ocean / through that Region / made by Lieut. Jno. G. Parke, Corps Top^l Eng^{rs} / under orders from / the Honble Jefferson Davis, Sec^y of War. / 1854 / drawn by H. Custer Ass^t / Lith. by Bien & Sterner 90 Fulton St. N. Y. / 66.3 x 169.2 cm. Scale: five miles to one inch. [11] Profile of Route / from / Pimas Villages on the Rio Gila / to / Mesilla on the Rio Bravo. / 1854. / Horizontal Scale—Five miles to an Inch. / [diagrammatic scale] / Vertical Scale —One thousand feet to an Inch. / Distortion 26.4 times / Jno. G. Parke / Lt. Corps Top. Eng^{rs}· / Lith. by Bien & Sterner 90 Fulton St. N Y. / 45.4 x 206 cm. (page size). Scale as above. [12] General Map / of a Survey in California / in connection with examinations for / Railroad Routes to the Pacific Ocean / made by order of the War Department / by Lieut. R. S. Williamson, U. S. Top^t[!] Eng^{rs} assisted by / Lieut. J. G. Parke, U. S. Top^t Eng^{rs} / and / Mr Isaac Williams Smith, C. E. / drawn by Charles Preuss. / [thick and thin rules] / Scale 1/600,000 / [diagrammatic scale: 9 1/2 miles to one inch] / 61.1 x 183.2 cm. Scale as above. [13] Profile of Walkers Pass. / . . . / Profile of Hum-pah-ya-mup Pass. / . . . / Profile of Tah-ee-chay-pah Pass. / . . . / Profile of route from summit of Tah-ee-chay-pah Pass to the Tejon Depot Camp. / . . . / Profile of New Pass. / . . . / Profile of San Fernando Pass. / . . . / 71.2 x 50 cm. Scale: horizontal, 1:120,000; vertical, 1:24,000. [14] Profile of Cajon Pass. / . . . / Profile of San Francisquito Pass. / . . . / Profile of San Gorgonio Pass. / . . . / Profile of the Colorado Desert from Station 15 of San Gorgonio Pass to the wagon-road. / . . . / Profile of Warner's Pass. / . . . / 71.5 x 54.8 cm. Scale as in preceding map. Three volumes, calf, leather labels on backstrips.

Ref.: Howes P3 see; Wagner-Camp 261–67; Wheat (*Transmississippi*) 842, 851, 857, 861–63, 872–73, 876

The two volumes of text comprise the following sections:

Pages [1]–24: general title-page and index for Executive Documents.

Pages [i–ii], [1]–[40]: 33d Congress, [vertical bracket] House of Representatives. [vertical bracket] Ex. Doc. / 1st Session. No. 129. / [double rule] / Report 3 of / the Secretary of War / Communicating the several / Pacific Railroad Explorations. / [short rule] / In Three Volumes. / [short rule] / Washington: / A. O. P. Nicholson, Printer. / 1855. /

Pages [1]–116: An Examination / by Direction of the / Hon. Jefferson Davis, Secretary of War, / of the / Reports of Explorations for Railroad Routes from the / Mississippi to the Pacific, Made under the Orders / of the War Department in 1853–'54, / and of the / Explorations Made Previous to that time, which have a bearing / upon the subject: / By / Capt. A. A. Humphreys & Lieut. G. K. Warren, / Corps Topographical Engineers. / [rule] / Washington: / Printed by A. O. P. Nicholson. / 1855. /

Pages [i–ii]: Note [by Capt. Humphreys regarding typographical errors.]

Pages [1]–4: [double rule] / Report / of / Maj. General Thos. S. Jesup, / Quartermaster General U. S. Army, / upon the / Cost of Transporting Troops and Supplies / to / California, Oregon, New Mexico, / etc., etc. / [double rule] /

Pages [i]–[xvi], [1]–[600], [i]–[xvi]: [double rule] / Report / of / Exploration of a Route for the Pacific Railroad, / near the Forty-seventh and Forty-ninth Parallels, / from / St. Paul to Puget Sound. / [short rule] / By I. I. Stevens, / Governor of Washington Territory. / [double rule] /

Volume II:

Pages [1]–24: identical with first twenty-four pages of first volume.

Pages [i–ii]: title-page as in first volume, verso blank; page [iii] Contents, resolution on verso; page [iv] [double rule] / Report / of / Exploration of a Route for the Pacific Railroad, / near the 38th and 39th Parallels of Latitude, / from / the Mouth of the Kansas to Sevier River, in the Great Basin. / [short rule] / By Lieut. E. G. Beckwith, / Third Artillery. / [double rule] /; page [v] blank; page [vi] Contents, verso blank; pages 1–152 text.

Pages [1]–136: [double rule] / Report / of / Explorations for the Pacific Railroad, / on the Line of the / Forty-first Parallel of North Latitude. / [short rule] / By Lt. E. G. Beckwith. / Third Artillery. / 1854. / [double rule] / 1 f /

Pages [1]–154, [i]–vi, [i]–ii: [double rule] / Report / of / Explorations for a Railway Route, / near the Thirty-fifth Parallel of Latitude, / from / the Mississippi River to the Pacific Ocean. / [rule] / By Lieut. A. W. Whipple, / Corps of Topographical Engineers. / [double rule] / 1 a /

Pages [1]–324: [double rule] / Report / of / Exploration of a Route for the Pacific Railroad, / near the Forty-second Parallel of Latitude, / from / the Red River to the Rio Grande, / [rule] / By Brevet Captain John Pope, / Corps of Topographical Engineers. / [double rule] / 1 c /

The work was intended to have been issued in three volumes of text and one volume of maps.

It is doubtful that the third volume was issued in regular form, although there is an incomplete copy in the Library of Congress and possibly another copy (complete?) in the library of the Geological Survey. The reports were issued and printed separately and apparently bound together at a later time. It will be noted that the general title-pages are dated 1854, but that at least one of the reports bears the date 1855 on its title-page.

4436 UNITED STATES. WAR DEPART-MENT.

. . . REPORT OF THE SECRETARY OF WAR, COMMUNICATING . . . INFORMATION RESPECTING THE PURCHASE OF CAMELS FOR THE PURPOSES OF MILITARY TRANSPORTATION. WASHINGTON: A. O. P. NICHOLSON, PRINTER, 1857.

[1]–238. 22.4 x 14.2 cm. 21 plates listed, figures in text unlisted. Black cloth, blind embossed sides, title in gilt on backstrip.

Ref.: Greenly (*Camels*)

34th Congress, 3rd Session, Senate, Executive Document No. 62, Serial 881.

4437 UNITED STATES. WAR DEPART-MENT

THE EXECUTIVE DOCUMENTS . . . SECOND SESSION, THIRTY-FIFTH CONGRESS, 1858–'59, AND SPECIAL SESSION OF THE SENATE OF 1859 . . . WASHINGTON: WILLIAM A. HARRIS, PRINTER, 1859.

[1]–50, [1]–670. 22.4 x 14.4 cm. Unlisted illustrations in text. Calf, red and green leather labels.

Ref.: Greenly (*Camels*); Wagner-Camp 296, 303, 314

One volume only.

Among the many reports to the Secretary of War are included a "Diary of a trip from Fort Bridger, Utah Territory, via Bridger's Pass / and Laramie Plain to Fort Laramie, Nebraska Territory, by Mr. / John Bartletson. /" pages 52–6. This is a small part of a long report on the state of affairs in Utah. Also included is a report by Randolph B. Marcy on his march from Camp Scott to New Mexico and return during the winter of 1857–58, pages 187–201.

There is also included the first part of the long report by G. K. Warren, pages 620–70, Wagner-Camp 314.

A fascinating volume, with many short and long reports on military affairs in the West.

Among the reports noted is a long section by Colonel B. L. E. Bonneville regarding activities among the Navajos. There is also a long illustrated essay by Hekekyan Bey on the care and handling of camels.

4438 UNITED STATES. WAR DEPART-MENT

[Caption title] . . . PROTECTION ACROSS THE CONTINENT. LETTER FROM THE SECRETARY OF WAR . . . TRANSMITTING INFORMATION RESPECTING THE PROTECTION OF THE ROUTES ACROSS THE CONTINENT TO THE PACIFIC FROM MOLESTATION BY HOSTILE INDIANS . . .

[1]–55, [56 blank]. 22.7 x 14.3 cm.

BOUND WITH:

[Caption title] ISLAND OF SAN JUAN. MESSAGE FROM THE PRESIDENT OF THE UNITED STATES . . . RELATIVE TO THE ISLAND OF SAN JUAN, IN WASHINGTON TERRITORY . . .

[1, 2 blank]. Two documents bound together in new red cloth.

Ref.:

39th Congress, 2nd Session, House Executive Document Nos. 23–24, Serial 1288. [Washington: Government Printing Office, 1867.]

Contains a number of letters relating to inspection of western forts by General William T. Sherman and a long, elaborate report made to Sherman by Colonel D. B. Sacket, Inspector General of the United States Army, including detailed descriptions of western forts.

The second piece is a refusal by the Secretary of State, William H. Seward, to allow Congress to publish the correspondence between the United States and Great Britain relative to their joint occupancy of the Island of San Juan.

4439 UNITED STATES. WAR DEPART-MENT

[Caption title] . . . LETTER OF THE SECRETARY OF WAR, COMMUNICATING . . . INFORMATION IN RELATION TO THE LATE INDIAN BATTLE ON THE WASHITA RIVER . . .

[1]–48. [1]–2. [1, 2 blank]. 22.7 x 14.5 cm. Three parts bound together in new red cloth.

Ref.:

40th Congress, 3rd Session, Senate, Executive Document No. 18, Parts 1–3, Serial 1360. [Washington: Government Printing Office, 1869.]

The operations described in this series of reports includes the famous attack of General Custer on the camp of Black Kettle.

4440 UNITED STATES. WAR DEPART-MENT.

[Caption title] . . . GEOGRAPHICAL AND GEOLOGICAL SURVEYS WEST OF THE MISSISSIPPI . . .

[1]–15, [16 blank]. 23.2 x 14.9 cm. Sewn, unbound.

Ref.:

43rd Congress, 1st Session, House, Executive Document No. 240, Serial 1614. [Washington: Government Printing Office, 1874.]

4441 UNITED STATES. WAR DEPART-MENT

[Caption title] MESSAGE . . . RELATING TO ABAN-DONED MILITARY RESERVATIONS, AND RENEWING HIS FORMER RECOMMENDATION, FOR LEGISLATION WHICH WILL PROVIDE FOR THE DISPOSAL OF SUCH RESERVATIONS NO LONGER NEEDED. DECEMBER 19, 1882 . . .

[1]–56. 22.8 x 14.6 cm. Three folding maps and plans: [all lines underlined] Plot of Military Reservation / Declared by the President April 11. 1859. embracing / Coal-Mines on Sulphur-Creek. Wyoming. / Area of Reservation 99 17/100 Acres. / Traced from official copy of the township plot. / [plan] / Plot Showing Location of Reservation Relative to Fort Bridger. / 38 x 25.7 cm. (paper size). Scale (upper map): two inches to one mile. Scale (lower map): 1/4 inch to one mile. Map: [Plan of Fort Bridger.] [lower left corner:] Made in Office of chief of Engineers Jan'y 16. 1882. / 24.2 x 33 cm. Scale: about 500 feet to an inch. Map: [Plan of Fort Dodge Military Reservation.] 60.5 x 41.5 cm. No scale given. Sewn, unbound, removed from bound volume.

Ref.:

47th Congress, 2nd Session, Senate, Executive Document Number 20, Serial 2073. [Washington: Government Printing Office, 1882.]

4442 UNITED STATES. WAR DEPART-MENT. (Surgeon-General's Office)

CIRCULAR NO. 4. WAR DEPARTMENT, SURGEON GENERAL'S OFFICE, WASHINGTON, DECEMBER 5, 1870. A REPORT ON BARRACKS AND HOSPITALS, WITH DESCRIPTIONS OF MILITARY POSTS. WASHING-TON: GOVERNMENT PRINTING OFFICE, 1870.

[i]–xxxiii, [xxxiv blank], [1]–494. 29.5 x 23 cm. One illustration and twelve plans. Original tan printed wrappers.

Prov.: Presentation copy from John S. Billings.

Ref.: Howes B450

Report prepared by John S. Billings, Assistant Surgeon United States Army.

4443 UNITED STATES. WAR DEPART-MENT. (Surgeon-General's Office)

CIRCULAR NO. 8. WAR DEPARTMENT, SURGEON-GENERAL'S OFFICE, WASHINGTON, MAY 1, 1875. A REPORT ON THE HYGIENE OF THE UNITED STATES ARMY, WITH DESCRIPTIONS OF MILITARY POSTS. WASHINGTON: GOVERNMENT PRINTING OFFICE, 1875.

[i]–lix, [lx blank], [1]–567, [568 blank]. 29.2 x 23 cm. Folding map and 12 plans. Map: Map of the / Western Military Departments, / of the / United States, / Showing Military Posts and Principal Routes. / 1874. / The Graphic Co. Photo-Lith. 39 & 41 Park Place, N. Y. / 28.6 x 34.1 cm. Scale: 160 miles to one inch. Original tan printed wrappers.

Ref.: Howes B450

Ninety-five posts were added in the five years between 1870 and 1875 and a few were discontinued.

4444 UNITED STATES BOUNTY LAND OFFICE

SELECTED LOCATIONS OF SOLDIERS' BOUNTY LANDS, WITH MAPS, DESCRIPTION AND UNITED STATES DEEDS. MANHATTAN FALLS, IN THE COUNTIES OF LINN, DELAWARE AND JONES, STATE OF IOWA. GOVERNMENT VALUE OF PUBLIC LANDS FOR CASH, 40 ACRES --------- $ 50 00 80 " --------- 100 00 160 " --------- 200 00 SECURED BY THE WAR-RANT AND BY THE SURVEYS MADE BY NICHOLAS HAIGHT. UNITED STATES BOUNTY LAND OFFICE . . . NEW-YORK: CASPER C. CHILDS, PRINTER, 1852.

[1]–[20]. 22 x 12.9 cm. Buff printed wrappers with title on front wrapper, stabbed.

Ref.:

The maps mentioned on the title-page do not accompany the present copy and probably were not published. They are mentioned in the first paragraph of text as "exhibited at the office."

4445 UNITED STATES CAVALRY ASSO-CIATION

JOURNAL OF THE UNITED STATES CAVALRY ASSOCI-ATION. VOLUME I. FORT LEAVENWORTH, KANSAS, 1888.

[i–vi], [i–ii], [143]–267, [268 blank], [1]–426, [i–iv], [1]–433, [434 blank]. 22.3 x 14.3 cm. Three illustrations unlisted. Six parts bound together, contemporary brown half morocco.

Ref.:

Comprises Parts 2–3 of Volume I and 4–7 of Volume II, i.e., parts are numbered consecutively. Title-page of Volume II present.

Included is ' "The Days of the Empire"— Arizona, 1866–1869' by C. C. C. Carr, Volume II, No. 4, pages [3]–22.

4446 UNITED STATES GAZETTE, THE.
Philadelphia

[Newspaper] THE UNITED STATES GAZETTE. PUB-LISHED (DAILY) BY HART & CHANDLER . . . VOL. LXV. PHILADELPHIA—THURSDAY MORNING, NO-VEMBER 15, 1827. NO. 9866 . . .

Newspaper, [1–4]. 51.6 x 38.5 cm. Unbound. Fold repaired.

Ref.: Wagner-Camp 35 see

On page [2], columns 3–4 under the heading West of the Rocky Mountains. / there is printed Jedidiah Smith's account of crossing the deserts of Utah and Nevada to Southern California. *The United States Gazette* reprinted the account from its appearance in the *Missouri Republican*, October 11, 1827. The printing described by Wagner-Camp is a French translation of 1828.

4447 UPHAM, CHARLES W.

LIFE EXPLORATIONS AND PUBLIC SERVICES OF JOHN CHARLES FREMONT . . . BOSTON: TICKNOR AND FIELDS, M.DCCC.LVI.

[i]–viii, [9]–366, [367–70 blank, yellow leaf, [1]–[12] advertisements]. 18.3 x 11.7 cm. Illustrations unlisted. Black cloth, blind panels and fillets on sides, gilt backstrip.

Ref.: Wagner-Camp 282 see

Editions: Boston, 1856.

4448 URREA, JOSE

DIARIO DE LAS OPERACIONES MILITARES DE LA DIVISION QUE AL MANDO DEL GENERAL JOSE URREA HIZO LA CAMPANA DE TEJAS. PUBLICALO SU AUTOR CON ALGUNAS OBSERVACIONES PARA VINDICARSE ANTE SUS CONCIUDADANOS. VICTORIA DE DURANGO: IMPRENTA DEL GOBIERNO A CARGO DE MANUEL GONZALEZ, 1838.

[1]–136. 19.2 x 12.2 cm. Rebound in bright green semi-limp leather.

Prov.: Booklabel of Carlos R. Linga.

Ref.: Howes U31; Rader 3516; Raines p. 208; Sabin 98152; Streeter 940

4449 UTAH TERRITORY. Governor (Brigham Young)

[Broadside] PROCLAMATION BY THE GOVERNOR. CITIZENS OF UTAH—WE ARE INVADED BY A HOSTILE FORCE WHO ARE EVIDENTLY ASSAILING US TO ACCOMPLISH OUR OVERTHROW AND DESTRUCTION . . . GIVEN UNDER MY HAND AND SEAL AT GREAT SALT LAKE CITY, TERRITORY OF UTAH, THIS FIFTH DAY OF AUGUST, A.D. EIGHTEEN HUNDRED AND FIFTY SEVEN AND OF THE INDEPENDENCE OF THE UNITED STATES OF AMERICA THE EIGHTY SECOND. BRIGHAM YOUNG.

Broadside, 28 x 19 cm. Text, 23.8 x 14.3 cm.

Ref.:

By this proclamation, Brigham Young declared the Territory under martial law.

4450 UTAH TERRITORY. Legislative Assembly. House

[Caption title] RULES FOR CONDUCTING BUSINESS IN THE HOUSE OF REPRESENTATIVES OF THE TERRITORY OF UTAH . . .

[1]–4. 20.9 x 14 cm. Unbound leaflet. In a blue cloth case.

Ref.: McMurtrie (*Utah*) 25

Page 4: [thick and thin rules] / 100 Copies: Published by Authority. / Joseph Cain, Public Printer. /

Cain was public printer in 1854 and 1855.

V

4451 VAIL, A. L.

A MEMORIAL OF JAMES M. HAWORTH, SUPERINTENDENT OF UNITED STATES INDIAN SCHOOLS . . . KANSAS CITY: PRESS OF H. N. FAREY & CO., 1886.

[1]–178. 21 x 17.5 cm. Portrait. Black cloth, blind fillet bands on sides, name of subject on front cover in gilt, gilt edges.

Ref.: Howes V3

Errata slip, 7.6 x 16.5 cm., inserted at page 171.

Haworth lived in Kansas, Iowa, Texas, and the Indian country in general.

4452 VALCARCEL Y BAQUERIZO, DOMINGO

[Caption title] . . . INSTRUCCION DEL PAPEL SELLADO . . .

[A–B]². 1–7, [8 blank]. 28 x 19.8 cm. Bound with Number 9.

Ref.:

Dated at the end 1782, probably printed at Mexico City.

4453 VALLEY TAN, THE

[Newspaper] THE VALLEY TAN . . . VOLUME 2. GREAT SALT LAKE CITY, WEDNESDAY, FEBRUARY 29, 1860. NUMBER 16 . . .

[1–4]. 45.1 x 30.7 cm. Unbound.

Ref.:

This last number of *The Valley Tan* contains on pages [2–3], columns 4–5, 1–3 William H. Rogers: The Mountain Medows[!] Mas-/sacre. /

Editor and publisher: Stephen De Wolfe.

4454 VAN BUREN, A. DE PUY

JOTTINGS OF A YEAR'S SOJOURN IN THE SOUTH; OR, FIRST IMPRESSIONS OF THE COUNTRY AND ITS PEOPLE; WITH A GLIMPSE OF DISTINGUISHED MEN . . . BATTLE CREEK, MICHIGAN, 1859.

[i]–x, [11]–320. 19.5 x 12.5 cm. Gray cloth, blind embossed sides, title in gilt on sides.

Ref.: Clark III 503; Howes V15

Van Buren looked at everything through rose-colored glasses and made the mistake of picturing the entire Southern region as he found it on a few ideal plantations in the Yazoo basin.—Clark

4455 VAN CLEVE, CHARLOTTE OUIS-CONSIN

"THREE SCORE YEARS AND TEN," LIFE-LONG MEMO-RIES OF FORT SNELLING, MINNESOTA, AND OTHER PARTS OF THE WEST . . . 1888.

[1]–176. 20.2 x 15 cm. Portrait. Brown cloth, title in gilt on front cover and backstrip.

Ref.: Bradford 5550

Printed in Minneapolis by Harrison & Smith.

A printed copyright notice is mounted at the foot of the verso of the title-page.

4456 VANCOUVER, GEORGE

A VOYAGE OF DISCOVERY TO THE NORTH PACIFIC OCEAN, AND ROUND THE WORLD; IN WHICH THE COAST OF NORTH-WEST AMERICA HAS BEEN CARE-FULLY EXAMINED AND ACCURATELY SURVEYED . . . LONDON: PRINTED FOR G. G. AND J. ROBINSON, 1798.

[*]⁴, a–d⁴, A², [**]¹, B–3I⁴. [1–8, 8 blank], [i]–[xxxviii], [1]–432. [*]², A², [**]¹, B–3S⁴. [i–x, x blank], [1]–504. [*]², A², [**]¹, B–3S⁴, [3T]². [i–x, x blank], [1]–[508]. 29.3 x 23 cm. 34 plates and maps listed. Map: Hergest's Islands / Discovered by the Daedalus Store Ship / Lieuᵗ Hergest Commander / and Surveyed by / Mʳ Gooch Astronomer. / [upper right:] XVIII / [lower centre:] London: Published May 1ˢᵗ 1798, by J. Edwards Pall Mall and G. Robinson Paternoster Row. / [lower right:] J. Warner sc. / 23.9 x 18.9 cm. No scale given. ATLAS contains sixteen maps, charts and views as follows: Map: A Chart / Shewing part of the / S. W. Coast of New Holland / With the Tracks of / His Majesty's Sloop / Discovery and Armed Tender Chatham, / Commanded by George Vancouver Esqʳ in the Year 1791 / [swelled rule] / Engraved by T. Foot, Weston Place / Battle Bridge / [upper right:] N⁰ 1 / [lower centre:] London. Published May 1ˢᵗ 1798, by J. Edwards Pall Mall and G. Robinson Paternoster Row. / 61.7 x 78.3 cm. Scales as indicated. *Inset:* A Survey / of / King George IIIᵈ Sound. / on the / S. W. Coast of New Holland. / 14.9 x 18.8 cm. Scale: two miles to one inch. *Inset:* Dusky Bay in New England / Copied from a sketch of Captain Cook's with such / Addi-

tions and Improved as where[!] made by the / Discovery and Chatham, / in the Year / 1791. / 29 x 35.2 cm. No scale given. *Inset:* Pickersgill Harbour /. 8.8 x 7.5 cm. Scale: about 225 fathoms to one inch. *Inset:* Anchor Island Harbour /. 12.2 x 19.3 cm. Scale: 300 fathoms to one inch. *Inset:* Facile Harbour /. 8.5 x 19.3 cm. Scale: 30 fathoms to one inch. *Inset:* A Sketch / of / the Snares / with the Track of the Chatham between them /. 8.2 x 19.3 cm. Scale: two miles to one inch. *Inset:* Chatham Island /. 15.2 x 20.9 cm. Scale: two leagues to one inch. *Inset:* The / Island of Oparo /. 13.8 x 20.9 cm. Scale: about 2 1/2 miles to one inch. Map: A Chart / Shewing Part of the / Coast of N. W. America, / With the Tracks of / His Majesty's Sloop / Discovery and Armed Tender Chatham, / Commanded by George Vancouver Esq. and prepared / under his immediate inspection by Lieuᵗ Joseph Baker, / in Which the / Continental Shore has been finally traced and determined from Latᵈ 38°. 15′N. / and Longᵈ 237°. 27′E. to Latᵈ 45°. 46′N. and Longᵈ 236°. 15′E. / [two-line note] / Engraved by B. Baker Islington / [upper right:] Plate 3. / [lower centre:] London published May 1. 1798 by J. Edwards Pall Mall, and G. Robinson Paternoster Row. / 77.5 x 62.5 cm. No scale given. *Inset:* Bay of Trinidad /. 16.6 x 16.7 cm. Scale: 1/2 mile to one inch. Map: A Chart / shewing part of the / Coast of N. W. America, / with the tracks of His Majesty's Sloop / Discovery and Armed Tender Chatham; / Commanded by George Vancouver Esqʳ and prepared / under his immediate inspection by Lieuᵗ Joseph Baker, in which / the Continental Shore has been traced and determined from / Lat: 45″30 N. and Long. 236″12 E. to Lat: 52″15 N. and Long. 232″40 E. / at the different periods shewn by the Tracks / [two lines of notes] / Warner Sculp. / [upper right:] 5 / [lower centre:] London: Published May 1ˢᵗ 1798, by J. Edwards Pall Mall & G. Robinson Paternoster Row. / 78.3 x 62 cm. No scale given. *Inset:* Entrance / of / Columbia River /. 13.8 x 22.2 cm. Scale: 1 1/3 leagues to one inch. *Inset:* Gray's Harbour /. 18.5 x 18.2 cm. Scale: two leagues to one inch. *Inset:* Port Discovery /. 18.5 x 14.8 cm. Scale: two leagues to one inch. Map: A Chart / shewing part of the / Coast of N. W. America / with the tracks of His Majesty's Sloop / Discovery and Armed Tender Chatham / Commanded by George Vancouver Esq. and prepared / under his immediate inspection by Lieuᵗ Joseph Baker in which the / Continental Shore has been correctly traced and determined from / Lat. 51:45 N. and Long. 232:08 E. to Lat. 57.30 N. and Long. 226:44 E. / at the periods shewn by the Tracks. / [two lines of notes] / Warner Sculp. / [upper right:] 7 / [lower centre:] [same as preceding]. 75.3 x 61.4 cm. No scale given. *Inset:* A Survey / of / Port Stewart /. 14.7 x 10.7 cm. Scale: 9/16 inches to one inch. Map: A Chart / Shewing part of the / Coast of N. W. America / With the Tracks of / His Majesty's Sloop / Discovery and Armed Tender Chatham; / Commanded by George Vancouver Esq. and prepared / under his immediate inspection by Lieu^t Joseph Baker; / in Which the / Continental Shore has been correctly traced and determined from Lat^{de} 30°.00. N. and / Long^d 244°.32 E. to Lat^d 38°.30 N. and Long^d 237°.13. E. / [swelled rule] / [three lines of notes] / Engraved by T. Foot, Weston Place, / Battle Bridge. / [upper right:] N° 8 / [lower centre:] [same as preceding]. 78 x 62 cm. No scale given. *Inset:* Entrance / of / Port S^n Francisco. / 21.3 x 25.6 cm. Scale: two miles to one inch. *Inset:* Port S^n Diego /. 21.3 x 15.7 cm. Map: A Chart / Shewing Part of the / Coast of N. W. America, / with the Tracks of / His Majesty's Sloop / Discovery and Armed Tender Chatham; / Commanded by George Vancouver Esqr and prepared / under his immediate inspection by Lieu^t Joseph Baker; / in Which the / Continental Shore has been correctly traced and determined. / from Lat^{de} of 59°.30 North & Long^{de} 207°20 East; / to Cape Douglas in Lat^{de} 58°.52' North & Long^{de} 207°20 East. / [two-line note] / Engraved by S. J. Neele 352 Strand. / [lower centre:] London Published May 1st 1798, by T. R. Edwards Pall Mall & C. Robinson Pater Noster Row. / 78 x 62.6 cm. No scale given. *Inset:* A Survey / of / Fort Chatham /. 20.3 x 18.5 cm. Scale: 1 1/2 miles to one inch. Map: A Chart / Shewing part of the / Coast of N. W. America / With the Tracks of / His Majesty's Sloop / Discovery and Armed Tender Chatham / Commanded by George Vancouver Esqr and prepared / under his immediate inspection by Lieu^t Joseph Baker, / in Which the / Continental Shore has been correctly traced and determined from Lat^d 59°.45' N. and / Long^d 219°.30' E. to Lat^d 59°.56' N. and Long^d 212°.08 E. / at the periods shewn by the Track / [upper right:] N° 11 / [lower centre:] London. Published May 1st 1798, by J. Edwards, Pall Mall & G. Robinson, Paternoster Row. / [lower right:] Engraved by T. Foot, Weston Place, St Pancras. / 55 x 73.6 cm. No scale given. *Inset:* A Survey / of / Port Chalmers /. 23 x 24 cm. Scale: two miles to one inch. Map: A Chart / Shewing part of the / Coast of N. W. America / With the Tracks of / His Majesty's Sloop / Dis-

covery and Armed Tender Chatham / Commanded by George Vancouver Esqr and prepared / under his immediate inspection by Lieu^t Joseph Baker, / in Which the / Continental Shore has been correctly traced and determined from the Lat^{de} 57°.07 1/2 N. and / Long^d 227°.00. E. to Lat^d 59°.59. N. and Long^d 219°.00. E. / at the periods shewn by the Track. / [swelled rule] / Engraved by T. Foot, Weston Place, / St Pancras. / [upper right:] N° 12 / [lower centre:] London: Published May 1st 1798, by J. Edwards Pall Mall and G. Robinson Paternoster Row. / 73.6 x 62.3 cm. No scale given. *Inset:* Entrance / into / Cross Sound /. 20.9 x 14.8 cm. Scale: about 1 1/8 leagues to one inch. *Inset:* A Survey / of / Port Conclusion /. 20.2 x 14.7 cm. Scale: 2/3 mile to one inch. *Inset:* A Survey / of / Port Protection /. 20.2 x 14.9 cm. Scale: one-half mile to one inch. Map: A Chart / shewing part of the / Coast of N. W. America / with the tracks of His Majesty's Sloop / Discovery and Armed Tender Chatham / Commanded by George Vancouver Esqr and prepared / from the foregoing Surveys under his immediate inspection by Lieu^t Edwd Roberts in which the / Continental Shore has been correctly Traced and Determined, / From Lat. 29°.54 N. and Long: 244°.33 E. to Cape Douglas in Lat. 58°.52 N. and Long. 207°.20 E. / during the Summers of 1792, 1793 and 1794. / [three lines of notes] / Warner Sculp. / [upper right:] 14 / [lower centre:] London: Published May 1st 1798, by J. Edwards Pall Mall & G. Robinson Paternoster Row. / 77 x 60.1 cm. No scale given. Map: A Chart / of the / Sandwich Islands / as Surveyed during the Visits of His Majesty's Sloop / Discovery and Armed Tender Chatham / Commanded by George Vancouver Esq. / in the Years 1792 1793 & 1794. / and prepared under his immediate inspection by / Lieu^t Joseph Baker. / Engraved by J. Warner / [upper right:] 15. / [lower centre:] [same as preceding]. 55 x 77.8 cm. No scale given. *Inset:* Part of the Gallapagos Isles /. 32.6 x 20 cm. No scale given. *Inset:* The / Island of Cocoas. / 18.5 x 18.3 cm. Scale: one mile to one inch. Three volumes of text and one of atlas, full contemporary mottled calf, gilt borders, gilt backs, green morocco labels, mottled edges. Atlas in marbled brown boards, plain calf corners and back, labeled in gilt.

Ref.: Cowan p. 655; Cox II pp. 30–31; Howes V23; Jones 667; Sabin 98443; Smith 10469; Staton & Tremaine 688; Wagner (*Cart. of N.W. Coast*) pp. 209 et seq.

The great voyage was accomplished in 1790 to 1795.

4457 VAN DERSAL, SAMUEL

VAN DERSAL'S STOCK GROWERS' DIRECTORY OF MARKS AND BRANDS FOR THE STATE OF SOUTH DAKOTA, 1902 . . . COMPILED AND PUBLISHED EXPRESSLY FOR THE DAKOTA FARMER, ABERDEEN, SOUTH DAKOTA . . .

[1]–[166], [167–216 advertisements], plus inserts as follows: [1–4] before front fly-leaf, [1–4] after front fly-leaf, 1–[2] between pages [2]–3. 23.2 x 15 cm. Black cloth, title stamped in gilt on front cover and backstrip, advertisements on endpapers and fly-leaves.

Ref.: Adams (*Ramp. Herd*) 2394 see

Published at Aberdeen in 1902.

Unpaginated advertisements inserted within text.

The edition described by Adams differs somewhat from the present copy.

4458 VAN DE VENTER, C.

LETTER, SIGNED. 1825 June 4, Department of War. One page, 24.5 x 19.8 cm. To Thomas Mather. In Mather Papers.

Covering letter for his appointment as Commissioner of the Santa Fé Road Commission.

4459 VAN DIEST, P. H.

THE GRAND ISLAND MINING DISTRICT, OF BOULDER COUNTY, COLORADO . . . DENVER, COLORADO: THE MINING REVIEW PUBLISHING COMPANY, 1876.

[1]–25, [26 blank]. 21.9 x 14.1 cm. Folding map: Map / of the / Caribou- and Idaho-Hills / Grand Island Mining District, / Boulder County Colorado / by / H. J. van Wetering & P. H. van Diest / May 1876. / 23.6 x 41.7 cm. Scale: about 265 feet to one inch. In lower section, one view and four diagrams. Cream printed wrappers with title on front wrapper, and advertisements on verso of front and recto and verso of back wrapper.

Ref.: Howes V29; McMurtrie & Allen (*Colorado*) 312

4460 VAN SICKEL, S. S.

A STORY OF REAL LIFE ON THE PLAINS . . . CEDAR RAPIDS, IA.: T. S. METCALF, BOOK AND JOB PRINTER, 1892.

[3]–50. 19.7 x 13.4 cm. Portrait. Light blue printed wrappers, with title on front wrapper. In a brown cloth case.

Ref.: Howes V42

An episode in the life of a buffalo hunter; includes account of the Adobe Walls fight.—Howes

Editions: N.p. [1875]. Chicago, 1876. Topeka, 1877. Harper, Kans. [1885?]. Various places 1892, 1895, 1896.

4461 VANSYCKE, J. M.

AUTOGRAPH LETTER, SIGNED. 1857 May 15, San Francisco. Five pages, 25 x 19.8 cm. To A. W. Francisco.

A fine letter about the Crabb filibustering expedition to Sonora, Mexico. The letter describes the local reaction to the massacre at Caborca and includes a list of the chief figures, McCoun, Wood, Dr. Oxley, etc. The recipient was a newspaperman on the Cincinnati *Daily Enquirer*.

The letter accompanies the collection of letters by Dr. T. W. Oxley.

4462 VAN TRAMP, JOHN C.

PRAIRIE AND ROCKY MOUNTAIN ADVENTURES; OR, LIFE IN THE WEST . . . COLUMBUS: PUBLISHED AND SOLD EXCLUSIVELY BY SUBSCRIPTION, BY J. & H. MILLER, 1858.

[i]–vi, [7]–640. 21.5 x 14 cm. 61 plates, unlisted. Dark brown embossed leather, marbled edges.

Ref.: Howes V43; Rader 3523; Wagner-Camp 312

Some copies have an added note on page 640; this one does not. There is a variant (later) imprint dated from St. Louis, 1859.

4463 VAN WOERT, WILLIAM T.

FIFTEEN YEARS OF FRONTIER LIFE; AN AUTOBIOGRAPHICAL SKETCH . . . DUBUQUE, IOWA: PUBLISHED FOR THE AUTHOR, 1870.

[1]–80. 21.3 x 14 cm. Green printed wrappers with title on front wrapper. Lacks back wrapper, last leaf defective.

Ref.: Howes V46

Deals with experiences in Minnesota, Montana, etc. and the Civil War.—EDG

4464 VAN ZANDT, NICHOLAS B.

A FULL DESCRIPTION OF THE SOIL, WATER, TIMBER, AND PRAIRIES OF EACH LOT, OR QUARTER SECTION OF THE MILITARY LANDS BETWEEN THE MISSISSIPPI AND ILLINOIS RIVERS . . . WASHINGTON CITY: PRINTED BY P. FORCE, 1818.

[i]–iv, [1]–127, [128 blank]. 22.1 x 12.9 cm. Folding map: A / General Plat / of the / Military Lands, / between the / Mississippi & Illinois Rivers / from the Official Surveys / and drawn upon a scale of four miles to an inch / [vignette; below vignette:] Cone & Freeman. Sculp.^{t} Baltimore. / By / Nicholas Biddle Van Zandt / late a Clerk in the General Land Office of the United States / Washington City. / Entered according to Act of Congress. / 107 x 72.2 cm. Scale: as above. Cut into 30 panels, 21.5 x 12.6 cm., mounted on linen. Marbled boards, black leather

back and corners, lettered in gilt on backstrip, edges tinted yellow.

Ref.: Buck 127; Howes V48; Sabin 98590
Very few copies are found with the map.

4465 VAUGHAN, ISAAC P., & ROBERT H. SAUNDERS

[Broadside] TO THE PUBLIC. FOR SOME TIME PAST SLANDEROUS REPORTS RELATIVE TO THE CHARACTER OF OUR PROFESSIONAL "CHARGES," HAVE BEEN SO INDUSTRIOUSLY CIRCULATED, THAT JUSTICE TO OURSELVES REQUIRES THEY SHOULD BE STOPPED AT ONCE . . . SOME TIME LAST YEAR A "BILL OF CHARGES" WAS MUTUALLY ENTERED INTO BY THE PHYSICIANS OF KEYTESVILLE, CHARITON AND GLASGOW, . . . ISAAC P. SAUNDERS. ROBT. H. SAUNDERS . . . SIGNED: DOCTOR ARTHUR SCOTT; . . . BENSON & GREEN, PRINTERS—"TIMES OFFICE," FAYETTE. [MAY 1, 1841.]

Broadside, 25 x 20.4 cm. Text, 21.1 x 17.3 cm.
Ref.:
The broadside contains a list of charges which Drs. Vaughan and Saunders considered slanderous.

With the broadside is a photograph labeled: Dr. Vaughan / made by Brown, Glasgow, Mo. Also a newspaper clipping (June 13, 1940) "Interesting Items from the Files of the Glasgow Weekly Times in 1858" noting Dr. Vaughan's successes in plastic surgery.

4466 VAUGHN, ROBERT

THEN AND NOW; OR, THIRTY-SIX YEARS IN THE ROCKIES. PERSONAL REMINISCENCES OF SOME OF THE FIRST PIONEERS OF THE STATE OF MONTANA. INDIANS AND INDIAN WARS. THE PAST AND PRESENT OF THE ROCKY MOUNTAIN COUNTRY. 1864–1900 . . . MINNEAPOLIS: TRIBUNE PRINTING COMPANY, 1900.*

[7]–461, [462 blank]. 21.4 x 14.5 cm. 58 illustrations listed. Green pictorial cloth.
Ref.: Howes V60

4467 VAUGHAN & CO., W. R.

A POCKET ACCOUNT BOOK AND DIARY FOR 1872 AND 1873, FROM KANSAS CITY WEST . . . COUNCIL BLUFFS, IOWA: PRINTED AT BLUFF CITY BOOK AND JOB PRINTING HOUSE, 1872.

[1]–72. Eight leaves of ruled paper inserted between pages 32 and 33. 14.2 x 10.3 cm. Buff printed wrappers with title on front wrapper, advertisements on verso of front and recto and verso of back wrapper.
Ref.: Howes V58
Contains business directories and sketches of thirty towns in Missouri, Kansas, Wyoming, and Colorado.

The seven stanza verses in manuscript on the first two inserted leaves are amusing. They are verses to Lilly Tyler—pure doggerel.

4468 VELASCO, JOSE FRANCISCO

NOTICIAS ESTADISTICAS DEL ESTADO DE SONORA, ACCOMPANADAS DE LIGERAS REFLECSIONES, DEDUCIDAS DE ALGUNOS DOCUMENTOS Y CONOCIMIENTOS PRACTICOS ADQUIRRIDOS EN MUCHOS ANOS, CON EL FIN DE DARLAS AL PUBLICO, Y DE QUE LOS SABIOS ESTADISTAS PUEDAN HACER USO DE LAS QUE LES PAREZCAN OPORTUNAS . . . MEXICO: IMPRENTA DE IGNACIO CUMPLIDO, 1850.

[I]–IX, [X blank], [11]–350. 21 x 13.7 cm. Folding map: Plano / de la Rada de Guaymas / en el golfo de California, / Levantado en Marzo de 1840 á bordo de la corbeta francesa la Danaid, / por los Sres. Fisquet y Garnault, / bajo la direccion del Sr. T. de Rosamel, command.te de la espedicion. / . . . [decorative rule] / [below border at right:] Litog. de Cumplido. / 20.5 x 28.4 cm. Scale: about 3250 metres to one inch. Full contemporary mottled calf, gilt back.
Ref.: Cowan pp. 656–57; Howes V66; Jones 1254
Pages [320]–335 comprise an itinerary of D. José Elias: Jornadas / Seguidas por D. José Elias para la Alta California, / desde la villa de Guadalupe ó el Altar. /

4469 VELASCO, JOSE FRANCISCO

SONORA: ITS EXTENT, POPULATION, NATURAL PRODUCTIONS, INDIAN TRIBES, MINES, MINERAL LANDS, ETC., ETC. TRANSLATED . . . BY WM. F. NYE. SAN FRANCISCO: H. H. BANCROFT AND COMPANY, 1861.

[i]–vi, [7]–190. 17.7 x 11.6 cm. Brown cloth, blind embossed sides, title in gilt on backstrip.
Ref.: Howes N231
This is an abridged translation of the author's *Noticias . . . del estado de Sonora . . .* 1850. The interesting itinerary at the end of the original printing is not given in the translation.

4470 VENEGAS, MIGUEL

NOTICIA DE LA CALIFORNIA, Y DE SU CONQUISTA TEMPORAL, Y ESPIRITUAL HASTA EL TIEMPO PRESENTE . . . EN MADRID: EN LA IMPRENTA DE LA VIUDA DE MANUEL FERNANDEZ, M.D.CCLVII.

¶–¶¶¶⁴, A–Gg⁴. ¶⁴, A–Aaaa⁴, Bbbb². ¶⁴, A–Hhh⁴, Iii². [i–xxiv], 1–240. [i–viii], 1–564. [i–viii], 1–436. 19.9 x 14.5 cm. Four maps: Map: Mapa / de la / California / su Golfo, y Provincias / fronteras en el Continente / de Nueva / España. / [lower left of cartouche:] I.ª Peña sculp. M.ʰ / 31.2 x 20.1 cm. (neat line of map). No scale given. Three sides bordered by ten illustrations and cartouche. Decorative cartouche carrying dedication on face of map: Al Rey N.S. / la Provincia / de la Compañia / de JHS de / Nueva españa / lo O. D. y C. / 1757. / Map: Seno de California, y su costa ori-/ental nuevamente descubierta, / y registrada desde el Cabo đ las / Virgenes, hasta su termino, que es / el Rio Colorado año 1747. por el / P. e Ferdinando Consag. de la / Compª de IHS, Missioñ en la California. / 31 x 28.6 cm. Scale: 8 1/2 Spanish leagues to one inch. Map: Viage de Ansòn. Lib. 3. Cap. 8. pag. 305. Mapa 33. / Carta / de la Mar del Sur, ò Mar pacifico, / entre el Equador, y 39 1/2 de latitud sep-/tentrional / hallada por el Almirante Jorge An son en el Galeon de Philipinas, que / apresò. / [lower right:] Joseph Gonzᶻ sculpᵗ Mʰ / 23.5 x 22.8 cm. No scale given. Map: Mapa / de la America Septent.l. / Asia Oriental y Mar del Sur / Intermedio Formado / sobre las Memorias mas recientes / y exactas hasta el / Año de 1754. / [lower left:] Manuel. Rodriguez. Sculst- / [lower right:] M. A. de 1756 /. 29.9 x 36 cm. Scale: about 25 maritime leagues to one inch. Lower portion contains three cartouches against pictorial ground. Three volumes, contemporary limp vellum, with manuscript titles on backstrips, faintly mottled edges.

Ref.: Barrett 2539; Cowan p. 659; Field 1599; Howes V69; Jones 491; Medina (*BHA*) 3855; Sabin 98848; Stevens (*Nuggets*) 2736; Streit III 663; Wagner (*SS*) 132; Zamorano Eighty 78

Wagner attributes the text to Father Andrés Marcos Burriel.

4471 VENEGAS, MIGUEL

A NATURAL AND CIVIL HISTORY OF CALIFORNIA . . . LONDON: PRINTED FOR JAMES RIVINGTON AND JAMES FLETCHER, 1759.

A⁸, a², B–Ff⁸, Gg². A⁴, B–Bb⁸, Cc². [i–xx], [1]–455, [456 blank]. [i–vii, viii blank], [1]–387, [388 blank]. 22.2 x 14 cm. Map and four plates. Map: An / accurate Map / of / California, / Drawn by / the Society of Jesuits, / & dedicated to the / King of Spain. / 1757 [upper right:] Vol: I. page 13. / [lower right:] J. Gibson Sculp: / 31.1 x 20 cm. No scale given. Two volumes, contemporary tan boards with mottled brown calf backstrips and corners, red leather labels on backstrips, entirely uncut and mostly unopened. In a blue cloth case.

Ref.: Barrett 2536; Cowan p. 658; Field 1600; Howes V69; Jones 499; Sabin 98845; Stevens (*Nuggets*) 2737; Wagner (*SS*) 132a; Zamorano Eighty 78 note

A remarkably fine copy of the first English edition.

4472 VENEGAS, MIGUEL, & JUAN FRANCISCO LOPEZ

MANUALITO DE PARROCOS, PARA LOS AUTOS DEL MINISTERIO MAS PRECISOS, Y AUXILIAR A LOS ENFERMOS . . . NUEVO MEXICO: IMPRENTA DEL PRESBITERO ANTONIO JOSE MARTINEZ A CARGO DE J. M. BACA, 1839.

[i–iv], 1–52. 13.5 x 8.6 cm. Rebound in old black cloth, blind fillets on sides, with title (largely obliterated) on front cover in gilt. In a black cloth case.

Ref.: AII (*New Mexico*) 14; McMurtrie (*New Mexico*) 16; Wagner (*New Mexico*) 14

A fragment of another religious work is used as a front endleaf.

Streit lists several other editions, but not this one.

4473 VER PLANCK, VIRGINIA D.

THE ADVENTURES OF TEDDY JOHNSON; OR, EARLY LIFE ON THE PRAIRIE . . . FISHKILL-ON-HUDSON, N. Y.: EDWARD VER PLANCK, 1901.

[i–iv], [1]–54, [55–56 blank]. 14.7 x 9.9 cm. Pale yellow printed wrappers, with title on front wrapper.

Ref.:

An amusing amateur job of publishing.

The action in this tale takes place in Iowa near Fort Dodge, so the author says, but I believe it derives entirely from the author's imagination.—EDG

4474 VERAX, *pseud.*

AN EXPOSTULATORY EPISTLE TO THE WELCH[!] KNIGHT, ON THE LATE REVOLUTION IN POLITICKS . . . LONDON: PRINTED FOR J. ROBINSON, 1745.

[A]–D⁴. [1]–32. 19.4 x 11.7 cm. Bound with Number 3115.

Ref.:

An attack on Sir Watkin Williams Wynn by an unidentified political opponent.

4475 VETANCURT, AUGUSTIN DE

ART DE LENGUA MEXICANA . . . CON LICENCIA, EN MEXICO POR FRANCISCO RODRIGUEZ LUPERCIO. 1673.

[*]⁴, A–P⁴. [i–vi], 1–14, 14–49, [50–57] LEAVES. [i.e., pages [i–xii, 1–116]. (Leaf 29 misfoliated 19.) 20.4 x 14.6 cm. Contemporary limp vellum, with leather ties. Title in manuscript on backstrip.

Prov.: Branded on top and bottom edges, but brand is indistinguishable.

Ref.: Butler (*Nahuatl*) 237; Medina (*Mexico*) 1103; Pilling 4002; Sabin 99385; Stevens (*Nuggets*) 2750; Streit II 2326 note

4476 VETANCURT, AUGUSTIN DE

CHRONICA DE LA PROVINCIA DEL SANTO EVAN-
GELIO DE MEXICO . . . EN MEXICO, POR DONA
MARIA DE BENAVIDES VIUDA DE IUAN DE RIBERA.
ANO DE 1697.

[ʃ]², ʃʃ², ʃʃʃ², A–Eeee². [i]–xii, [1]–136, [137–
38], [i–ii], [1]–156. (In the first part, page 75 is
mispaginated 65 and 136 is mispaginated 1361.)
27.6 x 20.6 cm.

Ref.: Howes V83; Jones 302; Medina (*Mexico*) 1684; Sabin 99386; Stevens (*Nuggets*) 2751;
Wagner (*SS*) 68

BOUND WITH:

[Caption title:] TRATADO DE LA CIUDAD DE MEXI-
CO, Y LAS GRANDEZAS QUE LA ILUSTRAN DESPUES
QUE LA FUNDARON ESPANOLES. . . .

A–O². 1–56.

Ref.: Medina (*Mexico*) 1716; Wagner (*SS*) 70
Rebound in full nineteenth century Spanish
calf, leather labels, sprinkled edges.

Prov.: Gilt label of Dr. Mariano Padilla on
backstrip and his embossed bookstamp on front
endleaf.

A prime authority for the history of New
Mexico.—Wagner

In the Newberry-Ayer copy, the mispagination 65 for 75 is present, but the mispagination
of 136 has been corrected.

The *Chronica* is present in the Ayer collection
as the fourth part of the same author's *Teatro
Mexicano*, in which the *Tratado* . . . is also
found.

4477 VICTOR, FRANCES FULLER

THE RIVER OF THE WEST. LIFE AND ADVENTURE IN
THE ROCKY MOUNTAINS AND OREGON . . . HART-
FORD, CONN.: R. W. BLISS & COMPANY, 1870.

[1–2], [i]–xxii, [23]–602. 21.9 x 14.2 cm. 31 illustrations listed. Brown cloth, with gilt vignette on
front cover and title in gilt on backstrip.

Prov.: Inscribed on blank leaf at front: Dʳ
Fredᵏ Dally / from the / Author. / [dash] /.

Ref.: Bradford 5586; Howes V89; Smith
10555

4478 VICTOR, WILLIAM B.

LIFE AND EVENTS . . . CINCINNATI: APPLEGATE &
CO., 1859.

[i]–viii, [9]–232, [233–40 advertisements]. 21.7 x
14.3 cm. Brown cloth, blind embossed sides,
title in gilt on backstrip.

Ref.: Howes V90; Raines p. 209
Contains material relating to the financing of
Austin's Texas colony through the efforts of
Joseph H. Hawkins.

4479 VIGIL, DONACIANO

[Wrapper title] BREVE EXPOSICION QUE DA AL
PUBLICO EL CIUDADANO DONACIANO VIGIL, CAPI-
TAN DE LA COMPANIA DEL BADO, COMO VOCAL DE
LA EXMA. ASAMBLEA, MANIFESTANDO LOS MOTIVOS
QUE LE IMPELIERON A VOTAR POR EL EMPRESTITO
FORZOZO A QUE A PEDIMENTO DEL EXMO . . . SR
GOBERNADOR Y COMMANDANTE GRAL. D. MARIANO
MARTINEZ DECRETO LA MISMA HONORABLE ASAM-
BLEA EN 14 DE FEBRERO DEL CORRIENTE ANO. DE
1845. IMPRENTA PARTICULAR A CARGO DE J. M. B.

[1–14]. 19.5 x 14 cm. Yellow printed wrappers
with title on front wrapper, stabbed and stitched.
Repaired.

Ref.:
Jesús María Baca maintained his printing
office in Santa Fé in 1845.
No other copy has been located.

4480 VIGILANTE COMMITTEE

[Broadside] BRUTUS GUARDS 22D COMPANY V. C.
Broadside badge printed in black on silk ribbon,
15.4 x 5.9 cm.

Ref.:
Used in 1856. Probably printed in San Francisco.

4481 VIGILANTES OF MONTANA (?)

CARTE-DE-VISITE PHOTOGRAPH OF THE HANGING
OF TWO MEN BY VIGILANTES, PROBABLY MONTANA.
Photograph, 10 x 5.8 cm. Card, 10.6 x 6.3 cm.

The photograph is similar to, and was undoubtedly taken at the same time as, an illustration in Langford's *Vigilante Days and Ways* . . .
Acquired from Langford's daughter in 1951.
—EDG

4482 VIGILANTES OF WYOMING

ORIGINAL PHOTOGRAPH OF THREE HANGED MEN,
CON WEIGER, ASA MOORE, AND BIG ED BARNARD.
On verso: Geo. W. McFadden, / [flourish]
Photographer. [flourish] / Laramie City, W. /
Printed in sepia, mounted on stiff card. Print,
9.6 x 5.5 cm. Card, 10.6 x 6.3 cm.

Ref.: Bancroft (*Popular Tribunals*) I 717
In manuscript, on the face of the print: No
3 / No 2 / No 1 /. On verso: No 1 Con Weiger /
″2 Asa Moore / ″3 Big Ed Barnard /. Also pencil note: Hanged by Wyo. / vigilantes Oct
1868 /.

From collection of Nathaniel P. Langford
through his daughter.

4483 VILAPLANA, HERMENEGILDO DE

VIDA PORTENTOS DEL AMERICANO SEPTENTRIONAL
APOSTOL EL V. P. FR. ANTONIO MARGIL DE JESUS . . .

EN LA IMPRENTA DE LA BIBLIOTHECA MEXICANA, 1763.

¶4+1, ¶¶–¶¶¶¶4, A–Tt4. [i]–xxxiv, [1]–336. 20 x 14.4 cm. Portrait. Contemporary vellum, title in manuscript on backstrip.

Ref.: Clark I 166; Howes V98; Jones 510; Medina (*Mexico*) 4862; Sabin 99614; Streit III 806; Wagner (*SS*) 142

See also Espinosa, Isidoro Felix de for another biography of Antonio Margil de Jesus.

4484 VILLAGRA, GASPAR DE

HISTORIA DE LA NUEVA MEXICO . . . EN ALCALA: POR LUYS MARTINEZ GRANDE, 1610.

[*]8, ¶–¶¶8, A–Nn8. [1]–48, 1–287 numbered LEAVES, leaf with colophon. 14.3 x 9.4 cm. (Folios 74 and 162 are misnumbered 34 and 152, no foliation for 92.) Contemporary limp vellum. Lacks front endleaf.

Prov.: Signature inside front cover: RʰD: Waddilone / Madrid 1788 / [underline] /. Bookplate of Henry Huth.

Ref.: Jones 173; Medina (*BHA*) 566; Rader 3538; Raines p. 210; Sabin 99641; Stevens (*Nuggets*) 2764; Wagner (*SS*) 14

Wagner calls for unfoliated leaves 18 and 28, which are foliated in this copy.

4485 VILLAGRA, GASPAR DE

[Caption title] FOL. I. SERUICIOS QUE A SU MAGESTAD HA HECHO EL CAPITAN GASPAR DE VILLAGRA, PARA QUE V. M. LE HAGA MERCED . . .

A4. 1–4 LEAVES. 29.6 x 20.5 cm.

Ref.: Wagner (*SS*) 19

This copy differs slightly from the Wagner copy. Note the caption title; nine lines on last page; no signatures on last page.

4486 VILLARD, HENRY

THE PAST AND PRESENT OF THE PIKE'S PEAK GOLD REGIONS . . . ST. LOUIS, MO.: SUTHERLAND & MCEVOY, PUBLISHERS, 1860.

[1]–112. 20.6 x 13.3 cm. Folding map: Routes to the Pikes Peak Gold Regions. / [lower left:] A. Mᶜ Lean Lith 3ᵈ & Pine. St. Louis, Mo. / 22.1 x 55.7 cm. (neat line). No scale indicated. Lacks one other map and frontispiece view. Original brown cloth, with title on front cover.

Prov.: Presentation copy from the author to his wife inscribed in pencil on front blank leaf: To my dearly loved Fanny— / Harry. / Munich —November 23d 1866. /

Ref.: Howes V101; Wagner-Camp 366

The only perfect copies are in the Coe Collection at Yale, and the Library of Colorado State College.

4487 VILLARD, HENRY

MEMOIRS . . . 1835–1900 . . . BOSTON: HOUGHTON, MIFFLIN AND COMPANY, 1904.*

[i]–xi, [xii blank], [1]–393, [394 colophon]. [i]–vi, [1]–393, [394 colophon]. 22 x 14.8 cm. Four illustrations and eight maps listed. Two volumes, blue ribbed cloth, gilt tops, uncut.

Ref.: Howes V100

4488 VILLAVICENCIO, JUAN JOSEPH DE

VIDA, Y VIRTUDES DE EL VENERABLE, Y APOSTOLICO PADRE JUAN DE UGARTE DE LA COMPANIA DE JESUS . . . IMPRESSA . . . EN MEXICO, EN LA IMPRENTA DE REAL, Y MAS ANTIGUO COLEGIO DE SAN ILDEFONSO, 1752.

[*]2, *2, **2, A–Hhh2. [i–xii], 1–214, [215–16 Index]. 19.9 x 14.3 cm. Contemporary limp vellum, with leather ties. Manuscript title on backstrip.

Prov.: Bookplate of Biblioteca del General Riva Palacio.

Ref.: Barrett 2554; Cowan p. 661; Diaz Mercado 932 (in Bolton's *Guide to Archives of Mexico*); Howes V104; Jones 472; Medina (*Mexico*) 4105; Sabin 99694; Wagner (*SS*) 126

Father Juan de Ugarte lived among the California Indians for thirty years. His explorations about the Gulf of California helped dispel the belief that California was an island.

4489 VILLIERS DU TERRAGE, MARC, BARON DE

. . . LA DECOUVERTE DU MISSOURI ET L'HISTOIRE DU FORT D'ORLEANS (1673–1728). PARIS: LIBRAIRIE ANCIENNE HONORE CHAMPION, 1925.*

[i–iv], 1–138, [139 colophon, 140 blank]. 23.4 x 18 cm. Two maps listed. Marbled boards, maroon levant morocco back, tinted top, uncut. Original front wrapper bound in.

Ref.: Howes V105; Rader 3540

Limited to 300 copies.

4490 VINTON, STALLO

JOHN COLTER, DISCOVERER OF YELLOWSTONE PARK. AN ACCOUNT OF HIS EXPLORATION IN 1807 AND OF HIS FURTHER ADVENTURES AS HUNTER; TRAPPER; INDIAN FIGHTER; PATHFINDER AND MEMBER OF THE LEWIS AND CLARK EXPEDITION . . . NEW YORK: EDWARD EBERSTADT, 1926.

[1]–114, [115 blank, 116 colophon]. (Pages [1–4] blank.) 24.1 x 16 cm. Frontispiece. Gray boards, white vellum back, uncut, unopened.

Ref.: Howes V114; Smith 10603

Limited to 30 copies on Large Paper, signed by the author.

4491 VISCHER, EDWARD

BRIEFE EINES DEUTSCHEN AUS CALIFORNIEN . . .
SAN FRANCISCO, CALIFORNIEN, 1873.

[1]–31, [32 blank]. 24 x 15.1 cm. Cream printed
wrappers with title on front wrapper.

Ref.: Calif. Hist. Soc. Quarterly, Vol. XIX,
No. 3, Sept., 1940, pp. 193–216; Cowan p. 661;
Howes V128a

The letters published here described Vischer's
first visit to California in 1842. Most of them
were published in four installments of *Allgemeine
Zeitung* (Munich) late in January, 1846.
They were picked up and printed again in the
California Chronik (San Francisco), and then
published separately in the present pamphlet
form.

The letters have been translated and published
in the *California Historical Society Quarterly*
by Erwin Gustav Gudde. Gudde states that
"The two versions are identical, except that the
reprint has a fifth installment and that many
names are supplied or their misspelling corrected
. . . Important and interesting . . . is an
additional letter, which describes Vischer's journey
aboard the California as a fellow passenger
with a number of Micheltorena's convict soldiers."

4492 VISCHER, EDWARD

VISCHER'S PICTORIAL OF CALIFORNIA LANDSCAPE,
TREES AND FOREST SCENES. GRAND FEATURES OF
CALIFORNIA SCENERY, LIFE, TRAFFIC AND CUSTOMS.
SAN FRANCISCO: PRINTED BY JOSEPH WINTERBURN
& COMPANY, 1870.

[i–iv], [1]–4, [129]–131, [132 blank], [5–12], [60
pages of photographs], [title, verso blank], [14
pages of photographs], [leaf without photographs],
[title, verso blank], [46 pages of photographs],
[title, verso blank], [6 pages of photographs].
Illustrations listed, except as noted below.
Original full black morocco, gilt, gilt edges.
Photographs and fly-titles mounted, each leaf
attached to cloth stub.

Ref.: Cowan p. 662; Howes V131

The Contents leaf calls for Geology of the
High Sierra (pages 117–119) and the Yosemite
Valley (pages 119–127) but these are not present.

Pages 8–9 list the California landscapes.

Page 11 lists four series of plates, i.e., Californian
Landscape; Trees and Forest Scenes;
Grand Features of Californian Scenery; Life,
Traffic and Customs. Two photographs are missing
from the third group, but there is an unlisted
map.

The titles are present for parts 1–3. The fourth
and fifth parts have title-pages as follows:

[Part IV:] Review / of / California's Progress.
Compilation / of Technical Topographic and
Pictorial Subjects, Mining, Agriculture and Industry,
/ Traffic, Commerce and Shipping. /
[decoration] / Reduced original Photographs, /
Copies of Maps and Lithographic Illustrations,
with Photographs of Drawings. / San Francisco,
1867. Edward Vischer, / [decorative rule] / Review
of California's Progress; / (Vischer's Miscellaneous
Views of California, Copyright
1863.) / [ornamental rule] / Author's own Drawings,
or Illustrations from his Sketches, entered
according to act of Congress, in the year 1867, by
Edward Vischer, in the Clerk's Office / of the
District Court of the United States for the
Northern District of California. / [title printed
in red within gold rule border].

[Part V:] Early Industrial Progress in California.
/ Exhibition / at the / Mechanic's Industrial
Fair / Selection from C. E. Watkins' Stereoscopic
Views, / San Francisco. / 1864. / Contribution
to Vischer's Miscellaneous Views thankfully
acknowledged. E. V. / [within decorative
border, printed in purple].

The fourth part contains fifteen listed photographs
and thirty-one unlisted photographs.

The unlisted photographs are as follows:
Crystal Spring, Casa del Pablo de Robles, View
of the Convent of Santa Barbara, Encampment
of Mexican "Arrieros," North View of the
Church and Ex-Mission of Santa Ines, South
View of . . . San Buenaventura, Californian
Method of Killing Cattle, Scene at a California
Rodeo, Emigrant Encampment . . . Sierra Nevada,
Monitor Comanche, Carcass of a Whale,
Arch in the Rock, [Coast scene], Richardson's
Bay, Nugget of gold, Miner's Own Book,
Miner's Own Book (another version), Mount
Diablo Coal-Mines, New Almaden Quicksilver
Mine [i], New Almaden Quicksilver Mine [ii],
Sierra Buttes-Mines, Topographical Map . . .
Eureka Lake Water Co. . . . , [Five mining
scenes in one photograph], Map of St. Helena
Mountain Range, Topographical and Railroad
Map of the Central Part of the State of California
. . . 1865, [Six Napa Valley views].

The final section comprises seven photographs.

Few copies contain precisely the same number
of plates.—Cowan

4493 VISSCHER, WILLIAM L.

A THRILLING AND TRUTHFUL HISTORY OF THE
PONY EXPRESS; OR, BLAZING THE WESTWARD WAY
AND OTHER SKETCHES AND INCIDENTS OF THOSE
STIRRING TIMES . . . CHICAGO: RAND, McNALLY &
CO.*

[1]–98. 24.8 x 16.8 cm. Illustrations unlisted. Gray pictorial cloth.

    Ref.: Cowan p. 662; Rader 3548
Copyrighted 1908.

    Wright Howes tells me that when he came to Chicago in 1913 Colonel Visscher was impecunious and dependent to a large extent on his younger friends for drinks and food. His boon companion at that time was Opie Reed. Upon Visscher's death, about 1916, there was found a cache of 200 or 300 copies of this Pony Express book in his living quarters. These copies were bought by Powner, the book dealer for whom Howes at that time worked, and sold for $1.50 per copy. When his supply was exhausted, Powner used the plates, which he had also bought, to print or have printed a further supply (quantity unknown). Question? Has any difference been detected between copies of the two editions?—EDG

4494 [VIZETELLY, HENRY]

FOUR MONTHS AMONG THE GOLD-FINDERS IN ALTA CALIFORNIA; BEING THE DIARY OF AN EXPEDITION FROM SAN FRANCISCO TO THE GOLD DISTRICTS. BY J. TYRWHITT BROOKS, M. D. LONDON: DAVID BOGUE, MDCCCXLIX.*

[i]–xviii, [1]–207, [208 blank]. 19.9 x 12.1 cm. Map. Red cloth, blind embossed sides, title stamped in gilt on backstrip, uncut.

    Ref.: Cowan p. 75; Howes V134; Vizetelly (*Glances Back through Seventy Years*, London, 1893); Watson, D. S. (in *California Historical Society Quarterly*, March 1932, p. 65)

    Watson's article describes this work as spurious Californiana, but the author thinks Vizetelly did not tell the whole truth when he described the writing and printing of the book in his autobiography. Vizetelly does not mention using Colonel Mason's famous report published in December, 1848, but states he used Colonel Frémont's reports for his imaginary adventures. The book was readily accepted on publication and even as late as 1914 the work was usually accepted as authentic. However, Vizetelly had exposed the fraud and it had been redescribed in 1908 by Courtney in his *Secrets of Our National Literature.*—EDG

4495 VOICE OF THE PEOPLE

[Newspaper] VOICE OF THE PEOPLE. VOL. I. CHICAGO, FRIDAY, JULY 27, 1838. NO. V . . .

[1–4]. 44 x 29.4 cm. Unbound.

    Ref.:

    At the foot of the last column on page [3]: Published Weekly at / The Office of the American. / Chicago, Illinois, / Until after the Ensuing August Election. / (By the Whig Young Men's Association.) /

    The fourth page is a poster comprising the slate of the People's Ticket.

4496 [VOLLMER, CARL G. W.]

CALIFORNIEN UND DAS GOLDFIEBER. REISEN IN DEM WILDEN WESTEN NORD-AMERIKA'S, LEBEN UND SITTEN DER GOLDGRÄBER, MORMONEN UND IN-DIANER . . . BERLIN: VERLAG VON THEODOR THIELE, 1863.

[i–vi], [1]–744. 22 x 14.6 cm. Eight colored lithographs and 51 illustrations in the text. Mottled boards, red leather backstrip and corners, back gilt, marbled edges.

    Ref.: Cowan p. 701; Howes V140

4497 VON LEICHT, FERDINAND, & J. D. HOFFMANN

[Map] TOPOGRAPHICAL MAP / OF / LAKE TAHOE / AND / SURROUNDING COUNTRY, / COMPILED FROM THE BEST AUTHORITIES, / BY / FERDINAND VON LEICHT, & J. D. HOFFMANN, / CIVIL ENGINEERS. / 432 MONTGOMERY ST. S. F. / 1874. / SCALE 2 MILES TO 1 INCH. / [diagrammatic scale] / ENTERED AC-CORDING TO AN ACT OF CONGRESS IN THE YEAR 1873 BY FERD. VON LEICHT IN THE OFFICE OF THE LIBRARIAN OF CONGRESS IN WASHINGTON, D. C. / *Two small inset views:* Lake Tahoe and Donner Lake, both in lower right corner.

Folding map, 61.8 x 52.7 cm. Scale: 2 miles to one inch. Folded into original black cloth covers, 16.5 x 10.3 cm., with gilt title on front cover: Map of / Lake Tahoe. / 1874. /

    Ref.: Phillips p. 836

4498 VOORHEES, LUKE

PERSONAL RECOLLECTIONS OF PIONEER LIFE ON THE MOUNTAINS AND PLAINS OF THE GREAT WEST . . .*

[1]–75, [76 blank]. 21.4 x 14.5 cm. Portrait. Black cloth.

    Ref.: Howes V142; Smith 5708

    The leaf headed: In Appreciation / is dated Cheyenne, Wyo., July 1, 1920.

    This also appears as the second part of Lathrop, G.: *Some Pioneer Recollections . . .* Philadelphia, 1927.

4499 [VOSE, J. H.]

[Caption title] . . . REPORT FROM THE SECRETARY OF WAR . . . ON THE SUBJECT OF DISTURBANCES WITH THE INDIANS ON THE FRONTIER OF ARKAN-SAS . . .

[1]–4. 22.2 x 13.8 cm. Stapled into gray boards, black cloth backstrip, typed white label on front cover.

    Ref.:

25th Congress, 2nd Session, Senate, Document No. 487, Serial 319. [Washington, 1838.]

Contains two letters by Lieutenant Colonel J. H. Vose regarding disturbances between Indians and whites on the Red River near Fort Towson. "The white people were undoubtedly the aggressors, as is generally the case in all Indian difficulties."

Printer's imprint, lower left corner, pages [1]: [short rule] / Blair & Rives, printers. /

4500 VROOM, JAMES W.

GRANT OF THE RIO DE LAS ANIMAS IN COLORADO. TO CORNELIO VIGIL AND CERAN ST. VRAIN, MADE DECEMBER 9, 1843, AND THE OPINION OF JAMES W. VROOM AS TO THE CHARACTER AND VALIDITY OF THE SAME.

[1]–44. 21 x 14.3 cm. Removed from bound volume, unbound. Remnants of orange wrappers.
Ref.:
Dated on page 37: Denver, November 6, 1888.

W

4501 WADDINGTON, ALFRED

[Wrapper title] THE FRAZER MINES VINDICATED; OR, THE HISTORY OF FOUR MONTHS . . . VICTORIA: PRINTED BY P. DE GARRO, 1858.

[1]–49, [50 blank], [51 appendix, 52 blank]. 21.4 x 13.3 cm. Tan printed wrappers, with title on front wrapper. In a dark blue morocco case.
Ref.: Sabin 100899; Smith 10624; Staton & Tremaine 3871

Issue two without erratum note at end of Appendix for an error on page 6, error corrected. Several manuscript corrections in text.

4502 WADSWORTH, WILLIAM

THE NATIONAL WAGON ROAD GUIDE, FROM ST. JOSEPH AND COUNCIL BLUFFS, ON THE MISSOURI RIVER, VIA SOUTH PASS OF THE ROCKY MOUNTAINS, TO CALIFORNIA . . . SAN FRANCISCO: WHITTON, TOWNE & CO., PRINTERS AND PUBLISHERS, 1858.

[i blank, ii frontispiece, iii]–viii, [9]–160. 16.8 x 11.1 cm. Vignettes in text, map: Map / of the Overland Route / [lower left:] Kuchel & Dresel lith. 176. Clay St. S. F. / 13 x 44.7 cm. No scale given. Manuscript note on face of map by A. J. Murphy: Spent / 2 years in / Salt lake /. Pink printed wrappers with title on front wrapper, advertisements on recto and verso of back wrapper. Manuscript label pasted onto backstrip. In a red half morocco case.
Prov.: In black ink at the top of the front

wrapper and on page [vii]: A J Murphy /. In red ink on front wrapper: Andrew J Murphy /. Andrew J. Murphy is said to have been a Roman Catholic priest who went overland to California and died there.
Ref.: Cowan p. 665; Greenwood 1029; Howes W3; Jones 1405; Sabin 100930; Wagner-Camp 313

The Wagner-Camp collation is slightly faulty. The pagination of the first section on the "Overland Route" is [9]–72, "The National Wagon Road Guide" runs from [73] to 132, "Valedictory Advice" pages [133] to 136 and "Appendix" from [137] to 160.

Most of the vignette illustrations are amusing in character. They may have been the work of Charles Nahl.

4503 WAGGONER, GEORGE A.

STORIES OF OLD OREGON . . . SALEM, OREGON: STATESMAN PUBLISHING CO., 1905.*

[i–iv], [1]–292. 18.9 x 13.9 cm. Illustrations unlisted. Pictorial gray-green cloth.
Prov.: Inscribed in pencil on fly-leaf: With regard / G A Waggoner /.
Ref.: Smith 10642

4504 WAGNER, HENRY R.

CALIFORNIA IMPRINTS: AUGUST 1846—JUNE 1851 . . . BERKELEY, CALIFORNIA, 1922.

[i–viii], 1–97, [98 blank]. 25.4 x 17.7 cm. 20 photostats, unlisted. White boards, white vellum backstrip, title in gilt on backstrip.
Ref.:
Limited to 150 copies of which twenty-five are specially bound with photostats.

4505 WAGNER, HENRY R.

THE PLAINS AND THE ROCKIES: A BIBLIOGRAPHY OF ORIGINAL NARRATIVES OF TRAVELS AND ADVENTURES, 1800–1865 . . . SAN FRANCISCO: JOHN HOWELL, 1921.

[i–viii], 1–193, [194 blank]. 25.3 x 17.3 cm. 40 unlisted reproductions of title-pages. Gray boards, vellum back. In buckram slip case.
Limited to 50 copies, extra-illustrated.
Editions: San Francisco, 1920.

4506 WAGNER, HENRY R., & CHARLES L. CAMP

. . . THE PLAINS AND THE ROCKIES . . . COLUMBUS, OHIO: LONG'S COLLEGE BOOK COMPANY, 1953.*

[i–viii], [602 blank]. 23.5 x 15.4 cm. Illustrations unlisted. Decorated boards, tan cloth back, printed paper labels. In board slip case.
Prov.: Laid in is a card from the publisher

announcing the gift of the De Luxe Edition from the editor.

Ref.:

De Luxe Edition.

Editions: San Francisco, 1920, 1921, 1937.

4507 WAGNER, HENRY R.

THE SPANISH SOUTHWEST, 1542–1794 . . . ALBUQUERQUE: THE QUIVIRA SOCIETY, 1937.

[1]–270. [271]–553, [554 blank]. 24.8 x 16.5 cm. 114 illustrations listed. Two volumes, brown boards with white cloth backstrips.

Ref.:

Limited to 401 copies.

Editions: Berkeley, 1924.

4508 WAGON MASTER'S TRAIN BOOK

[Cover title] TRAIN, GENERAL NO. [in manuscript: 1] [in manuscript: Edward Boulware] WAGON MASTER. LEFT [in manuscript: June 5th 65] RETURNED [in manuscript: July 5] [three lines of manuscript: 2nd Trip July 11 Returned Augt 17 Left on 3rd trip 19 Augt].

[1]–8, [i–iv], [unpaginated page,] 1, 1, 2, 2, 3, 3, etc. to 36, 36, 37, 38, 39, 41, 42, 43, 44, 45, 46–65, 72–77. 59 leaves, irregularly paginated, as above. 19.5 x 13 cm. Sheep, with leather flap and cloth tie, with title on front cover as above.

Ref.:

An exceedingly interesting printed and manuscript Wagon Train Master's book.

The contents comprise the following material:

Pages [1]–3: Wagon-Masters and Others, / In Charge of Trains of [dotted rule] / Will be Governed by the Following / Rules and Regulations. / [diamond rule] / . . .

Pages [4]–8: Instructions / to / Wagon-Masters, / and all Employees Connected for Transporting Trains. / [decorative rule] / . . .

Pages [i–iv]: manuscript index on lined pages.

Page unpaginated: blank except for ruled lines.

Pages 1, 1–27, 27: manuscript accounts with individual employees.

Pages 28, 28, 29, 29: blank except for ruled lines.

Pages 30, 30–33, 33, 34, 35: lists of sacks, boxes, etc. carried in each wagon, including weights.

Pages 36, 36, 37, 38: blank except for ruled lines.

Page 39: part of an account with Jacob Waggonseller.

Page 41: accounting for loss of three head of cattle.

Pages 42, 42: headed Cattle Account, but without entries.

Pages 43–46: headed Outfit Account, includes printed list of outfit and manuscript numbers, additions, etc.

Pages 47–48: headed Orders, but without entries.

Pages 49–52: headed Receipts for Cattle, but without entries.

Pages 53–56: headed Receipts for Outfitting, and other Property, but without entries.

Pages 57–58: headed Train Expense, with manuscript entries.

Pages 59–60: headed Rations, &c., with manuscript entries.

Page 61: headed Medicine Chest, with manuscript entries.

Page 62: headed Ammunition, with manuscript entries.

Pages 63–65: headed Miscellaneous, but without manuscript entries.

Pages 72–77: headed Miscellaneous, without entries on pages 72–74, and pages 75–77 filled with manuscript entries of payments made.

At points above where pages are omitted, the leaves have been torn out. An indeterminate number of leaves are missing after page 77, probably two.

The Wagon Master, according to the front cover, was Edward Boulware. He was employed by M. W. Payne on the run from Nebraska City to Fort Kearney or Fort MacPherson.

Accompanying the volume is a printed and manuscript broadside agreement, signed by Wagon-Masters, Assistants, and Teamsters; [thick and thin rule] / We, the undersigned, Wagon-Masters, Assistants, and Teamsters, in the employ of [dotted rule above which in manuscript: M W] / [dotted rule above which in manuscript: Payne] / agree, that we will faithfully perform all the duties incumbent upon us, as / good Teamsters, and that we will not use profane language, get drunk, gamble, or be cruel to animals. / [eight lines] / [double rule] / [double vertical rule] [ten signatures in right column] /. Broadside, 31.7 x 19.6 cm. Text, 28 x 17.3 cm. Blue ruled paper. The document provides for fifty dollars per month for teamsters.

4509 WAGSTAFF, ALEXANDER E.

LIFE OF DAVID S. TERRY. PRESENTING AN AUTHENTIC, IMPARTIAL AND VIVID HISTORY OF HIS EVENTFUL LIFE AND TRAGIC DEATH . . . SAN FRANCISCO, CAL.: CONTINENTAL PUBLISHING COMPANY, 1892.

[i]–xvi, 15–526. 21.9 x 14.7 cm. Frontispiece and four plates. Full sheepskin, black and red skiver labels on backstrip, marbled edges.

Ref.: Cowan p. 666; Howes W14

4510 WAKEFIELD, JOHN A.

HISTORY OF THE WAR BETWEEN THE UNITED STATES AND THE SAC AND FOX NATIONS OF INDIANS, AND PARTS OF OTHER DISAFFECTED TRIBES OF INDIANS, IN THE YEARS EIGHTEEN HUNDRED AND TWENTY-SEVEN, THIRTY-ONE, AND THIRTY-TWO . . . JACKSONVILLE, ILL.: PRINTED BY CALVIN GOUDY, 1834.

[i]–x, [1]–142. 16.6 x 9.9 cm. Brown linen. Lacks flyleaves. In a brown half leather case.

Ref.: Byrd 213; Howes W19; Sabin 100978

One of the most important contemporary sources on these Indian troubles. Also contains an account of the captivity of the Hall girls.

4511 WALGAMOTT, CHARLES S.

REMINISCENCES OF EARLY DAYS. A SERIES OF HISTORICAL SKETCHES AND HAPPENINGS IN THE EARLY DAYS OF SNAKE RIVER VALLEY . . .

[i–iv], [1]–[128]. [1]–[128]. 22.9 x 15 cm. Illustrations unlisted. Two volumes, first in red cloth, second in purple.

Prov.: Signed by the author under the portrait, Volume I page [iv]: C. S. Walgamott / June 19th 1930 /.

Ref.: Howes W31

Printed at Twin Falls, Idaho, copyrighted 1926 and 1927.

4512 WALKER, ADAM

A JOURNAL OF TWO CAMPAIGNS OF THE FOURTH REGIMENT OF U. S. INFANTRY, IN THE MICHIGAN AND INDIANA TERRITORIES, UNDER THE COMMAND OF COL. JOHN P. BOYD, AND LT. COL. JAMES MILLER DURING THE YEARS 1811, & 12 . . . KEENE, N. H.: PRINTED AT THE SENTINEL PRESS, BY THE AUTHOR, 1816.

A–M6. [1]–143, [144 blank]. (Page 14 mispaginated 11.) 19 x 11.7 cm. Gray boards, tan paper back, printed white paper label. In a red half morocco case.

Prov.: Bookplates of Marshall Library (Buffalo Historical Society) and John W. Lowe. And with G. D. Smith's bill to J. W. Lowe for purchase at the Marshall Sale pasted in.

Ref.: Field 1619; Howes W33; Jones 783; Sabin 101032; Thomson 1173

The sections on Harrison's campaign, the retaking of Detroit, and the defeat of Proctor are particularly interesting.

4513 WALKER, JUDSON E.

CAMPAIGNS OF GENERAL CUSTER IN THE NORTHWEST, AND THE FINAL SURRENDER OF SITTING BULL . . . NEW YORK: JENKINS & THOMAS, 1881.

[1]–139, 1–[10]. 23 x 14.9 cm. Seven illustrations. Pink printed wrappers, with title on front wrapper, verso of back wrapper: portrait of Sitting Bull. In blue cloth slip case.

Ref.: Howes W40; Jones 1613; Rader 3567

4514 WALKER, THOMAS

JOURNAL OF AN EXPLORATION IN THE SPRING OF THE YEAR 1750 . . . BOSTON: LITTLE, BROWN, AND COMPANY, 1888.*

[1]–69, [70 blank]. 19.5 x 14.5 cm. Frontispiece. Tan printed boards with title on front cover.

Prov.: Bookplates of Charles Edwin Stratton and Edwin Stanton Fickes.

Ref.: Bradford 5657; Clark I 169; Howes W43

Walker visited Kentucky long before Boone arrived. His account is thought to be the first extant report by a white man.

4515 WALKER, W. S.

GLIMPSES OF HUNGRYLAND; OR, CALIFORNIA SKETCHES COMPRISING SENTIMENTAL AND HUMOROUS SKETCHES, POEMS, ETC, A JOURNEY TO CALIFORNIA AND BACK AGAIN, BY LAND AND WATER . . . CLOVERDALE, CAL.: REVEILLE PUBLISHING HOUSE, 1880.

[1]–78, [79–82 advertisements]. 19.5 x 12 cm. Pink printed wrappers with title on front wrapper, uncut.

Ref.: Cowan p. 677 see

Cowan lists an 1885 edition under a slightly different title and does not mention this 1880 edition.

4516 WALKER, WILLIAM

THE UNITY OF ART. AN ADDRESS, DELIVERED BEFORE THE ALUMNI SOCIETY OF THE UNIVERSITY OF NASHVILLE, OCTOBER 3RD, 1848 . . . NASHVILLE: PRINTED BY A. NELSON, 1848.

[1]–31, [32 blank]. 21.3 x 13.7 cm. Removed from a bound volume.

Ref.: AII (*Tennessee*) 338

The author was William Walker, the Central American filibusterer.

4517 WALKER, WILLIAM

THE WAR IN NICARAGUA . . . MOBILE: S. H. GOETZEL, & CO., 1860.

[i]–xii, [13]–431, [432 blank, 433 advertisement, 434 blank]. 18.5 x 12.3 cm. Portrait and map: Colton's / Nicaragua / Guatemala, Honduras, San Salvador / & Costa Rica. / Revised, Enlarged / —and— / Published by S. H. Goetzel & Co. / Mobile, Ala. / [lower right:] Entered according to the Act of Congress in the year 1860 by J. H. Colton in the Clerks Office of the Dis-

trict Court of the United States for the Southern District of New York / *Inset:* Colton's / Map of the / Republic of / Nicaragua. / 13.5 x 18.4 cm. Scale: about 38 miles to one inch. *Inset:* Harbor of / San Juan de Nicaragua. / 3.4 x 5.4 cm. Scale: 2 2/3 miles to one inch. *Inset:* Manzanilla I. / Aspinwall City / Navy Bay. / 4.2 x 4.4 cm. Scale: 2000 feet to 7/16 inches. *Inset:* City / of / Panama /. 3.2 x 4.4 cm. No scale indicated. 31 x 39.6 cm. including border. Scale: about 80 miles to one inch. Dark gray cloth.

Ref.:

A remarkably impersonal and accurate account of a fantastic episode in American history.

An earlier (1856) edition of this map was used in Wells: *Walker's Expedition* . . . New York, 1856.

4518 WALKER, WILLIAM F.

PRESENTMENT OF THE REV. WILLIAM F. WALKER, HIS ANSWER, AND THE VERDICT OF THE COURT. PRIVATE IMPRESSION. CHICAGO: GEER & WILSON, MDCCCXLVI.

[1]–98. 22.2 x 14.2 cm. Pale blue printed wrappers with title on front wrapper, note on verso of front wrapper.

Ref.: Byrd 1256; McMurtrie (*Chicago*) 130

The wrapper is dated 1847 and the verso is dated [January 6], 1847.

The Rev. Mr. Walker was found guilty of "an unchristian temper" on two of eleven specifications; on the other nine he was found not guilty. A most fascinating case.

4519 WALL, OSCAR G.

RECOLLECTIONS OF THE SIOUX MASSACRE. AN AUTHENTIC HISTORY OF THE YELLOW MEDICINE INCIDENT, THE FATE OF MARSH AND HIS MEN, OF THE SIEGE AND BATTLES OF FORT RIDGELY, AND OF OTHER IMPORTANT BATTLES AND EXPERIENCES. TOGETHER WITH A HISTORICAL SKETCH OF THE SIBLEY EXPEDITION OF 1863 . . . 1909.*

[1–2], [i]–v, [vi blank], [9]–282, [283–84 blank], [i]–iii Index, [iv blank]. 19.3 x 13.3 cm. Two maps in text, several small text portraits, eight pages of inserted illustrations, six of which are included in pagination. Red cloth.

Prov.: Signature in pencil inside front cover: S J Browne / Sept 8 / 1910/. Pencil notes in same hand on front fly-leaf and a few marginal notes in text. A typed slip tipped to inner front cover reads: This book is from the library of S. J. Brown, noted half-breed scout, and bears his autograph.

Ref.: Howes W46

Published at Lake City, Minnesota.

4520 WALLA WALLA [Washington Territory]. BOARD OF IMMIGRATION

[Wrapper title] EASTERN WASHINGTON TERRITORY; OR, THE WALLA WALLA COUNTRY. A GENERAL DESCRIPTION OF ITS CLIMATE, SOIL, PRODUCTIONS AND ADVANTAGES. WALLA WALLA, W. T.: "WALLA WALLA UNION" JOB PRINTING ESTABLISHMENT, 1875.

[1]–14, [lacks 15–16]. 23 x 15.1 cm. Printed wrappers, probably gray, with title on front wrapper, advertisements on verso of front and recto of back wrapper, officers of the Walla Walla Board of Immigration on verso of back wrapper.

Ref.:

Page [1] carries the statement in the text that the pamphlet was compiled and published under the direction of the Board of Immigration. The final leaf may have had a form or coupon on page [16].

4521 WALLACE, CHARLES

THE CATTLE QUEEN OF MONTANA. A STORY OF THE PERSONAL EXPERIENCE OF MRS. NAT. COLLINS, FAMILIARLY KNOWN TO WESTERN PEOPLE AS "THE CATTLE QUEEN OF MONTANA" OR "THE COWBOYS' MOTHER," IN WHICH IS INCLUDED NARRATIVES OF THRILLING ADVENTURES, RECITALS OF STIRRING EVENTS, TALES OF HARDSHIPS AND PRIVATIONS, ANECDOTES OF PERSONAL EXPERIENCE, AND DESCRIPTIONS OF THE PLAINS, THE MINES, CATTLE RAISING INDUSTRY AND OTHER FEATURES OF WESTERN LIFE . . . ST. JAMES, MINN.: C. W. FOOTE, PUBLISHER, 1894.

[IX]–XIII [XIV blank], [15]–249, [250 blank]. 19.2 x 13.1 cm. 32 illustrations. Pink printed wrappers, with title on front wrapper. Lacks back wrapper. In a maroon cloth case.

Prov.: Auerbach copy.

Ref.: Adams 1038; Adams (*Ramp. Herd*) 2423; Howes C596

The printer's imprint on the verso of the title-leaf reads: Printed and Bound by / Donohue & Henneberry, / Chicago /.

4522 WALLACE, HENRY

LETTERS TO THE FARM FOLK . . . DES MOINES, IOWA: THE WALLACE PUBLISHING COMPANY, 1915.

[1]–96. 22.9 x 15 cm. Portrait. Tan wrappers, punched, tied with brown silk cord, wallet edges.

Ref.:

4523 WALLACE, HENRY

UNCLE HENRY'S OWN STORY OF HIS LIFE. PERSONAL REMINISCENCES . . . DES MOINES, IOWA: THE WALLACE PUBLISHING COMPANY, 1917 [–1919].

[1]–119 (including [1–2] blank and one plate), [120 blank]. [1]–129 (including [1–2] blank), [130–34 blank]. [1]–114 (including [1–2] blank). 23.3 x 15.3 cm. Illustrations unlisted. Three volumes, gray green, and tan printed wrappers, punched, brown, green and tan silk cord ties, wallet edges.

Ref.: Howes W52

4524 WALLACE, WILLIAM H.

CLOSING SPEECH FOR THE STATE MADE BY WM. H. WALLACE, ESQ., PROSECUTING ATTORNEY OF JACKSON COUNTY, MO. IN THE TRIAL OF FRANK JAMES FOR MURDER, HELD AT GALLATIN, DAVIESS CO., MO., IN AUG. AND SEPT., 1883. PUBLISHED BY CITIZENS OF GALLATIN, MISSOURI. KANSAS CITY, MO.: PRESS OF RAMSEY, MILLETT & HUDSON, 1883.

[1]–65, [66 blank]. 22.3 x 14.5 cm. Buff printed wrappers, with title on front wrapper, uncut.

Ref.: Adams 1040; Howes W56

4525 WALLEN, HENRY D.

[Caption title] . . . REPORT OF THE SECRETARY OF WAR, COMMUNICATING . . . THE REPORT OF CAPTAIN H. D. WALLEN OF HIS EXPEDITION, IN 1859, FROM DALLES CITY TO GREAT SALT LAKE, AND BACK . . .

[1]–51, [52 blank]. 22.5 x 14.6 cm. Map: Map / of a Reconnoissance for a Military Road / from / The "Dalles" of the Columbia River / to / Great Salt Lake / under the command of / Capt. H. D. Wallen, 4.ᵗʰ Inf. / by / Lieut. Joseph Dixon, T. Eng⁽ʳ⁾ˢ / 1859. / [upper right:] Senate Ex. Dec.[!] Nº 34—36ᵗʰ Cong. 1ˢᵗ. Sess. / [lower right:] Lith. of J. Bien 180 Broadway N. Y. / 41.1 x 55.3 cm. Scale: 25 miles to one inch. Rebound in new red cloth.

Ref.: Howes W57; Wagner-Camp 367

36th Congress, 1st Session, Senate, Executive Document No. 34, Serial 1041. [Washington, 1860.]

4526 WALTON, JOSIAH P., *Editor*

SCRAPS OF MUSCATINE HISTORY; CONTAINING FACTS AND STORIES TOLD AT OLD SETTLERS' MEETINGS AND OTHER PLACES, BY REV. A. B. ROBBINS, CAPT. W. L. CLARK, JOHN MAHIN, J. A. PARVIN, T. S. PARVIN, G. W. VAN HORNE, J. BRIDGMAN, PETER JACKSON, E. U. COOK, S. W. STEWART, W. S. FULTZ AND J. P. WALTON; WITH LISTS OF OLD SETTLERS . . . 1893.

[i–iv], [1]–4, 17–22, 29–38, [1]–4, [1–8], [1]–[4, 4 blank], [1]–8, [1]–8, [1]–12, [1]–6, [1–6], [7–8 blank], [1]–6, [7–8 blank], [1]–[8, 8 blank], [1]–6, [1]–8,[1]–[4, 4 blank]. 22.3 x 14.9 cm. Brown cloth, title in gilt on front cover.

Ref.: Howes W79

Printed at Muscatine. The earlier of two printings comprising 112 pages.

4527 WALTON, WILLIAM

LIFE AND ADVENTURES OF BEN THOMPSON, THE FAMOUS TEXAN . . . AUSTIN: PUBLISHED BY THE AUTHOR, 1884.

[1]–229, [230 blank]. 16.3 x 11.5 cm. Portrait and 14 plates. Rebound in half black calf.

Ref.: Adams 1048; Clements Library (*Texas*) 47; Howes W82; Rader 3584; Raines p. 212

The subject of this engaging sketch was a Texas desperado and gambler who looked at life a good deal of the time down the sights of a gun. On occasion he was a Texas Ranger; he was also hired once as a guard by the Atchison, Topeka and Santa Fé against the deviltries of the Denver and Rio Grande Railroad.

4528 WALWORTH, REUBEN H., & OTHERS

OPINION OF HON. REUBEN H. WALWORTH, "GREENE C. BRONSON, WM. CURTIS NOYES, ESQ., AND JOHN M. BARBOUR," UPON THE POWER OF CONGRESS TO REPEAL THE ACT GRANTING LANDS TO THE TERRITORY OF MINNESOTA FOR RAILROAD PURPOSES. APPROVED, JUNE 29, 1854. SAINT PAUL: PRINTED AT THE MINNESOTIAN OFFICE, 1854.

[1]–26, [27–28 blank]. 22 x 14.6 cm. Light gray wrappers. Lacks front wrapper.

Ref.: AII (*Minnesota*) 83

4529 WANDELL, C. W.

HISTORY OF THE PERSECUTIONS!! ENDURED BY THE CHURCH OF JESUS CHRIST OF LATTER DAY SAINTS, IN AMERICA . . . SYDNEY: PRINTED BY ALBERT MASON.

[1]–64. Bound with Number 3346.

Ref.: Howes W84

Published about 1852.

4530 WARD, DILLIS B.

[Wrapper title] ACROSS THE PLAINS IN 1853 . . . SEATTLE, WASH.

[i–ii], [1]–55, [56 blank]. 17.5 x 11.6 cm. Portrait. Buff printed wrappers, punched and tied with brown cord.

Prov.: Inscribed in pencil on page [i]: To be sent to R. A. W. / when read— / Sis— /. Inscribed in pencil on front wrapper: Katharine Ward [?] / from / Mrs. Ward / of Madison /

Ref.: Howes W94; Smith 4243

The Preface is signed by Edmond S. Meany, University of Washington, Seattle, September, 1911. Imprint of Bull Bros. [Seattle] on page 55.

Started from Arkansas, followed the Santa Fé trail to Colorado, then north to the Overland trail and Oregon.—Howes

4531 [WARD, NAHUM]

A BRIEF SKETCH OF THE STATE OF OHIO, ONE OF THE UNITED STATES IN NORTH AMERICA . . . GLASGOW: PRINTED BY J. NIVEN, AND SOLD BY A. PENMAN & CO., 1822.

[1]–16. 19.8 x 11.6 cm. Map: Map / of / Ohio, / One of the United States of / North America. / [below neat line:] Watson's Lithog. 169, George st. Glasgow. / 31.4 x 30.6 cm. Scale not given. Rebound in half sprinkled calf, red leather label. In a half morocco case.

Prov.: With the bookplates of George Brinley (4583) and C. G. Littell.

Ref.: Bradford 5680; Sabin 47394, 101319; Thomson 1370

4532 WARD, S. E.

BRASS TOKEN, stamped: S. E. Ward, Sutler U. S. A. / [diamond] Fort Laramie D. T. [diamond] / Good for / 50: / in Sutlers / Goods /. 3.4 cm. in diameter.

4533 WARD, S. E.

BRASS TOKEN, same as above except: 25ⁿ /. Measures 2.9 cm. in diameter.

4534 WARE, EUGENE F.

AUTOGRAPH LETTER, SIGNED. No date, Topeka, Kansas. One page, 26.2 x 19.9 cm. To T. J. Majors.

Marked "strictly private," the letter refers to "drinking the health of the man who will kick Rosewater out of the State."

Laid in Ware: *The Lyon Campaign in Missouri* . . . 1907.

4535 WARE, EUGENE F.

TYPEWRITTEN LETTER, SIGNED. 1893 January 3, Fort Scott, Kansas. One page 14.9 x 21.1 cm. To O. J. Smith.

Regarding a series of articles which Smith had asked Ware to write.

Laid in Ware: *The Indian War of 1864* . . . 1911.

4536 WARE, EUGENE F.

THE INDIAN WAR OF 1864 BEING A FRAGMENT OF THE EARLY HISTORY OF KANSAS, NEBRASKA, COLORADO, AND WYOMING . . . TOPEKA, KAN.: CRANE & COMPANY, 1911.*

[i]–[xii], 1–601, [602 blank]. (Page [i] blank, [ii] frontispiece.) 19 x 13.7 cm. 31 illustrations listed. Blue cloth, title in gilt on front cover and backstrip.

Ref.: Howes W103

Laid in is a Typewritten Letter, signed by the author. 1893 January 3.

4537 WARE, EUGENE F.

THE LYON CAMPAIGN IN MISSOURI. BEING A HISTORY OF THE FIRST IOWA INFANTRY AND OF THE CAUSES WHICH LED UP TO ITS ORGANIZATION, AND HOW IT EARNED THE THANKS OF CONGRESS, WHICH IT GOT . . . TOPEKA, KANSAS: PRINTED BY CRANE & COMPANY, 1907.

[i]–[xii, xii blank], 1–377, [378 blank]. 19.2 x 13.4 cm. Facsimile, two maps and two portraits, unlisted. Light blue cloth, title in gilt on front cover and backstrip.

Ref.:

Laid in is an Autograph Letter, signed by the author. No date, Topeka, Kansas.

4538 WARE, JOSEPH E.

THE EMIGRANT'S GUIDE TO CALIFORNIA, CONTAINING EVERY POINT OF INFORMATION FOR THE EMIGRANT—INCLUDING ROUTES . . . ALTITUDES, WITH A LARGE MAP OF ROUTES, AND PROFILE OF COUNTRY, &C.,—WITH FULL DIRECTIONS FOR TESTING AND ASSAYING GOLD. ST. LOUIS, MO., PUBLISHED BY J. HALSALL.

[i]–vi, [7]–56. 13.5 x 8.7 cm. Map: Map / of the / Route to California, / Compiled / from Accurate Observations / and / Surveys by Government. / Engraved by Joseph E. Ware, / No. 31 Locust Street, St. Louis. / [Copyright secured by Law.] / 35.2 x 117.9 cm. No scale given. *Inset:* Diagram of the / Shortest Routes / to the Frontier, / at Independence & St. Joseph. / 12.5 x 8.5 cm. (neat line, irregular shape). No scale given. *Inset across top:* Profile / of the Routes, / from the Mouth of the Kansas, to San Francisco, California. / 5.2 x 113.4 cm. Mounted on cloth and in cloth case. Black cloth, with white printed label on front cover. Label largely worn away, new end-papers. In a brown half morocco case.

Ref.: AII (*Missouri*) 629; Cowan p. 669; Howes W104; Sabin 101405; Wagner-Camp 175; Wheat (*Transmississippi*) 649; Wheat (*Gold Region*) 133; Wheat (*Gold Rush*) 220

Imprint on verso of title-leaf: St. Louis, Mo. / Printed at the Union Office: / 1849. /

Oddly enough, Ware had not himself made the trip, but compiled his "guide" from published sources—Fremont and probably Hastings, Bryant and Clayton.—Wheat (*Gold Rush*)

4539 WARNER, FRANK W., Compiler

MONTANA TERRITORY. HISTORY AND BUSINESS DIRECTORY, 1879 . . . HELENA, FISK BROTHERS, PRINTERS AND BINDERS.

[i–xiv], [1]–218, [219 advertisement, 220 blank]. (Pages [i] and [220] pasted to inner front and back covers respectively.) (Six pages of advertisements preceding title page, thirty-two pages of unpaginated advertisements interspersed, advertisement on inner back cover.) 21.1 x 14.5 cm. Five full-page illustrations, four of which are not included in pagination, numerous illustrations in text, folding map. Map: [Map of Helena and Vicinity.] 23.1 x 18.3 cm. Scale: 45 miles to one inch. Gray printed boards with black leather backstrip and cloth fore edges, advertisements on front and back covers, with title above and below rule borders, gilt title on backstrip.

Prov.: Signature on front cover: Cha.ˢ, Warren Stoddard / Helena, Mon / Aug – 4ᵗʰ / 85" /.

Ref.: Howes W108; McMurtrie (*Montana*) 121; Smith 10725

The preface, signed by Warner, is dated from Helena, Montana, April 1st, 1879. The work is copyrighted 1879.

The sketch of the Vigilantes is from Dimsdale.

4540 [WARNER, JUAN J., BENJAMIN HAYES, & J. WIDNEY]

AN HISTORICAL SKETCH OF LOS ANGELES COUNTY, CALIFORNIA. FROM THE SPANISH OCCUPANCY, BY THE FOUNDING OF THE MISSION SAN GABRIEL ARCHANGEL, SEPTEMBER 8, 1771, TO JULY 4, 1876 . . . LOS ANGELES, CAL.: MIRROR PRINTING, RULING AND BINDING HOUSE, 1876.*

[1]–88. 21.5 x 14 cm. Rebound in maroon half morocco. Original front wrapper mounted and bound in.

Ref.: Blumann & Thomas 1133; Cowan p. 669; Howes W110

Prepared by the Literary Committee of the Los Angeles Centennial Celebration, 1776, largely from previously unused sources. Dr. J. S. Griffin's overland diary is included. Griffin was with Kearny's command.

4541 WARNER, M. M.

WARNER'S HISTORY OF DAKOTA COUNTY, NEBRASKA, FROM THE DAYS OF THE PIONEERS AND FIRST SETTLERS TO THE PRESENT TIME . . . DAKOTA CITY, NEB.: LYONS MIRROR JOB OFFICE, 1893.

[vii]–[xxiv], [31]–387, [388 advertisements]. 21.1 x 14.5 cm. Illustrations unlisted. Blue cloth, gilt title on front cover.

Ref.: Howes W111

Based on personal interviews with pioneers of the county.

4542 WARNER, OPIE L.

A PARDONED LIFER: LIFE OF GEORGE SONTAG . . .

[1]–211, [212 blank]. 18.6 x 12.5 cm. Portrait. Red cloth, title in black on front cover and backstrip.

Ref.: Adams 1057; Cowan p. 669

Printed by The Index Print at San Bernardino, California; copyrighted 1909. Sontag was a train robber.

4543 WARRE, HENRY J.

SKETCHES IN NORTH AMERICA AND THE OREGON TERRITORY . . . LITHOGRAPHED, PRINTED AND PUBLISHED BY DICKINSON & CO.

[i–iv], [1]–5, [6 blank]. 54.2 x 36.2 cm. 16 leaves of plates, (two illustrations on each of four leaves, one on each of twelve) and map. Map: [Route of Captain Warre.] 20.8 x 49.6 cm. No scale given. All except map colored. Green cloth, green leather corners and back, gilt title on cover and backstrip, gilt edges.

Prov.: Bookplate of Sir Henry Allen Johnson.

Ref.: Bradford 5686; Howes W114; Sabin 101455; Smith 10727; Wagner-Camp 157

Made, in 1845, when war between England and the United States over the Oregon boundary seemed imminent, this trip by Capt. Warre across the northern Rockies to Puget Sound must have had some military purpose. However, any report of that nature became waste-paper on his return to London, as an amicable adjustment had then been made; but a better fate attended the views he had painted and were here magnificently reproduced; they remain the only western color plates comparable in beauty to those by Bodmer accompanying Maximilian's *Travels.* The dedication forming prelim. p. 3 and 4 was not issued in all copies.—Howes

Published at London in 1848.

4544 WARREN, ELIZA SPALDING

MEMOIRS OF THE WEST. THE SPALDINGS . . .*

[1]–153, [154 blank]. 19.1 x 13.4 cm. Illustrations unlisted. Green cloth.

Ref.: Howes W117; Smith 10731

Dated at end of the Foreword, December 1st, 1916. Imprint of March Printing Company, Portland, Oregon, on verso of title-leaf.

The author's parents came to Oregon in 1836 with Dr. Whitman and his wife. The author was born at the Lapwai Mission in 1837 and at the age of ten was present at the Whitman Massacre. She gives her mother's diary of the overland trip to Oregon in 1836, pages 54–71, and letters from Oregon written by her father from 1842–1855, pages 72–100.—EDG

4545 WARREN, GOUVERNEUR K.

CARTE-DE-VISITE PHOTOGRAPH, head in profile to his left, body three-quarters to his left, in Army uniform. Photograph, 8.8 x 5.6 cm. Stiff card, 10.1 x 6.1 cm. Printed in sepia.

Signed along lower margin, on card, G K Warren /. At lower left corner of photograph, in another hand: Genl /.

4546 WARREN, GOUVERNEUR K.

. . . EXPLORATIONS IN THE DACOTA COUNTRY, IN THE YEAR 1855 . . . WASHINGTON: A. O. P. NICHOLSON, SENATE PRINTER, 1856.

[i–ii], [1]–79, [80 blank], [i]–vi. 23.4 x 14.3 cm. Two illustrations in text, unlisted, one unlisted map and two listed maps and one listed profile. Map: Sketch / of the / Blue Water Creek / embracing the field of action of the force / under the command of / Bvt. Brg. Genl. W. S. Harney / in the attack of the 3ʳᵈ Sept. 1855, / on the "Brule" band of the Indian Chief / Little Thunder / [double rule] / made by / Lieut. G. K. Warren, / Topᵗ Engʳ of the Expedition. / Sept. 3ʳᵈ. / [upper left:] Sen. Ex. Doc. 76–1. Sess. 34. Cong. / [upper right:] Page 74. / [lower right:] P. S. Duval & Co's lith. Philadᵃ / 22 x 14 cm. Scale: 1 7/20 miles to one inch. Map: Section of Map / Compiled in P. R. R. Office / with additions designed to illustrate / Lᵗ Warrens Report of Military Reconnaissances / in the Dacota Country / 1855 / Scale of 1:3000000 / [rule] / Compiled by Lᵗ Warren, T. E. / Drawn by E. Freyhold. / [upper right:] [Senate Ex. Doc. Nᵒ 76 1. Sess. 34. Cong.] / [lower right:] P. S. Duval & Co's. Lithʸ Philᵃ / 38.6 x 48. 2 cm. Scale as above. Map: Reconnoissances / in the / Dacota Country / by / G. K. Warren, / Lieut: Topᵗ Engʳˢ U. S. A. / made while attached to the Staff of Bvt Brigʳ Genᵗ Harney, Commander of the Sioux Expedition in 1855. / assisted by Mr. Paul Carrey on the Route from Fort Pierre to Fort Kearney, and by the voluntary ser-/-vices of Lieut: G. T. Baleh, U. S. Ord: on the route from Fort Laramie to Fort Pierre. The Sketch from Fort / Pierre to the Mouth of White River is by Lieut: D. Curtis 2ⁿᵈ Inf:. This Map contains, in addition, all / authentic Explorations within the limits comprised by it. They are those of Major Long, Nicollet, Capᵗ / Fremont and Capᵗ Stansbury. / [lower left:] P. S. Duval & Co. Lith: Philadᵃ / [right margin:] Profile of Route from Fort Pierre to Fort Kearney, / made by Lieut: G. K. Warren, Topogrᵗ Engineers, 1855. / 17.4 x 82.4 cm. 91 x 145 cm. Scale: 10 miles to one inch. Rebound in blue buckram.

Ref.: Howes W118; Wagner-Camp 283; Wheat (*Transmississippi*) 871

34th Congress, 1st Session, Senate, Executive Document No. 76, Serial 822.

4547 WARREN, HENRY

STATEMENT OF HENRY WARREN, CLAIMS FOR INDIAN DEPREDATIONS, KIOWA AND CHEYENNE TRIBES. WEATHERFORD, TEXAS, 1872.

[1]–8. 21.8 x 14.5 cm. Unbound leaflet.
Ref.:

4548 WASEURTZ, G. M.

A SOJOURN IN CALIFORNIA BY THE KING'S ORPHAN . . . 1842–1843. EDITED . . . BY HELEN PUTNAM VAN SICKLEN. SAN FRANCISCO: PRINTED AT THE GRABHORN PRESS, MCMXLV

[i]–[xii], [1]–[90], [91 colophon, 92 blank]. 32.6 x 22.8 cm. 30 illustrations and maps listed, four in color. Decorated boards, cloth back, printed paper label, fore and lower edges uncut.
Ref.: Howes W125
Limited to 300 copies on unwatermarked laid paper.

4549 WASEURTZ, G. M.

ANOTHER COPY.

[i]–[xii], [1]–[90]. 33 x 22.8 cm. Marbled boards, red morocco back, fore and lower edges uncut.
Prov.: Inscribed on front fly-leaf: for Everett from Ed Grabhorn / printers proof Copy /.
Printed on Vidalon wove paper.

4550 WASHBURN, CEPHAS

REMINISCENCES OF THE INDIANS . . . RICHMOND: PRESBYTERIAN COMMITTEE OF PUBLICATION.

[1]–5, vi–viii, 9–236. 18.6 x 11.6 cm. Black cloth, blind fillets on sides, title in gilt on backstrip.
Ref.: Field 1622; Howes W127; Rader 3588
Note on inner front cover by Edward Eberstadt, in pencil: undoubtedly this is / much scarcer than / we (or I) have realized / E /. Washburn was superintendent of the Dwight Mission among the Cherokees of Arkansas.

This was reprinted (in effect) by Emmet Starr as *Cherokee West* . . . 1910.

4551 WASHBURNE, E. B.

HISTORICAL SKETCH OF CHARLES S. HEMPSTEAD . . . TO WHICH IS APPENDED A MEMOIR OF EDWARD HEMPSTEAD . . . BY HON. THOMAS H. BENTON. GALENA: GAZETTE BOOK AND JOB PRINTING HOUSE, 1875.

[1]–29, [30 blank]. 21 x 13.9 cm. Removed from bound volume, unbound.
Ref.:

4552 WASHBURNE, E. B.

SKETCH OF EDMUND COLES . . . CHICAGO: JANSEN, McCLURG & COMPANY, 1882.

[1]–253, [254 blank], [255–56 advertisements]. 20.8 x 14.2 cm. Portrait and facsimiles unlisted. Dark brown cloth.

Ref.:

4553 WASHINGTON, GEORGE

THE JOURNAL OF MAJOR GEORGE WASHINGTON . . . WILLIAMSBURGH PRINTED, LONDON, REPRINTED FOR T. JEFFERYS, 1754.

[A]–D⁴. [1]–32. 19.4 x 11.7 cm. Map: Map / of the Western parts / of the Colony of / Virginia, / as far as the / Mississipi[!]. / 23.3 x 35.4 cm. No scale given. Bound with Number 3315.

Ref.: Howes W134; Sabin 101710

The map shows the reading, in the lower right corner: The Shawanons are the same with y̆. Senekas / one of the Six Nations. /

Editions: Williamsburgh, 1754.

4554 WASHINGTON TERRITORY. Governor (Isaac I. Stevens)

MESSAGE OF THE GOVERNOR OF WASHINGTON TERRITORY. ALSO, THE CORRESPONDENCE WITH THE SECRETARY OF WAR, MAJOR GEN. WOOL, THE OFFICERS OF THE REGULAR ARMY, AND OF THE VOLUNTEER SERVICE OF WASHINGTON TERRITORY. OLYMPIA. EDWARD FURSTE, PUBLIC PRINTER, 1857.

[1–4], [I]–XVII, [XVIII blank], [XIX–XX blank], [1]–406, [1–2], [I]–XVII, [XVIII–XX blank]. (First page [1] is title-page, pages [2–4] blank.) 21.9 x 14.2 cm. Plain blue wrappers. In a blue buckram case.

Ref.: AII (*Washington*) 28; Sabin 101911

4555 WATERS, CHARLES O.

ADDRESS AND POEM; DELIVERED AT THE LAYING OF THE CORNER STONE OF THE IOWA FEMALE COLLEGIATE INSTITUTE, BY THE GRAND LODGE OF I. O. OF O. F. OF IOWA, IN IOWA CITY, OCT. 27TH, 1853. IOWA CITY, IOWA: PRINTED AT THE REPORTER OFFICE, 1853.

[i–ii]. [1]–[38]. 21.8 x 13.8 cm. Apparently removed from bound volume.

Ref.: Moffit 142

The poem occupies pages [21]–36 and is captioned: Woman's Rights. / [double rule] / A Poem / By Richard H. Sylvester. / [double rule] / . . .

4556 [WATERS, WILLIAM E.(?)]

LIFE AMONG THE MORMONS, AND A MARCH TO THEIR ZION: TO WHICH IS ADDED A CHAPTER ON THE INDIANS OF THE PLAINS AND MOUNTAINS OF THE WEST . . . NEW YORK: MOORHEAD, SIMPSON & BOND, 1868.

[i]–[xvi, xvi blank], [1]–219, [220 blank], [221–23 advertisements, 224 blank]. 18.8 x 12.3 cm. Four plates, unlisted. Brown cloth, title in gilt on backstrip.

Prov.: Inscribed on inner front cover: From publishers to / Isaac Davega /.

Ref.: Howes W157

Dale Morgan speaks well of this book in his *The Great Salt Lake* . . . [1947], pages 352–53: "distinguished by its temperate spirit and exact observation."

4557 WATKINS, BEN

COMPLETE CHOCTAW DEFINER, ENGLISH WITH CHOCTAW DEFINITION . . . VAN BUREN, ARK.: J. W. BALDWIN, PRINTER & PUBLISHER, 1892.

[1]–[95], [96 blank]. 20 x 14 cm. Black cloth.

Ref.:

4558 WATSON, DOUGLAS S.

WEST WIND. THE LIFE STORY OF JOSEPH REDDEFORD WALKER . . . LOS ANGELES, CALIFORNIA: PERCY H. BOOTH, 1934.

[i–viii, viii blank], 1–[112]. 26.3 x 18.9 cm. Six illustrations and a map listed. Brown boards, red leather back, fore and lower edges uncut.

Prov.: Inscribed on front endleaf: For Ed. Grabhorn: / So that you will possess another of / the 50 Books in addition to the / six the American Institute of Graphic / Arts chose of your own making, I / am sending you this copy of West Wind. / Douglas S Watson / Dec. 21, 1934. / for E. D. Graff— / I was supposed to print / this but— / Yours / Ed Grabhorn / March 9/39 /.

Ref.: Howes W165

Limited to 100 copies.

4559 [WATSON, JAMES T.]

[Caption title] ACROSS THE CONTINENT IN A CARAVAN. RECOLLECTIONS OF A JOURNEY FROM NEW YORK THROUGH THE WESTERN WILDERNESS AND OVER THE ROCKY MOUNTAINS TO THE PACIFIC IN 1846 . . .

617–632. 26.2 x 19.6 cm. Nine illustrations unlisted. Stapled into gray boards, black cloth back, typed label on front cover.

Ref.:

Excerpt from *Journal of American History*, Vol. I, 1907.

4560 WATTS, WILLIAM J

[Wrapper title] CHEROKEE CITIZENSHIP AND A BRIEF HISTORY OF INTERNAL AFFAIRS IN THE CHEROKEE NATION, WITH RECORDS AND ACTS OF

NATIONAL COUNCIL FROM 1871 TO DATE . . .
MULDROW, INDIAN TERRITORY: REGISTER PRINT,
1895.

[i–iv], [1]–[146]. (Pages [i–ii] blank.) 14.9 x 13
cm. Two portraits, in text. Pale blue printed
wrappers, with title on front wrapper and advertisement on verso of back wrapper.

Prov.: Huntington duplicate, stamped on
recto of back wrapper.

Ref.: Foreman p. 48; Howes W180

The author was president of the Cherokee
Indian Citizenship Association.

4561   WAUGH, LORENZO

AUTOBIOGRAPHY OF LORENZO WAUGH . . . OAK-
LAND, CAL.: PACIFIC PRESS, 1883.

[i]–[xii], [13]–311, [312 blank]. 19 x 13.2 cm. Illustrations unlisted. Blue cloth.

Ref.: Cowan p. 672; Howes W181

4562   WEAVER, BENJAMIN

THE FIRST SETTLING OF KANSAS, IN . . . 1854 . . .

[1]–41, [42–43 blank], [44]. 13.4 x 9.3 cm. Blue
printed wrappers, with title on front wrapper,
cut of frog riding bicycle on verso of back
wrapper.

Ref.: Howes W185

The imprint, within a decorative box, appears
on the verso of the title-page: Published / by /
Eugene B. Weaver, / St. Joseph, Mo. / 1898 /.

4563   [WEBB, THOMAS H.]

ORGANIZATION, OBJECTS, AND PLAN OF OPERA-
TIONS, OF THE EMIGRANT AID COMPANY: ALSO A
DESCRIPTION OF KANSAS. FOR THE INFORMATION OF
EMIGRANTS . . . BOSTON: PRINTED BY ALFRED
MUDGE & SON, 1854.

[1]–24. 20.7 x 12.9 cm. Stabbed, unbound. In a
red cloth case.

Ref.: Howes W192; Sabin 22474; Wagner-
Camp 247

Contains George H. Park: "Notes of a Trip
up Kansas River, Including Observations on the
Soil, Climate, Scenery, &c." pages 9–18.

The organization was known as the New
England Emigrant Aid Society.

Editions: Boston, 1854 (22 pages).

4564   WEBBER, CHARLES W.

ADVENTURES IN THE CAMANCHE COUNTRY, IN
SEARCH OF A GOLD MINE . . . GLASGOW: PUB-
LISHED BY R. GRIFFIN & CO., MDCCCXLVIII.

[i]–vi, [7]–299, [300 blank]. (Page 299 mispaginated 296.) 16.5 x 10.4 cm. Black cloth, blind
embossed sides, title in gilt on backstrip, uncut,
mostly unopened.

Ref.: Howes W198; Sabin 102247; Wagner-
Camp 158

A pirated edition of *Old Hicks the Guide.*

4565   WEBBER, CHARLES W.

THE GOLD MINES OF THE GILA. A SEQUEL TO OLD
HICKS THE GUIDE . . . NEW YORK: DEWITT &
DAVENPORT, 1849.

[i–viii], 1–134, [i–iv], [135]–263, [264 blank].
18.6 x 12.1 cm. Two volumes bound in one,
black cloth, blind embossed sides, title in gilt on
backstrip.

Ref.: Dobie p. 157; Howes W195; Sabin
102247; Wagner-Camp 176; Wright I 2687

A more lurid tale, but based in part either on
the author's experiences or the adventures of
men he knew.

4566   WEBBER, CHARLES W.

OLD HICKS THE GUIDE; OR, ADVENTURES IN THE
CAMANCHE COUNTRY IN SEARCH OF A GOLD MINE
. . . NEW YORK: HARPER & BROTHERS, 1848.

[i]–x, [11]–356, [357 advertisement, 358 blank].
18.7 x 12.5 cm. Brown cloth, blind embossed
sides, gilt title on backstrip.

Ref.: Howes W198; Rader 3597; Sabin
102249; Wagner-Camp 158; Wright I 2690

A lurid tale of Texas.

4567   WEBBER, CHARLES W.

TALES OF THE SOUTHERN BORDER. PHILADELPHIA:
J. B. LIPPINCOTT & CO., 1868.

[1]–400. 21 x 13.8 cm. Eight illustrations and
two vignettes, unlisted. Maroon cloth, blind
embossed sides, title in gilt on backstrip.

Ref.: Howes W199; Raines p. 216; Wright II
2672

Editions: Philadelphia, 1852, 1853, 1856.

4568   WEBSTER, DANIEL

SPEECH OF MR. WEBSTER, IN THE SENATE, IN REPLY
TO MR. CALHOUN'S SPEECH . . . DELIVERED ON THE
16TH OF FEBRUARY, 1833. WASHINGTON: PRINTED
BY GALES AND SEATON, 1833.

[1]–48. Bound with Number 1084.

Ref.: Sabin 102283.

4569   WEBSTER, DELIA ANN

BY-LAWS OF THE WEBSTER KENTUCKY FARM AS-
SOCIATION, WITH A BRIEF DESCRIPTION OF ITS
ORIGIN AND SUBJECT. BOSTON: PRESS OF GEO. C.
RAND & AVERY, 1858.

[1]–24. 19.2 x 12.2 cm. Glazed white printed
wrappers with title on front wrapper.

Ref.:

The Association was formed "for the purpose
of saving a valuable estate from the grasp of the
Slave Power."

4570 WEBSTER, DELIA ANN

KENTUCKY JURISPRUDENCE. A HISTORY OF THE TRIAL OF MISS DELIA A. WEBSTER. AT LEXINGTON, KENTUCKY, DEC'R 17–21, 1844 . . . ON A CHARGE OF AIDING SLAVES TO ESCAPE FROM THAT COMMON-WEALTH . . . VERGENNES: E. W. BLAISDELL, PRINT-ER, 1845.*

[1]–84. 18.2 x 11.5 cm. Removed from a bound volume.

Ref.: Howes W201

Inflammatory propaganda.

4571 WEBSTER, KIMBALL

THE GOLD SEEKERS OF '49. A PERSONAL NARRATIVE OF OVERLAND TRAIL AND ADVENTURES IN CALI-FORNIA AND OREGON FROM 1849 TO 1854 . . . MANCHESTER, N. H.: STANDARD BOOK COMPANY, 1917.

[1]–240. (Pages [1]–4] blank.) 19.5 x 13.3 cm. 16 illustrations listed. Red cloth, printed white paper label on front cover.

Prov.: Edward E. Ayer's copy, with annotations, one signed in the text.

Ref.: Cowan p. 673; Smith 10815

4572 WEEKLY PACIFIC NEWS, THE

[Newspaper] THE WEEKLY PACIFIC NEWS. VOL. I. SAN FRANCISCO, FRIDAY MORNING, MARCH 1, 1850. NO. 16. FOR THE STEAMER OREGON OF FIRST MARCH . . .

[1–4]. 57 x 44 cm. Unbound.

Ref.:

Edited by F. C. Ewer, who inserts the following note: This edition of the "Pacific News" for the Steamer, for want of any other kind to be obtained in California, is printed on a very nice quality of wrapping paper . . .

The newspaper was intended for the States.

4573 WEEKLY PACIFIC NEWS, THE

[Newspaper] WEEKLY PACIFIC NEWS. PER STEAMER TENNESSEE.—SAN FRANCISCO, CAL., MONDAY, JULY 15, 1850. THE PACIFIC NEWS. MONDAY MORNING, JULY 8, 1850 . . .

[1–4] 54.5 x 38 cm. Unbound.

Ref.:

Edited by J. Winchester.

4574 WEEKLY PACIFIC NEWS, THE

THE SAME . . . PER STEAMER PANAMA FOR PAN-AMA.—SAN FRANCISCO, CAL., THURSDAY, AU-GUST 1, 1850. DAILY PACIFIC NEWS. J. WINCHES-TER, EDITOR. THURSDAY MORNING, JULY 25, 1850 . . .

[1–4]. 60.6 x 46 cm. Unbound.

Ref.:

See also under *The Pacific, The Pacific News,* and *Steamer Pacific News.*

The *Steamer Pacific News* and *The Pacific News* were also edited by J. Winchester, but the other paper appears to be a rival.

4575 THE WEEKLY REGISTER

THE WEEKLY REGISTER. CONTAINING POLITICAL, HISTORICAL, GEOGRAPHICAL, SCIENTIFICAL, AS-TRONOMICAL, STATISTICAL, AND BIOGRAPHICAL, DOCUMENTS, ESSAYS, AND FACTS . . . BALTIMORE: RE-PRINTED AND PUBLISHED BY THE EDITOR, AT THE FRANKLIN PRESS. 1816 [–1840].

59 volumes. Many volumes contain supplements, which are included in pagination. There are some errors in pagination, not recorded here. Sizes of volumes vary from 24.4 x 15.7 to 30.7 x 20.9 cm.

1: [i–iv], [1]–480. Supplement to No. 4 [65]–72; to No. 10 [167]–176; to No. 10 [177]–184; to No. 11 [201]–208; to No. 15 [273]–280; to No. 17 [313]–320; to No. 19 [353]–360; to No. 23 [425]–432.

2: [i–iv], [1]–432. Supplement to No. 29 [49]–56; to No. 39 [217]–224.

3: [i–iv], [1]–416, [417]–480 Appendix, [1]–16 Addendum. With folding plate at end of Addendum.

4: [i–iv], [1]–432. Supplement to No. 2 [33]–40; Appendix [425]–432. Map on p. 413.

5: [i–iv], [1]–432, [1]–192. Supplement to volume. Supplements to No. 109 [81]–88; to No. 9 [153]–160.

6: [i–iv], [1]–448. Supplements to No. 1 [17]–24; to No. 145 [249]–256; to No. 149 [321]–328; to No. 153 [393]–400.

7: [i–iv], [1]–416, [i–ii], [1]–192.

8: [i]–viii, [417]–432, [17]–452, [i–ii], [1]–192. Supplement to No. 191 [153]–160; to No. 12 [209]–216; to No. 17 [297]–304; to No. 204 [385]–388.

9: [i]–vii, [viii blank], [1]–452, [1]–192, [1]–8. Supplement to No. 22 [381]–388.

10: [i]–viii, [1]–436. Supplement to No. 8 [129]–136; to No. 16 [365]–372. Map on page 121.

11: [i]–viii, [1]–432. Supplement to No. 19 [313]–320. Map on page 183.

12: [i]–viii, [1]–416.

13: [i]–viii, [1]–436. Supplement to No. 17 [273]–280; to No. 24 [397]–404.

14: [i]–viii, [1]–440. Supplement to No. 5 [65]–72; to No. 10 [169]–176; to No. 16 [273]–280.

15: [i]–viii, [1]–470, [1]–192. Supplement to No. 11 [177]–184; to No. 13 [317]–224; to No. 15 [257]–264; to No. 15 [265]–272; to

No. 17 [304]–312; to No. 18 [329]–336; to No. 19 [353]–360; to No. 20 [377]–384.

16: [i]–viii, [1]–440, [i–ii], [1]–192. Supplement to No. 3 [57]–64.

17: [i]–viii, [1]–456. Supplement to No. 15 [241]–248; to No. 16 [265]–272; to No. 21 [353]–360; to No. 22 [377]–384; to No. 23 [401]–408.

18: [i]–viii, [1]–464. Supplement to No. 1 [17]–24; to No. 4 [73]–80; to No. 7 [129]–136; to No. 11 [201]–208; to No. 16 [289]–296; to No. 21 [377]–384.

19: [i]–viii, [1]–432. Supplement to No. 16 [257]–264; to No. 20 [329]–336.

20: [i]–viii, [1]–416.

21: [i]–viii, [1]–416.

22: [i]–viii, [1]–424. Supplement to No. 26 [417]–424.

23: [i]–viii, [1]–416, [i–ii], [1]–192.

24: [i]–viii, [1]–416.

25: [i]–viii, [1]–416.

26: [i]–viii, [1]–432. Supplement to No. 11 [177]–184; to No. 19 [313]–320.

27: [i]–viii, [1]–416.

28: [i]–viii, [1] 416.

29: [i]–viii, [1]–432. Supplement to No. 22 [353]–360; to No. 24 [393]–400.

30: [i]–viii, [1]–456. Supplement to No. 4 [65]–72; to No. 7 [121]–136; to No. 15 [265]–280.

31: [i]–viii, [1]–416.

32: [i]–viii, [1]–432. Supplement to No. 4 [65]–80.

33: [i]–viii, [1]–440. Supplement to No. 20 [321]–328; to No. 21 [315]–352; to No. 25 [417]–424.

34: [i]–viii, [1]–424. Supplement to No. 5 [81]–88.

35: [i]–viii, [1]–440. Supplement to No. 17 [273]–280; to No. 23 [377]–384.

36: [i]–viii, [1]–424. Supplement to No. 13 [209]–216.

37: [i]–viii, [1]–440. Supplement to No. 19, 32 pages, No. 22, 24 pages.

38: [i]–viii, [1]–460, [i–ii], 1–210. Supplement to No. 9 [169]–176; to No. 13 [245]–252. Nos. 1–2, 5, 24 pp. No. 10, 20 pp.

39: [i]–viii, [1]–472. Supplement to No. 2 [33]–40; Septennial Number [457]–472. Nos. 16, 17, 20, 24—24 pp.

40: [i]–viii, [1]–464. Nos. 1, 6, 12, 16, 20, 22—24 pp.

41: [i]–viii, [1]–480, 1–64. Nos. 11–20 misnumbered 10–19. Nos. 3, 5, 10, 17, 20, 25—24 pp., No. 6–32 pp.

42: [i]–viii, [1]–464, [1]–16, [17]–24, 9–16, 33–39 [40 blank].

43: [i]–viii, [1]–440, [i–ii], [1]–264.

44: [i]–viii, [1]–432.

45: [i]–viii, [1]–440.

46: [i]–viii, [1]–456. Includes No. 27, August 30. Nos. 10, 15, 16—24 pp.

47: [i]–viii, [1]–456.

48: [i]–vii, [viii blank], [1]–464.

49: [i]–viii, [1]–464.

50: [i]–viii, [1]–440.

51: [i]–viii, [1]–416.

52: [i]–vii, [viii blank], [1]–416.

53: [i]–viii, [1]–416.

54: [i]–viii, [1]–416.

55: [i]–vii, [viii blank], [1]–416.

56: [i]–viii, [1]–416.

57: [i]–xv, [xvi blank], [1]–432. Includes 27 numbers.

58: [i]–xvi, [1]–416.

Vol. 1, p. 314—map; Vol. 3, p. 16 of addendum—folding plate; Vol. 10, p. 121—map; Vol. 11, p. 183—map. 59 volumes (including Index Vols. I–XII, described below), full contemporary calf or roan. One volume rebound in full morocco.

Ref.: Sabin 55314

Volumes 42–58 have not been collated fully, since practice of supplementary numbers was discontinued. From Volume 38 to 58, the number of pages in the parts varied occasionally. The set is divided into five series, but the whole number is also given.

ACCOMPANIED BY:

GENERAL INDEX TO THE FIRST TWELVE VOLUMES, OR FIRST SERIES, OF NILES' WEEKLY REGISTER . . . FROM SEPTEMBER, 1811, TO SEPTEMBER, 1817 . . . BALTIMORE: PRINTED AND PUBLISHED BY THE EDITOR, AT THE FRANKLIN PRESS, 1818. [i–ii], [1]–232, 1–22.

4576 WEIGHTMAN, RICHARD H.

SPEECH OF HON. RICHARD H. WEIGHTMAN, OF NEW MEXICO, DELIVERED IN THE HOUSE OF REPRESENTATIVES, MARCH 15, 1852: VINDICATORY OF THE COURSE OF GOVERNOR JAMES S. CALHOUN, OF NEW MEXICO . . . EXPOSING THE CHARACTER OF THE MILITARY GOVERNMENT . . . AND THE MACHINATIONS OF THE AMERICAN AND FOREIGN ANTI-SLAVERY SOCIETY TO STIR UP THE NEW MEXICANS . . . WASHINGTON: PRINTED AT THE CONGRESSIONAL GLOBE OFFICE, 1852.

[1]–29, [30–32 blank]. 22 x 14.3 cm. Removed from bound volume, unbound.

Ref.: Howes W223

4577 WELBY, ADLARD

A VISIT TO NORTH AMERICA AND THE ENGLISH SETTLEMENTS IN ILLINOIS, WITH A WINTER RESIDENCE AT PHILADELPHIA; SOLELY TO ASCERTAIN THE AC-

TUAL PROSPECTS OF THE EMIGRATING AGRICUL-
TURALIST, MECHANIC, AND COMMERCIAL SPECULA-
TOR . . . LONDON: PRINTED FOR J. DRURY, 1821.

[i]–xii, [1]–224. 22.5 x 13.7 cm. 14 plates. Gray
boards with white printed label, 4.5 x 2.5 cm., on
backstrip. In a red cloth case.
    Ref.: Buck 150; Howes W229; Jones 836;
Sabin 102514; Thomson 1197
    Errata slip tipped in at back.
    Welby visited the English settlement in Illi-
nois and reported disappointment with it.

4578 WELLES, ALONZO M.

REMINISCENT RAMBLINGS . . . DENVER, COLO.: THE
W. F. ROBINSON PRINTING CO., 1905.*

[1]–459, [460 blank]. 18.6 x 12.3 cm. Illustrations unlisted, printed in blue-green. Red buckram.
    Prov.: Inscribed on the front fly-leaf: Com-
pliments of / The Author / [flourish] /.
    Ref.: Howes W238; Munk (Alliot) p. 227
    The author's *Ramblings* were in Arizona,
New Mexico, and Colorado, particularly among
mines.

4579 WELLES, GIDEON

LINCOLN AND SEWARD. REMARKS UPON THE ME-
MORIAL ADDRESS OF CHAS. FRANCIS ADAMS, ON THE
LATE WM. H. SEWARD, WITH INCIDENTS AND COM-
MENTS ILLUSTRATIVE OF THE MEASURES AND POL-
ICY OF THE ADMINISTRATION OF ABRAHAM LIN-
COLN . . . NEW YORK: SHELDON & COMPANY,
1874.

[i]–viii, [7]–215, [216 blank]. 18.4 x 12.4 cm.
Dark orange cloth, stamped in black and gilt.
    Ref.: Monaghan 938

4580 WELLS, CHARLES W.

A FRONTIER LIFE; BEING A DESCRIPTION OF MY EX-
PERIENCE ON THE FRONTIER THE FIRST FORTY-TWO
YEARS OF MY LIFE, WITH SKETCHES AND INCIDENTS
OF HOMES IN THE WEST; HUNTING BUFFALO AND
OTHER GAME; TROUBLE WITH THE INDIANS, AND
MY EARLY WORK IN THE MINISTRY . . . CINCIN-
NATI: PRESS OF JENNINGS & PYE.*

[1]–313, [314 blank]. 18.3 x 12.1 cm. Blue cloth.
    Ref.: Howes W244
    Copyrighted 1902.
    Wells' frontier was Nebraska and the Black
Hills in the 1860's.

4581 WELLS, EDMUND W.

ARGONAUT TALES. STORIES OF THE GOLD SEEKERS
AND INDIAN SCOUTS OF EARLY ARIZONA . . . NEW
YORK: FREDERICK H. HITCHCOCK.*

[1]–478. (Pages [1–2] blank.) 22 x 14.6 cm. Ten
illustrations listed. Green ribbed cloth, gilt top,
uncut.
    Prov.: Inscribed on the page [1]: To my genial
friend / George H. Smalley. / Compliments of /
Edmund Wells / December 25, 1927. /
    Ref.: Rader 3602
    Copyrighted 1927.

4582 WELLS, JAMES M.

"WITH TOUCH OF ELBOW;" OR, DEATH BEFORE DIS-
HONOR. A THRILLING NARRATIVE OF ADVENTURE
ON LAND AND SEA . . . PHILADELPHIA: THE JOHN
C. WINSTON CO., 1909.

[1–2], i–[viii], 1–362. 18.8 x 12.7 cm. 16 illustrations listed. Blue pictorial cloth.
    Ref.: Howes W249
    Cavalry service in the Civil War, preceded by
freighting experiences on the plains in the
'fifties.—Howes

4583 WELLS, JOHN G.

WELLS' POCKET HAND-BOOK OF IOWA; PAST, PRES-
ENT, AND PROSPECTIVE . . . NEW YORK: JOHN G.
WELLS, 1857.

[i]–vi, [7]–136. 14.5 x 36.9 cm. Folding map attached to inside front cover: Iowa / Scale of
Miles / [diagrammatic scale: 25 miles to one
inch.] / 29.1 x 36.9 cm. Scale as above. Gray
cloth, title in gilt on front cover.
    Ref.: Howes W250; Mott (*Iowa*) p. 61

4584 WELLS, JOHN G.

WELLS' POCKET HAND-BOOK OF NEBRASKA PAST,
PRESENT, AND PROSPECTIVE . . . NEW YORK: JOHN
G. WELLS, 1857.

[1]–iv, [9]–90, [91–100 advertisements]. 14.4 x
9.2 cm. Map: Wells' / New Sectional Map / of /
Nebraska / From the last Government Surveys / J. G. Wells / 11 Beekman St. New York. /
J P. Snow / Land Agent / Otoe Nebraska / Scale
of Miles / [diagrammatic scale: 10 miles to one
inch] / [lower right:] Lith. V. Keil 181 William
St. N Y. / [centre, below border:] Entered according to Act of Congress, in the year 1857, by
J. G. Wells, in the Clerk's Office of the District
Court of the Southern District of New York. /
72.2 x 54 cm. (including border). Map: Great
Direct Route! / New York and Erie Railroad /
and its Connections. / 11.8 x 26.2 cm. No scale
given. On verso is full-page advertisement for
the railroad line. Map: Southern Iowa and
Southern Nebraska, / with Part of Kansas and
Missouri. / A Correct Geographical View of the
Country, together with all the Principal Roads
now Constructed, / and Showing the Great

Overland Emigrant Route, / From Burlington and Fort Madison on the Mississippi River, Otoe, Bennett's Ferry to Fort Kearney, connecting with the Government Wagon Road through the South Pass to California. / [nine lines of text below map] / [lower right:] Fisk, Levis, & Russell, Eng^s 15 Spruce St. N. York / 13.1 x 31.4 cm. No scale given. Dark green cloth with blind embossed borders on sides, title in gilt on front cover.

Ref.: Howes W251

Pages [v–viii] are not present in this copy and they may not have been published. There is no evidence that they were ever present in this copy.

4585 [WELLS, POLK]

LIFE AND ADVENTURES OF POLK WELLS (CHARLES KNOX POLK WELLS), THE NOTORIOUS OUTLAW, WHOSE ACTS OF FEARLESSNESS AND CHIVALRY KEPT THE FRONTIER TRAILS AFIRE WITH EXCITEMENT, AND WHOSE ROBERIES[!] AND OTHER DEPREDATIONS IN THE PLATTE PURCHASE AND ELSEWHERE, HAVE BEEN A MOST FREQUENT DISCUSSION TO THIS DAY . . . PUBLISHED BY G. A. WARNICA.

[1]–259, [260 blank]. 22 x 14.8 cm. 20 illustrations listed. Blue cloth.

Ref.: Adams 1067

Neither place nor date of publication is given.

4586 WELLS, PROCTOR R.

MEMORIES OF EARLY DAYS . . . SAN JOSE, CAL.: PRESS OF FRANK M. ELEY, 1904.

[1]–39, [40 blank]. 17.1 x 13 cm. Portrait. Gray printed wrappers, with title on front wrapper.

Prov.: At top of page [40]: P. R. Wells / Return to 580 South / 5 St San Jos /.

Ref.: Howes W252

Grabhorn told me this was published in an exceedingly small edition and consequently it is scarce and much sought after in California.— EDG

4587 WELLS, WILLIAM V.

WALKER'S EXPEDITION TO NICARAGUA; A HISTORY OF THE CENTRAL AMERICAN WAR; AND THE SONORA AND KINNEY EXPEDITIONS . . . NEW YORK: STRINGER AND TOWNSEND, 1856.

[i]–vi, 11–316. 18.2 x 12.3 cm. Portrait and map: Central America / 1856. / Published by J. H. Colton & Co. N° 172 William St New York / [lower left:] Entered according to Act of Congress, in the Year 1856, by J. H. Colton & Co. in the Clerks Office of the District Court of the United States for the Southern District of New York /. *Inset:* Isthmus / of / Panama /. 8.2 x 6.4 cm. Scale: 18 miles to one inch. *Inset:* Harbor of / San Juan de Nicaragua. / 3.4 x 5.4 cm. Scale: 2 2/3 miles to one inch. *Inset:* The "Nicaragua Route" /. 4.2 x 16.3 cm. Scale: 20 miles to one inch. *Inset:* Manzanilla I. / Aspinwall City / Navy Bay. / 4.2 x 4.4 cm. Scale: 2000 feet to 7/16 inch. *Inset:* City / of / Panama /. 3.2 x 4.4 cm. Scale not indicated. 31.5 x 40 cm. (including border). Scale: About 80 miles to one inch. Black cloth.

Ref.: Howes W256; Rader 3604

For a later edition of the map, see Walker, William: *The War in Nicaragua.*

4588 WELSH, HERBERT

REPORT OF A VISIT TO THE NAVAJO, PUEBLO, AND HUALAPAIS INDIANS OF NEW MEXICO AND ARIZONA . . . PHILADELPHIA: PUBLISHED BY THE INDIAN RIGHTS ASSOCIATION, 1885.*

[1]–48. 23 x 14.6 cm. Tan printed wrappers, with title on the front wrapper.

Ref.: Munk (Alliot) p. 227; Rader 3608; Saunders 1348

4589 WELTON, E. W.

[Manuscript map] MAP / OF THE / CALIFORNIA STATE TELEGRAPH, / AND / [vignette of stage coach and of telegraph line] / OVERLAND MAIL ROAD / AUSTIN TO GREAT SALT LAKE CITY. / FROM ACTUAL SURVEY, AUG., 1866. / DRAWN BY E. W. WELTON. /

Manuscript map, 37.7 x 90.5 cm. (paper size). 33.4 x 86.4 cm. (neat line). Scale: 11 miles to one inch. In a metal tube.

The California State Telegraph Company (the first of its kind in California) received a franchise on May 3, 1852. Work on the first segment connecting Marysville and Stockton and Sacramento was started the same year and was completed the following year. Operations leading to a line to Salt Lake City were started in May of 1861 and the connection between Placerville, Nevada, and Salt Lake City was completed within five months. Western Union secured the subsidy offered by the Congress of the United States in 1860 and started construction of a line from Omaha to Salt Lake City, arriving there in October, 1861. Western Union had offered to divide the subsidy if the California State Telegraph Company and its subsidiaries would consolidate with Western Union. Eventually, this was effected.

The map has been mounted on cloth and the edges have been bound with brown ribbon. On the verso is the following inscription: Austin, Nevada, Dec. 6, 1860 / E. W. Welton /.

4590 WE'RE A BAND OF FREEMEN

[Broadside] WE'RE A BAND OF FREEMEN. THE TEETOTALERS ARE COMING . . . PLACERVILLE AMERICAN PRINT—PLACERVILLE.

Broadside, 33.5 x 15.3 cm. Text, 29 x 9.6 cm.
Ref.:
There were three Placervilles—in California, Colorado, and Idaho. There is no indication as to which this is nor as to the date.

4591 WERICH, J. LORENZO

PIONEER HUNTERS OF THE KANKAKEE . . . BY J. LORENZO WERICH, 1920.*

[i–iv], [9]–[197], [198 blank]. 18.7 x 13.2 cm. 20 plates listed. Red cloth, concealed staples, with title in black on front wrapper.
Ref.:
No place of printing indicated.

4592 WERNER, HERMAN

ON THE WESTERN FRONTIER WITH THE UNITED STATES CAVALRY FIFTY YEARS AGO . . .

[1]–98. (Page [1] copyright notice, page [2] frontispiece.) 21 x 13.8 cm. Portrait. Light brown printed wrappers, with title on front wrapper.
Ref.: Howes W259
Copyrighted 1934. No indication of place of publication.
The Modoc war, Montana operations, etc.—Howes

4593 WERTH, JOHN J.

A DISSERTATION ON THE RESOURCES AND POLICY OF CALIFORNIA: MINERAL, AGRICULTURAL AND COMMERCIAL, INCLUDING A PLAN FOR THE DISPOSAL OF THE MINERAL LANDS . . . BENICIA, CAL.: ST. CLAIR & PINKHAM, PUBLISHERS, 1851.

[i]–viii, [1]–87, [88 blank]. 19.6 x 12.7 cm. Cream printed wrappers with title on front wrapper. In a blue cloth case.
Ref.: AII (*California*) 184; Bradford 5751; Cowan pp. 675–76; Howes W262; Sabin 102640; Wagner (*California Imprints*) 139
These letters had appeared in the Alta and the introduction contains correspondence of August 16 and 20 relative to reprinting them in pamphlet from, The Alta of October 16 notices the pamphlet.—Wagner
One of the earliest works descriptive of California, prepared by a local observer. It is usually cited as the first work to be printed in Benicia, but the sermon of Dr. Woodbridge antedates it by several months.—Cowan
Howes calls for an errata leaf [neither AII (*California*), Cowan, nor Wagner mentions it], but in the present copy, the list of errata appears at the foot of page viii,

4594 WEST, G. R.

[Caption title] COMMERCE OF DUBUQUE IN 1853. DUBUQUE, IOWA, DEC. 31ST. 1853. . . .

[1]–4. 21.5 x 14.5 cm. Unbound. Removed from a bound volume.
Ref.:
Two paragraphs on page 4 indicate the leaflet is a reprint from the *Herald*. Imprint on page 4: Printed at the Herald Book and Job Office.

4595 WEST, G. R.

[Caption title] STATISTICS OF THE COMMERCIAL AND BUSINESS IMPORTANCE OF THE CITY OF DUBUQUE, IOWA, FOR THE YEAR ENDING DECEMBER 31ST, 1854 . . .

[1]–[6]. 22.7 x 14.5 cm. Unbound. Removed from bound volume.
Ref.:
Page [6] carries a full-page advertisement for the G. R. West & Co., Forwarding and Commission Merchants. The advertisement is dated Dubuque, January 1st, 1855.

4596 WEST, GEORGE M.

THE EMIGRANT'S COMPANION AND GUIDE FROM LIVERPOOL IN ENGLAND TO THE CONTINENT OF NORTH AMERICA: AND MORE ESPECIALLY TO THE FERTILE REGION OF OHIO, IN THE WESTERN TERRITORY . . . LIVERPOOL. PRINTED BY HODGSON AND CO.

[i]–iv, [5]–48. 17.9 x 10.5 cm. Tan printed wrappers, with title on front wrapper, advertisement on verso of back wrapper.
Ref.: Howes W274; Sabin 102721
Published in 1830.

4597 WEST, HARRIET CLINE

THE LIFE AND TRAVELS OF HARRIET CLINE WEST. REVIEWED AND PREPARED FOR THE PRESS BY JAMES M. HIATT . . . KAHOKA, MO.: BY HARRIET CLINE WEST, 1910.

[1]–[177], [178 blank]. (Pages [1–2] blank.) 16.5 x 11.1 cm. Ten illustrations, unlisted. Dark green-gray wrappers, title printed on front wrapper in black with an overlay of gilt (mostly worn off). In a green buckram case.
Ref.: Howes W276
With her husband, the author left West Virginia for Kahoka, Missouri, in 1865. In 1872 they made a trip to Kansas by wagon and settled in Russel, Kansas, where her husband went into the cattle business. Indians, buffalo, locusts, etc. lent variety to life in Russel, which they left in 1880 to return to Kahoka. Trips to Texas and the great Northwest in 1905–06 gave the author an opportunity to describe her adventures there.
—EDG

4598 WEST, SIMEON H.

LIFE AND TIMES OF S. H. WEST. WITH AN APPENDIX ON EVOLUTION, RELIGION, AND SPIRITUAL PHENOMENA. LEROY, ILL.

[1]–298. 22.2 x 15.4 cm. 11 illustrations, unlisted. Dark red cloth.

Prov.: Inscribed on front endleaf: Presented / to / W. R. Berry / With / Compliments / of / S. H. West. / The initials under W. R. have been erased and the new initials supplied in indelible pencil.

Ref.: Howes W281
Copyrighted 1908.

West traveled to California via New Orleans, Vera Cruz, and overland to Acapulco in 1852. He went overland to California in 1859–60. He was, in later years, a convinced believer in spiritualism.

4599 WESTERN COLLEGE, Cedar Rapids, Iowa

[Broadside] RULES AND REGULATIONS OF WESTERN COLLEGE. THE STUDENTS OF THIS INSTITUTION ARE EXPECTED TO OBSERVE THE FOLLOWING RULES: . . . STUDY HOURS FROM 5 O'CLOCK, A.M., TO 6, FROM 7 TO 12, FROM 1, P.M. TO 4, AND FROM 7 TO 9. SOME ORAL RULES MAY, FROM TIME TO TIME, BE GIVEN THE STUDENTS. THESE WILL BE CONSIDERED AS BINDING AS THE WRITTEN OR PRINTED ONES. TIMES PRINT, FRANKLIN BLOCK, CEDAR RAPIDS, IOWA.

Broadside (edges trimmed) on green paper, 27.8 x 21.8 cm. Text, 27.6 x 21.7 cm.

Ref.:
The *Times* was started in 1855, which would put this broadside after that year.

4600 WESTERN JOURNAL, THE

THE WESTERN JOURNAL, OF AGRICULTURE, MANUFACTURES, MECHANIC ARTS, INTERNAL IMPROVEMENT, COMMERCE, AND GENERAL LITERATURE . . . VOL. I [–XIV]. ST. LOUIS: CHARLES & HAMMOND, PRINTERS, 1848 [–1855].

I: [i]–xii, [3]–144, [i]–ii, [115]–230, [i]–ii, [231]–288, [i]–ii, [289]–346, [i]–ii, [347]–636, [i]–ii, [637]–[694]. II: [i–ii], [i]–ii, [i]–ii, [i]–ii, [i]–ii, [1]–210, [i]–ii, [211]–440, [i]–viii. III: [i–iv], [1]–418 [last leaf inverted and reversed]. (No title-page; first number is October, 1849, Vol. III, No. 1.) IV: 1–416, [i]–vi. (No title-page; first number is April, 1850, Vol. IV, No. 1.) V: [i]–v, [vi–viii blank], [1]–70, [72]–141, [143]–212, [143]–352. (Note on page [ii] regarding mispaginations.) VI: [i]–v, [vi blank], 1–414. VII: [i–ii], [i]–iii, [iv blank], 1–[436]. (No title-page.) VIII: [i–ii], [i]–iii, [iv blank], 1–440. IX: [1–2], [i]–iii, [iv blank], 1–254, 253–438. X: [1–2], [i]–

iv, 1–228, [227]–378, [377]–446. (Page 387 mispaginated 487.) XI: [1–2], [i]–iv, 1–152, [157]–454. XII: [1–2], [i]–iv, [1]–450. (Pages 159, 447 mispaginated 59, 44.) XIII: [1–2], [i]–iv, [1]–[78], [i]–ii, [77]–[154], [i]–ii, [153]–230], [i]–ii, [229]–[306], [i]–ii, [303]–376, [i]–[vi], [377]–444, [i]–ii. (Seemingly erratic pagination is caused by advertisements at ends of parts.) XIV: [1–2], [i]–iv, 1–74, [1–4], [i]–ii, [75]–148, [1–4], [i]–ii, [149]–222, [1–4], [i]–ii, [223]–296, [1–4], [i]–ii, [297]–370, [1–4], [i]–ii, [371]–438, [i]–ii. (Page 141 mispaginated 14; 144, 44; 239, 29; 143 unpaginated.) 20.3 x 12.4 cm. Folding plan facing page 252, Vol. I. Folding map after title-leaf, Vol. II: Skeleton Map / Showing the / Rail Roads / Completed and in progress in the / United States / Jul^g Hutawa Lith^r N. Second St. N° 45 St. Louis, Mo. /. 27.6 x 41.1 cm. No scale given. Two woodcuts on each of pages 145, 218, [219], 252, 289, 345, 435 of Vol. VII. Vol. VIII: Lithograph portrait of J. O'Fallon, Lith by Schaerff & Bro. 71 Market Str. St. Louis /. Vol. IX: Lithograph portrait of Thomas Allen. Engraved expressly / for the / Western Journal and Civilian / Dagu. by Long St. Louis. Lith. by Schaerff & Bro. 4th Str. N° 52. /. Woodcuts on pages 165, 294, 385. Vol. X: Lithograph E. & C. Robyn Lithogr^s N° 44, 2nd St. St. Louis Mo. [at right:] Drawn from nat & engr. on Stone by E. Robyn / St. Louis Mo. / Entered according to act of Congress A.D. 1852 by E. & C. Robyn in the Clerk's Office of the District Court of Missouri /. Woodcut on pages 275, 399. Vol. VII: facing page 1: Atala / Lith. by Schanti (?) & Bro. Atala / 71 Market Str. St. Louis /. 14 volumes, rebound in brown boards, brown cloth backs, red leather labels.

Ref.:
Issues for June–August, Vol. II, not published because of cholera and a fire. Some title-page differences from volume to volume. M. Tarver and T. F. Risk were the editors and proprietors.

Contains considerable material on the Plains, the Rockies, Fur trade, the Southwest, and California.

4601 WESTERN LITERARY MESSENGER, THE

THE WESTERN LITERARY MESSENGER. A WEEKLY JOURNAL OF LITERATURE, BIOGRAPHY, NEWS, ART, SCIENCE, AND AMUSEMENT. VOLUME II [–III] . . . BUFFALO: THOMAS NEWELL, PRINTER, 1842–3 [–1843–4].

[i–iv], [1]–177, [185]–412. [i–iv], [1]–414. 31.3 x 24.1 cm. At end of Vol. II: Map: Map / of the / United States / Territory of Oregon / West of the Rocky Mountains. / Exhibiting the various

Trading Depots or Forts / occupied by the British Hudson Bay Company con-/nected with the Western and northwestern Fur Trade. / [swelled rule] Compiled in the Bureau of Topographical / Engineers from the latest authorities un-/der / the direction of Col. J. J. Abert by / Wash: Hood. / 1838. / M. H. Stansbury del. / [rule] / W. J. Stone Sc. Wash^n / 44.3 x 51.9 cm. Scale: about 16 miles to one inch. Two volumes, contemporary marbled boards, sheep backstrips and corners.

Ref.: Wagner-Camp 94

Edited by J. S. Chadbourne and J. Clement.

The two volumes contain the W. A. Ferris narrative, starting in the issue for January 11, 1843, and continuing through May 18, 1844.

4602 WESTERN MAGAZINE, THE

THE WESTERN MAGAZINE. A LITERARY MONTHLY . . . EDITED BY WM. ROUNSEVILLE. VOLUME I. CHICAGO: ROUNSEVILLE, & CO., 1845-6.

[i–iv], [1]–384. (Pages 89–96 mispaginated 88–95, page 125 mispaginated 1.) 24.2 x 15.7 cm. One inserted woodcut, several text illustrations and full-page woodcuts (versos blank) on four pages. Half brown straight-grain leather. Lacks fly-leaves.

Ref.:

The periodical comprises twelve numbers of 32 pages each. There is a substantial number of original contributions to the magazine, although much of the material is copied from other publications.

4603 WESTERN MAGAZINE, THE

[Wrapper title] WESTERN MAGAZINE VOL. 1. N^0 3. CHICAGO, ILL.: ROUNSEVILLE & CO., DECEMBER, 1845.*

[65]–95. 25.1 x 16.5 cm. Woodcut view facing page [65], cuts in text. Buff printed wrappers, with title on front wrapper, advertisements on verso of back wrapper.

4604 WESTERN MAGAZINE, THE

SAME. VOL. 1. N^0 11 . . . AUGUST, 1846.*

[321]–352. 23.6 x 16.6 cm. Full-page woodcut on page [321]. Buff printed wrappers with title on front wrapper and advertisements on verso of back wrapper.

Ref.:

Front wrapper of No. 5 (February, 1846) laid in.

4605 WESTERN MONTHLY, THE

[Wrapper title] VOL. IV. JULY, 1870. NO. 19. THE WESTERN MONTHLY DEVOTED TO LITERATURE, BIOGRAPHY, AND THE INTERESTS OF THE WEST . . . CHICAGO: THE WESTERN MONTHLY COMPANY.

[1]–80, 1–8 advertisements. 24 x 15.3 cm. Portrait. Tan printed wrappers with title on front wrapper and advertisements on verso of front and recto and verso of back wrapper. Rebacked, back wrapper repaired.

Ref.:

Contains: The Valley of the Upper Yellowstone. / By C. W. Cook. / pages 60–67. And: San Xavier del Bac. / By Josephine Clifford. / pages 28–34.

4606 WESTERN MONTHLY REVIEW, THE

THE WESTERN MONTHLY REVIEW . . . CINCINNATI: PUBLISHED BY E. H. FLINT, 1828–1830.

[i]–viii, [9]–756, [757–60 advertisements]. [i–iv], [9]–704. [i–iv], [1]–668. 21.2 x 13.2 cm. Three volumes, contemporary half calf.

Ref.: Rusk I pp. 168–70

Edited by Timothy Flint. Two months were skipped between the first and second volumes and one month between the second and third volumes. The set contains many fine articles about the West—including some material about the Transmississippi West.

4607 WESTERN MOUNTAINEER, THE

[Newspaper] THE WESTERN MOUNTAINEER. GEORGE WEST . . . EDITOR & PUBLISHER. VOL. I. GOLDEN CITY, JEFFERSON, WEDNESDAY, DECEMBER 14 [–21], 1859. NO. 2 [–3] . . .

Two issues, each [1–4]. 39.5 x 24.3 cm. Unbound.

Ref.: McMurtrie & Allen (*Colorado*) p. 271.

The paper ran for about a year, closing on December 20, 1860, because of "a deficiency in the bank account."

4608 WESTERN REVIEW AND MISCELLANEOUS MAGAZINE, THE

THE WESTERN REVIEW AND MISCELLANEOUS MAGAZINE . . . VOLUME FIRST [–IV] . . . LEXINGTON, KENTUCKY: PUBLISHED BY WILLIAM GIBBES HUNT, 1820 [–1821].

Each volume: [i–iv], [1]–384. (Numerous errors in pagination.) 21.3 x 13 cm. Four volumes bound in two, contemporary half sheep, red leather labels.

Ref.: Rusk I pp. 165–67, 201, II, pp. 7, 21, 22, 25, 33

The Western Review was the earliest attempt to establish a literary periodical of its sort in the West.

4609 WESTERN STAGE COMPANY

[Broadside] WESTERN STAGE CO. GREAT WESTERN & SOUTHERN MAIL & PASSENGER ROUTES! IMPORTANT TO PASSENGERS GOING WEST AND SOUTH OF DUBUQUE. REGULAR DAILY LINES OF FOUR HORSE POST COACHES, LEAVE DUBUQUE EVERY MORNING . . . THE COMPANY ASSURE THE TRAVELING PUBLIC THAT THEIR STOCK IS OF SUPERIOR QUALITY; THEIR DRIVERS CAREFUL AND EXPERIENCED, AND THEIR COACHES NEW, ROOMY, AND OF THE BEST MANUFACTURE, AND THEIR AIM IS SAFETY, SPEED & COMFORT . . . WM. JACKSON, AGENT . . . EXPRESS AND HERALD JOB PRINT, DUBUQUE.

Broadside, 35.2 x 17.3 cm. Text, 33.1 x 14.5 cm. Border at foot bled.

Ref.:

4610 WESTERN STAGE COMPANY

[Broadside] WESTERN STAGE CO. THROUGH TO IOWA CITY IN ONE DAY. LEAVE DAVENPORT ON ARRIVAL OF MORNING TRAIN OF CARS FROM CHICAGO FOR BLUE GRASS, MUSCATINE, WEST LIBERTY AND IOWA CITY . . . J. Y. & W. D. PORTER, AGENTS ON THE CARS. R. LOUNSBERRY, AGENT. GENERAL STAGE OFFICE, LE CLAIRE HOUSE, DAVENPORT, IOWA, SEPT., 1855. RAYMOND'S PRINTING HOUSE, ROCK ISLAND.

Broadside, 24.8 x 15 cm. Text, 22.9 x 13.5 cm.
Ref.: Byrd 2362

4611 WESTERN TOWN COMPANY

[Caption title] THE FIRST ANNUAL REPORT OF THE WESTERN TOWN COMPANY . . .

[1]–3, [4 blank]. 20 x 13.5 cm. Unbound leaflet.
Ref.:
Signed and dated on page 3: George P. Waldron, Secretary. / Dubuque, Iowa. October 1st 1857.

Apparently this company developed plans for and established Sioux Falls, Iowa.

Lawrence K. Fox of the South Dakota State Historical Society suggests that the title quoted in the second paragraph, "History of the States and Territories of the Great West" is probably Ferris, Jacob: *The States and Territories of the Great West* . . . New York, 1856. The vicinity of Sioux Falls is described by Ferris.

4612 WESTERN TRAVELLER'S POCKET DIRECTORY, THE . . .

THE WESTERN TRAVELLER'S POCKET DIRECTORY AND STRANGER'S GUIDE. SCHENECTADA[!]: PRINTED AT THE REFLECTOR OFFICE, 1836.

[1]–[96]. 10.8 x 7.5 cm. Yellow boards, green cloth back, printed paper label on front cover. Lacks fly-leaf at back.

Ref.: Howes T331; Sabin 103024

An earlier edition carried the title *The Traveller's Pocket Directory and Stranger's Guide* . . . Schenectady, 1831.

Editions: Schenectady, 1831, 1833, 1834. New York, 1832.

4613 WESTON, SILAS

FOUR MONTHS IN THE MINES OF CALIFORNIA; OR, LIFE IN THE MOUNTAINS . . . PROVIDENCE: BENJAMIN T. ALBRO, PRINTER, 1854.

[1]–[48]. 22.4 x 13.9 cm. Tan printed wrappers, with title on front wrapper. In a brown cloth case.

Ref.: Cowan p. 676; Howes W292; Sabin 103053

The first edition appeared the same year under the title *Life in the Mountains* . . . Providence, 1854.

4614 WETMORE, ALPHONSO

[Caption title] . . . MEMORIAL OF ALPHONSO WETMORE, FOR A RECONSIDERATION OF HIS CLAIM ON ACCOUNT OF LOSSES IN THE SERVICE OF THE UNITED STATES . . .

[1]–5, [6–8 blank]. 22.1 x 14.4 cm. Rebound in new red cloth.

Ref.: Wagner-Camp 69

24th Congress, 1st Session, Senate, Document No. 368, Serial 283. [Washington, 1836.]

Wetmore here gives a sketch of his life and services on the Western Frontier from 1815 onward. He had lost an arm in the service yet was asking for only $15 per month pension.—EDG

Printer's imprint on page [1]: [short rule] / [Gales & Seaton, print.] /

4615 WETMORE, ALPHONSO

GAZETTEER OF THE STATE OF MISSOURI. WITH A MAP OF THE STATE, FROM THE OFFICE OF THE SURVEYOR-GENERAL, INCLUDING THE LATEST ADDITIONS AND SURVEYS TO WHICH IS ADDED AN APPENDIX, CONTAINING FRONTIER SKETCHES, AND ILLUSTRATIONS OF INDIAN CHARACTER . . . ST. LOUIS: PUBLISHED BY C. KEEMLE, 1837.

[i]–xvi, [17]–382. (Pages [i–iv] blank.) 21.8 x 13.6 cm. Engraved frontispiece and folding map: Keemle & Wetmore's / Map / of the / State of Missouri: / With the latest additions and surveys from / the Office of the Surveyor General. / February 1837. / [decorative rule] / Entered according to Act of Congress. / 58.6 x 60.7 cm. Scale: 12 miles to an inch. Red cloth, printed paper label, 5.5 x 3.2 cm., on backstrip.

Ref.: AII (*Missouri*) 210; Howes W296; Rader 3616; Sabin 103064; Wagner-Camp 69

Pages 307–34 contain: "Sketch of Mountain Life. By a Trapper."

4616 WETMORE, HELEN CODY

LAST OF THE GREAT SCOUTS. THE LIFE STORY OF COL. WILLIAM F. CODY ("BUFFALO BILL") . . .

[1–2], [i]–xiii, [xiv blank], [1]–267, [268 blank]. 21.5 x 14.7 cm. 19 full-page illustrations listed. Blue cloth, front cover embossed, title in gilt.

Prov.: Bookplate of John Thomas Lee.
Ref.: Howes W297; Rader 3617

Printed in Duluth, Minnesota, 1899. Mrs. Wetmore was Cody's sister.

Laid in at front is an Autograph Letter, signed, by William F. Cody. 1887 February 15, New York.

4617 WHARTON, JUNIUS E.

HISTORY OF THE CITY OF DENVER FROM ITS EARLIEST SETTLEMENT TO THE PRESENT TIME . . . DENVER, COLORADO: BYERS & DAILEY, PRINTERS, 1866.

[1]–184. 20.6 x 12.1 cm. Green printed wrappers, with title on front wrapper with advertisements at top, bottom, and on both outer sides of border, advertisement on recto of front wrapper. Back wrapper supplied. In a red cloth folder.

Ref.: Bradford 5765; Howes W303; Jones 1497; McMurtrie & Allen (*Colorado*) 73; Wilcox p. 122

The text of the history appears on the rectos only, advertisements on the versos. A *Directory* by D. O. Wilhelm occupies pages 102–126, with a General Directory, pages 128–176. The Addenda occupy pages [177]–184.

4618 [WHEAT, MARVIN T.]

TRAVELS ON THE WESTERN SLOPE OF THE MEXICAN CORDILLERA, IN THE FORM OF FIFTY-ONE LETTERS, DESCRIPTIVE OF MUCH OF THIS PORTION OF THE REPUBLIC OF MEXICO . . . SAN FRANCISCO: WHITTON, TOWNE & CO., 1857.*

[i]–xvi, [17]–438. 18.2 x 11.1 cm. Frontispiece (or pictorial title-page) and five illustrations. Brown cloth, title in gilt on backstrip. In red cloth folder and case.

Ref.: Howes W313; Munk (Alliot) p. 50

Contains considerable material about Arizona, including Washburn's trip from Fort Yuma up the Gila, to Tucson and back by way of Alter and Sonoita in 1856, travels in the Gadsden Purchase, the Tepic Conspiracy, copper mining, practicability of a railroad, American filibustering expedition, etc.

4619 WHEATON, W. G.

REPORT UPON THE PRELIMINARY SURVEY OF THE FIRST TWO DIVISIONS OF THE SHEFFIELD & SAVANNAH RAILROAD: WITH A MAP SHOWING ITS CONNECTIONS . . . ROCK ISLAND: FROM T. R. RAYMOND'S PRINTING HOUSE, 1856.

[i–ii], [1]–14, [15], [16 blank], [17–18 blank]. 20.6 x 14.2 cm. Folding map at back: Map of / Sheffield and Savannah / Rail-Road / W. G. Wheaton / Peoria Civil Engineer / [lower right corner:] Acheson lith / Chicago /. 69.2 x 54.1 cm. No scale given. Stabbed in yellow printed wrappers, with title on front wrapper.

Ref.: Byrd 2551

Page [15] is headed: Act of Incorporation. /

4620 WHEELER, D. H. & CO., Plattsmouth, Nebraska Territory

[Trade card] D. H. WHEELER. J. W. MARSHALL. E. C. LEWIS. D. H. WHEELER & CO., REAL ESTATE AGENTS, PLATTSMOUTH, N. T. . . .

Broadside, 5.1 x 8.9 cm., on stiff card.
Ref.:

4621 WHEELER, HOMER W.

THE FRONTIER TRAIL; OR, FROM COWBOY TO COLONEL . . . LOS ANGELES: PUBLISHED BY TIMES-MIRROR PRESS, 1923.*

[i–iv, iv blank], [1]–334. 22.7 x 15.2 cm. 15 plates listed and one unlisted facsimile. Light brown pictorial cloth.

Ref.: Adams (*Ramp. Herd*) 2500; Howes W322

4622 WHEELOCK, ELEAZAR

A CONTINUATION OF THE NARRATIVE OF THE INDIAN CHARITY-SCHOOL, BEGUN IN LEBANON, IN CONNECTICUT; NOW INCORPORATED WITH DARTMOUTH-COLLEGE . . . HARTFORD: PRINTED IN THE YEAR 1773.

[A]–D8, [E]2. [1]–68. 20.3 x 12.6 cm. Stabbed, uncut, unopened. In new blue wrappers. In a blue cloth case.

Ref.: Evans 13077; Field 1644; Howes W331; Sabin 103211

Wheelock's seventh narrative covers the period September 26, 1772, to September 26, 1773. Pages 44–68 carry an "Abstract of a Journal of a Mission to the Delaware Indians, West of the Ohio, June 19, 1772 to Oct. 2, 1773 by David MacClure and Levi Frisbie."

4623 [WHEELOCK, THOMPSON B.]

DOCUMENTS COMMUNICATED TO CONGRESS BY THE PRESIDENT, AT THE OPENING OF THE SECOND SESSION OF THE TWENTY-THIRD CONGRESS, ACCOMPANYING THE REPORT OF THE SECRETARY OF WAR.

[i–ii], 49–94. 22.2 x 14.1 cm. Extracted from bound volume and rebound in new red cloth.

Ref.: Howes K161 note see; Wagner-Camp 51

23rd Congress, 2nd Session, Senate Executive Document No. 1, Serial 266. [Washington, 1854.]

Pages 49–93 comprise Document No. 1, the Report from the Major General of the Army. Included is Captain Thompson B. Wheelock's journal of Colonel Henry Dodge's expedition from Fort Gibson to the Pawnee Indian villages, June to August, 1854, pages 73–93.

4624 WHEILDON, WILLIAM W.

. . . SCIENTIFIC EXCURSION ACROSS THE STATE OF IOWA, FROM DUBUQUE TO SIOUX CITY AND SPRING-VALE . . . CONCORD, MASS.: PREPARED AT THE REQUEST OF THE PARTY, 1873.

[i–ii (ii blank)], [1]–11, [12–14 blank]. 23.3 x 14.8 cm. Yellow printed wrappers, with title on front wrapper.

Ref.:

Appendix to the *Proceedings* (August, 1872) of the American Association for the Advancement of Science.

4625 WHIG BATTERING-RAM, THE

[Newspaper] THE WHIG BATTERING-RAM; OR, STRAIGHTOUT REVIVED. VOLUME 1. CITY OF COLUMBUS, FRIDAY, SEPT. 6, 1844. NUMBER 5 . . .

[1–4]. 47.5 x 34.3 cm. Unbound.

Ref.:

The newspaper was edited by Rufus B. Sage, author of *Scenes in the Rocky Mountains.* Although only one short article is signed by Sage, the editor probably supplied most if not all of the text. The paper was rabidly anti-Locofoco.

Laid in the paper-bound copy of Sage's book.

4626 WHIG PARTY. Wisconsin

[Broadside] MILWAUKEE COUNTY WHIG MEETING . . . HELD . . . MILWAUKEE, ON THE 26TH DAY OF JUNE, 1841 . . . JAMES CLYMAN, CHAIRMAN. E. K. COLLINS, SECRETARY.

Broadside, 55.5 x 20.1 cm. Text, 47 x 12.1 cm.

Ref.:

Resolution in opposition to the appointment of James Duane Doty as governor.

4627 WHILLDIN, M.

A DESCRIPTION OF WESTERN TEXAS, PUBLISHED BY THE GALVESTON, HARRISBURG & SAN ANTONIO RAILWAY COMPANY, THE SUNSET ROUTE . . . GALVESTON, TEXAS: PRINTED AT THE "NEWS" STEAM BOOK & JOB OFFICE, 1876.

[i–ii, ii blank], [1]–120. 18.5 x 11.8 cm. 29 plates, unlisted. Colored pictorial wrappers bound into original blue cloth, title in gilt on front cover, red mottled edges, map on inner front wrapper.

Ref.: Howes W338; Winkler & Friend 3913

The lithographed plates are especially interesting.

4628 WHITE, ELIJAH

[Wrapper title] A CONCISE VIEW OF OREGON TERRITORY, ITS COLONIAL AND INDIAN RELATIONS; COMPILED FROM OFFICIAL LETTERS AND REPORTS, TOGETHER WITH THE ORGANIC LAWS OF THE COLONY . . . WASHINGTON: T. BARNARD, PRINTER, 1846.

[1]–72. 22.7 x 14.5 cm. Blue printed wrappers, with title on front wrapper.

Prov.: Inscribed on front wrapper: Hon J. F. Simmons U. S. Senate /.

Ref.: Bradford 5790; Cowan (1914) p. 247; Howes W349; Smith 10916; Wagner-Camp 144 see

Describes the initial establishment of organized society in that region. Consists of letters written by White to government authorities at Washington, printed previously in various documents.—Howes

4629 WHITE, ELIJAH

TESTIMONIALS AND RECORDS, TOGETHER WITH ARGUMENTS IN FAVOR OF SPECIAL ACTION FOR OUR INDIAN TRIBES . . . WASHINGTON: PRINTED BY R. A. WATERS, 1861.

[1–4], [i]–[iv], [5]–84. 22.6 x 14.5 cm. Tan printed wrappers with title on front wrapper. Lacks back wrapper.

Ref.: Howes W350

Very poor paper.

4630 WHITE, H. L.

[Caption title] KNOX COUNTY, JULY 30TH 1817. FELLOW-CITIZENS, . . .

[A]². [1–3], [4 blank]. 33.5 x 20.4 cm. Unbound leaflet.

Prov.: Inscribed on page [4]: H L White /.

Ref.:

Probably printed in Knoxville, certainly in 1817. Not listed in AII (*Tennessee*). The text expounds White's views and intentions in regard to land laws and solicits the suffrage of the voters at the approaching election.

4631 WHITE, JOHN, of Kentucky

[Caption title] SPEECH OF MR. WHITE, OF KENTUCKY, . . . JUNE 5, 1840 . . . IN OPPOSITION TO THE SUB-TREASURY BILL . . .

[1]–48. Bound with Number 1084.

Ref.:

Printed in Washington in 1844.

4632 WHITE, JOHN, of Kentucky

[Caption title] SPEECH OF THE HON. JOHN WHITE, OF KENTUCKY, IN DEFENCE OF MR. CLAY . . . DELIVERED IN THE HOUSE OF REPRESENTATIVES . . . APRIL 23, 1844 . . .

[1]–8. Bound with Number 1084.
Ref.:
Printed in Washington in 1844.

4633 WHITE, JOHN

SKETCHES FROM AMERICA. PART I.—CANADA PART
II.—A PIC-NIC TO THE ROCKY MOUNTAINS . . .
LONDON: SAMPSON LOW, SON, AND MARSTON,
1870.

[i]–viii, [1]–373, [374 blank]. 21.7 x 13.7 cm.
Blue cloth, gilt title on backstrip.
Ref.: Howes W358
Includes a trip from Chicago to Cheyenne
and Denver.

4634 WHITE, JOHN M.

THE NEWER NORTHWEST . . . A DESCRIPTION OF
THE HEALTH RESORTS AND MINING CAMPS OF THE
BLACK HILLS OF SOUTH DAKOTA AND BIG HORN
MOUNTAINS IN WYOMING . . . ST. LOUIS, MO.: PUB-
LISHED BY SELF-CULTURE PUBLISHING CO., 1894.

[i–viii], [1]–205, [206–225 advertisements, 226
blank]. 19.3 x 13.7 cm. Numerous illustrations
from photographs, some woodcuts, etc. White
printed wrappers, with title on front wrapper,
advertisement on verso of front wrapper. Back
wrapper and backstrip supplied, final leaf defective.
Prov.: Elliott Coues, / Sept. 1895. / on title-
page.
Ref.: Howes W360; Jennewein 200

4635 [WHITE, WILLIAM F.]

A PICTURE OF PIONEER TIMES IN CALIFORNIA. IL-
LUSTRATED WITH ANECDOTES AND STORIES TAKEN
FROM REAL LIFE . . . SAN FRANCISCO: PRINTED BY
W. M. HINTON & CO., 1881.

[i]–[viii, viii blank], [1]–677, [678 blank]. 21.9 x
14 cm. Black cloth, title stamped in gilt on front
cover and backstrip.
Prov.: Signature of the author in pencil on
front endleaf: W$_{\#}^{m}$ F White /. Author's name
"Grey" crossed out on title-page and F. White /
supplied in manuscript. Author's name crossed
out at end of Introduction and signature supplied in manuscript: W$_{\#}^{m}$ F. White /.
Ref.: Cowan p. 680; Howes W372
Author's copy.

4636 WHITE & MORRIS

MANUSCRIPT RECEIPT, SIGNED: White & Morris.
1811 April 6, New Orleans. One page, 9.9 x 20
cm. Receipt to Robert McKnight.

4637 WHITE PINE MINING DISTRICT, Nevada

[Map] WHITE PINE M. DISTRICT /.

Manuscript map, 94 x 52 cm. On tracing linen.
Shows claims and lodes, May 28, 1870, to
March 24, 1884, with table, listing names, etc.,
nos. 37–110.

4638 WHITEHOUSE, JOHN H.

ADDRESS OF THE BISHOP OF THE DIOCESE OF ILLI-
NOIS, A. D. 1854 . . . NEW-YORK: PUDNEY & RUS-
SELL, PRINTERS, 1854.

[1]–26, [27–28 blank]. 20.8 x 13.4 cm. Removed
from bound volume, unbound.
Ref.:
Accompanying the pamphlet is an anonymous pamphlet referred to in the *Address*, page
20: [caption title] The Proposed Cathedral in
Illinois / . . .

4639 WHITELY, ISAAC H.

RURAL LIFE IN TEXAS . . . ATLANTA, GEORGIA: JAS.
P. HARRISON & CO., PRINTERS, 1891.

[i–iv advertisements], [1]–82, [83–86 advertisements, 87–88 blank]. 20.9 x 23.5 cm. Illustrations unlisted. Yellow printed wrappers with
title on front wrapper, advertisements on verso
of front wrapper and verso of back wrapper.
Ref.: Clements Library (*Texas*) 49; Howes
W377
This autobiographical sketch probably
should be taken with a generous sprinkling of
salt. It purports to be an account of the author's
attempts to make a living by hook or by crook,
in Texas in the 1870's and 1880's. His experiences ranged from selling patent medicine (water
colored red and pills made from Texas mud) to
speculating in shady land deals (from which he
profited enough to acquire a "vehicle agency").
The copyright notice appears on an inserted
slip, 11.5 x 23 cm., and was held by George W.
Harrison, 1891.

4640 WHITMAN, E. B., & A. D. SEARL

[Map] MAP / OF / EASTERN KANSAS / BY / E. B.
WHITMAN & A. D. SEARL, / GENERAL LAND
AGENTS / LAWRENCE, KANSAS / 1856. / BOSTON,
PUBLISHED BY J. P. JEWETT AND C^{O}. / ENTERED AC-
CORDING TO ACT OF CONGRESS IN THE YEAR 1856
BY E. B. WHITMAN & A. D. SEARL, IN THE CLERKS
OFFICE OF THE DISTRICT COURT OF MASS. / L. M.
BRADFORD & CO'S LITH, BOSTON. / *Inset:* [Plan of
the area around Fort Riley]. 15.3 x 15.6 cm. No
scale given. *Insets:* Three small views in Law-
rence and Topeka.

Map, 67.9 x 52.7 cm. Scale: 13 miles to an inch. Brown cloth covers, 16 x 10 cm., with title on front cover in gilt.

Ref.: Phillips p. 346

Inside the front cover is mounted a yellow broadside signed by Whitman & Searl, dated Lawrence, Kansas, June 15, 1856, comprising proposals to establish an "Emigrant's Intelligence Office."

4641 [WHITMER, DAVID]

AN ADDRESS TO ALL BELIEVERS IN CHRIST . . . RICHMOND, MISSOURI: DAVID WHITMER, 1887.

[1]–75, [76 blank]. 21.6 x 14.8 cm. Gray printed wrappers, with title on front wrapper.

Ref.: Howes W381; Morgan III 50

This pamphlet is one of the most influential and important works produced by any of the Mormon factions, and it continues to be a standard source book for students of Mormonism . . .—Morgan

4642 WHITNEY, ASA

A PROJECT FOR A RAILROAD TO THE PACIFIC . . . NEW YORK: PRINTED BY GEORGE W. WOOD, 1849.

[i]–viii, [1]–112. 23 x 14.2 cm. Two maps. [Map of the World.] [above neat line, centre:] Nº 1 / [at foot, centre:] This Map was prepared by Mʳ Whitney for Mʳ Breese's / report to the Senate, U. S. 29 Congress. / [lower right:] Miller's Lith. 102 Broadway, N. Y. / [below neat line, centre:] 1235 /. 31.8 x 52.3 cm. No scale given. Map: [Map of the North America.] [above neat line, centre:] Nº 2 / [lower right:] Miller's Lith. 102 Broadway, N. Y. / 37.6 x 45.3 cm. No scale given. Green printed wrappers with title on front wrapper. In a blue half morocco case.

Ref.: Cowan p. 680; Howes W383; *Railway Economics* p. 288; Smith 10963

This was the culmination of Whitney's promotion of his scheme for a transcontinental railroad. The opposition was so great, despite his own prodigious labors, that he abandoned his plans and retired. He lived, however, to see the completion of one such railroad and the inauguration of three others.

4643 WHITNEY, E. C. & T. H.

HISTORY AND CAPTURE OF GERONIMO AND APACHE INDIANS . . . ST. AUGUSTINE, FLA.: FLORIDA TIMES-UNION PRINT, 1887.

[1]–48. 15.2 x 11.2 cm. Six vignettes in text. Pale yellow printed wrappers with title on front wrapper, advertisements on recto and verso of back wrapper.

Prov.: W. J. Holliday copy.

Ref.: Howes W385

Pages [3] and 4 are a Business Directory for St. Augustine. There are advertisements on pages 35–48.

4644 WHITNEY, HENRY C.

LIFE ON THE CIRCUIT WITH LINCOLN. WITH SKETCHES OF GENERALS GRANT, SHERMAN AND McCLELLAN, JUDGE DAVIS, LEONARD SWETT, AND OTHER CONTEMPORARIES. BOSTON: ESTES AND LAURIAT, PUBLISHERS.

[i]–viii, 1–601, [602 blank]. 22.6 x 16.6 cm. 67 illustrations listed. Dark red cloth, title in gilt on front cover and backstrip, gilt top.

Ref.: Howes W386; Monaghan 1112

Copyrighted 1892.

4645 WHITNEY, JOEL P.

[Wrapper title] SILVER MINING REGIONS OF COLORADO. WITH SOME ACCOUNT OF THE DIFFERENT PROCESSES NOW BEING INTRODUCED FOR WORKING THE GOLD ORES OF THAT TERRITORY . . . NEW YORK: D. VAN NOSTRAND, 1865.

[1]–107, [108 blank]. 18.5 x 12.1 cm. Buff printed wrappers, with title on front wrapper.

Ref.: Howes W388; Wagner-Camp 427; Wilcox p. 123

4646 WHITNEY, JOSIAH D.

. . . THE YOSEMITE BOOK; A DESCRIPTION OF THE YOSEMITE VALLEY AND THE ADJACENT REGION OF THE SIERRA NEVADA, AND OF THE BIG TREES OF CALIFORNIA . . . PUBLISHED BY AUTHORITY OF THE LEGISLATURE. NEW YORK: JULIUS BIEN, 1868.

[1]–116, [117–18]. 30 x 24.2 cm. 28 photographs, mounted, and two maps mounted on linen. Full green morocco, gilt, gilt edges.

Ref.: Bradford 5811; Cowan p. 702; Farquhar 7a; Howes W389

Limited to 250 copies. (See footnote on page 13.) Part of the Geological Survey of California.

4647 WHITON, H. J.

AUTOGRAPH LETTER, SIGNED. 1870 March 25, Chapman Nebraskey. To George W. Whiton. One page, 22.8 x 13.4 cm.

Describes briefly his journey from Ohio, via Chicago, and the first few days after his arrival in Chapman. Written on the verso of a broadside by J. E. Morrill. With the original stamped envelope.

4648 WIED-NEUWIED, MAXIMILIAN ALEXANDER PHILIPP, PRINZ VON

REISE IN DAS INNERE NORD-AMERIKA IN DEN JAHREN 1832 BIS 1834 . . . COBLENZ: BEI J. HOELSCHER, 1839 [–1840].

[I]–XVI, [1]–[654], [655 colophon, 656 blank]. [I]–[XXIV], [1]–687, [688 colophon]. 33.3 x 27.2

cm. Illustrated. Original dark orange wrappers, uncut, unopened.

Ref.: Howes M443a; Rader 3652; Sabin 47017; Wagner-Camp 76

4649 WIED-NEUWIED, MAXIMILIAN ALEXANDER PHILIPP, PRINZ VON

TRAVELS IN THE INTERIOR OF NORTH AMERICA . . . LONDON: ACKERMANN AND CO., MDCCCXLIII.* (Atlas only)

[i]–[xii], [1]–520. 31.2 x 24.4 cm. 81 colored vignettes and illustrations and a folding map. Plates after C. Bodmer, each large plate with the embossed stamp of Bodmer in the margin. Map: [title in three columns in German, French, and English] Map / to / illustrate the Route of / Prince Maximilian / of / Wied / in the interior of / North America / From Boston to the / Upper Missouri &c. / in / 1832, 33 & 34. / 42 x 81 cm. Scale: about 33 miles to one inch. *Inset:* Great / Falls / of the / Missouri / . 6.4 x 25.2 cm. No scale given. Plates listed in text and on a single leaf in the Atlas. Two volumes, dark green cloth, green leather corners and backstrips, gilt edges. One volume folio and the other imperial folio.

Ref.: Field 1036; Howes M443a; Jones 1076; Rader 3652 note; Sabin 47017; Wagner-Camp 76

The title-page of the Atlas reads as follows: Illustrations / to / Maximilian Prince of Wied's / Travels / in / the Interior of / North America / London. / Ackermann & Comp.ᵞ 96 Strand. / MDCCCXLIV. / [i–iv], [81 plates]. 60.7 x 44.3 cm.

4650 WIERZBICKI, FELIX P.

CALIFORNIA AS IT IS AND AS IT MAY BE; OR, A GUIDE TO THE GOLD REGION . . . SAN FRANCISCO: PRINTED BY WASHINGTON BARTLETT, 1849.

[1]–[62]. 21.6 x 15.3 cm. Glazed lavender wrappers. Wrappers defective, part of back wrapper missing. In a black half morocco case.

Prov.: C. G. Littell copy, with bookplate. Inscribed on page [3]: The first Book Printed North of / Mexico or West of the Rocky Mountains / Presented to J. A. Tucker / By his Brother / [and in another hand:] Presented to Milton Tucker / by his Grandmother Tucker / on January first 1917. /

Ref.: AII (*California*) 114; Blumann & Thomas 3914; Cowan p. 682; Hanna-Powell p. 26; Howes W405; Jones 1322; Sabin 103893; Wagner (*California Imprints*) 44

First California-printed English book of original nature; this, with its highly interesting contents, renders it the most important and prized of all books printed there, with the possible exception of Figueroa's *Manifesto.*—Howes

4651 WIERZBICKI, FELIX P.

THE SAME. SECOND EDITION.

[i]–[vi, vi blank], [5]–76, [77 errata, 78 blank]. 21.7 x 14.2 cm. Rebound in brown half morocco, partly unopened, uncut.

Ref.: AII (*California*) 115; Blumann & Thomas 3915; Jones 1323, others as above

Editions: San Francisco, 1849.

4652 WIGGIN, C. P.

[Map] MACLEAN & LAWRENCES / SECTIONAL MAP / OF / KANSAS TERRITORY / COMPILED FROM THE U. S. SURVEY'S[!] / BY / C. P. WIGGIN. / I HEREBY CERTIFY THAT THE ABOVE MAP WAS COMPILED / FROM THE FIELD NOTES OF THE SURVEYS ON FILE IN THIS OFFICE. / L. A. MACLEAN, / CHIEF CLERK / SURVEYOR GENERAL OFFICE / LECOMPTON, K. T. APRIL 1857. / WM. SCHUCHMAN & BRO. LITH. PITTSBURGH, PA. /

Map, 100.5 x 101 cm. (including border). Scale not given. Folded into black cloth covers, 16.6 x 11.4 cm., with title in gilt on front cover.

Ref.: Phillips p. 346

4653 WILHELM, THOMAS

HISTORY OF THE EIGHTH U. S. INFANTRY, FROM ITS ORGANIZATION, IN 1838 . . . PRINTED AT HEADQUARTERS, EIGHTH INFANTRY, 1873.

[i]–xiv, [5]–430. [i]–xiv, [7]–431, [432 blank], [I]–VII, [VIII blank]. 19 x 14.6 cm. 41 illustrations listed. Frontispiece portrait and pictorial title-page of first volume not present. Two volumes, mottled board sides, black leather backstrips and corners, title in gilt on backstrips, also name of former owner.

Prov.: Stamped on backstrips: Col. Jno. E. Smith / U. S. A. /

Ref.: Howes W413; Nicholson p. 927

The first edition had appeared under the title *Synopsis of the History of the Eighth U. S. Infantry . . . 1871.*

4654 WILHELM, THOMAS

[Caption title] MEMORANDUM FROM THE ADJUTANT'S OFFICE, 8TH INFANTRY . . .

[1]–117, [118 blank]. (Two blank leaves at front, one at back.) 20.9 x 13.9 cm.

Ref.: Howes W413 note

Probably printed on the Army press at Fort Whipple, 1874.

On page [1]: Dec. 2.—We have just yesterday closed our last volume on the "History of the Eighth Regiment."

Manuscript note laid in: Memorandum from the Adjutant's Office / 8ᵗʰ / Infantry / [double rule] / A / Diary / Covering Events From / Dec. 2, 1873 to October 5, 1874 / Including / Activities at Fort Russell; a History and / minute Description of that Place; Post of / Beaver; Camp Stambaugh; A Journey / from Fort Russell to Independence Mountain / in North Park and the most Practical Route / Thereto; Sketch of Gen. J. V. Bamford; Daily / Diary of the Journey from Fort Russell through / the Black Hills and Sioux Country to / Spotted Tail's Agency with an Account of / the Natives and Country Encountered, also, / Descriptions of Fort Laramie, Red Cloud's / Agency, etc.; Return to Fort Russell; Removal / from Duty in the Platte Department to Assignment / in the Division of the Pacific; Train to San / Francisco; Steamer for the Mouth of the Colorado; / Fort Yuma; Fort Mojave; March to Fort Whipple / with account of the Hardships Suffered through / Heat & Lack of Water; Description of Fort Whipple. / By / The Judge Advocate of the 8ᵗʰ Infantry. / [ornament] / Fort Whipple, A. T., Army Press, 1874 /.

4655   [WILHELM, THOMAS]

SYNOPSIS OF THE HISTORY OF THE EIGHTH U. S. INFANTRY. AND THE MILITARY RECORD OF OFFICERS ASSIGNED TO THE REGIMENT, FROM ITS ORGANIZATION, JULY, 1838, TO SEPT. 1871. DAVID'S ISLAND, NEW YORK HARBOR, 1871.

[i–vi], [1]–484, [485–86 blank], [487–88 Appendix], 485–91, [492 blank], [i–iii index], [iv blank]. (Pages 381–446 bound with outer margins at inner edge.) 18.6 x 13.1 cm. Half black morocco.

Ref.: Howes W413; Nicholson p. 927

The introductory note is signed Thomas Wilhelm, Adjutant Eighth Infantry.

The imprint on the second preliminary leaf reads: Printed at Regimental Headquarters, / Eighth Infantry, / David's Island New York Harbor. / MDCCCLXXI. / The last page bears the following note: Charles H. Fernald, Richard N. Hall, Privates, Company "I" Eighth U. S. Infantry, Printers.

A frontispiece portrait appears in most copies.

4656   WILKES, CHARLES

WESTERN AMERICA, INCLUDING CALIFORNIA AND OREGON . . . PHILADELPHIA: LEA AND BLANCHARD, 1849.

[i]–ix, [x blank], 3–130, [131–32 blank], [1–32 advertisements]. (Pages [i–ii] blank.) 23.3 x 14.7 cm. Three folding maps: A Correct Map / from Actual Surveys and Examinations / Embracing a Portion of / California / between Monterey and the Pacific Butes[!] / In the Valley of the /

Sacramento / Shewing the Placeres / 1849 / Drawn by F. D. Stuart. / [lower centre:] Entered according to act of Congress in the year 1849, by Lea & Blanchard, in the Clerk's office of the district Court of the Eastern district of Pennsylvania. / 59.6 x 43.1 cm. Scale: about 7 miles to one inch. Map: Map / of / Upper California / by the / Best Authorities / 1849. / 21.7 x 29.3 cm. No scale given. Map: Map / of the / Oregon Territory / from the / Best Authorities. / 1849. [lower right:] Edwᵈ Yeager Sc. / 21.2 x 33.5 cm. No scale given. *Inset:* Columbia River / Reduced from a Survey / Made by the / U. S. Ex. Ex. / 1841 / 19.1 x 7.8 cm. Scale: 30 miles to one inch. Gray printed wrappers with title on front wrapper, advertisement on verso of back wrapper. New backstrip. In a brown cloth case.

Ref.: Cowan p. 683; Howes W416; Jones 1224; Sabin 103995; Wheat (*Transmississippi*) 654, 655; Wheat (*Gold Rush*) 134, 135

Written from material gathered by the author on his famous government exploring expedition of 1832–34, but not included in his official *Narrative*, as this region was not then United States public domain. In a sense it constitutes the first Pacific coast guide; De Smet contributed some geographical information to it.—Howes

4657   WILKES, GEORGE

THE HISTORY OF OREGON, GEOGRAPHICAL AND POLITICAL . . . NEW YORK: WILLIAM H. COLYER, 1845.

[1]–[128]. 22.8 x 14.1 cm. Map: [Map of Part of Oregon, Washington, and Part of British Columbia.] 21 x 27.8 cm. No scale given. Gray printed wrappers, with title on front wrapper, advertisement on verso of back wrapper. In a dark blue cloth case.

Ref.: Bradford 5849; Howell 332; Howes W418; Sabin 103997; Smith 11005; Wagner-Camp 119; Wheat (*Transmississippi*) 501

George Wilkes was a crusading journalist who sponsored causes which kept him in hot water . . . This is his brief on the rights of the United States to the Oregon Country.—Jones

4658   WILKIE, FRANC B.

DAVENPORT PAST AND PRESENT; INCLUDING THE EARLY HISTORY, AND PERSONAL AND ANECDOTAL REMINISCENCES OF DAVENPORT . . . DAVENPORT: PUBLISHING HOUSE OF LUSE, LANE & CO., 1858.

[1]–[334]. 21.6 x 13.9 cm. Eight portraits and six illustrations, including lithographed double-page frontispiece. Black cloth, blind embossed borders on sides, title in gilt on backstrip.

Ref.: Bradford 5850; Moffit 402; Mott (*Iowa*) p. 55

4659   WILKIE, FRANC B.

THE IOWA FIRST. LETTERS FROM THE WAR . . .
DUBUQUE: PRINTED AT THE HERALD BOOK AND JOB
ESTABLISHMENT, 1861.

[1]–114. 21.7 x 13.7 cm. Blue printed wrappers
with title on front cover.
   Prov.: Rubber stamped name, De Los W.
Guyot / twice on front wrapper both crossed
out. Inscribed in manuscript: [double rule] /
J. A Woods / Politeness of a / member of the /
[printed line:] "The Iowa First." / [decorative
rule] / [manuscript double rule] /.
   Ref.: Howes W422
   Pages [54]–60: "the first [and last] issue of
'Our Whole Union, or Missouri Valley Register,' Edited and Published by a Squad of Printers of the First Regiment of Iowa Volunteers,
while encamped at Macon City, Missouri."
   These thirty-two letters, written April 24
through August 10, 1861, by Wilkie, the only
regular correspondent to accompany the First
Iowa Regiment, originally appeared in the Dubuque *Herald.*—EDG

4660   WILKIE, FRANC B.

THE SAME.
20.6 x 13.4 cm. Contemporary half leather.

4661   WILKINS, BEN C.

CRUISE OF THE "LITTLE NAN;" FIVE HUNDRED
MILES DOWN THE MISSISSIPPI RIVER . . . HURON,
DAKOTA: HURONITE PUBLISHING HOUSE, 1886.

[1]–88, [89 note, 90–92 blank]. (Page [1] blank,
page [2] frontispiece.) 15.1 x 11.6 cm. Nine illustrations and three vignettes. Printed pictorial
wrappers with title on front wrapper. In a black
half leather case.
   Ref.: Howes W424
   According to an introductory note, the first
edition, printed five years earlier was produced
from a small hand press for friends and was a
limited edition.
   Editions: Huron, 1881.

4662   WILKINS, JOHN

AUTOGRAPH LETTER, SIGNED. 1770 July 28, Fort
Chartres. One page, 24.1 x 18.6 cm. To James
Rumsey.
   Regarding the quality of whiskey left at Fort
Chartres by a Mr. Bradley. Wilkins was then
British commandant at Fort Chartres in the
Illinois Country.
   Laid in Buttricke, George: *Affairs at Fort
Chartres,* 1768–1781 . . . 1864.

4663   WILKINSON, JAMES

AUTOGRAPH LETTER, SIGNED. 1791 April 15,
Frankfort in Kentucky. Three pages, 18.3 x 15
cm. To Philip Nolan.
   A fascinating letter about credit and the sale
of tobacco. There are two postscripts signed
with initials and one unsigned postscript. The
last phrase in the letter reads: Be extremely
cautious how you write to me.

4664   WILKINSON, JAMES

AUTOGRAPH LETTER, SIGNED "Your—Big Boned
Friend." 1800 August 28, Washington. Three
pages, 25 x 20.1 cm. To Jonathan Williams.
   A rather coyly expressed invitation to Williams to assume that a military appointment to
be offered was initiated by Wilkinson. The following year, Williams was appointed by Jefferson as Inspector of Fortifications. He later became Superintendent at West Point. The letter is
undated, but the stamped postmark of August 28
appears on the fourth page.

4665   WILKINSON, JAMES

AUTOGRAPH LETTER, RETAINED COPY. 1806 May
6, St. Louis. Three pages, 32.6 x 20 cm. Silked.
To Colonel Thomas H. Cushing.
   Letter of instruction regarding his appointment as commandant of the military establishments west of the Mississippi River. Cushing
was to be stationed at Natchitoches.

4666   WILKINSON, JAMES

LETTER, RETAINED COPY. 1806 May 8, St. Louis.
32.4 x 20.2 cm. Silked. To Colonel Thomas H.
Cushing.
   Further instructions following his letter of
May 6. There are a few corrections in Wilkin-
son's hand. The letter is signed with initials:
J: W: / but not in Wilkinson's hand.

4667   WILKINSON, JAMES

EXTRACT OF A LETTER. 1806 September 8,
Natchez. Four pages, 26.3 x 20.8 cm. Silked. To
Henry Dearborn.
   Outline of plans to counter Spanish plans in
the Southwest.

4668   WILKINSON, JAMES

AUTOGRAPH MEMORANDUM. No place, no date.
One page, 32.1 x 19.4 cm. Silked.
   Wilkinson's copy of part of the cypher used
for the Burr-Wilkinson correspondence. According to an unsigned note by Wilkinson on the
verso, the explanation of the cypher was written by Captain Campbell Smith in 1794–96
when he was acting as Wilkinson's aide-de-

camp. To the original memorandum, Wilkinson added a cypher for the alphabet and numbers for himself and Burr. On the verso, Wilkinson's docket appears: 5 / Memo—to be / kept carefully— / — W /.

4669 WILKINSON, JAMES

MEMOIRS OF GENERAL WILKINSON. VOLUME II. WASHINGTON CITY: PRINTED FOR THE AUTHOR, 1811.

[*]¹, [**]², a–b⁴, [1]²⁺¹, 2–12⁴, 13², 1–17⁴. [i–iv], [1]–136. 23.2 to 22.8 x 14.7 to 13.1 cm. Gray boards, white paper backstrip discolored to tan, white printed paper label, 3.1 x 2.2 cm., uncut. In a brown cloth case.

Ref.: Howes W428; Sabin 104028

The following title-page appears after the general title: Burr's Conspiracy / Exposed: / and / General Wilkinson / Vindicated / against the Slanders of his Enemies / on that / Important Occasion. / [short thick and thin rules] / 1811. /

Autograph Letter signed by Thomas Power laid in.

Editions: Washington, 1810.

4670 WILKINSON, JAMES

MEMOIRS OF MY OWN TIMES . . . PHILADELPHIA: PRINTED BY ABRAHAM SMALL, 1816.

[a*]–b*⁴, A–5P⁴, (A)–(E)⁴, (F)². [i]–[xvi, xvi blank], [1]–855, [856 blank]. [1–44]. [*]², A–4C⁴, 4D², (A)–(Ii)⁴, (Kk)². [i–iv], [1]–578, [579–80 blank]. [1–260]. [*]², A–3Q⁴, (A)–(G)⁴. [i–iv], [1]–496, [1–62 (63–4 blank)]. 22.4 x 14 cm. Three facsimiles, ten tables, and Atlas described below. Three volumes, gray boards, white paper backs, with two original printed white paper labels, 5.4 x 5.9 cm.: Wilkinson's / Memoirs. / [thick and thin rules] / Vol. II [–III]. / [ornamental band at top and foot], uncut. Two volumes rebacked.

Prov.: Broadside "Conditions and Regulations of the Library of the Woburn Young Men's Society" on inner front cover of each volume, with additional oval label. Signature of W. R. Cutter in each volume.

Ref.: Howes W429; Sabin 104029; Shaw & Shoemaker 39822

Atlas: Diagram and Plans, / Illustrative / of the / Principal Battles and Military Affairs, / Treated of in / Memoirs of My Own Times. / [thick and thin rules] / By James Wilkinson, / Late a Major General in the Service of the United States. / [thin and thick rules] / Philadelphia: / Printed by Abraham Small. / 1816. / [*]⁴. [1–8 (2, 4, 5, 7 blank)]. 28.5 x 22.5 cm. 19 maps and plans: Sketch of the / Rivers Sᵗ Law-

rence / and Soriel, / from their confluence, up to / Laprarie & Sᵗ Johns. / [upper left:] Vol. I. Page 56. / [upper right:] Nº I / [lower right:] H. S. Tanner / 11.1 x 19.3 cm. Scale: about 2 1/2 leagues to one inch. [2] Sketch of / Trenton / as it was / Decʳ 26ᵗʰ 1776. / [dash] / [upper left:] Vol. I. Page 128. / [upper right:] Nº 2 / [lower right:] H. S. Tanner /. 11 x 20.4 cm. Scale: 1000 yards to one inch. [3] Part of / New Jersey, / embracing Trenton & Princeton; to exhibit the operations of the / American & British Armies, / Janʸ 1ˢᵗ 2ⁿᵈ & 3ʳᵈ 1777 with / Genˡ Washington's / previus[!] movements, against the Hessians, under / Colˡ Rahl, at Trenton, / Decʳ 25ᵗʰ & 26ᵗʰ 1776. / [upper left:] Vol. I Pages 134 / [upper right:] Nº 3, 4, 5 / 33.8 x 33.6 cm. Scale: One mile to one inch. [4] Affair of / Princeton / January 3ʳᵈ 1777. / [upper left:] Page 141 / [upper right:] Nº 6 / [lower right:] H. S. Tanner / 21.3 x 15.8 cm. Scale: 20 chains to one inch. [5] Part / of the / River Sᵗ Lawrence / [upper left:] Vol. III. Page 187 / [upper right:] Nº 7 / [lower right:] H. S. Tanner / 10.8 x 19.4 cm. Scale: one mile to one inch. [6] Sketch of the / Sᵗ Lawrence / from Cornwall to Grand River. / [upper left:] Vol. III. Page 361. / [upper right:] Nº 8 / [lower right:] H. S. Tanner / 11.7 x 15.9 cm. Scale: 10 miles to one inch. Accompanied by a leaf headed: Explanation of the Diagram, No. VIII. [7] Disposition of the / American Troops / on the 30ᵗʰ March 1814, before / La Cole Mill; / a stone Building, 60 by 40 feet, 3 stories / high, Cannon proof, fortified / and Garrisoned with 600 Men. / [double rule] / [upper left:] Vol. III. Page 432 / [upper right:] Nº 9 / [lower right:] H. S. Tanner / 11.2 x 18.8 cm. Scale not indicated. [8] Sackets Harbor / [upper right:] Nº 10 / 11.1 x 22.7 cm. Scale: about 550 yards to one inch. [9] [Plan of the engagement on the Niagara River, July 4, 1814] [upper left:] Vol. I. / [upper right:] Nº 11 /. 15.4 x 10.7 cm. Scale: about 400 yards to one inch. [10] Battle of / Bridgewater / View 1ˢᵗ / [upper left:] Vol. I. / Nº 12. / 25.5 x 16.8 cm. Scale: 200 yards to one inch. [11] Battle of / Bridgewater / View 2ⁿᵈ / [upper left:] Vol. I. / [upper right:] Nº 13. / 25 x 16.5 cm. Scale: 200 yards to one inch. [12] Battle of / Bridgewater / View 3ʳᵈ / [upper left:] Vol. I / [upper right:] Nº 14 /. 25.3 x 16.5 cm. Scale: 200 yards to one inch. [13] Battle of / Bridgewater / View 4ᵗʰ / [upper left:] Vol. I / [upper right:] Nº a 14 / 25.1 x 16.7 cm. Scale: 200 yards to one inch. [14] Map / of the / Straights of Niagara / from Lake Erie to Lake Ontario. / [upper right:] Nº 15 /. 38.4 x 18 cm. Scale: 2 miles to one inch. *Inset:* Vertical Section of the great slope which occasions the Falls. / 5.3 x 17.1 cm. Scale: one mile to one inch. [15] Map of Maj: Gen: Ross's route, with the British Column, from Benedict, on the Patuxent River, to the City of Washington, August 1814. / Nº 16. / 34.5 x 40.1 cm. Scale: 2 1/2 miles to one inch. Title appears above neat line in upper margin. [16] The Affair of / Bladensburg / August 24.ᵗʰ 1814. / [upper right:] Nº 17. / 15.5 x 18 cm. Scale: 500 yards to one inch. Accompanied by a leaf headed: Explanation of the Diagram, No. XVII. [17] [White Marsh to Philadelphia] [upper right:] Nº 18 / [upper left:] Vol. /. 15.7 x 11.1 cm. Scale: about 2 1/3 miles to one inch. [18] Plan of / Rouses Point / at the foot of / Lake Champlain. / [double rule] / [upper left:] Vol. III. Page 225. / [upper right:] N.º 19. / [lower right:] H. S. Tanner /. 19.1 x 11 cm. Scale: 400 yards to one inch. [19] Part of / Vermont / [upper left:] Vol. III, Page 495. / [upper right:] Nº 20. / [lower right:] H. S. Tanner /. 19.1 x 11.6 cm. Scale: about 1 1/2 miles to an inch. Tan boards, uncut.

Prov.: Signatures on title-page: T. Sedgwick / Susan A. L. Sedgwick /.

Wilkinson's *Memoirs* is one of the most difficult books of the early nineteenth century to use as source material. The author's style is "turgid and confused" and he is far from impartial, yet the work must be used for any clear knowledge of the period and of the events with which Wilkinson was involved. Every statement he makes, and every letter he quotes, must be checked and rechecked for accuracy.

4671 WILLCOX, O. B.

[Wrapper title] ANNUAL REPORT . . . DEPARTMENT OF ARIZONA, FOR 1878–79. WHIPPLE BARRACKS, PRESCOTT, 1879.

[1]–[9], [10 blank]. 19.8 x 12.4 cm. White printed wrappers with title on front wrapper.

Ref.:

Pages [7–9] comprise Brief of Scouts / Made in the / Department of Arizona, / during the Fiscal Year, 1878–79. /

4672 WILLCOX, O. B.

[Wrapper title] ANNUAL REPORT . . . DEPARTMENT OF ARIZONA, FOR THE YEAR 1881–82. WHIPPLE BARRACKS, PRESCOTT, A. T.: OFFICE OF THE ASSISTANT ADJUTANT GENERAL, 1882.

[1]–17, [18 blank]. 20 x 12.6 cm. White printed wrappers with title on front wrapper. Removed from bound volume. Lacks back wrapper.

Prov.: In red ink at foot of wrapper title: Col. A. G. Bruckett. / 3d. Cav. / [Probably not signed by Bruckett but for him.]

Ref.:

Printed at Prescott.

The Report contains descriptions of actions against the Indians of New Mexico and Arizona, principally against the bands of Loco and Nantia-tish. Geronimo was present at several engagements, but is not mentioned.

4673 WILLCOX, R. N.

REMINISCENCES. OF CALIFORNIA LIFE . . . AVERY, OHIO: WILLCOX PRINT, 1897.

[i–ii], [1]–290. 21 x 13.7 cm. Half-tone portrait with caption mounted on blank leaf preceding title-page. (Howes believes this was printed about 1901.) Black cloth, title stamped in gilt on backstrip.

Ref.: Cowan p. 684; Howes W436

4674 WILLIAMS, ALBERT

A PIONEER PASTORATE . . . SAN FRANCISCO: BACON & COMPANY, 1882.

[i]–xvi, [1]–255, [256 blank]. 21 x 13.8 cm. Portrait. Green cloth, black decorative bands on sides, title stamped in gilt on backstrip.

Prov.: Inscribed on front fly-leaf: Rev. Eldridge Mix D. D. / with respects / Albert Williams / West Orange / 18 Sept. 1890 /.

Ref.: Cowan p. 686

Second Edition, with an added chapter.

Editions: San Francisco, 1879.

4675 WILLIAMS, C. M.

[Wrapper title] THE EXPERIENCE OF A MAIL CARRIER IN A DAKOTA BLIZZARD . . . KANSAS CITY, MO., RIGBY-RAMEY PRINTING CO.

[1–8]. 14.7 x 10.4 cm. Pink printed wrappers with title on front wrapper and two vignette portraits on verso of back wrapper.

Ref.:

No date of publication is given, nor obtainable from the text.

Williams says he was on the road without sleep for 103 hours, on a mail route from Fort Thompson to Wessington Springs, in a blizzard. As a result, he lost both legs below the knees.

4676 WILLIAMS, ELLEN

THREE YEARS AND A HALF IN THE ARMY; OR, HISTORY OF THE SECOND COLORADOS . . . NEW YORK: PUBLISHED FOR THE AUTHOR BY FOWLER & WELLS COMPANY.

[i–iv, iv blank], [1]–178, [1]–8 advertisements. 18.5 x 12.4 cm. Portrait. Scarlet pictorial cloth, title on front cover and backstrip.

Ref.: Howes W452; Nicholson p. 928; Wilcox p. 124

Copyrighted 1885.

4677 WILLIAMS, HENRY L.

"BUFFALO BILL" (THE HON. WILLIAM F. CODY) RIFLE AND REVOLVER SHOT; PONY EXPRESS RIDER; TEAMSTER; BUFFALO HUNTER; GUIDE AND SCOUT . . . LONDON: GEORGE ROUTLEDGE AND SONS, 1887.

[i]–vi, [7]–192. 21.3 x 14 cm. Frontispiece portrait. Pictorial wrappers printed in color, text on front wrapper, advertisements on verso of front and recto and verso of back wrapper. In a red buckram case.

Ref.: Howes W454

4678 WILLIAMS, JESSE

A DESCRIPTION OF THE UNITED STATES LANDS OF IOWA: BEING A MINUTE DESCRIPTION OF EVERY SECTION AND QUARTER SECTION . . . NEW-YORK: PUBLISHED BY J. H. COLTON, 1840.

[1]–180, [i advertisement, ii–iv blank]. 15 x 9.8 cm. Map: Map / Of the Surveyed part of / Iowa; / Exhibiting the Sections, Townships & Ranges / Compiled from the United States Surveys / By Jesse Williams, / Late a Clerk in the Surveyor General's Office, Cincinnati. / [rule] / Scale of 6 miles to the inch. / [rule] / New York / Published by J. H. Colton / 1840 /. [lower centre:] Engraved by / Sherman & Smith / New York. / [below border:] Entered according to Act of Congress, in the year 1840, by J. H. Colton, in the Clerk's Office of the District Court of the Southern District of New York. / 81 x 52.9 cm. Scale as above. *Inset:* Map of / Rock Island Rapids / Of the Mississippi River. / [rule] / Scale 2 miles to an Inch. / [rule] / 10.8 x 20.4 cm. Scale as above. *Inset:* Map of / Des Moines Rapids / of the Mississippi River. / 18 x 10.2 cm. Scale: two miles to one inch. Green cloth, blind embossed borders on sides, with title in gilt on front cover.

Ref.: Howes W459; Mott (*Iowa*) p. 61; Sabin 104241

4679 WILLIAMS, JOHN G.

THE ADVENTURES OF A SEVENTEEN-YEAR-OLD LAD AND THE FORTUNES HE MIGHT HAVE WON . . . BOSTON: PRINTED FOR THE AUTHOR BY THE COLLINS PRESS, 1894.

[i]–x, [11]–308. 23.2 x 15.2 cm. Illustrations unlisted. Dark red cloth, title in gilt on front cover and on backstrip.

Prov.: Inscribed on front endleaf: Dr. A. C. Posey / Compliments of / J. G. Williams / 37 Sever St. / Charlestown / Mass. /

Ref.: Cowan p. 687; Howes W465

Williams came to California in 1849. Pages 174–308 are devoted to his experiences here.—Cowan

Williams also mined in the Fraser River district.

4680 WILLIAMS, JOHN R.

BIOGRAPHICAL SKETCH OF THE LIFE OF WILLIAM G. GREENE OF MENARD COUNTY, ILL. . . . PUBLISHED BY W. R. BRINK & CO., 1874.

1–18. 19.8 x 14.8 cm. Three portraits. Green cloth, title in gilt on front cover.

Prov.: Signature of E. M. Haines on front fly-leaf.

Ref.:

Place of publication not given.

Haines was a prominent Illinois politician and historian.

4681 WILLIAMS, JOHN S., *Editor*

[Wrapper title] THE AMERICAN PIONEER, A MONTHLY PERIODICAL . . . CINCINNATI, O.: EDITED AND PUBLISHED BY JOHN S. WILLIAMS, 1842.

[1]–48. 26.2 x 14.7 cm. Four gatherings, in original folded sheets, uncut, unopened, laid in printed white wrappers, with title on front wrapper.

Ref.: Howes W469

No other copy of the first part of Volume II has been found with the date 1842.

As a repository of material on the Ohio valley pioneer events ranks with Craig's *Olden Time.*—Howes

4682 WILLIAMS, JOSEPH

NARRATIVE OF A TOUR FROM THE STATE OF INDIANA TO THE OREGON TERRITORY, IN THE YEARS 1841–2 . . . CINCINNATI: PRINTED FOR THE AUTHOR, 1843.

[1]–48. 21.2 x 12.8 cm. Rebound in new calf. In a light brown cloth case.

Ref.: Bradford 5887; Howes W471; Sabin 104304; Wagner-Camp 105

Account of the 1841 overland expedition, the first to be made by actual settlers. His return in 1842 was over the southern route via Taos and Bent's Fort.—Howes

4683 WILLIAMS, LOREN L.

AUTOGRAPH MANUSCRIPT JOURNALS, SIGNED. 1851 to 1880, various places. Five volumes (973 pages), folio, blue lined paper, black leather backstrips, leather corners and marbled board sides. Considerably worn.

An extraordinarily interesting journal of pioneer life in Oregon, Washington, Idaho, and Montana.

The first volume, entitled: Early Reminiscences of South / Western Oregon. By L. L. Williams /, is a narrative of Williams' earliest years in Oregon including an account of his seven and one-half years of ill health as the result of an Indian arrow imbedded in his abdomen. The battle in which he was wounded is vividly described. Inserted in this volume, as in the other volumes, are numerous printed and manuscript materials relating to Williams' career as hunter, surveyor, county clerk, homesteader, captain in the Oregon Volunteers, traveler, guide, lumberman, etc.

Volume I contains the following inserted materials:

Broadside: In Memoriam. / . . . This is a set of memorial resolutions on the death of L. L. Williams by his I. O. O. F. Lodge.

Manuscript: Lettered manuscript headed: Family Record / [1868?] no place. One page, 30.3 x 40.3 cm. Apparently compiled and lettered by L. L. Williams. The last date used in the record is December 21, 1868, the date of the death of Xury Williams, father of Loren L.

Map: [Survey of Cape Blanco.] 24.8 x 17.5 cm. Manuscript. Surveyed in 1857.

Prints, newspaper clippings, printed illustrations: Throughout the five volumes there are inserted numerous (hundreds) of pieces relating to the text. In only a few instances will these be noted further.

Map: [Survey of the Port Orford area.] 39.5 x 24.8 cm. Manuscript. Surveyed in 1857.

Map: [Survey of the area near the mouth of the Rogue River.] 39.4 x 24.8 cm. Manuscript.

Map: [Survey of the area near the mouth of the Coquille River.] 37.8 x 24.3 cm. Manuscript.

Drawing: This is it. Full size, as it appeared after it worked out /. [Drawing of an Indian arrowhead and part of shaft.] 24.7 x 16 cm.

Map: [Survey of Entrance to Coose[!] Bay.] 39 x 24.8 cm. Manuscript. Surveyed in 1857.

Manuscript: Document signed by B. J. Burns, S. F. Chadwick, John Nicholson, and by or for 39 others. 1851, December 23, Scottsburg, Oregon.

Map: [Survey of Umpqua River near Scottsburg.] 24.8 x 39.4 cm. Manuscript. Surveyed in 1856.

Volume II: Covers the years 1859 to 1862 and includes several trips into the back country, surveying expeditions, a cattle drive, etc.

Map: [Section of the Des Chutes River.] 24.8 x 17 cm. Manuscript. To illustrate an escape from the Indians.

Also, included in the text are sketch maps, a view of Mt. St. Hellens, etc.

Five printed and manuscript county warrants for Douglas County, Oregon, 1862 April 8 to 1866 May 23, Roseburg, Oregon.

Volume III: Covers the years 1862 to January 6, 1866 and includes exploratory trips, trouble with Indians, enlistment in the Oregon Volunteers as captain, service in the field, etc.

Map: [Photograph, tinted, of] Map / of / Umpqua County / 1863 / L. L. W. [within a decorative frame] 12.6 x 19.6 cm., on a cardboard mount 15 x 22.2 cm.

Printed and manuscript receipt by Lord & Peters, 1863 July 10, Oakland.

Manuscript: Manuscript received by R. H. Dearborn, 1863 April 1.

Manuscript: Autograph Letter signed by Xury Williams. 1864 July 26.

Broadside: Instructions to Enrolling Officers . . . Filled in in manuscript for 1st District, Oregon, September 21, 1863.

Manuscript: Autograph Letter, signed by A. A. Skinner. 1865 January 10.

Manuscript: Autograph Letter, signed by Jesse Applegate. 1865 January 12.

Manuscript: Autograph Letter, signed by Xury Williams. 1864 October 16.

Leaflet: General Orders, No. 2 . . . War Department, / Adjutant General's Office, / Washington, January 7, 1865.

Broadside: General Orders, / No. 24 . . . War Department, / Adjutant General's Office, / Washington, February 21, 1865.

Broadside: Head-Quarters, District of Oregon, Fort Vancouver, W. T., March 24th, 1865. General Orders, No. 14 . . .

Commission: Printed and manuscript document, signed by Addison C. Gibbs, Governor of Oregon, and James E. May and Cyrus A. Reed. 1865 March 4, Salem, Oregon. Williams' commission as captain in the First Regiment of the Oregon Infantry.

Manuscript: Autograph manuscript, unsigned, of a four-line stanza. 10.8 x 20.2 cm. With small pen sketch in upper left corner. Writer unidentified. Docketed on back: Received February 15—1865 / Roseburg Ogn [small bracket] L L W /.

Manuscript: Document, signed by F. B. White. 1865 May 1.

Manuscript: Document, signed by Charles Hobart for F. B. White. 1865 April 26.

Broadside: General Orders, / No. 67 . . . War Department, / Adjutant General's Office, / Washington, April 16, 1865. /

Broadside: General Orders, / No. 3 . . . War Department, / Adjutant General's Office, / Washington, January 14, 1865. /

Broadside: General Orders, / No. 4 . . . War Department, / Adjutant General's Office, / Washington, January 16, 1865.

Broadside: General Orders, / No. 60 . . . War Department, / Adjutant General's Office, / Washington, April 7, 1865.

Broadside: Head Quarters Department of Pacific, / San Francisco, Cal., March 7, 1865. / General Orders, / No. 15 . . .

Broadside: Head Quarters Department of Pacific, / San Francisco, Cal., April 20, 1865. / General Orders, / No. 28 . . .

Broadside: Head Quarters, Department of the Columbia, / Fort Vancouver, W. T., February 24, 1866 . . . General Orders, No. 4 . . .

Broadside: General Orders, / No. 101. War Department, / Adjutant General's Office, / Washington, May 30, 1865.

Map: Route of Scouting Expedition N*o*. 1 / Consisting of 40 men of 1$\underline{st}$ *Ogn. Cav.* Co. "G" / and 40 men of C*o*. "H" 1$\underline{st}_{''}$ Ogn *Infy.* / from May 23$\underline{d}$ to June 6$\underline{st}$[!] 1865 / 39 x 31.7 cm. Scale: four miles to one inch. Manuscript.

Broadside: General Orders, / No. 108. War Department, / Adjutant General's Office, / Washington, D. C., June 2, 1865.

Manuscript: Document (copy). 1865 June 15, War Department, Adjutant General's Office, Washington, D. C.

Map: Scout N^o· 2 / By / Company "H" / From June 14 to June 25$\underline{th}$ 1865 /. 30.7 x 37.9 cm. Scale: four miles to one inch. Manuscript.

Map: [Scout No. 3 commencing Aug. 1, 1865]. 42.3 x 33.7 cm. (paper size). No scale given. Manuscript, unfinished?

Manuscript: Autograph Letter, signed by Mineeba Callison. 1865 August 2.

Manuscript: Autograph Document, signed by L. L. Williams. 1865 September 1, Hd Qrs Silvies River Expedition / In the Field (Head of Beaver Creek) . . . / One page, 15.5 x 20 cm. General Order No. 1.

Manuscript: Autograph Document, signed by L. L. Williams. 1865 Sept. 2 Hd Qrs Silvies River Expedition / In the field, head of Beaver Creek Ogn . . . / Two pages, 31.2 x 20 cm. General Order No. 2.

Map: Diagram / of / Route from Camp Dahlgreen to Indian Springs /. 40.5 x 31.7 cm. Scale: four miles to one inch. Manuscript.

Map: Diagram / of / Route from Indian Springs to Camp Wright /. 32 x 39.7 cm. Scale: four miles to one inch. Manuscript.

Manuscript: Document, signed by W. J. Sanborn. 1865 September 20. Headquarters Department of the Columbia, Fort Vancouver, W. T.

Map: [Plan of] Camp Wright / Oregon / — 1865 66 /. 31.1 x 38.8 cm. (neat line). Scale: 25 feet to one inch. Manuscript.

Manuscript: Autograph Document, signed by Capt. Williams. 1865 Oct. 5, Hd Qrs Silvies River Expedition / Camp on Silvies River, Ogn . . . / One page, 23.5 x 19.2 cm. General Order No. 4.

Manuscript: Autograph Document, signed by Capt. Williams. 1866[!] Oct. 5, place as in preceding. One page, 23.5 x 19.2 cm. General Order No. 5.

Manuscript: Autograph Document, signed by Capt. Williams. 1865 Oct. 6, Camp Wright, Oregon. Four pages, 30.3 x 19.8 cm. General Order No. 7.

Manuscript: Autograph Document, signed by Capt. Williams. 1865 Oct. 20, place as in preceding. Two pages, 30 x 18.8 cm. General Order No. 9.

Manuscript: Autograph Document, signed by Capt. Williams. One page, 31.2 x 20 cm. 1865 Oct. 20, Camp Wright, Oregon. Special Order No. 10.

Map: [Route of scout, Nov. 7 to 23, 1865]. 32.2 x 40.8 cm. Scale: four miles to one inch. Manuscript.

Manuscript: Autograph Letter, signed by Capt. Williams. 1865 Nov. 13, Camp Wright, Ore. One page, 24.9 x 20 cm. To the commanding officer at Fort Vancouver. Recommending the use of bloodhounds in tracking "renegade Indians."

Manuscript: Document, signed by W. J. Sanborn. 1865 December 1.

Manuscript: Document, signed by Charles S. Lovell. 1865 December 1.

Map: Scout / From Camp Wright Oregon / to / Middle and South forks of Malheur River / . . . 39 x 32 cm. Scale: four miles to one inch. Manuscript.

Manuscript: Autograph Document, signed by Capt. Williams. Two pages, 31.1 x 19.8 cm. 1865 December 28, Camp Wright, Ore. General Orders No. 15.

Volume IV covers the period January 7, 1866 to November 9, 1875 and contains the following inserted materials:

Manuscript: Autograph Letter, signed (copy) by Capt. Williams. 1876 July 22, Roseburg, Ore. Twelve pages, 24.8 x 19.7 cm. To his nephew. Describing a trip to the Yellowstone River country.

Map: Diagram / of / Oregon. / 46.3 x 60.2 cm. No scale indicated. An extremely interesting map partially printed and partially in manuscript by Williams.

Manuscript: Autograph Manuscript, signed by Capt. Williams. 1866 February 20, Camp Wright, Ore. Three pages, 31.2 x 19.8 cm. Proceedings of a Council of Administration convened at Camp Wright . . .

Manuscript: Document, signed by Simeon Francis. 1866 July 16.

Manuscript: Autograph Letter, signed (copy) by Capt. Williams. 1866 October 16, Roseburg, Ore. One page, 24.7 x 19.8 cm. To the Adjutant General, Washington, D.C.

Map: [two maps on one sheet] [1:] Diagram of Harney Lake Ford . . . / 31.8 x 24 cm. Scale: about 60 feet to one inch. [2:] Diagram of Scout to S. side of Harney Lake . . . / 31.8 x 16.5 cm. Scale: four miles to one inch.

Manuscript: Autograph Document, signed by Capt. Williams. 1866 February 8, Camp Wright. Four pages, 31.2 x 19.8 cm. Orders No. 11.

Broadside: Head Quarters Military Division of the Pacific, / San Francisco, Cal., February 28, 1866. / General Orders, / No. 7.

Manuscript: Document, signed (copy of extract) by D. W. Applegate for W. J. Sanborn. 1866 May 1.

Manuscript: Copy of a Document, signed. 1866 April 19, Washington, D. C. Special Orders No. 178 (extract).

Manuscripts: Twenty-six printed and manuscript documents (receipts, forms, returns, records, etc.) relating to Capt. Williams' accounts during his service. Various places and dates, signed by various officers.

Photograph: [Portrait of L. L. Williams.] 14.7 x 10.2 cm., mounted on card, 16.5 x 10.7 cm. Buchtel & Stolte. B. and S. Portland, Oregon. / Full-face vignette portrait, bust length, in uniform. Signed (?) in pencil.

Manuscript: Autograph Letter, signed by Xury Williams. 1867 September 3.

Manuscript: Autograph Letter, signed by Xury Williams. 1868 May 26.

Manuscript: Autograph Letter, signed by Xury Williams. 1868 May 19.

Manuscript: Autograph Letter, signed by Xury Williams. 1867 April 20.

Manuscript: Autograph Document, by L. L Williams, signed by M. M. Melvin. 1868 July 11, Roseburg, Oregon. Lists of Moneys on deposit in Clerks Office Douglas County / Oregon, and turned over by L. L. Williams County Clerk on / the 10-day of July 1868, to M. M. Melvin his successor. /

Pamphlet: Nelson's Pictorial Guide-Books. / [rule] / Salt Lake City . . . London: T. Nelson and Sons.

Map: Map of the / Pacific Railroad. / [rule] / Western P. R. R. . . . / Central P. R. R. . . . / Union P. R. R. . . .

Manuscript: Document, signed by E. L. Applegate. 1871 January 9.

Manuscript: Autograph Letter, signed by Capt. Williams (copy in pencil). 1872 Dec. 10, Roseburg, Ore. Two pages, 24.7 x 19.7 cm. To H. P. Baldwin. Covering letter for a donation to the Michigan Fire victims.

Manuscript: Autograph Letter, signed by H. P. Baldwin. 1872 January 10.

Manuscript: Autograph Manuscript, document signed by J. R. Ellison. 1872 April 16.

Broadside: Republican Ticket. July 1872 election.

Broadside: National / Republican / Ticket.

Manuscript: Autograph Letter, signed by J. H. Egan. 1873 March 1.

Manuscript: Autograph Note, signed by D. B. Denison. 1873 Nov. 25.

Manuscript: Autograph Letter, signed by L. H. Cann. 1873 December 9.

Manuscript: Autograph Letter, signed by H. H. Luse. 1873 April 28.

Telegram: Telegram from F. Sutherlin, W. Willson and others. 1874 April 15.

Manuscript: Autograph Letter, signed (copy in pencil), by Capt. Williams. 1874 April 15. One page, 21.4 x 13.2 cm. To Sutherlin, Willson and others. Refusing offer to run as candidate.

Broadside: In Memoriam. / [short broken rule] / Mary Ellen Hamblock . . .

Photograph: [Arch Rock, Mackinac, Michigan]. 15.4 x 20.4 cm. Four men are on the rock, one of them may be Capt. Williams. Labeled in manuscript by Williams.

Volume V covers the period 1875 to Oct. 16, 1880:

Broadside: Republican Ticket. [Oregon] /

Leaflet: [Roseburg (?)] Public School / [flourishes] / [ornament] Entertainment [ornament] / [flourish] / —at— / Central School, / Friday Eve., June 23, 1876.

Broadside: Grand Dramatic / and / Musical Concert! / Benefit of Junction City Church.

The volume contains a large number of newspaper clippings relating to Indian troubles, including the Modoc War, etc.

Scattered through the last three volumes are several newspaper clippings of articles by Capt. Williams. Probably the most interesting and important is a series of three about the Yellowstone Park waterworks.

4684 WILLIAMS, JOSEPH S.

OLD TIMES IN WEST TENNESSEE . . . MEMPHIS, TENN.: W. G. CHEENEY, PRINTER AND PUBLISHER, 1873.

[1]–6, [1]–4, [7]–295, [296 blank]. 18.9 x 12 cm. Dark blue cloth.

Ref.: Howes W472

The collation given by DLC is: 2 p. l., 295 p.

4685 WILLIAMS, MARY ANN BARNES

PIONEER DAYS OF WASHBURN, N. DAK. AND VICINITY . . .

[i–iv], 1–120. 20.7 x 14.9 cm. Illustrations and text illustrations unlisted. White printed wrappers.

Prov.: Inscribed on verso of front wrapper: June 15–'38 / To Cousin Louise / Nourse / Compliments of the Author / — /

Ref.: Howes W474

Copyrighted Dec. 1936. Published by Washburn Leader, Washburn, N. D.

Of particular value are sections on Fort Stevenson, 1867–83, and mail carrying through Washburn in the Eighties.

4686 WILLIAMS, R. H.

WITH THE BORDER RUFFIANS. MEMORIES OF THE FAR WEST 1852—1868 . . . NEW YORK: E. P. DUTTON AND COMPANY, 1907.*

[i]–xviii, [1]–478. 21.6 x 14 cm. Six illustrations listed. Red pictorial cloth, gilt top, uncut.

Ref.: Adams 1099; Howes W475

After a lurid frontier apprenticeship in Kansas, this young Englishman ranched in Western Texas and served with the Rangers.—Howes

Editions: London, 1907.

4687 WILLIAMS, WELLINGTON

THE TRAVELLER'S AND TOURIST'S GUIDE THROUGH THE UNITED STATES OF AMERICA, CANADA, ETC. CONTAINING THE ROUTES OF TRAVEL BY STEAMBOAT, STAGE AND CANAL . . . PHILADELPHIA: LIPPINCOTT, GRAMBO & CO., MDCCCLI.

[i]–iv, [5]–216, 1–20. 14.1 x 9 cm. Map: A New Map / of the / United States. / Upon which are Delineated its Vast Works of / Internal communication, / Routes across the Continent &c. / Showing also / Canada / and the / Island of Cuba. / By W. Williams. / Philadelphia. / Published by Lippincott, Grambo & Co. No. 14 N.

Fourth S^t / 1851. / Scale of Miles / [diagrammatic scale: about 65 miles to an inch.] / [lower left:] Entered, according to Act of Congress, in the year 1851, by W. Williams in the Clerk's Office of the District Court of the Eastern District of Pennsylvania. / 61.8 x 74.8 cm. Scale as above. *Inset:* Map of the / Niagara River / and / Falls. / 9.4 x 8.6 cm. No scale given. *Inset:* City & Harbor / of / Havana. / 7.8 x 6.4 cm. No scale given. *Inset:* Map of the / Island of Cuba. / Scale of Miles. / [diagrammatic scale] /. 7.6 x 23.1 cm. Scale: about 78 miles to an inch. *Inset:* Map of / California, / Oregon, / New Mexico, / Utah &c. / 26.8 x 23.2 cm. Scale: about 140 miles to an inch. Brown leather, front cover with pictorial design in gilt, including title, same on back cover in blind, text attached at inner edge and with front endpaper to front cover, backstrip of pamphlet and last leaf protected by marbled paper wrapper, map attached to inner back cover.

Ref.: Clark III, 434; Sabin 104392 see; Wheat (*Gold Region*) 235; Wheat (*Transmississippi*) 769

The map described by Wheat is dated 1852, but copyrighted 1851.

4688 WILLIAMS, W. H.

MANITOBA AND THE NORTH-WEST; JOURNAL OF A TRIP FROM TORONTO TO THE ROCKY MOUNTAINS . . . TORONTO: HUNTER, ROSE & COMPANY, 1882.

[i]–xi, [xii blank], [9]–258. 22.1 x 14.4 cm. Gray printed wrappers, with title on front wrapper.

Ref.: Peel 495

Accompanied the Marquess of Lorne's party.

4689 WILLIAMS, WILLIAM

JOURNAL OF THE LIFE, TRAVELS, AND GOSPEL LABOURS OF WILLIAM WILLIAMS, A MINISTER OF THE SOCIETY OF FRIENDS . . . DUBLIN: REPRINTED BY WEBB AND CHAPMAN, 1839.

[i]–[x, x blank], [1]–195, [196 blank]. 18.4 x 11 cm. Dark brown cloth.

Ref.: Howes W490; Sabin 104411

Editions: Cincinnati, 1828.

4690 WILLIAMS, XURY

AUTOGRAPH LETTER, SIGNED. 1864 July 26, Grand Blanc, Michigan. Four pages, 20.5 x 12.5 cm. To Loren L. Williams.

Inserted in Manuscript Journals of Loren L. Williams, Volume III.

4691 WILLIAMS, XURY

AUTOGRAPH LETTER, SIGNED. 1864 October 16, Grand Blanc, Michigan. Two pages, 20 x 12.4 cm. To Loren L. Williams.

Inserted in Manuscript Journals of Loren L. Williams, Volume III.

4692 WILLIAMS, XURY

AUTOGRAPH LETTER, SIGNED. 1867 September 3, Grand Blanc, Michigan. Four pages, 19.7 x 12.6 cm. To Loren L. Williams.

Family news. Inserted in Manuscript Journals of Loren L. Williams, Volume IV.

4693 WILLIAMS, XURY

AUTOGRAPH LETTER, SIGNED. 1868 May 26, Grand Blanc, Michigan. Two pages, 19.7 x 12.6 cm. To Loren L. Williams.

On the third and fourth pages there is an Autograph Letter by Mrs. Xury Williams to her step-son Loren. Inserted in Manuscript Journals of Loren L. Williams, Volume IV.

4694 WILLIAMS, XURY

AUTOGRAPH LETTER, SIGNED. 1868 May 19. No place. One page, 24.8 x 19.4 cm. To Loren L. Williams.

Note in margin by Loren L. Williams: My Fathers last Letter. / Inserted in Manuscript Journals of Loren L. Williams, Volume IV.

4695 WILLIAMS, XURY

AUTOGRAPH LETTER, SIGNED. 1867 April 20, Grand Blanc, Michigan. One page, 24.6 x 19.7 cm. To Loren L. Williams.

Inserted in Manuscript Journals of Loren L. Williams, Volume IV.

4696 WILLIAMSON, JOHN P.

ENGLISH-DAKOTA VOCABULARY. WASICUN IAPI IESKA WOWAPI . . . SANTEE AGENCY, NEB.: EDWARD R. POND, MAZAEHDE, 1871.

[i–vi, vi blank], 1–137, [138 blank]. 19 x 11.4 cm. Half blue leather, marbled sides.

Prov.: Inscribed on title-page: Gen¹ McCook / Secy Dak. Ter / With Compliments of / Editor. / and lower: Col Wᵐ M. Ferry / Compliments of Cousin Sarah /. Inside front cover: MᶜCook /

Ref.: AII (*Nebraska*) 241; Butler (*Dakota*) 153; Pilling 4154

4697 WILLIAMSON, JOHN P.

AN ENGLISH-DAKOTA SCHOOL DICTIONARY. WASICUN QA DAKOTA IESKA WOWAPI . . . YANKTON AGENCY, D. T.: IAPI OAYE PRESS, 1886.

[i–vi], [1]–144. 18.7 x 12.8 cm. Black leather backstrip and corners, black cloth sides, title in gilt up backstrip.

Ref.: Allen (*Dakota*) 476; Butler (*Dakota*) 151

One of the two Ayer copies is partly on pink paper.

Editions: Santee Agency, 1871.

4698 WILLRICH, GEORG

ERINNERUNGEN AUS TEXAS . . . LEIPZIG, VERLAG VON CHRISTIAN ERNST KOLLMANN, 1854.

[1]–173, [174 advertisement]. [1]–176. [1]–174, [175–76 advertisements]. 16.7 x 10.5 cm. Three volumes, green printed wrappers, with title on front wrappers, advertisements on versos of back wrappers, uncut. Corner of one wrapper (back) torn off affecting text. In a green cloth case.

Ref.: Howes W509; Raines p. 220

4699 WILLS, JOHN A.

[Wrapper title] CHORPENNING CASE. BEFORE THE 43D CONGRESS, 1ST SESSION. IN THE MATTER OF THE AWARD OF POSTMASTER GENERAL CRESSWELL[!] IN FAVOR OF GEORGE CHORPENNING VS. THE UNITED STATES. COULD CONGRESS LEGALLY OR CONSTITUTIONALLY REPEAL OR SET ASIDE THAT AWARD, &C.? ARGUMENT OF JOHN A. WILLS, OF COUNSEL. WASHINGTON, D. C., M'GILL & WITHEROW, PRINTERS.

[1]–40. 21.6 x 14.4 cm. Lavender printed wrappers with title on front wrapper, removed from bound volume. With other Chorpenning materials in a red cloth box.

Ref.:

Published in Washington.

Signed on page 40: John A. Wills, / Of Counsel for George Chorpenning. /

4700 [WILSON, ALEXANDER]

[Caption title] FOR THE PORT FOLIO. PARTICULARS OF THE DEATH OF CAPT. LEWIS. THE FOLLOWING LETTER, FROM THE AUTHOR OF AMERICAN ORNITHOLOGY . . .

33–48. (Text of Wilson's letter occupies 34–47.) 21 x 13.1 cm. Removed from bound volume, unbound.

Ref.:

Extracted from: The Port Folio. Vol. 7. Philadelphia: Publish'd by Bradford & Inskeep, 1811.

Wilson's letter is dated Natchez, Mississippi Ter., May 28th, 1811. It was published in the issue for January, 1812, Vol. VII, No. 1.

4701 WILSON, EDWARD

AN UNWRITTEN HISTORY. A RECORD FROM THE EXCITING DAYS OF EARLY ARIZONA . . .

[1]–[78]. 17.3 x 12.2 cm. Red cloth, stapled under cloth, red edges, rounded corners.

Prov.: Signature on front endleaf and bookplate inside front cover of E. A. Brininstool, both dated January, 1919.

Ref.: Howes W519

Uncopyrighted. Published at Phoenix in 1915.

4702 WILSON, ELIJAH N.

AMONG THE SHOSHONES . . . SALT LAKE CITY, UTAH: SKELTON PUBLISHING COMPANY.

[1]–222. 20.2 x 13.5 cm. Eight illustrations unlisted. Red cloth.

Ref.: Howes W520

Copyrighted 1910.

A good narrative of Rocky Mountain trapping. Most of the edition was suppressed according to Howes.—EDG

A two and one-half-page manuscript note starting on page 222 is dated Aug. 19, 1912. It consists of personal reminiscences by I. K. King of his experiences with "Uncle Nick."

4703 WILSON, H. T.

HISTORICAL SKETCH OF SANTA FE, NEW MEXICO . . . CHICAGO: PUBLISHED BY THE HOTEL WORLD PUBLISHING CO.

[1]–[100]. 22 x 14.9 cm. Illustrations unlisted. Gray pictorial wrappers, with title on front wrapper, advertisements on verso of front and recto of back wrapper, vignette and border on verso of back wrapper.

Ref.: Howes W523

Probable date of publication is 1880.

Pages [77–9] comprise a Business Directory of Santa Fé and pages [80–100] carry advertisements.

4704 WILSON, JAMES C.

ADDRESS ON THE OCCASION OF REMOVING THE REMAINS OF CAPTAINS WALKER AND GILLESPIE, ON THE TWENTY-FIRST OF APRIL, A. D. 1856 . . . PRINTED AT THE OFFICE OF THE SAN ANTONIO LEDGER.

[1]–18, [19–20 blank]. 21.3 x 13.5 cm. Light yellow printed wrappers with title on front wrapper. Lacks back wrapper.

Ref.: Winkler 805

Published at San Antonio in 1856.

Walker and Gillespie, both Texas Rangers, were killed fighting in Mexico. Gillespie died in Monterrey in 1846 and Walker at Huamantla, Tlaxcala. Walker was the man who helped Samuel Colt develop the "Walker Colt."

4705 WILSON, JAMES T. D.

[Map] A NEW & CORRECT / MAP [Texas star] OF / TEXAS / COMPILED FROM THE / MOST RECENT SURVEYS & AUTHORITIES TO THE YEAR / 1845 [last numeral changed in manuscript to 6] / BY JAMES T. D. WILSON. / PUBLISHED BY R. W. FISHBOURNE NEW-ORLEANS. / SCALE OF MILES. / [diagrammatic scale: 30 miles to one inch] / [lower left:] ENTERED ACCORDING TO AN ACT OF CONGRESS, IN THE YEAR 1845, BY R. W. FISHBOURNE, IN THE CLERK'S OFFICE OF THE U. S. DISTRICT COURT, DISTRICT OF LOUISIANA. / [lower right:] FISHBOURNE LITHOGRAPHER, 46, CANAL STREET, NEW ORLEANS. /

Map, 55.6 x 70.6 cm. Scale as above. Folded into board folder, 15.4 x 9.8 cm., with red roan backstrip, and printed paper label on front cover, 2.4 x 4.5 cm.

Ref.: Phillips p. 844

4706 WILSON, LYCURGUS A.

LIFE OF DAVID W. PATTEN THE FIRST APOSTOLIC MARTYR . . . COPYRIGHTED 1900. SALT LAKE CITY, UTAH: THE DESERET NEWS, 1904.

[i]–viii, [1], 72. 15.7 x 12 cm. Dark gray printed wrappers, stapled, black cloth back.

Ref.:

Patten was killed in 1838 near Far West, Missouri.

4707 WILSON, OBED G.

MY ADVENTURES IN THE SIERRAS . . . FRANKLIN, OHIO: THE EDITOR PUBLISHING CO., 1902.*

[i–ii], 1–115, [116 blank]. 18.6 x 12.5 cm. Dark red cloth.

Ref.: Cowan p. 689; Howes W533

In 1854 the author met and had a long visit with Jim Beckwourth.—EDG

4708 [WILSON, RICHARD L.]

NOTES OF A SANTA FE TOUR. CAMP SKETCHES. NO. 1 [–6]. Newspaper clippings mounted on five pages of a discarded manuscript account book, 31.6 x 20 cm., three columns per page.

Three of the articles are headed: For the Juliet Courier. / and the series is presumed to have been published in Joliet, Illinois before 1843. They are extracts from Wilson's *Short Ravelings from a Long Yarn* . . . Chicago, 1847, Chapts. I–IV. But each of the articles is signed D.

4709 WILSON, RICHARD L.

SHORT RAVELINGS FROM A LONG YARN; OR, CAMP AND MARCH SKETCHES, ON THE SANTA FE TRAIL . . . CHICAGO: GEER & WILSON, 1847.

[1]–64. 22.5 x 14.1 cm. Text illustrations. Salmon printed boards with title on front cover and advertisement on back, black roan backstrip. First two leaves in facsimile, new backstrip. In a black cloth case.

Prov.: Gift of Warren Howell and EDG to the Graff Collection, 1962.

Ref.: Byrd 1253; Howes T45; McMurtrie (*Chicago*) 128; Wagner-Camp 142

The text was prepared for the press by Benjamin F. Taylor. Wilson was on the Santa Fé

Trail with Captain Houck's party in 1841. There is an exceptionally fine account of a buffalo hunt included in the text.

4710 WILSON, VEAZIE

GUIDE TO THE YUKON GOLD FIELDS. WHERE THEY ARE AND HOW TO REACH THEM . . . SEATTLE: THE CALVERT COMPANY, 1895.

[i]–[xvi (xvi blank)], [17]–[73], [74 blank], [i–ii], 1–13 advertisements, [14 blank], [i–ii], 1–22 Juneau Business Directory. 22.1 x 14.7 cm. 27 illustrations and three maps listed. Map: V. Wilson's Map / of the / Routes to the Gold Fields / of the Yukon River. / [lower right:] Curtis & Guptil, Eng. / Seattle, Wash. / [lower left:] Copyrighted by the Calvert Co. Seattle, Wash. / 37.1 x 20.6 cm. Scale: 20 miles to an inch. Map: V. Wilson's Map / of the / Forty-Mile / Mining-District / 1895 / Yukon River / [lower left:] Copyrighted by V. Wilson. / 38.1 x 25 cm. No scale given. Map: V. Wilson's Map / of the / Birch-Creek / Mining-District / 1895 / Yukon River / [lower left:] Copyrighted by V. Wilson /. 38.2 x 24.9 cm. No scale given. Buff printed pictorial wrappers, with title on front wrapper. In a light brown cloth case.

Ref.: Howes W541; Smith 11103; Wickersham 3996

Wilson died towards the end of 1894 before this book was published. The book is based on extensive personal travel and observation. It was one of the first reliable guides to that country.—EDG

4711 [WINCHESTER, JAMES]

HISTORICAL DETAILS, HAVING RELATION TO THE CAMPAIGN OF THE NORTH-WESTERN ARMY, UNDER GENERALS HARRISON AND WINCHESTER, DURING THE WINTER OF 1812–13 . . . LEXINGTON K.: PRINTED BY WORSLEY & SMITH, 1818.

[A]–L⁴. [1]–88. 23.2 to 22 x 14.7 to 14.3 cm. Stabbed, uncut. In a brown cloth case, leather label.

Prov.: Bookplate of C. G. Littell.

Ref.: AII (*Kentucky*) 696; Bay p. 324; Howes W555; Sabin 32047, 104738

Attempt by the author to answer McAfee's allegations against his conduct at the river Raisin, etc.—Howes

4712 WINCHESTER, JAMES D.

CAPT. J. D. WINCHESTER'S EXPERIENCE ON A VOYAGE FROM LYNN, MASSACHUSETTS TO SAN FRANCISCO, CAL. AND TO THE ALASKAN GOLD FIELDS . . . SALEM, MASS.: NEWCOMB & GAUSS, PRINTERS, 1900.*

[1]–251, [252 blank]. 23.6 x 15.4 cm. 37 illustrations listed. Dark blue cloth.

Prov.: Tipped in at the front is a stiff card (6.1 x 10.2 cm.) inscribed: Please Receive this / Book With / Capt. James Daly Winchester's / Compliments /.

Ref.: Howes W556; Smith 11106; Wickersham 80

Laid in is a prospectus for the book, 21.5 x 13.7 cm., a broadside headed: Synopsis of Capt. J. D. Winchester's experience in the / Alaskan Gold Fields. / [rule] / [18 lines] / [rule] / Price $1.00. Paid on delivery of Book. /

4713 WINGET, D. H.

ANECDOTES OF BUFFALO BILL WHICH HAVE NEVER BEFORE APPEARED IN PRINT . . . CLINTON, IOWA, 1912.

[1]–224. (Pages [1–3] blank). 19 x 13.4 cm. Illustrations unlisted. Gray pictorial cloth.

Ref.: Howes W564

4714 WINSLOW, DAMON A.

HISTORY OF ST. JOSEPH, MICHIGAN . . . SINCE 1669 . . . CHICAGO: BEACH & BARNARD, 1869.

[1]–98. 15.7 x 10.6 cm. Tan printed boards with short title on front cover and advertisement on back cover, brown cloth backstrip, advertisements on inner covers. Lacks fly-leaves.

Prov.: Inscription inked in over pencil on front cover: Compliments of D. A. W. /, and with signature below: N. Bacon /.

Ref.: Howes W574

Based mainly on the recollections of pioneers.

4715 WINTHROP, THEODORE

THE CANOE AND THE SADDLE, ADVENTURES AMONG THE NORTHWESTERN RIVERS AND FORESTS; AND ISTHMIANA . . . BOSTON: TICKNOR AND FIELDS, 1863.

[i blank, ii advertisement], [1]–375, [376 blank], [1]–16 advertisements dated November 1862. 18.1 x 11.4 cm. Dark brown cloth, embossed designs on sides, title stamped in gilt on backstrip.

Ref.: Howes W584; Smith 11130

4716 WISCONSIN TERRITORY. Laws, Statutes, etc.

[Caption title] AN ACT FOR THE PARTITION OF THE HALF-BREED LANDS, & FOR OTHER PURPOSES . . .

[1]–4. 25.9 x 15.4 cm. Unbound leaflet.

Ref.:

On page 4: Approved January 16th, 1838. / Henry Dodge. /

Acts of the Legislature of Wisconsin, passed during the Winter Session of 1837–8, and the special session of June, 1838, in the city of Burlington, were printed by James G. Edwards in Burlington, Iowa in 1838. This act appears as

No. 54 on pages 101–08. This four-page leaflet is a re-set job and not just an offprint.

4717 WISCONSIN TERRITORY. Laws, Statutes, etc.

ACTS OF THE LEGISLATURE OF WISCONSIN, PASSED DURING THE WINTER SESSION OF 1837-8, AND THE SPECIAL SESSION OF JUNE, 1838, IN THE CITY OF BURLINGTON . . . BURLINGTON, IOWA: PRINTED BY JAMES G. EDWARDS, 1838.

[1]–372. 21.9 x 13.9 cm. Contemporary half sheepskin, tan board sides, red leather label.
Ref.: McMurtrie (*Wisconsin*) 14; Moffit 2

4718 WISCONSIN TERRITORY. Legislative Assembly. Council

JOURNAL OF THE COUNCIL OF THE FIRST LEGISLA-TIVE ASSEMBLY OF WISCONSIN, BEGUN AND HELD AT BELMONT, ON THE TWENTY-FIFTH DAY OF OC-TOBER, ONE THOUSAND EIGHT HUNDRED AND THIRTY-SIX. BELMONT: JAMES CLARKE, TERRI-TORIAL PRINTER, 1836.

[1]–104. 23.5 x 15.2 cm. Tan printed wrappers with title on front wrapper, uncut, unopened.
Ref.: AII (*Wisconsin*) 12; Jones 992; McMur-trie (*Wisconsin*) 7
Belmont was the first state capital.

4719 WISCONSIN TERRITORY. Legislative Assembly. House. Committee Appointed to Examine into the Condition of the Banks of the Territory

[Caption title] REPORT OF THE COMMITTEE AP-POINTED TO EXAMINE INTO THE CONDITION OF THE BANKS OF THE TERRITORY . . .

[1]–4. 32.6 x 20.2 cm. Unbound leaflet, uncut.
Ref.:
The report was also printed on pages 101 to 105 of the *Journal* of the 1837–38 Legislative Assembly preceded by the statement, under date of November 27, 1837: "Mr. Sheldon, chairman of the select committee appointed to investigate the condition of the several banks in this Territory, made the following report, which was read, and on motion of Mr. Quigley, fifty copies were or-dered to be printed."
James Clarke & Co. of Burlington, Iowa, were printers to the House in November, 1837. However, in December the question of a printer was argued several times. The 1837–38 *Journal* was printed by Charles S. Sholes of Green Bay.

4720 WISCONSIN TERRITORY. Legislative Assembly. House. Select Committee on Sale of Lots in Potosi

[Caption title] . . . REPORT OF THE SELECT COM-MITTEE TO WHOM WAS REFERRED THE REPORT OF THE COMMISSIONERS, AND OTHER PAPERS RELATIVE TO SURVEY AND SALE OF LOTS IN POTOSI . . .

[1]–16. 19.5 x 14.4 cm. Stabbed, unbound, fore-edge uncut.
Ref.: AII (*Wisconsin*) 329; McMurtrie (*Wis-consin*) 235
Printed in Madison in 1846. 5th Legislature, 1st Session.
The Receiver's Report is dated at the end on page 16: Lancaster, Grant County, W.T. Dec. 30, 1845.
The House ordered 200 copies printed.

4721 WISE, HENRY A.

[Caption title] OPINIONS OF HON. HENRY A. WISE, UPON THE CONDUCT AND CHARACTER OF JAMES K. POLK . . .

[1]–8. Bound with Number 1084.
Ref.: Sabin 104890
Printed in Washington in 1844.

4722 WISLEZENUS, FREDERICK A.

EIN AUSFLUG NACH DEN FELSEN-GEBIRGEN IM JAHRE 1839 . . . ST. LOUIS, MO.: GEDRUCKT BEI WILH. WEBER, 1840.

[1]–[126]. (Page 56 mispaginated 65.) 17.7 x 12 cm. Map: [Northwest United States, from the forks of the Platte to the Pacific and from the Arkansas River to Canada] [lower right:] on Stone engraved by Rassau & Michaud, St. Louis M.º. /. 26.8 x 43.2 cm. No scale given. Brown marbled boards, red leather label on backstrip stamped in gold, reading down: [thick and thin vertical rules] / Wislezenus Ausfl. n. d. Felsen-gebirgen. / [thin and thick vertical rules] /. In a dark gray cloth case.
Prov.: Small rubber stamp on title-page (German).
Ref.: Howes W596; Rader 3712; Sabin 104905; Wagner-Camp 83
A very rare book and one covering a very interesting period of western history.—Wagner.
The author, a St. Louis physician, traveled the Oregon trail in 1839 with a group of traders. He went to the rendezvous on the Green River, on to Fort Hall, and then returned to Missouri via North Park, Cache la Poudre, Bent's Fort, and the Santa Fé trail.

4723 WISLEZENUS, FREDERICK A.

. . . MEMOIR OF A TOUR TO NORTHERN MEXICO, CONNECTED WITH COL. DONIPHAN'S EXPEDITION, IN 1846 AND 1847 . . . WASHINGTON: TIPPIN & STREEPER, PRINTERS, 1848.*

[1]–141, [142 blank]. 22.7 x 14.4 cm. Three maps: Map: Profile of Elevations above the Level of the Sea. / [upper left:] Senate, Mis§ doc.

N⁰ 26 / [three horizontal sections: Route from Independence Mo. to Santa Fé. Route from Santa Fé to Chihuahua. Route from Chihuahua to Reynosa on the Rio Grande.] 42 x 58.5 cm. (paper size). Scale: 36 miles to one inch. Map: Geological Sketch. / [upper left:] Senate Mis⁵ doc. no. 26 /. 30.7 x 27.7 cm. No scale given. Map: Map / of a tour from Independence to / Santa Fe, Chihuahua, / Monterey and Matamoros / By A. Wislezenus, / in 1846 and 1847. / Lith. by E. Weber & Co. Balto / Explanation of signs: / [six lines] / Scale of 50 miles to one inch. / [upper left:] Senate, Mis⁵ doc. N⁰ 26 /. 49.8 x 40.4 cm. Scale as above. Removed from bound volume and inserted in a Gaylord binder, red cloth backstrip.

Ref.: Howes W597; Rader 3715; Wagner-Camp 159

30th Congress, 1st Session, Senate, Miscellaneous Document No. 26, Serial 511.

According to Wagner-Camp, the Huntington and Streeter copies have a special title-page, but it is not clear whether or not this is in place of the present title-page.

4724   WISTAR, ISAAC J.

AUTOBIOGRAPHY OF ISAAC JONES WISTAR, 1827–1905 . . . PHILADELPHIA: PRINTED BY THE WISTAR INSTITUTE OF ANATOMY AND BIOLOGY, 1914.

[i]–[x, x blank], 1–341, [342 blank]. [i]–[vi, vi blank], 1–191, [192 blank]. 28.5 x 20 cm. Eight illustrations and one map listed. Map: Accompanying / Autobiography of General Isaac J. Wistar / [short rule] / Sketch Map of Route across Continent / in 1849. / [six lines of notes] / [diagrammatic scale: about 120 miles to one inch] /. 23.8 x 45 cm. Scale as above. Two volumes, maroon cloth backstrips, gray board sides, white printed label on front covers, uncut.

Prov.: Presentation bookplate from the Wistar Institute of Anatomy and Biology to Richard Wistar Davids.

Ref.: Cowan p. 692; Howes W598

Limited to 250 copies.

Includes an overland narrative in 1849.

4725   WISTER, OWEN

THE VIRGINIAN. A HORSEMAN OF THE PLAINS . . . NEW YORK: THE MACMILLAN COMPANY, 1902.

[i]–[xiv, xiv blank], 1–504, [505–10 advertisements]. 18.9 x 12.9 cm. Eight illustrations listed. Yellow pictorial cloth, fore and lower edges uncut. In a red cloth jacket.

Ref.: Dobie p. 124; Johnson (Blanck) p. 547

4726   WITTEN, ROBERT R.

PIONEER METHODISM IN MISSOURI AND THE MISSION OF METHODISM . . . OCTOBER 7, 1906 . . .

[1]–98. 16.5 x 11.2 cm. Five illustrations, four of them portraits. Brown printed wrappers, cloth backstrip.

Ref.:

No place of printing given.

4727   WIXSON, FRANKLIN

THE MINER'S MANUAL. A READY-RECKONER, AND REFERENCE-BOOK OF USEFUL INFORMATION, FOR THE CONVENIENCE OF MINERS AND ALL DEALERS IN NATIVE GOLD . . . YANKTON, DAKOTA: THE DAKOTA HERALD PRINT, 1877.

[1]–15, [16 blank]. 13 x 8 cm. Stitched.

Ref.:

4728   WOGAN, BARON EMILE DE

VOYAGES ET AVENTURES . . . PARIS: COLLECTION HETZEL.

[i–iv], 1–[327], [328 blank]. 17.5 x 11.1 cm. Purple cloth, purple morocco back, gilt.

Ref.: Howes W609; Monaghan 1489

Published in 1863.

Entirely devoted to adventures in California in 1850.

4729   WOLFE, J. M., *Compiler*

GUIDE, GAZETTEER AND DIRECTORY OF NEBRASKA RAILROADS, COMPRISING THE UNION PACIFIC, SIOUX CITY AND PACIFIC, MIDLAND PACIFIC, BURLINGTON AND MISSOURI RIVER IN NEBRASKA, OMAHA AND NORTHWESTERN, OMAHA AND SOUTHWESTERN, AND BROWNVILLE, FT. KEARNEY & PACIFIC RAILROADS . . . OMAHA, NEB.: J. M. WOLFE, COMPILER AND PUBLISHER, 1872.

[i–ii advertisements], [1]–160, [1–64 advertisements]. 19.2 x 13.3 cm. 16 illustrations and a folding map. Map: Cram's / Rail Road & Township Map / of / Nebraska / Issued by / J. M. Wolfe, / Publisher of / Nebraska Railway Guide, Gazetteer & Directory. Mailed to any address on receipt of price, Bound $2, Paper $1. / Omaha, Neb. / 1872. / 38.6 x 51.7 cm. No scale given. Pictorial wrappers, yellow ground, with title on front wrapper, advertisements on verso of front and recto and verso of back wrapper, advertisements in color on verso of back wrapper, advertisement on backstrip reading up. In a dark blue buckram case.

Ref.: AII (*Nebraska*) 290; Bradford 5980; Howes W614; *Railway Economics* p. 161

Advertising leaves on colored paper interspersed throughout, not included in pagination.

4730   WOLFE, J. M., *Compiler*

NEBRASKA CITY DIRECTORY, FOR 1870, CONTAIN-
ING A HISTORICAL AND COMMERCIAL SKETCH OF
THE CITY . . . NEBRASKA CITY, NEB.: J. M. WOLFE,
PUBLISHER, 1870.

[1]–26, [33]–152. 21.8 x 13.8 cm. Tan printed
boards with black leather backstrip, title at top
of front cover, with advertisements below, advertisements on verso of front and recto and
verso of back covers and end leaves.

Ref.: AII (*Nebraska*) 177; Howes N29
Advertisements interspersed throughout,
mostly on colored paper, none included in
pagination.

Probably not printed in Nebraska City.—AII
(*Nebraska*). Wolfe's principal office was at Dubuque, Iowa.

4731   [WOLL, ADRIAN]

EXPEDICION HECHA EN TEJAS, POR UNA PARTE DE
LA 2. DIVISION DEL CUERPO DE EGERCITO DEL
NORTE. MONTEREY: IMPRESO POR FRANCISCO
MOLINA, 1842.

[1]–60. (Verso of page 13 paginated 15 and recto
of 16 paginated 14.) 18.9 x 12.8 cm. Two folding
tables. New full red morocco.

Ref.: Clements Library (*Texas*) 24; González
& Gómez 403; Howes W619; Sabin 104992;
Streeter 989
General Adrian Woll is described by George
W. Kendall as a Frenchman in the Mexican service under Santa Anna. In 1842, he led about 1500
men into Texas, captured San Antonio de Bejar,
pressed on, and was stopped by a small force at
the Salado River. The *Expedicion* comprises a
series of official reports of the venture. Two lists
of captured Texans are given on pages 20–21 and
47.

4732   WOOD, JOHN

JOURNAL OF JOHN WOOD, AS KEPT BY HIM WHILE
TRAVELING FROM CINCINNATI TO THE GOLD DIG-
GINGS IN CALIFORNIA, IN THE SPRING AND SUMMER
OF 1850 . . . CHILLICOTHE: PRESS OF ADDISON
BOOKWALTER, 1852.

[i–ii blank], [1]–76, [77–8 blank] 17.1 x 11.3 cm.
Buff printed wrappers, with title on front wrapper, Table of Distances on verso of back wrapper. In a blue cloth case.

Ref.: Cowan p. 693; Howes W633; Jones
1290; Wagner-Camp 220
Described by Wagner in California Historical
Society *Quarterly*, December, 1927.

4733   WOOD, JOHN

THE SAME . . . COLUMBUS: NEVINS & MYERS, BOOK
AND JOB PRINTERS, 1871.

[1]–112. 16.7 x 11.4 cm. Yellow printed wrappers, with title on front wrapper. Back wrapper
supplied in photostat. In a blue cloth case.
Second Edition.

4734   WOOD, L. K.

[Wrapper title] THE DISCOVERY OF HUMBOLDT
BAY . . .

[i–iv blank], [1]–22, [23–4 blank]. 18.8 x 14.6
cm. Cream printed wrappers with title on front
wrapper, stapled through covers.

Ref.:
Published first in the *Humboldt Times* (Union,
Calif.), April 26 to May 31, 1856. Later in
Maysville Eagle (Maysville, Ky.), June 19, 1856
to August 19, 1856; *Humboldt Times* (Eureka,
Calif.), Feb. 7, 1863, and succeeding numbers;
West Coast Signal (Eureka, Calif.), March 30,
1873, and succeeding numbers; and *Humboldt
Standard* (Eureka), December, 1901.

The present pamphlet is a reprint from the
setting in the last listed paper. The son of the
author, stated in a letter to Warren Howell that
there were about 100 copies printed for the author's friends.

4735   WOOD, LEONARD

[Caption title] REPORT OF ASSISTANT SURGEON
LEONARD WOOD, U. S. ARMY. FORT BOWIE, A. T.,
SEPTEMBER 8, 1886. TO BRIGADIER GENERAL N. A.
MILES, U. S. A., ALBUQUERQUE, NEW MEXICO.
SIR'[!] I HAVE THE HONOR TO FORWARD THE FOL-
LOWING REPORT, RELATING TO THE RECENT EX-
PEDITION IN SONORA AGAINST THE HOSTILE
APACHES . . .

[1]–7, [8 blank]. 19.6 x 12.9 cm. White printed
wrappers with title on front wrapper.

Prov.: This copy was sent by Lawton to his
friend R. G. Carter and is found in the Lawton
Scrap-book, and is inscribed on front wrapper:
Sent to me by Lawton. /

Ref.:

4736   WOOD, R. E.

LIFE AND CONFESSIONS OF JAMES GILBERT JENKINS:
THE MURDERER OF EIGHTEEN MEN . . . AS NAR-
RATED BY HIMSELF TO COL. C. H. ALLEN, SHERIFF
OF NAPA COUNTY, WHILE IN JAIL UNDER SENTENCE
OF DEATH FOR THE MURDER OF PATRICK O'BRIEN.
PHONOGRAPHICALLY REPORTED AND ARRANGED
FOR THE PRESS BY R. E. WOOD. SAN FRANCISCO:
PRINTED BY WILLIAM P. HARRISON & CO., 1864.

[1]–56. 22.9 x 14.7 cm. Portrait frontispiece and
one plate. Buff printed wrappers, with title on
front wrapper, advertisements on verso of back
wrapper.

Ref.: Adams 1121; Cowan p. 312; Howes
W635

The dispensation of justice in that day was not impeded by iniquitous technicality, nor disturbed by false sentiment. This abandoned wretch was arrested Jan. 19, 1864, and hanged on March 18 of the same year.—Cowan

4737 WOODMAN, DAVID, JR.

GUIDE TO TEXAS EMIGRANTS . . . BOSTON: PRINTED BY M. HAWES, 1835.

[i]–vi, [13]–192. 18.1 x 11.1 cm. Engraved plate and map. Map: Map / of the Colonization Grants to / Zavala, Vehlein & Burnet / in / Texas, / Belonging to / the Galveston Bay: / Texas Land Cº / Scale of Miles. / [diagrammatic scale: about 57 miles to one inch.] / [lower right:] S. Stiles & Co. N. Y. / 22.9 x 29.9 cm. Scale as above. *Inset:* Plan / of the Port of / Galveston, / Made by order of the / Mexican Government. / By / Alexander Thompson / of the / Mexican Navy in 1828. / 13.8 x 8 cm. No scale given. Light blue cloth, with title in gilt on backstrip. Lacks blank leaf at end and back endleaf.

Ref.: Bradford 6000; Clements Library (*Texas*) 12; Howes W647; Phillips p. 413; Rader 3731; Raines p. 222; Sabin 105111; Streeter 1177

The Austins were not the only supporters of immigration to Texas. One of the other groups was the Galveston Bay and Texas Land Company, which controlled the Burnet, Vehlein, and Zavala grants. The present volume contains, as part of the text, all of a promotional pamphlet issued by the company.

4738 WOODMAN, GEORGE

MAP OF THE BOISE AND OWYHEE MINES . . . SAN FRANCISCO: PUBLISHED AND SOLD BY A. GENSOUL, 1864.

[1]–4. 14.5 x 10.1 cm. Folding map: Map / of the Mining Sections of / Idaho & Oregon / embracing the Gold and Silver mines of / Boise & Owyhee / By Geo: Woodman / compiled chiefly from notes of his travels and Surveys / during the last 18 months. / [rule] / Published by A. Gensoul / Bookseller & Stationer / 511 Montgomery St: San Francisco. / [double rule] / Lith. by B. F. Butler San F. 1864. / [lower centre:] Entered according to Act of Congress, in the year 1864 in the month of Febr: by Geo: Woodman, in the Clerk's Office of the District Court of the Northern District of California. / 57.2 x 70 cm. (including border). Scale: 20 miles to one inch. Mounted on linen. Brown cloth folders, 15 x 10.2 cm., with green paper label on front cover, text tipped along inner edge to front

cover, map pasted to inner back cover, Gensoul advertisement on inner front cover.

Ref.: Wagner-Camp 429 see

4739 WOODRUFF, GEORGE H.

FIFTY YEARS AGO: OR, GLEANINGS RESPECTING THE HISTORY OF NORTHERN ILLINOIS A FEW YEARS PREVIOUS TO, AND DURING THE BLACK HAWK WAR . . . JOLIET: JOLIET REPUBLIC AND SUN PRINT, 1883.

[1]–62, [63–4 blank]. 21.7 x 14.6 cm. Gray printed wrappers, with title on front wrapper.

Ref.: Howes W648

4740 WOODRUFF, GEORGE H.

FORTY YEARS AGO! A CONTRIBUTION TO THE EARLY HISTORY OF JOLIET AND WILL COUNTY. TWO LECTURES DELIVERED BEFORE THE HISTORICAL SOCIETY OF JOLIET . . . DECEMBER 17TH, 1873, AND MARCH 24TH, 1874. JOLIET: JOLIET REPUBLICAN STEAM PRINTING HOUSE, 1874.

[i]–iv, [1]–108. 22.4 x 14.5 cm. Dark green printed wrappers with title on front wrapper printed in gold. In a blue cloth folder.

Prov.: Inscribed in pencil on title-page: F. H. Hastings / from Geo H. Woodruff / Aug— 1874— /.

Ref.: Buck 1136; Howes W648

4741 WOODS, DANIEL B.

SIXTEEN MONTHS AT THE GOLD DIGGINGS . . . NEW YORK: HARPER & BROTHERS, 1851.*

[i]–viii, [9]–199, [200 blank], [1]–6 advertisements, [1–2 advertisements]. (Pages [i–ii] blank.) 18.7 x 11.2 cm. Plum cloth, blind embossed sides, title stamped in gilt on backstrip.

Ref.: Blumann & Thomas 4744; Cowan p. 694; Howes W651; Sabin 105123

4742 WOODS, JOHN

TWO YEARS' RESIDENCE IN THE SETTLEMENT ON THE ENGLISH PRAIRIE, IN THE ILLINOIS COUNTRY, UNITED STATES . . . LONDON: PRINTED FOR LONGMAN, HURST, REES, ORME, AND BROWN, PATERNOSTER-ROW. 1822.

[1]–2, [1]–2, [1]–2, [1]–2, [1]–8 advertisements, front endleaf, [i–iv, iv blank], [1]–310. 20.8 x 13 cm. Two maps. Map: Map of / Illinois. / English Miles. / [diagrammatic scale: about 62 miles to one inch] / [lower centre:] London, Published by Longman, Hurst, Rees, Orme & Brown, Paternoster Row. March, 1822. / [lower right:] Sidʸ Hall, sc Bury Strᵗ Bloomsbʸ / 16.7 x 22.5 cm. *Inset:* Environs / of / Albion. / English Miles. / [diagrammatic scale: 18 miles to one inch.] / 7.5 x 22.5 cm. Map: English Prairie / Divided into Sections / [lower centre:] London, Pub. by Longman & Cº March, 1822. / [lower

right:] Sid.ᵞ Hall, sc. / 16.8 x 10.8 cm. Scale: one and one-half English miles to an inch. Blue boards, tan paper backstrip, with white paper label, 2.8 x 2.4 cm., uncut. In a brown cloth case.

Ref.: Bradford 6007; Buck 153; Church 1322; Howes W654; Jones 846; Sabin 105125

4743 WOODS, W. H.

[Wrapper title] HISTORICAL SKETCH OF AN ORIGINAL PORTRAIT OF GOVERNOR MERIWETHER LEWIS BY M. FAVRET DE SAINT MEMIN . . . RICHMOND, VA.: WHITTET & SHEPPERSON, PRINTERS, 1890.

[1]–22, [23–4 blank]. 23.3 x 15 cm. Gray wrappers, with title as above on front cover. In a brown half morocco case.

Ref.:

Accompanying the pamphlet is a photograph (sepia) dated 1890 taken by Prince, Washington, D.C., of the St. Memin portrait.

4744 WOODWARD, THOMAS S.

WOODWARD'S REMINISCENCES OF THE CREEK, OR MUSCOGEE INDIANS, CONTAINED IN LETTERS TO FRIENDS IN GEORGIA AND ALABAMA . . . MONTGOMERY, ALA.: BARRETT & WIMBISH, 1859.

[1]–168. 22.6 x 14 cm. Light brown printed wrappers with title on front wrapper, copyright notice on verso of front wrapper, printer's advertisement on recto of back wrapper. Rebacked. In a green half morocco case.

Ref.: Howes W665; Rader 3735

Woodward's *Reminiscences* comprises the judgments of the most knowledgeable man of his day on the Creek Indians.

4745 WOOLLEY, LELL H.

CALIFORNIA, 1849–1913; OR, THE RAMBLING SKETCHES AND EXPERIENCES OF SIXTY-FOUR YEARS' RESIDENCE IN THAT STATE . . . OAKLAND, CALIFORNIA: DEWITT & SNELLING, 1913.

[1]–48. 22.8 x 15.2 cm. Frontispiece portrait. Gray printed wrappers, with title on front wrapper, advertisement on verso of back wrapper.

Ref.: Cowan p. 695

4746 WOOLWORTH, JAMES M.

NEBRASKA IN 1857 . . . OMAHA CITY, N. T.: PUBLISHED BY C. C. WOOLWORTH, 1857.

[1]–105, [106–28 advertisements, last seven pages being for Nebraska Territory advertisers]. 16.8 x 11.4 cm. Map: Nebraska / and / Kanzas. / Prepared by J. H. Colton & C.ᵒ, 172, William S.ᵗ, New York, / for / Woolworth's Nebraska in 1857. / Scale of Miles. / [diagrammatic scale: 80 miles to one inch] / [lower left:] Entered according to Act of Congress in the Year 1855 by J. H. Colton & Co. in the Clerks Office of the Dist. Court of the U. S. for the South.ⁿ Dist. of New

York. / 32.4 x 39 cm. (including border). Scale as above. *Inset:* Map of the Surveyed Portion of Nebraska /. 16 x 10.7 cm. (neat line, irregular shape). No scale given. Buff printed wrappers with title on front wrapper, advertisement on verso of back wrapper. In a brown cloth case.

Ref.: AII (*Nebraska*) 15; Bradford 6018; Howes W670; Sabin 105220; Wagner-Camp 295

Although the imprints are for Omaha, the volume was stereotyped and printed in New York. Both stereotyper's and printer's imprint appear on the verso of the title-page.

At the time of publication, Nebraska Territory included Montana and Idaho. The author compiled much of his work from personal observation and, as General Land Agent, he probably knew what he was writing about.

4747 WORKMAN, JAMES

ESSAYS AND LETTERS ON VARIOUS POLITICAL SUBJECTS . . . NEW-YORK: PRINTED AND PUBLISHED BY I. RILEY, 1809.

[*]², A–N⁶, O⁴. [1]–165, [166 blank]. 16 x 9.5 cm. Original or contemporary tan boards, calf back and corners.

Ref.: Howes W676; Sabin 105480

Although this volume is styled Second American Edition on the title-page, only portions had appeared previously.

4748 WORKMAN, JAMES, & LEWIS KERR, Trials

THE TRIALS OF THE HONB. JAMES WORKMAN, AND COL. LEWIS KERR, BEFORE THE UNITED STATES' COURT, FOR THE ORLEANS DISTRICT, ON A CHARGE OF HIGH MISDEMEANOR, IN PLANNING AND SETTING ON FOOT, WITHIN THE UNITED STATES, AN EXPEDITION FOR THE CONQUEST AND EMANCIPATION OF MEXICO. NEW-ORLEANS: PRINTED BY BRADFORD & ANDERSON, 1807.

[A]–P⁶. [1]–180. 18.2 x 10.8 cm. Old boards, new calf backstrip and corners.

Ref.: Howes C226; Sabin 105484

Both Judge Workman and Colonel Lewis had been involved in the Burr-Wilkinson conspiracy and each had incurred the enmity of Wilkinson. The present work is a record of their two trials, at the end of the second of which each was acquitted.

4749 WORTH, JOSEPH

ADVENTURES AND NARROW ESCAPES IN NICARAGUA . . . IN 1866 AND 1867. SAN FRANCISCO: SPAULDING & BARTO, 1872.

[1]–52. 17.5 x 11.4 cm. Cream printed wrappers with title on front wrapper.

Ref.:

4750 [WORTLEY, VICTORIA STUART]

A YOUNG TRAVELLER'S JOURNAL OF A TOUR IN NORTH AND SOUTH AMERICA DURING THE YEAR 1850 . . . LONDON: T. BOSWORTH, M.DCCC.LII.

[i]–[xii], [1]–260. 17 x 10.3 cm. 16 plates listed. Pink cloth, blind embossed borders on sides, title in gilt on backstrip, uncut.

Ref.: Howes W688

The author was the eldest daughter (aged twelve at the time) of Lady Emmeline Stuart-Wortley. Part of the trip of which this is a diary took the party down the Ohio and Mississippi Rivers.

4751 WREDE, FRIEDRICH W. VON

LEBENSBILDER AUS DEN VEREINIGTEN STAATEN VON NORDAMERIKA UND TEXAS . . . CASSEL: IN COMMISSION BEI THEODOR FISCHER, 1844.

[1–4], [I]–[VI, VI blank], [1]–324. 19.3 x 11.5 cm. Contemporary brown marbled boards, brown cloth back and corners, front cover of original printed green wrapper mounted on front cover.

Ref.: Buck 305; Clark III 259; Howes W690; Rader 3743

There was also an edition in two parts paginated [6] 160; [6] 161–324. Clark repeats this.

The foreword is signed Emil Drescher; on the front cover and title-page his last name is filled in in manuscript.

4752 WRIGHT, DAVID

MEMOIR OF ALVAN STONE, OF GOSHEN, MASS . . . BOSTON: GOULD, KENDALL AND LINCOLN, 1837.

[1–4], [9]–256. 14.6 x 9 cm. Brown cloth, title in gilt on backstrip.

Ref.: Buck 232; Howes W692; Rusk II p. 125; Sabin 105571

Includes extracts from Stone's diary and letters written from the time he left home, May 2, 1831, until his death in Alton, Illinois, February 13, 1833. These contain descriptions of the country and notes on the life and religious condition of the people.—EDG

4753 [WRIGHT, GEORGE B.]

COARSE FODDER, (BRAN, CHIPS AND SAWDUST MOSTLY) RAKED UP BY OLD SETTLER, BEING FACTS, FIGURES AND THINGS RELATING TO FERGUS FALLS, MINN. MINNEAPOLIS: JOHNSON, SMITH & HARRISON, 1881.

[1]–24. 22.5 x 15 cm. Folding map before title-page and maps on pages 7 & 11. Folding map: New / Township and Railroad Map / of the / State of / Minnesota / Published for the / North Pacific, Fergus & Black Hills R. R. / [lower right:] Lith. Pioneer Press Co. St. Paul / 50.1 x 43.2 cm. No scale given. Pale blue printed wrappers, with title on front wrapper, advertisements on verso of front wrapper and recto of back, map from page 11 repeated on verso of back wrapper.

Ref.:

The Wrights, George B. of Minneapolis, and Charles J. of Fergus Falls, advertised city lots and farm lands for sale.

4754 WRIGHT, GEORGE G.

[Wrapper title] AN ADDRESS DELIVERED BEFORE THE PIONEER ASSOCIATION OF VAN BUREN COUNTY, AUGUST 28TH, 1872 . . . AT KEOSAUQUA, IOWA. KEOSAUQUA REPUBLICAN PRINT.

[1]–36. 20.8 x 14.8 cm. Blue printed wrappers bound into tan buckram, gilt top.

Ref.: Mott (*Iowa*) p. 81

Published at Keosauqua in 1872.

4755 WRIGHT, J. S.

[Map] CHICAGO. / DRAWN BY / J. S. WRIGHT, / ACCORDING TO SURVEY. / 1834. / [lower left:] P. A. MESIER'S LITH. 28 WALL S.T N. YORK. /

Map, 48.5 x 38.6 cm. Scale: 600 feet to one inch. Broadside, unbound, printed on white wove paper, mounted (1958) on white laid paper.

Ref.:

The second printed map of Chicago. There are some manuscript changes and additions in red ink.

Removed from J. A. Wills' copy of a collection of pamphlets relating to the Bates vs. Illinois Central case.

4756 WRIGHT, ROBERT M.

DODGE CITY, THE COWBOY CAPITAL, AND THE GREAT SOUTHWEST IN THE DAYS OF THE WILD INDIAN, THE BUFFALO, THE COWBOY, DANCE HALLS, GAMBLING HALLS AND BAD MEN . . .

[1]–344. 19.5 x 12.6 cm. 40 illustrations, unlisted. Green pictorial cloth.

Ref.: Howes W706; Rader 3758

Copyrighted 1913. Printer's imprint appears on the recto of the frontispiece. Printed at Wichita, Kansas.

There was no ghost writer. This book has the real savor of Western Frontier Days.—EDG

4757 WRIGHT, WILLIAM

HISTORY OF THE BIG BONANZA: AN AUTHENTIC ACCOUNT OF THE DISCOVERY, HISTORY, AND WORKING OF THE WORLD RENOWNED COMSTOCK SILVER LODE OF NEVADA . . . HARTFORD, CONN.: AMERICAN PUBLISHING COMPANY, 1876.

[i]–xvi, 17–569, [570 blank]. 22 x 14.4 cm. 91 illustrations listed, but plate 44 is not present;

believed to have been omitted from all copies. Gray-brown cloth, stamped in gilt and black on front cover and in blind on back, title in gilt and black on backstrip.

Ref.: Howes W710

Contains a one-page introduction by Mark Twain.

The author is better known under the name Dan De Quille.

4758 [WRIGHT, WILLIAM]

A HISTORY OF THE COMSTOCK SILVER LODE & MINES, NEVADA AND THE GREAT BASIN REGION; LAKE TAHOE AND THE HIGH SIERRAS . . . VIRGINIA, NEVADA: PUBLISHED BY F. BOEGLE.

[i]–x, 11–158. 17.4 x 12.7 cm. Printed wrappers bound into gray boards, yellow cloth back.

Ref.: Howes W711

Copyrighted 1889.

4759 [WRIGHT, WILLIAM, & JOHN W.]

RECOLLECTIONS OF WESTERN TEXAS; DESCRIPTIVE AND NARRATIVE. (INCLUDING AN INDIAN CAMPAIGN) 1852–55. INTERSPERSED WITH ILLUSTRATIVE ANECDOTES . . . LONDON: W. & F. G. CASH, 1857.

[1]–88. 18.4 x 12.3 cm. Tan printed boards, brown cloth backstrip, with cover title, advertisements on back cover. In green cloth case.

Ref.: Howes W709; Wagner-Camp 295a

Erratum slip, 5.9 x 10.6 cm., pasted to page [3].

4760 WRIGHT HOUSE, Chamberlain, Dakota

[Broadsheet] WRIGHT HOUSE, GEO. WRIGHT, PROPRIETOR. CHAMBERLAIN, DAKOTA. ITS ADVANTAGES. THIS HOTEL HAS BEEN BUILT AND ARRANGED FOR SPECIAL COMFORT AND CONVENIENCE OF THE TRAVELING PUBLIC. ON ARRIVAL, EACH GUEST WILL BE ASKED HOW HE LIKES THE SITUATION, AND IF HE SAYS THE HOTEL OUGHT TO HAVE BEEN PLACED NEARER THE RAILROAD DEPOT, THE LOCATION OF THE HOUSE WILL BE CHANGED. CORNER FRONT ROOMS, UP ONLY ONE FLIGHT, FOR EACH GUEST . . . SPECIAL ATTENTION GIVEN TO PARTIES WHO CAN GIVE "INFORMATION AS TO HOW THESE THINGS ARE DONE IN YEWRUP."

Broadsheet, 25.5 x 13.9 cm.

Ref.:

The humorous rules of the house are followed on the second page by a mock menu, including such delicacies as Elephant, a la Tusk Sauce; Turkey, stuffed with Rubber Shoes; Baked Chignons; and Sawdust Pudding, a la Pine Sauce.

4761 [WRISTON, JENNIE ATCHESON]

A PIONEER'S ODYSSEY. PRIVATELY PRINTED, 1943.

[i]–xii, [1]–92. 19 x 13 cm. Frontispiece map. Dark blue cloth.

Ref.:

This overland trip took place in 1873. The route was through Kansas and the party followed the Republican river to Red Cloud, Nebraska, north to Hastings and Fort Kearney, up the Platte to Cherry Creek in Colorado. They had come by railroad in 1863 from New York State to Missouri and in 1873 went by wagon overland.—EDG

4762 WYANDOTT CITY COMPANY

[Broadside] WYANDOTT CITY COMPANY. NO. [in manuscript: Thos H Swope] IS ENTITLED TO ONE SHARE OF TEN LOTS . . . WYANDOTT CITY, KANSAS TERRITORY. [in manuscript: Nov 21st], A. D. 1857 [7 obscured by manuscript 9] [in manuscript: Silas Armstrong], PRESIDENT. [in manuscript: W B Robins] SECRETARY. KANSAS CITY ENTERPRISE PRINT.

Broadside, 14.6 x 20.5 cm. Text, 11.6 x 19.7 cm.

Ref.:

On the verso in manuscript are locations of the lots, and receipts for the sale of the lots by Swope and a later owner.

The Swope family was prominent in early Kansas City, Missouri, history and the name is memorialized in one of the city's most important parks.

4763 WYETH, JOHN B.

OREGON; OR, A SHORT HISTORY OF A LONG JOURNEY FROM THE ATLANTIC OCEAN TO THE REGION OF THE PACIFIC, BY LAND . . . CAMBRIDGE: PRINTED FOR JOHN B. WYETH, 1833.

[i]–iv, [1]–87, [88 blank]. 19.1 x 12.3 cm. Tan printed wrappers with title on front wrapper. In a green half morocco case.

Ref.: Bradford 6038; Cowan (1914) p. 254; Howell 344; Howes W717; Jones 946; Sabin 105649; Smith 11236; Wagner-Camp 47

First printed account of the first emigrant party to cross the plains.—Howes

4764 WYETH, NATHANIEL J.

SOURCES OF THE HISTORY OF OREGON. VOLUME I, PARTS 3 TO 6 INCLUSIVE. THE CORRESPONDENCE AND JOURNALS OF CAPTAIN NATHANIEL J. WYETH, 1831–6 . . . EDITED BY F. G. YOUNG . . . EUGENE, ORE.: UNIVERSITY PRESS, 1899.*

[i]–xix, [xx blank], [1]–262. 24.6 x 16.8 cm. Two folding sketch maps and one map in text. Gray-green printed wrappers, with title on front wrap-

per, list of publications on verso, statement of aims of Society on recto of back wrapper, and list of officers on verso. In olive-green cloth case.

    Ref.: Howes W718; Smith 11238

4765 WYLIE, W. W.

YELLOWSTONE NATIONAL PARK; OR, THE GREAT AMERICAN WONDERLAND, A COMPLETE DESCRIPTION OF ALL THE WONDERS OF THE PARK . . . KANSAS CITY, MO.: PUBLISHING HOUSE OF RAMSEY, MILLETT & HUDSON, 1882.

[i–iv], [1]–99, [100 blank, 101–10 advertisements]. (Page [i] blank, pages [ii–iii] advertisements, page [iv] frontispiece.) 16.5 x 12.7 cm. Illustrations unlisted. Brown cloth, with gilt title and vignette on front cover.

    Ref.:

4766 WYOMING. Live Stock Commissioners, Board of

OFFICIAL BRAND BOOK OF THE STATE OF WYOMING . . . LARAMIE, WYOMING: THE LARAMIE REPUBLICAN COMPANY, 1913.

[i–iv], 1–252. 19.6 x 11 cm. Limp dark green leather, speckled edges, rounded corners.

    Ref.: Adams (*Ramp. Herd*) 2607
    Printed on India paper.

4767 WYOMING. Live Stock Commissioners, Board of

OFFICIAL BRAND BOOK OF THE STATE OF WYOMING AND A COMPILATION OF LAWS AFFECTING LIVE STOCK . . . DENVER, SMITH-BROOKS CO.

[i–iv], 1–450. 19.1 x 9.8 cm. Limp red leather, red edges, rounded corners.

    Ref.: Adams (*Ramp. Herd*) 2608
    Printed on thin paper. Published in 1916.

4768 WYOMING. Live Stock Commissioners, Board of

SUPPLEMENT NO. 2 TO THE 1916 WYOMING STATE BRAND BOOK . . . DENVER, SMITH-BROOKS CO.

[i–ii], 1–113, [114–26 blank]. 19.7 x 10.9 cm. Red wrappers.

    Ref.:
    Brand records and changes to August 1, 1917.

4769 WYOMING. Live Stock Commissioners, Board of

OFFICIAL BRAND BOOK OF THE STATE OF WYOMING AND A COMPILATION OF LAWS AFFECTING LIVE STOCK . . . LARAMIE, WYOMING: THE LARAMIE REPUBLICAN COMPANY, 1919.

[1]–639, [640 blank]. 20 x 11 cm. Limp green leather, rounded corners.

    Ref.: Adams (*Ramp. Herd*) 2609

4770 WYOMING. Live Stock Commissioners, Board of

OFFICIAL BRAND BOOK OF THE STATE OF WYOMING . . . CASPER, WYOMING, S. E. BOYER AND COMPANY.

[i–iv], 1–446. 20.3 x 10.5 cm. Limp red leather, red edges, rounded corners.

    Ref.: Adams (*Ramp. Herd*) 2610
    Published after July 1, 1927.

4771 WYOMING. Live Stock and Sanitary Board

OFFICIAL BRAND BOOK OF THE STATE OF WYOMING . . . SHERIDAN, WYOMING: PUBLISHED BY THE MILLS COMPANY.

[i–vi (vi blank)], 1–446. 20 x 15.7 cm. Limp black leather, rounded corners.

    Ref.: Adams (*Ramp. Herd*) 2611
    Published after June 30, 1936.

4772 WYOMING TERRITORY. Constitutional Convention, 1889

MEMORIAL TO THE PRESIDENT AND CONGRESS FOR THE ADMISSION OF WYOMING TERRITORY TO THE UNION. WITH APPENDICES SHOWING THE ACTION TAKEN BY THE PEOPLE, AND THE CONSTITUTION, AS ADOPTED. CHEYENNE, WYOMING: BRISTOL & KNABE PRINTING COMPANY, 1889.

[i]–xiv, [xv–xvi fly title], [1]–[76]. 22.9 x 14.5 cm. Tan printed wrappers with title on front wrapper. Back wrapper supplied. In a yellow cloth case.

    Ref.: AII (*Wyoming*) 150

4773 WYOMING TERRITORY. GOVERNOR (J. A. Campbell)

MESSAGE OF GOVERNOR CAMPBELL TO THE THIRD LEGISLATIVE ASSEMBLY, OF WYOMING TERRITORY, CONVENED AT CHEYENNE, NOVEMBER 4TH, 1873. CHEYENNE, WYOMING TERRITORY: H. GLAFCKE, PRINTER, 1873.

[1]–17, [18 blank]. 21.5 x 14.2 cm. Yellow printed wrappers, with title on front wrapper.

    Ref.: AII (*Wyoming*) 13

4774 WYOMING STOCK GROWERS' ASSOCIATION

CATTLE BRANDS OWNED BY MEMBERS OF THE WYOMING STOCK GROWERS' ASSOCIATION . . . CHICAGO: THE J. M. W. JONES STATIONERY & PRINTING CO., 1882.

[1]–57, [58 blank]. [i]–ii Index. 16.4 x 10.5 cm. Sheepskin with wallet flap.

    Ref.: Adams (*Ramp. Herd*) 2579; Howes W727

The first Wyoming brand book. First state. Without the two extra leaves at the end.

4775 WYOMING STOCK GROWERS' AS-SOCIATION

THE SAME.

[1]–57, [2 blank pages], 58–9, [60 blank], [i]–ii Index. 16.4 x 10.5 cm. Sheepskin.

Ref.: Adams (*Ramp. Herd*) 2579; Howes W727

Second state. With two additional leaves before Index.

4776 WYOMING STOCK GROWERS' AS-SOCIATION

THE SAME. CHICAGO: THE J. M. W. JONES STATIONERY & PRINTING CO., 1883.

[1]–81, [82–102 blank], [I]–II Index. 16.6 x 10.5 cm. Sheepskin, pink edges.

Ref.: Adams (*Ramp. Herd*) 2580; Howes W727

Correction slip pasted over page 81.

4777 WYOMING STOCK GROWERS' AS-SOCIATION

BRAND BOOK FOR 1884 . . . CHEYENNE: NORTHWESTERN LIVE STOCK JOURNAL.

[1–132]. 18.9 x 10.7 cm. Sheepskin.

Ref.: Adams (*Ramp. Herd*) 2581; Howes W727

Published in 1884.

4778 WYOMING STOCK GROWERS' AS-SOCIATION

THE SAME FOR 1885 . . . CHEYENNE: NORTHWESTERN LIVE STOCK JOURNAL.

[1–122 pages]. 18.9 x 10.7 cm. Cream cloth.

Ref.: Adams (*Ramp. Herd*) 2582; Howes W727

Correction slip tipped to entry for George D. Rainsford.

4779 WYOMING STOCK GROWERS' AS-SOCIATION

BRAND BOOK PUBLISHED BY THE WYOMING STOCK GROWERS ASSOCIATION. 1887 . . . CHEYENNE: THE NORTHWESTERN LIVE STOCK JOURNAL.

[3]–125, [126 blank]. 19.9 x 10.9 cm. Cream cloth.

Ref.: Adams (*Ramp. Herd*) 2583

4780 WYOMING STOCK GROWERS' AS-SOCIATION

[On verso of front endpaper] WYOMING STOCK GROWERS' / ASSOCIATION. / [decorative rule] / [dotted line, with Spring in manuscript] ROUND UP, 188 [4 in manuscript]. / DISTRICT NO. [dotted line with 13 in manuscript] / [dotted line with Saml Moses in manuscript] FOREMAN. / [dotted line with Chris Stortz in manuscript] ASSISTANT. /

[1]–[96]. 17.5 x 12.3 cm. Brown cloth, wallet flap at fore-edge; paper label on flap, filled in in manuscript: No. 13 / Spring / 1884 /. Abbreviation No. printed.

Ref.:

Pasted to the inside front cover is a printed slip of instructions for District No. 13. Two pages of Record of Mavericks have been filled in and signed by Samuel Moses. The affidavit on page [47] has not been filled in; two leaves of Foreman's Bill of Sale (original and duplicate) have been torn out.

The manuscript date 1887 appears on the front cover.

4781 WYOMING STOCK GROWERS' AS-SOCIATION

THE SAME, but a different printing. [For Spring Round Up, 1885. James Preston, Foreman. Wm Booker Assistant. Round-Up No. 1. District not indicated.]

[1]–94. 17.7 x 11.3 cm. Brown cloth with wallet flap at fore-edge, manuscript label on flap: No. 1 / Spring / 1885 /. Abbreviation No. printed in red.

Ref.:

Pasted to the inside front cover is a printed slip of instructions for Roundup No. 1. Sixteen pages of Record of Mavericks have been filled in; the affidavit on page [47] is filled in and notarized; eight leaves of Foreman's Bill of Sale (original and duplicate) have been torn out along perforations.

4782 WYOMING STOCK GROWERS' AS-SOCIATION

THE SAME, but a different printing. [Inside front cover not filled in.]

[1]–[100]. 17.5 x 11.1 cm. Cream cloth with wallet flap along fore-edge. Worn.

Ref.:

Printed slip pasted to inside front cover bearing instructions for Roundup No. 17. Eight pages of the Record of Mavericks have been used; the affidavit on page [50] has been filled in and notarized; twelve leaves of Foreman's Bill of Sale (original and duplicate) have been torn out along perforations.

4783 WYOMING STOCK GROWERS' ASSOCIATION

LETTERS FROM OLD FRIENDS AND MEMBERS OF THE WYOMING STOCK GROWERS ASSOCIATION. CHEYENNE, WYOMING: THE S. A. BRISTOL COMPANY.

[1]–55, [56 blank]. 22.8 x 14.9 cm. Each letter signed in facsimile. Tan printed wrappers, title on front wrapper printed in brown.

Ref.: Adams (*Ramp. Herd*) 2601

The letters are addressed to Harry E. Crain, Chairman of the Historical Committee of the Association. They were published in 1923.

X

4784 XANTUS, JANOS

. . . LEVELEI EJSZAKAMERIKABOL . . . PESTEN: LAUFFER ES STOLP KIADO KONYVKERESKEDESE TULAJDONA.

[1]–175, [176 advertisements]. 22.2 x 14.8 cm. 12 plates, with tinted backgrounds. Green ribbed cloth.

Ref.: Howes X1

The title is *Letters from North America.* Published at Buda-Pesth in 1858.

Unauthorized edition of letters by a Hungarian exile and scientist who accompanied a railroad survey through the Southwest and California. The incompetent editor, Prépost, produced rather chaotic information, much of it borrowed from Marcy's Red River report.—Howes

4785 XANTUS, JANOS

UTAZAS: KALIFORNIA DELI RESZEIBEN . . . PESTEN: KIADJAK LAUFFER ES STOLP, 1860.

[i–x], 1–191, [192–94 advertisements]. 22.3 x 14.2 cm. Folding map and eight lithographed plates with tinted grounds. Map: Kalifornia / déli részei / Legújabb kútfök után szerkesztette és rajzolta. / Xántus János / 1858 / Mérték: 1:6,000,000. / [diagrammatic scale] / [lower left:] Kiadják Lauffer és Stolp Pesten. 1860. [lower right:] Nyomt. Haske és Társa, Pest 1859. / 32.7 x 32.1 cm. Scale as above. Gray printed boards, with title on front cover and backstrip, two lines of text on back cover.

Ref.: Barrett 2681; Cowan p. 697; Howes X2

The title is *Travels in Southern California.* Published at Buda-Pesth in 1860.

Authorized edition of this scientist's letters on California; they embody, without acknowledgement, much from the reports of Abert and Emory.—Howes

Y

4786 YAVAPAI COUNTY STOCK GROWERS' ASSOCIATION

BRAND BOOK OF THE YAVAPAI CO. STOCK GROWERS' ASSOCIATION, PREPARED MAY 1, 1885 . . . KANSAS CITY, MO.: ISAAC P. MOORE, PRINTER AND BINDER, 1885.

[1–2], [I]–IV, [5]–44. 16.9 x 9.6 cm. Calf. Apparently lacks front endleaf.

Ref.:

4787 [YOUNG, FRANK C.]

ACROSS THE PLAINS IN '65. A YOUNGSTER'S JOURNAL, FROM "GOTHAM" TO "PIKE'S PEAK." . . . DENVER, COLORADO, NOVEMBER, 1905. THIS (SOUVENIR) EDITION PRIVATELY PRINTED.*

[1–6], [i]–[x], [1]–224. 16.9 x 13 cm. Dark red cloth, gilt top. Folding map.

Ref.: Howes Y25

Limited to 200 copies.

Day-by-day journal of a trip from Atchison to Julesburg and Denver.—Howes

Tipped in before the limitation leaf is a small slip (6.7 x 12 cm.) regarding association with *Echoes from Arcadia.* There is a copyright notice in favor of the author on a small slip (1.9 x 3.8 cm.) pasted to the page facing the title-page.

4788 [YOUNG, FRANK C.]

ECHOES FROM ARCADIA. THE STORY OF CENTRAL CITY, AS TOLD BY ONE OF "THE CLAN." . . . FOR PRIVATE CIRCULATION. DENVER, COLO., 1903.*

[1–4], [i–x, x blank], [1]–220. 16.9 x 13.2 cm. Dark red cloth, gilt top.

Prov.: Inscribed on first blank leaf: Eugene H. Feats— / with the sincere regards of / F. C. Young. / April 29/08. /

Ref.: Howes Y26; Wilcox p. 127

Limited to 200 copies.

Minute record of fifteen golden years, reviving a unique social life and a ghost-town's departed glory.—Howes

4789 YOUNG, HARRY

HARD KNOCKS: A LIFE STORY OF THE VANISHING WEST . . . PORTLAND, OREGON, 1915.

[1]–240. 19.5 x 13.5 cm. 25 illustrations listed. Yellow printed wrappers. In green cloth case.

Ref.: Howes Y27; Smith 11274

4790 YOUNG, JOHN H.

[Map] MITCHELL'S / TRAVELLERS GUIDE / THROUGH THE / UNITED STATES. / A MAP / OF THE / ROADS, DISTANCES, STEAM BOAT / & CANAL ROUTES &C. / BY J. H. YOUNG / PHILADELPHIA. / PUB-

LISHED BY / S. AUGUSTUS MITCHELL. / 1833. / ENGRAVED ON STEEL BY J. H. YOUNG & D. HAINES. / [lower right:] ENTERED ACCORDING TO ACT OF CONGRESS, IN THE YEAR 1832, BY S. AUGUSTUS MITCHELL, IN THE CLERKS OFFICE OF THE DISTRICT COURT, OF THE EASTERN DISTRICT, OF PENNSYLVANIA. / *Inset:* Vicinity / of / Cincinnati. / 7.3 x 7.3 cm. *Inset:* Vicinity / of / Albany. / 7.3 x 7.3 cm. *Inset:* Vicinity / of / New / Orleans. / 5.7 x 9.2 cm. *Inset:* Vicinity / of / Boston. / 8.9 x 6.6 cm. *Inset:* Vicinity / of / New York. / 8.9 x 6.6 cm. *Inset:* Vicinity / of / Philadelphia. / 8.9 x 6.6 cm. *Inset:* Vicinity / of / Baltimore / and / Washington. / 8.9 x 6.6 cm. *Inset:* Vicinity / of / Charleston. / 8.9 x 6.6 cm. *Inset:* Vicinity / of the / Falls / of / Niagara. / 6.1 x 6.3 cm.

Map, 43.4 x 55 cm. Scale: about 78 miles to an inch (no scale indicated for insets). Dark blue leather, 13.6 x 8.2 cm., gilt borders, gilt panel in centre of front cover with title.

Ref.: Phillips p. 886

Attached to the inside front cover is a broadside, folded, 45.4 x 57.3 cm., with nine boxes containing the following headings: Index. / Steam-Boat and Canal Routes. / Statistical Table of the United States. / Different Classes of Inhabitants—1830. / Length of the Principal Rail-roads, (Finished or in Progress,) / in the United States. / Lengths of the Principal Canals, (Finished or in Progress,) / in the United States. / Table / Showing the Distance from Washington to the Capital or Largest Town of each State; / also from each Capital or Largest Town to each of the Others. /

4791 YOUNG, JOHN H.

[Map] A / NEW MAP OF / TEXAS, / WITH THE CONTIGUOUS / AMERICAN & MEXICAN STATES / BY J. H. YOUNG. / PHILADELPHIA: / PUBLISHED BY S. AUGUSTUS MITCHELL. / 1835 / ENTERED ACCORDING TO ACT OF CONGRESS IN THE YEAR 1835 BY S. AUGUSTUS MITCHELL IN THE CLERKS OFFICE OF THE DISTRICT COURT OF THE EASTERN DISTRICT OF PENNSYLVANIA. / [lower centre:] ENGRAVED BY J. H. YOUNG / [lower left of cartouche:] SOLD BY / MITCHELL & HINMAN / N.º 6 NORTH FIFTH STREET. / SCALE OF MILES. / [diagrammatic scale: 55 miles to one inch] /.

Map, 32.5 x 39 cm. Scale as above. Folded into dark green roan folder, 12.4 x 7.6 cm., gilt borders, title in gilt on front cover.

Ref.: Phillips p. 841; Streeter 1178

4792 YOUNG, JOHN H.

[Map] THE / TOURIST'S POCKET MAP / OF THE / STATE OF ILLINOIS / EXHIBITING ITS / INTERNAL IMPROVEMENTS / ROADS DISTANCES &C. / BY / J. H. YOUNG / PHILADELPHIA: / PUBLISHED BY / S. AUGUSTUS MITCHELL. / 1837 / [lower left:] ENTERED ACCORDING TO ACT OF CONGRESS IN THE YEAR 1834 BY S. AUGUSTUS MITCHELL IN THE CLERKS OFFICE OF THE DISTRICT COURT OF THE EASTERN DISTRICT OF PENNSYLVANIA. / [lower right:] ENGRAVED BY F. F. WOODWARD /.

Map, 37.7 x 31.3 cm. Scale: 30 miles to an inch. Folded into black leather covers, 12.4 x 7.7 cm., with title in gilt on front cover.

Ref.: Phillips p. 327 see

Inside front cover is pasted a printed statement headed: Public Lands. /

Editions: Philadelphia, 1834.

4793 YOUNG, JOHN H.

[Map] UNITED STATES / [below neat line:] J. H. YOUNG SC. /

Map, 20.1 x 24.3 cm. Scale: 350 miles to an inch. Folded and mounted on inner back cover of a brown leather folder, 9 x 5.5 cm., with gilt title on front cover. In a black silk protective bag.

Ref.:

Philadelphia, about 1837.

Outside neat line, in lower right corner, are the engraved numerals XXIX /.

Also appears in Malte-Brun: *A New General Atlas* . . . Philadelphia, 1837.

4794 YOUNG, JOHN R.

MEMOIRS OF JOHN R. YOUNG, UTAH PIONEER. 1847 . . . SALT LAKE CITY, UTAH: THE DESERET NEWS, 1920.

[i]–vi, [9]–341, [342 blank]. 18.7 x 13.2 cm. Four portraits. Dark blue cloth, with title in gilt on front cover and backstrip. Probably lacks pages vii–viii.

Prov.: Inscribed on front fly-leaf: Presented with good wishes / to / Isabel C Prescoot / Teacher at Kayenta / For Her Civility and Kindness / to / My Utah Friends / John R Young / Blanding Utah / April 30—1928—My 91—Birthday /.

Ref.: Howes Y29

Born in 1837 at Kirtland, Ohio, this Mormon nephew of Brigham Young was at Nauvoo, Winter Quarters, and made the trip overland to Utah with the Saints in 1847. In 1858, returning from Hawaii, he went overland from San Francisco to Utah. In 1862 he was called on to transport immigrants from Omaha to Utah at which time he had many adventures with Indians. He is quite sincere and frank as to his plural marriages.—EDG

4795 YOUNGBLOOD, CHARLES L.

ADVENTURES OF CHAS. L. YOUNGBLOOD DURING TEN YEARS ON THE PLAINS . . . BOONVILLE, IND.: BOONVILLE STANDARD CO., PRINTERS, 1882.

[1]–199, [200 blank]. 19.2 x 13.4 cm. Portrait. Blue cloth, gilt title on front cover and backstrip.

Ref.: Howes Y34; Rader 3780

This edition should not be confused with the rather common later Chicago edition wherein the narrative is dragged out through some 400 pages by a hack writer.—EDG

4796 YOUNGER, COLE

THE STORY OF COLE YOUNGER. BY HIMSELF . . . CHICAGO: THE HENNEBERRY COMPANY, 1903.

[1]–[124], [125 advertisement, 126–28 blank]. 22.1 x 14.3 cm. 34 illustrations listed. White printed wrappers, with title on front wrapper and backstrip. In a red cloth case.

Ref.: Adams 1131; Howes Y35

Z

4797 ZIEBER & CO., Philadelphia

[Map] CALIFORNIA, / TEXAS, / MEXICO, / AND PART OF THE / UNITED STATES. / COMPILED FROM THE LATEST AND BEST AUTHORITIES. /

Map, 21.8 x 25.4 cm. Scale: about 195 miles to one inch. Folded into pale blue printed boards, 9.3 x 7.8 cm., with title on front cover.

Ref.:

Published before March, 1847, since that date appears in manuscript in an inscription on the inner front cover.

4798 ZIEGENFUSS, C. O.

WESTERN MONTANA. A REVIEW OF THE MINERAL, TIMBER AND AGRICULTURAL RESOURCES OF THE COUNTIES OF SILVER BOW, JEFFERSON, MADISON, BEAVERHEAD, DEER LODGE AND MISSOULA WITH SPECIAL REFERENCE TO BUTTE CITY . . . BUTTE, MONTANA: PRESS OF INTER MOUNTAIN PUBLISHING COMPANY, 1886.

[1]–176. (Pages [1–2] advertisements.) 21.1 x 13.8 cm. Folding map: Map / Showing Location / —of— / Surveyed Mining Claims / in the Vicinity / —of— / Butte City, M. T. / January 1st, 1886. / [decorative rule] / Kornberg & Hoff, / Civil Engineers and Surveyors, / Butte City, M. T. / 20 x 33 cm. No scale given. Gray printed wrappers, with title on front wrapper. In a brown half morocco box.

Ref.: Howes Z10

Advertising matter interspersed throughout included in pagination.

4799 ZINCKE, F. BARHAM

AUTOGRAPH MANUSCRIPT, SIGNED, of A winter in the United States. / by / F. Barham Zwincke[!] / Vicar of Wherestead, & Chaplain in Ordinary to the Queen. / Murray—1868. / This M. S. was written in the summer of 1868; the greater part of it during a fit of / gout. I had made no notes of the excursion it describes. The only memoranda I had for facts / & dates were contained in the letters I had in its course from time to time written to my wife. / Some of the most illegibly written pages of the M.S. she recopied for me, to save time. / These will be found in in[!] her handwriting— /

363 pages, 22.7 x 18.5 cm. Bound in red cloth almost matching the cloth of the printed work.

The manuscript was used by the printer for the original (and only) edition.

4800 ZINCKE, F. BARHAM

LAST WINTER IN THE UNITED STATES, BEING TABLE TALK COLLECTED DURING A TOUR THROUGH THE LATE SOUTHERN CONFEDERATION, THE FAR WEST, THE ROCKY MOUNTAINS, &C. . . . LONDON: JOHN MURRAY, 1868.

[i]–xvi, [1]–314, [1]–6 advertisements. 19.5 x 12.2 cm. Red cloth, blind borders on covers, title gilt on backstrip, uncut.

Ref.: Clark (*New South*) I 245; Howes Z15

4801 ZUNIGA, IGNACIO

RAPIDA OJEADA AL ESTADO DE SONORA . . . MEJICO: IMPRESO POR JUAN OJEDA, 1835.

[1]–66. 20.2 x 14.6 cm. Rebound in marbled wrappers. In a brown cloth case.

Ref.: Howes Z25; Sabin 106402

Account of his attempt to establish a colony in present Arizona [on the Colorado and Gitos] with a view of uniting New Mexico and California.—Howes

Index

The following index is designed to guide the reader in using the catalogue. It contains the names of all individuals mentioned in the text, except those used as main entries of the catalogue and those of bibliographers cited under the heading *Ref*. Publishers and printers, where known, have been included. Places mentioned in the text of the catalogue and places of particular importance in the texts of the books described are listed. While large areas (Northeast, Northwest Territory, Southwest, etc.) appear in the index, we have also tried to define areas more specifically, i.e., Illinois, Kansas, Chicago, etc. Territories and states are listed in each instance under the final state name.

Subjects treated in the books described are indexed as far as is practical; certainly, most of the important subjects are noted whether or not they are mentioned on the title pages. But it is patently impossible to include all subjects mentioned. For instance, in noting that General George Crook was in Arizona after the Civil War, Crook and Arizona are entered, but not the Civil War. Certain portmanteau subject headings have been unavoidable, such as *Ranching*, which includes works about cattle, grass, range lands, etc. It has unfortunately been impossible to break down further many of these portmanteau entries, long as they are, because of the aforementioned fact that most of the books cover a variety of topics and because further subdivision would have made an index already long and complex even longer and more cumbrous.

Index entries in italics are book titles. Italicized entries within quotation marks are titles of maps or engravings. Roman entries within quotation marks are usually titles of essays, articles, or extracts; in some instances, quotation marks appear in publishers' entries, as in "Daily News" Printing House.

Adjutant General, U.S. Army, Washington, D.C. Sir:—As the Chiricahua Apache Campaign Has Ended . . . 1886 4362
Adjutant General's Office: See also U.S. Army 4253–4266
Admission of New States 3737
Adobe Walls, Tex. 183, 3264, 4460
Adventures and Experience of Joseph H. Jackson . . . 1846 2176
Adventures and Explorations in New and Old Mexico . . . 1861 372
Adventures and Narrow Escapes in Nicaragua . . . 1872 4749
Adventures and Recollections of General Walter P. Lane . . . 1887 2384
Adventures in Mexico 3614
Adventures in Mexico and the Rocky Mountains . . . 1847 3620, 3621, 3622
Adventures in Texas . . . 1841 2575
Adventures in the Apache Country . . . 1869 437
Adventures in the Camanche Country . . . 1848 4564
Adventures in the Canyons of the Colorado . . . 1920 204
Adventures in the Pacific . . . 1845 886
"Adventures in the Rocky Mountains" 54
Adventures in the Rocky Mountains in 1834 54
Adventures of a Seventeen-Year-Old Lad and the Fortunes He Might Have Won . . . 1894 4679
Adventures of Antelope Bill in the Indian War of 1862 . . . 1898 3241
Adventures of Big-Foot Wallace . . . 1871 1187
Adventures of Chas. L. Youngblood . . . 1882 4795
Adventures of Huckleberry Finn . . . 1885 760
Adventures of James Capen Adams . . . 1860 1912
Adventures of My Grandfather . . . 1867 3265
Adventures of Teddy Johnson . . . 1901 4473
Adventures of the First Settlers on the Oregon or Columbia River . . . 1849 3576, 3577
Adventures of Two Alabama Boys . . . 1912 937
Adventures on the Columbia River . . . 1831 893
Adventures on the Plains . . . 1922 582
Adventures on the Western Coast of South America . . . 1847 886
Adventures with Indians and Game 44
Advertisements 2055
Advertiser, The 3208
Advertiser Book and Job Office 527
Advertiser Print 1467, 2966
"Advocate" Book and Job Office, Print 3478
Advocates for Devils Refuted . . . 1845 2021
"*Affair of Bladensburg*" 4670
"*Affair of Princeton*" 4670
Affairs at Fort Chartres, 1768–1781 . . . 1864 530, 4662

Affecting Narrative of the Captivity and Sufferings of Mrs. Mary Smith . . . 1815 3862, 3863
Affleck, I. D. 3676
Afoot and Alone . . . 1873 1804, 3339
Africa 409, 699, 2536, 3250, 3946
After Forty Years . . . ca. 1906 1595
After Having Resisted the Open Efforts of the Enemy . . . 1815 4364
After 60 Years . . . 1925 2858, 3134
"'*After the Chase*'" 2000
Aftermath . . . 1896 2461
Agassiz, A. 42
Age Water Power Print 2095
Agencies 4326, 4327
Agriculture: See also Farming 2231, 2912, 4234, 4492
Agriculture Library, Department of 1030
Aguayo, Marques de San Miguel de 3242
Aguayo Expedition 3242
Aguilar, Josefa 1261
Aitken, R. 895
Aitkin, Jane 3639
"Ajax" 1810, 3051
Akademische Buchhandlung 3099
Akron, O. 2383
Al Perfecto del Candado de . . . 1865 3004
Alabama 409, 735, 937, 1649, 2794, 3417, 3591, 4118, 4299, 4300, 4384, 4744
Alabama, Senator from 755
Alamo, Fall of the 4220
Alamo, The 2503, 2695, 2696
Alamo Printing Co. 2727
Alamos, Sonora, Mexico 3891
Alarick, Rafael & Liandro 47
Alaska 22, 28, 91, 120, 406, 407, 449, 450, 562, 570, 583, 681, 763, 805, 876, 901, 905, 908, 1029, 1083, 1143, 1303, 1440, 1678, 1821, 1832, 2346, 2357, 2362, 2363, 2402, 2452, 2506, 2557, 2572, 2626, 2697, 2848, 2937, 3074, 3169, 3281, 3282, 3287, 3288, 3507, 3602, 3708, 3794, 3888, 3937, 3938, 3999, 4096, 4199, 4203, 4356, 4710, 4712
Alaska . . . 1895 449
Alaska Exploring Expedition of 1883 3708
"*Alaska Peninsula and Aleutian Islands*' 450
Alaskan Gold Fields 4712
Albany, N.Y. 1241, 4062, 4790
Albany County, Wyo. 1945
Albany, Fort 1840
Albany River 1840
Albemarle Sound 2202
Alberquerque: See Albuquerque
Albert, Duke of Saxe-Gotha 2506
Albion, Ill. 1367, 4742
Albro, B. T. 4613
Albuquerque 101, 108, 2420, 2743, 2990, 4231, 4735
Alcala, Martin 2455
Alcatraz Island, Calif. 4356
"*Alcatraz Island, Cal.*" 4356
Alcohol 3742
Alden, I. 1317
Alden, I. S. 1317

Alden, J. B. 1666
Alden, W. 1317
Aldrich, D. 2601
Aldrich Party 2600
Alert (ship) 372, 3271
Aleutian Islands 416, 450
Alexander, C. 4363
Alexander College 3270
Alexander, Fort 3215
"Alexander von Humboldt's Correspondence with Jefferson, Madison, and Gallatin" 3290, 3291, 3292
Alexandre's . . . Compendium . . . 1901 34
Alexandria, La. 1357
Alexis, Grand Duke 35
Algodon, Cloth of 3910
Algodon, Spain 3910
Algona Bee . . . 1922 2108
Algona, Ia. 2108
Allegan County, Mich. 860, 1244
Allegany Towns 2532
Alleghany Mountains 1556, 2185, 2780, 2781, 2806, 3266, 3462
Alleghany River 97, 2954, 3707
Allegheny, Penna. 902
Allen, C. 17
Allen, C. H. 4736
Allen, E. 1794
Allen, F. P. 222
Allen, J. 2397, 3698, 3703, 3704
Allen, J. L. 2461
Allen, P. 2477
Allen, T. 43, 4381
Allen, W. 4062
Allen, W. D. 2486
Allen, W. H. 1694
Allen, Z. 4183
"Allen, Montana" 44
Allen broadside 3703, 3704
Alley, B. F. 2385
Allgemeine Zeitung (Munich) 4491
Alling, W. 2031
Allison, C. 183
Allison, Scout E. H. 479
Allison Ranch 531
Allsop, F. W. 802
Alma, Nebr. 1905
Almanac 649, 1194, 1201, 3031, 3526, 3816, 4183
Almanac and Traveler's Guide for 1851 . . . 3816
Almaden Mining Case 3666
Almon, J. 2029, 3341
Along Alaska's Great River . . . 1885 3708
Alonzo 4005
Alta, Calif. 634
Alta California 3525
Alta California 539, 637, 4593
Alta California Job Office 1038
Altar, El 4468
Altemus, H. 876
Alter, Calif. 4618
Alton, Ill. 1706, 3191, 3237, 3381, 3608, 3729, 4752
Alton Observer—Extra . . . 1838 2078
Alton Riots 1380
Altowan . . . 1846 3986
Alturas County, Ida. 3485

Alturas Mining Reporter and Key to the Mammoth Cabinet of Ores . . . 1883 3485
Alumni Society of the University of Nashville 4516
Alvarado, Mex. 1092, 1094
Alvarez, Manuel 47, 3004
Alvin, Tex. 2293
Alvord, B. 4352
Amateur Newspaper 1529
Ambrose Island 812
Ambrosio de Letinez . . . 1842 1502
Amelia Island 4378, 4409
"Amendments to the Organic Act" (Dakota) 986
America, Discovery of 3867
"Americae Descrip." 1471
American, Office of the 4495
American, Yr . . . 1840 692
American-Anderson Galleries 475
American Antiquarian Society 35, 1146, 1454, 1647, 1786, 2408
American Antiquarian Society, Proceedings of the 1368, 1454
American Association for the Advancement of Science 413, 4624
American Baptist Board of Foreign Missions, Press of 285
American Baptist Flag Office 167
American Baptist Publication Society 129, 4200
American Bible Society 287
American Bisons . . . 1876 42
American Board of Commissioners for Foreign Missions 2827
American, Chicago 969
American Colonization Society 1209
American Family Robinson . . . 1854 238
American Flat, Nev. 1882
American Freeman 781
American Freeman Print 1679
American Frontier Government 3760
American Fur Company 1996
American Fur Trade of the Far West . . . 1902 696
American Geographical & Statistical Society 2921, 3976
American Geographical Society Library 52
American Historical Association Journal 1022
American Home Missionary Society 3587, 3660, 4208
American Institute 2388
American Institute of Graphic Arts 4558
American Instructor . . . 1826 2285
American Ivy pamphlet 1700
American Journal of Science and Arts . . . 1859 321
American Missionary Establishment 1216
American Monthly Journal of Geology 924
American Museum, or, Universal Magazine 51
American News Co. 560, 1093, 1237
American Office 1933
American Ornithology 4700
American Phalanx 2195
American Philosophical Society 2779

American Photo-Lithographic Co. 1111, 1449
American Pioneer . . . 1842 4681
American Printing Co. 1895
American Publishing Co. 762, 4757
American Quarterly Register 135
American Reform Tract and Book Society 322
American Register and Magazine 3141, 4149
American-Russian Relations 879
American Sketch Book . . . 1879 52
American Society 3720
"American Society" 3935
American Society for Encouraging the Settlement of the Oregon Territory 2288
American Society for Promoting the Civilization and General Improvement of the Indian Tribes within the United States 3007
American State Papers 290, 2874
American Tales 1237
American Technical Book 2362
American Turf Register and Sporting Magazine 54
Amerikanische Jagd- und Reiseabenteuer . . . 1858 4015, 4016
Amerman, J. W. 330
Amherst, Mass. 331
Amis, C. 3013
Amity College Association 56
"Ammunition" 4508
Among the Cotton Thieves . . . 1867 131
Among the Indians . . . 1868 341, 342
Among the Shoshones . . . 1910 4702
Among the Sioux of Dakota . . . 1881 3315
Amos Wright (ship) 2308
Amsterdam 3099
Amsterdam, Ile d' 3250
Amusing and Thrilling Adventures . . . 1854 2244, 2245, 3273, 3274
Anaconda 1846
Anahuac Mountains 1294, 1295
Analectic Magazine . . . 1820 58
Analysis of Theology, Law, Religion, and the Rights of Man . . . 1855 3563
Anarchism 3808
Anatomy 4724
Ancestors and Descendants of Isaac Alden and Irene Smith . . . 1903 1317
Anchor Island 4456
"Anchor Island Harbour" 4456
Anchor Publishing Co. 237
"Ancient Fortification on the Missouri" 2480, 2481
Ancient York Masons 1417
Andele; or, the Mexican-Kiowa Captive . . . 1899 2764
Anderson, A. 3258
Anderson, A. C. 59
Anderson, Bill 1213
Anderson, E. I. 2620
Anderson, H. C. 3107, 3108, 3109
Anderson, M. B. 2253, 2405, 2406
Anderson, T. J. 2266
Anderson, W. M. 54
Anderson, W. T. 1585

Anderson Galleries 2619
Andreas, A. T. 351, 560
Andrew County, Mo. 1642
Andrew Jackson Potter, the Noted Parson of the Texan Frontier . . . 1883 1618
Andrews, E. A. 2908
A'Neals, J. W., & Co. 3342
Anecdotes of Buffalo Bill . . . 1912 4713
Angel Island, Calif. 4356
"Angel Island, Cal." 4356
Angelo, V. 3054
Anian, Strait of 460
Anjouan, Ile d' 3250
"Anecdotes of the Mines" 637
Ann Onymous 4202
Annales de la Propagation de la Foi pour le Diocèse de Montreal . . . 1874–76 3887
Annals of a Western Missionary . . . 1853 65
Annals of Chicago . . . 1840 151
Annals of Iowa 1488, 2918, 4129
Annals of Old Fort Cummings New Mexico . . . n.d. 3197
Annals of San Francisco . . . 1855 3901
Annals of the City of Kansas . . . 1858 3917, 3918
Annals of the Minnesota Historical Society . . . 1851, 1852, 1853 2822–2824
Annals of the Propagation of the Faith . . . 1877–83 3885
Annapolis Royal 2855
"Annapolis Royal" 650
"Annexation of Texas, The" 1492
Annie: A Tragic Dramina . . . 1869 441
Annin & Smith 1786
Anniversary Exercises of the Omaha Public Schools . . . 1873 3111
Annual 1741
Annual Message of Mark W. Izard . . . 1855 2963
Annual Message to the Legislative Assembly of Nebraska . . . 1857 2957
Annual Register of Indian Affairs . . . 1836, 1837, 1838 2586–2588
Annual Report . . . Auditor and Treasurer of the Territory of Montana . . . 1887 2862
Annual Report . . . Chief Quartermaster 2320
Annual Report . . . Colonization Society of the State of Iowa . . . 1857 813
Annual Report . . . Commissioner of Indian Affairs 48
Annual Report . . . (Crook) . . . 1883, 1885 928, 929
Annual Report . . . Department of Arizona . . . 1875, 1876, 1877, 1879, 1882, 1886, 1887, 1888 2277–2279, 2785–2787, 4671, 4672
Annual Report . . . Department of the Columbia . . . 1879 1980
Annual Report . . . Department of the Missouri, 1889 2760
Annual Report . . . (Graham) . . . 2082

Browning, O. H. 226, 2281
Brown's Flat Mining Laws 1844
Brown's Marysville Directory . . . 1861 434
Brownson, Elder 3346
Brownson, O. A., Jr. 1160
Brownsville 3778
Brownville, Nebr. 228, 766, 973, 1467, 2967, 2968, 3412, 4729
Brownville, 1st December, 1817. To Major General Brown. My Dear Sir . . . 3997
Brownville, Ft. Kearney & Pacific Railroad 4729
Bruce, J. P. 2868
Bruce & Wright 2733
"Bruce's Map of Alaska, M. W." 450
Bruckett, A. G. 4672
Brulé Agency, Mont. 4327
"Brulé" Band 4546
Brulé Index 1154
Brulé Sioux 46
Brumfield, W. H. 2121
Bruns, J. H. 1175
Brunt, Walter N., Co. 3305
Brussels, Court of 3670
Brutus Guards, 22d Company, V. C. 4480
Bruyset Ainé et Buynand 3254
Bryan, F. T. 2228, 4416
Bryan, G. M. 557
Bryan, W. S. 4069
Bryan & Millar 2793
Bryan, Brand & Co. 1213, 2441, 3435
Bryanites 3061
Bryan's Pass 4416
Bryant, E. 1486, 4538
Bryant, T. 459
Bryant, Wm. C., & Co. 4249–4251
Buache, P. 2363
Buccaneer, The 4005
Buchanan, J. 2863
Buchanan, James 637, 2035, 2568, 4414, 4416, 4417
Buchanan, W. 2587
Buchanan County, Nebr. 2460
Buchmeyer, Mrs. A. J. 2246
Buchtel & Stolte 4683
Buck, J. J. 202
Bucking the Sagebrush . . . 1904 3957
Buck-Molina Co. 456
"Buckskin Bill" 623, 3421
Buckskin Clothing 124
Buckskin Mose . . . 1873 3252
Budd, Sir Cecil L. 826
Budd, J. G. 1517
Buechner, L. 2757, 3835
Buell, B. S. 1558, 1929, 3344
Buell & Blanchard 3308
Buena Vista, Mex. 1799
Buena Vista County, Ia. 200
Buffalo, N. Y. 1009, 1958, 2233, 2524, 3056, 3255, 3816, 4183
Buffalo Bill: See Cody, W. F.
"Buffalo Bill" 4616, 4677
"Buffalo Bill" from Prairie to Palace . . . 1893 486
"Buffalo Bill" (The Hon. William F. Cody) Rifle and Revolver Shot . . . 1887 4677
Buffalo Bill's Wild West 486, 784, 785
Buffalo Bill's Wild West . . . 1893 784

Buffalo Bill's Wild West. America's National Entertainment . . . 1884 785
Buffalo Child Long Lance 470, 471
Buffalo Country 1788
" 'Buffalo Family Big Dry Creek' " 2000
" 'Buffalo Grazing in the Big Open, North Montana, 1880' " 2000
Buffalo Hunters 183, 4460, 4677
Buffalo Hunting 1073, 2190, 4580
Buffalo Hunts 277, 1013, 1073, 1889, 2190, 4580, 4709
Buffalo Jones' Forty Years of Adventure . . . 1899 2233
Buffalo Lake, Minn. 591
" 'Buffalo near Smoky Butte, North Montana' " 2000
Buffalo Range 1112, 1113
"Buffalo to Council Bluffs, St. Louis to Toronto" 1009
Buffalo Wallow 183
Buffaloes 20, 35, 183, 277, 768, 785, 864, 1013, 1112, 1113, 1178, 1342, 1788, 1889, 2000, 2233, 2512, 2668, 2669, 4460, 4597, 4677, 4709, 4756
Bufford's Lith., J. H. 867
Buford, Camp near Fort 4293
Buford, Fort 46, 343, 479, 4327, 4293
Bugle, The 2918
Bugle Office 1362
Buillemin, A. 2361
Buisson, F. 2735, 2736, 3524
Bulfinch, C. 4380
Bull, J. P. 3968
Bull Bros. 4530
Bulletin de la Société de Géographie . . . 1835 3884
Bulletin Office 1242
"Bulletin" Steam Book and Job Printing Rooms 18
Bullion, Ida. 3485
Bullock, T. 716, 717
Bullock, W. 2163, 2167
Bunky 1534
Bunny 2030
Burch, I. H. 226
Burch, J. C. 2739
Burch, Mary W. 226
Burdette Co. 1535
Burdick, U. P. 46, 1451
Bure l'Aîné 2462
Bureau County, Ill. 1379, 2715, 2716, 2719
Bureau de Publication de la Bibliothèque d'Education 3044
Bureau of Immigration, N. Mex. 2990, 2991, 3513
Bureau of Indian Affairs 4384
Bureau of Statistics 4423–4425
Bureau of Topographical Engineers: See United States. Army. Engineers, Corps of
Burfurst, Otto 2850
Burgess, H. 637
Burgess, Stringer & Co. 2464
Burke, J. M. 486, 785
Burke, T. 3367
Burke, W. S. 2266
Burke, Boykin & Co. 2529
Burkley Envelope and Printing Co. 489

Burleigh, W. A. 315
Burley, A. H. 2072, 2073
Burley, A. H. & C. 1745, 4229
Burlington, Ia. 371, 517, 1489, 1856, 1889, 2121, 2376, 2456, 2457, 2555, 3013–3015, 3392, 3422, 3570, 3657, 3658, 4233, 4584, 4716, 4717, 4719, 4729
Burlington, N.J. 924
Burlington, Wis. 2799
Burlington and Missouri River Railroad 4729
Burlington, Cedar Rapids, & Northern Railway 1943
Burlington Hawk-Eye Print 3013, 3014
Burlington Route 682
Burnet, D. G. 1497, 1975
Burnet Grant 4737
Burnett, W. B. 1690
Burney, D. 497
Burnham 1762
Burns, B. J. 4683
Burntwood River 3698
Burntwood (or Broulé) River 3698
Burpee, L. J. 1853, 2403, 2937
Burr, A. 673, 732, 1056, 1176, 1613, 2625, 2690, 3338, 4408, 4669
Burr, D. H. 335, 1653
Burr Printing House 1870
Burr-Wilkinson Conspiracy 502–506, 673, 732, 1056, 1175, 1176, 1613, 1713, 2625, 2690, 3338, 4373, 4376, 4408, 4668, 4669, 4748
Burr-Wilkinson Correspondence 4668
Burr-Wilkinson Cypher 4668
Burriel, Father Andres Marcos 4470
Burros 785
Burroughs, H. N. 2839, 2841
Burrows, J. M. D. 1924
Burrows Block 1924
Burr's Conspiracy Exposed . . . 1811 4669
Burt, A. 509
Burton, R. F. 2677
Burton, W. E. 513
Burton's Gentleman's Magazine . . . 1840 513
Bush, A. 3121, 3122
Bushnell's Business & Residence Directory of Council Bluffs . . . 1868 515
Bushwhackers 1883, 1884, 4332
Business Advertiser and General Directory of the City of Chicago, for the Year 1845–6 . . . 1845 3028
Business & Residence Directory of Council Bluffs . . . 1868 515
Business Card 3221
"Business Directory" (Princeton, Ill.) 3848
"Business Directory for St. Augustine" 4643
"Business Directory of Santa Fe" 4703
Bussey, W. 1110
Bute, Lord 3916
Butler, B. F. 4738
Butler, Gov. 3245
Butler, J. 143
Butler, J. D. 1368
Butler, Mrs. Pierce 2299

Butler, Ruth Lapham 2883
Butler, S. T. 3006
Butler, W. H. 3378
Butler, W. H. & S. G. 665
Butler & Bowman 3723
Butler & Lambdin 3212
Butler, Sir William, An Autobiography . . . 1911 521
Butte, Mont. 3277, 4798
Butte Bystander 3277
Butte County, Calif. 293
Butte Miner Company 451
Butterfield, B. 4144
Butterfield, C. W. 1841
Butterfield Overland Mail Company 3403
Butterfield Stage 2213, 4204
Buttricke, G. 4662
Butts, O. 4129
Buyer's Book of Memorandums . . . 1870 2417
"By-Gone Days" 1705
By-Laws, Articles of Incorporation and House Rules . . . the Cheyenne Club . . . 1888 674
By Laws of Boonville R. A. Chapter No. 3 . . . 1844 1419
By-Laws of Clarksville Lodge No. 17 . . . ca. 1837 1420
By-Laws of Palmyra Lodge, No. 18 . . . 1837 1421
By-Laws of St. Louis Lodge, No. 1 . . . 1835 1422
By-Laws of St. Paul Lodge, No. 1 . . . 1849 1418
By-Laws of Stock Board District No. 6 . . . 1880 2056
By-Laws of the Rocky Mountain Medical Association . . . 1875 3541
By-Laws of the Webster Kentucky Farm Association . . . 1858 4569
By-Laws of Wyandotte Lodge, No. 3 . . . 1858 1417
By Ox Team to California . . . 1910 3325
By Ox-Team to California . . . 1916 2016
Byers, W. N. 3543
Byers & Dailey 4617
Bytown, Mgr. l'Evêque de 3887

C., A.N.J. 3540
C., M. 1582
C. F. Smith, Fort 954, 2520, 4099
CK Ranch 1095
Cabet, E. 2039
Cabin Book . . . 1844, 1852 3718, 3719
Cabo de las Virgenes 4470
Caborca 3151
Cabrillo, Juan Rodriguez 4072
Cache La Poudre 4243, 4416, 4722
Cache La Poudre River 3140
Caddoes 48, 208
Cadell & Davies 416, 1840, 2630, 2631
Cadiack Island 2506
Cadmus Book Shop 3836
Cadwalader, A. 534
Cady, Ellen D. 1017
Caffrey, D. Mc., & McLoughlin, E. Frank 684

Cage, J. 2250
Cain, J. 4450
Cairo, Ill. 3638
Caiter, O. M. 4312
Cajon Pass 4435
Calamity Jane 483, 484
Calaveras, Calif. 1844
Calaveras County, Calif. 2101, 3403
Calcraft, J. H. 3115
Calderon, La Viuda de Bernardo 3681
Caldwell, E. 3565
Caldwell, F. 740
Caldwell, J. 2184, 2185
Caldwell, Kans. 1411, 3906
Caledonia 2831
Calendar, The 2917
Calhoun, F. C. S. 3690
Calhoun, J. C. 40, 290, 1084, 3858
Calhoun, J. S. 2997, 3003, 4576
Calhoun, S. H. 1639
Calhoun & Woodruff 2971
Calhoun Printing Company 785
Calhoun's Speech 4568
California 1, 2, 9, 11, 29, 59, 67, 78, 83, 102, 111, 114, 122, 125, 127, 137, 139, 188, 193, 197, 198, 199, 209, 215, 219, 240, 245, 252, 253, 261, 269, 272, 291–293, 298, 328, 338, 358, 359, 364, 370, 390, 391, 393, 396, 403, 404, 408, 412, 416, 425, 429, 431, 434, 437, 457, 458, 472, 494, 531, 536, 539, 550, 565, 571, 580, 582, 590, 604, 606, 609, 618, 619, 623, 625, 629, 633–635, 637, 641, 643, 694, 700, 726, 727, 729, 733, 742, 746, 747, 754, 762, 764, 769, 794–796, 799, 801, 812, 835, 839, 841–844, 851, 868–870, 879, 880, 882, 884, 886, 897, 909, 910, 921, 937, 965, 994, 995, 998, 1018, 1020, 1024, 1027, 1042–1044, 1050, 1059, 1075, 1077, 1078, 1091, 1142, 1143, 1146, 1149, 1169, 1178, 1179, 1184, 1189, 1190, 1195, 1216, 1225, 1228, 1250, 1252, 1262, 1264, 1273, 1281, 1286, 1293–1295, 1305, 1306, 1308, 1315, 1316, 1318, 1319, 1338, 1347, 1350, 1377, 1387, 1390, 1391, 1400–1402, 1429–1431, 1433–1436, 1443–1448, 1525, 1539, 1541, 1546, 1550, 1551, 1554, 1556, 1570, 1575, 1581, 1585, 1595, 1601, 1609, 1610, 1614, 1625, 1626, 1632, 1635, 1652, 1653, 1674, 1688, 1696, 1697, 1716, 1724–1726, 1743, 1746, 1761, 1783, 1784, 1799, 1812, 1815, 1837, 1844, 1848, 1874, 1888, 1895, 1899, 1901, 1910–1912, 1919, 1952–1954, 1964, 2003–2006, 2008, 2012, 2016–2018, 2022, 2026–2028, 2059, 2101, 2106, 2160, 2162, 2169–2171, 2180, 2181, 2205, 2211, 2221, 2223–2225, 2229, 2236, 2244, 2254–2256, 2258, 2284, 2290, 2291, 2293, 2298, 2315, 2329, 2333, 2341, 2343, 2344, 2352, 2355, 2361, 2383, 2385, 2390–2392, 2397, 2429, 2443, 2447, 2461, 2469, 2516, 2518, 2519, 2521, 2523, 2562, 2564, 2565, 2598, 2600–2602, 2610, 2611, 2614, 2615, 2632, 2648, 2651, 2664, 2670, 2676, 2677, 2685,

2686, 2693, 2698, 2711, 2720, 2721, 2728, 2739, 2758, 2761, 2771, 2777, 2791, 2813, 2839, 2841, 2885, 2909, 2919, 2923, 2929, 2943, 2951, 2985, 2986, 3016, 3020, 3024, 3042, 3045, 3056, 3098, 3131, 3132, 3151, 3154, 3157, 3173, 3175, 3178–3180, 3201, 3204, 3211, 3216, 3217, 3252, 3255, 3257, 3259–3263, 3269, 3271–3274, 3279, 3304, 3305, 3309, 3324, 3325, 3333, 3334, 3339, 3345, 3365, 3403, 3431, 3433, 3450, 3473–3475, 3488, 3491, 3503, 3504, 3525, 3527, 3551, 3553, 3558, 3562, 3565, 3597, 3598, 3626, 3633–3635, 3637, 3652, 3653, 3664–3667, 3669, 3687, 3688, 3691–3693, 3695, 3705, 3723, 3744, 3745, 3760, 3783, 3786, 3788, 3791, 3793, 3811, 3814, 3836, 3865, 3884, 3901, 3926, 3927, 3939, 3954, 3959, 3962–3966, 3968, 3972, 3983, 3988, 4007, 4013, 4021, 4031, 4040, 4041, 4047–4049, 4051, 4059, 4060, 4068, 4072–4074, 4084, 4103, 4104, 4114, 4124, 4132, 4134, 4136, 4138, 4143, 4157, 4185, 4201, 4204, 4207, 4225, 4230, 4252, 4254, 4317, 4318, 4356, 4388, 4416, 4434, 4446, 4468, 4470, 4471, 4480, 4488, 4491, 4492, 4494, 4496, 4497, 4502, 4504, 4509, 4515, 4538, 4540, 4548, 4549, 4558, 4559, 4561, 4571, 4572–4574, 4584, 4586, 4589, 4590, 4593, 4598, 4600, 4613, 4635, 4646, 4650, 4654, 4656, 4673, 4674, 4679, 4682, 4687, 4707, 4728, 4732, 4733, 4735, 4736, 4741, 4745, 4784, 4785, 4797, 4801
"*California . . . 1839*" 1377
California . . . 1848 2003
California . . . 1850 1347
"*California 1854*" 580
California . . . 1856 2022
California, a Trip across the Plains, in the Spring of 1850 . . . 1850 1
California, Alta 4468
California and Its Gold Regions . . . 1849 835, 3527
California and Oregon Trail . . . 1849 3201
California As It Is . . . 1851 1716
California As It Is and As It May Be . . . 1849 4650, 4651
California As She Was: As She Is: As She Is to Be . . . 1850 269
California Chronik (San Francisco) 4491
California Coast 2205, 2632
California, Conquest of 637, 1142, 2003, 2564, 3173, 3474, 3475
California Constitutional Convention 540, 548
California Crusoe . . . 1854 3488
California, Department of 3601, 4254, 4355, 4388
California, 1849–1913 . . . 1913 4745
California Emigrants 3790
California Express, Office of the 2698
California, First Volunteer Infantry of 4268
California 49er . . . 1903 2632
California '46 to '88 . . . 1888 1783

"[*California from below Los Angeles to above San Francisco*]" 1387
California Gold . . . 1894 425
California Gold Region 835
California, Gulf of 1059, 4468, 4488
California Historical Society 582, 769
California Historical Society Quarterly 3250, 4491, 4732, 4733
California Illustrated . . . 1852 2469
California Imprints . . . 1922 4504
California in 1837 . . . 1890 1216
"California in 1837" 1216
California in 1850 . . . 1851 4007
California in 1851 . . . 1933 727
California in '41. Texas in '51 . . . 1901 1027
California Indian War Debt 1697
California Indians 4488
California: Its History, Population, Climate, Soil, Productions, and Harbors 3173
California Joe 467
California Land Commission 2514
"California Landscapes" 4492
"California Lion and a Pirate" 637
California, Location of State Capitol 543
California, Lower 246, 747
California Mines 2
California Mining District (Colo.) 148
California Missions 625, 1250
California Overland Express . . . 1865 4059
California Phalanx 11
"*California per P. Ferdinandum Consak*" 137
California Pioneers 1812
California Scenes . . . 1855 2027
California (ship) 460, 3154, 4491
California Sketches . . . 1850 2343
California State Telegraph Company 4589
"*California, Texas, Mexico, and Part of the United States*" 1195, 4797
California, University of 137
California Volunteers, Company K, First Infantry, 3263
California, Voyage of the 460
California Water 3250
Californian . . . 1847 550
"*Californian Method of Killing Cattle*" 4492
"Californiana" 637
Californias 3063
"*Californias: Antigua y Nueva*" 3179
"*Californie, La, d'après une très grande Carte Espagnole*" 460
Californie Devoilee, La . . . 1850 4185
Californien und das Goldfieber . . . 1863 4496
Californische Skizzen . . . 1856 1541
Calkins & Co., C. W. 4054
"*Callicum et Maquilla*" 2736
Callison, Mineeba 4683
Calumet, The 232, 555
Calvert Company 4710
Calvinism 439, 2021
Calvo, C. A., Jr. 3709
Camanche: See also Comanche
Camanche Country 4566

Camas, Ida. 3485, 4330
Camas Prairie and Wood River Colonization Co. (Ida.) 3485
Cambridge, Washington Co., N.Y. 3537
Cambridge Academy 3537
Cambridge University Press 49, 2598
Camels 4436, 4437
Cameron & Fall 3985
Cameron, Ill. 3034
Cameron, Fort 4327
Camp, C. L. 2850, 3282, 4506
Camp, J. G. 3073
Camp, T. C. 2991
Camp, W. M. 2804
Camp and Prison Journal . . . 1867 1455
"*Camp Apache, A. T.*" 4356
Camp Baker, Mont. 4327
"*Camp Bidwell, Cal.*" 4356
"*Camp Bowie, A. T.*" 4356
Camp Brown, Wyo. 4327
Camp Cooke, Dak. 4293
Camp Dahlgreen, Ore. 4683
Camp Douglas, Tenn. 877
Camp Douglas, Utah 2037, 4327
Camp Floyd, Utah 3791
"*Camp Gaston, Cal.*" 4356
"*Camp Grant, A. T.*" 4356
"*Camp Halleck, Nev.*" 4356
Camp Harney, Ore. 4290, 4356
"*Camp Harney, Ogn.*" 4356
"*Camp Howard, I. T.*" 4356
"*Camp Huachuca, A. T.*" 4356
"*Camp John A. Rucker, A. T.*" 4356
"*Camp Lowell, A.T.*" 4356
"*Camp McDermit, Nev.*" 4356
"*Camp McDowell, A.T.*" 4356
Camp McGarry, Nev. 4334
Camp Missouri, Missouri River 290
"*Camp Mojave, A.T.*" 4356
Camp near Fort Berthold 4293
Camp near Fort Buford 4293
Camp No. 2, U.P.R.R., Buffalo Co., Neb. 4240
Camp on Crazy Woman Fork 2420
Camp on Fresh Water Fork, Brazos River, Tex. 2420
"*Camp Reynolds, Angel Island, Cal.*" 4356
Camp Robinson, Nebr. 2420, 4327
Camp Scott 4437
Camp Sheridan, Nebr. 4327
Camp Stambaugh, Wyo. 4327, 4654
Camp Supply, Ind. Ter. 4327
Camp Thomas, Ariz. 4356
"*Camp Verde, A.T.*" 4356
Camp Walbach, Dak. 4246, 4250
Camp Watson, Ore. 554
"'*Camp—Weld*' C. T." 3344
Camp Wood, Tex. 2190
Camp Wright, Ore. 4683
Camp Yuma, Ariz. 3809
Campaign Biography 296
Campaign in New Mexico with Colonel Doniphan . . . 1847 1210
Campaigning against the Sioux . . . 1906 2257
Campaigning with Crook . . . 1890 2326
Campaigns of General Custer in the Northwest . . . 1881 4513

Campbell, A. H. 4435
Campbell, D. P. 1495
Campbell, H. 3260
Campbell, H., Jr. 3260
Campbell, H. J. 3737
Campbell, J. A. 3260, 4773
Campbell, J. L. 560
Campbell, Jas., & Co. 2310, 3028
Campbell, R. 2948, 3260
Campbell, R. A. 119
Campbell, R. I. 3013, 3014
Campbell, Robert, F.R.G.S. 562
Campbell, Robert, R.M.F.C. 562
Campbell, T. 2416
Campbell, W. J. 3696
Campbell & Hoogs' Directory . . . 1850 565, 2211
Campbell, Malcolm, Sheriff . . . 1932 1012, 2750
"Campbell's Map of Idaho" 560
Camping Parties 4348
Campos, Jose Maria 194
Canada 22, 28, 59, 100, 103, 113, 130, 133, 153, 154, 187, 320, 321, 327, 357, 460, 518–520, 522, 524, 537, 560, 562, 567–570, 588, 642, 643, 650, 651, 669, 681, 805, 835, 867, 876, 893, 900, 952, 1005, 1029, 1038, 1098, 1133, 1255, 1283, 1325, 1400, 1401, 1406, 1407, 1457, 1538, 1554, 1607, 1621, 1622, 1624, 1652, 1653, 1763, 1786, 1832, 1840, 1853, 1858–1864, 1866, 1874, 1892–1894, 1947, 1977, 2189, 2243, 2255, 2262, 2331, 2332, 2345, 2354, 2362–2366, 2403–2406, 2432, 2433, 2527, 2572, 2604, 2609, 2612, 2626, 2630, 2631, 2640, 2646, 2666, 2705, 2712, 2808, 2809, 2855, 3042, 3043, 3124, 3181, 3215, 3250, 3256, 3287, 3288, 3314, 3341, 3415, 3426, 3493, 3495, 3527, 3532, 3554, 3555, 3576–3580, 3627, 3763, 3785–3787, 3794, 3825–3827, 3829, 3831, 3885–3888, 3937, 3938, 4025, 4052, 4053, 4070, 4079, 4122, 4163, 4164, 4199, 4203, 4232, 4369, 4501, 4512, 4633, 4687, 4688, 4711, 4715, 4722
"*Canada and Part of the United States*" 2712
Canada Lode 4180
Canadian Border 3359
Canadian Pacific Railway 187
Canadian Pacific Railway, an Appeal to Public Opinion . . . 1885 569
Canadian Rebellion of 1837 3042
Canadian Red River Exploring Expedition 1894
Canadian River 3264, 3790
Canadian Rockies 519, 520, 1538
Canadienne, Imprimerie 4070
Canadiens de l'Ouest . . . 1878 4070
Canal Commissioners (Chicago) 4058
Canal Trustees (Chicago) 2075
Canals 105, 1084, 1869, 2074, 2075, 2952, 4058
Canby, E. R. S. 326, 4266, 4337, 4338
Canby, Fort 4356
"*Canby, W. T., Fort*" 4356
Canby Massacre 1458

Cancelada, Juan Lopez 3296
Canchalagua 1525
Cane, A. 3103
Cane-Hill Murders 95
Canfield, Emily 572
Cañizares, José de 3179
Cann, L. H. 4683
Cannibalism 1081, 1460, 1461, 2610
Canning, G. 2167
Cannon, F. J. 2371
Cannon, Geo. Q., & Sons Co. 426, 2370
Canoe and the Saddle . . . 1863 4715
Canoe Journey 3287
Canon City, Colo. 3344, 3668, 3905
Canonsburg, Penna. 3033
Canterbury, Archbishop of 658
Canton, China 2736
Canton, Fulton County, Ill. 4045
Canton, Miss. 4216
Canton, Nebr. 577
Canton, O. 322
Canton: Its Pioneers and History . . . 1871 4045
Cantor, M. 2442
Cantova, I. A. 2356
Canyons of the Colorado . . . 1895 3335
Cape Blanco, Wash. 4683
"*Cape Disappointment, W.T.*" 4356
Cape Douglas, Wash. 4456
Cape Horn 193, 245, 637, 812, 835, 998, 1688, 3474, 3475
"Cape Horn and Cooperative Mining in '49" 637
Cape Mendocino 1377
Cape Verde Islands 844
Capitaine Paul . . . 1838 1172
Capital Book Co. 912
Capital News Job Rooms 575
Capitol at Washington 2412
Capitol Hill, Des Moines, Ia. 4218
"*Capitulation . . . 1812*" 1388
Capron, J. P. 644
Captain Gray's Company . . . 1859 1180
Captain J. Allen's Expedition . . . 1846 41
Capt. J. D. Winchester's Experience on a Voyage from Lynn, Mass. . . . 1900 4712
Captain Jeff . . . 1906 2667
Captain John Baptiste Saucier . . . 1901 3880
Captain John Baptiste Saucier at Fort Chartres . . . 1901 3883
Captain Thornton Parker Fife Drum and Bugle Corps 3197
Capt. W. F. Drannan, Chief of Scouts . . . 1910 1148
Captive Maidens 3045
Captivity 903
Captivity and Massacre of the Oatman Family! . . . ca. 1857 3632, 4006
Capture and Escape . . . 1870 2399
Captured by the Indians . . . 1907 591
Carafa, Francesco 747
Carbery, I. I. 2566
Carbery, J. P. 2566
"*Carcass of a Whale*" 4492
Card, B. C. 4295

Cardelle, Clara 1073
Carey, H. C., & I. Lea 2188, 2280
Carey, J. M., & Bro. 1095
Carey, M. 51, 1518, 1520, 1521, 3839, 3840, 3994
Carey, M., & Son 303
Carey & Hart 584, 1210, 2112, 3633–3635, 3869, 4147
Carey, Lea & Blanchard 2157–2160
Carey, Ohio 393
Careys American Edition of Guthries Geography Improved 3839
Caribbees 650, 651, 1470, 1471
Cariboo 2646, 3215
"Cariboo" 1977
Caribou Mining District, Colo. 4459
Caricatures 3432
Carl Ehrlichkeit . . . 1869 442
Carleton, G. H. 585
Carleton, J. H. 793, 3141, 4336, 4338–4342, 4344–4347, 4399
Carleton, L. C. 1237
Carlin Hunting Party 1890
Carlinville, Macoupin County, Ill. 4160
Carlisle, D. 2876
Carlisle, Penna. 121
Carlton, R. 1723
Carlton & Porter 617, 1722, 2926
Carlton, Fort 2243
"*Carlton's Sectional Map of Iowa*" 585
Carmen, Presidio del 461, 462, 463
"Carnival Ball at Monterey in 1829" 637
Carolinas 1136, 1137, 2463, 2780, 2781, 2855, 4154
Caroline . . . 1870 443
Caroline, Susanna 1081
Caroline Islands 2356
Carondelet, Francisco Luis Hector, Baron de 3338
Carpenter, T. 506
Carpenters 353, 354, 355
Carpet-Bagger in Tennessee . . . 1869 202
Carr, C. C. C. 4445
Carr, E. 589
Carr, E. A. 4349
Carr, F. I. 1558
Carr, T. J. 71, 862
Carrasco, Francisco 693
Carrascoso (printer) 3279
Carrey, Paul 4546
Carrillo, Antonio Garcia 2765
Carrington, A. 3947
Carrington, E. 1056
Carrington, Frances C. 2924
Carrington, H. B. 305, 592, 596, 597, 598, 1312, 2520, 3297
Carroll, W. 4116
Carrollton (Ill.) Press 459
Carrothers, Mrs. Helen 4069
Carruth, J. A. 1341
Carruth, J. H. 3281, 3282
Carrying on for 50 Years with the Courage of Custer . . . 1926 2858
Carson, C. 206, 467, 1341, 1425, 1788, 1914, 1969, 2711, 3144, 3630, 3631, 4340
Carson City, Nev. 3056
Carson-Harper Co. 2212

Carson, Kit: See Carson, C.
Carson, Kit, Days . . . 1914 3629–3631
Carson's, Kit, Fight . . . 1878 3264
Carson's, Kit, Own Story . . . 1926 603
Carson Pass 880
Carson Valley 3791
Carson's Creek, Calif. 3403
Carta a los Habitantes de la Provincia de la Luisiana . . . 1780 2538
"*Carta de la Bahia del Espiritu Sto.*" 3242
"*Carta de la Mar del Sur, o Mar pacifico*" 4470
"*Carta de los Caminos*" 1092
"*Carta de los reconocimientos hechoes en 1602*" 1262
Carta del P. Fernando Consag . . . 1748 2355
"*Carta della California*" 747
"*Carta Esférica de los Reconocimientos hechos en la Costa N.O. de America*" 1262
Carta General de la República Mexicana de García Cubas 2765
"*Carta Geografica delle Diocesi delle Citta Vescovili*" 2732
"*Carte de la Bay et Detroit d'Hudson*" 133
"*Carte de la Baye de Hudson*" 650
"*Carte de l' Accadie*" 650
"*Carte de la Côte de l' Amérique*" 1169
"*Carte De la Côte N.O. d'Amérique*" 2736
"*Carte de la Découverte de la Terre d'Ielmer*" 4122
"*Carte de la découverte faite l'an 1663 dans l'Amérique Septentrionale*" 4122
"*Carte de La Louisiane*" 650, 1173, 2462
"*Carte de la Louisiane et du Cours du Mississipi*" 2507
"*Carte de la Mer Pacifique du Nord*" 2736
"*Carte de la nouuelle france*" 642
"*Carte de la Nouuelle France et de la Louisiane*" 1858
"*Carte de la Partie Intérieure de l'Amérique Septentrionale*" 2736
"*Carte de la Partie Orientale de la Nouvelle France*" 650
"*Carte de la Province Ecclesiastique de l'Oregon*" 3044
"*Carte de la Riviere de Richelieu et du Lac Champlain*" 650
"*Carte de la Riviere Longue*" 2365
"*Carte de la Route*" 2009
"*Carte de la Sonore et de la Basse Californie*" 2361
"*Carte de la Vallée de Mexico*" 2009
"*Carte de L'Amerique Septentrionale*" 650
"*Carte, de l'Embouchure Septentrionale du Canal de la Reine Charlotte*" 3250
"*Carte de l'Isle de Ieso*" 460
"*Carte de l'Isle de Montreal*" 650
"*Carte de l'Isle de Terre-neuve*" 650
"*Carte de l'Isle d'Orleans*" 650

Cattle Queen of Montana . . . 1894
4521
Cattle-Raising on the Plains of North America . . . 1885 3499
Cattle Rustling 182
Cattle Trade 210
Cattle Trails 242, 2275, 2443, 3294
Cattlemen 2486
Caumartin, Louis-Urbain Le Fevre 4122
Cavalry Band, Second 4283
Cavalry Band, Tenth 4284
Cavalry, 1st Nebraska 2515
Cavalry, First U.S. 1551
Cavalry, Second U.S. 3544
Cavalry, Fourth Ohio 3286
Cavalry, Fourth U.S. 4279, 4280–4282
Cavalry, Fifth U.S. 3361
Cavalry, Kentucky 3714
Cavalry Life in Tent and Field . . . 1894 374
Cavalry School for Practice 121
Cavalry Service 4582
Cavalry, Sixth U.S. 614
Cavalry, 7th U.S. 2927, 2928
Cavalry, Tenth U.S. 1571, 3529, 4278
Cavelier de la Salle de Rouen . . . 1871 1624
Cavendish, T. 1582
Caxton Club 74, 2253, 2405, 3964
Caxton Press 1798, 4020
Caxton Printers 2580, 3694
Caygua 2304, 2305, 2306
Cayme Press 4096
Cayuse Indians 417, 418
Ceazar 2825
Cedar Point, O. 2901
Cedar Rapids, Ia. 65, 599, 1244, 2152, 2421, 4599
Censorship 2455
Census Bureau 4396
Centennial, The . . . 1876 632
"Centennial Address at the Philadelphia Exhibition in 1876" 3950
Centennial Exhibition . . . n.d. 2274
Centennial Exposition 1268
Centennial Historical Oration . . . 1876 94
Centennial History and Directory of La Porte City, Blackhawk County, Iowa . . . 1876 3210
Centennial History of Gage County, Nebraska . . . 1876 3890
Centennial History of Pawnee County . . . 1876 1215
Centennial History of Sarpy County . . . 1876 157
'Centennial' Sketch of Clay County . . . 1876 738
Centerville, Ida. 2055
Central America 364, 409, 1447, 1448, 3147, 4230, 4517
"Central America" 837
"*Central America 1856*" 4587
Central American Filibusterer 4516
Central American War 4587
Central and South America 1470, 1471
Central and Southwestern Arizona . . . 1889 1288

Central City, Colo. 188, 970, 3344, 4788
"*Central City, Col'o. Ter.*" 3344
Central Gold Region . . . 1860 1556
Central Idaho Stock Growers' Association 2057
Central Iowa Farms and Herds . . . 1873 3672
Central Mexico 746
Central Mining Company 3538
Central National Highway 274
Central New Mexico Cattle Growers' Association 3006
Central Pacific Railroad 2977, 3155, 4304, 4683
Central Pacific Railroad Excursion . . . 1866 634
Central Pacific Railroad, of California 2255, 2256
Central Publishing Company 126, 1646
Central Route . . . 1854 1836, 1837, 3551
Centralia Massacre 1585
Century Co. 637, 2684
Century Magazine 3345
"*Cerographic Map of Iowa*" 2907
Cerro Colorado, Ariz. 3893
Cerro Gordo County, Ia. 3672
"*Cerro Roblero*" 1673
Certificate, Land 577
Certificate, Membership 53
Chacon, Urbano 3541
Chadbourne, J. S. 4601
Chadwick, S. F. 500, 4683
Chalmers, Port 4456
Chambaye, Gulf of 3161
Chamber of Commerce, St. Louis 3645
Chamberlain, Dak. 4760
Chambers, Charlotte 1512
Chambers, J. 2143, 2144
Chambers, J. H., & Co. 4196
Chambers, R. P. 3902
Chambers & Knapp 43, 3644, 3646
Chambers, Harris & Knapp 3309
Chambers' Prairies 640
Chambers's Journal of Popular Literature Science and Arts . . . 1855 641
Chambon (engraver) 1173
Champaign Public Library 3866
Champ-d'Asile . . . 1819 2487
"*Champ-d'Asile ou Carte des Etablissments fondés dans l'Amérique Septentrionale*" 2487
Champion, Honoré 4198, 4459
Champion and Press Book and Job Printing Establishment 388
Champlin, T. A. P. 3790
Champney, C. H. 1452
Chandler, G. A. 3459
Chandler, H. 1982
Chandler, J. B. 3982
"Change of Location West of Omaha" 4249
Changuion, Chez 362
Chaplain in Ordinary to the Queen 4799
Chaplin, Spafford & Mathison 889
Chapman, C. C., & Co. 1665
Chapman, J. 3201

Chapman, S. 1389
Chapman & Hall 246, 566, 1403, 2298, 2354, 2449, 3453, 3751
Chapman, Nebr. 2897
Chapman, Nebraskey 2897, 4647
Chappel, Ella A. 2918
Chappell, W. 3413
"Character of the Constitutional Government of the United States" 4216
Charakeys (Cherokees) 2855
Charbonneau, Jean Baptiste 743
Charbonneau, Lizette 743
Charbonneau, Toussaint 743
Chariton, Mo. 4465
Charles III of Spain 3910–3914
Charles IV of Spain 3915, 3916
Charles & Hammond 2536, 4600
Charles A. Loren, vs. Henry E. Benson . . . n.d. 266
Charles County, Md. 3417
Charles O'Malley 2304, 2305, 2306
Charles Town in Carolina 2855
Charles W. Quantrell . . . n.d. 477
Charless, J. 2540
Charless & Paschall 207, 2066, 2067
Charless' Missouri & Illinois Magazine Almanac . . . 1818 649
Charleston, Ill. 2856
Charleston, S.Car. 1058, 1241, 2336, 4062, 4790
"*Charleston*" 4062
Charlestown, Mass. 2780, 2781, 4679
Charlestown Company 2614
Charley 3294
Charlie Reynolds . . . 1914–15 3459
Charlmonte . . . 1856 220
"*Chart from the 14th to the 16th Degree of South Latitude*" 2356
"*Chart from the South Point of Formoso to Great Lieuchieux*" 416
"*Chart of a Great Part of the Great Pacific Ocean*" 2397
"*Chart of Beering's Straits*" 2356
"*Chart of Matagorda Bay*" 2308
"*Chart of the Bay of Vera Cruz*" 1092
"*Chart of the Caroline Islands*" 2356
"*Chart of the Coast from Behrings Bay to Sea Otter Bay*" 2506
"*Chart of the Columbia River*" 4380
"*Chart of the Discoveries in the Seas of Chican and Tartary*" 2397
"*Chart of the Galapagos*" 812
"*Chart of the Internal Part of Louisiana*" 3290, 3291, 3292
"*Chart of the Interior Part of North America*" 2734
"*Chart of the Islands of Radack and Ralick*" 2356
"*Chart of the N.E. Coast of Asia*" 416
"*Chart of the N.W. Coast of America and N.E. Coast of Asia*" 2734
"*Chart of the North-West Coast of America*" 2397
"*Chart of the Northern Pacific Ocean*" 2734
"*Chart of The Northwest Part of the Great Ocean*" 2358
"*Chart of the Sandwich Islands*" 4456
"*Chart of the World*" 2397, 2506

Clark, F. 4202
Clark, G. R. 2235, 2416
Clark, G. R. H. 743, 2478
Clark, H. A. 351
Clark, J. 1722, 3231
Clark, J. C. 4327
Clark, Julia 2478
Clark, M. 3259
Clark, M. H. 3101
Clark, O. S. 183
Clark, W. 423, 743, 1384, 2219, 2411, 2477, 2478–2485, 2699, 3312, 3686, 4411
Clark, W. A. 3950
Clark, W. L. 4526
Clark, W. P. 4283
Clark, W. R. C., & Co. 3260
Clark, William, Papers 552
Clark Stanley's Snake Oil Liniment 3942
Clark, Wing, & Brown 345
Clark, Fort (Mo.) 377
Clark, Fort (Tex.) 2420, 4327
Clarke, C. 867, 1538
Clarke, J. 2130, 2146, 4718
Clarke, J., & Co. 115, 1935, 4719
Clarke, M. St. C. 3596
Clarke, R., & Co. 523, 524, 734, 780, 1472, 1645, 1681, 1834, 2729, 3174, 4241
Clarke, S. 4189
Clarke, W. 2488
Clarke & Bro. 2966
Clarke Publishing Co., S. J. 2314
Clark's Fork 2243, 4329
Clarks's Miscellany . . . 1812 735
Clarkson, J. J. 4186
Clarksville Lodge No. 17 1420
Claudine Lavalle . . . 1853 3608
Claxton, Remsen & Haffelfinger 1187, 2283, 2399, 3924
Clay, H. 1084, 3858
Clay, M. J. 3880
Clay Allison of the Washita . . . 1920 739
Clay Co. Globe 738
Clay County, Nebr. 738
Clayes, O. M. 83
Clayton, J. M. 4414
Clayton, Kit 2863
Clayton, W. 1170, 4538
Clayton & Co. 3426
Clayton County, Ia. 932
"Clayton's, G. W., Store" 3344
Clear Creek County, Colo. 3953
Clear Water, Ore. 3919
Clearfield County, Pa. 2461
Cleaveland, J. R. 1558
Cleaves & Vaden 106
Cleeve, C. W. 3346
Clem, J. 4214
Clemens, J. 3742
Clemens, O. 2984, 3034, 4233
Clemens, S. L. 760–762, 2385, 4757
Clemens Boys 3056
Clement, J. 4601
Clements, A. 1213
Clements, A. H. 1668
Clements, W. L. 3849
Clements Library 46, 2901
Clerke, Captain 3501

Clerk's Office, Cook County, Ill. 4058
Cleveland, G. 3581
Cleveland, Nebr. 766
Cleveland, O. 1192, 3258
Cleveland & Russell 4065
Cleveland & Toledo Railroad Co. 765, 2082, 4211
Cleveland, Columbus & Cincinnati Railroad Co. 765, 2082
Cleveland Land Company . . . 1858 766
Clevenger, R. A. 1012
Clevenger, S. V. 4327
Clifford, Josephine 4605
Clifton, Ariz. 826, 3285
"Climate and Resources of Montana" 2292
"Climatology of Minnesota" 2819, 2820
"Climatology of the Saskatchewan District and of British Oregon" 2819, 2820
Clinton, D. 2280
Clinton County, Ia. 767
Clinton Herald . . . 1856 767
Clipper Office 1844
Clogher, W. 3445
Closing Speech for the State . . . 1883 4524
Clothing and Cost of Camp Equipage 4256
Clover, S. T. 1875
Clowes & Sons, Ltd., W. 826
Clubb, H. S. 3068, 3069
Clum, J. 4214
Clyman, J. 4626
Clyman, James, American Frontiersman . . . 1928 769
Coahuila 1210, 1211, 1336, 1337, 1424, 1498, 1943, 1945, 2769, 4107
Coahuila y Tejas 2768
Coal Fields 1010, 1162
Coal Mines 4441
Coale, H. K. 1748
Coale & Maxwell 377
Coarse Fodder, (Bran, Chips and Sawdust Mostly) . . . 1881 4753
"Coast Scene" 4492
"Coasts of Guatimala and Mexico" 1377
Cobbett, W. 302, 1366, 3867
Coble, J. C. 1957
Coburn, W. S., John Patterson & A. K. Shaw 3743
Coburn & Newman Publishing Co. 631
Cocoas Island 4456
Cocos Island 812
Codsiogo 3765
Cody, J. 2055
Cody, W. F. [Buffalo Bill] 467, 486, 783, 862, 1013, 2030, 2117, 2664, 2895, 4616, 4677, 4713
Cody and Salsbury 784
Cody's Sister 4616
Coe Collection 2459, 4486
Coeur d'Alene 2341, 2798
Coeur d'Alene, Fort 4356
"Coeur d'Alene, I. T., Fort" 4356
Coeur d'Alene Labor Riots 3802
Coeur d'Alene Lake 2932

Coeur d'Alene Mission 2932
Coffee, J. 4370
Coffee, Fort 2531
Coffeen, H. A. 791
Coffey, T. J. 1316
Coffeyville, Kans. 1235
Coffeyville Journal Print 1235
Coffin, E. H. 240
Coffin, G. B. 794
Coffin, N. 2087
Cogan, D. 552
Cohahuila: See Coahuila
Colburn, Henry 1734, 2391, 3786, 4174
Colburn, Henry, & Richard Bentley 2201
Colby, L. W. 2649, 2650
Cole 3229
Cole, S. 1135
Cole, Mr. & Mrs. W. 2055
Coleccion de Constituciones de los Estados Unidos Mexicano . . . 1828 2768
Coleccion de Documentos Relativos al Departamento de Californias . . . 1845 625
Coleccion de varios documentos para la Historia de la Florida y Tierras Adyacentes . . . 1857 3866
Colegio Caroli 3132
Colegio de la Santa-Cruz de Queretaro 85
Colegio Seminario 3733
Coleman, R. 3501
Coleman, W. T. 637
Coles, W. 2590
Cole's Creek, La. 504
Coleson's Narrative, Miss. . . . 1864 803
Colfax, S. 370
Colima, Mex. 1169
Collamer, J. 1084
Collection de Cartes Geographiques . . . 1797 2736
Collection de Precis Historiques Melanges Litteraires et Scientifiques . . . 1853 4105
Collection of General Orders, Circulars, Reports, and Courts Martial Reports, Department of Texas, 1874–1882 4366
Collection of Sacred Hymns . . . 1841 3844
Collections of the Georgia Historical Society . . . 1848 1540
Collector, The 4081
College at Puebla 1287
College of Physicians and Surgeons of the Upper Mississippi 3671
College Springs, Ia. 56
Collet, C. 642
Collier, D. C. 821
Collier & Cleaveland Lith. Co. 819
Collier & Hall 3550
Colliers' Magazine 2420
Collins, C. 26
Collins, E. K. 4626
Collins, I. 2235
Collins, J. 743
Collins, J. S. 2910
Collins, J. W. 810
Collins, M. 4310

Commissioner of Indian Affairs 1344, 1531, 3643, 4305
Commissioner to Collect the Laws and Archives of Oregon 3121
Commissioners of the Santa Fé Road Commission 180, 2629, 3446, 3447
Commissioners to Locate the Seat of Government (Nebraska) 2955
Committee . . . Act for Establishing Trading Houses with the Indians 4375
Committee Appointed to Examine into the Condition of the Banks of the Territory (Wisconsin) 4719
Committee of Citizens of Santa Fe 2992, 2993
Committee of Commerce and Manufactures 4371
Committee of Secrecy 1469, 3115
Committee of the People of the State of Texas 4107
Committee of Vigilance 2521, 4104
Committee . . . on . . . Compensation . . . to Captain . . . Pike 4374
Committee on Foreign Affairs 4381
Committee on Indian Affairs 99, 290, 1274, 2592
Committee on Internal Improvements 544
Committee on Invitations 4197
Committee on Military Affairs 3243, 4379, 4391
Committee on Private Land Claims 4385, 4386
Committee on Public Buildings and Grounds 543
Committee on Public Lands 545, 4110, 4390
Committee on Territories 4382, 4383
Committee . . . on the Conduct of John Smith 4373
Committee on the Conduct of the War (Colorado) 824, 825
Committee . . . on the Introduction of Slaves from Amelia Island 4378
Committee on the Judiciary 311
Committee to Inquire into the Conduct of General Wilkinson 4376
Committee to Prepare an Address 2136
"Commodore Jones War" 3271
Commonwealth, Office of the 823
Commonwealth Printing Company 3961
Communication from C. S. Drew . . . 1860 1150, 1151
Communication from Captain Samuel Adams . . . 1870 17
Communication from the Secretary of the Territory (Iowa) . . . 1840 2146
Communication Relative to the Location of the U.P.R.R. across the Rocky Mountains . . . 1867 3550
Communism 532, 2039, 2040
"Communism. History of the Experiment at Nauvoo of the Icarian Settlement" 2040

Communist Colony 532
Compagnia Inglesa 3062
Compagnie des Indes 1397
Compagnie du Scioto 2467
Companion to the Botanical Magazine . . . 1835 1947
Comparative, Chronological Statement . . . 1845 845
Compensation for Whiskey, Gunpowder, Horse and Mules 4377
Complete Account of the John Morgan Raid . . . 1863 3780, 3781
Complete Choctaw Definer . . . 1892 4557
Complete City Directory of La Salle and Peru . . . 1876 1865
Complete Guide to the Gold Districts of Kansas & Nebraska . . . 1859 3229
Complete List of the Lots and Lands Conveyed to the Trustees of the Illinois and Michigan Canal . . . 1850 2074
Complimentary, Ogden House Opening and Reception . . . 1869 3077
Comprehensive History of the Church of Jesus Christ of Latter-Day Saints . . . 1930 4081
Compton's Fort, Ill. 1576
Comstock Club 1589
Comstock Club . . . 1891 1588
Comstock Silver Lode 3200, 4757, 4758
Comte de Raousset-Boulbon et l'Expedition de la Sonore . . . 1859 2361
Con Real Órden de primero de Diciembre próximo 9
Conant, A. H. 811
Conant, H. N. 2571
Concanen & Lee 3302
Concho, Fort 4327
Concise Account of North America . . . 1765 3554
Concise History of the Mormon Battalion . . . 1881 4226
Concise View of Oregon Territory . . . 1846 4628
Concise View of the Number, Resources, and Industry of the American People . . . 1842 2838
Concklin, G. 1167, 1815, 3989
Conclusion, Port 4456
Concord Association 175
Concord General Assembly (Baptists) 159
Concordia, Kans. 2206
Condensed Geography and History of the Western States . . . 1828 1353
Condensed History of the Apache and Comanche Indian Tribes . . . 1899 2246
Conder, T. 2091
Condition and Resources of Southern Dakota . . . 1872 398
"Conditions and Regulations of the Library of the Woburn Young Men's Society" 4670
Conduct of the War (Colorado), Committee on the 824, 825
Cone & Freeman 4464

Confederacy 60, 473, 936, 993, 1034, 1455, 1764, 1850, 2213, 2227, 2241, 2299, 2529, 2724–2726, 2812, 4118, 4268
Confederate Army 60
Confederate Cruisers 473
Confederate Imprint 4118
Confederate Novel 936
Confederate Prisons 1455
Confederate Soldier 993
Confederate Spy . . . 1866 936
Confederate Texan Troops 4268
Confession of Faith (Presbyterian) 942, 943
Confession of Jereboam O. Beauchamp . . . 1826 220
Confessions of Geo. P. Beale and Geo. Baker . . . 1865 217
"Confirming the Gold Discovery" 637
Conger, O. T. 3278, 3565
Congregational Church 322, 1218, 3352, 3440, 3990, 4208
Congregational Church, Morris, Ill. 4208
Congregational House 195
Congregational Iowa 3440
Congregational Pioneer Society of Topeka 3484
Congregational Publishing Society 14
Congregational Sunday-School and Publishing Society 3313, 3331
Congreso Constituyente 774
Congress, U.S. 5, 6, 17, 41, 48, 98, 99, 100, 104, 128, 214–216, 290, 337, 350, 437, 544, 558, 559, 700, 870, 906, 907, 913, 1016, 1059, 1096, 1097, 1150, 1249, 1306, 1323, 1332–1334, 1429–1434, 1436, 1437, 1531, 1609, 1611, 1625, 1653, 1946, 1989, 1990, 2107, 2125, 2126, 2228, 2335, 2378, 2573, 2592, 2593, 2675, 2678, 2703, 2704, 2782, 2783, 2805, 2834, 2932, 3022, 3071, 3320, 3429, 3506, 3581, 3596, 3600, 3646, 3703, 3754, 3776, 3789, 3790, 3792, 3809, 3867, 3947, 4107, 4142, 4293, 4370–4443, 4499, 4525, 4537, 4546, 4568, 4576, 4589, 4614, 4623, 4723
Congress of Rough Riders 784
Congressional Globe Office 272, 563, 1697, 3149, 3776, 3979, 4576
Conkey, W. B., Co. 2402, 2751, 3074, 3802
Connecticut 1816, 1828, 4622
Connecticut Mutual Life Insurance Co. 3021
Connecticut Reserve 135, 1828
Connelley, W. E. 3562
Connelly, H. 2998, 2999
Connelly Collection 601, 3746
Connor 912
Connor & Hussey 4033
Conn's Job Office 1178
Conquering our Great American Plains . . . 1930 1868, 1966
Conquering the Wilderness . . . 1883 4195
Conquest of California 637, 869, 965, 2059, 3474, 3475, 4135
Conquest of California . . . 1896 4135

Coos Bay, Wash. 4683
"Copia del plano del puerto de S. Diego" 3652
Copiado del Mapa de S. Mc. L. Staples 2765
Copper 826, 2101, 4618
Copper Mine River 1840
Copper Mines 2101
Copper Mining 4618
Copy of a Report of Major D. Fergusson . . . 1863 1306
Copy of My Journal from Fort Union 109
Copy of Report of Brigadier General George Crook 4362
Copy of the Evidence Taken at Denver and Fort Lyon, Colorado Territory . . . 1867 4292
Copy of the Official Journal of Lieutenant Colonel Philip St. George Cooke . . . 1849 870
Copy of the Report and Journal of Captain Medorem Crawford . . . 1863 913
Coquille River, Wash. 4683
Cora, C. 1286
Corbin, H. C. 4369
Cordano 1262
Cordova, J. de: See De Cordova, J.
Cordts, Anst. von H. 3099
Corey & Fairbank 1740, 2089
Coriolanus . . . 1870 443
Cormandel 2519
Cornet 4321
Cornish, Lamport & Co. 844
Cornplanter 4162
Cornwall 4670
Coronado, Francisco Vasquez 181, 1023
Corps of Topographical Engineers: See United States Army. Engineers, Corps of
Correct Account of the Murder of Generals Joseph and Hyrum Smith . . . 1845 1001, 1002
"Correct Map from Actual Surveys and Examinations Embracing a Portion of California between Monterey and the Pacific Butes" 4656
"Correct Map of the Pennsylvania Central Rail Road" 3741
Correct Time Cards . . . 1877 689
Correspondence . . . (Fisher) . . . 1919 1328
Correspondence and Official Proceedings . . . 1855 3122
Correspondence of Bishop George Miller . . . 1855 2799
Correspondence on the Occasion of the Presentation by Major-General Sanford . . . 1862 3670
Correspondencia que ha mediado entre la legacion extraordinaria de Mexico y el departamento de estado de los estados-unidos . . . 1837 2772
Cortes, Hernando 1376, 3356
Coruba, R. C. & R. 2619
Corwin, T. 1556
Corydon, Ind. 2395
Çosalá, Mex. 1265

Cose, O. D. 1634
Cosmopolitan Book Corporation 471
Cossitt, H. D.La: See La Cossitt, H. D.
"Cost of Transporting Troops and Supplies to California, Oregon New Mexico" 4435
Costa Azia la Veracruz 3242
Costa Rica 105, 4517
Costanzo, Miguel 2009
Coster, J. H. 4356
Costilla Estate 318
Cote, A., & Cie. 2705
Cotes, R. 1470, 1471
Cotta, J. G. 1682, 3218, 4015
Cotten, G. B. 118
Cotton 131, 297, 2113, 3094
Cotton Kingdom . . . 1861 3094
Cotton Thievery 131
Cottonwood Springs, Nebr. 579
Couch, W. L. 2174
Couchman, E. 1947
Coues, E. 2484, 4019, 4634
Coulter, Edith M. 795
Council Bluff Agency 2918
Council Bluff City, Ia. 2836
Council Bluffs, Ia. 58, 149, 150, 287, 334, 487, 515, 694, 726, 974, 1009, 1061, 1236, 1362, 1395, 1952–1954, 2300, 2836, 3056, 3077, 3078, 3192–3195, 3243, 3553, 3761, 4068, 4129, 4226, 4502
Council Bluffs Agency Ferry 1952, 1953, 1954
Council Bluffs & Davenport Railroad 2136
Council Bluffs, Iowa . . . n.d. 887
Council Journal of the First Legislative Assembly of Montana . . . 1866 2860
Council of the Indies 3915
"Counterfeit Editions" 1331
"Country around Fort Gibson" 4433
"Country between the Red River Settlement and the Rocky Mountains" 3167
"Country Drained by the Mississippi" 2188
"Country of the Mississippi below the 33d deg. N. Lat." 2188
"County & Township Railroad Map of the States of Missouri, Iowa, Illinois and Wisconsin" 3032
County Clerk 4683
County Commissioners' Court, Cook County, Ill. 866, 4144
County Directory Publishing Co. 2985
"County Map of Nebraska, Kansas and Parts of Iowa and Missouri" 836
County Warrants 1135
Courant Book & Job Office 1396
Courier Book & Job Print 2401
Courier Office 2810, 3198, 3199
Courier Steam Book & Job Printing House 894, 2857
Courier Steam Press Print 3608
Courier Steam Printing House 1751
"Course of the River Mississippi . . . 1772 3584

Court Guide, for the Second Judicial District, Nebraska Territory . . . 1856 2965
Court Martial 935, 1432, 4255, 4335, 4341
Court Proceedings in the Trial of Dakota Indians . . . 1927 3682
Courtney, F. 592, 4494
Courts District (Iowa) 4397
Courts, District, (Texas) 4114
Courts. Sixth Judicial District 2128
Courts of Inquiry 4292
Covens, Jean et Corneille Mortier 2507
Cover, Jr., J. 1583
Covered Wagon . . . 1922 1965
Covered Wagon Days . . . 1929 1082
"Cow" 962
Cow Creek, Ore. 4224
Cow Creek Station, Kans. 4275
Cow Puncher 2030
Cowan, R. E. 191, 544, 1387, 1541, 3665, 4014
Cowboy, The . . . 1922 3557
Cowboy and Indian Trader . . . 1951 3694
Cowboy Detective . . . 1912 3802
Cowboys 8, 13, 410, 428, 605, 739–741, 748, 749, 779, 785, 808, 863, 1076, 1129, 1515, 1898, 1957, 1967, 2030, 2032, 2194, 2471–2473, 2616, 3294, 3314, 3328, 3329, 3455–3460, 3500, 3557, 3694, 3722, 3802–3807, 3942, 4026, 4039, 4145, 4158, 4521, 4621, 4639, 4725, 4756, 4795
"Cowboys' Mother" 4521
Cowdery, O. 708
Cowdery, O., & Co. 708
Cowen, D. S. 107
Cowlitz Valley, Wash. 573
Cowperthwait & Co., H. 106
Cox, G. 2184, 2185
Cox, J. 2857
Cox, John, & Co. 1975
Cox & Holloway 330
Cox, Port 2734, 2736
Coxe, T. 3289, 3867
Coyle, W. H., & Co. 3908
Coyottes 785
Cozans, M. T. 418
Crabb, H. A. 23, 3151, 4417, 4461
Crabb Expedition 23, 3151, 4414, 4461
Cragin, F. W. 1490, 2438
Craig, I. 2185
Craig, J. R. 1886
Craig, N. B. 2185, 3089, 3992
Craig, Fort 4327, 4335
Craighead, R. 663, 4205
Craig's *Olden Time* 4681
Crain, H. E. 4783
Cram, 4729
Cram, C. F., Lith. 2659
Cramer, H. P., & Co. 3118
Cramer, Z. 946, 947, 2954
Cramer & Speer 1877
Cramer, Spear & Eichbaum 379, 944
"Cram's Sectional Map of Colorado" 904
Crandall, L. 985
Crane & Co. 564, 864, 1025, 1129, 2116, 2233, 4536, 4537

Daily Reese River Reveille Office
2982
Daily Republican Office 3162
Daily Republican, Press of the 4148
Daily Rocky Mountain News 510
Daily Sentinel 694
Daily Sentinel Print 2203, 2204, 4191
Daily Sentinel Steam Power Press
454, 694
Daily Snort . . . 1859 973
Daily State Sentinel Office 4036
Daily Telegraph . . . 1861 974
Daily Times, Huron, Dak. 213
Daily Times Book and Job Printing
House 4083
Daily Times Print 3082, 3573
Daily Tribune Book and Job Office
2090
Daily Tribune Office 2847
Daily Tribune Print 1483, 3352,
3896
Daily Whig Book & Job Office 636
Daily Wisconsin Steam Press 1101
Dairyman's Daughter . . . 1847 1278,
3498
Dakin Pub. Co. 28
Dakota: See also Dacota, Dahkota
Dakota, North, South & Territory
24, 26, 46, 86, 89, 90, 188, 205, 315–
317, 398, 427, 479, 482, 551, 688,
690, 748, 749, 768, 769, 806, 912,
933, 934, 953, 959, 961, 975, 990,
1030, 1031, 1039, 1040, 1110, 1111,
1114, 1118, 1154, 1192, 1203, 1237,
1332, 1335, 1389, 1451, 1452, 1501,
1577, 1771, 1773, 1827, 1834, 1838,
1839, 1842, 1878, 1907, 1913, 1932,
1936, 1950, 2038, 2110, 2189, 2207,
2209, 2210, 2257, 2276, 2282, 2283,
2360, 2368, 2386, 2387, 2399, 2439,
2499, 2548, 2578, 2639, 2658, 2660,
2668, 2669, 2672, 2778, 2942, 2974,
3048, 3110, 3113, 3117, 3138, 3230,
3262, 3293, 3313, 3315, 3369, 3394,
3395, 3407, 3419, 3420, 3423, 3425,
3437, 3483, 3575, 3579, 3580, 3601,
3717, 3737, 3805, 3837, 3874, 3903,
3975, 4000, 4001, 4061, 4089–4093,
4198, 4217, 4242, 4250, 4293, 4295,
4303, 4327, 4328, 4546, 4580, 4634,
4654, 4675, 4685, 4727, 4760
Dakota . . . 1884 1192
Dakota & Great Southern Railway
1192
Dakota, Chief Quartermaster,
Department of, 4295
Dakota City 558, 559, 2672
*Dakota Constitutional Convention . . .
1883* 987
Dakota County . . . 1868 2842
Dakota County, Minn. 1166, 2842
Dakota County, Nebr. 4541
Dakota, Department of 46, 3601,
4293–4298
Dakota Farmer 4457
Dakota First Reading Book . . . 1839
3505
Dakota Friend . . . 1852 988
Dakota Herald 3737
Dakota Herald Print 4727
"*Dakota in Miniature*" 1389
Dakota Indian Reservation 3519

Dakota Indians 1932, 2822, 3262,
3423, 3505, 3682, 3683, 3876,
4061, 4696, 4697
"Dakota Language" 2822
Dakota, Military Division of 980
Dakota Mission 988
Dakota Southern Railroad 398
*Dakota Territorial Agricultural
Society . . . 1877* 989
Dakota War Whoop . . . 1863 2578
Dakota-Wyoming-Montana Frontier
3315
Dale, E. E. 27
Dallas, A. J. 4420
Dallas, Tex. 525
Dallas County 1956
Dalles, The 2243
Dalles City, Ore. 4525
Dalles, Fort 2932
Dallison, J. K. 431
Dally, F. 4477
Dalmatie, Duc de 1169
Dalton Gang 1235
Daly, J. 1627
Daly, O. J. 2055
Damon, S. C. 1443, 1444
Danaid (ship) 4468
Dance Halls 4756
Dane, G. E. 3204
*Danenhower's Chicago City Di-
rectory . . . 1851* 999
Danforth, Wright & Co. 1375
*Dangerous Crossing and What
Happened on the Other Side . . .
1924* 1887
Dangers of the Country . . . 1807
3289, 3971
Daniel Boone . . . ca. 1886 1717
Danite Band 1879, 3449
*Dans Les Montagnes Rocheuses . . .
1884* 2669
Darby, J. G. 1488
Dardanelle Baptist Association 160
Darley, F. O. C. 2628
Darmstadt 3889
Dartmouth College 4622
"*Dash*" 3619
Dashaway Hall 4031
Dashwood, S. S. 363
"Date of the Discovery of the
Yosemite" 637
*Datos de los Trabajos Astronomicos
y Topograficos, Dispuestos en
forma de diario . . . 1850* 3652
*Daughter of the Middle Border . . .
1921* 1507
Daughters of the American Revolu-
tion, Esther Reed Chapter 1041
Dauphin, Port 650
Dauzats, Adrien 323
Davega, I. 4556
Davenport, G. 351, 392, 2431
Davenport, G. L. 1011
Davenport, Margaret 1008
Davenport, R. D. 2326
Davenport, Ia. 392, 508, 849, 867,
1008, 1194, 1489, 1924, 2302,
2431, 3391, 3421, 3442, 3678,
4610, 4658
*Davenport, Manufacturing Facilities
and Business Wants . . . 1874* 1010

Davenport Past and Present . . . 1858
4658
"*Davenport's Block, Geo. L.*" 1924
David (binder) 3849
David, E. T. 1095
David, R. B. 2750
*David S. Maynard and Catherine T.
Maynard . . . 1906* 3368
Davids, R. W. 4724
Davidson, J. S. 3992
Davidson, J. W. 4278
Davidson, V. L. 694
Davidson, W. 353, 1578
Davidson County, Tenn. 4116
Davies, D. 656, 3379
Davies, H. E. 1013
Davies, J. T. 1013
Davies & Jones 2995
Davis 291
Davis, C. F. 4197
Davis, D. 4644
Davis, D. L. 1877
Davis, F. 4322
Davis, F. W. 372
Davis, Florence H. 2439
Davis, G. 1084, 4382
Davis, H. K. 1474, 1475
Davis, H. S. 2400
Davis, Jefferson 974, 1527, 2227,
4435
Davis, Mrs. J. A. 3938
Davis, J. C. 4197
Davis, L. W. 4222
Davis, O. F. 4238
Davis, S. H. 654, 664, 666, 1413,
3373, 3376, 3377, 3379
Davis, S. M. 663
Davis, T. O. 2069
Davis, V. Jefferson 2241
Davis, Varina A. 2227
Davis, W. 915
Davis, W. A. 4420, 4428
Davis County, Ia. 1266, 2884
Davis, Fort 1675, 4327
Davis Mountains, Tex. 3416
Dawes, H. L. 1110, 4392
Dawson, E. B. 141, 4062
Dawson, G. 1190
Dawson, H. B. 1533, 2217
Dawson, S. J. 1894
Dawson, T. F. 861, 2742
Dawson & Napier 1894
Dawson City, Alaska 1303, 3169
Dawson County, Tex. 2845
Dawson's Book Shop 918, 2951
Day, G. & Elizabeth 4200
Day, H. 543
Day, H. N. 135
Day, M., & Co. 2386, 2387
Day & Haghe 2663
Day County, Dak. 1192
Day, Egbert & Fidlar 1851
Day Publishing Co., Luella 1029
Day of the Cattleman . . . 1929 3133
Day with the Cow Column in 1843 74
'"Days of the Empire"—Arizona,
1866–1869' 4445
*Days on the Road Crossing the Plains
in 1865 . . . 1902* 1870
Dayton, O. 46, 2561
Deadwood, Dak. 2420, 4242
Deadwood, Mont. 317

Dean-Hicks Company 152
Deane, C. 3145
Deane, R. 111, 112
Dear Doctor: I Am Making a Study of Midwifery . . . n.d. 3197
Dearborn, H. 3289, 4667
Dearborn, R. H. 4683
Dearborn, Fort 2339, 2340, 4377
Dearborn River 2932
Dearing, M. F. 165
Dease, P. W. 3794
Dease & Simpson 3415
Death Comes to the Archbishop 1992
Death Valley 2670, 2758, 3926, 3972
Death Valley in '49 . . . 1894 2670
Death Valley Scotty 2758
Debrett, J. 2091
Decatur and Rush County Emigrants 4140
Decatur County, Ind. 4140
December Lode, Colo. 2051
Decherd, Ark. 2846
Decision of the Supreme Court, of the State of Iowa . . . 1852 2139
Decker, J. H. 2960
Decker, P. 3421, 4064
Decker, W. R. 3138
"Declaration of Rights" 2103
Decline and Fall of Samuel Sawbones . . . 1900 2452
De Cordova, J. 920, 1119, 2232
De Cordova & Frazier 1036
Decouverte du Missouri et l'Histoire du Fort d'Orleans . . . 1925 4489
Découvertes et Établissements de Cavelier de la Salle . . . 1870 1623, 1624
Decreto Numero 110 (Coahuila and Texas) . . . 1830 771
Decreto Numero 187 (Coahuila and Texas) . . . 1832 770
Dedication Ball, at the Seltzer House . . . 1876 3726
Deed 1361
Deer 785
Deer Lodge, Mont. 3041
Deer Lodge County, Mont. 2863, 4798
Deer Lodge County Recorder's Office 2863
Deer Park, Ill. 1239
Deerfoot 3302
Deering, F. C. 1323
Defence of Gen. Sidney Sherman . . . 1859 3754
Defence of Kenyon College . . . 1831 660
Defence of Mr. Clay 4632
Defiance, Fort 215, 216
Deficiency in the Bank Account 4607
De Forrest, C. H. 4336, 4341
Defrémery, M. 1623, 1624
De Garro, P. 4501
Degrand, P. P. F. 3365
De Guerra Family 3525
De Kalb County, Ill. 3468
De Krafft, E. 4409, 4410
Del Lib. 2 De Alvarez 47
Del Norte County 328
Del Tomo Tercero de Alvarez 47
Delafield, Wisc. 694
De Lachapelle, A. 2361

Delahaye l'Aîné 460
Delaney, D. 217
Delaney, Theresa 1605
Delanglez, Jean 1173
Delaware 409, 2202
Delaware County, Ia. 4444
Delaware Language 3240
Delawares 286, 2235, 3330, 4139
Delgado, Francisco 3064
Delisle, Guillaume 460, 2363
Dellenbaugh, F. S. 216, 498, 1762
Demerara, British Guiana 4212
Demilt, A. 1338
Democracy 1492
Democrat Office 676, 1477, 1478, 2074
Democrat, Office of the 2070
Democratic Argus Extra 1134
Democratic Meeting . . . 1843 1046
Democratic Party 3208
"Democratic Press" Steam Printing House 3717
Democratic State Journal Office 2909
Demoine Navigation & Railroad Company 2671
Demun, J. 4410
Denison, D. B. 4683
Denison's, E. S., Yosemite Views . . . 1881 1050
Denmark 3346, 3876
Denmark and Des Moines River Associations 3440
Dent, F. T. 3790
Dentu, E. 2361
Denver 188, 192, 299, 578, 633, 683, 684, 724, 731, 1055, 1251, 1252, 1385, 1386, 1412, 1490, 2178, 2273, 2276, 2349, 2400, 2643, 2743, 3036, 3140, 3144, 3344, 3955, 3982, 4241, 4251, 4292, 4426, 4617, 4633, 4787
Denver, Governor 2270
Denver and Rio Grande Railroad 4527
"Denver City, Col. Ter." 3344
Denver Mountaineer Print 2050–2053, 3764
"*Denver Pacific Railway Map*" 1054
Denver Post 280
Denver Public Library 1899, 3344, 3540, 3542
Denver Tribune 1028
Denver Tribune Association Print 1055
Denver Tribune Print 1392
Department General Orders No. 17 . . . 1863 4341
Department of Arizona, Lieutenant-Colonel George Crook, Commanding . . . 1872 4270
Departamento de Arispe 3063
Depôt des Cartes et Plans de la Marine 650
Dépôt Général de la Marine 699
Dépôt Hydrographique 2009
Depredations and Massacre by the Snake River Indians . . . 1861 1531
DeQuille, Dan 64, 4757, 4758
Derachés, Father 3655
Derbishire, S. 1894
Derby, Lt. 3809

Derby, G. H., & Co. 1435, 1513, 1896
Derby & Jackson 296, 372, 2338, 2340, 3868
Dernieres Decouvertes dans l'Amerique Septentrionale de M. de La Sale . . . Paris 1697 4163, 4164
Derrotero de la Expedicion en la Provincia de los Texas . . . 1722 3242
Desbarats, G. 1894
Desbruslins 650
Des Chutes River, Wash. 4683
Description de la Louisiane . . . 1683, 1688 1858, 1859
"*Description of a Day on Lake Erie*" 3619
"Description of California" 3788
Description of Central Iowa . . . 1858 2122
"Description of Fort Whipple" 4654
Description of Jacksonville . . . 1853 2087
Description of Keokuk . . . 1855 3443
Description of Louisiana . . . 1880 1860
Description of Oregon and California . . . 1849 2839
"Description of Outfitting Points" 560
Description of the Bounty Lands in the State of Illinois . . . 1819 996
Description of the City of Keokuk . . . 1854 2749, 3441
"Description of the Principal Roads and Routes . . . 1819" 996
Description of the United States Lands of Iowa . . . 1840 4678
Description of Western Texas . . . 1876 4627
"Descriptions of Fort Laramie, Red Cloud's Agency, etc." 4654
Descriptive, Historical, Commercial, Agricultural and Other Important Information . . . 1874 3664
Descriptive Pamphlet. No. 1 . . . 1860 4083
Descriptive Pamphlet of Knox County, Neb. . . . 1883 1456
Descriptive Review of Cass County, Nebraska . . . 1879 3162
Descriptive Sketch of the Spirit Lake Region . . . 1885 1943
Descubierta, La (ship) 2009
Desengaño, Puerto del 1262
Deseret News 1062, 4063, 4706, 4794
Deseret News Co. 2891
Deseret News Office 2525
Deseret News Print 3656
Deseret News Publishers 2372
"*Design for Jubilee College*" 3379
Desilver, C. 1855
De Smedt, P. J.: See Smet, P. J. de
De Smet, P. J.: See Smet, P. J. de
Des Moines, Ia. 560, 2122, 2150, 2671, 4218
Des Moines County, Ia. 1825, 1826, 2376, 3353
"*Des Moines, Iowa, from Capitol Hill*" 4218
Des Moines Land Assoc. 1489

Desmoines Navigation & Railroad Company 2671
Des Moines Rapids 4678
Des Moines River 41, 585, 1066, 4383
Des Moines River Improvement 2137
"*Des Moines River Improvement*" 585
Des Moines Valley 1060
De Soto, Hernando 181, 1902, 1948, 3700
De Soto Lode, Enterprise District, Colo. 1558, 1564
Desperadoes of the South-West . . . 1847 95
Des Plaines River 7
Destereu, Mademoiselle 4164
"Destiny of the Indian Tribes" 2822
Destroy All Previous Time Schedules . . . 1868 4237
"*Detail of Area about Fort Smith*" 4433
Detailed Account of the Massacre by the Dakota Indians of Minnesota in 1862 . . . 1923 3683
Detailed Description of the Scenes and Incidents . . . 1871 1524
Detectives 3803, 3804–3807, 4277
De Terra, Helmut 3290, 3291, 3292
Detroit, Dak. 1192
Detroit, Mich. 145, 331, 409, 475, 476, 1057, 1269, 1388, 2570, 2900, 2901, 3213, 4512
Detroit River 1070
Detroit Tribune 1070, 2082
"*Deutsches Sogen. West-Falen Settle-ment im Missouri-Staate am Osage*" 1873
Development and Resources of Beadle County . . . 1889 213
Devil's Gate, Nev. 1882
Devil's Lake, N. Dak. 93
"Devil's Lake" 1452
Devine, T. 1894
Devol & Haines 1071
DeVoto, B. 54
Dew Drops . . . 1900 4215
Dewing, J., Publishing Co. 2373
DeWitt & Davenport 1387, 4565
Dewitt & Snelling 4745
De Wolfe, S. 4453
Dexter, Hamilton & Co. 1237
Dey, P. A. 4236, 4251
"*Denver, Colorado, Showing the Location of Depot Grounds & the Right of Way*" 1054
Dheulland (engraver) 650
Diagram and Plans, Illustrative of The Principal Battles and Military Affairs, Treated of in Memoirs of My Own Times . . . 1816 4670
"*Diagram of Corner Stones*" 3463
"*Diagram of Harney Lake Ford . . .*" 4683
"*Diagram of Oregon*" 4683
"*Diagram of Route from Camp Dahlgreen to Indian Springs*" 4683
"*Diagram of Route from Indian Springs to Camp Wright*" 4683
"*Diagram of Scout to S. Side of Harney Lake . . .*" 4683

"*Diagram of the City of Salem*" 424
"*Diagram of the Shortest Routes to the Frontier*" 4538
"*Diagram of the State of Alabama*" 4384
"*Diagram of the State of Missouri*" 4384
Dialogue between Josh. Smith & the Devil . . . n.d. 3346, 3347
"Diamond Dick" 623, 3421, 4064
Diario de las operaciones militares de la division que al mando del General Jose Urrea . . . 1838 4448
Diario de Viage la Comision de Limites . . . 1850 278
Diario Historico . . . 1770 884
Diary (Breen) . . . 1946 396
Diary (Hunton) . . . 1956–1959 2023
Diary (Longsworth) . . . 1927 2530
Diary (Moore) . . . 1946 2883
Diary and Letters . . . (Cook) . . . 1919 865
"Diary Covering Events from Dec. 2, 1873 to October 5, 1874" 4654
Diary of a Forty-Niner . . . 1906 571
Diary of a Journey from Missouri to California in 1849 . . . 1928 730
Diary of a Journey from the Mississippi to the Coasts of the Pacific . . . 1858 2849
Diary of a Journey Through Arizona . . . 1866 108
"Diary of a Trip from Fort Bridger, Utah Territory, via Bridger's Pass and Laramie Plain to Fort Laramie, Nebraska Territory" 4437
"Diary of an Excursion to the Ruins of Abó, Quarra, and Gran Quivira in New Mexico" 4399
Diary of the Siege of Detroit . . . 1860 1970
Diary of the Washburn Expedition to the Yellowstone and Firehole Rivers . . . 1905 2389
"Diary of Thomas Scantlebury" 3690
Dibble, W. E., & Co. 846, 847, 3934
Dickens County, Tex. 2845
Dickenson, G. D. 1078
Dickinson, J. 1841
Dickinson & Co. 4543
Dickman, T. 1231
Dicks, J. 3715
Dictamen de la Comision de Puntos Constitucionales . . . 1830 773
Dictation Exercises . . . 1855 3033
Dictionary of American Biography 2185
Dictionary of Dakota . . . 1889 3903
Dictionary of the Sioux Language . . . 1866 2037
Dictionary of Ute Indian Language . . . n.d. 3725
Didot, François 133, 699
Diedrich, R. 3582
Dienst, A. 4113
Dietz, A. A. 1083
Dietz Opera House, Oakland . . . 1877 783
"Different Classes of Inhabitants—1830" 4790

Dighton, D. 2163, 2167
Dillingham, J. E. 3344
Dillon, J. F. 1924
Dilly, C. 622
Dimsdale, T. J. 2733, 4153, 4539
Dinwiddie, Mrs. G. T. 1570
Diploma 3197
Directories 66, 219, 282, 371, 388, 400, 424, 431, 433, 434, 487, 488, 515, 525, 531, 556, 565, 648, 758, 759, 806, 841–843, 999, 1101, 1155, 1156, 1166, 1243, 1248, 1276, 1296, 1310, 1311, 1339, 1396, 1484, 1485, 1530, 1586, 1655, 1706, 1707, 1727–1729, 1745, 1818, 1823, 1824, 1844, 1854, 1865, 1903, 1921, 1930, 1977, 2209, 2210, 2282, 2307, 2321, 2322, 2417, 2561, 2570, 2571, 2584, 2606, 2652, 2662, 2666, 2752, 2802, 2811, 2857, 2936, 2985, 3012, 3027–3031, 3041, 3150, 3210, 3220, 3408, 3441, 3564, 3664, 3673, 3799, 3848, 3870, 3900, 3950, 3968, 4036, 4037, 4065, 4118, 4132, 4141, 4192–4194, 4229, 4467, 4539, 4612, 4617, 4643, 4703, 4710, 4730
Directory, Business Mirror and Historical Sketches of Randolph County . . . 1859 2857
Directory for the Village of Rochester . . . 1827 1243
Directory of Chicago for the Year 1858 . . . 1858 4065
Directory of Grass Valley . . . 1865 531
"Directory of Keokuk" 3441
"Directory of Laramie City" 4191
Directory of Marengo County . . . 1861 4118
Directory of the City of Council Bluffs . . . 1866 487
Directory of the City of Dallas . . . 1875 525
Directory of the City of Detroit . . . 1837 2570
Directory of the City of Milwaukee . . . 1847, 1848 2571, 2811
Directory of the City of Nevada and Grass Valley . . . 1861 4132
Directory of the City of Placerville . . . 1862 1339
Directory of the County of Placer . . . 1861 3968
Disbursing Records 4293
Discourse (Belknap) . . . 1792 3867
Discourse (Bradstreet) . . . 1807 3289
Discourse, Delivered at Hopkinton . . . 1807 386
Discourse, Delivered at the Funeral of Hon. Joseph Duncan . . . 1844 4024
Discourse, Intended to Commemorate the Discovery of America . . . 1792 239
"Discoveries of Gold" 2122
"*Discoveries of the Honble Hudson's Bay Cos. Arctic Expedition* 3415, 3794
Discoveries of the World . . . 1601 1493
Discovery 1493
Discovery (ship) 3501, 3502, 4456

Engineer Office, Headquarters Department of Arizona. Whipple Barracks, Prescott, September 25, 1886 3928
Engineer School, Press of the 3734
Engineers, Corps of: See U.S. Army. Engineers, Corps of
Engineer's Report. To Le Grand Byington and Others . . . 1850 1009
England 573, 1224, 1283, 1973, 2030, 2061, 2094, 2323, 2734, 2855, 3314, 3359, 3372, 3619, 3956, 4154, 4438, 4543
Engles, S. 1775
English-American His Travail by Sea and Land . . . 1648 1470
English Colony 300, 304
English-Dakota School Dictionary . . . 1886 4697
English-Dakota Vocabulary . . . 1871 4696
English Emigrants 1677
English Family Robinson . . . 1852 3452
English Grammar Simplified . . . 1846 1438
English Prairie, Ill. 3304, 4742
"English Prairie" 4742
"English Prairie and Adjacent Country" 303
English Settlement in Illinois 1366, 1367, 4577
English Settlements 4076
English Sportsman in the Western Prairies . . . 1861 277
"Enlarged Map of Chilkoot, Chilkat and White Pass Routes" 805
"Enlarged Map of Klondike Mining District" 805
Enos, A. F. 1252
"Enquirer" Office 2662
Enquiry into the Causes of the Alienation of the Delaware and Shawanese Indians . . . 1759 3330, 4139
Enquiry into the Principles on Which a Commercial System . . . Should be Founded . . . 1787 895, 3867
Ensayo Cronologico . . . 1713 181
Ensign & Thayer 3269
Ensign & Thayer's Travellers' Guide through the States of Ohio, Michigan, Indiana, Illinois, Missouri, Iowa, and Wisconsin . . . 1852 1253
Ensign, Bridgman & Fanning's Lake and River Guide . . . 1856 1254
Ensigns & Thayer 3269
Ensign Peak 608
Enterprise Book and Job Printing House 4035
Enterprise District (De Soto Lode), Colo. 1558
"Entire Territory of Wisconsin" 4, 3869
"Entrance into Cross Sound" 4456
"Entrance of Columbia River" 4456
"Entrance of Port San Francisco" 4456
"Entrée des Détroits de Jean de Fuca" 2736

Entrée du Port de San Francisco 1169
Envelope 1929
"Environs of Albany" 4062
"Environs of Albion" 4742
"Environs of Baltimore and Washington" 4062
"Environs of Boston" 4062
"Environs of Detroit" 141
"Environs of Lexington" 141
"Environs of Mobile" 141
"Environs of Nashville" 141
"Environs of New York" 4062
"Environs of Pensacola" 141
"Environs of Philadelphia and Trenton" 4062
"Environs of St. Louis" 141
"Environs of Savannah" 4062
Ephraim 4129
Erbgrossherzogs von Hessen 1228
Erhard, Chez 1119, 1121
Erie, Lake: See Lake Erie
Erinnerungen Aus Texas . . . 1854 4698
Ermatinger's, Edward, York Factory Express Journal . . . 1912 1255
Ernest W. 2161
Ernst, H. 219
Erste Reise Nach dem Nordlichen Amerika . . . 1835 3218
Erwin, J. 2025
Escalante, Tomas 1265, 1797, 3791
Escalante y Arvisu, Manuel 3065
"Escape of Deerfoot the Indian Runner from the Chippeways" 3302
Escmo. Sr. Puesta en Conocimiento del Honorable Congreso . . . 1830 3891
Escudero, José Agustin de 3297
Esmerelda 2711
Espejo, Antonio de 85, 1023, 1582
Espinosa, Isidoro Felix 4483
Espionage 1654, 1782
Espiritu Santo, Bahia del 3242
Esposicion Al Publico Sobre Los Asuntos De Tejas . . . 1835 116
Esposicion dirigida al Supremo Gobierno por los Comisionados . . . 1848 2775
Esposicion que el Presbitero Antonio Jose Martinez . . . 1843 2694
Esquisse de la Situation Politique et Civile de la Louisiane . . . 1804 1263, 3524
"Esquisse de l'Anse des Amis" 2736
"Esquisse de l'Anse du Radeau" 2736
"Esquisse du Port Cox" 2736
Esquisse sur le Nord-Ouest de l'Amerique . . . 1869 4052
"Esquisse sur le Nord-Ouest de l'Amerique" 3887
"Essai d'une Carte que Mr. Guillaume Delisle" 460
Essai Politique sur le Royaume de la Nouvelle-Espagne . . . 1811 2009, 2010
Essays and Letters on Various Political Subjects . . . 1809 4747
Essex Institute 3197
Estado-Mayor-General 3296
Estado que Manifiesta la Fuerza . . . 1828 2771

Estaing, Comte d' 1280
Estes & Lauriat 4644
Estes Park, Colo. 3557
Estienne Robinot, Chez 2251
Estracto de Noticias del Puerto de Monterrey . . . 1770 1264
Estrada, Father 67
Establissement de la Foi . . . 1691 2433
Etablissement Géographique de Bruxelles 3831
Ethnological Society 3619
Etoile du Kansas et de l'Iowa, L' 70
Eugene City, Ore. 72, 3810
Eureka, Calif. 4734
Eureka Publishing Company 76
Europe 1626, 2536, 2948
Evacuation of Texas . . . 1837 1321
Evangelist Book & Job Office 1051
Evans, D. 2112
Evans, De L. 3614
Evans, E. 3121
Evans, G. G. 2113
Evans, G. S., & Co. 733
Evans, J. 822, 824
Evans, J. A. 4246, 4249, 4250
Evans, J. O. 1008
Evans, J. W. 1883, 1884
Evans, L. 3341
Evans, W. G. 2483
Evanston, Ill. 3273, 3274, 3314
Evansville (Ind.) Journal 2951
Evansville (Ind.) Journal 2951
Evening Capital News 3969
Evening Concert . . . 1879 4284
Evening Democrat Print 1149
Evening Globe Print 334
Evening Journal—Extra . . . 1871 1271
Evening News Press 1915
Evening Post . . . 1871 1272
Evening Press Publishing Co. 1031
Evening Telegraph 19
Eventful Narratives . . . 1887 1273
Everett, E. 1353, 4258
Everett House . . . 1870 1275
Everts & Co., L. H. 4134
Evidence in Relation to Land Titles . . . 1840 4110
Evidence Reported to the Senate, by the Committee Appointed to Inquire into the Facts Relating to the Conduct of John Smith . . . 1807 4373
Evidence Taken on the Trial of Mr. Smith . . . 1843 3859
Evil of Intoxicating Liquor . . . 1844 1278, 3731
Evolution 4598
Evolution of a State . . . 1900 3872
Ewbank, Mrs. 824
Ewer, F. C. 4572
Ewing, C. A. 395
Ewing, C. N. 1849, 2730
Ewing, F. 942
Ewing, M. C. 4380
Ewing, T. E. 4276, 4277
Examination of the Principles . . . 1749 1224, 3115
"Examination of the Reports of Explorations for Railroad Routes from the Mississippi to the Pacific" 4435

Farro, J. 4410
Farrow, Lieutenant 1983
Farrow & Dennett 4118
Farthest West 1443
Farwell, C. H. 3901
Farwell, Fredy B. 1963
Farwell, W. B. 637
Fashion Restaurant 2055
Fassett, S. M. 2493
"Father Clark" . . . *1855* 3231
Father Taylor . . . *1924* 2109
Faulconer, M. A. 3466, 3467
Faulk, A. J. 977–981
Faulkner, Mr. 796
Faulkner & Allen 3154
Fausett, T. 1699
Faust First Premium Printing
  House 3067
Faux, W. 1301
Favour, A. H. 1742
Fay, W. 3228
Fayette, Me. 516
Fayette, Mo. 2707, 3446, 3447,
  3772, 4465
Fayetteville, Ark. 1660
Feather River 3962
Feather River Party 1044
Featherstonhaugh, G. W. 924
Feats, E. H. 4788
Federal Government 1889
Federal Mining Laws 2982
Federal Union Book & Job Printing
  Office 2843
Federurbian . . . *1834* 1974
Feenan Papers 1302
Felix Island 812
Felloes & Faust 3969
Fellowes, W. D. 2167, 3409–3411,
  3535
Fellowship Meetinghouse 174
Femme de Loth 2736
Fenian Brotherhood, Idaho Circle
  2055
Fenian Brotherhood, John Mitchel
  Circle 2055
Fenzo, M. 747
Fergus, G. H. 2716
Fergus, Robert 12, 1727, 1745,
  2098, 2606, 3027, 3029, 3214
Fergus Falls, Minn. 4753
Fergus Printing Co. 3214
Fergus Reprints 151, 435
Ferguson, R. D. 2981
"Fern Frond" 962
Fernald, C. H. 4655
Fernandez, Domingo 3675
Fernandez, La Viuda de Manuel
  4470
Fernandez de Taos, Taos County,
  N. Mex. 2991
Fernandina, Floridas 1364
Ferrall, S. A. 3072
Ferrelo, Bartolome 4072
Ferrett & Co., E. 991
Ferribault, Pelagie 3940
Ferris, A. C. 637
Ferris, A. J. 3519
Ferris, J. 4611
Ferris, W. A. 4601
Ferris Bros. 1184
Ferry, W. M. 4696
Ferslew & Co. 1310

Festoons of Fancy . . . *1814* 2508
Fetter & Co., G. G. 2213
Fetterman, W. J. 305
Fetterman, Fort 4327
Fetterman Massacre 592, 1312, 1458
"Few Words of Consolation for the
  'Globe' " 3858
Fick, J. -G. 1541
Fickes, E. S. 2747, 4514
Fiction 184, 254, 255, 256, 258, 402,
  513, 516, 538, 695, 755, 756, 760,
  803, 936, 956, 991, 1180, 1199,
  1223, 1237, 1354, 1355, 1360, 1426,
  1502, 1503, 1506–1509, 1511, 1537,
  1598, 1710, 1711, 1713, 1732, 1733,
  1738, 1741, 1792, 1793, 1805, 1948,
  1965–1967, 2114–2116, 2237, 2240,
  2471–2473, 2487, 2508, 2529, 2556,
  2577, 2607, 2873, 2939, 3251, 3316,
  3452, 3453, 3486, 3488, 3516, 3595,
  3608, 3624, 3641, 3715, 3925, 3986,
  3987, 4473, 4564–4567, 4725
Fidlar & Chambers 392
Field, A. P. 2069
Field, E. 1598
Field, Mr. & Mrs. 1313
Field and Farm 3036
*Field Notes, Crossing the Prairies
  and Plains* . . . *1865* 3982
Fields, J. 743
Fields, R. 743
Fields, Osgood & Co. 793, 1805
Fifteen Thousand Miles by Stage . . .
  1911 3999
Fifteen Years of Frontier Life . . .
  1870 4463
*Fifteen Years' Residence with the
  Mormons* . . . *1876* 1640
*Fifth Annual Report of the Board of
  Regents of the Smithsonian Insti-
  tution* . . . *1851* 4398
*Fifth Calvary in the Sioux War of
  1876* . . . *1880* 2327
*Fifty-One Year's Reminiscences of
  Texas* 52
Fifty Years Ago . . . *1883* 4739
*Fifty Years and Over of Akron and
  Summit County* . . . *1892* 2383
Fifty Years in Both Hemispheres . . .
  1854 3026
Fifty Years in Camp and Field . . .
  1909 1908
Fifty Years in Iowa . . . *1888* 508
50 Years in the Saddle . . . *1942* 3500
*Fifty Years' Observation of Men and
  Events* . . . *1884* 2315
Fifty Years of Public Life . . . *1856*
  3868
Fifty Years on the Mississippi . . . *1889*
  1602
Fifty Years on the Old Frontier . . .
  1923 863
Fifty Years on the Trail . . . *1889*
  3128
*Fighting Indians in the 7th U.S.
  Cav.* . . . *1878* 2927, 2928
Figueroa's *Manifesto* 4650
Filibustering 23, 1132, 2195, 2361,
  3151, 3333, 3988, 4204, 4417, 4517,
  4587, 4618, 4749
Filings from an Old Saw . . . *1956*
  1142

Filley & Ballard 1322
Fillmore, Millard 4363, 4415
Fillmore, Andrew County, Mo. 3871
Fillmore County, Nebr. 1767, 2627
Fillmore County News 2627
Fillmore, Fort 2619–2621
Finance 3026
Finch, C. S. 3804
Finch & McCabe 65
Fink, Mike 4146, 4147
Finlayson, D. 3076
Finley, H. S. 1924
Fire Insurance 922
Firehole River 2389
First Annual Directory of Fort Scott
  . . . *1875* 556
First Annual Exhibit . . . *1858* 2563
First Annual Message . . . *to the
  Legislative Assembly (Dakota)* . . .
  1866 977
First Annual Report . . . *of the
  Central University of Iowa* . . .
  1854 636
*First Annual Report of the Officers
  of the Denver Pacific Railway &
  Telegraph Co.* . . . *1869* 1054
*First Annual Report of the President
  and Directors to the Stockholders
  of the Iowa Central Air Line Rail-
  road Company* . . . *1858* 2151
*First Annual Report of the Sonora
  Exploring and Mining Company*
  . . . *1857* 3892
*First Annual Report of the Union
  Colony of Colorado* . . . *1871* 4235
*First Annual Report of the Western
  Town Company* . . . *1857* 4611
First Baby in Camp . . . *1893* 263
First Baptist Church (Burlington,
  Ia.) 2457
First Church of Christ (Sacramento)
  269
First Citizen of Prescott . . . *1929*
  1742
"First Emigrant Train to California"
  637
*First Eight Months of Oklahoma
  City* . . . *1890* 1534
*"First Part of Captn. Pike's Chart
  of the Internal Part of Louisiana"*
  3290, 3291, 3292
First Presbyterian Church (Chicago)
  955
"First Presbyterian Church—(New
  School)" 2662
*First Regiment of New York
  Volunteers* . . . *1882* 733
First Settling of Kansas . . . *1898*
  4562
First Victoria Directory . . . *1860*
  2666
First Ward School, Dubuque 1160
Fischer, Theodor 4751
Fish, H. 2342
Fish, Mr. & Mrs. H. 3716
Fishbourne, R. W. 4705
Fisher, G. 2514, 2653
Fisher, G. P. 4032
*Fisher, George, Secretary and
  Translator* . . . *1853–54* 2514
Fisher, H. 1798
Fisher's Party, W. S. 3949

Franklin, W. B. 4413
Franklin, W. M. 2933
Franklin, Mo. 2683
Franklin, Tenn. 877, 2309, 4370
Franklin (Tenn.), Citizens of 2309
Franklin County, Ia. 3672
Franklin County, Kans. 1636
Franklin County, N.Y. 3310
Franklin Expedition from First to Last . . . 1855 2331
Franklin Hudson Publishing Co. 801, 2414, 2550, 2944
Franklin Press 4575
Franks, J. W., & Sons 1909
Fraser, R. 4163
Fraser, W. 3987
Fraser Mines 4501
Fraser River 59, 2572, 2819, 2820, 3215, 4501
Fraser River District 4679
"Fraser River from New Westminster to below Fort Alexander" 3215
Fraser River Gold Rush 881
Fraud 3636, 4084, 4494
Frazer Mines Vindicated . . . 1858 4501
Frazier, E. 1409
Frazier, R. 743
Frechette, J. -B., Père 340
Frechette & Cie. 3886
Fred Bennett, The Mormon Detective . . . 1887 260
Fred Steele, Fort 4327
Frederic, J. 1490
Frederick County, Va. 423
Free Lands of Dakota . . . 1876 933
Free-Lecture Course 3197
Free Press Print 4107
Free Press Steam Book and Job Printing House 131
Freedom of the Press 3675
Freeman, J. 671, 3115
Freeman, J. W. 1412
Freeman & Bro. 1533
Freeman's Almanac 1296
Freeman's Journal 380, 418, 438
Freemasons 1413–1423, 1619, 2055, 2417, 2540, 3343, 4186
Freeport, Ill. 3358
Freewater, Ore. 3402
Freighting 287, 2350, 2664, 3008, 3676, 3955, 4033, 4508, 4582
Freiheitskampf in Texas . . . 1844 1227
Frémont, J. C. 6, 36, 37, 270, 296, 381, 618, 619, 637, 1184, 1204, 1427, 1437, 1837, 1979, 2841, 2986, 3022, 3260, 3261, 3360, 3553, 4447, 4538, 4546
Frémont, J. C. & J. B. 1425
Frémont, Jessie B. 602, 637, 1436
Fremont, Miss 3655
Fremont, Nebr. 1951, 2972
Fremont County, Colo. 3905
Fremont County, Ia. 2502
"Fremont in the Conquest to California" 637
Fremont: The West's Greatest Adventurer . . . 1928 2986
Fremont Tribune 1833
Frémont's Battalion 1783

Fremont's 1845–46 Explorations 3791
Fremont's Reports 4494
French, Mrs. 2055
French, S. G. 2228
French & Indian War 1699, 3554, 3555, 3849, 3992, 4154
French and Indians of Illinois River . . . 1874 2713, 2714
French Colony (Alabama) 4118
French Creek, Dak. 26, 3707
French Emigrant 2654
French Fleet off Newport 668
French in Mexico 323
French Mormon 281
French Settlers 1345
French's Party 2791
Frénzeny, Paul 3128
Frères L'Honoré, Chez les 2365
Fresh Water Fork, Brazos River, Tex. 2420
Fresh Water Fork, Camp on 2420
Fresno, Calif. 385
Freyhold, E. 2932, 2933, 4309, 4546
Freytas, Nicolas de 1307
Friedenwald 1039
Friedrichsburg, Tex. 3889, 4017
Friedrichsburg, Die Colonie des Deutschen Fursten-Vereins in Texas . . . 1867 4017
Friend, The 994, 1443, 444
Friend & Aub 1130, 1856, 1857, 2776
Friendly, Aunt 695
Friendly Cove 2734
"Friendly Hint to Missouri" 3858
Friends 1949, 4689
Friend's Intelligencer 1949
Friends Press 2512
Friendship's Offering . . . 1858 3478
Friesen, F. 2009
Friesen, Oltmanns et Thulier 2009
Frisbie, L. 4622
Froben, Louis von 4327
Froebel, G., Verlag von 3582
Frog Lake, Saskatchewan 1605
Frog Lake Massacre 1605
From Cattle Range to Cotton Patch . . . 1902 297
From England to California . . . 1868 2761
From Everglade to Canon with the Second Dragoons . . . 1875 3544
From Home to Home . . . 1885 900, 1886
From Kirtland to Salt Lake City . . . 1890, 1891 2510, 4226
"From Our Front Window Looking North" 1749
From the Atlantic Surf to the Golden Gate . . . 1869 2008
From the Atlantic to the Pacific, Overland . . . 1866 188
From the Gold Mine to the Pulpit . . . 1904 2249
From Yorktown to Santiago . . . 1900 614
Frommann, M. 3889
Froncoso, Diego 3179
Fronteras 2771

Frontier and Indian Life . . . 1895, 1897 4090, 4091
Frontier Army Sketches . . . 1883 3960, 3961
Frontier County, Nebr. 2790
Frontier Days . . . 1917 2360
Frontier Guardian . . . 1851 1450, 3643
Frontier Index 1533, 4283
Frontier Lady . . . 1932 3598
Frontier Legend . . . 1954 206
Frontier Life . . . 1879, 1902 3762, 4580
Frontier Newspaper Humor 973
Frontier Phoenix 1533
Frontier Scout . . . 1864 1451, 1452, 2889
Frontier Service During the Rebellion . . . 1885 3263
Frontier Theory 4209
Frontier Trail . . . 1923 4621
Frontier Trails . . . 1930 576
Frontier Years 2000
Frost, D. 2639
Frost, D. M. 2285
Frost, J. H. 2440
Frost, M. 2990
Frost's Son, S. A. 2639
Froude, J. A. 512
Frozen Sea 1862
Fruit of Home Missions . . . ca. 1865 50, 3587, 4208
Fruits of Mormonism . . . 1851 3814
Fry's Traveler's Guide, and Descriptive Journal . . . 1865 1457
Fuerte Valley, Sonora 1225
Fugitive 3289
Fugitive Slave Case . . . 1850 1409
Full and Authentic Account of the Murder of James King . . . 1856 1286
Full Description of the Soil, Water, Timber, and Prairies of Each Lot, or Quarter Section of the Military Lands . . . 1818 4464
Fuller, Emeline 2002, 4388
Fuller, H. B. 811
Fuller, N. W. 2513
Fulton, F. R. 2564
Fulton, R. 2488
Fulton & Co. 1999
Fulton, Ark. 2675
Fulton County, Ill. 4045
Fultz, W. S. 4526
"Funeral Dirge" 1418
Funeral Discourse . . . 1849 3213
"Funeral of Col. Hardin" 1779
Funeral Services. The Funeral of Hon. T. B. Cuming . . . 1858 945
Funter, M. 2734, 2736
Fur Hunters of the Far West . . . 1855 3578
Fur Trade 32, 54, 88, 98–100, 154, 290, 298, 341, 342, 347, 377–379, 567, 631, 696, 697, 745, 768, 769, 776, 846, 847, 893, 897, 938, 1098, 1106, 1147, 1148, 1182, 1193, 1274, 1338, 1400, 1401, 1538, 1603, 1611, 1742, 1759, 1786, 1853, 1866, 1914, 1942, 1996, 2158–2161, 2193, 2212, 2234, 2359, 2403, 2404, 2461, 2527, 2609, 2630, 2631, 2640, 2664, 2688

2705, 2903, 2948, 2974, 3071, 3168, 3192, 3193–3195, 3243, 3271, 3506, 3522, 3532, 3576–3578, 3610, 3611, 3686, 3875, 4085–4093, 4130, 4232, 4380, 4381, 4411, 4429, 4462, 4463, 4466, 4490, 4498, 4558, 4591, 4600, 4601, 4615, 4702, 4707
Furnace Bomb Ketch 1098
Furnas, R. W. 2957, 2967
Furnas County, Nebr. 1468
Furste, E. 4554
Further Papers Relative to the Exploration by the Expedition Under Captain Palliser 3167
Further Report, A . . . 1742 3115
Further Report from the Committee of Secrecy . . . 1742 1469
"Future of Democracy, The" 1492

G. 1492
G., W. D. 1872
G.A.R. Encampment in San Francisco 3667
"*G. W. Claytons Store*" 3344
Gadsden, J. 1625
Gadsden Purchase 1225, 2004–2006, 3893, 3894, 4618
Gadsden Treaty 836, 1625
Gage, D. W. 2495
Gage County, Nebr. 3890
Gage Papers 2901
Gager, J., & Co. 687, 1311
Gaines, E. P. 2772
Gainesville, Fla. 3175
Galapagos Islands 812, 4456
Gale, S. F. 2072, 2073
Galena, Ill. 644, 672, 971, 1484, 1485, 1576, 2072, 2073, 2642, 3070, 3380, 3761, 3899, 4183, 4551
"*Galena and Chicago Union Rail Road the Only Rail-Road Route*" 1479
Galena City Directory . . . 1854, 1858 1484, 1485
Gales & Seaton 104, 290, 337, 804, 1084, 1212, 1274, 1436, 2335, 2592, 2593, 2782, 2830, 2834, 2886, 3071, 3998, 4067, 4384, 4421, 4568, 4614
Galesburg, Ill. 2490, 2606, 3034, 3564, 3565
Galesburg City Directory . . . 1861 3564
Galesburg, Monmouth, Knoxville and Abingdon Directories . . . 1857 2606
Galindo, Ygnacio 2765
Gallagher, W. D. 457, 1872
Galland's Iowa Emigrant . . . 1840 1488
"*Galland's Map of Iowa*" 1488
Gallatin, A. 49
Gallatin, Mo. 2608, 4524
Gallatin Saddle 1490
Gallego, Juan 3675
Galvan, Imprenta de 2768
Galveston, Tex. 3398, 4737
Galveston Bay 1494, 1495, 1496, 1497
Galveston Bay & Texas Land Co. 4737

Galveston Bay and Texas Land Company, Notice . . . 1835 1495
Galveston, Harrisburg & San Antonio Railway Company 4627
Galvez, Matias de 2492
Gamble, A. 2707
Gamble Gulch, Colo. 2097
Gambler, Reformed 1638
Gambling 1071, 1638, 4756
Gambling Halls 4756
Gambling Unmasked! . . . 1847 1638
Gammel, H. P. N., & Co. 1188
Gammel's Book Store 2192, 3872
Gantt, D. 2964
Garbanati, H. 970
Garcia Conde, Diego 2009
Garcia-Conde, Pedro 3652
García Cubas 2765
Garcilaso de la Vega 181
Garddet, J. C. 2049
Garden of the World . . . 1856 995
Garden Valley of Nebraska . . . 1880 2238
Gardiner, Abigail 2442
Gardiner, G. W. 3031
Garland, Lieutenant 1363
Garland, Fort 4327
Garnavillo, Ia. 932
Garnier Frères 3637
Garote, Calif. 1844
Garrard, K. 4435
Garraty, M. 2055
Garrett, Emma N. 2557
Garrett, P. 2475, 2476
Garrison, G. P. 1199
Garrison, W. L. 2704
Garrison Belle Vue, Ia. 2219
Garrisoning of Western Posts and Forts 4254
Garry, Fort 519, 520, 1894, 2243
Garside, J. 3340
Gary, G. W., & Co. 776
Garza County, Tex. 2845
Gaspésie 2432, 2433
Gasconade 743
Gast, A., & Co.'s New Process 2238
Gast, Aug., Bank Note & Litho. Company 3730
Gast, John, & Co. 2759
Gast, Leopold, & Brother 3412
Gass, P. 743
Gaston, Camp 4356
"Gate City," Lee County, Ia. 3443
Gate City, Press of the 4197
Gate City Print 2316, 2317
Gateway Printing Co. 3134
Gatewood, Lieutenant Charles B. . . . and the Surrender of Geronimo . . . 1929 1523
Gaubil, R. P. 460
Gaume Frères 1119
Gavit, E. C. 2431
Gaxiola, Jesus 1265
Gaxiola, José Maria 3066
Gazeta de Mexico . . . 1729 1528
Gazette, The . . . 1848 1529
Gazette Book and Job Printing House 4551
Gazette Co. 1010
Gazette (Galena), Daily 971
Gazette Office 3710
Gazette Publishing Co. 672

Gazetteer 224, 433, 923, 1297, 1310, 1706, 1707, 1727, 1823, 1824, 3150, 3232, 3233, 3237, 3526, 3712, 3713, 4615, 4729
Gazetteer and Directory of Jackson County, Iowa . . . 1878 3150
Gazetteer and Intelligencer Prints 3565
Gazetteer of Illinois . . . 1834, 1837, etc. 3232, 3233, 3237, 3526
Gazetteer of Madison County . . . 1866 1706
Gazetteer of the State of Missouri . . . 1837 4615
Gazetteer of the States of Illinois and Missouri . . . 1823 224
Gazlay's San Francisco Business Directory for 1861 1530
Geary, J. W. 1486
Gebow, J. A. 2217
Gedney, J. F. 1334, 2281, 3177
Geer & Wilson 3031, 4518, 4709
Geer's Print 1703, 1704
Geffs 1534
Gelderland, The Netherlands 1931
Gellibrand, W. 2654
Gem, A. "The City of the Plains." . . . 1887 1535
Gem City Business College, Quincy, Ill. 1768
Gemmell, J. 3358
Gems of Rocky Mountain Scenery . . . 1869 2708
Gems of Thought and History of Shoshone County . . . 1940 1915
Genealogical History of the Duncan Stuart Family in America . . . 1894 4020
Genealogy 1244, 1317, 1390, 1631, 1827, 2021, 2295, 2582, 2878, 2895, 3860, 3861, 4020, 4544
General Assembly (Louisiana) 2542
Gen. Austin's Map of Texas 2880
General Baptist Publishing House 892
General Circular (Kelley) 3935
General Circular (Oregon) 53
General Circular to All Persons of Good Character . . . 1831 2286, 2288
"General Crook in the Indian Country" 637
General Directory and Business Advertiser of the City of Chicago, for the Year 1844 . . . 1844 3027
General Directory of Sioux City . . . 1880 3799
General Epistle from the Council . . . n.d. 715
"General Expenses of the Indian Department" 4420
General Field Orders 1980, 4293
Gen. Hunt's Letter to Senator Sam Houston . . . 1849 2015
General: I Have the Honor to Submit for the Information of . . . 1869 4325
General Index to the First Twelve Volumes . . . 1818 4575
General Instructions for the Government of the Consular and Commercial Agents . . . 1838 4111

General Instructions. Office of the
Surveyor General of Wisconsin
and Iowa . . . n.d. 4419
General Joseph Smith's Appeal to
the Green Mountain Boys . . . 1843
3855
General Land Agent 4746
General Land Office 1505, 2017,
2460, 4395, 4464
"General Map of a Survey in Cali-
fornia" 4435
"General Map of British North
America" 2809
"General Map of New France" 2364
"General Map of the Northern Pa-
cific States and Territories" 2933
"General Map of the United States
and Mexico" 387
"General Map Showing the Countries
Explored & Surveyed by the
United States & Mexican Bound-
ary Commission" 198, 3901
General; or, Twelve Nights in the
Hunter's Camp . . . 1869 196
General Orders, U.S. Army: See also
U.S. Army. General Orders
General Orders and Circulars . . .
1856–61 4254
General Orders and Circulars, 1867
to 1874 and 1883 to 1884 4293
General Orders and Circulars, 1867–
1882 4360
General Orders, Circulars and Ros-
ters, Issued from Headquarters
Dep't of Dakota, 1884 . . .
1885 4293
General Orders, Circulars and Ros-
ters. Dep't of Dakota, 1883 . . .
1884 4293
General Orders, Circulars, Annual
Report, and Rosters, Issued from
Headquarters Department of Da-
kota. 1895 4298
"General Outline Map of Arizona"
2583
"General Plat of the Military Lands,
between the Mississippi & Illinois
Rivers" 4464
"General Profile of the Union Pa-
cific Railway" 3177
"General Profile from Westport near
the Western Border of the State
of Missouri to the Sevier River
(Great Basin)" 4435
General Regulations of the Illinois
State Troops 1239
General Scott Lode, Colo. 2182
General Sheridan's Squaw Spy . . .
1869 1537
General Smith's Views of the Powers
and Policy of the Government of
the United States . . . 1844 1084,
3856
"General View of the Falls of Niaga-
ra" 2746
Geneva, Ia. 2801
Geneva, Ill. 1310
Geneva, Wisc. 3782
"Geneva and Adjacent Country" 2801
Geneva Lake Herald, Office of 3782
"Geneva, Wayne County, Ioway Dis-
trict Wisconsin Territory" 2801

Genoa, Calif. 3791
Gensoul, A. 80, 1882, 4738
Gentleman's Magazine . . . 1840 513
Gentlemen's Magazine . . . 1790 1538
Gent's Furnishing Goods 332
"Geografia dei luoghi delle missioni
nei territorj di Wisconsin e di
Michigan" 2732
Geographer of the United States
2029
Geographical and Geological Sur-
veys West of the Mississippi . . .
1874 4390, 4440
Geographical and Statistical History
of the County of Hennepin . . .
1869 2844
Geographical and Topographical De-
scription of Wisconsin . . . 1844
2398
Geographical Catechism of Pennsyl-
vania and the Western States . . .
1836 3605
Geographical Club . . . n.d. 3614
"Geographical Description of Min-
nesota" 2819, 2820
Geographical, Geological and Sta-
tistical Chart of Wisconsin &
Iowa . . . 1837 4
Geographical, Historical, Political,
Philosophical and Mechanical Es-
says . . . 1750 1270
Geographical, Historical, Political,
Philosophical and Mechanical Es-
says, Number II . . . 1756 1270
Geographical Memoir Upon Upper
California . . . 1848 1429
Geographical Sketch of that Part of
North America, Called Oregon . . .
1831 2286
Geographical Sketch of that Part of
North America, Called Oregon . . .
1830 2287, 2288
Geographical Sketches on the West-
ern Country . . . 1819 997
Geographical Statistics . . . 1850
4149
"Geographically Correct Map of
Kansas & Colorado" 3818, 3819
"Geographically Correct Map of the
Kansas Pacific Railway" 2276
Geography 272, 460, 510, 1353,
1356, 1429, 1556, 1852, 4390, 4440
Geography and Resources of Arizona
& Sonora . . . 1859 2921
Geological Formation 534
"Geological Map of South-West
Branch Pacific Rail Road" 4043
Geological Report of the Country
Along the Line of the Southwest-
ern Branch of the Pacific Railroad
. . . 1859 3645, 4043
"Geological Section through Treas-
ure Hill, East & West" 4056
"Geological Sketch" 4723
"Geological Sketch of the Lead
Mine District of Missouri" 3701
Geological Survey 4435
Geological Survey of California
4646
Geology 324, 510, 534, 3549, 3645,
3701, 4043, 4056, 4435, 4440,
4646, 4723

"Geology of the High Sierra" 4492
George, H. 228
George, S. 1817
George & Cos. Lithography 3576,
3577
George C. Bates v. the Illinois Cen-
tral Railroad Co. Argument . . .
1859 2084
George C. Bates vs. Ill. Central
Rail Road Co. Ejectment 2085
George Fisher, Secretary and Trans-
lator . . . 1853–54 2514
George, Fort 2609
"Geo. L. Davenport's Block" 1924
George, Lake: See Lake George
George Mason . . . 1829 1355
Georgetown, Calif. 1339
Georgetown, Colo. 632
Georgetown Courier Steam Print-
ting House & Blank Book Manu-
factory 1453
Georgia 10, 409, 485, 1136, 1137,
1540, 2299, 2450, 2946, 2947,
3094, 3096, 3280, 3310, 3318,
3738, 3924, 4076, 4154, 4299,
4300, 4744
"Georgia and Alabama" 141
"Georgia und Alabama" 409
Gerault, Baron 3947
Gere, C. H. 4123
Gere, T. D. 4333
Gere & Brownlee 2497
German Colonization of Texas 1843
German Doctor, A 2466
Germantown, Penna. 2557
Germany 743, 3346, 3932
Geronimo 156, 356, 367, 928–931,
1523, 2419, 2420, 2785, 3186,
3928, 4336, 4362, 4643,
4672
Geronimo Campaign 3186
Getchell & Neilsen 482
Getwins, J. 1952, 1953, 1954
Geysers 3944
Gibbes, C. D. 61, 604
Gibbon, 2461
Gibbon, J. 3759
Gibbon, Laura R. 2461
Gibbs, A. C. 4683
Gibbs, Mrs. G. A. 3494
Gibbs, I. L. 4044
Gibson, G. 743
Gibson, H. G. 733
Gibson, J. 4471
Gibson, T. 3543
Gibson, W. 3346
Gibson, W. F. 2215
Gibson & Morrison 1276
Gibson, Miller & Richardson 244
Gibson, Fort 1885, 2531, 3529, 3756,
4306, 4327, 4433, 4623
Giddings, J. R. 1084
Gide, Chez 323
Gideon, G. S. 3976, 3977
Gideon, J. & G. S. 620, 621, 765,
1084, 2082
Giffart, P. -F. 650
Gifford, L. 2461
Giguet et Michaud 2792
Gihon, J. H. 3901

Greene, Mary 1995
Greene, M. W. 3739
Greenfield, Ill. 459
Greenhill, Elizabeth 2467
Greenland 3161
Greenly, A. H. 1343
Green's Historical Series . . . 1912
1636
Greenup, C. 2309
Greenville, Me. 1606
Greenville, O. 743, 1231
Greenwood, W. H. 3177, 4327
Gregg, J. 2765, 3998
Gregg, Stella D. 1666
Gregg, T. 1116, 1117
Gregg, W. 1213
Gregg & Brown 3606
Gregg Party 328
Gregory, J. F. 4330
Gregory Diggings 724
Gregory District, Colo. 1558, 1667
Gregory District (Seger Lode) 1558
Gregory Gold Mining Co. 1667
Gregory Gulch, Colo. 3540
Grey, W. 498
Grey Bull River 4329
Greyslaer 220
Gridley 996
Gridley, E. G. 1296
Grierson, B. H. 930, 1204, 1808,
2175, 3529, 3755, 3756, 4310,
4312, 4313, 4362
Grierson Papers 1204, 1808, 2175,
3529, 4310, 4312, 4313
Grierson's Copy 4313
Griffin, J. S. 4540
Griffin, P. 1948
Griffin, R., & Co. 4564
Griffin, Fort 4327
Griffith, L. A. 247
Griffith, S. M. 2040
Grigg & Elliot 3233
Griggs, S. C., & Co. 1380, 3870
Griggs, Watson & Day 3929
Grim Chieftain of Kansas . . . 1885
1327
Gringo, El . . . 1857 1021
Grinnell, Ia. 1679
Grinnell College 1679, 1680
Griswold, D. S. 3406
Griswold, M. V. B. 1391
Grit Printery 4023
Grizzly Bear 15, 16, 109, 1912
Grizzly Bear Hunter 1912
Grocery Business 3955
Grondel, Jean-P. Gougon de 3359
Groner, "Con" 785
Grosseherzogliche Luxemburgische
409
Grossmann, G. 2009
Grothé, L. Emile 2251
Grouard, F. 1035
Groundplan of Indian Key 3255
Groveland Belle Company 1899
Grover, F. R. 1748
Grover, L. F. 3119, 3121
Grover & Baker 3437
Groves, K. 3346
Grubbs, J. W. 3198
Grummond, G. W. 592
Grundy County, Ia. 3672
Grupps, J. W. 3198, 3199

Guadalajara, Audiencia de 3279
Guadalupe, Mexico 4468
Guadalupe Hidalgo, Mexico 2775,
3652
Guadalupe, Victoria Mexico 2770
Guajardo, General 2695, 2696
Gual, P. 1364
Guatemala 1377, 4485, 4517
Guayardo, Jesus 1287
Guaymas, Mexico 245, 1169, 4468
Guerard, N. 1858
Guerreu, C. 2037
Guerrillas 477, 850, 1213, 1585,
1883, 1884, 2418, 2581, 3746, 4332
Guerrillas of the West . . . 1876 76
Gudde, E. G. 4491
Guibert 2487
Guide (profession) 4677, 4683
*Guide Book on Kiowa, Comanche, and
Apache Reservation . . . 1901* 3463
Guide Books: See also Directories and
Gazetteers 1, 4, 57, 141, 200, 224,
267, 318, 324, 335, 336, 345, 346,
433, 457, 458, 536, 560, 751, 752,
763, 805, 828, 833, 834, 838, 876,
878, 946, 947, 953, 957, 963, 964,
996, 997, 1038, 1044, 1091, 1092,
1163–1165, 1167, 1192, 1208, 1246,
1247, 1253, 1254, 1288, 1289, 1297,
1309, 1334, 1457, 1488, 1550, 1650,
1681, 1682, 1685–1687, 1690, 1693,
1706, 1707, 1716, 1724–1727, 1735,
1739, 1767, 1768, 1806, 1815, 1820,
1830, 1867, 1873, 1916, 1934, 1935,
1943, 1952–1956, 1959, 1977, 2017,
2029, 2061, 2091, 2092, 2203, 2207,
2221, 2284, 2287, 2288, 2433, 2434–
2437, 2676, 2677, 2697, 2722, 2740,
2751, 2752, 2754, 2757, 2794, 2839,
2840, 2842–2845, 2853, 2867, 2879,
2914, 2933, 3011, 3012, 3015, 3021,
3034, 3037, 3041, 3048, 3074, 3084,
3091, 3092, 3099, 3112, 3113, 3153,
3162, 3188, 3189, 3191, 3205, 3206,
3219, 3229, 3232–3237, 3267–3269,
3304, 3358, 3419, 3420, 3437, 3448,
3463, 3582, 3605, 3679, 3695, 3712,
3713, 3721, 3724, 3788, 3793, 3816,
3818, 3819, 3838–3840, 3852–3854,
3889, 3965–3967, 3969, 4000, 4001,
4011, 4035, 4068, 4121, 4182, 4183,
4192–4194, 4199, 4211, 4400, 4401,
4502, 4538, 4583, 4584, 4596, 4612,
4687, 4710, 4729, 4737, 4746, 4765
Guide for Emigrants . . . 1831 141,
3234
*Guide for Emigrants to Minnesota
. . . 1857* 1685
*Guide for the Territory of Iowa . . .
1839* 833, 834
*Guide from the Lakes to the Rocky
Mountains . . . 1868* 4211
*Guide, Gazetteer and Directory of
Nebraska Railroads . . . 1872* 4729
*Guide Map of the Best and Shortest
Cattle Trail to the Kansas Pacific
Railway . . . n.d.* 2275
*Guide through Ohio, Michigan, Indi-
ana, Illinois, Missouri, Wisconsin
& Iowa* 421, 3852–3854
Guide to Texas Emigrants . . . 1835
4737

*Guide to the City of Chicago . . .
1868* 1686, 1687
*Guide to the Great Coeur d'Alene
Gold Field* 2798
*Guide to the Kansas Gold Mines at
Pike's Peak . . . 1859* 1693
*Guide to the New Gold Region of
Western Kansas and Nebraska . . .
1859* 3092
*Guide to the Republic of Texas . . .
1839* 2017
*Guide to the Union Pacific Railroad
Lands . . . 1873* 2408, 4238
*Guide to the Yukon Gold Fields . . .
1895* 4710
Guignard, Jean 4164
Guignes, M. de 460
Guild, H. A. 2969
Guilford, N. & G., & Co. 1352, 1741
Guinea 4163
Guion, Captain 4383
Gulager, Susan Train 1017
Gulf of Chambaye 3161
Gulf of Mexico 650, 651, 1167,
2251–2253, 2426, 3359
Gulf of Mexico . . . 1859 2426
Gulf Stream 2426
Gunfighters 951
Gunfights 4042
Gunn, Elizabeth 1688
Gunn, Elizabeth Le Breton 1688
*"Gunn & Mitchell's New Map of
Kansas and the Gold Mines"* 1691,
1692
Gunnison, J. W. 3947, 4435
*"Gunn's New Map of Kansas and
the Gold Mines"* 1690
Gunter's Landing, Tenn. 4299
Gunther, C. F. 1483
Gurley, J. A. 3552
Guthrie, Okla. 1423, 2649
*Guthrie Lodge of Perfection, No. 1,
to the Venerable Master . . . n.d.*
1423
Guthrie's Geography Improved 3839
Guyot, De Los W. 4659, 4660
Guzman, Juan 2766
Gwin, Lucy 2920
Gwin, W. McK. 108, 2602
Gwinn, J. P. 3081

H., E. P. 1991
*Hace Algunos Dias que Estaba por
Decidirme a . . . 1835* 2996
Hackett, S. E. 2400
Hacq. 1169
Hadley, T. B. J. 119
Hafen, L. R. 1690, 3884
Hagerty, F. H. 976, 3903
Haggard, J. V. 3297
Hahn, K. 1916
Haight, N. 4444
Hailey, Ida. 3485
Hailman Printing Co. 2614
Haines 2282
Haines, E. M. 7, 2250, 3482, 4680
Haiti 1195
Hakluyt, R. 1259, 1493
Halderman, J. A. 2430
Hale, Mary King 1715
Hale, P. C. 2398
Hale, W. P. 1431

773

Harrison & Smith 4455
Harrison & Sons 4216
Harrison County, O. 432
Harry, J. 1081
Harsh, L. 1361
Harsha, W. 2570
Harsha & Willcox 3213
Hart, Mrs. B. F. 102
Hart, J. 1802, 1803
Hart & Chandler 4446
Harte, F. B. 3339
Hartford, Conn. 1241, 4171
Hartford Publishing Co. 2011
Harthill, A., & Co. 1806
Hartmann 2487
Hartsuff, Fort 4327
Harvard College 42, 2042, 2953, 3707
Harvey, G. A. 248, 1891
Harvey, Sir John 3614
Hartzoff, M. 2478
Haseltine, T. H. 2713
Haske es Tarsa 4785
Haskell, D. 1786
Haslar Hospital, Gosport 3492
Haslam, R. H. 4214
Hastings, F. H. 4740
Hastings, F. S. 4050
Hastings, L. W. 4538
Hastings, R. 2308
Hastings, Minn. 1166
Hastings, Nebr. 4761
Hatch, E. A. C. 2819, 2820
Hatch, E. W. 712
Hathaway, G. 2655
Hauser 1039
Havana, Cuba 1610, 2901, 2947, 4687
Havers, E. A. 782
Havre de Grace 650
"*Havre de Milfort*" 650
Hawaii 796, 837, 879, 893, 994, 1391, 1443, 1444, 1463, 3250, 4173, 4174, 4434, 4456, 4794
"*Hawaiian Group or Sandwich Islands*" 837
Hawes, M. 4737
Hawes & Stow, Mirror Office 2567
Hawk-Eye Book & Job Office Print 3393
Hawk-Eye Office 2086, 2456
Hawk-Eye Steam Print 1460, 1461
Hawkeye Book & Job Establishment 371
Hawkeye Book & Job Printing House 491
Hawkeye Pioneer Association 1826
Hawkins, B. 1540
Hawkins, J. H. 4478
Hawkins, W. W. 204
Hawkins Family 1827
Hawley, J. 1243
Hawley, J. R., & Co. 3286
Hawleyville, Ia. 1585
Haworth, J. M. 4451
Hay, M. 2522
Hayday (binder) 2939
Hayden, B. F. 1421
Hayden's Party 1344
Hayes, B. 4540
Hayes, J. L. 3511
Hayes's River 3532

"Hayfield Fight" 2520
Hayman, R. G. 3198
Haynes, J. E. 2389
Hays, J. G. 629
Hays, Mayor 3889
Hays, Fort 2297, 4327
Hayward, G. 1794
Haywood, J. 2734
Hazard, W. P. 238
Hazel, Harry 2237
Hazzard, J. L. 1855
Head, C. A. 1545
Head of Beaver Creek 4683
Head Quarters: See also U.S. Army. Headquarters
Head Quarters. Parish of Iberville, September 8th, 1816, Militia General Orders. 2547
Headless Horseman . . . 1866 3453
Heald, H. 744
Heald, N. 2411
Health Resorts 4634
Heap, D. P. 4327
Heap, G. H. 3551
Heart Whispers . . . 1859 106
Heartman, C. F. 3839
Heartman's Historical Series 2700
Heath, H. H. 3005
Heath, W. 4333
Heath, W. M. 3085
Hebard, Grace R. 593, 743
Heckewelder, J. G. E. 944
Heclawa 1890
Hector, J. 3167
Hedderich, G. 46
Heidemann, Elizabeth 3833
Heilmann, J. A. 1923
Heinemann, W. 2346
Heintzelman, Maj. 1225
Heintzelman Mine 3893
"*Heintzelman Mine, at Cerro Colorado, near Tubac, Arizona*" 3893
Heirs & Russell 3436
Heiskell, F. S. 439
Heiskell & Brown 1198
Heiss' Gallery 4099
Hekekyan Bey 4437
Held, P. T. 2420, 4279–4282
Helena, Mont. 309, 373, 1085, 1845, 1846, 2871, 3041, 3950, 4539
Helena Directory . . . 1884 3950
Helena Independent 309
Helena Theatre! . . . 1866 1845
Helena's Social Supremacy . . . 1894 1846
Heliograph System 1674, 3928
Heliotype Printing Co. 760
Hell on the Border . . . 1898 1785
Helldorado . . . 1928 395
Helps to the Study of Presbyterianism . . . 1834 439
Hempstead, E. 4551
Henckel, G. 2660
Henderson, Sarah F. 1328
Henderson, Senator 4385
Henderson, Mr., Made the Following Report . . . 1845 4385
Henley, J. C. 2042
Henneberry Co. 2753, 4796
Hennepin County, Minn. 2844
Hennesey, P. 1411
Henry, A. 270

Henry, G. F. 2109
Henry, G. T. 2110
Henry, S. 1966
Henry & Cohen 3549
Henry County Directory . . . 1859 371
Henry County Historical Society 3199
Henry Farnam . . . 1922 1292
Henshall, T. 1362
Heppenheimer, Fr. 3092
"Her Life, Adventures and Sufferings Among the Apachee & Mohave Indians" 3060
Herald & Book & Job Printer 171
Herald Book & Job Establishment 4659, 4660
Herald Book & Job Office 2796, 2797, 4594
Herald Book & Job Printing Establishment 1941
Herald Book & Job Rooms 514
Herald Co. 1063
Herald Office 160, 1589, 3153, 3343, 3398, 3440
Herald Print 69, 1617, 2097, 2972, 3276, 3784
Herald Printing & Electrotyping House 3485
Herald Printing & Publishing Company, Limited 3680
Herald Printing House 3737
Herald Publishing Co. 745
Herald Steam Book & Job Printing House 243, 4192, 4193
Herald Steam Book Office 3465
Herald Steam Printing House 2988
Herederos de Doña María de Rivera 1504
Herges Printing Company 375
Hergest, Lieut. 4456
"*Hergest's Islands*" 4456
Herington Sun Press 2333
Herle, P., & Co. 1873
Herline & Hensel, Lith. 1127
Hermenegildo Garces, Francisco Tomas 401
Herndon, W. H. 3583, 4172
Herndon's Lincoln . . . 1889 1871
Heroes 4195
Heroes and Incidents of the Mexican War . . . 1903 1539
Heroes of the Plains . . . 1881 467
Heroine du Texas . . . 1819 2487
Herold, D. E. 2248
Herran, Tomas 3891
Herrera, José Antonio 3062
Herriman, A. H. 2357
Herschel, Sir John 140
Hervey, W. H. 1362
Herz, N. 2367
Hesperian; or, Western Monthly Magazine . . . 1828–1829 1872
Hesperos . . . 1850 1976
Hessen, Erbgrossherzogs von 1228
Hessians 4670
Hetzel Collection 281, 4728
Heubach, E. 4310
Hewitt, Emily E. 1876
"Hexcombe War" 3434
Hezlep, G. 3651
Hiatt, J. M. 4597

Hibernicus . . . *1828* 1877
Hickman, N. 3634
Hickok, J. B. 852
Hickok, W. 467, 468, 1868
Hicks, D., & Co. 3155
Hicks Printing Company 2205
Hiett, Mrs. Geo. W. 4103
Higgins, C. S. 4222
Higgins, S. W. 3966
High Misdemeanor 4748
High School Literary Society. Closing Exercises . . . 1875 3106
High Sierras 4758
Highland, Colo. 1386, 3344
Highland, Ill. 1706
Highland, O. 4133
Highland Park, Ill. 4213–4215, 4217
Higuera, Prudencia 637
Hijar, José 1319, 1320
Hildesheim 1256
Hildreth, S. P. 944
Hill, A. J. 2528, 3835
Hill, A. S. 900
Hill, E. J. 1748
Hill, I. 2285
Hill, J. E. 1816
Hill, T. & W. 1213
Hill City, S. Dak. 3048
Hilliard & Brown 3923
Hilliard, Gray, Little & Wilkins 1355, 3874
Hillsboro Gazette Job Room 4133
Himes, G. H. 3574
Himes the Printer 1218
Hines, G. 417
Hinckley, Clarissa N. 3565
Hindman, L. 1895
Hindman, R. L. 1895
Hinkle, J. T. 1135
Hinman, C. 1899
Hinman, R. 1986
Hinman, Sarah H. 1899
Hinman, W. R. 599
Hinman & Dutton 4, 3869
Hinton, H. L. 3252
Hinton, R. J. 3437
Hinton, W. M., & Co. 4157, 4635
Hirschfeld, F. 682
His Imperial Highness the Grand Duke Alexis in the United States of America . . . 1872 35
"*Hispania Nova*" 1471
Histoire de la Conqueste de la Floride . . . 1685 1902
Histoire de la Louisiane . . . 1758 2462
Histoire de L'Amerique Septentrionale . . . 1722 133
Histoire des Comites de Vigilance aux Attakapas . . . 1861 182
Histoire des Terres Nouuellement Descouuertes . . . 1586 1259
Histoire et Description Generale de la Nouvelle France . . . 1744 650
Histoire Raisonee des Operations Militaires et Politiques de la Derniere Guerre . . . 1783 2230
Historia . . . (González de Mendoza) 1259
Historia Breve de la Conquista de los Estados Independientes del Imperio Mejicano . . . 1839 1424

Historia de la Nueva Mexico . . . 1610 4484
Historia General y Natural de las Indias . . . 1851–55 3147
Historic Sketches of the Cattle Trade . . . 1874 2594
Historical Account of the Doings and Sufferings of the Christian Indians in New England, in the Years 1675, 1676, 1677 . . . 1836 49
Historical and Biographical Record of the Cattle Industry . . . 1895 891
Historical and Descriptive Sketch of Sonoma County, Calif. . . . 1877 4134
Historical & Philosophical Society of Ohio 1999, 3020, 3213, 3277
Historical and Statistical Sketches, of Lake County, State of Illinois . . . 1852 7, 1703, 1704
Historical Committee of the Association (Wyoming Stock Growers') 4783
Historical Details, Having Relation to the Campaign of the North-Western Army . . . 1818 4711
Historical Narrative of the Civil and Military Services of Major-General William H. Harrison . . . 1824 1026
Historical Publishing Co. 466
Historical Record . . . 1886–90 2891, 2892
Historical Reminiscences . . . 1857 4218
Historical Review of Belleville, Illinois . . . 1870 1891
Historical Sketch and Review of the the Business of the City of Leavenworth . . . 1857 1822
Historical Sketch of an Original Portrait of Governor Meriwether Lewis . . . 1890 4743
"Historical Sketch of Anderson County, Texas" 52
Historical Sketch of Cass County, Illinois . . . 1876 3740
Historical Sketch of Charles S. Hempstead . . . 1875 4551
Historical Sketch of Dodge County, Minnesota . . . 1870 2843
Historical Sketch of Jersey County, Illinois . . . 1876 1751
Historical Sketch of Los Angeles County . . . 1876 4540
Historical Sketch of Lyon County, Iowa . . . 1873 2036
Historical Sketch of Parker County and Weatherford, Texas . . . 1877 3873
Historical Sketch of Rio Vista, Cal. . . . 1914 3175
Historical Sketch of Santa Fe . . . 1880 4703
Historical Sketch of Scott County, Illinois . . . 1876 2348
Historical Sketch of the Catholic Church in New Mexico . . . 1887 1037
Historical Sketch of the Flathead Indian Nation . . . 1890 3559

Historical Sketch of the Omaha Tribe of Indians in Nebraska . . . 1885 1348
Historical Sketch of the Origin, Progress, and Wants, of Illinois College . . . 1832 147
"Historical Sketch of the Upper Mississippi, Galena, and the Lead Trade" 1485
Historical Sketch of Washington and Jefferson College . . . 1890 2852
Historical Sketches of Jackson County, Illinois . . . 1894 3018
Historical Sketches of New Mexico 1883 3363
Historical Society (Iowa) 2138
Historical Society of Joliet 4740
Historical Society of Montana . . . 1874 2870
Historical Society of New Mexico 3681
Historie of the Great and Mightie Kingdom of China . . . 1588 1582
"Histories of Monroe County and Rochester" 1243
History and Capture of Geronimo . . . 1887 4643
History and Directory of Green Lake and Waushara Counties . . . 1869 1396
History and Directory of Laramie City . . . 1875 4191
History and Directory of Nevada County, California . . . 1867 219
History and Geography of the Mississippi Valley . . . 1832 1356
History and Resources of Dakota, Montana, and Idaho . . . 1866 90
History and Statistics of Brown Co., Kansas . . . 1876 2896
History Company 155
"History of a Western Trapper" 1633
"History of Adams County" 1791
History of Antelope County, Nebraska . . . 1909 2428
History of Baptist Indian Missions . . . 1840 2586, 2589
History of Bloomington and Normal . . . 1879 499
History of California . . . 1854 580
History of Cheyenne and Northern Wyoming . . . 1876 4192, 4193
History of Chicago . . . 1876 415
History of Cooper County, Missouri . . . 1876 2470
History of Dakota County . . . 1893 4541
History of Davis County, Iowa . . . 1876 2884
History of Door County, Wisconsin . . . 1881 2692
History of Early Steamboat Navigation on the Missouri River . . . 1903 697
History of Fannin County . . . 1885 612
History of Fort Bend County . . . 1904 3908
History of Fremont County, Iowa . . . 1877 2502

778

Knox County, Nebr. 1456
Knox County, Tenn. 4630
Knox County News 1456
Knoxville, Ill. 2606
Knoxville, Tenn. 1198, 2424, 2425
Kodiak 2506
Koenen, Fr. 136
Koester, T. 2179
Kolecki, Theodore 2932
Kollman, Christian Ernst 4698
Konsag, F. 747, 2355, 3132
Kootanie Pass 320, 321, 2243, 3167
"Kootanie and Boundary Passes"
  3167
*"Kootanie and Boundary Passes of
  the Rocky Mountains"* 320
Kootenais Pass: See Kootanie Pass
Kootenie Pass: See Kootanie Pass
Korea 416
Kornberg & Hoff 4798
Kossuth, Des Moines County, Ia.
  3353
Kotzebue, M. O. de 699
Kotzebue Sound 2357
Kowetah Mission 2531
Krafft, C. de 1230
Kramm, G. 2423
Kromegay, W. H. 670
Kruger's Verlagshandlung, K. M.
  3970
Krull, C. 2330
Krusenstern, Ivan Federovich 2506
Ku Klux Klan . . . 1884 2465
Kuchel & Dresel 4502
Kuiper 1256
Kuykendall, J. M. & H. L. 2360
Kyle Stuart . . . 1834 2617

L., A. C. 1127
L., G. 2917
L., H. O. 2385
L. D. Saints' Book and Millenial
  Star Depot 2197, 2198
La Barge, J. 697
Labels 2055
LaBiche, F. 743
Labors of Mgr. A. Ravoux . . . 1897
  3423
Labrador 650
"Lac de Nicaragua" 2009
Lac Supérieur 460
*"Lac Supérieur et autres lieux ou
  sont les Missions"* 2416
Lacock, A. 3146
La Cole Mill 4670
Lacon, Ill. 3156
La Cossitt, H. D. 172, 353, 2156
LaCrosse, Wisc. 52
*Ladies and Officers of the United
  States Army . . . 1880* 1646
Ladies' College 1924
Ladies of Idaho City 2055
Lafayette and Missouri River Rail
  Road 2121
Lafferty, L. D. 8
La Font, Colo. 1393
La France, Joseph 1098
La Grande Printing Co. 949, 950
La Grange, Calif. 1844
Laguna, N.Mex. 3354, 3355
Laguna Mission 3354, 3355
Laguna Mission Press 3354, 3355

La Harpe, Ill. 2063
Lahcotah 2037
Lahontan, Louis Armand de Lom
  d'Arce, Baron de 3636
Lahure, Ch. 63
Laird & Lee 260, 2248
La Jolla, Calif. 3629
Lake, Mr. 597
Lake, Sir James Winter 2527
Lake, W. 2686
Lake and River Guide . . . 1856 1254
Lake Bennett, Alaska 1303
Lake Champlain 650, 1608, 2082,
  4670
Lake County, Colo. 148
Lake County, Ill. 1703, 1704, 1748,
  2071
Lake County Company of Illinois
  726
Lake County Leader . . . 1881 2368
Lake Erie 1608, 2029, 2082, 2202,
  3619, 3707, 4670
Lake George 2746
Lake Huron 650, 2029
Lake Maurepas 131
Lake Michigan 620, 621, 1057, 1093,
  1608, 2029, 2082, 2810
Lake Minnetonka 2092
"Lake Minnetonka and Vicinity"
  2092
Lake of the Woods 2280
Lake Ontario 1608, 2082, 2527,
  3707, 4670
Lake St. Clair 1608, 2082
Lake Street Fire 3748
Lake Superior 460, 573, 650, 1093,
  1538, 1685, 1894, 2354, 2416,
  2738, 2933, 3167, 3521
Lake Tahoe 4035, 4497, 4758
"Lake Tahoe" 4497
"Lake Tahoe and Vicinity" 4035
Lake Utah 3791
Lake Winnepeek 2280
Lakeside Classics 2792
Lakeside Library 2658
Lakeside Press 401, 510, 1718, 1719,
  2428, 3026, 3319
Lakeside Press Memorial Library
  2658
LaLande, Baptiste 2903
Lamb, G. 2186
Lamb, Miss H. G. 2707
Lambach, H. 1924
Lambdin 3212
Lamberson, D. B. 1955, 1956
Lambert, J. 4327, 4416
Lambert & Lane 2180, 2181
Lambrite, J. 1924
Lancaster, Nebr. 2955
Lancaster, Grant County, Wisc.
  4720
Land Agent 4584
Land Cases 1919
Land Certificate 1362
Land Claims 3920, 4385, 4386
Land Claims, Committee on Pri-
  vate 4385, 4386
Land Commissioner 517
Land Deals 4639
Land Department, Burlington &
  Missouri R. R. Co. 492, 493

Land Department, Union Pacific
  Railroad 4238
Land Grant, Repeal of 4528
Land Grants 4109, 4110, 4116, 4167,
  4500, 4737
Land Laws 118, 119, 2017, 2887,
  4630
Land of Golden Grain . . . 1883 1123
Land of Little Rain . . . 1903 114
Land of Gold . . . 1855 1848
Land of Nome . . . 1902 2626
*Land of Ophir, Ideal and Real . . .
  1853* 125
Land of the Aztecs . . . 1859 3750
"Land of the Shoshones" 2686
Land Office 1386, 2308, 3412, 3582,
  3889
Land Office at Fairfield 4422
Land Office, Brownville, Nebr. 3412
Land Office in Denver 1386
Land Office of Texas 2308, 3582
Land Sales 2035, 2079, 2081, 2155,
  2238, 2318, 2319, 2460, 3259,
  3508, 3651, 3758, 4238, 4611,
  4720, 4753
Land Share 577, 3058
Land Title 3784
*Land Warrants. A Constant Supply
  and Warranted Genuine . . . 1848*
  2376
Landauer, Mrs. Bella C. 1555
Lander, F. W. 558, 559
*Landreise (Scharmann's) nach
  Californien . . . 1905* 3692
Lane, Eliza S. 3020
Lane, J. 3149
Lane, J. H. 1327
Lane, Lydia Spencer 289
Lane, Squire 2184
Lane, W. C. 4393
Lane & Scott 1233
Lane & Tippett 2925, 3847
Laneuville, A. 2541, 2543–2547
Lang, H. O. 2385
Langdon, J. J. 999, 1818, 3494
Langdon & Goff 973
Lange, Georg Gustav, Verlag von
  2352
Lange, Henry 2851
Langford, N. P. 1370, 4481, 4482
Langford, Dak. 1878
Langley, H. G. 1658–1663
Langley, J. 1662
Langley, J. H. 3538
Lanier, Mrs. 2344
Lanier, S. 878
Lanphere, G. C. 107
Lanphier & Walker 2063
Lantao 2736
Lanuville, A.: See Laneuville, A.
La Pérouse, Jean François de Ga-
  laup, Comte de 416, 1840
Lapham, I. A. 2810, 2811
La Platte River: See Platte River
La Porte, Ind. 1252
La Porte City, Ia. 3210
Laprarie River, Canada 4670
"Lapwai, I. T., Fort" 4356
Lapwai Mission 4544
Lara, José M. F. de 2772, 2775

Life and Adventures of the American Cow-Boy . . . 1897 3942
Life and Adventures of the Genuine Cowboy . . . 1900 4026
Life and Adventures of Wilburn Waters . . . 1878 776
Life and Adventures of William Filley . . . 1867 1322
Life and Confession of Aaron Todd . . . 1840 4160
Life and Confessions of James Gilbert Jenkins . . . 1864 4736
Life and Events . . . 1859 4478
Life and Exploits of John Goodall . . . 1931 478
Life and Labors of Bishop Hare . . . 1911 1987
Life and Labour in the Far, Far West . . . 1884 187
Life and Letters of William Beaumont 222
Life and Marvelous Adventures of Wild Bill . . . 1880 468
Life and Military Services of Gen. William Selby Harney . . . 1878 3435
Life and Ministerial Labors of Eld. R. J. Coleman . . . 1894 802
Life and Public Services of Hon. Abraham Lincoln . . . 1860 2490
Life and Scenery in Missouri . . . 1890 3080
Life and Services of Gen. Ben McCulloch . . . 1888 2596, 3572
Life and Times of Gen'l John A. Sutter . . . 1895 3705
Life and Times of Patrick Gass . . . 1859 2183
Life and Times of S. H. West . . . 1908 4598
Life and Travels (Branstetter) . . . 1913 391
Life and Travels of Addison Coffin . . . 1897 792
Life and Travels of Harriet Cline West . . . 1910 4597
Life and Travels of Josiah Mooso . . . 1888 2885
Life and Travels of Thomas Simpson . . . 1845 3785
Life and Writings of Adolphus F. Monroe . . . 1857 2856
Life Explorations and Public Services of John Charles Fremont . . . 1856 4447
Life History . . . 1886 909
Life in California . . . 1846, n.d. 122, 3525
"Life in California before the Gold Discovery" 637
Life in the "Far West" . . . 1848, 1849 3619, 3623
Life in the Mountains . . . 1854 4613
Life in the New World . . . 1844 3720
Life in the Wilds of America . . . 1880 126
Life, Letters and Papers of William Dunbar . . . 1930 1174, 1175
Life, Letters and Travels of Father Pierre-Jean de Smet, S.J. . . . 1905 3824
Life of a Pioneer . . . 1900 426

Life of a Rover . . . 1926 2877
Life of Abraham Lincoln . . . 1872 2374
Life of Alfred B. Meacham . . . 1883 326, 4266
Life of David S. Terry . . . 1892 4509
Life of David W. Patten . . . 1904 4706
Life of Dr. Wm. F. Carver . . . 1878 623, 3421, 4064
Life of Elisha Tyson . . . 1825 4227
Life of General Stand Watie . . . 1915 60
Life of Governor Evans . . . 1924 2643
Life of Henry Dodge . . . 1890 3657–3659
Life of Hon. William F. Cody . . . 1879 786
Life of Isaac Ingalls Stevens . . . 1900 3974
Life of J. C. Adams . . . 1860 15, 16
Life of John Ledyard . . . 1828 3923
"Life of John Proctor" 3845, 3846
Life of John Wesley Hardin . . . 1896 1780
Life of Joseph Bishop . . . 1858 1628
Life of Ma-Ka-Tai-Me-She-Kia-Kiak . . . 1833 313
Life of Martha Morgan 1610
Life of Mrs. Emily J. Harwood . . . 1903 2294
Life of Pat F. Garrett . . . 1908 3689
Life of Rev. John Clark . . . 1856 1722
Life of Rev. L. B. Stateler . . . 1907 3240, 3945
Life of Sile Doty . . . 1880 798
Life of the Marlows . . . 1892 2682
Life of the Right Reverend Joseph P. Machebeuf . . . 1908 1992
Life of Thomas Hawley Canfield . . . 1889 572
Life of Thomas Steed . . . 1935 3956
Life of Tom Candy Ponting . . . 1907 3314
Life of Tom Horn . . . 1904 1957
Life of Ven. Padre Junipero Serra . . . 1884 3178
"Life on the Border" 783
Life on the Circuit with Lincoln . . . 1892 4644
Life on the Plains and Among the the Diggings . . . 1854 1042
Life on the Plains of the Pacific . . . 1852 1896
Life Sketch of Pierre Barlow Cornwall . . . 1906 880
Life Sketches of a Jayhawker of '49 . . . 1916 3972
Life, Three Sermons, Some of the Miscellaneous Writings of Rev. Jesse Greene . . . 1852 1649
Life, Times and Treacherous Death of Jesse James . . . 1882 4196
"Life, Traffic and Customs" 4492
Life, Travels and Adventures of an American Wanderer . . . 1883 1338
Life, Travels and Opinions of Benjamin Lundy . . . 1847 1195
Life, Trial, Death, and Confession

of Samuel H. Calhoun . . . 1862 1639
Life's Voyage . . . 1898 1463
Light & Horton 3285
Lillie, G. W. 1076
Lincoln, Abraham 1045, 1075, 1654, 1807, 1829, 1871, 1988, 2088, 2248, 2353, 2374, 2375, 2490, 2495, 2498, 2522, 2597, 2955, 3090, 3114, 3247, 3317, 3337, 3583, 3927, 3973, 4032, 4172, 4579, 4644
Lincoln, Mary Todd 2493
Lincoln, Nebr. 55, 2496, 2497, 2950, 3758
Lincoln & Douglas Debates 2495
Lincoln & Edmands 2591, 3234
Lincoln and Seward . . . 1874 4579
Lincoln County War 2668
Lincoln, Fort A. 4327
Lincoln Lode, Colo. 3764
Lincoln, the Capital of Nebraska . . . 1870 55
Lindeman, H. R. 4426
Lind, Jenny 3954
Linder, U. F. 1003
Lindsay & Blakiston 871–873, 4151
Lindsey, B., Sr. 1494
"Lines & Stations of Heliograph System" 1674
Linforth, J. 3346
Linga, Carlos R. 4448
Linguistics: See Indian Linguistics
Lindley, John 21
Linley: See Lindley, John
Linn, L. F. 4380
Linn County, Ia. 1774, 4444
Linn, Mr., Submitted the Following Report . . . 1838 4380
Linstadt, Mrs. F. 2055
Linton, J. F. 229
Lintot, Frances 2504, 2505
Lintot, Nancy 2504
"Lion marin ou Eléphant de mer" 3250
Lipman, L. 1389
Lippincott, J. B., & Co. 288, 378, 592, 598, 755, 756, 2220, 2222, 2241, 2381, 2382, 2574, 2576, 2974, 3793, 4028, 4029, 4221, 4567
Lippincott, Grambo & Co. 1200, 1694, 1837, 2225, 3556, 3699, 3700, 3789, 3947, 4687
Lippman, Mrs. J. 1588
Lipscomb, A. A. 1132
Lipsey, J. J. 3689
Liquor Traffic 4097
Lisa, Manuel 290, 377
Lisiansky's Isle 2506
List of Lots and Lands in and about Chicago . . . 1853 2075
List of Members of the Constitutional Convention . . . 1859 2271
"List of Mineral Claims Shown upon Parkinson's Map of the Comstock Lode" 3200
Lista de los Ciudadanos . . . 1834 3675
Lista General de los Ciudadanos . . . 1828 2455
"Liste des Cartes" 460

Loup City, Nebr. 264
Loup City Northwestern Print 264
Louthian Book Company 1957
Loutre, la 2736
Loutre de Mer, Port la 2736
Love, Capt. 1344
Love, J. 3660
Lovejoy, Amelia 2549
Lovejoy Murder 1017
Lovejoy Riot 1380
Lovell, C. S. 4286, 4683
Lovell, J. 1893, 1894
Lovell, J. W., Co. 1338
Lovering, L. A. 3601
Loving Publishing Co. 2784
Lovingood, Sut 1068
Low, Sampson: See Sampson Low, etc.
Lowe, E. 3100
Lowe, J. 3107–3109
Lowe, J. W. 4512
Lowell, Alice J. 694
Lowell, John A., & Co. 2621
Lowell Bleachery Finish 2759
Lowell, Camp 4356
Lower California: See Baja California and California
"Lower Falls of the Columbia" 2480, 2481
Lowman & Hanford Stationery & Printing Co. 449, 450, 3368
Loyal Legion, Colorado Commandery 1108
Loyalty on the Frontier . . . 1863 306
Lubbock County, Tex. 2845
Lucas, R. 2136
Lucas, S. 1164
Luck of a Wandering Dane . . . 1885 2562
Luck of Roaring Camp . . . 1870 1805
Ludditt Press, A. J. 192
Luddy, Mr. 3346
Ludlow, W. 4327
Luke Darrell, the Chicago Newsboy . . . 1866 2556
Lumbering 1343, 4683, 4798
Lundy, B. 1195, 4227
Luney, M. 2055
Lupercio, Francisco Rodriguez 4475
Luse, H. H. 4683
Luse & Co. 1194
Luse, Lane & Co. 3301, 3678, 4658
Lusk Herald 2409
Luttig, J. 743
Lyle, J. 1572, 2654
Lyle, J. R. 3850
Lyle, John, and Lyle Farm, 1925 1572
Lyman 640
Lyman, P. 1816
Lynam, R. 230, 231
Lynching 2312, 2856, 2935, 4481, 4482
Lynde & Hough Co. 2357
Lynn, Mass. 4712
Lynn County, Tex. 2845
Lyon, N. 1850
Lyon Campaign in Missouri . . . 1907 4534, 4537
Lyon County, Ia. 2036
Lyon County, Kans. 1636

Lyon County, Minn. 3241
Lyon, Fort 4292, 4327, 4389
Lyon's Campaign 4537
Lyons City, Iowa; Its Position and Resources . . . 1858 2567
Lyons Mirror Job Office 4541

M., W. H. 2707
McAfee, J. B. 2266
McAfee, R. B. 4711
Macao 2736
Macbeth 1960
McCaleb, W. F. 3434
McCall, J. G., & Co. 2357
M'Cary, B. 2064
McCarty 1411
McCarty, J. 2150
McCleery 1578
McClellan, G. B. 121, 2675, 3141, 4644
McClellan, R. 3934
McClelland, C. P. 3273, 3274
McClinnon & Crooks 290
M'Cloud, R. 2832
MacClure, D. 4622
McClure, J. 2951
McClure Company 410
McClurg, A. C. 922
McClurg, A. C., & Co. 1772, 1773, 1971, 2375, 3630, 3631
McConnel, J. 2347
McCook, Gen. 4696
McCoppin, F. 1189
McCormack, T. J. 2353
McCormick, L. J. 1745, 2582
McCormick, R. C. 80
McCormick, S. J. 417, 1180
McCormick Bros. 1037
McCormick Family 2582
McCoun 4461
McCoy, A. 1213
MacCoy, J. C. 525, 1098, 1259, 1863, 1864, 2252, 2432, 4163
McCreery, Alice Richards 1484
McCulloch, B. 1639, 3572, 3973
McCulloch, H. 4144
McCulloch's Rangers 3451
McCullough, H. 1075
McDade, T. M. 803
McDermit, Camp 4356
McDermott, J. F. 2792
Macdonald 1578
McDonald, A. 3787
Macdonald, A. B. 2191, 4042
McDonald, F. A. 2515
McDonald, J. 701, 702, 996, 1277
McDonald, R. H. 2598
Macdonald, S. D. 1417
McDonald, W., & Co. 227
M'Donald & Sherman 934
McDonald, Gill & Co. 2012
McDonell, J. 2782
M'Donnel, C. 3571
McDonnell, A. 29
McDonnell, E. 2600, 2601
McDonogh, M. 2489, 2637, 2638
McDowell, I. 4315, 4356
McDowell, J. 1633
McDowell, Camp 4356
"McDowell Reservation, Fort" 1673
McDuffee, J. 1084
McEvoy, H. N. 4036

McEwen, T. 601
McFadden, G. W. 4482
McGarry, Camp 4334
McGehee, M. 637
McGill, T. 3978
M'Gill & Witherow 700, 3244, 4699
McGillycuddy, V. T. 2207
McGraw, Mr. 2261
McGraw-Hill Co. 3565
McGregor, A. W. 2431
McGregor's Hall 2055
McGuffey's Newly Revised Third Reader . . . n.d. 2613
Machen, Mr. 2184
McHenry, E. J. M. 2258
McHenry County, Ill. 2250
Machuël, Père Jean Baptiste 133
McIlvaine, Caroline 2717
McIntire, Jas. 2616
M'Intosh (printer) 186
McIntosh, Fort 4327
McIntyre, James 2616
M'Intyre & Foster 1389
McIntyre Bros. 3495
McIntyre Publishing Co. 2616
Mackal, J. B. 4327
McKarett, Fort 4327
McKeeber, C. 1110
McKenney, W. L. 2707
M'Kenny, J. H. 2121, 2146
Mackenzie, Quin 3636
Mackenzie, R. 366, 2582, 3141, 3186, 3756
McKenzie County Farmer 478
Mackenzie's Fight 1552, 2420
Mackenzie's Last Fight with the Cheyennes . . . 1890 366
Mackinac, Mich. 113, 2901, 4683
Mackinac, Fort 1057
McKinney, B. A. 3843
McKinney, Fort 4330
McKinstry, G. 2410, 3337
McKissack, W. M. D. 4434
McKittrick, J. L. 2515
McKnight, James 2635, 3902
McKnight, R. 245, 552, 2603, 2898, 2903, 2904, 3517, 4410, 4636
McLane, L. 2710
McLaughlin, C. H. 2270
McLaughlin, D. 3101
McLaughlin, J. 3919
McLean, A. 4486
McLean, A., Lith. 578
McLean, J. 2083, 2085
McLean, Judge 2082
Maclean, L. A. 4652
McLean, N. C. 2083
"Maclean & Lawrences Sectional Map of Kansas Territory" 4652
Maclean, Roger & Co. 568
McLean County, Ill. 499
Maclear & Co., Liths. 1894
McLellan, D. 198, 3094, 3852–3854
McLeod, M. 3787
McLeure, Lewis 390
McLoughlin Bros. 799
McMahon, T. J. 2836
McMaster Printing Co. 1534
Macmillan, Sir Frederick 797
Macmillan Company 102, 1506, 1507, 1511, 1712, 2117, 2609, 2706, 3288, 4039, 4725

McMurtrie, D. C. 4283
McNally, J. 560
McNally's System of Geography 90
McNeal, H. 743
McNeal, S. D. 1203
McNeill, Captain 2572
Macomb, J. W. 1096
Macomb County, Mich. 46
Macon, N. 4372
Macon City, Mo. 3139, 4659, 4660
Macoupin County, Ill. 4160
McPherson, Fort 35, 2743, 4327, 4508
McQueen Lode, Colo. 2097
McRae, Fort 4327
M'Vickar, A. 2483
Mad Rush for Gold in Frozen North . . . 1914 1083
Madeira 844
Madison, James 2541–2545
Madison, Dak. 2368
Madison, Ind. 2395, 2561
Madison, Wisc. 209, 1186, 1743, 3038
Madison County, Ill. 1706
Madison County, Mont. 1769, 4798
Madison County, Nebr. 2238
Madison, Fort 1489, 2219, 2445, 3547, 4584
Madisonian, The . . . 1844 1329, 2653
Madisonian Print 2302
Madjicosemah 416
Madrid, Spain 1259, 4484
Madrid (Iowa) Historical Society 2554
Madrigal, Pedro 1259
Magazine of Travel . . . 1857 2655
Magellan, Straits of 2519
Magoffin, J. & S. 245
Magruder, T. 3920
Mahaska County, Ia. 1371, 1920, 3672
Mahin, J. 4526
Mahony, D. A., & J. B. Dorr 2142
"Maid of Matamoras" 2114
Mail Carrier 4675
Mail Coach 4275
Mail Contractor 4044
Mail Routes 2933, 4044, 4357, 4403
Main-Travelled Roads . . . 1891 1508
Maine 2860, 3269
Maissin, E. 323
Major, D. C. 4305
Major & Knapp 4250
Major Brown (ship) 4151
Major General Scott, of the United States Army, Sends to the Cherokee People . . . 1838 4300
Majors, A. J. 2555
Majors, T. F. 2515
Majors, T. J. 4534
Ma-Ka-Tai-Me-She-Kia-Kiak 313
Makin, J. 2127
"Making of California" 637
Malabar 2519
Malan, C. 1278
Malcolm Campbell, Sheriff . . . 1932 1012, 2750
Malheur River, Ore. 4290, 4683

Malignity Exposed . . . 1847 664, 3303
Mallandaine, Edw., & Co. 2666
Mallery, G. 1110
Malone, Ia. 1154
Malta, Mont. 779
Malte-Brun 4793
Mammoth Tree from California . . . 1858 21
"*Mamoth tel qu'il existe au Musaeum à Philadelphie*" 3254
Man, S. 3902
Man in Earnest . . . 1868 811
Man in the Moon 917
Man Without a Country . . . 1865 1710, 1711
Manchester, Penna. 902
Manchester Conference 3346
Mandan District, Ore. 4062
Mandans 723, 743
Manhattan, Kans. 1850
Manhattan Falls, Ia. 4444
Manifesto . . . 1855 1320
Manifesto del Honorable Congreso, a los Habitantes del Estado Senorenses . . . 1825 3065
Manifiesto a la Republica Mejicana . . . 1835 1319
Manifiesto que a los Pueblos . . . 1829 3064
Manila, R. P. 2397, 2420, 2736, 3677
Manitoba 187, 4688
Manitoba and the North-West . . . 1882 4688
Manitoba Free Press Print 562
Manley, B. 955
Manliness of the Christian Soldier . . . 1925 3197
Manlius, N.Y. 509
Manualito de Parrocos . . . 1839 4472
Manly, W. L. 2670, 3972
Mann, Mrs. 1950
Manner, M. M. 2863
Manners 77
Manners and Customs of Several Indian Tribes . . . 1823 2019
Manual for Emigrants to America . . . 1832 828
Manual for the Use of the Legislative Assembly of the Territory of Dakota . . . 1866 986
Manual of Arms for Light Infantry . . . 1860, 1861 1239, 1240
Manual para Administrar los Santos Sacramentos . . . 1760 1504
Manufacturer's, Farmer's, & Mechanic's Guide . . . 1822 1849
Manufacturing, Agricultural and Industrial Resources of Iowa . . . 1872 2034
"*Manuscript Map of the Route from the Western U.S. Border to Taos*" 2707
"*Manzanilla I., Aspinwall City, Navy Bay*" 4517, 4587
Manzanillo, Fort del 1169
Maouna, Island of 2397
Map and Description of Texas . . . 1840 2880

Map and Guide to the White Pine Mines . . . 1869 534
"*Map and Profile Sections Showing the Railroads of the United States*" 2536
"*Map, Describing the Country about the Mouth of the Platte River*" 1597
"*Map Drawn to Illustrate the Travels & from the Documents of the Abbé Domenech*" 1121
"*Map Drawn upon Stag-skins*" 2364
"*Map Exhibiting Mr. Hearne's Tracks*" 1840
"*Map Illustrating Baldwin Möllhausen's Travels*" 2849
"*Map Illustrating the Advantages of the Central Transit Route through Mexico to the Pacific Ocean*" 3512
"*Map Illustrating the Author's Route from the Suez Canal to Zanzibar & Ujiji*" 3946
"*Map Illustrating the Plan of the Defences of the Western & Northwestern Frontier, As Proposed by Charles Gratiot*" 4432
"*Map Illustrating the Plan of the Defences of the Western & Northwestern Frontier, As Proposed by the Hon. J. R. Poinsett*" 4432
"*Map Illustrative of Report of Capt. Fisk*" 1334
"*Map No. 1. El Paso & Fort Yuma Wagon Road*" 558, 559
"*Map No 1. Reconnaissance and Survey of a Railway Route from Mississippi River near 35th Parallel North Lat.*" 4435
"*Map No. 2 of the El Paso & Fort Yuma Wagon Road*" 558, 559
"*Map, No. 2. Showing a Continuation of Details of Fort Smith and Santa Fe Route*" 3790
"*Map No. 3, Showing Continuation of Details of Fort Smith and Santa Fe Route*" 3790
"*Map No. 4. Colonies During the Revolutionary War*" 1986
"*Map No. 4. Showing Continuation of Fort Smith and Santa Fe Route*" 3790
"*Map No. 6. War of 1812*" 1986
"*Map of a Large Country Newly Discovered*" 1862
"*Map of a New World Between New Mexico and the Frozen Sea*" 1862
"*Map of a Reconnoissance between Fort Leavenworth on the Missouri River and the Great Salt Lake*" 3947
"*Map of a Reconnoissance for a Military Road*" 4525
"*Map of a Tour from Independence to Santa Fe, Chihuahua, Monterey and Matamoros*" 4723
"*Map of Ab-sa-ra-ka*" 596
Map of Alaska . . . 1895 450
"*Map of Alaska*" 905
"*Map of America*" 2630, 2631
"*Map of an Exploring Expedition to the Rocky Mountains*" 1436

Martin County, Tex. 4106
Martinez, Andres 2764
Martinez, Antonio Jose 2995, 4472
Martinez, Esteban Josef 3653
Martinez, F. 2771
Martinez, Mariano 4479
Martinez, M. J. 2765
Martinique 3524
Martinsville, Ind. 1445
Marvelous Country . . . 1873 898
Mary Knox Lode, Colo. 4179
Maryland 409, 2029, 2202, 2248
Maryland Historical Society 2730
Marysville, Calif. 434, 746, 2295, 2698, 4589
Marysville Directory for the Year 1861 . . . 1861 434
Masi, W. M. 4192, 4193
Mason, A. 4529
Mason, Colonel 3695, 4494
Mason, E. C. 1980
Mason, J. 349
Mason, J. D. 64
Mason, J. W. 4273
Mason, R. B. 547, 679, 680, 2080, 2082
Mason, T. 1232, 1233
Mason, T. B. 376
Mason Bros. 3094, 3095
Mason City, Ia. 3603
Mason Collection 3866
Mason County, Ill. 3114
Masonic Literature 4186
Masonic Oration 2540
Masons 1413–1423, 1619, 2540, 4186
Massac, Fort 1176
Massachusetts 1828, 2701, 3723, 3935
Massachussets Emigrant Aid Company 4563
Massachusetts Home Mission Society 195
Massachusetts Missionary Society 2806
Massachusetts State Texas Committee 2704
Massacre at Caborca 4461
Massacre at Mountain Meadows 4418
Massacre, Creek du 2397
Massacre of Cheyenne Indians . . . 1865 4389
Massacres 103, 1181, 3933, 4389, 4418, 4461
Massacres of the Mountains . . . 1886 1181
Massey, S. L. 946
Massey, Hill County, Tex. 1952–1954
Massingberd, R. 2364
Massassoit House 4033
Master William Mitten . . . 1864 2529
Matamay Island 416
Matamoras 2661, 4723
Material Resources of Marion County, Oregon . . . 1876 2752
Mather, Mrs. 2707
Mather, T. 430, 1500, 1993, 2629, 2707, 3311, 3446, 3447, 3766–3774, 4458
Mathison, J. 2712

Matias Moreno, José 401
Matlack & Harvey 2562
Matthews, H. M. 954
Maupin, J. 1213
Maupin, T. 1213
Maurelle, Francisco Antonio 2397, 2919
Maurepas, Comte de 650
Maurepas, Lake: See Lake Maurepas
Mauro, P. 1331
Mauvaises Terres 4398
Maverick, M. A. 878
Maverick, Mary 3608
Maverick, P. 3707
"Maverick" 2727
Mawman, J. 2780, 2781
Maxey, S. B. 3983
Maximilian, Prinz von Wied-Neuwied: See Wied-Neuwied, Maximilian Alexander Philipp
Maxwell, J. 58, 2019
Maxwell, John, & Co. 4016
May, J. 2431
May, J. E. 1545, 4683
Maynadier, H. E. 3429, 4303
Maynard, Catherine T. 3368
Maynard, D. S. 3368
Mayo Valley, Ariz. 1225
Mayotte, Iles de 3250
Maypole, M. 2058
Maysville, Ky. 4734
Maysville Eagle 4734
Mazatlan, Mexico 245, 1169, 1819, 2632
Meacham, A. B. 326
Meade, C. 504
Meador Publishing Company 305
Meadville Theological School 3678
Meagher, Brigadier-General Thomas Francis . . . 1870 2566
Meany, E. S. 4530
Meares, John 2736
Meares, Port 2734, 2736
Mears, E. B. 2615
Mears, O. 2212
"Measures of Adjustment" . . . 1134
Mechanics' Circulating Library 2185
Mechanic's Industrial Fair 4492
Mechlin, J. P. 3791
Medal of Honor 144, 183
Medary, J. 3037
Medary, S. 2271
Medary, S. A. 558, 559, 840
Medical Director, Department of Arizona, Whipple Barracks, Prescott, A. T. Sir: . . . 1883 4274
Medical Practice 3151
Medical Repository . . . 1803–07 2737
Medicine 222, 223, 1555, 2218, 2325, 2618, 2737, 3427, 3443, 3541, 3671, 3757, 3795, 4274, 4465
Medicine Bow Mountains 3140
"Medicine Chest" 4508
Medicine-Lodge Cresset 3906
Mediterranean Sea 3161
Meeker, E. M. 3981
Meeker, J. 284, 286, 2586
Meeker County, Minn. 3834
Meeker *Journal* 2586
"Meffert's Day!" 2055

Megrue, C. G. 4392
Meier Expedition 1187
Meine, F. J. 2508
Meine Reise Nach Nord-Amerika . . . 1845 3661
Meisel, A., Lith. 42
Meisel Bro's 1386
Melcher & Rogers 3075
Melish, J. 303, 327
Mellen, J. 2097
Mellette, A. C. 983, 3904
Mellon, W. L. 2400
Mellon, Thomas, and His Times . . . 1885 2747
Melton Mowbray and Other Memories . . . 1924 1442
Melvin, M. M. 4683
Memoir (Mowry) . . . 1857 2921
"Memoir" (Kennicott) 681
Memoir and Writings (Perkins) . . . 1851 3249
Memoir, Historical, and Political, on the North-West Coast of North America . . . 1840 1653
Memoir of a Tour to Northern Mexico . . . 1848, 1850 4723, 3582
Memoir of Abijah Hutchinson . . . 1843 2031
Memoir of Alvan Stone . . . 1837 4752
Memoir of Charlotte Chambers . . . 1856 1512
Memoir of Rev. Joseph Badger . . . 1851 135
Memoir of Rev. Levi Spencer . . . 1856 322
"Memoir of the History and Physical Geography of Minnesota" 2822
Memoir of the Late Hon. Daniel P. Cook . . . 1857 436
Memoir of the Life and Public Services of John Charles Fremont . . . 1856 296
Memoir of the Proposed Territory of Arizona . . . 1857 2922
"Memoir of the Selkirk Settlement on the Red River of the North" 2819, 2820
Memoir on the Recent Surveys, Observations, and Internal Improvements, in the United States . . . 1829 4062
"Mémoire (Tonty) . . ." 1283
Memoire, ou, Coup d'Oeil Rapide . . . 1802 2792
Memoire sur les Moeurs, Coustumes et Religion des Sauvages . . . 1864 3256
Me'moire sur le Pays & La Mer . . . 1754 2363
Memoires de l'Amerique Septentrionale 2365
Memoires de Paul Jones . . . 1798 2242
Memoires du Capitaine Peron . . . 1824 3250
Memoires d'un Mormon . . . 1862 281
Memoires et Documents . . . 1879–1888 2680
Memoires Historiques sur la Louisiane . . . 1753 1173

Morgan, E. B. 1028
Morgan, G. H. 3645
Morgan, J. 1610, 2631, 3780
Morgan, J. C. 3634
Morgan, P. 884
Morgan, R. P. 1009, 1483
Morgan, W. J., & Co. 148
Morgan & M'Kenny 1409, 1415, 2140, 3422
Morgan, Shepard Co. 571
Morgan, Williams, & Co. 2569
Morgan County, Ill. 1851, 2088
Morgan Journal, Jacksonville, Ill. 1779
Morgan's Manual of the U.S. Homestead and Townsite Laws . . . 1893 2887
Morgan's Raid 3780
Morgenstjernen . . . 1882–85 2891, 2892
Morley, James Henry: 1824–1889. A Memorial . . . 1891 2893
Mormon Battalion 426, 869, 2525, 2526, 4226, 4434
Mormon Factions 4641
Mormon Newspaper 1450
Mormon Station, Carson Valley 641
Mormon Trail 4207
Mormon Trek 2263–2265, 2370, 2371, 2415, 2510
Mormon Way-Bill to the Gold Mines . . . 1851 536
Mormonism 1346, 1796, 1985, 2013, 2441, 2799, 3346, 3814, 4641
Mormonism . . . 1844 2013
Mormonism Portrayed . . . 1841 1796
Mormonism Triumphant! . . . 1849 1346, 3346
Mormonism Unvailed . . . 1834 1985
Mormonism Unveiled . . . 1877 2441
Mormons 25, 96, 203, 260, 262, 263, 281, 351, 370, 419, 426, 512, 586, 627, 646, 707–721, 736, 737, 751, 752, 857, 859, 868, 869, 899, 1001, 1002, 1017, 1061, 1062, 1221, 1273, 1299, 1308, 1346, 1380, 1450, 1587, 1596, 1610, 1615, 1640, 1648, 1665, 1666, 1694, 1753, 1796, 1879, 1985, 2008, 2013, 2068, 2176, 2177, 2186, 2197, 2198, 2215, 2234, 2263–2265, 2323, 2347, 2370, 2371, 2415, 2441, 2446, 2500, 2501, 2509–2511, 2560, 2755, 2761, 2799, 2833, 2836, 2891, 2892, 2930, 2931, 2953, 3185, 3273, 3274, 3331, 3346–3351, 3449, 3461, 3465–3467, 3488, 3585, 3608, 3814, 3844, 3855–3861, 3876–3879, 3931, 3932, 3956, 4003, 4004, 4051, 4063, 4081, 4082, 4129, 4156, 4165, 4187, 4206, 4226, 4418, 4434, 4449, 4453, 4496, 4529, 4556, 4641, 4706, 4794
Mormons . . . 1850 2263–2265, 3346
Mormons at Home . . . 1856 1308
Mormons, or Knavery Exposed . . . 1841 737
Mormons; or, Latter-Day Saints . . . 1852 1694
Morning Chronicle 3614
Morning Globe Print 3665
Morning Post 3614
Morrell, B. 207
Morrill, J. E. 4647

Morrill, J. E., Leake & Reed 2897
Morrill, J. S. 4251
Morrill Family 2895
Morrills and Reminiscences . . . 1918 2895
Morris, C. A. F. 2757
Morris, Colonel 1336
Morris, G. 3289
Morris, J. 174
Morris, T. 2900
Morris, Ill. 4208
Morrison, C. C. 4348
Morrison, J. 810
Morrison, J. S. 1675
Morrison, W. M. 2589
Morrison, Ill. 2549
Morrow (photographer) 927
Morrow, J. 3052, 3732
Morrow, W. 808
Morse, B. S. 676
Morse, H. 3234
Morse, J. 3007
Morse, J. F. 841
Morse, L. F. 4252
Morse, S. E. 1659–1663, 2398
Morse, S. F. 2765
Morse, S. W. 2515
Morsman, Cap. 2910
Morsman, E. M. 2910
Morsman, J. J. 2910
Morsman, W. 2910
Mortimer, J. 3641
Morton, A. S. 2609
Morton, C. S. 2021
Morton, G. E. 3803
Morton, G. M. 808
Morton, J. S. 2968, 2969
Morton, John P., & Co. 3927
Morton & Griswold 62, 1073, 4109
Morton, Longwell & Co. 2458
Moseley, W. D. 1363
Moses, J. 2348
Moses, S. 4780
Mosquito Coast 409
Motto of Jubilee College . . . 1851 2916, 2917
"Mouillage de la Mission de Sta. Barbara" 1169
"Mouillage de San Pedro" 1169
Moulton, R. 1497
Mound Builders 1472
Mounds 3790
"Mount Diablo Coal-Mines" 4492
Mount Pleasant, Ia. 66, 172
"Mount Pleasant City Directory" 66
Mount Morris, Ill. 3537
Mt. St. Hellens 4861
Mt. Sterling, Ill. 1592
Mount Vernon, Ia. 1460, 1461, 2002
Mount Washington Company 4021
Mountain Bugle . . . 1849 2918
Mountain Lions 785
Mountain Meadows Massacre 586, 899, 2441, 2446, 2511, 3185, 4453
"Mountain Medows Massacre" 4453
Mountain Sheep 785, 2000
" 'Mountain Sheep' " 2000
Mountaineering in the Sierra Nevada . . . 1874 2329
Mountains and Molehills . . . 1855 2685
"Mountains near Canon City" 3344

Mounted Riflemen 4363
Mounted Volunteers (Florida) 1363
Mounted Volunteers (Illinois) 107
Mourer, W. J. 3567, 3568
Moutard, Chez 3523
"Mouth of Columbia River" 2480–2482
Mouth of the Kansas River 4435
"Mouth of the Mississippi River" 2462, 2463
Movement of Troops 4368
Mowry, J. 2313
Mowry, S. 350
Mowry, W. A. 592
Moxos or Moxes 2519
Moyle, Geo. W., Publishing Co. 1888
Muddy Creek 4250
Muddy Fork 1436
Mudge, Alfred, & Son 4563
Mule Train 2443
Mulford, P. L. 2928
Mulford, Lee & A. F. 2927
Mulford's, Prentice, Story . . . 1889 2929
Mulgrave, Port 1262
Mullan, J. 1096
Mumey, N. 1690, 1693, 3344
Mumford, M. 1214
Munk Collection 1807
Munroe, J. 3000–3004
Munroe, J., & Co. 1594
Munroe & Francis 2874
Munsell, J. 1841, 1970, 2343
Munsell's Historical Series 1970
Muquardt, C. 630
Murchison, Sir R. I. 321
Murden, M. 1364
Murder 217, 351, 1001, 1002, 1286, 1342, 1391, 1614, 1639, 1957, 2312, 2554, 2906, 2935, 3102, 3681, 4155, 4160, 4187, 4188, 4509, 4524, 4736
Murder of M. V. G. Griswold . . . 1858 1391
Murillo Velarde 47
Murphy, A. J. 4502
Murphy, J. 3424
Murphy, J. S. 2515
Murphy, John, & Co. 2730, 3166
Murphy, R. 1046, 1047
Murphy, T. B. 231
Murphy, Thos. D., Company 3427
Murphy, Virginia Reed 637
Murphy's Camp, Calif. 3403
Murray, John 130, 1406, 1407, 2167, 3168, 3565, 3620–3622, 4800
Murray's Colonial & Home Library 3620–3622
Muscatine, Ia. 353, 1006, 1489, 2173, 2662, 3086–3088, 3207, 4526, 4610
Muscatine City Directory . . . 1856 2662
Muscle-Shell River 2160
Muscogee Indians 4744
Museum f. Länder- u. Völkerkunde Linden-Museum Stuttgart 2848
Museum of New Mexico, Santa Fe 704
Music 3567–3569, 4279–4284, 4321
Musical Evening Entertainment . . . 1875 4321

"*National Map of the American Republic or United States of North America*" 2838

"*National Map of the Territory of the United States*" 2281

"*National Map of the United States*" 3269

National Military Order of San Fernando 3618

National Museum 4398

National Park 3944

National Police Gazette 968

National Printing Co. 809, 810

National Publishing Company 212

National Railroad Bill 1697

National Railway Publication Co. 4238

National Republican Ticket . . . 1872 3469

National Republican Ticket . . . n.d. 4683

National Salute 4336

National Wagon Road Guide . . . 1858 4502

"*Native Clergy and Candidates*" 3395

Natural and Civil History of California . . . 1759 4471

Natural History 3640

Natural History of Western Wild Animals . . . 1875 616

Nau, A. 3289–3292

Nautical Magazine, and Naval Chronicle 3619

Nauvoo, Ill. 25, 351, 532, 627, 709, 710, 712–714, 1001, 1002, 1084, 1796, 2039, 2041, 2068, 2176, 2177, 2186, 2323, 2415, 2799, 2930, 2931, 2953, 3350, 3351, 3585, 3844, 3855, 3856, 3858, 3859, 3956, 4081, 4156, 4794

Nauvoo, Ill.: See Icarian Community; Mormons

Nauvoo Legion 2953

Nauvoo, Mayor of 3860, 3861

Nauvoo, Municipal Court of 3859

Navajo and His Blanket . . . 1903 1939

Navajo Country 2228, 3789

Navajo Reservation 1672, 1673

Navajos 402, 1939, 2004–2006, 2228, 3005, 3789, 4051, 4340, 4437, 4588

Naval Biography . . . 1815 2569

Naval Operations 2230

Naval Power 896

Navarro, Juan 278

Navarro, Juan R. 3652

Navarro, Martin 2537, 2538

Navigation of the Western Rivers 3646

Navigator . . . 1808 947, 2954

Navy 1184, 1836, 2242, 2309, 2569, 2602, 4582

Navy Bay 4517, 4587

Navy, French 1280

Naypes, Los 1499

Neale Publishing Company 2, 3434, 3676

Near East 3161

"*Near the Toll Gate*" 2178

Nebenzahl, K. 3304

Nebraska 19, 24, 35, 55, 90, 92, 142, 157, 211, 228, 243, 264, 282, 366, 376, 468, 469, 489, 492–494, 517,

577, 579, 682, 724, 738, 750, 766, 801, 806, 836, 861, 862, 945, 1007, 1012, 1013, 1018, 1067, 1068, 1110, 1129, 1177, 1200, 1206, 1207, 1215, 1292, 1304, 1335, 1348, 1369, 1374, 1375, 1433–1435, 1437, 1456, 1457, 1465–1467, 1552, 1576, 1597, 1690–1692, 1695, 1709, 1721, 1724–1726, 1767, 1770, 1810, 1833, 1905, 1936, 1951, 2110, 2230, 2378, 2408, 2414, 2427, 2428, 2460, 2496, 2497, 2515, 2627, 2702, 2743, 2759, 2778, 2790, 2836, 2853, 2854, 2895, 2897, 2911–2913, 2918, 2941, 2950, 2955–2966, 2968, 2978, 3058, 3092, 3100–3111, 3113, 3145, 3162, 3165, 3191, 3229, 3245, 3246, 3273, 3274, 3340, 3412, 3437, 3519, 3633–3635, 3647, 3752, 3758, 3815, 3835, 3837, 3852–3854, 3890, 3897, 3898, 3947, 3993, 4009, 4044, 4119, 4120, 4123, 4182, 4217, 4238, 4327, 4333, 4359, 4361, 4394, 4536, 4541, 4580, 4584, 4620, 4647, 4729, 4730, 4746

Nebraska Advertiser.—Extra 2967, 2968

Nebraska Advertiser Print 2965

Nebraska and Kansas . . . 1854 2702

"*Nebraska and Kansas*" 836

"*Nebraska and Kanzas*" 2853, 2854, 3437, 4746

Nebraska as It Is . . . 1869 1810

Nebraska Central Land Agency 3758

Nebraska. Citizens' Committee 2969

Nebraska City 579, 596, 597, 1721, 1809, 2912, 2913, 2969, 3245, 3412, 4044, 4508, 4730

Nebraska City Directory, for 1870 . . . 1870 4730

Nebraska City, N.T., Jan. 5th, 1858. Hon. Thomas A. Hendricks—Commissioner of the General Land Office: Sir:— 4044

Nebraska City News 1809

Nebraska Commandery of the Military Order of the Loyal Legion 3170

Nebraska, East Sub-district of 4333

Nebraska, Her Resources . . . 1885 1466

Nebraska Historical Society 4123

Nebraska in 1857 . . . 1857 4746

Nebraska—Indian Treaties—and the Rights of Citizens . . . 1844 2970

Nebraska, Its Characteristics and Prospects . . . 1873 517

Nebraska, Its Cheap Lands, Homesteads, etc. . . . 1870 2496

Nebraska, Kansas, Dakota, Colorado and Montana . . . 1866 90

Nebraska National Guard 2971

Nebraska Press Printing Office 1007

Nebraska Republican 806

Nebraska State Fair 1721

Nebraska Volunteers, 1st Reg. 1927

Needham, E. 3882

Needham, F. J. 2929

Neele, 2358, 2397, 2479–2481, 2780, 2781

Neele, S. 416, 1840, 2202, 4456

Neely Co. 2452

Neff, I. H. 3102

Negroes 1792, 1793, 2825

Nelson, A. 4516

Nelson, J. Y. 3128

Nelson, Johnny 3128

Nelson, Mrs. Mary A. 345

Nelson, T., & Sons 2977, 4683

Nelson River 1098, 3532

Nelson's Pictorial Guide-Books 4683

Nemaha County . . . 1902 1177

Nemaha Land District, Nebr. 228

Nemaha Valley Journal . . . 1858 2978

Neosho Valley, Kans. 1768

Nesmith, J. W. 1152

Netherclift, J., & Son 3786

Netherlands, The 1931

Neuer praktischer Wegweiser für Auswanderer nach Nord-Amerika . . . 1848 3695

Neuner Company 390

Neuville, Alexdr. la: See Laneuville, A.

Neva (ship) 2506

Nevada 63, 64, 188, 295, 338, 370, 385, 428, 437, 534, 762, 806, 831, 899, 1074, 1075, 1724–1726, 1830, 1882, 1980–1984, 3056, 3200, 3491, 3503, 4035, 4056, 4252, 4334, 4446, 4589, 4637, 4757, 4758

Nevada, Calif. 4132

Nevada, Colo. 3344

Nevada City, Calif. 219, 431, 694, 3151

Nevada County, Calif. 2985

Nevada County Directory, for 1871–72 . . . 1871 2985

Nevada, District of 4334

Nevada, Grass Valley and Rough and Ready Directory . . . 1856 431

Nevada Orientale Géographie . . . 1867 63

Nevada State Mining Law . . . 1866 2982

Neve, Felipe de 546

Nevill, R. 2304–2306

Nevin, Ia. 2987

Nevins & Myers 4733

New, S. 720

New Albany Ledger 1

"*New Almaden Quicksilver Mine*" 4492

"*New & Correct Map of Texas*" 4705

New and Short Route Open to the Gold Regions . . . 1859 1770

New and Short Route to the Gold Mines of the Black Hills . . . 1865 315

New and True Religion . . . 1897 3955

New Archangel 1169

New Bedford, Mass. 245, 3933, 4183

New Book, Washington Territory West of the Cascade Mountains . . . 1870 2741

New Boston, Ill. 3023

New Braunfels, Tex. 3889

New Brunswick, Nova Scotia 996

New Castle, Dela. 673

New York City and County Lode, Gregory District, Colo. 1558, 1568, 1569
"New York Company, The" 1489
New York Courier & Enquirer 3596
New York Herald 309, 1615, 2923, 3008, 3346
New-York Historical Society 1555, 2568, 2654
New-York Monthly Magazine 2349
New York Popular Publishing Co. 3009
New York Public Library 211, 343, 1835
New York Regiment 3983
New York Society Library 3170
New York Society of the Order of the Founders and Patriots of America 4219
New York State 3228, 4761
New York Tribune 1651, 1679, 2583
New York World 2923
"New York und Umgebungen" 279
New-Yorker Staats-Zeitung 3692
New Zealand 409
Newark, Dak. 1192
Newberry, E. 3502
Newberry, W. L. 3812
Newberry Library 476, 2883
Newbury 2075
Newbury, Mass. 3321
Newbury Port, Mass. 2063
Newby, T. C. 1765, 2022, 3624
Newcastle, Duke of 1224
Newcastle, Ind. 3199
Newcomb, C. F. 295
Newcomb & Gauss 4712
Newell, R. 3121
Newell, T. 4601
Newer Northwest . . . 1894 4634
Newfoundland 650
"Newhall's New Map of Iowa" 3013, 3014
Newman 743, 3025
Newmark, M. H. 3016
Newmark, M. R. 3016
Newport, R. I. 668
"News" Book and Job Office 3754
News (Buffalo Lake, Minn.) 591
News Power Press Print 495
News Print 3472
News Printing Company 4426
News Printing Co. Press 3344
"News" Steam Book & Job Establishment 3227
"News" Steam Book & Job Office 4627
Newsham, John, of Chadshunt 1471
"Newsletter" Publication Office 440
Newson, Moore, Foster & Company 4079
Newton, Ellen Huldah 3020
Newton, H. 2207
Newton, Ia. 1595, 3674
Neylan, J. F. 2321, 2322
Nez Perces 343, 1980, 2551, 3759, 3944, 4034, 4291
"Nez-Percé Campaign" 1982
Nez Perce Joseph . . . 1881 1982
Niagara, N.Y. 1986, 2612, 3056, 4687
Niagara Falls 1241, 2746, 4790

"Niagara Falls" 837
Niagara Frontier 475
Niagara River 3707, 4670, 4687
Nicaragua 580, 637, 1132, 2195, 2469, 3333, 3988, 4517, 4587, 4749
"Nicaragua, Guatemala, Honduras, San Salvador & Costa Rica" 4517
Nicaragua, Lac de 2009
" 'Nicaragua Route' " 4587
Nicholas, T. 1470, 1471
Nicholl, R. J. 4237
Nichols, C. D. 1457
Nichols & Hall 3271
Nicholson, A. O. P. 4399, 4435, 4436, 4546
Nicholson, C. 826
Nicholson, J. 4683
Nicholson, W. L. 4403
Nickajack, Battle of 1514
Nicolet, J. 524
Nicollet, J. N. 3022, 4546
"Nieuwe Kaert des grondgebieds van den Oregon" 3825
"Night Watch" 111
Niles, J. 700
Niles, N. 2193
Niles, Mich. 726
Niles Register 2242, 2951, 4575
Nimmo, J., Jr. 4423–4425
Nimmo, W. P. 2599
Ninckley & Hartwell 3905
Nininger City . . . 1856 1127
Niobrara, Nebr. 315, 2110, 3394, 3395, 3797, 4394
Nion, Jean-Luc 133
Nipon 460
Nisbet, J. 3901
Nisbet, J., & Co. 153
Nisbet, J. M. 53
Nisqualli Indians 4202
Nitschke Bros. 1986
Niven, J. 4531
Nixon, G. H. 3412
Nixon-Jones Printing Co. 1602, 3575, 4061
Niza 1023
Nobili, Nicolao de 668
Noble, C. W. 3634
Noble Plow . . . 1866 3023
Nobles, W. H. 558, 559
Nolan, P. 423, 497, 673, 1174, 1708, 1710–1713, 2014, 2504, 2505, 2825, 4663
Nolin, J. B. 882
Nome, Alaska 1303
Non-Intervention 2978
Nonpareil Job Printing & Publishing House 1163
Nonpareil Printing Co. 487, 515
Nonpareil Steam Print 3078
" 'Noon Camp on Big Dry River Montana' " 2000
Nootka, Alaska 416, 1169, 1262, 2734, 2736, 3250, 3653, 3936
Nootka Sound 812, 1285, 2734, 2736
"Nord-America" 409
Nordamerika Vorzuglich Texas im Jahre 1849 . . . 1850 3970
Nordamerikanische Freistaat Texas . . . 1851 3582
Norfolk, Nebr. 4064

Norfolk, O. 2532
Norfolk, Va. 1171
Norfolk Sound 2506
Normal, Ill. 499
Norman, B. M. 3634
Norman, Remington Co. 3728
Norris, T. W. 2181
Norris, W., & Co., 316
Norris & Taylor 3030
North, F. 785, 2515
North America 113, 362, 363, 409, 460, 622, 650, 651, 1098, 1283, 1556, 2744, 2745, 3322, 3554, 3555, 3947, 4025, 4076, 4122, 4750
"North America" 837
North Carolina: See also Carolinas 10, 2029, 2091, 2582, 3096, 3428, 3839, 4299, 4300
North Dakota: See also Dakota 93, 572, 976, 1123, 1166, 1326, 2439, 2548, 3752, 4085–4088, 4685
North Dakota, State Historical Society of 2439
"North Island and Peninsula, San Diego" 1674
North Missouri Railroad 1824, 3645
"North Missouri Rail Road Map" 3032
North Missourian Press 2608
North of 36 . . . 1923 1966
North Pacific 2572
North Pacific, Fergus & Black Hills R. R. 4753
"North Pacific Ocean and the Adjacent Coasts" 1653
North Park 4654, 4722
"N. Part of Maine" 3269
North Platte, Nebr. 19, 785, 1369, 4252
North Platte and Its Associations . . . 1910 19
North Platte Post, Nebr. 4327
"North Platte Route to the Gold Mines" 487
North Saskatchewan 1605
North Sea 2630, 2631
"North View of the Church and Ex-Mission of Santa Ines" 4492
Northampton, Mass. 3197
Northeast 642, 1256, 1301, 1624, 1765, 1828, 1926, 2838, 4648, 4649
Northeast Passage 2356
"Northern America" 3415, 3794
Northern Border Brigade . . . 1926 2110
Northern Boundary of Missouri . . . 1842 4383
Northern Counties Gazetteer and Directory, for 1855–6 . . . 1855 1727
Northern Cross Rail Road Schedule 757
Northern Frontier, Commission to Investigate the 2765
Northern Indiana Railroad 4211
Northern Iowa . . . 1858 1163
Northern Islander 2799
Northern Nebraska as a Home for Immigrants . . . 1875 3113

Private Land Claims 4385, 4386
Private Letters of Parmenas Taylor Turnley . . . 1863 4216
Private Life of the Late Benjamin Franklin . . . 1793 1405
Proceedings . . . 1872 4624
Proceedings . . . Baptist General Association of Texas . . . 1868 176
Proceedings . . . Baptist Missionary and Educational Convention of the Indian Territory . . . 1886–1889 170, 171
Proceedings . . . Concord General Association . . . 1868 159
Proceedings . . . Dardanelle Baptist Association . . . 1868 160
Proceedings in the Case of the United States versus William Christy . . . 1836 706
Proceedings of a Convention, Held at Carthage . . . 1845 857
Proceedings of a Convention of Delegates . . . 1836 856
Proceedings of a Council of Administration Convened at Camp Wright . . . 1866 4683
Proceedings of a General Court Martial for the Trial of Major Osborne Cross . . . 1860 935
Proceedings of a Great Democratic Meeting . . . 1843 1047
Proceedings of a Pacific Railroad Convention . . . 1853 3156
"Proceedings of a Public Meeting Held at St. Anthony" 2819, 2820
Proceedings of a Public Meeting of Citizens of Minnesota . . . 1859 3648
"Proceedings of Public Meetings Held at St. Paul, Minnesota" 2819, 2820
Proceedings of the American Philosophical Society . . . 1959 3290, 3291, 3292
Proceedings of the Annual Meeting and Dinner of the Order of Indian Wars of the United States . . . 1929 1523
Proceedings of the Antiquarian and Historical Society of Illinois . . . 1828 2076
Proceedings of the Benton County Agricultural Society . . . 1854 275
Proceedings of the Centennial Reunion of the Moore Family . . . 1882 2878
Proceedings of the Convention to Consider the Opening of the Indian Territory . . . 1888 858
Proceedings of the Friends of a Rail-Road to San Francisco . . . 1849 3365
Proceedings of the Grand Lodge . . . 1847 1413
Proceedings of the Harbor and River Convention . . . 1847 1776
Proceedings of the Historical Society of Linn County, Iowa . . . 1905–1907 1774
Proceedings of the Illinois Educational Convention . . . 1834 2088

Proceedings of the International Council of Indians . . . 1887 2104
Proceedings of the Johnson County Old Settlers Association from 1866 to 1899 2132
Proceedings of the Mass Meeting of the National Democracy of Texas . . . 1860 2949
Proceedings of the National Ship-Canal Convention . . . 1863 2952
Proceedings of the Nebraska Territorial Convention 1695
Proceedings of the Pioneer Settlers' Association, of Louisa County, Iowa . . . 1861 3300
Proceedings of the Pioneer Settlers' Association, of Scott County, Iowa . . . 1859 3301
Proceedings of the Rapids Convention, Held at Burlington, Iowa . . . 1852 3422
Proceedings of the Second Convocation of the Clergy and Laity . . . 1854 3397
Proceedings of the State Historical Society of Wisconsin, 1913 4207
Proclamacion del Gobernador . . . 1861 2999
Proclamacion, por cuanto que el Pueblo de Nuevo-Mejico . . . 1850 3001
Proclamation (Dakota) . . . 1868, 1889 981, 983
Proclamation (Idaho) . . . 1889 2046
Proclamation (New Mexico) . . . 1850, 1869 3000, 3005
Proclamation by the Governor (New Mexico) . . . 1861 2998
Proclamation by the Governor (Utah) . . . 1857 4449
Proclamation! In Consequence of the Great Calamity . . . 1871 679
Proclamation! The Preservation of the Good Order and Peace . . . 1871 680
Proclamation to the People of California . . . 1849 548
Proclamation! To the People of Dakota Territory . . . 1876 980
Proclamation! To the People of the Coasts and Islands of the Pacific . . . n.d. 3346, 3349
Proctor, A. P. 861
Proctor, Henry 4512
Proctor, J. 3845, 3846
"*Profile of a Route from San Pedro on the Pacific Coast to Memphis on the Mississippi River*" 4435
"*Profile of Cajon Pass*" 4435
"*Profile of Elevations above the Level of the Sea*" 4723
"*Profile of Line from Mouth of Weber Cañon*" 4250
"*Profile of Route from Fort Pierre to Fort Kearney*" 4546
"*Profile of Route from Pimas Villages on the Rio Gila to Mesilla on the Rio Bravo*" 4435
"*Profile of Section of Weber Cañon*" 4250
"*Profile of the Route*" 1436
"*Profile of the Routes, from the*

Mouth of the Kansas, to San Francisco, California" 4538
"*Profile of the Traveling Route from the South Pass*" 1429, 1431
"*Profile of Walkers Pass*" 4435
"*Profile or Vertical Section of the Country*" 2188
Programme. First Ward School . . . 1870 1160
Programme for Retreat, at Fort Sill, I.T. . . . 1877 4279–4282
Programme of Evening Serenade . . . 1873 4283
Progress Print 3210
Progressive Times 65
Prohibition 4097
Project for a Railroad to the Pacific . . . 1849 2536, 4642
Proofs of the Corruption of Gen. James Wilkinson . . . 1809 732
Propagation de la Foi, Association de l' 3887, 4052
Prophet, The 744, 1026, 2411
Prophet of Palmyra . . . 1890 1664, 1666
Proposal for a Charter to Build a Railroad . . . 1847 621
Proposed Cathedral in Illinois . . . ca. 1853 3366
"Proposed Cathedral in Illinois" 4638
Proposed Certificate of Inspection . . . ca. 1850 2119
"*Proposed Reservation for Hualpais Indians*" 4273
Propper, G. N. 315
Prose and Poetry of the Live Stock Industry . . . 1905 1412
Prose Sketches and Poems . . . 1834 3285
Prospect from the Congress-Gallery . . . 1796 777, 3867
Prospecto, con la Dura Cruz de la Firme Oposicion . . . ca. 1870 3208
Prospectors' Manual . . . 1886 4199
Prospects of Vallejo . . . 1871 1910
Prospectus, Geological Survey and Report of the Gregory Gold Mining Company . . . 1863 1667
Prospectus for the "Little Fort Porcupine and Democratic Banner" . . . 1845 2513
Prospectus of a Series of North American Views 1407
Prospectus of Belden: The White Chief 236
Prospectus of Lewis and Clark's Tour to the Pacifick Ocean . . . 1807 3323
Prospectus of the Fort Collins Agricultural Colony of Colo. . . . 1873 1385
Prospectus of the Fountain Colony of Colorado . . . 1871 1392
Prospectus of the Mining Bureau of Montana . . . 1866 2866
Protection Across the Continent . . . 1867 4438
Protection Afforded by Volunteers of Oregon and Washington Territories to Overland Immigrants in 1854 . . . 1859 4387

Swett, L. 4644
Swift, C. S. 1494
Swigert, J. 3714
Swigert, S. M. 3714
Swinburne, J. E. 845
Swine 2030, 4155
Swisher, Bella French 52
Swisher, J. M. 52
Swiss Peasant . . . 1848 1278, 2665
Swope, T. H. 4762
Swope Family 4762
Swords, T. & J. 2737
Swords, Thomas 4434
Swormstedt, L., & A. Poe 265
Swormstedt, L., & J. H. Power 2902, 4008
Syd Dakota Ekko's Trykkeri 3903
Sydenham's Island 3933
Sykes, M. 2200
Sylverio (engraver) 3242
Sylvester, R. H. 4555
Sylvester, Harrison & Bro. 813, 1606
Syms-York Co., Inc. 1702, 3610, 3611
Synod of Iowa 4233
Synopsis of Capt. J. D. Winchester's Experience in the Alaskan Gold Fields 4712
Synopsis of Indian Scouts and Their Results, for the Year 1864. General Orders, Number 4 4346
Synopsis of the History of the Eighth U.S. Infantry . . . 1871 4653, 4655
Synopsis of the Indian Tribes within the United States East of the Rocky Mountains, and the British and Russian Possessions of North America 49
"Synopsis of the March of the First Cavalry Division from Triune to Decherd" 2846
Syria 3161

"T T" Ball 2055
T, T W 4019
Tabb, H. B. 787
Table of Distances in the Department of Dakota . . . 1875 4295
Table of Distances of the Overland Daily Stage Line . . . 1863 3140
Table of Distances, Published for the Information of the Troops . . . 1878 4348
"Table of Travelling Distances" 3341
Table Rock, S. Dak. 3420
"Table Showing the Distance from Washington" 4790
Tables of Distances 1204, 2029, 3140, 3230, 3341, 3527, 4295, 4326, 4348
Taché, Msgr., Évêque de St. Boniface 3887
Tacoutché Tessé 2009
Tagebuch einer Reise vom Mississippi nach den Kusten der Sudsee . . . 1858 2851
Tah-ee-chay-pah Pass 4435
Tah-Gah-Jute . . . 1851 2730
Tahoe, Lake: See Lake Tahoe
Tailoc Tow 2736
Tait, Denman & Co. 4057
Tait, J. Selwyn, & Sons 374
Tait, W. & C. 1351

Talbert Raid 1411
Talcott, E. B. 4058
Tale of Home and War . . . 1888 1991
Tale of Two Oceans . . . 1893 193
Tales from Buffalo Land . . . 1940 479
Tales of the Chuck Wagon . . . 1926 4145
Tales of the Northwest . . . 1830 3874
Tales of the Southern Border . . . 1868 4567
Tales of the Trail . . . 1898 2116
Tales of Travels West of the Mississippi . . . 1830 3875
Tallagassee Mission, Ark. 2531
Tallequah 2902
Tama County, Ia. 648
Tamos, Cayetano 3476
Tampico, Mexico 1092, 1329
"*Tampico and its Environs*" 1092
Tanner, H., Jr. 2880
Tanner, H. S. 117, 141, 947, 2423, 2744, 2745, 3055, 4670
Tanner, J. 2189
Tanner, R. J. 623
"*Tanner's Map of U States*" 2423
Tanto Que se Saco de Una Carta . . . 1730 250
Taos, N.Mex. 270, 602, 2694, 2707, 2996, 3766, 4682
Taos County, Report to the Bureau of Immigration . . . 1881 2991
Taos Trail 1513
Taos, Valley of, New Mex. 2707, 3766
Tappan, L. N. 1386
"*Tappan & Co.*" 3344
Tardieu, Ambroise 699
Tardieu, B. 2487
Tardieu, J. B. 1519, 3524
Tarros, D. Raimondo 747
"Tarrying in Nicaragua" 637
Tartary 2397
Tarte, L. J., & Frère 3507
Tarver, M. 4600
Tatanka Yotanka 3797
Ta-ton-ka-i-yo-ton-ka 3797
Tator, C. 3102
Taxes 1683
Taylor 3230
Taylor, B. F. 4709
Taylor, "Buck" 785
Taylor, F. 1213
Taylor, Father 2109
Taylor, H. 1848
Taylor, H. W. 1832
Taylor, J. 712–714, 1001, 1002, 1084, 3346, 3350, 3351, 3856, 3858, 4081
Taylor, J. H. 1818
Taylor, J. W. 2819, 2820
Taylor, John S., & Co. 3958
Taylor, N. G. 2281
Taylor, S., Jr. 2386, 2387
Taylor, Scout 309
Taylor, W. C. 2147
Taylor, W. H. 4120
Taylor, Wm., & Co. 3634
Taylor, Zachary 1799, 4414
Taylor & Taylor 742
Taylor & Tracy 2089
Taylor & Woodruff 3855
Taylor, Fort 2932
Tayohaia Bay 2506

Tazous 2364
Tchangk 2519
Teamster 4677
Teatro Mexicano 4476
Tebbetts, G. P. 1746
Tecumseh 1026, 3245
Teesdale, J. 2129
Teesdale, Elkins & Co. 647
Teetotalers 4590
Tehuantepec, Isthmus of 1169
Tejas y los Estados-Unidos de America . . . 1837 4167
Tejon Pass, Calif. 108, 1697
Tejon Depot Camp, Calif. 4435
Telegram Print 2885
Telegraph Company 4589
Telegraph (Omaha), Daily 974
Telegraph Office 1329, 3380, 4114
Telegraph Printing Co. 1052, 2457
Télégraphe, Imprimerie du 1263
Telegraphic Circular . . . 1883 4293
Tello, M. 1307
Temperance 1006, 2826, 4097
Temperance Crusader . . . 1854 4097
Tempest, S. 2463
Temple, Tex. 4113
Templeton, G. M. 954, 2613, 3033, 4098, 4101
Ten Days on the Plains . . . 1872 1013
Ten Eyck, Frances 592, 595
Ten Mile, Colo. 3819
Ten Squaws . . . 1870 448
Ten Thousand Miles of Travel, Sport, and Adventure . . . 1869 4175
Ten Years a Cowboy . . . 1886, 1888 3328, 3329
Ten Years in Oregon . . . 1844, 1848 36, 37, 2440
Ten Years in the Ranks . . . 1914 2778
Ten Years on a Georgia Plantation . . . 1883 2450
Ten Years on the Iowa Frontier . . . ca. 1915 2111
Tennal Lode 1756
Tennessee 175, 202, 268, 383, 384, 409, 433, 439, 526, 529, 589, 735, 942, 943, 1034, 1198, 1269, 1439, 1514, 1628, 1649, 1734, 1739, 2091, 2574, 2617, 2633, 2780, 2781, 3417, 3595, 3707, 3721, 3839, 3840, 3864, 4102, 4154, 4299, 4300, 4370, 4630, 4684
Tennessee (ship) 3954, 4573
Tennessean . . . 1827 3595
Tenney Bros. 817, 819, 2401
" *Tent in Mexico*' " 3619
Tenth Convention of the Nebraska Sunday School Association . . . 1877 2972
Tepic Conspiracy 4618
Teran, General 117
Ternaux-Compans, H. 626
"*Terra Firma et Novum Regnum Granatense et Popaian*" 1471
"*Terre Australe decouuerte l'An 1644*" 4122
Terre d'Ielmer 4122
Terre de Iesso 1863, 1864
Terre Haute, Alton and St. Louis Railroad Line 3437
Terre-Neuve 650

Waldie's Select Circulating Library
1357
Waldron, G. P. 4611
Wales 692, 3309
Wales, W. W. 2092
Wales & Roberts 589, 2102
Walhalla, N. Dak. 2439
Walker, G. 3987
Walker, G. H. 1351
Walker, J. 545, 2097
Walker, J. & C. 1283, 2061
Walker, J. P. 4327
Walker, J. R. 4558
Walker, R. J. 920, 1644, 2232, 4422
Walker, W., Gov. 240, 1132, 1695,
2195, 3988, 4204, 4587, 4749
Walker & Gillespie 4704
"Walker Colt" 4704
Walker Litho. and Printing Co. 46
Walker's Expedition . . . 1856 4517,
4587
Walker's Filibustering Expedition
240, 3333, 4517, 4587
Walkers Pass, Calif. 4435
Walkup, W. B., & Co. 1204
Wall, J. H. 1579, 1580
Wall, Judge 264
Walla Walla, Wash. 417, 949, 950,
1096, 3192–3195, 3360, 4520
Walla Walla Board of Immigration
4520
Walla Walla Bulletin 950
Walla Walla, Fort 456, 2932, 3677,
4356
"*Walla Walla, W. T., Fort*" 4356
"Walla Walla Union" Job Printing
Establishment 4520
Walla-Walla Valley 2342
Wallace 1645
Wallace, Bigfoot 1187
Wallace, F. T. 1305
Wallace, W. H. 339, 2121
Wallace, Fort 4327
Wallace Publishing Company 4522,
4523
Wallamet, Ore. 3247
Waller, E. 3227
Walling, A. G. 3326, 4034
Walling-Lith 2798
Wallowa, Wash. 1982
Wallowa Valley Indian Question
3119
Walpole, Robert, Earl of Orford 1469
Walsh 2634
Walsh, Captain 1280
Walsh, J. R. 560
Walter, J. 2734
Walter Bray's Dramatic and Concert
Troupe 1845
Walters, Mrs. 1506
Walters & Weber 1330, 4160
Walton, J. 1135
Walton, E. P., Jr. 1084
Walton, Mrs. E. P. 1084
Walton, J. P. 353, 4526
Wandell, C. W. 3346
Wanderings in Minnesota . . . 1867
3690
Wanderings of an Artist . . . 1859
2262
Wapello County, Ia. 2312, 3672
Wapsinonoc Township, Ia. 1655
War College 305

War Department 180, 452, 593, 1017,
2256, 2629, 2707, 2874, 2932, 3289,
3429, 4253–4369, 4427–4443, 4458,
4683
War Department, Adjutant General's
Office 4683
War Department Library 4296, 4297
War Department, Republic of Texas
4115
War Eagle 2499
"War Eagle," Office of the 2193
War in Nicaragua . . . 1860 4517,
4587
War of 1812 103, 135, 1026, 1388,
1526, 1649, 1738, 1986, 2112, 2541–
2546, 2568, 2569, 2607, 2681, 3073,
3850, 4364, 4512, 4670, 4711
War Scout of 1812 . . . 1850 351
War, Secretary of 4258, 4259, 4307,
4384, 4413, 4416, 4430, 4431, 4435,
4437, 4440, 4554
*War Sketches . . . of Arkansaw . . .
1895* 312
War with Mexico . . . 1907 851
Ward, Katharine 4530
Ward, M. E. 820
Ward, Mrs. 4530
Ward, Ned 1845
Ward, Lock, & Tyler 1948
Ward Ritchie Press 189
Ware, E. F. 4534, 4535
Ware, W. W. 4176–4181
"*Warehouse 54, Fort D. A. Russell*"
3612
Warm Springs, Ida. 2055
Warm Springs Pavilion 2055
Warner, 4456
Warner, B. R., & Co. 1847
Warner, E. 3145
Warner, J. 4456
Warner, W. 743
Warner, W. H. 1249
Warner, Beers & Co. 2448
Warner's Pass, Calif. 4435
Warnica, G. A. 4585
"Warning, A" 2807
Waronzow-Daschkaw, Comte de 699
War-Path and Bivouac . . . 1890 1325
Warpath & Cattle Trail . . . 1928 808
Warpenton 743
Warr, J. & W. W. 117, 2880
Warren, E. 3987
Warren, G. K. 3437, 4308, 4309,
4435, 4437
Warren, R. P. 220
Warren & Buell 1309
Warren, Edward . . . 1854 3987
Warren, O. 2532
Warsaw, Ill. 2445, 3342
Warsaw Signal . . . 1845 4187
Washakie, Fort 4330
Washburn, C. 3951
Washburn, N. Dak. 4685
Washburn Leader 4685
Washburn Party 1277
Washburn's Trip 4618
Washburne, E. B. 2093, 2974
Washington, George 777, 983, 1323,
1699, 2228, 2488, 3115, 4670
Washington, J. M. 3789
Washington 87, 338, 370, 409, 438,
465, 573, 806, 907, 913, 914, 949,
950, 1041, 1053, 1090, 1096, 1158,

1202, 1208, 1241, 1267, 1268, 1386,
1400–1402, 1457, 1531, 1551, 1575,
1652, 1653, 1695, 1698, 1724–1726,
1747, 1750, 1827, 1980, 1982, 1983,
2018, 2160, 2259, 2292, 2341, 2342,
2377, 2380, 2390, 2407, 2420, 2461,
2486, 2551, 2572, 2587, 2699, 2707,
2740, 2741, 2753, 2754, 2932, 2933,
2936, 3192–3195, 3250, 3290–3292,
3367, 3397, 3491, 3974, 3976–3981,
4013, 4034, 4046, 4052, 4053, 4062,
4202, 4244, 4254, 4293, 4316, 4319,
4320, 4372, 4387, 4416, 4435, 4438,
4520, 4554, 4592, 4657, 4683, 4715
"*Washington*" 4062
Washington, D.C. 349, 620, 1651,
1654, 1656, 1675, 1829, 1986, 2112,
2297, 2420, 2674, 2738, 2812, 3024,
3073, 3588, 3589, 3595, 3666, 4062,
4392, 4414, 4628, 4664, 4670, 4790
Washington, South Yuba River,
Calif. 3151
Washington & Jefferson College 2852
Washington Chronicle 3650
Washington County, Ida. 1791
Washington County, Mo. 2831
Washington County, Nebr. 243
Washington Historical Quarterly 1053
"*Washington Islands*" 2506
Washington (ship) 1653
Washington Standard 1876
*Washington Territory . . . 1865, 1870,
1877* 1268, 2741, 2754
*Washington Territory West of the
Cascade Mountains . . . 1870* 2740
Washington University 294
Washington, University of 901, 2754,
4530
Washington Volunteers 4554
Washington's Expeditions . . . 1910
1699
Washingtonea Gigantea 21
Washita, Fort 218
Washita River 1357, 4406, 4407
Washita River, Battle on the 4439
Washoe, Nev. 188
Washoe Mining Claims 3200
Wasicun Iapi Ieska Wowapi . . . 1871
4696
*Wasicun Qa Dakota Ieska Wowapi
. . . 1886* 4697
Wa-Si-Cu Tam-a-He-Ca 912
Waterloo, Ill. 2193
Waters, B. E. 1347
Waters, F. R. 2018
Waters, R. A. 4629
Waters, W. 776
Watertown, Wisc. 3413
Watie, Stand 60
Watkins 4123
Watkins, H. 2064
Watkins, Mr. & Mrs. 1997
Watkins & Smead 2659
Watkins' Stereoscopic Views, C. E.
4492
Watson, D. 3179
Watson, D. S. 4494
Watson, Rev. Mr. 945
Watson, Camp 554
Watson's Lithog. 4531
Watsonville, Calif. 2257
Watt, G. D. 3346